Civil Aircraft and Glider
Registers Of
United Kingdom & Ireland 2003

USERS' GUIDE

There are a number of purposes to this annual volume. The primary one is to list all aircraft on the current civil aircraft registers, giving full details of types and previous identities, registered ownership and/or operator, probable home base and certification of airworthiness status. This information reproduces, expands upon and amplifies the official country registers. However, we go well beyond that; included are all other known, but no longer currently registered, UK and Irish aircraft noted in a reasonably identifiable condition and which are displayed or on/for rebuild. Some of these are held for instructional, fire or spares use. The majority of these are in located in the UK and Ireland but a few are resident abroad. In addition we detail the extensive numbers of foreign registered aircraft now located in both the UK and Ireland, some of which may aspire to G- & EI- registrations in due course. Finally, we include a comprehensive listing of all gliders in use throughout the area in order to present an all-inclusive guide of the civil aviation scene.

Secondly on a more technical level, we cater for the aviation specialist and historian who wishes to know more about a particular aircraft by providing detailed information such as non-standard engine power and reasons for that aircraft's non-airworthy state, if applicable and where known. It has been the policy for some years to record engine details in the text, for example the modification of an airframe to receive a non standard engine has to be approved by the CAA and is then recorded in their Register.We also record this change. When microlights first appeared in 1981 there was little standardisation and, consequently, we recorded all engine information. Now that the majority of microlight are commercially produced, either in whole or kit form, engine fitment has become more standard to type but not in all cases. A similar situation exists for BMAA and PFA approved types.

A guide to the main text is as follows:

Registration (Regn)   Registrations are set out in alphabetic order. Aircraft no longer currently registered are marked with an asterisk (*). A few aircraft, either real or static reproductions are identified in fictitious UK civil marks for display purposes and are shown in the Index. Those marks which have been re-issued or re-allotted, particularly either if the first holder or allottee did not use the marks or they were not allocated at the time, are shown with a suffix, for example (2) after the registration.

Type   We adopt the official type description as set down by the manufacturer or designer. Where there is doubt, reference is made to the relevant issue of "Jane's All the Worlds Aircraft", "Airlife's World Aircraft" and the annual "World Directory of Leisure Aviation". Indication is given if the manufacturer is a successor company or a licence builder - although not always if it is merely a sub-contractor. Under this column, we show engine types in parenthesis if the engine is non-standard, for all PFA & BMAA approved SLA types and for those vintage and classic aircraft where engines can vary. Additional explanatory notes show details of any unrepaired accidents and comments on the airframe's identity and where the true position is at variance with the official records.

Constructors' Number (C/N)   This is the often referred to as the Manufacturers' Serial Number and is generally quoted in the official registers. Some aircraft have more than one c/n, for example PFA and BMAA approved types can have the home-builders' own reference number as well as an official sequential number allotted by these organisations plus, on occasion, a manufacturers' plan or kit number. All are shown where known. Those homebuilds and microlights which have been registered without a c/n are identified by the CAA using owners' initials following by "01" These numbers are replaced if the correct c/n is identified. Although manufacturers often identify weightshift microlights with separate c/ns for the Trike unit and for the Wing respectively the CAA usually only records the latter c/n. For example, manufacturers Hornet, Mainair and Medway issue a composite c/n comprising both units. Both c/ns are identified, if known, with the c/n for the Trike unit preceding that for the Wing.

Previous Identities (P/I)   These are set out in reverse order with the most recent identity first. Some of these may have been issued several times and are noted with a suffix, for example (2), after the registration. Those registrations shown in parenthesis were allotted but believed never officially used. The nationality of foreign military serials is indicated only where it may not be apparent. Manufacturers' test marks, also known as "B Conditions" identities are given where known.

Registration Date (Date)   This is the date of the original registration for those particular marks even where subsequently removed and restored.

Owner/Operator   This is the registered owner for current aircraft as recorded in CAA records. Where the operator is known to be different this is shown in parenthesis. Included under this column are details of the latest reported status, for example if the C of A is not current or the aircraft is known to be under repair plus details of any names and, in particular, any military colour schemes and marks worn. Some aircraft are shown as temporary un-registered ("Temp unregd"); this is where the CAA has not received an application from a new owner following a sale. Usually the CAA gives a period of discretion and if no response is received the Certificate is cancelled and the aircraft is not permitted to fly. Such action usually stimulates the new owner to produce the relevant documentation.

Probable Base   The information in this column is not guaranteed: there is no official information. Reports by members and other readers who visit airfields and strips are perused to compile this column. Aircraft change base frequently. Balloons are generally shown as being based at the owner's registered address. When the location is uncertain the owner's hometown is shown in parenthesis except in the case of balloons. Readers are reminded that the identification of a base, particularly if it is a private strip, is not an invitation to visit and in a number of cases visiting is actively discouraged because of previous abuses. We recognise the need for privacy in this area and consequently not all information held is published. Readers are also directed to the ABIX Bases data-base which has current details of airfields and listings of occupants. This is updated frequently.

C of A Expiry   Information is taken from the monthly and annual details published by the CAA. The expiry date indicates the currency of the aircraft's Certificate and details of the suffix letters applied are set out below. Where a C of A has expired or lapsed and an aircraft has been reported since that date further details are shown.

UK CERTIFICATES OF AIRWORTHINESS (C of A) STATUS

The coding after the date of expiry indicates the Certification category. The absence of code letter indicates that the aircraft holds Private category C of A of one or three year duration.

Codings used in this book are follows:-

A   **Aerial Work:**
          Normally indicating aerial advertising & banner towing.

NE   **Non-Expiring:**
          Hot Air Balloons were, until recently, usually certified as such. The suffix in parenthesis indicates whether it is an Aerial Work, Private or Transport certificate. Non-Expiring exemptions were also given a few years ago to certain early microlights. These are being progressively upgraded. Any without a date should be considered to have lapsed.

P   **Permit to Fly:**
          Introduced in 1950 covering homebuilder, vintage and microlight aircraft - normally issued for one year.

S   **Special:**
          Mainly lapsed now and replaced by permits to fly but sometimes still used for manufacturers trials aircraft, particularly for overseas demonstration.

T   **Transport (Passenger):**
          Issued to any aircraft operated for hire or reward, usually for either one or three years duration, and

T(C) **Transport (Cargo):**
          As above, but aircraft restricted to carrying cargo for hire or reward. Few aircraft fall into this category.

GLOSSARY of TERMS and ABBREVIATIONS

AA	Automobile Association
AB	Aktiebolaget (1)
AAC	Army Air Corps
AAIU	Aircraft Accident Investigation Unit
AC	Awaiting Certification
AERONCA	Aeronautical Corpn of America
AESL	Aero Engine Services Ltd
AIRCO	Aircraft Manufacturing Co
ALAT	Aviation Légère de l'Armée de Terre
AMD-BA	Avions Marcel Dassault-Breguet & Aviation
ANEC	Air Navigation & Engineering Co
ANG	Air National Guard
APSS	Aviation Preservation Society of Scotland
ASS	Air Signals School
AVIA	Azionara Vercellese Ind.Areo
A/c	Aircraft
Aka	also known as
Assn	Association

BA	British Aircraft Manufacturing Co Ltd
BAC	British Aircraft Company
BAC	British Aircraft Corporation
BAT	British Aerial Transport Co Ltd
BoBMF	Battle of Britain Memorial Flight
BMAA	British Microlight Aircraft Association
BV	Besloten Vennootschap (2)

CAARP	Coopérative des Ateliers a Aeronautiques de la Région Parisienne
CAF	Candian Air Force
CASA	Construcciones Aeronáuticas SA
CC	County Council
CCF	Canadian Car & Foundry
CEA	Centre Est Aviation
CZAL	Ceskoslovenske Zavody Automobilove a Letecke
Corp	Corporation
c	circa
C of A	Certificate of Airworthiness
C of R	Certificate of Registration
c/s	Colour scheme

DBF	Destroyed by fire
DEFRA	Department for Environment, Food & Rural Affairs
DOSAAF	Dobrovol'noe Obshchestvo Sodeistviya Armii, Aviasii i Flotu

EMBRAER	Empresa Brasileira de Aeronautica SA
Eng	Engineering
EoN	Elliotts of Newbury Ltd
ERCO	Engineering & Research Corporation
ETPS	Empire Test Pilots' School
Ets	Etablissement

FAA	Fleet Air Arm
FLPH	Foot Launched Propelled Hang-glider
FTS	Flying Training School
f/f	First flight
fsm	Full Scale Model

GAF	Government Aircraft Factory
GC	Gliding Club
GmbH	Gesellschaft mit beschrankter Haftung (3)

HAB	Hot-Air Balloon

IAR	Industria Aeronautica Romania
IAV	Intreprinderea deAvioane
ICA	Intreprinderea de Constructii Aeronautice
ICAO	International Civil Aviation Organisation
III	Initiziative Industriali Italian
IMCO	Intermountain Manufacturing Co
IWM	Imperial War Museum
Intl	International

JAA	Joint Aviation Authorities
JAR	Joint Aviation Regulations
JEFTS	Joint Elementary Flying Training School

KG	Kommanditgesellschaft (4)
KK	Kabushiki Kaisha (5)

LAK	Litovskaya Aviatsyonnaya Konstruktsiya
LET	Letecky Narodny Podnik
LLC	Limited Liability Corporation (6)
LLP	Limited Liability Partnership (7)
LVG	Luft-Verkehrs Gesellschaft
Lsg	Leasing
Ltd	Limited (8)

MBB	Messerschmitt-Bölkow-Blohm
MLB	Minimum Lift Balloon
MPA	Man Powered Aircraft

NV	Naamloze Vennootschap (9)
NK	Not known
Ntu	Not taken up
n/w	nose-wheel

OGMA	Oficinas Gerais de Material Aeronautico
Op	Operated by

PFA	Popular Flying Association
PIK	Polytecknikkojen Ilmailukerho
PLC	Public Limited Company (10)
PRC	Peoples' Republic of China
PT	Pesawat Terbang (11)

PWFU	Permanently WFU
PZL	Panstwowe Zaklady Lotnicze (State Aviation Works)
Qv	Which See
R	Reservation
RAF	Royal Aircraft Factory
RAF	Royal Air Force
RAFC	RAF College
RCAF	Royal Candian Air Force
Rep	Reproduction
RFC	Royal Flying Corps
RN	Royal Navy
RNAS	Royal Naval Air Service
RSAF	Royal Saudi Air Force
RTS	Reduced to spares
SA	Société Anonyme (12)
SA	Sociedad Anónima (13)
SA	Spoika Akeyjna (14)
SAAC	Society of Amateur Aircraft Constructors
SAI	Skandinavsk Aero Industri
SAN	Société Aeronautique Normande
SAR	Search and Rescue
SIPA	Société Industrielle pour l'Aéronautique
SNCAC	Société Nationale de Constructions Aéronautiques du Centre
SNCAN	Société Nationale de Constructions Aéronautiques du Nord
SOCATA	Société de Construction d'Avions de Tourisme et d'Affaires
SoS	Secretary of State
SRL	Société Anonyme à Responsabilité Limitée (14)
SpA	Societa per Azioni (16)
SPP	Strojirny Prvni Petiletky
SEAE	School of Electrical & Aeronautical Engineering
Srs.	Series
SS	Special Shape
SZD	Szybowcowy Zaklad Dowswiadczalny
TAD	Technical Aid & Demonstrator
TBA	To be advised
TEAM	Tennessee Engineering & Manufacturing
TWU	Tactical Weapons Unit
t/a	Trading as
tr	Trustee of
t/w	tail-wheel
UAS	University Air Squadron
USAAC	United States Army Air Corps
VW	Volkswagen
WACO	Weaver Aircraft Corp
WFU	Withdrawn from Use

Company Constitution Notes

(1)	Sweden	Joint Stock
(2)	Netherlands	Private
(3)	Germany	Private Limited
(4)	Germany	Limited Partnership
(5)	Japan	
(6)	USA	Limited Partnership
(7)	UK	Limited Partnership
(8)	UK	Private Limited
(9)	Belgian/Netherlands	
(10)	UK	Public Limited
(11)	Indonesia	
(12)	France/Romania	Public Limited
(13)	Spain	Public Limited
(14)	Poland	
(15)	Italy	Public Limited Company
(16)	Italy	Public Limited Company

CAA DATA

UNITED KINGDOM REGISTER OF CIVIL AIRCRAFT @ 1st JANUARY 2003

CLASS	CERTIFICATION STATUS							TOTAL
	T [1]	TC [2]	A [3]	PRIVATE	SPECIAL	PERMIT	NOT CERTIFICATED	
FIXED WING MTOW > 5700 KG	984 *(974)*	9 *(7)*	17 *(20)*	17 *(20)*	- -	29 *(27)*	153 *(133)*	1209 *(1181)*
FIXED WING MTOW > 2730 KG <= 5700 KG	152 *(149)*	- -	10 *(9)*	43 *(48)*	- -	68 *(71)*	100 *(101)*	373 *(378)*
FIXED WING MTOW <= 2730 KG EXCL MICROLIGHTS	2292 *(2229)*	- -	19 *(18)*	2505 *(2571)*	2 *(3)*	1345 *(1398)*	2083 *(1991)*	8246 *(8210)*
MICROLIGHTS INC FLPH	- -	- -	- -	- -	- -	2119 *(2161)*	1506 *(1360)*	3625 *(3521)*
GLIDERS	-	-	-	-	-	-	1 *(1)*	1 *(1)*
HELICOPTERS	785 *(749)*	- -	1 *(0)*	139 *(154)*	- -	34 *(32)*	175 *(155)*	1134 *(1090)*
GYROPLANES	-	-	-	-	-	72 *(64)*	172 *(178)*	244 *(242)*
GAS FILLED AIRSHIPS	2 *(1)*	- -	- -	- -	- -	- -	3 *(3)*	5 *(4)*
HOT AIR AIRSHIPS	- -	- -	12 *(12)*	- -	- -	- -	14 *(12)*	26 *(24)*
GAS FILLED BALLOONS	- -	- -	1 *(1)*	- -	- -	- -	12 *(10)*	13 *(11)*
HOT AIR BALLOONS	185 *(153)*	- -	525 *(479)*	40 *(27)*	- -	- -	931 *(1017)*	1681 *(1676)*
GAS/HOT AIR BALLOONS	- -	- -	- -	- -	- -	- -	6 *(7)*	6 *(7)*
MINIMUM LIFT BALLOONS	- -	- -	- -	- -	- -	- -	99 *(118)*	99 *(118)*
TOTALS	4400 *(4255)*	9 *(7)*	585 *(539)*	2744 *(2820)*	2 *(3)*	3667 *(3753)*	5255 *(5096)*	16662 *(16473)*

Key:

1	T	Transport Passenger
2	TC	Transport Cargo
3	A	Aerial

Data produced by CAA Aircraft Registration Section, Kingsway, London WC2

SECTION 1

PART 1 – FIRST PERMANENT UNITED KINGDOM REGISTER

The Air Board was formed in May 1916 and established the Civil Aerial Transport Committee (CATC) a year later. The CATC's primary brief was to report on the measures necessary to develop aviation for civil and commercial purposes. Meantime the Air Force Bill received the Royal Assent in November 1917 leading to the creation of the Air Council and Air Ministry. Although the Armistice was negotiated in November 1918 official restrictions on civil flying were not lifted as, technically, a state of war continued until the signing of the Peace Treaty in July 1919.

There were no international regulations controlling the registration of civil aircraft within the United Kingdom at the end of the First World War. Consequently the Air Ministry's Civil Air Department specified a system of temporary registration marks in May 1919. This ran until July 1919. Two registers were established for (i) military aircraft sold for civil purposes and already bearing Service serials - they would be allocated their serials as registration marks with the Service ring markings obliterated and (ii) new aircraft and those built from spares - they were allocated marks in a special Service sequence commencing at K100. Subsequently, a number of these aircraft were re-allocated registrations in the first Permanent United Kingdom Register of Civil Aircraft which replaced the two Temporary Registers. This was inaugurated on 31st July 1919 and ran until 29th July 1928 when the registration G-EBZZ had been issued. With the growth of international civil aviation new regulations commenced on 1st January 1929 - see below.

Meantime the civil use of Airships and Balloons came under the supplementary air traffic regulations of the Air Navigation Act 1911-1919. A separate Lighter-than-Air Register (G-FAAA-FAAZ) was established until the end of 1928 when the Director-General of Civil Aviation decided to terminate it and authorise that all airships and balloons would be registered in the new sequence of registration marks commencing at G-AAAA. The fresh series of registrations was introduced retrospectively from 30th July 1928 - see SECTION 1, Part 2.

Regn	Type	C/n	P/I		Date	Owner/Operator	Probable Base	CA Expy
G-EAAA - G-EAZZ								
G-EASD	Avro 504L	E.5	S-AHAA		26. 3.20	G.M.New	Breighton	
	(Le Clerget 130hp)		S-AAP/G-EASD/(RAF)			*(New owner 2.02)*		
G-EBAA - G-EBZZ								
G-EBHX	de Havilland DH.53 Humming Bird	98	No.8		22. 9.23	The Shuttleworth Trust	Old Warden	12. 7.03P
	(ABC Scorpion II)		(Lympne 1923)			*"L'Oiseau-Mouche"*		
G-EBIA	R.A.F. SE-5A	654/2404	F904		26. 9.23	The Shuttleworth Trust	Old Warden	26. 5.03P
	(Wolseley Viper 200hp)		"D7000"/G-EBIA/F904			*(As "F904/H" in 56 Sqdn RFC c/s)*		
G-EBIR	de Havilland DH.51	102	VP-KAA		22. 1.24	The Shuttleworth Trust	Old Warden	31. 5.02P
	(ADC Renault 120hp)		G-KAA/G-EBIR			*"Miss Kenya"*		
G-EBJO	ANEC II	2	No.7		17. 7.24	The Shuttleworth Trust	Old Warden	30.11.35
			(Lympne 1924)			*(Rebuild nearing completion 12.00)*		
G-EBKY	Sopwith Pup	w/o 3004/14	"N5180"		27. 3.25	The Shuttleworth Trust	Old Warden	9. 5.03P
	(Le Rhone 80hp) *(ex Sopwith Dove)*		"N5184"/G-EBKY			*(As "N6181" in 3 Sqdn RNAS c/s) "Happy"*		
G-EBLV	de Havilland DH.60 Moth	188			22. 6.25	BAE Systems (Operations) Ltd	Old Warden	21. 6.03P
	(ADC Cirrus III)					*(On loan to The Shuttleworth Trust)*		
G-EBNV	English Electric S.1 Wren	4	(BAPC.11)		9. 4.26	The Shuttleworth Trust	Old Warden	23. 6.87P
	(ABC 398cc)					G-EBNV*(Composite aircraft - principally c/n 3 rebuilt 1955/56: as "No.4": no marks carried: noted 5.01)*		
G-EBQP	de Havilland DH.53 Humming Bird	114	J7326		?. 4.27	M.C.Russell tr G-EBQP Syndicate	Hatch	
	(Bristol Cherub III)					*(On rebuild 9.02: will use wings ex Martin Monoplane G-AEYY & carry "J7326")*		
G-EBWD	de Havilland DH.60X Moth	552			2. 3.28	The Shuttleworth Trust	Old Warden	24. 4.03P
	(ADC Hermes 2)							
G-EBXU	de Havilland DH.60X Moth	627			2. 5.28	D.E.Cooper-Maguire	Goodwood	17. 4.02P
	(DH Gipsy II)							

PART 2 – SECOND PERMANENT UNITED KINGDOM REGISTER

The transition to a second series of registrations, commencing from G-AAAA onwards, was made with effect from 30th July 1928. Registrations were usually allocated in alphabetical sequence until the late 1970s although there have been numerous sporadic exceptions to this rule throughout the period. The G-AAAA-AZZZ series were all allocated by July 1972 and a new series G-BAAA onwards was used in the same month: this series became exhausted in June 2001. Notwithstanding this, and commencing in 1974, many registrations were issued ahead of the natural alphabetical sequence and came from all of the forthcoming G-Bxxx to G-Zxxx series, examples being Concorde G-BSST (5.68), Accountant G-BTEL (8.57) and Harrier G-VSTO (6.71).

All the advance G-Bxxx registrations have been now subsumed within the proper sequence and the new G-Cxxx series came into use, formally, in June 2001. However, some G-Cxxx registration series, namely G-CAAA to G-CAXP was allocated to Canada from April 1920 until January 1929 whilst G-CYAA to G-CYZZ and G-CYUA to G-CYZZ-were allocated to Canadian military aircraft from June 1920 until 1931. Consequently, with the onset of the new series, the Civil Aviation Authority will not be allocating any further registrations from the G-CAxx range. Nine advance registrations, which were issued between December 1977 and March 1999, remain. None of these was ever allocated previously, although two of them were reserved in 1928.

In addition, a number of special registration series were allocated as follows:
   a) G-N81AC and G-N94AA to N94AE, specific alpha-numeric marks, were used for British Airways' Concordes in 1979 & 1980,
   b) G-FYAA-FYZZ were dedicated for minimum lift balloons from January 1982 until 1997, and
   c) G-MBAA-MBZZ, G-MGAA-MGZZ, G-MJAA-MJZZ, G-MMAA-MNZZ, G-MTAA-MTZZ & G-MYAA-MZZZ were dedicated for microlight aircraft from 1981 to 1998 until the CAA decided to allocate new registrations from the current series.

Regn	Type	C/n	P/I	Date	Owner/Operator	Probable Base	CA Expy
G-AAAA - G-AAZZ							
G-AADR(2)	Moth Corporation DH.60GM Moth (DH Gipsy I)	138	NC939M	2. 6.86	H.F.Moffatt	Woodlow Farm, Bosbury	16. 8.02P
G-AAEG	de Havilland DH.60G Moth	1027	D-EUPI D-1599/G-AAEG	4. 2.29	I.B.Grace *(New owner 1.02)*	(Ada, MI, USA)	
G-AAHI	de Havilland DH.60G Moth *(DH Gipsy I) (Original fuselage used in 1953 rebuild of G-AAWO)*	1082		25. 5.29	N.J.W.Reid	Lee-on-Solent	30. 6.02P
G-AAHY	de Havilland DH.60M Moth (DH Gipsy I)	1362	HB-AFI G-AAHY	10. 5.29	D.J.Elliott *(Brooklands Flying Club titles)*	Thruxton	13. 8.03P
G-AAIN	Parnall Elf II (ADC Hermes 2)	2 & J.6		11. 6.29	The Shuttleworth Trust	Old Warden	10. 7.03P
G-AALY	de Havilland DH.60G Moth *(DH Gipsy I) (Composite: rebuilt from components*	1175	F-AJKM G-AALY	9. 9.29	K M Fresson	Hill Farm, Durley	15. 5.05T
G-AAMY(2)	Moth Corporation DH.60GMW Moth (Wright Gipsy L320)	86	N585M NC585M	2. 5.80	Totalsure Ltd	Seppe-Hoeven, The Netherlands	29. 7.03P
G-AANG(2)	Bleriot Type XI (Anzani 25hp) *(1910 original)*	14	BAPC3	29.11.81	The Shuttleworth Trust *(No external marks: noted 5.02)*	Old Warden	
G-AANH(2)	Deperdussin Monoplane (Anzani Y 35hp) *(Possibly c/n 143)*	43	BAPC4	29.10.81	The Shuttleworth Trust *(No external marks: noted 5.02)*	Old Warden	14. 5.83P
G-AANI(2)	Blackburn 1912 Monoplane (Gnome 683 50hp)	725	BAPC5 No.9	29.10.81	The Shuttleworth Trust *(No external marks)*	Old Warden	13. 6.03P
G-AANJ(2)	Luft-Verkehrs Gesellschaft C.VI (Benz 230hp) *(Composite aircraft including parts from LVG 1594: captured 1916/17 and allotted RFC serial "XG7")*	4503	9239M C7198/18/"1594"/C7198/18	29.10.81	The Shuttleworth Trust *(As "7198/18" in German Air Force c/s)*	Old Warden	16. 5.03P
G-AANL(2)	de Havilland DH.60M Moth (DH Gipsy I) *(Composite rebuild)*	1446	OY-DEH RDAF S-357/S-107	26. 6.87	A.L.Berry *(National Flying Services titles)*	(Dunfermline)	9. 5.03P
G-AANM(2)	Bristol F.2b (RR Falcon)	"67626"	BAPC166	16. 7.87	Aero Vintage Ltd *(Noted as "D7889" 5.02)*	Old Warden	
G-AANV(2)	Morane Saulnier Moth 60M (DH Gipsy I)	13	HB-OBU CH-349/F-AJNY	8. 3.84	R.A.Seeley	Longwood Farm, Morestead	13. 9.03P
G-AAOK(2)	Curtiss-Wright Travel Air CW-12Q (Warner Scarab @ 125hp)	12Q-2026	N370N NC370N/NC352M	18.11.81	Shipping & Airlines Ltd	Rushett Farm, Chessington *(Damaged in gales Rijeka, Yugoslavia 21.10.83: on rebuild 5.01)*	18. 1.84P
G-AAOR(2)	de Havilland DH.60G Moth (DH Gipsy I) *(C/n uncertain: probably a composite)*	1075	EC-AAO	15. 4.85	V.S.E.Norman	Rendcomb	20. 5.03P
G-AAPZ	Desoutter I (ADC Hermes)	D.25		?. ?.31	The Shuttleworth Trust *(National Flying Services titles)*	Old Warden	12. 4.01P
G-AAUP	Klemm L 25-1a (Salmson AD9)	145		19. 2.30	J I.Cooper t/a Newbury Aeroplane Co *"Clementine"*	Denford Manor, Hungerford	21.11.84P
G-AAWO	de Havilland DH.60G Moth *(DH Gipsy I) (1953 rebuild substituted original fuselage of G-AAHI)*	1235		2. 5.30	N.J.W.Reid & L.A.Fenwick	Lee-on-Solent	10. 2.03P
G-AAXK*	Klemm L 25-1a	182		?. 5.30	C.C.Russell-Vick *(Damaged White Waltham 3.62: cancelled by CAA 18.3.91) (Fuselage stored 3.00)*	Orpington	29.11.60
G-AAYX	Southern Martlet (AS Genet Major 1A)	202		14. 5.30	The Shuttleworth Trust	Old Warden	16. 5.03P
G-AAZG	de Havilland DH.60G Moth	1253	EC-AAE EC-MMA/M-CMMA/MW-133/G-AAZG *(Valid CofR 1.03)*	23. 5.30	J.A.Pothecary	Old Sarum	
G-AAZP	de Havilland DH.80A Puss Moth (DH Gipsy Major)	2047	HL537 G-AAZP/SU-AAC/G-AAZP	4. 6.30	R.P.Williams *"British Heritage"*	Denford Manor, Hungerford	29. 5.03

G-ABAA - G-ABZZ

G-ABAG	de Havilland DH.60G Moth	1259		23. 6.30	The Shuttleworth Trust	Old Warden	2. 5.03P
	(DH Gipsy I)						
G-ABDX	de Havilland DH.60G Moth	1294	HB-UAS	22. 8.30	M.D.Souch	Hill Farm, Durley	28. 7.99P
	(DH Gipsy I)		G-ABDX				
G-ABEV(2)	de Havilland DH.60G Moth	1823	N4203E	10. 3.77	S.L.G.Darch	East Chinnock, Yeovil	9.10.97P
	(DH Gipsy I)		G-ABEV(2)/HB-OKI/CH-217		*(Noted Chilbolton 10.01)*		
G-ABLS	de Havilland DH.80A Puss Moth	2164		7. 5.31	R.C.F.Bailey	(Ledbury)	24. 9.03P
	(DH Gipsy Major)						
G-ABNT	Civilian CAC.1 Coupe	O.2.3		10. 9.31	Shipping & Airlines Ltd	Biggin Hil	16. 9.02P
	(AS Genet Major 1A) *(C/n also quoted as O.3)*						
G-ABNX	Robinson Redwing 2	9		2. 7.31	R.J.Burgess	Redhil	12. 5.03P
					tr Redwing Syndicate		
G-ABOX(2)	Sopwith Pup	-	N5195	2. 9.84	C.M.D. & A.P.St.Cyrien	AAC Middle Wallop	22. 4.93P
	(Le Rhone 80hp)				*(On loan to Museum of Army Flying) (As "N5195")*		
G-ABSD	de Havilland DH.60G Moth	1883	A7-96	21.11.31	M.E.Vaisey	(Hemel Hempstead)	
	(Identity unconfirmed		VH-UTN/G-ABSD		*(On rebuild following import from USA in 1985) (Valid CofR 1.03))*		
G-ABUS	Comper CLA.7 Swift	S.32/4		27. 2.32	R.C.F.Bailey	(Ledbury)	19. 6.79P
	(Pobjoy Niagara 3)				*(On rebuild 1989: valid CofR 1.03)*		
G-ABVE	Arrow Active 2	2		19. 3.32	R.A.Fleming	Breighton	1. 5.03P
	(DH Gipsy III)						
G-ABWP	Spartan Arrow 1	78		?. 4.32	R.E.Blain	Redhil	27. 3.03P
	(Cirrus Hermes 2)						
G-ABXL	Granger Archaeopteryx	3A		3. 6.32	J.R.Granger	Radcliffe-on-Trent	22. 9.82P
	(Cherub III)				*(New owner 4.02)*		
G-ABYA	de Havilland DH.60G Moth	1906		?. 7.32	D A Hay & J.F.Moore	Biggin Hill	17. 2.05
	(DH Gipsy I)						
G-ABZB(2)	de Havilland Moth Major	5011	SE-AEL	11. 9.80	R.Earl & B.Morris	Folley Farm, Hungerford	15. 8.03P
	(DH Gipsy Major 1C)		OY-DAK				

G-ACAA - G-ACZZ

G-ACAA(2)	Bristol F.2b	7434	F4516	25.10.91	Patina Ltd	Duxford	25. 4.01P
	(RR Falcon) (Restored as original but rebuilt from various components)				*(Op The Fighter Collection as "D8084/S")*		
G-ACCB	de Havilland DH.83 Fox Moth	4042		24. 1.33	E.A.Gautrey	(Nuneaton)	20. 7.57
					(Crashed off Southport 25.9.56 & on rebuild 10.95: current status unknown)		
G-ACDA	de Havilland DH.82A Tiger Moth	3175	BB724	6. 2.33	B.D.Hughes	Denford Manor, Hungerford	26. 6.82
			G-ACDA		*(Crashed & burned out near Cirencester 27.6.79 - fuselage reported stored 10.01)*		
G-ACDC	de Havilland DH.82A Tiger Moth	3177	BB726	6. 2.33	The Tiger Club (1990) Ltd	Headcorn	15. 4.05T
	(Composite airframe)		G-ACDC				
G-ACDI	de Havilland DH.82A Tiger Moth	3182	BB742	6. 2.33	J.A.Pothecary	NewtonToney, Salisbury	AC
	(Composite rebuild)		G-ACDI		*(On rebuild 2002)*		
G-ACDJ	de Havilland DH.82A Tiger Moth	3183	BB729	6. 2.33	de Havilland School of Flying Ltd	White Waltham	16. 8.04T
			G-ACDJ				
G-ACEJ	de Havilland DH.83 Fox Moth	4069		21. 4.33	Janice I.Cooper	(Lee on Solent)	14. 8.04
					t/a Newbury Aeroplane Co *(Scottish Motor Traction titles)*		
G-ACET	de Havilland DH.84 Dragon	6021	2779M	21. 4.33	M.D.Souch	(Hedge End, Southampton)	
			AW171/G-ACET		*(On rebuild 1.00: composite based on original wings)*		
G-ACGT*	Avro 594B Avian IIIA	R3/CN/171	EI-AAB	?. 5.33	Not known	(Leeds)	21. 7.39
					(Cancelled 1.1.39 as sold as revealed during 1938 census) (On rebuild 4.00)		
G-ACGZ	de Havilland Moth Major	5038	VT-AFW	30. 5.33	N.H.Lemon	(Maidenhead)	
			G-ACGZ		*(Restored 28.9.99: on rebuild 2000)*		
G-ACLL	de Havilland DH.85 Leopard Moth	7028	AW165	16. 1.34	D.C.M. & V.M.Stiles	Jurby, Isle of Man	6.12.95P
			G-ACLL		*(New owners 1.03)*		
G-ACMA	de Havilland DH.85 Leopard Moth	7042	BD148	14. 3.34	S.J.Filhol	Headcorn	3. 2.94P
			G-ACMA		*(Stored 2.95: current status unknown)*		
G-ACMD(2)	de Havilland DH.82A Tiger Moth	3195	N182DH	20. 1.88	M.J.Bonnick	Rectory Farm, Abbotsley	18. 7.05
			EC-AGB/Sp AF 33-5 *(Provenance doubtful: EC-AGB had interim Spanish AF serial 30-104)*				
G-ACMN	de Havilland DH.85 Leopard Moth	7050	X9381	?. 4.34	M.R.& K.E.Slack	Duxford	25. 7.03
			G-ACMN				
G-ACNS	de Havilland Moth Major	5068	ZS-???	?. 3.34	R.I.& D.Souch	Hill Farm, Durley	12. 8.05
			G-ACNS				
G-ACOJ(2)	de Havilland DH.85 Leopard Moth	7035	F-AMXP	5. 6.87	A.J.Norman	Rendcomb	3. 9.04
	(Composite with wings from HB-OXO)				tr Norman Aeroplane Trust		
G-ACSP	de Havilland DH.88 Comet	1994	CS-AAJ	21. 8.34	K.Fern & T.M.Jones	Egginton, Derby	
			G-ACSP/E-1		*(On rebuild 9.02 based on some original components)*		
G-ACSS	de Havilland DH.88 Comet	1996	K5084	4. 9.34	The Shuttleworth Trust	Old Warden	2. 6.94P
	(DH Gipsy Queen 2)		G-ACSS		*"Grosvenor House/34" (Active 2002)*		
	(i) Two static replicas exist, both as "G-ACSS", with identities BAPC.216 & BAPC.257 - see SECTION 4						
	(ii) Flying replica built Repeat Aircraft, Riverside CA, USA 1993 for T J Wathen regd N88XD [T7] is also as "G-ACSS"						
G-ACTF	Comper CLA.7 Swift	S.32/9	VT-ADO	24. 5.34	The Shuttleworth Trust	Old Warden	29. 4.99P
	(Pobjoy Niagara 2)				*"The Scarlet Angel"*		
G-ACUS(2)	de Havilland DH.85 Leopard Moth	7082	HB-OXA	17.11.77	R.A.& V.A.Gammons	RAF Henlow	18.12.05
	(Composite incl parts ex HB-OXO c/n 7045)		(G-ACUS)				
G-ACXB(2)	de Havilland Moth Major	5098	EC-ABY	24. 1.89	D.F.Hodgkinson	(Gravesend)	
			EC-BAX/Sp AF 30-53/EC-YAY		*(On rebuild 2000)*		
G-ACXE	British Klemm L 25c1 Swallow	21		29.10.34	J.G.Wakeford	(Bexhill-on-Sea)	7. 4.40
	(On rebuild since 1989 using components to re-draw plans and produce a substantially "new-build" airframe: progress continuing 2002 with some						
	mainspar build sub-contracted to Denford Manor)						
G-ACZE	de Havilland DH.89A Dragon Rapide	6264	G-AJGS	20.11.34	Wessex Aviation & Transport Ltd	Haverfordwest	8. 8.95
			G-ACZE/Z7266/G-ACZE		*(Stored 9.00)*		

G-ADAA - G-ADZZ

G-ADEV(2)	Avro 504K (Le Rhone 110hp)	R3/LE/61400	G-ACNB "E3404"	18. 4.84	The Shuttleworth Trust (As "H5199")	Old Warden	24. 4.03P
	(P/i not confirmed but, if correct, full p/i is 3118M/BK892/G-ADEV/H5199)						
G-ADFV*	Blackburn B.2	5920/8	2893M G-ADFV	3. 4.35	Not known	(St.Ives, Huntingdon)	26. 6.41
	(To 574 ATC Sqdn Caterham School, Surrey as 2893M on 17.2.42: cut up in 1950, rear fuselage preserved: reconstruction commenced in 1967: *forward fuselage for rebuild 3.00)*						
G-ADGP	Miles M.2L Hawk Speed Six	160	G-ADGP	20. 5.35	R.A.Mills	Booker	7. 5.03P
G-ADGT	de Havilland DH.82A Tiger Moth	3338	BB697 G-ADGT	23. 5.35	Jillian Franks & M.Dalton (Southburgh, Thetford, Norfolk)		10.11.05T
G-ADGV	de Havilland DH.82A Tiger Moth	3340	(D-E...) G-ADGV/(G-BACW)/BB694/G-ADGV	23. 5.35	K.J. & P.J.Whitehead	Whitchurch Hill, Reading	23. 7.05
G-ADGZ*	de Havilland DH.82A Tiger Moth	3344		23. 5.35	Not known	Hill Farm, Durley	
					(Cancelled 17.9.40: to RAF as BB700 in 9.40) (Reported 5.02)		
G-ADHD(2)	de Havilland Moth Major *(Rebuild of ex Spanish components ex USA)*	5105	EC-... Spanish AF 34-5/EC-W32	17. 2.88	M.E.Vaisey *(Noted 7.02)*	RAF Henlow	
G-ADIA	de Havilland DH.82A Tiger Moth	3368	BB747 G-ADIA	13. 8.35	S.J. Beaty	Wold Lodge, Finedon	5. 5.05
G-ADJJ	de Havilland DH.82A Tiger Moth	3386	BB819 G-ADJJ	29. 8.35	J.M.Preston *(On rebuild 8.02)*	Chilbolton	20. 3.75
G-ADKC	de Havilland DH.87B Hornet Moth	8064	X9445 G-ADKC	27. 3.36	A.J.Davy	RAF Marham	20.12.04
G-ADKK	de Havilland DH.87B Hornet Moth	8033	W5749	9.11.35	R M & D R Lee	Kemble	10. 8.03
G-ADKL	de Havilland DH.87B Hornet Moth	8035	F-BCJO G-ADKL/W5750/G-ADKL	?.11.35	P.R.& M.J.F.Gould	Coulommiers, Seine-et-Marne, France	8. 7.05
G-ADKM	de Havilland DH.87B Hornet Moth	8037	W5751 G-ADKM	12.11.35	L.V.Mayhead	Hill Farm, Durley	6. 7.01
G-ADLY	de Havilland DH.87B Hornet Moth	8020	W9388 G-ADLY	5.10.35	Totalsure Ltd	Seppe-Hoeven, The Netherlands	24. 5.04
G-ADMT	de Havilland DH.87B Hornet Moth	8093		8. 5.36	P.A.D.Swoffer "Curlew"	Popham	19. 5.04
G-ADND	de Havilland DH.87B Hornet Moth	8097	W9385 G-ADND	4. 8.36	The Shuttleworth Trust (As "W9385/YG-L/3" in 502 Sqdn c/s)	Old Warden	25. 4.03P
G-ADNE	de Havilland DH.87B Hornet Moth	8089	X9325 G-ADNE	10. 3.36	G-ADNE Ltd "Ariadne"	Lee-on-Solent	25. 4.03
G-ADNL	Miles M.5 Sparrowhawk	239		12. 8.35	A.G.Dunkerley	(Bristol)	13. 5.58S
	(On rebuild 6.00 from components discarded from the reconstruction in 1953 as M.77 Sparrowjet)						
G-ADNZ(2)	de Havilland DH.82A Tiger Moth	85614	6948M DE673	10.10.74	D.C.Wall (As "DE673")	Old Buckenham	1. 8.03
G-ADPC	de Havilland DH.82A Tiger Moth	3393	BB852 G-ADPC	24. 9.35	D J Marshall	Charity Farm, Baxterley	2. 8.03
G-ADPJ	BAC Drone 2 (Douglas Sprite)	7		21. 8.35	N.H.Ponsford	(Selby)	17. 5.55
	(Crashed Leicester 3.4.55: on rebuild 12.99 using parts from G-AEJR c/n 22)						
G-ADPS	BA Swallow 2 (Pobjoy Cataract 2)	410		4. 9.35	J.F.Hopkins	Watchford Farm, Yarcombe	2. 9.03P
G-ADRA(2)	Pietenpol Air Camper (Continental A65)	PFA 1514		10. 4.78	A.J.Mason "Edna May"	Finmere	11. 4.03P
G-ADRH(2)	de Havilland DH.87A Hornet Moth	8038	(ZK-ANR) G-ADRH/F-AQBY/HB-OBE	6. 8.82	R G Grocott (On rebuild 2000)	Mandeville, New Zealand	
G-ADRR(2)	Aeronca C.3	A.734	N17423 NC17423	6. 9.88	S.J.Rudkin *(Stored 1992: wings @ Skycraft/Spalding 11.01)*	Roughay Farm, Bishops Waltham	
G-ADUR	de Havilland DH.87B Hornet Moth	8085		10. 3.36	R.A.Seeley	Phoenix Farm, Lower Upham	1. 8.04
G-ADWJ	de Havilland DH.82A Tiger Moth	3450	BB803 G-ADWJ	9.12.35	C.Adams *(Under restoration 3.97: Valid CofR @ 4.02)*	(Madley)	
G-ADWT	Miles M.2W Hawk Trainer	215	CF-NXT G-ADWT/NF750/G-ADWT	18.11.35	R.Earl & B.Morris (On rebuild 10.01)	Denford Manor, Hungerford	15 .6.62
G-ADXT	de Havilland DH.82A Tiger Moth *(Mainly a rebuild of components)*	3436		9.12.35	J.R.Hanauer *(Forced landed & overturned Fishbourne 22.6.01)*	Goodwood	18. 7.03T
G-ADYS	Aeronca C.3 (Aeronca E113C)	A.600		?. 1.36	Janice I Cooper *(London Air Park Flying Club titles)*	Rendcomb	3.10.02P

G-AEAA - G-AEZZ

G-AEBB	Mignet HM.14 Pou-Du-Ciel	KWO.1		24. 1.36	The Shuttleworth Trust *(Noted 5.01)*	Old Warden	31. 5.39
G-AEBJ	Blackburn B.2 (DH Gipsy Major)	6300/8		4. 2.36	BAE Systems (Operations) Ltd	Warton	20. 6.03
G-AEDB	BAC Drone 2 (Cherub III)	13		18. 3.36	P.L.Kirk & R E Nerou	Hucknall	26. 5.87P
					(Registered as BGA2731 31.3.81: composite with wings of G-AEJH & tail of G-AEEN: noted 7.01)		
G-AEDU(2)	de Havilland DH.90A Dragonfly	7526	N190DH G-AEDU/ZS-CTR/CR-AAB	4. 6.79	A.J.Norman tr Norman Aeroplane Trust	Langham	22. 7.05
G-AEEG	Miles M.3A Falcon Major	216	SE-AFN Fv913/SE-AFN/G-AEEG/U-20	14. 3.36	P.R.Holloway	Old Warden	18. 6.04
G-AEFG*	Mignet HM.14 Pou-Du-Ciel (Scott Flying Squirrel)	JN.1	BAPC.75	27. 3.36	N.H.Ponsford	(Selby)	31. 3.38
					(Cancelled in 31.3.38 census: rebuilt using 65% of original incl engine: on rebuild 1.00)		
C-AEFT	Aeronca C.3	A.610		1/. 4.36	N.C.Chittenden	Combrook	1. 8.02P
	(JAP J.99)(Rebuilt in 1976 with major parts of G-AETG (qv) & carries c/n AB.110 thereof)						
G-AELO	de Havilland DH.87B Hornet Moth	8105	AW118 G-AELO	30. 7.36	M.J.Miller	Little Gransden	9. 5.03
G-AEML	de Havilland DH.89 Dragon Rapide	6337	X9450 G-AEML	1. 9.36	Amanda Investments Ltd "Proteus"	Rendcomb	22. 5.05
G-AEMY*	Mignet HM.14 Pou-Du-Ciel	NMB.1		25. 8.36	N.Ponsford *(Cancelled 31.7.37) (Small parts stored 12.99)*	(Selby)	

G-AENP(2)	Hawker Afghan Hind	41H/81902	(BAPC.78)	29.10.81	The Shuttleworth Trust	Old Warden	6. 5.02P
	(Kestrel V)		R.Afghan AF		(As "K5414 "in 15 Sqdn c/s)		
G-AEOA	de Havilland DH.80A Puss Moth	2184	ES921	1.10.36	A. & P.A.Wood	Audley End	27. 6.95P
	(DH Gipsy Major)		G-AEOA/YU-PAX/UN-PAX		t/a P & A Wood (Current status unknown)		
G-AEOF(2)	Rearwin 8500 Sportster	462	N15863	1.12.81	Shipping & Airlines Ltd	Biggin Hill	5.10.01P
	(Le Blond 5DF 85hp)		NC15863				
G-AEPH	Bristol F.2b	7575	D8096	13.11.36	The Shuttleworth Trust	Old Warden	18. 9.03P
	(RR Falcon 3) (Original c/n 3746 & rebuilt c.1931)		G-AEPH/D8096		(As "D8096")		
G-AERV	Miles M.11A Whitney Straight	307	EM999	30.12.36	R.A.Seeley	Hill Farm, Durley	9. 4.66
			G-AERV		(New owner 5.02)		
G-AESB(2)	Aeronca C.3	A.638	N15742	5. 8.88	R.J.M.Turnbull	Rydinghurst Farm, Cranleigh	
			NC15742		(For rebuild 2002)		
G-AESE	de Havilland DH.87B Hornet Moth	8108	W5775	13. 1.37	J.G.Green	White Ox Mead, Bath	4.10.01
			G-AESE		"Sheena"		
G-AESZ	Chilton DW.1	DW.1/1		?. 1.37	R.E.Nerou	Rendcomb	13. 8.03P
	(Carden Ford 32hp)						
G-AEUJ	Miles M.11A Whitney Straight	313		19. 2.37	R.E.Mitchell (Stored 4.02)	RAF Cosford	4. 6.70
G-AEVS	Aeronca 100	AB.114		3.37	A.M.Lindsay & N.H.Ponsford	Breighton	4. 9.03P
	(JAP J.99) (Composite including parts of original G-AEXD)				"Jeeves"		
G-AEXD	Aeronca 100	AB.124		1. 4.37	M A & R W Mills (Brickhouse Farm, Frogland Cross)		20. 4.70P
	(JAP J.99) (Mainly comprises parts of G-AESP after rebuild in 1958: stored B R Cox 1998: current status unknown)						
G-AEXF	Percival P.6 Mew Gull	E.22	ZS-AHM	18. 5.37	R.A.Fleming	Breighton	7. 7.03P
	(Rebuilt as c/n PFA 13-10020)						
G-AEXT	Dart Kitten II	123		?. 4.37	A.J.Hartfield	Marsh Hill Farm, Aylesbury	27. 6.03P
	(JAP J.99)						
G-AEXZ	Piper J-2 Cub	997		5. 2.38	J.R. & Mrs M.Dowson	(Leicester)	2.11.78S
	(Continental A75)				(On rebuild 3.00)		
G-AEZF*	Short S.16 Scion 2	PA.1008	M-5	18. 6.37	R.Jackson/Acebell Aviation Ltd	Redhill	5. 5.54
			G-AEZF		(On rebuild 6.00)		
G-AEZJ	Percival P.10 Vega Gull	K.65	SE-ALA	2. 7.37	R.A.J.Spurrell	White Waltham	10. 6.04
			D-IXWD/PH-ATH/G-AEZJ				
G-AEZX(2)	Bücker Bü.133C Jungmeister	1018	N5A	10. 5.88	A.J.E.Ditheridge	Moat Farm, Milden	27. 7.00P
			PP-TDP		(As "LG+03" in Luftwaffe c/s)		

G-AFAA - G-AFZZ

G-AFAX	BA Eagle 2	138	VH-ACN	26.10.37	J.G.Green & M.J.Miller	Audley End	9. 5.05P
	(DH Gipsy Major)		G-AFAX				
G-AFCL	BA L.25c Swallow II	462		3.11.37	M.Mordue & C.P.Bloxham	Shotteswell	20. 8.03P
	(Pobjoy Niagara 3)						
G-AFDO(2)	Piper J-3C-65 Cub	2593	N21697	7. 6.88	R.Wald "Butter Cub"	Hill Farm, Durley	27. 7.99P
	(Frame No.2633)		NC21697		(On rebuild 12.02)		
G-AFEL(2)	Monocoupe 90A	A.782	N19432	7. 6.82	M.Rieser	(Germany)	24.11.03P
	(Lambert R266)		NC194323				
G-AFFD	Percival P.16A Q-Six	Q.21	(G-AIEY)	12. 2.38	B.D.Greenwood	Sywell	31. 8.56
			X9407/G-AFFD		(On rebuild 2002)		
G-AFFH	Piper J-2 Cub	1166	EC-ALA	26. 3.38	M.J.Honeychurch	(Pewsey)	29. 8.53
	(Continental A40)		G-AFFH		(On rebuild 10.01)		
G-AFGC	BA L.25c Swallow II	467	BK893	4. 4.38	G E.Arden	Thorns Cross Farm, Chudleigh	20. 3.51
	(Pobjoy Niagara 3)		G-AFGC		(Stored 1.98: current status unknown)		
G-AFGD*	BA L.25c Swallow II	469	BK897	4. 4.38	A.T.Williams, B.Arden, C.A.Cook, J.Hughes & M.Barmby		
	(Pobjoy Cataract 3)		G-AFGD		tr South Wales Swallow Group	Shobdon	9. 4.01P
					(Cancelled 6.4.01 by CAA)		
G-AFGE	BA L.25c Swallow II	470	BK894	4. 4.38	G.R.French "	Benson's Farm, Laindon	27. 7.98P
	(Pobjoy Niagara 2)		G-AFGE		"Maggie (Stored 8.01)		
G-AFGH	Chilton DW.1	DW.1/2		20. 3.38	M.L. & G.L.Joseph	Denford Manor, Hungerford	7. 7.83P
	(Lycoming O-145-A2) (To be re-engined with Carden-Ford)				(On rebuild 10.01)		
G-AFGI	Chilton DW.1	DW.1/3		30. 3.38	J.E. & K.A.A. McDonald	White Waltham	25. 6.03P
	(Walter Mikron 2)						
G-AFGM(2)	Piper J-4A Cub Coupe	4-943	N26895	30.12.81	P.H.Wilkinson	Carlisle	9.11.99P
			NC26895		(Noted 1.02)		
G-AFGZ	de Havilland DH.82A Tiger Moth	3700	G-AMHI	9. 5.38	M.R.Paul & P.A.Shaw	Lee-on-Solent	16. 3.03
			BB759/G-AFGZ				
G-AFHA(2)	Mosscraft MA.1	MA.1/2		27. 2.67	C.V.Butler	(Allesley, Coventry)	
					(Small components only stored)		
G-AFIN	Chrislea LC.1 Airguard	LC.1	BAPC.203	7. 7.38	N H Wright	Queach Farm, Bury St Edmunds	
					(On rebuild 12.01 using original wings, tailplane & metal fittings)		
G-AFIR	Luton LA-4 Minor	JSS.2		7. 7.38	A.J.Mason	(Aylesbury)	30. 7.71
	(JAP J-99)				(Damaged near Cobham 14.3.71 & on rebuild 2000)		
G-AFIU*	Parker CA-4 Parasol	CA-4		19.10.82	S P Connatty	Barton	
	(Luton Minor variant with reserved marks from 1938)				(Cancelled 31.3.99 by CAA) (Stored 2.00)		
G-AFJA	Taylor-Watkinson Dingbat	DB.100		2. 8.38	K.Woolley	(Berkswell, Coventry)	23. 6.75
	(Carden-Ford 32hp)				(Damaged Headcorn 19.5.75 and partially rebuilt: stored 12.01)		
G-AFJB	Foster-Wikner GM.1 Wicko	5	DR613	15. 8.38	J.Dibble	Hill Farm, Durley	12. 7.63
	(DH Gipsy Major 1)		G-AFJB		(On rebuild 5.02)		
G-AFJV(2)	Mosscraft MA.2	MA.2/2		27. 2.67	C.V.Butler	(Allesley, Coventry)	
					(Small components only stored)		
G-AFLW*	Miles M.17 Monarch	792		2.11.38	N.I.Dalziel	White Waltham	30. 7.98
					(Cancelled 3.5.01 by CAA)		
G-AFNG	de Havilland DH.94 Moth Minor	94014	AW112	2. 5.39	D.Saunders	Carnmore, Galway	21.10.98P
			G-AFNG		tr The Gullwing Trust (Noted 2.03)		
G-AFNI	de Havilland DH.94 Moth Minor	94035	W7972	11. 5.39	J.Jennings	Fenland	26. 5.67
			G-AFNI		(On rebuild 2002)		

G-AFOB	de Havilland DH.94 Moth Minor	94018	X5117 G-AFOB	16. 5.39	K.Cantwell *(New owner 2.02)*	(Royston)	11. 5.93P
G-AFOJ	de Havilland DH.94 Moth Minor *(Cabin)*	9407	E-1 E-0236/G-AFOJ	21. 7.39	R.M.Long *"Bugs 2"* *(On loan to De Havilland Heritage Museum) (Valid CofR 4.02)*	London Colney	27. 8.69P
G-AFPN	de Havilland DH.94 Moth Minor *(Now regd with c/n 94016)*	94044	X9297 G-AFPN	23. 5.39	J.W. & A.R.Davy	Redhill	2. 7.05
G-AFRZ	Miles M.17 Monarch	793	G-AIDE W6463/G-AFRZ	24. 3.39	R.E.Mitchell *(Believed stored 4.02)*	RAF Cosford	29. 6.70
G-AFSC	Tipsy Trainer 1 *(Walter Mikron 2)*	11		15. 7.39	D.M.Forshaw	Panshanger	2. 7.03P
G-AFSV	Chilton DW.1A *(Train 45hp)*	DW.1A/1		5. 4.39	R.E.Nerou *(For rebuild 8.02)*	(Coventry)	12. 7.72
G-AFSW*	Chilton DW.2	DW.2/1		6. 4.39	R.I.Souch	(Hedge End, Southampton)	
	(Not completed originally: fuselage box in poor condition: stored 1.00: current status unknown)						
G-AFTA	Hawker Tomtit *(Mongoose 3C)*	30380	K1786 G-AFTA/K1786	26. 4.39	The Shuttleworth Trust *(As "K1786")*	Old Warden	3. 7.03P
G-AFUP(2)	Luscombe 8A Master *(Continental A65)*	1246	N25370 NC25370	7. 6.88	R.Dispain *(Restored CofR 5.01)*	Chilbolton	12. 3.97P
G-AFVE(2)	de Havilland DH.82A Tiger Moth	83720	T7230	1. 2.78	W.N.Gibson t/a Tigerfly *(As "T-7230")*	Booker	30. 4.04T
G-AFVN	Tipsy Trainer 1 *(Walter Mikron 2)*	12		15. 7.39	D.F.Lingard	Fenland	2. 1.03P
G-AFWH(2)	Piper J-4A Cub Coupe *(Continental A65)*	4-1341	N33093 NC33093	14. 1.82	C.W.Stearn & R.D.W.Norton *(Stored 7.01)*	Southery	2. 7.01P
G-AFWI	de Havilland DH.82A Tiger Moth	82187	BB814 G-AFWI	19. 7.39	E.Newbigin Brown Shutters Farm, Norton St Philips, Somerset		12. 8.03
G-AFWT	Tipsy Trainer 1 *(Walter Mikron 2)*	13		1. 8.39	J.M.Lovell	Chilbolton	4. 4.03P
G-AFYD(2)	Luscombe 8AF Silvaire *(Continental C90)*	1044	N25120 NC25120	29. 7.75	J.D.Iliffe	Hampstead Norreys	14. 9.03
G-AFYO(2)	Stinson HW-75 Model 105 *(Continental C90)*	7039	F-BGQP NC22586 *(Probably ex Fr.Mil with identity "22586")*	25. 4.77	R.N.Wright Red House Farm, Gedney Marsh, Holbeach		8. 5.03P
G-AFZA(2)	Piper J-4A Cub Coupe *(Continental A65)*	4-873	N26198 NC26198	27. 6.84	P.G.R.Brown *(On rebuild Cheriton Bishop 11.02)*	(Crediton)	2.12.02P
G-AFZK(2)	Luscombe 8A Master *(Continental A65)*	1042	N25118 NC25118	24.10.88	M.G.Byrnes *(Current status unknown)*	Walkeridge Farm, Overton	29. 5.97P
G-AFZL(2)	Porterfield CP-50 *(Continental A50)*	581	N25401 NC25401	18. 3.82	P.G.Lucas & S.H.Sharpe tr The Skinny Bird Flyers	White Waltham	29. 6.03P
G-AFZN(2)	Luscombe 8A Master *(Continental A65)*	1186	N25279 NC25279	5.10.81	A.L.Young	Henstridge	2.12.02P

G-AGAA - G-AGZZ

G-AGAT(2)	Piper J-3F-50 Cub *(Franklin 4AC-150)*	4062	N26126 NC26126	17. 7.87	O.T.Taylor & C.J.Marshall	(Newark)	30. 4.02P
G-AGEG(2)	de Havilland DH.82A Tiger Moth	82710	N9146 D-EDIL/R.Neth AF A-32/PH-UFK/A-32/R4769	16. 8.82	A.J.Norman tr Norman Aeroplane Trust	Rendcomb	15. 5.04
G-AGFT(2)	Avia FL.3 *(CNA D4S)*	176	I-TOLB MM....	21. 8.84	K.Joynson & K.Cracknell *(As "W7" in Italian Co-Belligerent AF c/s)*	Sandtoft	4.12.03P
G-AGHY(2)	de Havilland DH.82A Tiger Moth *(On rebuild from ex Rollason airframe/components)*	82292	N9181	17. 2.88	P.Groves *(Current status unknown)*	Stubbington	
G-AGIV(2)	Piper J-3C-65 Cub (L-4J-PI) *(Frame No.12506)*	12676	OO-AFI OO-GBA/44-80380	13. 8.82	P.C. & F.M.Gill	Waits Farm, Belchamp Walter	2.10.02P
G-AGJG	de Havilland DH.89A Dragon Rapide	6517	X7344	25.10.43	M.J. & D.J.T.Miller *(On rebuild 2001)*	Duxford	15.11.74
G-AGLK	Taylorcraft Auster 5D	1137	RT475	25. 8.44	C R Harris	Rochester	13. 4.04
G-AGMI(2)	Luscombe 8A Master *(Continental A65)*	1569	N28827 NC28827	15.11.88	P.R.Bush	RAF Kinloss	9. 4.03P
G-AGNJ(2)	de Havilland DH.82A Tiger Moth *(Built DH Australia)*	660	VP-YOJ ZS-BGF/SAAF 2366	21. 2.89	B.P., A.J. & P.J.Borsberry *(On rebuild 6.95) (Current status unknown)*	Kidmore End, Reading	
G-AGOH	Auster V J/1 Autocrat	1442		19. 4.45	Leicestershire County Council Museums *(Valid CofR 4.02) (On loan to Newark Air Museum)*	Winthorpe	24. 8.95
G-AGOY	Miles M.48 Messenger 3	4690	EI-AGE G-AGOY/HB-EIP/G-AGOY/U-0247 *(On rebuild 4.92: as "U-0247")*	5. 6.45	P.A.Brook	West Chiltington, Pulborough	25.11.53
G-AGPK(2)	de Havilland DH.82A Tiger Moth	86566	N657DH F-BGDN/Fr AF/PG657	27.10.88	Delta Aviation Ltd *(Fitted with wings, tailplane, fin & rudder ex G-ANLH 2002)*	Sywell	23. 4.05T
G-AGSH	de Havilland DH.89A Dragon Rapide 6	6884	EI-AJO G-AGSH/NR808	25. 7.45	Techair London Ltd *"Jemma Meeson"* *(BEA titles)*	Bournemouth	11. 7.04
G-AGTM	de Havilland DH.89A Dragon Rapide 6	6746	JY-ACL D-ABP/G-AGTM/NF875	19. 9.45	Aviation Heritage Ltd	Coventry	11. 5.03T
G-AGTO	Auster V J/1 Autocrat	1822		2.10.45	M.J.Barnett & D.J.T.Miller	Duxford	22. 2.03
G-AGTT	Auster V J/1 Autocrat	1826		2.10.45	R.Farrer *(Stored 12.97) (Current status unknown)*	(Bromham, Bedford)	11. 2.93
G-AGVG	Auster V J/1 Autocrat *(Lycoming O-360-A2A + modified tail surfaces)*	1858		7.12.45	S.J.Riddington	Leicester	15. 6.03
G-AGVN	Auster V J/1 Autocrat	1873	EI-CKC G-AGVN	18. 1.46	R J Bentley Pallas West, Toomywvara, Co.Tipperary		28. 9.05
G-AGVV(2)	Piper J-3C-65 Cub (L-4H-PI)	11163	F BCZK Fr.AF/43-29872	10. 2.81	M.Molina-Ruano	(Malaga, Spain)	2. 9.03P
G-AGXN	Auster J/1N Alpha	1963		22. 1.46	Gentleman's Aerial Touring Carriage Syndicate Ltd 	Barton Ashes	16. 5.05
G-AGXU	Auster J/1N Alpha	1969		24. 1.46	B.H.Austen	Oaksey Park	25. 4.03
G-AGXV	Auster V J/1 Autocrat	1970		1. 2.46	B.S.Dowsett *"Pamela IV"*	Little Gransden	7. 9.03
G-AGYD	Auster J/1N Alpha	1985		4. 2.46	P.R.Hodson *(Damaged near Felthorpe 25.11.90: on rebuild 4.94: current status unknown)*	(Norwich)	24.11.90

G-AGYK	Auster V J/1 Autocrat	2002		4. 2.46	M.C.Hayes tr Autocraft Syndicate	Shobdon	25. 6.04
G-AGYT	Auster J/1N Alpha	1862		18. 1.46	P.J.Barrett	(Lightwater, Surrey)	27. 2.91
					(On overhaul 6.94: current status unknown)		
G-AGYU	de Havilland DH.82A Tiger Moth	85265	DE208	10. 1.46	P.L.Jones *(As "DE208")*	Ronaldsway	11. 8.04
G-AGYY(2)	Ryan ST3KR (PT-21-RY)	1167	N56792	15. 6.83	J.J.van Egmond	Hoogeveen, The Netherlands	19. 7.03P
	(Kinner R56)		41-1942		tr Nostalgic Flying *(As "27" in USAAC c/s)*		
G-AGZZ(2)	de Havilland DH.82A Tiger Moth	T256 & 926	N3862	14. 5.82	R.C.Mercer	(Pewsey)	23. 4.04
	(Built DH Aircraft Pty Ltd, Australia)		VH-BTU/VH-RNM/VH-BMY/A17-503				

G-AHAA - G-AHZZ

G-AHAG	de Havilland DH.89A Dragon Rapide	6926	RL944	31. 1.46	Pelham Ltd *(On rebuild 10.01)*	Membury	15. 7.73
G-AHAL	Auster J/1N Alpha	1870		31. 1.46	Wickenby Flying Club Ltd	Wickenby	7. 6.04T
G-AHAM	Auster V J/1 Autocrat	1885		21. 1.46	C.P.L.Jenkins	Rush Green	24.10.02
G-AHAN(2)	de Havilland DH.82A Tiger Moth	86553	N90406	31. 5.85	Tiger Associates Ltd	White Waltham	1. 6.04T
			F-BGDG/Fr.AF/PG644				
G-AHAP	Auster V J/1 Autocrat (Rover V-8)	1887		8. 2.46	M.J.Kirk *(New owner 6.02)*	Haverfordwest	20. 2.91P
G-AHAU	Auster V J/1-160 Autocrat	1850	(HB-EOL)	11. 2.46	A.C.Webber	Andreas, Isle of Man	13. 4.03
	(Lycoming O-320-A) *(Built-up fin/fuselage fillet)*						
G-AHAV*	Auster V J/1 Autocrat	1863	(HB-EOM)	13. 2.46	C.J.Freeman	Headcorn	21. 6.75
					(Cancelled 22.2.99 by CAA) (Fuselage stored 4.00)		
G-AHBL	de Havilland DH.87B Hornet Moth	8135	P6786	6. 2.46	H.D.Labouchere	Blue Tile Farm, Langham	9. 5.03
			CF-BFN				
G-AHBM	de Havilland DH.87B Hornet Moth	8126	P6785	6. 2.46	P.A. & E.P.Gliddon	Redhil I	21. 6.02
			CF-BFJ/(CF-BFO)/CF-BFJ				
G-AHCK*	Auster J/1N Alpha	1973		25. 3.46	Not known	Thwing, Great Driffield	
	(Orig regd as J/1 Autocrat)				*(Damaged in arson attack Ingoldmells 14.9.91: cancelled 22.4.94 by CAA) (Noted 3.02)*		
G-AHCL	Auster J/1N Alpha	1977	G-OJVC	13. 5.46	Electronic Precision Ltd	RAF Mona	10.10.91
			G-AHCL		*(On rebuild 8.92 with Lycoming 0-320: current status unknown)*		
G-AHCR	Gould-Taylorcraft Plus D Special	211	LB352	15. 4.46	D.E.H.Balmford & D.R.Shepherd	Dunkeswell	12. 9.03P
	(Continental C90)				tr Wagtail Flying Group		
G-AHEC(2)	Luscombe 8A Silvaire	3428	N72001	28.10.88	P.G.Baxter	Hill Farm, Nayland	17. 6.03P
	(Continental A65)		NC72001				
G-AHGD	de Havilland DH.89A Dragon Rapide	6862	NR786	1. 4.46	R.Jones t/a Southern Sailplanes	Membury	20. 9.92
					(Destroyed near.Audley End 30.6.91: components for possible rebuild 8.97)		
G-AHGW	Taylorcraft Plus D	222	LB375	2. 9.46	C.V.Butler	Shenington	3. 5.96P
					(Op Military Auster Flight) (As "LB375")		
G-AHGZ	Taylorcraft Plus D	214	LB367	24. 4.46	M.Pocock	Duxford	13.10.02
					(As "LB367") (To Stephen White mid 2001)		
G-AHHH	Auster 5 J/1N Alpha	2011	F-BAVR	11. 5.46	H.A.Jones	RAF Coltishall	2. 8.02P
			G-AHHH				
G-AHHT	Auster 5 J/1N Alpha	2022		11. 5.46	A.C.Barber & N.J.Hudson Durleighmarsh Farm, Rogate		31. 5.04
					tr Southdowns Auster Group		
G-AHIP(2)	Piper J-3C-65 Cub (L-4H-PI)	12122	OO-GEJ(2)	3. 7.85	A.R.M.Cot-Croft	Rayne Hall Farm, Rayne	11.12 03P
	(Frame No.11950)		OO-ALY/44-79826				
	(Officially regd with c/n 12008: see G-AJAD)						
G-AHIZ	de Havilland DH.82A Tiger Moth	86533	PG624	23. 4.46	CFG Flying Ltd	Cambridge	1. 6.03T
	(Regd with fuselage no.4610)						
G-AHKX	Avro 19 Srs.2	1333		18. 5.46	BAE Systems (Operations) Ltd	Old Warden	14.10.02P
G-AHLK	Taylorcraft E Auster III	700	NJ889	1. 5.46	E.T.Brackenbury *On rebuild 1.02)*	Leicester	21. 9.97
G-AHLT	de Havilland DH.82A Tiger Moth	82247	N9128	2. 5.46	K.J.Jarvis	Seppe, The Netherlands	1. 6.03
G-AHNR(2)	Taylorcraft BC-12D	7204	N43545	15.11.88	T.P.Hancock	Leicester	2. 6.03P
	(Continental A65)		NC43545				
G-AHOO(2)	de Havilland DH.82A Tiger Moth	8615	6940M	6. 6.85	J.T. & A.D.Milsom	Pewsey	10. 8.03
	(Regd with c/n 86149)		EM967				
G-AHPZ	de Havilland DH.82A Tiger Moth	83794	EI-AFJ	22. 5.46	N.J.Wareing	Goodwood	30. 4.04
			G-AHPZ/T7280				
G-AHRO(2)	Cessna 140	8069	N89065	25. 1.82	R.H.Screen	Ashcoft Fam, Winsford	20. 7.03
			NC89065				
G-AHSA	Avro 621 Tutor	-	K3215	21. 6.46	The Shuttleworth Trust	Old Warden	1. 5.03P
	(Lynx IVM)		G-AHSA/K3215		*(As "K3215")*		
G-AHSD	Taylorcraft Plus D	182	LB323	1. 7.46	A.L.Hall-Carpenter	(Thetford)	10. 9.62
					(On rebuild 8.95: current status unknown)		
G-AHSO	Auster 5 J/1N Alpha	2123		8. 8.46	W.P.Miller	Mavis Enderby	6. 4.95T
					(On rebuild 8.98: current status unknown))		
G-AHSP	Auster V J/1 Autocrat	2134	F-BGRO	8. 8.46	R.M.Weeks	Earls Colne	27. 9.03
			G-AHSP				
G-AHSS	Auster J/1N Alpha	2136		8. 8.46	A.M.Roche	Great Massingham	6. 7.03
G-AHST*	Auster J/1N Alpha	2137		8. 8.46	A.C.Frost	Standalone Farm, Meppershall	3. 7.03
					(Cancelled 24.7.01 by CAA)		
G-AHTE	Percival P.44 Proctor 5	Ae58		26. 6.46	D.K.Tregilgas	Great Oakley, Clacton	10. 8.61
					(Stored for rebuild 7.02)		
G-AHUF(2)	de Havilland DH.82A Tiger Moth	86221	A2123	26. 2.85	Dream Ventures Ltd	Bagby	22. 8.03T
			NL750		*(As "T7997")*		
G-AHUG	Taylorcraft Plus D	153	LB282	5. 6.46	D.Nieman	(Thame)	12. 7.70
G-AHUJ*	Miles M.14A Hawk Trainer 3	1900	R1914	6. 6.46	Not known	Strathallan	9. 7.98P
					(Cancelled 19.11.99 as WFU) (Stored 12.01 as "R1914")		
G-AHUV	de Havilland DH.82A Tiger Moth	3894	N6593	24. 6.46	A.D.Gordon	Blair Atholl	10. 7.00
G-AHVU	de Havilland DH.82A Tiger Moth	84728	T6313	14. 8.46	R.A.L.Hubbard *(As "T6313")*	West Meon	17. 3.03
G-AHVV	de Havilland DH.82A Tiger Moth	86123	EM929	24. 6.46	B.M.Pullen	Thruxton	18. 1.03
G-AHWJ	Taylorcraft Plus D	165	LB294	20. 6.46	M.Pocock *(New owner 1.03)*	Kemble	30. 6.71
G-AHXE	Taylorcraft Plus D	171	LB312	9. 7.46	Jenny M.C.Pothecary *(As "LB312")*	AAC Netheravon	17. 7.03P

G-AIAA - G-AIZZ

Reg	Type	c/n	Prev ID	Date	Owner	Location	Date
G-AIBH	Auster 5 J/1N Alpha	2113		19. 8.46	M.J.Bonnick	Standalone Farm, Meppershall	17. 7 02P
G-AIBM	Auster V J/1 Autocrat	2148		2. 9.46	D.G.Greatrex	Thatcham	9.11.04
G-AIBR	Auster V J/1 Autocrat	2151		2. 9.46	K.L.Clarke	(Horncastle)	24. 7.02T
G-AIBW	Auster J/1N Alpha	2158		2. 9.46	W.B.Bateson (*Stored 12.01*)	Blackpool	4. 5.97T
G-AIBX	Auster V J/1 Autocrat	2159		2. 9.46	B.H.Beeston tr The Wasp Flying Group	Little Gransden	5.12.05
G-AIBY	Auster V J/1 Autocrat	2160		2. 9.46	D.Morris	Sherburn in Elmet	13. 4.81
					(Stored 6.97) (Current status unknown)		
G-AICX(2)	Luscombe 8A Silvaire	2568	N71141	27. 1.88	R.V.Smith	Henstridge	8. 7.03P
	(Continental A65)		NC71141		*"Easy Grace"*		
G-AIDL	de Havilland DH.89A Dragon Rapide 6	6968	TX310	23. 8.46	Atlantic Air Transport Ltd (*Air Caernarfon titles*)	Coventry	13. 6.05T
G-AIDS	de Havilland DH.82A Tiger Moth	84546	T6055	22. 8.46	K.D.Pogmore & T.Dann	Benson's Farm, Laindon	24. 7.03
					"The Sorcerer"		
G-AIEK	Miles M.38 Messenger 2A	6339	U-9 2	7. 8.46	J.Buckingham	New Farm, Felton, Bristol	29. 8.03
					(As "RG333" in 2 TAF Comm Sqdn c/s)		
G-AIFZ	Auster J/1N Alpha	2182		2.11.46	M.D.Anstey	Rushett Manor, Chessington	20. 8.01
G-AIGD	Auster V J/1 Autocrat	2186		2.11.46	R.B.Webber	Trenchard Farm, Eggesford	5. 6.03P
	(Officially regd incorrectly as J/1N Alpha)						
G-AIGF	Auster J/1N Alpha	2188		5.11.46	A.R.C.Mathie	(Southampton)	17.11.05
G-AIGR*	Auster J/1N Alpha	2172		12.10.46	C.J.Baker	Carr Farm, Thorney, Newark	25. 4.88
	(Rebuilt 1953 with spare fuselage no.TAY/R/308G)				*(Damaged in gales Cranfield 3.86: cancelled 20.1.96 by CAA) (Original frame noted 1.03)*		
G-AIGT	Auster J/1N Alpha	2176		12.10.46	R.R.Harris (*New owner 4.02*)	Crowfield	22.10.76
G-AIGU*	Auster J/1N Alpha	2180		12.10.46	Not known		
						Fontenay-en-Contentin, Lower Normandy, France	5. 9.74S
					(Cancelled 1.7.92 as TWFU) (Unconfirmed frame noted 9.02)		
G-AIIH	Piper J-3C-65 Cub (L-4H-PI)	11945	44-79649	14. 9.46	J.A.de Salis	Oxford	6. 1.03P
G-AIJI*	Auster J/1N Alpha	2307		15. 4.47	C.J.Baker	Carr Farm, Thorney, Newark	
	(Originally regd as J/1 Autocrat)				*(Damaged in gales Humberside 12.1.75: cancelled 12.3.75 as WFU) (Frame for spares 1.03)*		
G-AIJM	Auster V J/4	2069	EI-BEU	13.11.46	N.Huxtable *"Priscilla"*	Cheddington	28. 3.97
			G-AIJM		*(Damaged near Tring 5.1.97: stored pending overhaul/repairs)*		
G-AIJT	Auster V J/4 Srs.100	2075		13.11.46	J.L.Thorogood	Pittrichie Farm, Whiterashes	5. 5.05
	(Continental O-200-A)				tr The Aberdeen Auster Flying Group		
G-AIKE	Taylorcraft J Auster 5	1097	NJ728	15.11.46	C.J.Baker	Carr Farm, Thorney, Newark	3. 2.66
	(Frame No.TAY 2450)				*(Crashed Luton 1.9.65 & dismantled 1.03) (Valid CofR @ 4.02)*		
G-AIPR	Auster V J/4	2084		9. 1.47	R.W. & Mrs M.A.Mills	Church Farm, North Moreton	27. 5.00P
					tr The MPM Flying Group		
G-AIPV	Auster V J/1 Autocrat	2203		9. 1.47	W.P.Miller *"Buttercup"*	Mavis Enderby	7. 2.05
G-AIRC	Auster V J/1 Autocrat	2215		13. 1.47	A.Noble	Perth	14. 1.04
G-AIRI*	de Havilland DH.82A Tiger Moth	3761	N5488	22.10.46	E.R.Goodwin	Little Gransden	9.11.81
					(Cancelled 3.4.89 as WFU) (Stored 10.01)		
G-AIRK	de Havilland DH.82A Tiger Moth	82336	N9241	22.10.46	R.C.Teverson, R.W.Marshall & C.E.McKinney		
						Waits Farm, Belchamp Walter	5. 7.04
G-AISA	Tipsy B Srs.1	17		24. 4.47	A.A.M. & C.W.N.Huke	RAF Shawbury	18. 2.03P
G-AISC	Tipsy B Srs.1	19		24. 4.47	D.R.Shepherd	Cumbernauld	23. 5.79P
					tr Wagtail Flying Group (*Stored 1.02*)		
G-AISS(2)	Piper J-3C-65 Cub (L-4H-PI)	12077	D-ECAV	3. 9.85	K.W.Wood & F.Watson	Insch	25. 6.97P
	(Frame No.11904)		SL-AAA/44-79781		*(Airframe & wings stored separately 3.02)*		
G-AIST	Supermarine 300 Spitfire IA	WASP/20/2	AR213	25.10.46	Sheringham Aviation UK Ltd	Booker	26. 3.02P
	(Built Westland Aircraft) (Also Heston Aircraft Company c/n HA1 6S/5 139)				*(As "AR213/PR-D" in 609 Sqdn c/s)*		
G-AISX	Piper J-3C-85 Cub (L-4H-PI)	11663	43-303722	8.10.46	A M Turney	Booker	21. 5.03P
	(Frame No.11489) (Rebuilt with ex Spanish airframe)				t/a Cubfly		
G-AIUA	Miles M.14A Hawk Trainer 3	2035	T9768	11.11.46	R.Trickett (*On rebuild 9.00*)	(King's Lynn)	13. 7.67P
	(Crashed Roborough 26.9.65: fuselage stored 1995 for long term rebuild: orig. centre section used to rebuild G-AKPF: wings fitted in 1960's from G-ANWO)						
G-AIUL*	de Havilland DH.89A Dragon Rapide 6	6837	NR749	8.11.46	I.Jones	Ley Farm, Chirk	29. 9.67
					(Cancelled 6.4.73 as WFU) (Fuselage noted 2.00)		
G-AIXJ	de Havilland DH.82A Tiger Moth	85434	DE426	28.11.46	D.Green	Goodwood	13. 8.03
	(Probably composite airframe rebuilt by Newbury Aeroplane Co 1991)						
G-AIXN	Automobilove Zavody Mraz M.1C Sokol	112	OK-BHA	22. 4.47	A.J.Wood	Breighton	5. 2.03P
G-AIYG(2)	SNCAN Stampe SV-4B	21	OO-CKZ	31. 8.89	R.Lageirse & H.Ewaut	(Drongen, Belgium)	7. 6.03
	(DH Gipsy Major)		F-BCKZ/Fr Mil				
G-AIYR	de Havilland DH.89A Dragon Rapide	6676	HG691	11.12.46	Spectrum Leisure Ltd	Clacton/Duxford	1. 5..05T
					(Op Classic Wings) "Classic Lady"		
G-AIYS	de Havilland DH.85 Leopard Moth	7089	YI-ABI	16.12.46	R.A.& V.A.Gammons	RAF Henlow	16. 4.04
			SU-ABM				
G-AIZU	Auster V J/1 Autocrat	2228		31. 1.47	C.J. & J.G.B.Morley	Popham	19. 6.03
G-AIZY	Auster V J/1 Autocrat	2233		31. 1.47	B.J.Richards (Brunel Technical College, Bristol)		20. 9.78S
					(Damaged Portskewett, Caldicot 8.89: on rebuild 6.91: current status unknown)		

G-AJAA - G-AJZZ

Reg	Type	c/n	Prev ID	Date	Owner	Location	Date
G-AJAD(2)	Piper J-3C-65 Cub (L-4H-PI)	12008	OO-GEJ(1)	26. 6.84	C R Shipley	(Bristol)	20.12.02P
	(Frame No.11835) (Regd with c/n 11700)				*44-79712 (Airframe has original fuselage of OO-GEJ discarded in a rebuild in 70s: OO-GEJ was rebuilt using Frame No.11950 (c/n 12122) ex OO-ALY/44-79826 & is now G-AHIP: OO-ALY was rebuilt from c/n 11700 ex OO-TON/43-30409)*		
G-AJAE	Auster J/1N Alpha	2237		4. 2.47	J Cooke tr Lichfield Auster Group	(Lichfield)	5. 7.03
G-AJAJ*	Auster J/1N Alpha	2243		4. 2.47	R.B.Lawrence	Trenchard Farm, Eggesford	18. 4.94
					(Stored 6.01: cancelled 24. 1.03 by CAA)		
G-AJAM	Auster V J/2 Arrow	2371		8. 2.47	D.A.Porter	Griffins Farm, Temple Bruer	14. 6.03P
G-AJAP(2)	Luscombe 8A Silvaire	2305	N45778	26. 1.89	R J Thomas	Hamilton Farm, Bilsington	1. 8.03P
	(Continental A65)		NC45778				
G-AJAS	Auster J/1N Alpha	2319		14. 3.47	C.J.Baker	Carr Farm, Thorney, Newark	11. 4.90
					(Valid CofR 4.02: noted 1.03)		

Reg	Type	c/n	Prev ID	Date	Owner	Location	Last
G-AJBJ*	de Havilland DH.89A Dragon Rapide	6765	NF894	20. 1.47	John Pierce Aviation Ltd	Ley Farm, Chirk	14 .9.61T
	(Cancelled 16.12.91 by CAA) (Under rebuild 9.00)						
G-AJCL(2)*	de Havilland DH.89A Dragon Rapide	6722	NF851	7. 9.48	John Pierce Aviation Ltd	Ley Farm, Chirk	
	(WFU Shobdon 11.1.71 &:broken up: cancelled 24.5.71) (Noted 10.01)						
G-AJCP(2)	Rollason-Druine D.31 Turbulent	PFA 512		9. 2.59	B.R.Pearson	Eaglescott	4. 9.78S
	(Ardem 4C02)				tr Turbulent Group *(Stored 10.95) (Current status unknown)*		
G-AJEE*	Auster V J/1 Autocrat	2309		14. 3.47	A.R.Carillo De Albornoz	Ronaldsway	10. 7.89
	(Stored 8.92: cancelled 1.9.00 by CAA) (Current status unknown)						
G-AJEH	Auster J/1N Alpha	2312		14. 3.47	J.T.Powell-Tuck *(Current status unknown)* (Pontypool)		28. 5.90
G-AJEM*	Auster V J/1 Autocrat	2317	F-BFPB	14. 3.47	K.A.Jones	Haverfordwest	18. 2.72
			G-AJEM		*(Cancelled 1.9.00 by CAA)*		
G-AJES(2)	Piper J-3C-65 Cub (L-4H-PI)	11776	OO-ACB	21. 9.84	G.W.Jarvis	Shifnal	24. 7.03P
	(Frame No.11602)		43-30485		*(As "330485/44/C" in USAAC c/s)*		
G-AJGJ	Taylorcraft J Auster 5	1147	RT486	31. 1.47	D.Gotts & E.J.Downing	Bournemouth	19. 7.03
					tr Auster RT486 Flying Group *(As "RT486/PF-A")*		
G-AJHS	de Havilland DH.82A Tiger Moth	82121	N6866	12. 2.47	J.M.Voeten & H.Van Der Pauw		
					(Op Vliegend Museum) Seppe, The Netherlands		18. 6.03
G-AJHU*	de Havilland DH.82A Tiger Moth	83900	T7471	12. 2.47	(P Siegwald)	Orbigny, Indre-et-Loire, France	23. 8.98T
					(As "T7471" 8.00: on rebuild 2001: cancelled 4.4.02 by CAA)		
G-AJIH	Auster V J/1 Autocrat	2318		2. 4.47	A.H.Diver	Newtownards, Co.Down	19.11.94
					(Stored 3.01: cancelled 23.4.02 by CAA)		
G-AJIS	Auster J/1N Alpha	2336		30. 4.47	J.D.Smith & J.M.Hodgson	Baxby Manor, Husthwaite	25. 5.03
					tr Husthwaite Auster Group		
G-AJIT	Auster V J/1 Kingsland	2337		30. 4.47	A.J.Kay	Netherthorpe	14. 6.03P
	(Continental O-200-A)				tr G-AJIT Group		
G-AJIU	Auster V J/1 Autocrat	2338		30. 4.47	M.D.Greenhalgh	Netherthorpe	20. 6.03
G-AJIW	Auster J/1N Alpha	2340		30. 4.47	Truman Aviation Ltd	Nottingham	22. 8.04
G-AJJS(2)	Cessna 120	13047	8R-GBO	7. 1.87	R.W.Marchant, I.D.Ranger & S.C.Parsons		
	(Continental O-200-A)		VP-GBO/VP-TBO/N1106M/YV-T-CTA/NC2786N tr Robhurst Flying Group			Little Robhurst Farm, Woodchurch		8. 5.03P
	(Thought rebuilt 1994 with new imported airframe)						
G-AJJT(2)	Cessna 120	12881	N2621N	27. 1.88	J.S.Robson	Franklyns Field, Chewton Mendip	27.11.03P
	(Continental C85)		NC2621N				
G-AJJU(2)	Luscombe 8E Silvaire	2295	N45768	10. 1.89	S.C.Weston & R.J.Hopcraft	Enstone	20. 8.02P
	(Continental C85)		NC45768				
G-AJKB(2)	Luscombe 8E Silvaire	3058	N71631	4. 1.89	A.F.Hall & S.P.Collins	Tibenham	23. 8.99P
	(Continental C85)		NC71631		*(Noted 6.02)*		
G-AJOA	de Havilland DH.82A Tiger Moth	83167	T5424	29. 4.47	Aero Antiques	Durley	22. 5.03
	(Badly damaged landing Lotmead Farm, Wanborough, Swindon 13.5.01: sold 10.01 for rebuild)						
G-AJOE	Miles M.38 Messenger 2A	6367		28. 4.47	P.W.Bishop	Kemble	18.10.04
G-AJON(2)	Aeronca 7AC Champion	7AC-2633	OO-TWH	3. 1.86	A.Biggs & J.L.Broad	Shenington	30. 6.02P
					tr Oscar November 92 Syndicate		
G-AJPI	Fairchild F.24R-46A Argus 3	851	HB614	26. 4.47	K.A.Doornbos	(Eelde, The Netherlands)	30. 1.04
	(UC-61A-FA)		43-14887		*(As "314887" in USAAF c/s)*		
G-AJRB	Auster V J/1 Autocrat	2350		12. 5.47	RB Aeroclub Ltd tr RB Flying Group	Sywelll	8. 3.04
G-AJRC	Auster V J/1 Autocrat	2601		12. 5.47	M Barker	Willy Howe Farm, Wold Newton	14. 7.02
G-AJRE	Auster V J/1 Autocrat	2603		12. 5.47	R.R.Harris *(On rebuild 1.03)*	(Stowmarket)	8. 8.02
G-AJRS	Miles M.14A Hawk Trainer 3	1750	P6382	30. 4.47	The Shuttleworth Trust	Old Warden	14. 8.03P
	(Composite a/c which flew as "G-AJDR" 1.54/3.71)		G-AJDR/G-AJRS/P6382		*(As "P6382/C" in 16 EFTS c/s)*		
G-AJTW	de Havilland DH.82A Tiger Moth	82203	N6965	21. 5.47	J.A.Barker *(As "N6965/FL-J")*	Tibenham	9. 9.00
	(Crashed landing Raydon near Ipswich 7.6.99 & extensively damaged) (Current status unknown)						
G-AJUD*	Auster V J/1 Autocrat	2614		5. 6.47	C.L.Sawyer	(Bromham, Bedford)	18. 5.74
	(On rebuild 12.97: cancelled 31.3.99 by CAA) (Noted for sale 2000)						
G-AJUE	Auster V J/1 Autocrat	2616		5. 6.47	P.H.B.Cole	Craysmarsh Farm, Melksham	31.10.02
G-AJUL	Auster J/1N Alpha	2624		18. 6.47	M.J.Crees	Halstead, Essex	11. 9.81
					(On rebuild 12.90)		
G-AJVE	de Havilland DH.82A Tiger Moth	85814	DE943	28. 5.47	R.A.Gammons	RAF Henlow	10. 6.03
	(Composite 1981 rebuild including substantial parts of G-APGL c/n 86460/NM140)						
G-AJVH*	Fairey Swordfish II	---	LS326	28. 5.47	Royal Navy Historic Flight	RNAS Yeovilton	
	"City of Liverpool" (Cancelled 30.4.59 as restored to RN) (As "LS326/L2" in 836 Sqdn c/s)						
G-AJWB	Miles M.38 Messenger 2A	6699		17. 6.47	G.E.J.Spooner	Earls Colne	23. 1.05
G-AJXC*	Taylorcraft J Auster 5	1409	TJ343	11. 6.47	J.Graves	Scotland Farm, Hook	2. 8.82
	(Damaged Hook in gales 16.10.87) (Cancelled 3.4.89 by CAA) (Stored 9.94: fuselage noted 10.02)						
G-AJXV	Taylorcraft G Auster 4	1065	F-BEEJ	8. 9.47	Barbara A.Farries	Carr Farm, Thorney, Newark	27. 2.05
			G-AJXV/NJ695		*(As "NJ695") "Little Lulu"*		
G-AJXY	Taylorcraft G Auster 4	792	MT243	4. 5.48	D.A.Hall	(Melton Mowbray)	10.11.70
					(On rebuild 1993: new owner 7.00)		
G-AJYB	Auster J/1N Alpha	847	MS974	3. 2.49	P.J.Shotbolt	Ingthorpe Farm, Great Casterton, Lincs	25. 7.02

G-AKAA - G-AKZZ

Reg	Type	c/n	Prev ID	Date	Owner	Location	Last
G-AKAT	Miles M.14A Hawk Trainer 3	2005	F-AZOR	2. 7.47	J.D.Haslam	Breighton	31. 7.03P
			G-AKAT/T9738		*(As "T9738")*		
G-AKAZ(2)	Piper J-3C-65 Cub	AN.1 & 8499	F-BFYL	19. 4.82	Frazerblades Ltd	Duxford	26. 7.03P
	(L-4A-PI) *(Frame No.8616)*		Fr Mil/42-36375		*(As "57-H" in 83rd FS/78th FG USAAF c/s)*		
G-AKBO	Miles M.38 Messenger 2A	6378		15. 7.47	P.R.Holloway	Old Warden	3. 8.03
G-AKDN	de Havilland DHC.1A Chipmunk 10	11		14. 8.47	P.S.Derry	Bagby	17. 5.03
G-AKDW	de Havilland DH.89A Dragon Rapide	6897	F-BCDB	25. 8.47	De Havilland Aircraft Museum Trust Ltd	London Colney	8. 5.59
			G-AKDW/YI-ABD/NR833		*"City of Winchester" (On rebuild 3.02)*		
G-AKEZ	Miles M.38 Messenger 2A	6707		27. 8.47	P.G.Lee	Fanners Farm, Great Waltham, Essex	15.11.68
					(Noted on rebuild 10.01)		
G-AKGD*	Miles M.65 Gemini 1A	6492		11. 9.47	Miles Aircraft Collection	(NK)	14.11.66
					(Cancelled 22.11.73 as WFU) (Parts only stored off-site 2.00)		
G-AKHP	Miles M.65 Gemini 1A	6519		3.10.47	P.A.Brook	Shoreham	11. 6.03

G-AKHW*	Miles M.65 Gemini 1A	6524	ZK-KHW	21.10.47	(S Smith)	(Dairy Flat, New Zealand)	
					(Shipped to New Zealand 16.5.91 & cancelled 9.12.94: noted 2.00 as "G-AKHW")		
G-AKHZ*	Miles M.65 Gemini 7	6527		21.10.47	The Miles Aircraft Collection	(NK)	8. 1.64
					(Composite airframe with parts from G-ALMU, G-ALUG & G-AMME: on rebuild 5.01)		
G-AKIB(2)	Piper J-3C-90 Cub	12311	OO-RAY	18. 4.84	M.C.Bennett	Bodmin	20. 8.03P
	(L-4H-PI) *(Frame No.12139)*		44-80015		*(As "480015/M/44" in USAAC c/s)*		
G-AKIF	de Havilland DH.89A Dragon Rapide	6838	LN-BEZ	24. 9.47	Airborne Taxi Services Ltd	(London SW1)	19. 8.03T
			G-AKIF/NR750				
G-AKIN	Miles M.38 Messenger 2A	6728		19. 9.47	D.L.Sentance tr Sywell Messenger Group	Sywell	10.10.05
G-AKIU	Percival P.44 Proctor 5	Ae129		20. 2.48	Air Atlantique Ltd *(Current status unknown)*	Coventry	24. 1.65
G-AKKB	Miles M.65 Gemini 1A	6537		28.10.47	J.Buckingham	New Farm, Felton, Bristol	29. 4.05
					(Air Total c/s)		
G-AKKH	Miles M.65 Gemini 1A	6479	OO-CDO	23. 7.48	J.S.Allison	RAF Halton	13.11.03T
G-AKOE*	de Havilland DH.89A Dragon Rapide 4	6601	X7484	3.12.47	J.E.Pierce	Ley Farm, Chirk	25. 7.82
					(British Airways titltes) (Stored 2.00) (Cancelled 18.6.02 by CAA)		
G-AKPF	Miles M.14A Hawk Trainer 3	2228	V1075	27. 1.48	P.R.Holloway (As "V1075" in RAF c/s)	Old Warden	9. 4.03P
	(i) Rebuilt 1955 as composite with centre-section from G-AIUA, fuselage from G-ANLT, wings from G-AHYL)						
	(ii) Rebuilt 1970/80 with about 10% of fuselage from G-AKPF: tail unit also from G-ANLT)						
G-AKRA(2)	Piper J-3C-65 Cub	11255	I-FIVI	15. 6.84	W.R.Savin	(Cambridge)	
	(L-4H-PI) *(Frame No.11080)*		43-29964		*(On rebuild 9.00)*		
G-AKRP	de Havilland DH.89A Dragon Rapide 4	6940	CN-TTO	26. 1.48	R.H.Ford	Sywell	26. 6.03
			(F-DAFS)/G-AKRP/RL958		c/o Fordaire Aviation Ltd "Northamptonshire Rose"		
G-AKSY	Taylorcraft J Auster 5D	1567	F-BGOO	10. 2.48	A.Brier	Breighton	22. 3.04
			G-AKSY/TJ534		*(As "TJ534")*		
G-AKSZ	Taylorcraft J Auster 5C	1503	F-BGPQ	10. 2.48	P.W.Yates & R.G.Darbyshire	(Chorley)	9. 5.02
	(DH Gipsy Major 1) *(Large fin & rudder)*		G-AKSZ/TJ457				
G-AKTH(2)	Piper J-3C-65 Cub (L-4J-PI)	13211	OO-AGL	14. 7.86	G.J.Harry, The Viscount Goschen		
	(Frame No.13041) (Regd with incorrect c/n 13047)		PH-UCR/45-4471			Bradleys Lawn, Heathfield	14. 4.03P
G-AKTI(2)	Luscombe 8A Silvaire	4101	N1374K	27. 5.87	M.W.Olliver	Farley Farm, Romsey	3.3.02P
	(Continental A65)		NC1374K				
G-AKTK(2)	Aeronca 11AC Chief	11AC-1017	N9379E	13. 3.89	R.W.Marshall, G.C.Jones & R Lloyd		
	(Continental A65)		NC9379E			Waits Farm, Belchamp Walter	11.9.03P
G-AKTN(2)	Luscombe 8A Silvaire	3540	N77813	22. 7.88	D.Taylor	Clacton	9. 1.03P
	(Continental A65)		NC77813				
G-AKTO(2)	Aeronca 7BCM Champion	7AC-940	N8515X	19. 5.88	D.C.Murray	Lee-on-Solent	26. 9.03P
	(Continental A75) *(Modified ex 7AC standard 1950)*		N82311/NC82311				
G-AKTP(2)	Piper PA-17 Vagabond	17-82	N4683H	24. 6.88	P.J.B.Lewis	Swansea	5. 8.03P
	(Continental C85)		NC4683H		tr Golf Tango Papa Group		
G-AKTR(2)	Aeronca 7AC Champion	7AC-3017	N58312	19. 6.89	C.Fielder	New Farm, Felton	18. 7.03P
			NC58312		"Eddie"		
G-AKTS(2)	Cessna 120	11875	N77434	26. 5.88	W.Fairney	Kemble	17. 6.03P
			NC77434		"Southern Belle"		
G-AKTT(2)	Luscombe 8A Silvaire	3279	N71852	21. 7.88	S.J.Charters	(Leeds)	23. 6.92P
	(Continental A65)		NC71852		*(Crashed 6.7.91: stored 1.96) (Current status unknown)*		
G-AKUE(2)	de Havilland DH.82A Tiger Moth	P.68	ZS-FZL	12. 2.86	D.F.Hodgkinson	(Redhill)	4. 4.04T
	(Built OGMA)		CR-AGM/FAP				
G-AKUF(2)	Luscombe 8F Silvaire	4794	N2067K	1. 8.88	E.J.Lloyd	Cardington	7. 8.03P
	(Continental C90)		NC2067K				
G-AKUG(2)	Luscombe 8A Silvaire	3689	N77962	21. 7.88	P Groves	Lee-on-Solent	26. 3.03P
	(Continental A65)		NC77962		tr G-AKUG Group		
G-AKUH(2)	Luscombe 8E Silvaire	4644	N1917K	24.10.88	I.M.Bower	Leicester	18.10.02P
	(Continental O-200-A)		NC1917K		"Lucy Too"		
G-AKUI(2)	Luscombe 8E Silvaire	2464	N45937	24.10.88	D.A.Sims	Yeatsall Farm, Abbots Bromley	17. 3.03P
	(Continental O-200-A)		NC45937				
G-AKUJ(2)	Luscombe 8E Silvaire	5282	N2555K	4. 8.88	R.C.Green	Coventry	8.11.03P
	(Continental C85)		NC2555K				
G-AKUK(2)	Luscombe 8A Silvaire	5793	N1166B	28.10.88	N.B.Brown	Leckhampstead Farm, Newbury	21. 6.02P
	(Continental A65)		NC1166B		tr Leckhampstead Flying Group		
G-AKUL(2)	Luscombe 8A Silvaire	4189	N1462K	9. 2.89	E.A.Taylor	Southend	21. 5.90P
	(Continental A65)		NC1462K		*(Noted 2.03)*		
G-AKUM(2)	Luscombe 8F Silvaire	6452	N2025B	17. 2.88	D A Young	North Weald	7.11.03P
	(Continental C90)						
G-AKUN(2)	Piper J-3C-85 Cub	6914	N38304	13. 1.89	W.R.Savin	Cold Harbour Farm, Willingham	29. 4.02P
			NC38304				
G-AKUO(2)	Aeronca 11AC Chief	11AC-1376	N9730E	16. 1.89	L.W.Richardson	Denham	17. 9.32P
			NC9730E				
G-AKUP(2)	Luscombe 8E Silvaire	5501	N2774K	9. 5.89	D.A.Young	North Weald	
	(Lycoming O-320)		NC2774K		*(Stored 3.97: on rebuild 12.02)*		
G-AKUR(2)	Cessna 140	13819	N1647V	26. 1.89	J.Greenaway & C.A.Davis	Popham	21. 9.95
			NC1647V		*(Current status unknown)*		
G-AKUW	Chrislea CH.3 Srs.2 Super Ace	105		8. 3.48	J & S Rickett	North Coates	15. 5.03P
G-AKVF	Chrislea CH.3 Srs.2 Super Ace	114	AP-ADT	8. 3.48	B.Metters	Bourne Park, Hurstbourne Tarrant	15. 4.03P
			G-AKVF				
G-AKVM(2)	Cessna 120	13431	N3173N	10. 1.89	N.Wise & S.Walker	Croft-on-Tees, Darlington	5. 6.03P
			NC3173N				
G-AKVN(2)	Aeronca 11AC Chief 11	AC-469	N3742B	13. 1.89	C.E.Ellis	Priory Farm, Tibenham	27 5.03P
			NC3742B		tr Breckland Aeronca Group		
G-AKVO(2)	Taylorcraft BC-12D	9845	N44045	10. 1.89	R.J.Whybrow & M.J.Steward	Priory Farm, Tibenham	16 4.03P
	(Continental A65)		NC44045		tr Albion Flyers		
G-AKVP(2)	Luscombe 8A Silvaire	5549	N2822K	21. 7.48	J M Edis	Charity Farm, Baxterley	4.11.02P
	(Continental A65)		NC2822K				
G-AKVR	Chrislea CH3 Srs.4 Skyjeep	125	VH-OLD	8. 3.48	N.D.Needham	Old Manor Farm, Anwick	
			VH-RCD/VH-BRP/G-AKVR		*(New owner 3.01)*		
G-AKVZ	Miles M.38 Messenger 4B	6352	RH427	25. 6.48	Shipping & Airlines Ltd	Biggin Hil	l4.10.03

G-AKWS	Auster 5A-160	1237	RT610	1. 4.48	Fast Aerospace Ltd	Crowfield	4. 6.03
	(Lycoming O-320)				*(As "RT610")*		
G-AKWT*	Taylorcraft J Auster 5	998	MT360	1. 4.48	C.J.Baker	Carr Farm, Thorney, Newark	22. 7.49
	(Crashed Tollerton 7.8.48) (Derelict frame stored 1.03)						
G-AKXP	Taylorcraft J Auster 5	1017	NJ633	13. 4.48	M.Pocock	RAF Keevil	19.12.70
	(Crashed St.Mary's, Isles of Scilly 9.4.70: noted less wings 2.03 as NJ633)						
G-AKXS	de Havilland DH.82A Tiger Moth	83512	T7105	13. 4.48	J. & G.J.Eagles	Oaksey Park	21. 3.03
	(Spun into ground White Waltham 21.7.02 & destroyed)						
G-AKZN*	Percival P.34A Proctor III	K.386	8380M	24. 5.48	Royal Air Force Museum Reserve Collection		
			Z7197		*(As "Z7197")*	RAF Stafford	29.11.63
	(Cancelled 27.9.63 as Marks WFU & reverted to Military Marks)						

G-ALAA - G-ALZZ

G-ALAH*	Miles M.38 Messenger 4A	-	RH377	28. 5.48	Not known	Sabadell, Barcelona, Spain	18. 4.65
	(WFU 18.4.65) (Stored as "G-ALAH" 3.95: noted 11.01)						
G-ALBD	de Havilland DH.82A Tiger Moth	84130	T7748	27. 5.48	C.H.Schoonbeek	Midden Zeeland, The Netherlands	31.10.81
	(Damaged Leopoldsburg, Belgium 24.5.81: noted 9.02 with Gyrocopter Aviation being rebuilt for static display)						
G-ALBJ	Taylorcraft J Auster 5	1831	TW501	3. 6.48	P.N.Elkington	Bloxholm, Sleaford	23. 8.03
G-ALBK	Taylorcraft J Auster 5	1273	RT644	3. 6.48	S.J.Wright	(Boston)	17. 4.03
G-ALEH(2)	Piper PA-17 Vagabond	17-87	N4689H	17. 8.81	A.D.Pearce	White Waltham	28. 3.03P
	(Continental A65)		NC4689H				
G-ALFA	Taylorcraft J Auster 5	1236	RT607	20.10.48	S.P.Barrett	Sturgate	14. 9.04
	(P/i uncertain as c/n 1236 considered sold as HB-EOC 4.48: reported as c/n 826 (MS958) but doubtful) tr Golf Alfa Auster Group						
G-ALGA(2)	Piper PA-15 Vagabond	15-348	N4575H	3.12.86	G.A.Brady	Enstone	7.10.03P
	(Lycoming O-145)		NC4575H				
G-ALGT	Supermarine 379 Spitfire F.Mk.XIVc	6S/432263	RM689	9. 2.49	Rolls-Royce plc	Filton	
			"RM619"/G-ALGT/RM689		*(Destroyed in crash Woodford 27.6.92: under restoration 2002)*		
G-ALIJ(2)	Piper PA-17 Vagabond	17-166	N4866H	13. 2.87	A.S.Cowan	Popham	19. 3.02P
	(Continental A65)				tr Popham Flying Group G-ALIJ		
G-ALIW	de Havilland DH.82A Tiger Moth	82901	N27WB	17. 8.81	D.I.M.Geddes & F.R.Curry	Shoreham	14. 8.03
			ZK-ATI/NZ899/R5006		tr Provost Flying Group		
G-ALJF	Percival P.34A Proctor 3	K.427	Z7252	3. 3.49	J.F.Moore	Biggin Hill	8. 7.04
G-ALJL	de Havilland DH.82A Tiger Moth	84726	T6311	7. 3.49	D & R I Souch	Hill Farm, Durley	28. 9.50
	(On long term rebuild from components 8.00)						
G-ALNA	de Havilland DH.82A Tiger Moth	85061	T6774	11. 4.49	R.J.Doughton	Vendee Air Park, France	11.11.01T
	(Brooklands Aviation titles)						
G-ALND	de Havilland DH.82A Tiger Moth	82308	N9191	12. 4.49	J.T.Powell-Tuck	Abergavenny	11. 4.82
	(As "N9191" in RN c/s) (Crashed Panshanger 8.3.81 & on rebuild 3.96)						
G-ALNV*	Taylorcraft J Auster 5	1216	RT578	21. 4.49	C.J.Baker	Carr Farm, Thorney, Newark	4. 7.50
	(WFU & frame stored 1.03)						
G-ALOD(2)	Cessna 140	14691	N2440V	14.10.83	J.R.Stainer	Whitehall Farm, Benington	11. 1.05
G-ALRI	de Havilland DH.82A Tiger Moth	83350	ZK-BAB	2. 5.51	Wessex Aviation & Transport Ltd	Chalmington	19. 8.94
			G-ALRI/T5672		*(As "T5672" in RAF c/s) (For restroration 2003)*		
G-ALTO(2)	Cessna 140	14253	N2040V	19. 1.82	J.M.Edis	Charity Farm, Baxterley	3. 7.04
	(Continental C85)						
G-ALTW*	de Havilland DH.82A Tiger Moth	84177	T7799	13. 6.49	A.Mangham	Denford Manor, Hungerford	8. 6.70
	(Crashed Panshanger 5.11.69: cancelled 7.9.81 by CAA) (Tailplane & wings stored 10.01)						
G-ALUC	de Havilland DH.82A Tiger Moth	83094	R5219	28. 6.49	D.R. & Mrs M.Wood		
					Fowle Hall Farm, Paddock Wood, Kent		7.11.04
G-ALVP*	de Havilland DH.82A Tiger Moth	82711	R4770	26. 9.49	D & R Leatherland	(Nottingham)	15. 2.61
	(CofA expired & WFU 1961) (On rebuild 2002)						
G-ALWB	de Havilland DHC.1 Chipmunk 22A	C1/0100	OE-ABC	28.12.49	D J Neville & P A Dear-Neville	(Royston)	18. 5.03
			G-ALWB				
G-ALWS	de Havilland DH.82A Tiger Moth	82415	N9328	24. 1.50	A.P.Beynon	Welshpool	
	(Officially regd with c/n 82413)				*(On rebuild 8.00)*		
G-ALWW	de Havilland DH.82A Tiger Moth	86366	NL923	24. 1.50	D.E.Findon	Bidford	11. 3.03
					tr Stratford-upon-Avon Tiger Moth Group		
G-ALXZ	Taylorcraft J Auster 5-150	1082	D-EGOF	1. 2.50	M.F.Cuming	Sackville Farm, Riseley	12. 7.03
	(Lycoming O-320) (Frame No.TAY24070)		PH-NER/G-ALXZ/NJ689				
G-ALYG	Taylorcraft J Auster 5D	835	MS968	14. 3.50	A.L.Young	Henstridge	19. 1.70
	(Officially regd with incorrect identity MT968:)				*(Frame stored 8.02: for rebuild as Auster 5)*		
G-ALYW(2)	de Havilland DH.106 Comet 1	06009	(G-ALYV)	18. 9.51	RAF Exhibition Production & Transportation Team		
	(BU 6.55: fuselage converted to "Nimrod MRA.4" guise as "XV238/41") RAF Cranwell						14. 6.54

G-AMAA - G-AMZZ

G-AMAW	Luton LA-4 Minor	JRC.1 & SA.I		29. 4.50	R.H.Coates	Breighton	6. 8.88P
	(Bristol Cherub 3) (Aka as Swalesong SA.I)				*(Stored 3..02)*		
G-AMBB	de Havilland DH.82A Tiger Moth	85070	T6801	1. 5.50	J.Eagles	Oaksey Park	
	(Composite rebuild - parts to "G-MAZY" ? - see SECTION 9, PART 2(i): on rebuild 6.95) (Current status unknown)						
G-AMCA	Douglas C-47B-30DK Dakota 3	16218/32966	KN487	1. 6.50	Atlantic Air Transport Ltd	Coventry	10.12.00A
			44-76634		*(Partially dismantled 1.02)*		
G-AMCK	de Havilland DH.82A Tiger Moth	84641	N65N	15. 6.50	Avia Special Ltd	Sherburn-in-Elmet	15. 3.04T
			C-GBBF/SLN-05/D-EGXY/HB-UAC/G-AMCK/T6193				
G-AMCM	de Havilland DH.82A Tiger Moth	85295	DE249	14.12.50	A K & J.I Cooper	Denford Manor, Hungerford	28. 5.56
	(Regd with c/n "89259")				*(Crashed near Somerton 25.9.55: rear fuselage frame on restoration 10.01 but not original G-AMCM!)*		
G-AMEN(2)	Piper PA-18 Super Cub 95 (L-18C-PI)	18-1998	(G-BJTR)	29.12.81	A.Lovejoy & W.Cook	Popham	26. 7.03P
	(Frame No.18-1963) (Italian rebuild c/n OMA.71-08)		MM52-2398 "EI.71"/I-EIAM/MM52-2398/52-2398 tr Sierra Golf Flying Group				
G-AMHF	de Havilland DH.82A Tiger Moth	83026	R5144	6. 2.51	Wavendon Social Housing Ltd	Sywell	14. 9.03
	(Rebuilt with components from G-BABA c/n 86584 ex F-BGDT/PG687)						

Reg	Type	c/n	Prev id	Date	Owner	Location	Date
G-AMHJ*	Douglas C-47A-25DK Dakota 6	13468	SU-AZI	6. 2.51	Atlantic Air Transport Ltd	Coventry	5.12.00A

G-AMHJ/ZS-BRW/KG651/42-108962
(Partially dismantled 1.02: to go to Assault Glider Association, RAF Shawbury: cancelled 23. 1.03 as wfu)

Reg	Type	c/n	Prev id	Date	Owner	Location	Date
G-AMIU	de Havilland DH.82A Tiger Moth	83228	T5495	9. 4.51	M D Souch	Hill Farm, Durley	9. 9.71

(Crashed Booker 15.10.69: frame reported on restoration Denford Manor 10.01: now departed for completion)

Reg	Type	c/n	Prev id	Date	Owner	Location	Date
G-AMIV*	de Havilland DH.82A Tiger Moth	83105	R5246	9. 4.51	G Turner	(Cheltenham)	

(WFU 12.11.65: cancelled 15.6.73 as WFU) (Stored for rebuild 2002)

Reg	Type	c/n	Prev id	Date	Owner	Location	Date
G-AMKL*	Auster B.4	2983	XA177	3. 7.51	C.J.Baker	Carr Farm, Thorney, Newark	

G-AMKL/G-25-2
(Dismantled Rearsby 1956 & cancelled 24.9.58) (New fuselage 1.03)

Reg	Type	c/n	Prev id	Date	Owner	Location	Date
G-AMKU	Auster 5 J/1B Aiglet	2721	ST-ABD	10. 7.51	P.G.Lipman	Romney Street Farm, Sevenoaks	5. 7.03

SN-ABD/G-AMKU

Reg	Type	c/n	Prev id	Date	Owner	Location	Date
G-AMMS	Auster J/5K Aiglet Trainer	2745		11.10.51	A.J.Large *(Noted 6.01)*	Trenchard Farm, Eggesford	19.10.98
G-AMNN	de Havilland DH.82A Tiger Moth	86457	NM137	24.12.51	M.Thrower *"Spirit of Pashley"*	Shoreham	20. 7.03T

t/a Northbrook College of Aeronautical Engineering

(Composite from unidentified airframe: original G-AMNN may have been absorbed into G-BPAJ)

Reg	Type	c/n	Prev id	Date	Owner	Location	Date
G-AMPG(2)	Piper PA-12 Super Cruiser	12-985	N2647M	25. 3.85	R.Simpson	Preston Court, Ledbury	17. 6.03P

(Hoerner wing-tips) NC2647

Reg	Type	c/n	Prev id	Date	Owner	Location	Date
G-AMPI(2)	SNCAN Stampe SV-4C	213	N6RA	13. 2.84	T.W.Harris	Booker	14. 6.03

F-BCFX

Reg	Type	c/n	Prev id	Date	Owner	Location	Date
G-AMPY	Douglas C-47B-15DK Dakota 3	15124/26569	(EI-BKJ)	8. 3.52	Atlantic Air Transport Ltd	Coventry	5. 1.02A

G-AMPY/N15751/G-AMPY/TF-FIO/G-AMPY/JY-ABE/G-AMPY/KK116/43-49308 *(Op Atlantic Airlines)*

Reg	Type	c/n	Prev id	Date	Owner	Location	Date
G-AMPZ	Douglas C-47B-30DK Dakota 4	16124/32872	EI-BDT	8. 3.52	Air Service Berlin CFH GmbH	Berlin Templehof	29. 4.04T

G-AMPZ/TF-AIV/G-41-3-66/PH-RIC/G-AMPZ/OD-AEQ/G-AMPZ/KN442/44-76540

Reg	Type	c/n	Prev id	Date	Owner	Location	Date
G-AMRA	Douglas C-47B-15DK Dakota 6	15290/26735	XE280	8. 3.52	Atlantic Air Transport Ltd	Coventry	13. 7.03T

G-AMRA/KK151/43-49474

Reg	Type	c/n	Prev id	Date	Owner	Location	Date
G-AMRF	Auster J/5F Aiglet Trainer	2716	VT-DHA	20. 3.52	A.I.Topps	East Midlands	2. 1.04

G-AMRF

Reg	Type	c/n	Prev id	Date	Owner	Location	Date
G-AMRK	Gloster Gladiator 1	-	L8032	16. 5.52	The Shuttleworth Trust	'Old Warden'	1. 8.03P

(Bristol Mercury XXX) "K8032"/G-AMRK/L8032   *(As "423-Port/427-Starboard" in R.Nor AF c/s)*

Reg	Type	c/n	Prev id	Date	Owner	Location	Date
G-AMSG	SIPA 903	77	OO-VBL	25.11.81	S.W.Markham	Valentine Farm, Odiham	1. 5.03P

F-BGHB

Reg	Type	c/n	Prev id	Date	Owner	Location	Date
G-AMSV	Douglas C-47B-25DK Dakota 3	16072/32820	(F-BSGV)	15. 5.52	Atlantic Air Transport Ltd	Inverness	13. 8.03A

G-AMSV/KN397/44-76488   *(Op Atlantic Airlines)*

Reg	Type	c/n	Prev id	Date	Owner	Location	Date
G-AMTA	Auster J/5F Aiglet Trainer	2780		24. 5.52	N.H.J.Cottrell	Headcorn	3. 8.03
G-AMTF	de Havilland DH.82A Tiger Moth	84207	ZK-AVE	11. 6.52	M.Lageirse & P.Winters	RAF Marham	19. 7.04

G-AMTF/T7842   *(As "T-7842")*

Reg	Type	c/n	Prev id	Date	Owner	Location	Date
G-AMTK	de Havilland DH.82A Tiger Moth	3982	N6709	18. 6.52	S.W.McKay & M.E.Vaisey	(Berkhamsted)	27. 5.66

(Stored 12.99: CofR @ 4.02)

Reg	Type	c/n	Prev id	Date	Owner	Location	Date
G-AMTM	Auster V J/1 Autocrat	3101	G-AJUJ	3. 7.52	R.J.Stobo	Oaklands Farm, Stonesfield, Oxon	27. 6.03P

(Auster rebuild - originally c/n 2622)

Reg	Type	c/n	Prev id	Date	Owner	Location	Date
G-AMTV	de Havilland DH.82A Tiger Moth	3858	OO-SOE	5. 8.52	M.A.Wray	(Wotton-Under-Edge)	16. 1.04

G-AMTV/N6545   tr Tango Victor Flying Group

Reg	Type	c/n	Prev id	Date	Owner	Location	Date
G-AMUF	de Havilland DHC.1 Chipmunk 21	C1/0832		2. 9.52	Redhill Tailwheel Flying Club Ltd	Redhill	5. 2.05
G-AMUI	Auster J/5F Aiglet Trainer	2790		29. 8.52	R B Webber	Trenchard Farm, Eggesford	15.2.66T

(Restored 7.02)

Reg	Type	c/n	Prev id	Date	Owner	Location	Date
G-AMVD	Taylorcraft J Auster 5	1565	F-BGTF	6.10.52	M.Hammond	Airfield Farm, Hardwick	14. 5.04

G-AMVD/TJ565   *(As "TJ565")*

Reg	Type	c/n	Prev id	Date	Owner	Location	Date
G-AMVP	Tipsy Junior	J.111	OO-ULA	23.10.52	A.R.Wershat	Sandown	22. 6.94P

(Walter Mikron 2)   *(Damaged Wroughton 4.7.93: stored 7.02)*

Reg	Type	c/n	Prev id	Date	Owner	Location	Date
G-AMVS	de Havilland DH.82A Tiger Moth	82784	OO-SOJ	12.11.52	J.T.Powell-Tuck	(Pontypool)	21.12.53

G-AMVS/R4852   *(On rebuild 8.92: current status unknown)*

Reg	Type	c/n	Prev id	Date	Owner	Location	Date
G-AMYD	Auster J/5L Aiglet Trainer	2773		13. 2.53	G.H.Maskell	Duckend Farm, Wilstead, Bedford	3. 9.04
G-AMYL(2)	Piper PA-17 Vagabond	17-30	N4613H	24. 4.87	P.J.Penn-Sayer	Scaynes Hill, Haywards Heath	20. 6.89P

(Continental C75) NC4613H   t/a The Fun Airplane Co *"Yankee Lady"*
(Stored 9.97: current status unknown)

Reg	Type	c/n	Prev id	Date	Owner	Location	Date
G-AMZI	Auster J/5F Aiglet Trainer	3104		4. 5.53	J.F.Moore	Rexden, Rye	9. 1.04
G-AMZT	Auster J/5F Aiglet Trainer	3107		28. 5.53	D.Hyde, J.W.Saull & J.C.Hutchinson	Standalone Farm, Meppershall	25. 5.04
G-AMZU	Auster J/5F Aiglet Trainer	3108		28. 5.53	J.A.Longworth, A.R.M. & C.B.A.Eagle	White Waltham	25. 9.05

tr Flying Flicks

G-ANAA - G-ANZZ

Reg	Type	c/n	Prev id	Date	Owner	Location	Date
G-ANAF	Douglas C-47B-35DK Dakota 3	16688/33436	N170GP	17. 6.53	Atlantic Air Transport Ltd	Coventry	27. 2.03A

G-ANAF/KP220/44-77104   *(Op Thales for radar & electronic trials)*

Reg	Type	c/n	Prev id	Date	Owner	Location	Date
G-ANCS	de Havilland DH.82A Tiger Moth	82824	R490	12. 9.53	C.E.Edwards & E.A.Higgins	Rush Green	7.10.05
G-ANCX	de Havilland DH.82A Tiger Moth	83719	T7229	15. 9.53	D.R.Wood	Fowle Hall Farm, Paddock Wood	28. 7.02
G-ANDE	de Havilland DH.82A Tiger Moth	85957	EM726	23. 9.53	A.J.West	Redhill	4. 4.03T
G-ANDM	de Havilland DH.82A Tiger Moth	3946	EI-AGP	23. 9.53	N.J.Stagg	Bristol	14. 8.03

G-ANDM/EI-AGP/G-ANDM/(G-ANDI)/N6642

Reg	Type	c/n	Prev id	Date	Owner	Location	Date
G-ANDP	de Havilland DH.82A Tiger Moth	82868	D-EBEC	22. 9.53	A.H.Diver	Newtownards, Co.Down	27. 3.05

N9920F/G-ANDP/R4960

Reg	Type	c/n	Prev id	Date	Owner	Location	Date
G-ANEH	de Havilland DH.82A Tiger Moth	82067	N6797	29. 9.53	G.J.Wells *(As "N-6797")*	(Booker)	24. 7.04
G-ANEL	de Havilland DH.82A Tiger Moth	82333	N9238	1.10.53	R A G Lucas	Redhill	29.10.05
G-ANEM	de Havilland DH.82A Tiger Moth	82943	EI-AGN	1.10.53	P.J.Benest	Hamstead Marshall	16. 7.02

G-ANEM/R5042

Reg	Type	c/n	Prev id	Date	Owner	Location	Date
G-ANEN	de Havilland DH.82A Tiger Moth	85418	OO-ACG	2.10.53	A.J.D.Douglas-Hamilton	Goodwood	13. 4.05

G-ANEN/DE410

Reg	Type	c/n	Prev id	Date	Owner	Location	Date
G-ANEW	de Havilland DH.82A Tiger Moth	86458	NM138	6.10.53	A.L.Young *(Frame stored 8.02)*	Henstridge	18. 6.62T
G-ANEZ	de Havilland DH.82A Tiger Moth	84218	T7849	20.10.53	C.D.J.Bland	Sandown	18. 8.05
G-ANFC	de Havilland DH.82A Tiger Moth	85385	DE363	13.10.53	J.E.Pierce	Welshpool	9.10.03T
G-ANFI	de Havilland DH.82A Tiger Moth	85577	DE623	16.10.53	G.P.Graham *(As "DE623")*	Shobdon	2. 2.03

(Another Tiger Moth "DE623", alias D-EDON, is displayed @ Auto und Technik Museum, Sinsheim, Germany)

Reg	Type	c/n	Prev id	Date	Owner	Location	Date
G-ANFL	de Havilland DH.82A Tiger Moth	84617	T6169	22.10.53	R.P.Whitby tr IDA Flying Group	Swanton Morley	13. 6.04
G-ANFM	de Havilland DH.82A Tiger Moth	83604	T5888	22.10.53	L.S.Mitton, A.J.Coker & N.H.Lemon tr Reading Flying Group	White Waltham	15. 8.04
G-ANFP	de Havilland DH.82A Tiger Moth	82530	N9503	28.10.53	G D Horn *(Frame only 1.00)*	(Fordingbridge)	1. 7.63
G-ANFV	de Havilland DH.82A Tiger Moth	85904	DF155	1.12.53	R.A.L.Falconer	Shempston Farm, Elgin	4. 2.01
					(As "DF155") (On rebuild 11.02)		
G-ANGK(2)	Cessna 140A	15396	N9675A	10. 3.89	G.A.Copeland	Popham	12. 8.04
G-ANHK	de Havilland DH.82A Tiger Moth	82442	F-BHIM G-ANHK/N9372	4.12.53	J.D.Iliffe	Hampstead Norreys	19. 3.03
G-ANHR*	Taylorcraft J Auster 5	759	MT19	25.12.53	C.G.Winch	Rushett Farm, Chessington	20. 7.86
					(Cancelled 4.4.02 by CAA) (Stored 2002)		
G-ANHS	Taylorcraft G Auster 4	737	MT197	5.12.53	R.G.Tomlinson tr Tango Uniform Group	Spanhoe	22. 8.04
G-ANHU	Taylorcraft G Auster 4	799	EC-AXR G-ANHU/MT255	5.12.53	D.J.Baker	Carr Farm, Thorney, Newark	22.10.66
					(Valid CofR 4.02: dismantled 1.03)		
G-ANHW*	Taylorcraft J Auster 5D *(Originally regd as Auster 5)*	1396	TJ320	5.12.53	D.J.Baker	Carr Farm, Thorney, Newark	9. 3.70
					(Forced landed Carlton Manor, Norfolk 1970: WFU 15.12.71) (Derelict fuselage stored 1.03)		
G-ANHX	Taylorcraft J Auster 5D	2064	TW519	5.12.53	D.J.Baker	Carr Farm, Thorney, Newark	2.11.73
					(Crashed 28.3.70: dismantled 1.03) (Valid CofR 4.02)		
G-ANIE	Taylorcraft J Auster 5	1809	TW467	5.12.53	S.J.Partridge	Bassingbourn	27.11.05
					(Op Military Auster Flight) (As "TW467/ROD-F" in 664 Sqdn c/s)		
G-ANIJ	Taylorcraft J Auster 5D	1680	TJ672	5.12.53	M.Pocock	Kemble	5. 5.71
					(As "TJ672" in 657 Sqdn c/s: noted 12.00)		
G-ANJA	de Havilland DH.82A Tiger Moth	82459	N9389	7.12.53	P.Aukland *(As "N9389")*	Seething	6. 6.05
G-ANJD	de Havilland DH.82A Tiger Moth	84652	T6226	8.12.53	I.Laws	Audley End	7. 8.03
G-ANKK	de Havilland DH.82A Tiger Moth	83590	T5854	24.12.53	P A.Cambridge tr Halfpenny Green Tiger Group *(As "T5854")*	Charity Farm, Baxterley	20. 6.04
G-ANKT	de Havilland DH.82A Tiger Moth	85087	T6818	24.12.53	The Shuttleworth Trust *(As "T6818")*	Old Warden	16. 8.03
G-ANKZ	de Havilland DH.82A Tiger Moth	3803	(N) F-BHIO/G-ANKZ/N6466	30.12.53	D.W.Graham	Hill Farm, Durley	15. 4.99
					(As "N6466") (New CofR 5.02)		
G-ANLD	de Havilland DH.82A Tiger Moth	85990	OO-DPA G-ANLD/EM773	30.12.53	K.Peters	Rushett Manor, Chessington	17.12.05
					(Crashed Old Warden 23.6.01 & substantially damaged)		
G-ANLH	de Havilland DH.82A Tiger Moth *(Fuselage No. MCO/de Havilland DH.4623)*	86546	N3744F OO-EVO/G-ANLH/PG637	4. 1.54	I.M.Castle *(See G-AGPK)*	Sywell	16. 5.03T
G-ANLS	de Havilland DH.82A Tiger Moth	85862	DF113	7. 1.54	P.A.Gliddon	Great Fryup, Egton, Whitby	29. 6.03
G-ANMO	de Havilland DH.82A Tiger Moth	3255	F-BHIU G-ANMO/K4259	22. 1.54	E. & K.M.Lay	White Waltham	17. 8.03
					(As "K-4259/71")		
G-ANMV	de Havilland DH.82A Tiger Moth	83745	F-BHAZ G-ANMV/T7404	22. 1.54	B.P.Sanders t/a Tigerfly	Booker	26. 6.01T
					(Dismantled 7.01 & sold to Germany 2002)		
G-ANMY	de Havilland DH.82A Tiger Moth	85466	OO-SOL "OO-SOC"/G-ANMY/DE470	22. 1.54	F.P.Le Coyte tr Lotmead Flying Group *(As "DE470/16" in RAF c/s)*	Lotmead Farm, Wanborough, Swindon	3. 9.04
G-ANNB	de Havilland DH.82A Tiger Moth	84233	N6037 D-EGYN/G-ANNB/T6037	22. 1.54	G.M.Bradley *(On rebuild 2002)*	(Colchester)	12. 6.58
G-ANNE(2)	de Havilland DH.82A Tiger Moth	"83814"		15. 4.94	C.R.Hardiman	Shobdon	30. 5.58
	(G-ANNE(1) ex T7418, sold as OO-CCI/90-CCI/9Q-CCI) (Composite airframe: on rebuild 9.02)						
G-ANNG	de Havilland DH.82A Tiger Moth	85504	DE524	22. 1.54	P.F.Walter	Farnborough	18. 5.01
G-ANNI	de Havilland DH.82A Tiger Moth	85162	T6953	22. 1.54	A.R.Brett *(As "T6953")*	Little Gransden	6. 9.03
G-ANNK	de Havilland DH.82A Tiger Moth	83804	F-BFDO G-ANNK/T7290	22. 1.54	D.R.Wilcox *(New owner 5.02)*	Sywell	25. 9.87
G-ANOH	de Havilland DH.82A Tiger Moth	86040	EM838	22. 2.54	N.Parkhouse	Redhill	30.10.05T
G-ANOK*	SAAB 91C Safir	91311	SE-CAH	22. 4.54	A.F.Galt & Co Ltd	(Yarrow Ford)	5. 2.73
					(Cancelled 15.10.81 by CAA) (Stored 6.00)		
G-ANOM	de Havilland DH.82A Tiger Moth	82086	N6837	2. 3.54	A.L.Creer	(Bristol)	3. 5.62T
					(Crashed Fairoaks 17.12.61: on rebuild 6.00)		
G-ANON	de Havilland DH.82A Tiger Moth	84270	T7909	4. 3.54	R.C.Hields t/a Hields Aviation *(As "T7909")*	Sherburn-in-Elmet	23. 2.03T
G-ANOO	de Havilland DH.82A Tiger Moth	85409	DE401	11. 3.54	R.K.Packman	Compton Abbas	12. 9.02
G-ANPE	de Havilland DH.82A Tiger Moth	83738	G-IESH G-ANPE/F-BHAT/G-ANPE/T7397	27. 3.54	I.E.S.Hudleston	Duxford	23.11.02
G-ANPK*	de Havilland DH.82A Tiger Moth	3571	L6936	4. 4.54	A.D.Hodgkinson	Thruxton	10. 7.97T
					(Damaged Jaywick Sands, Clacton 18.8.96: on rebuild 2002: cancelled 7.1.03 by CAA)		
G-ANPP*	Percival P.34 Proctor III	H.264	HM354	8. 4.54	P Jeffery	(Cutlers Green, Essex)	5. 5.69
					(Cancelled 3.4.89 by CAA) (Stored 2000)		
G-ANRF	de Havilland DH.82A Tiger Moth	83748	T5850	24. 5.54	C.D.Cyster	Glenrothes	24. 8.04
G-ANRM	de Havilland DH.82A Tiger Moth	85861	DF112	8. 6.54	Spectrum Leisure Ltd *(Op Classic Wings) (As "DF112")*	Clacton/Duxford	28. 7.04T
G-ANRN	de Havilland DH.82A Tiger Moth	83133	T5368	24. 5.54	J.J.V.Elwes	Rush Green	26. 4.04
G-ANRP	Taylorcraft J Auster 5	1789	TW439	21. 5.54	I.C.Naylor & P.G.Wood *(As "TW439")*	Bagby	16.12.02
G-ANSM	de Havilland DH.82A Tiger Moth	82909	R5014	3. 6.54	R.M.Kimbell	Sywell	17. 8.03T
G-ANTE	de Havilland DH.82A Tiger Moth	84891	T6562	20. 9.54	P Reading *(As "T-6562")*	Sywell/White Waltham	16. 7.05T
G-ANWB	de Havilland DHC.1 Chipmunk 21	C1/0987	G-5-17	15. 2.55	G.Briggs	Blackpool	17.12.04T
G-ANWO	Miles M.14A Hawk Trainer 3	718	L8262	31.12.58	A.G.Dunkerley	West Chiltington, Pulborough	18. 4.63
	(DBR Kirton-in-Lindsey 21.4.62 & cancelled as damaged: although restored 24.6.87 unlikely little residue: wings to G-AIUA in 1960s & fuselage remnants slight of substance: notwithstanding has valid CofR @ 4.02)						
G-ANXC	Auster J/5R Alpine	3135	5Y-UBD VP-UBD/G-ANXC/(AP-AHG)/G-ANXC tr Alpine Group	4.12.54	R.B.Webber	Trenchard Farm, Eggesford	2. 8.98
G-ANXR	Percival P.31C Proctor 4	H.803	RM221	14.12.54	L.H.Oakins *(As "RM221")*	Biggin Hill	14.12.03
G-ANZT	Thruxton Jackaroo	84176	T7798	4. 3.55	D.J.Neville & P.J.Dear	Rush Green	14. 8.05
G-ANZU	de Havilland DH.82A Tiger Moth	3583	L6938	9. 3.55	P.A.Jackson *(Stored 1994)*	Brookfield Farm, Great Stukeley	17. 3.91
G-ANZZ	de Havilland DH.82A Tiger Moth	85834	DE974	14. 3.55	J.I.B.Bennett & P.P.Amershi *(Current CofR 3.02)*	(Hatfield)	28. 2.69T

G-AOAA - G-AOZZ

Reg	Type	c/n	Prev id	Date	Owner	Location	Date
G-AOAA	de Havilland DH.82A Tiger Moth	85908	DF159	14. 3.55	R.C.P.Brookhouse	Thruxton	8.12.91T
	(Damaged Redhill 4.6.89: under restoration 2002)						
G-AOBG*	Somers-Kendall SK-1	1		30. 3.55	A.J.E.Smith	Breighton	26. 6.58
	(WFU after engine turbine failure 11.7.57: stored 12.02)						
G-AOBH	de Havilland DH.82A Tiger Moth	84350	T7997	31. 3.55	P.Nutley	Thruxton	25. 5.03
	(Regd with c/n 83818 ex T7439)				*(As "NL750" which belongs to G-AHUF once regd to this owner)*		
G-AOBO	de Havilland DH.82A Tiger Moth	3810	N6473	23. 4.55	J.S. & J.V.Shaw	Cubert, Newquay	28. 8.69T
	(On rebuild 10.97: current status unknown)						
G-AOBU	Hunting Percival P.84 Jet Provost T.1	P84/6	XM129	2. 5.55	T.J.Manna	North Weald	26. 2.03P
			G-AOBU/G-42-1		t/a Kennet Aviation *(As "XD693/Z-Q" in 2 FTS c/s)*		
G-AOBX	de Havilland DH.82A Tiger Moth	83653	T7187	26. 4.55	S.Bohill-Smith	Uffley Common, Odiham	4.12.05
					tr David Ross Flying Group		
G-AOCP(2)*	Taylorcraft J Auster 5	1800	W462	25. 5.56	C.J.Baker	Carr Farm, Thorney, Newark	
	(WFU 22.6.68) (Fuselage frame noted 1.03)						
G-AOCR(2)	Taylorcraft J Auster 5D	1060	EI-AJS	25. 5.56	G.J.McDill	Park Farm, Eaton Bray	2. 5.05
			G-AOCR/NJ673		*(As "NJ673")*		
G-AOCU(2)	Taylorcraft J Auster 5	986	MT349	8. 6.56	S.J.Ball *(On rebuild 1.02)*	Leicester	22. 2.04
G-AODT	de Havilland DH.82A Tiger Moth	83109	R5250	4. 8.55	R.A.Harrowven	Tibenham	30. 4.01
G-AOEH	Aeronca 7AC Champion	7AC-2144	N79854	8. 9.55	R.A. & S.P.Smith	(Great Yeldham)	24. 3.03P
	(Continental A65)		OO-TWF				
G-AOEI	de Havilland DH.82A Tiger Moth	82196	N6946	14. 9.55	CFG Flying Ltd	Cambridge	11. 7.05T
	(Regd with fuselage no.MCO/DH3409 which should correspond to ex DE298 [85332]: a/c is probably composite airframe)						
G-AOES	de Havilland DH.82A Tiger Moth	84547	T6056	6.10.55	K.A.& A.J.Broomfield	Charity Farm, Baxterley	15. 6.02
G-AOET	de Havilland DH.82A Tiger Moth	85650	DE720	7.10.55	Techair London Ltd	Oaklands Farm, East Tytherley	1.11.02
G-AOEX	Thruxton Jackaroo	86483	NM175	10.10.55	A.T.Christian	Walkeridge Farm, Overton	3. 2.68T
					(On rebuild 10.01)		
G-AOFE	de Havilland DHC.1 Chipmunk 22A	C1/0150	WB702	13. 9.56	W.J.Quinn *(As "WB702")*	(Goodwood)	8.10.04
G-AOFJ(2)*	Auster Alpha 5	3401		3.10.56	R.Drew	Perth	20. 9.79
	(Cancelled 3.4.89 by CAA) (Stored dismantled 11.00)						
G-AOFM	Auster J/5P Autocar	3178		16. 6.55	S.J.Cooper *(New owner 1.02)*	(Lincoln)	13. 5.05
G-AOFS	Auster J/5L Aiglet Trainer	3143	EI-ALN	28.10.55	P.N.A.Whitehead	Leicester	26. 4.04
			G-AOFS				
G-AOGI	de Havilland DH.82A Tiger Moth	85922	(N)	14.12.55	W.J.Taylor	(Skegness)	23. 8.91
			OO-SOA/G-AOGI/DF186		t/a Lincs Aerial Spraying Co *(Stored 10.92)*		
G-AOGR	de Havilland DH.82A Tiger Moth	84566	XL714	20. 1.56	M.I.Edwards	Grange Farm, Boughton	16. 9.96T
			G-AOGR/T6099		*(As "XL714": noted 5.02)*		
G-AOGV	Auster J/5R Alpine	3302		2. 2.56	R.E.Heading	Walnut Tree Farm, Thorney, Whittlesey	17. 7.72
					(Stored 12.97: current status unknown)		
G-AOHL*	Vickers 802 Viscount	161		2. 1.56	London-Southend Airport Co Ltd	Southend	11. 4.80T
	(WFU 6.2.81 as cabin services trainer: cancelled 27.3.81:) (For spares 1992: derelict @ 1.94: Fire Service trainer 2.03)						
G-AOHY*	de Havilland DH.82A Tiger Moth	3850	N6537	23. 2.56	M.Somerton-Rayner	AAC Middle Wallop	20. 8.60
					tr AAC Reserve Collection Trust		
					(On rebuild 9.00: cancelled 5.3.01 as temporarily WFU)		
G-AOHZ	Auster J/5P Autocar	3252		28. 2.56	A.D.Hodgkinson	Thruxton	25. 9.03
G-AOIL	de Havilland DH.82A Tiger Moth	83673	XL716	20. 8.56	C.D.Davidson	Lee-on-Solent	17. 9.05
			G-AOIL/T7363		*(As "XL-716")*		
G-AOIM	de Havilland DH.82A Tiger Moth	83536	T7109	27. 8.56	D.A.Hardiman	Shobdon	8. 4.04
G-AOIR	Thruxton Jackaroo	82882	R4972	13. 1.56	K.A.& A.J.Broomfield	Charity Farm, Baxterley	1. 4.05
G-AOIS	de Havilland DH.82A Tiger Moth	83034	R5172	13. 1.56	J.K.Ellwood	Sherburn in Elmet	10. 7.04
G-AOIY	Auster J/5V-160 Autocar	3199		1. 3.56	J.B.Nicholson	Trenchard Farm, Eggesford	26. 8.90
	(Lycoming O-320)				*(On rebuild 1.03)*		
G-AOJH	de Havilland DH.83C Fox Moth	FM.42	AP-ABO	29. 3.56	Connect Properties Ltd	Kemble	17.10.02
G-AOJJ	de Havilland DH.82A Tiger Moth	85877	DF128	5. 4.56	E.& K.M.Lay *(As "DF128/RCO-U")*	White Waltham	26. 7.03
	(Swung on take-off Goodwood 8.7.01, stuck parked aircraft, wings and tail broken off: new owners 10.01)						
G-AOJK	de Havilland DH.82A Tiger Moth	82813	R4896	5. 4.56	R.J.Willies	Top Farm, Croydon, Royston	18. 8.05
G-AOJR	de Havilland DHC.1 Chipmunk 22	C1/0205	SE-BBS	9. 4.56	G J G-H Caubergs & N Marien	Grimbergen, Belgium	28. 7.05
			OY-DFB/D-EGIM/G-AOJR/D-EGIM/G-AOJR/WB756				
G-AOKH*	Percival P.40 Prentice 1	PAC/212	VS251	11. 4.56	J.F.Moore	Biggin Hill	2. 8.73
					(Cancelled 17.6.92 by CAA) (Stored 12.00)		
G-AOKL	Percival P.40 Prentice 1	PAC/208	VS610	13. 4.56	The Shuttleworth Trust	Old Warden	20. 9.96
					(As "VS610/K-L") (Under restoration 5.01)		
G-AOLK	Percival P.40 Prentice 1	PAC/225	VS618	25. 4.56	A.Hilton	Southend	14. 6.04
G-AOLU	Percival P.40 Prentice 1	B3/1A/PAC/283	EI-ASP	25. 4.56	N.J.Butler	(Montrose)	14. 6.04
	(Regd with c/n 5830/3)		G-AOLU/VS356		t/a Montrose Air Station Museum *(As "VS356")*		
G-AORB(2)	Cessna 170B	20767	OO-SIZ	13. 2.84	A.R.Thompson	Hawley Farm, Tadley	2. 3.03
			N2615D		tr Hawley Farm Group		
G-AORG	de Havilland DH.114 Heron	214101	XR441	1. 5.56	Duchess of Brittany (Jersey) Ltd	Jersey	23. 4.03
	(Built as Sea Heron C.1)		G-AORG/G-5-16		*(Jersey Airlines titles) "Duchess of Brittany"*		
G-AORW	de Havilland DHC.1 Chipmunk 22A	C1/0130	WB682	28. 5.56	Bushfire Investments Ltd "Kate"	Booker	3.11.02
G-AOSF	de Havilland DHC.1 Chipmunk 22	C1/0023	D-EIIZ	25.10.02	D.Mercer	Porta Westfalica, Germany	25.10.02
			G-AOSF/HB-TUA/G-AOSF/WB571 *(As "WB571/34")*				
G-AOSK	de Havilland DHC.1 Chipmunk 22A	C1/0178	WB726	26. 6.56	E.J.Leigh	Audley End	23.11.02
					(As "WB726/E" in Cambridge UAS c/s)		
G-AOSO	de Havilland DHC.1 Chipmunk 22	C1/0227	WD288	26. 6.56	The Earl of Suffolk & Berkshire & J.Hoerner	Charlton Park, Malmesbury	19.10.03
					(As "WD288")		
G-AOSU	de Havilland DHC.1 Chipmunk 22	C1/0217	WB766	28. 6.56	T.Holloway	Easterton	28. 6.03
	(Lycoming O-360)				tr RAFGSA *(Op Fulmar Gliding Club)*		
G-AOSY	de Havilland DHC.1 Chipmunk 22	C1/0037	WB585	29. 6.56	B.A.Webster	Seething	26. 6.05
					tr WFG Chipmunk Group *(As "WB585/M")*		
G-AOTD	de Havilland DHC.1 Chipmunk 22	C1/0040	WB588	30. 6.56	S.Piech	Old Sarum	4.10.03
					(As "WB588/D" in Oxford UAS c/s)		

G-AOTF	de Havilland DHC.1 Chipmunk 23 (Lycoming O-360)	C1/0015	WB563	2. 7.56	T.Holloway tr RAFGSA	Bicester	17. 10.04
G-AOTK	Druine D.53 Turbi (Walter Mikron 3)	1 & PFA 230		1.11.56	T.J.Adams	RAF Henlow	9.12.02P
G-AOTR	de Havilland DHC.1 Chipmunk 22	C1/0045	HB-TUH D-EGOG/G-AOTR/WB604	12. 7.56	M.R.Woodgate	Belfast	30. 3.03
G-AOTY	de Havilland DHC.1 Chipmunk 22	C1/0522	AWG472	12. 7.56	A.A.Hodgson (As "WG472" in RAF c/s)	(Abergele)	22. 1.04T
G-AOUO	de Havilland DHC.1 Chipmunk 22 (Lycoming O-360)	C1/0179	WB730	10. 8.56	T.Holloway tr RAFGSA	RAF Cosford	16. 3.03
G-AOUP	de Havilland DHC.1 Chipmunk 22	C1/0180	WB731	10. 8.56	A.R.Harding	(Newton Green, Sudbury)	24.10.02
G-AOVS*	Bristol 175 Britannia 312F	13430	(G-BRAC)	28. 2.58	(Redcoat Airlines) (Broken up 10.79: fuselage for Fire Service use 3.00)	Luton	31 .7.79T
G-AOVW	Taylorcraft J Auster 5	894	MT119	16.11.59	B.Marriott	Ropsley Heath Farm, Grantham	1.10.03
G-AOXN	de Havilland DH.82A Tiger Moth	85958	EM727	31.10.56	S.L.G.Darch	East Chinnock, Yeovil	21.12.01
G-AOZH	de Havilland DH.82A Tiger Moth	86449	NM129	18. 1.57	M.H.Blois-Brooke (As "K2572")	Redhill	28. 9.02T
G-AOZL	Auster J/5Q Alpine	3202		5. 2.57	R.M.Weeks (On rebuild 7.02)	Earls Colne	28. 5.88
G-AOZP	de Havilland DHC.1 Chipmunk 22A	C1/0183	WB734	14. 2.57	H.Darlington	High Easter	27. 3.05

G-APAA - G-APZZ

G-APAF	Auster Alpha 5	3404	G-CMAL G-APAF	25. 3.57	J J J Mostyn (As "TW511")	Henstridge	1. 8.05
G-APAH	Auster Alpha 5	3402		29. 3.57	T.J.Goodwin	Great Oakley, Clacton	5. 4.04
G-APAL	de Havilland DH.82A Tiger Moth	82102	N6847	3. 4.57	Avia Special Ltd (As "N6847")	Barton	9. 7.03T
G-APAM	de Havilland DH.82A Tiger Moth	3874	N6580	3. 4.57	R.P.Williams Denford Manor, Hungerford tr Myth Group "Myth"		8. 7.04
G-APAO	de Havilland DH.82A Tiger Moth	82845	R4922	3. 4.57	Spectrum Leisure Ltd (Op Classic Wings)	Clacton	24. 9.05T
G-APAP	de Havilland DH.82A Tiger Moth	83018	R5136	3. 4.57	J.Romain (As "R5136")	Duxford	30. 4.04
G-APBE	Auster Alpha 5	3403		7. 5.57	G.C.Deacon	(High Wycombe)	6.12.04
G-APBI	de Havilland DH.82A Tiger Moth	86097	EM903	16. 5.57	A.Wood Halstead, Essex (Damaged Audley End 7.7.80: on rebuild 12.90: current status unknown)		19. 4.82
G-APBO	Druine D.53 Turbi (Continental C75)	PFA 229		3. 6.57	R.C.Hibberd	(Devizes)	13. 5.03P
G-APBW	Auster Alpha 5A	3405		23. 5.57	N.Huxtable	Cheddington, Bucks	1. 6.03
G-APCB	Auster J/5Q Alpine	3204		5. 6.57	A.A.Beswick & I.A.Freeman	Thruxton	7. 3 04
G-APCC	de Havilland DH.82A Tiger Moth	86549	PG640	11. 6.57	L.J.Rice	Bishopstrow Farm, Warminster	25. 5.03
G-APDF*	de Havilland DH.106 Comet 4	6407		2. 2.57	Not known (Chipping Campden) (To RAE as XV814 3.67 & cancelled) (Nose only 3.00)		
G-APFA	Druine D.52 Turbi (Continental A65)	PFA 232		5. 2.57	F.J.Keitch	Smiths Farm, Brixham	22. 9.92P
G-APFG*	Boeing 707-436	17708	N5094K	7. 8.59	Phoenix Aviation (Cancelled 11.68 as WFU) (Nose only 4.00)	Bruntingthorpe	24. 5.81T
G-APFU	de Havilland DH.82A Tiger Moth	86081	EM879	28. 8.57	Leisure Assets Ltd	Goodwood	11. 4.03T
G-APGL	de Havilland DH.82A Tiger Moth	86460	NM140	6. 9.57	K.A.Broomfield Charity Farm, Baxterley (Not previously converted: on rebuild 3.97: see G-AJVE)		
G-APIE	Tipsy Belfair (Walter Mikron 2)	535	(OO-TIE)	22.10.57	D.Beale	Witchford	15. 4.03P
G-APIH	de Havilland DH.82A Tiger Moth	82981	N111DH OY-DGJ/D-EMEX/G-APIH/R5086	25.10.57	K.Stewering	Borken-Gemen, Germany	23. 3.03
G-APIK	Auster Alpha	3375		11.11.57	J.H.Powell-Tuck	Gloucestershire	14.12.02
G-APIZ	Rollason-Druine D.31 Turbulent (Volkswagen 1600)	PFA 478		22.11.57	E J I Musty "Witch Lady"	White Waltham	29.10.03P
G-APJB	Percival P.40 Prentice T.1	PAC/086	VR259	28.11.57	Atlantic Air Transport Ltd (As "VR259/M" in 2 ASS c/s)	Coventry	10. 7.05T
G-APJO	de Havilland DH.82A Tiger Moth (C/n quoted as "17712":) (	86446	NM126	23.12.57	D.R. & Mrs M.Wood Tunbridge Wells Crashed Ross-on-Wye 5.8.58: on rebuild & may include components from G-APJR)		27. 3.59T
G-APJZ	Auster Alpha	3382	5N-ACY (VR-NDR)/G-APJZ	3. 1.58	P.G.Lipman Romney Street Farm, Sevenoaks (Damaged Thornicombe 10.11.75: on rebuild 12.97: current status unknown)		15. 7.77
G-APKH	de Havilland DH.85 Leopard Moth	PPS.85/1/DH7131		23. 1.58	A R Tarleton Konstanz, Germany (Composite rebuild of c/n 7002 [G-ACGS/PH-ALM/G-ACGS] & c/n 7040 [G-ACLZ/AW121/G-ACLZ] - mainly the latter)		14. 8.03P
G-APKM*	Auster Alpha	3385		27. 1.58	C.J.Baker Carr Farm, Thorney, Newark (Cancelled 9.10.91 as TWFU) (Dismantled 1.03)		9. 1.89
G-APKN	Auster Alpha	3387		27. 1.58	P.R.Hodson tr The Felthorpe Auster Group Felthorpe (Destroyed in arson attack 18.2.03)		9. 8.05
G-APLO	de Havilland DHC.1 Chipmunk 22	C1/0144	AEI-AHU WB696	1. 5.58	Lindholme Aircraft Ltd (As "WD379/K" in Cambridge UAS c/s)	Jersey	2.11.03T
G-APLU	de Havilland DH.82A Tiger Moth	85094	VR-AAY F-OBKK/G-APLU/T6825	2. 4.58	R.A.Bishop & M.E.Vaisey	Rush Green	14. 8.04
G-APMB*	de Havilland DH.106 Comet 4B	6422		15. 4.58	Gatwick Handling Ltd Gatwick (Cancelled 19.1.79 as WFU) (Ground Trainer airframe 9.00)		18. 5.79
G-APMH	Auster J/1U Workmaster	3502	F-OBOA G-APMH	15. 4.58	J.L.Thorogood	Insch	19. 5.04
G-APMX	de Havilland DH.82A Tiger Moth	85645	DE715	9. 5.58	M.A.Broughton	Popham	21.10.02
G-APNJ*	Cessna 310	35335	EI-AJY N3635D	2. 6.58	Northbrook College Shoreham (Cancelled 5.12.83 as WFU) (As instructional airframe 1.02)		28.11.74
G-APNS	Garland-Bianchi Linnet (Continental C90)	001		17. 6.58	P.M.Busaidy Scaynes Hill, Haywards Heath (Stored 6.95) (Current status unknown) (Valid CoR 4.02)		6.10.78S
G-APNT	Bellamy Currie Wot (Continental PC60) (Regd with c/n P.6,399)	HAC/3		18. 6.58	B.J.Dunford Longwood Farm, Morestead "Airymouse"		1. 8.03P
G-APNZ	Rollason-Druine D.31 Turbulent (Ardem 4C02)	PFA 482		17. 4.58	J.Knight Hailsham (Damaged River Rother near Iden 3.9.95: on rebuild)		13.12.95P
G-APOD*	Tipsy Belfair (Walter Mikron 2)	536	(OO-TIF)	16. 7.58	L.F.Potts (Bannockburn) (Under restoration 6.00: cancelled 6.9.00 by CAA)		23. 8.88P

Reg	Type	C/n	Prev id	Date	Owner/Operator	Location	Date
G-APOI	Saunders-Roe Skeeter	Srs.8	S2/5081	29. 7.58	B.Chamberlain	Otley, Ipswich	2. 8.00P
G-APOL*	Druine D.31 Turbulent	PFA 439		31. 7.58	A.Gregori & S.Tinker	Charterhall	18. 6.94P
	(Ardem 4C02)				*(Damaged Charterhall 24.7.93: stored 6.00: cancelled 13.9.00 as WFU)*		
G-APPA	de Havilland DHC.1 Chipmunk 22	C1/0792	N5073E	11. 9.58	D.M.Squires	(Wellesbourne Mountford)	14. 7.85
			G-APPA/WP917		*(On slow rebuild 1.03)*		
G-APPL	Percival P.40 Prentice 1	PAC/013	VR189	7.10.58	Susan J.Saggers	Biggin Hill	1.10.03
G-APPM	de Havilland DHC.1 Chipmunk 22	C1/0159	WB711	14.10.58	Freston Aviation Ltd *(As "WB711")*	Crowfield	15. 8.05
G-APPN	de Havilland DH.82A Tiger Moth	83839	T7328	17.10.58	E.G.Waite-Roberts	Longwood, Southampton	18. 4.04
					(Crashed Mendlesham 14.7.64: rebuilt 2000/01 as "T7328": believed to be same aircraft as G-DHTM (qv))		
G-APRF	Auster Alpha 5	3412	VR-LAF	8.12.58	W.B.Bateson	Blackpool	14.11.00
			G-APRF		*(Stored 8.02)*		
G-APRJ	Avro 694 Lincoln B.2	-	RF342	29.12.58	D.Copley	Sandtoft	
			G-36-3/G-29-1/G-APRJ/RF342				
			(Confirmed most parts present dismantled and in open storage 2001: fuselage still bearing "G-29-1" & wings "RF342")					
G-APRR	CZL Super Aero 45 Srs.04	04-014	OK-KFQ	5. 1.59	R.H.Jowett	Ronaldsway	26. 9.03
G-APRS	Scottish Aviation Twin Pioneer 3	561	G-BCWF	9. 1.59	Bravo Aviation Ltd	Coventry	15. 7.03T
			XT610/G-APRS/(PI-C430)		*(Op Atlantic Air Transport Ltd) (ETPS titles)*		
G-APRT	Taylor JT.1 Monoplane	PFA 537		15. 1.59	D.A.Slater	Rushett Farm, Chessington	26. 5.03P
	(Ardem 4C02)						
G-APSA	Douglas DC-6A	45497	4W-ABQ	12. 2.59	Atlantic Air Transport Ltd	Coventry	11. 4.05T
			HZ-ADA/G-APSA/CF-MC		*(Op Air Atlantique)*		
G-APSO*	de Havilland DH.104 Dove 5	04505	(N1046T)	16. 2.59	Cormack (Aircraft Services) Ltd	Kemble	8. 7.78T
			G-APSO		*(To Devonair) (Cancelled 2.5.01 as WFU)*		
			(Wings fitted to G-BWWC: forward part of fuselage fitted with stub wings & used as engine test-bed by 4.00)					
G-APSR	Auster J/1U Workmaster	3499	OO-HXA	22. 4.59	D & K Aero Services Ltd	Namur-Temploux, Belgium	20.10.05A
			G-APSR/VP-JCD/G-APSR/(F-OBHR)		*(Op P.De Liens)*		
G-APTP	Piper PA-22-150 Tri-Pacer	22-5009	EI-AJN	20. 3.59	Comunica Industries International Ltd		
	(Modified to PA-20 Pacer configuration)					Roughay Farm, Bishops Waltham	1. 5.03
G-APTR	Auster Alpha	3392		15. 4.59	C.J.& D.J.Baker	Carr Farm, Thorney, Newark	11. 4.87
					(Complete 1.03)		
G-APTU	Auster Alpha 5	3413		20. 4.59	A.J. & J.M.Davis	Leicester	8. 6.98
					tr G-APTU Flying Group *(On rebuild 3.00)*		
G-APTY	Beech G35 Bonanza	D-4789	EI-AJG	4. 6.59	G.E.Brennand	Blackpool	23. 3.03
G-APTZ	Rollason-Druine D.31 Turbulent	PFA 508		18. 3.59	Tiger Club (1990) Ltd	Headcorn	19. 5.03P
	(Volkswagen 1600)						
G-APUE	Orlican L-40 Meta-Sokol	150708	OK-NMB	2. 6.59	S.E. & M.J.Aherne	Top Farm, Croydon, Royston	18. 5.03
G-APUR	Piper PA-22-160 Tri-Pacer	22-6711		3. 7.59	L F Miller	Kildare	20. 8.04
G-APUW	Auster J/5V Srs.160 Autocar	3273		23. 6.59	E.A.J.Hibbard	Hill Farm, Nayland	18.12.03
G-APUY	Druine D.31 Turbulent	PFA 509		24. 6.59	C.Jones	Barton	10. 6.86P
	(Volkswagen 1300)				*(Stored 2.00)*		
G-APUZ	Piper PA-24-250 Comanche	24-1094	N6000P	3. 7.59	Tatenhill Aviation	Tatenhill	23. 1.02
G-APVF	Putzer Elster B	006	D-EEQX	29.12.83	A.& E.A.Wiseman	Breighton	2. 5.03P
	(Continental O-200-A)		97+04/D-EJUH		*(As "97+04" in Luftwaffe c/s)*		
G-APVG	Auster J/5L Aiglet Trainer	3306	(ZK-BQW)	10. 7.59	R.Farrer	Cranfield	20. 3.00
G-APVL	Saunders-Roe P531-2	S2/5311	XP166	23. 7.59	R.E.Dagless	Yaxham, Dereham	
			G-APVL				
G-APVN	Druine D.31 Turbulent	PFA 511		24. 7.59	R.Sherwin	Swanborough Farm, Lewes	24. 6.94P
	(Volkswagen 1600)				*(Stored 3.97: current status unknown)*		
G-APVS	Cessna 170B	26156	N2512C	7. 8.59	N.Simpson *"Stormin' Norman"*	East Kirkby	23. 6.03
G-APVU	Orlican L-40 Meta-Sokol	150706	OK-NMI	21. 8.59	S.A. & M.J.Aherne	(St.Albans)	27. 6.79
					(Damaged Manchester 12.9.78: on rebuild 1993)		
G-APVZ	Rollason-Druine D.31 Turbulent	PFA 545		23. 7.59	I.D.Daniels	Maypole Farm, Chislet	18. 3.03P
	(Ardem 4C02)						
G-APWL	EoN AP.10 460 Standard Srs.1A	EoN/S/001	BGA.1172/BRK	2. 9.59	D.G.Andrew	Eaglescott	
			G-APWL/RAFGSA.268/G-APWL				
G-APWP	Druine D.31 Turbulent	PFA 497		14. 9.59	C.F.Rogers *(Current status unknown)*	(Wheathamstead)	27. 6.67
G-APXJ	Piper PA-24-250 Comanche	24-291	VR-NDA	11.12.59	T.Wildsmith	Gamston	15.11.02
			N10F				
G-APXR	Piper PA-22-160 Tri-Pacer	22-7172	N10F	29. 1.60	A.Troughton	Belfast	2.12.04
G-APXT	Piper PA-22-150 Tri-Pacer	22-3854	N4545A	16. 2.60	A E Cuttler	(Wokingham)	5. 7.87T
			(Damaged Southend 26.12.85 & on rebuild to PA-20 Pacer configuration: new owner 12.01)					
G-APXU	Piper PA-22-150 Tri-Pacer	22-474	N1723A	10. 2.60	The Scottish Aero Club Ltd	Perth	20. 2.85
					"The Cloth Bomber" (Rebuild nearing completion 11.00)		
G-APXY	Cessna 150	17711	N7911E	15. 1.60	The Merlin Flying Club Ltd	Hucknall	1. 4.05T
G-APYB	Tipsy T.66 Nipper 3	T66/S/39		28. 1.60	B.O.Smith	Yearby	12. 6.96P
	(Built Avions Fairey SA) (Volkswagen 1834)				*(On rebuild 1.02)*		
G-APYG	de Havilland DHC.1 Chipmunk 22	C1/0060	OH-HCB	11.11.60	E.J.I.Musty & P.A.Colman	White Waltham	5. 7.04
			WB619				
G-APYI	Piper PA-22-135 Tri-Pacer	22-2218	N8031C	8. 2.60	B.T. & J.Cullen	Ballyboy, Co.Meath	16. 8.03
	(Modified to PA-20 Pacer configuration)						
G-APYN	Piper PA-22-160 Tri-Pacer	22-6797	N2804Z	24. 2.60	S.J.Raw	Morgansfield, Fishburn	21. 6.02
G-APYT	Champion 7FC Tri-Traveler7		FC-387	9. 5.60	B.J.Anning	Watchford Farm, Yarcombe	16. 9.02P
G-APZJ	Piper PA-18-150 Super Cub	18-7233	N10F	29. 1.60	R.Jones t/a Southern Sailplanes	Membury	15. 5.03
					(Rebuilt 1986 after accident 12.6.83 using un-identified new fuselage frame)		
G-APZL	Piper PA-22-160 Tri-Pacer	22-7054	EI-ALF	27. 1.60	B.Robins	Dunkeswell	14. 5.99
			N10F				
G-APZR*	Cessna 150	17861	N6461T	31. 3.60	Avtech Ltd	Biggin Hill	4. 4.81
					(Damaged Biggin Hill 14.1.81: front fuselage used as engine test-bed: noted 12.00)		
G-APZX	Piper PA-22-150 Tri-Pacer	22-5181	N7420D	28. 4.60	Applied Signs Ltd	Tatenhill	20. 6.03
	(Modified to PA-20 Pacer configuration)						

G-ARAA - G-ARZZ

Reg	Type	c/n	Prev id	Date	Owner	Location	Date
G-ARAI	Piper PA-22-160 Tri-Pacer	22-7421	N10F	17. 5.60	J.Mann	(Cheshunt)	14.11.04
G-ARAM	Piper PA-18-150 Super Cub	18-7312	N10F	17. 5.60	Spectrum Leisure Ltd	Clacton	22. 6.02T
G-ARAN	Piper PA-18-150 Super Cub	18-7307	N10F	28. 4.60	A.P.Docherty	Clacton	8. 6.04
					(Dismantled 8.02 after force landing post 5.02)		
G-ARAO	Piper PA-18 Super Cub 95	18-7327	N10F	17. 5.60	R.G.Manton *(As "607327/L/09" in USAAC c/s)*	Denham	30. 1.05
G-ARAS	Champion 7FC Tri-Traveler	7FC-396		12. 9.60	G.J.Taylor	(Lichfield)	22. 6.01P
					tr Alpha Sierra Flying Group		
G-ARAT	Cessna 180C	50827	N9327T	18. 5.60	C.Buck	Felthorpe	14. 6.04
G-ARAW	Cessna 182C Skylane	52843	N8943T	18. 5.60	R.P.Beck, G.& R.L.McLean	Sherburn-in-Elmet	8.12.05T
					t/a Ximango UK		
G-ARAX	Piper PA-22-150 Tri-Pacer	22-3830	N4523A	22. 4.60	J.J.Bywater	Old Sarum	14. 4.02
G-ARAY*	Avro 748 Srs.1A/200	1535	OY-DFV	21. 4.60	Air Salvage International	Alton	16. 6.90T
		G-11/G-ARAY/PI-C784/G-ARAY/VP-LIO/G-ARAY/PP-VJQ/G-ARAY/YV-C-AMC/G-ARAY					
		(WFU 17.10.89 & broken up 5.92) (Cancelled 2.11.95 as WFU) (Nose only 1.02)					
G-ARAZ	de Havilland DH.82A Tiger Moth	82867	R4959	25. 3.60	D.A.Porter	Griffins Farm, Temple Bruer	28. 5.04
					(As "R4959/59" in RAF c/s)		
G-ARBE	de Havilland DH.104 Dove 8	04517		6. 5.60	M.Whale & M.W.A.Lunn	Kemble	3.10.02
G-ARBG	Tipsy T.66 Nipper 2	ABAC.1 & 57		11. 5.60	J.Horovitz & J.McLeod	Felthorpe	17. 8.84P
	(Built Avions Fairey SA) (Volkswagen 1834 Acro)				*(Damaged Felthorpe 6.5.84: on rebuild 5.91)*		
G-ARBM	Auster 5 J/1B Aiglet	2792	EI-AMO	8. 6.60	A.D.Hodgkinson	Dunkirk Farm, Canterbury	6. 6.03
			G-ARBM/VP-SZZ/VP-KKR				
G-ARBN*	Piper PA-23-160 Apache	23-1385	EI-AKI	1. 6.60	Busy Bee Aviation Ltd	Sibson	25. 8.86T
			N3421P		*(Damaged Sibson 8.86: cancelled 5.1.89 as WFU) (Fuselage stored unmarked 10.01)*		
G-ARBO	Piper PA-24-250 Comanche	24-2117	N10F	15. 6.60	Arrow Aviation Services Ltd	Exeter	27. 5.84
					(Force landed Morecambe Bay 27.4.83: new owner 6.01)		
G-ARBP	Tipsy T.66S Nipper 2	54		7. 6.60	F.W.Kirk	Seighford	14. 6.03P
	(Built Avions Fairey SA) (Volkswagen 1834)						
G-ARBS	Piper PA-22-160 Tri-Pacer	22-6858	N2868Z	24. 8.60	S.D.Rowell	Valley Farm, Winwick	22. 1.05
	(Modified to PA-20 Pacer configuration)				*"Greta"*		
G-ARBV	Piper PA-22-160 Tri-Pacer	22-5836	N8633D	29. 6.60	D.J.Sheen tr Oaksey Pacers	Oaksey Park	19. 7.03
					(Rebuilt 1983/84 using fuselage of G-ARDP c/n 22-4254)		
G-ARBZ	Rollason-Druine D.31 Turbulent	PFA 553		6. 5.60	G.Richards	Headcorn	15.10.99P
	(Ardem 4C02)				*(New owner 2.03)*		
G-ARCC	Piper PA-22-150 Tri-Pacer	22-4006	N4853A	23. 6.60	A.S.Cowan	Popham	23. 5.03
					tr Popham Flying Group G-ARCC		
G-ARCF	Piper PA-22-150 Tri-Pacer	22-4563	N5902D	28. 6.60	M.J.Speakman	North Coates	20. 5.05
G-ARCI*	Cessna 310D	39266	N6966T	21.10.60	Not known	Blackpool	25. 4.84
					(Damaged Sandtoft 22.8.86: cancelled 3.1.89 by CAA) (Open store 8.02)		
G-ARCS	Auster D.6	Srs.180	3703	4. 7.60	E.A.Matty	Shobdon	3. 9.03
G-ARCT	Piper PA-18 Super Cub 95	18-7375	EI-AVE	6. 7.60	C.F.O'Neil	(Belfast)	21. 4.86
			G-ARCT/N10F		*(Damaged Mullaghmore 29.3.87: stored 1996)*		
G-ARCV	Cessna 175A Skylark	17556757	N8057T	7.11.60	R.Francis & C.Campbell	Sandtoft	3. 9.05
	(Continental O-300D)						
G-ARCW	Piper PA-23 Apache	23-796	N2187P	7. 7.60	F W Ellis	Water Leisure Park, Skegness	17. 4.04
	(Modified to PA-23-160 standard)						
G-ARDB	Piper PA-24-250 Comanche	24-2166	PH-RON	15. 8.60	P.Crook	Andrewsfield	7. 6.04
			G-ARDB/N7019P				
G-ARDD	Scintex CP.301C-1 Emeraude	549		4. 7.60	G.E.Livings	RAF Halton	26. 7.03P
	(Rebuilt EMK Aeroplanes with c/n EMK.004)						
G-ARDG*	Lancashire Aircraft EP-9 Prospector 2	47		14. 7.60	G.Pearce	Durrington, West Sussex	
					(Cancelled 28.5.82 as WFU) (Stored 8.01)		
G-ARDJ	Auster D.6 Srs.180	3704		15. 7.60	R.E.Neal t/a RN Aviation (Leicester Airport)	Leicester	7. 7.88T
					(Damaged near Leicester 30.5.86: dismantled 1.02)		
G-ARDO	Wassmer Jodel D.112J	146	F-PBTE	22. 8.60	W.R.Prescott	Kilkeel, Co.Down	18. 4.03P
	(Built Ets Couesnon)		F-BBTE/F-WBTE		*(Composite with fuselage of G-AYEO c/n 684 ex F-BIGG)*		
G-ARDS	Piper PA-22-150 Caribbean	22-7154	N3214Z	4. 9.60	A.C.Donaldson & C.I.Lavery	Newtownards, Co.Down	28. 5.03
G-ARDT	Piper PA-22-160 Tri-Pacer	22-6210	N9158D	15. 9.60	B.W.Haston	Cheyne Farm, Stonehaven	29. 6.05
G-ARDV	Piper PA-22-160 Tri-Pacer	22-7487	EI-APA	28. 7.60	R.W.Christie	(Ballymena, Co.Antrim)	2. 1.99
			G-ARDV/N10F		*(Damaged Ballymena 10.7.98: current status unknown)*		
G-ARDY	Tipsy T.66 Nipper 2	55		10. 8.60	D.Best	Enstone	12.12.00P
	(Built Avions Fairey SA) (Martlet Volkswagen)						
G-ARDZ*	SAN Jodel D.140A Mousquetaire	49		10.11.60	M.J.Wright	Cherry Tree Farm, Monewden	29.11.91
					(Cancelled 26.2.99 by CAA) (Noted 5.00)		
G-AREH	de Havilland DH.82A Tiger Moth	85287	(G-APYV)	4. 7.60	C.D.Cyster & A.J.Hastings	Glenrothes	19. 4.66T
			6746M/DE241		*(On rebuild & new owners 2.02)*		
G-AREI	Taylorcraft Auster III	518	9M-ALB	14.12.60	P.J.Stock *"Akyab"*	(Petersfield)	21. 4.03
			VR-RBM/VR-SCJ/MT438		*(Op Military Auster Flight) (As "MT438" in SEAC c/s)*		
G-AREL	Piper PA-22-150 Caribbean	22-7284	N3344Z	14. 9.60	H.H.Cousins	Fenland	8. 1.05
					t/a Fenland Aeroservices		
G-AREO	Piper PA-18-150 Super Cub	18-7407	N10F	24. 8.60	The Vale of the White Horse Gliding Club		
						Sandhill Farm, Shrivenham	17. 9.04
G-ARET	Piper PA-22-160 Tri-Pacer	22-7590	N10F	2. 9.60	I.S.Runnalls	Church Farm, North Moreton	20. 5.83T
					(On rebuild 5.99)		
G-AREV	Piper PA-22-160 Tri-Pacer	22-6540	N9628D	25.10.60	D.J.Ash *"Smart Cat"*	Barton	2. 1.04
G-AREX	Aeronca 15AC Sedan	15AC-61	CF-FNM	12. 9.60	R.J.M.Turnbull & P.Lowndes		
						Rydinghurst Farm, Cranleigh	4.10.04
G-ARFB	Piper PA-22-150 Caribbean	22-7518	N3625Z	8. 9.60	D.Shaw	Egginton, Derby	28. 2.03
G-ARFD	Piper PA-22-160 Tri-Pacer	22-7565	N3667Z	8. 9.60	J.R.Dunnett	Priory Farm, Tibenham	31. 5.04
G-ARFG	Cessna 175AX Skylark	56505	N7005E	15.11.60	P.K.Blair	Stapleford	28. 1.04T
	(Rebuilt to Cessna 172 standard 1988)				tr Foxtrot Golf Group		
G-ARFH	Piper PA-24-250 Comanche	24-2240	N7087P	13.10.60	A.B.W.Taylor	Great Massingham	25. 1.04

G-ARFI	Cessna 150A	15059100	N41836 G-ARFI/N7000X	1. 2.61	J.H.Fisher	Haverfordwest	19. 7.03
G-ARFL	Cessna 175B Skylark	17556868	N8168T	2. 2.61	A.J.Hobbs	Acle Bridge, Norfolk	7. 3.03
G-ARFO	Cessna 150A	15059174	N7074X	23. 3.61	Breakthrough Aviation Ltd	Leicester	25. 4.03T
G-ARFT	SAN Jodel DR.1050 Ambassadeur	170		27.10.60	R.Shaw	(Sowerby Bridge)	13.10.84
	(Damaged Prestwick 15.6.84: current status unknown)						
G-ARFV	Tipsy T.66 Nipper 2	44		5.10.60	C.J.Pidler	(Wellington)	29.11.01P
	(Built Avions Fairey SA) (Volkswagen 1834)						
G-ARGB*	Auster 6A Tugmaster	2593	VF635	12.10.60	C.J.Baker	Carr Farm, Thorney, Newark	21. 6.74
	(Dismantled fuselage 1.03)						
G-ARGG	de Havilland DHC.1 Chipmunk 22	C1/0247	WD305	19.10.60	B.Hook	Coventry	21. 4.96
	(As "WD305") (Stored w/o engine 5.00)						
G-ARGO	Piper PA-22-108 Colt	22-8034		18. 1.61	D R Smith	Sleap	18. 5.05
G-ARGV	Piper PA-18-150 Super Cub	18-7559	N10F	20.12.60	Wolds Gliding Club Ltd	Pocklington	17. 3.05
	(Lycoming O-360-A4)						
G-ARGY	Piper PA-22-160 Tri-Pacer	22-7620	G-JEST G-ARGY/N10F	20.12.60	D.H.& R.T.Tanner	Wellesbourne Mountford	7.12.02
	(Modified to PA-20 configuration)						
G-ARGZ	Rollason-Druine D.31 Turbulent	PFA 562		7.11.60	The Tiger Club (1990) Ltd	Headcorn	1310.03P
	(Volkswagen 1600)						
G-ARHB	Forney F-1A Aircoupe	5733		17. 4.61	A.V.Rash & D.R.Wickes	Earls Colne	7.11.02
					tr Aircoupe Hotel Bravo		
G-ARHC	Forney F-1A Aircoupe	5734		26. 5.61	A.P.Gardner	Little Gransden	21. 6.04
G-ARHF*	Forney F-1A Aircoupe	5737		26. 5.61	(R Ford)	Sywell	10. 5.94
	(Cancelled 10.11.95 by CAA) (On rebuild 8.01)						
G-ARHI	Piper PA-24-180 Comanche	24-2260	N7299P N10F	20.12.60	D.D.Smith	Norwich	27. 7.03
G-ARHL*	Piper PA-23-250 Aztec	27-402		3. 3.61	C.J.Freeman	Headcorn	23.11.79
	(On overhaul 4.00: cancelled 15.3.01 as WFU)						
G-ARHM	Auster 6A	2515	VF557	5. 1.61	R.C.P.Brookhouse	(London SW10)	9.12.01
G-ARHN	Piper PA-22-150 Caribbean	22-7514	N3622Z	10. 1.61	J.R.Lawrence	Nether Huntlywood Farm, Gordon	5. 3.03
	(Rebuilt with parts of G-ATXB - DBR 26.8.74)						
G-ARHP	Piper PA-22-160 Tri-Pacer	22-7549	N3652Z	10. 1.61	R.N.Morgan	Boones Farm, High Garrett, Braintree	22. 5.03
G-ARHR	Piper PA-22-150 Caribbean	22-7576	N3707Z	10. 1.61	A.R.Wyatt	Fowlmere	22.10.04
G-ARHU	Piper PA-22-160 Tri-Pacer	22-7602	N3726Z	10. 1.61	M.S.Bird *(New owner 1.02)*	(Salisbury)	10.12.98
G-ARHW	de Havilland DH.104 Dove	8 04512		10. 1.61	Pacelink Ltd	Fairoaks	14. 3.02T
G-ARHZ	Rollason-Druine D.62A Condor	PFA 247 RAE/602		13.12.60	T.J.Goodwin	Bounds Farm, Ardleigh	26. 7.95P
	(Continental O-200-A)				*(Damaged Damyns Hall, Upminster 4.9.94)*		
G-ARID	Cessna 172B Skyhawk	48209	N7709X	2. 2.61	L.M.Edwards	Sleap	25. 6.03
G-ARIF	Ord-Hume O-H 7 Minor Coupe	O-H 7 & PAL/1401		22. 8.60	N.H.Ponsford	Wigan	
	(Modified Luton LA-4C Minor)				*(Stored incomplete 3.96)*		
G-ARIH	Auster 6A	2463	TW591	23. 1.61	R.Tarder & J.J.Fisher	Yeatsall Farm, Abbots Bromley	14. 6.04
					tr India Hotel Group *(As "TW591" in 664 (AOP) Sqdn c/s)*		
G-ARIK	Piper PA-22-150 Caribbean	22-7570	N3701Z	26. 1.61	C.J.Berry	Booker	3. 5.03
G-ARIL	Piper PA-22-150 Caribbean	22-7574	N3705Z	26. 1.61	T.I.Carlin	City of Derry	21.12.01
G-ARIM	Druine D.31 Turbulent	PFA 510		27. 2.61	R M.White	(Chapel/High Kype Farm), Strathaven	
	(Current status unknown)						
G-ARIN*	Piper PA-24-250 Comanche	24-1182	N6084P	10. 2.61	NK	Walton New Road Business Park, Bruntingthorpe	22. 8.90
	(Crashed near Bodmin 20.5.90 on take-off: cancelled 29.8.90 as WFU) (Fuselage noted in scrapyard compound 12.01)						
G-ARJB	de Havilland DH.104 Dove	8 04518		29. 9.60	M.Whale & M.W.A.Lunn	Kemble	10.12.73T
					(JCB titles) "Exporter" (Stored 5.02)		
G-ARJE	Piper PA-22-108 Colt	22-8184		29. 3.61	C.I.Fray	(Disley)	29. 4.73
	(On rebuild 1993: new owner 10.00)						
G-ARJF	Piper PA-22-108 Colt	22-8199		23. 3.61	A.M.Noble	Pepperbox, Salisbury	17. 4.03
G-ARJH	Piper PA-22-108 Colt	22-8249		29. 3.61	A.Vine	Goodwood	10. 9.03
G-ARJS	Piper PA-23-160 Apache G	23-1977	N10F	3. 3.61	Bencray Ltd	Blackpool	12.11.03T
					(Op Blackpool & Fylde Aero Club)		
G-ARJT	Piper PA-23-160 Apache G	23-1981	N10F	3. 3.61	J.A.Cole	Netherthorpe	29. 1.01T
G-ARJU	Piper PA-23-160 Apache G	23-1984	N10F	3. 3.61	G.R.Manley	Biggin Hill	5. 3.03T
G-ARJV	Piper PA-23-160 Apache G	23-1985	N10F	3. 3.61	Metham Aviation Ltd	Thruxton	17. 6.05
G-ARJZ*	Rollason-Druine D.31 Turbulent	PFA 564		8. 2.61	C.J.Tilson	Great Massingham	4. 9.95P
	(Volkswagen 1700)				*(Stored 2.99: cancelled 11.9.00 by CAA)*		
G-ARKG	Auster J/5G Cirrus Autocar	3061	AP-AHJ VP-KKN	22. 2.61	G.C.Milborrow	Spanhoe	8. 8.04
G-ARKJ	Beech N35 Bonanza	D-6736		5. 5.61	P.A.Brook	Shoreham	20. 1.05
G-ARKK	Piper PA-22-108 Colt	22-8290		12. 4.61	R.D.Welfare	Fairoaks	7.11.03
G-ARKM	Piper PA-22-108 Colt	22-8313		12. 4.61	D.Dytch & J.Moffat	Perth	1.12.04T
G-ARKN	Piper PA-22-108 Colt	22-8327		9. 5.61	R.Redfern	Egginton, Derby	8. 8.05
G-ARKP	Piper PA-22-108 Colt	22-8364		19. 5.61	C.J.& J.Freeman	Headcorn	20.12.04T
G-ARKS	Piper PA-22-108 Colt	22-8422		7. 6.61	R.A.Nesbitt-Dufort	Bradleys Lawn, Heathfield	28.11.04
	(Lycoming O-320)						
G-ARLG	Auster D.4/108	3606		4. 4.61	R.D.Helliar-Symons	Bourne Park, Hurstbourne Tarrant	14. 5.03P
					tr Auster D4 Group		
G-ARLK	Piper PA-24-250 Comanche	24-2433	EI-ALW G-ARLK/N10F	25. 5.61	Gibad Aviation Ltd	Stapleford	2. 4.05
G-ARLP(2)	Beagle A.61 Terrier 1	3724(1)	VX123	11. 4.61	D.R.Whitby tr Gemini Flying Group	(Fakenham)	31.10.91
	(C/n officially quoted as 2573/VF631 which became G-ARLM(2)/G-ASDK)				*(Damaged Truleigh Farm, Edburton 4.8.91: on rebuild 2000)*		
G-ARLR	Beagle A.61 Terrier 2	3721 & D.601	VW996	11. 4.61	M. Palfreman	Bagby	9. 9.01
G-ARLX	SAN Jodel D.140B Mousquetaire II	66	(VH-...)	12. 4.61	J.S & S.V.Shaw	Dunkeswell	30. 5.04T
G-ARLY*	Auster J/5P Autocar	3271		14. 4.61	Not known	(Switzerland)	6. 6.71
	(Sold in Switzerland 11.87 & cancelled 25.2.99 by CAA) (On rebuild to D.6/180 standard using parts ex Airedale G-ARNR & wings ex J/5R G-APAA 1.03)						
G-ARLZ	Rollason-Druine D.31A Turbulent	RAE/578		7. 4.61	Little Bear Ltd	Exeter	18. 7.03P
	(Ardem 4C02)						
G-ARMA	Piper PA-23-160 Apache G	23-1967	N4448P	8. 5.61	C J Hopewell *(Stored 10.01)*	Sibson	22. 7.77
G-ARMB	de Havilland DHC.1 Chipmunk 22A	C1/0099	WB660	26. 4.61	I.M.Castle *(As "WB660")*	Sywell	20. 5.05

Reg	Type	c/n	Prev id	Date	Owner/Operator	Location	Date
G-ARMC	de Havilland DHC.1 Chipmunk 22A	C1/0151	WB703	26. 4.61	J.T.H.Henderson	White Waltham	7. 6.02
					(As "WB703" in RAF c/s)		
G-ARMD	de Havilland DHC.1 Chipmunk 22A	C1/0237	WD297	26. 4.61	D M Squires (Stored 1.03)	(Redditch)	5. 6.76
G-ARMF	de Havilland DHC.1 Chipmunk 22A	C1/0394	WG322	26. 4.61	D.M.Squires	(Redditch)	12.10.98
					(As "WZ868") (Damaged 1996: stored 1.03))		
G-ARMG	de Havilland DHC.1 Chipmunk 22	C1/0575	AWK558	26. 4.61	D.K.Keays tr The MG Group	Bidford	1. 3.04
G-ARML	Cessna 175B Skylark	17556995	N8295T	12. 7.61	R.W.Boote	RAF Lyneham	31. 3.02
G-ARMN	Cessna 175B Skylark	17556994	N8294T	18. 8.61	B.R.Nash	Lower Wasing Farm, Brimpton	13. 6.05
G-ARMO	Cessna 172B Skyhawk	48560	N8060X	12. 6.61	G.M.Jones	Little Staughton	21. 3.05
G-ARMR	Cessna 172B Skyhawk	48566	N8066X	12. 6.61	Sunsaver Ltd	Barton	16. 8.03
G-ARMS*	de Havilland DH.82A Tiger Moth	85698	DE784	25. 4.61	Not known	Krugersdorp, South Africa	
			(Struck trees & crashed George airfield, George, South Africa 27.5.61: cancelled?) (On rebuild 12.02)					
G-ARMZ	Rollason-Druine D.31 Turbulent	PFA 565		2. 5.61	J.Mickleburgh & D.Clark	Headcorn	11.12.03P
	(Volkswagen 1500)						
G-ARNB	Auster J/5G Cirrus Autocar	3169	AP-AHL	18. 5.61	R.F.Tolhurst	Lenham, Maidstone	19. 2.77
			VP-KNL		(Possibly on rebuild 1995: current status unknown)		
G-ARND	Piper PA-22-108 Colt	22-8484		6. 6.61	E.J.Clarke	Seighford	4. 8.99
G-ARNE	Piper PA-22-108 Colt	22-8502		15. 6.61	T.D.L.Bowden	Knettishall	7. 6.04
	(Lycoming O-320)						
G-ARNG	Piper PA-22-108 Colt	22-8547		26. 6.61	F.B.Rothera	Stoneacre Farm, Farthing Corner	10. 1.04
	(Lycoming O-320)						
G-ARNJ	Piper PA-22-108 Colt	22-8587		3. 8.61	R.A.Keech	Woodvale	18. 1.03
G-ARNK	Piper PA-22-108 Colt	22-8622		5. 9.61	N.G. & A.N.M.McDonald	RAF Coltishall	5.11.04
	(Reported as converted to PA-20 configuration with Lycoming O-320 as "Super Colt" although CAA records identify as "modified" whilst retaining Lycoming O-235)						
G-ARNL	Piper PA-22-108 Colt	22-8625		3. 8.61	Miss J.A.Dodsworth	White Waltham	19. 9.03
G-ARNN	Globe GC-1B Swift	1272	VP-YMJ	11. 5.61	K.E.Sword	(Leicester)	11. 7.74
			VP-RDA/ZS-BMX/NC3279K		(Crashed Hucknall 1.9.73: current status unknown)		
G-ARNO	Beagle A.61 Terrier 1	3722	VX113	8. 5.61	R.Webber	Trenchard Farm, Eggesford	19. 6.81
	(Official p/i now shown as VX115)				(Frame noted 11.01) (New CofR 2.03)		
G-ARNP	Beagle A.109 Airedale	B.503		10. 5.61	S.T. & M.Isbister	North Weald	5. 4.03
	(Original regd with c/n A109-P1)						
G-ARNY	SAN Jodel D.117	595	F-BHXQ	13. 6.61	P.Jenkins	Inverness	9. 4.03P
G-ARNZ	Rollason-Druine D.31 Turbulent	PFA 579		28. 6.61	The Tiger Club (1990) Ltd	Headcorn	25.11.03P
	(Volkswagen 1600)						
G-AROA	Cessna 172B Skyhawk	48628	N8128X	19. 9.61	D.E.Partridge	Rayne Hall Farm, Rayne	29. 8.03T
					tr The D & P Group		
G-AROC	Cessna 175BX Skylark	1756997	G-OTOW	2.10.61	A.J.Symms	High Ham, Yeovil	3. 2.03
	(Modified to 172 configuration)		G-AROC/N8297T				
G-AROJ*	Beagle A.109 Airedale	B.508	HB-EUC	17. 5.61	C.J.Baker	Carr Farm, Thorney, Newark	8. 1.76
	(Originally regd with c/n A.109-1)		G-AROJ		(Cancelled 21.1.80) (Stored dismantled 1.03)		
G-ARON	Piper PA-22-108 Colt	22-8822		23.11.61	R.W.Curtis	(Warminster)	5. 7.01
G-AROO	Forney F.1A Aircoupe	5750	N25B	3.11.61	W.J.McMeekan	Newtownards, Co.Down	21.11.04
G-AROW	SAN Jodel D.140B Mousquetaire II	71		13. 9.61	A.R.Crome	Great Oakley, Clacton	3. 4.03
G-AROY	Boeing-Stearman A75N1(PT-17) Kaydet	75-4775	N56418	6. 6.61	W.A.Jordan	Spanhoe	17. 9.03
	(Pratt & Whitney R985)		42-16612				
G-ARPK*	de Havilland DH.121 Trident 1C	2111		13. 4.61	Fire School	Manchester	17. 5.82T
					(WFU 24.5.82: cancelled.1.98) (Noted @ fire dump 10.02)		
G-ARPL*	de Havilland DH.121 Trident 1C	2112		13. 4.61	Not known	Glasgow	13. 8.84T
					(WFU 24.5.82) (Cockpit section on fire training ground 1.03)		
G-ARPO(2)*	de Havilland DH.121 Trident 1C	2116	(G-ARPP)	23. 3.64	International Fire Training Centre	Teesside	12. 1.86T
					(WFU 12.12.83) (To Fire School: extant 7.01)		
G-ARPP(2)*	de Havilland DH.121 Trident 1C	2117	(G-ARPR)	23. 3.64	Glasgow Airport Ltd	Glasgow	16. 2.86T
					(WFU 2.83 & cancelled) (For Training use 1.03)		
G-ARRD	SAN Jodel DR.1051 Ambassadeur	274		20. 7.61	D.J.Taylor & J.P.Brady	(Bicester)	30.11.02P
G-ARRE	SAN Jodel DR.1050 Ambassadeur	275		20. 7.61	A.Luty & M.P.Edwards	Barton	17. 6.05
G-ARRG*	Cessna 175B Skylark	17556999	N8299T	5.10.61	Not known	Little Staughton	4. 5.73
			(Damaged Great Yarmouth 3.11.70: cancelled 7.12.70 as destroyed) (Fuselage stored unmarked 9.00)					
G-ARRI	Cessna 175B Skylark	17557001	N8301T	5.10.61	R.D.Fowden	Pembury	2. 5.04
G-ARRL	Auster 5 J/1N Alpha	2115	VP-KFK	13. 6.61	A.C.Ladd	Romney Street Farm, Sevenoaks	22. 7.05
			VP-KPF/VP-VFK/VP-UAK				
G-ARRO	Beagle A.109 Airedale	B.507	EI-AYL(2)	16. 6.61	M.& S.W.Isbister	Spanhoe	17. 1.74
	(Originally regd with c/n A.109-P5)		G-ARRO/(EI-AVP)/G-ARRO		(Stored 4.01)		
G-ARRS	Menavia Piel CP.301A Emeraude	226	F-BIMA	29. 6.61	Julia P.Drake	Sherburn-in-Elmet	8. 7.03P
G-ARRT	Wallis WA-116/Mc	2		28. 6.61	K.H.Wallis	Reymerston Hall, Norfolk	26. 5.83P
	(McCulloch 4318A) (Orig regd as a Wallis Gyroplane then became WA-116/Mc)				(Noted 8.01)		
G-ARRX	Auster 6A	2281	VF51	24. 7.61	J.E.D.Mackie	Popham	7. 6.03
					(As "VF512/PF-M" in 43 OTU c/s) "Peggy Too"		
G-ARRY	SAN Jodel D.140B Mousquetaire II	72		13. 9.61	Fictionview Ltd	(Lichfield)	11.11.04
G-ARRZ	Rollason-Druine D.31 Turbulent	PFA 580		21. 8.61	C.I.Jefferson "Tarzan"	Hingham, Norfolk	21.12.90P
	(Ardem 4C02)				(Damaged Horley, Surrey 21.7.90: on rebuild 9.97: current status unknown)		
G-ARSB(2)*	Cessna 150A	15059337	N7237X	25. 9.61	Not known	Little Staughton	10. 6.88
					(Cancelled 1.8.94 by CAA) (Fuselage stored 2.00)		
G-ARSG	Roe Triplane Type IV rep	HAC.1	(BAPC.1)	29.10.81	The Shuttleworth Trust	Old Warden	21. 8.03P
	(ADC Cirrus III) (Also c/n TRI.1)				(No external marks)		
G-ARSL	Beagle A.61 Terrier 2	2539	VF581	13. 7.61	D.J.Colclough (As "VF581")	Trenchard Farm, Eggesford	10. 9.03
G-ARSU	Piper PA-22-108 Colt	22-8835	EI-AMI	23.11.61	D.P.Owen	Thruxton	11. 6.03
			G-ARSU				
G-ARSW*	Piper PA-22-108 Colt	22-8858		23.11.61	Not known	(Maidenhead)	30. 1.97
			(Fuselage donated for construction of Leyat Helica (or "Propeller car") replica with 55hp Lycoming engine: cancelled 27.11.02 by CAA)					
G-ARTH	Piper PA-12 Super Cruiser	12-3278	EI-ADO	22. 9.61	R.I.Souch & B.J.Dunford	Hill Farm, Durley	21. 4.95P
					(Stored 12.01)		
G-ARTJ*	Bensen B.8M	7		22. 9.61	M A Stewart	(Cupar)	
	(Volkswagen 1600) (Originally regd with c/n 8-104-100)				(Cancelled 6.6.75 as WFU) (Stored 6.00: current status unknown)		

G-ARTL	de Havilland DH.82A Tiger Moth		"T7281"	22. 9.61	F G Clacherty	Longwood Farm, Morestead	25. 5.03
	(P/i is doubtful - if correct the c/n is 83795)				*(As "T7281" in RAF c/s)*		
G-ARTM*	Beagle A.61 Terrier 1	3723	WE536	9.10.61	C.J.Baker	Carr Farm, Thorney, Newark	13.11.71
	(Crashed Priory Farm, Turvey, Beds 28.5.70) (Cancelled 12.9.73 as WFU) (Fuselage 1.03)						
G-ARTZ(2)	McCandless M.4	M4/1		24.10.61	W.R.Partridge *(Noted 10.00)*	St.Merryn	13.10.69P
	(Volkswagen 1500)				*(Note G-ARTZ (1) is located at Ulster Folk & Transport Museum, Belfast)*		
G-ARUG	Auster J/5G Cirrus Autocar	3272		2. 1.62	D.P.H.Hulme	Biggin Hill	18. 4.03
G-ARUI	Beagle A.61 Terrier 1	2529	VF57	19. 3.62	T.W.J.Dann	Southend	18. 2.05
G-ARUL	LeVier Cosmic Wind	103	N22C	28.11.61	P.G.Kynsey *"Ballerina"*	Duxford	4. 7.03P
	(Continental O-200-A) (Rebuilt 1973 as c/n PFA 1511: contains little of original as fuselage, wings & data plate for original held elsewhere)						
G-ARUO*	Piper PA-24-180 Comanche	24-2427	N7251P	16. 1.62	J.B.W.Dore		
						Walton New Road Business Park, Bruntingthorpe	22. 8.00
	(Cancelled 18.7.00 by CAA) (Fuselage noted in scrapyard compound 12.01)						
G-ARUR*	Piper PA-28-160 Cherokee	28-133		16. 1.62	M.Jarrett	Crowland	12.10.92
	(Damaged in forced landing near Redhill on 14.9.92: cancelled 27.11.92 as destroyed) (Fuselage stored 6.00)						
G-ARUV	Piel CP.301 Emeraude Srs.1	PFA 700		2. 2.62	P.O'Fee	RAF Keevil	22. 4.03P
	(Continental C90)				*"Emma"*		
G-ARUY	Auster J/1N Alpha	3394		2. 2.62	D Burnham	Andrewsfield	27.11.05
G-ARUZ	Cessna 175C Skylark	17557080	N8380T	23. 2.62	S.R.Page & M.Lowe	Cardiff	25. 3.03
					tr Cardiff Skylark Group		
G-ARVO	Piper PA-18 Super Cub 95	18-7252	D-ENFI	18. 1.83	Northamptonshire School of Flying Ltd	Sywell	20.11.04T
			N3376Z				
G-ARVT	Piper PA-28-160 Cherokee	28-379		21. 3.62	Red Rose Aviation Ltd	Liverpool	11. 4.04
G-ARVU	Piper PA-28-160 Cherokee	28-410	PH-ONY	30. 3.62	Barton Mudwing Ltd	Barton	2. 5.04
			G-ARVU				
G-ARVV	Piper PA-28-160 Cherokee	28-451		11. 7.62	G.E.Hopkins	Shobdon	10. 4.04
G-ARVZ	Rollason-Druine D.62B Condor	RAE/606		6.12.61	R.N.Wilkinson	RAF Shawbury	8. 5.03P
G-ARWB	de Havilland DHC.1 Chipmunk 22A	C1/0621	WK611	2. 1.62	P.G.Alston	Thruxton	4.11.05
					tr Thruxton Chipmunk Flying Group *(As "WK611")*		
G-ARWO	Cessna 172C Skyhawk	49187	N1487Y	10. 4.62	J.J.Sheeran	(Naas, Co.Kildare)	20. 3.03
G-ARWR	Cessna 172C Skyhawk	49172	N1472Y	13. 4.62	M.McCann	Insch	26. 7.04
					tr Devanha Flying Group		
G-ARWS	Cessna 175C Skylark	17557102	N8502X	12. 4.62	B.A.I.Torrington	Swansea	28. 8.04
G-ARXB	Beagle A.109 Airedale	B.509	EI-BBK	5. 2.6	M.Isbister	Spanhoe	9. 9.76
	(Originally regd with c/n A.109-2)		G-ARXB/EI-ATE/G-ARXB		*(Stored awaiting rebuild 12.01)*		
G-ARXC*	Beagle A.109 Airedale	B.510	EI-ATD	9. 4.62	C.J.Baker	Carr Farm, Thorney, Newark	27. 6.76
	(Originally regd with c/n A.109-3)		G-ARXC		*(Cancelled 12.4.89 as WFU) (Fuselage on rebuild 1.03)*		
G-ARXD	Beagle A.109 Airedale	B.511		19. 4.62	D.Howden	Lumphanan	13. 6.86
	(Originally regd with c/n A.109-4)				*(Under restoration 6.00)*		
G-ARXG	Piper PA-24-250 Comanche	24-3154	N10F	21. 2.62	R.F.Corstin t/a Fairoaks Comanche	Fairoaks	24. 7.05
G-ARXH	Bell 47	G 40	N120B	13. 2.62	A.B.Searle	Cranfield	6. 7.90
			NC120B		*(Noted 7.00)*		
G-ARXP	Phoenix Luton LA-4A Minor	PAL/1119 & PFA 816		23. 2.62	E.Evans	Benson's Farm, Laindon	17.10.95P
	(Walter Mikron 3)				*(Wings stored 8.01: fuselage elsewhere)*		
G-ARXT	SAN Jodel DR.1050 Ambassadeur	355		14. 3.62	M.F.Coy	Wellesbourne Mountford	13.11.04
					tr CJM Flying Group		
G-ARXU	Auster 6A	2295	VF526	5. 3.62	E.C.Tait & M.Pocock	AAC Netheravon	16. 9.05
					(As "VF526/T" in Army c/s)		
G-ARXW	Morane MS.885 Super Rallye	100		30. 3.62	M.J.Kirk	Haverfordwest	4. 5.04
G-ARYF	Piper PA-23-250 Aztec B	27-2065	N10F	11. 4.62	D.A.Hitchcock *(New owner 6.02)*	Biggin Hill	11. 6.05
G-ARYH	Piper PA-22-160 Tri-Pacer	22-7039	N3102Z	9. 3.62	C.Watt	Crosland Moor	12. 5.02
G-ARYI	Cessna 172C	49260	N1560Y	13. 7.62	Joyce Rhodes	Blackbushe	10. 8.03T
G-ARYK	Cessna 172C	49288	N1588Y	13. 7.62	G.W.Goodban	Lydd	30. 9.03T
G-ARYR	Piper PA-28-160 Cherokee	B28-770		12. 7.62	R.P.Synge & C.S.Wilkinson	Turweston	4. 5.03
					tr GARYR Flying Group		
G-ARYS	Cessna 172C Skyhawk	49291	N1591Y	13. 7.62	D.J.Squires, C.J & J.Hill	Coventry	31. 8.03
G-ARYV	Piper PA-24-250 Comanche	24-2516	N7337P	17. 4.62	D.C.Hanss	Elstree	30. 7.05T
G-ARYZ	Beagle A.109 Airedale	B.51		29. 4.62	C.W.Tomkins	Spanhoe	26. 2.01
G-ARZB	Beagle-Wallis WA-116 Srs.1 Agile	B.203	XR943	18. 4.62	K.H.Wallis *"Little Nellie"*	Reymerston Hall, Norfolk	29. 6.93P
	(McCulloch 4318A)		G-ARZB				
	(Flown as "XR943" for evaluation 1962 & remained on UK Register: used in 1966 for James Bond film "You Only Live Twice") (Noted 8.01)						
G-ARZE*	Cessna 172C	49388	N1688Y	22. 6.62	Black Knight Parachute Centre		
						Bank End Farm, Cockerham	16. 3.77
	(Damaged beyond repair Brawdy 11.9.76 & cancelled) (Training airframe 2.00)						
G-ARZN	Beech N.35 Bonanza	D-6795	N215DM	23. 5.62	D.W.Mickleburgh	(Oakham)	5. 9.04
G-ARZS	Beagle A.109 Airedale	B.515	EI-BAL	11. 5.62	M.& S.W.Isbister	Spanhoe	23. 5.75
			G-ARZS		*(Stored 4.01)*		
G-ARZW	Phoenix Currie Wot	1 & HAC/5		25. 5.62	B.R.Pearson	Eaglescott	7. 1.89P
	(Walter Mikron 3)				*(Damaged near Headcorn 12.2.88: on rebuild 10.99 as Pfalz D.VII scale rep)*		

G-ASAA - G-ASZZ

G-ASAA	Phoenix Luton LA-4A Minor	O-H/4		19. 4.62	M.J.Aubrey	(Kington, Hereford)	7. 6.01P
	(JAP J.99)				*(Noted 2002)*		
G-ASAI	Beagle A.109 Airedale	B.516		26. 6.62	K.R.Howden *(On rebuild 6.00)*	(Lumphanan)	20. 5.77S
G-ASAJ	Beagle A.61 Terrier 2	B.605	WF569	26. 6.62	R.Skingley tr G-ASAJ Flying Group	Bassingbourn	19. 8.01
	(Initially allocated c/n 3732)				*(As Auster T.7 "WF569") (Op Military Auster Flight)*		
G-ASAK	Beagle A.61 Terrier 2	B.604	WE591	26. 6.62	J.H.Oakins *(As "WE591/Y")*	Persan-Beaumont, France	8. 6.05
G-ASAL(2)	Scottish Aviation Bulldog Srs.120/124	BH120/239	(G-BBHF)	5. 9.73	Pioneer Flying Co Ltd	Prestwick	22. 2.03P
			G-31-17				
G-ASAN*	Beagle A.61 Terrier 2	B.608	VX928	26. 6.62	R.J.Bentley	Haverfordwest	28. 6.96
					(On rebuild 4.97: cancelled 12.9.00 by CAA: current status unknown)		
G-ASAT	Morane MS.880B Rallye Club	178		21. 6.62	M.Cutovic	Croft Farm, Defford	2.11.03

G-ASAU	Morane MS.880B Rallye Club	179		21. 6.62	L.O.Queen	(Manchester)	10. 9.03
G-ASAX	Beagle A.61 Terrier 2	B.609	TW533	12. 6.62	P.G.Morris	Cheyene Farm, Stonehaven	1. 9.96
	(Converted from Auster 6 c/n 1911)				"The Jacobite Air Force" (Under restoration 6.00)		
G-ASAZ	Hiller UH-12E-4	2070	N5372V	18. 6.62	R.C.Hields	Sherburn-in-Elmet	14. 7..05T
					t/a Hields Aviation (Noted 10.02 as "XS165/37")		
G-ASBA	Phoenix Currie Wot	AE.1 & PFA 3005		16. 8.62	C.C.& J.M.Lovell	Chilbolton	6. 5.03P
	(Continental C90)						
G-ASBH	Beagle A.109 Airedale	B.519		26. 6.62	D.T.Smollett	Bratton Clovelly, Okehampton	19. 2.99
G-ASBU*	Beagle A.61 Terrier 2	3733(1) & B.613	WE570	12. 7.62	P G Morris	Cheyene Farm, Stonehaven	5. 7.82
	(Damaged Netherley 12.8.80: cancelled 16.10.85 as WFU) (Stored for spares 6.00)						
G-ASBY	Beagle A.109 Airedale	B.523		23. 7.62	F.A.Forster (New owner 4.02)	Lydd	22. 3.80
G-ASCC	Beagle E.3 Mk.11	B.701	(G-25/12)	23. 7.62	P.T.Bolton	South Lodge Farm, Widmerpool	31. 7.03P
			XP254		(As "XP254")		
G-ASCJ*	Piper PA-24-250 Comanche	24-2368	5N-AEB	2. 8.62	NK Walton New Road Business Park, Bruntingthorpe		2.10.88
			N7197P				
	(DBR landing Bournemouth 10.9.86: cancelled 8.1.87 as WFU) (Fuselage in scrapyard compound 12.01)						
G-ASCM	Isaacs Fury II	PFA 2002/1B & 1		1. 8.62	E.C.& P.King	Kemble	24.10.02P
	(Built J O Isaacs) (Lycoming O-290) (PFA c/n = Builder's membership no.?)				(As "K2050" in pre-war RAF c/s)		
G-ASCU	Piper PA-18A-150 Super Cub	18-6797	VP-JBL	31. 8.62	M.A.Recht	Aboyne	20.11.03
G-ASCZ	Menavia Piel CP.301A Emeraude	233	F-BIMG	1.10.62	P.Johnson	Goodwood	20.11.03P
G-ASDF*	Edwards Gyrocopter	NAFE.1		17.10.62	M.J.Aubrey	(Kington, Hereford)	
	(Triumph T110) (Mod. Adams-Wilson XH-1 Hobbycopter)				(Cancelled in 1963 as not completed) (Noted 2002)		
G-ASDK	Beagle A.61 Terrier 2	B.702	G-ARLM(2)	26.10.62	J.Swallow	(Leeds)	5. 8.99
	(Converted from Auster AOP.6 c/n 2573)		G-ARLP(1)/VF631		(New owner 8.02)		
G-ASDL	Beagle A.61 Terrier 2	B.703	G-ARLN(2)	26.10.62	N.C.Metcalfe	Church Farm, Shotteswell	30. 5.03
	(Also c/ns 3727 (1) & B.632 (1))		WE558		tr G-ASDL Group		
G-ASDY	Beagle-Wallis WA-116/F	B.205	XR944	9.11.62	K.H.Wallis	Reymerston Hall, Norfolk	28.10.97P
	(Franklin 2A-120-B)		(G-ARZC(1))		(Noted 8.01)		
	(Regd with c/n B.204 as Beagle-Wallis WA.116 Srs 1 & powered by McCulloch 4318A: fitted with 990cc Hillman Imp engine 1965 & known as WA.119: re-engined 1971 with 60hp 2-cylinder Franklin 2A-120-A & re-designated)						
G-ASEA	Phoenix Luton LA-4A Minor	PAL/1154		14.11.62	J.Bradstock	(Bath)	16. 8.89P
	(JAP J.99) (Regd with c/n PFA 1154: c/n also quoted as PFA 1319 which corresponds to EAA Biplane G-AYFY) (Stored 10.00)						
G-ASEB	Phoenix Luton LA-4A Minor	PAL/1149		26.11.62	S.R.P.Harper	Walkeridge Farm, Hannington	29.10.82P
	(Lycoming O-145)				(Under restoration 10.01)		
G-ASEO	Piper PA-24-250 Comanche	24-3367	(G-ASDX)	23. 1.63	M.Scott	Southampton	18.10.03
			N10F		t/a Pixies Day Nursery		
G-ASEP	Piper PA-23-235 Apache	27-541		28. 1.63	Air Warren Ltd (Maxim titles)	Denham	10. 7.05
G-ASEU	Rollason-Druine D.62A Condor	RAE/607		12. 2.63	W.M.Grant	Inverness	4. 5.03P
G-ASFA	Cessna 172D Skyhawk	17250182	N2582U	21. 2.63	D.Halfpenny	Maypole Farm,Chislet	18. 6.04
G-ASFD	LET L-200A Morava	170808	OK-PHH	26. 2.63	M.Emery (New CofR 12.02)	(Redhill)	12. 7.84T
G-ASFK	Auster J/5G Cirrus Autocar	3276		7. 3.63	T.D.G.Lancaster	Poplar Hall Farm, Elmsett	24. 5.03
G-ASFL	Piper PA-28-180 Cherokee B	28-1170		7. 3.63	J.Simpson & D.Kennedy	Lee-on-Solent	2. 1.04
G-ASFR	Bölkow Bö.208C Junior	522	D-EGMO	12. 3.63	S.T.Dauncey (Stored 1.02)	Yearby	29. 3.90P
G-ASFX	Druine D.31 Turbulent	PFA 513		18. 3.63	E.F.Clapham & W.B.S.Dobie	Oldbury-on-Severn	16. 8.02P
	(Volkswagen 1600)						
G-ASHH	Piper PA-23-250 Aztec	27-63	N455SL	25. 3.63	C.Fordham & L.Barr	Leicester	29. 8.03
			N4557P				
G-ASHS	SNCAN Stampe SV-4C	265	F-BCFN	23. 4.63	M & B Tools Ltd	Liverpool	6. 2.05T
	(DH Gipsy Major)				(Orig fuselage for rebuild of G-AWEF 1980: rebuilt 1984 with fuselage of G-AZIR c/n 452 ex F-BCXR)		
G-ASHT	Rollason-Druine D.31 Turbulent	PFA 1610		23. 4.63	C.W.N.Huke	Dinton, Wiltshire	19.12.02P
	(Volkswagen 1600)						
G-ASHU	Piper PA-15 Vagabond	15-46	N4164H	1. 5.63	T.J.Ventham	Little Bredy	3. 5.03P
	(Rotax 912UL)		NC4164H		"Calybe"		
G-ASHV*	Piper PA-23-250 Aztec B	27-2347	N10F	1. 5.63	Alderney Airport Fire Service	Alderney	22. 7.85T
					(Cancelled 20.6.88 as WFU) (On fire dump 12.01)		
G-ASHX	Cessna F172D Skyhawk	F172-0006	F-WLIR	3. 5.63	Powertheme Ltd	Barton	29. 5.05
G-ASIB	Cessna F172D Skyhawk	F172-0006	F-WLIR	9. 5.63	R.G.Jones & D.A.Smart	Hawarden	18. 4.04
	(Built Reims Aviation SA) (Wichita c/n 17250091)				tr G-ASIB Flying Group		
G-ASII	Piper PA-28-180 Cherokee B	28-1264		21. 5.63	T.R.Hart & R.W.S.Matthews	Exeter	13. 6.04
G-ASIJ	Piper PA-28-180 Cherokee B	28-1333	N7445W	21. 5.63	G.R.Moore tr G-ASIJ Group	Andrewsfield	1. 3.04T
G-ASIL	Piper PA-28-180 Cherokee B	28-1350	N7461W	21. 5.63	J.Dickenson & C.D.Powell	Leicester	8.11.04
G-ASIT	Cessna 180	32567	N7670A	24. 5.63	A. & P.A.Wood	Audley End	8.12.00
G-ASIY	Piper PA-25-235 Pawnee	25-2446		30. 5.63	T.Holloway tr RAFGSA	Bicester	18. 1.05
G-ASJL	Beech H35 Bonanza	D-5132	N5582D	14. 6.63	A.J.Orchard	(London W4)	24. 7.05
G-ASJO	Beech 23 Musketeer	M-518		18. 6.63	K A Boon tr G-ASJO Syndicate	Bembridge	12. 2.01
G-ASJV	Supermarine 361 Spitfire LF.IXB	CBAF.IX.552	OO-ARA	3. 7.63	Merlin Aviation Ltd	Duxford	3. 5.03P
					Belgian AF SM-41/Fokker B-13/R Neth H-68/H-105/MH434 (Op The Old Flying Machine Co)		
					(As "MH434/ZD-B" in 316 Sqdn c/s)		
G-ASJY	Gardan GY-80-160 Horizon	13		9. 7.63	P.D.Bradbury & S.M.Derbyshire	Bagby	2. 7.05
G-ASJZ	SAN Jodel D.117A	826	F-BITD	5. 7.63	W.J.Siertsema	Church Farm, North Moreton	7. 7.03P
G-ASKJ*	Beagle A.61 Terrier 1	3730	(EI-AMC)	16. 7.63	C.C.Irvine	Gamlingay	7. 2.85
			VX926		(On rebuild 1.96 in T.7 configuration as "VX926" in 664 Sqdn c/s: cancelled 7.8.00 by CAA)		
G-ASKL	SAN Jodel 150 Mascaret	27		18. 7.63	J.M.Graty	Nuthampstead	14. 7.05
G-ASKP	de Havilland DH.82A Tiger Moth	3889	N6588	22. 7.63	The Tiger Club (1990) Ltd	Headcorn	4. 3.03T
G-ASKT	Piper PA-28-180 Cherokee B	28-1410	N7497W	24. 7.63	T.J.Herbert	(Wallington)	10. 9.05
G-ASKV	Piper PA-25-235 Pawnee	25-2272	9Q-CHV	31. 7.63	Southdown Gliding Club Ltd	Parham Park	18. 4.05
			G-ASKV/ST-ACW/G-ASKV/ST-ACF/G-ASKV/N6700Z				
G-ASLP*	Bensen B.7	11		3. 9.63	R Light & T Smith	Stockport	
					(Cancelled 4.9.73 as WFU) (Stored 12.00)		
G-ASLR*	Agusta-Bell 47J-2 Ranger	2057		3. 9.63	Harley's American Night Club		7. 3.96T
						Avenida Espana, Playa de las Americas, Tenerife	
	(Damaged on take-off Bristol 31.1.96) (Cancelled 28.2.97 as WFU) (Noted @ 2.03 minus tail rotor: regn not carried but visible on c/n plate through canopy)						
G-ASLV	Piper PA-28-235 Cherokee	28-10048		11. 9.63	I.L.Harding	Sackville Farm, Riseley	10. 2.05
					tr Sackville Flying Group		

Reg	Type	c/n	Prev id	Date	Owner/Operator	Location	Date
G-ASLX	Menavia Piel CP.301A Emeraude	292	F-BISV	12. 9.63	P White	(Fethard, Co.Tipperary)	16. 1.03P
G-ASMA	Piper PA-30 Twin Comanche	30-143	N10F	17. 9.63	A.J.Mew & M.F.Oliver	White Waltham	5. 1.03
	(Modified to PA-39 C/R status)				tr Mike Alpha Group *"Double Trouble"*		
G-ASME	Bensen B.8M	12		24. 9.63	R.M.Harris & R.T.Bennett	(Nottingham)	9. 7.03P
	(Arrow GT500R)						
G-ASMF	Beech D95A Travel Air	TD-565		26. 9.63	M.J.A.Hornblower	Southend	3.10.02T
G-ASMJ	Cessna F172E	F172-0029		25.10.63	Aeroscene Ltd	Sherburn-in-Elmet	20. 5.04T
	(Built Reims Aviation SA) *(Wichita c/n 17250584)*						
G-ASML	Phoenix Luton LA-4A Minor	PAL/1148 & PFA 802		28.10.63	B.A.Schussler	Cowbit, Spalding	20.12.99P
	(Volkswagen 1600)				tr West Kesteven Flyers *(Stored 11.01)*		
G-ASMM	Rollason-Druine D.31 Turbulent	PFA 1611		31.10.63	W.J. Browning	Redhill	4.11.02P
	(Ardem 4C02)				*"Mouche Miel"*		
G-ASMO*	Piper PA-23-160 Apache	G 23-1995	5N-AAU 5N-ADB/N4473P	30.10.63	Not known	Wallington Green	14. 7.99T
	(WFU Bournemouth 2.9.81: cancelled 17.11.82) (Stored behind "Surrey Guns" shop @ junction of A237/A212 @ 3.00)						
G-ASMS	Cessna 150A	15059204	N7104X	18.11.63	P.J.Husband	Barton	8. 2.04
G-ASMT	Fairtravel Linnet 2	004		20.11.63	A.F.Cashin	Maypole Farm, Chislet	25. 9.01P
G-ASMU*	Cessna 150D	15060252	N4252U	26.11.63	Not known	(Moss-Side, Manchester)	3.11.85T
	(Damaged in gales Barton 13.2.89: on rebuild 1991: cancelled 17.12.93 by CAA) (Current status unknown)						
G-ASMV*	Scintex CP.1310-C3 Super Emeraude	919		22.11.63	P.F.D.Waltham	Leicester	7.11.94
	(Stored 10.97: cancelled 8.8.00 by CAA)						
G-ASMW	Cessna 150D	15060247	N4247U	26.11.63	Aviation Business Centres Ltd	Humberside	4. 7.04T
G-ASMY*	Piper PA-23-160 Apache H	23-2032	N4309Y	3.12.63	R.D. & E.Forster	Beccles	25.11.95T
	(Stored 10.01) (Cancelled 13.12.01 by CAA)						
G-ASMZ	Beagle A.61 Terrier 2	B.629	G-35-11 VF516	4.12.63	B.Andrews	Trenchard Farm, Eggesford	30. 3.03
	(Conversion of Auster AOP.10 c/n 2285)				*(As "VF516")*		
G-ASNB	Auster 6A Tugmaster	3725(2)	VX118	6.12.63	C J Harrison *(As "VX118")*	Church Farm, Shotteswell	29. 4.05T
G-ASNC	Beagle D.5/180 Husky	3678		9.12.63	Peterborough & Spalding Gliding Club Ltd	Crowland	13.11.03
G-ASND	Piper PA-23-250 Aztec	27-134	N4800P	10.12.63	J.R.Grange	Alderney	6. 7.03T
G-ASNI	Scintex CP.1310-C3 Super Emeraude	925		20.12.63	D.Chapman	(Louth)	22.12.02
G-ASNK	Cessna 205	205-0400	N8400Z	27.12.63	Justgold Ltd *(Op Blackpool Air Centre)*	Blackpool	10. 1.03T
G-ASNW	Cessna F172E	F172-0031		13. 1.64	B.M.Tremain	Draycott Farm, Chiseldon	8. 5.04
	(Built Reims Aviation SA) *(Wichita c/n 17250613)*				tr G-ASNW Group		
G-ASOC*	Auster 6A Tugmaster	2544	VF603	21. 1.64	R.J.McCarthy	Haverfordwest	18. 5.02
					tr Auster 6 Group *(Cancelled 16.8.02 by CAA)*		
G-ASOH	Beech 95-B55A Baron	TC-656		31. 1.64	G.S.Goodsir tr GMD Group	Biggin Hill	14. 6.04
G-ASOI	Beagle A.61 Terrier 2	B.627	G-35-11 WJ404	31. 1.64	N.K. & C.M.Geddes tr Ranfurly Flying Group	South Barnbeth Farm, Bridge of Weir	19. 6.98
G-ASOK	Cessna F172E	F172-0057		31. 1.64	D.W.Disney	Egginton, Derby	18. 9.05
	(Built Reims Aviation SA)						
G-ASOM	Beagle A.61 Terrier 2	B.622	G-JETS G-ASOM/G-35-11/VF505	3. 2.64	D.Humphries	Biggin Hill	15. 3.02
G-ASON*	Piper PA-30-160 Twin Comanche	30-312	(N7273Y)	4. 2.64	Not known	Elstree	30.11.91
	(Cancelled 9.7.92 by CAA) (Stored WFU 1.00)						
G-ASOX*	Cessna 205A	205-0556	N4856U	3. 2.64	A.Turnbull	Bournemouth	1. 8.92
	(On rebuild 1.99: cancelled 15.8.00 by CAA)						
G-ASPF	Jodel Wassmer D.120 Paris-Nice	02	F-BFNP	26. 2.64	T.J.Bates	Dairy House Farm, Worleston	19. 6.03P
G-ASPK	Piper PA-28-140 Cherokee	28-20051		28. 2.64	Westward Airways (Lands End) Ltd	St.Just	10. 4.05T
G-ASPP	Bristol Boxkite rep	BOX.1 & BM.7279	(BAPC.2)	29.10.81	The Shuttleworth Trust	Old Warden	10. 7.03P
	(Continental O-200-B)				*"(As No.12A")*		
G-ASPS	Piper J-3C-65 Cub Special	22809	N3571N NC3571N	2. 3.64	A.J.Chalkley	Rhoshirwaun, Pwllheli	30. 5.03P
	(Frame No.21971)						
G-ASPU	Druine D.31 Turbulent	PFA 1623		4. 3.64	M.K.Field	Sleap	21. 2.03P
	(Volkswagen 1500)						
G-ASPV(2)	de Havilland DH.82A Tiger Moth	84167	T7794	5. 3.64	B.S.Charters	Benson's Farm, Laindon	31. 8.97
	(P/I obscure - original G-ASPV sold Norway 7.75 & rebuilt as LN-MAX)				*(Stored 8.01)*		
G-ASRB	Rollason-Druine D.62B Condor	RAE/608		11. 3.64	T.J.McRae & H.C.Palmer	Shoreham	1.11.98
G-ASRC	Rollason-Druine D.62C Condor	RAE/609		11. 3.64	C.R.Isbell	Andrewsfield	7. 5.03P
G-ASRK	Beagle A.109 Airedale	B.538		26. 3.64	Bio Pathica Ltd	(London EC4)	21. 6.04
G-ASRO	Piper PA-30 Twin Comanche	30-395	N10F	31. 3.64	D.W.Blake tr Five Star Flying Group	Gloucestershire	14. 7.05
G-ASRR	Cessna 182G Skylane	18255135	(G-CBIL) EI-ATF/G-ASRR/N3735U	2. 4.64	P.Ragg	(Schwaz, Austria)	5. 7.05
G-ASRT	SAN Jodel 150 Mascaret	45		6. 4.64	P.Turton *(Current status unknown)*	Welshpool	6. 6.94P
G-ASRW	Piper PA-28-180 Cherokee B	28-1606	N11C	21. 4.64	Alliance Aerolink Ltd	Andrewsfield	10. 7.03T
G-ASSB*	Piper PA-30 Twin Comanche	30-432	N10F	22. 4.64	Brooklands Technical College	Weybridge	11. 3.93T
					(Cancelled 25.8.92 as WFU) (Instructional airframe 2.00)		
G-ASSE*	Piper PA-22-108 Colt	22-9832	N5961Z	28. 4.64	A.Ingold	(Birmingham)	12. 6.00
					tr G-ASSE Flying Group *(Cancelled 14.8.01 as WFU)*		
G-ASSF	Cessna 182G Skylane	18255593	N2493R	5. 5.64	B.W.Wells	Baxterley	5. 3.01
G-ASSP	Piper PA-30 Twin Comanche	30-458	N10F	7. 5.64	P.H.Tavener	Redhill	9. 8.03
G-ASSS	Cessna 172E	17251467	N5567T	7. 5.64	D.H.N.Squires & P.R.March	Filton	27. 5.03
G-ASST	Cessna 150D	15060630	N5930T	7. 5.64	F.R.H.Parker Pear Tree Farm, Marsh Gibbon, Bicester		1. 8.04
G-ASSV	Kensinger KF	02	N23S	11. 5.64	C.I.Jefferson	Deopham Green	30. 7.69P
	(Continental C85)				*(Crashed Wolverhampton 2.7.69: on rebuild 5.98: amended CofR 9.02)*		
G-ASSW	Piper PA-28-140 Cherokee	28-20055	N11C	11. 5.64	G S Stone	Biggin Hill	9. 7.04
G-ASSY	Druine D.31 Turbulent	PFA 586		12. 5.64	D.Silsbury	Dunkeswell	20. 4.84P
	(Volkswagen 1500)				*(Noted 5.93: current status unknown)*		
G-ASTA	Druine D.31 Turbulent	152	F-PJGH	12. 5.64	P.A.Cooke	RAF Brize Norton	13.11.97P
	(Ardem 4C02)						
G-ASTG	Nord 1002 Pingouin II	183	F-BGKI Fr.AF 183	21. 5.64	L.M.Walton	Duxford	26.10.73S
					(On rebuild - in primer fuselage & unmarked 10.01)		
G-ASTI	Auster 6A Tugmaster	3745	WJ359	27. 5.64	C.C.Burton	Combrook	12. 7.03
G-ASUB	Mooney M.20E Super	21397	N7158U	24. 6.64	S.C.Coulbeck	North Coates	10. 4.04
G-ASUD	Piper PA-28-180 Cherokee B	28-1654	N7673W	29. 6.64	S.J.Rogers & M.N.Petchey	Andrewsfield	28.11.03

G-ASUE	Cessna 150D	15060718	N6018T	30. 6.64	D.Huckle	West Thurrock	1. 8.90
					(Stored 6.94: valid CofR 4.02: current status unknown)		
G-ASUI	Beagle A.61 Terrier 2	B.641	VF628	6. 7.64	R.J.Bentley	(Nenagh, Co Tipperary)	11. 1.06
	(Conversion of Auster AOP.10 c/n 2570)						
G-ASUP	Cessna F172E	F172-0071		22. 7.64	P.T. & L.E.Trivett	Cardiff	14. 6.03
	(Built Reims Aviation SA)				t/a G-ASUP Air		
G-ASUR	Dornier Do.28A-1	3051	D-IBOM	28. 7.64	P R Dyson	Thruxton	22. 5.03
G-ASUS	Jurca MJ.2E Tempete	PFA 2001		28. 7.64	D.G.Jones	Coventry	3. 8.03P
	(Continental O-200-A)						
G-ASVG	Rousseau Piel CP.301B Emeraude	109	F-BILV	7. 8.64	K.S.Woodard *"Emma II"*	Priory Farm, Tibenham	24. 5.03P
G-ASVM	Cessna F172E	F172-0077		11. 8.64	R Seckington	(Fareham)	27. 1.03
	(Built Reims Aviation SA)						
G-ASVN	Cessna 206 Super Skywagon	206-0275	N5275U	12. 8.64	D.& L.Johnston	(Kerrville, Texas, USA)	21. 2.03
G-ASVO*	Handley Page HPR.7 Dart Herald 214	185	PP-SDG	13. 8.64	Perth College	Perth	14. 1.00T
			G-ASVO/G-8-3	*(WFU after collision Hurn 8.4.97: cancelled 25.9.01 by CAA) (Cockpit only 3.02)*			
G-ASVP	Piper PA-25-235 Pawnee	25-2978	N10F	17. 8.64	Aquila Gliding Club Ltd	Hinton in the Hedges	27. 3.05
G-ASVZ	Piper PA-28-140 Cherokee	28-20357	N11C	24. 8.64	J.S.Garvey	Tatenhill	19. 7.03
G-ASWB*	Beagle A.109 Airedale	B.543		25. 8.64	A.E.F.Bryant	Antwerp-Deurne	27. 6.97
					(Cancelled 10.6.98 by CAA) (Open storage 8.00)		
G-ASWF*	Beagle A.109 Airedale	B.537		26. 8.64	C.J.Baker	Carr Farm, Thorney, Newark	24. 7.83
					(Cancelled 3.2.89 by CAA) (Dismantled 1.03)		
G-ASWL	Cessna F172F	F172-0087		10. 9.64	J.A.Clegg	Swansea	10. 6.04
	(Built Reims Aviation SA)						
G-ASWN	Bensen B.8M	14		15. 9.64	D.R.Shepherd *(Partially built 12.00)*	(Prestwick)	
G-ASWP*	Beech A23 Musketeer II	M-587		22. 9.64	J.Holden & G.Benet	(Hastings)	27. 4.95
				(Damaged Sedlescombe 5.3.94: cancelled 17.8.00 by CAA: current status unknown)			
G-ASWW	Piper PA-30 Twin Comanche	30-556	N7531Y	1.10.64	R.Jenkins	Bournemouth	10. 6.03
			N10F		t/a RJ Motors		
G-ASWX	Piper PA-28-180 Cherokee C	28-1932	N11C	1.10.64	A.F.Dadds	Biggin Hill	16. 4.03
G-ASXC	SIPA 903	8	F-BEYK	6.10.64	M.K.Dartford & M.Cookson	(Andrewsfield)	21.11.01P
	(Continental C90) (Wide-track sprung-steel undercarriage)						
G-ASXD	Brantly B.2B	435		7.10.64	Lousada plc Crawley Park, Husborne Crawley, Bedford		2. 7.05
G-ASXF*	Brantly 305	1014		7.10.64	Not known Amen Corner, Binfield, Bracknell		16 .2.79
					(Cancelled 24.5.82 as WFU) (Stored 10.02)		
G-ASXI	Tipsy T.66 Nipper 3	56	VH-CGH	13.10.64	B.Dixon	Bagby	6. 5.03P
	(Built Avions Fairey SA) (Jabiru 2200A)		OO-KOC/(VH-CGC)				
G-ASXJ	Phoenix Luton LA-4A Minor	PFA 801		14.10.64	M.R.Sallows	Damyns Hall, Upminster	28. 4.03P
	(Lycoming O-145)				*"Pride & Joy"*		
G-ASXR	Cessna 210	57532	5Y-KPW	16.10.64	A.Schofield	Barton	3. 1.93
			VP-KPW/N6532X		*(Dismantled 5.01: current status unknown)*		
G-ASXS	SAN Jodel DR.1050 Ambassadeur	133	F-BJNG	19.10.64	R.A.Hunter	Finmere	2. 8.03
G-ASXU	Jodel Wassmer D.120A Paris-Nice	196	F-BKAG	19.10.64	M.G.Porter	Croft Farm, Defford	12. 3.03P
					tr The Jodel Group Defford		
G-ASXY	SAN Jodel D.117A	914	F-BIVA	27.10.64	P.A., R.A.Davies & D.G.Claxton	Cardiff	18. 2.03P
G-ASXZ	Cessna 182G Skylane	18255738	N3238S	28.10.64	Last Refuge Ltd Gedney Marsh Farm, Gedney, Wells		20. 7.03
G-ASYG	Beagle A.61 Terrier 2	B.637	VX927	3.11.64	G.Rea *(On rebuild 1.95)*	Turweston	19. 2.70T
G-ASYJ	Beech D95A Travel Air	TD-595	N8675Q	6.11.64	Crosby Aviation (Jersey) Ltd	Jersey	31.10.04
G-ASYP	Cessna 150E	15060794	N6094T	23.11.64	A.C.Melmore tr Henlow Flying Group	RAF Henlow	10.10.03
G-ASZB	Cessna 150E	15061113	N3013J	16.12.64	R.J.Scott	Blackbushe	19. 4.04
G-ASZD	Bölkow Bö.208A2 Junior	563	D-FNKI	16.12.64	M.J.Ayres	Full Sutton	23. 6.03P
G-ASZE	Beagle A.61 Terrier 2	B.636	VF552	17.12.64	P.J.Moore	Lee-on-Solent	9. 8.02
	(Conversion of Auster 6 c/n 2510)						
G-ASZR	Fairtravel Linnet 2	005		5. 1.65	R.Palmer & D.Scott	Swanborough Farm, Lewes	9. 8.03P
G-ASZS	Gardan GY-80-160 Horizon	70		6. 1.65	L.R.Burton tr ZS Group	Wellesbourne Mountford	25.11.04
G-ASZU	Cessna 150E	15061152	N3052J	13. 1.65	T.H.Milburn	Blackbushe	15. 5.05
G-ASZV	Tipsy T.66 Nipper 2	45	5N-ADE	14. 1.65	J.M.Gough	(Sale)	23. 5.90P
	(Volkswagen 1835) (Built Avions Fairey SA)		5N-ADY/VR-NDD		*(Stored 9.97: new owner 5.01)*		
G-ASZX	Beagle A.61 Terrier 1	3742	(SE-ELO)	18. 1.65	R.B.Webber	Exeter	11. 9.03
			WJ368				

G-ATAA - G-ATZZ

G-ATAA*	Piper PA-28-180 Cherokee C	28-2055	(OO-...)	20. 1.65	Not known	Southend	16. 5.87
			G-ATAA/(CN-...)/G-ATAA/N11C				
			(Damaged near Melan, France: 12.9.86: cancelled 24.11.86 by CAA) (Wreck stored dismantled 1.03)				
G-ATAF	Cessna F172F	F172-0135		25. 1.65	P.J.Thirtle	Humberside	23. 5.04T
	(Built Reims Aviation SA)						
G-ATAG	CEA Jodel DR.1050 Ambassadeur	226	F-BKGG	25. 1.65	T.M.Dawes-Gamble	Oxford	4.10.02
G-ATAS	Piper PA-28-180 Cherokee C	28-2137	N11C	4. 2.65	R Osborn tr Atlas Group	Andrewsfield	17. 8.03
G-ATAU	Rollason-Druine D.62B Condor	RAE/610		10. 2.65	M.A.Peare Siege Cross Farm, Thatcham		16.11.02
					tr Golf Alpha Uniform Group		
G-ATAV	Rollason-Druine D.62C Condor	RAE/611		10. 2.65	J.R.Hornby *(New owner 11.02)*	(Market Rasen)	6. 8.94
G-ATBG	Nord 1002 Pingouin II	121	F-BGVX	24. 2.65	T.W.Harris	Booker	5.11.03P
			F-OTAN-5/Fr.Mil		*(As "NJ+C11" in Luftwaffe c/s)*		
G-ATBH	CZL Aero 145	172015		24. 2.65	P.D.Aviram	Kingston-upon-Thames	26.10.81
					(On rebuild 1997: current status unknown)		
G-ATBI	Beech A23 Musketeer II	M-696		26. 2.65	A.C.Dent tr Three Musketeers Flying Group	Enstone	2. 6.03
G-ATBJ	Sikorsky S-61N	61-269	N10043?	12. 3.65	Veritair Ltd t/a British International	(Sherborne)	2. 6.03T
G-ATBL	de Havilland DH.60G Moth	1917	HB-OBA	2. 3.65	J.M.Greenland	Blackacre Farm, Holt, Wilts	23. 7.03P
	(DH Gipsy I)		CH-353				
G-ATBP	Alpavia Fournier RF3	59		11. 3.65	D.McNicholl	Inverness	19.10.02
G-ATBS	Druine D.31 Turbulent	PFA 1620		16. 3.65	J.A.Lear	Wigtown	24. 11.03P
	(Volkswagen 1500)				*"Fly Baby Fly"*		

Reg	Type	c/n	Prev id	Date	Owner	Location	Date
G-ATBU	Beagle A.61 Terrier 2	B.635	VF611	17. 3.65	D.M.Snape	Hucknall	2. 6.05
	(Conversion of Auster 6 c/n 2552)				tr K9 Flying Group		
G-ATBW	Tipsy T.66 Nipper 2	52	OO-MAG	19. 3.65	S.Bloomfield & C.Firth	Stapleford	14.10.02P
	(Built Cobelavia) (Volkswagen 1834 Acro)				tr Stapleford Nipper Group		
G-ATBX	Piper PA-20-135 Pacer	20-904	VP-KRX	19. 3.65	G.D. & P.M.Thomson Standalone Farm, Meppershall		17 .6.05
			VR-TCH/VP-KKE				
G-ATCC	Beagle A.109 Airedale	B.542		25. 3.65	J.R.Bowden	Headcorn	24. 3.05
G-ATCD	Beagle D.5/180 Husky	3683		25. 3.65	D.J.O'Gorman	Enstone	12. 3.03
G-ATCE	Cessna U206 Super Skywagon	U206-0380		25. 3.65	Pathcircle Ltd t/a British Parachute Schools	Langar	15. 7.05
G-ATCJ	Phoenix Luton LA-4A Minor PAL/1163 & PFA 812		N2180F	5. 4.65	P.R.Diffey Top Farm, Croydon, Royston		8. 6.01P
	(Volkswagen 1600)			*(Force landed Moggerhanger, Beds 10.11.01: damage to wing, propeller, cowling and undercarriage)*			
G-ATCL	Victa Airtourer 100	93		5. 4.65	A.D.Goodall	Cardiff	25. 7.05
G-ATCN*	Phoenix Luton LA-4A Minor	PAL/1118		7. 4.65	J.C.Gates & C.Neilson *(Cancelled 6.6.01 by CAA)*		
	(Lycoming O-145)					Comarques Farm, Thorpe-Le-Soken	26. 6.98P
G-ATCU	Cessna 337 Super Skymaster	3370133	N2233X	22. 4.65	The Committee for Aerial Photography,		
					University of Cambridge	Cambridge	25. 4.05A
G-ATCX	Cessna 182H Skylane	18255848	N3448S	26. 4.65	K.J.Fisher	St.Merryn	23. 8.03
				(Note fuselage of cancelled G-OLSC is also marked as "G-ATCX")			
G-ATDA	Piper PA-28-160 Cherokee	28-206	EI-AME	27. 4.65	Portway Aviation Ltd	Shobdon	27. 9.02
			(G-ARUV)				
G-ATDB	SNCAN 1101 Noralpha	186	F-OTAN-6	27. 4.65	J.W.Hardie	Glenrothes	22.11.78S
			Fr.Mil		*(Note "F-OTAN-6" used on G-BAYV) (Fuselage noted 3.02)*		
G-ATDN	Beagle A.61 Terrier 2	B.638	TW641	7. 5.65	Susan J.Saggers	Biggin Hill	8. 7.04T
	(Conversion of Auster 6 c/n 2499)				*(As "TW641")*		
G-ATDO	Bölkow Bö.208C Junior	576	D-EGZU	10. 5.65	P.Thompson	(Huddersfield)	4. 7.03P
G-ATEF	Cessna 150E	15061378	N3978U	25. 5.65	A.J.White & B.M.Scott t/a Swans Aviation	Blackbushe	12.11.05
G-ATEM	Piper PA-28-180 Cherokee C	28-2329	N11C	26. 5.65	Chiltern Valley Aviation Ltd	Bovingdon	11. 4.04
G-ATEP*	EAA Biplane	PFA 1301		28. 5.65	E.L.Martin Sausmarez Park, Guernsey		18. 6.73
	(Continental C75)				*(Cancelled 14.7.86 by CAA) (Frame stored 12.01)*		
G-ATES*	Piper PA-32-260 Cherokee Six	2-20		31. 5.65	Stirling Parachute Centre *(Ceased operations 2000)*		
					(Easter Poldar Farm, Thornhill)		11. 6.83
	(Crashed near Kinglassie 8.2.81: cancelled 22.10.84 as WFU) (Used as para-trainer 6.00: current status unknown)						
G-ATEV	CEA Jodel DR.1050 Ambassadeur	18	F-BJHL	31. 5.65	J.C.Carter & J.L.Altrip	(Cambridge)	13. 8.71
					(On rebuild 9.00: current status unknown)		
G-ATEW	Piper PA-30 Twin Comanche	30-719	N7640Y	3. 6.65	Air Northumbria (Woolsington) Ltd	Newcastle	26. 7.04
G-ATEX	Victa Airtourer 100	110	(VH-MTU)	3. 6.65	A K Smart tr Halton Victa Group (Sunbury-on-Thames)		12.10.02
G-ATEZ	Piper PA-28-140 Cherokee	28-21044	N11C	8. 6.65	EFI Aviation Ltd	Norwich	18. 5.03T
G-ATFD	CEA Jodel DR.1050 Ambassadeur	311	F-BKIM	14. 6.65	V.Usher	Wickenby	21. 2.04
G-ATFF	Piper PA-23-250 Aztec C	27-2898	N5769Y	16. 6.65	Neatspin Ltd	Tatenhill	15. 5.05
G-ATFM	Sikorsky S-61N Mk.II	61-270	CF-OKY	21. 6.65	Veritair Ltd Port Stanley, Falkland Islands		1.10.03T
			N10052 (USA P/I not confirmed)				
G-ATFR	Piper PA-25 Pawnee	25-135	OY-ADJ	28. 6.65	Borders (Milfield) Gliding Club Ltd	Milfield	29. 5.03
			N10F				
G-ATFV*	Agusta-Bell 47J-2A Ranger	2093	9J-ACX	1. 7.65	Not known Ley Farm, Chirk		8. 8.92T
			G-ATFV/MM80417		*(Cancelled 22.12.92 by CAA) (Stored 9.00)*		
G-ATFX*	Cessna F172G	F172-0196		8. 7.65	No.2157 Sqdn Air Cadets	Croydon	12. 2.92
	(Built Reims Aviation SA)				*(Damaged Booker 25.1.90: cancelled 22.3.91 by CAA) (Noted 3.00)*		
G-ATFW	Phoenix Luton LA-4A Minor	PFA 811		2. 7.65	P.A.Rose	(Walney, Barrow-in-Furness)	2.12.97P
	(Lycoming O-145)						
G-ATFY	Cessna F172G	F172-0199		8. 7.65	H.Cowan	Abbeyshrule, Co.Longford	25. 5.01
	(Built Reims Aviation SA)						
G-ATGE	SAN Jodel DR.1050 Ambassadeur	114	F-BJJF	9. 7.65	L.S.& K.L.Johnson Lodge Farm, St.Osyth, Clacton		14. 2.04
G-ATGO	Cessna F172G	F172-0181		12. 7.65	Poetpilot Ltd	Sherlowe	19. 7.04
	(Built Reims Aviation SA)						
G-ATGY	Gardan GY-80-160 Horizon	121		20. 7.65	P.W.Gibberson	Wellesbourne Mountford	1. 3.03
G-ATGZ	Griffiths GH-4 Gyroplane	G.1		20. 7.65	R.W.J.Cripps	(Shardlow, Derby)	
					(Stored 7.91: current status unknown)		
G-ATHD	de Havilland DHC.1 Chipmunk 22	WP971	G-ATHD	26. 7.65	O.L.Cubitt & K.P.A.Lewis	Denham	30. 6.03
		C1/0837	WP971		tr Spartan Flying Group *(As "WP971")*		
G-ATHK	Aeronca 7AC Champion 7	AC-971	N82339	2. 8.65	T.P.McDonald, T.Crawley & E.Walker	Crosland Moor	9. 4.03P
	(Continental A75)		NC82339				
G-ATHM	Wallis WA-116/F	402 & 211	4R-ACK	3. 8.65	Wallis Autogyros Ltd Reymerston Hall, Norfolk		23. 5.93P
	(Originally McCulloch - 60hp Franklin fitted in 1974)		G-ATHM		*(Noted 8.01)*		
G-ATHN*	SNCAN 1101 Noralpha	84	F-BFUZ	5. 8.65	E.L.Martin St.Peter Port, Guernsey		27. 6.75S
			Fr.Mil		*(Cancelled 16.12.91 by CAA) (Stored 12.01 in container)*		
G-ATHR	Piper PA-28-180 Cherokee C	28-2343	EI-AOT	11. 8.65	Britannia Airways Ltd	Luton	10. 8.04T
			N11C				
G-ATHT	Victa Airtourer 115	120		16. 8.65	D.A.Beese	Badminton	23.12.02
G-ATHU	Beagle A.61 Terrier 1	AUS/127/FM	7435M	16. 8.65	J.A.L.Irwin Park Farm, Eaton Bray		24. 9.04
			WE539				
G-ATHV	Cessna 150F	15062019	N8719S	16. 8.65	S.Greenwood	Sherburn in Elmet	2. 2.03
					tr Cessna Hotel Victor Group		
G-ATHZ*	Cessna 150F	15061586	(EI-AOP)	20. 8.65	E. & R.D.Forster	Beccles	27.3.98T
			N6286R		*(Noted 10.01) (Cancelled 13.12.01 by CAA)*		
G-ATIA	Piper PA-24-260 Comanche	24-4049	N8650P	20. 8.65	L.A.Brown	Leicester	22.10.04
			N10F		tr The India Alpha Partnership		
G-ATIC	CEA Jodel DR.1050 Ambassadeur	6	F-BJCJ	23. 8.65	R.E.Major	(St.Agnes, Cornwall)	1 .6.81
					(On overhaul 1993: current status unknown)		
G-ATIG*	Handley Page HPR.7 Dart Herald	214	PP-SDI	25. 8.65	Nordic Oil Services Ltd	Norwich	14.10.97T
		177	G-ATIG		*(Cancelled 29.10.96 as WFU: stored 5.00: current status unknown)*		
G-ATIN	SAN Jodel D.117	437	F-BHNV	8. 9.65	G.G.Simpson *(On rebuild 6.00)* Muirhouses Farm, Errol		18. 4.96P
G-ATIR	AIA Stampe SV-4C	1047	F-BNMC	9. 9.65	Austin Trueman Ltd	(St Albans)	29. 6.03
			G-ATIR/F-BMKQ/Aeronavale/F-BCDM/Aeronavale				
G-ATIS	Piper PA-28-160 Cherokee C	28-2713	N11C	9. 9.65	J.C.Holland	(Hungerford)	10. 2.03

Reg	Type	C/n	Prev id	Date	Owner/Operator	Location	Date2
G-ATIZ	SAN Jodel D.117	636	F-BIBR	15. 9.65	D.K.Shipton	Deenethorpe	17. 6.03P
G-ATJA	SAN Jodel DR.1050 Ambassadeur	378	F-BKHL	15. 9.65	D.A.Head & G.W.Cunningham	Bicester	13. 1.03
					tr Bicester Flying Group		
G-ATJC	Victa Airtourer 100	125		16. 9.65	Aviation West Ltd	Cumbernauld	14.12.03T
G-ATJG	Piper PA-28-140 Cherokee	28-21299		20. 9.65	C.A.McGee	North Weald	8.12.05T
G-ATJL	Piper PA-24-260 Comanche	24-4203	N8752P N10F	23. 9.65	M.J.Berry & T.R.Quinn	Blackbushe	20. 5.03
G-ATJM	Fokker DR.1 Triplane rep (Siemens SH-14A-165)	002	N78001 EI-APY/G-ATJM	23. 9.65	R.J.Lamplough Manor Farm, East Garston, Berks (*As "152/17") (Noted 12.00)*		10. 9.93P
G-ATJN	Dormois Jodel D.119	863	F-PINZ	23. 9.65	R.L.Wademan tr Oxenhope Flying Group	Oxenhope	17. 6.03P
G-ATJT	Gardan GY-80-160 Horizon	108		4.10.65	N.Huxtable	Cheddington	28. 5.05
G-ATJV	Piper PA-32-260 Cherokee Six	32-103	TF-GOS G-ATJV/N11C	7.10.65	Wingglider Ltd	Hibaldstow	15. 2.04A
G-ATKF	Cessna 150F	15062386	N3586L	20.10.65	J P A Freeman	Headcorn	4. 9.03T
G-ATKG*	Hiller UH-12B	496	103 Thai AF	21.10.65	Not known (*Cancelled 21.1.80) (Noted dumped 11.01)*	Eshott	28.11.69
G-ATKH	Phoenix Luton LA-4A Minor (Lycoming O-145)	PFA 809		25.10.65	H.E.Jenner (*Stored 1.96: current status unknown)*	Brenchley, Kent	24. 6.92P
G-ATKI	Piper J-3C-65 Cub (Continental A75)	17545	N70536 NC70536	25.10.65	C.O'Donnell (Kinsale, Co.Cork) tr KI Group		23. 4.03P
G-ATKT	Cessna F172G (*Built Reims Aviation SA)*	F172-0206		9.11.65	P.J.Megson	Goodwood	15. 5.05
G-ATKX	SAN Jodel D.140C Mousquetaire III	163		19.11.65	A.J.White & G.A.Piper (*Op Acebell Aviation)*	Redhill	23. 5.04T
G-ATKZ	Tipsy T.66 Nipper 2 (*Built Cobelavia) (Volkswagen 1834)*	72		24.11.65	J.W.Macleod (*Destroyed in arson attack 18.2.03)*	Felthorpe	29. 4.02P
G-ATLA	Cessna 182J Skylane	18256923	N2823F	24.11.65	J W & J T Whicher	Full Sutton	18.10 05
G-ATLB	SAN Jodel DR.1050M Excellence	78	F-BIVG	29.11.65	B.Lumb tr La Petit Oiseau Syndicate	Breighton	24. 8.05
G-ATLH*	Fewsdale Tigercraft Gyroplane	F.T5		6.12.65	Not known (*Cancelled 10.2.82 as WFU: stored 12.00)*	(Stockport)	
G-ATLM	Cessna F172G (*Built Reims Aviation SA)*	F172-0252		6.12.65	Airfotos Ltd	Newcastle	3. 3.03T
G-ATLP	Bensen B.8M (*McCulloch 4318F)*	17		9.12.65	R.F.G.Moyle	(Penryn)	19. 5.97P
G-ATLT	Cessna U206A Super Skywagon	U206-0523	N4823F	13.12.65	A.I.M & A.J. Guest	Dunkeswell	10. 6.05T
G-ATLV	Jodel Wassmer D.120 Paris-Nice	224	F-BKNQ	15.12.65	L.S.Thorne	(Lichfield)	8. 7.03P
G-ATMC	Cessna F150F (*Built Reims Aviation SA) (Wichita c/n 15062849)*	F150-0020		28.12.65	G.H.Farrah & D.Cunnane	Abbeyshrule, Co Longford	1. 7.04
G-ATMH	Beagle D.5/180 Husky	3684		3. 1.66	Dorset Gliding Club Ltd	Gallows Hill, Bovington	18. 7.03
G-ATMI*	Hawker Siddeley HS.748 Srs.2A/225	1592	VP-LIU G-ATMI/VP-LIU/G-ATMI/VP-LIU/G-ATMI/VP-LIU/G-ATMI	4. 1.66	Emerald Airways Ltd (*Cancelled 30.7.01 as WFU) (Fuselage on fire dump 12.01)*	Blackpool	18. 5.00T
G-ATMJ	Hawker Siddeley HS.748 Srs.2A/225	1593	VP-LAJ G-ATMJ/6Y-JFJ/G-ATMJ	4. 1.66	Emerald Airways Ltd	Liverpool	7. 9.03T
G-ATML	Cessna F150F (*Built Reims Aviation SA) (Wichita c/n 15062722)*	F150-0014		6. 1.66	G.I.Smith	Eddsfield	4.10.04
G-ATMM	Cessna F150F (*Built Reims Aviation SA) (Wichita c/n 15062775)*	F150-0016		6. 1.66	Skytrax Aviation Ltd	(Atherstone)	18. 4.04T
G-ATMN(2)	Cessna F150F (*Built Reims Aviation SA) (Wichita c/n 15063526)*	F150-0060	(G-ATNE)	6. 1.66	C.R.Hardiman (*Ditched off Isle of Grain 11.5.84 & salvaged: cancelled as destroyed 22.8.85) (New CofR 12.02)*	(Cardigan)	
G-ATMT	Piper PA-30 Twin Comanche	30-439	XW938 G-ATMT/N7385Y	10. 1.66	Montagu-Smith & Co Ltd	Hinton in-the Hedges	11. 7.05
G-ATMU*	Piper PA-23-160 Apache G	23-2000	N4478P	11. 1.66	P.K.Martin & R.W.Harris (*Stored dismantled 10.01: cancelled 6.3.02 by CAA)*	Sibson	14. 4.90T
G-ATMW	Piper PA-28-140 Cherokee	28-21486		11. 1.66	Bencray Ltd (*Op Blackpool & Fylde Aero Club)*	Blackpool	15. 3.04T
G-ATMY	Cessna 150F	15062642	SE-ETD N8542G	13. 1.66	A.Dobson	(Newark)	15. 9.03
G-ATNB	Piper PA-28-180 Cherokee C	28-3057	N11C	20. 1.66	M A Tidmarsh tr Bravo-180 Group	Tatenhill	31. 3.03
G-ATNE	Cessna F150F (*Built Reims Aviation SA) (Wichita c/n 15063252)*	F150-0042		20. 1.66	A.D.Revill	Leicester	14.12.03
G-ATNL	Cessna F150F (*Built Reims Aviation SA) (Wichita c/n 15063652)*	F150-0066		25. 1.66	G.A.Lauf Lower Upham Farm, Chiseldon tr G-ATNL Flying Group		24. 7.05
G-ATNV	Piper PA-24-260 Comanche	24-4350	N8896P	28. 1.66	B.S.Reynolds	Bourne	14.11.04
G-ATOA	Piper PA-23-160 Apache G	23-1954	N4437P	31. 1.66	Oscar Alpha Ltd	Stapleford	13. 6.03
G-ATOD	Cessna F150F (*Built Reims Aviation SA) (Wichita c/n 15062342)*	F150-0003		1. 2.66	J.H.A.Boyns, E.Watson & G.Bold	St.Just	14. 6.05
G-ATOH	Rollason-Druine D.62B Condor	RAE/612		3. 2.66	J Cooke tr Three Spires Flying Group	(Lichfield)	14. 6.03P
G-ATOI	Piper PA-28-140 Cherokee	28-21556	N11C	3. 2.66	R.W.Nash	RAF Brize Norton	27. 5.05
G-ATOJ	Piper PA-28-140 Cherokee	28-21584	N11C	3. 2.66	A Flight Aviation Ltd (*Op Prestwick Flying Club)*	Prestwick	29. 8.03T
G-ATOK	Piper PA-28-140 Cherokee	28-21612	N11C	3. 2.66	G.T.S.Done & P.R.Harrison tr ILC Flying Group	White Waltham	8. 3.04
G-ATOL	Piper PA-28-140 Cherokee	28-21626	N11C	3. 2.66	L.J.Nation & G.Alford tr G-ATOL Flying Group	Cardiff	23. 1.98
G-ATOM	Piper PA-28-140 Cherokee	28-21640	N11C	3. 2.66	A Flight Aviation Ltd (*Op Prestwick Flying Club)*	Prestwick	27. 8.04T
G-ATON	Piper PA-28-140 Cherokee	28-21654	N11C	3. 2.66	R.G.Walters	Shobdon	18. 9.04
G-ATOO	Piper PA-28-140 Cherokee	28-21668	N11C	3. 2.66	A.K.Komosa (*Noted airworthy 8.02)*	(Lingfield)	24. 9.84
G-ATOP	Piper PA-28-140 Cherokee	28-21682	N11C	3. 2.66	P.R.Coombs tr The Aero 80 Flying Group	Popham	22. 5.05
G-ATOR	Piper PA-28-140 Cherokee	28-21696	N11C	3. 2.66	D.Palmer tr Aligator Group	Shobdon	22. 6.03
G-ATOT	Piper PA-28-180 Cherokee C	28-3061	N11C	3. 2.66	Totair Ltd "Totty"	Shipdham	22. 6.03T
G-ATOU	Mooney M.20E Super	21961	N5946Q	3. 2.66	A.C.Mate tr M20 Flying Group	Sherburn-in-Elmet	28. 5.03
G-ATOZ	Bensen B.8M (*Rotax 503)*	18		7. 2.66	N.C.White & W.Stark (*Substantially rebuilt in 1986, original airframe stored Wimborne)*	Sorbie Farm, Kingsmuir	13. 8.03P

G-ATPD	Hawker Siddeley HS.125 Srs.1B/522	25085	5N-AGU G-ATPD	11. 2.66	Wessex Air (Holdings) Ltd	Bournemouth	14.10.98T
	(WFU 1997 - towed to fire dump & derelict 12.02)						
G-ATPN	Piper PA-28-140 Cherokee	28-21899	N11C	18. 2.66	R.W.Harris, M.F.Hatt, P.E.Preston & A.Jahanfar		
					(Op Southend Flying Club)	Southend	25. 3.05T
G-ATPT	Cessna 182J Skylane	18257056	N2956F	22. 2.66	G.B.Scholes tr Papa Tango Group	Elstree	11. 8.04
G-ATPV	Barritault JB.01 Minicab	01	F-PJKA	22. 2.66	C.F.O'Niell	Newtownards, Co.Down	28. 4.99P
	(Continental C90) (Rebuild of GY-20 F-PHUC c/n A.155)						
G-ATRG	Piper PA-18-150 Super Cub	18-7764	5B-CAB N4985Z	1. 3.66	Lasham Gliding Society Ltd	Lasham	31. 5.04
	(Lycoming O-360-A4)						
G-ATRI	Bölkow Bö.208C Junior	602	D-ECGY	3. 3.66	S.Alexander t/a Interesting Aircraft Co	Bidford	22. 4.01
G-ATRK	Cessna F150F	F150-0049	(G-ATNC)	4. 3.66	G.G. & J.G.Armstrong	Wigtown	19. 8.02
	(Built Reims Aviation SA) (Wichita c/n 15063381)				t/a Armstrong Aviation		
G-ATRM	Cessna F150F	F150-0053	(G-ATNJ)	4. 3.66	J.Redfearn	Morgansfield, Fishburn	26. 6.04T
	(Built Reims Aviation SA) (Wichita c/n 15063454)						
G-ATRO	Piper PA-28-140 Cherokee	28-21871	N11C	4. 3.66	J.S.Jewell & H.A.Aldous	Hardwick	20. 7.03
G-ATRP*	Piper PA-28-140 Cherokee	28-21885	N11C	4. 3.66	JRB Aviation Ltd	Southend	20. 9.84
	(Damaged Boughton Monchelsea 16.10.81: cancelled 10.11.86 as WFU) (Wreck stored 1.03)						
G-ATRR	Piper PA-28-140 Cherokee	28-21892	N11C	4. 3.66	Marham Investments Ltd	Ronaldsway	1.11.03T
					(Op Manx Flyers Aero Club)		
G-ATRW	Piper PA-32-260 Cherokee Six	32-360	N11C	8. 3.66	Moxley & Frankl Ltd & J.Pringle	Seething	31. 7.04
G-ATRX	Piper PA-32-260 Cherokee Six	32-390	N11C	8. 3.66	Central Aviation Ltd	Nottingham	4.10.04T
G-ATSI	Bölkow Bö.208C Junior	605	D-EFNU	14. 3.66	R.S.Jordan tr G-ATSI Group	Shipdham	15. 2.03
G-ATSL	Cessna F172G	F172-0260		16. 3.66	L.McMullin	Belfast	28. 8.04
	(Built Reims Aviation SA)						
G-ATSM	Cessna 337A Super Skymaster	337-0434	N5334S	23. 3.66	I.J. & H.R.Jones	Thruxton	10. 7.97T
					t/a Landscape & Ground Maintenance *(Current status unknown)*		
G-ATSR	Beech M35 Bonanza	D-6236	EI-ALL	29. 3.66	C.B.Linton tr G-ATSR Group	Gloucestershire	7. 2.05
G-ATSX	Bölkow Bö.208C Junior	608	D-EJUC	7. 4.66	R.J.Campbell & M.H.Goley	Westbury-sub-Mendip	1. 7.02
G-ATSY	Wassmer WA.41 Super Baladou IV	117		12. 4.66	R.L.& K.P.McLean	Rufforth	23.11.91
					t/a McLean Aviation *(Spares use for G-ATZS 5.01)*		
G-ATSZ	Piper PA-30 Twin Comanche B	30-1002	EI-BPS	13. 4.66	Sierra Zulu Aviation Ltd	Cambridge	16. 7.05T
				G-ATSZ/(AN-...)/G-ATSZ/(EI-BBS)/G-ATSZ/N7912Y				
G-ATTB	Wallis WA-116/F	214		19. 4.66	D.A.Wallis	Reymerston Hall, Norfolk	18. 5.98P
	(Franklin 2A) (Rebuild of WA-116 G-ARZC(2)/XR944 c/n 205)				*(As "XR944") (Noted 8.01)*		
	(Orig regd as Wallis WA.116 Srs 1 with McCulloch engine: fitted with Franklin 2A 1981 and renamed WA-116/F: reverted to XR944 for Service participation)						
G-ATTD	Cessna 182J Skylane	18257229	N3129F	19. 4.66	M.Brennan, M.A.Griggs & P.J.Ackerley	Blackpool	1. 4.05
G-ATTF*	Piper PA-28-140 Cherokee	28-21939	N11C	25. 4.66	D.H.Fear	Biggin Hill	10. 6.00
	(Cancelled 25.3.02 by CAA) (Noted wrecked 4.02)						
G-ATTI	Piper PA-28-140 Cherokee	28-21951	N11C	24. 4.66	T.Marsh tr G-ATTI Flying Group	(Locking)	26. 9 04T
G-ATTK	Piper PA-28-140 Cherokee	28-21959	N11C	25. 4.66	D.J.E.Fairburn tr The G-ATTK Flying Group	Southend	3. 5.04
G-ATTM	CEA Jodel DR.250 Srs.160	65		26. 4.66	R.W.Tomkinson	Seletar, Singapore	15.12.01
G-ATTR	Bölkow Bö.208C Junior	612	D-EHEH	28. 4.66	S.Luck	Audley End	1.10.03
G-ATTV	Piper PA-28-140 Cherokee	28-21991	N11C	2. 5.66	N.E.Leech tr G-ATTV Group	Andrewsfield	14. 2.05
G-ATTX	Piper PA-28-180 Cherokee C	28-3390	PH-VDP (G-ATTX)/N11C	2. 5.66	IPAC Aviation Ltd	Earls Colne	25. 1.03
G-ATUB	Piper PA-28-140 Cherokee	28-21971	N11C	2. 5.66	R.H.Partington & M.J.Porter	Wombleton	18. 3.05
G-ATUD	Piper PA-28-140 Cherokee	28-21979	N11C	2. 5.66	J.J.Ferguson	(Bideford)	24. 8.03T
G-ATUF	Cessna F150F	F150-0040		4. 5.66	D.P.Williams	Weeley Heath	16. 5.05
	(Built Reims Aviation SA) (Wichita c/n 15063229)				*"Honeysuckle"*		
G-ATUG	Rollason-Druine D.62B Condor	RAE/614		4. 5.66	R.Crosby	Watchford Farm, Yarcombe	7. 7.03P
G-ATUH	Tipsy T.66 Nipper	16	OO-NIF	4. 5.66	M.D.Barnard & C.Voelger	RAF Henlow	16. 4.03P
	(Built Avions Fairey SA) (Volkswagen 1600)						
G-ATUI	Bölkow Bö.208C Junior	611	D-EHEF	4. 5.66	A.W.Wakefield	Stapleford	26.11.05
G-ATUL	Piper PA-28-180 Cherokee C	28-3033	N9007J	6. 5.66	Kirkland Ltd	Ronaldsway	21. 6.05
G-ATVF	de Havilland DHC.1 Chipmunk 22	C1/0265	WD327	25. 5.66	T.M.Holloway	RAF Syerston	9. 5.04
	(Lycoming AEIO-360)				tr RAFGSA *(Op Four Counties Gliding Club)*		
G-ATVK	Piper PA-28-140 Cherokee	28-22006	N11C	27. 5.66	Broadland Flyers Ltd	Norwich	11. 12.04T
G-ATVL*	Piper PA-28-140 Cherokee	28-22013	N11C	27. 5.66	White Waltham Airfield Ltd	White Waltham	8. 9.00T
	(Cancelled 22.11.01 as destroyed) (For fire practice 11.01)						
G-ATVO	Piper PA-28-140 Cherokee	28-22020	N11C	27. 5.66	G.R.Bright	Little Gransden	13. 2.03T
G-ATVS	Piper PA-28-180 Cherokee C	28-3041	N9014J	1. 6.66	S.M.Patterson	Sandown	26.10.03T
G-ATVW	Rollason-Druine D.62B Condor	RAE/615		7. 6.66	G.G.Roberts	Rayne Hall Farm, Rayne	24. 5.04
G-ATVX	Bölkow Bö.208C Junior	615	D-EHER	9. 6.66	D.E.Thomas & R.G.Morris t/a D & G Aviation	Swansea	24.10.03P
G-ATWA	SAN Jodel DR.1050 Ambassadeur	296	F-BKHA	10. 6.66	P.J.Charnell, J.D.Atkinson, H.R.Browning & C.Clarke		
						Popham	13.12.05
G-ATWB	SAN Jodel D.117	423	F-BHNH	10. 6.66	C.R.Isbell	Andrewsfield	18. 7.03P
					tr Andrewsfield Whiskey Bravo Group		
G-ATWE*	GEMS MS.892A Rallye Commodore 150	10634		13. 6.66	D.I.Murray	(Newport, Gwent)	15. 2.82
	(Damaged near Taunton 29.3.81) (Cancelled 17.2.99 by CAA) (Stored 10.01)						
G-ATWJ	Cessna F172F	F172-0095	EI-ANS	21. 6.66	C.J. & J.Freeman	Headcorn	21. 5.04T
	(Built Reims Aviation SA)				t/a Weald Air Services		
G-ATWR*	Piper PA-30-160 Twin Comanche B	30-1134	N8025Y	30. 6.66	NK Walton New Road Business Park, Bruntingthorpe		22.12.94T
	(Damaged in crash Crosland Moor 14.9.93: cancelled 18.4.95 as TWFU) (Fuselage in scrapyard compound 12.01)						
G-ATXA	Piper PA-22-150 Tri-Pacer	22-3730	N4403A	8. 7.66	S.Hildrop	Top Farm, Croydon, Royston	17. 5.04
	(Modified to PA-20 Super Pacer configuration)						
G-ATXD	Piper PA-30 Twin Comanche B	30-1166	N8053Y	12. 7.66	LGH Aviation Ltd	Fairoaks	26. 4.03T
G-ATXM	Piper PA-28-180 Cherokee C	28-2759	N8809J	19. 7 66	M.J.Stack tr G-ATXM Flying Group	Stapleford	12.10.02
G-ATXN	Mitchell-Procter Kittiwake	1		19. 7.66	R.G.Day	Biggin Hill	17. 3.03P
	(Lycoming O-290)	1 & PFA 1306					
G-ATXO	SIPA 903	41	F-BGAP	19. 7.66	S.A. & D.C.Whitehead *"La Pirouette"*	Eaglescott	22. 7.03P
G-ATXZ	Bölkow Bö.208C Junior	624	D-ELNE	28. 7.66	M.R.Kaye tr G-ATXZ Group	Tatenhill	23. 5.03P
G-ATYM*	Cessna F150G	F150-0074		15. 8.66	J.F.Perry	Rochester	28. 9.92
	(Built Reims Aviation SA)				t/a J.F.Perry & Co *(Stored 7.02: cancelled 24.1.03 by CAA)*		
G-ATYS	Piper PA-28-180 Cherokee C	28-3296	N9226J	19. 8.66	E.Baker tr G-ATYS Flying Group	Headcorn	24. 5.03

G-ATZK	Piper PA-28-180 Cherokee C	28-3128	N9090J	21. 9.66	B.H. & E.F.Austen	Oaksey Park	21.10.02T
			(D-EFUN)/N9090J		tr Zulu Kilo Group		
G-ATZM	Piper J-3C-90 Cub Special	20868	N2092M	26. 9.66	R.W.Davison	Holywell	14.11.03P
	(Frame No.21310)		NC2092M				
G-ATZS	Wassmer WA.41 Super Baladou IV	128		30. 9.66	Temporal Songs Ltd & Anti Climb Guards Ltd	Rufforth	28.11.02
G-ATZY	Cessna F150G	F150-0135		14.10.66	Aircraft Engineers Ltd	Edinburgh	1. 7.00T
	(Built Reims Aviation SA)				*(Op Edinburgh Air Centre) (New owner 4.02)*		

G-AVAA - G-AVZZ

G-AVAR	Cessna F150G	F150-0122		27.10.66	J.A.Rees	Haverfordwest	25. 9.04T
	(Built Reims Aviation SA)						
G-AVAU	Piper PA-30 Twin Comanche B	30-1328	N8230Y	8.11.66	Enrico Ermano Ltd	Fairoaks	19. 6.05
			N10F				
G-AVAW	Rollason-Druine D.62C Condor	RAE/617		10.11.66	S.Banyard tr Condor Aircraft Group	Tibenham	25. 5.03
G-AVAX	Piper PA-28-180 Cherokee C	28-3798	N11C	11.11.66	J.J.Parkes	Wolverhampton	30. 5.05
G-AVBG	Piper PA-28-180 Cherokee C	28-3801	N11C	11.11.66	R.A.Cayless & R.D.B.Severn	White Waltham	9. 4.03
					tr G-AVBG Flying Group		
G-AVBH	Piper PA-28-180 Cherokee C	28-3802	N11C	11.11.66	T.R.Smith (Agricultural Machinery) Ltd		
						New Lane Farm, North Elmham	18. 5.03
G-AVBS	Piper PA-28-180 Cherokee C	28-3938	N11C	14.11.66	A.G.Arthur	Perranporth	1. 7.04T
G-AVBT	Piper PA-28-180 Cherokee C	28-3945	N11C	14.11.66	J.F.Mitchell	Shoreham	31. 5.04T
G-AVCM	Piper PA-24-260 Comanche B	24-4520	N9054P	5.12.66	R.F.Smith	Stapleford	26. 6.05
G-AVCN	Britten-Norman BN-2A-8 Islander	3	N290VL	6.12.66	Airstream International Group Ltd	Bembridge	5.11.76T
	(Originally regd as BN-2)		F-OGHG/G-AVCN		*(For restoration to flying status by Britten-Norman Aircraft Preservation Society)*		
G-AVCV	Cessna 182J Skylane	18257492	N3492F	15.12.66	The University of Manchester Institute of Science & Technology		
						Woodford	22. 2.04
G-AVCX	Piper PA-30 Twin Comanche B	30-1302	N8185Y	16.12.66	J H West	(Exeter)	12. 8.03
G-AVCY*	Piper PA-30 Twin Comanche B	30-1367	N8241Y	16.12.66	NK	Walton New Road Business Park, Bruntingthorpe	26. 7.93
		(Crashed on take-off Cardiff 9.3.91)			*(Cancelled 17.7.91 as WFU) (Fuselage in scrapyard compound 11.01)*		
G-AVDA	Cessna 182K Skylane	18257959	N2759Q	16.12.66	F.W.Ellis	Water Leisure Park, Skegness	17. 6.01
G-AVDB*	Cessna 310L	310L0079	N2279F	20.12.66	Not known	Coventry	8. 7.79
					(WFU Perth 8.7.79) (Cancelled 6.8.79) (Noted 1999: port wing @ Perth 1.00)		
G-AVDF*	Beagle B.121 Pup Srs.100	B.121-001		28.12.66	D Collings	Brimpton	22. 5.68
	(Originally registered as B.121C c/n B.151, became B.121 Srs.100 2.69)				*(Cancelled 22.5.68 as WFU) (Stored 1.03)*		
G-AVDG	Wallis WA-116 Srs.1 Agile	215		28.12.66	K.H.Wallis	Reymerston Hall, Norfolk	23. 5.92P
	(Variously powered by McCulloch: Fuji 440, Norton twin-rotor Wankel & now Rotax 532) (Stored 8.01)						
G-AVDS*	Beech 65-B80 Queen Air	LD-337	A40-CS	5. 1.67	Brunel Technical College	Filton	26. 8.77
			G-AVDS		*(Cancelled 1.3.89 as WFU) (Dumped 9.01 as "G-A...")*		
G-AVDT	Aeronca 7AC Champion	7AC-6932	N3594E	5. 1.67	D.Cheney & G.Moore	(Newry, Co.Armagh)	10. 7.90P
			NC3594E		*(Current status unknown)*		
G-AVDV	Piper PA-22-150 Tri-Pacer	22-3752	N4423A	5. 1.67	S C.Brooks	Wellcross Grange, Slinfold	23.10.03
	(Modifed to PA-20 Super Pacer configuration)						
G-AVDY	Phoenix Luton LA-4A Minor			10. 1.67	M.Stoney	Stapleford	9. 8.00P
	(Lycoming O-145)	PAL/1183 & PFA 808			*(Damaged landing Stapleford 18.12.99: stored 12.01)*		
G-AVEC	Cessna F172H	F172-0405		13. 1.67	Quick Flight Images LLP	Fairoaks	11. 5.05
	(Built Reims Aviation SA)						
G-AVEF	SAN Jodel 150 Mascaret	16	F-BLDK	19. 1.67	Heavy Install Ltd	Headcorn	20. 6.05T
G-AVEH	SIAI-Marchetti S.205-20R	346		20. 1.67	R.E.Gretton, K.Fear, A.D.F.Flintoft & R.L.F.Darby		
						Crowland	30. 3.03
G-AVEM	Cessna F150G	F150-0198		23. 1.67	T.D.& J.A.Warren	Goodwood	30. 5.03
	(Built Reims Aviation SA)						
G-AVEN	Cessna F150G	F150-0202		23. 1.67	Lawgra (No.386) Ltd	Cranfield	8.12.05
	(Built Reims Aviation SA)				t/a International Aerospace Engineeering		
G-AVER	Cessna F150G	F150-0206		23. 1.67	LAC (Enterprises) Ltd	Barton	19.12.04T
	(Built Reims Aviation SA)				*(Op Lancashire Aero Club)*		
G-AVEU	Wassmer WA.41 Super Baladou IV	136		27. 1.67	H & S Roberts	Enstone	10. 5.05
G-AVEX	Rollason-Druine D.62B Condor	RAE/616		31. 1.67	C.A.Macleod	Hinton in the Hedges	15. 4.03P
G-AVEY	Phoenix Currie Super Wot	SE.100 & PFA 3006		31. 1.67	B.J.Anning	Watchford Farm, Yarcombe	14. 8.02P
	(Pobjoy "R")						
G-AVFE*	Hawker Siddeley HS.121 Trident 2E	2144		1. 2.67	Belfast Airport Fire Service	Belfast	6. 5.85T
					(WFU 20.3.85: noted 5.00)		
G-AVFG*	Hawker Siddeley HS.121 Trident 2E	2146		1. 2.67	Fire School	Manchester	2. 7.85T
					(WFU 24.5.85) (Noted as "G-SMOKE" 10.02)		
G-AVFJ*	Hawker Siddeley HS.121 Trident 2E	2149		1. 2.67	International Fire Training Centre	Teesside	18. 9.83T
					(WFU 6.82: cancelled 9.7.82) (Front fuselage extant 7.01)		
G-AVFK*	Hawker Siddeley HS.121 Trident 2E	2150		1. 2.67	Royal Air Force	RAF Lyneham	15. 8.83T
					(WFU 31.12.81 & cancelled 12.5.82) (For Rescue training 1.00)		
G-AVFM*	Hawker Siddeley HS.121 Trident 2E	2152		1. 2.67	Brunel Technical College	Bristol	2. 6.84T
					(WFU 30.3.83) (Instructional Airframe 7.02)		
G-AVFP	Piper PA-28-140 Cherokee	28-22652	N11C	1. 2.67	Rebecca L.Howells	Barton	6. 8.05
G-AVFR	Piper PA-28-140 Cherokee	28-22747	N11C	1. 2.67	R.R.Orr	(Dromore, Co.Down)	5. 6.05
G-AVFU	Piper PA-32-300 Cherokee Six	32-40182	N11C	1. 2.67	M.J.Hoodless	Castlerock, Co Londonderry	30. 4.03T
G-AVFX	Piper PA-28-140 Cherokee	28-22757	N11C	1. 2.67	R.A.Irwin tr Wessex Flyers Group	Thruxton	26. 7.04
G-AVFZ	Piper PA-28-140 Cherokee	28-22767	N11C	1. 2.67	C.M.Toyne tr G-AVFZ Flying Group	Yeovil	25. 9.04
G-AVGA	Piper PA-24-260 Comanche B	24-4489	N9027P	31. 1.67	M.D.Crooks, J.R.Butterworth & V.R.Dennay	Biggin Hill	19. 1.03
					tr Conram Aviation Group *"C'est Si Bon"*		
G-AVGC	Piper PA-28-140 Cherokee	28-22777	N11C	31. 1.67	A.P.H.Hay	Popham	7. 5.04
G-AVGD	Piper PA-28-140 Cherokee	28-22782	N11C	31. 1.67	N.Morland	Denham	25. 8.05T
G-AVGE	Piper PA-28-140 Cherokee	28-22787	N11C	31. 1.67	A.J.Cutler	Bournemouth	11. 4.04T
G-AVGG*	Piper PA-28-140 Cherokee	28-22797	N11C	31. 1.67	Yorkshire Light Aircraft Ltd	Duxford	3. 7.71
		(Crashed Papplewick, Notts 10.8.70: cancelled 16.3.73 as WFU) (Wrecked cabin only 9.00)					
G-AVGI	Piper PA-28-140 Cherokee	28-22822	N11C	31. 1.67	D.G.Smith & C.D.Barden tr Golf India Group	Liverpool	16.12.04

G-AVGK	Piper PA-28-180 Cherokee C	28-3639	N9516J	2. 2.67	I.R.Chaplin	Andrewsfield	14.10.02T
G-AVGU	Cessna F150G	F150-0199		8. 2.67	Coulson Flying Services Ltd	Little Staughton	13. 2.04T
	(Built Reims Aviation SA)						
G-AVGY	Cessna 182K Skylane	18258112	N3112Q	17. 2.67	R.M.C.Sears & R.N.Howgego	Stoke Ferry	28. 3.03
			(Ran into ditch landing Maney, Cambs 2.4.00: damage to fuselage, wing and propeller)				
G-AVGZ	CEA Jodel DR.1050 Sicile	341	F-BKPR	14. 2.67	D.C.Webb *(Stored 10.00)*	Bagby	13. 7.97
G-AVHH	Cessna F172H	F172-0337		20. 2.67	Avon Aviation Ltd	Bristol	2. 2.05T
	(Built Reims Aviation SA)				t/a The Bristol & Wessex Aeroplane Club		
G-AVHL	SAN Jodel DR.105A Ambassadeur	90	F-BIVY	23. 2.67	A.P.Walsh & P.J.McMahon	Ludham	17. 8.03
G-AVHM	Cessna F150G	F150-0181		24. 2.67	M.Murphy tr M & N Flying Group	(Epsom)	31. 1.05T
	(Built Reims Aviation SA)			*(Rebuilt 1997 with fuselage from G-ATRL [F150-0050]: old fuselage dumped Shoreham 12.99)*			
G-AVHT*	Beagle E.3 (Auster AOP.9M)	-	WZ711	1. 3.67	M.Somerton-Raynor	AAC Middle Wallop	29. 4.01
	(Lycoming O-360)				*(As "WZ711") (Cancelled 10.4.01 by CAA: stored 2000)*		
G-AVHY	Sportavia Fournier RF4D	4009		10. 3.67	I K G Mitchell	Halesland	12. 2.03P
G-AVIA	Cessna F150G	F150-0184		10. 3.67	Cheshire Air Training Services Ltd	Liverpool	21.11.03T
	(Built Reims Aviation SA)						
G-AVIB	Cessna F150G	F150-0180		10. 3.67	James D Peace & Co	Edinburgh	22. 8.03T
	(Built Reims Aviation SA)				*(Op Edinburgh Air Centre)*		
G-AVIC	Cessna F172H	F172-0320	N17011	10. 3.67	Leeside Flying Ltd	Cork, Co.Cork	9. 5.04
	(Built Reims Aviation SA)						
G-AVID	Cessna 182K	18257734	N2534Q	10. 3.67	Jaguar Aviation Ltd *(Op Fife Parachute Centre)*	Eroll	18. 4.03
G-AVII	Agusta-Bell 206B JetRanger II	8011		10. 3.67	Bristow Helicopters Ltd "Brighton Belle"	Redhill	4. 1.04T
G-AVIL	Alon A.2 Aircoupe	A.5	N5471E	14. 3.67	D.J.Hulks *(As "VX147" in RAF c/s)*	Headcorn	16. 8.04
G-AVIN	SOCATA MS.880B Rallye Club	884		14. 3.67	P.Bradley	(Dorchester)	25. 5.02
G-AVIP	Brantly B.2B	471		14. 3.67	N.J.R.Minchin	Hill Top Farm, Hambledon	18.10.01
G-AVIS	Cessna F172H	F172-0413		14. 3.67	J P A Freeman	Headcorn	20. 1.05T
	(Built Reims Aviation SA)						
G-AVIT	Cessna F150G	F150-0217		14. 3.67	S.Vint	Manston	26. 9.04
	(Built Reims Aviation SA)				tr Invicta Flyers		
G-AVIZ	Scheibe SF-25A Motorfalke	4552	(D-KOFY)	21. 3.67	T.J.Wiltshire tr Spilsby Gliding Trust	Spilsby	19. 9.91
G-AVJE	Cessna F150G	F150-0219		29. 3.67	T.F.Fisher	Hinton in the Hedges	24. 5.04
	(Built Reims Aviation SA)				tr G-AVJE Syndicate		
G-AVJF	Cessna F172H	F172-0393		31. 3.67	J.A. & G.M.Rees	Haverfordwet	1. 1.04T
	(Built Reims Aviation SA)						
G-AVJH*	Druine D.62 Condor	PFA 603		31. 3.67	R Chapman	East Grinstead	4.11.83P
	(Continental O-200-A)			*(Crashed Nefyn, Gwynedd 31.7.83: cancelled 5.1.89) (As spares 4.00 for rebuild of G-AXGU qv)*			
G-AVJJ	Piper PA-30 Twin Comanche B	30-1420	N8285Y	7. 4.67	A.H.Manser	Gloucestershire	30. 7.04T
G-AVJK	SAN Jodel DR.1050M Excellence	453	F-BLJH	7. 4.67	M.H.Wylde	Long Marston	20. 7.05
	(Originally built as DR.1051)						
G-AVJO	Fokker E.III rep PPS/FOK/1 & PPS/REP/6			12. 4.67	Bianchi Aviation Film Services Ltd	Booker	12. 5.03P
	(Continental C85) (Regd as c/n PPS/FOK/6)				*(As "E.III 422/15" in German c/s)*		
G-AVJV	Wallis WA-117 Srs.1	K/402/X		12. 4.67	K.H.Wallis	Reymerston Hall, Norfolk	21. 4.89P
	(RR Continental O-200-B) (Used major parts of G-ATCV c/n 301)				*(Stored 8.01)*		
G-AVJW	Wallis WA-118/M Meteorite	K/502/X		12. 4.67	K.H.Wallis	Reymerston Hall, Norfolk	21. 4.83P
	(Meteor Alfa 1) (Originally regd as Wallis WA.118 Srs 2: used major components of G-ATPW c/n 401) (Stored 8.01)						
G-AVKB	Brochet MB.50 Pipistrelle	02	F-PFAL	17. 4.67	W.B.Cooper	Walkeridge Farm, Hants	30.10.96P
	(Walter Mikron 3)						
G-AVKD	Sportavia Fournier RF4D	4024		19. 4.67	R.E.Cross tr Lasham RF4 Group	Lasham	30. 5.03P
G-AVKG	Cessna F172H	F172-0345		21. 4.67	Aerogroup 98 Ltd	Ronaldsway	10.10.03
	(Built Reims Aviation SA) (Rebuilt with fuselage of G-AVDC c/n F172-0382 in 1986)						
G-AVKI	Slingsby Nipper T.66 RA.45 Srs.3	S.102/1586		24. 4.67	J.M.Greenway	(Wolverhampton)	7. 8.91P
	(Ardem 4C02) (Tipsy c/n 31)						
G-AVKK	Slingsby Nipper T.66 RA.45 Srs.3	S.104/1588	EI-BJH	24. 4.67	C.Watson	Newtownards, Co.Down	6. 4.03P
	(Ardem 4C02) (Tipsy c/n 74)		G-AVKK				
G-AVKL	Piper PA-30 Twin Comanche B	30-1418	OY-DHL	25. 4.67	Bravo Aviation Ltd	Jersey	11. 6.05
			G-AVKL/N8284Y				
G-AVKM*	Rollason-Druine D.62B Condor	RAE/620		26. 4.67	M Hobson	(Cruden Bay, Peterhead)	30. 6.82
			(Damaged in gales Wilkieston Farm, Cupar, Angus 2/3.3.82) (Stored 6.00: current status unknown)				
G-AVKN	Cessna 401	401-0082	(N3282Q)	26. 4.67	Law Leasing Ltd	Rochester	19. 6.05
G-AVKP	Beagle A.109 Airedale	B.540	SE-EGA	26. 4.67	D.R.Williams	Peplow	26. 9.03
G-AVKR	Bölkow Bö.208C Junior	648	D-EGRA	28. 4.67	A.C.Dufton & S.F.Jeffery	Bournemouth	10.10.04
G-AVKT*	Tipsy Nipper T.66 Srs.3	70	OO-HEL	1. 5.67	Not known	Yearby	
	(Built Cobelavia)		OO-DEL				
			(Crashed Constable Burton, Paull, Yorks 19.9.72) (Cancelled 14.2.73 as destroyed) (Frame noted 1.02)				
G-AVLB	Piper PA-28-140 Cherokee	28-23158	N11C	8. 5.67	M.Wilson	Sywell	2.12.03
G-AVLC*	Piper PA-28-140 Cherokee	28-23178	N11C	8. 5.67	NE Wales Institute of Higher Education	Welshpool	25. 9.98
					(Cancelled 20.3.02 as WFU)		
G-AVLD	Piper PA-28-140 Cherokee	28-23193	N11C	8. 5.67	S.H.A.Petter	White Waltham	30. 5.03
					tr The West London Strut Flying Group		
G-AVLE	Piper PA-28-140 Cherokee	28-23223	N11C	8. 5.67	G.E.Wright South Lodge Farm, Widmerpool		22.12.04
					t/a Video Security Services		
G-AVLF	Piper PA-28-140 Cherokee	28-23268	N11C	8. 5.67	G.H.Hughesdon	White Waltham	18. 2.04T
G-AVLG	Piper PA-28-140 Cherokee	28-23358	N11C	8. 5.6	C.H.R.Hewitt	(Ipswich)	23. 8.03
G-AVLH*	Piper PA-28-140 Cherokee	28-23368	N11C	8. 5.67	M.B.Rothschild	North Weald	18. 8.00
					(Cancelled 23.4.02 by CAA)		
G-AVLI	Piper PA-28-140 Cherokee	28-23388	N11C	8. 5.67	Lima India Aviation Ltd	Southend	11. 4.04
G-AVLJ	Piper PA-28-140 Cherokee	28-23393	9H-AAZ	8. 5.67	Cherokee Aviation Holdings Jersey Ltd	(Jersey)	5. 8.05T
			G-AVLJ/N11C				
G-AVLM	Beagle B.121 Pup 2	B121-003		8. 5.67	T.M. & D.A.Jones	Egginton, Derby	29. 4.69S
					(On slow restoration 1.03)		
G-AVLN	Beagle B.121 Pup 2	B121-004		8. 5.67	A.P.Marks	Sywell	9. 7.04S
G-AVLO	Bölkow Bö.208C Junior	650	D-EGUC	8. 5.67	P.J.Swain	Sandford Hall, Knockin	8. 6.03P

Reg	Type	C/n	Prev id	Date	Owner/Operator	Location	CofR
G-AVLT	Piper PA-28-140 Cherokee	28-23328	G-KELC G-AVLT/N11C	9. 5.67	RB Aeroclub Ltd tr RB Flying Group	Sywell	20. 9.04T
G-AVLW	Sportavia Fournier RF4D	4025		9. 5.67	J.C.A.C.da Silva	Damyns Hall, Upminster	1. 2.01
G-AVLY	Jodel Wassmer D.120A Paris-Nice	331		11. 5.67	N.V.de Candole	Loders Hill Farm, Bridport	3. 5.03P
G-AVMA	SOCATA GY-80-180 Horizon	196		12. 5.67	B.R.Hildick	Shenstone Hall Farm, Shenstone	3. 4.04
G-AVMB	Rollason-Druine D.62B Condor	RAE/621		12. 5.67	L.J.Dray *"Spirit of Silver City"*	Watchford Farm, Yarcombe	4. 9.03P
G-AVMD	Cessna 150G	15065504	N2404J	16. 5.67	T.A.White t/a Bagby Aviation	Bagby	16. 8.04
G-AVMF	Cessna F150G *(Built Reims Aviation SA)*	F150-0203		17. 5.67	J.F.Marsh	Newton Green, Sudbury	21. 7.03
G-AVMJ*	British Aircraft Corporation One-Eleven 510ED	BAC.138		11. 5.67	European Aviation Ltd *(WFU 6.94) (Cancelled 11.5.01 by CAA: used as cabin trainer 5.01)*	Bournemouth	17.11.94T
G-AVMK*	British Aircraft Corporation One-Eleven 510ED	BAC.139		11. 5.67	Gravesend College *(Cancelled 1.3.02 as destroyed: fuselage noted 2.02)*	Gravesend	8. 8.00T
G-AVMN	British Aircraft Corporation One-Eleven 510ED	BAC.142		11. 5.67	European Aviation Ltd *(AB Airlines c/s) (To Aviation Museum 5.01)*	Bournemouth	21. 6.00T
G-AVMP*	British Aircraft Corporation One-Eleven 510ED	BAC.144		11. 5.67	European Aviation Ltd *"The Madrid Express" (Stored 5.01: cancelled 12.11.02 by CAA)*	Bournemouth	6. 4.01T
G-AVMS	British Aircraft Corporation One-Eleven 510ED	BAC.146		11. 5.67	European Aviation Ltd *"The London Express" (New CofR 10.02)*	Bournemouth	26. 2.01T
G-AVMT	British Aircraft Corporation One-Eleven 510ED	BAC.147		11. 5.67	European Aviation Ltd *(European Minardi F1 titles) (Op Minardi F1 team)*	Bournemouth	5.12.03T
G-AVMY	British Aircraft Corporation One-Eleven 510ED	BAC.152		11. 5.67	European Aviation Ltd *(Stored 5.01)*	Bournemouth	28. 6.01T
G-AVMZ	British Aircraft Corporation One-Eleven 510ED	BAC.153 (5N-OSA)/G-AVMZ		11. 5.67	European Aviation Ltd *(Stored 5.01)*	Bournemouth	17.10.02T
G-AVNC	Cessna F150G *(Built Reims Aviation SA)*	F150-0200		18. 5.67	J.R.Alderson	Popham	24. 5.04
G-AVNN	Piper PA-28-180 Cherokee C	28-4049	N11C	26. 5.67	J.Acres tr G-AVNN Flying Group	Trenchard Farm, Eggesford	21. 3.03
G-AVNO	Piper PA-28-180 Cherokee C	28-4105	N11C	26. 5.67	Allister Flight Ltd	Southend	11.10.04T
G-AVNP*	Piper PA-28-180 Cherokee C	28-4113	N11C	26. 5.67	R W Harris, P E Preston, M F Hatt & M Jahanfar *(Op Southend Flying Club)* *(Force landed near Nayland 28.4.01: cancelled 27.11.01 as destroyed) (Wreck noted 2.03)*	Southend	25.10.04T
G-AVNS	Piper PA-28-180 Cherokee C	28-4129	N11C	26. 5.67	I.R.Chaplin	Andrewsfield	13. 7.03T
G-AVNU	Piper PA-28-180 Cherokee C	28-4153	N11C	26. 5.67	O.Durrani	Lydd	11. 2.04T
G-AVNW	Piper PA-28-180 Cherokee C	28-4210	N11C	26. 5.67	Len Smith's School & Sports Ltd	Fairoaks	6. 7.03T
G-AVNX	Sportavia Fournier RF4D	4026		26. 5.67	R.Davies & J.A.Hallam	Bicester	16. 4.03P
G-AVNZ	Sportavia Fournier RF4D	4030		26. 5.67	V.S.E.Norman	Rendcomb	18. 6.05
G-AVOA	SAN Jodel DR.1050 Ambassadeur	195	F-BJYY	31. 5.67	D.A.Willies	Anwick	5. 9.03
G-AVOC	CEA Jodel DR.221 Dauphin	67		2. 6.67	D.T.Kaberry & J.Paulson	Barton	21. 3.05
G-AVOH	Rollason-Druine D.62B Condor	RAE/622		6. 6.67	Halegreen Associates Ltd	Hinton in the Hedges	1. 5.05T
G-AVOM	CEA Jodel DR.221 Dauphin	65		6. 6.67	M.A.T.Mountford	Maypole Farm, Chislet	21. 8.03
G-AVOO	Piper PA-18-150 Super Cub *(Lycoming O-360-A4)*	18-8511	N10F	7. 6.67	London Gliding Club Pty Ltd *"Terry Mac"*	Dunstable	27. 3.03
G-AVOZ	Piper PA-28-180 Cherokee C	28-3711	N9574J	13. 6.67	P.Hoskins & R.Flavell tr Oscar Zulu Flying Group	Booker	30. 5.04
G-AVPD	Jodel D.9 Bebe *(Volkswagen 1500)*	521/MAC.1/PFA 927		15. 6.67	S.W.McKay *(Stored 12.99: Valid CofR @ 4.02)*	(Berkhamsted)	6. 6.75S
G-AVPH*	Cessna F150G *(Built Reims Aviation SA)*	F150-0197		20. 6.67	Zero 9 Flight Academy *(Fuselage noted 3.00: cancelled 26.3.02 by CAA)*	Beccles	9. 4.86T
G-AVPJ	de Havilland DH.82A Tiger Moth	86326	NL879	20. 6.67	C C.Silk	Bericote Farm, Blackdown, Leamington Spa	13. 8.04
G-AVPM	SAN Jodel D.117	593	F-BHXO	20. 6.67	J.C.Haynes	Breighton	10. 6.02P
G-AVPO	Hindustan HAL-26 Pushpak *(Continental C90)*	PK-127	9M-AOZ VT-DWL	31. 3.83	J.A.Coutts & W.G.Mitchell-Hudson	Cherry Tree Farm, Monewden	11. 9.03P
G-AVPS	Piper PA-30 Twin Comanche B	30-1548	N8393Y	27. 6.67	J.M.Bisco	Farley Farm, Romsey	11.11.05
G-AVPV	Piper PA-28-180 Cherokee C	28-2705	9J-RBP N11C	27. 6.67	K.A.Passmore	Rayne Hall Farm, Rayne	8. 3.03
G-AVPY	Piper PA-25-235 Pawnee C	25-4330	N4636Y N10F	7. 7.67	Aeros Holdings Ltd *(Crashed Lower Radbourne Farm, Ladbroke, Warwicks 25.6.76: on rebuild 12.02)*	Gloucestershire	14.10.77
G-AVRK	Piper PA-28-180 Cherokee C	28-4041	N11C	11. 7.67	J.Gama	Tatenhill	9. 3.03
G-AVRP	Piper PA-28-140 Cherokee	28-23153	N11C	14. 7.67	R J Guest t/a Trent-199	Tatenhill	6. 6.03
G-AVRS	SOCATA GY-80-180 Horizon	224		14. 7.67	Air Venturas Ltd *(Damaged landing Throstle Nest Farm, Cleveland 12.9.99)*	Bagby	7. 8.00
G-AVRU	Piper PA-28-180 Cherokee C	28-4025	N11C	17. 7.67	D.J.Rowell tr G-AVRU Partnership	Clacton	11.12.05
G-AVRW	Barritault JB-01 Minicab *(Continental C90)*	OH-1549 & PFA 1800		18. 7.67	D.J.Smith tr Kestrel Flying Group	Hucknall	28. 8.02P
G-AVRY	Piper PA-28-180 Cherokee C	28-4089	N11C	24. 7.67	Brigfast Ltd	Popham	6. 4.03
G-AVRZ	Piper PA-28-180 Cherokee C	28-4137	N11C	24. 7.67	Mantavia Group Ltd	Guernsey	26.11.05
G-AVSA	Piper PA-28-180 Cherokee C	28-4184	N11C	24. 7.67	J.Walker tr G-AVSA Flying Group	Barton	5. 5.05
G-AVSB	Piper PA-28-180 Cherokee C	28-4191	N11C	24. 7.67	D.L.Macdonald	Denham	2. 5.05
G-AVSC	Piper PA-28-180 Cherokee C	28-4193	N11C	24. 7.67	MSC019 Ltd	White Waltham	26. 4.03T
G-AVSD	Piper PA-28-180 Cherokee C	28-4195	N11C	24. 7.67	Landmate Ltd	Haverfordwest	18. 5.04
G-AVSE*	Piper PA-28-180 Cherokee C	28-4196	N11C	24. 7.67	G.Cotrulia *(Cancelled 18.5.99 by CAA) (Noted 5.00)*	Kildare, Co.Kildare	30. 4.00T
G-AVSF	Piper PA-28-180 Cherokee C	28-4197	N11C	24. 7.67	S.E.Pick & D.A.Rham tr Monday Club	Blackbushe	6. 4.03
G-AVSI	Piper PA-28-140 Cherokee	28-23148	N11C	24. 7.67	C.M.Royle tr G-AVSI Flying Group	White Waltham	29. 2.04
G-AVSP	Piper PA-28-180 Cherokee C	28-3952	N11C (PJ-ACT)	8. 8.67	Airways Flight Training (Exeter) Ltd	Exeter	4. 1.04T
G-AVSR	Beagle D.5/180 Husky	3689		8. 8.67	A.L.Young	Henstridge	19.10.02A
G-AVSZ	Agusta-Bell 206B JetRanger II	8032	VH-BEQ PK-HBZ/VR-BCR/PK-HBD/VR-BCR/G-AVSZ	8. 8.67	Patriot Aviation Ltd *(Amended CofR 3.02)*	Cranfield	16. 6.99T
G-AVTP	Cessna F172H *(Built Reims Aviation SA)*	F172-0458		17. 8.67	A.S.Watkins & M.J.Green tr Tango Papa Group	White Waltham	11. 7.04

Reg	Type	c/n	Prev id	Date	Owner	Location	Date
G-AVTT*	Ercoupe 415D	4399	SE-BFZ	21. 8.67	Wright Farm Eggs Ltd	Cherry Tree Farm, Monewden	20. 1.86
	(Continental C85)		NC3774H		*(Stored 6.00) (Cancelled 12.4.02 as temporarily WFU)*		
G-AVTV	SOCATA MS.893A Rallye Commodore 180	10725		24. 8.67	D.B.& M.E.Meeks	Seighford	6. 8.03
G-AVUD	Piper PA-30 Twin Comanche B	30-1515	N8422Y	5. 9.67	P.M.Fox	Biggin Hill	11. 7.04
			N9???N		t/a FM Aviation		
G-AVUG	Cessna F150H	F150-0234		11. 9.67	V.J.Larkin & P.Woodburn	Netherthorpe	9. 6.05
	(Built Reims Aviation SA)				tr Skyways Flying Club		
G-AVUH	Cessna F150H	F150-0244		11. 9.67	C.M.Chinn	North Coates	6. 8.04
	(Built Reims Aviation SA)						
G-AVUO	Phoenix Luton LA.4A Minor	PAL/1313		21. 9.67	M.E.Vaisey	(Hemel Hempstead)	
	(Initially not completed: parts used in construction of G-AXKH - possible long-term build project)						
G-AVUS	Piper PA-28-140 Cherokee	28-24065	(G-AVUT)	25. 9.67	D.J.Hunter	Norwich	6.12.04T
			N11C				
G-AVUT	Piper PA-28-140 Cherokee	28-24085	(G-AVUU)	25. 9.67	Bencray Ltd	Blackpool	17. 5.04T
			N11C		*(Op Blackpool & Fylde Aero Club)*		
G-AVUU	Piper PA-28-140 Cherokee	28-24100	(G-AVUS)	25. 9.67	R.W.Harris, A.Jahanfar, P.E.Preston & M.F.Hatt		
			N11C		*(Op Southend Flying Club)*	Southend	11. 5.03T
G-AVUZ	Piper PA-32-300 Cherokee Six	32-40302	N11C	29. 9.67	Ceesix Ltd	Jersey	23. 4.03
G-AVVC	Cessna F172H	F172-0443		29. 9.67	M.Turnbull	(Bedlington)	21.10.01T
	(Built Reims Aviation SA)						
G-AVVF*	de Havilland DH.104 Dove 8	04541		2.10.67	Not known	Gloucestershire	11. 2.88
	(Cancelled 26.6.91 as WFU) (Wreck on fire dump 4.01)						
G-AVVJ	SOCATA MS.893A Rallye Commodore 180	10752		6.10.67	M.Powell	Tibenham	29. 7.05
G-AVVL	Cessna F150H	F150-0257		6.10.67	N.E.Sams *"Samurai"*	Cranfield	11. 3.89T
	(Built Reims Aviation SA) (Wilksch WAM-120)				t/a International Aerospace Engineering		
G-AVWA	Piper PA-28-140 Cherokee	28-23660	N11C	19.10.67	SFG Ltd	Shipdham	19.12.02T
G-AVWD	Piper PA-28-140 Cherokee	28-23700	N11C	19.10.67	C.Bentley & B.Marlowe t/a Evelyn Air	Leeds-Bradford	30. 9.04T
G-AVWE*	Piper PA-28-140 Cherokee	28-23720	N11C	19.10.67	Not known	Blackpool	22. 4.82T
	(WFU & cancelled 8.6.89 by CAA) (Fuselage noted 3.00: current status unknown)						
G-AVWG	Piper PA-28-140 Cherokee	28-23760	N11C	19.10.67	Bencray Ltd	Blackpool	11. 8.91T
	(Damaged Tal y Fan, Conwy, Gwynedd 11.12.88: components used to rebuild G-BBEF in 1998/99 (qv): wings only 8.02)						
G-AVWI	Piper PA-28-140 Cherokee	28-23800	N11C	19.10.67	Mrs.L.M.Middleton	Cranfield	17. 2.03
G-AVWJ	Piper PA-28-140 Cherokee	28-23940	N11C	19.10.67	A.M.Harrhy	Sandown	29. 7.04
G-AVWL	Piper PA-28-140 Cherokee	28-24000	N11C	19.10.67	B.W.Griffiths & R.Fraser-Duthie	Coventry	4.10 04
					t/a Bobev Aviation		
G-AVWM	Piper PA-28-140 Cherokee	28-24005		19.10.67	A.Jahanfar, P.E.Preston, M.F.Hatt & R.W.Harris		
					(Op Southend Flying Club)	Southend	18. 6.04T
G-AVWN	Piper PA-28R-180 Cherokee Arrow	28R-30170	N11C	19.10.67	Vawn Air Ltd	Jersey	10. 4.05
G-AVWO	Piper PA-28R-180 Cherokee Arrow	28R-30205	N11C	19.10.67	I.L.Whittle tr The Whisky Oscar Group	(Woking)	15.11.03
G-AVWR	Piper PA-28R-180 Cherokee Arrow	28R-30242	N11C	19.10.67	S.J.French tr SJ French & Partners	Dunkeswell	31. 8.03
G-AVWT	Piper PA-28R-180 Cherokee Arrow	28R-30362	N11C	19.10.67	Cloudbase Aviation Ltd	Barton	21. 5.03
G-AVWU	Piper PA-28R-180 Cherokee Arrow	28R-30380	N11C	19.10.67	Arrow Flyers Ltd	Booker	18. 5.01
G-AVWV	Piper PA-28R-180 Cherokee Arrow	28R-30404	N11C	19.10.67	R.V.Thornton & R.Barron	Perth	18. 6.05
					tr Strathtay Flying Group		
G-AVWY	Sportavia Fournier RF4D	4031		26.10.67	P Turner	Halesland	4. 7.03P
G-AVXA	Piper PA-25-235 Pawnee C	25-4244	N4576Y	26.10.67	South Wales Gliding Club Ltd	Usk	5. 4.03
	(Re-built using new frame - c/n unknown)						
G-AVXC	Slingsby Nipper T.66 RA.45 Srs.3	S.108/1605		26.10.67	D.S.T.Eggleton	Waits Farm, Belchamp Walter	2. 5.03P
	(Ardem 4C02)						
G-AVXD	Slingsby Nipper T.66 RA.45 Srs.3	S.109/1606		26.10.67	R.L.Fraser	Dundee	29.10.02P
	(Volkswagen 1834 Acro)				tr Tayside Nipper Group		
G-AVXF	Piper PA-28R-180 Cherokee Arrow	28R-30044	N11C	26.10.67	J.A.Lunness	Top Farm, Croydon, Royston	25. 6.04
					tr JDR Arrow Group		
G-AVXI*	Hawker Siddeley HS.748 Srs.2A/238	1623		2.11.67	Hanningfield Metals	Templewood, Stock	30. 8.98T
	(Cancelled 24.10.01 by CAA) (Fuselage noted 8.02)						
G-AVXJ*	Hawker Siddeley HS.748 Srs.2A/238	1624		2.11.67	Emerald Airways Ltd	Exeter	22. 8.98T
	(External storage 11.01: cancelled 17.1.03 as wfu)						
G-AVXW	Rollason-Druine D.62B Condor	RAE/625		3.11.67	A.J.Cooper	Rochester	30. 9.01
G-AVXY	Auster AOP.9	AUS.10/92	XK417	7.11.67	G.J. Siddall	South Lodge Farm, Widmerpool	9. 7.00P
	(Officially regd as c/n AUS/120)				*(As "XK417" in Army c/s)*		
G-AVYK	Beagle A.61 Terrier 3	B.642	WJ357	20.11.67	J.P.Roland *(Stored 6.01)*	Eggington	28. 8.93
G-AVYL	Piper PA-28-180 Cherokee D	28-4622	N11C	24.11.67	N.E.Binner	Full Sutton	23. 5.05
G-AVYM	Piper PA-28-180 Cherokee D	8-4638	N11C	24.11.67	Carlisle Aviation (1985) Ltd	Carlisle	14. 5.04T
G-AVYP	Piper PA-28-140 Cherokee	28-24211	N11C	4.11.67	K.Hobbs t/a Aldergrove Flight Training Centre	Belfast	14. 2.04T
G-AVYR	Piper PA-28-140 Cherokee	28-24226	N11C	24.11.67	P.J. Huxley tr SAS Flying Group	Thruxton	18. 6.03
G-AVYS	Piper PA-28R-180 Cherokee Arrow	28R-30456	N11C	24.11.67	A.M.Playford	Poplar Hall Farm, Elmsett	2. 2.03
G-AVYT	Piper PA-28R-180 Cherokee Arrow	28R-30472	N11C	24.11.67	J.R.Tindale	Blackpool	7. 6.03
G-AVYV	Jodel Wassmer D.120A Paris-Nice	252	F-BMAM	27.11.67	A.J.Sephton	Brickhouse Farm, Frogland Cross	30. 8.93P
	(Stored 4.96) (Current status unknown)						
G-AVZI	Bölkow Bö.208C Junior	673	D-EGZF	19.12.67	C.F.Rogers	(Wheathampstead)	24. 7.76
	(Stored @ home 10.00)						
G-AVZN	Beagle B.121 Pup 1	B121-006		19.12.67	D J Mounter	Shipdham	16. 8.04
					tr Shipdham Aviators Flying Group		
G-AVZP	Beagle B.121 Pup 1	B121-008		19.12.67	T.A.White	Bagby	21. 6.04
G-AVZR	Piper PA-28-180 Cherokee C	28-4114	N4779L	19.12.67	Lincoln Aero Club Ltd	Sturgate	4. 5.03T
G-AVZU	Cessna F150H	F150-0283		29.12.67	R.D. & E.Forster	Beccles	23.12.05T
	(Built Reims Aviation SA)				*(Op Norfolk & Norwich Aero Club)*		
G-AVZV	Cessna F172H	F172-0511		29.12.67	E.L. & D.S.Lightbown	Crosland Moor	3.12.03
	(Built Reims Aviation SA)						
G-AVZW	EAA Model P Biplane	PFA 1314		29.12.67	R.G.Maidment & G.R.Edmondson	(Goodwood)	19. 9.02P
	(Lycoming O-290)						
G-AVZX	SOCATA MS.880B Rallye Club	1165		29.12.67	J.Nugent	(Glengeary, Co.Dublin)	19.11.02

G-AWAA - G-AWZZ

Reg	Type	C/n	Prev id	Date	Owner	Location	Status
G-AWAA*	SOCATA MS.880B Rallye Club	1174		29.12.67	P.A.Cairns	NK	4. 8.91
	(Stored 10.95: cancelled 4.3.99 by CAA) (Noted 8.01)						
G-AWAC	SOCATA GY-80-180 Horizon	234		29.12.67	Gardan Party Ltd *"Le Fantome"*	Popham	11. 6.04
G-AWAH	Beech D55 Baron	TE-540		1. 1.68	B.J.S.Grey	Duxford	2. 7.03
G-AWAJ	Beech D55 Baron	TE-536		1. 1.68	Standard Hose Ltd	Blackpool	19. 6.04
G-AWAT	Rollason-Druine D.62B Condor	RAE/627		8. 1.68	Tamwood Ltd	Shoreham	16. 7.04
G-AWAX	Cessna 150D	15060153	OY-TRJ N4153U	5. 1.68	H.H.Cousins	Fenland	14. 8.04
	(Tail-wheel conversion)						
G-AWAZ	Piper PA-28R-180 Cherokee Arrow	28R-30512	N11C	8. 1.68	R.Z.Staniszewski	Barton	28. 8.05
G-AWBA	Piper PA-28R-180 Cherokee Arrow	28R-30528	N11C	8. 1.68	A.Taplin & G.A.Dunster	Stapleford	16. 2.03
					tr March Flying Group		
G-AWBB	Piper PA-28R-180 Cherokee Arrow	28R-30552	N11C	8. 1.68	R.Warner	(Whittlesford)	24. 6.05
G-AWBC	Piper PA-28R-180 Cherokee Arrow	28R-30572	N11C	8. 1.68	Anglo Aviation (UK) Ltd	Bournemouth	28.12.03
G-AWBE	Piper PA-28-140 Cherokee	28-24266	N11C	8. 1.68	B.E.Boyle	Shenington	24.11.05
G-AWBG	Piper PA-28-140 Cherokee	28-24286	N11C	8. 1.68	G.D.Cooper	Rochester	26. 4.04T
G-AWBH	Piper PA-28-140 Cherokee	28-24306	N11C	8. 1.68	Proofgolden Ltd t/a Mainstreet Aviation	Newcastle	30.10.04T
G-AWBJ	Sportavia Fournier RF4D	4055		12. 1.68	J.M.Adams	RAF Syerston	6. 4.03P
G-AWBM	Druine D.31A Turbulent	PFA 1647		17. 1.68	A.D.Pratt	North Coates	20. 7.95P
	(Volkswagen 1700)						
G-AWBN	Piper PA-30 Twin Comanche B	30-1472	N8517Y	18. 1.68	Stourfield Investments Ltd	Jersey	2.12.05
G-AWBS	Piper PA-28-140 Cherokee	28-24331	N11C	22. 1.68	M.A.English & T.M.Brown	Little Snoring	18.12.05
G-AWBT*	Piper PA-30 Twin Comanche B	30-1668	N8508Y	22. 1.68	Cranfield University	Cranfield	25. 3.89
	(Damaged Humberside 10.3.88: cancelled 15.7.88 as WFU) (Derelict airframe 6.02)						
G-AWBU	Morane-Saulnier Type N Rep	PPS/REP/7		22. 1.68	Bianchi Aviation Film Services Ltd	Booker	29. 6.01P
	(Continental C90-8F)				*(As "MS824" in French AF c/s)*		
G-AWBX	Cessna F150H	F150-0286		22. 1.68	J.Meddings	Tatenhill	20.12.02
	(Built Reims Aviation SA)						
G-AWCM	Cessna F150H	F150-0281		25. 1.68	R.Garbett	Wolverhampton	14. 8.99T
	(Built Reims Aviation SA)						
G-AWCN	Reims FR172E Rocket	FR17200020		25. 1.68	R.C.Lunnon & A.J.Speight	Stapleford	4. 7.04
G-AWCP	Cessna F150H	F150-0354		29. 1.68	C.E.Mason	Shobdon	12. 2.03
	(Built Reims Aviation SA) (Tail-wheel conversion)						
G-AWDA	Slingsby Nipper T.66 RA.45 Srs.3	S.117/1624		7. 2.68	J.A.Cheesbrough	Ottringham	4. 6.03P
	(Volkswagen Acro 1834)						
G-AWDO	Druine D.31 Turbulent	PFA 1649		21. 2.68	R.N.Crosland	Deanland, Hailsham	9. 5.03P
	(Volkswagen 1600)						
G-AWDP	Piper PA-28-180 Cherokee D	28-4870	N11C	21. 2.68	B.H. & P.M.Illston	Norwich	12. 2.05T
					(Op Norwich School of Flying)		
G-AWDR	Reims FR172E Rocket	FR17200004		21. 2.68	B.A.Wallace	Nuthampstead	9. 4.04
G-AWDU	Brantly B.2B	481		23. 2.68	B.M.Freeman	(Stourport-on-Severn)	22. 7.01
G-AWDW	Campbell-Bensen CB.8MS	DS.1330		26. 2.68	M.R.Langton	(Taplow)	7.10.71P
	(McCulloch.4318C)				*(Stored 12.00)*		
G-AWEF	SNCAN Stampe SV-4C	549	F-BDCT	29. 3.68	The Tiger Club (1990) Ltd	Headcorn	19.12.04T
	(DH Gipsy Major)						
G-AWEI	Rollason-Druine D.62B Condor	RAE/628		6. 3.68	J.M.C.Coyle	Roughay Farm, Bishops Waltham	10.11.98T
					(Stored 6.01)		
G-AWEL	Sportavia Fournier RF4D	4077		7. 3.68	A.B.Clymo	Wolverhampton	14.11.02P
G-AWEM	Sportavia Fournier RF4D	4078		7. 3.68	B.J.Griffin	Wickenby	11. 6.03P
G-AWEN*	SAN Jodel DR.1050 Ambassadeur	67	F-BIVD	8. 3.68	(Skycraft Ltd)	(Spalding)	8.11.85
	(Crashed Crosland Moor 11.8.83: cancelled 28.11.91 by CAA) (Stored 11.01)						
G-AWEP	Barritault JB-01 Minicab	PFA 1801		12. 3.68	A.Louth	(Boston)	20.11.02P
	(Continental C90)						
G-AWES	Cessna 150H	15068626	N22933	20. 3.68	P.Montgomery-Stuart	Leicester	5. 8.84
	(Damaged in gale @ Glenrothes 2.10.81: on rebuild 1.97: current status unknown)						
G-AWET	Piper PA-28-180 Cherokee D	28-4871	N11C	21. 3.68	Broadland Flying Group Ltd	Old Buckenham	25. 5.03
G-AWEV	Piper PA-28-140 Cherokee	28-24460	N11C	21. 3.68	Norflight Ltd	Ludham	6. 1.01
G-AWEX	Piper PA-28-140 Cherokee	28-24472	N11C	21. 3.68	N.D. Wyndow	Coventry	10. 5.04
					tr Sir W.G.Armstrong-Whitworth Flying Group		
G-AWEZ	Piper PA-28R-180 Cherokee Arrow	28R-30592	N11C	21. 3.68	T.R.Leighton, R.G.E.Simpson & D.A.C.Clissett		
						Stapleford	7.12.02
G-AWFB	Piper PA-28R-180 Cherokee Arrow	28R-30689	N11C	21. 3.68	J.C.Luke	Filton	17. 4.05
G-AWFC	Piper PA-28R-180 Cherokee Arrow	28R-30670	N11C	21. 3.68	B.J.Hines	White Waltham	23. 8.04
G-AWFD	Piper PA-28R-180 Cherokee Arrow	28R-30669	N11C	21. 3.68	D.J.Hill	Cambridge	19. 5.02
G-AWFF	Cessna F150H	F150-0280		25. 3.68	West Wales Airport Ltd	Gloucestershire	17.10.05T
	(Built Reims Aviation SA)						
G-AWFJ	Piper PA-28R-180 Cherokee Arrow	28R-30688	N11C	26. 3.68	Parplon Ltd	Barton	24 3.05
G-AWFN	Rollason-Druine D.62B Condor	RAE/629		27. 3.68	P.B.Lowry	Deanland	17. 6.03P
G-AWFO	Rollason-Druine D.62B Condor	RAE/630		27. 3.68	R.E.Major	Porthtowan, Cornwall	5.11.03P
G-AWFP	Rollason-Druine D.62B Condor	RAE/631		27. 3.68	D.J.Taylor	White Waltham	22. 5.04
					t/a Blackbushe Flying Club		
G-AWFR*	Druine D.31 Turbulent	SU.001 & PFA 1652		27. 3.68	J.R.Froud	(Edenbridge, Kent)	
	(Reported as under construction 2000) (Cancelled 15.3.02 as WFU)						
G-AWFT	Jodel D.9 Bebe	PFA 932		29. 3.68	W.H.Cole	Spilsted Farm, Sedlescombe	22. 7.69P
	(Volkswagen 1200)				*(Noted 5.01)*		
G-AWFW	SAN Jodel D.117	599	PH-VRE F-BHXU	2. 4.68	C.J.Rodwell	(Keighley)	30. 8.03P
G-AWFZ	Beech 19A Musketeer Sport	MB-323	N2811B	3. 4.68	K A W Ashcroft	(St Neots)	18.12.05T
G-AWGA*	Beagle A.109 Airedale	B.535	EI-ATA G-AWGA/D-ENRU	3. 4.68	Not known	Biggin Hill	
	(WFU 3.7.86: cancelled 30.9.86 as WFU) (Noted 4.01?)						
G-AWGD	Cessna F172H	F172-0503		5. 4.68	R.P.Vincent	Shoreham	18. 7.03T
	(Built Reims Aviation SA)						

G-AWGK	Cessna F150H	F150-0347		8. 4.68	G.E.Allen	(Lincoln)	1. 5.04
	(Built Reims Aviation SA)						
G-AWGN	Sportavia Fournier RF4D	4084		9. 4.68	M.P.Barley	(Huntingdon)	9. 6.03P
G-AWGZ	Taylor JT.1 Monoplane	M.1 & PFA 1406		17. 4.68	R.L.Sambell	Stoke Golding	21. 6.93P
	(Ardem 4C02)				*(Damaged Sleap 14.7.92: noted 3.02)*		
G-AWHB*	CASA C.2111D *(He.111H-16)*	049	Spanish AF B2I-57	14. 5.68	Not known	Great Massingham	
	(Officially quoted as c/n 167 Spanish AF ex B2I-37) (Cancelled 27.4.01 as sold USA) (Fuselage noted 9.02 - to create flyable Heinkel He111 for Flying						
	Heritage Collection, Seattle, USA with wings ex CASA 2.111 B21-39 & Junkers Jumo engines)						
G-AWHX	Rollason Beta B.2	RAE/04	(G-ATEE)	17. 4.68	S.G.Jones "Vertigo" (On rebuild 10.01)	Membury	14. 6.87P
G-AWHY	Falconar F-11-3	PFA 1322	G-BDPB	17. 4.68	B.E.Smith	Wellcross Grange, Slinford	21. 5.03P
	(Continental C90)		(G-AWHY)				
G-AWIF*	Brookland Mosquito	3 & LC.1		17. 4.68	Not known	St.Merryn	7. 1.82P
					(Cancelled 30.5.84 as WFU) (Stored 8.01)		
G-AWII	Supermarine 349 Spitfire LF.Vc	WASP/20/223	AR501	25. 4.68	The Shuttleworth Trust	Old Warden	15. 5.03P
	(Built Westland Aircraft)				*(As "AR501/NN-A" in 310 Sqdn c/s)*		
G-AWIP	Phoenix Luton LA-4A Minor			30. 4.68	J.Houghton	(North Ferriby)	8. 5.89P
	(Continental A65)	PAL/1308 & PFA 830			*(Damaged near Holme-on-Spalding Moor 20.7.88: stored 2000)*		
G-AWIR	Bushby-Long Midget Mustang	PFA 1315		30. 4.68	K.E.Sword	Leicester	6. 3.90P
	(Continental O-200-A)				*(On overhaul 1991: current status unknown)*		
G-AWIT	Piper PA-28-180 Cherokee D	28-4987	N11C	30. 4.68	Cherry Orchard Aparthotel Ltd	Ronaldsway	16. 6.02T
					(Op Manx Flyers Aero Club)		
G-AWIV	Airmark TSR.3	PFA 1325		30. 4.68	F.R.Hutchings "Stor"	St. Just	17. 6.03P
	(Continental PC60)						
G-AWIW	SNCAN Stampe SV-4B	532	F-BDCC	2. 5.68	R.E.Mitchell *(Believed stored 4.02)*	RAF Cosford	6. 5.73
G-AWJE	Slingsby Nipper T.66 RA.45 Srs.3	S.121/1628		8. 5.68	P.G.Kavanagh & K.G.G.Howe	Barton	14. 7.03P
	(Volkswagen 1834)						
G-AWJF*	Slingsby Nipper T.66 RA.45 Srs.3	S.122/1629		8. 5.68	S.Maric	(Glasgow)	7. 6.88P
					(Cancelled 17.9.91 by CAA) (Stored 6.00)		
G-AWJX	Moravan Zlin Z.526 Trener Master	1049		22. 5.68	P.A.Colman *(New owner 11.02)*		29. 5.85A
					Luxters Farm, Hambleden, Henley-on-Thames		
G-AWJY	Moravan Zlin Z.526 Trener Master	1050		22. 5.68	M.Gainza	White Waltham	26. 4.03
G-AWKD	Piper PA-17 Vagabond	17-192	F-BFMZ	27. 5.68	A.T. & Mrs.M.R.Dowie	Scotland Farm, Hook	12. 9.03P
	(Continental A65)		N4892H				
G-AWKM*	Beagle B.121 Pup 1	B121-017		11. 6.68	D.M.G.Jenkins	Bourne Park, Hurstbourne Tarrant	29. 6.84
					(Damaged Swansea 7.91: stored less wings 10.01: cancelled 28.5.02 by CAA) (Open storage 9.02)		
G-AWKO	Beagle B.121 Pup 1	B121-019		11. 6.68	E.C.Felix	Cambridge	7. 6.04T
G-AWKP*	CEA Jodel DR.253 Regent	130		14. 6.68	Blackpool Air Centre	Blackpool	1.10.98
					(Forced landed SE Waterford on 8.6.98: cancelled 13.10.98 by CAA) (Fuselage noted 8.02)		
G-AWKT	SOCATA MS.880B Rallye Club	1235		17. 6.68	A.Ringland & P.Keating	Donegal, Co.Donegal	5. 3.03
G-AWLA	Cessna F150H	F150-0269	N13175	27. 6.68	T.A.White	Bagby	28. 6.04T
	(Built Reims Aviation SA)				t/a Bagby Aviation		
G-AWLF	Cessna F172H	F172-0536		27. 6.68	Gannet Aviation Ltd	City of Derry	6 .7.03
	(Built Reims Aviation SA)						
G-AWLG	SIPA 903	82	F-BGHG	27. 6.68	S.W.Markham	Valentine Farm, Odiham	22. 8.79P
					(Stored 1997: current status unknown)		
G-AWLI	Piper PA-22-150 Tri-Pacer	22-5083	N7256D	1. 7.68	J.S.Lewery "Little Peach"	Shoreham	15. 8.02
G-AWLO	Boeing Stearman E75 (PT-13D) Kaydet	75-5563	5Y-KRR	9. 7.68	N.D.Pickard	Little Gransden	16 5.05
	(Pratt & Whitney R985)		VP-KRR/42-17400				
G-AWLP	Mooney M.20F Executive 21	680200		9. 7.68	I.C.Lomax	Ottringham	7. 7.00
G-AWLR	Slingsby Nipper T.66 RA.45 Srs.3	S.125/1662		9. 7.68	T.D.Reid	Newtownards, Co.Down	6. 7.01P
G-AWLS	Slingsby Nipper T.66 RA.45 Srs.3	S.126/1663		9. 7.68	G.A.Dunster & B.Gallagher	(Loughton, Essex)	25. 3.88P
					(Damaged Stapleford 14.1.88: on rebuild 1995: current status unknown)		
G-AWLZ	Sportavia Fournier RF4D	4099		12. 7.68	J.H.Taylor tr Nympsfield RF4 Group	Nympsfield	19. 2.03P
G-AWMD	Jodel D.11	PFA 904		19. 7.68	D.A.Barr-Hamilton	Shobdon	23. 4.03P
	(Continental C90)				"Moby Dick"		
G-AWMF	Piper PA-18-150 Super Cub	18-8674	N4356Z	23. 7.68	Booker Gliding Club Ltd	Booker	26. 8.03
	(Lycoming O-360-A4)						
G-AWMI	AESL Airtourer T.2 (115)	505		24. 7.68	M.Furse	Cardiff	10. 5.04
G-AWMN	Phoenix Luton LA-4A Minor	PFA 827		30. 7.68	B.J.Douglas	Kildare, Co.Kildare	26. 7.03P
	(Volkswagen 1800)						
G-AWMP	Cessna F172H	F172-0488		31. 7.68	R.J.D.Blois	Yoxford, Saxmundham	23.12.05
	(Built Reims Aviation SA)						
G-AWMR	Druine D.31 Turbulent	43 & PFA 1661		1. 8.68	M.J.Bond	RAF Kinloss	23.10.01P
	(Volkswagen 1390)				"Demelza"		
G-AWMT	Cessna F150H	F150-0360		1. 8.68	M.Paisley	(Bangor)	24. 6.00
	(Built Reims Aviation SA)						
G-AWNT	Britten-Norman BN-2A Islander	32		2. 8.68	Sterling Helicopters Ltd	Norwich	6. 8.04A
G-AWOA	SOCATA MS.880B Rallye Club	1258		2. 8.68	J.A.Rimmer	RAF Mona	19.11.05
G-AWOE	Aero Commander 680E	680E-753-41	N3844C	5. 8.68	J.M.Houølder t/a Elstree Flying Club	Elstree	19 3.03
G-AWOF	Piper PA-15 Vagabond	15-227	F-BETF	6. 8.68	C.M.Hicks	Barton	21. 5.03P
	(Continental C90)						
G-AWOH	Piper PA-17 Vagabond	17-191	F-BFMY	6. 8.68	W.M.Haley, D.Ridley & R.H.Ryle tr The High Flatts Flying Group		
	(Continental C90)		N4891H		High Flatts Farm, Chester-le-Street		24. 7.03P
G-AWOT	Cessna F150H	F150-0389		14. 8.68	S.J.French	(Brackley)	28. 1.04T
	(Built Reims Aviation SA)						
G-AWOU	Cessna 170B	25829	VQ-ZJA	16. 8.68	S.Billington	(Macclesfield)	27. 5.01
			ZS-CKY/CR-ADU/N3185A				
G-AWOX*	Westland Wessex 60 Srs.1	WA/686	G-17-2	28. 8.68	Paintball Adventure West	Bristol	13. 1.83
			G-AWOX/5N-AJO/G-AWOX/9Y-TFB/G-AWOX/VH-BHE(3)/G-AWOX/VR-BCV/G-AWOX/G-17-1				
					(Cancelled 23.11.82 as TWFU) (Extant 2.00)		
G-AWPH	Percival P.56 Provost T.1	PAC/F/003	WV420	6. 9.68	J.A.D.Bradshaw	Three Mile Cross, Reading	28. 6.03P
G-AWPJ	Cessna F150H	F150-0376		9. 9.68	W.J.Greenfield	Humberside	24. 4.05T
	(Built Reims Aviation SA)				*(Op Humberside Flying Club)*		

Reg	Type	C/n	Prev id	Date	Owner	Location	Expiry
G-AWPN	Shield Xyla	2 & PFA 1320		13. 9.68	K.R.Snell	Deanland, Hailsham	23. 6.03P
	(Continental A65)						
G-AWPP	Cessna F150H	F150-0348		13. 9.68	Coulson Flying Services Ltd	Cranfield	22. 7.01T
	(Built Reims Aviation SA)						
G-AWPS	Piper PA-28-140 Cherokee	28-20196	5N-AEK	16. 9.68	A.R.Matthews	Sittles Farm, Alrewas	19.11.03
G-AWPU	Cessna F150J	F150-0411		18. 9.68	LAC (Enterprises) Ltd	Barton	29.11.03T
	(Built Reims Aviation SA)				(Op Lancashire Aero Club)		
G-AWPW	Piper PA-12 Super Cruiser	12-3947	N78572	23. 9.68	AK Leasing (Jersey) Ltd	Jersey	5. 4.04
			NC78572				
G-AWPY	Campbell-Bensen B.8M	CA/314		20. 9.68	J.Jordan	Melrose Farm, Melbourne	
					(Current status unknown)		
G-AWPZ	Andreasson BA-4B	1	SE-XBS	24. 9.68	J.M.Vening	Goodwood	5. 11.03P
G-AWRK	Cessna F150J	F150-0410		8.10.68	Systemroute Ltd	Shoreham	23. 7.03T
	(Built Reims Aviation SA)						
G-AWRY	Hunting-Percival P.56 Provost T.1	PAC/F/339	XF836	29.10.81	Sylmar Aviation & Services Ltd		
			8043M			Lower Wasing Farm, Brimpton	22. 8.88P
	(As "XF836") (Damaged near Newbury 28.7.87: on rebuild 6.94: current status unknown)						
G-AWSH	Moravan Zlin Z.526 Trener Master	1052	OK-XRH	23.11.68	Avia Special Ltd	(Hatfield)	23.12.04T
			G-AWSH				
G-AWSL	Piper PA-28-180 Cherokee D	28-4907	N11C	30.10.68	Fascia Services Ltd	King's Farm, Thurrock	14.11.03
G-AWSM	Piper PA-28-235 Cherokee C	28-11125	N11C	30.10.68	N.A.Wright t/a Aviation Projects	(London SW20)	19. 4.04T
G-AWSN	Rollason-Druine D.62B Condor	RAE/632		31.10.68	M.K.A.Blyth	Little Gransden	14. 11.03P
	(RR Continental O-200A)						
G-AWSP	Rollason-Druine D.62B Condor	RAE/634		31.10.68	R.Q. & A.S.Bond	Enstone	23. 1.95
	(RR Continental O-200A)				(Stored 7.02)		
G-AWSS	Rollason-Druine D.62B Condor	RAE/636		31.10.68	N.J. & D.Butler	(Fordoun)	19.10.94P
	(Last sighted stored 3.98: current status unknown - at owner's home?) (Valid CofR 4.02)						
G-AWST	Rollason-Druine D.62B Condor	RAE/637		31.10.68	T.P.Lowe	(Abbots Ripton)	31. 5.03P
	(RR Continental O-200A)						
G-AWSW	Beagle D.5/180 Husky	3690	XW635	4.11.68	C.Tyers	Spanhoe	25. 5.05T
			G-AWSW		t/a Windmill Aviation *(As "XW635")*		
G-AWTJ	Cessna F150J	F150-0419		8.11.68	P.L.Jameson	Elstree	8.12.04T
	(Built Reims Aviation SA)						
G-AWTL	Piper PA-28-180 Cherokee D	28-5068	N11C	12.11.68	I.R.Chaplin	Andrewsfield	23. 7.04T
G-AWTS	Beech 19A Musketeer Sport	MB-412	OO-BGN	14.11.68	J.Holden & G.Benet	Lydd	15. 8.05T
			G-AWTS/N2763B				
G-AWTV	Beech 19A Musketeer Sport	MB-424	N2770B	14.11.68	J.Whittaker	Welshpool	11.10.03
G-AWTX*	Cessna F150J	F150-0404		18.11.68	R.D. & E.Forster	Beccles	25. 6.95T
	(Built Reims Aviation SA)				*(Noted 11.00) (Cancelled 13.12.01 by CAA)*		
G-AWUA*	Cessna P206D Super Skylane	P206-0550	N8750Z	21.11.68	Not known	Blackpool	4.12.87
	(Damaged Thruxton 16.10.87: cancelled 11.8.88 as destroyed) (Wreck stored 8.02)						
G-AWUB	Gardan GY-201 Minicab	A.205	F-PERX	22.11.68	R.A.Hand	RAF Barkston Heath	14. 2.03P
	(Built Aeronautique Havraise)						
G-AWUE	SAN Jodel DR.1050 Ambassadeur	299	F-BKHE	22.11.68	K.W. & F.M.Wood	Insch	17.10.87
					(On rebuild 4.97: noted 3.02)		
G-AWUG	Cessna F150H	F150-0299		25.11.68	Aircraft Engineers Ltd	Edinburgh	31. 1.03T
	(Built Reims Aviation SA)				(Op Edinburgh Air Centre)		
G-AWUJ	Cessna F150H	F150-0332		25.11.68	S.R.Hughes	Netherthorpe	14. 2.03
	(Built Reims Aviation SA)						
G-AWUL	Cessna F150H	F150-0346		25.11.68	C.A. & L.P.Green	Drayton St.Leonard	15. 9.05
	(Built Reims Aviation SA)						
G-AWUN	Cessna F150H	F150-0377		25.11.68	D.Valentine	Sturgate	22. 1.05
	(Built Reims Aviation SA)				tr C150 Group		
G-AWUO	Cessna F150H	F150-0380		25.11.68	S.Stevens	Popham	22. 5.04
	(Built Reims Aviation SA)				tr SAS Flying Group		
G-AWUT	Cessna F150J	F150-0405		25.11.68	S.J.Black	Sherburn-in-Elmet	19.10.03
	(Built Reims Aviation SA)						
G-AWUU	Cessna F150J	F150-0408	EI-BRA	25.11.68	A.L.Grey	Armshold Farm, Kingston, Cambs	15. 6.97
	(Built Reims Aviation SA)		G-AWUU				
G-AWUX	Cessna F172H	F172-0577		25.11.68	D.K.& K.Brian, A.M.Martin & C.Kelly	St.Just	25. 4.04
	(Built Reims Aviation SA)						
G-AWUZ	Cessna F172H	F172-0587		25.11.68	I.R.Judge	Shoreham	27.10.04
	(Built Reims Aviation SA)				tr G-BUJU Flying Group		
G-AWVA	Cessna F172H	F172-0597		25.11.68	Barton Air Ltd	Barton	29 6.03
	(Built Reims Aviation SA)						
G-AWVB	SAN Jodel D.117	604	F-BIBA	26.11.68	H.Davies	Swansea	31. 5.03P
G-AWVC	Beagle B.121 Pup 1	B121-026	(OE-CUP)	27.11.68	J.H.Marshall & J.J.West	Sturgate	17. 7.04
G-AWVE	CEA Jodel DR.1050/M1 Sicile Record	612	F-BMPQ	27.11.68	E.A.Taylor *(Noted 2.03)*	Southend	18. 5.00
G-AWVF	Hunting-Percival P.56 Provost T.1	PAC/F/375	XF877	28.11.68	Hunter Wing Ltd	Sandown	19. 7.02P
					(As "XF877/J-X")		
G-AWVG	AESL Airtourer T2 (115)	513	OO-WIC	29.11.68	C.J.Scholfield	Top Farm, Croydon, Royston	9. 7.04
			G-AWVG				
G-AWVN	Aeronca 7AC Champion	7AC-6005	N2426E	4.12.68	P.K.Brown	Rush Green	15. 4.03P
			NC2426E		tr Champ Flying Group		
G-AWVZ	Jodel D.112	898	F-PKVL	12.12.68	D.C.Stokes	Dunkeswell	16. 7.03P
G-AWWE	Beagle B.121 Pup 2	B121-022	G-35-032	12.12.68	J.N.Randle	Coventry	10. 5.03
G-AWWI	SAN Jodel D.117	728	F-BIDU	13.12.68	W.J.Evans	Rhigos	13. 6.03P
G-AWWM	Gardan GY-201 Minicab	A.195	F-BFOQ	1. 1.69	P J Brayshaw	Haddock Stone Farm, Markington	10.12.92P
					(Current status unknown)		
G-AWWN	SAN Jodel DR.1050 Sicile	398	F-BLJA	8. 1.69	R.A.J.Hurst	Nuthampstead	18. 6.04
G-AWWO	CEA Jodel DR.1050 Sicile	552	F-BLOI	8. 1.69	A.R.Grimshaw & A.A.Macleod	Barton	15. 5.03
					tr The Whiskey Oscar Group		
G-AWWP	Aerosport Woody Pusher Mk.3			7. 1.69	M.S.& Mrs R.D.Bird	Pepperbox, Salisbury	
		WA/163 & PFA 1323			(Stored 6.93)		

G-AWWT	Druine D.31 Turbulent	PFA 1653		15. 1.69	E.L.Phillips	Andrewsfield	23. 4.97P
	(Volkswagen 1600)				*(Damaged Andrewsfield 7.10.96: current status unknown)*		
G-AWWU	Reims FR172F Rocket	FR17200111		15. 1.69	Westward Airways (Lands End) Ltd	St.Just	16. 3.03T
G-AWWW	Cessna 401	401-0294	N8446F	19.12.68	Treble Whiskey Aviation Ltd	Blackpool	17. 6.02T
					(Op Westair Flying Services)		
G-AWXR	Piper PA-28-180 Cherokee D	28-5171	N11C	24. 1.69	Aero Club de Portugal	(Lisbon, Portugal)	14. 4.04
G-AWXS	Piper PA-28-180 Cherokee D	28-5283	N11C	24. 1.69	J.A.Hardiman	Shobdon	3. 3.03T
G-AWXY*	Morane-Saulnier MS.885 Super Rallye	5097	EI-AMG	29. 1.69	Not known	Hibaldstow	1. 2.97
					(Cancelled 9.5.01 by CAA) (Noted 7.02)		
G-AWXZ	SNCAN Stampe SV-4C	360	F-BHMZ Fr.Mil/F-BCOI	30. 1.69	Bianchi Aviation Film Services Ltd	Booker	1.10.05A
G-AWYB	Reims FR172F Rocket	FR17200075		30. 1.69	J.R.Sharpe	Southend	27. 8.04
G-AWYJ	Beagle B.121 Pup 2	B121-038	G-35-038	10. 2.69	H.C.Taylor	Popham	27. 4.02
G-AWYL	CEA Jodel DR.253B Regent	143		11. 2.69	K.Gillam	Radley, Hungerford	19. 4.03
G-AWYO	Beagle B.121 Pup 1	B121-041	G-35-041	11. 2.69	B.R.C.Wild	Popham	12.12.05
G-AWYV	British Aircraft Corporation One-Eleven 501EX	BAC.178		11. 2.69	European Aviation Ltd	Bournemouth	24. 6.04T
G-AWYX	SOCATA MS.880B Rallye Club	1311		11. 2.69	Marjorie J.Edwards	Henstridge	27. 6.86
					(Open storage 4.98) (Current status unknown)		
G-AWZR*	Hawker Siddeley HS.121 Trident 3B Srs.101	2318		14. 1.69	International Fire Training Centre	Teesside	9. 4.86T
					(WFU 27.9.85 & cancelled 26.3.86 as WFU) (Noted 7.01)		
G-AWZS*	Hawker Siddeley HS.121 Trident 3B Srs.101	2319		14. 1.69	International Fire Training Centre	Teesside	9. 9.86T
					(WFU 5.12.85 & cancelled 18.3.86 as WFU) (Noted 7.01)		
G-AWZU*	Hawker Siddeley HS.121 Trident 3B Srs.101	2321		14. 1.69	British Airways Authority	Stansted	3. 7.86T
					(Cancelled 18.3.86 as WFU) (Used for training 5.02)		

G-AXAA - G-AXZZ

G-AXAB	Piper PA-28-140 Cherokee	28-20238	EI-AOA N6206W	17. 2.69	Bencray Ltd	Blackpool	25. 6.04T
					(Op Blackpool & Fylde Aero Club)		
G-AXAN	de Havilland DH.82A Tiger Moth	85951	F-BDMM Fr.AF/EM720	21. 2.69	M.E.Carrell	Little Gransden	17. 3.99
	(Official c/n EM720-85)				*(As "EM720")*		
G-AXAS	Wallis WA-116-T/Mc	217		25. 2.69	K.H.Wallis	Reymerston Hall, Norfolk	15. 6.99P
	(McCulloch 4318A 72hp)				*(Noted 8.01)*		
	(Originally registered as Wallis WA-116-T two-seater tandem version: used major components from G-AVDH c/n 216)						
G-AXAT	SAN Jodel D.117A	836	F-BITJ	26. 2.69	P.S.Wilkinson	Insch	26. 3.03P
G-AXBF	Beagle D.5/180 Husky	3691	OE-DEW	17.10.84	C.M.Barnes	Garden Piece, Basingstoke	8. 8.03
G-AXBG	Bensen B.8M	RC.1		12. 3.69	R.Curtis *(Current status unknown)* (Bury St.Edmunds)		
G-AXBH	Cessna F172H	F172-0571		12. 3.69	D.F.Ranger	Popham	20. 3.03T
	(Built Reims Aviation SA)						
G-AXBJ	Cessna F172H	F172-0573		12. 3.69	S.E.Goodman	Leicester	25. 1.04
	(Built Reims Aviation SA)				tr BJ Flying Group		
G-AXBU*	Reims FR172F Rocket	FR17200073		12. 3.69	M.Hobson	(Cruden Bay, Peterhead)	23. 8.75
					(Crashed near Priestland, Darvel 13.10.74) (Cancelled 12.79: stored 6.00: current status unknown)		
G-AXBW	de Havilland DH.82A Tiger Moth	83595	6854M T5879	12. 3.69	Hunter Wing Ltd	Frensham	5. 4.04
					(As "T-5879/RUC-W")		
G-AXBZ	de Havilland DH.82A Tiger Moth	86552	F-BGDF Fr.AF/PG643	14. 3.69	W.J.de Jong Cleyndert	(Dereham)	3. 4.05
G-AXCA	Piper PA-28R-200 Cherokee Arrow	28R-35053	N11C	18. 3.69	R.A.Symmonds	Walton Hall, Purleigh	26. 3.03
G-AXCG	SAN Jodel D.117	510	PH-VRA F-BHXI	19. 3.69	C.A.White	Andrewsfield	20. 6.03P
					tr The Charlie Golf Group		
G-AXCL*	SOCATA MS.880B Rallye Club	1321		25. 3.69	P.P.Loucas	Seething	9. 7.00
					(Cancelled 5.3.02 as WFU)		
G-AXCM	SOCATA MS.880B Rallye Club	1322		25. 3.69	D.C.Maniford	Bidford	18.12.04
G-AXCX	Beagle B.121 Pup 2	B121-046	G-35-046	31. 3.69	L.A.Pink	Sandown	10. 7.94
					(On active restoration Wiltshire @ 1.03)		
G-AXCY	SAN Jodel D.117A	499	F-BHXB	31. 3.69	S. Marom	Whitehall Farm, Benington	31. 5.05P
G-AXCZ	SNCAN Stampe SV-4C	186	ZS-VFW G-AXCZ/F-BCFG	31. 3.69	J.Price	Trenchard Farm, Eggesford	10. 7.83
					(Stored 1.02)		
G-AXDI	Cessna F172H	F172-0574		14. 4.69	M.F. & J.R.Leusby	Maypole Farm, Chislet	29.12.02
	(Built Reims Aviation SA)				t/a Jeanair		
G-AXDK	CEA DR.315 Petit Prince	378		16. 4.69	M.R.Weatherhead & T.J.Thomas	Sywell	3.12.05
					tr Delta Kilo Flying Group		
G-AXDM	Hawker Siddeley HS.125 Srs.400B	25194		17. 4.69	GEC-Marconi Avionics (Holdings) Ltd	Edinburgh	7. 6.03
					(Op BAE Systems)		
G-AXDV	Beagle B.121 Pup 1	B121-049		18. 4.69	T.A.White	Bagby	28. 6.04
G-AXDW	Beagle B.121 Pup 1	B121-053		18. 4.69	I.Beaty, P.J.Abbott & J.R.A.Stevens	Cranfield	27. 3.05
					tr Cranfield Delta Whiskey Group		
G-AXED	Piper PA-25-235 Pawnee B	25-3586	OH-PIM OH-CPY/N7540Z	24. 4.69	Wolds Gliding Club Ltd	Pocklington	11. 3.03
G-AXEI*	Ward P.45 Gnome	P.45		25. 4.69	A.J.E.Smith & N.H.Ponsford	Breighton	
					(Cancelled 30.5.84 as WFU) (Noted 12.02)		
G-AXEO	Scheibe SF-25B Falke	4645	D-KEBC	1. 5.69	The Borders (Milfield) Gliding Club Ltd	Millfield	30. 4.04
G-AXEV	Beagle B.121 Pup 2	B121-070		6. 5.69	D.S.Russell & J.Powell-Tuck	Gloucestershire	21. 5.03
G-AXFN	Jodel D.119	980	F-PHBU	19. 5.69	D.M.Jackson & P.A.Munster	Netherthorpe	7. 8.03P
					tr Fox November Group		
G-AXGA*	Piper PA-18 Super Cub 95	18-2047	PH-NLE	22. 5.69	R.A.Yates	Sibsey	1. 8.89
	(L-18C-PI) *(Frame No.18-2059)*		(PH-CUB)/R.Neth.AF R-51/8A-51/52-2447				
					(Damaged Felthorpe 26.12.86: cancelled 29.5.87 as WFU) (Frame stored 8.00)		
G-AXGC*	SOCATA MS.880B Rallye Club	1349		23. 5.69	P.A.Crawford & M.C.Bennett	Elstree	12. 5.88
					(Stored 9.95: cancelled 21.9.00 as WFU)		
G-AXGE	SOCATA MS.880B Rallye Club	1353		23. 5.69	R.P.Loxton	(Bridport)	25. 9.04

Reg	Type	C/n	Prev id	Date	Owner	Location	Date2
G-AXGG	Cessna F150J	F150-0440		28. 5.69	S.G.Moores	Maypole Farm, Chislet	17. 8.03
	(Built Reims Aviation SA)						
G-AXGP	Piper J-3C-90 Cub (L-4J-PI)	12544	F-BGPS	2. 6.69	M.R.Keen	Liverpool	9. 8.02P
	(Frame No.12374) (Reported as c/n 9542 ex 43-28251)		F-BDTM/44-80248		tr Golf Papa Group		
G-AXGR	Phoenix Luton LA-4A Minor	PAL/1125		2. 6.69	B A Schlussler	Cawthorpe	22. 7.03P
	(JAP J.99)						
G-AXGS	Rollason-Druine D.62B Condor	RAE/638		3. 6.69	P.A.Kirkham	Wellcross Grange, Slinfold	7. 7.03P
					tr G-AXGS Condor Group		
G-AXGU*	Rollason-Druine D.62B Condor	RAE/640		3. 6.69	R Chapman	East Grinstead	22. 5.76
				(Crashed near Godalming, Surrey 31.3.75: cancelled 8.3.88 as WFU) (Stored 4.00)			
G-AXGV	Rollason-Druine D.62B Condor	RAE/641		3. 6.69	S.B.Robson	Watchford Farm, Yarcombe	18. 4.02P
G-AXGZ	Rollason-Druine D.62B Condor	RAE/643		3. 6.69	A J Cooper	Rochester	8. 5.03P
G-AXHA	Cessna 337A Super Skymaster	3370484	(EI-ATH)	5. 6.69	G.R.E.Evans	Little Staughton	30. 8.02
			N5384S				
G-AXHC	SNCAN Stampe SV-4C	293	F-BCFU	6. 6.69	D.L.Webley	Cranwell	26. 4.03
G-AXHE*	Britten-Norman BN-2A Islander	86	4X-AYV	6. 6.69	The Scottish Parachute Club	Strathallan	15. 4.94
			G-AXHE	*(Crashed Cark 5.2.94: cancelled 31.3.94 as WFU) (Rear fuselage for para-training 6.00)*			
G-AXHO	Beagle B.121 Pup 2	B121-077		9. 6.69	L.H.Grundy	(Thurrock)	24. 5.04
G-AXHP	Piper J-3C-65 Cub (L-4J-PI)	12932	F-BETT	9. 6.69	Witham (Specialist) Vehicles Ltd	(Grantham)	9. 8.02P
	(Frame No.12762)		NC74121/44-80636		*(As "480636 A-58" in US Army c/s)*		
	(Regd with c/n "AF36506" which is USAAC contract no)						
G-AXHR	Piper J-3C-65 Cub (L-4H-PI)	10892	F-BETI	9. 6.69	K.B.Raven & E.Cundy	Hill Farm, Nayland	5. 8.03P
			43-29601		tr G-AXHR Cub Group *(As "329601/D-44" in US Army c/s)*		
G-AXHS	SOCATA MS.880B Rallye Club	1357		9. 6.69	W.B.& A.Swales	Bagby	29. 5.03
G-AXHT	SOCATA MS.880B Rallye Club	1358		9. 6.69	K.J.Duthie tr Hotel Tango Group	(Henley-on-Thames)	19. 4.04
G-AXHV	SAN Jodel D.117A	695	F-BIDF	9. 6.69	J.S.Ponsford tr Derwent Flying Group	Hucknall	13.5.03P
G-AXIA	Beagle B.121 Pup 1	B121-078		17. 6.69	P.S.Shuttleworth	Leicester	7. 5.04T
G-AXIE	Beagle B.121 Pup 2	B121-087		17. 6.69	G.McD.Moir	Egginton, Derby	7. 6.04
G-AXIF	Beagle B.121 Pup 2	B121-088	(SE-FGV)	17. 6.69	J.A.Holmes & S.A.Self *"Susie II"*	Egginton, Derby	16. 9.05T
G-AXIG	Scottish Aviation Bulldog Srs.100/104	BH120/002		24. 6.69	A.A.Douglas-Hamilton	Archerfield Estate, Dirleton	6. 5.05
G-AXIO	Piper PA-28-140 Cherokee B	28-25764	N11C	26. 6.69	White Waltham Airfield Ltd	White Waltham	20. 3.05T
					(Op West London Aero Services)		
G-AXIR	Piper PA-28-140 Cherokee B	28-25795	N11C	26. 6.69	A.G.Birch	Weston Zoyland	10. 5.04
G-AXIW	Scheibe SF-25B Falke	4657	(D-KABJ)	3. 7.69	M.B.Hill	Nympsfield	20. 9.02
G-AXIX	AESL Airtourer T4 (150)	A.527		3. 7.69	J.C.Wood	Shobdon	1 .3.04
G-AXJB	Omega 84 HAB	04		9. 7.69	Semajan Ltd	Romsey, Hants	20. 8.73S
	(Initially flown as G-AXDT)				tr Southern Balloon Group *"Jester"*		
G-AXJH	Beagle B.121 Pup 2	B121-089		11. 7.69	D.Collings tr The Henry Flying Group	Popham	2. 5.04
G-AXJI	Beagle B.121 Pup 2	B121-090		11. 7.69	D.R.Vale	Egginton, Derby	3. 6.05
G-AXJJ	Beagle B.121 Pup 2	B121-091		11. 7.69	M.L., T.M., D.A & P.M.Jones	Egginton, Derby	24. 8.03T
G-AXJO	Beagle B.121 Pup 2	B121-094		11. 7.69	J.A.D.Bradshaw *"Joey"*	Three Mile Cross, Reading	9. 8.03
G-AXJR	Scheibe SF-25B Falke	4652	D-KICD	4. 7.69	R.I.Hey tr The Falke Syndicate	Nympsfield	16. 5.03
G-AXJV	Piper PA-28-140 Cherokee B	28-25572	N11C	14. 7.69	ATC (Lasham) Ltd	Lasham	7. 6.04T
G-AXJX	Piper PA-28-140 Cherokee B	28-25990	N11C	14. 7.69	Patrolwatch Ltd	Barton	2.10.04
G-AXKH	Phoenix Luton LA-4A Minor	PAL/1316 & PFA 823		21. 7.69	M.E.Vaisey	(Hemel Hempstead)	18. 4.84P
	(Volkswagen 1600)				*(Current status unknown)*		
G-AXKO	Westland-Bell 47G-4A	WA/720	G-17-5	22. 7.69	G.P.Hinkley	Channons Hall, Tibenham	27. 1.03
G-AXKX	Westland-Bell 47G-4A	WA/728	G-17-13	22. 7.69	South Yorkshire Aviation Ltd	(Worksop)	3. 6.04
G-AXKY	Westland-Bell 47G-4A	WA/729	G-17-14	22. 7.69	G.A.Knight & G.M.Vowles	Gamston	1. 8.02
G-AXLG	Cessna 310K	310K0204	N3804X	25. 7.69	Smiths (Harlow) Aerospace Ltd	Willingale	16. 7.04
G-AXLI	Slingsby Nipper T.66 RA.45 Srs.3	S.131/1707		25. 7.69	K.R.H.Wingate	Halwell, Totnes	20. 5.03P
G-AXLS	SAN Jodel DR.105A Ambassadeur	86	F-BIVR	31. 7.69	J.C.M.Robb tr Axle Flying Club	Popham	15. 3.04
G-AXLZ	Piper PA-18 Super Cub 95	18-2052	PH-NLB	31. 7.69	R.J.Quantrell	Low Farm, South Walsham	23. 4.00
	(L-18C-PI) (Frame No.18-2065)		R.Neth.AF R-45/8A-45/52-2452	*(Damaged Low Farm 14.8.97: current status unknown)*			
G-AXMA	Piper PA-24-180 Comanche	24-3467	N8214P	5. 8.69	J.A.Fletcher	(Louth)	18. 6.04
G-AXMN	Auster J/5B Autocar	2962	F-BGPN	14. 8.69	J.A. & S.M.Fletcher	(Louth)	30. 6.04
G-AXMT	Dornier Bücker Bü.133C Jungmeister	46	N133SJ	19. 8.69	R.A.Fleming	Breighton	23. 5.03P
			G-AXMT/HB-MIY/U-99		*(As "U-99")*		
G-AXMW	Beagle B.121 Pup 1	B121-101		19. 8.69	DJP Engineering (Knebworth) Ltd	Cambridge	3. 5.04
G-AXMX	Beagle B.121 Pup 2	B121-103	VH-UPT	19. 8.69	Susan A.Jones	(Cannes, France)	5.10.03T
			G-AXMX/G-35-103				
G-AXNJ	Jodel Wassmer D.120 Paris-Nice	52	F-BHYO	29. 8.69	D.I.Vernon tr Clive Flying Group	Sleap	4.11.02P
G-AXNL	Beagle B.121 Pup 1	B121-113		3. 9.69	CAVOK Ltd	White Waltham	7. 4.04T
G-AXNM	Beagle B.121 Pup 1	B121-114		3. 9.69	T.W.Anderson	Bembridge	17.10.02
G-AXNN	Beagle B.121 Pup 2	B121-104		3. 9.69	Gabrielle Aviation Ltd *"Gabrielle"*	Shoreham	13. 8.03
G-AXNP	Beagle B.121 Pup 2	B121-106		3. 9.69	J.W.Ellis & R.J.Hemmings	Ashcroft Farm, Winsford	24. 6.05
G-AXNR	Beagle B.121 Pup 2	B121-108		3. 9.69	J R Clegg	Raby's Farm, Great Stukeley	25. 3.05
					tr November Romeo Group		
G-AXNS	Beagle B.121 Pup 2	B121-110		3. 9.69	D Beckwith & D Long tr Derwent Aero Group	Gamston	8. 7.04
G-AXNW	SNCAN Stampe SV-4C	381	F-BFZX	11. 9.69	Carolyn S.Grace	Blooms Farm, Sible Hedingham	4. 5.02
			Fr.Mil				
G-AXNX	Cessna 182M	18259322	N70606	16. 9.69	D.B.Harper	Biggin Hill	12. 5.05T
G-AXNZ	Pitts S-1C Special	EB.1 & PFA 1383		16. 9.69	W.A.Jordan	(Sandy)	30. 8.91P
	(Lycoming IO-360) (C/n quoted as EB.2 also)				*(Stored 12.97: current status unknown)*		
G-AXOH	SOCATA MS.894A Rallye Minerva 220	11062	D-EAGU	17. 9.69	Bristol Cars Ltd	White Waltham	24. 5.03
G-AXOJ	Beagle B.121 Pup 2	B121-109	G-35-109	24. 9.69	T.J.Martin tr Pup Flying Group	Rochester	27. 3.04
G-AXOR	Piper PA-28-180 Cherokee D	28-5453	N11C	30. 9.69	Oscar Romeo Aviation Ltd	Redhill	1. 4.05
G-AXOS	SOCATA MS.894A Rallye Minerva 220	11079		3.10.69	A.V.Hurley tr Henlow Thunderbolts	RAF Henlow	14. 5.03
G-AXOT	SOCATA MS.893A Rallye Commodore 180	11433		3.10.69	P.Evans & J.C.Graves	Doncaster	26. 3.03
G-AXOZ	Beagle B.121 Pup 1	B121-115	N70290	7.10.69	R.J.Ogborn	Hawarden	12. 9.03
			G-AXOZ/G-35-115				
G-AXPA	Beagle B.121 Pup 1	B121-116	D-EATL	7.10.69	D.G.Lewendon	Manor Farm, Glatton	4.11.87
			G-AXPA/G-35-116		*(On rebuild 10.01)*		
G-AXPB	Beagle B.121 Pup 1	B121-117	G-35-117	7.10.69	M.J.K.Seary & R.T.Austin tr Beagle Flying Group Leicester		17. 1.05

Reg	Type	c/n	Prev id	Date	Owner	Location	Date
G-AXPC	Beagle B.121 Pup 1	B121-119	PH-VRS G-AXPC	7.10.69	T.A.White	Bagby	30. 8.03
G-AXPF	Reims/Cessna F150K	F15000543		14.10.69	D.R.Marks	Hinton in the Hedges	22. 4.02
G-AXPG	Mignet HM.293 (Volkswagen 1300)	PFA 1333		14.10.69	W.H.Cole (Noted 5.01)	Spilsted Farm, Sedlescombe	20. 1.77P
G-AXPM	Beagle B.121 Pup 1	B121-122	G-35-122	20.10.69	Pup Flyers Ltd	North Weald	29. 5.05
G-AXPN	Beagle B.121 Pup 2	B121-123	G-35-123	20.10.69	A G Fletcher	Breighton	28. 2.05
G-AXPZ	Campbell Cricket (Rotax 582)	CA/320		3.11.69	W.R.Partridge (Noted 10.00)	St.Merryn	27. 4.99P
G-AXRC	Campbell Cricket (Volkswagen 1600)	CA/323		3.11.69	L.R.Morris	(Newry, Co.Armagh)	18. 5.78S
					(Damaged Wittering 22.10.77: stored Tattershall Thorpe 7.91: new owner 12.02)		
G-AXRP	SNCAN Stampe SV.4A	554	F-BDCZ	7.11.69	C C Manning	Rotary Farm, Hatch	5. 6.76
	(Originally regd as SV.4C (Renault 4P): damaged Gransden 19.10.74: restored 2.85 as SV-4A G-BLOL with c/n SS-SV-R1: NTU and restored 9.94 *as G-AXRP but stored as "G-BLOL" 10.99: on rebuild with DH Gipsy Major 2 @ 2.01)*						
G-AXRR	Auster AOP.9	AUS.178 & B5/10/178	XR241 G-AXRR/XR241	7.11.69	R.J.Burgess *(As "XR241" in Army yellow c/s)*	Crowfield	16. 9.03P
G-AXRT	Reims/Cessna FA150K Aerobat (Tail-wheel conversion)	FA15000018		12.11.69	C.C.Walley	Elstree	25. 1.06T
G-AXRU*	Reims/Cessna FA150K Aerobat	FA15000020		12.11.69	Arrival Enterprises Ltd *(Cancelled 2.3.99 by CAA) (Noted 4.01)*	Haverfordwest	10.12.87
G-AXSC	Beagle B.121 Pup 1	B121-138	G-35-138	13.11.69	R.J.MacCarthy	Swansea	6. 3.04
G-AXSD	Beagle B.121 Pup 1	B121-139	G-35-139	13.11.69	T.A.White t/a Bagby Aviation	Bagby	1. 4.05
G-AXSF	Nash Petrel	PFA 1516 & P.003		17.11.69	Nash Aircraft Ltd	Lasham	? .4.94P
	(Lycoming O-360) (Second allocation of PFA 1516 has no connection with G-BACA)				*(Stored 10.95: current status unknown)*		
G-AXSG	Piper PA-28-180 Cherokee E	28-5605	N11C	17.11.69	Admiral Property Ltd	Old Buckenham	26. 6.05
G-AXSI	Reims/Cessna F172H	F17200687	G-SNIP G-AXSI	19.11.69	A.J.G.Davis tr St.Marys Flying Group	St.Mary's, Isles of Scilly	23. 7.04
G-AXSM	CEA Jodel DR.1051 Sicile	512	F-BLRH	20.11.69	T.R.G.Barnby & M.S.Regendanz *(New owners 6.01)*	Headcorn	3.10.98
G-AXSW	Reims/Cessna FA150K Aerobat	FA15000003		25.11.69	R.Mitchell	(Chalfont St.Giles)	2. 3.04
G-AXSZ	Piper PA-28-140 Cherokee B	28-26188	N11C	26.11.69	R.Gibson & B.Collins tr The White Wings Flying Group	White Waltham	24. 4.03
G-AXTA	Piper PA-28-140 Cherokee B	28-26301	N11C	26.11.69	P.J.Farrell tr G-AXTA Aircraft Group	Shoreham	25. 5.04
G-AXTC	Piper PA-28-140 Cherokee B	28-26265	N11C	26.11.69	W.J.Knott tr G-AXTC Group	Stubby	29.10.05
G-AXTH*	Piper PA-28-140 Cherokee B	28-26283	N11C	26.11.69	W Bateson	Blackpool	27.10.90T
	(Damaged in forced landing near Compton Abbas 28.2.88: .cancelled by CAA 13.7.95) (Wreck stored 7.02)						
G-AXTJ	Piper PA-28-140 Cherokee B	28-26241	N11C	26.11.69	K.Patel	Elstree	13. 2.04T
G-AXTL	Piper PA-28-140 Cherokee B	28-26247	N11C	26.11.69	Pegasus Aviation (Midlands) Ltd	Tatenhill	6.11.04
G-AXTO	Piper PA-24-260 Comanche C	24-4900	N9449P N9705N	28.11.69	Jean L.Richardson *"Betsy Baby"*	Turweston	23. 7.03
G-AXTP	Piper PA-28-180 Cherokee C	28-3791	OH-PID	1.12.69	C.W.R.Moore	Elstree	10. 1.04
G-AXUA	Beagle B.121 Pup 1	B121-150	G-35-150	4.12.69	P.Wood	Bourn	12. 6.03
G-AXUB	Britten-Norman BN-2A Islander	121	5N-AIJ G-AXUB/N859JA/G-51-47	4.12.69	Headcorn Parachute Club Ltd	Headcorn	15. 5.03
G-AXUC	Piper PA-12 Super Cruiser	12-621	5Y-KFR VP-KFR/ZS-BIN	5.12.69	J.J.Bunton	Maypole Farm, Chislet	21. 4.05
G-AXUE*	CEA Jodel DR.105A Ambassadeur	59	F-BKFX F-OBFX	9.12.69	L Lewis	(Redcar)	
					(Crashed Bagby 11.6.89) (Cancelled 23.4.90 as WFU: stored for rebuild 1.02)		
G-AXUF	Reims/Cessna FA150K Aerobat	FA15000043		9.12.69	W.B.Bateson	Blackpool	10. 1.03T
G-AXUK	SAN Jodel DR.1050 Ambassadeur	292	F-BJYU	11.12.69	G.J. Keegan tr Downland Flying Group (2KI)	(Lewes)	23. 8.03
G-AXUM*	Handley Page 137 Jetstream 1	245		12.12.69	IGF/Sodetag Training School Toussous-le-Noble, France *(Cancelled 20.1.99 as PWFU) (Noted 6.01)*		
G-AXVB	Reims/Cessna F172H	F17200703		22.12.69	R.& J.Turner	Charlton Park, Malmesbury	26. 5.04
G-AXVK	Campbell Cricket	CA/327		1. 1.70	P.C.Lovegrove *(Noted 8.02)*	Henstridge	8. 3.89P
G-AXVM	Campbell Cricket (Volkswagen 1834)	CA/329		1. 1.70	D.M.Organ	Stoke Orchard, Cheltenham	10. 7.03P
G-AXVN	McCandless M.4 Gyroplane (Volkswagen 1700)	M4/6		5. 1.70	W.R.Partridge *(Stored 8.96: current status unknown)*	St.Merryn	
G-AXWA	Auster AOP.9	B5/10/133	XN437	13. 1.70	M.L. & C.M.Edwards *(As "XN437") (Noted 2.00)*	North Weald	
G-AXWT	Jodel D.11 (Continental C90)	PFA 911		26. 1.70	R.C.Owen	Danehill	2. 6.00P
G-AXWV	CEA DR.253 Regent	104	F-OCKL	2. 2.70	R Friedlander & D C Ray	Grateley	26.11.04
G-AXWZ	Piper PA-28R-200 Cherokee Arrow	28R-35605	N11C	3. 2.70	P.Walkley	Pittrichie Farm, Whiterashes	7.10.05P
G-AXXC	Rousseau Piel CP.301B Emeraude	117	F-BJAT	4. 2.70	L.F.Clayton	Wellesbourne Mountford	15. 1.03P
G-AXXV	de Havilland DH.82A Tiger Moth	85852	F-BGJI Fr.AF/DE992	24. 2.70	C.N.Wookey *(As "DE992")*	France Farm, Upavon	17. 6.04
G-AXXW	SAN Jodel D.117	632	F-BIBN	26. 2.70	D.F.Chamberlain & J.M.Walsh	Haverfordwest	23. 8.03P
G-AXYK	Taylor JT.1 Monoplane (Volkswagen 1500)	PFA 1409		2. 3.70	D.J.Hulks *(New CofR 4.02)*	Little Robhurst Farm, Woodchurch	13.10.03P
G-AXYU	Jodel D.9 Bebe (Volkswagen 1600)	547	EI-BVE G-AXYU	5. 3.70	P.Turton & H.C.Peake-Jones	Ash House Farm, Winsford	13. 9.01P
G-AXYZ	WHE Airbuggy	1005		10. 3.70	B.Gunn	Melrose Farm, Melbourne	22.12.92P
	(Volkswagen 1600) *(Originally regd as McCandless M.4 Gyroplane)*				*(Current status unknown)*		
G-AXZA*	WHE Airbuggy	1006		10. 3.70	C Verlaan	(Lelystad, The Netherlands)	15. 8.96P
	(Volkswagen 1700) *(Originally regd as McCandless M.4 Gyroplane)*				*(Cancelled 19.9.00 by CAA) (Current status unknown)*		
G-AXZB	WHE Airbuggy	1007		10. 3.70	B.Gunn	Melrose Farm, Melbourne	18.11.86P
	(Originally regd as McCandless M.4 Gyroplane)				*(New CofR 6.02)*		
G-AXZD	Piper PA-28-180 Cherokee E	28-5609	N11C	12. 3.70	G.M.Whitmore	High Cross, Ware	15.10.04
G-AXZF	Piper PA-28-180 Cherokee E	28-5688	N11C	12. 3.70	E.P.C. & W.R.Rabson *(Op Carill Aviation)*	Compton Abbas	23. 7.04T
G-AXZK	Britten-Norman BN-2A-26 Islander	153	V2-LAD VP-LAD/G-AXZK/G-51-153	12. 3.70	P.Johnson	Hinton in the Hedges	16. 4.03

G-AXZM	Slingsby Nipper T.66 RA.45 Srs.3A	PFA 1378		16. 3.70	G.R.Harlow	Newcastle	24. 8.89P
	(Volkswagen 1600) *(Slingsby kit c/n S.133/1709)*				*(Damaged near Eshott 21.8.89: possible rebuild 5.90: current status unknown)*		
G-AXZO	Cessna 180	31137	N3639C	17. 3.70	J.C.King	Bourne Park, Hurstbourne Tarrant	17.10.05
					tr Bourne Park Flyers		
G-AXZP	Piper PA-E23-250 Aztec D	27-4464	N13819	17. 3.70	D.Barnett tr Aztec Flying Group G-AXZP	Bristol	22. 8.04T
G-AXZT	SAN Jodel D.117A	607	F-BIBD	17. 3.70	N.Batty	Bagby	30. 4.03P
G-AXZU	Cessna 182N Skylane	18260104	N92233	19. 3.70	C D Williams	Goodwood	16. 8.03

G-AYAA - G-AYZZ

G-AYAB	Piper PA-28-180 Cherokee E	28-5804	N11C	24. 3.70	Films Ltd	Fairoaks	16. 8.03
G-AYAC	Piper PA-28R-200 Cherokee Arrow	28R-35606	N11C	24. 3.70	G.A.J.Smith-Bosanquet	Knettishall	23. 4.04
					tr The Fersfield Flying Group		
G-AYAN	Slingsby Cadet	III003 & PFA 1385	BGA1224	6. 4.70	D.C.Pattison	Brunton	20. 8.02P
	(Volkswagen 1600)		RAFGSA.223		*"Thermal Hopper"*		
	(Converted from T.31B [Frame No.SSK/FF776])						
G-AYAR	Piper PA-28-180 Cherokee E	28-5797	N11C	8. 4.70	Seawing Flying Club Ltd & A.Jahanfar	Southend	13. 2 05T
G-AYAT	Piper PA-28-180 Cherokee E	28-5801	N11C	8. 4.70	J.B.R.Elliot tr G-AYAT Flying Group	Seething	18. 3.04T
G-AYAW	Piper PA-28-180 Cherokee E	28-5805	N11C	14. 4.70	R.C.Pendle & M.J.Rose	Blackbushe	19. 6.05T
G-AYBD	Reims/Cessna F150K	F15000583		7. 4.70	Apollo Aviation Advisory Ltd	Shoreham	12. 9.04T
G-AYBG	Scheibe SF-25B Falke	4696	(D-KECJ)	13. 4.70	H.H.T.Wolf *(New owner 6.01)*	Gallows Hill, Bovington	4. 4.97
G-AYBO	Piper PA-23-250 Aztec D	27-4510	N13874	15. 4.70	Twinguard Aviation Ltd	Denham	28. 3.03
G-AYBP	Jodel D.112	1131	F-PMEK	16. 4.70	G.J.Langston	Bidford	30.10.02P
G-AYBR	Wassmer Jodel D.112	1259	F-BMIG	16. 4.70	R.T.Mosforth	Netherthorpe	30.10.03P
G-AYCC	Campbell Cricket	CA/336		20. 4.70	D.J.M.Charity	Hinton in the Hedges	16. 5.03P
	(Rotax 582)						
G-AYCE	Scintex CP.301C1 Emeraude	530	F-BJFH	20. 4.70	S.D.Glover	Plymouth	5. 9.03P
G-AYCF	Reims/Cessna FA150K Aerobat	FA15000055		22. 4.70	E.J.Atkins	Thruxton	8. 6.03
G-AYCG	SNCAN Stampe SV-4C	59	F-BOHF	24. 4.70	Nancy Bignall	White Waltham	6. 6.04
			F-BBAE/Fr.Mil				
G-AYCJ	Cessna TP206D Turbo Super Skylane	P206-0552	N8752Z	27. 4.70	White Knuckle Airways Ltd	Leeds-Bradford	30. 4.03
	(Regd with c/n T206-0552)						
G-AYCK	AIA Stampe SV-4C	1139	G-BUNT	28. 4.70	J.F.Graham	Jersey	12. 9.04
	(DH Gipsy Major)		G-AYCK/F-BANE				
G-AYCN	Piper J-3C-65 Cub	"13365"	F-BCPO	28. 4.70	W.R. & B.M.Young *(Stored 4.91: current status unknown)*		
	(Frame No. not known: c/n quoted became PH-UCM in 11.46 and p/i is doubtful)				Furze Hill Farm, Rosemarket, Milford Haven		27. 1.89P
G-AYCO	CEA DR.360 Chevalier	362	F-BRFI	29. 4.70	P.L.Buckley t/r Charlie Oscar Club	(Colchester)	30.10.03
G-AYCP	Jodel D.112	67	F-BGKO	30. 4.70	D.J.Nunn	St.Just	28. 6.03P
G-AYCT	Reims/Cessna F172H	F17200724		1. 5.70	Haimoss Ltd & D.C.Scouller	Old Sarum	8.12.04T
					(Op Old Sarum Flying Club)		
G-AYDI	de Havilland DH.82A Tiger Moth	85910	F-BDOE	7. 5.70	R.B. & E.W.Woods & J.D.M.Barr	(Thatcham)	10. 1.03
			Fr.AF/DF174				
G-AYDR	SNCAN Stampe SV-4C	307	F-BCLG	13. 5.70	A.J.McLuskie	Bishopstrow Farm, Warminster	27. 3.75
					(Damaged 16.6.73: on rebuild 8.93: current status unknown)		
G-AYDX	Beagle A.61 Terrier 2	B.647	VX121	20. 5.70	R.A.Kirby	Spanhoe	12. 1.03
G-AYDY	Phoenix Luton LA-4A Minor	PAL/1302 & PFA 817		21. 5.70	T.Littlefair	Lymington, Hants	15. 8.97P
	(Volkswagen 1600)				*(On rebuild 3.00)*		
G-AYDZ	CEA Jodel DR.200	01	F-BLKV	21. 5.70	M.W.Albery	Enstone	29. 3.05
	(Lycoming O-235)		F-WLKV		tr Zero One Group		
G-AYEB	Wassmer Jodel D.112	586	F-BIQR	26. 5.70	C.H.G.Baulf	RAF Wattisham	26. 7.02P
G-AYEC	Menavia Piel CP.301A Emeraude	249	F-BIMV	26. 5.70	J.J.Shepherd	Netherthorpe	17. 3.03P
					tr Red Wing Flying Group *"Antoinette"*		
G-AYED	Piper PA-24-260 Comanche C	24-4923	N9417P	28. 5.70	J.V.Hutchinson	(Frangy, France)	21.11.05
G-AYEE	Piper PA-28-180 Cherokee E	28-5813	N11C	28. 5.70	Halegreen Associates Ltd	Hinton in the Hedges	24. 6.05T
G-AYEF	Piper PA-28-180 Cherokee E	28-5815	N11C	28. 5.70	J.C.Rideout & A.L.Beaumont	Barton	22.1.05
					tr G-AYEF Group		
G-AYEG	Falconar F-9	PFA 1321		29. 5.70	A L Smith	Sackville Farm, Riseley	28. 7.05P
	(Volkswagen 1600)						
G-AYEH	SAN Jodel DR.1050 Ambassadeur	455	F-BLJB	8. 6.70	J.W.Scott	Wellesbourne Mountford	17. 6.05
					tr John Scott Jodel Group *"Jemima"*		
G-AYEI*	Piper PA-31 Turbo Navajo	31-631	N6730L	29. 5.70	Not known	Southend	11. 5.89
					(Cancelled 5.6.92 as WFU) (Hulk on fire dump 2.03)		
G-AYEJ	SAN Jodel DR.1050 Ambassadeur	253	F-BJYG	1. 6.70	J.M.Newbold	Enstone	7. 1.04
G-AYEN	Piper J-3C-65 Cub (L-4H-PI)	12184	F-BGQD	4. 6.70	P.J.Warde & C.F.Morris	Grove Farm, Raveningham	10. 7.03P
	(Frame No.12012)		(F-BGQA)/Fr.AF/44-79888				
	(Official identity is c/n 9696/43-835 but fuselages probably exchanged with F-BGQA on conversion in 1952/53)						
G-AYEV	SAN Jodel DR.1050 Ambassadeur	179	F-BERH	10. 6.70	L.G.Evans	Redhill	10. 2.03
			F-OBTH/F-OBRH				
G-AYEW	CEA Jodel DR.1050 Sicile	443	F-BLMJ	11. 6.70	J.M.Gale & J.R.Hope	Westacott Farm, Crediton	16.11.03
G-AYFC	Rollason-Druine D.62B Condor	RAE/644		19. 6.70	A.R.Chadwick	Breighton	26.12.02P
G-AYFD	Rollason-Druine D.62B Condor	RAE/645		19. 6.70	B.G.Manning	Little Down Farm, Milson	3. 7.04
G-AYFE	Rollason-Druine D.62C Condor	RAE/646		19. 6.70	D.I.H.Johnstone & W.T.Barnard	Strathaven	6.12.01
G-AYFF	Rollason-Druine D.62B Condor	RAE/647		19. 6.70	G.P.Badham	Park Farm, Eaton Bray	9. 7.03P
					tr Condor Syndicate		
G-AYFG	Rollason-Druine D.62C Condor	RAE/648		19. 6.70	C Jobling & A J Mackay	St Ghislain, Belgium	28.10 02
G-AYFP	SAN Jodel D.140 Mousquetaire	18	F-BMSI	24. 6.70	A.R.Wood	Audley End	27. 5.05
			F-OBLH/F-WNDO				
G-AYFV	Crosby Andreasson Super BA.4B	002 & PFA 1359		26. 6.70	A.R.C.Mathie	RAF Coltishall	5. 7.95P
	(Lycoming IO-320)				*(Current status unknown)*		
G-AYGA	SAN Jodel D.117	436	F-BHNU	30. 6.70	R.L.E.Horrell	Oxenhope	10. 4.03P
G-AYGB*	Cessna 310Q	310Q0111	N7611Q	2. 7.70	Perth College	Perth	23.10.87T
					(Cancelled 23.6.94 by CAA) (Instructional airframe 3.02)		
G-AYGC	Reims/Cessna F150K	F15000556		2. 7.70	S.R.Cooper tr Alpha Aviation Group	Barton	21. 5.04

Reg	Type	c/n	Prev id	Date	Owner	Location	Date
G-AYGD	CEA Jodel DR.1050 Sicile	515	F-BLRE	3. 7.70	D.Street tr G-AYGD Flying Group	Netherthorpe	9.12.04
	(Damaged Grove Farm, Retford 24.6.99: current status unknown)						
G-AYGE	SNCAN Stampe SV-4C	242	F-BCGM	6. 7.70	I.L.J. & S.Proudfoot	Duxford	4. 6.03
G-AYGG	Jodel Wassmer D.120 Paris-Nice	184	F-BJPH	10. 7.70	J.M.Dean	Stoneacre Farm, Farthing Corner	5. 4.03P
G-AYGX	Reims FR172G Rocket	FR17200208		15. 7.70	D.Waterhouse tr Reims Rocket Group	Barton	13. 8.03
G-AYHA	American AA-1 Yankee Clipper	AA1-0396	N6196L	21. 7.70	S.J.Carr	(St.Andrews)	21. 3.05
G-AYHX	SAN Jodel D.117A	903	F-BIVE	23. 7.70	L.J.E.Goldfinch	Old Sarum	6. 5.03P
G-AYHY	Sportavia Fournier RF4D	4156		24. 7.70	P.J. & S.M.Wells	Booker	3. 8.03
G-AYIG	Piper PA-28-140 Cherokee C	8-26878	N11C	31. 7.70	Biggles Ltd	Booker	26.11.05T
G-AYII	Piper PA-28R-200 Cherokee Arrow	28R-35736	N11C	4. 8.70	P.W.J. & P.A.S.Gove	Exeter	22. 3.03
G-AYIJ	SNCAN Stampe SV-4B	376	F-BCOM	4. 8.70	T.C.Beadle	Spilsted Farm, Sedlescombe	16. 6.03
G-AYIM	Hawker Siddeley HS.748 Srs.2A/270	1687	G-11-687 CS-TAG/G-AYIM/G-11-5	11. 8.70	Emerald Airways Ltd	Liverpool	21.12.04T
G-AYIT	de Havilland DH.82A Tiger Moth	86343	F-BGEZ Fr.AF/NL896	20. 8.70	S.R.Pollitt & H.M.Eassie tr Ulster Tiger Group	Newtownards, Co.Down	15.11.04
G-AYJA	SAN Jodel DR.1050 Ambassadeur	150	F-BJJJ	8. 9.70	G.Connell	Navan, Co.Meath	7. 7.05
G-AYJB	SNCAN Stampe SV-4C	560	F-BDDF	8. 9.70	F.J.M. & J.P.Esson *"Odette"*	Bere Farm, Warnford	20. 6.04
G-AYJD	Alpavia Fournier RF3	11	F-BLXA	8. 9.70	E.Shouler	Beeches Farm, South Scarle	27. 8.03P
G-AYJP	Piper PA-28-140 Cherokee C	8-26403	N11C	15. 9.70	RAF Brize Norton Flying Club Ltd	RAF Brize Norton	9. 5.04T
G-AYJR	Piper PA-28-140 Cherokee C	28-26694	N11C	15. 9.70	RAF Brize Norton Flying Club Ltd	RAF Brize Norton	8. 1.04T
G-AYJW	Reims FR172G Rocket	FR17200225		17. 9.70	N.D.Wyndow tr Sir W.G. Armstrong-Whitworth Flying Group	Coventry	27. 7.03T
G-AYJY	Isaacs Fury II (RR Continental C90)	PFA 1373		23. 9.70	M.F.Newman	Wreningham, Norfolk	1.10.02P
G-AYKD	SAN Jodel DR.1050 Ambassadeur	351	F-BKHR	30. 9.70	B F Hill	Shenstone Hall Far, Shenstone	20. 6.03
G-AYKJ	SAN Jodel D.117A	730	F-BIDX	6.10.70	J.M.Alexander	Lichfield	20. 6.03P
G-AYKK	SAN Jodel D.117	378	F-BHGM	6.10.70	D.M.Whitham	Crosland Moor	2. 5.85S
	(On rebuild 11.99: current status unknown)						
G-AYKL	Reims/Cessna F150L	F15000676		6.10.70	M.A.Judge tr Aero Group 78	Netherthorpe	19.12.02T
G-AYKS	Leopoldoff L.7 Colibri (Continental A65)	125	F-PCZX F-APZQ	8.10.70	W.B.Cooper	Walkeridge Farm, Overton	11.11.03P
G-AYKT	SAN Jodel D.117	507	F-BGYY F-OAYY	9.10.70	D.I.Walker	Lower Upham Farm, Chiseldon	11. 8.03P
G-AYKW	Piper PA-28-140 Cherokee C	28-26931	N11C	12.10.70	B.A.Mills	Bourn	18.11.02T
G-AYKX	Piper PA-28-140 Cherokee C	28-26933	N11C	12.10.70	B.Malpas tr Robin Flying Group	Woodford	9. 1.04
G-AYKZ	SAI KZ-VIII (DH Gipsy Major 7)	202	HB-EPB OY-ACB	13.10.70	R.E.Mitchell	RAF Cosford	17. 7.81P
	(Stored 4.02)						
G-AYLA	AESL Airtourer T2 (115)	524		12.10.70	D.S.P.Disney	Bristol	30. 6.05
G-AYLC	CEA Jodel DR.1051 Sicile	536	F-BLZG	12.10.70	E.W.B.Trollope	Wing Farm, Longbridge Deverill	8. 9.03P
G-AYLF	CEA Jodel DR.1051 Sicile	547	F-BLZQ	14.10.70	L.Daglish tr Sicile Flying Group	(Harpenden)	18. 7.01
G-AYLL	CEA Jodel DR.1050 Ambassadeur	11	F-BJHK	27.10.70	C.Joly	Lee-on-Solent	18. 5.01
G-AYLP	American AA-1 Yankee	AA1-0445	EI-AVV G-AYLP	21.10.70	D.Nairn & E.Y.Hawkins	Henstridge	10. 2.02
G-AYLV	Wassmer Jodel D.120 Paris-Nice	300	F-BNCG	27.10.70	M.R.Henham *(Current status unknown)*	(London N2)	13. 9.83P
G-AYLZ	SPP CZL Super Aero 45 Srs.04	06-014	9M-AOF F-BILP	2.11.70	M.J.Cobb	(East Grinstead)	11. 6.76
	(Damaged Andrewsfield 2.1.76: stored 1997: new owner 3.01)						
G-AYME	Sportavia Fournier RF5	5089		6.11.70	R.D.Goodger	Laddington	7. 8.03P
G-AYMK	Piper PA-28-140 Cherokee C	28-26772	N11C (PT-DPU)	17.11.70	M.Wright tr The Piper Flying Group	Newcastle	8.10.04
G-AYMO	Piper PA-23-250 Turbo Aztec C	27-2995	5Y-ACX N5845Y/(N5844Y)	18.11.70	G.Kidger	(Worksop)	4. 4.04
G-AYMR	Lederlin 380L Ladybug EAA/55189 & PFA 1513 (Continental C90)			19.11.70	P.Brayshaw	(Harrogate)	
	(Last reported under construction 1992: current status unknown)						
G-AYMU	Wassmer Jodel D.112	1015	F-BJPB	23.11.70	M.R.Baker	Bradleys Lawn, Heathfield	5. 6.92P
	(Damaged Hailsham, East Sussex 7.1.92: on rebuild Eastbourne 7.92: current status unknown)						
G-AYMV	Western 20 HAB	002		23.11.70	R.F.Turnbull *"Tinkerbelle"*	Clyro, Hereford	
	(New owner 5.02)						
G-AYMW	Bell 206B JetRanger II	587	EI-BJR G-AYMW	25.11.70	PLM Dollar Group Ltd	Cumbernauld	21. 4.04T
G-AYNA	Phoenix Currie Wot (Continental A65)	PFA 3016		25.11.70	I.D.Folland	(Chipping Norton)	17. 7.03P
G-AYND	Cessna 310Q	310Q0110	N7610Q	2.12.70	Source Group Ltd	Bournemouth	25. 6.04T
G-AYNF	Piper PA-28-140 Cherokee C	28-26778	N11C (PT-DPV)	3.12.70	W.S.Bath, M.H.Jones & G.H.Round tr BW Aviation	Wellesbourne Mountford	25. 7.03T
G-AYNJ	Piper PA-28-140 Cherokee C	28-26810	N11C	3.12.70	R.H.Ribbons	Swansea	16. 5.03T
G-AYNN	Cessna 185B Skywagon	185-0518	8R-GCC VP-GCC/N2518Z	11.12.70	Bencray Ltd	Blackpool	26.12.03T
	(Op Blackpool & Fylde Aero Club)						
G-AYOW	Cessna 182N Skylane	18260481	N8941G	6. 1.71	D.W.Parfrey	Coventry	3. 5.04
G-AYOY	Sikorsky S-61N	61-476		7. 1.71	Veritair, t/a British International	(Sherborne)	21. 4.03T
G-AYOZ	Reims/Cessna FA150L Aerobat	FA15000085		7. 1.71	S.A.Hughes	Andrewsfield	12.12.03
G-AYPE	MBB Bö.209 Monsun 160RV	123	D-EFJA	11. 1.71	Papa Echo Ltd *"Buswells Spirit"*	Rochester	9.11.03
G-AYPG	Reims/Cessna F177RG Cardinal (Wichita c/n 17700102)	F177RG0007		11. 1.71	D.P.McDermott	Haverfordwest	17. 1 .05
G-AYPH	Reims/Cessna F177RG Cardinal (Wichita c/n 17700146)	F177RG0018		11. 1.71	M.R. & K.E.Slack	Cambridge	19. 4.04
G-AYPJ	Piper PA-28-180 Cherokee E	28-5821	N11C	12. 1.71	R.B.Petrie *(On rebuild 1.03)*	RAF Mona	1 .10.04T
G-AYPM	Piper PA-18 Super Cub 95 (L-18C-PI) *(Frame No.18-1282)*	18-1373	ALAT 18-1373 51-15373	13. 1.71	R.Horner	Trenchard Farm, Eggesford	28. 6.03P
G-AYPO	Piper PA-18 Super Cub 95 (L-18C-PI) *(RR Continental O-200-A)*	18-1615	ALAT 18-1615 51-15615	13. 1.71	A.W.Knowles	Bodmin	22. 6.03
	(Rebuilt 1984 using OO-TSJ c/n 18-1398 (Frame No.18-1325) & ex (LN-TSJ)/OO-HMH/51-15398)						
G-AYPR	Piper PA-18 Super Cub 95 (L-18C-PI)	18-1631	ALAT 18-1631 51-15631	13. 1.71	R.G.Manton	Booker	27.11.03T

G-AYPS	Piper PA-18 Super Cub 95	18-2092	ALAT 18-2092	13. 1.71	R.J.Hamlett, L.G & D.C.Callow	Andrewsfield	22. 5.03P
	(L-18C-PI)		52-2492				
G-AYPT	Piper PA-18 Super Cub 95	18-1533	(D-EALX)	13. 1.71	B.L.Proctor & T.F.Lyddon	Dunkeswell	27. 5.05
	(L-18C-PI) (RR Continental O-200-A) *(Frame No.18-1508)* ALAT 18-1533/51-15533						
G-AYPU	Piper PA-28R-200 Cherokee Arrow B	28R-7135005	N11C	13. 1.71	Monalto Investments Ltd	Jersey	14. 3.05
G-AYPV	Piper PA-28-140 Cherokee D	28-7125039	N11C	13. 1.71	Ashley Gardner Flying Club Ltd	Ronaldsway	6. 9.04T
G-AYPZ	Campbell Cricket	CA/343		13. 1.71	A.Melody	Hentsridge	20. 8.87P
	(Volkswagen 1600)				*(Noted 11.02)*		
G-AYRF	Reims/Cessna F150L	F15000665		14. 1.71	D.T.A.Rees	Haverfordwest	25.11.00T
					(Crashed Upper Welson Farm, Haverfordwest 13.3.99)		
G-AYRG	Reims/Cessna F172K	F17200761		14. 1.71	Comed Aviation Ltd	Netherthorpe	26. 7.00T
G-AYRH	GEMS MS.892A Rallye Commodore 150	10558	F-BNBX	14. 1.71	S.O'Ceallaigh & J.Barry	(Cork, Co.Cork)	13. 1.03
G-AYRI	Piper PA-28R-200 Cherokee Arrow B	28R-7135004	N11C	15. 1.71	A.E.Thompson & Delta Motor Co (Windsor) Sales Ltd	White Waltham	21. 8.05
G-AYRM	Piper PA-28-140 Cherokee D	28-7125049	N11C	19. 1.71	M.J.Saggers	Biggin Hill	7. 8.03T
G-AYRO	Reims/Cessna FA150L Aerobat	FA1500102		21. 1.71	F.E.Baldwin tr Fat Boys Flying Club Hinton in the Hedges		21. 5.04T
G-AYRS	Jodel Wassmer D.120A Paris-Nice	255	F-BMAV	22. 1.71	L.R.H.D'Eath	(Diss)	8. 5.03P
G-AYRT	Reims/Cessna F172K	F17200777		22. 1.71	P.E.Crees	Shobdon	8. 4.04
G-AYRU	Britten-Norman BN-2A-6 Islander	181	G-51-181	22. 1.71	G. Burton	AAC Netheravon	16. 6.03A
			OH-BNA/G-51-181		tr Army Parachute Association		
G-AYSB	Piper PA-30 Twin Comanche C	30-1916	N8760Y	1. 2.71	N.J.Goff	(Ashtead)	9. 9.05
G-AYSD	Slingsby T.61A Falke	1726		4. 2.71	P.W.Hextall	Tatenhill	29. 4.94
					(Stored 1.95: current status unknown)		
G-AYSH	Taylor JT.1 Monoplane	PFA 1413		10. 2.71	C.J.Lodge	Hill Farm, Nayland	13. 5.03P
	(Volkswagen 1600)						
G-AYSJ	Dornier Bücker Bü.133C Jungmeister	-	D-EHVP	12. 2.71	Patina Ltd	Duxford	10. 7.03P
			G-AYSJ/HB-MIW/Swiss AF U-91 *(Op The Fighter Collection) (As "LG+01" in Luftwaffe c/s)*				
G-AYSK	Phoenix Luton LA-4A Minor	PFA 832		17. 2.71	S.R.Smith	Barton	18. 2.03P
	(Continental A65)				tr Luton Minor Group		
G-AYSX	Reims/Cessna F177RG Cardinal	F177RG0024		17. 2.71	A.P.R.Dean	Hawarden	16. 5.05
	(Wichita c/n 17700175)						
G-AYSY	Reims/Cessna F177RG Cardinal	F177RG0026		17. 2.71	M.B.North	Full Sutton	31. 7.03
	(Wichita c/n 17700180)						
G-AYTR	Menavia Piel CP.301A Emeraude	229	F-BIMD	3. 3.71	R.K.King tr Croft Farm Flying Group Croft Farm, Defford		11. 6.03P
G-AYTT	Phoenix PM-3 Duet	PFA 841		4. 3.71	H.E.Jenner	Rochester	31. 8.02P
	(Continental C90) *(Officially regd as Luton Minor III Duet)*						
G-AYTV	Jurca MJ.2D Tempete	PFA 2002		10. 3.71	C W Kirk	Swanborough Farm, Lewes	21. 3.03P
	(Continental C90)				tr Shoestring Flying Group		
G-AYUA	Auster AOP.9	---	7855M	12. 3.71	P.T.Bolton	South Lodge Farm, Widmerpool	
	(Officially regd as c/n B5/10-119)		XK416		*(As "XK416") (New owner 10.99; current status unknown)*		
G-AYUB	CEA Jodel DR.253B Regent	185		15. 3.71	D.J.Clark	Sywell	14. 9.05
G-AYUH	Piper PA-28-180 Cherokee F	28-7105042	N11C	17. 3.71	C.S.Sidle	Sherburn-in-Elmet	7. 4.05
G-AYUI*	Piper PA-28-180 Cherokee F	28-7105043	N8557	17. 3.71	Ansair Aviation Ltd	Andrewsfield	5.11.93T
			G-AYUI/N11C		*(Cancelled 27.10.98 by CAA) (Dismantled & hangared 5.02)*		
G-AYUJ	Evans VP-1	PFA 1538		17. 3.71	T.N.Howard "Unforgettable Juliet"	Woodvale	28. 2.97P
					(Damaged Ainsdale Beach, Southport 16.6.96: current status unknown)		
G-AYUM	Slingsby T.61A Falke	1730		19. 3.71	N A Stone & M H Simms	Swanton Morley	10. 6.02
G-AYUN	Slingsby T.61A Falke	1731		19. 3.71	R.J.Watts tr G-AYUN Group	Rattlesden	15. 5.03
G-AYUP	Slingsby T.61A Falke	1735	XW983	19. 3.71	P.R.Williams	Bicester	15. 7.96
			G-AYUP		*(Stored 2.97: current status unknown)*		
G-AYUR	Slingsby T.61A Falke	1736		19. 3.71	R.Hannigan & R.Lingard	Strubby	7. 4.05
G-AYUS	Taylor JT.1 Monoplane	PFA 1412		19. 3.71	C.J.Bragg	(Wickford)	13.10.03P
	(Volkswagen 1600)						
G-AYUT	SAN Jodel DR.1050 Ambassadeur	479	F-BLJZ	22. 3.71	D.M.Whitham	Kirkbride	16. 6.05
G-AYUV	Reims/Cessna F172H	F17200752		26. 3.71	Justgold Ltd *(Stored 12.01)*	Blackpool	11. 3.00T
G-AYVO	Wallis WA-120 Srs.1	K/602/X		6. 4.71	K.H.Wallis	Reymerston Hall, Norfolk	31.12.75P
	(RR Continental O-240-B @ 130hp)				*(Stored 8.01)*		
G-AYVP	Aerosport Woody Pusher	181 & PFA 1344		6. 4.71	J.R.Wraight	Chatham	
					(Stored incomplete: current status unknown)		
G-AYVT*	Brochet MB.84	9	F-BGLI	13. 4.71	R.A.Yates	Sibsey	20. 7.77
					(Damaged 28.6.77: cancelled 3.9.81 as WFU: fuselage & wings stored 8.00)		
G-AYWA*	Avro 19 Srs.2	1361	OO-VIT	14. 4.71	Air Atlantic Historic Flight	Coventry	
			OO-DFA/OO-CFA		*(Cancelled 22.8.73 as PWFU) (On long term restoration 4.00)*		
G-AYWD	Cessna 182N Skylane	18260468	N8928G	15. 4.71	S.I.Zorb tr Wild Dreams Group	Leicester	5.12.05T
G-AYWE	Piper PA-28-140 Cherokee C	28-26826	N5910U	16. 4.71	Intelcomm (UK) Ltd	Denham	30. 5.05
G-AYWH	SAN Jodel D.117A	844	F-BIVO	16. 4.71	D.Kynaston & J.Deakin	Cambridge	23. 7.02P
G-AYWM	AESL Airtourer T5 (Super 150)	A.534		16. 4.71	H.E.Collett tr The Star Flying Group	Gloucestershire	24. 5.03
G-AYWT	AIA Stampe SV-4C	1111	F-BLEY	21. 4.71	J.A.Carr	Bournemouth	25. 1.03T
	(DH Gipsy Major 10)		F-BAGL				
G-AYXP	SAN Jodel D.117A	693	F-BIDD	27. 4.71	G.N.Davies	Vowchurch, Hereford	22. 7.03P
G-AYXS	SIAI-Marchetti S.205-18R	4-165	OY-DNG	28. 4.71	T.Montague-Moore	Denham	26. 6.04
G-AYXU	Champion 7KCAB Citabria	232-70	N7587F	28. 4.71	E.T.& P.A.Wild	(Loughborough)	21. 5.04
G-AYXW*	Evans VP-1	PFA 1544		30. 4.71	M.Howe	North Coates	15. 8.01P
	(Ardem 4C02)				*(Cancelled 7.6.02 by CAA)*		
G-AYYL	Slingsby T.61A Falke	1738		10. 5.71	C.Wood	(Aylesbury)	2. 6.83
					(Suffered gale damage Manston 15.12.82: on rebuild 7.90: current status unknown)		
G-AYYO	CEA Jodel DR.1050/M1 Sicile Record	622	EI-BAI	11. 5.71	D.J.M.White	Boscombe Down	28. 9.05
			G-AYYO/F-BMPZ		tr Bustard Jodel Group		
G-AYYT	CEA Jodel DR.1050/MI Sicile Record	587	F-BMGU	13. 5.71	W.R.Prescott tr Yankee Tango Group Kilkeel, Co.Down		21. 8.05
G-AYYU	Beech C23 Musketeer Custom	M-1353		14. 5.71	M.A.Webb tr The Beech Group	Sturgate	3. 5.04
G-AYYX	SOCATA MS.880B Rallye Club	1812		18. 5.71	J.G.MacDonald	Morgansfield, Fishburn	23. 1.02
G-AYZE	Piper PA-39 Twin Comanche C/R	39-92	N8934Y	20. 5.71	J.E.Balmer	Gloucestershire	29. 8.03
G-AYZI	SNCAN Stampe SV-4C	15	(EI-)	24. 5.71	W.H.Smout	Spanhoe	28. 7.95
			G-AYZI/F-BBAA/Fr mil		*(On rebuild 6.98: current status unknown)*		

G-AYZK	CEA Jodel DR.1050/M1 Sicile Record	590	F-BMGY	24. 5.71	D.G.Hesketh	Sittles Farm, Alrewas	18. 7.03
G-AYZS	Rollason-Druine D.62B Condor	RAE/650		4. 6.71	M.N.Thrush	Manor Farm, Inglesham	11.11.03P
G-AYZU	Slingsby T.61A Falke	1740		4. 6.71	R.G.Garner	Wellesbourne Mountford	10. 6.04
					tr The Falcon Gliding Group		
G-AYZW	Slingsby T.61A Falke	1743		4. 6.71	R.S.Jones & J.McGouldrick	Portmoak	10. 4.04
					tr Portmoak Falke Syndicate		

G-AZAA - G-AZZZ

G-AZAB	Piper PA-30 Twin Comanche B	30-1475	5H-MNM	8. 6.71	Bickertons Aerodromes Ltd	Denham	19. 8.04
			5Y-AGB				
G-AZAJ	Piper PA-28R-200 Cherokee Arrow	28R-7135116	N11C	18. 6.71	J.C.McHugh & P.Woulfe	Stapleford	22. 6.03
G-AZAW	Gardan GY-80-160 Horizon	104	F-BMUL	24. 6.71	J.W.Foley	(Inverness)	28. 5.05
G-AZBA	Tipsy T.66 Nipper Srs.3B	PFA 1390		30. 6.71	L.A. Brown	Swansea	19. 6.03P
	(Volkswagen 1834) *(Slingsby-built kit)*						
G-AZBB	MBB Bo 209 Monsun 160FV	137	D-EFJO	1. 7.71	G.N.Richardson Shelsley Beauchamp, Worcester		9. 7.04
					t/a GN Richardson Motors		
G-AZBE	AESL Airtourer T5 (Super 150)	A.535		5. 7.71	R.G.Vincent tr BE Flying Group	Gloucestershire	15.12.02
G-AZBI	SAN Jodel 150 Mascaret	43	F-BMFB	12. 7.71	F.M.Ward	AAC Dishforth	8. 2.03P
G-AZBL	Jodel D.9 Bebe	PFA 938		12. 7.71	J.Hill	(Dudley)	15.10.85P
	(Volkswagen 1500)				*(On rebuild 1993 ?: current status unknown)*		
G-AZBN	Noorduyn AT-16-ND Harvard IIB	14A-1431	PH-HON	13. 7.71	Swaygate Ltd	Goodwood	12. 7.01P
			R.Neth.AF B-97/FT391/43-13132 *(As "FT391")*				
G-AZBU	Auster AOP.9	AUS.183	7862M	15. 7.71	K. Brooks	(Nottingham)	19. 5.03P
			XR246		tr Auster Nine Group *(As "XR246" in RAE c/s)*		
G-AZCB	SNCAN Stampe SV-4C	140	F-BBCR	21. 7.71	M.L.Martin	Redhill	30. 4.96
	(DH Gipsy Major 1C)						
G-AZCE	Pitts S.1C Special	373.H & PFA 1527		26. 7.71	R J Oulton	(Chepstow)	18. 6.76S
	(Lycoming O-235)				*(Crashed Eastbach Farm 2.9.75) (Current status unknown)*		
G-AZCK	Beagle B.121 Pup 2	B121-153		30. 7.71	D.R.Newell	Newtownards, Co.Down	7. 5.04
G-AZCL	Beagle B.121 Pup 2	B121-154		30. 7.71	J.J.Watts & D.Fletcher	Old Sarum	8. 7.04T
G-AZCN	Beagle B.121 Pup 2	B121-156	HB-NAY	30. 7.71	D.M.Callaghan & I.C.Haywood	Egginton, Derby	20. 6.04
			G-AZCN				
G-AZCP	Beagle B.121 Pup 1	B121-158	(D-EKWA)	30. 7.71	T.J.Watson	Elstree	18. 7.04
			G-AZCP				
G-AZCT	Beagle B.121 Pup 1	B121-161		30. 7.71	J.Coleman	Sywell	1. 8.05T
G-AZCU	Beagle B.121 Pup 1	B121-162		30. 7.71	A.A.Harris	Shobdon	5. 8.04
G-AZCV	Beagle B.121 Pup 2	B121-163	HB-NAR	30. 7.71	N.R.W.Long	Compton Abbas	14. 8.05
			G-AZCV		*(Great Circle Design titles)*		
G-AZCZ	Beagle B.121 Pup 2	B121-167		30. 7.71	L. & J.M.Northover	Cardiff	9. 7.04T
G-AZDA	Beagle B.121 Pup 1	B121-168		30. 7.71	B.D.Deubelbeiss	Elstree	10. 1.03
G-AZDD	MBB Bö.209 Monsun 150FF	143	D-EBJC	3. 8.71	J D Hall & D Lawrence	Rochester	28. 6.04
					tr Double Delta Flying Group		
G-AZDE	Piper PA-28R-200 Cherokee Arrow	28R-7135141	N11C	3. 8.71	C.Wilson *(Flyteam Aviation titles)*	Elstree	3.10.05
G-AZDF(2)*	Cameron O-84 HAB	24		18. 8.71	K L C M Busemeyer	Aachen, Germany	9. 5.88A
					"Hanniball" (Cancelled 22.4.98 as WFU) (Noted 2000)		
G-AZDG	Beagle B.121 Pup 2	B121-145	(G-BLYM)	17. 6.85	J.R.Heaps	Elstree	14. 3.04
			HB-NAM/(VH-EPT)/G-35-145		*(DHL titles)*		
G-AZDJ	Piper PA-32-300 Cherokee Six D	32-7140068	OY-AJK	23. 8.71	Delta Juliet Ltd	Cardiff	19. 4.03T
			G-AZDJ/N5273S				
G-AZDK	Beech 95-B55 Baron	TC-1406		23. 8.71	Mirage Aircraft Leasing Ltd Poplar Hall Farm, Elmsett		10. 4.04
G-AZDX	Piper PA-28-180 Cherokee F	28-7105186	N11C	25. 8.71	M.Cowan	Hundon, Suffolk	26. 3.05
G-AZDY	de Havilland DH.82A Tiger Moth	86559	F-BGDJ	25. 8.71	J.B.Mills	(Cambridge)	18. 8.97
			Fr.AF/PG650		*(Current status unknown)*		
G-AZEE	Morane MS.880B Rallye Club	74	F-BKKA	1. 9.71	J.Shelton Water Leisure Park, Skegness		27. 9.98
	(Composite incl fuselage of G-AZNJ c/n 5375 in 1980: original fuselage stored South Scarle 9.94: for rebuild 6.01)						
G-AZEF	Jodel Wassmer D.120 Paris-Nice	321	F-BNZS	1. 9.71	D.A.Palmer	Bidford	24. 2.03P
G-AZEG	Piper PA-28-140 Cherokee D	28-7125530	N11C	1. 9.71	The Ashley Gardner Flying Club Ltd	Ronaldsway	3. 7.04T
G-AZEU	Beagle B.121 Pup 2	B121-130	VH-EPL	15. 9.71	G.M.Moir	Egginton, Derby	15. 2.03
			G-35-130				
G-AZEV	Beagle B.121 Pup 2	B121-131	VH-EPM	15. 9.71	C.J.Partridge	Popham	23. 8.05
			G-35-131				
G-AZEW	Beagle B.121 Pup 2	B121-132	VH-EPN	15. 9.71	K.Cameron	Headcorn	18. 5.03
			G-35-132				
G-AZEY	Beagle B.121 Pup 2	B121-136	HB-NAK	15. 9.71	M.E.Reynolds	(Stockbridge)	5.12.03
			G-AZEY/VH-EPP/G-35-136				
G-AZFA	Beagle B.121 Pup 2	B121-143	VH-EPR	15. 9.71	J.Smith	Sandown	22. 7.04
			G-35-143				
G-AZFC	Piper PA-28-140 Cherokee D	28-7125486	N11C	16. 9.71	M.L.Hannah	Blackbushe	28. 8.05
G-AZFF	Wassmer Jodel D.112	1175	F-BLFI	17. 9.71	D.J.Laughlin	Mullaghmore, Co.Sligo	17. 6.03P
G-AZFI	Piper PA-28R-200 Cherokee Arrow B	28R-7135160	N11C	21. 9.71	GAZFI Ltd	Sherburn-in-Elmet	6. 4.04
G-AZFM	Piper PA-28R-200 Cherokee Arrow B	28R-7135218	N11C	24. 9.71	P.J.Jenness	Bournemouth	1. 8 04
G-AZFR	Cessna 401B	401B0121	N7981Q	30. 9.71	R E Wragg	Blackpool	10. 9.05T
G-AZGA	Jodel Wassmer D.120 Paris-Nice	144	F-BIXV	30. 9.71	A.F.Vizoso	RAF Halton	29. 9.03P
G-AZGC*	SNCAN Stampe SV-4C	120	F-BCGE	4.10.71	V.Lindsay	Kidmore End, Reading	22. 2.91
	(As "120" in French A/F c/s) (Damaged Folly Farm, Hungerford 28.5.90: stored 6.95: cancelled 19.9.00 by CAA)						
G-AZGE	SNCAN Stampe SV-4C	576	F-BDDV	6.10.71	M.R.L.Asto	East Hatley, Tadlow	15. 8.94
					(Stored 3.97: current status unknown)		
G-AZGF	Beagle B.121 Pup 2	B121-076	PH-KUF	6.10.71	K.Singh	Barton	2. 5.98
			G-35-076				
G-AZGI	SOCATA MS.880B Rallye Club	1896		7.10.71	B.McIntyre	Mullaghmore, Co.Sligo	4. 2.05
G-AZGL	SOCATA MS.894A Rallye Minerva 220	119291		7.10.71	The Cambridge Aero Club Ltd	Cambridge	8.12.05T
G-AZGY	Rousseau CP.301B Emeraude	122	F-BRAA	12.10.71	D.J.Gibson	Breighton	21. 5.03P

Reg	Type	c/n	Prev id	Date	Owner	Location	Code
G-AZGZ	de Havilland DH.82A Tiger Moth	86489	F-BGCF Fr.AF/NM181	13.10.71	R.J.King *(As "NM181")*	Rush Green	4. 6.05
G-AZHB	Robin HR100/200B Royal	118		14.10.71	C. & P.P.Scarlett	Headcorn	6. 8.03
G-AZHC	Wassmer Jodel D.112	585	F-BIQQ	18.10.71	A.Galante tr Aerodel Flying Group	Netherthorpe	9. 8.03P
G-AZHD	Slingsby T.61A Falke	1753		18.10.71	Nicola J.Orchard-Armitage	(Deal)	3. 8.03
G-AZHH	K & S SA.102.5 Cavalier (Lycoming O-290)	PFA 1393		20.10.71	D.W.Buckle	Morton Carr Farm, Nunthorpe	20. 1.00P
G-AZHI	AESL Airtourer T5 (Super 150)	A.540		20.10.71	Flying Grasshoppers Ltd	Headcorn	9. 5.03T
G-AZHK	Robin HR100/200B Royal	113	G-ILEG G-AZHK	22.10.71	D.J.Sage	(Reigate)	20. 5.05
G-AZHR	Piccard Ax6 HAB	617	N17US	27.10.71	C.Fisher tr Halcyon Balloon Group *"Happiness"*	Sheffield	AC
G-AZHT	AESL Airtourer	T3525		29.10.71	Aviation West Ltd *(Damaged Glenforsa, Mull 29.4.88: stored 6.00)*	(Glasgow)	29. 1.89T
G-AZHU	Phoenix Luton LA-4A Minor (Volkswagen 1834)	PFA 839		1.11.71	W.Cawrey	Netherthorpe	17. 7.03P
G-AZIB	SOCATA ST-10 Diplomate	141		4.11.71	W.B.Bateson	Blackpool	21.12.03
G-AZID	Reims/Cessna FA150L Aerobat	FA15000083	N9447	8.11.71	Aerobat Ltd	Wolverhampton	18.11.02T
G-AZII	SAN Jodel D.117	A 848	F-BNDO F-OBFO	12.11.71	P J Brayshaw	Haddock Stone Farm, Markington	11. 4.01P
G-AZIJ	Robin DR360 Chevalier	634		15.11.71	K.J.Fleming	RAF Woodvale	4. 6.03
G-AZIK	Piper PA-34-200 Seneca	34-7250018	N2392T	15.11.71	Walkbury Aviation Ltd	Sibson	30. 4.05T
G-AZIL	Slingsby T.61A Falke	1756		16.11.71	D.W.Savage	Arbroath	20.11.05
G-AZIP	Cameron O-65 HAB	29		24.11.71	P.G.Dunnington tr Dante Balloon Group *"Dante" (Non-airworthy - stored 2.97)*	Hungerford	5. 5.81A
G-AZJC	Sportavia Fournier RF5	5108		30.11.71	W.S.V.Stoney	(Arezzo, Italy)	1. 5.03P
G-AZJE	Barritault JB.01 Minicab (Continental C90)	JBE.1 & PFA 1806		1.12.71	J.B.Evans *(Stored 1.98: current status unknown)*	Ventnor, Isle of Wight	7. 7.82P
G-AZJN	Robin DR300/140 Major	642		6.12.71	Wright Farm Eggs Ltd	Cherry Tree Farm, Monewden	5. 6.03
G-AZJV	Reims/Cessna F172L	F17200810		8.12.71	J.A. & A.J.Boyd	Cardiff	13. 2.03
G-AZJY	Reims/Cessna FRA150L Aerobat	FRA15000126		8.12.71	R.P.Smith	Barton	7. 6.04
G-AZKC	SOCATA MS.880B Rallye Club	1914		8.12.71	L.J.Martin	Sandown	2. 7.03
G-AZKE	SOCATA MS.880B Rallye Club	1950	(LX-SDT)	8.12.71	D.A.Thompson & S.H.Little	Trier, <u>Germany</u>	3. 2.03
G-AZKK	Cameron O-56 HAB	32		13.12.71	P.J.Green & C.Bosley tr Gemini Balloon Group *"Gemini"*	Newbury	23.12.82A
G-AZKN*	Robin Jodel HR.100/200B Royal	122		20.12.71	Not known	Hinton in the Hedges	6.12.96
	(Damaged in force-landing near Long Watton, Leics 1.9.95: cancelled 31.5.96 as WFU) (Dismantled wreck stored 10.01)						
G-AZKO	Reims/Cessna F337F Super Skymaster (Wichita c/n 33701380)	F33700041		20.12.71	Willpower Garage Ltd *"Bird Dog"*	Wellesbourne Mountford	10. 8.03
G-AZKP	SAN Jodel D.117	419	F-BHND	20.12.71	B.N.Stevens	North Connel, Oban	11. 4.03P
G-AZKR	Piper PA-24-180 Comanche	24-2192	N7044P	23.12.71	J.Van Der Kwast	Rochester	21. 6.04
G-AZKS	American AA-1A Trainer	0334	N6134L	23.12.71	M.D.Henson	Coventry	23. 8.03
G-AZKW	Reims/Cessna F172L	F17200806		23.12.71	J.C.C.Wright	Hinton in the Hedges	21. 6.03T
G-AZKZ	Reims/Cessna F172L	F17200814		23.12.71	R.D. & E.Forster *(Op Norfolk Flying Club)*	Beccles	14. 8.04T
G-AZLE	Boeing-Stearman E75 (N2S-5) Kaydet (Continental W670)	75-8543	CF-XRD N5619N/Bu43449	29.12.71	A.E.Poulsom tr Air Farm Flyers *(As "2"in US Army c/s)*	Manor Farm, Tongham	28. 5.04
G-AZLF	Jodel Wassmer D.120 Paris-Nice	230	F-BLFL	30.12.71	M.S.C.Ball	Garston Farm, Marshfield	20.11.03P
G-AZLH	Reims/Cessna F150L	F15000757		31.12.71	Coulson Flying Services Ltd	Cranfield	30.11.03T
G-AZLJ*	Britten-Norman BN-2A Mk.III-1 Trislander	319	G-OREG	31.12.71	Mike Collett/Atlantic Group	Coventry	2. 2.00T
	SX-CBN/G-OREG/G-OAVW/G-AZLJ/G-51-319 *(Cancelled as 1.3.01 temp WFU) (Used for spares)*						
G-AZLL*	Reims/Cessna FRA150L Aerobat	F1500135		31.12.71	Rankart Ltd	Hinton in the Hedges	19.11.01T
	(Crashed Turweston 4.2.99 & destroyed: cancelled 21.7.99) (Wreck noted 10.01)						
G-AZLN	Piper PA-28-180 Cherokee F	28-7105210	N11C	3. 1.72	Liteflite Ltd	Oxford	5. 3.04
G-AZLO*	Reims/Cessna F337F Super Skymaster (Wichita c/n 33701347)	F33700029		4. 1.72	Not known	Bourn	22. 4.82
	(WFU 4.82: cancelled 4.12.86 by CAA: unmarked rear-fuselage stored 1.01)						
G-AZLP*	Vickers 813 Viscount	346	(ZS-SBT) ZS-CDT	4. 1.72	International Fire Training Centre *(Cancelled 19.12.86 as WFU: fuselage only 7.01)*	Teesside	3. 4.82T
G-AZLS*	Vickers 813 Viscount	348	(ZS-SBV) ZS-CDV	4. 1.72	International Fire Training Centre *(Cancelled 19.12.86 as WFU: noted 7.01)*	Teesside	9. 6.83T
G-AZLV	Cessna 172K	17257908	4X-ALM N79138	10. 1.72	N.A.Baxter	Newcastle	8. 4.04
G-AZLY	Reims/Cessna F150L	F15000771		10. 1.72	Cleveland Flying School Ltd	Teesside	5.12.02T
G-AZLZ	Reims/Cessna F150L	F15000772		10. 1.72	A.G.Martlew	Haverfordwest	16. 7.00
G-AZMC	Slingsby T.61A Falke	1757		12. 1.72	Essex Gliding Club Ltd *(Stored 8.90: current status unknown)*	Challock	22. 9.86
G-AZMD	Slingsby T.61C Falke	1758		12. 1.72	R.A.Rice	Wellesbourne Mountford	1. 6.04
G-AZMF	British Aircraft Corporation One-Eleven 530FX	BAC.240	7Q-YKJ/G-AZMF/PT-TYY/G-AZMF	14. 1.72	European Aviation Ltd *(Op European VIP First) "The European Express"*	Bournemouth	22. 1.04T
G-AZMJ	American AA-5 Traveler	0019		27. 1.72	R.T.Love	St.Merryn	1. 5.04
G-AZMN*	AESL Airtourer T5 (Super 150)	A.550		28. 1.72	Not known	Oaksey Park	7. 5.89
	(Crashed near Glasgow 23.6.87: cancelled 14.9.88 by CAA: stored 5.00)						
G-AZMZ	SOCATA MS.893A Rallye Commodore 180	11927		8. 2.72	D R Wilcox	Lyveden	10. 5.03
G-AZNC*	Vickers 813 Viscount	352	(ZS-SBZ) ZS-CDZ	8. 2.72	Airport Fire Services *(WFU2.82: cancelled 27.10.88 as WFU) (Non-destructive training 3.02)*	Teesside	18. 5.83T
G-AZNK	SNCAN Stampe SV-4A (DH Gipsy Major 10)	290	F-BKXF F-BCGZ	15. 2.72	P.D.Jackson & R.A.G.Lucas *"Globird"*	Redhill	20. 5.04
G-AZNL	Piper PA-28R-200 Cherokee Arrow II	28R-7235006	N11C	16. 2.72	B.P.Liversidge	Earls Colne	8. 8.02T
G-AZNO	Cessna 182P Skylane	18261005	N7365Q	18. 2.72	Aeros Holdings Ltd	Gloucestershire	3. 5.03
G-AZNT	Cameron O-84 HAB	34		21. 2.72	N.Tasker *"Oberon"*	Bristol	5. 6.85
G-AZOA	MBB Bö.209 Monsun 150FF	183	D-EAAY	21. 2.72	M.W.Hurst	Seighford	14. 6.04
G-AZOB	MBB Bö.209 Monsun 150FF	184	D-EAAZ	21. 2.72	G.N.Richardson *(Crashed Droitwich 21.8.83: stored 8.92: current status unknown)*	Shelsley Beauchamp, Worcester	9. 7.84
G-AZOE	AESL Airtourer T2 (115)	528		21. 2.72	B.J.Edmondson & J.K.Smithson tr G-AZOE 607 Group	Newcastle	15. 8.03

Reg	Type	c/n	Prev id	Date	Owner/Operator	Location	Date
G-AZOF	AESL Airtourer T5 (Super 150)	A.549		21. 2.72	R.J.W.Bayliff & A.C.Hart tr Cirrus Flying Group	Kirknewton	17. 2.04
G-AZOG	Piper PA-28R-200 Cherokee Arrow II	28R-7235009	N11C	21. 2.72	Atromin Ltd t/a Southend Flying Club	Southend	8. 8.04
G-AZOL	Piper PA-34-200 Seneca	34-7250075	N4348T	28. 2.72	D.I.Barnes	Stapleford	28. 6.03
G-AZOO	Western O-65 HAB	015		1. 3.72	Semajan Ltd *"Carousel"* (On loan to British Balloon Museum & Library) (Valid CofR 4.02)	Newbury	6. 6.77S
G-AZOR	MBB Bö.105DB	S.20	EC-DOE G-AZOR/D-HDAC	1. 3.72	Bond Air Services Ltd (Op Welsh Air Ambulance)	Swansea	31. 5.02T
G-AZOS	Jurca MJ.5-H1 Sirocco (Lycoming O-320)	001 & PFA 2206		1. 3.72	P.J.Tanulak	Sleap	18. 3.03P
G-AZOT	Piper PA-34-200 Seneca	34-7250073	N4340T	3. 3.72	Northern Aviation Ltd	(Stockton-on-Tees)	13. 9.03T
G-AZOU	SAN Jodel DR.1050 Sicile	354	F-BJYX	7. 3.72	D.Elliott & D.Holl tr Horsham Flying Group	Wellcross Grange, Slinfold	30. 6.05
G-AZOZ	Reims/Cessna FRA150L Aerobat	FRA15000136		7. 3.72	Seawing Flying Club Ltd *"The Wizard of Oz"*	Southend	16. 7.05T
G-AZPA	Piper PA-25-235 Pawnee C	25-5223	N8797L N9749N	7. 3.72	Black Mountains Gliding Club Ltd	Talgarth	1. 5.04
G-AZPC	Slingsby T.61C Falke	1767		7. 3.72	The Surrey Hills Gliding Club Ltd	Kenley	31. 7.04
G-AZPF	Sportavia Fournier RF5	5001	D-KOLT	10. 3.72	R.Pye	Blackpool	31. 7.04P
G-AZPV	Phoenix-Luton LA-4A Minor (Lycoming O-145)	PFA 833		14. 3.72	J.R.Faulkner (Stored 3.01)	(Brize Norton)	18. 9.97P
G-AZPX	Western O-31 HAB	011		20. 3.72	B.L.King tr Eugena Rex Balloon Group *"Eugena Rex"*	Coulsdon	
G-AZRA	MBB Bö.209 Monsun 150FF	192	D-EAIH	21. 3.72	Alpha Flying Ltd	Booker	3. 5.04
G-AZRD	Cessna 401B	401B0218	N7999Q	22. 3.72	G.Hatton tr Romeo Delta Group	Blackpool	6. 4.03T
G-AZRH	Piper PA-28-140 Cherokee D	28-7125585	N11C	23. 3.72	H.B.Carter tr Trust Flying Group	Jersey	18. 7.05
G-AZRI	Payne HAB (56,500 cu.ft)	GFP.1		21. 3.72	C.A.Butter & J.J.T.Cooke t/a Aardvark Balloon Co *"Shoestring"*	Newbury/Southal	
G-AZRK	Sportavia Fournier RF5	5112		23. 3.72	A.B.Clymo & J.F.Rogers	Shenington	30. 9.03P
G-AZRL	Piper PA-18 Super Cub 95 (L-18C-PI) (Frame No.18-1213)	18-1331	OO-SBR OO-HML/ALAT 18-1331/51-15331	23. 3.72	M.G.Fountain	Leicester	16.10.04
G-AZRM	Sportavia Fournier RF5 (Volkswagen 1834)	5111		24. 3.72	A.R.Dearden & R.Speer	Upper Broyle Farm, Ringmer	2. 5.03P
G-AZRN	Cameron O-84 HAB	28		28. 3.72	C.J.Desmet (New owner 5.01)	Brussels, Belgium	4. 7.81A
G-AZRP	AESL Airtourer T2 (115)	529		28. 3.72	B.F.Strawford	Shobdon	19. 8.04
G-AZRR	Cessna 310Q	310Q0490	N9923F	28. 3.72	Routarrow Ltd	Seething	23. 4.04
G-AZRS	Piper PA-22-150 Tri-Pacer	22-5141	XT-AAH F-OCGZ/ALAT 22-5141/"FMKAC"/N10F	28. 3.72	R.H.Hulls *"Sandpiper"*	Trenchard Farm, Eggesford	5. 9.03
G-AZRV*	Piper PA-28R-200 Cherokee Arrow B	28R-7135191	N2309T	4. 4.72	Not known	Compton Abbas	
	(Crashed on take-off Compton Abbas 30.12.00: cancelled 20.6.01 as destroyed: fuselage & port wing dumped 10.02)						
G-AZRX*	Gardan GY-80-160 Horizon	14	F-BLIJ	4. 4.72	Adventure Island Pleasure Ground	Marine Parade, Southend-on-Sea	20. 2.92
	(Damaged Sandtoft 14.8.91: cancelled 21.10.91 by CAA) (On display in Crazy Golf Course, Seafront 2.03)						
G-AZRZ	Cessna U206F Stationair	U20601803	N9603G	4. 4.72	M.R.Browne & R.G.Wood t/a Hinton Skydiving Centre	Hinton in the Hedges	26. 5.03
G-AZSA	Stampe et Renard SV-4B (Official c/n is 64)	1203	V-61 Belgian AF	5. 4.72	J.K.Faulkner	Biggin Hill	31. 7.04P
G-AZSC	Noorduyn AT-16-ND Harvard IIB	14A-1363	PH-SKK B-19 R.Neth AF/FT323/43-13064 (As "43/SC" in USAAF c/s)	7. 4.72	Machine Music Ltd	North Weald	20.11.03P
G-AZSD	Slingsby T.29B Motor Tutor RGB 01/72 & PFA 1574 (Rebuild of Slingsby c/n 561)			7. 4.72	R.G.Boyton t/a Essex Aviation (Current status unknown: valid CofR 4.02)	Halstead, Essex	
G-AZSF	Piper PA-28R-200 Cherokee Arrow II	28R-7235048	N11C	10. 4.72	W.T.Northorpe t/a Flight Simulation Air Park	Coventry	22. 8.05
G-AZSW	Beagle B.121 Pup 1	B121-140	PH-VRT G-35-140	24. 4.72	J.R.Parry	RAF Mona	4.11.02
G-AZSZ*	Piper PA-23-250 Aztec D	27-4194	N6851Y	25. 4.72	Industrial Cladding Systems Ltd (Cancelled 24.1.03 by CAA)	Kemble	2. 6.01T
G-AZTA	MBB Bö.209 Monsun 150FF	190	D-EAIF	25. 4.72	K.T.Pierce	Elstree	20. 9.04T
G-AZTD*	Piper PA-32-300 Cherokee Six D	32-7140001	N8611N	26. 4.72	Presshouse Publications Ltd (Cancelled 11.4.01) (In open storage 7.02)	Enstone	16. 8.98T
G-AZTF	Reims/Cessna F177RG Cardinal	F177RG0054		28. 4.72	D.A.Wiggins	Denham	13. 8.04
G-AZTK	Reims/Cessna F172F	F17200116	PH-CON OO-SIR	27. 4.72	S.O'Ceallaigh	(Cork)	20.10.00
G-AZTR*	SNCAN Stampe SV-4C	596	F-BDEQ	28. 4.72	P.G.Palumbo (Cancelled 10.10.00 by CAA) (Dismantled 6.01)	Booker	15. 7.94
G-AZTS	Reims/Cessna F172L	F17200866		28. 4.72	C.E.Stringer	Bagby	17.12.03T
G-AZTV	Stolp SA.500 Starlet (Continental C90)	SSM.2 & PFA 1584		19. 5.72	G.G.Rowland (Damaged Manor Farm, Grateley, Hants 4.7.92: current status unknown)	(Christchurch)	19.11.92
G-AZTW	Reims/Cessna F177RG Cardinal	F177RG0043		28. 4.72	I.M.Richmond	Panshanger	15. 6.03
G-AZUM	Reims/Cessna F172L	F17200863		11. 5.72	L.R.Sullivan tr Fowlmere Flyers	Fowlmere	18.12.03
G-AZUP	Cameron O-65 HAB	36		11. 5.72	R.S.Bailey & A.B.Simpson *"Eight of Hearts"*	Aylesbury/Hemel Hempstead	23.10.77S
G-AZUT	SOCATA MS.893A Rallye Commodore 180	10963	VH-TCH	12. 5.72	J.Palethorpe tr Rallye Flying Group	Blakedown, Kidderminster	9.11.02
G-AZUY	Cessna 310L	310L0012	SE-FEC LN-LMH/N2212F	15. 5.72	W.B.Bateson	Blackpool	5.11.05T
G-AZUZ	Reims/Cessna FRA150L Aerobat	FRA15000146		16. 5.72	D.J.Parker	Netherthorpe	16.12.03
G-AZVA	MBB Bö.209 Monsun 150FF	177	(D-EAAQ)	16. 5.72	P.J.Fahie	Old Sarum	8. 9.03
G-AZVB	MBB Bö.209 Monsun 150FF	178	(D-EAAS)	16. 5.72	M.H.James & D.Shrimpton	Compton Abbas	14. 6.03
G-AZVF	SOCATA MS.894A Rallye Minerva 220	11999	(F-OCSR)	16. 5.72	L.Williams tr Minerva Flying Group	Upfield Farm, Usk	9. 3.02
G-AZVG	American AA-5 Traveler	AA5-0075		16. 5.72	Whelan Building & Development Ltd	(Luton)	15. 9.05T
G-AZVH	SOCATA MS.894A Rallye Minerva 220	12017		16. 5.72	P.L.Jubb	Poplar Hall Farm, Elmsett	17. 6.05
G-AZVI	SOCATA MS.892A Rallye Commodore 150	12039		6. 5.72	R.E.Knapton	Turweston	12. 8.04
G-AZVJ	Piper PA-34-200 Seneca	34-7250125	N4529T	16. 5.72	Andrews Professional Colour Laboratories Ltd	Lydd	21. 8.03A

G-AZVL	Jodel D.119 *(Built Ets Valladeau)*	794	F-BILB	19. 5.72	P.T.East tr Forest Flying Group	Stapleford	16.12.03P
G-AZVM	Hughes 369HS (500C)	61-0326S	N9091F	19. 5.72	GTS Engineering (Coventry) Ltd	Coventry	6. 9.03
G-AZVP	Reims/Cessna F177RG Cardinal	F177RG0057		22. 5.72	Cardinal Flyers Ltd	Denham	25. 6.04
G-AZWB	Piper PA-28-140 Cherokee E	28-7225244	N11C	5. 6.72	B.N.Rides & L.Connor	Kemble	19.12.03
G-AZWD	Piper PA-28-140 Cherokee E	28-7225298	N11C	6. 6.72	JCL Aviation Ltd	Bournemouth	6. 5.05T
G-AZWE	Piper PA-28-140 Cherokee E	28-7225303	N11C	6. 6.72	P.M.Tucker tr G-AZWE Flying Group	Dunkeswell	11. 4.03T
G-AZWF	SAN Jodel DR.1050 Ambassadeur	130	F-BJJT	7. 6.72	J A D Reedie	Inverness	5.11.04
	(Composite including fuselage of DR.1050M F-BLJX c/n 492)				tr Cawdor Flying Group		
G-AZWS	Piper PA-28R-180 Cherokee Arrow	28R-30749	N4993J	8. 6.72	G.S.Blair & I.Parkinson	Eshott	2. 5.03
					tr Arrow 88 Flying Group		
G-AZWT	Westland Lysander IIIA	Y1536	RCAF 1582	9. 6.72	The Shuttleworth Trust	Old Warden	13. 8.03P
			V9552		*(As "V9367/MA-B" in 161 Sqdn c/s)*		
G-AZWY	Piper PA-24-260 Comanche C	24-4806	N9310P	16. 6.72	Keymer, Son & Co Ltd	Biggin Hill	24. 4.03
G-AZXA	Beech 95-C55 Baron	TE-72	SE-EKZ	19. 6.72	Cobham Leasing Ltd	Bournemouth	20. 6.05A
G-AZXB	Cameron O-65 HAB	48		20. 6.72	R.J.Mitchener & P.F.Smart	Andover	6. 5.81A
					t/a Balloon Collection *"London Pride II"*		
G-AZXC	Reims/Cessna F150L	F15000793		20. 6.72	D.C.Bonsall	Netherthorpe	28. 4.03T
G-AZXD	Reims/Cessna F172L	F17200878		20. 6.72	Birdlake Ltd *(Op Birdlake Aviation)*	Leicester	26. 6.03T
G-AZXG*	Piper PA-23-250 Aztec D	27-4328	N6963Y	23. 6.72	Cranfield University	Cranfield	18. 9.94
				(Crashed Little Snoring 25.10.91: cancelled 6.5.93 by CAA) (Instructional airframe 6.02)			
G-AZYA	Gardan GY-80-160 Horizon	57	F-BLPT	7. 7.72	T.Twelvetree & M.L.Moore	Old Sarum	9. 8.03
G-AZYD	GEMS MS.893A Rallye Commodore 180	10645	F-BNSE	30. 6.72	P.Storey	Husbands Bosworth	8. 8.05
					t/a Storey Aviation Services		
G-AZYM	Cessna 310Q	310Q0507	N218Y	6. 7.72	C.Matthews & G.J.Tickton	Guernsey	16. 3.03P
			G-AZYM/N5893M/N4592L				
G-AZYS	Scintex CP.301C-1 Emeraude	568	F-BJAY	7. 7.72	C.G.Ferguson & D.Drew	Jericho Farm, Lambley	10. 5.03P
G-AZYU	Piper PA-23-250 Aztec E	27-4601	N13983	13. 7.72	L.J.Martin	Redhill/Sandown	16. 5.04
G-AZYY	Slingsby T.61A Falke	1770		12. 7.72	J.A.Towers	Yearby	19. 6.05
G-AZYZ	Wassmer WA.51A Pacific	30	F-OCSE	14. 7.72	C.R.Buxton	(Gourvillette, France)	28. 6.04
G-AZZG*	Cessna 188 Agwagon 230	188-0279	OY-AHT	12. 7.72	N.C.Kensington	(Bridge of Cally)	1. 5.81A
			N8029V		*(On rebuild 6.00: cancelled 21.9.00 by CAA)*		
G-AZZH*	Practavia Pilot Sprite 115	PFA 1532		13. 7.72	A.Moore	(Dagenham)	
					(Stored 8.01) (Cancelled 23.4.02 by CAA)		
G-AZZO	Piper PA-28-140 Cherokee	28-22887	N4471J	18. 7.72	R.J.Hind	Stapleford	6. 8.03
G-AZZR	Reims/Cessna F150L	F15000690	LN-LJX	24. 7.72	M.W.Smith tr G-AZZR Flying Group	Exeter	20. 7.04T
G-AZZV	Reims/Cessna F172L	F15000883		18. 7.72	D.J.Hockings	Rochester	7. 7.05T
G-AZZZ	de Havilland DH.82A Tiger Moth	86311	F-BGJE	27. 7.72	S.W.McKay	RAF Henlow	21.12.04
			Fr.AF/NL864				

G-BAAA - G-BAZZ

G-BAAD	Evans Super VP-1	PFA 1540		27. 7.72	K.Wigglesworth	Breighton	29.10.02P
	(Volkswagen 1600)				tr Breighton VP-1 Group		
G-BAAF	Manning-Flanders MF.1 rep	PPS/REP/8		27. 7.72	Bianchi Aviation Film Services Ltd	Booker	6. 8.96P
	(Continental C75)				*(No external marks)*		
G-BAAI	SOCATA MS.893A Rallye Commodore 180	10705	F-BOVG	31. 7.72	R.D.Taylor	Thruxton	11. 9.00
G-BAAL	Cessna 172A	47678	PH-KAP	31. 7.72	W.H.Knowles	(Yundum/Banjul, Gambia)	20. 5.04T
			D-ELGU/N9878T				
G-BAAT	Cessna 182P Skylane	18260835	N399JF	10. 8.72	Melrose Pigs Ltd	Melrose Farm, Melbourne	21. 5.03
			G-BAAT/N9295G				
G-BAAU	Enstrom F-28A-UK	092		10. 8.72	G.Firbank	(Macclesfield)	6. 5.02T
G-BAAW	Jodel D.119	366	F-BHMY	11. 8.72	P J Newson	Cherry Tree Farm, Monewden	25. 4.03P
	(Built Ets Valladeau) (Continental 0-200-A)				tr Alpha Whiskey Flying Group		
G-BAAX*	Cameron O-84 HAB	50		8. 8.72	Not known *"Holker Hall"*	NK	
					(Cancelled 11.5.93 as WFU) (Inflated 6.02)		
G-BABB	Reims/Cessna F150L	F15000830		15. 8.72	Seawing Flying Club	Southend	6. 7.03T
G-BABC	Reims/Cessna F150L	F15000831		15. 8.72	Fordaire Aviation Ltd	Little Gransden	17. 9.03T
G-BABD	Reims/Cessna FRA150L Aerobat	FRA1500153		3. 8.72	K.F.Mason & D.Featherby t/a Anglia Flight	Norwich	18. 2.04T
G-BABE	Taylor JT.2 Titch	PEB/01 & PFA 1394		3. 8.72	M.Bonsall	Netherthorpe	7. 5.98P
	(Continental O-200-A)				*(New owner 4.01)*		
G-BABG	Piper PA-28-180 Cherokee C	28-2031	PH-APU	15. 8.72	C.E.Dodge	Bristol	9.11.03
			N7978W		tr Mendip Flying Group		
G-BABH	Reims/Cessna F150L	F15000820	EI-CCZ	15. 8.72	D.B.Ryder & Co Ltd	(Welwyn Garden City)	1. 4.04T
			G-BABH				
G-BABK	Piper PA-34-200 Seneca	34-7250219	PH-DMN	18. 8.72	D.F.J.Flashman	Biggin Hill	24. 9.01
			G-BABK/N5203T				
G-BACB	Piper PA-34-200 Seneca	34-7250251	N5354T	25. 8.72	Northern Aviation Ltd	(Stockton-on-Tees)	11. 7.05T
G-BACC	Reims/Cessna FRA150L Aerobat	FRA1500157		16. 8.72	C.M. & J.H.Cooper	Cranfield	13.12.04
G-BACE	Sportavia Fournier RF5	5102	(PT-DVZ)	25. 8.72	R.W.K.Stead	Perranporth	27.11.04
			D-KCID		tr Clockwork Mouse Flying Group *"The Clockwork Mouse"*		
G-BACJ	Jodel Wassmer D.120 Paris-Nice	315	F-BNZC	1. 9.72	J.M.Allan tr Wearside Flying Association	Newcastle	21. 3.03P
G-BACL	SAN Jodel 150 Mascaret	31	F-BSTY	4. 9.72	G.R.French	Benson's Farm, Laindon	26. 6 .05
			CN-TYY				
G-BACN	Reims/Cessna FRA150L Aerobat	FRA1500161		4. 9.72	F.Bundy	Bodmin	14. 6.03T
G-BACO	Reims/Cessna FRA150L Aerobat	FRA1500163		4. 9.72	M.M.Pepper	Sibson	14. 5.04
G-BACP	Reims/Cessna F150L Aerobat	FRA1500164		4. 9.72	M.Markwick & C.Hounslow	Shoreham	14. 5.04T
	(Built as FRA150L)						
G-BADC	Rollason-Luton Beta B.2A	PFA 02-10140		7. 9.72	D.H.Greenwood *(New owner 10.00)*	Barton	31. 1.85P
	(Original c/n was JJF.1 & PFA/1384: adopted c/n of Beta G-BETA when cancelled 3.2.87 by CAA as not completed and presumably incorporated)						
G-BADH	Slingsby T.61A Falke	1774		6. 9.72	D.W.Smart	Gallows Hill, Bovington	7. 8.05
					tr Falke Flying Group		
G-BADI*	Piper PA-23-250 Aztec D	27-4235	N6885Y	5. 9.72	West London AeroServices Ltd	North Weald	29.10.92T
	(Cancelled 9.7.02 by CAA) (Fuselage noted with fictitious marks "G-ESKY" & "AIR AMBULANCE" titles 9.02)						

Reg	Type	c/n	Prev id	Date	Owner	Location	Date
G-BADJ	Piper PA-E23-250 Aztec E	27-4841	N14279	11. 9.72	C.Papadakis	Oxford	17.12.05T
G-BADM	Rollason-Druine D.62B Condor	AE/653 & PFA 49-11442		8. 9.72	M.Harris & J.StJ.Mehta	Yeldon Farm, Nutley	10. 3.03P
G-BADW	Aerotek Pitts S-2A Special	2035		21. 9.72	R.E.Mitchell *(Stored 4.02)*	RAF Cosford	16. 9.95T
G-BADZ*	Aerotek Pitts S-2A Special	2038		21. 9.72	A.F.D.Kingdon *(Cancelled 4.4.02 by CAA)*	Blackpool	5. 6.00
G-BAEB	Robin DR400/160 Knight	733		19. 9.72	P.D.W.King	Lydd	21. 3.04T
G-BAEC	Robin HR100/210 Royal	145	EI-BDG G-BAEC	15. 9.72	Datacorp Enterprises Pty Ltd	Denham	6. 4.03
G-BAEE	CEA Jodel DR.1050/M1 Sicile Record	579	F-BMGN	29. 9.72	R.Little	Shoreham	19. 6.03
G-BAEM	Robin DR400/125 Petit Prince	728		25. 9.72	M.A.Webb	Denham	31. 5.03
G-BAEN	Robin DR400/180 Regent	736		25. 9.72	European Soaring Club Ltd	Le Blanc, France	8.10.03
G-BAEO	Reims/Cessna F172M	F17200911		14. 9.72	L.W.Scattergood	Sherburn-in-Elmet	
	(Re-built with original fuselage & remains of G-YTWO)				*(Noted 1.01)*		
G-BAEP	Reims/Cessna F150L Aerobat	FRA1500170		14. 9.72	A.M.Lynn	Fenland	17. 5.04T
	(Built as FRA150L)				t/a Busy Bee		
G-BAER	LeVier Cosmic Wind	106 & PFA 1571		14. 9.72	R.S.Voice	Rushett Manor, Chessington	14. 5.03P
	(Continental O-200-A)				*"Filly"*		
G-BAET	Piper J-3C-65 Cub (L-4H-PI)	11605	OO-AJI 43-30314	26. 9.72	C.J.Rees	Valley Farm, Winwick	20. 5.03P
	(Frame No.11430)						
G-BAEU	Reims/Cessna F150L	F15000873		26. 9.72	L.W.Scattergood	Humberside	30. 1.04T
G-BAEV	Reims/Cessna FRA150L Aerobat	FRA1500173		27. 9.72	T.J.Richardson	Sibson	6 3.04
G-BAEY	Reims/Cessna F172M	F17200915		28. 9.72	Skytrax Aviation Ltd	Sibson	9. 3.03T
G-BAEZ	Reims/Cessna FRA150L Aerobat	FRA1500169		28. 9.72	Donair Flying Club Ltd	East Midlands	19. 6.03T
G-BAFA	American AA-5 Traveler	AA5-0201	N6136A	6.10.72	C.F.Mackley	Sleap	31. 8.01
G-BAFG	de Havilland DH.82A Tiger Moth	85995	F-BGEL Fr.AF/EM778	13.10.72	J.E. & P.E.Shaw	Nottingham	18. 8.05
G-BAFL	Cessna 182P Skylane	18261469	N21180	15. 8.72	Lawgra (No.386) Ltd	Cranfield	23. 7.01
					t/a International Aerospace Engineering		
G-BAFP	Robin DR400/160 Knight	735		19.10.72	T.A.Pugh	Pool Quay, Breidden	11. 3.04
					tr Breidden Flying Group		
G-BAFT	Piper PA-18-150 Super Cub	18-5340	(D-E...) ALAT 18-5340/N10F	3. 8.72	T.J.Wilkinson	Sackville Farm, Riseley	2. 5.03
G-BAFU	Piper PA-28-140 Cherokee	28-20759	PH-NLS	11.10.72	D.Matthews	Humberside	19. 4.03T
G-BAFV	Piper PA-18 Super Cub 95	18-2045	R.Neth AF R-40/8A-40/52-2445	11.10.72	T.F. & S.J.Thorpe	Coldharbour Farm, Willingham	1.10.04
	(L-18C-PI) *(Frame No.18-2055)*						
G-BAFW	Piper PA-28-140 Cherokee	28-21050	PH-NLT	24.10.72	R.S.Chance	Bowmore, Isle of Islay	6. 4.03
G-BAFX	Robin DR400/140 Earl	739		30.10.72	K.R.Gough & C.J.Mewis	Clutton Hill Farm, Clutton	4. 5.04
G-BAGB	SIAI-Marchetti SF.260	1-07	LN-BIV	20.10.72	British Midland Airways Ltd	East Midlands	27. 4.03
G-BAGC	Robin DR400/140 Earl	737		13.10.72	W.P.Nutt	(Scarborough)	15. 6.05
G-BAGF	Jodel D.92 Bebe	59	F-PHFC	13.11.72	E.Evans	Benson's Farm, Laindon	
					(Wings stored 8.01: fuselage elsewhere)		
G-BAGG(2)	Piper PA-32-300 Cherokee Six	32-7340186	N9562N	7.12.73	S.A.Fell & N.J.Falla tr G-BAGG Group	Guernsey	16. 2.04
G-BAGI*	Cameron O-31 HAB	56		25.10.72	D.C.Boxall	Bristol	19. 9.76S
					"Vital Spark" (Cancelled 10.10.01 by CAA)		
G-BAGL	Westland SA.341G Gazelle 1	1067		26.10.72	Foremans Aviation Ltd	Linley Hill, Leven	30. 8.03T
G-BAGN	Reims/Cessna F177RG Cardinal	F177RG0068		24.10.72	R.W.J.Andrews	Wolverhampton	2. 8.04
G-BAGO	Cessna 421B Golden Eagle	421B0356	N7613Q	24.10.72	M.S.Choksey	Coventry	15.10.03
G-BAGR	Robin DR400/140 Petit Prince	753		30.10.72	F.C.Aris & J.D.Last	Caernarfon	11. 4.04
G-BAGS	Robin DR400/100 2+2	760		30.10.72	M Whale & M M A Lunn	Kemble	16. 1.03T
G-BAGT	Helio H.295 Super Courier	1288	CR-LJG	31.10.72	B.J.C.Woodall Ltd	Rushett Manor, Chessington	11.11.04
G-BAGV	Cessna U206F Stationair	U20601867	N9667G	31.10.72	K.Brady tr The Scottish Parachute Club	Strathallan	14. 5.04
G-BAGX	Piper PA-28-140 Cherokee	28-23633	N3574K	30.10.72	J.R.Clayton tr The Golf X-Ray Group	Conington	28.11.05T
G-BAGY	Cameron O-84 HAB	54		17.10.72	P.G.Dunnington	Hungerford	16. 6.81A
					"Beatrice" (Stored 2.97: current status unknown)		
G-BAHD	Cessna 182P Skylane	18261501	N21228	25.10.72	J.W.Hardy	Jericho Farm, Lambley	13. 2.04
					tr Lambley Flying Group		
G-BAHE	Piper PA-28-140 Cherokee C	28-26494	N5696U	30.10.72	A.O.Jones & M W Kilvert	Welshpool	8. 6.95
					(Stored 5.96: new owner 10.00)		
G-BAHF	Piper PA-28-140 Flite Liner	28-7125215	N431FL	30.10.72	BJ Services (Midlands) Ltd	Coventry	27. 6.04T
G-BAHG	Piper PA-24-260 Comanche B	24-4306	5Y-AFX N8831P	2.11.72	D.G.Sheppard	Great Oakley, Clacton	31. 8.03
					(Overran runway landing Great Oakley 21.4.02: nosewheel collapsed with damage to propeller & engine cowling)		
G-BAHH	Wallis WA-121/Mc	K/701/X		7.11.72	K.H.Wallis	Reymerston Hall, Norfolk	27. 5.98P
	(Wallis modified McCulloch)				*(Noted 8.01)*		
G-BAHI	Cessna F150H	F150-0330	PH-EHA	6.11.72	M.Player	Elstree	4. 2.05
	(Built Reims Aviation SA)				t/a MJP Aviation & Sales		
G-BAHJ	Piper PA-24-250 Comanche	24-1863	PH-RED N6735P	6.11.72	K.Cooper	Wolverhampton	21. 8.04
G-BAHL	Robin DR400/160 Knight	704	F-OCSR	8.11.72	B.P.Young tr Robin Group	Dunkeswell	10. 4.03T
G-BAHO	Beech C23 Sundowner	M-1456		7.11.72	P.H.White & J.A.L.Staig	Bournemouth	22.11.02
G-BAHP	Volmer VJ.22 Sportsman	PFA 1313		9.11.72	G.K.Holloway	Aboyne	18.10.93P
	(Continental C90)				tr Seaplane Group *(Noted engine running 1.01)*		
G-BAHS	Piper PA-28R-200 Cherokee Arrow II	28R-7335017	N15147	9.11.72	A.R.N.Morris	Shobdon	20. 6.03
G-BAHX	Cessna 182P Skylane	18261588	N21363	16.11.72	A.P.Stone tr Dupost Group	Blackpool	15. 8.03
G-BAIG	Piper PA-34-200 Seneca	34-7250243	OY-BSU G-BAIG/N5257T	21.11.72	Mid-Anglia Flying Centre Ltd	Cambridge	27. 9.03T
					t/a Mid-Anglia School of Flying		
G-BAIH	Piper PA-28R-200 Cherokee Arrow II	28R-7335011	N11C	21.11.72	M.G.West	King's Farm, Thurrock	22. 6.04
G-BAII	Reims/Cessna FRA150L Aerobat	FRA1500178		22.11.72	Cornwall Flying Club Ltd	Bodmin	14. 6.03T
					(Force landed Hendra Farm, Bodmin 9.9.01 & severely damaged) (Wreck noted 4.02)		
G-BAIK	Reims/Cessna F150L	F15000903		22.11.72	Wickenby Aviation Ltd	Wickenby	9. 4.03T
					(Op Lincoln Flight Centre)		
G-BAIN	Reims/Cessna FRA150L Aerobat	FRA1500177		23.11.72	S.J.Windle	Bodmin	25. 7.04T
G-BAIP	Reims/Cessna F150L	F15000898		13.11.72	G. & S.A.Jones	Linley Hill, Leven	28. 9.97T
					(Damaged Linley Hill 30.5.95: current status unknown)		

G-BAIS	Reims/Cessna F177RG Cardinal	F177RG0069		13.11.72	R.M.Graham & E.P.Howard	Seething	22. 8.05
					tr Cardinal Syndicate		
G-BAIW	Reims/Cessna F172M	F17200928		14.11.72	W.J.Greenfield	Humberside	10. 1.04T
G-BAIX	Reims/Cessna F172M	F17200931		14.11.72	R.A.Nichols	Elstree	22.12.02
G-BAIZ	Slingsby T.61A Falke	1776		27.11.72	G.C.Rumsey & R.G.Sangster	Hinton in the Hedges	21. 5.03
					tr Falke Syndicate		
G-BAJA	Reims/Cessna F177RG Cardinal	F177RG0078		29.11.72	Don Ward Productions Ltd	Rochester	17. 1.03
G-BAJB	Reims/Cessna F177RG Cardinal	F177RG0080		29.11.72	C.M.Bain	Inverness	29. 8.03
G-BAJC	Evans VP-1 Srs.2	PFA 1548		30.11.72	S.J.Greer	Dunkeswell	22. 3.99P
	(Volkswagen 1834)				*(Damaged landing Bovingdon 4.3.99: on rebuild 8.02)*		
G-BAJE	Cessna 177 Cardinal	17700812	N29322	30.11.72	D.M.Dawson	Blackpool	3.10.03
G-BAJN	American AA-5 Traveler	AA5-0259		29.11.72	I.M.Snelson	Blackpool	16. 5.03
G-BAJO	American AA-5 Traveler	AA5-0260		29.11.72	P.J.Kelsall tr G-BAJO Flying Group	Blackpool	30. 5.04
G-BAJR	Piper PA-28-180 Challenger	28-7305008	N11C	1.12.72	D.P.Bannister & D.T.Given	Newtownards, Co.Down	5. 4.03
					tr Chosen Flew Flying Group		
G-BAJY	Robin DR400/180 Regent	758		4.12.72	J.H.Fenwick t/a Rolincs Aviation	Nuthampstead	28. 8.04
G-BAJZ	Robin DR400/125 Petit Prince	759		4.12.72	Weald Air Services Ltd	Headcorn	27. 7.03T
G-BAKD	Piper PA-34-200 Seneca	34-7350013	N1378T	28.11.72	Andrews Professional Colour Laboratories Ltd	Headcorn	7. 5.04A
					(Op Foto Flite)		
G-BAKH	Piper PA-28-140 Cherokee F	28-7325014	N11C	12.12.72	Marham Investments Ltd	Belfast	6. 9.03T
					(Op Ulster Flying Club)		
G-BAKJ	Piper PA-30 Twin Comanche B	30-1232	TJ-AAI TJ-ADH/N8122Y	13.12.72	G.D.Colover, R.Jones & N. O'Connor	Biggin Hill	3. 5.03T
G-BAKM	Robin DR400/140 Earl	755		15.12.72	D.V.Pieri	Carlisle	5. 2.04
G-BAKN	SNCAN Stampe SV-4C	348	F-BCOY	15.12.72	M.Holloway	(Chard)	29. 7.05
G-BAKR	SAN Jodel D.117	814	F-BIOV	27.12.72	R.W.Brown	Stoneacre Farm, Farthing Corner	7.11.02P
G-BAKV	Piper PA-18-150 Super Cub	18-8993	N9744N	22.12.72	A.J.B.Shaw, Western Air (Thruxton) Ltd & F.Taylor		
						Thruxton	15. 8.04T
G-BAKW	Beagle B.121 Pup 2	B121-175		15.12.72	H.Beavan	White Waltham	21. 6.03
G-BAKY	Slingsby T.61C Falke	1777		20.12.72	T.J.Wiltshire	Spilsby	7. 8.98
G-BALD	Cameron O-84 HAB	58		2. 1.73	C.A.Gould tr Inter-Varsity Balloon Club *"Puffin"*	Ipswich	2. 7.78S
					(WFU after severe damage 25.6.78: basket to G-PUFF: valid CofR 4.02)		
G-BALF	Robin DR400/140 Earl	772		5. 1.73	G.& D.A.Wasey	Kemble	5. 7.03
G-BALG	Robin DR400/180 Regent	771		5. 1.73	R.Jones t/a Southern Sailplanes	Aston Down	5. 8.04
G-BALH	Robin DR400/140B Earl	766		5. 1.73	C.Johnson tr G-BALH Flying Group	Fenland	21. 6.04
G-BALI	Robin DR400 2 + 2	764		5. 1.73	A.Brinkley	Standalone Farm, Meppershall	3. 9.88
					(On rebuild 3.96)		
G-BALJ	Robin DR400/180 Regent	767		5. 1.73	D.A.Batt & D.de Lacey-Rowe		
						Fridd Farm, Bethersden, Kent	31. 5.03
G-BALK*	SNCAN Stampe SV-4C	387	F-BBAN Fr.Mil	3. 1.73	J.ThorogoodInsch	NK	
					(No CofA/Permit & cancelled 4.12.96 by CAA) (Fuselage stored 3.02)		
G-BALN	Cessna T310Q	310Q0684	N7980Q	8. 1.73	O'Brien Properties Ltd	Shoreham	1. 5.00T
G-BALY	Practavia Pilot Sprite 150	PFA 05-10009		10. 1.73	A.L.Young t/a Aly Aviation	(Henstridge)	
					(Project part completed and stored 8.95: current status unknown)		
G-BALZ	Bell 212	30542	EC-GCR EC-931/G-BALZ/	10. 1.73	Bristow Helicopters Ltd *(Op UN)*	(Iraq)	5.10.03T
			9Y-TIL/G-BALZ/VR-BIB/N8069A/G-BALZ/N99040/G-BALZ/EI-AWK/G-BALZ/VR-BEK/N2961W				
G-BAMB	Slingsby T.61C Falke	1778		9. 1.73	C Kaminski tr G-BAMB Syndicate	Eaglescott	2.10.03
G-BAMC	Reims/Cessna F150L	F15000892		12. 1.73	K.Evans	Mid Wales Airport, Kilkewydd	24. 7.05T
G-BAMF	MBB Bö.105D	BS.36	D-HDAM	10. 1.73	Bond Air Services	Sullom Voe	20. 6.03T
					(Op Sullom Voe Harbour Trust)		
G-BAMG*	Avions Lobet Ganagobie	PFA 1336		11. 1.73	Not known	Yearby	
					(Cancelled 5.8.91 by CAA: dismantled but complete 1.02)		
G-BAMJ	Cessna 182P	18261650	N21469	10. 1.73	A.E.Kedros	Enstone	29. 5.03
G-BAML	Bell 206B JetRanger II	36	N7844S	5. 1.73	Heliscott Ltd	Walton Wood, Pontefract	1. 6.03T
G-BAMM	Piper PA-28-235 Cherokee	28-10642	SE-EOA	16. 1.73	D.Clare & P.Moderate tr Group 235	Goodwood	22. 1.05
G-BAMR	Piper PA-16 Clipper	16-392	F-BFMS CU-P339	12. 1.73	H.Royce	Bradleys Lawn, Heathfield	21. 8.04
	(Lycoming O-290)						
G-BAMS	Robin DR400/160 Knight	774		15. 1.73	G-BAMS Ltd	Biggin Hill	31. 5.03T
G-BAMU	Robin DR400/160 Knight	778		15. 1.73	J.W.L.Otty tr The Alternative Flying Group	Sywell	9. 7.03
G-BAMV	Robin DR400/180 Regent	777		15. 1.73	K.Jones & E.A.Anderson	Booker	3. 5.03
G-BAMY	Piper PA-28R-200 Cherokee Arrow II	28R-7335015	N11C	9. 1.73	G.R.Gilbert tr G-BAMY Group	Birmingham	29. 3.04
G-BANA	CEA Jodel DR.221 Dauphin	73	F-BOZR	22. 1.73	G.T.Pryor	Seething	21.10.05
G-BANB	Robin DR400/180 Regent	776		22. 1.73	D.R.L.Jones	Kemble	15. 3.03T
G-BANC	Gardan GY-201 Minicab	A.203	F-PCZV F-BCZV	22. 1.73	J.T.S.Lewis & J.E.Williams		
	(Continental C90)					Brickhouse Farm, Frogland Cross	31. 5.02P
G-BANF	Phoenix Luton LA-4A Minor	PFA 838		22. 1.73	W.J.McCollum	Coagh, Co.Londonderry	5. 6.92P
	(Continental A65)				*(Damaged Mullaghmore 27.6.92: noted 11.01)*		
G-BANU	Jodel Wassmer D.120 Paris-Nice	247	F-BLNZ	31. 1.73	W.M. & C.H.Kilner		
						Shacklewell Lodge Farm, Empingham	23. 7.03P
G-BANV	Phoenix Currie Wot	PFA 3010		25. 1.73	K.Knight	(Malvern)	26. 6.84P
	(Lycoming O-290)				*(Damaged near Leek, Staffs 15.9.83: current status unknown)*		
G-BANW	CAARP CP.1330 Super Emeraude	941	PH-VRF	30. 1.73	P.S.Milner	Popham	28. 6.03P
	(Lycoming 0-235-C1)						
G-BANX	Reims/Cessna F172M	F17200941		31. 1.73	Oakfleet 2000 Ltd	Biggin Hill	6. 8.03T
G-BAOB	Reims/Cessna F172M	F17200949		2. 2.73	R.H.Taylor & S.O.Smith	Andrewsfield	22. 4.04T
G-BAOH	SOCATA MS.880B Rallye Club	2250		6. 2.73	A.P.Swain	Haverfordwest	28. 7.01
G-BAOJ	SOCATA MS.880B Rallye Club	2252		6. 2.73	R.E.Jones	Emlyns Field, Rhuallt	13. 8.01
G-BAOM	SOCATA MS.880B Rallye Club	2255		6. 2.73	P.J.D.Feehan	Exeter	17. 4.03
G-BAOP	Reims/Cessna FRA150L Aerobat	FRA1500190		5. 2.73	S.A.Boyall	Hardwick	11. 4.02
G-BAOS	Reims/Cessna F172M	F17200946		6. 2.73	Wingtask 1995 Ltd	Seething	14. 8.03T
G-BAOU	Grumman-American AA-5 Traveler	AA5-0298		8. 2.73	R.C.Mark	Shobdon	18. 9.04
G-BAPB	de Havilland DHC-1 Chipmunk 22A	C1/0001	WB549	26. 2.73	G.V.Bunyan	Bidford	31. 5.98
G-BAPI	Reims/Cessna FRA150L Aerobat	FRA1500195		8. 2.73	Industrial Supplies (Peterborough) Ltd	Sibson	6. 3.04

Reg	Type	c/n	Prev id	Date	Owner/Operator	Location	Date
G-BAPJ	Reims/Cessna FRA150L Aerobat	FRA1500196		8. 2.73	M.D.Page	Manston	10. 6.05
G-BAPL	Piper PA-23-250 Turbo Aztec E	27-7304966	N14377	12. 2.73	Donington Aviation Ltd	East Midlands	27. 8.01T
G-BAPR	Jodel D.115	295 & PFA 914		14. 2.73	J.P.Liber & J.F.M.Bartlett	Kemble	17. 4.03P
	(Continental PC60)						
G-BAPV	Robin DR400/160 Knight	742	F-OCSR	19. 2.73	J.D. & M.Millne	Newcastle	22. 8.03
G-BAPW	Piper PA-28R-180 Cherokee Arrow	28R-30697	5Y-AIR	21. 2.73	P.S.Farren & I.W.Lindsey	Denham	7.12.03
			N4951J		tr Papa Whisky Flying Group		
G-BAPX	Robin DR400/160 Knight	789		21. 2.73	M.Stanton tr G-BAPX	Group Sywell	11. 6.03
G-BAPY	Robin HR100/210 Royal	153		21. 2.73	D.M.Hansell	Old Buckenham	19. 3.05
G-BARC	Reims FR172J Rocket	FR17200356	(D-EEDK)	5. 3.73	C.H.Porter	Croft Farm, Defford	10. 4.04
					tr Severn Valley Aviation Group		
G-BARD*	Cessna 337C Super Skymaster	3370857	SE-FBU	1. 3.73	Not known	North Coates	9. 1.97
			N2557S		*(Damaged North Coates 12.6.94: cancelled 7.2.96 as WFU: current status unknown)*		
G-BARF	Wassmer Jodel D.112	1019	F-BJPF	5. 3.73	J.J.Penney	Neath	21. 1.01P
G-BARG	Cessna E310Q	310Q0712	N8237Q	2. 3.73	Tibus Aviation Ltd	Blackbushe	8.12.02T
G-BARH	Beech C23 Sundowner	M-1473		2. 3.73	J.R.Pybus	Sherburn-in-Elmet	22. 2.04
G-BARN	Taylor JT.2 Titch	PFA 60-11136		5. 3.73	R.G.W.Newton	(Seaford)	9. 6.03P
	(Continental C90)						
G-BARP	Bell 206B JetRanger II	967	N18092	5. 3.73	South Western Electricity plc	Bristol	9. 5.03T
G-BARS	de Havilland DHC-1 Chipmunk 22	C1/0557	WK520	26. 2.73	J.Beattie	RNAS Yeovilton	7. 8.05
					(As "1377" in Portuguese AF c/s)		
G-BARV	Cessna 310Q	310Q-0774		7. 3.73	Old England Watches Ltd	Elstree	9. 8.04
G-BARZ	Scheibe SF-28A Tandem Falke	5724	(D-KAUK)	8. 3.73	K.Kiely	AAC Dishforth	1.12.02
G-BASG*	Grumman-American AA-5 Traveler	AA5-0320	N5420L	12. 3.73	(Skycraft Ltd)	(Spalding)	20. 1.00
					(Damaged Isle of Rothsay 3.9.00: cancelled 6.12.00 as PWFU) (Fuselage for sale/repairable 11.01)		
G-BASH	Grumman-American AA-5 Traveler	AA5-0319	EI-AWV	12. 3.73	G.Jenkins	Popham	30. 9.05T
			G-BASH/N5419L		tr BASH Flying Group		
G-BASJ	Piper PA-28-180 Cherokee Challenger	28-7305136	N11C	13. 3.73	T.J.McElwee tr Challenger Flying Group	Kemble	7.12.03T
G-BASL	Piper PA-28-140 Cherokee F	28-7325195	N11C	13. 3.73	Justgold Ltd	Blackpool	2. 8.04T
G-BASM	Piper PA-34-200 Seneca	34-7350120	N16272	13. 3.73	M.Gipps & J.R.Whetlor	Denham	21. 2.05
G-BASN	Beech C23 Sundowner	M-1476		13. 3.73	M.F.Fisher	Tatenhill	6.11.04
G-BASO	Lake LA-4-180 Amphibian	358	N2025L	16. 3.73	C.J.A.Macaulay	Farley Farm, Romsey	24. 6.02
G-BASP	Beagle B.121 Pup 1	B121-149	SE-FOC	14. 3.73	B.J.Coutts	Sywell	19. 7.04
			G-35-149				
G-BATC	MBB Bö.105	DBS.45	D-HDAW	9. 3.73	Bond Air Services	Clacton	22. 6.03T
	(Originally registered as Bö.105D: rebuilt using new MBB pod 1989 c/n unknown)				*(Op Essex Air Ambulance)*		
G-BATJ	Jodel D.119	287	F-PIIQ	21. 3.73	D.J. & K.S.Thomas	Fenland	21. 6.03P
	(Built Ecole Technique Aeronautique) (Continental C90)						
G-BATN	Piper PA-23-250 Aztec E	27-7304987	N14391	26. 3.73	Marshall of Cambridge Aerospace Ltd	Cambridge	9. 1.03T
G-BATR	Piper PA-34-200 Seneca	34-7250290	9H-ABH	23. 3.73	A.S.Bamrah	Biggin Hill	24. 4.05T
			G-BATR/LN-BDT		t/a Falcon Flying Services		
					(Overran landing Woodchurch 4.8.02: struck hedge & badly damaged)		
G-BATV	Piper PA-28-180 Cherokee F	28-7105022	N5168S	26. 3.73	J.N.Rudsdale	Sherburn-in-Elmet	11. 2.05
					tr The Scoreby Flying Group		
G-BATW	Piper PA-28-140 Cherokee Flite Liner	28-7225587	N742FL	26. 3.73	K Simons & R.Rudderham	North Weald	10.12.02
					t/a Tango Whiskey Flying Partnership		
G-BAUC	Piper PA-25-235 Pawnee C	25-5243	N8761L	26. 3.73	Southdown Gliding Club Ltd	Parham Park	29. 5.03
G-BAUH	Dormois Jodel D.112	870	F-BILO	29. 3.73	G.A. & D.Shepherd tr G-BAUH Flying Group	Seething	19.10.01P
G-BAUJ*	Piper PA-23-250 Aztec E	27-7304986	N14390	29. 3.73	S.Bramwell	Cranfield	25. 7.94T
					(Cancelled 31.10.02 by CAA) (in open storage Cranfield 6.02)		
G-BAUW	Piper PA-23-250 Aztec E	27-4814	N14253	9. 4.73	R.E.Myson Jersey/Hardings Farm, Ingatestone		22. 7.03
G-BAVB	Reims/Cessna F172M	F17200965		10. 4.73	C.P.Course Church Farm, Wellingborough		26. 5.05T
G-BAVH	de Havilland DHC-1 Chipmunk 22	C1/0841	WP975	10. 4.73	D.C.Murray	Lee-on-Solent	24. 3.96
	(Lycoming 350hp)				tr Portsmouth Naval Gliding Club *(Current status unknown)*		
G-BAVL	Piper PA-23-250 Aztec E	27-4671	N14063	10. 4.73	S.P. & A.V.Chilcott	Bagby	12. 6.04T
G-BAVO	Boeing-Stearman A75N-1 Kaydet	-	4X-AIH	13. 4.73	M.Shaw	Old Buckenham	28. 6.04T
	(Continental W670) (Registered with c/n "3250-1405" which is a part number: original identity unknown) (As "26" in US Army c/s)						
G-BAVR	Grumman-American AA-5 Traveler	AA5-0348		12. 4.73	G.E.Murray	Haverfordwest	25. 9.04
G-BAVZ	Piper PA-23-250 Aztec E	27-7305045	N40241	18. 4.73	Cheshire Flying Services Ltd	Liverpool	12. 3.04T
					t/a Ravenair		
G-BAWG	Piper PA-28R-200 Cherokee Arrow II	28R-7335133	N11C	18. 4.73	Solent Air Ltd	Goodwood	1. 3.04
G-BAWK	Piper PA-28-140 Cherokee Cruiser	28-7325243		24. 4.73	Newcastle upon Tyne Aero Club Ltd	Newcastle	3. 8.04T
G-BAWN*	Piper PA-30-160 Twin Comanche C	30-1948	N8790Y	24. 4.73	NK Walton New Road Business Park, Bruntingthorpe		3. 5.98
					(Cancelled as WFU 23.6.98: fuselage in scrapyard compound 12.01)		
G-BAWR	Robin HR100/210 Royal	156		27. 4.73	T.Taylor	Thruxton	8. 6.00
G-BAXE	Hughes 269A-1	113-0313	N8931F	2. 5.73	Reeve Newfields Ltd	Sywell	21.12.93S
					(Frame only noted 11.01: current CofR 4.02)		
G-BAXJ	Piper PA-32-300 Cherokee Six B	32-40763	N1362Z	8. 5.73	A.G.Knight	Old Buckenham	14. 6.03
			(N59RG)/N1362Z/G-BAXJ/4X-ANY/N5224S t/a Airlaunch					
G-BAXS	Bell 47G-5	7908	5B-CFB	11. 5.73	R.M.Kemp	Fairoaks	14.12.03T
			G-BAXS/N4098G		t/a RK Helicopters		
G-BAXU	Reims/Cessna F150L	F15000959		14. 5.73	M.A.Wilson	RAF Mona	11. 4.04
G-BAXV	Reims/Cessna F150L	F15000906		14. 5.73	G. & S.A.Jones	Linley Hill, Leven	17. 5.04T
G-BAXY	Reims/Cessna F172M	F17200905	N10636	15. 5.73	Eaglesoar Ltd	Humberside	9.10.04T
G-BAXZ	Piper PA-28-140 Cherokee C	28-26760	PH-NLX	15. 5.73	D.Norris & H.Martin	Turweston	8. 3.04T
			N11C		tr G-BAXZ Syndicate		
G-BAYC*	Cameron O-65 HAB	68	(HB-BOU)	17. 5.73	Not known	NK	
			G-BAYC		*(Cancelled 15.5.98 as WFU) (Noted 2000)*		
G-BAYL*	SNCAN Nord 1203 Norecrin VI	161	F-BEQV	18. 5.73	J.E.Pierce	Ley Farm, Chirk	
					(Cancelled 14.11.91 by CAA) (Fuselage only stored outside 9.00)		
G-BAYO	Cessna 150L	15074435	N19471	18. 5.73	J A, G M, D T A & J A Rees	Haverfordwest	27. 6.04T
					t/a Messrs Rees of Poyston West		
G-BAYP	Cessna 150L	15074017	N18651	18. 5.73	D.I.Thomas tr Yankee Papa Flying Group	Popham	22. 5.05T
G-BAYR	Robin HR100/210 Royal	164		18. 5.73	P.Chamberlain	Turweston	23. 5.03

G-BAZC	Robin DR400-160 Knight	824		29. 5.73	R.Jones t/a Southern Sailplanes	Membury	24. 6.88
					(Damaged Crosland Moor 21.5.88: stored 10.01)		
G-BAZJ*	Handley Page HPR.7 Dart Herald	209	4X-AHR	30. 5.73	Guernsey Airport Fire Service	Guernsey	24.11.84T
		183	G-8-1		*(Cancelled 4.1.85 as WFU:) (In open storage 12.01)*		
G-BAZM	Jodel D.11	PAL/1416 & PFA 915		31. 5.73	A.F.Simpson	Watchford Farm, Yarcombe	22. 7.03P
	(Continental O-200-A) (Identified as "D.113")				*"L'Oiseau Jaime"*		
G-BAZS	Reims/Cessna F150L	F15000954		1. 6.73	L.W.Scattergood	Humberside	18. 11.04T
G-BAZT	Reims/Cessna F172M	F17200996		1. 6.73	Exeter Flying Club Ltd	Exeter	22. 5.03T

G-BBAA - G-BBZZ

G-BBAW	Robin HR100/210 Royal	167		12. 6.73	J.R.Williams	Goodwood	1.10.03
G-BBAX	Robin DR400/140 Earl	835		12. 6.73	G.J.Bissex & P.H.Garbutt	New Farm, Felton	21.11.03
G-BBAY	Robin DR400/140 Earl	841		12. 6.73	D.S.Brown & V.H.R. Gray		6. 3.05
					tr Rothwell Group	Rothwell Lodge Farm, Kettering	
G-BBAZ*	Hiller UH-12E	2165	EC-DOR	13. 6.73	Not known	Gamlingay	23. 5.91
			G-BBAZ/N31707/CAF112276/RCAF10276 *(Cancelled 29.5.96 by CAA) (Stored for restoration 2.00)*				
G-BBBB	Taylor JT.1 Monoplane	SAM/01 & PFA 1422		4. 6.73	S.A.MacConnacher	(Northampton)	
	(Volkswagen 1600)				*(Uncompleted project for sale 2001)*		
G-BBBC	Reims/Cessna F150L	F15000864	N10635	14. 6.73	A.A.Gardner	Humberside	20. 1.05T
G-BBBI	Grumman-American AA-5 Traveler	AA5-0392		15. 6.73	J.C.McCaig	West Freugh	20.12.02
G-BBBK	Piper PA-28-140 Cherokee	28-22572	SE-EYF	18. 6.73	Bencray Ltd	Blackpool	8. 8.04
					(Op Blackpool & Fylde Aero Club)		
G-BBBN	Piper PA-28-180 Cherokee Challenger	28-7305365	N11C	20. 6.73	Estuary Aviation Ltd	Southend	16. 1.03T
G-BBBO	SIPA 903	67	F-BGBQ	16. 1.74	G.K.Brothwood	Liverpool	18. 6.03P
G-BBBW	Clutton FRED Srs.2	DLW.1 & PFA 1551		26. 6.73	M.Palfreman	Wathstow Farm, Newby Wiske	2. 4.03P
	(Volkswagen 1834)						
G-BBBX	Cessna 310L	310L0134	OY-EGW	28. 6.73	Atlantic Air Transport Ltd	Jersey/Coventry	30.10.05
			N3284X				
G-BBBY	Piper PA-28-140 Cherokee Cruiser	28-7325533	N9501N	28. 6.73	D.T.Wright & D.L.Holland	Wickenby	5. 5.03
					tr G-BBBY Syndicate		
G-BBCA	Bell 206B JetRanger II	1101	N18091	29. 6.73	Heliflight (UK) Ltd	Wolverhampton	17.10.04T
G-BBCB	Western O-65 HAB	018		29. 6.73	G.M.Bulmer *"Cee Bee"*	Hereford	19. 5.76S
G-BBCC	Piper PA-23-250 Aztec D	27-4317	N6953Y	29. 6.73	Richard Nash Cars Ltd	Norwich	11. 4.04T
G-BBCH	Robin DR400 2 + 2	850		4. 7.73	A.J.& S.P.Smith	Turweston	19. 3.04T
G-BBCI	Cessna 150H	15069282	N50409	4. 7.73	A L & F Alam	Elstree	9. 8.03T
G-BBCK	Cameron O-77 HAB	76		4. 7.73	W R Teasdale	Maidenhead	15. 6.89S
					"Mary Gloster" (Inflated 4.02)		
G-BBCN	Robin HR100/210 Royal	168		11. 7.73	S.J.Goodburn	Gloucestershire	6. 9.03
					tr Gloucestershire Flying Club		
G-BBCP*	Thunder Ax6-56 HAB	007		11. 7.73	J.M.Robinson	(Oxfordshire)	10. 7.81A
					"Jack Frost" (Cancelled.29.10.01 as WFU & stored)		
G-BBCS	Robin DR400/140B Earl	851		12. 7.73	A.N.Kaschevski	(Hastings)	12. 5.04
G-BBCY	Phoenix Luton LA-4A Minor	PFA 825		17. 7.73	G.I.Ciupka	(St. Albans)	13. 6.02P
	(Volkswagen 1600)						
G-BBCZ	Grumman-American AA-5 Traveler	AA5-0382		18. 7.73	Southern Flight Centre Ltd	Shoreham	29. 4.04T
G-BBDC	Piper PA-28-140 Cherokee Cruiser	28-7325437	N11C	18. 7.73	B.Scragg & A Wilkins tr G-BBDC Group	Andrewsfield	26. 4.04
G-BBDE	Piper PA-28R-200 Cherokee Arrow II	28R-7335250	(EI-...)	18. 7.73	R.L.Coleman & A.E.Stevens	Panshanger	25. 9.03
			G-BBDE/N11C				
G-BBDG*	British Aircraft Corporation-Aérospatiale Concorde 100	13523 & 100-002		7. 8.73	British Airways plc	Filton	1. 3.82P
					(Cancelled 12.81 as WFU) (Acquired by Bristol Aero Collection 2004)		
G-BBDH	Reims/Cessna F172M	F17200990		19. 7.73	J.D.Woodward	Westbury-sub-Mendip	29. 5.05
G-BBDL	Grumman-American AA-5 Traveler	AA5-0406		18. 7.73	W B Bateson	Blackpool	4. 2.02
G-BBDM	Grumman-American AA-5 Traveler	AA5-0407		18. 7.73	G.Christy tr The Jackaroo Aviation Group	(Andover)	1.10.04
G-BBDO	Piper PA-23-250 Aztec E	27-7305120	N40361	24. 7.73	J W Anstee tr G-BBDO Flying Group	(Filton)	24. 5.03T
G-BBDP	Robin DR400/160 Knight	853		25. 7.73	Robin Lance Aviation Associates Ltd	Rochester	11. 9.04
G-BBDS	Piper PA-31-310 Turbo Navajo B	31-7300956	N97RJ	26. 7.73	Elham Valley Aviation Ltd	Lydd	19. 2.03T
			G-SKKB/G-BBDS/N7565L				
G-BBDT	Cessna 150H	15068839	N23272	26. 7.73	C.I.Beilby tr Delta Tango Group	Sherburn-in-Elmet	19. 3.03
G-BBDV	SIPA 903	7/21	F-BEYY	30. 7.73	W.McAndrew	Sackville Farm, Riseley	11. 6.03P
	(Continental C90) (Originally ex F-BEYJ c/n 7 but rebuilt in 1978 from F-BEYY c/n 21)						
G-BBEA	Phoenix Luton LA-4A Minor	PFA 843		30. 7.73	R Q T Newns	White Waltham	29. 4.02P
	(Volkswagen 1600)				tr Luton Group		
G-BBEB	Piper PA-28R-200 Cherokee Arrow II	28R-7335292	N9514N	31. 7.73	R.D.W.Rippingale	Anvil Farm, Hungerford	22. 2.04
G-BBEC	Piper PA-28-180 Cherokee Challenger	28-7305478	N11C	30. 7.73	J.B.Conway	Ronaldsway	31. 5.04T
G-BBED	SOCATA MS.894A Rallye Minerva 220	12097		30. 7.73	C.A.Shelley	Alcester	13. 9.87T
					t/a Vista Products *(Stored 9.95: current status unknown)*		
G-BBEF	Piper PA-28-140 Cherokee Cruiser	28-7325527	N9500N	31. 7.73	Comed Flight Training Ltd	Blackpool	1. 4.05T
	(Rebuilt using components from damaged G-AVWG by 4.99)						
G-BBEN	Bellanca 7GCBC Citabria	496-73	(D-EAUT)	7. 8.73	C.A.G.Schofield	Harpsden, Henley-on-Thames	10. 5.02
			N36416				
G-BBEO	Reims/Cessna FRA150L Aerobat	FRA1500205		3. 8.73	Mid America (UK) Ltd	(Tain)	27. 6.04T
G-BBEV	Piper PA-28-140 Cherokee D	28-7125340	LN-MTM	8. 8.73	Comed Aviation Ltd *(In open storage 8.02)*	Blackpool	19. 9.01T
G-BBEX	Cessna 185A Skywagon	185-0491	EI-CMC	7. 8.73	V.M.McCarthy	Kildare, Co.Kildare	1. 1.06T
			G-BBEX/4X-ALD/N99992/N1691Z				
G-BBEY	Piper PA-23-250 Aztec E	27-7305160	LN-FOE	8. 8.73	M.Hall	Bagby	27. 1.05T
			G-BBEY/N40396				
G-BBFC*	Grumman-American AA-1B Trainer	AA1B-0245	(N9945L)	14. 8.73	Not known	Bournemouth	25.12.96
					(Damaged Perranporth 9.6.96: temp unregd 14.10.96: on rebuild 1.00)		
G-BBFD	Piper PA-28R-200 Cherokee Arrow II	28R-7335342	N9517N	8. 8.73	C.H.Rose & A.R.Annable	White Waltham	17. 4.04T

G-BBFL	SRCM Gardan GY-201 Minicab (Continental A65)	21	F-BHCQ	17. 8.73	R.Smith (Under complete rebuild 3.02)	Barton Ashes	21. 9.93P
G-BBFV	Piper PA-32-260 Cherokee Six	32-778	5Y-ADF	13. 8.73	A.G.Knight t/a Airlaunch	Old Buckenham	26. 2.03
G-BBGB	Piper PA-E23-250 Aztec E	27-7305004	N40206	16. 8.73	Cheshire Flying Services Ltd t/a Ravenair	Liverpool	21. 2.03T
G-BBGC	SOCATA MS.893E Rallye 180GT	12215	F-BUCV	16. 8.73	P M Nolan	Kilkenny, Co.Kilkenny	7. 6.04
G-BBGI	Fuji FA.200-160 Aero Subaru	228		21. 8.73	M.S.Bird	Pepperbox, Salisbury	17. 9.98
G-BBGL	Oldfield Baby Lakes 7223-B412-B & PFA 1593 (Continental C90)			22. 8.73	F.Ball	Fenland	21. 3.02P
G-BBGR	Cameron O-65 HAB	85		20. 8.73	M.L. & L.P.Willoughby "Jabberwock"	Reading	26. 5.81A
G-BBGX	Cessna 182P Skylane	18262350	N58861	30. 8.73	D.I.Sutton tr GX Group	Denham	2. 5.04T
G-BBGZ	Cambridge Hot-Air Ballooning Assn HAB (42,000 cu.ft) CHABA 42			31. 8.73	J.L.Hinton, G.Laslett & R.A.Laslett (On loan to British Balloon Museum & Library) "Phlogiston" (Inflated 4.02)	Newbury	
G-BBHE	Enstrom F-28A	153	EI-BSD G-BBHE	3. 9.73	Clarke Aviation Ltd	Waterford, Co.Waterford	21.11.04
G-BBHF	Piper PA-23-250 Aztec E	27-7305166	N40453	5. 9.73	G.J.Williams	Sherburn-in-Elmet	4. 7.05T
G-BBHI	Cessna 177RG Cardinal RG	177RG0225	5Y-ANX N1825Q	7. 9.73	T.G.W.Bunce	Belfast	26. 9.03
G-BBHJ	Piper J-3C-85 Cub (Frame No.16037)	16378	OO-GEC	7. 9.73	J.Stanbridge & R.V.Miller tr Wellcross Flying Group	Wellcross Grange, Slinfold	4. 6.03P
G-BBHK	Noorduyn AT-16-ND Harvard IIB	14-787	PH-PPS (PH-HTC)/R.Neth AF B-158/FH153/42-12540 (As "FH153") (Noted 9.02)	7. 9.73	R.F.Warner t/a Bob Warner Aviation	Egginton, Derby	7. 5.86
G-BBHL	Sikorsky S-61N Mk.II	61-712	N4032S	7. 9.73	Bristow Helicopters Ltd (Op Marine & Coastguard Agency) "Glamis"	Stornoway	4.12.04T
G-BBHY	Piper PA-28-180 Cherokee Challenger	28-7305474	EI-BBS G-BBHY/N9508N	7. 9.73	Air Operations Ltd	Guernsey	20. 6.05
G-BBIA	Piper PA-28R-200 Cherokee Arrow II	28R-7335287	N11C	7. 9.73	G.H.Kilby	Stapleford	11. 1.04
G-BBIF	Piper PA-23-250 Aztec E	27-7305234	N9736N	10. 9.73	D M Davies "Flying Miss Daisie"	Tatenhill	25. 9.04T
G-BBIH	Enstrom F-28A-UK	026	N4875	12. 9.73	Stephenson Marine Co Ltd	Goodwood	28. 6.02T
G-BBII	Fiat G.46-3B	44	I-AEHU MM52801	13. 9.73	R.P.W.Steele t/a Godshill Aviation (In Italian markings)	Sandown	30. 6.03P
G-BBIL	Piper PA-28-140 Cherokee	28-22567	SE-FAR N4219J	13. 9.73	R.Furlong & N.Alexander tr India Lima Flying Group	Andrewsfield	22. 5.04
G-BBIO	Robin HR100/210 Royal	178		14. 9.73	R.A.King	Headcorn	3. 1.05
G-BBIX	Piper PA-28-140 Cherokee E	28-7225442	LN-AEN	17. 9.73	Sterling Aviation Ltd	Elstree	28. 1.02T
G-BBJI	Isaacs Spitfire 2 & PFA 27-10055 (Continental O-200-A)			18. 9.73	T.E.W.Terrell (As "RN218/N")	(Atherstone)	2. 9.03P
G-BBJU	Robin DR400/140 Earl	874		19. 9.73	J.C.Lister tr Victor Sierra Aero Club	Valley Farm, Winwick	25. 5.04
G-BBJV	Reims/Cessna F177RG Cardinal RG	F177RG0098		20. 9.73	3GRCOMM Ltd	(Hereford)	11. 4.03
G-BBJX	Reims/Cessna F150L	F15001017		20. 9.73	L.W.Scattergood	Sherburn-in-Elmet	29 9.05T
G-BBJY	Reims/Cessna F172M Skyhawk II	F17201075		20. 9.73	J.Luccetti	Fenland	17. 6.02
G-BBJZ	Reims/Cessna F172M Skyhawk II	F17201035		20. 9.73	J.K.Green t/a Burks Green & Partners	Gamston	28. 2.04T
G-BBKA	Reims/Cessna F150L	F15001029		20. 9.73	W.M.Wilson & R.Campbell	(Doncaster)	7. 03T
G-BBKB	Reims/Cessna F150L	F15001030		20. 9.73	Justgold Ltd (Op Blackpool Air Centre)	Blackpool	10. 1.03T
G-BBKE	Reims/Cessna F150L	F15001026		20. 9.73	J.D.Woodward	Westbury-sub-Mendip	8. 8.04T
G-BBKF	Reims/Cessna FRA150L Aerobat	FRA1500222		20. 9.73	D.W.Mickleburgh (Stored 6.95: current status unknown)	Compton Abbas	13. 6.91T
G-BBKG	Reims FR172J Rocket	FR17200465		20. 9.73	R.Wright	Twycross/Coventry	1. 3.04
G-BBKI	Reims/Cessna F172M Skyhawk II	F17201069		20. 9.73	C.W. & S.A.Burman	East Winch	20.12.04
G-BBKL	Menavia Piel CP.301A Emeraude	237	F-BIMK	21. 9.73	R.K.Griggs tr Piel G-BBKL	Perth	13. 6.03P
G-BBKR	Scheibe SF-24A Motorspatz	4018	D-KECA	24. 9.73	P.I.Morgans Furze Hill Farm, Rosemarket, Milford Haven		30. 3.79S
G-BBKU	Reims/Cessna FRA150L Aerobat	FRA1500214		26. 9.73	T.Hartley & R.J.Stainer tr Penguin Group	Bodmin	19. 6.04T
G-BBKX	Piper PA-28-180 Cherokee Challenger	28-7305581	N9550N	26. 9.73	RAE Aero Club Ltd	Farnborough	11.10.04T
G-BBKY	Reims/Cessna F150L	F15000991		26. 9.73	Telesonic Ltd	Barton	7. 1.04
G-BBKZ	Cessna 172M	17261495	N20694	27. 9.73	R.S.Thomson tr KZ Flying Group	Exeter	26. 4.03T
G-BBLH	Piper J-3C-65 Cub (L-4B-PI) (Frame No.9838) (Regd with c/n 10549)	10006	F-BFQY Fr.Mil/43-1145	24. 9.73	Shipping & Airlines Ltd (As "31145/26/G" in 183rd Field Battalion US Army c/s)	Biggin Hill	9. 5.05T
G-BBLM	SOCATA Rallye 100S	2392		3.10.73	J.R.Rodgers	Wolverhampton	19.12.04
G-BBLS	Grumman-American AA-5 Traveler	AA5-0440	EI-AYM G-BBLS	8.10.73	A.D.Grant	Perth	23. 4.05
G-BBLU	Piper PA-34-200 Seneca	34-7350271	N55984	8.10.73	A.S.Bamrah t/a Falcon Flying Services	Biggin Hill	28 5.05T
G-BBMB	Robin DR400/180 Regent	848	5Y-ASB	27. 9.73	I.James tr Regent Flying Group King's Farm, Thurrock		13. 5.04
G-BBMH	EAA Sport Biplane Model P.1 (Continental C90-14F)	PFA 1348		11.10.73	I.S.Parker	Damyns Hall, Upminster	11. 6.03P
G-BBMJ	Piper PA-23-250 Aztec E	27-7305150	N40387	12.10.73	Nationwide Caravan Rental Services Ltd	(Holywell)	21. 9.05T
G-BBMN	de Havilland DHC-1 Chipmunk 22	C1/0300	WD359	12.10.73	R.Steiner "03"	North Weald	4. 4.04
G-BBMO	de Havilland DHC-1 Chipmunk 22	C1/0550	WK514	12.10.73	D.M.Squires (As "WK514")	Wellesbourne Mountford	10. 6.04
G-BBMR	de Havilland DHC-1 Chipmunk 22	C1/0213	WB763	12.10.73	P J Wood (New owner 1.02)	(Twyford, Bucks)	
G-BBMT	de Havilland DHC-1 Chipmunk 22	C1/0712	WP831	12.10.73	J.Evans & D.Withers	Graveley	26. 4.02
G-BBMV	de Havilland DHC-1 Chipmunk 22	C1/0432	WG348	12.10.73	P.J.Morgan (Aviation) Ltd (As "WG348")	Sywell	9. 4.03
G-BBMW	de Havilland DHC-1 Chipmunk 22	C1/0641	WK628	12.10.73	J.A.Challen & K.Sherwell tr Mike Whiskey Group (As "WK628")	Shoreham	15.12.04
G-BBMX	de Havilland DHC-1 Chipmunk 22	C1/0800	WP924	12.10.73	K.A.Doornbos	Teuge, The Netherlands	20. 8.05
G-BBMZ	de Havilland DHC-1 Chipmunk 22	C1/0563	WK548	12.10.73	P.C.G.Wyld tr The Wycombe Gliding School Syndicate	Booker	21. 9.03
G-BBNA	de Havilland DHC-1 Chipmunk 22 (Lycoming O-360)	C1/0491	WG417	12.10.73	Coventry Gliding Club Ltd "Carrie"	Husbands Bosworth	22. 6.03
G-BBND	de Havilland DHC-1 Chipmunk 22	C1/0225	WD286	12.10.73	W.Norton & D.Fradley tr Bernoulli Syndicate (As "WD286/J")	Little Gransden	19. 4.03
G-BBNG	Bell 206B JetRanger II	134	VH-BHX G-BBNG/VR-BEY/G-BBNG/PK-HBO/N6268N (Op Eagle Helicopters)	16.10.73	MB Air Ltd	Winchester Farm, Ouston	27 5.05T
G-BBNH	Piper PA-34-200 Seneca	34-7350339	N56492	16.10.73	A.L.Howell, A.P.Barrow & M.G.D.Baverstock	Bournemouth	15. 2.04

G-BBNI	Piper PA-34-200 Seneca	34-7350312	N56286	16.10.73	Noisy Moose Ltd	(London W5)	26. 3.04T
G-BBNJ	Reims/Cessna F150L	F15001038		16.10.73	Sherburn Aero Club Ltd	Sherburn-in-Elmet	19.11.05T
G-BBNV	Fuji FA.200-160 Aero Subaru	232		23.10.73	Caseright Ltd	Hinton in the Hedges	25. 4.99
G-BBNZ	Reims/Cessna F172M Skyhawk II	F17201054		23.10.73	R.E.Nunn	Pent Farm, Postling	24. 5.03
G-BBOA	Reims/Cessna F172M Skyhawk II	F17201066		23.10.73	J.D.& A.M.Black	Lodge Farm, St.Osyth, Clacton	18. 7.05
G-BBOC	Cameron O-77 HAB	86		24.10.73	J.A.B.Gray	Cirencester	6. 1.90A
					t/a Bacchus Balloons *"Bacchus"*		
G-BBOD	Thunder O.5 HAB	MLB 013		24.10.73	B.R. & M.Boyle *"Little Titch"*	Newbury	
					(On loan to British Balloon Museum & Library)		
G-BBOE	Robin HR200/100	26		24.10.73	R.J.Powell	(Wickham, Hants)	7. 7.02
	(Badly damaged striking hedge & concrete post landing Wells Cross Farm, Horsham 24.6.01: dismantled)						
G-BBOH	AJEP Pitts S-1S Special			25.10.73	Techair London Ltd	Popham	8. 9.97P
	(Lycoming IO-360) AJEP-PS1-S-1 & PFA 1570				*(Noted 7.02)*		
G-BBOL	Piper PA-18-150 Super Cub	18-7561	D-EMFE	26.10.73	N.Artt	(Bradley Stoke, Bristol)	12. 6.04
			N3821Z				
G-BBOO	Thunder Ax6-56 HAB	012		4.10.73	K.Meehan *"Tiger Jack"*	Much Wenlock, Shropshire	31. 5.03A
G-BBOR	Bell 206B JetRanger II	1197	(SE-)	30.10.73	M.J.Easey	Town Farm, Hoxne, Eye	29. 7.05T
			G-BBOR				
G-BBOX	Thunder Ax7-77 HAB	011		24.10.73	R.C.Weyda	Newbury	23.12.82A
					(On loan to British Balloon Museum & Library) "Rocinante"		
G-BBPN	Enstrom F-28A-UK	166		30.10.73	Smarta Systems Ltd	(Pencader)	8. 8.03T
G-BBPO	Enstrom F-28A	176		30.10.73	Wilco (Helicopters) Ltd	Shoreham	8. 6.03T
G-BBPS	SAN Jodel D.117	597	F-BHXS	30.10.73	A.Appleby	Burtenshaw Farm, Barcombe	26. 5.03P
G-BBPX	Piper PA-34-200 Seneca	34-7250262	N1202T	7.11.73	Richel Investments Ltd	Guernsey	15. 9.01
G-BBPY	Piper PA-28-180 Challenger	28-7305590	N9554N	8.11.73	Sunsaver Ltd	Barton	14. 8.05
G-BBRA	Piper PA-23-250 Aztec E	27-7305197	N40479	12.11.73	R.C.Lough	Stapleford	7. 5.03
G-BBRB	de Havilland DH.82A Tiger Moth	85934	OO-EVB	21.11.73	R.Barham	(Biggin Hill)	
			Belgian AF T-8/ETA-8/DF198		*(Damaged Biggin Hill 16.1.87: current status unknown)*		
G-BBRC	Fuji FA.200-180 Aero Subaru	235		8.11.73	G-BBRC Ltd	Blackbushe	26. 5.05T
G-BBRI	Bell 47G-5A	25158	N18092	8.11.73	Alan Mann Helicopters Ltd	Fairoaks	28. 7.02T
	(Composite following several major rebuilds)						
G-BBRN	Mitchell-Procter Kittiwake I	02 & PFA 1352	XW784	20.11.73	R.D.Dobree-Carey	Henstridge	25.11.03P
	(Continental O-200-A)				*(As "XW784/VL")*		
G-BBRV	de Havilland DHC-1 Chipmunk 22	C1/0284	WD347	13.11.73	J A Keen & H M Farrelly	Liverpool	17. 2.03T
					(As "WD347" in RAF grey & orange dayglo stripes)		
G-BBRX	SIAI-Marchetti S.205-18F	342	LN-VYH	13.11.73	R.C. & A.K.West	Popham	21.12.04
			OO-HAQ				
G-BBRY*	Cessna 210	57091	5Y-KRZ	15.11.73	Not known	Enstone	
			VP-KRZ/N7391E				
	(Crashed landing Epsom 2.4.78: cancelled 5.12.83 as destroyed) (In open storage 7.02)						
G-BBRZ	Grumman-American AA-5 Traveler	AA5-0471	(EI-AYV)	15.11.73	C.P.Osborne	Mullaghmore, Co.Sligo	30. 4.99
			G-BBRZ		*(Noted 8.01)*		
G-BBSA	Grumman-American AA-5 Traveler	AA5-0472		15.11.73	Usworth 84 Flying Associates Ltd	Newcastle	16. 4.05
G-BBSB	Beech C23 Sundowner 180	M-1516		15.11.73	Amalmay Ltd tr Sundowner Group	Blackpool	31. 7.05T
G-BBSC*	Beech B24R Sierra 200	MC-217		15.11.73	I.Millar & G.H.Emerson	Belfast	3. 6.99
					tr The Beechcombers Flying Group		
	(Cancelled 27.7.01 by CAA) (Noted in wrecked condition 10.01)						
G-BBSM	Piper PA-32-300 Cherokee Six	32-7440005	N9577N	14.11.73	P.R.Nott	Biggin Hill	21. 8.03T
G-BBSS	de Havilland DHC-1 Chipmunk 22	C1/0520	WG470	21.11.73	Coventry Gliding Club Ltd	Husbands Bosworth	1. 4.04
	(Lycoming O-360)						
G-BBSW	Pietenpol Air Camper	PFA 1506		21.11.73	J.K.S.Wills	(London SE3)	
G-BBTB	Reims/Cessna FRA150L Aerobat	FRA1500224		26.11.73	BBC Air Ltd *(Op Abbas Air)*	Compton Abbas	2.11.02T
G-BBTG	Reims/Cessna F172M Skyhawk II	F17201097		26.11.73	R.W. & V.P.J.Simpson	Redhill	15. 5.05
					tr Tango Golf Flying Group		
G-BBTH	Reims/Cessna F172M Skyhawk II	F17201089		26.11.73	K.Kwok-Kin Lee	Newtownards, Co.Down	22. 8.05
G-BBTJ	Piper PA-23-250 Aztec E	27-7305131	N40369	27.11.73	Cooper Aerial Surveys Ltd	Sandtoft	8. 4.04T
G-BBTK	Reims/Cessna FRA150L Aerobat	FRA1500230		27.11.73	Cleveland Flying School Ltd	Teesside	17.10.99T
G-BBTS	Beech V35B Bonanza	D-9551	N3051W	29.11.73	S Wenham t/a Eastern Air	Cannes-Mandelieu	5. 6.03
G-BBTT*	Reims/Cessna F150L Commuter	F15001055		30.11.73	Not known	Newtownards, Co.Down	12. 3.76
	(Crashed Newtownards 9.3.75: cancelled 6.1.84 as WFU: stored 2.01)						
G-BBTY	Beech C23 Sundowner 180	M-1525		29.11.73	A.W.Roderick & W.Price	Cardiff	6. 6.04
G-BBTZ	Reims/Cessna F150L	F15001063		30.11.73	Marham Investments Ltd	Cumbernauld	22. 6.03T
					(Op Cumbernauld Flying School)		
G-BBUE	Grumman-American AA-5 Traveler	0479		6.12.73	Hebog (Mon) Cyf	Caernarfon	10. 3.00
G-BBUF	Grumman-American AA-5 Traveler	0480		6.12.73	W.McLaren *(Op Tayside Aviation)*	Perth	22.12.02T
G-BBUG	Piper PA-16 Clipper	16-29	F-BFMC	6.12.73	J.Dolan	Enniskillen, Co.Fermanagh	19. 7.02
G-BBUJ	Cessna 421B Golden Eagle	421B0335	OY-RYD	7.12.73	Coolflourish Ltd	(Mansfield)	18. 5.00
G-BBUT	Western O-65 HAB	020		11.12.73	R.G.Turnbull	Clyro, Hereford	23. 4.97A
					"Christabelle II" (New owner 5.02)		
G-BBUU	Piper J-3C-75 Cub (L-4A-PI)	10529	F-BBSQ	14. 1.74	O.J.J.Rogers	Hulcote Farm, Salford, Beds	16. 5.03P
	(Frame No.10354)		F-OAEZ/Fr.AF/43-29238				
G-BBVA	Sikorsky S-61N Mk.II	61-718		12. 2.74	Bristow Helicopters Ltd	Lee-on-Solent	24. 2.03T
					(Op Marine & Coastguard Agency) "Vega"		
G-BBVG*	Piper PA-23-250 Aztec C	27-2610	ET-AEB	20.12.73	Colton Aviation Ltd	Gamston	10. 9.88T
			5Y-AAT/N5514Y		*(Cancelled 10.2.89 as WFU: stored 11.00)*		
G-BBVJ	Beech B24R Sierra 200	MC-230		21.12.73	E.J.Berek	(Sheffield)	7. 6.03
G-BBVO	Isaacs Fury II	PFA 11-10091		20.12.73	J Moore	(Great Yarmouth)	20. 6.02P
	(Lycoming O-320)				*(As Hawker Nimrod "S1579/571" of 408 Flight FAA, HMS Glorious)*		
G-BBWZ	Grumman-American AA-1B Trainer	AA1B-0334		4. 1.74	Teleco Trading Ltd	Popham	20. 8.03T
G-BBXB	Reims/Cessna FRA150L Aerobat	FRA1500236		16. 1.74	D.M.Fenton	Breighton	12. 7.98T
G-BBXH	Reims FR172F Rocket	FR1720113	SE-FKG	21. 1.74	D.Ridley	Chester-le-Street	8.11.03
G-BBXK	Piper PA-34-200 Seneca	34-7450056	N54366	21. 1.74	J.A.Rees	Haverfordwest	25. 5.05T
G-BBXL	Cessna 310Q II 310Q	1076	EI-CLX	21. 1.74	Appleton Aviation Ltd	Full Sutton	23. 7.04T
			G-BBXL/(N1223G)				

Reg	Type	c/n	Prev id	Date	Owner	Location	Expiry
G-BBXS	Piper J-3C-65 Cub (L-4H-PI) (Continental C90) (Frame No.12042)	12214	N9865F G-ALMA/44-79918	25. 1.74 *(Officially regd as c/n "9865") (Noted 11.01)*	M.J.Butler	Spanhoe	14. 9.00P
G-BBXY	Bellanca 7GCBC Citabria	614-74	N57639	1. 2.74	R.R.L.Windus	Truleigh Manor Farm, Edburton	12. 6.99
G-BBXZ	Evans VP-1 PFA (Volkswagen 1600)	1562		31. 1.74 *(Stored 5.99: current status unknown)*	R.W.Burrows	Swanton Morley	8. 3.96P
G-BBYB	Piper PA-18 Super Cub 95 (L-18C-PI) (Frame No.18-1628)	18-1627	PH-TMA (D-ENCH)/ALAT 18-1627/51-15627	4. 2.74	The Tiger Club (1990) Ltd	Headcorn	17. 7.04T
G-BBYH	Cessna 182P	18262814	N52744	6. 2.74	Croftmarsh Ltd	Poplar Farm, Croft, Skegness	1.12.02
G-BBYO*	Britten-Norman BN-2A Mk.III-1 Trislander	362	ZS-KMH G-BBYO/G-BBWR	27. 2.74	Aurigny Air Services Ltd	Guernsey	1. 5.92T
				(WFU 2.92 & cancelled 23.2.95 as WFU) (Noted 12.01 for possible rebuild with fuselage of c/n 1072/N3267J)			
G-BBYP	Piper PA-28-140 Cherokee F	28-7425158	N9620N	19. 2.74	Jersey Aircraft Maintenance Ltd	Jersey	6. 7.03T
G-BBYS	Cessna 182P Skylane	18261520	5Y-ATE N21256	14. 2.74	I.M.Jones	Gamston	1. 5.03
G-BBZF	Piper PA-28-140 Cherokee F	28-7425195	N9501N	19. 2.74	J.McGuinness & R.Stamp (Enniscorthy, Co.Wexford) t/a East Coast Aviation		23. 6.03
G-BBZH	Piper PA-28R-200 Cherokee Arrow II	28R-7435102	N9608N	22. 2.74	ZH Flying Ltd	Exeter	4. 6.04
G-BBZJ	Piper PA-34-200-2 Seneca	34-7450088	N40880	26. 2.74	General Technics Ltd	Poham	11. 8.03T
G-BBZN	Fuji FA.200-180 Aero Subaru	230		26. 2.74	J.Westwood & P.D.Wedd	Cambridge	17. 2.05T
G-BBZO	Fuji FA.200-160 Aero Subaru	238		26. 2.74	L.A.N.King & M.J.Herlihy tr G-BBZO Group	Redhill	26. 8.05
G-BBZV	Piper PA-28R-200 Cherokee Arrow II	28R-7435105	N9609N	11. 3.74	P.B.Mellor	Cambridge	25. 9.05T

G-BCAA - G-BCZZ

Reg	Type	c/n	Prev id	Date	Owner	Location	Expiry
G-BCAH	de Havilland DHC-1 Chipmunk 22	C1/0372	WG316	6. 5.74	A.W.Eldridge (As "WG316")	Leicester	25. 6.05T
G-BCAN*	Thunder Ax7-77 HAB	015		5. 3.74 *(Cancelled 27.9.01 by CAA) "Beacon"*	D.D.Owen	Wotton-Under-Edge	7. 8.88A
G-BCAZ	Piper PA-12 Super Cruiser	12-2312	5Y-KGK VP-KGK/ZS-BYJ/ZS-BPH	12. 3.74	A.D.Williams	Rhos-y-Gilwen Farm, Rhos Hill	21. 2.05
G-BCBG	Piper PA-23-250 Aztec E	27-7305224	VP-BBN VR-BBN/(VR-BDM)/G-BCBG/N40494	13. 3.74	M.J.L Batt	Booker	8.11.04
G-BCBH	Fairchild 24R-46A Argus III (UC-61K-FA)	975	(VH-AAQ) G-BCBH/ZS-AXH/HB737/43-15011	13. 3.74	Dreamticket Promotions Ltd	Old Hay, Paddock Wood	28. 6.03
G-BCBJ	Piper PA-25-235 Pawnee C	25-2380/R		18. 3.74	Deeside Gliding Club (Aberdeenshire) Ltd	Aboyne	2. 9.04
		(Rebuild of c/n 25-2380/G-ASLA/N6802Z, quoting c/n 25-5544 the new fuselage of G-ASLA !)					
G-BCBL	Fairchild 24R-46A Argus III (UC-61K-FA)	989	OO-EKE D-EKEQ/HB-AEC/HB751/43-15025	19. 3.74 *(As "HB751")*	F.J.Cox	Eaglescott	31. 3.96
G-BCBM	Piper PA-23-250 Aztec C	27-3006	N5854Y	19. 3.74	Hatton & Westerman Trawlers	Netherthorpe	12. 5.01
G-BCBR	AJEP/Wittman W.8 Tailwind (Continental O-200-A)	TW3-380		20. 3.74	D.P.Jones	Top Farm, Croydon, Royston	14. 7.03P
G-BCBX	Reims/Cessna F150L	F15001001	F-BUEO	25. 3.74	J.Kelly (Stored 1.02)	Belfast	19. 2.95T
G-BCBZ	Cessna 337C Super Skymaster (Robertson STOL conversion)	3370942	SE-FKB N2642S	28. 3.74	Envirovac 2000 Ltd	(Blackwood)	23. 4.05
G-BCCC	Reims/Cessna F150L	F15001041		8. 4.74	A.M.Chester tr Triple Charlie Flying Group	Denham	25. 4.04T
G-BCCD	Reims/Cessna F172M Skyhawk II	F17201144		8. 4.74	R.M.Austin t/a Austin Aviation	Rochester	28. 6.04T
G-BCCE	Piper PA-23-250 Aztec E	27-7405282	N40544	3. 4.74	Golf Charlie Echo Ltd	Shoreham	15. 8.05T
G-BCCF	Piper PA-28-180 Cherokee Archer	28-7405069	N9632N	3. 4.74	Topcat Aviation Ltd	Liverpool	27. 6.03
G-BCCG	Thunder Ax7-65 HAB	020		4. 4.74	N.H.Ponsford t/a Rango Balloon & Kite Co "Zephyr" (Active 1999)	Leeds	7.11.83A
G-BCCJ	Grumman-American AA-5 Traveler	AA5-0546		8. 4.74	T.Needham	Dunkeswell	18. 6.03
G-BCCK	Grumman-American AA-5 Traveler	AA5-0547		8. 4.74	Prospect Air Ltd	Manchester	19. 9.05
G-BCCR	Piel CP.301A EmeraudePFA (Continental O-200-A)	712		8. 4.74	J.H. & C.J.Waterman Armshold Farm, Kingston, Cambs		22. 2.03P
G-BCCX	de Havilland DHC-1 Chipmunk 22 (Lycoming O-360)	C1/0531	WG481	17. 4.74	T.Holloway tr RAFGSA (Op Clevelands Gliding Club)	AAC Dishforth	28. 3.03
G-BCCY	Robin HR200/100 Club	37		18. 4.74	Charlie Yankee Ltd	Filton	21. 4.05
G-BCDJ	Piper PA-28-140 Cherokee	28-24276	PH-NLV N1841J	29. 4.74	B.F.Graham tr Bristol Aero Club	Filton	26. 5.04T
G-BCDK(2)	Partenavia P68 Victor	32	A6-ALN G-BCDK	4. 7.75	Flyteam Aviation Ltd	Elstree	2. 5.05T
		(Officially regd as P68B Victor)					
G-BCDL	Cameron O-42 HAFB	115		24. 4.74	D.P. & Mrs B.O.Turner "Chums"	Bath	13. 7.83A
G-BCDY	Reims/Cessna FRA150L Aerobat	FRA1500237		7. 5.74	R.Turrell & P.Mason	Stapleford	11. 7.03T
G-BCEA	Sikorsky S-61N Mk.II	61-721		7. 6.74	Veritair Ltd	Port Stanley, Falkland Islands	13. 7.03T
G-BCEB	Sikorsky S-61N Mk.II	61-454	N4023S	2.10.74	Veritair Ltd "The Isles of Scilly"	Penzance	16.12.05T
G-BCEC	Reims/Cessna F172M Skyhawk II	F17201082		7. 5.74	Trim Flying Club Ltd	Trim, Co.Meath	9. 7.03T
G-BCEE	Grumman-American AA-5 Traveler	AA5-0571		7. 5.74	N.F.Harrison	Stapleford	15. 5.03
				(Force-landed Stapleford 16.2.02, damage to nosewheel, prop, exhaust & engine firewall)			
G-BCEF	Grumman-American AA-5 Traveler	AA5-0572		7. 5.74	J.Fitzpatrick	(Urrugne, France)	9. 6.05
G-BCEN	Fairey Britten-Norman BN-2A-26 Islander	403	4X-AYG SX-BFB/4X-AYG/N90JA/G-BCEN	6. 5.74 *(Op Marine & Coastguard Agency)*	Atlantic Air Transport Ltd	Manston	7.11.03A
G-BCEO*	American Aviation AA-5 Traveler	7. 5.74	AA5-0575		W Bateson	Blackpool	
				(Crashed near Selby Farm, Stanton, Morpeth 28.4.02: cancelled 11.07.02 as destroyed) (Wreck noted 7.02)			
G-BCEP	Grumman-American AA-5 Traveler	AA5-0576		7. 5.74	G.Edelmann	Blackbushe	8. 6.03
G-BCER	CAB GY-201 Minicab	8	F-BGJP	8. 5.74	D.Beaumont	West Freugh	2. 4.03P
G-BCEX	Piper PA-23-250 Aztec E	27-7305024	N40225	13. 5.74	Western Air (Thruxton) Ltd	Thruxton	14. 5.05T
G-BCEY	de Havilland DHC-1 Chipmunk 22	C1/0515	WG465	14. 5.74	T.C.B.Dehn & C.A.Robey tr Gopher Flying Group (As "WG465" in RAF c/s)	White Waltham	12. 9.05
G-BCEZ	Cameron O-84 HAB	107		13. 5.74	P.F.Smart & R.J.Mitchener t/a Balloon Collection "Stars & Bars"	Romsey/Andover	20. 7.82A
G-BCFF	Fuji FA.200-160 Aero Subaru	237		21. 5.74	C.D.Burleigh	(Salisbury)	2.12.03

G-BCFN	Cameron O-65 HAB	109		23. 5.74	W.G.Johnston & H.M.Savage *"Fireball"*	Edinburgh	15. 5.77S
					(Noted 6.00)		
G-BCFO	Piper PA-18-150 Super Cub	18-5335	(D-EIOZ)	29. 5.74	D.C.Murray	Lee-on-Solent	11. 4.04
			ALAT 18-5335/N10F		tr Portsmouth Naval Gliding Club		
G-BCFR	Reims/Cessna FRA150L Aerobat	FRA1500244		30. 5.74	Bulldog Aviation Ltd & Motorhoods Colchester Ltd	Earls Colne	13.12.02T
					(Op Essex Flying School)		
G-BCFU	Thunder Ax6-56 HAB	027	EI-BAF	17. 5.74	Zebedee Balloon Service Ltd	Hungerford	
			(G-BCFU)		*"Smithwicks"* *(Restored & noted 1.00)*		
G-BCFW	SAAB 91D Safir	91-437	PH-RLZ	29. 5.74	D.R.Williams	Peplow	22. 7.03
G-BCFY	Phoenix Luton LA-4A Minor PAL/1301 & PFA/824			29. 5.74	G.Capes	(Brough)	17. 1 92P
					(Stored Sywell 8.92: new owner 10.00)		
G-BCGB	Bensen B.8P	CL.14		3. 6.74	J.W.Birkett	(Bursledon)	5. 7.01P
	(Rotax 503)				*(Operates from Chilbolton)*		
G-BCGC	de Havilland DHC-1 Chipmunk 22	C1/0776	WP903	13. 3.74	J C Wright	RAF Henlow	26. 7.04T
					(As "WP903" in Queen's Flight c/s)		
G-BCGH	SNCAN NC.854S	122	F-BAFG	10. 6.74	T.J.N.H.Palmer	Hill Farm, Nayland	28. 5.03P
					tr Nord Flying Group		
G-BCGI	Piper PA-28-140 Cherokee Cruiser	28-7425283	N9573N	10. 6.74	J.C.,T.,T. & H.R.Dodd	Panshanger	8. 6.03T
G-BCGJ	Piper PA-28-140 Cherokee Cruiser	28-7425286	N9574N	10. 6.74	BCT Aircraft Leasing Ltd	Kemble	1. 8.03T
					(Op BCT Flying Club)		
G-BCGL	Jodel D.112	668	F-BIGL	24. 4.74	T.J.Maynard	Kemble	29. 6.01P
	(Built Ets Valladeu)						
G-BCGM	Jodel Wassmer D.120 Paris-Nice	50	F-BHQM	15. 7.74	J.Pool	Sturgate	7. 4.03P
			F-BHYM				
G-BCGN	Piper PA-28-140 Cherokee F	28-7425323	N9595N	10. 6.74	Golf November Ltd	Oxford	2. 9.05
G-BCGS	Piper PA-28R-200 Cherokee Arrow II	28R-7235133	N4893T	13. 6.74	S.Rayne	Cambridge	17. 2.03
					tr Arrow Aviation Group		
G-BCGT	Piper PA-28-140 Cherokee	28-24504	N6779J	17. 6.74	L.Maikowski	Shoreham	16. 7.03T
G-BCGW	Jodel D.11 CC.001 & EAA/61554 & PFA 912			14. 6.74	G.H.& M.D.Chittenden	Highwood Hall	30. 1.85P
	(Lycoming O-290)				*(Current status unknown)*		
G-BCHK	Reims/Cessna F172H	F17200716	9H-AAD	19. 6.74	D Darby	(Cowbridge)	23.11.03
G-BCHL	de Havilland DHC-1 Chipmunk 22	C1/0680	AWP788	20. 6.74	Shropshire Soaring Ltd *(As "WP788")*	Sleap	18.10.04
G-BCHM	Westland SA.341G Gazelle 1	1168	G-17-20	14. 6.74	MW Helicopters Ltd *(New owner 5.02)*	Stapleford	23. 8.99
G-BCHP	Scintex CP.1310-C3 Super Emeraude	902	G-JOSI	24. 6.74	G.Hughes & A.G.Just	Earls Colne	6. 8.02P
			G-BCHP/F-BJVQ				
G-BCHT	Schleicher ASK 16	16021	(BGA1996)	25. 6.74	D.E.Cadisch & K.A.Lilleywhite	Dunstable	31. 5.04
			D-KAMY		tr Dunstable K16 Group		
G-BCHX*	Scheibe SF-23A Sperling	2013	D-EGIZ	28. 6.74	R.L.McLean t/a DG Powered Sailplanes	Rufforth	29. 6.83P
					(Damaged 7.8.82: frame stored 9.01: cancelled 22.3.02 as WFU)		
G-BCID	Piper PA-34-200 Seneca	34-7250303	N1381T	3. 7.74	Shenley Farms (Aviation) Ltd	Headcorn	27. 7.01T
G-BCIE*	Piper PA-28-151 Cherokee Warrior	28-7415405	N9588N	3. 7.74	Perth College	Perth	19.12.99T
					(Extensively damaged Perth 27.5.99: cancelled 15.9.99 as destroyed) (Dumped 3.02)		
G-BCIH	de Havilland DHC-1 Chipmunk 22	C1/0304	WD363	3. 7.74	J.M.Hosey (As "WD363")	Audley End	10. 7.05
G-BCIJ	Grumman-American AA-5 Traveler	AA5-0603	N6143A	3. 7.74	D.G.Page t/a Arrow Association	Elstree	7. 6.03
G-BCIK	Grumman-American AA-5 Traveler	AA5-0604	N6144A	3. 7.74	Trent Aviation Ltd	Tatenhill	28. 5.03
G-BCIL*	Grumman-American AA-1B Trainer	0378	N6168A	5. 7.74	M.Hobson	(Cruden Bay, Peterhead)	2.10.88
		AA1B-0378			*(Crashed Auchnagatt, Aberdeen 14.6.86: cancelled 24.11.86 as WFU: stored 6.00)*		
G-BCIN	Thunder Ax7-77 HAB	030		5. 7.74	R.A., P.M.G. & N.T.M.Vale	Kidderminster	5. 5.84A
					tr Isambard Kingdom Brunel Balloon Group		
G-BCIR	Piper PA-28-151 Cherokee Warrior	28-7415401	N9587N	9. 7.74	P.J.Brennan	Southend	16.10.03
G-BCJH*	Mooney M.20F Executive 21	670126	N9549M	11. 7.74	P.J.Bossard	Bourn	30. 6.91
					(Cancelled 26.9.00 by CAA) (In open store 11.01)		
G-BCJM	Piper PA-28-140 Cherokee F	28-7425321	N9592N	17. 7.74	Topcat Aviation Ltd	Manchester	10.11.02T
					(Op Manchester School of Flying)		
G-BCJN	Piper PA-28-140 Cherokee Cruiser	28-7425350	N9618N	17. 7.74	Topcat Aviation Ltd	Barton	8. 9.05T
G-BCJO	Piper PA-28R-200 Cherokee Arrow II	28R-7435272	N9640N	17. 7.74	R.Ross	Pittrichie Farm, Whiterashes	9. 7.03
G-BCJP	Piper PA-28-140 Cherokee	28-24187	N1766J	15. 8.74	D.J. & D.Pitman tr Omletair Flying Group	Bournemouth	11. 4.04
G-BCKF*	K & S SA.102.5 Cavalier	71055 & PFA 1594		29. 7.74	K Fairness c/o R Collin	(Eyemouth)	
					(No Permit issued &.cancelled 8.7.91 by CAA) (Stored 2001)		
G-BCKN	de Havilland DHC-1 Chipmunk 22	C1/0707	WP811	5. 8.74	T.Holloway	RAF Cranwell	16. 2.04
	(Lycoming O-360)				tr RAFGSA *(Op Cranwell Gliding Club)*		
G-BCKS	Fuji FA.200-180AO Aero Subaru	FA200-250		2. 8.74	S.Bhagat	(Pafos, Cyprus)	30. 4.01T
G-BCKT	Fuji FA.200-180 Aero Subaru	FA200-251		2. 8.74	P Chilcott tr Kilo Tango Group	Shoreham	20. 5.05
G-BCKU	Reims/Cessna FRA150L Aerobat	FRA1500256		1. 8.74	Stapleford Flying Club Ltd	Stapleford	24.10.04T
G-BCKV	Reims/Cessna FRA150L Aerobat	FRA1500251		1. 8.74	Cleveland Flying School Ltd	Teesside	6. 1.03T
G-BCLC	Sikorsky S-61N Mk.II	61-737		9. 1.75	Bristow Helicopters Ltd	Sumburgh	12. 1.03T
					(Op Marine & Coastguard Agency) "Craigievar"		
G-BCLD	Sikorsky S-61N Mk.II	61-739		4. 2.75	Bristow Helicopters Ltd *"Slains" (Stored 2002)* Aberdeen		2. 2.03T
G-BCLI	Grumman-American AA-5 Traveler	AA5-0643		12. 8.74	P.J.Wagstaff	Elstree	13. 9.03T
G-BCLL	Piper PA-28-180 Cherokee C	28-2400		13. 8.74	J.Nash & D.F.Amos tr G-BCLL Group	Popham	23.10.04
G-BCLS	Cessna 170B	20946	N8094A	23. 8.74	N Simpson	(Lincoln)	27. 1.83
					(Stored 7.99: new owner 12.01)		
G-BCLT	SOCATA MS.894A Rallye Minerva 220	12003	EI-BBW	1. 8.74	K.M.Bowen	Upfield Farm, Whitson	17. 7.05
			G-BCLT/F-BTRL				
G-BCLU	SAN Jodel D.117	506	F-BHXG	28. 8.74	S.J.Wynne	Knettishall	2.10.03P
G-BCLV*	Bede BD-5A	4885 & PFA 14-10074		28. 8.74	R A Gardiner	(Bridge of Weir)	
					(Not completed & unfinished frame stored: cancelled 31.7.89 as WFU) (Noted 6.00)		
G-BCLW	Grumman-American AA-1B Tr2	AA1B-0463		29. 8.74	J R Faulkner	Tatenhill	22. 8.05T
G-BCMD	Piper PA-18 Super Cub 95	18-2055	OO-SPF	4. 9.74	P.Stephenson	Great Oakley, Clacton	30. 5.05
	(L-18C-PI) (Frame No.18-2071)		R.Neth AF R-70/52-2455				
G-BCMT	Isaacs Fury II	PFA 1522		9. 9.74	R.W.Burrows	Priory Farm, Tibenham	
	(Continental O-200-A)				*(New owner 2.02)*		
G-BCNC	Gardan GY-201 Minicab	A.202	F-BICF	9. 9.74	J.R.Wraight	(Chatham)	
G-BCNP	Cameron O-77 HAB	117		16. 9.74	P.Spellward *"Blue Fret"*	Bristol	28. 7.00A

Reg	Type	c/n	Prev id	Date	Owner	Location	Date
G-BCNX	Piper J-3C-65 Cub (L-4H-PI)	11168	F-BEGM	17. 9.74	K.J.Lord	Cherry Tree Farm, Monewden	10. 7.03P
	(Frame No.10993)		Fr AF/43-29877		tr The Grasshopper Flying Group *(As "540" in USAF c/s)*		
G-BCNZ	Fuji FA-200-160 Aero Subaru	257		16. 9.74	I.Kazi	(Cranbrook)	23. 1.05
G-BCOB	Piper J-3C-65 Cub (L-4H-PI)	10696	F-BCPV	19. 9.74	R.W. & Mrs.J.Marjoram	Low Farm, South Walsham	24. 5.03P
	(Frame No.10521)		43-29405		*(As "329405/A/23" in USAAC c/s)*		
G-BCOI	de Havilland DHC-1 Chipmunk 22	C1/0759	WP870	24. 9.74	D.S.McGregor	Rayne Hall Farm, Rayne	13. 8.04
G-BCOJ	Cameron O-56 HAB	124		25. 9.74	T.J.Knott & M.J.Webber	Rickmansworth	12. 7.87A
					tr Phoenix Balloon Group *"Red Squirrel"*		
G-BCOL	Reims/Cessna F172M Skyhawk II	F17201233		25. 9.74	A.H.Creaser	Old Manor Farm, Anwick	25. 5.03T
G-BCOM	Piper J-3C-90 Cub (L-4A-PI)	10478	F-BDTP	27. 9.74	D.S.Clarke & N.P.Cook *"Dougal"*	Shoreham	8. 7.02P
	(Frame No.10303)		F-BFQP/OO-ADI/43-29187		tr Dougal Flying Group		
	(Officially regd as c/n 12040 which is correct identity of G-BGPD: fuselages probably exchanged in France)						
G-BCOO	de Havilland DHC-1 Chipmunk 22	C1/0204	WB760	10.10.74	T.G.Fielding & M.S.Morton	Blackpool	10.11.03
G-BCOR	SOCATA Rallye 100ST	2544	F-OCZK	7. 1.75	P.R.W.Goslin, P.Nichamin & I.M.Speight	Henstridge	27. 9.04
G-BCOU	de Havilland DHC-1 Chipmunk 22	C1/0559	WK522	10.10.74	P.J.Loweth *"Thunderbird 5"*	(Billericay)	30. 3.95
					(As "WK522" in RAF c/s) (Current status unknown)		
G-BCOX	Bede BD-5A	HJC.4523		10.10.74	H.J.Cox & B.L.Robinson *(Noted 7.99)*	Chivenor	27.11.95P
G-BCOY	de Havilland DHC-1 Chipmunk 22	C1/0212	WB762	10.10.74	Coventry Gliding Club Ltd	Husbands Bosworth	23. 1.03
	(Lycoming O-360)						
G-BCPD	CAB GY-201 Minicab	18	F-BGKN	24.10.74	P.R.Cozens	Hinton in the Hedges	14. 7.03P
G-BCPG	Piper PA-28R-200 Cherokee Arrow	28R-35705	N4985S	16.10.74	A.G.Antoniades tr Roses Flying Group	Barton	24. 6.04
G-BCPH	Piper J-3C-65 Cub (L-4H-PI)	11225	F-BCZA	13.12.74	M.J.Janaway	Siege Cross Farm, Thatcham	2. 4.04P
	(Frame No.11050)		Fr.AF/43-29934		*(As "329934/B/72" in 25th AOP French Armoured Divn of US 3rd Army c/s)*		
G-BCPJ	Piper J-3C-65 Cub (L-4J-PI)	13206	F-BDTJ	5.11.74	S.Hollingsworth	Popham	17. 4.03P
	(Frame No.13036)		45-4466		tr Piper Cub Group		
G-BCPK	Reims/Cessna F172M Skyhawk II	F17201194	(D-ELOB)	21.10.74	D.C.C.Handley	Sywell	12. 1.01T
G-BCPN	Grumman-American AA-5 Traveler	AA5-0665	N6155A	21.10.74	G.K.Todd	Full Sutton	25.10.03
G-BCPU	de Havilland DHC-1 Chipmunk 22	C1/0839	WP973	24.10.74	P.Waller	Booker	6. 8.05
G-BCRB	Reims/Cessna F172M Skyhawk II	F17201259		29.10.74	D.E.Lamb	Fenland	7. 5.04
G-BCRE*	Cameron O-77 HAB	128		30.10.74	Not known	NK	
					(Cancelled 19.5.93 by CAA) (Inflated 6.02)		
G-BCRI	Cameron O-65 HAB	135		5.11.74	V.J.Thorne *"Joseph"*	Bristol	26. 8.81A
G-BCRK	K & S SA.102.5 Cavalier	PFA 01-10049		5.11.74	P.G.R.Brown	Trenchard Farm, Eggesford	14. 7.00P
	(Lycoming O-235)						
G-BCRL	Piper PA-28-151 Cherokee Warrior	28-7415689	N9564N	5.11.74	BCRL Ltd	Humberside	21. 6.03T
G-BCRP	Piper PA-E23-250 Aztec E	27-7305082	N40269	7.11.74	Airlong Charter Ltd *(Op Skydrift Ltd)*	Norwich	27. 9.03T
G-BCRR	Grumman-American AA-5B Tiger	AA5B-0006		7.11.74	N.A.Whatling	Deenethorpe	5.12.03
G-BCRT	Reims/Cessna F150M	F15001164		18.11.74	G.Matthews tr Blue Max Flying Group	Sywell	11. 6.05T
G-BCRX	de Havilland DHC-1 Chipmunk 22	C1/0232	WD292	22.11.74	Tuplin Ltd	White Waltham	1. 8.03
					(As "WD292" in RAF c/s)		
G-BCSA	de Havilland DHC-1 Chipmunk 22	C1/0691	WP799	25.11.74	T.Holloway	Bicester	14. 2.03
	(Lycoming O-360)				tr RAFGSA		
G-BCSL	de Havilland DHC-1 Chipmunk 22	C1/0524	WG474	26.11.74	Jalawain Ltd tr Barton Chipmunk Flyers	Barton	26. 3.05
G-BCST	SOCATA MS.893A Rallye Commodore 180	10748	F-BPQD	18.11.74	D R Wilcox	Sywell	5.12.03
G-BCSX	Thunder Ax7-77 HAB	031		2.12.74	C.Wolstenholme *"Woophski"*	Macclesfield	5. 7.86A
G-BCSY	Taylor JT.2 Titch	PFA 1504		5.12.74	I.L.Harding	Sackville Farm, Riseley	
	(Volkswagen 1600)				*(Construction abandoned at advanced state: stored 3.97: current status unknown)*		
G-BCTF	Piper PA-28-151 Cherokee Warrior	28-7515033	N9585N	11.12.74	E.Reed	Teesside	20.10.05T
	(Rebuilt 1989/90 using major components from G-BFXZ)				t/a St.George Flight Training		
G-BCTI	Schleicher ASK 16	16029	D-KIWA	23.12.74	A.J.Southard	Hinton in the Hedges	24. 7.04
					tr Tango India Syndicate		
G-BCTJ	Cessna 310Q II	310Q1072	N1219G	23.12.74	D.Pearce & P.Golding tr TJ Flying Group	Biggin Hill	12. 8.05T
G-BCTK	Reims FR172J Rocket	FR17200546		23.12.74	R.T.Love	Bodmin	13. 3.03
G-BCTT	Evans VP-1 PFA	1543		24.12.74	M.J.Watson	Knettishall	25. 6.99P
	(Volkswagen 1600)						
G-BCUB	Piper J-3C-65 Cub (L-4J-PI)	13370	F-BFBU	13.12.74	A.L.Brown	Bourn	13. 6.01P
	(Lippert Reed conversion)		45-4630				
	(Officially regd with c/n 13186 now known to be G-BDOL (qv): airframes possibly switched during conversion in UK)						
G-BCUF	Reims/Cessna F172M Skyhawk II	F17201279		3. 1.75	R.N.Howell	(Mablethorpe)	19. 7.03
					t/a Howell Plant Hire & Construction		
G-BCUH	Reims/Cessna F150M	F15001195		7. 1.75	M.G.Montgomerie tr G-BCUH Group	Elstree	10. 1.04T
G-BCUJ	Reims/Cessna F150M	F15001176		9. 1.75	BCT Aircraft Leasing Ltd	Full Sutton	11. 2.05T
G-BCUL	SOCATA Rallye 100ST	2545	F-OCZL	27. 1.75	C.A.Ussher & Fountain Estates Ltd	Bagby	8. 5.00
G-BCUO	Scottish Aviation Bulldog Srs.120/122	BH120/371	Ghana AF G-107	9. 1.75	Cranfield University	Cranfield	27. 4.04T
			G-BCUO				
G-BCUS	Scottish Aviation Bulldog Srs.120/122	BH120/373	Ghana AF G-109	9. 1.75	S.J.& J.J.Ollier	Tatenhill	29. 4.05
			G-BCUS				
G-BCUV	Scottish Aviation Bulldog Srs.120/122	BH120/376	Ghana AF G-112	9. 1.75	Dolphin Property (Management) Ltd	Old Sarum	17. 5.03T
			G-BCUV		*(As "CB733" in RAF c/s)*		
G-BCUW	Reims/Cessna F177RG Cardinal RG	F177RG0119	SE-GKL	10. 1.75	S.J.Westley	Cranfield	12. 5.00T
G-BCUY	Reims/Cessna FRA150M Aerobat	FRA1500029		14. 1.75	J.C.Carpenter	Clipgate Farm, Denton	8. 3.04
G-BCVB	Piper PA-17 Vagabond	17-190	F-BFMT	22. 1.75	A.T.Nowak	Popham	14. 7.03P
	(Continental A65)		N4890H				
G-BCVC	SOCATA Rallye 100ST	2548	F-OCZO	16. 1.75	N.R Vine	Popham	25. 1.05
G-BCVE*	Evans VP-2	V2-1015 & PFA 7210		16. 1.75	North Western PFA Strut	Barton	
					(Cancelled 9.6.93 as TWFU) (Noted 5.01)		
G-BCVF	Practavia Pilot Sprite 115	GBC.1 & PFA 1362		27. 1.75	D.G.Hammersley	Tatenhill	17. 6.02P
	(Continental C125)						
G-BCVG	Reims/Cessna FRA150L Aerobat	FRA1500245	(I-AFAD)	16. 1.75	I.G.Cooper tr G-BCVG Flying Group	Compton Abbas	19.12.03
G-BCVH	Reims/Cessna FRA150L Aerobat	FRA1500258		16. 1.75	D.J.Reece	(Swindon)	18.11.05T
G-BCVJ	Reims/Cessna F172M Skyhawk II	F17201305		16. 1.75	Rothland Ltd	RAF Woodvale	13.12.03
G-BCVY	Piper PA-34-200T Seneca II	34-7570022	N32447	28. 1.75	Oxford Aviation Services Ltd	Oxford	16. 3.03T
G-BCWB	Cessna 182P Skylane II	18263566	N5848J	29. 1.75	M.F.Oliver & A.J.Mew	White Waltham	21.12.05T

G-BCWH	Practavia Pilot Sprite 115	PFA 1366		3. 2.75	R.Tasker	Blackpool	31. 5.03P
	(Continental O-240-A)						
G-BCWK	Alpavia Fournier RF3	24	F-BMDD	7. 2.75	T.J.Hartwell & D.R.Wilkinson	Thurleigh	13. 8.02P
G-BCWO	Fairey Britten-Norman BN-2A-21 Islander	431	SE-LAX	13. 2.75	Cormack (Aircraft Services) Ltd	Cumbernauld	
			LN-MAC/G-BCWO		*(Stored 2.03)*		
G-BCXB	SOCATA Rallye 100ST	2546	F-OCZM	7. 2.75	A.Smails	Morgansfield, Fishburn	15. 3.04
G-BCXE	Robin DR400 2+2	1015		19. 2.75	Weald Air Services Ltd	Headcorn	11. 6.05T
G-BCXJ	Piper J-3C-65 Cub (L-4J-PI)	13048	F-BFFH	21. 2.75	W.Readman	Old Sarum	18. 8.03P
	(Frame No.12878)		OO-SWA/44-80752		*(As "480752/E-39" in USAAC c/s)*		
G-BCXN	de Havilland DHC-1 Chipmunk 22	C1/0692	WP800	7. 3.75	G.M.Turner	RAF Halton	7. 5.03
					(As "WP800/2" in Southampton UAS c/s)		
G-BCYH	DAW Privateer Mk.3 Motor Glider	2 & PFA 1568	BGA.1158	10. 3.75	D.B.Limbert	Crosland Moor	17. 6.02P
	(Volkswagen 1600)		RAFGSA.264/XA297				
	(Regd as Cadet III and is a converted Slingsby T.31B c/n 839: marked incorrectly as "RAFGSA.246")						
G-BCYJ	de Havilland DHC-1 Chipmunk 22	C1/0360	WG307	12. 3.75	Just Plane Trading Ltd Top Farm, Croydon, Royston		19.12.02
					(As "WG307")		
G-BCYM	de Havilland DHC-1 Chipmunk 22	C1/0598	WK577	13. 3.75	C.H.Nicholls tr G-BCYM Group	Kemble	6. 9.03
G-BCYR	Reims/Cessna F172M Skyhawk II	F17201288		20. 3.75	J. & L.Donne	Inverness	4.12.04T
					t/a Donne Enterprise *(Op Highland Flying Club)*		
G-BCZH	de Havilland DHC-1 Chipmunk 22	C1/0635	WK622	19. 3.75	A.C.Byrne Botany Bay, Horsford, Norwich		31. 7.87
			(As "WK622" in RAF c/s) (Crashed Pentney, Norfolk 6.9.87: stored 8.93: current CofR 4.02)				
G-BCZI	Thunder Ax7-77 HAB	037		24. 3.75	R.G.Griffin & R.Blackwell	Newbury	16. 3.86A
					tr North Hampshire Balloon Group *"Motorway"*		
G-BCZM	Reims/Cessna F172M Skyhawk II	F17201350		3. 4.75	Cornwall Flying Club Ltd	Bodmin	2. 1.04T
G-BCZN	Reims/Cessna F150M	F15001149		27. 3.75	Mona Aviation Ltd	RAF Mona	10.12.03T
G-BCZO	Cameron O-77 HAB	158		27. 3.75	W.O.T.Holmes *"Leo" (Inflated 6.02)*	Shrewsbury	11.10.86A

G-BDAA - G-BDZZ

G-BDAD	Taylor JT.1 Monoplane	PFA 1453		2. 4.75	J.Gunson tr G-BDAD Group	(Preston)	3. 4.92P
	(Volkswagen 1700)				*(Damaged Blackpool 21.7.91: current status unknown)*		
G-BDAG	Taylor JT.1 Monoplane	PFA1430		1. 4.75	C.P.Whitwell	Oak Farm, Cowbit	20. 5.00P
G-BDAH*	Evans VP-1	PFA 7007		2. 4.75	G.H.J.Geurts	Cranfield	26. 5.99
	(Volkswagen 1600)				*(Cancelled 12.4.00 as temporarily WFU)*		
G-BDAI	Reims/Cessna FRA150M Aerobat	FRA1500266		21. 4.75	D.F.Ranger	Popham	25. 7.04T
G-BDAK	Rockwell Commander 112A	252	N1252J	10. 4.75	R.A.Denton	Sherburn-in-Elmet	31. 8.03
G-BDAL	Rockwell Shrike Commander 500S	3226	N57134	25. 4.75	Xjet Ltd	Farnborough	5. 9.04
G-BDAM	Noorduyn AT-16-ND Harvard IIB	14-726	LN-MAA	10. 4.75	Silver Victory BVBA	(Brasschaat, Belgium)	6. 9.03P
			Fv16047/FE992/42-12479		*(As "FE992/K-T" in 5(P)AFU c/s)*		
G-BDAO	SIPA 91 (Continental C85)	2	F-BEPT	10. 4.75	S.B.Churchill	Eastbach Farm, Coleford	1. 8.00P
G-BDAP	AJEP/Wittman TW.8 Tailwind	0387 & PFA 3507		9. 4.75	J.Whiting	Bagby	22. 8.02P
	(Continental O-200-A)						
G-BDAR	Evans VP-1 Srs.2	PFA 1537 & PFA 62-10461		10. 4.75	R.B.Valler	(Waterlooville)	20. 7.84P
	(Volkswagen 1600)				*(Current status unknown) (Valid CofR 4.02)*		
G-BDAY	Thunder Ax5-42A HAB	042		8. 4.75	T.M.Donnelly *"Meconium"*	Doncaster	16. 1.93A
G-BDBD	Wittman W.8 Tailwind	133	N1198S	25. 4.75	W.S.Siebert & B.Ohrman Wellesbourne Mountford		13. 8.03P
	(Continental O-200-A)				tr Tailwind Group		
G-BDBF	Clutton FRED Srs.II	PFA 1528		15. 4.75	J.M.Brightwell & A.J.Wright	Hucknall	18. 3.98P
	(Volkswagen 1600)				*(Noted 7.01)*		
G-BDBH	Bellanca 7GCBC Citabria	758-74	OE-AOL	15. 4.75	C.J.Gray	Finmere	1. 2.04
G-BDBI	Cameron O-77 HAB	162		15. 4.75	C Jones *"Funny Money" (New owner 12.01)*	Reading	11. 7.87A
G-BDBJ	Cessna 182P Skylane II	18263646	N4644K	18. 4.75	H.C.Wilson	Great Ashfield, Suffolk	30. 1.03
G-BDBU	Reims/Cessna F150M	F15001174		30. 4.75	E.Veitch	Cumbernauld	6. 7.03
G-BDBV	Aero Jodel D.11A V.3		D-EGIB	23. 4.75	G.G.Long	Seething	31.10.03P
	(Continental C90)				tr Seething Jodel Group		
G-BDCC	de Havilland DHC-1 Chipmunk 22	C1/0258	WD321	25. 4.75	Coventry Gliding Club Ltd	Husbands Bosworth	24. 3.02
	(Lycoming O-360						
G-BDCD	Piper J-3C-65 Cub (L-4J-PI)	12429	OO-AVS	28. 4.75	S C Brooks Wellcross Grange, Slinfold		22. 7.00P
	(Continental C90) *(Frame No.12257)*		44-80133		*(As "480133/B/44" in US Army c/s)*		
G-BDCE*	Reims/Cessna F172H	F17200704	PH-EHB	5. 5.75	Copperplane Ltd	Bournemouth	26. 4.01T
					(Damaged in gales Bournemouth 3.1.99: fuselage stored 5.00: cancelled 12.11.02 as wfu)		
G-BDCI	Scanor Piel CP.301C Emeraude	503	F-BIRC	25. 4.75	D.L.Sentance Rothwell Lodge Farm, Kettering		22.11.02P
G-BDCL	Grumman-American AA-5 Traveler	AA5-0773	EI-CCI	5. 5.75	J.Crowe	Coventry	29.11.93T
			G-BDCL/EI-BGV/G-BDCL/N1373R		*(Stored w/o wings 5.00)*		
G-BDCO	Beagle B.121 Pup 1	B121-171		6. 5.75	R.J.Page & M.H.Simms	(Haywards Heath)	28. 7.97
					(New owner 4.01)		
G-BDCU*	Cameron O-77 HAB	126		11. 6.75	Not known *(Cancelled 4.8.98 by CAA: extant 2000)* NK		20. 2.86
G-BDDD	de Havilland DHC-1 Chipmunk 22	C1/0326	WD387	16. 5.75	RAE Aero Club Ltd	Farnborough	16. 8.02T
G-BDDF	Jodel Wassmer D.120 Paris-Nice	97	F-BIKZ	20. 5.75	A.J.Hobbs	Acle Bridge, Norfolk	10.11.03P
G-BDDG	Dormois Jodel D.112	855	F-BILM	20. 5.75	J Pool & D.G.Palmer	Sturgate	9. 8.02P
G-BDDS	Piper PA-25-260 Pawnee C	25-4757	CS-AIU	22. 5.75	T.J.Price	Rhigos	16. 5.05
			N10F		tr Vale of Neath Gliding Club		
G-BDDT	Piper PA-25-235 Pawnee C	25-5324	CS-AIX	22. 5.75	W.J.& A.E.Taylor	East Winch	8. 7.99A
			N8820L		t/a Pawneee Aviation *(Noted 12.01)*		
G-BDDZ	Menavia Piel CP.301A Emeraude	253	F-BIMZ	30. 5.75	E.C.Mort	(Warrington)	20. 6.84P
					(Damaged Cranwell North 3.6.84: on rebuild 1.01)		
G-BDEC	SOCATA Rallye 100ST	2552	F-OCZS	28. 5.75	M.Mulhall	Kilkenny, Co.Kilkenny	10. 8.03
G-BDEH	Jodel Wassmer D.120A Paris-Nice	239	F-BLNE	2. 6.75	M.D.Nichol tr EH Group	Oaksey Park	27. 8.03P
G-BDEI	Jodel D.9 Bebe	585 & PFA 936		2. 6.75	R.Q.T.Newns *"Noddy"*	White Waltham	9.12.02P
	(Volkswagen 1600)				tr The Noddy Group		
G-BDEU	de Havilland DHC-1 Chipmunk 22	C1/0704	WP808	17. 6.75	A.Taylor *(As "WP808")*	Manor Farm, Binham	28. 1.02

Reg	Type	c/n	Prev id	Date	Owner	Location	Expiry
G-BDEX	Reims/Cessna FRA150M Aerobat	FRA1500279		12. 6.75	R.A.Powell	Lower Wasing Farm, Brimpton	11. 5.03T
G-BDEY	Piper J-3C-65 Cub (L-4J-PI)	12538	OO-AAT	17. 6.75	W.J. & Mrs.J.Morecraft	Highfield Farm, Empingham	22. 4.03P
	(Frame No.12366)		OO-GAC/44-80242		tr Ducksworth Flying Club		
G-BDEZ	Piper J-3C-65 Cub (L-4J-PI)	12383	OO-SOC	17. 6.75	R.J.M.Turnbull	Rydinghurst Farm, Cranleigh	10. 6.03P
	(Frame No.12211)		OO-EPI/44-80087				
G-BDFB	Phoenix Currie Wot	PFA 3008		20. 6.75	J.Jennings	Fenland	9. 6.03P
	(Walter Mikron III)						
G-BDFG*	Cameron O-65 HAB	179		24. 6.75	N.A.Robertson	Combe Hay Manor, Bath	16. 4.88A
					"Golly II" (Cancelled 21.10.01 as WFU & stored)		
G-BDFH	Auster AOP.9	B5/10/176	XR240	24. 6.75	R.O.Holden	Booker	20. 9.02P
	(Frame No.AUS 177 FM)				*(As "XR240")*		
G-BDFJ	Reims/Cessna F150M	F15001182		25. 6.75	Cassandra J.Hopewell	Sibson	13. 7.02T
G-BDFR	Fuji FA.200-160 Aero Subaru	FA200-262		7. 7.75	A.Houghton tr Fugi Group	Blackpool	1.11.04
G-BDFS	Fuji FA.200-160 Aero Subaru	FA200-263		7. 7.75	B.Lawrence	Goodwood	24. 9.00T
G-BDFW	Rockwell Commander 112A	308	N1308J	18. 6.75	M.E.& E.G.Reynolds	Blackbushe	22.11.04
G-BDFX	Taylorcraft J Auster 5	2060	F-BGXG	9. 7.75	J.Eagles	Oaksey Park	3. 6.94T
			TW517		*(Damaged Oaksey Park 10.10.93: on rebuild 4.02)*		
G-BDFY	Grumman-American AA-5 Traveler	AA5-0806		10. 7.75	G.Robertson	Edinburgh	22. 8.03
					tr The Grumman Group *(Op Edinburgh Flying Club)*		
G-BDFZ	Reims/Cessna F150M	F15001184	(D-EIWB)	14. 7.75	L.W.Scattergood	Sherburn-in-Elmet	17. 5.03T
			(F-BXIH)				
G-BDGB	Barritault JB-01 Minicab	PFA 1819		23. 6.75	D.G.Burden	Armshold Farm, Kingston, Cambs	12. 6.01P
	(Continental PC-60)						
G-BDGH	Thunder Ax7-77 HAB	049		16. 7.75	R.J.Mitchener & P.F.Smart	Andover	30. 8.83A
					t/a Balloon Collection *"London Pride III"*		
G-BDGM	Piper PA-28-151 Cherokee Warrior	28-7415165	N41307	30. 7.75	Comed Aviation	Blackpool	23. 1.04T
G-BDGP*	Cameron V-65 HAB	658	(N.....)	2. 9.80	A.Mayes & V.Lawton	Leamington Spa	17.11.96A
			G-BDGP		t/a Warwick Balloons *(Ladbroke Motor Group titles) (Cancelled 10.10.01 by CAA)*		
G-BDGY	Piper PA-28-140 Cherokee	28-23613	N3536K	5. 8.75	S.J.Willcox	Compton Abbas	2. 9.02T
G-BDHK	Piper J-3C-65 Cub (L-4A-PI)	8969	F-PHFZ	24. 7.75	A.Liddiard	Eastbach Farm, Coleford	16. 9.03P
	(Frame No.9068)		42-38400		*(As "329417" in USAAC c/s)*		
	(Official c/n quoted as "261" with p/i 42-36414 but this corresponds to c/n 8538/N75366)						
G-BDIE	Rockwell Commander 112A	342	N1342J	14. 8.75	R.J.Adams	RAF Brize Norton	10. 7.04T
G-BDIG	Cessna 182P Skylane II	18263938	N9877E	26. 8.75	P.B.Barrett & A R Bruce	Sturgate	15. 8.05
	(Reims-assembled with c/n F18200020)				t/a Air Group 6		
G-BDIH	SAN Jodel D.117	812	F-BIOT	22. 8.75	N.D.H.Stokes	(Bath)	11. 7.03P
G-BDIJ	Sikorsky S-61N Mk.II	61-751	9M-AYF	3.10.75	Bristow Helicopters Ltd	Lee-on-Solent	31. 5.04T
	(SAR conversion)		G-BDIJ		*(Op Marine & Coastguard Agency) "Crathes"*		
G-BDJC	AJEP/Wittman W.8 Tailwind	387AW & PFA 3508		29. 8.75	M.A. Hales	Barton Ashes	10. 6.03P
	(Continental O-200-A)				*(Noted 3.02)*		
G-BDJD	Jodel D.112 *(Continental A65)*	PFA 910		3. 9.75	J.E.Preston *"Marianne"*	(Ottringham)	29. 5.03P
G-BDJG	Phoenix Luton LA-4A Minor	PFA 828		3. 9.75	S.C.Barry	White Waltham	5. 6.03P
	(Volkswagen 1835)				tr Very Slow Flying Club		
G-BDJP	Piper J-3C-65 Cub Special	22992	OO-SKZ	11.12.75	S.T.Gilbert	Enstone	18. 5.03T
	(Continental C90) (Frame No.21017)		PH-NCV/NC3908K				
G-BDJR	SNCAN NC.858S	2	F-BFIY	30. 9.75	R.F.M.Marson *(On rebuild 9.00)*	(Fleet)	23. 5.92P
G-BDKB*	SOCATA Rallye 150ST	2631		30. 9.75	N.C.Anderson	(North Devon)	4. 6.82
					(Damaged Coleraine 5.7.81: cancelled 18.2.99 by CAA) (On rebuild 2.00)		
G-BDKC	Cessna A185F Skywagon	185-02569	N1854R	30. 9.75	Bridge of Tilt Co Ltd	Blair Atholl	23. 4.04
G-BDKD	Enstrom F-28	A319		30. 9.75	M A Crook & A E Wright	(Warrington)	29. 5.05
G-BDKH	Menavia Piel CP.301A Emeraude	241	F-BIMN	15.10.75	P.N.Marshall	Insch	11. 6.01P
G-BDKJ	K & S SA.102.5 Cavalier	72207 & PFA 1458		14.10.75	D.A.Garner	(Swansea)	5. 6.95P
	(Continental O-240-A)				*(Damaged Gloucestershire 14.9.97: current status unknown)*		
G-BDKM	SIPA 903	98	F-BGHX	17.11.75	S.W.Markham	Valentine Farm, Odiham	30. 4.03P
G-BDKU*	Taylor JT.1 Monoplane	PFA 1456		22.10.75	B.N.Stevens & A.J.L.Eves	Bodmin	5. 8.03P
	(Volkswagen 1500) (Possibly incorporates PFA 55-10301)				*(Cancelled 21.10.02 by CAA) (Noted 10.02)*		
G-BDKW	Rockwell Commander 112	106	N1277J	3.11.75	Orwell Flying Ltd	Poplar Hall Farm, Elmsett	16. 7.03T
			ZS-MIB/N1106J				
G-BDLO	Grumman-American AA-5A Cheetah	AA5A-0026	N6154A	3.11.75	S. & J.Dolan	Elstre	19. 7.04
G-BDLS	Grumman-American AA-1B Tr.2	AA1B-0564	N6153A	3.11.75	P.Asbridge & C.R.Tilley	Sleap	28.10.04
G-BDLT	Rockwell Commander 112A	363	N1363J	4.11.75	D.L.Churchward	Popham	11. 6.05
G-BDLY	K & S SA.102.5 Cavalier	PFA 01-10011		14.11.75	P.R.Stevens	Thruxton	21. 4.03P
	(Lycoming O-290)						
G-BDMM*	Jodel D.11	PFA 901		5.11.75	P.N.Marshall	(Aboyne)	
					(Cancelled 27.1.97 by CAA) (Stored but removed late 2000: current status unknown)		
G-BDMO*	Thunder Ax7-77A HAB	053	(EC-...)	25.11.75	Not known	NK	
			G-BDMO		*(Cancelled as WFU 8.3.95 - to Spain with no regn issued - WFU) (Inflated 6.01)*		
G-BDMS	Piper J-3C-65 Cub (L-4J-PI)	13049	F-BEGZ	4.11.75	A.T.H.Martin	Old Sarum	10. 5.03P
			44-80753		*(As "FR886" in RAF c/s)*		
G-BDMW	SAN Jodel DR.100A Ambassadeur	79	F-BIVM	2.12.75	R.O.F.Harper	Yew Tree Farm, Lymm Dam	15. 8.05
					tr G-BDMW Flying Group		
G-BDNC	Taylor JT.1 Monoplane	PFA 1454		8.12.75	D.W.Mathie	(Diss)	6. 3.02P
	(Walter Mikron III)						
G-BDNG	Taylor JT.1 Monoplane	PFA 1405		12.12.75	S.B.Churchill	Eastbach Farm, Culeford	17. 9.03P
	(Volkswagen 1834)				*"The Red Sparrow"*		
G-BDNO	Taylor JT.1 Monoplane	PFA 1431		15.12.75	S.D.Glover	Bodmin	10. 6.03P
	(Volkswagen 1600)						
G-BDNT	Jodel D.92	397	F-PINL	2. 1.76	R.F.Morton	Kemble	28. 7.03P
	(Volkswagen 1600)						
G-BDNU	Reims/Cessna F172M Skyhawk II	F17201405		2. 1.76	J. & K.G.McVicar	Elstree	31. 3.03T
G-BDNW	Grumman-American AA-1B Trainer	AA1B-0588		8. 1.76	P.Mitchell	Humberside	16. 4.03
G-BDNX	Grumman-American AA-1B Trainer	AA1B-0590		8. 1.76	R.M.North	Kimbolton	23. 8.04
G-BDOC	Sikorsky S-61N Mk.II	61-765		20. 3.76	Bristow Helicopters Ltd *"Tolquhoun"*	Sumburgh	28.12.04T
	(SAR conversion)				*(Op Marine & Coastguard Agency)*		

Reg	Type	c/n	Prev id	Date	Owner	Location	Date
G-BDOD	Reims/Cessna F150M	F15001266		20. 1.76	D.M.Moreau	(Wickham)	2. 7.03
G-BDOE	Reims FR172J Rocket	FR1720559		20. 1.76	D. & P.A.Sansome	Little Chase Farm, Kenilworth	5. 1.03
G-BDOG	Scottish Aviation Bulldog Srs.200	BH200/381		18.12.75	D.C.Bonsall	Netherthorpe	27. 6.03P
					(Phoenix Flying Group titles)		
G-BDOL	Piper J-3C-65 Cub (L-4J-PI)	13186	F-BCPC	18.12.75	L.R.Balthazor	Lee-on-Solent	15. 3.03P
	(Frame No.13016)		45-4446				
	(Official c/n 13370 but has c/n & USAAC plates relating to c/n 13370/ex 45-4630 now G-BCUB: airframes switched during UK conversion)						
G-BDON	Thunder Ax7-77A HAB	063		17.12.75	M.J.Smith *"Fred"*	York	24. 6.94A
G-BDOT	Fairey Britten-Norman BN-2A Mk III-2 Trislander	1025	ZK-SFF	21. 1.76	Lyddair Ltd	Lydd	20. 2.03T
			N900TA/N903GD/N3850K/VH-BPB/G-BDOT				
G-BDOW	Reims/Cessna FRA150M Aerobat	FRA1500296		26. 1.76	Boldlake Ltd	Barton	3. 4.04T
G-BDPA	Piper PA-28-151 Cherokee Warrior	28-7615033	N9630N	26. 1.76	D.R.Allard	Prestwick	6.11.03
G-BDPJ	Piper PA-25-235 Pawnee B	25-3665	PH-VBF	2. 2.76	T.M.Holloway	Bicester	19.12.03
	(Lycoming O-540A1B5-@ 250hp)		SE-EPZ		tr RAFGSA		
G-BDPK	Cameron O-56 HAB	191		4. 2.76	N.H.Ponsford & A.M.Lindsay	Leeds	29.12.88A
					t/a Rango Balloon & Kite Co		
G-BDRD	Reims/Cessna FRA150M Aerobat	FRA1500289		9. 2.76	Prestwick Flight Centre Ltd	Prestwick	27. 6.03T
G-BDRG	Taylor JT.2 Titch	PFA 60-10295		19.12.78	D.R.Gray *(Current status unknown)*	(Wilmslow)	
G-BDRJ	de Havilland DHC-1 Chipmunk 22	C1/0742	WP857	19. 2.76	J.C.Schooling *(As "WP857/24")*	Elstree	4. 7.02
G-BDRK	Cameron O-65 HAB	205		12. 2.76	D.L.Smith *"Smirk"*	Eling Hill, Newbury	20. 6.86A
G-BDRL*	Stits SA-3A Playboy	P-689	N730GF	12. 2.76	O.C.Bradley	Mullaghmore, Co.Antrim	17. 6.98P
	(Continental C85)				*(Cancelled 11.5.01 by CAA) (Stored 10.02)*		
G-BDSA*	Clutton-Tabenor FRED Srs.II	EI-BFS		23. 2.76	W D M Turtle	Rich Hill, Co.Armagh	5. 7.79P
		LAS.1803 & PFA 29-10141	G-BDSA		*(Cancelled by CAA 29.9.00) (Current status unknown)*		
G-BDSB	Piper PA-28-181 Cherokee Archer II	28-7690107	N8221C	23. 2.76	Testfair Ltd	Fairoaks	19. 7.04
G-BDSE	Cameron O-77 HAB	210		27. 2.76	British Airways plc *"Concorde"*	Worplesdon	31. 3.90A
G-BDSF	Cameron O-56 HAB	209		1. 3.76	J.H.Greensides *"Itzuma"*	Hull	24. 5.93A
G-BDSH	Piper PA-28-140 Cherokee Cruiser	28-7625063	N9638N	1. 3.76	D.Jones	Nottingham	26. 8.02
					tr The Wright Brothers Flying Group		
G-BDSK	Cameron O-65 HAB	166		3. 3.76	Semajan Ltd	Romsey	9. 9.03A
					tr Southern Balloon Group *"Carousel II"*		
G-BDSL	Reims/Cessna F150M	F15001306		5. 3.76	D.C.Bonsall	Netherthorpe	24. 6.04T
G-BDSM	Slingsby T.31 Motor Cadet III	PFA 42-10507		5. 3.76	N.F.James	Husbands Bosworth	22. 5.02P
G-BDTB	Evans VP-1 Srs.2	PFA 7009		15. 3.76	J.A.Hanslip	Cowbit, Spalding	29.10.03P
	(Volkswagen 1834)						
G-BDTL	Evans VP-1	PFA 7012		17. 3.76	A.K.Lang	(Stoke-sub-Hamdon, Somerset)	5. 9.85P
	(Volkswagen 1600)				*(Stored 5.98: current status unknown)*		
G-BDTN	Fairey Britten-Norman BN-2A Mk III-2 Trislander	1026	S7-AAN	16. 3.76	Aurigny Air Services Ltd	Guernsey	10. 6.98T
			VQ-SAN/G-BDTN		*(Stored 12.02)*		
G-BDTO	Fairey Britten-Norman BN-2A Mk.III-2 Trislander	1027	G-RBSI	16. 3.76	Aurigny Air Services Ltd	Guernsey	31. 3.05T
			G-OTSB/G-BDTO/8P-ASC/G-BDTO/(C-GYOX)/G-BDTO *(Merrill Lynch titles)* *"Nessie"*				
G-BDTU	Van Den Bemden Omega III Gas Balloon (20,000 cu.ft)	VDB-35 & AFB.4		16. 3.76	R.G.Turnbull	Clyro, Hereford	4. 8.99A
					"Omega III"		
G-BDTV	Mooney M.20F Executive	22-1307	N6934V	16. 3.76	S.Redfearn	Gamston	15. 6.03
G-BDTW*	Cassutt Racer IIIM PFA	034-10102		18. 3.76	R.Mohlenkamp	Damme, Germany	1.11.99P
	(Continental C90)				*"The Thunder Box" (Cancelled 21.1.00 as WFU)*		
G-BDTX	Reims/Cessna F150M	F15001275		19. 3.76	S.L.Lefley & F.W.Ellis	Water Leisure Park, Skegness	7. 6.03T
G-BDUI	Cameron V-56 HAB	218		19. 3.76	D.C.Johnson *"True Brit"*	Farnham	6. 7.91A
G-BDUL	Evans VP-1	PFA 1557		25. 3.76	C.K.Brown	(Helston)	23. 4.03P
	(Volkswagen 1834)						
G-BDUM	Reims/Cessna F150M	F15001301	F-BXZB	29. 3.76	P.Barnett, J.Eyre & J.Brand	Earls Colne	3. 4.03
G-BDUN	Piper PA-34-200T Seneca II	34-7570163	(EI-BLR)	29. 3.76	Air Medical Ltd	Oxford	27. 2.04T
			G-BDUN/SE-GIA				
G-BDUO	Reims/Cessna F150M Commuter	F15001304		29. 3.76	C.B.Mellor t/a BM Aviation	Popham	25. 4.04T
G-BDUY	Robin DR400/140B Major	1120		5. 4.76	J.G.Anderson	Pittrichie Farm, Whiterashes	20. 1.03
G-BDUZ	Cameron V-56 HAB	213		30. 3.76	P.J.Bish	Hungerford	19. 2.00A
					t/a Zebedee Balloon Service *"Hot Lips"*		
G-BDVA	Piper PA-17 Vagabond	17-206	CN-TVY	23. 4.76	I.M.Callier	Liss	13. 8.03P
	(Continental C90)		F-BFFE				
G-BDVB	Piper PA-15 Vagabond	15-229	F-BHHE	23. 4.76	B.P.Gardner	Whittles Farm, Mapledurham	5. 6.03P
	(Continental C90)		SL-AAY/F-BETG				
G-BDVC	Piper PA-17 Vagabond	17-140	F-BFBL	29. 9.76	A.R.Caveen	Sandford Hall, Knockin	9. 9.02P
	(Continental C90)						
G-BDWA	SOCATA Rallye 150ST	2695		20. 4.76	J.T.Wilson	Bann Foot, Lough Neagh	7. 6.01
G-BDWE	Flaglor Sky Scooter			12. 4.76	D.R.Leggett	Fenland	17. 4.02P
	(Volkswagen 1600) KF-S-66 &DWE-01 & PFA 1332				tr Fenland Strut Flying Group		
G-BDWH	SOCATA Rallye 150ST	2697		20. 4.76	M.A.Jones	Upper Harford Farm, Bourton-on-the-Water	10. 10.04
G-BDWJ	Replica Plans SE-5A	PFA 20-10034	"C1904"	27. 4.76	D.W.Linney	(Langport)	18. 7.03P
	(Continental C90)		"F8010"		*(As "F8010/Z" in RFC c/s)*		
G-BDWL	Piper PA-25-235 Pawnee B	25-3575	PH-IPO	4. 5.76	Peterborough & Spalding Gliding Club Ltd	Crowland	31. 7.03
			N7531Z				
G-BDWM	Bonsall DB-1 Mustang	PFA 73-10200		3. 5.76	D.C.Bonsall	Netherthorpe	15. 6.98P
	(Lycoming IO-360)				*(As "FB226/MT-A" in RAF c/s) (Noted 3.00)*		
G-BDWO	Howes Ax6 HAB	RBH.2		5. 5.76	R.B. & Mrs C.Howes *"Griffin"*	Keysoe, Bedford	
					(Complete & extant 11.88 but never certified)		
G-BDWP	Piper PA-32R-300 Cherokee Lance	32R-7680176	N8784E	7. 5.76	W.M.Brown & B.J.Wood	Coventry	26.10.03
G-BDWX	Jodel Wassmer D.120A Paris-Nice	311	F-BNHT	13. 5.76	R.P.Rochester	Wombleton	21.10.03P
G-BDWY	Piper PA-28-140 Cherokee E	28-7225378	PH-NSC	14. 5.76	Comed Aviation Ltd	Blackpool	7. 3.03T
			N11C				
G-BDXB	Boeing 747-236B	21239	N8280V	13. 1.77	Snapdragon Ltd	(Hamilton, Bermuda)	15. 6.02T
G-BDXE	Boeing 747-236B	21350		23. 2.78	European Skybus Ltd	Bournemouth	4. 4.03T
					(Op European Aviation Air Charter) (Red bands)		
G-BDXF	Boeing 747-236B	21351		23. 3.78	European Skybus Ltd	Bournemouth	30. 4.03T
					(Op European Aviation Air Charter) (Green bands)		

G-BDXG	Boeing 747-236B	21536		16. 6.78	European Skybus Ltd	Bournemouth	30. 6.03T
					(Op European Aviation Air Charter) (Pink bands)		
G-BDXH	Boeing 747-236B	21635		23. 2.79	European Skybus Ltd	Bournemouth	2. 5.04T
					(Op European Aviation Air Charter) (Blue bands)		
G-BDXI	Boeing 747-236B	21830		21. 2.80	British Airways plc *(Stored 10.02)*	Cardiff	13. 3.04T
G-BDXJ	Boeing 747-236B	21831	N1792B	2. 5.80	European Skybus Ltd	Bournemouth	7. 5.04T
					(Op European Aviation Air Charter) (Yellow bands)		
G-BDXN	Boeing 747-236M	23735	N6046P	17. 3.87	British Airways plc	Mojave-Kem Co, Ca, USA	12. 4.03T
					(Stored 12.02)		
G-BDXO	Boeing 747-236B	23799	N6055X	22. 4.87	British Airways plc	Mojave-Kem Co, Ca, USA	14. 5.03T
					(Stored 12.02)		
G-BDXX	SNCAN NC.858S	110	F-BEZQ	17. 5.76	M.Gaffney & K.Davis *(On rebuild 12.00)*	North Weald	3. 7.96P
G-BDYD	Rockwell Commander 114	14014	N1914J	21. 5.76	M.B.Durkin	(Shifnal)	11. 9.03
G-BDYF	Cessna 421C Golden Eagle II	421C0055	N98468	24. 5.76	Airpoint Trading Ltd	(Ongar)	8. 8.03T
G-BDYH	Cameron V-56 HAB	233		24. 5.76	B.J.Godding *"Novocastrian"*	Didcot	25.11.90A
G-BDZA	Scheibe SF-25E Super Falke	4320	(D-KECW)	1. 6.76	D.C.Mason tr Hereward Flying Group	Crowland	3.10.04
G-BDZC	Reims/Cessna F150M	F15001316		1. 6.76	A.M.Lynn	Sibson	21. 7.05T
G-BDZD	Reims/Cessna F172M Skyhawk II	F17201478		1. 6.76	J.K.Haig & A.L.Jones tr Zephyr Group	(Gravesend)	20. 9.03T
G-BDZU	Cessna 421C Golden Eagle II	421C0094	N98791	14. 6.76	R.Richardson tr Eagle Flying Group	East Midlands	27. 4.03T

G-BEAA - G-BEZZ

G-BEAB	CEA Jodel DR.1051 Sicile	228	F-BKGH	18. 8.76	R.C.Hibberd	Draycott Farm, Chiseldon	9. 3.03
G-BEAC	Piper PA-28-140 Cherokee	28-21963	4X-AND	4. 6.76	C.E.Stringer tr Clipwing Flying Group	Bagby	4. 6.03T
G-BEAG	Piper PA-34-200T Seneca II	34-7670204	N9395K	18. 6.76	Oxford Aviation Services Ltd	Oxford	22.10.03T
G-BEAH	Auster V J/2 Arrow	2366	F-BFUV	28. 6.76	J.G.Parish	Bedwell Hey Farm, Little Thetford, Ely	16. 4.03P
	(Continental C85)		F-BFVV/OO-ABS		tr Bedwell Hey Flying Group *"Llewellyn"*		
G-BEBE	Grumman-American AA-5A Cheetah	AA5A-0154		28. 6.76	Bills Aviation Ltd	Biggin Hill	26.10.02T
G-BEBG	WSK-PZL SZD-45A Ogar	B-655		29. 6.76	D.W.Coultrip	Hinton in the Hedges	23. 9.02
					tr The Ogar Syndicate		
G-BEBN	Cessna 177B Cardinal	17701631	4X-CEW	1. 7.76	E.J.Lamb	Stapleford	22. 3.03
			N34031				
G-BEBS	Andreasson BA-4B	HA/01 & PFA 38-10157		7. 7.76	N.J.W.Reid	Lee-on-Solent	17. 10.03P
	(Continental O-200-A)						
G-BEBU	Rockwell Commander 112A	272	N1272J	8. 7.76	Cardiff Wales Aviation Services Ltd	Cardiff	19. 4.04T
G-BEBZ	Piper PA-28-151 Cherokee Warrior	28-7615328	N6193J	14. 7.76	Goodwood Road Racing Co Ltd	Goodwood	19. 4.03T
G-BECA	SOCATA Rallye 100ST	2751		14. 7.76	M.A.Neale & P.A.Brain tr Bredon Flying Group	Bidford	30. 6.03
G-BECB	SOCATA Rallye 100ST	2783		14. 7.76	A.J.Trible	Henscott Farm, Holsworthy	24. 5.05
G-BECC	SOCATA Rallye 150ST	2748		14. 7.76	G.R.E.Tapper *(New owner 4.02)*	(Blandford Forum)	15. 5.00
G-BECE*	Aerospace Developments AD-500 Srs.B.1 Airship	1214/1		14. 7.76	Airship Heritage Trust	(Huntington)	1. 4.79P
					(Damaged Cardington 9.3.79) (Gondola only 3.02)		
G-BECF	Scheibe SF-25A Motorfalke	4555	OO-WIZ	14. 7.76	North County Ltd	(Middleton)	1. 3.94P
			(D-KARA)		*(Current status unknown)*		
G-BECK	Cameron V-56 HAB	136		27. 7.76	M E White *"Joyride"*	Templeogue, Dublin	21. 3.00A
G-BECN	Piper J-3C-65 Cub	12776	F-BCPS	27. 7.76	G Denney	RayneHall Farm, Rayne	30. 8.05
	(L-4J-PI)		HB-OCI(1)/44-80480		*(As "80480/44/E" in US Army c/s)*		
G-BECS	Thunder Ax6-56A HAB	074		4. 8.76	A.Sieger	Munster, Germany	21. 5.03A
G-BECT	CASA I-131E Jungmann	"3974"	E3B-338	3. 8.76	G.M.S.Scott	Headcorn	5. 8.03P
					tr Alpha 57 Group *(As "A-57" in Swiss AF c/s)*		
G-BECW	CASA I-131E Jungmann	2037	E3B-423	3. 8.76	R.G.Meredith	Denham	4.11.03P
	(Incorporating parts of G-BECY ex E3B-459)				*(As "A-10" in Swiss AF c/s)*		
G-BECZ	Mudry/CAARP CAP.10B	68	F-BXHK	26. 7.76	Avia Special Ltd	White Waltham	18. 3.04T
G-BEDA*	CASA I-131E Jungmann Srs.2000	2099	E3B-504	3. 8.76	M.G.Kates & D.J.Berry Sheffield Park, Haywards Heath		2. 4.00P
					tr DA Group *(Cancelled 2.11.01 by CAA)*		
G-BEDB*	SNCAN 1203 Norecrin II	117	F-BEOB	5. 8.76	J.E.Pierce	Ley Farm, Chirk	11. 6.80P
					(Cancelled 14.11.91 by CAA) (Stored 9.00)		
G-BEDD	SAN Jodel D.117A	915	F-BITY	3. 8.76	P.B.Duhig	Fenland	4. 9.03P
G-BEDF	Boeing B-17G-105-VE Flying Fortress	8693	N17TE	5. 8.76	B-17 Preservation Ltd	Duxford	21. 5.03P
			F-BGSR/44-85784		*(As "124485/DF-A" in USAAC c/s) "Sally B" (Port)/"Memphis Belle" (Starboard)*		
G-BEDG	Rockwell Commander 112A	482	N1219J	5. 8.76	Hotels International Ltd	Blackbushe	13.12.05
G-BEDJ	Piper J-3C-65 Cub (L-4J-PI)	12890	N6193J	5. 8.76	R.Earl	Denford Manor, Hungerford	8.10.96P
	(Frame No.12720)		44-80594		*(As "44-805942" in USAAC c/s) (Stored 10.01)*		
G-BEDP	Fairey Britten-Norman BN-2A Mk.III-2 Trislander	1039	ZK-SFG	17. 8.76	Lyddair Ltd	Lydd	28. 5.03T
			N902TA/N1FY/N401JA/G-BEDP				
G-BEEG	Fairey Britten-Norman BN-2A-26 Islander	550	(C-GYUH)	25. 8.76	M.D.Carruthers & S.F.Morris	Cark	30. 3.04T
			G-BEEG		t/a North West Parachute Centre		
G-BEEH	Cameron V-56 HAB	250		24. 8.76	Sade Balloons Ltd *"Tywi"*	Coulsdon, Surrey	12. 4.02A
G-BEEI*	Cameron N-77 HAB	249		24. 8.76	Not known	(The Wirral)	11. 3.90
					(Cancelled 4.8.98 by CAA) (Extant 2000)		
G-BEER	Isaacs Fury II	PFA 1588		31. 8.76	R.S.C.Andrews	Bidford	5. 6.03P
	(Lycoming O-235)				*(As "K2075" in RAF c/s)*		
G-BEEU	Piper PA-28-140 Cherokee F	28-7325247	PH-NSE	9. 9.76	H & E Merkado	Panshanger	6. 3.03T
			N11C				
G-BEFA	Piper PA-28-151 Cherokee Warrior	28-7615416	N6978J	8. 9.76	M.A.Verran t/a Verran Freight	RAF Benson	6. 4.03
G-BEFF	Piper PA-28-140 Cherokee F	28-7325228	PH-NSF	27. 9.76	M.R.Tobin	Panshanger	19. 5.03
			N11C				
G-BEGA*	Westland-Bell 47G-3B1	WA/705	XW185	19.10.76	Reel-Time Entertainments Ltd Ahlen Heliport, Germany		21.4.99
					(Cancelled - sold as D-H... 26.7.01) (NTU & stored 2002)		
G-BEGG	Scheibe SF-25E Super Falke	4326	(D-KDFB)	15.10.76	R.Culley & A.Collett	Hall Farm, Turweston	17. 5.03
					tr G-BEGG Flying Group		
G-BEHH	Piper PA-32R-300 Cherokee Lance	32R-7680323	N6172J	29.10.76	K.Swallow	Sherburn-in-Elmet	5. 9.03
G-BEHU	Piper PA-34-200T Seneca II	34-7670265	N6175J	3.11.76	Pirin Aeronautical Ltd	Stapleford	21. 3.05T

Reg	Type	C/n	Prev id	Date	Owner/Operator	Location	Status
G-BEHV	Reims/Cessna F172N Skyhawk II	F17201541		3.11.76	Edinburgh Air Centre Ltd	Edinburgh	10. 9.05T
G-BEHX*	Evans VP-2	V2-2338 & PFA 7222		8.11.76	G.S.Adams	Stewartstown, Co.Tyrone	22. 1.90P
	(Volkswagen 1834)				*"Ulster Flyer" (Stored 11.01) (Cancelled 16.12.02 as wfu)*		
G-BEIA	Reims/Cessna FRA150M Aerobat	FRA1500317		8.11.76	Oxford Aviation Services Ltd	Oxford	27.10.03T
G-BEIF	Cameron O-65 HAB	259		17.11.76	C Vening	Kirdford	25. 3.90A
					(Op Balloon Preservation Group) "Solitaire"		
G-BEIG	Reims/Cessna F150M	F15001361		18.11.76	T.J.Chapman	(Beccles)	26. 6.05T
G-BEII	Piper PA-25-235 Pawnee D	25-7656059	N54918	16.11.76	Burn Gliding Club Ltd	Burn	7. 4.05T
G-BEIL	SOCATA Rallye 150T	2653	F-BXDL	1.12.76	J.I.Oakes & R.A.Harris	Hill Farm, Nayland	2. 4.04
					tr The Rallye Flying Group		
G-BEIP	Piper PA-28-181 Cherokee Archer II	28-7790158	N6628F	22.11.76	S.Pope	Barton	16. 9.04
G-BEIS	Evans VP-1	PFA 7029		25.11.76	P.J.Hunt	Thruxton	16. 7.90P
	(Volkswagen 1600)				*(Stored 2.99: current status unknown)*		
G-BEJD	Avro 748 Srs.1/105	1543	LV-HHE	17.12.76	Emerald Airways Ltd	Liverpool	29. 3.03T
			LV-PUF		*(Reed Aviation titles) "Sisyphus"*		
G-BEJK	Cameron S-31 HAB	256		1.12.76	N.H.Ponsford & A.Lindsay	Leeds	16. 2.92A
					t/a Rango Balloon & Kite Co *"L'Essence" (or "Esso")*		
G-BEJL	Sikorsky S-61N Mk.II	61-224	EI-BPK	30.12.76	CHC Scotia Ltd	Aberdeen	30. 9.98
			G-BEJL/N4606G		*(Stored 2002)*		
G-BEJV	Piper PA-34-200T Seneca II	34-7770062	N7657F	31.12.76	Oxford Aviation Services Ltd	Oxford	12. 4.03T
G-BEKL	Bede BD-4E-150	151 & BD4E/2	(G-AYKB)	11. 1.77	F.E.Tofield	(Farnborough)	14.10.80P
	(Lycoming O-320)				*(New owner 4.02)*		
G-BEKM	Evans VP-1	PFA 7025		12. 1.77	G.J.McDill	Westmoor Far, Thirsk	23. 3.95P
	(Volkswagen 1834)				*(Stored 7.98: new CofR 1.03)*		
G-BEKN	Reims/Cessna FRA150M Aerobat	FRA1500318		12. 1.77	A.L.Brown	Bourn	8.10.89T
					(Open store without engines 11.01: new owner 7.02)		
G-BEKO	Reims/Cessna F182Q Skylane	F182000037		12. 1.77	G.J. & F.J.Leese	Old Buckenham	11. 6.03
G-BELF	Fairey Britten-Norman BN-2A-26 Islander	823	D-IBRA	13. 1.77	The Black Knights Parachute Centre Ltd	Cumbernauld	12. 3.01
	(Built IRMA)		G-BELF		*(Derelict 2.03)*		
G-BELP	Piper PA-28-151 Cherokee Warrior	28-7715219	N9543N	18. 1.77	Aerohire Ltd	Wolverhampton	2. 8.04T
G-BELT	Cessna F150J	F150-0409X		26. 1.77	Aero-Dynamics Ltd	Gloucestershire	22. 8.04T
	(Built Reims Aviation SA) (Mainly rebuild of G-AWUV & parts of G-ATND)						
G-BELX*	Cameron V-56 HAB	261		31. 1.77	V. & A.M.Dyer	Launceston	15. 8.93A
					"Topsy Taffy" (Cancelled 15.10.01 by CAA)		
G-BEMB	Reims/Cessna F172M Skyhawk II	F17201487		27. 1.77	Stocklaunch Ltd	Goodwood	23. 4.04T
G-BEMM	Slingsby Cadet III	1247	BGA942	27. 1.77	B.J.Douglas	Newtownards, Co.Down	24. 3.03P
	(Volkswagen 1600) *(Converted from T.31B)*		RAFGSA 289/BGA942				
G-BEMU	Thunder Ax5-42 HAB	097		9. 2.77	M.A.Hall *"Chrysophylax"*	Stoneleigh	16. 1.99A
G-BEMW	Piper PA-28-181 Cherokee Archer II	28-7790243	N9566N	9. 2.77	Touch & Go Ltd	White Waltham	10. 9.03
G-BEMY	Reims/Cessna FRA150M Aerobat	FRA1500315		9. 2.77	A J Roper & P A L Baker	Rochester	12.11.04T
G-BEND	Cameron V-56 HAB	260		14. 2.77	P.J.Bish tr Dante Balloon Group *Le Billet"*	Hungerford	1. 1.94A
G-BENF*	Cessna T210L Turbo Centurion II	21061356	N732AE	17. 2.77	Not known	Cherry Tree Farm, Monewden	
			D-EIPY/N732AE		*(Crashed Ipswich 29.5.81: cancelled 25.3.85 as destroyed) (In open storage 6.00)*		
G-BENJ	Rockwell Commander 112B	522	N1391J	7. 3.77	E.J.Percival	Blackbushe	3. 8.03
G-BENK	Reims/Cessna F172M Skyhawk II	F17201509		2. 3.77	Graham Churchill Plant Ltd	Turweston	4. 6.03
G-BENN	Cameron V-56 HAB	278		4. 3.77	S.J.Hollingsworth & M.K.Bellamy	Bleasby, Notts	15. 3.87A
					"English Rose" (New owners 10.01)		
G-BEOE	Reims/Cessna FRA150M Aerobat	FRA1500322		21. 3.77	W.J.Henderson t/a Air Images	Carlisle	11. 7.03T
G-BEOH	Piper PA-28R-201T Turbo Cherokee Arrow III	28R-7703038	N1905H	11. 3.77	J.J.Evendon	Blackbushe	6. 7.04
					tr G-BEOH Group		
G-BEOI	Piper PA-18-150 Super Cub	18-7709028	N54976	11. 3.77	Southdown Gliding Club Ltd	Parham Park	17.12.04
	(Lycoming O-360-A4)						
G-BEOK	Reims/Cessna F150M	F15001366		14. 3.77	D.C.Bonsall	Netherthorpe	11. 5.03T
G-BEOL	Short SC.7 Skyvan 3 Var.100	SH.1954	ZS-OIO	16. 3.77	Invicta Aviation Ltd	Manston	11. 3.03T
			JA8803(2)/G-BEOL/G-14-122				
G-BEOY	Reims/Cessna FRA150L Aerobat	FRA1500150	F-BTFS	30. 3.77	R.W.Denny *(Op Crowfield Flying Club)*	Crowfield	27. 3.05T
G-BEPC	SNCAN Stampe SV-4C	64	F-BFUM	17.10.77	Papa Charlie's Flying Circus Ltd	Dunkeswell	24. 3.01T
			F-BFZM/Fr.Mil				
G-BEPF	SNCAN Stampe SV-4C	424	F-BCVD	30. 3.77	L.J.Rice *(Stored 4.02)*	Chilbolton	
G-BEPS	Short SC.5 Belfast C.1	SH.1822	G-52-13	6. 4.77	Heavylift Aviation Holdings Ltd	Southend	31. 8.02T
			XR368		*(Wfu & stored for spares 2.03)*		
G-BEPV	Fokker S.11.1 Instructor	6274	PH-ANK	13. 4.77	L.C.MacKnight	Spanhoe	15. 4.93P
			Dutch Navy 174/E-31 Dutch AF		*(As "174" Dutch Navy 3.02) (On overhaul 12.02)*		
G-BEPY	Rockwell Commander 112B	524	N1399J	20. 4.77	S.A.Pigden	Standalone Farm, Meppershall	28. 6.04
					tr G-BEPY Group		
G-BERA	SOCATA Rallye 150ST	2821	F-ODEX	13. 4.77	P.J.Bloore & J.M.Biles	Bidford	10. 8.03T
G-BERC	SOCATA Rallye 150ST	2858		13. 4.77	R S Jones tr The Severn Valley Aero Group	Welshpool	5. 8.05
G-BERD	Thunder Ax6-56A HAB	106		25. 4.77	P.M.Gaines *"Goldfinger"*	Stockton-on-Tees	24. 4.03A
					(Inflated 4.02)		
G-BERI	Rockwell Commander 114	14234	N4909W	6. 5.77	K.B.Harper	Blackbushe	12. 5.03
G-BERN	Saffery S.330 MLB	4		19. 4.77	B.Martin *"Beeze I" (Noted 9.02)*	Somersham, Cambs	
G-BERT	Cameron V-56 HAB	273		19. 4.77	Semajan Ltd tr Southern Balloon Group *"Bert"*	Romsey	15. 5.03A
G-BERW	Rockwell Commander 114	14214	N4884W	6. 5.77	Romeo Whisky Ltd	Old Buckenham	5. 5.04
G-BERY	Grumman-American AA-1B Trainer	0193	N9693L	27.10.77	R.H.J.Levi	Stapleford	20. 6.04
G-BETD	Robin HR200/100 Club	20	PH-SRL	28. 4.77	W.A.Stewart	North Connel, Oban	18. 2.02
G-BETE	Rollason Beta B.2A	PFA 02-10169		26. 4.77	T.M.Jones	Egginton, Derby	
	(Incorporates parts from PFA 1304)				*(Under construction 8.99: current status unknown)*		
G-BETG	Cessna 180K Skywagon	180-52873	N64146	17. 5.77	E.G.& N.S.C.English	North Weald	11. 6.03
G-BETL	Piper PA-25-235 Pawnee D	25-7656016	N54874	27. 5.77	Cambridge Gliding Club Ltd	Gransden Lodge	11.12.03
G-BETM	Piper PA-25-235 Pawnee D	25-7656066	N54927	5. 5.77	Yorkshire Gliding Club (Pty) Ltd	Sutton Bank	9. 4.04
G-BETO	Morane Saulnier MS.885 Super Rallye	34	F-BKED	18. 5.77	A.J. & A.Hawley	Farley Farm, Romsey	11.12.04
					tr G-BETO Group		
G-BETP*	Cameron O-65 HAB	286		3. 5.77	J.R.Rix & Sons Ltd *"Rix"*	Hull	12. 6.88A
					(Cancelled 2.11.01 as WFU & stored)		

Regn	Type	C/n	Prev id	Date	Owner	Base	Date
G-BETT	Piper PA-34-200 Seneca	34-7250011	EI-BCD PH-AVM/N1978T	20. 6.77	D.F.J.Flashman *(New CofR 6.02)*	Biggin Hill	28. 7.99A
G-BETW	Rand Robinson KR-2	PFA 129-10251		26. 4.77	S.C.Solley	Clipgate Farm, Denton	
	(Original c/n allocated as KR-2/TAW.1 but PFA project no issued to T A Wiffen as VP-1 [62-10251]: presume VP-1 abandoned in favour of KR-2 (PFA 129 srs.): valid CofR 4.02)						
G-BEUA	Piper PA-18-150 Super Cub (Lycoming O-360-A4)	18-8212	D-ECSY N4146Z	21. 6.77	London Gliding Club Pty Ltd	Dunstable	27. 2.03
G-BEUD	Robin HR100/285 Tiara	534	F-BXRC	8. 6.77	E.A. & L.M.C.Payton	Cranfield	11. 8.05
G-BEUI	Piper J-3C-65 Cub (L-4H-PI)	12174	F-BFEC F-OAJF/Fr.AF/44-79878	19. 5.77	B.W.Webb tr G-BEUI Group	(Canterbury)	25. 2.02P
	(Frame No.12002) (Regd as ex 43-29245)						
G-BEUM	Taylor JT.1 Monoplane (Volkswagen 1700)	PFA 1438		8. 6.77	J.M.Burgess	St Just	1. 8.02P
G-BEUN	Cassutt Racer IIIM (Continental C90)	PFA 34-10241		20. 2.78	R.McNulty *(Noted 1.03)*	Bourn	7. 7.97P
G-BEUP	Robin DR400/180 Regent	1228		19. 5.77	Legal Week Ltd t/a Samuels Aviation	Biggin Hill	4. 4.04T
G-BEUU	Piper PA-18 Super Cub 95 (L-18C-PI) *(Frame No.should be 18-1523)*	18-1551	F-BOUU ALAT 18-1551/51-15551	27. 6.77	F.Sharples	Sandown	1.10.03P
G-BEUX	Reims/Cessna F172N	F17201596		30. 5.77	Multiflight Ltd	Leeds-Bradford	16.11.03T
G-BEUY	Cameron N-31 HAB	283		31. 5.77	M.L. & L.P.Willoughby *(Typhoo Tea titles) (Inflated 4.02)*	Reading	17.10.90A
G-BEVB	SOCATA Rallye 150ST	2860		2. 6.77	N.R.Haines	RAF Hullavington	16. 5.05
G-BEVC	SOCATA Rallye 150ST	2861		2. 6.77	B.W.Walpole	Swanton Morley	6. 7.03
G-BEVG	Piper PA-34-200T Seneca II	34-7570060	VQ-SAM N32854	31. 5.77	A.G.& J.Wintle	Elstree	3.10-.05T
G-BEVO	Sportavia Fournier RF5	5107	5N-AIX D-KAAZ	27. 6.77	D.G.Hey & W.E.R.Jenkins *(New owners 2.02)*	Little Gransden	20. 8.96P
G-BEVR	Fairey Britten-Norman BN-2A Mk.III-2 Trislander	1056	6Y-JQE G-BEVR/XA-THE(2)/G-BEVR	10. 6.77	Cormack (Aircraft Services) Ltd *(Noted 2.03)*	Cumbernauld	6. 7.82S
G-BEVS	Taylor JT.1 Monoplane (Volkswagen 1835)	PFA 1429		8. 6.77	D.Hunter	Kemble	8. 8.03P
G-BEVT	Fairey Britten-Norman BN-2A Mk.III-2 Trislander	1057		10. 6.77	Aurigny Air Services Ltd *(Islands Insurance titles)*	Guernsey	15.11.03T
G-BEVV	Fairey Britten-Norman BN.2A Mk.111-2 Trislander	1059	6Y-JQK G-BNZD/G-BEVV	10. 6.77	Cormack (Aero Club Services) Ltd *(Noted 2.03)*	Cumbernauld	
G-BEVW	SOCATA Rallye 150ST	2928		2. 6.77	P.G.A.Sumner	Town Farm, Woolaston	27. 3.03
G-BEWN	de Havilland DH.82A Tiger Moth	952	VH-WAL RAAF A17-529	16. 6.77	H.D.Labouchere	Blue Tile Farm, Langham	18. 7.03
	(Built DH Australia - rebuild c/n T305)						
G-BEWO	Moravan Zlin Z.326 Trener Master	915	CS-ALU	23.11.77	P.A.Colman	Luxters Farm, Hambleden, Henley-on-Thames	2. 7.03
G-BEWP*	Reims/Cessna F150M	F15001426		13. 6.77	Perth College	Perth	12. 8.85
	(Crashed Aboyne 4.10.83: cancelled 5.12.83 as destroyed: instructional use 3.02)						
G-BEWR	Reims/Cessna F172N Skyhawk II	F17201613		13. 6.77	Cheshire Air Training Services Ltd	Liverpool	3. 5.04T
G-BEWX	Piper PA-28R-201 Cherokee Arrow III	28R-7737070	N5723V	23. 6.77	A.Vickers	North Weald	23. 5.03
G-BEWY	Bell 206B JetRanger II	348	G-CULL EI-BXQ/G-BEWY/9Y-TDF	27. 6.77	Polo Aviation Ltd	Bristol	13. 5.04T
G-BEXN	Grumman-American AA-1C Lynx	AA1C-0045	N6147A	7. 9.77	D.F.Hurn	Popham	6. 4.03
G-BEXO	Piper PA-23 Apache	23-213	OO-APH N1176P	4. 7.77	G.R.Moore & A.K.Hulme	Rayne Hall Farm, Rayne	13. 8.03
G-BEXW	Piper PA-28-181 Cherokee Archer II	28-7790521	N38122	11. 7.77	T.R.Kingsley	Norwich	23. 3.03T
G-BEXX	Cameron V-56 HAB	274		29. 6.77	K.A.Schlussler *"Rupert of Rutland"*	Bourne	2. 7.86A
G-BEXZ	Cameron N-56 HAB	294		7. 7.77	D.C.Eager & G.C.Clark *"Valor"*	Bracknell/Worcester	13. 4.97A
G-BEYA	Enstrom 280C Shark	1104		15. 8.77	Hovercam Ltd	Staddon Heights, Plymouth	11. 2.04T
G-BEYL	Piper PA-28-180 Cherokee Archer	28-7405098	PH-SDW N9518N	6. 9.77	J.Baker tr Yankee Lima Group	Compton Abbas	28. 3.04
G-BEYN*	Evans VP-2	V2-3167 & PFA 63-10271		1. 8.77	H P Vox & T Rayner	East Fortune	
	(Cancelled 2.9.91 by CAA) (Incomplete airframe stored in hangar roof 6.00)						
G-BEYO	Piper PA-28-140 Cherokee Cruiser	28-7725215	N9648N	14. 7.77	W.B.Bateson	Blackpool	30. 5.04T
G-BEYT	Piper PA-28-140 Cherokee	28-20330	D-EBWO N6280W	19. 7.77	B.A.Mills *(Noted 10.01)*	Bourne	
G-BEYV	Cessna T210M Turbo Centurion II	210-61583	N732KX	19. 7.77	P.J.W. & N.Austen t/a Austen Aviation	Guernsey	13. 4.04T
G-BEYW	Taylor JT.1 Monoplane RJS.100 & PFA 55-10279 (Volkswagen 1834)			22. 7.77	R.A.Abrahams *"Red Hot"*	Barton	22. 4.03P
G-BEYZ	CEA Jodel DR.1050/MI Sicile Record	588	F-BMGV	22. 7.77	M.L.Balding	Biggin Hill	4. 6.03
G-BEZC	Grumman-American AA-5 Traveler	AA5-0493	F-BUYN (N7193L)	29. 7.77	T.V.Montgomery	Elstree	25. 7.04
G-BEZE	Rutan VariEze (Continental O-200-A)	PFA 74-10207		26. 7.77	S.K.Cockburn *(New owner 6.02)*	Biggin Hill	2. 6.92P
G-BEZF	Grumman-American AA-5 Traveler	AA5-0538	F-BVJP	29. 7.77	RAF College Flying Club Ltd	RAF Cranwell	17.12.04T
G-BEZG	Grumman-American AA-5 Traveler	AA5-0561	F-BVRJ	29. 7.77	M.D.R.Harling	Andrewsfield	31. 5.05
G-BEZH	Grumman-American AA-5 Traveler	AA5-0566	F-BVRK N9566L	29. 7.77	L. & S.M.Sims	Fenland	6. 3.04
G-BEZI	Grumman-American AA-5 Traveler	AA5-0567	F-BVRL N9567L	29. 7.77	Heather Matthews tr The BEZI Flying Group	Cranfield	21. 6.04
G-BEZK(2)	Cessna F172H *(Built Reims Aviation SA)*	F172-0462	D-EBUD D-ENHC/SLN-07/N20462	17. 8.77	C.F.Strowger	Beccles	18. 7.02
G-BEZL	Piper PA-31 Navajo C	31-7712054	SE-GPA	1. 8.77	A.Jahanfar *(Op JRB Aviation)*	Southend	29. 6.03T
G-BEZO	Reims/Cessna F172M Skyhawk II	F17201392		24. 8.77	Gloucestershire Flying Services Ltd	Gloucestershire	1. 4.04T
G-BEZP	Piper PA-32-300 Cherokee Six	32-7740087	N38572	19. 8.77	W.D.McNab & T.P.McCormack	White Waltham	3. 4.04
G-BEZR	Reims/Cessna F172M Skyhawk II	F17201395		24. 8.77	Kirmington Aviation Ltd	Sandown	8. 5.04T
G-BEZS*	Reims FR172J Rocket	FR1720562	(I-CCAJ)	11. 8.77	Not known	Bourn	22. 9.79
	(Damaged near Stapleford 15.6.79: front fuselage stored 11.01)						
G-BEZV	Reims/Cessna F172M Skyhawk II	F17201474	(I-CCAY)	24. 8.77	A.T.Wilson tr Insch Flying Group	Insch	21. 4.04

G-BEZY	Rutan VariEze	1167 & PFA 74-10225		26. 7.77	I.J.Pountney	(Malvern)	18. 5.96P
	(Continental PC60)						
G-BEZZ	Jodel D.112	397	F-BHMC	12. 8.77	M.J.Coles	Barton	3. 8.03P
	(Built Passot Aviation)				tr G-BEZZ Jodel Group		

G-BFAA - G-BFZZ

G-BFAA	SOCATA GY-80-160 Horizon	78	F-BLVY	20.10.77	Mary Poppins Ltd	(Stoke-on-Trent)	18.11.90
					(Current status unknown)		
G-BFAF	Aeronca 7BCM Champion	7BCM-11	N797US	15. 8.77	D.C.W.Harper	Finmere	30. 8.01P
	(L-16A-AE)		N2552B/47-797		(As "7797" in US Army c/s)		
G-BFAH	Phoenix Currie Wot	PFA 3017		22. 8.77	R.W.Clarke	(Cheadle)	
	(Continental O-200A) (Initially allocated with PFA project no 3017)						
	(Now being built as Replica SE-5A in RFC c/s and regd officially as c/n PFA 58-11376 but probably confused with PFA 101-11376,						
	a Sopwith Pup replica by same former owner/builder)						
G-BFAI	Rockwell Commander 114	14304	N4984W	17. 8.77	G.Gore-Brown	Sherburn-in-Elmet	8.12.05
					tr Alpha India Flying Group		
G-BFAK	GEMS MS.892A Rallye Commodore 150	10595	F-BNNJ	9. 8.77	J.M.Hedges	Lower Upham Farm, Chiseldon	19. 4.04
G-BFAM*	Piper PA-31P Pressurised Navajo	31P-39	SE-GLV	1. 9.77	Middle East Business Club Ltd	(Guernsey)	
			OH-PNF		(Cancelled & to G-SASK 30.10.97 but noted as "G-BFAM" on repair Biggin Hill 12.00)		
G-BFAP	SIAI-Marchetti S.205-20R	4-213	I-ALEN	1. 9.77	A.O'Broin	Raby's Farm, Great Stukeley	11. 6.03
G-BFAS	Evans VP-1 Srs.2	PFA 7033		15. 8.77	A.I.Sutherland	Fearn	18. 3.03P
	(Volkswagen 1834)						
G-BFAW	de Havilland DHC-1 Chipmunk 22	C1/0733	8342M	31. 8.77	R.V.Bowles	Husbands Bosworth	23.10.03
			WP848				
G-BFAX	de Havilland DHC-1 Chipmunk 22	C1/0496	8394M	31. 8.77	A.C.Kerr	Strathaven	23. 6.05
			WG422		(As "WG422")		
G-BFBA	SAN Jodel DR.100A Ambassadeur	88	F-BIVU	12. 9.77	W.H.Sherlock	Drayton Manor, Drayton St.Leonard	24.10.05
G-BFBB	Piper PA-23-250 Aztec E	27-7405294	SE-GBI	1. 9.77	Air Training Services Ltd	Booker	16. 6.04T
G-BFBC	Taylor JT.1 Monoplane	PFA 55-10280		5. 9.77	G Heins	(Rochdale)	
	(Volkswagen 1600)				(Under construction 2.93: new owner 1.02)		
G-BFBE	Robin HR200/100	12	PH-SRK	9. 9.77	A.C.Pearson	Rochester	23. 3.02
G-BFBF	Piper PA-28-140 Cherokee F	28-7325240	EI-BMG	9. 9.77	Marham Investments Ltd	Belfast	9. 5.05T
			G-BFBF/PH-SRF		(Op Woodgate Executive Air Services)		
G-BFBM	Saffery S.330 MLB	7		1. 9.77	B.Martin "Beeze II" (Noted 9.02)	Somersham, Cambs	
G-BFBR	Piper PA-28-161 Cherokee Warrior II	28-7716277	N38845	15. 9.77	M.R.Paul t/a Malcolm R Paul Racing	(Shere)	13. 2.04T
G-BFBU	Partenavia P68B Victor	24	SE-FTM	25. 1.78	Premiair Charter Ltd	Bournemouth	24. 4.03T
	(C/n indicates P68 model)						
G-BFBY	Piper J-3C-65 Cub (L-4H-PI)	10998	F-BDTG	29. 9.77	U.Schuhmacher	Hahn, Germany	7. 9.01P
			43-29707				
G-BFCT	Cessna TU206F Turbo Stationair II	U20603202	(LN-TVF)	15. 9.77	Just Plane Trading Ltd	Top Farm, Croydon, Royston	26. 1.04
			N8341Q				
G-BFDC	de Havilland DHC-1 Chipmunk 22	C1/0525	7989M	15.11.77	N.F.O'Neill	Newtownards, Co.Down	12. 6.03
			WG475				
G-BFDF	SOCATA Rallye 235E	12834	F-GAKT	6.10.77	M.A.Wratten	Bourne Park, Hurstbourne Tarrant	2. 5.05
G-BFDI	Piper PA-28-181 Cherokee Archer II	28-7790382	N2205Q	5.10.77	Truman Aviation Ltd	Nottingham	1.10.04T
G-BFDK	Piper PA-28-161 Warrior II	28-7816010	N40061	23. 9.77	S.T.Gilbert	Enstone	9. 5.04T
G-BFDL	Piper J-3C-65 Cub (L-4J-PI)	13277	HB-OIF	30.11.77	A.F.Nicholson	Shempstone Farm, Lossiemouth	7. 4.03P
	(Continental O-200-A) (Frame No.13107)		45-4537		(As "454537/04-J" in US Army c/s)		
G-BFDO	Piper PA-28R-201T Turbo Cherokee Arrow III		N38396	3.10.77	A.J.Gow	Denham	12.11.05
		28R-7703212					
G-BFDV*	Westland WG.13 Lynx HC.28	WA/028	TAD.013	3.10.77	SEAE Princess Marina College	Arborfield	
	(Originally regd as "Lynx 02F")		Qatar AF 1/G-17-20		(Cancelled 6.78) (As instructional airframe "QP-30" 7.02)		
G-BFDZ	Taylor JT.1 Monoplane	PFA 55-10185		5.10.77	J.A.Hanslip	Fenland	8. 8.03P
	(Volkswagen 1600)						
G-BFEB	SAN Jodel 150 Mascaret	34	F-BMJR	14.10.77	A.W.Russell	Portmoak	17. 6.03P
			OO-LDY/F-BLDX		tr Jodel Syndicate		
G-BFEF	Agusta-Bell 47G-3B1	1541	XT132	11.10.77	M.P.Wilkinson	Sandtoft	8. 7.05T
G-BFEH	SAN Jodel D.117A	828	F-BITG	5.10.77	J.A.Crabb	Dunkeswell	18.11.03P
G-BFEK	Reims/Cessna F152 II	F152201442		11.10.77	Gloucestershire Flying Services Ltd	Gloucestershire	20. 2.04T
G-BFER	Bell 212	30835	N18099	7.11.77	Bristow Helicopters Ltd	(Kazakhstan)	27.11.05T
G-BFEV	Piper PA-25-235 Pawnee D	25-7756060	N82547	20.10.77	Trent Valley Aerotowing Club Ltd	Kirton-in-Lindsey	18. 4.04
G-BFEW	Piper PA-25-235 Pawnee D	25-7756062	N82553	20.10.77	Cornish Gliding & Flying Club Ltd	Perranporth	25. 3.04
G-BFFC	Reims/Cessna F152 II	F15201451		27.10.77	Multiflight Ltd	Leeds-Bradford	15.11.04T
G-BFFE	Reims/Cessna F152 II	F15201454		27.10.77	A.J.Hastings	Edinburgh	19. 4.98T
					(Damaged 13.3.97: on rebuild 5.01)		
G-BFFJ	Sikorsky S-61N Mk.II	61-777	N6231	17. 1.78	Veritair Ltd "Tresco"	Penzance	22. 3.03T
G-BFFP	Piper PA-18-150 Super Cub	18-8187	PH-OTC	9.11.77	East Sussex Gliding Club Ltd	Ringmer	7. 5.04
	(Lycoming O-360-A4) (Frame No.18-8402)		N10F				
G-BFFT	Cameron V-56 HAB	360		7.11.77	R.I.McKean Kerr & D.C.Boxall	Bristol	16. 2.03A
					tr The Red Section Balloon Group "Red Leader"		
G-BFFW	Reims/Cessna F152 II	F15201447		14.11.77	Tayside Aviation Ltd	Dundee	12. 6.04T
G-BFFY	Reims/Cessna F150M	F15001376		14.11.77	G.A.Rodmell	Linley Hill, Leven	26. 3.04T
G-BFFZ	Reims/Cessna FR172K Hawk XPII	FR17200603	F-WZDU	14.11.77	E.Francis	Compton Abbas	15. 6.03T
G-BFGD	Reims/Cessna F172N Skyhawk II	F17201545	F-WZDT	14.11.77	J.T.Armstrong	Fairoaks	4.10.04T
G-BFGG	Reims/Cessna FRA150M Aerobat	FRA1500321	F-WZDS	14.11.77	S.J.Windle	Bodmin	5. 4.04T
G-BFGH	Reims/Cessna F337G Skymaster II	F33700081		14.11.77	T.Perkins	Bagby	5. 7.02
	(Wichita c/n 33701754)						
G-BFGK	SAN Jodel D.117	644	F-BIBT	27. 6.78	B.F.J.Hope	Stoneacre Farm, Farthing Corner	19. 6.03P
G-BFGL	Reims/Cessna FA152 Aerobat	FA1520339		14.11.77	Multiflight Ltd	Leeds-Bradford	10. 5.04T
G-BFGO*	Fuji FA.200-160 Aero Subaru	219	PH-KDB	25.11.77	R.J.Everett	Cranfield	23. 8.92
					(Damaged Rush Green 18.8.93: stored 7.96: cancelled 31.10.00 by CAA: current status unknown)		

Reg	Type	C/n	Prev id	Date	Owner	Location	Date
G-BFGS	SOCATA MS.893E Rallye 180GT	12571	F-BXYK Fr.AF 12571 FSCAZ/"41-AZ"	31. 8.76	Chiltern Flyers Ltd	Park Farm, Eaton Bray	15. 9.03
G-BFGW	Cessna F150H (Built Reims Aviation SA)	F150-0370	PH-TGO	24.11.77	C.E.Stringer (Current status unknown)	Humberside	19.10.95T
G-BFGX	Reims/Cessna FRA150M Aerobat	FRA1500328	F-BUDX	28.11.77	Prestwick Flight Centre Ltd	Prestwick	27. 8.04T
G-BFGZ	Reims/Cessna FRA150M Aerobat	FRA1500329		28.11.77	C.M.Barnes	Garden Piece, Basingstoke	10. 3.03T
G-BFHH	de Havilland DH.82A Tiger Moth	85933	F-BDOH Fr.AF/DF197	25.11.77	P.Harrison & M.J.Gambrell	Swanborough Farm, Lewes	22.10.03
G-BFHI	Piper J-3C-65 Cub (L-4J-PI)	12532	F-BFBT 44-80236	25.11.77	N Glass & A J Richardson	Bann Foot, Lough Neagh	26. 1.00P
G-BFHP	Champion 7GCAA Citabria	114	HB-UAX	8.12.77	A.M.Read	Turweston	13.10.05T
G-BFHR	CEA Jodel DR.220 2 + 2	30	F-BOCX	1.12.77	J.E.Sweetman	Bourne Park, Hurstbourne Tarrant	19. 6.03
G-BFHT	Reims/Cessna F152 II	F15201441		7.12.77	Westward Airways (Lands End) Ltd	St.Just	14. 5.04T
G-BFHU	Reims/Cessna F152 II	F15201461		7.12.77	D.J.Cooke	Hawarden	11.10.04T
G-BFHV	Reims/Cessna F152 II	F15201470		21.12.77	A.S.Bamrah t/a Falcon Flying Services	Rochester	22.11.04T
G-BFHX	Evans VP-1 (Volkswagen 1600)	PFA 62-10283		2.12.77	A.D.Bohanna & D.I.Trussler	Popham	7. 4.99P
G-BFIB	Piper PA-31 Turbo Navajo	31-684	LN-NPE OY-DVH/LN-RTJ	21.12.77	Richard Hannon Ltd	Lee-on-Solent	26.12.03T
G-BFID	Taylor JT.2 Titch Mk.III (Continental O-200-A)	PFA 60-10311		13.12.77	N.A.Scully (Damaged Breighton 31.5.99)	Griffins Farm, Temple Bruer	23. 8.99P
G-BFIE	Reims/Cessna FRA150M Aerobat	FRA1500331		12. 1.78	G-BFIE Ltd	Manston	14.12.03T
G-BFIG	Reims/Cessna FR172K Hawk XPII	FR17200615		12. 1.78	Tenair Ltd	Barton	2. 1.04
G-BFIJ	Grumman-American AA-5A Cheetah	AA5A-0486	N6160A	1. 3.78	T.H.& M.G.Weetman	West Freugh/Prestwick	23. 1.04
G-BFIN	Grumman-American AA-5A Cheetah	AA5A-0520	N6145A	22. 3.78	Prestwick Flight Centre Ltd	Prestwick	2. 5.05T
G-BFIT	Thunder Ax6-56Z HAB	136		20.12.77	J A G Tyson "Folly" (New CofR 4.02)	Torphins	3. 5.91
G-BFIU	Reims/Cessna FR172K Hawk XP	FR17200591	N96098	12. 1.78	B.M.Jobling	Hinton in the Hedges	18. 5.03
G-BFIV	Reims/Cessna F177RG Cardinal RG II	F177RG0161	N96106	12. 1.78	Kingfishair Ltd	Blackbushe	27. 5.05
G-BFIX	Thunder Ax7-77A HAB	133		9.12.77	R.Owen "Animal Magic"	Wigan	23. 1.79S
G-BFIY	Reims/Cessna F150M	F15001381	OE-CMT	11. 1.78	R J Scott	(Bracknell)	23. 6.02T
G-BFJJ	Evans VP-1 (Volkswagen 1800)	PFA 62-10273		30.12.77	N.Clark (New owner 12.02)	Farley Farm, Romsey	23. 6.96P
G-BFJR	Reims/Cessna F337G Skymaster II (Wichita c/n 33701761)	F33700082	N46297 (N53658)	4. 1.78	Mannix Aviation	East Midlands	9. 4.05
G-BFJZ	Robin DR400/140B Major	1290		20. 1.78	Weald Air Services Ltd	Headcorn	26. 8.04T
G-BFKB	Reims/Cessna F172N Skyhawk II	F17201601	PH-AXO	16. 1.78	R.L.Clarke & D.Tench tr Shropshire Flying Group	(Crewe)	2. 3.03T
G-BFKC	Rand Robinson KR-2	KKC.5 & PFA 129-10809		20. 1.78	L.H.S.Stephens & I.S.Hewitt	(Littleover, Derby)	
G-BFKF	Reims/Cessna FA152 Aerobat	FA1520337		26. 1.78	Aerolease Ltd	Conington	27. 4.04T
G-BFKH	Reims/Cessna F152 II	F15201464		26. 1.78	TG Aviation Ltd (Op Thanet Flying Club)	Manston	26. 3.04T
G-BFKL	Cameron N-56 HAB	369		23. 1.78	Merrythought Ltd	Telford	17. 7.92A
G-BFKY	Piper PA-34-200 Seneca	34-7350318	PH-NAZ N56332	22. 2.78	SLH Construction Ltd	Biggin Hill	23. 1.05T
G-BFLH	Piper PA-34-200T Seneca II	34-7870065	N2126M	16. 2.78	Air Medical Ltd	Oxford	8. 6.03T
			(Landed with undercarriage retracted Oxford 17.1.02: damage to propellers, underside of fuselage& flaps)				
G-BFLI	Piper PA-28-201T Turbo Arrow III	28R-7803134	N2582M	16. 2.78	J.K.Chudzicki "Spirit of Rita May"	Elstree	11. 6.04
G-BFLP*	Amethyst Ax6-56 HAB	001		20. 2.78	K.J.Hendry "Amethyst" (Cancelled 22.11.01 as WFU &.stored)	Gillingham, Kent	
G-BFLU	Reims/Cessna F152 II	F15201433		15. 2.78	Bravo Aviation Ltd (Op Air Alpha/Dalcross Flying Club)	Inverness	17. 5.04T
G-BFLX	Grumman-American AA-5A Cheetah	AA5A-0524	N6147A	14. 3.78	G Force Two Ltd	Blackbushe	23.11.04
G-BFLZ	Beech 95-A55 Baron	TC-220	PH-ILE HB-GOV	16. 3.78	K.A.Graham t/a Caterite Food Service	Carlisle	23. 8.04
G-BFME*	Cameron V-56 HAB	371		17. 2.78	A.Mayes & V.Lawton t/a Warwick Balloons "Avon Lad" (Cancelled 10.10.01 by CAA)	Leamington Spa	29. 1.88A
G-BFMG	Piper PA-28-161 Cherokee Warrior II	28-7716160	N3506Q	11. 5.78	Stardial Ltd	Fairoaks	17.10.05T
G-BFMH	Cessna 177B Cardinal	17702034	N34836	18. 4.78	Span Aviation Ltd	Newcastle	16. 6.05T
G-BFMK	Reims/Cessna FA152 Aerobat	FA1520344		6. 3.78	RAF Halton Aeroplane Club Ltd	RAF Halton	20. 3.05T
G-BFMR	Piper PA-20 Pacer 125	20-130	N7025K	20. 2.78	J.Knight	Headcorn	14. 2.03
G-BFMX	Reims/Cessna F172N Skyhawk II	F17201732		24. 8.78	A2Z Wholesale Fashion Jewellery Ltd	Farley Farm, Romsey	1. 8.03
G-BFMZ	Payne Ax6-62 HAB	GFP.2		1. 3.78	E.G.Woolnough (Active 8.99)	Halesworth, Suffolk	
G-BFNG	Wassmer Jodel D.112	1321	F-BNHI	6. 3.78	M.T.Taylor	Griffins Farm, Temple Bruer	21.10.03P
G-BFNI	Piper PA-28-161 Warrior II	28-7816290	N9505N	8. 3.78	P.Elliott	Biggin Hill	26. 7.05
G-BFNJ	Piper PA-28-161 Warrior II	28-7816281	N9520N	8. 3.78	Fleetlands Flying Association Ltd	Lee-on-Solent	6. 6.04T
G-BFNK	Piper PA-28-161 Warrior II	28-7816282	N9527N	8. 3.78	Oxford Aviation Services Ltd	Oxford	9. 1.06T
G-BFNU*	Britten-Norman BN-2B-21 Islander (Built IRMA)	877		16. 3.78	Isles of Scilly Skybus Ltd (Cancelled 28.1.94 as WFU) (Dismantled 4.02)	St.Just	18. 8.89T
G-BFOD	Reims/Cessna F182Q Skylane II	F18200068		23. 3.78	G.N.Clarke	Alderney	6. 6.04
G-BFOE	Reims/Cessna F152 II	F15201475		23. 3.78	Redhill Air Services Ltd	Redhill	19.12.02T
G-BFOF	Reims/Cessna F152 II	F15201448		9. 3.78	Gloucestershire Flying Services Ltd	Gloucestershire	21. 6.05T
G-BFOG	Cessna 150M	15076223	N66706	13. 3.78	BBC Air Ltd	Compton Abbas	24. 4.04T
G-BFOJ	American AA-1 Yankee	AA1-0395	OH-AYB (LN-KAJ)/(N6195L)	4. 4.78	N.W.Thomas	Bournemouth	18.11.05
G-BFOM	Piper PA-31-325 Navajo C/R	31-7512017	EI-DMI G-BFOM/HB-LHH/N59933	17. 3.78	Ashton Air Services Ltd	(Evesham)	5. 3.05T
G-BFOP	Jodel Wassmer D.120 Paris-Nice	32	F-BHTX	23. 3.78	R.J.Wesley & G.D.Western "Jean"	Sampsons Hall, Kersey	20. 5.03P
G-BFOS	Thunder Ax6-56A HAB	147		20. 3.78	N.T.Petty "Milton Keynes"	Sudbury, Suffolk	25.11.93A
G-BFOU	Taylor JT.1 Monoplane	PFA 55-10333		17. 3.78	G.Bee (Current status unknown)	(Stockton-on-Tees)	
G-BFOV	Reims/Cessna F172N Skyhawk II	F17201675		18. 5.78	D.J.Walker	Shoreham	18.10.05
G-BFPA	Scheibe SF-25B Falke	46179	D-KAGM	29. 3.78	N.Meiklejohn & J.Steel	Falgunzeon	13. 9.98

G-BFPB	Grumman-American AA-5B Tiger	AA5B-0706		7. 4.78	P.Murphy & L.Peake	Coventry	1. 9.05
					tr Papa Bravo Flying Group		
G-BFPH	Reims/Cessna F172K	F17200802	PH-VHN	23. 3.78	M.Pollard tr Linc-Air Flying Group	Sturgate	14. 8.05
G-BFPM	Reims/Cessna F172N Skyhawk II	F17201384	PH-MIO	13. 4.78	M P Wimsey & J M Cope	Wickenby	22.12.02T
G-BFPO	Rockwell Commander 112B	530	N1412J	10. 5.78	J.G.Hale Ltd	Shoreham	9.11.03
G-BFPP	Bell 47J-2 Ranger	2851	F-BJAN	23. 5.78	M.R.Masters Phoenix Farm, Lower Upham		11.11.99
			TR-LKD/F-OCBU		*(New CofR 6.02)*		
G-BFPR	Piper PA-25-235 Pawnee D	25-7856007	SE-KGY	4. 4.78	Booker Gliding Club Ltd	Booker	23. 6.81
			I-TOZU/G-BFPR/N82591		*(New CofR 7.02)*		
G-BFPS	Piper PA-25-235 Pawnee D	25-7856013	N82598	4. 4.78	Kent Gliding Club Ltd	Challock	10. 2.03
G-BFRA*	Rockwell Commander 114	14292	N4972W	28. 3.78	Ischia Investments Ltd	Cascais, Portugal	24.10.00
					(Cancelled 15.2.00 by CAA)		
G-BFRD	Bowers FlyBaby 1A	PFA 16-10300		27. 1.78	R.A.Phillips *(Under construction 6.00)*	(Elgin)	
G-BFRF*	Taylor JT.1 Monoplane	PFA 55-10330		7. 4.78	E.R.Bailey	(Hockley, Essex)	
	(Volkswagen 1500)				*(Cancelled 3.2.03 as temporarily wfu)*		
G-BFRI	Sikorsky S-61N Mk.II	61-809		26. 5.78	Bristow Helicopters Ltd	Aberdeen	14. 6.04T
G-BFRR	Reims/Cessna FRA150M Aerobat	FRA1500326	LN-ALO	19. 4.78	S.Cosgrove tr Romeo Romeo Flying Group	Tatenhill	27. 7.03
G-BFRS	Reims/Cessna F172N Skyhawk II	F17201555	LN-ALP	19. 4.78	Poplar Models Ltd Poplar Hall Farm, Elmsett		2. 5.03T
G-BFRV	Reims/Cessna FA152 Aerobat	FA1520345		17. 4.78	Solo Services Ltd	Shoreham	25. 9.03T
G-BFRY	Piper PA-25-260 Pawnee D	25-7405789	SE-GIB	23. 5.78	Yorkshire Gliding Club (Pty) Ltd	Sutton Bank	15. 6.03
G-BFSA	Reims/Cessna F182Q Skylane II	F18200074	F-WZDG	17. 4.78	Clark Masts Teksam Ltd	Sandown	27.11.05
G-BFSC	Piper PA-25-235 Pawnee D	25-7656068	N82302	2. 6.78	Essex Gliding Club Ltd	North Weald	14. 6.04A
G-BFSD	Piper PA-25-235 Pawnee D	25-7656084	N82338	2. 6.78	Deeside Gliding Club (Aberdeenshire) Ltd	Aboyne1	18. 4.05
G-BFSR	Cessna F150J	F150-0504	OH-CBN	7. 7.78	S.Bourne	Crowfield	21. 6.04T
	(Built Reims Aviation SA)						
G-BFSS	Reims FR172G Rocket	FR17200167	OH-CDY	7. 7.78	J.R.,S.J.Goddard & F.West	Grateley, Andover	6. 4.03
					t/a Minerva Services		
G-BFSY	Piper PA-28-181 Cherokee Archer II	28-7890200	N9503N	19. 4.78	A.S.Domone t/a Downland Aviation	Goodwood	24. 5.05
G-BFTC	Piper PA-28R-201T Turbo Arrow III	28R-7803197	N3868M	19. 4.78	M.J.Milns	Sherburn-in-Elmet	22. 6.03
G-BFTF	Grumman-American AA-5B Tiger	AA5B-0879		7. 9.78	F.C.Burrow Ltd	Sherburn-in-Elmet	31. 5.03
G-BFTG	Grumman-American AA-5B Tiger	AA5B-0777		15. 5.78	D.Hepburn & G.R.Montgomery	Perth	15.10.05
G-BFTH	Reims/Cessna F172N Skyhawk II	F17201671		3. 5.78	J.Birkett	Wickenby	15. 9.05T
G-BFTT	Cessna 421C Golden Eagle II	421C-0462	N6789C	3. 5.78	M.A.Ward	(Chichester)	15. 5.03T
G-BFTX	Reims/Cessna F172N Skyhawk II	F17201715		2. 5.78	S.& R.J.Casey tr G-BFTX Group	Manston	28. 3.03
G-BFUB	Piper PA-32RT-300 Lance II	32R-7885052	N9509C	18. 5.78	Jolida Holdings Ltd	Jersey	3. 4.05
G-BFUD	Scheibe SF-25E Super Falke	4313	D-KLDC	19. 5.78	P.A.Lewis	Walney Island	13.12.04
					tr The Lakes Libelle Syndicate		
G-BFUG	Cameron N-77 HAB	394		15. 5.78	Cornwall Ballooning Adventures Ltd	Newquay	19. 4.99A
G-BFVF	Piper PA-38-112 Tomahawk	38-78A0055	N9691N	1. 6.78	Goodair Leasing Ltd	Cardiff	9.10.05T
G-BFVG	Piper PA-28-181 Cherokee Archer II	28-7890408	N31746	1. 6.78	M.S.Cornah	Blackpool	22. 6.05
			N9558N		tr G-BFVG Flying Group		
G-BFVH	Airco DH.2 rep	WA4	"5964"	1. 6.78	M.J.Kirk	Haverfordwest	20. 7.01P
	(Built Westward Airways) (125 hp Kinner B54)				*(As "5964")*		
G-BFVP	Piper PA-23-250 Aztec F	27-7854096	N63966	6. 7.78	Sub Marine Services Ltd	(Falmouth)	10. 9.05
G-BFVS	Grumman-American AA-5B Tiger	0784	N28736	11. 8.78	S.W.Biroth & T.Chapman	Denham	8.11.03
G-BFVU	Cessna 150L Commuter	15074684	N75189	10. 8.78	G.A.Luscombe	(Totnes)	12. 7.03T
G-BFWB	Piper PA-28-161 Cherokee Warrior II	28-7816584	N31752	22. 6.78	Mid-Anglia Flight Centre Ltd	Cambridge	17. 7.05T
					t/a Mid-Anglia School of Flying		
G-BFWD	Phoenix Currie Wot	PFA 3009		22. 6.78	F.R.Donaldson	Goodwood	6.10.96P
	(Walter Mikron 3)						
G-BFWE	Piper PA-23-250 Aztec E	27-4583	9M-AQT	13. 7.78	Air Navigation & Trading Co Ltd	Blackpool	15. 2.03T
			9V-BDI/N13968				
G-BFWK*	Piper PA-28-161 Warrior II	28-7816610	N9589N	23. 6.78	Marham Investments Ltd	Belfast	8.12.99T
					(Cancelled 26.5.98 as WFU) (Wrecked fuselage stored 10.01)		
G-BFWL*	Reims/Cessna F150L	F15000971	PH-KDC	4.10.78	P.Maher tr G-BFWL Flying Group	Barton	27. 3.00
					(Cancelled 21.2.00 as WFU) (Fuselage noted behind hangar 11.01)		
G-BFXF	Andreasson BA.4B	AAB-001 & PFA038-10351		10. 7.78	A.Brown	Sherburn-in-Elmet	13. 8.03P
G-BFXG	Druine D.31 Turbulent	PFA 1663		10. 7.78	E.J.I.Musty & M.J.Whatley	White Waltham	
					(Partially complete 6.00)		
G-BFXK	Piper PA-28-140 Cherokee F	28-7325387	PH-NSK	1. 8.78	I.Simpson	Kirkbride	24. 5.03
G-BFXR	Wassmer Jodel D.112	247	F-BFTM	27. 7.78	J.M.Pearson	Crosland Moor	30.11.03P
G-BFXS	Rockwell Commander 114	14271	N4949W	3. 8.78	G.L.Owens	Conington	22. 8.05
G-BFXW	Gulfstream AA-5B Tiger	AA5B-0940		21. 2.79	Campsol Ltd	Leeds-Bradford	19. 6.03
G-BFXX	Gulfstream AA-5B Tiger	AA5B-0917		3.10.78	W.R.Gibson	North Weald	22.11.03
G-BFYA	MBB Bö.105DB	S.321	D-HJET	31.10.78	Sterling Helicopters Ltd *(Op Norfolk Police)*	Norwich	12. 5.03T
G-BFYC	Piper PA-32RT-300 Lance II	32R-7885200	N36645	31. 7.78	A.A.Barnes t/a Cyril Silver & Ptnrs	Biggin Hill	24. 4.03
G-BFYI	Westland-Bell 47G-3BI	WA302	XT167	24. 1.79	B.Walker & Co (Dursley) Ltd	Nympsfield	28. 6.03
G-BFYK	Cameron V-77 HAB	433	EI-BAY	16. 8.78	Louise E.Jones	Worcester	31.12.99A
			G-BFYK				
G-BFYL	Evans VP-2	PFA 63-10146		15. 8.78	W.C.Brown	(Camberley)	17.12.98P
	(Volkswagen 1834)						
G-BFZA	Alpavia Fournier RF3	5	F-BLEL	14. 9.78	T.J.Hartwell	Sackville Farm, Riseley	
G-BFZB	Piper J-3C-65 Cub (L-4J-PI)	13019	D-ECEL	21. 9.78	N.Rawlinson	Eggington, Derby	6. 8.03P
	(Continental C85) *(Frame No.12849)*		HB-OSP/44-80723		*(As "44-80723/J-E5")*		
G-BFZD	Reims/Cessna FR182 Skylane RG II	FR18200010		9.10.78	R B Lewis t/a R B Lewis & Co	Sleap	1. 2.03
G-BFZH	Piper PA-28R-200 Cherokee Arrow	28R-35307	OY-BDB	25.10.78	S.Mason	Glasgow	25. 9.03
G-BFZK*	Embraer EMB.110P2 Bandeirante	110-200	PT-GLS	17.11.78	Air Salvage International	Alton	
					(Cancelled 17.5.84 - to N5071N 5.84 then OY-BNM) (Noted as "OY-BNM" 7.00)		
G-BFZM	Rockwell Commander 112TC-A	13191	N4661W	9.10.78	J A Hart & R.J.Lamplough	Filton	29. 8.03
G-BFZN	Reims/Cessna FA152 Aerobat	FA1520348		20.10.78	A.S.Bamrah t/a Falcon Flying Services	Biggin Hill	29.11.81T
					(Crashed Narborough, Leics 4.10.80: rebuilt 2.95: current status unknown)		
G-BFZO	Gulfstream AA-5A Cheetah	AA5A-0697		1.11.78	P.Young	City of Derry	12. 5.03
					t/a Coleraine Landscape Services		
G-BFZT	Reims/Cessna FA152 Aerobat	FA1520356		4. 7.79	Pooler-LMT Ltd	Sherlowe	14.11.03T

G-BFZU	Reims/Cessna FA152 Aerobat	FA1520355		29. 6.79	Redhill Air Services Ltd	Redhill	12. 3.05T
G-BFZV	Reims/Cessna F172M	F17201093	SE-FZR	2.11.78	R.Thomas	AAC Middle Wallop	16. 3.03T

G-BGAA - G-BGZZ

G-BGAA	Cessna 152 II	15281894	N67529	18. 7.78	PJC (Leasing) Ltd	Stapleford	24. 6.04T
	(Bounced on landing Henlow 18.2.02 causing nosewheel to collapse)						
G-BGAB	Reims/Cessna F152 II	F1521531		13.10.78	TG Aviation Ltd *(Op Thanet Flying Club)*	Manston	7. 4.03T
G-BGAD*	Reims/Cessna F152 II	F1521532		13.10.78	Not known	Belfast	
	(DBR in a landing accident Newtownards 5.7.01: cancelled 17.8.01 as destroyed) *(Noted as wreck 10.01)*						
G-BGAE	Reims/Cessna F152 II	F1521540		8.11.78	Aerolease Ltd	Conington	30. 4.03T
G-BGAF	Reims/Cessna FA152 Aerobat	FA1520349		13.10.78	M.F.Hatt, P.E.Preston, R.W.Harris, A.Jahanfar & D.S.Woolf		
					(Op Southend Flying Club)	Southend	16. 8.03T
G-BGAG	Reims/Cessna F172N Skyhawk II	F17201754	"G-KING"	13.10.78	A.S.Bamrah t/a Falcon Flying Services	Rochester	11. 5.02T
G-BGAJ	Reims/Cessna F182Q Skylane II	F18200096		13.10.78	Ground Airport Services Ltd	Guernsey	4. 5.03
G-BGAX	Piper PA-28-140 Cherokee F	28-7325409	PH-NSH	20.10.78	C.D.Brack	Breighton	15. 4.05
G-BGAZ	Cameron V-77 HAB	439		20.10.78	C.J.Madigan & D.H.McGibbon	Bristol	4. 8.01A
	(New envelope ?)				"Silicon Chip/Robocop"		
G-BGBA	Robin R2100A Club	133	F-OCBJ	2. 5.78	D.Faulkner	Headcorn	24. 5.03
G-BGBE	SAN Jodel DR.1050 Ambassadeur	260	F-BJYT	29.11.78	J.A. & B.Mawby	Gravely	11. 6.05
G-BGBF	Druine D.31A Turbulent	PFA 1658		24.10.78	R.S.Jordan	Shipdham	25.11.02P
	(Volkswagen 1600)						
G-BGBG	Piper PA-28-181 Archer II	28-7990012	N39730	2.11.78	Harlow Printing Ltd	Newcastle	24. 5.03
G-BGBI	Reims/Cessna F150L	F15000688	PH-LUA	28.11.78	A.S.Bamrah t/a Falcon Flying Services	Rochester	5. 4.04T
G-BGBK	Piper PA-38-112 Tomahawk	38-78A0433	N9738N	2.11.78	The Sherwood Flying Club Ltd	Nottingham	25. 7.05
G-BGBN	Piper PA-38-112 Tomahawk	38-78A0511	N9657N	29.11.78	Bonus Aviation Ltd	Cranfield	7. 8.03T
G-BGBR	Reims/Cessna F172N Skyhawk II	F17201772		8.11.78	A.S.Bamrah	Southend	16. 2.04T
					t/a Falcon Flying Services *(Op Willowair Flying Club)*		
G-BGBW	Piper PA-38-112 Tomahawk	38-78A0670	N9710N	8.11.78	Truman Aviation Ltd	Nottingham	10. 7.03T
G-BGBY	Piper PA-38-112 Tomahawk	38-78A0711	N9689N	8.11.78	Cheshire Flying Services Ltd	Liverpool	6. 2.04T
G-BGBZ	Rockwell Commander 114	14423	N5878N	9.10.78	R.S.Fenwick	Rochester	9. 8.04
G-BGCM	Gulfstream AA-5A Cheetah	AA5A-0835		23. 3.79	G. & S.A.Jones	Linley Hill, Leven	13. 9.04T
G-BGCO	Piper PA-44-180 Seminole	44-7995128	N2103D	20.12.78	J.R.Henderson	Warton	21. 8.03
					(Op BAE Systems (Operations) Ltd)		
G-BGCY	Taylor JT.1 Monoplane	PFA 55-10370		23.11.78	A.T.Lane	*(Peterborough)*	30. 4.02P
	(Volkswagen 1600)						
G-BGEA	Reims/Cessna F150M	F15001396	OY-BJK	22. 3.79	C.J.Hopewell	Sibson	28. 6.03T
G-BGED	Cessna U206F Stationair	U20602279	LN-BGQ	12.12.78	Chapman Aviation Ltd	Tilstock	11. 4.03
			N1911U		"Sky Diva"		
G-BGEE	Evans VP-1	PFA 62-10287		27.11.78	R E Holmes	*(Ely)*	16. 5.95P
	(Volkswagen 1679)				*(On rebuild 9.00: wings @ Priory Farm, Tibenham 8.97)*		
G-BGEH	Monnett Sonerai II	209 & PFA 15-10254		1.12.78	D.& V.T.Hubbard	*(Basingstoke)*	16. 8.96P
	(Volkswagen 2234)						
G-BGEI	Oldfield Baby Lakes	PFA 10-10016		1.12.78	M.T.Taylor	Griffins Farm, Temple Bruer	20.11.02P
	(Continental A65) *(Fuselage of PFA 1576 incorporated during construction)*						
G-BGEK	Piper PA-38-112 Tomahawk	38A0575	N9662N	13.12.78	Cheshire Flying Services Ltd t/a Ravenair	Liverpool	16. 4.03T
G-BGEW	SNCAN NC.854S	63	F-BFSJ	13.12.78	R.H.Ashforth	Gloucestershire	23. 6.03P
	(Continental A65)						
G-BGFC	Evans VP-2	V2-1278 & PFA 63-10441		15.12.78	S.W.C.Hollins	Llandegla	29. 9.93P
	(Volkswagen 1834)						
G-BGFF	Clutton FRED Srs.II	PFA 29-10261		18.12.78	I.Daniels	Popham	1. 8.03P
	(Volkswagen 1834)						
G-BGFG	Gulfstream AA-5A Cheetah	AA5A-0687	N6158A	25. 1.79	Plane Talking Ltd	Blackbushe	30. 5.03T
G-BGFH	Reims/Cessna F182Q Skylane II	F18200105		18. 1.79	Rayviation Ltd	*(Driffield)*	20. 4.04T
	(Rebuilt with fuselage of G-EMMA [F18200099] 1994/95: original fuselage scrapped)						
G-BGFI	Gulfstream AA-5A Cheetah	AA5A-0733	N6142A	5. 3.79	I.J.Hay & A.Nayyar tr GFI Group	Biggin Hill	25.10.03
G-BGFJ	Jodel D.9 Bebe	PFA 1324		11.12.78	M.D.Mold	Watchford Farm, Yarcombe	25.11.02P
	(Volkswagen 1600)						
G-BGFK*	Evans VP-1	PFA 62-10343		20.12.78	I.N.M.Cameron	Wathstones Farm, Newby Wiske	
					(Cancelled 7.4.99 by CAA) *(Stored 7.01)*		
G-BGFT	Piper PA-34-200T Seneca II	34-7870218	N9714C	17. 1.79	Oxford Aviation Services Ltd	Oxford	15. 8.03T
G-BGFX	Reims/Cessna F152 II	F15201555		28.12.78	A.S.Bamrah	Biggin Hill	23. 6.91T
					t/a Falcon Flying Services *(Spares use 2.95)*		
G-BGGA	Bellanca 7GCBC Citabria 150S	1104-79		5. 2.79	L.A.King	North Connel, Oban	24. 1.04
G-BGGB	Bellanca 7GCBC Citabria 150S	1105-79		7. 2.79	G.H.N.Chamberlain	Rattlesden	17. 3.05
G-BGGC	Bellanca 7GCBC Citabria 150S	1106-79		5. 2.79	R.P.Ashfield & J.M.Stone		
						Gorwell Farm, Littlebredy, Dorset	21. 9.03
G-BGGD	Bellanca 8GCBC Scout	284-78		5. 2.79	Bristol & Gloucestershire Gliding Club Ltd	Nympsfield	22. 6.04
G-BGGE	Piper PA-38-112 Tomahawk	38-79A0161	N9673N	10. 1.79	Truman Aviation Ltd	Nottingham	25. 6.03T
G-BGGG	Piper PA-38-112 Tomahawk	38-79A0163	N9675N	10. 1.79	Teesside Flight Centre Ltd	Teesside	28. 6.04T
G-BGGI	Piper PA-38-112 Tomahawk	38-79A0165	N9675N	10. 1.79	Truman Aviation Ltd	Nottingham	6. 3.04T
G-BGGL	Piper PA-38-112 Tomahawk	38-79A0169	N9696N	10. 1.79	Grunwick Processing Laboratories Ltd	Cranfield	27. 6.03T
					(Op Bonus Aviation)		
G-BGGM	Piper PA-38-112 Tomahawk	38-79A0170	N9698N	10. 1.79	Grunwick Processing Laboratories Ltd	Cranfield	16.11.03T
					(Op Bonus Aviation)		
G-BGGN	Piper PA-38-112 Tomahawk	38-79A0171	N9706N	10. 1.79	Domeastral Ltd	Pansahnger	31. 8.03T
G-BGGO	Reims/Cessna F152 II	F15201569		8. 3.79	East Midlands Flying School Ltd	East Midlands	13. 7.03T
G-BGGP	Reims/Cessna F152 II	F15201580		8. 3.79	East Midlands Flying School Ltd	East Midlands	12.10.03T
G-BGGU	Wallis WA-116 RR	702		28.12.78	K.H.Wallis	Reymerston Hall, Norfolk	
	(Subaru EA61)				*(Noted 8.01)*		
G-BGGV	Wallis WA-120 Srs.2	703		28.12.78	K.H.Wallis	Reymerston Hall, Norfolk	
					(Not completed: valid CofR 4.02)		

G-BGGW	Wallis WA-122 RR	704		28.12.78	K.H.Wallis	Reymerston Hall, Norfolk	24. 4.98P
	(RR Continental O-240-A)				*(Noted 8.01)*		
G-BGHE	Convair L-13A-CO	-	N1132V	4. 8.80	J.M.Davis	Wichita, USA	
			47-346		*(On long-term rebuild: current status unknown)*		
G-BGHI	Reims/Cessna F152 II	F15201560		15. 1.79	V.R.McCready	(Sutton)	18. 5.03T
G-BGHJ	Reims/Cessna F172N Skyhawk II	F17201777	EI-BVF	15. 1.79	M.D.N.Fisher/Castle Aviation Ltd	Coventry	26. 7.04T
			G-BGHJ		*(Op Almat Flying Club)*		
G-BGHM	Robin R1180T Aiglon	227		19. 2.79	H.Price	Blackpool	5.11.03
G-BGHP	Beech 76 Duchess	ME-190	N60132	16. 1.79	Magenta Ltd *(Op Airways Flight Training)*	Exeter	22. 4.03T
G-BGHS	Cameron N-31 HAB	501		15. 1.79	W.R.Teasdale "Baby Champion"	Newbury	17. 1.00A
					(On loan to British Balloon Museum & Library) *(Inflated 4.02)*		
G-BGHT	Falconar F-12	PFA 22-10040		17. 1.79	C.R.Coates	Sneaton Thorpe, Whitby	
	(Lycoming O-290)						
G-BGHU	North American T-6G-NF Texan	182-729	FAP1707	22. 1.79	C.E.Bellhouse	Headcorn	2. 5.03P
			Fr.AF 115042/51-15042		"Carly" (As "115042/TA-042" in USAF c/s)		
G-BGHV	Cameron V-77 HAB	483		12. 1.79	E.Davies	Penlan Farm, Llanwrda	28. 9.03A
					t/a Adeilad Claddings "Adclad"		
G-BGHW*	Thunder Ax8-90 HAB	175		30. 1.79	W G Johnston	Edinburgh	
					(Cancelled 19.5.93 by CAA) (Stored 2001)		
G-BGHY	Taylor JT.1 Monoplane	PFA 1455		12. 1.79	R.A.Hand	RAF Barkston Heath	27. 6.02P
	(Volkswagen 1600)				"Shy Talk"		
G-BGHZ	Clutton FRED Srs.II	PFA 29-10445		12. 1.79	D.J.Howell tr FRED Group	(Stourbridge)	
					(Under construction 1999: new owner 10.02))		
G-BGIB	Cessna 152 II	152-82161	N68169	3. 7.79	Redhill Air Services Ltd	Redhill	24. 2.04T
G-BGID	Westland-Bell 47G-3B1	WA/340	XT181	28. 2.79	J.G.Brudenell	Wombleton	27. 5.05
G-BGIG	Piper PA-38-112 Tomahawk	38-78A0773	N2607A	23. 1.79	Air Claire Ltd *(Op Glasgow Flying Club)*	Glasgow	8. 4.04T
G-BGIO	Montgomerie-Bensen B.8MR			11. 1.79	R.M.Savage	Carlisle	24. 7.03P
	(Rotax 503)	GJ.1 & PFA G/01-1259			tr Great Orton Group		
G-BGIP	Colt 56A HAB	038		2. 2.79	R.D.Allen & M.Walker "The Snake"	Bristol	23. 7.03A
G-BGIU	Cessna F172H	F172-0620	PH-VIT	26. 2.79	D.W.Clifton & M.Ruggieri tr Skyhawk Flying Group		
	(Built Reims Aviation SA)					Standalone Farm, Meppershall	8. 7.04
G-BGIX	Helio H.295 Super Courier	1467	(G-BGAO)	17.10.79	Caroline M.Lee Fanners Farm, Great Waltham, Essex		6. 2.05
			N68861				
G-BGIY	Reims/Cessna F172N Skyhawk II	F17201824		31. 1.79	Air Claire Ltd *(Op Glasgow Flying Club)*	Glasgow	12. 8.03T
G-BGJB	Piper PA-44-180 Seminole	44-7995112	G-ISFT	1. 2.79	Ostend Air College NV	Ostend, Belgium	22.10.03T
			EI-CHF/G-BGJB/N3046B				
G-BGJU	Cameron V-65 HAB	499		5. 2.79	Janet A.Folkes "Spoils"	Loughborough	4. 4.93A
G-BGKC	SOCATA Rallye 110ST	3262		25. 4.79	J.H.Cranmer & T.A.Timms	Bidford	8. 9.99
					(In open storage 4.02)		
G-BGKO	Gardan GY-20 Minicab	PFA 1827		14. 2.79	R.B.Webber	Trenchard Farm, Eggesford	
					(Stored incomplete 11.02)		
G-BGKS	Piper PA-28-161 Warrior II	28-7916221	N9562N	12. 2.79	Marham Investments Ltd	Belfast	6. 4.03T
					(Op Woodgate Executive Air Services)		
G-BGKT	Auster AOP.9	B5-10/137	XN441	28.12.78	G.M.Bauer	Wickenby	4. 4.02P
	(Officially regd as AUS/137)				*(As "XN441" in RAF c/s)*		
G-BGKU	Piper PA-28R-201 Arrow III	28R-7837237	N31585	8. 3.79	Aerolease Ltd	Conington	4. 2.04T
G-BGKV	Piper PA-28R-201 Cherokee Arrow III	28R-7737156	N44985	21. 5.79	R.Haverson & A.K.Lake	Shipdham	2. 3.04
G-BGKY	Piper PA-38-112 Tomahawk	38-78A0737	N9732N	2. 3.79	Top Cat Aviation Ltd	Manchester	7. 7.03T
G-BGKZ	Auster J/5F Aiglet Trainer	2776	F-BGKZ	15.12.78	R.B.Webber	Trenchard Farm, Eggesford	25. 2.95
					(New CofR 7.02) Noted dismantled 11.02		
G-BGLA	Piper PA-38-112 Tomahawk	38-78A0741	N9699N	9. 3.79	B.H. & P.M.Illston t/a Norwich School of Flying	Norwich	24. 8.03T
G-BGLF	Evans VP-1 Srs.2	PFA 62-10388		28. 2.79	J.C.Morris	North Coates	19. 9.02P
	(Volkswagen 1834)				*(New owner 10.02)*		
G-BGLG	Cessna 152 II	15282092	N67909	11. 4.79	L.W.Scattergood	Breighton	1. 7.04T
G-BGLJ	Bell 212	30548	EC-HCZ	5. 3.79	Bristow Helicopters Ltd *(New CofR 2.03)*	Aberdeen	
			"EC-HCP"/G-BGLJ/(EC-GHP)/EC-295/G-BGLJ/9Y-TIJ/G-BGLJ/5N-AJX/G-BGLJ/EP-HBZ/VR-BEJ/N2956W				
G-BGLK	Monnett Sonerai IIL	PFA 15-10304		24. 2.78	J.Bradley	(Coleraine, Co.Londonderry)	31.8.89P
					(New owner 5.02)		
G-BGLN	Reims/Cessna FA152 Aerobat	FA1520354		8. 3.79	Bflying Ltd	Bournemouth	24. 8.03T
					(Op Bournemouth Flying Club)		
G-BGLO	Reims/Cessna F172N Skyhawk II	F17201900		8. 3.79	Pulsar Yacht Services Ltd	Southend	10.12.03
G-BGLS	Oldfield Super Baby Lakes	PFA 10-10237		11.12.78	J.F.Dowe	(Ipswich)	18. 6.88P
	(Lycoming O-235)				*(Current status unknown)*		
G-BGLW	Piper PA-34-200 Seneca	34-7250132	(G-BFPF)	2. 6.78	London Executive Aviation Ltd	Stapleford	28. 8.03T
			OY-BDZ/SE-FYS				
G-BGLZ	Stits SA-3A Playboy	71-100	N9996	19. 6.79	S.A.Cooke	Mitchell's Farm, Wilburton	10. 1.03P
	(Continental C90)				tr Stitts Playboy (Fenland) Flying Group		
G-BGME*	SIPA 903	96	G-BCML	1. 1.81	M.Emery & C.A.Suckling	Guildford	17. 6.94P
			"G-BCHU"/F-BGHU		*(Stored 1995: cancelled 15.11.00 by CAA) (Current status unknown)*		
G-BGMJ	CAB GY-201 Minicab	12	F-BGMJ	19. 6.78	S.L. & A.W.Wakefield, J.F.Hawkins & N.Birchall	Sibson	20. 8.03P
G-BGMN	Hawker Siddeley HS.748 Srs.2A/347	1766	PK-OCH	9. 3.79	Emerald Airways Ltd	Liverpool	19.11.04T
			G-BGMN/9Y-TGH/G-BGMN/9Y-TGH				
G-BGMO	Hawker Siddeley HS.748 Srs.2A/347	1767	ZK-MCB	9. 3.79	Emerald Airways Ltd	Liverpool	22. 4.05T
			G-BGMO/9Y-TGI/V2-LDB/9Y-TGI/(G-BGMO)				
G-BGMP	Cessna F172G	F172-0240	PH-BNV	26. 3.79	R.W.Collings	Hinton in the Hedges	5. 7.04
	(Built Reims Aviation SA)						
G-BGMR	Barritault JB-01 Minicab	PFA 56-10153		12. 3.79	R.A.M.Smith	White Waltham	13. 8.03P
	(Continental C90)				tr Mike Romeo Flying Group		
G-BGMS	Taylor JT.2 Titch	MS.1 & PFA 60-10400		20.10.78	M.A.J.Spice	(Middlewich, Cheshire)	
G-BGMT	SOCATA Rallye 235E	13126		14. 9.78	C.G.Wheeler	Morgansfield, Fishburn	26.12.03
G-BGMU	Westland-Bell 47G-3B1	WA/514	XT807	14. 5.79	V.L.J. & V.English	Whittlesey, Peterborough	16.11.03
G-BGMV	Scheibe SF-25B Falke	4648	D-KEBG	15. 5.79	C.A.Bloom & A.P Twort	Ringmer	16.11.01
G-BGND	Reims/Cessna F172N Skyhawk II	F17201576	PH-AYI	3. 3.78	A.J.M.Freeman	Andrewsfield	7.10.05
			(F-GAQA)				

Reg	Type	c/n	Prev id	Date	Owner	Location	Expiry
G-BGNT	Reims/Cessna F152 II	F15201644		23.10.79	Aerolease Ltd	Conington	1. 3.04T
G-BGNV	Gulfstream GA-7 Cougar	GA7-0078	N790GA	20. 4.79	G.J.Bissex	Filton	6.12.03T
G-BGOD	Colt 77A HAB	040		4. 4.79	C. & M.D.Steuer "Harvey Wallbanger"	London NW1	18. 6.97A
G-BGOG	Piper PA-28-161 Warrior II	28-7916350	N9639N	8. 6.79	W.D.Moore	Cranfield	31.10.03
G-BGOI	Cameron O-56 HAB	526		4. 4.79	S.Ellis *"Skymaster" (Active 2002)*	Bristol	13. 5.87A
G-BGOJ	Reims/Cessna F150L	F1500931	G-MABI	19. 4.79	D.J.Hockings	Rochester	30. 7.97
			G-BGOJ/PH-KDA		*(Current status unknown)*		
G-BGOL	Piper PA-28R-201T Turbo Arrow III	28R-7803335	N36705	11. 4.79	Valley Flying Co Ltd	Valley Farm, Stafford	14. 5.03
G-BGON	Gulfstream GA-7 Cougar	GA7-0095	N9527Z	24. 4.79	J.P.E.Walsh	Elstree	13. 8.03T
					t/a Walsh Aviation *(Op Cabair)*		
G-BGOR	North American AT-6D-NT Harvard III	88-14863	FAP1508	28. 3.79	J.M.Sargeant	Goudhurst	5. 6.03P
	(Reported as c/n 88-14880)		SAAF 7504/EX935/41-33908		*(As "14863/TA-863" in USAAF c/s)*		
G-BGPA	Cessna 182Q Skylane II	18266538	C-GYBW	11. 7.79	Tindon Ltd	Little Snoring	22. 4.04
			(N94935)				
G-BGPB	CCF Harvard 4	CCF4-538	FAP1747	4. 4.79	J.Romain *(Op Aircraft Restoration Co)*	Duxford	22. 3.03
	(T-6J-CCF Texan)		West German AF BF+050/WGAF AA+050/53-4619 *(As "1747" in Portuguese AF c/s)*				
G-BGPD	Piper J-3C-65 Cub (L-4H-PI)	12040	F-BFQP	18. 4.79	P.R.Whiteman	Marsh Hill Farm, Aylesbury	7. 5.03P
	(Frame No.11867)		F-BDTP/44-79744				
	(Officially regd as c/n 10478 which is ex 43-29187/OO-ADI/F-BFQP: G-BGPD is ex 44-79744/F-BDTP: presumably fuselages exchanged in France – see G-BCOM) (As "479744/49/M" in 92nd Armoured FA Btn, US 9th Army c/s)							
G-BGPH	Gulfstream AA-5B Tiger	AA5B-1248	(G-BGRU)	14. 8.79	Shipping & Airlines Ltd	Biggin Hill	2. 1.05T
G-BGPI	Plumb BGP.1 Biplane	PFA 83-10359		26. 6.78	B.G.Plumb	Hinton in the Hedges	5.11.03P
	(Continental O-200A)						
G-BGPJ	Piper PA-28-161 Warrior II	28-7916288	N9602N	24. 4.79	West Lancs Warrior Co Ltd	Woodvale	24. 6.03
G-BGPL	Piper PA-28-161 Warrior II	28-7916289	N9603N	20. 4.79	TG Aviation Ltd *(Op Thanet Flying Club)*	Manston	12. 6.03T
G-BGPM*	Evans VP-2	PFA 63-10335		17. 4.79	M.G.Reilly	(Basingstoke)	29. 4.86P
	(Volkswagen 2075)				*(Open storage Old Sarum 9.91: cancelled 4.10.00 by CAA: current status unknown)*		
G-BGPN	Piper PA-18-150 Super Cub	18-7909044	N9750N	12. 4.79	D.McHugh & A.R.Darke	East Winch	25.11.05T
G-BGPU	Piper PA-28-140 Cherokee F	28-7325282	PH-GNT	25. 4.79	Air Navigation & Trading Co Ltd	Blackpool	17. 8.03T
G-BGPZ*	Morane MS.890A Rallye Commodore 145	10284	F-BLBD	3. 5.79	A.S.Cowan	Popham	28. 1.02
					tr Popham Flying Group G-BGPZ *(Cancelled 14.5.02 as WFU)*		
G-BGRC	Piper PA-28-140 Cherokee B	28-26208	SE-FHF	12. 6.79	Tecair Aviation Ltd & G.F.Haigh	Swanton Morley	26.10.97T
			N5501U		*(Current status unknown)*		
G-BGRE	Beech 200 Super King Air	BB-568		8. 5.79	Martin-Baker (Engineering) Ltd	Chalgrove	23.10.05T
G-BGRG	Beech 76 Duchess	ME-233		8. 5.79	S.J.Skilton	Bournemouth	7. 4.05T
					t/a Aviation Rentals *(Op Professional Air Training)*		
G-BGRH	Robin DR400 2+2	1411		21. 5.79	C.R.Beard	Grassthorpe Grange	5. 4.04
G-BGRI	CEA Jodel DR.1050 Sicile	540	F-BLZJ	27. 4.79	R.T.Gunn & J.R.Redhead		
						Mount Airey Farm, South Cave	14.12.03
G-BGRL	Piper PA-38-112 Tomahawk	38-79A0917	N9725N	25. 4.79	G.G.Mepham	Goodwood	18. 5.03T
G-BGRM	Piper PA-38-112 Tomahawk	38-79A1067	N9673N	1. 8.79	P.L.Buckley	Hill Farm, Nayland	30. 5.03T
G-BGRN*	Piper PA-38-112 Tomahawk	38-79A0897	N9684N	25. 4.79	Goodwood Road Racing Co Ltd	Goodwood	12. 2.00T
					(Donated to Fire Section 5.01: no outer wings: cancelled 30.8.01 as WFU)		
G-BGRO	Reims/Cessna F172M Skyhawk II	F17201129	PH-KAB	4. 5.79	A.N.Pirie	RAF Leuchars	14.12.03T
					t/a Cammo Aviation *(Op Leuchars Flying Club)*		
G-BGRR	Piper PA-38-112 Tomahawk	38-78A0336	OO-FLT	8. 5.79	Goodair Leasing Ltd	Cardiff	23. 9.05T
			N9685N				
G-BGRS	Thunder Ax7-77Z HAB	203		21. 5.79	P.M.Gaines	Stockton-on-Tees	26. 4.03A
G-BGRT	Steen Skybolt	RCT.001 & PFA 64-10171		12. 9.78	J.H.Kimber & O.Meier	(Austria)	17.11.03P
	(Lycoming O-360)						
G-BGRX	Piper PA-38-112 Tomahawk	38-79A0609	N9662N	11. 5.79	Bonus Aviation Ltd	Cranfield	31.10.03T
G-BGSA	SOCATA MS.892E Rallye 150GT	12838	F-GAKC	29. 5.79	D.H.Tonkin	Bodmin	14. 6.04
G-BGSH	Piper PA-38-112 Tomahawk	38-79A0562	N9719N	11. 5.79	Thistle Aero Ltd	Carlisle	8. 9.05T
G-BGSI	Piper PA-38-112 Tomahawk	38-79A0564	N9720N	18. 5.79	Cheshire Flying Services Ltd	Liverpool	29. 9.03T
					t/a Ravenair *(Had accident and for spares use by 8.01 apparently)*		
G-BGSJ	Piper J-3C-65 Cub (L-4A-PI)	8781	F-BGXJ	21. 5.79	A.J.Higgins	(Lanport)	11 11.03P
	(Frame No.8917)		Fr.AF/42-36657				
G-BGST*	Thunder Ax7-65 Bolt HAB	217		14. 5.79	J.L.Bond *"Black Fred"*	Billingshurst	23. 3.91A
					(Cancelled 7.12.01 by CAA) (Stored 2002)		
G-BGSV	Reims/Cessna F172N Skyhawk II	F17201830		1. 8.79	Southwell Air Services Ltd	Linley Hill, Leven	24. 1.04
G-BGSW	Beech F33 Bonanza	CD-1253	OH-BDD	30. 5.79	C.Wood	Wellesbourne Mountford	28. 4.02T
G-BGSY	Gulfstream GA-7 Cougar	GA7-0096		4. 6.79	Plane Talking Ltd	Biggin Hill	29. 4.05T
G-BGTC	Auster AOP.9	AUS/168	XP282	12.10.79	P.T.Bolton	South Lodge Farm, Widmerpool	9. 6.97P
					(As "XP282") (Damaged Widmerpool 2.10.96: current status unknown)		
G-BGTF	Piper PA-44-180 Seminole	44-7995287	N2131Y	20. 6.79	NG Trustees & Nominees Ltd	Jersey	26. 4.03
G-BGTG	Piper PA-23-250 Aztec F	27-7954061	N2454M	23. 5.79	Keen Leasing (IoM) Ltd	Belfast	21.10.03T
G-BGTI	Piper J-3C-65 Cub (L-4J-PI)	12940	F-BFFL	17. 5.79	A.P.Broad	Brandy Wharf, Waddingham	19. 9.03P
	(Rotax 582) (Frame No.12770)		44-80644				
G-BGTJ	Piper PA-28-180 Cherokee Archer	28-7405083	OY-BIO	3. 7.79	Serendipity Aviation Ltd	Gloucestershire	17.12.03
			SE-GAH				
G-BGTT	Cessna 310R II	310R1641	N1AN	13. 7.79	Capital Trading (Aviation) Ltd	Exeter	29. 5.04T
			(N2635D)				
G-BGTX	SAN Jodel D.117	698	F-BIDI	22. 6.79	C.Adams & H F Young	Shobdon	4.11.02P
					tr Madley Flying Group *(Cisavia)*		
G-BGUB(2)	Piper PA-32-300 Six	32 7940252	N2387U	29.11.79	A.J.Diplock	Biggin Hill	27. 2.04
G-BGUY	Cameron V-56 HAB	441		27. 9.78	J.L.Guy *"Good Guy"*	Skipton	13.10.95A
G-BGVB	CEA DR.315 Petit Prince	308	F-BPOP	20. 7.79	P.J.Leggo	Leicester	24.11.05
G-BGVE	Scintex CP.1310-C3 Super Emeraude	931	F-BMJE	8. 6.79	R.T.L.Arkell Little Battleflats Farm, Ellistown, Coalville		5.11.03P
					tr Victor Echo Group *"Mon Papillon"*		
G-BGVH	Beech 76 Duchess	ME-260		8. 6.79	W.J. & J.C.M.Golden	Bowerchalke, Salisbury	8. 7.04
					t/a Valco Marketing		
G-BGVK	Piper PA-28-161 Cherokee Warrior II	28-7816400	PH-WPT	13. 6.79	K.R.Holland	Coventry	29. 5.04
			G-BGVK/N6244C				
G-BGVN	Piper PA-28RT-201 Arrow IV	28R-7918168	N2846U	22. 6.79	C.Smith & S.Carrington tr G-BGVN Syndicate	Fairoaks	15.11.03

G-BGVS	Reims/Cessna F172M	F17200992	PH-HVS	3. 5.79	J.W.Tulloch	Kirkwall	14.12.03T
			(PH-LUK)		tr Kirkwall Flying Club		
G-BGVV	Gulfstream AA-5A Cheetah	AA5A-0750		27. 6.79	A.H.McVicar	Prestwick	28. 5.04T
G-BGVW	Gulfstream AA-5A Cheetah	AA5A-0774		21. 6.79	Computech Aviation Ltd	Biggin Hill	23. 8.03T
G-BGVY	Gulfstream AA-5B Tiger	AA5B-1080	(G-BGVU)	21. 8.79	R.J.C.Neal-Smith	Old Sarum	4.10.03
			(F-GBOO)				
G-BGVZ	Piper PA-28-181 Archer II	28-7990528	N2886A	12. 7.79	W.Walsh & S.R.Mitchell	Liverpool	3. 7.03T
G-BGWC	Robin DR400/180 Regent	1420		26. 6.79	P.R.Deacon	Frinsted	29. 5.04T
G-BGWH*	Piper PA-18-150 Super Cub	18-7605	ST-ABR	18. 6.79	V.D.Speck	Clacton	14. 6.93T
			G-ARSR/N10F		*(Damaged Clacton 7.7.92: cancelled 17.5.01 by CAA: under rebuild 8.02)*		
G-BGWJ	Sikorsky S-61N Mk.II	61-819		20. 8.79	Bristow Helicopters Ltd *"Monadh Mor"*	Faeroe Isles	4. 6.04T
G-BGWK	Sikorsky S-61N Mk.II	61-820	N1346C	10. 9.79	Bristow Helicopters Ltd	Aberdeen	28.11.05T
			G-BGWK		*"Dunrobin"*		
G-BGWM	Piper PA-28-181 Archer II	28-7990458	N2817Y	29. 6.79	Thames Valley Flying Club Ltd	Turweston	10. 5.03T
G-BGWN	Piper PA-38-112 Tomahawk	38-79A0918	N9693N	2. 7.79	E.Evans	Breighton	1. 7.05
G-BGWO	Jodel D.112	227	F-BHGQ	22. 6.79	R.C.Williams	Breighton	22.10.03P
	(Built Ets Valladeau)				tr G-BGWO Group		
G-BGWR	Cessna U206A Super Skywagon	U206-0653	G-DISC	6. 7.79	The Parachute Centre Ltd	Tilstock	25. 1.04
			G-BGWR/PH-OTD/N4953F				
G-BGWS	Enstrom 280C Shark	1050		8.11.76	R.L.Heath t/a Whisky Sierra Helicopters	Goodwood	6. 2.04T
G-BGWU	Piper PA-38-112 Tomahawk	38-79A0788	N9703N	2. 7.79	J.S. & L.M.Markey	Draycott Farm, Chiseldon	1. 2.04
G-BGWV	Aeronca 7AC Champion	7AC-4082	OO-GRI	23. 8.79	J.A.Webb tr RFC Flying Group	(Alton)	10.10.86P
			OO-TWR		*(Damaged Popham 8.6.86: current status unknown)*		
G-BGWW	Piper PA-23-250 Turbo Aztec E	27-4587	OO-ABH	15. 6.79	Keen Leasing (IoM) Ltd	Ronaldsway	28. 9.01T
			N13971		*(New owner 4.02)*		
G-BGWY	Thunder Ax6-56Z HAB	229		23. 8.79	P.J.Eley	Braintree	19. 8.95A
G-BGXA	Piper J-3C-65 Cub (L-4H-PI)	10762	F-BGXA	1. 3.78	E.C. & P.King	Eastbach Farm, Coleford	29.11.02P
	(Frame No.10587 - regd with c/n 11170)		Fr.AF/43-29471		tr G-XA Group *(As "329471/F/44" in USAAC c/s)*		
G-BGXB	Piper PA-38-112 Tomahawk	38-79A1007	N9728N	2. 7.79	Signtest Ltd	Cardiff	16. 8.04T
G-BGXC	SOCATA TB-10 Tobago	35		19.10.79	D.H.Courtley	Alderney	12. 8.04
G-BGXD	SOCATA TB-10 Tobago	39		19.10.79	D.F.P.Finan	Teesside	31. 5.04T
G-BGXJ	Partenavia P.68B	189		6. 9.79	P.T.Davy	(Rueil, France)	8.10.05
G-BGXO	Piper PA-38-112 Tomahawk	38-79A0982	N9703N	5. 7.79	Goodwood Road Racing Co Ltd	Goodwood	12. 2.02T
G-BGXR	Robin HR200/100	53	F-BVYH	1.10.79	M. Miles tr Exray Group	Southampton	27.11.01
G-BGXS	Piper PA-28-236 Dakota	28-7911198	N2836Z	12. 7.79	Bawtry Road Service Station Ltd	Gamston	3. 3.04T
G-BGXT	SOCATA TB-10 Tobago	40		3.10.79	D.A.H.Morris	Wolverhampton	30. 9.04
G-BGYN	Piper PA-18-150 Super Cub	18-7709137	N62747	19. 7.79	B.J.Dunford	Long Wood, Morestead	26. 4.01
G-BGYT	Embraer EMB-110P1 Bandeirante	110.234	N104VA	11.10.79	Keenair Charter Ltd	Blackpool	12. 1.02T
			G-BGYT/PT-SAA		*(Keenair titles)*		
G-BGZF	Piper PA-38-112 Tomahawk	38-79A1015	N9700N	26. 7.79	Metropolitan Services Ltd	Hawarden	15. 2.04T
G-BGZJ*	Piper PA-38-112 Tomahawk	38-79A0999	N9665N	7. 9.79	Midland Aircraft Maintenance Ltd	Bourne Park, Hurstbourne Tarrant	14. 6.92T
	(Damaged Cambridge 5.8.90: cancelled 25.2.97 by CAA: stored for spares 10.01)						
G-BGZL	Eiri PIK.20E	20218		21. 8.79	F.Casolari	(Castellarano, Italy)	9. 8.04
G-BGZW	Piper PA-38-112 Tomahawk	38-79A1068	N9674N	1. 8.79	Cheshire Flying Services Ltd	Liverpool	11.12.04T
					t/a Ravenair		
G-BGZY	Jodel Wassmer D.120 Paris-Nice	118	F-BIQU	17. 8.79	M.Hale	(La Trinite Sur Mer, France)	16. 7.03P
G-BGZZ	Thunder Ax6-56 Bolt HAB	220		10. 8.79	J M.Eaton & K A Wilmore	Milton-under-Wychwood	16. 7.94A
					(New owners 12.01)		

G-BHAA - G-BHZZ

G-BHAA	Cessna 152 II	15281330	N49809	12. 2.79	Herefordshire Aero Club Ltd	Shobdon	16. 3.03T
G-BHAC	Cessna A152 Aerobat	A1520776	N7595B	12. 2.79	Herefordshire Aero Club Ltd	Shobdon	17. 4.03T
G-BHAD	Cessna A152 Aerobat	A1520807	N7390L	12. 2.79	Shropshire Aero Club Ltd	Sleap	11. 4.03T
					(Substantially damaged Tatenhill 16.6.00)		
G-BHAI	Reims/Cessna F152 II	F15201625	(D-EJAY)	14. 8.79	James D.Peace & Co	Edinburgh	18. 2.05T
					(Op Edinburgh Air Centre)		
G-BHAJ	Robin DR400/160 Major 80	1430		22. 8.79	Rowantale Ltd	Rochester	15. 3.04T
G-BHAM*	Thunder Ax6-56 Bolt HAB	251		28. 1.80	D.M. & K.R.Sandford *"Levitation"*	Stockport	7. 4.86A
					(Cancelled 4.12.01 by CAA) (Inflated 6.02)		
G-BHAR	Westland-Bell 47G-3B1	WA/353	XT194	7. 8.79	J.Bird & R.Cove	Cranfield	16.11.03
G-BHAV	Reims/Cessna F152 II	F15201633		15. 8.79	T.M. & M.L.Jones	Egginton, Derby	14. 2.05T
					(Op Derby Aero Club)		
G-BHAW	Reims/Cessna F172N Skyhawk II	F17201858		15. 8.79	I.R.Chaplin	King's Farm, Thurrock	19. 6.04T
G-BHAX	Enstrom F-28C-2-UK	486-2	N5689N	22.10.79	J.L.Ferguson	Barton	21. 7.05
G-BHAY	Piper PA-28RT-201 Arrow IV	28R-7918213	N2910N	17. 8.79	Alpha Yankee Ltd	Newcastle	26. 3.04
G-BHBA	Campbell Cricket	SMI/1		15. 8.79	S.N.McGovern	Henstridge	13. 9.03P
	(Rotax 503)				*(Noted 8.02)*		
G-BHBE	Westland-Bell 47G-3B1	WA/422	XT510	29.10.79	T.R.Smith (Agricultural Machinery) Ltd	Dereham	21.12.01
	(Soloy conversion)				*(Current status unknown)*		
G-BHBF	Sikorsky S-76A II Plus	760022	N4247S	9.11.79	Bristow Helicopters Ltd *"Spirit of Paris"*	North Denes	2. 1.04T
G-BHBG*	Piper PA-32R-300 Cherokee Lance	32R-7780515	N408RC	18. 9.79	L.T.Halpin	Leicester	4. 6.00T
			N9590N		*(Cancelled 11.6.02 by CAA)*		
G-BHBI	Mooney M.20J (201)	24-0842	N4764H	24. 9.79	A.M.McGlone tr G-BHBI Group	Biggin Hill	10. 4.03
G-BHBT	Marquart MA-5 Charger	PFA 68-10190		3. 9.79	R.G. & C.J.Maidment	Jackals Farm, Sussex	6..9.02P
G-BHBZ	Partenavia P.68B Victor	191		10. 9.79	P.C.Hamer & P.C.W.Landau	Sturgate	17. 7.05
G-BHCA*	Fokker D.VIII rep	HA/01 & PFA 82-10358		7. 3.80	Not known	St Just	
	(As "124" in German A/F c/s) (Destroyed near White Waltham 21.8.81: cancelled 4.2.87 by CAA) (Wreck noted 4.02)						
G-BHCC	Cessna 172M Skyhawk II	17266711	(G-BGLY)	26.10.79	D.Wood-Jenkins	Gloucestershire	27. 6.05T
			N80713				
G-BHCE	SAN Jodel D.117A	381	F-BHME	1.10.79	D.M.Parsons	Gloucestershire	27. 2.85P
					tr Parwebb Flying Group *(Stored unmarked 4.01)*		

Reg	Type	C/n	Prev id	Date	Owner/Operator	Location	Expiry
G-BHCM	Cessna F172H	F172-0468	SE-FBD	25. 9.79	J.Dominic	Denham	24. 4.04
	(Built Reims Aviation SA)						
G-BHCP	Reims/Cessna F152 II	F15201640		31.10.79	D.Copley *(Current status unknown)*	Sandtoft	12.10.98T
G-BHCX*	Reims/Cessna F152 II	F15201642		24. 9.79	Not known	Biggin Hill	
	(Damaged in storms on 16.10.87: cancelled 27.6.94 as destroyed: wreck noted unmarked 4.01)						
G-BHCZ	Piper PA-38-112 Tomahawk	38-78A0321	N214MD	26. 9.79	Jennifer E.Abbott	Goodwood	2.10.03
G-BHDD	Vickers 668 Varsity T.1	-	WL626	18.10.79	G.Vale	East Midlands	
	(As "WL626/P": to East Midlands Aeropark) (Valid CofR 4.02)						
G-BHDE	SOCATA TB-10 Tobago	58		2. 1.80	Alpha-Alpha Ltd	Liverpool	8. 3.04
	(Went off end of runway landing Caernarfon 16.7.01: struck barbed-wire fence, damaging both wings & propeller)						
G-BHDM	Reims/Cessna F152 II	F15201684		15.10.79	Tayside Aviation Ltd	Perth	19. 4.04T
G-BHDP	Reims/Cessna F182Q Skylane	F18200131		15.10.79	Zone Travel Ltd	Turweston	21.12.02
G-BHDR	Reims/Cessna F152 II	F15201680		15.10.79	Tayside Aviation Ltd	Dundee	5. 7.04T
G-BHDS	Reims/Cessna F152 II	F15201682		15.10.79	Tayside Aviation Ltd	Dundee	14. 7.05T
G-BHDU	Reims/Cessna F152 II	F15201681		15.10.79	A.S.Bamrah t/a Falcon Flying Services	Biggin Hill	29. 5.04T
G-BHDV	Cameron V-77 HAB	585		1. 2.80	P.Glydon "Dormouse"	Barnt Green, Birmingham	30. 5.03A
G-BHDW	Reims/Cessna F152 II	F15201652		15.10.79	Tayside Aviation Ltd	Dundee	30. 5.04T
G-BHDX	Reims/Cessna F172N Skyhawk II	F17201889		5.10.79	J.Kilbride	North Weald	28. 6.04
G-BHDZ	Reims/Cessna F172N Skyhawk II	F17201911		3.12.79	Arrow Flying Ltd	Denham	15. 5.04T
G-BHEC	Reims/Cessna F152 II	F15201676		3.12.79	Stapleford Flying Club Ltd	Stapleford	19. 7.04T
G-BHED	Reims/Cessna FA152 Aerobat	FA1520359		3.12.79	TG Aviation Ltd *(Op Thanet Flying Club)*	Manston	1. 5.04T
G-BHEG	SAN Jodel 150 Mascaret	46	PH-ULS OO-SET	3. 7.80	D.M.Griffiths	RAF Mona	25. 6.03P
G-BHEH*	Cessna 310G	310G-0016	N1720 N8916Z	14. 4.80	Not known	Shoreham	9.12.96
	(Cancelled 24.8.00 as WFU: fuselage on fire dump 4.01)						
G-BHEK	Scintex CP.1315-C3 Super Emeraude	923	F-BJMU	11.10.79	D.B.Winstanley	Barton	9.11.00P
G-BHEL	SAN Jodel D.117	735	F-BIOA	8.10.79	N.Wright & C.M.Kettlewell	Queach Farm, Bury St.Edmunds	26. 6.03P
G-BHEM	Bensen B.8MV EK.14 & PFA G/01-1016			8.10.79	G.C.Kerr	(Great Orton)	5.10.00P
	(Rotax 503)						
G-BHEN	Reims/Cessna FA152 Aerobat	FA1520363		3. 1.80	Leicestershire Aero Club Ltd	Leicester	20. 1.05T
G-BHER	SOCATA TB-10 Tobago	60	4X-AKK G-BHER	19.10.79	Air Touring Ltd	Gloucestershire	20. 7.03T
G-BHEU	Thunder Ax7-65 Srs.1 HAB	238		16.10.79	D.G.Such "Polomoche"	Birmingham	31. 5.03A
G-BHEV	Piper PA-28R-200 Cherokee Arrow II	28R-7435159	PH-BOY N41244	23.10.79	P.Hardy	Gamston	12. 4.03T
					tr 7-Up Group		
G-BHEX	Colt 56A HAB	056		15.10.79	A.S.Dear, R.B.Green & W.S.Templeton	Fordingbridge	20. 4.03A
					tr Hale Hot-Air Balloon Group "Superwasp"		
G-BHEZ	SAN Jodel 150 Mascaret	22	F-BLDO	31. 1.80	A.Shorter tr Air Yorkshire Group	Sherburn-in-Elmet	20. 6.03P
G-BHFC	Reims/Cessna F152 II	1436		7. 4.78	TG Aviation Ltd *(Op Thanet Flying Club)*	Manston	1. 8.05T
G-BHFE	Piper PA-44-180 Seminole	44-7995324	ADAF 0052 G-BHFE/N2383U	2.10.79	Grunwick Ltd	Cranfield	24. 1.03T
					(Op Bonus Aviation)		
G-BHFF	Dormois Jodel D.112	322	F-BEKJ	19.10.79	P.A.Dowell	Garston Farm, Marshfield	28. 3.02P
	(Force landed near Marlborough 1.9.01: damage to port u/c, port wing & engine)						
G-BHFG	SNCAN Stampe SV-4C	45	F-BJDN Fr.Mil	31.10.79	Stormswift Ltd	Gloucestershire	20. 3.05T
G-BHFH	Piper PA-34-200T Seneca II	34-7970482	N8075Q	23.10.79	G-WATS Aviation Ltd	Wolverhampton	14. 2.04T
G-BHFI	Reims/Cessna F152 II	16852		2.10.79	R.Bilson & D.Turner	Blackpool	8. 4.04T
					tr BAe Warton Flying Club		
G-BHFJ	Piper PA-28RT-201T Turbo Arrow IV	28R-7931298	N8072R	22.10.79	J.K.Beauchamp	White Waltham	30. 9.04
G-BHFK	Piper PA-28-151 Cherokee Warrior	28-7615088	N8325C	12.12.79	Ilkeston Car Sales Ltd	Jericho Farm, Lambley	25. 3.04
G-BHFR	Eiri PIK-20E Srs.1	20228	(D-KHJR) G-BHFR	8.11.79	J.T.Morgan "FR"	Husbands Bosworth	23 4.05
G-BHFS	Robin DR400/180 Regent	1304		7. 3.78	C.J.Moss	Shoreham	26.11.05
G-BHGC	Piper PA-18-150 Super Cub	18-8793	PH-NKH N4447Z	3. 4.79	Vectis Gliding Club Ltd	Bembridge	28. 2.03
G-BHGF	Cameron V-56 HAB	574		5.11.79	P.Spellward "Biggles"	Bristol	29. 8.00A
G-BHGJ	Jodel Wassmer D.120 Paris-Nice	336	F-BOYB	15. 1.80	Q.M.B.Oswell	RAF Halton	12. 4.03P
G-BHGK	Sikorsky S-76A II Plus	760049	N1545Y	27. 3.80	CHC Scotia Ltd	Humberside	8. 5.03T
G-BHGO	Piper PA-32-260 Cherokee Six	32-7800007	PH-BGP N9656C	16.11.79	DDCS Ltd *(Op Cherokee Six Group)*	(Newcastle)	30. 9.04
	(Damaged in hangar fire 5.2.01, to Leeds by road 16.3.01 - current status unknown)						
G-BHGP	SOCATA TB-10 Tobago	100		17. 1.80	D.Suleyman	Stapleford	29. 5.05
G-BHGX*	Colt 56B HAB	057		22.11.79	M.N.Dixon "Prospect"	Bicester	22. 7.90A
	(Cancelled 6.11.01 as WFU & stored)						
G-BHGY	Piper PA-28R-200-2 Cherokee Arrow II	28R-7435086	PH-NSL N57365	23.11.79	R.J.Clark	(Berkhampsted)	5. 8.04
G-BHHB	Cameron V-77 HAB	170		26.11.79	R.M.Powell "Pax"	Stockbridge	5. 7.03T
G-BHHE	CEA Jodel DR.1051/M1 Sicile Record	628	F-BMZC	26. 4.80	P.Bridges	Hamilton Farm, Kent	6.12.04
G-BHHG	Reims/Cessna F152 II	F15201725		4. 3.80	TG Aviation Ltd *(Op Thanet Flying Club)*	Manston	5. 7.04T
G-BHHH	Thunder Ax7-65 Bolt HAB	245		5.12.79	C.A.Hendley (Essex) Ltd "Christmas"	Loughton	27. 9.87A
G-BHHK	Cameron N-77 HAB	547		5.12.79	I.S.Bridge "Shadowfax II"	Shrewsbury	7.12.87A
G-BHHN	Cameron V-77 HAB	549		29.11.79	P.Gooch	Alresford, Hants	12. 4.03A
					tr The Itchen Valley Balloon Group "Valley Crusader"		
G-BHHX	Jodel D.112	223	F-BFAJ	19. ? 80	B.P.Harrison	Dunkeswell	11.12.02P
	(Built Ets Valladeau)				tr Hotel X-Ray Flying Group		
G-BHHZ	Rotorway Scorpion	133	MSI.1195	12.12.79	L.W. & O.Underwood Stoneacre Farm, Farthing Corner		23. 9.81P
	(Rotorway 133)				*(Stored 12.94: current status unknown)*		
G-BHIB	Reims/Cessna F182Q Skylane II	F18200134		18.12.79	S.N.Chater & B.Payne	Sherburn-in-Elmet	16. 4.03
G-BHIC	Reims/Cessna F182Q Skylane II	F18200135		18.12.79	W W, J B & D S Alton	Sherburn-in-Elmet	4. 7.05
					t/a W.F.Alton & Son		
G-BHIG	Colt 31A Air Chair HAB	060	SE-... G-BHIG	12.12.79	P.A.Lindstrand	Upplands Vasby, Sweden	13. 3.00A
					(Op S.Ericsson)		
G-BHIH	Reims/Cessna F172N Skyhawk II	F17201945		3. 1.80	R.W.Cope tr Eighty Four Group	Netherthorpe	15. 8.04
G-BHII	Cameron V-77 HAB	548		10.12.79	R.V.Brown "Tosca"	Maidenhead	2. 9.96A

Reg	Type	C/n	Prev ID	Date	Owner	Location	Date
G-BHIK	Adam RA.14 Loisirs (Continental A65)	11-bis	F-PHLK	6. 2.80	L.Lewis	(Redcar)	20. 8.85P
					(Damaged near Lancaster 17.4.85: stored 1.02)		
G-BHIL	Piper PA-28-161 Warrior II	28-8016069	G-SSFT N80821	17.12.79	A.S.Bamrah t/a Falcon Flying Services	Elstreel	15. 3.04T
G-BHIN	Reims/Cessna F152 II	F15201715		28. 1.80	Cristal Air Ltd *(New owner 3.02)*	Rochester	7. 7.98T
G-BHIR	Piper PA-28R-200 Cherokee Arrow	28R-35614	SE-FHP	21. 2.80	Factorcore Ltd *(Op Manchester School of Flying)*	Woodford	6.12.04T
G-BHIS	Thunder Ax7-65 Bolt HAB	254		26.11.79	J.R.Wilson tr The Hedgehoppers Balloon Group "Yo-Yo"	Didcot	21. 3.96A
G-BHIT	SOCATA TB-9 Tampico	63		7.12.79	C.J.P.Webster	Biggin Hill	31. 1.01T
G-BHIY	Reims/Cessna F150K	F15000627	F-BRXR	18.12.79	G.J.Ball	Old Sarum	17. 4.04
G-BHJF	SOCATA TB-10 Tobago	83		2. 1.80	P.Crutchfield tr Flying Fox Group	Blackbushe	26. 9.03
G-BHJI	Mooney M.20J (201)	24-0925	N3753H	11. 2.80	Deep Cleavage Ltd	Exeter	4. 2.05T
G-BHJK	Maule M-5-235C Lunar Rocket	7296C	N56359	25. 2.80	T.P.Spurge	Great Oakley, Clacton	30. 5.05
G-BHJN	Sportavia Fournier RF4D	4021	F-BORH	3. 1.80	G.E.Reeman & G.R.Beers tr RF4 Flying Group	Enstone	19. 9.03P
G-BHJO	Piper PA-28-161 Cherokee Warrior II	28-7816213	OO-FLD N9507N/N6034H	4. 1.80	J.G.Chree, K.J.Utting & A.Sangster tr The Brackla Flying Group	Inverness	12. 5.04
G-BHJS	Partenavia P.68B	172	I-KLUB	28.12.79	J.J.Watts & D.Fletcher	Bournemouth	1. 7.04T
G-BHJU	Robin DR400 2+2	1288	D-ECDK	9. 1.80	J.Barlow & P.Crow tr Ageless Aeronauts	Lydd	29. 5.04
G-BHKE	Bensen B.8MS VW.1 & PFA G/01-1009			7. 1.80	N.B.Gray	(Great Orton)	
G-BHKH	Cameron O-65 HAB	592		7. 1.80	D.G.Body "Daisy" tr Mid-Bucks Farmers Balloon Group	Leighton Buzzard	11. 8.96A
G-BHKJ	Cessna 421C Golden Eagle III (Robertson STOL conversion)	421C0848	(N26596)	25. 1.80	Totaljet Ltd	Blackpool	10. 9.04T
G-BHKT	Wassmer Jodel D.112	1265	F-BMIQ	10. 1.80	K.A.Stewart & G.Oldfield tr The Evans Flying Group *(Current status unknown)*	Croft Farm, Darlington	19.10.01P
G-BHLE	Robin DR400/180 Regent	1466		25. 1.80	B.D.Greenwood	Ronaldsway	16. 5.04
G-BHLH	Robin DR400/180 Regent	1320	F-GBIG	11. 2.80	P.E.Davis & S.H.Petherbridge	Netherthorpe	1. 7.04
G-BHLJ	Saffery-Rigg S.200 Skyliner MLB	IAR/01		23. 1.80	I.A.Rigg "Skyliner"	Manchester	
G-BHLT	de Havilland DH.82A Tiger Moth (Regd as c/n "911")	84997	ZS-DGA SAAF2272/T6697	9. 6.80	P.J. & A.J.Borsberry *(On rebuild 8.90: current status unknown)*	Kidmore End, Reading	26. 2.90
G-BHLU	Alpavia Fournier RF3	79	F-BMTN	14. 4.80	Skyview Systems Ltd	(Sudbury)	5. 3.03P
G-BHLW	Cessna 120 (Continental C85)	10210	N73005 NC73005	24. 3.80	L.W.Scattergood "Sky Ranger"	Sherburn-in-Elmet	12. 9.02P
G-BHLX	Grumman-American AA-5B Tiger	AA5B-0573	OY-GAR	1. 2.80	M.D.McPherson	Cranfield	28. 6.04T
G-BHMA	SIPA 903	61	OO-FAE F-BGBK	13. 3.80	H.J.Taggart	Ballymoney, Co.Antrim	18. 5.98P
G-BHMG	Reims/Cessna FA152 Aerobat	FA1520368		10. 6.80	R.D.Smith	Popham	18. 6.05T
G-BHMH*	Reims/Cessna FA152 Aerobat	FA1520367		16. 5.80	Not known	Biggin Hill	
					(Damaged Hale Farm, Chiddingstone 22.9.86: cancelled 9.8.89 as WFU: noted 4.01)		
G-BHMI	Reims/Cessna F172N Skyhawk II	F17202036	G-WADE G-BHMI	6. 8.80	GMI Aviation Ltd	Blackpool	9. 3.02T
G-BHMJ	Avenger T.200-2112 MLB	002		29. 1.80	R.Light "Lord Anthony I"	Stockport	
G-BHMK	Avenger T.200-2112 MLB	003		29. 1.80	P.Kinder "Lord Anthony II"	Stockport	
G-BHMR	Stinson 108-3 Station Wagon	108-4352	F-BABO F-DABO/NC6352M	12. 2.80	D.G.French *(Stored 6.01)*	Sandown	23.11.90
G-BHMT	Evans VP-1 (Volkswagen 1834)	PFA 62-10473		18. 2.80	P.E.J.Sturgeon	Chestnut Farm, Tipps End	8. 7.03P
G-BHNA	Reims/Cessna F152 II	F15201683		12. 2.80	Sheffield Aero Club Ltd	Sturgate	19.12.03T
G-BHNC	Cameron O-65 HAB	588		7. 2.80	D. & C.Bareford "Hot N'Cold"	Kidderminster	5. 3.94A
G-BHND	Cameron N-65 HAB	582		7. 2.80	S.M.Wellband	Frome	24. 6.89A
G-BHNK	Jodel Wassmer D.120A Paris-Nice	243	F-BLNK	26. 3.80	D.A.Bates tr G-BHNK Flying Group	St.Marys, Isles of Scilly	26. 3.03P
G-BHNL	Wassmer Jodel D.112	1206	F-BLNL	30. 1.80	J.C.Mansell	Watchford Farm, Yarcombe	15.10.03P
G-BHNO	Piper PA-28-181 Archer II	28-8090211	N81413	7. 2.80	Airfluid Hydraulics & Pneumatics (Wolverhampton) Ltd	Sleap	28. 6.04
G-BHNP	Eiri PIK-20E Srs.1	20253		29. 2.80	D.A.Sutton "NP"	Sackville Farm, Riseley	26. 5.05
G-BHNV	Westland-Bell 47G-3B1	WA/700	F-GHNM G-BHNV/XW180	11. 3.80	Leyline Helicopters Ltd *(Noted 10.02)*	Trenholme Farm, Billingham	28. 5.89T
G-BHNX	SAN Jodel D.117	493	F-BHNX	7. 9.78	A.J.Chalkley *(On rebuild 4.91: current status unknown)*	(Pwllheli)	12. 1.87P
G-BHOA	Robin DR400/160 Major 80	1478		27. 1.80	Goudhurst Service Station Ltd	Goudhurst	1. 9.05
G-BHOG	Sikorsky S-61N Mk.II	61-825	PT-YEK G-BHOG/(LN-ONK)/G-BHOG	25. 3.80	Bristow Helicopters Ltd *(Exported 1.03)*	Aberdeen	
G-BHOH	Sikorsky S-61N Mk.II	61-827		25. 4.80	Bristow Helicopters Ltd "Ben Avon"	Aberdeen	20. 5.02T
G-BHOJ	Colt 14A Cloudhopper HAB	080		27. 2.80	J.A.Folkes	Oswestry	
					(Re-registered as Colt 12A 10.00)		
G-BHOL	CEA Jodel DR.1050 Ambassadeur	35	F-BJQL	6. 2.80	J.E.Sharkey "Nicolette"	Inverness	12.11.04
G-BHOM	Piper PA-18 Super Cub 95 (L-18C-PI) (Frame No.18-1272)	18-1391	OO-PIU OO-HMT/ALAT 51-15391	7. 3.80	J.R.Hannen & A.W.Kennedy Whitehall Farm, Benington tr Oscar Mike Flying Group		2. 4.03P
G-BHOO	Livesey-Purves Thunder Ax7-65 HAB	001		26. 2.80	D.Livesey & J.M.Purves "Scraps"	Crayke, York	
G-BHOR	Piper PA-28-161 Warrior II	28-8016331	N82162	12. 6.80	A.J.Harewood tr Oscar Romeo Flying Group	Biggin Hill	26. 6.04
G-BHOT	Cameron V-65 HAB	777		15. 9.81	J.A.Baker tr The Dante Balloon Group "Le Billet Doux"	Marsh Benham	8. 8.99A
G-BHOZ	SOCATA TB-9 Tampico	84		11. 3.80	G-BHOZ Management Ltd	Kemble	15. 5.04
G-BHPK	Piper J-3C-65 Cub (L-4A-PI)	8979	F-BEPK Fr.Mil/42-38410	26. 2.80	L.B.Smith tr L4 Group *(As "238410/44/A" in USAAF c/s)*	Priory Farm, Tibenham	15. 3.03P
	(Frame No.9098: official c/n is 12161/44-79865 which is F-BFYU)						
G-BHPL	CASA I-131E Jungmann	1058	E3B-350	17. 7.80	R.G.Gray *(As "E3B-350/05-97" in Spanish AF c/s)*	Thruxton	1. 8.02P
G-BHPM	Piper PA-18 Super Cub 95 (L-18C-PI) (Frame No.18-1469)	18-1501	F-BOUR ALAT 51-15501	10. 4.80	P.I.Morgans Furze Hill Farm, Rosemarket, Milford Haven *(Stored 5.95: current status unknown)*		

Reg	Type	C/n	Prev id	Date	Owner/Operator	Location	Code
G-BHPN	Colt 14A Cloudhopper HAB	081	(SE-) G-BHPN	6. 3.80	Lindstrand Balloons Ltd *(Op S.Ericsson)*	Upplands Vasby, Sweden	13. 3.00A
G-BHPS	Jodel Wassmer D.120A Paris-Nice	148	F-BIXI	11. 6.80	T.J.Price	Rhigos	15. 7.03P
G-BHPY	Cessna 152 II	15282983	N46009	26. 3.80	Halegreen Associates Ltd	Hinton in the Hedges	27. 9.04T
G-BHPZ	Cessna 172N Skyhawk II	17272017	N6411E	26. 3.80	O'Brien Properties Ltd	Shoreham	4.10.02T
G-BHRB	Reims/Cessna F152 II	F15201707		20. 3.80	LAC (Enterprises) Ltd *(Op Lancashire Aero Club)* Barton		18. 2.05T
G-BHRC	Piper PA-28-161 Warrior II	28-7916430	N9527N	3. 4.80	Sherwood Flying Club Ltd	Nottingham	25. 2.04T
G-BHRH	Reims/Cessna FA150K Aerobat	FA1500056	PH-ECB D-ECBL/(D-EKKW)	24. 3.80	Merlin Flying Club Ltd	Hucknall	25. 6.05T
G-BHRM	Reims/Cessna F152 II	F15201718	F-GCHR	8. 4.80	Aerohire Ltd	Wellesbourne Mountford	27. 9.02T
G-BHRN	Reims/Cessna F152 II	F15201728	F-GCHV	8. 4.80	James D.Peace & Co *(Op Edinburgh Air Centre)*	Edinburgh	31. 7.05T
G-BHRO	Rockwell Commander 112A	364	N1364J	20. 3.80	John Raymond Transport Ltd	Cardiff	17. 8.04
G-BHRP	Piper PA-44-180 Seminole	44-8095021	N81602	1. 4.80	M.S.Farmers	Leicester	5. 3.04T
G-BHRR	Menavia Piel CP.301A Emeraude	270	F-BISK	28. 3.80	T.W.Offen *(Stored 5.01)* Spilsted Farm, Sedlescombe		28. 5.87P
G-BHRW	CEA Jodel DR.221 Dauphin	93	F-BPCP	10. 7.80	M.F.Filer & D.H.Williams	Dunkeswell	13. 4.05
G-BHRY	Colt 56A HAB	030		2. 4.80	A.S.Davidson *"Turkish Delight"*	Burton-on-Trent	29. 4.95A
G-BHSA	Cessna 152 II	15283693	(N4889B)	1. 5.80	D.Copley *(Fuselage noted 7.02 for escape practice)*	Sandtoft	11. 4.98T
G-BHSB	Cessna 172N Skyhawk II	17272977	(N1225F)	25. 6.80	SB Aviation Ltd	(Ilkley)	5. 2.05T
G-BHSD	Scheibe SF-25E Super Falke	4357	D-KDGG	21. 7.80	S.J.Filhol	(Castlefreke, Co.Cork)	15. 5.05
G-BHSE	Rockwell Commander 114	14161	N4831W AN-BRL/(N4831W)	15. 5.80	604 Squadron Flying Group Ltd	Booker	30. 5.05
G-BHSL*	CASA I-131E Jungmann	1117	E3B-236 Spanish AF	18. 6.80	Not known Gloucestershire *(Damaged on take off Cranfield on 6.7.96. stored dismantled 6.02)*		19. 7.96P
G-BHSN	Cameron N-56 HAB	595		10. 4.80	I.Bentley	Bath	12. 7.02A
G-BHSP	Thunder Ax7-77Z HAB	272		15. 4.80	G.A.Fisher *"Chicago"*	Guildford	23. 2.94A
	(Originally built as D-TRIER c/n 221)						
G-BHSS	Pitts S-1C Special	C.1461M	N1704	19. 9.80	S.P.A.Hill	Long Marston	23.11.03P
	(Lycoming O-320)						
G-BHSY	CEA Jodel DR.1050 Sicile	546	F-BLZO	6. 5.80	T.R.Allebone	Easton Maudit	10.10.04
G-BHTA	Piper PA-28-236 Dakota	28-8011102	N8197H	22. 4.80	Dakota Ltd	Jersey	23. 9.04
G-BHTC	CEA Jodel DR.1051/M1 Sicile Record	581	F-BMGR	1. 5.80	G.Clark	Kemble	20.12.04
G-BHTG	Thunder Ax6-56 Bolt HAB	273		18. 4.80	F.R. & Mrs S.H.MacDonald *"Halcyon"* Newdigate, Surrey		18.12.91A
G-BHTH*	North American T-6G-NT Texan	168-176 49-3072A	N2807G	20. 5.80	(J.J.Woodhouse) Shoreham *(Damaged Bourne Park near Andover 13.3.95; on rebuild @ Northbrook College 4.02)*		11. 5.97T
G-BHUE	SAN Jodel DR.1050 Ambassadeur	185	F-BERM F-OBRM	21. 4.80	M.J.Harris	(Worcester)	19.10.92
G-BHUG	Cessna 172N Skyhawk II	17272985	N1283F	24. 6.80	F.G.Baulch t/a FGT Aircraft Hire	Taw Mill, Devon	24. 1.05T
G-BHUI	Cessna 152 II	15283144	N46932	27. 5.80	Galair International Ltd	Wellesbourne Mountford	16.12.04T
G-BHUJ	Cessna 172N Skyhawk II	17271932	N5752E	27. 5.80	Flightline Ltd	Southend	20. 5.05T
G-BHUM	de Havilland DH.82A Tiger Moth	85453	VT-DGA VT-DDN/RIAF/SAAF 4622/DE457	9. 6.80	S.G.Towers	Beckwithshaw, Harrogate	9.12.02
G-BHUR	Thunder Ax3 Mini Sky Chariot HAB	277		9. 5.80	B.F.G.Ribbans *"Ben Hur"* Newbury *(On loan to British Balloon Museum & Library)*		3. 4.03A
G-BHUU	Piper PA-25-260 Pawnee	25-8056035	N2440Q	28. 5.80	Booker Gliding Club Ltd	Booker	2.11.03
G-BHVB	Piper PA-28-161 Warrior II	28-8016260	N9638N	16. 5.80	Caine Aviation Ltd	Wolverhampton	30. 7.04T
G-BHVF	SAN Jodel 150A Mascaret	11	F-BLDF	28.10.80	J.D.Walton	Swanborough Farm, Lewes	12.11.02P
G-BHVP	Cessna 182Q Skylane II	18267071	N97374	15.12.80	R.J.W.Wood	Gregory Farm, Mirfield	20. 9.04T
G-BHVR	Cessna 172N Skyhawk II	17270196	N738SG	27. 5.80	M.G.Montgomerie tr G-BHVR Group	Elstree	7. 6.03T
G-BHVV	Piper J-3C-65 Cub (L-4A-PI)	8953	F-BGXF Fr Mil/42-38384	27. 6.80	C.A.Ward	Rochester	17. 4.03P
	(Frame No.9048)						
	(Regd with c/n 10291/43-1430 which was F-BEGF: frames probably exchanged in 1953 rebuild)						
G-BHWA	Reims/Cessna F152 II	F15201775		28. 3.80	M.Housley & J.H.Mills t/a Lincoln Aviation	Wickenby	2. 6.04T
G-BHWB	Reims/Cessna F152 II	F15201776	(G-BHWA)	14. 4.80	M.Housley & J.H.Mills t/a Lincoln Aviation	Wickenby	20. 8.04T
G-BHWH	Weedhopper JC-24A	0074		23. 4.80	G.A.Clephane *(As "Bu.126603" in US Navy c/s) "Dream Machine"*	Basingstoke	30.11.86E
	(Fuji-Robin EC-34-PM) (Modified to JC-24C)						
G-BHWK	SOCATA MS.880B Rallye Club	870	F-BONK	27. 8.80	L.L.Gayther	Shobdon	16.12.04
G-BHWY	Piper PA-28R-200-2 Cherokee Arrow II	28R-7435059	N56904	17. 6.80	P.R.Gould & R.B.Cheek tr Kilo Foxtrot Flying Group	Sandown	16. 5.05
G-BHWZ	Piper PA-28-181 Cherokee Archer II	28-7890299	N3379M	8. 4.80	M A Abbott	Bournemouth	3. 7.04T
G-BHXA	Scottish Aviation Bulldog Srs.120/1210	BH120/407	Botswana DF OD1 G-BHXA	9. 6.80	Air Plan Flight Equipment Ltd *(Deltair Aviation titles)*	Barton	25. 7.03T
G-BHXD	Jodel Wassmer D.120 Paris-Nice	258	F-BMIA	3. 7.80	J.M.Fforde & M.Roberts	(Brecon)	19. 9.02P
G-BHXK	Piper PA-28-140 Cherokee	28-21106	VR-HGB 9V-BAJ/(9M-AOM)	14. 7.80	J.Moreland Bourne Park, Hurstbourne Tarrant tr GXK Flying Group		1. 6.03
G-BHXS	Jodel Wassmer D.120 Paris-Nice	133	F-BIXS	27. 8.80	I.R.Willis	Glenrothes	16.10.02P
G-BHXY	Piper J-3C-65 Cub (L-4H-PI)	11905	F-DEAXY F-BFQX/44-79609	1. 7.80	F.W.Rogers *(As "479609/PR-L4" in USAAC c/s) "Heather"*	Dunkeswell	16.10.02P
	(Frame No.11733)						
G-BHYA	Cessna R182 Skylane RG II	R18200532	N1717R	10. 7.80	B.Davies	(Sandridge)	27. 3.05
G-BHYC	Cessna 172 RG Cutlass II	172RG0404	(N4868V)	24. 6.80	IB Aeroplanes Ltd	City of Derry	1. 5.05
G-BHYD	Cessna R172K Hawk XP II	R1722734	N736RS	11.12.80	Sylmar Aviation & Services Ltd	Lower Wasing Farm, Brimpton	16. 9.02
G-BHYE	Piper PA-34-200T Seneca II	34-8070233	N8225U	27. 6.80	Oxford Aviation Services Ltd	Oxford	10. 6.04T
G-BHYF	Piper PA-34-200T Seneca II	34-8070234	N8225V	27. 6.80	Oxford Aviation Services Ltd	Oxford	25.11.02T
G-BHYG	Piper PA-34-200T Seneca II	34-8070235	N8225X	30. 6.80	Oxford Aviation Services Ltd	Oxford	9.10.04T
G-BHYI	SNCAN Stampe SV-4A	18	F-BAAF Fr.Mil	11. 7.80	G.L.Brown & A.M.Plato	Spanhoe	22.10.03
G-BHYO	Cameron N-77 HAB	659		30. 6.80	Adventure Balloon Co Ltd *"Alcock & Sissons"* Kirdford *(Op Balloon Preservation Group) (Inflated 6.02)*		8. 5.97A
G-BHYP	Reims/Cessna F172M Skyhawk II	F17201108	OY-BFR	30. 6.80	Avior Ltd	Oxford	16. 6.05T
G-BHYR	Reims/Cessna F172M	F17200922	OY-DZH SE-FZH/(OH-CFQ)	30. 6.80	S.D.Undrill tr G-BHYR Group	Stapleford	10. 7.05

G-BHYV	Evans VP-1	LC.2 & PFA 1569		2. 7.80	L.Chiappi	White Waltham	
	(Volkswagen 1600)				*(Flown 5.89: noted 2.03)*		
G-BHYX	Cessna 152 II	15281832	N67434	4. 7.80	Stapleford Flying Club Ltd	Stapleford	10. 4.05T
G-BHZE	Piper PA-28-181 Cherokee Archer II	28-7890291	OO-FLR	4.11.80	Zegruppe Ltd	White Waltham	12.12.02T
			(OO-HCM)/N3053M				
G-BHZH	Reims/Cessna F152 II	F15201786		25. 7.80	Plymouth School of Flying Ltd	Plymouth	24. 9.04T
G-BHZK	Grumman-American AA-5B Tiger	AA5B-0743	N28670	8. 9.80	R.G.Seth-Smith tr Zulu Kilo Group	Elstree	29. 5.05
G-BHZO	Gulfstream AA-5A Cheetah	AA5A-0692	N26750	21. 7.80	A.H.McVicar *(Op Prestwick Flight Centre)*	Prestwick	23.12.04T
G-BHZR	Scottish Aviation Bulldog Srs.120/1210	BH120/410	OD4	23. 7.80	R Burgess	Haverfordwest	29. 6.03
			Botswana DF/G-BHZR				
G-BHZS	Scottish Aviation Bulldog Srs.120/1210	BH120/411	OD5	23. 7.80	Air Plan Flight Equipment Ltd	Barton	8. 2.99T
			Botswana DF/G-BHZS				
G-BHZT	Scottish Aviation Bulldog Srs.120/1210	BH120/412	OD6	23. 7.80	D.M.Curties	Kemble	14. 3.05T
			Botswana DF/G-BHZT				
G-BHZU	Piper J-3C-65 Cub (L-4B-PI)	9775	F-BETO	17. 7.80	J.K.Tomkinson	Brook Farm, Boylestone, Derbyshire	7. 5.03P
	(Continental O-200-A)		(F-BFKH)/43-914				
	(Regd with Frame No.9606 fitted to F-BETO in 1961 rebuild replacing c/n 13164 ex 45-4424)						
G-BHZV	Jodel Wassmer D.120A Paris-Nice	278	F-BMON	23. 7.80	K.J.Scott	Stoneacre Farm, Farthing Corner	26. 6.00P
G-BHZX	Thunder Ax7-69A HAB	288		25. 7.80	R.J. & H.M.Beattie *"After Eight"*	Aylesbury	10. 6.94A

G-BIAA - G-BIZZ

G-BIAC	SOCATA Rallye 235E Gabier	13323		17. 7.80	D.R.Watson & A.J.Haigh	Maypole Farm, Chislet	18. 6.05T
G-BIAH	Wassmer Jodel D.112	1218	F-BMAH	20. 8.80	T.K.Duffy	Dunnyvadden	22. 5.03P
G-BIAI	Wallingford WMB.2 Windtracker MLB	008		1. 7.80	I.Chadwick tr Unicorn Group *"Amanda I"*	Horsham	
G-BIAK	SOCATA TB-10 Tobago	150		17. 7.80	Westmead Business Group Ltd	Biggin Hill	13. 8.03
G-BIAP	Piper PA-16 Clipper	16-732	F-BBGM	25. 6.80	P.J.Bish	Draycott Farm, Chiseldon	19. 3.04
	(Frame No.16-733)		F-OAGS				
G-BIAR	Rigg Skyliner II MLB	AKC-59 & IAR/02		9. 7.80	I.A.Rigg	Manchester	
G-BIAX	Taylor JT.2 Titch	GFR-1 & PFA 3228		30. 7.80	J.T.Everest	Popham	26. 7.02P
	(Continental O-200)				*(Stored at owner's home during Winter)*		
G-BIAY	Grumman-American AA-5 Traveler	AA5-0423	OY-GAD	26. 8.80	S.Martin	Southend	30. 7.05
			N7123L				
G-BIBA	SOCATA TB-9 Tampico	149		17. 7.80	TB Aviation Ltd	Denham	14. 7.00
G-BIBB	Mooney M.20C Mark 21	2803	OH-MOD	22. 7.80	P.M. Breton	Oaksey Park	23. 6.05
G-BIBJ	Enstrom 280C-UK-2 Shark	1187		13. 8.80	Tindon Ltd	Little Snoring	18. 2.05
G-BIBN	Reims/Cessna FA150K Aerobat	FA1500078	F-BSHN	29.10.80	B.V.Mayo	Maypole Farm, Chislet	7. 1.05
G-BIBO	Cameron V-65 HAB	667		7. 8.80	I.Harris *"Diadem"*	Devizes	30. 6.89A
G-BIBS	Cameron P-20 HAB	671		14. 8.80	Cameron Balloons Ltd	Bristol	
G-BIBT	Gulfstream AA-5B Tiger	AA5B-1047	N4518V	8. 9.80	Vizor Tempered Glass Ltd	Swansea	12. 7.04
G-BIBW	Reims/Cessna F172N Skyhawk II	F17201756		13.10.78	P.T.Fellows & J.C.Waller	Rochester	7. 3.05
G-BIBX	Wallingford WMB.2 Windtracker MLB	9		18. 8.80	I.A.Rigg *"Bumble"*	Manchester	
G-BICD	Taylorcraft J Auster 5	735	F-BFXH	20. 8.80	T R Parsons	Beeches Farm, South Scarle	3. 8.03P
			MT166				
G-BICE	North American AT-6C-1NT Harvard IIA	88-9755	FAP1545	3. 9.80	C.M.L.Edwards	Cherry Tree Farm, Monewden	30. 3.00P
			SAAF 7084/EX302/41-33275		*(As "41-33275/CE" in US Army c/s)*		
G-BICG	Reims/Cessna F152 II	F15201796		3. 9.80	A.S.Bamrah t/a Falcon Flying Services	Biggin Hill	27. 3.05T
G-BICJ	Monnett Sonerai II	726 & PFA 15-10531		22. 8.80	I.Parr	(Berwick-on-Tweed)	20.10.90P
	(Volkswagen 1834)				*(On rebuild 1997: current status unknown)*		
G-BICM	Colt 56A HAB	095		1. 9.80	W.S.Templeton & R.B.Green	Fordingbridge	20. 4.03A
					tr The Avon Advertiser Balloon Club *"Ladybird"*		
G-BICP	Robin DR360 Chevalier	610	F-BSPH	2.10.80	A.E.Smith	Breighton	28. 5.05
G-BICR	Jodel Wassmer D.120A Paris-Nice	135	F-BIXR	5. 9.80	G.L.Perry tr Beehive Flying Group	White Waltham	4. 6.03P
G-BICS	Robin R2100A Club	128	F-GBAC	4.12.80	I.Young	Sandown	18. 5.03
G-BICT*	Evans VP-1	PFA 62-10455		12. 8.80	A.C.Combe & D.L.Tribe	RAF Upavon	20. 2.97P
	(Volkswagen 1600)			*(Damaged near Evesham 4.8.96: cancelled 30.4.01 as WFU) (Fuselage only noted 5.01)*				
G-BICU	Cameron V-56 HAB	680		9. 9.80	S.D.Bather *"Nobby"*	Melksham	20. 9.03A
G-BICW	Piper PA-28-161 Warrior II	28-7916309	N2091U	8.10.80	D.Gellhorn	Blackbushe	15. 2.03
G-BICX	Maule M-5-235C Lunar Rocket	7287C	(G-MAUL(1))	2. 2.81	A.T.Jeans & J.F.Clarkson		1. 7.05
			N56352			Compton Chamberlayne, Salisbury	
G-BICY	Piper PA-23-160 Apache	23-1640	PH-ACL	26. 9.80	A.M.Lynn *(Op Busy Bee)*	Netherthorpe	9. 7.04T
			N4010P/(PH-ACL)/N4010P/N10F				
G-BIDD	Evans VP-1	PFA 62-10974		27.10.78	Jane Hodgkinson	Thruxton	2.12.00P
	(Volkswagen 1600) *(Initially regd with c/n PFA 62-10167 and combined with both projects)*						
G-BIDF	Reims/Cessna F172P Skyhawk II	F17202045	(PH-JPO)	18. 9.80	C.J.Chaplin & N.J.C.Howard	Redhill	6. 3.03T
G-BIDG	SAN Jodel 150A Mascaret	08	F-BLDG	11. 9.80	D.R.Gray	Barton	26. 6.02P
G-BIDH	Cessna 152 II	15280546	G-DONA	12. 9.80	Hull Aero Club Ltd	Linley Hill, Leven	16. 7.05T
			G-BIDH/N25234				
G-BIDI	Piper PA-28R-201 Arrow III	28R-7837135	N3759M	11.11.80	Ambrit Ltd	Elstree	9. 5.02
G-BIDJ	Piper PA-18A-150 Super Cub	18-6007	PH-MAY	22. 9.80	Flight Solutions Ltd	Panshanger	13. 7.03T
	(Frame No.18-6089)		N7798D				
G-BIDK	Piper PA-18-150 Super Cub	"18-6591"	PH-MAI	22. 9.80	J.& M.A.McCullough	Newtownards, Co.Down	5. 6.05
	(L-21A-PI)		R.Neth AF R-211/51-15679/N7194K				
	(This is a composite aircraft - PH-MAI was originally c/n 18-6591 (Frame No.18-6714) ex LN-TVB/N9285D but was rebuilt in 1976 using Frame No.18-503						
	(c/n 18-565) and ex R.Neth AF R-211 as shown)						
G-BIDO	Piel CP.301A Emeraude	327	F-POIO	25. 3.81	A.R.Plumb	Hill Farm, Nayland	19. 8.03P
G-BIDU	Cameron V-77 HAB	660		8. 1.81	N.J.& S.L.Hill	(Lespias, Cezan, France)	19. 7.03A
G-BIDX	Dormois Jodel D.112	876	F-BIQY	19. 9.80	P.Turton & H.C.Peake-Jones		5. 8.03P
						Ash House Farm, Winsford	
G-BIEF	Cameron V-77 HAB	679		25. 9.80	D.S.Bush *"Daedalus"*	Hertingfordbury, Herts	6. 3.94A
G-BIEJ	Sikorsky S-76A II Plus	760097		21.10.80	Bristow Helicopters Ltd *"Glen Lossie"*	North Denes	21. 2.04T
G-BIEN	Jodel Wassmer D.120A Paris-Nice	218	F-BKNK	3. 6.81	C.A.J.Van Andel (Raamsdonksveer, The Netherlands)		11.12.03P
G-BIEO	Wassmer Jodel D.112	1296	F-BMOK	19. 3.82	S.C.Solley tr Clipgate Flyers	Clipgate Farm, Denton	6. 8.03P

Reg	Type	C/n	Prev id	Date	Owner/Operator	Location	Date
G-BIES	Maule M-5-235C Lunar Rocket	7334C	N56394	24. 7.81	W.Procter t/a William Procter Farms	Stowes Farm, Tillingham	25. 3.03
G-BIET	Cameron O-77 HAB	674		30. 9.80	G.M.Westley "Archimedes"	London SW15	11. 1.02A
G-BIEY	Piper PA-28-151 Cherokee Warrior	28-7715213	PH-KDH OO-HCB/N9540N	10.11.80	A.S.Bamrah t/a Falcon Flying Services	Southend	15. 2.04T
G-BIFA	Cessna 310R II	310R1606	N36868	29. 1.81	J.S.Lee	Denham	17. 9.03
G-BIFB	Piper PA-28-150 Cherokee C	28-1968	4X-AEC	6.10.80	N.A.Ayub	Biggin Hill	11. 4.05T
G-BIFN	Bensen B.8MR	KW.1 & PFA G/01-1010		7.10.80	B.Gunn (Current status unknown)	(North Ferriby)	
G-BIFO	Evans VP-1 (Volkswagen 1834)	PFA 62-10411		29. 9.80	R.Broadhead	Eddsfield	11. 9.02P
G-BIFY	Reims/Cessna F150L	F15000829	PH-CEZ	9.10.80	D.M.Nott t/a Astra Associates	Panshanger	26. 9.05T
G-BIFZ	Partenavia P.68C	229		24. 6.81	Eli Sud SRL	(Salerno, Italy)	22.12.02T
G-BIGF*	Thunder Ax7-77 Bolt HAB	295		20.10.80	M.D.Steuer & C.A.Allen "Low Rider" (Cancelled 6.11.01 as WFU: current status unknown)	Monmouth	6. 9.91A
G-BIGJ	Reims/Cessna F172M	F17200936	PH-SKT	2.12.80	V.D.Speck	Clacton	5. 8.02T
G-BIGK	Taylorcraft BC-12D (Continental A65)	8302	N96002 NC96002	29.10.80	N.P.St.J.Ramsay	Hamilton Farm, Bilsington	14.10.02P
G-BIGL	Cameron O-65 HAB	690		22.10.80	P.L.Mossman "Biggles"	Bristol	12.10.02A
G-BIGP	Bensen B.8M (McCulloch)	PFA G/01-1005		14.10.80	R.H.S.Cooper	Cross Houses, Shrewsbury	20.10.97P
G-BIGR	Avenger T.200-2122 MLB	004		6.10.80	R.Light	Stockport	
G-BIGU	Bensen B.8MR	JRM.1 & G/01-1032		5.11.80	I.B.Pitt-Steele	Felthorpe	18. 9.03P
G-BIGY*	Cameron V-65 HAB	655		4. 9.80	Not known "Gemma" (Cancelled 3.6.98 by CAA) (Extant 2000)	Hungerford	
G-BIGZ	Scheibe SF-25B Falke	46142	D-KCAI	22.12.80	P.J.Mcquie tr The Big-z Owners Group	(Henlow)	22. 7.05
G-BIHD	Robin DR400/160 Major 80	1510		29.10.80	A.J.Fieldman	King's Farm, Thurrock	4. 2.04
G-BIHE*	Reims/Cessna FA152 Aerobat	FA1520373		6.11.80	Walkbury Aviation Ltd (Damaged near Sheerness 10.3.99: cancelled as destroyed 21.7.99: substantial parts stored 10.01)	Spanhoe	5. 3.99T
G-BIHF	Replica Plans SE.5A (Continental O-200-A) (Plans No.079275)	PFA 20-10548		27.10.80	S.H.O'Connell "Lady Di" (As "F-943" in 92 Sqdn RFC c/s)	White Waltham	5. 1.01P
G-BIHI	Cessna 172M Skyhawk II	17266854	(G-BIHA) N1125U	18.11.80	L.R.Haunch t/a Fenland Flying School	Fenland	15. 5.05T
G-BIHN*	Airship Industries Skyship 500	1214/02		2.11.80	Airship Heritage Trust (Destroyed San Francisco, CA, USA 1985: cancelled 31.1.91 by CAA) (Gondola only Y 2.03)	(Huntingdon)	1. 4.79
G-BIHO	de Havilland DHC.6 Twin Otter 310	738	A6-ADB G-BIHO	9. 1.81	Isles of Scilly Skybus Ltd	St.Just	18. 4.03T
G-BIHP	Van Den Bemden 1000m3 Gas Balloon (C/n quoted as "18" on Belgian CofR: believed rebuilt with 600m3 canopy c/n VDB-47)	VDB-38	OO-VBA	19.12.80	J.J.Harris "Belgica"	London SW6	3. 5.01
G-BIHT	Piper PA-17 Vagabond (Continental A65)	17-41	N138N N8N/N4626H/NC4626H	9. 1.81	W.E.Willets	Droppingwell Farm, Bewdley	15. 5.01P
G-BIHU	Saffery S.200 MLB	25		5.11.80	B.L.King	Coulsdon	
G-BIHX	Bensen B.8MR (Rotax 503)	PFA G/01-1003		12.11.80	P.P.Willmott	(Grimsby)	10. 7.03P
G-BIIA	Alpavia Fournier RF3	51	F-BMTA	14.11.80	J.D.Webb & J.D.Bally (New owners 8.02)	(Hereford)	16. 7.87P
G-BIIB	Reims/Cessna F172M Skyhawk II	F17201110	PH-GRE	18.11.80	Civil Service Flying Club (Biggin Hill) Ltd	Biggin Hill	24. 4.03T
G-BIID	Piper PA-18 Super Cub 95 (L-18C-PI) (Frame No.18-1558)	18-1606	OO-LPA OO-HMK/ALAT 18-1606/51-15606	5. 1.81	D.A.Lacey	Cumbernauld	9. 7.03P
G-BIIE	Reims/Cessna F172P Skyhawk II	F17202051		31.12.80	Sterling Helicopters Ltd	Norwich	12. 3.05T
G-BIIG	Thunder AX6-56Z HAB	307		26.11.80	A.Spindler	(Cleish)	19. 8.01A
G-BIIK	SOCATA MS.883 Rallye	1151552	F-BSAP	28.11.80	K.M.Bowen	Upfield Farm, Whitson	5. 8.05
G-BIIL	Thunder Ax6-56 Bolt HAB	306		12.11.80	I.M.Ashpole	Ross-on-Wye	3. 9.03A
G-BIIP	Pilatus Britten-Norman BN-2B-27 Islander	2103	6Y-JQJ 6Y-JKJ/N411JA/G-BIIP	1.12.80	Hebridean Air Services Ltd (Op Air X)	Bournemouth	26. 3.03T
G-BIIT	Piper PA-28-161 Warrior II	28-8116052	N82744	1.12.80	Tayside Aviation Ltd	Dundee	1. 4.05T
G-BIIV	Piper PA-28-181 Archer II	28-7990028	N20875	19.12.80	E.Bensoussan	(Paris, France)	21. 8.03T
G-BIIZ	Great Lakes 2T-1A Sport Trainer (Warner Super Scarab 165D-5)	57	N603K NC603K	1. 4.81	Circa 42 Ltd (Damaged Upper Harford, Glos 8.8.98: current status unknown)	(Colchester)	4. 2.99P
G-BIJB	Piper PA-18-150 Super Cub	18-8009001	N23923 N2573H	18. 8.80	Essex Gliding Club Ltd	North Weald	3. 4.04
G-BIJD	Bölkow Bö.208C Junior	636	PH-KAE (PH-DYM)/OO-SIS/(D-EGFA)	9.12.80	P.Singh tr Sikh Syndicate	Leicester	1.10.04
G-BIJE	Piper J-3C-65 Cub (L-4A-PI) (Frame No.8504)	8367	F-BIGN Fr.AF/42-15248	5. 5.81	R.L.Hayward & A.G.Scott (On rebuild 4.91: current status unknown)	Cardiff	
G-BIJS	Phoenix Luton LA-4A Minor (Volkswagen 1600)	PAL/1348 & PFA 835		18. 5.78	I.J.Smith	Brook Farm, Boylestone	14.11.95P
G-BIJU	Menavia Piel CP.301A Emeraude	221	G-BHTX F-BIJU	10. 6.80	J.R.Large tr Eastern Taildraggers Flying Club	Stapleford	17. 7.03P
G-BIJV	Reims/Cessna F152 II	F15201813		22.12.80	A.S.Bamrah t/a Falcon Flying Services	Biggin Hill	21. 3.05T
G-BIJW	Reims/Cessna F152 II	F15201820		22.12.80	A.S.Bamrah t/a Falcon Flying Services	(Blackbushe)	26. 2.05T
G-BIJX	Reims/Cessna F152 II	F15201829		29.12.80	A.S.Bamrah t/a Falcon Flying Services	Goodwood	3. 6.05T
G-BIKC	Boeing 757-236	22174		31. 1.83	DHL Air Ltd	East Midlands	9. 2.03T
G-BIKE	Piper PA-28R-200 Cherokee Arrow II	28R-7335173	OY-DVT N55047	18. 4.80	R.V.Webb Ltd	Elstree	7.10.04
G-BIKF(2)	Boeing 757-236	22177	(G-BIKG)	28. 4.83	Barclays Mercantile Business Finance Ltd (Op DHL)	East Midlands	14. 9.03T
G-BIKG(2)	Boeing 757-236	22178	(G-BIKH)	26. 8.83	DHL Air Ltd	East Midlands	26. 8.03T
G-BIKJ(2)	Boeing 757-236	22181	(G-BIKK)	9. 1.84	DHL Air Ltd	East Midlands	11. 1.04T
G-BIKK(2)	Boeing 757-236	22182	(G-BIKL)	1. 2.84	DHL Air Ltd	East Midlands	1. 2.04T
G-BIKM(2)	Boeing 757-236	22184	N8293V (G-BIKN)	21. 3.84	DHL Air Ltd	East Midlands	22. 3.04T
G-BIKN(2)	Boeing 757-236	22186	(G-BIKP)	23. 1.85	Barclays Mercantile Business Finance Ltd (Op DHL)	East Midlands	22. 9.05T
G-BIKO(2)	Boeing 757-236	22187	(G-BIKR)	14. 2.85	Barclays Mercantile Business Finance Ltd (Op DHL)	East Midlands	18. 2.05T

G-BIKP(2)	Boeing 757-236	22188	(G-BIKS)	11. 3.85	DHL Air Ltd	East Midlands	14. 3.05T
G-BIKR(2)	Boeing 757-236	22189	(G-BIKT)	29. 3.85	European Air Transport NV/SA	East Midlands	2. 4.05T
					(Op DHL)		
G-BIKS(2)	Boeing 757-236	22190	(G-BIKU)	31. 5.85	Barclays Mercantile Business Finance Ltd		
					(Op DHL)	East Midlands	2. 6.05T
G-BIKT(2)	Boeing 757-236	23398		1.11.85	British Airways plc *(For disposal 10.02)*	Heathrow	3.11.05T
G-BIKU(2)	Boeing 757-236	23399		7.11.85	DHL Air Ltd	East Midlands	7.11.05T
G-BIKV	Boeing 757-236	23400		9.12.85	DHL Air Ltd	East Midlands	11.12.05T
G-BIKW	Boeing 757-236	23492		7. 3.86	European Air Transport NV/SA	East Midlands	21. 3.05T
G-BIKY	Boeing 757-236	23533		28. 3.86	European Air Transport NV/SA	Brussels, Belgium	31. 3.05T
G-BIKZ	Boeing 757-236	23532		15. 5.86	DHL Air Ltd	Brussels, Belgium	30. 9.04T
G-BILB	Wallingford WMB-2 Windtracker MLB	14		22. 1.81	B.L.King	Coulsdon	
G-BILE	Scruggs BL-2B MLB	81231		13. 3.81	P.D.Ridout	Botley	
G-BILG	Scruggs BL-2B MLB	81232		13. 3.81	P.D.Ridout	Botley	
G-BILI	Piper J-3C-65 Cub (L-4J-PI)	13207	F-BDTB	14. 1.81	S.C.Wilson & J A Goodridge	White Waltham	12. 6.03P
	(Frame No.13044)		45-4467		tr G-BILI Flying Group *(As "454467/J/44" in US Army c/s)*		
G-BILJ	Reims/Cessna FA152 Aerobat	FA1520376		31.12.80	Bflying Ltd	Bournemouth	4. 7.05T
					(Op Bournemouth Flying Club)		
G-BILL	Piper PA-25-235 Pawnee D	25-7856028	N9174T	3. 1.79	A E & W.J.Taylor t/a Pawnee Aviation	East Winch	28. 6.03A
	(Lycoming O-540-G2A5 @ 260hp)						
G-BILR	Cessna 152 II	15284822	N4822P	19. 3.81	Shropshire Aero Club Ltd	Sleap	8. 5.05T
G-BILS	Cessna 152 II	15284857	N4954P	3. 6.81	Keen Leasing (IoM) Ltd	Newtownards, Co.Down	5. 7.02T
G-BILU	Cessna 172 RG Cutlass II	172RG0564	N5540V	29. 1.81	R.M.English & Sons Ltd	Full Sutton	6. 7.03T
G-BILZ	Taylor JT.1 Monoplane	PFA 55-10244		15.12.80	A.Petherbridge	Sibsey	29. 2.91P
	(Volkswagen 1600) *(Regd as c/n PFA 55-10124)*				*(Damaged Ingoldmells 10.6.90: stored 8.00)*		
G-BIMK	Tiger T.200 Srs.1 MLB	7/MKB-01		22.12.80	M.K.Baron	Stockport	
G-BIMM	Piper PA-18-150 Super Cub	18-3868	PH-VHO	8. 1.81	Spectrum Leisure Ltd	Clacton	6. 8.04
	(L-21B-PI) *(Frame No.18-3881)*		R.Neth AF R-178/54-2468				
G-BIMN	Steen Skybolt	PFA 64-10329		31.12.80	P.J.Reed tr Skybolt Six	Dunkeswell	1. .03P
	(Lycoming IO-360)						
G-BIMO	SNCAN Stampe SV-4C	394	F-BADG	5. 3.81	R.A.Robert	Sparr Farm, West Sussex	17. 3.02
	(DH Gipsy Major 10)		Fr.Mil		*(As "394" in French AF c/s)*		
G-BIMT	Reims/Cessna FA152 Aerobat	FA1520361	N8062L	9. 1.81	Gloucestershire Flying Services Ltd	Gloucestershire	26. 5.05T
G-BIMU	Sikorsky S-61N Mk II	61-752	N8511Z	9. 1.81	Bristow Helicopters Ltd	Stornoway	23.10.05T
	(SAR conversion)		VH-CRU/N4042S		*(Op Marine & Coastguard Agency) "Stac Pollaidh"*		
G-BIMX	Rutan VariEze	PFA 74-10544		6. 1.81	D.G.Crew	Biggin Hill	15 5.03P
	(Continental O-200-A)						
G-BIMZ	Beech 76 Duchess	ME-169	N6021K	20. 3.81	Firfax Systems Ltd	Gloucestershire	15.12.02
G-BING	Reims/Cessna F172P Skyhawk II	F17202084		12. 1.81	M.P.Dolan	City of Derry	16. 4.05
G-BINL	Scruggs BL-2B MLB	81216		5. 2.81	P.D.Ridout	Botley	
G-BINM	Scruggs BL-2B MLB	81217		5. 2.81	P.D.Ridout	Botley	
G-BINR	Unicorn UE-1A MLB	81004		20. 1.81	I.Chadwick tr Unicorn Group *"Lady Diana"*	Horsham	
G-BINS	Unicorn UE-2A MLB	80002		22.12.80	I.Chadwick tr Unicorn Group *"Caroline"*	Horsham	
G-BINT	Unicorn UE-1A MLB	80001		22.12.80	D.E.Bint	(Downham Market)	
G-BINX	Scruggs BL-2B MLB	81219		5. 2.81	P.D.Ridout	Botley	
G-BINY	Oriental Air-Bag MLB	OAB-001		22. 1.81	J.L.Morton	Wokingham	
G-BIOA	Hughes 369D (500)	120-0880D	OO-HFS	9. 2.81	AH Helicopter Services Ltd	Newton Abbot	8. 5.03T
			LX-HLE/OO-HFS/G-BIOA				
G-BIOB	Reims/Cessna F172P Skyhawk II	F17202042		23. 1.81	Aerofilms Ltd	Cranfield	16. 4.05T
G-BIOC	Reims/Cessna F150L	F15000848	F-BUEC	3. 2.81	D.J.Gage & G.Burns tr Southside Flyers	Prestwick	27. 8.05T
G-BIOI	SAN Jodel DR.1050/M Excellence	477	F-BLJQ	21. 1.81	R.Pidcock	Fenland	21. 4.03P
G-BIOJ	Rockwell Commander 112TC-A	13192	N4662W	22. 1.82	A.T.Dalby	Sywell	13.12.02
G-BIOK	Reims/Cessna F152 II	F15201810		2. 2.81	Tayside Aviation Ltd	Dundee	18. 4.05T
G-BIOM	Reims/Cessna F152 II	F15201815		5. 2.81	A.S.Bamrah t/a Falcon Flying Services	Headcorn	25. 4.02T
G-BIOR	SOCATA MS.880B Rallye Club	1229	OO-SAF	3. 2.81	R.L. & K.P.McLean	Rufforth	26. 9.02
	(Composite rebuild with components from G-AZGJ)				t/a McLean Aviation		
G-BIOU	SAN Jodel D.117A	813	F-BIOU	9. 8.78	M.D.Howlett tr Dubious Group	Ilmer, Bucks	23. 5.03P
G-BIOW	Slingsby T.67A	1988		26. 2.81	A.B.Slinger tr Slingsby T67A Group	Sherburn-in-Elmet	31. 3.03
G-BIPA	Grumman-American AA-5B Tiger	AA5B-0200	OY-GAM	24. 3.81	J.Campbell	Walney Island	14. 6.05
G-BIPH	Scruggs BL-2B MLB	81224		10. 2.81	C.M.Dewsnap	Camberley	
G-BIPI	Everett Gyroplane (Volkswagen 1834)	001		30. 4.81	C A Reeves	Apperley, Glos	19. 6.01P
G-BIPN	Alpavia Fournier RF3	35	F-BMDN	26. 2.81	J.C.R.Rogers & I.F.Fairhead	Cranwell	20.12.02P
G-BIPO	Mudry/CAARP CAP.20LS-200	03	F-GAUB	5. 3.81	A.McClean tr The CAP 20 Group	White Waltham	28. 4.03S
G-BIPT	Wassmer Jodel D.112	1254	F-BMIB	11. 3.81	C.R.Davies	Allensmore, Hereford	13. 3.03P
G-BIPV	Gulfstream AA-5B Tiger	AA5B-0981	N28266	10. 3.81	Airtime Aviation Ltd	Bournemouth	20. 5.05T
G-BIPW	Avenger T200-2112 MLB	10		24. 2.81	B.L.King	Coulsdon	
G-BIPY	Montgomerie-Bensen B.8MR			25. 2.81	C.G.Ponsford	(Braintree)	13.10.95P
	(Rotax 532) AJW.01 & PFA G/01-1007						
G-BIRD	Pitts S-1D Special 707-H & PFA 1596			3.11.77	P Metcalfe	(Stockton-on-Tees)	22. 1.03P
	(Lycoming IO-360)						
G-BIRE	Colt Bottle 56SS HAB *(Satzenbrau Bottle)*	323		4. 3.81	K.R.Gafney *"Satzenbrau"*	Bracknell	10. 1.84A
G-BIRH	Piper PA-18-150 Super Cub	18-3853	PH-LET	19. 3.81	Aquila Gliding Club Ltd	Hinton in the Hedges	19. 6.05
	(L-21B-PI) (Lycoming O-360-A4) *(Frame No.18-3857)*		R Neth AF R-163/54-2453		*(As "R-163" in R.Neth AF c/s)*		
G-BIRI	CASA I-131E Jungmann	1074	E3B-113	14. 4.81	M.G. & J.R.Jefferies	Little Gransden	27. 9.01P
G-BIRL	Avenger T200-2112 MLB	008		10. 3.81	R.Light	Stockport	
G-BIRP	Ridout Arena Mk.17 Skyship MLB	01		13. 3.81	Annette S.Viel	Botley	
G-BIRT	Robin R1180TD Aiglon	276		25. 3.81	W.D'A.Hall	White Waltham	19.11.05
G-BIRZ	Zenair CH.250-100 2-454 & PFA 24-10459			10. 3.81	L.D.Johnston	Perth	5. 8.03P
	(Lycoming O-290-G)						
G-BISG	Clutton FRED Srs.III RAC 01-224 & PFA 29-10675			13. 3.81	T.Littlefair *"Fuzz Bee"*	Lymington	29.10.86P
	(Volkswagen 1600)				*(New owner 10.00)*		
G-BISH	Cameron V-65 HAB	707		16. 3.81	P.J.Bish & C.Hall *"Tsaritsa"*	Hungerford	31. 7.03A
					t/a Zebedee Balloon Service		

Reg	Type	C/n	Prev id	Date	Owner/Operator	Location	Date
G-BISJ	Cessna 340A II	340A0497	OO-LFK N6328X	10. 4.81	Midland Airline Transport Services Ltd	Birmingham	24. 7.05T
G-BISL	Scruggs BL-2B MLB	81233		13. 3.81	P.D.Ridout	Botley	
G-BISM	Scruggs BL-2B MLB	81234		13. 3.81	P.D.Ridout	Botley	
G-BISS	Scruggs BL-2C MLB	81235		13. 3.81	P.D.Ridout	Botley	
G-BIST	Scruggs BL-2C MLB	81236		13. 3.81	P.D.Ridout	Botley	
G-BISX	Colt 56A HAB	324		18. 3.81	C.D.Steel	St Boswells	18. 8.99A
G-BISZ	Sikorsky S-76A II Plus	760156		19. 3.81	Bristow Helicopters Ltd	Redhill	23.10.04T
G-BITA	Piper PA-18-150 Super Cub	18-8109037	N82585	24. 3.81	D.J.Gilmour t/a Intrepid Aviation Co	North Weald	23. 7.05
G-BITE	SOCATA TB-10 Tobago	193		7. 5.81	M.A.Smith	Fairoaks	19.12.05
G-BITF	Reims/Cessna F152 II	F15201822		27. 3.81	Tayside Aviation Ltd	Dundee	18. 6.03T
G-BITH	Reims/Cessna F152 II	F15201825		27. 3.81	Tayside Aviation Ltd	Dundee	31. 8.03T
G-BITK	Clutton FRED Srs.II (Volkswagen 1500)	PFA 29-10369		23. 3.81	D.J.Wood	(Dover)	
G-BITM	Reims/Cessna F172P Skyhawk II	F17202046		13. 4.81	Dreamtrade Ltd	Barton	6. 11.05T
G-BITO	Wassmer Jodel D.112D	1200	F-BIUO	20. 3.81	A.Dunbar	Barton	5. 9.02P
G-BITS	Drayton B-56 HAB	MJB-01/81		16. 3.81	M.J.Betts	Drayton, Norwich	
	(Op Eastern Region, British Balloon & Airship Club) "Hedger"						
G-BITW*	Short SD.3-30 Var.100	SH.3070	G-EASI (G-BITW)/G-14-3070	26. 3.81	Air Salvage International	Alton	9. 6.98T
	(WFU Coventry 7.97 & broken up 7.99: cancelled 20.7.99 as WFU) (Fuselage noted 1.02)						
G-BITX*	Short SD.3-30 Var.100	SH.3069	G-14-3069	26. 3.81	Air Salvage International	Alton	20. 7.90T
	(Cancelled 19.4.90 - to OY-MUB) (Fuselage noted as "OY-MUB" 4.02)						
G-BITY	Bell FD.31T Flying Dodo MLB	2604		25. 3.81	A.J.Bell	Luton	
G-BIUL*	Cameron Bellows 60SS HAB *(Expansion Joint Shape)*	703		27. 3.81	J Hayden	Abingdon	12. 5.91
	(Cancelled 26.6.98 by CAA) (Inflated 4.02)						
G-BIUM	Reims/Cessna F152 II	F15201807		3. 4.81	Sheffield Aero Club Ltd	Netherthorpe	31. 1.03T
G-BIUO*	Rockwell Commander 112A	281	OY-PRH N1281J	30. 3.81	Not known	Bristol	28.10.84
	(Collided with Cirrus BGA.2138 Longdon 12.5.84: cancelled 10.1.89 as destroyed) (Wreck dumped 9.00)						
G-BIUP	SNCAN NC.854	S54	(G-AMPE) G-BIUP/F-BFSC	4. 6.81	J.Greenaway & T.D.Cooper tr BIUP Flying Group	Popham	10. 7.03P
G-BIUV	Hawker Siddeley HS.748 Srs.2A/275LFD	1701	5W-FAN G-AYYH/G-11-8	11. 5.81	Emerald Airways Ltd "City of Liverpool"	Liverpool	16. 6.05T
G-BIUW	Piper PA-28-161 Warrior II	28-8116128	N9506N	14. 4.81	D.R.Staley	Sturgate	27. 6.05
G-BIUY	Piper PA-28-181 Archer II	28-8190103	N8318X	3. 4.81	J.S.Develin & Z.Islam	Shoreham	3. 1.05T
G-BIVA	Robin R2112	137	F-GBAZ	6. 5.81	P.A.Richardson	Conington	4. 11.05
G-BIVC	Wassmer Jodel D.112 (Continental A65)	1219	F-BMAI	1. 6.81	M.J.Barnby	Brickhouse Farm, Frogland Cross	13. 7.00P
G-BIVF	Scintex CP.301C3 Emeraude	594	F-BJVN	4.11.81	R.J.Moore	Sywell	3.12.02P
G-BIVK	Bensen B.8V (Volkswagen 1834) *(Regd as B.8M)*	PFA G/01-1008		10. 4.81	D.Hamilton-Brown "Skyrider"	Henstridge	19.11.03P
G-BIVV	Gulfstream AA-5A Cheetah	AA5A-0857	N26979	26. 5.81	R.Afia t/a Robert Afia Consulting Engineer	Denham	18. 7.05T
G-BIWA	Stevendon Skyreacher MLB	102		8. 6.81	S.D.Barnes	Botley	
G-BIWB	Scruggs RS.5000 MLB	81541		8. 6.81	P.D.Ridout	Botley	8.10.03P
G-BIWC	Scruggs RS.5000 MLB	81546		26. 6.81	P.D.Ridout "Waterloo"	Botley	
G-BIWF	Ridout Warren Windcatcher MLB	WW.013		3. 7.81	P.D.Ridout	Botley	
G-BIWG	Ridout Zelenski Mk.2 MLB *(Regd with c/n 2401)*	Z.401		3. 7.81	P.D.Ridout	Botley	
G-BIWJ	Unicorn UE-1A MLB	81014		14. 7.81	B.L.King	Coulsdon	
G-BIWK	Cameron V-65 HAB	719		22. 4.81	I.R.Williams & R.G.Bickerdike "Double Fantasy"	Bedford/Huntingdon	30. 3.99A
G-BIWL	Piper PA-32-301 Saratoga	32-8106056	N83684	23. 4.81	A.R.Ward	Southend	1. 7.05
G-BIWN	Wassmer Jodel D.112	1314	F-BNCN	5. 6.81	C.R.Coates	Sneaton Thorpe, Whitby	8.10.03P
G-BIWR	Mooney M.20F Executive	22-1339	N6972V	1. 6.81	A.C.Brink	Bourn	19.10.03
G-BIWU	Cameron V-65 HAB	717		15. 5.81	D.J.Groombridge "Bumble Bee"	Bristol	3.12.98A
G-BIWW	American AA-5 Traveler	AA5-0263	OY-AYV	2 .6.81	B.M.R. & K.R.Sheppard "Kit-Kat" tr B & K Aviation Group	Little Staughton	3. 9.05
G-BIXA	SOCATA TB-9 Tampico	205		7. 5.81	W.& K.J.C.Maxwell	Perth	30. 9.05
G-BIXB	SOCATA TB-9 Tampico	208		7. 5.81	Aerolease Ltd	Conington	7. 3.03T
G-BIXH	Reims/Cessna F152 II	F15201840		30. 4.81	The Cambridge Aero Club Ltd	Cambridge	28. 2.03T
G-BIXI	Cessna 172 RG Cutlass II	172RG0861	N7533B	7. 7.81	J.F.P.Lewis tr X India Group	Sandown	10. 6.05
G-BIXL	North American P-51D-20NA Mustang	122-38675	IDF/AF2343 Fv.26116/44-72216	3. 7.81	R.J.Lamplough "Miss Helen" Manor Farm, East Garston		23. 6.03P
	(As "472216/HO-M" in 487th Fighter Sqdn/352nd Fighter Group c/s)						
G-BIXN	Boeing-Stearman A75N1 (PT-17-BW) Kaydet (Continental W670)	75-2248	N51132 41-8689	15. 6.81	V.S.E.Norman	Rendcomb	3. 8.96
	(As "FJ777" in RCAF c/s)						
G-BIXV	Bell 212	30870	N16931	27. 5.81	Bristow Helicopters Ltd	(Kazakhstan)	22. 7.05T
G-BIXW	Colt 56B HAB	348		18. 5.81	N.A.P.Bates "Spam"	Tunbridge Wells	17. 8.97A
G-BIXX	Pearson Srs.II MLB	00327		8. 5.81	D.Pearson	Solihull	
G-BIXZ	Grob G-109	6019	D-KGRO	14. 5.81	D.L.Nind & I.Allum	Booker/ Enstone	10. 6.04
G-BIYI	Cameron V-65 HAB	722		21. 5.81	P.F.Smart tr The Sarnia Balloon Group "Penny"	Basingstoke	16. 4.97A
G-BIYJ	Piper PA-18 Super Cub 95 (L-18C-PI)	18-1000	MM51-15303 I-EIST/MM51-15303/51-15303	5. 6.81	S.Russel	Wilkieston Farm, Peat Inn	27. 8.03P
G-BIYK	Isaacs Fury II (Continental C90)	PFA 11-10418		20. 5.81	C.W.Wilkins	(Peterborough)	1. 4.03P
G-BIYP	Piper PA-20 Pacer 125	20-802	CN-TYP F-DACJ/OO-ADP	25. 5.83	A.W.Hoy & S.W.M.Johnson	(Farnham)	3. 6.05
G-BIYR	Piper PA-18-150 Super Cub (L-21B-PI) *(Frame No. 18-3843)*	18-3841	(G-BIYB) PH-GER R.Neth AF R-151/5G-96/54-2441	26. 5.81	B.H.& M.J.Fairclough Watchford Farm, Yarcombe tr The Delta Foxtrot Flying Group *(As "R-151" in R.Neth AF c/s)*		1. 6.04
G-BIYT	Colt 17A Cloudhopper HAB	344		13. 7.81	J-M Francois	Salles-Courbatiers, France	30. 7.03A
G-BIYU	Fokker S.11-1 Instructor	6206	(PH-HOM) R.Neth AF E-15	13. 5.81	C.Briggs *(As "E-15" in R.Neth AF c/s)*	Bagby	24.10.01P

G-BIYW	Wassmer Jodel D.112	1209	F-BLNR	26. 5.81	K.Balaam	Poplar Hall Farm, Elmsett	18. 9.03P	
					tr Pollard/Balaam/Bye Flying Group			
G-BIYX	Piper PA-28-140 Cherokee Cruiser	28-7625064	OY-BLD	19. 6.81	W.B.Bateson	Blackpool	4. 4.05T	
G-BIYY	Piper PA-18 Super Cub 95	18-1979	MM52-2379	2. 6.81	A.E. & W.J.Taylor	Fenland	6. 3.05T	
	(L-18C-PI) *(Frame No.18-1914)*		I-EIGA/MM52-2379/52-2379					
G-BIZE	SOCATA TB-9 Tampico	209	9H-ABJ	15. 6.81	C.Fordham	Bourn	3. 7.05	
			G-BIZE					
G-BIZF	Reims/Cessna F172P Skyhawk II	F17202070		16. 6.81	R.S.Bentley	Cambridge	12. 6.04	
G-BIZG	Reims/Cessna F152 II	F15201873		16. 6.81	M.A.Judge tr Aero Group 78	(Sheffield)	31. 5.03T	
G-BIZI	Robin DR400 2+2	1543		29. 5.81	BIZI Club Ltd	Standalone Farm, Meppershall	18. 4.03T	
G-BIZK	Nord 3202B1	78	N2255E	22.11.85	A.I.Milne	Little Snoring	4.11.03P	
			ALAT		*(All-yellow French AF c/s)*			
G-BIZM	Nord 3202B	91	N2256K	22.11.85	Global Aviation Ltd	Humberside	31.10.00P	
			ALAT		*(New owner 6.02)*			
G-BIZO	Piper PA-28R-200 Cherokee Arrow II	28R-7535339	OY-DLH	16. 6.81	P.J.Mason & J.F.Leather	(Bristol)	1. 2.03	
			N1578X		tr Lemas Air			
G-BIZR	SOCATA TB-9 Tampico	210	G-BSEC	15. 6.81	R M A Kedzlie & E S Murphy	Fenland	19. 7.04	
			G-BIZR		tr Fenland Flying Group			
G-BIZT*	Bensen B.8M	PFA G/01-1015		10. 6.81	J.Ferguson	Kilkerran	12. 8.88P	
	(Volkswagen 1835)				*(Cancelled 3.4.97 by CAA) (Stored 6.00)*			
G-BIZU	Thunder Ax6-56Z HAB	358		15. 6.81	M.J.Loades *"Greenall Whitley"*	Southampton	6. 7.03A	
G-BIZV	Piper PA-18 Super Cub 95	18-2001	EI-74	12. 6.81	B.Davies	(Chester)	27. 6.03P	
	(L-18C-PI)		I-EIDE/MM522401/52-2401		*(As "18-2001" in US Army c/s)*			
G-BIZW	Champion 7GCBC Citabria	0157	D-EGPD	16. 7.81	J.C.Read t/a G.Read & Sons	North Reston	30. 8.04	
G-BIZY	Wassmer Jodel D.112	1120	F-BKJL	13. 7.81	W.Tunley	Hinton in the Hedges	20. 5.03P	
					t/a Wayland Tunley & Associates			

G-BJAA - G-BJZZ

G-BJAD	Clutton FRED Srs.2	CA.1 & PFA 29-10586		11. 6.81	Newark (Nottinghamshire & Lincolnshire) Air Museum Ltd			
						Newark		
G-BJAE	Lavadoux Starck AS.80 Holiday	04	F-PGGA	17. 6.81	D.J. & Mrs S.A.E.Phillips	(Leamington Spa)	8. 8.92P	
	(Continental A65)		F-WGGA		*(Damaged Woburn 17.8.91: current status unknown)*			
G-BJAF	Piper J-3C-65 Cub (L-4A-PI)	8437	D-EJAF	23. 6.81	P.J.Cottle	Craysmarsh Farm, Melksham	4. 9.03P	
	(Frame No.8540)		HB-OAD/42-15318					
G-BJAG	Piper PA-28-181 Archer II	28-7990353	PH-LDB	23. 6.81	C.R.Chubb	Manston	18. 6.05T	
			(PH-BEG)/(OO-FLM)/N2244W					
G-BJAJ	Gulfstream AA-5B Tiger	AA5B-1177	N4532V	2. 7.81	A.H.McVicar	Prestwick	17. 5.03T	
					(Op Prestwick Flight Centre)			
G-BJAL	CASA I-131E Jungmann	1028	E3B-114	11. 9.78	I.C.Underwood & S.B.J.Chandler	Breighton	29. 6.03P	
	(Spanish AF serial no. conflicts with G-BUCC)							
G-BJAO	Montgomerie-Bensen B.8MR			28. 8.81	A.P.Lay	Henstridge	2. 4.01P	
	(Rotax 582)	GLS-01 & PFA G/01-1001	*(Regd with c/n GL5-01)*					
G-BJAP	de Havilland DH.82A Tiger Moth	0482 & PFA 157-12897		15. 6.81	K.Knight	Shobdon	24. 7.03P	
	(Composite rebuild)				*(As "K2587" in pre-war 32 Sqdn/CFS c/s)*			
G-BJAS	Rango NA-9 MLB	TL-19		22. 6.81	A.Lindsay	Twickenham		
G-BJAV	Gardan GY-80-160 Horizon	28	OO-AJP	8. 9.81	P.L.Lovegrove	Bournemouth	26.10.03	
			F-BLVB					
G-BJAW	Cameron V-65 HAB	745		19. 6.81	G.A.McCarthy *"Breezin"*	Shepton Mallet	16. 4.86A	
G-BJAY	Piper J-3C-65 Cub (L-4H-PI)	12086	F-BFBN	1.11.78	D W Finlay (Lamourache Nord, Acquitaine, France)		18. 7.02P	
	(Frame No.11914)		OO-EAC/44-79790					
G-BJBK	Piper PA-18 Super Cub 95	18-1431	F-BOME	21. 8.81	M.S.Bird	Pepperbox, Salisbury	30. 5.03P	
	(L-18C-PI) (Continental O-200-A)*(Frame No.18-1370)*		ALAT/51-15431					
G-BJBM	Monnett Sonerai I	MEA-117 & PFA 15-10022		2. 7.81	T.F.Harrison	(Wolverhampton)	9. 1.97T	
	(Volkswagen 2074)				tr Sonerai G-BJBM Group *(New owner 1.02)*			
G-BJBO	CEA Jodel DR.250/160 Capitaine	40	F-BNJG	24. 8.81	R.C.Thornton tr Wiltshire Flying Group	Oaksey Park	1. 8.03	
G-BJBW	Piper PA-28-161 Warrior II	28-8116280	N2913Z	22. 7.81	T.G.Phillips, C.Greenland & J.Page	Popham	11. 1.03	
					tr 152 Group			
G-BJBX	Piper PA-28-161 Warrior II	28-8116269	N8414H	17. 7.81	Haimoss Ltd *(Op Old Sarum Flying Club)*	Old Sarum	15. 3.03T	
G-BJBY*	Piper PA-28-161 Warrior II	28-8116270	N8415L	20. 7.81	Haimoss Ltd	Old Sarum	10.12.99T	
					(Damaged Old Sarum 23.11.97: cancelled 3.3.98 as WFU) (Fuselage noted 8.01)			
G-BJCA	Piper PA-28-161 Warrior II	28-7916473	N2846D	30. 7.81	Plane Sailing (South West) Ltd	Plymouth	17. 2.03T	
G-BJCF	Scintex CP.1310-C3 Super Emeraude	936	F-BMJH	19.11.81	K.M.Hodson & C.G.H.Gurney	Manor Farm, Binham	15. 7.02P	
G-BJCI	Piper PA-18-150 Super Cub	18-6658	N9388D	10. 9.81	The Borders (Milfield) Aero-Tow Club Ltd	Milfield	10. 7.03	
	(Lycoming O-360-A4)							
G-BJCW	Piper PA-32R-301 Saratoga SP	32R-8113094	N2866U	6. 8.81	Golf Charlie Whisky Ltd	Fairoaks	27. 5.05	
G-BJDE	Reims/Cessna F172M	F17200984	OO-MSS	25. 8.81	S.P.Heathfield	Cranfield	31. 8.03	
			D-EGBR		t/a Cranfield Aircraft Partnership			
G-BJDF	SOCATA MS.880B Rallye 100T	3000	F-GAKP	21. 9.81	A.J.Wilkinson	Coldharbour Farm, Willingham	28. 2.03	
					tr G-BJDF Group			
G-BJDJ	British Aerospace HS.125 Srs.700B	257142	G-RCDI	27. 7.81	Falcon Jet Centre Ltd	Farnborough	8.10.05T	
			G-BJDJ/G-5-12					
G-BJDK	Ridout European E.157 MLB	S.2		17. 8.81	E.Osborn t/a Aeroprint Tours	Southampton		
G-BJDO	Gulfstream AA-5A Cheetah	AA5A-0823	N26936	3. 8.81	J.J.Woodhouse t/a Flying Services	Sandown	11. 4.03T	
G-BJDT	SOCATA TB-9 Tampico	227		21. 8.81	M J Foggo	(Isleworth)	22. 5.03T	
G-BJDW	Reims/Cessna F172M Skyhawk II	F17201417	PH-JBE	10. 8.81	J.Rae	Earls Colne	16.12.02T	
G-BJEI	Piper PA-18 Super Cub 95	18-1988	EI-66	27. 7.81	H.J.Cox	Wendover Farm, Sheepwash	7. 7.03P	
	(L-18C-PI) *(Frame No.18-1938)*		I-EILO/MM522388/52-2388					
G-BJEL	SNCAN NC.854S	113	F-BEZT	7. 8.81	N.F. & S.G.Hunter	Wolvesnewton, Chepstow	5. 9.02P	
G-BJEV	Aeronca 11AC Chief	11AC-270	N85897	12. 8.81	R.F.Willcox	Eastbach Farm, Coleford	10. 6.03P	
			NC85897		*(As "E/897" in US Navy c/s)*			
G-BJEX	Bölkow Bö.208C Junior	690	F-BRHY	27. 8.81	G.D.H.Crawford	(Henley-on-Thames)	28. 1.88	
			D-EEAM		*(Current status unknown)*			

G-BJFC	Ridout European E.8 MLB	S.1			17. 8.81	P.D.Ridout	Botley	
G-BJFE	Piper PA-18 Super Cub 95 (L-18C-PI)	18-2022	EI-91 I-EISU/MM522422/52-2422		17. 8.81	P.H.Wilmot-Allistone	Kemble	29 9.03P
G-BJFL	Sikorsky S-76A II Plus	760056	N106BH N1546T/(G-BHRK)		28. 8.81	Bristow Helicopters Ltd "Glen Moray"	(Kazaskstan)	17. 9.05T
G-BJFM	Jodel Wassmer D.120 Paris-Nice	227	F-BLFM		8.10.81	J.V.George & P.A.Smith	Popham	29.11.02P
G-BJGK	Cameron V-77 HAB	696			3. 9.81	M E.Orchard	Bristol	14.12.02A
G-BJGM	Unicorn UE-1A MLB	81015			21. 8.81	D.Eaves & P.D.Ridout "Capricorn"	Southampton	
G-BJGV	Bell 212	31171	5N-ALT G-BJGV/9V-BMH		9. 9.81	Bristow Helicopters Ltd (To become ZJ965 4.03)	Aberdeen	2. 9.05T
G-BJGX	Sikorsky S-76A II Plus	760026	N103BH N4251S		4. 9.81	Bristow Helicopters Ltd "Glen Elgin"	North Denes	8.10.03T
G-BJGY	Reims/Cessna F172P Skyhawk II	F17202128			13.10.81	K.& S.Martin	Gunton Hall, Somerton	13. 4.03
G-BJHB	Mooney M.20J (201)	24-1190	N1145G		23.12.81	Zitair Flying Club Ltd	Booker	23 5.05T
G-BJHK	EAA Acro-Sport 1 (Lycoming IO-360)	PFA 72-10470			20. 3.80	M.R.Holden	Stoneacre Farm, Farthing Corner	7. 7.03P
G-BJHT*	Thunder Ax7-65 Bolt HAB	368			27. 8.81	A.H. & L.Symonds "Aura" (Cancelled 1.2.00 as WFU)	Chelmsford	
G-BJIA	Allport Aerostatics YUO-1A-1-DA MLB	01			2. 9.81	D.J.Allport	Bourne, Lincs	
G-BJIC	Eaves Dodo 1A MLB	DD.3			4. 9.81	P.D.Ridout	Botley	
G-BJID	Osprey Lizzieliner 1B MLB	AKC.28			4. 9.81	P.D.Ridout	Botley	
G-BJIG	Slingsby T.67A	1992			16. 9.81	D.Lacy tr G-BJIG Slingsby Syndicate	White Waltham	15. 4.04
G-BJIR	Cessna 550 Citation II	550-0296	N6888C		17. 9.81	Gator Aviation Ltd (Op Aviation Beauport Ltd)	Jersey	17. 1.03T
G-BJIV	Piper PA-18-150 Super Cub (Lycoming O-360-A4)	18-8262	N5972Z		17. 9.81	Yorkshire Gliding Club (Pty) Ltd	Sutton Bank	30. 7.03
G-BJKF	SOCATA TB-9 Tampico	240			30. 9.81	P.C.Churcher t/a Venue Solutions	Denham	8. 4.04
G-BJKW	Wills Aera 2	A3JKW			1. 3.78	J.K.S.Wills	London SE3	
G-BJKY	Reims/Cessna F152 II	F15201886			22. 9.81	Manx Aero Marine Management Ltd (Op Westair Flying Services)	Blackpool	14.10.04T
G-BJLB	SNCAN NC.854S	58	(OO-MVM) F-BFSG		5.11.81	N.F.Hunter (Crashed nr Newport,Gwent 29.7.84: stored 8.90: current status unkownn)	Wolvesnewton, Chepstow	30. 6.83P
G-BJLC	Monnett Sonerai IIL (Volkswagen 1835)	942L & PFA 15-10634			18. 9.81	A.R.Ansell "Elsie" (Noted 6.01)	AAC Netheravon	11. 5.98P
G-BJLF	Unicorn UE-1C MLB	81018			21. 9.81	I.Chadwick tr Unicorn Group	Horsham	
G-BJLG	Unicorn UE-1B MLB	81017			21. 9.81	I.Chadwick tr Unicorn Group	Horsham	
G-BJLH	Piper PA-18 Super Cub 95 (L-18C-PI) (Frame No.18-1513)	18-1541	F-BOUM ALAT 51-15541		26.10.81	Felthorpe Flying Group Ltd (As "K-33" in US Army c/s) (Destroyed in arson attack 18.2.03)	Felthorpe	13. 6.03P
G-BJLX	Cremer Cracker MLB	15.711 PAC			24. 9.81	P.W.May	Wilmslow	
G-BJLY	Cremer Cracker MLB	15.709 PAC			24. 9.81	P.Cannon	Luton	
G-BJML	Cessna 120 (Continental C90)	10766	N76349 NC76349		5.10.81	D.F.Lawlor	Inverness	7. 5.03P
G-BJMO	Taylor JT.1 Monoplane	PFA 55-10612			30. 9.81	R.C.Mark	(Ludlow)	
G-BJMR	Cessna 310R II	310R1624	N2631Z		16. 7.79	J.M.Robinson	Rufforth	29. 2.04
G-BJMW	Thunder Ax8-105 Srs.2 HAB	369			14.10.81	G.M.Westley	London SW15	11. 1.02A
G-BJMX	Ridout Jarre JR-3 MLB	81601			6.10.81	P.D.Ridout	Botley	
G-BJMZ	Ridout European EA-8A MLB	S.5			6.10.81	P.D.Ridout	Botley	
G-BJNA	Ridout Arena Mk.117P MLB	202			6.10.81	P.D.Ridout	Botley	
G-BJNB*	WAR Vought F-4U Corsair rep	PFA 118-10711			13.10.81	Not known (No Permit to Fly issued: cancelled 8.11.89 by CAA: on build 3.00)	Beeches Farm, South Scarle	
G-BJND	Chown Osprey Mk.1E MLB	AKC.53			7.10.81	A.Billington & D.Whitmore	Liverpool	
G-BJNF	Reims/Cessna F152 II	F15201882			21.10.81	D.M. & B.Cloke	(Yeovil)	10. 2.03T
G-BJNG	Slingsby T.67AM	1993			16.10.81	D.F.Hodgkinson (Fuselage noted 10.02)	Dunkeswell	23. 7.01T
G-BJNH	Chown Osprey Mk.1E MLB	AKC.57			8.10.81	D.A.Kirk	Manchester	
G-BJNN	Piper PA-38-112 Tomahawk	38-80A0064	N9684N		15.10.81	Thistle Aero Ltd	Carlisle	31. 1.05T
G-BJNY	Aeronca 11CC Super Chief	11CC-264	CN-TYZ F-OAEE		28.10.81	P.I.& D.M.Morgans (Stored 4.91)	Furze Hill Farm, Rosemarket, Milford Haven	9. 8.90P
G-BJNZ	Piper PA-23-250 Aztec F	27-7954099	G-FANZ N6905A/C-GTJG		5.10.81	Bonus Aviation Ltd	Cranfield	3. 8.01T
G-BJOA	Piper PA-28-181 Archer II	28-8290048	N8453H		29.10.81	Channel Islands Aero Services Ltd (Op Jersey Aero Club)	Jersey	21. 11.04T
G-BJOB	SAN Jodel D.140C Mousquetaire III	118	F-BMBD		2.11.81	T.W.M.Beck & M.J.Smith	Monks Gate, Horsham	20. 6.03
G-BJOE	Jodel Wassmer D.120A Paris-Nice	177	F-BJIU		12.11.81	J.F.Govan tr Forth Flying Group	East Fortune	8. 9.03P
G-BJOP	Pilatus Britten-Norman BN-2B-26 Islander	2132			29.10.81	Loganair Ltd (Colum t/s)	Kirkwall	5. 9.03T
G-BJOT	SAN Jodel D.117	688	F-BJCO CN-TVH/F-DABU		12.11.81	R, J & Z Meares-Davies	(Stafford)	19. 9.02P
G-BJOV	Reims/Cessna F150K	F15000558	PH-VSD		4. 2.82	J.A.Boyd	(Maidstone)	19. 7.03
G-BJPI	Bede BD-5G (Hirth 230R)	1 & PFA 14-10218			30.10.81	M.D.McQueen	(Beckenham, Kent)	
G-BJPL	Chown Osprey Mk.4A MLB	AKC-39			13.10.81	M.Vincent	Jersey	
G-BJRA	Chown Osprey Mk.4B MLB	AKC.87			23.10.81	E.Osborn	Southampton	
G-BJRG	Chown Osprey Mk.4B MLB	AKC.95			26.10.81	A.de Gruchy	Jersey	
G-BJRH	Rango NA-36/Ax3 MLB	NHP-23			4.11.81	N.H.Ponsford t/a Rango Balloon & Kite Co	Leeds	
G-BJRP	Cremer Cracker MLB	15.712 PAC			29.10.81	M.D.Williams	Dunstable	
G-BJRR	Cremer Cracker MLB	15.715 PAC			29.10.81	M.D.Williams	Houghton Regis	
G-BJRV	Cremer Cracker MLB	15.713 PAC			29.10.81	M.D.Williams	Dunstable	
G-BJSS	Allport YUO-1B-1-DA Neolithic Invader Superballoon Srs.2/20 MLB	01-8101002			9.11.81	D.J.Allport	Bourne, Lincs	
G-BJST	CCF Harvard 4	CCF4-...	MM53795 SC-66		21.12.81	Tuplin Holdings Ltd (On rebuild 4.99: new owner 8.00)	Little Gransden	
G-BJSU*	Bensen B.8M	PFA G/01-1026			11.11.81	J.D.Newlyn (No Permit to Fly issued: cancelled by CAA 24.1.96) (Stored in garden 5.00)	River, Dover	
G-BJSV	Piper PA-28-161 Warrior II	28-8016229	PH-VZL (OO-HLM)/N35787		25.11.81	Airways Flight Training (Exeter) Ltd	Exeter	9. 9.03T

Reg	Type	C/n	Prev ID	Date	Owner/Operator	Location	Status
G-BJSW	Thunder Ax7-65Z HAB	378		16.11.81	Sandicliffe Garage Ltd *"Sandicliffe Ford"*	Stapleford, Notts	30.12.02A
G-BJSZ	Piper J-3C-65 Cub (L-4H-PI) *(Regd with c/n 11874)*	12047	D-EHID (D-ECAX)/(D-EKAB)/PH-NBP/44-79751	20.11.81	H.Gilbert	Enstone	1. 8.03P
G-BJTB	Cessna A150M Aerobat	A1500627	(G-BIVN) N9818J	28.10.82	V.D.Speck	Clacton	6. 11.05T
G-BJTF	Kirk Skyrider Mk.1 MLB	KSR-01		18.11.81	D.A.Kirk	Manchester	
G-BJTN	Chown Osprey Mk.4B MLB	ASC-112		23.11.81	M.Vincent	Jersey	
G-BJTO	Piper J-3C-65 Cub (L-4H-PI) *(Frame No.11352)*	11527	F-BEGK OO-AAL/43-30236	1.12.81	K.R.Nunn	Fritton Decoy, Great Yarmouth	16. 4.03P
G-BJTP	Piper PA-18 Super Cub 95 (L-18C-PI)	18-999	EI-51 I-EICO/MM5115302/51-15302	26.11.81	J.T.Parkins *"Sittin' Duck"* *(As "115302/TP" in VMO-6 Sqdn, US Marines c/s)*	Bidford	20.10.03P
G-BJTY	Chown Osprey Mk.4B MLB	ASC-115		23.11.81	A.E.de Gruchy	Jersey	
G-BJUB	Wild BVS Special 01 MLB	VS/PW01		25.11.81	P.G.Wild	Linley Hill,Leven	
G-BJUC	Robinson R22HP	0228		13. 1.82	A.J. & J.F.Thomasson t/a HeliServices	Blackpool	15.10.03T
G-BJUD	Robin DR400/180R Remorqueur *(Rebuilt using new fuselage: original scrapped Membury 11.88)*	870	PH-SRM	27.11.81	Lasham Gliding Society Ltd	Lasham	5. 1.06
G-BJUE	Chown Osprey Mk.4B MLB	ASC-114		23.11.81	M.Vincent	Jersey	
G-BJUG*	SOCATA TB-9 Tampico	248		30.12.81	Not known *(Crashed Oaksey Park 16.9.96: cancelled 1.10.96 as WFU: fuselage stored 4.01)*	Biggin Hill	
G-BJUR	Piper PA-38-112 Tomahawk	38-79A0915	N9722N	5. 2.82	Truman Aviation Ltd *(Op Nottingham School of Flying)*	Nottingham	23.11.03T
G-BJUS	Piper PA-38-112 Tomahawk	38-80A0065	N9690N	10.12.81	Panshanger School of Flying Ltd	High Cross, Ware	21. 9.03T
G-BJUU	Chown Osprey Mk.4B MLB	ASC-113		23.11.81	M.Vincent	Jersey	
G-BJUV	Cameron V-20 HAB	792		9.12.81	P.Spellward *"Busy Bee" (Valid CofR 9.02)*	Bristol	
G-BJUY	Colt Ax7-77A HAB *(Special Golf Ball shape) (Rebuild of Colting Ax7-77A c/n 77A-003)*	384	EI-BDE	15.12.81	Balloon Sports HB *(Op P.Lesser)*	Partille, Sweden	
G-BJVB	Cremer Cremcorn Ax1-4 MLB	82029		11.12.81	P.A.Cremer	Camberley	
G-BJVC	Evans VP-2 *(Volkswagen 1911)*	PFA 63-10599		17. 2.82	C.J.Morris *(Current status unknown)*	(Andover)	19. 6.91P
G-BJVF*	Thunder Ax3 Maxi Sky Chariot HAB *(C/n duplicates G-SPOP)*	187		15.12.81	A.G.R.Calder *(Cancelled 23.11.01 as WFU:) (Current status unknown)*	California, USA	6.10.91A
G-BJVH	Reims/Cessna F182Q Skylane	F18200106	D-EJMO PH-AXU(2)	21.12.81	R.J.D.Cuming	Wolverhampton	31. 8.03
G-BJVJ	Reims/Cessna F152 II	F15201906		6. 1.82	The Cambridge Aero Club Ltd	Cambridge	31. 5.04T
G-BJVK	Grob G-109	6074		11. 3.82	B.A.Kimberley *(Current status unknown)*	(Banbury)	22. 5.92
G-BJVM	Cessna 172N Skyhawk II	17269374	N737FA	14.12.81	I.C.Maclennan	Gunton Hall, Somerton	1. 8.03T
G-BJVS	Scintex CP.1310-C3 Super Emeraude	903	F-BJVS	5. 1.79	A.P.Milton tr BJVS Group	(Sidmouth)	8.10.03P
G-BJVT	Reims/Cessna F152 II	F15201904		12. 1.82	The Cambridge Aero Club Ltd	Cambridge	7.12.03T
G-BJVU	Thunder Ax6-56 Bolt HAB	397		31.12.81	G.V.Beckwith *"Cooper"*	York	26. 4.91A
G-BJVV	Robin R1180TD Aiglon2	79		5.11.81	Medway Flying Group Ltd	Rochester	18. 6.03T
G-BJWC*	Saro Skeeter AOP.10	S2/3070	7840M XK482	30.11.82	D.A.George *(Op Sloane Helicopters Ltd) (Cancelled 23.2.94 by CAA: stored 3.00)*	Sywell	
G-BJWH	Reims/Cessna F152 II	F15201919		7. 5.82	Kestrel Aviation Services Ltd	(Cheshunt)	7. 9.03T
G-BJWI	Reims/Cessna F172P Skyhawk II	F17202172		14. 5.82	Bflying Ltd *(Op Bournemouth Flying Club)*	Bournemouth	28. 8.04T
G-BJWJ	Cameron V-65 HAB	802		25. 1.82	R.G.Turnbull & S.G.Farse *"Gawain"* Glasbury, Hereford		24.11.00A
G-BJWO	Fairey Britten-Norman BN-2A-26 Islander	334	4X-AYR SX-BBX/4X-AYR/G-BAXC	16. 2.82	Stravintower Ltd t/a Falcons Parachute Centre	Hacketstown, Co.Carlow	13. 3.03A
G-BJWT	Wittman W.10 Tailwind *(Lycoming O-290-G)*	PFA 31-10688		5. 1.82	J.F.Bakewell tr Tailwind Group	Hucknall	26.11.03P
G-BJWV	Colt 17A Cloudhopper HAB	391		22. 1.82	D.T.Meyes *"Bryant Homes"*	Leamington Spa	26. 3.97A
G-BJWW	Reims/Cessna F172P Skyhawk II	F17202148	(D-EFTV)	1. 2.82	Manx Aero Marine Management Ltd *(Op Westair Flying Services)*	Blackpool	17. 9.03T
G-BJWX	Piper PA-18 Super Cub 95 (L-18C-PI) (Continental O-200-A)	18-1985	EI-64 I-EIME/MM522385/52-2385	23. 2.82	R.A.G.Lucas tr G-BJWX Syndicate	Redhill	21.12.02P
G-BJWZ	Piper PA-18 Super Cub 95 (L-18C-PI) *(Frame No.18-1262)*	18-1361	OO-HMO ALAT 18-1361/51-15361	18. 1.82	R.C.Dean tr G-BJWZ Syndicate	Redhill	16. 1.03P
G-BJXA	Slingsby T.67A	1994		8. 2.82	Comed Aviation Ltd	Blackpool	5. 4.01T
G-BJXB	Slingsby T.67A	1995		8. 2.82	XRay Bravo Ltd	Barton	16. 9.04
G-BJXK	Sportavia Fournier RF5	5054	D-KINB	3. 2.82	R.Thompson & S.Jenkins tr G-BJXK Syndicate	Usk	12. 3.04
G-BJXP	Colt 56B HAB	393		29. 3.82	H.J.Anderson *"Bart"*	Oswestry	9. 9.00A
G-BJXX	Piper PA-23-250 Aztec E	27-4692	F-BTCM N14094	7. 4.82	V.Bojovic	(Biggin Hill)	23. 6.01
G-BJXZ	Cessna 172N Skyhawk II	17273039	PH-CAA N1949F	24. 3.82	T.M.Jones *(Op Derby Aero Club)*	Egginton, Derby	8.11.04T
G-BJYD	Reims/Cessna F152 II	F15201915		25. 3.82	Cleveland Flying School Ltd	Teesside	21. 9.03T
G-BJYF	Colt 56A HAB	401		1. 3.82	H.Dos Santos *"Fanta"*	Caxton, Cambs	15. 6.03A
G-BJYG	Piper PA-28-161 Warrior II	28-8216053	N8458B	4. 3.82	S.R.Mitchell	Liverpool	20. 6.03T
G-BJYK	Jodel Wassmer D.120A Paris-Nice	185	(G-BJWK) F-BJPK	11. 5.82	T.Fox & D.A.Thorpe	Crowland	9. 6.03P
G-BJYN	Piper PA-38-112 Tomahawk	38-79A1076	G-BJTE N24310/N9671N	12. 3.82	Panshanger School of Flying Ltd	High Cross, Ware	6. 3.00T
G-BJZA	Cameron N-65 HAB	820		4. 3.82	A.D.Pinner *"Digby"*	Northampton	3. 6.97A
G-BJZB	Evans VP-2 *(Volkswagen 1834)*	PFA 63-10633		10. 3.82	I.P.Manley & J.Pearce	Marsh Farm, Sidlesham	15. 1.03P
G-BJZF	de Havilland DH.82A Tiger Moth *(Built Norfolk Aerial Spraying Ltd from spares)*	NAS-100		8. 3.82	R.Blasi	White Waltham	21. 6.03P
G-BJZN	Slingsby T.67A	1997		31. 3.82	A.R.T.Marsland	Breighton	20. 8.04
G-BJZR	Colt 42A HAB	402		18. 3.82	A.F.Selby tr Selfish Balloon Group *"Selfish"*	Loughborough	24. 7.02A
G-BJZX*	Grob G-109	6109	(D-KGRO)	3. 9.82	Oxfordshire Sport Flying Ltd *(Wrecked fuselage noted 12.01: cancelled 18.3.02 as WFU)*	Blackpool	4. 9.00

G-BKAA - G-BKZZ

Reg	Type	C/n	Prev id	Date	Owner/Operator	Location	Status
G-BKAE	Jodel Wassmer D.120 Paris-Nice	200	F-BKCE	5. 5.82	S.J.Harris	RAF Mona	24. 9.03P
G-BKAF	Clutton FRED Srs.II (Volkswagen 1835)	PFA 29-10337		23. 3.82	J.M.Robinson	(Achill Island, Co.Mayo)	30. 5.97P
G-BKAM	Slingsby T.67M Firefly 160	1999		26. 4.82	R.C.P.Brookhouse	(London SW10)	19.12.05
G-BKAO	Wassmer Jodel D.112	249	F-BFTO	22. 3.82	R.Broadhead	Eddsfield	11. 4.03P
G-BKAS	Piper PA-38-112 Tomahawk	38-79A1075	N24291 N9670N	16. 4.82	E.Reed t/a St.George Flight Training	Teesside	22. 7.05T
G-BKAY	Rockwell Commander 114	14411	SE-GSN	28. 9.81	D.L.Bunning tr The Rockwell Group	Dunkeswell	16. 5.04
G-BKAZ	Cessna 152 II	15282832	N89705	27. 4.82	L.W.Scattergood	Breighton	27. 4.03A
G-BKBB	Hawker Fury rep (RR Kestrel 5)	WA/6	OO-HFU OO-XFU/G-BKBB	2. 4.82	Brandish Holdings Ltd (As "K1930" in 43 Sqdn c/s) (Flew 17.1.01)	Old Warden	AC
G-BKBD	Thunder Ax3 Maxi Sky Chariot HAB	418		5. 4.82	M.J.Casson	Kendal	
G-BKBF	SOCATA MS.894A Rallye Minerva 220	11622	F-BSKZ	8. 9.82	K A Hale & L C Clark	Draycott Farm, Chiseldon	15. 8.04
G-BKBH*	Hawker Siddeley HS.125 Srs.600B	256052	5N-DNL G-5-698	1. 4.82	Beamalong Ltd (Cancelled 15.7.99 by CAA: noted fire dump 9.00)	Southampton	
			5N-DNL/5N-NBC/G-5-698/G-BKBH/G-5-698/TR-LAU/G-BKBH/G-BDJE/G-5-11					
G-BKBN	SOCATA TB-10 Tobago	287		4. 6.82	The Nicholls Baxter Partnership Ltd	(Wakefield)	31. 7.04
G-BKBO	Colt 17A Cloudhopper HAB	342		1. 9.82	J.Armstrong, M.A.Ashworth & H.Davey "Captain Courageous"	Newquay	23. 1.00A
G-BKBP	Bellanca 7GCBC Scout	465-73	N8693	1. 6.82	M.G. & J.R.Jefferies t/a H.G.Jefferies & Son (Damaged Graveley, Herts 23.5.93: stored 9.95: new owner 10.00)	Little Gransden	8. 5.95T
G-BKBS	Bensen B.8MV	PFA G/01-1027		14. 4.82	C R Gordon	Carlisle	27.11.03P
G-BKBV	SOCATA TB-10 Tobago	288	F-BNGO	4. 6.82	The Studio People Ltd	Welshpool	3. 2.03
G-BKBW	SOCATA TB-10 Tobago	289		4. 6.82	P.J.Bramhall & D.F.Woodhouse tr Merlin Aviation	Bristol	1. 5.04
G-BKCC	Piper PA-28-180 Cherokee Archer	28-7405099	OY-BGY	13. 5.82	DR Flying Club Ltd	Gloucestershire	6. 9.04T
G-BKCE	Reims/Cessna F172P Skyhawk II	F17202135	N9687R	26. 4.82	M.O.Loxton	Parsonage Farm, Eastchurch	15. 5.03T
G-BKCI	Brugger MB.2 Colibri (Volkswagen 1600)	PFA 43-10692		22. 4.82	E.R.Newall "Bugsy"	Breighton	
G-BKCJ	Oldfield Baby Lakes (Continental O-200-A)	PFA 10-10714		12. 5.82	S.V.Roberts	Sleap	26. 1.99P
G-BKCL	Piper PA-30 Twin Comanche C	30-1982	G-AXSP N8824Y	12. 1.81	R.P.Hodson	Full Sutton	26. 1.00T
G-BKCN	Phoenix Currie Wot (Continental A65)	PFA 3018		27. 4.82	N.A.A.Pogmore	Benson's Farm, Laindon	13. 8.03P
G-BKCR	SOCATA TB-9 Tampico	297		6. 5.82	A.Whitehouse (Fuselage noted 1.03)	Haverfordwest	3. 8.98T
G-BKCV	EAA Acro Sport II (Lycoming 0-360)	430 & PFA 72A-10776		5. 5.82	M.J.Clark	Stoke Golding	9. 4.03P
G-BKCW	Jodel Wassmer D.120A Paris-Nice	285	(G-BKCP) F-BMYF	1. 6.82	M.K.McGreavey tr Dundee Flying Group	Perth	25. 2.03P
G-BKCX	Mudry/CAARP CAP-10B	149		28. 7.82	R.Ingleton	Popham	19. 8.04
G-BKCY*	Piper PA-38-112 Tomahawk II	38-81A0027	OO-XKU N25629	22. 5.82	Wellesbourne Aviation Ltd (Stored 12.97: cancelled 30.6.00 as WFU: current status unknown)	Welshpool	7.11.94T
G-BKCZ*	Jodel Wassmer D.120A Paris-Nice	207	F-BKCZ	23. 4.82	M.R.Baker (Cancelled 7.5.02 by CAA - no UK CofA or PtoF issued since imported) (Noted 6.02)	Popham	
G-BKDC	Monnett Sonerai IIL (Volkswagen 1834)	876 & PFA 15-10597		2. 7.82	K.J.Towell (Damaged Breighton 7.8.90: current status unknown)	(Guildford)	18. 6.90P
G-BKDH	Robin DR400/120 Dauphin 80	1582	PH-CAB	25. 5.82	Dauphin Flying Group Ltd	Draycott Farm, Chiseldon	6.12.04T
G-BKDI	Robin DR400/120 Dauphin 80	1583	PH-CAD	25. 5.82	Mistral Aviation Ltd	Goodwood	7. 5.04T
G-BKDJ	Robin DR400/120 Dauphin 80	1584	PH-CAC	25. 5.82	I.H.Taylor	Sherburn-in-Elmet	28. 4.04
G-BKDK	Thunder Ax7-77Z HAB	428		21. 6.82	A.J.Byrne "Cider Riser"	Thatcham	17. 9.95A
G-BKDP	Clutton FRED Srs.III	PFA 29-10650		24. 5.82	M.Whittaker	(Wolverhampton)	
G-BKDR	Pitts S-1S Special (Lycoming IO-360)	PFA 09-10654		14. 6.82	T.J.Reeve	North Lopham, Diss	18. 6.03P
G-BKDX	SAN Jodel DR.1050 Ambassadeur	55	F-BITX	1. 6.82	G.J.Slater (Fuselage noted & wings @ Siege Cross Farm, Thatcham 10.01)	Clench Common	10. 9.99
G-BKEK	Piper PA-32-300 Cherokee Six	32-7540091	OY-TOP	30. 6.82	P.H.Maynard	Turweston	5. 9.04T
G-BKEP	Reims/Cessna F172M Skyhawk II	F17201095	OY-BFJ	8. 7.82	S.W.Watkins tr G-BKEP Group	Trecorras Farm, Llangarron	8.10.04
G-BKER	Replica Plans SE.5A (Continental O-200A)	PFA 20-10641		15. 6.82	N.K.Geddes South Barnbeth Farm, Bridge of Weir (As "F5447/N")		11. 7.03P
G-BKET	Piper PA-18 Super Cub 95 (L-18C-PI)	18-1990	EI-67 I-EIBI/MM522390/52-2390	17. 6.82	H.M.MacKenzie	Inverness	22.11.00P
G-BKEU	Taylor JT.1 Monoplane (Volkswagen 1600)	PFA 55-10553		18. 6.82	R.J.Whybrow & J.M.Springham	Knettishall	20. 7.95P
G-BKEV	Reims/Cessna F172M Skyhawk	F17201443	PH-WLH OO-CNE	8. 7.82	A.G.Measey tr Echo Victor Group	(Countesthorpe)	8. 3.04T
G-BKEW	Bell 206B-3 JetRanger III	3010	D-HDAD	8. 7.82	N.R.Foster t/a Foster Associates	Biggin Hill	17. 7.03
G-BKEY	Clutton FRED Srs.III (Volkswagen 1600)	PFA 29-10208		27. 5.82	G.S.Taylor (Current status unknown)	(Bewdley,Worcs)	
G-BKFC	Reims/Cessna F152 II	F15201443	OO-AWD	1. 9.82	Sulby Aerial Surveys Ltd Sibbertoft, Husbands Bosworth		11.11.04T
G-BKFI	Evans VP-1 Srs.2 (Volkswagen 1834)	PFA 62-10491		24. 6.82	P.L.Naylor	Bagby	27. 8.03P
G-BKFK	Isaacs Fury II (Lycoming O-290-D)	PFA 11-10038		25. 6.82	G.C.Jones Waits Farm, Belchamp Walter "Cia San" (Persian AF c/s)		27. 8.02P
G-BKFL	Aerosport Scamp	PFA 117-10814		17. 8.82	J.Sherwood (Noted 2.01)	Breighton	
G-BKFM	QAC Quickie 1 (Rotax 503)	PFA 94-10570		28. 6.82	G.E.Meakin (Damaged on take off Cranfield 4.7.98: new owner 7.01)	(Ruddington)	29. 6.98P
G-BKFN	Bell 214ST Super Transport	28109	LZ-CAW G-BKFN/VH-BEE/VH-LHT/G-BKFN	16. 8.82	Bristow Helicopters Ltd "Loch Broome"	Aberdeen	24.10.04T

Reg	Type	c/n	Prev id	Date	Owner	Location	Status
G-BKFR	Scintex CP.301C Emeraude	519	F-BUUR F-BJFF	30. 6.82	D.G.Burgess tr Devonshire Flying Group	Trenchard Farm, Eggesford	27. 8.02P
G-BKFW	Percival P.56 Provost T.1	PAC/F/303	XF597	21. 9.82	Sylmar Aviation & Services Ltd *(As "XF597/AH" in RAF College c/s)* Lower Wasing Farm, Brimpton		19. 7.03P
G-BKFZ	Piper PA-28R-200 Cherokee Arrow II	28R-7635127	OY-BLE	17. 8.82	R.S.Watt tr Shacklewell Flying Group	Shacklewell Lodge, Empingham	14.11.03
G-BKGA	SOCATA MS.892E Rallye 150GT	13287	F-GBXJ	15. 7.82	P.F.Salter tr BJJ Aviation	Wadswick Manor Farm, Corsham	3. 8.03
G-BKGB	Jodel Wassmer D.120 Paris-Nice	267	F-BMOB	21. 6.82	B.A.Ridgway	Rhigos	21. 2.03P
G-BKGC	Maule M-6-235C Super Rocket	7413C	N56465	23. 7.82	D.W.Pennell	Gloucestershire	4. 6.03
G-BKGL	Beech D18S (3TM) *(Beech c/n A-764)*	CA-164	CF-QPD RCAF 5193/1564	14. 7.82	A T J Darrah *(As "1164" in 1942 USAAC c/s)*	Duxford	1.11.04
G-BKGM	Beech 3NM (D18S) *(Beech c/n A-853)*	CA-203	N5063N G-BKGM/CF-SUQ/RCAF 2324	14. 7.82	A.E.Hutton *(As "HB275" in RAF/SEAC c/s)*	Dunsfold Park	25. 6.03
G-BKGR	Cameron O-65 HAB	864		6. 8.82	K.Kidner & L.E.More *(Amended CofR 12.01)*	Newton Abbot	8. 5.93P
G-BKGT	SOCATA Rallye 110ST Galopin	3361		23. 7.82	A.G.Morgan tr Long Marston Flying Group	Wellesbourne Mountford	28.11.03
G-BKGW	Reims/Cessna F152 II	F15201878	N9071N	11. 8.82	Leicestershire Aero Club Ltd	Leicester	18. 6.04T
G-BKHD	Oldfield Baby Lakes (Continental O-200-A) 8133-F-802B & PFA 10-107182			5. 8.82	P.J.Tanulak *(Damaged Shrewsbury 22.10.95: current status unknown)*	Sleap	11. 4.96P
G-BKHG	Piper J-3C-65 Cub (L-4H-PI)	12062	F-BCPT NC79807/44-79766	13. 9.82	K.G.Wakefield *(As "479766/D-63" in HQ 9th Army, USAAC c/s) "Puddle Jumper"* Brickhouse Farm, Frogland Cross		13. 5.03P
G-BKHJ	Cessna 182P Skylane II *(Reims c/n F18200040)*	18264129	PH-CAT D-EATV/N6223F	25. 8.82	Augur Films Ltd	Swanton Morley	15. 7.05
G-BKHR	Luton LA-4A Minor *(Volkswagen 1834)*	PFA 51-10228		24. 8.82	C.B.Buscombe & R.Goldsworthy	Bodmin	6. 3.02P
G-BKHW	Stoddard-Hamilton Glasair IIRG *(Lycoming O-320)*	357 & PFA 149-11312		27.8.82	D.Callabritto	Stapleford	28. 8.03P
G-BKHY	Taylor JT.1 Monoplane *(Volkswagen 1600)*	PFA 1416		8. 9.82	B.C.J.O'Neill	Damyns Hall, Upminster	11. 6.03P
G-BKIA	SOCATA TB-10 Tobago	322		25. 8.82	M.F.McGinn	Prestwick	24. 8.04T
G-BKIB	SOCATA TB-9 Tampico	323		25. 8.82	G.A.Vickers	Hawarden	3. 1.05T
G-BKIE*	Short SD.3-30 Var.100	SH3005	G-SLUG G-BKIE G-METP/G-METO/G-BKIE/C-GTAS/G-14-3005	15. 9.82	International Fire Training Centre *(Cancelled 16.9.97 as PWFU) (Noted 3.00 as "G-JON")*	Teesside	22. 8.93T
G-BKIF	Fournier RF6B-100	3	F-GADR	8.10.82	D.J.Taylor & J.T.Flint	Kimbolton	20. 9.03
G-BKII	Reims/Cessna F172M Skyhawk II	F17201370	PH-PLO (D-EGIA)	8.10.82	M.S.Knight t/a Sealand Aerial Photography	Goodwood	20. 2.04T
G-BKIJ	Reims/Cessna F172M	F17200920	PH-TGZ	15.10.82	V.D.Speck	Clacton/Duxford	2. 9.00T
G-BKIN	Alon A-2A Aircoupe	B-253	N5453F	24. 9.82	D.W.Vernon Puyallup (Thun Field/Pierce County), WA, USA		8.10.00
	(Refurbished during 12.01; UK CofA not renewed: shipped to Montreal 17.1.02 & by road to Tacoma, WA for re-assembly: will fly in UK marks but is for sale)						
G-BKIR	SAN Jodel D.117	737	F-BIOC	30. 9.82	R.Shaw & D.M.Hardaker *(On rebuild 3.96: current status unknown)*	Birds Edge, Penistone	28. 8.92P
G-BKIS	SOCATA TB-10 Tobago	329		22. 9.82	R.A.Irwin tr Wessex Flyers Group	Thruxton	18. 6.05
G-BKIT	SOCATA TB-9 Tampico	330		22. 9.82	D.N.Garlick, P.D.Foreman, P.Johnson & K.Dowling	Southend	14. 6.04
G-BKIX*	Cameron V-31 Air Chair HAB	863	(G-BKGJ)	23. 9.82	Not known *(Cancelled 4.8.98 by CAA) (Inflated 4.02)*	NK	21. 9.95
G-BKJB	Piper PA-18-135 Super Cub (L-21A-PI) *(Frame No.18-522)*	18-574	PH-GAI R Neth AF R-204/51-15657/N1003A	1. 8.83	Haimoss Ltd	Old Sarum	6. 9.04T
G-BKJF	SOCATA MS.880B Rallye 100T	2300	F-BULF	16.12.82	Journeyman Aviation Ltd	Sywell	12. 7.04
G-BKJS	Jodel Wassmer D.120A Paris-Nice	191	F-BJPS	4.10.82	J.H.Leigh tr Clipgate Flying Group	Clipgate Farm, Denton	23. 7.03P
G-BKJT*	Cameron O-65 HAB	148	EI-BAN	2.11.82	Not known *(Cancelled 19.5.93 by CAA) (Noted active 2000)*	(Lancashire/Cheshire)	
G-BKJW	Piper PA-23-250 Aztec E	27-4716	N14153	3.11.78	Alan Williams Entertainments Ltd	Southend	26. 5.05
G-BKKN	Cessna 182R Skylane II	18267801	N6218N	30.11.82	R.A.Marven t/a Marvagraphic	Coleman Green, Herts	30. 4.04
G-BKKO	Cessna 182R Skylane II	18267852	N4907H	30.11.82	B & G Jebson Ltd	Crosland Moor	7. 4.05
G-BKKZ	Pitts S-1S Special	PFA 09-10525	(G-BIVW)	10.11.82	J.A.Coutts	Nut Tree Farm, Redenhall	15. 6.03P
G-BKLO	Reims/Cessna F172M Skyhawk II	F17201380	PH-BET D-EFMS	22. 3.83	Stapleford Flying Club Ltd	Stapleford	11. 6.04T
G-BKMA	Mooney M.20J (201)	24-1316	N1170N	13.12.82	C.A.White t/a Foxtrot Whisky Aviation	Cambridge	1. 5.04
G-BKMB	Mooney M.20J (201)	24-1307	N1168P	15.12.82	W.A.Cook, B.Pearson & P.Turnbull	Sherburn-in-Elmet	3.12.04
G-BKMG	Handley Page 0/400 rep	TPG-1		8.12.82	M.G.King tr The Paralyser Group (Wroxham, Norwich) *(Under construction 1993: current status unknown)*		
G-BKMI	Supermarine 359 Spitfire HF.VIIIc	6S/583793	A58-671 MV154	23.12.82	The Aerial Museum (North Weald) Ltd *(As "MT928/ZX-M" in 145 Sqdn c/s)*	Filton	9. 7.03P
G-BKMT	Piper PA-32R-301 Saratoga SP	32R-8213013	N8005Z	4. 2.83	P.R. & B.N.Lewis tr Severn Valley Aviation Group	Shobdon	9. 4.04
G-BKMU*	Short SD.3-30 Var.100	SH.3092	SE-IYO G-BKMU/G-14-3092/EI-BEH/EI-BEG/G-BKMU/G-14-3092	13.12.82	Air Salvage International *(Cancelled 15.7.92 - to EI-EXP 7.92) (Fuselage only as "EI-EXP" 1.00)*	Alton	
G-BKMX	Short SD.3-60 Var.100	SH.3608	G-14-3608	13.12.82	BAC Leasing Ltd *"City of Bristol"* *(Op BAC Express titles)*	Exeter	15. 3.03T
G-BKNA	Cessna 421	421-0097	F-BUYB HB-LDZ/N4097L	28. 1.83	Launchapart Ltd *(Damaged Penbridge, Hereford 3.8.97)*	Barton	13. 8.97
G-BKNB	Cameron V-42 HAB	887		10. 1.83	D.N.Close	Andover	17. 7.97A
G-BKNI	Gardan GY-80-160D Horizon	249	F-BRJN	28. 1.83	A.Hartigan tr Blue Horizon Flying Group *"Blue Lady"*	Bourn	13. 5.02
G-BKNO	Monnett Sonerai IIL *(Volkswagen 1834)*	792 & PFA 15-10528		11. 3.83	S.Hardy	(Hemel Hempstead)	15. 6.99P
G-BKNP	Cameron V-77 HAB	874		22.12.82	I.Lilja *"Winnie The Pooh"*	Kvanum, Sweden	9. 4.03A

G-BKNZ	Menavia Piel CP.301A Emeraude	296	F-BISZ	21. 1.83	C.J.Bellworthy	Finmere	17. 4.03P
G-BKOA	SOCATA MS.893E Rallye 180GT	12432	F-BOFB	2. 3.83	P.Howick	Bodmin	31.10.05
			F-ODAT/F-BVAT				
G-BKOB	Moravan Zlin Z.326 Trener Master	757	F-BKOB	28. 9.81	W.G.V.Hall	Old Sarum	17. 5.05
					(Damaged on take off Old Sarum 12.3.00: on rebuild 11.01)		
G-BKOT	Wassmer WA.81 Piranha	813	F-GAIP	17. 2.87	Barbara N.Rolfe *(Stored 9.01)*	Little Gransden	AC
G-BKOU	Hunting P.84 Jet Provost T.3	PAC/W/13901	XN637	17. 2.83	Seagull Formation Ltd	North Weald	21. 8.03P
					(As "XN637/03" in TWU/79 Sqdn c/s)		
G-BKPA	Hoffmann H-36 Dimona	3522		16. 6.83	A.Mayhew	Rochester	26. 6.05
G-BKPB	Aerosport Scamp	PFA 117-10736		23. 2.83	B.R.Thompson	Leicester	27.11.02P
	(Volkswagen 1834)						
G-BKPC	Cessna A185F AGcarryall	185-03809	N4599E	10. 7.80	The Black Knights Parachute Centre Ltd		
						Bank End Farm, Cockerham	11.10.04
G-BKPD	Viking Dragonfly	302 & PFA 139-10897		11. 3.83	E.P.Browne & G.J.Sargent	Cambridge	20. 1.00P
	(Revmaster 2100D)				*(Damaged Cambridge 17.7.99: current status unknown)*		
G-BKPE	CEA Jodel DR.250/160 Capitaine	35	F-BNJD	18. 3.83	J.S. & J.D.Lewer	Dunkeswell	16.12.04
G-BKPN	Cameron N-77 HAB	923		9. 3.83	R.H.Sanderson *"Do It All"*	Nuneaton	21. 5.87A
G-BKPS	Grumman-American AA-5B Tiger	AA5B-0007	OO-SAS	7. 3.83	A.E.T.Clarke	Manston	1.10.03
			OO-HAO/(OO-WAY)/N1507R				
G-BKPX	Jodel Wassmer D.120A Paris-Nice	240	F-BLNG	19. 1.84	D.M.Garrett & C.A.Jones	Little Down Farm, Milson	15. 4.03P
G-BKPZ	Pitts S-1T Special	PFA 09-10852		4. 3.83	Mary A.Frost	Downland Farm, Redhill	2. 7.03P
	(Lycoming AEIO-360)						
G-BKRA	North American T-6G-NH Texan	188-90	MM53664	19. 8.83	First Air Ltd	Gloucestershire	25. 6.03T
			RM-9/51-15227		*(As "51-15227/10" in US Navy c/s)*		
G-BKRF	Piper PA-18 Super Cub 95	18-1525	F-BOUI	7.11.83	K.M.Bishop	(Krefeld, Germany)	29. 9.98P
	(L-18C-PI) *(Frame No.18-1502)*		ALAT/51-15525		*(Amended CofR 3.02)*		
G-BKRG*	Beech C-45G-BH	AF-222	N75WB	5. 5.83	(A.A.Marshall & P.L.Turland)	Bruntingthorpe	
	(Regd as C-45H)		N9072Z/51-11665		*(Cancelled 27.4.98 as WFU: used as spares source for G-BKRN 3.02 qv)*		
G-BKRH	Brugger MB.2 Colibri	142 & PFA 43-10150		15. 3.83	M.R.Benwell	Hinton in the Hedges	5. 8.03P
	(Volkswagen 1835)						
G-BKRK	SNCAN Stampe SV-4C	57	Fr.Navy	30. 3.83	J.R.Bisset tr Strathgadie Stampe Group	Insch	28. 6.98
G-BKRL*	Chichester-Miles Leopard	001		21. 3.83	Chichester-Miles Consultants Ltd	(Old Sarum)	14.12.91P
	(Noel Penny 301)				*(Cancelled 25.1.99 as WFU: stored 10.01)*		
G-BKRN	Beech D.18S	A-675	CF-DTN	14. 4.83	A.A.Marshall & P.L.Turland	Bruntingthorpe	26. 6.83P
	(Offcial c/n is CA-75 & suggests Canadian rebuild)		RCAF A675/RCAF 1500		*(Under restoration 3.02)*		
G-BKRS	Cameron V-56 HAB	908		23. 3.83	D.N. & L.J.Close *"Bonkers"*	Andover	17. 7.97A
G-BKRV*	Hovey Beta Bird	PFA 135-10875		30. 3.83	M.J.Aubrey	(Kington, Hereford)	25.6.97P
	(Rotax 503)				*(Cancelled 18.6.98 by CAA) (Noted 2002) .*		
G-BKRZ	Dragon 77 HAB	001		11. 4.83	J.R.Barber *"Rupert"*	Newbury	5. 3.94A
					(On loan to British Balloon Museum & Library)		
G-BKSB	Cessna T310Q II	310Q0914	VR-CEM	22. 4.83	D.H.& P.M.Smith t/a G.H.Smith & Son	Bagby	4. 5.03
			G-BKSB/HB-LMO/OE-FYL/(N69680)				
G-BKSC*	Saro Skeeter AOP.12	S2/7157	XN351	23. 5.83	R.A.L.Falconer	(Ipswich)	8.11.84P
	(Official c/n S2/7076 but may be component identity)		*(As "XN351")*		On overhaul 10.96: cancelled 11.10.00 by CAA) (Current status unknown)		
G-BKSD	Colt 56A HAB	361		11. 4.83	M.J.Casson *"Entwhistle Green"*	Kendal	2. 6.96A
G-BKSE	QAC Quickie 1	PFA 94-10748		6. 4.83	M.D.Burns	(Bridge of Weir)	8. 5.89P
	(Onan B48M) *(Regd with c/n PFA 94-10784)*				*(Stored 6.00: current status unknown)*		
G-BKSH*	Colt 21A Cloudhopper HAB	510		16. 5.83	Not known *"Mekon"*	NK	
					(Cancelled 12.5.98 by CAA) (Extant 2000)		
G-BKSP	Schleicher ASK 14	14028	D-KOMO	25. 5.83	J.H.Bryson	Bellarena	16. 5.03
G-BKSS	SAN Jodel 150 Mascaret	48	F-BMFC	14. 9.83	D.H.Wilson-Spratt *(Noted 8.00)*	Ronaldsway	
G-BKST	Rutan VariEze	12718-001		20. 4.83	R.Towle	(Hexham)	
G-BKSX	SNCAN Stampe SV-4C	61	F-BBAF	16. 5.83	C.A.Bailey & J.A.Carr Trenchard Farm, Eggesford		15. 6.89
			Fr.Mil		*(Stored 8.90: current status unknown)*		
G-BKTA	Piper PA-18 Super Cub 95	18-3223	OO-HBA	10. 5.83	M.J.Dyson & M.T.Clark	Fradley	31. 7.03P
	(L-18C-PI) *(Frame No.18-3246)*		Belg AF OL-L49/L-149/53-4823				
G-BKTH	Hawker Sea Hurricane IB	CCF/41H/4013	Z7015	24. 5.83	The Shuttleworth Trust	Old Warden	10. 5.03P
	(Built CCF)				*(As "Z7015/7-L" in 880 Sqdn RN c/s)*		
G-BKTM	PZL SZD-45A Ogar	B-656		31. 5.83	Repclif Chemical Services Ltd	Sleap	13. 6.03
G-BKTR	Cameron V-77 HAB	951		6. 6.83	A.Palmer *"Diddlybopper"*	Tonbridge	1. 6.02A
G-BKTV	Reims/Cessna F152 II	F15201450	OY-BJC	8. 8.83	A.Jahanfar	Hill Farm, Nayland	11. 8.05T
					(Op Seawing Flying Club)		
G-BKTZ	Slingsby T.67M Firefly	2004	G-SFTV	26. 8.83	P.R.Elvidge	Blackpool	18. 8.02
G-BKUE	SOCATA TB-9 Tampico	369	F-BNGX	31. 5.83	Pool Aviation (NW) Ltd	Blackpool	6. 2.03T
G-BKUJ*	Thunder Ax6-56 Srs.1 HAB	520		17. 6.83	R.J.Bent *"Edward Bear"*	Torquay	28. 9.88A
					(Cancelled 10.10.01 by CAA)		
G-BKUR	Menavia Piel CP.301A Emeraude	280	(G-BKBX)	19.10.83	R.Wells	Shotton Colliery	21. 6.03P
			F-BMLX/F-OBLY				
G-BKUS*	Bensen B.8M	PFA G/01-1045		7. 7.83	A.Charles	Newbury	21. 6.88P
					(Cancelled 11.10.00 by CAA) (Current status unknown)		
G-BKUT*	Morane-Saulnier MS.880B Rallye Club	376	F-BKZT	22. 7.83	Not known	(West Scotland)	
			(Crashed Nayes Coppice Farm, Havant 16.2.92: cancelled 7.4.92 by CAA) (Instructional use 6.00: current status unknown)				
G-BKUU	Thunder Ax7-77 Srs.1 HAB	522		3. 8.83	M.A.Mould *"Tanglefoot"*	Winchester	12. 4.03A
G-BKVA	SOCATA Rallye 180T Galerien	3274	SE-GFS	30. 6.83	J.M.Airey	Saltby	7. 6.04T
			F-GBXA		tr Buckminster Gliding Club Syndicate		
G-BKVB	SOCATA Rallye 110ST Galopin	3258	OO-PIP	22. 6.83	A. & K.Bishop	(Swansea)	11.12.05
G-BKVC	SOCATA TB-9 Tampico	372	F-BNGQ	4. 7.83	H.P.Aubin-Parvu	Biggin Hill	26. 3.05
G-BKVF	Clutton FRED Srs.III	PFA 29-10791		29. 7.83	J.M.Brightwell & A.J.Wright	(Egginton, Derby)	
					(Current status unknown)		
G-BKVG	Scheibe SF-25E Super Falke	4362	(D-KNAE)	25. 8.83	G-BKVG Ltd	North Hill	4. 6.05
G-BKVK	Auster AOP.9	AUS/10/2	WZ662	8. 8.83	J.D.Butcher	AAC Netheravon	29. 9.00P
					(Op Military Auster Flight) (As "WZ662" in Army c/s)		
G-BKVL	Robin DR400/160 Major	1625		26. 7.83	Tatenhill Aviation Ltd t/a Tatenhill Aviation	Tatenhill	22. 7.02T

G-BKVM	Piper PA-18-150 Super Cub	18-849	PH-KAZ	26. 8.83	D.G.Caffrey *"Spirit of Goxhill"*	North Coates	13.10.05
	(L-21A-PI) *(Frame No.18-824)*		RNeth AF R-214/51-15684		*(As "115684/VM" in US Army c/s)*		
G-BKVO	Pietenpol Air Camper	PFA 47-10799		8. 8.83	M.C.Hayes	(Woonton, Hereford)	25. 5.99P
	(Continental A65)				*(New owner 6.01)*		
G-BKVP	Pitts S-1D Special	002 & PFA 09-10800		19. 8.83	S.W.Doyle	Leicester	21. 4.03P
	(Lycoming IO-360)						
G-BKVS	Campbell Cricket	PFA G/01-1047		11. 8.83	K.Hughes	(Amlwch)	22.10.03P
	(Volkswagen 1834)						
G-BKVT	Piper PA-23-250 Aztec F	27-7754002	G-HARV	6. 2.84	BKS Surveys Ltd	Belfast	3. 4.03T
			N62760				
G-BKVW	Airtour AH-56 HAB	AH.003		27. 6.84	L.D. & H.Vaughan *"Lunardi"*	Tring	
G-BKVX	Airtour AH-56C HAB	AH.002		27. 6.84	P.Aldridge	Halesworth, Suffolk	
					"Featherspin" or "Liebling" ?		
G-BKVY	Airtour B-31 HAB	AH.001		9. 8.83	M.Davies *"Day Dream"*	Callington, Cornwall	15. 8.01A
G-BKWD	Taylor JT.2 Titch	PFA 60-10232		17. 8.83	E.H.Booker	Valley Farm, Winwick	11. 6.02P
	(Continental PC60) *(Originally regd as c/n PFA 60-10143: presumed absorbed into both projects)*						
G-BKWR	Cameron V-65 HAB	970		26. 8.83	K.J.Foster *"White Spirit"*	Coleshill, Birmingham	9. 7.00A
G-BKWW	Cameron O-77 HAB	984		13. 9.83	A.M.Marten *"Kouros" (Valid CofR 9.02)*	Woking	18. 1.89A
G-BKWY	Reims/Cessna F152T	F15201940		22. 9.83	The Cambridge Aero Club Ltd	Cambridge	11. 12.05T
G-BKXA	Robin R2100	114	F-GAOS	24.11.83	M.Wilson *(New owner 8.01)*	Little Gransden	22.10.99
G-BKXD	Aérospatiale SA365N Dauphin 2	6088	F-WMHD	7. 9.83	CHC Scotia Ltd	Blackpool	8.12.04T
G-BKXF	Piper PA-28R-200 Cherokee Arrow II	28R-7335351	OY-DZN	10.11.83	P.L.Brunton	Caernarfon	22. 6.05T
			N56092				
G-BKXM	Colt 17A Cloudhopper HAB	531		3.10.83	R.G.Turnbull	Glasbury, Hereford	8.10.03A
G-BKXN	ICA IS-28M2A	48		24.10.83	D.C.Wellard	Kemble	3. 5.03
G-BKXO	Rutan LongEz	PFA 74A-10580		24.10.83	D.F.P.Finan	Teesside	27. 6.00P
	(Continental O-200-A)				*(Stored 12.01)*		
G-BKXP	Auster AOP.6	2830	A-14	12.10.83	B.J.Ellis	Thruxton	
	(Frame No.TAY841BJ)		Belg AF/VT987		*(On rebuild 7.91: new owner 12.01)*		
G-BKXR	Druine D.31A Turbulent	303	OY-AMW	1.11.83	M.B.Hill	Draycott Farm, Chiseldon	20.11.03P
	(Volkswagen 1700)						
G-BKXX*	Cameron V-65 HAB	1000	(OO-)	1. 9.83	L.J.H.Decabooter & L.P.Neirynck *"Hot Mille"*		24. 7.99A
			G-BKXX		*(Cancelled 28.11.01 as WFU)*	St.Niklaas, Belgium	
G-BKZB	Cameron V-77 HAB	995		11.11.83	K.B.Chapple	Reading	6. 7.01A
G-BKZE	Aérospatiale AS332L Super Puma	2102	F-WKQE	30. 9.83	Heliworld Leasing Ltd	Aberdeen	25. 9.05T
G-BKZF	Cameron V-56 HAB	246	F-BXUK	14.11.83	A.D.Brice *"Xplorer"*	Cowbridge	18. 3.97A
G-BKZG	Aérospatiale AS332L Super Puma	2106	HB-ZBT	30. 9.83	CHC Scotia Ltd	Aberdeen	25. 8.05T
			G-BKZG				
G-BKZI	Bell 206A JetRanger	118	(5B-CGC/'D?)	7.12.83	Dolphin Property (Management) Ltd	Thruxton	19. 9.04T
			G-BKZI/N6238N				
G-BKZM	Isaacs Fury II	PFA 11-10742		27. 9.83	B.Jones	Haverfordwest	1.10.90P
	(Continental O-200-A)				*(As "K2060": stored 8.96: current status unknown)*		
G-BKZT	Clutton FRED Srs.II	PFA 29-10715		20.10.83	U.Chakravorty	(Margate)	2. 7.02P
	(Volkswagen 1834)						
G-BKZV	Bede BD-4	380	ZS-UAB	31. 8.84	G.I.J.Thomson	Little Snoring	4. 9.03P
	(Lycoming O-320)						

G-BLAA - G-BLZZ

G-BLAC	Reims/Cessna FA152 Aerobat	FA1520370		25. 3.80	D.C.C.Handley	Bourn	26. 7.04T
G-BLAF	Stolp SA.900 V-Star	PFA 106-10651		13. 9.83	P.R.Skeels	Lymm Dam	6.11.03P
	(Continental O-200-A)						
G-BLAG	Pitts S-1D Special	PFA 09-10195		1.12.83	G.R.J.Caunter	(Sandhurst)	12. 4.04P
	(Lycoming AEIO-360)						
G-BLAH	Thunder Ax7-77 Srs.1 HAB	526		3.10.83	T.M.Donnelly *"Blah"*	Doncaster	19. 8.01A
G-BLAI	Monnett Sonerai IIL	PFA 15-10583		6.12.83	T.Simpson	Breighton	12. 1.99P
	(Regd with c/n PFA 15-10584)				*(Noted 12.01)*		
G-BLAM	CEA DR.360 Chevalier	345	F-BRCM	6. 2.84	D.J.Durell	Maypole Farm, Chislet	11. 8.05
G-BLAT	SAN Jodel 150 Mascaret	56	F-BNID	30. 1.84	S.A.Smith & D.K.Gliddon	(Dunfermline)	12. 6.03P
					tr G-BLAT Flying Group		
G-BLAX	Reims/Cessna FA152 Aerobat	FA1520385		11.10.83	Bflying Ltd	Bournemouth	28. 5.05T
					(Op Bournemouth Flying Club)		
G-BLCG	SOCATA TB-10 Tobago	61	G-BHES	17. 3.80	P.Hickey & M.E.Woodroffe	Shoreham	15. 7.04
					tr Charlie Golf Flying Group		
G-BLCH	Colt 56D HAB	392		14.11.83	Balloon Flights Club Ltd *"Geronimo"*	Leicester	
G-BLCI	EAA AcroSport P	P-10A	N6AS	29. 2.84	M.R.Holden	Stoneacre Farm, Farthing Corner	16. 6.97T
					"Bluebottle" (Damaged Farthing Corner 1996: current status unknown)		
G-BLCM	SOCATA TB-9 Tampico	194	OO-TCT	2.12.83	R.Frazer & P.Tyler	Liverpool	27. 6.05T
			(OO-TBC)				
G-BLCT	CEA Jodel DR.220 2+2	23	F-BOCQ	22.12.83	C.J.Snell	Shoreham	7. 8.05
					tr Christopher Robin Flying Group		
G-BLCU	Scheibe SF-25B Falke	4699	D-KECC	30.12.83	C.F.Sellers	Rufforth	19. 7.02
G-BLCV	Hoffmann H-36 Dimona	36113	EI-CJO	21. 3.84	R.& M.Weaver	(Walton-on-Thames)	9. 7.05
			G-BLCV				
G-BLCW	Evans VP-1	PFA 62-10835		19.12.83	M.Flint *"Le Plank"*	Fenland	30. 6.03P
	(Volkswagen 1600)						
G-BLCY	Thunder Ax7-65Z HAB	487		13. 1.84	C.M.George *"Warsteiner"*	Brixton, Plymouth	26. 2.99A
G-BLDB	Taylor JT.1 Monoplane	PFA 55-10506		28.12.83	C.J.Bush	Great Oakley, Clacton	15. 5.03P
	(Volkswagen 1600)						
G-BLDD	WAG-Aero CUBy AcroTrainer	PFA 108-10653		29.12.83	A.F.Stafford	Combrook	17. 3.03P
	(Lycoming O-320)						
G-BLDG	Piper PA-25-260 Pawnee C	25-4501	SE-FLB	9. 1.84	Ouse Gliding Club Ltd	Rufforth	23. 6.05
			LN-VYM				

Reg	Type	C/n	ID2	Date	Owner/Operator	Location	Date2
G-BLDK	Robinson R22	0139	C-GSGU	17. 1.84	Helicentre Ltd	Blackpool	28. 6.02T
G-BLDN	Rand-Robinson KR-2	PFA 129-10913		12. 1.84	S.C.Solley Mavis	Enderby	14. 6.02P
G-BLDV	Pilatus Britten-Norman BN-2B-26 Islander	2179	D-INEY	13. 1.84	Loganair Ltd *(Benyhone Tartan t/s)*	Kirkwall	18. 7.02T
			G-BLDV				
G-BLEB	Colt 69A HAB	537		20. 1.84	I.R.M.Jacobs *(New CofR 2.02)*	Reading	30. 3.85A
G-BLEJ	Piper PA-28-161 Cherokee Warrior II	28-7816257	N2194M	8. 2.84	Eglinton Flying Club Ltd	City of Derry	17. 4.05T
G-BLEP	Cameron V-65 HAB	102		27. 2.84	D.Chapman	Maidstone	10. 9.96A
					tr The Ground Hogs *"Manor Marquees"*		
G-BLES	Stolp SA.750 Acroduster Too 197 & PFA 89-10428			8.12.83	G.N.Davies	Enstone	9. 9.02P
	(Lycoming O-360)						
G-BLET	Thunder Ax7-77 Srs.1 HAB	539		16. 2.84	Servatruc Ltd *"Servatruc"*	Nottingham	15. 8.97A
G-BLEW	Reims/Cessna F182Q Skylane II	F18200039	F-GAQD	21. 6.78	Seager Publishing Ltd	Kemble	3. 9.03
G-BLEZ	Aérospatiale SA365N Dauphin 2	6131		24. 1.84	CHC Scotia Ltd	(Forties Oil Field)	28. 8.05T
					(Op First Aim Medevac)		
G-BLFI	Piper PA-28-181 Archer II	28-8490034	N4333Z	22. 2.84	Bonus Aviation Ltd	Cranfield	27. 7.03T
G-BLFW	Grumman-American AA-5 Traveler	AA5-0786	OO-GLW	22. 2.84	D.C.A.Milne	Draycott Farm, Chiseldon	10. 9.05
					tr Grumman Club		
G-BLFY	Cameron V-77 HAB	1030		16. 3.84	A.N.F.Pertwee *"Groupie"*	Frinton-on-Sea	5. 4.92A
G-BLFZ	Piper PA-31 Navajo C	31-7912106	PH-RWS	21. 3.84	London Executive Aviation Ltd	Stapleford	10. 7.03T
			(PH-ASV)/N3538W				
G-BLGB*	Short SD.3-60 Var.100	SH.3641	G-14-3641	24. 2.84	Air Salvage International	Lasham	31. 3.98T
			(Damaged Stornoway 9.2.98: cancelled 19.11.98 as PWFU) (Hulk remains dumped 7.01)				
G-BLGH	Robin DR300/180R Remorqueur	570	D-EAFL	10. 4.84	Booker Gliding Club Ltd	Booker	2. 3.03
G-BLGR	Bell 47G-4A	7501	N3236G	2. 5.84	H., J.R. & H.C.Wake & S.P.Broughton & Co Ltd		
			HC-ASQ/N1186W		t/a Courteenhall Farms	Courteenhall, Northampton	24. 6.02
G-BLGS	SOCATA Rallye 180T	3206		7. 7.78	A.Waters t/a London Light Aircraft	Dunstable	21. 5.99
G-BLGT	Piper PA-18 Super Cub 95	18-1445	D-EAGT	1. 6.84	Meridian Aviation Ltd	Bournemouth	7.10.03P
	(L-18C-PI) *(Frame No.18-1399)*		D-EOCC/ALAT 51-15445				
G-BLGV	Bell 206B JetRanger II	982	5B-JSB	2. 5.84	Heliflight (UK) Ltd	Wolverhampton	22. 5.05T
			C-FDYL/CF-DYL				
G-BLGX*	Thunder Ax7-65 HAB	551		16. 4.84	"The 45"	Uttoxeter	NE(A)
					(Cancelled 19.5.93 by CAA) (Stored 2001)		
G-BLHH	CEA DR.315 Petit Prince	324	F-BPRH	3. 7.84	Central Certification Service Ltd Tower Farm, Woolaston		6. 6.03
G-BLHI	Colt 17A Cloudhopper HAB	506		8. 9.86	Janet A.Folkes *"Hopping Mad"*	Loughborough	24.11.01A
G-BLHJ	Reims/Cessna F172P Skyhawk II	F17202182		26. 3.84	James D.Peace & Co	Edinburgh	18.12.05T
					(Op Edinburgh Air Centre)		
G-BLHK	Colt 105A HAB	576		19. 6.84	A.S.Dear, R.B.Green & W.S.Templeton	Fordingbridge	12. 7.97A
					tr Hale Hot-Air Balloon Group *"Gloworm"*		
G-BLHM(2)	Piper PA-18 Super Cub 95	18-3120	LX-AIM	23. 7.84	A.G.Edwards	(Llandegla)	8. 8.03P
	(L-18C-PI) *(Frame No.18-3088)*		D-EOAB/Belg AF OL-L46/L-46/53-4720				
G-BLHN	Robin HR100/285 Tiara	539	F-GABF	20. 2.78	N.P.Finch	Goodwood	17. 8.03
G-BLHR	Gulfstream GA-7 Cougar	GA7-0109	OO-RTI	12. 4.84	T.E.Westley	Fowlmere	9.12.02T
			(OO-HRC)/N751G				
G-BLHS	Bellanca 7ECA Citabria 115	1342-80	OO-RTQ	12. 4.84	N.J.F.Campbell & D.J.Lockett	Inverness	29. 4.05
					tr Hotel Sierra Group		
G-BLHW	Varga 2150A Kachina	VAC161-80		17. 7.84	W.D.Garlick	Damyns Hall, Upminster	10. 5.03
					tr Kachina Hotel Whiskey Group		
G-BLID	DH.112 Venom FB.50 (FB.1)	815	J-1605	13. 7.84	P.G.Vallance Ltd	Charlwood, Surrey	AC
	(Built F + W)				*(Gatwick Aviation Museum: as "J-1605" in Swiss AF c/s)*		
G-BLIH	Piper PA-18-135 Super Cub	18-3828	(PH-KNG)	12.11.84	I.R.F.Hammond	Stubbington	AC
	(L-21B-PI) *(Frame No.18-3827)*		R Neth AF R-138/(PH-KNG)/(PH-GRC)/R-138/54-2428				
G-BLIK	Wallis WA-116/F/S	K-218X		30. 4.84	K.H.Wallis	Reymerston Hall, Norfolk	24. 4.98P
	(Franklin 2A-120)				*(Noted 8.01)*		
G-BLIT	Thorp T-18CW	PFA 76-10550		24. 4.84	A.P.Tyrwhitt-Drake	Fairoaks	6.11.03P
	(Lycoming O-320)						
G-BLIW	Percival P.56 Provost T.53	PAC/F/125	IAC.177	12. 6.85	D.Mould & J.De Uphaugh	Shoreham	17. 1.03P
					tr Provost Flying Group *(As "177" in Irish Air Corps c/s)*		
G-BLIX	Saro Skeeter AOP.12	S2/5094	PH-HOF	3. 5.84	K.M.Scholes	Wilden	13. 9.02P
			(PH-SRE)/XL809		*(As "XL809"in Army c/s)*		
G-BLIY	SOCATA MS.892A Rallye Commodore 150	11639	F-BSCX	9. 5.84	A.J.Brasher	Church Farm, North Moreton	27. 7.03
G-BLJD	Glaser-Dirks DG-400	4-85		15. 6.84	M I Gee	Rufforth	29. 5.03
G-BLJF	Cameron O-65 HAB	1041		14. 5.84	M.D.& C.E.C.Hammond *"Fat Lady"*	Kirdford	16. 8.00A
					(Op Balloon Preservation Group)		
G-BLJH	Cameron N-77 HAB	1047		14. 5.84	K A Kent *"Daydream"*	Kirdford	27. 6.89A
					(Op Balloon Preservation Group)		
G-BLJM	Beech 95-B55 Baron	TC-1997	SE-GRT	3. 3.78	R.A.Perrot	Guernsey	22. 8.03
G-BLJO	Reims/Cessna F152 II	F15201627	OY-BNB	21. 6.84	Redhill School of Flying Ltd	Redhill	3.10.04T
					(Op Redhill Flying Club)		
G-BLKK	Evans VP-1	PFA 62-10642		15. 6.84	N.Wright	Queach Farm, Bury St Edmunds	27. 6.02P
	(Volkswagen 1834)						
G-BLKM	CEA Jodel DR.1051 Sicile	519	F-BLRO	26. 6.84	F.H.Lissimore tr Kilo Mike Group	(Bromley)	27. 6.02
G-BLKP	British Aerospace Jetstream Srs.3102	634	(G-BLEX)	9. 7.84	Global Aviation Ltd	Humberside	19. 4.03T
			G-31-634				
G-BLKY	Beech 58 Baron	TH-1440		22. 8.84	J.C.Hall	Guernsey	28. 6.03
G-BLKZ	Pilatus P.2-05600-45	A-125	U-125	30. 7.84	R.W.Hinton *(As "A-125" in Swiss AF c/s)*	Duxford	24. 1.01P
G-BLLA	Bensen B.8M	PFA G/01-1055		27. 6.84	K.T.Donaghey	Henstridge	26. 7.02P
	(Volkswagen 1834)						
G-BLLB	Bensen B.8MR (Rotax 532)	PFA G/01A-1059		4. 9.84	D.H.Moss *(Noted 12.02)*	Henstridge	14. 6.01P
G-BLLD	Cameron O-77 HAB	1060		16. 7.84	G.Birchall	Ormskirk	18. 6.03
G-BLLH	CEA Jodel DR.220A/B 2+2	131	F-BROM	17. 7.84	M.D.Hughes	Pauncefoot, Romsey	18. 6.03
G-BLLN	Piper PA-18 Super Cub 95	18-3447	D-ECLN	27. 6.84	P.L.Pilch & C.G.Fisher	(Wadhurst)	25. 1.04T
	(Continental O-200A) (L-18C-PI) *(Frame No.18-3380)*		96+23/PY+901/QZ+011/AC+507/AS+508/54-747				
G-BLLO*	PA-18-95 Super Cub	18-3099	D-EAUB	11. 7.84	D.G. & M.G.Margetts	Sleap	12.10.96P
	(L-18C-PI) *(Frame No 18-3058)*		Belg AF OL-L25/L-25/53-4699		*(Cancelled 15.11.00 by CAA) (Dismantled 12.01)*		

Regn	Type	C/n	Prev id	Date	Owner/Operator	Location	Date
G-BLLP*	Slingsby T.67B		2008	19. 7.84	Cleveland Flying School Ltd	Bagby	4.12.00T
					(Cancelled 20.8.02 by CAA) (Stored 10.02)		
G-BLLR	Slingsby T.67C Firefly	2011		19. 7.84	R.L.Brinklow	Gloucestershire	28.11.04T
	(Lycoming O-320) (Regd as "T.67B (mod)")				(Op Cotswold Aero Club) (www.cotswoldaeroclub.co.uk titles)		
G-BLLS	Slingsby T.67B Firefly	2013		19. 7.84	Western Air (Thruxton) Ltd	Thruxton	17. 2.03T
G-BLLW	Colt 56B HAB	578		11. 9.84	G.Fordyce, R.Wickens & S.A.Sawyer	Olney	3. 5.03A
					"Angel Clare"		
G-BLLZ	Rutan LongEz	PFA 74A-10830		16. 7.84	R.S.Stoddart-Stones	Henstridge	22. 6.94P
	(Lycoming O-235)						
G-BLMA	Moravan Zlin Z.526A Trener Master	922	F-BORS	23. 7.84	G.P.Northcott	Redhill	24. 6.01
G-BLME	Robinson R22HP	0032	N90261	16. 4.85	Heli Air Ltd	Liverpool	24.10.05T
G-BLMG	Grob G-109B	6322		27. 9.84	R.W.Littledale tr Mike Golf Syndicate	Enstone	7.11.05
G-BLMI	Piper PA-18 Super Cub 95	18-2066	D-ENWI	5. 6.84	R.Gibson	White Waltham	16. 4.03P
	(L-18C-PI) (Frame No.18-2086)		R Neth AF R-55/52-2466		tr G-BLMI Flying Group (As "R-55" in R Neth AF c/s)		
G-BLMN	Rutan LongEz	PFA 74A-10643		3. 7.84	S.E.Bowers	Thruxton	5. 6.03P
	(Lycoming O-235) (Regd as c/n PFA 74A-10648)				tr G-BLMN Flying Group		
G-BLMP	Piper PA-17 Vagabond	17-193	F-BFMR	15. 5.84	M.Austin	Longwood Farm, Morestead	29. 6.03P
	(Continental A65)		N4893H				
G-BLMR	Piper PA-18-150 Super Cub	18-2057	PH-NLD	29. 5.84	Southern Flight Centre Ltd	Shoreham	22. 7.05T
	(L-18C-PI) (Frame No.18-2070) (Lycoming O-320)		R Neth AF R-72/52-2457				
G-BLMT	Piper PA-18-135 Super Cub	18-2706	D-ELGH	12. 9.84	I.S.Runnalls	Church Farm, North Moreton	25. 9.05
	(Frame No.18-2724)		N8558C				
G-BLMW	Nipper T.66 RA45 Mk.IIIB	PFA 25-11020		31. 8.84	S.L.Millar	Crowland	5. 8.03P
	(Ardem 10)						
G-BLMZ	Colt 105A HAB	404		24. 9.84	Mandy D.Dickinson "Zulu"	Bristol	28. 3.97A
G-BLNJ	Pilatus Britten-Norman BN-2B-26 Islander	2189		3. 9.84	Loganair Ltd (Martha Masanabo/Ndebele t/s)	Kirkwall	3.12.03T
G-BLNL	Pilatus Britten-Norman BN-2T Islander	2191	PH-RPN	30. 1.03	Hebridean Air Services Ltd	Cumbernauld	
			G-BLNL/PH-RPN/G-BLNL		(Stored 2.03)		
G-BLNO	Clutton FRED Srs.III	PFA 29-10559		17.10.84	L.W.Smith (Current status unknown)	(Sale, Cheshire)	
G-BLOB	Colt 31A Air Chair HAB	599		11. 9.84	Jacques W.Soukup Enterprises Ltd South Dakota, USA		5. 6.91A
G-BLOL	SNCAN Stampe SV.4A				See entry for G-AXRP		
G-BLOR	Piper PA-30 Twin Comanche	30-59	HB-LAE	19. 7.85	R.L.C.Appleton	Sheepwash	21. 5.05T
			N7097Y/N10F				
G-BLOS	Cessna 185A Skywagon	185-0359	LN-BDS	17. 9.84	Elizabeth Brun	Great Massingham	24. 4.03
			N4159Y				
G-BLOT	Colt 56B HAB	424		11. 9.84	H.J.Anderson "Pathfinder"	Oswestry	17. 7.96A
G-BLOV	Thunder Ax5-42 Srs.1 HAB	590		11. 9.84	A.G.R.Calder "Puff The Magic Dragon"	London SE16	29.11.02A
G-BLPA	Piper J-3C-65 Cub	11327	OO-AJL	27. 9.84	A.C.Frost	Rectory Farm, Abbotsley	22. 8.03P
	(L-4H-PI) (Frame No.11152)		OO-JOE/43-30036				
G-BLPB	Turner TSW Hot Two Wot	PFA 46-10606		19.10.84	I.R.Hannah	Redhill	10. 7.03P
	(Lycoming O-320-A)						
G-BLPE	Piper PA-18 Super Cub 95 (L-18C-PI)	18-3084	D-ECBE	28. 9.84	A.A.Haig-Thomas	Thorpe-le-Soken	17. 6.03P
	(Continental O-200-A) (Also quoted as 18-3083)		Belg Army L-10/53-4684				
G-BLPF	Reims FR172G Rocket	FR17200187	N4594Q	29. 1.85	Prestwick Flight Centre Ltd	Prestwick	2. 5.03T
			D-EEFL				
G-BLPG	Auster J/1N Alpha	3395	G-AZIH	21. 5.82	D.Taylor (As "16693" in RCAF c/s)	Clacton	18. 3.04
G-BLPH*	Reims/Cessna FRA150L Aerobat	FRA1500239	EI-BHH	19. 9.84	G.K. & T.G.Solomon Kittyhawk Farm, Deanland		25. 6.00
			PH-ASH		tr The New Aerobat Group (Cancelled 25.8.00 as temp WFU)		
G-BLPI	Slingsby T.67B Firefly	2016		24. 9.84	RAF Wyton Flying Club Ltd	RAF Wyton	30. 7.03T
G-BLPM	Aerospatiale AS.332L Super Puma	2122	LN-ONB	5.10.84	Bristo Helicopters Ltd	Aberdeen	25. 1.00
			G-BLPM/C-GQCB/G-BLPM		(New CofR 2.03)		
G-BLPP	Cameron V-77 HAB	432		19. 9.78	L.P.Purfield "Merlin"	Leicester	30. 4.94A
G-BLRA	British Aerospace BAe 146 Srs.100	E1017	N117TR	3.10.84	BAE Systems (Operations) Ltd	Woodford	15.10.03T
			N462AP/CP-2249/N462AP/G-BLRA/G-5-02				
G-BLRC	Piper PA-18-135 Super Cub	18-3602	OO-DKC	27.11.84	S.Hornung tr Supercub Group	Seething	20.12.03
	(L-21B-PI) (Frame No.18-3790)		PH-DKC/R NethAF R-112/54-2402				
G-BLRD	MBB Bö.209 Monsun 150FV	101	D-EBOA	15.10.84	T.A.Crone	Turweston	16. 8.04
			(OE-AHM)				
G-BLRF	Slingsby T.67C Firefly	2014		30.11.84	R.C.Nicholls	Wellesbourne Mountford	10. 1.03T
G-BLRG	Slingsby T.67B Firefly	2020		30.11.84	R.L.Brinklow (New CorR 4.02)	Turweston	17. 7.00T
G-BLRJ*	CEA Jodel DR.1051 Sicile	502	F-BLRJ	8. 2.78	M.P.Hallam	Jackrells Farm, Horsham	17. 7.00
					(Cancelled 6.3.02 as WFU)		
G-BLRL	Scintex CP-301C1 Emeraude	552	(G-BLNP)	5.11.84	N.Thorne	Breighton	8.10.03P
			F-BJFT				
G-BLRM	Glaser-Dirks DG-400	4-107		5. 2.85	J.A.& W.S.Y.Stephen	Aboyne	19. 4.03
G-BLRN	de Havilland DH.104 Dove 8	04266	N531WB	30.10.84	J.F.M.Bleeker Midden Zeeland, The Netherlands		13. 3.96
			G-BLRN/WB531		(To Pionier Hangaar Collection: as "WB531" in RAF c/s) (Stored 4.01)		
G-BLRW*	Cameron Elephant 77SS HAB	1074	.	14.12.84	Forbes Europe Inc	Balleroy, Normandy	1.10.00A
					"Great Sky Elephant" (Cancelled 14.11.02 by CAA)		
G-BLRY	Aérospatiale AS332L Super Puma	2111	LN-ONA	5. 2.85	Bristow Helicopters Ltd	Aberdeen	17. 6.05T
			G-BLRY/LN-ONA/G-BLRY/P2-PHP/VR-BIJ/G-BLRY/C-GQGL/G-BLRY				
G-BLSD*	de Havilland DH.112 Venom FB.54	928	N203DM	20. 5.85	R.J.Lamplough	North Weald	
	(Built F + W)		G-BLSD/J-1758		(As "J-1758 in Swiss AF c/s)		
					(Cancelled 5.6.96 as WFU) (Open storage less booms & tail unit 9.02)		
G-BLSF	Gulfstream AA-5A Cheetah	AA5A-0802	G-BGCK	21. 2.83	Plane Talking Ltd	Elstree	15. 6.03T
G-BLSK*	Colt 77A HAB	617		29.11.84	R.D.MacKenzie	Gerrards Cross	22. 5.96A
					(Cancelled 5.7.00 by CAA)		
G-BLST	Cessna 421C Golden Eagle III	421C0623	N88638	29.11.78	Cecil Aviation Ltd	Cambridge	16.12.03T
G-BLTA	Colt 77A Coil HAB	525		8. 6.84	K.A.Schlussler "James Sadler"	Bourne, Lincs	7. 8.91A
G-BLTC	Druine D.31A Turbulent	PFA 48-10964		18.12.84	G.P.Smith & A.W.Burton	Little Down Farm, Milson	8. 5.03P
	(Volkswagen 1600)						
G-BLTF	Robinson R22 A lpha	0428	N8526A	10. 1.85	Brian Seedle Helicopters Ltd	Blackpool	5. 4.04T
G-BLTK	Rockwell Commander 112TC-A	13106	SE-GSD	11.12.84	B.Rogalewski	Denham	26. 5.03
G-BLTM	Robin HR200/100 Club	96	F-GAEC	21.11.84	J.S.Swale tr Barton Robin Group	Barton	30. 7.03

G-BLTN	Thunder Ax7-65 HAB	621		4. 1.85	J.A.Liddle "Frederica"	Reading	3. 9.88A
G-BLTR	Sportavia-Putzer Scheibe SF-25B Falke	4823	D-KHEC	23. 1.85	V.Mallon	RAF Bruggen	1. 4.94
G-BLTS	Rutan LongEz	PFA 74A-10741		14. 1.85	R.W.Cutler	(Thorverton, Exeter)	
G-BLTT	Slingsby T.67B Firefly	2023		16. 1.85	C.W.Ward	Cardiff	5. 8.00T
G-BLTU	Slingsby T.67B Firefly	2024		16. 1.85	RAF Wyton Flying Club Ltd	RAF Wyton	21. 9.03T
G-BLTV	Slingsby T.67B Firefly	2025		16. 1.85	R.L.Brinklow	Hinton in the Hedges	17. 10.05T
	(Crashed in field near Withycombe Farm, Drayton, Oxon. 3.11.02 & substantially damaged)						
G-BLTW	Slingsby T.67B Firefly	2026		16. 1.85	R.L.Brinklow	Turweston	14.10.02T
G-BLTY	Westland WG.30 Srs.160	019	VT-EKG	14. 1.85	D.Brem-Wilson	(Bromley)	AC
			G-17-9/G-BLTY/G-17-19				
G-BLUI	Thunder Ax7-65 HAB	553		22. 2.85	Susan Johnson "Rhubarb & Custard"	Blackpool	31. 7.00A
G-BLUL	CEA Jodel DR.1050/MI Sicile Record	601	F-BMPJ	7. 3.85	J.Owen	Spilsted Farm, Sedlescombe	24.10.91
	(On overhaul 11.01)						
G-BLUM	Aérospatiale SA365N Dauphin 2	6101		21. 1.85	CHC Scotia Ltd	Humberside	14. 4.05T
G-BLUN	Aérospatiale SA365N Dauphin 2	6114	PH-SSS	21. 1.85	CHC Scotia Ltd	Liverpool	5. 3.05T
			G-BLUN				
G-BLUV	Grob G-109B	6336		1. 2.85	R.J.Buckels & S.K.Durso	North Weald	6.12.05
					tr The 109 Flying Group		
G-BLUX	Slingsby T.67M-200 Firefly	2027	G-7-145	31. 1.85	R.L.Brinklow	Hinton in the Hedges	8. 8.04T
			G-BLUX/G-7-113		t/a Richard Brinklow Aviation		
G-BLUZ	de Havilland DH.82B Queen Bee	1435 & SAL.150	LF858	9. 4.85	C.I.Knowles & J.Flynn	RAF Henlow	9. 7.03P
					tr The Bee Keepers Group (As "LF858")		
G-BLVA	Airtour AH-31 HAB	AH.004		12. 2.86	A.van Wyk	London SE12	
G-BLVB	Airtour AH-56 HAB	AH.005		12. 2.86	R.W.Guild "Bluejay"	Vilharino do Bairo, Portugal	
G-BLVI	Slingsby T.67M Firefly II	2017	(PH-KIF)	1. 2.85	Babcock Support Services Ltd	RAF Barkston Heath	24. 1.03T
			G-BLVI		t/a Babcock HCS (Op JEFTS)		
G-BLVK	Mudry/CAARP CAP-10B	141	JY-GSR	11. 3.85	E.K.Coventry	Childerditch	8. 5.03
G-BLVL	Piper PA-28-161 Warrior II	28-8416109	N43677	11. 2.85	Marair (Jersey) Ltd	Jersey	15. 5.03
G-BLVS	Cessna 150M Commuter	15076869	EI-BLS	19. 2.85	R.Collier	(Boston)	30. 7.03T
			N45356				
G-BLVW	Cessna F172H	F172-0422	D-ENQU	16. 5.85	R & D Holloway Ltd	Stapleford	10. 7.00
	(Built Reims Aviation SA)						
G-BLWB*	Thunder Ax6-56 Srs 1 HAB	645		22. 2.85	Not known	NK	10.11.99
	(Cancelled 28.11.01 as wfu) (Noted 4.02)						
G-BLWD	Piper PA-34-200T Seneca II	34-8070334	ZS-KKV	14. 3.85	Acre 123 Ltd	Biggin Hill	7. 5.05T
			ZS-XAT/N8253E				
G-BLWE*	Colt 90A HAB	648		5. 3.85	Huntair Ltd "Rair Computers"	Aachen, Germany	11. 5.00A
	(Cancelled 20.6.02 as WFU)						
G-BLWF	Robin HR100/210 Safari	183	F-BUSR	8. 3.85	Starguide Ltd	Stapleford	7. 6.03
G-BLWH	Fournier RF6B-100	7	F-GADF	3. 4.85	I.R.March	Booker	5. 9.03
G-BLWP	Piper PA-38-112 Tomahawk	38-78A0367	OY-BTW	7. 6.85	J.C.,T.,T. &, H.R Dodd	Panshanger	8. 3.04T
G-BLWT	Evans VP-1 Srs.2	PFA 62-10639		27. 3.85	J.S.Peplow	Shobdon	21. 4.03P
	(Volkswagen 1834)						
G-BLWV	Reims/Cessna F152 II	F15201843	EI-BIN	25. 2.85	Redhill Aviation Ltd (Op Redhill Flying Club) Blackbushe		1. 6.03T
G-BLWW*	Aerocar Mini-Imp Model C	PFA 136-10880		1. 3.85	M.K.Field tr The Brize Group	Sleap	4. 6.87P
	(Continental O-200-A)				(Cancelled 13.10.00 by CAA) (Noted 10.00)		
G-BLWY	Robin R2160D	176	F-GCUV	15. 4.85	K.D.Boardman	Perth	23.10.03
			SE-GXE				
G-BLXA	SOCATA TB-20 Trinidad	284	SE-IMO	11. 4.85	Tango Bravo Aviation Ltd	Blackbushe	14. 6.03
			F-ODOH				
G-BLXF*	Cameron V-77 HAB	1144		2. 4.85	P.Lawman "Candytwist III"	Northampton	2. 4.97A
	(Cancelled 29.10.01 as WFU & stored for possible rebuild)						
G-BLXG	Colt 21A Cloudhopper HAB	605		2. 5.85	A.Walker "Britannia Park"	Richmond, Surrey	6. 5.98A
G-BLXH	Alpavia Fournier RF3	39	F-BMDQ	25. 3.85	A.Rawicz-Szczerbo	Eaglescott	28 6.03P
G-BLXI	Scintex CP.1310-C3 Super Emeraude	937	F-BMJI	1. 4.85	R.Howard	Grove Moor Farm, Grassthorpe	11. 4.03P
G-BLXO	SAN Jodel 150 Mascaret	10	F-BLDB	9. 5.85	P.R.Powell	Allensmore, Hereford	3. 11.03P
G-BLXP	Piper PA-28R-200 Cherokee Arrow II	28R-7235200	N5226T	29. 7.85	M.B.Hamlett	Le Plessis-Belleville, France	5. 8.03
G-BLXR	Aérospatiale AS332L Super Puma	2154		14. 5.85	Bristow Helicopters Ltd "Cromarty"	Aberdeen	1. 7.03T
G-BLYD	SOCATA TB-20 Trinidad	518		1. 5.85	Yankee Delta Corporation Ltd	Redhill	4. 4.04
G-BLYE	SOCATA TB-10 Tobago	521		1. 5.85	G.Hatton	Blackpool	6. 6.04T
G-BLYK	Piper PA-34-220T Seneca III	34-8433083	N4371J	30. 5.85	Oxford Aviation Services Ltd	Gloucestershire	31.10.03T
G-BLYP	Robin R3000/120	109		15. 5.85	Weald Air Services Ltd	Headcorn	5. 5.01T
G-BLYT	Airtour AH-77 HAB	AH.008		7. 7.87	I.J.Taylor & R.C Kincaid "Signal 2"	Bristol	9. 8.03A
G-BLZA	Scheibe SF-25B Falke	4684	D-KBAJ	22. 5.85	T.A.Lacey tr Chiltern Gliding Club	RAF Halton	21. 9.03
G-BLZE	Reims/Cessna F152 II	F15201579	G-CSSC	3. 5.85	Redhill Aviation Ltd	Redhill	12. 4.04T
			PH-AYF(2)		(Op Redhill Flying Club)		
G-BLZF	Thunder Ax7-77 HAB	660		3. 6.85	H.M.Savage "Hector"	Edinburgh	10. 9.03A
G-BLZH	Reims/Cessna F152 II	F15201965		21. 6.85	Plane Talking Ltd	Blackbushe	3. 5.04T
G-BLZN	Bell 206B JetRanger II	314	ZS-HMV	12. 7.85	Hughes Helicopter Co Ltd	Biggin Hill	9. 7.04T
			C-GWDH/N1408W		t/a Biggin Hill Helicopters		
G-BLZP	Reims/Cessna F152 II	F15201959		10. 7.85	East Midlands Flying School Ltd	East Midlands	16.11.03T
G-BLZS	Cameron O-77 HAB	479		22. 5.85	M.M.Cobbold "Rainbow Brite"	Plymouth	25. 8.03A
					(Henry Africa's Hothouse Restaurant titles)		
G-BLZT*	Short SD 3-60 Var.100	SH.3676	G-14-3676	18. 6.85	BAC Express Airlines Ltd	(Southend)	29. 8.01T
	(Cancelled 11.3.02 as WFU: moved to BAC area 3.02)						

G-BMAA - G-BMZZ

G-BMAD	Cameron V-77 HAB	1166		10. 6.85	M.A.Stelling "Nautilus"	Bedford	29. 9.99A
G-BMAL	Sikorsky S-76A II Plus	760120	F-WZSA	27.11.80	CHC Scotia Ltd	Humberside	9. 5.04T
			G-BMAL		(Tail boom struck ground North Denes 12.7.01 & damaged)		
G-BMAO	Taylor JT.1 Monoplane	PFA 1411		29. 7.85	S.J.Alston	Hinton in the Hedges	13. 5.03P
	(Volkswagen 1600)						
G-BMAV	Aérospatiale AS350B Ecureuil	1089		1. 6.79	PLM Dollar Croup Ltd	Inverness	4. 8.00T

G-BMAX	Clutton FRED Srs.II	PFA 29-10322		20.12.78	D.A.Arkley	(Chelmsford)	24. 8.99P
	(Volkswagen 1834)						
G-BMAY	Piper PA-18-135 Super Cub	18-3925	OO-LWB	3. 7.85	R.W.Davies	Little Robhurst Farm, Woodchurch	15.11.04T
	(L-21B-PI) *(Frame No.18-3961)*		"EI-229"/I-EIJZ/MM542525/54-2525				
G-BMBB	Reims/Cessna F150L	F15001136	OO-LWM	2. 8.85	R.Manning	Netherthorpe	15.11.02T
			PH-GAA				
G-BMBJ	Schempp-Hirth Janus CM	20/209	(G-BLZL)	9. 9.85	J.Hallam tr BJ Flying Group	(Ashby-de-la-Zouch)	20. 3.04
G-BMBS	Colt 105A HAB	704		18. 7.85	H.G.Davies	Cheltenham	27. 8.91A
G-BMBW	Bensen B.8MR	MV-001 & PFA G/01-1064		27. 8.85	M.E.Vahdat	Uxbridge	30. 6.93P
	(Rotax 503)						
G-BMBZ	Scheibe SF-25E Super Falke	4322	D-KEFQ	17. 7.85	Cornish Gliding & Flying Club Ltd	Perranporth	11.10.03
G-BMCC	Thunder Ax7-77 HAB	705		12. 7.85	A.K. & C.M.Russell *"Charlie Charlie"*	Stafford	23. 2.99A
G-BMCD	Cameron V-65 HAB	1234		26. 6.85	M.C.Drye *"My Second Fantasy"*	Winkfield	11. 6.02A
G-BMCG	Grob G-109B	6362	(EAF673)	25. 7.85	Lagerholm Finnimport Ltd	Booker	26. 7.04
G-BMCI	Reims/Cessna F172H	F17200683	OO-WID	19. 8.85	A.B.Davis *(Op Edinburgh Flying Club)*	Edinburgh	13.11.04T
G-BMCK*	Cameron O-77 HAB	1180		9. 7.85	D.L.Smith t/a Smith Smart Partnership	Newbury	20.10.92A
					"Touchy" (Cancelled 6.12.01 as WFU) (Stored 2002)		
G-BMCN	Reims/Cessna F152 II	F15201471	D-ELDM	7. 8.85	Lincoln Aero Club Ltd	Sturgate	24.11.04T
G-BMCS	Piper PA-22-135 Tri-Pacer	22-1969	5Y-KMH	6. 9.85	P.R.Deacon	Rochester	15. 7.01
			VP-KMH/ZS-DJI				
G-BMCV	Reims/Cessna F152 II	F15201963		2.10.85	Leicestershire Aero Club Ltd	Leicester	9. 4.04T
G-BMCW	Aérospatiale AS332L Super Puma	2161	F-WYMG	4.10.85	Bristow Helicopters Ltd	Aberdeen	7.11.05T
			G-BMCW		*"Monifieth"*		
G-BMCX	Aérospatiale AS332L Super Puma	2164		7.10.85	Bristow Helicopters Ltd *"Lossiemouth"*	Aberdeen	14.11.04T
G-BMDB	Replica Plans SE.5A	PFA 20-10931		12. 8.85	D.Biggs	Boscombe Down	5. 6.03P
	(Continental O-200-A)				*(As "F235/B" in RFC c/s)*		
G-BMDC	Piper PA-32-301 Saratoga	32-8006075	OO-PAC	13. 8.85	J.D.M.Tickell	Aberdeen	5.10.03T
			OO-HKK/N8242A		t/a MacLaren Aviation		
G-BMDD*	Slingsby T.29 Motor Tutor	PFA 42-11070		8. 8.85	A.R.Worters	(Dunoon)	7.10.88P
	(Volkswagen 1834)				*(On rebuild 6.00: cancelled 13.10.00 by CAA) (Current status unknown)*		
G-BMDE	Pietenpol Air Camper	PFA 47-10989		12. 8.85	P.B.Childs	New Farm, Felton	18. 8.03P
	(Continental O-200-A)						
G-BMDJ	Price Ax7-77S HAB	TPB.1 & 003		1. 8.85	R.A.Benham	Burton-on-Trent	
	(Regd as Price TPB.1)				*(New owner 10.01) "Wings of Phoenix"*		
G-BMDK	Piper PA-34-220T Seneca III	34-8133155	ZS-LOS	16. 9.85	Air Medical Ltd	Oxford	24.11.04T
			N84209/N9553N				
G-BMDP	Partenavia P.64B Oscar	20008	HB-EPQ	20. 8.85	S.T.G.Lloyd	(Blackwood)	25. 5.04
G-BMDS	Jodel Wassmer D.120 Paris-Nice	281	F-BMOS	12. 8.85	J.V.Thompson	Breighton	1.10.02P
G-BMEA	Piper PA-18 Super Cub 95	18-3204	(D-ECZF)	12. 8.85	M.J.Butler	Ranksborough Hall Farm, Langham	15.10.03P
	(L-18C-PI)		Belg AF OL-L07/L-130/53-4804				
	(Frame No. reported as 18-3206 [c/n 18-3194 ex OL-L20/L-120/53-4794]: c/n 3204 has Frame No.18-3216)						
G-BMEB	Rotorway Scorpion 145	2896	VR-HJB	10.12.85	P.Trainor	(Newry, Co.Armagh)	
					(Current status unknown)		
G-BMEE	Cameron O-105 HAB	1189		4. 9.85	A.G.R.Calder	Los Angeles, CA, USA	8.10.89A
G-BMEG	SOCATA TB-10 Tobago	530		23.10.85	P.Farmer	(Cents, Luxembourg)	17.11.04
G-BMEH	Jodel 150 Special Super Mascaret	PFA 151-11047		15. 8.85	R.J.& C.J.Lewis	Garston Farm, Marshfield	21. 5.03P
	(Lycoming O-235) *(Rebuild of incomplete SAN Jodel 150 Mascaret c/n 62)*						
G-BMET	Taylor JT.1 Monoplane	PFA 1465		4. 9.85	M.K.A.Blyth	Little Gransden	7.11.02P
	(Volkswagen 1600)						
G-BMEU	Isaacs Fury II	PFA 11-10179		11. 9.85	I.G. Harrison	Egginton, Derby	
	(Salmson 90hp)				*(90% complete 6.99: new owner 11.02)*		
G-BMEX	Cessna A150K Aerobat	A1500169	N8469M	18. 9.85	N.A.M.Brain & C.Butler	Netherthorpe	19. 5.05
G-BMFD	Piper PA-23-250 Aztec F	27-7954080	G-BGYY	6. 9.79	Gold Air International Ltd	Cambridge	5. 2.04T
			N6834A/N9741N				
G-BMFG	Dornier Do.27A-1	27-1003-342	FAP 3460	23. 9.85	R.F.Warner t/a Sigma Services	(Broughton, Norfolk)	
			AC+955		*(On rebuild 2.99: current status unknown)*		
G-BMFI	PZL SZD-45A Ogar	B-657		23. 9.85	S.L.Morrey	Andreas, Isle of Man	29. 4.05
G-BMFL	Rand Robinson KR-2	PFA 129-11050		24. 9.85	E.W.B.Comber & M.F.Leusby	(Huntingdon)	
G-BMFN	QAC Quickie Tri-Q 200	EMK-017 & PFA 94A1-11062		27. 9.85	A.H.Hartog	Thruxton	1. 5.02P
	(Continental O-200-A)						
G-BMFP	Piper PA-28-161 Warrior II	28-7916243	N3032L	1.11.85	T.J.Froggatt & C.A.Lennard	Blackbushe	8. 7.04
					tr Bravo Mike Fox Papa Group		
G-BMFU	Cameron N-90 HAB	628		1.10.85	J.J.Rudoni	Rugeley, Staffs	12. 12.02T
G-BMFY	Grob G-109B	6401		8.10.85	P.J.Shearer	Kirkwall	3. 7.04
G-BMFZ	Reims/Cessna F152 II	F15201953		3.12.85	Cornwall Flying Club Ltd	Bodmin	30. 1.04T
G-BMGB	Piper PA-28R-200 Cherokee Arrow II	28R-7335099		8.11.85	A.L.Ings t/a Malmesbury Specialist Cars	Kemble	16. 8.04
G-BMGC*	Fairey Swordfish II	-	G-BMGC	23.10.85	Royal Navy Historic Flight	RNAS Yeovilton	
	(Built Blackburn Aircraft)		RCN W5856		*"City of Leeds"*		
			RN W5856		*(Cancelled 2.9.91 by CAA) (As "W5856/A2A" in 810 Sqdn c/s)*		
G-BMGG	Cessna 152 II	15279592	OO-ADB	10.10.85	A S Bamrah	Biggin Hill	24.10.03T
			PH-ADB		t/a Falcon Flying Services		
			D-EHUG/F-GBLM/N757AT				
G-BMGR	Grob G-109B	6396		27.11.85	D.S.Hawes & M.Clarke tr BMGR Group	Lasham	9. 2.04
G-BMHA	Rutan LongEz	PFA 74A-10973		18.10.85	S.F.Elvins	(Bristol)	
G-BMHC	Cessna U206F Stationair II	U20603427	N10TB	17.11.76	Spectrum Leisure Ltd	Clacton	22. 8.97T
			G-BMHC/N8571Q		*(Under rebuild 8.02)*		
G-BMHJ	Thunder Ax7-65 Srs.1 HAB	743		2. 1.86	M.G.Robinson *"Kittylog"*	Great Milton, Oxon	19. 5.92A
G-BMHL	Wittman W.8 Tailwind	PFA 31-10503		28.11.85	C.W.N. & A.A.M.Huke	RAF Shawbury	18.12.02P
	(Continental O-200-A)						
G-BMHS	Reims/Cessna F172M	F17200964	PH-WAB	7. 4.86	R.A.Hall	Rayne Hall Farm, Rayne	21. 7.04
					tr Tango Xray Flying Group		
G-BMHT	Piper PA-28RT-201T Turbo Arrow IV	28R-8231010	ZS-LCJ	18.11.85	White Aviation Ltd	Leeds-Bradford	22. 4.04T
			N8462Y				
G-BMID	Jodel Wassmer D.120 Paris-Nice	259	F-BMID	18. 8.81	P.E.S.Latham tr G-BMID Flying Group	RAF Shawbury	8. 5.03P

Reg	Type	C/n	Prev ID	Date	Owner	Location	CofA
G-BMIG	Cessna 172N Skyhawk II	17272376	ZS-KGI (N48630)	13. 5.86	Walkbury Aviation Ltd	Sibson	21. 6.04T
G-BMIM	Rutan LongEz (Lycoming O-235)	8102/160	OY-CMT OY-8102	12.12.85	R.M.Smith	Biggin Hill	1. 8.02P
G-BMIO	Stoddard-Hamilton Glasair IIRG	PFA 149-11016		25.11.85	J.M.Ayres & S.C.Ellerton	Kemble	3.10.02P
G-BMIP	Wassmer Jodel D.112	1264	F-BMIP	7.12.78	M.T.Kinch tr The Inglesham Flying Group	Manor Farm, Inglesham	11. 9.02P
G-BMIR(2)*	Westland Wasp HAS.1	F.9670	XT788	24. 1.86	Park Aviation Supply Little Glovers Farm, Charlwood, Surrey		
	(Cancelled 22.12.95 by CAA) (Exhibited in Flightaid's travelling roadshow 2002 as "XT78?/316" in 'Royal Navy' c/s)						
G-BMIS	Monnett Sonerai II VR-HIS (Revmaster R2100DQ)	755 & PFA 15A-10813		26. 2.87	B.A.Bower *(Stored 2000)*	Middle Wyke, St Mary Bourne	26.10.89P
G-BMIV	Piper PA-28R-201T Turbo Cherokee Arrow III	28R-7703154	ZS-JZW N5816V	7. 1.86	Firmbeam Ltd	Booker	22. 5.04
G-BMIW	Piper PA-28-181 Archer II	28-8190093	ZS-KTJ N8301J	6.12.85	Oldbus Ltd	Shoreham	14. 5.04T
G-BMIY	Oldfield Baby Lakes (Continental O-200-A)	PFA 10-10194	G-NOME	3.12.85	J.B.Scott *(Stored 12.01)*	Blackpool	27. 8.87P
G-BMJA	Piper PA-32R-301 Saratoga SP	32R-8113019	ZS-KTH N8309E	23.12.85	H Merkado	Panshanger	15. 8.05T
G-BMJC	Cessna 152 II	15284989	N623AP	3. 2.86	The Cambridge Aero Club Ltd	Cambridge	22. 7.04T
G-BMJD	Cessna 152 II	15279755	N757HP	21.11.85	Donair Flying Club Ltd	Tatenhill	5. 7.04T
G-BMJG*	Piper PA-28R-200 Cherokee Arrow	28R-35046	ZS-TNS ZS-FYC/N9345N	23.12.85	Western Air (Thruxton) Ltd	Blackpool	4. 2.99T
	(Damaged Thruxton 11.10.98: cancelled 15.4.99 by CAA) (Fuselage noted 12.01)						
G-BMJL	Rockwell Commander 114	14006	A2-JRI ZS-JRI/N1906J	8. 1.86	D.J.& S.M.Hawkins	(Woking)	10. 7.03T
G-BMJM	Evans VP-1 (Volkswagen 1834)	PFA 62-10763		21.11.85	M.J.Veary	Sywell	16. 5.03P
G-BMJN	Cameron O-65 HAB	1212		6.12.85	P.M.Traviss "F'red"	Yarm	3. 5.03A
G-BMJO	Piper PA-34-220T Seneca III	34-8533036	N6919K N9565N	5.12.85	Oxford Aviation Services Ltd	Gloucestershire	9. 5.04T
G-BMJR	Cessna T337H Turbo Skymaster II	33701895	G-NOVA N1259S	10. 7.84	Eastcote Services Ltd	Cranfield	10.10.05
G-BMJS	Thunder Ax7-77 HAB	754		3.12.85	S.E.Burton	Northampton	7. 4.96A
G-BMJT	Beech 76 Duchess	ME-376	ZS-KMI N3718W	4.12.85	Mike Osborne Properties Ltd	Ronaldsway	30. 3.04
G-BMJX	Wallis WA-116/X Srs.1 (Limbach L-2000)	K/219/X		31.12.85	K.H.Wallis *(Stored 8.01)*	Reymerston Hall, Norfolk	1. 4.89P
G-BMJY	SPP Yakovlev C.18A	NK	(France) Egypt AF 627	21. 1.86	R.J.Lamplough *(As "07" (yellow) in Russian AF c/s)*	Manor Farm, East Garston	27.11.01P
G-BMJZ	Cameron N-90 HAB	1219		16.12.85	P.Spellward "Uvistat" tr Bristol University Hot-Air Ballooning Society *(Valid CofR 9.02)*	Bristol	31. 3.94A
G-BMKB	Piper PA-18-135 Super Cub (L-21B-PI) (Frame No.18-3818)	18-3817	OO-DKB PH-DKB/(PH-GRP)/R Neth AF R-127/54-2417	11.12.85	Cubair Flight Training Ltd	Redhill	21. 2.03T
G-BMKC	Piper J-3C-65 Cub (L-4H-PI) (Continental C90) (Frame No.10970)	11145	F-BFBA 43-29854	2. 1.86	J.W.Salter "Little Rockette Jnr" (Holywood, Co Down) *(As "329854/R/44" in USAAC 533rd BS/381st Bomb Group c/s)*		11.10.02P
G-BMKD	Beech C90A King Air	LJ-1069	N223CG N67516	30.12.85	A.E.Bristow	Fairoaks	13. 4.03
G-BMKF	CEA Jodel DR.221 Dauphin	96	F-BPCS	3. 2.86	L., S.T.Gilbert & L.M.Radcliffe	Enstone	6. 8.03
G-BMKG	Piper PA-38-112 Tomahawk II	38-82A0050	ZS-LGC N91544	3. 2.86	APB Leasing Ltd	Welshpool	13. 8.04T
G-BMKI	Colt 21A Cloudhopper HAB	753		30.12.85	A.C.Booth	Bristol	25. 7.02A
G-BMKJ	Cameron V-77 HAB	1235		2. 1.86	R.C.Thursby	Barry	4. 5.03A
G-BMKK	Piper PA-28R-200 Cherokee Arrow II	28R-7535265	ZS-JNY N9537N	16. 1.86	Comed Aviation Ltd	Blackpool	5. 1.01T
G-BMKP	Cameron V-77 HAB	724	(G-BMFX)	10. 1.86	R.Bayly "And Baby Makes 10"	Bristol	7. 8.93A
G-BMKR	Piper PA-28-161 Warrior II	28-7916220	G-BGKR N9561N	14. 6.84	D.R.Shrosbee tr Field Flying Group	Goodwood	6. 6.03
G-BMKW	Cameron V-77 HAB	608		29. 1.86	A.C.Garnett "Aorangi"	Guildford	21. 9.00A
G-BMKY	Cameron O-65 HAB	1246		4. 3.86	Ann R.Rich "Orion"	Hyde	13. 4.02A
G-BMLB	Jodel Wassmer D.120A Paris-Nice	295	F-BNCI	20. 1.86	D.Kember tr Headcorn Flyers	Headcorn	1.10.02P
G-BMLC	Short SD.3-60 Var.100	SH.3688	SE-LDA G-BMLC/G-14-3688	18. 2.86	Aurigny Air Services Ltd	Guernsey	24 .5.02T
G-BMLJ	Cameron N-77 HAB	1263		7. 3.86	C.J.Dunkley t/a Wendover Trailers "Mr Funshine"	Aylesbury	26. 3.03A
G-BMLK	Grob G-109B	6424		24. 2.86	J.J.Mawson tr Brams Syndicate	Rufforth	29. 5.04
G-BMLL	Grob G-109B	6420		13. 3.86	C.Rupasinha tr G-BMLL Flying Group	Denham	24. 7.04
G-BMLM	Beech 95-58 Baron	TH-405	N111LM G-BMLM/F-GEPV/3D-ADF/ZS-LOZ/G-BMLM/G-BBJF	2. 7.79	N.J.Webb	Cranfield	12.10.02
G-BMLS	Piper PA-28R-201 Cherokee Arrow III	28R-7737167	N47496	11. 2.86	R.M.Shorter	Booker	24. 4.05T
G-BMLT	Pietenpol Air Camper (Continental C90)	PFA 47-10949		28. 1.86	W.E.R.Jenkins	Waits Farm, Belchamp Walter	20. 5.02P
G-BMLW	Cameron O-77 HAB	813		6. 2.86	M.L. & L.P.Willoughby "Stelrad"	Reading	7. 8.95A
G-BMLX	Reims/Cessna F150L	F15000700	PH-VOV	21. 3.86	J P A Freeman	Headcorn	20.12.04T
G-BMMC	Cessna 310Q	310Q0041	YU-BCY N7541Q	11. 2.86	I T Cooper	Gloucestershire	30. 3.02
G-BMMD	Rand Robinson KR-2 (Volkswagen 1834 Acro)	PFA 129-10817		7. 2.86	D.J.Howell *(Noted 10.01) (Cancelled 30.8.02 by CAA)*	Panshanger	14. 6.01P
G-BMMF	Clutton FRED Srs.II (Volkswagen 1834)	PFA 29-10296		20. 2.86	E.C.King "Thankyou Girl"	Kemble	18. 7.03P
G-BMMI	Pazmany PL-4A (Continental PC 60)	PFA 17-10149		6. 2.86	P.I.Morgans	Haverfordwest	18. 7.03P
G-BMMK	Cessna 182P Skylane II (Reims-assembled c/n F18200038)	18264117	OO-AVU N6129F	24. 3.86	G.G.Weston	Denham	23. 8.04T

Reg	Type	C/n	Prev id	Date	Owner/Operator	Location	Date
G-BMML	Piper PA-38-112 Tomahawk	38-80A0079	PH-TMG OO-HKD/N9662N	2. 4.86	J.C.& C.H.Strong	Thruxton	19. 5.04T
G-BMMM	Cessna 152 II	15284793	N4652P	10. 9.86	A.S.Bamrah t/a Falcon Flying Services	Biggin Hill	20.10.04T
G-BMMP	Grob G-109B	6432		27. 6.86	E.W.Reynolds	Tatenhill	24. 5.05
G-BMMV	ICA IS-28M2A	57		10. 3.86	F.R.Temple-Brown	Henstridge	24. 8.03
G-BMMW	Thunder Ax7-77 HAB	782		10. 3.86	P.A.George *"Ethos"*	Princes Risborough	3. 6.96A
G-BMMY	Thunder Ax7-77 HAB	716		11. 3.86	S.M.Wade & Sheila E.Hadley *"Winco"*	Salisbury	1. 8.03A
G-BMNL	Piper PA-28R-200 Cherokee Arrow II	28R-7535040	N32280 (N18MW)/N32280	17. 9.86	Elston Ltd tr Arrow Flying Group	Elstree	29. 5.05
G-BMNP*	Piper PA-38-112 Tomahawk II	38-81A0133	N23352	24. 3.86	APB Leasing Ltd	Tatenhill	27. 6.98T
	(Dismantled 8.99: cancelled 19.10.99 as destroyed) (Fuselage dumped 9.02)						
G-BMNV	SNCAN Stampe SV-4C (Lycoming IO-360)	108	F-BBNI	14. 3.86	Wessex Aviation & Transport Ltd	Haverfordwest	29. 8.03P
G-BMOE	Piper PA-28R-200 Cherokee Arrow II	28R-7635226	PH-PCB OO-HAS/N9221K	20. 5.86	E.P.C.Rabson	Compton Abbas	22.11.05T
G-BMOF	Cessna U206G Stationair II	U20603658	N7427N	17. 4.86	D.M.Penny tr Wild Geese Skydiving Centre	Movenis, Co.Londonderry	12. 4.03
G-BMOG	Thunder Ax7-77 HAB	793		2. 4.86	R.M.Boswell	Bawburgh, Norwich	28. 8.95A
	(Amended CofR 12.01)						
G-BMOH	Cameron N-77 HAB	1270		2. 4.86	P.J.Marshall & M.A.Clarke *"Ellen Gee"*	Ruislip	20. 8.91A
G-BMOI	Partenavia P68B Victor	103	I-EEVA	4. 4.86	Simmette Ltd	Exeter	6.11.04
	(C/n indicates P68 model)						
G-BMOK	ARV1 Super 2	011		14. 4.86	R.E.Griffiths	Middle Stoke, Kent	17. 8.03
G-BMOM	ICA IS-28M2A	50		30. 6.86	R.M.Cust	Sandtoft	5. 9.04
	(Rebuilt 2001 with forward fuselage of G-BKAB)						
G-BMOT	Bensen B.8M (Volkswagen 1834)	PFA G/01-1066		17. 4.86	Austin Trueman Ltd	Henstridge	13. 8.01P
	(Noted 12.02)						
G-BMOV	Cameron O-105 HAB	1307		11. 4.86	Cheryl Gillott *"Up & Down"*	Stroud	1. 7.99A
G-BMPC	Piper PA-28-181 Cherokee Archer II	28-7790436	LN-NAT	23. 4.86	C.J. & R.J.Barnes	East Midlands	16. 3.05T
G-BMPD	Cameron V-65 HAB	1200		4. 6.86	D.E. & J.M.Hartland *"Second Dawn"*	Matlock	12. 8.01A
G-BMPL	Optica OA.7 Optica	016		14. 4.86	Aces High Ltd *(Amended CofR 3.02)*	North Weald	2. 8.97T
G-BMPP	Cameron N-77 HAB	1303		15. 4.86	P.F.Smart *"Tuppence"*	Basingstoke	14. 5.93A
	tr The Sarnia Balloon Group *(Inflated 4.02: new owner 5.02)*						
G-BMPR	Piper PA-28R-201 Arrow III	28R-7837175	ZS-LMF N417GH	22. 4.86	B.Edwards	Full Sutton	20. 5.05
G-BMPS	Strojnik S-2A	045		18. 4.86	G.J.Green *(Current CofR 4.02)*	(Matlock)	
G-BMPY	de Havilland DH.82A Tiger Moth	"82619"	ZS-CNR SAAF??	25. 4.86	S.M.F.Eisenstein	Sandford Hall, Knockin	27. 3.03
G-BMRA	Boeing 757-236	23710		2. 3.87	DHL Air Ltd	East Midlands	2. 8.03T
G-BMRB	Boeing 757-236	23975		25. 9.87	Barclays Mercantile Business Finance Ltd *(Op DHL)*	East Midlands	29. 9.03T
G-BMRC	Boeing 757-236	24072	(N)	2.12.87	Barclays Mercantile Business Finance Ltd *(Op DHL)*	East Midlands	26. 1.04T
G-BMRD	Boeing 757-236	24073	(N) G-BMRD	2.12.87	DHL Holdings (UK) Ltd	East Midlands	3. 3.04T
G-BMRE	Boeing 757-236	24074	(N)	2.12.87	British Airways plc *(Stored 10.02)*	Lasham	28. 3.04T
G-BMRF	Boeing 757-236	24101		13. 5.88	DHL Air Ltd	East Midlands	17. 5.04T
G-BMRH	Boeing 757-236	24266		21. 2.89	DHL Air Ltd *(Op DHL)*	East Midlands	28. 2.05T
G-BMRI	Boeing 757-236	24267		17. 2.89	Barclays Mercantile Business Finance Ltd *(Op DHL)*	East Midlands	23. 2.05T
G-BMRJ	Boeing 757-236	24268		6. 3.89	DHL Air Ltd	East Midlands	13. 3.05T
G-BMSA	Stinson HW-75 Model 105 (Continental O-200-A)	7040	G-BCUM F-BGQO/NC21189	26. 3.86	M.A.Thomas tr The Stinson Group *"Iron Eagle"*	Barton	16. 9.02P
G-BMSB	Supermarine 509 Spitfire XI	CBAF.7722	G-ASOZ IAC158/G-15-171/MJ627	3. 5.78	M.S.Bayliss *(As "MJ627/9G-P" in 441 Sqdn c/s)*	Coventry	25. 4.03P
	(Regd as c/n 6S/R/749433)						
G-BMSC	Evans VP-2 (Volkswagen 1834)	V2-482MSC & PFA 63-10785		25. 8.82	S.Whitehead *(New owner 12.01)*	(Melton Mowbray)	8.10.99P
G-BMSD	Piper PA-28-181 Cherokee Archer II	28-7690070	EC-CVH N9646N	2. 7.86	H Merkado	Panshanger	20. 9.04T
G-BMSE	Valentin Taifun 17E	1082	D-KHVA(17)	20. 5.86	A.J.Nurse	Kemble	19. 7.02
G-BMSF	Piper PA-38-112 Tomahawk	38-78A0126	N4277E	9. 2.79	B.Catlow	Haverfordwest	30. 6.99
G-BMSG	SAAB 32A Lansen	32028	Fv.32028	22. 7.86	J.E.Wilkie	Cranfield	
	(Open store in bare-metal finish.6.02)						
G-BMSL	Clutton FRED Srs.III (Volkswagen 1834)	PFA 29-11142		19. 5.86	A.C.Coombe	Long Marston	4. 7.01P
G-BMSU	Cessna 152 II	15279421	N714TN	29. 8.86	S.Waite tr G-BMSU Group	Bagby	27.10.02T
G-BMTA	Cessna 152 II	15282864	N89776	27. 8.86	Alarmond Ltd *(Op Prestwick Flight Centre)*	Prestwick	16. 6.05T
G-BMTB	Cessna 152 II	15280672	N25457	19. 8.86	Sky Leisure Aviation (Charters) Ltd	Shoreham	16. 7.03T
G-BMTJ	Cessna 152 II	15285010	N6389P	19. 6.86	The Pilot Centre Ltd	Denham	14. 6.04T
G-BMTN	Cameron O-77 HAB	1305		4. 6.86	Industrial Services (MH) Ltd t/a Flete Rental *"Fletie"*	Bristol	1. 6.97A
G-BMTO	Piper PA-38-112 Tomahawk II	38-81A0051	N25679	28.11.86	A.S.Bamrah t/a Falcon Flying Services	Biggin Hill	11. 8.05T
G-BMTR	Piper PA-28-161 Warrior II	28-8116119	N83179	19. 6.86	Aeros Leasing Ltd	Gloucestershire	27. 3.05T
G-BMTS	Cessna 172N Skyhawk II	17270606	N739KP	17. 7.86	A.S.Bamrah t/a Falcon Flying Services	(Blackbushe)	23. 8.04T
G-BMTU	Pitts S-1E Special (Lycoming O-360)	PFA 09-10801		4. 6.86	Aerodynamics Ltd	Gloucestershire	22. 5.02P
G-BMTX	Cameron V-77 HAB	733		19. 6.86	J.A.Langley *"Boondoggle"* *(Buses for Bristol titles)*	Stroud	31. 5.03A
G-BMUD	Cessna 182P Skylane	18261786	OY-DVS N78847	6.11.81	Mescal E.Taylor *(www.newbridge.com titles)*	Netherthorpe	31. 7.03T
G-BMUG	Rutan LongEz (Lycoming O-235)	PFA 74A-10987		17. 6.86	P.Richardson & J.Shanley	Croft Farm, Darlington	24. 6.02P
G-BMUJ	Colt Drachenfisch SS HAB (Futuristic shape)	835		3. 6.86	Virgin Airship & Balloon Co Ltd *"Drachenfisch"*	Telford	27. 7.91A

Reg	Type	c/n	Prev id	Date	Owner	Location	Date
G-BMUK	Colt UFO SS HAB *(Futuristic shape)*	836		3. 6.86	Virgin Airship & Balloon Co Ltd *"UFO/Dream Station"*	Telford	26. 4.95A
G-BMUL	Colt Kindermond SS HAB *(Futuristic shape)*	837		3. 6.86	Virgin Airship & Balloon Co Ltd *"Kindermond/Childrens' Moon"*	Telford	26. 9.91A
G-BMUO	Cessna A152 Aerobat	A1520788	4X-ALJ N7328L	4. 6.86	Sky Leisure Aviation (Charters) Ltd	Redhill	30. 8.04T
G-BMUT	Piper PA-34-200T Seneca II	34-7570320	EC-CUH N3935X	23. 1.87	High Flyers Aviation Ltd	Newcastle	14. 11.05T
G-BMUU	Thunder Ax7-77 HAB	827		1. 8.86	G.Anorewartha *"Fiesta"*	Kings Lynn	29.10.98A
G-BMUZ	Piper PA-28-161 Warrior II	28-8016329	EC-DMA N9559N	24. 7.86	Newcastle upon Tyne Aero Club Ltd	Newcastle	5. 3.05T
G-BMVA	Scheibe SF-25B Falke	46223	RAFGGA.512 D-KAEN	28. 7.86	M.L.Jackson	Bidford	19. 2.05
G-BMVB	Reims/Cessna F152 II	F15201974		10. 9.86	N.D.Plumb	Hinton in the Hedges	10. 2.00T
G-BMVG	QAC Quickie Q-1 *(Rotax 503)*	PFA 94-10749		11. 6.86	P.M.Wright	Coventry	1. 1.02P
G-BMVI	Cameron O-105 HAB	1326		19. 6.86	M.L.Gabb t/a Heart of England Balloons *"Securicor"*	Alcester	7. 7.95A
G-BMVL	Piper PA-38-112 Tomahawk	38-79A0033	N2391B	5. 9.86	Airways Aero Associations Ltd *(Op British Airways Flying Club) (Blue Poole t/s)*	Booker	20.12.04T
G-BMVM	Piper PA-38-112 Tomahawk	38-79A0025	N2359B	5. 9.86	Airways Aero Associations Ltd *(Op British Airways Flying Club) (Waves of the City t/s)*	Booker	4. 3.04T
G-BMVS	Cameron Benihana 70SS HAB *(Aka Chef's Hat)*	1252		27.10.86	Benihana (UK) Ltd	London W1	14. 8.96A
G-BMVT	Thunder Ax7-77A HAB	102	SE-ZYY	15. 7.86	M.L. & L.P.Willoughby *"Trygg Hansa"*	Reading	
G-BMVU	Monnett Moni *(KEF-107)*	PFA 142-10948		14. 8.86	N.J.Cowley	Old Sarum	20. 9.99P
G-BMVW	Cameron O-65 HAB	1331		27. 6.86	S.P.Richards *"Olau Ferries"* *(Amended CofR 8.02)*	Cranbrook	15. 8.91A
G-BMWA	Hughes 269C	14-0271	N8998F	1. 7.86	R.J.H.Strong	(Yeovil)	19.12.05T
G-BMWE	ARV1 Super 2	012		1. 7.86	R.J.N.Noble	Farnborough	16. 1.00
G-BMWF	ARV1 Super 2 *(Rotax 914 Turbo)*	013		1. 7.86	N.R.Beale *(Under re-build 7.96: current status unknown)*	Deppers Bridge, Warwick	2. 4.90T
G-BMWM	ARV1 Super 2 *(Hewland AE75)*	020		30. 3.87	J.D.Muldowney	(Braintree)	14. 7.03P
G-BMWN*	Cameron Temple 80SS HAB	1211		9. 7.86	Forbes Europe Inc *"Temple"* *(Noted 9.01) (Cancelled 14.11.02 by CAA)*	Balleroy, Normandy	17. 6.96A
G-BMWR	Rockwell Commander 112A	365	N1365J	23. 9.86	M. & J.Edwards	Fairoaks	6. 5.02
G-BMWU	Cameron N-42 HAB	1346		22.12.88	I.Chadwick *"Baby Helix"* *(Op Balloon Preservation Group) (Valid CofR 4.02)*	Partridge Green	
G-BMWV	Putzer Elster B	024	D-EEKB 97+14/D-EBGI	5. 8.86	E.A.J.Hibbard *(Noted 5.00)*	Hill Farm, Nayland	
G-BMXA	Cessna 152 II	15280125	N757ZC	14. 7.86	I.R.Chaplin	Andrewsfield	28. 9.05T
G-BMXB	Cessna 152 II	15280996	N48840	14. 7.86	H.Daines Electronics Ltd *(Current status unknown)*	(Beccles)	21. 3.93T
G-BMXC	Cessna 152 II	15280416	N24858	14. 7.86	Devon School of Flying Ltd	Dunkeswell	1. 4.05T
G-BMXD	Fokker F.27 Friendship 500	10417	TF-FLR HL5210/(HL5206)/PH-FOR	6.10.86	BAC Express Airlines Ltd *"Scottish Trader"*	Gatwick	12.12.04T
G-BMXJ	Reims/Cessna F150L	F15000853	F-BUBA	18. 7.86	R.Harman tr Arrow Aircraft Group	Tatenhill	20. 6.03
G-BMXL	Piper PA-38-112 Tomahawk	38-80A0018	N25060	4. 9.86	Airways Aero Associations Ltd *(Op British Airways Flying Club) (Benyhone Tartan t/s)*	Booker	17. 6.05T
G-BMXX	Cessna 152 II	15284953	N5469P	10. 9.86	Evensport Ltd	Southend	1. 9.02T
G-BMYA*	Colt 56A HAB	864		13. 8.86	J Hayden *"British Gas"* *(Cancelled 29.4.97 as WFU) (Inflated 4.02)*	Abingdon	2.12.92A
G-BMYC	SOCATA TB-10 Tobago	696		1. 9.86	Elizabeth A. Grady	Old Buckenham	29. 4.05T
G-BMYD	Beech A36 Bonanza	E-2350		28.11.86	Seabeam Partners Ltd	Coventry	21. 3.05
G-BMYF	Bensen B.8M	PE-01		18. 8.86	G.Callaghan	Rich Hill, Co.Armagh	
G-BMYG	Reims/Cessna FA152 Aerobat	FA1520365	OO-JCA (OO-JCC)/PH-AXG	23.10.86	Greer Aviation Ltd	Prestwick	13. 6.05T
G-BMYI	Grumman-American AA-5 Traveler	AA5-0568	EI-BJF F-BVRM/N9568L	1. 9.86	W.C. & S.C.Westran	Shoreham	24. 5.02T
G-BMYJ	Cameron V-65 HAB	726		8. 9.86	S.P.Harrowing *"Skylark II"*	Port Talbot	6. 9.03A
G-BMYN	Colt 77A HAB	873		2. 9.86	F.R.Batersby & J.Jones tr Spectacles Balloon Group *"Spectacles"*	Manchester	25. 3.03A
G-BMYP	Fairey Gannet AEW.3	F.9461	8610M XL502	16. 9.86	D.Copley *(As "XL502" in 849 Sqdn/"B" Flight RN c/s: external storage 7.01)*	Sandtoft	29. 9.89P
G-BMYS	Thunder Ax7-77Z HAB	887		3.11.86	J.E.Weidema *(Op Pinkel Balloons)*	Baambrugge, The Netherlands	1. 6.01A
G-BMYU	Jodel Wassmer D.120 Paris-Nice	289	F-BMY	23. 6.78	N.P.Chitty	Drayton St.Leonard	3.10.03P
G-BMZA	Air Command 503 Modac	0589 *(Probably c/n 0389)*		11. 2.87	R.W.Husband *(Stolen c 6.9.01 c/w trailer)*	Blackbrook Farm, Sheffield	17.12.01P
G-BMZB	Cameron N-77 HAB	1370		30.10.86	D.C.Eager *"Dreamland"*	Bracknell	30. 4.95A
G-BMZE	SOCATA TB-9 Tampico	708		5.12.86	T.W.Pullin	Liverpool	15. 8.05T
G-BMZN	Everett Gyroplane 1 (Volkswagen 1835)	008		13.11.86	K.Ashford	(Walsall)	2.12.02P
G-BMZP	Everett Gyroplane 1 (Volkswagen 1835)	010		14.11.86	D.H.Kirton	(Berkhampstead)	10. 4.02P
G-BMZS	Everett Gyroplane 1 (Volkswagen 1835)	012		13.11.86	L.W.Cload	St.Merryn	23.10.03P
G-BMZW	Bensen B.8MR (Rotax 532)	PFA G/01-1021		16.10.86	P.D.Widdicombe	Huntingdon, York	25. 8.99P

G-BNAA - G-BNZZ

Reg	Type	c/n	Prev id	Date	Owner	Location	Date
G-BNAD	Rand Robinson KR-2 (Volkswagen 1834)	PFA 129-11077		10.11.86	M.C.Davies *(Amended CofR 3.02)*	(Roade, Northants)	27. 2.90P
G-BNAG	Colt 105A HAB	906		31.10.86	R.W.Batchelor	Thame	19.12.89A

Reg	Type	C/n	Prev id	Date	Owner/Operator	Location	Status
G-BNAI	Wolf W-11 Boredom Fighter	PFA 146-11083		31.10.86	C.M.Bunn	Haverfordwest	7. 3.03P
	(Continental A65) *(Represents Spad rep)*				*(As "146-11083/5" in AEF France 94th Aero Sqdn c/s)*		
G-BNAJ	Cessna 152 II	15282527	C-GZWF	3.11.86	Galair Ltd	Biggin Hill	11. 3.05T
			(N69173)		*(Op Surrey & Kent Flying Club)*		
G-BNAN	Cameron V-65 HAB	1333		28.10.86	Anne M.Lindsay & N.H.Ponsford	Leeds	7. 7.01A
					t/a Rango Balloon & Kite Co *"Actually"*		
G-BNAR	Taylor JT.1 Monoplane	PFA 55-10569		14.11.86	A.P.Daines	(Halstead)	28.12.90P
	(Volkswagen 1600)				*(New owner 1.03)*		
G-BNAU	Cameron V-65 HAB	1395		13.11.86	Cherry L.E.Lewis	Colwyn Bay	7. 9.03A
G-BNAW	Cameron V-65 HAB	1366		24.10.86	A. & P.A.Walker	Richmond, Surrey	25. 6.95A
					(HMS Recruitment titles) "Hippo-Thermia"		
G-BNBL	Thunder Ax7-77 HAB	910		7. 1.87	D.G.Such	Redditch	31. 5.03A
G-BNBU	Bensen B.8MV	PFA G/01-1070		1.12.86	B.A.Lyford *(Current status unknown)*	(St Merryn)	
G-BNBV	Thunder Ax7-77 HAB	915		2.12.86	Jennifer M.Robinson *"Layla"*	Milton-under-Wychwood	29.11.01A
G-BNBW	Thunder Ax7-77 HAB	914		11.12.86	I.S. & S.W.Watthews *"Mutley"*	Grange-over-Sands	9. 9.99A
G-BNBY	Beech 95-B55A Baron	TC-1347	G-AXXR	14. 2.83	J.Butler	(Lisle Sur Tarn, France)	2. 6.04
G-BNBZ	LET L-200D Morava	171329	D-GGDC	16.12.86	C.A.Suckling	Rushett Manor, Chessington	15. 5.00
			EI-AOY/(D-GLIN)/EI-AOY/OK-SHB				
G-BNCB	Cameron V-77 HAB	1401		2.12.86	C.W.Brown	Melton Mowbray	3. 5.03A
G-BNCC	Thunder Ax7-77 HAB	924		11.12.86	Celia J.Burnhope *"Charlie"*	(USA)	9.10.99A
G-BNCE*	Grumman G159 Gulfstream I	9	N436M	7. 4.87	Dundee Airport Fire Service	Dundee	9. 4.92T
			N436/N436M/N43M/(N709G)				
	(WFU 10.91 due to corrosion & cannibalised: cancelled 4.5.93 as WFU) (Fuselage in use 2002)						
G-BNCJ	Cameron V-77 HAB	815		16.12.86	D.Scott *"Sunshine Desserts"*	Melksham	7. 3.03A
G-BNCO	Piper PA-38-112 Tomahawk	38-79A0472	N2482F	8. 1.87	Diane K.Watson	Leicester	25.11.04T
G-BNCR	Piper PA-28-161 Warrior II	28-8016111	G-PDMT	10.12.86	Airways Aero Associations Ltd	Booker	16. 5.05T
			ZS-LGW/N8103D		*(Op British Airways Flying Club) (Chelsea Rose t/s)*		
G-BNCS	Cessna 180	30022	OO-SPA	7. 1.87	C.Elwell Transport (Repairs) Ltd	Tatenhill	17. 2.95
			D-ENUX/N2822A				
G-BNCU	Thunder Ax7-77 HAB	928		7. 1.87	W.De Bock	Peterborough	14. 7.00A
G-BNCZ	Rutan LongEz	PFA 74A-10723		8. 1.87	P.A.Ellway *"Atlas..T"*	Sherburn-in-Elmet	4.10.94P
	(Lycoming O-235)				*(Dismantled 2.00)*		
G-BNDG	Wallis WA-201/R	Srs.1K/220/X		22. 1.87	K.H.Wallis	Reymerston Hall, Norfolk	3. 3.88P
	(Rotax 64hp x 2)				*(Stored 8.01)*		
G-BNDN	Cameron V-77 HAB	1443		8. 1.87	J.A.Smith	Bristol	22.10.93A
G-BNDO	Cessna 152 II	15284574	N5387M	11. 2.87	Simair Ltd *(Op Essex School of Flying)*	Andrewsfield	12. 9.05T
G-BNDP	Brugger MB.2 Colibri	PFA 43-10956		8. 1.87	J.P.Kynaston	Burcott Lodge Farm, Leighton Buzzard	25. 4.03P
	(Volkswagen 1834)						
G-BNDR	SOCATA TB-10 Tobago	740		12. 2.87	P.F.Rothwell	(Alderley Edge)	28. 2.03T
G-BNDT	Brugger MB.2 Colibri	PFA 43-10981		8. 1.87	H.Haigh	Bagby	14. 7.03P
	(Volkswagen 1834)				tr Colibri Flying Group		
G-BNDV	Cameron N-77 HAB	1427		25. 2.87	R.E.Jones *"English Lake Hotels"*	Lytham St.Annes	9. 5.93A
G-BNDW	de Havilland DH.82A Tiger Moth	3942	N6638	10.12.86	N.D.Welch	Shobdon	
					(Components stored 3.96: current status unknown)		
G-BNDY	Cessna 425 Conquest I	425-0236	N1262T	2. 6.87	Standard Aviation Ltd	Newcastle	14.10.05
G-BNED	Piper PA-22-135 Tri-Pacer	22-1640	OO-JEF	26. 1.87	P.Storey	Sywell	AC
			N3385A		*(Current status unknown)*		
G-BNEE	Piper PA-28R-201 Arrow III	28R-7837084	N630DJ	28. 1.87	Britannic Management (Aviation) Ltd	Turweston	8. 8.03
			N9518N				
G-BNEK	Piper PA-38-112 Tomahawk II	38-82A0081	N9096A	28. 1.87	APB Leasing Ltd	Welshpool	17. 5.00T
G-BNEL	Piper PA-28-161 Warrior II	28-7916314	N2246U	27. 4.87	S.C.Westran	Shoreham	17. 10.05T
G-BNEN	Piper PA-34-200T Seneca II	34-8070262	N8232V	18. 2.87	Warwickshire Aerocentre Ltd	Birmingham	12. 5.05T
G-BNEO	Cameron V-77 HAB	1408		9. 2.87	J.G.O'Connell *"Rowtate"*	Braintree	2.11.00
G-BNES	Cameron V-77 HAB	1426		19. 2.87	G.Wells	Congleton	7. 1.99A
					t/a Northern Counties Photographers		
G-BNET	Cameron O-84 HAB	1368		22. 1.87	C.& A.I.Gibson *"Gordon Bennett"*	Stockport	1. 6.03A
G-BNEV	Viking Dragonfly	PFA 139-10935		28.11.86	N.W.Eyre	(Wombleton)	
	(Volkswagen 1834)				*(Nearing completion 6.92: current status unknown)*		
G-BNEX	Cameron O-120 HAB	1414		3. 4.87	The Balloon Club Ltd	Bristol	6. 5.90A
					t/a Bristol Balloons *"Sue Sheppard Employment Agency"*		
G-BNFG	Cameron O-77 HAB	1416		5. 3.87	Capital Balloon Club Ltd *"Dolores"*	London NW1	13. 1.94A
G-BNFI	Cessna 150J	15069417	N50588	8. 1.87	A.Waters	(Banbury)	1. 5.03
G-BNFK*	Cameron Egg 89SS HAB	1436		20. 2.87	Forbes Europe Inc	Balleroy, Normandy	15. 7.02A
	(Faberge Rosebud Egg shape)				*"Faberge Easter Egg" (Cancelled 14.11.02 by CAA)*		
G-BNFM	Colt 21A Cloudhopper HAB	668		5. 3.87	M.E.Dworski	Vermenton, France	24. 7.01A
G-BNFN	Cameron N-105 HAB	1442		13. 3.87	P.Glydon	Barnt Green, Birmingham	17. 6.97T
G-BNFO	Cameron V-77 HAB	816		5. 3.87	J.King & T.Ellenrieder *"Funshine"* tr Fox Group	Bristol	16. 5.03A
G-BNFP	Cameron O-84 HAB	1474		29. 4.87	B.F.G.Ribbans *"Dragonfly"*	Woodbridge	29. 3.03A
G-BNFR	Cessna 152 II	15282035	N67817	8. 4.87	Eastern Executive Air Charter Ltd	Southend	25. 4.03T
G-BNFS	Cessna 152 II	15283989	N5545B	10. 4.87	C & S Aviation Ltd	Wolverhampton	9. 7.02T
G-BNFV	Robin DR400/120 Dauphin 80	1767		4. 3.87	J.P.A.Freeman	Headcorn	15. 7.02T
G-BNGE	Auster AOP.61925	7704M		18. 3.87	M.Pocock	AAC Middle Wallop	6. 5.03P
			TW536		*(Op Military Auster Flight) (As "TW536/TS-V" in 657 AOP Sqdn c/s)*		
G-BNGJ	Cameron V-77 HAB	1487		18. 3.87	Lathams Ltd *"Latham Timber"*	High Wycombe	31.12.02A
G-BNGN	Cameron N-77 HAB	817		3. 4.87	Catherine B.Leeder *"Falcon"*	Diss	13.10.02A
G-BNGO	Thunder Ax7-77 HAB	971		26. 3.87	J.S.Finlan *"Thunderbird"*	Hamilton, New Zealand	5. 4.03A
					tr The G-BNGO Group *(Philips titles)*		
G-BNGP	Colt 77A HAB	1033		30. 3.87	Cornwall Ballooning Adventures Ltd	Newquay	1. 8.99A
					"Headland Hotel II"		
G-BNGR	Piper PA-38-112 Tomahawk	38-79A0479	N2492F	26. 3.87	Teesside Flight Centre Ltd	Teesside	1. 8.03T
G-BNGS	Piper PA-38-112 Tomahawk	38-78A0701	N2463A	26. 3.87	Teesside Flight Centre Ltd	Teesside	
					(Noted dismantled 3.02)		
G-BNGT	Piper PA-28-181 Archer II	28-8590036	N149AV	29. 4.87	Edinburgh Flying Club Ltd	Edinburgh	18. 5.05T
			N9559N				

Reg	Type	C/n	Prev ID	Date	Owner/Operator	Location	Date
G-BNGV	ARV1 Super 2	021		4. 6.87	N.A.Onions	Andrewsfield	6. 3.03
G-BNGW	ARV1 Super 2	022		4. 6.87	Southern Gas Turbines Ltd	Manston	8. 7.90T
					(Stored 6.94: current status unknown)		
G-BNGY	ARV1 Super 2	019	(G-BMWL)	9. 6.87	O.A.Bridle	(Bracknell)	28.11.04
G-BNHB	ARV1 Super 2	026		13. 7.87	C.J.Challener	Barton	24. 7.04
G-BNHE*	ARV1 Super 2	029		14. 8.87	L.J.Joyce	Dunkeswell	7. 8.99
					(Wrecked 5.00: cancelled 7.8.01 by CAA)		
G-BNHG	Piper PA-38-112 Tomahawk II	38-82A0030	N91435	23. 3.87	D.A.Whitmore	Bicester	31. 5.03T
G-BNHI	Cameron V-77 HAB	1249		26. 3.87	C.J.Nicholls *"Fun-Der-Bird"*	Warwick	24. 6.03A
G-BNHJ	Cessna 152 II	15281249	N49418	4. 6.87	The Pilot Centre Ltd	Denham	19.12.05T
G-BNHK	Cessna 152 II	15285355	N80161	30. 3.87	J.P.Slack	(Loughborough)	7. 6.03T
G-BNHN*	Colt Ariel Bottle SS HAB	1045		30. 3.87	NK *(Cancelled 24.1.92 as WFU) (Inflated 5.02)*	NK	
G-BNHO*	Thunder Ax7-77 HAB	1057		30. 3.87	M.J.Forster *"Bloody Mary"*	Newcastle	16. 7.97A
					(Cancelled 15.11.01 by CAA & stored)		
G-BNHT	Alpavia Fournier RF3	80	(D-KITX) G-BNHT/F-BMTO	13. 4.87	D.G.Hey tr G-BNHT Group	Little Gransden	9. 4.03P
G-BNID	Cessna 152 II	15284931	N5378P	24. 4.87	M.J.Ireland	Wellesbourne Mountford	21. 5.03T
G-BNIF	Cameron O-56 HAB	1464		15. 4.87	D.V.Fowler *"Nifty"*	Cranbrook, Kent	19. 5.00A
G-BNII	Cameron N-90 HAB	1497		15. 4.87	S.Saunders tr Topless Balloon Group	Farnham	16. 8.01
G-BNIJ	SOCATA TB-10 Tobago	758		27. 4.87	L.B.& F.H.Hancock	Kemble	16. 8.04
G-BNIK	Robin HR200/120 Club	43	LX-AIK LX-PAA	15. 4.87	N.J.Wakeling	Leicester	17. 5.03
G-BNIM	Piper PA-38-112 Tomahawk	38-78A0148	N9631T	18. 6.87	Aurs Aviation Ltd *(Op Glasgow Flying Club)*	Glasgow	30. 3.03T
G-BNIN	Cameron V-77 HAB	1079	G-RRSG(1) (G-BLRO)	15. 4.87	M.K.Grigson tr Cloud Nine Balloon Group *"Cloud Nine"*	Shoreham	10. 6.02A
G-BNIO	Luscombe 8AC Silvaire (Continental A75)	2120	N45593 NC45593	15. 4.87	W.H.Bliss	(North Shields)	5. 3.03P
G-BNIP	Luscombe 8A Silvaire (Continental A65)	3547	N77820 NC77820	15. 4.87	S.Maric *(New CofR 5.02)*	Cumbernauld	10. 2.93P
G-BNIU	Cameron O-77 HAB	1499		28. 4.87	MC VH SA	Brussels, Belgium	3. 4.00A
G-BNIV	Cessna 152 II	15284866	N4972P	24. 4.87	Aerohire Ltd *(Op Halfpenny Green Flight Centre)*	Wolverhampton	17. 8.03T
G-BNIW	Boeing-Stearman A75NI (PT-17) Kaydet (Pratt & Whitney R985)	75-1526	N49291 41-7967	22. 4.87	R.C.Goold	East Midlands	17. 4.04
G-BNIZ	Fokker F.27 Friendship 600F	10405	OY-SRA G-BNIZ/9Q-CLQ/PH-FOD	1. 6.87	Dart Group plc t/a Channel Express	Bournemouth	3.11.03T
G-BNJA	WAG-Aero Wag-a-Bond (Continental O-200-A)	PFA 137-10886		3. 4.87	B.E.Maggs	Clutton Hill Farm, Clutton	3. 8.03P
G-BNJB	Cessna 152 II	15284865	N4970P	27. 4.87	Aerolease Ltd	Conington	20. 7.03T
G-BNJC	Cessna 152 II	15283588	N4705B	27. 4.87	Stapleford Flying Club Ltd	Stapleford	26. 8.05T
G-BNJD	Cessna 152 II	15282044	N67833	27. 4.87	Aircraft Engineers Ltd	Edinburgh	24. 5.03T
G-BNJG	Cameron O-77 HAB	1502		9. 5.89	A.M.Figiel	High Wycombe	4. 4.97
G-BNJH	Cessna 152 II	15285401	C-GORA (N93101)	21. 7.87	J.McAuley *(Op Prestwick Flight Centre)*	Prestwick	5. 9.03T
G-BNJL	Bensen B.8MR (Rotax 532)	PFA G/01-1020		30. 4.87	J.M.Cox	Henstridge	29. 3.03P
G-BNJM	Piper PA-28-161 Warrior II	28-8216078	N8015V	27. 5.87	Teesside Flight Centre Ltd	Biggin Hill	4. 6.90T
					(Damaged Middleton, Cumbria 18.5.89: fuselage only 5.01)		
G-BNJO	QAC Quickie Q2 (Revmaster 2100D)	2217	N17LM	6.10.87	J.D.McKay	Crowfield	14. 5.93P
G-BNJR	Piper PA-28RT-201T Turbo Arrow IV	28R-8031104	N8212U	8. 5.87	D.Crocker	Thruxton	14. 8.05
G-BNJT	Piper PA-28-161 Warrior II	28-8116184	N8360T	11. 6.87	B.J.Newman, B.C.Williams, T.Kermode & M.Jones tr Chester Flying Group	Hawarden	10.12.02T
G-BNJU	Cameron Bust 80SS HAB	1324		13. 5.87	Ballon Team Bonn GmbH & Co KG *(Noted 1.02)* *"Ludwig von Beethoven"*	Meckenheim, Germany	19. 1.03A
G-BNJZ	Cassutt Racer IIIM (Continental O-200-A)	PFA 34-11228		14. 5.87	J.Cull	(Eastleigh)	1. 7.03P
G-BNKC	Cessna 152 II	15281036	N48894	26. 5.87	Herefordshire Aero Club Ltd	Shobdon	23. 9.05T
G-BNKD	Cessna 172N Skyhawk II	17272329	N4681D	19. 5.87	Bristol Flying Centre Ltd	Bristol	17.10.03T
G-BNKE	Cessna 172N Skyhawk II	17273886	N6534J	20. 5.87	T.Jackson tr Kilo Echo Flying Group	Manchester	18. 4.03T
G-BNKH	Piper PA-38-112 Tomahawk II	38-81A0078	N25874	14. 5.87	Goodwood Road Racing Co Ltd	Goodwood	24. 7.05T
G-BNKI	Cessna 152 II	15281765	N67337	19. 5.87	RAF Halton Aeroplane Club Ltd	RAF Halton	6. 7.05T
G-BNKP	Cessna 152 II	15281286	N49460	18. 5.87	Spectrum Leisure Ltd	Clacton	21. 8.03T
G-BNKR	Cessna 152 II	15281284	N49458	18. 5.87	Keen Leasing (IoM) Ltd	Newtownards, Co.Down	10. 7.02T
G-BNKS	Cessna 152 II	15283186	N47202	18. 5.87	Shropshire Aero Club Ltd	Sleap	9. 5.05T
G-BNKT	Cameron O-77 HAB	1356		13. 2.87	British Airways plc *"Katie II"*	Gatwick	29.12.01A
G-BNKV	Cessna 152 II	15283079	N46604	18. 5.87	S.C.Westran	Shoreham	29.10.05T
G-BNLA	Boeing 747-436	23908	N60665	30. 6.89	British Airways plc	Gatwick	29. 6.05T
G-BNLB	Boeing 747-436	23909		31. 7.89	British Airways plc *(Stored 4.02)*	Cardiff	13. 3.05T
G-BNLC	Boeing 747-436	23910		21. 7.89	British Airways plc *(Colum t/s)*	Gatwick	26. 7.05T
G-BNLD	Boeing 747-436	23911	N6018N	5. 9.89	British Airways plc *(Delftblue Daybreak t/s)*	Heathrow	5. 9.05T
G-BNLE	Boeing 747-436	24047		14.11.89	British Airways plc	Heathrow	16.11.05T
G-BNLF	Boeing 747-436	24048		23. 2.90	British Airways plc	Heathrow	11.10.05T
G-BNLG	Boeing 747-436	24049		23. 2.90	British Airways plc	Heathrow	1.10.05T
G-BNLI	Boeing 747-436	24051		19. 4.90	British Airways plc *(Benyhone Tartan t/s)*	Heathrow	20. 4.03T
G-BNLJ	Boeing 747-436	24052	N60668	23. 5.90	British Airways plc *(Ndebele Martha t/s)*	Gatwick	24. 5.03T
G-BNLK	Boeing 747-436	24053	N6009F	25. 5.90	British Airways plc	Heathrow	28. 5.03T
G-BNLL	Boeing 747-436	24054		13. 6.90	British Airways plc *(Chelsea Rose t/s)*	Heathrow	13. 6.03T
G-BNLM	Boeing 747-436	24055	N6009F	28. 6.90	British Airways plc *(Ndebele Martha t/s)*	Gatwick	27. 6.03T
G-BNLN	Boeing 747-436	24056		26. 7.90	British Airways plc *(Nalanji Dreaming t/s)*	Heathrow	26. 7.03T
G-BNLO	Boeing 747-436	24057		25.10.90	British Airways plc	Heathrow	24.10.03T
G-BNLP	Boeing 747-436	24058		17.12.90	British Airways plc	Gatwick	10. 9.03T
G-BNLR	Boeing 747-436	24447	N6005C	15. 1.91	British Airways plc	Heathrow	16. 1.04T
G-BNLS	Boeing 747-436	24629		13. 3.91	British Airways plc *(Wanula Dreaming t/s)*	Heathrow	12. 3.04T
G-BNLT	Boeing 747-436	24630		19. 3.91	British Airways plc	Gatwick	14.11.03T

G-BNLU	Boeing 747-436	25406		28. 1.92	British Airways plc	Heathrow	27. 1.05T
G-BNLV	Boeing 747-436	25427		20. 2.92	British Airways plc *(Waves of the City t/s)*	Gatwick	19. 2.05T
G-BNLW	Boeing 747-436	25432		4. 3.92	British Airways plc *"City of Norwich"*	Heathrow	4. 3.05T
G-BNLX(2)	Boeing 747-436	25435		1. 4.92	British Airways plc	Heathrow	2. 4.05T
G-BNLY(3)	Boeing 747-436	27090	N60659	10. 2.93	British Airways plc	Heathrow	9. 2.03T
G-BNLZ(3)	Boeing 747-436	27091		4. 3.93	British Airways plc *(Animals & Trees t/s)*	Heathrow	3. 3.03T
G-BNMA	Cameron O-77 HAB	830		15.12.87	N.Woodham *"Finian" (New CofR 4.02)*	Bristol	7. 4.02A
G-BNMB	Piper PA-28-151 Cherokee Warrior	28-7615369	N6826J	6.10.87	Britannia Airways Ltd	Liverpool	26. 1.03T
					(Op Britannia Airways Flying Club)		
G-BNMC	Cessna 152 II	15282564	N69218	29. 5.87	M.L.Jones *(Op Derby Aero Club)*	Egginton, Derby	10. 8.03T
G-BNMD	Cessna 152 II	15283786	N5170B	28. 5.87	T.M.Jones *(Stored 9.02)*	Egginton, Derby	28. 7.01T
G-BNME	Cessna 152 II	15284888	N5159P	25. 9.87	Northamptonshire School of Flying Ltd	Sywell	19.12.05T
G-BNMF	Cessna 152T	15285563	N93858	21. 7.87	Aerohire Ltd *(Op Midland Flight Centre)*	Wolverhampton	22. 8.03T
G-BNMG	Cameron O-77 HAB	1500		27. 5.87	J.H.Turner	Bridgnorth	4. 4.03A
G-BNMH	Pietenpol Air Camper	NH-1-001		2. 6.87	N.M.Hitchman	(Stoke Gifford)	
G-BNMI	Colt Black Knight HAB	1096		1. 6.87	Virgin Airship & Balloon Co.Ltd	Telford	26. 9.91A
G-BNMK*	Dornier Do.27A-1	271	OE-DGO	14. 8.87	G.Mackie	Belfast	
			56+04/BD+397/BA+399		*(Noted 10.01) (Cancelled 8.4.02 by CAA)*		
G-BNML	Rand Robinson KR-2	PFA 129-11240		23. 6.87	R.F.Cresswell	(Alfreton)	17. 8.00P
	(Volkswagen 1834)						
G-BNMO	Cessna R182 Skylane RG II	R18200956	N738RK	3. 7.87	Kenrye Developments Ltd	Trim, Co.Meath	26. 4.03
G-BNMU	Short SD.3-60 Var.100	SH.3724	N161DD	18. 6.87	BAC Express Airlines Ltd	Exeter	22.11.03T
			G-BNMU/G-14-3724		*(Stored 2002)*		
G-BNMX	Thunder Ax7-77 HAB	1003		15. 6.87	S.A.D.Beard	Cheltenham	16. 6.03A
G-BNNA	Stolp SA.300 Starduster Too	1462	N8SD	29. 6.87	M.A.Simpson	Leicester	6. 8.03P
	(Lycoming O-360)				tr Banana Group		
G-BNNC*	Cameron N-77 HAB	1523		16. 6.87	T McCoy *(Cancelled 2.6.98 as WFU) (Stored 2002)* Bath		9.10.96
G-BNNE	Cameron N-77 HAB	1413		15. 6.87	Balloon Flights International Ltd *(Active 9.01)*	Bath	
G-BNNI	Boeing 727-276	20950	VH-TBK	10.12.86	Cougar Leasing Ltd	Southend	17. 3.02T
					"Lady Patricia". (Open store 2.03).		
G-BNNO	Piper PA-28-161 Warrior II	28-8116099	N8307X	15. 6.87	Tindon Ltd	Norwich	5. 8.05T
G-BNNR	Cessna 152 II	15285146	N40SX	15. 6.87	Sussex Flying Club Ltd	Shoreham	29.10.05T
			N40SU/N6121Q				
G-BNNS	Piper PA-28-161 Warrior II	28-8116061	N8283C	26. 6.87	M.J.Allen & R.Inskip	Fowlmere	29. 5.05
					tr Warrior Aircraft Syndicate		
G-BNNT	Piper PA-28-151 Cherokee Warrior	28-7615056	N7624C	12. 6.87	S.T.Gilbert & D.J.Kirkwood	Hinton in the Hedges	1. 7.04T
G-BNNU	Piper PA-38-112 Tomahawk II	38-81A0037	N25650	12. 6.87	Edinburgh Flying Club Ltd	Edinburgh	2.12.05T
G-BNNX	Piper PA-28R-201T Turbo Cherokee Arrow III						
		28R-7703009	N9005F	14. 7.87	J.G.Freeden	Sherburn-in-Elmet	4.12.05T
G-BNNY	Piper PA-28-161 Warrior II	28-8016084	N8092M	1. 9.87	A.S.Bamrah	Biggin Hill	14.12.05T
					t/a Falcon Flying Services *(Op Southern Air)*		
G-BNNZ	Piper PA-28-161 Warrior II	28-8016177	N8135Y	24. 7.87	A S Bamrah	Biggin Hill	21.10.05T
					t/a Falcon Flying Services		
G-BNOB	Wittman W.8 Tailwind	258/DH1 & PFA 3502		13. 7.87	M.Robson-Robinson	(Abbots Bromley)	14. 5.02P
	(Continental.PC60)				*"Imogen"*		
G-BNOE	Piper PA-28-161 Warrior II	2816013	N9121X	26. 6.87	Sherburn Aero Club Ltd	Sherburn-in-Elmet	12. 2.04T
			N9568N				
G-BNOF	Piper PA-28-161 Warrior II	2816014	N9122B	26. 6.87	Tayside Aviation Ltd	Dundee	29. 3.04T
G-BNOG	Piper PA-28-161 Warrior II	2816015	N9122D	26. 6.87	BAE Systems Flight Training (UK) Ltd Jerez, Cadiz, Spain		24. 9.05T
G-BNOH	Piper PA-28-161 Warrior II	2816016	N9122L	26. 6.87	Sherburn Aero Club Ltd	Sherburn-in-Elmet	25. 1.04T
G-BNOJ	Piper PA-28-161 Warrior II	2816018	N9122R	26. 6.87	R.D.Turner & W.M.Brown	Blackpool	13. 7.03T
					tr BAE (Warton) Flying Club		
G-BNOK	Piper PA-28-161 Warrior II	2816019	N9122U	26. 6.87	BAE Systems Flight Training (UK) Ltd Jerez, Cadiz, Spain		19. 2.05T
G-BNOM	Piper PA-28-161 Warrior II	2816024		26. 6.87	Sherburn Aero Club Ltd	Sherburn-in-Elmet	14. 2.04T
G-BNON	Piper PA-28-161 Warrior II	2816025		26. 6.87	Tayside Aviation Ltd	Dundee	8. 3.04T
G-BNOP	Piper PA-28-161 Warrior II	2816027		26. 6.87	R.D.Turner & F.J.Smith	Blackpool	14. 8.05T
					tr BAE (Warton) Flying Club		
G-BNOS	Piper PA-28-161 Warrior II	2816029		26. 6.87	BAE Systems Flight Training (UK) Ltd Jerez, Cadiz, Spain		28. 2.03T
G-BNOT	Piper PA-28-161 Warrior II	2816030		26. 6.87	BAE Systems Flight Training (UK) Ltd Jerez, Cadiz, Spain		24. 6.05T
G-BNOV	Piper PA-28-161 Warrior II	2816032		26. 6.87	BAE Systems Flight Training (UK) Ltd Jerez, Cadiz, Spain		18. 6.03T
G-BNOX	Cessna R182 Skylane RG II	R18201026	N756AW	24. 6.87	Lawgra (No.386) Ltd	Cranfield	2. 4.03
					t/a International Aerospace Engineering		
G-BNOZ	Cessna 152 II	15281625	EI-CCP	22. 6.87	Halfpenny Green Flight Centre Ltd	Wolverhampton	21. 3.05T
			G-BNOZ/N65570				
G-BNPE	Cameron N-77 HAB	1519	(G-BNPX)	25. 8.87	Zebedee Balloon Service Ltd	Hungerford	26. 6.03A
G-BNPF	Slingsby T.31M Cadet III	826 & PFA 42-11122	XA284	3.11.87	S.Luck, P.Norman & D.R.Winder *"Noddy"*	Audley End	10. 8.00P
	(Stark Stamo MS.1400A) *(Contains wings from XE791 which became OO-ZDQ)*						
G-BNPH	Hunting-Percival P.66 Pembroke C.1	P66/41	WV740	30. 6.87	M.J.Willing	Jersey	5. 5.03P
	(Regd with c/n "PAC66/027")				*(As "WV740" in 60 Sqdn RAF c/s)*		
G-BNPL	Piper PA-38-112 Tomahawk	38-79A0524	N2420G	28. 7.87	Cardiff-Wales Flying Club	Cardiff	30. 1.03T
G-BNPM	Piper PA-38-112 Tomahawk	38-79A0374	N2561D	28. 7.87	Papa Mike Aviation Ltd *(Op Bonus Aviation)* Blackbushe		10. 5.05T
G-BNPO	Piper PA-28-181 Cherokee Archer II	28-7890123	N47720	28. 7.87	Bonus Aviation Ltd	Cranfield	15. 6.03T
G-BNPU*	Hunting-Percival P.66 Pembroke C.1	P66/87	XL929	30. 6.87	Northbrook College	Shoreham	17. 5.88P
	(Regd with c/n "K66/089")				*(Cancelled 11.8.88 as WFU) (As "XL929") (Noted 2.02)*		
G-BNPV	Bowers Fly Baby 1B	PFA 16-11120		2. 7.87	J.G.Day & R.Gauld-Galliers Rushett Manor, Chessington		20.11.03P
G-BNPY	Cessna 152 II	15280249	N24388	30. 6.87	J.C.Birdsall t/a Traffic Management Services	Gamston	19.12.02T
G-BNPZ	Cessna 152 II	15285134	N6109Q	30. 6.87	Tatenhill Aviation Ltd	Tatenhill	17.10.02T
G-BNRA	SOCATA TB-10 Tobago	772		15. 7.87	M.Walshe	Nottingham	8. 5.03
					tr Double D Airgroup *"Triple One"*		
G-BNRG	Piper PA-28-161 Warrior II	28-8116217	N83810	7. 7.87	RAF Brize Norton Flying Club Ltd	RAF Brize Norton	26. 3.03T
G-BNRK	Cessna 152 II	15284659	N6297M	29. 7.87	Redhill Aviation Ltd *(Op Redhill Flying Club)*	Redhill	6. 2.03T
					(Made heavy landing Redhill 29.3.02: nose u/c collapsed: damage to u/c, propeller, wing tip, engine frame & firewall)		
G-BNRL	Cessna 152 II	15284250	N5084L	13. 7.87	Walkbury Aviation Ltd	Sibson	25. 4.03T
G-BNRP	Piper PA-28-181 Cherokee Archer II	28-7790528	N984BT	25.11.87	Bonus Aviation Ltd	Cranfield	25. 5.03T

Reg	Type	C/n	Prev id	Date	Owner/Operator	Location	Expiry
G-BNRR	Cessna 172P Skyhawk II	17274013	N5213K	13. 7.87	PHA Aviation Ltd	Elstree	15.12.02T
G-BNRX	Piper PA-34-200T Seneca II	34-7970336	N2898A	25.11.87	Truman Aviation Ltd	Nottingham	8. 3.03T
G-BNRY	Cessna 182Q Skylane II	18265629	N735RR	20. 7.87	Reefly Ltd	Booker	30. 5.03T
G-BNSG	Piper PA-28R-201 Arrow III	28R-7837205	N9516C	30. 7.87	Armada Aviation Ltd	Redhill	19. 2.06
G-BNSI	Cessna 152 II	15284853	N4945P	6. 8.87	Sky Leisure Aviation (Charters) Ltd	Shoreham	3.11.02T
G-BNSL	Piper PA-38-112 Tomahawk II	38-81A0086	N25956	21. 7.87	APB Leasing Ltd	Welshpool	1. 5.03T
G-BNSM	Cessna 152 II	15285342	N68948	23. 7.87	Cornwall Flying Club Ltd	Bodmin	26. 7.03T
G-BNSN	Cessna 152 II	15285776	N94738	21. 7.87	The Pilot Centre Ltd	Denham	5. 5.03T
G-BNSO	Slingsby T.67M Firefly II	2021		20. 8.87	Babcock Support Services Ltd t/a Babcock HCS (Op JEFTS)	RAF Barkston Heath	17. 2.03T
G-BNSP	Slingsby T.67M Firefly II	2044		20. 8.87	Babcock Support Services Ltd t/a Babcock HCS (Op JEFTS)	RAF Barkston Heath	15. 2.03T
G-BNSR	Slingsby T.67M Firefly II	2047		20. 8.87	Babcock Support Services Ltd t/a Babcock HCS (Op JEFTS)	RAF Barkston Heath	15. 5.03T
G-BNST	Cessna 172N Skyhawk II	17273661	N4670J	21. 9.87	J.Revill tr CSG Bodyshop	Netherthorpe	16. 4.03T
G-BNSU	Cessna 152 II	15281245	N49410	2.12.87	A.R.Brown t/a Channel Aviation Ltd (Op Rural Flying Corps)	Bourn	31. 8.03T
G-BNSV	Cessna 152 II	15284531	N5322M	4.12.87	A.R.Brown t/a Channel Aviation Ltd (Valid CofR 4.02)	Bourn	12. 7.97T
G-BNSY	Piper PA-28-161 Warrior II	28-8016017	N4512M	18. 8.87	Carill Aviation Ltd	Southampton	12. 3.03T
G-BNSZ	Piper PA-28-161 Warrior II	28-8116315	N8433B	20. 8.87	Carill Aviation Ltd	Compton Abbas	8.12.05T
G-BNTC	Piper PA-28RT-201T Turbo Arrow IV	28R-8131081	N83428	4.11.87	M.F.Lassan	Wolverhampton	20. 6.03T
G-BNTD	Piper PA-28-161 Cherokee Warrior II	28-7716235	N38490 N9539N	5. 8.87	A.M.& F.Alam	Elstree	7.11.05T
G-BNTP	Cessna 172N Skyhawk II	172-72030	N6531E	4. 9.87	Westnet Ltd	Barton	30. 1.03
G-BNTS	Piper PA-28RT-201T Turbo Arrow IV	28R-8131024	N8296R	6. 8.87	Nasaire Ltd	Liverpool	11. 2.03
G-BNTT	Beech 76 Duchess	ME-228	N54SB	8.10.87	S.J.Skilton t/a Aviation Rentals (Op Professional Air Training)	Bournemouth	22. 5.03T
G-BNTW	Cameron V-77 HAB	1574		13. 8.87	P.Goss "Cecilia"	Alton	6.11.99A
G-BNTZ	Cameron N-77 HAB	1518		27. 8.87	P.M.Watkins t/a Balloon Team	Chippenham	26. 8.02A
G-BNUC	Cameron O-77 HAB	1575		18. 8.87	T.J.Bucknall "Bridges Van Hire II"	Hawarden	
G-BNUI	Rutan VariEze (Continental O-200-A)	PFA 74-10960		12. 8.87	I.T.Kennedy & K.H.McConnell	Belfast	21. 1.03P
G-BNUL	Cessna 152 II	152-84486	N4852M	2.10.87	Big Red Kite Ltd	(High Wycombe)	3. 5.03T
G-BNUN	Beech 58PA Baron	TJ-256	N6732Y	19. 8.87	British Midland Airways Ltd	East Midlands	8. 5.05T
G-BNUO	Beech 76 Duchess	ME-250	N6635Y	29. 9.87	G.A.F.Tilley	Bournemouth	26. 5.05T
G-BNUS	Cessna 152 II	15282166	N68179	26. 8.87	Stapleford Flying Club Ltd	Stapleford	6. 7.03T
G-BNUT	Cessna 152 II	15279458	N714VC	26. 8.87	Stapleford Flying Club Ltd	Stapleford	1. 6.03T
G-BNUV	Piper PA-23-250 Aztec F	27-7854038	N97BB N63894	2.10.87	L.J.Martin	Sandown/Redhill	9. 1.05
G-BNUX	Hoffmann H.36 Dimona	36236		26. 8.87	G.Hill tr Buckminster Dimona Syndicate	Saltby	13. 6.03
G-BNUY	Piper PA-38-112 Tomahawk II	38-81A0093	N26006	10. 9.87	Cardiff-Wales Aviation Services Ltd	Cardiff	17. 8.03T
G-BNVB	Grumman-American AA-5A Cheetah	AA5A-0758	N26843	28. 8.87	V.R.Coultan tr Grumman Group	Turweston	23. 2.03T
	(Regd as such but plate indicates Gulfstream-American production)						
G-BNVD	Piper PA-38-112 Tomahawk	38-79A0055	N2421B	16.11.87	D.A.Whitmore	Turweston	19. 6.03T
G-BNVE	Piper PA-28-181 Archer II	28-8490046	N4338D	28. 8.87	S.Parrish t/a Steve Parrish Racing	Fowlmere	10.12.05T
G-BNVT	Piper PA-28R-201T Turbo Cherokee Arrow III	28R-7703157	N5863V	26. 1.88	T.Yeung tr Victor Tango Group (Op Glasgow Flying Club)	Glasgow	12.11.03T
G-BNVZ	Beech 95-B55 Baron	TC-2042	N17720	25. 9.87	W.J.Forrest	White Waltham	14. 6.04
G-BNWA	Boeing 767-336ER	24333	N6009F	19. 4.90	British Airways plc (Delftblue Daybreak t/s)	Heathrow	24. 4.03T
G-BNWB	Boeing 767-336ER	24334	N6046P	2. 2.90	British Airways plc (Chelsea Rose t/s)	Heathrow	12. 2.06T
G-BNWC	Boeing 767-336ER	24335		2. 2.90	British Airways plc (Rendezvous t/s) (Stored 10.02)	Mojave-Kem Co, Ca, USA	21. 2.03T
G-BNWD	Boeing 767-336ER	24336	N6018N	2. 2.90	British Airways plc (Ndebele Emmly t/s) (Stored 10.02)	Mojave-Kem Co, Ca, USA	29.11.02T
G-BNWH	Boeing 767-336ER	24340	N6005C	31.10.90	British Airways plc	Heathrow	30.10.03T
G-BNWI	Boeing 767-336ER	24341		18.12.90	British Airways plc	Gatwick	17.12.03T
G-BNWM	Boeing 767-336ER	25204		24. 6.91	British Airways plc	Manchester	24. 6.04T
G-BNWN	Boeing 767-336ER	25444		30.10.91	British Airways plc	Heathrow	29.10.04T
G-BNWO	Boeing 767-336ER	25442		2. 3.92	British Airways plc "City of Barcelona"	Gatwick	1. 3.05T
G-BNWR	Boeing 767-336ER	25732		20. 3.92	British Airways plc	Gatwick	19. 3.05T
G-BNWS	Boeing 767-336ER	25826	N6018N	19. 2.93	British Airways plc	Heathrow	18. 2.03T
G-BNWT	Boeing 767-336ER	25828		8. 2.93	British Airways plc (Benyhone Tartan t/s)	Birmingham	29.11.05T
G-BNWU	Boeing 767-336ER	25829		16. 3.93	British Airways plc (Blomstrang t/s)	Gatwick	15. 3.03T
G-BNWV	Boeing 767-336ER	27140		29. 4.93	British Airways plc (Colum t/s)	Heathrow	28. 4.03T
G-BNWW	Boeing 767-336ER	25831		3. 2.94	British Airways plc	Heathrow	2. 2.03T
G-BNWX	Boeing 767-336ER	25832		1. 3.94	British Airways plc (Used for Future Strategic Tanker Transport programme)	Cambridge	28. 2.03T
G-BNWY	Boeing 767-336ER	25834	N5005C	22. 4.96	British Airways plc	Birmingham	21. 4.05T
G-BNWZ	Boeing 767-336ER	25733		25. 2.97	British Airways plc	Heathrow	24. 2.03T
G-BNXC	Cessna 152 II	15285429	N93171	24. 9.87	N.D.Wyndon tr Sir W.G.Armstrong-Whitworth Flying Group	Coventry	8. 3.04T
G-BNXD	Cessna 172N Skyhawk II	17272692	N6285D	25. 9.87	Hedcray Co Ltd t/a Direct Helicopters (Op Southend School of Flying)	Southend	9. 5.04T
G-BNXE	Piper PA-28-161 Warrior II	28-8116034	N8262D	24. 9.87	M.S.Brown t/a Rugby Autobody Repairs	Coventry	23.12.02
G-BNXG*	Cameron DP 70 HA Airship	1558		23. 9.87	Not known (Cancelled 18.6.93 by CAA) (Extant 8.02)	NK	
G-BNXI	Robin DR400/180R Remorqueur	1021	SE-FNI	13.10.87	London Gliding Club Pty Ltd	Dunstable	8. 2.03
G-BNXK	Nott/Cameron/Airship Industries ULD/3 Explorer Rozier HAB	7 & 1110	(G-BLJN)	23. 9.87	J.R.P.Nott	London NW3	
	(Hot-air envelope in Twain Harte, California, USA 12.97 - helium inner envelope stored Bristol 1995)						
G-BNXL	Glaser-Dirks DG-400	4-216		2.10.87	J.McLaughlin tr G-BNXL Group	Rufforth	14. 4.03
G-BNXM	Piper PA-18 Super Cub 95 (L-21B-PI) (Continental O-200-A)	18-4019	MM54-2619 EI-276/I-EIVC/MM54-2619/54-2619 (Italian Frame rebuild No.0006)	23.11.87	R.Thorp tr G-BNXM Group	Gipsy Wood	3. 9.02P

Reg	Type	C/n	Prev id	Date	Owner/Operator	Location	Date
G-BNXR	Cameron O-84 HAB	1515		23. 9.87	J.A.B.Gray "Bacchus II"	Cirencester	22. 8.02T
G-BNXT	Piper PA-28-161 Cherokee Warrior II	28-7716168	N4047Q	23. 9.87	A.S.Bamrah	Biggin Hill	27.10.05T
					t/a Falcon Flying Services (Op Euroflyers)		
G-BNXU	Piper PA-28-161 Warrior II	28-7916129	N2082C	23. 9.87	D.J.G.Carphin & R.E.Woolsey	Newtownards, Co.Down	3. 2.03
					tr Friendly Warrior Group		
G-BNXV	Piper PA-38-112 Tomahawk	38-79A0826	N2399N	10.12.87	W.B.Bateson (New owner 10.02)	Blackpool	5.10.01T
G-BNXX	SOCATA TB-20 Trinidad	664	N20GZ	15. 9.87	D.M.Carr	Wellesbourne Mountford	12. 5.03
G-BNXZ	Thunder Ax7-77 HAB	1105		13.10.87	W.S.Templeton, R.B.Green & A.S.Dear	Fordingbridge	6. 7.00A
					tr Hale Hot-Air Balloon Group "Dragonfly"		
G-BNYB	Piper PA-28-201T Turbo Dakota	28-7921040	N2856A	27. 1.88	Rosetta Milestone Ltd	Blackbushe	11. 2.04T
			N9533N				
G-BNYD	Bell 206B JetRanger II	1911	N3254P	1.10.87	Sterling Helicopters Ltd	Norwich	12.11.05T
			C-GTWM/N49712				
G-BNYK	Piper PA-38-112 Tomahawk II	38-82A0059	N2376V	23.10.87	APB Leasing Ltd	Welshpool	17. 5.05T
G-BNYL	Cessna 152 II	15280671	N25454	6.10.87	V.J.Freeman	Headcorn	9.11.03T
G-BNYM	Cessna 172N Skyhawk II	17273854	N6089J	13.11.87	D.J.Skinner tr Kestrel Syndicate	AAC Netheravon	16. 4.03
G-BNYN	Cessna 152 II	15285433	N93185	2.10.87	Redhill Aviation Ltd	Redhill	17. 2.03T
G-BNYO	Beech 76 Duchess	ME-78	N2010P	28.10.87	R.E.Wragg t/a Harding Wragg	Blackpool	5. 7.04T
G-BNYP	Piper PA-28-181 Archer II	28-8490027	N4330K	19.10.87	R.D.Cooper (Op Sandra's Flying Group)	Cranfield	13. 3.03T
G-BNYV	Piper PA-38-112 Tomahawk	38-78A0073	N9364T	13.11.87	Goodair Leasing Ltd	Cardiff	2. 5.03T
G-BNYX	Denney Kitfox Model 1	PFA 172-11285		28.10.87	R.W.Husband	Birds Edge, Penistone	14. 3.95P
					(Stored 3.96: current status unknown)		
G-BNYZ	SNCAN Stampe SV-4E	200	F-BFZR	10.12.87	M.J.Heudebourck & D.E.Starkey	White Waltham	5.10.03
	(Lycoming O-360)		Fr Mil				
G-BNZB	Piper PA-28-161 Warrior II	28-7916521	N2900U	18.11.87	Falcon Flying Services Ltd	Biggin Hill	24. 1.03T
G-BNZC	de Havilland DHC-1 Chipmunk 22	C1/0778	G-ROYS	11.11.87	The Shuttleworth Trust	Old Warden	27. 9.03
			7438M/WP905		(As "18013" in RCAF c/s)		
G-BNZG	Piper PA-28RT-201T Turbo Arrow IV	28R-8031132	N82376	23.11.87	Photo Shop Ltd	(Selby)	18. 3.02
G-BNZK	Thunder Ax7-77 HAB	1104		10.11.87	T.D.Marsden "Shropshire Lass"	Grimsby	28. 5.97A
G-BNZL	Rotorway Scorpion 133	2839		2.11.87	J.R.Wraight	Stoneacre Farm, Farthing Corner	
					(Complete but stored 5.95: current status unknown)		
G-BNZM	Cessna T210N Turbo Centurion II	21063640	N4828C	9.11.87	A.J.M.Freeman	North Weald	13. 3.03
G-BNZO	Rotorway Executive	RW152/3535		9.11.87	D.Collins & R.Ayres	Street Farm, Takeley	4. 1.02P
	(Rotorway RW162)				"Bonzo" (Noted 2.03)		
G-BNZR	Clutton FRED Srs.II	PFA 29-10727		10.11.87	R.M.Waugh	Newtownards, Co.Down	25. 5.99P
	(Volkswagen 1834)						
G-BNZV	Piper PA-25-235 Pawnee D	25-7405649	C-GSKU	22. 2.88	Northumbria Gliding Club Ltd	Currock Hill	27. 4.03
			N9548P	(Landed long Currock Hill 9.11.02, struck bushes, overturned & badly damaged).				
G-BNZZ	Piper PA-28-161 Warrior II	28-8216184	N8253Z	17.11.87	Zooom Aviation Ltd	Denham	8. 3.03T

G-BOAA - G-BOZZ

Reg	Type	C/n	Prev id	Date	Owner/Operator	Location	Date
G-BOAA	British Aircraft Corporation-Aérospatiale Concorde 102	100-006	G-N94AA G-BOAA	3. 4.74	British Airways plc	Heathrow	24. 2.01T
G-BOAB	British Aircraft Corporation-Aérospatiale Concorde 102	100-008	G-N94AB G-BOAB	3. 4.74	British Airways plc	Heathrow	19. 9.01T
G-BOAC	British Aircraft Corporation-Aérospatiale Concorde 102	100-004	G-N81AC G-BOAC	3. 4.74	British Airways plc	Heathrow	16. 5.05T
G-BOAD	British Aircraft Corporation-Aérospatiale Concorde 102	100-010	G-N94AD G-BOAD	9. 5.75	British Airways plc	Heathrow	3.12.04T
G-BOAE	British Aircraft Corporation-Aérospatiale Concorde 102	100-012	G-N94AE G-BOAE	9. 5.75	British Airways plc	Heathrow	18. 7.05T
G-BOAF	British Aircraft Corporation-Aérospatiale Concorde 102	100-016	G-N94AF G-BFKX	12. 6.80	British Airways plc	Heathrow	11. 6.04T
G-BOAG	British Aircraft Corporation-Aérospatiale Concorde 102	100-014	G-BFKW	9. 2.81	British Airways plc	Heathrow	3. 4.05T
G-BOAH	Piper PA-28-161 Warrior II	28-8416030	N43401 N9554N	21. 1.88	N.Singh & H.Kaur	Prestwick	19. 3.03T
G-BOAI	Cessna 152 II	15279830	C-GSJH N757LS	8. 1.88	Galair Ltd	Biggin Hill	22. 5.03T
G-BOAL	Cameron V-65 HAB	1600		5.11.87	A.Lindsay "No Name Balloon"	Twickenham	7. 2.02A
G-BOAM	Robinson R22 Beta	0717		10.12.87	Plane Talking Ltd	Elstree	21.12.02T
G-BOAO	Thunder Ax7-77 HAB	1162		2.12.87	D.V.Fowler	Cranbrook, Kent	17.10.02A
G-BOAS	Air Command 503 Commander			3.12.87	R.Robinson	(Leighton Buzzard)	
	(Rotax 503)	0388 & PFA G/04-1094			(Current status unknown)		
G-BOAU	Cameron V-77 HAB	1606		10.12.87	G.T.Barstow	Llandrindod Wells	9.12.96A
					"Flying Colours/Duster I"		
G-BOBA	Piper PA-28R-201 Arrow III	28R-7837232	N31249	4. 1.88	Atlantic Air Transport Ltd	Coventry	4. 7.03T
					t/a Atlantic Flight Training		
G-BOBB	Cameron O-120 HAB	1609		24.11.87	Over The Rainbow Balloon Flights Ltd	Mansfield	15. 3.03A
G-BOBG*	Jodel D.150	PFA 151-11222		18.12.87	L.Lewis	(Redcar)	
					(No Permit to Fly issued & cancelled 29.12.95 by CAA) (Stored 1.02)		
G-BOBH	Airtour AH-77B HAB	009		2.12.87	J. & K.Francis "Gloworm"	Southampton	29. 6.02A
G-BOBL	Piper PA-38-112 Tomahawk II	38-81A0140	N91335	4. 1.88	Cardiff Wales Aviation Services Ltd	Cardiff	28. 9.03T
G-BOBR	Cameron N-77 HAB	1623		10.12.87	M.Morris & P.A.Davies (New owner 5.02)	Oswestry	15. 2.03A
G-BOBT	Stolp SA.300 Starduster Too	CJ-01	N690CM	15.12.87	S.C.Lever tr G-BOBT Group	White Waltham	28. 6.03P
	(Lycoming O-360)						
G-BOBU*	Colt 90A HAB	900		15.12.87	Prescott Hot Air Balloons Ltd	Cheltenham	26. 9.00A
					(Cancelled 10.12.02 by CAA)		
G-BOBV	Reims/Cessna F150M	F15001415	EI-BCV	14.12.87	Sheffield Aero Club Ltd	Netherthorpe	6. 4.03T
G-BOBY	Monnett Sonerai II	PFA 15-10223		26.10.78	R.G.Hallam	Netherthorpe	8.11.82P
	(Volkswagen 2233)				(Damaged nr Barton 31.10.82: stored 9.96: current status unknown)		
G-BOBZ	Piper PA-28-181 Archer II	28-8090257	N81671	21.12.87	Trustcomms International Ltd	Goodwood	9. 3.98T

Reg	Type	c/n	Prev id	Date	Owner/Operator	Base	Fate
G-BOCB*	Hawker Siddeley HS.125 Srs.1B/522	25106	G-OMCA	14. 9.87	Not known	NK	16.10.90T
			G-DJMJ/G-AWUF				
			5N-ALY/G-AWUF/HZ-BIN		*(WFU @ Luton 1994 for spares: cancelled 22.2.95 as WFU)*		
					(Became Instructional airframe @ Barry Technical College & on disposal nose section saved by local collector 2.01)		
G-BOCC	Piper PA-38-112 Tomahawk	38-79A0362	N2540D	14.12.87	S.Lovatt	(Nottingham)	1. 1.04T
G-BOCF	Colt 77A HAB	1178		4. 1.88	Lindstrand Balloons Ltd	Oswestry	25. 7.94T
					(Stored 9.95: current status unknown)		
G-BOCG	Piper PA-34-200T Seneca II	34-7870359	N36759	30.12.87	Oxford Aviation Services Ltd	Oxford	5.12.03T
G-BOCI	Cessna 140A (Continental C90)	15497	N5366C	17.11.87	J.B.Bonnell *"Whitey"*	Thruxton	12.11.05
G-BOCK	Sopwith Triplane rep	153 & NAW-1		26. 1.88	The Shuttleworth Trust	Old Warden	31. 7.03P
	(Clerget Rotary 9B 130 hp)				*(As "N6290" in RNAS 8 Sqdn c/s) "Dixie II"*		
G-BOCL	Slingsby T.67C Firefly	2035		5. 1.88	Richard Brinklow Aviation Ltd	Thruxton	31. 8.03T
G-BOCM	Slingsby T.67C Firefly	2036		5. 1.88	Richard Brinklow Aviation Ltd	Hinton-in-the-Hedges	15. 6.03T
G-BOCN	Robinson R22 Beta	0726	N...	8. 1.88	Professional IT (Logistics) Ltd	Booker	1. 2.03T
			G-BOCN				
G-BOCP	Piper PA-34-220T Seneca III	3433089		17.12.87	BAE Systems Flight Training (UK) Ltd	Jerez, Cadiz, Spain	13. 6.04T
G-BOCR	Piper PA-34-220T Seneca III	3433111		26. 2.88	BAE Systems Flight Training (UK) Ltd	Jerez, Cadiz, Spain	10.12.04T
G-BOCS	Piper PA-34-220T Seneca III	3433112		26. 2.88	BAE Systems Flight Training (UK) Ltd	Jerez, Cadiz, Spain	18. 2.05T
G-BOCT	Piper PA-34-220T Seneca III	3433113		26. 2.88	BAE Systems Flight Training (UK) Ltd	Jerez, Cadiz, Spain	1.11.03T
G-BOCU	Piper PA-34-220T Seneca III	3433114		26. 2.88	BAE Systems Flight Training (UK) Ltd	Jerez, Cadiz, Spain	20. 9.04T
G-BOCX	Piper PA-34-220T Seneca III	3433121	N9613N	29. 9.88	BAE Systems Flight Training (UK) Ltd	Jerez, Cadiz, Spain	31. 5.02T
G-BODA	Piper PA-28-161 Warrior II	2816037	N9601N	19. 1.88	Oxford Aviation Services Ltd	Oxford	7. 5.03T
G-BODB	Piper PA-28-161 Warrior II	2816042	N9606N	23. 2.88	Oxford Aviation Services Ltd	Oxford	28. 9.03T
G-BODC	Piper PA-28-161 Warrior II	2816041	N9605N	23. 2.88	Oxford Aviation Services Ltd	Oxford	12. 4.03T
G-BODD	Piper PA-28-161 Warrior II	2816040	N9604N	23. 2.88	Oxford Aviation Services Ltd	Oxford	24. 8.03T
G-BODE	Piper PA-28-161 Warrior II	2816039	N9603N	23. 2.88	Oxford Aviation Services Ltd	Oxford	22. 6.03T
G-BODF	Piper PA-28-161 Warrior II	2816038	N9602N	19. 1.88	Oxford Aviation Services Ltd	Oxford	15. 6.03T
G-BODG*	Slingsby Cadet III	PFA 42-11310	WT911	9. 6.88	H.P.Vox	East Fortune	
	(Conversion of T.31B c/n 706)				*(Op East Fortune Flying Group) (Cancelled 15.4.99 by CAA) (Stored incomplete 6.00)*		
G-BODH	Slingsby Cadet III	PFA 42-10108	BGA.474	5. 1.88	M.M.Bain *"Fochinell"*	East Fortune	13. 8.02T
	(Volkswagen 1834) *(If p/i is correct then converted ex T.8 Tutor c/n MHL/RT.13 ex G-ALNK/BGA.474)*						
G-BODI	Stoddard-Hamilton SH-3R Glasair III	EMK-030 & 3088	(HB-)	14. 4.89	G.M.Howard	(Coppet, Switzerland)	21.11.02P
	(Built Jackson Barr Ltd)		G-BODI				
G-BODM	Piper PA-28-180 Cherokee Challenger	28-7305519	N56016	2. 2.88	R.Emery	Clutton Hill Farm, Clutton	24. 10.05T
G-BODO	Cessna 152 II	15282404	N68923	29. 1.88	Annie R.Sarson	Popham	29. 5.03
G-BODP	Piper PA-38-112 Tomahawk II	38-81A0010	N25616	5. 1.88	J.R.Santamaria	Guernsey	17.12.03T
G-BODR	Piper PA-28-161 Warrior II	28-8116318	N8436B	5. 1.88	Airways Aero Associations Ltd	Booker	2. 9.03T
					(Op British Airways Flying Club) (Waves & Cranes t/s)		
G-BODS	Piper PA-38-112 Tomahawk	38-79A0410	N2379F	3. 2.88	Coulson Flying Services Ltd	Cranfield	11. 9.04T
G-BODT	Jodel D.18	173 & PFA 169-11290		14. 1.88	L.D.McPhillips	Portmoak	22. 5.03P
	(Rotax 912UL)				tr Jodel G-BODT Syndicate		
G-BODU	Scheibe SF.25C-2000 Falke	44434	D-KIAA	19. 1.88	Faulkes Flying Foundation Ltd	Dunstable	9. 5.03
G-BODX	Beech 76 Duchess	ME-309	N67094	26. 2.88	S.J.Skilton	Bournemouth	16. 8.03T
					t/a Aviation Rentals *(Op Professional Air Training)*		
G-BODY	Cessna 310R II	310R1503	N4897A	17.12.87	Atlantic Air Transport Ltd	Coventry	23. 2.03T
G-BODZ	Robinson R22 Beta	0729		8. 1.88	Langley Construction Ltd	Nottingham	21. 4.04
G-BOEE	Piper PA-28-181 Cherokee Archer II	28-7690359	N6168J	20. 1.88	T.B.Parmenter	Lodge Farm, St.Osyth, Clacton	13. 6.03
G-BOEG	Short SD.3-60 Var.100	SH.3733	D-CFXE	27. 1.88	BAC Express Airlines Ltd	Gatwick/Exeter	19.11.03T
			N163DD/N133PC/G-BOEG/G-14-3733 *(Op BAC Express) "City of Paris"*				
G-BOEH	Robin DR340 Major	434	F-BRVN	4. 1.88	G.Bowles	Bradleys Lawn, Heathfield	14. 6.04
					tr Piper Flyers Group		
G-BOEI	Short SD.3-60 Var.100	SH3735	D-CFLX	27. 1.88	BAC Express Airlines Ltd	Exeter	7. 3.03T
	(Originally regd as Var.300)		VP-BKL/VR-BKL/G-BOEI/(VR-B..)/G-BOEI/G-14-3735				
G-BOEK	Cameron V-77 HAB	1658		25. 1.88	A.J.E.Jones *"Secret One"*	Bristol	7. 8.97A
G-BOEM	Aerotek Pitts S-2A Special	2255	N31525	17. 2.88	Margaret Murphy	Spanhoe	21. 7.01
	(Lycoming AEIO-360)						
G-BOEN	Cessna 172M Skyhawk	17261325	N20482	12. 2.88	Just Plane Trading Ltd	Top Farm, Croyfon, Royston	27. 6.03T
G-BOER	Piper PA-28-161 Warrior II	28-8116094	N83030	21. 1.88	M. & W.Fraser-Urquhart	Blackpool	18. 4.03
G-BOET	Piper PA-28RT-201 Arrow IV	28R-8018020	G-IBEC	28. 1.88	B.C.Chambers	Jersey	4. 8.03
			G-BOET/N8116V				
G-BOEW	Robinson R22 Beta	0750		27. 1.88	Plane Talking Ltd	Cranfield	21. 3.03T
G-BOEZ	Robinson R22 Beta	0753		27. 1.88	Plane Talking Ltd *(Op London Helicopter Centre)*	Redhill	15. 3.03T
G-BOFC	Beech 76 Duchess	ME-217	N6628M	28. 1.88	Magenta Ltd *(Op Airways Flight Training)*	Exeter	9. 3.03T
G-BOFD	Cessna U206G Stationair II	U20604181	N756LS	27. 1.88	D.M.Penny *(Op Wild Geese Parachute Centre)*	Cark	16. 8.03
G-BOFE	Piper PA-34-200T Seneca II	34-7870381	N39493	22. 2.88	Alstons Upholstery Ltd	Poplar Hall Farm, Elmsett	8. 8.03T
G-BOFF	Cameron N-77 HAB	1666		26. 1.88	R.C.Corcoran *(Systems 80 titles)*	Bristol	23. 7.03A
G-BOFL	Cessna 152 II	15284101	N5457H	28. 1.88	Gem Rewinds Ltd	Coventry	27. 3.03T
G-BOFM	Cessna 152 II	15284730	N6445M	28. 1.88	Gem Rewinds Ltd	Coventry	14. 6.03T
G-BOFO*	Ultimate Aircraft 10 Dash 200	(HB-)		15. 2.88	M.Werdmuller	(Felton, Bristol)	16. 6.92T
	(Lycoming HIO-360) 10-200-004 & PFA 180-11319		G-BOFO		*(Cancelled 12.6.00 as WFU) (Current status unknown)*		
G-BOFW	Cessna A150M Aerobat	A1500612	N9803J	15. 2.88	D.F.Donovan	Elstree	12.10.03T
G-BOFX	Cessna A150M Aerobat	A1500678	N9869J	15. 2.88	K.Hobbs t/a Aldergrove Flight Training Centre	Belfast	27.11.00T
G-BOFY	Piper PA-28-140 Cherokee Cruiser	28-7425374	N43521	3. 2.88	BCT Aircraft Leasing Ltd	Filton	30. 4.04T
G-BOFZ	Piper PA-28-161 Cherokee Warrior II	28-7816255	N2189M	10. 2.88	R.W.Harris *(Op Willowair Flying Club)*	Southend	19. 1.05T
G-BOGC	Cessna 152 II	15284550	N5346M	8. 2.88	Keen Leasing (IoM) Ltd	(Castletown, Isle of Man)	29. 8.04T
G-BOGG	Cessna 152 II	15282960	N45956	15. 2.88	The Royal Artillery Aero Club Ltd	AAC Middle Wallop	26. 9.03T
G-BOGI	Robin DR400/180 Regent	1821		15. 2.88	A.L.M.Shepherd	Rochester	23. 5.03I
G-BOGK	ARV Super 2	K.006 & PFA 152-11138		10. 2.88	H.N.Stone	(Morpeth)	1. 5.03P
	(Hewland AE75)						
G-BOGM	Piper PA-28RT-201T Turbo Arrow IV	28R-8031077	N8173C	10. 2.88	R.J.Pearce t/a RJP Aviation	Wolverhampton	9.11.03T
G-BOGO	Piper PA-32R-301T Saratoga SP	32R-8029064	N8165W	6. 4.88	A.S.Doman	Biggin Hill	26. 7.03T
G-BOGP	Cameron V-77 HAB	896		30. 3.88	T.Gunn *"Dire Straits"*	Crowborough	10. 7.00A
G-BOGV*	Air Command 532 Elite	0399 & PFA G/04-1102		10. 3.88	G.M.Hobman	Heworth, York	10. 1.91P
	(Rotax 532)				*(Cancelled 1.2.00 as WFU)*		

Reg	Type	c/n	Prev id	Date	Owner/Operator	Location	
G-BOGY	Cameron V-77 HAB	1650		15. 2.88	R.A.Preston "Bella"	Bristol	12.10.01A
G-BOHA	Piper PA-28-161 Cherokee Warrior II	28-7816352	N3526M	16. 3.88	T.F.& M.I.Hall	Shoreham	12. 6.03T
G-BOHD	Colt 77A HAB	1214		4. 3.88	D.B.Court "Bluebird"	Ormskirk	5. 8.02A
G-BOHF	Thunder Ax8-84 HAB	1197		8. 4.88	J.A.Harris	Sturminster Newton	19. 9.94A
G-BOHH	Cessna 172N Skyhawk II	17273906	N131FR N7333J	19. 2.88	T.Scott	Gamston	23. 5.04T
G-BOHI	Cessna 152 II	15281241	N49406	29. 2.88	V.D.Speck	Clacton	16. 7.03T
G-BOHJ	Cessna 152 II	15280558	N25259	29. 2.88	A.G.Knight t/a Airlaunch	Old Buckenham	5. 3.05T
G-BOHL	Cameron A-120 HAB	1701		11. 3.88	T.J.Bucknall "Son of City of Bath"	Hawarden	12.10.02
G-BOHM	Piper PA-28-180 Cherokee Challenger	28-7305287	N55000	18. 2.88	B.F.Keogh & R.A.Scott Lockmead Farm, South Marston		23. 4.03
G-BOHN*	Piper PA-38-112 Tomahawk II	38-81A0151	N23593	19. 2.88	Not known	(Pathhead)	19. 6.94T
	(Crashed Cardiff 13.8.93: cancelled 1.11.95 as WFU) (Fuselage stored 6.00: current status unknown)						
G-BOHO	Piper PA-28-161 Warrior II	28-8016196	N747RH N9560N	25. 2.88	G.J.Craig & D.L.H.Barrel tr Egressus Flying Group	Cambridge	3. 9.03T
G-BOHR	Piper PA-28-151 Cherokee Warrior	28-7515245	C-GNFE	29. 2.88	M C Wilson	Top Farm, Croydon, Royston	13. 4.04
G-BOHS	Piper PA-38-112 Tomahawk	38-79A0988	N2418P	26. 2.88	A.S.Bamrah t/a Falcon Flying Services	Biggin Hill	1. 4.04T
G-BOHT	Piper PA-38-112 Tomahawk	38-79A1079	N25304 C-GAYW/N24052	14. 4.88	E.Reed t/a St.George Flight Training	Teesside	11. 9.03T
G-BOHU	Piper PA-38-112 Tomahawk	38-80A0031	N25093	26. 2.88	D.A.Whitmore	Turweston	1. 5.03T
G-BOHV	Wittman W.8 Tailwind (Continental O-200-A)	621 & PFA 31-11151		3. 3.88	R.A.Povall	Yearby	10. 9.03P
G-BOHW	Van's RV-4 (Lycoming O-320)	PFA 181-11309		16. 6.88	P.J.Robins	Deenethorpe	20. 8.03P
G-BOHX	Piper PA-44-180 Seminole	44-7995008	N36814	9. 3.88	Airpart Supply Ltd	Oxford	6. 8.03T
G-BOIA	Cessna 180K Skywagon II	18053121	N2895K	3. 3.88	R.E., P.E.R., J.E.R. & R.J.W.Styles tr Old Warden Flying & Parachute Group	Rush Green	10. 1.04
G-BOIB	Wittman W.10 Tailwind	PFA 31-10551		3. 3.88	R.F.Bradshaw	Valley Farm, Winwick	17. 4.03P
G-BOIC	Piper PA-28R-201T Turbo Arrow III	28R-7803123	N2336M	7. 4.88	M.J.Pearson	Stapleford	12. 7.03
G-BOID	Bellanca 7ECA Citabria	1092-75	N8676V	3. 3.88	D.Mallinson	Birds Edge, Penistone	14. 3.04
G-BOIG	Piper PA-28-161 Warrior II	28-8516027	N4390B N9519N	1. 3.88	D.Vallance-Pell	Gamston	5. 9.03
G-BOIJ	Thunder Ax7-77 Srs.1 HAB	964		11. 3.88	K.Dodman	Stowmarket	12.10.02A
G-BOIK	Air Command 503 Commander (Rotax 503)	0420 & PFA G/04-1087		8. 3.88	F.G.Shepherd	Alston, Cumbria	22. 1.90P
	(Officially regd as c/n PFA G/04-1090)						
G-BOIL	Cessna 172N Skyhawk II	17271301	N23FL N23ER/(N2494E)	2. 3.88	Upperstack Ltd	Barton	15. 6.03T
G-BOIO	Cessna 152 II	15280260	N24445	7. 3.88	AV Aviation Ltd (Op Tayside Aviation)	Perth	7. 8.04T
G-BOIP	Cessna 152 II	15283444	N49264	7. 3.88	Stapleford Flying Club Ltd	Stapleford	26. 5.91T
	(Damaged Uckington 11.1.90: stored 5.98: current status unknown)						
G-BOIR	Cessna 152 II	15283272	N48041	7. 3.88	Shropshire Aero Club Ltd	Sleap	13. 6.03T
G-BOIT	SOCATA TB-10 Tobago	810		10. 3.88	Buckland Newton Hire Ltd	Henstridge	21.11.04T
G-BOIU	SOCATA TB-10 Tobago	811		10. 3.88	R & B Aviation Ltd	Guernsey	20. 4.04
G-BOIV	Cessna 150M Commuter	15078620	N704HH	30. 3.88	M.J.Page	Seething	25.11.03
G-BOIX	Cessna 172N Skyhawk II	17271206	C-GMMX N2253E	9. 3.88	JR Flying Ltd	Bournemouth	6. 2.04T
G-BOIY	Cessna 172N Skyhawk II	17267738	N73901	9. 3.88	L.W.Scattergood	Sherburn-in-Elmet	27. 7.03T
G-BOIZ	Piper PA-34-200T Seneca II	34-8070014	N81081	25. 2.88	R.W.Tebby t/a S.F.Tebby & Son (Op Bristol Flying Centre)	Bristol	17. 8.03T
G-BOJB	Cameron V-77 HAB	1615		11. 3.88	R.M.Trotter	Bristol	16. 7.03A
G-BOJD	Cameron N-77 HAB	1653		11. 3.88	R.S.McDonald "Bluebird"	(Chesham)	5. 7.03
G-BOJF*	Air Command 532 Elite Two Seat (Built Skyrider Aviation) (Rotax 532)	0425		11. 3.88	C Verlaan Waits Farm, Belchamp Walter		4. 6.91P
	(Cancelled 20.10.00 by CAA) (Airframe stored: current status unknown)						
G-BOJI	Piper PA-28RT-201 Arrow IV	28R-7918221	N2919X	31. 3.88	T.A.Stoate & K.D.Head tr Arrow Two Group	Blackbushe	7. 5.03
G-BOJK	Piper PA-34-220T Seneca III	3433020	G-BRUF N9113D	11. 3.88	Redhill Aviation Ltd (Op Redhill Flying Club)	Blackbushe	11. 4.03T
G-BOJM	Piper PA-28-181 Archer II	28-8090244	N8155L	21. 3.88	R.P.Emms	(Doncaster)	12. 5.03
G-BOJR	Cessna 172P Skyhawk II	17275574	N64539	22. 4.88	Exeter Flying Club Ltd	Exeter	8. 5.03T
G-BOJS	Cessna 172P Skyhawk II	17274582	N52699	29. 3.88	I.S.H.Paul	Denham	25. 5.03T
G-BOJU	Cameron N-77 HAB	1718		21. 3.88	M.A.Scholes "GB Transport"	London SE25	7. 9.97A
G-BOJW	Piper PA-28-161 Cherokee Warrior II	28-7716038	N1668H	28. 3.88	Brewhamfield Farm Ltd	(Wantage)	5.12.03T
G-BOJZ	Piper PA-28-161 Warrior II	28-7916223	N2113J	28. 3.88	A.S.Bamrah t/a Falcon Flying Services	Rochester	2. 4.04T
G-BOKA	Piper PA-28-201T Turbo Dakota	28-7921076	N2860S	15. 3.88	CBG Aviation Ltd	Fairoaks	14. 5.03
G-BOKB	Piper PA-28-161 Warrior II	28-8216077	N8013Y	29. 3.88	Apollo Aviation Advisory Ltd	Shoreham	31. 7.03T
G-BOKD	Bell 206B-3 JetRanger III	3654	G-ISKY G-PSCI/G-BOKD/N3171A	30. 8.01	Sterling Helicopters Ltd	Norwich	13. 4.03T
G-BOKF	Air Command 532 Elite (Rotax 532)	0404 & PFA G/04-1101		28. 3.88	J.K.Padden	(Morpeth)	22. 9.99P
G-BOKH	Whittaker MW7 (Rotax 532) (Officially regd as PFA 171-11231)	PFA 171-11281	(G-MTWT)	21. 3.88	A.J.Gordon (New owner 4.02)	Thame	1. 7.96P
G-BOKJ*	Whittaker MW7 (Rotax 532)	PFA 171-11283	(G-MTWV)	21. 3.88	M.R.Payne Wing Farm, Longbridge Deverill		4. 6.97P
	(Cancelled 17.5.01 as WFU) (Parts noted 12.01)						
G-BOKK*	Piper PA-28-161 Warrior II	28-8116300	N8427L	6. 4.88	Not known	Blackpool	7. 6.97T
	(Damaged Hamgreen, Redditch 18.5.95: cancelled 8.9.95 as WFU: wreck noted 12.01)						
G-BOKL	Piper PA-28-161 Warrior II	2816044	N9607N	24. 3.88	BAE Systems Flight Training (UK) Ltd Jerez, Cadiz, Spain		27. 7.03T
G-BOKP	Piper PA-28-161 Warrior II	2816050	N9611N	24. 3.88	BAE Systems Flight Training (UK) Ltd Jerez, Cadiz, Spain		18. 6.03T
G-BOKS	Piper PA-28-161 Warrior II	2816052		24. 3.88	BAE Systems Flight Training (UK) Ltd Jerez, Cadiz, Spain		30. 3.03T
G-BOKT	Piper PA-28-161 Warrior II	2816053		24. 3.88	BAE Systems Flight Training (UK) Ltd Jerez, Cadiz, Spain		28. 5.04T
G-BOKX	Piper PA-28-161 Cherokee Warrior II	28-7816080	N39709	28. 3.88	Shenley Farms (Aviation) Ltd	Headcorn	31. 9.03T
G-BOKY	Cessna 152 II	15285298	N67409	6. 4.88	D.F.F.Poore	Bournemouth	17. 6.04T
G-BOLB	Taylorcraft BC-12-65 (Continental A65)	3165	N36211 NC36211	17. 5.88	A.D.Pearce, E.C.& P.King "Spirit of California"	Kemble	26. 6.03P
G-BOLC	Fournier RF6B-100	1	F-BVKS	28. 3.88	J.D.Cohen	Dunkeswell	26.12.03
G-BOLD	Piper PA-38-112 Tomahawk	38-78A0180	N9740T	8. 7.88	Harnett Air Services Ltd (New owner 2.03)	(St. Albans)	21. 1.96T

G-BOLE	Piper PA-38-112 Tomahawk	38-78A0475	N2506E	13. 7.88	J.& G.Stevenson	Nottingham	28. 5.04
G-BOLF	Piper PA-38-112 Tomahawk	38-79A0375	N583P	13. 7.88	Teesside Flight Centre Ltd	Teesside	19. 7.04T
			YV-583P/YV-133E/YV-1696P/N9666N				
G-BOLG	Bellanca 7KCAB Citabria	517-75	N8706V	25.11.88	B.R.Pearson t/a Aerotug	Eaglescott	22. 5.04
G-BOLI	Cessna 172P Skyhawk II	17275484	N63794	30. 3.88	W White tr BOLI Flying Club	Denham	11. 7.03T
G-BOLL	Lake LA-4-200 Skimmer	295	(F-GRMX)	4. 5.88	M.C.Holmes	City of Derry	14. 6.03
			G-BOLL/EI-ANR/N1133L				
G-BOLN	Colt 21A Cloudhopper HAB	1226		4. 5.88	G.Everett	Maidstone	20. 5.03A
G-BOLO	Bell 206B JetRanger II	1522	N59409	2.11.87	Hargreaves Leasing Ltd	Goodwood	2. 3.03T
					(Op Blades Helicopters)		
G-BOLP	Colt 21A Cloudhopper HAB	1227		4. 5.88	J.E.Rose	Abingdon	1. 5.02A
G-BOLR	Colt 21A Cloudhopper HAB	1228		3. 5.88	C.J.Sanger-Davies	Uttoxeter	7. 8.95A
G-BOLS	Clutton FRED Srs.II	PFA 29-10676		6. 4.88	I.F.Vaughan *"The Ruptured Uck"*	(Melton Mowbray)	
G-BOLT	Rockwell Commander 114	14428	N5883N	16.10.78	H. Gafsen	Elstree	4. 7.04T
G-BOLU	Robin R3000/120	106	F-GFAO	14. 4.88	I.W.Goodger t/a Classair	Biggin Hill	18. 7.03T
			SE-IMS				
G-BOLV	Cessna 152 II	15280492	N24983	8. 4.88	A.S.Bamrah t/a Falcon Flying Services	Biggin Hill	20.12.02T
G-BOLW	Cessna 152 II	15280589	N25316	9. 6.88	JRB Aviation Ltd *(Op Seawing Flying Club)*	Southend	30. 8.03T
G-BOLX	Cessna 172N Skyhawk II	17269099	N734TK	8. 4.88	R.J.Burrough	Lydd	20.11.03
G-BOLY	Cessna 172N Skyhawk II	17269004	N734PJ	31. 3.88	Simair Ltd	Andrewsfield	19. 4.04T
G-BOLZ	Rand Robinson KR-2	PFA 129-10866		6. 4.88	B.Normington	Coventry	24. 7.02P
	(Volkswagen 1834)						
G-BOMA*	British Aerospace BAe 146 Srs.100	E1091	G-5-091	8. 4.88	Air Salvage International	Alton	
					(Cancelled 16.12.88 -to A6-SMK) (Fuselage noted 4.02)		
G-BOMB	Cassutt Racer IIIM	PFA 34-10386		18.12.78	S.Adams *"Blind Panic"* RAF Weston-on-the-Green		23. 5.98P
	(Continental O-200-A)				*(Damaged Weston Park, Telford 22.6.97: current status unknown)*		
G-BOMG	Pilatus Britten Norman BN-2B-26 Islander	2205	D-IBNF	6. 4.88	Loganair Ltd	Glasgow	12. 9.03T
			G-BOMG				
G-BOMN	Cessna 150F	15063089	N6489F	25. 4.89	Auburn Air Ltd	(Greystones, Co.Wicklow)	28. 8.03T
G-BOMO	Piper PA-38-112 Tomahawk II	38-81A0161	N91324	8. 4.88	APB Leasing Ltd	Welshpool	17. 6.04T
G-BOMP	Piper PA-28-181 Cherokee Archer II	28-7790249	N8482F	8. 4.88	SRC Contractors Ltd & D Carter	Elstree	12. 2.04T
G-BOMS	Cessna 172N Skyhawk II	17269448	N737JG	11. 4.88	Almat Flying Club Ltd & Penchant Ltd	Coventry	25.10.04T
G-BOMT	Cessna 172N Skyhawk II	17270396	N739AU	12. 7.88	R.A.Witchell	Andrewsfield	6. 5.04T
G-BOMU	Piper PA-28-181 Cherokee Archer II	28-7790318	N1631H	8. 4.88	J.Sawyer & P.R.Kinge t/a RJ Aviation	Blackbushe	19. 7.03T
G-BOMY	Piper PA-28-161 Warrior II	28-8216049	N8457S	28. 6.88	D.Knight t/a Southern Care Maintenance	Headcorn	17. 1.04T
G-BOMZ	Piper PA-38-112 Tomahawk	38-78A0635	N2315A	30. 6.88	I.C.Barlow & G.W.G.Young tr BOMZ Aviation	Booker	25. 4.03T
G-BONC	Piper PA-28RT-201 Arrow IV	28R-7918007	C-GXYX	13. 5.88	Finglow Ltd	Fowlmere	7. 7.03T
			N3069K				
G-BONE	Pilatus P.2-06	600-62	Sw.AF	8. 7.81	G.B.E.Pearce	Shoreham	14. 8.02P
			U-142/U-113				
G-BONO	Cessna 172N Skyhawk II	17270299	C-GSMF	11. 5.88	R.Jadunandan	Denham	24. 9.03T
			N738WS		tr G-BONO Flying Group		
G-BONP	CFM Streak Shadow			4. 5.88	T.J.Palmer	Prestwick	23.10 03P
	(Rotax 582)	108, SS-01P & PFA 161A-11344					
G-BONR	Cessna 172N Skyhawk II	17268164	C-GYGK	18. 4.88	D.I.Claik	Biggin Hill	24. 8.03
			(N733BH)				
G-BONS	Cessna 172N Skyhawk II	17268345	C-GIUF	18. 4.88	M.G.Montgomerie tr G-BONS Group	Elstree	31. 8.03
G-BONT	Slingsby T.67M Firefly II	2054		3. 5.88	Babcock Support Services Ltd RAF Barkston Heath		26. 9.03T
					t/a Babcock HCS *(Op JEFTS)*		
G-BONU	Slingsby T.67B Firefly	2037		3. 5.88	R.L.Brinklow *(Noted 4.02)*	Hinton in the Hedges	29. 6.00T
G-BONW	Cessna 152 II	15280401	OY-CPL	15. 4.88	Lincoln Aero Club Ltd	Sturgate	17. 8.03T
			N24825				
G-BONY	Denney Kitfox Model 1	166 & PFA 172-11351		11. 5.88	A.P.Worbey	Turweston	17. 8.03P
	(Inscribed as "Mk.2")						
G-BONZ	Beech V35B Bonanza	D-10282	N6661D	6. 4.88	P.M.Coulten	Boughton, Norfolk	1. 8.03
G-BOOB	Cameron N-65 HAB	515		12.11.79	J.Rumming *"Cracker"*	Swindon	8. 4.90A
G-BOOC	Piper PA-18-150 Super Cub	18-8279	SE-EPC	29. 4.88	R.R. & S.A.Marriott	Meon	23. 8.03
G-BOOD	Slingsby T.31M Motor Tutor	PFA 42-11264		4. 5.88	K.A.Hale	Clench Common	11.12.02P
	(Fuji-Robin EC-44-2PM) *(Wings ex XE810 c/n 923)*						
G-BOOE	Gulfstream GA-7 Cougar	GA7-0093	N718G	7. 6.88	N.Gardner	Southampton	31. 7.03T
G-BOOF	Piper PA-28-181 Cherokee Archer II	28-7890084	N47510	16. 6.88	H Merkado	Panshanger	19.10.03T
G-BOOG	Piper PA-28RT-201T Turbo Arrow IV	28R-8331036	N4303K	6. 5.88	Simair Ltd	Andrewsfield	4. 4.05
G-BOOH	Jodel D.112	481	F-BHVK	16. 5.88	R.M. MacCormac	RAF Henlow	3. 6.03P
	(Built Ets Valladeau)						
G-BOOI	Cessna 152 II	15280751	N25590	22. 8.88	Stapleford Flying Club Ltd	Stapleford	23. 4.04T
G-BOOJ	Air Command 532 Elite II PB206 & PFA G/04-1098			4. 5.88	Roger Savage Gyroplanes Ltd	Kingsmuir Sorbie	6.12.91P
	(Rotax 532)						
G-BOOL	Cessna 172N Skyhawk II	17272486	C-GJSY	27. 4.88	Surrey & Kent Flying Club Ltd	Biggin Hill	16.12.03T
			N5271D				
G-BOON*	Piper PA-32RT-300 Lance II	32R-7885253	N361DB	25. 4.88	Not known	Andrewsfield	28. 5.00T
					(Damaged landing Connemara 10.10.97: cancelled 3.3.98 by CAA) (Wreck noted 5.02)		
G-BOOV	Aérospatiale AS355F2 Twin Squirrel	5374		3. 5.88	Plane Talking Ltd	Elstree	2.10.03T
G-BOOW	Aerosport Scamp	PFA 117-10709		10. 5.88	I.E.Bloys	Fenland	17. 8.02P
	(Volkswagen 1834)						
G-BOOX	Rutan LongEz	PFA 74A-10844		3. 5.88	I.R.Wilde	Deenethorpe	7. 3.03P
	(Lycoming O-235)						
G-BOOZ	Cameron N-77 HAB	904	(G-BKSJ)	21. 6.83	J.E.F.Kettley *"Bluebell"*	Chippenham	
	(New home built envelope c 6.98)						
G-BOPA	Piper PA-28-181 Archer II	28-8490024	N43299	28. 4.88	Flyco Ltd	Denham	4. 8.03
G-BOPC	Piper PA-28-161 Warrior II	28-8216006	N2124X	6. 5.88	Aeros Ltd	Gloucestershire	19. 7.03T
G-BOPD	Bede BD-4 (Lycoming O-320)	632	N632DH	25. 5.88	S.T.Dauncey	Yearby	17. 6.03P
G-BOPH	Cessna TR182 Turbo Skylane RG II	R18201031	N756BJ	11. 5.88	Grandsam Investments Ltd	Cambridge	31. 5.03T
G-BOPO	FLS OA.7 Optica 301	021	EC-FVM	17. 5.88	Aces High Ltd	North Weald	27. 5.96T
			EC-435/G-BOPO		*(Stored as "EC-FVM" 6.02 in Helisureste titles)*		

G-BOPR	FLS OA.7 Optica 301	023		17. 5.88	Aces High Ltd *(Amended CofR 3.02)*	North Weald	
G-BOPT	Grob G-115	8046		10. 5.88	LAC (Enterprises) Ltd *(Op Lancashire Aero Club)* Barton		7.12.03T
G-BOPU	Grob G-115	8059		10. 5.88	LAC (Enterprises) Ltd *(Op Lancashire Aero Club)* Barton		18. 7.03T
					(Force landed on golf course west of Barton 9.8.01: struck grass bank & n/wheel collapsed)		
G-BOPV	Piper PA-34-200T Seneca II	34-8070265	N82323	7. 6.88	G.J.Powell	Biggin Hill	11. 7.03T
G-BOPX	Cessna A152 Aerobat	A1520932	N761BK	11. 5.88	Aerohire Ltd	Bourne Park, Hurstbourne Tarrant	24. 1.98T
					(Stored 10.01 less wings)		
G-BORB	Cameron V-77 HAB	1348		24. 8.88	M.H.Wolff	Liskeard	7. 7.02A
G-BORD	Thunder Ax7-77 HAB	1164		26. 5.88	D.D.Owen *"Marvin"*	Wotton-under-Edge	11.12.99A
G-BORE	Colt 77A HAB	642		24. 5.88	J.D.Medcalf & C.Wilson	Enfield	24. 8.02A
					tr Little Secret Hot Air Balloon Group *"My Little Secret"*		
G-BORG	Campbell Cricket	PFA G/03-1085		8. 6.88	G.Davison & H.Hayes	Carlisle	1. 9.03P
	(Rotax 503)				*(Noted 1.02)*		
G-BORH	Piper PA-34-200T Seneca II	34-8070352	N8261V	7. 6.88	Aerolease Ltd	Conington	31. 1.04T
G-BORI	Cessna 152 II	15281672	N66936	8. 6.88	S.Copeland	(Corby)	16.10.03T
G-BORJ	Cessna 152 II	15282649	N89148	27. 5.88	Pool Aviation (NW) Ltd	Blackpool	19.12.03T
G-BORK	Piper PA-28-161 Warrior II	28-8116095	N83036	13. 6.88	A.W.Collett	Turweston	29.11.03T
G-BORL	Piper PA-28-161 Cherokee Warrior II	28-7816256	N2190M	28. 9.88	Westair Flying School Ltd	Blackpool	8. 1.04T
G-BORM*	Hawker Siddeley HS.748 Srs.2B/217	1670	RP-C1043	29. 7.88	Not known	Exeter	
			V2-LAA/VP-LAA/9Y-TDH		*(WFU - to Fire Service: cancelled 18.6.92 by CAA) (Noted 10.00)*		
G-BORN	Cameron N-77 HAB	1777		13. 5.88	I.Chadwick *"Ian"*	Partridge Green, West Sussex	21. 4.03A
G-BORO	Cessna 152 II	15283767	N5130B	27. 5.88	Tatenhill Aviation Ltd	Tatenhill	8. 2.04T
G-BORR	Thunder AX8-90 HAB	1256		13. 6.88	W.J.Harris	Cheltenham	19. 8.03A
G-BORS	Piper PA-28-181 Archer II	28-8090156	N8127C	31. 5.88	Modern Air (UK) Ltd	Fowlmere	29. 6.03T
G-BORT	Colt 77A HAB	1255		7. 6.88	J.Triquet	St. Gemmes-Le-Robert, France	10. 9.01A
G-BORW	Cessna 172P Skyhawk II	17274301	N51357	23. 8.88	Briter Aviation Ltd	Coventry	26. 7.04T
G-BORY	Cessna 150L	15072292	N6792G	27. 5.88	D.G.Bell & S.J.Green	Egginton, Derby	28. 6.05T
G-BOSB	Thunder Ax7-77 HAB	1199		7. 6.88	M.Gallagher	Consett	17. 9.99A
	(Regd as c/n 581 but built as above)						
G-BOSD	Piper PA-34-200T Seneca II	34-7570085	N33086	7. 6.88	Barnes Olson Aeroleasing Ltd	Bristol	11. 8.04T
					(Op Bristol Flying Centre)		
G-BOSE	Piper PA-28-181 Archer II	28-8590007	N143AV	17. 5.88	M.P.Barker & R.Wolf tr G-BOSE Group White Waltham)		23. 5.03T
G-BOSF*	Colt 69A HAB	1271		23. 6.88	Virgin Airship & Balloon Co Ltd	Telford	28. 1.93A
					"Lloyds Bank" (Cancelled 8.11.01 as WFU) (Stored)		
G-BOSG*	Colt 17A Cloudhopper HAB	1272		23. 6.88	Virgin Airship & Balloon Co Ltd	Telford	22. 5.89A
					"Lloyds Bank Cloudhopper" (Cancelled 8.11.01 as WFU) (Stored)		
G-BOSJ	Nord 3400	124	N9048P	26. 5.88	A.I.Milne	Etthornes Farm, Swaffham	1.11.94P
			ALAT "MOO"		*(As "124" in Fr.AF c/s) (Damaged Fenland 12.6.94: stored 9.02)*		
G-BOSM	CEA Jodel DR.253B Regent	168	F-BSBH	24. 5.88	S.H.Gibson	High Cross, Ware	11.12.04
					tr Sierra Mike (Ware) Group		
G-BOSN	Aérospatiale AS355F1 Twin Squirrel	5266	N2109L	22. 8.88	L.Smith	Booker	20. 2.03T
			5N-AYL/G-BOSN/5N-AYL		t/a Helicopter Services		
G-BOSO	Cessna A152 Aerobat	A1520975	N761PD	25. 5.88	J.S.Develin & Z.Islam	Blackbushe	20. 8.04T
G-BOSR	Piper PA-28-140 Cherokee	28-22092	N7464R	26. 5.88	C R.Guggenheim tr Sierra-Romeo Group	Bournemouth	27. 6.03T
G-BOSU	Piper PA-28-140 Cherokee Cruiser	28-7325449	N55635	19. 7.88	R.A.Sands	Oxford	8. 6.04
G-BOSV*	Cameron V-77 HAB	1320		17. 6.88	K.H.Greenaway *"Joyride II"*	Market Harborough	7. 6.97A
					(Cancelled 7.11.01 as WFU & stored)		
G-BOTD	Cameron O-105 HAB	1611		6. 6.88	P.J.Beglan	Belves, France	8. 8.02A
G-BOTF	Piper PA-28-151 Cherokee Warrior	28-7515436	C-GGIF	8. 6.88	D.S.Woolf	Southend	4.10.03T
					tr G-BOTF Group *(Op Southend Flying Club)*		
G-BOTG	Cessna 152 II	15283035	N46343	9. 6.88	Donington Aviation Ltd	East Midlands	27. 9.03T
G-BOTH	Cessna 182Q Skylane II	18267558	N202PS	9. 6.88	A.C.Hinton-Lever tr G-BOTH Group	Barton	28. 3.04
			N114SP/N5172N				
G-BOTI	Piper PA-28-151 Cherokee Warrior	28-7515251	C-GNFF	9. 6.88	A.J.Bamrah t/a Falcon Flying Services	(Biggin Hill)	29. 8.03T
	(Converted to 28--161 model)						
G-BOTK	Cameron O-105 HAB	1765		9. 6.88	F.R. & V.L.Higgins	Leigh Upon Mendip	12. 7.96T
					"Champagne Rides"		
G-BOTM	Bell 206B-3 JetRanger III	3881	N31940	9. 6.88	David McLean Homes Ltd	Cambridge	8. 8.03
G-BOTN	Piper PA-28-161 Warrior II	28-7916261	N2173N	9. 6.88	Apollo Aviation Advisory Ltd	Shoreham	25. 1.04T
G-BOTO	Bellanca 7ECA Citabria	939-73	N57398	9. 6.88	A.K.Hulme tr G-BOTO Group	Rayne Hall Farm, Rayne	7. 1.04
G-BOTP	Cessna 150J	15070736	N61017	2. 8.88	R.F.Finnis & C.P.Williams	Thruxton	20. 5.04
G-BOTU	Piper J-3C-65 Cub	19045	N98803	8. 7.88	T.L.Giles	Hitcham, Wattisham	23. 7.03P
	(Continental A75)		NC98803				
G-BOTV	Piper PA-32RT-300 Lance II	32R-7885153	N36039	7. 6.88	Robin Lance Aviation Associates Ltd	Rochester	7. 7.02
G-BOTW	Cameron V-77 HAB	1761		14. 6.88	M.R.Jeynes	(Worcester)	17. 6.03A
G-BOUD	Piper PA-38-112 Tomahawk II	38-82A0017	N91365	26. 7.88	A.J.Wiggins	(Longhope, Glos)	11. 7.05T
G-BOUE	Cessna 172N Skyhawk II	17273235	N6535F	8. 8.88	Castleridge Ltd	(Harrogate)	22. 2.04T
G-BOUF	Cessna 172N Skyhawk II	17271900	N5605E	24. 6.88	M.I. & B.P.Sneap	Ripley, Derby	5. 7.04T
					t/a Amber Valley Aviation		
G-BOUJ	Cessna 150M Commuter	15076373	N3058V	25. 8.88	R.D.Billins	Cranfield	11. 1.03T
G-BOUK	Piper PA-34-200T Seneca II	34-7570124	N33476	31. 8.88	C.J. & R.J.Barnes	East Midlands	10.10.05T
G-BOUL	Piper PA-34-200T Seneca II	34-7670157	N8936C	28. 6.88	Oxford Aviation Services Ltd	Oxford	5. 4.04T
G-BOUM	Piper PA-34-200T Seneca II	34-7670136	N8401C	3. 8.88	Oxford Aviation Services Ltd	Oxford	19. 8.04T
G-BOUP	Piper PA-28-161 Warrior II	2816059	N9139X	12. 7.88	Oxford Aviation Services Ltd	Oxford	2. 03T
G-BOUR	Piper PA-28-161 Warrior II	2816060	N9139Z	12. 7.88	Oxford Aviation Services Ltd	Oxford	14.10.03T
G-BOUT	Zenair Colomban MC-12 Cri-Cri	12-0135	N120JN	14. 6.88	C.K.Farley *(Current status unknown)*	Southampton	
G-BOUV	Montgomerie-Bensen B.8MR	PFA G/01-1092		23. 6.88	G.C.Kerr	(Great Orton)	13. 6.03P
	(Rotax 532)						
G-BOUZ	Cessna 150G	15065606	N2606J	15. 6.88	Atlantic Bridge Aviation Ltd	Lydd	16. 3.04T
G-BOVB	Piper PA-15 Vagabond	15-180	N4396H	23. 6.88	P.Laycock & J R Pike	Twineham	16. 5.03P
	(Lycoming O-145)		NC4396H		tr Oscar Flying Group		
G-BOVG*	Cessna F172H	F172-0627	OO-ANN	2. 8.88	No.1476 Squadron, ATC	Rayleigh, Essex	14. 9.91
	(Built Reims Aviation SA)		D-ELTR		*(Damaged Southend 1991: cancelled 26.9.95 as WFU) (Instructional airframe 2.03)*		
G-BOVK	Piper PA-28-161 Warrior II	28-8516061	N69168	7. 9.88	Auto Corporation Ltd	Hawarden	14. 5.04T

G-BOVR	Robinson R22HP	0176	N9069D	28. 6.88	J.O'Brien	(Gorey, Co.Wexford)	19. 8.00T
G-BOVS	Cessna 150M Commuter	15078663	N704KC	21. 7.88	Blue Skies Aviation Ltd	Exeter	21.12.03T
G-BOVT	Cessna 150M Commuter	15078032	N8962U	1.12.88	C.J.Hopewell	(Fenland)	15. 4.04T
G-BOVU	Stoddard-Hamilton Glasair III	3090		16. 9.88	B.R.Chaplin	Deenethorpe	4. 3.03P
	(Lycoming IO-540)						
G-BOVV	Cameron V-77 HAB	1724		26. 9.88	P.Glydon	Birmingham	12.10.02A
G-BOVW	Colt 69A HAB	1286		13. 7.88	V.Hyland *"Enderby-Hyland Painting"*	Nottingham	6. 4.94A
G-BOVX	Hughes 269C	38-0673	N58170	12. 7.88	P.E.Tornberg	Sywell	25. 9.04T
G-BOWB	Cameron V-77 HAB	1767		13. 7.88	R.C.Stone *"Richard's Rainbow"*	Reading	14. 5.03A
G-BOWD	Reims/Cessna F337G Skymaster	F33700084	N337BC	8. 7.88	Badgehurst Ltd	Biggin Hill	4. 4.01T
	(Wichita c/n 33701791)		G-BLSB/EI-BET/D-INAI/(N53697)				
G-BOWE	Piper PA-34-200T Seneca II	34-7870405	N39668	14. 7.88	Oxford Aviation Services Ltd	Oxford	1. 7.04T
G-BOWL	Cameron V-77 HAB	1780		26. 7.88	P.G. & G.R.Hall *"Matrix"*	Chard	12. 5.00A
G-BOWM	Cameron V-56 HAB	1781		26. 7.88	C.G.Caldecott & G.Pitt Newcastle-under-Lyme, Staffs		30. 7.00A
G-BOWN*	Piper PA-12 Super Cruiser	12-1912	N3661N	26. 7.88	R.W.Bucknell	Andrewsfield	26. 2.00T
	(Lycoming O-235)		NC3661N	*(Damaged in 10.01 gales: cancelled 11.10.02 by CAA) (Noted at rear of hangar 8.02)*			
G-BOWO	Cessna R182 Skylane RG II	R18200146	(G-BOTR)	20. 7.88	J.J.Feeney	Elstree	12.11.04
			N2301C				
G-BOWP	Jodel Wassmer D.120A Paris-Nice	319	F-BNZM	26. 7.88	N.Crisp & R.Morris	Old Sarum	18. 4.03P
	(Continental O-200-A)						
G-BOWU	Cameron O-84 HAB	1779		1. 8.88	C.F.Pooley & D.C.Ball	Gloucester	7. 8.01A
					tr St.Elmos Fire Syndicate *"Elmo"*		
G-BOWV	Cameron V-65 HAB	1800		24. 8.88	R.A.Harris *"Sigmund"*	Axminster	14. 5.02A
G-BOWY	Piper PA-28RT-201T Turbo Arrow IV	28R-8131114	N404EL	8. 8.88	J.S.Develin & Z.Islam	Redhill	17. 8.03T
			N83648				
G-BOWZ	Bensen B.80V	PFA G/01-1060		27. 7.88	M D Cole	Carlisle	27. 2.03P
	(Rotax 532)			*(Noted 1.02)*			
G-BOXA	Piper PA-28-161 Warrior II	2816075	N9149Q	1.11.88	Channel Islands Aero Services Ltd	Jersey	8. 1.04T
					t/a Jersey Aero Club		
G-BOXB	Piper PA-28-161 Warrior II	2816064	N9142H	12. 8.88	First Class Ltd	Jersey	6. 2.03T
G-BOXC	Piper PA-28-161 Warrior II	2816063	N9142D	12. 8.88	Channel Islands Aero Services Ltd	Jersey	15. 5.03T
					t/a Jersey Aero Club		
G-BOXG	Cameron O-77 HAB	1792		26. 8.88	R.A.Wicks	Norwich	16. 8.03A
G-BOXH	Pitts S-1S Special	MP4	N8LA	29. 7.88	Pittsco Ltd	Full Sutton	7. 8.03P
	(Lycoming O-360)						
G-BOXJ	Piper J-3C-65 Cub (L-4H-PI)	12193	OO-ADJ	1. 8.88	J.D.Tseliki	(Shoreham)	20. 3.91P
	(Continental C90) *(Frame No.12021)*		44-79897	*(Current status unknown)*			
G-BOXR	Grumman American GA-7 Cougar	GA7-0059	N772GA	19.10.88	Plane Talking Ltd	Biggin Hill	11. 9.03T
	(C/n plate shows manufacturer as Gulfstream American)						
G-BOXT	Hughes 269C	104-0367	SE-HMR	1. 8.88	Jetscape Leisure Ltd	Gloucestershire	15. 6.03T
			PH-JOH/D-HBOL				
G-BOXU	Grumman-American AA-5B Tiger	AA5B-0026	N1526R	28. 7.88	G.C.Baker tr Marcher Aviation Group	Welshpool	15. 5.04
G-BOXV	Pitts S-1S Special	7-0433	N27822	8. 8.88	G.R.Clark Yeatsall Farm, Abbots Bromley		12. 6.02P
	(Lycoming O-360)						
G-BOXW	Cassutt Racer IIIM	PFA 34-11317		11. 8.88	D.I.Johnson	(Leigh-on-Sea)	
G-BOYB	Cessna A152 Aerobat	A1520928	N761AW	29. 7.88	Northamptonshire School of Flying Ltd	Sywell	14.12.03T
G-BOYC	Robinson R22 Beta	0837		22. 8.88	M.D.Thorpe t/a Yorkshire Helicopters Coney Park, Leeds		9. 8.04T
G-BOYF	Sikorsky S-76B	760343		15. 9.88	Darley Stud Management Co Ltd	Cambridge	24.11.03T
					(Op Air Hanson)		
G-BOYH	Piper PA-28-151 Cherokee Warrior	28-7715290	N8795F	8. 8.88	Superpause Ltd	White Waltham	26. 4.04T
	(Converted to 28-161 model)				*(Op West London Aero Club)*		
	(Engine stalled and caught fire landing Thruxton 17.4.02: damage to engine & cowling)						
G-BOYI	Piper PA-28-161 Warrior II	28-7816183	N9032K	8. 8.88	S.J.Harris & A.Ware tr G-BOYI Group	Welshpool	3. 4.04
G-BOYL	Cessna 152 II	15284379	N6232L	11. 8.88	Aerohire Ltd	Wolvehampton	26. 2.01T
G-BOYM	Cameron O-84 HAB	1796		25. 8.88	M.P.Ryan *"Frontline"*	Newbury	
G-BOYO	Cameron V-20 HAB	1843		27. 9.88	J.M.Willard	Burgess Hill	
G-BOYP	Cessna 172N Skyhawk II	17270349	N738YU	22. 8.88	Guildtons Ltd	North Weald	3. 5.04
G-BOYR	Reims/Cessna FA.337G Super Skymaster	RA04147	9. 9.88	Tri-Star Farms Ltd	Newtownards		
	(Wichita c/n 33701589)	F33700070	G-BOYR/PH-RPE				
G-BOYS	Cameron N-77 HAB	1759		16. 6.88	J King	Bristol	15.11.02T
G-BOYU	Cessna A150L Aerobat	A1500497	N8121L	31. 8.88	Upperstack Ltd	Barton	1.10.03T
G-BOYV	Piper PA-28R-201T Turbo Cherokee Arrow III	N1143H	1. 9.88	Arrow Air Ltd	Wellesbourne Mountford		21. 3.04T
		28R-7703014					
G-BOYX	Robinson R22 Beta	0862	N90813	25. 8.88	R.Towle	Hexham	28. 9.91T
				(Damaged Teesside 18.7.90: current status unknown)			
G-BOZI	Piper PA-28-161 Warrior II	28-8116120	(G-BOSZ)	14. 7.88	Aerolease Ltd	Conington	25.11.03T
			N8318A				
	(Made heavy landing Conington 30.6.02: left main & nose u/c collapsed with damage to left wing, fuselage underside, engine and propeller)						
G-BOZN	Cameron N-77 HAB	1807		1. 9.88	Calarel Developments Ltd	Chipping Campden	17. 9.02A
					"Calarel Developments"		
G-BOZO	Gulfstream AA-5B Tiger	AA5B-1282	N4536Q	12. 8.88	Caslon Ltd	Elstree	14.12.03T
G-BOZR	Cessna 152 II	15284614	N6083M	7. 9.88	Gem Rewinds Ltd	Coventry	7. 1.04T
G-BOZS	Pitts S-1C Special	221-H	N10EZ	31. 8.88	T.A.S.Rayner	Perth	1. 8.03P
	(Lycoming O-320-A2B)						
G-BOZU	Aero Dynamics Sparrow Hawk MkII		12.12.88	R.V.Phillimore	(Bexhill-on-Sea)		
		PFA 184-11371					
G-BOZV	Robin DR340 Major	416	F-BRTS	9. 8.88	C.J.Turner & S.D.Kent	(Bristol)	21.12.03
G-BOZW	Bensen B.8MR	PFA G/01-1096		1. 9.88	M.E.Wills	Lytchett Matravers	7. 8.03P
	(Rotax 532)						
G-BOZY	Cameron RTW-120 HAB	1770		1. 9.88	Magical Adventures Ltd	West Bloomfield, Mi., USA	21. 4.97A
G-BOZZ	Gulfstream AA-5B Tiger	AA5B-1155	N4530N	22. 8.88	A.W.Matthews tr Solent Tiger Group	Southampton	1.11.03

G-BPAA - G-BPZZ

Reg	Type	C/N	Prev ID	Date	Owner/Operator	Location	Status
G-BPAA	Akro Advanced AA-001 & PFA 200-11528			26. 8.88	Acro Engines & Airframes Ltd	Yearby	27 6.03P
	(Volkswagen Acro 2100)						
G-BPAB	Cessna 150M Commuter	15077244	N63335	21. 9.88	M.J.Diggins	Rayne Hall Farm, Rayne	7. 8.04
G-BPAC	Piper PA-28-161 Cherokee Warrior II	28-7716112	N2567Q	21. 9.88	G.G.Pratt	High Cross	11. 4.04
G-BPAF	Piper PA-28-161 Cherokee Warrior II	28-7716142	N3199Q	6. 9.88	RAF Brize Norton Flying Club Ltd	RAF Brize Norton	30. 5.03T
G-BPAI	Bell 47G-3B-1	6528	N8588F	9. 9.88	LRC Leisure Ltd	Barton	29. 3.01
					(Op Manchester Helicopter Centre)		
G-BPAJ	de Havilland DH.82A Tiger Moth	83472	G-AOIX	5.11.80	P.A.Jackson	Raby's Farm, Great Stukeley	15. 6.03
	(Composite with "real" G-AMNN ? qv)		T7087				
G-BPAL	de Havilland DHC-1 Chipmunk 22	C1/0437	G-BCYE	29.10.86	K.F. & P.Tomsett	Popham	3. 8.03
			WG350		(As "WG350")		
G-BPAO*	Air Command 503 Commander 0424 & G 04-1097			8. 9.88	Not known	Croft Farm, Defford	8. 8.91P
	(Cancelled 23.2.99 as PWFU) (Noted 1.02)						
G-BPAS	SOCATA TB-20 Trinidad	283	A2-ADR	9.11.88	Syndicate Clerical Services Ltd	Exeter	1. 3.04T
			F-GDBO				
G-BPAV	Clutton FRED Srs.II PFA 29-10274			21.11.78	P.A.Valentine	(Uxbridge)	
	(Volkswagen 1600)				(Under construction 1990: current status unknown)		
G-BPAW	Cessna 150M Commuter	15077923	N8348U	5. 9.88	P.D.Sims	Popham	18.10.04
G-BPAX	Cessna 150M Commuter	15077401	N63571	5. 9.88	W.E.Rodwell & N.J.Smith	Shoreham	22. 5.04
					tr The Dirty Dozen		
G-BPAY	Piper PA-28-181 Archer II	28-8090191	N3568X	12. 9.88	Leicestershire Aero Club Ltd	Leicester	10. 4.04T
G-BPBG	Cessna 152 II	15284941	N5418P	16. 9.88	Tatenhill Aviation Ltd	Tatenhill	18. 7.04T
G-BPBJ	Cessna 152 II	15283639	N4793B	9. 9.88	W.Shaw & P.G.Haines Whaley Farm, New York, Lincs		28. 1.04
G-BPBK	Cessna 152 II	15283417	N49095	9. 9.88	N.D.Wyndom	Coventry	23. 1.04T
					tr Sir W.G.Armstrong-Whitworth Flying Group		
G-BPBM	Piper PA-28-161 Warrior II	28-7916272	N3050N	12. 9.88	Halfpenny Green Flight Centre Ltd	Wolverhampton	18. 1.04T
G-BPBO	Piper PA-28RT-201T Turbo Arrow IV	28R-8131195	N8431H	28. 9.88	Tile Holdings Ltd	Sandtoft	6. 6.04
G-BPBP	Brugger MB.2 Colibri Mk.II PFA 43-10246			6. 2.78	D.A.Preston	(Ulverston)	16. 5.03P
	(Volkswagen 1600)						
G-BPBU	Cameron V-77 HAB	1844		23. 9.88	M.C.Gibbons & J.E.Kite "Sky Maid"	Bristol	16. 6.02A
G-BPBV	Cameron V-77 HAB	1821		21. 9.88	S.J.Farrant "Sugar Plumb"	(Godalmimg)	
G-BPBW	Cameron O-105 HAB	1841		14.10.88	R.J.Mansfield "October Gold" Bowness-on-Windermere		15. 9.96A
					(Amended CofR 8.02)		
G-BPBY	Cameron V-77 HAB	1818	(G-BPCS)	9.12.88	Louise Hutley "Brewster's Toy"	Guildford	15. 8.97A
G-BPBZ	Thunder Ax7-77 HAB	1258		10.10.88	A.W.J.Weston	Ross-on-Wye	
G-BPCA	Pilatus Britten-Norman BN-2B-26 Islander	2198	G-BLNX	28. 1.88	Loganair Ltd "Chatham Historic Dockyard"	Kirkwall	16. 2.03T
G-BPCF	Piper J-3C-65 Cub	4532	N140DC	12. 5.89	T.I.Williams	Shoreham	10. 7.03P
	(Continental O-200-A)		N28033/NC28033		(Lippert Reed clipped-wing conversion - s/no.SA811SW)		
G-BPCG	Colt AS-80 Mk.II Hot-Air Airship	1300		14.10.88	N.Charbonnier "Greensport/Napapijri"	Aosta, Italy	10.10.96A
G-BPCI	Cessna R172K Hawk XP II	R1722360	N9976V	3. 1.89	P.A.Warner & E.S.Scotchbrook		
						Lower Wasing Farm, Brimpton	24. 5.05
G-BPCJ*	Cessna 150J	15070797	N61096	26. 9.88	Not known Amen Corner, Binfield, Bracknell		
	(Badly damaged in gales Compton Abbas 25.1.90: cancelled 4.7.90 by CAA) (Fuselage noted 10.02)						
G-BPCK	Piper PA-28-161 Warrior II	28-8016279	N8529N	26. 9.88	W.G.Booth	Compton Abbas	20. 8.04T
			C-GMEI/N9519N				
G-BPCL	Scottish Aviation Bulldog Srs.120/128	BH120/393	HKG-6	20. 9.88	Isohigh Ltd tr 121 Group	North Weald	12. 7.04T
			G-31-19		(As "HKG-6" in Hong Kong DF c/s)		
G-BPCM	Rotorway Executive	E.3293	N979WP	21. 9.88	R.J.Turner tr Aircare Group	Weavers Loft, Wem	25.11.91P
	(Rotorway RW152)				(Stored 7.96: current status unknown)		
G-BPCR	Mooney M.20K (231)	25-0532	N98433	23. 9.88	T. & R.Harris "Over The Moony"	Biggin Hill	15.11.04
G-BPCV	Montgomerie-Bensen B.8MR PFA G/01-1088			11.10.88	M.A.Hayward (New owner 2.03)	(Liskeard)	25. 7.91P
G-BPCX	Piper PA-28-236 Dakota	28-8211004	N8441S	25.10.88	G.E.J.Spooner	Andrewsfield	27. 6.04T
G-BPDF	Cameron V-77 HAB	1806		6.10.88	The Ballooning Business Ltd	Northampton	31. 7.00T
					"Burning Ambition"		
G-BPDG	Cameron V-77 HAB	1839		21.10.88	D.F.H.Smith "Pretty Damn Good"	Burnley	4. 9.00A
G-BPDJ	Chris Tena Mini Coupe	275	N13877	4.10.88	J.J.Morrissey	(Teddington)	
	(Volkswagen 1835)				(To owner's home mid 2002)		
G-BPDM	CASA I-131E Jungmann	2058	E3B-369	24.10.88	J.D.Haslam	(Northallerton)	22. 6.96P
					(As "E3B-369/781-32" in Spanish AF c/s)		
G-BPDT	Piper PA-28-161 Warrior II	28-8416004	N4317Z	22.12.88	Channel Islands Aero Services Ltd	Jersey	18.12.04T
					t/a Jersey Aero Club		
G-BPDU	Piper PA-28-161 Cherokee Warrior II	28-7716195	N5672V	30. 9.88	Shoreham Flight Centre Ltd	Shoreham	1. 8.05T
G-BPDV	Pitts S-1S Special	27P	N330VE	15. 9.88	J.Vize	Sywell	17. 6.03P
	(Lycoming O-360)						
G-BPEC	Boeing 757-236ER	24882		6.11.90	British Airways plc (Waves & Cranes t/s)	Gatwick	12.11.03T
G-BPED	Boeing 757-236	25059		30. 4.91	British Airways plc (Koguty Lowickie t/s)	Heathrow	29. 4.04T
G-BPEE	Boeing 757-236ER	25060		3. 5.91	British Airways plc	Gatwick	2. 5.04T
G-BPEF	Boeing 757-236ER	24120	G-BOHC	18. 5.92	British Airways plc	Gatwick	17. 5.05T
			EC-ELA/EC-516/G-BOHC/EC-ELA/EC-202/G-BOHC				
G-BPEI	Boeing 757-236	25806	(G-BMRK)	9. 3.94	British Airways plc	Heathrow	8.12.05T
					"Chatham Historic Dockyard"		
G-BPEJ	Boeing 757-236	25807	(G-BMRL)	22. 4.94	British Airways plc	Heathrow	24. 4.03T
G-BPEK	Boeing 757-236	25808	(G-BMRM)	17. 3.95	British Airways plc	Heathrow	16. 3.04T
G-BPEL*	Piper PA 28-151 Cherokee Warrior	28-7415172	C-FEYM	10.10.88	R.W.Harris & A.Jahanfar	Southend	8. 2.92T
	(Cancelled 28.2.02 as WFU) (Dismantled wreck stored 03)						
G-BPEM	Cessna 150K	15071707	N6207G	24.10.88	R.Strong & R.G.Lindsey	Netherthorpe	17. 6.04
G-BPEO	Cessna 152 II	15283775	C-GQVO	10.10.88	Hecray Co Ltd	Southend	30. 7.05T
			(N5147B)		t/a Direct Helicopters (Op Southend School of Flying)		
G-BPES	Piper PA 38-112 Tomahawk II	38-81A0064	N25728	2.11.88	Sherwood Flying Club Ltd	Nottingham	5. 1.04T
G-BPEZ	Colt 77A HAB	1324		14.10.88	J.E.F.Kettley & W.J.Honey	Chippenham	6. 6.01A

Reg	Type	C/n	Prev id	Date	Owner	Location	Expiry
G-BPFB	Colt 77A HAB	1334		26.10.88	S.Ingram	Oldham	1. 6.03A
G-BPFC	Mooney M.20C Ranger	20-1243	N3606H	21.10.88	D.P.Wring	Dunkeswell	20. 5.05
G-BPFD	Jodel D.112	312	F-PHJT	3.11.88	K.Manley	Swanborough Farm, Lewes	22. 5.03P
G-BPFF	Cameron DP-70 Hot-Air Airship	1831		24.10.88	John Aimo Balloons SAS	Mondovi, Italy	13. 7.03A
G-BPFH	Piper PA-28-161 Warrior II	28-8116201	N83723	3.11.88	Muriel H.Kleiser *(Op Edinburgh Flying Club)*	Edinburgh	4.12.03T
G-BPFI	Piper PA 28-181 Archer II	28-8090113	N8103G	5. 1.89	F.Teagle	Truro	12. 7.04
G-BPFL	Davis DA-2A (Continental O-200-A)	051	N72RJ	27.10.88	B.W.Griffiths	Coventry	18. 1.03P
G-BPFM	Aeronca 7AC Champion	7AC-4751	N1193E NC1193E	13.10.88	T.J.Roberts	Rochester	13. 6.03P
G-BPFN	Short SD.3-60 Var.100	SH.3747	N747HH N747SA/G-BPFN/G-14-3747	2.11.88	Loganair Ltd *(Benyhone Tartan t/s)*	Glasgow	8. 9.03T
G-BPFZ	Cessna 152 II	15285741	N94594	27.10.88	Devon School of Flying Ltd	Dunkeswell	24. 1.05T
G-BPGC	Air Command 532 Elite (Rotax 532)	0440 & PFA G/04-1108		11.10.88	G.A.Speich *(Active 9.02)*	Beausdale, Kenilworth	1. 8.91P
G-BPGD	Cameron V-65 HAB *(New envelope c 8.01 c/n 4969)*	2000		9. 9.88	Gone With The Wind Ltd *"Silver Lining"*	Bristol	4.12.99A
G-BPGE	Cessna U206C Super Skywagon	U2061013	N29017	7.11.88	K.Brady tr The Scottish Parachute Club	Strathallan	14. 5.04
G-BPGF	Thunder Ax7-77 HAB	1355		22.11.88	M.Schiavo *"Dovetail"*	Manchester	25. 8.95A
G-BPGH	EAA Acrosport II (Continental IO-346)	422	N12JE	14.11.88	G.M.Bradley	Crowfield	16. 9.03P
G-BPGK	Aeronca 7AC Champion (Continental A65)	7AC-7187	N4409E	7. 2.89	D.A.Crompton	Yeatsall Farm, Abbots Bromley	21. 3.03P
G-BPGM	Cessna 152 II	15284932	N5380P	14.11.88	James D.Peace & Co *(Op Edinburgh Air Centre)*	Edinburgh	14. 4.05T
G-BPGT	Colt AS-80 Mk.II HA Airship	1248	(I-) G-BPGT	14.11.88	P.Porati	Milan, Italy	20. 7.00A
G-BPGU	Piper PA-28-181 Archer II	28-8490025	N4330B	26.10.88	G.Underwood	Nottingham	30. 1.04
G-BPGV	Robinson R22 Beta	0887		3.11.88	R.J.Everett	Sproughton	21.11.03T
G-BPGX	SOCATA TB-9 Tampico Club	884		4.11.88	D.A.Lee	Denham	13. 2.03T
G-BPGY	Cessna 150H	15067325	N6525S	24. 1.89	Premiair Engineering Ltd	Shoreham	2.12.02T
G-BPGZ	Cessna 150G	15064912	N3612J	14.11.88	J.B.Scott	Blackpool	17. 5.04
G-BPHB	Piper PA-28-161 Warrior II	2816069	N9148G	14.11.88	M.J.Wade	Turweston	22. 2.04T
G-BPHD	Cameron N-42 HAB	1863		21. 2.89	P.J.Marshall & M.A.Clarke *"Ellen Gee II"*	Ruislip	9. 6.02A
G-BPHG	Robin DR400/180 Regent	1887		29.11.88	K.J. & M.B.White Homefield Farm, Crowhurst, Lingfield		6. 6.04
G-BPHH	Cameron V-77 HAB	1840		2.12.88	C.D.Aindow *"Office Angels"*	Tonbridge	27. 3.03A
G-BPHI	Piper PA-38-112 Tomahawk	38-79A0002	N2535T	22.11.88	J.S.Develin & Z.Islam	Blackbushe	12. 7.04T
G-BPHJ	Cameron V-77 HAB	1881		23.11.88	C.W.Brown *"Twiggy"*	Nottingham	11. 5.02A
G-BPHK	Whittaker MW7	PFA 171-11389		24.11.88	P.J.D.Kerr	(Bridgwater)	25.10.02P
G-BPHL	Piper PA-28-161 Warrior II	28-7916315	N555PY N2247U	2.12.88	Teesside Flight Centre Ltd	Teesside	19. 7.04T
G-BPHO	Taylorcraft BC-12D	8497	N96197 NC96197	10. 1.89	A.A.Alderdice Woodview, Armagh, Co.Armagh *"Spirit of Missouri"*		16. 4.03P
G-BPHP	Taylorcraft BC-12-65 (Continental A65)	2799	N33948 NC33948	12.12.88	P.Duffield *"Spirit of Mississippi"* *(Crash landed Wellesbourne Mountford 11.4.99) (New owner 4.02)*	(Mickleover)	2.11.99P
G-BPHR	DH 82A Tiger Moth *(Built de Havilland Aircraft Pty Ltd, Australia)*	45	N48DH VH-BLX/A17-48	3. 1.89	N.Parry Lotmead Farm, Wanborough, Swindon tr A17-48 Group *(As "A17-48" in RAAF c/s)*		11.10.01
G-BPHT	Cessna 152 II	15282401	N961LP	5.12.88	Evensport Ltd	(Rayleigh)	16. 8.01T
G-BPHU	Thunder Ax7-77 HAB	1365		19.12.88	R.P.Waite	St.Helens	28. 5.03A
G-BPHW	Cessna 140 (Continental C85)	11035	N76595 NC76595	13. 1.89	M.Day	White Waltham	18. 5.05
G-BPHX	Cessna 140 (Continental C85)	12488	N2252N NC2252N	2.12.88	M.McChesney *(Stored 2.93: re-regd to same owner 10.00)*	Enniskillen, Co.Fermanagh	23. 5.93
G-BPHZ	Morane-Saulnier MS.505 Criquet	53/7	F-BJQC Fr Mil	17. 4.89	G.A.Warner t/a The Aircraft Restoration Co *(As "TA+RC" in I/JG54 Luftwaffe c/s)*	Duxford	26. 4.99P
G-BPID	Piper PA-28-161 Warrior II	28-7916325	N2137V	16. 3.89	J.T.Nuttall	Liverpool	24. 5.04T
G-BPIF	Bensen-Parsons Two Place (Rotax 532)	UK-01		19.12.88	B.J.L.P.de Saar	Shipdham	28. 3.96P
G-BPII	Denney Kitfox Model 1 (IAME KFM 112)	213 & PFA 172-11496		15.12.88	P.Etherington tr G-BPII Group	Sturgate	19. 2.03P
G-BPIJ	Brantly B.2B	465	N2293U	23. 3.89	A.D.Whitehouse	(Crewkerne)	13. 7.98
G-BPIK	Piper PA-38-112 Tomahawk II	38-82A0028	N3947M ZP-EAP/N91423	2.12.88	Metropolitan Services Ltd	Hawarden	12. 7.03T
G-BPIL	Cessna 310B	35620	N620GS OO-SEF/N5420A	16.11.89	A.L.Brown *"Fast Lady"* *(New owner 6.02)*	Bourn	28. 4.00T
G-BPIN	Glaser-Dirks DG-400	4-242		14.12.88	J.N.Stevenson	Lasham	11. 4.04
G-BPIO	Reims/Cessna F.152 II	F15201556	PH-VSO PH-AXS	23. 1.89	I.D.McClelland	Biggin Hill	12. 9.04T
G-BPIP	Slingsby T.31 Cadet III (Volkswagen 1600)	PFA 42-10771		14.11.88	J.H.Beard	Bodmin	27. 9.96P
G-BPIR	Scheibe SF-25E Super Falke	4332	N25SF (D-KDFX)	15.12.88	K.E.Ballington	Yeatsall Farm, Abbots Bromley	5. 4.04
G-BPIT	Robinson R22 Beta	0907	N80011	22.12.88	NA Air Ltd	Hawarden	18. 7.05T
G-BPIU	Piper PA-28-161 Warrior II	28-7916303	N3028T	28.12.88	P.G.Doble & P.G.Stewart	Fairoaks	28. 3.04
G-BPIV	Bristol 149 Blenheim IV *(Built Fairchild Aircraft Ltd as Bollingbroke IVT)*	-	"Z5722" RCAF 10201	15. 2.89	G.A.Warner *"Spirit of Britain First"* t/a The Aircraft Restoration Co *(As "R3281/UX-N")*	Duxford	19. 6.03P
G-BPIZ	Gulfstream AA-5B Tiger	AA5B-1154	N4530L	14. 2.89	N.R.F.McNally	Shoreham	21. 8.04
G-BPJB	Schweizer Hughes 269C	S.1331	N75065	7.11.88	Elborne Holdings Ltd	Cascais, Portugal	5.11.05
G-BPJD	SOCATA Rallye 110ST	3253	OY-CAV	22.12.88	J.G.Murphy tr G-BPJD Rallye Group	Morgansfield, Fishburn	21. 6.04
G-BPJE	Cameron A-105 HAB	1864		8.11.88	J.S.Eckersley *"Burley Stables"*	Henley-on-Thames	6. 5.03A
G-BPJF*	Piper PA-38-112 Tomahawk	38-78A0021	N9312T	5. 4.89	S McNulty *(Crashed on take-off at Egginton, Derby 20.6.98: cancelled 2.10.98 by CAA) (For rescue training 5.00)*	Coventry	4.10.98
G-BPJG	Piper PA-18-150 Super Cub	18-8350	SE-EZG N4172Z	4. 1.89	M.W.Stein	Oaksey Park	8. 8.04

G-BPJH	Piper PA-18 Super Cub 95 (L-18C-PI)	18-1980	EI-59 I-EICA/MM522380/52-2380	24. 5.83	P.J.Heron	City of Derry	31. 1.02P
G-BPJK	Colt 77A HAB	1362		22.12.88	Saran UK Ltd	Cheltenham	7. 9.03A
G-BPJL	Cessna 152 II	15281296	N49473	28.12.88	Willowair Flying Club (1996) Ltd	Southend	10. 7.04T
G-BPJO	Piper PA-28-161 Cadet	2841014	N9153Z	15.12.88	Plane Talking Ltd *(Op Denham School of Flying)*	Denham	20.12.04T
G-BPJP	Piper PA-28-161 Cadet	2841015	N9154K	22.12.88	S.J.Skilton t/a Aviation Rentals	Bournemouth	27. 6.04T
G-BPJR	Piper PA-28-161 Cadet	2841024	N9154X	17. 1.89	J.P.E.Walsh t/a Walsh Aviation	Denham	21.12.04T
G-BPJU	Piper PA-28-161 Cadet	2841032	N9156Z	11. 1.89	S.J.Skilton t/a Aviation Rentals	Bournemouth	1. 4.04T
G-BPJV	Taylorcraft F-21	F-1005	N2004L	12. 1.89	P.Glennon tr TC Flying Group	Booker	17. 6.03P
G-BPJW	Cessna A150K Aerobat	A1500127	C-FAJX CF-AJX/N8427M	4. 1.89	G & S.A.Jones	Linley Hill, Leven	4. 6.03T
G-BPKF	Grob G-115	8075		3. 1.89	R.V.Morgan & J.F.W.Steventon t/a Steventon Morgan Aviation	Compton Abbas	14. 1.04
G-BPKK	Denney Kitfox Model 1 (Rotax 532) *(Laid down as a Model 2)*	264 & PFA 172-11411		19.12.88	D.Moffat	Lochview House, Limerigg	11.10.02P
G-BPKM	Piper PA-28-161 Warrior II	28-7916341	PH-CKO N2140X/N9630N	6. 1.89	M.J.Greasby	RAF Halton	12. 7.04T
G-BPKO	Cessna 140	8936	N89891 NC89891	12. 1.89	M.J.Patrick	(Chichester)	18. 5.03
G-BPKR	Piper PA-28-151 Cherokee Warrior	28-7515446	N4341X	13. 3.89	Aeros Leasing Ltd	Filton	5. 4.04T
G-BPKZ	Short SD.3-60 Var.100	SH.3756	D-CFXB N264GA/N830BE/(B-....)/G-BPKZ	18. 1.89	BAC Express Airlines Ltd	(Horley)	28.11.05T
G-BPLF	Cameron V-77 HAB	1903		16. 1.89	I.R.Warrington & R.A.Macmillan *"Star Attraction"*	Stamford	5. 6.01A
G-BPLH	CEA Jodel DR.1051 Sicile (Potez 4E20A)	401	F-BLAE	27. 2.89	D.W.Tovey *(Noted 10.02)*	Bodmin	24.11.01
G-BPLM	AIA Stampe SV-4C	1004	F-BHET Fr.Mil/F-BDKC	8. 2.89	C.J.Jesson	Headcorn	30. 9.05T
G-BPLR	Pilatus Britten-Norman BN-2B-26 Islander	2209	OY-BNT JA5298/G-BPLR	20. 1.89	Hebridean Air Services Ltd *(Op Air X)*	Bournemouth	12.12.02T
G-BPLV	Cameron V-77 HAB	1822		23. 1.89	MC VH SA	Brussels, Belgium	1. 2.00A
G-BPLY	Christen Pitts S-2B Special (Lycoming AEIO-540)	5149		25. 1.89	J.D.Haslam	Teesside	20. 6.04
G-BPLZ	Hughes 369HS	91-0342S	N126CM	15. 2.89	Pyramid Helicopters Ltd	Wolverhampton	18. 6.04
G-BPMB	Maule M-5-235C Lunar Rocket	7284C	N5635T	13. 8.79	Earth Products Ltd	Crosland Moor	23. 1.04
G-BPME	Cessna 152 II	15285585	N94021	24. 1.89	Eastern Executive Air Charter Ltd *(Op Seawing Flying Club)*	Southend	5. 8.04T
G-BPMF	Piper PA-28-151 Cherokee Warrior	28-7515050	C-GOXL	2. 2.89	L. & A.Hill	Blackpool	2. 5.04
G-BPML	Cessna 172M Skyhawk II	17267102	N1435U	17.11.89	N.A.Bilton & P.R.Bennett	Priory Farm, Tibenham	29. 5.03T
G-BPMM	Champion 7ECA Citabria	7ECA-498	N5132T	22. 3.89	J.Murray *(Current status unknown)*	(Ballymoney, Co.Antrim)	25. 2.97P
G-BPMR	Piper PA-28-161 Warrior II	28-8416119	N4373S N9620N	25. 1.89	B.McIntyre	Filton	17. 5.04T
G-BPMU	Nord 3202B	70	(G-BIZJ) N22546/ALAT	26. 1.89	A.I.Milne *"AIX" (Stored 9.97: current status unknown)*	Little Snoring	19.10.90P
G-BPMW	QAC Quickie Q2 (Revmaster R2100DQ)	PFA 94A-10790	G-OICI G-OGKN	13. 3.89	P.M.Wright *(Damaged nr Basingstoke 16.2.91: on repair 9.00: current status unknown)*	Enstone	17. 8.91P
G-BPMX	ARV1 Super 2 (Hewland AE75)	K.005 & PFA 152-11128		30. 1.89	T.P.Toth	Enstone	20. 8.02P
G-BPNA	Cessna 150L	15073042	N1742Q	10. 2.89	BBC Air Ltd *(Op Abbas Air)*	Compton Abbas	30. 3.03T
G-BPND	Boeing 727-2D3RE	21021	OK-EGK N500AV/G-BPND/PH-AHZ/N500AV/HI-452/JY-ADV *(Cougar titles) "Katie"*	18.12.87	Cougar Leasing Ltd	(Bishops Stortford)	10. 4.01T
G-BPNI	Robinson R22 Beta	0948		6. 2.89	Heliflight (UK) Ltd	Wolverhampton	8. 4.04T
G-BPNL	QAC Quickie Q2 (Revmaster 2100D)	PFA 94A-11014		6. 2.89	J.R.Jensen *(Noted 5.02)*	Kemble	16. 1.96P
G-BPNN	Montgomerie-Bensen B.8MR	MV-003		3. 2.89	M.E.Vahdat	(Uxbridge)	
G-BPNO	Moravan Zlin Z.526 Trener Master	930	F-BPNO	18. 2.86	J.A.S.Baldry & S.T.Logan	RAF Cranwell	17. 6.03
G-BPNT	British Aerospace BAe 146 Srs.300	E3126		4. 1.89	Flightline Ltd	Southend	31. 5.05T
G-BPNU	Thunder Ax7-77 HAB	1011		9. 2.89	M.J.Barnes *"Firefly"*	Ivybridge	16. 8.02T
G-BPOB	Tallmantz Sopwith Camel F.1 rep (Warner Scarab 165)	TM-10	N8997	14. 3.89	Bianchi Aviation Film Services Ltd *(As "B2458/R" in RFC c/s)*	Booker	2. 9.02P
G-BPOL	Pietenpol Air Camper	PFA 47-10941		16. 2.89	G.W.Postance *(Current status unknown)*	(Burgess Hill, Sussex)	
G-BPOM	Piper PA-28-161 Warrior II	28-8416118	N4373Q N9619N	15. 2.89	C.Dale tr POM Flying Group	(Brigg)	27. 3.05T
G-BPON	Piper PA-34-200T Seneca II	34-7570040	N675ES N32644	13. 2.89	Aeros Leasing Ltd	Gloucestershire	15. 6.04T
G-BPOO	Montgomerie-Bensen B.8MR	MV-002 & PFA G/01A-1109		3. 2.89	M.E.Vahdat *(Not constructed: valid CofR 4.02)*	(Uxbridge)	
G-BPOS	Cessna 150M	15075905	N66187	21. 2.89	T.Akeroyd	Bourn	29.12.02T
G-BPOT	Piper PA-28-181 Cherokee Archer II	28-7790267	N8807F	7. 2.89	F A Yeates tr Icarus Flying Group	Rochester	17.12.04
G-BPOU	Luscombe 8A Silvaire (Continental A65)	4159	N1432K NC1432K	14. 2.89	P.K.Jordan tr Luscombe Trio	(Aylesford)	4.11.02P
G-BPOV*	Cameron Magazine 90SS HAB *(Forbes Magazine shape)*	1890		10. 3.89	Forbes Europe Inc *"Forbes Capitalist Tool" (Cancelled 14.11.02 by CAA)*	Balleroy, Normandy	5. 7.01A
G-BPPA	Cameron O-65 HAB	1930		15. 2.89	Rix Petroleum Ltd *"Rix Petroleum"*	Hull	13. 9.03A
G-BPPD	Piper PA-38-112 Tomahawk	38-79A0457	N2456F	15. 2.89	S.Snodgrass & M.A.Wood t/a AS Belting Products	Kemble	26. 9.04T
G-BPPE	Piper PA-38-112 Tomahawk	38-79A0189	N2445C	15. 2.89	First Air Ltd	Cardiff	5. 9.04T
G-BPPF	Piper PA-38-112 Tomahawk	38-79A0578	N2329K	15. 2.89	D.J.Bellamy tr Bristol Strut Flying Group	Bristol	5.12.04
G-BPPJ	Cameron A-180 HAB	1924		2. 3.89	Heather R.Evans	Ross-on-Wye	12. 3.01T
G-BPPK	Piper PA-28-151 Cherokee Warrior	28-7615054	N7592C	10. 3.89	UK Technical Consultants Ltd	Biggin Hill	30. 6.05T
G-BPPM	Beech B200 Super King Air	BB-1044	N7061T C-GJJT/N815CE/(N815CF)/N815CE/N62895	16. 2.89	Gama Aviation Ltd *(Op Bond Air Services)*	Aberdeen	17.10.04T

Reg	Type	C/n	Prev id	Date	Owner	Location	Date
G-BPPO	Luscombe 8A Silvaire (Continental A65)	2541	N3519M N71114/NC71114	15. 2.89	I.K.Ratcliffe *(Noted 10.01)*	Deanland	28. 6.03P
G-BPPP	Cameron V-77 HAB	1700		29. 2.88	P.F.Smart *"Thruppence"* tr The Sarnia Balloon Group	Basingstoke	28. 6.97A
G-BPPR*	Air Command 532 Elite	0434 & PFA G/04-1105		22. 2.89	T.D.Inch *(Cancelled 10.3.99 by CAA) (Used as Gyro-glider 2000)*	Swansea	14. 5.91P
G-BPPS	Mudry/CAARP CAP.21	9	F-GDTD	3. 5.85	N.B.Gray & L.Van Vuuren	Teesside	14. 3.02S
G-BPPU	Air Command 532 Elite (Rotax 532)	0438 & PFA G/04-1120		22. 2.89	J.Hough	Alresford, Hants	18.10.91P
G-BPPY	Hughes 269B (300)	20-0448	N9554F	10. 3.89	A.Harvey & R.C.S.Timbrell *(Current status unknown)*	Whimple, Exeter	16. 4.05T
G-BPPZ	Taylorcraft BC-12D (Continental C85)	7988	N28286 NC28286	22. 3.89	J.Gordon & M.Hart tr Zulu Warriors Flying Group	Charterhall	20. 9.03P
G-BPRA	Aeronca 11AC Chief	11AC-1344	N9702E NC9702E	22. 3.89	P.L.Clements	Beeches Farm, South Scarle	29. 7.03P
G-BPRC	Cameron Elephant 77SS HAB	1871		21. 2.89	A.Schneider *"Elefant Benjamin"*	Borken, Germany	1. 4.03A
G-BPRD	Pitts S-1C Special (Lycoming O-360)	ZZ.1	N10ZZ	21. 2.89	Shiela M.Trickey	St Just	15. 5.01P
G-BPRI	Aérospatiale AS355F1 Twin Squirrel	5181	G-TVPA G-BPRI/N364E	22. 2.89	Quay Contracts Ltd	(Portsmouth)	5. 11.05T
G-BPRJ	Aérospatiale AS355F1 Twin Squirrel	5201	N368E	22. 2.89	PLM Dollar Group Ltd	Cumbernauld	14.12.04T
G-BPRL	Aérospatiale AS355F1 Twin Squirrel	5154	N368E	22. 2.89	Gas & Air Ltd *(Op Virgin Helicopters)*	Booker	19. 4.03T
G-BPRM	Reims/Cessna F172L	F17200825	G-AZKG	20. 4.88	BJ Aviation Ltd	Welshpoo)	7. 1.05
G-BPRN	Piper PA-28-161 Warrior II	28-8116109	N83112	6. 3.89	Air Navigation & Trading Co Ltd	Blackpool	2. 8.04T
G-BPRR	Rand Robinson KR-2	PFA 129-11105		1. 3.89	P.E.Taylor *(Under construction 6.01: new owner 1.03)*	(Ferndown)	
G-BPRS	Air Command 532 Elite	0432		14. 4.89	B.K.Snoxall *(Believed damaged: cancelled 3.3.99 by CAA: current status unknown)*	(Whitchurch, Hants)	
G-BPRX	Aeronca 11AC Chief (Continental A75)	11AC-94	N86288 NC86288	3. 3.89	D.J.Dumolo & C.R.Barnes *(On rebuild 12.01)*	(Selby)	23. 8.99P
G-BPRY	Piper PA-28-161 Warrior II	28-8416120	N4373Y N9621N	2. 3.89	R.C.White t/a White Wings Aviation	East Midlands	21. 6.04T
G-BPSH	Cameron V-77 HAB	1837		21. 2.89	P.G.Hossack *"Coconut Ice"*	Pewsey	5. 4.97T
G-BPSJ	Thunder Ax6-56 HAB	1479		13. 3.89	Capricorn Balloons Ltd	Loughborough	4. 4.99A
G-BPSK	Montgomerie-Bensen B.8M (Rotax 532)	PFA G/01-1100		15. 3.89	P.T.Ambrozik *(Current status unknown)*	(Great Orton)	25.11.99P
G-BPSL	Cessna 177 Cardinal	17701138	N659SR	3. 3.89	N.P.Bendle tr G-BPSL Group	Dunkeswell	14.11.04
G-BPSO	Cameron N-90 HAB	1959		10. 3.89	J.Oberprieler	Mauern, Germany	19. 7.03A
G-BPSP*	Cameron Ship 90SS HAB (Columbus "Santa Maria" shape)	1848		10. 3.89	Forbes Europe Inc *"Santa Maria" (Cancelled 14.11.02 by CAA)*	Balleroy, Normandy	17. 6.94
G-BPSR	Cameron V-77 HAB	1962		10. 3.89	K.J.A.Maxwell *"Norma Jean"*	Haywards Heath	30.10.02T
G-BPSS	Cameron A-120 HAB	1947		27. 2.89	T.J.Parker t/a Anglian Countryside Balloons	Burnham-on-Crouch	31. 3.03T
G-BPTA	Stinson 108-2 Station Wagon (Franklin 6A4)	108-3429	N429C NC429C	22. 3.89	M.L.Ryan	Garston Farm, Marshfield	1.10.04
G-BPTD	Cameron V-77 HAB	2001		14. 3.89	J.Lippett *"Visions 2001"*	South Petherton, Somerset	11. 8.01A
G-BPTE	Piper PA-28-181 Cherokee Archer II	28-7690178	N8553E	9. 3.89	J.S.Develin & Z.Islam	Blackbushe	9. 8.04T
G-BPTF	Cessna 152 II	15281979	N67715	9. 3.89	J.B.P.E.Fernandes	(Cascais, Portugal)	20. 8.04T
G-BPTG	Rockwell Commander 112TC	13067	N4577W	31. 3.89	Marita A.Watteau	Shoreham	25.10.03
G-BPTI	SOCATA TB-20 Trinidad	414	N41BM	21. 4.89	N.Davis	Blackbushe	3. 7.04
G-BPTL	Cessna 172N Skyhawk II	17268652	N733YJ	22. 3.89	Cleveland Flying School Ltd	Teesside	8. 4.05T
G-BPTS	CASA I-131E Jungmann	NK	E3B-153 "781-75"	23. 5.89	Aerobatic Displays Ltd *(Op The Old Flying Machine Co) (As "E3B-153/781-75" in Spanish AF c/s)*	Duxford	19.12.02P
G-BPTU	Cessna 152 II	15282955	N45946	22. 3.89	A.M.Alam	Elstree	23. 6.03T
G-BPTV	Bensen B.8	PFA G/01-1058		30. 3.89	C.Munro	(Colne)	
G-BPTX	Cameron O-120 HAB	1972		29. 3.89	S.J.Colin t/a Skybus Ballooning	Cranbrook	13. 3.03T
G-BPTZ	Robinson R22 Beta	0958		22. 3.89	J. Lucketti	Barton	16. 11.98
G-BPUA	EAA Sport Biplane (Lycoming O-235)	SAAC-02	EI-BBF	30. 3.89	Skyview Systems Ltd	Priory Farm, Tibenham	30. 4.03P
G-BPUB	Cameron V-31 Air Chair HAB	1114		15. 3.89	M.T.Evans	Bath	3. 6.94A
G-BPUC	QAC Quickie Q.235 (Lycoming O-235)	2583	N250CE	22. 3.89	S.R.Monkcom	(Limassol, Cyprus)	4. 6.03P
G-BPUE	Air Command 532 Elite (Rotax 532)	0441 & PFA G/04-1136		29. 3.89	A.H.Brent	Brough	11. 9.91P
G-BPUF	Thunder Ax6-56Z HAB	270	(G-BHRL)	30. 4.80	R.C. & M.A.Trimble *"Buf Puf"*	Henley-on-Thames	10. 2.90A
G-BPUG	Air Command 532 Elite (Rotax 532)	0401 & PFA G/04-1157		29. 3.89	T.A.Holmes *(Possibly moved to Spain by 2000: current status unknown)*	Melrose Farm, Melbourne	18. 4.91P
G-BPUJ	Cameron N-90 HAB	1977		17. 4.89	D.Grimshaw	Preston	29.12.02T
G-BPUL	Piper PA-18A-150 Super Cub (L-18C-PI) *(Frame No thought to be in 18-25xx srs.)*	18-2517	OO-LUL PH-NEV	12. 4.89	C.D.Duthy-James	(Presteigne)	14. 7.05
G-BPUM	Cessna R182 Skylane RG II	R18200915	N738DZ	2. 5.89	R.C.Chapman	Marley Hall, Ledbury	30. 4.04
G-BPUP	Whittaker MW7	PFA 171-11473		2. 8.89	J.H.Beard	(Buckfastleigh, Devon)	
G-BPUR	Piper J-3L-65 Cub *(Frame No.4764)*	4708	N30228 NC30228	14. 6.89	H.A.D.Monro *(On rebuild 2000)*	(Hastings)	
G-BPUS*	Rans S-9 (Rotax 532)	PFA 196-11487		7. 4.89	T.A.Wright *(Cancelled 22.11.01 by CAA)*	Blackspring Farm, Castle Bytham	21. 4.00P
G-BPUU	Cessna 140	13722	N4251N NC4251N	31. 3.89	Sherburn Aero Club Ltd	Sherburn-in-Elmet	28.11.02T
G-BPUW	Colt 90A HAB	1436		12. 4.89	Gefa-Flug GmbH	Aachen, Germany	16. 7.03A
G-BPVA	Cessna 172F Skyhawk	17252286	N8386U	13. 4.89	J.Pilkington & P.Makin tr South Lancashire Flyers Group	Barton	13. 7.03
G-BPVC	Cameron V-77 HAB	1302		7. 4.89	B.D.Pettitt	Bury St. Edmunds	24. 3.03A
G-BPVE	Bleriot XI 1909 rep *(Built R.D.Henry, Texas 1967)*	1	N1197	20. 6.89	Bianchi Aviation Film Services Ltd *(As "1197")*	Booker	29. 6.01P

G-BPVH	Piper Cub J-3 Prospector	178C	CF-DRY	7. 4.89	D.E.Cooper-Maguire	Findon, Worthing	18. 8.03P
	(Continental C85)						
G-BPVI	Piper PA-32R-301 Saratoga SP	3213021	N91685	24. 4.89	M.T.Coppen	Goodwood	16. 7.01
G-BPVK	Varga 2150A Kachina VAC	85-77	N4626V	4. 5.89	H.W.Hall	Southend	12.12.03P
G-BPVM	Cameron V-77 HAB	1970		4. 4.89	R.M. Tonkins	Chatham	6. 9.97A
					tr Royal Engineers Balloon Club *"Viscount"* *(New CofR 6.02)*		
G-BPVN	Piper PA-32R-301T Turbo Saratoga SP		N8178W	14. 4.89	Y.Leysen	Goodwood	23. 8.04P
		32R-8029073					
G-BPVO	Cassutt Racer IIIM	DG.1	N19DD	13. 4.89	A.J.Brown	Old Buckenham	9. 6.03P
	(Continental O-200-A)				*"VooDoo"*		
G-BPVU	Thunder Ax7-77 HAB	965		12. 4.89	B.J.Hammond	Chelmsford	28. 3.02T
G-BPVW	CASA I-131E Jungmann	2133	E3B-559	17. 5.89	C. & J.W.Labeij	(Pulborough)	29. 9.03P
G-BPVY	Cessna 172D Skyhawk	17250568	N2968U	20. 4.89	O.Scott-Tomlin	Denham	13. 6.05
G-BPVZ	Luscombe 8E Silvaire	5565	N2838K	9. 5.89	W.E.Gillham & P.Ryman	Croft Farm, Darlington	31. 5.03P
	(Continental C85)		NC2838K				
G-BPWA	Piper PA-28-161 Cherokee Warrior II	28-7816074	N47450	7. 4.89	S.Azario	Goodwod	15. 5.04T
G-BPWB	Sikorsky S-61N	61822	EI-BHO	4. 5.89	Bristow Helicopters Ltd	Portland	10. 7.04T
			G-BPWB/EI-BHO		*(Op Marine & Coastguard Agency) "Portland Castle"*		
G-BPWC	Cameron V-77 HAB	1986		12. 4.89	H.B.Roberts *"Hot Flush"*	Bristol	9. 5.03T
G-BPWD	Cessna 120	10026	N72839	14. 4.89	M.W.Albery tr Peregrine Flying Group	Hucknall	27. 8.03P
	(Continental O-240-E)		NC72839				
G-BPWE	Piper PA-28-161 Warrior II	28-8116143	N8330P	2. 5.89	RPR Associates Ltd	Swansea	22. 6.05T
G-BPWG	Cessna 150M	15076707	(G-BPTK)	10. 4.89	W.R.Spicer & I.D.Carling		
			N45029			Nanbeck Farm, Wilsford, Grantham	20. 8.04
G-BPWI	Bell 206B-3 JetRanger III	3087	9M-BSR	14. 4.89	M.J Coates t/a Warren Aviation	Goodwood	21. 8.04T
			VH-HXZ/ZK-HXX/XC-PFH				
G-BPWK	Sportavia Fournier RF5B Sperber	51036	N56JM	17. 4.89	S.L.Reed	Usk	26. 8.03P
			(D-KEAR)				
G-BPWL	Piper PA-25-235 Pawnee	25-2304	N6690Z	14. 4.89	Tecair Aviation Ltd	Shipdham	19. 4.03
			G-BPWL/N6690Z				
G-BPWM	Cessna 150L	15072820	N1520Q	17. 4.89	M.E.Creasey	Crowfield	11.11.05
G-BPWN	Cessna 150L	15074325	N19308	17. 4.89	S.A.M.Tooley	(Luton)	19.11.05T
G-BPWP	Rutan LongEz	PFA 74A-11132		17. 4.89	J.F.O'Hara & A.J.Voyle	Denham	27. 6.03P
	(Continental O-240)						
G-BPWR	Cessna R172K Hawk XPII	R1722953	N758AZ	21. 4.89	A.M.Skelton	Humberside	7.10.04
G-BPWS	Cessna 172P Skyhawk II	17274306	N51387	21. 4.89	Chartstone Ltd	Redhill	2. 8.04T
G-BPWV*	Colt 56A HAB	1444		21. 4.89	Not known *"Coopers Exeter"*	Newbury	
					(Cancelled 4.8.98 by CAA) *(Noted 2000)*		
G-BPXA	Piper PA-28-181 Archer II	28-8390064	N4305T	12. 5.89	D.Howdle & D.L.Heighington	Netherthorpe	4. 6.04
					tr Cherokee Flying Group		
G-BPXB	Glaser-Dirks DG-400	4-248		2. 5.89	G.C.Westgate	Parham Park	25. 7.05
					tr Guy Westgate & Syndicate Partners		
G-BPXE	Enstrom 280C Shark	1089	N379KH	21. 4.89	A.Healy	Littlehampden, Bucks	27. 2.05
			C-GMLH/N660H				
G-BPXF	Cameron V-65 HAB	2003		21. 4.89	D.Pascall *(New owner 10.02)*	Croydon	
G-BPXH	Colt 17A Cloudhopper HAB	667	OO-BWG	21. 4.89	Sport Promotion SRL	Belbo, Italy	8. 9.00A
G-BPXJ	Piper PA-28RT-201T Turbo Arrow IV	28R-8231023	N8061U	21. 4.89	K.M.Hollamby	Biggin Hill	6.10.05
G-BPXX	Piper PA-34-200T Seneca II	34-7970069	N923SM	21. 4.89	E.C.& S.G.D.Clark	Biggin Hill	24. 7.04T
			N9556N				
G-BPXY	Aeronca 11AC Chief	11AC-S-50	N3842E	10. 4.89	P.L.Turner	Morgansfield, Fishburn	29.10.03P
G-BPYI	Cameron O-77 HAB	1988		9. 5.89	N.J.Logue	Pembroke Dock	18. 7.02A
G-BPYJ	Wittman W.8 Tailwind	PFA 31-11028		12. 5.89	J.Dixon	Bagby	19.10.00P
	(Continental PC60)						
G-BPYK	Thunder Ax7-77 HAB	1166		15. 5.89	A.R.Swinnerton *"Yorick"*	London EC2	29. 5.93
G-BPYL	Hughes 369D	100-0796D	N65AM	10. 5.89	Morcorp (BVI) Ltd	Wolverhampton	8. 7.04T
			G-BPYL/HB-XKT				
G-BPYN	Piper J-3C-65 Cub	11422	F-BFYN	14. 3.79	D.W.Stubbs tr The Aquila Group	White Waltham	7. 8.02P
	(L-4H-PI)		HB-OFN/43-30131				
G-BPYO	Piper PA-28-181 Archer II	2890114	SE-KIH	22. 5.89	Sherburn Aero Club Ltd	Sherburn-in-Elmet	29. 7.04T
G-BPYR	Piper PA-31 Navajo C	31-7812032	G-ECMA	15. 5.89	West Wales Airport Ltd	Shobdon	28.11.02T
			N27493				
G-BPYS	Cameron O-77 HAB	2008		9. 5.89	D.J.Goldsmith *"Aqualisa II"*	Edenbridge	14.12.99A
G-BPYT	Cameron V-77 HAB	1984		9. 5.89	M.H.Redman	Sturminster Newton	
G-BPYV	Cameron V-77 HAB	1992		17. 5.89	R.J.Shortall *(Spa Vehicle Electrics titles)*	Bath	7. 4.03A
G-BPYZ	Thunder Ax7-77 HAB	1521		11. 5.89	J.E.Astall *"Axis"*	Hinton St.George	7. 7.96A
					(Stolen Crewkerne, Somerset 23.10.97: current status unknown)		
G-BPZA	Luscombe 8A Silvaire	4326	N1599K	18. 4.89	M.J.Wright	Rochester	4. 7.03P
	(Continental A65)		NC1599K				
G-BPZB	Cessna 120	8898	N89853	25. 5.89	C. & M.A.Grime	Headcorn	10. 7.03P
	(Continental C90)		NC89853				
G-BPZC	Luscombe 8A Silvaire	4322	N1595K	6. 6.89	C C Lovell	(Winchester)	5. 7.90P
	(Continental A65)		NC1595K				
					(Damaged by gales Cranfield 25.1.90: used for spares 10.96) *(Valid CofR 4.02: current status unknown)*		
G-BPZD	SNCAN NC.858S	97	F-BEZD	26. 1.79	S.J.Gaveston, G.Richards & M.S.Regendanz	Headcorn	10. 7.03P
	(Continental C90) *(Built as NC.854S with Continental C65)*						
G-BPZE	Luscombe 8E Silvaire	3904	N1177K	6. 6.89	B.A.Webster	Hardwick	7. 5.03P
	(Continental C85)		NC1177K		tr WFG Luscombe Associates		
G-BPZK	Cameron O-120 HAB	1982		7. 4.89	D.L.Smith *"Hot Stuff"*	Newbury	12. 5.97T
G-BPZM	Piper PA-28RT-201 Arrow IV	28R-7918230	G-ROYW	12. 5.89	Airways Flight Training (Exeter) Ltd	Exeter	9.10.04T
			G-CRTI/SE-ICY				
G-BPZP	Robin DR400/180R Remorqueur	1471	D-EFZP	4. 5.89	Lasham Gliding Society Ltd	Lasham	23. 5.04
G-BPZS	Colt 105A HAB	1312		25. 5.89	Magical Adventures Ltd	West Bloomfield, Mi., USA	12.10.03A
					"Chamonix"		
G-BPZU	Scheibe SF-25C-2000 Falke	44471	D-KIAV	21. 7.89	D.A.Hatfield tr G-BPZU Group	Parham Park	12. 8.04

| G-BPZY | Pitts S-1C Special (Lycoming O-320) | RN-1 | N1159 | 15. 5.89 | J.S.Mitchell | White Waltham | 9. 5.03P |
| G-BPZZ | Thunder Ax8-105 HAB | 1441 | | 25. 5.89 | Capricorn Balloons Ltd | Loughborough | 21. 4.03T |

G-BRAA - G-BRZZ

G-BRAF	Supermarine 394 Spitfire FR.XVIIIe	6S/663052	Indian AF HS877 SM969	29.12.78	Wizzard Investments Ltd *(As "SM969/D-A" ?)*	North Weald	23. 9.93P
G-BRAJ	Cameron V-77 HAB	1876		25. 5.89	A.W.J.& C.Weston	Ross-on-Wye	
G-BRAK	Cessna 172N Skyhawk II	17273795	C-GBPN (N5438J)	23. 6.88	Rangecycle Ltd t/a Masonair	Bodmin	14. 2.04T
G-BRAM*	Mikoyan MiG-21PF	--	Hung AF 503	22. 5.89	Neales Aviation	Bournemouth	
					(Cancelled 16.4.99 by CAA) (Stored 2002) (As "503" in Russian AF c/s)		
G-BRAR	Aeronca 7AC Champion	7AC-6564	N2978E NC2978E	14. 6.89	C.D.Ward	Wombleton	9.10.03P
G-BRAW	Pitts S-1C Special (Lycoming O-290)	52544	N24DB	24. 5.89	J W Macleod, P.G.Bond & R.Anderson *(Destroyed in arson attack 18.2.03)*	Felthorpe	3. 7.03P
G-BRAX	Payne Knight Twister 85B (Continental O-200-A)	203	N9792	4. 5.89	R.Earl *(Current status unknown)*	White Waltham	29. 9.93P
G-BRBA	Piper PA-28-161 Warrior II	28-7916109	N2090B	25. 5.89	R.Clarke & S.H.Pearce	Wolverhampton	29.11.04T
G-BRBB	Piper PA-28-161 Warrior II	28-8116030	N8260W	28. 6.89	Aeros Leasing Ltd	Gloucestershire	24.10.04T
G-BRBD	Piper PA-28-151 Cherokee Warrior	28-7415315	N41702	28. 6.89	W.E.Rispin tr Bravo Delta Group *"Shaftesbury Belle"*	Compton Abbas	10. 4.05
G-BRBE	Piper PA-28-161 Warrior II	28-7916437	N2815D	13. 6.89	Solo Services Ltd *(Op Sussex Flying Club)*	Shoreham	20. 1.05T
G-BRBG	Piper PA-28-180 Cherokee Archer	28-7505248	N3927X	12. 6.89	Ken MacDonald & Co	Stornoway	22. 8.04
G-BRBH	Cessna 150H	15069283	N50410	13. 6.89	J.Maffia	Panshanger	7. 8.04T
G-BRBI	Cessna 172N Skyhawk II	17269613	N737RJ	7. 7.89	M.D.Harcourt-Brown tr G-BRBI Flying Group	Popham	3. 9.04
G-BRBJ	Cessna 172M Skyhawk II	17267492	N73476	26. 5.89	L.C.Macknight	Elstree	12. 1.02
G-BRBK	Robin DR400/180 Regent	1915		31. 5.89	R.Kemp	Thruxton	17.10.04
G-BRBL	Robin DR400/180 Regent	1920		5. 7.89	C.A.Marren	Upavon	6. 3.04
G-BRBM	Robin DR400/180 Regent	1921		5. 7.89	R.W.Davies Little Robhurst Farm, Woodchurch		23. 1.05
G-BRBN	Pitts S-1S Special (Lycoming O-360)	G.3	N81BG	14. 7.89	D.R.Evans	Gloucestershire	14. 6.03P
G-BRBO	Cameron V-77 HAB	1877		30. 5.89	M B Murphy *"Patches"*	Cheltenham	31. 5.03A
G-BRBP	Cessna 152 II	15284915	N5324P	14. 6.89	Staverton Flying Services Ltd	Gloucestershire	24. 7.04T
G-BRBS	Bensen B.8M (Rotax 503)	PFA G/01-1039		30. 5.89	K.T.MacFarlane (Kilmacolm, Renfrew) *(Under construction 6.00)*		
G-BRBT	Trotter Ax3-20 HAB	RMT-001		13. 6.89	R.M.Trotter *(Current status unknown)*	Bristol	
G-BRBU*	Colt 17A Cloudhopper HAB	1506		12. 6.89	Virgin Airship & Balloon Co Ltd *"National Theatre" (Cancelled 8.11.01 as WFU & stored)*	Telford	29. 5.90A
G-BRBW	Piper PA-28-140 Cherokee Cruiser	28-7425153	N40737	3. 7.89	Full Sutton Flying Centre Ltd	Full Sutton	1.11.04
G-BRBX	Piper PA-28-181 Cherokee Archer II	28-7690185	N8674E	20. 7.89	M.J.Ireland t/a Archer Air	Leicester	25. 3.05T
G-BRBY	Robinson R22 Beta	1027		15. 6.89	D Brown	Cumbernauld	26. 7.04T
G-BRCA	Jodel D.112 *(Built Ets Valladeau)*	1203	F-BLIU	11. 7.89	R.C.Jordan	Turweston	9. 6.03P
G-BRCD	Cessna A152 Aerobat	A1520796	N7377L	8. 6.89	D.E.Simmons tr Charlie Delta Group	Shoreham	30. 8.04
G-BRCE	Pitts S-1C Special (Lycoming O-290)	1001	N4611G	22. 6.89	R.D.Rogers Hulcote Farm, Salford, Beds *(Op Skylark Aerobatic Co)*		25.11.97P
G-BRCF	Montgomerie-Bensen B.8MR (Rotax 532)	PFA G/01A-1131		12. 6.89	J.S.Walton	Mold	30.10.91P
G-BRCG	Grob G-109	6077	N64BG D-KGRO	15. 6.89	I.R.Taylor	Tatenhill	15. 1.04
G-BRCI	Pitts S-1C Special (Lycoming O-320)	4668	N351S	6. 7.89	G.L.A.Vandormael	Wevelgem, Belgium	18. 3.04P
G-BRCJ	Cameron H-20 HAB	2028		13. 6.89	P.de Cock	Waasmunster, Belgium	25. 7.99A
G-BRCM	Cessna 172L Skyhawk	17259960	N3860Q	19. 6.89	S.G.E.Plessis & D.C.C.Handley *(Op Osprey Flying Club)*	Cranfield	18. 9.05T
G-BRCO*	Cameron H-20 HAB	2030		19. 6.89	M.Davies *"Shell Unleaded"* *(Cancelled 27.11.01 by CAA)*	Callington, Cornwall	17. 6.97A
G-BRCT	Denney Kitfox Model 2	396 & PFA 172-11521		23. 6.89	M.L.Roberts	Bodmin	13. 1.03P
G-BRCV	Aeronca 7AC Champion (Continental A65)	7AC-282	N81661 NC81661	19. 9.89	J.M.Jacobs	(Taunton)	15. 7.03P
G-BRCW	Aeronca 11BC Chief (Continental C85)	11AC-366	N85954 NC85954	16.10.89	R.B.McComish Bow, Totnes *(Registered p/i & c/n match but correct p/i is N85964 c/n 11AC-386)*		4. 6.03P
G-BRDB	Zenair CH-701 STOL	PFA 187-11412		11. 7.89	D.L.Bowtell	(Ware)	
G-BRDC	Thunder Ax7-77 HAB	1547		26. 6.89	P.J.Bish & C.Kunert t/a Zebedee Balloon Service *"Purple Rising"*	Hungerford	18. 1.00A
G-BRDD	Mudry CAP.10	B224		3. 8.88	R.D.Dickson	Coal Aston/Gamston	14.12.03
G-BRDE	Thunder Ax7-77 HAB	1538		22. 6.89	C.C.Brash *"Veronica"*	Maidenhead	14. 4.03A
G-BRDF	Piper PA-28-161 Cherokee Warrior II	28-7716085	N1139Q	26. 6.89	White Waltham Airfield Ltd *(Op West London Aero Services)*	White Waltham	24. 6.05T
G-BRDG	Piper PA-28-161 Cherokee Warrior II	28-7816047	N44934	26. 6.89	White Waltham Airfield Ltd *(Op West London Aero Services)*	White Waltham	17. 1.05T
G-BRDJ	Luscombe 8A Silvaire (Continental A65)	3411	N71984 NC71984	28. 6.89	J.D.Parker Franklyn's Field, Chewton Mendip		30.11.03P
G-BRDM	Piper PA-28-161 Cherokee Warrior II	28-7716004	N8464F	26. 6.89	White Waltham Airfield Ltd *(Op West London Aero Services)*	White Waltham	4.12.04T
G-BRDN	SOCATA MS.880B Rallye Club	1212	OY-DTV	14. 7.89	A.J.Gomes	Redhill	27. 4.02
G-BRDO	Cessna 177B Cardinal II	17702166	N35030	13. 7.89	I.Jane & A.Lidster t/a Cardinal Aviation	Teesside	21.12.01
G-BRDT	Cameron DP-70 Hot-Air Airship (Konig SD 570)	2029		3. 7.89	Tim Balloon Promotion Airships Ltd	Bristol	23.10.01A
G-BRDW	Piper PA-24-180 Comanche	24-1733	N6612P	12. 3.90	I.P.Gibson	Southampton	19.12.02
G-BREA	Bensen B.8MR (Rotax 503)	PFA G/01-1006		6. 7.89	T.J.Deane *(Noted 11.02)*	Henstridge	24.10.00P
G-BREB	Piper J-3C-65 Cub	7705	N41094 NC41094	3. 7.89	L.W.& O.Usherwood	Rochester	22. 8.03P
G-BREE	Whittaker MW7 (Rotax 503)	PFA 171-11497		22. 6.89	P.J.Fell	Newton Peverill	16. 5.03P

Reg	Type	C/n	Prev ID	Date	Owner/Operator	Location	Date
G-BREH	Cameron V-65 HAB	2049		7. 7.89	S.E. & V.D.Hurst *"Promise"*	Mansfield	13.12.02A
G-BREM*	Air Command 532 Elite (Rotax 532)	0614 & PFA G/04-1139		20. 7.89	T.W.Freeman	Wimpole Royston	25. 3.91P
					(Stored 7.91: cancelled 16.11.01 by CAA) (Current status unknown)		
G-BRER	Aeronca 7AC Champion (Continental A65)	7AC-6758	N3157E NC3157E	12. 7.89	I.Sinnett tr Rabbit Flight	Bodmin	10. 7.03P
G-BREU	Montgomerie-Bensen B.8 (Rotax 582)	PFA G/01A-1137		20. 7.89	J.S.Firth	Sherburn-in-Elmet	30. 9.03P
G-BREY	Taylorcraft BC-12D	7299	N43640 NC43640	14. 7.89	R.J.Pitts tr BREY Group	Leicester	5. 6.02P
G-BRFB	Rutan LongEz (Lycoming O-290)	PFA 74A-10646		14. 7.89	R.Young	Perth	24. 5.03P
G-BRFE	Cameron V-77 HAB	1835		20. 7.89	D.L.C.Nelmes tr Esmerelda Balloon Syndicate *"Esmerelda"*	Bristol	30. 7.02A
G-BRFH*	Colt 90A HAB	1543		14. 7.89	Polydron International Ltd *"Polydron" (Cancelled 9.11.01 as WFU & stored)*	Kemble	14. 3.97A
G-BRFI	Aeronca 7DC Champion (Continental C85)	7AC-4609	N1058E NC1058E	1. 8.89	A.C.Lines *(Damaged 1990: on rebuild 4.96)*	Leicester	19. 2.91P
G-BRFJ	Aeronca 11AC Chief (Continental A65)	11AC-796	N9163E NC9163E	28. 7.89	J.M.Mooney *(Stored 2.03)*	Lochview House, Limerigg	11. 9.02P
G-BRFL	Piper PA-38-112 Tomahawk	38-79A0431	N2416F	17. 8.89	Teesside Flight Centre Ltd	Teesside	13. 8.02T
G-BRFM	Piper PA-28-161 Warrior II	28-7916279	N2234P	17.10.89	Atlantic Air Transport Ltd	Coventry	9. 1.05T
G-BRFN	Piper PA-38-112 Tomahawk	38-79A0397	N2326F	23.10.89	Light Aircraft Leasing (UK) Ltd	Norwich	10.12.03T
G-BRFO	Cameron V-77 HAB	2025		6. 7.89	N.J.Bland *"Lurcher"* tr Hedgehoppers Balloon Group	Oxford	31. 7.00A
G-BRFW	Montgomerie-Bensen B.8 Two-Seat (Rotax 582)	PFA G/01-1073		20. 7.89	A.J.Barker	(Dundee)	12. 6.03P
G-BRFX	Pazmany PL-4A (Volkswagen 1700)	PFA 17-10079		14. 7.89	D.E.Hills *(Current status unknown)*	(Ipswich)	
G-BRGD	Cameron O-84 HAB	2043		20. 7.89	J.R.H. & M.A.Ashworth	Newquay	
G-BRGF	Luscombe 8E Silvaire (Continental C85)	5475	N23FP N944BL/N2748K/NC2748K	20. 7.89	N.Surman tr Luscombe Flying Group	RAF Henlow	11. 5.02P
G-BRGG	Luscombe 8A Silvaire (Continental A65)	3795	N1068K NC1068K	20. 7.89	M.A.Lamprell	Popham	2. 9.03P
G-BRGI	Piper PA-28-180 Cherokee E	28-5827	N77VG NIIVG	24. 7.89	Redhill Air Services Ltd	Rochester	20. 6.05
G-BRGN	British Aerospace Jetstream Srs.3102	637	G-BLHC G-31-637	20. 3.87	Cranfield University	Cranfield	16. 5.03T
G-BRGO	Air Command 532 Elite (Rotax 532)	0615 & PFA G/04-1149		7. 8.89	A.McCredie *(Airframe noted 5.00)*	Kingsmuir Sorbie	13. 2.91P
G-BRGP*	Colt Flying Stork SS HAB	1409		25. 7.89	Not known *"Great Eggspectations"* *(Cancelled 10.3.95 by CAA: noted Albuquerque, New Mexico, USA 10.01)*	(USA)	NE(A)
G-BRGT	Piper PA-32-260 Cherokee Six	32-658	N3744W	7.11.89	P.Cowley	East Midlands	10. 7.05
G-BRGW	Barritault JB-01 Minicab (Continental O-200-A)	PFA 1823		13.11.78	R.G.White	Hildon-le-Noble, Hants	18. 6.03P
G-BRGX	Rotorway Executive (Rotorway RW 152D)	3597		3. 8.89	D.W.J.Lee	South Burlingham, Norwich	8. 12.03P
G-BRHA	Piper PA-32RT-300 Lance II	32R-7985076	N2093P	27. 7.89	D.J.Chatterton & P.MacKinnon tr Lance G-BRHA Group	Earls Colne/Southend	29.11.04
G-BRHB	Boeing-Stearman B75N1 (N2S-3) Kaydet		EC-AID 75-6508 ACN67955/Bu.05334	10. 8.89	P R Bennett & R Sage *(New owners 12.01)*	Priory Farm, Tibenham	AC
G-BRHC*	Cameron V-77 HAB	1842		3. 8.89	Golf Centres Balloons Ltd *"Green Dragon" (Cancelled 8.11.01 as WFU) (Current status unknown)*	Gargonza, Italy	30. 8.94T
G-BRHG	Colt 90A HAB	1568		11. 9.89	Bath University Students Union (*Badgerline* titles)	Bath	9. 8.02A
G-BRHL	Montgomerie-Bensen B.8MR (Rotax 503)	PFA G/01A-1123		7. 8.89	R.M.Savage & T.M.Jones	Carlisle	26. 8.03P
G-BRHO	Piper PA-34-200 Seneca	34-7350037	N15222	20. 9.89	D.A.Lewis	Luton	5. 9.04
G-BRHP	Aeronca O-58B Defender (Continental A65)	058B-8533	N58JR N46536/43-1923	2. 8.89	C.J.Willis *(As "3-1923" in US Army c/s)*	Dunkeswell	22. 2.01P
	(If US Army serial is correct, type should be L-3C-AE Grasshopper)						
G-BRHR	Piper PA-38-112 Tomahawk	38-79A0969	N2377P	21. 8.89	J.Davies	Hawarden	28. 9.04T
G-BRHT	Piper PA-38-112 Tomahawk	38-79A0199	N2474C	4. 8.89	P.A.Murphy tr Romeo Hotel Tango Group	RAF Mona	9. 8.04T
G-BRHW	de Havilland DH.82A Tiger Moth	85612	7Q-YMY VP-YMY/ZS-DLB/SAAF 4606/DE671	26. 7.89	P.J. & A.J.Borsberry *(On rebuild 6.95: current status unknown)*	Kidmore End, Reading	
G-BRHX	Luscombe 8E Silvaire (Continental C90)	5114	N176M N2387K/NC2387K	8. 8.89	J.Lakin	Eaglescott	1. 8.03P
G-BRHY	Luscombe 8E Silvaire (Continental C85)	5138	N2411K NC2411K	8. 8.89	A.R.W.Taylor	Sleap	29. 4.03P
G-BRHZ*	Stephens Akro (Lycoming IO-360) *(Aka "Astro 235")*	ZA-235	N35EJ	20.12.89	T.A.Shears *(Cancelled 22.5.01 by CAA) (Stored dismantled in hangar 5.02)*	Membury	16. 4.98P
G-BRIA	Cessna 310L	310L0010	N2210F	4. 8.89	B.J.Tucker & R.C.Pugsley	Kemble	15.10.01T
G-BRID*	Cessna U206A Super Skywagon	U2060574	N4874F	7. 5.87	British Skysports *Cancelled 4.10.93 as WFU) (Used as para-trainer 1.96: current status unknown)*	Grindale	20. 5.93
G-BRIE	Cameron N-77 HAB	2076		8. 8.89	S.F.Redman	Sturminster Newton	24. 6.03A
G-BRIF	Boeing 767-204ER	24736	(PH-AHM) G-BRIF	10. 3.90	Britannia Airways Ltd *"Lord Horatio Nelson"*	Luton	18.11.05P
G-BRIG	Boeing 767-204ER	24757	(PH-AHN) G-BRIG	10. 4.90	Britannia Airways Ltd *"Eglantyne Jebb"*	Luton	17. 4.03T
G-BRIH	Taylorcraft BC-12D (Continental A75)	7421	N43762 NC43762	24. 8.89	A.D.Duke	Leicester	11. 9.02P
G-BRII	Zenair CH-600 Zodiac	PFA 162-11392		18. 8.89	A.C.Bowdrey *(Under build 2000)*	(Hemel Hempstead)	
G-BRIJ	Taylorcraft F-19	F-119	N3863T	23. 8.89	K.E.Ballington	Yeatsall Farm, Abbots Bromley	12. 6.01P
G-BRIK	Nipper T.66S RA45 Srs.3B (Volkswagen 1834) *(Rebuild of G-AVKH)*	PFA 25-10174		26. 4.77	P.R.Bentley *(Fuselage away on rebuild 11.01)*	Roughay Farm, Bishops Waltham	1. 8.02P
G-BRIL	Piper J-5A Cub Cruiser (Continental A75)	5-572	N35183 NC35183	2. 8.89	P.L.Jobes	Spilhall Farm, Co.Durham	19.12.02P

Reg	Type	C/n	Prev id	Date	Owner/Operator	Location	Date
G-BRIM*	Cameron O-160 HAB	1856		10. 8.89	Golf Centres Balloons Ltd	Bridport	11. 8.93T
	(Cancelled 8.11.01 as WFU) (Current status unknown)						
G-BRIO	Turner Super T-40A PFA 104-10636			7. 8.89	R.W.L.Breckell tr BRIO Flyers	(Liverpool)	15. 8.00P
	(Continental O-200-A) *(Regd incorrectly as PFA 104-10736)*						
G-BRIR	Cameron V-56 HAB	2056		17. 8.89	H.G.Davies & C.Dowd	Cheltenham	6. 9.97A
					(Skyviews Windows titles) "Spirit of Century"		
G-BRIS	Steen Skybolt (Lycoming IO-360)	01	N870MC	30. 8.89	Little Bear Ltd	Exeter	16. 1.03P
G-BRIV	SOCATA TB-9 Tampico Club	939		24. 8.89	P.M.Harrison	Sturgate	10. 2.03T
G-BRIY	Taylorcraft DF-65	6183	N59687	1. 2.90	S R Potts	Eshott	10. 7.98P
	(Continental A65) *(Built as TG-6 glider)*		NC59687/42-58678		*(As "42-58678/IY" in L-2A USAAC c/s) (New owner 1.02)*		
G-BRJA	Luscombe 8A Silvaire	3744	N1017K	12. 9.89	A.D.Keen	Dunkeswell	18. 6.03P
	(Continental A65)		NC1017K				
G-BRJB	Zenair CH-600 Zodiac 6-1283 & PFA 162-11573			2. 8.89	D.J.Hunter *(On build 4.02)*	Priory Farm, Tibenham	
G-BRJC	Cessna 120	12077	N1833N	21. 8.89	One Twenty Flyers Ltd	Nottingham	21. 3.03P
	(Continental C85)		NC1833N				
G-BRJK	Luscombe 8A Silvaire	4205	N1478K	21. 8.89	C.J.L.Peat & M.Richardson	Popham	11. 4.02P
	(Continental A65)		NC1478K		*(Stored dismantled 9.02)*		
G-BRJL	Piper PA-15 Vagabond	15-157	N4370H	21. 8.89	C.P.Ware & A R Williams	Garston Farm, Marshfield	8. 7.03P
	(Continental C85)		NC4370H				
G-BRJN	Pitts S-1C Special (Lycoming O-320)	1-MA	N6A	23. 8.89	W.Chapel	Sherburn-in-Elmet	22. 4.03P
G-BRJR	Piper PA-38-112 Tomahawk	38-79A0144	N2598B	31. 8.89	Chester Aviation Ltd	Hawarden	27. 5.05T
G-BRJT	Cessna 150H	15068426	N44SS	31. 8.89	B.J.Christopher & R.J.C.Borchardt	Kemble	30. 8.04T
			N22649		tr Pink Panther Flying Group		
G-BRJV	Piper PA-28-161 Cadet	2841167	N9185G	24. 8.89	Newcastle upon Tyne Aero Club Ltd	Newcastle	30.12.04T
G-BRJW	Bellanca 7GCBC Citabria 150S	1200-80	OO-LPG	7. 4.82	F.A.L.Castleden & A.J.Sillis	Horham	24. 8.03
G-BRJY	Rand-Robinson KR-2 PFA 129-11308			22. 8.89	R.E.Taylor	(Bonar Bridge)	23. 5.96P
	(Revmaster 2100D)				*(Under restoration 6.00)*		
G-BRKA*	Luscombe 8F Silvaire	5084	N2357K	13. 3.89	H.Savage-Jones	Bodmin	1. 8.99P
	(Continental C90)		NC2357K		*(Cancelled 20.4.99 as destroyed) (On rebuild 8.01)*		
G-BRKC	Auster V J/1 Autocrat	2749	F-BFYT	31. 8.89	J.W.Conlon	High Easter	19. 9.03P
G-BRKD*	Piaggio P.149D	306	D-EAMS	15. 9.89	P.E.H.Scott Standalone Farm, Meppershall		5.11.92
			92+10/AC+457/AS+457		*(Cancelled 28.5.99 by CAA: noted 9.00)*		
G-BRKH	Piper PA-28-236 Dakota	28-7911003	N21444	30. 8.89	Dateworld Ltd	Bournemouth	28.12.04
G-BRKL	Cameron H-34 HAB	2075		29. 8.89	P.L.Harrison	Rushden, Northampton	30.12.02A
G-BRKO	Oldfield Baby Great Lakes	CMK.1	N8GL	18. 1.90	R.Trickett	(Downham Market)	9. 1.02P
G-BRKR	Cessna 182R Skylane II	18268468	N9896E	2. 6.89	A.R.D.Brooker	Springfield Farm, Ettington	27. 1.05
G-BRKW	Cameron V-77 HAB	2093		1. 9.89	T.J.Parker	Burnham-on-Crouch	19.12.02
G-BRKY	Viking Dragonfly Mk II PFA 139-11117			7. 9.89	G.D.Price	Deanland,.Hailsham	8. 6.94P
	(Volkswagen 2180)				*(Stored 3.97: current status unknown)*		
G-BRLB	Air Command 532 Elite	0622		4. 9.89	F.G.Shepherd	(Great Orton)	
					(Valid CofR 4.02: current status unknown)		
G-BRLF	Campbell Cricket PFA G/03-1077			6. 9.89	D.Wood	Holbeach	1.12.00P
	(Rotax 503)						
G-BRLG	Piper PA-28RT-201T Turbo Arrow IV	28R-8431027	N4379P	12. 9.89	C.G.Westwood	RAF Shawbury	11. 1.02
			N9600N				
G-BRLI	Piper J-5A Cub Cruiser	5-822	N35951	23. 8.89	Little Bear Ltd	Exeter	27. 6.03P
	(Lycoming O-290)		NC35951				
G-BRLL	Cameron A-105 HAB	2032		7. 9.89	Aerosaurus Balloons LLP	Exeter	27.11.02T
G-BRLO	Piper PA-38-112 Tomahawk	38-78A0621	N2397K	26.10.89	E.Reed	Teesside	25. 2.04T
			N9680N		t/a St George Flight Training		
G-BRLP	Piper PA-38-112 Tomahawk	38-78A0011	N9301T	4.10.89	P D Brooks	Inverness	5. 4.04T
G-BRLR	Cessna 150G	15064822	N4772X	4.10.89	D.Carr & M.R.Muter	Newcastle	10. 5.04
G-BRLS	Thunder Ax7-77 HAB	1603		29. 9.89	Elizabeth C.Meek	Oswestry	20. 5.03A
G-BRLT	Colt 77A HAB	1588		12. 9.89	D.Bareford *"Pro-Sport"*	Kidderminster	17. 6.03A
G-BRLV	CCF Harvard 4	CCF4-194	N90448	14. 9.89	Extraviation Ltd *"Texan Belle"*	North Weald	26.12.03P
			RCAF 20403		*(As "93542/LTA-542" in 6148th TCS USAF c/s)*		
G-BRME	Piper PA-28-181 Cherokee Archer II	28-7790105	OY-BTA	14. 9.89	Keen Leasing Ltd	Belfast	21. 4.02T
G-BRMG	Supermarine 384 Seafire F.XVI	FLWA.25488	A2055	19. 9.89	T.J.Manna	(Royston)	
			SX336		*(As "SX336") (Current status unknown)*		
G-BRMI	Cameron V-65 HAB	2104		14. 9.89	M.Davies *"Sapphire"*	Callington, Cornwall	25. 8.01A
G-BRMJ*	Piper PA-38-112 Tomahawk	38-79A0784	N2316N	15. 9.89	Aerohire Ltd	Wellesbourne Mountford	25. 4.96T
					(Op Wellesbourne Aviation) (Cancelled 24.10.00 by CAA)		
G-BRML	Piper PA-38-112 Tomahawk	38-79A1017	N2510P	3.10.89	P.H.Rogers	Wolverhampton	3. 6.02T
G-BRMS	Piper PA-28RT-201 Arrow IV	28R-8118004	N82708	25. 9.89	Fleetbridge Ltd	White Waltham	11. 6.05
G-BRMT	Cameron V-31 Air Chair HAB	2038		31. 8.89	T.C.Hinton	Tunbridge Wells	
G-BRMU	Cameron V-77 HAB	2109		19. 9.89	K.J. & G.R Ibbotson	Gloucester	12. 3.03A
G-BRMV	Cameron O-77 HAB	2103		25. 9.89	P.D.Griffiths *"Viscount"*	Southampton	10. 7.03A
G-BRMW	Whittaker MW7 (Rotax 532) PFA 171-11395			25. 9.89	G.S.Parsons	(Coventry)	21. 4.03P
G-BRNC	Cessna 150M Commuter	15078833	N704SG	29. 9.89	D.C.Bonsall	Netherthorpe	9. 9.05T
G-BRND	Cessna 152 II	15283776	N5148B	7.11.89	T.M. & M.L.Jones *(Op Derby Aero Club)* Eggington, Derby		18. 7.05T
G-BRNE	Cessna 152 II	15284248	N5082L	4.10.89	Redhill Air Services Ltd *(Op Sky Leisure)*	Shoreham	3. 3.03T
G-BRNJ	Piper PA-38-112 Tomahawk	38-79A0415	N2395F	22. 9.89	Cardiff Wales Aviation Services Ltd	Cardiff	15.12.05T
G-BRNK	Cessna 152 II	15280479	N24969	22. 9.89	Sheffield Aero Club Ltd	Netherthorpe	12. 3.05T
G-BRNM	Chichester-Miles Leopard	002		17.10.89	Chichester-Miles Consultants Ltd	Bournemouth	AC
G-BRNN	Cessna 152 II	15284735	N6452M	22. 9.89	Sheffield Aero Club Ltd	Netherthorpe	24. 1.05T
G-BRNT	Robin DR400/180 Regent	1935		3.10.89	M.J.Cowham Top Farm, Croydon, Royston		3. 1.05
G-BRNU	Robin DR400/180 Regent	1937		31.10.89	November Uniform Travel Syndicate Ltd White Waltham		19. 5.05
G-BRNV	Piper PA-28-181 Cherokee Archer II	28-7790402	N2537Q	7.12.89	B.S.Hobbs	Goodwood	10. 3.05
G-BRNW	Cameron V-77 HAB	2138		2.10.89	N.Robertson & G.Smith *"Mr Blue Sky"*	Truro/Bristol	31. 7.03A
G-BRNX	Piper PA-22-150 Tri-Pacer	22-2945	N2610P	3.10.89	C.A.Robbins	(Royston)	19.12.05
G-BRNZ	Piper PA-32-300 Cherokee Six B	32-40594	N4229R	7. 2.90	L.I.Bailey tr Longfellow Flying Group	(Daventry)	20 6.05T
G-BROB	Cameron V-77 HAB	2073		29. 8.89	J.W.Tomkinson	(Beaconsfield)	4. 5.03A
G-BROE	Cameron N-65 HAB	2098		5.10.89	R.H.Sanderson *"Lancia Dedra"*	Nuneaton	3. 8.97A
G-BROG	Cameron V-65 HAB	2121		6. 9.89	R.Kunert *"The Dodger"*	Wokingham	31. 7.02A

Reg	Type	C/n	Prev id	Date	Owner/Operator	Location	Status
G-BROH	Cameron O-90 HAB	2120		6.10.89	P.A.Wenlock *"Linde"*	Stretton, Staffs	1. 8.99T
G-BROI	CFM Streak Shadow K.115-SA & PFA 161-11586 (Rotax 532)			16.11.89	G.J.Forshaw	(Cheadle)	6. 8.03P
G-BROJ*	Colt 31A HAB	1468		6.10.89	Virgin Airship & Balloon Co Ltd *"Fly Virgin"* (Cancelled 8.11.01 as WFU & stored)	Telford	23. 9.92A
G-BROL	Colt AS-80 Mk.II Hot-Air Airship (Rotax 462)	1578		6.10.89	Ballonwerbung Hamburg GmbH	Hamburg, Germany	21. 6.03A
G-BROO	Luscombe 8E Silvaire (Continental PC.60)	6154	N75297 N1527B/NC1527B	28. 9.89	P.R.Bush *(New owner 7.02)*	RAF Kinloss	8. 5.00P
G-BROP	Van's RV-4 (Lycoming O-360)	3	N19AT	25.10.89	K.E.Armstrong	Armshold Farm, Kingston, Cambs	27. 8.03P
G-BROR	Piper J-3C-65 Cub (L-4H-PI)	10885	F-BHMQ 43-29594	7.12.89	J.H.Bailey & A.P.J.Wiseman tr White Hart Flying Group	Sturgate	25. 6.03P
G-BROX	Robinson R22 Beta	1127	N8061V	13.10.89	P.H.Marlow & G.T.Kozlowski	Redhill	9.11.04T
G-BROY	Cameron O-90 HAB	2173		6. 9.89	T.G.S.Dixon *(Dixon Furnace Division tiles)*	Bromsgrove	27. 9.02A
G-BROZ	Piper PA-18-150 Super Cub	18-6754	HB-ORC N9572D	20. 9.89	P.G.Kynsey	Rushett Manor, Chessington	7. 3.05T
G-BRPE	Cessna 120 (Continental C85)	13326	N3068N NC3068N	11.10.89	P.M.Ireland	South Lodge Farm, Widmerpool	16. 5.03P
G-BRPF	Cessna 120 (Continental C85)	9902	N72723 NC72723	11.10.89	D.Sharp	Breighton	15. 5.03P
G-BRPG	Cessna 120 (Continental C85)	9882	N72703 NC72703	11.10.89	I.C.Lomax	Ottringham	29. 8.94P
G-BRPH	Cessna 120 (Continental C85)	12137	N1893N NC1893N	11.10.89	J.A.Cook	Pent Farm, Postling, Kent	1. 8.03P
G-BRPJ	Cameron N-90 HAB	2071		11. 9.89	Paul Johnson *"Presto"* t/a Cloud Nine Balloon Co	Consett	10. 3.99T
G-BRPK	Piper PA-28-140 Cherokee Cruiser	28-7325070	N15449	17.11.89	J.P.A.Gomes	Cascais, Portugal	17. 6.05
G-BRPL	Piper PA-28-140 Cherokee Cruiser	28-7325160	N15771	13.10.89	Comed Aviation Ltd	Blackpool	6.11.05T
G-BRPM	Nipper T.66 Srs.3B	PFA 25-11038		4. 3.85	T.C.Horner *(Under construction 6.00)*	(Barrhead)	
G-BRPO	Enstrom 280C Shark	1092	N636H	13.10.89	D.Jones	(Chester)	4. 7.05
G-BRPP	Brookland Hornet (Volkswagen 1776)	DC-1		16.10.89	B.J.L.P.& W.J.A.L.de Saar *(For rebuild 2000)*	(Great Yarmouth)	19. 8.93P
G-BRPR	Aeronca L-3C Defender (Continental A65)	058B-8823	N49880 43-1952	17.10.89	C.S.Tolchard *(As "31952" in US Army c/s)*	Earls Colne	20. 6.02P
G-BRPS	Cessna 177B Cardinal	17702101	N34935	23.10.89	R.C.Tebbett	Shobdon	19. 3.05
G-BRPT*	Rans S-10 Sakota (Rotax 532)	PFA 194-11554		18.10.89	B.G.Morris *(Cancelled 6.3.02 as WFU) (Noted 11.02)*	Crowfield	17. 6.00P
G-BRPU	Beech 76 Duchess	ME-140	N6007Z	17.10.89	Leeds Flying School Ltd	Leeds-Bradford	4.10.04T
G-BRPV	Cessna 152 II	15285228	N6311Q	6.11.89	GEM Rewinds Ltd	Coventry	7. 3.05T
G-BRPX	Taylorcraft BC-12D (Continental A65)	6462	N39208 NC39208	12.12.89	R.A.C.Lees tr The BRPX Group	Leicester	11. 9.03P
G-BRPY	Piper PA-15 Vagabond (Continental C85)	15-141	N4356H NC4356H	23.10.09	J. & V.Hobday	(Preston)	13. 6.02P
G-BRPZ	Luscombe 8A Silvaire (Continental A65)	911	N22089 NC22089	13.12.89	S.L. & J.P.Waring	Shacklewell Lodge, Empingham	30. 5.02P
G-BRRA	Supermarine 361 Spitfire LF.IXc *(Regd as c/n CBAF.8185)*	CBAF.IX.1875	Belg AF SM.29 R.Neth AF H.59/H.119/Fokker B-1/MK912	10.10.89	Historic Flying Ltd *(As "MK912/SH-L" of 350 (Belgian) Squadron)*	Duxford	19. 9.03P
G-BRRB*	Luscombe 8E Silvaire (Continental C85)	2611	N71184 NC71184	23.10.89	G.Crocker *(Cancelled 13.9.01 by CAA)*	(Southampton)	14. 5.00P
G-BRRD	Scheibe SF-25B Falke	4811	D-KBAT	30.10.89	R.M.Murray tr The G-BRRD Syndicate	Hinton in the Hedges	9. 5.04
G-BRRF*	Cameron O-77 HAB	2101		24.10.89	D.G.Body *"Daisy Chain"* tr Mid-Bucks Farmers Balloon Group *(Cancelled 10.4.02 as WFU)*	Leighton Buzzard	25. 3.00T
G-BRRG	Glaser-Dirks DG-500M	5E7-M5		7.11.89	D.C.Chaplin *"492"* tr Glider Syndicate	Sutton Bank	16.10.03
G-BRRJ	Piper PA-28RT-201T Turbo Arrow IV	28R-8431021	N4353T	27.11.89	M.Stower	Elstree	6. 7.05
G-BRRK	Cessna 182Q Skylane II	18266160	N759PW	30.10.89	Werewolf Aviation Ltd	Elstree	7. 5.05
G-BRRL	Piper PA-18 Super Cub 95 (L-18C-PI) *(Regd using paperwork of wrecked D-EMKE [18-2050])*	18-1615	G-AYPO(1) ALAT 18-1615/51-15615	17. 9.90	A.J.White tr Acebell G-BRRL Syndicate *(On rebuild 4.93: current status unknown)*	Whitehall Farm, Benington	
G-BRRN	Piper PA-28-161 Warrior II	28-8216043	N84533	30.10.89	Bonway Ltd	(London NW4)	17. 2.05T
G-BRRO	Cameron N-77 HAB	2142		30.10.89	B.Birch *"Newbury Building Society II"*	Bath	12. 9.03A
G-BRRR	Cameron V-77 HAB	2070		13.10.89	K.P.& G.J Storey *"Breezy"*	(Sawbridgeworth)	27. 7.03A
G-BRRS	Pitts S-1S Special (Lycoming O-360)	TM-1	N18TM	1.11.89	R.C.Atkinson *(Stored 5.95: current status unknown)*	Ranksborough Farm, Langham	25. 6.93P
G-BRRU	Colt 90A HAB	1591		1.11.89	Reach For The Sky Ltd	Guildford	26. 7.03T
G-BRRW	Cameron O-77 HAB	2125		7.11.89	D.V.Fowler *"Mobiloon"*	Cranbrook	5. 4.03T
G-BRRY	Robinson R22 Beta	1193		14.11.89	P.W.Vellacott	Thruxton	7. 1.05T
G-BRSA(2)	Cameron N-56 HAB	2113		8.11.89	C.Wilkinson	Newcastle	17.10.92A
G-BRSC(2)	Rans S-10 Sakota (Rotax 532)	0589.051		8.11.89	P.Wilkinson *(Stored 12.01)*	Blackpool	12. 8.97P
G-BRSE(2)	Piper PA-28-161 Warrior II	28-8016276	N8163R	5.12.89	Aerohire Ltd *(Op Devon School of Flying)*	Dunkeswell	6. 3.05T
G-BRSF(2)*	Supermarine 361 Spitfire HF.IXc	56332	SAAF RR232	2.11.89	J.Peace *(Cancelled 23.6.94 by CAA) (As "RR232": on rebuild 10.01)*	(Exeter)	
	(Composite inc tail/parts ex Mk.VIII/JF629 from W.Australia & wings ex Mk.XIV/R.Thai AF U14-6/93/RAF RM873)						
G-BRSG(2)	Piper PA-28-161 Cadet	2841285	N92011	23.11.89	J.Appleton t/a Holmes Rentals *(Op Denham School of Flying)*	Denham	4. 1.05T
G-BRSH(2)	CASA I-131E Jungmann *(C/n also reported as 2140: Spanish AF serial conflicts with F-AZGG)*	2156	E3B-540	29.11.89	L.Ness *(As "781-25" in Spanish AF c/s)*	(Nannestad, Norway)	9. 5.03P
G-BRSJ(2)	Piper PA-38-112 Tomahawk II	38-81A0044	N25664	29.12.89	APB Leasing Ltd	Welshpool	25. 3.05T
G-BRSK	Boeing-Stearman B75N1 (N2S-3) Kaydet (Continental W670)	75-1180	N5565N Bu.3403	15.11.89	C.R.Lawrence t/a Wymondham Engineering *(On rebuild 12.01)*	(Wymondham)	20. 1.97
G-BRSN	Rand Robinson KR-2 (Volkswagen 1834)	PFA 129-11178		10.11.89	K.W.Darby	(Teignmouth)	
G-BRSO	CFM Streak Shadow K.133-SA & PFA 161A-11601 (Rotax 618)			16.11.89	D.J.Smith	Old Sarum	14.11.03P

Reg	Type	c/n	Prev id	Date	Owner/Operator	Location	CofA
G-BRSP	Air Command 532 Elite (Rotax 532)	0626 & PFA G/04-1158		13.11.89	G.M. Hobman	(York)	10. 1.92P
G-BRSW	Luscombe 8AC Silvaire (Continental A75)	3249	N71822 NC71822	15.11.89	P.H.Needham tr Bloody Mary Aviation *"Bloody Mary"*	Fenland	25. 6.03P
G-BRSX	Piper PA-15 Vagabond (Continental A65)	15-117	N4334H NC4334H	27.10.89	P.M.Newman Stoneacre Farm, Farthing Corner		4. 9.03P
G-BRSY	Hatz CB-1 (Lycoming O-290-D)	6	N2257J	15.11.89	J.P.Barrett t/a G.A.Barrett & Son	Breighton	23. 9.03P
G-BRTD	Cessna 152 II	15280023	N757UW	11. 1.90	R.G.Prince, T.G.Phillips & C.Greenland tr 152 Group	Popham	21. 6.05
G-BRTH	Cameron A-180 HAB *(Replacement envelope c/n 3199 fitted 1994)*	2016		21.11.89	The Ballooning Business Ltd *"Burning Ambition II"*	Northampton	13. 7.03T
G-BRTJ	Cessna 150F	15061749	N8149S	22.11.89	Avon Aviation Ltd	Bristol	24. 5.03T
G-BRTK	Boeing-Stearman E75 (PT-13D) Kaydet (Continental W670)	75-5949	N16716 42-17786/Bu.38728	29.11.89	Eastern Stearman Ltd *(Donating parts to N52485 [75-4494] @ 12.01 - see SECTION 5)*	Rendcomb	24. 4.93
G-BRTL	MD Helicopters Hughes 369E	0356E	(F-GHLF)	5. 1.90	Crewhall Ltd	Leatherhead	31. 3.05
G-BRTM	Piper PA-28-161 Warrior II	28-8416083	N4334L	12.12.89	Oxford Aviation Services Ltd	Oxford	3. 3.05T
G-BRTP	Cessna 152 II	15281275	N49448	28.11.89	Tatenhill Aviation Ltd	Tatenhill	22. 8.05T
G-BRTT	Schweizer Hughes 269C	S.1411		29.11.89	Technical Exponents Ltd Bennetts Field, Middlesex		30. 7.05T
G-BRTV	Cameron O-77 HAB	2182		1.12.89	M.C.Gibbons *"Solitaire II"*	Bristol	12. 7.03A
G-BRTW	Glaser-Dirks DG-400	4-259		22.12.89	I.J.Carruthers	(Great Orton)	4. 4.05
G-BRTX	Piper PA-28-151 Cherokee Warrior	28-7615085	N8307C	27.12.89	J.Phelan & D.G.Scott tr Spectrum Flying Group	Belfast	19. 4.04T
G-BRTZ*	Slingsby Cadet III (Volkswagen 1600)	PFA 42-10545		24. 1.90	R.R.Walters (Midden-Zeeland, The Netherlands) *(Stored 2001: cancelled 13.2.02 by CAA)*		14. 3.97P
G-BRUA	Cessna 152 II	15281212	N49267	11. 1.90	BBC Air Ltd *(Op Abbas Air)*	Compton Abbas	5.11.05T
G-BRUB	Piper PA-28-161 Warrior II	28-8116177	N8351Y	27.12.89	Flytrek Ltd	Compton Abbas	12. 1.03
G-BRUD	Piper PA-28-181 Archer II	28-8390010	N8300S	9. 2.90	Wilkins & Wilkins (Special Auctions) Ltd RAF Henlow t/a Henlow Flying Club		18. 3.05T
G-BRUE*	Cameron V-77 HAB	2183		15.12.89	NK *(Cancelled 13.3.01 as WFU) (Noted 8.01)* NK		26. 7.99
G-BRUG	Luscombe 8E Silvaire (Continental C85)	4462	N1735K NC1735K	15.12.89	P.A.Cain & N.W.Barratt	Compton Abbas	21. 3.03P
G-BRUH	Colt 105A HAB	1650		15.12.89	D.C.Chipping *(Amended CofR 3.02)*	Grantham	29. 7.93T
G-BRUI	Piper PA-44-180 Seminole	44-7995150	N2230E G-BRUI/N2230E	15.12.89	B.J.Tucker	Kemble	4.11.05T
G-BRUJ	Boeing-Stearman A75N1 (PT-17) Kaydet (Continental R670)	75-4299	N55557 42-16136	6. 4.90	M.Walker *(As "16136/205" in USN c/s)*	Liverpool	16. 7.04T
G-BRUM	Cessna A152 Aerobat	A1520870	N4693A	12. 3.86	Aerohire Ltd	Wolverhampton	6. 9.04T
G-BRUN	Cessna 120 (Continental C85)	9294	G-BRDH N72127/NC72127	29. 8.89	O.C.Brun	Great Massingham	21. 1.03P
G-BRUO	Taylor JT.1 Monoplane (Volkswagen 1600)	PFA 55-10859		15.12.89	P.M.Beresford	Crosland Moor	8. 2.02P
G-BRUU	EAA Biplane Model P1 (Lycoming O-360)	1	N41MW N4775G	22.12.89	E.C.Murgatroyd Sackville Lodge, Riseley *(Badly damaged in accident Sackville 30.9.00) (Current status unknown)*		17. 6.98P
G-BRUV	Cameron V-77 HAB	2100		16. 8.89	T.W.& R.F.Benbrook *"biG-BRUVver"*	Romford	22.10.02A
G-BRUX	Piper PA-44-180 Seminole	44-7995151	N2245E	8. 3.79	Hambrair Ltd	Nottingham	13.12.03
G-BRVB	Stolp SA.300 Starduster Too (Lycoming O-360)	409	N33MH	21.12.89	M.N.Petchey & S.Turner	Andrewsfield	23. 7.03P
G-BRVC	Cameron N-180 HAB	2180		15.12.89	The Balloon Club Ltd	Bristol	18. 7.01T
G-BRVE	Beech D17S Traveller (UC-43-BH)	6701	N1193V NC1193V/Bu.32874/FT475/44-67724/(Bu.23689)	12. 3.90	P.A.Teichman	(London NW2)	25. 2.05
G-BRVF	Colt 77A HAB	1651		19.12.89	The Ballooning Business Ltd *(NAPS titles)* Northampton		3. 5.03T
G-BRVG	North American SNJ-7C Texan	88-17676	N830X N4134A/Bu.90678/(42-85895)	24. 1.90	D.J.Gilmour t/a Intrepid Aviation Co Goodwood *(As "27" in VS-932 Sqdn, USN c/s)*		6. 6.05
G-BRVH*	Smyth Model S Sidewinder (Lycoming O-290)	PFA 92-11251		19.12.89	I.C.White Abbeville, France *(Cancelled 24.7.02 by CAA) (Noted 7.02)*		10. 5.02P
G-BRVI	Robinson R22 Beta	1240		27.12.89	P.M.Whitaker Addingham, Bradford		12. 5.05
G-BRVJ	Slingsby Cadet III (Volkswagen 1600) *(Modified ex T.31B)*	701 & PFA 42-11382	(BGA3360) WT906	24. 1.90	B.Outhwaite	Breighton	22. 8.03P
G-BRVL	Pitts S-1C Special (Lycoming IO-320)	559H	N2NW	10. 1.90	M.F.Pocock	RAF Mona	17. 6.03P
G-BRVN	Thunder Ax7-77 HAB	1614		28.12.89	D.L.Beckwith	Northampton	19. 6.03A
G-BRVO	Aérospatiale AS350B Ecureuil	2315		3. 1.90	Ferns Surfacing Ltd	Sandhurst, Kent	6. 5.05T
G-BRVR	Barnett Rotorcraft J4B-2	216-2		20. 2.90	M.Richardson t/a Ilkeston Contractors	Ilkeston	
G-BRVS	Barnett Rotorcraft J4B-2	210-2		20. 2.90	M.Richardson t/a Ilkeston Contractors	Ilkeston	
G-BRVT	Christen Pitts S-2B Special (Lycoming AEIO-540)	5189		6. 4.90	A.Caramella & R.Woollard *"The Tart"*	Biggin Hill	14. 1.03T
G-BRVU	Colt 77A HAB	1652		4. 1.90	J.K.Woods *"Concorde Watches"*	Chatham	25. 6.02A
G-BRVY	Thunder Ax8-90 HAB	1676		9. 1.90	G.E. & J.V.Morris *"Golden Gem"*	Cheltenham	14. 6.03A
G-BRVZ	SAN Jodel D.117	433	F-BHNR	22.12.89	M.K.Titman & J.K.Millard	(Banbury)	19. 6.03P
G-BRWA	Aeronca 7AC Champion	7AC-351	N81730 NC81730	20. 3.90	D.D.Smith & J.R.Edwards Scotland Farm, Hook		23.10.03P
G-BRWD	Robinson R22 Beta	1231	N8064U	15. 1.90	R.C.Hayward t/a Rotorways Helicopters	Manston	15. 5.05
G-BRWF	Thunder Ax7-77 HAB	1200		15. 1.90	D.R.& C.L.Firkins	Tewkesbury	6. 6.02A
G-BRWO	Piper PA-28-140 Cherokee Cruiser	28-7325548	N55985	11. 1.90	Spitfire Aviation Ltd	Bournemouth	17.11.02T
G-BRWP	CFM Streak Shadow (Rotax 532)	K.122 & PFA 161A-11596		17. 1.90	R Riffin	Perth	1.10.03P
G-BRWR	Aeronca 11AC Chief (Continental A65)	11AC-1319	N9676E	17. 1.90	A.W.Crutcher	Cardiff	2. 7.03P
G-BRWT	Scheibe SF-25C-2000 Falke	44480	D-KIAY	11. 1.90	Booker Gliding Club Ltd	Booker	5. 6.05
G-BRWU	Phoenix Luton LA-4A Minor (JAP J.99) *(Officially regd as PFA 1141: correct PFA No.not known)*	PAL/1141		18. 1.90	R.B.Webber & P.K.Pike Trenchard Farm, Eggesford		4. 6.03P
G-BRWV	Brugger MB.2 Colibri (Volkswagen 1834)	PFA 43-11027		18. 1.90	R.W.Chatterton	(Grantham)	13. 6.03P

G-BRWX	Cessna 172P Skyhawk II	17274729	N53363	17. 1.90	D.A.Abels	Oaksey Park	26.10.02T
G-BRWY*	Cameron H-34 HAB	2214		17. 1.90	E.Krafft	Annweiler, Germany	17. 4.94A
					(Cancelled 6.11.01 by CAA) (Current status unknown)		
G-BRWZ*	Cameron Macaw 90SS HAB	2206		29. 1.90	Forbes Europe Inc	Balleroy, Normandy	3. 9.00
					"Capitalist Tool" (Cancelled 14.11.02 by CAA)		
G-BRXA	Cameron O-120 HAB	2217		19. 1.90	R.J.Mansfield	Bowness-on-Windemere	19. 2.01T
					(New owner 5.02)		
G-BRXB	Thunder Ax7-77 HAB	1631		18. 1.90	H.Peel	Worcester	22. 7.02A
G-BRXC	Piper PA-28-161 Warrior II	28-8416043	N4339X	19. 2.90	Oxford Aviation Services Ltd	Oxford	10. 4.05T
			N9563N				
G-BRXD	Piper PA-28-181 Archer II	28-8290126	D-EHWN	19. 2.90	D.D.Stone	Wellesbourne Mountford	29. 3.03
			N9690N/N8203E				
G-BRXE	Taylorcraft BC-12D	9459	N95059	25. 1.90	Wendy J.Durrad	Eastbach Farm, Coleford	30. 9.03P
	(Continental A65)		NC95059		*"Flying Fishes"*		
G-BRXF	Aeronca 11AC Chief	11AC-1033	N9396E	25. 1.90	C.G.Nice tr Aeronca Flying Group	Andrewsfield	22. 6.03P
	(Continental A65)		NC9396E				
G-BRXG	Aeronca 7AC Champion	7AC-3910	N85178	1. 3.90	J.D.Webb	Hill Farm, Nayland	11. 9.03P
	(Continental A65)		NC85178		tr X-Ray Golf Flying Group		
G-BRXH	Cessna 120	10462	N76068	25. 1.90	A.C.Garside tr BRXH Group	Headcorn	1. 4.03P
	(Continental C85)		NC76068				
G-BRXL	Aeronca 11AC Chief	11AC-1629	N3254E	31. 1.90	G.Taylor	Hawarden	22. 9.99P
	(Continental A65)		NC3254E		*(As "42-78044" in US Army L-3F c/s) "Fat Bullet"*		
G-BRXN	Montgomerie-Bensen B.8MR	PFA G/01-1160		31. 1.90	C.M.Frerk	Henstridge	19. 8.03P
	(Rotax 532)				*(Noted 8.02)*		
G-BRXO	Piper PA-34-200T Seneca II	34-7970149	N111ED	12. 4.90	Aviation Services Ltd	Toussus-le-Noble, France	3. 9.05
			N9618N				
G-BRXP	SNCAN Stampe SV-4C	678	N33528	2. 2.90	T.Brown	Maypole Farm, Chislet	
	(Lycoming)		F-BGGU/FrAF 678/(F-BDNX)		*(Fuselage noted on rebuild 3.00)*		
G-BRXS	Howard Special T-Minus	REC-1	N2278C	14. 2.90	A.Shuttleworth	Barton	11.11.02P
	(Lycoming O-290) *(Modified Taylorcraft BC)*						
G-BRXU	Aérospatiale AS332L Super Puma	2092	VH-BHV	6. 3.90	Bristow Helicopters Ltd *"Crail"*	Aberdeen	11. 9.04T
			G-BRXU/HC-BMZ/C-GSLO				
G-BRXV	Robinson R22 Beta	1246		7. 2.90	J.W.F. & S.M.Tuke	Headcorn	31. 5.05T
					t/a Tukair Aircraft Charter		
G-BRXW	Piper PA-24-260 Comanche	24-4069	N8621P	16. 2.90	P.A.Jenkins tr Oak Group	Coventry	18. 1.03
					(Made belly landing Coventry 31.1.02 after u/c retracted instead of flaps: damage to prop & underside)		
G-BRXY	Pietenpol Air Camper	PFA 47-11416		7. 2.90	P.S.Ganczakowski	Great Eversden	25. 6.03P
	(Continental C90)						
G-BRYI	de Havilland DHC.8-311A	256	C-GEOA	26. 3.91	Brymon Airways Ltd	Bristol	27. 3.03T
					(Chelsea Rose t/s) "Northumberland/Drigantes"		
G-BRYJ	de Havilland DHC.8-311A	319	C-GEOA	27. 3.92	Brymon Airways Ltd *"Somerset/Gwlad-yr-Haff"*	Bristol	2. 4.03T
G-BRYU	de Havilland DHC.8-311A *(Q300)*	458	(9M-PGA)	4. 4.98	Brymon Airways Ltd *(Benyhone Tartan t/s)*	Bristol	3. 4.04T
			C-GFEN				
G-BRYV	de Havilland DHC.8-311A *(Q300)*	462	(9M-PGD)	10. 4.98	Brymon Airways Ltd *(Colum t/s)*	Bristol	9. 4.04T
			C-GFHZ				
G-BRYW	de Havilland DHC.8-311A *(Q300)*	474	(9M-PG.)	26. 5.98	Brymon Airways Ltd *(Koguty Lowickie t/s)*	Bristol	24. 5.04T
			C-GDIU				
G-BRYX	de Havilland DHC.8-311A *(Q300)*	508	C-GDOE	25. 9.98	Brymon Airways Ltd	Plymouth	27. 9.04T
G-BRYY	de Havilland DHC.8-311A *(Q300)*	519	C-FDHD	11.12.98	Brymon Airways Ltd *(Rendezvous t/s)*	Plymouth	10.12.04T
G-BRYZ	de Havilland DHC.8-311A *(Q300)*	464	C-FCSG	16.10.98	Brymon Airways Ltd	Plymouth	15.10.04T
G-BRZA	Cameron O-77 HAB	2231		7. 2.90	L. & R.J.Mold *"Breezy"*	High Wycombe	12. 2.01A
					(Phil Dunson/Wycombe Insurance titles)		
G-BRZB	Cameron A-105 HAB	2212		7. 2.90	Cornwall Ballooning Adventures Ltd	Newquay	13. 3.00A
					"Headland Hotel"		
G-BRZD	HAPI Cygnet SF-2A	PFA 182-11443		8. 2.90	C.I.Coghill	Popham	15. 3.02P
	(Volkswagen 2078)						
G-BRZE	Thunder Ax7-77 HAB	1633		8. 2.90	G.V.Beckwith & F.Schoeder *"Jenlain"*	York	31. 8.97A
G-BRZG	Enstrom F-28A	169	N9053	8. 2.90	Metropolitan Services Ltd	Hawarden	7. 4.03
G-BRZI	Cameron N-180 HAB	2215		8. 2.90	C.E.Wood t/a Eastern Balloon Rides	Witham	24. 2.00T
G-BRZK	Stinson 108-2 Voyager	108-2846	N9846K	17. 4.90	P.C.G.Wyld	Booker	13. 2.03
			NC9846K		tr Voyager G-BRZK Syndicate		
G-BRZL*	Pitts S-1D Special	01	N899RN	26. 2.90	R.T.Cardwell	Challock	2. 8.96P
	(Lycoming O-360)				*(Noted on rebuild 5.00: cancelled 25.10.00 by CAA)*		
G-BRZO	Jodel D.18	PFA 169-11275		14. 2.90	J.D.Anson	(Liskeard)	
G-BRZS	Cessna 172P Skyhawk II	17275004	N54585	2.10.90	H.Hargreaves & P.F.Hughes	Blackpool	24. 2.03
					tr G-BHYP Flying Group		
G-BRZT	Cameron V-77 HAB	2241		21. 2.90	Beverley Drawbridge *"Hoopla"*	Cranbrook, Kent	19. 2.01A
G-BRZV	Colt Flying Apple SS HAB	1662		26. 2.90	Obst Vom Bodensee Marketing Gbr		14. 9.97A
						Tettnang-Siggenweiler, Germany	
G-BRZW	Rans S-10 Sakota 0789.058 & PFA 194-11932			21. 2.90	D.L.Davies	Emlyn's Field, Rhuallt	6. 8.98P
	(Rotax 532)						
G-BRZX	Pitts S-1S Special (Lycoming O-320)	711-H	N272H	22. 2.90	J.L.Dixon	Sherburn-in-Elmet	21. 4.03P
G-BRZZ	CFM Streak Shadow K.135 & PFA 161A-11628			22. 2.90	T.Mooney tr Shetland Flying Group	Sumburgh	8.10.03P
	(Rotax 532)						

G-BSAA - G-BSZZ

G-BSAI	Stoddard-Hamilton Glasair III	3102		31. 1.90	K.J. & P.J.Whitehead	Booker	28. 5.03P
G-BSAJ	CASA I-131E Jungmann	2209	E3B-209	23. 1.90	P.G.Kynsey	Headcorn	15. 7.03P
G-BSAK	Colt 21A Sky Chariot HAB	1696		26. 2.90	K.Meehan t/a Northern Flights	Much Wenlock	31. 5.03A
G-BSAS	Cameron V-65 HAB	2191		27. 2.90	J.R.Barber	King's Lynn	31. 5.03A
G-BSAV	Thunder Ax7-77 HAB	1555		26. 2.90	E.A., H.A.Evans, I.G. & C.A.Lloyd	Chesterfield	22. 6.03A
					"Burnt Savings"		

Reg	Type	C/n	Prev id	Date	Owner/Operator	Location	Date
G-BSAW	Piper PA-28-161 Warrior II	28-8216152	N8203C YV-2265P/N8203C	27. 2.90	Carill Aviation Ltd	Southampton	6. 8.05T
G-BSAZ	Denney Kitfox Model 2	602 & PFA 172-11664	(G-BRVW)	5. 3.90	A.J.Lloyd, D.M.Garrett & J.T.Lane	(Bromyard)	26. 6.97P
G-BSBA	Piper PA-28-161 Warrior II	28-8016041	N2574U	1. 3.90	London Transport Flying Club Ltd	Fairoaks	15. 5.03T
G-BSBG	CCF Harvard 4 (T-6J-CCF Texan)	CCF4-483	1753 Moz.PLAF FAP 1753/BF+053/AA+053/52-8562	5. 3.90	A.P.St.John *(As "20310/310" in RCAF c/s)*	Liverpool	15. 7.03P
G-BSBI	Cameron O-77 HAB	2245		6. 3.90	D.M.Billing *"Calibre"*	Uckfield	18. 6.03A
G-BSBK*	Colt 105A HAB	1319		6. 3.90	Zebra Ballooning Ltd *(Cancelled 18.10.01 by CAA)*	Maidstone	12. 6.97T
G-BSBN	Thunder Ax7-77 HAB	1531		6. 3.90	B.Pawson *"Venus"*	Cambridge	9.12.93A
G-BSBR	Cameron V-77 HAB	2247		26. 2.90	R.P.Wade *"Honey"*	Wigan	19. 9.03A
G-BSBT	Piper J-3C-65 Cub	17712	N70694 NC70694	9. 3.90	R.W.H.Watson	Grimmet Farm, Maybole	11. 2.02P
G-BSBV	Rans S-10 Sakota (Rotax 532)	1089.064 & PFA 194-11769		9. 3.90	R.G.Cameron	Muirhouses Farm, Errol	20. 7.00P
G-BSBW	Bell 206B-3 JetRanger III	3664	N43EA N6498V/9Y-THC	12. 3.90	D.T.Sharpe	Sherburn-in-Elmet	21. 8.05T
G-BSBX	Montgomerie-Bensen B.8MR (Rotax 503)	PFA G/01A-1135		12. 3.90	R.J.Roan *(Noted 7.02)*	(Peterborough)	26. 5.93P
G-BSBZ	Cessna 150M	15077093	N63086	29. 3.90	D.T.Given t/a DTG Aviation	Newtownards, Co.Down	27. 6.05T
G-BSCA	Cameron N-90 HAB	2237		12. 3.90	P.J.Marshall & M.A.Clarke *"The Graduate"*	Ruislip	12. 6.03A
G-BSCB	Air Command 532 Elite (Rotax 532)	0627 & PFA G/04-1172		16. 3.90	P.H.Smith	Nottingham	18. 9.97P
G-BSCC	Colt 105A HAB	1006		15. 3.90	Capricorn Balloons Ltd	Loughborough	11. 3.03T
G-BSCE	Robinson R22 Beta	1245		15. 3.90	H.Sugden	Humberside	17. 3.05T
G-BSCF	Thunder Ax7-77 HAB	1537		14. 3.90	V.P.Gardiner *"Charlie Farley"*	Stoke-on-Trent	22.11.02A
G-BSCG	Denney Kitfox Model 2	PFA 172-11600		23. 4.90	N.L.Beever	Sibsey	30.10.01P
G-BSCH	Denney Kitfox Model 2	510 & PFA 172-11621		16. 3.90	R.B.Wilson	(Kendal)	3.10.03P
G-BSCI	Colt 77A HAB	1683		16. 3.90	J.L. & S.Wrigglesworth *"Brody"*	Ilminster	14. 8.03A
G-BSCK	Cameron H-24 HAB	2263		16. 3.90	J.D.Shapland *"Monacle"*	Wadebridge	11. 6.95A
G-BSCM	Denney Kitfox Model 2	638 & PFA 172-11745		28. 3.90	S.A.Hewitt	Sheepcote Farm	8. 7.03P
G-BSCN	SOCATA TB-20 Trinidad	1070	D-EGTC G-BSCN	27. 3.90	B.W.Dye	Biggin Hill	1. 6.02
G-BSCO	Thunder Ax7-77 HAB	1635		6. 3.90	F.J.Whalley *"Bluebell"*	Cleish	8. 9.02A
G-BSCP	Cessna 152 II	15283289	N48135	20. 3.90	Moray Flying Club (1990) Ltd	RAF Kinloss	6.10.05T
G-BSCR*	Cessna 172M Skyhawk II	17262182	N12693	20. 3.90	London Link Flying Ltd *(Crashed Clacton 19.6.99; cancelled 21.10.99 as WFU)*	Elstree	16. 1.00T
G-BSCS	Piper PA-28-181 Cherokee Archer II	28-7890064	N47392	3. 4.90	Wingtask 1995 Ltd	Seething	16. 5.05T
G-BSCV	Piper PA-28-161 Cherokee Warrior II	28-7816135	C-GQXW	22. 3.90	S.E.Burton tr Southwood Flying Group	Earls Colne	18.10.02
G-BSCW	Taylorcraft BC-65	1798	N24461 NC24461	22. 3.90	S.Leach *(Carries "C24461" on fin)*	(Honiton)	30. 6.03P
G-BSCX	Thunder Ax8-105 HAB	1748		21. 3.90	Balloon Flights Club Ltd *"Balloon Flights"*	Leicester	14. 7.99T
G-BSCY	Piper PA-28-151 Cherokee Warrior *(Converted to '28-161 model)*	28-7515046	C-GOBE	22. 3.90	A.S.Bamrah t/a Falcon Flying Services	Lydd	15. 7.05T
G-BSCZ	Cessna 152 II	15282199	N68226	22. 3.90	A.G.Nicholson	Booker	6. 7.03T
G-BSDA	Taylorcraft BC-12D (Continental A75)	7316	N43657 NC43657	15.11.90	D.G.Edwards	Shoreham	8.10.01P
G-BSDB	Pitts S-1C Special (Lycoming O-320)	01	(N1867) N77R	22. 3.90	J.T.Mielech *(New owner 5.01)*	(Frankfurt, Germany)	31. 5.99P
G-BSDD	Denney Kitfox Model 2	639 & PFA 172-11797		28. 3.90	D.C.Crawley *(New owner 6.02)*	(Calverton, Notts)	21. 6.96P
G-BSDH	Robin DR400/180 Regent	1980		18. 4.90	R.L.Brucciani	Leicester	7. 5.05
G-BSDI	Corben Junior Ace Model E (Continental A75)	3961	N91706	28. 3.90	T.K.Pullen & A.J.Staplehurst	Eaglescott	23.10.02P
G-BSDJ	Piper J-4E Cub Coupe (Continental C85)	4-1456	N35975 NC35975	13. 2.91	B.M.Jackson	(Thame)	29. 1.02P
G-BSDK	Piper J-5A Cub Cruiser (Continental A75)	5-175	N30337 NC30337	28. 3.90	S.Haughton & I.S.Hodge Field Farm, Great Missenden		4. 6.03P
G-BSDL	SOCATA TB-10 Tobago	156		7.10.80	P.Middleton & G.Corbin tr Delta Lima Group	Sherburn-in-Elmet	14. 6.03
G-BSDN	Piper PA-34-200T Seneca II	34-7970335	N2893A	2. 4.90	McCormick Consulting Ltd	Manchester	20. 6.05T
G-BSDO	Cessna 152 II	15281661	N65894	23. 5.90	L.W.Scattergood	Sherburn-in-Elmet	13. 7.03T
G-BSDP	Cessna 152 II	15280268	N24468	11. 6.90	I.S.H.Paul *(Op The Pilot Centre)*	Denham	27. 7.03T
G-BSDS	Boeing-Stearman E75 (PT-13A) Kaydet (Continental W670)	75-118	N57852 38-470	6. 4.90	A.Basso *(As "118" in US Army c/s)*	Biel, Switzerland	13. 5.03
G-BSDV	Colt 31A HAB	1722		30. 3.90	C.D.Monk *(Active 2001)*	Bath	8. 9.03A
G-BSDW	Cessna 182P Skylane II	18264688	N9125M	9. 4.90	Parker Diving Ltd	(Helston)	30. 5.05T
G-BSDX	Cameron V-77 HAB	2050		30. 3.90	D.K.Fish	Bedford	
	(Canopy fitted to G-SNOW and rebuilt with G-SNOW's original canopy, c/n 541)						
G-BSDZ	Enstrom 280FX	2051	OO-MHV (OO-JMH)/G-ODSC/G-BSDZ	3. 4.90	Avalon Group Ltd	Hawarden	25. 7.05
G-BSED	Piper PA-22-160 Tri-Pacer *(Hoerner wing-tips: tail-wheel conversion)*	22-6377	N9404D	7. 6.90	Tayflite Ltd	Perth	5. 9.03
G-BSEE	Rans S-9 (Rotax 532)	PFA 196-11635		2. 3.90	P.M.Semler	Buttermilk Farm, Easton Maudit	26.11.01P
G-BSEF	Piper PA-28-180 Cherokee C	28-1846	N7831W	18. 4.90	I.D.Wakeling Franklyns Field, Chewton Mendip		4.11.02
G-BSEG	Ken Brock KB-2 (Rotax 582) *(C/n possibly PFA G/06-1106)*	PFA G/01-1106		3. 4.90	S.J.M.Ledingham	Carlisle	2. 7.02P
G-BSEJ	Cessna 150M Commuter	15076261	N66767	4. 5.90	I.Shackleton	Wolverhampton	19.11.05T
G-BSEK	Robinson R22	0027	N45AD N90193	10. 4.90	Helicentre Ltd	Blackpool	28. 4.05T
G-BSEL	Slingsby T.61G Super Falke	1986		31. 3.80	T.Holloway tr RAFGSA *(Op Bannerdown Gliding Club)*	RAF Keevil	23. 5.04
G-BSEP	Cessna 172	46555	N6455E	12. 4.90	R.J.Watts tr EP Aviation	Biggin Hill	15. 3.05
G-BSER	Piper PA-28-160 Cherokee	B28-790	N5665W	19. 4.90	Yorkair Ltd	Sandtoft	17. 7.03T

Reg	Type	C/n	Prev id	Date	Owner/Operator	Location	Date
G-BSET	Beagle B.206 Basset CC.1	B.006	XS765	3.12.86	Lawgra (No.386) Ltd t/a International Aerospace Engineering (As "XS765" in RAF Transport Command c/s)	Cranfield	28. 7.98
G-BSEU	Piper PA-28-181 Cherokee Archer II	28-7890108	N47639	1. 5.90	Euro Aviation 91 Ltd	Blackbushe	25. 5.05
G-BSEV	Cameron O-77 HAB	2271		20. 4.90	The Ballooning Business Ltd	Northampton	12. 5.00A
G-BSEY	Beech A36 Bonanza	E-1873	N1809F	17. 5.90	K.Phillips Ltd	Coventry	10. 9.05
G-BSFA	Aero Designs Pulsar (Rotax 582) *(Tricycle u/c)*	176 & PFA 202-11754		18. 4.90	S.Eddison & R.Minett	Gloucestershire	7. 7.03P
G-BSFB	CASA I-131E Jungmann Srs.2000	2053	E3B-449	27. 4.90	C.D.Beal *(As "S5+B06" in Luftwaffe c/s)*	Andrewsfield	2. 1.03P
G-BSFD	Piper J-3C-65 Cub	16037	N88419 NC88419	25. 5.90	AJD Engineering Ltd	Milden	19.10.01P
G-BSFE	Piper PA-38-112 Tomahawk II	38-82A0033	N91452	26. 4.90	D.J.Campbell	Glasgow	19. 3.03T
G-BSFF	Robin DR400/180R Remorqueur	1295	D-ELMM	20. 4.90	Lasham Gliding Society Ltd	Lasham	11. 7.05
G-BSFK	Piper PA-28-161 Warrior II	28-8516062	N6918D	1. 5.90	Oxford Aviation Services Ltd	Oxford	10. 7.05T
G-BSFP	Cessna 152T	15285548	N93764	9. 5.90	Walkbury Aviation Ltd	Sibson	5. 8.05T
G-BSFR	Cessna 152 II	15282268	N68341	9. 5.90	Galair Ltd	Biggin Hill	8. 7.05T
G-BSFV	Woods Woody Pusher (Continental C85)	201	N16WP	30. 4.90	M.J.Wells *"Woody's Pusher"*	Watchford Farm, Yarcombe	7. 5.03P
G-BSFW	Piper PA-15 Vagabond (Continental A65)	15-273	N4484H NC4484H	26. 4.90	J.R.Kimberley	Bounds Farm, Ardleigh	18.12.02P
G-BSFX	Denney Kitfox Model 2	506 & PFA 172-11723		23. 4.90	H.Hedley-Lewis	Croft Farm, Defford	23. 9.03P
G-BSFY	Denney Kitfox Model 2	PFA 172-11632		16. 3.90	C.I.Bates	Long Marston	17. 4.02P
G-BSGB	Gaertner Ax4 Skyranger HAB	SR.0001		30. 3.90	B.Gaertner	Oxford	
G-BSGD	Piper PA-28-180 Cherokee E	28-5691	N3463R	4. 5.90	R.J.Cleverley	Draycott Farm, Chiseldon	6. 6.03
G-BSGF	Robinson R22 Beta	1383		1. 5.90	Hecray Co Ltd t/a Direct Helicopters	Southend	24. 6.05T
G-BSGG	Denney Kitfox Model 2 (Jabiru 2200A)	PFA 172-11666		1. 5.90	C.G.Richardson	Fulbeck, Lincs	6. 6.03P
G-BSGH	Airtour AH-56B HAB	014		1. 5.90	A.R.Hardwick *"Battle of Britain"*	Shefford	
G-BSGJ	Monnett Sonerai II (Volkswagen 1835)	300	N34WH	1. 5.90	G.A.Brady *(Noted 7.02)*	Enstone	6. 9.91P
G-BSGK	Piper PA-34-200T Seneca II	34-7870331	N36450	22. 5.90	R.Hope, M.J.Martin & B.W.Powell t/a GK Aviation	Manston	17.11.02
G-BSGL	Piper PA-28-161 Warrior II	28-8116041	N82690	10. 5.90	Keywest Air Charter Ltd *(Op Liverpool Flying School) "Liverbird V"*	Liverpool	4. 9.05T
G-BSGP	Cameron N-65 HAB	2293		1. 5.90	T.D.Gibbs	Billingshurst	27.10.03A
G-BSGR*	Boeing-Stearman E75 (PT-17) Kaydet *(Reported as c/n 75-6714 ex N66870/Bu.07110)*	75-4721	N75864 EC-ATY/N55050/42-16558	19. 6.90	A.G.Dunkerley *(Cancelled 10.3.99 by CAA) (Noted unmarked 12.00)*	Kemble	
G-BSGS	Rans S-10 Sakota (Rotax 532)	1289.076 & PFA 194-11724		9. 5.90	M.R.Parr	(Holmbrook, Cumbria)	2. 9.03P
G-BSGT	Cessna 210N Turbo Centurion II *(Reims-assembled c/n F2100020)*	21063361	LX-ATL D-EOGB/N5308A	21. 5.90	B.J.Sharpe	Booker	14. 1.06
G-BSGY	Thunder Ax7-77 HAB *(Envelope ex G-BROA c/n 1535)*	1760		18. 7.90	P.D.Kenington *"Bugsy"*	Winterbourne, Bristol	26. 7.03A
G-BSHA	Piper PA-34-200T Seneca II	34-7670216	N9707K	2. 5.90	Justgold Ltd	Blackpool	24. 7.99T
G-BSHC	Colt 69A HAB	1668		8. 5.90	Magical Adventures Ltd	West Bloomfield, Mi., USA	12.10.98A
G-BSHD	Colt 69A HAB	1736		8. 5.90	D.B.Court *"Jester"*	Ormskirk	1. 6.03A
G-BSHH	Luscombe 8E Silvaire (Continental C85)	3981	N1254K NC1254K	11. 5.90	G.M.Wightman	Shenington	5. 2.03P
G-BSHI	Luscombe 8DF Silvaire Trainer (Continental C90)	1821	N39060 NC39060	11. 5.90	Catcott Garage Ltd	Dunkeswell	14. 8.01P
G-BSHK	Denney Kitfox Model 2 (Rotax 532)	449 & PFA 172-11752		11. 5.90	D.Doyle & C.Aherne	Kildare	10. 7.03P
G-BSHO	Cameron V-77 HAB	2313		16. 5.90	D J Duckworth & C Stewart *(Peugeot/Talbot titles)*	Chesham	18. 5.03A
G-BSHS	Colt 105A HAB	1674	(D-OCAT) G-BSHS	16. 5.90	I.Novosad	Planegg, Germany	9. 9.01A
G-BSHT	Cameron V-77 HAB	2321		30. 5.90	E.C.Moore *"Buckshot II"*	Great Missenden	19. 11.03T
G-BSHV	Piper PA-18-135 Super Cub (L-18C-PI)	18-3123	OO-GDG Belg Army L-49/53-4723	16. 5.90	G.T Fisher	Northside, Thorney	20. 5.04
G-BSHY	EAA Acrosport 1 (Lycoming O-290)	PFA 72-10928		17. 4.90	R.J.Hodder	Eastfield Farm, Manby	15. 7.03P
G-BSHZ	Enstrom F-28	F427	N51702	16. 5.90	G.Birchmore	(Tiverton)	30.12.04
G-BSIC	Cameron V-77 HAB	2322		17. 5.90	J.M.& A.Cornwall	Brimington	22. 6.03A
G-BSIF	Denney Kitfox Model 2	563 & PFA 172-11886		5. 7.90	P.Annable	(Belper)	21. 3.03P
G-BSIG	Colt 21A Cloudhopper HAB	1322		18. 5.90	E.C. & A.J.Moore	Great Missenden	2.11.02A
G-BSIH	Rutan LongEz	1200-1 & PFA 74A-11492		31. 5.90	W.S.Allen	(Cheltenham)	
G-BSII	Piper PA-34-200T Seneca II	34-8070336	N8253N	16. 5.90	T Belso	Top Farm, Croydon, Royston	4. 8.02
G-BSIJ	Cameron V-77 HAB	2164		23. 5.90	A.S.Jones	Wolverhampton	19. 8.03A
G-BSIK	Denney Kitfox Model 1	51		5. 6.90	S.P.Collins	Hill Farm, Nayland	31. 1.01P
G-BSIM	Piper PA-28-181 Archer II	28-8690017	N9092Y	22. 5.90	Bobbington Air Training School Ltd	Wolverhampton	29. 8.05T
G-BSIO	Cameron Furness House 56SS HAB	2310		25. 5.90	R.E.Jones *"Pinkie"*	Lytham St.Annes	19. 3.03A
G-BSIU	Colt 90A HAB	1774		25. 5.90	S.Travaglia	Firenze, Italy	20.11.01A
G-BSIY	Schleicher ASK14	14005	5Y-AID D-KOIC	4. 6.90	E.V.Goodwin tr Winwick Flying Group	(Huntingdon)	20.10.96
G-BSIZ	Piper PA-28-181 Archer II	28-7990377	N2162Y	25. 5.90	A.M.L.Maxwell	Alderney	20. 6.05
G-BSJB	Bensen B.8	PFA G/01-1080		5. 6.90	J.W.Limbrick	(Bewdley)	
G-BSJU	Cessna 150M	15076430	N3230V	14. 6.90	A.C.Williamson *(Op Crowfield Flying Club)*	Crowfield	4. 4.04T
G-BSJW	Everett Gyroplane Srs.2 (Rotax 532)	020		6. 6.90	R.Sarwan	(Beccles)	25.10.91P
G-BSJX	Piper PA-28-161 Warrior II	28-8216084	N8036N	30. 5.90	D.A.Shields & L.C.Brekkeflat	Denham	23. 7.05T
G-BSJZ	Cessna 150J	15070485	N60661	7. 5.91	BCT Aircraft Leasing Ltd *(Op BCT Flying Club)*	Wellesbourne Mountford	25. 4.05T
G-BSKA	Cessna 150M	15076137	N66588	31. 7.90	H.Daines Electronics Ltd	(Beccles)	16. 3.03T
G-BSKD	Cameron V-77 HAB	2336		4. 6.90	M.J.Gunston *"Skulduggery"*	Camberley	29. 7.03A

Reg	Type	c/n	Prev id	Date	Owner	Location	Expiry
G-BSKE	Cameron O-84 HAB	1604	ZS-HYD	4. 6.90	S.F.Redman	(Sturminster Newton)	19. 8.03A
			G-BSKE				
G-BSKG	Maule MX-7-180 Star Rocket	11072C		7. 6.90	J.R.Surbey	Blockmoor Farm, Barway, Ely	6. 2.03
G-BSKI	Thunder Ax8-90 HAB	1623		18. 5.90	P.G.Ward	Camberley	17.10.01A
					tr G-BSKI Balloon Group *"Ski Maiden"*		
G-BSKK	Piper PA-38-112 Tomahawk	38-79A0671	N2525K	11. 6.90	A.S.Bamrah	Biggin Hill	20.11.05T
					t/a Falcon Flying Services		
G-BSKL	Piper PA-38-112 Tomahawk	38-78A0509	N4252E	11. 6.90	A.S.Bamrah	Birmingham	20.11.05T
					t/a Falcon Flying Services *(Op Warwickshire Aero Centre)*		
G-BSKO	Maule MXT-7-180 Star Rocket	14008C		7. 6.90	M.A.Ashmole	Perth	12. 5.03
G-BSKP	Supermarine 379 Spitfire F.XIVe	6S/663417	SG-31	27. 6.90	Historic Flying Ltd	Duxford	12. 6.03P
			Belg AF/RN201		*(As "RN201" in 41 Sqdn silver & red c/s)*		
G-BSKU	Cameron O-84 HAB	2330		8. 6.90	Alfred Bagnall & Sons (West) Ltd *"Bagnalls II"*	Bristol	7. 6.02A
G-BSKW	Piper PA-28-181 Archer II	2890138	N91940	1. 6.90	Shropshire Aero Club Ltd	Sleap	9. 4.03T
G-BSLA	Robin DR400/180 Regent	1997		22. 6.90	A.B.McCoig tr Robin Lima Alpha Group	Rochester	19. 3.05
G-BSLE	Piper PA-28-161 Warrior II	28-8116028	N8260L	25. 6.90	Oxford Aviation Services Ltd	Oxford	1.10.05T
G-BSLH	CASA I-131E Jungmann Srs.2000	2222	E3B-622	27. 7.90	P.Warden	Biel, Switzerland	20. 8.03P
	(Despite quoted c/n & p/i this is a new-build aircraft by Bücker Prado SL, Albacete, Spain who have acquired the rights and drawings from CASA)						
G-BSLI	Cameron V-77 HAB	2115		15. 6.90	J.D.C & F.E.Bevan *"Blackbird"*	Market Drayton	30. 7.00T
G-BSLK	Piper PA-28-161 Warrior II	28-7916018	N20849	15. 6.90	R.A.Rose	Wellesbourne Mountford	6. 4.03T
G-BSLM	Piper PA-28-160 Cherokee	28-308	N5262W	22. 6.90	A S Thorogate & K Richards	Old Sarum	6. 3.03
					tr Old Sarum Cherokee Group		
G-BSLT	Piper PA-28-161 Warrior II	28-8016303	N81817	19. 6.90	L.W.Scattergood	Old Sarum	25. 1.03T
G-BSLU	Piper PA-28-140 Cherokee	28-24733	OY-PJL	19. 6.90	D.J.Budden Ltd	Shobdon	22. 9.02
			OH-PJL/SE-FFA				
G-BSLV	Enstrom 280FX	2054	D-HHAS	26. 6.90	Keswick Outdoor Clothing Co Ltd	(Keswick)	10. 7.03T
			G-BSLV				
G-BSLW	Bellanca 7ECA Citabria	431-66	N9696S	16. 7.90	D.W.Mann tr Shoreham Citabria Group	Shoreham	6. 9.03
G-BSLX	WAR Focke-Wulf 190 rep	24	N698WW	19. 6.90	D.Featherby tr FW190 Gruppe	Norwich	2. 8.02P
					(As "1+4" in Luftwaffe c/s)		
G-BSMB	Cessna U206E Super Skywagon	U20601659	N9459G	25. 6.90	London Parachute School Ltd	Gloucestershire	9. 3.03
			C-GUUW/N9459G				
G-BSMD	SNCAN 1101 Noralpha	139	F-GDPQ	26. 6.90	R.J.Lamplough	North Weald	4. 5.96P
			F-YEEE/F-YCZK/CAN-11/Fr.Mil *(As "+14" in Luftwaffe c/s) (Stored 12.00*					
G-BSME	Bölkow Bö.208C Junior	596	D-ECGA	25. 6.90	D.J.Hampson	Fenland	17. 5.03
G-BSMG	Montgomerie-Bensen B.8M	PFA G/01-1170		22. 6.90	A.C.Timperley	(Aberfeldy)	16. 7.97P
	(Rotax 532)						
G-BSMK	Cameron O-84 HAB	2328		26. 6.90	D.F.Maine & D.M.Newton	Redditch	17. 6.03A
					tr G-BSMK Shareholders		
G-BSML	Schweizer Hughes 269C (300C)	S.1462	PH-HUH	10.10.90	K.P.Foster & B.I.Winsor	Bodmin	3. 4.03
			N134DM				
G-BSMM	Colt 31A Sky Chariot HAB	1779		27. 6.90	D.V.Fowler	Cranbrook, Kent	3.11.02A
G-BSMN	CFM Streak Shadow			26. 6.90	P.J.Porter	(Wincanton)	16. 9.03P
	(Rotax 582)	K.137-SA & PFA 161A-11656					
G-BSMO	Denney Kitfox (Rotax 582)	PFA 172-11773		16. 7.90	R.H.Taylor tr Kitfox Group	Seething	3. 4.03P
G-BSMS	Cameron V-77 HAB	2356		26. 6.90	Sade Balloons Ltd *"Sadie"*	Coulsdon	1. 6.02A
G-BSMT	Rans S-10 Sakota	1289.077 & PFA 194-11793		29. 6.90	P.J.Barker	Romney Street, Sevenoaks	6. 3.03P
	(Rotax 532)						
G-BSMU	Rans S-6 Coyote II	1089.090 & PFA 204-11732	G-MWJE	27. 6.90	G.C.Hutchinson	(Bedale)	12.11.02P
G-BSMV	Piper PA-17 Vagabond	17-94	N4696H	29. 6.90	A.Cheriton *"Sophie"*	Wellesbourne Mountford	5. 3.03P
	(Continental C85)		NC4696H				
G-BSMX	Bensen B.8MR	PFA G/01-1171		3. 7.90	J.S.E.R.McGregor	(Birmingham)	
					(Current status unknown)		
G-BSND	Air Command 532 Elite	PFA G/04-1180		16. 7.90	B Gunn & W.B.Lumb	Melrose Farm, Melbourne	
					(New owner 4.02)		
G-BSNE	Luscombe 8E Silvaire	5757	N1130B	2.11.90	N.Reynolds & C.Watts	(Guildford)	5. 8.03P
	(Continental C85)		NC1130B				
G-BSNF	Piper J-3C-65 Cub	3070	N23317	17. 8.90	D.A.Hammant	Bere Farm, Warnford, Southampton	17. 9.03P
	(Continental O-200-A) *(Frame No.3116)*		NC23317 *(Lippert Reed conversion)*					
G-BSNG	Cessna 172N Skyhawk II	17270192	N738SB	19. 7.90	A.J. & P.C.MacDonald	Edinburgh	4.11.05T
G-BSNJ	Cameron N-90 HAB	2335		6. 7.90	D.P.H.Smith	(France)	13. 5.03A
G-BSNL	Bensen B.8MR	PFA G/01-1181		16. 7.90	A.C.Breane	(Balleybofey, Co.Donegal)	20. 7.97P
	(Rotax 532)				*(Amended CofR 9.02)*		
G-BSNN*	Rans S-10 Sakota	PFA 194-11846		31. 7.90	O. & S.D.Barnard	Leicester	27. 6.00P
	(Rotax 532)				*(Noted 1.02: cancelled 9.4.02 by CAA)*		
G-BSNO*	Denney Kitfox	PFA 172-11813		29. 6.90	Not known	East Fortune	
	(Damaged Sweethope Farm, Kelso 9.7.97: cancelled 18.11.97 as destroyed) (Stored 2001)						
G-BSNP	Piper PA-28R-201T Turbo Cherokee Arrow III	28R-7703236	N38537	18. 7.90	D.F.K.Singleton	(Teck, Germany)	24. 9.05
G-BSNR	British Aerospace BAe 146 Srs.300	E3165	EC-FGT	13. 7.90	KLM UK Ltd *(Op Buzz)*	Stansted	20.11.03T
			EC-807/G-6-165/G-BSNR/N886DV/G-BSNR/(N886DV)/G-6-165					
G-BSNT	Luscombe 8A Master	1679	N37018	16. 7.90	P.K.Jordan	Stoneacre Farm, Farthing Corner	19. 2.03P
	(Built as 8C) (Continental A65)		NC37018		tr Luscombe Quartet		
G-BSNU	Colt 105A HAB	1811		23. 7.90	M.P.Rich tr Gone Ballooning *(New owner 1.03)*	Bristol	2. 2.97A
G-BSNV	Boeing 737-4Q8	25168		5. 2.92	British Airways plc	Gatwick	18. 2.05T
G-BSNW	Boeing 737-4Q8	25169		12. 3.92	British Airways plc	Gatwick	19. 3.05T
G-BSNX	Piper PA-28-181 Archer II	28-7990311	N3028S	19. 7.90	Halfpenny Green Flight Centre Ltd	Wolverhampton	21. 8.05T
G-BSNY	Bensen B.8M	PFA G/01-1176		16. 7.90	H.McCartney	Newtownards, Co.Down	6. 9.01P
	(Arrow GT500R)						
G-BSNZ	Cameron O-105 HAB	2364		16. 7.90	Zebedee Balloon Service Ltd	Hungerford	21. 9.02A
G-BSOE	Luscombe 8A Silvaire	4331	N1604K	22. 8.90	S.B.Marsden	Sturgate	
	(C/n would indicate Model 8E)		NC1604K		*(Stored dismantled as "N1604K" 4.00: current status unknown)*		
G-BSOF	Colt 25A Sky Chariot Mk.II HAB	1820		27. 7.90	L P Hooper *(Noted 1.02)*	Bristol	7.11.03A
G-BSOG	Cessna 172M Skyhawk II	17263636	N1508V	16. 7.90	B.Chapman & A.R.Budden	Goodwood	12.12.02

G-BSOJ	Thunder Ax7-77 HAB		1818	JA-... G-BSOJ	31. 7.90	R.J.S.Jones	Stourbridge	22. 4.03A
G-BSOK	Piper PA-28-161 Cherokee Warrior II	28-7816191		N9749K	19. 7.90	Aeros Leasing Ltd	Gloucestershire	20. 1.03T
G-BSOM	Glaser-Dirks DG-400		4-126	LN-GMC D-KGDG	12. 7.90	M.J.Watson tr G-BSOM Group *"403"*	Rufforth	4. 4.03
G-BSON	Green S-25 HAB		001		7. 6.90	J.J.Green *(Current status unknown)*	Newbury	
G-BSOO	Cessna 172F		17252431	N8531U	19. 7.90	P.W.Lawrence tr Double Oscar Flying Group	Seething	6.11.05
G-BSOR	CFM Streak Shadow K.131-SA & PFA 161A-11602 (Rotax 532)				23.10.89	A.Parr	(London W1)	9. 4.03P
G-BSOT	Piper PA-38-112 Tomahawk II	38-81A0053		N25682	23. 7.90	APB Leasing Ltd	Welshpool	26. 9.05T
	(Veered off runway landing Welshpool 6.9.01: damage to engine cowling, undercarriage & both wings)							
G-BSOU	Piper PA-38-112 Tomahawk II	38-81A0130		N23373	23. 7.90	D.J.Campbell	Glasgow	10. 9.00T
G-BSOX	Luscombe 8AE Silvaire (Continental C85)		2318	N45791 NC45791	7. 8.90	R.S.Lanary *"Bobby Sox"*	Sixpenny Handley, Dorset	19. 5.03P
G-BSOY	Piper PA-34-220T Seneca III		3433155	OY-CEU	1. 8.90	BAE Systems Flight Training (UK) Ltd	(Perth)	8. 4.04T
G-BSOZ	Piper PA-28-161 Warrior II	28-7916080		N30220	14. 8.90	The Moray Flying Club 1990	RAF Kinloss	28.12.05T
G-BSPA	QAC Quickie Q.2 (Revmaster R2100DQ)		2227	N227T	16. 8.90	G.V.Mckirdy & B.K.Glover	Enstone	21. 8.01P
G-BSPB	Thunder Ax8-84 HAB		1803		24. 7.90	Nigs Pertwee Ltd	Frinton-on-Sea	22. 9.00T
G-BSPC*	SAN Jodel D.140C Mousquetaire III		150	F-BMFN	2.11.81	Not known	Headcorn	31.10.85
	(Cancelled 15.8.94 by CAA) (On overhaul 9.97: derelict remains noted 10.00)							
G-BSPE	Reims/Cessna F172P Skyhawk II	F17202073			31.12.80	T.W.Williamson	(Richmond)	17. 6.05
G-BSPF*	Cessna T303 Crusader	T30300100		OY-SVH N3116C	31. 7.90	K P Gibben tr G-BSPF Crusader Group	Blackpool	
	(Crashed Burton Joyce, Notts 16.7.98: cancelled 25.8.98 as WFU:) (Wreck noted 12.01)							
G-BSPG	Piper PA-34-200T Seneca II	34-8070168		N8176S	8. 8.90	D.P.Hughes	Elstree	4.11.02
G-BSPI	Piper PA-28-161 Warrior II	28-8116025		N8258V	26. 7.90	Halegreen Associates Ltd	Hinton in the Hedges	9. 4.04T
G-BSPJ	Bensen B.8	PFA G/01-1061			3. 8.90	C.M.Jones	Carlisle	8. 1.03P
G-BSPK	Cessna 195A (Jacobs R-755-9)		7691	N1079D	14. 8.90	A.G. & D.L.Bompas	Biggin Hill	25. 4.03
G-BSPL	CFM Streak Shadow (Rotax 582)	K.140-SA			26. 7.90	R.D.Davidson	Perth	19. 3.03P
G-BSPM	Piper PA-28-161 Warrior II	28-8116046		N82679	27. 7.90	White Waltham Airfield Ltd *(Op West London Aero Services)*	White Waltham	11.10.03T
G-BSPN	Piper PA-28R-201T Turbo Cherokee Arrow III 28R-7703171			N5965V	31. 7.90	V.E.H.Taylor	(Carmarthen)	10. 1.03
G-BSPW*	Avid Speed Wing (Rotax 582)	PFA 189-11840			17. 7.90	M J Sewell *(Cancelled 20.9.00 by CAA) (Stored 12.01)*	Blackpool	27. 5.94P
G-BSPX	Neico Lancair 320 521-320-259FB & PFA 191-11865				31. 7.90	C.H.Skelt *(Current status unknown)*	(Reigate)	
G-BSRH	Pitts S-1C Special (Lycoming O-360)	LS-2		N4111	7. 8.90	M.R.Janney *(Carries "N4111" on rudder)*	Redhill	22. 6.03P
G-BSRI	Nelco Lancair 235 (Lycoming O-235) *(Tricycle u/c)*	PFA 191-11467			9. 8.90	G.Lewis	Liverpool	1. 8.03P
G-BSRJ	Colt AA-1050 Gas Balloon		1782		20. 8.90	Trezpark Ltd *"White Fang"* *(Op D Levin)*	Boulder, Colorado, USA	16. 8.32A
G-BSRK	ARV1 Super 2 (Hewland AE75)	K.007		ZK-FSQ	8. 8.90	D.M.Blair	RAF Mona	1. 6.03P
G-BSRL	Campbell Cricket Mk.4 rep	PFA G/03-1325			8. 8.90	I.Rosewall	Henstridge	17. 4.03P
	(Regd as, and rebuilt from, Everett Gyroplane Srs.2 c/n 0022 - converted by Peter Lovegrove)							
G-BSRP	Rotorway Executive (Rotorway RW 152)		3824		15. 8.90	R.J.Baker	Hawarden	8. 8.02P
G-BSRR	Cessna 182Q Skylane II		18266915	N96961	25. 7.90	C.M.Moore	(Buckingham)	10. 7.03
G-BSRT	Denney Kitfox Model 2	742 & PFA 172-11873			9. 8.90	A.J.Lloyd	Little Down Farm, Milson	18. 8.03P
G-BSRX	CFM Streak Shadow K.148-SA & PFA 206-11870 (Rotax 618)				15. 8.90	P.Williams	Netherthorpe	22. 5.03P
G-BSRZ	Air Command 532 Elite Two-Seat PFA G/05-1188				15. 8.90	A.S.G.Crabb *(Current status unknown)*	(Buxton)	
G-BSSA	Luscombe 8E Silvaire (Continental C85)		4176	N1449K NC1449K	15. 8.90	K.R.Old tr Luscombe Flying Group	White Waltham	12. 5.03P
G-BSSB	Cessna 150L Commuter		15074147	N19076	15. 8.90	D.T.A.Rees	Haverfordwest	14. 6.03T
G-BSSC	Piper PA-28-161 Warrior II	28-8216176		N81993 N9529N/N8234B	15. 8.90	Oxford Aviation Services Ltd	Gloucestershire	9. 2.03T
G-BSSE	Piper PA-28-140 Cherokee Cruiser	28-7525192		N33440	22.10.90	Comed Aviation Ltd	Blackpool	19. 5.05T
G-BSSF	Denney Kitfox Model 2	738 & PFA 172-11796			15. 8.90	A.M.Hemmings	Sandtoft	20.11.03P
G-BSSI	Rans S-6 Coyote II	0190.112 & PFA 204-11782		(G-MWJA)	17. 8.90	J.Currell *(New owner 9.01)*	(Bangor, Belfast)	16.11.99P
	(Rotax 582) *(Tricycle u/c)*							
G-BSSK	QAC Quickie Q.200 (Continental O-200-A)	PFA 94A-11354			5. 9.90	D.G.Greatrex *(Current status unknown)*	Enstone	23. 9.99P
G-BSSO	Cameron O-90 HAB		2255		23. 7.90	R.R. & J.E.Hatton *"Just So"*	Bristol	28. 6.03A
G-BSSP	Robin DR400/180R Remorqueur		2015		24. 9.90	Soaring (Oxford) Ltd *(Op Air Cadets Gliding School)*	RAF Syerston	8. 1.06
G-BSSV	CFM Streak Shadow K.129-SA & PFA 206-11657 (Rotax 532)				21. 8.90	R.W.Payne *(Current status unknown)*	Eddsfield	5. 5.98P
G-BSSW	Piper PA-28-161 Cherokee Warrior II	28-7816143		N47850	29. 8.90	R.L.Hayward *(Op Bristol Flying Club)*	Filton	5. 9.05T
G-BSSX	Piper PA-28-161 Warrior II	2816056		N9141H	11. 9.90	Airways Aero Associations Ltd *(Op British Airways Flying Club)*	Booker	14.12.05T
G-BSTC	Aeronca 11AC Chief (Continental A65)	11AC-1660		N3289E NC3289E	15.10.90	J Armstrong & D Lamb *(Damaged Henstridge 18.4.93: on rebuild 12.95: new owners 1.02)*	(Crook)	26. 6.93P
G-BSTE	Aérospatiale AS355F2 Twin Squirrel	5453			29. 8.90	Hygrade Foods Ltd	Biggin Hill	10. 8.03
G-BSTH	Piper PA-25-235 Pawnee C	25-5009		N8599L	25. 9.90	Scottish Gliding Union Ltd	Portmoak	15. 3.03
G-BSTI	Piper J-3C-65 Cub (Continental C85) *(Frame No.19073)*	19144		N6007H NC6007H	31. 8.90	G.L.Nunn & J.D.Barwick	North Lopham	5. 2.03P
G-BSTK	Thunder Ax8-90 HAB		1838		17. 9.90	M.Williams	Wadhurst, East Sussex	4. 5.95A
G-BSTL	Rand Robinson KR-2	PFA 129-11863			6. 9.90	C.S.Hales	Shenington	27. 6.03P
	(May incorporate G-BYLP qv)							

Reg	Type	C/n	Prev id	Date	Owner/Operator	Location	Date
G-BSTM	Cessna 172L Skyhawk	17260143	N4243Q	25. 9.90	A.H.Windle tr G-BSTM Group	Cambridge	1. 3.03
G-BSTO	Cessna 152 II	15282133	N68005	4. 9.90	Plymouth School of Flying Ltd	Plymouth	5.12.05T
G-BSTP	Cessna 152 II	15282925	N89953	4. 9.90	Cobham Leasing Ltd	Bournemouth	4.11.02T
G-BSTR	Grumman-American AA-5 Traveler	AA5-0688	OO-ALR	8.10.90	James Allan (Aviation & Engineering) Ltd		
			OO-HAN/(OO-WAZ)			Sorbie Farm, Kingsmuir	4.12.02
G-BSTT	Rans S-6 Coyote II	0190.115 & PFA 204-11880		5. 9.90	D.G.Palmer	Fetterangus	2.12.02P
	(Rotax 582)						
G-BSTV	Piper PA-32-300 Cherokee Six	32-40378	N4069R	13. 9.90	B.C.Hudson *(Open store 7.00)*	Popham	
G-BSTX	Luscombe 8A Silvaire	3301	EI-CDZ	10. 9.90	G.R.Nicholson	(Newry, Co.Armagh)	29.11.02P
			G-BSTX/N71874/NC71874				
G-BSTY	Thunder Ax8-90 HAB	394		12. 9.90	M.V.Farrant tr Shere Balloon Group *"Beastie"*	Billingshurst	19. 8.03A
G-BSTZ	Piper PA-28-140 Cherokee Cruiser	28-7725153	N1674H	10.10.90	Air Navigation & Trading Co Ltd	Blackpool	18.11.02T
G-BSUA	Rans S-6 Coyote II	PFA 204-11910		29.10.90	A.J.Todd	Abbey Warren Farm, Bucknall, Lincoln	4. 9.03P
	(Rotax 582)						
G-BSUB	Colt 77A HAB	1801		30.10.90	R.R.J.Wilson & M.P.Hill	Bristol	6. 4.03A
G-BSUD	Luscombe 8A Master	1745	N37084	14. 9.90	I.G.Harrison	Eggington, Derby	18.12.02P
	(Continental A65)		NC37084				
G-BSUE	Cessna U206G Stationair II	U20604334	N756TB	6. 9.90	R.A.Robinson	Little Gransden	7. 3.04
G-BSUF	Piper PA-32RT-300 Lance II	32R-7885240	N32PL	17. 9.90	S.T.Laffin	Blackbushe	21. 8.03
			ZP-PJQ/N9641N				
G-BSUH*	Cessna 140	8092	N89088	15.10.90	Not known	Abbeyshrule, Co.Longford	2. 5.94
	(Continental C85)		NC89088		*(Damaged Gowran Grange 6.93: cancelled 28.4.95 by CAA) (Airframe stored 5.00)*		
G-BSUJ	Brugger MB.2 Colibri	PFA 43-10726		17. 9.90	M.A.Farrelly	(Liverpool)	
G-BSUK	Colt 77A HAB	1374		21. 9.90	A.J.Moore	Northwood, Middlesex	2. 8.94A
G-BSUO	Scheibe SF-25C-2000 Falke	44501	D-KIOK	6.12.90	British Gliding Association Ltd	Bicester	22. 6.03
G-BSUR	Rotorway Executive 90	5003		21. 9.90	D.J.Kelly	(Mullingar, Co.Westmeath)	1.12.93P
	(Rotorway RI 162)				*(New owner 7.02)*		
G-BSUT	Rans S-6ESA Coyote II *(Tricycle u/c)*			2.10.90	J.Bell	Barton	15. 1.03P
	(Rotax 582)	0990.138 & PFA 204-11897					
G-BSUV	Cameron O-77 HAB	2407		26. 9.90	R.Moss	Banchory	8. 9.02A
G-BSUW	Piper PA-34-200T Seneca II	34-7870081	N2360M	26. 9.90	TG Aviation Ltd *(Op Thanet Flying Club)*	Manston	20.12.02T
G-BSUX	Carlson Sparrow II	PFA 209-11794		5.10.90	J.Stephenson	Wombleton	9. 6.03P
	(Rotax 532)						
G-BSUZ	Denney Kitfox Model 3	745 & PFA 172-11875		10. 9.90	M.J.Clark	Sedgwick	3. 9.02P
	(Rotax 582) *(Converted from Model 2)*						
G-BSVB	Piper PA-28-181 Archer II	2890098	N9155S	10. 9.90	K.A.Boost	(Broxbourne)	16. 1.03T
G-BSVE	Binder CP.301S Smaragd	113	HB-SED	27. 9.90	R.E.Perry tr Smaragd Flying Group	Halesland	26.11.03P
G-BSVG	Piper PA-28-161 Warrior II	28-8516013	C-GZAV	2.10.90	Airways Aero Associations Ltd	Booker	22.12.05T
					(Op British Airways Flying Club) (Colum t/s)		
G-BSVH	Piper J-3C-65 Cub	15360	N87702	2.10.90	A.R.Meakin	Eastbach Farm, Coleford	13. 8.01P
	(Continental A75) *(Frame No.15003)*		NC87702				
G-BSVI	Piper PA-16 Clipper	16-186	N5379H	7.11.90	I.R.Blakemore *"Spirit of St.Petersburg"*	Old Sarum	1.11.05
G-BSVK	Denney Kitfox Model 2	PFA 172-11731		2.10.90	C.M.Looney	(Leatherhead)	5. 4.94P
G-BSVM	Piper PA-28-161 Warrior II	28-8116173	N8351N	7.11.90	EFG Flying Services Ltd	Biggin Hill	2. 2.03T
G-BSVN	Thorp T-18	107	N4881	17. 9.90	J.H.Kirkham	Barton	18. 6.03P
	(Lycoming O-290)						
G-BSVP	Piper PA-23-250 Aztec F	27-7754115	N63787	9. 2.78	Transport Command Ltd	Shoreham	6. 8.05T
G-BSVR	Schweizer Hughes 269C (300C)	S.1236	OO-JWW	14.11.90	Martinair Ltd	Sherburn-in-Elmet	4. 6.04
			D-HLEB				
G-BSVS	Robin DR400/100 Cadet	2017		22.10.90	D.M.Chalmers	Upper Harford	22. 3.03
G-BSVV	Piper PA-38-112 Tomahawk	38-79A0723	N2492L	3.10.90	H & E Merkado	Panshanger	10. 6.03T
G-BSVW	Piper PA-38-112 Tomahawk	38-79A0149	N2606B	9.11.90	Cardiff Wales Aviation Services Ltd	Cardiff	25. .04T
G-BSVX	Piper PA-38-112 Tomahawk	38-79A0950	N2336P	10. 1.91	Cristal Air Ltd	Rochester	14. 5.03T
G-BSVZ	Pietenpol Air Camper	1008	N3265	6.11.90	G.F.M.Garner	(Wootton Rivers)	6. 9.93P
	(Regd as a Pietenpol/Challis Chaffinch)				*(On rebuild 2000)*		
G-BSWB	Rans S-10 Sakota	0489.046 & PFA 194-11560		8.10.90	F.A.Hewitt	Garston Farm, Marshfield	5. 6.03P
	(Rotax 532)						
G-BSWC	Boeing-Stearman E75 (PT-13D) Kaydet	75-5560	N17112	16.11.90	R.J.Thwaites	Gloucestershire	11. 9.03T
	(Lycoming R-680)		N5021V/42-17397		*(As "112" in US Army c/s)*		
G-BSWF	Piper PA-16 Clipper	16-475	N5865H	12.10.90	T.M.Storey	Newells Farm, Lower Beeding	24. 2.05
	(Lycoming O-320)						
G-BSWG	Piper PA-17 Vagabond	15-99	N4316H	8.10.90	P.E.J.Sturgeon	Queach Farm, Bury St Edmunds	24.10.03P
	(Continental A65-8)		NC4316H				
G-BSWH	Cessna 152 II	15281365	N49861	15.10.90	Airspeed Aviation Ltd	Egginton, Derby	14. 3.02T
G-BSWL	Slingsby T.61F Venture T.2	1974	EI-CCQ	15.10.90	K.Richards	Talgarth	11. 3.04
			G-BSWL/ZA655				
G-BSWM	Slingsby T.61F Venture T.2	1965	ZA629	12.10.90	P.S.Holmes tr Venture Gliding Group	Bellarena	26. 3.03
G-BSWR	Pilatus Britten-Norman BN-2T Turbine Islander			22.10.90	Police Authority for Northern Ireland	Belfast	2. 3.04T
		2245			*(Op Royal Ulster Constabulary)*		
G-BSWV	Cameron N-77 HAB	2369		22.10.90	S.Charlish *"Leicester Mercury"*	Leicester	16. 2.03A
G-BSWX	Cameron V-90 HAB	2401		22.10.90	B.J.Burrows *"Beeswax"*	Bristol	29. 6.01A
G-BSWY	Cameron N-77 HAB	2428		12.10.90	M.R.Nanda tr Nottingham Balloon Club	Nottingham	17. 8.03A
G-BSWZ	Cameron A-180 HAB	2419	C-FGWZ	22.10.90	G.C.Ludlow	Kirdford	19. 7.99T
			G-BSWZ		*(Op Balloon Preservation Group) "Keep Britain Farming"*		
G-BSXA	Piper PA-28-161 Warrior II	28-8416121	N4373Z	11.12.90	A.S.Bamrah	Biggin Hill	2. 8.03T
			N9622N		t/a Falcon Flying Services		
G-BSXB	Piper PA-28-161 Warrior II	28-8416125	N4374D	4.12.90	Aeros Leasing Ltd	Filton	13. 4.03T
			N9626N				
G-BSXC	Piper PA-28-161 Warrior II	28-8416126	N4374F	4.12.90	L.T.Halpin	Clutton Hill Farm, Clutton	2. 9.04T
			N9627N				
G-BSXD	Soko P-2 Kraguj	030	30146	22.10.90	L.C.MacKnight	Elstree	22. 4.99P
			Yugoslav Army		*(As "30146" in Yugoslav Army c/s)*		
G-BSXI	Mooney M.20E Chapparal	700056	N6766V	31.10.90	A.N.Pain	Southend	4. 5.03
G-BSXM	Cameron V-77 HAB	2446		5.11.90	C.A.Oxby *"Oxby"*	Doncaster	31. 8.03A

G-BSXN	Robinson R22 Beta	1611		14.11.90	Northumbria Helicopters Ltd	Newcastle	9. 2.03
G-BSXS	Piper PA-28-181 Archer II	28-7990151	N3055C	26.11.90	Jaxx Landing Ltd	Swansea	9.12.05T
G-BSXT	Piper J-5A Cub Cruiser	5-498	N33409	8.11.90	M.G. & K.J.Thompson	Belle Vue Farm, Yarnscombe	26. 7.03P
	(Continental C85)		NC33409				
G-BSXX	Whittaker MW7	PFA 171-11469		16.10.90	H.J.Stanley *(Current status unknown)*	(Abingdon)	
G-BSXZ	British Aerospace BAe 146 Srs.300	E3174	G-NJIB	14.11.90	Flightline Ltd	Exeter	11. 4.04T
			B-1776/G-BSXZ/G-6-174				
G-BSYA	Jodel D.18	PFA 169-11316		7.11.90	S.Harrison	Eshott	26. 6.02P
	(Volkswagen 1834)						
G-BSYB	Cameron N-120 HAB	2406		7.11.90	M.Buono	Mondovi, Italy	24. 7.03A
G-BSYC	Piper PA-32R-300 Lance	32R-7780159	N7745T	2. 4.91	M.N.Pinches	Wolverhampton	8. 5.03
			N1435H				
G-BSYD	Cameron A-180 HAB	2426		18.10.90	A.A.Brown t/a Balloon Company *"Discovery"*	Guildford	20. 9.02T
G-BSYF	Luscombe 8A Silvaire	3455	N72028	12.11.90	Atlantic Connexions Ltd	Little Gransden	6.10.03P
			NC72028		t/a Atlantic Aviation		
G-BSYG	Piper PA-12 Super Cruiser	12-2106	N3228M	12.11.90	E.R.Newall tr Fat Cub Group	Breighton	10. 7.03P
	(Lycoming O-235)		NC3228M				
G-BSYH	Luscombe 8A Silvaire	2842	N71415	13.11.90	N.R.Osborne	Insch	28.11.02P
	(Continental A65)		NC71415				
G-BSYI	Aérospatiale AS355F1 Twin Squirrel	5197	M-MJI	14.11.90	Lynton Aviation Ltd	Denham	28.11.05T
					t/a Signature Aircraft Charter		
G-BSYK*	Piper PA-38-112 Tomahawk II	38-81A0143	N23449	30. 1.91	Flychoice Ltd	Wolverhampton	
					(No CofA issued: cancelled 10.3.99 by CAA) (Stored 5.01)		
G-BSYL*	Piper PA-38-112 Tomahawk II	38-81A0172	N91333	23. 1.91	Flychoice Ltd	Wolverhampton	
					(No CofA issued: cancelled 10.3.99 by CAA) (Stored 5.01)		
G-BSYM*	Piper PA-38-112 Tomahawk II	38-82A0072	N2507V	30. 1.91	Flychoice Ltd	Wellesbourne Mountford	4. 9.94T
					(Damaged 27.7.94: cancelled 26.10.00 by CAA) (Dumped 9.02)		
G-BSYO	Piper J-3C-65 Cub (L-4B-PI)	12809	(G-BSMJ)	19. 2.91	C.R.Reynolds & J.D.Fuller Pent Farm, Postling, Kent		27. 3.03P
	(Continental O-200-A) *(Frame No.12639)*		(G-BRHE)/EC-AIY/HB-ODO/HB-OUA/44-80513				
	(Officially regd as c/n 10244 which is HB-OVG ex 43-1383/F-BFYF)				*(Force landed & overturned 1 mile NW Cranfield 23.6.00 due to engine failure)*		
G-BSYU	Robin DR400/180 Regent	2027		26.11.90	K.J.J.Jarman & P.D.Smoothy	Hinton in the Hedges	11. 4.03
G-BSYV	Cessna 150M	15078371	N9423U	16.11.90	L.R.Haunch t/a Fenland Flying School	Fenland	16. 3.03T
G-BSYW*	Cessna 150M	15078446	N9498U	16.11.90	J Cropper *(Cancelled 19.4.01 by CAA)*	Barton	25. 3.00
G-BSYZ	Piper PA-28-161 Warrior II	28-8516051	N6908H	22.11.90	S.W.Cowie tr Yankee Zulu Group	Glasgow	26. 9.03T
					(Op Glasgow Flying Club)		
G-BSZB	Stolp SA.300 Starduster Too	545	N5495M	3.12.90	D.T.Gethin	Haverfordwest	23. 9.03P
	(Lycoming O-360)						
G-BSZC	Beech C-45H-BH Expeditor	AF-258	N9541Z	14.12.90	A.A.Hodgson *"Southern Comfort"*	Bryngwyn Bach	1. 6.03
			51-11701		*(As "AF258/51-11701A" in USAF c/s)*		
	(Originally built as AT-7 42-2490 c/n 4166: re-manufactured 4.52)						
G-BSZD	Robin DR400/180 Regent	2029		21.11.90	R.J.Hitchman & M.Rowland	Draycott Farm, Chiseldon	4. 4.03
G-BS7F	CEA Jodel DR.250/160 Capitaine	32	F-BNJB	29.11.90	J.B.Randle	Church Farm, Piltdown	24. 4.03
G-BSZG	Stolp SA.100 Starduster (Lycoming O-320)	101	N70P	27.11.90	D.F.Chapman *(Noted 4.01)*	Headcorn	4. 7.00P
G-BSZH	Thunder Ax7-77 HAB	1848		27.11.90	P.K.Morris	Cleethorpes	3. 5.03T
G-BSZI	Cessna 152 II	15285856	N95139	17.12.90	Eglinton Flying Club Ltd	City of Derry	27. 2.03T
G-BSZJ	Piper PA-28-181 Archer II	28-8190216	N8373Z	6.12.90	R.D.Fuller & M.L.A.Pudney		3. 5.03
						St Lawrence, Bradwell-on-Sea	
G-BSZM	Montgomerie-Bensen B.8MR	PFA G/01-1193		30.11.90	A.McCredie	Carlisle	6. 9.02P
	(Rotax 582)						
G-BSZN	Bücker Bü.133D-1 Jungmeister	2002	N8103	30.11.90	A.J.Norman	Cambridge	25. 4.03P
	(Built Bitz) (Siemens Bramo SH14A)		D-ECAY(1)		tr Norman Aeroplane Trust		
G-BSZO	Cessna 152 II	15280221	N24334	30.11.90	Hecray Co Ltd	Southend	17.12.04T
					t/a Direct Helicopters *(Op Southend School of Flying)*		
G-BSZS	Robinson R22 Beta	1235	N8058J	13.12.90	A.Liddiard t/a Bladerunner Helicopters	Shobdon	3. 4.03T
G-BSZT	Piper PA-28-161 Warrior II	28-8116021	N8260D	31.12.90	Golf Charlie Echo Ltd	Shoreham	8. 4.03T
G-BSZU	Cessna 150F Commuter	15063481	N6881F	3.12.90	J.E.Jones	Bournemouth	18.12.05T
G-BSZV	Cessna 150F	15062304	N3504L	3.12.90	Kirmington Aviation Ltd	Sandown	17. 7.03T
G-BSZW	Cessna 152 II	15281072	N48958	3.12.90	Haimoss Ltd	Old Sarum	6.12.03T
G-BSZY*	Cameron A-180 HAB	2479		3. 1.91	K.H.Benning	Telgte, Germany	2. 1.96A
					(Cancelled 18.10.01 by CAA)		

G-BTAA - G-BTZZ

G-BTAB	British Aerospace BAe.125 Srs.800B	258088	G-5-563	12. 7.88	Aravco Ltd	Farnborough	6. 5.03T
			G-BOOA/(ZK-RHP)/G-5-563				
G-BTAD*	Macair Merlin	PFA 208-11661		6.11.90	Not known	Scotland Farm, Hook	
					(Under construction 5.95: cancelled 16.4.99 by CAA with no Permit to Fly issued) (Noted 2.03)		
G-BTAG	Cameron O-77 HAB	2454		12.11.90	R.A.Shapland *"Tag-Along"*	Petworth	13. 1.02A
G-BTAH	Bensen B.8M (Arrow GT500R)	PFA G/07-1196		13.12.90	C.J.Toner *(Noted 5.00)*	Abbeyshrule	31. 8.98P
G-BTAK	EAA Acrosport (Lycoming O-320)	21-468	N440X	27.12.90	P.G.Harrison *"The Duck"*	Sywell	15. 3.03P
G-BTAL	Reims/Cessna F.152 II	F15201444		7. 4.78	TG Aviation Ltd *(Op Thanet Flying Club)*	Manston	16. 3.03T
G-BTAM	Piper PA-28-181 Archer II	2890093	RA01765	10. 1.91	Tri-Star Farms Ltd	Ronaldsway	24. 4.03
			G-BTAM/N9153D				
G-BTAN	Thunder Ax7-65Z HAB	517		4. 5.83	A.S.Newnham	Southampton	8. 8.00A
G-BTAP	Piper PA-38-112 Tomahawk	38-78A0141	N9603T	8. 1.91	Western Air (Thruxton) Ltd	Thruxton	20. 7.03T
G-BTAR*	Piper PA-38-112 Tomahawk	38-79A0383	N2584D	13. 2.91	Aerohire Ltd	Blackpool	12. 3.00T
					(Damaged Liverpool 19.6.98: on rebuild 12.01) (Cancelled 9.4.02 by CAA)		
G-BTAS	Piper PA-38-112 Tomahawk	38-79A0545	F-GTAS	21. 2.91	Cardiff Wales Aviation Services Ltd	Cardiff	13. 6.03T
			G-BTAS/N2492G				
G-BTAT	Denney Kitfox Model 2	689 & PFA 172-11832		6.11.90	J M Keane	Deanland	8. 4.03P
G-BTAU	Thunder Ax7-77 HAB	1429		13.12.90	S.& G.Gebauer	Lippstadt, Germany	16. 4.03A
G-BTAW	Piper PA-28-161 Warrior II	28-8616031	N9259T	14.12.90	A.J.Wiggins	Gloucestershire	16. 5.03T
					(Op Gloucester & Cheltenham Flying School)		

Reg	Type	C/n	Prev ident	Date	Owner/Operator	Base	Expiry
G-BTAZ	Evans VP-2	PFA 63-11474		13.12.90	G.S.Poulter *(Noted complete 6.00)*	Norwich	
G-BTBA	Robinson R22 Beta	1717		18. 3.91	Heliflight (UK) Ltd	Wolverhampton	30. 4.03
G-BTBB	Thunder Ax8-105 Srs.2 HAB	1871		23.11.90	W.J.Brogan	Steiermark, Austria	16. 9.03T
G-BTBC	Piper PA-28-161 Warrior II	28-7916414	N28755	19.12.90	Wellesbourne Flyers Ltd	Wellesbourne Mountford	21. 4.03T
G-BTBF	Fisher FP.202 Super Koala	SK.067 & PFA 158-11954	(G-MWOZ)	24.12.90	E.A.Taylor	(Southend)	
	(Under construction 1.02)						
G-BTBG	Denney Kitfox Model 2	PFA 172-11845		18.12.90	P D Brookes	Long Marston	2. 1.03P
G-BTBH	Ryan ST3KR (PT-22-RY)	2063	N8541	8. 2.91	A.T.Hooper & C.C.Silk tr Ryan Group *(As "854" in US Army c/s)*		
	(Kinner R56)		N50993/41-20854			Bericote Farm, Blackdown, Leamington Spa	9.12.02P
G-BTBI	WAR P-47 Thunderbolt rep	0054	N47DL	8. 1.91	R.D.Myles	(Blairgowrie)	22.10.03P
	(Continental O-200-A) *(Marked as "Project No.52685A")*				*(As "85" in USAF c/s)*		
G-BTBJ	Cessna 190	16046	N4461C	2.10.91	P.Camus	(Dijon, France)	21. 8.03
	(Originally regd as Cessna 195B: re-designated 6.01 when fitted with Jacobs Aircraft & Engines R-755-B2)						
G-BTBL	Montgomerie-Bensen B.8MR Merlin			21.12.90	N.H.Collins	Cork Farm, Streethay	2. 9.01P
	(Rotax 532)	PFA G/01A-1183			t/a AES Radionic Surveillance Systems		
	(Lost power on take-off Roddidge, Alrewas 27. 4.01 & incurred substantial damage)						
G-BTBN	Denney Kitfox Model 2	686 & PFA 172-11859		31.12.90	R.C.Bowley	Croft Farm, Defford	19. 8.03P
G-BTBP	Cameron N-90 HAB	2464		21.12.90	Julia B.Turnau tr Chianti Balloon Club	Pianella, Italy	21. 6.00A
G-BTBR	Cameron DP-80 Hot-Air Airship	2344		21.12.90	Cameron Balloons Ltd	Bristol	15. 1.03A
G-BTBU	Piper PA-18-150 Super Cub	18-7509010	N9665P	3. 1.91	A.J.White tr G-BTBU Syndicate	Redhill	24. 7.03
G-BTBV	Cessna 140	12727	N2474N NC2474N	2. 4.91	M.S.Johnson	Enstone	6. 8.03
	(Continental C85)						
G-BTBW	Cessna 120	14220	N2009V NC2009V	24. 1.91	Melanie J.Willies	Top Farm, Croydon, Royston	25. 7.04
	(Continental C90)						
G-BTBX	Piper J-3C-65 Cub	6334	N35367 NC35367	29. 1.91	J.B.Hargrave & D.T.C.Collins	RAF Henlow	3.10.03
					tr Henlow Taildraggers		
G-BTBY	Piper PA-17 Vagabond (Continental C85)	17-195	N4894H	4. 1.91	G.J.Smith	Clipgate Farm, Denton	1. 5.03P
G-BTCA	Piper PA-32R-300 Lance	32R-7780381	N5941V	10. 1.91	R.Page tr Lance Group	Wolverhampton	26. 5.03
G-BTCB	Air Command 582 Sport	0634 & PFA G/04-1198		9. 1.91	G.Scurrah	Millom	
	(Nearing completion 5.95: current status unknown)						
G-BTCC	Grumman F6F-5K Hellcat	A-11286	(N10CN) N100T/FN80142/Bu.80141	31.12.90	Patina Ltd	Duxford	6. 7.03P
	(Composite with centre section from F6F-3 Bu.08831 c/n A-218)				*(Op The Fighter Collection)*		
					(As "Bu.40467/19" in VF-6 Sqdn/US Navy c/s)		
G-BTCD	North American P-51D-25NA Mustang	122-39608	N51JJ N6340T/RCAF 9568/44-73149	11. 1.91	Pelham Ltd	Duxford	2. 5.03P
					(Op The Old Flying Machine Co) "Ferocious Frankie"		
					(As "413704/B7-H" in 374th FG/USAAF c/s)		
G-BTCE	Cessna 152 II *(Tail-wheel conversion)*	15281376	N49876	10. 1.91	S.T.Gilbert	Enstone	11. 4.04T
G-BTCH	Luscombe 8E Silvaire	6403	N1976B NC1976B	11. 2.91	J.Grewcock & R.C.Carroll	Popham	16. 9.03P
	(Continental C85)						
G-BTCI	Piper PA-17 Vagabond	17-136	N4839H NC4839H	11. 1.91	T.R.Whittome	Inverness	15. 7.03P
	(Continental A65)						
G-BTCJ	Luscombe 8AE Silvaire	1869	N41908 NC41908	16. 1.91	Mrs J.M.Lovell	Chilbolton	9. 6.03P
	(Continental O-200A)						
G-BTCM	Cameron N-90 HAB	1306	(G-BMPW)	8. 5.86	Zebedee Balloon Service Ltd	Hungerford	10.10.00A
G-BTCR	Rans S-10 Sakota (Rotax 532)	PFA 194-11877		11. 1.91	B.J.Hewitt	Newtownards, Co.Down	11. 1.02P
G-BTCS	Colt 90A HAB	1895		11. 1.91	R.C.Stone "Rosie Rags"	Reading	20.12.02A
					(Variety Club of GB titles)		
G-BTCW	Cameron A-180 HAB	2458		17. 1.91	P.Clark t/a Bristol Balloons	Bristol	21. 7.00T
G-BTCZ*	Cameron Chateau 84SS HAB	2246		18. 1.91	Forbes Europe Inc	Balleroy, Normandy	7. 7.02
					"Chateau II" *(Cancelled 14.11.02 by CAA)*		
G-BTDA	Slingsby T.61F Venture T.2	1870	XZ550	17. 4.91	T.Holloway	RAF Wattisham	29. 5.03
					tr RAFGSA *(Op Anglia Gliding Club)*		
G-BTDC	Denney Kitfox Model 2	405 & PFA 172-11483		11. 1.91	O.Smith	Croft Farm, Darlington	
	(Current status unknown)						
G-BTDD	CFM Streak Shadow			14. 1.91	N.D.Ewer	Plaistows, St Albans	6. 3.03P
	(Rotax 582) K.127-SA & PFA 161A-11622						
G-BTDE	Cessna C-165 Airmaster	551	N21911 NC21911	18. 1.91	G.S.Moss	Popham	11.10.03
G-BTDF	Luscombe 8AF Silvaire	2205	N45678 NC45678	17. 4.91	R.Harrison	(Sunderland)	19. 8.93P
	(Continental C85)				tr Delta Foxtrot Group *(Current status unknown)*		
G-BTDN	Denney Kitfox Model 2	688 & PFA 172-11826		22. 1.91	S.D.Arnold tr Foxy Flyers Group	Long Marston	12. 6.03P
G-BTDP	Grumman TBM-3R Avenger	3381	N3966A Bu.53319	5. 2.91	A.Haig-Thomas	North Weald	28. 5.03P
					(As "53319/RB-319" in USN c/s)		
G-BTDR	Aero Designs Pulsar (Rotax 582)	PFA 202-11962		24. 1.91	R.A.Blackwell	North Weald	28. 7.03P
G-BTDS	Colt 77A HAB	1897		29. 1.91	CP Witter Ltd "Witters II"	Chester	18. 4.03A
G-BTDT	CASA I-131E Jungmann Srs.2000	2131	E3B-505	5. 2.91	T.A.Reed	Watchford Farm, Yarcombe	22. 5.02P
G-BTDV	Piper PA-28-161 Cherokee Warrior II	28-7816355	N3548M	25. 2.91	Southern Flight Centre Ltd	Shoreham	18. 6.04T
G-BTDW	Cessna 152 II	15279864	N757NC	25. 2.91	J.A.Blenkharn	Carlisle	18.10.03T
G-BTDX	Piper PA-18-150 Super Cub	18-7809098	N62595	28. 1.91	A.D.Hammond	Great Massingham	15. 3.04T
					t/a Hammond Aviation		
G-BTDZ	CASA I-131E Jungmann Srs.2000	2104	E3B-524	5. 2.91	R.J.Pickin & I.M.White	Headcorn	12. 6.03P
G-BTEA	Cameron N-105 HAB	284		31. 5.77	M.W.A.Shemilt "Big Red"	Henley-on-Thames	8. 5.99A
G-BTEE	Cameron O-120 HAB	2499		24. 1.91	W.H. & J.P.Morgan	Swansea	17. 5.02T
					"Y Ddraig Goch/The Red Dragon"		
G-BTEF	Pitts S-1 Special	515H	N88PR	19. 2.91	C.Davidson	Blackpool	28.10.97P
	(Lycoming IO-360)				*(Now CofR 3.02)*		
G-BTEI*	Everett Campbell Cricket Gyroplane Srs.3	023		31. 1.91	R A Jarvis	Sorbie Farm, Kingsmuir	21.12.98P
	(Damaged landing nr Great Orton 15.8.95: stored 2001: cancelled 23.5.01 by CAA)						
G-BTEK	SOCATA TB-20 Trinidad	1240		4. 2.91	M Northwood	Enstone	30. 6.05T
G-BTEL	CFM Streak Shadow K.125-SA & PFA 206-11667			31. 1.91	J.E.Eatwell	Boscombe Down	30. 8.03P
	(Rotax 618)						
G-BTES	Cessna 150H	15068371	N22575	29. 4.91	R.A.Forward	Spilsted Farm, Sedlescombe	19. 6.04
G-BTET	Piper J-3C-65 Cub	18296	N98141 NC98141	5. 2.91	R.M.Jones	Blackpool	9. 6.03P

Reg	Type	C/n	Prev id	Date	Owner	Location	CofA
G-BTEU	Aérospatiale SA365N2 Dauphin 2	6392		11. 2.91	CHC Scotia Ltd	Humberside	1. 4.04T
G-BTEW	Cessna 120 (Continental C90)	10238	CF-ELE	29. 4.91	Kay F.Mason	Norwich	28. 6.04
G-BTEX	Piper PA-28-140 Cherokee	28-23773	CF-XXL N3907K	24. 4.91	McAully Flying Group Ltd	Little Snoring	11. 4.04T
G-BTFA	Denney Kitfox Model 2 (Rotax 503)	566 & PFA 172-11520		13. 2.91	K.R.Peek Church Farm, North Moreton		6.10.94P
					(Damaged North Moreton 18.6.97: current status unknown)		
G-BTFC	Reims/Cessna F.152 II	F15201668		23. 5.79	Tayside Aviation Ltd	Dundee	29. 3.04T
G-BTFD*	Colt AS-105 Mk.II Hot-Air Airship	1856		13. 2.91	Media Fantasy Aviation UK Ltd	London SE16	
					(No CofA issued: cancelled 26.10.00 by CAA)		
G-BTFE	Parsons Gyroplane Model 1 (Rotax 582) *(Tandem Trainer)*	38		13. 2.91	J.R.Goldspink	Haverfordwest	27.10.01P
G-BTFF	Cessna T310R II	310R0718	N1363G	25. 2.91	Clear Prop Ltd	Blackbushe	29. 5.03
G-BTFG	Boeing-Stearman A75NI (N2S-4) Kaydet (Continental W670)	75-3441	N4467N Bu.30010	20. 2.91	TG Aviation Ltd *(As "441" in USN c/s)*	Manston	2. 7.05
G-BTFJ	Piper PA-15 Vagabond (Lycoming O-145)	15-159	N4373H NC4373H	13. 2.91	C.W.Thirtle & R.J.Court tr Vagabond FJ Flying Group	Old Sarum	8. 6.02P
G-BTFK	Taylorcraft BC-12D (Continental A65)	10540	N599SB N5240M	13. 2.91	M.Gibson (Raheen, Co.Limerick)		16. 2.00P
G-BTFL	Aeronca 11AC Chief	11AC-1727	N3403E NC3403E	18. 2.91	J.G.Vaughan Eastbach Farm, Coleford tr BTFL Group		26.11.03P
G-BTFM	Cameron O-105 HAB	2623		12. 8.91	P.Forster & J.Trehern tr Edinburgh University Hot-Air Balloon Club	Edinburgh	16.11.02A
G-BTFO	Piper PA-28-161 Cherokee Warrior II	28-7816580	N31728	12. 3.91	Flyfar Ltd	Blackpool	22. 5.03
G-BTFP	Piper PA-38-112 Tomahawk	38-78A0340	N6201A	17. 4.91	Teesside Flight Centre Ltd *(Stored 12.01)*	Teesside	6. 8.00T
G-BTFS	Cessna A150M Aerobat	A1500719	N20331	20. 2.91	P.A.James	Redhill	1. 5.03T
G-BTFT	Beech 58 Baron	TH-979	N2036W	14. 3.91	Fastwing Air Charter Ltd	Thruxton	8. 4.04T
G-BTFU	Cameron N-90 HAB	2391		28. 2.91	J.J.Rudoni & A.C.K.Rawson "Maltesers II" t/a Wickers World Hot Air Balloon Co	Stafford	12.12.02A
G-BTFV	Whittaker MW7 (Rotax 532)	PFA 171-11722		8. 2.91	S.J.Luck Tower Farm, Wollaston		6. 1.03P
G-BTFW	Montgomerie-Bensen B.8MR (Rotax 532)	PFA G/01A-1141		20. 2.91	J.R.J.Read	Henstridge	13. 6.03P
G-BTFX	Bell 206B JetRanger II	1648	N400MH N90219	20. 2.91	J.Selwyn Smith (Shepley) Ltd Shepley, Huddersfield		1. 5.03T
G-BTFY	Bell 206B JetRanger II	1714	(ZS-) G-BTFY/N49590	20. 2.91	Hughes Helicopter Co Ltd t/a Biggin Hill Helicopters *(Crashed Cudham 17.1.03 and substantially damaged)*	Biggin Hill	29. 5.04T
G-BTGD	Rand Robinson KR-2 (Volkswagen 1915)	PFA 129-11150		22. 2.91	A.P.Worbey	Turweston	19. 2.03P
G-BTGG	Rans S-10 Sakota (Rotax 582)	PFA 194-11944		20. 2.91	A.R.Cameron	Oaksey Park	22. 6.96P
G-BTGH	Cessna 152 II	15281048	N48919	2. 4.91	C & S Aviation Ltd	Wolverhampton	9. 4.04T
G-BTGI	Rearwin 175 Skyranger (Continental A75)	1517	N32308 NC32308	26. 2.91	A.H.Hunt Lower Botrea Farm, Newbridge, Penzance		27. 6.01P
G-BTGJ	Smith DSA-1 Miniplane (Continental A65)	NM.II	N1471	25. 3.91	G.J.Knowles *(Stored 4.99: current status unknown)*	Little Gransden	20. 5.94P
G-BTGL	Avid Speed Wing	PFA 189-11885		27. 2.91	I.Kazi	(Cranbrook, Kent)	4. 9.03P
G-BTGM	Aeronca 7AC Champion (Continental A65)	7AC-3665	N84943 NC84943	11. 3.91	G.P.Gregg	Shacklewell Lodge	16. 4.03P
G-BTGO	Piper PA-28-140 Cherokee D	28-7125613	N1998T	20. 2.91	Halegreen Associates Ltd Hinton in the Hedges		13. 7.03T
G-BTGP	Cessna 150M Commuter	15078921	N704WA	28. 2.91	Billins Air Services Ltd *(Op City Air)*	Cranfield	16. 5.03T
G-BTGR	Cessna 152 II	15284447	N6581L	28. 2.91	A.J.Gomes *(Op Sky Leisure Aviation)*	Shoreham	25. 7.00T
G-BTGS(2)	Stolp SA.300 Starduster Too (Lycoming O-320) EAA/50553 & PFA 35-10076		G-AYMA	30. 9.87	G.N.Elliott tr Mr.G.N.Elliott & Partners	(Steyning)	29. 5.03P
G-BTGT	CFM Streak Shadow K.164-SA & PFA 206-11964 (Rotax 582)		(G-MWPY)	1. 3.91	G.D.Bailey	(Winchester)	23. 7.03P
G-BTGU	Piper PA-34-220T Seneca III	34-8233106	N999PW N8160V	1. 3.91	Carill Aviation Ltd	Southampton	30. 5.03T
G-BTGV	Piper PA-34-200T Seneca II	34-7970077	N3004H	26. 3.91	Roper & Wreaks Ltd	Shobdon	3. 8.03T
G-BTGW	Cessna 152 II	15279812	N757KY	5. 3.91	Stapleford Flying Club Ltd	Stapleford	10. 8.03T
					(Struck tree in poor weather 12.11.01 & made forced landing Detling Show Ground: substantially damaged)		
G-BTGX	Cessna 152 II	15284950	N5462P	5. 3.91	Stapleford Flying Club Ltd	Stapleford	24. 8.03T
G-BTGY	Piper PA-28-161 Warrior II	28-8216199	N209FT N9574N	5. 3.91	Stapleford Flying Club Ltd	Stapleford	23. 6.03T
G-BTGZ	Piper PA-28-181 Cherokee Archer II	28-7890160	N47956	8. 4.91	Allzones Travel Ltd	Biggin Hill	17. 9.03T
G-BTHA	Cessna 182P	18263420	N2932P	22. 3.91	T.P.Hall tr Hotel Alpha Flying Group	Liverpool	21. 8.03
G-BTHD	Yakovlev Yak-3U *(Conversion of LET Yak C.11)*	170101	(France) EAF.533	7. 3.91	Patina Ltd *(Op The Fighter Collection) (On restoration 6.01)*	Duxford	
G-BTHE	Cessna 150L	15075340	N11348	7. 3.91	J.H.Loose & F.P.White Mount Airey Farm, South Cave tr Humberside Police Flying Club		8. 6.03T
G-BTHF	Cameron V-90 HAB	2543		7. 3.91	N.J. & S.J.Langley	Bristol	20. 8.03T
G-BTHH	CEA Jodel DR.100A Ambassadeur	5	F-BJCH	28. 2.91	H.R.Leefe Bourg-en-Bresse, France		1. 9.02
G-BTHI	Robinson R22 Beta	1732		26. 3.91	M.D.Thorpe Coney Park, Leeds t/a Yorkshire Helicopters		27. 7.03T
G-BTHJ	Evans VP-2	PFA 63-10901		14. 3.91	C.J.Moseley *(Under construction 8.92: current status unknown)*	Bournemouth	
G-BTHK	Thunder Ax7-77 HAB	1906		11. 3.91	M.J.Chandler	Cranbrook	22. 6.03A
G-BTHM	Thunder Ax8-105 HAB	1925		11. 3.91	J.K.Woods	Chatham	19. 6.03A
G-BTHN	Murphy Renegade 912	384 & PFA 188-12005		12. 3.91	F.A.Purvis "Spirit of England II"	Eshott	22. 8.03P
G-BTHP	Thorp T.211	101		13. 6.91	M.J.Newton	Barton	27.11.04P
G-BTHR	SOCATA TB-10 Tobago	1296		13. 3.91	P, A, A & J McRae	White Waltham	21. 4.05T
G-BTHU	Avid Flyer (Rotax 532)	PFA 189-11427		14. 3.91	R.C.Bowley	(Earls Croome, Worcester)	
					(Damaged Field Head Farm, Denholme, Bradford 7.6.92: on rebuild 5.95: current status unknown)		
G-BTHV	MBB Bö.105D	BS-4S.855	D-HMBV G-BTHV/D-HFHM	20. 3.91	Bond Air Services Ltd *(Op Gloucestershire Air Ambulance)*	Gloucestershire	12. 5.03T

Reg	Type	c/n	Prev id	Date	Owner/Operator	Location	Date
G-BTHW	Beech F33C Bonanza	CJ-130	PH-BNA N23787	18. 3.91	Robin Lance Aviation Associates Ltd	Rochester	20. 8.03
G-BTHX	Colt 105A HAB	1939		18. 3.91	R.Ollier	Northwich, Cheshire	15. 5.03A
G-BTHY	Bell 206B-3 JetRanger III	2290	N6606M VH-BIQ/ZK-HBQ/DQ-FEN/ZK-HLU	20. 3.91	Sterling Helicopters Ltd	Norwich	19. 5.03T
G-BTHZ	Cameron V-56 HAB	486	OO-BBC	20. 3.91	C.N.Marshall	Nairobi, Kenya	
	(Noted as "OO-BBC" 9.95: current status unknown)						
G-BTID	Piper PA-28-161 Warrior II	28-8116036	N82647	25. 6.91	Plymouth School of Flying Ltd	Plymouth	24. 5.03T
G-BTIE	SOCATA TB-10 Tobago	187		30. 3.81	Aviation Spirit Ltd	Clee Hill, Ludlow	18. 1.03T
G-BTIF	Denney Kitfox Model 3	684 & PFA 172-11862		27. 2.91	D.A.Murchie	(Blackwaterfoot, Arran)	10. 8.01P
	(Converted from Model 2)						
G-BTIG	Montgomerie-Bensen B.8MR (Rotax 532)	PFA G/01-1093		21. 3.91	K.Jarvis	Carlisle	15. 5.02P
G-BTII	Gulfstream AA-5B Tiger	AA5B-1256	N4560S	5. 6.91	S.A.Niechial & P.W.Gillott tr BTII Group	Biggin Hill	13. 5.05
G-BTIJ	Luscombe 8E Silvaire (Continental C85)	5194	N2467K NC2467K	3. 4.91	S.J.Hornsby	Compton Abbas	16. 9.03P
G-BTIK	Cessna 152 II	15282993	N46068	26. 3.91	I.R.Chaplin	Andrewsfield	12. 6.05T
G-BTIL	Piper PA-38-112 Tomahawk	38-80A0004	N24730	26. 3.91	B.J.Pearson	Eaglescott	AC
	(Fuselage noted 10.00 with Fresca titles)						
G-BTIM	Piper PA-28-161 Cadet	2841159	N9185D (SE-KIO)	24. 8.89	S.J.Skilton t/a Aviation Rentals	Bournemouth	25.10.04T
G-BTIO	SNCAN Stampe SV-4C	303	N73NS F-BCLC	28. 3.91	M.D. & C.F.Garratt	(Bushey, Watford)	8.10.05
G-BTIR	Denney Kitfox Model 2 (Hewland AE75)	PFA 172-11952		26. 3.91	R.B.Wilson	(Kendal)	5.10.03P
G-BTIS	Aérospatiale AS355F1 Twin Squirrel	5261	G-TALI	10. 4.91	J.P.E.Walsh t/a Walsh Aviation *(Op Cabair Helicopters)*	Elstree	9. 6.04T
G-BTIU	SOCATA MS.892A Rallye Commodore 150	10914	F-BPQS	7. 5.91	Battle Aviation Services Ltd	(St.Leonards-on-Sea)	16. 6.05
G-BTIV	Piper PA-28-161 Warrior II	28-8116044	N82697	10. 5.91	B.R.Pearson tr Warrior Group	Eaglescott	6. 7.03T
G-BTIZ	Cameron A-105 HAB	2546		11. 3.91	Wendy A.Board t/a Glen Board Promotions	Penshurst	8. 7.02A
G-BTJA	Luscombe 8E Silvaire (Continental C85)	5037	N2310K NC2310K	4. 4.91	M.W.Rudkin	Woodford	14. 7.03P
G-BTJB	Luscombe 8E Silvaire (Continental C85)	6194	N1567B NC1567B	4. 4.91	M.Loxton	Parsonage Farm, Eastchurch	21. 5.03P
G-BTJC	Luscombe 8F Silvaire (Lycoming O-290)	6589	N2162B	4. 4.91	Alison M.Noble	Thruxton	18.10.99P
	(Damged Glebe Farm, Stockton, Warminster 31.7.99: current status unknown)						
G-BTJD	Thunder Ax8-90 Srs.2 HAB	1865		28. 3.91	R.E.Vinten	Wellingborough	3. 5.03A
G-BTJF	Thunder Ax10-180 Srs.2 HAB	1952		28. 3.91	Airborne Adventures Ltd *"Yorkshire Lad"*	Skipton	4. 5.01T
G-BTJH	Cameron O-77 HAB	2559		3. 4.91	H.Stringer *"Oriel"*	Scarborough	3. 4.00T
G-BTJK	Piper PA-38-112 Tomahawk	38-79A0838	N2427N	3. 4.91	Western Air (Thruxton) Ltd	Thruxton	6. 9.03T
G-BTJL	Piper PA-38-112 Tomahawk	38-79A0863	N2477N	3. 4.91	J.S.Develin & Z.Islam	Shoreham	22. 8.04T
G-BTJN	Montgomerie-Bensen B.8MR (Rotax 532)	PFA G/01-1194		3. 4.91	A.Hamilton *(Operates from Strathaven)*	Stonehouse	9.12.00P
G-BTJO	Thunder Ax9-140 HAB	1948		3. 4.91	G.P.Lane	Gerrards Cross	28. 4.92A
G-BTJS	Montgomerie-Bensen B.8MR (Rotax 532)	PFA G/01-1083		8. 4.91	B.F.Pearson	(Newark)	18.10.00P
G-BTJU	Cameron V-90 HAB	2554		8. 4.91	C.W.Jones (Floorings) Ltd *(C W Jones Carpets titles)*	Bristol	9. 8.03A
G-BTJX	Rans S-10 Sakota (Rotax 582)	PFA 194-12014		9. 4.91	W.C.Dobson	Beeches Farm, South Scarle	25. 3.03P
G-BTKA	Piper J-5A Cub Cruiser	5-954	N38403 NC38403	11. 4.91	Janet M.Lister	Valley Farm, Winwick	9. 5.03P
G-BTKB	Murphy Renegade 912	376 & PFA 188-11876		11. 4.91	P.& J.Calvert	Rufforth	17. 7.03P
	(Rotax 912)						
G-BTKD	Denney Kitfox Model 4	853 & PFA 172-11941		15. 4.91	P.A.Howell	Long Marston	21. 5.03P
	(Rotax 582) *(Denney c/n indicates Model 3 & conflicts with N653CP)*						
G-BTKG	Avid Flyer (Rotax 582)	PFA 189-12037		16. 4.91	I.Holt	Drayton St Leonards	15. 8.03P
G-BTKL	MBB Bö.105DB-4	S.422	D-HDMU Swedish Army/D-HDMU	2. 5.91	Veritair Ltd *(Op Central Counties Police Air Operations Unit)*	Wolverhampton	2. 3.03T
G-BTKN	Cameron O-120 HAB	2579	OO-BQQ	24. 4.91	R.H.Etherington	Siena, Italy	16. 4.03A
G-BTKP	CFM Streak Shadow (Rotax 582)	K.174 & PFA 206-12036		24. 4.91	G.D.Martin	(Cambridge)	20. 8.02P
G-BTKT	Piper PA-28-161 Warrior II	28-8216218	N429FT N9606N	9. 5.91	Eastern Executive Air Charter Ltd & E.Alexander t/a General Aero Services	King's Farm, Thurrock	14. 7.97T
	(Damaged near Shoreham 8.8.95: fuselage only 9.99: current status unknown)						
G-BTKV	Piper PA-22-160 Tri-Pacer	22-7157	N3216Z	25. 4.91	R.A.Moore	Newtownards, Co.Down	1. 8.04
G-BTKW	Cameron O-105 HAB	2566		25. 4.91	P.Spellward tr Bristol University Hot Air Ballooning Society	Bristol	9. 3.01A
G-BTKX	Piper PA-28-181 Cherokee Archer II	28-7890146	N47866	14. 5.91	R.M.Pannell	Eaglescott	30. 4.03
G-BTKZ	Cameron V-77 HAB	2573		26. 4.91	S.P.Richards *"Lancaster Jaguar"* *(Amended CofR 8.02)*	Tonbridge	7. 6.97T
G-BTLB	Wassmer WA.52 Europa	42	F-BTLB	17. 4.89	A.S.Cowan tr Popham Flying Group G-BTLB	Popham	14. 6.04
G-BTLG	Piper PA-28R-200 Cherokee Arrow	28R-35811	N5045S	29. 4.91	W.B.Bateson	Blackpool	15. 3.04
G-BTLL*	Pilatus P.3-03	323-5	A-806	18. 4.91	Not known	Headcorn	23. 6.94P
	(Cancelled 27.10.95 by CAA) (As "A-806" in Swiss AF c/s: stored 10.00)						
G-BTLM	Piper PA-22-160 (Tail-wheel conversion)	22-6162	N9025D	16. 5.91	A.C.& M.D.N.Fisher	Fenland	12.10.03
G-BTLP	Grumman-American AA-1C Lynx	AA1C-0109	N9732U	13. 5.91	Partlease Ltd	Stapleford	23. 1.04
G-BTMA	Cessna 172N Skyhawk II	17273711	N5136J	2. 5.91	East of England Flying Group Ltd	North Weald	20. 9.03T
G-BTMH	Colt 90A HAB	1963		14. 5.91	European Balloon Corporation	Espinette, Belgium	19. 8.01A
G-BTMJ	Maule MX-7-180 Star Rocket	11073C		11. 6.91	C.M.McGill	White Waltham	4. 9.04
G-BTMK	Cessna R172K Hawk XP II	R1722787	N736TZ	10. 6.91	S.P. & A.C.Barker	East Midlands	12.12.03T
G-BTMN	Thunder Ax9-120 Srs.2 HAB	2003		17. 5.91	M.E.White *(Inflated 4.02)*	Dublin	8. 3 99T
G-BTMO	Colt 69A HAB	2004		20. 5.91	Cameron Balloons Ltd t/a Thunder & Colt *(Current CofR 4.02)*	Bristol	

Reg	Type	c/n	Prev id	Date	Owner/Operator	Base	Status
G-BTMP	Everett Campbell Cricket (Rotax 532)	024 & PFA G/03-1226		20. 5.91	P.W.McLaughlin	Henstridge	24.10.03P
G-BTMR	Cessna 172M Skyhawk II	17264985	N64047	20. 5.91	Linley Aviation Ltd	Linley Hill, Leven	15. 6.03T
G-BTMS	Avid Speed Wing	908 & PFA 189-12023	(CS-) G-BTMS	24. 4.91	F.Sayyah *(Operates from Redhill)*	(Crawley)	19. 2.03P
G-BTMT	Denney Kitfox Model 1	66		10. 5.91	M.D.Burns	Cumbernauld	16.10.03P
G-BTMV	Everett Gyroplane Srs.2	025		21. 5.91	L.Armes *(Current status unknown)*	Basildon	
G-BTMW	Zenair CH-701 STOL (Rotax 582)	PFA 187-11808		21. 5.91	L.Lewis *(Stored 1.02)*	Yearby	9. 4.96P
G-BTMX	Denney Kitfox Model 3 (Rotax 582)	916 & PFA 172-12079		13. 5.91	M.H.McKeown *(New owner 5.02)*	Enniskellen, Co.Fermanagh	18. 2.03P
G-BTNA	Robinson R22 Beta	1800		23. 5.91	Quay Contracts Ltd	Booker	13.10.05T
G-BTNC	Aérospatiale SA365N2 Dauphin 2	6409		21. 6.91	CHC Scotia Ltd	Humberside	9.10.04T
G-BTND	Piper PA-38-112 Tomahawk	38-78A0155	N9671T	23. 5.91	R.B.Turner	Gloucestershire	14. 3.05T
G-BTNE	Piper PA-28-161 Warrior II	28-8116212	N8379H	22. 7.91	D.Rowe	Wellesbourne Mountford	21. 6.04T
G-BTNI	British Aerospace ATP	2038	EC-GSE	29. 5.91	Trident Aviation Leasing Services (Jersey) Ltd Woodford		
			EC-GKJ/G-OEDI/G-BTNI/(N238JX)/G-BTNI/TC-THU/G-BTNI/(G-SLAM) *(Exported 1.03)*				
G-BTNJ*	Cameron V-90 HAB	2534		28. 5.91	NK *(Cancelled 3.7.97 as WFU) (Noted 8.01)*	NK	
G-BTNL	Thunder AX10-180 HAB	2006	(OO-...) G-BTNL	29. 5.91	M.P.A.Sevrin	Court St.Etienne, Belgium	29. 7.01T
G-BTNN	Colt 21A Cloudhopper HAB	2018		3. 6.91	A.E.Austin	(Naseby)	7. 3.03A
G-BTNO	Aeronca 7AC Champion	7AC-3132	N84441 NC84441	31. 5.91	D.B.Evans & A.McGarrell tr November Oscar Group	Netherthorpe	10. 7.02P
G-BTNR	Denney Kitfox Model 3 (Rotax 582)	921 & PFA 172-12035		31. 5.91	H.Thompson	(Kidderminster)	27. 8.03P
G-BTNS	WSK PZL-104 Wilga 80	CF.20890883	N71695	22. 7.91	D.Rowland	Shoreham	25. 6.04A
G-BTNT	Piper PA-28-151 Cherokee Warrior	28-7615401	N6929J	31. 5.91	Britannia Airways Ltd *(Op Britannia Airways Flying Club)*	Luton	24.11.03T
G-BTNU	British Aerospace BAe 146 Srs.300	E3155	EI-CLJ G-BTHU/(G-BSLS)/G-6-155	24. 1.03	Trident Jet (Jersey) Ltd *(Stored 2.03)*	Filton	
G-BTNV	Piper PA-28-161 Cherokee Warrior II	28-7816590	N31878	20. 6.91	D.E.Peet	(Claygate)	17. 7.03
G-BTNW	Rans S-6ESA Coyote II (Rotax 582)	0391.171 & PFA 204-12077		3. 6.91	B.Read	Ince Blundell	14. 6.02P
	(Rans' kit c/n incorrect as this became G-MWUM: possibly 0391.174)						
G-BTOA*	Mong Sport MS-2 (Continental C85)	FHC-1	N1067Z	3. 6.91	G.Gilding *(Cancelled 26.10.00 by CAA) (On rebuild 8.01)*	Swanton Morley	16. 9.94P
G-BTOC	Robinson R22 Beta	1801	N23004	10. 6.91	N.Parkhouse	Chelwood Gate, West Sussex	19. 6.03T
G-BTOD*	Piper PA-38-112 Tomahawk	38-78A0675	N2421A	7. 6.91	S.M.P & D.A.Adams *(Cancelled 21.1.03 as wfu)*	Gamston	18.10.03T
G-BTOG	de Havilland DH.82A Tiger Moth	86500	F-BGCJ Fr.AF/NM192	5. 9.91	P.T.Szluha *(Stored as "F-BGCJ" 8.02)*	Audley End	
G-BTOL	Denney Kitfox Model 3 (Rotax 582)	919 & PFA 172-12052		26. 6.91	P.J.Gibbs	Truro	17. 7.03P
G-BTON	Piper PA-28-140 Cherokee Cruiser	28-7425343	N43193	15. 7.91	S.R.Turner	Poplar Hall Farm, Elmsett	19. 7.04T
G-BTOO	Pitts S-1C Special	5215-24A	N37H	12. 6.91	G.H.Matthews *(On overhaul 5.92: current status unknown)*	Sandown	
G-BTOP	Cameron V-77 HAB	2484		14. 6.91	J.J.Winter *"Big Top"*	Cardiff	
G-BTOS	Cessna 140 (Continental C85)	8353	N89325 NC89325	7. 6.91	J.L.Kaiser *(Current status unknown)*	Nancy-Essey, France	1. 7.99
G-BTOT	Piper PA-15 Vagabond (Lycoming O-145)	15-60	N4176H NC4176H	22. 5.91	M.S.Rogerson tr Vagabond Flying Group	Ferryhill	24. 4.03P
G-BTOU	Cameron O-120 HAB	2606		2. 7.91	R.M.Horn	Hatfield Peverel	15.11.03T
G-BTOW	SOCATA Rallye 180T Galerien	3360	F-BNGZ	9.11.82	Cambridge Gliding Club Ltd	Gransden Lodge	11. 4.04
G-BTOZ	Thunder Ax9-120 Srs.2 HAB	2008		28. 6.91	H.G.Davies	Cheltenham	9. 9.03T
G-BTPA	British Aerospace ATP	2007	EC-HGC G-BTPA/EC-GYE/G-BTPA/(N377AE)	19. 8.88	Capital Bank Leasing 12 Ltd	Woodford	18.11.98T
G-BTPB	Cameron N-105 HAB	1536		6. 7.87	C.N.Rawnson tr Test Valley Balloon Group *"Phone Book"*	Stockbridge	21. 9.96A
G-BTPC	British Aerospace ATP	2010	EC-HGB G-BTPD/EC-GYF/G-BTPC/G-11-10/(N380AE)	1. 9.88	Capital Bank Leasing 1 Ltd	Woodford	29.12.98T
G-BTPD	British Aerospace ATP	2011	EC-HGD G-BTPC/EC-GYR/G-BTPD/(N381AE)	1. 9.88	Seaforth Marime (JARL) Ltd & Flexify Ltd t/a NWS2	Woodford	6. 2.99T
G-BTPE	British Aerospace ATP	2012	EC-HGE G-BTPE/EC-GZH/G-BTPE/(N382AE) *(New CorR 2.02)*	1. 9.88	Capital Bank Leasing 3 Ltd	Woodford	12. 3.99T
G-BTPF	British Aerospace ATP	2013	EC-HCY G-BTPF/G-11-013/G-BTPF/(N383AE) *(New CorR 2.02)*	2. 9.88	Capital Bank Leasing 5 Ltd	Woodford	17. 4.99T
G-BTPG	British Aerospace ATP	2014	EC-HEH G-BTPG/(N384AE) *(New CorR 2.02)*	2. 9.88	Capital Bank Leasing 5 Ltd	Woodford	22. 5.99T
G-BTPH	British Aerospace ATP	2015	EC-HFM G-BTPH/(N385AE) *(Stored.5.02)*	2. 9.88	Capital Bank Leasing 6 Ltd	Zaragoza, Spain	11. 6.99T
G-BTPJ	British Aerospace ATP	2016	EC-HFR G-BTPJ/(N386AE) *(New CorR 2.02)*	2. 9.88	Capital Bank Leasing 7 Ltd	Woodford	9. 7.99T
G-BTPK	British Aerospace ATP	2041	EC-GSG EC-GLC/G-BTPK/G-11-041 *(New CorR 2.02) (Exported 1.03)*	3.10.91	Trident Aviation Leasing Services (Jersey) Ltd	Woodford	
G-BTPL	British Aerospace ATP	2042	EC-HES G-BTPL/EC-GLH/G-BTPL/G-11-042 *(New CorR 2.02)*	3.10.91	Trident Aviation Leasing Services (Jersey) Ltd	Woodford	21.11.95T
G-BTPN	British Aerospace ATP	2044	EC-GSI EC-GNJ/G-BTPN/G-11-044 *(Stored 5.02)*	19.11.91	Trident Aviation Leasing Services (Jersey) Ltd	Zaragoza, Spain	19.12.98T
G-BTPT	Cameron N-77 HAB	2575		10. 6.91	Derbyshire Building Society	Derby	15.12.01A
G-BTPX	Thunder Ax8-90 HAB	1873		18. 6.91	E.Cordall	Chichester	22. 8.03
G-BTPZ	Isaacs Fury II	PFA 11-11927		1. 7.91	M.A.Farrelly *(As "85" in Portuguese AF c/s)*	Ormskirk	
G-BTRB	Colt Mickey Mouse SS HAB	1959		4. 7.91	Benedikt Haggeney GmbH *"Calibre"*	Ennigerloh, Germany	25 .6.03A
G-BTRC	Avid Speed Wing (BMW R100)	913 & PFA 189-12076		2. 7.91	Grangecote Ltd	Goodwood	18. 7.03P
	(Lost power after touch & go Trueleigh Farm, Brighton 22.6.01: substantially damaged in landing)						

Reg	Type	C/n	Prev id	Date	Owner/Operator	Location	Date
G-BTRE	Reims/Cessna F172H	F17200657	N10657	3. 7.91	M.L.J.Warwick	Stapleford	18.10.04T
G-BTRF	Aero Designs Pulsar (Rotax 582)	PFA 202-12051		4. 7.91	C.Smith	Spilsted Farm, Sedlescombe	19.10.03P
G-BTRG	Aeronca 65C Super Chief (Continental A65)	C4149	N22466 NC22466	4. 7.91	A.Welburn	South Cave, Hull	19. 8.03P
G-BTRH	Aeronca 7AC Champion (Continental A65)	7AC-2895	N84204 NC84204	4. 7.91	J.Horan	(Abbeyfeale, Co.Kerry)	15. 5.02P
G-BTRI	Aeronca 11CC Super Chief (Continental C85)	11CC-246	N4540E NC4540E	4. 7.91	P.A.Wensak	Bounds Farm, Ardleigh	17. 7.03P
G-BTRK	Piper PA-28-161 Warrior II	28-8216206	N297FT N9594N	8. 7.91	Stapleford Flying Club Ltd	Stapleford	26.10.03T
G-BTRL	Cameron N-105 HAB	2622		5. 7.91	J.Lippett *"Harrods"*	South Petherton, Somerset	24. 8.02A
G-BTRN	Thunder AX9-120 S2 HAB	1983		11. 7.91	P.B.D.Bird	Bristol	21. 6.02T
G-BTRO	Thunder Ax8-90 HAB	1872		11. 7.91	Capital Balloon Club Ltd	London NW1	17. 4.03A
G-BTRP	MD Helicopters Hughes 369E (500E)	0475E	N1607D	11. 7.91	P.C.Shann & P.C.Shann Management & Research Ltd	Fulford, York	25. 3.05
G-BTRR	Thunder Ax7-77 HAB	1905		12. 7.91	M.F.Comerford	(Stoke-on-Trent)	1.10.03A
G-BTRS	Piper PA-28-161 Warrior II	28-8116004	N8248V	12. 7.91	K.D.Taylor & T.Bailey tr Airwise Flying Group	Barton	4. 2.05
G-BTRT	Piper PA-28R-200 Cherokee Arrow II	28R-7535270	N1189X	24. 7.91	C.E.Yates	Barton	22. 1.04
G-BTRU	Robin DR400/180 Regent	2089		12. 7.91	R.H.Mackay	(Keith)	30. 1.04
G-BTRW	Slingsby T.61F Venture T.2	1968	ZA632	5. 7.91	G.B.Monslow tr The Falke Syndicate	Long Marston	3.12.03
G-BTRX*	Cameron V-77 HAB	1143	VH-HIH	12. 7.91	Not known *(Cancelled 2.5.97 as WFU) (Inflated 6.02)*	NK	
G-BTRY	Piper PA-28-161 Warrior II	28-8116190	N8363L	18. 7.91	Oxford Aviation Services Ltd	Oxford	6.12.04T
G-BTRZ	Jodel D.18 (Volkswagen 1834)	148 & PFA 169-11271		16. 7.91	R.M.Johnson & R.Collin	Midlem Farm, Midlem	29. 9.03P
G-BTSB	Corben Baby Ace D (Continental A65)	JC-1	N3599	16. 7.91	J.A.MacLeod	Stornoway	17. 6.03P
G-BTSC*	Evans VP-2 (Arrow GT500)	PFA 63-10342		20.10.78	G.B.O'Neill *(Stored 6.00: cancelled 20.1.03 by CAA)*	(Upwood, Cambs)	13. 2.96P
G-BTSJ	Piper PA-28-161 Cherokee Warrior II	28-7816473	N9417C	23. 7.91	Plymouth School of Flying Ltd	Plymouth	11. 1.04T
G-BTSL	Cameron Glass 70SS HAB *(Tennent's Lager Glass shape)*	1627		27. 1.88	M.R.Humphrey & J.R.Clifton *"Tennent's Glass"*	Brackley	25. 4.90A
G-BTSM	Cessna 180A	32678	P2-DEQ VH-DEQ/VH-DEC/N7781A	9. 7.91	C.Couston tr Sierra Mike Group	Church Farm, North Moreton	17. 4.05
G-BTSN	Cessna 150G	15065106	N3806J	30. 8.91	N.A.Bilton	Priory Farm, Tibenham	7. 5.05
G-BTSP	Piper J-3C-65 Cub	7647	N41013 NC41013	30. 8.91	J.A.Walshe & A.Corcoran	Strandhill, Sligo	24. 4.03P
G-BTSR	Aeronca 11AC Chief (Continental A65)	11AC-785	N9152E NC9152E	30. 8.91	R.D.& E.G.N.Morris	Perth	29. 4.03P
G-BTSV	Denney Kitfox Model 3 (Rotax 582)	PFA 172-11920		24. 7.91	M.G.Dovey	Popham	9. 6.03P
G-BTSW	Colt AS-105GD Hot-Air Airship	1999		24. 7.91	Gefa-Flug GmbH *(Adler Modemarkt titles)*	Aachen, Germany	17. 4.03A
G-BTSX	Thunder Ax7-77 HAB	2027		24. 7.91	C.Moris-Gallimore *(New Cof R 3.02)*	Sao Bras de Alportel, Portugal	18. 9.94
G-BTSZ	Cessna 177A Cardinal	17701198	N30332	30. 7.91	K.D.Harvey	Popham	27. 6.03T
G-BTTB	Cameron V-90 HAB	2624		22. 7.91	R.M.Tonkins tr Royal Engineers Balloon Club *"Sapper IV"*	Chatham	18. 8.03A
G-BTTD*	Montgomerie-Bensen B.8MR (Rotax 582)	PFA G/01-1204		31. 7.91	K.B.Gutridge *(Cancelled 18.3.02 by CAA)*	Carlisle	22. 7.02P
G-BTTE	Cessna 150L	15075558	N11602	31. 7.91	C.A.Wilson & W.B.Murray	Hill Farm, Nayland	19. 7.04T
G-BTTK*	Thunder Ax8-105 HAB	2036		9. 8.91	Tempowish Ltd *(Cancelled 31.10.02 as wfu)*	Frinton-on-Sea	11. 6.02A
G-BTTL	Cameron V-90 HAB	2649		12. 8.91	A.J.Baird *"Hyde Farm Dairy"*	Cheltenham	10. 8.02A
G-BTTO	British Aerospace ATP	2033	EC-HNA EC-GJU/G-BTTO/G-OEDE/G-BTTO/TC-THV/G-BTTO/S2-ACZ/G-11-033 *(Exported 1.03)*	16. 8.91	Trident Aviation Leasing Services (Jersey) Ltd	Woodford	
G-BTTP	British Aerospace BAe 146 Srs.300	E3203	G-6-203	20. 8.91	KLM UK Ltd *(Op Buzz)*	Stansted	11.11.03T
G-BTTR	Aerotek Pitts S-2A Special (Lycoming IO-360)	2208	N38MP	16. 8.91	C.Butler	Breighton	22. 3.04
G-BTTS	Colt 77A HAB	1861		16. 8.91	J.A.Lomas tr Rutland Balloon Club	Melton Mowbray	19. 8.03A
G-BTTW	Thunder Ax7-77 HAB	2016		27. 8.91	J.Kenny	Athlone, Co.Roscommon	13. 9.03A
G-BTTY	Denney Kitfox Model 2	PFA 172-11823		29. 7.91	K.J.Fleming *(Current status unknown)*	(Liverpool)	
G-BTTZ	Slingsby T.61F Venture T.2	1961	ZA625	30. 7.91	M.W.Olliver	Halesland	3. 9.03
G-BTUA	Slingsby T.61F Venture T.2	1985	ZA666	20. 8.91	C.Edmunds t/r Shenington Gliding Club	Shenington	17. 6.04
G-BTUB	LET Yakovlev C.11 *(Identity of 039 quoted)*	172623	(France) Egyptian AF 543	29. 8.91	M.G. & J.R.Jefferies *(Soviet AF c/s without serial)*	Little Gransden	27. 6.03P
G-BTUE	British Aerospace ATP	2039	EC-GSF EC-GKI/G-OEDH/(G-OGVA)/G-OEDH/G-BTUE/TC-THT/G-11-039/G-BTUE/G-11-039 *(Exported 1.03)*	5. 9.91	Trident Aviation Leasing Services (Jersey) Ltd	Woodford	
G-BTUG	SOCATA Rallye 180T	3208		10. 7.78	Herefordshire Gliding Club Ltd	Shobdon	28. 1.06
G-BTUH	Cameron N-65 HAB	1452		28. 8.91	B.J.Godding *(Zanussi titles)*	Didcot	
G-BTUJ	Thunder Ax9-120 HAB	2022		30. 8.91	ECM Construction Ltd	Great Missenden	20. 5.02T
G-BTUK	Aerotek Pitts S-2A Special (Lycoming AEIO-360)	2260	N5300J	2. 9.91	S.H.Elkington	Wickenby	24.10.03T
G-BTUL	Aerotek Pitts S-2A Special (Lycoming AEIO-360)	2200	N900RS	2. 9.91	J.M.Adams	Tatenhill	26. 2.04
G-BTUM	Piper J-3C-65 Cub (Continental C85) *(Frame No.19586)*	19516	N6335H NC6335H	6. 9.91	I.M.Mackay tr G-BTUM Syndicate *"Jingle-Belle"*	White Waltham	14. 7.03P
G-BTUR	Piper PA-18 Super Cub 95 (Continental C90) (L-18C-PI) *(Frame No.18-3218)*	18-3205	OO-LVM Belg AF OL-L08/L-131/53-4805	11. 9.91	A.P.Meredith	East Midlands	25. 3.05T
G-BTUS	Whittaker MW7 (Rotax 503)	PFA 171-11999		5. 9.91	C.T.Bailey	(Swindon)	1. 5.03P
G-BTUU	Cameron O-120 HAB	2669		16. 9.91	J.L.Guy	Skipton	13.12.01T

G-BTUV	Aeronca 65TAC Defender	C.1661TA	N36816	12. 9.91	M.B.Hamlett & R.E.Coates (Lagny de Sec, France)		
			NC36816		*(Partially rebuilt 1.00: new owners 9.01)*		
G-BTUW	Piper PA-28-151 Cherokee Warrior	28-7415066	N54458	12. 9.91	T.S.Kemp	Enstone	12. 7.04T
G-BTUX	Aérospatiale SA365N2 Dauphin 2	6424		12. 9.91	CHC Scotia Ltd	Humberside	1. 2.05T
G-BTUY	British Aerospace BAe 146 Srs.300	E3202	G-NJIC	17. 9.91	National Jet Italia S.p.A	Milan, Italy	25. 6.04T
			B-17811/B-1781/G-BTUY/G-6-202 9 *(Impounded 2002)*				
G-BTUZ	American General AG-5B Tiger	10075	N11939	3.10.91	Grocontinental Ltd	Sleap	26. 2.03
G-BTVA	Thunder Ax7-77 HAB	2009		16. 9.91	A.H.Symonds *"Bertie Bassett"*	Chelmsford	17. 6.03A
G-BTVB	Everett Gyroplane Srs.3 (Rotax 532)	026		24. 9.91	J.Pumford	Henstridge	18. 4.03P
G-BTVC	Denney Kitfox Model 2	PFA 172-11784		23. 9.91	P.Mitchell *"Zebedee"*	Long Marston	5. 9.02P
G-BTVE	Hawker Demon I (Kestrel V)	-	2292M	18. 9.91	Demon Displays Ltd	Rotary Farm, Hatch	AC
	(Composite of ex IAC Hector -front & K8203 -rear)		K8203		*(As "K8203" in 64 Sqdn c/s) (On rebuild 10.99)*		
G-BTVG*	Cessna 140	12350	N2114N	30. 8.91	V C Gover	Inverness	15. 4.99
	(Continental O-200-A)		NC2114N		*(Cancelled 18.5.01 by CAA) (Stored 2001)*		
G-BTVH*	Colt 77A HAB	1027	G-ZADT	24. 9.91	D.N. & L.J.Close	Andover	19. 8.97A
			G-ZBCA		*(Cancelled 18.10.01 by CAA)*		
G-BTVO	British Aerospace BAe 146 Srs.300	E3205	G-NJID	18. 9.91	Flightline Ltd	Exeter	18.10.03T
			B-1777/G-BTVO/G-6-205				
G-BTVR	Piper PA-28-140 Cherokee Cruiser	28-7625012	N4328X	16. 9.91	Full Sutton Flying Centre Ltd	Full Sutton	9. 4.04T
G-BTVU	Robinson R22 Beta	1937		26. 9.91	B.Enzo	Bologna, Italy	17. 3.03
G-BTVV	Reims/Cessna F337G Skymaster	F33700058	PH-RPD	25. 9.91	C. Keane	Weston, Dublin	12. 1.03T
	(Wichita c/n 33701476)		N1876M				
G-BTVW	Cessna 152 II	15279631	N757CK	23. 9.91	Halegreen Associates Ltd	Hinton in the Hedges	24. 1.05T
G-BTVX	Cessna 152 II	15283375	N48786	23. 9.91	J.C.Birdsall t/a Trafic Management Services	Gamston	2. 8.04T
G-BTWB*	Denney Kitfox Model 3	920 & PFA 172-12278	(G-BTTM)	21. 8.91	J.E.Tootell	East Fortune	
					(Cancelled 14.3.99 by CAA) (Under construction 8.01)		
G-BTWC	Slingsby T.61F Venture T.2	1975	ZA656	23. 9.91	T.M.Holloway tr RAFGSA	Upavon	21. 3.05
G-BTWD	Slingsby T.61F Venture T.2	1976	ZA657	23. 9.91	York Gliding Centre Ltd	Rufforth	26. 3.04
					t/a York Gliding Centre		
G-BTWE	Slingsby T.61F Venture T.2	1980	ZA661	23. 9.91	T.M.Holloway	RAF Syerston	13. 3.04
					tr RAFGSA *(Op Four Counties Gliding Club)*		
G-BTWF	de Havilland DHC-1 Chipmunk 22	C1/0564	WK549	30. 9.91	J.A. & V.G.Simms (As "WK549")	Breighton	24. 4.04
G-BTWI	EAA Acrosport I	230	N10JW	2.10.91	S.Alexander & W.M.Coffee	Bidford	1. 2.03P
	(Lycoming O-290)						
G-BTWJ	Cameron V-77 HAB	2670		3.10.91	S.J. & J.A.Bellaby *"Windy Jack"*	Nottingham	7. 6.03A
G-BTWL	Wag-Aero CUBy Acro Sport Trainer			3.10.91	I.M.Ashpole	Llangarron	7.10.03P
	(Lycoming O-235)	PFA 108-10893					
G-BTWM	Cameron V-77 HAB	2163		4.10.91	R.C.Franklin *"Aerolus"*	Chesham	12. 9.03A
G-BTWN	Maule MXT-7-180 Star Rocket	14025C		7.10.91	C.T.Rolls	Redhill	11. 7.04
G-BTWU	Piper PA-22-135 Tri-Pacer	22-2135	N3320B	10.10.91	Prestige Air (Engineers) Ltd	Haverfordwest	
					(Noted as "N3320B" 7.99: current status unknown)		
G-BTWV	Cameron O-90 HAB	2675		10.10.91	S.F.Hancke	Sunbury-on-Thames	30. 6.01A
G-BTWX	SOCATA TB-9 Tampico Club	1401		14.10.91	D.Weston t/a British Car Rentals	Bourn	20. 9.03T
G-BTWY	Aero Designs Pulsar	PFA 202-12040		15.10.91	M.Stevenson	Pepperbox, Salisbury	6. 8.03P
	(Rotax 582) *(Tail-wheel u/c)*						
G-BTWZ	Rans S-10 Sakota	PFA 194-12117		15.10.91	D.G.Hey *(Current status unknown)*	Little Gransden	8.11.99P
G-BTXB	Colt 77A HAB	2072		16.10.91	A Derbyshire *"Shellgas"* *(New owner 11.01)*	Telford	1. 8.99T
G-BTXD	Rans S-6ESA Coyote II *(Tail-wheel u/c)*	0591.191 & PFA 204-12104		22.10.91	M.Isterling	Insch	7. 7.03P
	(Rotax 582)						
G-BTXF	Cameron V-90 HAB	2692		2.10.91	G.Thompson	Ambleside	3. 3.03
G-BTXG	British Aerospace Jetstream Srs.3102	719	SE-FVP	23.10.91	Highland Airways Ltd	Inverness	9. 7.03T
			G-BTXG/OK-REJ/G-BTXG/OY-EEC/G-BTXG/N418MX/G-31-719				
G-BTXH	Colt AS-56 Hot-Air Airship	2078		23.10.91	L.Kiefer	March-Flugstetten, Germany	26. 3.93A
G-BTXI	Noorduyn AT-16-ND Harvard IIB	14-429	Fv.161052	5.10.91	Patina Ltd	Duxford	22. 8.02P
			RCAF FE695/FE695/42-892		*(Op The Fighter Collection) (As "FE695/94")*		
G-BTXK	Thunder Ax7-65 HAB	1910	ZS-HYP	28.10.91	T.M.Dawson	Woodford Green	5.12.96
			G-BTXK				
G-BTXM*	Colt 2IA Cloudhopper HAB	2082		29.10.91	Virgin Airship & Balloon Co Ltd	Telford	22. 8.97A
					"Virgin Megastore Hopper" (Cancelled 13.11.01 as WFU:) (Stored)		
G-BTXS	Cameron O-120 HAB	2141		16.10.91	Semajan Ltd tr Southern Balloon Group	Romsey	2. 6.03A
G-BTXT	Maule MXT-7-180 Star Rocket	14027C		7.10.91	H.Balfour-Paul	Inverness	4. 1.04
G-BTXV	Cameron A-210 HAB	2703		30.10.91	The Ballooning Business Ltd	Northampton	27. 3.99T
					"Burning Ambition III"		
G-BTXW	Cameron V-77 HAB	2717		31.10.91	P.C.Waterhouse	Wadhurst, East Sussex	20. 4.03A
					"Scott's Whisky"		
G-BTXX	Bellanca 8KCAB Decathlon	595-80	OY-CYC	1.10.91	Tatenhill Aviation Ltd	Tatenhill	4. 3.04T
			SE-IEP/N5063G				
G-BTXZ	Zenair CH.250 (Lycoming O-290)	PFA 113-12170		24.10.91	I.Parris & P.W.J.Hull	Hinton in the Hedges	31.10.03P
G-BTYC	Cessna 150L	15075767	N66002	4.11.91	Polestar Aviation Ltd	Jersey	5. 3.05T
G-BTYE	Cameron A-180 HAB	2704		5.11.91	K.J.A.Maxwell & D.S.Messmer	Haywards Heath	26. 3.00T
					"Rolling Rock"		
G-BTYF	Thunder Ax10-180 Srs.2 HAB	2086		7.11.91	P.Glydon	Barnt Green, Birmingham	5. 4.01T
G-BTYH	Pottier P.80S	PFA 160-11121		11.11.91	R.Pickett	Tatenhill	13. 10.03P
	(Volkswagen 1834)						
G-BTYI	Piper PA-28-181 Archer II	28-8190078	N8287T	15.11.91	C.E.Wright	Fenland	28. 2.04
			(Bounced on landing Fenland 10.4.02, nose u/c broke off, also causing damage to propeller)				
G-BTYK	Cessna 310R II	310R0138	N200VC	21.11.91	Revere Aviation Ltd	Jersey	12. 7.03
			N5018J				
G-BTYT*	Cessna 152 II	15280455	N24931	25.11.91	M.J.Green	Southend	20. 3.99T
					(Cancelled 19.9.00 by CAA) (Noted w/o engine 2.03)		
G-BTYW	Cessna 120	11725	N77283	27.11.91	C.J.Parker	Shacklewell Farm, Wittering	1.10.04
	(Continental C85)		NC77283		tr G-BTYW Group		
G-BTYX*	Cessna 140	11004	N76568	27.11.91	Not known	Rochester	23. 2.98T
			NC76568		*(Cancelled 10.4.01 by CAA) (Stored 7.02)*		

G-BTYY	Curtiss Robin	C-2475	N348K	8.10.91	R.R.L.Windus	Truleigh Manor Farm, Edburton	1. 9.97P
	(Continental W-670)		NC348K				
G-BTYZ	Colt 210A HAB	2083		17.10.91	T.M.Donnelly	Doncaster	1.12.02T
G-BTZA	Beech F33A Bonanza	CE-957	PH-BNT	22.11.91	H.Mendelssohn tr G-BTZA Group	Kirknewton	13. 4.04
G-BTZB	Yakovlev Yak-50	801810	DOSAAF 77	27.11.91	J.S.& J.S.Allison	Duxford	25. 9.03P
					(As "69" in Soviet AF c/s)		
G-BTZD	Yakovlev Yak-1 Srs.1	8188	1342	10.12.91	Historic Aircraft Collection Ltd	Audley End	AC
	(C/n stamped on engine bearers)		(Soviet AF)		(Salvaged from lake in N.Russia mid 1991 after forced landing c.1942: stored 3.96)		
G-BTZE	LET Yakovlev C.11	171312	(France)	11. 2.92	Bianchi Aviation Film Services Ltd	Booker	
			Egypt AF/OK-JIK		(Current status unknown)		
G-BTZG	British Aerospace ATP	2046	PK-MTV	11.12.91	Trident Aviation Leasing Services (Jersey) Ltd	Woodford	
			(PK-MAA)/G-BTZG		(Stored 12.01)		
G-BTZH	British Aeropsace ATP	2047	PK-MTW	11.12.91	Trident Aviation Leasing Services (Jersey) Ltd	Woodford	
			(PK-MAC)/G-BTZH		(Exported 1.03)		
G-BTZK	British Aerospace ATP	2050	PK-MTZ	11.12.91	Trident Aviation Leasing Services (Jersey) Ltd	Woodford	
			G-BTZK/(PK-MAF)/G-BTZK		(Exported 1.03)		
G-BTZL	Oldfield Baby Lakes	8506-M-28B	N2288B	12.12.91	K.P.Rusling	Little Gransden	18. 7.03P
	(Continental C85)						
G-BTZO	SOCATA TB-20 Trinidad	1409		18.12.91	P.R.Draper	Thruxton	2. 4.04
G-BTZP	SOCATA TB-9 Tampico Club	1421		18.12.91	M.W.Orr	Oxford	21. 8.04T
G-BTZR	Colt 77B HAB	2087		18.12.91	P.J.Fell "Bullet"	Maidenhead	26.12.02A
G-BTZS	Colt 77B HAB	2088		18.12.91	P.T.R.Ollivere "Petal"	Sutton	18. 6.03A
G-BTZU	Cameron Concept 60 HAB	2734		20.12.91	A.C.Rackham	Keswick	28. 1.96A
G-BTZV	Cameron V-77 HAB	2410		20.12.91	A.W.Sumner "Vulcan" (Amended CofR 8.02)	St.Ives	8. 9.01A
G-BTZX	Piper J-3C-65 Cub	18871	N98648	27. 2.92	D.A.Woodhams & J.T.Coulthard	Bidford	14. 2.03P
			NC98648				
G-BTZY	Colt 56A HAB	2084		17.10.91	T.M.Donnelly	Doncaster	13.10.94A
G-BTZZ	CFM Streak Shadow K.169-SA & PFA 206-12155			23.12.91	D.R.Stennett	Mendlesham	3. 8.03P
	(Rotax 582)						

G-BUAA - G-BUZZ

G-BUAA	Corben Baby Ace	D561	N516DH	19.11.91	M.W.Chamberlain	(Magor)	16. 5.02P
	(Continental A65)						
G-BUAB	Aeronca 11AC Chief	11AC-1759	N3458E	17. 1.92	J.Reed	Craysmarsh Farm, Melksham	19. 6.03P
	(Continental A65)		NC3458E				
G-BUAC	Slingsby Cadet III	PFA 42-12059	(ex??)	17. 1.92	D.A.Wilson & C.R.Partington	Brunton	4.10.94P
	(Volkswagen 1200) (Original identity unknown, possibly home-built)				(New owner 4.02)		
G-BUAF	Cameron N-77 HAB	2746		2. 1.92	T.H.Wadden "Ariston"	Ringwood	7. 5.03
	(Rebuilt from 5N-ATT)						
G-BUAG	Jodel D.18	PFA 169-11651		3. 1.92	A.L.Silcox	Bodmin	1. 7.03P
	(Volkswagen 1834)				(Noted 10.02)		
G-BUAI	Everett Gyroplane Srs.3	030		6. 1.92	C.G.Brown & D.H.Kirton	(Hinckley)	9. 4.32P
	(Rotax 532)				tr Pop-Corn Group		
G-BUAJ	Cameron N-90 HAB	2735		7. 1.92	J.R. & S.J.Huggins "Chunnel Plant Hire"	Dover	31. 5.01A
G-BUAM	Cameron V-77 HAB	2470		10. 1.92	N.Florence "J & E Page Flowers"	London SW11	17.12.02T
G-BUAN	Cessna 172N Skyhawk II	17270290	N738WH	23.12.91	Studio 916 Ltd	Kemble	2. 9.04T
G-BUAO	Luscombe 8A Silvaire	4089	N1362K	15. 1.92	S.L.Lewis	Draycott Farm, Chiseldon	3. 7.03P
	(Continental A65)		NC1362K				
G-BUAR	Supermarine 358 Seafire LF.IIIc	-	PP972-	21. 1.92	Wizzard Investments Ltd	Earls Colne	AC
	(Built Westland Aircraft Ltd)		Aeronavale/PP972		(Op David Arnold/Flying A Services) (As "PP972")		
G-BUAT	Thunder Ax9-120 HAB	2093		24. 1.92	J.Fenton "Calor"	Preston	17. 3.00T
G-BUAU*	Cameron A-180 HAB	2744		17. 1.92	C.J.Sandell	Sevenoaks	22. 3.96T
					t/a Out of this World Balloons (Cancelled by CAA 18.10.01)		
G-BUAV	Cameron O-105 HAB	2767		27. 1.92	C.D.Monk	Radstock	26. 3.97T
G-BUAX	Rans S-10 Sakota	PFA 194-11848		28. 1.92	S.P.Wakeham & N.Parsons	RAF St.Mawgan	30. 4.03P
	(Rotax 582)						
G-BUBN	Pilatus Britten-Norman BN-2B-26 Islander	2270		14. 2.92	Isles of Scilly Skybus Ltd	St.Just	18. 2.03T
G-BUBR	Cameron A-250 HAB	2779		5. 2.92	Balloon Flights International Ltd	Bath	2. 9.01T
					(Bath Building Society titles) "BIBS I"		
G-BUBS	Lindstrand LBL-77B HAB	144		10.10.94	Beaulah J.Bower "Bubbles Balloon"		
	(Possibly a new envelope c 9.95?)				Middle Wyke Farm, St.Mary Bourne, Andover		20. 8.02A
G-BUBT	Stoddard-Hamilton IIS RG Glasair			6. 2.92	M.D.Evans	Dunkeswell	7. 8.02P
	(Lycoming IO-320) 2026 & PFA 149-11633						
G-BUBU	Piper PA-34-220T Seneca III	34-8233060	N8043B	9. 7.87	Brinor (Holdings) Ltd	Poplar Hall Farm, Elmsett	3. 8.03
G-BUBW	Robinson R22 Beta	2048		7. 2.92	Forth Helicopter Services Ltd	Edinburgh	6. 9.04T
G-BUBY	Thunder Ax8-105 Srs.2 HAB	2115		3. 2.92	T.M.Donnelly "Jorvik Viking Centre"	Doncaster	10. 6.03T
G-BUCA	Cessna A150K Aerobat	A1500220	N5920J	14. 6.89	D.Featherby tr BUCA Group	Norwich	17. 3.05T
G-BUCB	Cameron H-34 HAB	2777		11. 2.92	A.S.Jones	Wolverhampton	14. 8.02A
G-BUCC	CASA I-131E Jungmann	1109	G-BUEM	11. 9.78	P.L.Gaze	Goodwood	2. 7.02P
	(Spanish AF serial conflicts with G-BJAL)		G-BUCC/E3B-114		(As "BU+CC" in Luftwaffe c/s)		
					(Made heavy landing Goodwood 31.1.02 & airframe distorted)		
G-BUCG	Schleicher ASW 20L	20396	BGA.3140	19. 2.92	W.B.Andrews	Booker	3. 8.03
	(Konig SD430)		I-FEEL		"344"		
G-BUCH	Stinson V 77 (AT-19) Reliant	77-381	N9570H	21. 2.92	Pullmerit Ltd	White Waltham	7. 9.02
			FB531(RN)				
G-BUCI*	Auster AOP.9	B5/10/150	XP242	10. 2.92	M.Somerton-Rayner	Middle Wallop	19. 5.00P
					t/a Historic Aircraft Flight Reserve Collection		
					(As "XP242" in Army Air Corps c/s) (Cancelled 5.3.01 as temporarily WFU)		
G-BUCJ	de Havilland DHC.2 Beaver AL.1	1442	XP772	23. 3.92	Propshop Ltd & G.Warner	Duxford	
					t/a British Aerial Museum (As "XP772" in Army)		
G-BUCK	CASA I-131E Jungmann Srs.1000	1113	E3B-322	11. 9.78	R.A.Cayless & J.G.Brander	White Waltham	7. 3.03P
					tr Jungmann Flying Group (As "BU+CK" in Luftwaffe c/s)		

Reg	Type	C/n	Prev ID	Date	Owner/Operator	Location	Date
G-BUCM	Hawker Sea Fury FB.11	-	VX653	26. 2.92	Patina Ltd	Duxford	
	(Op The Fighter Collection) (As "VX653")						
G-BUCO	Pietenpol Air Camper	PFA 47-11829		10. 2.92	A.James	Siege Cross Farm, Thatcham	8. 8.03P
	(Continental C90)						
G-BUCS	Cessna 150F	15062368	N3568L	25. 8.89	Atlantic Bridge Aviation Ltd	Lydd	1. 4.04T
G-BUCT	Cessna 150L	15075326	N11320	14. 6.89	Atlantic Bridge Aviation Ltd	Lydd	5.11.03T
G-BUDA	Slingsby T.61F Venture T.2	1963	ZA627	18. 2.92	T.M.Holloway tr RAFGSA	RAF Halton	26. 6.04
G-BUDB	Slingsby T.61F Venture T.2	1964	ZA628	18. 2.92	T.M.Holloway tr RAFGSA	Bicester	5. 9.04
G-BUDC	Slingsby T.61F Venture T.2	1971	ZA652	18. 2.92	I.P.Litchfield tr T.61 Group	Enstone	30. 8.02
G-BUDE	Piper PA-22-135 Tri-Pacer	22-980	N1144C	9. 4.92	B.A.Bower	Branscombe	1. 2.04
	(Tail-wheel conversion)						
G-BUDF	Rand-Robinson KR-2	PFA 129-11155		26. 2.92	M.Stott	(Bedford)	30. 8.01P
	(HAPI Magnum 75)						
G-BUDI	Aero Designs Pulsar	PFA 202-12185		25. 2.92	R.W.L.Oliver	Popham	18. 7.03P
	(Rotax 582)						
G-BUDK	Thunder Ax7-77 HAB	2076		2. 3.92	W.Evans	Wrexham	4. 4.03A
G-BUDL	Taylorcraft E Auster III	458	PH-POL	5. 3.92	M.Pocock	AAC Middle Wallop	
	(Regd with Frame No.TAY 5810)		8A-2/R Neth AF R-17/NX534		*(As "NX534") (On rebuild 6.98 for Military Auster Flight)*		
G-BUDN	Cameron Shoe 90SS HAB	2761		6. 3.92	Magical Adventures Ltd	West Bloomfield, Mi., USA	1. 8.00A
	(Converse Allstar Trainers shape)				*"Converse Allstar Boot"*		
G-BUDO	PZL-110 Koliber 150	03900045	(D-EIVT)	12. 3.92	A.S.Vine	Haverfordwest	27. 7.02
G-BUDR	Denney Kitfox Model 3	1086 & PFA 172-12107		16. 3.92	N.J.P.Mayled	Dunkeswell	17. 8.03P
	(Rotax 582)						
G-BUDS	Rand Robinson KR-2	PFA 129-10937		31.12.85	D.W.Munday	Popham	
					(Noted unmarked nearing completion 9.01)		
G-BUDT	Slingsby T.61F Venture T.2	1883	XZ563	30. 3.92	R.V.Andrews tr G-BUDT Group	Eaglescott	10. 7.04
G-BUDU	Cameron V-77 HAB	2447		16. 3.92	T.M.G.Amery	Llandeilo	18. 9.03A
G-BUDW	Brugger MB.2 Colibri	PFA 43-10644	G-GODS	19. 3.92	J.M.Hoblyn	Watchford Farm, Yarcombe	3.10.00P
	(Volkswagen 1600)				*(Crashed Taunton Racecourse 13.8.00: under repair 1.03)*		
G-BUEC	Van's RV-6	21015 & PFA 181C-11884		17. 3.92	A.H.Harper	Henstridge	27. 7.03P
	(Lycoming O-360)						
G-BUED	Slingsby T.61F Venture T.2	1979	ZA660	12. 3.92	D.J.Wood	Waldershare Park	4. 7.04
					tr SE Kent Civil Service Flying Club		
G-BUEE	Cameron A-210 HAB	2803		20. 3.92	The Balloon Club Ltd	Bristol	21. 7.00T
					t/a Bristol Balloons *(Wookey Hole Caves titles)*		
G-BUEF	Cessna 152 II	15280862	N25928	17. 3.92	A.L.Brown t/a Channel Aviation	Bourn	1. 9.05T
G-BUEG	Cessna 152 II	15280347	N24736	17. 3.92	Plymouth School of Flying Ltd	Plymouth	28.11.04T
G-BUEI	Thunder Ax8-105 HAB	2172		23. 3.92	Elinore French Ltd	Morpeth	14. 2.03A
					t/a Imagination Balloon Flights		
G-BUEK	Slingsby T.61F Venture T.2	1879	XZ559	30. 3.92	Norfolk Gliding Club Ltd	Tibenham	14.11.04
G-BUEL*	Colt Bottle II SS HAB	2141		26. 3.92	Not known *"Korbel Brut"*	USA	
	(Korbel California Champagne Bottle shape)				*(Cancelled 30.7.98 by CAA) (Noted 2000)*		
G-BUEN	VPM M.14 Scout	VPM14-UK101		19. 3.92	F.G.Shepherd	Carlisle	4.12.96P
	(Arrow GT1000R)				*(Noted 11.01)*		
G-BUEP	Maule MXT-7-180 Star Rocket	14023C		24. 3.92	G.M.Bunn	Goodwood	1. 5.04
G-BUEV	Cameron O-77 HAB	2810	EI-CFW	31. 3.92	R.R.McCormack	Belfast	21. 9.03A
			G-BUEV				
G-BUEW	Rans S-6 Coyote II	D-190111 & PFA 204-12021	G-MWYF	1. 4.92	M.F.Hadley	Lower Mountpleasant Farm, Chatteris	10.12.03P
			(EI-CEL)				
G-BUEX	Schweizer Hughes 269C (300C)	S.1412	G-HFLR	14. 4.92	EK Aviation Ltd	(Mildenhall)	17. 7.05T
G-BUEZ*	Hawker Hunter F.6A	S4U-3275	8736M	3. 4.92	Not known	Spanhoe	
	(Built Armstrong-Whitworth Aircraft)		XF375		*(Cancelled 28.8.01 as WFU) (Noted 11.02)*		
G-BUFA	Cameron R-77 Gas/HAB	2712		19. 3.92	Noble Adventures Ltd	(The Netherlands)	10. 6.93A
					(Stored 1996: current status unknown)		
G-BUFC	Cameron R-77 Gas/HAB	2823		19. 3.92	Noble Adventures Ltd	(The Netherlands)	23. 6.93A
					(Stored 1996: current status unknown)		
G-BUFE	Cameron R-77 Gas/HAB	2825		19. 3.92	Noble Adventures Ltd	(The Netherlands)	21. 6.93A
					(Stored 1996: current status unknown)		
G-BUFG	Slingsby T.61F Venture T.2	1977	ZA658	3. 4.92	Halegreen Associates Ltd	Hinton in the Hedges	16. 8.04
G-BUFH	Piper PA-28-161 Warrior II	28-8416076	N43520	15. 4.92	M.P.Rainford & J.E.Slee	Blackpool	3. 6.04T
					tr The Tiger Leisure Group		
G-BUFJ	Cameron V-90 HAB	2809		7. 4.92	S.P.Richards	Tonbridge	1. 7.03T
G-BUFK	Cassutt Racer IIIM	PFA 34-11069		7. 4.92	D.I.H.Johnstone & W.T.Barnard	(Lanark)	
					(Under construction 6.00)		
G-BUFN	Slingsby T.61F Venture T.2	1967	ZA631	8. 4.92	S.C.Foggin	Sandhill Farm, Shrivenham	3.10.04
					tr BUFN Group		
G-BUFR	Slingsby T.61F Venture T.2	1880	XZ560	9. 4.92	East Sussex Gliding Club Ltd	Ringmer	3. 6.04
	(Rollason RS Mk.2)						
G-BUFT	Cameron O-120 HAB	2814		9. 4.92	D.Bron	St Barthelemy, France	22. 6.03T
G-BUFV	Avid Speed Wing Mk.4	PFA 189-12192		15. 4.92	M.& B.Gribbin	(Antrim, Co.Antrim)	19. 6.02P
G-BUFX	Cameron N-90 HAB	2835		22. 4.92	Kerridge Computer Co Ltd *"Kerridge II"*	Newbury	3. 7.03A
G-BUFY	Piper PA-28-161 Warrior II	28-8016211	N130CT	14. 4.92	Bickertons Aerodromes Ltd	Denham	30. 6.04T
			N8TS/N3571K		*(Op The Pilots Centre)*		
G-BUGB	Stolp SA.750 Acroduster Too	PFA 89-11942		22. 4.92	R.M.Chaplin	Rochester	27. 8.03P
	(Lycoming O-360-A1D)						
G-BUGD	Cameron V-77 HAB	2195		23. 4.92	P.Haslett	Arcy sur Cure, France	16. 7.03A
G-BUGE	Bellanca 7GCAA Citabria	339-77	N4165Y	23. 4.92	V.Vaughan & N.O'Brien	Mullinahone, Co.Tipperary	13. 9.04T
G-BUGG	Cessna 150F	15062479	N8379G	24. 3.92	C.P.J.Taylor & D.M.Forshaw	Panshanger	28. 9.05
G-BUGH*	Rans S-10 Sakota	0790.110 & PFA 194-11899		24. 4.92	D.T.Smith	Bagby	31. 8.99P
	(Rotax 582)				*(Cancelled 3.8.01 by CAA)*		
G-BUGI	Evans VP-2	PFA 7201		16. 4.92	J.A.Rees	Haverfordwest	25.11.02P
	(Continental A65-8)						
G-BUGJ	Robin DR400/180 Regent	2137		28. 4.92	W.M.Patterson	(Manorcunningham)	19. 7.04
G-BUGL	Slingsby T.61F Venture T.2	1966	ZA630	29. 4.92	J.Edwards & B.L.Owen tr VMG Group	Tibenham	1. 6.04

Reg	Type	C/n	Prev id	Date	Owner/Operator	Location	Status
G-BUGM	CFM Streak Shadow K.176-SA & PFA 206-12069 (Rotax 582)			29. 4.92	D.Penn-Smith tr The Shadow Group	Sywell	29. 6.03P
G-BUGN*	Colt 210A HAB	2193		1. 5.92	R.W.Batchelor *(Cancelled 29.11.01 as WFU)*	Thame	31. 7.99T
G-BUGO	Colt 56B HAB	2143		18. 5.92	Escuela de Aerostacion Mica	Valencia, Spain	19. 7.00A
G-BUGP	Cameron V-77 HAB	2278	OO-BEE	10. 3.92	R. Churcher	Canterbury	14. 7.02A
G-BUGS	Cameron V-77 HAB	2482		14. 4.92	S.J.Dymond *"Bugs Bunny"*	Tidworth	14. 9.01T
G-BUGT	Slingsby T.61F Venture T.2	1871	XZ551	22. 4.92	R.W.Hornsey	Rufforth	5. 8.05
G-BUGV	Slingsby T.61F Venture T.2	1884	XZ564	28. 4.92	Oxfordshire Sportflying Ltd	Enstone	23.10.04
G-BUGW	Slingsby T.61F Venture T.2	1962	ZA626	22. 4.92	Halegreen Associates Ltd	Hinton in the Hedges	16. 8.04
G-BUGY	Cameron V-90 HAB	2800		9. 4.92	I.J.Culley tr Dante Balloon Group *"Florance"*	Bosham	31. 7.03A
G-BUGZ	Slingsby T.61F Venture T.2	1981	ZA662	22. 4.92	R.W.Spiller tr Dishforth Flying Group	AAC Dishforth	24. 5.02
G-BUHA	Slingsby T.61F Venture T.2	1970	ZA634	29. 4.92	K.E. Ballington *(As "ZA634/C")*	Saltby	19. 7.02
G-BUHK	Boeing 737-4Q8	26289		14. 6.93	British Airways plc	Heathrow	13. 6.03T
G-BUHM	Cameron V-77 HAB	2481		7. 5.92	L.A.Watts *"Blue Horizon"*	Pangbourne, Reading	10.12.02A
G-BUHO	Cessna 140 (Continental C90)	14402	N2173V	1. 5.92	W.B.Bateson	Blackpool	19.11.04T
G-BUHR	Slingsby T.61F Venture T.2	1874	XZ554	8. 5.92	S J Wright tr Denbeigh Falke Group	Lleweni Parc	16.10.05
G-BUHS	Stoddard-Hamilton Glasair I TD (Lycoming O-360)	149	C-GYMB	8. 5.92	E.J.Spalding	(Dingwall)	6. 9.00P
G-BUHU	Cameron N-105 HAB	2785		13. 5.92	Unipart Group Ltd tr Unipart Balloon Club	Cowley	21.11.96A
G-BUHY	Cameron A-210 HAB	2858		14. 5.92	Adventure Balloon Co Ltd	London W7	21. 9.99T
G-BUHZ	Cessna 120	14950	N3676V	1. 5.92	M R Houseman tr C140 Group	Spanhoe	20. 1.03P
G-BUIC	Denney Kitfox Model 2	PFA 172-11802		1. 5.92	C.R.Northrop & B.M.Chilvers	(Huntingdon/Wisbech)	
G-BUIE	Cameron N-90 HAB	2863		22. 5.92	B.Conway	Wheatley, Oxon	24. 1.01A
G-BUIF	Piper PA-28-161 Warrior II	28-7916406	N28375	29. 5.92	Newcastle upon Tyne Aero Club Ltd	Newcastle	8. 9.04T
G-BUIG	Campbell Cricket (Rotax 532)	PFA G/03-1173		27. 5.92	J.A.English	(Edinburgh)	29.10.03P
G-BUIH	Slingsby T.61F Venture T.2	1876	XZ556	29. 5.92	Yorkshire Gliding Club (Pty) Ltd	Sutton Bank	8. 6.04
G-BUIJ	Piper PA-28-161 Warrior II	28-8116210	N83784	3. 6.92	Tradecliff Ltd	Blackbushe	9. 7.04
G-BUIK	Piper PA-28-161 Warrior II	28-7916469	N2845P	2. 6.92	A.S.Bamrah t/a Falcon Flying Services	Shoreham	23. 8.04T
G-BUIL	CFM Streak Shadow K.182-SA & PFA 206-12121 (Rotax 582)			8. 5.92	P.N.Bevan & L.M.Poor *"Mr Bounce"*	Perth	7. 5.03P
G-BUIN	Thunder Ax7-77 HAB	1882		5. 6.92	P C Johnson	Gloucester	20. 9.02A
G-BUIO	British Aerospace Jetstream Srs.3202	835	OH-JAB G-BUIO/C-GZRT/G-31-835	1. 9.92	BAE Systems (Operations) Ltd *(Op Eastern Airways)*	Woodford	26. 4.03T
G-BUIP	Denney Kitfox Model 2	710 & PFA 172-11874		8. 6.92	Avcomm Developments Ltd	Enstone	1. 8.32P
G-BUIR	Avid Speed Wing Mk.4 (Rotax 582)	PFA 189-12213		9. 6.92	M.C.J.Myers *(Damaged nr Gainsborough 26.1.97: on rebuild 5.97: new owner 7.02)*	(Cheltenham)	29. 4.97P
G-BUIU	Cameron V-90 HAB	2641		11. 6.92	H.Micketeit	Bielefeld, Germany	18. 4.03A
G-BUJA	Slingsby T.61F Venture T.2	1972	ZA653	22. 5.92	T.M.Holloway tr RAFGSA *(Op Wrekin Gliding Club)*	RAF Cosford	8. 7.01
G-BUJB	Slingsby T.61F Venture T.2	1978	ZA659	21. 5.92	O.F.Vaughan & D.A.Fall tr Falke Syndicate	Shobdon	11. 7.04
G-BUJE	Cessna 177B Cardinal	17701920	N34646	10. 6.92	J.Flux tr FG93 Group	Old Sarum	5. 5.04
G-BUJH	Colt 77B HAB	2207		23. 6.92	R.P.Cross & R.Stanley	Luton/Harpenden	20.11.03A
G-BUJI	Slingsby T.61F Venture T.2	1882	XZ562	22. 5.92	Solent Venture Syndicate Ltd	Lee-on-Solent	28. 5.04
G-BUJJ	Avid Speed Wing	213	N614JD	20.10.92	C.Walsh	Bodmin	26. 9.03P
G-BUJK	Montgomerie-Bensen B.8MR Merlin (Rotax 582)	PFA G/01-1211		25. 6.92	K.J.Robinson	(Oxford)	12. 4.03P
G-BUJL	Aero Designs Pulsar	PFA 202-11892		16. 6.92	J.J.Lynch *(Current status unknown)*	(Dunstable)	
G-BUJM	Cessna 120 (Continental C85)	11784	N77343 NC77343	19. 6.92	M.Holliday tr Cessna 120 Flying Group	RNAS Yeovilton	28.10.02
G-BUJN	Cessna 172N Skyhawk II	17272713	N6315D	19. 6.92	Aerohire Ltd	Wolverhampton	30.11.95T
G-BUJO	Piper PA-28-161 Cherokee Warrior II	28-7716077	N1014Q	19. 6.92	A.S.Bamrah t/a Falcon Flying Services	Biggin Hill	24. 3.03T
G-BUJP	Piper PA-28-161 Warrior II	28-7916047	N21624	19. 6.92	White Waltham Airfield Ltd	White Waltham	27. 6.02T
G-BUJR	Cameron A-180 HAB	2821		22. 6.92	Dragon Balloon Company Ltd	(Hope Valley)	16.10.05T
G-BUJV	Avid Speed Wing Mk.4	PFA 189-12250		3. 7.92	C.Thomas *(Damaged Caernarfon 13.8.93: current status unknown)*	(Tamworth)	28. 7.94P
G-BUJW	Thunder Ax8-90 Srs.2 HAB	2208		6. 7.92	R.T.Fagan	Bath	6. 8.95T
G-BUJX	Slingsby T.61F Venture T.2	1873	XZ553	7. 7.92	J.R.Chichester-Constable	Burton Constable, Hull	19. 7.02
G-BUJZ	Rotorway Executive 90 (Rotorway RI 162)	5119		9. 7.92	M.P.Swoboda *(Damage on take-off near Purleigh, Essex 2.11.01: noted 2.03)*	Street Farm, Takeley	9.10.02P
G-BUKA	Fairchild SA.227AC Metro III	AC-706B	ZK-NSQ N27185/G-BUKA/N27185	24. 8.88	Atlantic Air Transport Ltd *(Atlantic Express titles)*	Coventry	11. 6.03T
G-BUKB	Rans S-10 Sakota (Rotax 582)	PFA 194-12078		13. 7.92	M.K.Blatch	RAF Keevil	15. 9.03P
G-BUKF	Denney Kitfox Model 4 (Rotax 582)	PFA 172A-12247		2. 6.92	A.G.V.McClintock tr Kilo Foxtrot Group	East Fortune	7. 3.03P
G-BUKH	Druine D.31 Turbulent (Volkswagen 1600)	PFA 48-11419		14. 8.92	P.M.Newman	Stoneacre Farm, Farthing Corner	6. 8.03P
G-BUKI	Thunder Ax7-77 HAB	2239		8. 7.92	Airxcite Ltd t/a Virgin Balloon Flights	(Wembley)	15. 1.03T
G-BUKJ	British Aerospace ATP	2052	EC-HCO G-BUKJ/EC-GLD/G-OEDF/G-BUKJ/TC-THZ/G-BUKJ *(Exported 1.03)*	5. 8.92	Trident Aviation Leasing Services (Jersey) Ltd	Woodford	
G-BUKK	Dornier Bücker Bü.133D Jungmeister	27	N44DD HB-MKG/Sw AF U-80	15.11.89	E.J.F.McEntee *(As "U-80" in Swiss AF c/s)*	Kirdford, Billingshurst	10.10.02P
G-BUKN	Piper PA-15 Vagabond	15-215	N4427H NC4427H	15. 7.92	B.F. & M.A.Goddard *(New owners 4.01)*	(Southampton)	
G-BUKP	Denney Kitfox Model 2 (Rotax 582)	PFA 172-12301		22. 7.92	S.Moreton	Shenstone	1. 7.03P
G-BUKR	SOCATA MS.880B Rallye 100T	2923	LN-BIY	27. 7.92	G.R.Russell tr G-BUKR Flying Group	Bridport	14.11.02
G-BUKS	Colt 77B HAB 2	241		6. 7.92	R.& M.Bairstow	Middlewich, Cheshire	24. 7.03A
G-BUKT	Luscombe 8E Silvaire (Continental C85)	2197	N45670 NC45670	30. 7.92	M.G.Talbot & J.N.Wilshaw	Sherburn-in-Elmet	13.11.02P

G-BUKU	Luscombe 8E Silvaire	4720	N1993K	30. 7.92	D.J.Warren tr Silvaire Flying Group	Rochester	11.12.03P
	(Continental C85)		NC1993K				
G-BUKV	Colt AS-105 Mk.II Hot-Air Airship	2212	ZS-HYO	3. 8.92	A.Ockelmann t/a Ballon Reisen	Buchholz, Germany	17. 4.02A
			G-BUKV				
G-BUKX	Piper PA-28-161 Cherokee Warrior II 28-7816674		N231PA	5. 8.92	LNP Ltd	Exeter	12.12.04T
G-BUKZ	Evans VP-2	PFA 63-10761		5. 8.92	P.R.Farnell *(Extant 7.02)*	Wombleton	
G-BULB	Thunder Ax7-77 HAB	1968		3. 7.92	Richard Nash Cars Ltd	Norwich	6. 4.03A
G-BULC	Avid Flyer Mk.4	PFA 189-12202		6. 7.92	C.Nice	Popham	3. 7.03P
	(Rotax 582)						
G-BULD	Cameron N-105 HAB	2136		6. 8.92	C.L.Jenkins	Bristol	27. 3.03T
G-BULE*	Price TPB.2 HAB	004		10. 8.92	A.G.R.Calder	London NW1	
					(Cancelled 23.11.01 as WFU)		
G-BULF	Colt 77A HAB	2043		10. 8.92	P.Goss & T.C.Davies	Christchurch	10. 5.03A
G-BULG	Van's RV-4	JRV4-1	C-FELJ	28. 7.92	M.J.Aldridge	Priory Farm, Tibenham	21. 5.03P
	(Lycoming O-320)						
G-BULH	Cessna 172N Skyhawk II	17269869	N738CJ	2. 7.92	Touchdown Properties Ltd	Blackpool	9. 9.02T
G-BULJ	CFM Streak Shadow K.191-SA & PFA 206-12199			10. 8.92	C.C.Brown	Lubenham	1. 8.03P
	(Rotax 582)						
G-BULK	Thunder Ax9-120 Srs.2 HAB	2237		3. 7.92	S.J.Colin t/a Skybus Ballooning	Cranbrook	12. 10.03T
G-BULL	Scottish Aviation Bulldog Srs.120/128	BH120/392	HKG-5	20. 9.88	Solo Leisure Ltd	Old Sarum	23. 9.04T
			G-31-18		*(As "HKG-5" in Hong Kong c/s)*		
G-BULM	Aero Designs Pulsar	PFA 202-12010		11. 8.92	J.Lloyd	(Wokingham)	1. 5.03P
	(Rotax 582) *(Tricycle u/c)*						
G-BULN	Colt 210A HAB	2265		13. 8.92	H.G.Davies	Cheltenham	31. 7.03T
G-BULO	Luscombe 8A Silvaire	4216	N1489K	13. 8.92	A.F.S.Caldecourt	Popham	23. 5.03P
	(Continental A65)		NC1489K				
G-BULR	Piper PA-28-140 Cherokee B	28-25230	HB-OHP	8. 7.92	R & H Wale (General Woodworks) Ltd	Little Gransden	13. 5.05T
			N7320F		*"Margaret Ann"*		
G-BULT	Everett Gyroplane Srs.1	PFA G/03A-1213		20. 8.92	A.T.Pocklington	(Bishops Stortford)	8.12.03P
	(Originally regd as Campbell Cricket c/n PFA G/03-1213: type & c/n officially amended 13.12.02)						
G-BULW*	Rans S-10 Sakota	PFA 194-11663		18. 8.92	J.L.M. van Hoesel	Lelystad, The Netherlands	
					(To PH-RNS 98R. cancelled 17.4.98: noted as "G-BULW" 6.01)		
G-BULY	Avid Flyer	PFA 189-12309		12. 8.92	D.R.Piercy	Newton Peverill	23. 7.03P
	(Rotax 582)				*"Lady Irene"*		
G-BULZ	Denney Kitfox Model 2	PFA 172-11546		31. 7.92	T.G.F.Trenchard	Newton Peverill	30.10.02P
G-BUMP	Piper PA-28-181 Cherokee Archer II 28-7790437		PH-MVA	17. 1.79	Marham Investments Ltd	Ronaldsway	20.11.03T
			OO-HCH/N3105Q		*(Op Manx Flyers Aero Club)*		
G-BUNB	Slingsby T.61F Venture T.2	1969	ZA633	25. 8.92	T.M.Holloway	RAF Cranwell	9. 1.05
					tr RAFGSA *(Op Cranwell Gliding Club)*		
G-BUNC	PZL-104 Wilga 35A	129444	SP-TWP	2. 9.92	R.F.Goodman	Husbands Bosworth	18. 6.05
G-BUND	Piper PA-28RT-201T Turbo Arrow IV 28R-8031107		N8219V	18. 7.88	Jenrick Ltd & A.Somerville	Blackbushe	20. 8.04
G-BUNG	Cameron N-77 HAB	2905		2. 9.92	A.Kaye	Wellingborough	18. 1.03A
					tr The Bungle Balloon Group *(Aspen titles) "Bungle"*		
G-BUNH	Piper PA-28RT-201T Turbo Arrow IV 28R-8031166		N8255H	26. 8.92	Jennifer A.Blenkharn	Carlisle	20. 1.05T
					t/a JB Consultants (Aviation)		
G-BUNI	Cameron Bunny 90SS HAB	2897		23. 9.92	Virgin Airship & Balloon Co Ltd	Telford	29.10.99A
					(Cadburys Caramel Bunny shape)		
G-BUNJ	K & S SA.102-5 Cavalier	PFA 01-10058		10. 9.92	J.A.Smith	Great Massingham	
					(Nearing completion 9.97: current status unknown)		
G-BUNM	Denney Kitfox Model 3	PFA 172-12111		15. 9.92	P.N.Akass	Inverness	18. 4.03P
	(Rotax 582) *(Floatplane)*				*(Overturned landing Beauly Firth 28.8.01: landing gear not retracted)*		
G-BUNO	Neico Lancair 320	PFA 191-12332		11. 9.92	J.Softley *(On build 2000)*	(Newbury)	
G-BUNS*	Reims/Cessna F150K	F15000648	F-BSIL	28. 8.92	R.W.H.Cole	Spilsted Farm, Sedlescombe	
					t/a Cole Aviation		
					(Noted stored 11.01: cancelled 13.5.02 as WFU - no UK CofA issued)		
G-BUNV	Thunder Ax7-77 HAB	1967		23. 9.92	R.M.Garnett *"Skylark"*	Eastleigh	12. 8.02A
G-BUNZ	Thunder Ax10-180 Srs.2 HAB	2271		7. 9.92	M.A.Scholes	Haywards Heath	10. 4.03T
G-BUOA	Whittaker MW6-S Srs.A Fatboy Flyer			25. 9.92	R.Blackburn	(Raphoe, Co.Donegal)	5.11.02P
	(Rotax 582)	PFA 164-11959					
G-BUOB	CFM Streak Shadow K.186-SA & PFA 206-12156			29. 9.92	A.M.Simmons	Belle Vue Farm, Yarnscombe	18. 7.03P
	(Rotax 582)						
G-BUOC	Cameron A-210 HAB	2924		5.10.92	Aerosaurus Balloons LLP	Exeter	12. 6.03T
G-BUOD	Replica Plans SE.5A	PFA 20-10474		5.10.92	M.D.Waldron	Kemble	11. 6.03P
	(Continental C90)				*(As "B595/W" in 56 Sqdn, RFC c/s)*		
G-BUOE	Cameron V-90 HAB	2938		6.10.92	B.& J.Smallwood	Chippenham	18. 4.03A
					t/a Dusters & Co *"Flying Colours 2"*		
G-BUOF	Druine D.62B Condor	PFA 49-11236		6.10.92	R.P.Loxton	Loxton Farm, Sherbourne	5. 8.03P
	(Continental O-200-A)						
G-BUOI	Piper PA-20-135 Pacer	20-571	OY-ALS	18. 9.92	R.A.L.Hubbard tr Foley Farm Flying Group	Meon	15. 5.05
	(Lycoming O-320) *(Hoerner wing-tips)*		D-EHEN/N7750K				
G-BUOJ	Cessna 172N Skyhawk II	17271701	N5064E	8.10.92	Falcon Flying Services Ltd	Biggin Hill	12. 7.04T
G-BUOK	Rans S-6-116 Coyote II			9.10.92	M.Morris	Fieldhead Farm, Denholme, Bradford	17. 9.03P
	(Rotax 912UL)	0692.314 & PFA 204A-12317					
G-BUOL	Denney Kitfox Model 3	PFA 172-12142		12.10.92	G.P.& F.C.Coleman	(Tattershall)	7. 7.03P
	(Rotax 582)						
G-BUON	Avid Aerobat (Rotax 582)	PFA 189-12160		13.10.92	S.R.Winder	(Bolton)	6.11.01P
G-BUOR	CASA I-131E Jungmann Srs.2000	2134	N89542	21.10.92	M.I.M.Schermer Voest	(Lelystad, The Netherlands)	13.11.95P
			EC-336/E3B-508		*(On rebuild 2001)*		
G-BUOS	Supermarine 394 Spitfire FR.XVIIIe	6S/672224	HS687	19.10.92	Historic Flying Ltd	Duxford	21. 8.03P
	(Regd as c/n 6S/676224)		Ind AF/SM845		*(Op Aircraft Restoration Company) (As "SM845/GZ-J")*		
G-BUOW	Aero Designs Pulsar XP	PFA 202-12206		22.10.92	T.J.Hartwell	Sackville Lodge, Riseley	8. 6.95P
	(Rotax 912)				*(New owner 7.01)*		
G-BUOX	Cameron V-77 HAB	2925		23.10.92	R.M.Pursey & C.M.Richardson	Newbury/Oxford	14. 5.00A
					"High Flyer"		

Reg	Type	c/n	Prev id	Date	Owner/Operator	Location	CofA
G-BUOZ	Thunder Ax10-180 HAB	1962	(SX-) G-BUOZ	29.10.92	Zebedee Balloon Service Ltd	Hungerford	5. 4.03T
G-BUPA	Rutan LongEz (Lycoming O-235)	750	N72SD	22. 9.92	N.G.Henry	Gloucestershire	13. 8.03P
G-BUPB	Stolp SA.300 Starduster Too (Lycoming IO-360)	RH.100	N8035E	3.11.92	J.R.Edwards tr Starduster PB Group	Popham	12. 2.03P
G-BUPC	Rollason Beta B2 (Continental C90)	PFA 02-12369		29.10.92	C.A.Rolph	Liverpool	3. 6.03P
G-BUPF	Bensen B.8MR (Rotax 532)	PFA G/01-1209		5.11.92	P.W.Hewitt-Dean	(Wootton Bassett)	1. 8.02P
G-BUPG	Cessna 180J Skywagon	18052490	N52086	15.10.92	T.P.A.Norman	Rendcomb	6.11.05
G-BUPI	Cameron V-77 HAB	1778	G-BOUC	28. 7.88	Sally A.Masey *"Bristol United Press"* (Western Daily Press/Evening Post titles)	Bristol	30. 4.00A
G-BUPJ	Sportavia Fournier RF4D	4119	N7752	10.11.92	M.R.Shelton *(Current status unknown)*	Tatenhill	
G-BUPM	VPM M-16 Tandem Trainer (Rotax 914)	VPM16-UK-102		16.10.92	Roger Savage Gyroplanes Ltd	Carlisle	29. 5.03P
G-BUPO*	Moravan Zlin Z.526F Trener Master	1267	YR-OAZ YR-ZAO	23.11.92	P.J.Behr & F.Mendelssohn (Sarreguemines/Strasbourg, France) *(Cancelled 2.10.00 as WFU: current status unknown)*		31. 1.96
G-BUPP	Cameron V-42 HAB	2789		21. 7.92	L.J.Schoeman	Basildon	28. 3.02A
G-BUPR	Jodel D.18 (Limbach L2000)	PFA 169-11289		23.11.92	R.W.Burrows	Priory Farm, Tibenham	1. 5.03P
G-BUPS	Aérospatiale/Alenia ATR 42-300	109	DQ-FEP F-WWEF	16.12.92	Titan Airways Ltd	Stansted	5. 6.05T
G-BUPT	Cameron O-105 HAB	2960		25.11.92	P.M.Simpson	Hemel Hempstead	23. 3.03A
G-BUPU	Thunder Ax7-77 HAB	2305		25.11.92	R.C.Barkworth & D.G.Maguire *"Puzzle"*	(USA)	26. 3.01A
G-BUPV	Great Lakes 2T-1A Sport Trainer (Gladden Kinner R55)	126	N865K NC865K	26.11.92	R.J.Fray	Sibson	28. 6.03P
G-BUPW	Denney Kitfox Model 3 (Rotax 912)	PFA 172-12281		22.10.92	G.M.Park tr Forfoxake Flyers	(Lochwinnoch)	10. 7.03P
G-BURD	Reims/Cessna F172N Skyhawk II	F17201677	PH-AXI	26. 4.78	M.O.Loxton	Parsonage Farm, Eastchurch *(Island Aviation - Historic Air Tours titles)*	12.12.05T
G-BURE	Jodel D.9 Bebe	PFA 944		30.11.92	Lucy J.Kingsford *(Noted 3.00)*	Headcorn	
G-BURF*	Rand Robinson KR-2 (Volkswagen 1834)	PFA 129-11345		30.11.92	P.J.H.Moorhouse & B.L.Hewart	(Stockport)	
			(Noted on a trailer Sunbury Cross 30.6.02) (Cancelled 14.8.02 by CAA - no PtoF issued)				
G-BURG	Colt 77A HAB	2042		12. 1.93	S.T.Humphreys *"Lily"*	Great Missenden	14. 8.03A
G-BURH	Cessna 150E	15061225	EI-AOO G-BURH/EI-AOO/N2125J	2.12.92	C.A.Davis & R F H Roberts tr BURH Flying Group	Thruxton	6.11.02
G-BURI	Enstrom F-28C	433	N51743	11.12.92	R.L.Heath tr India Helicopters Group	Goodwood	26. 5.05T
G-BURL	Colt 105A HAB	2297		18.11.92	J.E.Rose	Abingdon	5. 1.03T
G-BURN	Cameron O-120 HAB	2793		18. 2.92	Innovation Ballooning Ltd *"Innovations"*	Bath	1.8.03T
G-BURP	Rotorway Executive 90 (Rotorway RI 162)	5116		8.10.92	N.K.Newman *(Stored 7.99) (Amended CofR 3.02)*	(Buckingham)	13. 9.96P
G-BURS	Sikorsky S-76A II Plus	760040	(HP-) G-BURS/G-OHTL	4. 5.89	Lynton Aviation Ltd t/a Signature Aircraft Charter	Blackbushe	25.10.03T
G-BURT	Piper PA-28-161 Cherokee Warrior II	28-7716105	N2459Q	10. 6.81	B.A.Paul	Denham	2. 6.05T
G-BURU	British Aerospace Jetstream Srs.3202 *(Originally regd as Srs.3206)*	974	F-GMVH G-BURU/(F-OHFT)/G-31-974	14. 1.93	Trident Aviation Leasing Services (Ireland) Ltd *(Exported 1.03)*	(Dublin)	
G-BURZ	Hawker Nimrod II	41H-59890	K3661	22.12.91	Historic Aircraft Collection Ltd *(On rebuild 8.95: current status unknown)*	St.Leonards-on-Sea	
G-BUSB	Airbus Industrie A320-111 *(Originally flown as G-BRSA)*	0006	(G-BRAA) F-WWDD	30. 3.88	British Airways plc *(Koguty Lowickie t/s)*	Heathrow	19. 4.04T
G-BUSC	Airbus Industrie A320-111	0008	(G-BRAB) F-WWDE	26. 5.88	British Airways plc	Heathrow	1. 6.04T
G-BUSD	Airbus Industrie A320-111	0011	(G-BRAC) F-WWDF	21. 7.88	British Airways plc *"Isle of Mull"*	Heathrow	21. 7.04T
G-BUSE	Airbus Industrie A320-111	0017	F-WWDG	1.12.88	British Airways plc	Heathrow	30.11.04T
G-BUSF	Airbus Industrie A320-111	0018	F-WWDH	26. 5.89	British Airways plc	Heathrow	25. 5.05T
G-BUSG	Airbus Industrie A320-211	0039	F-WWDM	30. 5.89	British Airways plc	Heathrow	30. 5.05T
G-BUSH	Airbus Industrie A320-211	0042	F-WWDT	19. 6.89	British Airways plc	Heathrow	18. 6.05T
G-BUSI	Airbus Industrie A320-211	0103	F-WWDB	23. 3.90	British Airways plc *(Grand Union t/s)*	Heathrow	21. 3.03T
G-BUSJ	Airbus Industrie A320-211	0109	F-WWIC	6. 8.90	British Airways plc *(Water Dreaming t/s)*	Heathrow	5. 8.03T
G-BUSK	Airbus Industrie A320-211	0120	F-WWIN	12.10.90	British Airways plc	Heathrow	11.10.03T
G-BUSN	Rotorway Executive 90 (Rotorway RI 162)	5141		6. 1.93	J.A.McGinley	(Dublin)	6. 6.02P
G-BUSR	Aero Designs Pulsar (Rotax 582) *(Tail-wheel u/c)*	PFA 202-12356		15.12.92	S.S.Bateman & R.A.Watts	Cheddington	21. 6.03P
G-BUSS	Cameron Bus 90SS HAB	1685		11. 3.88	Magical Adventures Ltd *(National Express tiles)*	Oswestry	31. 1.96A
G-BUSV	Colt 105A HAB	2324		12. 1.93	M.N.J.Kirby	Northwich, Cheshire	13. 1.03
G-BUSW	Rockwell Commander 114	14079	N4749W	18. 1.93	J.M.J.Palmer *(New owner 3.02)*	(Swanley)	AC
G-BUSY	Thunder Ax6-56A HAB	111		20. 6.77	M.E.Hooker *"Busy Bodies"*	Whitchurch	27. 4.86A
G-BUTA	CASA I-131E Jungmann Srs.2000 *(Correct c/n not known)*	1101/A	E3B-336	20. 1.93	A.G.Dunkerley	Breighton	8. 2.02P
G-BUTB	CFM Streak Shadow K.190 & PFA 206-12243 (Hirth 2706 R05)			20. 1.93	S.Vestuti	Swansea	11. 4.03P
G-BUTD	Van's RV 6 (Lycoming O-320)	PFA 181-12152		21. 1.93	N.W.Beadle	Hardwick	2. 9.03P
G-BUTE	Anderson EA-1 Kingfisher Amphibian (Lycoming O-235) PFA 132-10798		G-BRCK	15. 8.91	T.Crawford	Cumbernauld	15.10.99P
G-BUTF	Aeronca 11AC Chief	11AC-1578	N3231E NC3231E	21. 1.93	N.J.Mortimore	Watchford Farm, Yarcombe	20.11.03P
G-BUTG	Zenair CH-601HD Zodiac (Continental C90)	PFA 162-12225		22. 1.93	J.M.Palmer	Coldharbour Farm, Willingham	12. 5.03P
G-BUTH	CEA Jodel DR.220 2+2	6	F-BNVK	10. 2.93	T.V.Thorp	Clench Common	6. 6.03T

G-BUTJ	Cameron O-77 HAB	2991		25. 1.93	A.J.A. & P.A.Bubb *"Purple Haze"*	Guildford	29. 6.02A
G-BUTK	Murphy Rebel	PFA 232-12091		25. 1.93	D.B.Almey	(Spalding)	10. 6.03P
	(Rotax 912-UL)						
G-BUTL	Piper PA-24-250 Comanche	24-2352	G-ARLB	4. 4.84	D.Heater	Blackbushe	28. 7.05
			N10F				
G-BUTM	Rans S-6-116 Coyote II	PFA 204A-12414		22. 1.93	N.D.White	Buttermilk Farm, Blisworth	2. 7.03
	(Rotax 912UL) *(Tailwheel u/c)*				tr G-BUTM Group		
G-BUTT*	Reims/Cessna FA150K Aerobat	FA1500029	G-AXSJ	18. 8.86	C.R.Guggenheim	Bournemouth	24.10.99T
	(Blown over in gales 1.99 & fuselage stored 5.00: cancelled 4.10.01 by CAA) (Current status unknown)						
G-BUTW	British Aerospace Jetstream Srs.3202	975	F-GMVI	23. 2.93	Trident Aviation Leasing Services (Ireland) Ltd	(Dublin)	
	(Originally regd as Srs.3206)		G-BUTW/(F-OHFU)/G-31-975		*(Exported 1.03)*		
G-BUTX	Bücker Bü.133C Jungmeister	NK	E1-4	3. 2.93	A.J.E.Smith	Leeward Air Ranch, Florida, USA	23.10.02P
	(Warner Super Scarab)		Span AF ES.1-4/35-4		*(Op Real Aeroplane Company)*		
	(Possibly c/n 1010 or a CASA built I-133L)						
G-BUTY	Brugger MB.2 Colibri	PFA 43-12387		30.11.92	R.M.Lawday	(Milford, Derby)	
G-BUTZ	Piper PA-28-180 Cherokee C	28-3107	G-DARL	23. 4.93	A.J. & J.M.Davis	Sywell	13. 7.03T
			4R-ARL/4R-ONE/SE-EYD				
G-BUUA	Slingsby T.67M Firefly II	2111		17. 3.93	Babcock Support Services Ltd	AAC Middle Wallop	22. 7.52T
					t/a Babcock HCS		
G-BUUB	Slingsby T.67M Firefly II	2112		17. 3.93	Babcock Support Services Ltd	AAC Middle Wallop	1. 6.05
					t/a Babcock HCS		
G-BUUC	Slingsby T.67M Firefly II	2113		17. 3.93	Babcock Support Services Ltd	AAC Middle Wallop	14. 8.05
					t/a Babcock HCS		
G-BUUD	Slingsby T.67M Firefly II	2114		17. 3.93	Babcock Support Services Ltd	RAF Barkston Heath	31. 8.05T
					t/a Babcock HCS *(Op JEFTS)*		
G-BUUE	Slingsby T.67M Firefly II	2115		17. 3.93	Babcock Support Services Ltd	RAF Barkston Heath	29. 9.05T
					t/a Babcock HCS *(Op JEFTS)*		
G-BUUF	Slingsby T.67M Firefly II	2116		17. 3.93	Babcock Support Services Ltd	RAF Barkston Heath	26.10.05T
					t/a Babcock HCS *(Op JEFTS)*		
G-BUUG	Slingsby T.67M Firefly II	2117		17. 3.93	Babcock Support Services Ltd	RAF Barkston Heath	19. 7.05T
					t/a Babcock HCS *(Op JEFTS)*		
G-BUUI	Slingsby T.67M Firefly II	2119		17. 3.93	Babcock Support Services Ltd	RAF Barkston Heath	18.11.02T
					t/a Babcock HCS *(Op JEFTS)*		
G-BUUJ	Slingsby T.67M Firefly II	2120		17. 3.93	Babcock Support Services Ltd	AAC Middle Wallop	20. 8.05T
					t/a Babcock HCS		
G-BUUK	Slingsby T.67M Firefly II	2121		17. 3.93	Babcock Support Services Ltd	RAF Barkston Heath	16. 1.03T
					t/a Babcock HCS *(Op JEFTS)*		
G-BUUL	Slingsby T.67M Firefly II	2122		17. 3.93	Babcock Support Services Ltd	RAF Barkston Heath	16. 1.03T
					t/a Babcock HCS *(Op JEFTS)*		
G-BUUM	Piper PA-28RT-201 Arrow IV	28R-7918090	N2145X	14. 1.93	J.Phelan & D.G.Scott	Belfast	3. 4.05
					tr Bluebird Flying Group		
G-BUUN	Lindstrand LBL-105A HAB	015		9. 2.93	Flying Pictures Ltd *"British Gas"*	Chilbolton	11. 3.02A
G-BUUO	Cameron N-90 HAB	2994		9. 2.93	M.P.Rich tr Gone Ballooning Group	Bristol	19. 6.03A
G-BUUP	British Aerospace ATP	2008	G-MANU	18. 2.93	Trident Aviation Leasing Services (Jersey) Ltd		
			G-BUUP/CS-TGA/G-11-8/(N378AE)			Woodford	24. 3.03T
G-BUUR	British Aerospace ATP	2024	EC-GUX	18. 2.93	Trident Aviation Leasing Services (Jersey) Ltd		
			G-OEDJ/G-BUUR/CS-TGC/G-BUUR/CS-TGC/G-11-024			Woodford	14. 8.98T
G-BUUS*	Skyraider Gyrocopter	P.01		9. 2.93	Sycamore Aviation Ltd	Healinks Farm, Clitheroe	11. 5.95P
	(Arrow GT500)				*(Cancelled 13.4.99 as WFU: stored 2000)*		
G-BUUT	Interavia 70TA HAB	04509-92		21. 1.93	Aero Vintage Ltd	Rye	
G-BUUX	Piper PA-28-180 Cherokee D	28-5128	OY-BCW	17. 2.93	M.A.Judge tr Aero Group 78	Netherthorpe	6.11.05T
G-BUUZ	British Aerospace Jetstream Srs.3202	976	F-GMVJ	10. 3.93	Trident Aviation Leasing Services (Ireland) Ltd	(Dublin)	
	(Originally regd as Srs.3206)		G-BUUZ/(F-OHFV)/G-31-976		*(Exported 1.3)*		
G-BUVA	Piper PA-22-135 Tri-Pacer	22-1301	N8626C	12. 2.93	K.W.Thomas tr Oaksey VA Group	Oaksey Park	18. 4.03
G-BUVB*	Colt 77A HAB	2041		22. 1.93	T.L.Regan *(Cancelled 17.9.01 by CAA)*	Newcastle	23. 3.94A
G-BUVC	British Aerospace Jetstream Srs.3202	970	F-GMVP	10. 3.93	Air Kilroe Ltd	Manchester	5. 3.04T
			F-GLPY/G-BUVC/F-GLPY/(F-OHFS)/G-BUVC/G-31-970				
G-BUVD	British Aerospace Jetstream Srs.3202	977	F-GMVK	10. 3.93	Air Kilroe Ltd *(Op Eastern Airways)*	Manchester	26. 4.04T
			G-BUVD/(F-OHFR)/(F-OHFW)/G-31-977				
G-BUVE	Colt 77B HAB	2376		8. 3.93	G.D.Philpot *"Trident"*	Hemel Hempstead	23. 3.03A
G-BUVG	Cameron N-56 HAB	3012		8. 3.93	Cameron Balloons Ltd	Bristol	22. 8.03A
					(Cameron Balloons titles)		
G-BUVL	Fisher Super Koala	PFA 228-11399		3. 3.93	A.D.Malcolm	Park Farm, Throwley, Faversham	24. 6.02P
	(Jabiru 2200)				*"Spirit of Throwley"*		
G-BUVM	CEA Jodel DR.250/160 Capitaine	54	OO-NJR	11. 3.93	G.G.Milton	Kimbolton	29.11.04
			F-BNJR				
G-BUVN	CASA I-131E-2000 Jungmann	2092	EC-333	12. 3.93	W.Van Egmond	Hoogeveen, The Netherlands	23. 7.03P
			E3B-487		*(As "BI-005" in R.Neth AF c/s)*		
G-BUVO	Reims/Cessna F182P Skylane II	F18200022	G-WTFA	10. 3.93	D.W.Wall tr BUVO Group	Southend	1. 6.05
			PH-VDH/D-EJCL				
G-BUVP	CASA I-131E-2000 Jungmann Srs.2000	2139	EC-338	12. 3.93	M.I.M.Schermer Voest	Lelystad, The Netherlands	14. 9.98P
	(Regd with c/n 2155)		E3B-539				
G-BUVR	Christen A-1 Husky	1162		12. 3.93	A.E.Poulsom	Manor Farm, Tongham	26. 4.05
G-BUVS	Colt 77A HAB	2381		12. 3.93	S.J.Chatfield	(Guildford)	13.11.02A
G-BUVT	Colt 77A HAB	2382		12. 3.93	N.A.Carr	Leicester	23. 3.03A
G-BUVW	Cameron N-90 HAB	3020		19. 3.93	Bristol Balloon Fiestas Ltd	Bristol	7. 2.01A
G-BUVX	CFM Streak Shadow SA			22. 3.93	G.K.R.Linney	Latch Farm, Kirknewton	27. 8.03P
	(Rotax 582)	K.214SA & PFA 206-12410					
G-BUVZ	Thunder Ax10-180 Srs.2 HAB	2380		24. 3.93	A.Van Wyk	Caxton, Cambs	13. 7.03T
G-BUWE	Replica Plans SE.5A	PFA 20-11816		25. 3.93	P.N.Davis & H.Wilebore	Stoke Golding	19. 8.03P
	(Continental C90)				tr Taildragger Classics *(As "C9533/M" in RFC c/s)*		
G-BUWF	Cameron N-105 HAB	3036		26. 3.93	R.E.Jones *"British Aerospace II"*	Lytham St.Annes	19. 3.02T
G-BUWH	Parsons Two-Place Gyroplane	PFA G/08-1215		1. 4.93	R.V.Brunskill	Melrose Farm, Melbourne	22. 8.95P
	(Rotax 532)						

Reg	Type	C/n	Prev id	Date	Owner	Location	Date
G-BUWI	Lindstrand LBL-77A HAB	023		5. 4.93	Capital Balloon Club Ltd *"Throw Up"*	London NW1	1. 4.03T
G-BUWJ	Pitts S-1C Special (Lycoming O-320)	2002	N110R	25. 3.93	R.P.Marks	Dunkeswell	20. 9.02P
G-BUWK	Rans S-6-116 Coyote II (Rotax 912)	PFA 204A-12448		7. 4.93	R.Warriner	Bradleys Lawn, Heathfield	12. 6.03P
G-BUWM	British Aerospace ATP	2009	CS-TGB G-BUWM/CS-TGB/G-11-9	19. 4.93	BAE Systems (Operations) Ltd *(Stored 12.01)*	Woodford	
G-BUWR	CFM Streak Shadow K.177-SA & PFA 206-12068 (Rotax 582)			26. 4.93	T.Harvey	Grove Farm, Raveningham	30. 9.03P
G-BUWS	Denney Kitfox Model 2	PFA 172-11831		26. 4.93	J.E.Brewis *(Current status unknown)*	(Castletown, Isle of Man)	
G-BUWT	Rand Robinson KR-2	PFA 129-10952		5. 4.93	Cynthia M.Coombe *(Current status unknown)*	(Greenford, Middx)	
G-BUWU	Cameron V-77 HAB	3053		27. 4.93	T.R.Dews	(Warminster)	20. 3.02A
G-BUWY	Cameron V-77 HAB	2961		27. 4.93	P.A.Sachs *"Pixel"*	West Byfleet	15. 5.03A
G-BUWZ	Robin HR200/120B	254		22. 4.93	A.N.Kaschevski	Lydd	13. 2.05T
G-BUXB	Sikorsky S-76A	760086	(F-GSJG) G-BUXB VR-CCZ/N399BB/N39RP	11. 6.93	Lynton Aviation Ltd t/a Signature Aircraft Charter	Blackbushe	16. 8.03T
G-BUXC	CFM Streak Shadow K.188 & PFA 206-12177 (Rotax 582)			20. 4.93	J.P.Mimnagh	(Wirral)	14. 2.03P
G-BUXD	Maule MXT-7-160 Star Rocket (Tricycle u/c)	17001C	N9231R	4. 5.93	S.Baigent	Jersey	12. 9.02
G-BUXI	Steen Skybolt (Lycoming IO-360)	PFA 64-10755		16. 3.93	M.Frankland	Caernarfon	9. 8.02P
G-BUXJ	Slingsby T.61F Venture T.2	1878	XZ558	6. 5.93	D.Mihailovic tr Venture Motor Glider Club	RAF Halton	9. 8.03
G-BUXK	Pietenpol Aircamper (Continental C90)	PFA 47-11901		12. 5.93	B.P.Hogan	Sywell	14. 7.01P
G-BUXL	Taylor JT.1 Monoplane	PFA 55-11819		12. 5.93	C.P.Whitwell *(New owner 1.03)*	(Oak Farm, Cowbit	
G-BUXN	Beech C23 Sundowner	M-1752	N9256S	13. 5.93	C.J.Addis tr Private Pilots Syndicate	Bournemouth	1.10.05
G-BUXO	Pober P-9 Pixie	PFA 105-10647		17. 5.93	J.Mangiapane tr P-9 Flying Group *(Nearing completion 2000)*	(Matlock)	
G-BUXR	Cameron A-250 HAB	3056		13. 5.93	D.S.King t/a Celebration Balloon Flights	Nottingham	18. 6.03T
G-BUXS	MBB Bö.105DBS-4 (Originally c/n S.41: rebuilt 1993)	S.913	G-PASA G-BGWP/F-ODMZ/G-BGWP/HB-XFD/N153BB/D-HDAS	19. 5.93	Bond Air Services *"Im Bru"*	Aberdeen	25. 5.05T
G-BUXT	Dornier 228-202K	8065	D-CBOL TC-FBM/D-CBOL	24. 5.93	Air Wales Ltd *(Stored 2002)*	Roskilde, Denmark	26. 5.04T
G-BUXU	Beech D17S (GB-2) Traveler	4823	N9113H Bu 33024	20. 5.93	S.J.Ellis *(Noted 5.02)*	Barton	5. 6.05
G-BUXV	Piper PA-22-160 Tri-Pacer (Super Pacer Tail-wheel conversion)	22-6685	N9769D	20. 5.93	T.McManus & W.Connor tr Bogavia Two	Weston, Dublin	11.10.03
G-BUXW	Thunder Ax8-90 Srs.2 HAB	2405		25. 5.93	J.M.Percival *"Silver Lady"*	Burton-on-the-Wolds	9. 7.03A
G-BUXX	Piper PA-17 Vagabond (Continental A75)	17-28	N4611H NC4611H	31. 3.93	R.H.Hunt	Old Sarum	16. 5.02P
G-BUXY	Piper PA-25-235 Pawnee	25-2705	C-GZCR N6959Z	18. 3.93	Bath, Wilts & North Dorset Gliding Club Ltd	Kingston Deverill	30. 1.04
G-BUYB	Aero Designs Pulsar (Rotax 582) (Tail-wheel u/c)	PFA 202-12193		28. 5.93	A.P.Fenn	Shobdon	1. 4.03P
G-BUYC	Cameron Concept 80 HAB	3095		28. 5.93	R.P.Cross	Luton	3.10.03A
G-BUYD	Thunder Ax8-90 HAB	2422		28. 5.93	Anglia Balloon School Ltd t/a Anglia Balloons *(KLM UK titles)*	Norwich	26.12.01A
G-BUYE*	Aeronca 7AC Champion (Continental A65)	7AC-4327	N85584 NC85584	30. 4.93	R.Mazey *(On rebuild 9.00: cancelled by 27.2.03 by CAA)*	(Bristol)	16.11.96P
G-BUYF	American Aircraft Falcon XP (Rotax 503)	600179	N512AA	13. 5.93	D.S.Bremner tr G-BUYF Syndicate	Barton	2. 1.03P
G-BUYG*	Colt Flying Gin Bottle 12 SS HAB (Gordon's Gin Bottle shape)	2331		28. 5.93	United Distillers plc *"Gordon's Gin"* *(Cancelled 7.11.01 by CAA) (Current status unknown)*	(Spain)	20. 5.96
G-BUYI*	Thunder Ax7-77 HAB	1266		20. 6.88	Chelmsford Management Ltd *"Elevation"* *(Cancelled 9.11.01 as WFU:) (Current status unknown)*	Chelmsford	18. 7.99A
G-BUYJ	Lindstrand LBL-105A HAB	039		1. 6.93	D.K.Fish	Bedford	7.11.03T
G-BUYK	Denney Kitfox Model 4 (Rotax 912UL)	PFA 172A-12214		1. 6.93	A.W.Shellis	Otherton, Cannock	2. 1.03P
G-BUYL	Rotary Air Force RAF 2000 (Rebuilt by Newtonair using parts from G-TXSE)	H2-92-361	C-FPFN	2. 6.93	Newtonair Gyroplanes Ltd	Dunkeswell	21. 3.03P
G-BUYN	Cameron O-84 HAB	1214	OE-KZG	4. 6.93	Reach For The Sky Ltd	(Guildford)	16.12.01A
G-BUYO	Colt 77A HAB	2398		4. 6.93	S.F.Burden	Noordwijk, The Netherlands	8. 5.03A
G-BUYR	Mooney M.20C Mark	212650	N1369W	7. 6.93	Charmaine R.Weldon	Haverfordwest	15. 9.00
G-BUYS	Robin DR400/180 Regent	2197		21. 6.93	F.A.Spear	Nuthampstead	7. 4.05
G-BUYT	Ken Brock KB-2 (Rotax 582)	PFA G/06-1214		7. 6.93	J.L.G.McLane & D.G.Chaplin	(York)	11. 3.03P
G-BUYU	Bowers Fly Baby 1A (Continental A65)	PFA 16-12222		7. 6.93	R.Metcalfe	Sparr Farm, Wisborough Green	18. 7.03P
G-BUYY	Piper PA-28-180 Cherokee B	28-1028	C-FXDP CF-XDP/N7214W	18. 3.93	A.J.Hedges & C.E.Yates tr G-BUYY Group	Bristol	4. 7.05T
G-BUZA	Denney Kitfox Model 3 1178 & PFA 172-12547 (Rotax 582)			10. 6.93	J.Thomas	Shefford	2. 4.03P
G-BUZB	Aero Designs Pulsar XP (Rotax 912) (Tail whool u/c)	PFA 202-12312		14. 6.93	S.M.Lancashire	Lymm Dam	21. 5.03P
G-BUZC	Everett Gyroplane Srs.3A	034		14. 7.93	M.P.Lhermette *(Damaged 7.94: stored Sproughton 12.95: current status unknown)*	(Faversham)	
G-BUZD	Aérospatiale AS332L Super Puma	2069	C-GSLJ N189EH/C-GSLJ/HC-BNB/C-GSLJ/PT-HRN/C-GSLJ	11. 2.93	CHC Scotia Ltd	Aberdeen	14.12.05T
G-BUZE	Avid Speed Wing	PFA 189-12047		16. 6.93	J.M.Fforde	(Talgarth)	24. 3.03P
G-BUZF	Colt 77B HAB	1993		16. 6.93	A.E.Austin	Naseby	12. 4.03A
G-BUZG	Zenair CH.601HD Zodiac (Continental O-200-A)	PFA 162-12457		17. 6.93	N.C.White	Sorbie Farm, Kingsmuir	26. 6.03P

G-BUZH	Star-Lite SL-1	119	N4HC	17. 6.93	C.A.McDowall	Farley Farm, Romsey	8. 9.00P
	(Built H M Cottle) (Rotax 447)			*(Damaged Farley Farm 10.8.00: in container 9.00 - fuselage only) (Current status unknown)*			
G-BUZJ	Lindstrand LBL 105A HAB	038		17. 6.93	Eastgate Motor Co Ltd	Bristol	6. 9.03A
					t/a Eastgate Mazda *(Mazda titles)*		
G-BUZK	Cameron V-77 HAB	2962		17. 6.93	J.T.Wilkinson	Calne	24. 6.03A
G-BUZL	VPM M-16 Tandem Trainer	VPM16-UK-105		18. 6.93	R.M.Savage	Carlisle	12. 3.02P
	(Rotax 914)				t/a Roger Savage (Photography)		
G-BUZM	Avid Speed Wing Mk.3	PFA 189-12179		30. 4.93	R.McLuckie & O.G.Jones	RAF Mona	6. 3.03P
	(Jabiru 2200)			*(Damaged nosewheel and propeller taxiing Caernarfon 13.5.01)*			
G-BUZN	Cessna 172H	17256056	N2856L	24. 6.93	H.Jones	Barton	26.11.05
G-BUZO	Pietenpol Aircamper	PFA 47-12408		28. 6.93	D.A.Jones	(Maidenhead)	
	(Salmson AD9)						
G-BUZR	Lindstrand LBL-77A HAB	044		29. 6.93	Lindstrand Balloons Ltd	Oswestry	5. 12.02A
G-BUZS	Colt Flying Pig SS HAB	2415		2. 7.93	Banco Bilbao Vizcaya	(Spain)	20. 5.96A
G-BUZT	Kolb Twinstar Mk.3			1. 7.93	A.C.Goadby	Sampsons Hall, Kersey	3. 4.03P
	Mainair Kit No K0009-0193 & PFA 205-12367						
G-BUZV	Ken Brock KB-2	PFA G/06-1152		1. 7.93	K.Hughes	(Amlwch, Gwynedd)	
G-BUZY	Cameron A-250 HAB	2936		29. 4.93	P.J.D.Kerr	Bridgwater	31. 5.02T
G-BUZZ	Agusta-Bell 206B JetRanger II	8178	F-GAMS HB-XGI/OE-DXF	13. 4.78	European Skytime Ltd	Gloucestershire	3. 7.05T

G-BVAA - G-BVZZ

G-BVAA	Avid Speed Wing Mk.4	PFA 189-12166		10. 6.93	D.T.Searchfield	(Aldershot)	4. 9.03P
G-BVAB	Zenair CH.601HDS Zodiac	PFA 162-12475		26. 5.93	N.J.Keeling, R.F.Mclachlan & J.A.Charlton	(Ashbourne)	22. 5.03T
	(Rotax 912UL)						
G-BVAC	Zenair CH.601HD Zodiac	PFA 162-12504		1. 6.93	A.G.Cozens	Goodwood	6. 9.03P
	(Rotax 912UL)						
G-BVAF	Piper J-3C-65 Cub	4645	OO-UBU N28199/NC28199	14. 6.93	N.M.Hitchman	Southwater, Sussex	18. 6.03P
	(Continental C85)						
G-BVAG	Lindstrand LBL-90A HAB	022		7. 7.93	R.Tillson & P.Ellis	Ilkeston	10. 6.03A
					tr Firefly Balloon Team *"Gee Tee"*		
G-BVAH	Denney Kitfox Model 3	PFA 172-12031		22.10.91	S.Allinson	(Napton, Southam)	10.11.03P
	(Rotax 912)						
G-BVAI	PZL-110 Koliber 150	03900040	OY-CYJ	7. 7.93	A.R.Howard	Gamston	15. 6.03
G-BVAM	Evans VP-1	PFA 62-12132		7. 7.93	R.F.Selby	(Littlehampton)	
G-BVAN	SOCATA MS.892E Rallye 150GT	12376	F-BVAN	21.11.88	A.J.A.Weal	(Goring-by-Sea)	17. 5.04T
G-BVAO	Colt 25A Sky Chariot HAB	2024		9. 7.93	Janice M.Frazer	Hexham, Northumberland	6. 5.03A
G-BVAW	Staaken Z-1 Flitzer	PFA 223-12058		12. 7.93	L.R.Williams	(Aberdare)	29. 6.99P
	(Volkswagen 1834)				t/a Flitzer Sportflugverein *(As "D692") (New owner 4.02)*		
G-BVAX	Colt 77A HAB	1213		30. 3.88	P.H.Porter *"Vax"*	Tenbury Wells	5. 8.95A
G-BVAY	Rutan VariEze	RS.8673/345	N5MS	3. 9.93	D.A.Young	(Sunderland)	11.11.02P
G-BVAZ	Montgomerie-Bensen B.8MR	PFA G/01-1190		12. 7.93	N.Steele	(Lisburn, Co.Down)	28. 4.03P
	(Rotax 582)						
G-BVBG	Piper PA-32R-300 Cherokee Lance	32R-7680151	N19BP	22. 7.93	R.K.Spence	Cardiff	7. 1.01T
G-BVBN	Cameron A-210 HAB	2904		2. 8.93	M.L. & S.M.Gabb t/a Heart of England Balloons	Alcester	10.10.01T
G-BVBP	Avro 683 Lancaster B.10	-	KB994 RCAF	4. 8.93	D Copley	North Weald	
	(Built Victory Aircraft, Canada as B.X)			*(Forward fuselage only hangared 8.01)*			
G-BVBR	Avid Speed Wing	PFA 189-12085		3. 8.93	N J Garbett	(Grantham)	16. 4.03P
G-BVBS	Cameron N-77 HAB	3128		4. 8.93	Marley Building Materials Ltd	Birmingham	7. 5.02A
G-BVBU	Cameron V-77 HAB	3076	(OO-BYS)	5. 8.93	J.Manclark *(Op Alba Ballooning)*	Haddington	26. 7.97A
G-BVBV	Avid Speed Wing	PFA 189-12187		4. 8.93	L.W.M.Summers	Popham/Sandown	19. 5.03P
G-BVCA	Cameron N-105 HAB	3129		11. 8.93	Unipart Group Ltd tr Unipart Balloon Club	Cowley	25. 6.00A
G-BVCB*	Rans S-10 Sakota	PFA 194-11882		11. 8.93	M.D.T.Barley	Cambridge	27. 9.02P
	(Rotax 912-UL)			*(Cancelled 5.12.02 by CAA)*			
G-BVCC	Monnett Sonerai 2LT	PFA 15-10547		12. 8.93	J.Eggleston	(Northallerton)	
G-BVCE	British Aerospace BAe 146 Srs.300	E3209	G-NJIE B-1778/G-BVCE/G-6-209	5.11.93	National Jet Italia SpA	Exeter	13. 7.04T
				(Stored 2002)			
G-BVCG	Van's RV-6 (Lycoming O-320)	PFA 181-11783		17. 8.93	C.J.F.Flint	Sleap	30. 5.03P
G-BVCJ	Agusta A109A II	7265	G-CLRL G-EJCB	23. 8.93	Castle Air Charters Ltd	Liskeard	5. 3.03T
G-BVCL	Rans S-6-116 Coyote II *(Tricycle u/c)*			25. 8.93	J Powell	(Fareham)	25. 6.03P
	(Rotax 912UL)	0493.486 & PFA 204A-12551					
G-BVCM	Cessna 525 CitationJet	525-0022	N1329N	2. 5.94	Kwik Fit plc	Edinburgh	22. 5.03
G-BVCO	Clutton Fred Srs.2	PFA 29-10947		25. 8.93	I.W.Bremner	(Dornoch, Sutherland)	15. 7.03P
G-BVCP	Piper CP.1 Metisse	PFA 253-12512		24. 6.93	C.W.R.Piper	Hinton in the Hedges	11.12.03P
	(Revmaster 2200)						
G-BVCS	Aeronca 7AC Champion	7AC-1346	N69BD N82702/NC82702	1. 9.93	P.C.Isbell	Cherry Tree Farm, Monewden	26.11.02P
	(Continental A65)						
G-BVCT	Denney Kitfox Model 4-1200			27. 8.93	A.F.Reid	Comber, Co Down	16. 7.03P
	(Rotax 912UL)	1761 & PFA 172A-12456					
G-BVCY	Cameron H-24 HAB	3136		3. 9.93	A.C.K.Rawson & J.J.Rudoni	Stafford	19. 1.02A
G-BVDB	Thunder AX7-77 HAB	2364	G-ORDY	6. 9.93	M.J.Smith & J.Towler	York	17.10.99A
G-BVDC	Van's RV-3 (Lycoming O-235)	PFA 99-12218		12. 7.93	J.A.A.Schofield	(Henley-on-Thames)	27. 5.00P
G-BVDD	Colt 69A HAB	2170		6. 9.93	R.M.Cambridge & D.Harrison-Morris	Oswestry	27. 8.02P
					"Delta Dawn Fantasia"		
G-BVDE	Taylor JT-1 Monoplane	PFA 55-11278		6. 9.93	S.G.Hammond	(Rushden)	31. 1.02P
	(Volkswagen 1834)						
G-BVDF*	Cameron Doll 105SS HAB	3112		7. 9.93	Cameron Balloons Ltd	(Germany)	3.11.94A
				(Cancelled 19.9.01 as WFU)			
G-BVDH	Piper PA-28RT-201 Arrow IV	28R-7918030	N2176L	13. 9.93	Goodair Leasing Ltd	Cardiff	18. 4.03T
G-BVDI	Van's RV-4 (Lycoming O-320)	2058	N55GJ	13. 9.93	D.F.Brown	Perth	10. 4.03P
G-BVDJ	Campbell Cricket (Rotax 582)	PFA G/03-1189		13. 9.93	Shirley Jennings	St Merren	24. 7.03P
G-BVDM	Cameron Concept 60 HAB	3141		15. 9.93	M.P.Young	Dover	31. 5.01A

Reg	Type	C/n	Prev id	Date	Owner/Operator	Location	Expiry
G-BVDN	Piper PA-34-220T Seneca III	34-8133185	G-IGHA G-IPUT/N8424D	16. 9.93	Convergence Aviation Ltd	Jersey	12. 8.04T
G-BVDO	Lindstrand LBL-105A HAB	055		16. 9.93	J.Burlinson *"West Lodge Hotel II"*	Aston Clinton	10. 2.03T
G-BVDP	Sequoia F8L Falco	PFA 100-10879		17. 9.93	T.G.Painter *(Noted 7.02)*	Parham Park	
G-BVDR	Cameron O-77 HAB	2452		21. 9.93	T.Duggan	Selby	7. 9.01T
G-BVDS	Lindstrand LBL-69A HAB	102		23. 9.93	Lindstrand Balloons Ltd	Oswestry	26. 6.01A
G-BVDT	CFM Streak Shadow SA-1 (Rotax 582)	K.223 & PFA 206-12462		23. 9.93	H.J.Bennet	North Connel, Oban	21. 4.03P
G-BVDW	Thunder Ax8-90 HAB	2507		30. 9.93	S.C.Vora *"Cosmic"*	Oadby	19. 6.03
G-BVDX	Cameron V-90 HAB	3159	OO-BMY G-BVDX	30. 9.93	R.K.Scott *"Merlin"*	Yeovil	11. 9.03A
G-BVDY	Cameron Concept 60 HAB	3167		30. 9.93	K.A. & G.N.Connolly	Monmouth	23. 3.96A
G-BVDZ	Taylorcraft BC-12D	9043	N96743 NC96743	21. 1.94	P.N.W.England *(Current status unknown)*	(Hove)	
G-BVEA	Nostalgair N.3 Pup (Mosler MM-CB35)	01-GB & PFA 212-11837	G-MWEA	7. 6.93	N.Lynch	Breighton	20. 8.02P
G-BVEH	Wassmer Jodel D.112	1294	F-BMOH	29.10.93	M.L.Copland	Breighton	20. 5.03P
G-BVEJ	Cameron V-90 HAB	3169		5.10.93	J.D.A.Snields & A.R.Craze *"1066"*	Battle	7. 6.03T
G-BVEK	Cameron Concept 80 HAB	3133		5.10.93	A.D.Malcolm	Devizes	23. 3.03A
G-BVEL*	Evans VP-1 Srs.2	PFA 62-11983		6.10.93	M.J. & S.J.Quinn *(Cancelled 22.3.99 by CAA) (Under construction 6.00)*	(Kilmacolm)	
G-BVEN	Cameron Concept 80 HAB	3164		6.10.93	Hildon Associates Ltd	Stockbridge	5. 7.03A
G-BVEP	Luscombe 8A Master	1468	N28707 NC28707	8.10.93	B.H.Austen	Oaksey Park	21.10.02
G-BVER	de Havilland DHC.2 Beaver 1	1648	G-BTDM XV268	13. 8.91	Seaflite Ltd *(As "XV268" in AAC c/s) (New owner 11.01)*	Lochearnhead	23. 4.95T
G-BVES	Cessna 340A II	340A0077	N1378G	8. 9.93	K.P.Gibbin & I.M.Worthington	Nottingham	9.12.02T
G-BVEU	Cameron O-105 HAB	3145		12.10.93	H.C.Wright	Kelfield, York	15. 2.03T
G-BVEV	Piper PA-34-200 Seneca	34-7250316	N1428T HB-LLN/D-GHSG/N1428T	8.10.93	R.W.Harris, M.F.Hatt & JRB Aviation Ltd *(Op Southend Flying Club)*	Southend	9. 8.03T
G-BVEW	Lindstrand LBL-150A HAB	057		14.10.93	A.Van Wyk	Cambridge	15. 8.02T
G-BVEY	Denney Kitfox Model 4-1200 (Rotax 582)	PFA 172A-12527		14.10.93	J.H.H.Turner	(Houston)	24. 5.03P
G-BVEZ	Hunting-Percival P.84 Jet Provost T.3A	PAC/W/9287	XM479	13.10.93	Newcastle Jet Provost Co Ltd *(As "XM479/54" in RAF c/s)*	Newcastle	27. 8.03P
G-BVFA	Rans S-10 Sakota (Rotax 582)	PFA 194-12298		7. 9.93	S.R.Wilgrove	Redlands, Swindon	20. 8.02P
G-BVFB	Cameron N-31 HAB	3175		20.10.93	Bath City Council *"Bath Heritage"*	Bath	7. 4.03A
G-BVFF	Cameron V-77 HAB	3161		26.10.93	I.R.Warrington	Stamford	18. 1.03A
G-BVFM	Rans S-6-116 Coyote II (Tricycle u/c) (Rotax 912UL)	0793.522 & PFA 204A-12579		2.11.93	J.Gorman	(Banstead)	17. 5.03P
G-BVFO	Avid Speed Wing	PFA 189-12053		9. 9.93	P.Chisman	Enstone	20. 4.03P
G-BVFP	Cameron V-90 HAB	3179		2.11.93	C.Duppa-Miller	Warwick	8. 4.03A
G-BVFR	CFM Streak Shadow (Rotax 582)	K.237-SA & PFA 206-12567		3.11.93	R.W.Chatterton	Griffins Farm, Temple Bruer	6. 3.02P
G-BVFS*	Slingsby T.31M Cadet III (Arrow) (Converted to Motor Tutor)	PFA 42-11387	ex RAF?	3.11.93	V.M.Crabb *(Stored dismantled 3.02: cancelled 22.3.02 by CAA)*	(Southend)	
G-BVFT	Maule M-5-235C Lunar Rocket	7183C	N6180M	5.11.93	Sunrise Air Services Ltd	Bodmin	6. 6.03T
G-BVFU	Cameron Sphere 105SS HAB	3137		18.11.93	Stichting Phoenix *(Greenpeace titles)*	Amsterdam, The Netherlands	25. 6.03A
G-BVFY	Colt 210A HAB	2493	DQ-BVF G-BVFY	30. 9.93	T.J.Bucknall *(Op Balloon Preservation Group) "Scotair"*	Malpas	11. 5.00T
G-BVFZ	Maule M-5-180C Lunar Rocket	8082C	N5664D	21. 2.94	C.N.White Franklyns Field, Chewton Mendip		7. 3.03
G-BVGA	Bell 206B-3 JetRanger III	2922	N54AJ VH-SBC	11.11.93	J.L Leonard t/a Findon Air Services	Shoreham	30. 1.03T
G-BVGB	Thunder Ax8-105 Srs.2 HAB 2	408		11.11.93	M.E.Dunstan-Sewell	Bristol	23. 7.03A
G-BVGE	Westland WS-55 Whirlwind HAR.10	WA/100	8732M XJ729	18.11.93	J.F.Kelly (Mullingar, Co.Westmeath) *(As "XJ729" in RAF Rescue c/s)*		18. 9.03P
G-BVGF	Europa Aviation Europa (Rotax 912) (Tri-gear u/c)	034 & PFA 247-12565		18.11.93	A.Graham & G.G.Beal *(F/f 15.8.96)*	Brunton	23.10.03P
G-BVGG	Lindstrand LBL-69A HAB	011		30.11.93	Lindstrand Balloons Ltd	Oswestry	6. 4.01A
G-BVGH	Hawker Hunter T.7 (Centre fuselage no.is HABL 003360)	HABL 004328	XL573	26.11.93	DAT Enterprises Ltd *(As "XL573")*	North Weald	10. 7.03P
G-BVGI	Pereira Osprey 2 (Lycoming O-320)	PFA 70-10536		29.11.93	A.A.Knight	North Connel, Oban	25.11.03P
G-BVGJ	Cameron Concept 80 HAB	3099		7.12.93	D.T.Watkins *"Pizza Express"*	Hexham	4. 8.02A
G-BVGO	Denney Kitfox Model 4-1200 (Rotax 582)	PFA 172A-12362		15.11.93	T.Marriott *(New owner 1.03)*	(Ilkeston)	8. 9.00P
G-BVGS	Robinson R22 Beta	2389	N2363S	9.12.93	Bristol & Wessex Helicopters Ltd	Bristol	25. 7.03T
G-BVGT	Crofton Auster V J/1A Special (Blackburn Cirrus 2) (Rebuild of unregd Auster J/1 Autocrat frame used as engine test rig)	PFA 00-220		19.11.93	P.N.Birch	RAF Coltishall	12. 9.03P
G-BVGW	Luscombe 8A Silvaire	4823	N2096K NC2096K	18.11.93	L.A.Groves	Lee-on-Solent	26. 9.02P
G-BVGY	Luscombe 8E Silvaire	4754	N2027K NC2027K	18.11.93	M.C.Burlock *(New owner 8.02)*	(Reading)	
G-BVGZ	Fokker DR 1 Triplane rep (Lycoming AIO-360)	VHB-10 & PFA 238-12654		20.12.93	R.A.Fleming *(German AF c/s)*	Breighton	7. 5.03P
G-BVHC	Grob G-115D-2 Heron	82005	D-EARG	14.12.93	VT Aerospace Ltd *(Op Royal Navy)*	Plymouth	30. 3.03T
G-BVHD	Grob G-115D-2 Heron	82006	D-EARJ	14.12.93	VT Aerospace Ltd *(Op Royal Navy)*	Plymouth	5. 6.03T
G-BVHE	Grob G-115D-2 Heron	82008	D-EARQ	14.12.93	VT Aerospace Ltd *(Op Royal Navy)*	Plymouth	27. 3.03T
G-BVHF	Grob G-115D-2 Heron	82011	D-EARV	14.12.93	VT Aerospace Ltd *(Op Royal Navy)*	Plymouth	18. 5.03T
G-BVHG	Grob G-115D-2 Heron	82012	D-EARX	14.12.93	VT Aerospace Ltd *(Op Royal Navy)*	Plymouth	8. 5.03T
G-BVHI	Rans S-10 Sakota (Rotax 582)	PFA 194-12608		20.12.93	P.D.Rowley	(Godalming)	2. 6.99P
G-BVHK	Cameron V-77 HAB	3209		23.12.93	Ann R.Rich *"Intel Inside"*	Hyde	7. 9.02

Reg	Type	C/n	Prev ID	Date	Owner/Operator	Location	Status
G-BVHL	Nicollier HN.700 Menestrel II	PFA 217-12614		24.12.93	W.Goldsmith	(Boldon Colliery)	
G-BVHM	Piper PA-38-112 Tomahawk	38-79A0313	G-DCAN N2490D	14.11.91	A.J.Gomes	Shoreham	18. 8.05T
	(Op Sky Leisure Aviation)						
G-BVHO	Cameron V-90 HAB	3158		29.12.93	N.W.B.Bews	Tenbury Wells	18. 7.03
G-BVHP	Colt 42A HAB	2533		31.12.93	Danny Bertels Ballooning BVBA	Wommelgem, Belgium	26. 7.03
G-BVHR	Cameron V-90 HAB	3174		5. 1.94	G.P.Walton	Bagshot	29. 7.03T
G-BVHS	Murphy Rebel	050 & PFA 232-12180		5. 1.94	J.R.Malpass	(Coal Aston)	9. 5.03P
	(Lycoming O-235)						
G-BVHT	Avid Speed Wing Mk.4	PFA 189-12226		28.10.93	R.S.Holt	Long Marston	17. 6.03P
G-BVHU*	Colt Flying Bottle 13 SS HAB	2499		6. 1.94	Bias International Ltd	Rio De Janeiro, Brazil	19. 2.95A
					"Kaiser" (Cancelled 22.10.01 by CAA)		
G-BVHV	Cameron N-105 HAB	3215		6. 1.94	Wye Valley Aviation Ltd	Ross-on-Wye	31.10.03T
					(New owner 5.02)		
G-BVHX*	Pilatus Britten-Norman BN-2T-4R Defender 4000	4003		21. 1.94	Britten-Norman Ltd	Bembridge	
					(Stored 8.99: cancelled 5.4.00 as WFU)		
G-BVHY	Pilatus Britten-Norman BN-2T-4R Defender 4000	4004		21. 1.94	B N Group Ltd	Bembridge	
					(Stored 11.00)		
G-BVIA	Rand Robinson KR-2	PFA 129-11004		14. 1.94	K.Atkinson	(Ulverston)	
G-BVIC	English Electric Canberra B.2/B.6	71105	XH568	25.10.93	Classic Aviation Projects Ltd	Bruntingthorpe	30. 1.97P
	(C/n relates to nose section ex WG788 from 1970 rebuild: XH568 has c/n 71399)				*(As "XH568") (Stored 9.97: current status unknown)*		
G-BVIE	Piper PA-18 Super Cub 95 (L-18C-PI)	18-1549	G-CLIK	26. 1.94	J.C.Best tr C'est La Vie Group	Andrewsfield	19. 3.03P
	(Continental O-200-A) (Frame No.18-1521)		(G-BLMB)/D-EDRB/ALAT 18-1549/51-15549		*"C'est La Vie"*		
G-BVIF	Montgomerie-Bensen B.8MR	PFA G/01A-1228		26. 1.94	R.M. & D.Mann	(Brodick, Arran)	21. 8.95P
	(Rotax 582)				*(Noted 4.00)*		
G-BVIG	Cameron A-250 HAB	3213		26. 1.94	Balloon Flights International Ltd	Bath	2. 9.01T
					(Bath Building Society titles) "BIBS II"		
G-BVIH	Piper PA-28-161 Warrior II	28-7916191	G-GFCE G-BNJP/N2212G	26.10.93	Ocean Developments Ltd	Redhill	23. 1.00T
					(New CofR 5.02)		
G-BVIK	Maule MXT-7-180 Star Rocket	14056C		31. 1.94	D S Simpson tr Graveley Flying Group	Graveley	17. 8.03
G-BVIL	Maule MXT-7-180 Star Rocket	14059C		31. 1.94	K. & S.C.Knight	Shobdon	5. 7.03
G-BVIN	Rans S-6ESA Coyote II	PFA 204-12533		25.10.93	T.J.Wilkinson	Sackville Lodge Farm, Riseley	5. 7.03P
	(Rotax 503)						
G-BVIR	Lindstrand LBL-69A HAB	079		2. 2.94	Aerial Promotions Ltd *(Vauxhall titles)*	Cannock	25. 5.01A
G-BVIS	Brugger MB.2 Colibri	PFA 43-10666		2. 2.94	B.H.Shaw	Spanhoe	9.12.02P
G-BVIT	Campbell Cricket (Rotax 582)	PFA G/03-1229		4. 2.94	D.R.Owen *(New owner 3.01)*	(Blackburn)	24. 7.97P
G-BVIV	Avid Speed Wing	PFA 189-12034		25.10.93	M.Burton	(Malpas)	17. 3.00P
G-BVIW	Piper PA-18-150 Super Cub	18-8277	SE-EPD	4. 2.94	T W M Beck	Partridge Green, Bolney	28. 6.03T
G-BVIX	Lindstrand LBL-180A HAB	082		8. 2.94	European Balloon Display Co Ltd	Great Missenden	31. 3.01T
					"Drifter"		
G-BVIZ	Europa Aviation Europa	052 & PFA 247-12601		24. 1.94	T.J.Punter & P.G.Jeffers	Booker	21. 3.03P
	(Rotax 912) (Monowheel u/c)				*(F/f 26.9.96)*		
G-BVJA	Fokker F.28 Mk.100 *(Fokker 100)*	11489	PH-EZE	22. 4.94	British Midland Airways Ltd	East Midlands	24. 4.03T
G-BVJB	Fokker F.28 Mk.100 *(Fokker 100)*	11488	PH-EZD	7. 7.94	British Midland Airways Ltd	East Midlands	6. 7.03T
G-BVJC	Fokker F.28 Mk.100 *(Fokker 100)*	11497	PH-EZJ	2.12.94	British Midland Airways Ltd	East Midlands	1.12.03T
G-BVJD	Fokker F.28 Mk.100 *(Fokker 100)*	11503	PH-EZO	14.12.94	British Midland Airways Ltd	East Midlands	13.12.03T
G-BVJE	Aérospatiale AS350B1 Ecureuil	1991	SE-HRS	3. 2.94	PLM Dollar Group Ltd	Inverness	24. 2.03T
G-BVJF	Montgomerie-Bensen B.8MR	PFA G/01-1082		18. 2.94	D.M.F.Harvey	(Yate, Bristol)	
G-BVJG	Cyclone AX3/K	C.3123187 & PFA 245-12663	G-69-14 (G-MYOP)	15. 2.94	T.D.Reid	Tandragee, Co.Armagh	31.10.03P
	(Rotax 582)						
G-BVJH	Aero Designs Pulsar (Rotax 582)	PFA 202-12196		22. 2.94	J.Stringer	(Broxbourne)	21. 3.01P
G-BVJK	Glaser-Dirks DG-800	A8-24-A21		30. 3.94	B.A.Eastwell	Ringmer	21. 8.03
G-BVJN	Europa Aviation Europa	066 & PFA 247-12666		2. 3.94	A.C.Beaumont	White Waltham	11.10.02P
	(Rotax 912) (Tri-gear u/c)				tr JN Europa Group *"Better by Redesign" (F/f 16.12.95)*		
G-BVJP	Aérospatiale/Alenia ATR 42-300	371	F-WWLN	7. 4.94	Aeronautix Leasing Ltd	Dinard, France	6. 4.03T
G-BVJT	Reims/Cessna F406 Caravan II	F406-0073		2. 2.94	P Madent & M Evans t/a Nor Leasing	Farnborough	29. 3.03
G-BVJU	Evans VP-1	PFA 62-10691		10. 3.94	Barbara A.Schlussler *(Current status unknown)*	(Bourne)	
G-BVJX	Marquart MA.5 Charger	PFA 68-11239		12. 1.94	E.Newsham	Breighton	8. 7.03P
	(Lycoming O-360)						
G-BVJZ	Piper PA-28-161 Cherokee Warrior II	28-7816248	N2088M	22. 3.94	A.R.Fowkes	Denham	24. 7.03T
G-BVKA	Boeing 737-59D	24694	SE-DNA (SE-DLA)	15. 2.94	British Midland Airways Ltd *"Vauxhall"*	East Midlands	28. 2.03T
G-BVKB	Boeing 737-59D	27268	SE-DNM	24. 3.94	British Midland Airways Ltd	East Midlands	11. 4.03T
G-BVKC	Boeing 737-59D	24695	SE-DNB (SE-DLB)	5. 5.94	British Midland Airways Ltd	East Midlands	15. 5.03T
G-BVKD	Boeing 737-59D	26421	SE-DNK	25.11.94	British Midland Airways Ltd	East Midlands	15.12.03T
G-BVKF	Europa Aviation Europa	050 & PFA 247-12638		11. 3.94	T.R.Sinclair	Lamb Holm Farm, Orkney	1. 6.03P
	(Rotax 912UL) (Tri-gear u/c)				*(F/f 2.3.96)*		
G-BVKH	Thunder Ax-8-90	HAB2574		15. 3.94	R.B.Gruzelier	Salisbury	10. 7.03
G-BVKJ	Bensen B.8M (Rotax GT500R)	PFA G/01-1221		17. 3.94	A.G.Foster	Grimsby	27. 8.99P
G-BVKK	Slingsby T.61F Venture T.2	1984	ZA665	22. 2.94	K.E.Ballington	Saltby	27. 3.05
G-BVKL	Cameron A-180 HAB	3255		17. 3.94	Dragon Balloon Company Ltd	(Hope Valley)	1. 4.01T
G-BVKM	Rutan VariEze (Continental O-200-A)	1933	N7137G	5. 4.94	J.P.G.Lindquist	(Kilchberg, Switzerland)	13. 8.02P
G-BVKR	Sikorsky S-76A	760115	734 RJordAF	4. 3.94	Bristow Helicopters Ltd	Aberdeen	8.12.03T
G-BVKU	Slingsby T.61F Venture T.2	1877	XZ557	22. 3.94	S.P.Wareham tr G-BVKU Syndicate	Kingston Deverill	6.12.04
G-BVKV*	Cameron N-90 HAB	3236		24. 3.94	Pringle of Scotland Ltd	Hawick	3. 2.97A
					(Cancelled 24.9.01 as WFU)		
G-BVKX	Colt 14A Cloudhopper HAB	2580		28. 3.94	H.C.J.Williams	Bristol	
G-BVKZ	Thunder Ax9-120 HAB	2547		23. 3.94	D.J.Head	Newbury	25. 7.00T
G-BVLC	Cameron N-42 HAB	3256		28. 3.94	Cameron Balloons Ltd	Bristol	26. 7.02A
G-BVLD	Campbell Cricket (Arrow GT500)	PFA G/01A-1163		29. 3.94	C.Berry	(Swansea)	8. 6.03P
G-BVLE	McCandless M.4	PFA G/10-1232		29. 3.94	H.Walls	Victoria Bridge, Strabane	
					(Under construction 11.01)		
G-BVLF	CFM Starstreak Shadow SS-D	K.250-SSD		4. 3.94	B.R.Johnson *(Current status unknown)*	(Farnham)	

Reg	Type	C/n	Prev id	Date	Owner	Location	Date
G-BVLG	Aérospatiale AS355F1 Twin Squirrel	5011	N57745	31. 3.94	PLM Dollar Group Ltd	Cumbernauld	6. 4.03T
G-BVLH	Europa Aviation Europa 013 & PFA 247-12491			30. 3.94	D.Barraclough	Brunton	5. 8.03P
	(Rotax 912) *(Monowheel u/c)*				*(F/f 15.7.01)*		
G-BVLI	Cameron V-77 HAB	5568	N9544G	30. 3.94	Janet Lewis-Richardson	Waiheke, New Zealand	4. 4.03A
G-BVLK	Rearwin 8125 Cloudster	803	N25403	6. 4.94	M.C.Hiscock	Titchfield, Hants	
			NC25403		*(On rebuild 2.96: current status unknown)*		
G-BVLL	Lindstrand LBL-210A HAB	101		9. 3.94	Aerial Promotions Ltd	Cannock	29. 7.03T
G-BVLP	Piper PA-38-112 Tomahawk II	38-82A0002	N91355	8. 4.94	Turweston Aero Club Ltd	Turweston	14. 5.03T
G-BVLR	Van's RV-4	PFA 181-12306		13. 4.94	S.D.Arnold & S.J.Moodey	(Coventry)	
	(Lycoming 0320-E2A s/n 46482-27A)				tr RV4 Group *(Under construction 7.99)*		
G-BVLS	Thunder Ax8-90 Srs.2 HAB	2577		13. 4.94	J.R.Henderson	Stratford-upon-Avon	25. 6.03A
G-BVLT	Bellanca 7GCBC Citabria 150S	1103-79	SE-GHV	6. 4.94	M.D.Hinge	Old Sarum	2. 9.05T
G-BVLU	Druine D.31 Turbulent	PFA 1604		18. 4.94	C.D.Bancroft	Litlte Down Farm, Milson	17.11.03P
G-BVLV	Europa Aviation Europa 039 & PFA 247-12585			10. 3.94	J.T.Naylor tr Euro 39 Group	Bidford	18. 4.03P
	(Rotax 912UL) *(Monowheel u/c)*				*(F/f 2.4.96)*		
G-BVLW	Avid Hauler Mk.4	PFA 189-12577		24. 3.94	D.M.Johnstone	Shobdon	13.10.03P
	(Hirth F30)						
G-BVLX	Slingsby T.61F Venture T.2	1973	ZA654	19. 4.94	T.M.Holloway tr RAFGSA	Easterton	11. 3.04
					(Op Fulmar Gliding Club)		
G-BVLZ	Lindstrand LBL-120A HAB	063		4. 3.94	Balloon Flights Club Ltd	Kings Norton, Leicester	6.10.03T
G-BVMA	Beech 200 Super King Air	BB-797	G-VPLC	22. 7.93	Manhattan Air Ltd	Blackbushe	21.10.04T
			N84B				
G-BVMC	Robinson R44 Astro	0060		15. 4.94	B.E.Llewllyn t/a Bell Commercials	Swansea	13. 7.03T
G-BVMD	Luscombe 8E Silvaire	5265	9Q-CGB	15. 4.94	P.J.Kirkpatrick	Top Farm, Croydon, Royston	30. 5.03P
			KAT-?/VP-YRB/ZS-BWC/NC2538K				
G-BVMF	Cameron V-77 HAB	3195		22. 4.94	P.A.Meecham	Milton-Under-Wychwood	28. 8.03A
G-BVMG*	Bensen B.80V	PFA G/01-1056		25. 4.94	Not known	Lochview House, Limerigg	
					(Cancelled by CAA 11.12.00 - no PtoF issued: stored 2.03)		
G-BVMH	Wag-Aero Sport Trainer	PFA 108-12647		28. 4.94	R.A.Durance	(Wellingore)	12. 6.02P
	(Continental C90-8)				*(As "624/D-39" in US Army c/s)*		
G-BVMI	Piper PA-18-150 Super Cub	18-4649	D-EIAC	6. 4.94	O.Cowley	(Shepperton)	7. 3.04
	(Frame No.18-4613)		(PH-WDP)/D-EIAC/D-EKAF/N10F				
	(Officially regd with c/n 18-8482 ex OH-PIN/N4262Z but rebuilt from D-EIAC [18-4649] after crash 15.8.95)						
G-BVMJ	Cameron Eagle 95SS HAB	3262		28. 4.94	R.D.Sargeant	Wollerau, Switzerland	29. 5.03A
G-BVML	Lindstrand LBL-210A HAB	094		29. 4.94	Ballooning Adventures Ltd	Hexham	18. 5.03T
G-BVMM	Robin HR200/100 Club	41	F-BVMM	18. 8.80	R.H.Ashforth	Gloucestershire	30. 7.04
G-BVMN	Ken Brock KB-2	PFA G/06-1218		29. 4.94	S.A.Scally	(Cockermouth)	4. 7.01P
	(Rotax 582)						
G-BVMR	Cameron V-90 HAB	3269		28. 3.94	I.R.Comley *"Midnight Rainbow"*	Gloucester	19. 5.04A
G-BVMU	Aerostar Yakovlev Yak-52	9211809	YR-013	11. 5.94	A.L.Hall-Carpenter	Shipdham	5. 9.03P
	(Official c/n is 9411809)				*(As "09" in DOSAAF c/s)*		
G-BVNG	de Havilland Moth Major	NK	EC-AFK	17. 5.94	(P Groves)	Lee-on-Solent	
			EE1-81/30-81		*(On rebuild 2003)*		
G-BVNI	Taylor JT.2 Titch	PFA 60-11107		20. 5.94	T.V.Adamson *(Noted 7.01)*	Rufforth	
G-BVNL	Rockwell Commander 114	14118	I-ECCE	13. 5.94	A.W.Scragg	Leicester	5. 7.03
			N4789W				
G-BVNM	Boeing 737-4S3	24163	G-BPKA	31. 3.92	British Airways plc	Gatwick	31. 3.05T
			9M-MJJ/G-BPKA				
G-BVNN	Boeing 737-4S3	24164	G-BPKB	18. 3.92	British Airways plc	Gatwick	18. 3.05T
			9M-MLA/G-BPKB				
G-BVNO	Boeing 737-4S3	24167	G-BPKE	18. 3.92	British Airways plc *(Benyhone Tartan t/s)*	Gatwick	14. 4.05T
			9M-MLB/G-BPKE				
G-BVNR	Cameron N-105 HAB	3288		24. 5.94	Liquigas SpA	Milan, Italy	11. 1.03A
	(New envelope c/n 4994 @ 1.01)						
G-BVNS	Piper PA-28-181 Cherokee Archer II	28-7690358	N6163J	13. 4.94	Scottish Airways Flyers (Prestwick) Ltd	Prestwick	11. 8.03T
G-BVNU	FLS Aerospace Sprint Club	004		25. 5.94	Aces High Ltd *(Amended CofR 3.02)*	Dunsfold Park	17.10.98T
G-BVNY	Rans S-7 Courier (Rotax 532)	PFA 218-11951		24. 5.94	P.C.Goodwin	RAF Keevil	24. 2.03P
G-BVOA	Piper PA-28-181 Archer II	28-7990145	N2132C	31. 5.94	M.J. & R.J.Millen	Rochester	20. 7.03T
					t/a Millen Aviation Services *(Cable Consult Ltd titles)*		
G-BVOB	Fokker F.27 Friendship 500	10366	PH-FMN	5. 7.94	BAC Express Airlines Ltd *"Euro Trader"*	Exeter	6.10.03T
			PT-LZM/F-BPNA/PH-FMN				
G-BVOC	Cameron V-90 HAB	3291		8. 6.94	Sally A.Masey	Bristol	11. 5.03A
					(Bristol Evening Post/Western Daily Press titles) "Scoop"		
G-BVOG*	Cameron RN-9 Gas/HAB	3285		14. 6.94	Cameron Balloons Ltd	Bristol	12.10.95A
					(Cancelled 16.1.02 by CAA) (Extant 8.02)		
G-BVOH	Campbell Cricket	PFA G/03-1220		14. 6.94	G.A.Speich	Beausale, Warwick	23. 6.03P
	(Rotax 532)						
G-BVOI	Rans S-6-116 Coyote II	PFA 204A-12712		14. 6.94	A.P.Bacon	Wick	31. 5.03P
	(Rotax 532)						
G-BVOK	Aerostar Yakovlev Yak-52	9111505	RA9111505	14. 6.94	T.Maloney, J.Ormerod & D.Treacher	Shoreham	9. 7.03P
			DOSAAF55		t/a Transair Aviation *(As "55" in DOSAAF c/s)*		
G-BVON	Lindstrand LBL-105A HAB	001	N532LB	16. 6.94	P.A.Lindstrand *"Phoenix"*	Dallas, Texas, USA	10. 8.03
			G-BVON				
G-BVOO	Lindstrand LBL-105A HAB	123		16. 6.94	T.G.Church	Blackburn	18. 1.01T
G-BVOP	Cameron N-90 HAB	3317		21. 6.94	October Gold Ballooning Ltd	Windermere	19. 2.01T
					t/a Mr.Lazenbys		
G-BVOR	CFM Streak Shadow K.238-SA & PFA 206-12695			31. 3.94	K.Fowler	(Basingstoke)	7. 7.03P
	(Rotax 582)						
G-BVOS	Europa Aviation Europa 003 & PFA 247-12562			11. 4.94	D.A.Young	Brunton	13. 8.03P
	(Mid-West AE100R) *(Monowheel u/c)*				tr Durham Europa Group *(F/f 3.10.98)*		
G-BVOU	Hawker Siddeley HS.748 Srs.2A/270	1721	CS-TAH	21. 6.94	Emerald Airways Ltd *(Lynx titles)*	Exeter	30. 7.04T
			G-11-6				
G-BVOV	Hawker Siddeley HS.748 Srs.2A/372	1777	CS-TAO	21. 6.94	Emerald Airways Ltd	Liverpool	11. 5.04T
			G-11-4				

G-BVOW	Europa Aviation Europa	084 & PFA 247-12679		27. 6.94	M.W.Cater	Husbands Bosworth	17. 7.03P
	(Rotax 912) *(Monowheel u/c)*				tr Europa Syndicate *(F/f 7.10.96)*		
G-BVOX	Taylorcraft F-22	2208	N221UK	20. 5.94	Jones Samuel Ltd	Leicester	22. 6.03
G-BVOY	Rotorway Executive 90	5238		17. 6.94	Southern Helicopters Ltd	Street Farm, Takeley	AC
	(Rotorway RI 162)				*(On rebuild 2.03)*		
G-BVOZ	Colt 56A HAB	2595		21. 6.94	Balloon School (International) Ltd	Petworth	27. 2.02A
					t/a British School of Ballooning		
G-BVPA	Thunder Ax8-105 Srs.2 HAB	2600		24. 6.94	J.Fenton t/a Firefly Balloon Promotions	Preston	30.12.02T
G-BVPD	CASA I-131E Jungmann	2086	F-AZNG	12. 7.94	D.Bruton	Abbeyshrule, Co.Longford	23. 1.03P
			E3B-482				
G-BVPK	Cameron O-90 HAB	3313		1. 7.94	D.V.Fowler	Cranbrook	10. 7.03T
G-BVPL	Zenair CH.601HD Zodiac	PFA 162-12693		4. 7.94	E.Burrows	(Dungannon, Co.Tyrone)	6. 8.03P
	(Continental O-200-A)						
G-BVPM	Evans VP-2 Coupe	V2-1016 & PFA 7205		6.11.78	P.Marigold	(Locking, Weston super Mare)	31. 5.94P
	(Continental A65)				*(Stored 7.95: current status unknown)*		
G-BVPN	Piper J-3C-65 Cub	6917	G-TAFY	6. 7.94	C.Willoughby	Turweston	19. 7.03P
			N31073/N38207/N38307/NC38307				
	(Regd as c/n 5298 but has Frame No.7002 which was N38207: probably used in rebuild of N31073 in early 1970s)						
G-BVPP	Folland Gnat T.1	FL.536	8620M	22. 4.94	T.J.Manna	North Weald	23.12.03P
			XP534		t/a Kennet Aviation *(As "XR993" in Red Arrows c/s)*		
G-BVPR	Robinson R22 Beta	1612	G-KNIT	17. 6.94	E.Bailey	Spoonley/Gloucestershire	4. 2.03T
G-BVPS	Jodel D.112	PFA 917		6. 7.94	P.J.Sharp *(Current status unknown)*	(Harpenden)	
G-BVPU*	Cameron A-140 HAB	3296		12. 7.94	Cameron Balloons Ltd	(Canada)	22. 7.97A
					(Cancelled 10.10.01 by CAA)		
G-BVPV	Lindstrand LBL-77B HAB	119		13. 7.94	A.R.Greensides	Burton Pidsea, Hull	23. 11.03A
					"Reverend Leonard"		
G-BVPW	Rans S-6-116 Coyote II *(Tricycle u/c)*			12. 7.94	J.G.Beesley	Halwell, Totnes	20.10.03P
	(Rotax 582)	029H.587 & PFA 204A-12737					
G-BVPX	Bensen B.8 Tyro Gyro Mk.II			13. 7.94	A.W.Harvey	Henstridge	9. 5.02P
	(Modified P Lovegrove) PCL125 & PFA G/011-1237						
G-BVPY	CFM Streak Shadow	K.204 & PFA 206-12375		14. 6.94	R.J.Mitchell	(Scalloway, Shetland)	27. 6.03P
	(Rotax 582)				*(Operates from Tingwall)*		
G-BVRA	Europa Aviation Europa	008 & PFA 247-12635		25. 7.94	N.E.Stokes *"Hummingbird"*	(Ellesmere)	24.10.03P
	(Rotax 912) *(Monowheel u/c)*				*(F/f 13.10.00)*		
G-BVRH	Taylorcraft BL-65	1657	N23929	15. 7.94	M.J.Smith	(Henfield)	25. 7.03
			G-BVRH/N24322/NC24322				
G-BVRI	Thunder Ax6-56 HAB	2622		2. 8.94	A.Van Wyk	Caxton, Cambs	30.11.02A
G-BVRK	Rans S-6ESA Coyote II	1193.566	G-MYPK	14. 7.94	J.Secular	(Beckenham)	
G-BVRL	Lindstrand LBL-21A HAB	130		3. 8.94	A.M.Holly t/a Exclusive Ballooning	Berkeley	24.10.03A
G-BVRR	Lindstrand LBL-77A HAB	133		9. 8.94	G.C.Elson t/a Lindstrand Balloon School	Ronda, Spain	23. 6.03A
G-BVRU	Lindstrand LBL-105A HAB	131		15. 8.94	Flying Pictures Ltd	Chilbolton	11. 3.02A
G-BVRV	Van's RV-4	793	N144TH	23. 6.94	A.Troughton	Armagh Field, Woodview	15. 4.03P
	(Lycoming AEIO-320)						
G-BVRZ	Piper PA-18 Super Cub 95	18-3442	SE-ITP	22.11.94	R.W. Davison	(Wirral)	25. 5.01
	(Regd with Frame No.18-3381)		LN-LJG/D-EDCM/96+19/QW+901/QZ+001/AC+507/AS+506/54-752				
					(Damaged on take off Kilrea 30.7.98: new owner 11.02)		
G-BVSB	TEAM mini-MAX 91A	PFA 186-12241		1. 7.94	D.G.Palmer	Fetterangus	2.12.02P
	(Rotax 503)						
G-BVSD	Sud SE.3130 Alouette II	1897	V-54	8. 9.94	M.J.Cuttell	Gloucestershire	17. 4.05
			Swiss AF		*(As "V-54" in Swiss AF c/s)*		
G-BVSF	Aero Designs Pulsar	PFA 202-12071		1. 7.94	S.N. & R.J.Freestone	Deanland	17. 6.03P
	(Rotax 582) *(Tricycle u/c)*						
G-BVSJ	Pilatus Britten-Norman BN-2T Islander	2286		31. 1.95	B-N Group Ltd *(To become EP-BFR 2003)*	Bembridge	17.12.03T
G-BVSL*	Pilatus Britten-Norman BN-2B-26 Islander	2288		31. 1.95	Britten-Norman Ltd	Bembridge	
					(Cancelled 12.10.00 as temporarily WFU)		
G-BVSM	Rotary Air Force RAF 2000	2000	EW-42	24. 8.94	S Ram *(Noted 7.02)*	(Lowestoft)	24. 1.97P
G-BVSN	Avid Speed Wing	PFA 189-12088		24. 8.94	A.S.Markey	Old Sarum	31.10.03P
G-BVSO	Cameron A-120 HAB	3339		25. 8.94	A.Kaye	Wellingborough	28. 7.02T
					t/a Khaos Ballooning *(Cameron Balloons titles)*		
G-BVSP	Hunting P.84 Jet Provost T.3A	PAC/W/6327	XM370	31. 8.94	H.G.Hodges & Son Ltd	Long Marston	2. 4.03P
G-BVSS	Jodel 150 Mascaret	118 & PFA 151-11878		22. 8.94	A.P.Burns	RAF Woodvale	19. 5.03P
G-BVST	Jodel 150 Mascaret	130 & PFA 235-12198		11. 8.94	A.Shipp	Full Sutton	24. 9.03P
	(Continental O-200-A)						
G-BVSV*	Cameron C-80 HAB	3194		5. 9.94	Cameron Balloons Ltd	Beirut, Lebanon	1. 9.95A
					(Cancelled 19.9.01 as WFU: current status unknown)		
G-BVSW*	Cameron C-80 HAB	3210		5. 9.94	Cameron Balloons Ltd	Beirut, Lebanon	1. 9.95A
					(Cancelled 19.9.01 as WFU: current status unknown)		
G-BVSX	TEAM mini-MAX 91A	PFA 186-12463		9. 9.94	J.A.Clark	(Sittingbourne)	18. 7.03P
	(Mosler MM CB-35)						
G-BVSY	Thunder Ax9-120 HAB	2631		16. 8.94	G.R.Elson t/a Lindstrand Balloon School	Ronda, Spain	6. 6.03T
G-BVSZ	Pitts S-1E(S) Special	PFA 09-11235		9. 9.94	R.C.F.Bailey	(Swinmore Farm, Ledbury)	11.11.02P
	(Lycoming AEIO-360)						
G-BVTA	Tri-R Kis	PFA 239-12450		26. 8.94	P.J.Webb	Dunkeswell	17.10.03P
G-BVTC	British Aircraft Corporation BAC.145 Jet Provost T.5A	XW333		7. 9.94	Global Aviation Ltd	Humberside	12. 2.03P
		EEP/JP/997			*(As "XW333")*		
G-BVTD	CFM Streak Shadow SA			14. 9.94	M.Walton	Old Sarum	6. 9.02P
	(Rotax 582)	K.159-SA & PFA 206-11972					
G-BVTJ	Aérospatiale/Alenia ATR 72-202	342	F-WWEV	7.12.94	Cityflyer Express Ltd *(Waves & Cranes t/s)*	Gatwick	6.12.04T
			F-GKOI/F-WWLX				
G-BVTK	Aérospatiale/Alenia ATR 72-202	357	F-WWEW	21.10.94	Cityflyer Express Ltd *(Chelsea Rose t/s)*	Gatwick	20.10.04T
			F-GKOJ				
G-BVTL	Colt 31A Air Chair HAB	2572		5. 7.94	A.Lindsay	Twickenham	15. 5.97
G-BVTM	Reims/Cessna F152 II	F15201827	G-WACS	31. 8.94	RAF Halton Aeroplane Club Ltd	RAF Halton	29. 8.04T
			D-EFGZ				

Reg	Type	C/n	Prev id	Date	Owner	Location	Date
G-BVTN	Cameron N-90 HAB	3361		16. 9.94	P.Zulehner	Peterskirchen, Austria	27. 9.02A
G-BVTO	Piper PA-28-151 Cherokee Warrior	28-7415253	G-SEWL D-EDOS/N9550N	19. 9.94	A.S.Bamrah t/a Falcon Flying Services	Lydd	7. 2.04T
G-BVTV	Rotorway Executive 90 (Rotorway RI 162)	5243		16. 9.94	H.G.Orchin	Street Farm, Takeley	16.12.02P
G-BVTW	Aero Designs Pulsar	PFA 202-12172		14. 9.94	J.D.Webb	(Hereford)	
G-BVTX	de Havilland DHC-1 Chipmunk 22A	C1/0705	WP809	2. 8.94	M.W.Cater	Husbands Bosworth	11.11.04
					tr TX Flying Group *(As "WP809/78" in RN c/s)*		
G-BVUA	Cameron O-105 HAB	3369		27. 9.94	D.C.Eager	Bracknell	28. 5.00A
G-BVUC	Colt 56A HAB	2608	G-639*	30. 9.94	Cameron Balloons Ltd t/a Thunder & Colt	Bristol	19. 9.01A
	("B" Conditions markings carried as such 9.94)*						
G-BVUG	Betts TB.1 (120hp Tigre G IV-A2) PFA 265-12770			3.10.94	William Tomkins Ltd	Spanhoe	20. 5.03P
	(Modified AIA Stampe SV.4C c/n1045 ex G-BEUS/F-BKFK/F-DAFK/Fr.Mil)						
G-BVUH	Thunder Ax6-65B HAB	243	JA-A0075	3.10.94	N.C.A.Crawley	Great Yarmouth	
G-BVUI	Lindstrand LBL-25A Cloudhopper HAB	148		5.10.94	J.W.Hole	Much Wenlock	10. 6.03A
G-BVUJ	Ken Brock KB-2 (Rotax 503)	PFA G/06-1244		10.10.94	R.J.Hutchinson	Kemble	17. 5.99P
G-BVUK	Cameron V-77 HAB	3372		11.10.94	H.G.Griffiths & W.A.Steel	Reading	11. 8.03A
G-BVUM	Rans S-6-116 Coyote II (Rotax 582)	PFA 204A-12685		11.10.94	M.A.Abbott	Newbigging Farm, Montrose	29. 9.03P
G-BVUN	Van's RV-43363 (Lycoming O-360)	UK & PFA 181-12488		11.10.94	A.E.Kay Parsons Farm, Waterperry Common, Oakley		7. 6.03P
G-BVUO	Cameron R-150 Gas/HAB	3365		13.10.94	M.Sevrin	Court St.Etienne, Belgium	21.12.95A
G-BVUT	Evans VP-1 Srs.2 (Volkswagen 1600)	PFA 62-12092		24.10.94	P.J.Weston	Pepperbox, Salisbury	29. 9.99P
	(Damaged on take off Pepperbox 13.3.99: current status unknown)						
G-BVUU	Cameron C-80 HAB	3383		11.10.94	T.M.C.McCoy "Ascent"	Bath	25. 9.03T
					(Op Ascent Balloons)		
G-BVUV	Europa Aviation Europa	141 & PFA 247-12762		23. 9.94	R.J.Mills	Gamston	8. 8.03P
	(Rotax 912) *(Monowheel u/c)*				*(F/f 8.5.99)*		
G-BVUZ	Cessna 120	11334	Z-YGH VP-YGH/VP-NAM/VP-YGH	20. 9.94	N.O.Anderson	(Trumpington, Cambridge)	
G-BVVA	Aerostar Yakovlev Yak-52	8776109	LY-ANN DOSAAF 52	24.10.94	T.W.Freeman	Litle Gransden	15. 7.02P
G-BVVB	Carlson Sparrow II (Rotax 532)	PFA 209-11809		26. 9.94	L.M.McCullen	North Connel, Oban	27. 8.03P
G-BVVC	Hawker Hunter F.6A (Built Armstrong-Whitworth Aircraft)	S4/U/3362	8685M XF516	28.10.94	Chivenor Memorial Flight Ltd	Exeter	16.10.02P
					(As "XF516/19" in 234 Sqdn c/s)		
G-BVVE	Wassmer Jodel D.112	1070	F-BKAJ	28.10.94	G.W.Jarvis	Shifnal	11 4.03P
G-BVVG	Nanchang CJ-6A (Yak 18)	2751219	(F-....) G-BVVG/Chinese PLAAF	10.10.94	K.E.Wells	White Waltham	9. 9.03P
					tr Peeking Duck Group *(As "2751219/88" in PRChina A/F c/s)*		
G-BVVH	Europa Aviation Europa	014 & PFA 247-12505		31.10.94	T.G.Hoult	Gamston	27. 8.03P
	(Rotax 912) *(Monowheel u/c)*				*(F/f 31.8.00)*		
G-BVVI	Hawker Audax I (Built Avro)	--	2015M K5600	3.11.94	Aero Vintage Ltd	St.Leonards-on-Sea	
					(On rebuild 8.95: current status unknown)		
G-BVVK	de Havilland DHC.6-310 Twin Otter	666	LN-BEZ	21.12.94	Loganair Ltd "Chatham Historic Dockyard"	Glasgow	12. 1.04T
G-BVVL	EAA Acrosport 2 (Lycoming O-360)	PFA 72A-10887		11.11.94	G.A.Breen	(Algarve, Portugal)	7. 7.03P
G-BVVM	Zenair CH.601HD Zodiac (Rotax 912UL)	PFA 162-12539		3.10.94	A.Rooker	Wickenby	9. 5.03P
G-BVVN	Brugger MB.2 Colibri (Volkswagen 1834)	PFA 43-10979		12.10.94	N.F.Andrews	Emlyns Field, Rhuallt	11. 9.02P
G-BVVP	Europa Aviation Europa	088 & PFA 247-12697		20. 9.94	I Mansfeld	Kemble	9.12.02P
	(Rotax 912) *(Monowheel u/c)*				*(F/f 7.8.96)*		
G-BVVR	Stits SA-3A Playboy (Continental A65)	P-736	N4620S	14.11.94	I.T.James	Enstone	14. 3.02P
G-BVVS	Van's RV-4 (Lycoming O-320)	PFA 181-12324		15.11.94	E.C. & N.S.C.English	North Weald	16.10.03P
G-BVVU	Lindstrand LBL Four SS HAB	155	HB-QAP G-BVVU	18.11.94	Magical Adventures Ltd	West Bloomfield, Mi., USA	6.12.01P
G-BVVW	IAV-Bacau Yakovlev Yak-52 (C/n plate shows c/n 833519)	844605	RA013611 DOSAAF15/DOSAAF95	6.11.94	J.E.Blackman	Monewden	5.12.03P
G-BVVX	Yakovlev Yak-18A	NK	307 Russian AF	11.11.94	J.M. & E.M.Wicks Boones Farm, High Garrett, Braintree		7. 5.03P
G-BVVZ	Corby CJ-1 Starlet (Volkswagen 1834)	PFA 134-12293		9.11.94	P.V.Flack	Fairoaks	18. 4.02P
G-BVwA*	SOCATA MS.880B Rallye 100T	2747	F-GACD	29.11.94	G.K.Brunwin *(Cancelled 23.10.02 as wfu)*	Kemble	14. 4.01
G-BVWB	Thunder Ax8-90 Srs.2 HAB	3000		2.12.94	M.A.Stelling, K.C.& K.Tanner	(Barton-Le-Clay)	21. 5.03
G-BVWC	English Electric Canberra B.2	71399	WK163	2.12.94	Classic Aviation Projects Ltd	Coventry	29. 5.01P
	(C/n relates to nose section originally fitted to XH568)				*(As "WK163") (Acquired by Mike Collett/Atlantic Group)*		
G-BVWE	Cameron C-80 HAB	3414		6.12.94	D.G.Body	Leighton Buzzard	18. 6.01T
					tr Mid-Bucks Farmers Balloon Group		
G-BVWK*	Air & Space 18-A Gyroplane	18-14	SE-HID N6108S	19.12.94	Whisky Mike (Aviation) Ltd	(Kinnettles, Forfar)	
					(Cancelled 18.10.00 as temporarily WFU)		
G-BVWL*	Air & Space 18-A Gyroplane	18-63	SE-HIE N90588/N6152S	19.12.94	Whisky Mike (Aviation) Ltd	(Kinnettles, Forfar)	
					(Cancelled 18.10.00 as temporarily WFU)		
G-BVWM	Europa Aviation Europa	070 & PFA 247-12620		14.12.94	A.Aubeelack	White Waltham	11. 9.03P
	(Rotax 912) *(Monowheel u/c)*				tr Europa Syndicate *(F/f 31.7.00)*		
G-BVWP	de Havilland DHC-1 Chipmunk 22	C1/0741	WP856	19.12.94	T.W.M.Beck	Monks Gate, Horsham	24. 5.04
					(As "WP856/904" in RN c/s)		
G-BVWW	Lindstrand LBL-90A HAB	169		28.12.94	Drawflight Ltd "Double Whiskcy"	Hastings	5. 9.03A
G-BVWX	VPM M-16 Tandem Trainer (Arrow GT1000R)	VPM16-UK-111		3. 1.95	M.L.Smith	Popham	17. 6.02P
G-BVWY	Porterfield CP.6 (Continental A65)	5720	N27223 NC27223	23.11.94	B.Morris	Oaksey Park	30. 7.03P
G-BVWZ	Piper PA-32-301 Saratoga	3206055	I-TASP N9184N	3. 1.95	N.N.Kenny	Lymm Dam	3.12.03
G-BVXA	Cameron N-105 HAB	3441		4. 1.95	R.E.Jones *(Ribby Hall titles)*	Lytham St.Annes	19. 3.03T

G-BVXB	Cameron V-77 HAB	3442		4. 1.95	J.A.Lawton *"Pat McLean"*	Godalming	21.10.03A
G-BVXC	English Electric Canberra B(I).8	6649	WT333	9. 1.95	Classic Aviation Projects Ltd	Bruntingthorpe	AC
	(As "WT333") (Current status unknown)						
G-BVXD	Cameron O-84 HAB	3432		5. 1.95	N.J.Langley *(Prudential titles)*	Bristol	11. 8.03A
G-BVXE	Steen Skybolt	PFA 64-11123	G-LISA	5. 1.95	J.Buglass	Sleap	7. 1.03P
	(Lycoming IO-360)						
G-BVXF	Cameron O-120 HAB	3400		21. 9.94	Off The Ground Balloon Co Ltd	Kendal	7. 6.03T
G-BVXG	Lindstrand LBL-90A HAB	110		5. 1.95	G.C.Elson t/a Lindstrand Balloon School	Ronda, Spain	16. 9.03A
G-BVXJ	Bücker Bü.133 Jungmeister	NK	Span AF E1-9	11. 1.95	J.D.Haslam	Bagby	15. 9.03P
	(Built CASA)		Span AF ES1-9/35-9		*(As "ES-9/G-BVXJ" in Spanish Air Force c/s)*		
G-BVXK	Aerostar Yakovlev Yak-52	9111306	RA44508(1)	12. 1.95	E.Gavazzi	White Waltham	5. 7.03P
			DOSAAF 26		*(As "26" in DOSAAF c/s)*		
G-BVXM	Aérospatiale AS350B Ecureuil	2013	I-AUDI	10. 1.95	The Berkeley Leisure Group Ltd	Sparkford	4. 3.04T
			I-CIOC				
G-BVXR	de Havilland DH.104 Devon C.2	04436	XA880	13. 1.95	M.Whale & M.W.A.Lunn	Kemble	
					(As "XA880" in RAE c/s) (Stored 5.02)		
G-BVXS	Taylorcraft BC-12D	9284	N96984	27. 1.95	Janet M.Allison *"Obsession"*	Swanton Morley	21. 8.02P
	(Continental A65)		NC96984				
G-BVXW	Short SC.7 Skyvan 3A-100	SH.1889	LX-DEF	15.11.95	Babcock Support Services Ltd t/a Babcock HCS		
			Arg.Coast Guard PA-52/G-14-61			RAF Weston-on-the-Green	30. 1.03T
G-BVYF	Piper PA-31-350 Navajo Chieftain	31-7952102	G-SAVE	8. 2.95	J.A., G.M, D.T.A. & J.A.Rees	Haverfordwest	23. 1.03T
			N3518T		t/a Messrs Rees of Poynston West		
G-BVYG	Robin DR300/180R	611	F-BSQB	9. 1.95	Ulster Gliding Club Ltd	Bellarena	9. 4.05
			F-BSPI				
G-BVYK	TEAM mini-MAX 91A	PFA 186-12598		13. 2.95	S.B.Churchill	Eastbach Farm, Coleford	4. 8.98P
	(Rotax 447)						
G-BVYM	Robin DR300/180R	656	F-BTBL	9.12.94	London Gliding Club Pty Ltd	Dunstable	19. 7.04
G-BVYO	Robin R2160	288		11. 1.95	Lifeskills Ltd	(Bromsgrove)	15. 4.04T
G-BVYP	Piper PA-25-235 Pawnee B	25-3481	N7475D	13. 2.95	Bidford Airfield Ltd	Bidford	16. 3.04
			OY-CLT/N7475Z				
G-BVYR	Cameron A-250 HAB	3411		2. 2.95	Voyager Balloons Ltd	Cambridge	14. 8.03T
G-BVYT*	QAC Quickie Q.2	2443	N3797S	18. 1.95	C.A.McGee *(Cancelled 7.1.03 by CAA)*	Enstone	2. 9.00P
G-BVYU	Cameron A-140 HAB	3544		17. 2.95	A.M.Holly t/a Exclusive Ballooning	Breadstone	14. 5.03T
G-BVYX	Avid Speed Wing Mk.4	PFA 189-12370		16. 2.95	G.J.Keen	Andrewsfield	15. 4.03P
G-BVYY	Pietenpol Aircamper	PFA 47-12559		20. 2.95	J.R.Orchard	Wolverhampton	28. 6.98P
G-BVYZ	Stemme S-10V	14-011	D-KGDD	6. 3.95	L.Gubbay & S.Sagar	Denham	26. 3.05
G-BVZD	Tri-R Kis *(Tricycle u/c)*	PFA 239-12416		21. 2.95	D.R.Morgan	Old Sarum	18. 6.03P
	(Canadian Air Motive CAM.100)						
G-BVZE	Boeing 737-59D	26422	SE-DNL	7. 3.95	British Midland Airways Ltd	East Midlands	22. 3.04T
G-BVZG	Boeing 737-5Q8	25160	SE-DNF	12. 4.95	British Midland Airways Ltd	East Midlands	1. 5.04T
G-BVZH	Boeing 737-5Q8	25166	SE-DNG	25. 4.95	British Midland Airways Ltd	East Midlands	26. 5.04T
					(Op bmibaby) "baby blue skies"		
G-BVZI	Boeing 737-5Q8	25167	SE-DNH	15. 5.95	British Midland Airways Ltd	East Midlands	11. 6.04T
					(Op bmibaby)		
G-BVZJ	Rand Robinson KR-2	PFA 129-11049		21. 2.95	J.P.McConnell-Wood	Phoenix Farm, Hants	
	(Revmaster)				*(Damaged landing Phoenix Farm 15.7.98: current status unknown)*		
G-BVZM	Cessna 210M Centurion II	21061674	OO-CNJ	28. 2.95	J.J.M.Feeney	Elstree	25. 3.04
			N732PV				
G-BVZN	Cameron C-80 HAB	3546		28. 2.95	Sally J.Langley	Bristol	3. 8.03A
					t/a Sky Fly Balloons *(Taywood Homes titles)*		
G-BVZO	Rans S-6-116 Coyote II *(Tricycle u/c)*			1. 3.95	P.Atkinson	Sandtoft	22. 7.03P
	(Rotax 582)	0494.606 & PFA 204A-12710					
G-BVZR	Zenair CH.601HD	PFA 162-12417		2. 3.95	J.D.White	Nottingham	5.11.03P
	(Rotax 912UL)						
G-BVZT	Lindstrand LBL-90A HAB	183		9. 3.95	F.W.Farnsworth Ltd	Nottingham	16. 8.03A
					t/a Pork Farms Bowyers *(Bowyers Pork Farms titles)*		
G-BVZV	Rans S-6-116 Coyote II	PFA 204A-12832		16. 2.95	A.G.Cameron & W.G.Dunn	(Winkleigh)	16. 5.03P
	(Rotax 582) (Nosewheel u/c)						
G-BVZX	Cameron H-34 HAB	3564		15. 3.95	Julia B.Turnau tr Chianti Balloon Club	Siena, Italy	21. 6.96A
G-BVZZ	de Havilland DHC-1 Chipmunk 22	C1/0687	WP795	5. 1.95	D.C.Murray	Lee-on-Solent	14. 6.04
					tr Portsmouth Naval Gliding Club *(As "WP795/901" in RN c/s)*		

G-BWAA - G-BWZZ

G-BWAA	Cameron N-133 HAB	3471		9. 3.95	C.& J.Bailey	Bristol	14.11.03T
					t/a Bailey Balloons *(Brunel Ford titles)*		
G-BWAB	Jodel D.140 Mousquetaire	PFA 251-12469		25. 1.95	W.A.Braim	(Driffield)	29.10.03P
G-BWAC	Waco YKS-7	4693	N50RA	19. 8.92	D.N.Peters	Little Gransden	19.10.04
	(Jacobs R-755)		N2896D/NC50				
G-BWAD	Rotary Air Force RAF 2000	147 & PFA G/13-1254		27. 2.95	Newtonair Gyroplanes Ltd	Henstridge	18. 9.03P
	(Two-seat trainer)				*(Op A Melody)*		
G-BWAE	Rotary Air Force RAF 2000	PFA G/13-1252		27. 2.95	D.P.Kearns	(Lichfield)	23. 7.03P
G-BWAF	Hawker Hunter F.6A	S4/U/3393	8831M	24. 2.95	RV Aviation Ltd	Bournemouth	
	(Built Armstrong-Whitworth Aircraft)		XG160		*(Noted 11.01 in natural metal finish)*		
G-BWAG	Cameron O-120 HAB	3478		3. 2.95	P.M.Skinner	Maidstone	31. 5.03T
G-BWAH	Montgomerie-Bensen B.8MR	PFA G/01-1208		16. 3.95	J.B.Allan *(Noted 11.02)*	Henstridge	11. 3.03P
G-BWAI	CFM Streak Shadow SA			21. 3.95	C.M.James	(Canterbury)	9. 5.01P
	(Rotax 582)	K.235SA & PFA 206-12556			*(New owner 6.02)*		
	(Originally allocated as BMAA/HB/052 c.1990)						
G-BWAJ	Cameron V-77 HAB	3579		22. 3.95	R.S. & S.H.Ham *"Robsel"*	Axbridge, Somerset	9. 8.01A
G-BWAO	Cameron C-80 HAB	3436		24. 3.95	Airxcite Ltd t/a Virgin Balloon Flights	(Wembley)	17. 7.03T
G-BWAP	Clutton FRED Srs.3	PFA 29-10959		24. 3.95	G.A.Shepherd *(Current status unknown)*	Seething	

G-BWAR	Denney Kitfox Model 3 (Rotax 582)	PFA 172-12432		16. 3.95	I.Wightman	Croft Farm, Defford	29. 9.03P
G-BWAT	Pietenpol Aircamper (Continental C90)	PFA 47-11594		15. 3.95	P.W.Aitchison	Shobdon	28. 7.02P
G-BWAU	Cameron V-90 HAB	3569		27. 3.95	K.M. & A.M.F.Hall	London N10	24. 4.03A
G-BWAV	Schweizer Hughes 269C (300C)	S.1204	SE-JAY LN-OTS/OY-HDW/N41S	28. 2.95	B.Maggs t/a Helihire	(Guildford)	29. 7.04T
G-BWAW	Lindstrand LBL-77A HAB	207		28. 3.95	D.Bareford *(Seton Healthcare titles)*	Kidderminster	17. 6.03A
G-BWBA	Cameron V-65 HAB	3456		27. 2.95	P.G.Dunnington tr Dante Balloon Group *(British Airways titles)*	Hungerford	19. 8.02A
G-BWBB	Lindstrand LBL-14A HAB	222		3. 4.95	Oxford Promotions (UK) Ltd *(Op F Prell)*	Kentucky, USA	
G-BWBC	Cameron N-90AS HAB	3574		12. 6.95	Wetterauer Montgolfieren EV "Zeppelin"	Budingen, Germany	21. 5.03A
G-BWBE	Colt Flying Ice Cream Cone SS HAB	3560		3. 4.95	Benedikt Haggeney GmbH	Ennigerloh, Germany	17. 4.03A
G-BWBF	Colt Flying Ice Cream Cone SS HAB	3561		3. 4.95	Benedikt Haggeney GmbH	Ennigerloh, Germany	17. 4.03A
G-BWBG	Cvjetkovic CA-65 Skyfly	PFA 1566		6. 4.95	T.White & M.C.Fawkes	Charity Farm, Baxterley	
G-BWBH*	Thunder Fork Lift Truck 90SS HAB	3472		6. 4.95	Jungheinrich AG *(Cancelled 24.1.03 as wfu)*	Hamburg, Germany	18. 4.01A
G-BWBI	Taylorcraft F-22A	2207	N22UK	3. 4.95	P.J.Wallace	Eshott	31. 5.05
G-BWBJ	Colt 21A HAB	3532		6. 4.95	U.Schneider	Giessen, Germany	12.12.02A
G-BWBO	Lindstrand LBL-77A HAB	157		10. 4.95	T.J.Orchard, N.J.Glover & S.R.Godfrey	Aylesbury	14.12.02A
G-BWBT	Lindstrand LBL-90A HAB	184		3. 4.95	British Telecommunications plc *(BT titles)*	Newbury	18. 4.03A
G-BWBV*	Colt Piggy Bank SS HAB	3535		19. 4.95	Iduna-Bausparkasse AG *(Cancelled 16.11.01 as WFU) (Preserved)*	(The Netherlands)	5. 4.01A
G-BWBY	Schleicher ASH26E	26076		30. 8.95	J.S.Wand	Aston Down	14.11.04
G-BWBZ	ARV1 Super 2 (Mid-West AE.100R)	PFA 152-12802		10. 3.95	P.I.Lewis	Sleap	9. 6.03P
G-BWCA	CFM Streak Shadow (Rotax 582)	K.160 & PFA 206-11985		19. 4.95	S.Woolmington	(Colchester)	1. 8.02P
G-BWCC	Van Den Bemden 460m3 (Gas) Free Balloon "022" *(C/n may be a corruption of Dutch CofR 622) (Dutch records indicate some parts came from OO-BGX which itself became G-BBFS)*		PH-BOX	5. 4.95	R.W.Batchelor *"Prof A.Piccard"* tr Piccard Balloon Group	Thame	
G-BWCG	Lindstrand LBL-42A HAB	223		25. 4.95	Oxford Promotions (UK) Ltd *(Op F Prell)*	Kentucky, USA	10. 1.97A
G-BWCK	Everett Gyroplane Srs.3 (Rotax 582)	036		26. 4.95	A.C.S.M.Hart	Farley Farm, Romsey	20. 2.03P
G-BWCO	Dornier Do.28D-2 Skyservant	4337	EI-CJU (N5TK)/5N-AOH/D-ILIF	19. 6.95	Wingglider Ltd *(Stored 8.00)*	Hibaldstow	19. 5.99A
G-BWCS	British Aircraft Corporation BAC.145 Jet Provost T.Mk.5	XW293 EEP/JP/957		28. 4.95	R.E.Todd *(As "XW293/Z") (Noted Bournemouth for engine change 12,02)*	Sandtoft	15. 3.02P
G-BWCT	Tipsy T.66 Nipper Srs.1 (Built Avions Fairey SA)	11	"OO-NIC" PH-MEC/D-EMEC/OO-NIC	27. 4.95	J.S.Hemmings & C.R.Steer	(Rye/Bexhill-on-Sea)	
G-BWCV	Europa Aviation Europa (Subaru EA-81/100) *(Monowheel u/c)*	041 & PFA 247-12591		4. 5.95	G.V.McKirdy *(F/f 22.3.97) (On rebuild 7.02)*	Enstone	14. 4.98P
G-BWCW	Barnett Rotorcraft J4B (Lycoming)	PFA G/14-1256		5. 5.95	S.H.Kirkby *(Noted 11.00)*	Sunny Down, Stockbridge	
G-BWCY	Murphy Rebel (Lycoming O-235)	PFA 232-12135		15. 5.95	A.Konieczek	St.Michaels	16. 9.03P
G-BWCZ	Revolution Helicopters Mini-500 (Rotax 582)	0010		1. 5.95	D.Nieman	(Thame)	
G-BWDE	Piper PA-31P Pressurised Navajo	31P-7400193	G-HWKN HB-LIR/D-IAIR/N7304L	12. 5.95	Tomkat Aviation Ltd *(Stored 10.97)*	Shoreham	18.12.96T
G-BWDF	WSK PZL-104 Wilga 35A	21950955		17. 5.95	Shivair Ltd *(Current status unknown)*	(London SE1)	30.11.98
G-BWDH	Cameron N-105 HAB	3549		22. 5.95	Bridges Van Hire Ltd	Awsworth, Nottingham	11. 6.01T
G-BWDM*	Lindstrand LBL-120A HAB	263		26. 5.95	G.D. & L.Fitzpatrick *(Cancelled 22.2.02 by CAA)*	Thame	14. 2.02T
G-BWDO	Sikorsky S-76B	760356	VR-CPN N9HM	2. 6.95	Haughey Air Ltd	(Newry, Co.Armagh)	8. 6.03T
G-BWDP	Europa Aviation Europa (Rotax 912) *(Monowheel u/c)*	062 & PFA 247-12637		7. 6.95	W.Hueltz *(F/f 16.11.95)* *(Suffered fire refuelling 14.5.00 - severe damage deforming fuselage: new owner 5.01 - & new fuselage/kit no??)*	(Bonn, Germany)	9. 8.03P
G-BWDR	Hunting-Percival P.84 Jet Provost T.3A	XM376 PAC/W/6603		6. 6.95	W.O.Bayazid *(As "XM376/27")*	Humberside	24.10.02P
G-BWDS	Hunting-Percival P.84 Jet Provost T.Mk.3A *(Correct c/n PAC/W/9231?)*	XM424 "PAC/W/932"	(N77506)?/XM424	6. 6.95	J.Sinclair *(As "XM424")*	North Weald	23. 5.01P
G-BWDT	Piper PA-34-220T Seneca III	34-8233045	PH-TWI G-BKHS/N8472H	21. 9.88	H.R.Chambers	Redhill	16. 8.03
G-BWDU	Cameron V-90 HAB	3143		19. 6.95	D.M.Roberts	Llandeilo	2. 8.03A
G-BWDV	Schweizer Hughes 269C	S.1712	N86G	16. 6.95	Oxford Aviation Services Ltd	Oxford	3. 9.04T
G-BWDX	Europa Aviation Europa (Rotax 912) *(Monowheel u/c)*	056 & PFA 247-12603		13. 6.95	J.B.Crane *(F/f 27.4.97)*	Fenland	23. 5.02P
G-BWDZ	Sky 105-24 HAB	002		13. 6.95	Skyride Balloons Ltd	King's Lynn	27. 5.03T
G-BWEA	Lindstrand LBL-120A HAB	252		14. 6.95	S.R.Seager *(Parrott & Coales titles)*	Aylesbury	8. 7.00T
G-BWEB	British Aircraft Corporation BAC.145 Jet Provost T.5A	XW422 EEP/JP/1044		19. 6.95	D.W.N.Johnson *(As "XW422".in red/white/blue RAF c/s)*	North Weald	26. 6.03P
G-BWED	Thunder Ax7-77 HAB	3575		20. 6.95	J.Tod	London WC2	20. 6.96
G-BWEE	Cameron V-42 HAB	3480		8. 3.95	Aeromantics Ltd	Bristol	
G-BWEF	SNCAN Stampe SV-4C (DH Gipsy Major 10)	208	G-BOVL N20SV/F-BHES/F-BBLC	13. 5.93	A.J.White tr Acebell BWEF Syndicate	Redhill	7. 3.04
G-BWEG	Europa Aviation Europa (Rotax 912) *(Conventional u/c)*	053 & PFA 247-12600		4. 4.95	B.A.Selmes & R.J.Marsh tr Wessex Europa Group *(F/f 29.3.97)*	Dunkeswell	10. 6.03P
G-BWEH	HOAC DV-20 Katana	20123		19. 6.95	Lowlog Ltd	Elstree	19. 7.04T
G-BWEL	Sky 200-24 HAB	003		27. 6.95	Hot Air Balloons Ltd	Henley-on-Thames	26. 3.03T
G-BWEM	Supermarine 358 Seafire L.III	-	IAC.157 RX168	28. 6.95	C.J.Warrilow & S.W.Atkins *(On rebuild 10.01)*	(Exeter)	
G-BWEN	Macair Merlin GT (Subaru EA81)	050194 & PFA 208A-12859		20. 6.95	B.W.Davies *(Noted 1.03)*	Fenland	7.12.95P

Reg	Type	C/n	Prev id	Date	Owner/Operator	Location	Date
G-BWEO	Lindstrand LBL-14M HAB	285		23. 6.95	Lindstrand Balloons Ltd	Oswestry	19. 5.00A
G-BWEP*	Lindstrand LBL-77M HAB	286		23. 6.95	Lindstrand Balloons Ltd	Oswestry	19. 5.00A
					(Cancelled 17.5.00 as WFU)		
G-BWER	Lindstrand LBL-14M HAB	287		23. 6.95	Lindstrand Balloons Ltd	Oswestry	4.11.97A
G-BWEU	Reims/Cessna F152 II	F15201894	EI-BNC	15. 6.95	Affair Aircraft Leasing Ltd	(Weatherby)	2. 9.04T
			N9097Y				
G-BWEV	Cessna 152 II	15283182	EI-BVU	28. 6.95	Haimoss Ltd	Old Sarum	10.10.04T
			N47184				
G-BWEW	Cameron N-105 HAB	3637		30. 6.95	Unipart Group Ltd	Cowley	17. 1.00A
					tr Unipart Balloon Club (Unipart titles)		
G-BWEY	Bensen B.8	PFA G/01-1197		3. 7.95	F.G.Shepherd	Alston, Cumbria	
G-BWEZ	Piper J-3C-85 Cub	6021	N29050	3. 7.95	J.G.McTaggart tr PJ L4 Group	Glasgow	31.10.03P
			NC29050		(As "FR887" in silver c/s)		
G-BWFD	HOAC DV-20 Katana	20127		5. 7.95	Diamond Aircraft UK Ltd	Gamston	30. 7.04T
G-BWFE	HOAC DV-20 Katana	20129		5. 7.95	Airways Ltd	Gamston	23. 7.04T
G-BWFG	Robin HR200/120	293		20. 7.95	Atlantic Air Transport Ltd	Coventry	7. 2.05T
G-BWFH	Europa Aviation Europa	201 & PFA 247-12842		14. 7.95	B.L.Wratten	(Crowborough)	29. 6.03P
	(Rotax 912) (Monowheel u/c)				(F/f 6.1.98)		
G-BWFI	HOAC DV-20 Katana	20128		17. 7.95	Lowlog Ltd	Elstree/Cranfield	12. 8.04T
G-BWFJ	Evans VP-1	PFA 62-10349		1. 9.78	P.A.West	Old Sarum	27. 1.93P
	(Volkswagen 1600)				(Stored 5.94: current status unknown)		
G-BWFK*	Lindstrand LBL-77A HAB	289		17. 7.95	Virgin Airship & Balloon Co Ltd "Orange"	Telford	24. 8.00A
					(Cancelled 2.3.01 as WFU)		
G-BWFM	Yakovlev Yak-50	781208	NX5224R	19. 7.95	Classic Aviation Ltd	Little Gransden	17. 4.03P
			DDR-WQX/DM-WQX		(Op The Old Flying Machine Co)		
G-BWFN	HAPI Cygnet SF-2A	PFA 182-11335		19. 7.95	T.Crawford (Under construction 5.02)	Cumbernauld	
G-BWFO	Colomban MC-15 Cri-Cri	PFA 133-11253		19. 7.95	O.G.Jones	(Llanbedr)	
	(JPX PUL-212)						
G-BWFP	IAV-Bacau Yakovlev Yak-52	855503	RA44501(1)	20. 7.95	M.C.Lee	Blackpool	27. 3.03P
	(C/n plate states 855606 [DOSAAF 61 (blue)] - composite?) DOSAAF 43						
G-BWFR	Hawker Hunter F.5841	H-697398	J-4031	24. 7.95	The Old Flying Machine Air Museum Co Ltd	Scampton	3. 8.99P
					(As "J-4031")		
G-BWFS	Hawker Hunter F.5841	H-697425	J-4058	24. 7.95	The Old Flying Machine Air Museum Co Ltd	Scampton	5. 7.99P
					(As "J-4058")		
G-BWFT	Hawker Hunter T.8M41	H-695332	XL602	24. 7.95	B.R.Pearson tr T8M Group	Exeter	23. 7.99P
					(As "XL602")		
G-BWFV	HOAC DV-20 Katana	20132		26. 7.95	J.P.E.Walsh t/a Walsh Aviation	Cranfield	29. 8.04T
G-BWFX	Europa Aviation Europa	038 & PFA 247-12586		26. 7.95	A.D.Stewart	Rayne Hall Farm, Rayne	21. 2.03P
	(Rotax 912) (Monowheel u/c)				(F/f 31.8.96)		
G-BWFY	Aérospatiale AS350B1 Ecureuil	1963	N518R	31. 7.95	PLM Dollar Group Ltd	Inverness	21. 7.04T
G-BWFZ	Murphy Rebel	PFA 232-12536	G-SAVS	19. 7.95	S.Beresford	(Gringley-on-the-Hill, Doncaster)	10. 7.03P
	(Lycoming O-235)						
G-BWGF	British Aircraft Corporation BAC.145 Jet Provost T.5A	EEP/JP/989	XW325	10. 8.95	J.W.Cullen	Blackpool	29. 7.03P
					tr Specialscope Jet Provost Group (As "XW325/E")		
G-BWGG	Max Holste MH.1521C1 Broussard	20	F-GGKG	10. 7.95	M.J.Burnett Jnr. & R.B.Maalouf	Rednall	21. 8.03
			F-WGKG/Fr mil		(As "315-SQ/20" in ALAT c/s)		
G-BWGJ	Chilton DW.1A	PFA 225-12615		11. 8.95	T.J.Harrison	Lower Upham, Hants	
	(Lycoming O-145-A2)				(Complete 5.00)		
G-BWGK	Hawker Hunter GA.11	HABL-003032	XE689	15. 8.95	B.R.Pearson tr GA11 Group	Exeter	11. 7.01P
	(Centre fuselage no.is 41HR HABL 003032)				(As "XE689/864/VL")		
G-BWGL	Hawker Hunter T.8C	HABL-003086	XF357	15. 8.95	Elvington Events Ltd	Elvington	8. 7.03P
	(Officially regd with c/n 41H-695946)				(As T.Mk.7 prototype "XJ615")		
G-BWGM	Hawker Hunter T.8C	HABL-003008	XE665	15. 8.95	B.J.Pover tr The Admirals Barge	Exeter	24. 6.98P
	(Officially regd with c/n 41H-695940)				(As "XE665/876/VL")		
G-BWGN	Hawker Hunter T.8C	41H-670689	WT722	15. 8.95	B.J.Pearson tr T8C Group	Exeter	3. 9.97P
					(As "WT722/878/VL")		
G-BWGO	Slingsby T.67M-200 Firefly	2048	SE-LBC	15. 8.95	R.Gray	Fairoaks	9. 6.05
G-BWGP	Cameron C-80 HAB	3631		17. 8.95	D.J.Groombridge	Bristol	29. 9.03A
					(London Camera Exchange titles)		
G-BWGR	North American TB-25N-NC Mitchell	108-34200	N9494Z	18. 8.95	D Copley	Sandtoft	
	(Official c/n 108-30925 - corruption of USAAF serial)		44-30925		(As "151632/N9494Z")		
G-BWGS	British Aircraft Corporation BAC.145 Jet Provost T.5A	XW310 EEP/JP/974		18. 8.95	Katharina K.Gerstorfer	North Weald	21. 7.03P
					(As "XW310/37")		
G-BWGT	Hunting-Percival P.84 Jet Provost T.4		8991M	21. 8.95	R.E.Todd (Op The Jet Provost Club)	Sandtoft	30. 5.03P
	(Reported as c/n PAC/W/19992)	PAC/W/21624	XR679				
G-BWGU	Cessna 150F	15062962	EI-CDU	18. 8.95	Goodair Leasing Ltd	Hill Farm, Nayland	31. 5.04
			N8862G				
G-BWGX	Cameron N-42 HAB	3633		21. 8.95	Newbury Building Society	Newbury	19. 1.00A
G-BWGY	HOAC DV-20 Katana	20134		22. 8.95	Plane Talking Ltd	Cranfield	12.10.04T
G-BWGZ	HOAC DV-20 Katana	20135		22. 8.95	Plane Talking Ltd	Cranfield	15.10.04T
G-BWHA*	Hawker Hurricane II	B41H/G5/21232	Z5053	23. 8.95	Historic Flying Ltd	(Audley End)	
	(Regd with c/n 41H-G3121232)		(Soviet AF)/Z5053		(As "Z5252/GO-B")		
					(On rebuild 8.95: cancelled 2.8.01 by CAA) (Current status unknown)		
G-BWHB	Cameron O-65 HAB	2759		24. 8.95	G.Aimo	Mondovi, Italy	11. 7.03A
G-BWHC	Cameron N-77 HAB	3647		25. 8.95	R.B.Craik (Travelsphere Holidays titles)	Northampton	5. 7.03A
G-BWHD	Lindstrand LBL-31A HAB	292		29. 8.95	J.C.E.Price	Portadown	12. 1.01A
					tr Army Air Corps Balloon Club		
G-BWHF	Piper PA-31-325 Navajo C/R	31-7612076	F-GECA	7. 9.95	Awyr Cymru Cyf	Shobdon	31.10.05T
			D-IBIS/N59862				
G-BWHG	Cameron N-65 HAB	3619		7. 9.95	M.Stefanini & F.B.Alaoui	Florence, Italy	4. 8.03A
G-BWHH	Piper PA-18-135 Super Cub	18-3605	PH-KNA	9. 8.95	J.W.Macleod	Felthorpe	8. 7.03
	(L-21B-PI) (Frame No.18-3789)		R.Neth AF R-115/54-2405		(As "44" in US Army c/s) (Destroyed in arson attack 18.2.03)		
G-BWHI	de Havilland DHC-1 Chipmunk 22	C1/0637	WK624	8. 9.95	N.E.M.Clare	Duxford	9. 12.04T
	(Hulk of WK624/M may have been used in rebuild of G-AOSY c 1998/99)				(As "WK624/M")		

Reg	Type	C/n	Prev id	Date	Owner	Location	Date
G-BWHK	Rans S-6-116 Coyote II *(Tricycle u/c)*			15. 9.95	D.A.Buttress	Wolverhampton	12. 5.03P
	(Rotax 582) 0695.834 & PFA 204A-12908						
G-BWHM	Sky 140-24 HAB	006		18. 9.95	C.J.S.Limon	London NW1	5. 4.03T
G-BWHP	CASA I-131E Jungmann	2109	E3B-513	18. 8.95	J.F.Hopkins	Watchford Farm, Yarcombe	16. 7.03P
					(As "S4+A07" in Luftwaffe c/s)		
G-BWHR	Tipsy Nipper T.66 Srs.1 PFA 25-12843		(OO-KAM)	19. 9.95	L.R.Marnef	(Koningshooikt, Belgium)	
	(Composite homebuild of orig Fairey build c/n 29 & 71) OO-69				*(Current status unknown)*		
G-BWHS	Rotary Air Force RAF.2000 PFA G/13-1253			25. 9.95	J M Cox	(Windsor)	2. 1.03P
	(Subaru EA82)						
G-BWHT	Everett Campbell Cricket	046		27. 9.95	D.Brown *(Current status unknown)*	(Newton Stewart)	
G-BWHU	Westland Scout AH.1	F.9517	XR595	27. 9.95	N.J.F.Boston	Oreston, Plymouth	27. 1.03P
					(As "XR595/M" in Army c/s)		
G-BWHV	Denney Kitfox Model 2 PFA 172-11857			28. 9.95	A.C.Dove	(Ashtead)	2. 4.03P
G-BWHW	Cameron A-180 HAB	3634		29. 9.95	Societé Bombard SARL	Meursanges, France	6. 10.03A
G-BWHY	Robinson R22	0098	N90366	24. 3.87	Finnigan-Wood Ltd	Blackpool	11. 6.05T
G-BWIA	Rans S-10 Sakota PFA 194-12044			15. 9.95	P.A.Beck	Cambridge	24. 9.01P
	(Rotax 582)						
G-BWIB	Scottish Aviation Bulldog Srs.120/122 BH120/227		Ghana AF G-103	10.10.95	B.I.Robertson	(Pontiac, Michigan, USA)	8. 5.04T
					(As "XX514")		
G-BWID	Druine D.31 Turbulent (Volkswagen 1200) 201		F-PHFR	16.10.95	A.M.Turney	Cheddington	28. 4.03P
G-BWII	Cessna 150G	15065308	N4008J	22. 9.95	J.D.G.Hicks	Beeches Farm, South Scarle	25. 2.05
			(G-BSKB)/N4008J				
G-BWIJ*	Europa Aviation Europa 006 & PFA 247-12513			19.10.95	R.Lloyd	Gloucestershire	
	(Mid-West AE100R) (Monowheel u/c)				*(Noted 9.99: cancelled 2.11.00 by CAA) (Current status unknown)*		
G-BWIK	de Havilland DH.82A Tiger Moth	86417	7015M	20.10.95	B.J.Ellis	Little Gransden	
			NL985		*(On rebuild as "NL985": current status unknown)*		
G-BWIL	Rans S-10 Sakota 1089.065 & PFA 194-11770		G-WIEN	4.10.95	J.C.Longmore	Netherthorpe	29. 1.02P
	(Rotax 582)						
G-BWIP	Cameron N-90 HAB	3668		20.10.95	S.H.Fell	Carlisle	27.10.96A
G-BWIR	Dornier 328-100	3023	D-CDXF	18.10.95	Suckling Airways (Norwich) Ltd	Cambridge	19.10.03T
			N328DA/D-CDHH		t/a Scot Airways		
G-BWIV	Europa Aviation Europa 210 & PFA 247-12871			27.10.95	T.G.Ledbury	White Waltham	9. 9.99P
	(Rotax 912) *(Monowheel u/c)*				*(F/f 20.8.96)*		
G-BWIW	Sky 180-24 HAB	008		1.11.95	J.A.Cooper	Ivybridge	16. 4.03T
G-BWIX	Sky 120-24 HAB	009		31.10.95	J.M.Percival *"Mayfly III"*	Loughborough	7. 1.03
G-BWJG	Mooney M.20J (201MSE)	24-3319	N1083P	7.11.95	Samic Ltd	Elstree	27 5.05
G-BWJH	Europa Aviation Europa 007 & PFA 247-12643			10.11.95	P.J.Rudling	Sandown	20. 9.02P
	(Rotax 912) *(Tri-gear u/c)*				*(F/f 22.3.97)*		
G-BWJI	Cameron V-90 HAB	3727		13.11.95	Calarel Developments Ltd	Chipping Camden	17. 9.02A
G-BWJK*	Rotorway Executive	CWT.1	G-OKIT	24.10.95	B.Singh	(Huddersfield)	
	(Rotorway RW 152)				*(No PtoF issued: cancelled 29.8.01 by CAA)*		
G-BWJM	Bristol M.1C rep	NAW-2		23.11.95	The Shuttleworth Trust	Old Warden	7. 5.03P
	(Built Northern Aeroplane Workshops)				*(As "C4918" in 72 Sqdn c/s)*		
G-BWJN	Montgomerie-Bensen B.8MR PFA G/01-1262			16.11.95	M.Johnston	Carlisle	26. 9.03P
	(Rotax 582)						
G-BWJP	Cessna 172C	17249424	N1824Y	21.11.95	T.W.R.Case *(New owner 8.01)*	(Sidmouth)	
G-BWJR	Sky 120-24 HAB	007		22.11.95	W.J.Brogan *"Filzmooser"*	Steiermark, Austria	21.12.96
					(New CofR 9.02)		
G-BWJT	Yakovlev Yak-50	812003	RA013852	3.11.95	D Bonucchi	(Watford)	10.11.03P
			DOSAAF50		*(www.YAKUK.Co.Uk titles)*		
G-BWJW	Westland Scout AH.1	F.9705	XV130	29.11.95	C.L.Holdsworth	Redhill	22. 4.03P
					(As "XV130/R" in 666 Sqdn c/s)		
G-BWJY	de Havilland DHC-1 Chipmunk 22	C1/0519	WG469	5.12.95	K.J.Thompson *(As "WG469")*	Newtownards, Co.Down	23. 5.03
G-BWKD	Cameron O-120 HAB	3773		8.12.95	K.E. & L.J.Viney *"Rainbow"*	Olney, Bucks	7. 3.03T
G-BWKE	Cameron AS-105GD Hot Air Airship	3685		8.12.95	W.Arnold	Kassel, Germany	4. 2.03A
G-BWKF	Cameron N-105 HAB	3736		8.12.95	R.M.M.Botti	Grosseto, Italy	12. 2.03A
G-BWKG	Europa Aviation Europa 004 & PFA 247-12451			28.11.95	E.H.Keppert	(Vienna, Austria)	8. 8.03P
	(Rotax 912) *(Monowheel u/c)*				*(F/f 30.9.99)*		
G-BWKJ	Rans S-7 Courier PFA 218-12918			14.12.95	R.W.Skelton	Portadown, Co.Armagh	17.10.03P
	(Verner SVS1400)				*"Festina Lente/Nihl Timeo"*		
G-BWKK	Auster AOP.9 AUS.166 & B5/10/165		XP279	30. 7.79	C.A.Davis & D.R.White	Popham	1. 8.96P
					(As "XP279" in Army c/s)		
G-BWKR	Sky 90-24 HAB	014		18.12.95	Beverley Drawbridge	Cranbrook	16. 3.03T
G-BWKT	Stephens Akro Lazer PFA 123-11421			19.12.95	P.D.Begley	Sywell	21. 3.03P
G-BWKU	Cameron A-250 HAB	3730		21.12.95	Balloon School (International) Ltd	Petworth	17. 7.03T
					t/a British School of Ballooning		
G-BWKV	Cameron V-77 HAB	3780		27.12.95	Poppies (UK) Ltd	Wootton Fitzpaine, Dorset	19. 8.03A
G-BWKW	Thunder Ax8-90 HAB	3770		28.12.95	Venice Simplon Orient Express Ltd	Frinton-on-Sea	9. 1.97A
					"Road to Mandalay"		
G-BWKX	Cameron A-250 HAB	3731		2. 1.96	Balloon School (International) Ltd	Petworth	17. 7.03T
					t/a Hot Airlines *(Hot Airlines titles)*		
G-BWKZ	Lindstrand LBL-77A HAB	340		21.12.95	J.H.Dobson	Reading	28. 6.03T
G-BWLD	Cameron O-120 HAB	3774	(I-....)	16. 1.96	D & P Pedri & C.Nicolodi	(Villa Lagarina, Italy)	10. 4.03A
G-BWLF	Cessna 404 Titan II	404-0414	G-BNXS	26.10.94	P.Maden & M Evans	Farnborough	19. 3.03
			HKG-4/(N8799K)		t/a Nor Leasing		
G-BWLJ	Taylorcraft DCO-65 O	4331	C-CUSA	16. 1.96	C.Evans	Hill Farm, Nayland	18.12.02P
G-BWLL	Murphy Rebel PFA 232-12499			22. 1.96	F.W.Parker	Richmond, N.Yorks	16. 7.02P
	(Lycoming O-235)						
G-BWLM	Sky 65-24 HAB	015		24. 1.96	W.J.Brogan	Steiermark, Austria	5. 2.97
G-BWLN	Cameron O-84 HAB	3737		24. 1.96	Reggiana Riduttori SRL	S.Polo d'Enza, Italy	14. 7.03A
G-BWLP	HOAC DV-20 Katana	20141	OE-UDV	6. 2.96	Plane Talking Ltd	Elstree	12.11.03T
G-BWLR	Max Holste MH.1521C1 Broussard	185	F-GGKJ	25. 1.96	Chicory Crops Ltd	Sywell	16. 3.03
			F-WGKJ/French AF		*(As "185/44-CA" in French AF c/s)*		
G-BWLS	HOAC DV-20 Katana 100	20142	OE-UHK	6. 2.96	M.Reed t/a Shadow Aviation	Elstree	19. 7.03T

Reg	Type	c/n	Prev id	Date	Owner	Location	Expiry
G-BWLT	HOAC DV-20 Katana	20149		6. 2.96	Plane Talking Ltd	Elstree	12.11.03T
G-BWLV	HOAC DV-20 Katana	20151		6. 2.96	Plane Talking Ltd	Elstree	23. 6.05T
G-BWLW	Avid Speed Wing Mk.4	PFA 189-12763		26. 1.96	P.C. & Susan A.Creswick	Weston Zoyland	
G-BWLX	Westland Scout AH.1	F.9709	XV134	29.12.95	B.J.Green	Draycott Farm, Chiseldon	4. 7.03P
					(As "XV134" in AAC c/s)		
G-BWLY	Rotorway Executive	5142		11. 1.93	P.W. & I.P.Bewley	Ley Farm, Chirk	17.10.02P
	(Rotorway RI 162)						
G-BWLZ	Wombat Gyrocopter	PFA G/09-1255		28.12.95	M.R.Harrisson	Guernsey	
					(Stored 3.98: new owner 10.00)		
G-BWMA	Colt 105A HAB	1853		31.10.90	L.Lacroix St Paul en Chablais, Haute-Savoie, France		24. 6.02A
G-BWMB	Jodel D.119	77-1492	F-BGMA	17. 2.78	C.Hughes	Finmere	19. 5.03P
	(Orig F-BGMA c/n 77 became F-PHQH & rebuilt as Larrieu JL.2: G-BWMB presumed to be rebuild using some components of c/n 77 & new build c/n 1492)						
G-BWMC	Cessna 182P Skylane II	18263117	N5462J	30. 1.96	P.F.N.Burrow & E.N.Skinner Trenchard Farm, Eggesford		11. 7.03
			G-BWMC/OO-RGM/(OO-RAN)/F-BVOU/N7333N tr Eggesford Eagles Flying Group					
G-BWMD	Enstrom 480	5013		5. 2.96	Lamindene Ltd	Goodwood	8. 7.02T
G-BWMF	Gloster Meteor T.7	G5/356460	7917M	15.12.95	M.Jones tr Meteor Flight	Yatesbury	
			WA591		(On rebuild 3.02)		
G-BWMG	Aérospatiale AS332L Super Puma	2046	OY-HMG	1. 2.96	Bristow Helicopters Ltd "Catterline"	Aberdeen	24. 6.03T
G-BWMH	Lindstrand LBL-77B HAB	152		7. 2.96	J.W.Hole	Much Wenlock	10. 6.03A
G-BWMI	Piper PA-28RT-201T Turbo Arrow IV	28R-8031131	F-GCTG	31. 1.96	Oxford Aviation Services Ltd	Oxford	18.12.05T
			N82482/N9571N				
G-BWMJ	Nieuport Scout 17/23 rep	PFA 121-12351		8. 2.96	R.Gauld-Galliers & Lisa J.Day	Popham	27. 7.03P
	(Warner Scarab 165)				(As "B3459/2" in RFC c/s)		
G-BWMK	de Havilland DH.82A Tiger Moth	84483	T8191	9. 2.96	APB Leasing Ltd (New owner 2.02)	Welshpool	AC
G-BWML	Cameron A-275 HAB	3725		12. 2.96	A.J.Street (Exeter Balloons titles)	Exeter	17. 8.01T
G-BWMN	Rans S-7 Courier	PFA 218-12446		14. 2.96	G.J.Knee & G.Keyser	Turweston	9. 4.03P
	(Rotax 912UL)						
G-BWMO	Oldfield Baby Lakes	JAL.3	G-CIII	14. 2.96	N.M.Robbins	Sleap	28. 2.03P
	(Continental C85)		N11JL				
G-BWMS	de Havilland DH.82A Tiger Moth	82712	OO-EVJ	14. 2.96	Foundation Early Birds (Nederhorst, The Netherlands)		
			T-29/R4771		(Current status unknown)		
G-BWMU	Cameron Monster Truck 105SS HAB	3607		20. 2.96	Magical Adventures Ltd West Bloomfield, Mi., USA		2. 8.01A
					"Skycrusher"		
G-BWMV	Colt AS-105 Mk.II Hot Air Airship	3775		22. 2.96	D.Stuber	Bad Krenznach, Germany	10. 7.02A
G-BWMX	de Havilland DHC-1 Chipmunk 22	C1/0481	WG407	19. 2.96	K.S.Kelso Top Farm, Croydon, Royston		2. 4.05
					tr 407th Flying Group (As "WG407/67")		
G-BWMY	Cameron Bradford & Bingley 90SS HAB	3808		23. 2.96	Magical Adventures Ltd West Bloomfield, Mi., USA		20. 4.00A
G-BWNB	Cessna 152 II	15280051	N757WA	23. 8.96	Galair International Ltd	Wolverhampton	13.11.05T
G-BWNC	Cessna 152 II	15284415	N6487L	23. 8.96	Galair International Ltd	Wellesbourne Mountford	24.11.02T
G-BWND	Cessna 152 II	15285905	N95493	23. 8.96	Galair International Ltd, M.R.Galiffe & G.Davis		
						Wellesbourne Mountford	21. 9.02T
G-BWNH	Cameron A-375 HAB	3553		28. 2.96	Noble Adventures Ltd (Amended CofR 12.01) Bristol		12. 5.97A
G-BWNI	Piper PA-24-180 Comanche	24-136	N5123P	15. 2.96	T.D.Cooper & D.F.Hunt	Popham	30. 7.05
G-BWNJ	Hughes 269C	86-0528	N42LW	29. 2.96	L.R.Fenwick Long Fosse House, Beelsby, Grimsby		12. 6.05
			N27RD/N7458F				
G-BWNK	de Havilland DHC-1 Chipmunk 22	C1/0317	WD390	4. 3.96	B.Whitworth (As "WD390")	Breighton	6. 4.03
G-BWNL*	Europa Aviation Europa 068 & PFA 247-12675			27. 2.96	H.Smith (F/f 10.9.97)	Morgansfield, Fishburn	
	(Subaru) (Tri-gear u/c)			(Damaged Fishburn 14.12.97: cancelled 11.12.00 by CAA - no PtoF issued) (Being rebuilt 2002)				
G-BWNM	Piper PA-28R-180 Cherokee Arrow	28R-30435	N934BD	5. 3.96	D.Houghton	Croft Farm, Defford	17.10.05
G-BWNO	Cameron O-90 HAB	3716		5. 3.96	M.A.Pratt & T Knight	Hertford	30. 8.02A
G-BWNP	Cameron Club-90 SS HAB	1717	EI-BVQ	6. 3.96	C.J.Davies & P.Spellward	Hope Valley	2. 5.00
	(Club Orange Soft Drink Can shape)						
G-BWNR	Piper PA-38-112 Tomahawk	38-78A0449	N2361E	6. 3.96	APB Leasing Ltd	Sleap	6. 5.05T
G-BWNS	Cameron O-90 HAB	3842		6. 3.96	Smithair Ltd "Hector"	Billingshurst	19. 8.03T
					(Self Assessment Tax titles)		
G-BWNT	de Havilland DHC-1 Chipmunk 22	C1/0772	WP901	7. 3.96	R.A.Stafford	East Midlands	24. 5.03T
					t/a Three Point Aviation (As "WP901")		
G-BWNU	Piper PA-38-112 Tomahawk	38-78A0334	N9294T	8. 3.96	Kemble Aero Club Ltd	Kemble	24. 9.05
G-BWNX*	Thunder Ax10-180 Srs.2 HAB	2352	G-OWBC	2. 1.96	MJN Balloon Management Ltd Longleat, Warminster		2. 4.01T
					(Cancelled 26.6.02 by CAA)		
G-BWNY	Aeromot AMT-200 Super Ximango	200-055		11. 6.96	H.G.Nicklin	Rufforth	31. 5.05
G-BWNZ	Agusta A109C	7654		3. 4.96	Anglo Beef Processors Ltd	(Ardlee, Co.Louth)	13. 4.05T
G-BWOA	Sky 105-24 HAB	027		13. 3.96	Akhter Group Holdings plc	Harlow	11. 7.02A
G-BWOB	Luscombe 8F Silvaire	6179	N1552B	14. 3.96	P.J.Tanulak & H.T.Law	(Shrewsbury)	
			NC1552B				
G-BWOD	IAV-Bacau Yakovlev Yak-52	833810	LY-ALY	14. 3.96	Insurefast Ltd	Sywell	16. 5.03P
			DOSAAF 139		(As "DOSAAF 139")		
G-BWOE	Yakovlev Yak-3U	1701231	(G-BUXZ)	14. 3.96	Classic Aviation Ltd	Duxford	
	(Converted from LET Yak C.11)		NX11SN/(France)/Egyptian AF		(New owner 2.03)		
G-BWOF	British Aircraft Corporation BAC.145 Jet Provost T.5	XW291		18. 3.96	Techair London Ltd	Bournemouth	23. 4.03P
		EEP/JP/955					
G-BWOK	Lindstrand LBL-105G HAB	370		19. 3.96	Lindstrand Balloons Ltd	Oswestry	31. 8.01A
G-BWOL*	Hawker Sea Fury FB.11	ES.3617 & 61631	D-CACY(2)	18. 3.96	The Old Flying Machine (Air Museum) Catfield, Norfolk		
			G-9-66/WG599 (On restoration for K Weeks 2.00: cancelled 4.1.01 by CAA: current status unknown)					
G-BWON	Europa Aviation Europa 112 & PFA 247-12720			29. 1.96	H.J.Fish	(Ripley)	1. 8.03P
	(Rotax 912) (Conventional u/c)				(F/f 22.7.97)		
G-BWOR	Piper PA-18-135 Super Cub	18-2547	OO-WIS	21. 3.96	C.D.Baird Roughay Farm, Bishops Waltham		12. 8.05
	(L-18C)		OO-HMF/ALAT/52-6229				
G-BWOT	Hunting P.84 Jet Provost T.3A	PAC/W/10138	XN459	25. 3.96	Red Pelicans Ltd	North Weald	27. 3.03P
	(Reported as c/n PAC/W/949267)				(As "XN459" in all-red Red Pelicans c/s)		
G-BWOU	Hawker Hunter F.58A	HABL.003067	J-4105	26. 3.96	The Old Flying Machine (Air Museum) Co Ltd Scampton		20. 1.99P
			G-9-315/A2565/XF303		(As "105")		
	(Regd with c/n 41H-003067 ex XF306/7776M/G-9-402 which became J-4133:- G-BWOU may be a composite)						

Reg	Type	C/n	Prev id	Date	Owner	Location	Status
G-BWOV	Enstrom F-28A	222	N690BR G-BWOV/F-BVRG	26. 3.96	A.P.Goddard	(Southampton)	16. 5.03T
G-BWOW	Cameron N-105 HAB	3805		31. 1.96	S.J.Colin *"Skybus"* t/a Skybus Ballooning	Cranbrook	8. 5.03T
G-BWOX	de Havilland DHC-1 Chipmunk 22	C1/0728	WP844	27. 3.96	J.St Clair-Quentin (As *"WP844"*)	Spanhoe	10. 7.00
G-BWOY	Sky 31-24 HAB	029		28. 3.96	C.Wolstenholme	Bristol	3.11.03A
G-BWOZ	CFM Streak Shadow SA (Rotax 582)	K.154SA & PFA 206-12988		1. 4.96	N.P.Harding	Plaistows Farm, St Albans	4.11.02P
G-BWPB	Cameron V-77 HAB	3866		1. 4.96	R.H. & N.K.Calvert t/a The Fair Weather Friends Ballooning Co	Bristol	16. 9.03A
G-BWPC	Cameron V-77 HAB	3867		1. 4.96	Helen Vaughan *"Olive"*	Tring	11. 1.03A
G-BWPE	Murphy Renegade Spirit UK	PFA 188-12791		2. 4.96	J.Hatswell (Active 9.02)	(Menton, France)	
G-BWPF	Sky 120-24 HAB	028		3. 4.96	Zebedee Balloon Service Ltd *"Whisper"*	Hungerford	19. 9.03T
G-BWPH	Piper PA-28-181 Cherokee Archer II	28-7790311	N1408H	4. 4.96	H & E Merkado	Panshanger	1. 5.05T
G-BWPJ	Steen Skybolt (Continental IO-346)	PFA 64-12854		9. 4.96	W.R.Penaluna	St Just	20.10.03P
G-BWPM*	Pilatus Britten-Norman BN-2T-4R Defender 4000	4007		24. 4.96	Britten-Norman Ltd (Cancelled 19.10.00 as temporarily WFU)	Bembridge	
G-BWPP	Sky 105-24 HAB	031		9. 4.96	P.F.Smart *"Fourpence"* tr The Sarnia Balloon Group	Basingstoke	17. 7.00A
G-BWPR	Pilatus Britten-Norman BN-2T-4S Defender 4000	4010		24. 4.96	B-N Group Ltd	Bembridge	AC
G-BWPS	CFM Streak Shadow SA (Rotax 618)	K.275SA & PFA 206-12954		9. 2.96	P.M.E.D.McNair-Wilson	Old Sarum	4. 8.03P
G-BWPT	Cameron N-90 HAB	3838		5. 3.96	G.Burrows	Sheffield	1. 5.00A
G-BWPV*	Pilatus Britten-Norman BN-2T-4S Defender 4000	4012		24. 4.96	Britten-Norman Ltd (Cancelled 19.10.00 as temporarily WFU)	Bembridge	
G-BWPW*	Pilatus Britten-Norman BN-2T-4S Defender 4000	4013		24. 4.96	Britten-Norman Ltd (Cancelled 19.10.00 as temporarily WFU)	Bembridge	
G-BWPX*	Pilatus Britten-Norman BN-2T-4S Defender 4000	4014		24. 4.96	Britten-Norman Ltd (Cancelled 19.10.00 as temporarily WFU)	Bembridge	
G-BWPY	HOAC DV-20 Katana 100	20158	OE-UDV	10. 6.96	S.Phillips t/a SAS Flight Services	(Amersham)	14. 6.04T
G-BWPZ	Cameron N-105 HAB	3889		19. 4.96	Flying Pictures Ltd *"Jaguar"*	Chilbolton	17. 4.02A
G-BWRA	Sopwith LC-1T Triplane rep (Warner Scarab 165)	PFA 21-10035	G-PENY	19. 4.96	S.M.Truscott & J.M.Hoblyn (As *"N500"* in RNAS c/s) Watchford Farm, Yarcombe/RNAS Yeovilton		10.11.02P
G-BWRC	Avid Hauler Mk.4 (Hirth F30)	PFA 189-12979		22. 2.96	B.Williams	Chilsfold Farm, Crawley	25. 5.03P
G-BWRM	Colt 105A HAB	3734		23. 4.96	N.Charbonnier	Aosta, Italy	24. 1.03A
G-BWRO	Europa Aviation Europa (Rotax 912) (Monowheel u/c)	196 & PFA 247-12849		22. 4.96	J.G.M.McDiarmid (F/f 22.9.97)	Bodmin	30. 5.03P
G-BWRP	Beech 58 Baron	TH-1737	VR-BVB N3217H	23. 4.96	Astra Aviation Ltd	Guernsey	8. 8.05
G-BWRR	Cessna 182Q Skylane II	18266660	N95861	29. 3.94	D.O.Halle	East Midlands	15. 8.03T
G-BWRS	SNCAN Stampe SV-4C	437	(N) F-BCVQ	24. 4.96	G.P.J.M.Valvekens	(Diest, Belgium)	
G-BWRT	Cameron Concept-60 HAB	3078	EI-BYP	22.10.96	W.R.Teasdale (Inflated 4.02)	Maidenhead	
G-BWRV	Lindstrand LBL-90A HAB	371		23. 4.96	Flying Pictures Ltd (Audi titles)	Chilbolton	24. 2.01A
G-BWRW*	Sky 220-24 HAB	032		23. 4.96	Sky Trek Ballooning Ltd (Cancelled 22.3.02 by CAA)	Longfield, Kent	30. 5.02T
G-BWRY	Cameron N-105 HAB	3817		24. 4.96	G.Aimo *"Ferodo"*	Mondovi, Italy	12. 7.03A
G-BWRZ	Lindstrand LBL-105A HAB	383		26. 4.96	Flying Pictures Ltd (Rover titles)	Chilbolton	17. 3.02A
G-BWSB	Lindstrand LBL-105A HAB	384		26. 4.96	Flying Pictures Ltd (MG titles)	Chilbolton	17. 3.02A
G-BWSC	Piper PA-38-112 Tomahawk II	38-81A0125	N23203	29. 4.96	APB Leasing Ltd	Long Marston	15. 7.02T
G-BWSD	Campbell Cricket	PFA G/03-1216		3. 5.96	R.F.G.Moyle	(Penryn)	
G-BWSG	British Aircraft Corporation BAC.145 Jet Provost T.5	EEP/JP/988	XW324	13. 5.96	R.M.Kay (As *"XW324"* in 6FTS c/s)	Jersey	17. 9.05P
G-BWSH	Hunting P.84 Jet Provost T.3A	PAC/W/10159	XN498	13. 5.96	Global Aviation Ltd	Humberside	8. 7.03P
G-BWSI	K & S SA.102.5 Cavalier (Lycoming O-235)	PFA 01-10624		18. 4.84	B.W.Shaw	Wathstow Farm, Newby Wiske	27. 8.03P
G-BWSJ	Denney Kitfox Model 3 (Rotax 582)	PFA 172-12204		15. 5.96	J.M.Miller	Sutton Meadows, Ely	20. 2.03P
G-BWSL	Sky 77-24 HAB	004		16. 5.96	The Balloon Co Ltd	Cheltenham	15. 1.02A
G-BWSN	Denney Kitfox Model 3 (Rotax 582)	PFA 172-12141		16. 5.96	W.J.Forrest	Siege Cross Farm, Thatcham	11. 9.03P
G-BWSO	Cameron Apple Sainsbury 90SS HAB	3915		17. 5.96	Flying Pictures Ltd *"Sainsbury's Apple"*	Chilbolton	11. 6.02A
G-BWSP	Cameron Carrots Sainsbury 80SS HAB	3914		17. 5.96	Flying Pictures Ltd *"Sainsbury's Carrots"*	Chilbolton	5. 7.02A
G-BWST	Sky 200-24 HAB	036		20. 5.96	S.A.Townley t/a Sky High Leisure	Wrexham	13. 8.03T
G-BWSU	Cameron N-105 HAB	3848		20. 5.96	A.M.Marten *"Wonder Bra"*	Guildford	23. 9.99A
G-BWSV	IAV-Bacau Yakovlev Yak-52	877601	DOSAAF 43	20. 5.96	P.Traynor	Wellesbourne Mountford	21.11.03P
G-BWSY	British Aerospace BAe 125 Srs.800B	258201	G-OCCI G-5-699	28. 5.96	BAE Systems (Operations) Ltd	Filton/Warton	26. 8.03
G-BWSZ	Montgomerie-Bensen B.8MR (Rotax 582)	PFA G/01-1268		14. 5.96	D.Cawkwell	Goole	6. 1.98P
G-BWTA	HOAC DV-20 Katana	20159	OE-UDV	10. 6.96	Plane Talking Ltd	Cranfield	21.10.05T
G-BWTB	Lindstrand LBL-105A HAB	374		29. 5.96	Servatruc Ltd	Nottingham	18. 5.03A
G-BWTC	Moravan Zlin Z.242L	0697		2. 8.96	Oxford Aviation Services Ltd	Oxford	17.11.05T
G-BWTD	Moravan Zlin Z.242L	0698		2. 8.96	Oxford Aviation Services Ltd	Oxford	4.11.05T
G-BWTE	Cameron O-140 HAB	3885		30. 5.96	R.J. & A.J.Mansfield	Bowness-on-Windermere	19. 2.01T
G-BWTF	Lindstrand Bear SS HAB	375		3. 6.96	Free Enterprise Balloons Ltd *"Mr Biddle"*	East Leroy, MI, USA	28. 4.03A
G-BWTG	de Havilland DHC-1 Chipmunk 22	C1/0119	WB671	4. 6.96	P.M.M. de Graaf tr Chipmunk 4 Ever Foundation (As *"WB671/910"*)	Teuge, The Netherlands	2. 8.03

Reg	Type	C/n	Prev id	Date	Owner/Operator	Location	Date2
G-BWTH	Robinson R22 Beta	1767	HB-XYD N4052R	5. 6.96	L.Smith t/a Helicopter Services	Booker	27. 6.05T
G-BWTJ	Cameron V-77 HAB	3917		7. 6.96	A.J.Montgomery	Yeovil	9. 5.03A
G-BWTK	Rotary Air Force RAF 2000 GTX-SE	PFA G/13-1264		7. 6.96	Terrafirma Services Ltd Lamberhurst Farm, Faversham		24. 6.03P
G-BWTN	Lindstrand LBL-90A HAB	357		12. 6.96	Clarks Drainage Ltd	Oakham	19. 8.03A
G-BWTO	de Havilland DHC-1 Chipmunk 22	C1/0852	WP984	5. 6.96	A.C.Eltis & P.L.Reilly (As "WP984/H")	(Fen Drayton)	21. 6.04
G-BWTR	Slingsby T.61F Venture T.2	1881	XZ561	12. 6.96	P.R.Williams	(Brackley)	
G-BWTU*	Lindstrand LBL-77A HAB	376		17. 6.96	Virgin Airship & Balloon Co Ltd	Telford	14. 1.02A
					(Land Rover titles) (Cancelled 3.1.03 as wfu)		
G-BWTW	Mooney M.20C	20-1188	EI-CHI N6955V	5. 6.96	R.C.Volkers	Henstridge	23.12.05
G-BWUA	Campbell Cricket	PFA G/03-1248		17. 6.96	R.T.Lancaster	Ash, Hants	
G-BWUB	Piper PA-18S-135 Super Cub	18-3986	N786CS	13. 6.96	Caledonian Seaplanes Ltd	Dunkeswell	2. 4.05T
	(L-21C) (Regd with c/n 18-3786)		G-BWUB/SX-AHB/EI-263/I-EIUO/MM54-2586/54-2586				
G-BWUE	Hispano HA-1112-M1L	223	N9938	14. 6.96	R.A.Fleming	Breighton	
	(Reported as c/n 172: C4K-155 was c/n 223)		G-AWHK/C4K-102		(On rebuild 12.02)		
G-BWUH	Piper PA-28-181 Archer III	2843048	N9272E (G-BWUH)	30. 8.96	B.K.Ambrose tr G-BWUH Flying Group	Fowlmere	7.10.05
G-BWUJ	Rotorway Executive 162F	6153		2. 7.96	Southern Helicopters Ltd	Street Farm, Takeley	3.12.03P
	(Rotorway RW.162F)						
G-BWUK	Sky 160-24 HAB	043		2. 7.96	Spotlight Group Ltd	Axbridge	7. 8.03T
G-BWUL	Noorduyn AT-16 Harvard IIB	14A-1415	N16NA	4. 7.96	Aereo Servizi Bresciana SRL	(Montichiari, Italy)	13.10.97
			G-BWUL/FT375/43-13116				
G-BWUM	Sky 105-24 HAB	038		5. 7.96	P.Stern & F.Kirchberger	Regen/Lam, Germany	30. 7.03
					"Wanninger"		
G-BWUN	de Havilland DHC-1 Chipmunk 22	C1/0253	WD310	5. 7.96	T.Henderson	Upper Broyle Farm, Ringmer	10. 1.03
					(As "WD310")		
G-BWUP	Europa Aviation Europa 104 & PFA 247-12703			3. 7.96	G.A.Haines	(Buckie)	6. 3.03P
	(Subaru EA81/100) (Conventional u/c)				(F/f 19.10.98)		
G-BWUR	Thunder Ax10-210 Srs.2 HAB	3910		11. 7.96	T.J.Bucknall "Kinetic"	Malpas	7. 4.01T
					(Op Balloon Preservation Group)		
G-BWUS	Sky 65-24 HAB	040		16. 7.96	N.A.P.Bates	Tunbridge Wells	25. 5.02A
G-BWUT	de Havilland DHC-1 Chipmunk 22	C1/0918	WZ879	4. 6.96	Aero Vintage Ltd (As "WZ879/73")	(Rye)	22. 3.03
G-BWUU	Cameron N-90 HAB	3954		17. 7.96	South Western Electricity plc	Bristol	27. 6.01A
G-BWUV	de Havilland DHC-1 Chipmunk 22A	C1/0655	WK640	18. 7.96	P.Ray (As "WK640/C")	Wombleton	16. 8.03
G-BWUW	British Aircraft Corporation BAC.145 Jet Provost T.5A	XW423		18. 7.96	Tindon Ltd	(Little Snoring)	14. 2.02P
		EEP/JP/1045			(As "XW423/14")		
G-BWUZ*	Campbell Cricket	PFA G/03-1267		24. 6.96	M.A.Concannon	Henstridge	20. 3.02P
	(Rotax 582)				(Cancelled 8.7.02 by CAA)		
G-BWVB	Pietenpol Aircamper	PFA 47-11777		24. 7.96	M.J.Whatley	Cranfield	1.11.03P
	(Continental O-200-A)						
G-BWVC	Jodel D.18	PFA 169-11331		29. 7.96	R.W.J. Cripps	(Spondon, Derby)	
G-BWVH	Robinson R44 Astro	0072	SX-HDE (D-HBBT)	10. 9.96	AG Aviation Ltd	(Naas, Co.Kildare)	9.10.05T
G-BWVI	Stern ST.80 Balade	PFA 166-11190		7. 8.96	M.P.Wakem	Barton	6. 8.03P
	(Volkswagen 1834)						
G-BWVL	Cessna 150M	15077229	N50NA N63286	13. 8.96	A.H.Shaw	Gloucestershire	18. 1.03T
G-BWVM	Colt AA-1050 Gas FB	3806		14. 8.96	B.B.Baxter Ltd Statesville, North Carolina, USA		4.10.02A
					(Op S Parks) "Moonshine"		
G-BWVN	Whittaker MW7	PFA 171-11839		19. 8.96	R.K.Willcox	(Bristol)	
G-BWVP*	Sky 160-24 HAB	044		21. 8.96	Not known "Balloons over Siam"	NK	
					(No CofA issued & cancelled 26.11.99 by CAA) (Extant 8.02)		
G-BWVR	IAV-Bacau Yakovlev Yak-52	878202	LY-AKQ DOSAAF 134	27. 8.96	J.H.Askew "52"	Barton	24. 7.02P
G-BWVS	Europa Aviation Europa 085 & PFA 247-12686			28. 8.96	D.R.Bishop	Kemble	9. 4.03P
	(Rotax 912) (Monowheel u/c)				(F/f 11.3.99)		
G-BWVT	de Havilland DHA.82A Tiger Moth	1039	N1350	27. 8.96	R.Jewitt	(Tunbridge Wells)	20. 6.05
	(Built DH Australia)		VH-SNZ/A17-604/VH-AIN/A17-604				
G-BWVU	Cameron O-90 HAB	3204		28. 8.96	J.Atkinson	Dorchester	26. 1.99A
G-BWVV	Jodel D.18	PFA 169-12699		29. 8.96	P.Cooper	Sherburn-in-Elmet	22.11.02P
	(Volkswagen 1834)						
G-BWVY	de Havilland DHC-1 Chipmunk 22	C1/0766	WP896	3. 9.96	P.W.Portelli (As "WP896/M")	White Waltham	17. 6.04
G-BWVZ	de Havilland DHC-1 Chipmunk 22	C1/0614	WK590	16. 7.96	D.Campion (As "WK590/69")	Grimbergen, Belgium	18.10.05
G-BWWA	Ultravia Pelican Club GS	PFA 165-12242		6. 9.96	T.J.Franklin & D.S.Simpson	(Hitchin)	17. 6.05P
	(Rotax 912-UL)						
G-BWWB	Europa Aviation Europa 080 & PFA 247-12670			9. 9.96	M.G.Dolphin "The Wheelbarrow"	RAF Syerston	21. 2.03P
	(Rotax 912) (Monowheel u/c)				(F/f 25.1.97)		
G-BWWC	de Havilland DH.104 Dove 7	04498	XM223	14. 6.96	Air Atlantique Ltd	(Coventry)	
	(Wings from G-APSO fitted early 2000)				(As "XM223") (Stored 6.02)		
G-BWWE	Lindstrand LBL-90A HAB	410		11. 9.96	B.J.Newman	Rushden, Northants	30.12.02T
G-BWWF	Cessna 185A Skywagon	185-0240	N4893K	13. 9.96	S M Craig Harvey	Hinton in the Hedges	15.10.03
			G-BWWF/9J-MCK/5Y-BBG/ET-ACI/N4040Y				
G-BWWG	SOCATA Rallye 235E Gabier	13121	EI-BIF HB-EYT/N344RA	23.10.96	J.J.Frew	(Ballymena, Co.Antrim)	18. 5.03
G-BWWH	Yakovlev Yak-50	853010	LY-ABL LY-XNI/DOSAAF	16. 9.96	De Cadenet Motor Racing Ltd	Little Gransden	7. 7.03P
					"853010"		
G-BWWI	Aérospatiale AS332L Super Puma	2040	OY-HMF (G-TIGT)	11. 9.96	Bristow Helicopters Ltd "Johnshaven"	Aberdeen	8.11.05T
G-BWWK	Hawker Nimrod I41	H-43617	S1581	13. 9.96	Patina Ltd	Duxford	16. 5.02P
	(RR Kestrel)				(As "S1581/573" in 802 Sqdn c/s)		
G-BWWL	Colt Flying Egg SS HAB	1813	JA-A0513	19. 9.96	Magical Adventures Ltd West Bloomfield, Mi., USA		2. 8.01A

Reg	Type	C/n	Prev id	Date	Owner/Operator	Location	Status
G-BWWN	Isaacs Fury II (Lycoming O-235-H2C)	PFA 11-10957		23. 9.96	F.J.Ball *(As "K8303/D")*	Priory Farm, Tibenham	13 .6.03P
G-BWWP	Rans S-6-116 Coyote II (Rotax 582) *(Tailwheel u/c)*	PFA 204A-12648		2.10.96	P.Lewis	(Leighton Buzzard)	20. 8.99P
G-BWWS	Rotary Air Force RAF 2000 GTX-SE	PFA G/13-1277		7.10.96	R.I.Grant	(Bristol)	3. 11.03P
G-BWWT	Dornier 328-110	3022	D-CDXO VT-VIG/D-CDHG	12.11.96	Suckling Airways (Luton) Ltd t/a Scot Airways	Cambridge	12.11.03T
G-BWWU	Piper PA-22-150 Tri-Pacer *(Hoerner wing-tips: tail-wheel conversion)*	22-5002	N7139D	9.10.96	J.D.Bally	(Builth Wells)	26. 5.02
G-BWWW	British Aerospace Jetstream Srs.3102	614	G-31-6141	8. 7.83	BAE Systems (Operations) Ltd	Warton	9. 2.01A
G-BWWX	Yakovlev Yak-50	853003	LY-AOI DOSAAF	11.10.96	J.L.Pfundt	Hilversum, The Netherlands	28. 3.03P
G-BWWY	Lindstrand LBL-105A HAB	411		14.10.96	M.J.Smith	Westow, York	28. 7.02T
G-BWWZ	Denney Kitfox Model 3 (Rotax 912)	PFA 172-13054		15.10.96	A.I.Eskander	Barton	20..6.03P
G-BWXA	Slingsby T.67M-260 Firefly	2236		19. 3.96	Babcock Support Services Ltd t/a Babcock HCS *(Op JEFTS)*	RAF Barkston Heath	27. 6.05T
G-BWXB	Slingsby T.67M-260 Firefly	2237		19. 3.96	Babcock Support Services Ltd t/a Babcock HCS *(Op JEFTS)*	RAF Barkston Heath	17. 7.05T
G-BWXC	Slingsby T.67M-260 Firefly	2238		19. 3.96	Babcock Support Services Ltd t/a Babcock HCS *(Op JEFTS)*	RAF Barkston Heath	18. 8.05T
G-BWXD	Slingsby T.67M-260 Firefly	2239		19. 3.96	Babcock Support Services Ltd t/a Babcock HCS *(Op JEFTS)*	RAF Barkston Heath	18. 8.05T
G-BWXE	Slingsby T.67M-260 Firefly	2240		19. 3.96	Babcock Support Services Ltd t/a Babcock HCS *(Op JEFTS)*	RAF Barkston Heath	28. 8.05T
G-BWXF	Slingsby T.67M-260 Firefly	2241		19. 3.96	Babcock Support Services Ltd t/a Babcock HCS *(Op JEFTS)*	RAF Barkston Heath	5. 9.05T
G-BWXG	Slingsby T.67M-260 Firefly	2242		19. 3.96	Babcock Support Services Ltd t/a Babcock HCS *(Op JEFTS)*	RAF Barkston Heath	23. 9.02T
G-BWXH	Slingsby T.67M-260 Firefly	2243		19. 3.96	Babcock Support Services Ltd t/a Babcock HCS *(Op JEFTS)*	RAF Barkston Heath	20.10.05T
G-BWXI	Slingsby T.67M-260 Firefly	2244		19. 3.96	Babcock Support Services Ltd t/a Babcock HCS *(Op JEFTS)*	RAF Barkston Heath	3.11.05T
G-BWXJ	Slingsby T.67M-260 Firefly	2245		19. 3.96	Babcock Support Services Ltd t/a Babcock HCS *(Op JEFTS)*	RAF Barkston Heath	1.12.05T
G-BWXK	Slingsby T.67M-260 Firefly	2246		19. 3.96	Babcock Support Services Ltd t/a Babcock HCS *(Op JEFTS)*	RAF Barkston Heath	13.11.05T
G-BWXL	Slingsby T.67M-260 Firefly	2247		19. 3.96	Babcock Support Services Ltd t/a Babcock HCS *(Op JEFTS)*	RAF Barkston Heath	12.12.05T
G-BWXM	Slingsby T.67M-260 Firefly	2248		19. 3.96	Babcock Support Services Ltd t/a Babcock HCS *(Op JEFTS)*	RAF Barkston Heath	26.11.02T
G-BWXN	Slingsby T.67M-260 Firefly	2249		19. 3.96	Babcock Support Services Ltd t/a Babcock HCS *(Op JEFTS)*	RAF Barkston Heath	4.12.02T
G-BWXO	Slingsby T.67M-260 Firefly	2250		19. 3.96	Babcock Support Services Ltd t/a Babcock HCS *(Op JEFTS)*	RAF Barkston Heath	21.12.02T
G-BWXP	Slingsby T.67M-260 Firefly	2251		19. 3.96	Babcock Support Services Ltd t/a Babcock HCS *(Op JEFTS)*	RAF Barkston Heath	8. 1.03T
G-BWXR	Slingsby T.67M-260 Firefly	2252		19. 3.96	Babcock Support Services Ltd t/a Babcock HCS *(Op JEFTS)*	RAF Barkston Heath	13. 1.03T
G-BWXS	Slingsby T.67M-260 Firefly	2253		19. 3.96	Babcock Support Services Ltd t/a Babcock HCS *(Op JEFTS)*	RAF Barkston Heath	29. 1.03T
G-BWXT	Slingsby T.67M-260 Firefly	2254		19. 3.96	Babcock Support Services Ltd t/a Babcock HCS *(Op JEFTS)* "6"	RAF Barkston Heath	5. 2.03T
G-BWXU	Slingsby T.67M-260 Firefly	2255		19. 3.96	Babcock Support Services Ltd t/a Babcock HCS *(Op JEFTS)*	RAF Barkston Heath	11. 2.03T
G-BWXV	Slingsby T.67M-260 Firefly	2256		19. 3.96	Babcock Support Services Ltd t/a Babcock HCS *(Op JEFTS)*	RAF Barkston Heath	21. 2.03T
G-BWXW	Slingsby T.67M-260 Firefly	2257		19. 3.96	Babcock Support Services Ltd t/a Babcock HCS *(Op JEFTS)*	RAF Barkston Heath	27. 2.03T
G-BWXX	Slingsby T.67M-260 Firefly	2258		19. 3.96	Babcock Support Services Ltd t/a Babcock HCS *(Op JEFTS)*	RAF Barkston Heath	12. 3.03T
G-BWXY	Slingsby T.67M-260 Firefly	2259		19. 3.96	Babcock Support Services Ltd t/a Babcock HCS *(Op JEFTS)*	RAF Barkston Heath	13. 3.03T
G-BWXZ	Slingsby T.67M-260 Firefly	2260		19. 3.96	Babcock Support Services Ltd t/a Babcock HCS *(Op JEFTS)*	RAF Barkston Heath	26. 3.03T
G-BWYB	Piper PA-28-160 Cherokee	28-263	N6374A G-BWYB/6Y-JLO/6Y-JCH/VP-JCH	16. 9.96	I.M.Latiff	Little Staughton	9. 8.03
G-BWYC	Cameron N-90 HAB	3994		17.10.96	Cameron Balloons Ltd *(Cameron Balloons titles)*	Bristol	14. 9.02A
G-BWYD	Europa Aviation Europa (Rotax 912) *(Monowheel u/c)*	072 & PFA 247-12621		28. 8.96	H.J.Bendiksen *(F/f 3.5.97)*	Biggin Hill	28. 8.03P
G-BWYE	Cessna 310R II	310R1654	F-GBPE (N26369)	6. 9.96	Air Charter Scotland Ltd	Edinburgh	8.12.02T
G-BWYG	Cessna 310R II	310R1580	F-GBMY (N1820E)	28.10.96	R.F.Jones t/a Kissair Aviation	Biggin Hill	20.11.03T
G-BWYH	Cessna 310R II	310R1640	F-GBPC N2634Y	28.10.96	Air Charter Scotland Ltd	Edinburgh	4. 6.03T
G-BWYI	Denney Kitfox Model 3 (Rotax 912)	PFA 172-12143		30.10.96	J.Adamson	Beeches Farm, South Scarle	1. 4.03P
G-BWYK	Yakovlev Yak-50	812004	RA01386 DOSAAF 51	9. 8.96	R.A.L.Hubbard tr Foley Farm Flying Group	Meon, Petersfield	14. 1.03P
G-BWYM	HOAC DV-20 Katana	20067	D-EWAU	27. 1.97	Plane Talking Ltd	Elstree	18. 6.03T
G-BWYN	Cameron O-77 HAB	1162	G-ODER	13.11.96	W.H.Morgan *"Hobo"*	Swansea	29. 4.01A

G-BWYO	Sequoia Falco F.8L (Lycoming O-320-E2A)	PFA 100-10920		7.11.96	N.G.Abbott & J.Copeland Flamstone Park, Bishopstone	17. 6.03P
G-BWYP	Sky 56-24 HAB	053		8.11.96	S.A.Townley t/a Sky High Leisure Wrexham	9.11.01A
G-BWYR	Rans S-6-116 Coyote II (Rotax 912-UL) (Tailwheel u/c)	PFA 204A-13058		8.11.96	R.C.Burden Bagby	26. 8.03P
G-BWYS	Cameron O-120 HAB	3997		30. 9.96	J.M.Stables t/a Aire Valley Balloons Knaresborough	1. 6.03T
G-BWYU	Sky 120-24 HAB	052		13.11.96	D.J.Tofton (Driving Prices Down titles) Warboys	16. 7.03A
G-BWYZ	Pilatus Britten-Norman BN-2B-20 Islander	2300		2.12.96	B-N Group Ltd (New owner 7.02) Bembridge	AC
G-BWZA	Europa Aviation Europa (Rotax 912S) (Monowheel u/c)	063 & PFA 247-12626		1.11.96	M.C.Costin Bidford (F/f 7.7.97)	13. 7.03P
G-BWZD	Avid Flyer Mk.4	PFA 189-12453		29.11.96	B.Moore (Keady, Co.Armagh)	
G-BWZE*	Hunting Percival P.84 Jet Provost T.3A	PAC/W/6605	XM378	29.11.96	Not known Weert, The Netherlands	
	(Damaged Lelystad, Netherlands 14.10.00: cancelled by CAA 17.5.01) (Dismantled & stored 12.01)					
G-BWZF	Pilatus Britten-Norman BN-2B-20 Islander	2301		12.12.96	B-N Group Ltd (New owner 7.02) Bembridge	AC
G-BWZG	Robin R2160	311	F-WZZZ	6.11.96	Sherburn Aero Club Ltd Sherburn-in-Elmet	17. 5.03T
G-BWZI	Agusta A109A II	7269	OH-HAD N109AK	29.11.96	P.W.Harris Pendley Farm, Aldbury, Tring t/a Pendley Farm	5. 3.03T
G-BWZJ	Cameron A-250 HAB	4021		2.12.96	Balloon School (International) Ltd Petworth t/a Balloon Club of Great Britain	17 7.03T
G-BWZK	Cameron A-210 HAB	4020		2.12.96	Balloon School (International) Ltd Petworth t/a Balloon Club of Great Britain	14. 7.03T
G-BWZP	Cameron Home Special 105SS HAB	4051		6.12.96	Flying Pictures Ltd (Barclays Mortgages titles) Chilbolton	10. 4.02A
G-BWZT	Europa Aviation Europa (Rotax 912) (Monowheel u/c)	115 & PFA 247-12727		9.12.96	A.M.Smyth tr G-BWZT Group Crowfield (F/f 10.8.97)	16. 9.03P
G-BWZU	Lindstrand LBL-90B HAB	418		12.12.96	K.D.Pierce Cranbrook, Kent	7. 9.03
G-BWZW	Bell 206B-3 JetRanger III	12	G-CTEK N7812S	26.11.96	R & M International Engineering Ltd Dereham	15. 6.98T
G-BWZX	Aérospatiale AS332L Super Puma	2120	F-WQDX	12.12.96	Bristow Helicopters Ltd "Muchalls" Aberdeen	5. 5.04T
			G-BWZX/F-WQDX/5V-MCD/5V-TAH/LN-OLE			
G-BWZY	Hughes 269A	95-0378	G-FSDT N269CH/N1336D/64-18066	4.12.96	Katharine B.Elliott Redhill	19. 6.04
G-BWZZ	Hunting Percival P.84 Jet Provost T.3A	PAC/W/9278	XM470	5. 9.96	Hunter Enterprises Ltd (Leuven, Belgium) (As "XM470/12" in 1 FTS c/s)	15. 5.03P

G-BXAA - G-BXZZ

G-BXAB	Piper PA-28-161 Warrior II	28-8416054	G-BTGK N4344C	7.10.96	TG Aviation Ltd Manston	25. 4.03T
G-BXAC	Rotary Air Force RAF 2000 GTX-SE	PFA G/13-1279		21.11.96	D.C.Fairbrass Fyfield	13. 6.03P
G-BXAD	Cameron Thunder Ax11-225 Srs.2 HAB	4052		18.12.96	M E White Dublin	22. 6.03T
G-BXAF	Pitts S-1D Special (Lycoming O-360)	PFA 09-12258		6.12.96	N.J.Watson (Tattershall)	2. 5.03P
G-BXAH	Piel CP.301A Emeraude (Continental C90)	AB.422	D-EBAH	29.10.96	G.E.Valler (Stafford)	16. 7.03P
G-BXAI	Cameron Colt 120A HAB	4056		20.12.96	E.F. & R.F.Casswell Maidstone	9. 6.00T
G-BXAJ	Lindstrand LBL-14A HAB	425		23.12.96	Oscair Project AB Taby, Sweden	
G-BXAK	IAV-Bacau Yakovlev Yak-52	811508	LY-ASC DOSAAF	23.12.96	J.G.McTaggart Cumbernauld (New owner 4.01)	30. 6.03P
G-BXAL	Cameron Bertie Bassett 90SS HAB	4034		13. 1.97	Trebor Bassett Ltd "Bertie Bassett" Kirdford (Op Balloon Preservation Group)	27. 1.02A
G-BXAM	Cameron N-90 HAB	4035		13. 1.97	Trebor Bassett Ltd "Bertie Junior" Howden, Yorks	28. 4.03A
G-BXAN	Scheibe SF-25C Falke 1700	44299	D-KDGQ	13. 1.97	E.R.Boyle tr C Falke Syndicate Winthorpe	15.10.03
G-BXAO	Jabiru Jabiru SK (Jabiru 2200A)	PFA 274-13066		14. 1.97	P.J.Thompson (Gaerwen) (Damaged Ledicot near Shobdon 3.5.98: current status unknown)	23. 4.99P
G-BXAR	British Aerospace Avro 146-RJ100	E3298	G-6-298	27. 3.97	Cityflyer Express Ltd Manchester (Delftblue Daybreak t/s)	29. 3.03T
G-BXAS	British Aerospace Avro 146-RJ100	E3301	G-6-301	23. 4.97	Cityflyer Express Ltd Birmingham	29. 4.03T
G-BXAU	Pitts S-1 Special (Lycoming O-320)	GHG.9	N9GG	22. 1.97	P J Tomlinson Gloucestershire	6. 6.02P
G-BXAV	Aerostar Yakovlev Yak-52	9111608	RA013252 DOSAAF 73	4. 1.97	Skytrace (UK) Ltd Wolverhampton tr G-BXAV Group (As "DOSAAF 72")	25. 3.03P
G-BXAY	Bell 206B-3 JetRanger III	3946	N85EA N521RC/N3210D	24. 1.97	Viewdart Ltd Conington	30. 7.03T
G-BXBA	Cameron A-210 HAB	4072		10. 1.97	Reach For The Sky Ltd Guildford	25. 7.03T
G-BXBB	Piper PA-20-135 Pacer	20-959	EC-AOZ N1133C	24. 1.97	M.E.R.Coghlan Farley Farm, Romsey (Noted as "EC-AOZ 3.03)	
G-BXBC	Anderson EA-1 Kingfisher Amphibian	PFA 132-11302		28. 1.97	S.Bisham Swanbister Farm, Orphir, Kirkwall	
G-BXBD	CASA I-131 Jungmann	1052	E3B-317	28. 1.97	P.B.Childs & B.L.Robinson Kemble	2. 7.03P
	(P/i uncertain as Jungmann "E3B-317" @ Musee de Jean Tinguely, Basel, Switzerland) (As "CW+BG/50" in Luftwaffe c/s)					
G-BXBG	Cameron A-275 HAB	4023		28. 1.97	M.L.Gabb Alcester	18. 2.03T
G-BXBH*	Hunting Percival P.84 Jet Provost T.3A	PAC/W/9241	XM365	29. 1.97	G-BXBH Provost Ltd Little Snoring (As "XM365") (Cancelled 10.10.02 by CAA)	31. 8.01P
G-BXBI	Hunting Percival P.84 Jet Provost T.3A	PAC/W/11799	XN510	29. 1.97	Global Aviation Ltd (Binbrook)	
G-BXBK	Mudry/CAARP CAP.10B	17	N170RC French AF "307-SO"	30. 1.97	S.Skipworth White Waltham	31. 7.03
G-BXBL	Lindstrand LBL-240A HAB	317		31. 1.97	J.Fenton t/a Firefly Balloon Promotions Preston	16. 7.03T
G-BXBM	Cameron O-105 HAB	3990		31. 1.97	P.Spellward (Beneficial Bank titles) Bristol tr Bristol University Hot Air Ballooning Society	2. 3.03A
G-BXBN	Rans S-6-116 Coyote II (Rotax 582) (Tricycle u/c)	PFA 204A-13062		31. 1.97	A.G.Foster North Coates (Crashed on approach c.7.01: noted dismantled in hangar 7.01)	17. 5.01P

Reg	Type	C/n	Prev id	Date	Owner	Location	Date
G-BXBP	Denney Kitfox Model 2	PFA 172-12149		3. 2.97	G.S.Adams	Enniskillen, Co.Fermanagh	18.11.03P
G-BXBR	Cameron A-120 HAB	1983	SE-ZDY	4. 2.97	M.G.Barlow	Skipton	
G-BXBT	Aérospatiale AS355F1 Twin Squirrel	5262	G-TMMC G-JLCO	11. 2.97	McAlpine Helicopters Ltd	Oxford	28. 9.04T
G-BXBU	Mudry/CAARP CAP.10B	103	N173RC French AF	11. 2.97	J.F.Cosgrave & H.R.Pearson	Denham	24. 6.03
G-BXBY	Cameron A-105 HAB	4077		13. 2.97	S.P.Watkins *(Op D Littlewood) (Bath Stone titles)*	Bath	7. 4.03T
G-BXBZ	WSK PZL-104 Wilga 80 *(C/n quoted officially as CF21930941)*	CF21910941	EC-GDA ZK-PZQ	13. 2.97	P.G.Marks	Dunstable	25. 6.03
G-BXCA	Hapi Cygnet SF-2A *(Rotax 912-UL)*	PFA 182-12921		22. 1.97	J N Harley	Popham	5. 9.03P
G-BXCC	Piper PA-28-201T Turbo Dakota	28-7921068	D-EKBM N2855A	19. 2.97	Greer Aviation Ltd	Kirknewton	25. 7.03T
G-BXCD	TEAM mini-MAX 91A	PFA 186-12393		18. 2.97	R.Davies	Bicester	26.10.02P
G-BXCG	CEA Jodel DR.250/160 Capitaine	60 & PFA 299-13146	D-EHGG	22. 5.97	A.B.Clarke tr CG Group	Cambridge	27. 8.03P
G-BXCH	Europa Aviation Europa *(Rotax 912) (Monowheel u/c)*	186 & PFA 247-12980		19. 2.97	D.M.Stevens *(F/f 19.9.97)*	Haverfordwest	26. 5.02P
G-BXCJ	Campbell Cricket (Rotax 532)	PFA G/03-1177		24. 2.97	F.Knowles	Henstridge	11. 7.03P
G-BXCK	Cameron Douglas-Lurpak Butterman 110SS HAB	4076		25. 2.97	Flying Pictures Ltd *(Lurpak Douglas titles)*	Chilbolton	8.10.02A
G-BXCL	Montgomerie Bensen B.8MR *(Rotax 582)*	PFA G/01-1287		26. 2.97	A.D.Gordon	Blair Atholl	21.10.03P
G-BXCM	Lindstrand LBL-150A HAB	443		26. 2.97	A M Holly t/a Exclusive Ballooning	Berkeley	10. 8.03T
G-BXCN	Sky 105-24 HAB	047		27. 2.97	Capricorn Balloons Ltd	Loughborough	16. 3.98T
G-BXCO	Colt 120A HAB	4086		3. 3.97	T.G.Church	Blackburn	17. 4.03T
G-BXCP	de Havilland DHC-1 Chipmunk 22	C1/0744	WP859	27. 2.97	S.Conlan *(As "WP859")*	Kildare	13. 5.03
G-BXCS	Cameron N-90 HAB	4122		4. 3.97	Flying Pictures Ltd *(Lurpak titles)*	Chilbolton	26. 3.03A
G-BXCT	de Havilland DHC-1 Chipmunk 22	C1/0145	WB697	3. 3.97	Wickenby Aviation Ltd *(As "WB697/95")*	Wickenby	2. 5.03T
G-BXCU	Rans S-6-116 Coyote II *(Rotax 912UL) (Tricycle u/c)*	PFA 204A-13105		6. 3.97	R.S.Gent	Redmoor Farm, North Duffield	15. 7.03P
G-BXCV	de Havilland DHC-1 Chipmunk 22	C1/0807	WP929	3. 3.97	Ocean Flight Holdings Ltd *(As "WP929/F")*	Duxford	22.10.03T
G-BXCW	Denney Kitfox Model 3	PFA 172-12619		6. 3.97	M.J.Blanchard	(Swanage)	
G-BXDA	de Havilland DHC-1 Chipmunk 22	C1/0747	WP860	7. 3.97	S.R.Cleary *(As "WP860/6")*	Cumbernauld	17. 6.03
G-BXDB	Cessna U206F Stationair	U20602233	G-BMNZ F-BVJT/N1519U	18.12.96	D.A.Howard	(Isle of Colonsay)	6. 8.04T
G-BXDD*	Rotary Air Force RAF 2000 GTX-SE	PFA G/13-1284		9. 1.97	R.M.Savage t/a Roger Savage (Photography) *(Cancelled 9.4.02 by CAA)*	Carlisle	4. 7.00P
G-BXDE	Rotary Air Force RAF 2000 GTX-SE	PFA G/13-1280		14. 1.97	A.McRedie	Carlisle	23. 1.02P
G-BXDF	Beech 95-B55 Baron	TC-2011	SE-IXG OY-ASB	7. 3.97	Chesh-Air Ltd	Liverpool	17. 1.03T
G-BXDG	de Havilland DHC-1 Chipmunk 22	C1/0644	WK630	7. 3.97	R.I.Warman	Holly Hill Farm, Guist	16. 8.04
G-BXDH	de Havilland DHC-1 Chipmunk 22	C1/0270	WD331	10. 3.97	Victory Workwear Ltd *(As "WD331")*	Kemble	17. 1.05
G-BXDI	de Havilland DHC-1 Chipmunk 22	C1/0312	WD373	10. 3.97	J.R.Gore *(As "WD373/12" in RAF c/s)*	Gloucestershire	31.10.03
G-BXDL	Hunting Percival P.84 Jet Provost T.3	PAC/W/9286	A8983M XM478	18. 3.97	G.P.Williams *(As "XM478")*	(Swansea)	25. 3.03P
G-BXDM	de Havilland DHC-1 Chipmunk 22	C1/0723	WP840	28. 2.97	The RAF Halton Aeroplane Club Ltd *(As "WP840/9")*	RAF Halton	25. 6.03T
G-BXDN	de Havilland DHC-1 Chipmunk 22	C1/0618	WK609	18. 3.97	W.D.Lowe & L.A.Edwards *(As "WK609/93")*	Booker	1.11.03
G-BXDO	Rutan Cozy *(Lycoming O-235-C2C)*	PFA 159-12032		21. 3.97	C.R.Blackburn	(Kirk Michael, Isle of Man)	18. 12.02P
G-BXDP	de Havilland DHC-1 Chipmunk 22	C1/0659	WK642	27. 2.97	T.A.McBennet & J.Kelly *(As "WK642")*	(Woodenbridge, Co.Wicklow)	11. 9.03
G-BXDR	Lindstrand LBL-77A HAB	441		25. 3.97	British Telecommunications plc *"Bright Future"*	(Thatcham, Berks)	10. 4.03A
G-BXDS	Bell 206B-3 JetRanger III	2734	G-OVBJ G-BXDS/OY-HDK/N661PS	19. 2.98	Sterling Helicopters Ltd	Norwich	24. 7.03T
G-BXDT	Robin HR200/120	B315		25. 3.97	Multiflight Ltd	Leeds-Bradford	3. 6.03T
G-BXDU	Aero Designs Pulsar	PFA 202-11991		25. 3.97	M.P.Beaton	(London E4)	
G-BXDV	Sky 105-24 HAB	049		26. 3.97	A.Parsons tr Loughborough Students Union Hot Air Balloon Club	Loughborough	6. 5.03
G-BXDY	Europa Aviation Europa *(Rotax 912) (Monowheel u/c)*	229 & PFA 247-12914		27. 3.97	D.G. & S.Watts *"The Rocketeer" (F/f 31.10.97)*	Laddingford	1. 2.03P
G-BXDZ*	Lindstrand LBL-105A HAB	437		4. 4.97	M.A.Webb *(Cancelled 2.3.00 by CAA)*	Yarcombe	14. 4.99A
G-BXEA	Rotary Air Force RAF 2000 GTX-SE	PFA G/13-1270		2. 4.97	R.Firth	Netherthorpe	11. 1.03P
G-BXEB	Rotary Air Force RAF 2000 GTX-SE	PFA G/13-1285		2. 4.97	Penny Hydraulics Ltd	Netherthorpe	11. 3.03P
G-BXEC	de Havilland DHC-1 Chipmunk 22	C1/0647	WK633	3. 4.97	K.P. & D.S.Hunt *(As "WK633/B")*	Redhill	27. 4.03
G-BXEE	Enstrom 280C Shark	1117	OH-HAN N336AT	9. 4.97	S.T.Raby	Grange Farm, Woodwalton	28. 6.04
G-BXEF	Europa Aviation Europa *(Jabiru 3300) (Monowheel u/c)*	159 & PFA 247-12790		7. 4.97	C.& W.P.Busuttil-Reynaud	(Emsworth, Hants)	
G-BXEJ	VPM M16 Tandem Trainer *(Arrow GT 1000)*	D-9302	D-MIFF	8. 4.97	N.H.Collins t/a AES Radionic Surveillance Systems	Cork Farm, Streethay	9. 5.03P
G-BXEN	Cameron N-105 HAB	4090		11. 4.97	G.Aimo	Mondovi, Italy	14. 6.02A
G-BXEP	Lindstrand LBL-14M HAB	460		14. 4.97	Lindstrand Balloons Ltd	Oswestry	19. 5.00A
G-BXER	Piper PA-46-350P Malibu Mirage	4636110		21. 7.97	Glasdon Group Ltd	Blackpool	3. 9.03
G-BXES	Hunting Percival P.66 Pembroke C.1 *(Regd with c/n PAC/W/3032)*	P66/101	N4234C 9042M/XL954	14. 4.97	Atlantic Air Transport Ltd *(As "XL954")*	Coventry	16. 4.03P
G-BXET	Piper PA-38-112 Tomahawk	38-80A0028	N25089	14. 4.97	APB Leasing Ltd	Welshpool	10. 8.03T
G-BXEX	Piper PA-28-181 Cherokee Archer II	28-7790463	N3562Q	16. 4.97	R.Mayle	Biggin Hill	12. 5.03T
G-BXEY	Colt AS-105GD Hot-Air Airship	3936		15. 4.97	D.Mayer	Felsberg, Germany	12. 9.03A

Reg	Type	C/n	Prev id	Date	Owner/Operator	Location	Exp
G-BXEZ	Cessna 182P Skylane II *(Reims assembled c/n F18200054)*	18264344	OH-CHJ N1479M	16. 4.97	Forhawk Ltd	Bodmin	6. 1.03T
G-BXFB	Pitts S-1 Special *(Lycoming O-360-A4A)*	9543	N77ZZ	16. 4.97	D.Dobson	Little Staughton	11. 2.03P
G-BXFC	Jodel D.18	PFA 169-11322		17. 4.97	B.S.Godbold	Little Gransden	24. 7.02P
G-BXFD	Enstrom 280C Shark	1084	N88MD N632H	18. 4.97	Buckland Newton Hire Ltd	Bournemouth	25. 7.03T
G-BXFE	Mudry/CAARP CAP.10B	135	N175RC French AF	18. 4.97	Avion Aerobatic Ltd	(London N1)	26. 3.04T
G-BXFG	Europa Aviation Europa *(Rotax 912) (Monowheel u/c)*	018 & PFA 247-12500		21. 4.97	A.Rawicz-Szczerbo *(F/f 10.11.99)*	Eaglescott	13. 5.03P
G-BXFI	Hawker Hunter T.7	41H-670815	WV372	24. 4.97	Fox-One Ltd *(As "WV372/R" in 2 Sqdn c/s)*	Kemble	16.10.03P
G-BXFK	CFM Streak Shadow *(Rotax 582)*	K.206 & PFA 206-12329		24. 4.97	S.J.M.French & T.I.Gorell	(Miltonn Keynes)	18.11.03P
G-BXFN	Cameron Colt 77A HAB	4145		25. 4.97	Cameron Balloons Ltd	Bristol	21. 7.03A
G-BXFP	British Aircraft Corporation BAC.167 Strikemaster Mk.87 EEP/JP/2873 & PS.165 or 171?		Botswana DF OJ5/Kenyan AF 602/G-27-192 *(As "NZ6361" in RNZAF c/s)*	29. 4.97	Strikemaster Films Ltd	(London NW4)	4. 8.03P
G-BXFU	British Aircraft Corporation BAC.167 Strikemaster Mk.83 EEP/JP/???? & PS.158		Botswana DF OJ1/ZG805/Kuwait AF 110/G-27-151 *(As "OJ-1")*	29. 4.97	Global Aviation Ltd	Humberside	6. 8.02P
G-BXFV	British Aircraft Corporation BAC.167 Strikemaster Mk.83 EEP/JP/???? & PS.173		Botswana DFOJ8/ZG811/Kuwait AF 119/G-27-188 *(As "OJ-8")*	29. 4.97	Global Aviation Ltd	Humberside	23. 6.03P
G-BXFY	Cameron Bierkrug-90 SS HAB	4133	D-OIBP G-BXFY	29. 4.97	Ballooning Bavaria	Ruhstorf, Germany	12. 9.03A
G-BXFZ*	Sky 65-24 HAB	065		22. 4.97	Aerial Promotions Ltd	Cannock	14. 5.99A
			(Stolen and recovered in damaged state 4.99: cancelled 2.11.01) (Current status unknown)				
G-BXGA	Eurocopter AS350B2 Ecureuil	2493	OO-RCH OO-XCH/F-WZFX	30. 4.97	PLM Dollar Group Ltd	Inverness	27. 8.03T
G-BXGC	Cameron N-105 HAB	4137		6. 5.97	Cliveden Ltd *(Op Ascent Balloons) (Royal Crescent Hotel titles)*	Bath	25.10.03T
G-BXGD	Sky 90-24 HAB	067		6. 5.97	Servo & Electronic Sales Ltd *(Ocean FM titles)*	Lydd	9. 6.03T
G-BXGE*	Cessna 152 II	15282700	N89283	8. 5.97	APB Leasing Ltd *(Noted 9.01 less wings: cancelled 22.3.02 as WFU)*	Tatenhill	16. 7.00T
G-BXGG	Europa Aviation Europa *(Rotax 912) (Monowheel u/c)*	178 & PFA 247-12803		29. 4.97	C.J.H & P.A.J.Richardson Bremridge Farm, Shillingford *(F/f 30.9.98)*		23. 9.02P
G-BXGH	Diamond DA-20-A1 Katana	10151		20. 5.97	Cumbernauld Flying School Ltd	Cumbernauld	21. 6.04T
G-BXGK	Lindstrand LBL-203M HAB	468		12. 5.97	Lindstrand Balloons Ltd	Oswestry	
G-BXGL	de Havilland DHC-1 Chipmunk 22	C1/0924	WZ884	12. 5.97	Airways Aero Associations Ltd *(Op British Airways Flying Club) (BOAC titles)*	Booker	26.10.03T
G-BXGM	de Havilland DHC-1 Chipmunk 22	C1/0806	WP928	9. 5.97	A.T.Stolton tr Chipmunk Golf Mike Group *(As "WP928/D" ARMY)*	Shoreham	28.10.03
G-BXGO	de Havilland DHC-1 Chipmunk 22	C1/0097	WB654	13. 5.97	A.Judd tr Trees Group *(As "WB654/U")*	Booker	26.10.03
G-BXGP	de Havilland DHC-1 Chipmunk 22	C1/0927	WZ882	12. 5.97	J.Pote tr Eaglescott Chipmunk Group *(As "WZ882/K" in "ARMY" c/s)*	Eaglescott	20. 8.04T
G-BXGS	Rotary Air Force RAF 2000 GTX-SE PFA G/13-1290			14. 5.97	C.R.Gordon	(Cupar)	21.12.01P
G-BXGT	III Sky Arrow 650T *(Rotax 912-UL)*	PFA 298-13085		7. 5.97	Sky Arrow (Kits) UK Ltd	Old Sarum	29. 6.02P
G-BXGV	Cessna 172R Skyhawk II	17280240	N9300F	7. 1.98	D.Varns tr Skyhawk Group	White Waltham	8. 2.04T
G-BXGW	Robin HR200/120	B317		16. 5.97	Multiflight Ltd *(Op Multiflight Flying Club)*	Leeds-Bradford	3.10.03T
G-BXGX	de Havilland DHC-1 Chipmunk 22	C1/0609	WK586	19. 5.97	Interflight (Air Charter) Ltd *(As "WK586")*	Blackbushe	24.10.03
G-BXGY	Cameron V-65 HAB	4125		18. 4.97	Gone With The Wind Ltd	Hungerford	1. 3.03A
G-BXGZ	Stemme S-10V	14-023	D-KSTE EC-GGD/D-KGDF	18. 8.97	D.Tucker & K.Lloyd "S10" *(Noted 5.01)*	Aston Down	10. 1.04
G-BXHA	de Havilland DHC-1 Chipmunk 22	C1/0801	WP925	20. 5.97	F.A.de Munck & C.S.Huijers (Seppe, The Netherlands) *(As "WP925/C" ARMY)*		28. 8.03
G-BXHD	Beech 76 Duchess	ME-284	OY-ARM N223JC	22. 5.97	S.J.Skilton *t/a Aviation Rentals (Op Professional Air Training)*	Bournemouth	7. 8.03T
G-BXHE	Lindstrand LBL-105A HAB	459		23. 5.97	L.H.Ellis	Princes Risborough	6. 8.03T
G-BXHF	de Havilland DHC-1 Chipmunk 22	C1/0808	WP930	28. 5.97	R.A.Wallis tr Hotel Fox Sydicate *(As "WP930/J")*	Redhill	23. 5.04
G-BXHH	Grumman-American AA-5A Cheetah	AA5A-0105	N9705U	3. 6.97	M.G.Greenslade t/a Oaklands Flying	Biggin Hill	6. 6.03T
G-BXHJ	Hapi Cygnet SF-2A *(Volkswagen 1835)*	PFA 182-12159		29. 5.97	I.J.Smith Brook Farm, Boylestone, Derby *(Current status unknown)*		
G-BXHL	Sky 77-24 HAB	055		29. 5.97	R.K.Gyselynck "Harlequin"	Port Erin, Isle of Man	30. 5.03
G-BXHO	Lindstrand Telewest Sphere SS HAB	474		30. 5.97	Magical Adventures Ltd	Oswestry	25. 2.03A
G-BXHP	Lindstrand LBL-105A HAB	458		30. 5.97	Flying Pictures Ltd "Britannia"	Chilbolton	10. 5.03A
G-BXHR	Stemme S-10V	14-030		23. 7.97	J.H.Rutherford	Rufforth	11. 9.03
G-BXHU	Campbell Cricket Mk.6 *(Rotax 503)*	PFA G/16-1293		3. 6.97	P.J.Began	Henstridge	28. 7.03P
G-BXHY	Europa Aviation Europa *(Rotax 912S) (Monowheel u/c)*	022 & PFA 247-12514		6. 6.97	A.L.Thorne & B.Lewis tr Jupiter Flying Group *(F/f 9.3.98)*	White Waltham	25. 2.03P
G-BXIA	de Havilland DHC-1 Chipmunk 22	C1/0056	WB615	9. 6.97	W.Askew, G.Bullock & C.Duckett t/a Dales Aviation *(As "WB615/E")*	Blackpool	18. 8.05T
G-BXIC	Cameron A-275 HAB	4162		9. 6.97	Aerosaurus Balloons LLP	Exeter	2.10.03T
G-BXID	IAV-Bacau Yakovlev Yak-52	888802	LY-ALG DOSAAF 74	10. 6.97	E.S.Ewen	Kemble	25. 2.02P
G-BXIE	Cameron Colt 77B HAB	4181		11. 6.97	The Aerial Display Co Ltd *(Michelin titles)*	Looe	19. 7.01A
G-BXIF	Piper PA-28-181 Cherokee Archer II	28-7690404	PH-SWM OO-HAY/N6827J	12. 6.97	Piper Flight Ltd	RAF Brize Norton	9. 7.03T
G-BXIG	Zenair CH-701 STOL *(Rotax 912-UL)*	PFA 187-12065		16. 6.97	A.J.Perry	Marsh Farm, Bracklesham	13. 6.03P
G-BXIH	Sky 200-24 HAB	076		16. 6.97	G.C.Ludlow	Hythe	13. 8.02P

Reg	Type	C/n	Prev id	Date	Owner/Operator	Location	Date
G-BXII	Europa Aviation Europa 175 & PFA 247-12812 (Rotax 912S) *(Conventional u/c)*			30. 4.97	D.A.McFadyean *(F/f 5.8.01)*	Long Marston	11. 6.03P
G-BXIJ	Europa Aviation Europa 076 & PFA 247-12698 (Rotax 912) *(Monowheel u/c)*			16. 6.97	D.G. & E.A.Bligh *"Bligh's Ballistic"* *(F/f 21.12.97)*	Inverness	17. 4.03P
G-BXIM	de Havilland DHC-1 Chipmunk 22	C1/0548	WK512	13. 5.97	P.R.Joshua & A.B.Ascroft *(As "WK512/A/ARMY")*	RAF Brize Norton	2. 7.03
G-BXIO	SAN Jodel DR.1050M Excellance	493	F-BNIO	16. 5.97	D.N.K. & M.A.Symon	Perth	3. 7.04
G-BXIT	Zebedee V-31 HAB	Z1/3999		8. 5.97	P.J.Bish t/a Zebedee Balloon Service	Hungerford	
G-BXIV	Agusta A109A	7135	F-GERU HB-XOK/D-HFZF	13. 6.97	Heli-Tele Ltd	North Weald	22.10.04T
G-BXIW	Sky 105-24 HAB	073		24. 6.97	L.A.Watts	Pangbourne, Reading	24. 5.03
G-BXIX	VPM M-16 Tandem Trainer (Arrow GT1000R)	PFA G/12-1292		13. 6.97	D.Beevers	Pocklington	12. 7.00P
G-BXIY	Blake Bluetit (Gnat 32hp) *(Pre-war composite from Spartans G-AAGN/G-AAJB & Avro 504K)*	01	BAPC.37	26. 6.97	J.Bryant *(On rebuild 8.02)*	Audley End	
G-BXIZ*	Lindstrand LBL-31A HAB	476		3. 7.97	Hyundai Car (UK) Ltd *(Cancelled 7.1.00 as WFU)*	High Wycombe	24. 7.00A
G-BXJA	Cessna 402B	402B0356	N5753M XA-RFK/N5753M	17. 7.97	Air Charter Scotland Ltd	Edinburgh	23. 1.04T
G-BXJB	IAV-Bacau Yakovlev Yak-52	877403	LY-ABR DOSAAF 15 "15"	30. 6.97	A.M.Playford, D.J.Young & N. Willson	Poplar Hall Farm, Elmsett	16. 5.03P
G-BXJC	Cameron A-210 HAB	419		12. 7.97	Balloon School (International) Ltd t/a British School of Ballooning	Petworth	3. 7.03T
G-BXJD	Piper PA-28-180 Cherokee C	28-4215	OY-BBZ	27. 6.97	BCT Aircraft Leasing Ltd *(Op Bristol Flying Club)*	Filton	14.11.03T
G-BXJG	Lindstrand LBL-105B HAB	478		11. 7.97	C.E.Wood	Witham	5. 7.02T
G-BXJH	Cameron N-42 HAB	4194		15. 7.97	B.Conway	Wheatley, Oxon	22. 9.01A
G-BXJI*	Tri-R Kis	PFA 239-12573		2. 7.97	R.M.Wakeford *(F/f 21.10.00) (Cancelled 20.2.03 as temporarily wfu)*	Cumbernauld	20. 5.03p
G-BXJM	Cessna 152 II	15282380	OO-HOQ F-GHOQ/N68797	15. 7.97	I.R.Chaplin	Rayne Hall Farm, Rayne	20. 8.03T
G-BXJO	Cameron O-90 HAB	4190		16. 7.97	Dragon Balloon Company Ltd	(Hope Valley)	1. 8.03T
G-BXJP	Cameron C-80 HAB	4171		17. 7.97	AR Cobaleno Pasta Fresca SRL	Perugia, Italy	23. 7.03A
G-BXJS	Schempp-Hirth Janus	CM35/265	OH-819	7. 7.97	R.A.Hall tr Janus Syndicate	Enstone	17. 8.03
G-BXJT	Sky 90-24 HAB	072		18. 7.97	J.G. O'Connell	Braintree	25. 1.02A
G-BXJU*	Sky 90-24 HAB	077		18. 7.97	Sky Operations Ltd *(Castrol titles) (Cancelled 26.6.01 by CAA)*	Thailand	24. 7.98A
G-BXJV	Dimona DA-20-A1 Katana	10152		23. 7.97	Tayside Aviation Ltd	Dundee	30. 7.03T
G-BXJW	Dimona DA-20-A1 Katana	10211	(OE-) N811CH	23. 7.97	Tayside Aviation Ltd	Dundee	15. 8.03T
G-BXJY	Van's RV-6 (Lycoming O-320-D3G)	PFA 181-12447		23. 7.97	D.J.Sharland	Popham	6. 5.03P
G-BXJZ	Cameron C-60 HAB	4168		23. 7.97	R.S.Mohr	Chippenham	22.10.03A
G-BXKA	Airbus Industrie A320-214	714	N714AW G-BXKA/F-WWIX	24.11.97	JMC Airlines Ltd	Manchester	23. 4.05T
G-BXKB	Airbus Industrie A320-214	716	N716AW G-BXKB/F-WWIZ	10.12.97	JMC Airlines Ltd	Manchester	5. 5.05T
G-BXKC	Airbus Industrie A320-214	730	F-WWBQ	15.12.97	JMC Airlines Ltd	Manchester	14.12.03T
G-BXKD	Airbus Industrie A320-214	735	F-WWBV	17.12.97	JMC Airlines Ltd	Manchester	25.10.03T
G-BXKF	Hawker Hunter T.7 (Regd with c/n 41H-003315)	HABL-003314	8676M XL577	28. 7.97	R.F.Harvey	Kemble	AC
G-BXKH	Cameron Colt Sparkasse Box 90SS HAB	4161		4. 8.97	Westfalisch-Lippischer Sparkassen und Giroverband *"Spardueschen"*	Münster, Germany	13. 8.03A
G-BXKJ	Cameron A-275 HAB	4215		4. 8.97	Ballooning Network Ltd	Bristol	25. 6.03T
G-BXKL	Bell 206B-3 JetRanger III	3006	N5735Y	8.10.97	Swattons Aviation Ltd	Thruxton	18.11.03T
G-BXKM	Rotary Air Force RAF 2000 GTX-SE	PFA G/13-1291		5. 8.97	J.R.Huggins	Lamberhurst Farm, Faversham	14. 7.03P
G-BXKO	Sky 65-24 HAB	083		11. 8.97	J-M.Reck	Evette-Salbert, France	14. 3.03
G-BXKU	Cameron Colt AS-120 Mk.II HA Airship	4165		15. 8.97	D.C.Chipping	Grantham	19. 4.01A
G-BXKW	Slingsby T.67M-200 Firefly	2061	VR-HZS HKG-13/G-7-129	15. 8.97	N.A.Whatling *(As "HKG-13")*	Deenethorpe	1. 5.04T
G-BXKX	Taylorcraft J Auster 5	803	D-EMXA HB-EOK/MS938	19. 8.97	A.L.Jubb	Orchard Farm, Sittingbourne	21. 5.04
G-BXLA	Robinson R22 Beta	1368	SE-HVX N4014G	12. 8.97	Fast Helicopters Ltd	Thruxton	27. 9.03T
G-BXLC	Sky 120-24 HAB	085		20. 8.97	A.F.Selby	Loughborough	5.10.99A
G-BXLF	Lindstrand LBL-90A HAB	487		3. 9.97	R. & J.Moffatt t/a Variohm Components *(Variohm Components titles)*	Towcester	4. 7.03A
G-BXLG	Cameron C-80 HAB	4250		5. 3.98	D. & L.S.Litchfield *"Borne Again"*	Reading	12. 8.03A
G-BXLI	Bell 206B-3 JetRanger III	4041	N206JR G-JODY	8. 9.97	Williams Grand Prix Engineering Ltd	Wantage	19.11.03T
G-BXLK	Europa Aviation Europa 071 & PFA 247-12613 (Rotax 912) *(Monowheel u/c)*			11. 9.97	R.G.Fairall *(F/f 31.5.98)*	Redhill	23. 2.03P
G-BXLN	Sportavia Fournier RF4D	4022	F-BORK	15. 9.97	R.W.Hornsey, A.Wiseman & N.Thorne	Breighton	27. 2.03
G-BXLO	Hunting Percival P.84 Jet Provost T.4	AC/W/19986	9032M XR673	14. 8.97	HCR Aviation Ltd *(As "XR673" in silver RAF c/s with yellow trainer bands)*	North Weald	30.11.02P
G-BXLP	Sky 90-24 HAB	084		18. 9.97	G.B.Lescott	Oxford	9.11.03A
G-BXLR	PZL-110 Koliber 160A	04980077	SP-WGF(2)	10. 6.98	Oakmast Systems Ltd	Wolverhampton	31.10.04T
G-BXLS	PZL-110 Koliber 160A	04980078	SP-WGG	23. 6.98	P.A.Rickells	Gamston	23. 9.04
G-BXLT	SOCATA TB-200 Tobago XL	1457	F-GRBB EC-FNX/EC-234/F-GLFP	28. 4.97	R.M.Shears	Blackbushe	25. 5.03
G-BXLY	Piper PA-28-151 Cherokee Warrior	28-7715220	G-WATZ N7641F	19. 9.97	Auto Corporation Ltd	Hawarden	16. 7.04T
G-BXLZ	Europa Aviation Europa 123 & PFA 247-12815 (Subaru EA81/100) *(Monowheel u/c)*			24. 6.97	A.R.Round *(F/f 31.7.98)*	Breighton	25. 4.03P

G-BXMF	Cassutt Racer IIIM	PFA 34-13003		19. 9.97	J.F.Bakewell	Hucknall	24. 1.03P
G-BXMG	Rotary Air Force RAF 2000 GTX	H2-92-3-59	PH-TEN	18. 8.97	P.A.Howell	(Alcester)	17.12.03P
G-BXMH	Beech 76 Duchess	ME-168	F-GDMO N6021Y	19. 9.97	R.Clarke	Wolverhampton	25. 2.04T
G-BXML	Mooney M.20A	1594	OY-AIZ	26. 9.97	G.Kay	Crosland Moor	19. 3.05
G-BXMM	Cameron A-180 HAB	4252		28.10.97	B.Conway	Wheatley, Oxon	3.11.00A
G-BXMN*	de Havilland DH.82A Tiger Moth	86243	N82RD N8353/ZS-IGJ/CR-AGL/FAP/NL772	2.10.97	L V Handley *(As "NL772")*	Welshpool	27. 7.02
	(Damaged landing Springwood, Blackburn 25.5.99: cancelled 13.11.99 as destroyed: wreck noted 8.00)						
G-BXMU	WSK PZL-104 Wilga 80	CF20890880	EC-GMH ZK-PZP/SP-FWP	9.10.97	D.J.S.McClean tr G-BXMU Group	City of Derry	2. 9.05
G-BXMV	Scheibe SF-25C Falke 1700	44223	D-KDFV	7. 8.97	J.B.Marett Sandhill Farm, Shrivenham tr Falcon Flying Group		23. 5.04
G-BXMW	Cameron A-275 HAB	4247		19. 2.98	Ballooning Network Ltd *"BIBS III"* *(Bath Building Society titles)*	Bristol	25. 6.03T
G-BXMX	Phoenix Currie Wot	PFA 58-13055		23. 9.97	M.J.Hayman	(Totnes)	
G-BXMY	Hughes 269C	74-0328	N9599F	20.10.97	DS Air Ltd	(Horsham)	7.12.03T
G-BXMZ	Diamond DA-20-A1 Katana	10236		4.12.97	Tayside Aviation Ltd	Dundee	12. 2.04T
G-BXNA*	Avid Flyer	118	N5531J	10.10.97	G Haynes	(Hemel Hempstead)	
	(Cancelled 25.5.01 by CAA - no PtoF issued) (Noted 11.01)						
G-BXNC	Europa Aviation Europa	122 & PFA 247-12970		13.10.97	J.K.Cantwell	(Ashton-under-Lyne)	
	"The Magic Leprechaun" (Current status unknown)						
G-BXND*	Cameron Thomas The Tank Engine 110SS HAB	4254	(JA-A0935)	2. 2.98	Virgin Airship & Balloon Co Ltd *(Cancelled 19.11.02)*	Telford	25. 6.02A
G-BXNG	Beech 58 Baron	TH-874	N18747	13.10.97	Bonanza Flying Club Ltd	Booker	4.11.03
G-BXNH	Piper PA-28-161 Cherokee Warrior II	28-7816314	N2828M	22.10.97	CC Management Associates Ltd	Redhill	7.12.03T
G-BXNM	Cameron A-210 HAB	4245		12.12.97	N.D.Hicks t/a Horizon Ballooning	Alton	19.11.03T
G-BXNN	de Havilland DHC-1 Chipmunk 22	C1/0849	WP983	4. 8.97	J.N.Robinson *(As "WP983/B" in RAF c/s)*	Old Sarum	27. 7.04
G-BXNS	Bell 206B-3 JetRanger III	2385	N16822	3.11.97	Sterling Helicopters Ltd	Norwich	19.12.03T
G-BXNT	Bell 206B-3 JetRanger III	2398	N94CA N123AL	11.11.97	Sterling Helicopters Ltd	Norwich	3.12.03T
G-BXNU*	Jabiru Jabiru SK *(Jabiru 2200A)*	PFA 274-13218		31.10.97	J.Smith	(Downham Market)	14. 7.01P
	(Crashed 7.00 & written off: fuselage converted into static exhibition: cancelled 23.1.03 as wfu).						
G-BXNV	Cameron Colt AS-105 GD Hot-Air Airship	4231		19. 2.98	The Sleeping Society	Edegem, Belgium	16. 7.03A
G-BXNX	Lindstrand LBL-210A HAB	318		3.11.97	Jane H.Cuthbert t/a Spirit of Adventure	Sevenoaks	19. 2.03T
G-BXOA	Robinson R22 Beta	1614	N41132 JA7832	10.11.97	MG Group Ltd	Sywell	25. 1.04
G-BXOB	Europa Aviation Europa *(Tri-gear u/c)*	209 & PFA 247-12892		6.11.97	S.J.Willett *(Current status unknown)*	(Maidstone)	
G-BXOC	Evans VP-2	PFA 63-10305		29. 9.97	H.J. & E.M.Cox *(Current status unknown)*	(Bideford)	
G-BXOF	Diamond DA-20-A1 Katana	10256		4.12.97	Cumbernauld Flying School Ltd	Cumbernauld	30. 1.04T
G-BXOI	Cessna 172R Skyhawk II	17280145	N9990F	17.11.97	J.S.& J.Q.Malcolm	Wolverhampton	2. 2.04T
G-BXOJ	Piper PA-28-161 Warrior III	2842010	N9265G	15.12.97	P.Foster	(Warwick)	15.12.00T
G-BXOM	Isaacs Spitfire	PFA 27-12768		25.11.97	J.H.Betton *(Current status unknown)*	(Ammanford)	
G-BXON	Auster AOP.9	AUS/10/60	WZ729	1.12.97	C.J.& D.J.Baker Carr Farm, Thorney, Newark *(As "WZ729") (On rebuild 1.03)*		
G-BXOO	Grumman-American AA-5A Cheetah	AA5A-0674	N26721	10.12.97	ENS-Entire Network Solutions Ltd	Blackbushe	15.12.03T
G-BXOR	Robin HR200/120	B321		1.12.97	L.Burrow	Leeds-Bradford	5. 3.04T
G-BXOS	Cameron A-200 HAB	4286		19. 2.98	Airborne Balloon Management Ltd	Beltring, Kent	19. 6.03T
G-BXOT	Cameron C-70 HAB	4200		21.10.97	Gone With The Wind Ltd *(Op Dante Balloon Group)*	Bristol	8. 2.03A
G-BXOU	CEA Jodel DR.360 Chevalier	312	F-BPOU	6.10.97	S.H. & J.A.Williams	Blackpool	11. 2.04
G-BXOV	Cameron Colt 105A HAB	4227		12.12.97	The Aerial Display Co Ltd *(Michelin titles)*	Looe	15.11.00A
G-BXOW	Cameron Colt 105A HAB	4228		9. 1.98	The Aerial Display Co Ltd *(Michelin titles)*	Looe	28. 9.03A
G-BXOX	Grumman American AA-5A Cheetah	AA5A-0694	F-GBDS	27. 2.98	R.L.Carter & P.J.Large	(Thame)	11. 4.04T
G-BXOY	QAC Quickie Q.235	PFA 94-12183		17.11.97	C.C.Clapham	Enstone	22. 8.03P
	(Originally regd as "Q.200")						
G-BXOZ	Piper PA-28-181 Cherokee Archer II	28-7790173	N6927F	14.10.97	Spritetone Ltd	White Waltham	15. 2.04T
G-BXPB	Diamond DA-20-A1 Katana	10257		4.12.97	C.R.Lear	RAF Keevil	21. 1.04T
G-BXPC	Diamond DA-20-A1 Katana	10258		4.12.97	Cubair Flight Training Ltd	Redhill	30. 1.04T
G-BXPD	Diamond DA-20-A1 Katana	10259		4.12.97	Cubair Flight Training Ltd	Redhill	5. 3.04T
G-BXPE	Diamond DA-20-A1 Katana	10263		4.12.97	Tayside Aviation Ltd	Dundee	5. 3.04T
G-BXPF	Venture Thorp T.211	105	N6524Y	8.12.97	AD Aviation Ltd	Carlisle	1. 4.04T
G-BXPH	Sky 220-24 HAB	096		4.12.97	J.Nolte	Aachen, Germany	1. 4.00
G-BXPI	Van's RV-4 *(Lycoming O-360-A1A)*	PFA 181-12426		2. 1.98	Cavendish Aviation Ltd	Gamston	31. 8.03P
G-BXPK	Cameron A-250 HAB	4226		2. 2.98	Richard Nash Cars Ltd *(Sign Express titles)*	Norwich	23. 3.03T
G-BXPL	Piper PA-28-140 Cherokee	28-24560	N7224J	10.12.97	C.R.Guggenheim	Bournemouth	21. 3.04T
G-BXPM	Beech 58 Baron	TH-1677	N207ZM	10.10.97	Foyle Flyers Ltd	City of Derry	21. 2.04
G-BXPO	Venture Thorp T.211	104	N6524Q	10.12.97	AD Aviation Ltd	Teesside	29. 3.04T
G-BXPP	Sky 90-24 HAB	092		17.12.97	Adam Associates Ltd *"Niceday"*	Thatcham, Berks	11. 6.01A
G-BXPR	Cameron Colt Can 110SS HAB	4218		2. 2.98	FRB Fleischwarenfabrik Rostock-Bramow Rostock, Germany		12. 2.03A
G-BXPS	Piper PA-23-250 Aztec C	27-3498	G-AYLY N6258Y	10.12.90	Wendy A.Moore	Redhill	11. 6.05T
G-BXPT	Ultramagic H-77 HADB	77-140		22.12.97	G.D.O.Bartram	Ordino, Andorra	11.10.03A
G-BXPV	Piper PA-34-220T Seneca III	3448035	A7-FCH N9198X	24.12.97	Oxford Aviation Services Ltd	Gloucestershire	7. 2.04T
G-BXPW	Piper PA-34-220T Seneca III	3448034	A7-FCG N9171R	9. 2.98	Oxford Aviation Services Ltd	Gloucestershire	3. 4.04T
G-BXPY	Robinson R44 Astro	0154	OY-HFV	22.12.97	O.Desmet & B.Mornie	Amougies, Belgium	25. 1.04

G-BXRA	Mudry/CAARP CAP.10B	3	FrAF 03	12.12.97	P.A.Soper	Fenland	17. 8.04
			F-TFVR				
G-BXRB	Mudry/CAARP CAP.10B	100	FrAF 100	12.12.97	T.T.Duhig Little Battleflats Farm, Ellistown, Coalville		9. 7.04
G-BXRC	Mudry/CAARP CAP.10B	134	FrAF 134	12.12.97	I.F.Scott tr Group	AlphaFenland	20. 3.05
G-BXRD	Enstrom 280FX	2012	PH-JVM	22.12.97	S.G.Oliphant-Hope	Shoreham	8. 2.04
			N213M		t/a Eastern Atlantic Helicopters		
G-BXRF	Scintex CP.1310-C3 Super Emeraude	935	OO-NSF	9. 1.98	D.T.Gethin	Swansea	28. 2.03
			F-BMJG				
G-BXRG	Piper PA-28-181 Archer II	28-7990036	PH-LEC	29. 1.98	Alderney Flying Training Ltd	Alderney	1. 3.04T
			N21173				
G-BXRH	Cessna 185A Skywagon	185-0413	HB-CRX	10.12.97	R.E.M.Holmes	Ronaldsway	4. 6.04
	(Hoerner wing-tips)		N1613Z				
G-BXRM	Cameron A-210 HAB	4237		23. 4.98	Dragon Balloon Company Ltd	(Hope Valley)	16. 3.02T
G-BXRO	Cessna U.206G Stationair II	U20604217	OH-ULK	9. 2.98	M.Penny	Movenis, Co.Londonderry	17. 4.04
			N756NE				
G-BXRP	Schweizer Hughes 269C	S.1334	OH-HSP	27. 1.98	C.W.Larner	Haverfordwest	21. 3.04T
			N7506U				
G-BXRR	Westland Scout AH.1	F.9740	XW612	28. 1.98	T.K.Phillips	Thruxton	8. 8.03P
G-BXRS	Westland Scout AH.1	F.9741	XW613	28. 1.98	B-N Group Ltd	Bembridge	7. 5.03P
G-BXRT	Robin DR400/180	2382		23. 2.98	R.A.Ford	White Waltham	26. 4.04
G-BXRV	Van's RV-4	PFA 181-12482		12. 1.98	B.J.Oke tr Cleeve Flying Group	Gloucestershire	9. 6.03P
G-BXRY	Bell 206B JetRanger II	208	N4054G	19. 3.98	Cross Lane Services Ltd	(Sleaford)	6. 8.04T
G-BXRZ	Rans S-6-116 Coyote II	PFA 204A-13195		3. 2.98	F.Gallacher	Perth	9.10.04A
G-BXSA	Cameron PM-80 HAB	4297		11. 3.98	Flying Pictures Ltd	(Dubai)	2. 6.00A
	(Coca Cola bottle)						
G-BXSC	Cameron C-80 HAB	4251		12.12.97	S.J.Coates *"Keepsake"* Barton-le-Clay, Bedford		11.10.02A
G-BXSD	Cessna 172R Skyhawk II	17280310	N431ES	12. 3.98	K.K.Freeman	Bodmin	29. 3.04
G-BXSE	Cessna 172R Skyhawk II	17280352	N9321F	19. 5.98	MK Aero Support Ltd	Bristol	12. 7.04T
					(Op Bristol & Wessex Flying Club)		
G-BXSG	Robinson R22 Beta-II	2789		3. 2.98	R.M.Goodenough	Wotton-under-Edge	1. 3.04T
G-BXSH	DG Flugzeugbau DG-800B	8-121B50		5. 2.98	R.O'Conor	Rufforth	4. 11.05
G-BXSI	Jabiru Jabiru SK	PFA 274-13204		5. 2.98	M.H.Molyneux	Wickenby	8. 5.03P
	(Jabiru 2200A)						
G-BXSJ	Cameron C-80 HAB	4330		24. 3.98	Balloon School (International) Ltd	Petworth	17. 7.03T
					t/a British School of Ballooning		
G-BXSM	Cessna 172R Skyhawk II	17280320	N432ES	10. 3.98	East Midlands Flying School Ltd	East Midlands	11. 4.04T
G-BXSP	Grob G-109B	6335	D-KNEA	25. 3.98	I.M.Donnelly	Aboyne	7. 4.04
G-BXSR	Reims/Cessna F172N	F17202003	PH-SPY	6. 2.98	S.A.Parkes	King's Farm, Thurrock	21. 4.04T
			D-EITH				
G-BXST	Piper PA-25-235 Pawnee C	25-4952	PH-BAT	9. 2.98	P.Channon	Porthtowan	5. 5.02A
	(Frame No.25-4971)		N8532L				
G-BXSU	TEAM mini-MAX 91A	PFA 186-12357	G-MYGL	20. 2.98	M.R.Overall	Wethersfield	11. 4.03P
	(Rotax 503)						
G-BXSV	SNCAN Stampe SV-4C	446	N21PM	10.10.02	B.A.Bower	(Seaton)	
			F-BDDB				
G-BXSX	Cameron V-77 HAB	4329		6. 4.98	D.R.Medcalf	(Bromsgrove)	24. 6.03A
G-BXSY	Robinson R22 Beta-II	2778		27. 1.98	N.M.G.Pearson	Bristol	5. 2.04T
G-BXTB	Cessna 152 II	15282516	OH-CMS	25. 2.98	Haimoss Ltd	Old Sarum	25. 4.04T
			N69151				
G-BXTC	Taylor JT.1 Monoplane	PFA 55-13142		25. 2.98	R.Holden-Rushworth	(Devizes)	
G-BXTD	Europa Aviation Europa	155 & PFA 247-12772		26. 2.98	P.R.Anderson	Hucknall	14. 5.03P
	(Rotax 912) (Monowheel u/c)				*(F/f 23.1.00)*		
G-BXTE	Cameron A-275 HAB	4028		30. 3.98	Adventure Balloon Co Ltd	Hook	19. 8.03T
G-BXTF	Cameron N-105SS HAB	4304		2. 4.98	Flying Pictures Ltd *"Sainsbury's Strawberry"* Chilbolton		8. 5.03A
G-BXTG	Cameron N-42 HAB	4305		2. 4.98	Flying Pictures Ltd *"Sainsbury"*	Chilbolton	26. 7.01A
G-BXTH	Westland SA.314D Gazelle HT.3	1120	XW866	13. 3.98	Flightline Ltd *(As "E" in RAF c/s: stored 2.03)* Southend		
G-BXTI	Pitts S-1S Special	NP-1	ZS-VZX	9. 3.98	A.B.Treherne-Pollock	White Waltham	25. 7.03P
			N96MM				
G-BXTJ	Cameron N-77 HAB	4332		6. 4.98	J M Albury (Chubb titles)	Cirencester	4. 1.03A
G-BXTK	Dornier Do.28	D-24080	D-IDBB	15. 5.98	R.Ebke	(Porta Westfalica, Germany)	
			58+05 German AF				
G-BXTL	Schweizer 269	C-10075		13. 3.98	Oxford Aviation Services Ltd	Oxford	2. 4.04T
G-BXTN	Aérospatiale/Alenia ATR 72-202	483	F-WWEV	24.10.97	Cityflyer Express Ltd *(Whale Rider t/s)*	Gatwick	23.10.03T
G-BXTO	Hindustan HAL-26 Pushpak	PK-128	9V-BAI	12. 2.98	A.M.Pepper tr Pushpak Flying Group	(Stone)	24. 2.03P
	(Continental C90-8F)		VT-DWM				
G-BXTP	Diamond DA-20-A1 Katana	10306	N636DA	10. 3.98	Diamond Aircraft UK Ltd	Gloucestershire	23. 4.04T
					(Op Cotswold Flying Club)		
G-BXTR	Diamond DA-20-A1 Katana	10307	N607DA	10. 3.98	Diamond Aircraft UK Ltd	Norwich	23. 4.04T
G-BXTS	Diamond DA-20-A1 Katana	10308	N638DA	10. 3.98	I.M.Armitage	(London W4)	21. 5.04T
G-BXTT	Grumman-American AA-5B Tiger	AA5B-0749	F-GBDH	27. 2.98	P.Curley & R.Bailes-Brown tr G-BXTT Group		14. 3.04
G-BXTU	Robinson R22 Beta-II	2790		3. 3.98	TDR Aviation Ltd	(Craigavon, Co.Armagh)	7. 4.04T
G-BXTV	Cope Bug	BUG.2		12. 3.98	B.R.Cope	(Bewdley)	
G-BXTW	Piper PA-28-181 Archer III	2843137	N41279	26. 5.98	J.N.Davison t/a Davison Plant Hire	Compton Abbas	17. 6.04
			(G-BXTW)/N41279				
G-BXTY	Piper PA-28-161 Cadet	2841179	PH-LED	11. 3.98	Bflying Ltd *(Op Bournemouth Flying Club)* Bournemouth		27. 6.04T
G-BXTZ	Piper PA-28-161 Cadet	2841181	PH LEE	11. 3.98	Bflying Ltd *(Op Bournemouth Flying Club)* Bournemouth		25. 3.04T
G-BXUA	Campbell Cricket Mk.5	PFA G/03-1272		12. 3.98	R.N.Bodley	Henstridge	1. 7.03P
G-BXUB	Lindstrand Syrup Bottle SS HAB	508		30. 4.98	Free Enterprise Balloons Ltd	Mason, Wi. USA	29. 4.03A
					"Mrs Butterworth"		
G-BXUC	Robinson R22 Beta	0908	OY-HFB	17. 3.98	R.C.Hields t/a Hields Aviation	Sherburn-in-Elmet	29. 3.04T
G-BXUE	Sky 240-24 HAB	098		30. 4.98	G.M.Houston t/a Scotair Balloons	Lesmahagow	5. 4.03T
G-BXUF	Agusta-Bell 206B JetRanger II	8633	EC-DUS	12. 5.98	SJ Contracting Services Ltd	Oxford	26. 7.04T
			OE-DXE				
G-BXUG	Lindstrand Baby Bel SS HAB	512		14. 5.98	Virgin Airship & Balloon Co Ltd *"Mr Cool"*	Telford	13. 4.01A

Reg	Type	C/n	Prev id	Date	Owner/Operator	Location	Date
G-BXUH	Lindstrand LBL-31A HAB	513		2. 6.98	Virgin Airship & Balloon Co Ltd *"Baby-Bel"*	Telford	12. 4.01A
G-BXUI	DG Flugzeugbau DG-800B	8-105-B39	BGA.4382 D-KKLC	12. 5.98	J.Le Coyte	Rufforth	28. 5.04P
G-BXUK	Robinson R44 Astro	0093	D-HIFF	19. 6.95	G.Elliott t/a Hertfordshire Helicopters	(Luton)	26. 6.04T
G-BXUL	Vought (Goodyear) FG-1D Corsair *(Officially regd as c/n P32823)*	3205	N55JP "NZ5611"/"NZ5648/Bu.88391	25. 3.98	The Old Flying Machine (Air Museum) Co *(P/i of Bu.88439 quoted) (As "92844/8" of VF-17 in US Navy c/s)*	Duxford	27. 5.03P
G-BXUM	Europa Aviation Europa *(Rotax 912) (Monowheel u/c)*	067 & PFA 247-12611		19. 3.98	D.Bosomworth *(F/f 19.4.99)*	RAF Lyneham	10. 5.03P
G-BXUO	Lindstrand LBL-105A HAB	520		27. 3.98	Lindstrand Balloons Ltd	Oswestry	27. 9.03A
G-BXUS	Sky 65-24 HAB	111		6. 4.98	K.Coate-Bond	Basingstoke	2. 7.03A
G-BXUU	Cameron V-65 HAB	4362		23. 4.98	R.G.A.Fulton	Wye, Ashford	5. 9.02A
G-BXUW	Cameron Colt 90A HAB	4317		23. 4.98	Zycomm Electronics Ltd	Ripley	1. 6.03A
G-BXUX	Brandli Cherry BX-2 *(Continental C90-12F)*	PFA 179-12571		4. 4.98	M.F.Fountain	Manston	28.10.03P
G-BXUY	Cessna 310Q	310Q0231	N137SA D-IHMT/N7731Q	16. 4.98	Massair Ltd	Liverpool	24.10.04
G-BXVA	SOCATA TB-200 Tobago XL	1325	F-GJXL F-WJXL	15. 4.98	H.R.Palser	Cardiff	28. 6.04
G-BXVB	Cessna 152 II	15282584	N69250	15. 4.98	PJC (Leasing) Ltd	Stapleford	25. 9.04T
G-BXVC*	Piper PA-28RT-201T Turbo Arrow IV	28R-7931113	D-ELIV N2152V	20. 4.98	J.S.Develin & I.Zahurul *(Cancelled 22.1.03 as wfu)*	Redhill	28. 6.01T
G-BXVD	CFM Streak Shadow SA *(Rotax 912)*	K.301SA & PFA 206-13304		1. 4.98	Rotech Frabrication Ltd *(Noted 2.02)*	Pittrichie Farm, Whiterashes	24. 8.01P
G-BXVE	Lindstrand LBL-330A HAB	492		6. 5.98	Adventure Balloon Co Ltd *(Adventure Balloons titles)*	London W7	24. 3.03T
G-BXVF	Thunder Ax11-250 Srs.2 HAB	4371		22. 5.98	T.J.Parker t/a Anglian Countryside Balloons	Burnham-on-Crouch	20. 4.03T
G-BXVG	Sky 77-24 HAB	99		28. 5.98	M.Wolf	Wallingford	27. 3.03
G-BXVH	Sky 25-16 HAB	120		23. 4.98	Flying Pictures Ltd *(AXA titles)*	Chilbolton	7. 3.02A
G-BXVI	Supermarine 361 Spitfire LF.XVIe	CBAF.IX.4644	6944M "RF114"/RW386	27.12.84	Wizzard Investments Ltd *(On rebuild 4.89: current status unknown)*	North Weald	
G-BXVJ	Cameron O-120 HAB	2201	PH-VVJ G-IMAX	12. 3.98	Aerosaurus Balloons LLP	Exeter	3. 3.03T
G-BXVK	Robin HR200/120	B326		1. 7.98	Northamptonshire School of Flying Ltd	Sywell	23. 6.04T
G-BXVL	Sky 180-24 HAB	113		16. 6.98	S.Stanley t/a Purple Balloons	Sudbury	18. 3.03T
G-BXVM	Van's RV-6A	PFA 181-13103		26. 2.98	J.G.Small	RAF Woodvale	22. 5.03P
G-BXVN*	Sky 105-24 HAB	115		17. 9.98	L.V.D. Avyle t/a Skydance *(Cancelled 23.10.00 by CAA - no CofA issued)*	Wachtebetie, Belgium	
G-BXVO	Van's RV-6A *(Lycoming O-320-D1A)*	PFA 181-12575		28. 4.98	P.J.Hynes & M.E.Holden	Sleap	24. 8.03P
G-BXVP	Sky 31-24 HAB	056		28. 4.98	L.Greaves	Doulting, Somerset	18.10.03A
G-BXVR	Sky 90-24 HAB	061		20. 7.98	P.Hegarty	Magherafelt, Co.Londonderry	21. 9.03
G-BXVS	Brugger Colibri MB.2 *(Volkswagen 1834)*	PFA 43-11948		5. 5.98	G.T.Snoddon	Newtownards, Co.Down	19. 5.03
G-BXVT	Cameron O-77 HAB	1444	PH-MKB	30. 7.98	R.P.Wade *(Current status unknown)*	Wigan	
G-BXVU	Piper PA-28-161 Cherokee Warrior II	28-7816063	N47372	5. 5.98	Lyddair Ltd	Lydd	17. 7.04T
G-BXVV	Cameron V-90 HAB	4369		5. 5.98	Floating Sensations Ltd	Thatcham	28. 4.03A
G-BXVW	Colt Piggy Bank SS HAB	4366		2. 7.98	G.Binder	Sonnennbuhl, Germany	2. 8.03A
G-BXVX	Rutan Cozy *(Lycoming O-320-E2A)*	PFA 159-12680		6. 5.98	G.E.Murray	Swansea	21.10.03P
G-BXVY	Cessna 152	15279808	N757KU	11. 5.98	Stapleford Flying Club Ltd	Stapleford	13.11.04T
G-BXVZ	WSK-PZL Mielec TS-11 Iskra	3H-1625	SP-DOF Polish AF?/SP-DOF	27. 3.98	J.Ziubrzynski *(Noted 7.02)*	Manston	AC
G-BXWA	Beech 76 Duchess	ME-232	OY-CYM (SE-IUY)/D-GBTD	8. 4.98	Plymouth School of Flying Ltd	Plymouth	23. 6.04T
G-BXWB	Robin HR100/200B Royale	08	HB-EMT	29. 4.98	W.A.Brunwin	Oaksey Park	25. 7.04T
G-BXWC	Cessna 152	15283640	N4794B	11. 5.98	PJC (Leasing) Ltd	Stapleford	12. 7.04T
G-BXWD	Agusta A109A-II	7266	N565RJ I-URIA/D-HEMZ/N109BD	14. 5.98	Castle Air Charters Ltd	Liskeard	AC
G-BXWE	Fokker F.28 Mk.0100 *(Fokker 100)*	11327	PH-CFE F-GJAO/PH-CFE/PH-EZL/(G-FIOX)/PH-EZL	6. 7.98	British Midland Airways Ltd *(Op bmi Regional)*	East Midlands	30. 8.04T
G-BXWF	Fokker F.28 Mk.0100 *(Fokker 100)*	11328	PH-CFF F-GKLX/PH-CFF/PH-EZM/(G-FIOY)/PH-EZM	13. 7.98	British Midland Airways Ltd *(Op bmi Regional)*	East Midlands	31. 8.04T
G-BXWG	Sky 120-24 HAB	114		28. 5.98	Airbourne Adventures Ltd	Skipton	25. 6.03T
G-BXWH	Denney Kitfox Model 4-1200 Sportster	PFA 172A-12343		4. 3.98	B.J.Finch	Croft Farm, Defford	23. 5.03P
G-BXWI	Cameron N-120 HAB *(Rebuilt 1999 but new canopy c/n not known)*	4395		12. 6.98	Flying Pictures Ltd *(Energis titles)*	Chilbolton	30. 7.02A
G-BXWK	Rans S-6ESA Coyote II *(Tricycle u/c) (Rotax 582)*	0298.1020 & PFA 204-13317		19. 5.98	R.J.Teal	Baxby Manor, Husthwaite	13.11.02P
G-BXWL	Sky 90-24 HAB	117		20. 7.98	I.S.Bridge t/a The Shropshire Hills Balloon Company	Shrewsbury	16.11.03A
G-BXWO	Piper PA-28-181 Archer II	28-8190311	D-ENHA(2) N8431C	22. 5.98	J.S.Develin & Z.Islam	Redhill	23. 7.04T
G-BXWP	Piper PA-32-300 Cherokee Six	32-7340088	N8143D G-BXWP/OE-DRR/N16452	26. 5.98	J.B.Tucker & D.J.Royle t/a Alliance Aviation	Barton	27. 7.04
G-BXWR	CFM Streak Shadow SA *(Rotax 912)*	K.289-SA & PFA 206-13205	G-MZMI	22. 5.98	M.A.Hayward	Bodmin	17. 3.03P
G-BXWT	Van's RV-6	PFA 181-12639		19. 7.96	R.C.Owen	Danehill	26. 7.03P
G-BXWU	FLS Aerospace Sprint 160	003		19. 6.98			
G-BXWV	FLS Aerospace Sprint 160	005	G-70-503	5. 6.98	Aces High Ltd *(Amended CofR 3.02)*	North Weald	
G-BXWX	Sky 25-16 HAB	082	G-70-505	5. 6.98	Aces High Ltd *(Amended CofR 3.02)*	North Weald	
G-BXXE	Rand Robinson KR-2S	PFA 129-10927		29. 5.98	Zebedee Balloon Service Ltd	Hungerford	14. 3.00A
G-BXXG	Cameron N-105 HAB	3662		8. 6.98	N.Rawlinson *(Under construction 5.99)*	(Leek)	
				19. 6.98	Allen Owen Ltd	Wotton-under-Edge	2. 4.02A

G-BXXH	Hatz CB-1	PFA 143-12445			9. 6.98	R.D.Shingler	Forest Farm, Welshpool	
G-BXXI	Grob G-109B	6400	F-CAQR F-WAQR		9. 6.98	M.N.Martin	Lyveden	23.10.04
G-BXXJ	Colt Flying Yacht SS HAB	1797	JA-A0515		10. 6.98	Magical Adventures Ltd	West Bloomfield, Mi., USA	7. 9.01A
G-BXXK	Reims/Cessna F172N	F17201806	D-EOPP		15. 6.98	I.R.Chaplin	Andrewsfield	22. 8.04T
G-BXXL	Cameron N-105 HAB	4408			16. 7.98	Flying Pictures Ltd (Blue Peter titles)	Chilbolton	17. 8.01A
G-BXXN	Robinson R22 Beta	0720	N720HH		16. 6.98	L.L.Smith t/a Helicopter Services	Booker	5. 7.04T
G-BXXO	Lindstrand LBL-90B HAB	534			6. 7.98	K.Temple (New owner 11.01)	Diss	7. 9.00A
G-BXXP	Sky 77-24 HAB	124			20. 7.98	C.J.James	Wincanton	7. 5.03A
G-BXXR	Lovegrove AV-8 Gyroplane	PFA G/15-1263			29. 6.98	P.C.Lovegrove	Didcot	
	(Registered as Lovegrove BGL Four Runner c/n PFA G/15-1273)							
G-BXXS	Sky 105-24 HAB	116			30. 7.98	L.D.& H.Vaughan	Tring	11. 1.03A
G-BXXT	Beech 76 Duchess	ME-212	(N212BE) F-GBOZ		17. 7.98	S.J.Skilton t/a Aviation Rentals	Cardiff	21. 7.04T
G-BXXU	Colt 31A HAB	4427			21. 8.98	Sade Balloons Ltd	Coulsdon	17.10.03
G-BXXW	Enstrom F-28	F771	G-SCOX N330SA/G-BXXW/JA7823		2. 7.98	G.Kidger	(Worksop)	22.10.04
G-BXYC	Schweizer 269C	S.1716	D-HFDZ		8. 7.98	Foremans Aviation Ltd	Linley Hill, Leven	20. 8.04T
G-BXYD	Eurocopter EC120B	1006			7. 7.98	Helimac Ltd	Carluke	13.12.04T
G-BXYE	Scintex CP.301-C1 Emeraude	559	F-BTEO F-PTEO/F-WTEO/F-BJFV		8. 7.98	D.T.Gethin	Swansea	
G-BXYF	Colt AS-105 GD Airship	4433			7. 8.98	LN Flying Ltd	Frinton-on-Sea	2.10.03A
G-BXYG	Cessna 310D	39089	HB-LSF F-GEJT/3A-MCA/F-BBOT/F-OBOT/(N6789T)		14. 8.98	Equitus SARL	Merville-Calonne, France	28. 1.05T
G-BXYJ	SAN Jodel DR.1050 Ambassadeur	143	F-BJNA		28. 7.98	J.Dickinson tr G-BXYJ Group	(Dinnington)	21.10.04
G-BXYK	Robinson R22 Beta	1579	N4037B		27. 7.98	D.N.Whittlestone	(Oxenhope)	16. 1.05T
G-BXYL	Cameron A-275 HAB	4450			22. 7.98	Ballooning Network Ltd	Bristol	14. 7.02T
G-BXYM	Piper PA-28-235 Cherokee B	28-10858	SE-FAM		18. 8.98	Ashurst Aviation Ltd	Shoreham	22.12.04T
G-BXYN	Van's RV-6	PFA 181-13265			29. 7.98	J.A.Tooley & R.M.Austin	(Thatcham)	
G-BXYO	Piper PA-28RT-201 Arrow IV	28R-8018046	PH-SDD N8164M		18. 8.98	Oxford Aviation Services Ltd	Oxford	1.12.04T
G-BXYP	Piper PA-28RT-201 Arrow IV	28R-8018050	PH-SBO N8168H		18. 8.98	Westflight Aviation Ltd	Gloucestershire	6.11.04T
G-BXYR	Piper PA-28RT-201 Arrow IV	28R-8018101	PH-SDA N8251B		3. 8.98	Oxford Aviation Services Ltd	Oxford	26.11.04T
G-BXYT	Piper PA-28RT-201 Arrow IV	28R-7918198	PH-SBN (PH-SBM)/OO-HLA/N2878W		3. 8.98	Oxford Aviation Services Ltd	Oxford	9. 9.04T
G-BXYU*	Reims/Cessna F152 II	F15201804	OH-CKD		31. 7.98	Exeter Flying Club Ltd	Dunkeswell	24. 8.01T
			SE-IFY (Cancelled 16.10.99 as destroyed Whiddon Down, Okehampton 2.8.99: fuselage noted 2.02)					
G-BXYX	Van's RV-6	22293	N2399C		31. 7.98	A G Palmer	Wellesbourne Mountford	3. 1.03P
	(Lycoming O-320-E2D)							
G-BXYY	Reims FR172E Rocket	FR17200016	OY-AHO F-WLIP		20. 4.98	Haimoss Ltd	Old Sarum	13. 6.04T
G-BXZA	Piper PA-38-112 Tomahawk	38-79A0864	N2480N		6. 8.98	P.D.Brooks	Inverness	30.10.04T
G-BXZB	Nanchang CJ-6A	2632019	Chin AF		18. 9.98	Wingglider Ltd (As "2632019")	Hibaldstow	31. 5.02P
G-BXZD	Westland SA.314C Gazelle HT.2	1174	XW895		25. 8.98	Middleton Miniature Mouldings Ltd	Teesside	18. 3.03P
			(As "XW895/51" in Royal Navy c/s)					
G-BXZF	Lindstrand LBL-90A HAB	575			8. 1.99	R.G.Carrell	Havant	19. .03A
G-BXZG	Cameron A-210 HAB	4424			21. 8.98	Société Bombard SARL Meursanges, Côte-d'Or, France		6.10.03A
G-BXZH	Cameron A-210 HAB	4423			21. 8.98	Société Bombard SARL Meursanges, Côte-d'Or, France		6.10.03A
G-BXZI	Lindstrand LBL-90A HAB	543			14. 8.98	S.Stanley t/a Purple Balloons	Sudbury	18. 6.03A
G-BXZK	MD Helicopters MD.900	900-00057	N9238T G-76-057		27. 8.98	Dorset Police Air Support Unit	Winfrith	17. 2.05T
G-BXZM	Cessna 182S	18280310	N2683L		8.10.98	Oxford Aviation Services Ltd	Oxford	8.10.01T
G-BXZN	Advanced Technologies Firebird CH1 ATI	00002	N8186E		25. 8.98	Intora-Firebird plc	Southend	
			(Stored 1.03 - unconfirmed)					
G-BXZO	Pietenpol Air Camper	PFA 47-12818			10. 7.98	P.J.Cooke	(Uckfield)	14. 7.03P
G-BXZS	Sikorsky S-76A II Plus	760287	N190AL N190AE/N153AE/N7265A		14. 9.98	Bristow Helicopters Ltd	Redhill	3. 5.05T
G-BXZT	MS.880B Rallye Club	1733	OO-EDG D-EBDG/F-BSVL		2. 9.98	Limerick Flying Club (Coonagh) Ltd Coonagh, Co.Limerick		11.12.04
G-BXZU	Micro Aviation Bantam B22 S	98-015	ZK-JJL		21. 9.98	M.E.Whapham & R.W.Hollamby Corn Wood Farm, Adversane		8. 5.03P
	(Rotax 582)							
G-BXZV	CFM Streak Shadow K.293SA & PFA 206-13357				18. 9.98	CFM Aircraft Ltd	Parham Park	30. 7.02P
	(Rotax 912-UL) (Originally regd as Streak Shadow SA: new desig 8.01: kit c/n unchanged)							
G-BXZY	CFM Streak Shadow DD	296-DD			21. 9.98	P.A.James t/a Cloudbase Aviation G-BXZY	Redhill	16.12.02P
	(Rotax 582)		(Bounced landing Redhill 16.2.02 & nose u/c collapsed causing damage to fuselage underside)					
G-BXZZ	Sky 160-24 HAB	109			14. 7.98	S.J.Colin t/a Skybus Ballooning	Cranbrook	29. 5.03T

G-BYAA - G-BYZZ

G-BYAA	Boeing 767-204ER	25058	PH-AHM G-BYAA/N60659		23. 4.91	Britannia Airways Ltd "Sir Matt Busby CBE"	Luton	13.11.05T
G-BYAB	Boeing 767-204ER	25139	(PH-AHN) G-BYAB		11. 6.91	Britannia Airways Ltd "Brian Johnston CBE MC"	Luton	26. 3.05T
G-BYAD	Boeing 757-204ER	26963			6. 5.92	Britannia Airways Ltd	Luton	22. 2.05T
G-BYAE	Boeing 757-204ER	26964			12. 5.92	Britannia Airways Ltd	Luton	26. 4.04T
G-BYAF	Boeing 757-204ER	26266			13. 1.93	Britannia Airways Ltd	Luton	19. 1.06T
G-BYAH	Boeing 757-204ER	26966			5. 2.93	Britannia Airways Ltd	Luton	10. 2.03T
G-BYAI	Boeing 757-204	26967			1. 3.93	Britannia Airways Ltd	Luton	4. 3.03T
G-BYAJ	Boeing 757-204ER	25623			4. 3.93	Britannia Airways Ltd	Luton	23. 1.05T
G-BYAK	Boeing 757-204	26267			6. 4.93	Britannia Airways Ltd	Luton	13. 4.03T
G-BYAL	Boeing 757-204	25626			13. 5.93	Britannia Airways Ltd	Luton	18. 5.03T

Reg	Type	C/n	Prev id	Date	Owner/Operator	Location	Date
G-BYAN	Boeing 757-204	27219		26. 1.94	Britannia Airways Ltd	Luton	14. 2.04T
G-BYAO	Boeing 757-204	27235		3. 2.94	Britannia Airways Ltd	Luton	2. 2.03T
G-BYAP	Boeing 757-204	27236		15. 2.94	Britannia Airways Ltd *"John Lennon"*	Luton	14. 2.03T
G-BYAS	Boeing 757-204	27238		9. 3.94	Britannia Airways Ltd	Luton	31. 1.05T
G-BYAT	Boeing 757-204	27208		21. 3.94	Britannia Airways Ltd	Luton	24. 3.04T
G-BYAU	Boeing 757-204	27220		18. 5.94	Britannia Airways Ltd	Luton	17. 5.03T
G-BYAV	Taylor JT.1 Monoplane (Volkswagen 1600)	PFA 55-11010		27. 8.98	T J Adams *(Noted 6.02)*	RAF Henlow	4.10.01P
G-BYAW	Boeing 757-204	27234		3. 4.95	Britannia Airways Ltd *"Eric Morecambe OBE"*	Luton	2. 4.04T
G-BYAX	Boeing 757-204	28834		24. 2.99	Britannia Airways Ltd	Luton	28. 2.05T
G-BYAY	Boeing 757-204	28836		13. 4.99	Britannia Airways Ltd	Luton	12. 4.05T
G-BYAZ	CFM Streak Shadow SA (Rotax 582)	K.244 & PFA 206-12656		1. 9.98	A.G.Wright	(Camberley)	6. 3.03P
G-BYBA	Agusta-Bell 206B-3 JetRanger III	8596	G-BHXV G-OWJM/G-BHXV	31. 3.98	R.Forests Ltd	White Waltham	5. 9.05T
G-BYBC	Agusta-Bell 206B JetRanger II	8567	G-BTWW EI-BJV/G-BTWW	31. 3.98	Proofgolden Ltd t/a Mainstreet Aviation	(Durham)	28. 6.03T
G-BYBD	Cessna F172H *(Built Reims Aviation SA)*	F172-0487	G-OBHX G-AWMU	6. 7.98	R Ross	Pittrichie Farm, Whiterashes	23. 6.02T
G-BYBE	Jodel Wassmer D.120A Paris-Nice	269	OO-FDP	24. 7.98	R.J.Page	Shipdham	15. 5.05
G-BYBF	Robin R2160i	329		1.10.98	D.J.R.Lloyd-Evans	Compton Abbas	2. 5.05T
G-BYBH	Piper PA-34-200T Seneca II	34-8070078	N119SA (G-BYBH)/N4023K/N3567B	9. 6.00	Goldspear (UK) Ltd	White Waltham	22 .8.03
G-BYBI	Bell 206B-3 JetRanger III	3668	ZS-RGP N5757M	19.10.98	Winkburn Air Ltd	Elstree	19. 7.05T
G-BYBJ	Medway Hybred 44XLR	MR156/135		22. 1.99	M Gardner	Rochester	25. 4.01P
G-BYBK	Murphy Rebel *(Built L A Dyer)* (Lycoming O-235-L2C)	260R	N95LD	19. 8.98	R.K..Hyatt	Bodmin	1. 4.03P
G-BYBL	Gardan GY-80 Horizon 160D	127	F-BMUY	25. 9.98	R.H.W.Beath	(Bath)	21.11.03
G-BYBM	Jabiru Jabiru SK (Jabiru 2200A)	PFA 274-13377		18. 9.98	P.J.Hatton	(Okehampton)	17. 9.03P
G-BYBN	Cameron N-77 HAB	3082	N6004M	30. 9.98	M.G.& R.D.Howard	Bristol	27. 9.03A
G-BYBO	Medway EclipseR (Jabiru 2200A)	155/134		14. 9.98	R.Skene	Rochester	26. 4.03P
G-BYBP	Cessna A185	F18503804	OO-DCD F-GDCD/F-ODIA/N4593E	15.10.98	G.M.S.Scott	Headcorn	28. 2 05
G-BYBR	Rans S-6-116 Coyote II *(Tricycle u/c)* (Rotax 912-UL)	0996.1042 & PFA 204A-13081		10. 7.98	J.B.Robinson	Blackpool	20. 8.03P
G-BYBS	Sky 80-16 HAB	136		27.10.98	K.B.Chapple	Reading	11. 8.03
G-BYBU	Murphy Renegade Spirit UK (Rotax 582)	PFA 188-13229		12.10.98	L.C.Cook *"Wayward Spirit"*	Sywell	30. 5.03P
G-BYBV	Mainair Rapier (Rotax 503-2V)	1183-1198-7 & W986		20.10.98	M.W.Robson	York	1.11.02P
G-BYBW	TEAM mini-MAX (Rotax 447)	PFA 186-12120		19.10.98	R.M.Laver	(Crawley)	22.11.00P
G-BYBX	Slingsby T.67M-260 Firefly	2261		21.10.98	Slingsby Aviation Ltd	Wombleton	
G-BYBY	Thorp T-18C Tiger	492	N77KK	17. 7.98	L.J.Joyce	Liverpool	21.11.03P
G-BYBZ	Jabiru Jabiru SK (Jabiru 2200A)	PFA 274-13290		7. 9.98	A.W.Harris	Coventry	27. 12.03P
G-BYCA	Piper PA-28-140 Cherokee D	28-7125223	PH-VRZ N11C	24. 9.98	A.Reay	(Ramsbottom, Bury)	8. 2.05T
G-BYCB	Sky 21-16 HAB	142		28.10.98	Zebedee Balloon Service Ltd	Hungerford	
G-BYCD	Cessna 140 (Continental O-200-A)	13744 NC4273N	N4273N	28. 9.98	G.P.James	Fenland	17. 4.05
G-BYCE	Robinson R44 Astro	0520		12.10.98	Walters Plant Hire Ltd	(Aberdare)	30.10.04T
G-BYCF	Robinson R22 Beta-II	2866		12.10.98	Teleology Ltd	(Todmorden)	9.12.04T
G-BYCJ	CFM Shadow DD (Rotax 582)	K.294-DD & PFA 161-13258		14.10.98	S.R.Winter	Hunsdon	30.11.02P
G-BYCL	Raj Hamsa X'Air 582	331 & BMAA/HB/088		15.10.98	D.O'Keefe, K.Rutter & A.J.Clarke	London Colney	28. 6.03P
G-BYCM	Rans S-6ES Coyote II (Rotax 503 DCDI)	PFA 204-13315		15. 9.98	E.W.McMullan	Dunnyvadden, Co.Antrim	7.11.00P
G-BYCN	Rans S-6ES Coyote I (Rotax 582-48)	PFA 204-13314		15. 9.98	J.K.Dunseath & T.J.Croskery	Mullaghmore, Co.Sligo	21. 3.03P
G-BYCO*	Rans S-6ES Coyote II	PFA 204-13318		17. 9.98	T J Croskery	City of Derry	8. 5.02P
	(Struck ground in practice forced landing Limavady 23.8.01: wreck noted 9.01: cancelled 3.1.02 as WFU)						
G-BYCP	Beech B200 Super King Air	BB-966	F-GDCS	15.10.98	London Executive Aviation Ltd	Stapleford	11. 2.03
G-BYCS	CEA Jodel DR.1051 Sicile	201	F-BJUJ	28.10.98	Fire Defence plc	Trenchard Farm, Eggesford	24. 5.05
G-BYCT	Aero L-29A Delfin	395142	ES-YLH Estonian AF/Soviet AF	29.10.98	Propeller BVBA *(OO-DDK reserved 2003))*	Wevelgem, Belgium	14. 5.03P
G-BYCU	Robinson R22 Beta	1094	G-OCGJ	3.11.98	M.Roebuck	(Stockport)	15. 9.04T
G-BYCV	Murphy Maverick (Rotax 503)	PFA 259-12925		24. 9.98	P.Shackleton	Old Sarum	5.11.03P
G-BYCX	Westland Wasp HAS.Mk.1	F.9754 & WA-B-Z3	ZK-HOX SA Navy 92	9.11.98	S.H.Tizzard, P.G.Lister & J.Chapman *"92"*	(Ringwood)	2. 5.03P
G-BYCY	III Sky Arrow 650T (Rotax 912-UL)	PFA 298-13332		10.11.98	K.A.Daniels	(South Wales)	17. 6.03P
G-BYCZ	Jabiru Jabiru SK (Jabiru 2200A)	PFA 274-13388		16.10.98	R.Scroby	(Leicester)	12. 9.03P
G-BYDA	McDonnell Douglas DC-10-30	46990	OY-CNO XA-SYE/F-GGMZ/C-GFHX/9V-SDA	25. 3.99	MyTravel Airways Ltd	Manchester	29. 3.05T
G-BYDB	Grob G-115B	8025	VH-JVL D-EFCG	26. 3.99	J.B.Baker	Tatenhill	16. 4.05
G-BYDD	Mooney M.20J	24-0847	D-EIWM	19.10.98	A.D.E.Eade	Old Sarum	19. 5.05T
G-BYDE	Supermarine 361 Spitfire IX	-	Sov AF PT879	11.11.98	A.H.Soper	(Romford)	

Reg	Type	C/n	Prev id	Date	Owner/Operator	Location	Status
G-BYDF	Sikorsky S-76A	760364	JA6615	9. 1.98	Brecqhou Development Ltd	Guernsey	8. 7.04T
G-BYDG	Beech C24R Sierra	MC-627	OY-AZL	9.11.98	Professional Air Training Ltd	Bournemouth	21. 5.05T
G-BYDI	Cameron A-210 HAB	4495		4. 2.99	N.J.Appleton t/a First Flight	Bristol	16. 2.02T
					(Park Furnishers titles)		
G-BYDJ	Colt 120A HAB	3527		17.11.98	D.K.Hempleman-Adams	Box, Wilts	19. 6.02A
G-BYDK	Stampe SV-4C	55	F-BCXY	20.11.98	Bianchi Aviation Film Services Ltd	Booker	
	(P/i quoted officially as F-BCXV which was c/n 298)						
G-BYDL	Hawker Hurricane IIB	-	Soviet AF Z5207	17.11.98	Retro Track & Air (UK) Ltd	(Dursley)	
					(New owner 12.01)		
G-BYDM	Pegasus Quantum 15-912	7488		18.11.98	P.Roberts	(Bideford)	5. 7.03P
G-BYDN	Fokker F.28 Mk.0100	11329	N13OML	4. 6.99	Stockholm Aircraft Finance IV BV *(Stored 10.01)*		
	(Fokker 100)		SE-DUF/PH-CFG/PH-EZV/(G-FIOZ)/PH-EZV			Woensdrecht, The Netherlands	3. 6.02T
G-BYDO	Fokker F.28 Mk.0100	11323	N131ML	17. 3.99	Stockholm Aircraft Finance IV BV *(Stored 10.01)*		
	(Fokker 100)		SE-DUB/PH-CFA/(PH-LNP)/PH-EZC/(G-FIOT)/PH-EZC			Woensdrecht, The Netherlands	25. 3.02T
G-BYDR	North American B-25D-30NC Mitchell II	100-20644	N88972	22. 3.99	Patina Ltd *"Grumpy"*	Duxford	25. 5.02P
	(C/n 100-23644 reported)		CF-OGQ/RCAF KL161/43-3318		*(Op The Fighter Collection as "VO-B" in 98 Sqdn RAF c/s)*		
G-BYDS	Messerschmitt Bf109E-3	1342	Luft'ffe	24.11.98	Alpine Deer Group Ltd	Not known	
					(On rebuild 11.99 for American Flying Heritage Collection, Seattle, Washington)		
G-BYDT	Cameron N-90 HAB	4499		28. 1.99	N.J.Langley	Bristol	19. 8.03A
G-BYDU*	Cameron Cart SS HAB	4500		28. 1.99	Virgin Airship & Balloon Co Ltd	Telford	29.11.00A
					(Tesco titles) (Cancelled 13.3.01 by CAA)		
G-BYDV	Van's RV-6	PFA 181-13264		3.12.98	R G Andrews	Rathcool, Co.Cork	8. 6.03P
	(Lycoming O-320-D1F)						
G-BYDW	Rotary Air Force RAF 2000 GTX-SE			4.12.98	R G Turck	Rayne Hall Farm, Rayne	20. 2.03P
		PFA G/13-1302					
G-BYDX	American General AG-5B Tiger	10051	N374SA	25. 3.99	A.J.Watson tr Bibit Group	Southampton	19. 4.05
			G-BYDX/F-GKBH/N1191Y				
G-BYDY	Beech 58 Baron	TH-1852	C-GBWF	10.11.98	J.F.Britten	Blackbushe	16.12.04
G-BYDZ	Pegasus Quantum 15-912	7493		22.12.98	W.McCormack	Broomhill Farm, West Calder	16. 4 03P
G-BYEA	Cessna 172P	17275464	PH-ILL N63661	7.10.98	Plane Talking Ltd	Redhill	19.10.04T
G-BYEB	Cessna 172P	17274634	PH-ILM N52917	7.10.98	Plane Talking Ltd	Elstree	18.10.04T
G-BYEC	DG Flugzeugbau DG-800B	8-102-B36	D-KSDG	13.11.98	P.R.Redshaw	Rufforth	9. 1.05
G-BYED	British Aircraft Corporation BAC.145 Jet Provost T.5A		N166A/XW302	23.11.98	M.A.Petrie & J.E.Rowley	(Ruthin)	23. 5.01P
		EEP/JP/966					
G-BYEE	Mooney M.20K (231)	25-0282	N231JZ	20. 7.88	R.J.Baker & W.Woods	Coventry	10. 4.04
					tr Double Echo Flying Group		
G-BYEH	CEA DR.250/160 Capitaine	15	OO-SOL F-BMZL	6.10.98	E.J.Horsfall	Blackpool	25. 8.02
G-BYEI	Cameron 90SS Chick	4519		1. 4.99	Bic UK Ltd *(Bic SoftFeel titles)*	Harefield	5.10.00A
G-BYEJ	Scheibe SF-28A Tandem Falke	5713	OE-9070 (D-KDAM)	18.12.98	D.Shrimpton	RAF Keevil	16. 9.05
G-BYEK	Stoddard-Hamilton GlaStar	PFA 295-13087		14. 9.98	G.M.New	Bagby	10. 7.03P
G-BYEL	Van's RV-6	PFA 181-12560		7. 1.99	D.Millar	Bidford	3. 7.03P
G-BYEM	Cessna R182 Skylane RG II	R18200822	N494 D-ELVI/N737FT	8. 1.99	Wycombe Air Centre Ltd	Booker	30. 1.05T
G-BYEO	Zenair CH.601HDS Zodiac	PFA 162-13345		11. 1.99	M.J.Diggins	White Waltham	16. 6.03P
	(Rotax 912-UL) (Tail-wheel u/c)				tr Cloudbase Flying Group		
G-BYEP	Lindstrand LBL 90B HAB	560		20.11.98	D.G Macguire	Pulborough	26. 3.01A
G-BYER	Cameron C-80 HAB	4513		19.11.98	Cameron Balloons Ltd *"E2"*	Bristol	11. 7.03A
G-BYES	Cessna 172P	17274514	PH-ILN N172TP/N52424	7.10.98	Plane Talking Ltd	Biggin Hill	24.10.04T
G-BYET	Cessna 172P	17275122	PH-ILP N55158	7.10.98	Plane Talking Ltd	Redhill	15.10.04T
G-BYEU*	Pegasus Quantum 15	7495		28. 1.99	T.C.Brown	Mill Farm, Shifnal	2. 3.03P
					(Cancelled 20.5.02 as WFU)		
G-BYEW	Pegasus Quantum 15-912	7499		15. 1.99	P.M.Coppola	East Fortune	15. 2.02P
G-BYEX	Sky 120-24 HAB	135		21. 1.99	Ballongflyg Upp & Ner AB	Stockholm, Sweden	19. 2.02A
G-BYEY	Lindstrand LBL-21 Silver Dream HAB	577		15. 1.99	Oscair Project Ltd	Taby, Sweden	
G-BYEZ	Dyn'Aéro MCR-01 Ban-bi	47 & PFA 301-13185		25.11.98	J.P.Davies	Leicester	28. 6.03P
	(Rotax 912)						
G-BYFA	Reims/Cessna F152 II	F15201968	G-WACA	19.11.98	A.J.Gomes	Biggin Hill	5. 5.96
G-BYFC	Jabiru Jabiru SK (Jabiru 2200A)	PFA 274-13344		5. 2.99	A.C.N.Freeman	Booker	7. 6.03P
G-BYFD	Grob G-115A	8100	EI-CCN G-BSGE	15. 1.99	D.Lewis	Popham	24. 5.03T
G-BYFE	Pegasus Quantum 15-912	7496		21. 6.99	J.L.Pollard	Knapthorpe Lodge, Caunton	23. 2.03P
					tr G-BYFE Flying Group		
G-BYFF	Pegasus Quantum 15-912	7500		1. 2.99	D.Young tr Kemble Flying Club	Kemble	8. 2.03P
G-BYFG	Europa Aviation Europa XS	396 & PFA 247-13407		22. 1.99	P R Brodie	(Guildford)	
	(Jabiru 3300) (Tri-gear u/c)				*(Under construction 5.02)*		
G-BYFH	Bede BD-5B	665		22. 1.99	G M J Monaghan	(Bury St Edmunds)	
					(Current status unknown)		
G-BYFI	CFM Starstreak Shadow SA	PFA 206-13300		11. 2.99	D.G.Cook	Leiston	
G-BYFJ	Cameron N-105 HAB	4545		4. 3.99	R.J.Mercer	Belfast	7. 6.03A
G-BYFK	Cameron Printer-105 SS HAB	4522		4. 3.99	Flying Pictures Ltd *(Samsung Printers titles)*	Chilbolton	26. 5.03A
G-BYFL	Diamond HK 36 TTS	36623		5. 2.99	C.N.J.Squibb	RNAS Culdrose	23. 6.05
					tr Seahawk Gliding Club		
G-BYFM	Jodel DR.1050-M1 Sicile Record rep PFA 304-13237			26. 2.99	P.M.Standen & A.J.Roxburgh	Barton	5. 6.03P
	(Continental O-200-A)						
G-BYFN	Thruster T600N	9029-T600N-030		8. 2.99	J.S.Manning	(Albufeira, Portugal)	30. 6.01P
	(Rotax 503-2V)						
G-BYFP	Piper PA-28-181 Archer III	2843238	N4137N G-BYFP/N41270	5. 7.99	B.Badley	Andrewsfield	5. 7.05T

G-BYFR	Piper PA-32R-301 Saratoga IIHP	3246133	N4135P	13. 4.99	Buckleton Ltd	(Jersey)	8. 7.04T
			G-BYFR/N9515N				
G-BYFT	Pietenpol Aircamper	PFA 47-13057		22.12.98	M W Elliott	(Tamworth)	
G-BYFU	Lindstrand LBL-105B HAB	594		9. 3.99	Balloons Lindstrand France	Curcay Sur Dive, France	4. 3.02A
G-BYFV	TEAM mini-MAX 91	PFA 186-13431		5. 2.99	W.E.Gillham	Croft Farm, Darlington	16. 7.03P
G-BYFX	Colt 77A HAB	4547		4. 3.99	Flying Pictures Ltd *(Agfa titles)*	Chilbolton	26. 3.03A
G-BYFY	Avions Mudry CAP.10B	263	F-GKKD	9. 3.99	R.W.H.Cole	Spilsted Farm, Sedlescombe	AC
					t/a Cole Aviation *(Noted 11.01)*		
G-BYGA	Boeing 747-436	28855		15.12.98	British Airways plc *(Chelsea Rose t/s)*	Heathrow	13.12.04T
G-BYGB	Boeing 747-436	28856		17. 1.99	British Airways plc *(Colum t/s)*	Heathrow	16. 1.02T
G-BYGC	Boeing 747-436	25823		19. 1.99	British Airways plc *(Chelsea Rose t/s)*	Heathrow	23. 10.04T
G-BYGD	Boeing 747-436	28857		26. 1.99	British Airways plc *(Rendezvous t/s)*	Heathrow	23. 10.04T
G-BYGE	Boeing 747-436	28858		5. 2.99	British Airways plc	Heathrow	4. 2.05T
G-BYGF	Boeing 747-436	25824		17. 2.99	British Airways plc *(Chelsea Rose t/s)*	Heathrow	16. 2.05T
G-BYGG	Boeing 747-436	28859		29. 4.99	British Airways plc *(Rendezvous t/s)*	Heathrow	28. 4.05T
G-BYHC	Cameron Z-90 HAB	4555		16. 3.99	A.M. Holly t/a Exclusive Ballooning	Bristol	25. 3.02T
G-BYHE	Robinson R22 Beta	2023	N82128	14. 1.99	L Smith t/a Helicopter Services	Booker	24. 2.05T
			LV-VAB				
G-BYHG	Dornier 328-100	3098	D-CDAE	7. 4.99	Suckling Aviation (Cambridge) Ltd	Cambridge	6. 4.03T
			D-CDXZ		t/a Scot Airways		
G-BYHH	Piper PA-28-161 Warrior III	2842050	N4126Z	15. 6.99	Stapleford Flying Club Ltd	Stapleford	19. 6.05T
			G-BYHH/N9527N				
G-BYHI	Piper PA-28-161 Warrior II	28-8116084	SE-IDP	4. 1.99	Haimoss Ltd	Old Sarum	25. 2.05T
G-BYHJ	Piper PA-28R-201 Arrow	2844020	N41675	25. 2.00	Bflying Ltd	Bournemouth	10. 4.03T
			G-BYHJ/N41675		*(Op Bournemouth Flying Club)*		
G-BYHK	Piper PA-28-181 Archer II	2843240	N4128V	20. 5.99	T-Air Services Ltd	(Kirk Michael, Isle of Man)	23. 6.05T
			(G-BYHK)/N9519N				
G-BYHL	de Havilland DHC-1 Chipmunk 22	C1/0361	WG308	15. 3.99	M.R.& I.D.Higgins	Gamston	18. 6.03
G-BYHM	British Aerospace BAe 125 Srs.800B	258233	VP-BTM	12. 2.99	Corporate Aircraft Leasing Ltd	Jersey	24. 2.03
			VR-BTM/(VR-BQH)/F-WQCD/D-CAVW/G-5-770				
G-BYHN	Mainair Blade 912	1191-0399-7 & W994		9. 4.99	R.Stone	(Stoke-on-Trent)	16. 3.03P
G-BYHO	Mainair Blade 912	1197-0599-7 & W1000		16. 3.99	P.J.Morton	St.Michaels	22. 3.03P
G-BYHP	CEA DR.253B Regent	161	OO-CSK	29. 3.99	D.A.Hood	Sywell	25. 8.05T
G-BYHR	Pegasus Quantum 15-912	7518		6. 4.99	I.D.Chantler	Long Acre Farm, Sandy	26. 7.03P
G-BYHS	Mainair Blade 912	1187-0299-7 & W990		11. 3.99	D.A.Bolton	Barton	26. 4.03P
G-BYHT	Robin DR400-180R Remorqueur	811	HB-EUU	9. 4.99	R.C.Wilson tr Deeside Robin Group	Aboyne	1. 9.05
G-BYHU	Cameron N-105 HAB	4567		30. 4.99	Freeup Ltd *(Iveco Ford Truck titles)*	Bristol	19. 8.03A
G-BYHV	Raj Hamsa X'Air 582	361 & BMAA/HB/090		25. 3.99	S.N.J.Huxtable	(Highbridge)	30. 4.03P
G-BYHW*	Cameron A-160 HAB	2848	D-OWEH	25. 3.99	R H Etherington	Siena, Italy	4. 9.02A
					(Cancelled 21.5.02 as WFU)		
G-BYHX	Cameron A-250 HAB	4565		16. 4.99	Global Ballooning Ltd	Uckfield	12. 2.03T
G-BYHY	Cameron V-77 HAB	4493		22. 3.99	P Spellward	Bristol	28. 3.03A
G-BYHZ	Sky 160-24			13. 5.99	Skyride Balloons Ltd	King's Lynn	27. 5.03T
G-BYIA	Jabiru Jabiru SK	PFA 274-13436		10. 2.99	G.M.Geary	Morgansfield, Fishburn	11. 5.03P
	(Jabiru 2200A)						
G-BYIB	Rans S-6ES Coyote II	PFA 204-13387		26. 3.99	G A Clayton	(Chesterfield)	19. 9.03P
	(Rotax 582-48)						
G-BYIC	Cessna U.206G Turbo Stationair	U20605476	OY-NUA	27. 4.99	D.M.Penney	Shotton Colliery	29. 7.05
			N113RS/N3RS/N6398U				
G-BYID	Rans S-6ES Coyote II *(Tricycle u/c)*			11. 5.99	J.A.E.Bowen	Davidstow Moor	23.10.03P
	(Rotax 582-48)	0498.1218 & PFA 204-13348					
G-BYIE	Robinson R22 Beta-II	2933		22. 4.99	J.W.Ramsbottom t/a Jepar Rotorcraft	(Preston)	22. 5.05T
G-BYII	TEAM mini-MAX	PFA 186-11820		22. 1.99	J S R Moodie	Rovie Farm, Rogart	
	(Rotax 447)				*(Current status unknown)*		
G-BYIJ	CASA I-131E Jungmann	2110	E3B-514	16. 7.90	P.R.Teager & R.N.Crosland	Deanland	29. 5.03P
G-BYIK	Europa Aviation Europa	154 & PFA 247-12771		2. 2.99	P.M.Davis	Oxford	12. 9.03P
	(Rotax 912) (Monowheel u/c)				*(F/f 13.8.99)*		
G-BYIL	Cameron N-105 HAB	4591		29. 4.99	Oakfield Farm Products Ltd	Broadway	17. 6.03A
					(Oakfield Farm Products titles)		
G-BYIM	Jabiru Jabiru UL *(Jabiru 2200A)* PFA 274A-13397			22.12.98	W J Dale	Langar	21. 3.03P
G-BYIN	Rotary Air Force RAF 2000 GTX-SE			19. 1.99	J.R.Legge	(Rossendale)	8. 8.03P
		PFA G/13-1305					
G-BYIO	Colt 105A HAB	4601		30. 4.99	N.Charbonnier *(Lindt titles)*	Aosta, Italy	24. 1.03A
G-BYIP	Aerotek Pitts S-2A	2244	N109WA	23. 2.99	D.P.Heather-Hayes	Perth	10.10.05T
	(Lycoming AE1O-360-A1E)		TC-ECN				
G-BYIR	Aerotek Pitts S-1S Special	1-0063	N103WA	23. 2.99	Hampshire Aeroplane Co.Ltd	Sancreed	14. 9.02
	(Lycoming AE1O-360-B4A)		TC-ECP				
G-BYIS	Pegasus Quantum 15-912	7508		25. 2.99	A.J.Ridell	Knapthorpe Lodge, Caunton	18. 4.03P
G-BYIT	Robin DR500/200i President	0010		27. 1.99	P.R.Liddle	Rochester	23. 5.05
	(Registered as DR400/500)						
G-BYIU	Cameron V-90 HAB	4552		6. 4.99	H.Micketeit	Bielefeld, Germany	29. 3.01A
G-BYIV	Cameron PM-80 HAB *(Coca Cola bottle)*	4595		14. 5.99	A.Schneider	Borken, Germany	1. 4.03A
G-BYIW	Cameron PM-80 HAB *(Coca Cola bottle)*	4596		14. 5.99	A.Schneider	Borken, Germany	1. 4.03A
G-BYIX	Cameron PM-80 HAB *(Coca Cola bottle)*	4597		14. 5.99	A.Schneider	Borken, Germany	1. 4.03A
G-BYIY	Lindstrand LBL-105B	601		26. 3.99	J.H.Dobson	Reading	27. 3.03A
G-BYIZ	Pegasus Quantum 15-912	7504		8. 2.99	J.D.Gray	Eshott	28. 2.03P
G-BYJA	Rotary Air Force RAF 2000 GTX-SE			6. 4.99	B.Errington-Weddle	Henstridge	18. 7.02P
		PFA G/13-1297			*(Damaged rolling-over late Summer 2001)*		
G-BYJB	Mainair Blade 912	1192-0499-7 & W995		6. 4.99	J.H.Bradbury	Arclid Green, Sandbach	11. 4.03P
G-BYJC	Cameron N-90 HAB	4562		30. 4.99	D.E.Bentley Ltd	Sheffield	16. 6.01A
G-BYJD	Jabiru Jabiru UL	PFA 274-13376		16. 4.99	M.W.Knights	Hinddeston	21. 5.03P
	(Jabiru 2200A) (PFA prefix "274" indicates model SK: a model UL shold be "274A")						
G-BYJE	TEAM mini-MAX 91	PFA 186-12327		6. 4.99	A.W.Austin	(Cheltenham)	
G-BYJF	Thorp T.211	107	N2545C	20. 5.99	AD Aviation Ltd	Liverpool	25. 7.05

Reg	Type	C/n	Prev id	Date	Owner/Operator	Location	Date
G-BYJG	Lindstrand LBL 77A HAB	600		16. 4.99	Lindstrand Balloons Ltd	Oswestry	9. 5.03A
G-BYJH	Grob G.109B	6512	D-KFRI	19. 5.99	A.J.Buchanan	Parham Park	26. 6.05
G-BYJI	Europa Aviation Europa F0004 & PFA 247-13010		G-ODTI	19. 4.99	P S Jones	Wolverhampton	22. 7.02P
	(Rotax 912) *(Monowheel u/c)*			*(F/f 4.6.96)*			
G-BYJJ	Cameron C-80 HAB	4436	SX-MAX	20. 4.99	Proxim Franchising SRL	Milan, Italy	12. 1.03A
G-BYJK	Pegasus Quantum 15-912	7524		7. 5.99	B S Smy	East Fortune	16. 5.03P
G-BYJL	Aero Designs Pulsar	PFA 202-13311		20. 4.99	F.A.H.Ashmead	(Sway)	4. 7.03P
G-BYJM	Cyclone AX2000	7523		25. 5.99	A.R.Hood Knapthorpe Lodge, Caunton		20. 5.03P
	(Rotax 582-48)				tr Caunton Ax2000 Syndicate		
G-BYJN	Lindstrand LBL-105A HAB	605		30. 4.99	B.Meeson	Pwllheli	29. 4.00A
G-BYJO	Rans S-6ES Coyote II *(Tail-wheel u/c)*			4. 3.99	G.Ferguson	King's Lynn	9. 6.03P
	(Rotax 582-48) 0498.1217 & PFA 204-13338						
G-BYJP	Aerotek Pitts S-1S Special	1-0064	N105WA	16. 3.99	T.Riddle tr Eaglescott Pitts Group	Eaglescott	14. 9.02
	(Lycoming AE1O-360-B4A)		TC-ECR				
G-BYJR	Lindstrand LBL-77B HAB	608		30. 4.99	C.D.Duthy-James	Presteigne	21. 4.03A
G-BYJS	SOCATA TB-20 Trinidad	1875	F-OIGE	15. 1.99	J K Sharkey	Denham	9. 5.05
G-BYJT	Zenair CH.601HD Zodiac	PFA 162-13130		4. 5.99	J.D.T.Tannock	Nottingham	5. 3.03P
	(Rotax 912S)						
G-BYJU	Raj Hamsa X'Air 582	429 & BMAA/HB/098		6. 5.99	C.W.Payne	Croft Farm, Defford	20. 4.02P
G-BYJV	Cameron A-210 HAB	4612		4. 6.99	Societe Bombard SRL	Beaune, France	6.10.03A
G-BYJW*	Cameron Sphere 105SS HAB	4585		15. 6.99	Forbes Europe Inc	Far Hills, NJ, USA	24. 4.03A
					(Cancelled 14.11.02 by CAA)		
G-BYJX	Cameron C-70 HAB	4580		30. 4.99	B.Perona	Torino, Italy	24. 4.03A
G-BYJZ	Lindstrand LBL 105A HAB	609		27. 5.99	M.A..Webb	Chard	26. 7.02A
G-BYKA	Lindstrand LBL-69A HAB	612		7. 5.99	Aerial Promotions Ltd *(Vauxhall titles)*	Cannock	6.10.03A
G-BYKB	Rockwell Commander 114	14121	SE-GSM	18. 5.99	A.Walton	Little Staughton	27. 5.05P
			N4801W				
G-BYKC	Mainair Blade 912	1196-0599-7 & W999		7. 5.99	D.Gabott	Ince Blundell	23. 6.03P
	(Rotax 912-UL)						
G-BYKD	Mainair Blade 912	1198-0599-7 & W1001		7. 5.99	D.C.Boyle	(Chorley)	21. 6.03P
	(Rotax 912-UL)						
G-BYKE	Rans S-6ESA Coyote II	PFA 204-13327		22. 1.99	C.Townsend	Kemble	6. 3.03P
	(Tricycle u/c)			*(Rolled to starboard on take-off Enstone 17.3.02, struck runway, caught fire & destroyed)*			
G-BYKF	Enstrom F-28	F725	JA7684	19. 5.99	Battle Helicopters Ltd	(Battle)	22.12.02T
G-BYKG	Pietenpol Aircamper	PFA 47-12827		17. 3.99	K.B.Hodge *(Nearing completion 2000)*	(Mold)	
G-BYKI*	Cameron N-105 HAB	4635		4. 6.99	Flying Pictures Ltd	Navan, Co.Meath	29. 7.02A
					(Cancelled 19.3.02 by CAA)		
G-BYKJ	Westland Scout AH.Mk.1	F.9696	XV121	6. 8.99	B.H.Austen	Oaksey Park	29. 9.03P
	(Pod build no.F8-6043)				t/a Austen Associates		
G-BYKK	Robinson R44 Astro	0572		4. 3.99	Banner Helicopters Ltd	(Heywood)	18. 3.05T
G-BYKL	Piper PA-28-181 Archer II	28-8090162	HB-PFB	15. 7.99	S.Gwilliam & D.J.McConnachie	Biggin Hill	18. 7.05T
			N8129Y		tr Metropolitan Police Flying Club (Biggin Hill)		
G-BYKN	Piper PA-28-161 Warrior II	28-7916307	HB-PDO	22. 6.99	Oxford Aviation Services Ltd	Oxford	2. 9.05T
			N2838C/N9613N				
G-BYKO	Piper PA-28-161 Warrior II	28-8516063	HB-PKA	22. 6.99	Oxford Aviation Services Ltd	Gloucestershire	1. 8.05T
			F-GECN/N6920C				
G-BYKP	Piper PA-28R-201T Turbo Arrow IV	28R-7931029	HB-PDB	22. 6.99	Oxford Aviation Services Ltd	Oxford	10. 9.05T
			N3010G				
G-BYKR	Piper PA-28-161 Warrior II	2816061	HB-PLM	22. 6.99	Oxford Aviation Services Ltd	Oxford	30. 7.05T
G-BYKS	Leopoldoff L.6 Colibri	129	N10LC	19. 4.99	I.M.Callier	(Basingstoke)	
			F-BGIT/F-WGIT		*(On restoration 10.01)*		
G-BYKT	Pegasus Quantum 15-912	7529		28. 5.99	D.A.Bannister & N.J.Howarth	Deenethorpe	26. 5.03P
G-BYKU	BFC Quad City Challenger II	PFA 177A-13252		25. 5.99	K.W.Seedhouse	Walsall	
	(BFC-supplied kit as distinct from Quad City version)						
G-BYKW	Lindstrand LBL 77B HAB	620		22. 6.99	P-J.Fuseau	(Chanteloup, France)	28. 5.03A
G-BYKX	Cameron N-90 HAB	4657		10. 8.99	G.Davis *"Knowledgepool"*	Reading	23. 5.03A
G-BYKZ	Sky 140-24 HAB	147		25. 2.99	D.J.Head	Newbury	5. 8.03T
G-BYLA	Clutton-Tabenor FRED Srs.3	PFA 29-10775		11. 5.99	R.Holden-Rushworth	(Devizes)	
G-BYLB	de Havilland DH.82A Tiger Moth	83286	T5595	24. 5.99	P.W. Payne	(Kingston upon Thames)	
G-BYLC	Pegasus Quantum 15-912	7528		25. 6.99	T.Marriott	(Park Hall Farm, Derbys)	21. 8.03P
G-BYLD	Pietenpol Aircamper	PFA 47-13392		27. 4.99	S.Bryan	(Banbury)	
G-BYLE	Piper PA-38-112 Tomahawk II	38-82A0031	N91437	18. 6.99	Surrey & Kent Flying Club Ltd	Biggin Hill	6. 3.03T
G-BYLF	Zenair CH.601HDS Zodiac	PFA 162-13179		3. 6.99	G.Waters	(Swansea)	
G-BYLG	Robin HR200/120	B336		20. 7.99	Building and Commercial Ltd	Gloucestershire	1. 8.05T
G-BYLH	Robin HR200/120	B335		9. 7.99	Multiflight Ltd	Leeds-Bradford	19. 7.05T
G-BYLI	NOVA Vertex 22	14319		9. 4.99	M Hay *(New owner 1.03)*	(Dundee)	
G-BYLJ	Letov LK-2M Sluka	PFA 263-13464		9. 6.99	N.E.Stokes	Dunkeswell	
	(Rotax 447)				*(Noted 4.00)*		
G-BYLL	Sequoia Falco F.8L	PFA 100-10843		6.12.85	N.J.Langrick	Breighton	6. 3.03P
	(Lycoming O-320-A3C)						
G-BYLM	Piper PA-46-350P Malibu Mirage	4636217		30. 7.99	Polestar Holdings Ltd	Alderney	5. 8.05T
G-BYLN	Raj Hamsa X'Air 532	430 & BMAA/HB/096		7. 7.99	R.Gillespie & S.P.McGirr	(Killygordon, Co.Donegal)	
G-BYLO	Tipsy Nipper T.66 Srs.1	04	OO-NIA	27. 4.99	M.J.A.Trudgill	RAF Henlow	13. 5.03P
	(Built Avions Fairey SA)						
G-BYLP	Rand Robinson KR-2	PFA 129-11431		19. 4.99	C.S.Hales *(See G-BSTL)*	(Walsall)	
G-BYLR	Cessna 404 Titan	404-0046	OH-CDC	14. 6.99	Air Charter Scotland Ltd	Edinburgh	19. 6.03T
			SE-GZH/N5428G				
G-BYLS	Bede BD-4	PFA 37-11288		13.12.90	G.H.Bayliss	Shobdon	17. 6.03P
	(Lycoming O-320-E2F)						
G-BYLT	Raj Hamsa X'Air 582	411 & BMAA/HB/095		8. 6.99	T.W.Phipps & B.G.Simons Craysmarsh Farm, Melksham		26. 6.03P
G-BYLV	Thunder Ax8-105 S2 HAB	4061		6. 7.99	Wind Line SRL	Iesolo, Italy	18. 9.03A
G-BYLW	Lindstrand LBL 77A HAB	615		11. 6.99	Associazione Gran Premio Italiano	Perugia, Italy	10. 6.00A
G-BYLX	Lindstrand LBL 105A HAB	614		11. 6.99	Italiana Aeronavi	Cervignano, Italy	10. 6.03A
G-BYLY	Cameron V-77 HAB	3375	G-ULIA(2)	16. 7.97	R.Bayly *(See G-ULIA)*	Bristol	30. 6.03A

G-BYLZ	Rutan Cozy Mk.4	PFA 159-12464		21. 5.99	E.R.Allen	(Billingshurst)	AC
G-BYMA	British Aerospace Jetstream Srs.3202	840	(G-OESU)	28. 7.99	Air Kilroe Ltd *(Op Eastern Airways)*	Humberside	1. 9.03T
	OH-JAE/N840JX/C-GSCS/G-31-840/N332QK/G-31-840						
G-BYMB	Diamond Katana DA.20-C1	C0051		9. 7.99	S.C.Brown t/a Enstone Flying Club	Enstone	15. 5.03T
G-BYMC	Piper PA-38-112 Tomahawk II	38-82A0034	N91457	18. 6.99	B W Gomez	Coventry	10. 5.03T
					(Force landed nr Alsager, Staffs 23.11.01 due to engine failure)		
G-BYMD	Piper PA-38-112 Tomahawk II	38-82A0009	N91342	18. 6.99	Surrey & Kent Flying Club Ltd	Biggin Hill	19. 8.05T
G-BYME	Gardan GY-80 Horizon 180	207	F-BPAA	24. 5.99	Air Venturas Ltd	Bagby	12.11.05
G-BYMF	Pegasus Quantum 15-912	7540		9. 7.99	G.R.Stockdale	Rufforth	16. 7.01P
G-BYMG	Cameron A-210 HAB	4631		17. 9.99	P.Johnson t/a Cloud Nine Balloon Co	Consett	16. 5.03T
G-BYMH	Cessna 152	15284980	N6127P	15. 7.99	PJC (Leasing) Ltd	Stapleford	25. 7.03T
G-BYMI	Pegasus Quantum 15	7533		9. 7.99	N.C.Grayson	Rufforth	13. 7.03P
G-BYMJ	Cessna 152	15285564	N93865	16. 7.99	PJC (Leasing) Ltd	Stapleford	26.11.05T
G-BYMK	Dornier 328-100	3062	LN-ASK	9. 6.99	Suckling Aviation (Cambridge) Ltd	Cambridge	8. 6.04T
			D-CDXE		t/a Scot Airways		
G-BYML	Dornier 328-100	3069	D-CDUL	27. 7.99	Suckling Aviation (Cambridge) Ltd	Cambridge	14. 8.04T
			LN-ASL/D-CDXT(2)		t/a Scot Airways		
G-BYMM	Raj Hamsa X'Air 582	417 & BMAA/HB/093		29. 4.99	R.W.F Boarder	Field Farm, Oakley	8. 8.03P
G-BYMN	Rans S-6ESA Coyote II	PFA 204-13477		16. 6.99	R.L.Barker	Brock Farm, Billericay	31.10.03P
	(Rotax 582-48) (Tricycle u/c)						
G-BYMO	Campbell Cricket	PFA G/03-1266		16. 7.99	D.G.Hill	(Stockton-on-Tees)	7. 7.03P
G-BYMP	Campbell Cricket Mk 1	PFA G/03-1265		16. 6.99	J.J.Fitzgerald	(Newtownards, Co.Down)	16. 5.03P
G-BYMR	Raj Hamsa X'Air 582	432 & BMAA/HB/094		18. 6.99	W.M/McMinn	(Craigavon)	6.11.03P
G-BYMT	Pegasus Quantum 15-912	7549		16. 7.99	S.A.Owen	Latch Farm, Kirknewton	30. 7.03P
G-BYMU	Rans S-6ES Coyote II	PFA 204-13424		25. 6.99	I.R.Russell & G.Frogley	Swinford	24. 5.03P
	(Tricycle u/c)						
G-BYMV	Rans S-6ES Coyote II	PFA 204-13444		25. 6.99	G.A.Squires	(Wakefield)	25. 7.03P
G-BYMW	Boland 52-12 HAB	001		25. 6.99	C.Jones	Reading	
G-BYMX	Cameron A-105 HAB	4629		16. 7.99	H.Reis	Aachen, Germany	23.10.03A
G-BYMY	Cameron N-90 HAB	4653		19. 7.99	Cameron Balloons Ltd *(Cameron Balloons titles)*	Bristol	17. 8.03A
G-BYNA	Cessna F172H	F172-0626	OO-VDW	15. 1.99	Heliview Ltd	Blackbushe	15. 4.05T
	(Built Reims Aviation SA)		PH-VDW/(G-AWTH)/F-WLIT				
G-BYND	Pegasus Quantum 15	7546		16. 7.99	M.C.Kerr	Clench Common	14. 9.03P
	(Rotax 582-40)						
G-BYNE	Pilatus PC-6/B2-H4 Turbo Porter	631	HB-FLW	10. 8.99	D.M.Penny	Le Luc, Cennes, France	1.10.05
			C-FRAV/N631SA/N62148/HS-.../N62148/XW-PFC/XW-PDK/HB-FCR				
G-BYNF	North American NA-64 Yale I	64-2171	N55904	10. 1.00	R.S.Van Dijk	Duxford	
			3349 RCAF		*(Dismantled & stored 3.00 as "3349")*		
G-BYNH	Rotorway Executive 162F	6323		5. 7.99	R.C.Mackenzie	(Saffron Walden)	7. 7.00P
	(Rotorway RI 162F)						
G-BYNI	Rotorway Executive 90	5216		16. 7.99	M.Bunn	Fundenhall, Norfolk	14. 3.03P
	(Rotorway RI 162)						
G-BYNJ	Cameron N-77 HAB	4661		26. 7.99	G.Aimo *(Primagaz titles)*	Mondovi, Italy	24. 4.03A
G-BYNK	Robin HR200/160	338		28. 7.99	M.& K.A.Whittaker	(Henley-on-Thames)	30. 9.05T
G-BYNL	Jabiru Jabiru SK	PFA 274-13328		20. 7.99	R.C.Daykin	Tatenhill	10. 3.03P
G-BYNM	Mainair Blade 912	1204-0799-7 & W1007		20. 7.99	M.W.Holmes	(Ilkeston)	27. 7.03P
	(Rotax 912)						
G-BYNN	Cameron V-90 HAB	4643		16. 7.99	M.K.Grigson *"Cloud Nine"*	(Shoreham)	5. 6.03
G-BYNO	Pegasus Quantum 15-912	7556		5. 8.99	R.J.Newsham & G.J.Slater	Clench Common	19. 8.02P
G-BYNP	Rans S-6ES Coyote II	PFA 204-13414		22. 7.99	R.J. Lines	(Scunthorpe)	5. 6.03P
G-BYNR	Jabiru Jabiru UL	0129	EI-MAT	23. 7.99	E.Bentley	Morgansfield, Fishburn	26. 9.02P
	(Jabiru 2200A)				*(Left runway after landing Sandtoft 2.3.02 & extensively damaged)*		
G-BYNS	Jabiru Jabiru SK	PFA 274-13235		23. 7.99	D.K.Lawry *(Current status unknown)*	(Diss)	
G-BYNT	Raj Hamsa X'Air Victor 2	457 & BMAA/HB/107		20. 7.99	G.R.Wallis Lower Mountpleasant Farm, Chatteris		13.12.02P
G-BYNU	Cameron Thunder AX7-77 HAB	3520		29. 7.99	Aerial Promotions Ltd	Cannock	30. 7.02A
G-BYNV	Sky 105-24 HAB	165		11. 8.99	Par Rovelli Construzioni SRL	Mazzini, Italy	18. 5.03
G-BYNW	Cameron H-34 HAB	4666		27. 7.99	Flying Pictures Ltd *(Energis titles)*	Chilbolton	30. 7.02A
G-BYNX	Cameron RX-105 HAB	4656		26. 7.99	Cameron Balloons Ltd	London	1.11.00A
G-BYNY	Beech 76 Duchess	ME-247	N247ME	4. 8.99	Magenta Ltd	Exeter	17.10.05T
			OE-FES/N6635H				
G-BYOA	Slingsby T.67M-260 Firefly	2262		8. 6.99	Babcock Support Services Ltd	RAF Barkston Heath	17.10.05T
					t/a Babcock HCS *(Op JEFTS)*		
G-BYOB	Slingsby T.67M-260 Firefly	2263		8. 6.99	Babcock Support Services Ltd	RAF Church Fenton	6.10.05T
					t/a Babcock HCS *(Op JEFTS)*		
G-BYOD	Slingsby T.67C Firefly	2265		13. 6.00	TDR Aviation Ltd Enniskellen, Co.Fermanagh		9.12.04T
G-BYOF	Robin R2160I	337		29. 7.99	Lifeskills Ltd	(Bromsgrove)	20.10.05T
G-BYOG	Pegasus Quantum 15-912	7555		15. 9.99	M.D.Hinge	Old Sarum	1.11.03P
G-BYOH	Raj Hamsa X'Air 582	443 & BMAA/HB/101		23. 7.99	P.H.J.Kent	Davidstow Moor	23. 3.03P
G-BYOI	Sky 80-16 HAB	163		5. 8.99	I.S.& S.W.Watthews	Cark-in-Cartmel	21. 8.03
G-BYOJ	Raj Hamsa X'Air 582	458 & BMAA/HB/108		23. 7.99	H.M.Owen	(Llanelli)	3. 3.03P
G-BYOK	Cameron V-90 HAB	3726		9. 8.99	D.S.Wilson	Norwich	6. 4.03A
G-BYOM	Sikorsky S-76C	760464	G-IJCB	25. 8.99	Starspeed Ltd	Blackbushe	26. 3.03T
G-BYON	Mainair Blade	1199-0599-7 & W1002		4. 8.99	S.Mills & G.M.Hobman	(North Ferriby)	19.10.02P
	(Rotax 503-2V)						
G-BYOO	CFM Streak Shadow SA	K.270 & PFA 206-12806		6. 8.99	C.I.Chegwen	Otherton, Cannock	4. 4.03P
	(Rotax 912-UL)						
G-BYOR	Raj Hamsa X'Air 582	472 & BMAA/HB/117		11. 8.99	S.C.Scrowther	(Brentwood)	19. 7.03P
	(3-blade Ivoprop)						
G-BYOS	Mainair Blade 912	1209-0899-7 & W1012		6. 8.99	J.L.Guy	(Gargrave)	15. 8.03P
	(Rotax 912-UL)						
G-BYOT	Rans S-6ES Coyote II *(Tricycle u/c)*			29. 7.99	H.F.Blakeman	Arclid Green, Sandbach	6. 9.02P
	(Rotax 503)	0498.1221 & PFA 204-13363					
G-BYOU	Rans S-6ES Coyote II *(Tricycle u/c)*			1. 6.99	J.R.Bramley	(Lincoln)	20.10.03P
	(Rotax 582)	1298.1288 & PFA 204-13460					

G-BYOV	Pegasus Quantum 15-912	7554		17. 8.99	K.W.A.Ballinger	(Wokingham)	4. 9.03P
G-BYOW	Mainair Blade	1207-0899-7 & W1010		9. 8.99	M.Forsyth	(Kelso)	23. 3.03P
	(Rotax 582-2V)						
G-BYOX	Cameron Z-90 HAB	4672		31. 8.99	Virgin Airship & Balloon Co.Ltd	Telford	11. 6.03A
G-BYOY	Canadair T-33AN Silver Star 3	T33-231	N36TH	8. 2.00	K.K.Gerstorfer	North Weald	AC
	N333DV/N134AT/N10018/N134AT/RCAF 21231 (Noted 9.02 as "N36TH "in USAF c/s)						
G-BYOZ	Mainair Rapier	1208-0899-7 & W1011		12. 8.99	M.Morgan	Arclid Green, Sandbach	11. 9.03P
	(Rotax 503-2V)						
G-BYPA	Aérospatiale AS355F2 Twin Squirrel	5348	G-NWPI	20. 8.99	Anglia Aviation plc	(Ipswich)	28. 3.03T
			F-GMAO				
G-BYPB	Pegasus Quantum 15-912	7566		3. 9.99	S.Graham	Clench Common	13. 7.03P
G-BYPC	Lindstrand LBL AS2 Gas	634		17. 8.99	Lindstrand Balloons Ltd	Plano, Texas, USA	
					(Super 2 - Superpressure titles)		
G-BYPD	Cameron A-105 HAB	4680		6. 1.00	Headland Hotel Co Ltd	Newquay	10. 1.02A
G-BYPE	Gardan GY-80 Horizon 160	180	F-BNYD	10. 8.99	H.I.Smith & P.R.Hendry-Smith	Little Snoring	4.11.02
G-BYPF	Thruster T600N (Rotax 582UL)	9089-T600N-034		17. 8.99	C.J.Powell tr Canary Syndicate	(Pentre)	3.10.03P
G-BYPG	Thruster T600N (Rotax 582UL)	9089-T600N-035		17. 8.99	J.I.Greeshields tr G-BYPG Syndicate	Dunkeswell	22. 3.03P
G-BYPH	Thruster T600N (Rotax 582UL)	9089-T600N-036		17. 8.99	Pickup & Son Property Maintenance Ltd	(Markfield)	11. 5.03P
	(Officially regd with incorrect c/n as 9099-T600N-036)						
G-BYPJ	Pegasus Quantum 15-912	7565		17. 9.99	P.J.Manders	Great Bromley	26. 9.03P
G-BYPL	Pegasus Quantum 15-912	7558		9. 9.99	I.T.Carlse	(Fowlmere)	26. 9.03P
G-BYPM	Europa Aviation Europa XS	407 & PFA 247-13418		16.12.98	P.Mileham	(Saffron Walden)	
	(Rotax 912S) (Tri-gear u/c)						
G-BYPN	SOCATA MS.880B Rallye Club	2043	F-BTPN	23. 7.99	R.& T.C.Edwards	Sturgate	19. 4.03
G-BYPO	Raj Hamsa X'Air 582	439 & BMAA/HB/111		25. 8.99	A Costello & D W Willis	Tarn Farm, Cockerham	24. 7.02P
G-BYPP	Medway Rebel SS	168/146		25.10.99	J.L. Gowens	(Maidstone)	17. 3.01P
G-BYPR	Zenair CH.601HD Zodiac	PFA 162-12816		25. 8.99	D.Clark	Portmoak	11. 2.03P
	(Lycoming O-235)						
G-BYPT	Rans S-6ES Coyote II (Tricycle u/c)			27. 8.99	S. H.Revelle	Hardwicke, Hay-on-Wye	3.11.03P
	(Jabiru 2200) 0499.1316 & PFA 204-13508						
G-BYPU	Piper PA-32R-301 Saratoga II HP	3246150	N4160K	2.12.99	S.C.Tysoe	East Midlands	1.12.02T
			G-BYPU/N9518N				
G-BYPW	Raj Hamsa X'Air 582	441 & BMAA/HB/113		1. 9.99	A.D.Worrall & B.J.Ellis	Tarn Farm, Cockerham	22.12.03P
					tr G-BYPW		
G-BYPY	Ryan ST3-KR	1001	F-AZEV	5.10.99	P.B.Rice	Breighton	9. 4.03P
			N18926		(As "001")		
G-BYPZ	Rans S-6-116 Super 6 (Tricycle u/c)			14. 7.99	R.A.Blackbourn	Perth	19. 6.01P
	(Rotax 912-UL) 0299.1304 & PFA 204A-13448						
G-BYRA	British Aerospace Jetstream Srs.3202	845	OH-JAG	26.10.99	Air Kilroe Ltd	Humberside	21.11.05T
			N845JX/N845AE/G-31-845		(Op Eastern Airways)		
G-BYRC	Westland Wessex HC.Mk.2	WA539	XT671	23. 9.99	D.Brem-Wilson	Honey Crock Farm, Redhill	
G-BYRE*	Rans S-10 Sakota	PFA 194-11729		23. 7.91	R J & M B Trickey	(Ythanbank)	
					(Cancelled 8.5.99 by CAA) (80% complete 4.02)		
G-BYRF*	Cameron N-77 HAB	4692		20. 9.99	AAA Entertainments Ltd	Richmond, Surrey	15 .9.00A
					(Cancelled 10.12.02 by CAA)		
G-BYRG	Rans S-6ES Coyote II (Tricycle u/c)			9. 9.99	W.H.Mills	Haverfordwest	18. 2.03P
	(Rotax 582) 1298.1289 & PFA 204-13518						
	(Made forced landing in field Whitland 28.7.02: nose u/c broke off & aircraft overturned, damaging the left wing, tailfin, propeller and engine cowling)						
G-BYRH	Medway Hybred 44XLR (Rotax 503)	MR165/143		25.10.99	M.R.Holland	(Pontyclun)	16. 2.03P
G-BYRJ	Pegasus Quantum 15-912	7548		24. 9.99	D A Chamberlain	Long Marston	27 .9.03P
G-BYRK	Cameron V-42 HAB	4662		14. 7.99	Gone With The Wind Ltd	Twain-Harte, Ca, USA	13. 8.03A
G-BYRM	British Aerospace Jetstream Srs.3202	847	OH-JAF	16.12.99	Air Kilroe Ltd (Op Eastern Airways)	Humberside	18. 1.03T
			N847JX/N847AE/N332QN/G-31-847				
G-BYRO	Mainair Blade	1210-0899-7 & W1013		20. 8.99	P.W.F.Coleman Corn	Wood Farm, Adversane	13 10.03P
	(Rotax 582)						
G-BYRP	Mainair Blade 912	1075-1295-7 & W877		15. 9.99	M.P.Middleton	(Llandrindod Wells)	15. 8.03P
	(Rotax 912-UL) (C/n amended to c/n 1075-0396-7 & W877)						
G-BYRR	Mainair Blade 912	1211-0999-7 & W1015		17. 8.99	G.R.Sharples	(Harrow)	2 .6.03P
	(Rotax 912-UL) (C/n amended to 1222-0999-7 & W1015 by Mainair)						
G-BYRS	Rans S-6ES Coyote II (Tricycle u/c)			17. 9.99	R.Beniston	Rufforth	9. 6.03P
	(Rotax 582) 0998.1266 & PFA 204-13425						
G-BYRU	Pegasus Quantum 15-912	7574		24. 9.99	V.R.March tr The Sarum QTM912 Group	Old Sarum	27 .9.03P
G-BYRV	Raj Hamsa X'Air 582	387 & BMAA/HB/106		10. 9.99	J.A.Greenhalgh	(Worcester)	4.11.02P
G-BYRX	Westland Scout AH.Mk.1	F.9640	XT634	5.10.99	Historic Helicopters Ltd (As "XT634")	Thruxton	2.11.03P
G-BYRY	Slingsby T.67M-200 Firefly	2042	B-HZQ	28. 9.99	T.R.Pearson	Tibenham	21. 3.03T
			VR-HZQ/HKG-11		(As "HKG-11")		
G-BYRZ	Lindstrand LBL 77M HAB	643		28. 9.99	Challenge Transatlantique	Metz, France	5.12.00A
	(Reported to be rebuild of G-BXDX)				"Conseil Régional de Lorraine"		
G-BYSA	Europa Aviation Europa XS	360 & PFA 247-13199		23. 8.99	B.Allsop	Bentley Farm, Cold Ashton	18. 4.03P
	(Rotax 912S) (Monowheel u/c)				(F/f 17.12.99)		
G-BYSE	Agusta-Bell 206B JetRanger II	8553	G-BFND	3.11.81	Alspath Properties Ltd	(Stratford-upon-Avon)	18. 9.05T
G-BYSF	Jabiru Jabiru UL	PFA 274A-13356		5.10.99	S.J.Marshall	Sittles Farm, Alrewas	7.11.03P
	(Jabiru 2200A)						
G-BYSG	Robin HR200/120B	339		22.11.99	Anglian Flight Centres Ltd	Earls Colne	22.12.05T
G-BYSI	PZL-110 Koliber 160A	04990081	SP-WGI	21. 1.00	J.& D.F.Evans	Gamston	15. 3.03
G-BYS.I	de Havilland DHC-1 Chipmunk 22	C1/0021	SE-BON	12.10.99	Silver Victory BVB	Antwerp-Deurne, Belgium	17. 8.03T
			WB569		(As "WB569")		
G-BYSK	Cameron A-275 HAB	4699		23. 2.00	Balloon School (International) Ltd	Petworth	17. 7.03T
					(British School of Ballooning titles)		
G-BYSL*	Cameron O-56 HAB	1269		10. 4.86	S.M.M.Askey (Cancelled 19.9.01 as WFU)	Tring	22. 8.96A
G-BYSM	Cameron A-210 HAB	4698		12. 4.00	Balloon School (International) Ltd	Bath	29. 7.03P
					(Op Heritage Balloons) "Bath Heritage"		
G-BYSN	Rans S-6ES Coyote II (Tricycle u/c)			19.10.99	A.L.& A.R.Roberts	(Coningsby)	13. 6.03P
	(Rotax 582) 1098.1270 & PFA 204-13459						

G-BYSP	Piper PA-28-181 Archer II	28-8590047	D-EAUL N6909D	12.10.99	Aerohire Ltd	Defford	21.11.05T
G-BYSR	Pegasus Quantum 15-912	7560		7. 3.00	J.Lane & P.R.Thomas	Clench Common	18. 4.03P
G-BYSS	Medway Rebel SS (Two Stroke International (2SI))	167/145		25.10.99	C.R.Stevens	(Ashford)	18 .6.03P
G-BYSV	Cameron N-120 HAB	4704		15.10.99	Cameron Balloons Ltd *(Cameron Balloons titles)* Bristol		25. 1.03T
G-BYSW	Enstrom 280FX Shark	2026	I-LUST N88CV	19. 9.00	D A Marks	(Bedford)	2.11.03
G-BYSX	Pegasus Quantum 15-912	7586		23.11.99	R.H.Braithwaite tr RAF Microlight Flying Association	RAF Wyton	14.11.03P
G-BYSY	Raj Hamsa X'Air 582	448 & BMAA/HB/109		21.10.99	J.M.Davidson	(Tewkesbury)	2. 5.03P
G-BYTA	Kolb Twinstar Mk.3 (Rotax 582)	PFA 205-13240		2. 9.99	R.E.Gray	(Oxted)	5. 7.03P
G-BYTB	SOCATA TB-20 Trinidad	2002	F-OILE	18. 5.00	Ottoman Empire Ltd	Biggin Hill	7 6.03P
G-BYTC	Pegasus Quantum Q2 Sport 15-912	7571		25.10.99	J.Hood	Eshott	25.10.02P
G-BYTD	Robinson R22 Beta-II	3003		25.10.99	Ace Air Flights Ltd	(Blackrock, Co.Dublin)	6.11.05T
G-BYTE	Robinson R22 Beta	1250		18. 4.90	Patriot Aviation Ltd	Cranfield	17. 6.02T
G-BYTG	Glaser-Dirks DG-400	4-211	D-KBBP	18.11.99	P.R.Williams & B.Sebestik	(Brackley)	23. 2.03
G-BYTH	Airbus Industrie A320-231	0429	C-GTDM	21. 1.00	MyTravel Airways Ltd	Manchester	7.11.05T
	G-BYTH/D-ASSR/(D-AUKT)/G-BYTH/EI-TLE/D-AORX/N429RX/F-WWIZ						
G-BYTI	Piper PA-24-250 Comanche	24-3489	D-ELOP N8297P/N10F	9.11.99	P.Marsden tr G-BYTI Syndicate	Netherthorpe	27. 3.03
G-BYTJ	Cameron Concept-80 HAB	4703		19.11.99	M.White *"Rapido"*	Cirencester	23. 8.03A
G-BYTK	Jabiru Jabiru UL	PFA 274A-13465		8.11.99	K.A.Fagan & S.R.Pike	Booker	28. 3.03P
G-BYTL	Mainair Blade 912	1224-0999-7 & W1017		19.10.99	M.E.Keefe	St. Michaels	17.10.03P
G-BYTM	Dyn'Aéro MCR-01 Ban-bi	PFA 301-13440		1.10.99	I.Lang	Gloucestershire	4. 9.03P
G-BYTN	de Havilland DH.82A Tiger Moth	3993	7014M N6720	18.11.99	B.D.Hughes *(On rebuild 10.01)*	(Rotary Farm, Hatch)	AC
G-BYTO	Aérospatiale/Alenia ATR 72-212	472	G-OILA F-WWEJ	17.11.99	Cityflyer Express Ltd	Gatwick	27. 3.05T
G-BYTP	Aérospatiale/Alenia ATR 72-212	473	G-OILB F-WWEG	30. 4.99	Cityflyer Express Ltd *(Colum t/s)*	Gatwick	29. 5.05T
G-BYTR	Raj Hamsa X'Air 582	460 & BMAA/HB/105		5.10.99	A.P.Roberts & R.Dunn	Dunkeswell	28. 8.03P
G-BYTS	Montgomerie Bensen B.8MR (Rotax 912)	MGM-2		22. 9.99	M.G.Mee	Carlisle	18. 7.03P
G-BYTT	Raj Hamsa X'Air 582	402 & BMAA/HB/100		22. 9.99	J.L.Pearson	(Roundwood, Co.Wicklow)	25. 7.03P
G-BYTU	Mainair Blade 912 (Rotax 912)	1225-1099-7 & W1018		26.11.99	L.Chesworth	(Malpas)	25. 7.03P
G-BYTV	Jabiru Jabiru UL	PFA 274A-13454		3.11.99	E.Bentley	Morgansfield, Fishburn	9. 4.03P
G-BYTW	Cameron O-90 HAB	4747		11. 4.00	Sade Balloons Ltd	London EC2	30.11.02A
G-BYTX	Whittaker MW6-S Fat Boy Flyer (Rotax 532)	PFA 164-12819		2.12.99	J.K.Ewing	(Poole)	20. 8.03P
G-BYTY	Dornier 328-100	3104	D-CDXJ 5N-BRI	2.12.99	Sucking Airways (Cambridge) Ltd t/a Scot Airways	Cambridge	8.12.03T
G-BYTZ	Raj Hamsa X'Air 582	486 & BMAA/HB/120		26.10.99	K.C.Millar	(Dromara, Co.Down)	24. 3.05P
G-BYUA	Grob G.115E Tutor	82086E	D-EUKB	22. 7.99	VT Aerospace Ltd *(Op Cambridge/London UAS)*	RAF Wyton	5. 8.05T
G-BYUB	Grob G.115E Tutor	82087E		22. 7.99	VT Aerospace Ltd *(Op University of Wales UAS)*	RAF St.Athan	5. 8.05T
G-BYUC	Grob G.115E Tutor	82088E		22. 7.99	VT Aerospace Ltd *(Op CFS/East Midlands UAS)*	RAF Cranwell	5. 8.05T
G-BYUD	Grob G.115E Tutor	82089E		22. 7.99	VT Aerospace Ltd *(Op Northrumbrian UAS)*	RAF Leeming	5. 8.05T
G-BYUE	Grob G.115E Tutor	82090E		12. 8.99	VT Aerospace Ltd *(Op CFS/East Midlands UAS)*	RAF Cranwell	30. 8.05T
G-BYUF	Grob G.115E Tutor	82091E		12. 8.99	VT Aerospace Ltd *(Op Cambridge/London UAS)*	RAF Wyton	30. 8.05T
G-BYUG	Grob G.115E Tutor	82092E		22. 9.99	VT Aerospace Ltd *(Op Universities of Glasgow & Strathclyde AS)*	Glasgow	27 .9.05T
G-BYUH	Grob G.115E Tutor	82093E		22. 9.99	VT Aerospace Ltd *(Op Bristol UAS)*	RAF Colerne	27 .9.05T
G-BYUI	Grob G.115E Tutor	82094E		24. 9.99	VT Aerospace Ltd *(Op Liverpool/Manchester UAS) (Code "UI")*	RAF Woodvale	27 .9.05T
G-BYUJ	Grob G.115E Tutor	82095E		24. 9.99	VT Aerospace Ltd *(Op Northrumbrian UAS)*	RAF Leeming	27 .9.05T
G-BYUK	Grob G.115E Tutor	82096E		18.10.99	VT Aerospace Ltd *(Op Cambridge/London UAS)*	RAF Wyton	28.10.05T
G-BYUL	Grob G.115E Tutor	82097E		18.10.99	VT Aerospace Ltd *(Op Cambridge/London UAS)*	RAF Wyton	28.10.05T
G-BYUM	Grob G.115E Tutor	82098E		18.10.99	VT Aerospace Ltd *(Op Southampton UAS)*	Boscombe Down	28.10.02T
G-BYUN	Grob G.115E Tutor	82099E		18.10.99	VT Aerospace Ltd *(Op Cambridge/London UAS)*	RAF Wyton	28.10.05T
G-BYUO	Grob G.115E Tutor	82100E		19.11.99	VT Aerospace Ltd *(Op Cambridge/London UAS)*	RAF Wyton	28.11.05T
G-BYUP	Grob G.115E Tutor	82101E		19.11.99	VT Aerospace Ltd *(Op Oxford UAS)*	RAF Benson	28.11.05T
G-BYUR	Grob G.115E Tutor	82102E		19.11.99	VT Aerospace Ltd *(Op Aberdeen, Dundee & St.Andrews UAS)*	RAF Leuchars	28.11.05T
G-BYUS	Grob G.115E Tutor	82103E		19.11.99	VT Aerospace Ltd *(Op Oxford UAS)*	RAF Benson	28.11.05T
G-BYUT	Grob G.115E Tutor	82104E		7.12.99	VT Aerospace Ltd *(Op Oxford UAS)*	RAF Benson	14.12.05T
G-BYUU	Grob G.115E Tutor	82105E		7.12.99	VT Aerospace Ltd *(Op Universities of Glasgow & Strathclyde AS)*	Glasgow	14.12.05T
G-BYUV	Grob G.115E Tutor	82106E		7.12.99	VT Aerospace Ltd *(Op Oxford UAS)*	RAF Benson	14.12.05T
G-BYUW	Grob G.115E Tutor	82107E		7.12.99	VT Aerospace Ltd *(Op Aberdeen, Dundee & St.Andrews UAS)*	RAF Leuchars	14.12.05T

G-BYUX	Grob G.115E Tutor	82108E	18. 1.00	VT Aerospace Ltd	RAF Woodvale	16. 12.05T
				(Op Liverpool/Manchester UAS) (Code "UX")		
G-BYUY	Grob G.115E Tutor	82109E	18. 1.00	VT Aerospace Ltd	RAF Leuchars	31. 1.03T
				(Op Aberdeen, Dundee & St.Andrews UAS)		
G-BYUZ	Grob G.115E Tutor	82110E	18. 1.00	VT Aerospace Ltd	RAF Woodvale	31. 1.03T
				(Op Liverpool/Manchester UAS) (Code "UZ")		
G-BYVA	Grob G.115E Tutor	82111E	18. 1.00	VT Aerospace Ltd	RAF Cranwell	31. 1.03T
				(Op CFS/East Midlands UAS)		
G-BYVB	Grob G.115E Tutor	82112E	17. 2.00	VT Aerospace Ltd	Glasgow	28. 2.03T
				(Op Universities of Glasgow & Strathclyde AS)		
G-BYVC	Grob G.115E Tutor	82113E	17. 2.00	VT Aerospace Ltd *(Op Bristol UAS)*	RAF Colerne	2. 3.03T
G-BYVD	Grob G.115E Tutor	82114E	17. 2.00	VT Aerospace Ltd	RAF Wyton	2. 3.03T
				(Op Cambridge/London UAS)		
G-BYVE	Grob G.115E Tutor	82115E	17. 2.00	VT Aerospace Ltd	Boscombe Down	2. 4.03T
				(Op Southampton UAS)		
G-BYVF	Grob G.115E Tutor	82116E	22. 2.00	VT Aerospace Ltd	Glasgow	28. 2.03T
				(Op Universities of Glasgow & Strathclyde AS)		
G-BYVG	Grob G.115E Tutor	82117E	22. 3.00	VT Aerospace Ltd	RAF Church Fenton	2. 4.03T
				(Op Yorkshire UAS)		
G-BYVH	Grob G.115E Tutor	82118E	22. 3.00	VT Aerospace Ltd	RAF Leuchars	4. 4.03T
				(Op Aberdeen, Dundee & St.Andrews UAS)		
G-BYVI	Grob G.115E Tutor	82119E	22. 3.00	VT Aerospace Ltd	RAF Leuchars	4. 4.03T
				(Op Aberdeen, Dundee & St.Andrews UAS)		
G-BYVJ	Grob G.115E Tutor	82120E	14. 4.00	VT Aerospace Ltd	RAF Wyton	25. 4.03T
				(Op Cambridge/London UAS)		
G-BYVK	Grob G.115E Tutor	82121E	14. 4.00	VT Aerospace Ltd	RAF Leuchars	25. 4.03T
				(Op Aberdeen, Dundee & St.Andrews UAS)		
G-BYVL	Grob G.115E Tutor	82122E	14. 4.00	VT Aerospace Ltd	RAF St.Athan	26. 4.03T
				(Op University of Wales UAS)		
G-BYVM	Grob G.115E Tutor	82123E	14. 4.00	VT Aerospace Ltd	RAF Leuchars	26. 4.03T
				(Op Aberdeen, Dundee & St.Andrews UAS)		
G-BYVN	Grob G.115E Tutor	82124E	18. 5.00	VT Aerospace Ltd *(Op Bristol UAS)*	RAF Colerne	31. 5.03T
G-BYVO	Grob G.115E Tutor	82125E	18. 5.00	VT Aerospace Ltd *(Op Birmingham UAS)*	RAF Cosford	31. 5.03T
G-BYVP	Grob G.115E Tutor	82126E	18. 5.00	VT Aerospace Ltd *(Op Oxford UAS)*	RAF Benson	31. 5.03T
G-BYVR	Grob G.115E Tutor	82127E	18. 5.00	VT Aerospace Ltd *(Op Oxford UAS)*	RAF Benson	31. 5.03T
G-BYVS	Grob G.115E Tutor	82128E	20. 6.00	VT Aerospace Ltd	RAF Wyton	29. 6.03T
				(Op Cambridge/London UAS)		
G-BYVT	Grob G.115E Tutor	82129E	20. 6.00	VT Aerospace Ltd	RAF Wyton	29. 6.03T
				(Op Cambridge/London UAS)		
G-BYVU	Grob G.115E Tutor	82130E	20. 6.00	VT Aerospace Ltd *(Op Oxford UAS)*	RAF Benson	29. 6.03T
G-BYVV	Grob G.115E Tutor	82131E	20. 6.00	VT Aerospace Ltd	RAF Church Fenton	29 .6.03T
				(Op Yorkshire UAS)		
G-BYVW	Grob G.115E Tutor	82132E	21. 7.00	VT Aerospace Ltd	RAF Church Fenton	6. 8.03T
				(Op Yorkshire UAS)		
G-BYVX	Grob G.115E Tutor	82133E	21. 7.00	VT Aerospace Ltd	RAF Church Fenton	6. 8.03T
				(Op Yorkshire UAS)		
G-BYVY	Grob G.115E Tutor	82134E	21. 7.00	VT Aerospace Ltd	RAF Church Fenton	6. 8.03T
				(Op Yorkshire UAS)		
G-BYVZ	Grob G.115E Tutor	82135E	21. 7.00	VT Aerospace Ltd	RAF Church Fenton	6. 8.03T
				(Op Yorkshire UAS)		
G-BYWA	Grob G.115E Tutor	82136E	21. 8.00	VT Aerospace Ltd	RAF St.Athan	30 .8.03T
				(Op University of Wales UAS)		
G-BYWB	Grob G.115E Tutor	82137E	21. 8.00	VT Aerospace Ltd *(Op Bristol UAS)*	RAF Colerne	30 .8.03T
G-BYWC	Grob G.115E Tutor	82138E	18. 9.00	VT Aerospace Ltd *(Op Bristol UAS)*	RAF Colerne	27 .9.03T
G-BYWD	Grob G.115E Tutor	82139E	18. 9.00	VT Aerospace Ltd	RAF Woodvale	27. 9.03T
				(Op Liverpool/Manchester UAS) (Code "WD")		
G-BYWE	Grob G.115E Tutor	82140E	18. 9.00	VT Aerospace Ltd *(Op Bristol UAS)*	RAF Colerne	27 .9.03T
G-BYWF	Grob G.115E Tutor	82141E	18. 9.00	VT Aerospace Ltd	RAF Cranwell	27 .9.03T
				(Op CFS/East Midlands UAS)		
G-BYWG	Grob G.115E Tutor	82142E	13.10.00	VT Aerospace Ltd *(Op Bristol UAS)*	RAF Colerne	29.10.03T
G-BYWH	Grob G.115E Tutor	82143E	13.10.00	VT Aerospace Ltd	RAF Leeming	29.10.03T
				(Op Northrumbrian UAS)		
G-BYWI	Grob G.115E Tutor	82144E	13.10.00	VT Aerospace Ltd *(Op Bristol UAS)*	RAF Colerne	29.10.03T
G-BYWJ	Grob G.115E Tutor	82145E	13.10.00	VT Aerospace Ltd	RAF Woodvale	29.10.03T
				(Op Liverpool/Manchester UAS) (Code "WJ")		
G-BYWK	Grob G.115E Tutor	82146E	17.11.00	VT Aerospace Ltd	RAF Cranwell	28.11.03T
				(Op CFS/East Midlands UAS)		
G-BYWL	Grob G.115E Tutor	82147E	17.11.00	VT Aerospace Ltd	RAF Woodvale	28.11.03T
				(Op Liverpool/Manchester UAS) (Code "WL")		
G-BYWM	Grob G.115E Tutor	82148E	17.11.00	VT Aerospace Ltd	RAF Cranwell	28.11.03T
				(Op CFS/East Midlands UAS)		
G-BYWN	Grob G.115E Tutor	82149E	17.11.00	VT Aerospace Ltd	RAF Woodvale	28.11.03T
				(Op Liverpool/Manchester UAS) (Code "WN")		
G-BYWO	Grob G.115E Tutor	82150E	7.12.00	VT Aerospace Ltd *(Op Birmingham UAS)*	RAF Cosford	14. 1.04T
G-BYWP	Grob G.115E Tutor	82151E	7.12.00	VT Aerospace Ltd	RAF Church Fenton	14. 1.04T
				(Op Yorkshire UAS)		
G-BYWR	Grob G.115E Tutor	82127E	18. 5.00	VT Aerospace Ltd	RAF Wyton	31. 5.03T
				(Op Cambridge/London UAS)		
G-BYWS	Grob G.115E Tutor	82153E	7.12.00	VT Aerospace Ltd	RAF Leeming	16. 1.04T
				(Op Northrumbrian UAS)		
G-BYWT	Grob G.115E Tutor	82154E	12.12.00	VT Aerospace Ltd	RAF Leeming	16. 1.04T
				(Op Northrumbrian UAS)		
G-BYWU	Grob G.115E Tutor	82155E	19. 1.01	VT Aerospace Ltd	RAF Wyton	28. 1.04T
				(Op Cambridge/London UAS)		

Reg	Type	C/n	Prev id	Date	Owner/Operator	Location	Date
G-BYWV	Grob G.115E Tutor	82156E		19. 1.01	VT Aerospace Ltd *(Op Birmingham UAS)*	RAF Cosford	28. 1.04T
G-BYWW	Grob G.115E Tutor	82157E		19. 1.01	VT Aerospace Ltd	RAF Cranwell	28. 1.04T
					(Op CFS/East Midlands UAS)		
G-BYWX	Grob G.115E Tutor	82158E		14. 2.01	VT Aerospace Ltd	RAF Wyton	25. 2.04T
					(Op Cambridge/London UAS)		
G-BYWY	Grob G.115E Tutor	82159E		14. 2.01	VT Aerospace Ltd	RAF Cranwell	25. 2.04T
					(Op CFS/East Midlands UAS)		
G-BYWZ	Grob G.115E Tutor	82160E		14. 2.01	VT Aerospace Ltd	RAF Cranwell	4. 3.04T
					(Op CFS/East Midlands UAS) (Code "WZ")		
G-BYXA	Grob G.115E Tutor	82161E		14. 2.01	VT Aerospace Ltd	RAF Woodvale	4. 3.04T
					(Op Liverpool/Manchester UAS) (Code "XA")		
G-BYXB	Grob G.115E Tutor	82162E		19. 3.01	VT Aerospace Ltd	Boscombe Down	1. 4.04T
					(Op Southampton UAS)		
G-BYXC	Grob G.115E Tutor	82163E		19. 3.01	VT Aerospace Ltd	RAF Cranwell	1. 4.04T
					(Op CFS/East Midlands UAS)		
G-BYXD	Grob G.115E Tutor	82164E		19. 3.01	VT Aerospace Ltd	RAF Cranwell	1. 4.04T
					(Op CFS/East Midlands UAS)		
G-BYXE	Grob G.115E Tutor	82165E		19. 3.01	VT Aerospace Ltd	RAF Church Fenton	1. 4.04T
					(Op Yorkshire UAS)		
G-BYXF	Grob G.115E Tutor	82166E		12. 4.01	VT Aerospace Ltd *(Op Birmingham UAS)*	RAF Cosford	25. 4.04T
G-BYXG	Grob G.115E Tutor	82167E		12. 4.01	VT Aerospace Ltd *(Op Birmingham UAS)*	RAF Cosford	25. 4.04T
G-BYXH	Grob G.115E Tutor	82168E		12. 4.01	VT Aerospace Ltd	RAF Wyton	29. 4.04T
					(Op Cambridge/London UAS)		
G-BYXI	Grob G.115E Tutor	82169E		12. 4.01	VT Aerospace Ltd	RAF Woodvale	29. 4.04T
					(Op Liverpool/Manchester UAS)		
G-BYXJ	Grob G.115E Tutor	82170E		16. 5.01	VT Aerospace Ltd	Boscombe Down	28. 5.04T
					(Op Southampton UAS)		
G-BYXK	Grob G.115E Tutor	82171E		16. 5.01	VT Aerospace Ltd	RAF St.Athan	28. 5.04T
					(Op University of Wales UAS)		
G-BYXL	Grob G.115E Tutor	82172E		16. 5.01	VT Aerospace Ltd *(Op Birmingham UAS)*	RAF Cosford	28. 5.04T
G-BYXM	Grob G.115E Tutor	82173E		16. 5.01	VT Aerospace Ltd	Boscombe Down	28. 5.04T
					(Op Southampton UAS)		
G-BYXN	Grob G.115E Tutor	82174E		8. 6.01	VT Aerospace Ltd	Boscombe Down	11. 6.04T
					(Op Southampton UAS)		
G-BYXO	Grob G.115E Tutor	82175E		8. 6.01	VT Aerospace Ltd *(Op Birmingham UAS)*	RAF Cosford	11. 6.04T
G-BYXP	Grob G.115E Tutor	82176E		8. 6.01	VT Aerospace Ltd	RAF Wyton	11. 6.04T
					(Op Cambridge/London UAS)		
G-BYXR	Grob G.115E Tutor	82177E		8. 6.01	VT Aerospace Ltd *(Op Oxford UAS)*	RAF Benson	11. 6.04T
G-BYXS	Grob G.115E Tutor	82178E		18. 7.01	VT Aerospace Ltd *(Op Oxford UAS)*	RAF Benson	29. 7.04T
G-BYXT	Grob G.115E Tutor	82179E		18. 7.01	VT Aerospace Ltd	RAF Cranwell	29. 7.04T
					(Op CFS/East Midlands UAS)		
G-BYXU	Piper PA-28-161 Cherokee Warrior II	28-7716097	EI-BXU	8. 1.99	F.P.McGovern & F.O'Sullivan	Waterford, Co.Waterford	25. 4.03
			G-BNUP/N2282Q				
G-BYXV	Medway EclipseR	162/140		25.10.99	K.A.Christie	(Laurencekirk)	25. 4.03P
	(Jabiru) (C/n not confirmed)						
G-BYXW	Medway EclipseR	166/147		25.10.99	T.D.Walker	Plaistows Farm, St Albans	22. 5.02P
	(Rotax 912S) (Officially registered as c/n 166/144)						
G-BYXX	Grob G.115E Tutor	82180E		18. 7.01	VT Aerospace Ltd	RAF Woodvale	29. 7.04T
					(Op Liverpool/Manchester UAS)		
G-BYXY	Grob G.115E Tutor	82181E		18. 7.01	VT Aerospace Ltd	RAF Leeming	29. 7.04T
					(Op Northrumbrian UAS)		
G-BYXZ	Grob G.115E Tutor	82182E		15. 8.01	VT Aerospace Ltd *(Op CFS)*	RAF Cranwell	17. 9.04T
G-BYYA	Grob G.115E Tutor	82183E		15. 8.01	VT Aerospace Ltd *(Op CFS)*	RAF Cranwell	23. 9.04T
G-BYYB	Grob G.115E Tutor	82184E		15. 8.01	VT Aerospace Ltd *(Op CFS)*	RAF Cranwell	17. 9.04T
G-BYYC	Hapi Cygnet SF-2A	PFA 182-12311		25.11.99	C.D.Hughes & G.H.Smith	Shenstone	7. 5.03P
G-BYYD	Cameron A-250 HAB	4712		31. 3.00	C & J.M.Bailey	Bristol	3. 7.03T
G-BYYE	Lindstrand LBL 77A HAB	151		25.11.99	D.J.Cook	Norwich	25. 6.02A
G-BYYF	Boeing 737-229C	21738	OO-SDR	11. 1.00	European Aviation Air Charter Ltd	Bournemouth	28. 2.04T
G-BYYG	Slingsby T.67C Firefly	2101	PH-SGI	30.11.99	B Dixon & S E Marples	Newcastle	12. 1.03T
G-BYYI	British Aerospace Jetstream Srs.3107	620	VH-JSW	1. 3.00	Vale Aviation Ltd	Southampton	
			G-31-620				
G-BYYJ	Lindstrand LBL 25A Cloudhopper HAB	651		10.12.99	A.M.Barton	Coulsdon	21. 8.03A
G-BYYK	Boeing 737-229C	20916	OO-SDK	11. 1.00	European Aviation Air Charter Ltd	Bournemouth	AC
					(Stored as "OO-SDK" 12.02)		
G-BYYL	Jabiru Jabiru UL	PFA 274A-13480		10.12.99	C.Jackson	Ince Blundell	13. 5.03P
	(Jabiru 2200A)						
G-BYYM	Raj Hamsa X'Air 582	476 & BMAA/HB/119		21.10.99	D.J.McCall & B.Pilling	Dunkeswell	1. 8.03P
G-BYYN	Pegasus Quantum 15-912	7601		6. 1.00	J.A.Robinson	Tarn Farm, Cockerham	14. 6.03P
G-BYYO	Piper PA-28R-201 Arrow II	2837061	(N182ND)	11. 2.00	Stapleford Flying Club Ltd	Stapleford	26. 4.03T
			N9249C/G-BYYO/N9249C				
G-BYYP	Pegasus Quantum 15	7603		11. 2.00	D.A.Linsey-Bloom	Kingston Seymour	16. 2.03P
	(Rotax 582-40)						
G-BYYR	Raj Hamsa X'Air 582	453 & BMAA/HB/115		23.12.99	T D Bawden	Weston Zoyland	
G-BYYT	Jabiru Jabiru UL	PFA 274A-13452		18.11.99	T.D.Saveker	Bodmin	12. 5.03P
G-BYYW	de Havilland DHC-1 Chipmunk T.20	57	CS-DAR	22 .2.00	R.Farrer	(Bedford)	
	(Built OGMA)		1367 Portuguese AF		*(Stored 2000)*		
G-BYYX	TEAM mini-MAX 91	PFA 186-13410		6. 1.00	P.L.Turner	(Darlington)	3. 4.03P
G-BYYY	Pegasus Quantum 15-912	7564		8.12.99	C.J.Finnigan	Knapthorpe Lodge, Caunton	30.12.02P
G-BYYZ	Staaken Z-21A Flitzer	PFA 223-13324		12.11.99	A.E.Morris	Fairoaks	27. 6.03P
G-BYZA	Aérospatiale AS355F2 Twin Squirrel	5518	JA6784	20.12.99	MMAir Ltd	(Saffron Walden)	17. 4.03T
			F-OHNK				
G-BYZD	Tri-R Kis Cruiser	PFA 302-13156		22.11.99	R.T.Clegg	Netherthorpe	23. 5.03P
G-BYZE	Aérospatiale AS350B2 Ecureuil	2773	F-OGVR	8. 2.00	V.H.L.Ellis	Booker	14. 3.03T
G-BYZF	Raj Hamsa X'Air <u>Victor 1</u>	461 & BMAA/HB/110		7. 1.00	R P Davies	(Harrogate)	

Reg	Type	C/n	Prev id	Date	Owner	Location	Date
G-BYZG	Cameron A-275 HAB	4706		23. 2.00	Horizon Ballooning Ltd *(Horizon titles)*	Alton	24. 4.03T
G-BYZJ	Boeing 737-3Q8	24962	G-COLE PP-VOX	11. 1.00	British Midland Airways Ltd *(Star Alliance c/s)*	East Midlands	20.11.04T
G-BYZL	Cameron GP-65 HAB	4494		6. 4.00	P.Thibo	(Junglinster, Luxemburg)	15. 7.03A
G-BYZM	Piper PA-28-161 Warrior II	28-8116317	HB-PNK N8436A	4. 2.00	Goodair Leasing Ltd	Biggin Hill	11. 5.03T
G-BYZO	Rans S-6ES Coyote II *(Tricycle u/c)* (Rotax 582) 1298.1287 & PFA 204-13560			14. 1.00	A.J.Boulton *(Crashed on landing Blackpool 4.8.02)*	Roddidge, Fradley	28. 5.03P
G-BYZP	Robinson R22 Beta-II	3018		9.12.99	Wallis & Son Ltd	Cambridge	22.12.02T
G-BYZR	III Sky Arrow 650TC	C001	D-ENGF I-TREI	24. 1.00	G.H.Jackson & R.Moncrieff	Egginton, Derby	12. 4.03P
G-BYZS	Jabiru Jabiru UL-450 (Jabiru 2200A)	PFA 274A-13489		25. 1.00	N.Fielding	Ince Blundell	31. 5.03P
G-BYZT	Nova Vertex 26	13345		21. 1.00	M Hay *(New owner 1.03)*	(Dundee)	
G-BYZU	Pegasus Quantum 15 (Rotax 582-40)	7613		15. 2.00	N I Clifton	East Fortune	16. 2.03P
G-BYZV	Sky 90-24 HAB	174		15. 8.00	P.Farmer	Wadhurst	19. 1.01
G-BYZW	Raj Hamsa X'Air 582	499 & BMAA/HB/129		19. 1.00	H.C.Lowther	Kirkbride	24 .6.03P
G-BYZX	Cameron R-90 HAB	4751		31. 3.00	D.K.Hempleman-Adams *"Britannic Challenge"*	Corsham	5. 9.03A
G-BYZY	Pietenpol Aircamper	PFA 47-12190		2.12.99	D.N.Hanchet	White Waltham	
G-BYZZ	Robinson R22 Beta-II	3000		1.12.99	Astra Helicopters Ltd	Bristol	3. 2.03T

G-BZAA - G-BZZZ

Reg	Type	C/n	Prev id	Date	Owner	Location	Date
G-BZAA	Mainair Blade 912 1142-0198-7 & W945 (Rotax 462) *(C/n amended to 1142-1299-7 & W945 by Mainair)*			22.11.99	R.Locke	(Newark)	19. 9.03P
G-BZAB	Mainair Rapier (Rotax 503) 1228-1299-7 & W1021			23.12.99	B.J.Mould	Mill Farm, Shifnal	7.1.03P
G-BZAD	Cessna 152	15279563	N303MA N714ZN	22. 3.00	Cristal Air Ltd	Shoreham	6.11.04T
G-BZAE	Cessna 152	15281300	N49480	22. 3.00	Jaxx Landing Ltd	Swansea	4 .5.03T
G-BZAF	Raj Hamsa X'Air 582	503 & BMAA/HB/130		18. 1.00	Y.A.Evans	Rufforth	5.10.03P
G-BZAG	Lindstrand LBL 105A HAB	542		29..2.00	A.M.Figiel	High Wycombe	19. 4.03A
G-BZAH	Cessna 208B Caravan I	208B0811	N5196U tr Army Parachute Association	28. 2.00	G Burton	AAC Netheravon	13. 4.03A
G-BZAI	Pegasus Quantum 15	7614		9. 2.00	D.Paget	Dunkeswell	9. 5.03P
G-BZAJ	PZL-110 Koliber 160A	04990082	SP-WGK	10. 2.00	PZL International Aviation Marketing & Sales plc	North Weald	16. 7.03T
G-BZAK	Raj Hamsa X'Air 582	477 & BMAA/HB/114		20. 1.00	R.J.Ripley	Field Farm, Oakley	5.11.02P
G-BZAL	Mainair Blade 912 1205-0799-7 & W1008 (Rotax 912-UL)			27. 1.00	K.Worthington	Tarn Farm, Cockerham	11. 5.03P
G-BZAM	Europa Aviation Europa 265 & PFA 247-12969 (Rotax 912) *(Monowheel u/c)*			6.12.99	D.Corbett *(F/f 7.1.01)*	Shobdon	21. 4.03P
G-BZAO	Rans S-12XL (Rotax 582)	PFA 307-13394		1. 2.00	M.L.Robinson	Kirkbride	AC
G-BZAP	Jabiru Jabiru UL-450	PFA 274A-13479		13.12.99	S.Derwin	Morgansfield, Fishburn	26. 6.03P
G-BZAR	Denney Kitfox Model 4-1200 Speedster (Rotax 912UL)	PFA 172B-12529	G-LEZJ	17. 2.00	C.E.Brookes Little Battleflats Farm, Ellistown, Coalvill *"Ol Red"*		30. 8.03P
G-BZAS	Isaacs Fury II (CAM100)	PFA 11-10837		10. 2.00	H.A.Brunt & H.Frick *(As "K5673") "Spirit of Dunsfold"*	Bournemouth	4. 7.03P
G-BZAT	British Aerospace Avro 146-RJ100	E3320	G-6-320	18.11.97	Cityflyer Express Ltd *(Waves of the City t/s)*	Birmingham	8. 1.04T
G-BZAU	British Aerospace Avro 146-RJ100	E3328		25. 4.98	Cityflyer Express Ltd *(Colum t/s)*	Birmingham	11. 6.04T
G-BZAV	British Aerospace Avro 146-RJ100	E3331		19. 5.98	Cityflyer Express Ltd	Birmingham	23. 7.04T
G-BZAW	British Aerospace Avro 146-RJ100	E3354		11. 6.99	Cityflyer Express Ltd	Birmingham	15. 7.05T
G-BZAX	British Aerospace Avro 146-RJ100	E3356		9. 7.99	Cityflyer Express Ltd	Manchester	16. 8.05T
G-BZAY	British Aerospace Avro 146-RJ100	E3368		15. 2.00	Cityflyer Express Ltd	Manchester	27. 3.03T
G-BZAZ	British Aerospace Avro 146-RJ100	E3369		15. 2.00	Cityflyer Express Ltd	Manchester	13. 4.03T
G-BZBC	Rans S-6ES Coyote II *(Tricycle u/c)* (Rotax 582) 0499.1314 & PFA 204-13525			2. 2.00	A.J.Baldwin	(Ripley)	16. 3.03P
G-BZBE	Cameron A-210 HAB	4708		9. 5.00	Dragon Balloon Company Ltd	(Hope Valley)	16. 2.03T
G-BZBF	Cessna 172M (Lycoming O-360)	17262258	N126SA G-BZBF/9H-ACV/N12785	20.12.99	L.W.Scattergood	Welshpool	9. 8.03T
G-BZBH	Thunder Ax7-65 Bolt HAB	173		28.11.78	R.B. & G.Craik *"Serendipity II"*	Northampton	19. 4.03A
G-BZBI	Cameron V-77 HAB	4740		4. 4.00	C.& A.I.Gibson *"Flying Colours"*	Stockport	1. 6.03A
G-BZBJ	Lindstrand LBL-77A HAB	646		29. 2.00	G.T.Restell	(Folkestone)	24. 8.02A
G-BZBL	Lindstrand LBL-120A HAB	676		23. 2.00	Flying Pictures Ltd *(betinternet.com titles)*	Chilbolton	17. 4.02A
G-BZBM	Cameron A-315 HAB	4741		7. 4.00	Listers of Coventry (Motors) Ltd	Alcester, Warks	30.4.02T
G-BZBN	Thunder AX9-120 S2	4786		21. 2.00	K Willie	Maldegem, Belgium	25.9.03A
G-BZBO	Stoddard-Hamilton Glasair III	3032		21. 2.00	M B Hamlett	Lagny le Sec, France	
G-BZBP	Raj Hamsa X'Air 582	470 & BMAA/HB/131		29. 2.00	K.Angel	Stoke, Kent	16.6.03P
G-BZBR	Pegasus Quantum 15-912	7631		26. 5.00	E.Lewis	Weston Zoyland	28. 9.03P
G-BZBS	Piper PA-28-161 Warrior III	2842080	N4180H G-BZBS/N9529N	10. 5.00	S.J.Skilton t/a Aviation Rentals *(Op Solent Flight Training)*	Southampton	9 .5.03T
G-BZBT	Cameron Hopper H-34 HAB	4730		18. 5.00	British Telecommunications plc	Thatcham	10.4.03A
G-BZBU	Robinson R22	0131	OH-HLB SE-HOH	23. 5.00	J.N.A.Cawoood	(Skipton)	28. 6.03T
G-BZBW	Rotorway Executive 162F (Rotorway RI 162F)	6415		23. 2.00	M Gardiner	(Crewkerne)	AC
G-BZBX	Rans S-6ES Coyote II *(Tricycle u/c)* PFA 204-13501			26. 1.00	R.Johnstone	Otherton, Cannock	20. 5.03P
G-BZBZ	Jodel D.9 Bébé *(Volkswagen 1600)* 519 *(Built Etienne de Schrevel, Gent 1970-77)*		OO-48	29. 2.00	S Marom Whitehall Farm, Benington *(Noted 8.01)*		
G-BZDA	Piper PA-28-161 Warrior III	2842087	N41814 G-BZDA/N41814	29. 6.00	S.J.Skilton t/a Aviation Rentals	Bournemouth	29. 6.03T
G-BZDB	Thruster T600T (Rotax 582)	0030-T600T-041		7. 3.00	M R Jones *"Snoopy"* Wing Farm, Longbridge Deverill *(Crashed 1.6.02 & on rebuild 2.03)*		12.3.03P

G-BZDC	Mainair Blade	1232-0100-7 & W1025			13. 3.00	E.J.Wells & P.J.Smith	Over Farm, Gloucester	14. 3.03P
	(Rotax 462)					*(Severely damaged landing Popham 5.5.02 - repair)*		
G-BZDD	Mainair Blade 912	1238-0200-7 & W1031			21. 1.00	T.Williams tr Barton Blade Group	Barton	14. 2.03P
G-BZDE	Lindstrand LBL 210A HAB	665			6. 3.00	Toucan Travel Ltd *(Toucan Travel titles)*	Basingstoke	24. 3.03T
G-BZDF	CFM Streak Shadow SA	K.241 & PFA 206-12609			7. 3.00	J.W.Beckett	(Bromsgrove)	15. 6.01P
	(Rotax 582)							
G-BZDI	Aero L-39C Albatros	031822	ES-ZLB		7. 6.00	M.Gainza & E.Gavazzi	North Weald	1. 7.03P
			Sov AF					
G-BZDJ	Cameron Z-105 HAB	4832			27. 6.00	BWS Security Systems Ltd	Bath	17. 6.03A
	(Carries incorrect ident tab as "N-105")					*(BWS Security Systems titles)*		
G-BZDK	Raj Hamsa X'Air 582	447 & BMAA/HB/124			8. 2.00	B.Park	Truro	27.11.03P
G-BZDL	Pegasus Quantum 15-912	7629			18. 4.00	D.M.Holman	(Northwich)	27. 5.03P
G-BZDM	Stoddard-Hamilton GlaStar	PFA 295-13283			13. 3.00	F.G.Miskelly	(London SW6)	23. 7.03P
G-BZDN	Cameron N-105 HAB	2840	D-OABB		26. 4.00	J.D.& K.Griffiths	Bingham	12.3.03T
			D-Saxonia(2)					
G-BZDP	Scottish Aviation.Bulldog Srs.120/121	BH120/244	XX551		31. 3.00	D.M.Squires *(As "XX551/E")*	Wellesbourne Mountford	8. 7.04
G-BZDR	Tri-R Kis	9403			8. 3.00	T.J.Johnson *(Noted 2002)*	Old Buckenham	
G-BZDS	Pegasus Quantum 15-912	7633			17. 4.00	J.M.Hardstaff	Rufforth	17. 4.03P
G-BZDT	Maule MXT-7-180 Star Rocket	14099C			11. 8.00	Strongcrew Ltd	(Tiverton)	23 .8.03
G-BZDU	de Havilland DHC-1 Chipmunk 22	C1/0714	WP833		31. 3.00	M.R.Clark	Newcastle upon Tyne	6. 7.03
G-BZDV	Westland SA.314C Gazelle HT.Mk.2	1150	3D-HXL		31. 3.00	MW Helicopters Ltd	Stapleford	AC
			G-BZDV/XW884			*(Noted 9.02)*		
G-BZDW	Westland SA.341G Gazelle HT.Mk.3	1906	3D-HVW		31. 3.00	MW Helicopters Ltd	Stapleford	10.11.03P
			G-BZDW/ZB626			*(Made heavy "run-on" landing Hadleigh 26.11.02: turned over & badly damaged)*		
G-BZDX	Cameron Colt Sugarbox-90 SS HAB	4814			17. 5.00	Stratos Ballooning GmbH & Co KG		
							Ennigerloh, Germany	7. 6.02A
G-BZDY	Cameron Colt Sugarbox-90 SS HAB	4815			22. 5.00	Stratos Ballooning GmbH & Co KG		
							Ennigerloh, Germany	8. 4.03A
G-BZDZ	Jabiru Jabiru SP	232	ZU-BVB		14. 5.01	R.M.Whiteside	Shoreham	18.8.03P
	(Jabiru 2200A)							
G-BZEA	Cessna A152	A1520824	N7606L		13. 3.00	Sky Leisure Aviation (Charters) Ltd	Redhill	23. 1.04T
G-BZEB	Cessna 152	15282772	N89532		31. 1.00	Sky Leisure Aviation (Charters) Ltd	Shoreham	24. 9.03T
G-BZEC	Cessna 152	15284475	N4655M		21. 1.00	Sky Leisure Aviation (Charters) Ltd	Redhill	14. 8.05T
G-BZED	Pegasus Quantum 15-912	7600			17. 3.00	M.P.Wimsey	(Louth)	18. 4.03P
G-BZEE	Agusta-Bell 206B JetRanger II	8554	G-OJCB		22 .2.00	Yateley Helicopters Ltd	Blackbushe	18.10.03T
G-BZEG	Mainair Blade	1239-0200-7 & W1032			3. 3.00	Mainair Microlight School Ltd	Ince Blundell	20. 3.03P
	(Rotax 912-UL)							
G-BZEH	Piper PA-28-235 Cherokee B	28-10838	9M-ARW		31. 3.00	A.D.Wood	Spanhoe	3. 5.04
			RP-C704/PI-C704/N9182W					
G-BZEI	Agusta A109E Power	11056			8. 6.00	Stolkin Helicopters Ltd	(London WC2)	11. 6.03T
G-BZEJ	Raj Hamsa X'Air 582	500 & BMAA/HB/134			31. 3.00	P.J.Perry tr X'Air Flying Group	Otherton, Cannock	19.9.03P
G-BZEK	Cameron C-70 HAB	4860			30. 5.00	Ballooning 50 Degrees Nord	Fouhren, Luxembourg	28. 5.02A
G-BZEL	Mainair Blade	1245-0300-7 & W1038			27. 3.00	M.W.Bush	(Ilfracombe)	17. 4.03P
	(Rotax 582)							
G-BZEM	Glaser-Dirks DG-800B	8-194-B116	BGA 4887		8. 5.00	I.M.Stromberg	Rufforth	19.12.05
			G-BZEM					
G-BZEN	Jabiru Jabiru UL-450	PFA 274-13272			4. 4.00	B.W.Stockil	Bagby	29. 5.03P
G-BZEP	Scottish Aviation Bulldog Srs.120/121	BH120/257	XX561		4. 4.00	I.D.McClelland *(As "XX561/7")*	Biggin Hill	25. 5.05T
G-BZER	Raj Hamsa X'Air BMW R100	526 & BMAA/HB/133			22. 3.00	N.P.Lloyd & H.Lloyd-Hughes	(Wrexham)	
G-BZES	Rotorway Executive 90	6191	G-LUFF		25. 4.00	Southern Helicopters Ltd	Street Farm, Takeley	
						(Noted 2.03)		
G-BZET	Robin HR200/120B	345	F-GTZG		9. 5.00	Anglian Flight Centres Ltd	Earls Colne	21. 5.03T
G-BZEU	Raj Hamsa X'Air 582	518 & BMAA/HB/140			20. 4.00	M.Bundy	Lower Mountpleasant Farm, Chatteris	25. 9.01P
G-BZEV	Vahdat Semicopter 1 Gyroplane	002			10.10.00	M.E.Vahdat	(Uxbridge)	
G-BZEW	Rans S-6ES Coyote II *(Tricycle u/c)*				5. 4.00	J.E.Gattrell & A.R.Trace	Sittles Farm, Alrewas	9. 9.03P
	(Rotax 582) 0998.1268.0199.ES & PFA 204-13450							
G-BZEX	Raj Hamsa X'Air BMW R100	530 & BMAA/HB/135			5. 4.00	J.M.McCullough & R.T.Henry	(Castlewellan)	
G-BZEY	Cameron N-90 HAB	4829			15. 5.00	The Ballooning Business Ltd	Northampton	15. 5.03T
						(Wrangler titles)		
G-BZEZ	CFM Streak Shadow DD	PFA 161-13503			1. 2.00	G.J.Pearce	Southwater, Sussex	7.11.02P
G-BZFB	Robin R2112A Alpha	175	EI-BIU		7. 4.00	M.R.Brown	Bidford	26. 6.03
G-BZFC	Pegasus Quantum 15 (Rotax 582)	7640			14. 4.00	G.Brown	East Fortune	2. 7.03P
G-BZFD	Cameron N-90 HAB	2725	OO-BFD		24. 5.00	David Hathaway Transport Ltd *(Noted 2002)*	Bristol	
G-BZFF	Raj Hamsa X'Air 582	521 & BMAA/HB/137			6. 4.00	A.L.H.Seed	Tarn Farm, Cockerham	12. 6.03P
						tr G-BZFF Flying Group		
G-BZFG	Sky 105 HAB	4842			27. 4.00	Virgin Airship & Balloon Co Ltd *(Benadryl titles)*	Telford	28. 4.03P
G-BZFH	Pegasus Quantum 15-912	7660			15. 5.00	J.S.Hamilton t/a Kent Scout Microlights	(Edenbridge)	17. 5.03P
G-BZFI	Jabiru Jabiru UL	PFA 274A-13497			27. 3.00	A.W.J.Findlay tr Group Family	Sywell	2. 4.03P
G-BZFJ	Westland SA.314C Gazelle HT.2	1098	XW861		9. 5.00	European Marine Ltd *(As "XW861/52")*	Goodwood	23. 6.03P
	(Pod no WA107) (If p/i correct c/n is 1102 but reported c/n is thought to be 1096 which corresponds to G-BBHV while c/n 1098 translates to G-BBHW)							
G-BZFK	TEAM mini-MAX	PFA 186-12060			17. 4.00	H.P.Brooks	Deanland	1. 9.03P
	(Rotax 447 or 377?)							
G-BZFN	Scottish Aviation Bulldog Srs.120/121	BH120/325	XX667		18. 4.00	Thomas Aviation Ltd *(As "XX667/16")*	Ashbourne	7.10.04T
G-BZFO	Mainair Blade	1235-0100-7 & W1028			29. 3.00	J.E.Walendowski	Crosland Moor	14. 5.03P
	(Rotax 503)							
G-BZFP	de Havilland DHC-6-310 Twin Otter	696	C-GGNF		11. 8.00	Loganair Ltd	Glasgow	13. 8.032T
			N712PV/N696WJ/F-ODUH/TR-LZN/C-GKIQ *"Chatham Historic Dockyard"*					
G-BZFR	Extra EA.300/L	203			26. 6.00	Powerhunt Ltd	Biggin Hill	17. 7.03T
	(Official c/n outside normal EA300L c/n batch at present: possibly ex D-EDGE with published c/n 03?)							
G-BZFS	Mainair Blade 912	1243-0300-7 & W1036			23. 3.00	S.P.Stone & F.A.Stephens	Baxby Manor, Husthwaite	12. 4.03P
G-BZFT	Murphy Rebel	PFA 232-13224			7. 4.00	N.A.Evans	Branscombe	1. 7.03P
G-BZFU	Lindstrand LBL HS-110 HA Airship	671			25. 4.00	PNB Entreprenad AB	Malmo, Sweden	11. 1.03A
G-BZFV	Zenair CH.601UL Zodiac	PFA 162A-13547			14. 4.00	T.R.Sinclair & T.Clyde	Lamb Holm Farm, Orkney	18. 1.03P
	(Rotax 912S)							

G-BZGA	de Havilland DHC-1 Chipmunk 22	C1/0608	WK585	31. 3.00	Propshop Ltd *(As "WK585")*		Duxford	30. 4.04T
G-BZGB	de Havilland DHC-1 Chipmunk 22	C1/0905	WZ872	31. 3.00	Chipmunk Aviation Ltd		Newcastle	6. 7.03
G-BZGC	Aérospatiale AS355F1 Twin Squirrel	5077	G-CCAO	26. 3.99	McAlpine Helicopters Ltd *(Police c/s)*		Warton	21.11.05T
			G-SETA/G-NEAS/G-CMMM/G-BNBJ/C-GLKH					
G-BZGD	Piper PA-18-150 Super Cub	18-8109049	N90943	15. 5.00	M.G.& S.J.White t/a Proline Aviation		Compton Abbas	4. 7.03T
G-BZGE	Medway EclipseR	159/139		6. 5.99	J.A.McGill		Rochester	30. 6.02P
	(Jabiru 2200A) (Believed to contain original sailwing of G-MZGE)							
G-BZGF	Rans S-6ES Coyote II			25. 4.00	D.F.Castle		London Colney	13. 7.03P
		0899.1334 & PFA 204-13594		*(Bounced on landing London Colney 22.7.01: damaged fuselage & prop)*				
G-BZGH	Reims/Cessna F172N Skyhawk II	F17201789	EI-BGH	1.12.98	D.Behan tr Golf Hotel Group		(Dublin)	4. 9.05
G-BZGI	Ultramagic M-145 HAB	145/12		9. 6.00	European Balloon Co Ltd		Great Missenden	13. 7.03T
G-BZGJ	Thunder AX10-180 S2 HAB	3956	LN-CBT	8. 5.00	M.Wady t/a Merlin Balloons		Hamstreet	8. 5.03T
G-BZGK	North American OV-10B Bronco	338-17	Luftwaffe 9932	9. 6.00	Invicta Aviation Ltd		Duxford	AC
			D-9561/Bu 158308		*(Op Aircraft Restoration Co) (As "99+32")*			
G-BZGL	North American OV-10B Bronco	338-11	Luftwaffe 9926	9. 6.00	Invicta Aviation Ltd		Duxford	AC
			D-9555/Bu 158302		*(Op Aircraft Restoration Co) (As "99+26")*			
G-BZGM	Mainair Blade 912	1247-0400-7 & W1040		14. 4.00	D.Young		(Alford)	1. 5.03P
G-BZGN	Raj Hamsa X'Air 582	445 & BMAA/HB/128		3. 5.00	C.S.Warr & P.A.Pilkington		North Coates	27.10.03P
	(Kit no. conflicts with G-HITM)							
G-BZGO	Robinson R44 Astro	0757		14. 4.00	P.Durkin		Blackpool	14. 5.03T
G-BZGP	Thruster T600N	0400-T600N-043		25. 4.00	M.L.Smith	Ginge Farm, Wantage		29. 8.03P
	(Rotax 582)							
G-BZGR	Rans S-6ES Coyote II *(Tricycle u/c)*			3. 5.00	J.M.Benton		(Hadzor, Worcs)	23. 7.03P
G-BZGS	*(Jabiru 2200)* 0999.1338.ES & PFA 204-13595							
G-BZGS	Mainair Blade 912	1242-0300-7 & W1035		10. 5.00	S.C.Reeve		Ashbourne	1.11.03P
	(Rotax 912)							
G-BZGT	Jabiru Jabiru UL-450	PFA 274A-13539		4. 5.00	P.H.Ronfel *(Noted 7.02)*		Crosland Moor	
G-BZGU	Raj Hamsa X'Air 582	512 & BMAA/HB/138		4. 5.00	C.Kiernan	(Mostrim, Co.Longford)		8.10.03P
G-BZGV	Lindstrand LBL 77A HAB	695		9. 5.00	J.H.Dryden		Okehampton	9. 8.03A
G-BZGW	Mainair Blade	1246-0400-7 & W1039		5. 5.00	C.S.M.Hallam		Barton	18 12.02P
	(Rotax 503)							
G-BZGX	Raj Hamsa X'Air Z.202	400 & BMAA/HB/099		2. 6.00	A.Crowe	(Ballyclare, Co.Antrim)		
				(Under construction 8.01)				
G-BZGY	Dyn'Aéro CR100C	21	F-TGCI	7. 6.00	D.Hayes	Spilsted Farm, Sedlescombe		13. 2.03P
G-BZGZ	Pegasus Quantum 15-912	7674		7. 6.00	W.H.J.Knowles		Weston Zoyland	25. 9.03P
G-BZHA	Boeing 767-336ER	29230	N60668	22. 5.98	British Airways plc *(Wings t/s)*		Heathrow	21. 5.04T
G-BZHB	Boeing 767-336ER	29231		30. 5.98	British Airways plc *(Delftblue Daybreak t/s)*		Heathrow	29. 5.04T
G-BZHC	Boeing 767-336ER	29232		29. 6.98	British Airways plc *(Waves & Cranes t/s)*		Heathrow	28. 6.04T
G-BZHE	Cessna 152	15281303	D-EAOC	20. 4.00	Two Seven Aviation Ltd		Denham	22. 6.03T
			N49484					
G-BZHF	Cessna 152	15283986	D-EMJA	20. 4.00	Two Seven Aviation Ltd		Earls Colne	11. 7.03T
			N4858H					
G-BZHG	Tecnam P92-EM Echo	PFA 318-13606		24. 5.00	M.& J Turner	Lower Mountpleasant Farm, Chatteris		2.12.02P
	(Jabiru 2200A)							
G-BZHI	Enstrom F-28A-UK	281	G-BPOZ	14.12.99	Tindon Ltd		Litle Snoring	20.6.05
			N246Q					
G-BZHJ	Raj Hamsa X'Air 582	482 & BMAA/HB/126		10. 5.00	T Harrison-Smith		Stoke, Kent	23.11.03P
G-BZHK	Piper PA-28-181 Archer III	2843347	N41647	14. 7.00	Meldform Metals Ltd	Top Farm, Croydon, Royston		13. 7.03T
			N9519N					
G-BZHL	Noorduyn AT-16 Harvard IIB	14A-1158	FT118	6. 6.00	R.H.Cooper & S.Swallow		Hemswell	
	(Built Noorduyn, Canada)		43-12859		*(Stored 1.02)*			
	(Officially quoted FT118 matches as above rather with quoted USAAF serial '43-12959')							
G-BZHN	Pegasus Quantum 15-912	7677		20. 6.00	P.L.Cummings t/a Eaglescott Microlights		Eaglescott	14. 6.03P
G-BZHO	Pegasus Quantum 15	7658		19. 5.00	N.D.Meer		Roddige, Fradley	15. 5.03P
	(Rotax 582)							
G-BZHP	Quad City Challenger II			11. 5.00	F.Payne	Plaistows Farm, St Albans		
	(Rotax 582) CH2-0995-CW-1398 & PFA 177-13153			*(CW denotes "clipwing" though a/c has standard wing configuration)*				
G-BZHR	Jabiru Jabiru UL-450	PFA 274A-13493		16. 5.00	G.W.Rowbotham		(Loughborough)	6. 8.03P
G-BZHS	Europa Aviation Europa	207 & PFA 247-12865		16. 5.00	P.Waugh		(Llangollen)	
	(Rotax) (Monowheel u/c)							
G-BZHT	Piper PA-18A-150 Super Cub	18-5886	ZK-BTF	25. 5.00	The Furness Gliding Club Proprietary		Walney	18.12.04
					t/a Lakes Gliding Club			
G-BZHU	Wag-Aero CUBy Sport Trainer	AACA/351	ZK-MPH	25. 5.00	P.J.Lawless tr Teddy Boys Flying Club		Gloucestershire	13. 6.03P
G-BZHV	Piper PA-28-181 Archer III	2843382	N41848	17.10.00	Dorset Aircraft Leasing Ltd		Bournemouth	19.10.03T
			G-BZHV/N41848					
G-BZHW	Piper PA-28-181 Archer III	2843409	N4184D	16. 2.01	Delta Kilo Services LLP		(Crawley)	22. 2.04T
			G-BZHW/N4184D					
G-BZHX	Thunder AX11-250 S2 HAB	4880		21. 6.00	T.H.Wilson *"Slim Your Bin"*		Diss	21. 8.03T
G-BZHY	Mainair Blade 912	1250-0500-7 & W1043		7. 6.00	M.Morris	Tarn Farm, Cockerham		29. 5.03P
G-BZIA	Raj Hamsa X'Air HK700	475 & BMAA/HB/116		1. 6.00	A.V.I.Hudson	Priory Farm, Tibenham		23. 9.03P
G-BZIB	Denney Kitfox Model 3	PFA 172-11898		4. 5.00	S.L.Symons		Leicester	
G-BZIC	Lindstrand LBL Sun SS HAB	702		8. 6.00	Ballongaventyr 1 Skane AB		Lund, Sweden	20. 6.02A
G-BZID	Montgomerie-Bensen B.8MR	PFA G/01-1315		31. 5.00	S.C.Gillies		(Buckie)	
	(Air Command Elite G-BOGW cannabalised to produce G-BZID)				*(New owner 10.02)*			
G-BZIF	Dornier 328-100	3053	F-GNBS	20. 6.00	Suckling Airways (Cambridge) Ltd		Cambridge	12. 7.04T
			D-CDXU		t/a Scot Airways			
G-BZIG	Thruster T600N	0400-T600N-042		25. 4.00	Ultra Air Ltd		Leicester	8. 5.03P
	(Rotax 582 UL)							
G-BZII	Extra EA.300/L	119		13. 9.00	J.A.Carr		Guernsey	18. 9.03T
G-BZIJ	Robin DR500/200i President	0023		9. 3.00	Rob Airways Ltd		Guernsey	13. 4.03
	(Registered as DR400/500 but c/n plate denotes type as DR.500/200)							
G-BZIK	Cameron A-250 HAB	4890		27. 6.00	Breckland Balloons Ltd		Dereham	11. 6.03T
G-BZIL	Cameron Colt 120A HAB	4876		7. 7.00	S.R.Seager		Aylesbury	11. 3.03T
					t/a Champagne Flights *(Parrott & Coales titles)*			

Reg	Type	C/n	Prev id	Date	Owner	Location	Date code
G-BZIM	Pegasus Quantum 15-912	7678		20. 6.00	H.J.W.Munckton	(Farnham)	17. 8.02P
G-BZIN	Robinson R44 Raven	0776		23. 6.00	Helicentre Ltd	Blackpool	12. 7.03T
G-BZIP	Montgomerie-Bensen B.8MR	PFA G/01A-1319		11. 5.00	S.J.Boxall	Askern, Yorks	12. 6.03P
G-BZIR	Mainair Blade 912	1251-0600-7 & W1044		4. 7.00	D.M.Law	(Chiseldon)	10. 7.01P
	(Rotax 912-UL or Motavia?)						
G-BZIS	Raj Hamsa X'Air 582	520 & BMAA/HB/142		12. 6.00	J.Way & R.Bonnett	Maypole Farm, Chislet	12.11.03P
					tr X'Air Group		
G-BZIT	Beech 95-B55 Baron	TC-564	HB-GBS	12. 6.00	G-BACB Ltd	Hintin in the Hedges	8. 1.04T
			I-ALGE/HB-GBS/N6845Q				
G-BZIV	Jabiru Jabiru UL	PFA 274A-13587		20. 6.00	V.R.Leggott	Coldharbour Farm, Willingham	30. 8.03P
G-BZIW	Pegasus Quantum 15-912	7681		17. 7.00	J.M.Hodgson	Baxby Manor, Husthwaite	23. 8.03P
G-BZIX	Cameron N-90 HAB	4867		3. 8.00	Sport Promotion SRL	La Morra, Italy	19. 9.03A
G-BZIY	Raj Hamsa X'Air 582	488 & BMAA/HB/141		19. 6.00	I.K.Hogg	Kirkbride	19. 9.03P
G-BZIZ	Ultramagic H-31 HAB	31/02		12. 6.00	G.D.O.Bartram	(Andorra la Vella)	9.11.02A
G-BZJA	Cameron Fire-90 SS HAB	4757		5. 5.00	J M Albury (Chubb titles)	Cirencester	8. 3.02A
	(Chubb Fire Extinguisher shape)						
G-BZJB	Aerostar Yakovlev Yak-52	811601	ZU-YAK	18. 9.00	D.Watt	(Yaxley)	22.10.03P
G-BZJC	Thruster T600N	0070-T600N-044		21. 6.00	Thruster Air Services Ltd	Sandown	8. 4.03P
	(A/c is Thruster Sprint)				(Op Solent Microlights)		
G-BZJD	Thruster T600T 450 Jabiru	0070-T600T-045		21. 6.00	Heart Of The Ocean Ltd	(Sark)	14. 5.03P
G-BZJF	Pegasus Quantum 15	7696		21. 7.00	R.S.McMaster	Sywell	20. 7.03P
	(Rotax 582)						
G-BZJH	Cameron Z-90 HAB	4920		10. 7.00	Cameron Balloons Ltd	Italy	24. 7.03A
G-BZJI	Nova X-Large	3718946		28. 6.00	M Hay (New owner 1.03)	(Dundee)	
G-BZJJ	Robinson R22 Beta	3081		12. 6.00	Helicentre Ltd	Liverpool	29. 6.03T
G-BZJK*	Robinson R22 Beta	3090		20. 6.00	Helicentre Ltd (Cancelled 27.8.02 as WFU)	Blackpool	12. 7.03T
G-BZJL	Mainair Blade 912S	1252-0600-7 & W1046		4. 7.00	D.N.Powell	(Bootle)	14. 2.03P
	(Rotax 912 ULS)						
G-BZJM	VPM M16 Tandem Trainer	PFA G/12-1301		19. 6.00	J.Musil (Noted 10.02) Mount Airey Farm, South Cave		
G-BZJN	Mainair Blade 912	1254-0600-7 & W1048		13. 7.00	R.M.Pickwick	Willingale	18. 7.03P
	(Rotax 912-UL)						
G-BZJO	Pegasus Quantum 15	7699		6. 9.00	J.D.Doran	(Mullingar, Co.Westmeath)	5. 9.03P
G-BZJP	Zenair CH.701UL	PFA 187-13579		30. 6.00	D.Jerwood	Upfield Farm, Whitson	8. 7.03P
G-BZJR	Montgomerie-Bensen B.8MR	PFA G/01-1320		11. 7.00	N.H.Collins	Sittles Farm, Alrewas	
					t/a AES Radionic Surveillance Systems		
G-BZJS	Taylor JT.2 Titch	PFA 60-13622		12. 7.00	R.W.Clarke	(Warminster)	
	(Wings & tail noted 10.01: construction abandoned temporarily?)						
G-BZJU	Cameron A-200 HAB	4810		30. 6.00	Leeds Castle Enterprises Ltd	Leeds Castle, Kent	19. 6.03T
	(Leeds Castle titles)						
G-BZJV	CASA 1-131E Jungmann Srs.1000	1075	Span AF E3B-367	31. 7.00	J.A.Sykes	Stretton	15.11.02P
G-BZJW	Cessna 150F	15062054	OO-WIH	27. 6.01	R.J.Scott	Fairoaks	AC
			OO-SIH/N8754S		(Stored 8.02)		
G-BZJX	Ultramagic N-250 HAB	250/12		4. 7.00	Hot Air Balloons Ltd	Henley-on-Thames	26. 3.03T
					(e-homes titles)		
G-BZJY*	Lindstrand LBL 69A HAB	715		28. 6.00	J.J.C.Bernardin	Curcay-sur-Dive, France	15. 6.03A
					(Cancelled 12.8.02 by CAA)		
G-BZJZ	Pegasus Quantum 15	7697		2. 8.00	S.Baker	Long Marston	3. 8.03P
G-BZKB	Reims/Cessna F172N Skyhawk II	F17201914	CS-AQW	3. 7.00	Stapleford Flying Club Ltd	Stapleford	10. 8.03T
			(G-BOJJ(1))/CS-AQW				
G-BZKC	Raj Hamsa X'Air 532	502 & BMAA/HB/144		12. 7.00	P.J.Cheyney	Ne wHouse Farm, Birds Edge	22. 4.03P
G-BZKD	Stolp SA.300 Starduster Too	1	N70DM	3. 7.00	P.& C.Edmunds	Enstone	14. 2.03P
G-BZKE	Lindstrand LBL 77B HAB	708		17. 7.00	P.M.Harrison	(Oswestry)	6. 9.02A
G-BZKF	Rans S-6ES Coyote II	PFA 204-13610		17. 7.00	A.W.Hodder	(Sleaford)	27.11.02P
G-BZKG	Extreme/Silex	E761 01A		17. 7.00	R.M.Hardy	(Baldock)	
G-BZKH	Flylight Airsports Doodle Bug/Target	DB023		17. 7.00	B.Tempest	(Halifax)	
G-BZKI	Flylight Airsports Doodle Bug/Target	DB063		17. 7.00	S.Bond	(Huddersfield)	
G-BZKJ	Flylight Airsports Doodle Bug/Target	DB067		17. 7.00	Flylight Airsports Ltd	Sywell	
G-BZKK	Cameron V-56 HAB	396		2. 8.78	P.J.Green & C.Bosley	Newbury	13. 8.96A
					tr Gemini Balloon Group "Gemini II"		
G-BZKL	Piper PA-28R-201 Cherokee Arrow III	28R-7737152	D-EFFZ	20. 7.00	Van Diemen International Racing Service Ltd		
			N40000			Old Buckenham	30. 8.03
G-BZKN	Campbell Cricket Mk.4	PFA G/03-1304		20. 7.00	G.R.Jones (New owner 3.02)	(Banbury)	
G-BZKO	Rans S-6ES Coyote II (Tricycle u/c)			20. 7.00	J.A.R.Hartley	Long Marston	21.11.03P
	(Rotax 912-UL) 0199.1293 & PFA 204-13564						
G-BZKP	Boeing 737-229C	20915	OO-SDJ	26. 7.00	European Aviation Air Charter Ltd	Bournemouth	AC
					(To 5Y-KQN 2.03)		
G-BZKR	Cameron Colt Sugarbox-90 SS HAB	4922		4. 8.00	Stratos Ballooning GmbH & Co KG		
						Enningerloh, Germany	27.11.02A
G-BZKS	Ercoupe 415CD	4834	EI-CIH	22. 8.00	M.D.& W.R.Horler	Haverfordwest	
			OO-AIA/(PH-NDO)/N94723/NC94723				
G-BZKT	Cyclone Pegasus Quantum 15	7711		23. 8.00	Rochester Microlights Ltd	Rochester	21. 8.03P
	(Rotax 582)						
G-BZKU	Cameron Z-105 HAB	4931		21. 7.00	Cameron Balloons Ltd	Bristol	31. 8.01P
G-BZKV	Cameron Sky 90-24 HAB	4857		5. 9.00	Omega Selection Services Ltd	Stonehouse	8. 8.03A
					(Omega titles)		
G-BZKW	Ultramagic M-77 HAB	77-179		25. 7.00	T.G.Church	Blackburn	8.12.02T
G-BZKX	Cameron V-90 HAB	4505		19. 7.00	Cameron Balloons Ltd	Dalien, PRC	26. 7.01A
G-BZKY	Focke-Wulf FW.189-A1	2100	Luftwaffe V7+1H	9. 8.00	M T Pearce-Ware	(Worthing)	
	(Built Aero-Avia)				(Restoration being undertaken in UK & Germany)		
G-BZKZ	Lindstrand LBL 25A Cloudhopper HAB	721		14. 8.00	Lindstrand Balloons Ltd	Oswestry	8. 1.03A
G-BZLA	Aérospatiale SA341G Gazelle 1	1392	N2TV	31. 7.00	P.J.Brown	Redhill	14.10.04T
			N49534		t/a PJ Brown Civil Engineering and Haulage		
G-BZLC	PZL-110 Koliber 160A	04980084	SP-WGL	13. 9.00	G.F.Smith	(Milton Keynes)	29. 4.05T
G-BZLD	Raj Hamsa X'Air 582	567 & BMAA/HB/145		3. 8.00	C.Blackburn	(Ballybofey, Co.Donegal)	28. 2.03P

Reg	Type	C/n	Prev id	Date	Owner	Location	Date/Status
G-BZLE	Rans S-6ES Coyote II	PFA 204-13608		12. 7.00	W.S.Long	Mayfield Farm, Stevenson	18. 9.03P
G-BZLF	CFM Shadow CD	K.236 & BMAA/HB/053		31. 7.00	D.W.Stacey	(St. Albans)	
G-BZLG	Robin HR200/120B	353		7. 7.00	G.S.McNaughton (Op Prestwick Flying Club)	Prestwick	19.10.03T
G-BZLH	Piper PA-28-161 Warrior II	28-8316075	N43069	23. 8.00	S.J.Skilton	Southampton	30. 8.03T
					t/a Aviation Rentals (Op Solent Flight Centre)		
G-BZLI	SOCATA TB-21 Tobago TC	500	F-GENI	29. 9.00	K.B.Hallam	(Woking)	2.10.03
G-BZLJ	Cameron N-90 HAB	2348	LX-BAG	4. 8.00	Gone With The Wind Ltd	Bristol	13. 8.03A
			LX-MTC				
G-BZLK	Slingsby T.31M Motor Tutor	PFA 42-13629		2. 8.00	I.P.Manley	(Chichester)	
	(Formerly T.31B BGA2976/EVA ex WT873 [683])						
	(Owner's website www.ivannn.flyer.co.uk/t31m.htm intends to record conversion to powered status)						
G-BZLL	Pegasus Quantum 15-912	7693		9. 8.00	J.J.Smith	Long Marston	24. 9.03P
G-BZLM	Mainair Blade	1257-0800-7 & W1051		8. 8.00	B.J.Palfreyman	Perth	16. 3.03P
	(Rotax 582)						
G-BZLO	Denney Kitfox Model 2	PFA 172-13630		8. 8.00	M.W.Hanley	(Truro)	9. 1.03P
G-BZLP	Robinson R44 Raven	0814		17. 7.00	Regentweb Ltd	(Lincoln)	14. 8.03P
G-BZLS	Cameron Sky 77-24 HAB	4858		17. 8.00	D.W. Young	(Stenhousemuir)	8. 9.02A
G-BZLT	Raj Hamsa X'Air 582	486 & BMAA/HB/125		10. 8.00	G.Millar	Moygashel, Co.Tyrone	24. 6.03P
G-BZLU	Lindstrand LBL 90A HAB	719		9. 8.00	A.E.Lusty	Bourne	9. 8.03A
G-BZLV	Jabiru Jabiru UL-450	PFA 274A-13537		15. 8.00	G.Dalton	Bodmin	6. 8.03P
G-BZLX	Pegasus Quantum 15-912	7714		30. 8.00	J.McCormack	Broomhill Farm, West Calder	16. 4.03P
G-BZLY	Grob G.109B	6242	D-KLMG	24. 8.00	M.Yolson	Egelsbach, Germany	14.11.04
			G-BZLY/OE-9230				
G-BZLZ	Pegasus Quantum 15-912	7721		13. 9.00	A.R.Way	Dunkeswell	5.10.03P
G-BZMB	Piper PA-28R-201 Arrow III	28R-7837144	HB-PBY	20. 4.00	D.S.Seex	King's Farm, Thurrock	19. 6.03T
			N3963M				
G-BZMC	Jabiru Jabiru UL	PFA 274A-13593		18. 8.00	J.R.Banks	(Douglas, Isle of Man)	16. 9.03P
G-BZMD	Scottish Aviation Bulldog Srs.120/121	BH120/347	XX554	18. 8.00	D.M.Squires (As "XX554/09")	(Wellesbourne Mountford)	13.11.04
G-BZME	Scottish Aviation Bulldog Srs.120/121	BH120/347	XX698	18. 8.00	B.Whitworth (As "XX698/9")	Breighton	2. 9.04
G-BZMF	Rutan LongEZ	PFA 74-10698		30. 8.00	R.A.Gardiner & A.McLaughlin	Cumbernauld	13. 6.03P
G-BZMG	Robinson R44 Raven	0815		16. 8.00	Ramsgill Aviation Ltd	Sherburn-in-Elmet	14. 9.03T
G-BZMH	Scottish Aviation Bulldog Srs.120/121	BH120/341	XX692	21. 8.00	M.E.J.Hingley & Co.Ltd	Wellesbourne Mountford	17.10.04
					(As "XX692/A")		
G-BZMI	Pegasus Quantum 15-912	7716		22. 9.00	T.W.Thiele	Newnham, Baldock	18.10.03P
G-BZMJ	Rans S-6ES Coyote II	PFA 204-13631		31. 8.00	J.Seddon & F.J.Lloyd	Tarn Farm, Cockerham	13. 6.03P
	(Tricycle u/c)				tr Heskin Flying Group		
G-BZML	Scottish Aviation Bulldog Srs.120/121	BH120/342	XX693	1. 9.00	I.D.Anderson (As "XX693/07")	Poplar Hall Farm, Elmsett	14.11.04
G-BZMM	Robin DR400/180R Remorqueur	918	OE-KIR	17. 7.00	N.A.C.Norman	Feshiebridge	5.10.03
			D-EAWR				
G-BZMO	Robinson R22 Beta	1219	N24282	31. 7.00	Sloane Helicopters Ltd	Sywell	4. 9.03T
			JA7814/N8056H				
G-BZMR	Raj Hamsa X'Air 582	480 & BMAA/HB/149		11. 9.00	M.Grime (Noted 2.03)	Brook Farm, Pilling	26.5.03P
G-BZMS	Mainair Blade	1256-0700-7 & W1050		2. 8.00	A.J.Tyler	Beccles	9. 9.03P
	(Rotax 582)						
G-BZMT	Piper PA-28-161 Warrior III	2842107	N4147D	29.11.00	S J Skilton	Wellesbourne Mountford	28.11.03T
			G-BZMT/N9519N/N4147D			t/a Aviation Rentals		
G-BZMV	Cameron Concept-80 HAB	4930		26. 9.00	Latteria Soresinese Soc Coop ARL	Soresina, Italy	23. 4.03P
G-BZMW	Pegasus Quantum 15-912	7720		26. 9.00	J.I.Greenshields	Dunkeswell	3.10.03P
G-BZMX	Cameron Z-90 HAB	4942		1. 9.00	Cameron Balloons Ltd (Cameron Balloons titles)	Bristol	27.10.02A
G-BZMY	SPP Yakovlev Yak C-11	171314	F-AZSF	4.10.00	E.G.Gavazzi	North Weald	24. 3.03P
			Egyptian AF		"1"		
G-BZMZ	CFM Streak Shadow	K265-CD & BMAA/HB/051		13. 9.00	J.F.Fouche	(London EC1)	
G-BZNA*	Lindstrand LBL 90A HAB	732		21. 9.00	Lindstrand Balloons Ltd	Abuja, Nigeria	28. 9.01A
					(Cancelled 5.2.03 by CAA)		
G-BZNB	Pegasus Quantum 15	7739		10.11.00	R.C.Whittall	Weston Zoyland	9.11.03P
	(Rotax 503)						
G-BZNC	Pegasus Quantum 15-912	7736		25.10.00	D.E.Wall	Long Marston	13. 2.03P
G-BZND	Sopwith Pup rep	PFA 101-11815		27. 9.00	B.F.Goddard	(Southampton)	
G-BZNE	Beech B300 Super King Air	FL-286	N4486V	17.10.00	G.Davies	Blackbushe	16.11.03
	(Aka "King Air 350")						
G-BZNF	Cameron Colt 120A HAB	4866		13.11.00	N. Charbonnier	Aosta, Italy	24. 1.03A
G-BZNG	Raj Hamsa X'Air J22	571 & BMAA/HB/147		4.10.00	G.L.Craig	Newtownards, Co.Down	1. 8.03T
G-BZNH	Rans S-6ES Coyote II (Tricycle u/c)			18.10.00	R.E.Quine & R.W.Cooper	Jurby, Isle of Man	21. 3.03P
	(Rotax 582)	0899.1333 &.PFA 204-13660					
G-BZNI	Bell 206B JetRanger II	2142	G-ODIG	4.10.00	Trimax Ltd	Manston	3. 1.04T
			G-NEEP/N777FW/N3CR				
G-BZNJ	Rans S-6ES Coyote II (Tailwheel u/c)			23.10.00	S.P.Read & M.H.Wise	Weston Zoyland	19. 4.03P
	(Rotax 582)	0700.1342 & PFA 204-13640					
G-BZNK	Morane Saulnier MS.315E D2	354	F-BCNY	2.11.00	R.H.Cooper & S.Swallow	(Stow, Lincs)	
			French AF		(Work continuing 11.01)		
G-BZNM	Pegasus Quantum 15	7754		20.11.00	M.Tomlinson	(Burton-on-Trent)	19.11.02P
	(Rotax 582)						
G-BZNN	Beech 76 Duchess	ME-343	N6133P	25.10.00	S.J.Skilton	Bournemouth	14.12.03T
			F-GHSU/N6722L		t/a Aviation Rentals (Op Bournemouth Flying Club)		
G-BZNO	Ercoupe 415C	2118	N99495	9.11.00	D.K.Tregilgas	Great Oakley, Clacton	
G-BZNP	Thruster T600N-450	0100-T600N-047		27.10.00	R.S.O'Carroll	(Craigavon, Co.Armagh)	3.12.03P
	(Rotax 582)						
G-BZNR	British Aerospace BAe 125 Srs.800B	258180	G-XRMC	30.10.00	RMC Group Services Ltd	Farnborough	11.12.04T
			G-5-675				
G-BZNS	Mainair Blade	1263-1000-7 & W1057		23.11.00	M.K.B.Molyneux	(Nantwich)	11. 2.03P
	(Rotax 582)						
G-BZNT	Aero L-29 Delfin	893019	ES-YLG	3.11.00	T.Carmichael	North Weald	29. 4.03P
			Estonian AF/Soviet AF		(New owner 3.02)		
G-BZNU	Cameron A-300 HAB	4960		29.11.00	Flying Pictures Ltd	Chilbolton	9. 5.03A
G-BZNV	Lindstrand LBL 31A HAB	741		12.12.00	G.R. Down	Gillingham	14. 4.03A

G-BZNW	Isaacs Fury II	PFA 11-13402		10.11.00	J.E.D.Rogerson	(Ferryhill)	
G-BZNX	SOCATA MS.880B Rallye Club	2113	F-BTVX	17.11.00	R.E.Knapton	Turweston	30. 1.04
G-BZNY	Europa Aviation Europa XS 401 & PFA 247-13355			14.11.00	A.K.Middlemas	Rufforth	1. 1.04P
	(Rotax 912S) (Tri-gear u/c)				(F/f 22.9.02)		
G-BZNZ	Lindstrand LBL Cake SS HAB	747		21.12.00	Oxford Promotions (UK) Ltd (Op F Prell) Kentucky, USA		3. 4.03A
G-BZOB	Slepcev Storch	PFA 316-13592		21.11.00	J.E.& A.Ashby	(Papworth Everard)	
	(Australian-built kit 3/4 scale rep.)				(Planned completion early 2003		
G-BZOC	Pegasus Quantum 15-912	7753		29.11.00	S.J.Doyle	(Liverpool)	28.11.02P
G-BZOD	Pegasus Quantum 15-912	7763		18.12.00	N.F.Mackenzie	East Fortune	28. 3.03P
G-BZOE	Pegasus Quantum 15	7723		14. 9.00	B.N.Thresher	Dunkeswell	2.10.03P
	(Rotax 582)						
G-BZOF	Montgomerie-Bensen B.8MR	MGM3/SJML		17.11.00	S.J.M.Ledingham	Carlisle	7. 8.03P
G-BZOG	Dornier 328-100	3088	D-CDXN(5)	19.12.00	Suckling Airways (Cambridge) Ltd	Cambridge	20.12.02T
			F-GNPR		t/a Scot Airways		
G-BZOH	Cameron Bull-110 SS HAB	4983		12. 1.01	Ballon Team Bonn GmbH & Co KG		
						Meckenheim, Germany	10. 1.03A
G-BZOI	Nicollier HN.700 Menestrel II	PFA 217-12604		27.10.00	S.J.McCollum	Newtownards, Co.Down	22. 5.03P
G-BZOL	Robin R3000/140	124	F-GEKZ	20.12.00	F.Swetenham	Poplar Hall Farm, Elmsett	6. 3.04T
G-BZOM	Rotorway Exececutive 162F	6243	N767SG	27. 3.01	J.A.Jackson (Noted 2.03)	Street Farm, Takeley	AC
G-BZON	Scottish Aviation Bulldog Srs.120/121	BH120/214	XX528	19.12.00	Roger Savage Gyroplanes Ltd (As "XX528/X") Carlisle		8. 7.04
G-BZOO	Pegasus Quantum 15-912	7702		15. 8.00	K.Brown	Sywell	16.11.03P
G-BZOP	Robinson R44	0958		11. 1.01	20:20 Logistics Ltd	(Stoke-on-Trent)	28. 1.04T
G-BZOR	TEAM mini-Max 91	PFA 186-13312		9. 8.00	A.Watt	Insch	13. 5.03P
G-BZOU	Pegasus Quantum 15-912	7768		22. 3.01	A.J.Gordon	Farnborough	3. 4.03P
G-BZOV	Pegasus Quantum 15-912	7769		22. 3.01	D.Turner	(Bicester)	29. 5.03P
G-BZOW	Whittaker MW7	PFA 171-13118		15.12.00	G.W.Peacock	(Doncaster)	
G-BZOX	Cameron Colt 90B HAB	10000		8. 2.01	D.J.Head	Newbury	13. 2.02P
G-BZOY	Beech 76 Duchess	ME-144	EC-ICJ	3.1.01	S.J. Skilton t/a Aviation Rentals	Bournemouth	31. 1.04T
			G-BZOY/F-GFFH/5T-AOH/F-ODJQ/F-GBLO				
G-BZOZ	Van's RV-6	PFA 181-12455		14. 9.00	V.Edmundson	(Blackburn)	
G-BZPA	Mainair Blade 912S	1264-1100-7 & W1058		13.12.00	J.McGoldrick	Newtownards, Co.Down	28. 1.03P
G-BZPB	Hawker Hunter GA.Mk.11	41H-670758	WV256	15. 1.01	B.R.Pearson	Exeter	17. 7.03P
					(As "WB188" Hunter prototype in its first form /duck-egg green c/s)		
G-BZPC	Hawker Hunter GA.Mk.11	HABL-003061	XF300	15. 1.01	B.R.Pearson	Exeter	AC
					(As "WB188" Hunter prototype in its second form/all-red c/s)		
G-BZPD	Cameron V-65 HAB	4700		10.11.00	Gone With The Wind Ltd	Bristol	
G-BZPE	Lindstrand LBL 310A HAB	746		16. 2.01	Aerosaurus Balloons LLP	Exeter	19. 9.03T
G-BZPF	Scheibe SF-24B Motorspatz 1	4028	PH-971	19. 1.01	D.Shrimpton	RAF Keevil	17. 2.05
			OE-9005/(D-KECO)				
G-BZPG	Beech C24R Sierra	MC-556	N23840	27. 3.01	S.J.Skilton t/a Aviation Rentals	Bournemouth	30. 4.04T
					(Op Professional Flight Training)		
G-BZPH	Van's RV-4	PFA 181-12867		6. 9.00	A.G.Truman tr G-BZPH RV-4 Group	Kemble	24.11.03P
G-BZPI	SOCATA TB-20 Trindad	1814	SX-ATT	20.12.00	K.M.Brennan	(Desford)	28. 1.04T
G-BZPJ	Beech 76 Duchess	ME-227	N6630Z	2. 3.01	S.J.Skilton t/a Aviation Rentals	Bournemouth	19. 3.04T
					(Op Bournemouth Flying Club)		
G-BZPK	Cameron C-80 HAB	4183		23. 2.01	Horizon Ballooning Ltd	Alton	19.11.03T
G-BZPL	Robinson R44	0948		10. 1.01	M.K.Shaw	San Bonet, Majorca	5. 2.04T
G-BZPM	Cessna 172S Skyhawk 172S	8561	N72760	11. 1.01	TDR Aviation Ltd	(Craigavon, Co.Armagh)	4. 3.04T
G-BZPN	Mainair Blade 912S	1268-0101-7 & W1062		25. 1.01	G.R.Barker	(Epping)	2. 3.03P
G-BZPP	Westand Wasp HAS.Mk.1	F9675	XT793	15. 1.01	S.L.Negus	Moat Farm, Otley	24. 2.03P
G-BZPR	Ultramagic N-210 HAB	210/14		16. 1.01	European Balloon Display Co Ltd	Great Missenden	15. 2.03T
G-BZPS	Scottish Aviation Bulldog Srs.120/121	BH120/316	XX658	8. 1.01	D.M.Squires	(Wellesbourne Mountford)	AC
					(As "XX658/03") (Noted 1.03)		
G-BZPT	Ultramagic N-210 HAB	210/15		16. 1.01	European Balloon Display Co. Ltd	Great Missenden	10. 2.03T
G-BZPU	Cameron V-77 HAB	5433	N20726	2. 5.01	J.Vonka	New Malden	
G-BZPV	Lindstrand LBL 90B HAB	727		17. 1.01	D.P.Hopkins	Pidley, Huntingdon	29. 5.03A
					(LakesideLodge Golf Centre titles)		
G-BZPW	Cameron V-77 HAB	6245	N4463V	2. 2.01	J.Vonka	New Malden	12. 7.03A
G-BZPX	Ultramagic S-105 HAB	105/78		12. 2.01	G.M.Houston t/a Scotair Balloons	Lesmahagow	18. 3.03T
G-BZPY	Ultramagic H-31 HAB	31/03		12. 2.01	G.M.Houston t/a Scotair Balloons	Lesmahagow	18. 3.03A
G-BZPZ	Mainair Blade (Rotax 582)	1265-1200-7 & W1059		23. 1.01	M C W Robertson	(Leek, Staffs)	13. 3.03P
G-BZRA	Rans S-6ES Coyote II (Rotax 912)	PFA 204-13683		16. 1.01	A.W.Fish	(Telford)	28. 3.03P
G-BZRB	Mainair Blade (Rotax 582)	1270-0201-7 & W1064		7. 3.01	S.B.Brady	(Stoke-on-Trent)	7. 3.03P
G-BZRC	de Havilland DH.115 Vampire T.Mk.11	15143	WZ584	26. 3.01	D.Copley	Sandtoft	
					(Dismantled & unconverted as "WZ584/K" 7.02)		
G-BZRD	de Havilland DH.115 Vampire T.Mk.11	15687	XH313	27. 3.01	D.Copley	Sandtoft	
					(Dismantled & unconverted as "XH313/E" 7.02)		
G-BZRE	Percival P.56 Provost T.Mk.1	PAC/F/234	7688M	15. 5.01	D.Copley	Sandtoft	
			WW421		(Dismantled & unconverted as "WW421" 7.02)		
G-BZRF	Percival P.56 Provost T.Mk.1	PAC/F/062	7698M	15. 5.01	D.Copley	Sandtoft	
			WV499		(Dismantled & unconverted as "WV499" 7.02)		
G-BZRG	Huntwing Avon	0009090 & BMAA/HB/154		16. 1.01	W.G.Reynolds	(Cromer)	
					(Frame only completed by 7.01)		
G-BZRJ	Pegasus Quantum 15-912	7783		5. 2.01	R.W.Goddin	Newnham, Baldock	11. 4.03P
G-BZRN	Robinson R44	0971		1. 2.01	Toriamos Ltd	(Naas, Co.Kildare)	15. 2.04T
G-BZRO	Piper PA-30 Twin Comanche C	30-1923	SE-IYL	2. 3.01	Comanche Hire Ltd	Gloucestershire	21. 5.04T
			D-GATI/I-KATI/N8767Y				
G-BZRP	Pegasus Quantum 15-912	7758		24. 1.01	R H Braithwaite	RAF Cosford	15. 2.03P
					tr RAF Microlight Flying Association		
G-BZRR	Pegasus Quantum 15-912	7727		4.10.00	R.E.Welch	Knapthorpe Lodge, Caunton	8.10.03P
					tr Syndicate Romeo Romeo		
G-BZRS	Eurocopter EC135-T1	0166		22. 3.01	Bond Air Services Ltd	Aberdeen	8. 4.04T
G-BZRT	Beech 76 Duchess	ME-89	EC-HYO	21. 3.01	S.J.Skilton t/a Aviation Rentals	Bournemouth	12.11.05T
			G-BZRT/F-GHBL/N2074G				

Reg	Type	C/n	Prev id	Date	Owner	Location	Date2
G-BZRU	Cameron V-90 HAB	10053		1. 5.01	Close Invoice Finance Ltd *"Close Encounter"*	Newbury	28. 5.03A
G-BZRV	Van's RV-6	PFA 181A-13573		12.10.00	E.Hicks & N.M.Hitchman	Garston Farm, Marshfield	11. 8.03P
G-BZRW	Mainair Blade 912S	1266-0101-7 & W1060		6. 2.01	N.D.Kube	(Groby, Leics)	1. 8.03P
G-BZRX	Ultramagic M-105 HAB	105/80		3. 5.01	Specialist Recruitment Group plc	Huntingdon	10. 8.03A
					(Interaction Recruitment/Dixon Finance Division titles)		
G-BZRY	Rans S-6ES Coyote II	PFA 204-13666		1. 2.01	S.Forman	Norwich	30. 7.03P
G-BZRZ	Thunder AX11-250 S2 HAB	10013		11.10.01	T.J.Bucknall	Chester	17.10.03T
					(Op Cheshire Balloon Flights) "Kinetic"		
G-BZSA	Pegasus Quantum 15	7784		25. 1.01	Cyclone Airsports Ltd t/a Pegasus Aviation	Manton	2.12.02P
G-BZSB	Pitts S-1S Special	PFA 09-13697		2. 2.01	D.W.Melville	(Newton Abbot)	
G-BZSC	Sopwith Camel F.1 rep	NAW-3		15. 1.01	The Shuttleworth Trust	Old Warden	AC
	(Built Northern Aeroplane Workshops)				*(Under consruction 3.02)*		
G-BZSD	Piper PA-46-350P Malibu Mirage	4636168	N838DB N333DB	14. 2.01	Harpin Ltd	(Nun Monkton, York)	13. 2.04T
G-BZSE	Hawker Hunter T.Mk.7	41H-670788	9096M WV322	6. 2.01	Towerdrive Ltd	Kemble	7. 4.03P
	(Off.regd as T.Mk.8B (c/n 41H-670792) see G-FFOX)						
	(Frames of WV318 & WV322 interchanged in RAF service:G-FFOX is c/n 41H-670792 & ex WV318 & has centre fuselage.ex WV322.						
	G-BZSE's c/n plate shows HABL/R/41H-670792 as per G-FFOX & has centre fuselage ex WV318)						
G-BZSF	Hawker Hunter T.Mk.8	BHABL-003150	9237M XF995	6. 2.01	Towerdrive Ltd	(Ashbourne)	AC
G-BZSG	Pegasus Quantum 15-912	7766		22. 2.01	K.J.Gay	(Bangor, Co.Down)	16. 3.03P
G-BZSH	Ultramagic H-77 HAB	77/191		12. 4.01	J.L.Hutsby	Oxhill, Warwicks	8. 4.03A
G-BZSI	Pegasus Quantum 15	7787		12. 3.01	B.& K.Yoxall	Rufforth	11. 3.03P
G-BZSL	Sky 25-16 HAB	138		31. 1.01	A.E.Austin	Naseby	8.10.03A
G-BZSM	Pegasus Quantum 15	7788		23. 2.01	S.J.Mawman	Knapthorpe Lodge, Caunton	26. 3.03P
G-BZSO	Ultramagic M-77C HAB	77/190		22. 3.02	C.C.Duppa-Miller	Warwick	12. 4.03A
G-BZSP	Stemme S.10	10-14	HB-2217 D-KDNE	10. 5.01	A.Flewelling, & L.Bleaken	Aston Down	22. 8.04
					"626"		
G-BZSR	Hawker Hunter T.Mk.7	41H-693832	A2617 XL601	15. 2.01	Stick & Rudder Aviation Ltd	(Meetkerke, Belgium)	
					(On rebuild 2002 in red & white livery of 4 FTS)		
G-BZSS	Pegasus Quantum 15-912	7770		6. 2.01	T.R.Marsh		
						Brown Shutters Farm, Norton St Philips, Somerset	29. 3.03P
G-BZST	Jabiru Jabiru UL	PFA 274A-13616		13. 2.01	G.Hammond	Headcorn	4. 9.03T
G-BZSU	Cameron A-315 HAB	10009		13. 6.01	Ballooning Network Ltd	Bristol	8. 4.03T
					(Bath Building Society titles)		
G-BZSV	Aherne Barracuda	631		20. 2.01	M.J.Aherne	(St. Albans)	AC
G-BZSX	Pegasus Quantum 15-912	7789		23. 2.01	J.B.Greenwood	Rufforth	22. 2.03P
G-BZSY	SNCAN Stampe SV-4A	677	N12426 F-BGGT/French AF	12. 3.01	G P J M Valvekens	Diest, Belgium	
G-BZSZ	Jabiru Jabiru UL	PFA 274A-13432		16. 2.01	M.C.J.Ludlow	Pent Farm, Postling	7. 8.03P
G-BZTA	Robinson R44	0968		20. 2.01	Thurston Helicopters Ltd	Headcorn	7. 3.04T
G-BZTC	TEAM mini-MAX 91	PFA 186-13336		23. 1.01	G G Clayton	Roche, Cornwall	11.12.02P
G-BZTD	Thruster T600T 450 JAB	0021-T600T-049		22. 2.01	B O & B C McCartan	(Banbridge, Belfast)	14. 5.03P
G-BZTE	Cameron A-275 HAB	10028		26. 6.01	Richard Nash Cars Ltd *(Richard Nash titles)*	(Norwich)	22. 3.03T
G-BZTF	IAV-Bacau Yakovlev Yak-52	866703	LY-AKE DOSAAF	28. 2.01	A.C.Pledger tr KY Flying Group	(Buntingford)	18. 4.03P
G-BZTG	Piper PA-34-220T Seneca V	3449126	EC-HGK N4141N	4. 4.01	L.R.Chiswell	Alderney	16. 4.04T
	(Made heavy landing Little Snoring 15.12.01: nosewheel collapsed, damaging nose cone, props, u/carriage & engines)						
G-BZTH	Europa Aviation Europa	010 & PFA 247-12494		21.12.00	T J Houlihan	Kemble	
	(Rotax 912) (Monowheel u/c)				*(F/f 22.12.02)*		
G-BZTI	Europa Aviation Europa XS	124 & PFA 247-13172		30. 3.01	W.Hoolachan	Kemble	12. 9.02P
	(Rotax 914) (Tri-gear u/c)				*(F/f 5.8.01)*		
G-BZTJ	CASA Bü.133C Jungmeister	41	Span AF ES1-41	7. 3.01	R.A.Seeley	Denham	
G-BZTK	Cameron V-90 HAB	10083		6. 3.01	Cameron Balloons Ltd	Bristol	5. 7.03A
G-BZTL	Cameron Colt Flying Ice Cream Cone SS HAB	10008		16. 5.01	Stratos Ballooning GmbH & Co KG		
						Ennigerloh, Germany	18. 4.03A
G-BZTM	Mainair Blade	1273-0201-7 & W1068		12. 2.01	L.Hogan	Glenrothes	12. 3.03P
G-BZTN	Europa Aviation Europa XS	504 & PFA 247-13715		16. 3.01	W.Pringle & J.Dewberry	(Worksop)	
	(Tri-gear u/c)						
G-BZTR	Mainair Blade	1276-0301-7 & W1071		8. 3.01	J.Lynch	Baxby Manor, Husthwaite	30. 3.03P
G-BZTS	Cameron Bertie Bassett-90 SS HAB	10050		3. 5.01	Trebor Bassett Ltd	Rickmansworth	17. 5.03A
G-BZTT	Cameron A-275 HAB	4953		28. 8.01	Spotlight Group Ltd	Axbridge	26. 8.03T
G-BZTU	Mainair Blade 912	1272-0201-7 & W1066		8. 2.01	A J Tyler t/a Cloudscape Microlights	Beccles	24. 3.03P
G-BZTV	Mainair Blade 912S	1278-0301-7 & W1073		2. 4.01	S.Dornan	Greenwall Farm, Forth	4. 4.03P
G-BZTW	Huntwing Avon	9906092 & BMAA/HB/136		17. 1.01	T.S.Walker	(Sandbach)	19. 5.03P
	(Rotax 582)						
G-BZTX	Mainair Blade 912	1267-0101-7 & W1061		9. 2.01	K.A.Ingham	(Wilmslow)	24. 3.03P
G-BZTY	Jabiru Jabiru UL	PFA 274A-13533		1. 3.01	R.P.Lewis	Southery	19. 7.03P
G-BZTZ	MD Helicopters MD 600N	RN056	N70412	15. 5.01	Helicorp Ltd	Kintore	15. 7.04T
G-BZUB	Mainair Blade	1274-0201-7 & W1069		27. 3.01	A.J.Lindsay	Newtownards, Co.Down	13. 6.03P
G-BZUC	Pegasus Quantum 15-912	7796		10. 4.01	G.Breen	(Lagos, Algarve, Portugal)	10. 4.03P
G-BZUD	Lindstrand LBL 105A HAB	780		27. 3.01	P.N.Rhodes	(Oswestry)	26. 3.02A
G-BZUE	Pegasus Quantum 15	7800		23. 4.01	D.J.& M.E.Walcroft	(Great Missenden)	7. 5.03P
G-BZUF	Mainair Rapier	1277-0301-7 & W1072		27. 3.01	S.J.Perry	(Sandbach)	1. 7.03P
G-BZUG	Tiger Cub RL7A XP Sherwood Ranger	PFA 237-13040		23. 3.01	S.P.Sharp	Old Sarum	4. 9.03p
					(In pseudo RAF c/s as fake serial "SR-XP020")		
G-BZUH	Rans S-6ES Coyote II	PFA 204-13716		26. 3.01	J.D.Sinclair-Day	(Ryton)	9. 7.03P
G-BZUI	Pegasus Quantum 15-912	7798		8. 5.01	A.Wales	Rufforth	21.10.02P
G-BZUK	Lindstrand LBL 31A HAB	776		7. 3.01	G.R.J.Luckett	Fort Collins, Co, USA	7.103.03A
G-BZUL	Jabiru Jabiru UL	PFA 274A-13678		28. 3.01	P.Hawkins	Rufforth	22. 8.03P
	(Jabiru 2200A)						
G-BZUM	Mainair Blade 912	1271-0201-7 & W1065		13. 3.01	R.B.Milton	(London E2)	21. 3.02P
G-BZUN	Mainair Blade 912	1279-0301-7 & W1074		18. 4.01	E.Paxton & A Jones	Ince Blundell	23. 4.03P

G-BZUO	Cameron A-340HL HAB	4952		18. 5.01	T.J.Parker Burnham-on-Crouch	3. 4.03T
					t/a Anglian Countryside Balloons	
G-BZUP	Raj Hamsa X'Air 582	624 & BMAA/HB/164		24. 4.01	A.A.J.Lappin Newtownards, Co.Down	31. 7.03P
G-BZUR	Gefa-Flug AS.105GD Airship	0021	D-OATV	19. 2.02	Tim Balloon Promotion Airships Ltd Ceva, Italy	15.2.03P
G-BZUU	Cameron O-90 HAB	10058		14. 6.01	D.C.Ball & C.F.Pooley London SE1	3. 6.02A
G-BZUV	Cameron H-24 HAB	2665	LX-JLW	27. 4.01	J.N.Race "The Gerkin" Lewes	10. 5.03A
G-BZUX	Pegasus Quantum 15	7819		22. 5.01	K.M.MacRae, J.D.& C.A.Capewell East Fortune	31. 5.03P
G-BZUY	Van's RV-6	PFA 181A-13471		23. 5.01	D.M.Gale & K.F.Crumplin Henstridge	15. 1.03P
G-BZUZ	Hunt Avon-Blade BMW R100	BMAA/HB/162		9. 2.01	J.A.Hunt (Abergavenny)	14. 6.03P
	(Mainair sailwing c/n W1067)					
G-BZVA	Zenair CH.701UL	PFA 187-13635		21. 3.01	M.W.Taylor Insch	17. 1.03P
	(Rotax 912)					
G-BZVB	Reims FR172H Rocket	FR17200327	G-BLMX	29. 8.00	R.& E.M.Brereton (King's Lynn)	13.11.03T
			PH-RPC			
G-BZVC	Mickleburgh L107	PFA 256-12549		21. 3.01	D.R.Mickleburgh (Milton Keynes)	
					(Exhibited incomplete at 1996 PFA Rally)	
G-BZVD	Cameron Colt Forklift-105 SS HAB	10084		15. 6.01	Stratos Ballooning GmbH & Co KG *"JungHeinrich"*	
					Ennigerloh, Germany	8. 4.03A
G-BZVE	Cameron N-133 HAB	10092		20. 6.01	Flying Pictures Ltd Chilbolton	15. 5.02A
G-BZVF	Cessna 182T Skylane	T18208009	N109LP	12. 6.01	R. Macaire t/a Denston Hall Estate Crowfield	8. 7.04T
G-BZVG	Eurocopter AS350B3 Ecureuil	3368	F-WQOR	5. 3.01	Finlay (Holdings) Ltd (Augher, Co.Tyrone)	3. 7.04
G-BZVH	Raj Hamsa X'Air 582	561 & BMAA/HB/160		20. 4.01	B.& D.Bergin Enniskillen, Co.Fermanagh	17. 4.03P
G-BZVI	Nova Vertex 24 Hang Glider	13379		24. 5.01	M Hay *(New owner 1.03)* (Dundee)	
G-BZVJ	Pegasus Quantum 15	7821		12. 6.01	W.T.Davis Perth	11. 6.03P
G-BZVK	Raj Hamsa X'Air 582	592 & BMAA/HB/152		22. 2.01	K.P.Taylor Whitehall Farm, Benington	20. 1.03P
G-BZVM	Rans S-6ES Coyote II	PFA 204-13705		1. 3.01	N.N.Ducker (Ashbourne)	14. 7.03P
G-BZVN	Van's RV-6	PFA 181-13188		25. 4.01	J.A.Booth Gamston	7. 8.02P
G-BZVO	Cessna TR182 Turbo Skylane RG	R18200990	D-EPOL	3. 4.01	Swiftair Ltd Elstree	AC
			N739CX			
G-BZVR	Raj Hamsa X'Air 582	566 & BMAA/HB/146		13. 3.01	R.P.Sims Davidstowe Moor	10. 9.03P
G-BZVS	CASA 1-131E Jungmann Srs.2000	2013	D-EHEP(2)	3. 5.01	W.R.M.Beesley Breighton/Lambley	14. 7.03P
	(Avco Lycoming-180hp)		D-EDEE/Spanish AF E3B-409			
G-BZVT	III Sky Arrow 650TC	PFA 298-13333		23. 3.01	D.J.Goldsmith *(New owner 7.02)* (Edenbridge)	
G-BZVU	Cameron Z-105 HAB	10078		9. 8.01	Prudential Investment Managers Ltd Bristol	8. 8.03A
					(The Mall titles)	
G-BZVV	Pegasus Quantum 15-912	7793		12. 3.01	A.Featherstone & D.C.Mott Knapthorpe Lodge, Caunton	18. 3.03P
G-BZVW	Ilyushin Il-2	1870710	Sov AF	16. 5.01	S.Swallow & R.H.Cooper (Stowe, Lincs)	
G-BZVX	Ilyushin Il-2	1878576	Sov.AF	16. 5.01	S.Swallow & R.H.Cooper (Stowe, Lincs)	
G-BZVZ	Eurocopter AS355N Twin Squirrel	5691		24. 4.01	Ilona Ltd *(Based on board MV Ilona)* (Jersey)	14. 6.04
G-BZWB	Mainair Blade 912	1284-0507-7 & W1079		26. 4.01	L.Cottle Baxby Manor, Husthwaite	2. 5.03P
G-BZWC	Raj Hamsa X'Air Falcon 912	587 & BMAA/HB/157		9. 5.01	G.A.J.Salter (Taunton)	29. 4.03P
G-BZWF	Colt AS-120 Mk.II HA Airship	10095	(HS-)	2. 5.01	MA Flying Ltd Andover	20. 6.02A
			G-BZWF			
G-BZWG	Piper PA-28-140 Cherokee Cruiser	28-7625188	N9656K	17. 5.01	H & E Merkado Panshanger	12. 7.04T
G-BZWH	Cessna 152	15281339	N49819	17. 5.01	J & H Aviation Services Ltd North Weald	14. 6.04T
G-BZWI	Medway EclipseR	170/148		3. 5.01	R.A.Keene Over Farm, Gloucester	28.11.03P
G-BZWJ	CFM Streak Shadow SA	PFA 206-13553		8. 5.01	T.A.Morgan (Carshalton)	
G-BZWK	Jabiru Jabiru SK	PFA 274-13292		8. 5.01	R.Thompson Redhill	6. 3.03P
G-BZWM	Solar Wings Pegasus XL-Q	7792		18. 5.01	D.T.Evans (Hereford)	17. 5.02P
G-BZWN	Van's RV-8	PFA 303-13692		14. 5.01	A.J.Symms & R.D.Harper Old Sarum	21. 1.03P
	(Tailwheel u/c)					
G-BZWR	Mainair Rapier	1275-0301-7 & W1070		7. 3.01	W.E.Ross Tarn Farm, Cockerham	18. 6.03P
G-BZWS	Pegasus Quantum 15-912	7813		26. 4.01	A.G.Quinn Knapthorpe Lodge, Caunton	3. 5.03P
G-BZWT	Tecnam P92-EM Echo	PFA 318-13681		17. 5.01	R.F.Cooper Field Farm, Oakley	19.12.03P
	(Jabiru 2200A) (Marked as P92S)					
G-BZWU	Pegasus Quantum 15-912	7831		19. 7.01	P.C.Hogg Long Acre Farm, Sandy	17. 8.03P
G-BZWV	Steen Skybolt	PFA 64-10751		30. 5.01	P.D.& K.Begley *(Noted 9.02)* Sywell	
G-BZWX	Whittaker MW5-D Sorcerer	PFA 163-13599		1. 6.01	G.E.Richardson Sywell	7. 4.03P
G-BZWY	CFM Streak Shadow SA	PFA 206-13601		31. 5.01	B.Cartwright (Craigavon)	
G-BZWZ	Van's RV-6	PFA 181A-13419		26. 4.01	J.Shanley (Middlesbrough)	
G-BZXA	Raj Hamsa X'Air Victor 2	560 & BMAA/HB/148		31. 5.01	D.W.Mullin Hawarden	25. 6.03P
G-BZXB	Van's RV-6	PFA 181A-13625		4. 6.01	B.J.King-Smith & D.J.Akerman Goodwood	21.2.03P
G-BZXC	Scottish Aviation Bulldog Srs.120/121	BH120/260	XX612	8. 6.01	P.J.M.& C.C.M.Squires (Wellesbourne Mountford)	17.12.05P
					(As "XX612/A03")	
G-BZXD	Rotorway Executive 162F	6494		5. 6.01	P.G.King (Gravesend)	AC
G-BZXE	de Havilland DHC-1 Chipmunk 22	C1/0722	WP839	5. 6.01	K.Moore Blackpool	
G-BZXF	Cameron A-210 HAB	4999		5. 2.02	Off The Ground Balloon Co Ltd Kendal	12. 3.03T
G-BZXG	Dyn'Aéro MCR-01 ULC	PFA 301B-13815		26.10.01	J.Rankin Perth	21. 7.03P
G-BZXH	Jodel D.150 Mascaret	149	F-PBUS	22. 6.01	E.J.Horsfall Blackpool	13. 5.03P
	(Built M.Busmey)					
G-BZXI	Nova Philou 26 Hang Glider	11207		16. 5.01	M Hay *(New owner 1.03)* (Dundee)	
G-BZXJ	Schweizer 269C	10128		20. 6.01	Helicentre Ltd Liverpool	22. 7.04T
G-BZXK	Robin HR200/120B	286	F-GNNV	12. 6.01	S.J. Skilton t/a Aviation Rentals Bournemouth	15. 7.04T
G-BZXL	Whittaker MW5-D Sorcerer	PFA 163-13738		7. 6.01	K.Wright (Douglas, Isle of Man)	24. 1.03P
G-BZXM	Mainair Blade 912	1283-0501-7 & W1078		20. 4.01	P.Harper St.Michaels	1. 5 03P
G-BZXN	Jabiru Jabiru UL-450	PFA 274A-13747		7. 6.01	J.Armstrong Lower Mountpleasant Farm, Chatteris	3.12.03P
G-BZXO	Cameron Z-105 HAB	10125		27. 6.01	Virgin Airship & Balloon Co Ltd Telford	23. 5.03A
					(Innogy/nPower titles)	
G-BZXP	Air Creation Kiss 400-582			14. 6.01	E.D.Deed Sywell	24.10.02P
	UK001, A00056-0054/T00100 & BMAA/HB/169					
G-BZXR	Cameron N-90 HAB	10124		3. 9.01	Derbyshire Building Society Belper	21. 8.02A
G-BZXS	Scottish Aviation Bulldog Srs.120/121	BH120/296	XX631	21. 6.01	K.J.Thompson Newtownards, Co.Down	AC
					(As "XX631/W") (Noted 11.01)	
G-BZXT	Mainair Blade 912	1286-0501-7 & W1081		25. 5.01	S.R.Vinsun tr Barton 912 Flyers Barton	5. 6.03P

Reg	Type	C/n	Prev id	Date	Owner/Operator	Base	
G-BZXV	Pegasus Quantum 15-912	7828		28. 6.01	S.Laws	Rufforth	3. 7.03P
G-BZXW	VPM M16 Tandem Trainer (Rotax 912S)	PFA G/12-1249	G-NANA	30. 4.01	S.J.Tyler	(Carlisle)	31. 8.00P
G-BZXX	Pegasus Quantum 15-912	7812		20. 4.01	R.R.Nichol	Carlisle	24. 4 03P
G-BZXY	Robinson R44 Raven	1027		12. 6.01	Extraviation Ltd	Booker	2. 7.04T
G-BZXZ	Scottish Aviation Bulldog Srs.120/121	BH120/294	XX629	1. 6.01	Air & Ground Aviation Ltd *(As "XX629/V")*	Sleap	11. 9.04T
G-BZYA	Rans S-6ES Coyote II	PFA 204-13529		12. 6.01	D.J.Clack	(West Malling)	5. 8.03P
G-BZYB	Westland SA.314D Gazelle HT.3	1272	XX382	14. 6.01	Aerocars Ltd	East Garston, Berks	9. 7.03P
G-BZYC	Westland SA.314B Gazelle AH.1	1208	XW903	14. 6.01	Aerocars Ltd *(Noted 6.02)*	East Garston, Berks	
G-BZYD	Westland SA.314B Gazelle AH.1 *(C/n 1652 quoted also)*	1648	XZ329	14. 6.01	Aerocars Ltd *(As "XZ329" in Army c/s)*	Filton	23. 4.03P
G-BZYE	Robinson R22 Beta	3231		15. 6.01	Plane Talking Ltd	Elstree	2. 7.04T
G-BZYG	DG Flugzeugbau DG-500MB	5E-220-B15		25. 9.01	R.C.Bromwich	(Blandford Forum)	15.11.04
G-BZYI	Nova Phocus 123 Hang Glider	9748		8. 6.01	M Hay *(New owner 1.03)*	(Dundee)	
G-BZYK	Jabiru Jabiru UL (Jabiru 2200A)	PFA 274A-13227		21. 6.01	A.S.Forbes	Kingston Seymour	28. 8.03P
G-BZYL	Rans S-6ES Coyote II	PFA 204-13718		22. 6.01	J.D.Harris	Kingston Seymour	8. 5.03P
G-BZYM	Raj Hamsa X'Air HK700	649 & BMAA/HB/172		21. 6.01	G.Fleck	(Troon)	
G-BZYN	Pegasus Quantum 15-912	7835		15. 8.01	K.Roberts	(Caernarfon)	31. 8.03P
G-BZYO	Colt 210A HAB	3523	D-OSPM	19. 7.01	P.M.Forster *(Op Alba Ballooning)*	Edinburgh	6. 1.03T
G-BZYP	British Aerospace Jetstream Srs.3200	978	F-GMVL F-OHFX/G-31-978	1. 8.01	Trident Aviation Leasing Services (Ireland) Ltd *(Exported 1.03)*	(Dublin)	
G-BZYR	Cameron N-31 HAB	10137		6. 8.01	Virgin Balloon & Airship Co Ltd *(Benadryl titles)*	Telford	11. 6.03A
G-BZYS	Micro Aviation Bantam B22S	94-001	ZK-JDO	12. 7.01	D.L.Howell	(Gillingham, Kent)	12. 9.02P
G-BZYT	Interavia 80TA	0430992		6. 7.01	N.G.Cranham	(Nottingham)	
G-BZYU	Whittaker MW6 Merlin (Rotax 582)	PFA 164-13647		2. 7.01	K.J.Cole	Over Farm, Gloucester	8. 7.03P
G-BZYV	Noble Hardman Snowbird Mk.V 582 BMAA/HB/175			5. 7.01	S.Jones	(Tregaron)	
G-BZYW	Cameron N-90 HAB	10134		6. 8.01	C.& J.M.Bailey t/a Bailey Balloons *(SWEB titles)*	Bristol	5. 8.02T
G-BZYX	Raj Hamsa X'Air HK700	653 & BMAA/HB/173		15. 6.01	A.G.Marsh *(Noted 7.02)*	Middle Stoke, Kent	
G-BZYY	Cameron N-90 HAB	10130		30. 8.01	Mason Zimbler Ltd *(Oracle titles)*	Bristol	3. 8.03A
G-BZZA	Boeing 737-3L9	26441	D-ADBA OY-MAL	17.11.99	KLM UK Ltd *(Op Buzz)*	Stansted	16. 1.03T
G-BZZB	Boeing 737-3L9	25125	D-ADBG OY-MMW/PP-SOR/OY-MMW	17.11.99	KLM UK Ltd *(Op Buzz)*	Stansted	17. 1.03T
G-BZZD	Reims/Cessna F172M Skyhawk II	F172O1436	G-BDPF	14. 4.98	R.H.M.Richardson-Bunbury	Bodmin	7. 8.05T
G-BZZE	Boeing 737-3Q8	26310	N14381	13.12.02	KLM UK Ltd *(Op Buzz)*	Stansted	17.12.05T
G-BZZF	Boeing 737-3Q8	26311	N19382	28. 1.03	KLM UK Ltd *(Op Buzz)*	Stansted	
G-BZZG	Boeing 737-3Q8	26312	N14383	3.03R	KLM UK Ltd *(Op Buzz) (Delivered 2.03)*	Stansted	
G-BZZH	Boeing 737-3Q8	26313	N14384	3.03R	KLM UK Ltd *(Op Buzz) (For delivery 3.03)*	Stansted	
G-BZZI	Boeing 737-3Q8	26314	N73385	3.03R	KLM UK Ltd *(Op Buzz) (For delivery 3.03)*	Stansted	
G-BZZJ	Boeing 737-3Q8	26321	N17386	3.03R	KLM UK Ltd *(Op Buzz) (For delivery 3.03)*	Stansted	

G-CAAA - G-CZZZ

Reg	Type	C/n	Prev id	Date	Owner/Operator	Base	
G-CAHA	Piper PA-34-200T Seneca II	34-7770010	N23PL SE-GPY/(D-IIIC)/SE-GPY	7. 7.98	H & R.Marshall	Sandtoft	9. 1.05T
G-CAIN	CFM Shadow CD (Rotax 503)	062	G-MTKU	26. 1.99	S.K.Starling	Suton, Norfolk	14. 2.03P
G-CALL	Piper PA-23-250 Aztec F	27-7754061	N62826	21.12.77	J.D.Moon	Ronaldsway	29. 5.04T
G-CAMB	Aérospatiale AS355F2 Twin Squirrel	5416RAF	N813LP	17.12.96	Cambridge & Essex Air Support Consortium	Wyton	3. 5.03T
G-CAMM	Hawker Cygnet rep (Mosler MM-CB35)	PFA 77-10245	(G-ERDB)	30. 5.91	D.M.Cashmore *"6" (On loan to The Shuttleworth Collection)*	Old Warden	18. 7.03P
G-CAMP	Cameron N-105 HAB	4546		24. 3.99	R D Parry *(Op Hong Kong Balloon & Airship Club)*	Hong Kong, PRC	7. 4.02A
G-CAMR	BFC Quad City Challenger II *(As a BFC Kit should carry PFA/177A type prefix)*	PFA 177-12569		26. 3.99	P R A Walker *(Current status unknown)*	Ringwood	
G-CAPI	Mudry/CAARP CAP.10B	76	G-BEXR	16. 3.99	Air Combat Experience Ltd	(Farnham)	20. 8.03
G-CAPX	Avions Mudry CAP.10B	280		21. 9.98	H J Pessall	Leicester	26. 3.05
G-CBAB	Scottish Aviation Bulldog Srs.120/121	BH120/235	XX543	14. 6.01	Propshop Ltd *(As "XX543/F")*	Duxford	14. 3.05
G-CBAD	Mainair Blade 912	1287-0601-7 & W1082		8. 6.01	D.Sykes	Rufforth	23. 6.03P
G-CBAE	British Aerospace BAe.146 Srs.200	E2057	SE-DRB N698AA/N146AC/G-5-057	30. 4.02	BAE Systems (Operations) Ltd *(Open storage 10.02 as "SE-DRB")*	(Hatfield)	
G-CBAF	Neico Lancair 320	PFA 191-13567		11. 6.01	R.W.Fairless	(Portsmouth)	17. 7.03P
G-CBAH	Raj Hamsa X'Air 582	640 & BMAA/HB/174		4. 7.01	D.N.B.Hearn	(Ventnor)	
G-CBAI	Flight Design CT2K (Rotax 912S)	01-02-04-07	G-69-52	4. 7.01	D.J.Goldsmith *(New owner 6.02)*	(Edenbridge)	
G-CBAJ	de Havilland DHC-1 Chipmunk 22	C1/0276	WD335	11. 7.01	J.Lamb	(Solihull)	
G-CBAK	Robinson R44 Clipper	1089		2. 8.01	J.Robinson	(Bridlington)	1. 8.04T
G-CBAL	Piper PA-28-161 Warrior II	28-8116087	LN-MAD N83007	25. 3.94	Britannia Airways Ltd	Filton	13. 4.03T
G-CBAN	Scottish Aviation Bulldog Srs.120/121	BH120/326	XX668	26. 7.01	C.J.D.Howcroft & C.Hilliker *(As "XX668/1")* RAF Colerne		4.10.04T
G-CBAO							
G-CBAP	Zenair CH.601UL	PFA 162A-13656		12. 7.01	L.J.Lowry	Lower Mountpleasant Farm, Chatteris	25.11.03P
G-CBAR	Stoddard-Hamilton GlaStar	PFA 295-13133		18. 5.01	C M Barnes *(Under construction 10.01)*	(Tadley)	
G-CBAS	Rans S-6ES Coyote II (Rotax 912) *(Tailwheel u/c)*	PFA 204-13688		4. 7.01	S.R.Green	Tates Farm, Winterbourne	15. 1.03P
G-CBAT	Cameron Z-90 HAB	10099		1. 6.01	British Telecommunications plc *(BT Ignite titles)*	Thatcham	10. 4.03A
G-CBAU	Rand Robinson KR-2	PFA 129-12789		11. 7.01	B.Normington	(Leamington Spa)	
G-CBAV	Raj Hamsa X'Air Victor 2	399 & BMAA/HB/127		7. 9.01	D.W.Stamp & G.J.Lampitt	Pound Green, Buttonoak, Kidderminster	3. 9.03P
G-CBAW	Cameron A-300 HAB	10148		16. 4.02	D.K.Hempleman-Adams	Corsham	

Reg	Type	c/n	Prev id	Date	Owner	Location	Status
G-CBAX	Tecnam P92-EM Echo	PFA 318-13698		26. 6.01	R.P.Reeves	Dunkeswell	22.10.03P
G-CBAY	Pegasus Quantum 15-912	7829		4. 6.01	P.R.Jones	Felthorpe	18. 6.02P
					(Destroyed in arson attack 18.2.03)		
G-CBAZ	Rans S-6ES Coyote II	PFA 204-13596		12. 7.01	G.V.Willder	Barton	11. 9.02P
G-CBBA	Robin DR400/180	2505		27. 7.01	A.P.Loch	North Weald	15. 8.04
G-CBBB	Pegasus Quantum 15-912	7827		22. 6.01	A.Rose	Knapthorpe Lodge, Caunton	21. 6.03P
					tr Charlie Bravo Group		
G-CBBC	Scottish Aviation Bulldog Srs.120/121	BH120/201	XX515	8. 6.01	Bulldog Flyers Ltd (As "XX515/4")	Blackbushe	15.11.04T
G-CBBF	Beech 76 Duchess	ME-352	OY-BED EI-BHS	23. 7.01	Liddell Aircraft Ltd	Bournemouth	6.11.04T
G-CBBG	Mainair Blade	1291-0601-7 & W1086		23. 7.01	P.J.Donoghue	Warrington	27.3.03P
G-CBBH	Raj Hamsa X'Air Victor 2	435 & BMAA/HB/143		19. 7.01	W.G.Colyer	(Tonbridge)	11.11.03P
G-CBBL	Scottish Aviation Bulldog Srs.120/121	BH120/243	XX550	8. 8.01	I.R.Bates (As "XX550/Z")	Fenland	16.10.04
G-CBBM	ICP MXP-740 Savannah J22	"Kit 3" & BMAA/HB/176		10. 8.01	P.J.Wilson & S.Whittaker	Sandtoft	
					t/a Sandtoft Ultralights Partnership (Noted 12.01)		
G-CBBN	Pegasus Quantum 15-912	7844		9. 8.01	C.D.Hogbourne	Long Acres Farm, Sandy	27. 8.02P
G-CBBO	Whittaker MW5-D Sorcerer	PFA 163-13443		23. 7.01	P.J.Gripton	(Sutton-on-the-Forest)	
G-CBBP	Pegasus Quantum 15-912	7843		31. 7.01	P.F.Warren	(Bridgwater)	30. 7.03P
G-CBBR	Scottish Aviation Bulldog Srs.120/121	BH120/290	XX625	8. 8.01	Elite Consultancy Corporation Ltd	Norwich	AC
					(As "XX625/01") (Noted 2.02)		
G-CBBS	Scottish Aviation Bulldog Srs.120/121	BH120/343	XX694	8. 8.01	Elite Consultancy Corporation Ltd	Egginton, Derby	AC
					(As "XX694/E") (In open storage 1.03)		
G-CBBT	Scottish Aviation Bulldog Srs.120/121	BH120/344	XX695	8. 8.01	Elite Consultancy Corporation Ltd	Egginton, Derby	AC
					(As "XX695/3") (In open storage 1.03)		
G-CBBU	Scottish Aviation Bulldog Srs.120/121	BH120/360	XX711	6. 8.01	Elite Consultancy Corporation Ltd	Egginton, Derby	AC
					(As "XX711/X") (In open storage 1.03)		
G-CBBV	Westland SA.341G Gazelle HT.3	1750	XZ940	28. 8.01	Elite Consultancy Corporation Ltd (Noted 1.02)	Norwich	
G-CBBW	Scottish Aviation Bulldog Srs.120/121	BH120/277	XX619	1. 8.01	S.E.Robottom-Scott (As "XX619/T")	Coventry	27. 8.03T
G-CBBX	Lindstrand LBL 69A HAB	805		2. 8.01	J.L.F.Garcia	Guadalajara, Spain	5. 8.02A
G-CBBZ	Pegasus Quantum 15-912	7840		14. 8.01	A.J.Irving	(St.Albans)	31 .8.03P
G-CBCA	Piper PA-32R-301T Saratoga II TC	3257244	N5338S	4.10.01	Thistle Aircraft Leasing Ltd	Cumbernauld	9.10.04T
G-CBCB	Scottish Aviation Bulldog Srs.120/121	BH120/223	XX537	25. 9.01	The General Aviation Trading Co Ltd	North Weald	28.11.04T
					(As "XX537/C")		
G-CBCC							
G-CBCD	Pegasus Quantum 15	7845		6. 8.01	I.A.Lumley	(Penrith)	8..8.03P
G-CBCE	CASA 1-131E Jungmann rep	PFA 242-13771		7. 8.01	E.B.Toulson	Breighton	
					(As "A 50" in pre-WW2 Swiss AF dark green/red c/s)		
G-CBCF	Pegasus Quantum 15-912	7846		23. 8.01	F.Beeson	Baxby Manor, Husthwaite	22. 8.03P
G-CBCH	Zenair CH.701UL	PFA 187-13568		8. 8.01	L.G.Millen	(Sittingbourne)	
G-CBCI	Raj Hamsa X'Air 582	659 & BMAA/HB/180		9. 8.01	D.Mcdonagh	Bagby	30. 1.03P
G-CBCJ	Rotary Air Force RAF 2000 GTX-SE	PFA G/13-1331		13. 8.01	J.P.Comerford	Henstridge	18. 9.03P
G-CBCK	Nipper T.66 RA45 Srs.3	PFA 25-11051	G-TEDZ	14. 8.01	N.M.Bloom	Abbots Hill Farm, Hemel Hempstead	13.12.03P
	(Jabiru 2200A) (Fairey c/n 30)						
G-CBCL	Stoddard-Hamilton GlaStar	PFA 295-13089		5. 9.97	A.H.Harper	(Langport)	
G-CBCM	Raj Hamsa X'Air HK 700	656 & BMAA/HB/177		23. 7.01	A.Hipkin	Droppingwell Farm, Bewdley	
G-CBCO	Scottish Aviation Bulldog Srs.120/121	BH120/238	XX546	9. 8.01	P.Stephenson (As XX546/03")	Great Oakley, Clacton	
G-CBCP	Van's RV-6A	PFA 181A-13643		6. 8.01	A.M.Smith tr G-CBCP Group	Crowfield	
G-CBCR	Scottish Aviation Bulldog Srs.120/121	BH120/351	XX702	5. 9.01	S.C.Smith (As "XX702/P")	Fenland	1. 7.05T
G-CBCS	British Aerospace Jetstream Srs.3200	842	SE-LHA N842JX/N842AE/G-31-842/N332QL/G-31-842	27. 9.01	Air Kilroe Ltd t/a Eastern Airways	Humberside	4.10.04T
G-CBCT	Scottish Aviation Bulldog Srs.120/121	BH120/302	XX664	23. 8.01	T.Brun (Noted 9.01)	(Paris, France)	
G-CBCU	Hawker Siddeley Harrier GR.3	712229	ZD668	9.11.01	Y.Dumortier Hannants Model Warehouse, Oulton Broad		
	(Officially quoted c/n is FL/41H-0250295 is forward fuselage no.)				(Noted 8.02)		
G-CBCV	Scottish Aviation Bulldog Srs.120/121	BH120/348	XX699	30. 8.01	Cheshire Aviators Ltd (As "XX699/F")	Liverpool	8. 7.05
G-CBCX	Pegasus Quantum 15	7848		10. 9.01	D.V.Lawrence	(Stourbridge)	9. 9.03P
G-CBCY	Beech C24R Sierra MC-491		N881RS PH-HLA	26. 9.01	Liddell Aircraft Ltd	Bournemouth	3. 3.05T
	(Officially regd as Musketeer Super R)						
G-CBCZ	CFM Streak Shadow	PFA 206-13586		13. 9.01	J.A.Hambleton *"Alana Rose"*	(Market Drayton)	10.11.03P
G-CBDA	British Aerospace Jetstream Srs.3217..	986	JA8590 G-31-986	30.10.01	Eastern Airways (UK) Ltd	Humberside	16. 4.03T
					(Op Air Kilroe)		
G-CBDC	Thruster T600N 450 Jab	0071-T600N-054		12. 7.01	D.Clarke	Great Massingham	14. 7.03P
					t/a David Clarke Microlight Aircraft		
G-CBDD	Mainair Blade	1293-0701-7 & W1088		1. 8.01	R.E.Dugmore	(Northwich)	24. 4.03P
G-CBDG	Zenair CH.601HD	PFA 162-13375		3. 9.01	R.E.Lasnier	(Moreton, Wirral)	
G-CBDH	Flight Design CT2K	01.07.02.17		4.10.01	J.Hosier	Kemble	18.10.02P
		(Pegasus c/n 7849)					
G-CBDI	Denney Kitfox Model 2	PFA 172-11888		4. 9.01	J.G.D.Barbour	Sherriff Hall Estate, Balgone	20. 3.03P
G-CBDJ	Flight Design CT2K	01-07-01-17		11.10.01	P.J.Walker	Griffins Farm, Temple Breuer	27.10.03P
		(Pegasus c/n 7850)					
G-CBDK	Scottish Aviation Bulldog Srs.120/121	BH120/259	XX611	26. 9.01	J.N.Randle (As "XX611")	Coventry	20.10.05
G-CBDL	Mainair Blade	1292-0701-7 & W1087		1. 8.01	D.Lightwood	(Macclesfield)	14.11.02P
G-CBDM	Tecnam P92-EM Echo	PFA 318-13756		11. 7.01	C.J.Willy & J.J.Cozens	(South Petherton)	
G-CBDN	Mainair Blade	1297-0801-7 & W1092		20. 9.01	A. & R.W.Osborne	Priory Farm, Tibenham	26. 9.03P
G-CBDO	Raj Hamsa X'Air 582	583 & BMAA/HB/170		12.11.01	R.T.Henry	Newtownards, Co.Down	22.10.03P
G-CBDP	Mainair Blade 912	1295-0801-7 & W1090		17. 8.01	D.S.Parker	Carlisle	16. 8.03P
G-CBDS	Scottish Aviation Bulldog Srs.120/121	BH120/356	XX707	27. 7.01	H R M Tyrell (As "XX707/4")	Sleap	6.12.04T
G-CBDT	Zenair CH.601HD	PFA 162-12474		17. 9.01	D.G.Watt	(Kirkby Stephen)	
G-CBDU	Quad City Challenger II	PFA 177-13000		14. 9.01	Hiscox Cases Ltd (Noted 11.01)	Otherton, Cannock	
G-CBDV	Raj Hamsa X'Air 582	616 & BMAA/HB/161		6. 8.01	R.J.Brown	Davidstow Moor	23. 4.03P
G-CBDW	Raj Hamsa X'Air J22	575 & BMAA/HB/150		18. 9.01	P.R.& V.C.Reynolds	Latch Farm, Kirknewton	18. 8.03P
G-CBDX	Pegasus Quantum 15	7857		11.10.01	C.C.Beck	(Croydon)	15.10.03P
G-CBDY	Raj Hamsa X'Air Victor 2	588 & BMAA/HB/155		26. 9.01	P.M.Stoney	Stock Farm, Billericay	
G-CBDZ	Pegasus Quantum 15-912	7852		11. 9.01	C.I.D.H.Garrison	Sutton Meadows, Ely	10. 9.03P

Reg	Type	C/n	Prev id	Date	Owner	Location	Status
G-CBEB	Air Creation Kiss 400-582 UK/FL003/135 & BMAA/HB/184			3.10.01	P.R.J.& A.R.R.Williams	(Bristol)	22. 4.03P
G-CBEC	Cameron Z-105 HAB	10105		16.10.01	A.L.Ballarino	Piedimonte Matese, Italy	3.10.02A
G-CBED	Cameron Z-90 HAB	10121		15.10.01	John Aimo Balloons SAS	Mondovi, Italy	17. 9.03A
G-CBEE	Piper PA-28R-200 Cherokee Arrow II	28R-7635055	N4479X	5.10.01	IHC Aviation Ltd	Biggin Hill	15.11.04T
G-CBEF	Scottish Aviation Bulldog Srs.120/121	BH120/286	XX621	3.10.01	M.A.Wilkinson (As "XX621/H")	Spanhoe Lodge	31. 1.05
G-CBEG	Robinson R44 Raven	1124		28. 9.01	J.Henderson	Kintore	11.10.04T
G-CBEH	Scottish Aviation Bulldog Srs.120/121	BH120/207	XX521	28. 9.01	R.E.Dagless (As "XX521/H")	Holly Hill Farm, Guist	9. 9.05
G-CBEI	Piper PA-22-108 Colt	22-9136	SE-CZR	5. 6.02	L.G.Appelbeck	East Winch	AC
G-CBEJ	Colt 120A HAB	10181		11.10.01	J.A.Gray	Cirencester	27. 6.03T
G-CBEK	Scottish Aviation Bulldog Srs.120/121	BH120/349	XX700	26. 9.01	S.Landregan (As "XX700/17")	Blackbushe	15.11.04T
G-CBEL	Hawker Iraqi Fury FB.Mk.11	37579	N36SF Iraqi AF 315	6. 8.01	J.A.D.Bradshaw "361/NAVY""	Kemble	30.10.03P
G-CBEM	Mainair Blade	1294-0801-7 & W1089		17. 8.01	M.Earp	(Macclesfield)	14.11.02P
G-CBEN	Pegasus Quantum 15-912	7855		8.10.01	B.J.Syson	Kemble	23.11.03P
G-CBEO							
G-CBEP	British Aerospace Jetstream 3206	980	F-GMVN G-31-980	23.11.01	Trident Aviation Leasing Services (Ireland) Ltd (Exported 1.03)	(Dublin)	
G-CBER	British Aerospace Jetstream 3206	982	F-GMVO G-31-982	12. 3.02	Trident Aviation Leasing Services (Ireland) Ltd (Exported 1.03)	(Dublin)	
G-CBES	Europa Aviation Europa 061 & PFA 247-12691 (Rotax 912) (Monowheel u/c)			27. 9.01	M R Hexley (F/f 22.7.02)	(Penmaenmawr)	5.8.03P
G-CBET	Mainair Blade 912S	1296-0801-7 & W1091		6. 9.01	R.Neale	(Chelmsford)	7. 9.03P
G-CBEU	Pegasus Quantum 15-912	7869		16.10.01	C.Lee	(Luton)	15.10.03P
G-CBEV	Pegasus Quantum 15-912	7854		16.10.01	B.J.Syson	(Luton)	15.10.03P
G-CBEW	Flight Design CT2K (Pegasus Aviation c/n)	7868		19.10.01	M.Clare	(Gayton, Northants)	16.11.02P
G-CBEX	Flight Design CT2K (Pegasus Aviation c/n)	7867		29.10.01	B.W.T.Rood	Sywell	14.11.02P
G-CBEY	Cameron C-80 HAB	10190		31.10.01	D.V.Fowler	(Cranbrook)	15.11.03A
G-CBEZ	Robin DR400/180	2511		26. 2.02	K.V.Field	Turweston	8. 4.05T
G-CBFA	Diamond DA40 Star	40063		25.10.01	Lyrastar Ltd	Redhill	5. 3.05T
G-CBFB	Diamond DA40 Star	40079		30. 4.02	Phantom Air Ltd	(Telford)	1. 7.05T
G-CBFC	Diamond DA40 Star	40062		22.10.01	Diamond Aircraft UK Ltd	Gamston	
G-CBFD	Westland SA.341C Gazelle HT.2	1158	XW887	24.10.10	Aerocars Ltd (Noted 6.02)	East Garston, Berks	AC
G-CBFE	Raj Hamsa X'Air Victor 2 636 & BMAA/HB/186			19.10.01	S.Whittle & M.L.Powell	Brook Farm, Pilling	16. 6.03P
G-CBFF	Cameron O-120 HAB	10167		20.11.01	T.M.C.McCoy (Op Ascent Balloons) "Ascent"	Bath	31.10.03T
G-CBFG	Cameron Thunder AX8-105 S2 HAB	10187		13.11.01	Master Ad (UK) Ltd	Bangkok, Thailand	28.10.02A
G-CBFH	Cameron Thunder AX8-105 S2 HAB	10188		13.11.01	Master Ad (UK) Ltd	Bangkok, Thailand	28.10.02A
G-CBFI	Piper PA-18-150 Super Cub	18-6279	SE-FDY LN-HHA/SE-CTA/N8675D	5.10.01	L.F.Appelbeck (Fuselage noted 8.02 as "SE-FDY")	East Winch	AC
G-CBFJ	Robinson R44 Raven	1131		7.11.01	Scotia Helicopters Ltd	Cumbernauld	8.11.04T
G-CBFK	Murphy Rebel	PFA 232-13340		13. 9.01	D.Webb (Noted 8.02)	Bidford	13.10.03P
G-CBFL	British Aerospace BAe.146 Srs.200	E2055	SE-DRF N697AA/N145AC/G-5-055/N145AC/G-5-055 (Open storage10.02)	25.10.01	BAE Systems (Operations) Ltd	Exeter	
G-CBFM	SOCATA TB-21 Trinidad GT	710	PH-BLM D-EFAK(4)	2. 1.02	Execflight Ltd	Southend	17. 3.05T
G-CBFN	Robin HR100/200B	112	F-BTBP	1. 3.02	A.C.Barton tr Foxtroy November Group	Blackbushe	11. 6.05
G-CBFO	Cessna 172S Skyhawk	172S8929	N3520A	22.10.01	Halegreen Associates Ltd	Hinton-in-the-Hedges	29.10.04T
G-CBFP	Scottish Aviation Bulldog Srs.120/121	BH120/306	XX636	29.10.01	I.D.McClelland (As "XX636/Y")	Biggin Hill	23. 1.05T
G-CBFR							
G-CBFT	Raj Hamsa X'Air 582 685 & BMAA/HB/190			6.11.01	P.Richardson	(Newark)	17. 6.03P
G-CBFU	Scottish Aviation Bulldog Srs.120/121	BH120/293	XX628	12.11.01	J.R.& S.J.Huggins Chalksole Green Farm, Alkham (As "XX628/9")		15. 4.05
G-CBFV	Comco Ikarus C42-FB-UK (Rotax 912ULS)	PFA 322-13774		5.11.01	P.A.D.Chubb	Mergate Hall, Bracon Ash	19. 2.03P
G-CBFW	Bensen B.8	PFA G/01-1312		6.11.01	B.F.Pearson	(Newark)	
G-CBFX	Rans S-6ES Coyote II (Rotax 582)	PFA 204-13820		8.11.01	N.C. Harper tr G-CBFX Group	(Norwich)	9. 6.03P
G-CBFY	Cameron Z-250 HAB	10023		9.11.01	Cameron Balloons Ltd	Bristol	1. 4.03A
G-CBFZ	Jabiru Jabiru UL-450	PFA 274-13617		8.11.01	A.H.King	(Orpington)	1. 4.03P
G-CBGA	PZL-110 Koliber 160A	04010086	SP-WGM	14.11.01	PZL International Aviation Marketing & Sales plc	North Weald	17. 1.05T
G-CBGB	Zenair CH.601UL	PFA 162A-13819		12.11.01	R.Germany	Knapthorpe Lodge, Caunton	21. 4.03P
G-CBGC	SOCATA TB-10 Tobago	1584	VH-YHB	21. 9.01	Tobago Aviation Ltd	Blackbushe	15.11.04T
G-CBGD	Zenair CH.701UL	PFA 187-13785		13.11.01	I.S. Walsh	(Ivybridge)	
G-CBGE	Tecnam P92-EM Echo	PFA 318-13680		9.11.01	T.C.Robson	Little Snoring	17. 7.03P
G-CBGF	Piper PA-31 Navajo 310	31-749	F-BTCP N7227L	2. 1 02	S J Skilton t/a Aviation Rentals	Blackpool	3. 3.05T
G-CBGG	Pegasus Quantum 15	7874		27.11.01	A.R.Cundill	Dunkeswell	2.12.03P
G-CBGH	Teverson Bisport	PFA 267-12784		7.11.01	R.C.Teverson Waits Farm, Belchanp Walter (Under construction 6.02)		
G-CBGI	CFM Streak Shadow	PFA 206-13559		30.10.01	M.W.W.Clotworthy	(Bath)	
G-CBGJ	Aeroprakt A22 Foxbat	PFA 317-13803		14.11.01	W.R.Davis-Smith	(Tarporley)	4. 4.03P
G-CBGK	Hawker Siddeley.Harrier GR.Mk.3 (Forward fuselage no.FL/41H-0150252)	41H-712218	9220M XZ995	13.12.01	Y.Dumortier Hannants Model Warehouse, Oulton Broad (Noted 8.02)		
G-CBGL	Max Holste MH.1521M Broussard	19	F-BMJO F-BNCN/Fr AF	3.12.01	A.I.Milne tr Broussard Flying Group	Horsford	AC
G-CBGM	Mainair Blade 912	1299-1001-7 & W1094		30.10.01	J.R.Pearce	Chilbolton	5.11.03P
G-CBGN	Van's RV-4	PFA 181-12443		16.10.01	G.A.Nash (Noted 11.02)	Kemble	
G-CBGO	Murphy Maverick 430	PFA 259-13470		24.10.01	C.R.Ellis & E.A.Wrathall	(Chapel-en-le-Frith)	12. 6.03P
G-CBGP	Comco Ikarus C42 FB UK	PFA 322-13741		22.11.01	A.R.Lloyd	(Hannington)	20. 5.03P
G-CBGR	Jabiru Jabiru UL-450 (Jabiru 2200A)	PFA 274A-13682		21.11.01	K.R.Emery	Sittles Farm, Alrewas	20..2.03P
G-CBGS	Cyclone AX2000 (HKS 700E)	7866		8. 3.02	G.J.Slater	Clench Common	12. 3.03P
G-CBGT	Mainair Blade 912	1300-1001-7 & W1095		30.10.01	J.A.Cresswell	(Sittles Farm, Alrewas)	5.11.03P

Reg	Type	C/n	Prev ID	Date	Owner	Location	Date2
G-CBGU	Thruster T600N 450 Jab	0121-T600N-055		21.11.01	K.Ford & M.Gill	(Spilsby)	6.12.02P
G-CBGV	Thruster T600N 450	0121-T600N-056		21.11.01	K.Tuck	(Dereham)	6. 1.03P
	(Jabiru 2200A)						
G-CBGW	Thruster T600N 450 Jab	0121-T600N-058		21.11.01	N.J.S.Pitman	Rochester	20. 2.03P
G-CBGX	Scottish Aviation Bulldog Srs.120/121	BH120/287	XX622	26.11.01	G.B.Pearce (As "XX622/B")	Wasington, West Sussex	7.10.05
G-CBGY	Mainair Blade 912	1304-1101-7 & W1099		28. 8.02	M.Talbot	Onecote, Leek	15. 9.03P
G-CBGZ	Westland SA.341C Gazelle HT.2	1923	ZB646	30.10.01	D.Weatherhead Ltd	(Knebworth)	19. 9.03P
G-CBHA	SOCATA TB-10 Tobago	1583	VH-YHA	6.11.01	D.P.Boyle	(Oldham)	9. 5.05P
G-CBHB	Raj Hamsa X'Air J22	189 & BMAA/HB/189		22.11.01	Marine Power Scotland Ltd	(Troon)	
G-CBHC	Rotary Air Force RAF 2000 GTX-SE			22.11.01	A.J.Thomas	(Sutton Coldfield)	
		PFA G/13-1326					
G-CBHD	Cameron Z-160 HAB	10225		1. 3.02	Ballooning 50 Degrees Nord	Fouhren, Luxembourg	10. 2.03A
G-CBHE	Slingsby T.67M-200 Firefly	2050	SE-LBE	28.12.01	R Swann	Bournemouth	AC
			LN-TFE/G-7-125		(Noted 6.01)		
G-CBHF							
G-CBHG	Mainair Blade 912S	1298-1001-7 & W1093		12.12.01	J.A.Horn	Shotton Colliery	17.12.02P
G-CBHH							
G-CBHI	Europa Aviation Europa XS	373 & PFA 247-13245		31.10.01	B.Price	(Southampton)	
	(Rotax 912S) (Monowheel u/c)						
G-CBHJ	Mainair Blade 912	1305-1201-7 & W1100		28. 1.02	B.C.Jones	(Altrincham)	22. 4.03P
G-CBHK	Pegasus Quantum 15 (HKS)	7871		6.12.01	B.Dossett	London Colney	3. 1.03P
G-CBHL	Eurocopter AS350B2 Ecureuil	2673	C-GKHS	28. 1.02	Bishop Avionics Ltd	(Reading)	19. 3.05P
			JA6123				
G-CBHM	Mainair Blade 912	1301-1100-7/W1096		3.12.01	W.T.Milburn	Barton	2.12.02P
G-CBHN	Pegasus Quantum 15-912	7872		6.12.01	G.G.Cook	Clench Common	1.1.03P
G-CBHO	Gloster Gladiator II	-	N5719	11.12.01	Retro Track & Air (UK) Ltd	(Dursley)	
			(P/i not confirmed)				
G-CBHP	Corby CJ-1 Starlet	PFA 134-12498		12.12.01	D.H.Barker (New owner 8.02)	(London SE10)	
G-CBHR	Stephens Akro Z	Q056	VH-IAC	31.12.01	D T Karbery	Barton	24. 3.03P
	(Built H Selvey)						
G-CBHT	Dassault Falcon 900EX	48	G-GPWH	3. 1.02	TAG Aviation (UK) Ltd	Farnborough	23.11.05T
			F-WWFP				
G-CBHU	Tiger Cub RL5A Sherwood Ranger	PFA 237-12477		12.12.01	M.J.Gooch	(Tarvin)	
G-CBHV	Raj Hamsa X'Air 582	525 & BMAA/HB/139		12.12.01	J.D.Buchanan	Coldharbour Farm, Willingham	15.10.03P
G-CBHW	Cameron Z-105 HAB	10217		16. 1.02	Bristol Chamber of Commerce, Industry and Shipping		
					(Bristol 2008 titles)	Bristol	8. 1.03A
G-CBHX	Cameron V-77 HAB	3950		19.12.01	N.A.Apsey "Irene"	Hazlemere	1. 1.03A
G-CBHY	Pegasus Quantum 15-912	7859		7. 1.02	M.W.Abbott	Enstone	6. 1.03P
G-CBHZ	Rotary Air Force RAF 2000 GTX-SE						
		PFA G/13-1321		2. 1.02	M P Donnelly	(Thurso)	
G-CBIB	Flight Design CT2K	7878/01-08-06-23		21. 1.02	J.A.Moss	(Harleston)	6. 3.03P
	(Regd with Pegasus c/n 7878: c/n carried as shown)						
G-CBIC	Raj Hamsa X'Air Victor 2	608 & BMAA/HB/156		2. 1.02	J T Blackburn & D R Sutton	Brook Farm, Pilling	3. 9.03P
G-CBID	Scottish Aviation Bulldog Srs.120/121	BH120/242	XX549	14.12.01	D.A.Steven (As "XX549/6")	White Waltham	22. 8.05
G-CBIE	Flight Design CT2K	01.09.01.23		10. 1.02	S.J.Page	Tower GFarm, Woolaston	17. 1.03P
		(Pegasus c/n 7879)					
G-CBIF	Jabiru Jabiru UL-450	PFA 274A-13789		3. 1.02	J A Iszard	Parham Park	17. 7.03P
G-CBIG	Mainair Blade 912	1303-1101-7 & W1098		29.11.01	J.H.Bradbury	(Sandbach)	1.12.02P
G-CBIH	Cameron Z-31 HAB	10243		4. 1.02	Cameron Balloons Ltd	Bristol	19. 7.03A
G-CBII	Raj Hamsa X'Air 582	676 & BMAA/HB/185		7. 1.02	A.Worthington	Tarn Farm, Cockerham	5. 3.03P
G-CBIJ	Comco Ikarus C42-FB-UK	PFA 322-13720		3. 1.02	A Jones	Newark	5. 3.03P
	(Rotax 912ULS)						
G-CBIK	Rotorway Executive 162F	6112		9. 1.02	J.Hodson	(Ashbourne)	AC
G-CBIL	Cessna 182K Skylane	18257804	(G-BFZZ)	9.10.78	E Bannister & J R C Spooner	East Midlands	3. 2.03T
			D-ENGO/N2604Q				
G-CBIM	Lindstrand LBL 90A HAB	817		28. 1.02	R.K.Parsons	South Petherton	14. 1.03A
G-CBIN	TEAM mini-MAX 91	PFA 186-13111		7. 1.02	D.E.Steade	(Kempsey, Worcs)	10.6.03P
G-CBIO	Thruster T600N	4500022-T600N-062		7. 1.02	G.J.Slater	Clench Common	18. 4.03P
	(Jabiru 2200A)						
G-CBIP	Thruster T600N	4500022-T600N-060		7. 1.02	A.H.Woolley	(Nuthall)	28. 5.03P
	(Jabiru 2200A)						
G-CBIR	Thruster T600N	4500022-T600N-061		7. 1.02	M.L.Smith	Popham	3. 4.03P
	(Jabiru 2200A)						
G-CBIS	Raj Hamsa X'Air 582	708 & BMAA/HB/199		15. 1.02	P.T.W.T.Derges	(Littleover)	2.10.03P
G-CBIT	Rotary Air Force RAF 2000 GTX-SE			27.11.01	Terrafirma Services Ltd	Lamberhurst Farm, Faversham	
		PFA G/13-1340					
G-CBIU	Cameron Flame-95 SS HAB	10222		6. 2.02	Flying Pictures Ltd	Chilbolton	22. 4.03A
					(British Gas-Think Energy titles)		
G-CBIV	Best Off Skyranger 912	BMAA/HB/201		25. 1.02	P.M.Dewhurst & S.N.Bond	Sywell	13. 8.03P
G-CBIW	Lindstrand LBL 310A HAB	821		24. 1.02	C.E.Wood	Witham	26.11.03P
G-CBIX	Zenair CH.601UL	PFA 162A-13765		24.12.01	M F Cottam	(Lincoln)	17. 4.03P
G-CBIY	Aerotechnik EV-97 Eurostar	PFA 315-13846		23. 1.02	E.M.Middleton	(Hereford)	4. 4.03P
G-CBIZ	Pegasus Quantum 15-912	7870		6.12.01	A.Ambler	(Market Rasen)	9.12.02P
G-CBJA	Air Creation Kiss 400-582			11.12.01	C W Lark	(Dursley)	22. 4.03P
	FL006, A01192-1194/T01101 & BMAA/HB/195						
G-CBJC							
G-CBJD	Stoddard-Hamilton GlaStar	PFA 295-13853		23. 1.02	K.F.Farey	(Bourne End, Bucks)	
G-CBJE	Rotary Air Force RAF 2000 GTX-SE						
		PFA G/13-1342		23. 1.02	K.F.Farey	(Bourne End, Bucks)	
G-CBJF	Eurocopter EC120B	1257		25. 1.02	Metroheli Ltd (EI-TOY allocated 6.02)	(Dublin)	12. 3.05T
G-CBJG	de Havilland DHC-1 Chipmunk Mk.20	63	CS-AZT	8. 2.02	C.J.Rees	(Oundle)	
	(Built OGMA)		Portuguese AF FAP 1373				
G-CBJH	Aeroprakt A22 Foxbat	PFA 317-13847		30. 1.02	H.Smith	Morgansfield, Fishburn	8. 9.03P
G-CBJI	Cameron N-90 HAB	4169		22. 3.02	C.D.H.Oakland	Bristol	10. 3.03A

Reg	Type	C/n	Prev id	Date	Owner	Location	
G-CBJJ	Scottish Aviation Bulldog Srs.120/121	BH120/211	XX525	3.12.01	Elite Consultancy Corporation Ltd	Norwich	
					(As "XX525/8") (Noted 2.02)		
G-CBJK	Scottish Aviation Bulldog Srs.120/121	BH120/362	XX713	3.12.01	Elite Consultancy Corporation Ltd	Norwich	
					(As "XX713/2") (Noted 1.02)		
G-CBJL	Air Creation Kiss 400-582			8. 2.02	R.E.Morris	(Kidwelly)	
	FL005, A01158-1164/T01099 & BMAA/HB/205						
G-CBJM	Jabiru Jabiru SP-470	PFA 274B-13769		11.12.01	A T Moyce	Newtownards	22. 5.03P
G-CBJN	Rotary Air Force RAF 2000 GTX-SE						
		PFA G/13-1335		30. 1.02	R.Hall	(Truro)	
G-CBJO	Pegasus Quantum 15-912	7861		10.12.01	J E Borill	(Fort William)	9.12.02P
G-CBJP	Zenair CH.601UL	PFA 162A-13590		31. 1.02	R.E.Peirse	(Royston)	19. 8.03P
G-CBJR	Aerotechnik EV-97 Eurostar	PFA 315-13845		31. 1.02	B.J.Crockett	(Hereford)	4. 4.03P
G-CBJS	Cameron C-60 HAB	10253		17. 4.02	J.M.Stables	Knaresborough	16. 4.03A
G-CBJT	Mainair Blade	1302-1101-7 & W1097		12.12.01	T.K.I.Dearden	(Tring)	17.12.02P
G-CBJU	Van's RV-7A	PFA 323-13868		1. 2.02	T.W.Waltham	(Salisbury)	
G-CBJV	Rotorway Executive 162F	6589		13. 2.02	K.S.Duddy	Street Farm, Takeley	4. 6.03P
G-CBJW	Comco Ikarus C42	PFA 322-13811		13. 2.02	T.J.Cale	(Malvern)	9. 4.03P
G-CBJX	Raj Hamsa X'Air Falcon J 22 622 & BMAA/HB/181			13. 2.02	M.R.Coreth	(Sherborne)	2.12.03P
G-CBJY	Jabiru Jabiru UL-450	PFA 274A-13613		14. 2.02	D.L.H.Person	(Bury St. Edmunds)	
G-CBJZ	Westland SA.341G Gazelle HT.Mk.3	1734	3D-HGW XZ932	13. 2.02	MW Helicopters Ltd	Stapleford	AC
G-CBKA	Westland SA.341G Gazelle HT.Mk.3	1746	XZ937	20. 2.02	MW Helicopters Ltd	Stapleford	AC
G-CBKB	Bucker Bu.181C Bestmann	121	F-PCRL F-BCRU	28. 1.02	W.R.& G.D.Snadden	(Alexandria)	
G-CBKC	Westland SA.341D Gazelle HT.Mk.3	1104	XW862	20. 2.02	MW Helicopters Ltd	Stapleford	AC
G-CBKD	Westland SA.341C Gazelle HT.Mk.2	1130	XW868	20. 2.02	MW Helicopters Ltd	Stapleford	AC
G-CBKE	Air Creation Kiss 400-582			18. 2.02	R.J. Howell	Henstridge	16. 6.03P
	FL010, A02014-2007/T02011 & BMAA/HB/206						
G-CBKF	Flying K Enterprises Easy Raider J22			24. 1.02	R.J.Creasey	(London NW1)	30.10.03P
	0003 & BMAA/HB/202						
G-CBKG	Thruster T600N	4500022-T600N-059		1. 3.02	G.E Hillyer-Jones	Shobdon	3. 3.03P
	(Jabiru 2200A)						
G-CBKH	Robinson R44 Raven	1168		15. 2.02	E.Wootton t/a E.F.Wootton and Son	Sywell	7. 3.05P
G-CBKI	Cameron Z-90 HAB	10236		22. 3.02	Wheatfields Park Ltd	Winscombe	10. 3.03A
G-CBKJ	Cameron Z-90 HAB	10251		6. 3.02	Du Pont (UK) Ltd (DuPont Solar Max titles)	Stevenage	5. 4.03A
G-CBKK	Ultramagic S-130 HAB	130/32		19. 3.02	Airborne Adventures Ltd (Co-Op Bank titles)	Skipton	25. 3.03T
G-CBKL	Raj Hamsa X'Air 582	682 & BMAA/HB/203		18. 2.02	J.Garcia	(Kilmarnock)	23. 9.03P
G-CBKM	Mainair Blade 912	1310-0102-7 & W1105		21. 1.02	N.Purdy	(Sutton-in-Ashfield)	17. 2.03P
G-CBKN	Mainair Blade 912	1316-0302-7 & W1111		11. 3.02	S.G.Ward	Chatham	17. 3.03P
G-CBKO	Mainair Blade 912S	1311-0102-7 & W1106		11. 2.02	I.Steele	(Wigton)	19. 2.03P
G-CBKP	Cameron C-70 HAB	10250		22. 2.02	Cameron Balloons Ltd	Bristol	
G-CBKR	Piper PA-28-161 Warrior III	2842143	N5334N	15. 3.02	Devon School of Flying Ltd	Dunkeswell	21. 3.05T
G-CBKS	Air Creation Kiss 400-582			28. 1.02	S.Kilpin	(Hackleton, Northants)	25. 9.03P
	FL007, A01193-1203/T01113 & BMAA/HB/197						
G-CBKU	Comco Ikarus C42-FB-UK			4. 3.02	R.G.Q. Kellett-Clarke	Old Sarum	4. 6.03P
	0112-6431 & PFA 322-13862						
G-CBKV	Cameron Z-77 HAB	4946		15. 3.02	J.F.Till	Welburn	10. 3.03A
G-CBKW	Pegasus Quantum 15-912	7892		25. 3.02	I.W.Trench	(Edinburgh)	3. 4.03P
G-CBKX	Cameron Z-210 HAB	10286		12. 3.02	Flying Circus Srl.	Madrid, Spain	10. 3.03A
G-CBKY	Jabiru Jabiru SP-470	PFA 274B-13764		6. 3.02	P.R.Sistern	Limavady, Co.Londonderry	6.10.03P
G-CBLA	Aero Designs Pulsar XP (Built J.L.Reeves)	367	N367JR	15. 2.02	J.P.Kynaston	(Luton)	12.11.03P
G-CBLB	Tecnam P92-EM Echo	PFA 318-13770		12. 3.02	M.A.Lomas (Noted 10.02)	Spanhoe	
G-CBLD	Mainair Blade 912S	1306-1201-7 & W1101		21. 3.02	N.E.King	Rufforth	24. 3.03P
G-CBLE	Robin R2120U	364		16. 4.02	Mistral Aviation Ltd	Goodwood	16. 7.05T
G-CBLF	Raj Hamsa X'Air 582	696 & BMAA/HB/194		18. 3.02	E.G.Bishop	(Minehead)	
G-CBLG	Robin R2160	1375		16. 4.02	West Wales Airport Ltd	Shobdon	15. 5.05T
G-CBLH	Raj Hamsa X'Air 582	673 & BMAA/HB/182		18. 3.02	S.Rance (Noted 10.02)	Newton Peverill	
G-CBLI	Aerostar Yakovlev Yak-52	867110	LY-ANU DOSAAF 136 yellow	9. 4.02	E.G.Gavazzi	North Weald	15. 5.03P
G-CBLJ	IAV-Bacau Yakovlev Yak-52	888615	RA444721 DOSAAF 57 yellow	9. 4.02	G.H.Wilson "Black/02"	Audley End	25. 4.03P
G-CBLK	Hawker Hind	41H-82971	Afghan AF L7181	20. 3.02	Aero Vintage Ltd	(Northiam)	
G-CBLL	Pegasus Quantum 15-912	7891		22. 3.02	Light Flight Ltd	Knapthorpe Lodge, Caunton	3. 4.03P
G-CBLM	Mainair Blade 912	1308-0102-7 & W1103		12. 2.02	J.Dearn tr G-CBLM Flying Group	Barton	17. 2.03P
G-CBLN	Cameron Z-31 HAB	10285		26. 4.02	Virgin Balloon & Airship Co Ltd (Benadryl titles)	Telford	7. 5.03A
G-CBLO	Lindstrand LBL 42A HAB	854		3. 4.02	Virgin Airship & Balloon Co Ltd (nPower titles)	Telford	9. 4.03A
G-CBLP	Raj Hamsa X'Air Falcon J22 646 & BMAA/HB/213			26. 3.02	M.J.Kaye & S.Litchfield	(Swinton)	
G-CBLR	Stemme S10-VT	11-002	D-KVIN	22. 3.02	C.R.Lear	RAF Keevil	11. 4.05P
G-CBLS							
G-CBLT	Mainair Blade 912	1315-0202-7 & W-1110		25. 4.02	S.J.Joseph	(Waltham Cross)	29. 4.03P
G-CBLU	Cameron C-90 HAB	10128		30. 4.02	A.G.Martin	Bristol	30. 4.03A
G-CBLV	Flight Design CT2K (Pegasus Aviation c/n)	7886		11. 4.02	A.K.Pickering	(Villefollett, Deux-Sèvres, France)	16. 4.03P
G-CBLW	Raj Hamsa X'Air Falcon V2 641 & BMAA/HB/209			13. 3.02	R.R.Hadley	Dunkeswell	
G-CBLX	Air Creation Kiss 400-582			3. 4.02	J H Hayday	(Great Missenden)	30.10.03P
	FL008, A02013-2003/T02010 & BMAA/HB/208						
G-CBLY	Grob G.109B	6403	D-KITZ(2) (F-WAQS)	12. 3.02	D.A.Smith tr G-CBLY Syndicate	Wing Farm, Longbridge Deverill	20. 5.05
G-CBLZ	Rutan LongEz	1046	F-PYYV	5. 6.02	R.P.H.Hancock	(Great Shelford)	9.10.03P
G-CBMA	Raj Hamsa X'Air 582	739 & BMAA/HB/204		14. 2.02	K.Angel (Noted 7.02)	Middle Stoke, Kent	
G-CBMB	Cyclone AX2000	7894		18. 6.02	York Microlight Centre Ltd	Rufforth	24. 6.03P
G-CBMC	Cameron Z-105 HAB	10274		30. 4.02	The Balloon Co Ltd t/a First Flight (Edward Ware Homes titles)	Bristol	17. 4.03T

Regn	Type	C/n	Prev id	Date	Owner/Operator	Location	CofA
G-CBMD	IAV-Bacau Yakovlev Yak-52	822710	RA44460	4.11.02	R.J.Hunter	(London SE3)	12.11.03P
			LY-AHE/DOSAAF 100 (Yellow)				
G-CBME	Reims/Cessna F.172M	F17201060	TF-FTV	28. 2.02	Skytrax Aviation Ltd	Egginton, Derby	2. 4.05T
			TF-POP/SE-FZP				
G-CBMF	BAE Systems Avro 146-RJ100	E3387		27. 3.02	BAe Systems (Operations) Ltd *(Stored 2.03)*	Filton	23. 6.03T
G-CBMG	BAE Systems Avro 146-RJ85	E2393		27. 3.02	BAe Systems (Operations) Ltd *(Stored 2.03)*	Filton	12. 8.03T
G-CBMH	BAE Systems Avro 146-RJ85	E2394		27. 3.02	BAe Systems (Operations) Ltd *(Stored 2.03)*	Filton	12. 8.03T
G-CBMI	IAV-Bacau Yakovlev Yak-52	855907	LY-AOZ	24. 7.02	A Burani	Elstree	25. 7.03P
			RA02050/DOSAAF 107(blue)		*(ETPS c/s)*		
G-CBMJ	RAF 2000 GTX-SE	PFAG/13-1336		22. 3.02	C.D.Upsall	(Stirling)	3.11.03P
G-CBMK	Cameron Z-120 HAB	10293		11. 4.02	Flying Pictures Ltd	Chilbolton	16. 4.03A
					(Woolwich Building Society titles)		
G-CBML	de Havilland DHC-6-310 Twin Otter	695	C-FZSP	5. 6.02	Isles of Scilly Skybus Ltd	St.Just	4. 6.05T
			HB-LSN/C-FZSP/TR-LZO/C-GJZK				
G-CBMM	Mainair Blade 912	1312-0202-7 & W1107		9. 9.02	M.R.Mosley	(Retford)	15. 9.03P
G-CBMO	Piper PA-28-180 Cherokee D	28-4806	ZS-ONK	16. 5.02	E.W. Guess (Holdings) Ltd	Sibson	23. 7.05T
			9J-RHN/N6391J				
G-CBMP	Cessna R182 Skylane RG	R18201325	ZS-MWT	9. 4.02	E.W.Guess (Holdings) Ltd	East Winch	AC
			N38MH/YV-2034P/N2286S				
G-CBMR	Medway Eclipser	172/150		27. 3.02	A.Bradfield	(Hornchurch)	3. 4.03P
G-CBMS	Medway Eclipser	173/151		27. 3.02	C.J.Draper t/a Medway Microlights	Middle Stoke, Kent	14. 7.03P
G-CBMT	Robin DR400/180 Regent	2538		3. 5.02	A.C.Williamson	Crowfield	26. 6.05T
G-CBMU	Whittaker MW6-S Fat Boy Flyer	PFA 164-13339		30. 4.02	F.J.Brown	(Flitwick)	
G-CBMV	Pegasus Quantum 15	7893		3. 5.02	B.Hamilton	(Alvechurch)	14. 5.03P
G-CBMW	Zenair CH.701 UL	PFA 187-13788		9. 4.02	C.Long	(Pontypool)	
G-CBMX	Air Creation Kiss 400-582			28. 3.02	D.L.Turner	(Sidcup)	14. 8.03P
	FL009, A02012-2004/T02009 & BMAA/HB/207						
G-CBMY							
G-CBMZ	Aerotechnik EV-97 Eurostar	PFA 315-13890		12. 4.02	P.Grenet & J.C.O'Donnell	(Banbury)	10. 7.03P
G-CBNA	Flight Design CT2K *(Pegasus Aviation c/n)*	7887		31. 5.02	D.M.Wood	(Banbury)	16. 6.03P
G-CBNB	Eurocopter EC120B	1040		8. 6.99	Arenberg Consultadoria e Servicos LDA	(Madeira, Portugal)	29. 6.05
G-CBNC	Mainair Blade 912	1319-0402-7 & W1114		17. 4.02	A.C.Rowlands	(Nether Heyford, Northants)	22. 4.03P
G-CBNF	Rans S-7 Courier	PFA 218-13762		12. 4.02	T.R.Grief *(Noted 7.02)*	Bagby	
G-CBNG	Robin R2112 Alpha	180	PH-ROL	20. 5.02	Solway Flyers Ltd	Carlisle	20. 6.05
			F-GCAF				
G-CBNI	Lindstrand LBL 90A HAB	857		16. 4.02	Cancer Research UK	(London WC2)	28. 4.02A
G-CBNJ	Raj Hamsa X'Air 912	680 & BMAA/HB/187		23. 4.02	M.K.Slaughter tr 912 X'Air Group	Farley Farm, Romsey	2.12.03P
G-CBNK	Aerotechnik EV-97 Eurostar	PFA 315-13888		17. 4.02	M.R.M.Welch	(Lewes)	7. 7.03P
G-CBNL	Dyn'Aéro MCR-01 Club	PFA 307A-13805		12. 4.02	D.H.Wilson	(Belper)	
	(C/n should be PFA 301A-13805)						
G-CBNM	North American P-51D Mustang	122-31590	SE-BKG	29. 4.02	Patina Ltd	Duxford	
	4X-AIM/Israeli DFAF 2338/Swedish AF Fv26158/44-63864 *(Op The Fighter Collection)*						
G-CBNN							
G-CBNO	CFM Streak Shadow	PFA 206-13809		8. 3.02	D.J.Goldsmith	(Crockham Hill)	9.10.03P
G-CBNS	Lindstrand LBL 180A HAB	824		23. 4.02	Lindstrand Espana SL	Madrid, Spain	7. 5.03P
G-CBNT	Pegasus Quantum 15-912	7860		14. 5.02	R.K.Watson	(Billericay)	17. 6.03P
G-CBNU	Supermarine 361 Spitfire LF.IX		Turkish AF	27. 8.02	M.Aldridge	(Ashford)	
	CBAF IX 2115		ML411				
G-CBNV	Rans S-6ES Coyote II	PFA 204-13817		23. 4.02	C.W.J.Davis	Sywell	6.10.03P
G-CBNW	Cameron N-105 HAB	10283		16. 5.02	C.& J.M.Bailey	Bristol	21. 4.03T
					t/a Bailey Balloons *(Bristol & West titles)*		
G-CBNX	Montgomerie-Bensen B.8MR	PFA G/01A-1345		26. 4.02	C.Hewer	(Carlisle)	8. 9.03P
G-CBNY	Air Creation Kiss 400-582			30. 4.02	R.Redman	(Grantham)	29. 9.03P
	FL013, A02051-2047/T02035 & BMAA/HB/218						
G-CBNZ	TEAM Minimax 1700R	PFA 272-13624		30. 4.02	J.J.Penney	(Neath)	
G-CBOA	Auster B.8 Agricola Srs.1	AIRP/860	ZK-BXO	22. 4.02	C.J.Baker	Carr Farm, Newark	AC
	(Built from spares by Airepair, New Zealand)		ZK-BMN				
G-CBOC	Raj Hamsa X'Air 582	623 & BMAA/HB/166		1. 5.02	A.J.McAleer	(Dungannon)	
G-CBOD	Comco Ikarus C42 FB UK	PFA 322-13854		30. 4.02	B.Hunter	Eddsfield	28. 8.03P
G-CBOE	Hawker Hurricane IIB	R30040	RCAF 5487	24. 5.02	Classic Aero Engineering Ltd	Thruxton	
	(Built CCF)						
G-CBOF	Europa Aviation Europa XS	431 & PFA 247-13462		1. 5.02	I.W.Ligertwood	(Liverpool)	
G-CBOG	Mainair Blade 912S	1309-0102-7 & W1104		26. 3.02	J.S.Littler	(Standish)	27. 3 03P
G-CBOK	Rans S-6ES Coyote II	PFA 204-13864		19. 4.02	C.J.Arthur	(Ryton)	2. 1.04P
G-CBOL	Mainair Blade	1320-0402-7 & W1115		3. 5.02	A.Anderson	Carlisle	17. 6.03P
G-CBOM	Mainair Blade 912	1314-0202-7 & W1109		30. 4.02	G.Suckling	(Saffron Walden)	30. 4.03P
G-CBON*	Cameron Bull-110 SS HAB	10261		14. 6.02	Ballonteam Bonn GmbH and Co KG	Meckenheim, Germany	7. 5.03A
					(Cancelled 16.1.03 as temporarily wfu)		
G-CBOO	Mainair Blade 912S	1317-0302-7 & W1112		4. 4.02	A.H.Walker	Carlisle	3. 4.03P
G-CBOP	Jabiru Jabiru UL-450	PFA 274A-13611		2. 5.02	D.W.Batchelor	(Immingham)	5.12.03P
G-CBOR	Reims/Cessna F172N Skyhawk II	F17201656	PH-BOR	28. 5.87	Pauline Seville	Barton	24. 5.03T
			PH-AXG(1)				
G-CBOS	Rans S-6ES Coyote II	PFA 204-13859		8. 5.02	R.Skene	Rochester	19. 8.03P
G-CBOT	Robinson R44 Raven	1194		11. 4.02	Heli Air Ltd *(Op Red Helicopters)*	Bournemouth	8. 5.05T
G-CBOU	Bensen-Parsons Two-Place Gyroplane	PFA G/08-1311		8. 5.02	R.Collin & M.S.Sparkes	(Gateshead)	
G-CBOV	Mainair Blade	1327-0502-7 & W1122		16. 5.02	J.C.Miller	Greenwall Farm, Forth	17. 6.03P
G-CBOW	Cameron Z-120 HAB	10302		7. 8.02	Associated Technologies Ltd	Banbury	5. 6.03A
G-CBOX							
G-CBOY	Pegasus Quantum 15-912	7898		17. 4.02	C.W.Laskey	Shobdon	16. 4.03P
G-CBOZ	IAV-Bacau Yakovlev Yak-52	811308	LY-AOC	15.11.02	T.M.Knight	Headcorn	21.11.03P
			DOSAAF 30				
G-CBPA							

Reg	Type	C/n	Prev id	Date	Owner/Operator	Location	Notes
G-CBPB	British Aircraft Corporation BAC.167 Strikemaster Mk.80A	EEP/JP/159	29. 5.02 R.Saudi AF 1108/G-27-27		Transair (UK) Ltd	North Weald	AC
G-CBPC	Sportavia-Putzer RF-5B Sperber	51013	OY-XKC-R5 D-KCIL	27. 6.02	J.Bennett tr Lee RF-5B Group	Lee-on-Solent	26. 8.05
G-CBPD	Comco Ikarus C42 FB UK	PFA 322-13863		14. 5.02	M.L.Robinson tr Ikarus Group	Kirkbride	
G-CBPE	SOCATA TB-10 Tobago	129	HB-EZR	13. 6.02	A.F.Welch	Little Staughton	25. 6.05T
G-CBPF							
G-CBPG	The Balloon Works Firefly 7 HAB	FS7-001	N9045C	14. 6.02	I.Chadwick tr Balloon Preservation Flying Group	Horsham	
G-CBPH	Lindstrand LBL 105A HAB	850		29. 5.02	Vastano Ivan	Florence, Italy	5. 6.03A
G-CBPI	Piper PA-28R-201 Arrow III	2844073	N53496	23. 5.02	Benair Aviation Ltd	(Jersey)	23. 7.05
G-CBPJ							
G-CBPK	Rand-Robinson KR-2	PFA 129-11461		22. 5.02	R.J.McGoldrick	(Biggin Hill)	
G-CBPL	TEAM Minimax 93	PFA 186-13100		24. 5.02	K.M.Moores	(Boston)	
G-CBPM	Yakovlev Yak-50	812101	LY-ASG DOSAAF 58 ?	10. 7.02	P.W.Ansell *"50"*	North Weald	11. 7.03P
G-CBPN	Thruster T600N 450 Jab	0052-T600N-065		23. 5.02	J.S.Webb	Old Sarum	1. 7.03P
G-CBPO	Yakovlev Yak-50	853101	LY-AOT	3.03R	(M Jefferies) *"59" (blue)*	(Little Gransden)	
G-CBPP	Jabiru Jabiru UL-450	PFA 274A-13607		23. 4.02	J.N.Pearson	(Walsall)	
G-CBPR	Jabiru Jabiru UL-450	PFA 274A-13492		16. 5.02	P.L.Riley & F.B.Hall	(Plymouth)	
G-CBPS							
G-CBPT	Robinson R22 Beta	3329		22. 5.02	Plane Talking Ltd	Blackbushe	10. 7.05T
G-CBPU	Raj Hamsa X'Air BMW R100 *(Officially regd as BMAA/HB/217(1) in error)*	BMAA/HB/123		27. 5.02	M.S.McCrudden & W.P.Byrne	(Holywood, Co.Down)	
G-CBPV	Zenair CH.601UL	PFA 162A-13689		28. 5.02	R.D. Barnard	(Stockport)	
G-CBPW	Lindstrand LBL 105A HAB	863		12. 6.02	Flying Pictures Ltd *(Samsung titles)*	Chilbolton	19. 6.03A
G-CBPX	IAV-Bacau Yakovlev Yak-52	8910004	RA02956 LY-ABV/DOSAAF 106 (yellow)	20.12.02	M. Richardson	Sibson	
G-CBPY	IAV-Bacau Yakovlev Yak-52	800708	RA44474 LY-AMP/DOSAAF 52	8. 1.03	Lyttondale Associates Ltd	Sherburn-in-Elmet	
G-CBPZ	Ultramagic N-300 HAB	300/04		25. 6.02	G.C.Ludlow t/a Kent & Canterbury Balloons	Ashford	28 06.03T
G-CBRB	Ultramagic S-105 HAB	105/103		19. 6.02	I.S.Bridge	Shrewsbury	17.10.03A
G-CBRC	Jodel D.18	PFA 169-11408		31. 5.02	B.W.Shaw *(Noted 9.02 on build)*	Wathstow Farm, Northallerton	
G-CBRD	Jodel D.18	PFA 169-11484		31. 5.02	J.D.Haslam	(Northallerton)	
G-CBRE	Mainair Blade 912	1330-0602-7 & W1125		19. 6.02	R.J.Davey	(Sleaford)	20. 6.03P
G-CBRF	Comco Ikarus C42 FB UK	PFA 322-13900		7. 6.02	T.W.Gale	(Portmarnock, Co.Dublin)	6.10.03P
G-CBRG	Cessna 560XL Citation Excel	560-5266	N5245D	13. 8.02	Stadium City Ltd	(Brough)	14. 8.03T
G-CBRH	IAV-Bacau Yakovlev Yak-52	844815	LY-ALO DOSAAF 135	6. 9.02	B.M.Gwynnett	Haverfordwest	12. 9.03P
G-CBRJ	Mainair Blade 912S	1321-0502-7 & W1116		24. 4.02	R.W.Janion	(Northwich)	10. 7.03P
G-CBRK	Ultramagic M-77 HAB	77/212		8. 7.02	R.T.Revel	High Wycombe	30. 7.03P
G-CBRL	IAV-Bacau Yakovlev Yak-52	833708	RA44468 LY-AOX/DOSAAF 122?	2.12.02	P.S. Mirams tr Norbert Group	Biggin Hill	23.12.03P
G-CBRM	Mainair Blade	1326-0502-7 & W1121		19. 6.02	M.H.Levy	(Northwich)	25. 6.03P
G-CBRN							
G-CBRO	Robinson R44 Raven	1221		17. 6.02	R.D.Jordan	Cranfield	8. 7.05T
G-CBRP							
G-CBRR	Aerotechnik EV-97 Eurostar	PFA 315-13919		18. 6.02	C.M.Theakstone	(Wellingborough)	1. 8.03P
G-CBRT	Murphy Elite	PFA 232-13461		19. 6.02	R.W.Baylie	(Hailsham)	
G-CBRU	IAV-Bacau Yakovlev Yak-52	888911	RA02042 DOSAAF 98 (yellow)	21. 1.03	S.M.Jackson tr Romeo Alpha 42 Group	Rochester	
G-CBRV	Cameron C-90 HAB	10323		31. 7.02	C.J.Teall	Salford, Chipping Norton	19. 7.03
G-CBRW	Aerostar Yakovlev Yak-52	9111415	RA44464 DOSAAF 50	4. 2.03	M A Gainza *(As "50")*	North Weald	
G-CBRX	Zenair CH.601UL Zodiac	PFA 162A-13833		21. 6.02	J.B.Marshall *(Noted 1.03)*	Eddsfield	
G-CBRY	Pegasus Quik	7902		24. 6.02	Cyclone Airsports t/a Pegasus Aviation	Manton	
G-CBRZ	Air Creation Kiss 400-582 FL015, A02086-2080/T02052 & BMAA/HB/226			21. 6.02	B.Chantry	(London E11)	
G-CBSA	Westland SA.341C Gazelle HT.Mk2	1007	XW845	6. 6.02	London Helicopter Centres Ltd *(As "XW845/47")*	Redhill	
G-CBSB	Westland SA.341C Gazelle HT.Mk2	1081	XW857	6. 6.02	London Helicopter Centres Ltd *(As "XW857/55")*	Redhill	
G-CBSC	Westland SA.341C Gazelle HT.Mk2	1148	XW871	6. 6.02	London Helicopter Centres Ltd *(As "XW871/44")*	Redhill	
G-CBSD	Westland SA.341C Gazelle HT.Mk2	1045	XW854	6. 6.02	London Helicopter Centres Ltd *(As "XW8545/46")*	Redhill	
G-CBSE	Westland SA.341C Gazelle HT.Mk2	1402	XX436	6. 6.02	London Helicopter Centres Ltd *(As "XW36/39")*	Redhill	
G-CBSF	Westland SA.341C Gazelle HT.Mk2	1924	ZB647	6. 6.02	London Helicopter Centres Ltd *(As "ZB647/40")*	Redhill	
G-CBSH	Westland SA.341G Gazelle HT.Mk.3	1344	XX406	28.10.02	London Helicopter Centres Ltd *(As "XX406/P")*	Redhill	
G-CBSI	Westland SA.341G Gazelle HT.Mk3	1736	XZ934	6. 6.02	London Helicopter Centres Ltd *(As "XZ934/U")*	Redhill	AC
G-CBSJ	Westland SA.341G Gazelle HT.Mk3	1792	ZA802	6. 6.02	London Helicopter Centres Ltd *(As "ZA802/W")*	Redhill	AC
G-CBSK	Westland SA.341G Gazelle HT.Mk3	1914	ZB627	6. 6.02	Knoland Aviation Ltd	Southend	16.10.03P
G-CBSL	IAV-Bacau Yakovlev Yak-52	822013	RA44534	13. 1.03	I.A.D.Acland	(Wareham)	
G-CBSM	Mainair Blade 912	1331-0602-7 & W1126		10. 5.02	Mainair Sports Ltd	Rochdale	
G-CBSN							
G-CBSO	Piper PA-28-181 Archer II	28-7690376	D-EOFL N9595N	18. 7.02	Archer One Ltd *(Op Lydd Aero Club)*	Lydd	12. 8.05T
G-CBSP	Pegasus Quantum 15-912	7903		9. 7.02	D.S.Carstairs	Perth	22. 7.03P
G-CBSR	IAV-Bacau Yakovlev Yak-52	877913	I Y-AQR DOSAAF 100 (yellow) ?	10. 7.02	L.Olivier tr Pegasus U2W	Wevelgem, Belgium	9. 7.03P
G-CBSS	IAV-Bacau Yakovlev Yak-52	833707	RA44475 LY-AIJ/DOSAAF 121?	19.2.03	M Chitty	White Waltham	20 .2.04P
G-CBST	Bell 412EP	36296	C-GLZU (N3033A)	25. 6.02	FB Leasing Ltd *(To become Griffin HC.2 ZJ703)*	RAF Akrotiri, Cyprus	AC
G-CBSU	Jabiru Jabiru UL	PFA 274A-13812		15. 7.02	P.K.Sutton	(Dudley)	
G-CBSV	Montgomerie-Merlin 912	PFA G/01A-1344		1. 7.02	J.A.McGill	Biggin Hill	
G-CBSW							

Reg	Type	c/n	Prev id	Date	Owner	Location	
G-CBSX	Air Creation Kiss 400-582			3. 7.02	N.Hartley	Baxby Manor, Husthwaite	
	FL014, A02085-2079/T02051 & BMAA/HB/225				*(Noted 11.02)*		
G-CBSZ	Mainair Blade 912S	1334-0602-7 & W1129		6. 8.02	D.M.Newton	(Douglastown, Forfar)	15. 8.03P
G-CBTA							
G-CBTB	III Sky Arrow 650TS	PFA 298-13832		25. 6.02	D.A.& J.A.S.T.Hood	(London W2)	
G-CBTC							
G-CBTD	Pegasus Quantum 15-912	7904		9. 7.02	D.Baillie	Carlisle	14. 7.03P
G-CBTE	Mainair Blade 912S	1328-0602-7 & W1123		10. 7.02	P.M.Ryder	Carlisle	22. 7.03P
G-CBTF							
G-CBTG	Comco Ikarus C42 FB UK	PFA 322-13849		25. 6.02	J.A.Way & R.Bonnett tr Ikarus Group	(Ramsgate)	
G-CBTH	Flying Pictures Elson Apoly1 44000 HAB	2002/07		1. 8.02	Flying Pictures Ltd	Chilbolton	
G-CBTI	Flying Pictures Elson Apoly1 44000 HAB	2002/08		1. 8.02	Flying Pictures Ltd	Chilbolton	
G-CBTK	Raj Hamsa X'Air 582	589 & BMAA/HB/168		9. 7.02	C.D.Wood	Dunkeswell	22. 9.03P
G-CBTL	Monnett Moni	PFA 142-11558		8. 7.02	G.Dawes	(Dover)	
G-CBTM	Mainair Blade	1322-0502-7 & W1117		2. 7.02	M.Furniss	(Macclesfield)	10. 7.03P
	(Rotax 582)						
G-CBTN	Piper PA-31 Navajo C	31-7812073	OO-VLH N27636	7. 8.02	C.& P.Wood t/a Durban Aviation Services	(Crowborough Hill)	10. 9.05T
G-CBTO	Rans S-6ES Coyote II	PFA 204-13910		16. 7.02	B.J.Mould	Mill Farm, Shifnal	6.10.03P
G-CBTR	Lindstrand LBL 120A HAB	733		22. 7.02	R.H.Etherington	Siena, Italy	22. 7.03A
G-CBTS	Gloster Gamecock rep	GA 97		17. 7.02	Retro Track & Air (UK) Ltd	(Dursley)	
	(Built Retro Track & Air (UK) Ltd)						
G-CBTT	Piper PA-28-181 Archer II	28-7890127	G-BFMM N47735	22. 7.02	Citicourt Aviation Ltd	Denham	4.10.04T
G-CBTU	Cessna 550 Citation II	550-0601	G-OCDB G-ELOT/(N1303M)	12. 8.02	Thames Aviation Ltd	Fairoaks	28. 2.03T
G-CBTV	Tri-R Kis	PFA 239-12467		14. 5.02	T.V.Thorp	(Marlborough)	
G-CBTW	Mainair Blade 912	1329-0602-7 & W1124		20. 6.02	D.Hyatt	Middle Stoke, Kent	25. 6.03P
G-CBTX	Denney Kitfox Mk2	PFA 172-11721		19. 7.02	G.I.Doake	(Craigavon, Co Armagh)	
G-CBTY	Raj Hamsa X'Air *Victor 2*	720 & BMAA/HB/222		19. 7.02	K.Quigley	(Newtownbalregan, Dundalk, Co Louth)	
G-CBTZ	Pegasus Quantum 15-912	7909		29. 7.02	Thames Valley Airsports Ltd	Chiltern Park, Ipsden, Wallingford	29. 7.03P
G-CBUA	Extra EA.230	009	N230KR N286PA	5. 9.02	G.C.J.Cooper	Sherburn-in-Elmet	AC
G-CBUB	Bell 412EP	36297	C-GADQ (N30338)	22. 7.02	FB Leasing Ltd *(To become Griffin HT.1 ZJ707)*	RAF Shawbury	AC
G-CBUC	Raj Hamsa X'Air 582	779 & BMAA/HB/228		22. 7.02	A.P.Fenn & D.R.Lewis	Shobdon	
G-CBUD	Pegasus Quantum 15-912	7906		30. 7.02	A.W.Rhodes	Yatesbury	30. 7.03P
G-CBUE	Ultramagic N-250 HAB	250/25		5.12.02	Elinore French Ltd t/a Imagination Balloon Flights	Morpeth	
G-CBUF	Flight Design CT2K *(Pegasus Aviation c/n)*	7901		26. 7.02	Cyclone Airsports Ltd t/a Pegasus Aviation	Manton	14. 8.03P
G-CBUG	Tecnam P92-EM Echo	PFA 318-13662		20. 6.01	R.C.Mincik	Bournemouth	30. 6.03P
	(Carries "P92-S" titles)						
G-CBUH	Westland Scout AH.Mk.1	F9475	XP849	5. 8.02	R.E.Dagless	Yaxham, Dereham	
G-CBUI	Westland Wasp HAS.Mk.1	F9590	XT420	5. 8.02	Military Helicopters Ltd	Thruxton	
G-CBUJ	Raj Hamsa X'Air 582	651 & BMAA/HB/212		1. 8.02	J.T.Laity tr G-CBUJ Flying Group	Kemble	
G-CBUK	Van's RV-6A	PFA 181A-13614		25. 7.02	P.G.Greenslade	(Billingshurst)	
G-CBUL							
G-CBUM							
G-CBUN	Barker Charade	PFA 166-13520		31. 7.02	P.E.Barker	(Bedford)	
G-CBUO	Cameron O-90 HAB	3353	CC-PMH	15. 8.02	W.J.Treacy & P.M.Smith	(Trim, Co.Meath)	27. 8.03A
G-CBUP	VPM M16 Tandem Trainer		ZU-AIH	28. 8.02	R.W.Husband	Blackbrook Farm, Sheffield	
	SA-M16-10M & PFA G/12-1346						
G-CBUR	Zenair CH 601UL	PFA 162A-13891		19. 7.02	R.J.Kelly	(London NW11)	18. 9.03P
G-CBUS	Pegasus Quantum 15	7916		29. 8.02	J.Liddiard	Ginge Farm, Wantage	15. 9.03P
G-CBUU	Pegasus Quantum 15-912	7917		27. 8.02	Smart Central Vacuums Ltd	(Nicholas, Hereford)	27. 8.03P
G-CBUV							
G-CBUW	Cameron Z-133 HAB	10322		29. 8.02	Balloon School (International) Ltd	Petworth	29. 8.03T
G-CBUX	Cyclone AX2000	7918		2.10.02	J.Madhvani	Plaistows Farm, St Albans	2.10.03P
G-CBUY	Rans S-6ES Coyote II	PFA 204-13954		13. 8.02	S.C.Jackson & J.S.Coster	Rufforth	30.10.03P
G-CBUZ	Pegasus Quantum 15	7907		31. 7.02	S.T.Allen	Yatesbury	30. 7.03P
	(Rotax 503)						
G-CBVA	Thruster T600N	4500082-T600N-068		14. 8.02	G.St.Clair Moseley	(Limavady, Co.Londonderry)	27. 8.03P
	(Jabiru 2200A)						
G-CBVB	Robin R2120U	365		26. 7.02	Mistral Aviation Ltd	Goodwood	AC
G-CBVC	Raj Hamsa X'Air 582	792 & BMAA/HB/230		15. 8.02	M.J.Male	(Chard)	6.10.03P
G-CBVD	Cameron C-60 HAB	10338		31.10.02	Phoenix Balloons Ltd	Bristol	19. 9.03
G-CBVE	Raj Hamsa X'Air Falcon 912	229 & BMAA/HB/229		19. 8.02	D.F.Hughes	(London SE9)	
G-CBVF	Murphy Maverick	PFA 259-12876		19. 8.02	J.Hopkinson	(Bradford)	
G-CBVG	Mainair Blade 912S	1338-0802-7 & W1133		27. 8.02	F.Godfrey	(South Shields)	15. 9.03P
G-CBVH	Lindstrand LBL 120A HAB	870		2. 9.02	Line Packaging & Display Ltd	Gillingham	11.11.03A
G-CBVI	Robinson R44 Raven	1259		21. 8.02	Heli Air Ltd	Wellesbourne Mountford	10. 9.05T
G-CBVK	Schroeder Fire Balloons G HAB	408	D-OVHS	30. 9.02	S.Travaglia t/a Idea Balloon	Fiorentino, Italy	
G-CBVL	Robinson R22 Beta	3353	N71650	23. 8.02	Helicopter Training & Hire Ltd	Newtownards	
G-CBVM	Aerotechnik EV-97 Eurostar	PFA 315-13932		8. 8.02	J.Cunliffe & A.Costello	Brook Farm, Pilling	28. 8.03P
G-CBVN	Pegasus Quik	7919		27. 8.02	Cyclone Airsports Ltd t/a Pegasus Aviation	Manton	
G-CBVO	Raj Hamsa X'Air 582	627 & BMAA/HB/227		27. 8.02	W.E.Richards	(Swindon)	
G-CBVP	Bell 412EP	36301	C-GLYY	2. 9.02	FB Leasing Ltd *(To become Griffin HT.Mk.1 ZJ708)*	RAF Shawbury	AC
G-CBVR	Best Off Skyranger 912	UK/209 & BMAA/HB/231		6. 9.02	R.H.J.Jenkins	(Liverpool)	
G-CBVS	Best Off Skyranger 912	UK/215 & BMAA/HB/234		19. 8.02	S.C.Cornock	(Birmingham)	
G-CBVT	IAV-Bacau Yakovlev Yak-52	9010305	LY-AGR	19. 9.02	Lancair Espana SL	(Alicante, Spain)	19. 9.03P
G-CBVU	Piper PA-28R-200 Cherokee Arrow II	28R-7135007	ZS-RER N11C	12. 9.02	E.W.Guess (Holdings) Ltd	Sibson	

Reg	Type	C/n	Prev id	Date	Owner	Location	
G-CBVV	Cameron N-120 HAB	10331		13. 9.02	John Aimo Balloons SAS	Mondovi, Italy	13. 8.03A
G-CBVW	Maule M5-210C Strata Rocket	6048C	A2-WNP ZS-LVB	12. 9.02	E.W.Guess (Holdings) Ltd	Sibson	
G-CBVX	Cessna 182P Skylane	18263419	ZS-IYZ N9653G	16.12.02	E.W.Guess (Holdings) Ltd	Sibson	
G-CBVY	Comco Ikarus C42 FB UK 0112-6436 & PFA 322-13835			4. 9.02	M.J.Hendra & R.Gossage	Ince Blundell	
G-CBVZ	Flight Design CT2K (*Pegasus Aviation c/n should be 7914*)	9714		19. 9.02	David Goode Sculpture Ltd	(Oxford)	1.10.03P
G-CBWA	Flight Design CT2K (*Pegasus Aviation c/n*)	7921		11.10.02	Leading Edge Aero Ltd	(Bourne End)	10.10.03P
G-CBWB	Piper PA-34-200T Seneca II	34-7770188	N2495Q	31.10.02	Fairoaks Airport Ltd	Fairoaks	10.12.05T
G-CBWC	Sikorsky S-61N	61740	OY-HDO LN-OSU	7.10.02	CHC Scotia Ltd	Aberdeen	
G-CBWD	Piper PA-28-161 Warrior III	2842160	N5357G	1.10.02	Plane Talking Ltd	Blackbushe	17.10.05T
G-CBWE	Aerotechnik EV-97 Eurostar	PFA 315-13958		16. 9.02	E.Clarke	Brook Farm, Pilling	21.10.03P
G-CBWF	Europa Aviation Europa XS T-G 551 &PFA 247-13879			17. 9.02	Celebrations Ltd	(Douglas, Isle of Man)	
G-CBWG	Aerotechnik EV-97 Eurostar	PFA 315-13918		17. 9.02	M.Rhodes	(Stoke-on-Trent)	11.11.03P
G-CBWH	Nott Nazca II HAB	8		18. 9.02	J.R.P.Nott	London NW3	
G-CBWI	Thruster T600N	4500102-T600N-071		20. 9.02	G.J.Slater	Clench Common	13.10.03P
G-CBWJ	Thruster T600N	4500092-T600N-069		20. 9.02	A.J.Turner	(Chelmsford)	7.10.03P
G-CBWK	Ultramagic H-77 HAB	77/218		4.11.02	H.C. Peel	Worcester	
G-CBWL	Best Off Skyranger 912	UK/208 & BMAA/HB/236		23. 9.02	P.J.Little	(Warrington)	
G-CBWM	Mainair Blade 912 1339-0802-7 & W1134 (Rotax 503) (*This is a rebuild, with new frame & c/n, of G-BZUM (1271-0201-7 & W1065)*).			22. 8.02	Mainair Sports Ltd	St.Michaels	15. 9.03P
G-CBWN	Campbell Cricket Mk.6	PFA G/16-1328		24. 9.02	G.J.Layzell	(Quedgeley)	
G-CBWO	Rotorway Executive 162F	6597		24. 9.02	Handyvalue Ltd		
G-CBWP	Europa Aviation Europa 233 & PFA 247-12930 (*Rotax 912) (Monowheel u/c*)			1.10.02	Thrifty Car Rental/Total garage, A23, Horley T.W.Greaves	(Hull)	AC
G-CBWR	Thunder Ax7-77 HAB	2348	N754TC	7.10.02	A.Lutz	Sudbury	14.10.03A
G-CBWS	Whittaker MW-6 Merlin	PFA 164-12863		7.10.02	D.W.McCormack	(Atherstone)	
G-CBWT	Bell 412EP	36304	C-GFNR	2.10.02	FB Leasing Ltd	RAF Shawbury	AC
G-CBWU	Rotorway Executive 162F	6416		4.10.02	F.A.Cavaciuti t/a Usk Valley Trout Farm	(Llanbadoc)	AC
G-CBWV	Falconar F-12A Cruiser	PFA 22-13904		7.10.02	A.Ackland	(Reading)	
G-CBWW	Best Off Skyranger 912	UK/210 & BMAA/HB/232		30. 8.02	R.L.& S.H.Tosswill	(Workington)	
G-CBWX	Slingsby T67M-260	2282	G-7-194	11.10.02	Slingsby Aviation Ltd (*For Bahrain Amiri Air Force as 401*)	Wombleton	10.12.05T
G-CBWY	Raj Hamsa X'Air 582	775 & BMAA/HB/244		17.10.02	T.Collins	(Chard)	
G-CBWZ	Robinson R22 Beta	3101	N141DC	23.10.02	Plane Talking Ltd	Elstree	13.11.05T
G-CBXA	Raj Hamsa X'Air 582	790 & BMAA/HB/245		18.10.02	N.Stevenson-Guy	(Beaminster)	
G-CBXB	Lindstrand LBL 150A HAB	878		23.10.02	M.A.Webb	Meifod	29.10.03A
G-CBXC	Comco Ikarus C42 FB UK	PFA 322-13955		23.10.02	A.R.Lloyd	(Hannington, Northants)	
G-CBXD	Bell 206L-3 Long Ranger III	51328	D-HAUA N21AH/N21830	22.10.02	Chester Air Maintenance Ltd	Hawarden	8.12.05T
G-CBXE	Flying K Enterprises Easy Raider J22 0006 & BMAA/HB/198			22. 8.02	A.Appleby	(Hailsham)	
G-CBXF	Flying K Enterprises Easy Raider J22 0001 & BMAA/HB/196			19.11.02	F.Colman	Eshott	
G-CBXG	Thruster T600N 450	0112-T600N-073		29.10.02	P.J.Fahie	Compton Abbas	27.11.03P
G-CBXH	Thruster T600N 450	0122-T600N-075		29.10.02	Thruster Air Services Ltd	Ginge Farm, Wantage	1.12.03P
G-CBXI							
G-CBXJ	Cessna 172S Skyhawk	172S8125	N2391J	30.10.02	Caernarfon Airworld Ltd	Caernarfon	19.12.05T
G-CBXK	Robinson R22 Mariner	2302M	N3052P LQ-BLD/N80524	4.11.02	County Garage (Cheltenham) Ltd	Gloucestershire	AC
G-CBXL	Bell 412EP	36306	C-GBUP	7.11.02	FB Leasing Ltd	Hurn	AC
G-CBXM	Mainair Blade	1335-0802-7 & W1130		19. 8.02	B.A.Coombe	(Billingshurst)	15. 9.03P
G-CBXN	Robinson R22 Beta	3385		11.11.02	N.M.Pearson	Bristol	27.11.05T
G-CBXO	Robinson R22 Beta	3402	N71909	15. 1.03	Plane Talking Ltd (*Op London Helicopters*)	Redhill	
G-CBXP	Piper PA-28-161 Cadet	2841210	N117ND	7.11.02	Plane Talking Ltd	Blackbushe	2.12.05T
G-CBXR	Raj Hamsa X'Air Falcon J22	612 & BMAA/HB/224		11.11.02	J.F Heath	(Annan)	
G-CBXS	Best Off Skyranger J22	UK/246 & BMAA/HB/248		13.11.02	C.J.Erith	(Reading)	
G-CBXT	Westland Gazelle HT.Mk.3	1191	XW898	26. 9.02	Flying Machinery Ltd	(Godalming)	AC
G-CBXU	TEAM miniMax 91A	PFA 186-13037		13.11.02	T.J.Shaw	(Grimsby)	
G-CBXV	Mainair Blade	1343-1002-7-W1138		4.10.02	G.Verity	(Northwich)	15.12.03P
G-CBXW	Europa Aviation Europa XS 494 & PFA 247-13674 (*Monowheel u/c*)			18.11.02	R.G.Fairall	Redhill	
G-CBXX	Robinson R44 Clipper	1264		9.10.02	M.J. Magowan & C.Lilburn	(Lisburn, Co.Antrim)	30.10.05T
G-CBXY	British Aerospace BAe 146 Srs.100	E1124	ZE702 G-6-124/ZE702/G-6-124	18.11.02	Tronos plc (*Noted 11.02*)	Southend	10.1.1992
G-CBXZ	Rans S-6ES Coyote II	PFA 204-13988		20.11.02	D.Tole	(Coventry)	
G-CBYA	Schweizer 269C	S-1773	OY-HSM N69A	15.11.02	F.Frandsen	Redhill	AC
G-CBYB	Rotorway Executive 162F	6623		20.11.02	T.Clark t/a Clark Contracting	(Amersham)	AC
G-CBYC							
G-CBYD	Rans S-6ES Coyote II	PFA 204-13871		21.11.02	R.Burland	(St. Andrews)	
G-CBYE	Pegasus Quik	7933		27. 1.03	A.D.Griffin	(Pershore)	
G-CBYF	Mainair Blade	1349-1202-7-W1144		2. 1.03	C.P.Lemon	(Chorley)	
G-CBYH	Aeroprakt A22 Foxbat	PFA 317-13902		2.12.02	G.C Moore tr G-CBYH Foxbat Group	(Crewe)	
G-CBYI	Pegasus Quantum 15	7931		2. 1.03	J.M.Hardy & M.C.Watson	Deenethorpe	
G-CBYJ	Steen Skybolt	PFA 64-13354		2.12.02	F.G Morris	(Armagh, Co.Armagh)	
G-CBYM	Mainair Blade 1323-0502-7 & W1118 (Rotax 582)			13. 9.02	A.Clarke	(Macclesfield)	22. 9.03P

G-CBYN	Europa Aviation Europa XS 518 & PFA 247-13751			5.12.02	A.B.Milne	(Reading)	
	(Rotax 912S) *(Tri-gear u/c)*						
G-CBYO	Pegasus Quik	7928		5.12.02	A.M.Dalgetty	Perth	15.12.03P
G-CBYP	Whittaker MW-6S Fat Boy Flyer	PFA 164-13131		6.12.02	R.J.Grainger	(Northampton)	
G-CBYR	Bell 412EP	36308	C-GBUK	20.12.02	FB Leasing Ltd	RAF Shawbury	
G-CBYS	Lindstrand LBL 21A HAB	156		17.12.02	J.J.C.Bernardin	Curcay-sur-Dive, France	16.12.03A
G-CBYT	Thruster T600N 450	0102-T600N-072		10.10.02	B.E.Smith	(Wallsend)	30.10.03P
G-CBYU	Piper PA-28-161 Cherokee Warrior III	2842173	N53606	12. 2.03	Stapleford Flying Club Ltd	Stapleford	AC
G-CBYV	Pegasus Quantum 15-912	7920		19. 9.02	I.A.Baker	Sywell	1.10.03P
G-CBYW	Hatz CB-1	PFA 143-13710		16. 1.03	T.A.Hinton	(Bristol)	
G-CBYX							
G-CBYY	Robinson R44 Clipper	1250	N71837	11. 9.02	Helicopter Training & Hire Ltd	Newtownards, Co.Down	3.10.05P
G-CBYZ	Tecnam P92-EM Echo-Super	PFA 318A-13984		17.12.02	M.& R.Rudd	(Dorchester)	
G-CBZA	Mainair Blade	1344-1002-7-W1139		28.10.02	G.Churton	(Stoke-on-Trent)	2. 1.04P
G-CBZB	Mainair Blade	1346-1102-7-W1141		6.12.02	A. Bennion	(Northwich)	
G-CBZC							
G-CBZD	Mainair Blade	1348-1102-7-W1143		12.12.02	J. Shaw	(Fleckney, Leics.)	
G-CBZE	Robinson R44 Clipper	1276		12.12.02	Heli Air Ltd	Wellesbourne Mountford	AC
	(Marked as "Raven")						
G-CBZF	Robinson R22 Beta	3393	N71878	6.12.02	Heli Air Ltd	Wellesbourne Mountford	AC
G-CBZG	Rans S-6ES Coyote II	PFA 204-13894		9. 1.03	N.McKenzie	(Carlisle)	
G-CBZH	Pegasus Quik	7934		30. 1.03	M.Bond	(Bias, France)	
G-CBZI	Rotorway Executive 162F	6718		3. 1.03	T.D.Stock	(London SE18)	AC
G-CBZJ	Lindstrand LBL 25A Cloudhopper HAB	892		9. 1.03	Lindstrand Balloons Ltd	Oswestry	
G-CBZK	Robin DR400/180 Regent	2543		12. 2.03	J Halley	(London SE1)	AC
G-CBZL	Westland SA.314G Gazelle HT.Mk.3	WA2010	ZB629	17. 1.03	London Helicopter Centres Ltd	Redhill	
G-CBZM	Jabiru Jabiru SPL-450	PFA 274A-13827		2. 1.03	M.E.Ledward	(Southampton)	
G-CBZN	Rans S-6ES Coyote II	PFA 204-13652		6. 1.03	A.James	(Sutton Coldfield)	
G-CBZO	Robinson R22 Beta	3390	N71881	23.12.02	Heli Air Ltd	Wellesbourne Mountford	AC
G-CBZP							
G-CBZR	Piper PA-28R-201 Arrow	2837029	EC-IJX N175ND	13. 1.03	S.J.Skilton t/a Aviation Rentals	Bournemouth	
G-CBZS	Lynden Aurora	PFA 313-13534		13. 1.03	J.Lynden	(Bolton)	
G-CBZT	Pegasus Quik	7936		6. 1.03	Cyclone Airsports Ltd t/a Pegasus Aviation	Rochdale	
G-CBZU	Lindstrand LBL 180A HAB	877		13. 1.03	Great Escape Ballooning Ltd	Olney	
G-CBZV							
G-CBZW	Zenair CH.701 UL	PFA 187-13731		13. 1.03	T.M.Siles	(Heathfield)	
G-CBZX	Dyn'Aero MCR-01 ULC Banbi	PFA 301B-13957		15. 1.03	S.L.Morris	(Salisbury)	
G-CBZY	Flylight Airsports Doodle Bug/Target	DB022		22.11.02	A.I.Calderhead-Lea	(Basildon)	
G-CBZZ	Cameron Z-275 HAB	10346		12. 2.03	A C K Rawson & J J Rudoni	Stafford|	
G-CCAB	Mainair Blade	1345-1002-7-W1140		28. 1.03	R.W.Street	(Edinburgh)	
G-CCAC	Aerotechnik EV-97 Eurostar	PFA 315-13979		26.11.02	P.J Ladd & J.S.Holden Craysmarsh Farm, Melksham		
G-CCAD	Pegasus Quik	7924		3.12.02	D.Seiler	(Ossett)	4.12.03P
G-CCAE	Jabiru Jabiru UL-450	PFA 274A-13938		17. 1.03	C.E.Daniels	(Felthorpe)	
G-CCAF	Best Off Skyranger 912	UK/212 & BMAA/HB/235		28.11.02	D.W.& M.L.Squire	(St. Austell)	
G-CCAG	Mainair Blade 912	1350-1202-7 & W1145		22.11.02	J.R.North	Ince Blundell	
G-CCAH							
G-CCAJ	TEAM Hi-MAX 1700R	PFA 272-13916		16.12.02	A.P.S.John	(Tewkesbury)	
G-CCAK	Zenair CH.601 HD	PFA 162-13469		11.12.02	A. Kinmond	(Blairgowrie)	
G-CCAL	Tecnam P92-EM Echo	PFA 318-13842		6.12.02	D. Cassidy	(Canterbury)	
G-CCAM	Mainair Blade	1347-1102-7-W1142		6.12.02	M.D. Peacock	(Leatherhead)	
G-CCAN	Cessna 182P Skylane	18264069	SE-LON OH-COZ/C-GWXC/(N6052F)	16. 1.03	100% Bikes Ltd	East Winch	
G-CCAP	Robinson R22 Beta	3413		11. 2.03	Heli Air Ltd	Wellesbourne Mountford	
G-CCAR	Cameron N-77 HAB	464		5.12.78	D.P.Turner (*Mitsubishi Cars titles*)	Bath	19. 7.02A
	(Rebuilt with envelope c/n 670 @ 8.1980: with c/n 2108 in 1989 & again with c/n 2658 in 1992)						
G-CCAS	Pegasus Quik	7935		11. 2.03	A W Buchan tr Quik Alpha Sierra	(Newark)	
G-CCAT	Gulfstream AA-5A Cheetah	AA5A-0893	G-OAJH G-KILT/G-BJFA/N27169	16. 1.92	Plane Talking Ltd	Cranfield	31.10.05T
G-CCAU	Eurocopter EC135-T1	0040	G-79-01	30. 6.98	West Mercia Constabulary	Wolverhampton	21. 7.04T
G-CCAV							
G-CCAW	Mainair Blade 912	1351-0103-7-W1146		5. 2.03	C A Woodhouse	(Nottingham)	9. 2.04P
G-CCAX	Raj Hamsa X'Air 582	791 & BMAA/HB/251		20. 1.03	N.Farrell	(Tarmonbarry, Co.Roscommon)	
G-CCAY	Cameron Z-42 HAB	10373		27. 2.03	P Stern	Deggendorf, Germany	
G-CCAZ	Pegasus Quik	7927		3.12.02	P.A. Bass	Sywell	4.12.03P
G-CCBA	Best Off Skyranger BMW R100	UK/277 & BMAA/HB/256		23. 1.03	R.M.Bremner tr Fourstrokes Group	(Winchester)	
G-CCBB	Cameron N-90 HAB	10085	G-TEEZ	11. 2.03	L E & S C A Craze	Leighton Buzzard	20. 9.03A
G-CCBC	Thruster T600N 450	0013-T600N-077		23. 1.03	Thruster Air Services Ltd	Ginge Farm, Wantage	
G-CCBD							
G-CCBE							
G-CCBF	Maule M5-235C Lunar Rocket	7276C	G-NHVH N5634N	29.11.02	M.D.N.Fisher	Sywell	27. 3.05
G-CCBG	Best Off Skyranger V2P	UK/214 & BMAA/HB/240		28. 1.03	G.R.Wallis	(March)	
G-CCBH	Piper PA-28-235 Cherokee	28-10648	PH-ABL F-BNFY/N9054W	29. 1.03	Mannix Aviation Ltd	(Derby)	
G-CCBI	Raj Hamsa X'Air HK 700	600 & BMAA/HB/192		4. 2.03	H Adams	(Ayr)	
G-CCBJ	Best Off Skyranger 912	UK/285 & BMAA/HB/262		4. 2.03	A T Hayward	(Broseley)	
G-CCBK	Aerotechnik EV-97 Eurostar	PFA 315-14025		5. 2.03	J A & G R Pritchard	(Hay-on-Wye)	
G-CCBL							
G-CCBM	Aerotechnik EV-97 Eurostar	PFA 315-14023		5. 2.03	W Graves	(Huntingdon)	
G-CCBN							
G-CCBO							
G-CCBP	Lindstrand LBL 60X HAB	908		12. 2.03	Lindstrand Balloons Ltd	Oswestry	

G-CCBR	Jodel Wassmer D.120 Paris-Nice	59	OO-JAL	18. 2.03	R R Walters	(Ipswich)	
			(OO-CMF)/F-BHYP				
G-CCBS							
G-CCBT							
G-CCBU	Raj Hamsa X'Air 582	758 & BMAA/HB/237		19. 2.03	M.L.Newton	(Whitstable)	
G-CCBV							
G-CCBW	Tiger Cub RL5A LW Sherwood Ranger			18. 2.03	P H Wiltshire	(Southampton)	
		PFA 237-13002					
G-CCBX							
G-CCBY	Jabiru Jabiru UL-450	PFA 274A-13528		21. 2.03	D.M.Goodman	(Driffield)	
G-CCBZ	Aero Designs Pulsar	1936	N4075X	17. 2.03	J M Keane	(Brighton)	
G-CCCA	Supermarine 509 Spitfire Trainer IX	CBAF.9590	G-TRIX	18. 2.03	Historic Flying Ltd	Duxford	13. 6.00P
			(G-BHGH)/Irish Air Corps 161/G-15-174/PV202				
G-CCCB	Thruster T600N 450	0033-T600N-078		24. 2.03	Thruster Air Services Ltd	Ginge, Wantage	
G-CCCC	Cessna 172H	17255822	SE-ELU	9. 2.79	Springbank Aviation Ltd	(Castletown, Isle of Man)	1. 5.04T
			N2622L				
G-CCDD							
G-CCCE	Aeroprakt A22 Foxbat	PFA 317-14002		16. 1.03	C.V.Ellingworth	(Wincanton)	
G-CCCF	Thruster T600N 450	0033-T600N-081		24. 2.03	Thruster Air Services Ltd	Ginge, Wantage	
G-CCCG							
G-CCCH	Thruster T600N 450	0033-T600N-079		24. 2.03	Thruster Air Services Ltd	Ginge, Wantage	
G-CCCI	Medway EclipseR	174/152		11. 2.03	C J Draper	(Rochester)	11. 2.04P
G-CCCJ	Nicollier HN.700 Menestrel II	PFA 217-13707		26. 2.03	R Y Kendall	(Newcastle upon Tyne)	
G-CCCK	Best Off Skyranger 912	UK/289 & BMAA/HB/265		26. 2.03	J S Liming & A U I Hudson	(Norwich)	
G-CCCM							
G-CCCN							
G-CCCO							
G-CCCP	IAV-Bacau Yakovlev Yak-52	899404	LY-AKV	30.11.93	A.H.Soper & P. Evans	North Weald	1. 7.03P
			DOSAAF16 (Yellow)				
G-CCCR							
G-CCCS							
G-CCCT							
G-CCCU							
G-CCCV							
G-CCCW							
G-CCCX							
G-CCCY							
G-CCCZ							
G-CCDA							
G-CCDB							
G-CCDC	Rans S-6ES Coyote II	PFA 204-13992		28. 1.03	G.N.Smith	Headcorn	
G-CCDD							
G-CCDE							
G-CCDF							
G-CCDG							
G-CCDH	Best Off Skyranger 912	UK/211 & BMAA/HB/233		5. 2.03	D M Hepworth	(West Linton)	
G-CCDJ	Raj Hansa X'Air Falcon 582	692 & BMAA/HB/214		18. 2.03	J M Spitz	(Bushey)	
G-CCDK							
G-CCDL							
G-CCDM							
G-CCDN							
G-CCDO							
G-CCDP							
G-CCDR							
G-CCDS							
G-CCDT							
G-CCDU							
G-CCDV							
G-CCDW							
G-CCDX	Aerotechnik EV-97 Eurostar	PFA 315-14013		18. 2.03	H F Breakwell & R A Morris	(Tamworth)	
G-CCDY							
G-CCDZ							
G-CCEA							
G-CCEB							
G-CCEC							
G-CCED							
G-CCEE							
G-CCEF							
G-CCEG							
G-CCEH							
G-CCEI							
G-CCEJ							
G-CCEK							
G-CCEL	Jabiru Jabiru UL-450	PFA 247A-13976		12. 2.03	R Piper	(Newtownards, Co.Down)	
G-CCEM	Aerotechnik EV-97 Eurostar	PFA 315-13987		19. 2.03	E.Atherden	E.Atherden	
G-CCEN							
G-CCEO							
G-CCEP							
G-CCER							
G-CCES							
G-CCET							
G-CCEU							
G-CCEV							
G-CCEW							

G-CCEX
G-CCEY
G-CCEZ
G-CCFA
G-CCFB
G-CCFC
G-CCFD
G-CCFE
G-CCFF
G-CCFG
G-CCFH
G-CCFI
G-CCFJ
G-CCFK
G-CCFL
G-CCFM
G-CCFM
G-CCFO
G-CCFP
G-CCFR
G-CCFS
G-CCFT
G-CCFU
G-CCFV
G-CCFW
G-CCFX
G-CCFY
G-CCFZ
G-CCGA
G-CCGB
G-CCGC
G-CCGD
G-CCGE
G-CCGF
G-CCGG
G-CCGH
G-CCGI
G-CCGJ
G-CCGK
G-CCGL
G-CCGM
G-CCGN
G-CCGO
G-CCGP
G-CCGR
G-CCGS
G-CCGT
G-CCGU
G-CCGV
G-CCGW
G-CCGX
G-CCGY
G-CCGZ
G-CCHA
G-CCHB
G-CCHC
G-CCHD
G-CCHE
G-CCHF
G-CCHG
G-CCHH
G-CCHI
G-CCHJ
G-CCHK
G-CCHL
G-CCHM
G-CCHN
G-CCHO
G-CCHP
G-CCHR
G-CCHS
G-CCHT
G-CCHU
G-CCHV
G-CCHW
G-CCHX
G-CCHY
G-CCHZ
G-CCIA
G-CCIB
G-CCIC
G-CCID
G-CCIE
G-CCIF

Reg	Type	C/n	Prev id	Date	Owner/Operator	Base	
G-CCIG							
G-CCIH							
G-CCII							
G-CCIJ							
G-CCIK							
G-CCIL							
G-CCIM							
G-CCIN							
G-CCIO							
G-CCIP							
G-CCIR							
G-CCIS							
G-CCIT							
G-CCIU							
G-CCIV							
G-CCIW							
G-CCIX*	Supermarine 361 Spitfire LF.IXe	CBAF.IX.558	G-BIXP	9. 4.85	K.Weeks *(As "TE517")*	Booker	
	(C/n is Firewall No.)		IDFAF2046/Czech AF/TE517		*(Cancelled 6.1.93 as TWFU: stored pending rebuild 3.00)*		
G-CCIY							
G-CCIZ							
G-CCLY	Bell 206B-3 JetRanger III	3594	G-TILT	26. 4.95	Ciceley Ltd	Samlesbury	30.10.04
			G-BRJO/N2295Z				
G-CCMY	Boeing 757-23A	24528	G-OBWS	16. 5.02	MyTravel Airways Ltd	Manchester	12. 7.04T
			PH-AHP/G-BXOL/SE-DSM/OO-ILI				
G-CCOZ	Monnett Sonerai II	0197 & PFA 15-10107		31. 5.78	P.R.Cozens	Hinton in the Hedges	21. 6.00P
	(Volkswagen 1900)						
G-CCST	Piper PA-32R-301 Saratoga II	3246182	HPN4180T	14. 2.01	A.K.Webb	(Onchan, Isle of Man)	22. 2.04T
G-CCUB	Piper J-3C-65 Cub	2362A	N33528	2. 4.81	Cormack (Aircraft Services) Ltd	Rothesay	
			NC33528/NX33528		*(On rebuild 2001)*		
G-CCVV*	Supermarine 379 Spitfire FR.XIVe	6S/649186	IAF"42"	18. 5.88	K.Weeks	Catfield, Norfolk	
			MV262		*(Cancelled 6.1.93 as TWFU) (On rebuild 12.99 as "MV262")*		
G-CDAV	Piper PA-34-220T Seneca	V3449033	N9284Q	27.11.97	Neric Ltd	Fowlmere	27.12.03T
			G-CDAV/N9284Q				
G-CDBS	MBB Bö.105DBS-4	S.738	D-HDRZ	29. 9.89	Bond Air Services Ltd	St.Mawgan	8.11.04T
			VH-MBK/N970MB/D-HDRZ		*(Op Cornwall Air Ambulance)*		
G-CDET	Culver LCA Cadet	129	N29261	10.11.86	H.B.Fox	Booker	11.11.03P
	(Continental O-200-A)		NC29261		*(As "29261" in USAAF c/s)*		
G-CDGA	Taylor JT.1 Monoplane	6020/1 & PFA 55-10382		28.12.78	R.M.Larimore	(Spondon, Derby)	
					(Current status unknown)		
G-CDON	Piper PA-28-161 Warrior II	28-8216185	N8254D	24. 5.88	East Midlands Flying School Ltd	East Midlands	17. 5.03T
G-CDPY	Europa Aviation Europa	303 & PFA 247-13029		8. 3.00	A.Burrill	(Reading)	
	(Rotax 912) (Monowheel u/c)						
G-CDRU	CASA I-131E Jungmann	2321	EC-DRU	19. 1.90	P.Cunniff "Yen a Bon"	White Waltham	30. 6.03P
			E3B-530				
G-CDUO	Boeing 757-236	24792	SE-DUO	20. 2.02	Britannia Airways Ltd	Luton	10. 3.05T
			G-BRJI/SX-BBZ/G-BRJI/SX-BBZ/G-BRJI/EC-FMQ/EC-786/EC-EVC/EC-446/G-BRJI				
G-CDUP	Boeing 757-236	24793	SE-DUP	30. 4.02	Britannia Airways Ltd	Luton	1. 5.05T
			G-OOOT/G-BRJJ/EC-490/G-BRJJ				
G-CDUX	Piper PA-32-300 Cherokee Six	32-7340074	EC-DUX	31. 7.02	D.J.Mason	(Peel)	17.12.05T
			F-BSGY/5T-TJR/N11C				
G-CEAA	Airbus Industrie A300B2-1C	062	F-WQGQ	2. 7.98	European Aviation Ltd	Bournemouth	AC
			F-BUAI		*(Open store 7.01)*		
G-CEAB	Airbus Industrie A300B2-1C	027	F-WQGS	15.11.99	European Aviation Ltd	Bournemouth	
			F-BUAH/F-WLGC/F-WLGB		*(Open store 7.01)*		
G-CEAC	Boeing 737-229	20911	OO-SDE	11. 6.99	European Aviation Air Charter Ltd	Bournemouth	25. 8.05T
			C-GNDX/OO-SDE/C-GNDX/OO-SDE *(Op Palmair European)*				
G-CEAD	Boeing 737-229	21137	OO-SDM	11.10.99	European Aviation Air Charter Ltd	Bournemouth	16.11.05T
G-CEAE	Boeing 737-229	20912	OO-SDF	25. 1.00	European Aviation Air Charter Ltd	Bournemouth	28. 2.03T
G-CEAF	Boeing 737-229	20910	G-BYRI	13. 1.00	European Aviation Air Charter Ltd	Bournemouth	3. 4.03T
			OO-SDD/EC-EEG/OO-SDD				
G-CEAG	Boeing 737-229	21136	OO-SDL	6. 6.00	European Aviation Air Charter Ltd	Bournemouth	14. 6.03T
			(OO-SDL)				
G-CEAH	Boeing 737-229	21135	OO-SDG	1. 8.00	European Aviation Air Charter Ltd	Bournemouth	14.11.03T
G-CEAI	Boeing 737-229	21176	OO-SDN	7. 3.01	European Aviation Air Charter Ltd	Bournemouth	28. 9.04T
			9M-MBP/OO-SDN/N8277V				
G-CEAJ	Boeing 737-229	21177	OO-SDO	5.12.00	European Aviation Air Charter Ltd	Bournemouth	22. 4.04T
G-CEAL	Short SD.3-60 Var.100	SH.3761	N161CN	11. 9.95	BAC Express Airlines Ltd	Exeter	12. 1.03T
			N161SB/G-BPXO		*"City of Belfast"*		
G-CEEE	Robinson R44 Raven II	10005		26.11.02	Heli Air Ltd	Wellesbourne Mountford	17.12.05T
G-CEGA	Piper PA-34-200T Seneca II	34-8070367	N8272B	30.12.80	Oxford Aviation Services Ltd	Oxford	22 .8.05T
G-CEGP	Beech 200 Super King Air	BB-726	G-BXMA	14. 5.01	Cega Aviation Ltd	Goodwood	7. 8.03T
			(N58AJ)/G-BXMA/N622JA/N522JA/N222JD				
G-CEGR	Beech 200 Super King Air	BB-351	N68CP	23. 7.97	Cega Aviation Ltd	Goodwood	18. 8.03T
			N351FW/N6666C/N6666K				
G-CEJA	Cameron V-77 HAB	2469	G-BTOF	17. 6.91	L. & C.Gray	Farnborough	22. 6.03A
G-CELS	Boeing 737-377	23660	VH-CZH	17. 5.02	Dart Group plc *(Op Jet 2)*	Leeds-Bradford	19. 6.05T
G-CELU	Boeing 737-377	23657	VH-CZE	13. 6.02	Dart Group plc *(Op Channel Express)*	Bournemouth	30. 7.05T
G-CELV	Boeing 737-377	23661	VH-CZI	2.10.02	Dart Group plc *(Op Jet 2)*	Leeds-Bradford	AC
G-CELX	Boeing 737-377QC	26354	VH-CZB	3.03R	Dart Group plc *(Op Jet 2)*	Leeds-Bradford	AC
G-CERT	Mooney M.20K (252TSE)	25-1134		5.10.87	K.A.Hemming	Fowlmere	24. 2.03
G-CEXA	Fokker F.27 Friendship 500RF	10503	N703A	19. 1.96	Dart Group plc *(Op Channel Express)*	Bournemouth	24. 3.05TC
			PH-EXK				
G-CEXB	Fokker F.27 Friendship 500RF	10550	N743A	15.11.95	Dart Group plc *(Op Channel Express)*	Bournemouth	30. 1.05TC
			PH-EXF				

Reg	Type	C/n	Prev ID	Date	Owner/Operator	Location	Status
G-CEXD	Fokker F.27 Friendship 600	10351	PH-KFE	18. 2.97	Dart Group plc *(Op Channel Express)*	Bournemouth	18. 2.03TC
			HB-AAX/PH-FLX				
G-CEXE	Fokker F.27 Friendship 500	10654	SU-GAF	2. 4.97	Dart Group plc *(Op Channel Express)*	Bournemouth	14. 5.03TC
			PH-EXJ				
G-CEXF	Fokker F.27 Friendship 500	10660	SU-GAE	2. 4.97	Dart Group plc *(Op Channel Express)*	Bournemouth	30. 6.03TC
			PH-EXC				
G-CEXG	Fokker F.27 Friendship 500	10459	G-JEAP	13.11.00	Dart Group plc *(Op Channel Express)*	Bournemouth	15. 6.04T
			9Q-CBI/OY-APF/9Q-CBI/PH-RUA/VH-EWR/F-BYAH/OY-APF/PH-EXD				
G-CEXH	Airbus Industrie A300B4-203F	117	D-ASAZ	30. 3.98	Dart Group plc *(Op Channel Express)*	Liege	1. 4.04T
			N14966/N966C/F-OGTB/9V-STA/F-WZER				
G-CEXI	Airbus Industrie A300B4-203	121	D-ASAA	3. 9.98	Dart Group plc *(Op Channel Express)*	Liege	3. 9.04T
			N15967/N967C/F-OGTC/9V-STB/F-WZEK				
G-CEXJ	Airbus Industrie A300B4-203F	147	N300FV	17. 3.00	Channel Express (Air Services) Ltd	(Bournemouth)	19. 3.03T
			F-WQIP/9M-MHD/F-WZMA				
G-CEXK	Airbus Industrie A300B4-103	105	PH-ABF	9. 4.02	Channel Express (Air Services) Ltd	(Bournemouth)	1. 8.05T
			N304FV/F-WQJR/SX-BEF/F-WZED				
G-CEXS	Lockheed L.188CF Electra	1091	N5539	14. 4.92	Dart Group plc *(Op Channel Express)*	(Bournemouth)	15. 4.05T
			N171PS/N971HA/N171PS				
G-CEYE	Piper PA-32R-300 Lance	32R-7780533	SE-KCD	24.10.02	M.J.Barton & I.Blamire	Lee-on-Solent	AC
			OH-PAS				
G-CFAA	BAE Systems Avro 146-RJ100	E3373		9. 5.00	Cityflyer Express Ltd	Manchester	15. 6.03T
G-CFAB	BAE Systems Avro 146-RJ100	E3377		23. 8.00	Cityflyer Express Ltd	Manchester	28.11.03T
G-CFAC	BAE Systems Avro 146-RJ100	E3379		23. 8.00	Cityflyer Express Ltd	Manchester	14.12.03T
G-CFAD	BAE Systems Avro 146-RJ100	E3380		23. 8.00	Cityflyer Express Ltd	Manchester	24. 1.04T
G-CFAE	BAE Systems Avro 146-RJ100	E3381		12. 1.01	Cityflyer Express Ltd	Birmingham	22. 2.04T
G-CFAF	BAE Systems Avro 146-RJ100	E3382		15. 1.01	Cityflyer Express Ltd	Birmingham	22. 3.04T
G-CFAH	BAE Systems Avro 146-RJ100	E3384		15. 1.01	Cityflyer Express Ltd	Birmingham	5. 6 04T
G-CFBI	Colt 56A HAB	570		11. 7.84	G.A.Fisher tr Out-of-the-Blue	Kirdford	24. 7.91A
					(Op Balloon Preservation Group) "Air O"		
G-CFLY*	Cessna 172F	17252635	PH-SNO	25. 8.78	Not known	Blackpool	13. 7.95
			N8731U		*(Cancelled 5.6.95 by CAA) (Stored 8.00)*		
G-CFME	SOCATA TB-10 Tobago	1795	F-GNHU	15. 4.98	Charles Funke Associates Ltd	Goodwood	12. 6.04T
G-CFRA	Cessna 560XL Citation Excel	560-5183	N5090V	5. 9.01	Cirrus Aviation Holding Ltd	(Douglas, Isle of Man)	5 .9.02T
G-CGHM	Piper PA-28-140 Cruiser	28-7425143	PH-NSM	25. 4.79	I.J.Sixsmith	(Haywards Heath)	15.10.03T
			N9614N				
G-CGOD	Cameron N-77 HAB	2647		5. 9.91	G.P.Lane *"Neptune"*	Waltham Abbey	24. 3.03A
G-CHAD	Aeroprakt A22 Foxbat	PFA 317-13909		30. 4.02	C.J.Rossiter	(Wolverhampton)	
G-CHAM	Cameron Pot 90SS HAB	2912		29. 9.92	B.J.Reeves & C.Walker	Brighouse	24. 7.03A
	(Chambourcy Pot shape)				t/a High Exposure Balloons *"Yogpot"*		
G-CHAP	Robinson R44 Astro	0326		9. 4.97	Brierley Lifting Tackle Co Ltd	Wolverhampton	4. 5.03T
G-CHAR	Grob G-109B	6435		21. 5.86	T.Holloway tr RAFGSA	Bicester	7. 5.05
G-CHAS	Piper PA-28-181 Archer II	28-8090325	N82228	18. 3.91	C.H.Elliott	Stapleford	29. 5.03
G-CHAV	Europa Aviation Europa 117 & PFA 247-12769			28.12.94	R.P.Robinson	(Hardwicke, Glos)	11.11.03P
	(Rotax 912UL) *(Monowheel u/c)*				*(F/f 3.4.00)*		
G-CHCD	Sikorsky S-76A II Plus	760101	OY-HEZ	16. 1.98	CHC Scotia Ltd	North Denes	28.11.04T
			G-CHCD/G-CBJB/N288SP/C-GIMN/YV-326C				
G-CHCF	Eurocopter AS332L2 Super Puma	2567		30.11.01	CHC Scotia Ltd	Aberdeen	15. 1.05T
G-CHEB	Europa Aviation Europa 263 & PFA 247-12967			16. 9.96	C.H.P.Bell	Brunton	12. 6.03P
	(NSI EA-81/100)				*(F/f 25.5.97)*		
G-CHEL	Colt 77B HAB	4823		18. 5.00	Chelsea Financial Services plc	Cirencester	26. 5.03P
					(Chelsea Financial Service titles)		
G-CHEM	Piper PA-34-200T Seneca II	34-8170032	N8292Y	26. 8.87	London Executive Aviation Ltd	Stapleford	2. 2.03T
G-CHER	Piper PA-38-112 Tomahawk II	38-82A0004	G-BVBL	19.12.00	Aerohire Ltd	Cardiff	23. 3.03T
			N91339				
G-CHET	Europa Aviation Europa Turbo XS			12. 2.98	H.P.Chetwynd-Talbot	Wombleton	19. 4.03P
	(Rotax 914) *(Tri-gear u/c)* 376 & PFA 247-13277				*(F/f 17.1.00)*		
G-CHEZ	Pilatus Britten-Norman BN-2B-20 Islander	2234	9M-TAM	30. 4.01	The Cheshire Police Authority	Liverpool	11. 8.05T
			G-BSAG				
G-CHIK	Reims/Cessna F152 II	F15201628	G-BHAZ	19.10.81	Stapleford Flying Club Ltd	Stapleford	14.11.03T
			(D-EHLE)				
G-CHIP	Piper PA-28-181 Archer II	28-8290095	N81337	22. 2.82	C.M.Hough	Fairoaks	26. 4.03
G-CHIS	Robinson R22 Beta	1740		5. 4.91	I.R.Chisholm t/a Bradmore Helicopter Leasing	Costock	8. 8.03T
G-CHIX	Robin DR400/500	0036	F-GXGD	29.11.01	P.A.& R.Stephens	Moor Farm, West Haslerton	9. 1.05
			F-WQPN				
G-CHKL*	Cameron Kookaburra 120SS HAB	3733		8.11.95	Eagle Ltd	Canowindra, Australia	21. 3.01A
					(Cancelled 30.3.01 by CAA)		
G-CHKN	Air Creation Kiss 400-582			18. 9.01	I.Tomkins	Sywell	6. 2.03P
	UK/FL002/134 & BMAA/HB/183						
G-CHLT	Stemme S-10	10-30	D-KGCD	3. 7.91	J.Abbess	Tibenham	3.12.03
G-CHMP	Bellanca 7ACA Champ	62-72	N68556	21.12.92	I.J.Langley	Bidford	
					(Stored 10.92: current status unknown)		
G-CHNX	Lockheed L.188AF Electra	1068	EI-CHO	1.11.94	Dart Group plc	Bournemouth	31.10.01T
			(G-CHNX)/N5535		*(Op Channel Express) (Stored 12.02)*		
G-CHOK	Cameron V-77 HAB	1752		25. 5.88	Amanda J.Moore *"S'il Vous Plait"*	Great Missenden	2.11.02A
G-CHOP	Westland-Bell 47G-3B1	WA/380	XT221	19.12.78	Dolphin Property (Management) Ltd	(Thruxton)	14. 3.05T
G-CHPY	de Havilland DHC.1 Chipmunk 22	C1/0093	WB652	7. 3.97	JGH Computer Services Ltd	Gloucestershire	15.10.01T
G-CHSU	Eurocopter EC135-T1	0079		4. 2.99	Thames Valley Police Authority	RAF Benson	12. 4.05T
					(Op Chiltern Air Support Unit)		
G-CHTA	Grumman-American AA-5A Cheetah	AA5A-0631	G-BFRC	3. 3.86	Quickspin Ltd	Biggin Hill	23. 2.03T
					(Op Biggin Hill School of Flying)		
G-CHTG	Rotorway Executive 90	5118	G-BVAJ	19.11.99	G.Cooper	Street Farm, Takeley	26.12.02P
	(Rotorway RI 162)						
G-CHTT*	Varga 2150A Kachina	VAC162-80		7. 9.84	H.W.Hall	Southend	6. 9.87
				(Damaged near Hatherleigh, Devon 27.4.86: cancelled 9.8.94 by CAA: wreck stored dismantled 2.03)			

G-CHUG	Europa Aviation Europa	260 & PFA 247-12960			29. 7.96	C.M.Washington	(Stoke-on-Trent)	15.12.03P
	(Rotax 912S) (Monowheel u/c)					(F/f 6.12.02)		
G-CHUK	Cameron O-77 HAB	2773			6. 3.92	L.C.Taylor	Burton-on-Trent	5. 4.93A
G-CHUM	Robinson R44 Raven	0839			2. 8.00	Vitapage Ltd	Elstree	7. 9.03T
G-CHYL	Robinson R22 Beta	1197			28.11.89	Caroline M.Gough-Cooper	Bournemouth	16. 1.05T
						(Op Bournemouth Helicopters)		
G-CHZN	Robinson R22 Beta	0884	G-GHZM		9. 4.99	Cloudbase Ltd	Shobdon	21.3.05T
			G-FENI					
G-CIAO	III Sky Arrow 650T	PFA 298-13095			23. 7.97	G Arscott	Popham	11.11.02P
	(Rotax 912-UL)							
G-CIAS	Pilatus Britten-Norman BN-2B-21 Islander	2162	HC-BNS		1. 5.91	Channel Island Air Search Ltd	Guernsey	11. 3.03
			G-BKJM					
G-CICI	Cameron R-15 Gas/HAB	673	(N)		11.11.80	Noble Adventures Ltd	Bristol	5. 6.91P
			G-CICI/(G-BIHP)					
G-CIDD	Bellanca 7ECA Citabria	1002-74	N86577		29.11.00	A.& P.West	(Calne)	4.10.04
G-CIFR	Piper PA-28-181 Cherokee Archer II	28-7790208	PH-MIT		18. 6.97	Shropshire Aero Club Ltd	Sleap	30. 8.03T
			OO-HBB/N7654F					
G-CIGY	Westland-Bell 47G-3B1	WA/350	G-BGXP		26.10.98	R.A.Perrot	Guernsey	16. 7.03
			XT191					
G-CIPI*	AJEP Wittman W.8 Tailwind	AJEP/2 & PFA 1363	G-AYDU		22. 7.87	N.R.Hurley	Cannes, France	15. 6.99P
	(Continental O-200-A)					(Cancelled 8.8.01 by CAA: wreck stored 3.00)		
G-CITI	Cessna 501 Citation I	501-0084	VP-CDM		21. 9.87	Euro Executive Jet Ltd	Bournemouth	22.05.03T
			VR-CDM/G-CITI/(N11JC)/(N463CJ)/N3160M					
G-CITR	Cameron Z-105 HAB	10278			22. 2.02	Flying Pictures Ltd (Citroën C3 titles)	Chilbolton	
G-CITY	Piper PA-31-350 Navajo Chieftain	31-7852136	N27741		12. 9.78	Woodgate Aviation (IoM) Ltd	Ronaldsway	5.11.03T
G-CIVA	Boeing 747-436	27092			19. 3.93	British Airways plc (Chelsea Rose t/s)	Heathrow	18. 3.03T
G-CIVB	Boeing 747-436	25811	(G-BNLY)		15. 2.94	British Airways plc (Chelsea Rose t/s)	Heathrow	14. 2.04T
G-CIVC	Boeing 747-436	25812	(G-BNLZ)		26. 2.94	British Airways plc (Delftblue Daybreak t/s)	Heathrow	25. 2.03T
G-CIVD	Boeing 747-436	27349			14.12.94	British Airways plc (Stored 10.02)	Cardiff	3. 8.03T
G-CIVE	Boeing 747-436	27350			20.12.94	British Airways plc	Heathrow	22. 8.03T
G-CIVF	Boeing 747-436	25434	(G-BNLY)		29. 3.95	British Airways plc	Gatwick	20. 4.04T
G-CIVG	Boeing 747-436	25813	N6009F		20. 4.95	British Airways plc	Heathrow	18. 4.04T
G-CIVH	Boeing 747-436	25809			23. 4.96	British Airways plc	Gatwick	22. 4.05T
G-CIVI	Boeing 747-436	25814			2. 5.96	British Airways plc	Gatwick	1. 5.04T
G-CIVJ	Boeing 747-436	25817			11. 2.97	British Airways plc	Heathrow	10. 9.05T
G-CIVK	Boeing 747-436	25818			28. 2.97	British Airways plc	Heathrow	30. 8.05T
G-CIVL	Boeing 747-436	27478			28. 3.97	British Airways plc	Heathrow	26.11.05T
G-CIVM	Boeing 747-436	28700			5. 6.97	British Airways plc (Waves & Cranes t/s)	Heathrow	4. 6.03T
G-CIVN	Boeing 747-436	28848			29. 9.97	British Airways plc (Delftblue Daybreak t/s)	Gatwick	28. 9.03T
G-CIVO	Boeing 747-436	28849	N6046P		5.12.97	British Airways plc (Benthone Tartan t/s)	Heathrow	4.12.03T
G-CIVP	Boeing 747-436	25850			17. 2.98	British Airways plc (Colum t/s)	Heathrow	16. 2.04T
G-CIVR	Boeing 747-436	25820			2. 3.98	British Airways plc (Waves & Cranes t/s)	Gatwick	21. 2.04T
G-CIVS	Boeing 747-436	28851			13. 3.98	British Airways plc (Whale Rider t/s)	Heathrow	12. 3.01T
G-CIVT	Boeing 747-436	25821	(G-CIVN)		20. 3.98	British Airways plc (Delftblue Daybreak t/s)	Heathrow	9.11.03T
G-CIVU	Boeing 747-436	25810	(G-CIVO)		24. 4.98	British Airways plc (Wings t/s)	Heathrow	23. 4.04T
G-CIVV	Boeing 747-436	25819	N6009F		23. 5.98	British Airways plc	Heathrow	10. 4.04T
			(G-CIVP)					
G-CIVW	Boeing 747-436	25822	(G-CIVR)		15. 5.98	British Airways plc	Heathrow	14. 5.04T
G-CIVX	Boeing 747-436	28852			3. 9.98	British Airways plc	Heathrow	2. 9.04T
G-CIVY	Boeing 747-436	28853			29. 9.98	British Airways plc (Whale Rider t/s)	Heathrow	28. 9.04T
G-CIVZ	Boeing 747-436	28854			31.10.98	British Airways plc (Benyhone Tartan t/s)	Heathrow	30.10.04T
G-CJAA	British Aerospace BAe 125 Srs.800B	258240	G-HCFR		28.11.02	Ourjet Ltd	Farnborough	16.12.03T
			HB-VLT/G-SHEA/G-BUWC/G-5-772					
G-CJAD	Cessna 525 Citationjet	525-0435	N525AD		28. 6.02	A.B.Davis t/a Davis Aircraft Operations	Edinburgh	27. 6.03T
			N5244F					
G-CJAE	Cessna 560 Citation V	560-0046	G-CZAR		28.11.02	Ourjet Ltd	Farnborough	3. 4.03T
			(N26656)					
G-CJBC	Piper PA-28-180 Cherokee D	28-5470	OY-BDE		28.11.80	J.B.Cave	Wolverhampton	29. 8.05
G-CJCI	Pilatus P.2-06	600-63	U-143		30. 7.84	J.Briscoe & P.G.Bond tr Pilatus P2 Flying Gp	Norwich	29. 6.01P
						(As "CC+43"" in Luftwaffe c/s in Arado Ar.96B guise)		
G-CJUD	Denney Kitfox Model 3	847 & PFA 172-11939			17. 1.91	N.H.Martin	Skipwith, Selby	14. 5.03P
	(Rotax 582)							
G-CKCK	Enstrom 280FX Shark	2071	OO-PVL		5. 5.95	Farmax Ltd (On slow rebuild 12.02	Bournemouth	14. 5.98T
G-CLAC	Piper PA-28-161 Warrior II	28-8116241	N8396U		18. 5.87	M.J.Steadman	Blackbushe	22. 12.05
G-CLAS	Short SD.3-60 Var.200	SH.3635	EI-BEK		28. 7.93	BAC Express Airlines Ltd "City of Cardiff"	Exeter	20. 7.05T
			G-BLED/G-14-3635					
G-CLAV	Europa Aviation Europa	060 & PFA 247-12641			11.10.02	G.Laverty	(Tobermory, Isle of Mull)	
	(Ritax 912) (Monowheel u/c)							
G-CLAX	Jurca MJ.5 Sirocco	PFA 2204	G-AWKB		22. 4.99	G.D.Claxton (Current status unknown)	(Pontyclun)	
G-CLAY	Bell 206B-3 JetRanger III	4409	G-DENN		16. 9.02	Claygate Distribution Ltd Paynetts Farm, Goudhurst		21. 7.05
			N75486/C-GFNO					
G-CLEA	Piper PA-28-161 Warrior II	28-7916081	N30296		28. 8.80	R.J.Harrison & A.R.Carpenter	Oaksey Park	19. 2.05
G-CLEE	Rans S-6ES Coyote II	PFA 204-13670			29. 6.01	R.Holt	Mill Farm, Shifnal	26. 9.03P
G-CLEM	Bölkow Bö.208A-2 Junior	561	G-ASWE		22. 9.81	J.J.Donely & A.D.P.Thompson	Coventry	9. 6.03P
			D-EFHE				tr Bölkow Group		
G-CLEW	Hawker Siddeley HS.748 Srs.2B/242	1647	ZS-OCF		.03R	Emeral Airways Ltd	Liverpool	
G-CLEO	Zenair CH.601HD Zodiac	PFA 162-13500			9. 8.99	K.M.Bowen (Current status unknown)	Goldcliff	
G-CLFC	Mainair Blade	1324-0502-7 & W1119			11. 6.02	G.N.Cliffe & G.Marshall	(Winsford)	16. 6.03P
G-CLHD	British Aerospace BAe 146 Srs.200	E2023	G-DEBF		2. 5.00	Business Midland Regional Ltd	Aberdeen	26. 9.05T
			N165US/N347PS				(Op BMI Commuter)		
G-CLIC	Cameron A-105 HAB	2557			18. 4.91	R.S.Mohr "Clic Trust"	Corsham	20. 8.02A
	(New envelope c/n 3395 @ 4.95)							
G-CLKE	Robinson R44 Astro	0185	G-HREH		22. 9.98	J.Clarke t/a Clarke Business	(Burnley)	10. 9.03T
			D-HREH					

G-CLOE	Sky 90-24 HAB	019		11. 3.96	C.J.Sandell *"Headfirst"*	Sevenoaks	14. 5.03T
G-CLOS	Piper PA-34-200T Seneca II	34-7870361	HB-LKE N36783	17. 6.86	P.S.Kirby	Coventry	3.10.04
G-CLOW	Beech 200 Super King Air	BB-821	N821RC TC-DBY/N144TM/F-GDCB	2.11.99	Clowes Estates Ltd	(Ashbourne)	7.11.05T
G-CLRK	Sky 77-24 HAB	101		3. 3.98	William Clark & Son (Parkgate) Ltd	(Dumfries)	2.12.99A
G-CLUB	Reims/Cessna FRA150M Aerobat	FRA15000347	OO-AWZ F-WZAZ/(F-WZDZ)	10. 2.83	D.C.C.Handley	Cranfield	24. 6.05T
G-CLUE	Piper PA-34-200T Seneca II	34-7970502	N8089Z	15. 9.92	Kilo Aviation Ltd	(Northwich)	4. 4.05T
G-CLUX	Reims/Cessna F172N Skyhawk II	F17201996	PH-AYG(3)	1. 5.80	J.G.Jackman & K.M.Drewitt t/a J & K Aviation	Hawarden	20. 8.04T
G-CMED	SOCATA TB-9 Tampico	1867	F-GSZK	19. 3.01	S.C.Brown t/a Enstone Flying Club	Enstone	28. 3.04T
G-CMGC	Piper PA-25-235 Pawnee D	25-7756042	G-BFEX N82525	19.11.91	Midland Gliding Club Ltd	Long Mynd	19. 4.04
G-CNAB	Jabiru Jabiru UL	PFA 274-13651		27. 9.00	W.A.Brighouse	(Whitby)	20.10.03P
	(Jabiru 2200A) (PFA prefix "274" indicates model SK: a model UL shold be "274A")						
G-CNDY	Robinson R22 Beta-II	2677	G-BXEW	15. 5.97	Testgate Ltd	Goodwood	8. 6.03T
G-COAI	Cranfield A.1-400 Eagle	001	G-BCIT	1. 6.98	Cranfield University	Cranfield	
					(Noted 7.99: current status unknown)		
G-COCO	Reims/Cessna F172M Skyhawk II	F17201373	PH-SMO OO-ADI	27.10.80	P.C.Sheard & R.C.Larder	North Reston, Louth	27. 3.05
G-CODE	Bell 206B-3 JetRanger III	3850	N222DM N84TC	27. 8.96	B.Wronski	Gloucestershire	26.11.05
G-COEZ	Airbus Industrie A320-231	0179	OY-CNH F-WWIS	10. 2.97	MyTravel Airways Ltd	Manchester	11. 2.03T
G-COIN	Bell 206B JetRanger II	897	EI-AWA	11. 3.85	C.Sarno	Cranfield	6. 7.03
G-COLA	Beech F33C Bonanza	CJ-137	G-BUAZ PH-BNH	31. 3.92	J R C Spooner & P M Scarratt	East Midlands	22.11.04
G-COLH	Piper PA-28-140 Cherokee	28-23143	G-AVRT N11C	13.10.00	J.G.O'Brien	Stapleford	28. 2.05
G-COLL	Enstrom 280C-UK-2 Shark	1223		17. 8.81	Taylor Air Services Ltd	(Cockermouth)	16. 5.04
G-COMB	Piper PA-30 Twin Comanche B	30-1362	G-AVBL N8236Y	14. 9.84	J.T.Bateson	Blackpool	27.11.04
G-CONB	Robin DR400/180 Regent	2176	G-BUPX	14. 4.93	C.C. & C.Blakey t/a Winchcombe Farm	Redhill	24. 2.05T
G-CONC	Cameron N-90 HAB	2139		13.11.89	British Airways plc *"Concorde"*	Heathrow	22. 9.02T
G-CONL	SOCATA TB-10 Tobago	173	F-GCOR	22.12.98	J.M.Huntington	Full Sutton	29. 6.05
G-CONV	Convair CV-440-54	484	CS-TML N357SA/N28KE/N28KA/N4402	19. 7.01	Atlantic Air Transport Ltd *(Emergency landing Coventry 29.10.01 - stored 2002)*	Coventry	AC
G-COOT	Taylor Coot A	EE-1A		16. 9.81	P.M.Napp	(Newcastle upon Tyne)	
G-COPS	Piper J-3C-65 Cub	11911	F-BFYC Fr.AF/44-79615	17. 7.79	R.W.Sproat & C.E.Simpson	Lennox Plunton Farm, Borgue	19.12.02P
	(L-4H-PI) (Frame No.11739)						
	(Regd as c/n 36-817 which is a USAAC Contract No)						
G-COPT*	Aérospatiale AS350B Ecureuil	2168	9M-FSA 9V-BOR	25. 2.98	Owenlars Ltd *(Cancelled 11.7.02 by CAA)*	(Odiham)	10. 4.04T
G-CORB	SOCATA TB-20 Trinidad	1178	F-GKUX	12. 4.99	G.D.Corbin	Flamstone Park, Bishopstone	2. 5.05
G-CORD	Slingsby Nipper T.66 RA.45 Srs.3	S.129/1676	G-AVTB	21. 3.88	A.V.Lamprell	Charity Farm, Baxterley	13. 6.03P
	(Rebuild from S.105/1565)						
G-CORN	Bell 206B-3 JetRanger III	3035	G-BHTR N18098	4. 6.99	John A.Wells Ltd	Costock	12. 4.04T
G-CORP	British Aerospace ATP	2037	G-BTNK N860AW/G-BTNK/G-11-037	2. 3.98	BAE Systems (Operations) Ltd	Warton	28. 3.03T
G-CORT	Agusta-Bell 206B-3 JetRanger III	8739		21. 6.96	Helicopter Training & Hire Ltd	Belfast	28. 7.05T
G-COSY	Lindstrand LBL-56A HAB	017		18. 2.93	D.D.Owen	Wotton-under-Edge	2. 4.03A
G-COTT	Cameron Flying Cottage 60SS HAB	687	"G-HOUS"	13. 2.81	M.R.Nanda tr Nottingham Hot-Air Balloon Club *"Cottage"*	Nottingham	15.12.98A
G-COUP	Ercoupe 415C	1903	N99280 NC99280	27. 5.93	S.M.Gerrard *"Jenny Lin"* *(Under rebuild 3.01)*	Bembridge	17. 7.99
	(Continental C75)						
G-COVE	Jabiru Jabiru UL	PFA 274A-13409		23. 7.99	A.A.Rowson	Lleweni Parc	28. 5.03P
	(Jabiru 2200A)						
G-COWS	ARV Super 2	K.009 & PFA 152-11182	(G-BONB)	27. 5.88	T.C.Harrold *(Destroyed in arson attack 18.2.03)*	Felthorpe	5. 9.03P
	(Hewland AE75)						
G-COZI	Rutan Cozy III	PFA 159-12162		19. 7.93	D.G.Machin	Lydd	14.10.03P
	(Lycoming O-320)						
G-CPCD	CEA Jodel DR-221 Dauphin	81	F-BPCD	11.12.90	D.J.Taylor	Enstone	10. 7.04
G-CPDA	de Havilland DH.106 Comet 4C	6473	XS235	10. 8.00	C.Walton Ltd	Bruntingthorpe	AC
G-CPEL	Boeing 757-236	24398	N602DF EC-EOL/EC-597/G-BRJE/EC-EOL/EC-278/G-BRJE	24. 8.92	British Airways plc *(Animals & Trees t/s)*	Heathrow	26.10.05T
G-CPEM	Boeing 757-236	28665		28. 3.97	British Airways plc	Heathrow	27. 3.03T
G-CPEN	Boeing 757-236	28666		23. 4.97	British Airways plc	Heathrow	22. 4.03T
G-CPEO	Boeing 757-236	28667		11. 7.97	British Airways plc	Heathrow	10. 7.03T
G-CPEP	Boeing 757-2Y0	25268	C-GTSU EI-CLP/N400KL/XA-TAE	16. 4.97	Air 2000 Ltd	Manchester	9. 7.03T
G-CPER	Boeing 757-236	29113		29.12.97	British Airways plc	Gatwick	28.12.03T
G-CPES	Boeing 757-236	29114		17. 3.98	British Airways plc	Heathrow	16. 3.04T
G-CPET	Boeing 757-236	29115		12. 5.98	British Airways plc	Heathrow	11. 5.04T
G-CPEU	Boeing 757-236	29941		1. 5.99	Air 2000 Ltd	Manchester	30. 4.05T
G-CPEV	Boeing 757-236	29943	(G-CPEW)	11. 6.99	Air 2000 Ltd	Manchester	10. 6.05T
G-CPFC	Reims/Cessna F152 II	F15201430		1.12.77	Willowair Flying Club (1996) Ltd	Southend	12. 7.04T
G-CPMK	de Havilland DHC.1 Chipmunk 22	C1/0866	WZ847	28. 6.96	Towerdrive Ltd *(As "WZ847")*	Sleap	24.10.05
G-CPMS	SOCATA TB-20 Trinidad	1607	F-GNHA	7. 4.98	Charlotte Park Management Services Ltd	Goodwood	1. 5.04T
G-CPOL	Aérospatiale AS355F1 Twin Squirrel	5007	N5775T C-GJJB/N5775T	30.11.95	MW Helicopters Ltd	Stapleford	30. 1.05T
G-CPSF	Cameron N-90 HAB	3747	G-OISK	21. 4.99	S.A.Simington & J.D.Rigden	Norwich	23. 3.03A
G-CPSH	Eurocopter EC135-T1	0209		8. 4.02	Thames Valley Police Authority	Booker	20. 6.05T

Reg	Type	c/n	Prev id	Date	Owner	Location	
G-CPTM	Piper PA-28-151 Cherokee Warrior	28-7715012	G-BTOE N4264F	9. 7.91	T.J.Mackay & C.M.Pollett	Woodford	14. 2.04T
G-CPTS	Agusta-Bell 206B JetRanger II	8556		1. 6.78	A.R.B.Aspinall	Skipton	27. 6.03
G-CPXC	CAP Aviation CAP.10C	301		11.12.01	I.Valentine	Kilrush, Co.Kildare	16. 7.05
G-CRAB	Best Off Skyranger 912	UK/245 & BMAA/HB/246		1.11.02	R.A.Bell	(Sleaford)	
G-CRAK*	Cameron N-77 HAB	2291		7. 6.90	Mobile Windscreens Ltd	Stafford	14. 7.97A
					"Mobile Windscreens" (Cancelled 20.11.01 as WFU by CAA) (Stored)		
G-CRAY	Robinson R22 Beta	0919		12. 1.89	F.C.Owen *(New CofR 2.03)*	(Burnley)	7. 4.98
G-CRES	Denney Kitfox Model 2 (Rotax 912)	PFA 172-11574		7. 6.90	K.M.James	Higher Barn Farm, Houghton	20.11.03P
G-CREW	Piper PA-46-350P Malibu Mirage	4636309	N41865	20.10.00	Longslow Dairy Ltd	Seething	22.10.03
G-CRIC	Colomban MC.15 Cri-Cri (JPX PUL.212)	PFA 133-10915		22. 7.83	R.S.Stoddart-Stones	(Caterham)	5. 5.99P
G-CRIL	Rockwell Commander 112B	521	N1388J	22. 6.79	J.W.Reynolds tr Rockwell Aviation Group	Cardiff	1.11.03
G-CRIS	Taylor JT.1 Monoplane	PFA 55-10318		5. 6.79	C.R.Steer	Spilsted Farm, Sedlescombe	
					(Bare fuselage noted 5.01)		
G-CROB	Europa Aviation Europa XS T-G (Jabiru 3300)	442 & PFA 247-13510		25. 4.02	R.G.Hallam	(Macclesfield)	
G-CROL	Maule MXT-7-180 Star Rocket	14032C	N9232F	24.11.93	N.G.P.Evans	Oaksey Park	4. 3.04
G-CROW	Robinson R44 Raven	0754		19. 4.00	Longmoore Ltd	(Godalming)	18. 5.03T
G-CROY	Europa Aviation Europa (Rotax 912-UL) *(Monowheel u/c)*	101 & PFA 247-12896		7. 2.97	A.Croy *(F/f 27.3.98)*	Kirkwall	9. 7.03P
G-CRPH	Airbus Industrie A320-231	0424	F-WQBB F-WWIV	10. 4.95	MyTravel Airways Ltd	Manchester	14. 4.04T
G-CRUM	Westland Scout AH.1 *(Pod No.F8-6151)*	F.9712	XV137	17. 3.98	Military Helicopters Ltd *(As "XV137") (New owner 7.02)*	Thruxton	25.11.03P
G-CRUZ	Cessna T303 Crusader	T30300004	N9336T	7.12.90	Bank Farm Ltd	Bank Farm, Benwick, Cambs	21. 6.03T
G-CSAV	Thruster T600N	4500032-T600N-064		14. 3.02	Thruster Air Services Ltd	Ginge Farm, Wantage	
G-CSBM	Reims/Cessna F150M	F15201359	PH-AYC	24. 5.78	Halegreen Associates Ltd	Hinton in the Hedges	6.12.03T
G-CSCS	Reims/Cessna F172N Skyhawk II	F17201707	PH-MEM (PH-WEB)/N9899A	28.11.86	Cheryl Sullivan	Stapleford	10. 6.05T
G-CSDJ	Jabiru Jabiru UL (Jabiru 2200A)	PFA 274A-13337		23. 3.99	D W, J Johnston, C D & S Slater	Kemble	22. 5.03P
G-CSFC	Cessna 150L	15075360	(G-BFLX) N11370	21. 3.78	I.G.McDonald tr Foxtrot Charlie Flying Group	RNAS Culdrose	6. 3.05
G-CSFD	Ultramagic M-90 HAB	90/56		12.12.02	L.A. Watts	Pangbourne	14.10.03A
G-CSFT*	Piper PA-23-250 Aztec B	27-4521	G-AYKU N13885	20. 9.84	Not known	North Weald	3.12.94T
					(Cancelled 5.6.96 as WFU) (Fuselage dumped behind hangar 9.02)		
G-CSIX	Piper PA-32-300 Cherokee Six	32-7840030	ZS-OMX Z-WJM/VP-WJM/HB-PCX/ZS-KBR/N9857K	15. 6.01	G.A.Ponsford	Goodwood	19 .7.04
G-CSMK	Aerotechnik EV-97 Eurostar	PFA 315-13813		4.12.01	Cosmik Aviation Ltd	Deppers Bridge, Warwick	4. 4.03P
G-CSNA	Cessna 421C Golden Eagle III	421C0677	(D-IOSS) N26522	11. 6.79	Air Montgomery Ltd	Leeds-Bradford	18. 8.O5T
G-CSPJ	Hughes 369HS	55-0745S	G-BXJF N99KS/N9KS	24. 7.97	The Hughes Helicopter Co Ltd	Biggin Hill	12. 9.03T
G-CSWH	Piper PA-28R-180 Cherokee Arrow	28R-30541	N4647J	5. 4.02	CSW Flying Hire Ltd	(Willenhall)	9. 9.05T
G-CTCL	SOCATA TB-10 Tobago	1107	G-BSIV	16. 7.90	MRS Ltd	Fairoaks	30. 9.05T
G-CTCT	Flight Design CT 2K (Rotax 912 ULS)	00-04-04-94	G-69-51	26. 6.00	Cyclone Airsports Ltd t/a Pegasus Aviation	Manton	AC
G-CTEC	Stoddard-Hamilton GlaStar	PFA 295-13260		9.11.99	B.N.C.Mogg	Bibberne Farm, Stalbridge	
G-CTEL	Cameron N-90 HAB	3933		27. 8.96	D.Triggse *"Gable Top"*	Alresford	12. 4.03A
G-CTFF	Cessna T206H Turbo Stationair	T20608150	N24309	29.10.01	Rajair Ltd	(Ellesmere)	4 11.04T
G-CTGR	Cameron N-77 HAB	1775		28. 8.97	T.G.Read *(Charles Church titles)*	Knutsford	13 9.03T
G-CTIO	SOCATA TB-20 Trinidad	2174	F-OIMH	7.11.02	Cityiq Ltd	(London EC3)	6.11.05T
G-CTIX	Supermarine 509 Spitfire T.IX *(Major rebuild from parts pre 1994)*	---	N462JC G-CTIX/IDFAF 2067/0607/MM4100/PT462	9. 4.85	A.A.Hodgson *(As PT462/SW-A")*	Bryngwyn Bach	2. 5.03P
G-CTKL	Noorduyn Harvard IIB *(C/n quoted as "76-80")*	07-30	(G-BKWZ) MM54137/RCAF3064	22.11.83	M.R.Simpson *(As "54137/69" in US Navy c/s)*	North Weald	11. 4.03P
G-CTLA	Airbus Industrie A321-211	1887	D-AVZC	11. 2.03	MyTravel Airways Ltd	Manchester	
G-CTOY	Denney Kitfox Model 3 (Rotax 582)	1176 & PFA 172-12150		14.10.91	B.McNeilly *(Current status unknown)*	Newtownards, Co.Down	10. 5.93P
G-CTPW	Bell 206B-3 JetRanger III	4374	(N9145B)	30.11.95	S.J.Skilton t/a Aviation Rentals *(Op Bournemouth Helicopters)*	Bournemouth	19. 2.05T
G-CTWW	Piper PA-34-200T Seneca II	34-7970191	G-ROYZ G-GALE/N3052X	21. 7.93	Centreline Air Charter Ltd	Southend	19. 1.03T
G-CTZO	SOCATA TB-20 Trinidad GT	2166	F-OIME	7.10.02	Trinidad Hire Ltd	(Leighton Buzzard)	6.10.05T
G-CUBB	Piper PA-18-150 Super Cub (L-18C-PI) *(Lycoming O-360-C2) (Frame No.18-3009)*	18-3111	PH-WAM Belgian AF OL-L37/53-4711	5.12.78	Bidford Airfield Ltd	Bidford	18. 4.04
G-CUBI	Piper PA-18-125 Super Cub (L-18C-PI)	18-3181	PH-GAV PH-VCV/R.Neth AF R-83/Belgian AF L-107/53-4781	26. 2.79	G.T.Fisher	(Thorney)	4.11.94T
					(Official c/n 18-559 related to PH-GAV prior to 1970 rebuild when it incorporated Frame No.18-3170 from PH-VCV: current status unknown)		
G-CUBJ	Piper PA-18-150 Super Cub (L-18C-PI) *(Frame No.18-2035)*	18-2036	PH-MBF PH-NLF/R.Neth AF R-43/8A-43/52-2436 *(As "18-5395/CDG" in French Army c/s)*	15.12.82	R.A.Fleming	Breighton	19.10.03
					(Regd with c/n 18-5395 after 1974 rebuild of PH-NLF which acquired data plate from, & took identity of, PH-MBF - note also G-SUPA carries this c/n)		
G-CUBP	Piper PA-18-150 Super Cub *(Frame No.18-8725)*	18-8482	N1136Z G-DVMI/OH-PIN/N4262Z	8. 8.96	D.W.Berger	(Torrington)	29. 4.05
					(Regd with c/n 18-8823 the "official" identity of N1136Z/D-EIAC: rebuilt 1984/85 with Frame No.18-4613 ex D-EKAF: this frame fitted to G-BVMI following accident on 15.8.95: repaired frame of G-BVMI has now become G-CUBP)		
G-CUBS	Piper J-3C-65 Cub *(Frame No.17792)*	"17792"	G-BHPT F-BSGQ/LX-AIH/N70688/NC70688	26.10.01	S.M.Rolfe t/a Sunbeam Aviation	Willington, Beds	15. 4.03P
					(Quoted p/i is suspect - possibly c/n 18105 ex NC71076/N71076)		
G-CUBW	Wag-Aero Acro Trainer	PFA 108-13581		26.11.02	B.G, N.D.Plumb & A.G. Bourne	Hinton in the Hedges	
G-CUBY	Piper J-3C-65 Cub *(Rebuilt with new fuselage 1996/97)*	16317	G-BTZW N88689/NC88689	2. 3.95	Claudine A.Bloom	Shoreham	24. 6.03P

Reg	Type	C/n	Prev id	Date	Owner	Location	Date
G-CUCU	Colt 180A HAB	3869		22. 4.96	S.R.Seager	Aylesbury	13. 7.03T
G-CUPN	Piper PA-46-350P Malibu Mirage	4636144		11. 2.98	Airpark Flight Centre Ltd	Coventry	25. 4.04
G-CURR	Cessna 172R Skyhawk II	17280143	G-BXOH N9989F	27. 5.98	JS Aviation Ltd	Booker	9. 4.04T
G-CURV	Avid Speed Wing	PFA 189-12169		28. 3.00	K.S.Kelso	(Baldock)	
G-CUTE	Dyn'Aéro MCR-01 Ban-bi	PFA 301-13511		7. 9.99	E.G.Shimmin	Cambridge	20.12.03P
G-CUTY	Europa Aviation Europa (Tri-gear u/c)	224 & PFA 247-12910		20. 8.96	D.J. & M.Watson	(Selby)	
G-CVBF	Cameron A-210 HAB	3588		2. 6.95	Airxcite Ltd t/a Virgin Balloon Flights	Wembley	15. 8.01T
G-CVIP	Bell 206B-3 JetRanger III	3228	SX-HDJ N824C/N824H/N3902L	29. 4.02	Sloane Helicopters Ltd	Sywell	30. 4.05T
G-CVIX	de Havilland DH.110 Sea Vixen D.3 (Regd as FAW.2 with c/n 10132)	10125	XP924	26. 2.96	De Havilland Aviation Ltd (As "XP924")	Bournemouth	29. 5.03P
G-CVLH	Piper PA-34-200T Seneca II	34-8070332	F-GCPK N8252D/N8250H	5. 9.02	Atlantic Aviation Ltd	Jersey	12. 9.05T
G-CVPM	VPM M-16 Tandem Trainer (Arrow GT1000R)	VPM16-UK-110		26. 3.98	C.S.Teuber	(Hannover, Germany)	24. 5.03P
G-CVYD	Airbus Industrie A320-231	0393	B-HYO VR-HYO/F-WWIR	24. 2.98	JMC Airlines Ltd	Manchester	25. 1.04T
G-CVYE	Airbus Industrie A320-231	0394	B-HYP VR-HYP/F-WWBB	23. 3.98	JMC Airlines Ltd	Manchester	24. 1.04T
G-CVYG	Airbus Industrie A320-231	0443	B-HYT VR-HYT/F-WWBV	10.11.98	JMC Airlines Ltd	Manchester	30.11.04T
G-CWAG	Sequoia Falco F.8L (Lycoming O-320)	PFA 100-10895		11. 5.92	I.R.Court & W.Jones	Leicester	3.12.02P
G-CWBM	Phoenix Currie Wot (Continental C85)	PFA 3020	G-BTVP	28. 3.94	B.V.Mayo	Maypole Farm., Chislet	25. 9.03P
G-CWFA	Piper PA-38-112 Tomahawk	38-78A0120	G-BTGC N9507T	17. 8.99	Cardiff-Wales Flying Club Ltd	Cardiff	7. 9.01T
G-CWFB	Piper PA-38-112 Tomahawk	38-78A0623	G-OAAL N4471E	13. 1.00	Cardiff Wales Aviation Services Ltd	Cardiff	26.12.03T
G-CWFD	Piper PA-38-112 Tomahawk	38-79A0038	G-BSVY N2396B	10. 8.00	Cardiff Wales Flying Club Ltd	Cardiff	22.10.03T
G-CWFE	Piper PA-38-112 Tomahawk	38-80A0020	G-BPBR N25082/N9652N	29.11.01	Cardiff Wales Flying Club Ltd	Cardiff	30. 6.01T
G-CWFY	Cessna 152 II	15284639	G-OAMY N6214M	13. 1.00	Cardiff Wales Aviation Services Ltd	Cardiff	14.11.03T
G-CWFZ	Piper PA-28-151 Cherokee Warrior	28-7715131	G-CPCH G-BRGJ/(G-BPGP)/N5425F	27.10.99	Cardiff Wales Flying Club Ltd	Cardiff	6. 6.03T
G-CWIZ	Aérospatiale AS350B Ecureuil	1847	CS-HDF G-DJEM/G-ZBAC/G-SEBI/G-BMCU	18.10.95	PLM Dollar Group Ltd	Cumbernauld	6. 4.05T
G-CWOT	Phoenix Currie Wot (Walter Mikron 2)	PFA 3019		31. 1.78	J.Beirne Boleybeg, Ballymore, Co.Westmeath tr G-CWOT Group "Jonah"		13. 1.03P
G-CXCX	Cameron N-90 HAB (Replacement envelope c/n 3332)	1242		14. 3.86	Cathay Pacific Airways (London) Ltd "Cathay Pacific IV" (Cancelled 23.8.02 by CAA)	Swindon	6. 7.03A
G-CXDZ	Cassutt Speed Two	PFA 34-13816		27.12.02	J.A.H. Chadwick	(London NW1)	
G-CXHK	Cameron N-77 HAB	4978		22. 2.01	Cathay Pacific Airways (London) Ltd	London SW1	11. 2.03A
G-CYLS	Cessna T303 Crusader	T30300005	N20736 G-BKXI/N303CC/(N9355T)	20.12.90	Gledhill Water Storage Ltd	Blackpool	29. 3.03
G-CYMA	Gulfstream GA-7 Cougar	GA7-0083	G-BKOM N794GA	15. 8.83	Cyma Petroleum (UK) Ltd	Elstree	13. 6.04
G-CYRA	Kolb Twinstar Mk.3 (Rotax 503)	PFA 205-12434	G-MYRA	30. 1.03	S.J.Fox	Popham	15. 5.03P
G-CZAG	Sky 90-24 HAB	171		5.10.99	S.McCarthy	Rothersthorpe	15. 5.03
G-CZCZ	Mudry/CAARP CAP.10B	54	OE-AYY F-WZCG/HB-SAK/F-BUDT	28. 7.94	P.R.Moorhead & M.Farmer	Garston Farm, Marshfield	21. 8.03

G-DAAA - G-DZZZ

Reg	Type	C/n	Prev id	Date	Owner	Location	Date
G-DAAH	Piper PA-28RT-201T Turbo Arrow IV	28R-7931104	N3026U	27. 4.79	R.Peplow	Wolverhampton	24. 5.03
G-DAAM	Robinson R22 Beta	2043		3. 6.92	Hecray Co Ltd t/a Direct Helicopters	Southend	10. 7.04T
G-DAAZ	Piper PA-28RT-201T Turbo Arrow IV	28R-7931247	N2896B	17. 1.03	Calais Ltd	Guernsey	
G-DABS	Robinson R22 Beta	3083		15. 5.00	B.Seymour	(Middlesbrough)	1. 6.03
G-DACA	Percival P.57 Sea Prince T.1	P57/12	WF118	6. 5.80	P.G.Vallance Ltd (Gatwick Aviation Museum as "WF118")	Charlwood, Surrey	17. 7.81P
G-DACC	Cessna 401B	401B-0112	N77GR N4488A/G-AYOU/N7972Q	1. 9.86	Niglon Ltd	Coventry	12. 3.05
G-DACF	Cessna 152 II	152-81724	G-BURY N67285	13. 6.97	T.M. & M.L.Jones (Op Derby Aero Club)	Egginton, Derby	17. 8.03T
G-DACS*	Short SD.3-30 Var.100	SH.3089	C-GLAL N330CG/G-BKDM/G-14-3089	6. 7.98	Blockair Ltd (Cancelled 15.8.02 as WFU) (Open store, engineless 2.03)	Southend	9..8.01T
G-DAEX	Dassault Falcon 900EX	78	F-WWFR	22. 2.01	Triair (Bermuda) Ltd	Farnborough	22. 2.03T
G-DAFY	Beech 58 Baron	TH-1591	N5684C	6.10.93	P.R.Earp	Gloucestershire	5.12.04
G-DAIR	Luscombe 8A Master (Diesel Air 100hp)	1474	G-BURK N28713/NC28713	3.10.97	D.F.Soul	Standalone Farm, Meppershall	19.10.99P
G-DAIV	Ultramagic H-77 HAB	77/184		2.11.00	D.Harrison-Morris	Ellesmere	
G-DAJB	Boeing 757-2T7ER	23770		26. 2.87	Monarch Airlines Ltd	Luton	13. 5.05T
G-DAJC	Boeing 767-31KER	27206		15. 4.94	MyTravel Airways Ltd	Manchester	14. 4.03T
G-DAKK	Douglas C-47A-35DL Skytrain	9798	(G-OFON) F-GEOM/Fr Navy 36/OK-WZB/OK-WDU/42-23936 (Stored 10.02)	26. 7.94	General Technics Ltd	Lee-on-Solent	23. 5.03T
G-DAKO	Piper PA-28-236 Dakota	28-7911187	PH-ARW (PH-MFB)/D-EECG/PH-ARW/OO-HCX/N29718	29. 7.99	Methods Application Ltd	(London WC2)	5.11.05T

Reg	Type	C/n	Prev id	Date	Owner	Base	CofA
G-DAMY	Europa Aviation Europa (Rotax 912-UL) (Tri-gear u/c)	105 & PFA 247-12781		21.10.94	Skyquest Aviation Ltd (F/f 25.9.96)	(Maidenhead)	18. 6.03P
G-DANA	Jodel DR.200 rep	PFA 304-13351	G-DAST	2.12.02	F.A.Bakir	Barton	
G-DAND	SOCATA TB-10 Tobago	72		5.12.79	Portway Aviation Ltd	Shobdon	20. 9.04
G-DANT	Rockwell Commander 114	14298	N4978W	9. 7.96	D.P.Tierney	Biggin Hill	17. 7.02
G-DANY	Jabiru Jabiru UL	PFA 274A-13588		28.12.00	D.A.Crosbie	(Sudbury)	
G-DANZ	Eurocopter AS355N Twin Squirrel	5658		14. 9.98	Frewton Ltd	Oxford	9. 2.05T
G-DAPH	Cessna 180K Skywagon II	18053016	N2620K	29. 1.92	M.R.L.Astor	East Hatley, Tadlow	18. 2.02
G-DARA	Piper PA-34-220T Seneca III	34-8333060	PH-TCT / N83JR/N4297J/N9632N	8.11.88	Sys (Scaffolding Contractors) Ltd	Gamston	11. 4.04
G-DARK	CFM Shadow DD (Rotax 582)	K.295 & PFA 161-13308		13. 7.00	R.W.Hussey	Old Sarum	20..8.03P
G-DASH	Rockwell Commander 112A	237	G-BDAJ / N1237J	31. 3.87	D.& M.Nelson	Bourn	26. 3.03
G-DASU	Cameron V-77 HAB	2300		6. 4.90	D. & L.S.Litchfield "Borne Free"	Reading	11. 8.97A
G-DATE	Agusta A109C	7633	G-RNLD / I-ANAG	30. 3.00	Datel Direct Ltd	Stone	8. 8.05
G-DATG	Reims/Cessna F182P Skylane	F18200013	D-EATG	8.11.01	Oxford Aeroplane Co Ltd	Oxford	14. 3.05T
G-DATH	Aerotechnik EV-97 Eurostar	PFA 315-13967		8.10.02	D.N.E.D'Ath	(Sandy)	
G-DAVD	Reims/Cessna FR172K Hawk XP	FR17200632	D-EFJT / (PH-ADL)/PH-AXO	23.12.99	D M Driver	Elstree	23.12.02T
G-DAVE	Jodel D.112 (Built Ets Valladeau)	667	F-BICH	16. 8.78	D.A.Porter	Griffins Farm, Temple Bruer	13. 8.03P
G-DAVO	Gulfstream AA-5B Tiger	AA5B-1226	G-GAGA / G-BGPG/(G-BGRW)	5. 1.96	Kadala Aviation Ltd	Elstree	12. 2.04T
G-DAVT	Schleicher ASH26E	26090		24. 4.96	D.A.Triplett	Sleap	10. 5.05
G-DAWG	Scottish Aviation Bulldog Srs.120/121	BH120/208	XX522	13. 3.02	R.H.Goldstone (As "XX522/06")	(Worsley)	
G-DAYI	Europa Aviation Europa (Monowheel u/c)	298 & PFA 247-13027		19. 8.96	A.F.Day	(West Wickham)	
G-DAYS	Europa Aviation Europa (Rotax 912-UL) (Monowheel u/c)	177 & PFA 247-12810		9. 5.95	D.J.Bowie (F/f 28.6.97)	Sleap	21. 7.03P
G-DAYZ	Pie7tenpol Aircamper	PFA 47-12342		22. 6.01	J.G.Cronk	(Chichester)	
G-DAZY	Piper PA-34-200T Saratoga II	34-7770335	N953A	4. 2.03	Centreline Air Charter Ltd	(Bristol)	AC
G-DBDB	VPM M16 Tandem Trainer	PFA G/12-1239		19.10.99	D.R.Bolsover	Lossiemouth	12. 6.03P
G-DBHH	Agusta-Bell 206B JetRanger II	8111	G-AWVO / VH-BHI/PK-HCA/G-AWVO/9Y-TDN/PK-HBG/G-AWVO	24. 5.96	UK Helicopter Charter Ltd	Rochester	22. 6.04T
G-DBYE	Mooney M.20M	27-0098	N91462	24. 3.98	A.J.Thomas	Cranfield	5. 4.04
G-DCAV	Piper PA-32R-301 Saratoga IIHP	3246075	N92864 / G-DCAV	8. 5.97	S.Dixon-Smith t/a Lyons Aviation	Fowlmere	15 .5.03T
G-DCDB	Bell 407	53137	C-FCDB / N7238A	19.10.99	Paycourt Ltd	Knocksedan, Co.Dublin	19.10.05T
G-DCEA	Piper PA-34-200T Seneca II	34-8070079	N3567D	13. 2.91	Bristol Flying Centre Ltd	Bristol	12. 7.03T
G-DCKK	Reims/Cessna F172N Skyhawk II	F17201589	PH-GRT / PH-AXA	19. 5.80	J.Maffia	Panshanger	24. 4.04T
G-DCPA	MBB BK-117C-1C	7511	D-HECU / D-HXXL/G-LFBA/D-HECU/D-HMBF	16.12.97	Devon & Cornwall Constabulary	Exeter	16. 6.05T
G-DCSE	Robinson R44 Astro	0659		23. 9.99	Foxtrot Golf Helicopters Ltd	Edinburgh	13.10.05T
G-DCXL	SAN Jodel D.140C Mousquetaire III	101	F-BKSM	27. 5.88	C.F.Mugford tr X-Ray Lima Group	Little Gransden	16. 3.03
G-DDAY	Piper PA-28R-201T Turbo Arrow III	28R-7703112	G-BPDO / N3496Q	24.11.88	K.E.Hogg tr G-DDAY Group	Tatenhill	15. 4.04
G-DDBD	Europa Aviation Europa XS	PFA 247-13569		11. 2.03	B.Davies	(Horsham)	
G-DDMV	North American T-6G-NF Texan	168-313	N3240N / Haitian AF 3209/49-3209	30. 4.90	E.A.Morgan (As "493209" in Califorian ANG c/s)	Gloucestershire	3. 2.03
G-DDOG	Scottish Aviation Bulldog Srs.120/121	BH120/210	XX524	18. 6.01	Gamit Ltd (As "XX524/04") (Noted 9.02)	North Weald	AC
G-DEAN	Solar Wings Pegasus XL-Q (Rotax 462)	SW-TE-0117 & SW-WQ-0123	G-MVJV	30.11.98	D.C.P.Cardey & G.D.Tannahill	Hereford	10. 9.01P
G-DEBE	British Aerospace BAe 146 Srs.200	E2022	N163US / N346PS	5. 8.96	Flightline Ltd	Southend	6. 8.05T
G-DEBR	Europa Aviation Europa (Tri-gear u/c)	232 & PFA 247-12922		31. 1.01	A J Calvert & C T Smallwood	(Buxton/Ripley)	
G-DECK	Cessna T210N Turbo Centurion	21064017	N958MK / D-ERDK/N4834Y	29. 2.00	R.J.Howard	Sherburn-in-Elmet	16. 3.03
G-DEER	Robinson R22 Beta-II	2827		17. 7.98	Westinbrook Ltd	Shoreham	28. 7.04T
G-DEFK	British Aerospace BAe 146 Srs.200	E2012	G-DEBK / C-FHAV/N601AW	22.10.99	Flightline Ltd (Op Clubair)	Montichiari, Italy	25. 4..05T
G-DEFL	British Aerospace BAe 146 Srs.200	E2014	G-DEBL / C-FHAX/N602AW	22.10.99	Clubair Sixgo SpA	Montichiari, Italy	28. 1.05T
G-DEFM	British Aerospace BAe 146 Srs.200	E2016	G-DEBM / C-FHAZ	22.10.99	Flightline Ltd	Aberdeen	16 .3.05T
G-DELF	Aero L-29A Delfin	194555	ES-YLM / Soviet AF 12 (Red)	28. 8.97	B.R.Green "12"	Manston	26. 9.01P
G-DELT	Robinson R22 Beta	0898		11.11.88	Flightworks (Midlands) Ltd	(Coventry)	22. 4.05T
G-DEMH	Reims/Cessna F172M Skyhawk II (Lycoming O-360)	F17201137	G-BFLO / PH-DMF/(EI-AYO)	18.11.91	M.Hammond	Airfield Farm, Hardwick	14. 6.04
G-DENA	Cessna F150G (Built Reims Aviation SA)	F150-0204	G-AVEO / EI-BOI/G-AVEO	14.12.95	W.M.Wilson & R.Campbell	Sandtoft	20. 1.02T
G-DENB	Cessna F150G (Built Reims Aviation SA)	F150-0136	G-ATZZ	14.12.95	Just Plane Trading Ltd	Top Farm, Croydon, Royston	11. 6.03T
G-DENC	Cessna F150G (Built Reims Aviation SA)	F150-0107	G-AVAP	14.12.95	M Dovey	Top Farm, Croydon, Royston	29. 9.05T
G-DEND	Reims/Cessna F150M	F15001201	G-WAFC / G-BDFI/(OH-CGD)	6. 6.97	C.N.Critchlow tr November Delta Group	(Honiton)	30. 9.04T
G-DENE	Piper PA-28-140 Cherokee	28-21710	G-ATOS / N11C	5. 2.98	Avon Aviation Ltd t/a The Bristol and Wessex Aeroplane Club	Bristol	11. 7.05T

Reg	Type	C/n	Prev id	Date	Owner	Location	Date
G-DENH	Piper PA-28-161 Warrior II	28-8216202	G-BTNH	14. 4.97	Plane Talking Ltd	Blackbushe	8. 3.04T
			N253FT/N9577N				
G-DENI	Piper PA-32-300 Cherokee Six	32-7340006	G-BAIA	7.12.95	A.Bendkowski	Rochester	29. 5.04T
			N11C				
G-DENR	Reims/Cessna F172N Skyhawk II	F17201839	G-BGNR	30. 4.97	A.P.Daines	(Great Yeldham)	9.10.05T
G-DENS	Binder CP.301S Smaragd	121	D-ENSA	20.11.85	G.E.Roe & I.S.Leader	Garston Farm, Marshfield	9. 9.03P
	(A/c also carries c/n AB.429 denoting completion as Amateur Build)						
G-DENT	Cameron N-145 HAB	4135		8. 4.97	Deproco UK Ltd	Dorking	11. 3.03A
G-DENZ	Piper PA-44-180 Seminole	44-7995327	G-INDE	3. 7.97	W.J.Greenfield	Humberside	3. 4.05T
			G-BHNM/N8077X				
G-DERB	Robinson R22 Beta	1005	G-BPYH	28. 6.95	S Thompson	(Coventry)	3. 7.04T
G-DERV	Cameron Truck 56SS HAB	1719		21. 3.88	J.M.Percival "Shell UK Truck"	Loughborough	22. 2.00A
G-DESS	Mooney M.20J (201)	24-1272	N11598	20.10.87	R.M.Hitchin	(Bath)	22. 3.03
G-DEST	Mooney M.20J	24-3429		6.11.98	Allegro Aviation Ltd	(Guernsey)	12. 1.05
G-DEVL	Eurocopter EC120B	1273		7. 6.02	Swift Frame Ltd	(Norwich)	4. 7.05T
G-DEVS	Piper PA-28-180 Cherokee B	28-830	G-BGVJ	5. 3.85	B.J.Hoptroff & J.M.Whiteley	Blackbushe	23. 1.05
			D-ENPI/N7066W		tr 180 Group		
G-DEXP	ARV1 Super 2	003 & PFA 152-11154		24. 4.85	W.G.McKinnon	Perth	22. 4.03P
	(Hewland AE75)						
G-DEXY	Beech E90 King Air	LW-136	N750DC	6. 4.89	Specsavers Aviation Ltd	Guernsey	2. 2.05
			N30CW/N84GA/N328TB/TR-LTT				
G-DEZC	British Aerospace HS.125 Srs.700B	257070	G-BWCR	28. 5.96	Bunbury Aviation Ltd	Guernsey	17. 7.03
			G-5-604/HB-VGG/G-5-604/HB-VGG				
G-DFKI	Westland SA.314C Gazelle HT.2	1216	XW907	12. 2.02	Leisure Park Management Ltd	Goodwood	26.12.03P
			G-BZOT				
G-DFLY	Piper PA-38-112 Tomahawk	38-79A0450	N9655N	15. 2.79	P.M.Raggett	Rochester	13. 6.03
G-DGCL	DG Flugzeugbau DG-800B	8-185-B109		27. 3.00	C.J.Lowrie	Parham Park	19. 4.03
G-DGDG	Glaser-Dirks DG-400-17	4-27		25. 3.83	M.Clarke tr DG-400 Flying Group	Lasham	28. 5.04
G-DGIV	DG Flugzeugbau DG-800B	8-145-B69		27.11.98	W.R.McNair	(Holywood, Co.Down)	23.11.04
G-DGWW	Rand Robinson KR-2	PFA 129-11044		7. 3.91	W.Wilson	Liverpool	27. 7.03P
	(Hapi Magnum 75)						
G-DHCB	de Havilland DHC.2 Beaver 1	1450	G-BTDL	20. 6.91	Seaflite Ltd	(Lochearnhead)	16. 9.97T
	(Floatplane)		XP779		*(Stored 2001)*		
G-DHCC	de Havilland DHC.1 Chipmunk 22	C1/0393	WG321	28. 5.97	Eureka Aviation NV (As "WG321")	Antwerp, Belgium	21. 9.03T
G-DHCI	de Havilland DHC.1 Chipmunk 22	C1/0884	G-BBSE	12. 7.89	Felthorpe Flying Group Ltd	Felthorpe	13.11.03
			WZ858		*(Destroyed in arson attack 18.2.03)*		
G-DHDV	de Havilland DH.104 Dove 8	04205	VP981	26.10.98	Air Atlantique Ltd (As "VP981")	Coventry	1. 4.03T
G-DHJH	Airbus Industrie A321-211	1238	D-AVZL	7. 6.00	MyTravel Airways Ltd	Manchester	6. 6.03T
G-DHLB	Cameron N-90 HAB	3261		20. 4.94	B.A.Bower	Seaton	28.10.96A
G-DHPM	de Havilland DHC-1 Chipmunk Mk.20	55	CS-AZS	28. 3.02	P.Meyrick	(Northwich)	27. 5.05
	(Built OGMA)		Portuguese AF FAP 1365				
G-DHSS	de Havilland DH.112 Venom FB.50 (FB.1)	836	J-1626	26. 3.99	D J L Wood	Bournemouth	22. 4.03P
	(Built F + W)				*(As "WR360" in white RAF c/s)*		
G-DHTM	de Havilland DH.82A Tiger Moth	PFA 157-11095		6. 1.86	E.G.Waite-Roberts	(Basingstoke)	
					(Believed parts consumed within rebuild of G-APPN qv)		
G-DHTT	de Havilland DH.112 Venom FB.50 (FB.1)	821	(G-BMOC)	17.10.96	D.J.Lindsay Wood	Bournemouth	17. 7.99P
	(Built F + W)		J-1611		*(As "WR421" in all-red c/s) (Stored 1.03)*		
G-DHUU	de Havilland DH.112 Venom FB.50 (FB.1)	749	(G-BMOD)	26. 2.96	D.J.Lindsay Wood	Bournemouth	24. 5.02P
	(Built F + W)		J-1539		*(As "WR410" in 6 Sqdn RAF c/s) (Stored1.03)*		
G-DHVV	de Havilland DH.115 Vampire T.55	55092	U-1214	5. 9.91	Lindsay Wood Promotions Ltd	Bournemouth	5. 6.03P
	(Built F + W) (Reported as built with c/n 974)				*(As "XE897" in 54 Sqdn RAF c/s)*		
G-DHWW	de Havilland DH.115 Vampire T.55	979	U-1219	5. 9.91	Lindsay Wood Promotions Ltd	Bournemouth	23. 4.03P
	(Built F + W)				*(As "XG775" in RN FOFT Yeovilton c/s)*		
G-DHXX	de Havilland DH.100 Vampire FB.6	682	J-1173	5. 9.91	Lindsay Wood Promotions Ltd	Bournemouth	14. 8.02P
	(Built F + W)				*(As "VT871" in 54 Sqdn RAF c/s) (Stored1.03)*		
G-DHYY*	de Havilland DH.115 Vampire T.11	15112	WZ553	17. 3.95	Lindsay Wood Promotions Ltd	Bournemouth	
					(As "WZ553/40") (Cancelled 7.11.02 by CAA) (Stored 1.03)		
G-DHZF	de Havilland DH.82A Tiger Moth	82309	G-BSTJ	7. 7.99	M.R.Parker (As "N9192" in RAF c/s)	Sywell	10.10.05
			OO-MEH/OO-GEB/OO-MOR/RNeth AF A-13/PH-UFB/A-13/N9192				
G-DHZZ	de Havilland DH.115 Vampire T.55	990	U-1230	5. 9.91	Lindsay Wood Promotions Ltd	Bournemouth	4. 8.03P
	(Built F + W)				*(As "WZ589" in 54 Sqdn RAF c/s)*		
G-DIAL	Cameron N-90 HAB	1851		7.11.88	A.J.Street "London"	Exeter	11. 5.00A
G-DIAT	Piper PA-28-140 Cherokee Cruiser	28-7425322	G-BCGK	19. 7.89	The RAF Benevolent Fund Enterprises Ltd	Bristol	22. 2.04T
			N9594N		*(Op Disabled Flyers Group/Bristol & Wessex Aeroplane Club)*		
G-DICK	Thunder Ax6-56Z HAB	159		6. 7.78	R.D.Sargeant "Dandag"	Wollerau, Switzerland	29. 5.03A
G-DIGI	Piper PA-32-300 Cherokee Six	32-7940224	D-EIES	13.10.98	D.Stokes tr Security UN Ltd Group	Stapleford	19.11.04T
			N2947M				
G-DIKY	Murphy Rebel	PFA 232-13182		13. 2.98	R.J.P.Herivel	Alderney	
G-DIMB	Boeing 767-31KER	28865		28. 4.97	MyTravel Airways Ltd	Manchester	27. 4.03T
G-DIME	Rockwell Commander 114	14123	N49829	9. 3.88	H.B.Richardson	Badminton	9. 9.04
G-DINA	Gulfstream AA-5B Tiger	AA5B-1218	N4555Y	27. 2.81	Portway Aviation Ltd	Shobdon	20. 6.05
G-DING	Colt 77A HAB	1862		28. 6.91	G.J.Bell "Dingbat"	Albuquerque, NM, USA	13 9.03A
G-DINK	Lindstrand Bulb SS HAB	785		28. 6.01	Dinkelacker-Schwaben Brau AG	Stuttgart, Germany	22. 7.02A
G-DINO	Pegasus Quantum 15	7225	G-MGMT	15.12.98	G.Van Der Gaag Lower Mountpleasant Farm, Chatteris		28. 7.03P
	(Rotax 582)						
G-DINT	Bristol 156 Beaufighter IF	STAN B1 184604	3858M	17. 6.91	T.E.Moore	Rotary Farm, Hatch	
			X7688		*(On rebuild from various ex Australian components 10.99)*		
G-DIPI	Cameron Tub 80SS HAB	1745		6. 5.88	R.A.Preston "KP Choc Dips Tub"	Bristol	11.12.98A
G-DIPM	Piper PA-46-350P Malibu Mirage	4636325	N5350V	20. 2.02	D.Priestley	Jersey	25. 2 05T
G-DIPS*	Taylor JT.1 Monoplane	PFA 55-10320		19.12.78	B.J.Halls	Sibsey	
	(Volkswagen 1500)				*(Cancelled 31.3.99 by CAA) (Fuselage stored 8.00)*		
G-DIRK	Glaser-Dirks DG-400	4-124	D-KEKT	18. 9.86	C.J.Lowrie	Rufforth	29. 1.05
G-DIRT*	Thunder Ax7-77Z HAB	345		23. 4.81	Not known	Auxerre, France	8.6.84
					(Cancelled 12.1.99 by CAA) (Extant 2002)		

Reg	Type	C/n	Prev id	Date	Owner	Location	Date
G-DISK	Piper PA-24-250 Comanche	24-1197	G-APZG EI-AKW/N10F	9. 8.89	G.A.Burtenshaw tr G-DIRK Syndicate	Guernsey	30. 5.03
G-DISO	SAN Jodel 150 Mascaret	24	9Q-CPK OO-APK/F-BLDT	16.12.86	P.F.Craven	Cumbernauld	5. 6.03P
G-DIVA	Cessna R172K Hawk XPII	R1723071	N758FX	10. 2.86	R.J.Harris	(Bicester)	3.10.04T
G-DIWY	Piper PA-32-300 Cherokee Six	32-40731	OY-DLW D-EHMW/N8931N	26.11.91	IFS Chemicals Ltd	East Winch	6. 6.04
G-DIXY	Piper PA-28-181 Archer III	2843195	N41284 G-DIXY/N41284	10.12.98	M.G.Bird	Fowlmere	16.12.04T
G-DIZO	Jodel Wassmer D.120A Paris-Nice	326	G-EMKM F-BOBG	30. 5.91	D.& E.Aldersea	Breighton	4. 3.03P
G-DIZY	Piper PA-28R-201T Turbo Cherokee Arrow III						
		28R-7703401	N47570	13.10.88	Calverton Flying Club Ltd	Cranfield	11. 4.04T
G-DIZZ	Hughes 369HE	89-0105E	N9029F	19. 2.97	H.J.Pelham	Cleeves Farm, Salisbury	19. 6.03
G-DJAE	Cessna 500 Citation I	500-0339	G-JEAN N300EC/N707US/G-JEAN/(N5339J)	3.11.98	Source Group Ltd	Bournemouth	27. 3.03T
G-DJAR	Airbus Industrie A320-231	0164	OY-CNE (D-ACSL)/OY-CNE/F-WWIE	18. 3.97	MyTravel Airways Ltd	Manchester	17. 3.03T
G-DJAY	Jabiru Jabiru UL-450	PFA 274A-13633		8. 8.00	D.J.Pearce	(Reading)	13 .5.03P
G-DJCR	Varga 2150A Kachina	VAC 155-80	EI-CFK G-BLWG/OO-HTD/N8360J	11. 4.96	D.J.C.Robertson	Perth	30. 4.99
G-DJEA	Cessna 421C Golden Eagle II	421C0654	TC-AAA N37379/(N24BS)/N37379	16. 4.98	Bettany Aircraft Holdings Ltd	Jersey	4. 2.05
G-DJJA	Piper PA-28-181 Archer II	28-8490014	N4326D	14. 9.87	B.Cheese & S.M.Price t/a Choice Aircraft (Op Modern Air)	Fowlmere	18.12.05T
G-DJNH	Denney Kitfox Model 3 (Rotax 582)	772 & PFA 172-11896		20. 9.90	D.J.N.Hall	Downwood, Dorset	29. 5.01P
G-DKDP	Grob G-109	6100	(G-BMBD) D-KAMS	9. 7.85	D.W. & J.E.Page	Tibenham	28.11.03
G-DKGF*	Viking Dragonfly Mk.1 (Volkswagen 1834)	PFA 139-10898		16.10.86	P.C.Dowbor (Cancelled 29.3.01 by CAA) (Dumped less engine 7.02)	Enstone	
G-DLCB	Europa Aviation Europa (Rotax 912-UL) (Monowheel u/c)	46 & PFA 247-12652		16.11.95	I.L.Griffith (F/f 23.4.96)	(Penarth)	8. 5.03P
G-DLDL	Robinson R22 Beta	1971		2. 1.92	Aeromega Ltd	Stapleford	5. 4.04T
G-DLFN	Aero L-29 Delfin	294872	ES-YLE Estonian AF/Soviet AF	28. 5.98	T.W.Freeman & N.Gooderham	Southend	26.11.01P
G-DLOM	SOCATA TB-20 Trinidad	1102	N2823Y	13.12.90	J.N.A.Adderley	Rochester	12. 7.04
G-DLTR	Piper PA-28-180 Cherokee E	28-5803	G-AYAV N11C	15. 3.96	BCT Aircraft Leasing Ltd (Op Bristol & Wessex Aero Club)	Bristol	18. 7.05T
G-DMAC	Jabiru Jabiru UL	PFA 274-13321		15.10.98	C.J.Pratt	Goodwood	29. 7.03P
	(Jabiru 2200A) *(PFA prefix "274" indicates model SK: a model UL shold be "274A")*						
G-DMAH	SOCATA TB-20 Trinidad GT	2039	F-OILY	2. 4.01	C.A.Ringrose	(Tadworth)	9. 4.04T
G-DMCA	McDonnell Douglas DC-10-30	48266	N3016Z	12. 3.96	Monarch Airlines Ltd (Stored 1.02)	Manchester	11. 3.03T
G-DMCD	Robinson R22 Beta	1201	G-OOLI G-DMCD	14.11.89	R.W.Pomphrett	Denham	18.12.04T
G-DMCS	Piper PA-28R-200 Cherokee Arrow II	28R-7635284	G-CPAC PH-SMW/OO-HAU/N75220	29. 5.84	W.G.Ashton & J Bingley t/a Arrow Associates	(Wokingham)	19. 4.05T
G-DMCT	Flight Design CT2K	01-04-02-12		10. 7.01	K.H.Negal	Sittles Farm, Alrewas	18. 7.02P
G-DMSS	Westland SA.341D Gazelle HT.3	1089	XW858	13. 7.01	MSS Holdings Ltd (As "XW858")	Blackpool	16. 7.03P
G-DMWW	CFM Shadow DD (Rotax 582)	304-DD		12.10.98	Microlight Sport Aviation Ltd	Lower Mountpleasant Farm, Chatteris	13. 5.02P
G-DNCN	Agusta-Bell 206A JetRanger	8185	9H-AAJ Libyan Arab Rep.AF 8185/5A-BAM	21.11.97	J.J.Woodhouse t/a Flying Services	Sandown	16. 1.04T
G-DNCS	Piper PA-28R-201T Turbo Arrow III	28R-7803024	N47841	3. 1.89	BC Arrow Ltd	Barton	11. 4.04
G-DNGR	Colt 31A HAB	10162		18.10.01	G.J.Bell	Wokingham	12.10.03A
G-DNLB	MBB Bö.105DBS-4 (Rebuilt with new pod S.850 1992)	S.60/850		10. 4.92	Bond Air Services Ltd	(Stromness)	23. 4.04T
	G-BTBD/VH-LCS/VH-HRM/G-BCDH/EC-DUO/G-BCDH/D-HDBK (Op Northern Lighthouse Board)						
G-DNOP	Piper PA-46-350P Malibu Mirage	4636303	N4174A	26. 7.00	Campbell Aviation Ltd	Denham	3. 8.03T
G-DNVT	Gulfstream Gulfstream IV	1078	(G-BPJM) N17589	29. 9.89	Shell Aircraft Ltd	Rotterdam, The Netherlands	28. 9.03T
G-DOCA	Boeing 737-436	25267		21.10.91	British Airways plc (Benyhone Tartan t/s)	Heathrow	20.12.03T
G-DOCB	Boeing 737-436	25304		16.10.91	British Airways plc (Wings t/s)	Gatwick	15. 2.04T
G-DOCD	Boeing 737-436	25349		6.11.91	British Airways plc (Animals & Trees t/s)	Heathrow	6. 5.04T
G-DOCE	Boeing 737-436	25350		20.11.91	British Airways plc (Blomsterang t/s)	Heathrow	6. 8.04T
G-DOCF	Boeing 737-436	25407		9.12.91	British Airways plc (Koguty Lowickie t/s)	Heathrow	9. 7.04T
G-DOCG	Boeing 737-436	25408		16.12.91	British Airways plc (Chelsea Rose t/s)	Gatwick	15. 8.04T
G-DOCH	Boeing 737-436	25428		19.12.91	British Airways plc (Grand Union t/s)	Heathrow	18. 8.04T
G-DOCI	Boeing 737-436	25839		8. 1.92	British Airways plc	Gatwick	7. 1.05T
G-DOCL	Boeing 737-436	25842		2. 3.92	British Airways plc (Ndebele Martha t/s)	Heathrow	1. 3.05T
G-DOCM	Boeing 737-436	25843		19. 3.92	British Airways plc (Rendezvous t/s)	Gatwick	18. 3.05T
G-DOCN	Boeing 737-436	25848		21.10.92	British Airways plc	Gatwick	20.10.05T
G-DOCO	Boeing 737-436	25849		26.10.92	British Airways plc	Gatwick	25.10.05T
G-DOCP	Boeing 737-436	25850		2.11.92	British Airways plc	Gatwick	1.11.05T
G-DOCR	Boeing 737-436	25851		6.11.92	British Airways plc (Waves of the City t/s)	Gatwick	5.11.05T
G-DOCS	Boeing 737-436	25852		1.12.92	British Airways plc	Gatwick	30.11.05T
G-DOCT	Boeing 737-436	25853		22.12.92	British Airways plc (Crossing Borders t/s)	Gatwick	23.12.05T
G-DOCU	Boeing 737-436	25854		18. 1.93	British Airways plc (Ndebele Martha t/s)	Heathrow	19. 1.06T
G-DOCV	Boeing 737-436	25855		25. 1.93	British Airways plc (Benyhone Tartan t/s)	Heathrow	24. 1.06T
G-DOCW	Boeing 737-436	25856		2. 2.93	British Airways plc (Rendezvous t/s)	Heathrow	3. 2.03T
G-DOCX	Boeing 737-436	25857		29. 3.93	British Airways plc (Colum t/s)	Gatwick	28. 3.03T
G-DOCY	Boeing 737-436	25844	OO-LTQ G-BVBY/TC-ALS/G-BVBY/(G-DOCY)	17.10.96	British Airways plc	Heathrow	17.10.05T
G-DOCZ	Boeing 737-436	25858	EC-FXJ EC-657/G-BVBZ/(G-DOCZ)	12.12.94	British Airways plc	Heathrow	11. 1.04T

Reg	Type	C/n	Previous identity	Date	Owner	Location	Expiry
G-DODB	Robinson R22 Beta	0911	N8005R	3. 5.96	Exmoor Helicopters Ltd	Withiel Farm, Minehead	5.12.05T
G-DODD	Reims/Cessna F172P Skyhawk II	F17202175		5.10.82	K.Watts	Denham	4.10.98
G-DODI	Piper PA-46-350P Malibu Mirage	4636019		26.10.95	CAVOK SRL	(Milan)	22. 2.04T
G-DODR	Robinson R22 Beta	1325	N80721	5. 6.96	Exmoor Helicopters Ltd	Withiel Farm, Minehead	25. 7.02T
G-DOEA	Gulfstream AA-5A Cheetah	AA5A-0895	G-RJMI N27170	30. 4.96	Critical Simulations Ltd	Elstree	28. 7.03T
G-DOFY	Bell 206B-3 JetRanger III	3637	N2283F	26. 8.87	Cinnamond Ltd (Op Cabair Helicopters)	Silver Springs, Denham	17 6.05T
G-DOGG	Scottish Aviation Bulldog Srs.120/121	BH120/308	XX638	3.10.01	P.Sengupta (As "XX638")	Bourne Park, Hurstbourne Tarrant	26. 3.05T
G-DOGZ	Rogerson Horizon 1 (Marked as "Fisher Super Koala")	PFA 241-13129		10. 8.98	J.E.D.Rogerson	Morgansfield, Fishburn	19. 9.03P
G-DOIT	Aérospatiale AS350B2 Ecureuil	1902	F-GMAZ LN-OTA/SE-JAC/LN-OBD/(F-GHYU)/LN-OBD/SE-JAC/HB-XPH	10.10.01	C.C.Blakey	Redhill	22.11.04T
G-DOLY	Cessna T303 Crusader	T30300107	N303MK G-BJZK/(N3645C)	20. 7.94	R.M.Jones	Blackpool	14. 9.03
G-DOME	Piper PA-28-161 Warrior III	2842062	N4160V	12. 1.00	Plane Talking Ltd	Elstree	16. 1.03T
G-DONI	Gulfstream AA-5B Tiger	AA5B-1029	G-BLLT OO-RTG/(OO-HRS)	20. 7.95	Southern Flight Centre Ltd	Shoreham	7.12.03
G-DONS	Piper PA-28RT-201T Turbo Arrow IV	28R-8131077	N8336L	22. 4.88	C.E.Griffiths	Blackbushe	8.10.03
G-DONZ	Europa Aviation Europa	032 & PFA 247-12545		1. 6.94	D.J.Smith & D.McNicholl (On build 2000)	Knockbain Farm, Dingwall	
G-DOOZ	Aérospatiale AS355F2 Twin Squirrel	5367	G-BNSX	13. 5.88	Lynton Aviation Ltd t/a Signature Aircraft Charter	Blackbushe	4. 4.03T
G-DORB	Bell 206B-3 JetRanger III	3955	SE-HTI TC-HBN	15. 8.90	Blue Anchor Leisure Ltd	(Ingoldmells)	28.11.02
G-DORN	Dornier EKW C-3605	332	HB-RBJ SwissAF C-552	15. 5.98	R.G.Gray (As "C-552")	Bournemouth	11.11.02P
G-DOVE	Cessna 182Q Skylane II	18266724	N96446	26. 6.80	J.Sinclair-Dean	Guernsey	24. 7.04
G-DOWN	Colt 31A Air Chair HAB	1570		3. 8.89	M.Williams "Up & Down"	Wadhurst, Sussex	8. 6.00A
G-DPSP	McDonnell Douglas DC-10-10	46646	OY-CNS SE-DHS/N913WA	12. 9.00	MyTravel Airways Ltd	Manchester	26.10.03T
G-DPST	Phillips ST-2 Speedtwin	PFA 207-12674		10. 5.96	Speedtwin Developments Ltd	Upper Cae Garw Farm, Trelleck, Monmouth	
G-DRAG	Cessna 152 II (Tail-wheel conversion)	15283188	G-REME G-DRAG/G-BRNF/N47217	27. 4.90	L.A.Maynard & M.E.Scouller (Op Old Sarum Flying Club)	Old Sarum	5. 8.05T
G-DRAM	Reims FR172F Rocket (Floatplane)	FR17200102	OH-CNS	18. 9.98	T.A.Crumpton t/a Clyde River Rats	(Lochearnhead)	11. 4.05T
G-DRAW	Colt 77A HAB	1830		31. 8.90	C.Wolstenholme	Oswestry	29. 6.02A
G-DRAY	Taylor JT-1 Monoplane	PFA 1452		13. 7.78	L.J.Dray	(Sidmouth)	
G-DRBG	Cessna 172M Skyhawk	17265263	G-MUIL N64486	18. 1.95	Wilkins & Wilkins (Special Auctions) t/a Henlow Flying Club Ltd	RAF Henlow	13. 5.04T
G-DREX	Cameron Saturn 110SS HAB	4217		28.10.97	LRC Products Ltd	Broxbourne, Herts	3.11.99A
G-DRGN	Cameron N-105 HAB	2024		13. 6.91	W.I.Hooker & C.Parker	Nottingham	4. 7.01T
G-DRGS	Cessna 182S	18280375	N2389X	17.11.98	D.R.G.Scott	Edinburgh	30. 1.05
G-DRHL	Eurocopter AS350B2 Ecureuil	3032		12. 1.98	Lytonworth Ltd	Wellesbourne Mountford	29. 4.04T
G-DRKJ	Schweizer Hughes 269C (300C)	S.1172	G-BPPW N3624J	19.10.00	D.R.Kenyon t/a Aviation Bureau	Shoreham	27. 9.04T
G-DRMM	Europa Aviation Europa (Tri-gear u/c)	362 & PFA 247-13201		27. 7.98	M.W.Mason	(Nantwich)	
G-DRNT	Sikorsky S-76A II Plus	760201	N93WW N3WQ/N3WL/N3121G	5. 4.90	CHC Scotia Ltd	North Denes	1. 5.03T
G-DROP	Cessna U206C Super Skywagon	U2061230	G-UKNO G-BAMN/4X-ALL/N71943	7. 8.87	Peterborough Parachute Centre Ltd	Sibson	2. 3.03
G-DRSV	Robin DR315X Petit Prince (Regd with c/n PFA 210-11765 following major rebuild)	624	F-ZWRS	7. 6.90	R.S.Voice	Rushett Manor, Chessington	14. 5.03P
G-DRUM*	Thruster TST Mk.1 (Rotax 503)	8068-TST-081	G-MVBR	12. 1.99	C.C.Mercer (Wings stored Longbridge Deverill 12.01) (Cancelled 16.10.02 by CAA)	Saltash	3. 3.01P
G-DRYI	Cameron N-77 HAB	2046		7. 8.89	C.A.Butter (New owner 2.01) (Barbour titles)	Marsh Benham	4. 6.94A
G-DRYS	Cameron N-90 HAB	3377		1.12.95	C.A.Butter (Barbour titles)	Marsh Benham	27. 7.03A
G-DRZF	CEA DR.360 Chevalier	451	F-BRZF	4. 9.91	P.K.Kaufeler	Earls Colne	6.12.03
G-DSFT	Piper PA-28R-200 Cherokee Arrow II	28R-7335157	G-LFSE G-BAXT/N11C	22.11.00	J.Jones	Biggin Hill	10. 4.05T
G-DSGC	Piper PA-25-260 Pawnee C	25-4890	OY-BDA	3. 5.95	Devon & Somerset Gliding Club Ltd	North Hill	24. 3.05
G-DSID	Piper PA-34-220T Seneca	3447001		21. 7.95	R.Howton	Biggin Hill	4. 9.04
G-DSLL	Pegasus Quantum 15-912	7836		5. 7.01	A.J.Slater	(Sandbach)	4. 7.03P
G-DSPI	Robinson R44 Astro	0661	G-DPSI	25.10.99	Focal Point Communications Ltd	(London SW6)	2111.05T
G-DTCP	Piper PA-32R-300 Lance	32R-7780255	G-TEEM N2604Q	26. 1.93	G-DTCP Aviation Ltd	(Luton)	22. 4.04
G-DTOO*	Piper PA-38-112 Tomahawk	38-79A0312	N9713N	15. 2.79	Not known (Damaged Seething 9.7.94: cancelled 31.1.95 as WFU) (Fuselage noted 8.02)	Panshanger	29. 7.94T
G-DUDE	Van's RV-8	PFA 303-13246		16. 7.99	W.M.Hodgkins	(Stadhampton)	
G-DUDS	CASA I-131E Jungmann (Enma Tigre G-1V-B)	2108	D-EHDS E3B-512	27. 6.90	B R Cox	(Bristol)	3. 6.00P
G-DUDZ	Robin DR400/180 Regent	2367	G-BXNK	3.12.97	D.H.Pattison	Lower Upham Farm, Chiseldon	26.11.03
G-DUGE	Comco Ikarus C42 FB UK	PFA 322-13855		30. 7.02	D.Stevenson	Plaistows Farm, St Albans	
G-DUGI	Lindstrand LBL 90A HAB	562		16. 8.99	D.J.Cook	Norwich	25. 6.02A
G-DUGS	Van's RV-9A	PFA 320-13966		21.10.02	D.M.Provost	(Salford)	
G-DUKK	Extra EA.300/L	125	D-EXAC	27.11.00	R.A.& K.M.Roberts t/a Puddleduck Plane Partnership	Goodwood	14.12.03
G-DUNG	Sky 65-24 HAB	125		20. 7.98	G.J.Bell	Albuquerque, NM, USA	12.10.03A
G-DUNN*	Zenair CH.200 (Lycoming O-320)	AD-1 & PFA 24-10450		5.10.78	A.Dunn tr Chevalier Flying Group (Under construction 1988: cancelled 23.1.03 as temporarily wfu)	(Lancing)	

Reg	Type	C/n	Prev id	Date	Owner	Location	Status
G-DURO	Europa Aviation Europa (Rotax 912-UL) *(Monowheel u/c)*	033 & PFA 247-12554		15.11.93	D.J.Sagar *(F/f 9.1.99)*	Bidford	9 .4.03P
G-DURX	Colt 77A HAB	1522		25. 5.89	V.Trimble *(Durex/Avanti titles)*	Henley-on-Thames	26. 6.02A
G-DUSK	de Havilland DH.115 Vampire T.Mk.11	15596	XE856	1. 2.99	R.M.A.Robinson & R.Horsfield *(On rebuild 10.99: current status unknown)*	RAF Henlow	
G-DUST	Stolp SA.300 Starduster Too JP-2 (Lycoming O-360)		N233JP	28. 4.88	J.V.George *(Damaged in collision with G-AKTM Badminton 16.7.89: on rebuild 2001)*	(Winchester)	22. 5.90P
G-DUVL	Reims/Cessna F172N Skyhawk II	F17201723	G-BFMU(1)	16. 8.78	A.J.Simpson	White Waltham	26. 2.04
G-DVBF	Lindstrand LBL 210A HAB	188		6. 3.95	Airxcite Ltd t/a Virgin Balloon Flights	Wembley	16. 7.99T
G-DVON	de Havilland DH.104 Devon C.2/2	04201	(G-BLPD) VP955	26.10.84	C.L.Thatcher tr The 955 Preservation Group *(As "VP955": stored 5.02)*	Kemble	29. 5.96
G-DWIA	Chilton DW.1A	PFA 225-12256		25. 1.93	D.Elliott	(Horsham)	
G-DWIB	Chilton DW.1B	PFA 225-12374		22.12.93	J.Jennings	(Bedford)	
G-DWMS	Jabiru Jabiru UL-450	0266 & PFA 274A-13491		21. 6.00	D.H.S.Williams	Sutton Meadows, Ely	8. 5.03P
G-DWPF	Technam P92-EM Echo	PFA 318-13838		17. 5.02	P.I.Franklin & D.J.M.Williams	(Guernsey)	9. 9..03P
G-DWPH	Ultramagic M-77 HAB	77/109		17. 3.95	Jennifer M.Robinson *"Miguel"* t/a Ultramagic UK	Chipping Norton	26. 6.03
G-DYNE	Cessna 414 Chancellor	414-0070	N8170Q	4. 8.87	Commair Aviation Ltd t/a Commodore International	Nottingham	23.10.03
G-DYNG	Colt 105A HAB	1721	G-HSHS	9. 2.98	M.J.Gunston *"High Society"*	Camberley	12.10.03A
G-DYOU*	Piper PA-38-112 Tomahawk	38-78A0436	N9737N	19.10.78	Not known *(Damaged Booker 23.7.92: cancelled 24.5.95 as WFU: hulk dumped 11.01)*	Booker	3. 3.94T

G-EAAA - G-EZZZ (see SECTION 1, PART 1 for original G-EA.. & G-EB..[1919 to 1928] registrations)

Reg	Type	C/n	Prev id	Date	Owner	Location	Status
G-EAGA(2)	Sopwith Dove rep (Le Rhone 80hp)	"3004/1"	(G-BLOO)	22.11.89	A.Wood *(On loan to The Shuttleworth Collection)*	Old Warden	16. 5.01P
	(Orig Dove G-EAGA, c/n 3004/1, exported to Australia & in use as K-157 by 11.12.19. Remains of unregistered Dove, thought to have been K-157, and which crashed Essendon, Victoria 9.3.30 brought to UK circa 1987/88, rebuilt as G-BLOO and subsequently re-registered as above)						
G-EAVX(2)	Sopwith Pup	PFA 101-10523	B1807	16. 1.87	K.A.M.Baker *(To carry "B1807/A7" in RFC c/s: valid CofR 1.03)*	(Winscombe, Somerset)	
	(Claimed as rebuild of original aircraft written-off Hendon 21.7.21 & cancelled)						
G-EBJI(2)	Hawker Cygnet rep	PFA 77-10240		9. 8.77	C.J.Essex *(Under construction 7.99: valid CofR 1.03)*	(Coventry)	
G-EBZN(2)	de Havilland DH.60X Moth (Cirrus I)	608	VP-NAA VP-YAA/ZS-AAP/G-UAAP	28.10.88	Jane Hodgkinson *(On rebuild from original components: valid CofR 1.03)*	(Gravesend)	
G-ECAB	Curtiss JN-4D (Curtiss OX-5)	1917	N2525	28. 5.99	V.S.E.Norman	Rendcomb	AC
G-ECAH	Fokker F.27 Friendship Mk.500	10669	G-JEAH VH-EWY/PH-EXL	14. 4.00	Euroceltic Airways Ltd	Dublin	14. 2.03T
G-ECAN	de Havilland DH.84 Dragon	2048	VH-DHX VH-AQU/RAAF A34-59	11. 1.01	A.J. Norman t/r Norman Aeroplane Trust *(On rebuild 2.03)*	Chilbolton	AC
	(Built de Havilland Aircraft Pty Ltd, Bankstown, Australia)						
G-ECAS	Boeing 737-36N	28554		16.12.96	British Midland Airways Ltd *(Op bmibaby) "golden jubilee baby"*	East Midlands	19.12.05T
G-ECAT	Fokker F.27 Friendship Mk.500	10672	G-JEAI VH-EWZ/PH-EXS	14. 4.00	Euroceltic Airways Ltd *(Skidded off end of runway landing Sligo 3.11.02)*	Dublin	16.12.02T
G-ECBH	Reims/Cessna F150K	F15000577	D-ECBH	16. 5.85	G.Harber tr ECBH Flying Group	Haverfordwest	8. 9.05T
G-ECDX	de Havilland DH.71 Tiger Moth rep (DH Gipsy I)	SP.7		1.11.94	M.D.Souch & N.Parkhouse *(Under build 2.03)*	Hill Farm, Durley	
G-ECGC	Reims/Cessna F172N Skyhawk II	F17201850		10.10.79	Euroair Flying Club Ltd	Cranfield	26. 7.04T
G-ECGO	Bölkow Bö.208C Junior	599	D-ECGO	24. 8.89	A Flight Aviation Ltd *(Op Prestwick Flying Club)*	Prestwick	30. 3.03T
G-ECHO	Enstrom 280C-UK-2 Shark	1017	G-LONS G-BDIB	28. 5.82	A.L.Pattinson t/a ALP Electrical (Maidenhead)	Oaksey Park	1. 6.03
G-ECJM	Piper PA-28R-201T Turbo Arrow III	28R-7803178	G-FESL G-BNRN/N321EC/N3561M	25. 9.90	Regishire Ltd	Southampton	4. 3.04
G-ECLI	Schweizer 269C	S 1784	N69A	16. 7.99	C.S.& C.A.Wright t/a Central Communications Group	(Sidmouth)	13.11.05
G-ECOS	Aérospatiale AS355F1 Twin Squirrel	5300	G-DOLR G-BPVB/OH-HAJ/D-HEHN	24. 9.92	Multiflight Ltd *(Op Northern Helicopters (Leeds) Ltd)*	Leeds-Bradford	20.11.03T
G-ECOX	Pietenpol Aircamper GN.1	WLAW.1 & PFA 47-10356		5.12.78	H.C.Cox *(Under construction 2001)*	(Bristol)	
G-ECVB	Pietenpol Aircamper	PFA 47-13014		20. 4.00	K.S.Matcham	Barton Ashes	7.10.03P
G-ECZZ	Eurocopter EC120B	1053		15.10.99	Kensington & Chelsea Aviation Ltd	Redhill	21.10.05T
G-EDAV	Scottish Aviation Bulldog Srs.120/121	BH120/220	XX534	8. 8.01	Edwalton Aviation Ltd *(As "XX534/B")*	(Nottingham)	6. 8.05
G-EDEN	SOCATA TB-10 Tobago	66		8. 1.80	N.G.Pistol tr Group Eden	Elstree	17. 4.05
G-EDFS	Pietenpol Aircamper	PFA 47-13206		24. 3.98	D.F.Slaughter	(Redhill)	
G-EDGE	Jodel 150 Mascaret (Continental O-200-A)	111 & PFA 151-11223		14. 9.88	A.D.Edge *(Under construction 2000)*	(Brampton, Huntington)	
G-EDGI	Piper PA-28-161 Warrior	28-7916565	D-EBGI N2941R	19. 1.99	R.A.Forster	Cardiff	26..3.05
G-EDMC	Pegasus Quantum 15-912	7513		11. 3.99	E.McCallum	Eshott	13. 4.03P
G-EDNA	Piper PA-38-112 Tomahawk	38-78A0364	OY-BRG	4. 9.84	D.J.Clucas	Woodford	17.12.05T
G-EDRV	Van's RV-6A	PFA 181A-13451		20. 8.99	E.A.Yates	(Harlow)	
G-EDTO	Reims FR172F Rocket	FR17200090	D-EDTQ	21. 3.01	N.G.Hopkinson	Fenland	29. 4.04
G-EDVL	Piper PA-28R-200 Cherokee Arrow II	28R-7235245	G-BXIN D-EDVL/N1243T	30. 6.97	J.S.Develin & Z.Islam *(Op Sky Leisure)*	Shoreham	24. 5.03T
G-EECO	Lindstrand LBL 25A Cloudhopper HAB	668		1. 2.00	P.A.Bubb & A.J.Allen	Guildford	7. 5.02A
G-EEGL	Christen Eagle II (Lycoming AEIO-360)	AES/01/0353	5Y-EGL	14.12.90	M.P.Swoboda	(Street Farm, Takeley)	20. 8.03P
G-EEGU	Piper PA-28-161 Warrior II	28-7916457	D-EEGU N2831A	7. 5.02	Premier Flight Training Ltd	Norwich	29. 8.05T
G-EEJE	Piper PA-31 Navajo B	31-825	OH-PNG	18. 5.01	Geeje Ltd	(Fadmoor, York)	6. 8.04T
G-EELS	Cessna 208B Caravan I	208B0619		3. 3.97	Glass Eels Ltd	Gloucestershire	26. 7.03T

Reg	Type	C/n	Prev Identity	Date	Owner	Location	Expiry
G-EENA	Piper PA-32R-301 Saratoga SP	32R-8013011	C-GBBU	3.10.97	Gamit Ltd	Andrewsfield	20. 6.04
G-EENI	Europa Aviation Europa	199 & PFA 247-12831		28. 7.98	M.P.Grimshaw *(Current status unknown)*	(London W5)	
G-EENY	Gulfstream GA-7 Cougar	GA7-0094	N721G	21. 6.79	J.P.E.Walsh	Cranfield	20. 7.03T
					t/a Walsh Aviation *(Op Cabair)*		
G-EERH	Ruschmeyer R90-230RG	003	D-EERH	5. 4.01	D.Sadler *(Noted 5.01)*	Perth	2. 5.04
G-EERV	Van's RV-6	PFA 181-13381	G-NESI	13. 9.01	C.B.Stirling	Damyns Hall, Upminster	20. 3 03P
G-EESA	Europa Aviation Europa	025 & PFA 247-12535	G-HIIL	9. 4.96	C.B.Stirling	Damyns Hall, Upminster	3. 6.03P
	(NSI EA-81/100) *(Monowheel u/c)*				*(F/f 20.11.96)*		
G-EESE*	Cessna U206G Stationair	U20603883	OO-DMA	28. 2.85	Not known	Movenis, Co.Londonderry	1. 4.91
			N7344C				
	(Crashed Magilligan, Co.Londonderry 31.12.88: cancelled 17.7.90 as destroyed) (Fuselage noted 9.01)						
G-EEST	British Aerospace Jetstream Srs.3102	781	SE-LGM	16. 8.00	Eastern Airways (Europe) Ltd	Humberside	23.10.03T
			OY-SVY/C-FASJ/G-31-781				
G-EEUP	SNCAN Stampe SV-4C	451	F-BCXQ	1. 9.78	A.M.Wajih	Redhill	11.10.02
G-EEYE	Mainair Blade 912	1313-0202-7 & W1108		13. 5.02	B.J.Egerton	(Bootle)	13.5.03
G-EEZS	Cessna 182P Skylane	18261338	D-EEZS	8.11.99	M.A.London & A.J.Buckhold	(Peterborough)	13. 1.03
			N63054/D-EEZS/(N20981)				
G-EFGH	Robinson R22 Beta	1487	G-ROGG	3. 5.01	Foxtrot Golf Helicopters Ltd	Edinburgh	16. 9.05T
G-EFIR	Piper PA-28-181 Archer II	28-8090275	D-EFIR	5. 5.99	Leicestershire Aero Club Ltd	Leicester	8. 6.05T
			N8179R				
G-EFRY	Avid Aerobat	PFA 189-12096		22. 3.93	P.A.Boyden	(Dunsfold)	27. 3.03P
G-EFSM	Slingsby T.67M-260 Firefly	2072	G-BPLK	16. 7.92	Pooler-LMT Ltd	Sleap	17.12.05T
G-EFTE	Bölkow Bö.207	218	D-EFTE	4. 1.90	L.J. & A.A.Rice	Bishopstrow Farm, Warminster	7.10.05
G-EGAL	Christen Eagle II	0042-86	SE-XMU	11. 3.96	J H Penfold	Swanborough Farm, Lewes	29. 4.02P
	(Lycoming AEIO-360)						
G-EGEE	Cessna 310Q	310Q0040	G-AZVY	14.11.83	P.G.Lawrence	(Taunton)	19. 7.03T
			SE-FKV/N7540Q				
G-EGEG	Cessna 172R Skyhawk	17280894	N7262H	4. 7.00	C.D.Lever	Elstree	6. 7.03
G-EGGI	Comco Ikarus C42 FB UK	PFA 322-13872		18. 4.02	A.G.& G.J.Higgins	Bitteswell	1. 8.03P
G-EGGS	Robin DR400/180 Regent	1443		15.11.79	R.Foot	Lasham	17. 7.04
G-EGHB	Ercoupe 415D	1876	N3414G	1. 9.95	P.G.Vallance	Rochester	23. 9.05
	(Continental O-200-A)		N99253/NC99253				
G-EGHH	Hawker Hunter F.58	41H-697450	J-4083	4. 7.95	G.R Lacey	Bournemouth	
					(With Bournemouth Aviation Museum for rebuild 1.03)		
G-EGHR	SOCATA TB-20 Trinidad	795	F-GGIQ	19.12.97	B.M.Prescott	Goodwood	13. 3.04T
G-EGJA	SOCATA TB-20 Trinidad	1101	N2807D	13.12.90	D.A.Williamson	Alderney	14.12.03
G-EGLD	Piper PA-28-161 Cadet	2841283	N92007	23.11.89	J.Appleton	Denham	6. 1.05T
					t/a Holmes Rentals *(Op Denham School of Flying)*		
G-EGLE	Christen Eagle II	F.0053		30. 3.81	S.J.Hampton tr Eagle Group	(London W4)	17. 9.03P
	(Built Airmore Aviation) (Lycoming AEIO-360)						
G-EGLS	Piper PA-28-181 Archer III	2843348	N4187C	5. 6.00	D.J.Cooke	Old Sarum	5. 6.03
G-EGLT	Cessna 310R II	310R1874	G-BHTV	9. 9.93	Capital Trading (Aviation) Ltd	Exeter	15. 1.05T
			N1EU/(N3206M)				
G-EGNR	Piper PA-38-112 Tomahawk	38-79A0233	OY-VIG	6.10.97	Metropolitan Services Ltd	Hawarden	8. 2.04T
			SE-KNI/N2570C				
G-EGTR	Piper PA-28-161 Cadet	2841281	G-BRSI	25. 4.98	Stars Fly Ltd	Elstree	23. 1.05T
			N92001				
G-EGUL	Christen Eagle II	Argence 0001	G-FRYS	19. 1.93	I.S.Smith tr G-EGUL Flying Group	RAF Coltishall	15. 8.03P
	(Built Argence EA) (Lycoming AEIO-360)		N66EA				
G-EGUY	Sky 220-24 HAB	103		24. 4.98	Sky Trek Ballooning Ltd	Longfield	17 12.03T
G-EHBJ	CASA I-131E Jungmann 2000	2150	E3B-550	19. 7.90	E.P.Howard	Priory Farm, Tibenham	6. 8.03P
G-EHGF	Piper PA-28-181 Archer II	28-7790188	D-EHGF	23.10.00	E.Stokes & J.Lamb tr Pegasus Flying Group	Barton	20. 2.04T
			N9534N				
G-EHLX	Piper PA-28-181 Archer II	28-8090317	D-EHLX	5.11.99	I.R.Carver, R.J.Barber & B.Cook	Seething	13. 1.06
			N8218S		t/a Carver-Barber-Cook		
G-EHMJ	Beech S35 Bonanza	D-7879	D-EHMJ	12. 1.99	A.L.Burton & A.J.Daley	Gamston	14. 3.05
G-EHMM	Robin DR400/180R Remorqueur	867	D-EHMM(1)	10.12.84	Booker Gliding Club Ltd	Booker	1. 4.03
G-EHMS	MD Helicopters MD.900	900-00068	N3212K	12. 7.00	Virgin HEMS (London) Ltd	Denham	11.10.03T
G-EHUP	Aérospatiale SA341G Gazelle 1	1407	F-GIJR	3.10.97	M W Helicopters Ltd	Stapleford	11. 1.04T
			N869GT/N869/N49523				
G-EHXP	Rockwell Commander 112	227	D-EHXP	27. 1.00	A.L.Stewart	Teesside	3. 2.03T
			N1227J				
G-EIBM	Robinson R22 Beta	1993	G-BUCL	25. 3.94	XL Aviation Ltd	Lower Baads Farm, Peterculter	5. 3.04T
					(Op HJS Helicopters)		
G-EIII	Extra EA.300	057	G-HIII	4.12.00	D Dobson	Little Staughton	16 .8.03T
	(Lycoming AEIO-540-L1B5)		D-ETYD				
G-EIIR*	Cameron N-77 HAB	358		16.11.77	D.V.Howard "Silver Jubilee"	Bath	14. 5.93A
					(Cancelled 23.10.01 by CAA)		
G-EIKY	Europa Aviation Europa	054 & PFA 247-12634		27. 9.94	J.D.Milbank	Insch	7. 6.03P
	(Rotax 912-UL) *(Monowheel u/c)*				*(F/f 20.7.97)*		
G-EIRE	Cessna T182T Turbo Skylane	T18208049	N3500U	24. 7.01	J.Byrne	Kemble	31. 7.04T
G-EISO	SOCATA MS.892A Rallye Commodore 150	10563	D-EISO	23. 1.01	T.E.Harry Simmons tr G-EISO Group	(Newport)	24. 5.04T
			F-BNSO				
G-EITE	Luscombe 8A Silvaire	3407	N71980	27. 7.88	S R H Martin	Denham	19 12.02P
G-EIWT	Reims/Cessna FR182 Skylane RG	FR18200052	D-EIWT	28. 1.86	P.P.D.Howard-Johnston	Glenrothes	10. 4.04T
			OO-BLI				
G-EJEL	Cessna 550 Citation II	550-0643	N747CR	19.12.01	A.J.& E.A.Elliott	(Huddersfield)	8. 1.05
			N643MC/PT-ODW/N13091/(N1259S)				
G-EJGO	Zlin Z.226 Trener 6HE Spezial	199	D-EJGO	7. 8.85	Aerotation Ltd	Rochester	14. 8.05
			OK-MHB				
G-EJMG	Cessna F150H	F150-0301	D-EJMG	27. 4.98	T.A.White tr Bagby Aviation	Teesside	14.11.04T
	(Built Reims Aviation SA)						
G-EJOC	Aérospatiale AS350B Ecureuil	1465	G-GEDS	21.12.94	E.& S.Vandyk	(Newbury)	8. 7.02T
			G-HMAN/G-SKIM/G-BIVP		t/a Leisure & Retail Helicopters		

G-EKIR	Piper PA-28-161 Cadet	2841157	SE-KIR (SE-KII)	17. 6.02	Aeros Leasing Ltd (Op Aeros Flying Club)	Gloucestershire	6. 8.05T
G-EKKL	Piper PA-28-161 Warrior II	28-8416087	D-EKKL N43588	24. 3.99	Apollo Aviation Advisory Ltd	Shoreham	21 6.04T
G-EKKO	Robinson R44 Raven	0821		18. 7.00	MC Air Ltd	Wellesbourne Mountford	3..8.03T

(Tail skid hit ground landing Wellesbourne Mountford 2.9.01: broke up & tail boom & rotors detached: cancelled 27.5.02 as destroyed) (Wreck noted 8.02)

G-EKMN	Zlin Z.242L	0652	SE-KMN	15. 5.01	R.C.Poolman	Gloucestershire	21. 6.04T
G-EKMW	Mooney M.20J (205)	24-3213	D-EKMW	13. 5.02	A.C.Armstrong	Jersey	16. 7.05T
G-EKOS	Reims/Cessna FR182 Skylane RG	FR18200017	D-EKOS	15. 7.98	S.Charlton	Sherburn-in-Elmet	12. 9.04
G-ELBC	Piper PA-34-200 Seneca	34-7350021	G-BANS N15110	4. 4.91	Stapleford Flying Club Ltd (Op LBC Radio @ "London Lookout")	Stapleford	27.12.03T
G-ELDR	Piper PA-32-260 Cherokee Six	32-7400027	SE-GBK	21. 1.03	Elder Aviation Ltd	Gloucestershire	
G-ELEE	Cameron Z-105 HAB	4882		11. 7.00	D.Eliot	Aberdeen	21. 9.03A
G-ELEN	Robin DR400/180	2363		16. 9.97	N.R. & E.Foster	Cannes, France	30.11.03T
G-ELIT	Bell 206L LongRanger	45091	SE-HTK N2652	28. 7.99	Henfield Lodge Aviation Ltd	(Henfield)	18. 8.05T
G-ELIZ	Denney Kitfox Model 2	717 & PFA 172-11835		19. 7.90	A.J.Ellis t/a Tiger Helicopters	Sandown	5.11.93P

(Damaged Brighstone, Isle of Wight 10.5.93: current status unknown)

G-ELKA	Christen Eagle II (Lycoming AEIO-360)	0001	N121DJ	18.10.94	P.J.Lawton "Ping Pong"	Blackbushe	7. 9.03P
G-ELKS	Avid Speed Wing Mk.4 (Jabiru 2200A)	PFA 189-13109		6. 1.98	H.S.Elkins	Garston Farm, Marshfield	9. 7.03P
G-ELLA	Piper PA-32R-301 Saratoga IIHP	3246050	N9279Q G-ELLA	13. 8.96	C.C.W.Hart	White Waltham	23.11.02
G-ELLE	Cameron N-90 HAB	4498		11. 1.99	N.D.Eliot	(London SW19)	18. 6.03A
G-ELLI	Bell 206B-3 JetRanger III	4231	D-HMOF	24. 6.97	RA Fleming Ltd	Brandon Hall, Leeds	6. 7.03T
G-ELMH	North American AT-6D-NT Harvard III	88-16336	FAP1662 EZ341/42-84555	22. 7.92	M.Hammond "Fools Rush-In" (As "42-84555/EP-H" in USAAC c/s)	Airfield Farm, Hardwick	25. 5.03P
G-ELNX	Bombardier CL600-2B19	7508	VH-KXJ C-FMNY	26. 4.02	Eurolynx Corporation	Stansted	23. 5.03
G-ELUN	Robin DR400/180R Remorqueur	1102	D-ELUN I-ALSA	29. 5.02	P.Harper-Little & I.A.Lane tr Cotswold DR400 Syndicate	Nympsfield	11. 7.05
G-ELZN	Piper PA-28-161 Warrior II	28-8416078	D-ELZN N9579N	20. 7.99	Northamptonshire School of Flying Ltd	Sywell	5. 9.05T
G-ELZY	Piper PA-28-161 Warrior II	28-8616027	D-ELZY N9095Z/(N163AV)/N9641N	13. 4.99	Goodwood Road Racing School Ltd	Goodwood	23. 5.05T
G-EMAS	Eurocopter EC135-T1	0107		6. 7.99	East Midlands Air Support Unit	Sibbertoft	7.10.05T
G-EMAX	Piper PA-31-350 Navajo Chieftain	31-7952029	N276CT SE-KKP/54202 Swedish Navy/SE-KKP/LN-PAI	8.12.98	AM & T Aviation Ltd (Op Air Mercia)	Bristol	14. 1.03T
G-EMAZ	Piper PA-28-181 Archer II	28-8290088	N8073W G-EMAZ/N8073W	26. 4.90	E.J.Stanley	RAF Woodvale	27.10.05T
G-EMBA	Embraer EMB-145EU	145.016	PT-SYM	17. 7.97	Port One Ltd	(Cep, Brazil)	14. 8.03T
G-EMBB	Embraer EMB-145EU	145.021	PT-SYR	27. 8.97	British Regional Airlines Ltd	East Midlands	1. 9.03T
G-EMBC	Embraer EMB-145EU	145.024	PT-SYU	1.10.97	British Airways Citiexpress Ltd (Koguty Lowickie t/s)	Ronaldsway	8.10.03T
G-EMBD	Embraer EMB-145EU	145.039		7. 1.98	British Airways Citiexpress Ltd (Animals & Trees t/s)	Ronaldsway	11. 1.04T
G-EMBE	Embraer EMB-145EU	145.042		3. 2.98	British Airways Citiexpress Ltd (Waves of the City t/s)	Ronaldsway	2. 2.04T
G-EMBF	Embraer EMB-145EU	145.088		10.11.98	British Airways Citiexpress Ltd (Grand Union t/s)	Ronaldsway	9.11.04T
G-EMBG	Embraer EMB-145EU	145.094		18.11.98	British Airways Citiexpress Ltd (Water Dreaming t/s)	Ronaldsway	17.11.04T
G-EMBH	Embraer EMB-145EU	145.107		20. 1.99	British Airways Citiexpress Ltd (Blomsterang t/s)	Birmingham	19. 1.05T
G-EMBI	Embraer EMB-145EU	145.126		23. 4.99	British Airways Citiexpress Ltd (Paitahni t/s)	Manchester	22. 4.05T
G-EMBJ	Embraer EMB-145EU	145.134		24. 5.99	British Airways Citiexpress Ltd (Youm-Al-Suq t/s)	Manchester	26. 5.05T
G-EMBK	Embraer EMB-145EU	145.167		26. 8.99	British Airways Citiexpress Ltd	Ronaldsway	25. 8.05T
G-EMBL	Embraer EMB-145EU	145.177		4.10.99	British Airways Citiexpress Ltd	Ronaldsway	3.10.05T
G-EMBM	Embraer EMB-145EU	145.196		22.11.99	British Airways Citiexpress Ltd	Ronaldsway	21.11.05T
G-EMBN	Embraer EMB-145EU	145.201		13. 1.00	British Airways Citiexpress Ltd	Ronaldsway	12. 1.06T
G-EMBO	Embraer EMB-145EU	145.219		14. 3.00	British Airways Citiexpress Ltd	Ronaldsway	13. 3.03T
G-EMBP	Embraer EMB-145EU	145.300		25. 8.00	British Airways Citiexpress Ltd	Ronaldsway	24. 8.03T
G-EMBS	Embraer EMB-145EU	145.357		20.12.00	British Airways Citiexpress Ltd	Ronaldsway	19.12.03T
G-EMBT	Embraer EMB-145EU	145.404		22. 3.01	British Airways Citiexpress Ltd	Ronaldsway	21. 3.04T
G-EMBU	Embraer EMB-145EU	145.458	PT-SVD	22. 6.01	British Airways Citiexpress Ltd	Ronaldsway	21. 6.04T
G-EMBV	Embraer EMB-145EU	145.482	PT-SXB	12. 9.01	British Airways Citiexpress Ltd	Ronaldsway	11. 9.04T
G-EMBW	Embraer EMB-145EU	145.546	PT-SZJ	19.12.01	British Airways Citiexpress Ltd	Southampton	18.12.04T
G-EMBX	Embraer EMB-145EU	145.573	PT-SBJ	21. 3.02	Brymon Airways Ltd	Plymouth	20. 3.05T
G-EMBY	Embraer EMB-145EU	145.617	PT-SDF	17. 7.02	British Airways Citiexpress Ltd	Ronaldsway	16. 7.05T
G-EMCM	Eurocopter EC120B	1160		20.11.00	C.R.W.Morrell	(London SW7)	28. 2.04
G-EMDM	Diamond DA-40-P9 Star	40009	OE-KPO OE-VPO	7.10.02	D.J.Munson	(Aylesbury)	20.10.05T
G-EMER	Piper PA-34-200 Seneca	34-7350002	N3081T	29. 7.91	Haimoss Ltd (Op Old Sarum Flying Club)	Old Sarum	26. 2.04T
G-EMHH	Aérospatiale AS355F2 Twin Squirrel	5169	G-BYKH SX-HNP/VR-CCM/N57967	3. 8.99	Hancocks Holdings Ltd	Costock	26. 7.05T
G-EMIN	Europa Aviation Europa (Rotax 912-UL) (Monowheel u/c)	083 & PFA 247-12673		1. 3.94	S.A.Lamb (F/f 26.5.97)	Rochester	27. 8.03P
G-EMJA	CASA I-131E-2000 Jungmann (Enma Tigre G-IV-B)	013 & PFA 242-12340	(Span.AF)	2. 9.94	P.J.Brand	High Cross, Ware	20. 5.03P

(Composite from Spanish spares imported in 1991)

G-EMLY	Pegasus Quantum 15 (Rotax 582-40)	7531		30. 6.99	A.R.White	(Farnham)	27. 6.03P
G-EMMS	Piper PA-38-112 Tomahawk	38-78A0526	OO-TKT N4414E	14. 9.79	Cheshire Flying Services Ltd t/a Ravenair	Liverpool	12.11.03T

G-EMMY	Rutan VariEze	577 & PFA 74-10222		21. 8.78	M.J.Tooze	Biggin Hill	18. 6.06P
	(Lycoming O-235)						
G-EMNI*	Phillips ST.1 Speedtwin Mk.2			25. 5.95	A.J.Clarry	(Pewsey, Wilts)	
		006 & PFA 207-12880			*(Cancelled 17.10.01 as WFU: no PtoF issued)*		
G-EMSI	Europa Aviation Europa	191 & PFA 247-12817		24. 1.95	P.W.L.Thomas	(York)	
	(Rotax 912S) *(Tri-gear u/c)*						
G-EMSL	Piper PA-28-161 Warrior II	28-8216117	G-TSFT	20. 2.02	Environmental Maintenance Services Ltd	Biggin Hill	14. 2.05T
			G-BLDJ/N9632N				
G-EMSY	de Havilland DH.82A Tiger Moth	83666	G-ASPZ	27. 6.91	B.E.Micklewright	Bourne Park, Hurstbourne Tarrant	24.10.03
	(Rebuilt with parts from OO-MOT)		D-EDUM/T7356				
G-ENCE	Partenavia P.68B	141	G-OROY	1. 6.84	J.J.H.& A.E.Hanna	(Budleigh Salterton)	28. 9.03T
			G-BFSU		t/a Bicton Aviation		
G-ENEE	CFM Streak Shadow	K.280 & PFA 206-13628		14. 8.00	T.Green	Wombleton	23. 4.03P
	(Rotax 912-UL)						
G-ENGO	Steen Skybolt	PFA 64-13429		15.11.00	C.Docherty	(Mount Pleasant, Falklands)	
G-ENIE	Nipper T.66 Srs.IIIB	PFA 25-10214		17. 3.78	E.J.Clarke	Seighford	11. 6.03P
	(Volkswagen 1800)						
G-ENII	Reims/Cessna F172M Skyhawk II	F17201352	PH-WAG	18. 1.79	J.Howley	Blackbushe	4.11.02T
			(D-EDQM)				
G-ENNI	Robin R3000/180	128	F-GGJA	5.10.99	F.R.Traynor	Wellesbourne Mountford	18 12.05T
G-ENNK	Cessna 172S Skyhawk	172S8538	N72729	15. 9.00	AK Enterprises Ltd	(London N8)	1.11.03T
G-ENNY	Cameron V-77 HAB	1399		1.12.86	B.G.Jones *"Crocks of Frome"*	Devizes	11. 7.03A
G-ENOA	Cessna F172F	F172-0138	G-ASZW	2. 9.81	M.K.Acors	King's Farm, Thurrock	17.10.03
	(Built Reims Aviation SA)						
G-ENRE	Jabiru Jabiru UL-450	PFA 274A-13755		28. 6.01	J.C.Harris	Rochester	4.11.03
G-ENRI	Lindstrand LBL-105A HAB	294		4. 8.95	P.G.Hall	Chard	7. 6.03T
					(Henry Numatic Vacuum Cleaners titles)		
G-ENRY	Cameron N-105 HAB	2096		26. 9.89	P.G. & G.R.Hal *"Henry"*	Chard	7. 7.94T
G-ENSI	Beech F33A Bonanza	CE-699	D-ENSI	17. 3.78	G.Garnett	Denham	19. 5.05
G-ENTT	Reims/Cessna F152 II	F15201750	G-BHHI	9.11.93	C.& A.R.Hyett	(Fleet)	31. 3.05T
			(PH-CBA)				
G-ENTW	Reims/Cessna F152 II	F15201479	G-BFLK	21. 1.93	Firecrest Aviation Ltd, W.Bagnall & M.Pevan	Elstree	15. 8.04T
G-ENVY	Mainair Blade	1260-1000-7 & W1054		20.12.00	D A Pollitt & P Millership	(Bolton)	17.12.02P
	(Rotax 912-UL)						
G-EOFM	Reims/Cessna F172N Skyhawk	F17201988	D-EOFM	2.11.01	20th Air Training Group Ltd	Dublin	7. 3.05T
G-EOFS	Europa Aviation Europa	296 & PFA 247-13033		22. 7.98	G.T.Leedham	Gunby Lea Farm, Overseal	24. 9.03P
	(Rotax 914-UL) *(Tri-gear u/c)*				*(F/f 31.7.99)*		
G-EOFW	Pegasus Quantum Q2 Sport 15-912	7582		15.10.99	G.C.Weighell	Long Marston	14.10.03P
G-EOHL	Cessna 182L Skylane	18259279	D-EOHL	4. 3.99	G.B.Dale & M.C.Terris	Enniskillen, Co.Fermanagh	10. 4.05
			N70505				
G-EOIN	Zenair CH.701UL	PFA 187-13490		19.11.99	D.G.Palmer	Fetterangus	11. 8.03P
	(Verner SVS1400)						
G-EOLD	Piper PA-28-161 Warrior II	28-8516030	D-EOLD	31. 3.00	Goodwood Road Racing Co Ltd	Goodwood	25. 5.03T
			N4390F/N9531N				
G-EOMA	Airbus Industrie A330-243	265	F-WWKU	26. 4.99	Monarch Airlines Ltd	Luton	25. 4.05T
G-EORD	Cessna 208B Grand Caravan	208B0935	N5263D	19. 3.02	Air Medical Ltd	Oxford	18. 4.05T
G-EORG	Piper PA-38-112 Tomahawk	38-78A0427	N9734N	18. 9.78	Airways Aero Associations Ltd	Booker	14. 7.03T
	(Rebuilt with new fuselage: old one stored 9.96)				*(Op British Airways Flying Club) (Whale Rider t/s)*		
G-EORJ	Europa Aviation Europa	347 & PFA 247-13139		23. 7.99	P.E.George	(Sutton Coldfield)	
	(Rotax 912S) *(Monowheel u/c)*				*(Current status unknown)*		
G-EPAR	Robinson R22 Beta-II	2781		26. 2.98	J.W.Ramsbottom t/a Jepar Rotorcraft & J.A.Bickerstaffe		
						Blackpool	26. 2.01T
	(Crashed on landing Blackpool 22.12.99 & severely damaged: pod stored 12.01) (New owners 12.02)						
G-EPDI	Cameron N-77 HAB	370		25. 1.78	R.Moss *"Pegasus"*	Banchory	29. 6.91A
G-EPED	Piper PA-31-350 Chieftain	31-8252040	G-BMCJ	22. 3.95	Pedley Furniture International Ltd	Duxford	17. 4.03T
			N121CF/N41060				
G-EPOL	Aérospatiale AS355F1 Twin Squirrel	5302	G-SASU	13. 1.98	Cambridge and Essex Air Support Unit	Boreham	12.11.05T
			G-BSSM/G-BMTC/G-BKUK				
G-EPOX	Aero Designs Pulsar XP	PFA 202-12355		27. 4.94	K.F.Farey	(Bourne End)	11. 9.02P
G-EPTR	Piper PA-28R-200 Cherokee Arrow II	28R-7235090	D-EPTR	26. 5.98	Tayflite Ltd	Perth	13. 8.04T
			OH-PTR/(SE-KVF)/N4558T				
G-ERAD	Beech C90A King Air	LJ-1565	N213NC	18. 7.01	G.R.Kinally	(Cranleigh)	25. 7.04
	(Marked as C90B)				t/a GKL Management Services Ltd		
G-ERBL	Robinson R22 Beta-II	2711		26. 6.97	G.V.Maloney	(Cavan, Co.Cavan)	27. 7.03T
G-ERCO	Ercoupe 415D	3210	N2585H	7. 4.93	A.R. & M.V.Tapp	Maypole Farm, Chislet	15. 8.05
	(Continental C85)		NC2585H				
G-ERDA	Staaken Z-21A Flitzer	PFA 223-13947		15. 1.03	J.Cresswell	(Lymington)	
G-ERDS	de Havilland DH.82A Tiger Moth	85028	ZS-BCU	27. 7.94	W.A.Gerdes	(Lee-on-Solent)	8. 7.04
			SAAF 2267/T6741				
G-ERFS	Piper PA-28-161 Warrior II	28-8216051	D-EPFS	29.11.02	S.Harrison	Lee-on-Solent	AC
			N84570				
G-ERIC	Rockwell Commander 112TC	13010	SE-GSA	26. 9.78	Atomchoice Ltd	Cranfield	11. 5.03
G-ERIK	Cameron N-77 HAB	1753		18. 5.88	T.M.Donnelly *"Norsewind"*	Doncaster	24. 2.00A
G-ERIS	Hughes 369D (500D)	11-0871D	G-PJMD	1. 3.96	R.J.Howard	Leeds	9. 9.04
	(Modified to 500E standard)		G-BMJV/N1110S				
G-ERIX	Boeing-Stearman E75 (PT-13D) Kaydet	75-5093	N5055V	9. 3.88	Flight Incentives NV	Antwerp, Belgium	22. 1.04
	(Pratt & Whitney R985)		42-16930		*(As "985" in US Navy c/s)*		
G-ERJA	Embraer EMB-145EP	145.229		25. 2.00	Brymon Airways Ltd	Bristol	24. 2.03T
G-ERJB	Embraer EMB-145EP	145.237	PT-SIC	13. 3.00	Brymon Airways Ltd	Bristol	12. 3.03T
G-ERJC	Embraer EMB-145EP	145.253		25. 4.00	Brymon Airways Ltd	Bristol	25. 4.03T
G-ERJD	Embraer EMB-145EP	145.290		20. 7.00	Brymon Airways Ltd	Bristol	19. 7.03T
G-ERJE	Embraer EMB-145EP	145.315	PT-SMG	15. 9.00	Brymon Airways Ltd	Bristol	14. 9.03T
G-ERJF	Embraer EMB-145EP	145.325		24.10.00	Brymon Airways Ltd	Bristol	23.10.03T
G-ERJG	Embraer EMB-145EP	145.394		8. 3.01	Brymon Airways Ltd	Bristol	7. 3.04T

G-ERMO	ARV Super 2 (Hewland AE75)	018	G-BMWK	7. 1.87	T.Pond	Sandtoft	19. 6.05
G-ERMS	Thunder AS-33 Hot Air Airship	A.1		28.11.78	B.R. & M.Boyle	Newbury	
					"Microbe" (On loan to British Balloon Museum & Library)		
G-ERNI	Piper PA-28-181 Archer II	28-8090146	G-OSSY	9.10.91	H.A.Daines	Beccles	8. 3.04
			N81215				
G-EROL	Westland SA.341G Gazelle 1	1108	G-NONA	18.10.02	Coin UK Ltd	Booker	21. 2.05T
			G-FDAV/G-RIFA/G-ORGE/G-BBHU				
G-EROM	Robinson R22 Beta	3383		19.11.02	Aeromega Ltd	Stapleford	27.11.05T
G-ERRI	Lindstrand LBL 77A HAB	811		20. 2.02	K.J.Baxter	Norton, Worcs	18. 7.03A
G-ERRY	Grumman-American AA-5B Tiger	AA5B-0725	G-BFMJ	20. 3.84	M.D.Savage & A.F.K.Horne	Shobdon	13. 6.05
					t/a Gemini Aviation		
G-ESAM	MBB Bö.105D	BS-4S.138/911	G-BUIB	7.12.00	Bond Air Services Ltd	Boreham	24. 6.02T
	(Remanufactured with new pod c/n S.911 c.1992)		G-BDYZ/D-HDEF		*(Op Essex Air Ambulance)*		
G-ESFT	Piper PA-28-161 Warrior II	28-7916060	G-ENNA	16. 5.97	Plane Talking Ltd	Elstree	21. 4.03T
			N22065				
G-ESKY	Piper PA-23-250 Aztec D	27-4172	G-BBNN	24.11.95	Systems & Research Ltd	(Haywards Heath)	5. 6.03T
			N6832Y	*(Fuselage @ North Weald 9.0 as "G-ESKY" & "AIR AMBULANCE" is that of G-BADI qv)*			
G-ESSX	Piper PA-28-161 Warrior II	28-8016261	G-BHYY	30. 7.82	S.Harcourt	Cardiff	16. 1.97T
			N9639N		t/a Courtenay Enterprises *(Noted 3.01)*		
G-ESSY	Robinson R44 Raven	1281		17. 1.03	Heli Air Ltd	Wellesbourne Mountford	
G-ESTA	Cessna 550 Citation II	550-0127	G-GAUL	24. 6.98	Executive Aviation Services Ltd	Gloucestershire	18. 8.03T
			N550TJ/(N29TG)/N29TC/N2631N				
G-ESTE	Gulfstream AA-5A Cheetah	AA5A-0780	G-GHNC	28. 4.87	Plane Talking Ltd	Elstree	8.12.04T
			N26877		*(Op Cabair Flying School)*		
G-ESTR	Van's RV-6	PFA 181A-13638		11. 9.00	R.M.Johnson	Midlem Farm, Midlem	
G-ESUS	Rotorway Executive 162F	6169		7.10.96	J.Tickner	Street Farm, Takeley	29. 7.02P
	(Rotorway RI 162F)						
G-ETAV	Piper PA-32-300 Cherokee Six D	32-7140008	G-MCAR	12. 2.01	H.Peck	(Sheffield)	26. 4.05T
			G-LADA/G-AYWK/N8616N				
G-ETBY	Piper PA-32-260 Cherokee Six	32-211	G-AWCY	13. 7.89	K.Richards-Green & M.B.Smithson	Oxford	25. 9.05
	(Rebuilt with spare Frame No.32-858S)		N3365W		tr G-ETBY Group		
G-ETCW	Stoddard-Hamilton GlaStar	5627	D-ETCW	12.12.01	P.G.Hayward	Little Snoring	16. 1.03P
	(Nosewheel u/c)						
G-ETDA	Piper PA-28-161 Warrior II	28-8116256	N84051	9. 3.88	T.Griffiths	Oaksey Park	13. 4.03
G-ETDC	Cessna 172P Skyhawk II	17274690	N53133	4. 5.88	Osprey Air Services Ltd	RAF Kinloss	20. 7.03T
					(Op Moray Flying Club)		
G-ETHU	Eurocopter EC135-T1	0198		17. 1.02	Helimand Ltd	Jethou, Channel Islands	24. 2.05
G-ETHY	Cessna 208B Caravan	20800293	N1295M	19.10.98	N.A.Moore	Movenis, Co.Londonderry	2 4.03T
			G-ETHY				
G-ETIN	Robinson R22 Beta	0853	N9081D	7. 9.88	Getin Helicopters Ltd	(Nazeing)	24. 9.03T
G-ETIV	Robin DR400/180	2454		12. 7.00	J.Macgilvray	North Connel, Oban	6. 8.03T
G-ETME	Nord 1002 Pingouin	274	N108J	18. 4.00	S.H.O'Connell & J.N.Pittock	White Waltham	20. 7.03
	(Renault 6Q)		F-BFRV/French AF 274		tr 108 Flying Group		
					(As "10/KG+EM" in WW2 Luftwaffe North Africa c/s)		
G-EUGN	Robinson R44 Raven	0822		19. 7.00	Twinlite Developments Ltd	(Maynooth, Co.Kildare)	13. 8.03T
G-EUOA	Airbus Industrie A319-131	1513	D-AVYE	15. 6.01	British Airways plc	Heathrow	14. 6.04T
G-EUOB	Airbus Industrie A319-131	1529	D-AVWH	4. 7.01	British Airways plc	Heathrow	3. 7.04T
G-EUOC	Airbus Industrie A319-131	1537	D-AVYP	16. 7.01	British Airways plc	Heathrow	15. 7.04T
G-EUOD	Airbus Industrie A319-131	1558	D-AVYJ	16. 8.01	British Airways plc	Heathrow	15. 8.04T
G-EUOE	Airbus Industrie A319-131	1574	D-AVWF	5. 9.01	British Airways plc	Heathrow	4. 9.04T
G-EUOF	Airbus Industrie A319-131	1590	D-AVYW	23.10.01	British Airways plc	Heathrow	22.10.04T
G-EUOG	Airbus Industrie A319-131	1594	D-AVWU	23.10.01	British Airways plc	Heathrow	22.10.04T
G-EUOH	Airbus Industrie A319-131	1604	D-AVYM	14.12.01	British Airways plc	Heathrow	13.12.04T
G-EUOI	Airbus Industrie A319-131	1606	D-AVYN	13.11.01	British Airways plc	Heathrow	12.11.04T
G-EUOJ	Airbus Industrie A319-...			R	British Airways plc *(For delivery 4.03)*	Heathrow	
G-EUOK	Airbus Industrie A320-...			R	British Airways plc		
G-EUOL	Airbus Industrie A320-...			R	British Airways plc		
G-EUOM	Airbus Industrie A320-...			R	British Airways plc		
G-EUON	Airbus Industrie A320-...			R	British Airways plc		
G-EUOO	Airbus Industrie A320-...			R	British Airways plc		
G-EUOP	Airbus Industrie A320-...			R	British Airways plc		
G-EUOR	Airbus Industrie A320-...			R	British Airways plc		
G-EUOS	Airbus Industrie A320-...			R	British Airways plc		
G-EUOT	Airbus Industrie A320-...			R	British Airways plc		
G-EUOU	Airbus Industrie A320-...			R	British Airways plc		
G-EUOV	Airbus Industrie A320-...			R	British Airways plc		
G-EUOW	Airbus Industrie A320-...			R	British Airways plc		
G-EUOX	Airbus Industrie A320-...			R	British Airways plc		
G-EUOY	Airbus Industrie A320-...			R	British Airways plc		
G-EUOZ	Airbus Industrie A320-...			R	British Airways plc		
G-EUPA	Airbus Industrie A319-131	1082	D-AVYK	6.10.99	British Airways plc	Birmingham	5.10.05T
G-EUPB	Airbus Industrie A319-131	1115	D-AVYT	9.11.99	British Airways plc	Heathrow	8.11.05T
G-EUPC	Airbus Industrie A319-131	1118	D-AVYU	12.11.99	British Airways plc	Birmingham	11.11.02T
G-EUPD	Airbus Industrie A319-131	1142	D-AVWG	10.12.99	British Airways plc	Birmingham	9.12.05T
G-EUPE	Airbus Industrie A319-131	1193	D-AVYT	27. 3.00	British Airways plc	Birmingham	26. 3.03T
G-EUPF	Airbus Industrie A319-131	1197	D-AVWS	30. 3.00	British Airways plc	Birmingham	29. 3.03T
G-EUPG	Airbus Industrie A319-131	1222	D-AVYG	25. 5.00	British Airways plc	Heathrow	24. 5.03T
G-EUPH	Airbus Industrie A319-131	1225	D-AVYK	23. 5.00	British Airways plc	Birmingham	22. 5.03T
G-EUPJ	Airbus Industrie A319-131	1232	D-AVYJ	30. 5.00	British Airways plc	Heathrow	29. 5.03T
G-EUPK	Airbus Industrie A319-131	1236	D-AVYO	30. 5.00	British Airways plc	Birmingham	29. 5.03T
G-EUPL	Airbus Industrie A319-131	1239	D-AVYP	8. 6.00	British Airways plc	Heathrow	7. 6.03T
G-EUPM	Airbus Industrie A319-131	1258	D-AVYR	30. 6.00	British Airways plc	Heathrow	29. 6.03T
G-EUPN	Airbus Industrie A319-131	1261	D-AVWA	10. 7.00	British Airways plc	Heathrow	9..7.03T
G-EUPO	Airbus Industrie A319-131	1279	D-AVYU	1. 8.00	British Airways plc	Heathrow	31. 7.03T

Reg	Type	Serial	Prev ID	Date	Owner/Operator	Location	Date
G-EUPP	Airbus Industrie A319-131	1295	D-AVWU	14. 8.00	British Airways plc	Heathrow	13. 8.03T
G-EUPR	Airbus Industrie A319-131	1329	D-AVYH	9.10.00	British Airways plc	Heathrow	8.10.03T
G-EUPS	Airbus Industrie A319-131	1338	D-AVYM	23.10.00	British Airways plc	Heathrow	22.10.03T
G-EUPT	Airbus Industrie A319-131	1380	D-AVWH	5.12.00	British Airways plc	Heathrow	4.12.03T
G-EUPU	Airbus Industrie A319-131	1384	D-AVWP	14.12.00	British Airways plc	Heathrow	13.12.03T
G-EUPV	Airbus Industrie A319-131	1423	D-AVYE	13. 2.01	British Airways plc	Heathrow	12. 2.04T
G-EUPW	Airbus Industrie A319-131	1440	D-AVYP	6. 3.01	British Airways plc	Birmingham	5. 3.04T
G-EUPX	Airbus Industrie A319-131	1445	D-AVWB	14.12.01	British Airways plc	Heathrow	13.12.04T
G-EUPY	Airbus Industrie A319-131	1466	D-AVYK	12. 4.01	British Airways plc	Heathrow	11. 4.04T
G-EUPZ	Airbus Industrie A319-131	1510	D-AVYY	7. 6.01	British Airways plc	Heathrow	6. 6.04T
G-EURA	Agusta-Bell 47J-2 Ranger	2061	G-ASNV	21. 7.83	L.Goddard	Thornicombe, Dorset	21. 1.04
G-EURX	Europa Aviation Europa XS T-G	482 & PFA 247-13661		15.12.00	C C Napier	Newtownards, Co.Down	
G-EUUA	Airbus Industrie A320-232	1661	F-WWIH	31. 1.02	British Airways plc	Heathrow	30. 1.05T
G-EUUB	Airbus Industrie A320-232	1689	F-WWBE	14. 2.02	British Airways plc	Heathrow	13. 2.05T
G-EUUC	Airbus Industrie A320-232	1696	F-WWIO	28. 2.02	British Airways plc	Heathrow	27. 2.05T
G-EUUD	Airbus Industrie A320-232	1760	F-WWBN	29. 4.02	British Airways plc	Heathrow	28. 4.05T
G-EUUE	Airbus Industrie A320-232	1782	F-WWDO	30. 5.02	British Airways plc	Heathrow	29. 4.05T
G-EUUF	Airbus Industrie A320-232	1814	F-WWIY	29. 7.02	British Airways plc	Heathrow	28. 7.05T
G-EUUG	Airbus Industrie A320-232	1829	F-WWIU	30. 8.02	British Airways plc	Heathrow	29. 8.05T
G-EUUH	Airbus Industrie A320-232	1665	F-WWIG	25.10.02	British Airways plc	Heathrow	24.10.05T
G-EUUI	Airbus Industrie A320-232	1871	F-WWBI	22.11.02	British Airways plc	Heathrow	21.11.05T
G-EUUJ	Airbus Industrie A320-232	1883	F-WWBQ	25.11.02	British Airways plc	Heathrow	24.11.05T
G-EUUK	Airbus Industrie A320-232	1899	F-WWDO	20.12.02	British Airways plc	Heathrow	AC
G-EUUL	Airbus Industrie A320-232	1708	F-WWIV	20.12.02	British Airways plc	Heathrow	AC
G-EUUM	Airbus Industrie A320-232	1907	F-WWDN	23.12.02	British Airways plc	Heathrow	AC
G-EUUN	Airbus Industrie A320-232	1910	F-WWDP	31. 1.03	British Airways plc	Heathrow	AC
G-EUUO	Airbus Industrie A320-232	1958	F-WWIS	4.03R	British Airways plc (For delivery 4.03)		
G-EUUP	Airbus Industrie A320-232	2038		7.03R	British Airways plc (For delivery 7.03)		
G-EUUR	Airbus Industrie A320-232	2040		7.03R	British Airways plc (For delivery 7.03)		
G-EUUS	Airbus Industrie A320-232			R	British Airways plc		
G-EUUT	Airbus Industrie A320-232			R	British Airways plc		
G-EUUU	Airbus Industrie A320-232			R	British Airways plc		
G-EUUV	Airbus Industrie A320-232			R	British Airways plc		
G-EVES	Dassault Falcon 900B	165	F-WWFD	13.11.97	Northern Executive Aviation Ltd	Manchester/Jersey	12.11.03T
G-EVET	Cameron Concept 80 HAB	3703		30.10.95	K.J.Foster	Coleshill, Birmingham	6. 7.03A
G-EVEY	Thruster T600N 450 Jab	0121-T600N-057		22.11.01	K J Crompton	(Bangor, Belfast)	9.12.03P
G-EVLN	Gulfstream Gulfstream IV	1175	N18WF	3. 6.02	Metropix Ltd	(London EC4)	5. 9.03T
			VH-CCA/(N1175B)/HB-ITJ/N17588				
G-EVVA	Piper PA-28R-200 Cherokee Arrow B	28R-7135151	G-BAZU	15.10.02	D.C.Woods	Elstree	17.12.04
			EI-AVH/N11C				
G-EWAN	Protech PT-2C-160 Prostar	PFA 249-12425		23. 6.93	C.G.Shaw	Truleigh Manor Farm, Edburton	7.11.03P
	(Lycoming O-320-B2B)						
G-EWBC	Jabiru Jabiru SK	PFA 274-13457		3.11.00	E.W.B.Comber	Fenland	22. 7.03P
G-EWFN	SOCATA TB-20 Trinidad	1009	G-BRTY	22. 1.90	Trinidair Ltd	Filton	21. 4.05T
G-EWIZ	Pitts S-2SE Special S	18	VH-EHQ	12.11.82	S.J.Carver	Netherthorpe	27. 2.03P
	(Lycoming AEIO-540)						
G-EXEA	Extra EA.300/L	082		9. 3.99	J.A.Carr	Guernsey	29.10.05T
	(Lycoming AEIO-540-L1B5)						
G-EXEC	Piper PA-34-200 Seneca	34-7450072	(G-EXXC)	11. 5.78	Sky Air Travel Ltd	Stapleford	13. 3.03T
			OY-BGU				
G-EXEX	Cessna 404 Titan II	404-0037	SE-GZF	3. 5.79	Atlantic Air Transport Ltd	Inverness	29. 7.03A
			(N5418G)		(Op DEFRA)		
G-EXIT	SOCATA MS.893E Rallye 180GT	12979	F-GARX	22. 9.78	M.A.Baldwin	Maypole Farm, Chislet	31. 5.04
G-EXPD	Stemme S.10-VT	11-063		5. 7.01	Global Gliding Expeditions Ltd	(Builth Wells)	30. 8.04
G-EXPL	American Champion 7GCBC Citabria	1220-96		9. 5.96	E.J.F.McEntee	Goodwood	24.11.02
G-EXPR	Colt 90A HAB	1064		17. 8.87	D.P.Hopkins	Pidley, Huntingdon	22. 4.01A
					t/a Lakeside Lodge Golf Centre		
G-EXPS	Short SD.3-60-100	SH.3661	TC-AOA	11. 5.99	ATA-Aerocondor Transportes Aereos SA		
			G-BLRT/SE-KRV/G-BLRT/G-14-3661			Cascais-Tires, Portugal	27 .5.05T
G-EXTR	Extra EA.260	004	D-EDID	10. 8.92	S.J.Carver	Netherthorpe	30 3.03P
	(Lycoming AEIO-540)						
G-EYAK	Yakovelev Yak-50	801894	RA01193	19. 2.03	P N A Whitehead	Leicster	AC
			DOSAAF?				
G-EYAS	Denney Kitfox Model 2	PFA 172-11858		3. 3.93	K.Hamnett	Long Marston	14. 3.03P
G-EYCO	Robin DR400/180 Regent	1949		12. 3.90	Charlie Oscar Ltd	Perth	25. 4.05
G-EYES	Cessna 402C II	402C0008	SE-IRU	16. 7.90	Atlantic Air Promotions Ltd	Inverness	15. 8.05T
			G-BLCE/N4648N		(Op Environment Agency)		
G-EYET	Robinson R44 Astro	0052	G-JPAD	30.11.98	Warwickshire Flight Training Centre Ltd	Coventry	18. 5.03T
G-EYLE	Bell 206L-1 LongRanger II	45232	G-OCRP	20.11.01	Eyles Construction Ltd	Manston	10. 8.03T
			V4-AAB/G-OCRP/G-BWCU/N2758A/C-FPET/N2758A/JA9234/N27545/JA9234				
G-EYNL	MBB Bö.105D	BS-5S.382	LN-OTJ	19. 8.96	Sterling Helicopters Ltd	Norwich	1112.05T
			D-HDLR/EC-DSO/D-HDLR				
G-EYOR	Van's RV-6	PFA 181A-13259		15.10.99	S.I.Fraser	Henstridge	14. 1.03P
G-EYRE	Bell 206L-1 LongRanger II	45229	G-STVI	12.11.90	Hideroute Ltd	Manston	13. 7.03T
			N60MA/N5091K				
G-EZAR	Pegasus Quik	7942		3.03R			
G-EZEL	Westland SA.341G Gazelle 1	1073	(F-GIVQ)	1.12.00	W R Pitcher/Regal Group UK	Leatherhead	14. 3.04T
			I-ATOM/F-BXPG/G-BAZL				
G-EZER	Cameron H-34 HAB	2366	LX-ROM	31.10.02	D.D.Maltby	Bristol	14.11.03A
G-EZJA	Boeing 737-73V	30235		13.10.00	EasyJet Airline Co Ltd	Luton	12.10.03T
G-EZJB	Boeing 737-73V	30236	N1787B	22.11.00	EasyJet Airline Co Ltd	Luton	21.11.03T
G-EZJC	Boeing 737-73V	30237		15.12.00	EasyJet Airline Co Ltd	Luton	13.12.03T
G-EZJD	Boeing 737-73V	30242		13. 7.01	EasyJet Airline Co Ltd	Luton	12. 7.04T

G-EZJE	Boeing 737-73V	30238		10. 8.01	EasyJet Airline Co Ltd	Luton	9. 8.04T
G-EZJF	Boeing 737-73V	30243		15. 8.01	EasyJet Airline Co Ltd	Luton	14. 8.04T
G-EZJG	Boeing 737-73V	30239		28. 9.01	EasyJet Airline Co Ltd	Luton	27. 9.04T
G-EZJH	Boeing 737-73V	30240		15.10.01	EasyJet Airline Co Ltd	Luton	14.10.04T
G-EZJI	Boeing 737-73V	30241		20.12.01	EasyJet Airline Co Ltd	Luton	AC
G-EZJJ	Boeing 737-73V	30245		30. 1.02	EasyJet Airline Co Ltd	Luton	29. 1.05T
G-EZJK	Boeing 737-73V	30246		7. 2.02	EasyJet Airline Co Ltd	Luton	6. 2.05T
G-EZJL	Boeing 737-73V	30247		12. 2.02	EasyJet Airline Co Ltd	Luton	11. 2.05T
G-EZJM	Boeing 737-73V	30248		24. 4.02	EasyJet Airline Co Ltd	Luton	23. 4.05T
G-EZJN	Boeing 737-73V	30249		8. 5.02	EasyJet Airline Co Ltd	Luton	7. 5.05T
G-EZJO	Boeing 737-73V	30244		6. 6.02	EasyJet Airline Co Ltd	Luton	5. 6.05T
G-EZJP	Boeing 737-73V	32412		11. 6.02	EasyJet Airline Co Ltd	Luton	10. 6.05T
G-EZJR	Boeing 737-73V	32413		20. 8.02	EasyJet Airline Co Ltd	Luton	19. 8.05T
G-EZJS	Boeing 737-73V	32414		23. 9.02	EasyJet Airline Co Ltd	Luton	20. 9.05T
G-EZJT	Boeing 737-73V	32415		19.12.02	EasyJet Airline Co Ltd	Luton	AC
G-EZJU	Boeing 737-73V	32416		21.12.02	EasyJet Airline Co Ltd	Luton	AC
G-EZJV	Boeing 737-73V	32417		3. 3.03	EasyJet Airline Co Ltd	Luton	
G-EZJW	Boeing 737-73V	32418		3.03R	EasyJet Airline Co Ltd *(For delivery 3.03)*	Luton	
G-EZJX	Boeing 737-73V	32419		5.03R	EasyJet Airline Co Ltd *(For delivery 5.03)*	Luton	
G-EZJY	Boeing 737-73V	32420		6.03R	EasyJet Airline Co Ltd *(For delivery 6.03)*	Luton	
G-EZJZ	Boeing 737-73V	32421		7.03R	EasyJet Airline Co Ltd *(For delivery 7.03)*	Luton	
G-EZOS	Rutan VariEze *(Continental O-200-A)*	002 & PFA 74-10221		10. 7.78	C.Moffat	Blackbushe	18.10.03P
G-EZYB	Boeing 737-3M8	24020	N797BB I-TEAA/OO-LTA/(OO-BTA)	17.10.96	EasyJet Airline Co Ltd	Luton	20.10.05T
G-EZYC	Boeing 737-3Y0	24462	G-BWJA	28. 5.97	EasyJet Airline Co Ltd	Luton	4. 4.05T
			EC-FJR/EC-897/G-TEAA/EI-BZQ/(N116WA)/EI-BZQ/EC-ENS/EC-244/N5573K				
G-EZYD	Boeing 737-3M8	24022	N798BB I-TEAE/OO-LTC/(OO-BTC)	5. 2.97	EasyJet Airline Co Ltd	Luton	10. 2.03T
G-EZYF	Boeing 737-375	23708	D-AGEX	3.11.97	EasyJet Airline Co Ltd	Luton	9.11.03T
			(G-EZYC)/4L-AAA/PT-TEC/(C-GZPW)				
G-EZYG	Boeing 737-33V	29331	N1768B	19. 8.98	EasyJet Airline Co Ltd	Luton	18. 8.04T
G-EZYH	Boeing 737-33V	29332		17. 9.98	EasyJet Airline Co Ltd	Luton	17. 9.04T
G-EZYI	Boeing 737-33V	29333	N1787B	24.11.98	EasyJet Airline Co Ltd	Luton	22.11.04T
G-EZYJ	Boeing 737-33V	29334		18.12.98	EasyJet Airline Co Ltd	Luton	17.12.04T
G-EZYK	Boeing 737-33V	29335		31. 1.99	EasyJet Airline Co.Ltd	Luton	30. 1.05T
G-EZYL	Boeing 737-33V	29336	N1787B	12. 3.99	EasyJet Airline Co Ltd	Luton	11. 3.05T
G-EZYP	Boeing 737-33V	29340		17. 9.99	EasyJet Airline Co Ltd	Luton	16 .9.05T
G-EZYR	Boeing 737-33V	29341	N1787B	20.10.99	EasyJet Airline Co.Ltd	Luton	18.10.05T
G-EZYT	Boeing 737-3Q8	26307	HB-IIE N721LF/(HB-IIE)	28. 6.00	EasyJet Airline Co Ltd	Luton	27. 6.03T
G-EZYU	Piper PA-34-200-2 Seneca	34-7450110	G-BCDB N41346	4. 7.01	P.A.S.Dyke	Elstree	30. 7.05T
G-EZZA	Europa Aviation Europa XS *(Rotax 914) (Monowheel u/c)*	537 & PFA 247-13841		10. 5.02	J.C.R.Davey	(Bicester)	

G-FAAA - G-FZZZ

G-FABB	Cameron V-77 HAB	822	LX-FAB	13.12.89	P.Trumper	Ashford, Kent	8. 5.03T
G-FABI	Robinson R44 Astro	0325		5. 4.97	J.Froggatt Ltd	(Dukinfield)	27. 4.03T
G-FABM	Beech 95B55A Baron	TC-2259	G-JOND G-BMVC/N66456	22. 2.91	F.B.Miles	Gloucestershire	17. 8.04
G-FACE	Cessna 172S Skyhawk	172S9194	N52733	24.10.02	Stanair Ltd t/a Ace Aviation	Shoreham	28.10.05T
G-FALC	Aeromere F.8L Falco	3224	G-AROT	19. 2.81	P.J.Jones	Oxford	28. 6.04
G-FALO	Sequoia F.8L Falco	1401		10. 5.02	M.J.& S.E.Aherne	Top Farm, Croydon, Royston	AC
G-FAME	CFM Starstreak Shadow SA-II *(Jabiru 2200)*	K.273SA & PFA 206A-12973		23. 5.96	T.J.Palmer *(Operates from Prestwick & Oban)*	(Symington)	23.11.03P
G-FAMH	Zenair CH.701 Stol *(Jabiru 2200A)*	PFA 187-13301		26. 6.98	G.T.Neale	Sandown	25.11.02P
G-FANC	Temco Fairchild 24R-46	R46-347	N77647 NC77647	16.10.89	A.T.Fines *(Destroyed in arson attack 18.2.03)*	Felthorpe	26. 5.03T
G-FANL	Cessna R172K Hawk XPII	R1722873	N736XQ	7. 6.79	J.A.Rees	Haverfordwest	2. 7.03T
G-FANN*	Hawker Siddeley HS.125 Srs.600B	256019	HZ-AA1	13. 2.89	British Airways Aircraft Recovery Unit	Dunsfold	
			G-BARR	*(No CofA issued: cancelled 29.3.93 as WFU: on fire dump 3.00 as "HZ-AA1")*			
G-FARM	SOCATA Rallye 235E	12832	F-GARF	10.10.78	Bristol Cars Ltd	White Waltham	27. 6.04
G-FARO	Star-Lite SL-1 (Rotax 447)	PFA 175-11359		19. 6.89	M.K.Faro	Henstridge	6.10.03P
G-FARR	SAN Jodel 150 Mascaret	58	F-BNIN	21. 7.81	G.H.Farr	Dairy House Farm, Worleston	19. 5.03P
G-FARY	QAC Quickie Tri-Q	PFA 94A-10951		2. 4.02	F.Sayyah	Enstone	17.10.03P
G-FATB	Commander Aircraft Commander 114B	14624	N6037Y	3. 7.96	James D.Peace & Co	(Kirkwall)	19. 8.05
G-FAYE	Reims/Cessna F150M	F15001252	PH-VSK	24. 1.80	Cheshire Air Training Services Ltd	Liverpool	5. 7.04T
G-FBAT	Aeroprakt A22 Foxbat *(Rotax 912-S)*	PFA 317-13591		16. 5.00	The Small Aeroplane Co Ltd	Otherton, Cannock	11. 2.03P
G-FBIX	de Havilland DH.100 Vampire FB.9	22100	7705M WL505	24. 7.91	D.G.Jones *(As "WL505") (On rebuild 1.01)*	(St Mary Hill, Bridgend)	
G-FBMW	Cameron N-90 HAB	3019		23. 4.93	K-J.Schwer	Erbach-Donaurieden, Germany	10. 9.03A
G-FBPI	ANEC IV Missel Thrush	PFA 312-13417		19. 1.99	R.Trickett *(Noted incomplete 3.02)*	(Wolverhampton)	
G-FBRN	Piper PA-28-181 Archer II	28-8290166	D-ERBN N82628	3. 8.98	Herefordshire Aero Club Ltd	Shobdon	26. 9.04T
G-FBWH	Piper PA-28R-180 Cherokee Arrow	28R-30368	SE-FCV	23. 8.78	F.T.Short	Whaley Farm, New York, Lincs	2. 4.04
G-FCDB	Cessna 550 Citation Bravo	550-0985	N5269J	10. 9.01	Eurojet Aviation Ltd	Belfast	9. 9.03T
G-FCLA	Boeing 757-28A	27621	N1789B	26. 2.97	JMC Airlines Ltd	Manchester	25. 2.03T
G-FCLB	Boeing 757-28A	28164	N751NA G-FCLB	25. 3.97	JMC Airlines Ltd	Manchester	29. 4.04T

Reg	Type	c/n	Prev id	Date	Owner/Operator	Location	Date
G-FCLC	Boeing 757-28A	28166		9. 5.97	JMC Airlines Ltd	Manchester	8. 5.03T
G-FCLD	Boeing 757-25F	28718		25. 4.97	JMC Airlines Ltd	Manchester	24. 4.03T
G-FCLE	Boeing 757-28A	28171		24. 5.98	JMC Airlines Ltd	Manchester	23. 5.04T
G-FCLF	Boeing 757-28A	28835		24. 3.99	JMC Airlines Ltd	Manchester	22. 3.05T
G-FCLG	Boeing 757-28A	24367	N701LF	18.12.98	JMC Airlines Ltd	Manchester	2..4.05T
			EI-CLM/N381LF/N240LA/C-GTSK/C-GNXI/G-GAWB				
G-FCLH	Boeing 757-28A	26274	N751LF	17. 2.99	JMC Airlines Ltd	Manchester	12. 5.05T
			EI-CLU/N161LF				
G-FCLI	Boeing 757-28A	26275	N651LF	17. 3.99	JMC Airlines Ltd	Manchester	1. 6.05T
			EI-CLV/N151LF				
G-FCLJ	Boeing 757-2Y0	26160	N160GE	26. 4.99	JMC Airlines Ltd	Manchester	25 .4.05T
			EI-CJX/N3519M/N1786B/(B-2830) *(Apple Vacations titles - Apple t/s)*				
G-FCLK	Boeing 757-2Y0	26161	N161GE	6. 4.99	JMC Airlines Ltd	Manchester	5. 4.05T
			EI-CJY/N3521N				
G-FCSP	Robin DR400/180 Regent	2022		24.10.90	F.C.Smith t/a FCS Photochemicals	Biggin Hill	22. 2.03
G-FCUK	Pitts S-1C Special	02	OH-XPB	9. 8.02	M.O'Hearne	Rufforth	
G-FEBE	Cessna 340A II	340A-0345	N405LS	12. 7.88	Eight Eight Aviation Services Ltd	(Jersey)	20. 6.04
			(N37320)				
G-FEBY	Robinson R22 Beta	3179		23. 4.01	Astra Helicopters Ltd	Bristol	25. 4.04T
G-FEDA	Eurocopter EC120B Colibri	1129	F-WQOD	2. 8.00	Federal Aviation Ltd	(Bury St.Edmunds)	22 .8.03T
G-FEFE	Scheibe SF-25B Falke	46126	EI-BVZ	11. 4.94	D.G.Roberts	Aston Down	1.11.02
			D-KADB		tr G-FEFE Syndicate		
G-FELL	Europa Aviation Europa	372 & PFA 247-13208		17. 3.98	R.Barton	(Spilsby)	28. 8.03P
	(Rotax 912UL) (Tri-gear u/c)						
G-FELT	Cameron N-77 HAB	1174		19. 7.85	Allan Industries Ltd *"Fuzzy Felt"*	Chinnor	30.12.02A
G-FERN	Mainair Blade 912	1342-1002-7-W1137		18.10.02	M.H.Moulai	North Coates	27.10.03P
G-FEZZ	Agusta Bell 206B JetRanger II	8317	SU-YAD	16. 9.98	L.Smith	Booker	4.10.04T
			YU-HAT		t/a Helicopter Services		
G-FFAB	Cameron N-105 HAB	4067		20. 2.97	L.Greaves *(Forever Friends titles)*	Shepton Mallet	17. 5.03A
G-FFEN	Reims/Cessna F150M	F15001204	PH-VGL	25. 8.78	R.J.Everett	Hill Farm, Nayland	19. 3.03T
G-FFFT	Lindstrand LBL 31A HAB	705		30. 5.00	The Aerial Display Co Ltd *(FT titles)*	Looe	10. 1.03A
G-FFOX	Hawker Hunter T.7B	41H-670788	WV318	10. 1.96	Delta Engineering Aviation Ltd	Kemble	14. 5.03P
	(Composite including components of WV322- see G-BZSE)				*(As "WV318/D" in all-black c/s)*		
G-FFRA	Dassault Falcon 20DC	132	N902FR	28. 5.92	Cobham Leasing Ltd	Bournemouth	20.10.05A
			(N23FR)/(N149FE)/N2FE/N560L/N4348F/F-WMKG				
G-FFRI	Aérospatiale AS355F1 Twin Squirrel	5120	G-GLOW	15. 4.93	ATC Trading Ltd	Lasham	5. 5.03T
			G-PAPA/G-CNET/G-MCAH				
G-FFTI	SOCATA TB-20 Trinidad	1065		23. 2.90	R Lenk	(Thetford)	19. 8.05T
G-FFTT	Lindstrand LBL Newspaper SS HAB	673		10. 7.00	The Aerial Display Co Ltd *(FT titles)*	Looe	17. 8.02A
G-FFUN	Pegasus Quantum 15	6655	G-MYMD	9. 6.99	J.B.Hobbs	Long Acre Farm, Sandy	12.12.03P
G-FFWD	Cessna 310R II	310R0579	G-TVKE	20. 2.90	R.J.Herbert (Engineering) Ltd	Marshland	19. 3.04
			G-EURO/N87468				
G-FGID	Vought FG-1D Corsair	3111	N8297	1.11.91	Patina Ltd	Duxford	12. 5.03P
	(Built Goodyear Aircraft Corporation)		N9154Z/Bu.88297		*(Op The Fighter Collection) (As "KD345/A-130" in 1850 Sqdn RN c/s)*		
G-FHAJ	Airbus Industrie A320-231	0444	D-ACAF	14.11.01	MyTravel Airways Ltd	Manchester	15.11.04T
			N444RX/TC-ONF/N444RX/F-WWBY				
G-FHAS	Scheibe SF-25E Super Falke	4359	(D-KOOG)	14. 5.81	Burn Gliding Club Ltd	Burn	30.12.05
G-FIAT	Piper PA-28-140 Cherokee F	28-7425162	G-BBYW	19. 7.89	Halegreen Associates Ltd	Hinton in the Hedges	31. 7.05T
			N9622N				
G-FIBS	Aérospatiale AS350BA Ecureuil	2074	JA9732	14. 6.94	Pristheath Ltd	Denham	8. 8.03T
G-FIFE	Reims/Cessna FA152 Aerobat	FA15200351	G-BFYN	15. 2.95	Tayside Aviation Ltd	Glenrothes	3. 2.03T
G-FIFI	SOCATA TB-20 Trinidad	688		16. 1.87	F.A.Saker	Denham	15. 7.02
G-FIGA	Cessna 152 II	15284644	N6243M	3. 6.87	Aerohire Ltd *(Op Midland Flight Centre)* Wolverhampton		23. 3.03T
G-FIGB	Cessna 152 II	15285925	N95561	16.11.87	Aerohire Ltd	Wellesbourne Mountford	12. 2.00T
G-FIJJ	Reims/Cessna F177RG Cardinal	F177RG0031	G-AZFP	29. 4.99	Middleton Miniature Mouldings Ltd	Teesside	15. 6.03
	(Wichita c/n 17700194)						
G-FIJR	Lockheed L.188PF Electra	1138	(EI-HCF)	12. 9.91	Atlantic Air Transport Ltd	Southend	12. 9.04T
			G-FIJR/C-FIJR/CF-IJR/N134US *(Atlantic Airlines titles)*				
G-FIJV	Lockheed L.188C Electra	1129	EI-HCE	29. 8.91	Atlantic Air Transport Ltd	Coventry	27. 9.04T
			G-FIJV/C-FIJV/CF-IJV/N7143C *(Atlantic Airlines titles)*				
G-FILE	Piper PA-34-200T Seneca II	34-8070108	N8140Z	23. 7.87	Barnes Olson Aeroleasing Ltd	Bristol	23.11.05T
G-FILL	Piper PA-31 Navajo C	31-7912069	OO-EJM	28. 6.96	P.V.Naylor-Leyland	Deenethorpe	23. 8.03
			N3521C				
G-FINA	Reims/Cessna F150L	F15000826	G-BIFT	12.10.93	D.Norris	Finmere	8.12.05T
			PH-CEW				
G-FIND	Reims/Cessna F406 Caravan II	F406-0045	OY-PEU	16. 8.90	Atlantic Air Transport Ltd	Coventry	4. 5.03T
			5Y-LAN/G-FIND/PH-ALV/F-WZDT				
G-FINZ	III Sky Arrow 650T	PFA 298-13824		8. 1.03	A.G.Counsell	(Banchory)	
G-FIRM	Cessna 550 Citation Bravo	550-0940	N5263S	29. 9.00	Marshall of Cambridge Aerospace Ltd	Cambridge	2.10.04T
G-FIRS	Robinson R22 Beta-II	2807		15. 4.98	M. & S.Chantler	(Crewe)	13. 5.04
G-FIRZ	Murphy Renegade Spirit UK	PFA 188-13494		10.12.99	P.J.Houtman	(St.Albans)	14.11.02P
	(Rotax 912-UL)						
G-FISH	Cessna 310R II	310R1845	N2740Y	8. 5.81	Air Charter Scotland Ltd	Edinburgh	28.10.05T
G-FISK*	Pazmany PL-4A	PFA 17-10129		14.12.88	K.S.Woodard	Little Snoring	11. 4.96P
	(Volkswagen 1834)				*(Stored 6.00: cancelled 8.11.00 by CAA)*		
G-FITZ	Cessna 335	335-0044	G-RIND	20. 4.95	D.S.Hodgetts	Wolverhampton	14. 3.05
			N2710L				
G-FIZU	Lockheed L.188CF Electra	2014	EI-CHY	6. 4.93	Atlantic Air Transport	Coventry	3. 1.05T
			G-FIZU/SE-IZU/(N857ST)/N857U/PH-LLG				
G-FIZY	Europa Aviation Europa XS	384 & PFA 247-13291	G-DDSC	16.12.99	G.Holland	(Bath)	
	(Jabiru 3300) (Tri-gear u/c)				*(Current status unknown)*		
G-FIZZ	Piper PA-28-161 Cherokee Warrior II	28-7816301	N2721M	1.12.78	Tecair Aviation Ltd	Shipdham	19.10.03T
G-FJET	Cessna 550 Citation II	550-0419	G-DCFR	7. 7.97	London Executive Aviation Ltd	London City	17. 1.03T
			G-WYLX/VH-JVS/G-JETD/N1217N				

Reg	Type	C/n	Prev ID	Date	Owner	Location	Date
G-FJMS	Partenavia P68B Victor *(C/n indicates P68 model)*	113	G-SVHA / OY-AJH	7.9.92	F.J.M.Sanders *(Stored 12.02)*	Bournemouth	13.6.05T
G-FKNH	Piper PA-15 Vagabond *(Continental C85)*	15-291	CF-KNH / N4517H/NC4517H	19.3.97	M.J.Mothershaw	RAF Woodvale	15.5.03
G-FLAG	Colt 77A HAB	2000		20.9.90	B.A.Williams	Maidstone	10.6.97T
G-FLAK	Beech E55 Baron	TE-1128	N4771M	26.9.89	D.Clark *"Red Baron"*	Great Massingham	29.7.05T
G-FLAP	Cessna A152 Aerobat	A1520856	G-BHJB / N4662A	14.6.02	Walkbury Aviation Ltd	Sibson	2.9.05T
G-FLAV	Piper PA-28-161 Warrior II	28-8016283	N8171X	7.4.94	S.W.Parker tr The Crew Flying Group	Leicester	23.5.03
G-FLCA	Fleet 80 Canuck	068	CS-ACQ / CF-DQP	18.7.90	E.C.Taylor *(On rebuild 3.01)*	(Balsall Common)	
G-FLCT	Hallam Fleche	PFA 309-13389		21.10.98	R G Hallam	(Macclesfield)	
G-FLEA	SOCATA TB-10 Tobago	235	PH-TTP / G-FLEA	31.7.81	J.J.Berry	Shoreham	26.7.05
G-FLEW	Lindstrand LBL-90A HAB	586		21.1.99	Lindstrand Balloons Ltd	Oswestry	30.6.03A
G-FLGT	Lindstrand LBL 105A HAB	888		5.12.02	Lindstrand Balloons Ltd	Oswestry	16.12.03A
G-FLII	Grumman-American GA-7 Cougar	GA7-0003	G-GRAC / C-GRAC/(N1367R)/N730GA	18.12.91	Plane Talking Ltd *(Op Capital Radio "Flying Eye")*	Elstree	23.10.04T
G-FLIK	Pitts S-1S Special *(Lycoming O-320)*	PFA 09-10513		7.1.81	R.P.Millinship	Leicester	22.5.03P
G-FLIP	Reims/Cessna FA152 Aerobat	FA15200375	G-BOES / G-FLIP	29.12.80	Walkbury Aviation Ltd	Sibson	9.5.03T
G-FLIT	Rotorway Executive 162F *(Rotorway RI 162F)*	6324		22.12.98	R.F.Rhodes	Street Farm, Takeley	7.11.02P
G-FLIZ	Staaken Z-21 Flitzer	006 & PFA 223-13115		24.3.97	M.A.Wood *(As "D-694")* Shempston Farm, Lossiemouth		
G-FLJA	Piper PA-32-260 Cherokee Six *(Rebuilt using spare Frame No.32-860S)*	32-219	G-AVTJ / N3373W	6.12.00	F L Avery	Dunkeswell	29.1.05T
G-FLKE	Scheibe SF-25C Falke	44673		5.10.01	Faulkes Flying Foundation Ltd	Lasham	18.10.04
G-FLKS	Scheibe SF-25C Falke	44662	D-KIEQ	16.10.00	Faulkes Flying Foundation Ltd	Dunstable Downs	19.10.03
G-FLOA	Cameron O-120 HAB	4006		4.10.96	Floating Sensations Ltd	Thatcham	2.10.03T
G-FLOR	Europa Aviation Europa *(Rotax 912-UL) (Monowheel u/c)*	171 & PFA 247-12793		11.11.98	A.F.C.Van Eldik *(F/f 13.8.99)*	Pent Farm, Kent	1.10.03P
G-FLOX	Europa Aviation Europa *(Jabiru 2200A) (Monowheel u/c)*	129 & PFA 247-12732		28.6.95	T.W.Eaton tr DPT Group *(F/f 19.6.98)*	Fowle Hall Farm, Laddingford	5.7.03P
G-FLPI	Rockwell Commander 112A	205	SE-FLP / (N1205J)	16.3.79	H.J.Freeman	Newcastle	22.3.03T
G-FLSI	FLS Sprint 160	001		20.8.93	Aces High Ltd *(Amended CofR 3.02)*	North Weald	AC
G-FLTA	British Aerospace BAe 146 Srs.200	E2048	N189US / N365PS	25.2.98	Flightline Ltd	Aberdeen	26.2.04T
G-FLTB	British Aerospace BAe 146 Srs.200	E2024	G-CLHA / G-DEBC/N166US/N348PS)	14.5.02	Flightline Ltd	Southend	22.5.05T
G-FLTG	Cameron A-140 HAB	4506		3.11.00	Floating Sensations Ltd	Thatcham	12.9.03T
G-FLTY	Embraer EMB-110P1 Bandeirante	110.215	G-ZUSS / G-REGA/N711NH/PT-GMH	28.8.92	Keenair Charter Ltd	Blackpool	12.7.03T
G-FLTZ	Beech 58 Baron	TH-1154	G-PSVS / N5824T/YV-266P	21.9.93	Flightline Ltd	Southend	16.8.04
G-FLUF	Lindstrand Bunny SS HAB	002		7.4.93	Lindstrand Balloons Ltd *(Not built: current CofR 4.02)*	(Oswestry)	
G-FLUX	Piper PA-28-181 Archer III	2843484	N5339U	13.3.02	TEC Air Hire Ltd	(Petersfield)	21.3.05T
G-FLVU	Cessna 501 Citation I	501-0178	N83ND / N4246A/LV-PML/N67749	11.6.98	Neonopal Ltd	Liverpool	23.6.04T
G-FLYA	Mooney M.20J (201SE)	24-3124		8.6.89	BRF Aviation Ltd	Full Sutton	18.2.05
G-FLYE	Cameron A-210 HAB	4216		12.12.97	A.M.Holly t/a Exclusive Ballooning	Berkeley	9.9.03T
G-FLYG	Slingsby T-67C	2074	PH-SGA / (PH-SBA)	23.8.02	G.Laden *(Exported 1.03)*	(North Ferriby)	
G-FLYH	Robinson R22 Beta	1932	CS-HEQ / G-BXMR/N923FM/N2306E	4.10.02	C.D. Cochrane t/a Cyclone Helicopters	Manston	3.10.05T
G-FLYI	Piper PA-34-200 Seneca	34-7250144	G-BHVO / SE-FYY	1.9.81	S Papi & R Ruiz tr G-FLYI Group *(Op Willowair Flying Club)*	Southend	29.6.03T
G-FLYP	Beagle B.206 Srs 2	B.058	N40CJ / N97JH/G-AVHO/VQ-LAY/G-AVHO	15.10.98	Key Publishing Ltd	Cranfield	29.4.02T
G-FLYS	Robinson R44 Astro	0347		5.6.97	Newmarket Plant Hire Ltd	Cambridge	21.6.03T
G-FLYT	Europa Aviation Europa *(NSI EA-81/100) (Conventional u/c)*	057 & PFA 247-12653		15.5.95	K.F.& R.Richardson *(F/f 7.8.96)*	Wellesbourne Mountford	6.5.00P
G-FLYY	British Aircraft Corporation BAC.167 Strikemaster Mk.80A	EEP/JP/163	R.Saudi AF 1112/G-27-31	3.9.01	D.T.Barber	City of Derry	AC
G-FLZR	Staaken Z-21 Flitzer	PFA 223-13219		21.9.01	J.F.Govan	East Linton	
G-FMAM	Piper PA-28-151 Cherokee Warrior	28-7415056	G-BBXV / N9603N	7.6.90	P B Anderson tr Lima Tango Flying Group	Southend	25.11.02T
G-FMGG	Maule M-5-235C Lunar Rocket	7260C	G-RAGG / N5632M	30.4.02	S.Bierbaum	Bodmin	18.4.05
G-FMKA	Diamond HK36 TC Super Dimona	36672		26.4.00	A.Bailey	Enstone	11.6.03
G-FMSG	Reims/Cessna FA150K Aerobat	FA15000081	G-POTS / G-AYUY	4.1.95	G.Owen	Humberside	9.11.03T
G-FNLD	Cessna 172N Skyhawk II	17270596	(G-BOUG) / N739KD	3.8.88	D.Wright & R.C.Laming tr Papa Hotel Flying Group	Fenland	26.2.04
G-FNLY	Reims/Cessna F172M	F17200910	G-WACX / G-BAEX	20.3.89	C.F.Dukes	Exeter	9.8.03T
G-FNPT	Piper PA-28-161 Warrior III	2842163	N5346Y	2.10.02	Chalrey Ltd	(Pinner)	17.10.05T
G-FOGG	Cameron N-90 HAB	1365		21.11.86	J.P.E.Money-Kyrle *"Phileas Fogg"*	Chippenham	25.9.96A
G-FOGY	Robinson R22 Beta	1020	N62991 / F-GGAI	5.7.99	M.N. Cowley t/a Dragonfly Aviation	(Daventry)	25.7.05T
G-FOLD	Avid Speed Wing *(Rotax 582)*	PFA 189-12041		30.10.92	B.W.& G.Evans	(Stoke-on-Trent)	2.6.01P

Reg	Type	C/n	Prev id	Date	Owner/Operator	Location	Date
G-FOLI	Robinson R22 Beta-II	2813		25. 4.98	K.Duckworth	Wolverhampton	7. 6.04
G-FOLY	Aerotek Pitts S-2A Special (Lycoming AEIO-360)	2213	N31477	26. 7.89	S.A.Laing	Perth	24. 2.02
G-FOPP	Neico Lancair 320 (Lycoming IO-320)	PFA 191-12319		14. 8.92	Airsport (UK) Ltd	Cranfield	19. 6.03P
G-FORC	SNCAN Stampe SV-4C	665	(G-BLTJ) F-BDNJ	6. 6.85	I.A.Marsh	Little Gransden	24. 5.03
G-FORD	SNCAN Stampe SV-4C (DH Gipsy Major 10)	129	F-BBNS	7. 2.78	P.H.Meeson *(Damaged East Tytherley 16.7.96: stored 4.02)*	Chilbolton	31. 7.98
G-FORR	Piper PA-28-181 Archer III	2843336	N4160Z G-FORR/N4160Z	20. 4.00	B.& A.E.Galt t/a Buchanan Partnership	Glenrothes	19. 4.03T
G-FORS	Slingsby T.67C-3 Firefly	2082	PH-SGD (PH-SBD)	17.11.99	V.R.Coultan, M.J.Golding, E.P.Dablin & M.Glazer t/a Open Skies Partnership	Turweston	18.12.05T
G-FORZ	Pitts S-1S	PFA 09-13393		3.11.98	N.W.Parkinson *(New owner 4.02)*	(High Wycombe)	
G-FOSY	SOCATA MS.880B Rallye Club	1304	G-AXAK	7.12.00	A.G.Foster	North Coates	17. 5.04
G-FOTO	Piper PA-E23-250 Aztec F	27-7654089	G-BJDH G-BDXV/N62614	27. 2.79	Aerofilms Ltd	Cranfield	10. 3.03A
G-FOWL	Colt 90A HAB	1198		11. 3.88	N.A.Fishlock *"Chicken"* tr G-FOWL Ballooning Group	Cheltenham	10. 8.02A
G-FOWS	Cameron N-105 HAB	3995		11.12.96	Fowlers of Bristol Ltd *(Fowlers Motorcycles titles)*	Bristol	5.12.02A
G-FOXA	Piper PA-28-161 Cadet	2841240	N9192B	17.11.89	Leicestershire Aero Club Ltd	Leicester	13. 5.02T
G-FOXB	Aeroprakt A22 Foxbat	PFA 317-13878		15. 3.02	M.Raflewski	(Omagh, Co Tyrone)	7. 8.03P
G-FOXC	Denney Kitfox Model 3 (Rotax 582)	773 & PFA 172-11900		8. 1.91	G.Hawkins *"Foxe Lady"*	(Wareham)	10. 9.01P
G-FOXD	Denney Kitfox (Rotax 582)	PFA 172-11618		22.11.89	M.Hanley	Deenethorpe	21. 8.02P
G-FOXF	Denney Kitfox Model 4	PFA 172-12399		24. 3.00	M.S.Goodwin	Bridge of Weir	5. 9.02P
G-FOXG	Denney Kitfox Model 2 (Rotax 532)	452 & PFA 172-11886		15. 8.90	A.C.Newman tr Kitfox Group	Romney Street Farm, Sevenoaks	12.11.03P
G-FOXI	Denney Kitfox Model 2 (Rotax 532)	PFA 172-11508		21. 9.89	B.Johns	Combrook	21. 8.03P
G-FOXM	Bell 206B JetRanger II	1514	G-STAK G-BNIS/N35HF/N135VG	5. 2.93	R.P.Maydon t/a Milton Keynes City Air *(Op CSE Helicopters - Fox FM Radio)*	Oxford	26. 1.03T
G-FOXS	Denney Kitfox Model 2	465 & PFA 172-11571		15. 8.90	S.P.Watkins & C.C.Rea	Sheepcote	28 7.03P
G-FOXZ	Denney Kitfox	PFA 172-11834		4.12.90	S.C.Goozee	(Wimborne)	19.10.98
G-FPIG	Piper PA-28-151 Cherokee Warrior	28-7615001	G-BSSR N1190X	22. 3.00	Birchland Financial Management Ltd	Bournemouth	14. 3.03
G-FPLA	Beech B200 Super King Air	BB-944	N31WL HB-GHZ/HL5260/N1824V	3.12.97	FR Aviation Ltd *(Op Flight Precision)*	Teesside	9. 3.04T
G-FPLB	Beech B200 Super King Air	BB-1048	N739MG N223MD/9Y-TGY	3.12.97	FR Aviation Ltd *(Op Flight Precision)*	Teesside	11. 1.04T
G-FPLC	Cessna 441 Conquest II	441-0207	G-FRAX G-BMTZ/N27280	14. 1.98	FR Aviation Ltd *(Op Flight Precision)*	Teesside	29. 3.03T
G-FPLD	Beech 200 Super King Air	BB-1433	N43CE N43AJ/C-CMEV/C-CMEH/N8043K	2.11.01	Flight Precision Ltd	Teesside	19.11.04T
G-FPSA	Piper PA-28-161 Warrior II	28-8616038	G-RSFT G-WARI/N9276Y	28.2.03	Deep Cleavage Ltd	Exeter	26. 2.04T
G-FRAF	Dassault Falcon 20E	295/500	N911FR I-EDIM/F-WRQQ	1. 9.87	Cobham Leasing Ltd *(Op FR Aviation)*	Bournemouth	18.10.02A
G-FRAG	Piper PA-32-300 Six	32-7940284	N3566L	21. 1.80	T.A.Houghton	Rochester	21. 5.04
G-FRAH	Dassault Falcon 20DC	223	G-60-01 N900FR/(N904FR)/N22FE/N4407F/F-WPUX	31. 5.90	Cobham Leasing Ltd *(Op FR Aviation)*	Teesside	7.10.02A
G-FRAI	Dassault Falcon 20E	270	N901FR N37FE/N4435F/F-WPUZ	17.10.90	Cobham Leasing Ltd *(Op FR Aviation)*	Teesside	18. 4.03A
G-FRAJ	Dassault Falcon 20DC	20	N903FR (N25FR)/N5FE/(N146FE)/N5FE/N367GA/N367/N842F/F-WMKJ	30. 4.91	Cobham Leasing Ltd *(Op FR Aviation)*	Bournemouth	12.12.05A
G-FRAK	Dassault Falcon 20DC	213	N905FR N32FE/N4390F/F-WJMM	9.10.91	Cobham Leasing Ltd *(Op FR Aviation)*	Bournemouth	13. 4.03A
G-FRAL	Dassault Falcon 20DC	151	N904FR (N24FR)/N3FE/(N148FE)/N3FE/N810PA/N810F/N4360F/F-WMK *(Op FR Aviation)*	17. 3.93	Cobham Leasing Ltd *(Op FR Aviation)*	Teesside	22.12.02A
G-FRAM	Dassault Falcon 20DC	224	N907FR N23FE/N4408F/F-WPUY	13. 5.93	Cobham Leasing Ltd *(Op FR Aviation)*	Bournemouth	26. 5.05A
G-FRAN	Piper J-3C-65 Cub (L-4J-PI) (Continental C90) (Frame No.12447)	12617	G-BIXY F-BDTZ/44-80321	14. 7.86	I.Dole tr Essex L-4 Group *(As "480321/H-44" in USAAC c/s)*	Rayne Hall Farm, Rayne	19. 4.02P
G-FRAO	Dassault Falcon 20DC	214	N906FR N33FE/N4400F/F-WNGO	23.10.92	Cobham Leasing Ltd *(Op FR Aviation)*	Bournemouth	28. 1.03A
G-FRAP	Dassault Falcon 20DC	207	N908FR N27FE/N4395F/F-WMKF	12. 7.93	Cobham Leasing Ltd *(Op FR Aviation)*	Bournemouth	19.10.05A
G-FRAR	Dassault Falcon 20DC	209	N909FR N28FE/N4396F/F-WLCX	2.12.93	Cobham Leasing Ltd *(Op FR Aviation)*	Bournemouth	15. 2.03A
G-FRAS	Dassault Falcon 20C	82/418	CAF117501 20501/F-WJMM	31. 7.90	Cobham Leasing Ltd *(Op FR Aviation)*	Bournemouth	1.12.05A
G-FRAT	Dassault Falcon 20C	87/424	CAF117502 20502/F-WJMJ	31. 7.90	Cobham Leasing Ltd *(Op FR Aviation)*	Teesside	21. 2.03A
G-FRAU	Dassault Falcon 20C	97/422	CAF117504 20504/F-WJMJ	31. 7.90	Cobham Leasing Ltd *(Op FR Aviation)*	Teesside	15.12.05A
G-FRAW	Dassault Falcon 20C	114/420	CAF117507 20507/F-WJMM	31. 7.90	Cobham Leasing Ltd *(Op FR Aviation)*	Bournemouth	9. 4.05A
G-FRAY	Cassutt Racer IIIM	PFA 34-11211		24.10.90	C.I.Fray	(Macclesfield)	
G-FRBA	Dassault Falcon 20C	178/459	OH-FFA F-WPXF	16. 7.96	FR Finances Ltd *(Op FR Aviation)*	Bournemouth	16 .5.03A
G-FRCE*	Folland Gnat T.1	FL.598	8604M XS104	28.11.89	Not known *(Cancelled 25.2.00 by CAA) (In open storage 6.00)*	Cranfield	17. 4.95P
G-FRGN	Piper PA-28-236 Dakota	2811046	N9244N	8. 2.96	Fregon Aviation Ltd	Enstone	11. 3.05T

G-FROH	Eurocopter AS350B2 Ecureuil	9024		16. 5.00	Specialist Helicopters Ltd	Nairn	18. 5.03T
G-FRYI	Beech 200 Super King Air	BB-210	G-OAVX	15. 3.96	London Executive Aviation Ltd	Stapleford	26. 3.03T
			G-IBCA/G-BMCA/N5657N				
G-FSHA	Denney Kitfox Model 2	PFA 172-11906		20. 9.99	P.P.Trangmar	(Hailsham)	
G-FSFT	Piper PA-44-180T Turbo Seminole	44-8207020	N8236B	5.11.82	D.B.Ryder & Co Ltd	(Welwyn Garden City)	12.10..04T
			N9615N				
G-FTAX	Cessna 421C Golden Eagle II	421C0308	N8363G	23. 8.84	Gold Air International Ltd	Cambridge	16. 5.01T
			G-BFFM/N8363G				
G-FTIL	Robin DR400/180 Regent	1825		10. 3.88	RAF Wyton Flying Club Ltd	RAF Wyton	5.10.03T
G-FTIM	Robin DR400/100 Cadet	1829		6. 5.88	M S Bird	Kemble	10. 5.04
G-FTIN	Robin DR400/100 Cadet	1830		6. 5.88	G.D.Clark & M.J.D.Theobald	Blackpool	10.10.03
					tr YP Flying Group		
G-FTSE	Fairey Britten-Norman BN-2A Mk.III-2 Trislander		G-BEPI	23. 5.00	Aurigny Air Services Ltd	Guernsey	18.12.05T
		1053			*(Hambros Banking titles)*		
G-FTUO	Van's RV-4	926	C-FTUQ	23.12.97	J.E. Singleton *"Raven"*	Hinton in the Hedges	21 3.03P
	(Lycoming IO-360-B4A)				tr G-FTUO Flying Group		
G-FTWO	Aérospatiale AS355F2 Twin Squirrel	5347	G-OJOR	27. 1.87	McAlpine Helicopters Ltd	Oxford	18. 3.05T
			G-FTWO/G-BMUS				
G-FUEL	Robin DR400/180 Regent	1537		15. 5.81	R.Darch	East Chinnock, Yeovil	3. 8.03
G-FULL	Piper PA-28R-200 Cherokee Arrow II		G-HWAY	26.11.84	Stapleford Flying Club Ltd	Stapleford	17.12.05T
		28R-7435248	G-JULI/(G-BKDC)/OY-POV/CS-AQF/N43128				
G-FUNK	Yakovlev Yak-50	852908	RA852908	27. 3.98	D.J.Gilmour t/a Intrepid Aviation Co	North Weald	1.11.02P
G-FUNN	Plumb BGP-1 Biplane	PFA 83-12744		16.10.95	J.D.Anson	(Liskeard)	
G-FUZY	Cameron N-77 HAB	1751		6. 5.88	Allan Industries Ltd *"Fuzzy Felt II"*	Chinnor	5.11.96A
G-FUZZ	Piper PA-18 Super Cub 95	18-1016	(OO-HMY)	11. 9.80	G.W.Cline	Gipsy Wood, Yorkshire	17. 3.03P
	(L-18C-PI) (Frame No.18-1086)		ALAT-FMBIT/51-15319		*(As "51-15319/A-319" in yellow US Army c/s)*		
G-FVBF	Lindstrand LBL-210A HAB	311		6.12.95	Virgin Balloon Flights Ltd	London SE16	22. 10.03T
					"Red November"		
G-FWPW	Piper PA-28-236 Dakota	2811018	N9145L	10.10.88	P.A. & F.C.Winters	Oxford	22.10.03
G-FXBT	Aeroprakt A22 Foxbat	PFA 317-13787		7. 2.02	R.H.Jago	(Poole)	8. 9.03P
G-FXII*	Supermarine 366 Spitfire F.XIIE	6S/197707	N224	4.12.89	P.R.Arnold	(Newport Pagnell)	
	(On rebuild from components 3.00 as "EN224")				t/a Peter R.Arnold Collection *(Cancelled 9.5.02 as temporarily WFU)*		
G-FYAN	Williams Westwind MLB	MDW-1		6. 1.82	M.D.Williams	Dunstable	
G-FYAO	Williams Westwind MLB	MDW-001		6. 1.82	M.D.Williams	Dunstable	
G-FYAU	Williams Westwind Two MLB	MDW-002		6. 1.82	M.D.Williams	Dunstable	
G-FYAV	Osprey Mk.4E2 MLB	ASC-247		12. 1.82	C.D.Egan & C.Stiles	Hounslow	
G-FYBD	Osprey Mk.1E MLB	ASC-136		20. 1.82	M.Vincent	Jersey	
G-FYBE	Osprey Mk.4D MLB	ASC-128		20. 1.82	M.Vincent	Jersey	
G-FYBF	Osprey Mk.5 MLB	ASC-218		20. 1.82	M.Vincent	Jersey	
G-FYBG	Osprey Mk.4G2 MLB	ASC-204		20. 1.82	M.Vincent	Jersey	
G-FYBH	Osprey Mk.4G MLB	ASC-214		20. 1.82	M.Vincent	Jersey	
G-FYBI	Osprey Mk.4H MLB	ASC-234		20. 1.82	M.Vincent	Jersey	
G-FYCL	Osprey Mk.4G MLB	ASC-213		9. 2.82	P.J.Rogers	Banbury	
G-FYCV	Osprey Mk.4D MLB	ASK-276		19. 2.82	M.Thomson	London SW11	
G-FYCZ	Osprey Mk.4D2 MLB	ASC-244		24. 2.82	P.Middleton	Colchester	
G-FYDF	Osprey Mk.4D MLB	ASK-278		22. 3.82	K.A.Jones	Thornton Heath	
G-FYDI	Williams Westwind Two MLB	MDW-005		29. 3.82	M.D.Williams	Dunstable	
G-FYDN	European 8C MLB	DD34/S.22		5. 4.82	P.D.Ridout	Botley	
G-FYDO	Osprey Mk.4D MLB	ASK-262		15. 4.82	N.L.Scallan	Hayes	
G-FYDP	Williams Westwind Three MLB	MDW-006		29. 3.82	M.D.Williams	Dunstable	
G-FYDS	Osprey Mk.4D MLB	ASK-261		15. 4.82	M.E.Scallan	Hayes	
G-FYEK	Unicorn UE-1C MLB	82024		2. 7.82	D. & D.Eaves	Southampton	
G-FYEO	Scallan Eagle Mk.1A MLB	001		20. 7.82	M.E.Scallan	Hayes	
G-FYEV	Osprey Mk.1C MLB	ASK-294		10. 8.82	M.E.Scallan	Hayes	
G-FYEZ	Scallan Firefly Mk.1 MLB	MNS-748		22. 9.82	M.E. & N.L.Scallan	Hayes	
G-FYFI	European E.84PS MLB	S.29		1.12.82	M.A.Stelling	Barton-le-Clay	
G-FYFJ	Williams Westwind Two MLB	MDW-010		14.12.82	M.D.Williams	Dunstable	
G-FYFN	Osprey Saturn 2 DC3 MLB	ATC-250/MJS-11		17. 2.83	J.Woods & M.Woods	Bracknell	
G-FYFW	Rango NA-55 MLB	NHP-40		8.10.84	N.H.Ponsford & A.M.Lindsay	Leeds	
	(Radio controlled)				t/a Rango Kite & Balloon Co *"Vaughan Williams"*		
G-FYFY	Rango NA-55RC MLB	AL-43		28. 2.85	A.M.Lindsay	Leeds	
	(Radio controlled)				*"Fifi"*		
G-FYGI	Rango NA-55RC MLB	NHP-54		26. 6.90	D.K.Fish	Bedford	
	(Radio controlled)						
G-FYGJ	Airspeed-300 MLB	001		8.10.91	N.Wells	Tunbridge Wells	
G-FYGM	Saffery/Smith Princess MLB	551		24.11.97	A. & N.Smith	Goole	
G-FZZA	General Avia F22-A	018		13. 8.98	APB Leasing Ltd	Welshpool	15.10.04T
	(Struck runway heavily in forced landing Welshpool 28.11.01: nose u/c collapsed causing damage to propeller & nose)						
G-FZZI	Cameron H-34 HAB	2105		30.10.89	Magical Adventures Ltd	West Bloomfield, Mi., USA	30. 7.96A

G-GAAA - G-GZZZ

G-GABD	Gulfstream GA-7 Cougar	GA7-0043	D-GABD	13. 4.82	C.B.Stewart *(Op Prestwick Flight Centre)*	Prestwick	5.12.02T
G-GACA	Hunting Percival P.57 Sea Prince T.1	P57/58	WP308	2. 9.80	P.G.Vallance Ltd	Charlwood, Surrey	4.11.80P
					(Gatwick Aviation Museum as "WP308/572")		
G-GAFA	Piper PA-34-200T Seneca II	34-7970218	D-GAFA	12.10.99	SRC Contractors Ltd	Luton	6.12.05T
			N2247Z				
G-GAFT	Piper PA-44-180 Seminole	4496162	N5324Q	24. 1.03	Atlantic Flight Training Ltd	Coventry	
G-GAFX	Boeing 747-245F	20827	N641FE	28. 8.99	Airfreight Express Ltd	Heathrow	9. 9.02T
			VP-BXP/N641FE/(N632FE)/N812FT/N702SW *(Op Cargolux)*				
G-GAII	Hawker Hunter GA.11	HABL-003028	XE685	7.12.94	DAT Enterprises Ltd	North Weald	24. 6.98P
	(Officially regd with c/n 41H-004038)				*(As "XE685/861/VL" in RN c/s)*		

Reg	Type	c/n	Prev id	Date	Owner	Location	Expiry
G-GAJB	Gulfstream AA-5B Tiger	AA5B-1179	G-BHZN N37519	6. 4.87	G.A.J.Bowles	Elstree	23 1.05T
G-GAJW	Bell 407	53186	N52245	15. 6.01	A.J.Walter (Aviation) Ltd	(Horsham)	15. 6.04T
G-GALA	Piper PA-28-180 Cherokee E	28-5794	G-AYAP N11C	31. 7.89	Flyteam Aviation Ltd	Elstree	10. 5.05T
G-GALB	Piper PA-28-161 Warrior II	28-8616021	D-EHMP N9097E/(N157AV)/N9635N	1. 9.00	Goodair Leasing Ltd	Cardiff	14.12.03T
G-GALL	Piper PA-38-112 Tomahawk	38-78A0025	G-BTEV N9315T	1. 6.00	C.W.Good	Cardiff	29. 1.05T
G-GAME	Cessna T303 Crusader	T30300098	(F-GDFN) N2693C	25. 2.83	P.Heffron	Swansea	14. 6.04
G-GAND	Agusta-Bell 206B JetRanger II	8073	G-AWMK 9Y-TFC/G-AWMK/(VR-BCV)/G-AWMK	11. 1.00	A & B Glass Co. Ltd	Earls Colne	6. 6.03T

(Airframe exchanged with 5N-AQJ during rebuild 1999 & became c/n 8051 ex 5N-AQJ/G-BLPL/VR-BDY/I-EVBU. by default, unofficially: 5N-AQJ was cancelled 1.00 on export as VH-JEF with c/n 8051)

Reg	Type	c/n	Prev id	Date	Owner	Location	Expiry
G-GANE	Sequoia F.8L Falco	906 & PFA 100-11100		25. 9.85	S.J.Gane	Kemble	13. 6.03P
	(Lycoming IO-320)						
G-GASC	Hughes 369HS (500)	110-0270S	G-WELD G-FROG/OO-KAR	11. 7.85	Crewhall Ltd	Effingham	11. 5.05T
G-GASP	Piper PA-28-181 Cherokee Archer II	28-7790013	N4328F	15.10.90	D.J.Turner tr G-GASP Flying Group	Fairoaks	21.12.02
G-GASS	Thunder Ax7-77 HAB	1746		19. 4.90	M.W.Axon	Brentwood	4. 7.03A
					tr Servowarm Balloon Syndicate "Travel Gas III"		
G-GAWA*	Cessna 140	9619	G-BRSM N72454/NC72454	17. 9.91	D.B.Almey	(Spalding)	11. 6.05
	(Continental C85)		(Cancelled 12.2.03 as wfu)				
G-GAZA	Aérospatiale SA341G Gazelle 1	1187	G-RALE G-SFTG/N87712	19. 6.92	The Auster Aircraft Co Ltd	Waltham, Leics	8. 8.04
G-GAZI	Aérospatiale SA341G Gazelle 1	1136	G-BKLU N32PA/N341VH/N90957	29. 6.90	Sharpness Dock Ltd	(Plymouth)	13. 6.05T
			(New owner 5.02)				
G-GAZL	Westland SA341C Gazelle	HT.21078	G-CBBY XW856	3. 4.02	R.M.Bailey	Addison Mains, Dalmahoy	21. 2.03P
G-GAZZ	Aérospatiale SA341G Gazelle 1	1271	F-GFHD YV-242CP/HB-XGA/F-WMHCUCC (Op Cheqair)	14. 3.90	Stratton Motor Co (Norfolk) Ltd & International Group Ltd	Stapleford	22. 6.02T
G-GBAO	Robin R1180TD Aiglon	277	F-GBAO	9. 9.81	J.Kay-Movat	Slinfold	10. 6.04
	(Rebuild of R.1180 prototype F-WVKU c/n 01)						
G-GBFF	Reims/Cessna F172N	F17201565	F-GBFF	16. 6.99	E.J.Watts	Bodmin	17 .6.05T
G-GBGA	Scheibe SF-25C Falke	44683	D-KIEJ	28. 8.02	British Gliding Association Ltd	Leicester	25. 9.05
G-GBHI	SOCATA TB-10 Tobago	19	F-GBHI	12.11.97	Robert Purvis Plant Hire Ltd	(Larbert)	30.11.03
G-GBLP	Reims/Cessna F172M Skyhawk II	F17201042	G-GWEN G-GBLP/N14496	9.11.84	Aviate Scotland Ltd	Edinburgh	8.11.03T
					(Op Edinburgh Air Centre)		
G-GBLR	Reims/Cessna F150L	F15001109	N961L (D-EDJE)	30. 4.85	G.Matthews tr Blue Max Flying Group	Coventry	11. 7.05T
G-GBRB	Piper PA-28-180 Cherokee C	28-2583	N8381W	2. 2.00	Border Air Training Ltd	Carlisle	24. 2.03T
G-GBSL	Beech 76 Duchess	ME-265	G-BGVG	27. 3.81	M.H.Cundey	Redhill/Alderney	29. 5.05
G-GBTA	Boeing 737-436	25859	G-BVIIA (G-GBTA)	7. 2.94	British Airways plc (Youm-Al-Suq t/s)	Gatwick	31.10.05T
G-GBTB	Boeing 737-436	25860	OO-LTS G-BVHB/OO-LTS/G-BVHB/(G-GRTR)	23.10.96	Aurigny Air Services Ltd	Guernsey	28.10.05T
G-GBUE	Robin DR400/120A Petit Prince	1354	G-BPXD F-GBUE	11. 5.89	J.A.Kane tr G-GBUE Group	Bagby	21. 6.04
G-GBXS	Europa Aviation Europa Turbo XS	F0005	"G-2000" G-GBXS	1. 4.98	Europa Aircraft Co Ltd	Wombleton	5. 6.03P
	(Rotax 914) (Monowheel u/c)		(F/f 1.5.98)				
G-GCAC	Europa Aviation Europa XS T-G	559 & PFA 247-13940		21. 8.02	G.J.Cattermole	(Dudley)	
	(Rotax 912S)						
G-GCAT	Piper PA-28-140 Cherokee B	28-26032	G-BFRH OH-PCA	22.10.81	H.Skelton tr Group CAT	Sturgate	5. 9.05
G-GCCL	Beech 76 Duchess	ME-322	(G-BNRF) N6714U	5. 8.87	Aerolease Ltd	Conington	10.12.05T
G-GCJL*	British Aerospace Jetstream Srs.4100	41001		5. 2.91	BAE Systems (Operations) Ltd	Woodford	29. 4.95S
					(Stored 12.01) (Cancelled 15.11.02 as wfu)		
G-GCKI	Mooney M.20K (231)	25-0401	N4062H	15. 8.80	B.Barr	Seething	15. 8.04
G-GCNZ*	Cessna 150M Commuter	15075933	C-GCNZ	8.11.88	Not known	Elstree	27. 3.98T
			(Cancelled 8.6.99 as destroyed) (Wreck noted 2.01)				
G-GCUB	Piper PA-18-150 Super Cub	18-7922	SE-GCO Swedish Army 51249/N10F	11. 2.99	N.J.Morgan	Tatenhill	6 .8.05
G-GCYC	Reims/Cessna F182Q Skylane	F18200157	F-GCYC	11. 2.00	G-GCYC Ltd	Barton	12. 4.03
G-GDAM*	Piper PA-18-135 Super Cub	18-3535	PH-PVW (PH-DKE)/R-107/54-2335	30. 6.81	Not known Siege Cross Farm, Thatcham		11. 8.91
	(L-21B-PI) (Frame No.18-3648)		(Cancelled by CAA 18.3.99) (Stored dismantled 10.01)				
G-GDER	Robin R1180TD	280	F-GDER	15. 5.97	Berkshire Aviation Services Ltd	Fairoaks	15. 5.03
G-GDEZ	British Aerospace BAe 125 Srs.1000B	259026	N9026 G-5-743/ZS-ACT/ZS-CCT/G-5-743	30.10.95	Frewton Ltd	Jersey	20.11.05
G-GDGR	SOCATA TB-20 Trinidad	378	F-GDGR	23. 7.97	Willwright Aviation Ltd	Liverpool	30. 8.03T
G-GDOG	Piper PA-28R-200 Cherokee Arrow II	28R-7635227	G-BDXW N9235K	17. 4.89	R.K.& S.Perry	Thruxton	7.11.05
G-GDRV	Van's RV-6	21367	C-GDRV	26.11.01	M.A.Jardim de Queiroz	(Worcester)	7. 4.03P
	(Built D.Piper)				tr G-GDRV Group (Noted 11.01)		
G-GDTU	Avions Mudry CAP.10B	193	F-GDTU (N.....)/F-GDTK/F-WZCI	27. 5.99	Sherburn Aero Club Ltd	Sherburn-in-Elmet	15 .9.05T
G-GEDI	Dassault Falcon 2000	49	VP-BEF F-WWMD	23. 7.98	Victoria Aviation Ltd	(Guernsey)	22. 7.03T
G-GEEP	Robin R1180TD Aiglon	266		9. 4.80	C.J.P.Green	Booker	7. 8.04
G-GEES	Cameron N-77 HAB	357		8.11.77	N.A.Carr	Leicester	31. 5.00A
G-GEEZ	Cameron N-77 HAB	1159		3. 5.85	Charnwood Forest Turf Accountants Ltd	Leicester	7. 4.96A
					"Tic Tac"		

Reg	Type	C/n	Prev ID	Date	Owner/Operator	Location	Date
G-GEGE*	Robinson R22 Beta-II	2994		19.10.99	C.& S.Hewgill	Wellesbourne Mountford	28.10.02T
					t/a CSL Industrial *(Cancelled 2.7.01 by CAA: noted 5.02)*		
G-GEHP	Piper PA-28RT-201 Arrow IV	28R-8218014	F-GEHP	24. 4.98	Aeros Leasing Ltd	Gloucestershire	4. 7.04T
			N82023				
G-GEMS	Thunder Ax8-90 Srs.2 HAB	2287	G-BUNP	6.11.92	B.Sevenich, B.& S.Harren & W.Christoph		
					(Stolen 7.6.00)	Aachen, Germany	2. 4.01T
G-GENN	Gulfstream GA-7 Cougar	GA7-0114	G-BNAB	2.12.94	Abraxas Aviation Ltd	Elstree	15. 1.04T
			G-BGYP				
G-GEOF	Pereira Osprey 2	PFA 70-10384		7. 9.78	G.Crossley	(Blackpool)	
G-GERY	Stoddard-Hamilton GlaStar	PFA 295-13475		6. 7.01	G.E.Collard	Popham	3. 7.03P
	(Tailwheel u/c)						
G-GFAB	Cameron N-105 HAB	2048		4. 8.89	The Andrew Brownsword Collection Ltd	Bath	17. 5.03A
G-GFCA	Piper PA-28-161 Cadet	2841100	N9174X	24. 4.89	Aeros Leasing Ltd	Gloucestershire	4.10.04T
G-GFCB	Piper PA-28-161 Cadet	2841101	N9175F	24. 4.89	AM & T Aviation Ltd	Bristol	11. 7.04T
G-GFCD	Piper PA-34-220T Seneca III	34-8133073	G-KIDS	31. 5.90	Stonehurst Aviation Ltd	Coventry	7. 4.05T
			N83745				
G-GFCF	Piper PA-28-161 Cadet	2841259	G-RHBH	28. 6.90	Aerohire Ltd	Dunkeswell	12. 2.05T
			N9193Z		*(Op Devon School of Flying)*		
G-GFEY	Piper PA-34-200T Seneca II	34-7870343	D-GFEY	13. 5.98	West Wales Airport Ltd	Shobdon	15. 1.05
			D-IFEY/N36599				
G-GFFA	Boeing 737-59D	25038	G-BVZF	10. 2.00	British Airways plc	Gatwick	2. 5.04T
			SE-DND/(SE-DNC)				
G-GFFB	Boeing 737-505	25789	LN-BRT	15. 2.00	British Airways plc	Gatwick	8. 5.03T
G-GFFC	Boeing 737-505	24272	LN-BRG	23. 3.00	British Airways plc	Manchester	8. 6.03T
G-GFFD	Boeing 737-59D	26419	LY-BFV	3. 7.00	British Airways plc	Manchester	13. 8.03T
			OY-SEG/G-OBMY/SE-DNI				
G-GFFE	Boeing 737-528	27424	LX-LGR	16. 6.00	British Airways plc	Gatwick	10. 7.03T
			(F-GJNP)				
G-GFFF	Boeing 737-53A	24754	G-OBMZ	2. 1.01	British Airways plc	Manchester	20. 9.05T
			SE-DNC				
G-GFFG	Boeing 737-505	24650	LN-BRC	20. 9.00	British Airways plc	Manchester	29.10.03T
			N5573K				
G-GFFH	Boeing 737-5H6	27354	VT-JAW	24.10.00	British Airways plc	Gatwick	23. 1.04T
			9M-MFG				
G-GFFI	Boeing 737-528	27425	LX-LGS	9.11.00	British Airways plc	Manchester	18.12.03T
			(F-GJNQ)				
G-GFFJ	Boeing 737-5H6	27355	VT-JAZ	19. 1.01	British Airways plc	Manchester	12. 3.04T
			9M-MFH				
G-GFKY	Zenair CH.250	34	C-GFKY	23. 4.93	J.J.Beal	(Aberdeen)	6. 6.03P
	(Lycoming O-235)						
G-GFLY	Reims/Cessna F150L	F15000822	PH-CES	28. 8.80	Tindon Ltd	Little Snoring	1.12.04T
G-GFTA	Piper PA-28-161 Warrior III	2842047	N4132L	1. 4.99	One Zero Three Ltd	Guernsey	31. 3.05T
			G-GFTA/N9525N				
G-GFTB	Piper PA-28-161 Warrior III	2842048	N4120V	7. 5.99	One Zero Three Ltd	Guernsey	6. 5.05T
			G-GFTB/N4120V				
G-GGCT	Flight Design CT2K *(Pegasus Aviation c/n)*	7938		18. 2.03	G.R.Graham	Carlisle	
G-GGGG	Thunder Ax7-77 HAB	162		2. 8.78	T.A.Gilmour *"Flying G"*	Stockbridge	17. 8.99A
					tr Flying G Group		
G-GGLE	Piper PA-22-108 Colt	22-8914	N5234Z	13. 5.93	M.& S.Leonard	Crowfield	2.10.05T
	(Frame No.108-915) (Tail-wheel conversion incorporating parts from G-AROM c/n 22-8805)						
G-GGOW	Colt 77A HAB	1542		19. 6.89	G.Everett *"Charles Rennie Mackintosh"*	Dartford	20. 5.03A
G-GGRR	Scottish Aviation Bulldog Srs.120/121	BH120/272	G-CBAM	11. 7.01	F.P.Corbett	White Waltham	2. 9.04
			XX614		*(As "XX614/V")*		
G-GGTT	Agusta-Bell 47G-4A	2538	F-GGTT	21. 8.97	Face & Fragrance Ltd	(Manchester)	8. 7.04
			I-ANDO				
G-GHEE	Aerotechnik EV-97 Eurostar	PFA 315-13840		14.12.01	C.J.Ball	(Cheltenham)	27. 5.03P
G-GHIA	Cameron N-120 HAB	2442		13.11.90	J.A.Marshall	Billingshurst	22. 8.03T
G-GHIN	Thunder Ax7-77 HAB	1802		16. 7.90	N.T.Parry *"Pegasus"*	Binfield	4. 9.00A
G-GHOW	Reims/Cessna F182Q Skylane	F18200151	OO-MCD	20. 2.01	G.How	Top Farm, Croydon, Royston	3. 4.04T
			F-BJCE				
G-GHPG	Cessna 550 Citation II	550-0897	EI-GHP	22. 2.02	MCP Aviation (Charter) Ltd	Stapleford	7. 3.03T
			N5079V				
G-GHRW	Piper PA-28RT-201 Arrow IV	28R-7918140	G-ONAB	8.12.83	Bonus Aviation Ltd	Cranfield	22.12.03T
			G-BHAK/N29555				
G-GHSI	Piper PA-44-180T Turbo Seminole	44-8107026	SX-ATA	2.12.94	M.G.Roberts	Bournemouth	1.12.97
			N8278Z		*(Damaged late 1994: on rebuild 8.95: current status unknown)*		
G-GHZJ	SOCATA TB-9 Tampico	941	F-GHZJ	4. 3.98	M.Haller	Little Snoring	30. 4.04
G-GIGI	SOCATA MS.893A Rallye Commodore 180	11637	G-AYVX	28. 9.81	D.J.Moore	Aston Down	13. 4.00
			F-BSFJ				
G-GILT	Cessna 421C Golden Eagle III	421C0515	G-BMZC	3. 7.97	Spearmint Rhino Companies (Europe) Ltd	Booker	9.10.03T
			N555WV/N555WW/N885WW/N885EC/N88541				
G-GINO	Auster V J/1 Autocrat				*See entry for G-AJEM*		
G-GIRA	British Aerospace HS.125 Srs.700B	257103	YL-VIR	16. 1.02	EAS Aeroserviza SAS	(Venice, Italy)	5. 5.03T
			YL-VIP/VP-BOJ/VR-BOJ/G-LTEC/G-BHSU/G-5-12				
G-GIRY	American General AG-5B Tiger	10146	F-GIRY	5. 2.99	Crestway Technologies Ltd	Denham	25. 4.05T
G-GISO	Piper PA-44-180T Turbo Seminole	44-8107065	D-GISO	25.10.01	G.Cockerton	Coventry	26.11.04T
			N82112/N9602N				
G-GIWT	Europa Aviation Europa XS 463 & PFA 247-13623			29. 3.01	A.Twigg	(Wootton Bassett)	
	(Monowheel u/c)						
G-GJCD	Robinson R22 Beta	0966		22. 2.89	J.C.Lane	Wolverhampton	21. 5.04T
G-GJKK	Mooney M.20K (252TSE)	25-1227	F-GJKK	26.11.93	Pergola Ltd	Weston, Dublin	15. 3.03
G-GKAT	Enstrom 280C Shark	1200	F-GKAT	26. 8.97	Elham Valley Aviation Ltd	Manston	8. 3.04
			N5694Y				

Reg	Type	c/n	Prev id	Date	Owner/Operator	Location	C of A
G-GKFC	Tiger Cub RL5A LW Sherwood Ranger (Jabiru 2200A) PFA 237-12947		G-MYZI	24.11.98	K.F.Crumplin	Franklyn's Field, Chewton Mendip	6. 1.03P
G-GLAD	Gloster Gladiator II	-	N5903	5. 1.95	Patina Ltd *(As "N2276") (Op The Fighter Collection: on rebuild 9.02)*	Duxford	
G-GLAW	Cameron N-90 HAB	1808		10.10.88	George Law Plant Ltd *"Law Civil Engineers"*	Kidderminster	29. 7.03A
G-GLED	Cessna 150M	15076673	C-GLED	6. 1.89	Firecrest Aviation Ltd	Elstree	26.11.04T
G-GLIB	Robinson R44 Raven	1226		12. 6.02	Helisport UK Ltd	(Chelmsford)	11. 7.05T
G-GLTT	Piper PA-31-350 Chieftain	31-8452004	N27JV XA-SVW/XA-SGZ/N606SM/N4115D	19. 9.97	E.K.Davies	Guernsey	18. 3.04T
G-GLUC	Van's RV-6 (Built L De Sandeleer)	20153	C-GLUC	15.10.99	Speedfreak Ltd	Crosland Moor	13 .6.03P
G GLUE	Cameron N-65 HAB	390		17. 3.81	L.J.M.Muir & G.D.Hallett *(Mobile Windscreens titles) "Tacky Jack/Jack of Herts"*	East Molesey	17. 7.90A
G-GLUG	Piper PA-31-350 Chieftain	31-8052077	N2287J G-BLOE/G-NITE/N3559A	1. 9.94	Champagne-Air Ltd	Newcastle	23.11.02T
G-GMAA	Learjet Learjet 45	45-167	N5012V	1. 5.02	Gama Aviation Ltd	Farnborough	30. 4.03T
G-GMAB	British Aerospace BAe 125-1000B	259034	N81HH N290H/G-BUWX/G-5-761	21.11.01	Gama Aviation Ltd	Farnborough	11. 3.03T
G-GMAX	SNCAN Stampe SV-4C	141	G-BXNW F-BBPB	19. 6.87	Glidegold Ltd *(Damaged in crash Booker 3.6.91: rebuild 5.96: current status unknown)*	Booker	29. 8.93T
G-GMPA	Aérospatiale AS355F2 Twin Squirrel	5409	G-BPOI	26. 9.89	Greater Manchester Police Authority	Barton	9. 1.05T
G-GMPB	Pilatus Britten-Norman BN-2T-4S Defender 4000	4011	G-BWPU/(9M-TPD)/G-BWPU	5. 4.02	B-N Group Ltd *(Op Greater Manchester Police)*	Bembridge	1. 7.03T
G-GMPS	MD Helicopters MD.900	900-00081	N7033K	8. 1.01	Greater Manchester Police Authority	Barton	12. 2.04T
G-GMSI	SOCATA TB-9 Tampico	145		18. 9.80	M.L.Rhodes	Wolverhampton	28. 5.03T
G-GNAT	Folland Gnat T.1	FL.595	8638M XS101	14. 4.82	Brutus Holdings Ltd *(As "XS101" in CFS c/s)*	Cranfield	18. 9.03P
G-GNJW	Comco Ikarus C42 (Rotax 912ULS)	PFA 322-13717		21. 8.01	I.R.Westrope	(Haverhill)	5. 3.03P
G-GNTB	SAAB-Scania SF.340A	340A-082	HB-AHL OK-RGS/SE-E82	30. 9.91	Swedish Aircraft Holdings AB	(Stockholm, Sweden)	13. 3.03T
G-GNTC	SAAB-Fairchild SF.340A	340A-020	HB-AHE SE-E20	25. 9.92	Aurigny Air Services Ltd	Guernsey	24. 9.05T
G-GNTF	SAAB-Scania SF.340A	340A-113	HB-AHO SE-F13	27.10.94	Swedish Aircraft Holdings AB	(Stockholm, Sweden)	27.10.01T
G-GNTG	SAAB-Scania SF.340A	340A-126	HB-AHR SE-F26	18.11.94	Loganair Ltd	Glasgow	18.11.03T
G-GNTZ	British Aerospace BAe 146 Srs.200	E2036	G-CLHB G-GNTZ/HB-IXB/N175LN/N355PS	31. 3.00	British Airways Citiexpress Ltd	Aberdeen	25.11.03T
G-GOBT	Colt 77A HAB	1815		13. 2.91	British Telecommunications plc *"Sky Piper"*	Thatcham	18. 3.00A
G-GOCX	Cameron N-90 HAB	2619		7. 8.91	R.D.Parry	Hong Kong, PRC	5. 1.02A
G-GOGW	Cameron N-90 HAB	3304		31. 8.94	S.E.Carroll	Reading	12. 7.03A
G-GOLF	SOCATA TB-10 Tobago	250		21.12.81	A.C.Scamell tr Golf Golf Group	Biggin Hill	6. 7.03
G-GOMD	Aviat Pitts S-2B	5213	F-GOMD N319JM	5. 4.02	Extreme Aerobatics Ltd	(Lewes)	14. 4.05T
G-GONE	de Havilland DH.112 Venom FB.50 (FB.1) (Built F + W)	752	J-1542	17. 9.84	D.G.Jones	Bournemouth	5. 6.03P
G-GONN	Eurocopter AS355N Ecureuil II	5557	HB-XIQ VR-BQM/G-BVNW/(D-HWPC)	20. 3.02	Gama Leasing Ltd	Farnborough	7. 4.05T
G-GOOD	SOCATA TB-20 Trinidad	1657	F-GNHJ	4.11.94	T.M.Sloan & M.P.Bowcock	Goodwood	10. 1.04T
G-GORE	CFM Streak Shadow K.138-SA & PFA 206-11646 (Rotax 532) (PFA project no duplicates TEAM mini-MAX G-MWFD)			12. 4.90	M.S.Clinton	Old Sarum	7. 8.03P
G-GORF	Robin HR200/120B	291	F-GORF	14. 1.00	J.A.Ingram	Nottingham	10. 2.03T
G-GOSL	Robin DR400/180 Regent	1974	G-BSDG	14. 1.02	R.M.Gosling	Stones Farm, Wickham St Pauls, Essex	23. 5.05
G-GOSS	CEA Jodel DR-221 Dauphin	125	F-BPRA	4.12.80	D.Oddy tr Avon Flying Group	Bidford	12. 5.03
G-GOTC	Gulfstream GA-7 Cougar	GA7-0074	G-BMDY OO-LCR/OO-HRA	25. 6.97	Wakelite Ltd *(Op Denham School of Flying)*	Denham	10. 3.05T
G-GOTO	Piper PA-32R-301T Saratoga II TC	3257026	N92965 G-GOTO/N92965	8. 1.98	J.A.Varndell	Blackbushe	21. 1.04
G-GOUP	Robinson R22 Beta	1663	G-DIRE	9. 1.01	Electric Scribe 2000 Ltd	(Aberdeen)	27. 3.03T
G-GPAG	Van's RV-6	PFA 181A-13306		18. 5.01	P.A.Green	(Romsey)	
G-GPAS	Jabiru Jabiru UL-450	PFA 274A-13823		15. 1.02	G.D.Allen	(Stowmarket)	21. 7.03P
G-GPEG	Cameron Sky 90-24 HAB	4849		31. 5.00	N.T.Parrry *"Pegasus"*	Bracknell	22. 6.03A
G-GPMW	Piper PA-28R-201T Turbo Arrow IV	28R-8031041	N3576V	3. 7.89	Calverton Flying Group Ltd	(London W4)	14. 5.04T
G-GPST	Phillips ST.1 Speedtwin	1 & PFA 207-11645		21. 6.90	Speedtwin Developments Ltd *(Continental O-200-A) (PFA project no duplicates Kolb Twinstar G-MWWM)*	Upper Cae Garw Farm, Trelleck, Monmouth	3.12.03P
G-GRAY*	Cessna 172N Skyhawk II	172-72375	N4859D	3.12.79	Not known *(Damaged ditching Firth of Forth, Musselburgh 2.4.93: cancelled 27.9.00 as WFU: noted dismantled 4.01)*	Nottingham	13. 2.95
G-GRGG	Cessna 525 CitationJet	525-0028	G-OHAT G-OICE/N1330S	18. 9.02	Houston Jet Services Ltd	Oxford	17.11.04T
G-GRID	Aérospatiale AS355F1 Twin Squirrel	5012	TG-BOS	28. 3.89	National Grid Co plc	Oxford	18. 6.04T
G-GRIF	Rockwell Commander 112TC-A	13258	G-BHXC N1005C	2.10.81	N.G.W.Cragg, E.T.N.Sutherland & C.Walker t/a Nicol Aviation	Gamston	28. 3.04
G-GRIN	Van's RV-6	PFA 181-12409		8. 1.98	A.Phillips	Boarhunt Farm, Fareham	23. 5.03P
G-GRIP	Colt Bibendum 110SS HAB	4224		5. 1.98	The Aerial Display Co Ltd *(Michelin titles)*	Looe	25. 1.02A
G-GROL	Maule MXT-7-180 Star Rocket	14091C		16. 6.98	D.C., C.& C.Croll	Southend	16.12.04
G-GRRC	Piper PA-28-161 Warrior II	2816076	G-BXJX HB-POM/D-EJTB/N9149X	9. 3.98	Goodwood Road Racing Co Ltd	Goodwood	2.11.03T
G-GRRR	Scotish Aviation Bulldog Srs.120/122	BH120/229	G-BXGU Ghana AF G-105	19.10.98	Horizons Europe Ltd *(As "XX614/V")*	Old Sarum	25. 5.05T
G-GRYZ	Beech F33A Bonanza	CE-1668	F-GRYZ D-ESNE/N80011/(OY-GEN)/N80011	4.10.99	J.Kawadri & M.Kaveh	Booker	13.11.05
G-GSCV	Comco Ikarus C42 FB UK	PFA 322-13939		5. 9.02	G.Sipson	(Coventry)	4.11.03P

G-GSFC	Robinson R22 Beta	0569	N2425J	3. 7.86	D.Sas	(Parma, Italy)	13 8.05
G-GSJH	Bell 206B-3 JetRanger III	3958	G-PENT	15. 3.02	S.J.Hanson t/a Interheli	Farleton, Lancaster	10. 6.05T
			G-IIRB/N903CA				
G-GSPG	Hughes 369HS	45-0738S	G-GEEE	17. 1.03	S.P.Giddings	(Newport Pagnell)	8.10.04
			G-BDOY		t/a S.Giddings Aviation		
G-GSSA	Boeing 747-47UF	29256	N495MC	23. 1.02	Global Supply Systems Ltd	Stansted	27. 1.05TC
			(N496MC)		(British Airways c/s)		
G-GSSB	Boeing 747-47UF	29252	N491MC	17. 1.03	Global Supply Systems Ltd	Stansted	
G-GTHM	Piper PA-38-112 Tomahawk II	38-81A0171	C-GTHM	17.11.86	Turweston Aero Club Ltd	Turweston	15.11.04T
			N91338				
G-GUAY	Enstrom 480	5036		1.12.98	Testactual Ltd t/a Heliway Aviation	(Fareham)	30.12.04T
G-GUCK	Beech C23 Sundowner 180	M-2221	G-BPYG	9. 4.92	J.T.Francis	Headcorn	25. 9.04
			N6638R				
G-GUFO	Cameron Saucer 80SS HAB	1641	C-GUFO	10. 6.98	Magical Adventures Ltd	Oswestry	6. 9.03A
			G-BOUB				
G-GULF	Lindstrand LBL-105A HAB	320		3.11.95	M.A.Webb	Chard	17. 7.02A
G-GULP	III Sky Arrow 650T	PFA 298-13664		4.12.00	Lord Rotherwick	(Chipping Norton)	24. 2.03P
G-GUMS	Cessna 182P Skylane	18261643	G-CBMN	11.11.02	A.C.Lees	Eddsfield	24. 6.05T
			ZS-KJS/N21458				
G-GUNS	Cameron V-77 HAB	2221		9. 5.90	Royal School of Artillery Hot Air Balloon Club	Larkhill	4. 4.03A
					"Guns"		
G-GURN	Piper PA-31 Turbo Navajo C	31-7912117	G-BHGA	20. 6.01	Neric Ltd	(Guernsey)	5. 4.03
			N3539M				
G-GURU	Piper PA-28-161 Warrior II	28-8316018	PH-SVJ	12. 2.02	Yankee Aviation Ltd	(London W1)	25. 2.05T
			N83085				
G-GUSS	Piper PA-28-151 Cherokee Warrior	28-7415497	G-BJRY	16. 8.95	M.J.Cleaver & J.M.Newman	Southend	7. 6.03T
			N43453				
G-GUST	Agusta-Bell 206B JetRanger II	8192	G-CBHH	30. 8.96	Gatehouse Estates Ltd	Sywell	11. 1.03T
			F-GALU/G-AYBE				
G-GUYS	Piper PA-34-200T Seneca II	34-7870283	G-BMWT	14. 7.87	R.J.& J.M.Z.Keel	Sturgate	3. 5.05
			N31984				
G-GVBF	Lindstrand LBL-180A HAB	250	PH-VBF	19. 5.95	Airxcite Ltd	Wembley	26 2.03T
			G-GVBF		t/a Virgin Balloon Flights		
G-GVPI	Evans VP-1	PFA 62-10668		9. 8.02	G.Martin	(Hinckley)	
G-GWIZ	Colt Clown SS HAB	1369	(G-BPWU)	25. 4.89	Magical Adventures Ltd	Oswestry	13. 4.99A
G-GWYN	Reims/Cessna F172M Skyhawk II	F17201217	PH-TWN	5. 3.81	D.J.Bruford	Exeter	27. 4.05
G-GYAK	Yakovlev Yak-50	852905	RA02246	9.12.02	M.V.Rijske & M.W.Levy	North Weald	23.12.03P
G-GYAT	Sud Gardan GY-80-160	136	D-EAZZ	13.12.02	J. Luck	Rochester	AC
			HB-DCL/F-BMUU				
G-GYAV	Cessna 172N Skyhawk II	17271362	C-GYAV	26. 8.87	Southport & Merseyside Aero Club (1979) Ltd	Liverpool	12. 3.03T
G-GYBO	Gardan GY-80-180 Horizon	228	OY-DTN	4. 8.98	M.J.Strother	Leeds-Bradford	23. 8.03T
			SE-FGL/OY-DTN				
G-GYMM	Piper PA-28R-200 Cherokee Arrow B		G-AYWW	22. 2.90	J.B.A.Ainsworth tr Gymm Group	Leicester	16.10.04
		28R-7135049	N11C				
G-GYRO	Campbell Cricket	PFA G/03-1046		26. 2.82	J.W.Pavitt	St.Merryn	11. 9.03P
	(Rotax 532) (Originally registered as Bensen B.8 (c/n 01 & PFA G/01-1046))						
G-GYTO	Piper PA-28-161 Warrior III	2842082	N160FT	11. 5.00	Wellesbourne Flyers Ltd	Wellesbourne Mountford	30. 5.03T
			N9511N		t/a Wellesbourne Aviation		
G-GZDO	Cessna 172N Skyhawk II	17271826	C-GZDO	11.10.88	G.Cambridge & G.W.J.Hall	Elstree	17. 5.04T
			(N5299E)		t/a Cambridge Hall Aviation (Op Firecrest Aviation)		
G-GZLE	Aérospatiale SA341G Gazelle 1	1145	G-PYOB	8. 5.01	R.G.Fairall	Redhill	19.12.03
			G-WELA/G-SFTD/G-RIFC/G-SFTD/N641HM/N341BB/F-WKQH				

G-HAAA - G-HZZZ

G-HACK	Piper PA-18-150 Super Cub	18-7168	SE-CSA	20.11.97	S.J.Harris	Kemble	2.12.03
			N10F				
G-HADA	Enstrom 480	5017		17. 9.96	W.B.Steele	Whitchurch, Shropshire	9.10.05
G-HAEC	Commonwealth CAC-18 Mustang 22		VR-HIU	1. 5.85	R.W.Davies	Little Robhurst Farm, Woodchurch	13. 6.03P
		CACM-192-1517	(RP-C651)/PI-C651/VH-FCB/A68-192 "Big Beautiful Doll" (Op The Old Flying Machine Ltd)				
	(Composite rebuilt 1974-76 using major components ex Philippine AF P-51D 44-72917) (As "472218/WZ-I" in 78th FG USAAF c/s)						
G-HAIG	Rutan LongEz	1983-L & PFA 74A-11149		20. 5.86	N.M.Robbins	(Oswestry)	9.12.03P
	(Lycoming O-235)						
G-HAIR	Robin DR400/180	2479		7.12.00	Arden Ridge Developments Ltd	(Southam)	25. 1.04T
					t/a Racoon International		
G-HAJJ	Glaser-Dirks DG-400	4-225		15. 2.88	P.W.Endean	Perranporth	21. 4.03
G-HALC	Piper PA-28R-200 Cherokee Arrow II	28R-7335042	N91253	26.11.90	Halcyon Aviation Ltd	Barton	18. 7.03
			C-FFQO/CF-FQO				
G-HALE	Robinson R44 Astro	0492		6. 8.98	Barhale Surveying Ltd	Elstree	19. 8.04T
G-HALJ	Cessna 140	8336	N89308	30. 4.96	H.A.Lloyd-Jennings	Old Sarum	8.10.05
	(Continental C85)		NC89308				
G-HALL	Piper PA-22-160 Tri-Pacer	22-7423	G-ARAH	8.11.79	F.P.Hall	Clipgate Farm, Denton	29. 6.03
			N10F				
G-HALP	SOCATA TB-10 Tobago	192	G-BITD	19. 8.81	D.Halpern (Valid CofR 4.02)	Booker	30. 5.97
G-HAMA	Beech 200 Super King Air	BB-303	N244JB	16.11.84	Gama Aviation Ltd	Farnborough	19.11.05T
	(To B200 status with 4 x blade propellers 1999)		N211JB/N3090C/N3030C/N200CA				
G-HAMI	Fuji FA.200-180 Aero Subaru	FA200-188	G-OISF	31. 1.92	K.G.Cameron	Biggin Hill	31. 3.05T
			G-BAPT				
G-HAMM	Yakovlev Yak-50	832409	LY-ANG	15.10.02	A.D.Hammond	North Weald	31.10.03P
			DOSAAF 81				
G-HAMP	Bellanca 7DCA Champ	30-72	N9173L	8. 8.88	K.Macdonald	Rushett Farm, Chessington	2. 9.03P
G-HANA	Westland Wessex HC.Mk.2	WA/624	XV729	9. 3.01	R.A.Fidler	Honeycrock Farm, Redhill	
	(C/n officially quoted as WA/513 but may be part of fuselage number)						

Reg	Type	C/n	Prev Id	Date	Owner/Operator	Location	Status
G-HANS	Robin DR400 2 + 2	1384		2. 3.79	T.A.White t/a Bagby Aviation	Teesside	20. 6.03T
G-HANY	Agusta Bell 206B-3 JetRanger III	8598	G-JEKP	5. 1.01	Swift Helicopters Ltd	(Macclesfield)	3. 4.03T
			D-HMSF/G-ESAL/G-BHXW				
G-HAPI	Lindstrand LBL 105A HAB	669		21. 3.00	Adventure Balloon Co Ltd	London W7	2. 7.03T
G-HAPR	Bristol 171 Sycamore HC.14	13387	8010M	15. 6.78	E.D.ap Rees	Weston-super-Mare	
			XG547		t/a The Helicopter Museum		
					(As "XG547/T-S" in CFS c/s) (Valid CofR 4.02)		
G-HAPY	de Havilland DHC.1 Chipmunk 22	C1/0697	WP803	3. 7.96	G-HAPY Ltd (As "WP803")	Booker	1.10.05
G-HARE	Cameron N-77 HAB	1467		12. 3.87	C.E. & J.Falkingham	Stevenage	22. 6.03A
G-HARF	Gulfstream Gulfstream IV	1117	N1761J	9.10.91	Fayair (Jersey) Co Ltd (Op Harrods)	Stansted/Jersey	20.12.05T
G-HARH	Sikorsky S-76B	760391	N7600U	30. 9.91	Air Harrods Ltd	Stansted	17. 1.05T
G-HARI	Raj Hamsa X'Air Victor 2	455 & BMAA/HB/103		11. 6.99	E Joplin	Lower Mountpleasant Farm, Chatteris	10 11.03P
G-HARN	Piper PA-28-181 Archer II	28-8290108	G-DENK	3. 2.00	Harnett Air Services Ltd	Elstree	15. 2.04T
			G-BXRJ/HB-PGO				
G-HART	Cessna 152 II	15279734	(G-BPBF)	2. 2.89	Atlantic Air Transport Ltd	Coventry	25. 6.04T
	(Tail-wheel u/c conversion)		N757GS				
G-HARY	Alon A-2 Aircoupe	A.188	G-ATWP	15. 3.93	R.E.Dagless	Holly Hill Farm, Guist	24. 5.04
G-HASI	Cessna 421B Golden Eagle	421B0654	G-BTDK	17. 2.98	Chester Air Maintenance Ltd	Hawarden	7. 3.02
			OY-BFA/N1558G				
G-HATF	Thorp T-18CW	PFA 76-11481		6.12.01	A.T.Fraser	(Crowthorne)	
G-HATZ	Hatz CB-1	17	N54623	11. 5.89	S.P.Rollason	Long Marston	28.10.03P
	(Lycoming O-320)						
G-HAUS	Hughes 369HM (500M)	52-0214M	G-KBOT	20. 7.99	J Pulford t/a Pulford Aviation	Sywell	21.10.05
			G-RAMM/EI-AVN/N9037F				
G-HAZE	Thunder Ax8-90 HAB	989		3. 8.88	T.G.Church	Blackburn	23. 6.97T
G-HBBC	de Havilland DH.104 Dove 8	04211	G-ALFM	24. 1.96	BBC Air Ltd	Compton Abbas	4. 7.04
			VP961/G-ALFM/VP961				
G-HBMW	Robinson R22	0170	G-BOFA	7. 7.94	Northumbria Helicopters Ltd	Newcastle	30. 9.03T
			N9068D				
G-HBOS	Scheibe SF-25C Rotax-Falke	44574	D-KTIN	26. 7.01	Coventry Gliding Club Ltd	Husbands Bosworth	29. 8.04
G-HBUG	Cameron N-90 HAB	1991		21. 6.89	R.T. & H.Revel "Humbug"	High Wycombe	4. 5.02A
G-HCSL	Piper PA-34-220T Seneca III	34-8133237	N84375	9. 5.91	Shoreham Flight Centre Ltd	Shoreham	16.11.03T
G-HDEW	Piper PA-32R-301 Saratoga SP	3213026	G-BRGZ	4.12.89	Plantation Stud Ltd	(Newmarket)	11. 3.04
			N91787				
G-HDIX	Enstrom 280FX	2076	N506DH	19. 2.98	D.H.Brown	(Burnley)	3. 5.04T
			D-HDIX				
G-HEBE	Bell 206B-3 JetRanger III	3745	CS-HDN	5. 2.97	MGGR (UK) Ltd	(Weston-super-Mare)	8. 6.03T
			N3179A				
G-HELE	Bell 206B-3 JetRanger III	3789	G-OJFR	21. 2.91	B E E Smith	White Waltham	12. 5.03T
			N18095				
G-HELN	Piper PA-18 Super Cub 95	18-3365	G-BKDG	10. 1.86	J.J.Anziani	Booker	5. 6.03P
	(L-21B-PI) (Frame No.18-3400)		MM52-2392/EI-69/EI-141/I-EIWB/MM53-7765/53-7765				
	(Regd as c/n 18-1992 but frame exchanged in Italian AF service: c/n 3365 was officially regd as N9837Q)						
G-HELV	de Havilland DH.115 Vampire T.55	975	U-1215	17. 9.91	Hunter Wing Ltd	Bournemouth	28. 5.03P
	(Built F + W)				(As "XJ771" in RAF c/s)		
G-HEMH	Eurocopter AS355N Twin Squirrel	5693	F-WQPV	18. 9.01	Hancocks Holdings Ltd	(Loughborough)	20.12.04T
G-HENT	SOCATA Rallye 110ST Galopin	3210	OO-MBV	28.11.01	R.J.Patton	Enniskillen, Co.Fermanagh	25. 2.05T
G-HENY	Cameron V-77 HAB	2486		9. 1.91	R.S.D'Alton "Henny"	Newbury	19. 8.02A
G-HEPY	Robinson R44 Astro	0695		11. 1.00	T.Everett	Thruxton	12. 1.03T
G-HERA*	Robinson R22 Beta	1426		26. 6.90	G.R.Day	Wolverhampton	21. 8.99T
				(Crashed on landing Blackpool 24.2.99 & cancelled same date as Destroyed - cabin stored 8.00)			
G-HERB	Piper PA-28R-201 Arrow III	28R-7837118	ZS-LAG	5. 6.86	Consort Aviation Ltd	(Leeds)	18.10.04
			N3504M				
G-HERC	Cessna 172S Skyhawk	172S8985	N5113P	10.12.01	The Cambridge Aero Club Ltd	Cambridge	15. 1.05T
G-HERD	Lindstrand LBL 77B	707		31. 7.00	S.W.Herd	Mold	5.10.03A
G-HERO*	Piper PA-32RT-300 Lance II	32R-7885086	G-BOGN	26. 4.88	Air Alize Communication	Biarritz, France	9. 7.97
			N33LV/N30573		(Noted 10.00) (Cancelled 10.4.02 by CAA)		
G-HEWI	Piper J-3C-65 Cub (L-4J-PI)	12566	G-BLEN	20. 7.84	R.Preston	Denham	16. 3.03
	(Continental C90) (Frame No.12396)		D-EBEN/HB-OFZ/44-80270		tr Denham Grasshopper Flying Group		
G-HEYY	Cameron Bear 72SS HAB	1244		21. 1.86	Magical Adventures Ltd	West Bloomfield, Mi., USA	30.11.98A
					(Hofmeister Lager Bear) "George"		
G-HFBM	Curtiss Robin C-2	352	LV-FBM	24. 4.90	D.M.Forshaw	High Cross, Ware	20. 8.02P
	(Continental W-670)		NC9279				
G-HFCA	Cessna A150L Aerobat	A1500381	N6081J	30. 8.91	Horizon Flying Club Ltd	Poplar Hall Farm, Elmsett	4.10.04T
	(Texas tail-wheel u/c conversion)						
G-HFCB	Reims/Cessna F150L	F15000798	G-AZVR	10. 2.87	Horizon Flying Club Ltd	Poplar Hall Farm, Elmsett	15. 3.03T
G-HFCI	Reims/Cessna F150L	F15000823	PH-CET	11. 9.80	A.Modi	Earls Colne	14. 2.05T
G-HFCL	Reims/Cessna F152 II	F15201663	G-BGLR	11.10.88	T.H.Hird	Earls Colne	24. 5.03T
G-HFCT	Reims/Cessna F152 II	F15201861		27. 1.81	Stapleford Flying Club Ltd	Stapleford	17. 6.05T
G-HFLA	Schweizer Hughes 269C (300C)	S.1428		8.12.89	Sterling Helicopters Ltd	Norwich	12. 3.05T
G-HFTG	Piper PA-23-250 Aztec E	27-7405378	G-BSOB	30. 4.87	Widehawk Aviation Ltd t/a Hawkair	Blackpool	6. 4.05T
			G-BCJR/N54040		(Ordnance Survey titles)		
G-HGPI	SOCATA TB-20 Trinidad	851		4. 8.88	M.J.Jackson	Bournemouth	23. 1.04
G-HHAA	Hawker Siddfeley Buccaneer S.Mk.2B	B3-01-73	9225M	6.12.02	Hawker Hunter Aviation Ltd	Scampton	
	(C/n officially quoted as B3-R-50-67)		XX885				
G-HHAB	Hawker Hunter F.Mk.58	41H-697439	Swiss AF J-4072	13. 1.03	Hawker Hunter Aviation Ltd	Scampton	
G-HHAC	Hawker Hunter F.Mk.58	41H-691770	G-BWIU	10.12.02	Hawker Hunter Aviation Ltd	Scampton	24. 2.99P
			Swiss AF J-4021		(As "XG232" in RAF c/s)		
G-HHAD	Hawker Hunter F.Mk.58	41H-697425	G-BWFS	10.12.02	Hawker Hunter Aviation Ltd	Scampton	
			Swiss AF J-4058				
G-HHAE	Hawker Hunter F.Mk.58	41H-697433	G-BXNZ	10.12.02	Hawker Hunter Aviation Ltd	Scampton	
	(C/n officially quoted as 41H-28364)		Swiss AF J-4066				
G-HHAF	Hawker Hunter F.Mk.58	41H-697448	G-BWKB	13. 1.03	Hawker Hunter Aviation Ltd	Scampton	
			Swiss AF J-4081				

Reg	Type	C/n	Prev id	Date	Owner/Operator	Base	Expiry
G-HHAV	SOCATA MS.894A Rallye Minerva 220	11620	G-AYDG	9.10.02	R.E.Dagless	Holly Hill Farm, Guist, Norfolk	25. 5.03T
G-HIBM	Cameron N-145 HAB	3197		8. 2.94	P.M.Forster (Op Alba Ballooning)	Edinburgh	15. 2.03T
G-HIEL	Robinson R22 Beta	1120		28. 9.89	R.C.Hields t/a Hields Aviation	Sherburn-in-Elmet	27. 9.03T
G-HIJK	Cessna 421C Golden Eagle III	421C-0218	G-OSAL G-HIJK/OY-BEC/SE-GZI/N5471G	25. 2.00	Oxford Aviation Services Ltd	Oxford	28.11.03T
G-HILO	Rockwell Commander 114	14224	N4894W	6. 2.98	F.H.Parkes	Stapleford	7. 4.04
G-HILS	Cessna F172H (Built Reims Aviation SA)	F172-0522	G-AWCH	20.12.88	B.F.W.Lowdon tr Lowdon Aviation Group	Blackbushe	29. 2.04
G-HILT	SOCATA TB-10 Tobago	298	(G-BMYB) EI-BOF/G-HILT	13. 5.82	Cheshire Aircraft Leasing Ltd	Hawarden	12.11.05T
G-HIND	Maule MT-7-235 Star Rocket	18037C		26. 3.98	R.G.Humphries	Bramshill Farm, Hatchgate	29. 4.04T
G-HINZ	Jabiru Jabiru SK	PFA 274-13441		1. 2.00	B.Faupel	Bourn	1. 8.03P
G-HIPE	Sorrell SNS-7 Hyperbipe (Lycoming IO-360)	209	N18RS	6. 4.93	T.A.S.Rayner	Stapleford	30. 6.01P
G-HIPO	Robinson R22 Beta	1719	G-BTGB	11. 9.92	Patriot Aviation Ltd	Cranfield	19. 5.03T
G-HIRE	Gulfstream GA-7 Cougar	GA7-0091	G-BGSZ N704G	10.12.81	London Aerial Tours Ltd	Rochester	26. 5.03T
G-HISS	Aerotek Pitts S-2A Special (Lycoming AEIO-360)	2137	G-BLVU SE-GTX	17. 3.92	L.V.Adams & J.Maffia "Always Dangerous"	Panshanger	24. 8.02T
G-HITM	Raj Hamsa X'Air Jab22 (Kit No. conflicts with G-BZGN)	445 & BMAA/HB/112		23. 2.00	J.A.C.Cockfield tr G-HITM Flying Group	RNAS Culdrose	16. 1.03P
G-HITS	Piper PA-46-310P Malibu	46-8508063	G-BMBE N6908W	24.10.00	Law 2000 Ltd	(London NW11)	11. 4.04T
G-HIUP	Cameron A-250 HAB	4464		16. 4.99	Bridges Van Hire Ltd	Nottingham	20. 8.03T
G-HIVA	Cessna 337A Super Skymaster	33700429	G-BAES SE-CWW/N5329S	28. 3.88	G.J.Banfield	Gloucestershire	28. 9.03
G-HIVE	Reims/Cessna F150M	F15001186	G-BCXT	19. 4.85	M.P.Lynn	(Fenland)	10. 5.04T
G-HJSM	Schempp-Hirth Nimbus 4DM	22/32	G-ROAM	19. 2.01	R.Jones tr 60 Group "60"	Lasham	29. 4.03
G-HJSS	AIA Stampe SV-4C	1101	G-AZNF F-BGJM/Fr Mil	7. 9.92	H.J.Smith	Shoreham	16. 6.05
G-HKHM	Hughes 369D	711019D	B-HHM VR-HHM/N50605	8. 4.99	Heli Air Ltd	Denham	25. 5.05
G-HLAA	Airbus Industrie A300B	4-203047	EI-TLN G-HLAA/N740SC/F-BVGJ/F-WUAX t/a Heavylift	6.10.97	HC Airlines	Stansted	7. 7.04T
G-HLAB	Airbus Industrie A300B4-203F	045	N743SC F-BVGI/F-WNDA	20. 2.98	Lombard Aviation Capital Ltd	Dublin	26. 2.04T
G-HLAD	Airbus Industrie A300B4-203	131	EI-TLQ 6Y-JMK/G-BIMB/F-WZEL	17. 5.01	Airplanes Finance Ltd	(Shannon, Co.Clare	5. 7.04T
G-HLCF	CFM Starstreak Shadow SA (Rotax 618)	K.256 & PFA 206-12796		10. 5.96	A B Atkinson	(York)	3.11.03P
G-HLFT	Short SC.5 Belfast C.1 (Mod.as Mk.2)	SH.1819	XR365	11. 9.81	Transpacific Pty Ltd	Mascot, Australia	20. 6.05T
G-HMAC	Hughes 369E	0357E	HB-XUO	3. 5.02	Helimac Ltd	Carluke	29. 5.05T
G-HMBJ	Commander Aircraft Commander 114B	14636	N6036F	30. 6.97	Bravo Juliet Aviation Ltd	Guernsey	24. 7.03
G-HMED	Piper PA-28-161 Warrior III	2842020	LX-III	21. 7.97	H.Faizal	Denham	12.12.03T
G-HMES	Piper PA-28-161 Warrior II	28-8216070	OY-CSN N8471N	21. 4.89	Cleveland Flying School Ltd (Op Teesside Aero Club)	Teesside	20. 8.01T
G-HMJB	Piper PA-34-220T Seneca III	34-8133040	N8356R	12. 7.89	Cross Atlantic Ventures Ltd	Blackpool	10.10.04
G-HMMV	Cessna 525 CitationJet	525-0358	N51564	16. 2.00	Gold Air International Ltd	Cambridge	5. 3.03T
G-HMPF	Robinson R44 Astro	0730		8. 3.00	Mightycraft Ltd	White Waltham	20. 3.03T
G-HMPH	Bell 206B JetRanger II	1232	G-BBUY N18090	20. 6.88	Sturmer Ltd	(Tring)	31. 3.05T
G-HMPT	Agusta-Bell 206B JetRanger II	8168	D-HARO	7.11.91	Helicopter Express Ltd	Dublin	3. 5.04T
G-HMSS	Bell 206B Jet Ranger II	1010	ZS-HMS C-GXOI/N58008	7. 5.02	Headshore Ltd	(Guildford)	
G-HNRY	Cessna 650 Citation VI	650-0219	N219CC N6829Z	23.10.92	Xjet Ltd	Farnborough	12. 1.03T
G-HOBO	Denney Kitfox Model 4 (Rotax 582)	PFA 172A-12140		10. 9.92	E M Woods "Navy Baby"	Lydney-St Briavals	29.10.03P
G-HOCK	Piper PA-28-180 Cherokee D	28-4395	G-AVSH N11C	15. 5.86	J.I.Simper tr G-HOCK Flying Group	Goodwood	12. 8.04T
G-HOFC	Europa Aviation Europa (Rotax 912UL) (Monowheel u/c)	119 & PFA 247-12736		25. 9.95	W.R.Mills (F/f 21.5.96) (Resides in personal trailer)	Upfield Farm, Whitson	7. 6.03P
G-HOFM	Cameron N-56 HAB	1245		21. 1.86	Magical Adventures Ltd (Op Balloon Preservation Group)	Kirdford	30.11.98A
G-HOGS	Cameron Pig 90SS HAB	4121		7. 4.97	Magical Adventures Ltd "Britannia Piggy Bank"	West Bloomfield, Mi., USA	1. 7.99A
G-HOHO	Colt Santa Claus SS HAB	1671		21.12.89	Oxford Promotions (UK) Ltd	Kentucky, USA	3. 4.03A
G-HOLY	SOCATA ST-10 Diplomate	108	F-BSCZ	31. 1.90	M.K.Barsham	Booker	26. 9.05
G-HOME	Colt 77A HAB	032		26. 2.79	Anglia Balloon School Ltd (On loan to British Balloon Museum & Library) "Tardis"	Newbury	27. 5.86A
G-HONG	Slingsby T.67M-200 Firefly	2060	VR-HZR HKG-12/G-7-128	24. 3.94	Babcock Support Services Ltd t/a Babcock HCS	AAC Middle Wallop	18.10.03T
G-HONI	Robinson R22 Beta	0871	G-SEGO N9081N	27. 1.00	Patriot Aviation Ltd	Cranfield	14.12.03T
G-HONK	Cameron O-105 HAB	1813		30. 9.88	T.F.W.Dixon & Son Ltd "Dixons"	Bromsgrove	14.9.971A
G-HONY	Lilliput Type 1 Srs.A MLB	L-01		31. 7.89	A.E. & D.E.Thomas	Honiton	
G-HOOD	SOCATA TB-20 Trinidad GT	2008	F-OILJ	25. 7.00	M.J.Hoodless	Blackbushe	31. 7.03
G-HOOT	Aérospatiale AS.355F2 Twin Squirrel	5346	G-SCOW ZS-HSW/G-POON/G-MCAL	27.11.02	Squirrel Helicopter Hire Ltd	(Weybridge)	14 .9.02T
G-HOOV	Cameron N-56 HAB	388		2. 3.78	Heather R.Evans "Hoover"	Ross-on-Wye	26. 5.89A
G-HOPE	Beech F33A Bonanza	CE-805	N2024Z	27. 2.79	Hurn Aviation Ltd	Bournemouth	2. 4.04
G-HOPI	Cameron N-42 HAB	2724		5.12.91	Ballonverbung Hamburg GmbH	Kiel, Germany	19. 7.02A
G-HOPS	Thunder Ax8-90 Srs.1 HAB	1220		11. 3.88	A.C. & B.Munn	Hastings	2. 9.01T
G-HOPY	Van's RV-6A (Lycoming O-320-B2B)	PFA 181-12742		4.12.95	R.C.Hopkinson	Booker	3. 4.03P

G-HORN	Cameron V-77 HAB	570		29.11.79	S.Herd	Mold	11.12.98A
G-HOST*	Cameron N-77 HAB	434		4. 9.78	D.Grimshaw *"Suzanna"*	Preston	18. 5.93A
	(Cancelled 13.11.01 as WFU) (Stored)						
G-HOTI	Colt 77A HAB	750		13. 7.87	R.Ollier *"Horace Hot One"*	Northwich, Cheshire	30. 9.90A
G-HOTT	Cameron O-120 HAB	2581		30. 4.91	D.L.Smith *"Floating Sensations"*	Newbury	17. 5.97T
G-HOTZ	Colt 77B HAB	2218		16. 6.92	C.J. & S.M.Davies	Castleton, Sheffield	18.10.03A
G-HOUS	Colt 31A Air Chair HAB	099		7.10.80	Anglia Balloon School Ltd t/a Anglia Balloons	Newbury	3. 5.90A
	(On loan to British Balloon Museum & Library) (Barratts titles) "K9"						
G-HOWE	Thunder Ax7-77 HAB	1340		10. 4.89	M.F.Howe *"Howie/Howzat"*	Linley Hill, Leven	15. 8.95A
G-HOWL	Rotary Air Force RAF 2000 GTX-SE	H2-95-6-164	N4994U	2. 7.01	C.J.Watkinson	Charity Farm, Baxterley	22. 7.02P
G-HPAD	Bell 206B JetRanger III	1997	G-CITZ	2. 9.02	Helipad Ltd	Nottingham	29. 7.05T
			G-BRTB/N9936K				
G-HPOL	MD Helicopters MD.900	900-00082	N70082	24. 1.01	Humberside Police Authority	Leconfield	3. 9.04T
G-HPSB	Commander Aircraft Commander 114B	14678	N6118R	24.10.01	Guernsey Enterprises Ltd	Guernsey	23.10.04T
G-HPSE	Commander Aircraft Commander 114B	14638	N6038V	26. 8.97	Al Nisr Ltd	Guernsey	16. 9.03A
G-HPUX	Hawker Hunter T.Mk.7	41H-693455	8807M	12. 3.99	Hawker Hunter Aviation Ltd	Duxford	
			XL587		(Partially rebuilt & stored 12.00) (New CofR12.02)		
G-HRHE	Robinson R22 Beta	1950	G-BTWP	24. 1.97	R.Whitear	(Hook)	18.12.03T
G-HRHI	Beagle B.206 Basset Srs.1	B.014	XS770	6. 7.89	Lawgra (No.386) Ltd t/a International Aerospace Engineering		
					(As "XS770" in Queens Flight c/s)	Cranfield	17.10.03
G-HRHS	Robinson R.44 Astro	0323		15. 4.97	Stratus Aviation Ltd	Redhill	16. 4.03
G-HRIO	Robin HR100/210 Safari	149	F-BTZR	22. 1.87	T.W.Evans	Southampton	17.12.04
G-HRLI	Hawker Hurricane	141H-136172	V7497	25. 4.02	Hawker Restorations Ltd	Milden	
G-HRLK	SAAB 91D/2 Safir	91376	G-BRZY	6. 3.90	Sylmar Aviation & Services Ltd		
			PH-RLK			Lower Wasing Farm, Brimpton	12. 5.04
G-HRLM	Brugger MB.2 Colibri	PFA 43-10118		28.12.78	M.W.Bodger	Yeatsall Farm, Abbots Bromley	21. 1.03P
	(Volkswagen 1834)				*"Titch"*		
G-HRNT	Cessna 182S Skylane	18280395	N2369H	29. 1.99	Dingle Star Ltd	Denham	6. 3.05
G-HROI	Rockwell Commander 112A	326	N1326J	19. 6.89	Intereuropean Aviation Ltd	Jersey	28. 4.04
G-HRON*	de Havilland DH.114 Heron 2B	14102	XR442	4. 4.91	M.E.R.Coghlan	Gloucestershire	
			G-AORH		(Cancelled 10.4.02 by CAA) (Stored unmarked 9.02)		
G-HRPN	Robinson R44 Raven II	10007		26.11.02	Harpin Ltd	(York)	AC
G-HRVD	CCF Harvard 4	CCF4-548	G-BSBC	8.12.92	K.F.Mason & D.Featherby t/a Anglia Flight	Norwich	
	(T-6J-CCF Texan)		Moz PLAF 1741/FAP 1741/BF+055/AA+055/53-4629 (On rebuild 1999: new owners 10.01)				
	(Possibly a composite with rear fuselage of Moz PLAF/FAP 1780/AA+614/53-4622)						
G-HRZN	Colt 77A HAB	536		14.12.83	A.J.Spindler *"Tequila Sunrise"*	Cleish	4. 5.88A
G-HSDW	Bell 206B JetRanger II	1789	ZS-HFC	16.12.85	Winfield Shoe Co Ltd & Stott Demolition Ltd	Rossendale	2. 2.05
G-HSLA	Robinson R22 Beta	1130	G-BRTI	22.11.01	Helicopter Support Ltd	(Ashleworth, Glos)	16. 4.03T
			EI-CDW/(EI-CFJ)/G-BRTI/N8044U				
G-HSLB	Agusta Bell 206B JetRanger II	8690	F-GUJR	4. 4.02	B3 Aviation Services Ltd	(Laxey, Isle of Man)	29. 5.05T
			SX-HEN/F-GRCY/I-ELEP				
G-HSOO	Hughes 369HE	109-0208E	G-BFYJ	3.11.93	Edwards Aviation Ltd	(Wilmslow)	27. 9.03T
			F-BRSY				
G-HTEL	Robinson R44 Raven	1155	N70319	25. 1.02	Forestdale Hotels Ltd	Burley, Ringwood	7. 2.05T
G-HTRL	Piper PA-34-220T Seneca III	34-8333061	G-BXXY	8. 2.00	Air Medical Ltd	Oxford	18. 2.04T
			PH-TLN/N4295X				
G-HUBB	Partenavia P68B Victor	194	OY-BJH	27. 5.83	G-HUBB Ltd	Denham	29. 7.04
			SE-GXL				
G-HUCH	Cameron Carrots 80SS HAB	2258	G-BYPS	13. 3.91	Magical Adventures Ltd	West Bloomfield, Mi., USA	2. 8.01A
					"Magic Carrots"		
G-HUEY	Bell UH-1H-BF Iroquois	13560	AE-413	23. 7.85	Argonauts Holdings Ltd	Bournemouth	12. 4.00P
			(Argentine Army)/73-22077		(Noted 12.02)		
G-HUFF	Cessna 182P Skylane II	18264076	PH-CAS	31.10.78	A.E.G.Cousins	Southend	31. 5.03T
	(Reims-assembled with c/n F18200033)		N6059F		(Op Seawing Flying Club)		
G-HUGG	Learjet Learjet 35A	35A-432	VR-CAD	9. 4.96	Northern Executive Aviation Ltd	Manchester	11. 4.03T
			N330BC/N4445Y/F-GDCN				
G-HUGO	Colt 260A HAB	2559		20. 1.94	P.G.Hall t/a Adventure Ballooning	Chard	7. 5.03T
G-HUGS	Robinson R22 Beta	1455	G-BYHD	27. 2.02	C.G.P.Holden	Gamston	19. 3.05T
			N900AB				
G-HUKA	MD Helicopters Hughes 369E (500E)	0298E	G-OSOO	12. 2.02	B.P.Stein	(London WC2)	16. 7.04T
G-HULL	Reims/Cessna F150M	F15001255	PH-TGR	19. 1.79	A.D.McLeod	Linley Hill, Leven	13. 9.04T
G-HUMF	Robinson R22 Beta	0534	N23743	18. 2.86	Plane Talking Ltd	Redhill	24. 1.05T
					(Op London Helicopter Centre)		
G-HUNI	Bellanca 7GCBC Scout	541-73	OO-IME	21.10.96	T.I.M.Paul	Denham	9. 7.04T
	(Officially regd as "Scout" although 7GCBC = Citabria)		D-EIME				
G-HUNK	Lindstrand LBL 77A HAB	551		9. 9.98	Lindstrand Balloons Ltd	Oswestry	23. 9.00A
G-HUPW	Hawker Hurricane 1	G5-92301	R4118	21. 8.01	P.J. & P.M.A.Vacher	(Abingdon)	
	(Built Gloster Aircraft Co.Ltd)				t/a Minmere Farm Partnership		
G-HURI	Hawker Hurricane XIIA (IIB)	72036	RCAF 5711	9. 6.83	Historic Aircraft Collection Ltd	Duxford	11. 7.03P
	(Built Canadian & Car Foundry Co)				(Op The Fighter Collection) (As "Z7381/XR-T" in 71 Sqdn RAF c/s)		
	(Composite - probably includes parts from c/n 44019/RCAF 5424, RCAF 5625 and RCAF 5547)						
G-HURN	Robinson R22 Beta	1441		18. 7.90	The Flightworks Group Ltd	Booker	3.12.03T
G-HURR	Hawker Hurricane XII (IIB)	52024	RCAF 5589	30. 7.90	R.A.Fleming	Breighton	18. 4.03P
	(Built Canadian & Car Foundry Co)				(As "BE417/AL-X")		
G-HURY	Hawker Hurricane IV	-	(Israel)	31. 3.89	Patina Ltd	Duxford	AC
	(RAF p/i unlikely as KZ321 was written off 23.5.43)		Yugoslav AF/KZ321		(Op The Fighter Collection) (As "KZ321":on rebuild 10.02)		
G-HUSK	Aviat A-18 Husky	2214		2. 1.03	Aviat Aircraft (UK) Ltd	(Telford)	
G-HUTT	Denney Kitfox Model 2	509 & PFA 172-11634		24. 1.90	P.C.E.Roberts	Truro	23. 2.03P
	(Rotax 582)						
G-HVAN	Tiger Cub RL5A LW Sherwood Ranger			10.12.98	H.T.H.Van Neck	(Wirral)	
		PFA 237-13074					
G-HVBF	Lindstrand LBL-210A HAB	372		23. 5.96	Airxcite Ltd t/a Virgin Balloon Flights	Wembley	29. 5.03T
G-HVIP	Hawker Hunter T.68	HABL-003215	J-4208	7. 7.95	Golden Europe Jet De Luxe Club Ltd	Bournemouth	16. 5.02P
			G-9-415/Fv.34080/G-9-56		(Op Dr.Karl Theurer)		

Reg	Type	c/n
G-HVRD	Piper PA-31-350 Navajo Chieftain	31-7305052
G-HXTD	Robin DR400/180	2510
G-HYAK	IAV-Bacau Yakovlev Yak-52	9011107
G-HYLT	Piper PA-32R-301 Saratoga SP	32R-8213001
G-HYST	Enstrom 280FX Shark	2082

G-IAAA - G-IZZZ

Reg	Type	c/n
G-IAFT	Cessna 152 II	15285123
G-IAGD	Robinson R22 Beta	0918
G-IANB	DG Flugzeugbau DG-800B	8-246B159
G-IANG	Bell 206L LongRanger	45132
G-IANH	SOCATA TB-10 Tobago	1843
G-IANI	Europa Aviation Europa XS T-G (Rotax 914)	505 & PFA 247-13714
G-IANJ	Reims/Cessna F150K	F15000548
G-IANW	Eurocopter AS350B3 Ecureuil	3447
G-IARC	Stoddard-Hamilton GlaStar	PFA 295-13261
G-IASL	Beech 60 Duke	P-21
G-IATU	Cessna 182P Skylane	18261436
G-IBBC	Cameron Sphere 105SS HAB	4082
G-IBBO	Piper PA-28-181 Cherokee Archer II	28-7790107
G-IBBS	Europa Aviation Europa (Rotax 912-UL) (Monowheel u/c)	118 & PFA 247-12745
G-IBED	Robinson R22 Alpha	0500
G-IBET	Cameron Can 70SS HAB	1625
G-IBFC	BFC Quad City Challenger II	CH2-0898-UK-1774 & PFA 177B-13369
G-IBFW	Piper PA-28R-201 Arrow III	28R-7837235
G-IBHH	Hughes 269C	74-0327
G-IBIG	Bell 206B JetRanger III	2202
G-IBLU	Cameron Z-90 HAB	4913
G-IBRI	Eurocopter EC120B	1073
G-IBRO	Reims/Cessna F152 II	F15201957
G-IBSF	Dassault Falcon 2000	151
G-IBZS	Cessna 182S Skylane	18280529
G-ICAB	Robinson R44 Astro	0086
G-ICAS	Aviat Pitts S-2B Special	5344
G-ICBM	Stoddard-Hamilton Glasair III Turbine (Allison 250-B17B)	3337
G-ICCL	Robinson R22 Beta	1608
G-ICES	Thunder Ax6-56 SP.1 HAB (Ice Cream special shape)	283
G-ICEY	Lindstrand LBL-77A HAB	043
G-ICKY	Lindstrand LBL-77A HAB	029
G-ICOI	Lindstrand LBL 105A HAB	564
G-ICOM	Reims/Cessna F172M Skyhawk II	F17201212
G-ICON	Rutan Long-EZ	PFA 74A-11104
G-ICRS	Comco Ikarus C42 FB UK (Rotax 912ULS)	PFA 322-13873
G-ICSG	Aérospatiale AS355F1 Twin Squirrel	5104
G-ICWT	Pegasus Quantum 15-912	7632
G-IDAY	Skyfox CA-25N Gazelle (Rotax 912)	CA25N-028
G-IDDI	Cameron N-77 HAB	2383
G-IDII	Dan Rihn DR.107 One Design (Lycoming O-360)	PFA 264 12953
G-IDSL	Flight Design CT2K *(Pegasus Aviation c/n)*	7922
G-IDUP	Enstrom 280C Shark	1163
G-IDWR	Hughes 369HS	69-0101S
G-IEIO	Piper PA-34-200T Seneca II	34-7670274
G-IEJH	SAN Jodel 150A Mascaret	02

Prev ident	Date	Owner	Base	Expiry
G-BEZU SE-GDP/N74920/N9666N	11. 6.87	N.Singh	Glasgow	7.12.03T
	24.10.01	Hayley Aviation Ltd	(Banstead)	12.12.04T
LY-ALU DOSAAF 124	27. 8.02	Goodridge (UK) Ltd	Exeter	27. 8.03P
N84588	23. 4.86	G.R.Balls	(South Croydon)	31. 1.05
	9. 7.98	Patten Helicopter Services Ltd	Barton	8.10.04
EI-BVW N6093Q	20. 6.95	Marham Investments Ltd *(Op Woodgate Executive Air Services)*	Newtownards, Co.Down	14. 8.04T
N2018Y G-DRAI/N8808V	16.11.99	M.Kenyon & A.Ingham t/a A & M Engineering	Blackpool	28.11.02T
	12. 3.02	I.S.Bullous	(Newcastle upon Tyne)	25. 9.05
SE-HSV PH-HMH/N16845	22. 1.98	Lothian Helicopters Ltd	(Pathhead, Oxenfoord Castle)	15. 2.04T
F-OILI	13. 3.00	XD Flight Management Ltd	(Horsham)	26. 3.03T
	20. 4.01	I.F.Rickard & I.A.Watson	(Woking)	
G-AXVW	19. 5.98	J.A.,G.M.,D.T.A. & J.A.Rees t/a Messrs Rees of Poyston West	Haverfordwest	19. 8.04T
F-WQPU	18. 9.01	Cairnsilver Ltd	(London SW1)	20. 1.05T
	9.11.99	A.A.Craig	Prestwick	9. 7.03P
G-SING D-IDTA/SE-EXT	18. 4.97	Applied Sweepers Ltd	Perth	13. 4.04
G-BIRS G-BBBS/N21131	8. 1.03	Auto Corporation Ltd	Liverpool	19. 4.04T
	2. 4.97	R.S.Kent tr Balloon Preservation Group	Lancing	17. 7.03A
D-EPCA N5389F	17.12.98	M.Gibbon	Panshanger	31. 1.05
	8. 9.94	R.H.Gibbs *(F/f 6.3.97)*	Popham	14. 4.03P
G-BMHN	7. 9.93	B.C.Seedle t/a Brian Seedle Helicopters *(New owner 7.02)*	Blackpool	30. 9.94
	25. 1.88	M.R.Humphrey & J.R.Clifton *"Carling Black Label"*	Brackley	25. 8.02A
	9.11.98	K.N.Dickinson	(Lytham St. Annes)	
N31534	22. 1.79	A.W.Collett	Wolverhampton	25. 8.03T
G-BSCD PH-HSH/SE-HFG	20. 8.99	The Hughes Helicopter Co Ltd t/a Biggin Hill Helicopters	Biggin Hill	11. 7.03T
G-BORV C-GVTY/N16763	20. 3.02	Big Heli-Charter Ltd	Manston	5. 5.05T
	4. 8.00	Blu SpA	Rome, Italy	11. 7.03A
LX-HCR	7. 2.02	Colibri Aviation Ltd	Kintore	19. 3.05T
EI-BRO	11.10.95	Leicestershire Aero Club Ltd	Leicester	14. 3.05T
F-WWVI	1.10.01	Marconda Services Ltd	Luton	19.11.05T
N7269A	11.12.99	Patrick Eddery Ltd	Oxford	9.12.05
	28.11.94	JR Clark Ltd	Culverthorpe, Grantham	25. 1.04
N511P	19. 6.97	J.C.Smith	Sherburn-in-Elmet	10. 7.03T
	18.12.00	G V Waters & D N Brown	Attleborough	AC
G-ORZZ	25.11.93	JK Aviation Services Ltd	Headcorn	20. 2.03T
	3. 7.80	British Balloon Museum & Library Ltd *"Ashfords"*	Newbury	3. 6.94A
	11. 8.93	G.C.Elson t/a Lindstrand Balloon School	Ronda, Spain	6. 6.03A
	19. 5.93	M.J.Green	Shrewsbury	15.11.02T
(D-O) G-ICOI	3.11.98	F.Schroeder	Mulheim Ruhr, Germany	20. 3.03A
G-BFXI PH-ABA/D-EEVC	25. 4.94	C G Elesmore	Manston	23. 6.03T
	29.11.00	S.J.& M.A.Carradice	(Sheffield)	
	11. 3.02	Ikarus Flying Group Ltd	(Aylesbury)	1. 8.03P
G-PAMI G-BUSA	6. 4.93	M W Helicopters Ltd	Stapleford	7. 2.05T
	7. 4.00	C.W.Taylor	Mill Farm, Shifnal	7. 4.03P
VH-RCR	29. 4.96	The Anglo-Pacific Aircraft Co (UK) Ltd & G.Horne	Perth	20. 6.03T
	21. 8.90	PSH Skypower Ltd *(Allen & Harris - Royal Sun Alliance titles)*	Pewsey	11. 9.03P
	16. 6.99	C.Darlow	Jericho Farm, Lambley	11. 9.02P
	28.10.02	D.S.Luke	Kemble	27.10.03P
G-BRZF N5687D	11. 5.92	Antique Buildings Ltd	Hunterswood Farm, Dunsford	7. 6.04
G-AXEJ	26. 5.81	M.A.& M.Gradwell	Barton	16.12.04
EI-EIO N6257J	6.12.02	Jade Air plc	Shoreham	AC
G-BPAM F-BLDA/F-WLDA	28. 2.95	A.Turner & D.Worth	Crowfield	18. 4.02P

Reg	Type	C/n	Prev id	Date	Owner/Operator	Location	Date
G-IEYE	Robin DR400/180 Regent	2123		29. 1.92	E.Hopper	Sherburn-in-Elmet	28. 6.04
G-IFAB	Reims/Cessna F182Q Skylane	F18200127	N61AN	6. 1.98	Tindon Ltd	Little Snoring	25.5.01
			G-IFAB/OO-ELM/(OO-HNU)				
G-IFDM	Robinson R44 Astro	0707		24. 1.00	Intex Computers Ltd	Sherburn-in-Elmet	3. 2.03T
G-IFFR	Piper PA-32-300 Cherokee Six	32-7340123	G-BWVO	1. 4.97	D.J.D & G.D.Ritchie & J.C.Gilbert	RAF Henlow	20. 3.03
			OO-JPC/N55520				
G-IFIT	Piper PA-31-350 Chieftain	31-8052078	G-NABI	31.12.85	Dart Group plc	Bournemouth	4.11.05T
			G-MARG/N3580C		(Op Channel Express)		
G-IFLI	Gulfstream AA-5A Cheetah	AA5A-0831	N26948	7. 7.82	I-Fly Ltd	(Cottingham)	20.10.03T
G-IFLP	Piper PA-34-200T Seneca II	34-8070029	N81WS	4. 1.88	Tayflite Ltd	Perth	25. 6.03T
			N81149				
G-IFTE	British Aerospace HS.125 Srs.700B	257037	G-BFVI	16. 5.96	Albion Aviation Management Ltd	Gatwick	17. 8.03T
			G-5-18				
G-IFTS	Robinson R44 Astro	0366		16. 9.97	Context GB Ltd t/a Aviation In Context	Blackpool	24. 9.03T
G-IGGL	SOCATA TB-10 Tobago	146	G-BYDC	26. 3.99	M.P.Perkin tr G-IGGL Flying Group	White Waltham	3. 1.05T
			F-GCOL				
G-IGHH	Enstrom 480	5034		1.12.98	G.H.Harding	(Whitchurch)	16. 1.05T
G-IGIE	SIAI Marchetti F.260	2-42	D-EHGB	13. 3.02	D.Fletcher & J.J.Watts	(Fordingbridge)	AC
G-IGII	Europa Aviation Europa	011 & PFA 247-12506		9. 4.02	W.C.Walters	Kemble	
	(NSI Subaru) (Conventional u/c)				(Noted 11.02)		
G-IGLA	Colt 240A HAB	2228		3. 7.92	M.L. & S.M.Gabb	Alcester	29. 8.03T
					t/a Heart of England Balloons (Barclaycard titles)		
G-IGLE	Cameron V-90 HAB	2609		11. 6.91	A.A.Laing "Giggle"	Aberdeen	19. 8.01A
G-IGLZ	Champion 8KCAB Super Decathlon	914-2003		18. 2.03	Blue Yonder Aviation Ltd	(Wickford)	
G-IGOA	Boeing 737-3YO	24678	EI-BZK	16. 7.98	Orix Aviation Systems	Stansted	19. 7.04T
					(Op Go Fly Ltd) "Go again/Let's Go" (Turquoise c/s)		
G-IGOB	Boeing 737-36Q	28660	EC-GNU	17.12.01	Go Fly Ltd (Easyjet titles)	Stansted	24.1.05T
G-IGOC	Boeing 737-3Y0	24546	EI-BZH	1. 5.98	Orix Aviation Systems	Stansted	7. 5.04T
					(Op Go Fly Ltd) "Go today/Just Go" (Purple c/s)		
G-IGOE	Boeing 737-3Y0	24547	EI-BZI	19. 5.98	Orix Aviation Systems	Stansted	20. 5.04T
					(Op Go Fly Ltd) "Go together/Ready to Go" (Pink c/s)		
G-IGOF	Boeing 737-3Q8	24698	PK-GWF	2. 4.98	Go Fly Ltd	Stansted	3 .6.04T
					"Go now/All Go" (Aqua Green c/s)		
G-IGOG	Boeing 737-3Y0	23927	F-GLLE	3. 9.98	Go Fly Ltd (Easyjet titles)	Stansted	3. 9.04T
			PT-TEK				
G-IGOH	Boeing 737-3Y0	23926	F-GLLD	6.11.98	Go Fly Ltd (Easyjet titles)	Stansted	12.12.04T
			PT-TEJ				
G-IGOI	Boeing 737-33A	24092	G-OBMD	30.12.98	Go Fly Ltd (Easyjet titles)	Stansted	13. 2.05T
G-IGOJ	Boeing 737-36N	28872	N1795B	11.11.98	Go Fly Ltd (Easyjet titles)	Stansted	20.11.04T
G-IGOK	Boeing 737-36N	28594		24. 4.99	Go Fly Ltd	Bristol	23. 4.05T
					"Go as you are/Get set Go" (Purple Blue c/s)		
G-IGOL	Boeing 737-36N	28596	N1015X	26. 6.99	Go Fly Ltd	Stansted	25.6.05T
					"Go exploring/Love to Go" (Terracota c/s)		
G-IGOM	Boeing 737-36N	28599		13. 7.99	Go Fly Ltd	Stansted	12. 7.05T
					"Go for a break/Off we Go" (Purple c/s)		
G-IGOO	Boeing 737-36N	28557	G-SMDB	15. 3.02	Go Fly Ltd (Easyjet titles)	Stansted	20. 3.03T
G-IGOP	Boeing 737-36N	28602		12. 8.99	Go Fly Ltd	Bristol	11. 8.05T
					"Go ahead/Away we Go" (Pink c/s)		
G-IGOR	Boeing 737-36N	28606		22.10.99	Go Fly Ltd	Stansted	20.10.05T
					"Go to work/Off you Go" (Turquoise c/s)		
G-IGOS	Boeing 737-3L9	27336	D-ADBH	21. 2 01	Go Fly Ltd (Easyjet titles)	Stansted	9. 3.04T
			OY-MAO				
G-IGOT	Boeing 737-3L9	24571	N2393W	12. 7.01	Go Fly Ltd	Stansted	11. 7.04T
			TC-IAE/D-ADBF/OY-MMF		"Go celebrate/Here we Go" (Terracota c/s)		
G-IGOU	Boeing 737-3L9	27337	D-ADBI	9. 5.01	Go Fly Ltd (Easyjet titles)	Stansted	14. 5.04T
			OY-MAP				
G-IGOV	Boeing 737-3M8	25017	N250GE	13. 9.01	Go Fly Ltd	Stansted	13. 9.04T
			LZ-BOF/N250GE/9V-TRD/N760BE/N35030/(OO-LTH)		"Go discover/Got to Go" (Purple c/s)		
G-IGOW	Boeing 737-3YO	23923	N923AP	24. 8.01	Go Fly Ltd	Stansted	23. 8.04T
			(G-OBWW)/N923AP/LZ-BOE/EC-FJZ/EC-898/EI-BZP/EI-CEE/G-TEAB/(N117AW)/EI-BZP/(LN-AEQ)/EI-BZP/EC-EIA/EC-152				
					"Go escape/Hasta lue Go" (Yellow c/s)		
G-IGOX	Boeing 737-3L9	24219	N219TY	21. 3.02	Go Fly Ltd	Stansted	20.3.05T
			PH-TSW/OY-MMO/G-BOZB/OY-MMO/N1786B "Go Euro/Atte lo Go" (White c/s)				
G-IGOY	Boeing 737-36N	28570	CS-TGQ	21.03.02	Go Fly Ltd (Easyjet titles)	Stansted	10.4.05T
G-IGOZ	Boeing 737-3Q8	24692	G-OBWZ	13.03.02	Go Fly Ltd (Easyjet titles)	Stansted	27. 3.03T
			N699PU/PK-GWG				
G-IGPW	Eurocopter EC120B	1027	G-CBRI	31. 7 99	J.Havakin	(Darlington)	30. 5.05T
G-IHSB	Robinson R22 Beta	0982		16. 3.89	P.Masters	(Highbridge)	6. 2.04T
G-IIAC	Aeronca 11AC Chief	11AC-169	(G-BTPY)	2. 7.91	G.R.Moore	Black Spring Farm, Castle Bytham)	4. 3.02P
	(Continental A65)		N86359/NC86359				
G-IIAN	Aero Designs Pulsar	PFA 202-12123		10. 9.91	I.G.Harrison	(Ripley, Derbyshire)	
					(Under construction 2000)		
G-IICI	Aviat Pitts S-2C	6017	N113PS	20. 5.02	D.G.Cowden	Redhill	15. 7.05
G-IICM	Extra EA.300/L (Lycoming AEIO-540)	100		19.11.99	Phonetiques Ltd "Charlie Macaw II"	Denham	27.11.05T
G-IIDI	Extra EA.300/L (Tail-wheel u/c)	047	G-XTRS	5.10.01	Power Aerobatics Ltd	Old Sarum	13. 3.05T
	(Lycoming AEIO-540)		D-EXJH		(Op Extreme Team)		
G-IIDY	Aerotek Pitts S-2B Special	5000	G-BPVP	11.11.02	R.P.Millinship tr The S-2B Group	Leicester	17. 5.95
			N5302M		(Damaged Clacton 19.6.92: on rebuild 5.93)		
G-IIFR	Robinson R22 Beta-II	2841		2. 9.98	R C Hields t/a Hields Aviation	Sherburn-in-Elmet	22.11.04T
G-IIID	Dan Rihn DR.107 One Design	PFA 264-12766		6. 7.00	D.A.Kean	(Cheltenham))	
G-IIIG	Boeing-Stearman A75N1 (PT-17) Kaydet	75-4354	G-BSDR	25. 3.91	F.& S.Vormezeele "Annie"	(Brasschaat, Belgium)	11. 6.03T
	(Continental W670)		N61827/42-16191				
G-IIII	Pitts S-2B Special	5010	N5330G	6. 1.89	R.J.Allan, A.J.Maxwell & N.Jones	Barton	5. 7.04T
	(Lycoming AEIO-540)						

Reg	Type	Serial	Prev id		Owner	Base	
G-IIIL	Pitts S-1T Special (Lycoming AEIO-360)	008	OH-XPT G-IIIL/N15JE	15. 2.89	The Sywell Boys Toy Box Ltd	Sywell	2. 9.03P
G-IIIR	Pitts S-1S Special (Lycoming IO-360)	604	N27M	21. 1.93	R.O.Rogers	Hulcote Farm, Salford, Bucks	20.12 01P
G-IIIT	Aerotek Pitts S-2A Special (Lycoming AEIO-360)	2222	N7YT	16. 1.89	Aerobatic Displays Ltd	Booker	9. 8.01A
G-IIIV	Pitts Super Stinker 11-260	PFA 273-13005		4. 2.97	G G Ferriman	Jericho Farm, Lambley	
G-IIIX	Pitts S-1S Special (Lycoming O-360)	AJT	G-LBAT G-UCCI/G-BIYN/N455T	22. 5.89	Jenks Air Ltd	RAF Halton	12. 3.03P
G-IILI	Extra EA.300/L	140	D-EXLB	23. 4.01	Firebird Aerobatics Ltd (Microlease titles)	Denham	3. 5.04T
G-IIMI	Extra EA.300/L	141	D-EXLE	2. 5.01	Firebird Aerobatics Ltd (Microlease titles)	Denham	17 .5.04T
G-IIPM	Aérospatiale AS350B Ecureuil	1790	G-GWIL	18.12.96	Kis Associates Ltd	(Bristol)	28.11.05T
G-IIPT	Robinson R22 Beta	2506	G-FUSI N83306	10. 5.01	P.R.Thorne	Aston Clinton	16. 5.04
G-IIRG	Stoddard-Hamilton Glasair IIS RG (Lycoming IO-360)	PFA 149-11937		29. 6.93	A.C.Lang	(Ottery St.Mary)	10.6.03P
G-IISI	Extra EA.300/200	014	D-EXWE	5. 7.01	I.A.Scott	(Vaxholm, Sweden)	15. 7.04T
G-IITI	Extra EA.300 (Lycoming O-360)	018	D-EFRR	12. 5.92	Aerobatic Displays Ltd (International Watch Company titles)	Booker	24.6.05A
G-IIXX	Montgomerie-Parsons Two Place (Rotax 912)	PFA G/08-1225		13.10.93	J.M.Montgomerie (Noted 2.98 unmarked: current status unknown)	(Crosshill)	
G-IIYK	Yakovlev Yak-50	842706	LY-AFZ DOSAAF 24	15.10.02	D.A.Hammant Bere Farn, Warnford, Southampton		22.10.03P
G-IIZI	Extra EA.300	037	JY-RNB D-ETXA	12.12.96	S.G.Jones, G.Archer & Power Aerobatics Ltd Old Sarum (Op Extreme Team)		11. 2.04T
G-IJAC	Avid Speed Wing Mk.4	PFA 189-12095		31.12.92	I.J.A.Charlton	(Petworth)	
G-IJBB	Enstrom 480	5010		17. 9.99	J.B.Booth	Barton	6.11.04
G-IJMC	VPM M-16 Tandem Trainer (Arrow GT1000R)	VPM16-UK-106	G-LIVA N900SA/G-PBTT/JA6169	10. 6.98	I.J.McTear	Carlisle	3. 6.02P
G-IJOE	Piper PA-28RT-201T Turbo Arrow IV	28R-8031178	G-POSA G-BVJM	14. 8.90	P.Randall	Sturgate	22. 7.05
G-IJYS	British Aerospace Jetstream Srs.3102	715	G-BTZT N416MX/G-31-715	5.10.92	Air Kilroe Ltd (Op Eastern Airways) "Flying Scotsman"	Humberside	18.11.03T
G-IKAP	Cessna T303 Crusader	T30300182	N63SA D-IKAP/N9518C	4. 3.99	T.M.Beresford	Cambridge	29. 4.05T
G-IKBP	Piper PA-28-161 Warrior II	28-8216132	N81762	16. 7.90	K.B.Page	Shoreham	24.10.05
G-IKIS	Cessna 210M Centurion II (Reims-assembled c/n F2100002)	21061754	N732TD	15. 5.78	R & H Trust Co Ltd tr Chapple Investment Trust	(Jersey)	25.12.04
G-IKRK	Europa Aviation Europa 220 & PFA 247-12903 (Rotax 912S) (Monowheel u/c)			16. 4.02	K.R.Kesterton	(Dunmow)	
G-IKRS	Comco Ikarus C42	PFA 322-13719		1. 8.01	P.G. Walton	Morgansfield, Fishburn	19.2.03P
G-ILDA	Supermarine 361 Spitfire HF.IX	CBAF.10164	G-BXHZ SAAF???/SM520	11. 7.02	P.W.Portelli (On rebuild in Oxfordshire 6.97: current status unknown)	(London SW10)	
G-ILEA	Piper PA-31 Navajo C	31-7812117	(8P-) G-ILEA/D-ILEA/N27775	7. 7.97	I.G.Fletcher	(London SW1)	7. 8.03
G-ILEE	Colt 56A Duo Chariot HAB	2624		29. 7.94	G.I.Lindsay "Gillie"	Pulborough	15. 6.03A
G-ILLE	Boeing-Stearman E75 (PT-13D) Kaydet (Continental W670)	75-5028	N68979 42-16865/Bu.60906	7. 3.90	M.Minkler (As "379" in USAAC c/s)	Oaksey Park	7. 6.02T
G-ILLY	Piper PA-28-181 Cherokee Archer II	28-7690193	SE-GND	21. 2.80	A.G.& K.M.Spiers Ltd (CofR restored 4.02)	Hinton in the Hedges	19.12.93
G-ILRS	Comco Ikarus C42 FB UK	PFA 322-13927		19. 6.02	Knitsley Mill Leisure Ltd	(Consett)	6.10.03P
G-ILSE	Corby CJ-1 Starlet (HAPI Magnum 1915cc)	PFA 134-10818		9. 1.84	S.Stride	Dromwich	7. 5.03P
G-ILTS	Piper PA-32-300 Six	32-7940215	G-CVOK OE-DOH/N2941C	28. 3.90	Foremans Aviation Ltd	Full Sutton	24. 2.05T
G-ILUM	Europa Aviation Europa XS 467 & PFA 247-13565 (Tri-gear u/c)			15. 6.00	A.R.Haynes	(Stevenage)	
G-IMAB	Europa Aviation Europa XS 331 & PFA 247-13128 (Rotax 912S) (Monowheel u/c)			1. 2.00	A.H.Brown (F/f 20.10.02)	Morgansfield, Fishburn	5.11.03P[
G-IMAN	Colt 31A Sky Chariot HAB	2605		23. 6.94	Benedikt Haggeney GmbH	Ennigerloh, Germany	16. 2.00A
G-IMBI	QAC Quickie 1 (Rotax 503)	484	G-BWIT N4482Z	7.10.02	J.D.King	(Bromley)	15. 7.03P
G-IMBY	Pietenpol Air Camper	PFA 47-12402		22.12.93	P.F.Bockh	(Horsham)	
G-IMGL	Beech B200 Super King Air	BB-1564	VP-CMA N205JT	9. 8.99	IM Aviation Ltd	Coventry	6. 9.05T
G-IMIC	IAV-Bacau Yakovlev Yak-52	8910001	RA021492 DOSAAF 103 (Yellow)	1. 8.02	C.Vogelgesang & R.Hockey	Booker	27. 8.03P
G-IMLI	Cessna 310Q	310Q0491	G-AZYK N4182Q	3. 4.86	W.R.M.Beesley	Nottingham	5. 6.03T
G-IMOK	Hoffmann HK-36R Super Dimona	36317	I-NELI OE-9352	31. 7.97	A.L.Garfield	Dunstable	3. 8.03
G-IMPX	Rockwell Commander 112B	512	N1304J	25.10.90	J.C.Stewart	(Calne)	27. 4.03
G-IMPY	Avid Flyer C	PFA 189-11439		10. 4.89	T.R.C.Griffin	Haverfordwest	6. 5.03P
G-INAV	Aviation Composites Europa	AC.001		23. 2.87	I.Shaw	(York)	
G-INCA	Glaser-Dirks DG-400	4-199		22. 1.87	K.D.Hook "CA"	Portmoak	17. 3.05
G-INDC	Cessna T303 Crusader	T30300122	G-BKFH N4766C	28. 6.83	Crusader Aviation Ltd	Oxford	10. 4.05
G-INDY	Robinson R44 Astro	0071		11. 7.94	M.B.Oastler t/a Lincoln Aviation	(Bicester)	19.10.03
G-INGA	Thunder Ax8-84 HAB	2149		16. 6.92	M.L.J.Ritchie	Weybridge	14. 9.94A
G-INGE	Thruster T600N Sprint (Jabiru 2200A)	9039-T600N-033		23. 2.99	Thruster Air Services Ltd	Ginge Farm, Wantage	23. 8.03P
G-INIS	Robinson R22 Beta	1982	G-UPMW	31. 5.00	EBG (Helicopters) Ltd	Redhill	13. 3.04T
G-INNI	Wassmer Jodel D.112	540	F-BHPU	30. 8.94	V.E.Murphy	(Fethard, Co.Tipperary)	5.12.03P

Reg	Type	C/n	Previous identity	Date	Owner	Location	Expiry
G-INNY	Replica Plans SE.5A (Continental C90)	PFA 20-10439		18.12.78	K.S.Matcham *(As "F5459/Y" in RFC c/s)*	Barton Ashes	15. 5.03P
G-INOW	ARV Monnett Moni (KEF 107)	223 & PFA 142-10953		30. 3.84	W.C.Brown *(Stored 8.97: current status unknown)*	Fairoaks	20. 8.88P
G-INSR	Cameron N-90 HAB	4320		23. 4.98	M.J.Betts & The Smith & Pinching Group Ltd	(Norwich)	18.6.03A
G-INTL	Boeing 747-245F	20826	N640FE (N631FE)/N811FT/N701SW	8.12.00	Airfreight Express Ltd *(Stored 2002l)*	Hahn, Germany	14. 3.04T
G-INVU	Agusta-Bell 206B JetRanger II	8530	G-XXII G-GGCC/G-BEHG	1. 3.95	Elmtree Estates Ltd	(Highbridge)	21. 4.03T
G-IOCO	Beech 58 Baron	TH-1783		6. 6.96	Arenberg Consultadoria E Servicos LDA	(Madeira, Portugal)	20. 6.05
G-IOIT*	Lockheed L.1011-385-1 Tristar 200	193N-1145	G-CEAP SE-DPM/G-BEAL	6. 5.98	Classic Airways *(Cancelled 1.10.98 by CAA) (Stored 5.01)*	Stansted	
G-IOOI	Robin DR400/160 Major 80	1700		31. 5.85	N.B.Mason & S.J.O'Rourke	Rendcomb	15.01.05
G-IONA	Aérospatiale/Alenia ATR 42-300	017	N971NA F-WWER	19.12.02	Highland Airways Ltd	Inverness	19.12.05T
G-IOPT	Cessna 182P Skylane	18261731	N182EE D-ECVM/N21585	9. 6.98	M.J.Valentine & P.R.Davis	Elstree	26. 9.04
G-IORG	Robinson R22 Beta	1679	OH-HRU G-ZAND	28. 1.00	G.M.Richardson t/a Commission-Air	(Market Deeping)	19. 4.03T
G-IOSI	CEA Jodel DR.1050 Sicile	526	F-BLRS	6.10.80	G.A.Saxby tr Sicile Flying Group	Bidford	9. 7.05
G-IOSO	CEA Jodel DR.1050 Ambassadeur	46	OO-VDV F-BJUE	13. 7.00	A.E.Jackson	Sibson	19.10.03
G-IOWE	Europa Aviation Europa XS (Rotax 912) *(Tri-gear u/c)*	388 & PFA 247-13303		30. 7.99	P.A.Lowe *(F/f 17.2.01)*	Wolverhampton	26. 3.03P
G-IPDM	Robinson R22 Beta-II	2738	G-OMSG	22. 5.02	A.J.& P.D.Morgan t/a Morhire	(Usk)	15. 5.04T
G-IPSI(2)	Grob G-109B	6425	G-BMLO	29. 5.86	D.G.Margetts	Vaynor Farm, Llanidloes, Powys	12. 6.05
G-IPSY	Rutan VariEze (Continental PC60)	1512 & PFA 74-10284	(G-IPSI)	19. 6.78	R.A.Fairclough	Biggin Hill	8. 7.03P
G-IPUP	Beagle B.121 Pup 2	B121-036	HB-NAC G-35-036	17. 7.95	R.G.Hayes & S.Tvietan tr Skyway Group	North Weald	18.10.04T
G-IRAF	Rotary Air Force RAF 2000 GTX-SE	PFA G/13-1278		17. 6.96	M.S.R.Allen	(Oakham)	16.10.03P
G-IRAN	Cessna 152 II	15283907	OH-CKM C-GBJY/(N6150B)	19. 8.97	I.R.Chaplin	Andrewsfield	23. 4.04T
G-IRIS	Gulfstream AA-5B Tiger	AA5B-1184	G-BIXU N4533N	14.12.87	A.H.McVicar *(Op Carlisle Flight Centre)*	Carlisle	17. 5.03T
G-IRJX*	BAE Systems Avro 146-RJX100	E3378		24. 5.00	BAE Systems (Operations) Ltd *(Cancelled 20.2.03 as wfu - for display)*	Manchester	
G-IRKB	Piper PA-28R-201 Cherokee Arrow III	28R-7737071	D-EJDS N5814V	7. 3.00	R.K.Brierley	Andrewsfield	31. 5.03
G-IRLY	Colt 90A HAB	1620		28.12.89	S.A.Burnett & L.P.Purfield "Air Canada Cargo II"	Leicester	6. 8.94A
G-IRPC	Cessna 182Q Skylane II	18266039	G-BSKM N559CT/N759JV	15. 5.91	J.W.Halfpenny	Cambridge	23. 7.05T
G-IRTH	Lindstrand LBL 150A HAB	772		20. 6.02	A.M.Holly	Berkeley	8. 7.03T
G-ISAX	Piper PA-28-181 Archer III	2843453	N5325G	28. 6.01	Singer & Frielander Commercial Finance Ltd	Glasgow	27. 6.04T
G-ISCA	Piper PA-28RT-201 Arrow IV	28R-8118012	N8288Y N6608N	12. 2.91	D.J. & P.Pay	Exeter	25. 5.03
G-ISDB	Piper PA-28-161 Cherokee Warrior II	28-7716074	G-BWET SX-ALX/D-EFFQ/N9612N	19. 2.96	Action Air Services Ltd	White Waltham	11. 4.04T
G-ISDN	Boeing-Stearman B75N1 (N2S-3) Kaydet *(Officially regd as model A75N1)*	75-1263	N4197X XB-WOV/Bu.3486	6. 2.95	D.R.L.Jones *(As "14" in US Army c/s)*	Rendcomb	18. 6.05
G-ISEH	Cessna 182R Skylane II	18267843	G-BIWS N6601N	9.11.90	Hadsley Ltd	King's Farm, Thurrock	29. 5.03
G-ISFC	Piper PA-31 Turbo Navajo B	31-7300970	G-BNEF N7574L	23. 3.94	G.R.E.Evans	Little Staughton	16. 5.03
G-ISIS	de Havilland DH.82A Tiger Moth	86251	G-AODR NL779	20.12.83	D.R. & M.Wood *(Crashed Nympsfield 18.9.61: on rebuild: current status unknown)*	Tunbridge Wells	29. 3.62
G-ISKA	WSK-PZL Mielec TS-11 Iskra	1H1018	Polish AF 1018	11. 5.00	P.C.Harper (Noted 3.02)	Bruntingthorpe	
G-ISLA	Britten-Norman BN-2A-26 Islander	206	PH-PAR G-BNEA/SE-FTA/G-51-206	7. 5.97	Hoe Leasing Ltd *(Op Macrins Hotel)*	Islay	21. 6.03T
G-ISMO	Robinson R22 Beta	0870	OH-HOR G-ISMO/N8214T	14.10.88	Moy Motorsport Ltd	Sywell	7.8.05T
G-ISSY	Eurocopter EC120B	1236	G-CBCG F-WQPT	11.10.01	D R Williams	(Brentwood)	3.12.04T
G-ISTT	Thunder Ax8-84 HAB	1787		12. 6.90	RAF Halton Hot Air Balloon Club "RAF Halton"	RAF Halton	7.9.03A
G-ITII	Aerotek Pitts S-2A Special (Lycoming AEIO-360)	2223	I-VLAT	5. 7.95	Aerobatic Displays Ltd	Booker	21.1.05A
G-ITOI	Cameron N-90 HAB	4785		14. 1.00	A.E.Lusty	(Bourne)	27..3.02A
G-ITON	Maule MX-7-235 Star Rocket	10050C	N5670R	11. 9.96	J.R.S.Heaton	Hawksbridge Farm, Oxenhope	19.12.02
G-ITUG	Piper PA-28-180 Cherokee C	28-4121	G-AVNR N11C	14. 8.02	S.I.Tugwell	(Barnet)	25.10.04T
G-IUAN	Cessna 525 CitationJet	525-0324	N5163C (N428PC)	30. 6.99	RF Celada SpA	(Milan, Italy)	23. 3.05
G-IVAC	Airtour AH-77B HAB	012		28.11.89	T.D.Gibbs	Billingshurst	27.10.03A
G-IVAN	Shaw Twin-Eze (Norton NR642 x 2)	39 & PFA 74-10502		11. 9.78	A.M.Aldridge "Mistress" (Noted 2000)	Ostend, Belgium	5.10.90P
G-IVAR	Yakovlev Yak-50	791504	D-EIVI (N5219K)/DDR-WQT/DM-WQT	24. 2.89	R.A.L.Hubbard & S.Whitcombe tr Foley Farm Flying Group	Meon	21. 3.03P
G-IVDM	Schempp-Hirth Nimbus 4DM	39/55	D-KABV	18.10.02	G.W. Lynch	(Sudbury)	AC
G-IVEL	Sportavia Fournier RF4D	4029	G-AVNY	29. 6.95	V.S.E.Norman (St.Ivel/Utterly Butterly titles)	Rendcomb	14. 4.01A
G-IVER	Europa Aviation Europa XS (Convertible u/c)	486 & PFA 247-13632		14. 8.00	I.Phillips	(Orpington)	

G-IVET	Europa Aviation Europa	020 & PFA 247-12511		23. 5.97	K.J.Fraser	(Abingdon)	
	(Rotax 912S) *(Conventional u/c)*				*(Current status unknown)*		
G-IVIV	Robinson R44 Astro	0016	(N803EH)	2. 8.93	Montage (Presentation Services) Ltd	(London N1)	23. 7.05
G-IVOR	Aeronca 11AC Chief	11AC-1035	EI-BKB	18. 6.82	P.R.White & C.P.Matthews	Bodmin	17. 3.03P
			G-IVOR/EI-BKB/N9397E		tr South Western Aeronca Group		
G-IVYS	Parsons Two Place Gyroplane	PFA G/08-1275		11. 1.00	R.M.Harris	(Nottingham)	
	(Mazda RX-7)						
G-IWON	Cameron V-90 HAB	2504	G-BTCV	17. 2.92	D.P.P.Jenkinson *"Twenty One"*	Tring	21. 7.00A
G-IWRC	Eurocopter EC135 T1	0241	D-HECA	9. 9.02	Proflight Ltd	(Banbury)	13.11.05T
G-IXII	Christen Eagle II	T0001	G-BPZI	9. 1.03	A.J.& M.A.N.Newall *"Thunder Eagle"*	Bagby	18. 4.02P
	(Lycoming IO-360)		N48BB				
G-IXIX	III Sky Arrow 650T	PFA 298-13257		24.10.00	W.J.De Gier	Old Sarum	2. 2.03P
G-IXTI	Extra EA.300/L	121		15. 9.00	Sundance Aviation Ltd	North Weald	29. 9.03T
G-IYAK	SPP Yakovlev Yak.C11	171103	OK-JIM	12. 1.94	E.K.Coventry	Earls Colne	25. 5.01P
			(Fr AF/Egypt AF)				
G-IYCO	Robin DR500/200i President	0031		23. 2.01	L.M.Gould	Jersey	21. 3.04
	(Registered as DR400/500)						
G-IZIT	Rans S-6-116 Coyote II	PFA 204A-12965		7. 3.96	J.R.Caylow	Nottingham	4. 6.03P
	(Rotax 912UL) *(Tailwheel u/c)*						
G-IZOD	Jabiru Jabiru UL	PFA 274A-13541		26. 5.00	D.A.Izod	Damyn's Hall, Upminster	4. 9.03P
G-IZZI	Cessna T182T Turbo Skylane	T18208100	N51197	19. 3.02	T.J. & P.S.Nicholson	Maypole Farm, Chislet	7.5.05T
G-IZZS	Cessna 172S Skyhawk	172S8152	N952SP	1. 7.99	Rankart Ltd	Hinton in the Hedges	26. 9.05T
G-IZZY	Cessna 172R Skyhawk II	17280419	G-BXSF	7. 9.99	R.Parsons	(Carmarthen)	30. 5.04T
			N9967F				

G-JAAA - G-JZZZ

G-JABA	Jabiru Jabiru UL	189 & PFA 274-13297		14.12.99	A P Gornall	Booker	19. 6.03P
	(Jabiru 2200A) *(PFA prefix "274" indicates model SK: a model UL shold be "274A")*						
G-JABB	Jabiru Jabiru UL-450	PFA 274-13555		27. 4.00	D.J.Royce	Ludham	2. 1.03P
	(Jabiru 2200A)						
G-JABO	WAR Focke-Wulf FW190-A3 rep	PFA 81-11786		23. 8.01	S.P. Taylor	(Crediton)	
G-JABS	Jabiru Jabiru UL-450	PFA 274-13704		27. 6.02	P.E.Todd tr Jabiru Flyer Group	(Andover)	
	(PFA c/n prefix should be '274A)						
G-JABY	Jabiru Jabiru SPL-450	PFA 274A-13672		2. 2.01	J.T.Grant	(Norwich)	
G-JACA	Piper PA-28-161 Warrior III	2842139	N5328Q	28. 2.02	Channel Islands Aero Services Ltd	Jersey	6. 3.05T
G-JACB	Piper PA-28-181 Archer III	2843278	G-PNNI	23. 7.02	Channel Islands Aero Services Ltd	Jersey	24.10.05T
			N41651				
G-JACC	Piper PA-28-181 Archer III	2843222	G-GIFT	23.12.02	Channel Islands Aero Services Ltd	Jersey	6.11.05T
			G-IMVA/SE-KIH/N9524N/N4166F				
G-JACK	Cessna 421C Golden Eagle III	421C1411	N421GQ	29. 4.97	JCT 600 Ltd	Leeds-Bradford	28. 4.04
			N125RS/N12028				
G-JACO	Jabiru Jabiru UL	PFA 274A-13371		14. 4.99	R Hatton	(Douglas, Isle of Man)	2.10.03P
	(Jabiru 2200A)						
G-JACS	Piper PA-28-181 Archer III	2843078	N9287J	15. 4.97	Vector Air Ltd	Fowlmere	17. 5.03T
			(G-JACS)				
G-JADJ	Piper PA-28-181 Archer III	2843009	N49TP	27. 7.99	S.J.Skilton	Bournemouth	28. 7.05T
	(Originally intended as c/n 2890240)		N92552		t/a Aviation Rentals *(Op Solent Flight Training)*		
G-JAEE	Van's RV-6A	PFA 181A-13571		16. 9.02	J.A.E.Edser	(Luton)	
G-JAGS	Reims/Cessna FRA150L Aerobat	FRA1500167	G-BAUY	24.10.01	P.A.Moslin	RAF Coltishall	19. 3.05T
			N10633		tr RAF Coltishall Flying Club		
G-JAHL	Bell 206B-3 JetRanger III	3565	N666ST	2. 1.98	D.T.Gittins t/a Jet Air Helicopters	Shobdon	22. 2.04T
G-JAIR	Mainair Blade	1249-0500-7 & W1042		11. 7.00	J.Loughran	(Stoke-on-Trent)	23. 1.03P
	(Rotax 582-2V)						
G-JAJB	Grumman AA-5A Cheetah	AA5A-0590	OY-CJE	30. 4.02	J.Bradley	RAF Upavon	29.5.05
			N26434				
G-JAJK	Piper PA-31-350 Chieftain	31-8152014	G-OLDB	16.12.99	Keen Leasing (IoM) Ltd	Belfast	24. 7.03T
			OY-SKY/G-DIXI/N40717				
G-JAJP	Jabiru Jabiru UL	PFA 274A-13627		1.12.00	J.W.E.Pearson & J.Anderson Plaistows Farm, St Albans		26. 9.03P
G-JAKE	de Havilland DHC.1 Chipmunk 22	C1/0584	G-BBMY	21. 1.80	K.Ritter	(Bangor)	11.12.01
			WK565				
G-JAKI	Mooney M.20R Ovation	29-0030		7. 2.95	J.M.Moss & D.M.Abrahamson	(Dublin)	11. 4.04
G-JAKS	Piper PA-28-160 Cherokee	28-339	G-ARVS	2. 7.99	K.Harper	Stapleford	18. 1.04
G-JALC	Boeing 757-225	22794	N504EA	6. 3.95	MyTravel Airways Ltd	Manchester	22. 4.04T
G-JAMP	Piper PA-28-151 Cherokee Warrior	28-7515026	G-BRJU	3. 4.95	ANP Ltd *(Op West London Aero Club)* White Waltham		27. 6.04T
			N44762		*(Nose u/carriage collapsed on heavy landing White Waltham 3.4.02)*		
G-JAMY	Europa Aviation Europa XS 449 & PFA 247-13557			5. 1.01	J P Sharp	Rayne Hall Fam, Rayne	13. 6.03P
	(Rotax 912 ULS)				*(F/f 1.5.01)*		
G-JANA	Piper PA-28-181 Archer II	28-7990483	N2838X	12. 2.87	C.Dashfield t/a Croaker Aviation	Stapleford	3. 6.05
G-JANN	Piper PA-34-220T Seneca III	3433133	N9154W	23. 6.89	MBC Aviation Ltd	Fairoaks	30. 8.04T
G-JANO	Piper PA-28RT-201T Arrow IV	28R-7918091	SE-IZR	14. 5.98	Abertawe Aviation Ltd	Swansea	24. 6.04T
			N2146X				
G-JANS	Reims FR172J Rocket	FR17200414	PH-GJO	11. 8.78	I.G.Aizlewood	Rush Green	29.10.04
			D-EGJO				
G-JANT	Piper PA-28-181 Archer II	28-8390075	N4297J	23. 2.87	Janair Aviation Ltd	Denham	1. 4.05T
	(Originally built as c/n 28-8290117/N81992/YV-2234P: not delivered and re-manufactured as c/n stated)						
G-JARA	Robinson R22 Beta	1837		11. 6.91	S.G.Simpson t/a HJS Helicopters		
					Culter Helipad, Lower Baads Farm, Peterculter		18. 7.03T
G-JARV	Aérospatiale AS355F1 Twin Squirrel	5164	G-OGHL	15.10.01	PLM Dollar Group Ltd	Inverness	27. 5.03T
			N5796S				
G-JASE	Piper PA-28-161 Warrior II	28-8216056	N8461R	13. 2.91	Mid-Anglia Flight Centre Ltd	Cambridge	24. 7.04T
					t/a Mid-Anglia School of Flying		

Reg	Type	Serial
G-JAVO	Piper PA-28-161 Warrior II	28-8016130
G-JAWC	Pegasus Quantum 15-912	7692
G-JAWZ	Pitts S-1S Special (Lycoming AEIO-360)	PFA 09-12846
G-JAXS	Jabiru Jabiru UL	PFA 274A-13548
G-JAYI	Auster V J/1 Autocrat	2030
G-JAZZ	Gulfstream AA-5A Cheetah	AA5A-0819
G-JBBS	Robinson R44 Raven	0784
G-JBDB	Agusta-Bell 206B JetRanger II	8238
G-JBDH	Robin DR400/180 Regent	1901
G-JBEN	Mainair Blade 912	1337-0802-7 & W1132
G-JBJB	Colt 69A HAB	1274
G-JBKA	Robinson R44 Raven	1175
G-JBPR	Wittman W.10 Tailwind	PFA 31-11490
G-JBRN	Cessna 182S Skylane	18280029
G-JBSP	Jabiru Jabiru SP-470 (Jabiru 2200A)	PFA 274B-13486
G-JBBZ	Eurocopter AS.350B3 Ecureuil	3580
G-JCAR	Piper PA-46-350P Malibu Mirage	4636223
G-JCAS	Piper PA-28-181 Archer II	28-8690036
G-JCBA	Sikorsky S-76B	760352
G-JCBJ	Sikorsky S-76C	760502
G-JCBX	Dassault Falcon 900EX	108
G-JCKT	Stemme S-10VT	11-004
G-JCMW	Rand Robinson KR-2	PFA 129-11064
G-JCUB	Piper PA-18-135 Super Cub (L-21B-PI) (Frame No.18-3630)	18-3531
G-JDBC	Piper PA-34-200T Seneca II	34-7570150
G-JDEE	SOCATA TB-20 Trinidad	333
G-JDEL	Jodel 150 Mascaret	112 & PFA 151-11276
G-JDFW	Airbus Industrie A320-212	0299
G-JDIX	Mooney M.20B Mark 21	1866
G-JDJM	Piper PA-28-140 Cherokee C	28-26877
G-JEAD	Fokker F.27 Friendship 500	10627
G-JEAE	Fokker F.27 Friendship 500 (Freighter conversion)	10633
G-JEAJ	British Aerospace BAe 146 Srs.200	E2099
G-JEAK	British Aerospace BAe 146 Srs.200	E2103
G-JEAM	British Aerospace BAe 146 Srs.300	E3128
G-JEAO	British Aerospace BAe 146 Srs.100	E1010
G-JEAS	British Aerospace BAe 146 Srs.200	E2020
G-JEAT	British Aerospace BAe 146 Srs.100	E1071
G-JEAU	British Aerospace BAe 146 Srs.100	E1035
G-JEAV	British Aerospace BAe 146 Srs.200	E2064
G-JEAW	British Aerospace BAe 146 Srs.200	E2059
G-JEAX	British Aerospace BAe 146 Srs.200	E2136
G-JEAY	British Aerospace BAe 146 Srs.200	E2138
G-JEBA	British Aerospace BAe 146 Srs.300	E3181
G-JEBB	British Aerospace BAe 146 Srs.300	E3185
G-JEBC	British Aerospace BAe 146 Srs.300	E3189
G-JEBD	British Aerospace BAe 146 Srs.300	E3191
G-JEBE	British Aerospace BAe 146 Srs.300	E3206
G-JECA	Canadair CL600-2B19 (CRJ 200)	7345
G-JECB	Canadair CL600-2B19 (CRJ 200)	7393

Prev ident	Date	Owner	Location	Expiry
G-BSXW / N8119S	17.9.97	Victor Oscar Ltd	Wellesbourne Mountford	25.6.03T
	21.7.00	A.W.Chester	(Brentwood)	20.7.03P
	6.11.95	A.R.Harding	(Newton Farm, Sudbury)	15.11.01P
	10.12.99	C A Palmer	Kemble	27.6.03P
OY-ALU / D-EGYK/OO-ABF	5.2.93	Bravo Aviation Ltd *(Op Air Atlantique)*	Coventry	12.8.02
N26932	30.3.82	R.W.Taylor tr Jazz Club	Southend	7.10.05
	14.9.00	Fredat Ltd	Elstree	1.10.03T
G-OOPS / G-BNRD/Oman AF 602	11.4.96	Brad Helicopters Ltd	Denham	21.12.02T
	17.3.89	W.A.Clark	Netherthorpe	23.5.04
	13.9.02	G.J.Bentley	(Chester)	16.9.03P
	26.7.88	Justerini & Brooks Ltd *"J & B Jeremy"*	London SW1	19.5.02A
	12.3.02	Heli Air Ltd	Wellesbourne Mountford	26.3.05T
	25.5.89	P.A.Rose & J.P.Broadhurst	Walney Island	
N432V / G-RITZ/N9872F	11.6.99	Parallel Flooring Accessories Ltd	Wickenby	9.3.04
	12.10.99	C.R.James	Ludham	10.6.03P
F-WQDE / F-WQPV	13.1.03	McAlpine Helicopters Ltd	Oxford	
N4148N	17.12.99	Aquarelle Investments Ltd	Jersey	21.12.05T
N9093N / (N170AV)/N9648N	12.6.89	Charlie Alpha Ltd	Jersey	19.6.04T
N95UT / N95LT/N120PP/N120PM	25.11.99	J C Bamford Excavators Ltd	East Midlands	10.2.03
	9.7.99	J C Bamford Excavators Ltd	East Midlands	21.7.03
F-WWFF	23.9.02	J.C.Bamford Excavators Ltd	East Midlands	22.9.03
	8.4.98	J.C.Taylor	(Castletown, Isle of Man)	13.5.04
	3.2.99	M.Wildish & J.Cook	(Gainsborough)	
PH-VCH / R.Neth AF R-103 /54-2331	21.1.82	N.Cummins & S.Bennett	Weston, Dublin	28.7.05T
G-BDEF / N33695	9.10.02	Bowdon Aviation Ltd	(Cheadle)	24.10.05T
G-BKLA / F-BNGX	1.5.84	A W Eldridge & J A Heard	Leicester	12.6.05
G-JDLI	19.9.95	K.F. & R.Richardson	(Solihull)	
OY-CNW / G-JDFW/G-SCSR/F-WWIQ	20.11.95	MyTravel Airways Ltd *(New CofR 12.02)*	Manchester	24.4.99T
G-ARTB	28.11.85	A.L.Hall-Carpenter *(In open storage 7.02)*	Shipdham	16.1.00
(G-HSJM) / G-AYIF/N11C	11.10.00	R.Jackson-Moore & D.J.Street tr The Hare Flying Group	Booker	17.7.04
VH-EWU / PH-EXL	14.11.90	BAC Group Ltd *(Op BAC Express)* "Midland Trader"	(Horley)	21.11.05T
VH-EWV / PH-FSO	2.1.91	BAC Express Airlines Ltd *(Op BAC Express)*	Exeter	15.1.03T
G-OLCA / G-5-099	20.9.93	Jersey European Airways (UK) Ltd *"Pride of Guernsey" (flybe.com titles)*	Gatwick	17.7.05T
G-OLCB / G-5-103	18.3.93	Jersey European Airways (UK) Ltd *"Pride of Birmingham" (Op Air France Express)*	Gatwick	20.6.05T
G-BTJT / HS-TBK/G-11-128	24.5.93	Jersey European Airways (UK) Ltd *"Pride of Jersey" (Op Air France Express)*	Heathrow	23.5.03T
G-UKPC / C-GNVX/N802RW/G-5-512/PT-LEP/G-BKXZ/PT-LEP *(Stored 2.03)*	19.9.94	Trident Aviation Leasing Services (Jersey) Ltd	Filton	4.6.05T
G-OLHB / G-BSRV/G-OSUN/C-FEXN/N604AW *(Op Air France Express)*	13.2.96	Jersey European Airways (UK) Ltd	Heathrow	13.7.03T
N171TR / J8-VBB/G-BVUY/B-2706/G-5-071 *(Op Air France Express)*	11.10.96	Jersey European Airways (UK) Ltd	Heathrow	23.10.05T
N135TR / J8-VBC/G-BVUW/B-584L/B-2704/G-5-035 *(Op Air France Express)*	30.12.96	Jersey European Airways (UK) Ltd	Heathrow	24.1.03T
N764BA / CC-CEN/N414XV/G-5-064/N404XV	17.6.97	Jersey European Airways (UK) Ltd	Gatwick	19.6.03T
(N759BA) / CC-CEJ/N401XV/G-5-059/N401XV/G-5-059 *(flybe.com titles)*	21.7.97	Jersey European Airways (UK) Ltd	Gatwick	21.8.03T
N136JV / C-FHAP/N136TR/N882DV/(N719TA)/N882DV/G-5-136 *(Op Air France Express)*	16.2.98	Jersey European Airways (UK) Ltd	Heathrow	19.2.04T
SE-DRL / N138JV/C-FHAA/N138TR/(N719TA)/N883DV/G-5-138	27.3.01	Jersey European Airways (UK) Ltd	Gatwick	26.3.04T
HS-TBL / G-6-181/G-BSYR/G-6-181 *(Op Air France Express)*	16.6.98	Jersey European Airways (UK) Ltd	Heathrow	27.7.04T
HS-TBK / G-6-185 *(Op Air France Express)*	26.6.98	Jersey European Airways (UK) Ltd	Heathrow	1.11.04T
HS-TBO / G-6-189	4.6.98	Jersey European Airways (UK) Ltd	Gatwick	1.7.04T
HS-TBJ / G-6-191	14.7.98	Jersey European Airways (UK) Ltd	Gatwick	17.9.04T
HS-TBM / G-6-206	28.5.98	Jersey European Airways (UK) Ltd	Gatwick	25.6.04T
	29.10.99	Jersey European Airways (UK) Ltd *(Op Air France Express)*	Heathrow	28.10.05T
C-GGKI / C-FMNQ	2.6.00	Jersey European Airways (UK) Ltd *(British European titles)*	Gatwick	1.6.03T

Reg	Type	C/n	Prev Reg	Date	Owner	Location	Date
G-JECC	Canadair CL600-2B19 *(CRJ 200)*	7434	C-FMKV	13.10.00	Jersey European Airways (UK) Ltd	Gatwick	26.10.03T
G-JECD	Canadair CL600-2B19 *(CRJ 200)*	7469	C-FMLI	19. 1.01	Jersey European Airways (UK) Ltd	Gatwick	31. 3.04T
					(Op Air France Express)		
G-JEDC	de Havilland DHC-8-311A *(Q300)*	532	C-GEOA	1.10.99	Jersey European Airways (UK) Ltd	Gatwick	30. 9.05T
G-JEDD	de Havilland DHC-8-311A *(Q300)*	533		21.10.99	Jersey European Airways (UK) Ltd	Gatwick	25.10.52T
G-JEDE	de Havilland DHC-8-311A *(Q300)*	534	C-GERL	25.11.99	Jersey European Airways (UK) Ltd	Gatwick	2.12.52T
G-JEDF	de Havilland DHC-8-311A *(Q300)*	548	C-GDIW	10. 7.00	Jersey European Airways (UK) Ltd	Gatwick	9. 7.03T
G-JEDG	de Havilland DHC-8-402Q *(Q300)*			R	Jersey European Airways (UK) Ltd	Gatwick	
G-JEDH	Robin DR400/180 Regent	2343		3. 2.97	J.B.Hoolahan	Rochester	16. 5.03
G-JEDI	de Havilland DHC-8-402Q *(Q400)*	4052	C-GFOD	25.10.01	Jersey European Airways (UK) Ltd	Gatwick	24.10.04T
G-JEDJ	de Havilland DHC-8-402Q *(Q400)*	4058	C-FDHZ	23. 1.02	Jersey European Airways (UK) Ltd	Gatwick	4. 2.05T
G-JEDK	de Havilland DHC-8-402Q *(Q400)*	4065	C-GEMU	23. 4.02	Jersey European Airways (UK) Ltd	Gatwick	30. 4.05T
					(flybe.com titles)		
G-JEDL	de Havilland DHC-8-402Q *(Q400)*	4067	C-GEOZ	17. 6.02	Jersey European Airways (UK) Ltd	Gatwick	30. 6.05T
G-JEDS	Andreasson BA-4B HA/02 & PFA 38-10158		G-BEBT	17.12.02	S.B.Jedburgh	Deanland, Hailsham	4. 7.03P
	(Lycoming O-235)						
G-JEDX	de Havilland DHC-8-201B *(Q200)*	541	C-FDHV	16. 2.00	Jersey European Airways (UK) Ltd	Gatwick	16. 2.03T
G-JEDY	de Havilland DHC-8-201B *(Q200)*	542	C-FNGB	27. 3.00	Jersey European Airways (UK) Ltd	Gatwick	6. 4.03T
G-JEDZ	de Havilland DHC-8-201B *(Q200)*	547	C-GDIU	7. 6.00	Jersey European Airways (UK) Ltd	Gatwick	13. 6.03T
G-JEET	Reims/Cessna FA152 Aerobat	FA15200369	G-BHMF	10.12.87	Willowair Flying Club (1996) Ltd	Southend	18.10.04T
G-JEFA	Robinson R44 Astro	0710		7. 2.00	Simlot Ltd	Denham	27. 4.03T
G-JEJE	RAF 2000 GTX-SE	PFA G/13-1352		21. 1.03	J.W.Erswell	(South Brent)	
G-JEMY	Lindstrand LBL 90A HAB	742		22.11.00	J.A.Lawton	(Godalming)	30.12.02A
G-JENA	Mooney M.20J (201)	24-1304	N1168D	5. 7.82	P.Leverkuehn	Antwerp-Deurne, Belgium	14.11.03
					t/a Mooney Partnership		
G-JENI	Cessna R182 Skylane RG II	R18200267	N3284C	17. 9.87	R.A.Bentley	Stapleford	23. 4.03
G-JENN	Gulfstream AA-5B Tiger	AA5B-1187	N4533T	7.12.81	M. Reed t/a Shadow Aviation	Elstree	23. 3.03T
G-JERL	Agusta A109E Power	11118		29. 5.01	Perment Ltd	(Clitheroe)	6 .6.04T
G-JERO	Europa Aviation Europa XS 492 & PFA 247-13691			13. 6.02	B.Robshaw & P.Jenkinson	(Pickering)	16.12.03P
	(Rotax 914) (Tri-gear u/c)						
G-JERS	Robinson R22 Beta	1610		21.12.90	Sloane Helicopters Ltd	Sywell	7. 6.03T
G-JESS	Piper PA-28R-201T Turbo Arrow III	28R-7803334	G-REIS	18. 9.95	N.E. & M.A.Bedggood	White Waltham	22. 5.03
			N36689				
G-JETC	Cessna 550 Citation II	550-0282	G-JCFR	28. 5.81	Ability Air Ltd	Stapleford	24. 3.03T
			G-JETC/N68644T				
G-JETG	Learjet Learjet 35A	35A-324	G-JETN	5. 3.98	Gama Aviation Ltd	Farnborough	31. 7.02T
			G-JJSG				
G-JETH	Armstrong-Whitworth Sea Hawk	FGA.6	"XE364"	10. 8.83	P.G.Vallance Ltd	Charlwood, Surrey	
	(Composite with WM983/A2511)		XE489		*(Gatwick Aviation Museum as "XE489")*		
G-JETI	British Aerospace BAe 125 Srs.800B	258056	G-5-509	9. 7.86	Ford Motor Co Ltd	Stansted	12.11.03T
G-JETJ	Cessna 550 Citation II	550-0154	G-EJET	9. 2.93	Citation Flying Services Ltd	Liverpool	15. 8.02T
			G-DJBE/(N8887N)				
G-JETM	Gloster Meteor T.7	-	VZ638	10. 8.83	P.G.Vallance Ltd	Charlwood, Surrey	
					(Gatwick Aviation Museum as "VZ638" in RN/FRU c/s)		
G-JETU	Aérospatiale AS355F2 Twin Squirrel	5450	VR-CET	18. 4.96	Summit Aviation Ltd	Oxford	22. 5.05T
			JA6623				
G-JETX	Bell 206B-3 JetRanger III	3208	N3898L	9. 2.88	Heli Charter Ltd	Manston	17. 5.03T
G-JETZ	MD Helicopters Hughes 369E (500E)	0450E	VR-HJI	26. 3.97	John Matchett Ltd	Sywell	15. 6.03
G-JFWI	Reims/Cessna F172N Skyhawk II	F17201622	PH-DPA	1. 9.80	Staryear Ltd	Barton	30. 1.03T
			PH-AXY				
G-JGBI	Bell 206L-4 LongRanger IV	52257	N91285	13. 8.01	Dorbcrest Homes Ltd	(Wigan)	16. 9.04
			C-GBUP				
G-JGMN	CASA I-131E Jungmann Srs.2000	2011	E3B-407	17. 4.91	P.D.Scandrett	Rendcomb	12. 9.03P
	(C/n as officially regd but carries c/n plate 2104 in rear cockpit: c/n 2011 is regd as N65522)						
G-JGSI	Pegasus Quantum 15-912	7515		19. 4.99	J.G.Spinks	Swinford, Rugby	31. 5.03P
G-JHAC	Reims/Cessna FRA150L Aerobat	FRA1500160	EI-BRX	16. 9.02	J.H.A.Clarke	(Bromham, Chippenham)	31. 3.88T
			G-BACM/EI-BRX/G-BACM		*(Current status unknown)*		
G-JHEW	Robinson R22 Beta	0672	N23677	20. 7.87	Burbage Farms Ltd	Hinckley	8.12.05
G-JHYS	Europa Aviation Europa 314 & PFA 247-13307			6. 3.01	J.D.Boyce & G.E.Walker	Burnham-on-Crouch	4. 6.03P
	(Tri-gear u/c)				*(F/f 16.10.01)*		
G-JIGS	Lindstrand LBL 90A HAB	656		9. 3.00	Jigsaw Connections Ltd	Reading	20. 7.02A
G-JIII	Stolp SA.300 Starduster Too	2-3-12	N9043	27. 5.93	J.G.McTaggart	Archerfield Estate, Dirleton	1. 7.03P
	(Lycoming IO-360)				t/a VTIO Company		
G-JILL	Rockwell Alpine Commander 112TC-A	13304	(OO-HPB)	25. 7.80	P M & P A O'Hare	Humberside	19. 2.05T
			G-JILL/N8070R/HB-NCW				
G-JILY	Robinson R44	0959		5. 1.01	AG Aviation Ltd	Naas, Co Kildare	27. 2.04
G-JIMB	Beagle B.121 Pup 1	B121-033	G-AWWF	7. 4.94	P.G.Fowler	Enstone	10. 5.04T
G-JIVE	MD Helicopters Hughes 369E (500E)	0486E	G-DRAR	24. 5.01	Sleekform Ltd	(Sowerby Bridge)	8.11.04T
			N101LH/N1608Z				
G-JJAN	Piper PA-28-181 Archer II	2890007	N9105Z	28. 3.88	Redhill Aviation Ltd t/a Redhill Flying Club	Redhill	4. 5.03T
G-JJEN	Piper PA-28-181 Archer III	2843370	N4190D	25. 8.00	J.E.Jenkins	Jersey	24. 8.03
G-JJMX	Dassault Falcon 900EX	112	F-WWFK	17.10.02	J.Hargreaves t/a J-Max Air Services	(Preston)	16.10.03T
G-JJWL	Robinson R44	0980		25. 1.01	Willbeth Ltd	Goodwod	8. 2.04T
G-JLCA	Piper PA-34-200T Seneca II	34-7870428	G-BOKE	3. 9.97	C.A.S.Atha	Teesside	25. 1.04T
			N21030				
G-JLEE	Agusta-Bell 206B-3 JetRanger III	8588	G-JOKE	10. 2.88	J S Lee	Booker	5.10.03
			G-CSKY/G-TALY				
G-JLHS	Beech A36 Bonanza	E-2571	N8046U	30.11.90	I.G.Meredith	Lydd	21. 2.03
G-JLMW	Cameron V-77 HAB	1768		23. 6.88	J.L.M.Watkins	Ivybridge	26. 2.99T
G-JLRW	Beech 76 Duchess	ME-165	N60206	4.11.87	Magenta Ltd *(Op Airways Flight Training)*	Exeter	19. 1.03
G-JMAA	Boeing 757-3CQ	32241		24. 4.01	JMC Airlines Ltd	Manchester	23 .4.04T
G-JMAB	Boeing 757-3CQ	32242		14. 5.01	JMC Airlines Ltd	Manchester	13. 5.04T
G-JMAC	British Aerospace Jetstream Srs.4100	41004	G-JAMD	12. 6.92	BAE Systems (Operations) Ltd	Liverpool	6.10.97A
			G-JXLI		*(For display by Wirral Aviation Society 1.03)*		

Reg	Type	C/n	Prev id	Date	Owner/Operator	Location	Date2
G-JMAN	Mainair Blade 912S	1290-0601-7 & W1085		12. 7.01	J.Manuel	(Southport)	15. 7.02P
G-JMCD	Boeing 757-25F	30757		26. 5.00	JMC Airlines Ltd *(Op Ryan International)*	Manchester	26. 5.03T
G-JMCE	Boeing 757-25F	30758		24. 6.00	JMC Airlines Ltd *(Op Ryan International)*	Manchester	22. 6.03T
G-JMCF	Boeing 757-28A	24369	C-FOOE	20. 5.00	JMC Airlines Ltd	Manchester	26. 5.03T
G-JMCG	Boeing 757-2G5	26278	D-AMUQ	27. 4.00	JMC Airlines Ltd	Manchester	1. 6.03T
G-JMDI	Schweizer Hughes 269C (300C)	S.1398	G-FLAT	24. 9.91	J.J.Potter	Sherburn-in-Elmet	25. 4.05T
G-JMKE	Cessna 172S Skyhawk	172S9248	N53012	17.12.02	115CR(146) Ltd	Wellesbourne Mountford	17.12.05T
G-JMTS	Robin DR400/180 Regent	2045		29.11.90	J.R.Whiting	Exeter	20. 6.03
G-JMTT	Piper PA-28R-201T Turbo Arrow III	28R-7803190	G-BMHM N3735M	8. 7.86	Jonathan Dunn	(Milton Keynes)	9. 5.05T
G-JMXA	Agusta A109E Power	11156		31. 5.02	J.J.Hargreaves (J-Max Air Services)	(Preston)	30. 5.05T
G-JNAS	Grumman American AA-5A Cheetah	AA5A-0604	SE-GEI LN-KLE	28.11.00	J.R.Nutter & A.L.Shore	Popham	17. 1.04T
G-JNET	Robinson R22 Beta	3195		6. 4.01	R.L.Hartshorn	(Matlock)	25. 4.04T
G-JNNB	Colt 90A HAB	2063		20.12.91	Justerini & Brooks Ltd *"J&B"*	London SW1	19. 5.02A
G-JODL	SAN Jodel DR.1050/M Excellence	99	F-BJJC	28. 4.86	D.Silsbury *(New owner 10.01)*	Dunkeswell	26.11.99
G-JOEL	Bensen B.8M	PFA G/03-1300		6. 7.99	G.C.Young	Swansea	
	(Converted from Air Command) (Note PFA type allocated as Cricket Mk.4 which aligns with correct PFA project no.srs.)						
G-JOEM	Airbus Industrie A320-231	0449	G-OUZO EI-VIR/N449RX/SX-BSV/N449RX/F-WWIG	17. 4.00	MyTravel Airways Ltd	Manchester	7.11.04T
G-JOEY	Fairey Britten-Norman BN-2A Mk.III-2 Trislander	1016	G-BDGG C-GSAA/G-BDGG	27.11.81	Aurigny Air Services Ltd *"Joey"*	Guernsey	26. 8.02T
G-JOJO	Cameron A-210 HAB	2674		20. 9.91	A.C.Rawson & J.J.Rudoni	(Little Haywood)	29. 4.03T
G-JOLY	Cessna 120 (Continental C85)	13872	OO-ACE	3. 9.81	B.V.Meade	Garston Farm, Marshfield	13. 6.03P
G-JONB	Robinson R22 Beta-II	2593		29. 4.96	J.Bignall	Mistletoe Farm, Pinner	27. 5.05
G-JONE	Cessna 172M Skyhawk II	17264490	N9724V	2.12.80	W.Bagnall	Southend	29. 3.03
G-JONH	Robinson R22 Beta	2170		3. 6.93	Productivity Computer Solutions Ltd	Sherburn-in-Elmet	22. 8.05T
G-JONI	Reims/Cessna FA152 Aerobat	FA15200346	G-BFTU	6. 7.84	R.F.& J.S.Pooler	Sleap	7. 7.03
G-JONO	Colt 77A HAB	1086		22. 6.87	The Sandcliffe Motor Group Ltd *"Sandcliffe Ford"*	Stapleford, Notts	17. 9.95A
G-JONY	Cyclone AX2000 HKS (HKS.700E)	7503		12. 3.99	K.R.Matheson *(USAF c/s)*	Sandtoft	11. 3.03P
G-JONZ	Cessna 172P Skyhawk II	17276233	N97835	28. 9.89	Truman Aviation Ltd	Nottingham	26. 5.05T
G-JOOL	Mainair Blade 912 (Rotax 912-UL)	1262-1000-7 & W1056		8.12.00	J R Gibson	Ince Blundell	13.12.02P
G-JOON	Cessna 182D	18253067	(N) G-JOON/OO-ACD/N9967T	9. 6.81	G.Jackson	Sibson	14.10.05T
G-JOPF*	Smyth Model S Sidewinder	PFA 92-12313		19. 4.01	Skycraft	Spalding	
	(Noted 10.02) (Cancelled 6.12.02 as wfu, no PtoF issued)						
G-JOSH	Cameron N-105 HAB	1319		13. 8.86	M.White	Cirencester	16. 8.96T
G-JOSS	Aérospatiale AS350B Ecureuil	1205	F-WQJY 3A-.../G-WILX/G-RAHM/G-UNIC/G-COLN/G-BHIV	31. 8.99	M.Burby	Jersey	29.10.05T
G-JOST	Europa Aviation Europa (Rotax 912) *(Tri-gear u/c)*	234 & PFA 247-12916		17. 6.98	J.A.Austin *(Current status unknown)*	(Bangor)	
G-JOYT	Piper PA-28-181 Archer II	28-7990132	G-BOVO N2239B	13. 2.90	John K.Cathcart Ltd	St. Angelo	30. 3.03T
G-JOYZ	Piper PA-28-181 Archer III	2843018	N9262R (G-JOYZ)	19. 1.96	S.W. & Joy E.Taylor	Biggin Hill	7. 2.05
G-JPAL	Aérospatiale AS355N Twin Squirrel	5692	F-GSJP	9.10.01	JPM Ltd	(Horsham)	6.11.04T
G-JPAT	Robin HR200/100 Club	76	G-BDJN	13. 9.00	M.Nash	(Forres)	29. 4.04
G-JPMA	Jabiru Jabiru UL (Jabiru 2200A) (Jabiru 2200A)	PFA 274A-13399		24. 5.99	J.P.Metcalfe *"Sheila"*	Lydd	12.11.03P
G-JPOT	Piper PA-32R-301 Saratoga SP	32R-8113065	G-BIYM N8385X	1. 8.94	S.W.Turley	Wickenby	29. 8.05T
G-JPRO	British Aircraft Corporation BAC.145 Jet Provost T.5A	XW433 EEP/JP/1055		10. 8.95	Edwalton Aviation Ltd *(As "XW433" in CFS c/s)*	Humberside	9. 4.03P
G-JPSI	Dassault Falcon 50EX	313	F-WWHR	12. 9.01	Sorven Aviation Ltd	Gloucestershire	11. 9.04T
G-JPTT	Enstrom 480	5032	G-PPAH	10. 4.02	Eastern Atlantic Helicopters Ltd	Shoreham	18. 5.04T
G-JPTV	British Aircraft Corporation BAC.145 Jet Provost T.5A *(C/n '...1002' reported)*	XW355 EEP/JP/1005		2. 5.96	Seagull Formation Ltd	North Weald	21. 8.03P
G-JPVA	British Aircraft Corporation BAC.145 Jet Provost T.5A	XW289 EEP/JP/953	G-BVXT	22. 2.95	T.J.Manna t/a Kennet Aviation *(As "XW289/73")*	North Weald	22. 5.03P
G-JREE	Maule MX-7-180 Star Rocket	11096C	N99MX N30051	13. 4.01	J.M.P.Ree	(Newbury)	19. 4.04A
G-JRME	Jodel D.140E	PFA 251-13155		13.11.02	J.E.& L.L. Rex	(Goole)	
G-JSAK	Robinson R22 Beta-II	2959		30. 6.99	S.M.& J.W.F.Tuke t/a Tukair Aircraft Charter	Headcorn	7. 7.05T
G-JSAR	Eurocopter AS.332L2 Super Puma	2576	F-WQRE	3. 9.02	Bristow Helicopters Ltd	Aberdeen	18.12.05T
G-JSAT	Pilatus Britten-Norman BN-2T Islander	2277	G-BVFK	5. 2.98	A.Wright tr Rhine Army Parachute Centre	RAF Weston-on-the-Green	5. 3.05A
G-JSJX	Airbus Industrie A321-213	0808	(EC-) D-AVZP	3. 4.98	MyTravel Airways Ltd	Manchester	27. 4.04T
G-JSON	Cameron N-105 HAB	2933		21. 5.92	Up & Away Ballooning Ltd *"Jason"*	High Wycombe	17. 8.03A
G-JSPC	Pilatus Britten-Norman BN-2T Islander	2264	G-BUBG	21.12.94	A.Wright tr Rhine Army Parachute Centre	Sennelager, Germany	13. 2.03A
G-JSPL	Jabiru Jabiru SPL-450	PFA 274A-13604		27.12.00	J A Lord	Knettishall	13. 5.03P
G-JTCA	Piper PA-23-250 Aztec E	27-7305112	G-BBCU N40297	29.12.80	J.D.Tighe t/a Eastern Air Executive	Sturgate	8.11.03T
G-JTCM	Aérospatiale AS350B Ecureuil	1836	G-HLEN G-LOLY/JA9897/N5805T/HP-1084P/HP-1084/N5805T	1. 3.02	Ardore Ltd	(Dungannon, Co.Tyrone)	29. 5.05T
G-JTPC	Aeromot AMT-200 Super Ximango	200-067		28. 5.97	J.T.Potter & P.G.Cowling tr G-JTPC Falcon 3 Group	Rufforth	22. 6.03
G-JTWO	Taylor J-2 Cub (Continental A65)	1754	G-BPZR N19554/NC19554	23.10.89	C.C.Silk Bericote Farm, Blackdown, Leamington Spa		16. 1.03P

Reg	Type	c/n	Prev identity	Date	Owner	Location	Expiry
G-JTYE	Aeronca 7BM Champion (Continental C85) *(Modified ex 7AS standard)*	7AC-4185	N85445 NC85445	26. 9.91	G.D.Horn *(Damaged Longwood Farm, Southampton 2.8.98: current status unknown)*	Old Sarum	17. 6.99P
G-JUDD	Jabiru Jabiru UL-450 (Jabiru 2200A)	PFA 274A-13570		9. 8.00	C.Judd	Lark Engine Farmhouse, Prickwillow, Ely	16. 1.03P
G-JUDE	Robin DR400/180 Regent	1869		14.10.88	Bravo India Flying Group Ltd	RAF Woodvale	15. 2.04
G-JUDI	North American AT-6D-NT Harvard III *(Regd as c/n "EX915-326165")*	88-14722	FAP 1502 SAAF7439/EX915/41-33888	17.11.78	A.A.Hodgson *(As "FX301/FD-NQ")*	Bryngwyn Bach	5. 6.03P
G-JUDY	Grumman-American AA-5A Cheetah	AA5A-0620	(G-BFWM) N26480	31. 8.78	Plane Talking Ltd	Biggin Hill	26.11.05T
G-JUIN	Cessna T303 Crusader	T30300014	OO-PEN N9401T	29. 2.88	M.J. & J M Newman	Denham	8. 5.03
G-JULL	Stemme S.10VT	11-039		10. 2.00	J.P.C.Fuchs	Rufforth	25. 4.03
G-JULU	Cameron V-90 HAB	3611		7. 7.95	N.J.Appleton	Bristol	4. 8.03A
G-JULZ	Europa Aviation Europa (Rotax 914) *(Monowheel u/c)*	312 & PFA 247-13045		8.10.96	M.Parkin *(F/f 31.10.02)*	Wombleton	8.12.03
G-JUNG	CASA I-131E Jungmann	1121	E3B-143	23.11.88	K.H.Wilson	White Waltham	25. 6.03P
G-JUPP	Piper PA-32RT-300 Lance II	32R-7885098	G-BNJF N31539	3.10.02	Jupp Air LLP	Wolverhampton	5.12.05T
G-JURA	British Aerospace Jetstream Srs.3102	772	SE-LDH OY-SVK/C-FAMJ/G-31-772	21. 5.01	Highland Airways Ltd *"City of Inverness"*	Inverness	14. 6.04T
G-JURE	SOCATA TB-10 Tobago	597	N106U	6.11.92	P.M.Ireland	South Lodge Farm, Widmerpool	14. 1.05
G-JURG	Rockwell Commander 114A GT *(Laid-down as c/n 14449)*	14516	N4752W	19. 9.79	Oxford Aviation Services Ltd	Oxford	28. 8.04
G-JUST	Beech F33A Bonanza	CE-1165	N334CW	11.10.00	Budge It Aviation Ltd	Elstree	14. 2.04
G-JVBF	Lindstrand LBL-210A HAB	265		5. 6.95	Airxcite Ltd t/a Virgin Balloon Flights	Wembley	6. 8.03T
G-JWBB	CEA Jodel DR.1050 Sicile	534	G-LAKI F-BLZD	17. 8.92	B.F.Baldock	Maypole Farm, Chislet	30. 6.05
G-JWBI	Agusta-Bell 206B JetRanger II	8435	G-RODS G-NOEL/G-BCWN	3. 4.96	J.W.Bonser	Walsall	26. 9.05T
G-JWCM	Scottish Aviation Bulldog Srs.120/1210	BH120/408	G-BHXB Botswana DF OD2/G-BHXB	19.10.99	M.L.J.Goff	Old Buckenham	16. 8.03T
G-JWDS	Cessna F150G *(Built Reims Aviation SA)*	F150-0216	G-AVNB	15.12.88	C.R. & S.A.Hardiman *(Noted unmarked 4.01)*	Gloucestershire	29. 9.94T
G-JWFT	Robinson R22 Beta	0989		16. 3.89	J.P.O'Brien	(Gorey, Co.Wexford)	10. 5.04
G-JWIV	CEA Jodel DR.1051 Sicile	431	F-BLMD	6. 9.78	C.M.Fitton	Trenchard Farm, Eggesford	9. 1.03P
G-JWLS	Bell 206B JetRanger II	1114	G-BSXE N40EA/C-GMVM/N83150	8. 1.99	Autospeed Helicopters Ltd	(Sevenoaks)	20. 1.03T
G-JWXS	Europa Aviation Europa XS T-G	517 & PFA 247-13743		5. 6.01	J.Wishart *(Owner deceased & project not commenced @ 2.03)*	(Carluke)	
G-JYAK	Yakovlev Yak-50 *(Correct p.i is RA01294)*	853001	RA01493	26.11.02	J.W.Stow	North Weald	12.12.03P

G-KAAA - G-KZZZ

Reg	Type	c/n	Prev identity	Date	Owner	Location	Expiry
G-KAAT	MD Helicopters MD.900	900-00056	G-PASS N9234P	22. 2.00	Police Aviation Services Ltd *(Op Kent Air Ambulance Trust)*	Marden	19. 4.05T
G-KAFE	Cameron N-65 HAB	1505		18. 5.87	J.R.Rivers-Scott	Loughborough	11. 5.02A
G-KAIR	Piper PA-28-181 Archer II	28-7990176	N3075D	28.12.78	Keen Leasing (IoM) Ltd	Belfast	2.10.03T
G-KAMM	Hawker Hurricane XIIA *(Built CCF)*	CCF/R32007	BW881	23. 2.95	Alpine Deer Group Ltd *(Rebuilt for American Flying Heritage Collection, Seattle, WA 11.99)*	Wanaka, NZ	AC
G-KAMP	Piper PA-18-135 Super Cub (L-18C)	18-3451	D-EDPM 96+27/NL+104/AC+502/AS+501/54-751	9. 5.97	S.N.Gregory & J.R.G.Furnell	(Lochearnhead)	29. 7.04T
G-KAOM	Scheibe SF.25C Falke	4417	D-KOAM	3. 2.98	Cambridge Gliding Club Ltd	Gransden Lodge	25. 3.05
G-KAPW	Percival P.56 Provost T.1	PAC/F/311	XF603	22. 9.97	The Shuttleworth Trust *(As "XF603/H")*	Old Warden	17. 4.03P
G-KARA	Brugger MB.2 Colibri (Volkswagen 1834)	PFA 43-10980		1. 6.95	Cara L.Reddish	Netherthorpe	27. 6.03P
G-KARI	Fuji FA.200-160 Aero Subaru	236	G-BBRE	19.12.84	The Scottish Civil Service Flying Club Ltd	Perth	10. 4.03T
G-KART	Piper PA-28-161 Warrior II	28-8016088	N8097B	10. 7.91	Newcastle upon Tyne Aero Club Ltd	Newcastle	24. 1.04T
G-KATI	Rans S-7 Courier (Jabiru 2200A)	0795.151 & PFA 218-12917		5. 3.96	S.M. & K.E.Hall	Netherthorpe	6. 3.03P
G-KATS	Piper PA-28-140 Cherokee Cruiser	28-7325022	G-BIRC OY-BGE	26. 8.83	A.G.Knight t/a Airlaunch	Old Buckenham	7. 8.05T
G-KATT	Cessna 152 II	15285661	G-BMTK N94387	10. 6.93	Aerohire Ltd	Wolverhampton	1. 7.02T
G-KATZ	Flight Design CT2K	7900		10. 7.02	A.N.D.Arthur	(London SW13)	11. 8.03P
G-KAUR	Colt 315A HAB	2536		1. 3.94	Balloon School (International) Ltd t/a Balloon Safaris	Petworth	17. 7.03T
G-KAWA	Denney Kitfox Model 2	PFA 172-11822		11. 3.91	J.W.Barr	Long Marston	22.10.02P
G-KAWW	Westland Wasp HAS Mk.1 *(Correct p/i is NZ3908)*	F9663	NZ3907 XT781	29. 3.99	G.P.Williams *(As "XT781/426")*	(Swansea)	6. 8.03P
G-KAXF	Hawker Hunter F.6A *(Built Armstrong-Whitworth Aircraft)*	S4/U/3361	8830M XF515	20.12.95	T.J.Manna t/a Kennet Aviation *(As "XF515/R")*	North Weald	8. 9.03P
G-KAXL	Westland Scout AH.1 *(Regd with c/n F8-7976)*	F9715	XV140	16.11.95	T.J.Manna t/a Kennet Aviation *(As "XV140/K")*	Newsells, Herts	12. 7.03P
G-KAXT	Westland Wasp HAS.1	F9669	NZ3905 XT787	5. 3.02	T.J.Manna	(Royston)	29.4.03P
G-KAYH	Extra EA 300/L	144		9. 4.02	Integrated Management Practices Ltd	(Maarheeze, The Netherlands)	16. 5.05T
G-KAZZ	Robinson R44	1135		21.12.00	Viking Office Supplies Ltd	(Lichfield)	21. 2.05T
G-KBKB	Thunder Ax8-90 Srs.2 HAB	2089		30.10.91	G.Boulden *"KB Cars"*	Aldershot	14. 9.03A

G-KBPI	Piper PA-28-161 Cherokee Warrior II	28-7816468	G-BFSZ N9556N	21. 5.81	Goodwood Road Racing Co Ltd	Goodwood	1. 9.05T
G-KBWW	Comper CLA.7 Swift rep	PFA 103-13554		3. 2.00	Hurstgate Ltd	(London W4)	
G-KCIG	Sportavia Fournier RF5B Sperber	51005	D-KCIG	19. 6.80	J.R.Bisset tr Deeside Fournier Group	Aboyne	29. 9.03P
G-KDET	Piper PA-28-161 Cadet	2841158	(SE-KIR) N9184Z	8. 8.89	Rapidspin Ltd (Op Biggin Hill School of Flying)	Biggin Hill	6.12.04T
G-KDEY	Scheibe SF-25E Super Falke	4325	D-KDEY	8. 1.99	J.French tr Falke Syndicate	Aston Down	14. 8.05
G-KDFF	Scheibe SF-25E Super Falke	4330	D-KDFF	25. 4.83	Bowland Forest Gliding Club Ltd Lower Cock Hill Farm, Chipping, Preston		16. 1.05
G-KDIX	Jodel D.9	PFA 54-10293		23.11.78	P.M.Bowden	(Stockport)	11. 6.03P
	(Volkswagen 1600)						
G-KDLN	LET Zlin Z.37A-2 Cmelak	19-05	OK-DLN	14. 8.95	J.Richards	Henstridge	27.10.02
G-KDMA	Cessna 560 Ultra	560-0553	N5145V	4. 4.01	Gamston Aviation Ltd	Gamston	3. 4.05T
G-KDOG	Scottish Aviation Bulldog Srs.120/121	BH120/289	XX624	18. 6.01	Gamit Ltd (As "XX624/E") (Noted 9.02)	North Weald	AC
G-KEAB*	Beech 65-B80 Queen Air	LD-344	G-BFEP/F-BRNR/OO-VDE	27. 9.87T	(N Franklin)	Bruntingthorpe	
					(Cancelled 24.5.91 as WFU: Fuselage noted 3.02)		
G-KEAC*	Beech 65-A80 Queen Air	LD-176	G-REXY G-AVNG/D-ILBO	3. 8.88	(E.A.Prentice) (Cancelled by CAA 3.4.01) (Stored 11.01)	Little Gransden	18. 9.89T
G-KEEN	Stolp SA.300 Starduster Too	800	PH-HAB (PH-PET)/G-KEEN/N800RE	19. 7.78	H.Sharp t/a Sharp Aerobatics	Belfast	25. 2.03P
	(Lycoming IO-540)						
G-KEES	Piper PA-28-180 Cherokee Archer	28-7505025	OO-AJV OO-HAC/N32102	29. 5.97	C.N.Ellerbrook	Wicklewood	7. 9.03
G-KELL	Van's RV-6	PFA 181-12845		16. 5.95	I.R.Thomas	(Pulborough)	15. 2.03P
	(Lycoming O-320-B2C)						
G-KELS	Van's RV-7	PFA 323-13801		22. 2.02	J.D.Kelsall	(Mansfield)	
G-KEMC	Grob G-109	6024	D-KEMC	19.10.84	D.L.H.Person, G.H.N.Chamberlain & R.S.Kiddy t/a Eye-Fly	Rattlesden	11. 9.03
G-KEMI	Piper PA-28-181 Archer III	2843180	N41493	28.10.98	R.B.Kempster	Fowlmere	27.10.04T
G-KENW	Robin DR400/500 President	39		20. 2.03	K.J.White	(Crowhurst)	
G-KENB	Air Command 503 Commander	PFA G/04-1153		7.11.89	K.Brogden	Heywood, Lancs	24. 9.93P
	(Rotax 503)						
G-KENI*	Rotorway Executive 152	3599		14. 3.89	A.J.Wheatley	Street Farm, Takeley	13. 3.03P
	(Rotorway RW 152)						
G-KENM	Luscombe 8EF Silvaire	2908	N21NK N71481/NC71481	9. 1.91	M.G.Waters	Compton Abbas	18.10.03P
G-KENN*	Robinson R22 Beta	0715		10.12.87	Barkham Antiques	Barkham, Berks	1. 1.97T
					(Damaged Sandtoft 31.10.94: cancelled 31.1.95 as WFU:) (Noted 7.01)		
G-KEST	Steen Skybolt	1	G-BNKG G-RATS/G-RHFI/N443AT	11. 6.91	B.Tempest tr G-KEST Syndicate	Leicester	20.10.03P
	(Lycoming IO-360)						
G-KEVB	Piper PA-28-181 Archer III	2843098	N9289E	29. 8.97	Palmair Ltd	Elstree	6. 9.03T
G-KEYS	Piper PA-23-250 Aztec F	27-7854052	N63909	6.10.78	T.M.Tuke & W.T.McCarter	City of Derry	1. 6.03T
G-KEYY	Cameron N-77 HAB	1748	G-BORZ	14. 6.88	B.N.Trowbridge	Egginton, Derby	3. 5.03A
G-KFAN	Scheibe SF-25B Falke	46301	D-KFAN	14. 5.96	R.G & J.A.Boyes (Current status unknown)	Eaglescott	29. 5.99
G-KFOX	Denney Kitfox Model 2	298 & PFA 172-11447		11.10.88	I.R.Lawrence	Eaglescott	25. 6.03P
G-KFRA	Piper PA-32-300 Six	32-7840182	G-BGII N20879	9. 9.97	M.Drake & W.Rankin tr West India Flying Group	Weston, Dublin	10.11.03
G-KFZI	Williams KFZ-1 Tigerfalck	PFA 153-11054		2. 2.89	L.R.Williams	(Aberdare)	
	(Continental C90) (Originally laid-down as Kestrel Sport c/n PFA 1530)						
G-KGAO	Scheibe SF-25C Falke 1700	44386	D-KGAG	30. 7.99	C.R.Ellis tr Falke 2000 Group	(Bishops Castle)	8. 8.05
G-KHOM	Aeromot AMT-200 Super Ximango			5. 5.98	O.C.Masters & K.M.Haslet	Waterford, Co.Waterford	21. 5.04
G-KHRE	SOCATA Rallye 150SV Garnement	2931	F-GAYR	25. 3.82	D.M.Gale & K.F.Crumplin Franklyn's Field, Chewton Mendip		28.12.03
G-KICK	Pegasus Quantum 15-912	7679		28. 6.00	G.D.Hall	Lower Mountpleasant Farm, Chatteris	27. 6.03P
G-KIMB	Robin DR300/140 Major	470	F-BPXX F-WPXX	23. 3.90	R.M.Kimbell	Sywell	8. 5.03
G-KIMK	Partenavia P68B Victor	27	G-BCPO	23. 2.01	M.Konstantinovic	(Brentwood)	29. 6.01
	(C/n indicates P68 model)						
G-KIMM	Europa Aviation Europa XS	404 & PFA 247-13404		20. 7.99	P.A.D.Clarke	Kemble	28.11.03P
	(Rotax 912ULS) (Monowheel u/c)				(F/f 14.11.01)		
G-KIMY	Robin DR400/140B Major	1401	PH-SRX	7. 6.00	D.C.Writer	Rochester	4. 7.03T
G-KINE	Gulfstream AA-5A Cheetah	AA5A-0896	N27173	20. 7.82	J.P.E.Walsh t/a Walsh Aviation (Op London School of Flying)	Biggin Hill	27. 7.03T
G-KIRK	Piper J-3C-65 Cub	10536	F-BBQC Fr AF/43-29245	28. 2.79	M.J.Kirk	(Australia)	17. 5.01P
	(Frame No.12490)						
G-KISS	Rand-Robinson KR.2	PFA 129-10899		2. 8.83	E.A.Rooney	(Whitstable)	
	(Volkswagen 1835)						
G-KITE	Piper PA-28-181 Archer II	28-8490053	N4338X	12. 4.88	L.G.Kennedy	Bournemouth	18. 4.03T
G-KITF	Denney Kitfox Model	1156	N156BH	10. 5.89	P Smith	Long Marston	22. 5.03P
G-KITI	Pitts S-2E Special	002	N36BM	21. 6.90	B.R.Cornes "Super Turkey II"	RAF Colerne	17. 4.01P
	(Lycoming IO-360)						
G-KITS	Europa Aviation Europa XS	468 & PFA 247-12844		13. 6.94	J.R.Evernden	Bidford	29.10.02P
	(Mid-West AE.100R) (Tri-gear u/c) (Kit No.003 originally quoted - presumably re-worked as 468) (F/f 19.7.95)						
G-KITT	Curtiss TP-40M Kittyhawk	27490	F-AZPJ	4. 3.98	Patina Ltd (Op The Fighter Collection)	Duxford	31.10.02P
			N1009N/N1233N/RCAF 840/43-5802 (As "49/Bengal Tiger" in US Army c/s)				
	(Officially c/n quoted as "31423")						
	(C/n 31423 was P-40N 43-23484/RCAF 877/N1009N(1) which was scrapped in 1965 when identity adopted by RCAF 840)						
G-KITY	Denney Kitfox Model 2	456 & PFA 172-11565		18. 8.89	J.P.Jenkins	South Lodge Farm, Widmerpool	2. 1.03P
	(IAME KFM112)				tr Kitfox KFM Group		
G-KITZ	Europa Aviation Europa XS T-G			17. 2.00	Europa Aircraft Co Ltd	Wombleton	11. 7.03P
	(Rotax 914UL)	460 & PFA 247-13578			(F/f 6.7.01)		
G-KKER	Jabiru Jabiru UL	PFA 274A-13474		1.10.99	W.K.Evans	Swansea	3. 4.03P
	(Jabiru 2200A)						
G-KKES	SOCATA TB-20 Trinidad	1316	G-BTLH	2. 3.92	Island Brokers Ltd	(Blackpool)	16. 5.04T
G-KKKK	Scottish Aviation Bulldog Srs.120/121	BH120/199	XX513	2.10.01	Drumforce Ltd (As "XX513/10")	Meppershall	16. 1.05T

Reg	Type	C/n	Prev ID / Date	Owner	Location	Expiry
G-KNAP	Piper PA-28-161 Warrior II	28-8116129	G-BIUX 15. 2.90	Keen Leasing (IoM) Ltd	Belfast	28. 4.02T
	N9507N *(Crashed on take off Stevensons Field, Letterkenny, Co Donegal 13.7.99: wreck stored 2.01)*					
G-KNEK	Grob G.109B	6437	D-KNEK 22. 5.00	R.A.Winley tr Syndicate 109	Currock Hill	7. 6.03
G-KNIB	Robinson R22 Beta	3145	30.10.00	C.G.Knibb	Sywell	26.11.03T
G-KNNY	Aérospatiale/Alenia ATR-42		3.03R	Air Wales *(For delivery 3.03)*		
G-KNOB	Lindstrand LBL-180A HAB	065	20.12.93	Wye Valley Aviation Ltd	Ross-on-Wye	16. 4.01T
G-KNOT	Hunting Percival P.84 Jet Provost T.Mk.3A	PAC/W/13893	G-BVEG 9. 6.99	R.S.Partridge-Hicks	North Weald	3. 8.03P
	XN629 *(As "XN629/49" in RAF c/s)*					
G-KNOW	Piper PA-32-300 Six	32-7840111	N9694C 21. 9.88	Hi Fly Ltd	(London W1)	15. 6.04
G-KNYT	Robinson R44 Astro	0723	13. 3.00	C.Bootman t/a Aircol	Cranfield	13. 3.03T
G-KODA	Cameron O-77 HAB	1448	26. 3.87	N.J.Milton *(Kodasnap titles)*	Bristol	
G-KOFM	Glaser-Dirks DG-600/18M	6-66M16	D-KOFM 13. 7.99	A.Mossman	(Feshiebridge)	28. 7.05
G-KOHF	Scheicher ASK-14	14033	D-KOHF 4. 9.01	J. Houlihan	(Hollywood, Co Down)	6.11.04
G-KOKL	Hoffmann H-36 Dimona	36276	D-KOKL 4. 3.98	R.Smith & R.Stembrowicz	Rufforth	5. 4.04
G-KOLB	Kolb Twinstar Mk.3A (Rotax 912UL)	PFA 205-12228	30. 6.93	J.L.Moar	Wick	29. 9.03P
G-KOLI	PZL-110 Koliber 150	03900038	23. 7.90	J.R.Powell	Perth	1. 2.05
G-KOMI	Yakovlev Yak-52	855509	LY-ALS 3.03R	(M Jefferies)	(Litle Gransden)	
	DOSAAF 69/DOSAAF 49 *(DOSAAF 69 not confirmed)* "69"					
G-KONG	Slingsby T.67M-200 Firefly	2041	VR-HZP 24. 3.94	Babcock Support Services Ltd	RAF Barkston Heath	3. 8.03T
	HKG-10/G-7-119			t/a Babcock HCS *(Op JEFTS)*		
G-KOOL	de Havilland DH.104 Devon C.2/2	04220	"G-DOVE" 12. 1.82	K.P.Hunt c/o 135 Sqdn (Reigate & Redhill) ATC	Redhill	AC
	VP967			*(Noted 12.02)*		
G-KORN	Cameron Berentzen Bottle 70SS HAB	1655	10. 5.88	A D & R.S.Kent, I M Martin & I Chadwick	Kirdford	23. 6.00A
				tr Balloon Preservation Flying Group *"Berentzen"*		
G-KOTA	Piper PA-28-236 Dakota	28-8011044	N8130R 23.12.88	D.J.Fravigar	Clough Farm, Croft, Skegness	14. 3.05
				t/a JF Packaging		
G-KPAO	Robinson R44 Astro	0382	G-SSSS 19.11.98	Avonline Ltd	Bristol	20.11.03T
G-KPTT	SOCATA TB-20 Trinidad	1821	F-GRBI 13. 6.01	Chartfleet Ltd	Fenland	23. 8.04T
G-KRAY	Robinson R22HP	0266	EI-CEF 25. 5.95	Sloane Helicopters Ltd	Sywell	4. 7.04T
	G-BOBO/N712BH/N100GV/N90763					
G-KRES	Stoddard-Hamilton Glasair IIS RG	PFA 149-12984	12. 6.96	G.Kresfelder	Shoreham	17. 2.03P
G-KRII	Rand Robinson KR-2	PFA 129-10934	4. 8.89	M.R.Cleveley	(Halesworth, Suffolk)	
G-KRIS	Maule M-5-235C Lunar Rocket	7357C	N56420 21. 4.81	A.C.Vermeer	(Antrim, Co.Antrim)	25. 1.04
G-KRNW	Eurocopter EC135-T1	0175	9. 7.01	Bond Air Services Ltd	Aberdeen	11. 7.04T
G-KSIR	Stoddard-Hamilton Glasair IIS RG (Lycoming IO-360)	2151 & PFA 149-12137	15. 4.94	The Hon R.Cayzer	Oxford	19. 6.03
G-KSKS	Cameron N-105 HAB	4963	21. 3.01	A.M Holly t/a Exclusive Ballooning	Bristol	26. 2.03T
				(Kwik Save titles)		
G-KSKY	Sky 77-24 HAB	170	15.10.99	J.R.Howard	Poulton-le-Fylde	6. 7.03A
G-KSVB	Piper PA-24-260 Comanche B	24-4657	G-ENIU 8.11.91	S.Juggler	Stapleford	28. 5.04
	G-AVJU/N9199P/N10F					
G-KTCC	Schempp-Hirth Ventus 2cM	33/57	D-KTCC 29. 4.02	D.Heslop	(Brentwood)	29. 5.05
G-KTEE	Cameron V-77 HAB	2177	28.12.89	D.C. & N.P.Bull *"Katie"*	Aylesbury	21. 9.03A
G-KTKT	Sky 260-24 HAB	110	19. 5.98	T.M.Donnelly *"Kit Kat"*	Doncaster	15. 5.03T
G-KTOL	Robinson R44 Clipper	0780	10.10.02	K.N.Tolley t/a JNK 2000	(Bromyard)	5. 7.03T
G-KUBB	SOCATA TB-20 Trinidad GT	2026	F-OILS 1.12.00	Offshore Marine Consultants Ltd	Gamston	7.12.03
G-KUKI	Robinson R22 Beta	1802	G-BTNB 15. 8.02	Kuki Helicopters Ltd	Gamston	24. 7.03T
	N23006					
G-KUTU	QAC Quickie Q.2 (Limbach L2000)	PFA 94A-10758	8. 3.82	J.Parkinson & R.Nash	Booker	29. 4.86P
	(Damaged Cranfield 18.5.85: stored 4.99: current status unknown)					
G-KVBF	Cameron A-340HL HAB	4313	6. 4.98	Airxcite Ltd t/a Virgin Balloon Flights	Wembley	22. 8.03T
G-KVIP	Beech 200 Super King Air	BB-487	17. 5.02	Capital Trading (Aviation) Ltd	Filton	29. 5.03T
	G-PLAT/N8PY/VH-PIL/N198SC/PT-OYR/N40QN/VH-NIC/N40QN/N400N/N243KA					
G-KWAK	Scheibe SF-25C Falke	44581	D-KWAK 8. 1.03	Mendip Gliding Club Ltd	Halesland	5. 1.03T
G-KWAX	Cessna 182E Skylane	18253808	N9902 18. 5.78	D.R.Graves	(Newton Abbot)	5. 1.03T
	YV-T-PTS/N2808Y					
G-KWIK	Partenavia P.68B	152	27. 9.78	ACD Cidra NV	Wevelgem, Belgium	11. 6.03T
G-KWKI	QAC Quickie Q.200 (Continental O-200-A)	PFA 94-12158	22.10.91	B.M.Jackson	Enstone	17. 9.03P
G-KWLI	Cessna 421C Golden Eagle II	421C0168	G-DARR 13.11.98	Langley Holdings plc	Gamston	25. 1.02
	G-BNEZ/N87386					
G-KYAK	SPP Yakovlev Yak C-11	171101	F-AZQI 21.12.78	M.Gainza *"36"*	North Weald	3.12.03P
	G-KYAK/F-AZHQ/G-KYAK/Israeli DFAF/Egyptian AF 590/Czech AF					
G-KYDD	Robinson R.44 Astro	0106	N2123E 16. 9.99	EK Aviation Ltd	Cambridge	3.10.05T
	D-HDLW					
G-KYNG	Aviamilano F.8L Falco 1	105	I-KYNG 6. 8.97	A E Hutton	North Weald	19. 6.04
	HB-UOH/I-STRI					

G-LAAA - G-LZZZ

Reg	Type	C/n	Prev ID / Date	Owner	Location	Expiry
G-LABS	Europa Aviation Europa (Rotax 912) (Monowheel u/c)	049 & PFA 247-12595	1. 3.94	C.T.H.Pattinson	(Bicester)	15.12.03P
				(F/f 3.11.02)		
G-LACA	Piper PA-28-161 Cherokee Warrior II	28-7816036	N44883 22. 6.90	LAC (Enterprises) Ltd *(Op Lancashire Aero Club)*	Barton	18. 3.05T
G-LACB	Piper PA-28-161 Warrior II	28-8216035	N8450A 12. 6.90	LAC (Enterprises) Ltd *(Op Lancashire Aero Club)*	Barton	9. 7.05T
G-LACD	Piper PA-28-181 Archer III	2843157	G-BYBG 11.11.98	D.H.Brown t/a David Brown Aviation	(Burnley)	22.10.04T
	N47BK					
G-LACE	Europa Aviation Europa (Monowheel u/c)	256 & PFA 247-12962	15. 4.96	J.H.Phillingham	(Wallingford)	
				(Current status unknown)		
G-LACR	Denney Kitfox	PFA 172-11945	4.12.90	C.M.Rose *(Under construction 6.00)*	(Edinburgh)	
G-LADD	Enstrom 480	5037	20. 5.99	Combi-Lift Ltd	(Clontibret, Co.Monaghan)	9. 7.05T
G-LADE	Piper PA-32-300 Six	32-7940030	N3008L 21.11.80	B.E.Bergabo *"Harry O"*	Denham	18. 6.05T

Reg	Type	Serial	Prev ID	Date	Owner	Location	Expiry
G-LADI	Piper PA-30 Twin Comanche	30-334	G-ASOO N10F	8. 4.94	S.H.Eastwood	Blackbushe	3.10.05T
G-LADS	Rockwell Commander 114	14314	N4994W (N114XT)/N4994W	6.12.90	D.F.Soul	Emberton, Olney	5. 1.03
G-LAGR	Cameron N-90 HAB	1628		25. 1.88	J.R.Clifton	Brackley	11.10.03A
G-LAIN	Robinson R22 Beta	1992		7. 2.92	Deadline Programming Ltd	Booker	4. 6.04T
G-LAIR	Stoddard-Hamilton Glasair IIS	2106		12. 9.91	A.I.O'Broin & S.T.Raby	Raby's Farm, Great Stukeley	
					(New owner 5.02)		
G-LAKE	Lake LA-250 Renegade	70	(EI-PJM) G-LAKE/N8415B	12. 7.88	P.J.McGoldrick	Lough Derg Marina, Killaloe	10. 6.05
G-LAMA	Aérospatiale SA315B Lama	2348	SE-HET	17. 3.98	PLM Dollar Group Ltd	Cumbernauld	19. 3.04T
G-LAMM	Europa Aviation Europa	244 & PFA 247-12941		20.11.95	S.A.Lamb	(Paddock Wood)	
	(Monowheel u/c)				*(Current status unknown)*		
G-LAMP	Cameron Lightbulb-110 SS HAB	4899		21. 7.00	LE Electrical Ltd	Norwich	18. 6.03A
G-LAMS	Reims/Cessna F152 II	F15201431	N54558	23. 6.68	Jaxx Landing Ltd	Swansea	2.10.03T
G-LAND	Robinson R22 Beta	0639		29. 4.87	Helicopter Training & Hire Ltd	Belfast	29. 3.02T
G-LANE	Reims/Cessna F172N Skyhawk II	F17201853		27. 6.79	G.C.Bantin	Sproatley	4. 6.03
G-LAOK	IAV-Bacau Yakovlev Yak-52	877404	LY-AOK DOSAAF 16 (yellow) (?)	22. 1.03	I.F.Vaughan & J.P.Armitage	Humberside	
G-LAOL	Piper PA-28RT-201 Cherokee Arrow IV	28R-7918211	D-EAOL N2903Y	6.10.99	G.P.Aviation Ltd	Goodwood	13. 1.03T
G-LAPN	Avid Aerobat	PFA 189-12146		4. 3.93	R.M. & A.P.Shorter	White Waltham	20. 8.03P
G-LARA	Robin DR400/180 Regent	2050		14. 2.91	K.D. & C.A.Brackwell	Goodwood	23. 4.03
G-LARE	Piper PA-39 Twin Comanche C/R	39-16	N8861Y	20. 2.91	Glareways (Neasden) Ltd	Biggin Hill	23. 4.03
G-LARK	Helton Lark 95	9517	N5017J	3.12.85	J.Fox	Booker	26. 3.02P
G-LASR	Stoddard-Hamilton Glasair II	2027		8. 1.90	G.Lewis *(Current status unknown)*	(Heswall, Wirral)	
G-LASS	Rutan VariEze	PFA 74-10209		20. 9.78	J.Mellor	(Neston, Cheshire)	12. 6.03P
	(Continental O-200-A)						
G-LAST	Cessna 340 II	340-0305	G-UNDY G-BBNR/N69452	2. 9.96	Prospect Developments (Northern) Ltd	Manchester	15. 8.03
G-LASU	Eurocopter EC135	T1 0228		3. 9.02	Lancashire Constabulary Air Support Unit	Warton	15.10.05T
G-LATK	Robinson R44 Astro	0064	G-BVMK	18. 7.94	Holly Aviation Ltd	Gloucestershire	27. 8.03T
G-LAVE	Cessna 172R Skyhawk	17280663	G-BYEV N2377J/N41297	10. 3.99	Connect Air Ltd	(Addlestone)	17. 4.05
G-LAWS	Sikorsky S-61N Mk.II	61-824	G-BHOF LN-ONK/G-BHOF/LN-ONK/G-BHOF	7. 7.99	Laws Helicopter Ltd	Aberdeen	9. 7.04T
G-LAZA	Lazer Z.200	PFA 123-12682		15. 6.95	M.Hammond	Airfield Farm, Hardwick	8.12.03P
	(Lycoming AEIO-360)						
G-LAZL	Piper PA-28-161 Warrior II	28-8116216	D-EAZL N9536N	9. 6.99	S.Bagley & K.J.Amies	Coventry	25. 7.05T
					t/a Hawk Aero Leasing		
G-LAZR	Cameron O-77 HAB	2240		6. 3.90	Laser Civil Engineering Ltd	Pershore	10. 6.97A
					"Laser Engineering"		
G-LAZY	Lindstrand LBL Armchair SS HAB	129		18. 9.94	The Air Chair Co Ltd	Westville, Indiana, USA	27. 4.03A
					"The Chair"		
G-LAZZ	Stoddard-Hamilton GlaStar	PFA 295-13059		31.10.96	A.N.Evans	(Congleton)	30.10.03P
G-LBLI	Lindstrand LBL 69A HAB	010		4.11.92	N.M.Gabriel	Kimberley, Notts	13. 4.03A
G-LBMM	Piper PA-28-161 Cherokee Warrior II	28-7816440	N6940C	28.11.89	Flexi-Soft Ltd	Wellesbourne Mountford	8. 5.05T
G-LBRC	Piper PA-28RT-201 Arrow IV	28R-7918051	N2245P	20. 7.88	D.J.V.Morgan	Wolverhampton	17. 1.04
G-LCGL	Comper CLA.7 Swift rep	PFA 103 11089		1.7.92	J.M.Greenland	Blackacre Farm, Holt, Wilts	15.11.03P
	(Pobjoy Niagara 1A)						
G-LCOC	Britten-Norman BN-2A Mk.III-1 Trislander	366	G-BCCU 4X-CCK/G-BCCU/9L-LAR/G-BCCU/(LN-VIV)	30. 7.01	AirX Ltd t/a Lecocqs.com	Alderney	6. 1.04T
G-LCON	Eurocopter AS355N Twin Squirrel	5572		28. 6.94	Lancashire Constabulary	Warton	26.10.03T
					(Op Lancashire Air Support Unit)		
G-LCRC	Boeing 757-23AER	24636	G-IEAB	27.10.93	MyTravel Airways Ltd	Manchester	9. 5.05T
G-LCYA	Dassault Falcon 900EX	105	F-WWFC	5. 8.02	London City Airport Jet Centre Ltd	London City	4. 8.05T
G-LDAH	Best Off Skyranger 912	UK/216 & BMAA/HB/241		8.10.02	A.S.Haslam & L.Dickinson	(Warwick)	
G-LDYS*	Thunder Ax6-56Z HAB	347		18. 5.81	P.Glydon & M.J.Myddelton	Keynsham	27. 3.00A
	(Regd as Colt 56A)				*"Gladys"* *(Cancelled 25.6.02 by CAA)*		
G-LEAF	Reims/Cessna F406 Caravan II	F406-0018	EI-CKY PH-ALN/OO-TIW/F-WZDX	7. 3.96	Atlantic Air Transport Ltd	Inverness	20. 5.03T
					(Op Highland Airways) (Atlantic Airlines c/s)		
G-LEAM	Piper PA-28-236 Dakota	28-8011061	G-BHLS N35650	1. 7.80	C.S.Doherty	Gamston	8. 7.04
G-LEAP	Pilatus Britten-Norman BN-2T Islander	2183	G-BLND	19. 8.87	G Burton	AAC Netheravon	18. 4.03A
					tr Army Parachute Association		
G-LEAR	Learjet Learjet 35A	35A-265	G-ZEST N1462B	20. 8.79	Northern Executive Aviation Ltd	Manchester	10. 1.03T
G-LEAS	Sky 90-24 HAB	158		4. 5.99	Leasing Group plc	Reading	28. 6.03A
					(The Leasing Group LNG fuel...the natural choice titles)		
G-LEAU	Cameron N-31 HAB	761		5. 8.81	P.L.Mossman *"Perrier" (Inflated 4.02)*	Bristol	24. 2.97A
G-LEBE	Europa Aviation Europa	237 & PFA 247-12927		17. 5.01	P.Atkinson	(Carnforth)	
	(Wilksch WAM-120) (Monowheel u/c)						
G-LECA	Aérospatiale AS355F1 Twin Squirrel	5043	G-BNBK C-GBKH	6. 2.87	South Western Electricity plc	Bristol	24. 7.05T
G-LEDA	Robinson R22 Beta	1938	G-IFOX	12.11.98	Pentacle Ltd	Denham	13.11.00T
G-LEED	Denney Kitfox Model 2	450 & PFA 172-11577		24. 4.91	M.J.Beding	(St. Austell)	4. 9.03P
	(Swung to left off runway Compton Abbas 16.9.02, went through wire fence & struck parked car: substantially damaged)						
G-LEEE	Jabiru Jabiru UL	PFA 274A-13516		18. 1.00	J.N.Fugl	Heathfield	20. 8.03P
G-LEEN	Aero Designs Pulsar XP	PFA 202-12147	G-BZMP G-DESI	16. 7.01	R.B.Hemsworth	(Bideford)	
G-LEES	Glaser-Dirks DG-400	4-238		4.10.88	J Bradley	RAF Upavon	14. 3.04
G-LEEZ	Bell 206L-1 LongRanger II	45761	G-BPCT D-HDBB/N3175G	22. 1.92	Pennine Helicopters Ltd	(Oldham)	7.12.03T
G-LEGG	Reims/Cessna F182Q Skylane II	F18200145	G-GOOS	26. 6.96	P.J.Clegg	Barton	19.12.02

Reg	Type	C/n	Prev id	Date	Owner/Operator	Base	Date2
G-LEGO	Cameron O-77 HAB	1975		14. 4.89	P.M.Traviss *"Jigsaw II"*	Yarm	3. 5.03A
G-LEIC	Reims/Cessna FA152 Aerobat	F15200416		16. 9.86	Leicestershire Aero Club Ltd	Leicester	8. 8.05T
G-LELE	Lindstrand LBL 31A HAB	806		16. 8.01	L.E.Electrical Ltd	Norwich	19. 8.02A
G-LENA	IAV-Bacau Yakovlev Yak-52	833901	LY-AMU DOSAAF 42 (red)	5.11.02	Yak-52 Ltd	(Salisbury	AC)
G-LEND*	Cameron N-77 HAB	2012		25. 5.89	Southern Flight Co Ltd	Southampton	12. 9.96T
					"Southern Finance Co/Glenda" (Cancelled 8.10.01 as WFU)		
G-LENI	Aérospatiale AS355F1 Twin Squirrel	5311	G-ZFDB G-BLEV	9. 8.95	Grid Aviation Ltd	Denham	21. 4.03T
G-LENN	Cameron V-56 HAB	1833		29. 9.88	A.E.Austin	Naseby	30.10.03A
G-LENS	Thunder Ax7-77Z HAB	168		3.11.78	R S Breakwell	(Bridgnorth)	13. 2.02A
G-LENX	Cessna 172N Skyhawk II	17272232	G-BMVJ N9347E	15. 2.02	M.W.Glencross	(Luton)	25. 2.02T
G-LENY	Piper PA-34-220T Seneca III	34-8233205	N111PS (OK-MKN)/PH-SMS/(PH-CCC)/D-GAPN/N82396	26. 7.00	Air Medical Ltd	Oxford	3. 8.03T
G-LEOS	Robin DR400/120 Dauphin 2+2	1884		29.11.88	P.G.Newens	Fairoaks	3. 4.04
G-LESJ	Denney Kitfox Model 3 (Rotax 582)	PFA 172-12001		4.10.94	P.Whittingham	Otherton, Cannock	21. 3.03P
G-LESZ	Denney Kitfox Model 5	PFA 172C-12822		25.10.02	L.A.James	Wharf Farm, Market Bosworth	
G-LEVI	Aeronca 7AC Champion	7AC-4001	N85266 NC85266	17. 4.90	Jean P.A.Pumphrey tr G-LEVI Group *("NC85266" on fin)*	White Waltham	2.10.03P
G-LEXI	Cameron N-77 HAB	438		26.10.78	T.Gilbert *(Rolls Royce/Jaguar titles)*	Weston-Super-Mare	18. 7.03A
G-LEXX	Van's RV-8	PFA 303-13896		11. 4.02	A.A.Wordsworth	(Sutton-in-Ashfield)	
G-LEZE	Rutan LongEz (Continental O-200-A)	PFA 74A-10702		31. 3.82	K.G.M.Loyal, A.J.Draper, J.R.J.Giesler & C.McGeachy	Wombleton	5.11.01P
G-LEZZ	Stoddard-Hamilton GlaStar (Lycoming O-320) *(Tricycle u/c)*	PFA 295-13241	G-BYCR	4.11.98	L.A.James	Wharf Farm, Market Bosworth	17. 6.03P
G-LFIX	Supermarine 509 Spitfire Trainer 9 *(C/n is firewall plate no)*	CBAF.8463	IAC162	1. 2.80	Carolyn S.Grace *"Nicholson Leslie"*	Duxford	16. 4.03P
			G-15-175/ML407 (As "ML407/OU-V" (stbd) in 485 Sqdn c/s & "ML407/"NL-D" (port) in 341 Sqdn c/s)				
G-LFSA	Piper PA-38-112 Tomahawk	38-78A0430	G-BSFC N9739N	22.10.90	Liverpool Flying School Ltd	Liverpool	15. 3.03T
G-LFSB	Piper PA-38-112 Tomahawk	38-78A0072	G-BLYC D-ELID/N9715N	20.10.94	Spencer Davies Engineering Ltd	(Burry Port)	7.10.03T
G-LFSC	Piper PA-28-140 Cherokee Cruiser	28-7425005	G-BGTR OY-BGO/SE-GDS	4. 9.95	M.B.North	Linley Hill, Leven	27.10.04T
G-LFSD	Piper PA-38-112 Tomahawk II	38-82A0046	G-BNPT N91522	21.10.96	Liverpool Flying School Ltd	Liverpoo	I1. 6.03T
G-LFSF	Cessna 150M	15077651	G-BSRC N6337K	9. 7.99	Gems Europe SA	Charleroi, Belgium	27. 5.03T
G-LFSG	Piper PA-28-180 Cherokee E	28-5799	G-AYAA N11C	19. 6.00	Liverpool Flying School Ltd	Liverpool	3.11.04T
G-LFSH	Piper PA-38-112 Tomahawk	38-78A0352	G-BOZM N6247A	16. 7.01	Liverpool Flying School Ltd	Liverpool	19. 6.04T
G-LFSI	Piper PA-28-140 Cherokee C	28-26850	G-AYKV N11C	14. 7.89	M.J.Green, P.S.Hoyle & S.Merriman	Humberside	13. 3.05T
G-LFSJ	Piper PA-28-161 Warrior II	28-7916536	G-BPHE N2911D	4.11.02	Leeds Flying School Ltd	Leeds-Bradford	26. 3.04T
G-LFVB	Supermarine 349 Spitfire LF.V	CBAF.2403	8070M 5377M/EP120	9. 5.94	Patina Ltd *"City of Winnipeg"*	Duxford	31. 8.02P
					(Op The Fighter Collection as "EP120/AE-A" in 402 Sqdn c/s)		
G-LFVC	Supermarine 349 Spitfire L.Vc	----	ZK-MKV A58-178/JG891	28. 9.99	Historic Flying Ltd	(Duxford)	
G-LGLG	Cameron Z-210 HAB	10258		11. 3.02	Flying Circus SRL	Madrid, Spain	25. 2.03A
G-LGNA	SAAB-Scania SF.340B	340B-199	N592MA SE-F99	11. 6.99	Loganair Ltd *(Benyhone Tartan t/s)*	Glasgow	13. 6.03T
G-LGNB	SAAB-Scania SF.340B	340B-216	N595MA SE-G16	8. 7.99	Loganair Ltd *(Waves of the City t/s)*	Glasgow	8. 7.03T
G-LGNC	SAAB-Scania SF.340B	340B-318	SE-KXC F-GTSF/EC-GMI/F-GMVZ/SE-KXC/SE-C18	9. 6.00	Loganair Ltd *"Chatham Historic Dockyard"*	Glasgow	11. 6.03T
G-LGND	SAAB-Scania SF.340B	340B-169	G-GNTH N588MA/SE-F69	7. 9.01	Loganair Ltd	Glasgow	4. 2.03T
G-LGNE	SAAB-Scania SF.340B	340B-172	G-GNTI N589MA/SE-F72	31. 8.01	Loganair Ltd	Glasgow	5. 2.03T
G-LGNF	SAAB-Scania SF340B	340B-192	N192JE G-GNTJ/N591MA/SE-F92	8. 8.02	Loganair Ltd	Glasgow	7. 8.03T
G-LGNG	SAAB-Scania SF.340B	340B-327	SE-C27 VH-CMH/SE-C27	16.12.02	Loganair Ltd	Glasgow	16.12.03
G-LGTE	Boeing 737-3Y0	24908	TC-SUP	25. 1.01	British Airways plc	Gatwick	26. 3.04T
G-LGTF	Boeing 737-382	24450	N115GB TC-IAC/CS-TIE	7. 3.01	British Airways plc	Gatwick	30. 4.04T
G-LGTG	Boeing 737-3Q8	24470	N696BJ SX-BFT/N470KB/PK-GWD	4. 4.01	British Airways plc	Gatwick	14. 6.04T
G-LGTH	Boeing 737-3Y0	23924	OO-LTV XA-SEM/G-BNGL	4. 4.01	British Airways plc	Gatwick	8. 6.04T
G-LGTI	Boeing 737-3Y0	23925	OO-LTY XA-SEO/G-BNGM	2. 4.01	British Airways plc	Gatwick	25. 7.04T
G-LGTJ	Boeing 737-3..			R	British Airways plc	Gatwick	
G-LGTK	Boeing 737-3..			R	British Airways plc	Gatwick	
G-LGTL	Boeing 737-3..			R	British Airways plc	Gatwick	
G-LHCA	Robinson R22 Beta	2947	N299FA	28.10.02	Rotorcraft Ltd	Redhill	28.11.05T
G-LHPL	Aérospatiale AS350 Ecureuil	2189	N612LH 9M-BAZ/ZK-HJW/JA9808	11. 5.99	Lloyd Helicopters (Pte) Ltd	Redhill	31. 5.05T
G-LIBB	Cameron V-77 HAB	2463		21. 6.91	R.J.Mercer	Belfast	7. 6.03A
G-LIBS	Hughes 369HS (500C)	43-0469S	N9147F	20. 8.85	A.R.Smith	Gloucestershire	28. 6.04T

Reg	Type	C/n	Prev id / date	Owner	Location	Date
G-LICK	Cessna 172N Skyhawk II	17270631	N172AG 17. 7.02	Leeds Flying School Ltd	Leeds-Bradford	16. 9.05T
			G-LICK/G-BNTR/N739LQ			
G-LIDA	Hoffman HK.36R Super Dimona	36355	15. 4.92	Bidford Airfield Ltd	Bidford	6.12.04
G-LIDE	Piper PA-31-350 Navajo Chieftain	31-7852156	(G-VIDE) 26.10.78	Keen Leasing (IoM) Ltd	Ronaldsway	27.10.04T
			N27800			
G-LIDR	Hoffmann H-36 Dimona	36208	G-BMSK 1. 4.96	B.Kerry tr G-LIDR Flying Group	Bidford	23. 1.05
G-LIDS	Robinson R22 Beta-II	2808	21. 4.98	Plane Talking Ltd	Elstree	7. 5.04T
G-LIFE	Thunder Ax6-56Z HAB	135	11. 1.78	D.P.Hopkins	Pidley	11.12.02A
				t/a Lakeside Lodge Golf Centre "Golden Delicious"		
G-LILP	Europa Aviation Europa XS	487 & PFA 247-13802	22. 5.02	G.L.Jennings	(Shoreham-by-Sea)	
	(Monowheel u/c)					
G-LILY	Bell 206B-3 JetRanger III	4107	14. 3.95	T.S.Brown	Twineham	11. 4.05T
			C-FIJD			
G-LINC	Hughes 369HS	43-0467S	C-FDUZ 14. 5.87	Sleekform Ltd	(Sowerby Bridge)	13. 3.03T
			CF-DUZ			
G LINE	Eurocopter AS355N Twin Squirrel	5566	22. 3.94	National Grid Co plc	Oxford	12. 5.03T
G-LION	Piper PA-18-135 Super Cub	18-3857	PH-KLB 29. 9.80	J.G.Jones "Grin'i Bare It"	(Corwen)	18.11.02
	(L-21B-PI) (Frame No.18-3841)		(PH-DKG)/R.Neth AF R-167/54-2457 t/a JG Jones Haulage (As "R-167" in R.Neth AF c/s)			
G-LIOT	Cameron O-77 HAB	2378	7. 8.90	N.D.Eliot	London SW19	5. 6.02A
G-LIPE	Robinson R.22 Beta	1882	G-BTXJ 23. 1.92	F.C.Owen	Blackpool	7. 3.04T
G-LIPS	Cameron Lips-90 SS HAB	4846	G-BZBV 15.11.00	Flying Pictures Ltd (Polaroid JoyCam titles)	Chilbolton	30. 7.02A
G-LISE	Robin DR500/200i President	0001	27. 7.98	J.Marks	Goodwood	26. 9.04
	(Registered as DR400/500)					
G-LITE	Rockwell Commander 112A	291	OY-RPP 13. 6.80	J.E.Dixon	Norwich	19.10.03
G-LITZ	Pitts S-1E Special	PFA 09-11131	3. 3.92	P.J.Caruth "Glitz"	(Yeovil)	2. 5.03P
	(Lycoming IO-360)					
G-LIVH	Piper J-3C-65 Cub	11529	OO-JAN 31. 3.94	M.D.Cowburn	Barton	22. 5.03
	(L-4H-PI) (Frame No.11354)		OO-AAT/AO-PAX/43-30238	(As "330238/A-24" in US Army c/s)		
G-LIVR	Enstrom 480	5038	14. 7.99	Soil Tech BV	Meer, Belgium	16. 9.05T
G-LIZA	Cessna 340A II	340A1021	G-BMDM 15. 2.90	Tayflite Ltd	Perth	12. 6.05T
			ZS-KRH/N4620N			
G-LIZI	Piper PA-28-160 Cherokee	28-52	G-ARRP 26. 1.89	R.J.Walker & J.R.Lawson	Cranwell	1. 8.05
			N5050W			
G-LIZZ	Piper PA-E23-250 Aztec E	27-7405268	G-BBWM 26. 7.93	T.J.Nathan	Fairoaks	28. 1.03
			N40532			
G-LJCC	Murphy Rebel	PFA 232-13355	8. 7.98	P.H.Hyde	(Biggleswade)	
G-LJET	Learjet Learjet 35A	35A-643	(N35NK) 2.12.88	Gama Aviation Ltd	Farnborough	19. 9.02T
			G-LJET/N39418			
G-LKTB	Piper PA-28-181 Archer III	2843496	N5339X 18.12.01	Top Cat Aviation Ltd	Manchester	19.12.04T
G-LLEW	Aeromot AMT-200S Super Ximango	200126	15.11.00	Lleweni Parc Ltd	Lleweni Parc	1. 3.04
G-LMAX	Sequoia F.8L Falco	PFA 100-13423	28.10.02	J. Maxwell	(Ascot)	
G-LMLV	Dyn'Aéro MCR-01 Club	PFA 301A-13524	25.10.99	L.& M.La Vecchia	Cambridge	7.11.03P
	(Rotax 912 ULS)					
G-LNAA	MD Helicopters MD.900	900-00074	G-76-0742 6. 9.00	Police Aviation Services Ltd	RAF Waddington	27.11.03T
			G-LNAA/N7030B	(Op Lincs & Notts Air Ambulance)		
G-LNDS	Robinson R44 Raven	1157	12. 2.02	MC Air Ltd	Wellesbourne Mountford	3. 3.05T
G-LNTI	Robinson R44 Astro	0457	G-TPTS 11. 4.00	LNT Aviation Ltd	Coney Park, Leeds	6. 5.04T
G-LNYS	Reims/Cessna F177RG Cardinal	F177RG0120	G-BDCM 30.11.92	J.W.Clarke	Tatenhill	28.12.02
			OY-BIP			
G-LOAD	Dan Rihn DR.107 One Design	PFA 264-13776	7. 6.02	M.J.Clark	(Horsham)	
G-LOAN	Cameron N-77 HAB	1434	9. 1.87	P.Lawman	Northampton	8. 5.01A
				(Newbury Building Society titles)		
G-LOBL	Bombardier BD-700-1A10 Global Express	9038	G-52-24 22. 2.02	1427 Ltd	Manchester	21. 2.03T
			C-GFJR			
G-LOBO	Cameron O-120 HAB	3389	3. 1.95	C.A.Butler t/a Solo Aerostatics	Newbury	26. 7.03A
G-LOCH	Piper J-3C-90 Cub	12687	HB-OCH 10.12.84	J.M.Greenland	Blackacre Farm, Holt, Wilts	5.11.03P
	(L-4J-PI) (Frame No.12517)		44-80391			
G-LOFA*	Lockheed L.188CF Electra	2002	N359Q 10. 2.94	Atlantic Air Transport Ltd	(Coventry)	9. 2.00T
			F-OGST/N359AC/TI-LRM/N359AC/HC-AVX/N359AC/VH-ECA			
			(Cancelled 29.7.98 as WFU) (Noted in fire practice area 4.02)			
G-LOFB	Lockheed L.188CF Electra	1131	N667F 28. 6.94	Atlantic Air Transport Ltd	Coventry	28. 6.03T
			N133AJ/CF-IJW/N131US			
G-LOFC	Lockheed L.188CF Electra	1100	N665F 15. 6.95	Atlantic Air Transport Ltd	Coventry	10. 7.04T
			N289AC/N6123A			
G-LOFD	Lockheed L.188CF Electra	1143	LN-FOG 12. 6.97	Atlantic Air Transport Ltd	Coventry	15. 6.03T
			LN-MOD/N9745C/(CF-IJC)/N9745C			
G-LOFE	Lockheed L.188CF Electra	1144	EI-CET 5. 1.99	Atlantic Air Transport Ltd	Coventry	19. 3.05T
			(G-FIGF)/N668Q/N668F/N24AF/N138US (Interlink Ireland titles)			
G-LOFF	Lockheed L-188C Electra	1128	LN-FON(2) 21. 6.00	Atlantic Air Transport Ltd	Coventry	AC
			N342HA/N417MA/OB-R-1138/HP-684/N417MA/CF-ZST/N7142C			
			(For Test bed use 5.02 - remains as "LN-FON")			
G-LOFG	Lockheed L-188C Electra	1116	LN-FOL(2) 21. 6.00	Atlantic Air Transport Ltd	Coventry	
			N669F/N404GN/N6126A	(Not converted - remains as "LN-FOL" & stored 4.02)		
G-LOFM	Maule MX-7-180A Star Rocket	20027C	N31110 19. 7.95	Atlantic Air Transport Ltd	Coventry	10. 9.04T
G-LOFT	Cessna 500 Citation I	500-0331	LN-NAT 12. 1.95	Atlantic Air Transport Ltd	Jersey	25. 3.03T
			EC-FUM/EC-500/LN-NAT/N40AC/N96RE/N86RE/N331CC/(N5331J)			
			(Atlantic Executive Aviation c/s)			
G-LOGO	MD Helicopters Hughes 369E (500E)	0454E	G-BWLC 4.10.96	R.M.Briggs	Brough	25. 7.05T
			HB-XIJ/SE-JAM			
G-LOIS	Jabiru Jabiru UL	0144 & SAAC-68	EI-JAK 14. 9.00	D.J.Abbott	Plaistows Farm, St Albans	30. 4.03P
	(Jabiru 2200A) (C/n officially shown as 'PFA 274A-0144')					
G-LOKM	PZL-110 Koliber 160A	04990080	G-BYSH 26.11.99	PZL International Aviation Marketing & Sales plc		
			SP-WGH		Earls Colne	16. 1.03T
G-LOLA	Beech A36 Bonanza	E-2116	N67501 18. 2.02	J.H. & L.F.Strutt	(Bishops Stortford)	11. 4.05P

Reg	Type	C/n	Prev id	Date	Owner/Operator	Location	Date
G-LOLL	Cameron V-77 HAB	2964		4.12.92	C.N.Rawnson	Stockbridge	31. 8.00A
					tr Test Valley Balloon Group		
G-LOOP	Pitts S-1C Special (Lycoming O-320)	850	5Y-AOX	11. 5.78	D.Shutter	Gamston	7. 6.03P
G-LOOS	Cameron Tissue Pack-100 SS HAB	4767		17. 5.00	Flying Pictures Ltd *(Quilted Velvet titles)*	Chilbolton	14. 5.02A
G-LOOT*	Embraer EMB.110P1 Bandeirante	110-223	G-BNOC	17. 1.91	Hanningfield Metals	Templewood, Stock	5.10.90T
			PT-GMP		*(Cancelled as WFU 10.5.94) (Unmarked fuselage noted 9.02)*		
G-LORA	Cameron A-250 HAB	3828		22. 2.96	Global Ballooning Ltd	Uckfield	12. 3.03T
G-LORC	Piper PA-28-161 Cadet	2841339	D-ESTC	12. 1.99	Sherburn Aero Club Ltd	Sherburn-in-Elmet	12. 3.05T
			N9184W/(N620FT)/(SE-KMP)				
G-LORD	Piper PA-34-200T Seneca II	34-7970347	N2908W	6. 5.88	Carill Aviation Ltd & R.P.Thomas	Southampton	8. 5.03T
G-LORN	Avions Mudry CAP.10B	282		4. 3.99	J.D.Gailey	Old Sarum	10. 5.05
G-LORR	Piper PA-28-181 Archer III	2843037	N9268X	19. 4.96	VA Technology Ltd	Wolverhampton	13. 6.05
			G-LORR				
G-LORT	Avid Speed Wing Mk.4	1124 & PFA 189-12219		12. 2.92	G.E.Laucht	Long Marston	23. 6.03P
G-LORY	Thunder Ax4-31Z HAB	171		28.11.78	A.J.Moore *"Glory"*	Northwood, Middx	
G-LOSI	Cameron Z-105 HAB	1001		15. 1.01	Aeropubblicita Vicenza SRL	(Caldogno, Italy)	24. 5.03A
G-LOSM	Armstrong-Whitworth Meteor NF.11	S4/U/2342	WM167	8. 6.84	Hunter Wing Ltd	Bournemouth	6. 8.03P
					(Op Jet Heritage Ltd) (As "WM167" in 141 Sqdn c/s)		
G-LOST	Denney Kitfox Model 3	PFA 172-12055		10. 8.95	J.H.S.Booth	Perth	6. 8.01P
	(Rotax 618) *(Floatplane)*						
G-LOTA	Robinson R44 Raven	1232		8. 7.02	Rahtol Ltd	Redhill	10. 7.05
G-LOTI	Bleriot Type XI rep	PFA 88-10410		21.12.78	Brooklands Museum Trust Ltd	Brooklands	19. 7.82P
	(ABC Scorpion II)				*(Valid CofR 4.02)*		
G-LOUN	Eurocopter AS355N Twin Squirrel	5627		24. 1.97	Firstearl Ltd	Oxford	15. 6.03T
G-LOVB	British Aerospace Jetstream Srs.3102	622	VH-HSW	12. 8.99	London Flight Centre (Stansted) Ltd	Stansted	5.10.00T
			G-31-622/G-BLCB/G-31-622		*(Op Love Air)*		
G-LOWA*	Colt 77A HAB	1451		14. 4.89	K.D.Peirce *(Cancelled 25.9.01 by CAA)*	Cranbrook	7. 6.97A
G-LOWE*	Monnett Sonerai I	367 & PFA 15-10344		16.11.78	Not known	Shennington	
					(Cancelled 16.9.97 as TWFU) (On assembly 6.01)		
G-LOWS	Sky 77-24 HAB	025		19. 3.96	A.J.Byrne & D.J.Bellinger *"Dawn Treader"*	Thatcham	22. 4.03
G-LOYA	Reims FR172J Rocket	FR17200352	G-BLVT	4. 8.89	T.R.Scorer	Earls Colne	31. 5.03
			PH-EDI/D-EEDI				
G-LOYD	Aérospatiale SA341G Gazelle 1	1289	G-SFTC	19. 6.85	I.G.Lloyd	Ripley, Derbyshire	7. 6.03
	(Rebuilt 1990 with major components of N6957 c/n 1060) N47298						
G-LPAD	Lindstrand LBL 105A HAB	632		5. 8.99	Line Packaging & Display Ltd	Gillingham	14. 4.03A
G-LPGI	Cameron A-210 HAB	4196		13. 8.97	A.Derbyshire	Stretton	2.11.02T
G-LRBW	Lindstrand HS-110 HA Airship	253		2. 8.95	Croymark Ltd *(New CofR 12.02)*	Ottawa, Canada	
G-LRSN	Robinson R44 Raven	0984		28. 3.01	Larsen Manufacturing Ltd	Belfast	4. 4.04T
G-LSFI	Gulfstream AA-5A Cheetah	AA5A-0770	G-BGSK	13. 2.84	A.D.Prothero Mount Airey Farm, South Cave		20. 7.03
					tr G-LSFI Group		
G-LSFT	Piper PA-28-161 Warrior II	28-8516008	G-BXTX	10.11.99	B.Peppercorn	(Upminster)	2. 4.04T
			PH-LEH/N130AV/N43682				
G-LSHI	Colt 77A HAB	1264		20. 7.88	J H Dobson	Streatley, Berks	12. 7.95A
					(Lambert Smith & Hampton titles)		
G-LSMI	Reims/Cessna F152 II	F15201710		1. 2.80	A.S.Bamrah t/a Falcon Flying Services	(Blackbushe)	4. 4.05T
G-LSTR	Stoddard-Hamilton GlaStar	PFA 295-13093		20. 4.98	R.Y.Kendal	Brunton	27. 6.03P
	(Tail-wheel u/c)						
G-LTFB	Piper PA-28-140 Cherokee	28-23343	G-AVLU	28. 2.97	London Transport Flying Club Ltd	Fairoaks	11. 4.04T
			N11C				
G-LTFC	Piper PA-28-140 Cherokee B	28-26259	G-AXTI	8. 6.94	London Transport Flying Club Ltd	Fairoaks	11. 9.03T
			N11C				
G-LTRF	Sportavia Fournier RF7	7001	G-EHAP	10.12.97	Skyview Systems Ltd Waits Farm, Belchamp Walter		3. 7.03P
			(G-BGVC)/D-EHAP/F-WPXV				
G-LTSB	Cameron LTSB-90SS HAB	4483		15. 1.99	Virgin Airship & Balloon Co Ltd	Telford	14.11.02A
					(Lloyds TSB titles)		
G-LUBE	Cameron N-77 HAB	1127		25. 2.85	A.C.Rawson *"Lubey Loo"*	Stafford	6. 4.03A
G-LUCK	Reims/Cessna F150M	F15001238	PH-LEO	13.12.79	Taylor Aviation Ltd	Sywell	23. 6.04T
			D-EHRA				
G-LUED	Aero Designs Pulsar (Rotax 582)	PFA 202-12122		9. 3.92	J.C.Anderson	Sturgate	1. 8.02P
G-LUFT	Putzer Elster C	011	G-BOPY	31. 3.92	A.& E.A.Wiseman	(Rufforth)	
			D-EDEZ		*(On rebuild 1.01)*		
G-LUKE	Rutan LongEz	PFA 74A-10978		4. 7.84	S.G.Busby	Booker	14. 8.03P
	(Lycoming O-235)						
G-LUKI	Robinson R44 Raven	0818	G-BZLN	20.10.00	Marcella Air Ltd	Panshanger	5.11.03T
G-LUKY	Robinson R44 Astro	0357		10. 7.97	English Braids Ltd	Gloucestershire	11. 9.03T
G-LULU	Grob G-109	6137		6. 9.82	A.P.Bowden	Enstone	15. 5.04
G-LUMA	Jabiru Jabiru SP-430	PFA 274B-13458		11. 5.99	B.Luyckx	Keuheuvel, Belgium	14. 7.03P
	(Jabiru 2200A)						
G-LUNA	Piper PA-32RT-300T Turbo Lance II	32R-7987108	N2246Q	19. 3.79	D.C.Settrington	Humberside	19. 4.03T
G-LUSC	Luscombe 8E Silvaire	3975	D-EFYR	1.11.84	M.Fowler	Bruntingthorpe	
			LN-PAT/(NC1248K)		*(On rebuild 9.97: current status unknown)*		
G-LUSH	Piper PA-28-151 Cherokee Warrior	28-7515201	OH-PAB	25. 7.01	T.P.W.Hyde tr Lush Group	Conington	1.11.04T
G-LUSI	Temco Luscombe 8F Silvaire	6770	N838B	3.10.89	J.P.Hunt & D.M.Robinson		
	(Continental C85)				Bourne Park, Hurstbourne Tarrant		12. 5.03P
G-LUST	Luscombe 8E Silvaire	6492	N2065B	9.11.89	M.Griffiths	Gloucestershire	9. 7.98P
	(Continental C85)		NC2065B		*(Noted 10.02)*		
G-LUVY	Aérospatiale AS355F1 Twin Squirrel	5134	N358E	25. 2.00	DNH Helicopters Ltd	Biggin Hill	18. 6.03T
			ZS-HUA/(G-BPDP)/D-HOCH/N358E/N5792M				
G-LUXE	British Aerospace BAe 146 Srs.300	E3001	G-5-300	9. 4.87	BAE Systems (Operations) Ltd	Woodford	8. 5.98S
			G-SSSH/(G-BIAD)				
G-LVES	Cessna 182S Skylane	18280741	G-ELIE	19. 8.02	R.W.& A.M.Glaves	East Midlands	23. 8.03T
			N23754				
G-LWAY	Robinson R44 Raven	1244	N71822	22. 8.02	Heli Air Ltd (Clontibret, Co.Monaghan)		15. 9.05T
					(Op Lantway Properties Ltd)		

Reg	Type	c/n	Prev id	Date	Owner	Location	Expiry
G-LWNG	Aero Designs Pulsar (Rotax 582) *(Tricycle u/c)*	PFA 202-11866	G-OMKF	14.10.02	R.O'Donnell	(Chulmleigh)	22. 8.03P
G-LYAK	IAV-Bacau Yakovlev Yak-52	822113	LY-AGN	18.12.02	Lee52 Ltd *(Poke Software titles)*	Popham	22.12.03P
			Ukraine AF 140 (yellow)/DOSAAF 40 (yellow)				
G-LYDA	Hoffmann H-36 Dimona	3515	OE-9213	5. 4.94	M.A.Holmes & M.J.Philpott tr G-LYDA Flying Group	Booker	9.10.03
G-LYDD*	Piper PA-31 Turbo Navajo	31-537	G-BBDU	8. 5.89	Not known	Blackpool	12. 5.89T
			N6796L	*(Damaged Lydd 17.7.91: cancelled 30.3.93 as WFU) (Fuselage on fire dump 12.01)*			
G-LYFA	Yakovlev Yak-52	822608	LY-AFA DOSAAF 110	3.30R	(M Jefferies) *"110" (Noted 3.03)*	(Little Gransden)	
G-LYNC	Robinson R22 Beta	3069		5. 5.00	Whirlybirds Ltd	(Birmingham)	20. 7.03T
G-LYND	Piper PA-25-235 Pawnee D *(Rebuild of G-ASFZ [25-2246] with new frame)*	"25-6309"	SE-IXU	8. 9.93	York Gliding Centre Ltd	Rufforth	18.11.05
G-LYNK	CFM Shadow DD (Rotax 582)	303-DD	G-BSFZ/N6672Z	12.10.98	J.Walton	(Southport)	16. 7.03P
G-LYPG	Jabiru Jabiru UL-450 (Jabiru 2200A)	PFA 274A-13466		6. 7.99	P.G.Gale	Fitzroy Farms, Bratton, Wilts	13. 5.03P
G-LYTE	Thunder Ax7-77 HAB	1113		29. 9.87	G.M.Bulmer *"Crispen"*	Hereford	19. 5.91A
G-LZZY	Piper PA-28RT-201T Turbo Arrow IV	28R-8031001	G-BMHZ ZS-KII/N8096D	8. 5.01	J.C.Lucas	Popham	28.5.05

G-MAAA - G-MZZZ

Reg	Type	c/n	Prev id	Date	Owner	Location	Expiry
G-MAAH	British Aircraft Corporation One-Eleven 488GH	BAC.259	VP-CDA	6.10.98	Aravco Ltd	Farnborough	27..4.03T
			G-MAAH/PK-TAL/G-BWES/PK-TAL/G-BWES/5N-UDE/LX-MAM/HZ-MAM				
G-MAAN	Europa Aviation Europa XS T-G	PFA 247-14009		7. 1.03	P.S.Maan	(Desborough)	
G-MABE	Reims/Cessna F150L	F15001119	G-BLJP N962L	20. 6.97	Herefordshire Aero Club Ltd	Shobdon	18. 6.03T
G-MABR	British Aerospace BAe 146 Srs.100	E1015	G-DEBN	13. 1.00	British Regional Airlines Ltd	Aberdeen	22.12.04T
			EC-GEP/EC-971/N568BA/XA-RST/N461AP/G-5-01				
G-MACH	SIAI-Marchetti SF.260	1-14	F-BUVY OO-AHR/OO-HAZ/(OO-RAB)	29.10.80	Cheyne Motors Ltd	Old Sarum	29. 5.05
G-MACK	Piper PA-28R-200 Cherokee Arrow II	28R-7635449	N5213F	18. 8.78	Haimoss Ltd	Old Sarum	18.12.04T
G-MAFA	Reims/Cessna F406 Caravan II	F406-0036	G-DFLT F-WZDZ	2. 6.98	Directflight Ltd *(Op DEFRA)*	Exeter	6. 6.04T
G-MAFB	Reims/Cessna F406 Caravan II	F406-0080	F-WWSR	27. 5.98	Directflight Ltd *(Op DEFRA)*	Prestwick	28. 9.04T
G-MAFE	Dornier 228202K	8009	G-OALF G-MLDO/PH-SDO/D-IDON	21.12.92	FR Aviation Ltd *(Op DEFRA)*	Bournemouth	4.11.05T
G-MAFF	Pilatus Britten-Norman BN-2T Islander	2119	G-BJED	20. 4.82	Cobham Leasing Ltd *(Op DEFRA)*	Teesside	25. 9.05T
G-MAFI	Dornier 228-202K	8115	D-CAAE	16. 2.87	Cobham Leasing Ltd *(Op DEFRA)*	Bournemouth	15. 7.05T
G-MAGC	Cameron Grand Illusion SS HAB	4000		19. 1.95	Magical Adventures Ltd	West Bloomfield, Mi., USA	16. 8.03A
G-MAGG	Pitts S-1SE Special (Lycoming O-360)	PFA 09-10873		17. 3.83	C.A.Boardman	Little Gransden	2. 4.03P
G-MAGL	Sky 77-24 HAB	164		14. 7.99	RCM SARL	Stuppicht, Luxembourg	13. 6.03
G-MAIE	Piper PA-32R-301T Saratoga IITC	3257046	N47BK N41283	1.12.00	B R Sennett	Jersey	30.11.03
G-MAIK	Piper PA-34-220T Seneca IV	3448078	N73BS	17.11.97	TEL (IoM) Ltd	Ronaldsway	7.12.03
G-MAIN	Mainair Blade 912 (Rotax 912-UL)	1202-0699-7 & W1005		16. 6.99	G.D.Ritchie	East Fortune	4. 7.03P
G-MAIR	Piper PA-34-200T Seneca II	34-7970140	N3029R	15. 2.89	Barnes Olson Aeroleasing Ltd *(Op Bristol Flying Centre)*	Bristol	10. 4.04T
G-MAJA	British Aerospace Jetstream Srs.4100	41032	G-4-032	22. 4.94	British Airways Citiexpress Ltd *(Op Eastern Airways)*	Humberside	24. 5.05T
G-MAJB	British Aerospace Jetstream Srs.4100	41018	G-BVKT N140MA/G-4-018	1. 6.94	British Airways Citiexpress Ltd *(Op Eastern Airways)*	Humberside	8. 6.03T
G-MAJC	British Aerospace Jetstream Srs.4100	41005	G-LOGJ	12. 9.94	British Airways Citiexpress Ltd) *(Op Eastern Airways)*	Humberside	20.12.03T
G-MAJD	British Aerospace Jetstream Srs.4100	41006	G-WAWR	27. 3.95	British Airways Citiexpress Ltd *(Op Eastern Airways)*	Humberside	2. 3.04T
G-MAJE	British Aerospace Jetstream Srs.4100	41007	G-LOGK	12. 9.94	British Airways Citiexpress Ltd *(Op Eastern Airways)*	Humberside	24. 2.03T
G-MAJF	British Aerospace Jetstream Srs.4100	41008	G-WAWL	6. 2.95	British Airways Citiexpress Ltd *(Op Eastern Airways)*	Humberside	18. 3.02T
G-MAJG	British Aerospace Jetstream Srs.4100	41009	G-LOGL	16. 8.94	British Airways Citiexpress Ltd *(Op Eastern Airways)*	Humberside	30. 3.02T
G-MAJH	British Aerospace Jetstream Srs.4100	41010	G-WAYR	4. 4.95	British Airways Citiexpress Ltd *(Op Eastern Airways)*	Humberside	13. 4.03T
G-MAJI	British Aerospace Jetstream Srs.4100	41011	G-WAND	20. 3.95	British Airways Citiexpress Ltd *(Op Eastern Airways)*	Humberside	27. 4.04T
G-MAJJ	British Aerospace Jetstream Srs.4100	41024	G-WAFT G-4-024	27. 2.95	British Airways Citiexpress Ltd *(Op Eastern Airways)*	Humberside	28.10.05T
G-MAJK	British Aerospace Jetstream Srs.4100	41070	G-4-070	27. 7.95	British Airways Citiexpress Ltd *(Op Eastern Airways)*	Humberside	2. 9.03T
G-MAJL	British Aerospace Jetstream Srs.4100	41087	G-4-087	1. 4.96	Eastern Airways (UK) Ltd *"R J Mitchell"*	Humberside	16. 5.03T
G-MAJM	British Aerospace Jetstream Srs.4100	41096	G-4-096	23. 9.96	British Airways Citiexpress Ltd *(Op Eastern Airways)*	Humberside	29.10.05T
G-MAJR	de Havilland DHC.1 Chipmunk 22	C1/0699	WP805	25. 9.96	C.Adams t/r Chipmunk Shareholders *(Current status unknown)*	(Gosport)	
G-MAJS	Airbus Industrie A300B4-605R	604	F-WWAX	26. 4.91	Monarch Airlines Ltd	Luton	25. 4.05T
G-MALA	Piper PA-28-181 Archer II	28-8190055	G-BIIU N82748	6. 3.81	D.C. & M.E.Dowell t/a M & D Aviation	Kemble	16. 4.05T
G-MALC	Grumman-American AA-5 Traveler	AA5-0664	G-BCPM N6170A	19.11.79	B.P.Hogan	Sywell	7. 6.03

G-MALK*	Reims/Cessna F172N Skyhawk II	F17201886	PH-SVS	1. 7.81	Edinburgh Airport Fire Service	Edinburgh	
			PH-AXF(3)				
	(Crashed near Lochgilphead 23.7.97: cancelled 23.12.97 as destroyed) (Fuselage for instructional use 2001)						
G-MALS	Mooney M.20K (231)	25-0573	N1061T	16. 8.84	J.Houlberg tr G-MALS Group	Blackbushe	25. 4.05
G-MALT	Colt Flying Hop SS HAB	1447		14. 4.89	P.J.Stapley *"Hoppie"*	London Colney	11. 9.97A
					(CofR restored 20.11.01)		
G-MAMC	Rotorway Executive 90	5057		24. 5.94	J.R.Carmichael	(Inverary)	19. 2.99P
	(Rotorway RI 162)				*(Damaged landing Cumbernauld 22.9.98 and removed: current status unknown)*		
G-MAMD	Beech B200 Super King Air	BB-1549	N1069S	16. 7.99	Gamston Aviation Ltd	Gamston	16. 7.05
G-MAMK	Robinson R44 Clipper	1201		17. 4.02	M. J.Hayward t/a M& M Aviation	Coventry	13. 5.05T
G-MAMO	Cameron V-77 HAB	1616		17.11.87	The Marble Mosaic Co Ltd *"Osprey"*	Portishead	27. 8.03A
G-MANA	British Aerospace ATP	2056	G-LOGH	21. 2.94	British Airways Citiexpress Ltd	Ronaldsway	21. 3.04T
			G-11-056		*(Op Manx Airlines)*		
G-MANB	British Aerospace ATP	2055	G-LOGG	14. 9.94	British Airways Citiexpress Ltd	Ronaldsway	26. 9.05T
			G-JATP/G-11-055		*(Op Manx Airlines)*		
G-MANC	British Aerospace ATP	2054	G-LOGF	7.11.94	British Airways Citiexpress Ltd	Ronaldsway	20.10.03T
			G-11-054				
G-MANE	British Aerospace ATP	2045	G-LOGB	7. 6.94	British Airways Citiexpress Ltd	Ronaldsway	26. 2.04T
			G-11-045				
G-MANF	British Aerospace ATP	2040	G-LOGA	19. 9.94	British Airways Citiexpress Ltd	Ronaldsway	5.11.04T
G-MANG	British Aerospace ATP	2018	G-LOGD	22. 8.94	British Airways Citiexpress Ltd	Ronaldsway	28. 9.04T
G-MANH	British Aerospace ATP	2017	G-LOGC	16.11.94	British Airways Citiexpress Ltd	Ronaldsway	14. 8.05T
G-MANI	Cameron V-90 HAB	3038		8. 3.93	M.P.G.Papworth	Ilkley	3. 7.01A
G-MANJ	British Aerospace ATP	2004	G-LOGE	6. 9.94	British Airways Citiexpress Ltd	Ronaldsway	14. 4.04T
G-MANL	British Aerospace ATP	2003	G-ERIN	3.10.94	British Airways Citiexpress Ltd	East Midlands	25. 5.05T
			G-BMYK				
G-MANM	British Aerospace ATP	2005	G-OATP	17.10.94	British Regional Airlines Ltd	Ronaldsway	20. 3.05T
			G-BZWW/(N375AE)/G-BZWW		*"Elaine Griffiths"*		
G-MANN	Aérospatiale SA341G Gazelle 1	1295	G-BKLW	14. 4.86	MW Helicopters Ltd	Stapleford	31. 5.04T
			N4DQ/N4QQ/N444JJ/N47316/F-WKQH				
G-MANO	British Aerospace ATP	2006	OK-TFN	28.11.94	Manx Airlines Ltd *(Rendezvous t/s)*	Ronaldsway	18. 1.05T
			G-MANO/G-UIET/G-11-5/(N376AE)				
G-MANP	British Aerospace ATP	2023	OK-VFO	28.10.94	Manx Airlines Ltd	Ronaldsway	25.10.03T
			G-MANP/G-PEEL				
G-MANS	British Aerospace BAe 146 Srs.200	E2088	G-CLHC	22. 5.00	British Regional Airlines Ltd	Aberdeen	25. 4.03T
			G-MANS/G-CHSR/G-5-088				
G-MANT*	Cessna 210L Centurion II	21060970	G-MAXY	22. 5.85	Sea-Front Crazee Golf	Great Yarmouth	2.10.94
			N550SV		*(Damaged near Oxford 16.2.92: cancelled 3.4.92 by CAA: noted 7.01)*		
G-MANW	Tri-R Kis	PFA 239-12628		12. 9.96	M.T.Manwaring	(Barking)	
G-MANX	Clutton FRED Srs.II	PW.2 & PFA 29-10327		31. 5.78	S.Styles	(Birmingham)	17. 8.82P
	(Ardem 4C02)				*(Crashed near Ronaldsway 30.10.81: on rebuild Wellesbourne Mountford 7.90)*		
G-MAPL	Robinson R44 Raven	0929	G-BZVP	7. 6.02	M.P.Lafuente	(Monte Carlo, Monaco)	2. 5.04T
G-MAPP	Cessna 402B	402B0583	D-INRH	16. 4.99	Simmons Mapping (UK) Ltd	Cranfield	5.10.05T
			N1445G	05.10.05			
G-MAPR	Beech A36 Bonanza	E-2713	N55916	17. 9.92	Moderandum Ltd	(Guernsey)	2. 9.04
G-MARA	Airbus Industrie A321-231	0983	D-AVZB	31. 3.99	Monarch Airlines Ltd	Luton	30. 3.05T
G-MARE	Schweizer Hughes 269C	S-1320		12. 8.88	The Earl of Caledon	Caledon Castle, Co.Tyrone	17.12.03
G-MASC	SAN Jodel 150A Mascaret	37	F-BLDZ	1. 2.91	K.F. & R.Richardson	Wellesbourne Mountford	10. 7.02P
G-MASF	Piper PA-28-181 Cherokee Archer II	28-7790191	OY-EPT	24. 6.97	Mid-Anglia Flight Centre Ltd	Cambridge	6. 8.03T
			LN-NAP		t/a Mid-Anglia School of Flying		
G-MASH	Westland-Bell 47G-4A	WA/725	G-AXKU	3.11.89	Defence Products Ltd	Redhill	21. 4.05
			G-17-10		*(US Army c/s)*		
G-MASS	Cessna 152 II	15281605	G-BSHN	6. 3.95	MK Aero Support Ltd	Denham	2. 5.05T
			N65541		*(Op The Pilot Centre)*		
G-MASX	Masquito Masquito M.80	03		19. 6.98	Masquito Aircraft NV	(Roosdaal, Belgium)	
G-MASY	Masquito Masquito M.80	02		19. 6.98	Masquito Aircraft NV	(Roosdaal, Belgium)	
G-MASZ	Masquito Masquito M.58	01		29. 4.97	Masquito Aircraft NV	(Roosdaal, Belgium)	AC
G-MATE	Moravan Zlin Z.50LX	0068		26.10.90	J.H.Askew	Breighton	5. 7.04
G-MATS	Colt GA-42 Gas Airship	738	JA1009	11. 6.87	P.A.Lindstrand	Oswestry	23. 5.90A
			G-MATS		*(New owner 6.01)*		
G-MATT	Robin R2160	97	G-BKRC	7. 5.85	D.J.Nicholson	East Midlands	27. 3.03
			F-BZAC/F-WZAC				
G-MATZ	Piper PA-28-140 Cherokee Cruiser	28-7325200	G-BASI	11.12.90	R.B.Walker,	Coventry	19.10.03T
			N11C		t/a Midland Air Training School		
	(Control lost during landing Coventry 27.3.02 & struck Precision Approach Path Indicator: damage to prop, engine & fuselage)						
G-MAUD	British Aerospace ATP	2002	(G-MANK)	14.12.93	British Airways Citiexpress Ltd	East Midlands	13. 6.04T
			G-MAUD/G-BMYM		*(Blue Poole t/s)*		
G-MAUK	Colt 77A HAB	901		16. 2.87	B.Meeson *"Mondial Assistance"*	Walsall	4. 6.92A
G-MAVI	Robinson R22 Beta	0960		7. 2.89	The Flightworks Group Ltd	Booker	26. 4.04T
G-MAXG	Pitts S-1S Special	PFA 09-13233		27. 4.01	T.P.Jenkinson	(Radlett)	
G-MAXI	Piper PA-34-200T Seneca II	34-7670150	N8658C	11. 2.81	Draycott Seneca Syndicate Ltd	Kemble	15. 5.03T
G-MAXV	Van's RV-4	PFA 181-13266		20. 1.00	R.S.Partridge-Hicks	(Bury St. Edmunds)	15. 5.03P
G-MAYO	Piper PA-28-161 Cherokee Warrior II	28-7716278	G-BFBG	20. 2.81	M.P.Catto t/a Jermyk Engineering	Fairoaks	11. 4.04T
			N38848				
G-MBAA	Hiway Skytrike Mk.II/Excalibur	01		23. 4.81	M.J.Aubrey	Kington, Hereford	
	(Hiro Delta 22)				*(Noted 2002)*		
G-MBAB	Hovey WD-II Whing Ding II			26. 5.81	M.J.Aubrey	Kington, Hereford	1. 2.98P
	(Konig SC340)	MA-59 & PFA 116-10706			*(Noted 2002)*		
G-MBAW	Pterodactyl Ptraveler	017		14. 7.81	J.C.K.Scardifield	(Lymington)	31. 8.86E
	(Cuyana 430R)				*(Current status unknown)*		
G-MBBB	Wheeler Scout II	0388W		3. 8.81	A.J.& B.Chalkley	(Pwllheli)	
	(Pixie 173)				*(Current status unknown)*		
G-MBBM	Eipper Quicksilver MX	10960		11. 9.81	J.Brown	(Markfield, Leics)	9.12.84E
	(Cuyana 430R)				*(In storage: current status unknown)*		

G-MBCJ	Mainair Tri-Flyer/Solar Wings Typhoon S		30. 9.81	R.A.Smith	(Doncaster)	30. 4.86E
		JRN-1 & T881-225	*(May have replacement wing T382-390L) (Current status unknown)*			
G-MBCK	Eipper Quicksilver MX	GWR-10962	30. 9.81	P.Rowbotham	(Loughborough)	17.11.86E
	(Rotax 503)		*(Current status unknown)*			
G-MBCL	Hiway Skytrike 160/Solar Wings Typhoon		30. 9.81	P.J.Callis	(Kibworth, Leicester)	N/E
		2332 & T1181-307	*(Current status unknown)*			
G-MBCU	American Aerolights Double Eagle (Amphibian)		5.10.81	J.L.May	(Portsmouth)	29. 9.03P
	(Rotax 377)	3181				
G-MBCX	Hornet 250/Airwave Nimrod 165 H090 & 0090 LJH		12.10.81	M.Maylor	(Louth)	31.12.87E
	(Fuji-Robin EC-25-PS)		*(Current status unknown)*			
G-MBDG	Eurowing Goldwing	E.20	19.10.81	B.Fussell	(Llanelli)	14.12.94P
	(Konig SC430)		*(Current status unknown)*			
G-MBDM	Southdown Sigma/Southdown trike	SST/001	26.10.81	A.R.Prentice	(Dartford)	4.12.88E
	(Fuji-Robin EC-25-PS)		*(Current status unknown)*			
G-MBET	MEA Mistral Trainer	MEA.103	10.11.81	B.H.Stephens	Old Sarum	27. 9.98E
	(Fuji-Robin EC-44-PM)		*(Noted in trailer 2002)*			
G-MBEU	Chargus T.250/Hiway Demon	T.250/06	10.11.81	R.C.Smith	(Clacton)	31. 5.86E
	(Fuji-Robin EC-25-PS)		*(Current status unknown)*			
G-MBFK	Hiway Skytrike/Demon 175	LR17D	16.11.81	D.W.Stamp	(Kidderminster)	9. 3.89E
	(Fuji-Robin EC-25-PS)		*(Current status unknown)*			
G-MBFO	Eipper Quicksilver MX	MLD-01	17.11.81	J.C.Larkin	(Maryport, Cumbria)	20. 8.93P
	(Cuyuna 430R)		*(Current status unknown)*			
G-MBFS*	American Aerolights Eagle	RF-01	19.11.81	M.J.Aubrey	Kington, Hereford	
	(Fuji-Robin EC-25-PS)		*(Cancelled 24.5.90 as WFU) (Noted 2002)*			
G-MBFZ	MSS Eurowing Goldwing	MSS-01	25.11.81	D.G.Palmer	Fetterangus	5. 9.00P
	(Fuji-Robin EC-34-PM)		*(Under active rebuild 2001)*			
G-MBGA	Mainair Tri-Flyer/Flexiform Solo Sealander	001	25.11.81	D.A.Caig	(Southport)	14. 9.97P
	(Originally regd as Mainair Tri-Flyer/Solar Wings Typhoon with same c/n)		*(Current status unknown)*			
G-MBGF	Twamley Trike/Birdman Cherokee	RWT-01	26.11.81	T.B.Woolley *(Current status unknown)*	(Leicester)	
G-MBGL*	Flexiform Sealander HF-1		1.12.81	Not known	Halwell, Totnes	
			(Cancelled as WFU 25.10.88) (Trike stored 2.01)			
G-MBGS	Rotec Rally 2B	PCB-1	2.12.81	P.C.Bell *(Current status unknown)*	(Yalding, Kent)	
G-MBGX	Southdown Lightning DS	RBDB-1	7.12.81	T.Knight	(Newton Abbot)	7. 3.92E
	(Sachs-Dolmar 340?) *(Believed fitted with UAS Storm Buggy trike ex G-MBKD)*		*(Current status unknown)*			
G-MBHE	American Aerolights Eagle	4210	18.12.81	R.J.Osborne	Long Marston	12.10.96P
	(Cuyuna 430R)		*(Current status unknown)*			
G-MBHK	Mainair Tri-Flyer 330/Flexiform Solo Striker		30.12.81	K.T.Vinning	(Stratford-upon-Avon)	11. 8.98P
	(Fuji-Robin EC-34-PM) EB-1 & 036-241181		*(Current status unknown)*			
	(Original Tri-Flyer 250 trike c/n 036 replaced by Tri-Flyer 330 c/n 060-382 in 1982)					
G-MBHZ	Pterodactyl Ptraveler	TD-01	6. 1.82	J.C.K.Scardifield	(Lymington)	28. 2.86E
	(Cuyuna 430R)		*(Current status unknown)*			
G-MBIA	Hiway Skytrike/Flexiform Sealander		6. 1.82	I.P.Cook	(Oldham)	9. 4.90E
	(Fuji-Robin EC-34-PM)	6172349/336	*(Current status unknown)*			
G-MBIT	Hiway Skytrike/Demon	2501	18. 1.82	K.S.Hodgson	(Yarm)	5.12.87E
	(Fuji-Robin EC-25-PS)		*(Reported as taken to Canada 9.89 but new owner 6.00!)*			
G-MBIY	Ultrasports Tripacer/Southdown Lightning Phase II		19. 1.82	J.W.Burton	Tarn Farm, Cockerham	18. 4.99P
	(Fuji-Robin EC-34-PM) *(Wing c/n L170-439)* 330		*(Stored 2.03)*			
G-MBIZ	Mainair Tri-Flyer 250/Hiway Vulcan		20. 1.82	E.F.Clapham, W.B.S.Dobi, S.P.Slade & D.M.A.Templeman		
	(Fuji-Robin EC-25PS) 039-251181 & SD9V		*(Current status unknown)*	(Bristol)		
G-MBJD	American Aerolights Eagle 215B	4169	21. 1.82	R.W.F.Boarder	(Tring)	9. 7.88E
	(Zenoah G25B1)		*(Current status unknown)*			
G-MBJF	Hiway Skytrike Mk.II/Vulcan C	80-00099	22. 1.82	C.H.Bestwick	(Nottingham)	31. 1.87E
	(Fuji-Robin EC-25-PS) *(C/n is engine serial no)*		*(Current status unknown)*			
G-MBJG	Chargus T.250/Airwave Nimrod UP CMT165045		25. 1.82	D.H.George	Sandown	16.12.03P
	(Fuji-Robin EC-25-PS)					
G-MBJK	American Aerolights Eagle	2742	16. 1.82	B.W.Olley	(Ely)	
	(Chrysler 820)		*(In store 2000)*			
G-MBJL	Hornet/airwave Nimrod	JSRM-01	26. 1.82	A.G.Lowe	(Aberdeen)	20.10.96P
	(Fuji-Robin EC-25-PS)		*(Noted at owner's home 4.02)*			
G-MBJM	Striplin Lone Ranger	LR-81-00138	26. 1.82	C.K.Brown	(Loughborough)	
	(Fuji-Robin) *(C/n 81-00138 is engine serial no)*		*(Current status unknown)*			
G-MBKY	American Aerolights Eagle 215B	BF-01	12. 2.82	M.J.Aubrey	(Kington, Hereford)	
	(Twin Chryslers)		*(Noted 2002)*			
G-MBKZ	Hiway Skytrike/Super Scorpion	EC25P8-04	12. 2.82	S.I.Harding	(Camberley)	
	(Fuji-Robin EC-25-PS) *(C/n is corruption of engine type)*		*(Current status unknown)*			
G-MBLK*	Ultrasports Tripacer/Southdown Lightning DS		18. 2.82	M.J.Aubrey	(Kington, Hereford)	
	(Fuji-Robin EC-44)	DS-390	*(Cancelled 23.6.97 as WFU) (Noted 2002).*			
G-MBLU	Ultrasports Tripacer/Southdown Lightning L195		26. 2.82	C.R.Franklin	(Barnstaple)	28.11.87E
	(Fuji-Robin EC-25-PS)	L195/191	*(Current status unknown)*			
G-MBMG	Rotec Rally 2B	RJP-01	3. 3.82	J.R.Pyper	(Craigavon, Co Armagh)	
			(Current status unknown)			
G-MBMT	Mainair Tri-Flyer/Southdown Lightning 195		8. 3.82	A.G.Rodenburg & T.Abro	(Tillicoultry)	25. 4.87E
	(Fuji-Robin EC-25-PS) TRY-01	*(Wing c/n L195-195?)*	*(Current status unknown)*			
G-MBOF	Pakes Jackdaw	LGP-01	26. 3.82	L.G.Pakes	(Ryde, Isle of Wight)	
			(Current status unknown)			
G-MBOH	MEA Mistral Trainer	008	29. 3.82	N.A.Bell	(Fordingbridge)	5. 9.88E
	(Fuji-Robin EC-44-PM)		*(Current status unknown)*			
G-MBPB(2)	Pterodactyl Ptraveller	PEB-01	7. 4.82	N.A.Bell *(For rebuild 12.01)*	(Fordingbridge)	
G-MBPG	Mainair Tri-Flyer/Solar Wings Typhoon		13. 4.82	S.D.Thorpe	Otherton, Cannock	14. 6.01P
	(Fuji-Robin EC-25-PS) 189-1983 & T381-105		*(Original trike was c/n 067-582 and may have been used for G-MMGT)*			
G-MBPJ	Centrair Moto-Delta G.11	001	14. 5.82	J.B.Jackson *(Current status unknown)*	(Chester)	
G-MBPU	Hiway Skytrike 250/Demon	DSS-01	21. 4.82	D.Hines *(New owner 10.02)*	(Crewe)	30. 4.00P
G-MBPX	Eurowing Goldwing SP	EW-42	21. 4.82	A.R.Channon	(Sawston, Cambridge)	6.11.96P
	(Konig SC430)		*(Current status unknown)*			

G-MBPY	Ultrasports Tripacer 330/Wasp Gryphon II RKP-01			21. 4.82	D.Hawkes & C.Poundes	(Milton Keynes)	12. 4.03P
	(Fuji-Robin EC-34-PM)						
G-MBRB	Electraflyer Eagle Mk.I	E.2229		9.12.81	R.C.Bott (Current status unknown)	(Tywyn)	
G-MBRD	American Aerolights Eagle 215B	E.2635		20. 4.82	R.J.Osborne	(Tiverton)	31. 8.85E
	(Fuji-Robin EC-25-PS)				(Current status unknown)		
G-MBRE	Wheeler Scout	73962		21. 4.82	C.A.Foster (Current status unknown)	(Leicester)	
G-MBRH	Ultraflight Mirage Mk.II	83-009 & RALH-01		20. 4.82	R.W.F.Boarder	Field Farm, Oakley	8. 1.01P
	(Rotax 447)						
G-MBRS	American Aerolights Eagle 215B	RWC.1		23. 4.82	W.J.Phillips	Haverfordwest	31. 8.85E
	(Zenoah G25B1)				(Stored 6.90: current status unknown)		
G-MBST	Mainair Gemini/Sprint	141-29383		10. 4.84	G.J.Bowen	(Llanelli)	25. 5.03P
	(Fuji-Robin EC-44-PM) (Fitted with Trike from G-MJXA)						
G-MBSX	Ultraflight Mirage II (Rotax 447)	240		14. 6.82	P.J.Careless & P.Samal	Sandy	30. 5.03P
G-MBTF	Mainair Gemini/Sprint	168-30683		26. 4.82	D.E.J.McVicar	(Antrim, Co.Antrim)	26. 3.00P
	(Fuji-Robin EC-44-PM)						
G-MBTH	Whittaker MW4	001 & T1081-262L	(G-MBPB(1))	6. 4.82	L.Greenfield & M.Whittaker	Otherton, Cannock	12. 7.03P
	(Fuji-Robin EC-34-PM)				tr The MW4 Flying Group		
G-MBTJ	Ultrasports Tripacer/Solar Wings Typhoon			2. 4.82	H.A.Comber	(Poole)	13. 9.93P
	(Fuji-Robin EC-25-PS)	CSRS-01	(Wing c/n may be T1081-286L)		(Current status unknown)		
G-MBTW	Aerodyne Vector 600	1188		10. 5.82	W.I.Fuller	Cambridge	5. 5.89E
	(Zenoah G25B1)				(Current status unknown)		
G-MBUA	Hiway Skytrike/Hiway Demon	RJN-01		30. 4.82	R.J.Nicholson (Current status unknown)	(Lightwater)	
G-MBUS*	MEA Mistral Trainer	FGJ-01		7. 5.82	(N.A.Bell)	(Fordingbridge)	
					(Cancelled 25.10.88 as destroyed) (For spares 12.01)		
G-MBUZ	Wheeler (Skycraft) Scout II	0366		4. 5.82	A.C.Thorne (Current status unknown)	(Yelverton)	
G-MBVS	Hiway Skytrike II/Super Scorpion	25T3		14. 5.82	M.A.Brown (Noted 7.01)	Swinford	
G-MBVW	Skyhook Cutlass/TR2	TR2/23		14. 5.82	M.Jobling	(Harrogate)	28. 5.87E
	(Solo 210 x 2)				(Current status unknown)		
G-MBWE*	American Aerolights Eagle	2937		18. 5.82	M.J.Aubrey	(Kington, Hereford	
	(Fuji-Robin EC-25-PS)				(Cancelled 24.3.99 by CAA) (Noted 2002)		
G-MBWG	Huntair Pathfinder 1	006		19. 5.82	T.Mahmood	(Aberdeen)	14. 7.99P
	(Fuji-Robin EC-34-PM)				(New owner 6.02)		
G-MBWH*	Jordan Duet 1	D82001		20. 5.82	Designability Ltd	Kemble	
					(Noted 1.02: cancelled 22.3.02 as WFU)		
G-MBWI*	Lafayette Hi-Nuski Mk.1	30680		8. 6.82	N H Ponsford	(Selby)	
					(Cancelled 13.6.90 by CAA). (Stored 12.01)		
G-MBXX	Ultraflight Mirage II	111		21. 1.82	E.J.Girling	St Just	14.11.88E
	(Kawasaki TA440)				(Stored 5.94: current status unknown)		
G-MBYH*	Maxair Hummer	001		4. 6.82	Not known	Doynton	31.12.87P
					(Cancelled 19.5.97 by CAA) (Noted derelict 2.03)		
G-MBYI	Ultraflight Lazair IIIE	A464/001		4. 6.82	M.Sumner	(Market Drayton)	5. 3.99P
	(Rotax 185 x 2) (Built AMF Microflight Ltd from kit as c/n A522) (C/n amended during rebuild after accident 28.8.82) (Current status unknown)						
G-MBYL	Huntair Pathfinder 1	009		4. 6.82	A.R.Hobbins	(Limavady, Co.Londonderry)	17. 2.02P
	(Fuji-Robin EC-44-PM)						
G-MBYM	Eipper Quicksilver MX	JW-01		4. 6.82	M.P.Harper & L.L.Perry	Priory Farm, Tibenham	21. 9.96P
	(Cuyuna 430R)				(Current status unknown)		
G-MBZH	Eurowing Goldwing	EW-50		14. 6.82	J.Spavins	Long Acre Farm, Sandy	31. 3.03P
	(Fuji-Robin EC-34-PM)						
G-MBZJ	Southdown Puma/Lightning	L170-415		14. 6.82	A.K.Webster	(Wallingford)	1. 8.98P
	(Fuji-Robin EC-34-PM)				(Stolen 24.8.97 from Chiltern Park: current status unknown)		
G-MBZK*	Ultrasports Tripacer 250/Solar Wings Typhoon			14. 6.82	J A Crofts	(Carmarthen)	14. 2.00P
	(Fuji-Robin EC-25-PS)	AAL-01 & T381-104L			(Cancelled 10.4.02 by CAA)		
G-MBZO	Mainair Tri-Flyer/Flexiform Medium Striker			15. 6.82	A.N.Burrows	(Kirkmichael, Isle of Man)	15. 4.98P
	(Fuji-Robin EC-34-PM)	GRH-01 & 021-101081			(Current status unknown)		
G-MBZV	American Aerolights Eagle 215B	4227-Z		16. 6.82	A.R.Lewis (Current status unknown)	White Waltham	N/E
G-MCAP	Cameron C-80 HAB	10186		30. 7.02	L.D.Thurgar (Mencap titles)	(Bristol)	15. 9.03A
G-MCEA	Boeing 757-225	22200	N510EA	6. 2.95	MyTravel Airways Ltd	Manchester	23. 3.04T
G-MCEL	Pegasus Quantum 15-912	7858		10.10.01	F.Hodgson	Sywell	12.10.03P
G-MCCF	Thruster T600N Sprint	0100-T600N-048		25. 4.01	C.C.F.Fuller	Craysmarsh Farm, Melksham	26. 5.03P
	(Jabiru 2200)						
G-MCJL	Pegasus Quantum 15-912	7497		16. 3.99	A.Gillett	(Southampton)	18. 6.02P
G-MCMS	Aero Designs Pulsar	PFA 202-11982		3. 2.93	B.R.Hunter	Easter Poldar Farm, Thornhill	19. 5.02P
	(Rotax 582)						
G-MCOX	Fuji FA.200-180AO Aero Subaru	296	(G-BIMS)	29.12.81	West Surrey Engineering Ltd	Fairoaks	7. 6.03
G-MCOY	Flight Design CT2K	01-04-01-12		25. 7.01	D.Young	Kemble	24. 7.03P
					t/a Pegasus Flight Training (Cotswolds)		
G-MCPI	Bell 206B-3 JetRanger III	3191	G-ONTB	4. 4.90	D.A.C.Pipe	Westbury-sub-Mendip	12. 3.03T
			N3896C				
G-MCXV	Colomban MC-15 Cri-Cri	371	F-PYVA	1. 3.00	H.A.Leek	(Melton Mowbray)	
	(Built J.P.Lorre)						
G-MDAC	Piper PA-28-181 Archer II	28-8290154	N8242T	6.11.87	B.R.McKay tr Alpha Charlie Flying Group	Compton Abbas	18. 5.03
G-MDBC	Pegasus Quantum 15-912	7814		4. 5.01	D.B.Caiden	East Fortune	24. 8.03P
G-MDBD	Airbus Industrie A330-243	266	F-WWKG	24. 6.99	MyTravel Airways Ltd	Manchester	24..6.05T
G-MDKD	Robinson R22 Beta	1247		18. 4.90	B.C.Seedle t/a Brian Seedle Helicopters	Blackpool	20. 5.02T
G-MEAH	Piper PA-28R-200 Cherokee Arrow II	28R-7435104	G-BSNM	14. 6.91	Stapleford Flying Club Ltd	Stapleford	6. 4.03T
			N46PR/G-BSNM/N46PR/N54439				
G-MEDA	Airbus Industrie A320-231	480	N480RX	12.10.94	British Mediterranean Airways Ltd	Heathrow	11.10.03T
			F-WWDU		(Whale Rider t/s)		
G-MEDB	Airbus Industrie A320-231	376	3B-RGY	19. 3.97	Debis Aircraft Leasing VII BV		7. 4.03T
			F-OHMB/(XA-SGB)/F-WWIK		(To VT-EYA 2003) Amsterdam, The Netherlands		
G-MEDD	Airbus Industrie A320-231	386	3B-RGZ	19. 3.97	British Mediterranean Airways Ltd	Heathrow	1. 4.03T
			F-OHMC/(XA-SGC)/F-WWBI		(Crossing Borders t/s)		
G-MEDE	Airbus Industrie A320-232	1194	F-WWDY	25. 4.00	British Mediterranean Airways Ltd	Heathrow	24..4.03T
G-MEDF	Airbus Industrie A321-231	1690	D-AVZX	28. 2.02	British Mediterranean Airways Ltd	Heathrow	27. 2.05T

Reg	Type	C/N	Prev ID	Date	Owner	Location	Status
G-MEDG	Airbus Industrie A321-231	1711	D-AVZK	5. 4.02	British Mediterranean Airways Ltd	Heathrow	4. 4.05T
G-MEDH	Airbus Industrie A321-231	1922	F-WWBX	3.03R	British Mediterranean Airways Ltd	Heathrow	
G-MEGA	Piper PA-28R-201T Turbo Arrow III	28R-7803303	N999JG	13. 2.86	Multi Ltd	Breighton	7. 1.05T
G-MEGG	Europa Aviation Europa XS 358 & PFA 247-13202			14. 6.00	M.E.Mavers	(Macclesfield)	
	(Rotax 912S) *(Monowheel u/c)*						
G-MELT	Cessna F172H	F172-0580	G-AWTI	23. 9.83	G.B.Kingham	Goodwood	27. 2.03
	(Built Reims Aviation SA)						
G-MELV	SOCATA Rallye 235E Gabier	13328	G-BIND	21. 5.86	J.W.Busby	Grove Fields Farm, Wasperton	21.12.02
G-MEME	Piper PA-28R-201 Arrow	2837051	N9219N	17. 8.90	Henry J.Clare Ltd	Bodmin	6.10.05
G-MEOW	CFM Streak Shadow K.172 & PFA 206-12025			23. 4.93	G.J.Moor	Craysmarsh Farm, Melksham	12. 6.03P
	(Rotax 582)						
G-MERC	Colt 56A HAB	842		11. 6.86	A.F. & C.D.Selby	Loughborough	16. 6.00A
G-MERE	Lindstrand LBL-77A HAB	092		7. 4.94	R.D.Baker *(Current status unknown)*	Canterbury	4. 3.03A
G-MERF	Grob G-115A	8091	EI-CAB	24. 7.95	G.Wylie tr G-MERF Group	White Waltham	24. 5.03
G-MERI	Piper PA-28-181 Archer II	28-8090267	N8175J	17. 7.80	A H McVicar	Carlisle	27.10.05T
G-MERL	Piper PA-28RT-201 Arrow IV	28R-7918036	N2116N	27. 6.86	M.Giles	Cardiff	22. 8.04
G-MEUP	Cameron A-120 HAB	2117		5.10.89	Innovation Ballooning Ltd	Bath	18. 8.02T
					(Sopwith Aviation Co titles)		
G-MEYO	Enstrom 280FX	2059	SX-HCN	13. 1.95	J.N.Ainsworth	(West Drayton)	17. 5.04T
G-MFAC	Cessna F172H	F172-0387	G-AVBZ	23. 8.01	Springbank Aviation Ltd	(Castletown, Isle of Man)	16. 5.03T
	(Built Reims Aviation SA)						
G-MFEF	Reims FR172J Rocket	FR17200426	D-EGJQ	19.10.00	M.& E.N.Ford	Partridge Green	19.11.03
G-MFHI	Europa Aviation Europa	202 & PFA 247-12841		14.11.97	M.F.Howe	Wombleton	26.10.02P
	(Rotax 912-UL) *(Monowheel u/c)*			*(F/f 28.7.98)*			
G-MFHT	Robinson R22 Beta-II	2601	N8334H	20. 6.96	MFH Helicopters Ltd	Blackpool	3. 7.05T
G-MFLI	Cameron V-90 HAB	2650		14. 8.91	J.M.Percival *"Mayfly"* (Mouldform titles)	Loughborough	12. 7.03A
G-MFMF	Bell 206B-3 JetRanger III	3569	G-BJNJ	4. 6.84	South Western Electricity plc	Bristol	16.11.03T
G-MFMM	Scheibe SF-25C Falke	4412	(G-MBMM)	20. 4.82	J.E.Selman	(Ardagh, Co.Limerick)	11. 1.03T
			D-KAEU				
G-MGAA	Quad City Challenger II			18. 8.97	P.Gibbs	Plaistows Farm, St Albans	22.12.02P
	(Rotax 582) CH2-0297-1568 & PFA 177A-13124						
G-MGAG	Aviasud Mistral 532GB 0587-045 & BMAA/HB/009			20. 6.89	M.Raj	Otherton, Cannock	27. 6.00P
G-MGAN	Robinson R44 Astro	0588		10. 5.99	Meegan Motors Ltd	(Castleblayney, Co.Monaghan)	9. 7.05T
G-MGCA	Jabiru Jabiru UL	PFA 274A-13228		8. 5.98	P.A.James	Redhill	15. 3.03P
	(Jabiru 2200A) *(Regd as PFA 274-13228)*				t/a Cloudbase Aviation		
G-MGCB	Solar Wings Pegasus XL-Q SW-TE-0344 & 7267			16.10.96	M.G.Gomez	Roddige, Fradley	25. 3.00P
	(Rotax 462) *(Trike ex G-MWUT)*						
G-MGDL	Pegasus Quantum 15	7400		17. 2.98	I.Fernihough	Bradley	15. 5.03P
	(Rotax 582)						
G-MGDM*	Pegasus Quantum 15-912	7406		19. 3.98	R.Jeffes *(Cancelled 5.12.01 by CAA)*	(London SW13)	18. 4.00P
G-MGEC	Rans S-6ESD Coyote II XL PFA 204-13209			13.10.97	P.Crowhurst	Sywell	29. 9.03P
	(Rotax 503-2V) *(Tricycle u/c)*						
G-MGEF	Pegasus Quantum 15-912	7261		18. 9.96	G.D.Castell	Long Acre Farm, Sandy	5.12.02P
G-MGFK	Pegasus Quantum 15-912	7396		2. 2.98	F.A.A.Kay	(Chorleywood)	9. 9.03P
G-MGGG	Pegasus Quantum 15-912	7377		3.11.97	R.A.Beauchamp	Shenstone	13. 5.03P
G-MGGT	CFM Streak Shadow SA-M			3. 6.94	R K & J.Hyatt	(Newquay)	5. 9.03P
	(Rotax 618) K.252 & PFA 206-12723						
G-MGGV	Pegasus Quantum 15-912	7484		12.10.98	R.W.Krake	Clench Common	30. 5.03P
G-MGMC	Pegasus Quantum 15-912	7430		28. 4.98	G.J.Slater	Clench Common	10. 6.03P
G-MGMG	Cessna 206H Statioair	20608181	N5076D	18.10.02	115CR(146) Ltd	Wellesbourne Mountford	28.10.05T
G-MGND	Rans S-6ESD Coyote II XL PFA 204-13152			27. 6.97	P.Vallis	(Alfreton)	23. 9.03P
	(Rotax 503)						
G-MGOD	Medway Raven X	MRB110/106		6. 7.93	P.C.Collins & T A Hinton	Doynton	1. 5.00P
	(Rotax 447)				*(Noted 2.03)*		
G-MGOM	Medway Hybred 44XLR	MR125/103		22.11.91	B.A.Showell	Middle Stoke, Kent	3. 9.01P
	(Rotax 503)						
G-MGOO	Murphy Renegade Spirit UK			14.11.89	A.R.Max	White Waltham	2. 5.03P
	(Rotax 582) 301 & PFA 188-11580						
G-MGPD	Solar Wings Pegasus XL-R	6905		9. 1.95	P.C.Davis	Weston Zoyland	15. 2.03P
	(Rotax 462)						
G-MGPH	CFM Streak Shadow SA-M		G-RSPH	27.11.97	R.S.Partridge-Hicks	(Bury St.Edmunds)	29. 7.00P
	(Rotax 582) K.286 & PFA 206-13166			*(Force landed Cockfield, Suffolk 29.7.01: damage to prop, nose u/c & port flap)*			
G-MGRH	Quad City Challenger II	CH2-1189-0482		20. 2.90	R.A. & B.M.Roberts	Griffins Farm, Temple Bruer	16. 2.00P
	(Hirth 2705.R06)						
G-MGTG	Pegasus Quantum 15-912	7369A	G-MZIO	19.12.97	R.B.Milton	Plaistows Farm, St Albans	21.10.02P
	(Original c/n 7369 amended after rebuild 11.98)						
G-MGTR	Huntwing/Experience	BMAA/HB/067		24. 7.97	A.C.Ryall	(Cardiff)	
	(Listed as "Huntwing Avon" in BMAA's records)				*(Current status unknown)*		
G-MGTV	Thruster T600N	4500052-T600N-070		14. 3.02	R.I.Blain	(Newtownards, Co.Down)	15. 8.03P
	(Jabiru 2200A)						
G-MGTW	CFM Shadow DD	K.287 & 287-DD		23. 1.98	G.T.Webster	Glenrothes	17. 8.03P
	(Rotax 582)						
G-MGUN	Cyclone AX2000	7284		18.12.96	I.Lonsdale	Tarn Farm, Cockerham	3. 5.03P
	(Rotax 582/48)						
G-MGUY	CFM Shadow CD	078		23.11.87	F.J.Luckhurst & R.G.M.Proost	(Old Sarum)	16. 8.91P
	(Rotax 447)				*(Crashed Home Farm, Pontisbury, Shrewsbury 20.7.91: current status unknown)*		
G-MGWH	Thruster T300	9013-T300-507		8.12.92	S.Bell & D.J.Flower	Baxby Manor, Husthwaite	18. 4.03P
	(Rotax 582)						
G-MGWI	Robinson R44 Astro	0663	G-BZEF	4. 5.00	T.J.French	(Cronberry, Cumnock)	9. 5.03T
G-MHCB	Enstrom 280C Shark	1031	N892PT	11.10.95	Springbank Aviation Ltd	(Castletown, Isle of Man)	14.10.02T
G-MHCD	Enstrom 280C-UK Shark	1112		12. 7.96	S.J.Ellis	Bryngwyn Bach	25. 9.04T
G-MHCE	Enstrom F-28A	150	G-BBHD	22. 8.96	Wyke Commercial Services Ltd	Barton	3. 7.05T
G-MHCF	Enstrom 280C-UK Shark	1149	G-GSML	19. 9.96	K., H.K. & D.Collier	Barton	30. 7.04T
			G-BNNV/SE-HIY		t/a HKC Helicopter Services		

Reg	Type	C/n	Prev id	Date	Owner	Location	Date
G-MHCG	Enstrom 280C-UK Shark	1155	G-HAYN / G-BPOX/N51776	7. 3.97	E.Drinkwater	Barton	5. 9.03
G-MHCH*	Enstrom 280C Shark	1043	N557H	19. 5.97	J.& S.Lewis Ltd *(Cancelled 15.1.02 as WFU)*	Barton	15.11.03T
G-MHCI	Enstrom 280C Shark	1152	N100WZ	20. 5.97	B & B Helicopters Ltd	Barton	17. 9.03T
G-MHCJ	Enstrom F-28C-UK	453	G-CTRN	30. 3.98	P.E.Toleman t/a Paradise Helicopters	Hawarden	21. 6.04T
G-MHCK	Enstrom 280FX	2006	G-BXXB / ZK-HHN/JA7702	5. 6.98	N., C. & N.C. Bailey / t/a Manchester Helicopter Centre	Barton	16. 9.04T
G-MHCL	Enstrom 280C Shark	1144	N51740	30. 6.98	Altolink Ltd	Hawarden	24.11.01T
G-MICH	Robinson R22 Beta	0647	G-BNKY	3. 9.87	Tiger Helicopters Ltd	Shobdon	10.10.05T
G-MICI	Cessna 182S Skylane	18280546	G-WARF / N7089F	14. 6.01	DI Aviation LLP	(Slough)	25. 7.05T
G-MICK	Reims/Cessna F172N Skyhawk II	F17201592	PH-JRA / PH-AXB	9. 1.80	S.J.Gronow / tr G-MICK Flying Group	Blackpool	23. 8.04
G-MICY	Everett Gyroplane Srs.1 (Volkswagen 1835)	018	(G-BOVF)	26. 2.90	D.M.Hughes	St.Merryn	2. 5.92P
G-MIDA	Airbus Industrie A321-231	806	D-AVZQ	31. 3.98	British Midland Airways Ltd	East Midlands	30. 3.04T
G-MIDC	Airbus Industrie A321-231	835	D-AVZZ	12. 6.98	British Midland Airways Ltd	East Midlands	11. 6.04T
G-MIDD	Piper PA-28-140 Cherokee Cruiser	28-7325444	D-BBDD / N11C	20. 1.97	R.B.Walker / t/a Midland Air Training School	Coventry	25. 5.04T
G-MIDE	Airbus Industrie A321-231	864	D-AVZB	14. 8.98	British Midland Airways Ltd	East Midlands	13. 8.04T
G-MIDF	Airbus Industrie A321-231	810	D-AVZS	24. 4.98	British Midland Airways Ltd	East Midlands	24. 4.04T
G-MIDG	Bushby-Long MM-1 Midget Mustang (Lycoming O-320)	385	N11DE	14. 3.90	C.E.Bellhouse	Headcorn	25. 6.03P
G-MIDH	Airbus Industrie A321-231	968	D-AVXZ	22. 3.99	British Midland Airways Ltd	East Midlands	21. 1.05T
G-MIDI	Airbus Industrie A321-231	974	D-AVZA	26. 3.99	British Midland Airways Ltd	East Midlands	25. 3.05T
G-MIDJ	Airbus Industrie A321-231	1045	D-AVZO	16. 7.99	British Midland Airways Ltd *(Stored 1.02)*	East Midlands	15. 7.05T
G-MIDK	Airbus Industrie A321-231	1153	D-AVZF	12. 1.00	British Midland Airways Ltd *(Star Alliance titles)*	East Midlands	11. 1.06T
G-MIDL	Airbus Industrie A321-231	1174	D-AVZH	22. 2.00	British Midland Airways Ltd *(Star Alliance titles)*	East Midlands	21. 2.03T
G-MIDM	Airbus Industrie A321-231	1207	D-AVZR	18. 4.00	British Midland Airways Ltd	East Midlands	17. 4.03T
G-MIDN	Airbus Industrie A321-231R			.03R	British Midland Airways Ltd	East Midlands	
G-MIDO	Airbus Industrie A321-231R			.03R	British Midland Airways Ltd	East Midlands	
G-MIDP	Airbus Industrie A320-232	1732	F-WWBK	24. 5.02	British Midland Airways Ltd	East Midlands	23. 5.05T
G-MIDR	Airbus Industrie A320-232	1697	F-WWIQ	22. 4.02	British Midland Airways Ltd	East Midlands	21. 4.05T
G-MIDS	Airbus Industrie A320-232	1424	F-WWBO	21. 3.01	British Midland Airways Ltd	East Midlands	20. 3.04T
G-MIDT	Airbus Industrie A320-232	1418	F-WWBI	14. 3.01	British Midland Airways Ltd	East Midlands	13. 3.04T
G-MIDU	Airbus Industrie A320-232	1407	F-WWDC	27. 2.01	British Midland Airways Ltd	East Midlands	26. 2.04T
G-MIDV	Airbus Industrie A320-232	1383	F-WWIQ	30. 1.01	British Midland Airways Ltd	East Midlands	29. 1.04T
G-MIDW	Airbus Industrie A320-232	1183	F-WWDT	29. 3.00	British Midland Airways Ltd *(Star Alliance titles)*	East Midlands	28. 3.03T
G-MIDX	Airbus Industrie A320-232	1177	F-WWDP	21. 3.00	British Midland Airways Ltd *(Star Alliance titles)*	East Midlands	20. 3.03T
G-MIDY	Airbus Industrie A320-232	1014	F-WWDQ	28. 6.99	British Midland Airways Ltd	East Midlands	27. 6.05T
G-MIDZ	Airbus Industrie A320-232	934	F-WWII	19. 1.99	British Midland Airways Ltd	East Midlands	18. 1.05T
G-MIFF	Robin DR400/180 Regent	2076		31. 5.91	J.C.Harvey / tr Westfield Flying Group	Spilsted Farm, Sedlescombe	16.10.03
G-MIGG	WSK PZL-Mielec Lim-5	1C1211	G-BWUF / Polish AF 1211	17. 1.03	D.Miles *(In North Vietnamese c/s)*	Bournemouth	
G-MIII	Extra EA.300/L (Lycoming AEIO-540)	013	D-EXFI	5. 9.95	Firebird Aerobatics Ltd *(Firebirds titles)*	Denham	26. 9.04T
G-MIKE	Brookland Hornet (Volkswagen 1830)	MG.1		15. 5.78	M.H.J.Goldring *(Current status unknown)*	St.Merryn	25. 9.92P
G-MIKG	Robinson R22 Mariner	3332M		5. 6.02	Direct Timber Ltd	(Coalville)	26. 6.05T
G-MIKI	Rans S-6ESA Coyote II (Tricycle u/c) (Rotax 912-UL)	0996.1040 & PFA 204-13094		28. 2.97	S.P.Slade	Kemble	16. 6.03P
G-MILA	Reims/Cessna F172N Skyhawk II	F17201686	D-EGHC(2) / PH-AYJ	9. 6.98	P.J.Miller	Cuckoo Tye Farm, Long Melford	28. 8.04A
G-MILE	Cameron N-77 HAB	2411		26. 9.90	Miles Air Ltd *(Miles Architectural Ironmongery Ltd titles)*	Bristol	14. 7.03A
G-MILI	Bell 206B-3 JetRanger III	2275	C-GGAR / 5H-MPV	5.10.94	Shropshire Aviation Ltd	(Telford)	1.10.04T
G-MILN	Cessna 182Q Skylane	18265770	N735XQ	9. 7.99	Meon Hill Farms (Stockbridge) Ltd	Thruxton	22. 8.05T
G-MILY	Grumman American AA-5A Cheetah *(C/n plate shows Gulfstream American details)*	AA5A-0672	G-BFXY	2. 9.96	Plane Talking Ltd	Elstree	17.10.05T
G-MIMA	British Aerospace BAe 146 Srs.200	E2079	G-CNMF / G-5-079	3. 3.93	Manx Airlines Ltd *(Op Manx Airlines)*	Ronaldsway	25.11.04T
G-MIME	Europa Aviation Europa (Rotax 912-ULS) (Monowheel u/c)	203 & PFA 247-12850		26. 9.97	N.W.Charles *(F/f 17.8.01)*	Kemble	12.10.03P
G-MIND	Cessna 404 Titan II	404-0004	G-SKKC / G-OHUB/SE-GMX/(N3932C)	27. 4.93	Atlantic Air Transport Ltd *(Op Highlands Airways Ltd)*	Inverness	13. 2.03T
G-MINN	Lindstrand LBL 90A HAB	883		30.10.02	S.M. & D.Johnson	Bromley	
G-MINS	Nicollier HN.700 Menestrel II	PFA 217-12354		23.10.92	R.Fenion	West Freugh	8.11.02P
G-MINT	Pitts S-1S Special (Lycoming AEIO-360)	PFA 09-10292		7. 2.83	T.G.Sanderson	Leicester	14.11.03P
G-MIOO	Miles M.100 Student 2	M1008	G-APLK	26.10.84	Aces High Ltd	(Woking)	6. 5.86P
		G-MIOO/G-APLK/XS941/G-APLK/G-35-4 *(On rebuild as "G-APLK" 3.02)*					
G-MISH	Cessna 182R Skylane II	18267888	G-RFAB / G-BIXT/N6397H	16. 6.95	M.J.Joslin	Redhill	1. 4.03
G-MISS	Taylor JT.2 Titch	PFA 3234		18.12.78	P.L.Brenen *(Noted 10.02)*	RAF Halton	
G-MITT	Jabiru Jabiru SK	PFA 274-13427		29. 2.00	N.C.Mitton	Goodwood	28. 8.03P
G-MIWS	Cessna 310R II	310R1585	G-ODNP / N19TP/N2DD/N1836E	1. 2.96	R.W.F.Warner	RAF Shawbury	9. 9.02P
G-MJAE	American Aerolights Eagle *(C/n not confirmed)*	1021		12. 7.82	T.B.Woolley *(Current status unknown)*	(Leicester)	

G-MJAJ	Eurowing Goldwing	EW-36		18. 6.82	R.D.J Brixton tr Canard Flyers Group	(Hyssington)	6. 8.03P
	(Fuji-Robin EC-44-PM)						
G-MJAM	Eipper Quicksilver MX	JCL-01		18. 6.82	J.C.Larkin	Maryport, Cumbria	20. 8.93P
	(Cuyuna 430)				*(Current status unknown)*		
G-MJAN	Hiway Skytrike I/Flexiform Hilander			21. 6.82	G.M.Sutcliffe	(Stockport)	4. 3.92E
	(Valmet)	RPFD-01 & 21U9			*(Current status unknown)*		
G-MJAV	Hiway Skytrike II/Hiway Demon 175	817003		23. 6.82	J.N.J.Roberts	Long Acre Farm, Sandy	10. 5.90E
	(Fuji-Robin 250)				*(Current status unknown)*		
G-MJAY	Eurowing Goldwing	EW-58		23. 6.82	M.Anthony	(Alfreton)	24. 7.90E
	(Fuji-Robin EC-34-PM)				*(Current status unknown)*		
G-MJAZ	Vector 627SR Ultravector	1251	PH-1J1	23. 6.82	B.Fussell	(Swansea)	23. 9.93E
	(Konig SC430)		G-MJAZ		*(Stored 1.97: current status unknown)*		
	(Originally regd as Aerodyne Vector 610 but converted 4.88 when PH-1J1)						
G-MJBK	Swallow AeroPlane Swallow B	582007-2		18.11.83	M.A.Newbould	(Harrogate)	N/E
	(Rotax 447)				*(Current status unknown)*		
G-MJBL	American Aerolights Eagle	2892		25. 6.82	B.W.Olley	(Ely)	16. 9.03P
	(Chrysler 820)						
G-MJBS	UAS Storm Buggy	JL814S		29. 6.82	G.I.Sargeant	(Bridgwater)	
					(BMAA records as damaged in 1982) (Current status unknown)		
G-MJBV	American Aerolights Eagle 215B	RSP-001		1. 7.82	B.H.Stephens	(Southampton)	11. 8.96P
	(Fuji-Robin EC-25-PS)				*(Current status unknown)*		
G-MJBZ	Huntair Pathfinder 1	PK-17		2. 7.82	J.C.Rose	Eastbach Farm, Coleford	28.12.93P
	(Fuji-Robin EC-34-PM)				*(Current status unknown)*		
G-MJCE	Ultrasports Puma/Southdown Sprint X	RGC-01		5. 7.82	L.I.Bateup	(Salisbury)	25. 8.01P
	(Fuji-Robin EC-44-PM) *(Designation amended by BMAA 1990)*						
G-MJCF*	Hill (Maxair) Hummer	SMC-01		5. 7.82	Not known	Doynton	N/E
	(Fuji-Robin EC-25-PS)				*(Cancelled 24.1.95 by CAA) (Noted derelict 2.03)*		
G-MJCN	Southern Flyer Mk.1	005		5. 7.82	C.W.Merriam	(Billingshurst)	11. 6.99P
	(Fuji-Robin EC-44-PM)				*(Current status unknown)*		
G-MJCU	Tarjani/Solar Wings Typhoon	SCG-01 & T982-610		7. 7.82	J.K.Ewing	Old Sarum	1. 9.94P
	(Fuji-Robin EC-25-PS)				*(Current status unknown)*		
G-MJCX	American Aerolights Eagle 215B	2759		7. 7.82	J.Channer	(Nottingham)	11. 8.94P
	(Chrysler 820?) *(May have Cuyana fitted)*				*(Current status unknown)*		
G-MJDE	Huntair Pathfinder 1	020		9. 7.82	P.Rayson	(Swadlincote)	1. 8.03P
	(Fuji-Robin EC-34-PM)						
G-MJDH*	Huntair Pathfinder 1	015		9. 7.82	T.Mahmood	Insch	12. 8.01P
	(Fuji-Robin EC-44-PM)				*(Dismantled 3.02) (Cancelled 10.6.02 as WFU)*		
G-MJDJ	Hiway Skytrike/Demon	VW17D		9. 7.82	A.J.Cowan *(Current status unknown)*	(Billingham)	
G-MJDP	Eurowing Goldwing	GW-001		12. 7.82	B.L.Keeping	Davidstow Moor	15.11.92P
	(Fuji-Robin EC-34-PM)				tr G-MJDP Flying Group *(New owner 1.03)*		
G-MJDR	Hiway Skytrike/Demon	PJB-01		14. 7.82	D.R.Redmile *(Current status unknown)*	(Leicester)	
G-MJDU	Eipper Quicksilver MXII	14002		15. 7.82	J.Brown	Markfield, Leics	17.11.86E
	(Rotax 503)				*(Current status unknown)*		
G-MJDW	Eipper Quicksilver MXII	RI-01		15. 7.82	J.A.Brumpton	(Horncastle)	29. 3.03P
	(Cuyuna 430)	*(C/n noted as 3506)*					
G-MJEB	Southdown Puma Sprint	SN1231/0041		18. 4.85	R.J.Shelswell	(Warwick)	1. 5.96P
	(Rotax 447)				*(Current status unknown)*		
G-MJEE	Mainair Tri-Flyer 250/Solar Wings Typhoon			20. 7.82	M.F.Eddington	(Wincanton)	11.11.00P
	(Fuji-Robin EC-25-PS)	038-251181					
G-MJEG	Eurowing Goldwing	GJS-01		20. 7.82	G.J.Stamper	Barton	23. 4.89E
	(Fuji-Robin EC-34-PM)				*(Stored 9.01)*		
G-MJEO	American Aerolights Eagle 215B	4562		26. 7.82	A.M.Shaw	(Stoke-on-Trent)	25. 6.93E
	(Zenoah G25B1)				*(Current status unknown)*		
G-MJER	Ultrasports Tripacer/Flexiform Solo Striker			23. 7.82	D.S.Simpson	Radwell, Letchworth	26.12.00P
	(Rotax 447)	DSD-01					
G-MJEY	Mainair Tri-Flyer 440/Southdown Lightning DS			27. 7.82	M.McKenzie	Insch	7. 6.96P
	(Fuji-Robin EC-44-PM)	085-26782 & PMC-01			*(Trike only stored 3.02)*		
G-MJFB	Ultrasports Tripacer/Flexiform Solo Striker			27. 7.82	B.Tetley	(Cowes)	27.10.03P
	(Fuji-Robin EC-34-PM)	AJK-01					
G-MJFM	Huntair Pathfinder 1	ML-0		12. 9.82	R.Gillespie & S.P.Girr	Mullaghmore, Co.Antrim	23. 7.99P
	(Fuji-Robin EC-34-PM)				*(Current status unknown)*		
G-MJFX	Skyhook TR1/Sabre	TR1/38		2. 8.82	M.R.Dean	(Hebden Bridge)	28. 2.87E
	(Hunting HS.525A)				*(Current status unknown)*		
G-MJGK*	Eurowing Goldwing	040		3. 8.82	Not known	Rufforth	
	(Fuji-Robin EC-34-PM)				*(Cancelled 13.6.90 by CAA) (Noted less wings 7.01)*		
G-MJHC	Ultrasports Tripacer 330/Southdown Lightning Mk II			9. 8.82	E.J.Allen	(Cambridge)	12.12.89E
	(Fuji-Robin EC-34)	82-00044	*(C/n is engine serial no)*		*(Current status unknown)*		
G-MJHR	Mainair Dual Tri-Flyer/Southdown Lightning			12. 8.82	B.R.Barnes	(Bristol)	
		GNS-01			*(Current status unknown)*		
G-MJHV	Hiway Skytrike II/Hiway Demon	AG-17		13. 8.82	A.G.Griffiths	(Avenchurch, Birmingham)	
					(Current status unknown)		
G-MJHX	Eipper Quicksilver MXII	1033		13. 8.82	P.D.Lucas	(Needham, Harleston)	14. 5.95P
	(Rotax 503)				*(Stored 9.97: current status unknown)*		
G-MJIA	Ultrasports Tripacer/Flexiform Solo Striker	SE-007		13. 8.82	D.G.Ellis	(Tamworth)	20. 9.96P
	(Rotax 377)				*(Current status unknown)*		
G-MJIC	Ultrasports Tripacer/Flexiform Solo Striker			13. 8.82	J.Curran	(Newry, Co.Armagh)	15.10.94P
	(Fuji-Robin EC-34-PM)	82-00043			*(Current status unknown)*		
G-MJIF	Mainair Tri-Flyer/Flexiform Striker "E-1 EC25PS-04"			16. 8.82	R.J.Payne	(Newmarket)	31.10.91E
	(Fuji-Robin EC-34-PL) *(C/n was original engine type)*				*(Current status unknown)*		
G-MJIR	Eipper Quicksilver MXII	1392		18. 8.82	H.Feeney	Long Marston	26. 1.95P
	(Rotax 503)				*(Stored 8.96: current status unknown)*		
G-MJIY	Ultrasports Puma/Southdown Sprint X	002 CSRS		23. 8.82	M.I.McClelland	Old Sarum	10. 7.00P
	(Fuji-Robin EC-34-PM) *(Originally regd as Ultrasports Tripacer/Flexiform Striker)*				t/a McClelland Aviation		
G-MJJA	Huntair Pathfinder 1	031		23. 8.82	R.D.Bateman & J.M.Watkins	Davidstow Moor	25. 8.02P

G-MJJF*	Ultrasports Tripacer/Solar Wings Large Typhoon		25. 8.82	G.Ravichandran	(London N13)	1. 4.01P
	(Fuji-Robin EC-34-PM) JGS-01 & 116-108 & T784-1152L			*(Cancelled 14.11.02 by CAA)*	
G-MJJK	Eipper Quicksilver MXII	3397	25. 8.82	M.J.O'Malley	(Northolt)	13.10.02P
	(Rotax 503)				
G-MJKB	Striplin Sky Ranger	ST 161	2. 9.82	A.P.Booth	(Newbury)
	(Officially quoted as c/n SRI-6-I)			*(Current status unknown)*	
G-MJKF	Hiway Demon	WGR-01	2. 9.82	S.D.Hill *(Current status unknown)*	(Henley-on-Thames)
G-MJKH*	Eipper Quicksilver MXII	1020	28. 1.83	D.O'Neill	Long Marston	23. 8.96P
	(Rotax 503)			*(Cancelled 6.11.00 by CAA) (Stored 8.01)*	
G-MJKO	Hiway Skytrike/Gold Marque Gyr 188	90030P	7. 9.82	M.J.Barry	(Bridgwater)	18.11.91E
	(Fuji-Robin EC-25-PS) *(Assembled from spares by Windsports)*			*(Current status unknown)*	
G-MJKX	Skyrider Airsports Phantom	PH.82005	14. 9.82	C.G.Johns	Droppingwell Farm, Bewdley	1. 8.98P
	(Fuji-Robin EC-50)			*(New owner 5.01)*	
G-MJLK*	Dragon Dragonfly 250-II	D.105	10. 9.82	Not known	Breighton
				(Cancelled 18.4.90 as WFU) (Dismantled 12.02)	
G-MJMB*	Weedhopper JC-24	846	23. 9.82	M.J.Aubrey	(Kington, Hereford)
	(Chotia 460)			*(Cancelled 7.9.94 by CAA). (Noted 2002)*	
G-MJMD	Hiway Skytrike II/Demon 175	OE17D	27. 9.82	T.A.N.Brierley	Baxby Manor, Husthwaite	1. 8.97P
	(Fuji-Robin EC-34-PM)			*(Current status unknown)*	
G-MJME*	Ultrasports Tripacer/Moyes Mega II	WIA	27. 9.82	Not known	Southwick, Trowbridge
				(Cancelled 29.1.88 as WFU) (Stored in workshop 2001)	
G-MJMN	Mainair Tri-Flyer/Flexiform Striker	087-04882	29. 9.82	K.Medd	(Manchester)	2. 6.01P
	(Fuji-Robin EC-34-PM)			*(Stored dismantled 1.02) (New owner 9.02)*	
G-MJMR	Mainair Tri-Flyer 250/Solar Wings Typhoon		30. 9.82	J.C.S.Jones	Emlyn's Field, Rhuallt
	DR-01 & 048-5182			*(Stored 12.97: current status unknown)*	
G-MJMS	Hiway Skytrike II/Demon 175	EEW-01	30. 9.82	D.E.Peace *(Current status unknown)*	(Rawdon, Leeds)
G-MJMU	Hiway Skytrike II/Demon 175	817003	1.10.82	P.Hunt	(Bishop Auckland)
	(Fuji-Robin EC-25-PS) *(C/n duplicates several a/c incl G-MJOI & PH-1B2 and is suspect!) (Current status unknown)*				
G-MJNK	Hiway Skytrike II/Demon 175	EA17D	14.10.82	S.W.Barker	Baxby Manor, Husthwaite	28.10.96P
	(Fuji-Robin EC-34-PM)			*(New owner 10.01)*	
G-MJNM	American Aerolights Double Eagle	430B	25.11.82	B.H.Stephens	(Southampton)	19. 9.93P
	(Cuyuna 430R)702			*(Current status unknown)*	
G-MJNO	American Aerolights Double Eagle Amphibian		24.11.82	R.S.Martin	(Gosport)	23. 6.03P
	(Rotax 447)	703			
G-MJNU	Skyhook TR1/Cutlass	TR1/17	19.10.82	R.W.Taylor *(Current status unknown)*	(Sheffield)
G-MJNY	Skyhook TR1/Sabre	TR1/35	3.11.82	P.Ratcliffe *(Current status unknown)*	(Sheffield)
G-MJOC	Huntair Pathfinder	048	25.10.82	A.J.Glynn	Gerpins Lane, Upminster	31. 7.99P
	(Fuji-Robin EC-34-PM)			*(Current status unknown)*	
G-MJOE	Eurowing Goldwing	EW-55	29.10.82	R.J.Osborne	(Tiverton)	19.11.88E
	(Rotax 377)			*(Current status unknown)*	
G-MJPA	Rotec Rally 2B	AT-01	5. 1.83	R.Boyd *(Current status unknown)* (Armagh, Co. Armagh)	
G-MJPE	Mainair Tri-Flyer 330/Demon 175		10.11.82	E.G.Astin	(Whitby)	7. 8.96P
	(Fuji-Robin EC-34-PM) 117-151282 & OG17D			*(Current status unknown)*	
G-MJPV	Eipper Quicksilver MX	JBW-01	30.11.82	F.W.Ellis	Water Leisure Park, Skegness	1. 2.95P
	(Cuyuna 430R)			*(Current status unknown)*	
G-MJRL	Eurowing Goldwing	EW-79 & SWA-5K	30.12.82	M.Daniels	(Heanor)	15. 6.00P
	(Rotax 377)				
G-MJRO	Eurowing Goldwing	EW-77 & SWA-04	31.12.82	H.P.Welch	(Taunton)	22. 9.99P
	(Rotax 447)			*(Current status unknown)*	
G-MJRR	Reece SkyRanger Srs.1	JR-3	26. 4.82	J.R.Reece *(Current status unknown)*	(Formby)
G-MJRS	Eurowing Goldwing	EW-80 & SWA-6K	5. 1.83	G.B.Gratton & J.L.Macfarlane	Chilbolton	12.10.01P
	(Rotax 377)				
G-MJRU	MBA Tiger Cub 440	SO.86	6. 1.83	D.J.Short *(Current status unknown)*	(Nailsea, Bristol)	31. 1.86E
G-MJSE	Skyrider Airsports Phantom	SF-101	24. 1.83	C.L.Betts	(Hove)	20. 5.02P
	(Fuji-Robin EC-40-PL)				
G-MJSF	Skyrider Airsports Phantom	SF-105	SE-...	24. 1.83	B.J.Towers	(Pershore)
	(Rotax 462)		G-MJSF		*(On rebuild 5.00)*	
G-MJSL	Dragon Light Aircraft Dragon 200	0018	24. 2.83	G.Kingston	Long Marston	22. 9.99P
	(Rotax 503)			*(New owner 1.02)*	
G-MJSO	Hiway Skytrike III/Demon 175	SA17D	1. 2.83	D.C.Read	(Ledbury)	N/E
	(Hiro 22)			*(Current status unknown)*	
G-MJSP	Romain MBA Super Tiger Cub Special 440	S0.54	7. 2.83	A P Chapman	North Coates	31. 1.86E
	(Tricycle u/c)			*(Fuselage only 12.00)*	
G-MJST	MEA Pterodactyl Ptraveler	GCS-01	2.12.81	C.H.J.Goodwin	(Bedford)	7. 5.99P
	(Fuji-Robin EC-34-PM)			*(Current status unknown)*	
G-MJSV*	MBA Tiger Cub 440	SO.87/2	2. 2.83	Not known	(Kinloss)
	(Officially regd with c/n SO.287)			*(Cancelled 9.11.89 by CAA) (Stored 2001)*	
G-MJSY	Eurowing Goldwing	EW-63	8. 2.83	A.J.Rex	(Wrexham)	5. 1.01P
	(Rotax 377)				
G-MJSZ	Harker DH Wasp	HA.5	10. 2.83	J.J.Hill	Baxby Manor, Husthwaite	24. 3.01P
	(Rotax 447)				
G-MJTC	Ultrasports Tri-Pacer/Typhoon	T1282-677	14. 2.83	V.C.Redhead *(Current status unknown)*	(Saxmundham)
G-MJTD	Gardner T-M Scout	83/001	14. 2.83	D.Gardner	(Rugby)
	(Thomas-Morse S4 Scout 2/3rd rep) (Possibly c/n PFA 111-10664)			*(As "41386" in US Army Signal Corps c/s) (Current status unknown)*	
G-MJTE	Skyrider Airsports Phantom	SF-106	15. 2.83	M.R.Jones	Wing Farm, Longbridge Deverill	11. 6.02P
	(Fuji-Robin EC-44-PM)				
G-MJTM	Southdown Aerostructure Pipistrelle P2B		21. 2.83	K.S.Matcham	Barton Ashes	16. 2.02P
	(KFM-107ER) 019 & SAL/P2B/002				
G-MJTP	Mainair Tri-Flyer/Flexiform Dual Sealander		25. 2.83	P.Milton	(Bedford)	22. 8.00P
	(Fuji-Robin EC-44-PM) AJDH-01 & 139-7383			*(Possibly fitted with Dual Striker wing after accident 29.10.87)*	
G-MJTR	Southdown Puma DS Mk.1	H362	9. 3.83	A.G.Rodenburg & T.Abro	(Tillicoultry)	15. 7.96P
	(Fuji-Robin EC-44-PM)			*(Current status unknown)*	
G-MJTX	Skyrider Airsports Phantom	SF-110	1. 3.83	P.D.Coppin	(Fareham)	22. 4.96P
	(Fuji-Robin EC-44-PM)			*(CofR restored 14.11.01)*	

Reg	Type	C/n	Date	Owner	Location	Status
G-MJTZ	Skyrider Airsports Phantom	MBS-01	29. 4.83	B.J.Towers	(Pershore)	N/E
	(Fuji-Robin EC-44-PM) *(Eng No.82-00119)*			*(Current status unknown)*		
G-MJUF*	MBA Super Tiger Cub 440	MCT-01	8. 3.83	D G Palmer	Fetterangus	
	(Fuji-Robin EC-44)			*(Cancelled 27.4.90 by CAA) (Stored 7.01)*		
G-MJUH*	MBA Tiger Cub 440	JEJ-01	9. 3.83	The Flix Public House	Bridge St, Girvan	5. 8.92P
	(Fuji-Robin EC-44)			*(Cancelled 2.7.96 as WFU: noted 6.00)*		
G-MJUO*	Eipper Quicksilver MX II	104C	22. 3.83	A Hamilton	Strathaven	
				(Cancelled 24.1.95 by CAA: noted 8.00)		
G-MJUU	Eurowing Goldwing	EW-70	28. 3.83	E.F.Clapham	(Oldbury-on-Severn)	3. 5.97P
	(Fuji-Robin EC-344-PM)			*(Current status unknown)*		
G-MJUV	Huntair Pathfinder Mk.1	045	18. 5.83	S.J.Overton	(Colchester)	31. 7.99P
	(Fuji-Robin EC-44-PM)					
G-MJUW	MBA Tiger Cub 440	SO.69	29. 3.83	D.G.Palmer	Fetterangus	7. 6.02P
	(Fuji-Robin EC-44-PM)					
G-MJUX	Skyrider Airsports Phantom	RFF-01 & PH00094	29. 2.84	K.H.A.Negal	Sittles Farm, Alrewas	10. 3.02P
	(Fuji-Robin EC-44-PM)					
G-MJUZ*	Dragon 150	015	30. 3.83	G.S.Richardson	North Coates	28. 2.87E
	(Fuji-Robin EC-51)			*(Stored 8.00: cancelled 15.11.02 by CAA)*		
G-MJVE	Medway Hybred 44XL/Solar Wings Typhoon XLII		19. 4.83	T.A.Clark	(Rheda-Wiedenbrueck, Germany)	5. 6.00P
	(Fuji-Robin EC-44-PM) 4483/1 & T483-761XL		*(Original wing c/n T283-703XL)*			
G-MJVF	CFM Shadow	CD002	12. 4.83	J.A.Cook	(Thorpeness)	15. 3.03P
	(Rotax 503)					
G-MJVN	Ultrasports Tripacer/Flexiform Striker		18. 4.83	R.McGookin	(West Kilbride)	5.10.93P
	(Fuji-Robin EC-44-PM) 82-00030-PR1		*(Original Trike & engine fitted in G-MJRP) (Current status unknown)*			
G-MJVP	Eipper Quicksilver MXII	1149	19. 4.83	G.J.Ward	(Dorchester)	10. 7.96P
	(Rotax 503) *(Original c/n 1124 became G-MTDO?)*			*(Current status unknown)*		
G-MJVU	Eipper Quicksilver MX II	1118	3. 4.84	F.J.Griffith	(Denbigh)	23. 6.02P
	(Rotax 503)					
G-MJVX	Skyrider Airsports Phantom	JAG-01 & SF-102	27. 4.83	J.R.Harris	Droppingwell Farm, Bewdley	19. 6.03P
	(Fuji-Robin EC-44-PM)					
G-MJVY	Dragon 150	D.150/013	4. 5.83	J.C.Craddock	(Freshwater, Isle of Wight)	21. 9.02P
	(Rotax 503)					
G-MJWB	Eurowing Goldwing	EW-59	24. 5.83	D.G.Palmer	Fetterangus	25. 8.93P
	(Fuji-Robin EC-34-PM)			*(Noted 7.01)*		
G-MJWF	MBA Tiger Cub 440	BRH-001 & SO.79	4. 5.83	T & R L Maycock *(New owners 6.02)*	(Glasgow)	
G-MJWJ	MBA Tiger Cub 440	013/191	9. 5.83	J.W.Barratt	(Langport)	18. 3.96P
	(Fuji-Robin EC-44-PM)			*(Current status unknown)*		
G-MJWK	Huntair Pathfinder 1	JWK-01	1.10.82	D.Young tr Kemble Flying Club	Kemble	26. 5.03P
	(Rotax 447)					
G-MJWZ	Solar Wings Panther XL-S	T583-781XL	9. 9.85	A.L.Davies	(Holywell)	27. 1.01P
	(Fuji-Robin EC-44-2PM)			*(New owner 10.02)*		
G-MJXF*	MBA Tiger Cub 440	EJH-01	1. 6.83	Not known	Southwater, Sussex	
				(Cancelled 5.9.94 by CAA) (Stored 8.01)		
G-MJXS*	Huntair Pathfinder II	134	25. 5.83	A.E.Sawyer	Melrose Farm Melbourn	
				(Stored 5.00) (Cancelled 11.4.02 by CAA)		
G-MJXY	Hiway Demon II/Skytrike 330	KQ17D	31. 5.83	H.C.Lowther	(Penrith)	25. 7.00P
	(Fuji-Robin EC-34-PM)					
G-MJYD	MBA Tiger Cub 440	SO.179	1. 6.83	R.A.Budd	(Ashbourne)	30. 7.92P
	(Fuji-Robin EC-44-PM)			*(New CofR 6.02)*		
G-MJYF	Mainair Gemini/Flash	305-585-3-W45	18. 4.85	W.D.Crooks	Newtownards, Co.Down	15. 6.01P
	(Fuji-Robin EC-44-PM)					
G-MJYJ*	MBA Tiger Cub	SO.177	6. 6.83	Not known	Spilsted Farm, Sedlescombe	
	(Regd as c/n OS.177)		*(Cancelled 23.6.93 by CAA) (Purchased for engine and dumped in barn 5.01)*			
G-MJYP	Mainair Gemini/Flexiform Dual Striker 167-13683		7. 6.83	M.S.Whitehouse	(Solihull)	23. 7.02P
	(Fuji-Robin EC-44-PM)					
G-MJYV	Mainair Rapier1 + 1/Flexiform Solo Striker		23.11.83	L.H.Phillips	(Solihull)	1.12.02P
	(Fuji-Robin EC-34-PM) 175-19783					
G-MJYW	Lancashire Micro-Trike Dual 330/Wasp Gryphon III		28. 6.83	P.D.Lawrence	(Munlochy, Ross-shire)	
	2/330PM/PGK/6.83/K			*(Dismantled & Trike used on G-MMPL::parts noted 7.01)*		
G-MJYX	Mainair Tri-Flyer/Hiway Demon	108-251182	9. 6.83	K.A.Wright	North Coates	22. 8.03P
	(Fuji-Robin EC-33-PM)					
G-MJZD	Mainair Gemini/Flash	311-585-3 & W50	18. 4.85	A.R.Gaivoto	Popham	14. 8.03P
	(Fuji-Robin EC-44-PM)					
G-MJZE	MBA Tiger Cub 440	SO.168	14. 6.83	J.E.D.Rogerson	Morgansfield, Fishburn	31. 1.86E
				tr Fishburn Flying Tigers *(Current status unknown)*		
G-MJZK(2)	Southdown Puma Sprint	SN1111/0081	3. 3.86	R.J.Osborne	(Tiverton)	18.10.91P
	(Fuji-Robin EC-44-PM)			*(Current status unknown)*		
G-MJZL	Eipper Quicksilver MXII	EEW-01	15. 6.83	T.Scarborough	(Boston)	6. 9.03P
	(Rotax 503)					
G-MJZO	Lancashire Micro-Trike/Flexiform Solo Striker		24. 6.83	J.W.Coventry	Davidstow Moor	2.11.01P
	(Fuji-Robin EC-34-PM) 1/330PM/LM/683/2					
G-MJZU	Mainair Gemini/Flexiform Dual Striker		21. 6.83	M.J.J.Dunning & C.B.Godfray	(Baginton)	3. 6.99P
	(Fuji-Robin EC-44-PM) 214-41183 & JDR-02		*(Gemini trike from G-MMVX(1) fitted) (Current status unknown)*			
G-MKAK	Colt 77A HAB	2039	15. 8.91	Virgin Airship & Balloon Co Ltd	Telford	21. 9.01T
				(Current status unknown)		
G-MKAS	Piper PA-28-140 Cherokee Cruiser	28-7425338	30. 4.98	MK Aero Support Ltd	Andrewsfield	14.11.04T
		OY-BGV				
G-MKIA	Supermarine 300 Spitfire I	6S-30565	16.11.00	S.J.Marsh	(Castelcucco, Italy)	
		P9374				
G-MKIV*	Bristol 149 Bolingbroke IVT	-	26. 3.82	G.A.Warner *(As "V6028/GB-D" in 105 Sqdn c/s)* Duxford		28. 5.88P
		RCAF 10038	*(Crashed Denham 21.6.87: cancelled 1.11.88 as destroyed: on rebuild 3.00 as static)*			
G-MKSF	Agusta A.109A II	7275	11.12.01	Markoss Aviation Ltd	Biggin Hill	30. 1.05T
		N18SF				
		F-GDPR				
G-MKSS	British Aerospace HS.125 Srs.700B	257175	29. 3.01	Markoss Aviation Ltd	Biggin Hill	4. 4.05T
		VP-BEK				
		VP-CEK/N770TJ/C9-TAC/(C9-TTA)				

Reg	Type	C/n	Prev ID	Date	Owner / status	Location	Date
G-MKVB	Supermarine 349 Spitfire LF.Vb	CBAF.2461	5718M / BM597	2. 5.89	Historic Aircraft Collection Ltd *(As "BM597/JH-C" in 317 Sqdn c/s)*	Duxford	25. 3.03P
G-MKVI	de Havilland DH.100 Vampire FB.6 *(Built F + W)*	676	J-1167	2. 6.92	T.C.Topen *(As "WL505" in 614 Sqdn c/s)* *(To De Havilland Aviation Ltd) : stored 3.97: current status unknown)*	Swansea	14. 9.95P
G-MLFF	Piper PA-23-250 Aztec E	27-7305194	G-WEBB / G-BJBU/N40476	31. 1.90	K.J.Bill	Wolverhampton	28.11.02T
G-MLGL	Colt 21A Cloudhopper HAB	527		3. 4.84	H.C.J.Williams *(Current status unknown)*	Bristol	
G-MLJL	Airbus Industrie A330-243	254	F-WWKT	15. 6.99	MyTravel Airways Ltd *"Ben Crossland"*	Manchester	14 .5.05T
G-MLTI	Dassault Falcon 900B	164	F-WWFC	13. 6.97	Multiflight Ltd	Leeds-Bradford	12. 6.03T
G-MLTY	Aérospatiale AS365N2 Dauphin	6431	N365EL / JA6673	4. 6.99	Multiflight Ltd	Leeds-Bradford	6. 6.03
G-MLWI	Thunder Ax7-77 HAB	1000		3. 9.86	M.L. & L.P.Willoughby *"Mr Blue Sky"*	Reading	12. 8.03A
G-MMAC	Dragon Srs.200 *(Fuji-Robin EC-44-PM)*	003	OY-... / G-MMAC	14. 7.82	J.F.Ashton & J.Kirwan *(Current status unknown)*	(Liverpool)	14. 5.87E
G-MMAE	Dragon Srs.200 *(Fuji-Robin EC-44-PM)*	005		7. 9.82	P.J.Sheehy & K.S.Matcham *(Noted 3.02)*	Barton Ashes	29. 7.96P
G-MMAG	MBA Tiger Cub 440 *(Fuji-Robin EC-44-PM)*	SO.47		22. 6.83	M.J.Aubrey *(Noted 2002)*	(Kington, Hereford)	14. 9.93P
G-MMAH*	Eipper Quicksilver MX II *(Also Eng No.14805)*	TM.1016		23. 6.83	Not known *(Cancelled 26.10.95 by CAA) (Derelict 2.03)*	Doynton	
G-MMAI	Dragon Srs.150 *(Fuji-Robin EC-44-PM)*	0032		1. 7.83	G.S.Richardson	(Cleethorpes)	13. 7.97P
				(Dismantled & parts split between North Coates and owner's home) (New CofR 6.01)			
G-MMAL*	Mainair Tri-Flyer/Flexiform Dual Striker *(Fuji-Robin EC-44-PM)*	DHM-01		20. 9.83	Tina E.Simpson	(Bewdley, Worcs)	1. 4.94P
				(On rebuild 10.97: cancelled 27.4.00 by CAA) (Current status unknown)			
G-MMAN	Mainair Tri-Flyer 330/Flexiform Solo Striker	192-6983		27. 9.83	K.F.Gittins	Rufforth	14.10.02P
G-MMAO*	Southdown Puma Sprint X	HS.549		28.12.83	P A Kershaw *(Cancelled 31.5.01 by CAA) (Stored 8.01)*	Ince Blundell	14. 3.00P
G-MMAR	Mainair Gemini/Puma Sprint MS *(Fuji-Robin EC-44-PM)*	195-11083-2		23. 9.83	A.R. & J.Fawkes *(Current status unknown)*	(Newbury)	17. 9.98P
G-MMAW	Mainair Rapier 1+1/Flexiform Solo Striker *(Fuji-Robin EC-34-PM)*	131/2-10283		18. 7.83	G.B.Hutchison *(New owner 8.01)*	(Doncaster)	
G-MMAX	Garland Trike/Flexiform Dual Striker *(Fuji-Robin EC-44-PM)*	0011		5. 8.93	M T Wells	(Newcastle-under-Lyme, Staffs)	18. 2.02P
G-MMAZ	Southdown Puma Sprint X *(Fuji-Robin EC-44-PM)*	MAPB-01		5. 8.83	A.R.Smith *(Current status unknown)*	(Chelmsford)	22. 7.96P
G-MMBL	Ultrasports Puma/Southdown Lightning DS *(Fuji-Robin EC-44-PM)*	80-00083		4. 7.83	B.J.Farrell *(Current status unknown)*	(Preston)	7. 3.92E
			(C/n is engine serial no.)				
G-MMBN	Eurowing Goldwing *(Rotax 447)*	EW-89		28. 6.83	E.H.Jenkins *(Current status unknown)*	(Newcastle upon Tyne)	27. 8.92E
G-MMBT	MBA Tiger Cub 440 *(Probably either c/n PFA 140-10924 or 10990)*	SO.131 & TA.01		19. 7.83	B.Chamberlain *(Stored 1.91: current status unknown)*	(Otley, Ipswich)	31. 1.86E
G-MMBU	Eipper Quicksilver MXII (Rotax 503)	CAL-222		8. 7.83	D.A.Norwood	Ash House Farm, Winsford	11. 6.03P
G-MMBV	Huntair Pathfinder *(Fuji-Robin EC-44-PM)* *(New sailwing 1999)*	044		8. 7.83	P.J.Bishop	Tarn Farm, Cockerham	5.10.03P
G-MMBY	Solar Wings Panther XL *(Fuji-Robin EC-44-PM)*	T483-759XL		20. 7.83	R.M.Sheppard & P.Huddleston	(Wantage/Marlborough)	3. 8.03P
G-MMBZ	Solar Wings Typhoon P *(Fuji-Robin EC-34-PM)*	T981-5217		20. 7.83	S.C.Mann *(Current status unknown)*	(Kirbymoorside)	28. 4.96P
		(Originally believed to have had sailwing c/n T781-217 - 5217 almost certainly a corruption of S217 for Typhoon Small - and then rebuilt as c/n T981-228)					
G-MMCI	Ultrasports Puma Sprint X *(Fuji-Robin EC-44-PM)*	DMP-01 & P.421		28. 9.83	R.J.Webb	Long Marston	24. 6.03P
G-MMCV	Hiway Skytrike II/Solar Wings Typhoon *(Fuji-Robin EC-34-PM)*	T583-783		27. 7.83	G.Addison *(Current status unknown)*	(Kinross)	8. 6.97P
G-MMCX	MBA Super Tiger Cub 440	MU.002		8. 8.83	D.Harkin *(Current status unknown)*	(Johnstone, Renfrew)	
G-MMCZ	Mainair Tri-Flyer/Flexiform Dual Striker *(Fuji-Robin EC-44-PM) (Mainair Trike c/n 180-6883)*	TE-01		10. 8.83	T.D.Adamson	Wombleton	24. 4.03P
G-MMDE	Mainair Tri-Flyer 250/Solar Wings Typhoon S	DES-1 & 025-211081-6		12. 8.83	D.J.Moore	(Oakington)	11. 6.01P
G-MMDF	Southdown Wild Cat Mk.II/Lightning Phase II *(Fuji-Robin EC-34-PM)*	007		24. 8.83	J.C.Haigh	(Tonbridge)	4. 11.03P
G-MMDK	Mainair Merlin/Striker *(Fuji-Robin EC-34-PM)*	181-16883		7. 9.83	P.E.Blyth *(Current status unknown)*	(Rotherham)	30. 5.99P
G-MMDN	Mainair Tri-Flyer 330/Flexiform Dual Striker	197-983 & RPO.12		30. 9.83	M.G.Griffiths *(Current status unknown)*	(Monmouth)	14. 9.89E
		(Mainair c/n not confirmed)					
G-MMDP	Mainair Gemini/Sprint X *(Fuji-Robin EC-44-PM)*	183-22883		20. 9.83	G.V. Cowle *(New owner 6.02)*	(Port St.Mary, Isle of Man)	25. 1.95P
G-MMDR	Huntair Pathfinder II *(Rotax 377)*	137		30. 8.83	C.Dolling *(To UAE 11.84: current status unknown)*	(United Arab Emirates)	
G-MMDY	Ultrasports Panther Sprint I *(Fuji-Robin EC-44-PM)*	S.064		7. 9.83	C.Duffin *(Current status unknown)*	(Portlaoise, Co.Laois)	20.11.90E
G-MMEJ	Mainair Tri-Flyer/Flexiform Striker	215-41183 & FF/LAI/83/JDR/03		15. 9.83	R.B.Tweedie *(Current status unknown)*	(Stoke-on-Trent)	9. 11.97P
G-MMEK	Medway Hybred 44XL/Solar Wings Typhoon XL2 *(Fuji-Robin EC-44-PM)*	12983/6		16. 9.83	M.G.J.Bridges	(Exeter)	28..8.00P
		(Typhoon sailwing c/n either T883-884XL or '887XL - both originally supplied to Medway for G-MMEK & G-MMEN)					
G-MMFD	Mainair Tri-Flyer 440/Flexiform Dual Striker	210-31082-2 & FF/LAI/83/JDR/12		20. 9.83	M.E.& W.L.Chapman	(Oldham)	6.12.93P
		(Trike unit is believed to be c/n 210-31083-2)					
G-MMFE	Mainair Tri-Flyer/Flexiform Striker *(Fuji-Robin EC-44-PM)*	FF/LAI/83/JDR/13		20. 9.83	W.Camm *(Current status unknown)*	(Barnsley)	16. 6.94P
		(Trike unit replaced by c/n 256-784-2 & probably now podded to 440 Gemini standard)					
G-MMFG	Lancashire Micro-Trike/Flexiform Dual Striker *(Fuji-Robin EC-44-PM)*	FF/LAI/83/JDR/15		20. 9.83	M.G.Dean & M.J.Hadland *(Current status unknown)*	Tarn Farm, Cockerham	18. 3.93E

G-MMFN*	MBA Tiger Cub 440	SO.113	31.10.83	J.S.Skipp	(Bromyard, Hereford)	30.11.95P
	(Fuji-Robin EC-44-PM)			*(Cancelled 12.7.01 as temporarily WFU)*		
G-MMFS	MBA Tiger Cub 440	SO.64	1.11.83	G.S.Taylor	(Shrewsbury)	27. 7.01P
	(Fuji-Robin EC-44-PM)					
G-MMFY	Cliff Sims Aztec trike/Dual Striker	AZT001CS	14.12.83	K.R.M.Adair & S.R.Browne	(Arundel)	10. 9.90E
				(Current status unknown)		
G-MMFZ*	Striplin (AES) Sky Ranger	HAW-01	18.11.83	M.J.Aubrey	(Kington, Hereford)	
	(Cuyana 430)			*(Cancelled 3.10.01.by CAA) (Noted 2002)*		
G-MMGF	MBA Tiger Cub 440	SO.124	18.11.83	J.G.Boxall	Pittrichie Farm, Whiterashes	22. 8.02P
	(Fuji-Robin EC-44-PM)					
G-MMGL	MBA Tiger Cub 440	SO.148 & BMAA/HB/050	23.11.83	H.E.Dunning	(Knaresborough)	30. 3.03P
	(Fuji-Robin EC-44-PM)					
G-MMGS	Solar Wings Panther XL	T1283-939XL	28.12.83	D.W.Bock	(Saltash)	12. 8.98P
	(Fuji-Robin EC-44-PM)			*(Current status unknown)*		
G-MMGT	Huntwing/Pegasus Classic	JAH-7	28.11.83	H.Cook	(Newport)	20. 5.03P
	(BMW R100) *(Currently with Trike c/n SW-TB-1228 ex G-MTOH)*			*(Amended CofR 3.02)*		
G-MMGU	SMD Gazelle/Flexiform Sealander	30-4883	1.12.83	A.D.Cranfield	(Wincanton)	19. 9.93E
	(Fuji-Robin EC-44-PM)			*(Current status unknown)*		
G-MMGV	Microknight Whittaker MW5 Sorcerer Srs.A	001	2.12.83	G.N.Haffey & M.W.J.Whittaker	(Chatham/Doncaster)	1. 9.02P
G-MMHG*	Hiway Skytrike 250/Solar Wings Storm	DRB-01	13.12.83	M.J.Aubrey	(Kington, Hereford)	
	(Fuji-Robin EC-25-PM)			*(Cancelled 22.9.93 by CAA) (Noted 2002)*		
G-MMHL	Hiway Skytrike II/Super Scorpion	KSC.84	19.12.83	E.J.Blyth	(Pickering)	9.12.91E
	(Fuji-Robin EC-44)			*(Current status unknown)*		
G-MMHN	MBA Tiger Cub 440	SO.136	19.12.83	M.J.Aubrey	(Kington, Hereford)	
	(Fuji-Robin EC-44)			*(Noted 2002)*		
G-MMHS	SMD Gazelle/Flexiform Dual Striker	104-11283	21.12.83	C.J.Meadows	(Shepton Mallet)	
				(Current status unknown)		
G-MMIB*	MEA Mistral Trainer	DH-01	3. 2.84	Not known	Old Sarum	
				(Cancelled 5.12.95 by CAA) (Stored 12.01)		
G-MMIE	MBA Tiger Cub 440	G7-7	3. 1.84	B.W.Olliver	(Telford)	31. 1.86E
	(Fuji-Robin EC-44)			*(Current status unknown)*		
G-MMIH	MBA Tiger Cub 440	SO.130	25. 4.84	R.A.Davis	(Gloucester)	19. 8.93P
	(Fuji-Robin EC-44-PM)			*(Current status unknown)*		
G-MMIL	Eipper Quicksilver MXII	1046	6. 1.84	C.K.Brown	(Loughborough)	24. 3.94P
	(Rotax 503)			*(Current status unknown)*		
G-MMIM	MBA Tiger Cub 440	SO.28 & BMAA/HB/060	11. 1.84	T.J.Bidwell	(Newtown, Powys)	26. 3.00P
	(Fuji-Robin EC-44-PM)					
G-MMIR	Mainair Gemini/Sprint	051-20182	25. 1.84	J.P.Wilson	Long Marston	15. 8.97P
	(Fuji-Robin EC-44-PM)			*(Stored 10.00)*		
	(Regd with orig Trike c/n ex G-MBKX then G-MJDO: rebuilt with Trike 314-585-3 ex G-MMZK: wing ex G-MMTI: orig Trike frame (c/n 051) gone by 10.00)					
G-MMIW	Southdown Puma Sprint	590	9. 2.84	J.Ryland	(Swanley)	4.11.02P
	(Fuji-Robin EC-44-PM)					
G-MMIX	MBA Tiger Cub 440	MBCB-01	14. 2.84	N.J.McKain	(Dumfries)	11.11.90E
	(Fuji-Robin EC-44-PM)			*(To Dumfries & Galloway Museum)*		
G-MMIZ	Southdown Lightning Mk.II	CB-01	24. 2.84	R.G.Earp	(Peterborough)	
G-MMJD	Southdown Puma Sprint	SP/1001	28. 6.83	C.A.Sargent	Wickhambrook, Newmarket	9. 2.03P
	(Fuji-Robin EC-44-PM)					
G-MMJF	Solar Wings Panther Dual XL-S		27. 2.84	K.J.Hoare & J.D.Nelson	Plaistows Farm, St Albans	2. 8.03P
	(Fuji-Robin EC-44-PM) PXL842-150 & T284-988XL					
G-MMJG	Mainair Tri-Flyer/Flexiform Dual Striker	185-1983	31. 9.83	A.Strang	(Larkhall)	10. 9.03P
	(Fuji-Robin EC-44-PM)					
G-MMJM	Southdown Puma Sprint 440		27. 2.84	R.J.Sanger	(Wickford)	31. 5.97P
		PD.500 & SN1111/001		*(Current status unknown)*		
G-MMJT	Mainair Gemini/Sprint X	JBT-01	20.12.83	W.F.Murray	Swinford, Rugby	11. 7.03P
	(Fuji-Robin EC-44-PM) *(No Mainair identity & probably plans built by J B Tate)*					
G-MMJV	MBA Tiger Cub 440	SO.195 & PFA 140-1090	25. 3.84	D.G.Palmer	Fetterangus	9. 5.93P
	(Fuji-Robin EC-44-PM)			*(Noted 7.01)*		
G-MMJX	Teman Mono-Fly	01	6. 3.84	M.Ingleton	Cripps Barn, Eastchurch	17. 7.02P
	(Rotax 377)					
G-MMKA	Solar Wings Panther Dual XL	T284-986XL	8. 3.84	R.S.Wood	(Wallacestone, Falkirk)	30. 4.86E
	(Fuji-Robin EC-44-PM)			*(Current status unknown)*		
G-MMKE	Birdman WT-11 Chinook	01817	2. 4.84	D.M.Jackson	(Belper)	31.12.87E
	(Rotax 277)			*(Current status unknown)*		
G-MMKG	Medway Hybred 44XL/Solar Wings Typhoon XL2		9. 3.84	G.P.Lane	(Bristol)	18. 7.97P
	(Fuji-Robin EC-44-PM)	22284/7		*(Reported with wing marked "G-MNYX" 8.96) (Current status unknown)*		
	(Typhoon sailwing c/n T-?84-1035XL - either '384 or '484)					
G-MMKH	Medway Hybred 44XL/Solar Wings Typhoon XL		9. 3.84	C.Richardson	Baxby Manor, Husthwaite	16.10.01P
	(Fuji-Robin EC-44-PM)	22284/8	*(Typhoon sailwing c/n T.?84-1047XL - either '384 or '484)*			
G-MMKK	Mainair Gemini/Flash	240-384-2	12. 3.84	M.Whittle	Shotton Colliery	20.12.02P
	(Fuji-Robin EC-44)					
G-MMKL	Mainair Gemini/Flash	238-384-2-W11	12. 3.84	D.W.Cox	(Kenilworth)	29 .9.93P
	(Fuji-Robin EC-44-PM)			*(Current status unknown)*		
G-MMKM	Mainair Gemini/Flexiform Dual Striker	221-184-2	12. 3.84	S.W.Hutchinson	(Northallerton)	11. 6.99P
	(Fuji-Robin EC-44-PM) *(Regd/stamped with c/n 221-0184-0002)*					
	(Orig fitted with Mainair 440 Tri-Flyer trike [210-1083] & part- exchanged for 440 Gemini as fitted: rebuild of trike originally exported to USA & re-imported)					
G-MMKP	MBA Tiger Cub 440	SO.203	13. 3.84	J.W.Beaty *(Current status unknown)*	(Kettering)	
G-MMKR	Mainair Tri-Flyer/Southdown Lightning DS		14. 3.84	C.R.Madden	(Great Orton)	7. 6.03P
	(Fuji-Robin EC-44)	209-171083 & CM-01	*(Regd as G-MNDK in error and then restored as G-MMKR)*			
G-MMKV	Southdown Puma Sprint X	P.521	24. 4.84	A.L.Flude	(Saxmundham)	28. 8.02P
	(Fuji-Robin EC-44-PM)					
G-MMKX	Skyrider Airsports Phantom 330	PH-107R	18. 3.85	C A James	Doynton	17. 6.01P
	(Fuji-Robin EC-34-PL-02)			*(Noted 2.03)*		
G-MMKY*	Jordan Duet Srs.1	CHS-01	19. 3.84	Not known	Field Farm, Oakley	
	(Rotax 503)			*(Cancelled by CAA 1.9.95: composite airframe being assembled 7.02 from this & G-MNIN)*		

Regn	Type / construction details	Date	Owner	Location	Exp/Status
G-MMLE	Eurowing Goldwing SP EW-81	21. 3.84	B.K.Harrison *(Current status unknown)*	(Glasgow)	
G-MMLH	Hiway Skytrike Mk.II 330/Demon PMH-01 & DJL-01	28. 3.84	P.M.Hendry & D.J.Lukey *(Current status unknown)*	(Folkestone)	
G-MMMB	Mainair Tri-Flyer/Sprint CR-01/170 & 170-16583 (Fuji-Robin EC-44-PM) *(Trike unit ex G-MJYU)*	5. 4.84	K.Birkett	(Southampton)	22. 9.02P
G-MMMG	Eipper Quicksilver MXL 1383 (Rotax 447)	5. 6.84	J.G.Campbell	(Barnsley)	19. 8.03P
G-MMMH	Hadland Willow/Flexiform Striker MJH 383 (BMW R80/7)	9.12.83	M.J.Hadland	(Wigan)	14. 9.03P
G-MMML	Dragon Srs.150 D150/002 OY-... (Fuji-Robin EC-44-PM) G-MMML	28. 6.83	R.G.Huntley South Wraxall, Bradford-on-Avon *(Noted 3.02)*		6. 8.00P
G-MMMN	Solar Wings Panther Dual XL-S (Fuji-Robin EC-44-2PM) PXL 843-150 & T484-105?XL *(probably '1059)*	4. 4.84	C.Downton	(Newton Abbot)	16. 7.03P
G-MMMR*	Ultrasports Tripacer/Flexiform Striker MAR-01 (Fuji-Robin EC-34-PM)	14. 3.84	H.A.Lloyd-Jennings *(Cancelled 19.11.01 by CAA)*	(London SW6)	31. 3.00P
G-MMNB	Eipper Quicksilver MX 4286 (Cuyuna 430R)	30. 3.84	J.M Lindop *(New owner 6.01)*	Long Marston	12.10.97P
G-MMND	Eipper Quicksilver MXII Q2 1038 (Rotax 503)	30. 3.84	G.B.Burby *(Dismantled 8.96: current status unknown)*	(Burnley)	13.11.94P
G-MMNH	Dragon Srs.150 D150/42 (Fuji-Robin EC-44-PM)	27. 7.83	T.J.Barlow *(Current status unknown)*	Dromore	30. 3.93E
G-MMNN	Sherry Buzzard 1	6. 4.84	E.W.Sherry *(Current status unknown)*	(Stoke-on-Trent)	
G-MMNS	Mitchell Super Wing U-2 PFA 114-10690	11. 4.84	C.Baldwin & J.C.Lister Valley Farm, Winwick *(Current status unknown)*		
G-MMNT	Flexiform trike/Flexiform Solo Striker SSL-1 (Rotax 277)	16. 4.84	C.R.Thorne *(Current status unknown)*	(Lyndhurst, Hants	)8. 7.88E
G-MMOB	Mainair Gemini/Sprint 244-584-2(K) & EM-01 (Fuji-Robin EC-44-PM) *(C/n 'K' denotes Kit built)*	11. 5.84	D.Woolcock	St.Michaels	24. 3.03P
G-MMOH	Solar Wings Pegasus XL-R SW-TB-1450 & T484-1054XL *(Trike fitted replacing one formerly on G-MBTT: new Trike now fitted ex G-MYGA)*	4. 5.84	T.H.Scott Rayne Hall Farm, Rayne *(Current status unknown)*		
G-MMOI*	MBA Tiger Cub 440 SO.92 (Fuji-Ribin EC-44M) *(C/n reported as S0.59)*	8. 5.84	P Talbot *(Cancelled 13.7.93 by CAA) (Noted dismantled @ owner's home 6.01)*	(Cromer)	31. 1.86E
G-MMOK	Solar Wings Panther XL-S (Fuji-Robin EC-44-PM) PXL844-157 & T584-1066XL	9. 5.84	R.F. & A.J.Foster	(Woodbridge)	23. 8.03P
G-MMOW	Mainair Gemini/Flash 246-684-3 & W06 (Fuji-Robin EC-44-PM)	21. 5.84	J.Wakelin	Davidstow Moor	3. 6.02P
G-MMPG	Southdown Puma Sprint NEA-01 (Fuji-Robin EC-34-PM) (Tripacer/Lightning Mk.II)	8. 6.84	T.J.Hector	(Royston)	15. 4.01P
G-MMPH	Southdown Puma Sprint P.545 (Fuji-Robin EC-44-PM)	20. 6.84	S.Whittle	(Wigan)	26. 8.02P
G-MMPI*	Pterodactyl Ptraveler 108 (Fuji-Robin EC-25)	23. 5.84	M.J.Aubrey *(Cancelled 24.8.94 as WFU) (Noted 2002) .*	(Kington, Hereford)	
G-MMPL	Lancashire Micro-Trike 440/Flexiform Dual Striker (Fuji-Robin EC-44-PM) PDL-02 & 2/330PM/PGK/683/K *(Trike unit from G-MJYW: maybe flown with exchangeable sailwings)*	5.12.83	P.D.Lawrence	Insch	13. 7.03P
G-MMPO	Mainair Gemini/Flash 325-785-3 & W65 (Fuji-Robin EC-44-PM)	18. 4.85	F H Cook	(Whitchurch)	28. 9.02P
G-MMPU	R J Heming Trike/Typhoon S4 (Fuji-Robin EC-34-PM) RJH-01 & T782-553L	5. 6.84	J.T.Halford *(Current status unknown)*	(Holt, Norfolk)	22. 5.96P
G-MMPZ	Teman Mono-Fly JWH-01 (Rotax 447)	2. 7.84	P.B.Kylo	(Consett)	15. 6.02P
G-MMRK	Ultrasports/Solar Wings Panther XL-S PXL846-175 & T684-1107XL	9. 7.84	J.A.Churchill *(Current status unknown)*	(Worthing)	28. 9.95P
G-MMRL	Ultrasports/Solar Wings Panther XL-S (Fuji-Robin EC-44-PM) PXL846-174 & T684-1102XL	17. 7.84	R.J.Hood	London Colney	18. 8.03P
G-MMRN	Southdown Puma Sprint P.544 (Fuji-Robin EC-44-PM)	16. 7.84	D.C.Read	(Ledbury)	18. 4.01P
G-MMRP	Mainair Gemini/Sprint 259-884-2-P.561 (Fuji-Robin EC-44-PM)	7. 2.85	J.C.S.Jones	Emlyn's Field, Rhuallt	8. 7.03P
G-MMRW	Mainair Gemini 440/Flexiform Dual Striker LAI/DS/25 & 216-71283	5. 1.84	M.D.Hinge *(Current status unknown)*	Salisbury	N/E
G-MMRZ*	Solar Wings Panther XL-S (Fuji-Robin EC-44-PM) PXL847-168 & T684-1099XL	16. 7.84	A.L.Lyall *(Stored 10.00: cancelled 24.4.02 as WFU)*	(Edinburgh)	20. 6.00P
G-MMSA	Solar Wings Panther XL-S (Fuji-Robin EC-44-2PM) PXL847-189 & T184-1142XL *(C/n probably T784-1142XL)*	9. 8.84	T.W.Thiele & G.Savage *(Current status unknown)*	(Baldock)	27. 5.98P
G-MMSG	Solar Wings Panther XL-S T884-1165XL (Fuji-Robin EC-44-2PM) *(Regd with c/n 8841/65XC which appears to be a corruption of Typhoon sailwing c/n style: 'XC may indicate exchange sailwing hence the apparent duplication with that known to be on G-MMTT)*	6. 9.85	R.W.McKee	(Deeside)	4. 6.01P
G-MMSH	Solar Wings Panther XL-S (Fuji-Robin EC-44-PM) PXL847-192 & T884-1163XL	28. 5.85	I.J.Drake *(Current status unknown)*	(Billericay)	7. 5.90P
G-MMSO	Mainair Gemini/Sprint 255-784-2-P.539 (Fuji-Robin EC-44-PM)	14. 1.86	K.A.Maughan *(Current status unknown)*	Sandtoft	26. 7.99P
G-MMSP	Mainair Gemini/Flash 265-984-2 (Fuji-Robin EC-44-PM) *(Original sailwing c/n W03 later sold to G-MNGF 1998: current sailwing identity not yet known)*	17. 8.84	J.Whiteford	East Fortune	24. 4.01P
G-MMSZ	Medway Half Pint/aerial Arts 130SX 2/21385 (JPL PUL425)	27. 3.85	P.Sykes *(Current status unknown)*	(Bournemouth)	N/E
G-MMTA	Solar Wings Panther XL-S (Rotax 462HP) PXL848-194 & T884-1164XL	25.10.84	P.A.McMahon	(Dun Laoghaire, Co.Dublin)	29. 6.03P
G-MMTC	Solar Wings Pegasus XL-R (Rotax 447) SW-TB-1037 & T684-1101XL	28. 9.84	T.L.Moses Llansaint, Carmarthen *(Original Trike was Ultrasports c/n PXL847-170 & later fitted to G-MNHH) (Dismantled 2.03)*		8. 2.02P
G-MMTD	Mainair Tri-Flyer/Hiway Demon 175 (Fuji-Robin EC-34-PM) 150-30583 & EIA-01 *(Trike originally exported to Denmark)*	16. 8.84	W.E.Teare	(Ramsey, Isle of Man)	10. 9.03P
G-MMTG	Mainair Gemini/Southdown Sprint 267-984-2 & P.577 *(Originally regd as Mainair Tri-Flyer with c/n RPWJ-01; type amended on 12.10.84) (New CofR 1.03)*	21. 8.84	J.C.F.Dalton	(St. Neots)	13.8.94P

G-MMTI	Southdown Puma Sprint	SN1221/0005	13. 9.84	S.A.Jackson	(Polegate)	26. 5.02P
	(Fuji-Robin EC-44-PM)	(C/n duplicates ZS-VLZ)		(See G-MMIR - possibly fitted with new wing)		
G-MMTJ	Southdown Puma Sprint	SN1221/0006	17. 1.85	P J Kirwan	(Geashill, Co.Offaly)	16. 4.00P
	(Fuji-Robin EC-44-PM)					
G-MMTL	Mainair Gemini/Sprint	268-1084-2-P.576	3.10.84	R.Hatton	(Douglas, Isle of Man)	18. 7.03P
	(Fuji-Robin EC-44-PM)					
G-MMTR	Solar Wings Pegasus XL-R	KND-03	27. 9.84	P.M.Kelsey	(Rufforth)	5.11.03P
	(Rotax 447)	(Orig fitted with Ultrasports trike/Typhoon wing c/n T984-1211XL: trike replaced by Solar Wings XL c/n SW-TB-1092 circa 8.86)				
G-MMTS	Solar Wings Panther XL	T784-1157XL	18. 9.84	A.S.Wason	(Wootton Bassett)	1. 6.03P
	(Fuji-Robin EC-44-PM)					
G-MMTT	Ultrasports/Solar Wings Panther XL-ST684-1165XL		12.12.84	C.T.H.Tenison	(Abergavenny)	7.11.97P
	(Fuji-Robin EC-44-PM) (C/n possibly T884-1165XL but duplicates G-MMSG)			(Current status unknown)		
	(Solar Wings records show sailwing as G-MMTT when returned for repair: G-MMSG possibly had a replacement wing)					
G-MMTV	American Aerolights Eagle 215B Seaplane SGP-1		25. 5.84	P.J.Scott	(Seaview, Isle of Wight)	21.11.96P
	(Fuji-Robin EC-25-PS)			(Current status unknown)		
G-MMTX*	Mainair Gemini/Sprint	275-1284-2-P.590	25. 3.85	P.C.Askew	Tarn Farm, Cockerham	6.11.00P
	(Fuji-Robin EC-44-PM) (Original fitted with wing P.577 now from G-MMTG)			(Cancelled 14.11.02 by CAA)		
G-MMTY	Fisher FP202U	2140	28. 9.84	B.E.Maggs	Brickhouse Farm, Frogland Cross	
				(Stored 4.96: current status unknown)		
G-MMTZ	Eurowing Goldwing	EW-60 & SWA-7	28. 9.84	R.B.D.Baker	(Torquay)	15. 7.03P
	(Rotax 447)					
G-MMUA*	Southdown Puma Sprint	SN1221/0007	21.12.84	C.R.Gale	(Kirk Michael, Isle of Man)	21. 8.00P
	(Fuji-Robin EC-44-PM)			(Cancelled 19.4.00 by CAA) (Stored 2001)		
G-MMUH	Mainair Tri-Flyer/Sprint	270-1084-2-P.579	8.11.84	J.P.Nicklin	(Hayling Island)	26. 8.03P
	(Fuji-Robin EC-44-PM)					
G-MMUL*	Ward Elf	E-47	16.10.84	N H Ponsford	Breighton	
				(Cancelled 12.4.89 by CAA) (Noted 12.02)		
G-MMUM	MBA Tiger Cub 440	SO.019	8. 3.83	Coulson Flying Services Ltd	(Skegness)	
	(Fuji-Robin EC-44)			(Current status unknown)		
G-MMUO	Mainair Gemini/Flash	272-1084-2 & W08	29.10.84	B.D.Bastin & D.R.Howells	Long Marston	13.10.02P
	(Fuji-Robin EC-44-PM)					
G-MMUR	Hiway Skytrike II/Solar Wings Storm	SLI.80180	28.12.84	R.J.Ripley	Field Farm, Oakley	
	(Fuji-Robin EC-25)			(Stored owner's house 1998)		
G-MMUT	Mainair Gemini/Flash II	235-484-2* &-W04	5.10.84	S.C.Briggs	East Fortune	5. 7.01P
	(Fuji-Robin EC-44-PM) (Original c/n 62-884-2 & W04: fitted with new Trike* first used on G-MMFC(3) & wing W73 @ 6.98- also see G-MNAC)					
G-MMUV	Southdown Puma Sprint	SN1121/0010	7.11.84	D.C.Read	(Ledbury)	2.11.89P
	(Fuji-Robin EC-44-PM)			(Current status unknown)		
G-MMUW	Mainair Gemini/Flash II	60-784-2 & W13	17. 1.85	J.C.K.Scardifield	(Lymington)	23. 3.87P
	(Fuji-Robin EC-44-PM)			(Current status unknown)		
	(Mainair Trike c/n 260 built as 440 Gemini with Sprint sailwing & regd G-MMSC. Sailwing sold & used on Puma in 1985. & trike fitted with Flash 1 sailwing and complete unit sold to Portugal in 1987)					
G-MMVA	Southdown Puma Sprint	SN1121/0011 & P.588	7.11.84	C.H.Tomkins	(Kettering)	26. 3.92P
	(Fuji-Robin EC-44-PM)			(Current status unknown)		
G-MMVC*	Solar Wings Panther XL-S	T684-1106XL	13.11.84	E.R.Holton	(Lichfield)	18. 1.90P
	(Fuji-Robin EC-44-PM)			(Cancelled 3.10.02 by CAA)		
G-MMVH	Southdown Raven X	SN2122/0015	10. 1.85	G.W. & K.M.Carwardine	(Isle of Grain)	29. 4.01P
	(Rotax 447)					
G-MMVI	Southdown Puma Sprint	SN1121/0012	28.11.84	G.R.Williams	(Haverfordwest)	2.11.97P
	(Fuji-Robin EC-44-PM)			(Current status unknown)		
G-MMVO	Southdown Puma Sprint	SN1232/0017	20. 3.85	D.M.Pearson	Chilton Park, Wallingford	20. 4.03P
	(Rotax 447)					
G-MMVP	Mainair Gemini/Flash II	76-1284-2 & W12	17.12.84	S.C.McGowan	(Rufforth)	16.12.02P
	(Fuji-Robin EC-44-PM)					
G-MMVS	Skyhook Pixie/Zeus (Solo 210)	TR1/52	28. 2.85	B.W.Olley (Current status unknown)	(Ely)	18.11.91E
G-MMVX	Southdown Puma Sprint	41183 & P.452	29.11.83	M.P.Jones	Haverfordwest	5. 4.03P
	(Fuji-Robin EC-44-PM)					
	(Original trike c/n quoted is corruption of Mainair 440 Tri-Flyer c/n 214-41183. Re-configured as a podded trike & became Gemini. This was re-fitted to G-MJZU: current trike believed, therefore, to be a Southdown)					
G-MMVZ	Southdown Puma Sprint	SN1121/0016	15. 1.85	M.J.Devane	(Killarney, Co.Kerry)	2. 8.03P
	(Fuji-Robin EC-44-PM)					
G-MMWA	Mainair Gemini/Flash II	271-1184-1 & W07	22.11.84	D.Muir	St.Michaels	14. 8.03P
	(Fuji-Robin EC-44-PM) (Trike c/n stamped as "KR271-1184-2")					
G-MMWC	Eipper Quicksilver MXII	1041	22.10.84	J.S.Harris & M.Holmes	Old Sarum	27. 7.03P
	(Rotax 503)					
G-MMWG	P Greenslade Trike/Flexiform Solo Striker		17.12.84	C.R.Green	(Redruth)	26. 6.99P
	(Rotax 377)	FF/LAI/83/JDR/11		(Current status unknown)		
	(Trike originally fitted to G-MJGN: wing no. duplicates G-MMFC)					
G-MMWL	Eurowing Goldwing	SWA-09 & EW-91	9. 4.85	P.J.Brookman	Knapthorpe Lodge, Caunton	14. 5.03P
	(Rotax 447)					
G-MMWN	Mainair Tri-Flyer/Flexiform Striker	1283.NH	21.11.84	D.H.George	(Sandown)	30. 3.97P
	(Rotax 377) (Originally fitted with Ultrasports Tripacer trike)			(Current status unknown)		
G-MMWS	Ultrasports Tripacer/Flexiform Solo Striker 983.SH		21.11.84	P.H.Risdale	Tower Farm, Wollaston	7. 6.03P
	(Rotax 377) (Originally fitted with Mainair trike) (Original owners of G-MMWN & 'MMWS were Nigel & Sally Huxtable& believed trikes were inter-changed)					
G-MMWT	CFM Shadow C (Rotax 503)	B.009	27. 3.85	J.A.C.du Plessis	Enstone	5. 7.03P
G-MMWX	Southdown Puma Sprint	SN1121/0047	10. 4.85	A.P.Aspinall	(Bassingbourn)	11. 5.03P
	(Fuji-Robin EC-44-PM)					
G-MMXD	Mainair Gemini/Flash II	282-185-3 & W20	28.12.84	W A Bibby	Brook Farm, Pilling	28. 3.03P
	(Rotax 447)					
G-MMXG	Mainair Gemini/Flash II	288-485-1 & W32	17. 1.85	T.Birch	(Wolverhampton)	15. 6.01P
	(Fuji-Robin EC-44-PM)			(Damaged c6.00 - trike used to rebuild G-MNBD & rest to store)		
G-MMXJ	Mainair Gemini/Flash II	289-185-3 & W22	17. 1.85	R.Meredith-	Hardy Radwell, Letchworth	6. 8.96P
	(Rotax 447)			(Current status unknown)		
G-MMXK	Mainair Gemini/Flash II	274-485-2 & W35	17. 1.85	G.K.Thornton	Higher Barn Farm, Houghton	12. 6.00P
	(Fuji-Robin EC-44-PM)					

G-MMXL	Mainair Gemini/Flash II (Fuji-Robin EC-44-PM)	292-385-3 & W36	17. 1.85	J.M.Marshall *(Current status unknown)*	(Urmston)	16. 5.97P
G-MMXN*	Southdown Puma Sprint (Fuji-Robin EC-44-PM)	SN1121/0021	24. 1.85	N.Green *(Cancelled 7.3.02 by CAA)*	(Shrewsbury)	31. 7.00P
G-MMXO	Southdown Puma Sprint (Fuji-Robin EC-44-PM)	SN1121/0018	23. 1.85	D.J.Tasker	Swinford, Rugby	9. 2.03P
G-MMXT*	Mainair Gemini/Flash (Fuji-Robin EC-44-PM)	302-485-3 & W41	29. 1.85	L.R.Orriss *(Cancelled 5.12.01 by CAA)*	(Rotherham)	16. 4.00P
G-MMXU	Mainair Gemini/Flash II (Fuji-Robin EC-44-PM)	254-784-2 & W21	29. 1.85	T.J.Franklin	Graveley Farm, Herts	14. 7.01P
G-MMXV	Mainair Gemini/Flash II (Fuji-Robin EC-44-PM)	298-385-3 & W37	29. 1.85	S.Brader	Tarn Farm, Cockerham	17. 3.02P
G-MMXW	Mainair Gemini/Sprint (Fuji-Robin EC-44-PM)	286-185-3-P.597	23. 1.85	A.Hodgson	(Milton Keynes)	4. 6.02P
G-MMYA	Solar Wings Pegasus XL-R/Se (Rotax 447) XL-P Proto & T784-1151XL		30. 1.85	E.G.Cartwright	(Belper)	5. 8.03P
G-MMYF	Southdown Puma Sprint (Fuji-Robin EC-44-PM)	SN1121/0026	28. 3.85	E.Smith	Swinford, Rugby	9. 7.03P
G-MMYL	Cyclone 70/Aerial Arts 130SX (Rotax 277)	CH.01	8. 3.85	A.G.Smith & J.T.Halford	Holt, Norfolk	17. 1.02P
G-MMYN	Solar Wings Panther XL-R (Rotax 447)	T784-1158XL	27. 2.85	B.& D.Bergin	(Athenry, Co.Galway)	16. 4.00P
G-MMYO	Southdown Puma Sprint (Fuji-Robin EC-44-PM) *(Fitted with rainbow Medway sailwing c3.96 after accident 20.9.95)*	SN1121/0037	11. 4.85	P.R.Whitehouse	Otherton, Cannock	29. 8.00P
G-MMYR	Eipper Quicksilver MXII (Rotax 503)	3345	27. 2.85	P.A.Pilkington	North Coates	17. 6.01P
G-MMYT	Southdown Puma Sprint (Fuji-Robin EC-44-PM) SN1121/0046 & T569/P621		15. 4.85	J.K.Divall *(Current status unknown)*	(Chichester)	25. 3.94P
G-MMYU	Southdown Puma Sprint (Rotax 447)	SN1231/0045	11. 6.85	M.V.Hearns	Glenrothes	21. 4.02P
G-MMYV	John Webb trike/Flexiform Striker (Rotax 277)	JW-2	22. 3.85	S.B.Herbert *(Current status unknown)*	(Presteigne)	20.12.95P
G-MMYY	Southdown Puma Sprint (Rotax 447)	SN1231/0042	18. 7.85	C.P.Davis & P.Bottrill	(Sutton Coldfield)	12. 7.03P
G-MMYZ*	Southdown Puma Sprint (Rotax 447)	SN1231/0034	28. 2.85	M.Bodill	Roddige, Fradley	19. 2.99P
	(Damaged in gales Roddidge 1.98: trike, less sailwing, stored 10.00: cancelled 31.5.01 by CAA)					
G-MMZA	Mainair Gemini/Flash II (Fuji-Robin EC-44-PM)	266-984-3 & W60	4. 3.85	G.T.Johnston	(Craigavon, Co Armagh)	30. 6.00P
G-MMZB	Mainair Gemini/Flash (Fuji-Robin EC-44-PM)	319-685-3 & W58	4. 3.85	M.A.Nolan	(Great Orton)	23. 5.02P
G-MMZF	Mainair Gemini/Flash II (Fuji-Robin EC-44-PM)	299-485-3 & W38	4. 3.85	A.R.Rhodes *(Operates from Kirkbride)*	(Annan)	13. 9.03P
G-MMZG	Solar Wings Panther XL-S (Fuji-Robin EC-44-PM) SW-TA-1008 & SW-WA-1022		12. 8.85	P.A.Jones	North Coates	13. 4.02P
G-MMZI	Medway Half Pint Srs.1/Aerial Arts 130SX (JPX PUL425) 2385/1 & 130SX-057		6. 3.85	J.Messenger *(Current status unknown)*	(Workington)	28. 3.93E
G-MMZJ	Mainair Gemini/Flash (Rotax 462)	312-585-3 & W51	18. 3.85	P.J.Glover	North Coates	15. 1.03P
G-MMZK	Mainair Gemini/Flash (Fuji-Robin EC-44-PM) *(Trike ex G-MMEZ: originally regd with trike c/n 314-585-3: to G-MMIR) (Current status unknown)*	326-785-3 & W53	18. 3.85	G.Jones & B.Lee	(Warrington)	3.11.99P
G-MMZM	Mainair Gemini/Flash (Fuji-Robin EC-44-PM)	304-585-3 & W44	18. 3.85	H.Brown	(Dunbar)	27.11.02P
G-MMZN	Mainair Gemini/Flash II (Fuji-Robin EC-44-PM)	283-185-3 & W23	18. 3.85	W.K.Dalus *(Current status unknown)*	(Keyworth)	28. 9.93P
G-MMZP	Solar Wings Panther XL (Built H Phipps) HP-01 (Fuji-Robin EC-44-PM) *(Possibly original trike from G-MJWZ)*		14. 3.85	B.Richardson *(Current status unknown)*	(Sunderland)	12. 1.94P
G-MMZR	Southdown Puma Sprint (Fuji-Robin EC-44-PM) SN1121/0039 & T560/P622		4. 7.85	J.E.Hicks tr International Animal Rescue *(Current status unknown)*	Dunkeswell	6.12.93P
G-MMZV	Mainair Gemini/Flash (Rotax 447)	313-585-3 & W52	18. 4.85	P.R.M.Spengler	(Bracknell)	12. 5.02P
G-MMZW	Southdown Puma Sprint (Fuji-Robin EC-44-PM) SN1121/0043 & T566/P620		28. 3.85	M.G.Ashbee *(Damaged c.8.00)*	(Cranbrook)	30. 9.00P
G-MMZX	Southdown Puma Sprint (Rotax 447)	SN1231/0051	17. 4.85	J.V.Rozentals *(Current status unknown)*	(Sutton-in-Ashfield)	10. 4.95P
G-MMZZ* ..	Maxair Hummer (Fuji-Robin EC-25)-	0010	8. 4.82	M.J.Aubrey *(Cancelled 12.6.00 by CAA) (Noted 2002*	(Kington, Hereford)	
G-MNAC	Mainair Gemini/Flash (Rotax 503) *(C/n now verified as 262-884-2 & W04 ex G-MMUT qv)*	335-885-3 & W72	18. 4.85.	R.A.Wells	(Earls Croome)	30. 7.03P
G-MNAE	Mainair Gemini/Flash (Rotax 447)	343-885-3 & W77	18. 4.85	G.C.Luddington	(Bletsoe)	29. 7.00P
G-MNAH	Solar Wings Panther XL-S (Fuji-Robin EC-44-PM) SW-TA-1002 & SW-WA-1002		24. 4.85	J.H.Button & G.A.Harman *(Current status unknown)*	(Sandy)	18. 9.99P
G-MNAI	Solar Wings Panther XL-S (Fuji-Robin EC-44-PM) SW-TA-1003 SW-WA-1003		15. 5.85	R.G.Cameron *(Current status unknown)*	Muirhouses Farm, Errol	23. 6.98P
G-MNAK	Solar Wings Panther XL-S (Fuji-Robin EC-44-PM) SW-TA-1005 & SW-WA-1005		15. 5.85	F.J.McVey	Insch	5. 5.03P
G-MNAR	Solar Wings Pegasus XL-R (Rotax 447) SW-TB-0014 & SW-WA-1011		6. 8.85	D.A.Cansdale	(Harlow)	3. 3.03P
G-MNAV	Southdown Puma Sprint (Fuji-Robin EC-44-PM)	SN1121/0033	28. 2.85	G.P.Morling	(Douglas, Isle of Man)	31. 8.03P
G-MNAW	Solar Wings Pegasus XL-R (Rotax 447) SW-TB-1010 & SW-WA-1014		16. 8.85	D.J.Harber	(Henley-on-Thames)	3. 6.02P
G-MNAX	Solar Wings Pegasus XL-R (Rotax 447) SW-TB-1011 & SW-WA-1015		16. 8.85	B.J.Phillips *(Current status unknown)*	(Newbury)	21. 7.96P

Reg	Type	C/n		Date	Owner	Location	Date
G-MNAY	Solar Wings Pegasus XL-R (Rotax 447)	SW-TB-1015 & SW-WA-1016		6. 8.85	A.Seaton *(New owner 5.02)*	(Sleaford)	11. 9.99P
G-MNAZ	Solar Wings Pegasus XL-R (Rotax 447)	SW-TB-1016 & SW-WA-1017		6. 8.85	R.W.Houldsworth	(Rochford)	15. 4.03P
G-MNBA	Solar Wings Pegasus XL-R (Rotax 447)	SW-TB-1024 & SW-WA-1018		6. 9.85	K.D.Baldwin *"Tigerfish"*	Graveley Farm, Herts	24. 6.03P
G-MNBB	Solar Wings Pegasus XL-R (Rotax 447)	SW-TB-1020 & SW-WA-1019		20. 9.85	A.Bishop	St Michaels	7. 7.03P
G-MNBC	Solar Wings Pegasus XLCJ (Rotax 503)	SW-TB-1026 & SW-WA-1020		11.10.85	M.Bastin	(Swindon)	9. 9.03P
G-MNBD	Mainair Gemini/Flash	162-683 & W42	G-MMSN	6. 1.86	P.Woodcock	Sittles Farm, Alrewas	2. 7.02P

Fuji-Robin EC-44-PM) (Originally built as Mainair 440 Tri-Flyer c/n 341-585-3 & W42. Unsold &.reworked by Mainair as c/n 162-683 & fitted to G-MMSN. This was podded to become a Gemini & used in rebuild of G-MNBD after late 1996 accident)

Reg	Type	C/n		Date	Owner	Location	Date
G-MNBE	Southdown Puma Sprint (Rotax 447)	SN1121/0050		17. 5.85	J.Liversuch & C.Hershaw	Doynton	2. 3.03P
G-MNBF*	Mainair Gemini/Flash (Fuji-Robin EC-44-PM)	306-585-3 & W46		2. 5.85	H.G.Denton *(Cancelled 14.11.02 as wfu)*	Knapthorpe Lodge, Caunton	5. 5.01P
G-MNBG	Mainair Gemini/Flash (Rotax 447)	347-585-3 & W66		9. 5.85	T.Barnett	(Redcar)	11. 9.03P
G-MNBI	Solar Wings Panther XL-S (Fuji-Robin EC-44-PM) PXL884-178 & T884-1161XL		G-MMVF?	3. 5.85	G.R.Cox	(Northampton)	29. 4.97P

(G-MMVF never received Permit before cancellation in 1990) (Current status unknown)

Reg	Type	C/n		Date	Owner	Location	Date
G-MNBJ*	Skyhook TR1 Pixie (Solo 210) *(Skyhook c/n TR1-56+ Zeus C wing)*	HLC-01		7. 5.85	Not known *(Cancelled by CAA 20.8.93) (Stored 2002)*	(Holmfirth)	
G-MNBM	Southdown Puma Sprint (Rotax 447)	SN1231/0058		25. 6.85	D.A.Hopewell *(New owner 6.02)*	(Newcastle-under-Lyme, Staffs)	7.10.01P
G-MNBN	Mainair Gemini/Flash (Fuji-Robin EC-44-PM)	303-485-3 & W43		11. 6.85	I.H.Gates	(Hastings)	18. 5.03P
G-MNBP	Mainair Gemini/Flash (Fuji-Robin EC-44-PM)	338-885-3 & W75		15. 5.85	N.L.Zaman	(London Colney)	30. 3.02P
G-MNBR*	Mainair Gemini/Flash (Rotax 447)	345-985-3 & W79		15. 5.85	N.A.P.Gregory *(Cancelled 31.5.00 by CAA: stored 10.00)*	Long Marston	5. 2.94P
G-MNBS	Mainair Gemini/Flash (Fuji-Robin EC-44-PM)	308-585-3 & W48		15. 5.85	P.A.Comins *(Current status unknown)*	(Nottingham)	20. 6.94P
G-MNBT	Mainair Gemini/Flash (Rotax 503)	322-685-3 & W62		15. 5.85	N.Williams-Jones	(Preston)	6. 3.03P
G-MNBV	Mainair Gemini/Flash (Rotax 447)	333-685-3 & W70		15. 5.85	J.Walshe	(Newtownards, Co.Down)	30. 7.03P
G-MNBW	Mainair Gemini/Flash (Rotax 447) *(C/n now SW-WF-0005 & W95 ex G-MNJI)*	332-685-3 & W69		15. 5.85	G.A.Brown & N.S.Brotherton	Weston Zoyland	10. 9.03P
G-MNCF	Mainair Gemini/Flash (Rotax 447)	321-685-3 & W61		3. 6.85	M.Elgey	(Fraserburgh)	4. 4.03P
G-MNCG	Mainair Gemini/Flash (Rotax 503)	320-685-3 & W59		3. 6.85	J E F Fletcher *(Rebuilt c2000)*	Tarn Farm, Cockerham	24. 8.02P
G-MNCI	Southdown Puma Sprint (Rotax 447)	SN1231/0059		7. 6.85	R.M.Wait & N.Hewitt	(Stourbridge)	4. 3.02P
G-MNCJ	Mainair Gemini/Flash (Fuji-Robin EC-44)	351-785-3 & W83		3. 6.85	R.S.McLeister	(Accrington)	16.11.93P

(Orig trike stolen , new one c/n 282-1284-2 ex G-MMXF fitted c.12.89) (Current status unknown)

Reg	Type	C/n		Date	Owner	Location	Date
G-MNCM	CFM Shadow C (Rotax 503)	006		31. 5.85	K.G.D.Macrae	Drummiard Farm, Bonnybank	23. 5.03P
G-MNCO	Eipper Quicksilver MX II	1045		3. 6.85	S.Lawton *(CofR restored 4.02)*	(Barnoldswick)	
G-MNCP	Southdown Puma Sprint (Rotax 447)	SN1231/0071		24. 6.85	S.Baker & D.M.Lane t/a Freedom Sports Aviation	(Barton under Needwood)	10. 4.00P
G-MNCS	Skyrider Airsports Phantom (Fuji-Robin EC-44-PM)	PH.00098		2. 1.86	C.G.Johns	(Bewdley, Worcs)	25. 7.03P
G-MNCU	Medway Hybred/Solar Wings Typhoon 44XL	26485/10 & SW-WA-1029		13. 6.85	A.Thornley	(Louth)	2. 5.03P
G-MNCV	Medway Hybred/Solar Wings Typhoon 44XL (Fuji-Robin EC-44-PM) 26485/11 & SW-WA-1030			13. 6.85 *(Pegasus XL-R wing)*	P.D.Mickleburgh	Swinford, Rugby	29.11.03P
G-MNDC	Mainair Gemini/Flash	336-885-3 & W73		12. 6.85	M.Medlock	(Guildford)	31. 8.03P
G-MNDD	Mainair Scorcher (Rotax 447)	358-885-1 & W85		12. 6.85	J.M.M.Bowles	Ince Blundell	14. 2.03P
G-MNDE	Medway Half Pint/Aerial Arts 130SX (JPL PUL425) *(Wing ex G-MNBZ)*	3/8685		19. 6.85	C.D.Wills	(Andover)	3.10.03P
G-MNDF	Mainair Gemini/Flash (Rotax 447)	327-785-3 & W67		25. 6.85	M.Ellis	Sandtoft	6. 6.02P
G-MNDG	Southdown Puma Sprint (Fuji-Robin EC-44-PM)	SN1121/0057		18. 7.85	P.J.Kirwan *(Current status unknown)*	(Geashill, Co.Offaly)	14. 6.99P
G-MNDO	Solar Wings Pegasus/Flash (Rotax 447) *(Trike is c/n SW-TB-1012 & Mainair sailwing c/n W86)*	SW-WF-0001		2. 7.85	R.H.Cooke	(Southampton)	27.07.03P
G-MNDU	Midland Ultralights Sirocco 377GB (Rotax 377)	MU-011		22. 7.85	M.A.Collins	(St. Neots)	18. 8.01P
G-MNDW	Midland Ultralights Sirocco 377GB (Rotax 377)	MU-014		30. 7.85	L.G.Horne	(Ashford)	24. 4.01P
G-MNDY	Southdown Puma Sprint (Fuji-Robin EC-44-PM) *(Trike rebuilt c4.99)*	DY-01 & P.536		2. 5.84	A.M.Marshall	(Oswestry)	19. 6.03P
G-MNDZ*	Southdown Puma Sprint (Rotax 447) *(Fitted with trike from G-MNCK)*	SN1121/0062		28. 6.85	Wendy A.Guest *(Cancelled 5.7.01 by CAA)*	(Bridgnorth)	6. 1.01P
G-MNEF	Mainair Gemini/Flash (Rotax 447)	344-885-3 & W78		8. 7.85	P.Greaves	(Currie)	23. 4.03P
G-MNEG	Mainair Gemini/Flash (Rotax 447)	360-885-3 & W92		8. 7.85	T.McDowell *(Current status unknown)*	(Kells, Co.Meath)	18.10.99P
G-MNEH	Mainair Gemini/Flash (Rotax 503)	361-885-3 & W90		8. 7.85	I.Rawson	St.Michaels	2. 7.03P
G-MNEI	Medway Hybred/Solar Wings Typhoon/XL-R (Fuji-Robin EC-44-PM) 8785/12 & SW-WA-1035			9. 7.85	L.G.Thompson *(Damaged 28.11.92 & stored 8.96: current status unknown)*	Long Marston	26. 7.93P

G-MNEK	Medway Half Pint/Aerial Arts 130S	4/8785	12. 7.85	M.I.Dougall	(Maidstone)	25. 9.94P
	(JPX PUL425)			*(Damaged Stoke 6.7.93: current status unknown)*		
G-MNER	CFM Shadow CD	008	15. 7.85	F.C.Claydon	Wickhambrook, Newmarket	6. 3.03P
	(Rotax 462)					
G-MNET	Mainair Gemini/Flash	349-885-3 & W81	23. 7.85	I P Stubbins	North Coates	29. 7.03P
	(Fuji-Robin EC-44-PM)					
G-MNEV	Mainair Gemini/Flash	362-1085-3 & W108	23. 7.85	C.A.Denver	St.Michaels	28. 3.03P
	(Rotax 447)					
G-MNEY	Mainair Gemini/Flash	365-1085-3 & W94	23. 7.85	D.A.Spiers	East Fortune	13. 8.03P
	(Rotax 447)					
G-MNFB	Southdown Puma Sprint	SN1231/0077	22. 7.85	C.Lawrence	(Highbridge)	9. 8.03P
	(Rotax 447)					
G-MNFE	Mainair Gemini/Flash	350-885-3 & W82	29. 7.85	D.R.Kennedy	East Fortune	20.10.01P
	(Fuji-Robin EC-44-PM)					
G-MNFF	Mainair Gemini/Flash	371-1185-3 & W110	29. 7.85	R.P.Cook & C.H.Spencer	St Michaels	24. 5.02P
	(Rotax 447)					
G-MNFG	Southdown Puma Sprint	SN1231/0078	31. 7.85	A.C.Hing	Long Acre Farm, Sandy	12. 6.03P
	(Rotax 447)					
G-MNFH	Mainair Gemini/Flash	364-1085-3 & W93	6. 8.85	K.Glynn	(Loughrea, Co.Galway)	30. 6.95P
	(Rotax 447)			*(Current status unknown)*		
G-MNFL	AMF Microflight Chevvron 2-32A	CH.002	19. 8.85	P.W.Wright	Saltby	13.12.OOP
	(Konig SD570)					
G-MNFM	Mainair Gemini/Flash	366-1085-3 & W98	10.10.85	P.M.Fidell	Wombleton	25. 7.03P
	(Rotax 447)					
G-MNFN	Mainair Gemini/Flash	367-1085-3 & W99	6.11.85	J.R.Martin	(Bedale)	30. 4.94P
	(Rotax 447)			*(Current status unknown)*		
G-MNFP	Mainair Gemini/Flash	368-1085-3 & W100	23.10.85	S.Farnsworth & P.Howarth	Tarn Farm, Cockerham	22. 5.03P
	(Rotax 447)					
G-MNFW	Medway Hybred 44XL	10885/13	15. 8.85	A.T.Palmer	(Plymouth)	15. 8.99P
	(Fuji-Robin EC-44-PM)			*(Current status unknown)*		
G-MNFX	Southdown Puma Sprint	SN1231/0079	14. 8.85	A.M.Shaw	(Stoke-on-Trent)	6. 9.03P
	(Rotax 447)					
G-MNGD	Ultrasports Tripacer/Solar Wings Medium Typhoon		13. 8.85	F.H.Cook	(Whitchurch)	3. 9.00P
	(Fuji-Robin EC-34-PM)	012 & T681-171				
G-MNGF	Solar Wings Pegasus/Flash		21. 8.85	P.J.Harrison	Beccles	23. 6.03P
	(Rotax 447)	W-TB-1022 & SW-WF-0003		*(Correct trike c/n is SW-TB-1022 plus Mainair sailwing c/n W87)*		
G-MNGG	Solar Wings Pegasus XL-R	T784-1159XL	21. 8.85	T.Peckham	(Faversham)	13. 5.03P
	(Rotax 447) *(Trike c/n is US.TPR.0002)*					
G-MNGK	Mainair Gemini/Flash	374-1085-3 & W112	5. 9.85	G.W.Dear	(Bournemouth)	30. 8.03P
	(Rotax 447)					
G-MNGL	Mainair Gemini/Flash	376-1085-3 & W114	5. 9.85	G.Cusden	Davidstow Moor	15.11.02P
	(Rotax 447)					
G-MNGM	Mainair Gemini/Flash	394-1285-3 & W109	5. 9.85	J.E.Caffull & D.R.Beale	Over Farm, Gloucester	27. 6.03P
	(Rotax 447) *(Originally supplied with Mainair trike c/n 377. However, this & sailwing from G-MNIO stolen from Popham overnight 15/16.3.86. Consequently, the trike of G-MNIO is fitted with the sailwing of G-MNGM)*					
G-MNGN	Mainair Gemini/Flash	378-1185-3 & W115	5. 9.85	T.B.Margetts	(Poole)	17. 6.99P
	(Rotax 447)			*(Current status unknown)*		
G-MNGS	Southdown Puma/Lightning 195	GJS-02	8. 5.84	R.J.Turner	(Spalding)	14. 8.02P
	(Fuji-Robin EC-34-PM) *(Tripacer Trike from G-MJRF)*					
G-MNGT	Mainair Gemini/Flash	372-1085-3 & W106	30. 9.85	J.W.Biegus	Arclid Green, Sandbach	7. 6.02P
	(Rotax 447)					
G-MNGU	Mainair Gemini/Flash	373-1085-3 & W111	30. 9.85	J.A.Ellis	(Dagenham)	)4. 6.02P
	(Rotax 503)					
G-MNGW	Mainair Gemini/Flash	386-1185-3 & W121	30. 9.85	D.G.Baker	Colemore Common, Hants	23. 4.03P
	(Rotax 447)					
G-MNGX	Southdown Puma Sprint	SN1231/0088	26. 9.85	R.J.Morris	(Ely)	24. 6.03P
	(Rotax 447)					
G-MNHB	Solar Wings Pegasus XL-R/Se		1.11.85	P.J.Soukup	(Winkleigh)	23. 3.03P
	(Rotax 447)	SW-TB-1031 & SW-WA-1045				
G-MNHC	Solar Wings Pegasus XL-R		31.10.85	C.Thomas	Haverfordwest	12. 3.02P
	(Rotax 447)	SW-TB-1032 & SW-WA-1046/2	*(Original sailwing [SW-WA-1046] damaged so planned rebuild as 'SW-WA-1058' for G-MNHO never came to fruition: replaced by SW-WA-1065, probably so marked on the sailwing, but re-numbered as SW-WA-1046/2)*			
G-MNHD	Solar Wings Pegasus XL-R		5.11.85	P.D.Stiles	(Ashley Down, Bristol)	22. 6.03P
	(Rotax 447)	SW-TB-1033 & SW-WA-1047				
G-MNHE	Solar Wings Pegasus XL-R/Se		11.12.85	J.R.Austin	Davidstow Moor	2. 8.02P
	(Rotax 447)	SW-TB-1036 & SW-WA-1048		*(Noted 11.01)*		
G-MNHH	Solar Wings Pegasus XL-S	SW-WA-1051	22. 1.86	F.J.Williams	(Shefford, Beds)	24. 6.01P
	(Fuji-Robin EC-44-PM) *(Trike is an Ultrasports unit c/n PXL847-170)*					
G-MNHI	Solar Wings Pegasus XL-R		8. 1.86	I.D.R.Hyde	Enstone	13. 7.95P
	(Rotax 447)	SW-TB-1042 & SW-WA-1052		*(Current status unknown)*		
G-MNHJ	Solar Wings Pegasus XL-R		11. 3.86	S.J.Woodd	(Oxford)	26. 6.93P
	(Rotax 447)	SW-TB-1056 & SW-WA-1053		*(Current status unknown)*		
G-MNHK	Solar Wings Pegasus XL-R		9. 7.86	R.D.Proctor	(Stamford)	13. 6.92P
	(Rotax 462)	SW-TE-0005 & SW-WA-1054		*(Current status unknown)*		
G-MNHL	Solar Wings Pegasus XL-R		9. 7.86	S B Walters	(Sidcup)	14. 5.03P
	(Rotax 447)	SW-TB-1077 & SW-WA-1055				
G-MNHM	Solar Wings Pegasus XL-R		11. 7.86	R.Noble	(Bracknell)	28. 8.02P
	(Rotax 447)	SW-TB-1078 & SW-WA-1056				
G-MNHN	Solar Wings Pegasus XL-R		11. 8.86	P.K.Peppard	(Doncaster)	14. 2.03P
	(Rotax 447)	SW-TB-1079 & SW-WA-1057				
G-MNHR	Solar Wings Pegasus XL-R		7. 8.86	B.D.Jackson	(Wincanton)	15. 3.03P
	(Rotax 447)	SW-TB-1081 & SW-WA-1060				
G-MNHS	Solar Wings Pegasus XL-R		21. 8.86	M.D.Packer	(Highbridge)	12.10.03P
	(Rotax 447)	SW-TB-1082 & SW-WA-1061				

Reg	Type	c/n	Prev id	Date	Owner	Location	Expiry
G-MNHT	Solar Wings Pegasus XL-R			4. 8.86	J.W.Coventry	Davidstow Moor	3.11.02P
	(Rotax 447)	SW-TB-1084 & SW-WA-1062					
G-MNHU*	Solar Wings Pegasus XL-R			4. 8.86	B.A.Wright & D.Lyon	Dunkeswell	16. 1.99P
	(Rotax 447)	SW-TB-1085 & SW-WA-1063			*(Cancelled 11.6.01 by CAA)*		
G-MNHV	Solar Wings Pegasus XL-R			18. 8.86	E.Jenkins	(Crymych, Dyfed)	31. 7.99P
	(Rotax 447)	SW-TB-1095 & SW-WA-1064			*(Current status unknown)*		
G-MNHZ	Mainair Gemini/Flash	310-585-3 & W118		15.10.85	I.O.S.Ross	(Cowie)	26. 8.01P
	(Fuji-Robin EC-44-PM)						
G-MNIA	Mainair Gemini/Flash	370-1185-3 & W105		10.10.85	A.E.Dix	Long Marston	10. 4.89P
	(Rotax 447)				*(Noted wrecked 1990)*		
G-MNIE	Mainair Gemini/Flash	388-1185-3 & W123		21.11.85	G.M.Hewer	(Cheltenham)	8. 7.02P
	(Rotax 447)						
G-MNIF	Mainair Gemini/Flash	403-286-4 & W147		7. 1.86	R.A.Needham	(Kendal)	15. 8.03P
	(Rotax 447)						
G-MNIG	Mainair Gemini/Flash	391-1285-3 & W129		9. 1.86	I.S.Everett	(Astwood)	22. 5.03P
	(Rotax 447)						
G-MNIH	Mainair Gemini/Flash	379-1185-3 & W116		10.12.85	A.R.Richardson	(Barnsley)	14. 1.03P
	(Rotax 447)						
G-MNII	Mainair Gemini/Flash	390-1285-3 & W128		6.11.85	R.F.Finnis	(Guildford)	6. 9.91P
	(Rotax 447)				*(Trike reported at St.Michaels 9.96: current status unknown)*		
G-MNIK	Solar Wings Pegasus Photon			29.10.85	C.D.C.Ashdown	Prestwick	31. 7.03P
	(Solo 210)	SW-TP-0002 & SW-WP-0002					
G-MNIL	Southdown Puma Sprint	SN1231/0094		4.11.85	P.L.Speakman	(Prescot)	17. 3.03P
	(Rotax 447)						
G-MNIM	Maxair Hummer	PJB-01		29.10.85	K.Wood *(Current status unknown)*	(Leicester)	
G-MNIN*	Designability (Jordan) Duet	018		7.11.85	Not known	Field Farm, Oakley	
	(Cancelled by CAA 25.9.95)			*(Composite airframe being assembled 3.00 from this & G-MMKY qv)*			
G-MNIP*	Mainair Gemini/Flash	393-1285-3 & W134		6.11.85	G.S.Bulpitt	Chilbolton	18. 8.00P
	(Rotax 447)				*(Cancelled 12.4.02 by CAA)*		
G-MNIS	CFM Shadow C	014		11.11.85	R.W.Payne	(Peterborough)	25. 4.92P
	(Rotax 503)				*(Current status unknown)*		
G-MNIT	Aerial Arts Alpha Mk.II/130SX	130SX/176		27. 2.86	M.J.Edmett	(London N3)	15. 8.99
	(Originally regd as Hiway Skytrike II with same c/n)			*(New owner 5.02)*			
G-MNIU	Solar Wings Pegasus Photon			27.11.85	S.Ferguson	(Bearsden)	17. 1.90E
	(Fuji-Robin EC-34) SW-TP-0003 & SW-WP-0003			*(Damaged & stored 3.90: new owner 10.02))*			
G-MNIW	Mainair Tri-Flyer/Airwave Nimrod 165	050/19181	EI-BOB	29.11.85	J.A.McIntosh & R.W.Mitchell	(Perth)	4. 9.00P
	(Fuji-Robin EC-25-PS)			*(Cancelled 8.5.02 by CAA)*			
G-MNIX	Mainair Gemini/Flash	395-1285-3 & W136		29.11.85	S.Farnworth	(Kempston, Bedford)	11. 7.98P
	(Rotax 447)				*(Current status unknown)*		
G-MNIZ	Mainair Gemini/Flash	392-1285-3 & W130		26. 2.86	A.G.Power	(Darwen)	3. 9.03P
	(Rotax 447)						
G-MNJB	Southdown Raven X	SN2232/0098		10.12.85	T.A.Simpson	Long Acre Farm, Sandy	26. 5.03P
	(Rotax 447)						
G-MNJC	MBA Tiger Cub 440	SO.215		8. 6.84	J.G.Carpenter	(Romsey)	20. 9.90E
	(Fuji-Robin EC-44)				*(Current status unknown)*		
G-MNJD	Mainair Tri-Flyer 440/Sprint	243-10484-2-P.537		2. 4.84	M.E.Smith	(Verwood)	8. 8.00P
	(Fuji-Robin EC-44-PM)						
G-MNJF	Dragon Srs.150	0068	(OY) 9-17	2. 1.86	B.W.Langley	South Wraxall, Bradford-on-Avon	14. 7.02P
	(Fuji-Robin EC-44-PM)						
G-MNJG	Mainair Gemini Sprint MS			29. 9.83	P.Batchelor	(Crawley)	16. 8.03P
	(Fuji-Robin EC-44-PM) SA.2030 & 251-684-2-P.593						
G-MNJH	Solar Wings Pegasus/Flash			22.10.85	C.P.Course	Church Farm, Wellingborough	18. 8.02P
	(Rotax 447)	SW-TB-1023 & SW-WF-0004	*(Mainair sailwing c/n W89)*				
G-MNJJ	Solar Wings Pegasus/Flash			22.10.85	P.A.Shelley	Sutton Meadows, Ely	26.11.96P
	(Rotax 447)	SW-TB-1029 & SW-WF-0006	*(Mainair sailwing c/n W96)*		*(Current status unknown)*		
G-MNJL	Solar Wings Pegasus/Flash			21.10.85	S.D.Thomas	(Bilston)	11.11.94P
	(Rotax 447)	SW-TB-1028 & SW-WF-0008	*(Mainair sailwing c/n W101)*		*(Current status unknown)*		
G-MNJN	Solar Wings Pegasus/Flash			19.11.85	D.Thorn	(St. Austell)	11. 1.03P
	(Rotax 447)	SW-TB-1034 & SW-WF-0010	*(Mainair sailwing c/n W103)*				
G-MNJO	Solar Wings Pegasus/Flash			19.11.85	S.Clarke	Long Marston	22. 3.03P
	(Rotax 447)	SW-TB-1035 & SW-WF-0011	*(Mainair sailwing c/n W126)*				
G-MNJR	Solar Wings Pegasus/Flash			30.12.85	M.G.Ashbee	(Cranbrook)	16. 4.03P
	(Rotax 447)	SW-TB-1041 & SW-WF-0013	*(Mainair sailwing c/n W133)*				
G-MNJS	Southdown Puma Sprint	SN1231/0085		18. 9.85	J.B.Mayes	Sutton Meadows, Ely	20. 6.03P
	(Rotax 447)						
G-MNJT	Southdown Raven X (Rotax 447)	SN2232/0087		20. 9.85	R.C.Hinkins	RAF Henlow	31. 3.03P
G-MNJU	Mainair Gemini/Flash	384-1185-3 & W119		20. 9.85	E.J.Wells	Over Farm, Gloucester	3. 6.03P
	(Rotax 447)						
G-MNJX	Medway Hybred 44XL	15885/14		9.12.85	H.A.Stewart	(Sittingbourne)	23. 7.98P
	(Fuji-Robin EC-44-PM)				*(Current status unknown)*		
G-MNKB	Solar Wings Pegasus/Photon			14. 1.86	M.E.Gilbert	Drummaird Farm, Bonnybank	3. 5.03P
	(Solo 210)	SW-TP-0005 & SW-WP-0005					
G-MNKC	Solar Wings Pegasus/Photon			14. 1.86	E.H.Jenkins	(Newcastle upon Tyne)	31. 8.97P
	(Solo 210)	SW-TP-0006 & SW-WP-0006			*(Current status unknown)*		
G-MNKD	Solar Wings Pegasus/Photon	SW-WP-0007		14. 1.86	D.Glasper	(Darlington)	28. 8.92P
	(Solo 210) *(Originally allocated trike c/n SW-TP-0007 but believed exported: current trike is possibly c/n SW-TP-0016) (New CofR 2.03)*						
G-MNKE	Solar Wings Pegasus/Photon			14. 1.86	M.J.Olsen	(Middlesbrough)	5. 5.03P
	(Solo 210)	SW-TP-0008 & SW-WP-0008					
G-MNKG	Solar Wings Pegasus/Photon			28. 1.86	T.W.Thompson	Eshott	11. 6.95P
	(Solo 210)	SW-TP-0010 & SW-WP-0010			*(Trike stored 9.97: current status unknown)*		
G-MNKI*	Solar Wings Pegasus/Photon		(EI-)	28. 1.86	T.Shivner	Salthill, Galway	24. 3.00P
	(Solo 210)	SW-TP-0012 & SW-WP-0012	G-MNKI		*(Cancelled 22.11.01 by CAA)*		
G-MNKK	Solar Wings Pegasus/Photon			28. 1.86	M.E.Gilbert	(Inverkeithing)	7. 5.95P
	(Fuji-Robin EC-34-PM) SW-TP-0014 & SW-WP-0014 *(To be fitted with Zanzottera 340cc engine) (Current status unknown)*						

Reg	Type	C/n	Date	Owner	Location	Date2
G-MNKM	MBA Tiger Cub 440 (Fuji-Robin EC-44-PM)	SO.213	30.12.85	R.Barcis	Brook Farm, Pilling	18. 2.02P
G-MNKN*	Wheeler (Skycraft) Scout Mk.III/3/R (Fuji-Robin EC-25)	410	6. 1.86	M.J.Aubrey *(Cancelled 19.2.99 as WFU).(Noted 2002)*	(Kington, Hereford)	
G-MNKO	Solar Wings Pegasus XL-Q (Rotax 447) SW-TB-1158 & SW-WX-0001		2. 1.86	G.Sharp	Eshott	13. 7.03P
G-MNKP	Solar Wings Pegasus/Flash (Rotax 447) SW-TB-1043 & SW-WF-0014 *(Mainair sailwing c/n W131)*		9. 1.86	C.Hasell	Graveley Farm, Herts	16. 2.03P
G-MNKR	Solar Wings Pegasus/Flash (Rotax 447) SW-TB-1045 & SW-WF-0015		14. 1.86	C.I.D.H.Garrison	Sutton Meadows, Ely	16. 7.03P
G-MNKS	Solar Wings Pegasus/Flash (Rotax 447) SW-TB-1044 & SW-WF-0016 *(Mainair sailwing c/n W132)*		9. 1.86	W.J.Walker	Drummaird Farm, Bonnybank	8. 4.03P
G-MNKU	Southdown Puma Sprint (Rotax 447)	SN1231/0100	29. 1.86	S.P.O'Hannrachain	(Coolaney, Co.Sligo)	30. 8.03P
G-MNKV	Solar Wings Pegasus/Flash (Rotax 447) SW-TB-1047 & SW-WF-0017 *(Mainair sailwing c/n W137)*		15. 1.86	P.C.Bishop tr G-MNKV Group	(Chard)	15. 4.03P
G-MNKW	Solar Wings Pegasus/Flash (Rotax 447) SW-TB-1049 & SW-WF-0018 *(Mainair sailwing c/n W140)*		28. 1.86	J.M.Macdonald Mill Farm, Hughley, Much Wenlock		19. 6.03P
G-MNKX	Solar Wings Pegasus/Flash Rotax 447) SW-TB-1054 & SW-WF-0019 *(Mainair sailwing c/n W139)*		28. 2.86	P.Samal	(Sandy)	15.12.02P
G-MNKZ	Southdown Raven X (Rotax 447)	SN2232/0102	4. 2.86	G.B.Gratton	Chilbolton	13. 7.03P
G-MNLB	Mainair 582 Gemini/Southdown Raven X (Rotax 582) 664-688-6 & SN2232/0117 *(Officially regd as Southdown Raven X (Modified Gemini F2A trike))*		11. 4.86	R.M.Cornwell	(Malmesbury)	25. 6.03P
G-MNLE	Southdown Raven X (Rotax 447)	SN2232/0128	30. 4.86	I.D. & P.G.Cresswell *(Current status unknown)*	(Rochester)	6.10.98P
G-MNLH	Romain Cobra Biplane (Midwest AE50R)	001	23. 1.86	J.W.E.Romain	(Welwyn)	13. 8.03P
G-MNLI	Mainair Gemini/Flash II (Rotax 503)	407-286-4 & W152	28. 1.86	C.E. & P.M.Fessi	(Bolton)	30. 6.02P
G-MNLK	Southdown Raven X (Rotax 447)	SN2232/0108	4. 2.86	M.J.Robbins *(Current status unknown)*	(Tunbridge Wells)	27. 7.98P
G-MNLM	Southdown Raven X (Rotax 447)	SN2232/0110	6. 2.86	A.P.White *(Current status unknown)*	(Exmouth)	9. 6.93P
G-MNLN	Southdown Raven X (Rotax 447)	SN2232/0111	6. 2.86	A.S.Windley	(Matlock)	27.12.00P
G-MNLT	Southdown Raven X (Rotax 447)	SN2232/0115	6. 2.86	J.L.Stachini	Middle Stoke, Kent	12. 8.01P
G-MNLU*	Southdown Raven X (Rotax 447)	SN2232/0116	6. 2.86	D.J.Ainsworth *(Cancelled 12.4.02 by CAA)*	(Preston)	24. 7.00P
G-MNLV	Southdown Raven X (Rotax 447)	SN2232/0118	6. 2.86	J.Murphy	(Tonbridge)	26. 5.02P
G-MNLY	Mainair Gemini/Flash (Rotax 503)	406-386-4 & W151	14. 2.86	A.McGlone	Ince Blundell	23.10.02P
G-MNLZ	Southdown Raven X (Rotax 447)	SN2232/0123	6. 2.86	E.L.Jenkins	(Bexleyheath)	12. 6.02P
G-MNMC	Mainair Gemini/Puma Sprint MS 222-284-2-P.524 (Fuji-Robin EC-44-PM)		20. 3.84	J.J.Milliken *(Current status unknown)*	(Winchester)	20. 9.96P
G-MNMD	Southdown Raven X	SN2000/0121	10. 2.86	P.G.Overall	(Crawley)	31. 5.03P
	(Rotax 447) *(Originally regd with c/n SN2232/0121) (SN2000 sailwing c/n prefix indicates sold without trike& suggests this may have changed also)*					
G-MNME*	Hiway Skytrike/Demon (Rotax 377)	WTP-01 & 3535009	12. 2.86	M.J.Aubrey *(Cancelled 28.4.00 by CAA) (Noted 2002) .*	(Kington, Hereford)	10.6.93
G-MNMG	Mainair Gemini/Flash II (Rotax 447)	419-386-4 & W177	11. 2.86	N.A.M.Beyer-Kay *(Current status unknown)*	(Southport)	20. 8.94P
G-MNMI	Mainair Gemini/Flash II (Fuji-Robin EC-44) *(Trike & engine ex G-MMZL following accident 8.9.91)*	317-685-3 & W178	11. 2.86	A.D.Bales	(Norwich)	9. 8.03P
G-MNMJ	Mainair Gemini/Flash II (BMW R80)	387-1185-3 & W122	11. 2.86	P.K.Appleton *(Current status unknown)*	Weston Zoyland	18. 9.99P
G-MNMK	Solar Wings Pegasus XL-R (Rotax 447) SW-TB-1021 & SW-WA-1038		19. 8.85	A.F.Smallacombe	(Okehampton)	2. 7.00P
G-MNML	Southdown Puma Sprint (Fuji-Robin EC-44-PM)	SN1111/0065	4. 8.83	R.C.Carr *(Current status unknown)*	(Launceston)	14. 7.97P
G-MNMN	Medway Hybred 44XLR (Rotax 447)	8286/16	7. 3.86	D.S Blofeld	Middle Stoke, Kent	31. 5.03P
G-MNMU	Southdown Puma Raven X (Fuji-Robin EC-44-PM)	SN2232/0127	17. 2.86	M.J.Curley	(London Colney)	20. 5.01P
G-MNMV	Mainair Gemini/Flash (Rotax 447)	375-1085-3 & W113	3. 3.86	B.Light	Tarn Farm, Cockerham	11. 5.03P
G-MNMW	Whittaker MW6-1-1 Merlin (Rotax 582)	PFA 164-11144	16. 4.86	E.F.Clapham, tr G-MNMW Flying Group	Otherton, Cannock	23. 7.02P
G-MNMY	Cyclone 70/Aerial Arts 110SX (Rotax 277)	CH-02	6. 3.86	N.R.Beale	Deppers Bridge, Warwick	26. 9.03P
G-MNNA	Southdown Raven X (Rotax 447)	SN2232/0129	4. 3.86	D. & G.D.Palfrey *(Current status unknown)*	(Tiverton)	20. 7.88P
G-MNNB	Southdown Raven (Fuji-Robin EC-44-PM)	SN2122/0130	4. 3.86	J.F.Horn	(Yelverton)	3. 6.03P
G-MNNC	Southdown Raven X (Rotax 447)	SN2232/0131	4. 3.86	S.A.Sacker	Deenethorpe	5. 8.00P
G-MNNF	Mainair Gemini/Flash II (Rotax 447)	402-286-4 & W148	28. 2.86	W.J.Gunn *(Stored 1.98: current status unknown)*	Long Marston	8. 4.97P
G-MNNG	Squires Lightfly/Solar Wings Photon SW-WP-0019 (Rotax 277) *(Trike may be Mainair Tri-Flyer c/n 032-221181 ex G-MJKY?)*		25. 2.86	C.C.Bilham	Huntingdon	4. 8.02P
G-MNNI	Mainair Gemini/Flash II (Rotax 503)	427-486-4 & W170	28. 2.86	J.C.Miller *(Amended CofR 3.02)*	(Edinburgh)	2. 6.98P

G-MNNJ	Mainair Gemini/Flash II	405-286-4 & W150		28. 2.86	R.Wilson & B.Skidmore	Tarn Farm, Cockerham	29. 7.03P
	(Rotax 503) *(ID Plate mis-marked as G-MNNZ)*						
G-MNNL	Mainair Gemini/Flash II	429-486-4 & W186		28. 2.86	D.Wilson	(Nottingham)	14. 9.03P
	(Rotax 503)						
G-MNNM	Mainair Scorcher Solo	424-486-1 & W182	(G-MNPE)	20. 3.86	S.R.Leeper & L.L.Perry	Priory Farm., Tibenham	8. 9.91P
	(Rotax 447)				*(New owners12.02)*		
G-MNNO	Southdown Raven X	SN2232/0133		26. 3.86	M.J.Robbins	(Tunbridge Wells)	16.12.01P
	(Rotax 447)						
G-MNNR	Mainair Gemini/Flash II	430-586-4 & W188		6. 3.86	W.A.B.Hill	Davidstow Moor	9. 6.02P
	(Rotax 503) *(Wing originally quoted as c/n W157)*						
G-MNNS	Eurowing Goldwing	EW-74		8. 4.86	J.S.R.Moodie	Rovie Farm, Rogart	
	(Rotax 377)				*(Current status unknown)*		
G-MNNV	Mainair Gemini/Flash II	431-586-4 & W187		10. 3.86	M.J.Lea	Tarn Farm, Cockerham	11. 4.02P
	(Rotax 503)						
G-MNNY	Solar Wings Pegasus/Flash			14. 3.86	M.J.& B.L.Edwards	(Penzance)	10. 9.02P
	(Rotax 447)	SW-TB-1059 & SW-WF-0023	*(Mainair sailwing c/n W161)*				
G-MNNZ	Solar Wings Pegasus/Flash II			24. 4.86	R.D.A.Henderson	(Exeter)	1. 4.98P
	(Rotax 447)	SW-TB-1060 & SW-WF-0101	*(Mainair sailwing c/n W162)*		*(Current status unknown)*		
G-MNPA	Solar Wings Pegasus/Flash II			18. 4.86	N.T.Murphy	(Rathongon, Co.Kildare)	30. 5.98P
	(Rotax 462)	SW-TB-1061 & SW-WF-0102			*(New owner 9.01)*		
	(Originally Mainair sailwing c/n W174 but now acquired W210 from G-MNZA)						
G-MNPC	Mainair Gemini/Flash II	423-586-4 & W181		17. 3.86	M.S.McGimpsey	Newtownards, Co Down	29. 7.03P
	(Rotax 462)						
G-MNPG	Mainair Gemini/Flash II	437-686-4 & W204		20. 3.86	P.Kirton	East Fortune	7. 7.02P
	(Rotax 447)						
G-MNPV	Mainair Scorcher Solo	432-586-1 & W189		24. 3.86	A.W.Fish	(Telford)	17. 5.98P
	(Rotax 447)				*(New owner 10.02)*		
G-MNPY	Mainair Scorcher Solo	452-886-1 & W229		25. 3.86	R.N.O.Kingsbury	(Tunbridge Wells)	31. 7.03P
	(Rotax 447)						
G-MNPZ	Mainair Scorcher Solo	449-886-1 & W226		25. 3.86	S.Stevens	(North Shields)	4. 9.93P
	(Rotax 503) *(3-Blade Propeller Test a/c)*				*(Current status unknown)*		
G-MNRD*	Ultraflight Lazair IIIE	81		17. 6.83	Not known	Sywell	15.9.99P
					(Cancelled 5.12.01 by CAA) (Noted 9.02)		
G-MNRE	Mainair Scorcher Solo	453-886-1 & W230		25. 3.86	A.P.Pearce	Wickhambrook, Newmarket	3. 3.03P
	(Rotax 447)						
G-MNRF	Mainair Scorcher Solo	461-986-1 & W238		25. 3.86	Flylight Airsports Ltd	Sywell	1. 8.02P
	(Rotax 447)						
G-MNRG	Mainair Scorcher	462-986-1 & W239		25. 3.86	C.Murphy	Ince Blundell	23.1.01P
	(Rotax 447)						
G-MNRI	Hornet Dual Trainer/Southdown Raven			26. 3.86	D.A.Robinson	Sandtoft	2. 8.02P
	(Rotax 462)	HRWA 0051 & SN2000/0119					
G-MNRK	Hornet Dual Trainer/Southdown Raven			26. 3.86	R.K.Beynon	(Balmedie)	30. 7.95P
	(Rotax 462?)	HRWA 0053 & SN2000/0183			*(Current status unknown)*		
G-MNRL*	Hornet Dual Trainer/Southdown Raven			26. 3.86	A.G.Ward	Long Acre Farm, Sandy	18. 1.01P
	(Rotax 462)	HRWA 0054 & SN2000/0184			*(Cancelled 21.11.01 by CAA)*		
G-MNRM	Hornet Dual Trainer/Southdown Raven			26. 3.86	R.I.Cannan	(Ramsey, Isle of Man)	26.12.02P
	(Rotax 462?)	HRWA 0055 & SN2000/0214					
G-MNRP	Southdown Raven X	SN2232/0135		7. 4.86	C.Moore	(Egremont)	5. 7.95P
	(Rotax 447)				*(Current status unknown)*		
G-MNRS	Southdown Raven X	SN2232/0137		7. 4.86	M.C.Newman	(St.Leonards-on-Sea)	28. 7.03P
	(Rotax 447)						
G-MNRT	Midland Ultralights Sirocco 377GB	MU-016		1. 4.86	R.F.Hinton	(Mansfield)	18. 8.01P
G-MNRW	Mainair Gemini/Flash II	411-486-4 & W156		7. 4.86	T.J.Gayton-Polley	(Billingshurst)	12.10.03P
	(Rotax 462)						
G-MNRX	Mainair Gemini/Flash II	434-686-4 & W220		8. 4.86	J.H.Peet	St.Michaels	8. 5.03P
	(Rotax 503)						
G-MNRY	Mainair Gemini/Flash II	418-486-4 & W169		7. 4.86	M.Carolan	(Coalisland, Dungannon)	13. 8.01P
	(Rotax 462)						
G-MNRZ	Mainair Scorcher Solo	426-586-1 & W184		4. 4.86	R Pattrick	Barton	27. 1.03P
	(Rotax 447)						
G-MNSA	Mainair Gemini/Flash II	442-786-4 & W219		18. 4.86	R.E.Morris	(Kidwelly, Dyfed)	7. 8.01P
	(Rotax 503)						
G-MNSB	Southdown Puma Sprint	539 & SN1121/0066		15. 6.83	T.D.Gibson	(Ledbury)	17. 7.00P
	(Fuji-Robin EC-44-PM)						
G-MNSD	Ultrasports Tripacer 250/Solar Wings Typhoon S4			23. 4.86	A.Strydom	(London WC1)	N/E
	(Hunting HS.260A)	T182-341L			*(New owner 10.02)*		
G-MNSH	Solar Wings Pegasus Flash II			14. 4.86	M.J.Aubrey	(Kington, Hereford)	15. 6.01P
	(Rotax 447)	SW-TB-1063 & SW-WF-0104	*(Mainair sailwing c/n W163)*				
G-MNSI	Mainair Gemini/Flash II	445-786-4 & W213		9. 4.86	A J Foster	Gravely Farm, Herts	9. 6.03P
	(Rotax 462)						
G-MNSJ	Mainair Gemini/Flash II	443-886-4 & W223		11. 4.86	T.K.Duffy	Dunnyvadden	15.12.02P
	(Rotax 503)						
G-MNSL	Southdown Raven X	SN2232/0145		17. 4.86	P.B.Robinson	(Ely)	11. 8.00P
	(Rotax 447)				*(New CofR 5.02)*		
G-MNSN	Solar Wings Pegasus Flash II			25. 4.86	F.R. & V.L.Higgins	Weston Zoyland	19. 4.97P
	(Rotax 447)	SW-TB-1066 & SW-WF-0105	*(Mainair sailwing c/n W173)*		*(Stored in wrecked condition 5.98: current status unknown)*		
G-MNSR*	Mainair Gemini/Flash II	399-486-4 & W144	(G-MNLJ)	17. 4.86	A.M.Bell	(Rufforth)	22. 5.00P
	(Rotax 503)				*(Cancelled 12.4.02 by CAA)*		
G-MNSX	Southdown Raven X	SN2232/0148		30. 4.86	S.F.Chave	(Honiton)	18. 7.03P
	(Rotax 447)						
G-MNSY	Southdown Raven X	SN2232/0149		30. 4.86	L.A.Hosegood	(Swindon)	8. 3.03P
	(Rotax 447)						
G-MNTC	Southdown Raven X	SN2232/0150		30. 4.86	D.S.Bancalari	(Norwich)	12.10.92P
	(Rotax 447)				*(New owner 11.01)*		

Reg	Type	C/n	Date	Owner	Location	Status
G-MNTD	Aerial Arts Chaser/110SX	110SX/255	24. 4.86	B.Richardson	(Sunderland)	
	(C/n duplicates G-MTSF)			*(Current status unknown)*		
G-MNTE	Southdown Raven X (Rotax 447)	SN2232/0151	30. 4.86	E Foster	St.Michaels	27. 6.03P
G-MNTI	Mainair Gemini/Flash II (Rotax 503)	447-886-4 & W231	8. 5.86	R.T.Strathie	(Melrose)	19. 8.01P
G-MNTK	CFM Shadow CD (Rotax 503)	024	8. 5.86	A.B.Potts	Eshott	17. 8.02P
G-MNTM	Southdown Raven X (Rotax 447)	SN2232/0154	19. 5.86	D.M.Garland	(Atherstone)	24. 7.01P
G-MNTN	Southdown Raven X (Rotax 447)	SN2232/0155	2. 6.86	J.Hall	(Wolverhampton)	31.12.03P
G-MNTP	CFM Shadow C (Rotax 462)	K.022	19. 5.86	E.G.White	Lower Upham Farm, Chiseldon	23. 9.03P
G-MNTS	Mainair Gemini/Flash II (Rotax 462)	450-886-4 & W227	3. 4.86	J.A.Colley	Over Farm, Gloucester	16. 1.02P
G-MNTT	Medway Half Pint/Aerial Arts 130SX (Rotax 462)	12/1486	7. 4.86	P.Sykes	(Bournemouth)	20. 6.03P
G-MNTU	Mainair Gemini/Flash II (Rotax 462?)	460-886-4 & W233	9. 7.86	S.Cogger	(Wickford)	15. 7.03P
G-MNTV	Mainair Gemini/Flash II (Rotax 462)	455-886-4 & W241	9. 7.86	D.R.Coles	Davidstow Moor	10.10.02P
G-MNTX	Mainair Gemini/Flash II (Rotax 503)	415-486-4 & W166	20. 5.86	S.S.Thornton	St.Michaels	19. 9.03P
G-MNTY	Southdown Raven X (Rotax 447)	SN2232/0157	29. 5.86	S.Phillips	(Snodland)	21. 5.02P
G-MNTZ	Mainair Gemini/Flash II (Rotax 503)	457-886-4 & W243	3. 6.86	R.W.Trenholm	Otherton, Cannock	4. 4.03P
G-MNUA	Mainair Gemini/Flash II (Rotax 462)	458-886-4 & W235	29. 5.86	J.McCullough	Castlewellan, Co.Down	16. 2.03P
G-MNUD	Solar Wings Pegasus Flash II (Rotax 462) SW-TE-0003 & SW-WF-0110		10. 6.86	P.G.H.Milbank	Sutton Meadows, Ely	20. 9.03P
	(Mainair sailwing c/n W195)					
G-MNUE	Solar Wings Pegasus Flash II (Rotax 462) SW-TE-0002 & SW-WF-0108		10. 6.86	P.M.Rogers	(Rochdale)	20.11.03P
	(Originally Mainair sailwing c/n W193 but fitted with W209 (ex original G-MNYA)					
G-MNUF	Mainair Gemini/Flash II (Rotax 503)	472-786-4 & W252	13. 6.86	C.Hannaby	Guy Lane Farm, Waverton	6. 8.03P
G-MNUG	Mainair Gemini/Flash II (Rotax 462)	465-986-4 & W245	13. 6.86	K.D.Adams	(Wirral)	22. 7.02P
G-MNUI	Mainair Tri-Flyer/Skyhook Cutlass (Fuji-Robin EC-44-PM)	MH-01	21. 5.86	M.Holling	(Goole)	28. 2.87E
	(Current status unknown)					
G-MNUL*	Midland Ultralights SX130/Firefly SX130/315 & MU-F013		9. 7.86	Not known	Sywell	
	(Cancelled by CAA 12.9.94) (Trike noted stored 9.02)					
G-MNUM	Mainair Gemini Sprint MS	226-184-2-P.508	12. 3.84	J.A.Sims	(Farnham)	18.10.03P
	(Fuji-Robin EC-44-PM) *(Trike originally allocated to G-MNMC)*					
G-MNUO	Mainair Gemini/Flash II (Rotax 462)	421-586-4 & W179	9. 7.86	P.S.Taylor	(Weybridge)	11. 5.02P
G-MNUR	Mainair Gemini/Flash II (Rotax 503)	470-986-4 & W250	14. 8.86	J.C.Greves	(Cobham)	30. 3.90P
				(Current status unknown)		
G-MNUU	Southdown Raven X (Rotax 447)	SN2232/0162	26. 6.86	P.N.Jackson	Davidstow Moor	10. 9.02P
G-MNUX	Solar Wings Pegasus XL-R (Rotax 447) SW-TB-1072 & SW-WA-1076		24. 6.86	A.M.Smith	(Newcastle upon Tyne)	3. 5.03P
G-MNUY	Mainair Gemini/Flash II (Rotax 503)	422-586-4 & W180	23. 6.86	M.Nymark	Newtownards, Co.Down	12.10.03P
G-MNVB	Solar Wings Pegasus XL-R (Rotax 447) SW-TB-1073 & SW-WA-1077		7. 7.86	M.J.Melvin	(Spalding)	13. 8.03P
G-MNVC	Solar Wings Pegasus XL-R (Rotax 447) SW-TB-1074 & SW-WA-1078		7. 7.86	M.N.C.Ward	Shobdon	11. 6.00P
G-MNVE	Solar Wings Pegasus XL-R (Rotax 447) SW-TB-1075 & SW-WA-1079		19. 6.86	M.P.Aris	(Welwyn)	11. 8.00P
G-MNVG	Solar Wings Pegasus Flash II (Rotax 447) SW-TB-1069 & SW-WF-0109		11. 6.86	D.J.Ward	Low Farm, South Walsham	6. 8.03P
	(Mainair sailwing c/n W194)					
G-MNVH	Solar Wings Pegasus Flash II (Rotax 462) SW-TE-0001 & SW-WF-0122		23. 6.86	J.A.Clarke & C.Hall	(London N22/E8)	9. 4.97P
	(Mainair sailwing c/n W260)		*(Current status unknown)*			
G-MNVI	CFM Shadow C (Rotax 503)	026	17. 6.86	D.R.C.Pugh	(Caersws, Powys)	17. 9.03P
G-MNVJ	CFM Shadow CD (Rotax 503)	028	17. 6.86	V.C.Readhead	(Saxmundham)	4. 5.02P
G-MNVK	CFM Shadow CD (Rotax 503)	029	17. 6.86	M.Cheetham	(Cuffley)	31. 7.02P
G-MNVL	Medway Half Pint/Aerial Arts 130SX (JPX PUL 425) 3/21585 & 130SX-100	G-MNBZ	22. 9.86	R.E.Symonds	(Woking)	5. 3.03P
G-MNVN	Southdown Puma Raven (Fuji-Robin EC-44-PM)	SN2132/0165	27. 6.86	P.A.Jones	North Coates	16.11.02P
G-MNVO	Hovey Whing-Ding II	CW-01	14. 8.86	C.Wilson *(New CofR 5.02)*	(Basildon)	
G-MNVP	Southdown Raven X (Rotax 447)	SN2232/0166	(EI-) G-MNVP	23. 6.86	N.Furlong	(Stradbally, Co.Laois)	19.12.03P
				(New owner 11.02)		
G-MNVT	Mainair Gemini/Flash II (Rotax 503)	477-786-4 & W258	27. 6.86	A.C.Barker,	Hinton in the Hedges	28. 7.87P
				t/a ACB Hydraulics *(Stored 4.90: current status unknown)*		
G-MNVU	Mainair Gemini/Flash II (Rotax 503)	468-986-4 & W248	26. 6.86	W.R.Marsh	Newhouse Farm, Hardwicke, Hereford	28. 6.99P
				(Current status unknown)		
G-MNVV	Mainair Gemini/Flash II (Rotax 503)	467-986-4 & W247	26. 6.86	R.P.Hothersall	St.Michaels	1. 5.02P
				(Op Northern Microlight School)		
G-MNVW	Mainair Gemini/Flash II (Rotax 503)	466-986-4 & W246	26. 6.86	J.C.Munro-Hunt	Little Down Farm, Milson	20. 9.98P
				(Current status unknown)		
G-MNVZ	Solar Wings Pegasus Photon (Solo 210) SW-TP-0021 & SW-WP-0021		27. 6.86	J.J.Russ	Eshott	27. 6.94P
				(Current status unknown)		

G-MNWA	Southdown Raven X (Rotax 447)	SN2232/0167	26. 6.86	P.R.Miller	(St. Neots)	9.11.02P
G-MNWD	Mainair Gemini/Flash II (Rotax 462)	474-986-4 & W254	27. 6.86	M.B.Rutherford	Swinford, Rugby	7. 7.01P
G-MNWG	Southdown Raven X (Rotax 447)	SN2232/0170	4. 8.86	D.Murray	(Clevedon)	28. 1.02P
G-MNWI	Mainair Gemini/Flash II (Rotax 503)	478-986-4 & W264	9. 7.86	W.H.Gilbertson	(Manchester)	10. 5.02P
G-MNWK	CFM Shadow C (Rotax 503)	030	9. 7.86	J.E.Hunt (Current status unknown)	(Welling, Kent)	19. 8.98P
G-MNWL	Arbiter Services Trike/Aerial Arts 130S	130SX/333	23. 7.86	E.H.Snook (Current status unknown)	(Newport Pagnell)	
G-MNWP	Solar Wings Pegasus/Flash II (Rotax 447)	SW-TB-1083 & SW-WF-0113 (Mainair sailwing c/n W198)	4. 8.86	P.J.Harrison (Cancelled 28.8.02 by CAA)	(Beccles)	19. 3.03P
G-MNWU	Solar Wings Pegasus/Flash II (Rotax 462)	SW-TE-0006 & SW-WF-0111 (Mainair sailwing c/n W196)	4. 8.86	F.J.E.Brownshill & W.Parkin	Field Farm, Oakley	26. 4.03P
G-MNWV	Solar Wings Pegasus/Flash II (Rotax 447)	SW-TB-1090 & SW-WF-0121 (Mainair sailwing c/n W206)	4. 8.86	A.T.Palmer tr Pegasus Group	Davidstow Moor	17. 8.03P
G-MNWW	Solar Wings Pegasus XL Tug (Rotax 462)	SW-TE-0008 & SW-WA-1085	8.10.86	N.P.Chitty tr Chiltern Flyers Aero Tow Group	Ginge Farm, Wantage	3. 8.03P
G-MNWY	CFM Shadow C (Rotax 503)	K.021 & PFA 161-11130	28. 7.86	N.E.Gormley (New owner 9.02)	(Dublin)	19. 8.03P
G-MNWZ	Mainair Gemini/Flash II (Rotax 503)	436-686-4 & W203 (G-MNXV)	19. 8.86	W.T.Hume (Current status unknown)	(Newmilns)	16. 6.98P
G-MNXA	Southdown Raven X (Rotax 447)	SN2232/0180	5. 8.86	B.D.Acres	(Maidstone)	28. 6.02P
G-MNXB	Mainair Tri-Flyer/Solar Wings Photon (Fuji-Robin EC-34-PM)	016-29981 & SW-WP-0022	29. 7.86	G.W.Carwardine (Current status unknown)	(Uckfield)	16. 6.98P
G-MNXE	Southdown Raven X (Rotax 447)	SN2232/0202	7. 8.86	A.E.Silvey	Wilburton, Ely	30.11.02P
G-MNXF	Southdown Puma Raven (Fuji-Robin EC-44-PM)	SN2132/0176	2. 9.86	D.E.Gwenin (Current status unknown)	(Tring)	13. 5.99P
G-MNXG	Southdown Raven X (Rotax 447)	SN2232/0181	3. 9.86	M.A.Williams	(Tonbridge)	22. 7.02P
G-MNXI	Southdown Raven X (Rotax 447)	SN2232/0179	19. 8.86	A.M.Yates (Current status unknown)	(Wisbech)	13. 7.96P
G-MNXO	Medway Hybred 44XLR (Rotax 447)	29786/19	3. 9.86	D.L.Turner	(Chatham)	6. 7.02P
G-MNXP	Solar Wings Pegasus Flash II (Rotax 447)	SW-TB-1094 & SW-WF-0117 (Mainair sailwing c/n W207)	16. 9.86	D.Harrison (Current status unknown)	(Bewdley)	6. 8.96P
G-MNXS	Mainair Gemini/Flash II (Rotax 462)	480-986-4 & W267	8. 9.86	F.T.Rawlings (Believed exported to Portugal c1988?: valid CofR 3.02)	(Hereford)	16. 3.89P
G-MNXU	Mainair Gemini/Flash II (Rotax 503)	482-1086-4 & W272	18. 8.86	J.M.Hucker (Current status unknown)	(Abertillery)	10. 3.98P
G-MNXX	CFM Shadow CD (Rotax 503)	K.027	13. 8.86	M.Oddone	Old Sarum	9. 2.03P
G-MNXZ	Whittaker MW5 Sorcerer (Fuji-Robin EC-34-PM)	PFA 163-11156	13. 8.86	P.J.Cheyney	Newhouse Farm, Loughborough	3. 6.02P
G-MNYA	Solar Wings Pegasus Flash II (Rotax 447)	SW-TB-1098 & SW-WF-0119 (Originally laid down with Mainair sailwing c/n W209 but changed to W259 - see G-MNUE)	3. 9.86	P.C.Stappleton	(Mold)	19. 1.02P
G-MNYB	Solar Wings Pegasus XL-R (Rotax 447)	SW-TB-1096 & SW-WA-1089	8. 9.86	O.P.Farrell	Drogheda, Co.Meath	8. 7.03P
G-MNYC	Solar Wings Pegasus XL-R (Rotax 447)	SW-TB-1097 & SW-WA-1090	3. 9.86	A.N.Papworth	Sutton Meadows. Ely	16. 7.03P
G-MNYD	Aerial Arts Chaser/110SX (Rotax 377)	110SX/320	19. 8.86	B.Richardson	(Sunderland)	25. 7.02P
G-MNYE	Aerial Arts Chaser/110SX (Rotax 337)	110SX/321	19. 8.86	R.J.Ripley (New owner 6.00)	(Oakley, Beds)	18.11.99P
G-MNYF	Aerial Arts Chaser/110SX (Rotax 377)	110SX/322	19. 8.86	B.Richardson	(Sunderland)	26. 7.03P
G-MNYG	Southdown Puma Raven (Fuji-Robin EC-44-PM)	SN2122/0172	19. 8.86	K.Clifford	(Stanmore)	3. 7.00P
G-MNYJ	Mainair Gemini/Flash II (Rotax 462)	485-1086-4 & W275	8. 9.86	G.B.Jones	Otherton, Cannock	13. 7.03P
G-MNYK	Mainair Gemini/Flash II	494-1086-4 & W296	11. 9.86	J.J.Ryan (Current status unknown)	(Enniscorthy, Co.Wexford)	4.10.95P
G-MNYL	Southdown Raven X (Rotax 447)	SN2232/0195	2. 9.86	A.D.F.Clifford (Current status unknown)	Broadmeadow Farm, Hereford	9. 6.98P
G-MNYM	Southdown Raven X (Rotax 447)	SN2232/0196	2. 9.86	A.D.Montriou & C.E.Arter	Dunkeswell	13. 8.00P
G-MNYP	Southdown Raven X (Rotax 447)	SN2232/0207	3. 9.86	A.G.Davies	(Bristol)	14. 5.01P
G-MNYS	Southdown Raven X/Se (Rotax 447)	SN2232/0208	8. 9.86	B.Ward (Current status unknown)	(Sheerness)	9. 1.99P
G-MNYU	Solar Wings Pegasus XL-R/Se (Rotax 447)	SW-TB-1100 & SW-WA-1092	16. 9.86	A.M.Sutton	(Stourbridge)	22. 4.03P
G-MNYW	Solar Wings Pegasus XL-R (Rotax 447)	SW-TB-1102 & SW-WA-1094	11. 9.86	M.P.Waldock (Current status unknown)	(Selsdon, Surrey)	7. 8.98P
G-MNYX	Solar Wings Pegasus XL-R (Rotax 462)	SW-TE-0009 & SW-WA-1095	19. 9.86	P.Mayes & J.P.Widdowson (See G-MMKG)	(Bridgnorth)	15. 6.03P
G-MNYZ	Solar Wings Pegasus Flash II (Rotax 462)	SW-TE-0010 & SW-WF-0114 (Mainair sailwing c/n W199)	11. 9.86	A.C.Bartolozzi	(Ely)	9. 3.00P
G-MNZB	Mainair Gemini/Flash II (Rotax 503)	483-1086-4 & W273	8. 9.86	P.A.Ryde	(Knebworth)	13. 2.03P
G-MNZC	Mainair Gemini/Flash II (Rotax 503)	484-1086-4 & W274	6. 9.86	C.J.Whittaker (New CofR 11.02)	(Ledbury)	19. 1.89P
G-MNZD	Mainair Gemini/Flash II (Rotax 503)	493-1086-4 & W295	8. 9.86	N.D.Carter (Stored 9.96: current status unknown)	Little Gransden	4. 4.96P
G-MNZE	Mainair Gemini/Flash II (Rotax 503) (Wing regd as W279 - see G-MTEK)	495-1086-4 & W297	8. 9.86	K.J.Hughes	Tarn Farm, Cockerham	16. 7.01P
G-MNZF	Mainair Gemini/Flash II (Rotax 503)	496-1186-4 & W291	8. 9.86	A.L.Wright	Swinford, Rugby	29. 5.03P
G-MNZJ	CFM Shadow CD (Rotax 503)	033	19. 9.86	T.E.P.Eves tr G-MNZJ Shadow Group	Baxby Manor, Husthwaite	11. 5.03P
G-MNZK	Solar Wings Pegasus XL-R/Se (Rotax 447)	SW-WA-1096	24. 9.86	J.G.Campbell & P.J.Perkins	Sandtoft	23. 7.02P

Reg	Type	c/n	Prev id	Date	Owner	Location	Status
G-MNZO	Solar Wings Pegasus Flash II	SW-TE-0012 & SW-WF-0125	*(Mainair sailwing c/n W218)*	30. 9.86	K.B.Woods & D.Johnson	Newnham, Baldock	13.10.03P
	(Rotax 462)						
G-MNZP	CFM Shadow BD	K.039 & PFA 161-11206		19. 9.86	J.G.Wakeford	Deanland, Hailsham	21. 6.03P
	(Rotax 447)						
G-MNZR	CFM Shadow BD	040		19. 9.86	J.S.Wilson	Priory Farm, Tibenham	24. 7.03P
	(Rotax 447)						
G-MNZS	Aerial Arts Alpha/130SX	130SX/376		23. 9.86	N.R.Beale	Deppers Bridge, Warwick	1. 8.00P
	(Rotax 277)						
G-MNZU	Eurowing Goldwing	EW-88		24. 9.86	H.B.Baker	Chilbolton	11.10.02P
	(Fuji-Robin EC-34-PM)						
G-MNZW	Southdown Raven X	SN2232/0220		17.10.86	C.A.James	Doynton	7. 7.02P
G-MNZX	Southdown Raven X	SN2232/0221		10.10.86	B.F.Hole	(East Grinstead)	3. 7.03P
	(Rotax 447)						
G-MNZZ	CFM Shadow CD	036		19. 9.86	P.J.Lynch	(Farnborough)	26. 7.03P
	(Rotax 503)						
G-MOAC	Beech F33A Bonanza	CE-1349	N1563N	25. 5.89	R.L.Camrass	Alderney	30. 5.04
G-MOBI	Aérospatiale AS355F1 Twin Squirrel	5260	G-MUFF G-CORR	11.11.93	Faiman Aviation Ltd	Redhill	18. 4.03T
G-MODE	Eurocopter EC120B	1295		19. 8.02	N.J.Ferris t/a Brilliant	(Chipping Norton)	17.11.05T
G-MOFB	Cameron O-120 HAB	4275		13. 1.98	D.M.Moffat	Chateaux d'Oex, Switzerland	5. 1.03A
G-MOFF	Cameron O-77 HAB	2040		27. 7.89	D.M.Moffat *"Moff"*	Alveston, Bristol	7. 9.95A
					(Current status unknown)		
G-MOFZ	Cameron O-90 HAB	3350		7. 9.94	D.M.Moffat	Alveston, Bristol	6. 1.03A
G-MOGI	Grumman-American AA-5A Cheetah	AA5A-0630	G-BFMU	1. 5.86	J.G.Stewart tr MOGI Flying Group	(Milton Keynes)	16.12.05
G-MOGY	Robinson R22 Beta	0899		23.11.88	S.G.Simpson Culter Helipad, Lower Baads, Peterculter		25. 1.04T
					t/a HJS Helicopters		
G-MOHS	Piper PA-31-350 Chieftain	31-8152115	G-BWOC N40898/CP-1665	29. 4.96	Sky Air Travel Ltd	Stapleford	28. 9.03T
G-MOJO	Airbus Industrie A330-243	301	F-WWYE	8.11.99	MyTravel Airways Ltd	Manchester	7.11 05T
G-MOKE	Cameron V-77 HAB	3686		4.10.95	D.D.Owen	Wotton-under-Edge	22.12.02A
G-MOLE	Taylor JT.2 Titch	PFA 60-10725		20. 1.87	S.R.Mowle	(Kenley)	
	(Continental O-200-A)				*(Under construction 10.90: current status unknown)*		
G-MOLI	Cameron A-250 HAB	3429		26. 1.95	J.J.Rudoni	Malpas	15.10.03T
					(Op Balloon Preservation Group) "Molly"		
G-MOLL	Piper PA-32-301T Turbo Saratoga	32-8024040	N82535	25. 3.91	N.A.M. & R.A.Brain	Netherthorpe	12. 5.03
G-MOLY	Piper PA-23-160 Apache	23-1686	EI-BAW G-APFV/EI-ALK/N10F	7. 6.79	R.R. & M.T.Thorogood	Henstridge	28. 2.05
G-MOMO	Agusta A109E Power	11154		30. 4.02	Air Harrods Ltd	Stansted	30. 4.05T
G-MONB	Boeing 757-2T7ER	22780		7. 3.83	Monarch Airlines Ltd	Luton	1. 2.03T
G-MONC	Boeing 757-2T7ER	22781	PH-AHO D-ABNY/G-MONC/EC-211/G-MONC	15. 4.83	Monarch Airlines Ltd	Luton	29. 4.05T
G-MOND	Boeing 757-2T7	22960	D-ABNZ G-MOND	28. 4.83	Monarch Airlines Ltd	Luton	13. 5.05T
G-MONE	Boeing 757-2T7ER	23293		27. 2.85	Monarch Airlines Ltd *(Renaissance Cruise titles)*	Luton	25. 2.03T
G-MONI	Monnett Moni	PFA 142-10925		12. 1.84	R.M.Edworthy	(Littleover)	16. 4.02P
	(IAME KFM.107)						
G-MONJ	Boeing 757-2T7ER	24104		26. 2.88	Monarch Airlines Ltd	Luton	23. 1.03T
G-MONK	Boeing 757-2T7ER	24105		26. 2.88	Monarch Airlines Ltd	Luton	31. 5.05T
G-MONR	Airbus Industrie A300B4-605R	540	VH-YMJ G-MONR/F-WWAT	15. 3.90	Monarch Airlines Ltd	Luton	2. 4.05T
G-MONS	Airbus Industrie A300B4-605R	556	VH-YMK G-MONS/F-WWAY	17. 4.90	Monarch Airlines Ltd	Luton	23. 3.03T
G-MONW	Airbus Industrie A320-212	391	F-WWDO	24. 2.93	Monarch Airlines Ltd	Luton	7. 3.03T
G-MONX	Airbus Industrie A320-212	392	F-WWDR	19. 3.93	Monarch Airlines Ltd	Luton	17. 3.03T
G-MOOR	SOCATA TB-10 Tobago	82	G-MILK	23. 7.91	M.Watkin	(Sheffield)	31.10.04
G-MOOS	Hunting-Percival P.56 Provost T.1	PAC/F/335	G-BGKA 8041M/XF690	5. 4.91	T.J.Manna	North Weald	17. 6.02P
					t/a Kennet Aviation *(As "XF690" in RAF c/s)*		
G-MOPB	Diamond DA40 Star	40067		19.11.01	Papa Bravo Aviation Ltd	Teesside	5. 3.05T
G-MOSS	Beech D55 Baron	TE-548	G-AWAD	12. 6.95	A.G.E.Camisa	Elstree	5. 6.03
G-MOSY	Cameron O-84 HAB	2315	EI-CAO	17. 4.96	P.L.Mossman	Bristol	30.5.03A
G-MOTA	Bell 206B-3 JetRanger III	4494	N81521	20.10.98	J W Sandle	Runcton Holme, King's Lynn	28.10.04T
G-MOTH	de Havilland DH.82A Tiger Moth	85340	7035M DE306	31. 1.78	M.C.Russell	Audley End	3. 4.05
	(Composite rebuild to DH.82 standard)				*(As "K-2567")*		
G-MOTI	Robin DR500/200i President	0006		23.11.98	O.Graham-Flatebo & The Lord Saville of Newdigate		11.02.05
	(Registered as DR400/500)				tr The Tango India Flying Group	Biggin Hill	
G-MOTO	Piper PA-24-180 Comanche	24-3239	G-EDHE N51867/G-ASFH/EI-AMM/N7998P	24. 3.87	L.T. & S.Evans	Sandown	11.11.05
G-MOUL	Maule M-6-235C Super Rocket	7518C		1. 5.90	M.Klinge	Prestwick	11. 5.03
G-MOUN	Beech B200 Super King Air	BB-1734	N123NA JA200N/N123NA	27. 9.02	G.& H.L.Mountain	(Ilkley)	7.11.05T
G-MOUR	Folland Gnat T.1	FL.596	8624M XS102	16. 5.90	R.F.Harvey & M.J.Gadsby *(New owners 6.02)*	Kemble	29. 4.99P
					tr Yellowjack Group *(As "XR991" in Yellowjacks c/s)*		
G-MOVE	Piper Aerostar 601P	61P-0593-7963263	OO-PKB G-MOVE/N8144J	5. 1.79	A. Kazaz	Leicester	6. 8.05
G-MOVI	Piper PA-32R-301 Saratoga SP	32R-8313029	G-MARI N8248H	6. 2.89	G-BOON Ltd	Cranfield	22. 2.03T
G-MOZZ	Avions Mudry CAP.10B	256		30.10.90	N.Skipworth & J.R.W.Luxton	Booker	2. 5.03
G-MPAC	Pelican PL	PFA 165-12944		6. 4.00	M.J.Craven	Rayne Hall Farm, Rayne	12. 6.03P
G-MPBH	Reims/Cessna FA152 Aerobat	FA15200374	G-FLIC G-BILV	8.12.88	The Moray Flying Club (1990)	RAF Kinloss	18. 8.05T
G-MPBI	Cessna 310R II	310R0584	F-GEBB HB-LMD/N87473	21. 7.97	M.P.Bolshaw & Co Ltd	Elstree	15. 8.03
G-MPCD	Airbus Industrie A320-212	379	C-GZCD	14. 3.94	Monarch Airlines Ltd	Luton	1. 5.04T
			G-MPCD/C-FTDU/G-MPCD/C-FTDU/G-MPCD/C-FTDU/G-MPCD/C-FTDU/G-MPCD/F-WWDY				

Reg	Type	C/n	Prev id	Date	Owner/Operator	Location	Date
G-MPRL	Cessna 210M Centurion	21061892	EC-GKD N732YY	5. 8.02	Myriad Public Relations Ltd		
						Top Farm, Croydon, Royston	17.10.05T
G-MPWH*	Rotorway Executive	3579		22. 6.90	Thistle Aviation Ltd	Henley-on-Thames	
					(Cancelled 28.3.00 by CAA - no Permit or CofA issued: believed stored incomplete)		
G-MPWI	Robin HR100/210	163	F-GBTY F-ODFA/F-BUPD	3. 3.80	Propwash Investments Ltd	Swansea	9. 5.05
G-MPWT	Piper PA-34-220T Seneca III	34-8333068	N4294X N888DB/N4294X/N9539N/N8218K	26. 9.88	Modern Air (UK) Ltd *"Duke 2"*	Fowlmere	19. 5.04T
	(Originally built as c/n 34-8233163)						
G-MRAJ	MD Helicopters Hughes 369E (500E)	0010E	N51946	19. 3.98	A.Jardine	Sywell	10. 6.06
G-MRAM	Mignet HM-1000 Balerit (Rotax 582)	134		15.11.99	R.A.Marven Tower Hill Lane, Coleman Green, Herts		17.11.02P
G-MRED	Elmwood CA-05 Christavia Mk.1 PFA 185-12935			2. 8.96	E.Hewett *(Current status unknown)*	(Fareham)	
G-MRJJ	Pegasus Quik	7941		3.03R			
G-MRKT	Lindstrand LBL-90A HAB	037		7. 6.93	Marketplace Public Relations (London) Ltd *"Kaytee"*		
						Crowthorne, Berks	21. 2.03A
G-MRLN	Sky 240-24 HAB	161		4. 8.99	M.Wady t/a Merlin Balloons	Hamstreet	8.5.03T
G-MRMR	Piper PA-31-350 Navajo Chieftain	31-7952092	OH-PRE G-WROX/G-BNZI/N3517T	21. 8.97	I.D. & P.J.Margetson-Rushmor, t/a MRMR Flight Services	Stapleford	22.12.03T
G-MROC	Pegasus Quantum 15-912	7498		22. 1.99	M.Convine	Tower Farm, Wollaston	13. 4.03P
G-MROY	Comco Ikarus C42	PFA 322-13758		9.10.01	D.M.Jobbins & K.R.Rowland	(Northampton)	9. 1.03P
G-MRSG	Canadair CL600-2C10 *(CRJ 700)*	10052	C-GIAR	2. 8.02	Maersk Air Ltd	Birmingham	5. 8.05T
G-MRSH	Canadair CL600-2C10 *(CRJ 700)*	10048	C-GIAI	31. 7.02	Maersk Air Ltd	Birmingham	30.7.05T
G-MRSI	Canadair CL600-2C10 *(CRJ 700)*	10039	C-GICL	9. 4.02	Maersk Air Ltd	Birmingham	11.4.05T
G-MRSJ	Canadair CL600-2C10 *(CRJ 700)*	10029		20.11.01	Maersk Air Ltd	Birmingham	21.11.04T
G-MRSK	Canadair CL600-2C10 *(CRJ 700)*	10028	C-GIBG	16.10.01	Maersk Air Ltd	Birmingham	17.10.04T
G-MRSN	Robinson R22 Beta	1654		21. 1.91	M D Thorpe, t/a Yorkshire Helicopters	Coney Park, Leeds	11. 6.03T
G-MRST	Piper PA-28RT-201 Arrow IV	28R-7918068	9H-AAU 5B-CEC/N3019U	27.11.86	Calverton Flying Group Ltd	(London W4)	8. 4.05T
G-MRTN	SOCATA TB-10 Tobago	62	G-BHET	9. 7.98	Underwood Kitchens Ltd	Turweston	30. 4.04
G-MRTY	Cameron N-77 HAB	1008		24. 4.84	R.A, P.M.G. & N.T.M. Vale *"Marty"*	Kidderminster	19. 5.96A
					(New owners 7.01)		
G-MSAL	Morane-Saulnier MS.733 Alcyon	143	F-BLXV Fr.Mil	16. 6.93	North Weald Flying Services Ltd	North Weald	
					(As "143" in Aeronavale c/s) (Dismantled 6.02)		
G-MSFC	Piper PA-38-112 Tomahawk II	38-81A0067	N25735	11. 5.90	Sherwood Flying Club Ltd	Nottingham	28.10.05T
G-MSFT	Piper PA-28-161 Warrior II	28-8416093	G-MUMS N118AV	2. 4.97	N.E.Dauncey	Compton Abbas	1. 5.03T
G-MSIX	DG Flugzeugbau DG-800B	8-156B80		21. 4.99	E.Coles	Dunstable	29. 5.05
	(New fuselage c/n 274 fitted c8.02)				tr G-MSIX Group		
	(Struck hedge making forced landing Cropthorne near Bidford 15.6.02 due to engine failure: substantial damage to fuselage & tailplane)						
G-MSKK	Canadair CL600-2B19 *(CRJ 200)*	7226	OY-MBO G-MSKK/C-GCBS/C-FMKZ	25. 5.98	Maersk Air Ltd	Birmingham	14.10.05T
G-MSKR	Canadair CL600-2B19 *(CRJ 200)*	7373	C-FMNB	24. 2.00	Maersk Air Ltd	Birmingham	27. 3.03T
G-MSKS	Canadair CL600-2B19 *(CRJ 200)*	7386	C-FMNW	3. 4.00	Maersk Air Ltd	Birmingham	5. 4.03T
G-MSKT	Canadair CL600-2B19 *(CRJ 200)*	7436	C-FMKZ	23.10.00	Maersk Air Ltd	Birmingham	24.10.03T
G-MSKU	Canadair CL600-2B19 *(CRJ 200)*	7442	C-GHTK C-FMLU	10.11.00	Maersk Air Ltd	Birmingham	12.11.03T
G-MSKV	Canadair CL600-2B19 *(CRJ 200)*			R	Maersk Air Ltd	Birmingham	
G-MSKY	Comco Ikarus C42	PFA 322-13722		3.10.01	C.K.Jones	Sywell	20. 1.03P
G-MSPY	Pegasus Quantum 15-912	7625		17. 3.00	J.Madhvani & R.K.Green	Plaistows Farm, St Albans	15. 3.03P
G-MSTC	Gulfstream AA-5A Cheetah	AA5A-0833	G-BIJT N26950	30. 1.95	Ardlui Ltd	(Douglas, Isle of Man)	19. 2.05T
G-MSTG	North American P-51D-25-NT Mustang 124-48271		NZ2427 45-11518	2. 9.97	M.Hammond *"Janie"*	Airfield Farm, Hardwick	19. 8.03P
					("414419/LH-F" in USAAF c/s of 350th Fighter Sqdn/353rd Fighter Gp)		
G-MSTR	Cameron Monster-110SS HAB	4957	G-OJOB	18. 7.01	Virgin Airship & Balloon Co Ltd	Telford	16.12.02P
G-MTAA	Solar Wings Pegasus XL-R			15.10.86	R.Scott	London Colney	30. 5.02P
	(Rotax 447) SW-TB-1108 & SW-WA-1102						
G-MTAB	Mainair Gemini/Flash II	492-1086-4 & W290		8.10.86	C.Thompson	(Wolverhampton)	2. 6.02P
	(Rotax 503)						
G-MTAC	Mainair Gemini/Flash II	486-1086-4 & W278		15.10.86	L.A.Le Roux	St.Michaels	15. 5.03P
	(Rotax 503)						
G-MTAE	Mainair Gemini/Flash II	500-1186-4 & W302		15.10.86	M.Fowler	(Camborne)	26. 6.03P
	(Rotax 503)						
G-MTAF	Mainair Gemini/Flash II	499-1186-4 & W301		5.10.86	P.A.Long	St Michaels	10.11.02P
	(Rotax 503)				*(Op North Lancs Micro School)*		
G-MTAG	Mainair Gemini/Flash II	487-1086-4 & W281		15.10.86	M.J.Cowie & J.P.Hardy	(Upton, Wirral)	7. 5.03P
	(Rotax 503)						
G-MTAH	Mainair Gemini/Flash II	488-1086-4 & W282		16.10.86	T.G.Elmhirst	St.Michaels	15. 9.03P
	(Rotax 503)						
G-MTAI	Solar Wings Pegasus XL-R			14.10.86	D.Ruston	(Sheffield)	27. 1.02P
	(Rotax 503) SW-TB-1109 & SW-WA-1103						
G-MTAJ	Solar Wings Pegasus XL-R			16.10.86	G.A. & S.D.Batchelor	(Launceston)	31. 7.02P
	(Rotax 447) SW-TB-1110 & SW-WA-1104						
G-MTAL	Solar Wings Pegasus Photon			15.10.86	R.P.Wilkinson	(Bath)	29.10.95P
	(Solo 210) SW-TP-0023 & SW-WP-0023				*(Being converted to Rotax 277)(Current status unknown)*		
G-MTAO	Solar Wings Pegasus XL-R			21.10.86	S.P.Disney & R.Jones	Swinford, Rugby	26. 6.01P
	(Rotax 447) SW-TB-1107 & SW-WA-1107						
G-MTAP	Southdown Raven X	SN2232/0225		15.10.86	M.C.Newman	(St.Leonards-on-Sea)	13. 6.98P
	(Rotax 447)				*(Current status unknown) (New owner 9.02)*		
G-MTAR	Mainair Gemini Flash II	504-1286-4-W307		16.10.86	J.B.Woolley	(Madrid, Spain)	31. 5.03P
	(Rotax 462)						
G-MTAS	Whittaker MW5 Sorcerer	PFA 163-11166		14.10.86	M.J.Badham	(Woodbridge)	30. 6.03P
	(Rotax 503-IV) *(May be Model MW5C?)*						
G-MTAT*	Solar Wings Pegasus XL-R			28.10.86	J.Ryan	(Enniscorthy, Co.Wexford)	4. 7.01P
	(Rotax 447) SW-TB-1113 & SW-WA-1108				*(Cancelled 15.8.01 by CAA)*		

Registration	Type / (Engine)	C/n	Date	Owner	Location	Date
G-MTAV	Solar Wings Pegasus XL-R (Rotax 447) SW-TB-1115 & SW-WA-1110		21.10.86	Susan Fairweather & Carolyn L.Harris (Nottingham/Warrington)		19. 5.03P
G-MTAW	Solar Wings Pegasus XL-R (Rotax 447) SW-TB-1116 & SW-WA-1111		21.10.86	M.G.Ralph	Weston Zoyland	13. 7.03P
G-MTAX	Solar Wings Pegasus XL-R (Rotax 447) SW-TB-1117 & SW-WA-1112		27.10.86	G Hawes	Great Glen	31. 7.03P
G-MTAY	Solar Wings Pegasus XL-R (Rotax 447) SW-TB-1118 & SW-WA-1113		27.10.86	S.A.McLatchie	Enstone	13. 8.03P
G-MTAZ	Solar Wings Pegasus XL-R (Rotax 447) SW-TB-1119 & SW-WA-1114		28.10.86	J.P.Whitehead Llansalnt, Carmarthen *(Noted 2.03)*		25. 3.01P
G-MTBA	Solar Wings Pegasus XL-R (Rotax 447) SW-TB-1120 & SW-WA-1115		27.10.86	R.J.W.Franklin & M.C.Buffery (Cheltenham) *(Wrecked 5.97: current status unknown)*		24. 6.93P
G-MTBB	Southdown Raven X (Rotax 447)	SN2232/0226	16.10.86	A.Miller	(Woking)	15.10.02P
G-MTBD	Mainair Gemini/Flash II 498-1186-4 & W299 (Rotax 447) *(Wing regd as W229)*		16.10.86	J.Williams	(Mansfield)	9. 8.03P
G-MTBE	CFM Shadow CD (Rotax 462HP)	K.035	16.10.86	S.K.Brown	Old Sarum	19.10.02P
G-MTBH	Mainair Gemini/Flash II 524-187-5 & W327 (Rotax 462)		28.10.86	T.& P.Sludds	(Enniscorthy, Co.Wexford)	5. 7.03P
G-MTBI*	Mainair Gemini/Flash II 508-1286-4 & W311 (Rotax 462)		27.10.86	A.Ormson (Rochdale) *(Flood damage late 2000) (Cancelled 15.11.00 as WFU) (Stored 1.02)*		29. 5.01P
G-MTBJ	Mainair Gemini/Flash II 509-1286-4 & W312 (Rotax 503)		27.10.86	R.M. & P.J.Perry Otherton, Cannock *(Op Staffordshire Aero Club)*		6. 7.02P
G-MTBK	Southdown Raven X (Rotax 503)	SN2232/0230	28.10.86	R.J.Grimwood Sywell *(Current status unknown)*		27. 6.99P
G-MTBL	Solar Wings Pegasus XL-R (Rotax 447) SW-TB-1121 & SW-WA-1117		6.11.86	R.N.Whiting Lower Mountpleasant Farm, Chatteris		15. 6.03P
G-MTBN	Southdown Raven X (Rotax 447)	SN2232/0227	28.10.86	A.J. & S.E.Crosby-Jones	Hailsham	9. 9.03P
G-MTBO	Southdown Raven X (Rotax 447)	SN2232/0233	28.10.86	J.Liversuch	Doynton	27.10.02P
G-MTBP	Aerotech MW-5B Sorcerer SR102-R440B-02 (Fuji-Robin EC-44-PM)		28.10.86	G.Bennett (Caister-on-Sea) *(Current status unknown)*		21. 9.94P
G-MTBR	Aerotech MW-5B Sorcerer SR102-R440B-03 (Fuji-Robin EC-44-PM)		20. 1.87	P.W.Hastings	Long Marston	31.10.02P
G-MTBS	Aerotech MW-5B Sorcerer SR102-R440B-04 (Fuji-Robin EC-44-PM)		27.10.86	T B Fowler	(Newent)	27. 9.03P
G-MTBU	Solar Wings Pegasus XL-R (Rotax 447) SW-TB-1122 & SW-WA-1118		13.11.86	R.P.R.Staveley	(Alfreton)	4. 1 .03P
G-MTBW*	Mainair Gemini/Flash II 520-187-5 & W322		6.11.86	Not known Otherton, Cannock *(Crashed Old Airfield, Aldridge 15.4.97 & cancelled by CAA 23.2.98) (Noted 4.01)*		
G-MTBX	Mainair Gemini/Flash II 510-1286-4 & W313 (Rotax 447)		6.11.86	R.K.W.Moss	(Northwich)	4. 3.03P
G-MTBY	Mainair Gemini/Flash II 507-1286-4-W310 (Rotax 447)		6.11.86	A.Worthington (Chorley) *(Current status unknown)*		5. 4.97P
G-MTBZ	Southdown Raven X (Rotax 447)	SN2232/0232	10.11.86	C A M Anderton Tarn Farm, Cockerham *(Damaged & stored 2.03)*		15.10.01P
G-MTCA	CFM Shadow C (Rotax 503)	K.011	6.11.86	J.R.L.Murray	East Fortune	26. 7.02P
G-MTCC*	Mainair Gemini/Flash II 497-1186-4 & W298 (Rotax 503)		13.11.86	J.Madhvani Plaistows Farm, St.Albans *(Damaged trike noted 9.00: cancelled 4.10.00 as WFU)*		21.10.96P
G-MTCE	Mainair Gemini/Flash II 511-1286-4 & W314 (Rotax 462)		2.12.86	R.S.Acreman Hatherton, Cannock *(Current status unknown)*		23. 5.99P
G-MTCG	Solar Wings Pegasus XL-R/Se (Rotax 447) SW-TB-1125 & SW-WA-1123		16.12.86	M K Nicholson	Eshott	11.12.02P
G-MTCH	Solar Wings Pegasus XL-R (Rotax 447) SW-TB-1126 & SW-WA-1124		28.11.86	R.E.H.Harris Davidstow Moor *(Current status unknown)*		29.11.95P
G-MTCK	Solar Wings Pegasus Flash II (Rotax 447) SW-TB-1127 & SW-WF-0127 *(Mainair sailwing c/n W263)*		11.12.86	S.Suckling	(Worthing)	16. 9.01P
G-MTCM	Southdown Raven X (Rotax 447)	SN2232/0239	11.12.86	J.C Rose Field Farm, Oakley *(New owner 9.01)*		2. 7.97P
G-MTCN	Solar Wings Pegasus XL-R (Rotax 447) SW-TB-1128 & SW-WA-1126		16.12.86	S.R.Hughes	(Gloucester)	18. 5.03P
G-MTCO	Solar Wings Pegasus XL-R (Rotax 447) SW-TB-1129 & SW-WA-1127		7. 1.87	A.J.Nesom	Baxby Manor, Husthwaite	8. 1.03P
G-MTCP	Aerial Arts Chaser/110SX 110SX/476 (Rotax 377)		16.12.86	B.Richardson	(Sunderland)	28. 6.00P
G-MTCR	Solar Wings Pegasus XL-R (Rotax 447) SW-TB-1130 & SW-WA-1128		16.12.86	P.J.Bates	Rufforth	26. 8.03P
G-MTCT	CFM Shadow CD (Rotax 503)	042	16.12.86	F.W.McCann	Cumbernauld	25. 8.03P
G-MTCU	Mainair Gemini/Flash IIA 451-1286-4 & W228 (Rotax 503)		5. 1.87	T.J.Philip	(Sale)	28. 5.03P
G-MTCW	Mainair Gemini/Flash II 502-1186-4 & W304 (Rotax 462)		5. 1.87	R.A.Watering	(Bourne, Lincs)	20. 1.03P
G-MTCX	Solar Wings Pegasus XL-R (Rotax 447) SW-TB-1131 & SW-WA-1129		9. 1.87	A.L.Davies Emlyn's Field, Rhuallt *(Current status unknown)*		30. 6.99P
G-MTDD	Aerial Arts Chaser/110SX 110SX/437 (Rotax 377)		26. 1.87	B.Richardson	(Sunderland)	4. 7.00P
G-MTDE	Aerial Arts Chaser/110SX 110SX/438 (Rotax 377) *(May now have Rotax 330)*		5. 1.87	M.N.Hudson	(Alford)	28. 3.03P
G-MTDF	Mainair Gemini/Flash II 515-287-5 & W319 (Rotax 503)		5. 1.87	S.R.Dalby	(Rossendale)	1. 5.03P

G-MTDG	Solar Wings Pegasus XL-R/Se		20. 1.87	E.W.Laidlaw	(Turriff)	7. 7.01P
	(Rotax 447) SW-TB-1132 & SW-WA-1130			*(Noted 8.00)*		
G-MTDH	Solar Wings Pegasus XL-R		22. 1.87	M.Shiner	Lamb Holm Farm, Orkney	5. 4.03P
	(Rotax 447) SW-TB-1133 & SW-WA-1131					
G-MTDI	Solar Wings Pegasus XL-R/Se		22. 1.87	W.Wood	Eshott	13. 5.91P
	(Rotax 447) SW-TB-1134 & SW-WA-1132			*(Stored 9.97: current status unknown)*		
G-MTDK	Aerotech MW-5B Sorcerer	SR102-R440B-06	22. 1.87	R.R.Hadley	Dunkeswell	23. 6.00P
	(Fuji-Robin EC-44-PM) *(To be converted to Rotax 447)*					
G-MTDN	Ultraflight Lazair IIIE	A465/002	22. 1.87	M.J.Broom	Long Marston	27. 6.97P
	(Rotax 185)			*(New owner 6.01)*		
G-MTDO	Eipper Quicksilver MXII	1124	27. 2.87	D.L.Ham	(Honiton)	5.11.87E
	(Rotax 503)			*(Current status unknown)*		
G-MTDR	Mainair Gemini/Flash II	516-287-5 & W276	26. 1.87	J.W. & C.Richardson	Baxby Manor, Husthwaite	25. 7.02P
	(Rotax 503)					
G-MTDU	CFM Shadow CD	K.037	26. 1.87	R.C.Osler	(Cheltenham)	5. 6.03P
	(Rotax 503-2V)					
G-MTDW	Mainair Gemini/Flash II	517-387-5 & W212	2. 2.87	S.R.Leeper	Priory Farm, Tibenham	29. 8.03P
	(Rotax 503)					
G-MTDX*	CFM Shadow BD	K.043	10. 2.87	L.Fekete	(Ellesmere Port)	4. 6.00P
	(Rotax 503)			*(Cancelled 12.4.02 by CAA)*		
G-MTDY	Mainair Gemini/Flash II	513-187-5 & W317	11. 2.87	S.Penoyre	(Windlesham)	13.10.00P
	(Rotax 462)					
G-MTEB*	Solar Wings Pegasus XL-R		9. 2.87	F.Watt	(Insch)	10. 7.00P
	(Rotax 447) SW-TB-1141 & SW-WA-1139			*(Cancelled 12.3.02 by CAA)*		
G-MTEC	Solar Wings Pegasus XL-R		9. 2.87	R.W.Glover	Kemble	11. 6.94P
	(Rotax 447) SW-TB-1142 & SW-WA-1140			*(Trike noted 2000)*		
G-MTED	Solar Wings Pegasus XL-R		9. 2.87	D.Marsh	Charminster, Bournemouth	31. 8.01P
	(Rotax 447) SW-TB-1143 & SW-WA-1141					
G-MTEE	Solar Wings Pegasus XL-R		13. 2.87	R.Foster	(Cannock)	25. 8.03P
	(Rotax 447) SW-TB-1144 & SW-WA-1142					
	(C/n plate incorrectly shows SW-WA-1144 & SW-WA-1142) (New wing ? - see G-MTLG)					
G-MTEJ	Mainair Gemini/Flash II	522-387-5 & W277	18. 2.87	G.J.Moore	Ince Blundell	2. 5.01P
	(Rotax 462)					
G-MTEK	Mainair Gemini/Flash II	523-387-5 & W279	3. 3.87	M.O'Hearne & G.M.Wrigley	Rufforth	17. 6.03P
	(Rotax 503)					
G-MTEN	Mainair Gemini/Flash II	527-487-5 & W285	25. 2.87	B.Bennison	(Brough)	14. 1.03P
	(Rotax 503)					
G-MTER	Solar Wings Pegasus XL-R/Se		19. 2.87	I.Stratford	(Stoke-on-Trent)	7. 4.02P
	(Rotax 447) SW-TB-1146 & SW-WA-1144					
G-MTES	Solar Wings Pegasus XL-R		19. 2.87	N.P.Read	Davidstow Moor	21. 8.03P
	(Rotax 447) SW-TB-1147 & SW-WA-1145					
G-MTET	Solar Wings Pegasus XL-R		19. 2.87	P.A.S.Talbot	(Camborne)	2. 5.00P
	(Rotax 447) SW-TB-1148 & SW-WA-1146					
G-MTEU	Solar Wings Pegasus XL-R/Se		19. 2.87	B.Harris	(Northwich)	)9. 4.01P
	(Rotax 447) SW-TB-1149 & SW-WA-1147					
G-MTEW	Solar Wings Pegasus XL-R/Se		19. 2.87	R.W. & P.J.Holley	(Shifnal)	4. 5.02P
	(Rotax 447) SW-TB-1151 & SW-WA-1149					
G-MTEX	Solar Wings Pegasus XL-R		19. 2.87	C.M.& K.M.Bradford	(Marlborough)	26. 8.02P
	(Rotax 447) SW-TB-1152 & SW-WA-1150					
G-MTEY	Mainair Gemini/Flash II	518-387-5 & W217	20. 2.87	A.Wells	Baxby Manor, Husthwaite	4. 6.98P
	(Rotax 503)			*(Current status unknown)*		
G-MTFA	Solar Wings Pegasus XL-R		24. 2.87	I.Armistead	(Kendal)	14. 3.94P
	(Rotax 462) SW-TB-1158 & SW-WA-1156			*(New CofR 11.02)*		
G-MTFB*	Solar Wings Pegasus XL-R		24. 2.87	I.D.Stokes	(Camelford)	20. 3.00P
	(Rotax 462) SW-TE-0015 & SW-WA-1157			*(Cancelled 12.4.02 by CAA)*		
G-MTFC	Medway Hybred 44XLR	22087/24	23. 3.87	J.K.Masters	(Chigwell)	25. 7.97P
	(Rotax 447)			*(Current status unknown)*		
G-MTFE	Solar Wings Pegasus XL-R		6. 3.87	D.A.Eastough	(Chellaston)	17. 5.02P
	(Rotax 447) SW-TB-1157 & SW-WA-1155	*(New sailwing fitted 1999)*				
G-MTFF	Mainair Gemini/Flash II	528-487-5 & W286	12. 3.87	T.N.Taylor	(Sidcup)	19. 4.96P
	(Rotax 503)			*(Current status unknown)*		
G-MTFG	AMF Chevvron 2-32C	CH.004	9. 3.87	R.Gardner	(Stratford-upon-Avon)	28. 7.03P
	(Konig SD570)					
G-MTFI	Mainair Gemini/Flash II	531-487-5 & W289	12. 3.87	M.Carolan	Annaghmore, Co.Tyrone	7. 6.03P
	(Rotax 503)					
G-MTFJ	Mainair Gemini/Flash II	532-487-5 & W320	12. 3.87	G.Souch & M.D.Peacock	(Leatherhead/Guildford)	3. 7.03P
	(Rotax 503)					
G-MTFL	Ultraflight Lazair IIIE (Rotax 185 x 2)	A466/003	12. 3.87	P.J.Turrell *(Current status unknown)*	(Halesowen)	26. 9.89P
G-MTFM	Solar Wings Pegasus XL-R		13. 3.87	P.R.G.Morley	Newnham, Baldock	20. 4.03P
	(Rotax 462) SW-TE-0016 & SW-WA-1158					
G-MTFN	Whittaker MW5 Sorcerer	PFA 163-11207	13. 3.87	K.Southam	(Newcastle upon Tyne)	21. 2.03P
	(Fuji-Robin EC-44-PM) *(May be Model MW5B)*					
G-MTFO	Solar Wings Pegasus XL-R/Se		18. 3.87	A.Gonzalez & W.Highton	Carlisle	1. 5.02P
	(Rotax 447) SW-TB-1159 & SW-WA-1159					
G-MTFP	Solar Wings Pegasus XL-R		18. 3.87	C.Rickards	(Swansea)	2. 3.03P
	(Rotax 447) SW-TB-1160 & SW-WA-1160					
G-MTFR	Solar Wings Pegasus XL-R/Se		18. 3.87	S.Ballantyne	(Blanefield)	19. 9.99P
	(Rotax 447) SW-TB-1161 & SW-WA-1161			*(Current status unknown)*		
G-MTFT	Solar Wings Pegasus XL-R		18. 3.87	A.T.Smith	Hughley, Much Wenlock	30. 7.00P
	(Rotax 447) SW-TB-1163 & SW-WA-1163					
G-MTFU	CFM Shadow BD	K.034	18. 3.87	G.R.Eastwood	Full Sutton	13. 8.00P
	(Rotax 447)					
G-MTFZ	CFM Shadow CD	053	24. 3.87	R.P.Stonor	Long Marston	26. 3.03P
	(Rotax 503)					

G-MTGA	Mainair Gemini/Flash II (Rotax 503)	535-587-5 & W293	26. 3.87	B.S.Ogden	Tarn Farm, Cockerham	3. 5.03P
G-MTGB	Thruster TST Mk.1 (Rotax 503)	837-TST-011	10. 4.87	G.Arthur	Tarn Farm, Cockerham	11. 9.00P
G-MTGC	Thruster TST Mk.1 (Rotax 503)	837-TST-012	10. 4.87	B.Foster & P.Smith	Gerpins Lane, Upminster	31. 5.03P
G-MTGD	Thruster TST Mk.1 (Rotax 503)	837-TST-013	10. 4.87	W.J.Lister	Fenland	31. 8.03P
G-MTGE	Thruster TST Mk.1 (Rotax 503)	837-TST-014	10. 4.87	G.W.R.Swift *(Current status unknown)*	(Hartfield)	17.10.99P
G-MTGF	Thruster TST Mk.1) (Rotax 503)	837-TST-015	10. 4.87	B.Swindon	(Chesham)	16. 9.03P
G-MTGH	Mainair Gemini/Flash II (Rotax 462)	536-587-5 & W294	31. 3.87	J.R.Gillies	(Hunsdon)	26. 5.03P
G-MTGJ	Solar Wings Pegasus XL-R (Rotax 447) SW-TB-1165 & SW-WA-1165		1. 4.87	M.S.Taylor	(Gillingham)	17. 2.02P
G-MTGK	Solar Wings Pegasus XL-R (Rotax 447) SW-TB-1166 & SW-WA-1166		1. 4.87	I.A.Smith *(Current status unknown)*	(Canterbury)	1. 8.91P
G-MTGL	Solar Wings Pegasus XL-R (Rotax 447) SW-TB-1167 & SW-WA-1167		1. 4.87	P.J.& R.Openshaw	(Warrington)	15. 4.03P
G-MTGM	Solar Wings Pegasus XL-R (Rotax 447) SW-TB-1168 & SW-WA-1168		1. 4.87	J.Needham	(Birmingham)	20. 8.03P
	(Original trike destroyed in gales 1.98 Roddige: fitted with trike from G-MNYT (c/n SW-TB-1099)					
G-MTGN	CFM Shadow BD (Rotax 447)	K.041	31. 3.87	N.G.Price	Bricket Wood, Radlett	15. 6.03P
G-MTGO	Mainair Gemini/Flash IIA (Rotax 462)	550-587-5 & W336	10. 4.87	P.Jephcott	(Solihull)	6. 7.03P
G-MTGP*	Thruster TST Mk.1 (Rotax 503)	847-TST-016	10. 4.87	L.A.Hosegood South Wraxall, Bradford-on-Avon *(Cancelled 30.12.02 by CAA)*		15. 3.03P
G-MTGR	Thruster TST Mk.1 (Rotax 503)	847-TST-017	10. 4.87	M.R.Grunwell	(Brentwood)	30.11.03P
G-MTGS	Thruster TST Mk.1 (Rotax 503)	847-TST-018	10. 4.87	R.Dennett	Barton	21. 8.03P
G-MTGT	Thruster TST Mk.1 (Rotax 503)	847-TST-019	10. 4.87	A.W.Paterson & P.McVay	(Mauchline)	28.11.02P
G-MTGU	Thruster TST Mk.1 (Rotax 503)	847-TST-020	10. 4.87	W Doyle	Eshott	13. 9.03P
G-MTGV	CFM Shadow CD (Rotax 503)	052	8. 4.87	V.R.Riley	(Amlwch)	11. 3.01P
G-MTGW	CFM Shadow CD (Rotax 503)	054	8. 4.87	J.O.Kane	(Halstead)	26 5.03P
G-MTGX	Hornet Dual Trainer/Southdown Raven (Rotax 462) HRWA 0061 & SN2000/0270		13. 4.87	M.A.Pantling *(New owner 4.02)*	Weston Zoyland	11. 4.97P
G-MTHB	Aerotech MW-5B Sorcerer SR102-R440B-08 (Fuji-Robin EC-44-PM)		10. 4.87	F.R.Wilson	(Stone)	11. 7.02P
G-MTHC	Raven Aircraft Raven X (Rotax 447)	SN2232/0257	15. 4.87	J.Channer	(Nottingham)	18. 3.02P
G-MTHG	Solar Wings Pegasus XL-R (Rotax 447) SW-TB-1170 & SW-WA-1171		13. 4.87	H.E.Paterson *(Current status unknown)*	(Poynton)	12. 3.03P
G-MTHH	Solar Wings Pegasus XL-R (Rotax 447) SW-TB-1171 & SW-WA-1172		13. 4.87	J.Palmer	(Winkleigh)	28.12.98P
G-MTHI	Solar Wings Pegasus XL-R (Rotax 447) SW-TB-1172 & SW-WA-1173		13. 4.87	J.R.Bowman	(Oxford)	16. 2.03P
G-MTHJ	Solar Wings Pegasus XL-R (Rotax 447) SW-TB-1173 & SW-WA-1174		13. 4.87	S.A.Watson	Long Acre Farm, Sandy	13.10.02P
G-MTHN	Solar Wings Pegasus XL-R (Rotax 447) SW-TB-1177 & SW-WA-1178		13. 4.87	G.E.Murphy	Haverfordwest	2. 9.01P
G-MTHS*	CFM Shadow CD (Rotax 582)	059	22. 4.87	A.J.McMenmamin Field Farm, Oakley *(Cancelled 11.6.99 by CAA) (Noted 5.00)*		17. 5.97P
G-MTHT	CFM Shadow CD (Rotax 503)	058	22. 4.87	B.J.Topham	Old Sarum	13. 4.03P
G-MTHV	CFM Shadow BD (Rotax 447)	K.049	7. 5.87	K.R.Bircher *(Noted 10.01)*	Over Farm, Gloucester	24. 7.00P
G-MTHW	Mainair Gemini/Flash II (Rotax 462)	540-587-5 & W325	14. 5.87	M.D.Kirby	Chase Farm, Billericay	4. 9.03P
G-MTHZ	Mainair Gemini/Flash IIA (Rotax 503)	541-587-5 & W329	14. 5.87	S.Bond & D.E.Lord	Crosland Moor	14. 2.03P
G-MTIA	Mainair Gemini/Flash IIA (Rotax 503)	544-687-5 & W332	14. 5.87	E.B.Atalay	(Kimbolton)	4. 8.02P
G-MTIB	Mainair Gemini/Flash IIA (Rotax 503)	545-687-5 & W333	14. 5.87	K.P.Hayes	St Michaels	5.12.03P
G-MTID	Raven Aircraft Raven X (Rotax 447)	SN2232/0276	18. 5.87	R.G.Featherby *(Cancelled 13.6.01 by CAA)*	(King's Lynn)	23. 2.99P
G-MTIE	Solar Wings Pegasus XL-R (Rotax 462) SW-TE-0019 & SW-WA-1183		18. 5.87	A.H.Paterson & I.M.Vass	(Wick)	28. 6.02P
G-MTIH	Solar Wings Pegasus XL-R (Rotax 447) SW-TB-1183 & SW-WA-1186		18. 5.87	C.R.Cawley & B.Chapman	(Clemsford)	16. 4.03P
G-MTIJ	Solar Wings Pegasus XL-R/Se (Rotax 447) SW-TB-1185 & SW-WA-1188		18. 5.87	M.J.F.Gilbody *(Current status unknown)*	(Urmston, Manchester)	1. 4.98P
G-MTIK	Raven Aircraft Raven X (Rotax 447)	SN2232/0272	19. 5.87	G A Oldershaw	(Ely)	23.11.03P
G-MTIL	Mainair Gemini/Flash IIA (Rotax 462)	549-687-5 & W338	21. 5.87	G.Turner	(Preston)	15. 8.02P
G-MTIM	Mainair Gemini/Flash IIA (Rotax 503)	553-687-5 & W341	21. 5.87	W.M.Swan	East Fortune	1. 5.03P

Reg	Type	C/n	Prev id	Date	Owner	Location	CofA
G-MTIN	Mainair Gemini/Flash IIA (Rotax 503)	547-687-5 & W335		1. 6.87	S.J.Firth	(Dallerie, Crieff)	3. 5.03P
G-MTIO	Solar Wings Pegasus XL-R (Rotax 447)	SW-TB-1187 & SW-WA-1190		26. 5.87	M.A.Coe	(Kettering)	5. 7.02P
G-MTIP	Solar Wings Pegasus XL-R (Rotax 447)	SW-TB-1188 & SW-WA-1191		26. 5.87	M.P.Jones	(Stafford)	15. 7.03P
G-MTIR	Solar Wings Pegasus XL-R/Se (Rotax 447)	SW-TB-1189 & SW-WA-1192		26. 5.87	D.Raybould	(Chesterfield)	6. 7.03P
G-MTIS	Solar Wings Pegasus XL-R (Rotax 447)	SW-TB-1190 & SW-WA-1193		26. 5.87	N.P.Power	(Eastbourne)	7. 4.02P
G-MTIU	Solar Wings Pegasus XL-R (Rotax 447)	SW-TB-1191 & SW-WA-1194		26. 5.87	D.Burdett	(Chatteris)	21. 8.03P
G-MTIV	Solar Wings Pegasus XL-R (Rotax 447)	SW-TB-1192 & SW-WA-1195		26. 5.87	P.J.Culverhouse, tr Syndicate IV	Sittles Farm, Alrewas	18.11.02P
G-MTIW	Solar Wings Pegasus XL-R (Rotax 447)	SW-TB-1193 & SW-WA-1196		26. 5.87	G.S.Francis	(Bristol)	10. 9.03P
G-MTIX	Solar Wings Pegasus XL-R (Rotax 447)	SW-TB-1194 & SW-WA-1197		26. 5.87	S.Pickering	Sutton Meadows, Ely	15. 1.01P
G-MTIY	Solar Wings Pegasus XL-R (Rotax 447)	SW-TB-1195 & SW-WA-1198		26. 5.87	P.J.Tanner	Weston Zoyland	25. 3.03P
G-MTIZ	Solar Wings Pegasus XL-R (Rotax 447)	SW-TB-1196 & SW-WA-1199		26. 5.87	S.L.Blount	Sutton Meadows. Ely	22.10.03P
G-MTJA	Mainair Gemini/Flash IIA (Rotax 503)	551-687-5 & W339		15. 6.87	R.Noble	(Bracknell)	6.12.03P
G-MTJB	Mainair Gemini/Flash IIA (Rotax 462)	554-687-5 & W343		2. 6.87	A.Dixon	Tarn Farm, Cockerham	5. 4.03P
G-MTJC	Mainair Gemini/Flash IIA (Honda BF52 @ 808cc)	555-687-5 & W344		1. 6.87	T.A.Dockrell	Kingston Seymour	2. 7.02P
G-MTJD	Mainair Gemini/Flash IIA (Rotax 462)	552-687-5 & W340		5. 6.87	D.J.Richards	(Nivillac, France)	19.10.02P
G-MTJE	Mainair Gemini/Flash IIA (Rotax 503)	556-687-5 & W345		24. 6.87	C.J.Dyke	Redlands, Swindon	10. 8.02P
G-MTJG	Medway Hybred 44XLR (Rotax 447)	22587/25		16. 6.87	Margaret A.Trodden *(Current status unknown)*	Tupton, Chesterfield	24. 2.99P
G-MTJH	Solar Wings Pegasus/Flash (Rotax 447)	SW-TB-1050 & W342-687-3 *(Trike previously fitted to G-MMUF)*		17. 6.87	C.L.Parker	Ampthill	3. 7.02P
G-MTJK*	Mainair Gemini/Flash IIA (Rotax 503)	559-787-5 & W348		17. 6.87	R.C.White *(Cancelled 10.6.02 by CAA)*	Aldermaston	16. 6.00P
G-MTJL	Mainair Gemini/Flash IIA (Rotax 503)	548-687-5 & W337		17. 6.87	D.J.Tuplin & B.G.M.Chapman	Sandtoft	27. 9.03P
G-MTJM	Mainair Gemini/Flash IIA (Rotax 462)	560-787-5 & W349		24. 6.87	K.J.Regan	(Teddington)	6. 8.00P
G-MTJN	Midland Ultralights Sirocco 377GB (Rotax 377)	MU-020		23. 6.87	S.Armstrong *(New owner 7.01)*	(Canterbury)	19. 3.94P
G-MTJP	Medway Hybred 44XLR (Rotax 447)	25687/27		6. 7.87	I.J.Alexander & P.Fitzsimmons	Plaistows Farm, St Albans	1. 7.02P
G-MTJS	Solar Wings Pegasus XL-Q (Rotax 462)	SW-TE-0022 & SW-WX-0013		6. 7.87	R.J.H.Hayward	(Belmont)	22. 9.02P
G-MTJT	Mainair Gemini/Flash IIA (Rotax 462)	558-787-5 & W347		16. 7.87	D.T.A.Rees	Haverfordwest	23. 2.03P
G-MTJV	Mainair Gemini/Flash IIA (Rotax 503)	562-787-5 & W351		16. 7.87	N.Charles & J.Richards	Swinford, Rugby	5. 7.03P
G-MTJW	Mainair Gemini/Flash IIA (Rotax 503)	563-787-5 & W352		16. 7.87	J.F.Ashton *(Current status unknown)*	(Liverpool)	4.10.95P
G-MTJX	Hornet Dual Trainer/Southdown Raven (Rotax 462)	HRWA 0063 & SN2000/0279		5. 8.87	J.P.Kirwan *(Current status unknown)*	(Liverpool)	31. 3.99P
G-MTJZ	Mainair Gemini/Flash IIA (Rotax 462)	561-787-5 & W350		16. 7.87	A.Robinson & J.Williams	Long Marston	19. 5.03P
G-MTKA	Thruster TST Mk.1 (Rotax 503)	867-TST-021		21. 7.87	C.M.Bradford & D.Marsh	Clench Common	19. 8.03P
G-MTKB	Thruster TST Mk.1 (Rotax 503)	867-TST-022		21. 7.87	M.Hanna	Rathfriland, Co.Down	13.10.01P
G-MTKD	Thruster TST Mk.1 (Rotax 503)	867-TST-024		21. 7.87	A.J.Hartung	(Lucan, Co.Dublin)	27.10.02P
G-MTKE	Thruster TST Mk.1 (Rotax 503)	867-TST-025		21. 7.87	M.R.Jones	Wing Farm, Longbridge Deverill	27. 8.03P
G-MTKG	Solar Wings Pegasus XL-R/Se Rotax 447)	SW-TB-1199 & SW-WA-1201		13. 7.87	W.J.Hodgins	Deenethorpe	19. 6.03P
G-MTKH	Solar Wings Pegasus XL-R (Rotax 447)	SW-TB-1200 & SW-WA-1202		13. 7.87	K.Brooker	(Horsham)	19. 6.03P
G-MTKI	Solar Wings Pegasus XL-R	SW-TB-1201 & SW-WA-1203		13. 7.87	I.D.A.Spanton	Malvern	22. 3.03P
G-MTKN	Mainair Gemini/Flash IIA (Rotax 503)	566-887-5 & W355		15. 7.87	A.J.Taylor	(Colne)	4. 6.03P
G-MTKR	CFM Shadow CD (Rotax 503)	067	9H-ABL G-MTKR	20. 7.87	P.A.James t/a Cloudbase Aviation	Redhill	4. 5.03P
G-MTKV	Mainair Gemini/Flash IIA (Rotax 503)	565-887-5 & W354		26. 8.87	L.A.Davidson	Sandtoft	22. 5.02P
G-MTKW	Mainair Gemini/Flash IIA (Rotax 503)	569-887-5 & W358		13. 7.87	R.T.Henry	Newtownards, Co.Down	3. 3.03P
G-MTKX*	Mainair Gemini/Flash IIA (Rotax 503)	568-887-5 & W357		13. 7.87	A.S.Leach *(Cancelled 27.12.02 by CAA)*	(Warrington)	27. 8.00P
G-MTKZ	Mainair Gemini/Flash IIA (Rotax 503)	571-887-5 & W360		31. 7.87	J.A.Ewens	East Fortune	9.10.03P

Reg	Type	C/n		Date	Owner	Location	Date2
G-MTLB	Mainair Gemini/Flash IIA (Rotax 503)	573-887-5 & W362		31. 7.87	D.N.Bacon	Hucknall	16. 3.01P
G-MTLC	Mainair Gemini/Flash IIA (Rotax 503)	574-887-5 & W363		31. 7.87	R.J.Alston	(Cromer)	13. 7.02P
G-MTLD	Mainair Gemini/Flash IIA (Rotax 503)	575-887-5 & W364		31. 7.87	I.A.Forrest	East Fortune	28. 3.03P
G-MTLG	Solar Wings Pegasus XL-R (Rotax 447)	SW-TB-1207 & SW-WA-1211		31. 7.87	D.Young tr Kemble Flying Club	Kemble	4.11.03P
G-MTLI	Solar Wings Pegasus XL-R (Rotax 447)	SW-TB-1209 & SW-WA-1213		31. 7.87	M.McKay *(Current status unknown)*	(Robertsbridge)	6. 6.97P
G-MTLJ	Solar Wings Pegasus XL-R/Se (Rotax 447)	SW-TB-1210 & SW-WA-1214		31. 7.87	R.E.Pratt	Sandtoft	14. 4.03P
G-MTLL	Mainair Gemini/Flash IIA (Rotax 503)	578-987-5 & W367		14. 8.87	M.S.Lawrence	Mill Farm, Shifnal	30. 6.03P
G-MTLM	Thruster TST Mk.1 (Rotax 503)	887-TST-027		5. 8.87	E.F.Howells tr Chloe's Flying Group *"Chloe"*	Manor Farm, Croughton	4. 6.02P
G-MTLN	Thruster TST Mk.1 (Rotax 503)	887-TST-028		5. 8.87	A.G.E.Smith	Doynton	14. 7.02P
G-MTLR	Thruster TST Mk.1 (Rotax 503)	887-TST-031		5. 8.87	G.A.McKay	(Linlithgow)	17. 5.01P
G-MTLT	Solar Wings Pegasus XL-R (Rotax 447)	SW-TB-1212 & SW-WA-1216		12. 8.87	S.P.MacDonald	Crowland	10.10.03P
G-MTLU	Solar Wings Pegasus XL-R/Se (Rotax 447)	SW-TB-1213 & SW-WA-1217		12. 8.87	M.W.Riley	(Morpeth)	22. 9.02P
G-MTLV	Solar Wings Pegasus XL-R (Rotax 447)	SW-TB-1214 & SW-WA-1218		12. 8.87	D.E.Watson	Long Marston	28. 8.02P
G-MTLX	Medway Hybred 44XLR (Rotax 447)	20687/26		14. 8.87	D.A.Coupland	RAF Wyton	28. 6.03P
G-MTLY	Solar Wings Pegasus XL-R (Rotax 462)	SW-TE-0026 & SW-WA-1220		12. 8.87	I.Johnston *(Current status unknown)*	(Bolton)	5. 7.92P
G-MTLZ	Whittaker MW5 Sorcerer (Rotax 377)	PFA 163-11241		13. 8.87	M.J.Davenport	Weston Zoyland	1. 8.03P
G-MTMA	Mainair Gemini/Flash IIA (Rotax 503)	579-987-5 & W368		14. 8.87	D.Bussell	St.Michaels	5. 7.03P
G-MTMC	Mainair Gemini/Flash IIA (Rotax 503)	581-987-5 & W370		14. 8.87	A.R.Johnson	Brenzett, Kent	25. 5.03P
G-MTME	Solar Wings Pegasus XL-R (Rotax 447)	SW-TB-1216 & SW-WA-1221		18. 8.87	M.T.Finch	Sutton Meadows, Ely	22.11.02P
G-MTMF	Solar Wings Pegasus XL-R (Rotax 447)	SW-TB-1217 & SW-WA-1222		18. 8.87	J.T.W.Smith	(Mallaig)	6. 6.03P
G-MTMG	Solar Wings Pegasus XL-R (Rotax 447)	SW-TB-1218 & SW-WA-1223		18. 8.87	C.W. & P.E.F.Suckling	(Rushden)	18. 8.00P
G-MTMI	Solar Wings Pegasus XL-R/Se (Rotax 447)	SW-TB-1220 & SW-WA-1225		18. 8.87	D.Crozier	Eshott	18. 1.03P
G-MTMK	Raven Aircraft Raven X (Rotax 447)	SN2000/0289		2. 9.87	D.W.Thomas	Long Marston	1. 8.02P
G-MTML	Mainair Gemini/Flash IIA (Rotax 462)	582-1087-5 & W371		27. 8.87	J.F.Ashton	(Liverpool)	30. 7.00P
G-MTMO	Raven Aircraft Raven X (Rotax 447)	SN2232/0278	(G-MTKL)	11. 9.87	H.Tuvey	(South Ockendon)	28. 8.03P
G-MTMP	Hornet Dual Trainer/Southdown Raven (Rotax 462)	HRWA 0064 & SN2000/0288		28. 8.87	P.G.Owen *(Current status unknown)*	Baxby Manor, Husthwaite	6. 8.99P
G-MTMR	Hornet Dual Trainer/Southdown Raven (Rotax 462)	HRWA 0065 & SN2000/0297		28. 8.87	D.J.Smith	Hucknall	13. 7.03P
G-MTMT	Mainair Gemini/Flash IIA (Rotax 462)	583-1087-5 & W372		3. 9.87	C.Pickvance	Tarn Farm, Cockerham	3. 8.02P
G-MTMV	Mainair Gemini/Flash IIA (Rotax 503)	585-1087-5 & W374		3. 9.87	M.F.Botha	Baxby Manor, Husthwaite	8. 4.03P
G-MTMW	Mainair Gemini/Flash IIA (Rotax 503)	587-1087-5 & W376		9. 9.87	J.C.Higham	(Willenhall)	13. 6.03P
G-MTMX	CFM Shadow CD (Rotax 503)	070		4. 9.87	D.R.White	(Chesham)	30. 5.03P
G-MTMY	CFM Shadow CD (Rotax 503)	071		4. 9.87	R.F.Learney tr G-MTMY Syndicate	Redhill	1. 2.03P
G-MTNC	Mainair Gemini/Flash IIA (Rotax 503)	588-1087-5 & W377		15. 9.87	D.J.Kelly & M Titmus	Shobdon	27. 8.03P
G-MTNE	Medway Hybred 44XLR (Rotax 447) *(Fitted with new trike as original was transferred to G-MVDC in 1988)*	7987/32		12.10.87	A.G.Rodenburg	(Tillicoultry)	25. 7.03P
G-MTNF	Medway Hybred 44XLR (Rotax 447)	1987/31		12.10.87	P.A.Bedford	(Tewkesbury)	12. 2.00P
G-MTNG	Mainair Gemini/Flash IIA (Rotax 503)	590-1087-5 & W379		21. 9.87	A.N.Bellis	Shobdon	25. 7.03P
G-MTNH	Mainair Gemini/Flash IIA (Rotax 462)	589-1087-5 & W378		17. 9.87	J.R.Smart	Over Farm, Gloucester	20. 5.02P
G-MTNI	Mainair Gemini/Flash IIA (Rotax 503)	595-1187-5 & W384		18. 9.87	D.Gatland	Rufforth	25.11.02P
G-MTNJ	Mainair Gemini/Flash IIA (Rotax 462)	593-1187-5 & W382		17. 9.87	S.F.Kennedy	(Market Harborough)	8.12.02P
G-MTNK	Weedhopper JC-24B (Fuji-Robin EC-34-PM) *(Test flown under "B" Conditions 29.6.00 as "G-???")*	1936		28. 9.87	P.Scott *(Current status unknown)*	Kemble	N/E
G-MTNL	Mainair Gemini/Flash IIA (Rotax 503)	591-1187-5 & W380		21. 9.87	R.A.Matthews	Otherton, Cannock	14. 1.03P
G-MTNM	Mainair Gemini/Flash IIA (Rotax 503)	592-1187-5 & W381		22. 9.87	C.J.Janson	Shobdon	7. 8.03P

G-MTNO	Solar Wings Pegasus XL-Q		23. 9.87	A.F.Batchelor	Rayne Hall Farm, Rayne	24. 6.03P
	(Rotax 447)	SW-TB-1252 & SW-WQ-0001				
G-MTNP	Solar Wings Pegasus XL-Q		23. 9.87	G.G.Roberts	Rayne Hall Farm, Rayne	17. 8.03P
	(Rotax 447)	SW-TB-1253 & SW-WQ-0002				
G-MTNR	Thruster TST Mk.1	897-TST-032	1.10.87	S.C.Briggs	East Fortune	7. 8.03P
	(Rotax 503)					
G-MTNS	Thruster TST Mk.1	897-TST-033	1.10.87	G.& B.W.Evans	Archlid Green, Sandbach	25. 5.02P
	(Rotax 503)					
G-MTNT	Thruster TST Mk.1	897-TST-034	1.10.87	G.Bennett	Blofield, Norfolk	11. 3.01P
	(Rotax 503)					
G-MTNU	Thruster TST Mk.1	897-TST-035	1.10.87	T.Jackson	Chase Farm, Bristol	15. 9.02P
	(Rotax 503)					
G-MTNV	Thruster TST Mk.1	897-TST-036	1.10.87	J.B.Russell	Larne, Co.Antrim	11.10.88P
	(Rotax 503)			*(Current status unknown)*		
G-MTNX	Mainair Gemini/Flash IIA	606-1187-5 & W393	29. 9.87	C.Evans	RAF Wyton	24. 6.02P
	(Rotax 503)					
G-MTNY	Mainair Gemini/Flash IIA	594-1187-5 & W383	2.10.87	R.C.Granger	(Burnham-on-Crouch)	8. 8.03P
	(Rotax 503)					
G-MTOA	Solar Wings Pegasus XL-R		15. 9.87	R.A.Bird	East Hunsbury, Northampton	8. 8.01P
	(Rotax 447)	SW-TB-1221 & SW-WA-1226				
G-MTOB	Solar Wings Pegasus XL-R		15. 9.87	P.S.Lemm	Hatherton, Cannock	1.10.97P
	(Rotax 447)	SW-TB-1222 & SW-WA-1227		*(Current status unknown)*		
G-MTOD*	Solar Wings Pegasus XL-R		15. 9.87	T A Gordon	(Liskeard)	3. 9.00P
	(Rotax 447)	SW-TB-1224 & SW-WA-1229		*(Cancelled 30.1.03 by CAA)*		
G-MTOE	Solar Wings Pegasus XL-R		15. 9.87	K.J.Bright	Old Sarum	13. 7.03P
	(Rotax 447)	SW-TB-1225 & SW-WA-1230				
G-MTOG	Solar Wings Pegasus XL-R		15. 9.87	D.S.F.McNair	(Lochgilphead)	25. 4.03P
	(Rotax 447)	SW-TB-1227 & SW-WA-1232				
G-MTOH	Solar Wings Pegasus XL-R		15. 9.87	H.Cook	(Pontypool)	2. 3.02P
	(Rotax 447)	SW-TB-1228 & SW-WA-1233				
G-MTOI	Solar Wings Pegasus XL-R		15. 9.87	M.P.Kingston	Deopham Green	20. 6.03P
	(Rotax 447)	SW-TB-1229 & SW-WA-1234				
G-MTOJ	Solar Wings Pegasus XL-R/Se		15. 9.87	D.S.Main	Old Sarum	29. 9.01P
	(Rotax 447)	SW-TB-1230 & SW-WA-1235				
G-MTOK	Solar Wings Pegasus XL-R		2.10.87	W.S.Davis	Oxton, Nottingham	13. 2.02P
	(Rotax 447)	SW-TB-1231 & SW-WA-1236				
G-MTOL	Solar Wings Pegasus XL-R		2.10.87	H M Manning	Rochester	3. 6.00P
	(Rotax 447)	SW-TB-1232 & SW-WA-1237				
G-MTOM	Solar Wings Pegasus XL-R/Se		2.10.87	R.J.Hood	London Colney	27. 7.01P
	(Rotax 447)	SW-TB-1233 & SW-WA-1238	*(Original sailwing now written off & shares with that from G-MMRL)*			
G-MTON	Solar Wings Pegasus XL-R		2.10.87	D.J.Willett	(Malpas)	8.10.03P
	(Rotax 447)	SW-TB-1234 & SW-WA-1239				
G-MTOO	Solar Wings Pegasus XL-R		2.10.87	G.W.Bulmer	Chase Farm, Bristol	15. 7.02P
	(Rotax 447)	SW-TB-1235 & SW-WA-1240				
G-MTOP	Solar Wings Pegasus XL-R/Se		2.10.87	P.D.Larkin	Field Farm, Oakley	13.10.01P
	(Rotax 447)	SW-TB-1236 & SW-WA-1241				
G-MTOR	Solar Wings Pegasus XL-R		9.10.87	W.F.G.Panayiotiou	(Llanelli)	28. 7.03
	(Rotax 447)	SW-TB-1237 & SW-WA-1242				
G-MTOS	Solar Wings Pegasus XL-R		9.10.87	C.McKay	Strathaven	16.10.03P
	(Rotax 447)	SW-TB-1238 & SW-WA-1243				
G-MTOT	Solar Wings Pegasus XL-R		9.10.87	G.J.Howley	(Coleford)	25. 3.03P
	(Rotax 447)	SW-TB-1239 & SW-WA-1244				
G-MTOU	Solar Wings Pegasus XL-R/Se		9.10.87	D.T.Smith	(Thornaby)	1. 3.03P
	(Rotax 447)	SW-TB-1240 & SW-WA-1245				
G-MTOX	Solar Wings Pegasus XL-R		19.10.87	T.P.Wright	(Ilkeston)	6. 1.01P
	(Rotax 447)	SW-TB-1243 & SW-WA-1248				
G-MTOY	Solar Wings Pegasus XL-R		19.10.87	C.M.Bradford tr G-MTOY Group	Yatesbury	8. 8.03P
	(Rotax 447)	SW-TB-1244 & SW-WA-1249				
G-MTOZ	Solar Wings Pegasus XL-R		19.10.87	P.J.McCool	Enstone	9. 6.02P
	(Rotax 447)	SW-TB-1245 & SW-WA-1250				
G-MTPA	Mainair Gemini/Flash IIA	598-1187-5 & W394	13.10.87	P.G.Eastlake	(Harlow)	14. 8.03P
	(Rotax 462)					
G-MTPB*	Mainair Gemini/Flash IIA	599-1187-5 & W387	15.10.87	Not known	St.Michaels	26.10.98P
	(Rotax 503)			*(Cancelled 18.1.00 by CAA) (Stored 9.02)*		
G-MTPC	Raven Aircraft Raven X	SN2232/0309	15.10.87	G.W.Carwardine	(Uckfield)	3.11.90P
	(Rotax 582) *(Modified to "Phillips Swphift" standard 1999)*			*(Current status unknown)*		
G-MTPE	Solar Wings Pegasus XL-R		21.10.87	J.Basset		29. 3.03P
	(Rotax 503)	SW-TB-1258 & SW-WA-1260		Brown Shutters Farm, Norton St Philips, Somerset		
G-MTPF	Solar Wings Pegasus XL-R		21.10.87	K.J.Mahon	Halwell, Totnes	3. 8.03P
	(Rotax 447)	SW-TB-1259 & SW-WA-1261				
G-MTPG	Solar Wings Pegasus XL-R		21.10.87	J.Sullivan	(Chipping Camden)	16. 7.03P
	(Rotax 447)	SW-TB-1260 & SW-WA-1262				
G-MTPH	Solar Wings Pegasus XL-R		30.10.87	L.M.Sams	Long Marston	9. 6.03P
	(Rotax 447)	SW-TB-1261 & SW-WA-1263				
G-MTPI	Solar Wings Pegasus XL-R/Se		30.10.87	R.J.Bullock	Long Marston	4. 8.02P
	(Rotax 447)	SW-TB-1262 & SW-WA-1264				
G-MTPJ	Solar Wings Pegasus XL-R		30.10.87	D.A.Whittaker	Roddige, Fradley	1. 7.02P
	(Rotax 447)	SW-TB-1263 & SW-WA-1265				
G-MTPK	Solar Wings Pegasus XL-R		30.10.87	S.H.James	Deenethorpe	21.10.01P
	(Rotax 447)	SW-TB-1264 & SW-WA-1266				
G-MTPL	Solar Wings Pegasus XL-R		30.10.87	I.R.F.King	(Tunbridge Wells)	)2. 9.99P
	(Rotax 447)	SW-TB-1265 & SW-WA-1267		*(Current status unknown)*		
G-MTPM	Solar Wings Pegasus XL-R		30.10.87	D.K.Seal	Roddige, Fradley	9. 9.01P
	(Rotax 447)	SW-TB-1266 & SW-WA-1268				

Reg	Type	Constructor's No	Date	Owner/Operator	Location	Notes
G-MTPN	Solar Wings Pegasus XL-Q		21.10.87	B.& D.Bergin	Athenry, Co.Galway	23. 6.02P
	(Rotax 447) SW-TB-1267 & SW-WQ-0004					
G-MTPP	Solar Wings Pegasus XL-R		21.10.87	P Molyneux	(Southport)	2.10.00P
	(Rotax 447) SW-TB-1257 & SW-WA-1259					
G-MTPR	Solar Wings Pegasus XL-R		21.10.87	T.Kenny	(Ballygar)	16. 6.96P
	(Rotax 447) SW-TB-1256 & SW-WA-1257			*(Current status unknown)*		
G-MTPS	Solar Wings Pegasus XL-Q		23.10.87	G.Tyler	(Cambridge)	5. 7.03P
	(Rotax 462) SW-TE-0021 & SW-WX-0011					
G-MTPT	Thruster TST Mk.1	8107-TST-038	23.10.87	J.T.Kendrick	Popham	3.11.96P
	(Rotax 503)			*(Current status unknown)*		
G-MTPU	Thruster TST Mk.1	8107-TST-039	23.10.87	D.R.Sims	Halwell, Totnes	27. 7.03P
	(Rotax 503)					
G-MTPV*	Thruster TST Mk.1	8107-TST-040	23.10.87	E.Bentley & A.Maxwell	Morgansfield, Fishburn	30. 5.01P
	(Rotax 503)			*(Cancelled 10.2.03 by CAA)*		
G-MTPW	Thruster TST Mk.1	8107-TST-041	23.10.87	T.A.Jones	Sittles Farm, Alrewas	4. 5.01P
	(Rotax 503)					
G-MTPX	Thruster TST Mk.1	8107-TST-042	23.10.87	T.Snook	Long Marston	2. 5.93P
	(Rotax 503)			*(Current status unknown)*		
G-MTPY	Thruster TST Mk.1	8107-TST-043	23.10.87	P.C.Appleton	Davidstow Moor	26. 7.03P
	(Rotax 503)					
G-MTRA	Mainair Gemini/Flash IIA	605-1187-5 & W395	28.10.87	E.N.Alms	Guy Lane Farm, Waverton	2. 2.03P
	(Rotax 503)			"Yellow Bird"		
G-MTRC	Midland Ultralights Sirocco 377GB	MU-021	2.11.87	D.Thorpe	Grantham	13. 4.03P
	(Rotax 377)					
G-MTRL	Hornet Dual Trainer/Southdown Raven		4.11.87	J.McAlpine	(Largs)	10.12.02P
	(Rotax 462) HRWA 0068 & SN2000/0326					
G-MTRM	Solar Wings Pegasus XL-R		10.11.87	D.B.Jones	Long Acre Farm, Sandy	26.6.03P
	(Rotax 462) SW-TE-0030 & SW-WA-1276					
G-MTRN	Solar Wings Pegasus XL-R		2.12.87	K.McCoubrey	(Stoke-on-Trent)	3. 8.01P
	(Rotax 447) SW-TB-1270 & SW-WA-1269					
G-MTRO	Solar Wings Pegasus XL-R/Se		2.12.87	H.Lloyd-Hughes	Emlyn's Field, Rhuallt	22. 4.03P
	(Rotax 447) SW-TB-1271 & SW-WA-1270					
G-MTRS	Solar Wings Pegasus XL-R		2.12.87	J.J.R.Tickle	Llanerchymedd, Gwynedd	13. 6.01P
	(Rotax 447) SW-TB-1274 & SW-WA-1273					
G-MTRT	Raven Aircraft Raven X	SN2232/0325	12.11.87	D.HinesFordhall	Villa Farm, Ternhill	14. 9.03P
	(Rotax 447)					
G-MTRU	Solar Wings Pegasus XL-Q		10.11.87	A.L.S.Routledge	Rufforth	15.10.00P
	(Rotax 447) SW-TB-1275 & SW-WQ-0009			*(Noted wrecked 7.01)*		
G-MTRV	Solar Wings Pegasus XL-Q		10.11.87	R.P.Speight	Clench Common	10. 9.02P
	(Rotax 477) SW-TB-1276 & SW-WX-0010					
G-MTRW	Raven Aircraft Raven X	SN2232/0328	12.11.87	P.K.J.Chun	Rochester	4.11.03P
	(Rotax 447)					
G-MTRX	Whittaker MW5 Sorcerer	PFA 163-11202	11.11.87	W.Turner	Otherton, Cannock	13. 2.95P
	(Rotax 447)			*(Stored 8.96: current status unknown)*		
G-MTRZ	Mainair Gemini/Flash IIA	611-1287-5 & W400	17.11.87	D.F.G.Barlow	(Morecambe)	18.8.03P
	(Rotax 503)					
G-MTSC	Mainair Gemini/Flash IIA	618-188-5 & W407	17.11.87	M.Walker	(Chester)	4. 6.02P
	(Rotax 503)					
G-MTSD*	Raven Aircraft Raven X	SN2232/0312	24.11.87	D.Turner	Field Farm, Oakley	10. 3.01P
	(Rotax 447)			*(Cancelled 18.10.02 as wfu)*		
G-MTSG	CFM Shadow CD	079	24.11.87	C.A.Purvis	Plaistows Farm, St Albans	22. 4.03P
	(Rotax 503)					
G-MTSH	Thruster TST Mk.1	8117-TST-044	3.12.87	R R Orr	Dromore, Co.Down	1. 6.03P
	(Rotax 503)					
G-MTSJ	Thruster TST Mk.1	8117-TST-046	3.12.87	P.J.Mogg	Sturminster Newton	28. 4.03P
	(Rotax 503)					
G-MTSK	Thruster TST Mk.1	8117-TST-047	3.12.87	J.S.Pyke	Westfield Farm, Hailsham	15. 5.03P
	(Rotax 503)					
G-MTSM	Thruster TST Mk.1	8117-TST-049	3.12.87	Environment Agency, Thames Region		
	(Rotax 503)				Field Farm, Oakley	14. 5.02P
G-MTSN	Solar Wings Pegasus XL-R		14.12.87	G.P.Lane	Doynton	15. 4.03P
	(Rotax 447) SW-TB-1278 & SW-WA-1280					
G-MTSO	Solar Wings Pegasus XL-R/Se		14.12.87	P.Wibberley	(Chesterfield)	20. 5.03P
	(Rotax 447) SW-TB-1279 & SW-WA-1281					
G-MTSP	Solar Wings Pegasus XL-R		14.12.87	R.J.Nelson	Swinford, Rugby	19.10.02P
	(Rotax 447) SW-TB-1280 & SW-WA-1282					
G-MTSR	Solar Wings Pegasus XL-R		14.12.87	J.Norman	Long Acre Farm, Sandy	13.10.02P
	(Rotax 447) SW-TB-1281 & SW-WA-1283					
G-MTSS*	Solar Wings Pegasus XL-R		14.12.87	T.M.Evans	(Haywards Heath)	31. 7.02P
	(Rotax 462) SW-TE-0031 & SW-WA-1284			*(Cancelled 21.8.02 by CAA)*		
G-MTSU	Solar Wings Pegasus XL-R		4. 1.88	L.Earls	(Drogheda, Co.Louth)	23.11.02P
	(Rotax 447) SW-TB-1289 & SW-WA-1285					
G-MTSV*	Solar Wings Pegasus XL-R		4. 1.88	R.J.Bowden	Dunkeswell	20. 8.00P
	(Rotax 447) SW-TB-1290 & SW-WA-1286			*(Cancelled 12.3.02 as WFU)*		
G-MTSX	Solar Wings Pegasus XL-R		4. 1.88	F.J.Bridges	Sittles Farm, Alrewas	30. 5.01P
	(Rotax 447) SW-TB-1282 & SW-WA-1288					
G-MTSY	Solar Wings Pegasus XL-R/Se		14. 1.88	N.F.Waldron	Swinford, Rugby	24. 5.99P
	(Rotax 447) SW-TB-1283 & SW-WA-1289			*(Current status unknown)*		
G-MTSZ	Solar Wings Pegasus XL-R/Se		14. 1.88	J.R.Appleton	(Colne)	18.10.03P
	(Rotax 447) SW-TB-1284 & SW-WA-1290					
G-MTTA	Solar Wings Pegasus XL-R		14. 1.88	J.J.McMennum	Kemble	4. 9.00P
	(Rotax 462) SW-TE-0035 & SW-WA-1291			*(Noted 12.01)*		
G-MTTB	Solar Wings Pegasus XL-R		14. 1.88	P.M.Golden	Siege Cross Farm, Thatcham	31.10.02P
	(Rotax 447) SW-TB-1285 & SW-WA-1292					

Reg	Type	Construction No.	Date	Owner	Location	Status
G-MTTD*	Solar Wings Pegasus XL-Q		15. 1.88	R.S.Noremberg	(Clacton-on-Sea)	18. 5.02P
	(Rotax 447) SW-TB-1286 & SW-WQ-0011			*(Cancelled 23.8.02 by CAA)*		
G-MTTE	Solar Wings Pegasus XL-Q		15. 1.88	L.G.Wray	(Knaresborough)	12. 5.03P
	(Rotax 462?) SW-TB-1287 & SW-WQ-0012					
G-MTTF	Whittaker MW6 Merlin	PFA 164-11273	14.12.87	P.Cotton	Long Marston	29. 3.95P
	(Rotax 532)			*(Current status unknown)*		
G-MTTH	CFM Shadow BD	K.061	15.12.87	G.F.Hill & A.Y-T.Leung	(Shenstone)	12. 5.02P
	(Rotax 447)					
G-MTTI	Mainair Gemini/Flash IIA	620-188-5 & W409	14.12.87	S.M.Savage	(Guildford)	19. 7.96P
	(Rotax 503)			*(Current status unknown)*		
G-MTTL*	Tri-Pacer 330/Excalibur	EXS-872	23. 3.88	M.J.Aubrey	(Kington, Hereford)	
	(Fuji-Robin EC-34-PM)			*(Cancelled 20.11.95 by CAA) (Noted 2002) .*		
G-MTTM	Mainair Gemini/Flash IIA	609-1287-5 & W398	5. 1.88	R.K.Woods	(Sheffield)	14. 1.03P
	(Rotax 503)					
G-MTTN	Skyrider Airsports Phantom	PH.00100	22. 1.88	K.H.A.Negal	Sittles Farm, Alrewas	N/E
	(Officially registered as Ultralight Flight Phantom)			*(New owner 10.01)*		
G-MTTP	Mainair Gemini/Flash IIA	612-188-5 & W401	18. 1.88	A.Ormson	St.Michaels	20. 6.03P
	(Rotax 462)					
G-MTTR	Mainair Gemini/Flash IIA	614-188-5 & W403	27. 1.88	A.Westoby	Hucknall	22. 7.00P
	(Rotax 462)					
G-MTTU	Solar Wings Pegasus XL-R		25. 2.88	C.G.Jarvis	Clench Common	25. 7.03P
	(Rotax 447) SW-TB-1332 & SW-WA-1294					
G-MTTW	Mainair Gemini/Flash IIA	622-188-5 & W411	15. 1.88	N.G.Woodall	Tarn Farm, Cockerham	11. 5.03P
	(Rotax 462)					
G-MTTX	Solar Wings Pegasus XL-Q		15. 2.88	M.J.Sunter	(Leyburn)	4. 5.03P
	(Rotax 447) SW-TB-1293 & SW-WQ-0013					
G-MTTZ	Solar Wings Pegasus XL-Q		21. 1.88	J.Haskett	(King's Lynn)	2. 8.03P
	(Rotax 462) SW-TE-0039 & SW-WQ-0015					
G-MTUA	Solar Wings Pegasus XL-R/Se		15. 1.88	P.A.Allwood	Rochester	5. 7.03P
	(Rotax 447) SW-TB-1294 & SW-WA-1295					
G-MTUB	Thruster TST Mk.1)	8018-TST-050	15. 1.88	Sligo Light Aviation Club Ltd	(Sligo, Co.Sligo	18. 7.03P
	(Rotax 503)					
G-MTUC	Thruster TST Mk.1	8018-TST-051	15. 1.88	E.J.Girling	Davidstow Moor	10. 1.03P
	(Rotax 503)					
G-MTUD	Thruster TST Mk.1	8018-TST-052	15. 1.88	A.J.Best	(Huby, York)	5.10.03P
	(Rotax 503)					
G-MTUF	Thruster TST Mk.1	8018-TST-054	15. 1.88	P.Stark	Strathaven	25.11.02P
	(Rotax 503)					
G-MTUI	Solar Wings Pegasus XL-R/Se		21. 1.88	C.S.Garrett & G.Butcher	Enstone	15. 2.03P
	(Rotax 447) SW-TB-1296 & SW-WA-1296					
G-MTUJ	Solar Wings Pegasus XL-R		21. 1.88	R.W.Pincombe	(Chumleigh, Devon)	31. 5.94P
	(Rotax 447) SW-TB-1297 & SW-WA-1297			*(Current status unknown)*		
G-MTUK	Solar Wings Pegasus XL-R		21. 1.88	G.L.Hall	Rufforth	7. 9.03P
	(Rotax 447) SW-TB-1298 & SW-WA-1298					
G-MTUL	Solar Wings Pegasus XL-R/Se		21. 1.88	P.J.Wood	(Worcester)	13. 4.03P
	(Rotax 447) SW-TB-1299 & SW-WA-1299					
G-MTUN	Solar Wings Pegasus XL-Q		20. 1.88	C.Hastings	Long Marston	10. 4.03P
	(Rotax 447) SW-TB-1301 & SW-WQ-0016		*(Fitted with Wing from G-MVUK?)*			
G-MTUP	Solar Wings Pegasus XL-Q		20. 1.88	S.J.Allen	Blisworth, Northampton	25. 8.03P
	(Rotax 447) SW-TB-1303 & SW-WA-0018					
G-MTUR	Solar Wings Pegasus XL-Q		20. 1.88	G.Ball	(Tewkesbury)	26. 3.03P
	(Rotax 447) SW-TB-1304 & SW-WQ-0019					
G-MTUS	Solar Wings Pegasus XL-Q		20. 1.88	A.I.McPherson	Glenrothes	4.11.02P
	(Rotax 447) SW-TB-1305 & SW-WQ-0020					
G-MTUT	Solar Wings Pegasus XL-Q		21. 1.88	L.F.Tanner & D.D.Lock	Sutton Meadows, Ely	15. 7.03P
	(Rotax 462) SW-TE-0040 & SW-WQ-0021					
G-MTUU	Mainair Gemini/Flash IIA	623-288-5 & W412	10. 2.88	M.Harris	Eshott	27. 7.00P
	(Rotax 503)					
G-MTUV	Mainair Gemini/Flash IIA	624-288-5 & W413	28. 1.88	J.F.Bolton	(Watford)	7.10.03P
	(Rotax 462)					
G-MTUX	Medway Hybred 44XLR	241287/33	2. 2.88	P.A.R.Wilson	Baxby Manor, Husthwaite	29. 8.99P
	(Rotax 503)			*(Current status unknown)*		
G-MTUY	Solar Wings Pegasus XL-Q		28. 1.88	H.C.Lowther	(Penrith)	1. 4.01P
	(Rotax 462) SW-TE-0041 & SW-WQ-0022					
G-MTVB	Solar Wings Pegasus XL-R		28. 1.88	J.Williams	(Worcester)	15.11.03P
	(Rotax 447) SW-TB-1307 & SW-WA-1302					
G-MTVG	Mainair Gemini/Flash IIA	628-388-6 & W417	12. 2.88	D.A.Whitworth & L.L.Perry	(Woodbridge)	29. 8.03P
	(Rotax 503)					
G-MTVH	Mainair Gemini/Flash IIA	626-288-6 & W415	17. 2.88	D.K.May	Tarn Farm, Cockerham	22. 5.03P
	(Rotax 503)					
G-MTVI	Mainair Gemini/Flash IIA	629-388-6 & W416	12. 2.88	R.A.McDowell	(Slough)	10. 5.92P
	(Rotax 503)			*(Current status unknown)*		
G-MTVJ	Mainair Gemini/Flash IIA	627-388-6 & W418	12. 2.88	D.M.Waller	(Keighley)	3. 5.02P
	(Rotax 503)					
G-MTVK	Solar Wings Pegasus XL-R		15. 2.88	J D MacNamara	(Crediton)	17. 3.98P
	(Rotax 447) SW-TB-1311 & SW-WA-1306			*(Current status unknown)*		
G-MTVL	Solar Wings Pegasus XL-R/Se		15. 2.88	K.P.Roper	Weston Zoyland	17. 6.03P
	(Rotax 447) SW-TB-1312 & SW-WA-1307					
G-MTVM	Solar Wings Pegasus XL-R		15. 2.88	M.D.Howard	(Great Yarmouth)	23.9.03P
	(Rotax 447) SW-TB-1313 & SW-WA-1308					
G-MTVN	Solar Wings Pegasus XL-R		15. 2.88	A.I.Crighton	Lower Mountpleasant Farm, Chatteris	11.10.03P
	(Rotax 447) SW-TB-1314 & SW-WA-1309					
G-MTVO	Solar Wings Pegasus XL-R		15. 2.88	D A Payne	Long Marston	19. 4.03P
	(Rotax 447) SW-TB-1315 & SW-WA-1310					

G-MTVP	Thruster TST Mk.1	8028-TST-056	10. 2.88	J.M.Evans	(Abingdon)	13. 3.03P
	(Rotax 503) *(C/n plate marked incorrectly as 8208-TST-056)*					
G-MTVR	Thruster TST Mk.1	8028-TST-057	10. 2.88	D.B.Southworth	(York)	19. 7.03P
	(Rotax 503)					
G-MTVS	Thruster TST Mk.1	8028-TST-058	10. 2.88	W.J.Burrell	(Banbridge, Co.Down)	2. 5.03P
	(Rotax 503)					
G-MTVT	Thruster TST Mk.1	8028-TST-059	10. 2.88	M.L.Walsh & A.T.Farmer	Mill Farm, Shifnal	2. 5.03P
	(Rotax 503)					
G-MTVV	Thruster TST Mk.1	8028-TST-061	10. 2.88	S.Wylie	(Coalisland, Co.Tyrone)	22.10.02P
	(Rotax 503)					
G-MTVX	Solar Wings Pegasus XL-Q		3. 3.88	M.O.O'Brien	Rufforth	4. 8.03P
	(Rotax 462HP) SW-TE-0042 & SW-WQ-0025					
G-MTWA	Solar Wings Pegasus XL-R		25. 2.88	A.P.Watkins,	Roddidge, Fradley	18. 4.02P
	(Rotax 447) SW-TB-1317 & SW-WA-1311			tr G-MTWA Flying Group		
G-MTWB	Solar Wings Pegasus XL-R		25. 2.88	M.W.A.Shemilt	(Henley-on-Thames)	13.11.98P
	(Rotax 447) SW-TB-1342 & SW-WA-1312		*(Originally fitted with trike c/n SW-TB-1318: latter damaged, repaired & resold with sailwing*			
	c/n SW-WA-1330 as SE-YOK)		*(Current status unknown)*			
G-MTWC	Solar Wings Pegasus XL-R		25. 2.88	J.Clark	Davidstow Moor	8. 6.02P
	(Rotax 447) SW-TB-1321 & SW-WA-1313					
G-MTWD	Solar Wings Pegasus XL-R		25. 2.88	J.C.Rawlings	(Olney)	7. 9.03P
	(Rotax 447) SW-TB-1320 & SW-WA-1314					
G-MTWF	Mainair Gemini/Flash IIA	630-388-6 & W419	25. 2.88	W.Porter	Knapthorpe Lodge, Caunton	19. 6.03P
	(Rotax 503)					
G-MTWG	Mainair Gemini/Flash IIA	631-288-6 & W420	25. 2.88	N.Mackenzie & P.S.Bunting	(Southport)	28. 7.00P
	(Rotax 503)					
G-MTWH	CFM Shadow CD	K.064	25. 2.88	V.A.Hutchinson	(Nuneaton)	17. 8.03P
	(Rotax 503)					
G-MTWK	CFM Shadow CD	073	25. 2.88	R.C.Fendick	Westbury-sub-Mendip	25. 9.03P
	(Rotax 503)					
G-MTWL	CFM Shadow BD	076	25. 2.88	M.J.Gray	Manor Farm, Croughton	19.10.02P
	(Rotax 447)					
G-MTWN	CFM Shadow CD	081	25. 2.88	P.W.Heywood	Davidstow Moor	26. 7.03P
	(Rotax 503)					
G-MTWR	Mainair Gemini/Flash IIA	632-388-6 & W421	3. 3.88	J.B.Hodson	Arclid Green, Sandbach	8. 4.03P
	(Rotax 503)					
G-MTWS	Mainair Gemini/Flash IIA	633-388-6 & W422	3. 3.88	K W Roberts	Sandtoft	25. 8.02P
	(Rotax 503)					
G-MTWX	Mainair Gemini/Flash IIA	634-488-6 & W423	11. 3.88	M.Warmerdam	(Leyland)	5. 6.02P
	(Rotax 503)					
G-MTWY	Thruster TST Mk.1	8038-TST-062	15. 3.88	M.F.Eddington	(Wincanton)	20. 4.03P
	(Rotax 503)					
G-MTWZ	Thruster TST Mk.1	8038-TST-063	15. 3.88	A.Makepeace	Walkeridge Farm, Hannington	8. 9.03P
	(Rotax 503)					
G-MTXA	Thruster TST Mk.1	8038-TST-064	15. 3.88	A.Maxwell	Morgansfield, Fishburn	21. 7.02P
	(Rotax 503)					
G-MTXB	Thruster TST Mk.1	8038-TST-065	15. 3.88	J.J.Hill	Baxby Manor, Husthwaite	30. 8.03P
	(Rotax 503)					
G-MTXC	Thruster TST Mk.1	8038-TST-066	15. 3.88	Joan A.Huntley	South Wraxall, Bradford-on-Avon	14. 7.02P
	(Rotax 503)					
G-MTXD	Thruster TST Mk.1	8038-TST-067	15. 3.88	S.Hoyle	Baxby Manor, Husthwaite	28. 3.03P
	(Rotax 503)					
G-MTXE	Hornet Dual Trainer/Southdown Raven		11. 3.88	F.J.Marton t/a Charter Systems	Long Marston	22. 5.00P
	(Rotax 462) HRWA 0070 & SN2000/0332					
G-MTXH	Solar Wings Pegasus XL-Q		11. 3.88	J.Rhodes	(Pontefract)	21. 7.97P
	(Rotax 447) SW-TB-1328 & SW-WQ-0030			*(Current status unknown)*		
G-MTXI	Solar Wings Pegasus XL-Q		11. 3.88	R.Lewis-Evans	(Poole)	20. 8.02P
	(Rotax 447) SW-TB-1329 & SW-WQ-0031					
G-MTXJ	Solar Wings Pegasus XL-Q		11. 3.88	J.E.Wright	Biggin Hill	4. 9.03P
	(Rotax 447) SW-TB-1330 & SW-WQ-0032					
G-MTXK	Solar Wings Pegasus XL-Q		11. 3.88	M.J.McManamon	(Inverurie)	4. 8.02P
	(Rotax 447) SW-TB-1331 & SW-WQ-0033					
G-MTXL	Noble Hardman Snowbird Mk.IV	SB-006	4. 5.88	P.J.Collins	(Dublin)	12. 6.00P
	(Rotax 532)			*(New owner 12.02)*		
G-MTXM	Mainair Gemini/Flash IIA	636-488-6 & W425	10. 5.88	W.Archibald	(Burntisland)	5.10.03P
	(Rotax 503))					
G-MTXO	Whittaker MW.6 Merlin	PFA 164-11326	11. 3.88	S.J.Whyatt	(Chipping Norton)	4. 8.98P
	(Rotax 503)			*(New CofR 12.02)*		
G-MTXP	Mainair Gemini/Flash IIA	637-488-6 & W426	23. 3.88	M.B.Buttle	St.Michaels	26.12.01P
	(Rotax 503)					
G-MTXR	CFM Shadow CD (Rotax 503)	K.038	23. 3.88	M.E.H.Quick	Old Sarum	9. 8.03P
G-MTXS	Mainair Gemini/Flash IIA	638-488-6 & W427	23. 3.88	S.E.Wilks	(Nottingham)	30. 4.03P
	(Rotax 503)					
G-MTXU	Noble Hardman Snowbird Mk.IV	SB-007	3. 5.88	J.A.Rees	Haverfordwest	16. 5.89P
	(Rotax 532)			*(Current status unknown)*		
G-MTXY*	Hornet Dual Trainer/Southdown Raven		30. 3.88	J.McAvoy	(Bishopton)	17. 8.02P
	(Rotax 462) HRWA 0073 & SN2000/0354			*(Cancelled 23.9.02 by CAA)*		
G-MTXZ	Mainair Gemini/Flash IIA	641-588-6 & W430	10. 5.88	P.Cave	(Caerphilly)	18. 6.03P
	(Rotax 503)					
G-MTYA	Solar Wings Pegasus XL-Q		29. 3.88	I.Clarkson	Long Marston	22. 9.03P
	(Rotax 462HP) SW-TE-0047 & SW-WQ-0037					
G-MTYC	Solar Wings Pegasus XL-Q		30. 3.88	C.I.D.H.Garrison	Sutton Meadows, Ely	20. 9.03P
	(Rotax 462) SW-TE-0049 & SW-WQ-0039					
G-MTYD	Solar Wings Pegasus XL-Q		29. 3.88	D.Young c/o Pegasus Flight Training (Cotswolds)		
	(Rotax 462) SW-TE-0050 & SW-WQ-0040				Kemble	19.10.03P

Reg	Type	C/n	Prev id	Date	Owner	Location	Expiry
G-MTYE	Solar Wings Pegasus XL-Q			29. 3.88	K.L.Chorley & A.Cook	Enstone	26. 5.03P
	(Rotax 462) SW-TE-0051 & SW-WQ-0041						
G-MTYF	Solar Wings Pegasus XL-Q			29. 3.88	J.Hyde	(Spalding)	20. 6.03P
	(Rotax 462) SW-TE-0052 & SW-WQ-0042						
G-MTYH	Solar Wings Pegasus XL-Q			7.11.88	P.R.Hanman	(Gloucester)	18. 6.03
	SW-TE-0054 & SW-WQ-0044						
G-MTYI	Solar Wings Pegasus XL-Q			30. 3.88	R.H.Stokes	(Warboys)	12. 9.03P
	(Rotax 462) SW-TE-0055 & SW-WQ-0045						
G-MTYL	Solar Wings Pegasus XL-Q			30. 3.88	E.T.H.Cox	(Church Stretton)	20.10.02P
	(Rotax 462) SW-TE-0058 & SW-WQ-0048			*(Original sailwing c/n SW-WQ-0048 replaced by c/n 6412)*			
G-MTYP	Solar Wings Pegasus XL-Q			30. 3.88	J L Ker	Eshott	15.12.02P
	(Rotax 462) SW-TE-0062 & SW-WQ-0052						
G-MTYR	Solar Wings Pegasus XL-Q			30. 3.88	M.E.Grafton	(Hay-on-Wye)	30. 4.99P
	(Rotax 462) SW-TE-0063 & SW-WQ-0053				*(New owner 5.01)*		
G-MTYS	Solar Wings Pegasus XL-Q			30. 3.88	R.G.Wall	Caerleon	28. 3.03P
	(Rotax 462) SW-TE-0064 & SW-WQ-0054						
G-MTYT	Solar Wings Pegasus XL-Q			30. 3.88	M.G.Walsh	Rufforth	13. 9.99P
	(Rotax 462HP) SW-TE-0065 & SW-WQ-0055				*(CofR restored 2.11.01)*		
G-MTYU	Solar Wings Pegasus XL-Q			30. 3.88	N.I.Garland & M.Powell	Dunkeswell	14. 4.03P
	(Rotax 462HP) SW-TE-0066 & SW-WQ-0056						
G-MTYV	Raven Aircraft Raven X	SN2232/0341		8. 4.88	R.E.J.Pattenden	(Maidstone)	7. 5.03P
	(Rotax 447)						
G-MTYW	Raven Aircraft Raven X	SN2232/0344		8. 4.88	R.Solomans	Middle Stoke, Kent	12. 7.03P
	(Rotax 447)						
G-MTYX	Raven Aircraft Raven X	SN2232/0345		8. 4.88	J.C.Hawkins	(Selsey)	15. 8.00P
	(Rotax 447)						
G-MTYY	Solar Wings Pegasus XL-R	SW-WA-1326		6. 5.88	G.J.Slater	Clench Common	3. 2.02P
	(Rotax 447)						
G-MTZA	Thruster TST Mk.1	8048-TST-068		13. 4.88	R.Bingham	(Craigavon, Co Armagh)	6. 5.03P
	(Rotax 503)						
G-MTZB	Thruster TST Mk.1	8048-TST-069		13. 4.88	S.J.O.Tinn	(Weymouth)	26. 2.03P
	(Rotax 503)						
G-MTZC	Thruster TST Mk.1	8048-TST-070		13. 4.88	R.W.Marshal	I(Armagh)	30. 6.03P
	(Rotax 503)						
G-MTZD	Thruster TST Mk.1	8048-TST-071		13. 4.88	G.H.Hills	(Alton)	8.10.99P
	(Rotax 503)				*(Current status unknown)*		
G-MTZE	Thruster TST Mk.1	8048-TST-072		13. 4.88	M R Jones	Wing Farm, Longbridge Deverill	26. 8.01P
	(Rotax 503)				*(Under rebuild 12.01)*		
G-MTZF	Thruster TST Mk.1	8048-TST-073		13. 4.88	D.Large tr Zulu Fox Group	Long Marston	4. 9.03P
	(Rotax 503)						
G-MTZG	Mainair Gemini/Flash IIA	642-588-6 & W431		10. 5.88	T.G.Greenhill	Swinford, Rugby	18. 6.03P
	(Rotax 503)						
G-MTZH	Mainair Gemini/Flash IIA	643-588-6 & W433		9. 6.88	D.C.Hughes	St.Michaels	17. 7.01P
	(Rotax 462)						
G-MTZK	Solar Wings Pegasus XL-R			6. 5.88	D.J.Brixton	Bishops Castle	23.10.03P
	(Rotax 447) SW-TB-1336 & SW-WA-1329				tr Shropshire Tow Group		
G-MTZL	Mainair Gemini/Flash IIA	645-588-6 & W435		10. 5.88	N.S.Brayn	Popham	31. 7.03P
	(Rotax 503)						
G-MTZM	Mainair Gemini/Flash IIA	646-588-6 & W436		3. 5.88	K.L.Smith	(Leicester)	27. 8.03P
	(Rotax 503)						
G-MTZO	Mainair Gemini/Flash IIA	649-688-6 & W439		6. 5.88	R.C.Hinds	(Newnham, Glos)	25. 6.03P
	(Rotax 462)						
G-MTZP	Solar Wings Pegasus XL-Q			6. 5.88	Island Micro Aviation Ltd	Sandown	25. 6.03P
	(Rotax 447) SW-TB-1337 & SW-WQ-0059						
G-MTZR	Solar Wings Pegasus XL-Q			6. 5.88	P.J.Hatchett	Emlyn's Field, Rhuallt	19. 8.98P
	(Rotax 447) SW-TB-1338 & SW-WQ-0060				*(Current status unknown)*		
G-MTZS	Solar Wings Pegasus XL-Q			6. 5.88	P.A.Darling	(Wilmslow)	15. 7.93P
	(Rotax 447) SW-TB-1339 & SW-WQ-0061				*(Current status unknown)*		
G-MTZT	Solar Wings Pegasus XL-Q			6. 5.88	M.Y.Brown	Eshott	28. 6.02P
	(Rotax 447) SW-TB-1340 & SW-WQ-0062						
G-MTZV	Mainair Gemini/Flash IIA	650-688-6 & W440		6. 5.88	G.J.Donnellon	Barton	26. 3.03P
	(Rotax 503)						
G-MTZW	Mainair Gemini/Flash IIA	651-688-6 & W441		25. 5.88	L.McIntyre	Ince Blundell	11.10.02P
	(Rotax 503)						
G-MTZX	Mainair Gemini/Flash IIA	652-688-6 & W442		23. 6.88	R.G.Cuckow & J.C.Thompson	(Wetherby)	2. 3.03P
	(Rotax 503)						
G-MTZY	Mainair Gemini/Flash IIA	653-688-6 & W443		24. 5.88	P.K.Dale	Bagby	13. 4.03P
	(Rotax 503)						
G-MTZZ	Mainair Gemini/Flash IIA	654-688-6 & W444		14. 6.88	P.J.Litchfield	Tarn Farm, Cockerham	14. 4.01P
	(Rotax 503)				*(Noted 2.03)*		
G-MUFY	Robinson R22 Beta	1248	D-HICH	13.12.96	Helicentre Liverpool Ltd	Liverpool	22.12.02T
G-MUIR	Cameron V-65 HAB	2037		23. 6.89	Lindsay J.M.Muir *"Muriel"*	East Molesey	6. 5.03A
G-MUNI	Mooney M.20J (201SE)	24-3118		12. 5.89	H.A.Daines	Beccles	15.10.04
	(Lost power on take-off Fairoaks 6.7.02, force-landed in field, damaged both wings, fuselage & propeller: new owner 1.03)						
G-MURI*	Learjet LearJet 35A	35A-646	N712JB	19. 2.98	Not known	Lyon/St Exupery, France	18. 2.00T
			N717JB/N646EA/XA-UMA/N3812G				
	(Crashed Lyon/Satolas, France 2.5.00 & destroyed: cancelled 20.6.00 as destroyed) (Wreck dumped 7.01)						
G-MURR	Whittaker MW6 Merlin	PFA 164-12501		16. 4.99	D.Murray	Bristol	
	(PFA Plans No duplicates G-SHIM)				*(Current status unknown)*		
G-MURY	Robinson R44 Astro	0201		19. 7.95	Simlot Ltd *(Op Jennifer Murray)*	Denham	17. 5.04T
G-MUSO	Rutan LongEz	PFA 74A-10590		11. 6.83	P.A.Willis	(Boston)	5. 8.03P
	(Lycoming O-235-C2A)						
G-MUTE	Colt 31A Air Chair HAB	2099		2.12.91	K.Temple	Eye	11.11.99A
G-MUVG	Cessna 421C Golden Eagle III	421C1064	N421DD	13. 1.97	Air Montgomery Ltd	Leeds-Bradford	12. 3.05T

Reg	Type	C/n	Prev	Date	Owner	Location	Status
G-MVAA	Mainair Gemini/Flash IIA (Rotax 503)	655-688-6 & W445		8. 6.88	G.F.J.Field	(Hucknall)	23. 2.03P
G-MVAB	Mainair Gemini/Flash IIA (Rotax 503)	656-688-6 & W446		10. 5.88	W.Anderson	Glenrothes	15. 9.03P
G-MVAC	CFM Shadow CD (Rotax 503)	K.077		12. 5.88	C.A.S.Powell	Insch	15. 9.02P
G-MVAD	Mainair Gemini/Flash IIA (Rotax 503)	657-688-6 & W447		10. 5.88	N.G.Woodall	Tarn Farm, Cockerham	10. 8.02P
G-MVAF	Southdown Puma Sprint (Fuji-Robin EC-44-2PM)	P.455	G-MBAF	24. 6.87	J.F.Horn	(Yelverton)	10. 5.03P
G-MVAG	Thruster TST Mk.1 (Rotax 503)	8058-TST-074		18. 5.88	W.A.Stephenson	(Newry, Co.Armagh)	22. 3.03P
G-MVAH	Thruster TST Mk.1 (Rotax 503)	8058-TST-075		18. 5.88	M.W.H.Henton *"Times Four"*	Popham	18. 8.03P
G-MVAI	Thruster TST Mk.1 (Rotax 503)	8058-TST-076		18. 5.88	D.J.Townsend	(Norwich)	14. 4.03P
G-MVAJ	Thruster TST Mk.1 (Rotax 503)	8058-TST-077		18. 5.88	A.T.Harvey	Long Marston	16. 6.02P
G-MVAK	Thruster TST Mk.1 (Rotax 503)	8058-TST-078		18. 5.88	P.A.Gasson	(Woking)	24. 8.03P
G-MVAL	Thruster TST Mk.1 (Rotax 503)	8058-TST-079		18. 5.88	G.C.Brooke	(Colchester)	7. 8.96P
G-MVAM	CFM Shadow CD (Rotax 503)	082		18. 5.88	C.P.Barber	Brook Farm, Pilling	12.10.02P
G-MVAN	CFM Shadow CD (Rotax 503)	K.048 & PFA 161-11219		18. 5.88	I.Brewster	Bourn	17. 8.03P
G-MVAO	Mainair Gemini/Flash IIA (Rotax 503)	658-688-6 & W448		24. 5.88	S.J.Robson *(Op Brook Farm Microlight Centre)*	Brook Farm, Pilling	24. 7.03P
G-MVAP	Mainair Gemini/Flash IIA (Rotax 503)	659-688-6 & W449		24. 5.88	R.J.Miller	Long Marston	31.10.02P
G-MVAR	Solar Wings Pegasus XL-R (Rotax 447)	SW-TB-1343 & SW-WA-1331		24. 5.88	A.J.Johnson	(Peterborough)	20. 9.02P
G-MVAT	Solar Wings Pegasus XL-R (Rotax 447)	SW-TB-1345 & SW-WA-1333		24. 5.88	P.Burtwistle	Perth	26. 2.03P
G-MVAV	Solar Wings Pegasus XL-R (Rotax 447)	SW-TB-1347 & SW-WA-1335		24. 5.88	D.J.Utting	(Bungay)	16. 2.03P
G-MVAW	Solar Wings Pegasus XL-Q (Rotax 447)	SW-TB-1348 & SW-WQ-0064		24. 5.88	G.Sharman	Sywell	23. 4.03P
G-MVAX	Solar Wings Pegasus XL-Q (Rotax 447)	SW-TB-1349 & SW-WQ-0065		24. 5.88	S.J.Rogers & D.W.Power	(Saundersfoot)	26. 8.02P
G-MVAY	Solar Wings Pegasus XL-Q (Rotax 447)	SW-TB-1350 & SW-WQ-0066		24. 5.88	V.O.Morris *(Current status unknown)*	(Swansea)	16. 4.97P
G-MVBB	CFM Shadow BD (Rotax 447)	K.051		24. 5.88	R.Garrod	(Mendlesham)	8.10.00P
G-MVBC	Mainair Tri-Flyer/Aerial Arts 130SX	130SX-616		24. 5.88	D.Beer	(Ilfracombe)	
	(Believed to be using Mainair Tri-Flyer 250 Trike from G-MJIX)				*(Current status unknown)*		
G-MVBD	Mainair Gemini/Flash IIA (Rotax 462)	660-688-6 & W450		8. 6.88	J.Batchelor	(Benfleet)	12. 6.02P
G-MVBF	Mainair Gemini/Flash IIA (Rotax 462) *(Original trike* now fitted to G-MNLB qv)*	662-688-6* & W452		14. 6.88	P.& C.Moore	(Corby)	19.10.02P
G-MVBG	Mainair Gemini/Flash IIA (Rotax 503)	663-688-6 & W453		25. 5.88	M.P.Edwards	Shifnal	27. 7.03P
G-MVBI	Mainair Gemini/Flash IIA (Rotax 503)	665-788-6 & W455		7. 6.88	P.Thomas	(Barrow-in-Furness)	26. 9.03P
G-MVBJ	Solar Wings Pegasus XL-R (Rotax 462)	SW-TE-0033 & SW-WA-1338		7. 6.88	R.J.O.Page	Old Sarum	4. 8.02P
G-MVBK	Mainair Gemini/Flash IIA (Rotax 462)	666-788-6 & W456		7. 6.88	C.S.Bowen & M.D.Carruthers	Manor Farm, Inskip	31. 3.03P
G-MVBL	Mainair Gemini/Flash IIA (Rotax 503)	669-788-6 & W459		7. 6.88	P.M.Wright	Higher Barn Farm, Houghton	15.11.01P
G-MVBM	Mainair Gemini/Flash IIA (Rotax 503)	667-788-6 & W457		7. 6.88	A.M.Wood	(Chelmsford)	9. 8.03P
G-MVBN	Mainair Gemini/Flash IIA (Rotax 503)	668-788-6 & W458		8. 6.88	M.Frankcom *(Current status unknown)*	(Darwen)	2. 6.99P
G-MVBO	Mainair Gemini/Flash IIA (Rotax 503)	671-788-6 & W461		8. 6.88	R.Brasher	(Rugeley)	17.11.03P
G-MVBP	Thruster TST Mk.1 (Rotax 503)	8068-TST-080		14. 6.88	K.J.Crompton	Newtownards, Co.Down	12. 3.03P
G-MVBT	Thruster TST Mk.1 (BMW R100)	8068-TST-083		14. 6.88	E.L.Everitt	Ley Farm, Chirk	23.11.03P
G-MVBY	Solar Wings Pegasus XL-R (Rotax 447)	SW-TB-1357 & SW-WA-1344		17. 6.88	J.E.Harman *tr Pigs R Us Flying Group*	(Napton)	6. 1.02P
G-MVBZ	Solar Wings Pegasus XL-R (Rotax 447)	SW-TB-1358 & SW-WA-1345		17. 6.88	A.G.Butler	Shenstone Hall Farm, Shenstone	11. 4.03P
G-MVCA	Solar Wings Pegasus XL-R (Rotax 447)	SW-TB-1359 & SW-WA-1346		17. 6.88	R.Walker	Sutton Meadows, Ely	2. 8.03P
G-MVCB	Solar Wings Pegasus XL-R (Rotax 447)	SW-TB-1360 & SW-WA-1347		17. 6.88	G.T.Clipstone	(Ipswich)	18. 6.00P
G-MVCC	CFM Shadow CD (Rotax 503)	K.045		17. 6.88	K.D.Mitchell	Shoreham	9. 5.03P
G-MVCD	Medway Hybred 44XLR (Rotax 447) *(Marked as "Raven") (Original sailwing transferred to G-MVOS: new wing c/n not yet known)*	MR001/34		14. 6.88	J.Thompson	Long Acre Farm, Sandy	27. 7.03P
G-MVCE	Mainair Gemini/Flash IIA (Rotax 503)	672-788-6 & W462		23. 6.88	J.D.Berry *(Current status unknown)*	Ince Blundell	5. 4.99P

G-MVCF	Mainair Gemini/Flash IIA	673-788-6 & W463	14. 7.88	J.L.Hamer	(Hartpury, Glos)	23. 7.02P
	(Rotax 462)					
G-MVCI	Noble Hardman Snowbird Mk.IV	SB-011	11.10.88	W.L.Chapman	Tarn Farm, Cockerham	13. 4.95P
	(Rotax 532)			*(Current status unknown)*		
G-MVCJ	Noble Hardman Snowbird Mk.IV	SB-012	11.10.88	C.W.Buxton	Barton	14. 9.03P
	(Rotax 532)					
G-MVCK	Cosmos Trike/La Mouette Profil 19	SDA-01	19. 7.88	S.D.Alsop *(Current status unknown)*	(Bath)	
G-MVCL	Solar Wings Pegasus XL-Q		27. 6.88	T.E.Robinson	Insch	1. 9.03P
	(Rotax 462HP)	SW-TE-0069 & SW-WQ-0075				
G-MVCM	Solar Wings Pegasus XL-Q		27. 6.88	M.M.Coggan	Sandtoft	7. 4.03P
	(Rotax 462)	SW-TE-0070 & SW-WQ-0076				
G-MVCN	Solar Wings Pegasus XL-Q		27. 6.88	S.R.S.Evans	(Chelmsford)	20. 3.01P
	(Rotax 462)	SW-TE-0071 & SW-WQ-0077				
G-MVCP	Solar Wings Pegasus XL-Q		27. 6.88	J.R.Fulcher	(Whittlesford)	27. 6.03P
	(Rotax 462)	SW-TE-0073 & SW-WQ-0079				
G-MVCR	Solar Wings Pegasus XL-Q		27. 6.88	A.V.Dunne	Plaistows Farm, St.Albans	30. 5.03P
	(Rotax 462)	SW-TE-0069 & SW-WQ-0080				
G-MVCS	Solar Wings Pegasus XL-Q		27. 6.88	J.J.Sparrow	Sywell	19. 7.02P
	(Rotax 462)	SW-TE-0075 & SW-WQ-0081				
G-MVCT	Solar Wings Pegasus XL-Q		27. 6.88	G.J.Lampitt	Pound Green, Buttonoak, Kidderminster	22. 8.03P
	(Rotax 462)	SW-TE-0076 & SW-WQ-0082				
G-MVCV	Solar Wings Pegasus XL-Q	SW-WQ-0084	27. 6.88	G.E.& B.T.Nunn	Long Acre Farm, Sandy	20. 4.02P
	(Rotax 462) *(Original trike c/n SW-TE-0078 damaged & replaced by SW-TE-0108: later repaired & fitted with sailwing SW-WQ-0105 & regd G-MVHP)*					
G-MVCW	CFM Shadow BD	084	28. 6.88	W.A.Douthwaite	Tarn Farm, Cockerham	1. 8.03P
	(Rotax 447)					
G-MVCY	Mainair Gemini/Flash IIA	674-788-6 & W464	14. 7.88	A.M.Smith	Otherton, Cannock	1. 5.03P
	(Rotax 503)					
G-MVCZ	Mainair Gemini/Flash IIA	675-788-6 & W465	26. 8.88	B.Hall	Tarn Farm, Cockerham	27.11.89P
	(Rotax 503)			*(New owner 1.03)*		
G-MVDA	Mainair Gemini/Flash IIA	676-788-6 & W466	13. 7.88	C.Tweedley	(Great Orton)	9. 7.03P
	(Rotax 462)					
G-MVDB	Medway Hybred 44XLR	MR005/36	28. 7.88	G.P.Barnes & J.W.Davies	Sywell	2. 5.02P
	(Rotax 447)					
G-MVDD	Thruster TST Mk.1	8078-TST-086	12. 7.88	D.J.Love	(Witton, Norwich)	9.11.99P
	(Rotax 503)			*(Current status unknown)*		
G-MVDE	Thruster TST Mk.1	8078-TST-087	12. 7.88	R.H.Davis	Doynton	26. 8.99P
	(Rotax 503)			*(Derelict 2.03)*		
G-MVDF	Thruster TST Mk.1	8078-TST-088	12. 7.88	J.Walsh & A.R.Sunley	Rayne Hall Farm, Rayne	2. 5.03P
	(Rotax 503)					
G-MVDG	Thruster TST Mk.1	8078-TST-089	12. 7.88	D.G.,P.M. & A.B.Smith	Popham	26. 7.00P
	(Rotax 503)					
G-MVDH	Thruster TST Mk.1	8078-TST-090	12. 7.88	P.E.Terrell	(Plymouth)	15. 8.02P
	(Rotax 503)					
G-MVDJ	Medway Hybred 44XLR	MR010/38	20. 7.88	W.D.Hutchings	(Nottingham)	15. 5.03P
	(Rotax 447)					
G-MVDK	Aerial Arts Chaser S	CH.702	5. 8.88	S.Adams	Leicester	29.11.98P
	(Rotax 377)			*(Noted 9.01)*		
G-MVDL	Aerial Arts Chaser S	CH.701	11. 8.88	J.R.Hall	Bibberne Farm, Stalbridge	18. 8.02P
	(Rotax 462)					
G-MVDN*	Aerial Arts Chaser S	CH.704	11. 8.88	Not known	St.Michaels	11. 2.94P
	(Rotax 377)			*(Cancelled 18.5.00 by CAA) (For rebuild 9.02)*		
G-MVDP	Aerial Arts Chaser S	CH.706	11. 8.88	P.Corke	Long Acre Farm, Sandy	9.11.02P
	(Rotax 447)					
G-MVDR	Aerial Arts Chaser S	CH.708	11. 8.88	S.B.Walters	(Northampton)	8. 3.03P
	(Rotax 447)					
G-MVDT	Mainair Gemini/Flash IIA	670-788-6 & W460	20. 7.88	D.C.Stephens	(Coleford, Glos)	26. 5.00P
	(Rotax 503)					
G-MVDU	Solar Wings Pegasus XL-R		13. 7.88	D.R.Western	Weston Zoyland	25.10.03P
	(Rotax 447)	SW-TB-1361 & SW-WA-1348				
G-MVDV	Solar Wings Pegasus XL-R		13. 7.88	E.J.Blyth & L.D.Benson	(Pickering)	24. 8.97P
	(Rotax 447)	SW-TB-1362 & SW-WA-1349		*(Current status unknown)*		
G-MVDW	Solar Wings Pegasus XL-R		13. 7.88	R.P.Brown	Long Acre Farm, Sandy	20. 7.97P
	(Rotax 447)	SW-TB-1363 & SW-WA-1350		*(Current status unknown)*		
G-MVDX	Solar Wings Pegasus XL-R		13. 7.88	C.Kett	Weston Zoyland	8. 8.98P
	(Rotax 447)	SW-TB-1364 & SW-WA-1351		*(Current status unknown)*		
G-MVDY	Solar Wings Pegasus XL-R		13. 7.88	C.G.Murphy	Biggin Hill	1. 6.92P
	(Rotax 447)	SW-TB-1365 & SW-WA-1352		*(Current status unknown)*		
G-MVDZ	Solar Wings Pegasus XL-R		12. 7.88	A.K.Pickering	(Robertsbridge)	19. 5.00P
	(Rotax 447)	SW-TB-1366 & SW-WA-1353				
G-MVEC	Solar Wings Pegasus XL-R		20. 7.88	J.A.Jarvis	Davidstow Moor	18.4.03P
	(Rotax 447)	SW-TB-1369 & SW-WA-1356				
G-MVED	Solar Wings Pegasus XL-R/Se		20. 7.88	P.A.Sleightholme	Baxby Manor, Husthwaite	24. 5.03P
	(Rotax 447)	SW-TB-1370 & SW-WA-1357				
G-MVEE	Medway Hybred 44XLR	MR004/35	22. 7.88	D.S.L.Evans	(Gravesend)	8. 6.01P
	(Rotax 447) *(Trike c/n same as G-MYMJ and suggests this has a replacement unit)*					
G-MVEF	Solar Wings Pegasus XL-R		19. 7.88	E.J.Blyth	(Pickering)	15.11.93P
	(Rotax 462)	SW-TE-0079 & SW-WA-1358		*(Current status unknown)*		
G-MVEG	Solar Wings Pegasus XL-R		19. 7.88	A.W.Leadley	(Strabane, Co.Tyrone)	15. 5.99P
	(Rotax 462)	SW-TE-0080 & SW-WA-1359		*(Current status unknown)*		
G-MVEH	Mainair Gemini/Flash IIA	677-788-6 & W468	26. 8.88	M.R.Coleman	(Windermere)	31. 7.03P
	(Rotax 503)					
G-MVEI	CFM Shadow CD (Rotax 503)	085	26. 7.88	R.H.Faux	(Penrith)	29.12.02P
G-MVEJ	Mainair Gemini/Flash IIA	678-888-6 & W469	27. 7.88	M.Thornburn & S.Mair	(Moffat/Lockerbie)	22.11.01P
	(Rotax 462)					

Reg	Type	C/n	Date	Owner	Location	
G-MVEK	Mainair Gemini/Flash IIA (Rotax 503)	679-888-6 & W470	27. 7.88	D.R.Gooby	Henstridge	20. 9.03P
G-MVEL	Mainair Gemini/Flash IIA (Rotax 503)	680-888-6 & W471	27. 7.88	M.R.Starling	Swanton Morley	25. 7.03P
G-MVEN	CFM Shadow CD (Rotax 503)	K.047	26. 7.88	D.J.Burton	(Brighton)	4. 8.03P
G-MVEO	Mainair Gemini/Flash IIA (Rotax 503)	682-888-6 & W472	28. 7.88	S.Macmillan	East Fortune	5. 2.03P
G-MVER	Mainair Gemini/Flash IIA (Rotax 503)	684-888-6 & W474	28. 7.88	J.R.Davis	(Cheltenham)	25. 4.03P
G-MVES	Mainair Gemini/Flash IIA (Rotax 503)	685-888-6 & W475	5. 8.88	F.W.McLean & S.H.Mitchell	East Fortune	4. 4.03P
G-MVET	Mainair Gemini/Flash IIA (Rotax 503)	686-888-6 & W476	19. 8.88	T.Bailey	Otherton, Cannock	14. 2.03P
G-MVEV	Mainair Gemini/Flash IIA (Rotax 503)	687-888-6 & W477	5. 8.88	C.Allen	(Alderley Edge)	8. 7.01P
G-MVEW	Mainair Gemini/Flash IIA (Rotax 503)	688-988-6 & W478	16. 9.88	N.A.Dye *(Current status unknown)*	Swanton Morley	27. 7.98P
G-MVEX	Solar Wings Pegasus XL-Q (Rotax 462)	SW-TE-0082 & SW-WQ-0088	5. 8.88	D. Maher	₊(Nenagh, Co Tipperary)	26. 5.02P
G-MVEZ	Solar Wings Pegasus XL-Q (Rotax 462)	SW-TE-0084 & SW-WQ-0090	9. 8.88	P.W.Millar *(Current status unknown)*	(Newnham)	13. 6.99P
G-MVFA	Solar Wings Pegasus XL-Q (Rotax 462HP)	SW-TE-0085 & SW-WQ-0091	9. 8.88	A.Johnson	Deenethorpe	23. 6.03P
G-MVFB	Solar Wings Pegasus XL-Q (Rotax 462)	SW-TE-0086 & SW-WQ-0092	9. 8.88	M.O.Bloy	(King's Lynn)	14. 4.02P
G-MVFC	Solar Wings Pegasus XL-Q (Rotax 462)	SW-TE-0087 & SW-WQ-0093	9. 8.88	D.R.Joint *(Current status unknown)*	(Bournemouth)	25. 6.95P
G-MVFD	Solar Wings Pegasus XL-Q (Rotax 462)	SW-TE-0088 & SW-WQ-0094	9. 8.88	C.D.Humphries	Long Marston	25. 5.01P
G-MVFE	Solar Wings Pegasus XL-Q (Rotax 462)	SW-TE-0089 & SW-WQ-0095	9. 8.88	S.J.Weeks	Kemble	30. 4.00P
G-MVFF	Solar Wings Pegasus XL-Q (Rotax 462)	SW-TE-0090 & SW-WQ-0096	9. 8.88	A.Makepeace	(Guildford)	31. 5.03P
G-MVFG	Solar Wings Pegasus XL-Q (Rotax 462)	SW-TE-0091 & SW-WQ-0097	9. 8.88	R.J.Vaughan	(Northwich)	5.10.00P
G-MVFH	CFM Shadow CD (Rotax 447)	086	9. 8.88	G.R.Read	(Mendlesham)	26. 1.03P
G-MVFJ	Thruster TST Mk.1 (Rotax 503)	8088-TST-092	11. 8.88	B.E.Renehan tr Kestrel Flying Group	Popham	22. 3.03P
G-MVFK	Thruster TST Mk.1 (Rotax 503)	8088-TST-093	11. 8.88	A.M.Commons	(Mentone, Victoria, Australia)	12. 3.03P
G-MVFL	Thruster TST Mk.1 (Rotax 503)	8088-TST-094	11. 8.88	C.Scoble tr G-MVFL Group	(Poole)	22. 5.02P
G-MVFM	Thruster TST Mk.1 (Rotax 503)	8088-TST-095	11. 8.88	W.J.H.Orr	(Blandford Forum)	24. 5.02P
G-MVFN	Thruster TST Mk.1 (Rotax 503-2V)	8088-TST-096	11. 8.88	A.G.Ward	Long Acre Farm, Sandy	29. 5.03P
G-MVFO	Thruster TST Mk.1 (Rotax 503-2V)	8088-TST-097	11. 8.88	A.L.Higgins & D.H.King tr G-MVFO Group	(Newport Pagnell)	22. 3.03P
G-MVFP	Solar Wings Pegasus XL-R (Rotax 447)	SW-TB-1371 & SW-WA-1365	9. 8.88	D J Brixton tr Shropshire Tow Group	Bishops Castle, Shropshire	24. 3.03P
G-MVFR	Solar Wings Pegasus XL-R (Rotax 447)	SW-TB-1372 & SW-WA-1366	9. 8.88	P.Newton *(Current status unknown)*	(Macclesfield)	21.11.99P
G-MVFS	Solar Wings Pegasus XL-R/Se (Rotax 447)	SW-TB-1373 & SW-WA-1367	9. 8.88	A.Cordes	(Leighton Buzzard)	20. 6.03P
G-MVFT	Solar Wings Pegasus XL-R (Rotax 447)	SW-TB-1374 & SW-WA-1368	9. 8.88	S.J.Whalley	Roddidge, Fradley	24.10.02P
G-MVFV	Solar Wings Pegasus XL-R (Rotax 447)	SW-TB-1376 & SW-WA-1370	9. 8.88	N.Sullivan & C.J.Munton	(Corby)	18. 5.02P
G-MVFW	Solar Wings Pegasus XL-R (Rotax 447)	SW-TB-1377 & SW-WA-1371	9. 8.88	S.F.Chaplin	Deenethorpe	28. 8.00P
G-MVFY	Solar Wings Pegasus XL-R (Rotax 447)	SW-TB-1379 & SW-WA-1373	9. 8.88	L.Luscombe	Weston Zoyland	19. 1.02P
G-MVFZ	Solar Wings Pegasus XL-R (Rotax 447)	SW-TB-1380 & SW-WA-1374	9. 8.88	R.K.Johnson	Popham	25. 5.03P
G-MVGA	Aerial Arts Chaser S (Rotax 508)	CH.707 *(C/n now CH.859)*	11. 8.88	F.Bastin *(Current status unknown)*	(Liskeard)	29. 7.99P
G-MVGB	Medway Hybred 44XLR (Rotax 447)	MR011/39	1. 9.88	R.Graham	Rochester	28. 8.02P
G-MVGC	AMF Chevvron 2-32C (Konig SD570)	010	2. 9.88	A.E.Dobson	Broadmeadow Farm, Hereford	8. 4.02P
G-MVGD	AMF Chevvron 2-32 (Konig SD570)	011	5. 9.88	T.R.James	(Southam)	19. 7.03P
G-MVGE	AMF Chevvron 2-32C (Konig SD570)	012	26. 9.88	J.P.Bennett *(Noted in trailer 2002)*	Old Sarum	20. 4.03P
G-MVGF	Aerial Arts Chaser S (Rotax 377)	CH.720	2. 9.88	J.H.Cooling "The Dingbat" (Noted 10.01)	Fenland	11.11.00P
G-MVGG	Aerial Arts Chaser S (Rotax 377)	CH.721	2. 9.88	J.B.Allan	Chase Farm, Billericay	16. 5.03P
G-MVGH	Aerial Arts Chaser S (Rotax 447)	CH.722	2. 9.88	J.E.Orbell *(Operates from Oban)*	(Spean Bridge)	14.11.03P
G-MVGL	Medway Hybred 44XLR (Rotax 447)	MR012/40	1. 9.88	W.Stacey	(Chelmsford)	21. 8.03P

Reg	Type	C/n		Date	Owner	Location	Status
G-MVGM	Mainair Gemini/Flash IIA (Rotax 503)	691-988-6 & W481		25. 8.88	A.R.Pitcher	(Cranbrook, Kent)	27.10.03P
G-MVGN	Solar Wings Pegasus XL-R/Se (Rotax 447)	SW-TB-1381 & SW-WA-1377		23. 8.88	M D Gregory	(Bideford)	10. 5.03P
G-MVGO	Solar Wings Pegasus XL-R (Rotax 447)	SW-TB-1382 & SW-WA-1378		23. 8.88	J.B.Peacock	Lower Mountpleasant Farm, Chatteris	14. 6.03P
G-MVGP	Solar Wings Pegasus XL-R (Rotax 447)	SW-TB-1383 & SW-WA-1379	(EC-) G-MVGP	23. 8.88	J.P.Cox	(Kettering)	9. 6.00P
G-MVGS*	Solar Wings Pegasus XL-R (Rotax 447)	SW-TB-1385 & SW-WA-1381		23. 8.88	J.J.Featherstone (Cancelled 21.1.03 as wfu)	Long Marston	30. 6.01P
G-MVGT*	Solar Wings Pegasus XL-Q (Rotax 462)	SW-TE-0092 & SW-WQ-0099		23. 8.88	R.Saunders (Cancelled 5.10.01 as WFU)	RAF Wyton	16. 7.00P
G-MVGU	Solar Wings Pegasus XL-Q (Rotax 462)	SW-TB-0092 & SW-WQ-0100		23. 8.88	T.D.Turner	Redlands, Swindon	21. 6.03P
G-MVGW	Solar Wings Pegasus XL-Q (Rotax 462)	SW-TE-0095 & SW-WQ-0102		23. 8.88	M.J.L.de Carvalho & V.V.P.Pedro tr G-MVGW Group (Current status unknown)	Lagos, Algarve	8. 2.92P
G-MVGY	Medway Hybred 44XLR (Rotax 447)	MR015/41		31. 8.88	D.G.Baker	(Petersfield)	21. 8.03P
G-MVGZ	Ultraflight Lazair IIIE (Rotax 185 x 2)	A.338	(ex?)	21.10.88	D.M.Broom	(Towcester)	25. 3.03P
G-MVHA	Aerial Arts Chaser S-1000 (Mosler CB-38)	CH.729		24. 8.88	R.Meredith-Hardy	Radwell Lodge, Baldock	24. 7.01P
G-MVHB	Powerchute Raider (Rotax 447)	80105		26. 8.88	A.E.Askew	(Melton Mowbray)	16. 6.03P
G-MVHC	Powerchute Raider (Rotax 447)	80106		26. 8.88	N.& S.A.Melrose	(Ripley)	19. 7.03P
G-MVHD	CFM Shadow CD (Rotax 503)	088		8. 9.88	S R Groves	Plaistows Farm, St Albans	31. 7.03P
G-MVHE	Mainair Gemini/Flash IIA (Rotax 503)	692-988-6 & W482		4.10.88	B.R.Thomas	East Fortune	31.10.03P
G-MVHF	Mainair Gemini/Flash IIA (Rotax 503)	693-988-6 & W483		4.10.88	M.G.Nicholson	(Kendal)	9. 5.03P
G-MVHG	Mainair Gemini/Flash IIA (Rotax 503)	694-988-6 & W484		14.10.88	C.A.J.Elder	(Bo'ness)	19. 3.03P
G-MVHH	Mainair Gemini/Flash IIA (Rotax 503) (Original trike 695.-.. replaced by 607-... ex G-MTSA 1995)	607-1187-5 & W485		24.10.88	G.Addison	East Fortune	27. 9.03P
G-MVHI	Thruster TST Mk.1 (Rotax 503)	8098-TST-100		26. 9.88	C.P.Fox (Under restoration 8.02)	Wing Farm, Longbridge Deverill	14.10.00P
G-MVHJ	Thruster TST Mk.1 (Rotax 503)	8098-TST-101		26. 9.88	R.C.Barnett	Margaretting	3. 4.03P
G-MVHK	Thruster TST Mk.1 (Rotax 503)	8098-TST-102		27. 9.88	D.J.Gordon	(St.Austell)	24. 6.03P
G-MVHL	Thruster TST Mk.1 (Rotax 503)	8098-TST-103		27. 9.88	G.Jones	(Llanfairfechan)	16. 7.02P
G-MVHN	Aerial Arts Chaser S (Rotax 377)	CH.728		9. 9.88	J.E.Sweetingham	Benson's Farm, Laindon	10. 6.01P
G-MVHO	Solar Wings Pegasus XL-Q (Rotax 462HP)	SW-TE-0097 & SW-WQ-0104		23. 9.88	S.J.Barkworth	Rufforth	29. 3.01P
G-MVHP	Solar Wings Pegasus XL-Q (Rotax 462)	SW-TE-0078 & SW-WQ-0105		23. 9.88	J.B.Gasson	Lower Mountpleasant Farm, Chatteris	9. 8.03P
	(Damaged trike from G-MVCV repaired and fitted to sailwing)						
G-MVHR	Solar Wings Pegasus XL-Q (Rotax 462)	SW-TE-0099 & SW-WQ-0106		23. 9.88	J.M.Hucker (Current status unknown)	Full Sutton	26. 5.98P
G-MVHS	Solar Wings Pegasus XL-Q (Rotax 462)	SW-TE-0100 & SW-WQ-0107		23. 9.88	C.L.Lebeter	(Derby)	14. 7.03P
G-MVHT*	Solar Wings Pegasus XL-Q (Rotax 462)	SW-TE-0104 & SW-WQ-0108		23. 9.88	A.M.Gould (Cancelled 21.5.01 as WFU)	(Bristol)	15.12.01P
G-MVHU*	Solar Wings Pegasus XL-Q (Rotax 462HP)	SW-TE-0182 & SW-WQ-0109		23. 9.88	A.McDermid (Cancelled 20.7.01 by CAA) (Trike only noted 7.02)	Field Farm, Oakley	30. 7.00P
	(Originally allocated trike c/n SW-TE-0102 but sale aborted & married with sailwing c/n SW-WQ-0115 as SE-YOP)						
G-MVHW	Solar Wings Pegasus XL-Q (Rotax 462)	SW-TE-0101 & SW-WQ-0111		23. 9.88	Ultralight Training Ltd	Roddige, Fradley	31. 8.02P
G-MVHX	Solar Wings Pegasus XL-Q (Rotax 462HP)	SW-TE-0105 & SW-WQ-0112		23. 9.88	E.F.Pipe	(Woodbridge)	31. 5.03P
G-MVHY	Solar Wings Pegasus XL-Q (Rotax 462HP)	SW-TE-0106 & SW-WQ-0113		23. 9.88	R.P.Paine	(Mansfield)	14. 8.03P
G-MVHZ	Hornet Dual Trainer/Southdown Raven (Rotax 462)	HRWA 0076 & MHR-101		26. 9.88	B.G.Colvin	East Winch	3. 8.03P
G-MVIA	Solar Wings Pegasus XL-R (Rotax 462)	SW-TE-0107 & SW-WA-1375		4.10.88	K.Parkyn	St.Just	14. 6.01P
G-MVIB	Mainair Gemini/Flash IIA (Rotax 503)	700-1088-4 & W490		14.10.88	LSA Systems Ltd	Arclid Green, Sandbach	13. 5.02P
G-MVIC*	Mainair Gemini/Flash IIA (Rotax 503)	699-1188-4 & W489		4.10.88	G.Tomlinson (Cancelled 29.11.01 by CAA)	Eshott	11. 4.00P
G-MVIE	Aerial Arts Chaser S (Rotax 377)	CH.732		14.10.88	T.M.Stiles (Current status unknown)	(Heathfield)	6. 6.97P
G-MVIF	Medway Raven X (Rotax 447) (Originally regd as Hybred 44XLR)	MR020/43		4.10.88	J.R.Harrison	(Bolsover)	1. 9.03P
G-MVIG	CFM Shadow B (Rotax 447)	K.044		5.10.88	M.P.& P.A.G.Harper (Damaged 1993: stored 8.93: current status unknown)	Priory Farm, Tibenham	20. 1.94P
G-MVIH	Mainair Gemini/Flash IIA (Rotax 503)	697-1088-6 & W487		14.10.88	T.M.Gilsenan	(Eaton Bray)	30. 5.03P
G-MVIL	Noble Hardman Snowbird Mk.IV (Rotax 582)	SB-014		6. 2.89	G.R.Graham	Kirkbride	13. 2.03P
G-MVIN	Noble Hardman Snowbird Mk.IV (Rotax 582) (Rebuilt to Mk.V standard)	SB-016		6. 2.89	R.S.W.Jones	Haverfordwest	23. 4.03P

G-MVIO	Noble Hardman Snowbird Mk.IV (Rotax 532)	SB-017		12. 4.89	B.Mason-Baker tr Mobility Advice Line	Shifnal	3. 5.03P
G-MVIP	AMF Chevvron 2-32 (Konig SD570)	008		11. 5.88	G.A.Furness & G.Sturgeon (Walney, Barriw-in-Furness)		21. 1.03P
G-MVIR	Thruster TST Mk.1 (Rotax 503) *(C/n plate marked as 8118-TST-104)*	8108-TST-104		21.10.88	T D Gardner	Kingsclere, Hannington	14. 8.03P
G-MVIT	Thruster TST Mk.1 (Rotax 503)	8108-TST-106	(C-) G-MVIT	21.10.88	A.P.Trumper	(Grantham)	10.10..03P
G-MVIU	Thruster TST Mk.1 (Rotax 503) *(Rebuilt as T.300)*	8108-TST-107		21.10.88	R.J.Humphries	Popham	12. 4.02P
G-MVIV	Thruster TST Mk.1 (Rotax 503)	8108-TST-108		21.10.88	P.J.Sears	(Ivybridge)	24. 6.01P
G-MVIW	Thruster TST Mk.1 (Rotax 532)	8108-TST-109		21.10.88	J.M.Nicholson	(Denham)	4. 6.01P
G-MVIX	Mainair Gemini/Flash IIA (Rotax 503)	702-1088-6 & W492		14.10.88	R.S.T.MacEwen	East Fortune	19.10.03P
G-MVIY	Mainair Gemini/Flash IIA (Rotax 503)	701-1088-6 & W491		14.10.88	J.J.Valentine	Ince Blundell	15. 7.02P
G-MVIZ	Mainair Gemini/Flash IIA (Rotax 503)	703-1088-6 & W493		14.10.88	A.J.Geary	(Pickering)	7. 7.03P
G-MVJA	Mainair Gemini/Flash IIA (Rotax 503)	696-988-6 & W486		5.12.88	J.R.Harrison	(Wisbech)	21. 7.03P
G-MVJC	Mainair Gemini/Flash IIA (Rotax 503)	705-1088-6 & W495		24.10.88	B.Temple	Priory Farm, Tibenham	16.10.02P
G-MVJD	Solar Wings Pegasus XL-R (Rotax 462) SW-TE-0109 & SW-WA-1386			24.10.88	R.S.Finlay	Kemble	30. 4.02P
G-MVJE	Mainair Gemini/Flash IIA (Rotax 503)	706-1188-6 & W496		21.10.88	G.Evans	Arclid Green, Sandbach	19.11.02P
G-MVJF	Aerial Arts Chaser S (Rotax 377)	CH.743		21.11.88	N.R.Andrew *(Noted 2.03)*	Doynton	17.10.99P
G-MVJG	Aerial Arts Chaser S (Rotax 377)	CH.749		22.11.88	T.H.Scott	Rayne Hall Farm, Rayne	13. 6.03P
G-MVJH	Aerial Arts Chaser S (Rotax 377)	CH.751		14.11.88	M.Van Rompaey	(Scunthorpe)	1. 9.03P
G-MVJI	Aerial Arts Chaser S (Rotax 377)	CH.752		17.11.88	T.Beckham	(Newcastle-upon-Tyne)	1.11.03P
G-MVJJ	Aerial Arts Chaser S (Rotax 508))	CH.753		14.11.88	C.W.Potts	(Newcastle-upon-Tyne)	24. 8.03P
G-MVJK	Aerial Arts Chaser S (Rotax 377)	CH.754		14.11.88	T.L.Travis	(Stafford)	23. 4.03P
G-MVJL	Mainair Gemini/Flash IIA (Rotax 503)	698-1188-6 & W488		21.10.88	F.Huxley	(Morpeth)	20. 5.01P
G-MVJM	Microflight Spectrum (Rotax 503)	007		21.10.88	S.E.Matthews tr Poppy Syndicate	Otherton, Cannock	18. 7.03P
G-MVJN	Solar Wings Pegasus XL-Q (Rotax 462) SW-TE-0110 & SW-WQ-0116			26.10.88	J.W.Wall *(Stored 7.02)*	Enstone	18. 2.96P
G-MVJO	Solar Wings Pegasus XL-Q (Rotax 462) SW-TE-0111 & SW-WQ-0117			26.10.88	J.D.Hoyland	(Winchester)	1. 6.03P
G-MVJP	Solar Wings Pegasus XL-Q (Rotax 462) SW-TE-0112 & SW-WQ-0118			26.10.88	S.H.Bakowski	Headcorn	18. 4.03P
G-MVJR	Solar Wings Pegasus XL-Q (Rotax 462) SW-TE-0113 & SW-WQ-0119			26.10.88	A.D.Woodroffe *(Current status unknown)*	(Henley-on-Thames)	30. 8.97P
G-MVJS	Solar Wings Pegasus XL-Q (Rotax 462) SW-TE-0114 & SW-WQ-0120			26.10.88	S.D.Morley	Rayne Hall Farm, Rayne	16.11.02P
G-MVJT	Solar Wings Pegasus XL-Q (Rotax 462HP) SW-TE-0115 & SW-WQ-0121			26.10.88	A.S.Johnson & T.M.Wakeley	(Poole)	11. 7.03P
G-MVJU	Solar Wings Pegasus XL-Q (Rotax 462) SW-TE-0116 & SW-WQ-0122			26.10.88	G.B.Hutchison	Sandtoft	19. 8.03P
G-MVJW	Solar Wings Pegasus XL-Q (Rotax 462) SE-TE-0118 & SW-WQ-0124			26.10.88	R.Dainty & D.W.Stamp Pound Green, Buttonoak, Kidderminster		4. 1.03P
G-MVKB	Medway Hybred 44XLR (Rotax 447) MR023/45			11.11.88	J.Newby	Sandtoft	11. 9.00P
G-MVKC	Mainair Gemini/Flash IIA (Rotax 503)	709-1188-6 & W499		16.11.88	R.L.Bladon	(Burntwood)	13. 7.03P
G-MVKF	Solar Wings Pegasus XL-R (Rotax 447) SW-TB-1389 & SW-WA-1392			14.11.88	B.Shaw	(Northampton)	7. 6.03P
G-MVKH	Solar Wings Pegasus XL-R (Rotax 447) SW-TB-1393 & SW-WA-1396			14.11.88	K.M.Elson	Roddige, Fradley	14.11.03P
G-MVKJ	Solar Wings Pegasus XL-R (Rotax 462) SW-TE-0132 & SW-WA-1398			14.11.88	G.V.Warner	Croughton	7. 6.02P
G-MVKK	Solar Wings Pegasus XL-R (Rotax 462) SW-TE-0131 & SW-WA-1397			14.11.88	P.G.Sayers	Graveley Farm, Herts	29. 6.03P
G-MVKL	Solar Wings Pegasus XL-R (Rotax 447) SW-TB-1391 & SW-WA-1394			14.11.88	J.Powell-Tuck	(Pontypool)	6. 6.91P
	(Although pod marked as "XL-Q" it remains a XL-R model) (Current status unknown)						
G-MVKM	Solar Wings Pegasus XL-R (Rotax 462) SW-TE-0136 & SW-WA-1399			14.11.88	R J Coppin	Hereford	6. 1.03P
	(Trike originally ordered as c/n SW-TB-1396 with Rotax 447: fitted with Rotax 462, hence SW-TE-prefix: data plate continues to record as "SW-TB-0136")						
G-MVKN	Solar Wings Pegasus XL-Q (Rotax 462) SW-TE-0120 & SW-WQ-0126			14.11.88	T.A.Colman	(London NW8)	17. 6.03P
G-MVKO	Solar Wings Pegasus XL-Q (Rotax 462HP) SW-TE-0121 & SW-WQ-0127			14.11.88	B.J.Lyford	(Swanage)	19. 9.02P
G-MVKP	Solar Wings Pegasus XL-Q (Rotax 462) SW-TE-0122 & SW-WQ-0128			14.11.88	J.Urwin	Eshott	22. 9.03P
G-MVKS	Solar Wings Pegasus XL-Q (Rotax 462) SW-TE-0124 & SW-WQ-0130			14.11.88	K.S.Wright *(Stored 8.95: current status unknown)*	Long Marston	13. 5.94P

G-MVKT	Solar Wings Pegasus XL-Q		14.11.88	N.C.Williams	Enstone 25. 5.03P
	(Rotax 462)	SW-TE-0125 & SW-WQ-0131			
G-MVKU	Solar Wings Pegasus XL-Q		14.11.88	J.R.F.Shepherd	Long Acre Farm, Sandy 17. 7.03P
	(Rotax 462)	SW-TE-0126 & SW-WQ-0132			
G-MVKV	Solar Wings Pegasus XL-Q		14.11.88	M D Callan	(Dundalk, Co.Louth) 8.12.02P
	(Rotax 462)	SW-TE-0127 & SW-WQ-0152	*(Original sailwing c/n SW-WQ-0133 damaged 14.8.91 & replaced by '-0152)*		
G-MVKW	Solar Wings Pegasus XL-Q		14.11.88	A.T.Scott	(London SW17) 16. 8.03P
	(Rotax 462)	SW-TE-0128 & SW-WQ-0134			
G-MVKX*	Solar Wings Pegasus XL-Q		14.11.88	G.R.Soper	Popham 2. 5.00P
	(Rotax 462)	SW-TE-0129 & SW-WQ-0135		*(Cancelled 20.11.01 as WFU)*	
G-MVKY	Aerial Arts Chaser S	CH.755	5.12.88	R.W.Whitehead	Swinford, Rugby 3. 7.02P
	(Rotax 377)				
G-MVKZ	Aerial Arts Chaser S	CH.756	5.12.88	J.Cresswell	Sittles Farm, Alrewas 23.10.02P
	(Rotax 377)				
G-MVLA	Aerial Arts Chaser S	CH.762	12.12.88	T.Birch	(Wolverhampton) 3. 9.03P
	(Rotax 377)				
G-MVLC	Aerial Arts Chaser S	CH.764	22.11.88	B.R.Barnes	(Bristol) 10. 5.03P
	(Rotax 377)				
G-MVLD	Aerial Arts Chaser S	CH.765	22.11.88	G.F.Atkinson	Rufforth 7. 5.00P
	(Rotax 377)				
G-MVLE	Aerial Arts Chaser S	CH.766	5.12.88	R.G.Hooker	Eshott 20.4.03P
	(Rotax 377)				
G-MVLF	Aerial Arts Chaser S	CH.767	11. 1.89	A.M.Buchanan	(Glasgow) 1. 8.03P
	(Rotax 508)				
G-MVLG	Aerial Arts Chaser S	CH.768	14.11.88	P.G.Richards	(Dumfermline) 25.11.96P
	(Rotax 377)			*(New owner 9.02)*	
G-MVLH	Aerial Arts Chaser S)	CH.769	22.11.88	A.W.Cove	(Wellingborough) 13.11.97P
	(Rotax 377)				
G-MVLJ	CFM Shadow CD	092	11.11.88	R.S.Cochrane	Sutton Meadows, Ely 11. 1.03P
	(Rotax 503)				
G-MVLL	Mainair Gemini/Flash IIA	708-1188-6 & W498	23.11.88	J.W.Peake	Otheron, Cannock 27.10.02P
	(Rotax 503)	*(Sailwing c/n now W396 ex G-MTSA)*			
G-MVLP	CFM Shadow C	095	22.11.88	D.Bridgland & D.T.Moran	Old Sarum 15.12.02P
	(Rotax 447)				
G-MVLR	Mainair Gemini/Flash IIA	713-1288-6 & W503	30.11.88	K.B.A.Judson	(Colchester) 18.11.00P
	(Rotax 503)				
G-MVLS	Aerial Arts Chaser S	CH.773	21. 2.89	T.C.Brown	Mill Farm, Shifnal 18. 2.03P
	(Rotax 377)				
G-MVLT	Aerial Arts Chaser S	CH.774	5.12.88	B.D.Searle	(Portsmouth) 31. 5.03P
	(Rotax 377)				
G-MVLW	Aerial Arts Chaser S	CH.778	28.12.88	E.W.P.van Zeller	(Ashford) 5. 9.99P
	(Rotax 377)			*(Current status unknown)*	
G-MVLX	Solar Wings Pegasus XL-Q		30.11.88	J.F.Smith	(High Wycombe) 25. 6.03P
	(Rotax 462)	SW-TE-0133 & SW-WQ-0114			
G-MVLY	Solar Wings Pegasus XL-Q		5.12.88	I.B.Osborn	Manston 28. 9.03P
	(Rotax 462)	SW-TE-0137 & SW-WQ-0142			
G-MVMC	Solar Wings Pegasus XL-Q		5.12.88	P.G.Becker	Hougham, Lincs 10. 4.02P
	(Rotax 462HP)	SW-TE-0141 & SW-WQ-0146			
G-MVMD	Powerchute Raider	80924	15.12.88	S.M.Paulin	(Reading) 13. 7.90P
	(Rotax 447)			*(Current status unknown)*	
G-MVME	Thruster TST Mk.1	8128-TST-110	12.12.88	R.C.Whittall	Weston Zoyland 22. 4.03P
	(Rotax 503)				
G-MVMG	Thruster TST Mk.1	8128-TST-112	12.12.88	P.A.Durrans	(Craigavon, Co.Armagh) 5. 5.03P
	(Rotax 503)				
G-MVMI	Thruster TST Mk.1	8128-TST-114	12.12.88	G.J.Johnson	North Coates 6. 1.03P
	(Rotax 503)				
G-MVML	Aerial Arts Chaser S	CH.781	28.12.88	G C Luddington	Wilden, Beds 29. 7.00P
	(Rotax 377)				
G-MVMM	Aerial Arts Chaser S	CH.797	21. 2.89	D.Margereson	(Chesterfield) 21. 7.03P
	(Rotax 377)				
G-MVMO	Mainair Gemini/Flash IIA	715-1288-6 & W507	12.12.88	K.Austwick	(Penrith) 12. 9.03P
	(Rotax 503)				
G-MVMR	Mainair Gemini/Flash IIA	717-1288-6 & W509	9. 1.89	P.W.Ramage	(Rufforth) 20. 9.96P
	(Rotax 503)			*(Current status unknown)*	
G-MVMT	Mainair Gemini/Flash IIA	718-189-6 & W510	22.12.88	R.F.Sanders	Hatherton, Cannock 25. 9.98P
	(Rotax 503)			t/a Independent Financial Advisory Service *(Current status unknown)*	
G-MVMU	Mainair Gemini/Flash IIA	719-189-6 & W511	22.12.88	M.J.A.New & A.Clift Mill Farm, Hughley, Much Wenlock	26. 8.03P
	(Rotax 503)			*"Icarus"*	
G-MVMV	Mainair Gemini/Flash IIA	720-189-6 & W512	22.12.88	M.J.A.New & A.Clift Mill Farm, Hughley, Much Wenlock	15. 3.03P
	(Rotax 503)				
G-MVMW	Mainair Gemini/Flash IIA	710-1188-6 & W500	11.11.88	K.Downes & B.Nock	(Wolverhampton) 31. 7.03P
	(Rotax 503)				
G-MVMX	Mainair Gemini/Flash IIA	721-189-6 & W513	23.12.88	D.A.Johns	Tarn Farm, Cockerham 13. 6.03P
	(Rotax 462) *(Trike stamped incorrectly as "W512")*				
G-MVMY	Mainair Gemini/Flash IIA	722-189-6 & W514	22.12.88	N.G.Leteney	(Congleton) 4.10.01P
	(Rotax 503)				
G-MVMZ	Mainair Gemini/Flash IIA	723-189-6 & W515	22.12.88	S.Richards	Otherton, Cannock 24. 5.02P
	(Rotax 503)				
G-MVNA	Powerchute Raider	81230	12. 7.89	B.Gorvett	(Swansea) 24. 5.93P
	(Rotax 447)			*(Current status unknown)*	
G-MVNC	Powerchute Raider	81232	12. 7.89	W.R.Hanley	(Edinburgh) 25. 7.00P
	(Rotax 447)				
G-MVNI	Powerchute Raider	90625	12. 7.89	N.J.Staib	Kemble 13. 7.02P
	(Rotax 447)				

G-MVNK	Powerchute Raider (Rotax 447)	90623		12. 7.89	J.Cunliffe *(Current status unknown)*	(Stoke-on-Trent)	16. 7.95P
G-MVNL	Powerchute Raider) (Rotax 447)	90624		12. 7.89	S.Penoyre	(Windlesham)	17. 3.01P
G-MVNM	Mainair Gemini/Flash IIA (Rotax 503)	725-189-6 & W517		6. 1.89	M.Castle & T.Hartwig	(Shrewsbury)	8. 6.00P
G-MVNN	Aerotech MW-5(K) Sorcerer (Rotax 447) 5K-0003-02 & BMAA/HB/022			28. 3.90	W S S Lubbock	(Callington)	21. 5.03P
G-MVNO	Aerotech MW-5(K) Sorcerer (Rotax 447)	5K-0004-02		4. 5.89	R.L.Wadley	Middle Stoke, Kent	31. 5.03P
G-MVNP	Aerotech MW-5(K) Sorcerer (Rotax 447)	5K-0005-02		13. 7.89	A M Edwards *(Current status unknown)*	(Wokingham)	24. 9.96P
G-MVNR	Aerotech MW-5(K) Sorcerer (Rotax 447)	5K-0006-02		4. 5.89	F.Jones	Ley Farm, Chirk	23. 8.01P
G-MVNS	Aerotech MW-5(K) Sorcerer (Rotax 447)	5K-0007-02		19. 7.89	R.D.Chiles	Shenstone Hall Farm, Shenstone	15. 7.03P
G-MVNT	Aerotech MW-5(K) Sorcerer (Rotax 447)	5K-0008-02		28. 3.90	P.E.Blyth	Wombleton	25 10.03P
G-MVNU	Aerotech MW-5(K) Sorcerer (Rotax 447)	5K-0009-02		4. 5.89	J.C.Rose	Field Farm, Oakley	21. 6.03P
G-MVNW	Mainair Gemini/Flash IIA (Rotax 503)	726-189-6 & W518		25. 1.89	A.Weatherall	(Preston)	6. 5.03P
G-MVNX	Mainair Gemini/Flash IIA (Rotax 503)	727-289-6 & W519		10. 1.89	I.Sidebotham	Barton	16. 6.03P
G-MVNY	Mainair Gemini/Flash IIA (Rotax 462)	724-189-6 & W516		11. 1.89	M.K.Buckland	(Daventry)	25. 7.03P
G-MVNZ	Mainair Gemini/Flash IIA (Rotax 503)	728-289-6 & W520		11. 1.89	B.Crouch	Oxton, Nottingham	8.11.03P
G-MVOA	Aerial Arts Chaser S (Rotax 462) *(Reported as Aerial Arts Alligator)*	CH.780		16. 1.89	A.B.Potts	Broomhill Farm, West Calder	7. 9.02P
G-MVOB	Mainair Gemini/Flash IIA (Rotax 503)	729-289-6 & W521		16. 1.89	B.J.Bader	(Taunton)	19. 4.03P
G-MVOD	Aerial Arts Chaser/110SX (Rotax 377)	110SX/653		16. 1.89	M.A.Hodgson	Baxby Manor, Husthwaite	29. 8.02P
G-MVOF	Mainair Gemini/Flash IIA (Rotax 503)	730-289-6 & W522		31. 1.89	D.Haynes	Beccles	27.11.03P
G-MVOH	CFM Shadow CD (Rotax 503)	K.090		23. 1.89	D.I.Farmer	Dunkeswell	2. 9.02P
G-MVOJ	Noble Hardman Snowbird Mk.IV (Rotax 532)	SB-019		26. 7.89	T.D.Thwaites tr The HFC Group *(Current status unknown)*	(Penrith)	28. 7.99P
G-MVOL	Noble Hardman Snowbird Mk.IV (Rotax 532)	SB-021		29. 8.89	E.J.Lewis tr Swansea Snowbird Fliers	(Swansea)	26. 1.02P
G-MVON	Mainair Gemini/Flash IIA (Rotax 503)	731-289-6 & W523		30. 1.89	J.V.Bailey	(Leigh, Lancs)	14. 7.02P
G-MVOO	AMF Chevvron 2-32C (Konig SD570)	014		10. 1.89	I.R.F.Hammond	Lee-on-Solent	1. 8.02P
G-MVOP	Aerial Arts Chaser S (Rotax 377)	CH.787		21. 2.89	D.Thorpe	Long Acre Farm, Sandy	4. 5.03P
G-MVOR	Mainair Gemini/Flash IIA (Rotax 462)	732-289-6 & W524	(EC-) G-MVOR	6. 2.89	P.T. & R.M.Jenkins	Dunkeswell	5.10.03P
G-MVOT	Thruster TST Mk.1 (Rotax 503)	8029-TST-116		17. 2.89	B.L.R.J.Keeping	Davidstow Moor	19. 9.03P
G-MVOU	Thruster TST Mk.1 (Rotax 503)	8029-TST-117		17. 2.89	S.Hoyle	(Thirsk)	2. 5.03P
G-MVOV	Thruster TST Mk.1 (Rotax 503)	8029-TST-118		17. 2.89	D.A.Duthie	Otherton, Cannock	26. 8.03P
G-MVOW	Thruster TST Mk.1 (Rotax 503)	8029-TST-119		17. 2.89	J.Short & B.J.Merret	Dunkeswell	17. 7.00P
G-MVOX	Thruster TST Mk.1 (Rotax 503)	8029-TST-120		17. 2.89	J.E.Davies	Haverfordwest	22. 6.03P
G-MVOY	Thruster TST Mk.1 (Rotax 503)	8029-TST-121		17. 2.89	G.R.Breaden	Tarn Farm, Cockerham	5.10.03P
G-MVPA	Mainair Gemini/Flash IIA (Rotax 503)	735-289-7 & W527		29. 3.89	J.E.Milburn *(Current status unknown)*	Eshott	30. 8.95P
G-MVPB	Mainair Gemini/Flash IIA (Rotax 503)	736-389-7 & W528		29. 3.89	P Harrison	(Ripon)	30. 7.03P
G-MVPD	Mainair Gemini/Flash IIA (Rotax 503)	738-389-7 & W530		7. 2.89	A.S.Bates	(Ashton-under-Lyne)	7. 9.03P
G-MVPE	Mainair Gemini/Flash IIA (Rotax 503)	739-389-7 & W531		7. 2.89	E.A.Wrathall	St.Michaels	10. 2.03P
G-MVPF	Medway Hybred 44XLR (Rotax 447)	MR036/52		27. 2.89	G H Crick	Plaistows Farm, St Albans	20. 6.03P
G-MVPG	Medway Hybred 44XLR Rotax 447)	MR026/53		15. 2.89	M.A.Jones *(Current status unknown)*	(Wigan)	30.12.98P
G-MVPH	Whittaker MW6-S Fatboy Flyer (Rotax 503)	PFA 164-11404		7. 2.89	A.A.Rowson *(Amended CofR 8.02)*	Emlyn's Field, Rhuallt	23. 8.99P
G-MVPI	Mainair Gemini/Flash IIA (Rotax 503)	740-389-7 & W532		9. 2.89	R.J.Bowden	Dunkeswell	26. 4.03P
G-MVPJ	Rans S-5 Coyote (Rotax 447)	88.083 & PFA 193-11470		15. 2.89	J.E.D.Rogerson *(New owner 3.02)*	Morgansfield, Fishburn	2. 8.99P
G-MVPK	CFM Shadow BD (Rotax 447)	K.091		15. 2.89	P.Sarfas *(Operates from Margaretting)*	(Billericay)	26. 7.02P
G-MVPL	Medway Hybred 44XLR (Rotax 447)	MR034/50		1. 3.89	J.N.J.Roberts *(Current status unknown)*	Long Acre Farm, Sandy	30. 4.98P

G-MVPM	Whittaker MW6 Merlin PFA 164-11272	21. 2.89	P.R.A. & S.Elliston	RAF Mona	30. 4.03P
	(Rotax 503) *(Reported as Type MW6-T)*				
G-MVPN	Whittaker MW6 Merlin PFA 164-11280	21. 2.89	A.M.Field	(Glastonbury)	18. 5.93P
	(Rotax 503)		*(Current status unknown)*		
G-MVPO	Mainair Gemini/Flash IIA 741-389-7 & W533	3. 3.89	A.H. & C.I.King	(Rye)	9. 8.99P
	(Rotax 503)		*(Current status unknown)*		
G-MVPR	Solar Wings Pegasus XL-Q	14. 3.89	R.S.Swift	Finmere	3.06.03P
	(Rotax 462) SW-TE-0149 & SW-WQ-0163				
G-MVPS	Solar Wings Pegasus XL-Q	14. 3.89	B.R.Chamberlain	London Colney	2. 9.03P
	(Rotax 462HP) SW-TE-0143 & SW-WQ-0140				
G-MVPU	Solar Wings Pegasus XL-Q	29. 3.89	I.B.Smith	(Peterborough)	2. 9.03P
	(Rotax 462) SW-TE-0150 & SW-WQ-0164				
G-MVPW	Solar Wings Pegasus XL-R	28. 3.89	C.A.Mitchell	(Newport, Gwent)	24.10.98P
	(Rotax 462) SW-TE-0177 & SW-WA-1411		*(Current status unknown)*		
G-MVPX	Solar Wings Pegasus XL-Q	28. 3.89	M.M.P.Evans	Plaistows Farm, St Albans	20. 3.03P
	(Rotax 462) SW-TE-0144 & SW-WQ-0158				
G-MVPY	Solar Wings Pegasus XL-Q	28. 3.89	G.H.Dawson	(Swavesey, Cambridge)	6. 8.02P
	(Rotax 462) SW-TE-0178 & SW-WQ-0188				
G-MVRA	Mainair Gemini/Flash IIA 743-489-7-W535	10. 4.89	D.Slassor	Eshott	6.11.03P
	(Rotax 503)7				
G-MVRB*	Mainair Gemini/Flash 747-489-7 & W539	29. 3.89	M.J.Burns & P.A.McGivern	Newtownards, Co.Down	17. 4.00P
	(Rotax 503)		*(Cancelled 5.12.01 by CAA)*		
G-MVRC	Mainair Gemini/Flash IIA 748-489-7 & W540	29. 3.89	M.O'Connell	Rufforth	16. 5.03P
	(Rotax 503)				
G-MVRD	Mainair Gemini/Flash IIA 749-489-7 & W541	9. 5.89	A.R.Helm	(Accrington)	14. 8.03P
	(Rotax 503)				
G-MVRE*	CFM Shadow CD K.087	10. 4.89	J.Madhvani	Plaistows Farm, St Albans	21.10.02P
	(Rotax 503)		*(Cancelled 13.8.02 by CAA)*		
G-MVRF	Rotec Rally 2B AIE-01	28. 4.89	A.I.Edwards *(Current status unknown)*	(Stafford)	
G-MVRG	Aerial Arts Chaser S (Rotax 377) CH.798	14. 4.89	J.P.Kynaston *(Current status unknown)*	(Luton)	31. 8.99P
G-MVRH	Solar Wings Pegasus XL-Q	10. 4.89	K.Farr	Swinford, Rugby	7. 9.03P
	(Rotax 462) SW-TE-0160 & SW-WQ-0177				
G-MVRI	Solar Wings Pegasus XL-Q	10. 4.89	P.Martin	(Stevenage)	23. 3.03P
	(Rotax 462) SW-TE-0145 & SW-WQ-0159				
G-MVRJ	Solar Wings Pegasus XL-Q	10. 4.89	M.A.Potter & J.Goldsmith-Ryan	(Barnstaple)	23. 3.03P
	(Rotax 462HP) SW-TE-0172 & SW-WQ-0165				
G-MVRL	Aerial Arts Chaser S CH.801	18. 4.89	C.N.Beale	Mill Farm, Shifnall	22. 7.02P
	(Rotax 447)				
G-MVRM	Mainair Gemini/Flash IIA 752-489-7 & W545	12. 4.89	I.H.Barbour	East Fortune	27. 9.03P
	(Rotax 462)				
G-MVRO	CFM Shadow BD K.105	3. 4.89	K.H.Creed	(Langar)	28.11.03P
	(Rotax 447)				
G-MVRP	CFM Shadow CD 097	7. 4.89	D.R.G.Whitelaw	North Connel, Oban	27. 7.03P
	(Rotax 503)				
G-MVRR	CFM Shadow CD 098	7. 4.89	S.Fairweather & S.P.Christian	Hougham, Lincs	28. 9.03P
	(Rotax 503)				
G-MVRT	CFM Shadow BD 104	7. 4.89	S.C.Cornock	(Lichfield)	13.10.03P
	(Rotax 447)				
G-MVRU	Solar Wings Pegasus XL-Q	12. 4.89	P.J.Edwards	(Newmarket)	9. 7.03P
	(Rotax 462) SW-TE-0166 & SW-WQ-0183				
G-MVRV	Powerchute Kestrel (Rotax 503) 90210	28. 4.89	G.M.Fletcher *(Current status unknown)*	(Chesterfield)	3. 2.97P
G-MVRW	Solar Wings Pegasus XL-Q	12. 4.89	L Harland	(Queenborough)	28. 8.03P
	(Rotax 462) SW-TE-0161 & SW-WQ-0178		*(Rebuilt 1999 including new factory supplied sailwing)*		
G-MVRX	Solar Wings Pegasus XL-Q	12. 4.89	M.Everest	(Hailsham)	18. 6.03P
	(Rotax 462HP) SW-TE-0151 & SW-WQ-0165				
G-MVRY	Medway Hybred 44XLR MR049/56	12. 4.89	K.Dodman	(Cambridge)	4. 3.99P
	(Rotax 447)		*(Current status unknown)*		
G-MVRZ	Medway Hybred 44XLR MR043/57	9. 5.89	I.Oswald	(London SE9)	13.11.01P
	(Rotax 503)				
G-MVSB	Solar Wings Pegasus XL-Q	18. 4.89	M.J.Olsen	Wombleton	23.11.02P
	(Rotax 462) SW-TE-0184 & SW-WQ-0193				
G-MVSD	Solar Wings Pegasus XL-Q	18. 4.89	M.T.Aplin tr G-MVSD Group	Dunkeswell	7. 6.03P
	(Rotax 462) SW-TE-0186 & SW-WQ-0195				
G-MVSE	Solar Wings Pegasus XL-Q	18. 4.89	A Gulliver	Thirsk	14. 8.03P
	(Rotax 462) SW-TE-0187 & SW-WQ-0196				
G-MVSG	Aerial Arts Chaser S CH.804	24. 4.89	M.Roberts	(Melksham)	20. 8.00P
	(Rotax 377)				
G-MVSI	Medway Hybred 44XLR MR040/58	18. 4.89	G.Cousins	(Maidstone)	
			(CofR restored 4.02)		
G-MVSJ	Aviasud Mistral 532GB 072 & BMAA/HB/013	18. 4.89	A.J.Record	(Selby)	25. 9.03P
G-MVSK*	Aerial Arts Chaser S CH.806	27. 4.89	G.A.Inch	(Bristol)	8. 1.00P
	(Rotax 377)		*(Cancelled 21.10.02 by CAA)*		
G-MVSM	Midland Ultralights Sirocco 377GB MU-023	21. 4.89	J.S.Seddon-Harvey	(Ross-on-Wye)	1. 8.03P
	(Rotax 377)				
G-MVSN	Mainair Gemini/Flash IIA 754-589-7 & W547	28. 4.89	D.Morrison	(Kelso)	16.11.02P
	(Rotax 503)				
G-MVSO	Mainair Gemini/Flash IIA 755-589-7 & W548	27. 4.89	P.W.Taylor	Swanton Morley	24. 7.03P
	(Rotax 503)				
G-MVSP	Mainair Gemini/Flash IIA 756-589-7 & W549	27. 4.89	D.R.Buchanan	Pulborough	4. 4.03P
	(Rotax 503)				
G-MVSR*	Medway Hybred 44XLR MR038/59	15. 5.89	G.Tate	Carlisle	4. 5.01P
	(Rotax 447)		*(Cancelled 25.7.01 by CAA)*		
G-MVST	Mainair Gemini/Flash IIA 750-589-7 & W543	12. 6.89	A.Raithby, A.Bower & N.McCusker	Rufforth	15. 5.03P
	(Rotax 462)				

G-MVSU	Microflight Spectrum 008 (Rotax 503)		4. 5.89	G.Wilkinson	Otherton, Cannock	9. 5.03P
G-MVSV	Mainair Gemini/Flash IIA 757-589-7 & W550 (Rotax 503)		11. 5.89	P.Shelton	St.Michaels	27. 9.03P
G-MVSW	Solar Wings Pegasus XL-Q (Rotax 462HP) SW-TE-0189 & SW-WQ-0198		17. 5.89	G.F.Ryland	Oxton, Notts	31.12.02P
G-MVSX	Solar Wings Pegasus XL-Q (Rotax 462) SW-TE-0190 & SW-WQ-0199		11. 5.89	A.R.Law	Davidstow Moor	14. 7.03P
G-MVSY	Solar Wings Pegasus XL-Q (Rotax 462) SW-TE-0191 & SW-WQ-0200		11. 5.89	C.M.Jones	(Yelverton)	30. 6.02P
G-MVSZ	Solar Wings Pegasus XL-Q (Rotax 462HP) SW-TE-0192 & SW-WQ-0201		11. 5.89	D.M.Goldsmith & R.M.Gill	Rufforth	31. 3.03P
G-MVTA	Solar Wings Pegasus XL-Q (Rotax 462) SW-TE-0193 & SW-WQ-0202		11. 5.89	A.Garlick	Knapthorpe Lodge, Caunton	20. 9.03P
G-MVTC	Mainair Gemini/Flash IIA 759-689-7 & W552 (Rotax 503)		30. 5.89	B.D.Bowen	Shobdon	8. 7.02P
G-MVTD	Whittaker MW6 Merlin PFA 164-11367 (Rotax 503)		11. 5.89	G.J.Green (Current status unknown)	(Matlock)	28. 4.97P
G-MVTI	Solar Wings Pegasus XL-Q (Rotax 462) SW-TE-0217 & SW-WQ-0206		25. 5.89	A.M.Prentice	(Great Shelford)	31. 8.03P
G-MVTJ	Solar Wings Pegasus XL-Q (Rotax 462) SW-TE-0197 & SW-WQ-0207		25. 5.89	P.D.Rowe	Dunkeswell	3.11.01P
G-MVTK	Solar Wings Pegasus XL-Q (Rotax 462) SW-TE-0198 & SW-WQ-0208		25. 5.89	S.Davis & S.E.Strangeway	(Hungerford)	18. 5.03P
G-MVTL	Aerial Arts Chaser S CH.809 (Rotax 337)		13. 6.89	R.W.Whitehead	Swinford, Rugby	22.12.02P
G-MVTM	Aerial Arts Chaser S CH.810 (Rotax 447)		13. 6.89	E.W.Laidlaw	Carlisle	25. 7.03P
G-MVUA	Mainair Gemini/Flash IIA 760-689-7 & W553 (Rotax 462)		14. 6.89	T.V.Almomd & K.Atherton	Ince Blundell	31. 5.03P
G-MVUB	Thruster T.300 089-T300-373 (Rotax 532)		13. 6.89	M.K.Ashmore	Siege Cross Farm, Thatcham	26. 6.03P
G-MVUD	Medway Hybred 44XLR (Rotax 503) MR037/55		19. 6.89	T.W.Nelson	Carlisle	19. 8.01P
G-MVUF	Solar Wings Pegasus XL-Q (Rotax 462) SW-TE-0203 & SW-WQ-0213		13. 6.89	G.& S.Simons	(Rustington)	24. 4.03P
G-MVUG	Solar Wings Pegasus XL-Q (Rotax 462) SW-TE-0204 & SW-WQ-0214		13. 6.89	E.D.Deed	Sywell	14. 9.03P
G-MVUH*	Solar Wings Pegasus XL-Q (Rotax 462) SW-TE-0205 & SW-WQ-0215		13. 6.89	A.Davis (Temporary WFU 16.5.00) (Dismantled for spares?)	(Macclesfield)	17. 8.99P
G-MVUI	Solar Wings Pegasus XL-Q (Rotax 462) SW-TE-0206 & SW-WQ-0216 (Wing marked incorrectly as c/n SW-TE-0216)		13. 6.89	J.K.Edgecombe	(Coalville)	10.11.02P
G-MVUJ	Solar Wings Pegasus XL-Q (Rotax 462) SW-TE-0207 & SW-WQ-0217		13. 6.89	J.H.Cooper	Enstone	17. 7.03P
G-MVUL	Solar Wings Pegasus XL-Q (Rotax 462HP) SW-TE-0209 & SW-WQ-0219		13. 6.89	P.J.Emery	(Waterlooville)	9. 6.01P
G-MVUM	Solar Wings Pegasus XL-Q (Rotax 462HP) SW-TE-0210 & SW-WQ-0220		13. 6.89	P.B.Howson	Arclid Green, Sandbach	7. 6.03P
G-MVUO	AMF Chevvron 2-32C (Konig SD570) 015		14. 6.89	D.Beevers	Melrose Farm, Melbourne	18. 7.01P
G-MVUP	Aviasud Mistral 532GB 1087-48 & BMAA/HB/003	83-CQ	10. 8.89	C.J.& B.W.Foulds	Ashbourne	1. 8.02P
G-MVUR	Hornet RS-ZA HRWA-0050 & ZA107 (Rotax 532) (Originally regd as c/n HRWA-0076: HRWA-0050 was ex G-MVLK)		3. 7.89	T.J.Gayton-Polley	(Billingshurst)	30.11.03P
G-MVUS	Aerial Arts Chaser S CH.813 (Rotax 377)		3. 7.89	H.Poyzer	Eshott	16.12.01P
G-MVUT	Aerial Arts Chaser S CH.814 (Rotax 377)		4. 7.89	A.J.Tyler	Beccles	21. 4.02P
G-MVVH	Medway Hybred 44XLR MR047/63 (Rotax 447)		11. 7.89	M.S.Henson	(Portsmouth)	17. 8.03P
G-MVVI	Medway Hybred 44XLR MR050/64 (Rotax 447 but now 503?)		12. 7.89	D.W.Allen	(London E6)	26.10.02P
G-MVVK	Solar Wings Pegasus XL-R (Rotax 447) SW-TB-1414 & SW-WA-1423		11. 7.89	A.J.Weir	(Bath)	30. 6.03P
G-MVVM	Solar Wings Pegasus XL-R (Rotax 447) SW-TB-1416 & SW-WA-1425		12. 7.89	N.B.Mehew	Oxton, Nottingham	7.10.01P
G-MVVN	Solar Wings Pegasus XL-Q (Rotax 462) SW-TE-0214 & SW-WQ-0226		11. 7.89	M.J.Hall	(Rugeley)	5.11.03P
G-MVVO	Solar Wings Pegasus XL-Q (Rotax 462) SW-TE-0215 & SW-WQ-0227		11. 7.89	A.L.Scarlett	Clench Common	20. 6.03P
G-MVVP	Solar Wings Pegasus XL-Q (Rotax 462) SW-TE-0216 & SW-WQ-0228		11. 7.89	M.P.Wimsey	(Louth)	2. 5.03P
G-MVVR	Medway Hybred 44XLR MR058/66 (Rotax 503)		20. 7.89	C.J.Meadows (New owner 12.02)	Franklyn's Field, Chewton Mendip	9. 9.96P
G-MVVT	CFM Shadow CD K.101 & PFA 161-11569 (Rotax 503)		26. 7.89	R.R.Armstrong	(Headcorn)	30. 5.03P
G-MVVU	Aerial Arts Chaser S (Rotax 462) CH.816		19. 7.89	S.Bradie	East Fortune	1. 6.03P
G-MVVV	AMF Chevvron 2-32C 016 (Konig SD570)	PH-1W9 G-MVVV	11. 5.89	P.R.Turton	Broomhill Farm, West Calder	16. 2.03P
G-MVVZ	Powerchute Raider 90628 (Rotax 447)		25. 7.89	J.H.Cadman	(Melton Mowbray)	13. 7.02P
G-MVWH*	Powerchute Raider 90736 (Rotax 447)		25. 7.89	M.H.Nice (Cancelled 10.02.03 by CAA)	(Taunton)	11. 8.00P
G-MVWJ	Powerchute Raider 90738 (Rotax 447)		25. 7.89	N.J.Doubek	(Stanford-le-Hope)	24. 5.03P
G-MVWN	Thruster T300 089-T300-374 (Rotax 503)		26. 7.89	T.B.Reakes tr Whisky November Group	Franklyns Field, Chewton Mendip	4. 6.03P

Reg	Type (Engine)	C/n	Date	Owner	Location	Status
G-MVWR	Thruster T300 (Rotax 503)	089-T300-377	26. 7.89	A.Allan	North Connel, Oban	20. 9.03P
G-MVWS	Thruster T300 (Rotax 503)	089-T300-378	26. 7.89	R.J.Humphries *(Current status unknown)*	(Southampton)	15. 8.95P
G-MVWV	Medway Hybred 44XLR (Rotax 447)	MR060/69	24. 7.89	K.Smith	(Rainham)	17. 8.03P
G-MVWW	Aviasud Mistral 532GB	0389-81 & BMAA/HB/005	25. 7.89	P.S.Balmer & B.H.D.Minto	Tarn Farm, Cockerham	19.10.03P
G-MVWX	Microflight Spectrum	009	24. 7.89	G.S.Taylor, tr Spectrum Otherton Syndicate	Otherton, Cannock	3. 4.03P
G-MVWZ	Aviasud Mistral 532GB	1288-70 & BMAA/HB/008	2. 8.89	B.R.Underwood	Little Battleflats Farm, Ellistown, Coalville	14. 5.03P
G-MVXA	Whittaker MW6 Merlin (Fuji-Robin EC-44-PM)	PFA 164-11337	17. 8.89	I.Brewster	Little Gransden	21. 4.03P
G-MVXB	Mainair Gemini/Flash IIA (Rotax 462)	762-789-7 & W555	3. 8.89	D.J.Cook	Northwich	19. 6.03P
G-MVXC	Mainair Gemini/Flash IIA (Rotax 503)	763-889-7 & W556	4. 8.89	D.Wood	Arclid Green, Sandbach	27.10.02P
G-MVXD	Medway Hybred 44XLR (Rotax 503)	MR061/70	3. 8.89	P.R.Millen	Clench Common	6. 5.03P
G-MVXE	Medway Hybred 44XLR (Rotax 447)	MR063/71	23. 8.89	A.M.Brittle	Sittles Farm, Alrewas	31. 7.00P
G-MVXI	Medway Hybred 44XLR (Rotax 447)	MR064/72	9. 8.89	G.R.Roach	Middle Stoke, Kent	11. 5.02P
G-MVXJ	Medway Hybred 44XLR (Rotax 447)	MR065/73	25. 8.89	P.J.Wilks *(Current status unknown)*	(Edenbridge)	26..9.90P
G-MVXL	Thruster TST Mk.1 (Rotax 503)	8089-TST-122	18. 8.89	A.J.Smith	(Cardiff)	30. 8.00P
G-MVXM	Medway Hybred 44XLR (Rotax 503) *(Reported as Medway Raven)*	MR055/75	17. 8.89	T.Thomson *(Current status unknown)*	(Hereford)	2. 8.97P
G-MVXN	Aviasud Mistra 532GB	065 & BMAA/HB/002	18. 8.89	B.M.Roberts	(Lincoln)	25. 8.03P
G-MVXR	Mainair Gemini/Flash IIA (Rotax 462)	764-889-7 & W557	22. 8.89	D M Bayne	East Fortune	28. 7.03P
G-MVXS	Mainair Gemini/Flash IIA (Rotax 503)	766-889-7 & W559	22. 8.89	J.W.Wood	Tarn Farm, Cockerham	25. 7.02P
G-MVXV	Aviasud Mistral 532GB	092 & BMAA/HB/004	22. 8.89	R.Bilson tr Mistral G-MVXV Group	Tarn Farm, Cockerham	5. 1.03P
G-MVXW	Rans S-4 Coyote (Rotax 447)	89.098 & PFA 193-11545	22. 8.89	M.R.C.Sims & A.A.Castleton	Dunkeswell	9.12.02P
G-MVXX	AMF Chevvron 2-32 (Konig SD570)	018	27. 7.89	C.K.Brown	(Loughborough)	24. 3.03P
G-MVYC	Solar Wings Pegasus XL-Q (Rotax 462HP)	SW-TE-0224 & SW-WQ-0239	8. 9.89	P.E.L.Street	(Lincoln)	1.10.03P
G-MVYD	Solar Wings Pegasus XL-Q (Rotax 462)	SW-TE-0225 & SW-WQ-0240	8. 9.89	T.M.Wakeley	Clench Common	26. 7.03P
G-MVYE	Thruster TST Mk.1 (Rotax 503)	8089-TST-123	13. 9.89	G.Elwes	Graveley Farm, Herts	24. 6.03P
G-MVYI	Hornet R-ZA (Rotax 462) *(Trike unit with c/n HRWB-0074 amended to HRWB-0081 was noted at Popham 4.96) (Current status unknown)*	HRWB-0074 & ZA122	22. 9.89	N.J.Warner	(Redditch)	21. 9.95P
G-MVYJ	Hornet R-ZA (Rotax 462) *(Trike unit shows deleted c/n HRWB-0070)*	HRWB-0075 & ZA111	22. 9.89	L.R.Hodgson	Kirkbride	21. 5.03P
G-MVYK	Hornet R-ZA (Rotax 462)	HRWB-0076 & ZA117	22. 9.89	P.Asbridge *(Current status unknown)*	Emlyn's Field, Rhuallt	22. 7.99P
G-MVYL	Hornet R-ZA (Rotax 462)	HRWB-0077 & ZA115	22. 9.89	J.L.Thomas *(Noted 10.01)*	Kingston Seymour	2. 3.03P
G-MVYN	Hornet R-ZA (Rotax 462)	HRWB-0079 & ZA136	22. 9.89	W.M.Studley	Weston Zoyland	26. 4.03P
G-MVYP	Medway Hybred 44XLR (Rotax 447)	MR071/77	19. 9.89	P.R.Chapman	(Swanley)	23. 3.03P
G-MVYR	Medway Hybred 44XLR (Rotax 447)	MR068/76	19. 9.89	K.J.Clarke	(Hockley)	24. 4.03P
G-MVYS	Mainair Gemini/Flash IIA (Rotax 503)	770-989-7 & W563	19. 9.89	B Hall	Tarn Farm, Cockerham	8. 2.03P
G-MVYT	Noble Hardman Snowbird Mk.IV (Rotax 532)	SB-022	26. 9.89	D.T.A.Rees	Haverfordwest	23. 2.03P
G-MVYU	Noble Hardman Snowbird Mk.IV (Rotax 532)	SB-023	7.11.89	B.Foster, W.Lagoda & P.Meah	(London E13)	26.6.99P
G-MVYV	Noble Hardman Snowbird Mk.IV (Rotax 532)	SB-024	21. 8.90	D.W.Hayden tr G-MVYV Group	(Swansea)	13. 4.03P
G-MVYW	Noble Hardman Snowbird Mk.IV (Rotax 532)	SB-025	22.10.90	T.J.Harrison	(Dalton-in-Furness)	15. 7.03P
G-MVYX	Noble Hardman Snowbird Mk.IV (Rotax 532)	SB-026	25.11.91	R.McBlain	Kilkerran	9. 7.01P
G-MVYY	Aerial Arts Chaser S (Rotax 508)	CH.824	26. 9.89	P.Kneeshaw	(Alford)	13. 1.03P
G-MVYZ	CFM Shadow BD (Rotax 447)	121	25. 9.89	K.W.Brunnenkant	(Lincoln)	2.10.03P
G-MVZA	Thruster T300 (Rotax 503)	089-T300-379	26. 9.89	C.C.Belcher	Popham	21. 9.02P
G-MVZB*	Thruster T300 (Rotax 503)	089-T300-380	26. 9.89	J.F.Kenyon *(Cancelled 28.5.02 by CAA)*	(Holsworthy)	29. 6.00P
G-MVZC	Thruster T300 (Rotax 532)	089-T300-381	26. 9.89	R.A.Knight	Chilbolton	17. 6.03P
G-MVZD	Thruster T300 (Rotax 532)	089-T300-382	26. 9.89	T.Pearce tr G-MVZD Syndicate	(Twickenham)	28. 8.03P

G-MVZE	Thruster T300 (Rotax 532)	089-T300-383	26. 9.89	T.L.Davis	(Graiguenamanagh, Co.Kilkenny)	9. 7.02P
G-MVZG	Thruster T300 (Rotax 532)	089-T300-385	26. 9.89	R.Lewis-Evans	Newton Peverill	31. 8.03P
G-MVZI	Thruster T300 (Rotax 503)	089-T300-387	26. 9.89	R.R.R.Whittern	South Wraxall, Bradford-on-Avon	17. 7.03P
G-MVZJ	Solar Wings Pegasus XL-Q (Rotax 462)	SW-TE-0226 & SW-WQ-0241	26. 8.89	P.Mansfield	(Peterborough)	3. 9.03P
G-MVZK	Quad City Challenger II UK (BMW R.100)	PFA 177-11498	28. 9.89	M.J.Downes	Breidden	13. 8.03P
G-MVZL	Solar Wings Pegasus XL-Q (Rotax 462)	SW-TE-0227 & SW-WQ-0242	4.10.89	P.R.Dobson	(Brentwood)	3. 6.03P
G-MVZM	Aerial Arts Chaser S (Rotax 377)	CH.825	2.11.89	P.S.Herbert	Godalming	12. 7.03P
G-MVZO	Medway Hybred 44XLR (Rotax 503)	MR072/78	25.10.89	D.L.Wright	(Northampton)	16. 3.03P
G-MVZP	Murphy Renegade Spirit UK (Rotax 582)	256 & PFA 188-11630	17.10.89	R.Germany *tr Zulu Papa Group (New owner 2.03)*	Knapthorpe Lodge, Caunton	7. 8.95P
G-MVZR	Aviadsud Mistral 532GB	090 & BMAA/HB/011	9.10.89	S.E. & J.A.Robinson	Tarn Farm, Cockerham	7. 6.01P
G-MVZS	Mainair Gemini/Flash IIA (Rotax 503)	771-1089-7 & W564	17.10.89	R.L.Beese	(Tarporley)	22. 5.03P
G-MVZT	Solar Wings Pegasus XL-Q (Rotax 462HP)	SW-TE-0228 & SW-WQ-0243	6.10.89	C.J.Meadows	Franklyn's Field, Chewton Mendip	25. 8.02P
G-MVZU	Solar Wings Pegasus XL-Q (Rotax 462)	SW-TE-0229 & SW-WQ-0244	6.10.89	R.D.Proctor	RAF Wittering	27.10.03P
G-MVZV	Solar Wings Pegasus XL-Q (Rotax 462HP)	SW-TE-0230 & SW-WQ-0245	6.10.89	I.M.Gibson	(Horsham)	12. 7.03P
G-MVZW	Hornet R-ZA (Rotax 462)	HRWB-0063 & ZA142	27.10.89	K.W.Warn	Popham	9. 8.02P
G-MVZX	Murphy Renegade Spirit UK (Rotax 582)	PFA 188-11590	18.10.89	G.Holmes	(Pickering)	22. 5.03P
G-MVZY	Aerial Arts Chaser S (Rotax 377)	CH.827	2.11.89	C.N.A.Batchelor-Wylam	Brook Farm, Pilling	12.10.02P
G-MVZZ	AMF Chevvron 2-32 (Konig SD570)	019	27. 7.89	D.Patrick	(Carlisle)	22. 5.03P
G-MWAB	Mainair Gemini/Flash IIA (Rotax 503)	772-1089-7 & W565	24.10.89	C.G.Deeley	(Lichfield)	28. 7.03P
G-MWAC	Solar Wings Pegasus XL-Q (Rotax 462)	SW-TE-0236 & SW-WQ-0260	25.10.89	P.A.Tabberer	Emlyn's Field, Rhuallt	2.10.03P
G-MWAD	Solar Wings Pegasus XL-Q (Rotax 462)	SW-TE-0237 & SW-WQ-0261	25.10.89	J.G.McNally	Sutton Meadows, Ely	14. 4.03P
G-MWAE	CFM Shadow CD (Rotax 503)	130	24.10.89	D.J.Adams	North Coates	12. 5.02P
G-MWAF	Solar Wings Pegasus XL-R (Rotax 447)	SW-TB-1422 & SW-WA-1441	30.10.89	A.Butterworth	(Poynton)	29. 5.03P
G-MWAG	Solar Wings Pegasus XL-R (Rotax 447)	SW-TB-1423 & SW-WA-1442	30.10.89	D.Foster	(Leek)	24. 4.02P
G-MWAI*	Solar Wings Pegasus XL-R (Rotax 462)	SW-TE-0238 & SW-WA-1443	1.11.89	A.G.Spurway *(Cancelled 20.12.02 by CAA)*	(Chard)	12.10.00P
G-MWAJ	Murphy Renegade Spirit UK (BMW R.100RS)	PFA 188-11438	1.11.89	M.Mailey	(Antrim)	28. 3.02P
G-MWAL	Solar Wings Pegasus XL-Q (Rotax 462)	SW-TE-0240 & SW-WQ-0263	2.11.89	A.W.Hill	Bluntisham	24. 6.03P
G-MWAN	Thruster T300 (Rotax 532)	089-T300-389	14.11.89	S.Croydon-Fowler	(Bodmin)	25. 6.02P
G-MWAP	Thruster T300 (Rotax 503)	089-T300-391	14.11.89	S.F.Chave & A.G.Spurway *"Wanda"*	Honiton/Chard	21. 7.03P
G-MWAR	Thruster T300 (Rotax 532)	089-T300-392	14.11.89	S.M.Birbeck	Popham	8.12.02P
G-MWAT	Solar Wings Pegasus XL-Q (Rotax 462)	SW-TE-0241 & SW-WQ-0265	13.11.89	D.G.Seymour	Yatesbury	21. 6.02P
G-MWAU	Mainair Gemini/Flash IIA (Rotax 582)	773-1189-7 & W566	7.12.89	L.Roberts	(Ammanford)	10. 5.03P
G-MWAV	Solar Wings Pegasus XL-R (Rotax 447)	SW-TB-1424 & SW-WA-1444	13.11.89	S.P.Waine *(See note under G-MWBL)*	(Fordingbridge)	6. 9.03P
G-MWAW	Whittaker MW6 Merlin (Rotax 503)	PFA 164-11460	10.11.89	J.A.Hindley	Brook Farm, Pilling	19. 6.02P
G-MWBI	Medway Hybred 44XLR (Rotax 503)	MR073/79	21.11.89	G.E.Coates	(Birmingham)	17. 7.03P
G-MWBJ	Medway Puma Sprint (Rotax 447)	MS003/1	21.11.89	C.C.Strong	(Buaes)	14. 7.00P
G-MWBK	Solar Wings Pegasus XL-Q (Rotax 462)	SW-TE-0248 & SW-WQ-0271	16.11.89	P.J.Harrison	Bracknell	26. 2.03P
G-MWBL	Solar Wings Pegasus XL-R/Se (Rotax 447)	SW-TB-1424 & SW-WA-1446	16.11.89	J.A.Valentine	(Blaydon-on-Tyne)	17. 4.03P
	(Trike c/n appears to have been duplicated with G-MWAV so two '1424s exist)					
G-MWBM	Hornet R-ZA (Rotax 462)	HRWB-0082 & ZA141	29.11.89	K.D.Shadforth *(Current status unknown)*	AAC Dishforth	2. 5.94P
G-MWBO	Rans S-4 Coyote (Rotax 447)	89.097 & PFA 193-11583	29.11.89	D.S.Coutts, tr G-MWBO Group	(Linlithgow)	30. 5.03P
G-MWBP	Hornet R-ZA (Rotax 462)	HRWB-0083 & ZA144	29.11.89	J.Rossall	Tarn Farm, Cockerham	13. 4.03P
G-MWBR	Hornet RS-ZA (Rotax 462)	HRWB-0084 & ZA145	29.11.89	I.A.Clark	(Grimsby)	29. 4.03P
G-MWBS	Hornet R-ZA (BMW R100)	HRWB-0085 & ZA146	29.11.89	P.D.Jaques *(Current status unknown)*	Sandtoft	23. 4.98P

G-MWBU	Hornet R-ZA	HRWB-0087 & ZA148	29.11.89	A R Mikolajczyk	(Mansfield)	2.11.02P
	(Rotax 462HP)					
G-MWBW	Hornet R-ZA	HRWB-0089 & ZA150	29.11.89	C.G.Bentley	(Chesterfield)	15. 5.00P
	(Rotax 462)					
G-MWBY	Hornet R-ZA	HRWB-0091 & ZA152	29.11.89	G.P.Austin	Mill Farm, Shifnal	19. 6.03P
	(Rotax 462)					
G-MWCB	Solar Wings Pegasus XL-Q		1.12.89	M.Foreman	(Telford)	4. 8.03P
	(Rotax 462) SW-TE-0250 & SW-WQ-0273					
G-MWCC	Solar Wings Pegasus XL-R/Se		1.12.89	C.King	(Ryton)	8. 1.03P
	(Rotax 447) SW-TB-1387 & SW-WA-1447		*(Trike ex G-MVKD when latter's sailwing sold)*			
G-MWCE	Mainair Gemini/Flash IIA 775-1289-7 & W568		19.12.89	B.A.Tooze	Shobdon	28. 3.03P
	(Rotax 503)					
G-MWCF	Solar Wings Pegasus XL-Q		13.12.89	J.D.Amos tr G-MWCF Group	(Marlborough)	20. 9.03P
	(Rotax 462) SW-TE-0252 & SW-WQ-0276					
G-MWCG	Microflight Spectrum 011		15.12.89	The Small Aeroplane Co. Ltd	Otherton, Cannock	18. 7.03P
	(Rotax 503-2V)					
G-MWCH	Rans S-6ESD Coyote II		15.12.89	W.Lucy & J.Burns	Morgansfield, Fishburn	26. 8.03P
	(Rotax 503) 0989.067 & PFA 204-11632		*(PFA c/n duplicates Kitfox G-BSFY)*			
G-MWCI	Powerchute Kestrel 91245		3. 1.90	E.G.Bray	Clacton	17. 1.02P
	(Rotax 503)					
G-MWCJ	Powerchute Kestrel 91246		3. 1.90	B.A.Dowland	(Thorney)	13. 7.02P
	(Rotax 503)					
G-MWCK	Powerchute Kestrel 91247		3. 1.90	A.Evans	(Wolverhampton)	21.10.02P
	(Rotax 503)					
G-MWCN	Powerchute Kestrel 91250		3. 1.90	H.J.Goddard	(Fleet)	22. 6.02P
	(Rotax 503)					
G-MWCO	Powerchute Kestrel 91251		3. 1.90	T.F.Bakker	(Fairford)	17. 5.93P
	(Rotax 503)			*(Current status unknown)*		
G-MWCP	Powerchute Kestrel 91252		3. 1.90	I Fraser	(Corgarff, Strathdon)	20.10.01P
	(Rotax 503)					
G-MWCR	Southdown Puma Sprint P.516 & SN1121/0070		24. 2.84	S.R.Hall	(Stroud)	2. 8.02P
	(Fuji-Robin EC-44-PM)					
G-MWCS	Powerchute Kestrel (Rotax 503) 91253		3. 1.90	B.J.L.Clark t/a Fly High (KSPT)	(Maidstone)	25.10.98P
				(Current status unknown)		
G-MWCU	Solar Wings Pegasus XL-R		27.12.89	C.M.Walters	(Chesterfield)	19.12.02P
	(Rotax 447) SW-TB-1412 & SW-WA-1449					
G-MWCV	Solar Wings Pegasus XL-Q		27.12.89	M.G.Taylor	(Stony Stratford)	20. 5.01P
	(Rotax 462HP) SW-TE-0256 & SW-WQ-0278					
G-MWCW	Mainair Gemini/Flash IIA 776-0190-7 & W569		29.12.89	A J Thomas	(Nottingham)	24. 6.03P
	(Rotax 462)					
G-MWCX	Medway Hybred 44XLR MR076/80		8. 1.90	P.A.Harris	(Petersfield)	31. 3.96P
	(Rotax 503)			*(Current status unknown)*		
G-MWCY	Medway Hybred 44XLR MR077/81		15. 1.90	J.K.Masters	(Chigwell)	17. 8.03P
	(Rotax 503)					
G-MWCZ	Medway Hybred 44XLR MR078/82		10. 1.90	A.Titcombe	(Aylesford)	29. 5.03P
	(Rotax 503)					
G-MWDB	CFM Shadow CD 100		3. 7.89	M.D.Meade	(St. Albans)	2. 5.03P
	(Rotax 503)					
G-MWDC	Solar Wings Pegasus XL-R/Se		5. 1.90	A.N.Edwards	(Great Orton)	23. 4.01P
	(Rotax 462) SW-TE-0255 & SW-WA-1450					
G-MWDD	Solar Wings Pegasus XL-Q		15. 1.90	A.L.Brown	Long Marston	16. 5.03P
	(Rotax 462) SW-TE-0258 & SW-WQ-0280					
G-MWDE	Hornet RS-ZA HRWB-0094 & ZA126		10. 1.90	H.G.Reid	Roddige, Fradley	13. 6.98P
	(Rotax 532)			*(Trike unit noted 10.00)*		
G-MWDI	Hornet RS-ZA HRWB-0098 & ZA158		10. 1.90	R.J.Perrin	Tarn Farm, Cockerham	6.11.00P
	(Rotax 532)			*(Noted 9.02)*		
G-MWDJ	Mainair Gemini/Flash IIA 777-0190-7 & W570		17. 1.90	M.Gardiner	Crosland Moor	27. 6.03P
	(Rotax 503)					
G-MWDK	Solar Wings Pegasus XL-Q		17. 1.90	T.Wicks	(Devizes)	27. 5.03P
	(Rotax 462) SW-TE-0259 & SW-WQ-0281					
G-MWDL	Solar Wings Pegasus XL-Q		17. 1.90	P.K.Dean	Sutton Meadows, Ely	31. 3.03P
	(Rotax 462) SW-TE-0260 & SW-WQ-0282					
G-MWDM	Murphy Renegade Spirit UK		18. 1.90	P.A.Hill tr Doctor & the Medics	Long Marston	3. 4.03P
	(Jabiru 2200A) 319 & PFA 188A-11628		*(PFA c/n duplicates Streak Shadow G-BRZZ)*			
G-MWDN	CFM Shadow CD K.102		17. 1.90	A.A.Duffus	(Unst, Shetland)	3. 8.03P
	(Rotax 503)					
G-MWDP	Thruster TST Mk.1 8129-TST-124		30. 1.90	J.Walker	(Ballymena, Co.Antrim)	5. 5.95P
	(Rotax 503)			*(Current status unknown)*		
G-MWDS	Thruster T300 089-T300-395		30. 1.90	M.D.Tulloch	Milltimber, Aberdeen	14. 1.03P
	(Rotax 532)					
G-MWDZ	Eipper Quicksilver MXL Sport II 022		29. 1.90	R.G.Cook	Cranfield	8. 6.03P
	(Rotax 503)					
G-MWEE	Solar Wings Pegasus XL-Q		12.12.88	R.J.Sharp	Rochester	2. 9.01P
	(Rotax 462) SW-TE-0175 & SW-WQ-0147					
G-MWEF	Solar Wings Pegasus XL-Q		30. 1.90	N.R.Williams	Long Marston	3. 7.03P
	(Rotax 462HP) SE-TE-0261 & SW-WQ-0283					
G-MWEG	Solar Wings Pegasus XL-Q		30. 1.90	S.P.Michlig	Long Marston	8. 9.03P
	(Rotax 462) SW-TE-0262 & SW-WQ-0284					
G-MWEH	Solar Wings Pegasus XL-Q		7. 2.90	K.A.Davidson	(Leuchars)	27. 1.02P
	(Rotax 462HP) SW-TE-0264 & SW-WQ-0286					
G-MWEK	Whittaker MW5 Sorcerer PFA 163-11284		20. 2.90	J.T.Francis	(Crowthorne)	15.10.00P
	(Rotax 447)					
G-MWEL	Mainair Gemini/Flash IIA 780-0290-7 & W573		13. 2.90	B.L.Benson	(Malpas)	12.11.01P
	(Rotax 503)					

G-MWEN	CFM Shadow CD	K.113		20. 2.90	P.Anning	(Torquay)	8. 8.01P
	(Rotax 503)						
G-MWEO	Whittaker MW5 Sorcerer	PFA 163-11263		21. 2.90	P.Stewart	(Portrush, Co.Antrim)	1.12.00P
	(Fuji-Robin EC-34-PM)						
G-MWEP	Rans S-4 Coyote	89.096 & PFA 193-11616		21. 2.90	E.J.Wallington	(Canterbury)	1.10.02P
	(Rotax 447)						
G-MWER	Solar Wings Pegasus XL-Q			1. 3.90	S.V.Stojanovic	(Swansea)	21. 8.02P
	(Rotax 462)	SW-TE-0265 & SW-WQ-0287					
G-MWES	Rans S-4 Coyote	89.099 & PFA 193-11737		1. 2.90	G.Scott	(London E18)	18. 2.03P
	(Rotax 447)			*(Wears "N89099" on tail which matches c/n but is not a p/i)*			
G-MWEU	Hornet RS-ZA	HRWB-0100 & ZA160		21. 2.90	K.H.Hicks	(March)	11.11.01P
	(Rotax 532)						
G-MWEY	Hornet R-ZA	HRWB0104 & ZA135		21. 2.90	J.Kidd	Tarn Farm, Cockerham	24. 9.00P
	(Rotax 462)						
G-MWEZ	CFM Shadow CD	136		22. 2.90	M.Fitch	Plaistows Farm, St Albans	5. 3.03P
	(Rotax 503)						
G-MWFA	Solar Wings Pegasus XL-R			27. 2.90	A.W.Edwards	Davidstow Moor	23. 6.02P
	(Rotax 447)	SW-TB-1406 & SW-WA-1454					
G-MWFB	CFM Shadow CD	K.119		1. 3.90	K.Hopkinson	(West Bridgford)	5.10.01P
	(Rotax 503)						
G-MWFC	TEAM mini-MAX	294 & PFA 186-11648	G-BTXC	1. 3.90	A.E.Sellers	Fenland	22. 4.03P
	(Rotax 447)		G-MWFC				
G-MWFD	TEAM mini-MAX	293 & PFA 186-11646		1. 3.90	M.A.Bolshaw	Brook Farm, Pilling	25. 7.01P
	(Rotax 447) *(PFA c/n duplicates Shadow G-GORE)*			*(Dismantled 2.03)*			
G-MWFF	Rans S-5 Coyote	89.106 & PFA 193-11639		10. 1.90	T.S.Arnup	(Hexham)	21. 2.02P
	(Rotax 447)						
G-MWFL	Powerchute Kestrel	00363		20. 3.90	A.Vincent	Fenland	31. 3.02P
	(Rotax 503)						
G-MWFS	Solar Wings Pegasus XL-Q			14. 3.90	C.P.Hughes	(Holywell)	22. 4.03P
	(Rotax 462)	SW-TE-0267 & SW-WQ-0289					
G-MWFT	MBA Tiger Cub 440	WFT-02		24.11.83	J.R.Ravenhill	Kemble	20. 4.03P
	(Fuji-Robin EC-44-PM)						
G-MWFU	Quad City Challenger II UK	PFA 177-11654		16. 3.90	M.E.Chamberlain	Higher Barn Farm, Houghton	29. 4.02P
	(Rotax 503)						
G-MWFV	Quad City Challenger II UK	PFA 177-11655		16. 3.90	W.D.Gordon	Falgunzeon	23. 8.02P
	(Rotax 503)						
G-MWFW	Rans S-4 Coyote	89.107 & PFA 193-11662		16. 3.90	C.C.B.Soden	Dunkeswell	14. 9.99P
	(Rotax 447)			*(Noted 11.01)*			
G-MWFX	Quad City Challenger II UK			20. 3.90	I.M.Walton	Wellesbourne Mountford	5. 6.03P
	(Rotax 462) CH2-1189-UK-0485 & PFA 177-11706						
G-MWFY	Quad City Challenger II UK	PFA 177-11668		20. 3.90	P.J.Ladd	Craysmarsh Farm, Melksham	1. 4.03P
	(Rotax 503)						
G-MWFZ	Quad City Challenger II UK			20. 3.90	A.Slade	(Enfield)	
	CH2-0190-UK-0506 & PFA 177-11707			*(Current status unknown)*			
G-MWGA	Rans S-5 Coyote	89.092 & PFA 193-11810		20. 3.90	G.N.Smith	Headcorn	23. 9.03P
	(Rotax 447)						
G-MWGC	Medway Hybred 44XLR	MR087/85		26. 3.90	I.Nicholls	Middle Stoke, Kent	12. 4.02P
	(Rotax 503)						
G-MWGG	Mainair Gemini/Flash IIA	785-0390-7 & W578		26. 3.90	D.Lopez	(Disley)	24. 4.03P
	(Rotax 462)						
G-MWGI	Aerotech MW5-K Sorcerer	5K-0012-02		28. 3.90	B.Barrass	Sywell	3. 9.91P
	(Rotax 447) *(Wings transferred to G-MTBT by 7.96)*			*(Noted 9.02)*			
G-MWGJ	Aerotech MW-5(K) Sorcerer	5K-0014-02		6. 9.90	V.J.Morris	Truro	20. 5.03P
	(Rotax 447)						
G-MWGK	Aerotech MW-5(K) Sorcerer	5K-0015-02	(G-MWLV)	19. 9.90	R.M.Thomas	Wombleton	10. 4.03P
	(Rotax 447)						
G-MWGL	Solar Wings Pegasus XL-Q			28. 3.90	J.Walker	Deenethorpe	7. 6.03P
	(Rotax 462)	SW-TE-0270 & SW-WQ-0293					
G-MWGM	Solar Wings Pegasus XL-Q			28. 3.90	P.J. & L.S.Kirkpatrick	(Cambridge)	2. 5.00P
	(Rotax 462)	SW-TE-0271 & SW-WQ-0294					
G-MWGN	Rans S-4 Coyote	89.113 & PFA 193-11709		26. 3.90	R.H.S.Cattle	Plaistows Farm, St Albans	31. 7.02P
	(Rotax 447)						
G-MWGO	Aerial Arts 110SX/Chaser	110SX/566		28. 3.90	B.Nicolson	(Middlesbrough)	28. 4.97P
	(Rotax 377)			*(Current status unknown)*			
G-MWGR	Solar Wings Pegasus XL-Q			6. 4.90	M.Booth	(Gloucester)	8. 7.02P
	(Rotax 462)	SW-TE-0272 & SW-WQ-0296					
G-MWGT	Powerchute Kestrel (Rotax 503)	00367		26. 4.90	G.McAleer	Newtownards, Co.Down	23. 6.01P
G-MWGU	Powerchute Kestrel (Rotax 503)	00368	(9H-)	26. 4.90	M.Pandolfino *(Current status unknown)*	Luqa, Malta	19. 7.91P
			G-MWGU				
G-MWGV*	Powerchute Kestrel (Rotax 503)	00369		26. 4.90	E.G.Bray *(Cancelled 6.6.01 by CAA)*	(Clacton)	20. 1.00P
G-MWGW	Powerchute Kestrel (Rotax 503)	00370		26. 4.90	S.P.Tomlinson *(Current status unknown)*	(Leominster)	13. 7.97P
G-MWGY*	Powerchute Kestrel (Rotax 503)	00372		26. 4.90	C.N.Bond *(Cancelled 8.8.02 by CAA)*	RAF Manston	29. 7.00P
G-MWGZ	Powerchute Kestrel (Rotax 503)	00373		26. 4.90	L.J.Lynch *(Status unknown)*	(Ventnor, Isle of Wight)	27. 5.97P
G-MWHC	Solar Wings Pegasus XL-Q			24. 4.90	P.J.Lowery	Long Acre Farm, Sandy	14. 5.99P
	(Rotax 462)	SW-TE-0274 & SW-WQ-0304		*(Current status unknown)*			
G-MWHD*	Microflight Spectrum	012		18. 4.90	P.B.& M.A.Howson	Arclid Green, Sandbach	14.12.00P
	(Rotax 503)			*(Cancelled 15.2.01 by CAA)*			
G-MWHF	Solar Wings Pegasus XL-Q			24. 4.90	N.J.Troke & S.Cox	Swinford, Rugby	10.11.02P
	(Rotax 462)	SW-TE-0275 & SW-WQ-0305					
G-MWHG	Solar Wings Pegasus XL-Q			24. 4.90	I.A.Lumley	(Great Orton)	4. 2.03P
	(Rotax 462)	SW-TE-0276 & SW-WQ-0306					
G-MWHH	TEAM mini-MAX	326 & PFA 186-11814		23. 4.90	B.F.Crick	(Desborough)	4. 8.00P
	(Rotax 447)						

G-MWHL	Solar Wings Pegasus XL-Q		1. 5.90	T.G.Jackson	(London SW11)	4. 6.03P
	(Rotax 462)	SW-TE-0278 & SW-WQ-0308				
G-MWHM	Whittaker MW6-S Fatboy Flyer	PFA 164-11463	18. 5.90	G.H.Davies	(Walsall)	2. 4.03P
	(Rotax 532)					
G-MWHO	Mainair Gemini/Flash IIA	778-0190-5 & W571	10. 5.90	B.Epps	Arclid Green, Sandbach	9. 3.01P
	(Rotax 503)					
G-MWHP	Rans S-6ESD Coyote II *(Tricycle u/c)*		8. 5.90	J.F.Bickerstaffe	Higher Barn Farm, Houghton	21. 1.03P
	(Rotax 532)	1089,093 & PFA 204-11768				
G-MWHR	Mainair Gemini/Flash IIA	787-0590-7 & W580	16. 5.90	B.Brazier	Brook Farm, Pilling	31.10.03P
	(Rotax 503)					
G-MWHT	Solar Wings Pegasus Quasar TC		15. 5.90	E.H.Gatehouse & D.M.Walters		
	(Rotax 503)	SW-TQ-0005 & SW-WQQ-0314			Pound Green, Buttonoak, Kidderminster	13. 8.03P
G-MWHU	Solar Wings Pegasus Quasar		15. 5.90	A.F.Frost & S.J.Park	Sywell	13.11.02P
	(Rotax 503)	SW-TQ-0006 & SW-WQQ-0315				
G-MWHW	Solar Wings Pegasus XL-Q		15. 5.90	N C Leonard	(Rowlands Gill)	16. 4.03P
	(Rotax 462)	SW-TE-0279 & SW-WQ-0317				
G-MWHX	Solar Wings Pegasus XL-Q		15. 5.90	N.P.Kelly	Trim, Co.Meath	15. 7.03P
	(Rotax 462)	SW-TE-0280 & SW-WQ-0318				
G-MWIA	Mainair Gemini/Flash IIA	789-0690-7 & W582	21. 5.90	M.Raj	Otherton, Cannock	27. 3.01P
	(Rotax 503)					
G-MWIB	Aviasud Mistral 532GB	094 & BMAA/HB/010	16. 5.90	N.W.Finn-Kelcey	Weston Underwood, Olney	14. 6.03P
				"Weston Belle"		
G-MWIC	Whittaker MW5-C Sorcerer	PFA 163-11224	20. 2.90	H.Lammers *"Freyja"*	(Liskeard)	24. 9.02P
	(Rotax 447)					
G-MWIE	Solar Wings Pegasus XL-Q		30. 5.90	R.Mercer	Long Marston	23. 3.03P
	(Rotax 462)	SW-TE-0282 & SW-WQ-0325				
G-MWIF	Rans S-6ESD Coyote II *(Tricycle u/c)*		30. 5.90	J.H.Cooling	Fenland	15. 4.03P
	(Rotax 503)	1089.095 & PFA 204-11749				
G-MWIG	Mainair Gemini/Flash IIA	790-0690-7 & W583	4. 6.90	D.R.Purslow	Shifnal	1. 8.03P
	(Rotax 462)					
G-MWIH	Mainair Gemini/Flash IIA	791-0690-5 & W584	4. 6.90	J.P.Kennedy	(Grimsby)	6. 2.03P
	(Rotax 503)					
G-MWIL	Medway Hybred 44XLR	MR096/90	8. 6.90	J.W.Savage	(St Albans)	13. 9.95P
	(Rotax 447)			*(Current status unknown)*		
G-MWIM	Solar Wings Pegasus Quasar TC		11. 6.90	P.J.Bates & T.S.Smith	Long Marston	13. 9.01P
	(Rotax 503)	SW-TQ-0008 & SW-WQQ-0326				
G-MWIO	Rans S-4 Coyote	90.117 & PFA 193-11774	11. 6.90	T.L.Aydon	(Buckley)	29.10.02P
	(Rotax 447)					
G-MWIP	Whittaker MW6 Merlin	PFA 164-11360	7. 6.90	D.Beer & B.J.Merrett	(Ilfracombe)	12. 4.01P
	(Rotax 582)					
G-MWIR	Solar Wings Pegasus XL-Q		8. 6.90	C.E.Dagless	Yaxham, Dereham	14. 7.03P
	(Rotax 462HP)	SW-TE-0283 & SW-WQ-0330				
G-MWIS	Solar Wings Pegasus XL-Q		8. 6.90	M.Mazure	(Edgware)	5. 9.03P
	(Rotax 462HP)	SW-TE-0284 & SW-WQ-0331				
G-MWIT	Solar Wings Pegasus XL-Q		8. 6.90	G.F.Ryland	Oxton, Nottingham	16. 2.02P
	(Rotax 462)	SW-TE-0285 & SW-WQ-0332				
G-MWIU	Solar Wings Pegasus Quasar TC		8. 6.90	D.G.Bond	(Reading)	29. 3.03P
	(Rotax 503)	SW-TQ-0010 & SW-WQQ-0333				
G-MWIV	Mainair Gemini/Flash	792-0690-5 & W585	15. 6.90	P.& J.Calvert	(Pickering)	14. 7.03P
	(Rotax 503)					
G-MWIW	Solar Wings Pegasus Quasar		18. 6.90	T.Yates	(Alfreton)	24. 6.03P
	(Rotax 503)	SW-TQ-0011 & SW-WQQ-0334				
G-MWIX	Solar Wings Pegasus Quasar TC		18. 6.90	T.D.Neal	Shobdon	26. 6.01P
	(Rotax 503)	SW-TQ-0012 & SW-WQQ-0335				
G-MWIY	Solar Wings Pegasus Quasar TC		22. 6.90	C.J.Gordon	Perth	2. 1.03P
	(Rotax 503)	SW-TQ-0014 & SW-WQQ-0336				
G-MWIZ	CFM Shadow CD (Rotax 462)	096	22.11.88	T.P.Ryan	Plaistows Farm, St Albans	13.10.02P
G-MWJD	Solar Wings Pegasus Quasar		22. 6.90	A.J.Blackwell	Long Marston	30. 9.99P
	(Rotax 503)	SW-TQ-0016 & SW-WQ-0339		*(Trike stored 4.02)*		
G-MWJF	CFM Shadow CD (Rotax 447)	K.123	26. 6.90	R.H.Cooke	(Southampton)	24. 7.02P
G-MWJG	Solar Wings Pegasus XL-R		26. 6.90	M.J.Piggott	Little Gransden	18. 6.03P
	(Rotax 447)	SW-TB-1415 & SW-WA-1472 *(Uses Trike ex G-MVVL)*				
G-MWJH	Solar Wings Pegasus Quasar		29. 6.90	N.J.Braund	(Bristol)	2.11.02P
	(Rotax 503)	SW-TQ-0017 & SW-WQQ-0340				
G-MWJI	Solar Wings Pegasus Quasar		29. 6.90	L.Luscombe	Weston Zoyland	10. 5.03P
	(Rotax 503)	SW-TQ-0018 & SW-WQQ-0341				
G-MWJJ	Solar Wings Pegasus Quasar		29. 6.90	R.Langham	Carlton Moor	26. 5.03P
	(Rotax 503)	SW-TQ-0019 & SW-WQQ-0342				
G-MWJK	Solar Wings Pegasus Quasar		29. 6.90	M.Richardson	(Swansea)	8. 4.03P
	(Rotax 503)	SW-TQ-0020 & SW-WQQ-0343				
G-MWJN	Solar Wings Pegasus XL-Q		29. 6.90	J.C.Corrall	Lower Mountpleasant Farm, Chatteris	18. 8.03P
	(Rotax 462)	SW-TE-0288 & SW-WQ-0344				
G-MWJO	Solar Wings Pegasus XL-Q		29. 6.90	C.Serra	Wareham, Dorset	23. 7.02P
	(Rotax 462HP)	SW-TE-0289 & SW-WQ-0345				
G-MWJP	Medway Hybred 44XLR	MR097/91	29. 6.90	D.W.Beach	Middle Stoke, Kent	13.12.02P
	(Rotax 503)					
G-MWJR	Medway Hybred 44XLR	MR098/92	28. 6.90	J.Stokes	Middle Stoke, Kent	7 .7.96P
	(Rotax 503)			*(Current status unknown)*		
G-MWJS	Solar Wings Pegasus Quasar TC		6. 7.90	R.J.Milward	Sywell	19. 3.03P
	(Rotax 503)	SW-TQ-0021 & SW-WQQ-0349				
G-MWJT	Solar Wings Pegasus Quasar TC		16. 7.90	K.V.Rands-Allen	Sywell	16. 2.03P
	(Rotax 503)	SW-TQ-0022 & SW-WQQ-0350				
G-MWJU	Solar Wings Pegasus Quasar		6. 7.90	S.Baker	Long Marston	3.11.03P
	(Rotax 503)	SW-TQ-0023 & SW-WQQ-0351				

G-MWJV	Solar Wings Pegasus Quasar		6. 7.90	A.Davies	Halwell, Totnes	4.10.03P
	(Rotax 503) SW-TQ-0024 & SW-WQQ-0352					
G-MWJW	Whittaker MW5 Sorcerer		11. 5.90	S.Badby	Tibenham	25. 9.02P
	(Fuji-Robin EC-44-PM) JDW-02 & PFA 163-11186					
G-MWJX	Medway Puma Sprint (Rotax 447) MS009/3		17. 7.90	R.Potter	Pound Green, Buttonoak, Kidderminster	13. 2.03P
G-MWJY	Mainair Gemini/Flash IIA 797-0790-7 & W590		16. 7.90	M.D.Walton	(Ware)	5. 4.02P
	(Rotax 503)					
G-MWJZ*	CFM Shadow CD K.132		19. 7.90	D.Mahajan	Lower Mountpleasant Farm, Chatteris	23. 7.99P
	(Rotax 503)		*(Severely damaged Chatteris during 1999: engine & wings removed & stored 7.02)*			
G-MWKA	Murphy Renegade Spirit UK PFA 188-11864		26. 7.90	C.E.Neill tr Downlands Flying Group	Deanland	8. 4.01P
	(Rotax 582) *(Incorporates project PFA 188-11690)*			"Spirit of Lewes"		
G-MWKE	Hornet RS-ZA HRWB-0108 & ZA167		30. 7.90	D.R.Stapleton	Tarn Farm, Cockerham	8.11.03P
	(Rotax 532) *(Trike c/n overstamped on HRWB-0107)*					
G-MWKO	Solar Wings Pegasus XL-Q		31. 7.90	D.D.Wardrope & G.W.Boyes	Carlisle	27. 8.03P
	(Rotax 462) SW-TE-0290 & SW-WQ-0357					
G-MWKP	Solar Wings Pegasus XL-Q		31. 7.90	K.H.Smalley	(Lincoln)	5. 7.03P
	(Rotax 462HP) SW-TE-0291 & SW-WQ-0358					
G-MWKW	Microflight Spectrum 015		3. 8.90	P.B. & M.Robinson	Sutton Meadows, Ely	29. 1.03P
	(Rotax 503)					
G-MWKX	Microflight Spectrum 016		3. 8.90	C.R.Ions	Eshott	3. 1.03P
	(Rotax 503)					
G-MWKY	Solar Wings Pegasus XL-Q		3. 8.90	C.R.Wright	Roddige, Fradley	16. 7.02P
	(Rotax 462HP) SW-TE-0292 & SW-WQ-0362					
G-MWKZ	Solar Wings Pegasus XL-Q		3. 8.90	T Bale & A Martin	(Barnstaple)	2. 2.03P
	(Rotax 462HP) SW-TE-0293 & SW-WQ-0363		*(Another unit noted with same c/n almost certainly G-MWEG with manufacturer's incorrect I/D plate)*			
G-MWLA	Rans S-4 Coyote 89.114 & PFA 193-11787		3. 8.90	B.J.Dowdle	(Middlesbrough)	1. 6.02P
	(Rotax 447)					
G-MWLB	Medway Hybred 44XLR MR104/93		15. 8.90	M.W.Harmer	Long Acre Farm, Sandy	11.10.02P
	(Rotax 503)					
G-MWLD	CFM Shadow CD 106		9. 5.89	P.C.Avery	Shipdham	1.11.01P
	(Rotax 503)					
G-MWLE	Solar Wings Pegasus XL-R		9. 8.90	D.Stevenson	Plaistows Farm, St Albans	13. 5.02P
	(Rotax 447) SW-TB-1425 & SW-WA-1474					
G-MWLF	Solar Wings Pegasus XL-R		9. 8.90	G.Rainey	Weston Zoyland	22. 8.01P
	(Rotax 447) SW-TB-1426 & SW-WA-1475					
G-MWLG	Solar Wings Pegasus XL-R		9. 8.90	N.Hay	(London W3)	2.10.03P
	(Rotax 447) SW-TB-1427 & SW-WA-1476					
G-MWLH	Solar Wings Pegasus Quasar		9. 8.90	R.A.Duncan	Drummaird Farm, Bonnybank	3. 7.03P
	(Rotax 503) SW-TQ-0030 & SW-WQQ-0364					
G-MWLI	Solar Wings Pegasus XL-Q G-65-8		9. 8.90	G.H.Betz & B.Cordi	(Royston)	29.10.03P
	(Rotax 503) SW-TB-1162 & SW-WQQ-0365 G-MWLI		*(Built as Quasar with trike c/n SW-TQ-0031 @ 8.90, modified to Quasar TC @ 10.91, to TL-Q (Rotax 447) @ 10.92 and rebuilt @ 4.99 with trike from G-MTFS following accident 5.4.96) (Trike '0081 to G-MWVM?)*			
G-MWLJ	Solar Wings Pegasus Quasar		9. 8.90	C.G.Rouse	Chandlers Ford	18. 9.03P
	(Rotax 503) SW-TQ-0032 & SW-WQQ-0366					
G-MWLK	Solar Wings Pegasus Quasar TC		9. 8.90	K.N.Cobb	(Bristol)	29. 6.01P
	(Rotax 503) SW-TQ-0033 & SW-WQQ-0367					
G-MWLL	Solar Wings Pegasus XL-Q		16. 8.90	J.Bacon	Botany Bay, Horsford	15. 8.03P
	(Rotax 462) SW-TE-0287 & SW-WQ-0338					
G-MWLM	Solar Wings Pegasus XL-Q		17. 8.90	P.J.Dale	(Chesham)	26. 5.03P
	(Rotax 462) SW-TE-0286 & SW-WQ-0322					
G-MWLN	Whittaker MW6-S Fatboy Flyer PFA 164-11844		16. 8.90	S.J.Field	(Bridgwater)	5. 6.92P
	(Rotax 503)			"Red Lips" *(Current status unknown)*		
G-MWLO	Whittaker MW6 Merlin PFA 164-11373		21. 8.90	S.P.Ganecki & L.Prew	Otherton, Cannock	6. 6.02P
	(Rotax 503)					
G-MWLP	Mainair Gemini/Flash 801-0990-5 & W594		24. 8.90	J.S.Potts	(Kilmarnock)	24. 8.99P
	(Rotax 503)			*(Current status unknown)*		
G-MWLS	Medway Hybred 44XLR MR081/95		29. 8.90	M.Liptrot	Carlisle	28. 6.03P
	(Rotax 503)					
G-MWLT	Mainair Gemini/Flash IIA 804-0990-7 & W597		31. 8.90	S.A.Sacker	Deenethorpe	18. 7.03P
	(Rotax 503)					
G-MWLU	Solar Wings Pegasus XL-R/Se		6. 9.90	T.P.G.Ward	(Great Orton)	14.10.91P
	(Rotax 462) SW-TE-0294 & SW-WA-1478		*(Trike c/n corrected from '0304 which is G-MWNC) (Stored 9.97: current status unknown)*			
G-MWLW	TEAM mini-MAX PFA 186-11717		14. 9.90	R.Wheeler	Field Farm, Oakley	24. 7.03P
	(Rotax 377)					
G-MWLX	Mainair Gemini/Flash IIA 805-0990-7 & W598		5.10.90	G.Good & E.J.Robson	East Fortune	27. 1.01P
	(Rotax 503)					
G-MWLZ	Rans S-4 Coyote 90.116 & PFA 193-11887		8.10.90	B.O.McCartan	(Banbridge, Co.Down)	3. 6.00P
	(Rotax 447)			*(New owner 18.10.02)*		
G-MWMB	Powerchute Kestrel 00399		7.11.90	D.J.Whysall	Ripley, Derbyshire	13. 7.02P
	(Rotax 503)					
G-MWMC	Powerchute Kestrel 00400		7.11.90	K.James	Kemble	30. 6.01P
	(Rotax 503)					
G-MWMD	Powerchute Kestrel 00401		7.11.90	D.J.Jackson	(Melton Constable)	20.11.91P
	(Rotax 503)			*(Current status unknown)*		
G-MWMG	Powerchute Kestrel 00404		7.11.90	M.D.Walton	(Tregaron)	26.10.02P
	(Rotax 503)					
G-MWMH	Powerchute Kestrel 00405		7.11.90	E.W.Potts	(Crymych)	31. 3.02P
	(Rotax 503)					
G-MWMI	Solar Wings Pegasus Quasar		21. 9.90	M.A.Evans	Weston Zoyland	30. 5.03P
	(Rotax 503) SW-TQ-0043 & SW-WQQ-0383					
G-MWMJ	Solar Wings Pegasus Quasar		21. 9.90	D.Webb	Kemble	24. 4.03P
	(Rotax 503) SW-TQ-0044 & SW-WQQ-0384					
G-MWMK	Solar Wings Pegasus Quasar		21. 9.90	M.E.Lloyd	(Bath)	14. 5.02P
	(Rotax 503) SW-TQ-0045 & SW-WQQ-0385					

G-MWML	Solar Wings Pegasus Quasar		21. 9.90	S.C.Key	Deopham Green	28. 9.03P
	(Rotax 503)	SW-TQ-0046 & SW-WQQ-0386				
G-MWMM	Mainair Gemini/Flash IIA	800-0890-7 & W593	24. 8.90	R.H.Church	Croft Farm, Defford	11. 5.03P
	(Rotax 462)					
G-MWMN	Solar Wings Pegasus XL-Q		2.10.90	N.A.Rathbone & P.A.Arnold	Swinford, Rugby	23. 2.03P
	(Rotax 462HP)	SW-TE-0297 & SW-WQ-0387				
G-MWMO	Solar Wings Pegasus XL-Q		2.10.90	R.S.Wilson	Insch	13. 7.03P
	(Rotax 462)	SW-TE-0298 & SW-WQ-0388				
G-MWMP	Solar Wings Pegasus XL-Q		2.10.90	D.M.Orrock & F.E.Hall	(Rushden)	28. 7.02P
	(Rotax 462HP)	SW-TE-0299 & SW-WQ-0389				
G-MWMR*	Solar Wings Pegasus XL-R		2.10.90	J.A.Crofts	Meidrim, Carmarthen	13. 3.00P
	(Rotax 462)	SW-TE-0300 & SW-WA-1483		*(Cancelled 16.4.02 by CAA)*		
G-MWMS	Mainair Gemini/Flash	807-1090-5 & W600	3.10.90	H N Barott	East Fortune	18.12.02P
	(Rotax 503)					
G-MWMT	Mainair Gemini/Flash IIA	808-1090-7 & W601	3.10.90	K.Sene	(Warrington)	23. 8.03P
	(Rotax 503)					
G-MWMU	CFM Shadow CD	150	2.10.90	A.J.Burton	Wickenby	12. 4.03P
	(Rotax 503) *(Manufacturer's records show as c/n 142 - with c/n 150 sold to Namibia)*					
G-MWMV	Solar Wings Pegasus XL-R		5.10.90	G.M.Stevens	Kemble	14. 5.03P
	(Rotax 462)	SW-TE-0307 & SW-WA-1484				
G-MWMW	Murphy Renegade Spirit UK		21. 8.89	H.Feeney *"Spirit of Cornwall"*	Long Marston	26. 7.02P
	(Rotax 532)	254 & PFA 188-11544				
G-MWMX	Mainair Gemini/Flash IIA	810-1090-7 & W603	17.10.90	L.Campbell	Swords, Co.Dublin	28.11.02P
	(Rotax 462)					
G-MWMY	Mainair Gemini/Flash IIA	809-1090-7 & W602	17.10.90	C.W.Lowe	Grove Farm, Raveningham	24. 6.03P
	(Rotax 462)					
G-MWMZ	Solar Wings Pegasus XL-Q		8.10.90	P.C.Ockwell	Redlands, Swindon	10. 8.03P
	(Rotax 462)	SW-TE-0301 & SW-WQ-0393				
G-MWNA	Solar Wings Pegasus XL-Q		8.10.90	S.Dixon	(Prudhoe)	17. 6.02P
	(Rotax 462)	SW-TE-0302 & SW-WQ-0394				
G-MWNB	Solar Wings Pegasus XL-Q		8.10.90	P.F.J.Rogers	(London SW17)	25. 6.02P
	(Rotax 462)	SW-TE-0303 & SW-WQ-0395				
G-MWNC	Solar Wings Pegasus XL-Q		8.10.90	G.S.Sage	(Sleaford)	9. 6.03P
	(Rotax 462HP)	SW-TE-0304 & SW-WQ-0396				
G-MWND	Tiger Cub RL5A Sherwood Ranger		9.10.90	D.A.Pike	Brook Farm, Pilling	13. 6.03P
	(Rotax 532)	001 & PFA 237-12229				
G-MWNE	Mainair Gemini/Flash IIA	803-1090-7 & W596	17.10.90	T.C.Edwards	(Ware)	11. 5.03P
	(Rotax 503)					
G-MWNF	Murphy Renegade Spirit UK	PFA 188-11853	15.10.90	D.J.White	Bodmin	1. 5.03P
	(Rotax 582)					
G-MWNG	Solar Wings Pegasus XL-Q		17.10.90	H.C.Thomson	Perth	3.11.03P
	(Rotax 462HP)	SW-TE-0305 & SW -WQ-0399				
G-MWNK	Solar Wings Pegasus Quasar TC		1.11.90	G.S.Lyon	RAF Wyton	1. 8.03P
	(Rotax 503)	SW-TQA-0054 & SW-WQQ-0403				
G-MWNL	Solar Wings Pegasus Quasar		1.11.90	Creation Company Films Ltd	Popham	30. 7.00P
	(Rotax 503)	SW-TQ-0055 & SW-WQQ-0404				
G-MWNO	AMF Chevvron 2-32	025	12.11.90	I.K.Hogg	Kirkbride	30. 4.03P
	(Konig SD570)					
G-MWNP	AMF Chevvron 2-32C	026	31.10.90	R.S.Tingle	(Burgess Hill)	18. 7.03P
	(Konig SD570)					
G-MWNR	Murphy Renegade Spirit UK	PFA 188-11926	12.11.90	J.J.Lancaster	Cublington	27. 8.03P
	(Rotax 582)					
G-MWNS	Mainair Gemini/Flash IIA	811-1190-7 & W604	6.11.90	G.M.Baker	(Spalding)	24. 6.03P
	(Rotax 503)					
G-MWNT	Mainair Gemini/Flash IIA	812-1190-7 & W605	6.11.90	C.G.Rodger	East Fortune	3. 6.03P
	(Rotax 582)					
G-MWNU	Mainair Gemini/Flash IIA	813-1190-5 & W606	6.11.90	C.C.Muir	(Bristol)	7. 5.03P
	(Rotax 503)					
G-MWNV	Powerchute Kestrel	00406	12.11.90	K.N.Byrne *(Current status unknown)*	(Colonsay)	13. 3.92P
G-MWNX	Powerchute Kestrel	00408	12.11.90	J.H.Greenroyd	(Hebden Bridge)	24. 9.02P
	(Rotax 503)					
G-MWOC	Powerchute Kestrel	00413	12.11.90	K.J.Foxall	(Tamworth)	10. 8.02P
	(Rotax 503)					
G-MWOD	Powerchute Kestrel	00414	12.11.90	T.Morgan	(Kidderminster)	4.10.00P
	(Rotax 503)					
G-MWOE	Powerchute Kestrel	00415	12.11.90	E.G.Woolnough & P.K.Reason	(Halesworth)	21. 1.02P
	(Rotax 503)					
G-MWOF	Microflight Spectrum	018	13.11.90	P.Williams	Otherton, Cannock	7. 4.03P
	(Rotax 503)					
G-MWOH	Solar Wings Pegasus XL-R/Se		28.11.90	P.Scammell	Kemble	18. 3.03P
	(Rotax 447)	SW-TB-1429 & SW-WA-1485				
G-MWOI	Solar Wings Pegasus XL-R		29.11.90	A.S.Wason	Yatesbury	17. 6.03P
	(Rotax 447)	SW-TB-1430 & SW-WA-1486				
G-MWOJ	Mainair Gemini/Flash IIA	814-1290-7 & W608	6.12.90	C.J.Pryce	(Port Sunlight)	18. 3.03P
	(Rotax 503)					
G-MWOK	Mainair Gemini/Flash IIA	815-1290-7 & W609	6.12.90	J.C.Miller	(Edinburgh)	19. 8.02P
	(Rotax 462)					
G-MWOL	Mainair Gemini/Flash IIA	816-1290-7 & W610	6.12.90	I.V.Watters	(Swansea)	31. 1.94P
	(Rotax 503)			*(Current status unknown)*		
G-MWOM	Solar Wings Pegasus Quasar TC		1. 3.91	T.J.Williams	(Tuam, Co.Galway)	31. 8.03P
	(Rotax 503)	SW-TQ-0060 & SW-WQQ-0412				
G-MWON	CFM Shadow CD (Rotax 503)	K.128	18.12.90	R.E.M.Gibson-Bevan	Wickenby	14. 7.03P
G-MWOO	Murphy Renegade Spirit UK		14. 9.90	R.C.Wood	Lower Mountpleasant Farm, Chatteris	12. 7.02P
	(Rotax 582)	318 & PFA 188-11811				

G-MWOP	Solar Wings Pegasus Quasar TC			31.12.90	A.Baynes	Sywell	2.10.02P
	(Rotax 503) SW-TQC-0059 & SW-WQQ-0410						
G-MWOR	Solar Wings Pegasus XL-Q			21.12.90	M.J.Saich	(Stevenage)	29. 7.02P
	(Rotax 462) SW-TE-0308 & SW-WQ-0411						
G-MWOV	Whittaker MW6 Merlin	PFA 164-11301		9. 1.91	D.J.Pennack	Weston Zoyland	13 8.02P
	(Rotax 503)						
G-MWOW	CFM Shadow B	K.007	83-AG	16. 9.85	E.M.Jackson	Old Sarum	14.10.03P
	(Rotax 447)						
G-MWOX	Solar Wings Pegasus XL-Q			7. 1.91	D.G.Matthews	(Epping)	19. 4.03P
	(Rotax 462) SW-TE-0309 & SW-WQ-0413						
G-MWOY	Solar Wings Pegasus XL-Q			7. 1.91	R.V.Barber	(Saffron Walden)	11.10.02P
	(Rotax 462HP) SW-TE-0310 & SW-WQ-0414						
G-MWPA*	Mainair Gemini/Flash IIA	817-0191-7 & W611		9. 1.91	T.Beckham	Eshott	4. 7.00P
	(Rotax 462)				(Cancelled 16.4.02 by CAA)		
G-MWPB	Mainair Gemini/Flash IIA	823-0191-7 & W617		3. 1.91	J.Fenton	St.Michaels	11. 7.03P
	(Rotax 503)						
G-MWPC	Mainair Gemini/Flash IIA	826-0191-7 & W620		3. 1.91	I.Shaw	Arclid Green, Sandbach	30. 4.03P
	(Rotax 503)						
G-MWPD	Mainair Gemini/Flash IIA	824-0191-7 & W618		9. 1.91	C.J.Roper	East Fortune	1. 2.02P
	(Rotax 503)						
G-MWPE	Solar Wings Pegasus XL-Q			9. 1.91	E.C.R.Hudson	Upper Stow, Weedon	26. 5.03P
	(Rotax 462HP) SW-TE-0096 & SW-WQ-0416		(Trike ex G-MVGX)				
G-MWPF	Mainair Gemini/Flash IIA	825-0191-7 & W619		11. 1.91	Gemini Aviation Ltd	Mill Farm, Shifnal	30. 5.03P
	(Rotax 503)						
G-MWPG	Microflight Spectrum	019		9. 1.91	D. Payn	Eshott	3. 1.03P
	(Rotax 503)				tr G-MWPG Group		
G-MWPH	Microflight Spectrum	020		9. 1.91	S.B.Mance & K.R.Wootton	(Millington)	29.10.00P
	(Rotax 503)						
G-MWPJ	Solar Wings Pegasus XL-Q			17. 1.91	D.S.Parker	Carlisle	14. 5.03P
	(Rotax 462) SW-TE-0312 & SW-WQ-0418						
G-MWPK	Solar Wings Pegasus XL-Q			17. 1.91	M.Harris	(Caversham)	31. 5.03P
	(Rotax 462) SW-TE-0313 & SW-WQ-0419						
G-MWPN	CFM Shadow CD	K.147		22. 1.91	W.R.H.Thomas	(Swansea)	11. 6.99P
	(Rotax 503)				(Current status unknown)		
G-MWPO	Mainair Gemini/Flash IIA	827-0191-7 & W621		29. 1.91	R.P.McGann	(Alfreton)	11. 8.03P
	(Rotax 503)						
G-MWPP	CFM Streak Shadow M		G-BTEM	14. 2.91	W.C.Yates	Higher Barn Farm, Houghton	1. 8.03P
	(Rotax 582) K.166-SA & PFA 206-11992						
G-MWPR	Whittaker MW6 Merlin	PFA 164-11260		16.10.90	S.F.N.Warnell (New owner 10.01)	(Staines)	
G-MWPS	Murphy Renegade Spirit UK	PFA 188-11931		18. 2.91	M.D.Stewart	(Leicester)	1. 7.98P
	(Rotax 582)				(New owner 6.01)		
G-MWPT	Hunt Avon/Huntwing	JAH-8 & BMAA/HB/015	EI-CKF	18. 2.91	M.Leyden & S.Cronin	(Ennis, Co.Clare)	10. 5.97P
	(Fuji-Robin EC-44-PM)		G-MWPT		(Current status unknown)		
G-MWPU	Solar Wings Pegasus Quasar TC			20. 2.91	R.L.Flowerday	(Exeter)	6. 7.02P
	(Rotax 503) SW-TQC-0062 & SW-WQQ-0426						
G-MWPW	AMF Chevvron 2-32C	027		26.11.90	E.L.T.Westman	Broadford, Isle of Skye	5.11.03P
	(Konig SD570)						
G-MWPX	Solar Wings Pegasus XL-R			27. 2.91	R.J.Wheeler	Haverfordwest	21. 7.03P
	(Rotax 462) SW-TE-0315 & SW-WA-1488						
G-MWPZ	Murphy Renegade Spirit UK	PFA 188-11631		18. 3.91	J.Ievers	Pains Castle	24. 2.99P
	(Rotax 582)				(Current status unknown)		
G-MWRB	Mainair Gemini/Flash IIA	819-0191-7 & W613		5. 2.91	A.S.Harvey	(Yeovil)	25. 4.01P
	(Rotax 503)				(Amended CofR 8.02)		
G-MWRC	Mainair Gemini/Flash IIA	820-0191-7 & W614		5. 2.91	D.R.Talbot	Chilton Park, Wallingford	23. 8.02P
	(Rotax 503)						
G-MWRD	Mainair Gemini/Flash IIA	821-0191-7 & W615		5. 2.91	P.Hassett	Ince Blundell	13. 2.03P
	(Motavia)						
G-MWRE	Mainair Gemini/Flash IIA	822-0191-7 & W616		5. 2.91	A.Simon	(Dingwall)	4. 8.03P
	(Rotax 503)						
G-MWRF	Mainair Gemini/Flash IIA	829-0191-7 & W623		4. 2.91	R.D.Ballard	(Bexhill)	15. 5.03P
	(Rotax 503)						
G-MWRG	Mainair Gemini/Flash IIA	830-0191-7 & W624		5. 2.91	S.A.Clarehugh	Eshott	20. 7.03P
	(Rotax 503)						
G-MWRH	Mainair Gemini/Flash IIA	831-0191-7 & W625		5. 2.91	E.G.Astin	Eshott	5. 7.03P
	(Rotax 503)						
G-MWRI*	Mainair Gemini/Flash IIA	828-0191-7 & W622		1. 3.91	R.N.Scarr	Clench Common	12.12.99P
	(Rotax 462)				(Cancelled 16.4.02 by CAA)		
G-MWRJ	Mainair Gemini/Flash IIA	832-0291-7 & W626		28. 2.91	J.S.Walton	(Mold)	26. 3.03P
	(Rotax 503)						
G-MWRK*	Rans S-6 Coyote II 0191.154 & PFA/204-11930			13. 2.91	R.H.Bambury	Breighton	10. 5.99P
	(Rotax 503) (Tricycle u/c)				(Damaged Easingwold 4.7.99: cancelled 19.5.00 by CAA) (Remains noted 12.02)		
G-MWRL	CFM Shadow CD (Rotax 503)	K.152		13. 2.91	A.E.Southern "Shadow Hawk"	Clench Common	18. 8.01P
G-MWRM	Medway Hybred 44XLR	MR086/94/91/S	G-MWLC	26. 2.91	M.A.Jones	(Wigan)	9.11.02P
	(Rotax 503)						
G-MWRN	Solar Wings Pegasus XL-R			5. 3.91	D.T.MacKenzie	(Glasgow)	28. 3.03P
	(Rotax 462) SW-TE-0316 & SW-WA-1489						
G-MWRP	Solar Wings Pegasus XL-R			1. 3.91	J.Liddiard	(Didcot)	16. 2.03P
	(Rotax 462) SW-TE-0318 & SW-WA-1491						
G-MWRR	Mainair Gemini/Flash IIA	834-0391-7 & W628		7. 3.91	G.P.Wiley	(Wolverhampton)	10. 4.03P
	(Rotax 503)						
G-MWRS	Ultravia Super Pelican	E001-201		9. 5.84	T.B.Woolley	(Narborough, Leics)	9. 9.87P
					(Current status unknown)		
G-MWRT	Solar Wings Pegasus XL-R			15. 3.91	G.L.Gunnell	Sywell	10. 9.03P
	(Rotax 447) SW-TB-1431 & SW-WA-1492						

G-MWRU	Solar Wings Pegasus XL-R		15. 3.91	J.McIver	(West Kilbride)	25. 8.96P
	(Rotax 447) SW-TB-1432 & SW-WA-1493			*(Current status unknown)*		
G-MWRV	Solar Wings Pegasus XL-R		15. 3.91	M.S.Adams	Roddige, Fradley	20. 4.03P
	(Rotax 447) SW-TB-1433 & SW-WA-1494					
G-MWRW	Solar Wings Pegasus XL-Q		25. 3.91	M Peters	Weston Zoyland	31. 8.03P
	(Rotax 462) SW-TE-0320 & SW-WQ-0431					
G-MWRX	Solar Wings Pegasus XL-Q		25. 3.91	C.D.Humphries	Long Marston	23. 8.03P
	(Rotax 462) SW-TE-0321 & SW-WQ-0432					
G-MWRY	CFM Shadow CD	K.162	26. 3.91	A.W.Hodder	Belle Vue Farm, Yarnscombe	26.10.01P
	(Rotax 503) *(Initially reserved as c/n K.158 which became G-MWSZ)*					
G-MWRZ	AMF Chevvron 2-32C (Konig SD570) 028		10. 4.91	M.J.Barrett	Davidstow Moor	4. 7.03P
G-MWSA	TEAM mini-MAX PFA 186-11855		8. 4.91	S.Hutchinson	(Scampton)	26. 3.03P
	(Rotax 377)					
G-MWSB	Mainair Gemini/Flash IIA 837-0591-7 & W631		30. 4.91	R.S.Benner	(Burton Joyce)	18.10.03P
	(Rotax 582)					
G-MWSC	Rans S-6ESD Coyote II PFA 204-12019		13. 5.91	E.M.Lear	(Langport)	30. 6.96P
	(Rotax 503) *(Tricycle u/c)*			*(Current status unknown)*		
G-MWSD	Solar Wings Pegasus XL-Q		6. 3.91	A.M.Harley	Sutton Meadows, Ely	18. 7.03P
	(Rotax 462) SW-TE-0319 & SW-WQ-0430					
G-MWSE	Solar Wings Pegasus XL-R		10. 4.91	Ultra Light Training Ltd	Roddige, Fradley	10. 5.03P
	(Rotax 462) SW-TE-0323 & SW-WA-1496			*(Fitted with trike unit from G-MTJR)*		
G-MWSF	Solar Wings Pegasus XL-R		10. 4.91	V.A.M.Bourne	Long Newnton, Malmesbury	15. 7.03P
	(Rotax 462) SW-TE-0324 & SW-WA-1497					
G-MWSH	Solar Wings Pegasus Quasar TC		30. 4.91	B.Kirkland	Tarn Farm, Cockerham	11. 9.01P
	(Rotax 503) SW-TQC-0064 & SW-WQ-0435					
G-MWSI	Solar Wings Pegasus Quasar TC		23. 5.91	J.A.Ganderton	Sywell	18.10.03P
	(Rotax 503) SW-TQC-0065 & SW-WQ-0436					
G-MWSJ	Solar Wings Pegasus XL-Q		12. 4.91	R.A.Barrett	Sutton Meadows, Ely	6. 7.03P
	(Rotax 462) SW-TE-0326 & SW-WQ-0437					
G-MWSK	Solar Wings Pegasus XL-Q		12. 4.91	J.Doogan t/a Scottglass	(Galashiels)	26. 5.02P
	(Rotax 462) SW-TE-0327 & SW-WQ-0438					
G-MWSL	Mainair Gemini/Flash IIA 835-0491-7 & W629		16. 4.91	C.W.Frost	Rufforth	11. 6.98P
	(Rotax 503)			*(Current status unknown)*		
G-MWSM	Mainair Gemini/Flash IIA 836-0491-7 & W630		16. 4.91	R.M.Wall & P.A.Garside	St.Michaels	23. 3.03P
	(Rotax 503)					
G-MWSO	Solar Wings Pegasus XL-R		25. 4.91	M.A.Clayton	(New Romney)	22. 5.03P
	(Rotax 462) SW-TE-0329 & SW-WA-1503					
G-MWSP	Solar Wings Pegasus XL-R		25. 4.91	P.A.Ashton	Knapton Lodge, Caunton	23.10.03P
	(Rotax 462) SW-TE-0330 & SW-WA-1504					
G-MWSR	Solar Wings Pegasus XL-R		25. 4.91	M.E.T.Taylor	(Lilleshall, Newport)	7. 8.03P
	(Rotax 462) SW-TE-0331 & SW-WA-1505					
G-MWSS	Medway Hybred 44XLR MR117/97		7. 5.91	F.S.Ogden	West Hoathly, Haywards Heath	20. 9.03P
	(Rotax 503)					
G-MWST	Medway Hybred 44XLR MR118/98		8. 5.91	A.Ferguson	(Sconser, Skye)	3. 9.01P
	(Rotax 503)					
G-MWSU	Medway Hybred 44XLR MR119/99		1. 5.92	T.D.Walker	Plaistows Farm, St Albans	26. 7.02P
	(Rotax 503)					
G-MWSW	Whittaker MW6 Merlin PFA 164-11328		15. 2.91	S.N.F.Warnell	Staines	
				(Current status unknown)		
G-MWSX	Aerotech MW5 Sorcerer PFA 163-11549		3. 5.91	D.R.Drewett	(Worthing)	10.10.03P
	(Rotax 447)					
G-MWSY	Aerotech MW5 Sorcerer PFA 163-11218		3. 5.91	J.E.Holloway	Saltash	19. 9.03P
	(Rotax 447)					
G-MWSZ	CFM Shadow CD K.158 (G-MWRY)		4. 4.91	P.G.Bibbey	Old Sarum	27. 9.03P
	(Rotax 503)					
G-MWTA	Solar Wings Pegasus XL-Q		8. 5.91	C D Arnold	Craysmarsh Farm, Melksham	21. 5.03P
	(Rotax 462) SW-TE-0332 & SW-WQ-0444					
G-MWTB	Solar Wings Pegasus XL-Q		8. 5.91	G.S.Highley	(Corby)	2. 9.03P
	(Rotax 462) SW-TE-0333 & SW-WQ-0445					
G-MWTC	Solar Wings Pegasus XL-Q		8. 5.91	P.Nicholson	(London SE18)	2. 9.03P
	(Rotax 462) SW-TE-0334 & SW-WQ-0446					
G-MWTD	Microflight Spectrum 022		13. 5.91	J.V.Harris tr Group Delta	Ashbourne	18. 4.00P
	(Rotax 503)					
G-MWTE	Microflight Spectrum 023		13. 5.91	R.Kirkland	RAF Halton	20. 6.03P
	(Rotax 503)					
G-MWTG	Mainair Gemini/Flash IIA 838-0591-7 & W632		16. 5.91	G.Keenan	(Warrington)	22. 4.03P
	(Rotax 582)					
G-MWTH	Mainair Gemini/Flash IIA 839-0591-7 & W633		21. 5.91	G.M.Hughes	(Edinburgh)	23. 1.03P
	(Rotax 503)					
G-MWTI	Solar Wings Pegasus XL-Q		23. 5.91	A.Crozier	Latch Farm, Kirknewton	15. 5.03P
	(Rotax 462HP) SW-TE-0251 & SW-WQ-0274					
G-MWTJ	CFM Shadow CD (Rotax 503) K.167		16. 5.91	T.D.Wolstenholme	Brook Farm, Pilling	27.10.02P
G-MWTK	Solar Wings Pegasus XL-R/Se		28. 5.91	A.J.Thomas	(Nottingham)	23. 4.03P
	(Rotax 462) SW-TE-0335 & SW-WA-1507					
G-MWTL	Solar Wings Pegasus XL-R		28. 5.91	B.Lindsay	(Chipping Sodbury)	25. 3.03P
	(Rotax 462) SW-TE-0336 & SW-WA-1508					
G-MWTM	Solar Wings Pegasus XL-R SW-WA-1509		28. 5.91	I.R.F.King	(Tunbridge Wells)	31. 3.02P
	(Rotax 462) SW-TE-0337 & SW-WA-1509					
G-MWTN	CFM Shadow CD K.153		23. 5.91	M.J.Broom	Long Marston	28. 7.99P
	(Rotax 503)			*(Current status unknown)*		
G-MWTO	Mainair Gemini/Flash IIA 840-0591-7 & W634		28. 5.91	J.Greenhalgh	St.Michaels	13. 6.03P
	(Rotax 503)					
G-MWTP	CFM Shadow CD K.107		23. 5.91	R.E.M.Gibson-Bevan	Wickenby	10. 6.03P
	(Rotax 503)					

G-MWTR	Mainair Gemini/Flash IIA (Rotax 582)	842-0591-7 & W636	31. 5.91	A.A.Howland	(Battle)	26.11.02P
G-MWTT	Rans S-6ESD Coyote II *(Tricycle u/c)* (Rotax 503) 20391.175 & PFA 204-12016		30. 4.91	L.E.Duffin *"Warrior 2"*	Insch	9. 2.02P
G-MWTU	Solar Wings Pegasus XL-R (Rotax 447) SW-TB-1435 & SW-WA-1501		21. 6.91	S.Woods	(Banagher, Co.Offaly)	2. 9.01P
G-MWTY	Mainair Gemini/Flash IIA (Rotax 503)	843-0691-7 & W637	12. 6.91	A.McGing & J.C.Townsend	(Bootle)	23. 9.02P
G-MWTZ	Mainair Gemini/Flash IIA (Rotax 503)	844-0691-7 & W638	12. 6.91	C.W.R.Felce	Riseley, Bedford	23. 6.03P
G-MWUA	CFM Shadow CD (Rotax 503)	K.161	10. 6.91	P.A.James t/a Cloudbase Aviation G-MWUA	Redhill	7. 6.03P
G-MWUB	Solar Wings Pegasus XL-R (Rotax 462) SW-TE-0338 & SW-WA-1510		12. 6.91	T.R.L.Bayley	(Edenbridge)	2. 6.03P
G-MWUC	Solar Wings Pegasus XL-R (Rotax 462) SW-TE-0339 & SW-WA-1511		12. 6.91	R.C.Best	(Lincoln)	26.10.02P
G-MWUD	Solar Wings Pegasus XL Tug (Rotax 462) SW-TE-0340 & SW-WA-1512		12. 6.91	M.J.Taggart	Clench Common	28. 6.03P
G-MWUF	Solar Wings Pegasus XL-R (Rotax 447) SW-TB-1439 & SW-WA-1514		13. 6.91	J.G.Jackson	Enstone	27. 7.03P
G-MWUH	Murphy Renegade Spirit UK (Built Canada/Saudi Arabia) (Rotax 582)	343	12. 6.91	Choicesource Ltd	Inverness	16. 9.00P
G-MWUI	AMF Chevvron 2-32C (Konig SD570)	029	2. 7.91	N.D.A.Graham	(Lochgilphead)	26. 4.03P
G-MWUK	Rans S-6ESD Coyote II *(Tricycle u/c)* (Rotax 503) 0491.187 & PFA 204-12090		1. 7.91	G.K.Hoult	Long Marston	18.10.02P
G-MWUL	Rans S-6ESD Coyote II *(Tricycle u/c)* (Rotax 503) 0391.172 & PFA 204-12054		10. 6.91	C.K.Fry	(Lychett Minster)	16. 8.03P
G-MWUN	Rans S-6ESD Coyote II *(Tricycle u/c)* (Rotax 503) 0695.841 & PFA 204-12075 *(Rebuilt with new Rans airframe as stated)*		10. 6.91 *(ZS-...?)*	M.L.Robinson tr Coyote Flying Group	Kirkbride	11. 4.03P
G-MWUO	Solar Wings Pegasus XL-Q (Rotax 462) SW-TE-0296 & SW-WQ-0379		26. 6.91	A.P.Slade	Field Farm, Oakley	7. 9.03P
G-MWUP	Solar Wings Pegasus XL-R (Rotax 462) SW-TE-0341 & SW-WA-1517		21. 6.91	R.G.Mulford	Gillingham	22. 7.03P
G-MWUR	Solar Wings Pegasus XL Tug (Rotax 462) SW-TE-0342 & SW-WA-1518		21. 6.91	A.W.Buchan & C.D.Creasey tr Nottingham Aerotow Club Knapthorpe Lodge, Caunton		19. 8.03P
G-MWUS	Solar Wings Pegasus XL-R (Rotax 462) SW-TE-0343 & SW-WA-1519		21. 6.91	H.R.Loxton	Weston Zoyland	29. 8.00P
G-MWUU	Solar Wings Pegasus XL-R (Rotax 462) SW-TE-0346 & SW-WA-1521		28. 6.91	B.R.Underwood & P.E.Hadley	Swinford, Rugby	26. 6.03P
G-MWUV	Solar Wings Pegasus XL-R (Rotax 462) SW-TE-0347 & SW-WA-1522		28. 6.91	A.D.Taylor	Carlisle	28.12.02P
G-MWUX	Solar Wings Pegasus XL-Q SW-WQ-0454 (Rotax 462HP) *(Originally supplied as a sailwing only - trike origin unknown)*		28. 6.91	B.D.Attwell	Caerphilly	27. 3.03P
G-MWUY	Solar Wings Pegasus XL-Q (Rotax 462) SW-TE-0345 & SW-WQ-0455		28. 6.91	M.J.Sharp	(Kilmarnock)	11. 1.03P
G-MWUZ	Solar Wings Pegasus XL-Q (Rotax 462) SW-TE-0350 & SW-WQ-0456		28. 6.91	A.P.Bratt	(Kenilworth)	1.11.02P
G-MWVA	Solar Wings Pegasus XL-Q (Rotax 462) SW-TE-0351 & SW-WQ-0457		28. 6.91	P.C.Hancox	Croft Farm, Defford	17. 2.03P
G-MWVE	Solar Wings Pegasus XL-R (Rotax 447) SW-TB-1441 & SW-WA-1524		18. 7.91	W.A.Keel-Stocker	Long Marston	3. 6.03P
G-MWVF	Solar Wings Pegasus XL-R/Se (Rotax 447) SW-TB-1442 & SW-WA-1525		18. 7.91	J.B.Wright	(Tamworth)	9. 4.00P
G-MWVG	CFM Shadow CD (Rotax 503)	151	5. 8.91	Shadow Aviation Ltd	Old Sarum	16.10.03P
G-MWVH	CFM Shadow CD (Rotax 503)	181	5. 8.91	J.Rochead & J.McAvoy tr Connel VH Group	North Connel, Oban	13. 6.03P
G-MWVK	Mainair Mercury (Rotax 503)	849-0891-5 & W643	13. 8.91	S.J.Robertson	(Newton Abbot)	18. 7.03P
G-MWVL	Rans S-6 ESD Coyote II *(Tricycle u/c)* (Rotax 503) 0892.341 & PFA 204-12118 *(Orig built with frame c/n 0491-186: damaged, repaired & fitted as a replacement frame to G-MZAH)*		13. 8.91	J.T., A., A. & O.D.Lewis	(Bakewell)	23. 6.03P
G-MWVM	Solar Wings Pegasus Quasar IITC (Rotax 503) SW-TQ-0031 & SW-WX-0020 *(Trike c/n duplicates G-MWLI)*		G-65-8 2. 9.91	J.D.Jones & A.A.Edmonds	(Shrewsbury)	13. 2.03P
G-MWVN	Mainair Gemini/Flash IIA (Rotax 503)	850-0891-7 & W644	19. 8.91	J.McCafferty	Enstone	20.11.03P
G-MWVO	Mainair Gemini/Flash IIA (Rotax 582)	852-0891-7 & W646	27. 8.91	P.M.Knight	(Elm Farm, Wickford)	11 7.03P
G-MWVP	Murphy Renegade Spirit UK (Rotax 582)	PFA 188-11735	22. 8.91	P.D.Mickleburgh *(New owner 2.03)*	Swinford, Rugby	29. 4.94P
G-MWVR	Mainair Gemini/Flash IIA (Rotax 503)	855-0991-7 & W650	30. 8.91	G.Cartwright	Northampton	20. 4.02P
G-MWVS	Mainair Gemini/Flash IIA (Rotax 503)	856-0991-7 & W651	30. 8.91	J.A.Brown	Otherton, Cannock	10. 1.03P
G-MWVT	Mainair Gemini/Flash IIA (Rotax 503)	860-1091-7 & W655	2. 9.91	J.Barlow & C.Osiejuk	Oxton, Nottingham	6.12.02P
G-MWVU	Medway Hybred 44XLR (Rotax 503)	MR123/102	18. 9.91	H.M.Manning	Rochester	24. 1.02P
G-MWVW	Mainair Gemini/Flash IIA (Rotax 503)	853-0891-7 & W647	9. 9.91	W.O'Brien	Arclid Green, Sandbach	29. 7.02P
G-MWVY	Mainair Gemini/Flash IIA (Rotax 503)	854-0991-7 & W649	4. 9.91	J.D.Hinton	(Tunbridge Wells)	4. 5.02P
G-MWVZ	Mainair Gemini/Flash IIA (RotaBx 503)	863-1091-7 & W658	4. 9.91	K.T.Leach	(Skelmersdale)	1.11.02P

G-MWWB	Mainair Gemini/Flash IIA (Rotax 503)	864-1091-7 & W659		18. 9.91	J.H.Bradbury	Arclid Green, Sandbach	20. 6.02P
G-MWWC	Mainair Gemini/Flash IIA (Rotax 582)	868-1191-7 & W663		23. 9.91	A. & D.Margereson	(Chesterfield)	21. 7.03P
G-MWWD	Murphy Renegade Spirit UK 344 & PFA 188-11719 (Rotax 582)			23. 9.91	F.Overall *"Winning Spirit"*	Wethersfield	31. 5.03P
G-MWWE	TEAM mini-MAX (Rotax 447)	PFA 186-11925		1.10.91	J.Entwistle *(Dismantled & stored 2.03)*	Tarn Farm, Cockerham	23. 7.97P
G-MWWG	Solar Wings Pegasus XL-Q (Rotax 462HP) SW-TE-0355 & SW-WQ-0468			3.10.91	A.W.Guerri	Rufforth	17. 8.03P
G-MWWH	Solar Wings Pegasus XL-Q (Rotax 462) SW-TE-0356 & SW-WQ-0469			3.10.91	M.R.Dunnett	Ludham	17. 7.03P
G-MWWI	Mainair Gemini/Flash IIA (Rotax 503)	870-1291-7 & W665		11.10.91	R.J.Vaughan	(Northwich)	2.10.03P
G-MWWJ	Mainair Gemini/Flash IIA (Rotax 503)	865-1191-7 & W660		22.10.91	S.B.Walsh & S.Lysaght	Tarn Farm, Cockerham	6.10.03P
G-MWWK	Mainair Gemini/Flash IIA (Rotax 582)	866-1191-7 & W661		22.10.91	J.C.Boyd tr JDS Group	Davidstow Moor	23. 6.03P
G-MWWL	Rans S-6ESD Coyote II (Rotax 503) *(Tricycle u/c)*	PFA 204-11849	(G-BTXD)	17.10.91	D.W.Lloyd	Long Acre Farm, Sandy	12. 6.03P
G-MWWM	Kolb Twinstar Mk.2 (Rotax 503) *(PFA Plans no duplicates G-GPST)*	PFA 205-11645	(G-BTXC)	17.10.91	D.Jordan	RAF Brize Norton	21. 6.02P
G-MWWN	Mainair Gemini/Flash IIA (Rotax 503)	872-1291-7 & W667		22.10.91	G A J Edwards	Dunkeswell	23. 3.03P
G-MWWP	Rans S-4 Coyote (Rotax 447)	90.115 & PFA 193-12073		21.10.91	R.McKinlay	Strathaven	1. 8.00P
G-MWWR	Microflight Spectrum (Rotax 503)	024		23.10.91	B.Fukes	North Coates	18. 5.03P
G-MWWS	Thruster T300 (Rotax 532)	089-T300-370	EI-BYW	4.11.91	S.P.McCaffrey *(Stored 3.97: current status unknown)*	Ginge Farm, Wantage	7. 7.95P
G-MWWV	Solar Wings Pegasus XL-Q (Rotax 462HP) SW-TE-0357 & SW-WQ-0470			30.10.91	R.W.Livingstone	Enniskillen, Co.Fermanagh	11. 4.03P
G-MWWX*	Microflight Spectrum (Rotax 503)	025		25.10.91	P.Turnbull & B.Smith *(Sustained accident 7.4.00) (Cancelled 21.9.00 as WFU)*	Eshott	13. 5.00P
G-MWWZ	Cyclone Chaser S (Rotax 447)	CH.829		29.10.91	P.J.Burrow	(Crediton)	28. 6.02P
G-MWXB	Mainair Gemini/Flash IIA (Rotax 503)	869-1191-7 & W664		6.11.91	N.W.Barnett	Sittles Farm, Alrewas	11. 8.02P
G-MWXC	Mainair Gemini/Flash IIA (Rotax 503)	874-0192-7 & W669		6.11.91	G.Dufton-Kelly	(Wirral)	28. 1.02P
G-MWXF	Mainair Mercury (Rotax 503)	867-1191-5 & W662		12.11.91	J.G.I.Muncey	(Witham)	12. 2.03P
G-MWXG	Solar Wings Pegasus Quasar IITC (Rotax 503) SW-TQC-0074 & SW-WQT-0471			7.11.91	J.E.Moseley	Saffron Walden	15. 7.03P
G-MWXH	Solar Wings Pegasus Quasar IITC (Rotax 503) SW-TQC-0075 & SW-WQT-0472			7.11.91	R.P.Wilkinson	Charmy Down, Bath	25. 5.03P
G-MWXJ	Mainair Mercury (Rotax 503)	861-1091-5 & W656		15.11.91	P.J.Taylor	(Scunthorpe)	11. 3.03P
G-MWXK	Mainair Mercury (Rotax 503)	862-1191-5 & W657		15.11.91	M.P.Wilkinson *(Current status unknown)*	Sandtoft	18. 7.96P
G-MWXL	Mainair Gemini/Flash IIA (Rotax 582)	859-1091-7 & W654		12.12.91	S.N.Catchpole	Beccles	23. 9.03P
G-MWXN	Mainair Gemini/Flash IIA (Rotax 582)	878-0192-7 & W673		20.11.91	P.I.Miles	(Chesterfield)	30. 5.03P
G-MWXO	Mainair Gemini/Flash IIA (Rotax 503)	880-0192-7 & W675		25.11.91	T.P.Wright	(Ilkeston)	19. 9.02P
G-MWXP	Solar Wings Pegasus XL-Q (Rotax 462) SW-TE-0359 & SW-WQ-0475			26.11.91	A.P.Attfield *(Current status unknown)*	Sutton Meadows, Ely	18. 8.99P
G-MWXR	Solar Wings Pegasus XL-Q (Rotax 462) SW-TE-0360 & SW-WQ-0476			26.11.91	G.W.Craig	Insch	9. 6.02P
G-MWXU	Mainair Gemini/Flash IIA (Rotax 582)	882-0192-7 & W677		9.12.91	C.M.Mackinnon	Cumbernauld	23. 1.03P
G-MWXV	Mainair Gemini/Flash IIA (Rotax 582)	879-1291-7 & W674		9.12.91	Launch Link Systems Ltd	Sutton Meadows, Ely	21. 5.02P
G-MWXW	Cyclone Chaser S (Rotax 377)	CH.830		9.12.91	K.C.Dodd	Roddige, Fradley	7. 5.03P
G-MWXX	Cyclone Chaser S (Rotax 447)	CH.831	(G-MWEB) (G-MWCD)	9.12.91	R.E.J.Pattenden	Maidstone	21. 7.03P
G-MWXY	Cyclone Chaser S (Rotax 447)	CH.832	(G-MWEC)	19.12.91	C A Benjamin	(Bedford)	1. 8.03P
G-MWXZ	Cyclone Chaser S (Rotax 508)	CH.836		31.12.91	N.R.Beale *"Daedalus"*	Deppers Bridge, Warwick	27. 4.01P
G-MWYA	Mainair Gemini/Flash IIA (Rotax 462)	886-0292-7 & W681		3. 1.92	R.F.Hunt	St.Michaels	28. 8.03P
G-MWYB	Solar Wings Pegasus XL-Q (Rotax 462) SW-TE-0364 & SW-WQ-0485			15. 1.92	P.D.Myer	Kemble	3.11.03P
G-MWYC	Solar Wings Pegasus XL-Q (Rotax 462) SW-TE-0365 & SW-WQ-0486			15. 1.92	N.J.Duckworth	(Bovington)	28. 6.03P
G-MWYD	CFM Shadow C (Rotax 503)	K.179		8. 1.92	J.Anderson	Plaistows Farm, St Albans	28. 5.03P
G-MWYE	Rans S-6ESD Coyote II *(Tricycle u/c)* (Rotax 503) 0591.189 & PFA 204-12223			10. 1.92	G A M Moffat	(Manchester)	5. 3.02P
G-MWYG	Mainair Gemini/Flash IIA (Rotax 582)	884-0292-7 & W679		15. 1.92	F.Tumelty & E.C.R.Brown	(Castlewellan, Co.Down)	14. 7.02P

G-MWYH	Mainair Gemini/Flash IIA 887-0292-7 & W682		15. 1.92	A.G.Carter & D.C.Jackson	(Giltbrook, Notts)	14. 8.03P
	(Rotax 503)					
G-MWYI	Solar Wings Pegasus Quasar IITC		30. 1.92	T.S.Chadfield	Graveley Farm, Herts	1. 4.02P
	(Rotax 503) SW-TQC-0083 & SW-WQT-0488					
G-MWYJ	Solar Wings Pegasus Quasar IITC		24. 1.92	J.W.Edwards	(Kingswinford)	28. 3.03P
	(Rotax 503) SW-TQC-0084 & SW-WQT-0489					
G-MWYL	Mainair Gemini/Flash IIA 877-0192-7 & W672		17. 1.92	A.J.Hinks	(South Queensferry)	29. 5.03P
	(Rotax 503)					
G-MWYM	Cyclone Chaser S 1000 CH.838		21. 1.92	C J Meadows	(Shepton Mallet)	16.12.01P
	(Mosler MM-CB35) *(Reported as rebuild of G-MVJI - perhaps trike only?)*					
G-MWYN	Rans S-6ESD Coyote II *(Tricycle u/c)*		22. 1.92	W.R.Tull	(Chipping Norton)	6. 5.00P
	(Rotax 503) 0491.185 & PFA 204-12168					
G-MWYS	CGS Arrowflight Hawk I Arrow		17. 2.93	D.W.Hermiston-Hooper	(Ryde, Isle of Wight)	
	(Rotax 447) H-T-470-R447 & BMAA/HB/020			t/a Civilair *(Current status unknown)*		
G-MWYT	Mainair Gemini/Flash IIA 881-0392-7 & W676		3. 2.92	M.A.Hodgson	Baxby Manor, Husthwaite	17. 9.03P
	(Rotax 503)					
G-MWYU	Solar Wings Pegasus XL-Q		30. 1.92	N.Hammerton	(Oxted)	12. 5.01P
	(Rotax 462) SW-TE-0364 & SW-WQ-0491					
G-MWYV	Mainair Gemini/Flash IIA 896-0392-7 & W691		3. 2.92	J.N.Whitworth	(Chesterfield)	4. 7.02P
	(Rotax 582)					
G-MWYY	Solar Wings Pegasus XL-Q		17. 2.92	R.D.Allard	Deenethorpe	31. 7.03P
	(Rotax 462) SW-TE-0365 & SW-WQ-0492					
G-MWYZ	Solar Wings Pegasus XL-Q		20.11.91	A.Boston	(Milton Keynes)	7. 6.03P
	(Rotax 462HP) SW-TE-0358 & SW-WQ-0474					
G-MWZA	Mainair Mercury 888-0292-5 & W683		7. 2.92	A.J.Malham	Rufforth	9. 2.03P
	(Rotax 503)					
G-MWZB	AMF Chevvron 2-32C 033		10. 2.92	A.J.Pickup	(Didcot)	24. 9.03P
	(Konig SD570)					
G-MWZC	Mainair Gemini/Flash IIA 899-0492-7 & W694		7. 2.92	L.W.Fowler	(Rochdale)	8. 4.03P
	(Rotax 503)					
G-MWZD	Solar Wings Pegasus Quasar IITC		2. 3.92	A.J.Blackwell	Long Marston	18. 4.03P
	(Rotax 503) SW-TQC-0086 & SW-WQT-0494					
G-MWZE	Solar Wings Pegasus Quasar IITC		17. 2.92	H.Lorimer	(Mauchline)	18. 7.01P
	(Rotax 503) SW-TQC-0087 & SW-WQT-0495					
G-MWZF	Solar Wings Pegasus Quasar IITC		17. 2.92	R.G.T.Corney	Clench Common	30. 7.03P
	(Rotax 582/40) SW-TQD-0108 & SW-WQT-0496 *(Trike c/n duplicates G-MYEK)*					
	(Data plate is stamped as above but G-MWZF built & flown originally with trike c/n SW-TQC-0088 & fitted with Rotax 503: then used to prove Rotax 582					
	with trike c/n SW-TQD-108 but re-numbered in manufacturer's build records as SW-TQD-0102)					
G-MWZG	Mainair Gemini/Flash IIA 889-0392-7 & W684		7. 2.92	P.L.Braniff	Newtownards, Co.Down	9. 9.03P
	(Rotax 582)					
G-MWZH	Solar Wings Pegasus XL-R		17. 2.92	P.A.Ord	(Redcar)	17. 4.00P
	(Rotax 462) SW-TE-0366 & SW-WA-1532					
G-MWZI	Solar Wings Pegasus XL-R		17. 2.92	K.Slater & S.Reader	(Burton-on-Trent)	9.10.03P
	(Rotax 462) SW-TE-0367 & SW-WA-1533					
G-MWZJ	Solar Wings Pegasus XL-R/Se		17. 2.92	P.Kitchen	Shotton Colliery	20. 2.02P
	(Rotax 462) SW-TE-0368 & SW-WA-1534					
G-MWZL	Mainair Gemini/Flash IIA 900-0492-7 & W695		17. 2.92	D.Renton	East Fortune	3. 7.03P
	(Rotax 582)					
G-MWZM	TEAM mini-MAX 91 PFA 186-12211 G-BUDD		18. 2.92	C.Leighton-Thomas *"My Buddy"*	(Bath)	29. 7.02P
	(Mosler MM-CB40) G-MWZM					
G-MWZN	Mainair Gemini/Flash IIA 902-0492-7 & W697		25. 2.92	K.J.Rexter	(Cumbernauld)	13. 2.03P
	(Rotax 582)					
G-MWZO	Solar Wings Pegasus Quasar IITC		26. 2.92	R.Oseland	Roddige, Fradley	16. 3.03P
	(Rotax 503) SW-TQC-0089 & SW-WQT-0498					
G-MWZP	Solar Wings Pegasus Quasar IITC		26. 2.92	M.G.Taylor	Long Acre Farm, Sandy	23. 8.02P
	(Rotax 503) SW-TQC-0090 & SW-WQT-0499					
G-MWZR	Solar Wings Pegasus Quasar IITC		26. 2.92	J.A.Robinson	Tarn Farm, Cockerham	29. 7.03P
	(Rotax 503) SW-TQC-0091 & SW-WQT-0500					
G-MWZS	Solar Wings Pegasus Quasar IITC EI-CIP		26. 2.92	A.W.King	(Dublin)	5. 7.03P
	(Rotax 503) SW-TQC-0092 & SW-WQT-0501 G-MWZS					
G-MWZT	Solar Wings Pegasus XL-R		26. 2.92	J.R.Lowman	Sutton Meadows, Ely	14. 8.03P
	(Rotax 462) SW-TE-0370 & SW-WA-1535					
G-MWZU	Solar Wings Pegasus XL-R		26. 2.92	D.W.Palmer	(Bexhill)	8. 6.03P
	(Rotax 462) SW-TE-0371 & SW-WA-1536					
G-MWZV	Solar Wings Pegasus XL-R		26. 2.92	D.J.Newby	Clench Common	16. 8.03P
	(Rotax 462) SW-TE-0372 & SW-WA-1537					
G-MWZW	Solar Wings Pegasus XL-R		26. 2.92	G.R.Puffett	Yatesbury	17. 6.03P
	(Rotax 462) SW-TE-0373 & SW-WA-1538					
G-MWZX	Solar Wings Pegasus XL-R		26. 2.92	N.M.S.Waters	(Arundel)	13. 8.03P
	(Rotax 462) SW-TE-0374 & SW-WA-1539					
G-MWZY	Solar Wings Pegasus XL-R		26. 2.92	S.J.Barkworth	Rufforth	14. 5.03P
	(Rotax 462) SW-TE-0375 & SW-WA-1540					
G-MWZZ	Solar Wings Pegasus XL-R		26. 2.92	M.P.Shea	Roddige, Fradley	18. 6.03P
	(Rotax 503) SW-TE-0376 & SW-WA-1541					
G-MXVI	Supermarine 361 Spitfire LF.XVIe CBAF.IX.4394 6850M		17. 2.89	De Cadenet Motor Racing Ltd	North Weald	30. 5.02P
	TE184			*(As "TE184/D" in Free French & 328 Squadron RAF c/s)*		
G-MYAB	Solar Wings Pegasus XL-R/Se		26. 2.92	A.N.F.Stewart	Long Marston	18. 6.03P
	(Rotax 462) SW-TE-0377 & SW-WA-1542					
G-MYAC	Solar Wings Pegasus XL-Q		26. 2.92	M.A.Garner	Thetford	13. 7.02P
	(Rotax 462) SW-TE-0378 & SW-WQ-0502					
G-MYAD	Solar Wings Pegasus XL-Q		26. 2.92	P.Byrne	Hacketstown, Co.Carlow	19. 6.03P
	(Rotax 462HP) SW-TE-0379 & SW-WQ-0503					
G-MYAE	Solar Wings Pegasus XL-Q		26. 2.92	R.J.Waller	Redlands, Swindon	15. 1.03P
	(Rotax 462) SW-TE-0380 & SW-WQ-0504					

G-MYAF	Solar Wings Pegasus XL-Q		26. 2.92	K.N.Rigley	(Newark)	23. 9.03P
	(Rotax 462) SW-TE-0381 & SW-WQ-0505					
G-MYAG	Quad City Challenger II PFA 177-12167		25. 2.92	J.W.G.Andrews	(Welwyn)	21.10.02P
	(Rotax 503)					
G-MYAH	Whittaker MW5 Sorcerer PFA 163-11233		2. 3.92	W.G.Tait	Dunkeswell	8. 7.03P
	(Rotax 447)					
G-MYAI	Mainair Mercury 892-0392-5 & W687		11. 3.92	J.Ellerton	(Hazel Grove)	6. 5.03P
	(Rotax 503)					
G-MYAJ	Rans S-6ESD Coyote II (Tail-wheel u/c)		3. 3.92	A.J.Fraley	Kingston Seymour	18. 7.03P
	(Rotax 503) 1291.248 & PFA 204-12227					
G-MYAK	Solar Wings Pegasus Quasar IITC	D-M...?	5. 3.92	I.E.Brunning	(Wigan)	1. 9.03P
	SW-TQC-0093 & SW-WQT-0506	G-MYAK				
G-MYAM	Murphy Renegade Spirit UK PFA 188-11907		6. 3.92	A.F.Reid	Newtownards, Co.Down	14. 9.01P
	(Rotax 582)					
G-MYAN	Aerotech MW-5(K) Sorcerer 5K-0017-02	(G-MWNI)	24. 3.92	J.Hollings	Melbourne, Derbyshire	1. 7.03P
	(Rotax 447) (Full Lotus floats)					
G-MYAO	Mainair Gemini/Flash IIA 894-0392-7 & W689		11. 3.92	R.H.Downe	(Edinburgh)	15. 5.02P
	(Rotax 503)					
G-MYAP	Thruster T300 9022-T300-501		12. 3.92	W.Fletcher	Clench Common	1. 5.03P
	(Rotax 582)					
G-MYAR	Thruster T300 9022-T300-502		12. 3.92	H.G.Denton	Knapthorpe Lodge, Caunton	22. 8.03P
	(Rotax 503)					
G-MYAS	Mainair Gemini/Flash IIA 895-0392-7 & W690		11. 3.92	A.N.Duncanson	Redlands, Swindon	1. 6.03P
	(Rotax 503)					
G-MYAT	TEAM mini-MAX PFA 186-12017		6. 3.92	M.A.Perry	Elm Farm, Wickford	14. 8.03P
	(Rotax 447)					
G-MYAU	Mainair Gemini/Flash IIA 890-0392-7 & W685		25. 3.92	P.P.Allen	(Ely)	26. 8.01P
	(Rotax 462)					
G-MYAV	Mainair Mercury 893-0392-5 & W688		23. 3.92	J.Lynch	East Fortune	20. 5.03P
	(Rotax 503)					
G-MYAY	Microflight Spectrum 027		13. 3.92	S.A.Clarehugh	Eshott	21.12.00P
	(Rotax 503)					
G-MYAZ	Murphy Renegade Spirit UK PFA 188-12027		16. 3.92	R.Smith	Kilkerran	10.10.03P
	(Rotax 582)					
G-MYBA	Rans S-6ESD Coyote II PFA 204-12210		12. 3.92	M.R.Cann	Dunkeswell	7. 7.03P
	(Rotax 503) (Tail-wheel u/c)			tr Climsland Climber Society		
G-MYBB	Maxair Drifter MD.001 & BMAA/HB/014		10. 4.92	M.Ingleton	(Sheerness)	12. 6.92P
	(Rotax 503)			(Current status unknown)		
G-MYBC	CFM Shadow CD BMAA/HB/047		18. 3.92	M.E.Gilbert	Drummaird Farm, Bonnybank	24. 5.03P
	(Rotax 503) (Originally regd with c/ns K.195 & PFA 206-12221 - PFA project no. indicates Streak Shadow)					
G-MYBD	Solar Wings Pegasus Quasar IITC		26. 3.92	A.M.Brumpton	(Horncastle)	3. 7.03P
	SW-TQC-0094 & SW-WQT-0511					
G-MYBE	Solar Wings Pegasus Quasar IITC		26. 3.92	M.Robson	(Sunderland)	25. 8.03P
	SW-TQC-0095 & SW-WQT-0512					
G-MYBF	Solar Wings Pegasus XL-Q		26. 3.92	K.H.Pead	(Ipswich)	7.12.02P
	(Rotax 462) SW-TE-0384 & SW-WQ-0513					
G-MYBG	Solar Wings Pegasus XL-Q		26. 3.92	P.A.Henretty & M.Aylett	(Northampton)	9. 7.03P
	(Rotax 462) SW-TE-0385 & SW-WQ-0514					
G-MYBI	Rans S-6ESD Coyote II (Tricycle u/c)		26. 3.92	A Cook & S Richens	Clench Common	16 7.03P
	(Rotax 503) 1291.249 & PFA 204-12186					
G-MYBJ	Mainair Gemini/Flash IIA 908-0593-7 & W706		2. 4.92	C.Nicholson	Sandtoft	12. 9.00P
	(Rotax 462)					
G-MYBL	CFM Shadow CD K.194		2. 4.92	J.P.Pullin	Henstridge	19.10.02P
	(Rotax 503)			(No external registration)		
G-MYBM	TEAM mini-MAX 91 PFA 186-12212		3. 4.92	B Hunter	Brook Farm, Pilling	18. 2.03P
	(Mosler MM-CB35)					
G-MYBN	Hiway Skytrike mkII/Demon 175 BRL-01		14. 4.92	B.R.Lamming (Current status unknown)	Seaton, Hull	
G-MYBO	Solar Wings Pegasus XL-R		16. 4.92	D W Pearce	Enstone	27. 1.03P
	(Rotax 447) SW-TB-1445 & SW-WA-1545					
G-MYBP	Solar Wings Pegasus XL-R/Se		16. 4.92	S.H.Williams	(Kidderminster)	2. 8.03P
	(Rotax 447) SW-TB-1446 & SW-WA-1546					
G-MYBS	Solar Wings Pegasus XL-Q		16. 4.92	J.L.Parker	(Maidstone)	21. 7.03P
	(Rotax 462) SW-TE-0387 & SW-WQ-0518					
G-MYBT	Solar Wings Pegasus Quasar IITC		16. 4.92	K.Wood	(Kingswinford)	4. 9.03P
	(Rotax 503 SW-TQC-0097 & SW-WQT-0519					
G-MYBU	Cyclone Chaser S CH.837	G-69-15	28. 4.92	R.L.Arscott	(Taunton)	21. 1.00P
	(Rotax 447)	G-MYBU				
G-MYBV	Solar Wings Pegasus XL-Q		5. 5.92	G.M.Balaam & F.A.Spiniello	Long Acre Farm, Sandy	23. 3.03P
	(Rotax 462) SW-TE-0393 & SW-WQ-0522					
G-MYBW	Solar Wings Pegasus XL-Q		5. 5.92	J.S.Chapman	Baxby Manor, Husthwaite	22. 8.02P
	(Rotax 462) SW-TE-0394 & SW-WQ-0523					
G-MYBY	Solar Wings Pegasus XL-Q		5. 5.92	P.R.Brooker	Smarden, Kent	12. 8.03P
	(Rotax 462) SW-TE-0396 & SW-WQ-0525					
G-MYBZ	Solar Wings Pegasus XL-Q		5. 5.92	J.M.Todd	Long Marston	27. 9.97P
	(Rotax 462) SW-TE-0397 & SW-WQ-0526			(Current status unknown)		
G-MYCA	Whittaker MW6-T Merlin PFA 164-11821		14. 5.92	R.A.L.Harris	(Andover)	2. 8.03P
	(Rotax 532)					
G-MYCB	Cyclone Chaser S (Rotax 447) CH.839		18. 5.92	P.Sykes	(Wimborne)	15.11.03P
G-MYCE	Solar Wings Pegasus Quasar IITC		14. 5.92	S.W.Barker	(Scarborough)	27. 6.03P
	(Rotax 503 SW-TQC-0098 & SW-WQT-0527					
G-MYCF*	Solar Wings Pegasus Quasar IITC		14. 5.92	I.J.Bratt	(Telford)	23. 1.01P
	(Rotax 503 SW-TQC-0099 & SW-WQT-0528			(Cancelled 9.11.01 by CAA)		
G-MYCJ	Mainair Mercury 906-0592-5 & W704		19. 5.92	W.Gray	East Fortune	28.11.02P
	(Rotax 503)					

Registration	Type (Engine)	Construction No.	Date	Owner/Operator	Location	Status
G-MYCK	Mainair Gemini/Flash IIA (Rotax 462)	909-0592-7 & W707	19. 5.92	J.P.Hanlon & A.C.McAllister	Ince Blundell	18.10.01P
G-MYCL	Mainair Mercury (Rotax 503)	910-0592-5 & W708	19. 5.92	Palladium Leisure Ltd	RAF Wyton	11. 5.03P
G-MYCM	CFM Shadow CD (Rotax 503)	196	20. 5.92	T.Jones *(Current status unknown)*	Redhill	20. 5.99P
G-MYCN	Mainair Mercury (Rotax 503)	901-0492-5 & W696	22. 5.92	P Lowham	Newtownards, Co.Down	27. 9.03P
G-MYCO	Murphy Renegade Spirit UK (Rotax 582)	PFA 188-12020	28. 5.92	V.A. & C.V.Brierley	(Dover)	26. 8.03P
G-MYCP	Whittaker MW6 Merlin (Rotax 532)	PFA 164-11505	2. 6.92	A C Jones	(Bilston)	9. 9.03P
G-MYCR	Mainair Gemini/Flash IIA (Rotax 503)	875-0192-7 & W670	10. 6.92	I.G.Webster	(Stoke-on-Trent)	10. 2.32P
G-MYCS	Mainair Gemini/Flash IIA (Rotax 503)	911-0592-7 & W710	12. 6.92	G.Penson tr Husthwaite Alpha Group	Baxby Manor, Husthwaite	11. 9.03P
G-MYCT	TEAM mini-MAX 91 (Rotax 447)	PFA 186-12163	30. 3.92	S.R.Roberts	Priory Farm, Tibenham	14 1.03P
G-MYCU	Whittaker MW6 Merlin (Rotax 532) *(PFA Plans No.duplicates Streak Shadow G-ORAF)*	PFA 164-11627	9. 6.92	R.D.Thomasson	London Colney	3.12.02P
G-MYCV	Mainair Mercury (Rotax 503)	913-0792-5 & W712	12. 6.92	D.P.Creedy	(Crewe)	6. 6.03P
G-MYCW	Powerchute Kestrel (Rotax 503)	00420	15. 6.92	C.D.Treffers	(Basildon)	30. 4.02P
G-MYCX	Powerchute Kestrel (Rotax 503)	00421	15. 6.92	R.S.McFadyen tr British Powered Paragliding Association	(Tamworth)	19.10.02P
G-MYCY	Powerchute Kestrel) (Rotax 503)	00422	15. 6.92	D.R.M.Powell	(Llandysul)	26. 7.02P
G-MYDA	Powerchute Kestrel (Rotax 503)	00424	15. 6.92	K.J.Greatrix	(Sleaford)	17.11.02P
G-MYDC	Mainair Mercury (Rotax 503)	916-0792-5 & W715	23. 6.92	D.J.Boylan & D.Gordon	Rufforth	10. 3.03P
G-MYDD	CFM Shadow CD (Rotax 503)	K.197	22. 6.92	C.H.Gem *(Current status unknown)*	(Marbella, Spain)	22.11.95P
G-MYDE	CFM Shadow CD (Rotax 503)	K.187	24. 6.92	D.N.L.Howell	Upper Colwall	11. 5.03P
G-MYDF	TEAM mini-MAX 91 (Rotax 447)	PFA 186-12129	24. 6.92	W.W.Vinton	(Westbury-on-Severn)	30. 8.02P
G-MYDI	Solar Wings Pegasus XL Tug (Rotax 462HP)	SW-TE-0402 & SW-WA-1557	26. 6.92	W.Greenwood tr Southern Hang Gliding Aerotow Group	Swanborough	3. 3.03P
G-MYDJ	Solar Wings Pegasus XL Tug (Rotax 462)	SW-TE-0403 & SW-WA-1558	1. 7.92	E.A.Potter & P.Stevens tr Cambridgeshire Aerotow Club	Sutton Meadows, Ely	24. 5.03P
G-MYDK	Rans S-6ESD Coyote II *(Tricycle u/c)* (Rotax 503)	0392.276 & PFA 204-12239	21. 4.92	J.W.Caush	(Whitley Bay)	18. 7.03P
G-MYDM	Whittaker MW6-S Fatboy Flyer (Rotax 582)	PFA 164-12105	26. 6.92	K.Gregan	(Dublin)	2. 7.03P
G-MYDN	Quad City Challenger II UK (Rotax 462)	CH2-1091-UK-0736 & PFA 177-12245	30. 6.92	T.C.& R.Hooks	Newtownards, Co.Down	8.10.02P
G-MYDO	Rans S-5 Coyote (Rotax 447)	89.110 & PFA 193-12274	6. 7.92	B.J.Benton	Long Marston	24.10.02P
G-MYDP	Kolb Twinstar Mk.3 (Rotax 503)	K0002-1291 & PFA 205-12231	15. 7.92	G.C.Reid	Deenethorpe	6. 8.02P
G-MYDR	Thruster T300 (Rotax 582)	9072-T300-505	21. 7.92	H.G.Soper	(Lewes)	24. 7.03P
G-MYDS	Quad City Challenger II UK (Rotax 503)	CH2-1289-UK-0500 & PFA 177-11716	6. 3.90	A.C.Ryall	(Swansea)	4.11.02P
G-MYDU	Thruster T300 (Rotax 582)	9072-T300-504	21. 7.92	J.A.Davison	(Portadown, Co.Armagh)	9. 6.02P
G-MYDV	Mainair Gemini/Flash IIA (Rotax 462)	917-0892-7 & W716	29. 7.92	A.Gibson *(Op Northern Microlight School)*	St.Michaels	3.10.02P
G-MYDW	Whittaker MW6 Merlin (Rotax 503)	PFA 164-12184	27. 7.92	A.Chidlow	Mansfield	2. 9.03P
G-MYDX	Rans S-6ESD Coyote II (Rotax 503) *(Tricycle u/c)*	PFA 204-12238	27. 7.92	R.J.Goodburn *"The Ruptured Duck"*	Spanhoe	17. 5.03P
G-MYDZ	Mignet HM-1000 Balerit (Rotax 582)	66	3. 8.92	D S Simpson	Graveley	7. 6.03P
G-MYEA	Solar Wings Pegasus XL-Q (Rotax 462HP)	SW-TE-0404 & SW-WQ-0537	28. 7.92	A.M.Taylor	Long Marston	3.11.03P
G-MYEC	Solar Wings Pegasus XL-Q (Rotax 462HP)	SW-TE-0406 & SW-WQ-0539	28. 7.92	D.Young tr Pegasus Flight Training	Kemble	31. 8.02P
G-MYED	Solar Wings Pegasus XL-R (Rotax 462HP)	SW-TE-0407 & SW-WA-1559	28. 7.92	A.J.Kentzer	(Sheffield)	28. 3.03P
G-MYEE*	Thruster TST Mk.1	8089-TST-206	11. 8.92	(M Jones)	Westbury, Wilts	1.12.98P
	(Regd as c/n 087-TST-206) (Ex ZK-FRW? & imported 12.90) (Noted as wreck 7.98: cancelled 16.10.98 as destroyed) (Wings, tail & fuse parts noted 12.01)					
G-MYEG	Solar Wings Pegasus XL-R (Rotax 447)	SW-TB-1447 & SW-WA-1560	4. 8.92	D.G.Matthews	(London Colney)	15.10.01P
G-MYEH	Solar Wings Pegasus XL-R (Rotax 447)	SW-TB-1448 & SW-WA-1561	4. 8.92	P.H.Woodward tr G-MYEH Flying Group	Roddidge, Fradley	18. 6.03P
G-MYEI	Cyclone Chaser S (Rotax 447)	CH.841	18. 8.92	T.J.Barley	(Sawbridgeworth)	11. 5.03P
G-MYEJ	Cyclone Chaser S (Rotax 447)	CH.842	18. 8.92	D.A.Cochrane	Newnham, Baldock	3. 4.00P
G-MYEK*	Solar Wings Pegasus Quasar IITC (Rotax 582/40)	SW-TQD-0108 & SW-WQT-0540	7. 8.92	B.A.McWilliams *(See G-MWZF) (Cancelled 8.3.02 by CAA)*	Long Marston	17. 7.00P

G-MYEM	Solar Wings Pegasus Quasar IITC		7. 8.92	D.J.Moore	Oakington, Cambs	26. 8.01P
	(Rotax 582/40) SW-TQD-0101 & SW-WQT-0542					
G-MYEN	Solar Wings Pegasus Quasar IITC		7. 8.92	P.R.Jeffcoat & D.Johnson	Long Marston	11. 5.02P
	(Rotax 582/40) SW-TQD-0105 & SW-WQT-0543					
G-MYEO	Solar Wings Pegasus Quasar IITC		7. 8.92	A.G.Curtis	Deenethorpe	11. 7.03P
	(Rotax 582/40) SW-TQD-0106 & SW-WQT-0544					
G-MYEP	CFM Shadow CD	K.205	13. 8.92	E.M.Middleton	(Hereford)	15. 4.03P
	(Rotax 503)					
G-MYER	Cyclone AX2000	B.1052901 & CA.001	G-69-27 19. 8.92	G.M.Douglas	Insch	3. 7.03P
	(Rotax 582/48)		G-MYER/G-69-5/59-GF			
G-MYES	Rans S-6ESD Coyote II *(Tricycle u/c)*		3. 7.92	F.J.Percival	Dairy House Farm, Worleston	9. 7.03P
	(Rotax 503) 0392.283 & PFA 204-12254			tr Dairy House Flyers		
G-MYET	Whittaker MW6 Merlin	PFA 164-12318	19. 8.92	G.Campbell	(Dorchester)	1.10.02P
	(Rotax 503)					
G-MYEU	Mainair Gemini/Flash IIA	918-0892-7 & W718	1. 9.92	G.J.Webster & P.J.Palmer	Mill Farm, Shifnal	15. 5.03P
	(Rotax 503)					
G-MYEV	Whittaker MW6 Merlin	PFA 164-11250	25. 8.92	M.J.Batchelor	Wickwar	
				(Valid CofR 4.02: noted active 2.03)		
G-MYEW	Powerchute Kestrel	00417	28. 8.92	J.Weston	(Grantham)	13. 7.02P
	(Rotax 503) *(Fitted with Harley Ram-air parachute)*					
G-MYEX	Powerchute Kestrel	00426	28. 8.92	R.S.McFadyen	(Tamworth)	17.11.02P
	(Rotax 503)					
G-MYFA	Powerchute Kestrel	00429	28. 8.95	D.A.Gardner	(Balfron)	23. 3.98P
	(Rotax 503)			*(Current status unknown)*		
G-MYFE	Rans S-6ESD Coyote II	PFA 204-12232	1. 9.92	K.A.Mitchell	(Henley-in-Arden)	22. 9.03P
	(Rotax 503)					
G-MYFH	Quad City Challenger II UK		9. 9.92	P.S.Fossey	(Bristol)	7.10.03P
	(Rotax 503) CH2-0292-0798 & PFA 177-12282					
G-MYFI	Cyclone AX3	C.3093159 & CA.002	9. 9.92	C.Childs	(Rochester)	11. 5.03P
	(Rotax 503)			t/a Medway Airsports		
G-MYFK	Solar Wings Pegasus Quasar IITC		11. 9.92	L.M.Bassett	(Bedford)	24. 9.02P
	(Rotax 582/40) SW-TQD-0113 & SW-WQT-0553					
G-MYFL	Solar Wings Pegasus Quasar IITC		11. 9.92	S.B.Wilkes	Roddige, Fradley	9. 6.03P
	(Rotax 582/40) SW-TQD-0103 & SW-WQT-0541/A		*(Orig regd as c/n SW-WQT-0554: replacement wing fitted to trike G-MYEL after wing stolen 1.1.93)*			
G-MYFM	Murphy Renegade Spirit UK	PFA 188-12249	9. 9.92	A.C.Cale	Long Marston	14.11.02P
	(Rotax 582)					
G-MYFN	Rans S-5 Coyote	89.112 & PFA 193-12273	16. 9.92	P.Doran	(Monaghan, Co.Monaghan)	7. 8.03P
	(Rotax 447)					
G-MYFO	Cyclone Chaser S	CH.843	22. 9.92	D.M.Broom	(Towcester)	29. 5.02P
	(Rotax 377)					
G-MYFP	Mainair Gemini/Flash IIA	920-0992-7 & W719	2.10.92	J.S.Hill & G.H.S.Skilton	(Stone)	13. 7.03P
	(Rotax 503)					
G-MYFR	Mainair Gemini/Flash IIA	921-0992-7 & W720	30. 9.92	P.G.Bright	(Hull)	16. 2.03P
	(Rotax 503)					
G-MYFT	Mainair Scorcher	922-0992-3 & W234	30. 9.92	N.Crowther-Wilton	Enstone	17. 1.03P
	(Rotax 503)					
G-MYFU	Mainair Gemini/Flash IIA	924-1092-7 & W722	7.10.92	P.E.Hudson	Tarn Farm, Cockerham	24. 7.02P
	(Rotax 462)					
G-MYFV	Cyclone AX3	C.2083050	6.10.92	J.K.Sargent	(Maidstone)	17. 9.03P
	(Rotax 503)					
G-MYFW	Cyclone AX3	C.2083051	13.10.92	B.J.Palfreyman	(Newthorpe, Notts.)	4. 8.02P
	(Rotax 503)					
G-MYFX	Solar Wings Pegasus XL-Q		25. 6.93	M.M.Danek	Redlands, Swindon	6. 8.01P
	(Rotax 462) SW-TE-0295 & SW-WQ-0378					
G-MYFY	Cyclone AX3	C.2083047	1.10.92	T.A.Simpson	Long Acre Farm, Sandy	15. 7.03P
	(Rotax 503)					
G-MYFZ	Cyclone AX3	C.2083048	20.10.92	M.L.Smith tr Buzzard Flying Group	Popham	6.12.02P
	(Rotax 503)					
G-MYGD	Cyclone AX3	C.2083049	21.10.92	D.Young tr Kemble Flying Club	Kemble	3.12.03P
	(Rotax 503)					
G-MYGE	Whittaker MW6 Merlin	PFA 164-11650	20.10.92	M.D. & S.M.North	Manor Farm, Croughton	24. 6.97P
	(Rotax 532)			*(Current status unknown)*		
G-MYGF	TEAM mini-MAX 91	PFA 186-12175	22.10.92	R.D.Barnard	Ley Farm, Chirk	31. 7.01P
	(Rotax 447)					
G-MYGH	Rans S-6ESD Coyote II		30.10.92	A.J.Alexander, K.G.Diamond & B.Knight	Redhill	22. 7.03P
	(Rotax 503) 0692.318 & PFA 204-12335					
G-MYGI	Cyclone Chaser S 447	CH.844	2.11.92	B.Richardson	(Morpeth)	6. 1.03P
	(Rotax 447)					
G-MYGJ	Mainair Mercury	923-0992-7 & W721	5.10.92	R.G.Jeffery	Arclid Green, Sandbach	19.12.02P
	(Rotax 503)					
G-MYGK	Cyclone Chaser S	CH.846	3.11.92	P.C.Collins	(Bath)	14.11.95P
	(Rotax 508)			*(Current status unknown)*		
G-MYGM	Quad City Challenger II UK		6.11.92	J.White & G.J.Williams	Mill Farm, Shifnall	20. 8.03P
	(Rotax 503) CH2-0391-UK-0662 & PFA 177-12261					
G-MYGO	CFM Shadow CD	K.114	28. 7.92	R.C.S.Mason	Sywell	30. 3.03P
	(Rotax 503)					
G-MYGP	Rans S-6ESD Coyote II *(Tail-wheel u/c)*		10.11.92	A.N.Hughes	(Somerton)	22. 8.03P
	(Rotax 503) 0992.349 & PFA 204-12368					
G-MYGR	Rans S-6ESD Coyote II	PFA 204-12378	16.11.92	R.B.M.Etherington	(Totnes)	5. 9.03P
	(Rotax 503)					
G-MYGT	Solar Wings Pegasus XL Tug		13.11.92	J.J.Hoer tr Condors Aerotow Syndicate	Dunkeswell	29. 3.03P
	(Rotax 462) SW-TE-0413 & SW-WA-1569					
G-MYGU	Solar Wings Pegasus XL-R		13.11.92	G.J.Boyer	(Highbridge)	7. 9.03P
	(Rotax 462) SW-TE-0414 & SW-WA-1570					

G-MYGV	Solar Wings Pegasus XL Tug			13.11.92	D.J.Brixton	Bishops Castle, Shropshire	16. 6.03P
	(Rotax 462HP) SW-TE-0415 & SW-WA-1571				tr Shropshire Tow Group		
G-MYGZ	Mainair Gemini/Flash IIA	928-1192-7 & W726		18.11.92	M Ryall	(Stockport)	3. 6.03P
	(Rotax 582)						
G-MYHF	Mainair Gemini/Flash IIA	929-1092-7 & W727		25.11.92	P.J.Bloor	(Knutsford)	6.10.03P
	(Rotax 503)						
G-MYHG	Cyclone AX3	C.2103070		27.11.92	I.McDiarmid	Strathaven	22. 8.02P
	(Rotax 503)				tr G-MYHG Flying Group		
G-MYHH	Cyclone AX3	C.2103069 & CA.006		30.11.92	M.L.Smith	Popham	23. 6.02P
	(Rotax 503)						
G-MYHI	Rans S-6ESD Coyote II (Tailwheel u/c)			8.12.92	M.Mills	Otherton, Cannock	11.12.01P
	(Rotax 503) 0692.312 & PFA 204-12279						
G-MYHJ	Cyclone AX3	C.2103073		11.12.92	J.S.Melville	(Chippenham)	13. 5.03P
	(Rotax 503) (Reported as c/n C.3093157 - see G-MYME)						
G-MYHK	Rans S-6ESD Coyote II (Tricycle u/c)			3.12.92	M.R.Williamson	Sutton Meadows, Ely	30. 7.03P
	(Rotax 503) 0692.311 & PFA 204-12349						
G-MYHL	Mainair Gemini/Flash IIA	932-0193-7 & W730		21.12.92	P.J.Lomax & J.A.Robinson	(Chorley)	7. 2.03P
	(Rotax 503)						
G-MYHM	Cyclone AX3	C.2103068 & CA.007		18.12.92	A.J.Bergman	Popham	27. 6.03P
	(Rotax 503)						
G-MYHN	Mainair Gemini/Flash IIA	933-0193-7 & W731		29.12.92	T.J.Widdison	(King's Lynn)	18. 5.03P
	(Rotax 582)						
G-MYHP	Rans S-6ESD Coyote II (Tricycle u/c)			8. 1.93	S F Winter "Grass Stripper"	(Calne)	17. 7.03P
	(Rotax 503) 0892.315 & PFA 204-12406						
G-MYHR	Cyclone AX3	C.2103071	G-68-8	15. 1.93	G.Humphrey	Long Marston	27. 6.03P
	(Rotax 503)		G-MYHR		tr G-MYHR Flying Group		
G-MYHS	Powerchute Kestrel	00433		26. 1.93	R.Kent	(Newark)	6. 4.01P
	(Rotax 503) (Frame No.00433/Parachute No.931013/Engine No.4104716)						
G-MYHX	Mainair Gemini/Flash IIA	930-1292-7 & W728		2.12.92	C.P.Simmons	(London N10)	23. 4.01P
	(Rotax 582)						
G-MYIA	Quad City Challenger II UK	PFA 177-12400		21. 1.93	I.J.Arkieson	Ley Farm, Chirk	3.10.00P
	(Rotax 503)						
G-MYIE	Whittaker MW6-S Fatboy Flyer	PFA 164-11800		26. 1.93	T.C.Viner	Long Marston	1. 6.03P
	(Rotax 532)						
G-MYIF	CFM Shadow CD	217		2. 2.93	L.Walsh	(Huntingdon)	18. 4.03P
	(Rotax 503)						
G-MYIH	Mainair Gemini/Flash IIA	937-0293-7 & W734		9. 3.93	C.A.Murray	(Loughton, Essex)	27. 5.03P
	(Rotax 582)				tr G-MYIH Flying Group		
G-MYII	TEAM mini-MAX 91	PFA 186-12119		10.11.92	S.A.Wilson	(Dromore)	5.11.02P
	(Mosler CB40)						
G-MYIJ	Cyclone AX3	C.2103072		8. 2.93	Ultralight Training Ltd	(Coventry)	29. 5.03P
	(Rotax 503)						
G-MYIK	Kolb Twinstar Mk.3	PFA 205-12220		13. 1.93	J.Latimer	Barton	19. 6.03P
	(Rotax 582)						
G-MYIL	Cyclone Chaser S	CH.849		3. 3.93	R.A.Rawes "Fricky"	Over Farm, Gloucester	14. 2.03P
	(Rotax 508)						
G-MYIM	Solar Wings Pegasus Quasar IITC		(EI-...)	22. 2.93	D.Forde	Clare Galway, Co.Galway	31. 8.03P
	(Rotax 582) SW-TQD-0122 & SW-WQT-0579		G-MYIM				
G-MYIN	Solar Wings Pegasus Quasar IITC			22. 2.93	W.P.Hughes	Long Acre Farm, Sandy	1. 8.03P
	(Rotax 582/40) SW-TQD-0123 & SW-WQT-0580						
G-MYIO	Solar Wings Pegasus Quasar IITC			22. 2.93	K.W.Brock	(London SW19)	1. 5.03P
	(Rotax 582/40) SW-TQD-0124 & SW-WQT-0581						
G-MYIP	CFM Shadow CD	K.198		16. 3.93	S.Marshall & A.Halsall	(Southport)	18.11.03P
	(Rotax 503)						
G-MYIR	Rans S-6ESD Coyote II (Tricycle u/c)			17. 3.93	P.Vergette	North Coates	1. 9.03P
	(Rotax 503) 0892.344 & PFA 204-12458						
G-MYIS	Rans S-6ESD Coyote II	PFA 204-12382		31.12.92	I.R.Henderson	Moss Side Farm, Carluke	20. 8.02P
	(Rotax 503) (Tricycle u/c)						
G-MYIT	Cyclone Chaser S	CH.850		19. 3.93	R.Barringer	Ravensthorpe, Northampton	28. 3.99P
	(Rotax 508)				(Current status unknown)		
G-MYIU	Cyclone AX3/503	C.3013084		22. 3.93	G.R.Hill	(Belfast)	21. 3.03P
	(Zanzottera Z-202)						
G-MYIV	Mainair Gemini/Flash IIA	938-0393-7 & W735		30. 3.93	P.S.Nicholls	Finmere	5. 6.03P
	(Rotax 582)						
G-MYIX	Quad City Challenger II UK			5. 1.93	A.Studley	(Crewkerne)	24. 4.03P
	(Rotax 503) CH2-0191-UK-0615 & PFA 177-12260						
G-MYIY	Mainair Gemini/Flash IIA	942-0493-7 & W737		1. 4.93	I.C.Macbeth	Arclid Green, Sandbach	22. 6.00P
	(Rotax 503)						
G-MYIZ	TEAM mini-MAX 91	PFA 186-12347		31. 3.93	S.E.Richardson	Escrick, York	26. 5.03P
	(Rotax 447)						
G-MYJB	Mainair Gemini/Flash IIA	943-0593-7 & W738		7. 4.93	T.J.Dutton	RAF Wyton	31 5.03P
	(Rotax 503)						
G-MYJC	Mainair Gemini/Flash IIA	944-0593-7 & W739		7. 4.93	R G Hearsey	(Rye)	14. 4.03P
	(Rotax 462)						
G-MYJD	Rans S-6ESD Coyote II (Tail-wheel u/c)			23. 4.93	D.R.Collier	(Staines)	22.11.03P
	(Rotax 503) 0792.324 & PFA 204-12360						
G-MYJF	Thruster T.300	9013-T300-509		14. 4.93	B.McConville	(Craigavon, Co Armagh)	5. 8.03P
	(Rotax 503)						
G-MYJG	Thruster Super T.300	9043-ST300-510		14. 4.93	J.E.L.Goodall	(Broadway)	5. 9.02P
	(Rotax 582) (Single-seat conversion)						
G-MYJJ	Solar Wings Pegasus Quasar IITC			27. 4.93	R.J.Collins	(Bideford)	26. 2.03P
	(Rotax 582/40) SW-TQD-0131 & SW-WQT-0591						
G-MYJK	Solar Wings Pegasus Quasar IITC			27. 4.93	D.J.Myers	Insch	20. 6.03P
	(Rotax 582/40) SW-TQD-0132 & SW-WQT-0592						

G-MYJM	Mainair Gemini/Flash IIA (Rotax 582)	945-0593-7 & W740		29. 4.93	S.McMaster	(Ballynahinch, Co.Down)	27. 9.02P
G-MYJO	Cyclone Chaser S (Rotax 508)	CH.851		30. 4.93	J.F.Phillips *(Current status unknown)*	(Liskeard)	24. 7.99P
G-MYJP	Murphy Renegade Spirit UK (Rotax 582)	357 & PFA 188-12045		3. 4.91	E.J.Pels	(Sainte-Alvere, Dordogne, France)	21. 2.03P
G-MYJR	Mainair Mercury (Rotax 503)	947-0593-7 & W742		12. 5.93	C.J.Johnson	(Hornchurch)	15 7.03P
G-MYJS	Solar Wings Pegasus Quasar IITC (Rotax 582)	6581		19. 5.93	P.R.Saunders	Long Acre Farm, Sandy	1. 5.02P
G-MYJT	Solar Wings Pegasus Quasar IITC (Rotax 582/40)	6582		19. 5.93	I.M.Bunce	(Forfar)	27. 6.03P
G-MYJU	Solar Wings Pegasus Quasar IITC (Rotax 582)	6573		19. 5.93	P.G.Penhaligon	Brook Farm, Pilling	30. 5.03P
G-MYJW	Cyclone Chaser S508 (Rotax 508)	CH.856		19. 5.93	T.Hudson	(Wellingborough)	7. 6.03P
G-MYJY	Rans S-6ESD Coyote II *(Tricycle u/c)* (Rotax 503)	0692.317 & PFA 204-12346		24. 5.93	F.N.Pearson	Baxby Manor, Husthwaite	27. 6.03P
G-MYJZ	Whittaker MW5-D Sorcerer (Rotax 447)	PFA 163-12385		22. 4.93	P.A.Aston *(Current status unknown)*	(Newton Abbot)	2.12.99P
G-MYKA	Cyclone AX3 (Rotax 503)	C.3013086		25. 5.93	K.R.Haskell	(Blandford Forum)	27. 1.02P
G-MYKB	Kolb Twinstar Mk.3 (Rotax 582)	K0007-0193 & PFA 205-12398		31. 3.93	D.Young	Eastbach Farm, Coleford	1. 9.00P
G-MYKC	Mainair Gemini/Flash IIA (Rotax 582)	948-0593-7 & W743		26. 5.93	S.D.Gray *(New owner 4.02)*	(Liverpool)	7. 5.03P
G-MYKD	Cyclone Chaser S (Rotax 447)	CH.857		26. 5.93	J.V.Clewer	(Ashford, Kent)	30.10.03P
G-MYKE	CFM Shadow BD (Rotax 447)	K.031		14. 1.88	M.Hughes Emlyn's Field, Rhuallt t/a MKH Engineering *(Current status unknown)*		26.10.96P
G-MYKF	Cyclone AX3 (Rotax 503)	C.3013083		8. 6.93	P.Jones *(Dismantled & stored 2.03)*	Brook Farm, Pilling	10. 7.01P
G-MYKG	Mainair Gemini/Flash IIA (Rotax 582)	950-0693-7 & W745		21. 6.93	P.G.Angus	Higher Barn Farm, Houghton	15.12.01P
G-MYKH	Mainair Gemini/Flash IIA (Rotax 582)	951-0693-7 & W746		21. 6.93	K.G. & G.F.Atkinson t/a F.Atkinson & Sons	Rufforth	9.11.03P
G-MYKI	Mainair Mercury (Rotax 503)	953-0693-7 & W748		21. 6.93	M.Wilkinson	East Fortune	3. 1.03P
G-MYKJ	TEAM mini-MAX (Rotax 508)	PFA 186-12215		10. 6.93	P.I.Frost	Guilsborough, Northampton	19. 5.03P
G-MYKL	Medway Raven X (Rotax 447)	MRB116/104		6. 7.93	S.Hutchinson	RAF Wyton	22.10.02P
G-MYKN	Rans S-6ESD Coyote II *(Tricycle u/c)* (Rotax 503)	0892.338 & PFA 204-12361		23. 6.93	S.E. & L.Hartles Lower Mountpleasant Farm, Chatteris *"Captain Airfix"*		21. 5.03P
G-MYKO	Whittaker MW6-S Fatboy Flyer (Hirth 2706)	PFA 164-11919		25. 6.93	J.Glover	(Bristol)	30. 7.03P
G-MYKP	Solar Wings Pegasus Quasar IITC (Rotax 582/40)	6627		7. 7.93	J.Mayer	(Stoke-on-Trent)	24.10.03P
G-MYKR	Solar Wings Pegasus Quasar IITC (Rotax 582/40)	6635		7. 7.93	C.Stallard	Larkins Farm, Laindon	26. 8.02P
G-MYKS	Solar Wings Pegasus Quasar IITC (Rotax 582/40)	6636		7. 7.93	M.Hurn	Graveley	28. 4.03P
G-MYKT	Cyclone AX3 (Rotax 503)	C.3013082		5. 7.93	P.J.Hepburn	Middle Stoke, Kent	5. 8.03P
G-MYKV	Mainair Gemini/Flash IIA (Rotax 503)	954-0793-7 & W749		13. 7.93	J.White & P.Gulliver	Mill Farm, Shifnal	14. 9.03P
G-MYKW	Mainair Mercury (Rotax 503)	960-0893-7 & W755		9. 7.93	I G Dunn & E.D Bailey	(Cramlington)	4. 4.03P
G-MYKX	Mainair Mercury (Rotax 503)	961-0893-7 & W756		3. 9.93	N.P.Hurst	East Fortune	14. 5.02P
G-MYKY	Mainair Mercury (Rotax 503)	962-0893-7 & W757		6. 8.93	R.P.Jewit	(York)	9.11.03P
G-MYKZ	TEAM mini-MAX 91 (Rotax 503)	PFA 186-11841	G-BVAV	26. 7.93	J.S.Harris	Old Sarum	21. 5.02P
G-MYLB	TEAM mini-MAX 91 (Rotax 532)	PFA 186-12419		2. 8.93	J.G.Burns	(Gateshead)	19.11.03P
G-MYLC	Pegasus Quantum 15 (Rotax 503)	6634		9. 8.93	G.C.Weighell tr G-MYLC Microlight Group	Enstone	24. 7.03P
G-MYLD	Rans S-6ESD Coyote II (Rotax 503) *(Tail-wheel u/c)*	PFA 204-12394		1. 3.93	E.Griffin	(Limerick, Co.Limerick)	27.10.03P
G-MYLE	Pegasus Quantum 15 (Rotax 503)	6609		9. 8.93	Susan E.Powell	Enstone	18. 9.03P
G-MYLF	Rans S-6ESD Coyote II *(Tricycle u/c)* (Rotax 503)	0493.483 & PFA 204-12544		4. 8.93	S J Honeybourne *"Low Flyer"*	(Grantham)	6. 1.03P
G-MYLG	Mainair Gemini/Flash IIA (Rotax 503)	959-0893-7 & W754		6. 8.93	J.D.& N.G.Philp	(Frome)	7. 6.03P
G-MYLH	Pegasus Quantum 15 (Rotax 503)	6632		27. 8.93	A.R.Ashworth	(Radstock)	21. 7.03P
G-MYLI	Pegasus Quantum 15 (Rotax 503)	6645		11. 8.93	A.M.Keyte	(West Wickham)	11. 5.03P
G-MYLJ	Cyclone Chaser S (Rotax 447)	CH.858		24. 8.93	B.W.Atkinson	North Coates	13. 7.03P
G-MYLK	Pegasus Quantum 15 (Rotax 503)	6602		27. 8.93	C.L.Minter tr G-MYLK Group	Deenethorpe	25. 9.03P

G-MYLL	Pegasus Quantum 15 (Rotax 462HP)	6650		31. 8.93	P.R.Mowbray	(Horncastle)	21. 4.03P
G-MYLM	Pegasus Quantum 15 (Rotax 582/40)	6651	(EC-) G-MYLM	31. 8.93	A.Young	Knapthorpe Lodge, Caunton	29. 7.03P
G-MYLN	Kolb Twinstar Mk.3 K0010-0193 & PFA 205-12430 (Rotax 582)			3. 9.93	C.D.Hatcher	Deenethorpe	25. 7.03P
G-MYLO	Rans S-6ESD Coyote II *(Tricycle u/c)* (Rotax 503) 0692.313 & PFA 204-12334			9. 9.93	A.Thornton	Ince Blundell	4.12.02P
G-MYLP	Kolb Twinstar Mk.3 K0005-0992 & PFA 205-12391 (Rotax 582)		(G-BVCR)	9. 9.93	R.Thompson *(Current status unknown)*	(Bristol)	27. 5.99P
G-MYLR	Mainair Gemini/Flash IIA 964-0993-7 & W759 (Rotax 582)			17. 9.93	L.Allen-McNaught & N.A.Angus	East Fortune	21. 8.03P
G-MYLS	Mainair Mercury 966-0993-7 & W761 (Rotax 503)			5.10.93	D.Burnell-Higgs	Shobdon	28. 3.03P
G-MYLT	Mainair Blade 967-1093-7 & W762 (Rotax 912)			23. 9.93	A.R.Walsh	Ince Blundell	29. 5.02P
G-MYLV	CFM Shadow CD (Rotax 503)	220		24. 9.93	G.Gilhead & R.G.M.Proost tr Aviation for Paraplegics & Tetraplegics Trust	Old Sarum	30. 3.03P
G-MYLW	Rans S-6ESD Coyote II *(Tricycle u/c)* (Rotax 503) 1292.401 & PFA 204-12560			4. 8.93	M.J.Phillips	Priory Farm, Tibenham	26. 8.03P
G-MYLX	Medway Raven X MRB113/109 (Rotax 447) *(Sailwing c/n also quoted for G-MYVV)*			6.10.93	T.M.Knight	(Luton)	12. 2.00P
G-MYLY	Medway Raven X) MRB001/108 (Rotax 447) *(Sailwing c/n also quoted for G-MYVU)*			23. 9.93	C.R.Smith *(Current status unknown)*	(Stanford-le-Hope)	3.10.94P
G-MYLZ	Pegasus Quantum 15 (Rotax 462)	6672		6.10.93	W.G.McPherson	Perth	21.11.03P
G-MYMB	Pegasus Quantum 15 (Rotax 582/40)	6674		6.10.93	C.A.Green *"Firebird"*	(Winterborne Earls)	19. 4.03P
G-MYMC	Pegasus Quantum 15 (Rotax 582/40)	6675		6.10.93	M.Brown	(Barnard Castle)	16. 2.03P
G-MYME	Cyclone AX3 C.3093157 (Rotax 503)			13.10.93	M.L.Smith *(See G-MYHJ)*	Popham	17.11.02P
G-MYMF	Cyclone AX3 (Rotax 503) C.3093158 (Rotax 503)			18.10.93	M.McClelland t/a McClelland Aviation	Old Sarum	8.11.02P
G-MYMH	Rans S-6ESD Coyote II *(Tricycle u/c)* (Rotax 503) 0793.520 & PFA 204-12576			20.10.93	A.R.Cattell	(Reading)	19. 6.03P
G-MYMI	Kolb Twinstar Mk.3 K0016-0693 & PFA 205-12537 (Rotax 582)			21.10.93	K.A.Wright	North Coates	27. 8.03P
G-MYMJ	Medway Raven X MRB004/110 (Rotax 447) *(Sailwing c/n also quoted for G-MYVX)*			28.10.93	N.Brigginshaw	RAF Wyton	26.10.02P
G-MYMK	Mainair Gemini/Flash IIA 968-1193-7 & W763 (Rotax 582)			29.10.93	A.Britton	(Rickmansworth)	14.12.02P
G-MYML	Mainair Mercury 969-1193-7 & W765 (Rotax 503)			29.10.93	D.J.Dalley	(Weymouth)	7. 6.01P
G-MYMM	Air Creation Ultraflight Fun 18S GT bis 93/001 (Rotax 503)			30. 9.93	W.H.Greenwood *(New owner 8.02)*	Swanborough Farm, Lewes	23. 8.01P
G-MYMN	Whittaker MW6 Merlin PFA 164-12124 (Rotax 582)			29.10.93	K.J.Cole	Over Farm, Gloucester	25. 11.03P
G-MYMO	Mainair Gemini/Flash IIA 955-0793-7 & W750 (Rotax 503)			24. 6.93	T.Jones	(Nantwich)	16. 9.02P
G-MYMP	Rans S-6ESD Coyote II *(Tricycle u/c)* (Rotax 503) 1291.250 & PFA 204-12436		(G-CHAZ)	5.11.93	R.J.D'Arcy	(Heathfield)	10. 7.03P
G-MYMR	Rans S-6ESD Coyote II *(Tricycle u/c)* (Rotax 503) PFA 204-12580			17.11.93	J.Neilands	(Ballybofey, Co.Donegal)	11. 5.03P
G-MYMS	Rans S-6ESD Coyote II *(Tricycle u/c)* (Rotax 503) 0893.526 & PFA 204-12581			17.11.93	M.R.Johnson & P.G.Briscoe	Long Marston	30.10.02P
G-MYMT	Mainair Mercury 970-1193-7 & W766 (Rotax 503)			19.11.93	W. & C.A.Bradshaw	St.Michaels	9.12.02P
G-MYMV	Mainair Gemini/Flash IIA 971-1193-7 & W767 (Rotax 503)			26.11.93	A.Szczepanek	Droppingwell Farm, Bewdley	8. 4.03P
G-MYMW	Cyclone AX3 C.3093156 (Rotax 503)			23.11.93	L.J.Perring	Field Farm, Oakley	1. 5.03P
G-MYMX	Pegasus Quantum 15 (Rotax 582/40)	6705		1.12.93	N.F.McKenzie	Insch	23. 6.03P
G-MYMY	Cyclone Chaser S CH.860 (Rotax 508)			7. 9.93	D.L.Hadley	(Canterbury)	29. 5.03P
G-MYMZ	Cyclone AX3 C.3093154 (Rotax 503)			7.12.93	The Microlight School (Lichfield) Ltd	Roddige, Fradley	28. 9.01P
G-MYNA	CFM Shadow C K.023 (Rotax 503)			10. 2.88	D.D.Parry	(Ware)	3. 9.03P
G-MYNB	Pegasus Quantum 15 6719 (Rotax 582/40)			14.12.93	D.M.Savage & J.P.Briggs	(MirfieLd)	14. 6.02P
G-MYNC	Mainair Mercury K973-1293-7 & W769 (Rotax 503) *(Supplied as Mainair Kit)*			17.12.93	A.Brotheridge	Redlands, Swindon	21. 8.03P
G-MYND	Mainair Gemini/Flash IIA 841-0591-7 & W635 (Rotax 503)			28. 5.91	P.D.Daniel & C.O'Brian	Sandtoft	23. 4.03P
G-MYNE	Rans S-6ESD Coyote II PFA 204-12497 (Rotax 503) *(Tail-wheel u/c)*			25. 6.93	J N W Moss	Sywell	7. 7.03P
G-MYNF	Mainair Mercury 974-1293-7 & W770 (Rotax 503)			17. 1.94	B.Walker tr G-MYNF Group	Eshott	24. 1.03P
G-MYNH	Rans S-6ESD Coyote II *(Tail-wheel u/c)* (Rotax 912) 0493.487 & PFA 204-12616			30.12.93	E.F. & V.M.Clapham	Oldbury-on-Severn	29. 3.01P
G-MYNI	TEAM mini-MAX 91 PFA 186-12314 (Mosler MM-CB35)			22. 2.93	J.J.Penney *(Current status unknown)*	(Neath)	17.11.99P

G-MYNJ	Mainair Mercury	K972-1293-7 & W768		14. 1.94	S.M.Buchan	(Leamington Spa)	10. 8.03P
	(Rotax 503) *(Supplied as Mainair Kit)*						
G-MYNK	Pegasus Quantum 15		6614	17.11.93	N.D.Azevedo	(London N5)	3.10.02P
	(Rotax 582/40)						
G-MYNL	Pegasus Quantum 15		6648	17.11.93	R.J.Murphy	East Fortune	6.10.02P
	(Rotax 582/40)						
G-MYNN	Pegasus Quantum 15		6679	17.11.93	P.H.E.Woodliffe-Thomas	Field Farm, Oakley	22.12.01P
	(Rotax 582/40)						
G-MYNO	Pegasus Quantum 15)		6724	10. 1.94	S.J.Baker	Sutton Meadows, Ely	20. 4.03P
	(Rotax 582/40)						
G-MYNP	Pegasus Quantum 15		6688	17.11.93	R.H.Braithwaite	RAF Henlow	30. 5.03P
	(Rotax 582/40)				tr RAF Microlight Flying Association		
G-MYNR	Pegasus Quantum 15		6692	17.11.93	P.R.Grady	Old Sarum	13. 4.05P
	(Rotax 582/40)						
G-MYNS	Pegasus Quantum 15		6694	17.11.93	E.G.Cartwright	(Belper)	18. 4.03P
	(Rotax 582/40)						
G-MYNT	Pegasus Quantum 15		6693	17.11.93	P.A.Vernon	Craysmarsh Farm, Melksham	13.11.03P
	(Rotax 582/40)						
G-MYNV	Pegasus Quantum 15		6725	10. 1.94	H.M.Smith	(Bampton)	7. 6.02P
	(Rotax 582/40)						
G-MYNX	CFM Streak Shadow SA-M			15. 6.92	T.J. & M.D.Palmer	(Symington)	23.11.03P
	(Rotax 618)	K.193-SA-M & PFA 206-12268			*(Operates from Oban)*		
G-MYNY	Kolb Twinstar Mk.3	K0014-0693 & PFA 205-12478		22.11.93	B.Alexander	Swinford, Rugby	25. 8.98P
	(Rotax 582)				*(Current status unknown)*		
G-MYNZ	Pegasus Quantum 15		6709	18. 1.94	N.S.Lynall	Otherton, Cannock	14. 9.02P
	(Rotax 582/40)						
G-MYOA	Rans S-6ESD Coyote II *(Tricycle u/c)*			23.11.93	M.D.Baylis tr Orcas Syndicate	Otherton, Cannock	17. 2.03P
	(Rotax 503)	0793.523 & PFA 204-12578					
G-MYOB	Mainair Mercury	976-1293-7 & W772		8.12.93	J.C. & B.E.Barnes	(Wisbech)	16.11.01P
	(Rotax 503)						
G-MYOF	Mainair Mercury	975-1293-7 & W771		3.12.93	A.R.Walker	Doncaster	12. 4.02P
	(Rotax 503)						
G-MYOG	Kolb Twinstar Mk.3	K0011-0193 & PFA 205-12449		19. 1.94	A.P. de Legh	Redhill	28. 7.03P
	(Hirth 2706)						
G-MYOH	CFM Shadow CD		K.201	27. 1.94	D.W.Bayliss	Popham	21. 5.02P
	(Rotax 503)						
G-MYOI	Rans S-6ESD Coyote II *(Tailwheel u/c)*			3. 2.94	J.Meijerink	Priory Farm, Tibenham	18.11.03P
	(Rotax 503)	1292.409 & PFA 204-12503					
G-MYOL	Air Creation Ultraflight Fun 18S GT bis	94/001		7. 2.94	I.R.Scott	Roddige, Fradley	7. 7.01P
	(Rotax 447)						
G-MYOM	Mainair Gemini/Flash IIA	981-0294-7 & W777		14. 2.94	J.G.Callan	Newtownards, Co.Down	3. 8.03P
	(Rotax 582)						
G-MYON	CFM Shadow CD		240	12. 1.94	D.W.& S.E.Suttill	Breighton	28. 2.02P
	(Rotax 503)						
G-MYOO	Kolb Twinstar Mk.3M			11. 5.92	P.D.Coppin	Colemore Common	5.11.03P
	(Rotax 582)	K0004-0192 & PFA 205-12200					
G-MYOR	Kolb Twinstar Mk.3	PFA 205-12602		16. 2.94	J.J.Littler	Chichester	3.10.03P
	(Rotax 582)						
G-MYOS	CFM Shadow CD		246	18. 2.94	E.J. & C.A.Bowles	Craysmarsh Farm, Melksham	10. 5.03P
	(Rotax 503)						
G-MYOT	Rans S-6ESD Coyote II *(Tail-wheel u/c)*			21. 2.94	D.E.Wilson	(Wadebridge)	15. 7.03P
	(Rotax 503)	0893.525 & PFA 204-12668					
G-MYOU	Pegasus Quantum 15		6726	1. 3.94	B.Dossett	London Colney	24. 8.03P
	(Rotax 582/40)						
G-MYOV	Mainair Mercury	K979-0294-7 & W775		1. 3.94	A.Davis	(Macclesfield)	26. 8.02P
	(Rotax 503) *(Supplied as Mainair Kit)*						
G-MYOW	Mainair Gemini/Flash IIA	983-0294-7 & W779		16. 3.94	A.J.A.Fowler	Corn Wood Farm, Adversane	16. 4.03P
	(Rotax 503)						
G-MYOX	Mainair Mercury	K984-0294-7 & W780		23. 2.94	A.D.Dudding	Sandtoft	11. 7.03P
	(Rotax 503) *(Supplied as Mainair Kit)*						
G-MYOY	Cyclone AX3		C.3123191	23. 2.94	A.McRoberts	(Bilston)	10. 6.03P
	(Rotax 503)						
G-MYOZ	BFC Quad City Challenger II UK			24. 2.94	T.J.Wickham	(Bordon, Hants)	10. 6.03P
	(Rotax 503)	CH2-1093-1045 & PFA 177A-12640					
G-MYPA	Rans S-6ESD Coyote II *(Tail-wheel u/c)*			24. 2.94	L.J.Dutch	Tarn Farm, Cockerham	11.11.03P
	(Rotax 503)	0893.527 & PFA 204-12678					
G-MYPC	Kolb Twinstar Mk.3	K0012-0199 & PFA 205-12437		2. 3.94	J.Young & S.Hussain	(Wolverhampton)	5. 9.01P
	(Rotax 582)						
G-MYPD	Mainair Mercury	982-0294-7 & W778		11. 3.94	R.D.McManus	(Stoke-on-Trent)	29.10.03P
	(Rotax 462)						
G-MYPE	Mainair Gemini/Flash IIA	985-0394-7 & W781		11. 3.94	G.Kerr	East Fortune	18. 4.03P
	(Rotax 582)						
G-MYPH	Pegasus Quantum 15		6764	11. 3.94	P.M.J.White	Wombleton	15. 6.03P
	(Rotax 582/40)						
G-MYPI	Pegasus Quantum 15		6767	11. 3.94	P.L.Jarvis	(Ruislip)	2. 8.03P
	(Rotax 582/40)						
G-MYPJ	Rans S-6ESD Coyote II *(Tricycle u/c)*			18. 3.94	G.P.Jones	(Stoke-on-Trent)	12. 8.03P
	(Rotax 503)	1293.569 & PFA 204-12692					
G-MYPL	CFM Shadow CD	K.213 & BMAA/HB/080		14. 2.94	G.I.Madden	(Milton Keynes)	8. 10.03P
	(Rotax 503)						
G-MYPM	Cyclone AX3		C.3123188	23. 3.94	Microflight Ireland Ltd	Mullaghmore, Co.Antrim	26. 6.03P
	(Rotax 503)						
G-MYPN	Pegasus Quantum 15		6727	12. 4.94	A.H.McBreen	(Rugby)	14. 6.02P
	(Rotax 582/40)						

Reg	Type	Construction		Date	Owner	Location	Date2
G-MYPP	Whittaker MW6-S Fat Boy Flyer	PFA 164-12413		11. 4.94	D.S.L.Evans *(Current status unknown)*	(Ashford)	
G-MYPR	Cyclone AX3 (Rotax 503)	C.3123190		13. 4.94	N.E.Ashton	Ince Blundell	7. 4.03P
G-MYPS	Whittaker MW6 Merlin (Rotax 503)	PFA 164-11585		19. 4.94	I.S.Bishop	Bicester	18. 9.03P
G-MYPT	CFM Shadow CD (Rotax 503)	K.212		22. 4.94	M.G. & S.A.Collins	(Oldbury-on-Severn)	25. 6.03P
G-MYPV	Mainair Mercury (Rotax 582)	986-0394-7 & W782		18. 3.94	J.J.Brex	(Milton Keynes)	13. 6.03P
G-MYPW	Mainair Gemini/Flash IIA (Rotax 582)	991-0494-7 & W787		3. 5.94	R.E.Parker	(Harlow)	22. 4.03P
G-MYPX	Pegasus Quantum 15 (Rotax 582/40) *(Believed to have used "B Conditions" marks "G-69-29" during trials)*	6785		28. 4.94	P.J.Callis & M.Aylett	Halwell, Totnes	3. 5.02P
G-MYPY	Pegasus Quantum 15 (Rotax 582/40)	6786		12. 5.94	G.& G.Trudgill	Shotton Colliery	27. 4.02P
G-MYPZ	BFC Quad City Challenger II UK (Hirth 2706) CH2-1093-UK-1046 & PFA 177A-12689 *(Regd incorrectly as CH2-0194-UK-1046)*			2. 3.94	E.G.Astin t/a BFC	Whitby	30. 8.01P
G-MYRB	Whittaker MW5 Sorcerer	PFA 163-11543		14. 4.94	P.J.Careless *(Valid CofR 4.02: current status unknown)*	(Sandy)	
G-MYRC	Mainair Blade (Rotax 462)	988-0594-7 & W784		1. 6.94	C.D.Connor	(Telford)	16. 8.03P
G-MYRD	Mainair Blade (Rotax 582)	989-0594-7 & W785		20. 5.94	W.J.Walker	Drummiard Farm, Bonnybank	21. 2.03P
G-MYRF	Pegasus Quantum 15 (Rotax 462HP)	6795		13. 5.94	A.O.Sutherland	Latch Farm, Kirknewton	23. 1.03P
G-MYRG	TEAM mini-MAX (Rotax 447)	PFA 186-11891		17. 5.94	D.G.Burrows	Shobdon	9. 6.03P
G-MYRH	BFC Quad City Challenger II UK (Rotax 582) CH2-1093-1044 & PFA 177A-12690			10. 3.94	D.M.Robbins	Thorney Island	4. 3.03P
G-MYRI	Medway Hybred 44XLR (Rotax 503)	MR180/841		23. 5.94	B.D.Acres	(Maidstone)	1. 9.00P
G-MYRJ	BFC Quad City Challenger II UK (Rotax 582) CH2-1093-1042 & PFA 177A-12658			28. 3.94	A.Watson	(Thatcham)	12. 8.03P
G-MYRK	Murphy Renegade Spirit UK 215 & PFA 188-11425 (Rotax 582)			3.10.89	P.Crowhurst	Sywell	2.10.03P
G-MYRL	TEAM mini-MAX 91 (Rotax 447)	PFA 186-11967		17. 5.94	J.N.Hanson	Brook Farm, Pilling	15. 9.03P
G-MYRM	Pegasus Quantum 15 (Rotax 582/40)	6800		26. 5.94	T.Read	Old Sarum	22. 6.03P
G-MYRN	Pegasus Quantum 15 (Rotax 582/40)	6801		26. 5.94	B.Robertson	Perth	23.11.02P
G-MYRO	Cyclone AX (Rotax 503)	3C.4043211		6. 6.94	R.I.Simpson & R.Tarplee	Rochester	22. 8.03P
G-MYRP	Letov LK-2M Sluka 829409x09? & PFA 263-12725 (Rotax 447)			6. 6.94	R.M.C.Hunter	Hindolveston	26. 9.03P
G-MYRR	Letov LK-2M Sluka (Rotax 447)	829409x05?		10. 6.94	B.C.McCartan	(Banbridge)	5. 8.03P
G-MYRS	Pegasus Quantum 15 (Rotax 582/40)	6803		13. 6.94	R.M.Summers	Insch	18. 5.03P
G-MYRT	Pegasus Quantum 15 (Rotax 582/40)	6732		1. 3.94	M.C.Taylor	(Coleford)	29. 4.02P
G-MYRU	Cyclone AX3 (Rotax 503)	C.4043210		7. 6.94	S.Fraser	(Newcastle upon Tyne)	3.11.01P
G-MYRV	Cyclone AX3 (Rotax 503)	C.4043209		8. 6.94	M.Gardiner	Rufforth	4. 7.03P
G-MYRW	Mainair Mercury (Rotax 503)	999-0694-7 & W795		17. 6.94	G.C.Hobson *(Op Northern Microlight School)*	St.Michaels	5. 7.03P
G-MYRY	Pegasus Quantum 15 (Rotax 582/40)	6813		15. 6.94	M.J.Hall	Roddige, Fradley	19. 8.02P
G-MYRZ	Pegasus Quantum 15 (Rotax 582/40)	6812		15. 6.94	G.D.Black	(Perth)	27. 6.02P
G-MYSA	Cyclone Chaser S (Rotax 508)	CH.864		15. 6.94	P.Nicholls	(Ludlow)	23. 3.03P
G-MYSB	Pegasus Quantum 15 (Rotax 582/40)	6809		22. 6.94	N.Harford	(Horley)	9.11.02P
G-MYSC	Pegasus Quantum 15 (Rotax 582/40)	6811		22. 6.94	K.R.White	Dunkeswell	28. 8.03P
G-MYSD	BFC Quad City Challenger II CH2-1093-1043 & PFA 177A-12688			23. 6.94	C.E.Bell *(Current status unknown)*	(Oakham)	
G-MYSG	Mainair Mercury (Rotax 582) *(Supplied as Mainair Kit)*	K993-0694-7 & W790		12. 7.94	M.Donnelly	(Northwich)	23. 7.03P
G-MYSI	Mignet HM.14/93	PFA 255-12700		18. 7.94	A.R.D.Seaman *(Current status unknown)*	Dagenham	
G-MYSJ	Mainair Gemini/Flash IIA (Rotax 503)	1001-0894-7 & W797		2. 8.94	E M Christoffersen	Baxby Manor, Husthwaite	10. 3.03P
G-MYSK	TEAM mini-MAX 91 (Rotax 447)	PFA 186-12203		25. 7.94	A.D.Bolshaw *(Op Brook Farm Microlight Centre)*	Brook Farm, Pilling	1. 8.02P
G-MYSL	Aviasud Mistral 582GB	066 & BMAA/HB/007	83-DE	27. 2.92	P.C.Piggott & M.E.Hughes Little Battleflats Farm, Ellistown, Coalville		9. 8.03P
G-MYSM	CFM Shadow CD (Rotax 503)	K.243 & BMAA/HB/049		22. 3.94	L.W.Stevens	(Grantham)	10.10.03P
G-MYSO	Cyclone AX3 (Rotax 503)	C.4043215		1. 8.94	M.L.Smith	Popham	25. 3.03P
G-MYSP	Rans S-6ESD Coyote II *(Tricycle u/c)* (Rotax 582) 0392-284 & PFA 204-12265			26. 5.92	H.F.Breakwell & J.M.Swash	Sittles Farm, Alrewas	13. 7.03P

G-MYSR	Pegasus Quantum 15 (Rotax 582)	6837		3. 8.94	J.G.Watson	Perth	31. 3.02P
G-MYSU	Rans S-6ESD Coyote II (Rotax 503)	PFA 204-12753		5. 8.94	K.W.Allan	Drummaird Farm, Bonnybank	17. 2.03P
G-MYSV	Aerial Arts Chaser S (Rotax 377)	CH.812	(ex Korea)	24. 8.94	R J Sims & I G Reason	(Salisbury)	30. 4.03P
G-MYSW	Pegasus Quantum 15 (Rotax 582)	6834		13. 7.94	D.A.Southern	Tarn Farm, Cockerham	19. 7.03P
G-MYSX	Pegasus Quantum 15 (Rotax 503)	6832		13. 7.94	J.L.Treves	Long Acre Farm, Sandy	29. 7.03P
G-MYSY	Pegasus Quantum 15 (Rotax 582)	6864		15. 8.94	F.Wilson	(Stone)	29. 3.03P
G-MYSZ	Mainair Mercury (Rotax 503) *(C/n confirmed but see G-MYYY)*	1006-0894-7 & W802		2. 9.94	R.G.McCron	Shobdon	29. 9.03P
G-MYTB	Mainair Mercury (Rotax 582)	1004-0894-7 & W800		19. 8.94	P.J.Higgins	Fenland	17. 8.03P
G-MYTC	Solar Wings Pegasus XL-Q	SW-WQ-0246	(ex...)	28. 9.94	M.J.Edmett *(New owner 5.02)*	(London N3)	
G-MYTD	Mainair Blade (Rotax 582)	1002-0894-7 & W798		18. 8.94	M.P.Law & B.E.Warburton	Barton	10. 7.03P
G-MYTE	Rans S-6ESD Coyote II (Rotax 503) *(Tail-wheel u/c)*	PFA 204-12718		22. 7.94	J.A.Way tr The Rans Flying Group	Lydd	9.11.02P
G-MYTG	Mainair Blade (Rotax 582)	1008-0994-7 & W804		16. 9.94	G.T.Snoddon	Newtownards, Co.Down	14. 2.03P
G-MYTH	CFM Shadow CD (Rotax 503)	089		7.11.88	J.E.Neil	Sherriff Hall Estate, Balgone	27. 9.03P
G-MYTI	Pegasus Quantum 15 (Rotax 582/40)	6874		6.10.94	J.Madhvani	Plaistows Farm, St Albans	23. 2.03P
G-MYTJ	Pegasus Quantum 15 (Rotax 582/40)	6877		29. 9.94	K.Laud	Roddige, Fradley	4. 6.03P
G-MYTK	Mainair Mercury (Rotax 503)	1009-1094-7 & W805		29. 9.94	D.A.Holroyd	(London W14)	30. 5.03P
G-MYTL	Mainair Blade (Rotax 582)	1010-1094-7 & W807		4.10.94	S.Ostrowski	Davidstow Moor	16. 6.03P
G-MYTM	Cyclone AX3 (Rotax 503)	C.3123189		13. 4.94	J P Gardiner	(Farnworth)	27. 8.03P
G-MYTN	Pegasus Quantum 15 (Rotax 503)	6878		30. 9.94	M.Hoggett & M.F.Ambrose	(Little Stukeley)	29. 4.03P
G-MYTO	Quad City Challenger II UK (Hirth 2705.R06)	PFA 177-12583		22. 7.94	R.W.Sage	Priory Farm, Tibenham	16. 4.01P
G-MYTP	CGS Arrow Flight Hawk II (Rotax 503) 215, H-CGS-489-P & PFA 266-12801		N215 *(C/n 215 believed to relate to p/i N215) (Current status unknown)*	6.10.94	R.J.Turner	Otherton, Cannock	8. 5.97P
G-MYTR	Solar Wings Pegasus Quasar IITC (Rotax 582/40)	6880		11.10.94	M.E.Grafton	(Hay-on-Wye)	22. 5.02P
G-MYTT	Quad City Challenger II (Rotax 503) CH2-0394-UK-111 & PFA 177-12761			11.10.94	R.J.Shave tr Challenger G-MYTT	Dunkeswell	19. 4.03P
G-MYTU	Mainair Blade (Rotax 582)	1011-1094-7 & W808		21.10.94	C.J.Barker	(Bagthorpe, Notts)	6. 6.03P
G-MYTV	Huntwing Avon (Rotax 503)	9204010 & BMAA/HB/029		13.10.94	P.J.Sutton	(Hereford)	15.11.03P
G-MYTX	Mainair Mercury (Rotax 503) *(Supplied as Mainair Kit)*	K1003-0894-7 & W799		23. 9.94	R.Steel	Rufforth	31. 8.03P
G-MYTY	CFM Streak Shadow M (Rotax 912UL)	K.242 & PFA 206-12607		11. 7.94	K.H.A.Negal	Enstone	6. 6.02P
G-MYTZ	Air Creation Ultraflight Fun 18S GT bis (Rotax 503)	94/003		7.11.94	S.N.Bond & D.E.Lord	(Huddersfield)	12. 7.032P
G-MYUA	Air Creation Ultraflight Fun 18S GT bis (Rotax 503)	94/002		8.11.94	J.Leden	(Buxton)	9. 7.03P
G-MYUB	Mainair Mercury (Rotax 503)	1014-1194-7 & W812		14.12.94	T.A.Ross	Arclid Green, Sandbach	10.10.01P
G-MYUC	Mainair Blade (Rotax 462)	1015-1294-7 & W813		16.11.94	A.D.Clayton	St.Michaels	4.11.03P
G-MYUD	Mainair Mercury (Rotax 582)	1016-1294-7 & W814		24.11.94	S.A.Noble	(Audley End)	30. 4.03P
G-MYUE	Mainair Mercury (Rotax 582)	1017-1294-7 & W815		22.11.94	R.J.Speight	(Amersham)	22. 7.01P
G-MYUF	Murphy Renegade Spirit (Jabiru 2200A)	PFA 188-12795		16.11.94	M.A.Pantling	Weston Zoyland	31. 7.03P
G-MYUH	Solar Wings Pegasus XL-Q (Rotax 462)	6810		28.11.94	K.S.Daniels	(London Colney)	13. 4.03P
G-MYUI	Cyclone AX3 (Rotax 503) *(C/n carried is C.102822 and probably results from a changed monopole)*	C.4043213		13.12.94	R. & M.Bailey	Plaistows Farm, St Albans	21. 4.03P
G-MYUK	Mainair Mercury (Rotax 462)	1020-0195-7 & W818		12.12.94	S.Lear	(London N15)	4. 3.03P
G-MYUL	Quad City Challenger II UK (Rotax 503) CH2-1293-UK-1063 & PFA 177-12687			10. 1.95	P.Knott	(Bradford)	24. 5.02P
G-MYUM	Mainair Blade (Rotax 582)	1018-1294-7 & W816		24.11.94	K.Horrobin	(Wigan)	19. 6.03P
G-MYUN	Mainair Blade (Rotax 582)	1019-0195-7 & W817		5.12.94	G.A.Barratt	(Preston)	7. 2.03P
G-MYUO	Pegasus Quantum 15 (Rotax 582)	6911		23. 1.95	D.S.Tompkins	Sywell	1. 7.03P
G-MYUP	Letov LK-2M Sluka (Rotax 447) 829409x24, UK.2 & PFA 263-12785			20.12.94	C J Meadows	(Shepton Mallet)	2. 4.03P
G-MYUR	Huntwing Avon (Rotax 582)	9409030 & BMAA/HB/034		24. 1.95	S.D.Pain	Rayne Hall Farm, Rayne	27. 3.03P

Reg	Type	C/n	Prev id	Date	Owner	Location	Expiry
G-MYUS	CFM Shadow CD (Rotax 503)	257		26. 1.95	G.Gilhead & R.G.M.Proost tr Aviation for Paraplegics & Tetraplegics Trust	Old Sarum	15. 7.03P
G-MYUU	Pegasus Quantum 15 (Rotax 462)	6917		30. 1.95	S.B.Williams	Headcorn	6. 7.03P
G-MYUV	Pegasus Quantum 15 (Rotax 582)	6918		6. 2.95	I.W.Barlow	(Ilkeston)	14. 7.03P
G-MYUW	Mainair Mercury (Rotax 503)	1024-0295-7 & W822		7. 2.95	D.M.Merritt-Holman	(Northwich)	3. 9.03P
G-MYUZ	Rans S-6ESD Coyote II *(Tricycle u/c)* (Rotax 503)	1293.568 & PFA 204-12741		5. 1.95	B.Davies	Sittles Farm, Alrewas	29. 4.03P
G-MYVA	Kolb Twinstar Mk.3 (Rotax 582)	PFA 205-12756		13. 2.95	A.S.Milner	(Southport)	16. 4.03P
G-MYVB	Mainair Blade (Rotax 582)	1021-0195-7 & W819		15.12.94	J.Rodgers	(Bury)	24. 4.03P
G-MYVC	Pegasus Quantum 15 (Rotax 582)	6904		13. 2.95	G.Lace	(Liverpool)	19. 5.02P
G-MYVE	Mainair Blade (Rotax 582)	1027-0295-7 & W825		8. 2.95	R.D.Serle & P.M.Jennings	Shobdon	15. 4.03P
G-MYVG	Letov LK-2M Sluka (Rotax 447)	829409x26 & PFA 263-12786		15. 2.95	N.P.Sleigh	Ince Blundell	14. 6.03P
G-MYVH	Mainair Blade (Rotax 582)	1028-0295-7 & W826		21. 2.95	J.Kennedy	Mill Farm, Shifnal	27. 3.03P
G-MYVI	Air Creation Ultraflight Fun 18S GT bis (Rotax 503)	94/004		17. 2.95	P.Osborne tr Northampton Aerotow Club	(Northampton)	11. 9.01P
G-MYVJ	Pegasus Quantum 15 (Rotax 582/40)	6974		24. 2.95	P.W.Davidson & A.I.McPherson	Glenrothes	27. 4.03P
G-MYVK	Pegasus Quantum 15 (Rotax 582/40)	6970		27. 2.95	J.Hammond	(Minehead)	20. 5.03P
G-MYVL	Mainair Mercury (Rotax 462)	1030-0395-7 & W828		1. 3.95	P.J.Judge *(New CofR 6.02- noted 7.02)*	Davidstowe Moor	7. 7.99P
G-MYVM	Pegasus Quantum 15 (Rotax 582/40)	6893	G-69-17 G-MYVM	9. 3.95	A.F.A.Marreiros *(Current status unknown)*	Lisboa, Portugal	27. 4.97P
G-MYVN	Cyclone AX3 (Rotax 503)	C.4043212		16. 3.95	F.Watt	Insch	5.10.03P
G-MYVO	Mainair Blade (Rotax 582)	1013-1194-7 & W811		8.11.94	S.S.Raines	Shobdon	29. 3.03P
G-MYVP	Rans S-6ESD Coyote II *(Tricycle u/c)* (Rotax 503)	0294.593 & PFA 204-12828		27. 3.95	C.E.Hormaeche	Eshott	23. 7.03P
G-MYVR	Pegasus Quantum 15 (Rotax 582)	6980		21. 3.95	I.W.Barlow	(Ilkeston)	25. 3.03P
G-MYVS	Mainair Mercury (Rotax 462)	1037-0495-7 & W835		12. 4.95	P.S.Flynn	Sandtoft	25. 4.03P
G-MYVT	Letov LK-2M Sluka (Rotax 447)	829409x25 & PFA 263-12835		17. 3.95	J.Hannibal	(Kidderminster)	11.11.03P
G-MYVV	Medway Hybred 44XLR (Rotax 503) *(Sailwing c/n also quoted for G-MYLX)*	MR127/109		3. 4.95	S.Perity	(Wisbech)	21. 8.02P
G-MYVW	Medway Raven X (Rotax 447) *(Sailwing c/n also quoted for G-MYMJ)*	MRB128/110		15. 5.95	J.C.Woolgrove *(Current status unknown)*	(Beckenham	5. 6.97P
G-MYVX	Medway Hybred 44XLR (Rotax 503)	MR129/111		3. 4.95	A.R.Fricker	(South Ockendon)	4. 6.02P
G-MYVY	Mainair Blade (Rotax 582)	1033-0495-7 & W831		29. 3.95	S.P.Maxwell	(Scunthorpe)	12.10.02P
G-MYVZ	Mainair Blade (Rotax 582)	1034-0495-7 & W832		31. 3.95	R.Llewellyn	(Chester)	22. 5.03P
G-MYWA	Mainair Mercury (Rotax 503)	1035-0495-7 & W833		30. 3.95	D.James	(Neath)	12. 5.03P
G-MYWC	Huntwing Avon (Rotax 503)	9409038 & BMAA/HB/043		3. 4.95	F.J.C.Binks	Sutton Meadows, Ely	21. 8.03P
G-MYWD	Thruster T.600N (Rotax 582)	9035-T600-511	(G-MYOJ)	18. 4.95	K.Draper	Middle Stoke, Kent	16. 8.03P
G-MYWE	Thruster T.600T (Rotax 503)	9035-T600-512	(G-MYOK)	18. 4.95	V.Goddard	Yatesbury	1. 3.03P
G-MYWF	CFM Shadow CD (Rotax 503)	K.248 & BMAA/HB/068		18. 4.95	M.A.Newman	(Saxmundham)	25. 1.03P
G-MYWG	Pegasus Quantum 15 (Rotax 582/40)	6998		20. 4.95	M.R.Bishop	(Dunstable)	18.10.03P
G-MYWH	Huntwing Experience	9409025 & BMAA/HB/037		20.12.94	G.N.Hatchett *(Current status unknown)*	North Connel, Oban	
G-MYWI	Pegasus Quantum 15 (Rotax 582)	7006		1. 5.95	J.R.Fulcher	(Whittlesford)	20. 2.03P
G-MYWJ	Pegasus Quantum 15 (Rotax 582)	6919		24. 1.95	P.A.Banks	Long Acre Farm, Sandy	25. 9.03P
G-MYWK	Pegasus Quantum 15 (Rotax 582)	7011		1. 5.95	M.S.McCrudden	Newtownards, Co.Down	25. 9.03P
G-MYWL	Pegasus Quantum 15 (Rotax 582)	6995		2. 5.95	J.L.Richards	Plaistows Farm, St. Albans	25. 3.03P
G-MYWM	CFM Shadow CD (Rotax 503)	K.227 & BMAA/HB/056		9. 5.95	N.J.Mckinley	(London N12)	25. 7.03P
G-MYWN	Cyclone Chaser S (Rotax 508)	CH.865		9. 5.95	G.M.Yule	Shobdon	1. 9.03P
G-MYWO	Cyclone Pegasus Quantum 15 (Rotax 582)	6932		9. 5.95	J.W.Cope	Wickenby	25.10.03P
G-MYWP	Kolb Twinstar Mk.3 (Rotax 582/40)	K0017-0993 & PFA 205-12561		7. 3.95	P.R.Day	(Southampton)	19. 8.03P

Reg	Type (Engine)	C/n	Date	Owner	Location	Expiry
G-MYWR	Cyclone Pegasus Quantum 15 (Rotax 582/40)	7002	10. 5.95	A P Watkins & R Horton	Roddidge, Fradley	11. 8.03P
G-MYWS	Cyclone Chaser S (Rotax 447)	6946 & CH.866	17. 5.95	M.H.Broadbent	(Bexhill-on-Sea)	25. 7.03P
G-MYWT	Pegasus Quantum 15 (Rotax 582)	6997	19. 5.95	J.Dyer	(Ware)	1. 8.03P
G-MYWU	Pegasus Quantum 15 (Rotax 582)	7024	25. 5.95	J.R.Buttle	Dunkeswell	23. 7.03P
G-MYWV	Rans S-4C Coyote (Rotax 447)	093.212 & PFA 193-12826	30. 5.95	A.H.Trapp	(Bewdley, Worcs)	7. 7.03P
G-MYWW	Pegasus Quantum 15 (Rotax 503)	7021	30. 5.95	C.W.Bailie	Newtownards, Co.Down	10. 8.03P
G-MYWX	Pegasus Quantum 15 (Rotax 582)	7019	6. 6.95	D.J.Revell	Lower Mountpleasant Farm, Chatteris	26. 7.02P
G-MYWY	Pegasus Quantum 15 (Rotax 582)	6982	20. 3.95	D.Young	Kemble	29. 9.03P
G-MYWZ	Thruster TST Mk.1 (Rotax 503)	8128-TST-115 G-MVMJ	22. 2.93	W.H.J.KNowles	Yundum/Banjul, Gambia	24. 9.03P
G-MYXA	TEAM mini-MAX 91 (Rotax 447)	PFA 186-12266	13. 6.95	L.H.S.Stephens	(Saltash)	14. 8.02P
G-MYXB	Rans S-6ESD Coyote II *(Tricycle u/c)* (Rotax 503)	1293.567 & PFA 204-12787	20. 6.95	P.R.Day	(Southampton)	3. 4.03P
G-MYXC	BFC Quad City Challenger II UK (Hirth H2706)	CH2-0294-UK-1099	16. 5.95	K.N.Dickinson	Higher Barn Farm, Houghton	
G-MYXD	Pegasus Quasar IITC (Rotax 582)	7029	21. 6.95	A.Cochrane	Long Acre Farm, Sandy	30. 8.03P
G-MYXE	Pegasus Quantum 15 (Rotax 582)	7061	23. 6.95	D.Little	(Crawley)	7. 9.03P
G-MYXF	Air Creation Ultraflight Fun 18S GT bis (Rotax 503)	94/005	23. 6.95	T.A.Morgan	Popham	15. 1.01P
G-MYXG	Rans S-6ESD Coyote II (Rotax 503) *(Tricycle u/c)*	PFA 204-12879	29. 6.95	G.H.Lee	Higher Barn Farm, Houghton	20. 6.01P
G-MYXH	Cyclone AX3 (Rotax 503)	7028	3. 7.95	G.M.Brown	Craysmarsh Farm, Melksham	27. 9.03P
G-MYXI	Cook Aries 1 *(Design awaiting finalisation 10.01- planned engine fit is BMW R80)*	BMAA/HB/048	4. 7.95	H.Cook	(Newport, Gwent)	
G-MYXJ	Mainair Blade (Rotax 582)	1048-0795-7 & W846	17. 7.95	L Seddon	(Cramlington)	22.11.03P
G-MYXK	BFC Quad City Challenger II (Rotax 503)	CH2-1194-1254 & PFA 177A-12877	11. 7.95	V.Vaughan	(Mullinahone, Co.Tipperary)	31. 7.03P
G-MYXL	Mignet HM-1000 Balerit (Rotax 582)	112	11. 7.95	R.W.Hollamby	Bardown, Wadhurst	17. 7.03P
G-MYXM	Mainair Blade (Rotax 582)	1047-0795-7 & W845	19. 7.95	S.C.Hodgson	(Chesterfield)	21. 7.03P
G-MYXN	Mainair Blade (Rotax 582)	1046-0795-7 & W844	27. 7.95	M.R.Sands	Shotton Colliery	19. 7.03P
G-MYXO	Letov LK-2M Sluka (Rotax 447)	8295s001 & PFA 263-12873	27. 7.95	G.W.Allport	(Kingswinford)	1. 1.02P
G-MYXP	Rans S-6ESD Coyote II (Rotax 503) *(Tail-wheel u/c)*	PFA 204-12886	31. 7.95	R S Amor	Weston Zoyland	14. 8.03P
G-MYXR	Murphy Renegade Spirit UK	PFA 188-12755	2. 8.95	S.Hooker *(Current status unknown)*	Ashford, Kent	
G-MYXS	Kolb Twinstar Mk.3 (Rotax 582)	K0015-0693 & PFA 205-12528	4. 5.94	R.Coar	Higher Barn Farm, Houghton	21. 4.03P
G-MYXT	Pegasus Quantum 15 (Rotax 582)	7073	4. 8.95	W.A.Donnelly	Latch Farm, Kirknewton	3. 8.02P
G-MYXU	Thruster T.300 (Rotax 582)	9024-T300-513	16. 8.95	D.W.Wilson	(Collone, Co.Armagh)	2. 9.03P
G-MYXV	Quad City Challenger II UK (Rotax 503)	CH2-1194-UK-1243	19. 7.95	S.G.Beeson	(Stoke-on-Trent)	8.11.02P
G-MYXW	Pegasus Quantum 15 (Rotax 582)	7090	24. 8.95	D.Martin	Perth	17. 7.03P
G-MYXX	Pegasus Quantum 15 (Rotax 582)	7081	25. 8.95	J.H.Arnold	Milverton, Taunton	5. 5.03P
G-MYXY	CFM Shadow CD (Rotax 503)	K.245 & BMAA/HB/059	29. 8.95	N.H.Townsend	Old Sarum	21. 7.03P
G-MYXZ	Pegasus Quantum 15 (Rotax 582)	7023	21. 6.95	T.P.Wright	(Ilkeston)	26 8.03P
G-MYYA	Mainair Blade (Rotax 462)	1052-0995-7 & W850	1. 9.95	D.E.Bassett	(Marple Bridge)	18.10.03P
G-MYYB	Pegasus Quantum 15 (Rotax 582)	7079	4. 9.95	A.L.Johnson	Long Acre Farm, Sandy	17.10.01P
G-MYYC	Pegasus Quantum 15 (Rotax 582)	7094	12. 9.95	M.Wills & R.Jones	Tarn Farm, Cockerham	17. 8.02P
G-MYYD	Cyclone Chaser S (Rotax 447)	CH.7099	15. 9.95	C Surman	(Cranleigh)	7.11.02P
G-MYYE	Huntwing Avon 462	9409035 & BMAA/HB/041	21. 9.95	N.S.Payne	(Hereford)	18. 8.02P
G-MYYF	Quad City Challenger II UK (Rotax 503)	PFA 177-12811	27. 9.95	G.Ferries	Insch	16.11.03P
G-MYYG	Mainair Blade (Rotax 462) *(Believed supplied as Mainair Kit, if so c/n K1054...)*	1054-0995-7 & W852	4.10.95	D.Guild tr Yankee Golf Syndicate	(Colchester)	23.10.02P
G-MYYH	Mainair Blade (Rotax 582)	1056-1095-7 & W854	3.10.95	D.Travers	(Scunthorpe)	21. 4.03P
G-MYYI	Pegasus Quantum 15 (Rotax 582)	7101	28. 9.95	S.Etches *(Current status unknown)*	Sandtoft	23. 7.99P

G-MYYJ	Huntwing Avon (Rotax 503)	9409033 & BMAA/HB/033	29. 9.95	M.J.Slater	(Marlborough)	
				(Completed 5.95 & stored 5.97: current status unknown)		
G-MYYK	Pegasus Quantum 15 (Rotax 582)	7100	2.10.95	L.Scarse	(Melksham)	18. 2.03P
G-MYYL	Cyclone AX3 (Rotax 503)	7110	4.10.95	P.M.Dewhurst & K.Meredith-Jones	Sywell	14.11.02P
G-MYYN	Pegasus Quantum 15 (Rotax 582)	7022	3.10.95	A.Gibbon & C.Cruickshank	(Dundee)	28.12.01P
G-MYYO	Medway Raven X (Rotax 447)	MRB134/114	5.10.95	J.R.Harrison	(Chesterfield)	30. 5.01P
G-MYYP	AMF Chevvron 2-32C (Konig SD570)	036	31.10.95	M.A.Sheehan	Roddige, Fradley	15.11.01P
G-MYYR	TEAM mini-MAX 91 (Rotax 447)	PFA 186-12724	31.10.95	J.J.James *(Noted 5.01)*	East Kirby	7.11.03P
G-MYYS	TEAM mini-MAX	PFA 186-11989	7.11.95	J.R.Hopkinson *(Current status unknown)*	(Chesterfield)	
G-MYYU	Mainair Mercury (Rotax 503)	1062-1295-7 & W862	17.11.95	J.T. & A.C.Swannick	Sandtoft	5. 4.02P
G-MYYV	Rans S-6ESD Coyote IIXL *(Tricycle u/c)* (Rotax 503) 0896.1026XL & PFA 204-12943		17.11.95	B.W.Drake	(Gloucester)	16. 7.01P
G-MYYW	Mainair Blade (Rotax 582)	1051-0895-7 & W849	8. 8.95	M.J.Naylor	(Leicester)	12.10.01P
G-MYYX	Pegasus Quantum 15 (Rotax 582)	7126	17.11.95	G.J.Rae	(Tranent)	5. 4.03P
G-MYYY	Mainair Blade (Rotax 582)	1031-0495-7 & W829	15. 3.95	E.D.Locke	Barton	31. 3.03P
G-MYYZ	Medway Raven X (Rotax 447)	MRB135/116	10. 1.96	J W Leaper	(Lincoln)	7. 6.03P
G-MYZA	Whittaker MW6 Merlin (Rotax 582)	PFA 164-11396	17. 7.95	D.C.Davies	Over Farm, Newent	25.11.03P
G-MYZB	Pegasus Quantum 15 (Rotax 582)	7124	22.11.95	N G Barbour	(Sleaford)	11. 3.03P
G-MYZC	Cyclone AX3 (Rotax 503)	7125	5.12.95	A.B.Simpson	Brook Farm, Pilling	2. 6.03P
				(Op Brook Farm Microlight Centre)		
G-MYZE	TEAM mini-MAX 91 (Global GMT-35)	PFA 186-12570	28. 9.95	R.B.M.Etherington	Totnes	6. 6.02P
G-MYZF	Cyclone AX3 (Rotax 503)	7133	11.12.95	Microflight (Ireland) Ltd	(Portrush, Co.Antrim)	6. 7.03P
G-MYZG	Cyclone AX3/503	7137	11. 1.96	R.A.Johns	Weston Zoyland	9. 1.00P
G-MYZH	Chargus Titan 38	JPA-1	16. 1.96	P.A.James *(Current status unknown)*	(Crawley)	
G-MYZJ	Pegasus Quantum 15 (Rotax 582)	7150	24. 1.96	P.Millar	Latch Farm, Kirknewton	28. 4.03P
G-MYZK	Pegasus Quantum 15 (Rotax 582)	7157	5. 2.96	J.Douglas	East Fortune	26. 5.03P
G-MYZL	Pegasus Quantum 15 (Rotax 582)	7158	5. 2.96	N.A.Harwood	(Littlehampton)	28. 7.03P
	(Original sailwing, with trike c/n 7230, believed sold to Australia as T2-2906: wing ex G-MZHH fitted to G-MYZL: previous marks noted underneath G-MYZL @ Shobdon 8.99: believed trike only of G-MZHH was sold to France 1.98 with another sailwing fitted)					
G-MYZM	Pegasus Quantum 15 (Rotax 582/40)	7159	5. 2.96	D.Hope	(Uckfield)	29. 4.03P
G-MYZN	Whittaker MW6-S-LW Fatboy Flyer (Rotax 582) PFA 164-12431		31. 1.96	M.K.Shaw	RAF Halton	8. 5.03P
G-MYZO	Medway Raven X (Rotax 447)	MRB136/115	12. 1.96	M.C.Arnold	Rochester	24. 5.02P
G-MYZP	CFM Shadow DD (Rotax 582)	249 & PFA 161-12914	7. 2.96	R.M.Davies & P.I.Hodgson	(Amersham)	19. 4.02P
G-MYZR	Rans S-6ESD Coyote II XL (Rotax 503) *(Tricycle u/c)*	PFA 204-12958	9. 2.96	S.E.J.McLaughlin Lark Engine Farmhouse, Prickwillow, Ely		30. 5.02P
G-MYZV	Rans S-6ESD Coyote II XL *(Tricycle u/c)* (Rotax 503) 0795.849 & PFA 204-12946		26. 2.96	B.W.Savory	Long Marston	8. 7.03P
G-MYZW	Cyclone Chaser S (Rotax 508)	7165	27. 2.96	P.J.Sheehy	(Warsash, Southampton)	18. 6.03P
G-MYZY	Pegasus Quantum 15 (Rotax 582)	7156	8. 2.96	D.D.Appleford	Kemble	16. 6.03P
G-MZAA	Mainair Blade (Rotax 462)	1059-1195-7 & W857	24.10.95	J.C.Kitchen	Plaistows Farm, St Albans	26. 2.03P
G-MZAB	Mainair Blade (Rotax 582)	1043-0695-7 & W841	26. 5.95	A.Meadley	(Northallerton)	12.10.02P
G-MZAC	BFC Quad City Challenger II (Rotax 503) CH2-0294-1100 & PFA 177A-12716		21. 7.95	M.N.Calhaem	Fradswell, Stafford	18. 6.03P
G-MZAE	Mainair Blade (Rotax 582)	1063-1295-7 & W863	4.12.95	C.M.Mackinnon	Castle Mains Estate, Braco	9. 5.03P
G-MZAF	Mainair Blade (Rotax 582)	1045-0795-7 & W843	1.12.95	G.C.Brown	Barton	3. 7.01P
G-MZAG	Mainair Blade (Rotax 582)	1042-0695-7 & W840	26. 5.95	R.D.Kay	St.Michaels	2. 5.03P
G-MZAH	Rans S-6ESD Coyote II *(Tricycle u/c)* (Rotax 503) 0393.470 & PFA 204-12553		3. 9.93	C.J.Collett	Long Marston	30. 7.02P
	(Originally built as tail-wheel u/c: repaired with frame 0491-186 [G-MWVL])					
G-MZAI	Mainair Blade (Rotax 912UL)	1065-0196-7 & W867	4.12.95	P.& M.Boultby	Nottingham	8. 1.02P
				(Noted 9.01)		
G-MZAJ	Mainair Blade (Rotax 582)	1067-0196-7 & W869	20.12.95	M.P.Daley	Arclid Green, Sandbach	24. 6.02P
G-MZAK	Mainair Mercury (Rotax 503)	1070-0296-7 & W872	15. 1.96	A.Munro	(Bishop's Stortford)	11. 5.03P
G-MZAL*	Mainair Blade (Rotax 503)	1076-0396-7 & W878	21. 2.96	T.Dunn	(Nottingham)	4. 4.01P
				(Cancelled 20.11.02 by CAA)		

G-MZAM	Mainair Blade (Rotax 582)	1044-0695-7 & W842	31. 5.95	B.M.Marsh & N.Cox		Shobdon	4. 8.03P
G-MZAN	Pegasus Quantum 15 (Rotax 582/40)	7188	7. 3.96	C.G.Veitch tr Zanco Syndicate		Dunkeswell	20. 6.03P
G-MZAO	Mainair Blade (Rotax 912UL)	1069-0296-7 & W871	15. 3.96	S.W.Dow		(Cuffley)	7. 4.00P
G-MZAP	Mainair Blade 912 (Rotax 912UL)	1036-0495-7 & W834	31. 3.95	J.W.McCarthy		(Southport)	27. 6.03P
G-MZAR	Mainair Blade (Rotax 582)	1072-0296-7 & W874	13. 2.96	T.R.Southall		Shobdon	20. 3.03P
G-MZAS	Mainair Blade (Rotax 582)	1049-0895-7 & W847	15. 8.95	T.Carter	Pound Green, Buttonoak, Kidderminster		1. 9.03P
G-MZAT	Mainair Blade (Rotax 582)	1060-1195-7 & W860	29.11.95	F.Henderson		(Wrexham)	10. 5.02P
G-MZAV	Mainair Blade (Rotax 462)	1078-0396-7 & W881	11. 3.96	B.B.Boniface		St Michaels	8. 5.03P
G-MZAW	Pegasus Quantum 15 (Rotax 503)	7160	14. 2.96	S.Stone & R.Atkinson		(Dursley)	22. 3.03P
G-MZAX	Pegasus Quantum 15 (Rotax 582)	7152	11. 3.96	D.W.Beach		(Harlow)	30. 1.03P
G-MZAY	Mainair Blade (Rotax 462)	1077-0396-7 & W880	15. 3.96	M.D.Harris	Earls Barton, Northampton		7. 4.03P
G-MZAZ	Mainair Blade (Rotax 462)	1040-0595-7 & W838	26. 5.95	P.Brown		St.Michaels	6. 6.03P
G-MZBA	Mainair Blade (Rotax 912UL)	1068-0296-7 & W870	15. 3.96	D J Cross		Redlands, Swindon	23. 3.03P
G-MZBB	Pegasus Quantum 15 (Rotax 582/40)	7139	13. 3.96	T.W.Pelan		Perth	27. 8.03P
G-MZBC	Pegasus Quantum 15 (Rotax 582)	7077	15. 8.95	B.M.Quinn		Barlow, Sheffield	10. 2.03P
G-MZBD	Rans S-6ESD Coyote II XL *(Tricycle u/c)* (Rotax 503) 0795.850XL & PFA 204-12957		15. 3.96	S P Yardley		Otherton, Cannock	26. 3.03P
G-MZBE	CFM Streak Shadow SA-M (Rotax 618) K.271 & PFA 206-12905		18. 3.96	N.J.Bushell		Old Sarum	11.12.02P
G-MZBF	Letov LK-2M Sluka (Rotax 447)	PFA 263-12881	18. 3.96	T.D.Reid		(Craigavon)	30. 7.03P
G-MZBG	Whittaker MW6-S Fatboy Flyer (Rotax 503)	PFA 164-12891	20. 3.96	M.W.Kilvert & I.Rowlands-Jones		(Newtown)	1. 6.01P
G-MZBH	Rans S-6ESD Coyote II (Rotax 503) *(Tricycle u/c)*	PFA 204-12244	21. 3.96	D.Sutherland		Breighton	18. 7.03P
G-MZBI	Pegasus Quantum 15 (Rotax 582/40)	7189	21. 3.96	B.C.Blackburn		Perth	31. 5.03P
G-MZBK	Letov LK-2M Sluka (Rotax 447)	8295s002 & PFA 263-12872	26. 3.96	R.J.Porter		Insch	26 .7.03P
G-MZBL	Mainair Blade (Rotax 582)	1080-0496-7 & W883	11. 4.96	J.R.Webster		(Ormskirk)	4. 7.03P
G-MZBM	Pegasus Quantum 15	7196	12. 4.96	C.S.Mackenzie		East Fortune	15. 6.03P
G-MZBN	CFM Shadow CD K069 & BMAA/HB/073 (Rotax 503) *(BMAA c/n issued for rebuild of Shadow BD G-MTWP)*		22. 4.96	P.A.James t/a Cloudbase Aviation G-MZBN		Redhill	19. 6.03P
G-MZBO	Pegasus Quantum 15 (Rotax 582)	7218	3. 5.96	A.M.Dalgetty		Perth	24. 7.03P
G-MZBR	Southdown Raven X	SN2232/0082	24. 5.96	D.M.Lane *(Current status unknown)*		(Stourbridge)	
G-MZBS	CFM Shadow D K.274 & PFA 161-13008 (Rotax 582/47)		14. 5.96	S.K.Ryan	Plaistowes Farm, St. Albans		25. 5.03P
G-MZBT	Pegasus Quantum 15-912	7224	22. 5.96	T.M.Clark		(Guildford)	3. 7.03P
G-MZBU	Rans S-6ESD Coyote II XL (Rotax 503)	PFA 204-12992	30. 5.96	C.Clark & R.S.Marriott		(Scunthorpe)	11.11.02P
G-MZBV	Rans S-6ESD Coyote II XL *(Tricycle u/c)* (Rotax 503) 0396.950XL & PFA 204-13009		30. 5.96	L.C.Barham & R.I.Cannan		Jurby	25. 3.03P
	(Heavy landing Jurby 6.9.01, damaging nose, port u/c & propeller)						
G-MZBW	Quad City Challenger II UK (Rotax 582) CH2-0795-UK-1367 & PFA 177-12971		19. 2.96	R.T.L.Chaloner		Dunkeswell	10.11.03P
G-MZBX	Whittaker MW6-S-LW Fatboy Flyer (Rotax 503)	PFA 164-12563	16. 5.96	S.Rose & P.Tearall	Gerpins Lane, Upminster		21. 1.03P
G-MZBY	Pegasus Quantum 15 (Rotax 582)	7227	30. 5.96	S.E.Dancaster		(Warrington)	9. 6.03P
G-MZBZ	Quad City Challenger II UK (Hirth 2706)	PFA 177-12928	11. 3.96	J.Flisher		Dunkeswell	17.10.02P
G-MZCA	Rans S-6ESD Coyote II XL *(Tricycle u/c)* (Rotax 503) 0396.953XL & PFA 204-12997		31. 5.96	S.J.Everett, K.Kettles & F.Williams		(Stratford-upon-Avon)	11. 8.03P
G-MZCB	Cyclone Chaser S (Rotax 447)	7220	4. 6.96	G.P.Hodgson		Rufforth	2. 8.03P
G-MZCC	Mainair Blade (Rotax 912UL)	1086-0696-7 & W889	7. 6.96	D.E.McGauley		Ince Blundell	15. 5.03P
G-MZCD	Mainair Blade (Rotax 582)	1087-0696-7 & W890	10. 6.96	G.Evans	Arclid Green, Sandbach		23. 9.03P
G-MZCE	Mainair Blade K1088-0696-7 & W891 (Rotax 462) *(Supplied as Mainair Kit)*		17. 6.96	P.Hayes		Ince Blundell	7. 4.02P
G-MZCG	Mainair Blade (Rotax 462)	1090-0696-7 & W893	17. 6.96	C.I.Poole		(Southport)	3. 9.03P
G-MZCH	Whittaker MW6-S Fatboy Flyer (Rotax 503)	PFA 164-12131	7. 6.96	B.G.King & J.T.Moore		Halwell, Totnes	5.11.02P
G-MZCI	Pegasus Quantum 15 (Rotax 582)	7231	10. 6.96	P.H.Risdale	Tower Farm, Wollaston		17. 8.03P
G-MZCJ	Pegasus Quantum 15 (Rotax 582/40)	7233	14. 6.96	A.W.Hay		Insch	19. 7.03P

Reg	Type	C/n	Prev id	Date	Owner	Location	Date2
G-MZCM	Pegasus Quantum 15 (Rotax 582) *(Unfaired trike)*	7219		3. 5.96	A.J.Harper	Croughton	10. 6.03P
G-MZCN	Mainair Blade (Rotax 582)	1079-0396-7 & W882		27. 6.96	K.Cockersol & K.J.Ratcliffe	Ince Blundell	10.10.02P
G-MZCO	Mainair Mercury (Rotax 462)	1091-0796-7 & W894		26. 6.96	E.Rush	(Congleton)	25. 2.03P
G-MZCP	Solar Wings Pegasus XL-Q (Rotax 462)	SW-TE-0434 & SW-WQ-0576		11. 2.93	C.Hamblin	Clench Common	13. 9.03P
G-MZCR	Pegasus Quantum 15 (Rotax 503)	7234		28. 6.96	J.E.P.Stubberfield	(Kenley)	30. 5.03P
G-MZCS	TEAM mini-MAX 91 (Rotax 377)	PFA 186-12646		20.12.95	D.T.J.Stanley	Kemble	3. 9.02P
G-MZCT	CFM Shadow CD (Rotax 503)	277		11. 7.96	W.G.Gill	Plaistows Farm, St Albans	20. 6.03P
G-MZCU	Mainair Blade (Rotax 462)	1082-0496-7 & W885		1. 5.96	C.E.Pearce	Beccles	6. 5.03P
G-MZCV	Pegasus Quantum 15 (Rotax 503)	7235		11. 7.96	B.S.Toole	Emlyn's Field, Rhuallt	6. 9.03P
G-MZCX	Huntwing Avon Skytrike (Rotax 503)	9510055 & BMAA/HB/072		17. 7.96	G.R.Coghill & W.Mccarthy tr Huntwing Group	(Wick)	1. 5.03P
G-MZCY	Pegasus Quantum 15 (Rotax 582)	7236		19. 7.96	M.H.Owen	Weston Zoyland	30. 8.32P
G-MZCZ*	Huntwing Experience	9409024 & BMAA/HB/039		24. 7.96	C.Kiernan	(Mostrim, Co.Longford)	
	(BMAA records show as Hunt Wing/Avon 462) (Completed & taxi-trials undertaken but not flown) (Cancelled 1.8.01 by CAA)						
G-MZDA	Rans S-6ESD Coyote II XL *(Tricycle u/c)* (Rotax 503)	0396.951 & PFA 204-13019		29. 7.96	W.C.Lombard	Newby Wiske	16. 8.03P
G-MZDB	Pegasus Quantum 15-912	7237		31. 7.96	M.J.Reed & D.C.Sollom	Clench Common	21. 4.03P
G-MZDC	Pegasus Quantum 15 (Rotax 582)	7246		2. 8.96	M.T.Jones	Long Marston	11.11.02P
G-MZDD	Pegasus Quantum 15 (Rotax 503)	7114	G-69-23	11. 7.96	C.D.Reeves	Weston Zoyland	15.11.03P
G-MZDE	Pegasus Quantum 15 (Rotax 582)	7238		12. 7.96	D.J.Taylor	(St.Neots)	15. 3.03P
G-MZDF	Mainair Blade (Rotax 462)	1093-0896-7 & W896		15. 8.96	T.D.Thompson	(Knutsford)	24. 4.03P
G-MZDG	Rans S-6ESD Coyote II XL *(Tricycle u/c)* (Rotax 503) 0696.1002.1100 & PFA 204-13030 *(Veered on take-off Barton 17.3.02: nose u/c collapsed damaging prop, engine cowling & cockpit frame)*			7. 8.96	M.J.Rhodes, tr Barton Heritage Flying Group	Barton	1. 5.03P
G-MZDH	Pegasus Quantum 15-912	7248		12. 8.96	V.G. & D.Concannon	(Nottingham)	14.11.03P
G-MZDI	Whittaker MW6-S Fatboy Flyer Srs.A (Rotax 503)	PFA 164-11929	G-BUNN	15. 8.96	J.M.Brooks	(Bromsgrove)	19. 2.02P
G-MZDJ*	Medway Raven X (Rotax 447)	MRB138/119		19. 8.96	R.Bryan & S.Digby *(Cancelled 28.12.01 by CAA) (Noted 2.03)*	Doynton	1. 5.00P
G-MZDK	Mainair Blade (Rotax 582) *(C/n reported as 1084-0696-7)*	1084-0596-7 & W887		9. 5.96	K.J.Miles	St.Michaels	29. 5.03P
G-MZDL	Whittaker MW6-S Fatboy Flyer (Hirth 2706)	PFA 164-12412		19. 8.96	C.D. & S.J.Wills	Chilbolton	11..8.03P
G-MZDM	Rans S-6ESD Coyote II XL *(Tricycle u/c)* (Rotax 503)	0396.954XL & PFA 204-13022		2. 9.96	M.E.Nicholas	Chilbolton	11. 4.01P
G-MZDN	Pegasus Quantum 15 (Rotax 582)	7255		5. 9.96	P.G.Ford	(Ely)	28. 9.03P
G-MZDO	Cyclone AX3 (Rotax 503)	7252		11. 9.96	W.H.J.Knowles	Yundum/Banjul, Gambia	24. 9.03P
G-MZDP	AMF Chevvron 2-32C (Konig SD570)	020		3. 4.90	F.Overall *(Damaged mid 1995: stored 2001: new owner 6.02)*	Whitehall Farm, Wethersfield	16. 3.96P
G-MZDR	Rans S-6ESD Coyote II XL (Rotax 503)	PFA 204-13012		8. 8.96	J.D.Gibbons	(Newry, Co.Armagh	21. 3.03P
G-MZDS	Cyclone AX3 (Rotax 503)	7253		16. 9.96	D.S.Paton	Sywell	29.11.03P
G-MZDT	Mainair Blade (Rotax 582)	1096-0996-7 & W899		19. 9.96	V.T.Betts	Otherton, Cannock	8. 7.03P
G-MZDU	Pegasus Quantum 15-912	7260		19. 9.96	G.A.Breen	(Lagos, Portugal)	26.10.03P
G-MZDV	Pegasus Quantum 15 (Rotax 582)	7199		9. 4.96	P.M.Wilkinson	(Great Orton)	5. 6.01P
G-MZDX	Letov LK-2M Sluka (Rotax 447 1-V)	PFA 263-12882		30. 9.96	R.P.Stonor	(London W3)	2. 9.03P
G-MZDY	Pegasus Quantum 15 (Rotax 462HP)	7263		2.10.96	R.Bailey	Sutton Meadows, Ely	7.10.02P
G-MZDZ	Hunt Avon/Wing	9501042 & BMAA/HB/045		23.10.96	E.W.Laidlaw *(Under construction 2001)*	(Turriff)	
G-MZEA	BFC Quad City Challenger II (Hirth 2706)	CH2-0294-1101 & PFA 177A-12728		22. 4.96	G.S.Cridland	Wymeswold	28. 2.02P
G-MZEB	Mainair Blade (Rotax 462)	1074-0396-7 & W876		22. 7.96	G.R.Barker	(Epping)	21. 7.02P
G-MZEC	Pegasus Quantum 15 (Rotax 582/40)	7278		24.10.96	A.B.Godber	Bradley Ashbourne, Derby	19.11.02P
G-MZED	Mainair Blade (Rotax 582)	1092-0796-7 & W895		3. 7.96	C.W.Potts	(Newcastle upon Tyne)	20.10.01P
G-MZEE	Pegasus Quantum 15 (Rotax 582)	7245		9. 8.96	B.J.Marsh	(Hemel Hempstead)	28. 8.03P
G-MZEG	Mainair Blade (Rotax 582)	1095-0896-7 & W898		8. 8.96	J.Jasinczuk	Otherton, Cannock	5. 9.03P
G-MZEH	Pegasus Quantum 15 (Rotax 582/40)	7259		19. 9.96	P.S.Hall	Sywell	16.10.03P
G-MZEI	Whittaker MW5-D Sorcerer (Rotax 447)	PFA 163-12011		28.10.96	W.G.Reynolds *(US Navy c/s)*	Overstrand	28. 8.02P

G-MZEJ	Mainair Blade	1097-0996-7 & W900		8.10.96	A.D.R.Huddleston	(Liverpool)	27. 7.02P
	(Rotax 462)						
G-MZEK	Mainair Mercury	1098-1096-7 & W901		14.10.96	M.Whiteman-Heywood	(Bewdley)	15.11.02P
	(Rotax 462)						
G-MZEL	Cyclone AX3	7250		30.10.96	T.I.Bull	Tarn Farm, Cockerham	16.10.03P
	(Rotax 503)						
G-MZEM	Pegasus Quantum 15-912	7277		8.11.96	M.Howland	Clench Common	8.11.03P
G-MZEN	Rans S-6ESD Coyote II *(Tricycle u/c)*			9. 7.96	C.Slater	(Dronfield)	23. 9.03P
	(Rotax 503)	1294.705 & PFA 204-12823					
G-MZEO	Rans S-6ESD Coyote II XL	PFA 204-13046		19.11.96	J.R.Dobson tr G-MZEO Group	Eshott	26. 8.03P
	(Rotax 503)						
G-MZEP	Mainair Rapier	1103-1296-7 & W906		13.12.96	A.C.Shields	(Douglas, Isle of Man)	19. 6.03P
	(Rotax 503)						
G-MZER	Cyclone AX2000	7251	G-69-28	4.12.96	B.H.Stephens tr Sarum AX2000 Group	Old Sarum	18. 3.03P
	(Rotax 582)		G-MZER				
G-MZES	Letov LK-2M Sluka	8296K10 & PFA 263-13064		5.12.96	J.L.Self	Lower Mountpleasant Farm, Chatteris	15.10.02P
	(Rotax 447)						
G-MZET	Cyclone Pegasus Quantum 15	7288		9.12.96	D.L.Walker	(Luxembourg)	13. 2.03P
	(Rotax 582)						
G-MZEU	Rans S-6ESD Coyote II XL	PFA 204-13023		23.12.96	T.E.Owen & G.P.Gibson	RAF Mona	17. 3.03P
	(Rotax 503) *(Tricycle u/c)*						
G-MZEV	Mainair Rapier	1101-1296-7 & W904		7. 1.97	I.D.Woolley	Barton	11. 6.03P
	(Rotax 503)						
G-MZEW	Mainair Blade	1105-0197-7 & W908		13. 1.97	S.J.Meehan	Sittles Farm, Alrewas	11. 4.03P
	(Rotax 462)						
G-MZEX	Pegasus Quantum 15	7292		19.11.96	J.Wittering	(Uttoxeter)	4. 3.03P
	(Rotax 582)						
G-MZEY	Micro Aviation B.22S Bantam	96-002	ZK-TII	7. 1.97	F.D.Hatton	Pound Green, Kidderminster	11.10.02P
	(Rotax 582)				tr Pound Green Syndicate		
G-MZEZ	Pegasus Quantum 15-912	7285		8.11.96	L.G.White	Field Farm, Oakley	2. 8.03P
G-MZFA	Cyclone AX2000	7301		17.12.96	P.J.Howard & M.Kerrison	(Ennis, Co.Clare)	2. 3.02P
	(Rotax 582/48)						
G-MZFB	Mainair Blade	1108-0197-7 & W911		7. 1.97	S.Chapman	(Bootle)	6. 5.03P
	(Rotax 462)						
G-MZFC	Letov LK-2M Sluka	8296K009 & PFA 263-13063		7. 1.97	P.B.Merritt	(Kingsclere)	24. 8.03P
	(Rotax 447)						
G-MZFD	Mainair Rapier	1109-0197-7 & W912		24. 1.97	R.Gill	Knapthorpe Lodge, Caunton	3. 6.03P
	(Rotax 462)						
G-MZFE	Huntwing Avon	9507049 & BMAA/HB/061		16. 1.97	G.J.Latham	Sittles Farm, Alrewas	15. 3.03P
	(Rotax 503)						
G-MZFF	Huntwing Avon 503 (3)	9604058 & BMAA/HB/074		22. 1.97	B.J.Adamson	(Stockport)	16.1 .03P
G-MZFG	Pegasus Quantum 15	7305		21. 1.97	A.M.Prentice	Yundum/Banjul, Gambia	6.12.01P
	(Rotax 582/40)						
G-MZFH*	AMF Chevvron 2-32C	039		27. 3.97	Finish Design Ltd t/a Air-Share	Membury	21. 4.98P
	(Konig SD570)				*(Cancelled by CAA 20.4.01) (Stored de-rigged with Aviation Enterprises 10.01)*		
G-MZFI	Lorimer Iolaire	BMAA/HB/035		30. 1.97	H.Lorimer	(Switzerland)	
	(BMW)				*"Iolaire" (Current status unknown)*		
G-MZFK	Whittaker MW6 Merlin	PFA 164-11626		10. 2.97	G.J.Chadwick,	Tarn Farm, Cockerham	9. 2.02P
	(Rotax 532)				tr G-MZFK Flying Group		
G-MZFL	Rans S-6ESD Coyote II XL *(Tricycle u/c)*			12. 2.97	D.L.Robson & U.Y.S.O'Reilly	Eshott	19. 8.03P
	(Rotax 503)	0696.999XL & PFA 204-13041					
G-MZFM	Pegasus Quantum 15	7310		21. 2.97	T.Holford	(Cannock)	28. 9.03P
	(Rotax 582/40)						
G-MZFN	Rans S-6ESD Coyote II	PFA 204-12977		26. 2.97	C.J. & W.R.Wallbank	Ley Farm, Chirk	27.11.02P
	(Rotax 503)						
G-MZFO	Thruster T.600N	9037-T600N-001		4. 3.97	J.Berry	Barton	13. 4.03P
	(Rotax 503)						
G-MZFP	Thruster T.600T	9047-T600T-002		4. 3.97	T.R.Villa	Priory Farm, Tibenham	12. 5.03P
	(Rotax 503) *(Noted with nosewheel configuration = T600N)*						
G-MZFR	Thruster T.600N	9047-T600N-003		4. 3.97	M.Firman tr Blue Bird Syndicate	Shobdon	28. 3.03P
	(Rotax 503)						
G-MZFS	Mainair Blade	1110-0297-7 & W913		8. 1.97	P.Green	(Louth)	11. 3.03P
	(Rotax 582) *(Officially regd with trike c/n 1010-0297-7)*						
G-MZFT	Pegasus Quantum 15-912	7264		2.10.96	J.F.Woodham	Hollow Hill Farm, Granborough	25. 4.03P
G-MZFU	Thruster T.600N	9047-T600N-004		4. 3.97	G J Slater	Clench Common	30. 1.03P
	(Rotax 503)						
G-MZFV	Pegasus Quantum 15-912	7324		13. 3.97	A.J.Geary	Baxby Manor, Husthwaite	22. 4.03P
G-MZFX	Cyclone AX2000 (Rotax 582/48)	7322		14. 3.97	Flylight Airsports Ltd	Sywell	7. 6.03P
G-MZFY	Rans S-6ESD Coyote II XL *(Tricycle u/c)*			17. 3.97	L.G.Tserkezos	(Reigate)	23. 6.03P
	(Rotax 503)	0696.1003 & PFA 204-13043					
G-MZFZ	Mainair Blade	1119-0497-7 & W922		2. 4.97	M J Day tr Blade G-MZFZ Flying Group	(Bungay)	8.12.02P
	(Rotax 582/2V)						
G-MZGA	Cyclone AX2000	7303		17.12.96	Microflight Ireland Ltd	Mullaghmore, Co.Antrim	26. 6.03P
	(Rotax 582)						
G-MZGB	Cyclone AX2000	7302		28. 1.97	P.Hegarty	(Magherafelt, Co.Londonderry)	28. 6.03P
	(Rotax 582)						
G-MZGC	Cyclone AX2000	7304		20.12.96	Carol E.Walls	Mullaghmore, Co.Antrim	11. 4.03P
	(Rotax 582)						
G-MZGD	Rans S-5 Coyote	89.095 & PFA 193-13096		1. 4.97	A.G.Headford	Barton	5, .8.03P
	(Rotax 447)						
G-MZGE*	Medway Hybred 44XLR	MR143/125		8. 4.97	Eclectic Computer Software Ltd	Stoke, Kent	27. 5.99P
					(Cancelled 9.7.01 by CAA) (Displayed Microlight Trade Fair, Popham 5.02)		
G-MZGF	Letov LK-2M Sluka	8296K008 & PFA 263-13073		8. 4.97	G.Lombardi	RAF Wyton	13. 5.03P
	(Rotax 447)						

G-MZGG	Pegasus Quantum 15	7327	10. 4.97	R.W.Partington	Sywell	17. 4.03P
	(Rotax 503)					
G-MZGH	Huntwing Avon 462	9406021 & BMAA/HB/070	20.10.96	J.H.Cole	(Rugeley)	27. 7.03P
G-MZGI	Mainair Blade	1117-0397-7 & W920	11. 4.97	H.M.Roberts	St.Michaels	6. 8.03P
	(Rotax 912UL)					
G-MZGJ	Kolb Twinstar Mk.3	K0008-0193 & PFA 205-12421	16. 4.97	P.Coppock	Kemble	29. 4.03P
	(Hirth 2705 R06)					
G-MZGK	Pegasus Quantum 15	7331	30. 4.97	A.J.Wells	Sywell	11.10.03P
	(Rotax 582/40)					
G-MZGL	Mainair Rapier	1104-0197-7 & W907	18.12.96	L.R.Fox	(Aylesbury)	4.. 5.03P
	(Rotax 503)					
G-MZGM	Cyclone AX2000	7334	1. 5.97	W.G.Dunn	Winkleigh, Devon	3. 8.03P
	(Rotax 582/48)					
G-MZGN	Pegasus Quantum 15	7332	2. 5.97	R.J.Townsend	Long Acre Farm, Sandy	22. 6.03P
	(Rotax 503)					
G-MZGO	Pegasus Quantum 15	7320	20. 3.97	S.F.G.Allen	Barton	5. 7.03P
	(Rotax 582/40)					
G-MZGP	Cyclone AX2000	7333	7. 5.97	D.G.Palmer	Fetterangus	12. 6.03P
	(Rotax 582/48)			tr Buchan Light Aeroplane Club		
G-MZGS	CFM Shadow DD	K.284 & PFA 161-13050	8. 5.97	D.Harris	(South Croydon)	27. 5.03P
	(Rotax 447)					
G-MZGT	RH7B Tiger Light	PFA 230-13013	10. 3.97	J.B.McNab	Dunkeswell	AC
	(5/8ths scale Tiger Moth) (Assembled for PFA approval to test fly @ 11.01)					
G-MZGU	Arrowflight Hawk II (UK)	PFA 266-13075	8. 5.97	P.Duffin	Mullaghmore, Co.Antrim	3. 5.02P
	(Rotax 503)					
G-MZGV	Pegasus Quantum 15	7339	12. 6.97	R.E.Kilby tr G-MZGV Syndicate	Dunkeswell	21. 3.03P
	(Rotax 582/40)					
G-MZGW	Mainair Blade	1112-0297-7 & W915	19. 2.97	R.Almond	Wickhambrook, Newmarket	2.10.03P
	(Rotax 462)					
G-MZGX	Thruster T.600N	9057-T600N-005	28. 4.97	R.L.Barton	Ginge Farm, Wantage	29. 7.02P
	(Rotax 503)					
G-MZGY	Thruster T.600N	9057-T600N-006	28. 4.97	M.J.& A.R.Wolldridge	Siege Cross Farm, Thatcham	9. 9.03P
	(Rotax 503)					
G-MZGZ	Thruster T.600N	9057-T600N-005	28. 4.97	K.Hanson tr G-MZGZ Group	Dunkeswell	17. 7.02P
	(Rotax 503)					
G-MZHA	Thruster T.600T	9057-T600T-008	28. 4.97	R.V.Buxton	Feshiebridge	22. 4.03P
	(Rotax 503)					
G-MZHB	Mainair Blade	1114-0297-7 & W917	19. 2.97	R.J.Butler	Guy Lane Farm, Waverton	22. 4.03P
	(Rotax 462)					
G-MZHC	Thruster T.600T	9067-T600T-009	13. 5.97	S.W.Tallamy	Davidstow Moor	12. 6.02P
	(HKS 700E)					
G-MZHD	Thruster T.600T	9067-T600T-010	13. 5.97	B.E.Foster	(Tain)	13. 7.02P
	(Rotax 503)					
G-MZHE	Thruster T.600N	9067-T600N-011	13. 5.97	C.Kemp & S.St.John	(Horsham)	7. 5.03P
	(Rotax 503)					
G-MZHF	Thruster T.600N	9067-T600N-012	13. 5.97	M.F.Cottam	(Lincoln)	3. 7.03P
	(Rotax 582)					
G-MZHG	Whittaker MW6-T	PFA 164-11420	16. 6.97	M.G.Speers	(Douglas, Isle of Man)	10. 6.03P
	(Rotax 532)					
G-MZHI	Pegasus Quantum 15	7337	27. 5.97	P R Hope	Knapthorpe Lodge, Caunton	3. 7.03P
				tr Quantum HI Group *(Op Derbyshire & Nottingham Microlight Club)*		
G-MZHJ	Mainair Rapier	1123-0697-7 & W926	17. 6.97	D.J.King	(Blackburn)	15. 6.03P
	(Rotax 462)					
G-MZHK	Pegasus Quantum Super Sport 15	7352	24. 6.97	A.D.S.Grant	Rufforth	3. 8.03P
	(Rotax 582/40)					
G-MZHL	Mainair Rapier	1126-0797-7 & W929	30. 6.97	K Mallin	(Halesowen)	13. 8.03P
	(Rotax 503)					
G-MZHM	TEAM hi-MAX 1700R	PFA 272-12912	8. 1.97	M.H.McKeown	(Gorey, Co.Wexford)	25. 6.03P
	(Robin 440)					
G-MZHN	Pegasus Quantum 15	7351	27. 6.97	T.G.Jones	Emlyn's Field, Rhuallt	20. 9.03P
	(Rotax 462HP)					
G-MZHO	Quad City Challenger II	PFA 177-12936	15. 7.97	J.Pavelin	Barling, Essex	10. 7.03P
	(Rotax 503)					
G-MZHP	Pegasus Quantum 15	7353	15. 7.97	A.S.Findley	Long Acre Farm, Sandy	20. 8.03P
	(Rotax 582)					
G-MZHR	Cyclone AX2000	7307	7. 3.97	J.Leden & C.P.Dawes	(Buxton)	1. 5.03P
	(Rotax 582)					
G-MZHS	Thruster T.600T	9077-T600T-013	4. 7.97	D.Mahajan	Lower Mountpleasant Farm, Chatteris	20.10.03P
	(Rotax 582)					
G-MZHT	Whittaker MW6 Merlin	PFA 164-11244	12. 6.97	S.J.Smith	Kemble	17. 6.02P
	(Rotax 503)					
G-MZHU	Thruster T.600T	9077-T600T-019	4. 7.97	M.S.Shelton	Stoneacre Farm, Farthing Corner	27. 8.02P
	(Rotax 503-2V)					
G-MZHV	Thruster T.600T)	9077-T600T-018	4. 7.97	L.G.M.Maddick tr Hotel Victor Group	Leicester	9. 9.03P
	(Rotax 503-UL) *(Officially regd as T.600N)*					
G-MZHW	Thruster T.600N	9077-T600N-017	4. 7.97	P.Turnbull	Eshott	28. 3.03P
	(Rotax 503-2V)					
G-MZHY	Thruster T.600N	9077-T600N-015	4. 7.97	J.P.Beeley	(Caernarfon)	11. 5.03P
	(Rotax 503)					
G-MZHZ	Thruster T.600N	9077-T600N-014	4. 7.97	B.S.Waycott Pound Green, Buttonoak, Kidderminster		29. 6.03P
	(Rotax 503UL)			tr Red Arrow Syndicate		
G-MZIA	TEAM hi-Max 1700R	PFA 272-13020	25. 4.97	I.J.Arkieson	(Meols, Wirral)	
G-MZIB	Pegasus Quantum 15	7354	15. 7.97	S.Murphy	Trim, Co.Meath	2. 9.00P
	(Rotax 582/40)					

G-MZIC	Pegasus Quantum 15 (Rotax 503)	7348		24. 6.97	Helen M.Squire & C.F.Two t/a Swansea Airsports Services	(Swansea)	6. 8.03P
G-MZID	Whittaker MW6 Merlin (Rotax 503)	PFA 164-11383		15. 7.97	M.G.A.Wood	(Tadcaster)	27 .9.02P
G-MZIE	Pegasus Quantum 15 (Rotax 582/40)	7359		6. 8.97	Flylight Airsports Ltd	Sywell	25. 8.03P
G-MZIF	Pegasus Quantum 15 (Rotax 503)	7355		16. 7.97	V.Grayson	(Sittingbourne)	25. 8.03P
G-MZIH	Mainair Blade (Rotax 462)	1128-0797-7 & W931		16. 7.97	E.Scarisbrick (Op Brook Farm Microlight Centre)	Brook Farm, Pilling	12. 9.01P
G-MZII	TEAM mini-MAX 88 (Rotax 447)	PFA 186-11842		19. 3.97	G.F.M.Garner	Clench Common	13. 8.01P
G-MZIJ	Pegasus Quantum 15 (Rotax 582/40)	7362		14. 8.97	C.M.Saysell	Plaistows Farm, St Albans	7.10.03P
G-MZIK	Pegasus Quantum 15 (Rotax 582/40)	7368		8. 9.97	N.J.Holt	Weston Zoyland	7. 6.03P
G-MZIL	Mainair Rapier (Rotax 462)	1132-0897-7 & W935		1. 9.97	A.J.Varga	Rufforth	5.10.03P
G-MZIM	Mainair Rapier (Rotax 462)	1124-0697-7 & W927		9. 6.97	M.J.McKegney	Newtownards, Co.Down	21. 7.03P
G-MZIR	Mainair Blade (Rotax 582)	1134-0997-7 & W937		18. 9.97	S.W.Tallamy	Davidstow Moor	29. 6.03P
G-MZIS	Mainair Blade (Rotax 462)	1115-0397-7 & W918		17. 2.97	K.R.McCartney	Baxby Manor, Husthwaite	23. 4.03P
G-MZIT	Mainair Blade (Rotax 912UL)	1129-0897-7 & W932		16. 7.97	P.M.Horn	Shotton Colliery	11. 5.03P
G-MZIU	Pegasus Quantum 15 (Rotax 582/40)	7371		15.10.97	S.F.Winter	Redlands, Swindon	16.12.02P
G-MZIV	Cyclone AX2000 (Rotax 582/48)	7372		21.10.97	C.J.Tomlin	Knapthorpe Lodge, Caunton	6.12.02P
G-MZIW	Mainair Blade (Rotax 462)	1127-0797-7 & W930		16. 7.97	N.E.J.Hayes	(Chorley)	11. 9.03P
G-MZIX	Mignet HM-1000 Balerit (Rotax 582)	130		23. 9.97	P.E.H.Scott	(Stockbridge)	13. 2.01P
G-MZIY	Rans S-6ESD Coyote II XL *(Tricycle u/c)* (Rotax 503) 1050.1050XL & PFA 204-13184			29. 9.97	P.A.Bell *(Rebuilt with new fuselage frame c.1998)*	Barton	10.12.02P
G-MZIZ	Murphy Renegade Spirit UK 257 & PFA 188-11701 (Rotax 582)		G-MWGP	21.10.92	G Long	Plaistows Farm, St Albans	25. 2.03P
G-MZJA	Mainair Blade (Rotax 582)	1135-0997-7 & W938		30. 9.97	R.C.McArthur	Ince Blundell	18. 3.03P
G-MZJB	Aviasud Mistral	047 (ex ?)		30. 9.97	D.M.Whitham *(Current status unknown)*	Crosland Moor	
G-MZJD	Mainair Blade (Rotax 503)	1130-0897-7 & W933		7. 8.97	A.F.Longhurst	(Rochdale)	20. 8.03P
G-MZJE	Mainair Rapier (Rotax 503)	1136-1097-7 & W939		17.10.97	J.E.Davies	(Southport)	2. 8.02P
G-MZJF	Cyclone AX2000 (Rotax 582/48)	7378		2.12.97	A.J.Blackwell	Long Marston	21.12.02P
G-MZJG	Pegasus Quantum 15 (Rotax 462)	7335		2. 5.97	J.Gamlen	Field Farm, Oakley	28. 5.03P
G-MZJH	Pegasus Quantum 15 (Rotax 503)	7350		25. 6.97	D.W.Ormond	Deenethorpe	27.11.03P
G-MZJI	Rans S-6ESD Coyote II XL *(Tricycle u/c)* (Rotax 503) 1096.1046XL & PFA 204-13221			3.11.97	B.S.Keene	(Blandford Forum)	15. 8.03P
G-MZJJ	Murphy Maverick (Jabiru 2200A)	PFA 259-13016		5.11.97	W.S.Warren	Dunkeswell	17. 4.03P
G-MZJK	Mainair Blade (Rotax 582)	1100-1196-7 & W903		19.11.96	A.H.Kershaw	(Bury)	15. 7.01P
G-MZJL	Cyclone AX2000 (Rotax 503)	7363		11. 8.97	A.J.Longbottom	Smeathorpe, Honiton	28.10.00P
G-MZJM	Rans S-6ESD Coyote II XL (Rotax 503-2V) 1096.1049XL & PFA 204-13215			19.11.97	R.J.Hopkins	Popham	17. 4.03P
G-MZJN	Pegasus Quantum 15 (Rotax 582/40)	7376		11.11.97	J.Nelson *(Op Derbyshire & Nottingham Microlight Club)*	Knapthorpe Lodge, Caunton	16.11.02P
G-MZJO	Pegasus Quantum 15 (Rotax 582/40)	7338		17. 6.97	D.J.Cook	Eaglescott	30. 9.03P
G-MZJP	Whittaker MW6-S Fatboy Flyer (HKS 700E)	PFA 164-13049		21.10.97	D.J.Burton & C.A.J.Funnell *(Current status unknown)*	(Brighton)	
G-MZJR	Cyclone AX2000 (HKS 700E)	7385		11.11.97	N.A.Martin tr Marlborough Aerotow Group	Clench Common	15. 1.04P
G-MZJS	Murphy Maverick 430 (Jabiru 2200A)	PFA 259-13017		12.12.97	R.D.Barnard	(Stockport)	22. 4.03P
G-MZJT	Pegasus Quantum 15-912	7399		23.12.97	M.A.McClelland	Old Sarum	23.12.02P
G-MZJV	Mainair Blade (Rotax 912)	1141-0198-7 & W944		7. 1.98	M.A.Roberts *(Current status unknown)*	West Malling	3. 2.99P
G-MZJW	Pegasus Quantum 15-912	7390		27. 1.98	W.H.J.Knowles	Yundum/Banjul, Gambia	18.10.03P
G-MZJX	Mainair Blade (Rotax 503-2V)	1139-0198-7 & W942		9. 1.98	R.H.H.Munro	(Sevenoaks)	7. 5.02P
G-MZJY	Pegasus Quantum 15-912	7394		23.12.97	S.G Payne tr Yankee Syndicate Long Acre Farm, Sandy		23.12.02P
G-MZJZ	Mainair Blade (Rotax 912UL)	1121-0597-7 & W924		23. 6.97	P.Crosby	Ince Blundell	22. 6.03P
G-MZKA	Pegasus Quantum 15 (Rotax 912)	7380		1.12.97	A.S.R.McSherry	West Kilbride	11.12.02P
G-MZKC	Cyclone AX2000 (Rotax 582-48)	7398		22. 1.98	W.E.Corps tr Broad Farm Flyers	Broad Farm, Eastbourne	20. 2.03P

G-MZKD	Pegasus Quantum 15 (Rotax 912)	7404		19. 3.98	S.J.E.Smith	(Newcastle upon Tyne)	9. 8.03P
G-MZKE	Rans S-6ESD Coyote II XL (Rotax 503-2V)	PFA 204-13248		19. 1.98	I.Findlay	Eshott	30. 5.03P
G-MZKF	Pegasus Quantum 15 (Rotax 912)	7407		21. 1.98	T.A.Howe	(Margate)	23. 8.03P
G-MZKG	Mainair Blade (Rotax 582-2V)	1145-0198-7 & W948		23. 1.98	N.S.Rigby	(Liverpool)	17.12.00P
G-MZKH	CFM Shadow DD (Rotax 582)	292-DD		23. 1.98	K.D.Mitchell	Shoreham	5. 5.03P
G-MZKI	Mainair Rapier (Rotax 503-2V)	1147-0298-7 & W950		12. 2.98	C.K.Richardson	East Fortune	18. 5.03P
G-MZKJ	Mainair Blade (Rotax 582)	1039-0595-7 & W837		19. 5.95	L.G.M.Maddick	Leicester	11. 9.03P
G-MZKK	Mainair Blade (Rotax 912)	1140-0198-7 & W943		12. 2.98	G.R.Hall	Lydd	13. 2.03P
G-MZKL	Pegasus Quantum 15 (Rotax 582/40)	7360		18. 8.97	P.S.Underwood	Over Farm, Gloucester	31. 8.03P
G-MZKM	Mainair Blade (Rotax 912UL)	1133-0897-7 & W936		15. 8.97	C.Bodill	(Nottingham)	7. 4.03P
G-MZKN	Mainair Rapier (Rotax 503-2V)	1138-1297-7 & W941		12.12.97	G.Craig	Newtownards, Co.Down	7. 6.03P
G-MZKO	Mainair Blade (Rotax 503)	1131-0897-7 & W934		5. 8.97	A.M.Durose	(Nottingham)	19. 9.03P
G-MZKR	Thruster T.600N (Rotax 582UL)	9038-T600N-021		27. 1.98	R.J.Arnett	(Albuferia, Portugal)	1 .3.03P
G-MZKS	Thruster T.600N (HKS 700E)	9038-T600N-022		27. 1.98	S.Jeffrey	Insch	3.10.03P
G-MZKT	Thruster T.600T (Rotax 582UL)	9038-T600T-023		27. 1.98	M.J.O'Connor	Stock Farm, Billericay	12 7.03P
G-MZKU	Thruster T.600T (Rotax 503UL)	9038-T600T-024		27. 1.98	A.S.Day	RAF Wyton	24. 9.03P
G-MZKV	Mainair Blade (Rotax 912)	1144-0198-7 & W947		28. 1.98	M.P.J.Moore	(Stoke-on-Trent)	15. 5.03P
G-MZKW	Quad City Challenger II (Hirth 2705 R06)	PFA 177-12518		22. 3.94	K.W.Warn	Siege Cross Farm, Thatcham	10.12.02P
G-MZKX	Pegasus Quantum 15 (Rotax 582-40)	7395		15. 1.98	M.G.Evans	(Milton Keynes)	14. 2.03P
G-MZKY	Pegasus Quantum 15 (HKS 700E)	7403		16. 1.98	G.N.S.Farrant	Drayton St Leonard	31. 5.03P
G-MZKZ	Mainair Blade (Rotax 582) *(Supplied as Mainair Kit)*	K1137-0298-7 & W940		18. 2.98	R.P.Wolstenholme	(Warrington)	10. 5.03P
G-MZLA	Pegasus Quantum 15 (Rotax 582)	7415		27. 2.98	D.A.Morgan	Dunkeswell	30. 3.03P
G-MZLB	Huntwing Experience	BMAA/HB/058		25. 2.98	M.Ffrench *(Current status unknown)*	(New Ross, Co.Wexford)	
G-MZLC	Mainair Blade (Rotax 912)	1146-0298-7 & W949		26. 2.98	M J Rummery	Ince Blundell	6. 4.03P
G-MZLD	Pegasus Quantum 15-912	7416		24. 3.98	B.Kirkland	Tarn Farm, Cockerham	14. 8.02P
G-MZLE	Murphy Maverick 430 (Jabiru 2200A)	PFA 259-12955	G-BXSZ	27. 2.98	A.A.Plumridge	Bodmin	14. 5.03P
G-MZLF	Pegasus Quantum 15 (Rotax 503)	7417		30. 3.98	J.H.Tope & B J Harper	(Newton Abbot)	11. 5.03P
G-MZLG	Rans S-6ESD Coyote II XL *(Tricycle u/c)* (Rotax 503-2V) 0897.1143XL & PFA 204-13192			3. 3.98	M.Rhodes	(Stoke-on-Trent)	5. 6.03P
G-MZLH	Pegasus Quantum 15 (Rotax 582-40)	7426		1. 4.98	R.J.Philpotts Pound Green, Buttonoak, Kidderminster		16. 9.03P
G-MZLI	Mignet HM-1000 Balerit (Rotax 582)	133		5. 3.98	A.G.Barr	(Llandudno)	10. 3.03P
G-MZLJ	Pegasus Quantum 15 (Rotax 503)	7421		20. 3.98	M.H.Colin	Otherton, Cannock	29. 3.03P
G-MZLK	Ultrasports Tripacer/Solar Wings Typhoon (Fuji-Robin EC-34-PM) T285-1471*(Trike unit ex G-MJEC & Sailwing is Typhoon S4+ (ex-hanglider) s/n T785-1471M)*			9. 3.98	J.A.Jones	(Winchester)	29. 9.02P
G-MZLL	Rans S-6ESD Coyote II (Rotax 503)	PFA 204-13067		23. 9.97	J.A.Willats & G.W.Champion	(Crawley)	6. 9.03P
G-MZLM	Cyclone AX2000 (Rotax 582-48) *(Modified to hang-glider tug version)*	7425		22. 4.98	P.Bennett	Swinford, Rugby	11. 5.03P
G-MZLN	Pegasus Quantum 15 (Rotax 503)	7431		14. 4.98	P.Thomson tr G-MZLN Flying Group	Deenethorpe	24. 4.03P
G-MZLO*	CFM Shadow D Srs.SS (Rotax 912-UL)	K.298-D		1. 4.98	CFM Aircraft Ltd *(Cancelled 4.2.03 by CAA)*	Leiston	2.10.01P
G-MZLP	CFM Shadow D Srs.SS (Rotax 912-UL)	K.299-D		1. 4.98	C.S.Robinson	Newtownards, Co.Down	21. 9.03P
G-MZLR*	Solar Wings Pegasus XL-Q (Rotax 462HP) *(Trike c/n SW-TB-1040 ex G-MNJP fitted with new sailwing c/n 7441)*	7441		28. 5.98	T.I.Courtney Knapthorpe Lodge, Caunton *(Cancelled 13.9.02 by CAA)*		31. 5.02P
G-MZLS	Cyclone AX2000 (HKS 700E V3)	7428		6. 7.98	G.Forster	North Coates	3. 8.02P
G-MZLT	Pegasus Quantum 15-912	7438		24. 4.98	C.S.Bourne	(Stone)	28. 4.03P
G-MZLU	Cyclone AX2000 (HKS 700E V3)	7439		28. 7.98	M.L.Smith	(Verwood)	6. 7.03P
G-MZLV	Pegasus Quantum 15 (Rotax 503)	7437		29. 4.98	A.L.Rudge	(Bridgwater)	6. 7.02P
G-MZLW	Pegasus Quantam 15 (Rotax 582-40)	7440		28. 4.98	S.P.Murphy	Sywell	23. 5.03P

G-MZLX	Micro Aviation B.22S Bantam	97-013	ZK-JIV	9.12.97	D.L.Howell	Long Acre Farm, Sandy	25. 9.03P
	(Rotax 582)						
G-MZLY	Letov LK-2M Sluka	PFA 263-13065		20. 4.98	W.McCarthy	Wick	8.10.03P
	(Rotax 447 1V)						
G-MZLZ	Mainair Blade	1154-0498-7 & W957		21. 4.98	S.R.Winter	Hunsdon	14. 5.03P
	(Rotax 912)						
G-MZMA	Pegasus Quasar IITC	6611		1. 9.93	A.C.Barnes & D.J.Parsons	(Ashington)	13. 4.03P
	(Rotax 582/40)						
G-MZMB	Mainair Blade	1149-0398-7 & W952		5. 3.98	J T Hearle	(Blackburn)	11. 4.02P
	(Rotax 462)						
G-MZMC	Pegasus Quantum 15-912	7206		10. 5.96	J.J.Baker	Deenethorpe	20. 5.03P
G-MZMD	Mainair Blade	1148-0398-7 & W951		5. 3.98	T.Gate	(Clitheroe)	22. 4.03P
	(Rotax 912)						
G-MZME	Medway Hybred 44XLR EclipseR	151/129E	G-582	8. 4.98	T.Bowles	Ince Blundell	1.11.03P
	(Jabiru 2200A) *(Test flown with "B" conditions marks as shown)*						
G-MZMF	Pegasus Quantum 15(HKS)	7387		30. 4.98	A.J.Tranter	(Aberdeen)	11. 9.03P
	(HKS 700E V3)						
G-MZMG	Pegasus Quantum 15	7446		27. 5.98	J M Pattison	Weston Zoyland	5.7.03P
	(Rotax 503)						
G-MZMH	Pegasus Quantum 15-912	7402		27. 1.98	M.Hurtubise	(Leamington Spa)	29. 3.03P
G-MZMJ	Mainair Blade	1155-0598-7 & W958		8. 5.98	S.Miles	(Sutton-in-Ashfield)	1. 8.02P
	(Rotax 912)						
G-MZMK	AMF Chevvron 2-32C	040		19. 5.98	K.D.Calvert	Park Farm, Eaton Bray	20. 9.03P
	(Konig SD 570)						
G-MZML	Mainair Blade	1158-0698-7 & W961		19. 5.98	M.J.Allan	Latch Farm, Kirknewton	16. 7.03P
	(Rotax 912)						
G-MZMM	Mainair Blade	1162-0698-7 & W965		19. 5.98	J.F.Shaw	Baxby Manor, Husthwaite	30. 7.03P
	(Rotax 912 or 462?)						
G-MZMN	Pegasus Quantum 15-912	7445		21. 5.98	L.A.Hosegood	Redlands, Swindon	16.12.01P
G-MZMO	TEAM mini-MAX 91	PFA 186-12951		20. 5.98	I.M.Ross	Insch	9 .5.03P
	(Rotax 447)						
G-MZMP	Mainair Blade	1160-0698-7 & W963		20. 5.98	D.Jessop	(Sleaford)	28.11.02P
	(Rotax 582-2V)						
G-MZMS	Rans S-6ES Coyote II *(Tricycle u/c)*			26. 5.98	D.G.Matthews	Long Marston	28.11.03P
	(Rotax 503) 1298.1203ES & PFA 204-13294						
G-MZMT	Pegasus Quantum 15	7449		18. 6.98	B.J.Kitson	Sutton Meadows, Ely	19. 7.03P
	(Rotax 582-40)						
G-MZMU	Rans S-6ESD-XL Coyote II	PFA 204-13242		5. 6.98	S.Cox	(Hinckley)	2.10.03P
	(Rotax 503-2V)						
G-MZMV	Mainair Blade	1152-0496-7 & W955		30. 3.98	P.R.Whitehouse	Otherton, Cannock	13. 5.03P
	(Rotax 462)					tr Blade Runners Syndicate		
G-MZMW	Mignet HM-1000 Balerit	125		2.10.96	M.E.Whapham	Corn Wood Farm, Adversane	21. 8.03P
	(Rotax 582)						
G-MZMX	Cyclone AX2000	7451		8. 9.98	R.H.Braithwaite	RAF Halton	18.10.03P
	(HKS 700E V3)					tr RAF Microlight Flying Association		
G-MZMY	Mainair Blade	1153-0498-7 & W956		16. 3.98	C.J.Millership	St.Michaels	18. 5.03P
	(Rotax 462)						
G-MZNA	Quad City Challenger II UK	CH2-0894-UK-1193	EI-CLE	19. 3.98	S.Hennessy	(Dublin)	8. 9.03P
	(Rotax 503)						
G-MZNB	Pegasus Quantum 15-912	7456		17. 7.98	F.Gorse	(Caernarfon)	7.12.02P
G-MZNC	Mainair Blade	1161-0698-7 & W964		22. 6.98	A.Costello	Brook Farm, Pilling	22. 6.03P
	(Rotax 912)						
G-MZND	Mainair Rapier	1170-0898-7 & W973		24. 6.98	S.D.Hutchinson	St Michaels	13. 7.03P
	(Rotax 912)						
G-MZNE	Whittaker MW6-S Fatboy Flyer	PFA 164-13120		26. 6.98	P.E.Owen	(Barnstaple)	21 .6.02P
	(Rotax 582-47)						
G-MZNG	Pegasus Quantum 15-912	7457		11. 8.98	G.G.Rowley	(Carlisle)	1. 1.03P
G-MZNH	CFM Shadow DD	K.297-DD		30. 6.98	P.A.James	Redhill	29. 7.03P
	(Rotax 582)						
G-MZNI	Mainair Blade	1163-0698-7 & W966		3. 7.98	V.D.Carmichael	(Dundonald, Belfast)	10. 4.03P
	(Rotax 912)						
G-MZNJ	Mainair Blade	1168-0798-7 & W971		6. 7.98	G.E.Cole	Over Farm, Gloucester	16. 8.03P
	(Rotax 462)						
G-MZNK	Mainair Blade	1164-0798-7 & W967		6. 7.98	D.S.Taylor & Taylor Refrigeration Ltd	(Maidstone)	22. 6.03P
	(Rotax 912)						
G-MZNL	Mainair Blade	1165-0798-7 & W968		6. 7.98	R.P.Taylor & Taylor Refrigeration Ltd	Rochester	22. 6.03P
	(Rotax 912)						
G-MZNM	TEAM mini-MAX 91	PFA 186-12304		10. 7.98	N.P.Thomson	(Falkirk)	
	(Fuji-Robin EC-44)					*(Amended CofR 3.02)*		
G-MZNN	TEAM mini-MAX 91	PFA 186-13125		10. 7.98	D.M.Dronsfield	Brook Farm, Pilling	17. 6.02P
	(Rotax 447)					*(Op Brook Farm Microlight Centre)*		
G-MZNO	Mainair Blade	1167-0798-7 & W970		9. 6.98	R.C.Colclough	(Stoke-on-Trent)	27. 9.03P
	(Rotax 462)						
G-MZNP	Pegasus Quantum 15-912	7466		22. 7.98	O.W.Achurch	(Northampton)	12. 9.03P
G-MZNR	Pegasus Quantum 15	7465		17. 8.98	E.S.Wills	(Paignton)	2. 8.03P
	(Rotax 503)						
G-MZNS	Pegasus Quantum 15-912	7473		31. 7.98	P.G.Leonard	(Luton)	3.11.03P
G-MZNT	Pegasus Quantum 15-912	7470		25. 9.98	M.P.Lewis	(Market Harborough)	27. 1.02P
G-MZNU	Mainair Rapier	174-0898-7 & W977		5. 8.98	D.N.Carnegie	(St.Bees)	21. 9.03P
	(Rotax 503-2V)						
G-MZNV	Rans S-6ESD Coyote II *(Tricycle u/c)*			7. 8.98	A.P.Thomas	Lower Wasing Farm, Brimpton	22.10.02P
	(Rotax 503-2V) 1294.704 & PFA 204-12884						
G-MZNX	Thruster T.600N	9098-T600N-026		10. 8.98	M H Moulai	North Coates	4.11.02P
	(Rotax 503UL-2V)						

G-MZNY	Thruster T.600N	9098-T600N-027		10. 8.98	Mainair Microlight School Ltd	Barton	26. 6.03P
	(Rotax 582)						
G-MZNZ	Letov LK-2M Sluka	8295s015 & PFA 263-13274		21. 4.98	K.T.Vinning	Long Marston	20. 5.03P
	(Rotax 447)						
G-MZOC	Mainair Blade	1172-0898-7 & W975		10. 8.98	R.A.Carr	(Alnwick)	1. 9.03P
	(Rotax 912)						
G-MZOD	Pegasus Quantum 15-912	7435		28. 4.98	J.W.Mann	Enstone	26. 4.03P
G-MZOE	Cyclone AX2000	7472		17. 9.98	York Microlight Centre Ltd	Rufforth	18. 3.03P
	(HKS 700E V3)						
G-MZOF	Mainair Blade	1122-0697-7 & W925		5. 6.97	A.P.S.John, T.D.Holland-Martin & P.J.Bossom		
	(Rotax 462)				t/a Overbury Farms	(Tewkesbury)	28. 7.03P
G-MZOG	Pegasus Quantum 15	7471		12.10.98	J.F.Leather	Weston Zoyland	13. 4.03P
	(Rotax 503)						
G-MZOH	Whittaker MW-5-D Sorcerer	PFA 163-13060		14. 8.98	D.M.Precious	(Camelford)	20.11.03P
	(Fuji-Robin EC-44) (Officially recorded as Rotax 377)						
G-MZOI	Letov LK-2M Sluka	8296s012 & PFA 263-13238		17. 8.98	M.C.Reed	(Loughborough)	5. 9.02P
	(Rotax 447 1V)						
G-MZOJ	Pegasus Quantum 15	7478		9.11.98	A.C. Lane	Long Acre Farm, Sandy	15.11.02P
	(Rotax 582-40)						
G-MZOK	Whittaker MW6 Merlin	PFA 164-11568		24. 8.97	R.K.Willcox	Chase Farm, Bristol	6. 7.03P
	(Rotax 582)						
G-MZOM	CFM Shadow DD	302-DD		8. 9.98	P.S.Winteron & P.Tidd tr Side-Stick Syndicate		
	(Rotax 582)				Lower Mountpleasant Farm, Chatteris		23. 2.03P
G-MZON	Mainair Rapier	1180-1098-7 & W983		11. 9.98	K.A.Armstrong	Brough	20. 2.03P
	(Rotax 503-2V)						
G-MZOP	Mainair Blade	1178-0998-7 & W981		11. 9.98	P.Barrow	Arclid Green, Sandbach	19.11.03P
	(Rotax 912)						
G-MZOR	Mainair Blade	1173-0898-7 & W976		21. 9.98	D.L.Foxley	Barton	7.10.01P
	(Rotax 912)						
G-MZOS	Pegasus Quantum 15-912	7458		6.10.98	Skyglobe Microlights Ltd	(London SE10)	15. 1.03P
	(Rotax 912)						
G-MZOT	Letov LK-2M Sluka	PFA 263-13346		21. 9.98	J.R.Walter	Quilkieston Farm, Stair	13 .8.03P
	(Rotax 447 1V)						
G-MZOV	Pegasus Quantum 15	7512		9. 3.99	J.C.Tunstall	Enstone	17. 3.02P
	(Rotax 503)						
G-MZOW	Pegasus Quantum 15-912	7502		9. 3.99	W.P.Byrne	Newtownards, Co.Down	31 .3.03P
G-MZOX	Letov LK-2M Sluka	PFA 263-13415		15. 2.99	C.M.James	(Canterbury)	
	(Rotax 447)				(Current status unknown)		
G-MZOY	TEAM mini-MAX 91	PFA 186-12526		29. 3.99	E.F.Smith (Current status unknown)	(Egremont)	
G-MZOZ	Rans S-6ESD Coyote II XL (Tricycle u/c)			20. 5.98	D.C.& S.G.Emmons	(Reading)	2. 9.03P
	(Rotax 582)	1096.1052XL & PFA 204-13168		(Officially recorded with Rotax 503 but '582 fitted)			
G-MZPB	Mignet HM-1000 Balerit	124		4.10.96	J.K.Evans	(Lamport)	27 8.03P
	(Rotax 582)						
G-MZPD	Pegasus Quantum 15	7013		9. 5.95	P.M.Dewhurst	Sywell	5. 6.02P
	(Rotax 582)						
G-MZPH	Mainair Blade	1177-0998-7 & W980		26. 8.98	C L G Innocent	Hadfold Farm, Billinghurst	11.10.03P
	(Rotax 582-2V)						
G-MZPJ	TEAM mini-MAX 91	PFA 186-12277		23.11.92	P.R.Jenson	Sittles Farm, Alrewas	21.11.02P
	(Rotax 503)						
G-MZPW	Pegasus Quasar IITC	6892		26.10.94	D.R.Griffiths	Weston Zoyland	3. 6.03P
	(Rotax 582)						
G-MZRC	Pegasus Quantum 15	7482		25.11.98	M.Hopkins	Rufforth	23. 2.03P
	(Rotax 582-40)						
G-MZRH	Pegasus Quantum 15	7269		11.10.96	R.J.Ware	Sittles Farm, Alrewas	28.12.02P
	(Rotax 582/40)						
G-MZRM	Pegasus Quantum 15-912	7455		10. 7.98	M.R.Mosley	(Retford)	2. 8.03P
G-MZRS	CFM Shadow CD	141		4. 4.90	M.R.Lovegrove	Croft Farm, Defford	29. 4.02P
	(Rotax 503)						
G-MZSC	Pegasus Quantum 15	7370		3.10.97	R.J.Greaves	Sywell	10. 9.03P
	(Rotax 503)						
G-MZSD	Mainair Blade	1179-0998-7 & W978		21. 8.98	D.Sampson	East Fortune	5.12.02P
	(Rotax 912)						
G-MZSM	Mainair Blade	1000-0794-7 & W796		15. 7.94	P.R.Anderson	Oxton, Nottingham	10. 9.03P
	(Rotax 582)						
G-MZTA	Mignet HM-1000 Balerit	120		14. 5.96	A.Fusco tr Sky Light Group	(Burwash)	8. 5.01P
	(Rotax 582)						
G-MZTS	Aerial Arts Chaser S	CH703	G-MVDM	19. 3.96	D.G.Ellis	(Tamworth)	26.10.02P
	(Rotax 377)						
G-MZUB	Rans S-6ESD Coyote II XL	PFA 204-13244		30. 4.98	B.O.Dowsett	Astwood	30. 7.03P
	(Rotax 503-2V) (Tricycle u/c)						
G-MZZT	Kolb Twinstar Mk.3	K0006-0992 & PFA 205-12596		1. 5.98	D.E.Martin	Plaistows Farm, St Albans	12. 6.03P
	(Rotax 582)						
G-MZZY	Mainair Blade	1050-0895-7 & W848		13.11.95	A.Mucznik	Oxton, Nottingham	18. 1.03P
	(Rotax 912UL)						

G-NAAA - G-NZZZ

G-NAAA	MBB Bö.105DBS-4	S.34/912	G-BUTN	6. 4.99	Bond Air Services Ltd	Blackpool	21. 2.05T
	(Rebuilt with new pod S.912 c.1993)		G-AZTI/EI-BTE/G-AZTI/EC-DRY/G-AZTI/D-HDAN (Op Lancashire Air Ambulance/AA)				
G-NAAB	MBB Bö.105DBS-4	S.416	D-HDMO	23. 3.99	Bond Air Services Ltd	Henstridge	8..4.05T
			D-HSTP/D-HDMO		(Op Dorset & Somerset Air Ambulance/AA)		
G-NAAS	Aérospatiale AS355F1 Twin Squirrel	5203	G-BPRG	23. 3.90	Northumbria Ambulance Service NHS Trust	Blyth	17. 7.05T
			G-NWPA/G-NAAS/G-BPRG/N370E (Op North East Air Ambulance)				

Regn	Type	C/n	Prev Id	Date	Owner	Base	CofA
G-NAAT*	Folland Gnat T.1	FL.507	XM697	27.11.89	Hunter Flying Club	Exeter	
	(Cancelled 10.4.93 as WFU) (For rebuild to static display condition 2003)						
G-NACA	Norman NAC-2 Freelance 180	2001		23.11.87	NDN Aircraft Ltd	Coventry	AC
	(Stored 6.99: current status unknown)						
G-NACI	Norman NAC-1 Freelance 180	NAC.001	G-AXFB	20. 6.84	L.J.Martin *(Stored 6.01)*	Sandown	7. 4.94P
G-NADS	TEAM mini-MAX 91 (Rotax 447)	PFA 186-12995		8. 2.99	S.Stockill	RAF Halton	22. 4.03P
G-NAPO	Pegasus Quantum 15-912	7799		6. 4.01	V.Causey & F.G.Green	Knapthorpe Lodge, Caunton	26. 5.03P
G-NARO	Cassutt Racer (Continental O-200-A)	M.14372	G-BTXR N68PM	14. 4.98	D.A.Wirdnam	Redhill	7.10.00P
	(Aka Musso Racer Original)						
G-NATT	Rockwell Commander 114A	14538	N5921N	14. 1.80	Northgleam Ltd	Hawarden	3.10.04T
G-NATX	Cameron O-65 HAB	1681		3. 3.88	A.G.E.Faulkner	Willenhall	5. 5.91T
	(National Express Rapide titles"						
G-NBAA	British Aerospace BAe 146 Srs.300	E3386		1. 8.01	BAE Systems (Operations) Ltd	Filton	23.6.03T
	(Avro 146-RJ100)				*(F/f 28.8.01: stored 2.03)*		
G-NBDD	Robin DR400/180 Regent	1103	F-BXVN	26. 9.88	J.N.Binks & I.H.Taylor	Sherburn-in-Elmet	11. 1.04
G-NCFC	Piper PA-38-112 Tomahawk	38-81A0107	N737V G-BNOA/N23272	14. 1.99	Light Aircraft Leasing (UK) Ltd	Norwich	21. 9.02T
G-NCFE	Piper PA-38-112 Tomahawk	38-80A0081	G-BKMK OO-GME/(OO-HKD)/N9676N	1. 7.99	R.M.Browes	(North Walsham)	19. 7.04T
G-NCFR	British Aerospace BAe 125 Srs.700B	257054	G-BVJY RA02802/G-BVJY/C6-BET	28. 4.97	Chauffair Ltd	Farnborough	27. 3.02T
G-NCUB	Piper J-3C-65 Cub (L-4H-PI)	11599	G-BGXV F-BFQT/AO-GAB/43-30308	6. 7.84	R S Basinger	(Norwich)	2. 9.03P
G-NDGC	Grob G-109	6150		7. 4.83	J.E.Bedford & M.Mathieson	Tibenham	28. 8.05
G-NDNI	Norman NDN-1 Firecracker	001		30. 3.77	N.W.G.Marsh *(Stored 5.00)*	Coventry	AC
G-NDOL	Europa Aviation Europa 044 & PFA 247-12594 (Subaru EA81) (Monowheel u/c)			30.11.93	S.Longstaff	(Sheffield)	5. 8.03P
					(F/f 18.11.95)		
G-NDOT	Thruster T600N (Jabiru 2200A)	0052-T600N-066		18. 6.02	P.C.Bailey	(Over, Cambridge)	1. 7.03P
G-NEAL	Piper PA-32-260 Cherokee Six	32-1048	G-BFPY N5588J	7.11.83	V.Walker tr VSD Group	Wolverhampton	14. 9.03
G-NEAT	Europa Aviation Europa 065 & PFA 247-12642 (Rotax 912UL) (Monowheel u/c)			28. 6.94	M.Burton	Nympsfield	21. 5.03P
					(F/f 11.10.96)		
G-NEEL	Rotorway Executive 90 (Rotorway RW 162)	5002		7. 8.90	M.B.Sims	Street Farm, Takeley	17. 6.98P
					(Noted 11.01)		
G-NEGS	Thunder Ax7-77 HAB	1059		18. 3.87	M.Rowlands *"Hot-Shot"*	Ashton-in-Makerfield	2. 8.03A
G-NEIL	Thunder Ax3 Maxi Sky Chariot HAB	379		2.12.81	N.A.Robertson *"Neil" (Op A Moore)*	Great Missenden	4. 9.03A
G-NELI	Piper PA-28R-180 Cherokee Arrow	28R-31011	OH-PWW D-EMWE/N7693J	9. 2.01	The Newcastle upon Tyne Aero Club Ltd	Newcastle	8. 4.04T
G-NEON	Piper PA-32-300B Cherokee Six	32-40683	D-EMKW N4246R	7. 4.00	S.C.A.Lever	Fairoaks	24. 5.03T
G-NERC	Piper PA-31-350 Navajo Chieftain	31-7405402	G-BBXX N66869	26. 4.94	Natural Environment Research Council	Coventry	29. 5.04T
					(Op Air Atlantique)		
G-NERI*	Piper PA-28-181 Cherokee Archer II	28-7890483	G-BMKO N31880	19. 3.93	Not Known	Bristol	10. 4.98T
	(Cancelled 24.11.98 as destoyed) (Wreck stored 2.00)						
G-NESA	Europa Aviation Europa XS T-G 450 & PFA 247-13544			17. 4.01	K.G.& V.E.Summerhill	(Boston)	
G-NESU	Pilatus Britten-Norman BN-2B-20 Islander	2260	G-BTVN	30. 5.95	Northumbria Police Authority	Teesside	20. 2.03T
					(Op North East Air Support Unit)		
G-NESV	Eurocopter EC135-T1	0067		4. 2.99	Northumbria Police Authority	Newcastle	30. 3.05T
					(Op North East Air Support Unit)		
G-NESW	Piper PA-34-220T Seneca III	34-8233072	D-GAMO N8064M	13.12.02	Scot Wings Ltd	(Elgin)	AC
G-NESY	Piper PA-18 Super Cub 95	18-7482	N124SA SE-CUG	18. 8.00	V.Fisher	North Side, Thorney	28. 8.03
G-NETA	Cessna 560XL Citation Excel	560-5230	N5085E	19. 2.02	Houston Air Taxis Ltd	Oxford	25. 2.03T
G-NETY	Piper PA-18-150 Super Cub	1809108	N4159K	8. 9.95	N.B.Mason	Rendcomb	27. 3.05
G-NEUF	Bell 206L-1 LongRanger II	45548	G-BVVV D-HUGO/OE-KXT/C-GLMM	20.11.98	Yendle Roberts Ltd	Booker	13. 9.04T
G-NEVS	Aero Designs Pulsar XP	PFA 202-12283		12.11.93	N.Warrener	(Stockport)	
G-NEWR	Piper PA-31-350 Navajo Chieftain	31-7952129	N35251	23. 8.79	MAS Airways Ltd	Biggin Hill	8. 1.03T
G-NEWS	Bell 206B-3 JetRanger III	2547	N18098	29.11.78	Abington Aviation Ltd	Cambridge	3. 4.03T
G-NEWT	Beech 35 Bonanza (Continental E-185 = C35 status)	D-1168	G-APVW EI-BIL/G-APVW/N9866F/4X-ACI/IDFAF 0604/ZS-BTE	28. 2.90	J.S.Allison	RAF Abingdon	16. 7.05
G-NEWZ	Bell 206B-3 JetRanger III	4475	C-GBVZ	28. 1.98	Peter Press Ltd	Blackbushe	1. 4.04T
G-NFLC	HP.137 Jetstream 1	222	G-AXUI G-8-9	12.12.95	Cranfield University	Cranfield	3. 6.03T
					(Op National Flying Laboratory Centre)		
G-NFNF	Robin DR400/180 Regent	2047	VP-BNU VR-BNU/G-BTDU	15.11.02	N.French	(Aldermaston)	3.12.05
G-NGBI*	American Aviation AA-5B Tiger	AA5B-1104	G-JAKK G-BHWI/N3752E	5. 3.85	Not known	Elstree	
	(Crashed landing Thurrock 12.7.90: cancelled 7.11.96 as WFU: wreck noted 5.00)						
G-NGRM	Spezio DAL-1 Tuholer (Lycoming O-290-G)	134	N6RM	14. 8.90	S.H.Crook	Redhill	7. 2.00P
					(Crashed near Le Touquet 24.7.99 following engine failure)		
G-NHRH	Piper PA-28-140 Cherokee	28-22807	OY-BIC SE-EZP	19. 5.82	J.E.Parkinson	Newcastle	22. 5.04
G-NHRJ	Europa Aviation Europa XS 333 & PFA 247-13112 (Tri-gear u/c)			30. 9.99	D.A.Lowe	(Telford)	
G-NIDG	Aerotechnik 99 Eurostar 990609 & PFA 315-13580 (Rotax 912-UL) (Regd as Aerotechnik EV-97 Eurostar)			29. 2.00	Skydrive Ltd	Shotteswell	6. 8.02P
	(Forced landing in Lecht ski area 7.6.02: fuselage & wings extensively damaged)						
G-NIGC	Jabiru Jabiru UL-450	PFA 274A-13703		3. 5.01	N.Creeney	Brook Farm, Pilling	9. 8.03P
G-NIGE	Luscombe 8E Silvaire (Continental C85)	3525	G-BSHG N72098/NC72098	6. 6.90	Gardan Party Ltd	Popham	3.12.02P
G-NIGL	Europa Aviation Europa 147 & PFA 247-12775 (Rotax 912) (Conventional u/c)			6. 7.95	N.M.Graham	(Southampton)	
					(Current status unknown)		

Reg	Type	C/n	Prev id	Date	Owner/Operator	Location	Notes
G-NIGS	Thunder Ax7-65 HAB	1663		30. 1.90	A.N.F.Pertwee *"Bang Sai"*	Frinton-on-Sea	22. 9.00A
G-NIKE	Piper PA-28-181 Archer II	28-8390086	N4315N	4. 7.89	Key Properties Ltd	White Waltham	23. 9.04T
G-NIKO	Airbus Industrie A321-211	1250	D-AVZA	21. 6.00	MyTravel Airways Ltd	Manchester	20. 6.03T
G-NINA	Piper PA-28-161 Cherokee Warrior II	28-7716162	G-BEUC N3507Q	29. 7.88	P.A.Layzell	Old Buckenham	16.11.03T
G-NINB	Piper PA-28-180 Cherokee Challenger	28-7305234	SE-KHR OY-DLR/CS-AHY/N11C	16. 7.99	P.A.Layzell	East Winch	21. 8.05T
G-NINC	Piper PA-28-180 Cherokee G	28-7205016	SE-KVH N2166T	2. 2.00	P.A.Layzell	Old Buckenham	28. 3.03T
G-NINE	Murphy Renegade 912 448 & PFA 188-12191 (Rotax 912)			16. 6.93	R.F.Bond	Garston Farm, Marshfield	29. 5.03P
G-NIOL	Robinson R44 Raven	1291		12. 2.03	Heli Air Ltd	Wellesbourne Mountford	
G-NIOS	Piper PA-32R-301 Saratoga SP	32R-8513004	N4381Z N105DX/N4381Z	28. 9.90	D.J.Everett & R.R.Alderslade t/a Plant Aviaton	Stapleford	19. 5.05
G-NIPA	Slingsby Nipper T.66 RA.45 Srs.3 (Volkswagen 1834 (Acro))	S.120/1627	G-AWDD	7. 6.96	R.J.O.Walker	North Lopham	3.11.93P
G-NIPP	Slingsby Nipper T.66 RA.45 Srs.3 (Volkswagen 1834) *(Tipsy c/n 32)*	S.103/1587	G-AVKJ	17. 1.00	T.Dale *(On rebuild 12.02)*	Breighton	21. 8.97P
G-NIPY	Hughes 369HS	124-0676S	OH-HMD SE-JAK/N65BL/N9232F	26.11.97	Jet Aviation (Northwest) Ltd	Blackpool	26. 4.04T
G-NITA	Piper PA-28-180 Cherokee C *(Used spare Frame No.28-3807S)*	28-2909	G-AVVG N7517W	16. 1.84	T.Clifford *(Wreck noted 6.02)*	Cranfield	17.11.97T
G-NJAG	Cessna 207 Skywagon	20700093	D-EMDN (N91152)	2. 8.78	G.H.Nolan	Biggin Hill	17. 6.03T
G-NJSH	Robinson R22 Beta	0780		19. 4.88	A J.Hawes	Sywell	29. 6.03
G-NLEE	Cessna 182Q Skylane II	18265934	G-TLTD N759EL	1.12.93	J.S.Lee	Booker	27. 9.02
G-NLYB	Cameron N-105 HAB *(Pink Elephant Head Shape)*	10012		19. 4.01	P.H.E.Van Overwalle	Nazareth, Belgium	11. 2.03A
G-NMHS	Eurocopter AS355N Twin Squirrel	5502	G-DPPS F-WYMM	26. 3.98	North Midlands Helicopter Support Unit	Buttersley	28. 5.04T
G-NMOS	Cameron C-80 HAB	4966		5. 1.01	C J Thomas & M C East	Godalming/Alton	23. 7.03A
G-NNAC	Piper PA-18-135 Super Cub (L-21B-PI) *(Frame No.18-3820)*	18-3820	PH-PSW R.Neth AF R-130/54-2420	19. 5.81	P.A.Wilde t/a PAW Flying Services	Bagby	11. 4.04T
G-NNON	Mainair Blade	1318-0302-7 & W1113		24. 4.02	A.Gannon	East Fortune	13. 5.03P
G-NOBI	Spezio HES-1 Tuholer Sport (Continental C125)	162	N1603	28.11.90	A.D.Pearce	(Lydney)	27. 7.00P
G-NOCK	Reims/Cessna FR182 Skylane RG II	FR18200036	G-BGTK (D-EHZB)	18. 1.94	F.J.Whidbourne	Blackbushe	6. 3.04
G-NODE	Gulfstream AA-5B Tiger	AA5B-1182	N4533L	22. 5.81	Strategic Telecom Networks Ltd	Blackbushe	5. 7.05T
G-NODY	American General AG-5B Tiger	10076	N1194C	3.10.91	Curd & Green Ltd *(Op Cabair)*	Elstree	12. 3.04T
G-NOIR	Bell 222	47031	G-OJLC G-OSEB/G-BNDA/A40-CG	9. 8.91	Arlington Securities plc	Blackbushe	31. 5.05T
G-NOMO	Cameron O-31 HAB *(Previously unregistered in Italy from 1976)*	241		31.10.00	Tim Balloon Promotion Airships Ltd	Bristol	5. 8.03A
G-NONI	Grumman-American AA-5 Traveler	AA5-0383	G-BBDA (EI-AYL)/G-BBDA	1. 8.88	P.T.Harmsworth tr November India Flying Group	Exeter	9. 5.04T
G-NOOK	Mainair Blade 912S	1281-0401-7 & W1076		11. 6.01	P.J.Hughes	(Chelmsford)	13. 9.03P
G-NOOR	Commander Aircraft Commander 114B	14656		6. 2.98	As-Al Ltd	Zell-am-See, Austria	31. 5.04
G-NORD	SNCAC NC.854	7	F-BFIS	20.10.78	W.J.McCollum *(Remains noted 11.01)*	Coagh, Co.Londonderry	27. 5.82P
G-NORT	Robinson R22	3404		7. 1.03	B.J.North t/a North Helicopters	Redhill	12. 2.06T
G-NOSE	Cessna 402B	402B0823	N98AR G-MPCU/SE-IRL/OO-TAT/(OO-SEL)/N3946C	23. 4.96	Atlantic Air Transport Ltd	Coventry	11. 5.03T
G-NOTE	Piper PA-28-181 Archer III	2843082	D-ESPI N9282N	19. 9.97	The General Aviation Trading Co Ltd	Elstree	27. 9.03T
G-NOTR	MD Helicopters MD 500N	LN018	N520MD	26. 2.01	Chartfleet Ltd	Spanhoe	27. 3.04T
G-NOTT	Nott ULD/2 HAB	06		11. 6.86	J.R.P.Nott	London NW3	
G-NOTY	Westland Scout AH.1	F.9630	XT624	5.11.97	R.P.Coplestone	Draycott Farm, Chiseldon	17. 3.03P
G-NOVO	Colt AS-56 Hot-Air Airship	1067		20. 5.87	J.R.Huggins	Dover	29. 4.97A
G-NOWW	Mainair Blade 912 (Rotax 912S)	1227-1299-7 & W1020		10.12.99	C Bodill	Nottingham	27.11.03P
G-NPKJ	Van's RV-6	PFA 181-13138		12. 2.98	K.Jones	Netherthorpe	21. 2.02P
G-NRDC*	Norman NDN-6 Fieldmaster	004		8. 6.81	Not known *(Cancelled 3.2.95 by CAA) (Wreck noted 7.02)*	Sandown	17.10.87P
G-NROY	Piper PA-32RT-300 Lance II	32R-7985070	G-LYNN G-BGNY/N3024L	26.11.93	R.L.West t/a Roy West Cars	Norwich	28. 2.05T
G-NRRA	SIAI-Marchetti SF.260W	116	F-GOBF BF8431/OO-SMB	29.11.00	G.N.Richardson	Shelsley Beauchamp, Worcester	AC
G-NRSC	Piper PA-23-250 Aztec E	27-7305142	N250MC (N244AR)/N250MC/EI-BXP/G-BSFL/PH-NOA/9M-AUS/PH-NOA/N40378	23. 6.00	Air Reconnaisance Ltd	(Leicester)	25. 6.03
G-NSEW	Robinson R44 Astro	0615		6. 7.99	Pebblestar Ltd	Harefield	11. 7.05T
G-NSOF	Robin HR200-120B	334		4. 6.99	Northamptonshire School of Flying Ltd	Sywell	20. 6.05T
G-NSTG	Cessna F150F *(Built Reims Aviation SA) (Wichita c/n 15063499) (Tail-wheel conversion)*	F150-0058	G-ATNI	16. 8.89	N.S.Travers-Griffin *"Iris"*	Coventry	23. 8.04
G-NSUK	Piper PA-34-220T Seneca V	3449256	N126RB(2	27. 2.03	Genus Management Services Ltd	Bournemouth	AC
G-NUDE	Robinson R44 Astro	0743	G-NSYT	16. 1.02	The Last Great Journey Ltd	(London SW3)	6. 4.03T
G-NULA	Flight Design CT2K (Pegasus Aviation c/n)	7913		17.10.02	R.C.Skidmore tr G-NULA Flying Group	(Daventry)	22.10.03P
G-NUTS	Cameron Mr Peanut 35SS HAB	711		18. 2.81	Balloon Flights International Ltd *"Mr Peanut II"* c/o Bristol Balloons *(New Cof R 3.02)*	Bristol	7. 4.86A
G-NUTY	Aérospatiale AS350B Ecureuil	1490	G-BXKT F-GXRT/N333FH/N5797V	20. 7.98	Arena Aviation Ltd	Redhill	5.10.03T
G-NVBF	Lindstrand LBL-210A HAB	249		19. 5.95	Airxcite Ltd t/a Virgin Balloon Flights	Wembley	14. 5.00T

G-NVSA	de Havilland DHC-8-311A (Q300)	451	C-GDNG	20.11.98	Brymon Airways Ltd	Plymouth	20.11.04T
G-NVSB	de Havilland DHC-8-311A (Q300)	517	C-GHRI	14. 1.99	Brymon Airways Ltd	Plymouth	13. 1.05T
G-NWPR	Cameron N-77 HAB	1181		15. 8.85	D.B.Court	(Ormskirk)	
	(Rebuilt with new envelope c/n 1667)				*(CofR restored 4.02)*		
G-NWPS	Eurocopter EC135-T1	0063		15.10.98	North Wales Police Authority	Boddelwydden	11. 2.05T
G-NYMF	Piper PA-25-235 Pawnee D	25-7556112	OO-PAL	8. 2.02	The Bristol Gliding Club Pty Ltd	Nympsfield	3. 3.05
			N267JW/N9799P				
G-NYTE	Reims/Cessna F337G Skymaster	F33700056	G-BATH	12. 5.86	I.M.Latiff	Little Staughton	9. 6.03T
	(Wichita c/n 33701465)		N10631				
G-NZGL	Cameron O-105 HAB	1361		3. 9.86	R.A., P.M.G. & N.T.M.Vale *"Nazgul"*	Kidderminster	28. 5.00A
G-NZSS	Boeing-Stearman E75 (N2S-5) Kaydet	75-8611	N4325	31. 1.89	D.L.H.Barrell	(Cambridge)	27. 6.05T
	(Lycoming R-680)		Bu.43517/42-109578		*(As "343251/27" in USAAC c/s)*		

G-OAAA - G-OZZZ

G-OAAA	Piper PA-28-161 Warrior II	2816107	N9142N	8. 9.93	Halfpenny Green Flight Centre Ltd	Wolverhampton	17. 9.05T
G-OAAC	Airtour AH-77B HAB	010		13. 9.88	Director, Army Air Corps, Historic Aircraft Board of Management		
					"Go AAC"	AAC Middle Wallop	10. 1.00A
G-OABB	SAN Jodel D150 Mascaret	01	F-BJST	21. 1.97	A.B.Bailey	Popham	19. 3.03
			F-WJST				
G-OABC	Colt 69A HAB	1159		17.11.87	P.A.C.Stuart-Kregor	Newbury	26. 6.00A
G-OABO	Enstrom F-28A	097	G-BAIB	10. 7.98	ABO Ltd	Goodwood	13.11.04T
G-OABR	American General AG-5B Tiger	10124	C-GZLA	15. 4.98	Vulcan House Management Ltd	(Wallington)	26. 4.04T
			N256ER				
G-OACA	Piper PA-44-180 Seminole	44-7995202	G-GSFT	31.07.02	Plane Talking Ltd	Elstree	19.12.04T
			EI-BYZ/N2193K				
G-OACB	Piper PA-44-180 Seminole	44-7995084	G-JSFT	21. 5.02	Plane Talking Ltd *(Op Cabair)*	Bournemouth	1. 8.04T
			D-GNFJ/PH-SYB/(PH-PLU)/N2118A				
G-OACC	Piper PA-44-180 Seminole	44-7995190	G-FSFT	15. 1.03	Plane Talking Ltd *(Op Cabair)*	Bournemouth	12.10.04T
			EI-CCO/N2135G				
G-OACE	Valentin Taifun 17E	1017	D-KCBA	22. 1.87	J.E.Dallison	Enstone	27. 4.02
G-OACG	Piper PA-34-200T Seneca II	34-7870177	G-BUNR	10. 3.94	Cega Aviation Ltd	Goodwood	26.11.04T
			EI-CFI/N9245C				
G-OACI	SOCATA MS.893E Rallye 180GT	13086	G-DOOR	5. 5.98	A.M.Quayle	Alderney	6. 4.04
			EI-BHD/F-GBCF				
G-OACP	de Havilland DHC.1 Chipmunk 22	2035	(CS-DAO)	20. 8.96	Aeroclub de Portugal	(Lisbon, Portugal)	14. 3.03
	(Built OGMA) (Lycoming O-360)		FAP 1345				
G-OADY	Beech 76 Duchess	ME-56	N5022M	27.10.86	Multiflight Ltd	Leeds-Bradford	31. 1.05T
G-OAER	Lindstrand LBL-105A HAB	359		4. 3.96	T.M.Donnelly *"Aero"*	Doncaster	25. 6.01A
G-OAFT	Cessna 152 II	15285177	G-BNKM	19. 4.88	Evensport Ltd	Walton Hall, Purleigh	18.11.02T
			N6161Q				
G-OAHC	Beech F33C Bonanza	CJ-133	G-BTTF	2. 9.91	V.D.Speck	Clacton	18. 7.04
			PH-BND				
G-OAJB	Cyclone AX2000	7281	G-MZFJ	16. 2.99	R.S.McMaster	Sywell	21. 5.03P
	(Rotax 582-48)						
G-OAJS	Piper PA-39 Twin Comanche C/R	39-15	G-BCIO	9. 3.94	Go-AJs Ltd	Sherburn-in-Elmet	16. 3.04
			N49JA/N57RG/G-BCIO/N8860Y				
G-OAKJ	British Aerospace Jetstream Srs.3202	795	G-BOTJ	20. 7.89	Air Kilroe Ltd	Manchester	31. 8.03T
			G-OAKJ/G-BOTJ/G-31-795				
G-OALB	Aero L-39C Albatros	931523	ES-ZLD	27. 6.00	Rocket Seat Ltd	North Weald	29.10.03P
			Soviet Air Force				
G-OALD	SOCATA TB-20 Trinidad	490	N54TB	17. 3.88	D.A.Grief t/a Gold Aviation	Biggin Hill	24. 5.03
			F-GBLL				
G-OALH	Tecnam P92-EA Echo	PFA 318-13675		12. 6.01	L.Hill	(Ulverston)	20. 3.03P
G-OAMF	Pegasus Quantum 15-912	7764		20.12.00	T.Southwell	(Spalding)	16. 3.03P
G-OAMG	Bell 206B-3 JetRanger III	2901	G-COAL	25. 2.86	Alan Mann Helicopters Ltd	Fairoaks	31. 5.04T
G-OAMI	Bell 206B JetRanger II	464	G-BAUN	15. 3.01	Stephenson Marine Co Ltd	Goodwood	10. 2.05T
			5N-BAY/G-BAUN/5N-AOU/VR-BIA/G-BAUN/N2261W				
G-OAML	Cameron AML-105 HAB	3881		4.12.96	Stratton Motor Co (Norfolk) Ltd	Long Stratton	9. 5.03A
G-OAMP	Reims/Cessna F177RG Cardinal	F177RG0006l	G-AYPF	30.11.93	G.Hamilton & R.Sheldon	Liverpool	2. 8.03
	(Wichita c/n 17700098)				tr Vale Aero Group		
G-OAMT	Piper PA-31-350 Navajo Chieftain	31-7752105	G-BXKS	23. 1.98	AM & T Solutions Ltd	Bristol	18.12.03T
			N350RC/EC-EBN/N27230				
G-OANI	Piper PA-28-161 Warrior II	28-8416091	N43570	8. 1.91	J.F.Mitchell	Oxford	8. 9.97
					(Damaged Upton Farm, Dover 16.6.96: wreck noted 9.96: current status unknown)		
G-OANN	Zenair CH.601HDS Zodiac	PFA 162-12932		2. 2.96	P.Noden	(Stoke-on-Trent)	8. 6.03P
	(Rotax 912-UL)						
G-OAPE	Cessna T303 Crusader	T30300245	N303MF	3. 2.99	C.Twiston-Davies & P.L.Drew	Jersey	25. 2.05
			D-INKA/N9960C/M303HW/N9960C				
G-OAPR	Brantly B-2B	446	(G-BPST)	21. 4.89	E.D.ap Rees	Weston-super-Mare	1. 7.04
			N2280U		t/a Helicopter International Magazine		
G-OAPW	Glaser-Dirks DG-400	4-268		17. 4.90	D.Bonucchi	(Watford)	10. 6.05
G-OARA	Piper PA-28R-201 Arrow	2837002	N802ND	28.10.98	S.Evans t/a Airsure	Denham	19.11.04T
			N9622N				
G-OARG	Cameron C-80 HAB	3379		20.10.94	G. & R.Madelin *"Argent"*	Farnham/London SW15	3.11.02A
G-OARI	Piper PA-28R-201 Arrow	2837005	N170ND	14.10.02	Plane Talking Ltd	Elstree	12.11.05T
G-OARO	Piper PA-28R-201 Arrow	2837006	N171ND	30.10.01	Plane Talking Ltd	Elstree	5.11.04T
G-OART	Piper PA-23-250 Aztec D	27-4293	G-AXKD	26.11.93	Levenmere Ltd	Old Buckenham	20. 3.03T
			N6936Y		*(Op Skydrift)*		
G-OARU	Piper PA-28R-201 Arrow	2837026	N174ND	24. 5.02	Plane Talking Ltd	Bournemouth	17. 7.05T
					(Op Cabair)		
G-OARV	ARV-1 Super	2001 & PFA 152-11060		18. 6.84	N.R.Beale	Sproughton	12.10.87P
	(Hewland AE75) *(Rebuilt with Kit No.008 1986)*				*(Stored 1.91: current status unknown)*		

Reg	Type	C/n	Prev ID	Date	Owner/Operator	Base	Status
G-OASH	Robinson R22 Beta	0761	N2627Z	13. 6.88	J.C.Lane *(Op Heliflight)*	Wolverhampton	21. 6.03T
G-OASP	Aérospatiale AS355F2 Twin Squirrel	5479	F-GJAJ F-WYMH	3. 8.95	Avon & Somerset Constabulary & Gloucestershire Constabulary *(Op Western Counties Police)*	Filton	14.10.04T
G-OATS	Piper PA-38-112 Tomahawk	38-78A0007	N9659N	14. 3.78	Truman Aviation Ltd	Nottingham	28. 9.03T
G-OATG	Advanced Technologies AT-10	1001		29.11.01	Advanced Technologies Group Ltd	Cardington	
G-OATV	Cameron V-77 HAB	2149		14. 2.90	W.G.Andrews	Plymouth	23.10.93A
G-OAVA	Robinson R22 Beta	3303		8. 3.02	J.G.M.McDiarmid	Bodmin	2. 4.05T
G-OAWS	Cameron Colt 77A HAB	4340		23. 4.98	Auto Windscreens Ltd	Chesterfield	23. 6.03A
G-OBAK	Piper PA-28R-201T Turbo Cherokee Arrow III	28R-7703054	D-EFOR N1146Q	27. 8.02	D R Freeth t/a DP Group Aviation	Popham	22. 9.05
G-OBAL	Mooney M.20J (201LM)	24-1601	N56569	27.11.86	Britannia Airways Ltd *(Op Britannia Flying Club)*	Luton	3. 4.05T
G-OBAM	Bell 206B-3 JetRanger III	4511	N6379U	25. 5.99	Cherwell Tobacco Ltd	(Whitchurch)	4 .7.05T
G-OBAN	SAN Jodel D.140B Mousquetaire II	80	G-ATSU F-BKSA	20. 2.92	S.R.Cameron	North Connel, Oban	21. 5.O4
G-OBAX	Thruster T600N 450 Jab	0051-T600N-053		12. 7.01	J.D.Smith t/a Baxby Airsports Club	Baxby Manor, Husthwaite	14. 7.02P
G-OBAY	Bell 206B JetRanger II	276	G-BVWR C-GNXQ/N4714R	27. 7.98	CI Motors Ltd *(Crashed 5.1.01: wreck noted 4.01) (New CofR2.03)*	(Preston)	6. 3.03T
G-OBBC	Colt 90A HAB	1358		11. 5.89	R.A. & M.A.Riley *"Beeb"* *(BBC in the Midlands titles)*	Bromsgrove	16. 7.01A
G-OBBJ	Boeing 737-8DR	32777	N379BJ	29.11.01	Multiflight Ltd	Leeds-Bradford	28.11.04
G-OBBO	Cessna 182S Skylane	18280534	N7274Z	8. 6.99	F.Friedenberg	Denham	21. 6.05
G-OBBY	Robinson R44	0939		4.12.00	P.C.& J.A.Twigg *(Noted dismantled 5.02)*	Wellesbourne Mountford	2. 1.04T
G-OBDA	Diamond DA-20-A1 Katana	10260		2. 7.98	Oscar Papa Ltd	Wolverhampton	30. 7.04T
G-OBEI	SOCATA TB-20O Tobago XL	2096	F-OIUX	26. 6.02	C.A.Hawkins	(Wokingham)	26. 6.05T
G-OBEN	Cessna 152 II	15281856	G-NALI G-BHVM/N67477	16. 8.93	Airbase Aircraft Ltd	Shoreham	29. 3.03T
G-OBET	Sky 77-24 HAB	178		22. 2.00	Flying Pictures Ltd *(Victor Chandler titles)*	Chilbolton	22. 2.01A
G-OBEV	Europa Aviation Europa *(Rotax 912S) (Monowheel u/c)*	188 & PFA 247-12813		3. 2.98	M.B.Hill & N.I.Wingfield *(Current status unknown)*	(Dursley)	
G-OBFC	Piper PA-28-161 Warrior III	2816118	N9252X	15. 7.96	Bflying Ltd *(Op Bournemouth Flying Club)*	Bournemouth	4. 8.05T
G-OBFS	Piper PA-28-161 Warrior III	2842039	N41274	4.12.98	Plane Talking Ltd	Elstree	3.12.04T
G-OBGC	SOCATA TB-20 Trinidad	1898		13. 5.99	Bidford Airfield Ltd	Bidford	29. 5.05T
G-OBHD	Short SD.3-60 Var.100	SH.3714	G-BNDK G-OBHD/G-BNDK/G-14-3714	20. 1.87	Emerald Airways Ltd	Liverpool	5. 3.03T
G-OBHI	Robinson R44 Clipper	1256		13. 9.02	Barnard Hamilton Aviation Ltd	(Wokingham)	1.10.05T
G-OBHL	Aérospatiale AS355F2 Twin Squirrel	5364	G-HARO G-DAFT/G-BNNN	7. 4.00	Richer Jet Ltd	Stapleford	20. 1.06T
G-OBIB	Colt 120A HAB	4229		9. 1.98	The Aerial Display Co Ltd *(Michelin titles)*	Looe	25 .1.02A
G-OBIL	Robinson R22 Beta	0792		10. 5.88	C.A.Rosenberg	Abergavenny	24. 8.03T
G-OBIO	Robinson R22 Beta	1402	N7724M	29. 6.98	A.E.Churchill	(Huntingdon)	7. 8.04
G-OBJB	Lindstrand LBL 90A HAB	640		12.11.99	B.J.Bower	Andover	15. 1.03A
G-OBJP	Pegasus Quantum 15-912	7847		29. 8.01	B.J.Partridge	Sutton Meadows, Ely	28. 2.03P
G-OBJT	Europa Aviation Europa *(Wilksch WAM-120) (Tri-gear u/c)*	055 & PFA 247-12623	G-MUZO	16.11.00	B.J.Tarmar	(Fordingbridge)	
G-OBLC	Beech 76 Duchess	ME-249	N6635R	3. 6.87	Pridenote Ltd	Sturgate	12.12.05T
G-OBLK	Short SD.3-60 Var.100	SH.3712	G-BNDI G-OBLK/G-BNDI/G-14-3712	20. 1.87	BAC Express Airlines Ltd *"City of Liverpool"*	(Horley)	11. 2.03T
G-OBLN	de Havilland DH.115 Vampire T.11 *(Regd with Nacelle No.DHP.48700)*	15664	XE956	14. 9.95	De Havilland Aviation Ltd *(As "XE956") (On rebuild 1.01)*	(St Mary Hill, Bridgend)	
G-OBLU	Cameron H-34 HAB	4914		4. 8.00	Blu SpA .	Rome, Italy	15. 7.03A
G-OBMI	Mainair Blade	1289-0601-7 & W1084		19. 6.01	I.G.Webster & P.Clark	(Crewe)	26. 7.03P
G-OBMM	Boeing 737-4Y0	25177		4.12.91	British Midland Airways Ltd	East Midlands	6. 4.05T
G-OBMP	Boeing 737-3Q8	24963		8. 1.92	British Midland Airways Ltd *"baby ET"* *(Op bmibaby)*	East Midlands	19. 3.05T
G-OBMS	Reims/Cessna F172N Skyhawk II	F17201584	OO-BWA (OO-HWA)/D-EBYX	16. 4.84	D.Beverley, A.J.& A.P.Ransome	Sherburn-in-Elmet	3. 7.05
G-OBMW	Grumman-American AA-5 Traveler	AA5-0805	G-BDFV	4. 7.79	Fretcourt Ltd	Sherburn-in-Elmet	3. 4.03
G-OBNA	Piper PA-34-220T Seneca V	3449002	N9281D (N338DB)	25. 5.00	Palmair Ltd	Elstree	31. 5.03
G-OBPL	Embraer EMB-110P2 Bandeirante	110.199	PH-FVB G-OEAB/G-BKWB/G-CHEVI/(PT-GLR)	27.11.98	BAC Leasing Ltd	Southend	12.12.01T
					(Open store w/o engines 2.03) (Fictitious marks 'G-OBWB' on starboard side 2.03)		
G-OBRI	Medway EclipseR	171/149		25.10.01	B.D.Campbell	(Maidstone)	
G-OBRY	Cameron N-180 HAB	3010		1. 3.93	A.C.K.Rawson & J.J.Rudoni *(New owner 4.02)*	(Stafford)	11. 3.03T
G-OBSF*	American Aviation AA-5A Cheetah	AA5A-0374	G-ODSF G-BEUW/N6158A	21. 9.88	Not known	Elstree	
					(Crashed on landing Blackbushe 8.2.97: repaired & re-regd as G-ODAE 11.97: cancelled [no date]: wreck identified as G-OBSF 5.00 but see G-ODAE)		
G-OBTS	Cameron C-80 HAB	3589		18. 4.95	Bedford Tyre Service (Chichester) Ltd *"Hi-Q"*	Chichester	14. 7.03A
G-OBUN	Cameron A-250 HAB	4711		29. 2.00	A.C.K.Rawson & J.J.Rudoni	(Stafford)	14 .1.03T
G-OBUS*	Piper PA-28-181 Archer II	28-7990242	G-BMTT N3002K	4. 8.86	Northbrook College	Shoreham	14. 8.89T
					(Crashed Goodwood 18.4.89: cancelled 30.8.89 as destroyed: fuselage used as instructional airframe 3.00)		
G-OBWD*	British Aircraft Corporation One-Eleven 518FG	BAC.203	G-BDAE G-AXMI	14. 1.93	British World Airlines *(Open store 2.03)*	Southend	14. 4.02T
G-OBWP	British Aerospace ATP	2051	G-BTPO G-5-051	8.10.99	Trident Aviation Leasing Services (Jersey) Ltd *(Noted for freight conversion 2.03)*	Exeter	17.10.02T
G-OBWR	British Aerospace ATP	205	G-BUWP G-11-053	8.10.99	Trident Jet (Jersey) Ltd	Woodford	20. 4.03T
G-OBYB	Boeing 767-304ER	28040		17. 5.96	Britannia Airways Ltd *"Bobby Moore OBE"*	Luton	16. 5.05T
G-OBYC	Boeing 767-304ER	28041	D-AGYC G-OBYC/D-AGYC/G-OBYC	21. 5.96	Britannia Airways Ltd *"Roy Castle OBE"*	Luton	7.11.03T

Reg	Type	C/n	Prev ID	Date	Owner/Operator	Location	Date2
G-OBYD	Boeing 767-304ER	28042	SE-DZG G-OBYD	4. 3.97	Britannia Airways Ltd	Luton	2. 5.04T
G-OBYE	Boeing 767-304ER	28979	D-AGYE G-OBYE	26. 2.98	Britannia Airways Ltd *"Bill Travers"*	Luton	28.10.05T
G-OBYF	Boeing 767-304ER	28208	D-AGYF G-OBYF	8. 6.98	Britannia Airways Ltd	Luton	30. 4.04T
G-OBYG	Boeing 767-304ER	29137		13. 1.99	Britannia Airways Ltd	Luton	12. 1.05T
C-OBYH	Boeing 767-304ER	28883	SE-DZO D-AGYH/G-OBYH	4. 2.99	Britannia Airways Ltd	Luton	24. 4.05T
G-OBYI	Boeing 767-304ER	29138		1. 2.00	Britannia Airways Ltd	Luton	31. 1.06T
G-OBYJ	Boeing 767-304ER	29384		20. 2.00	Britannia Airways Ltd	Luton	18. 2.03T
G-OBYT	Agusta-Bell 206A JetRanger	8237	G-BNRC Oman AF 601	30. 1.95	R.J.Everett	(Sproughton)	12. 7.03T
G-OCAD	Sequoia Falco F8L (Lycoming IO-320)	PFA 100-12114		8. 6.92	C.W.Garrard tr Falco Flying Group	Leicester	19.12.03P
G-OCAM	Gulfstream AA-5A Cheetah	AA5A-0741	G-BLHO OO-RTJ/OO-HRN	24. 3.94	Plane Talking Ltd *(Op Cabair)*	Cranfield	11.10.03T
G-OCAR	Colt 77A HAB	1099		6. 8.87	S.C.J.Derham *"Toyota"*	(Bridgnorth)	25. 8.00A
G-OCBI	Schweizer 269C-1	0139	N86G	14. 8.02	Oxford Aviation Services Ltd	Oxford	26. 9.05T
G-OCBS	Lindstrand LBL 210A HAB	602		21. 7.99	G.Binder	Sonnenbuhl, Germany	11. 6.03A
G-OCDS	Aviamilano F.8L Falco Srs.II	114	G-VEGL OO-MEN/I-VEGL	6. 9.85	C.O.P.Barth	(The Netherlands)	21.11.05
G-OCEA	Short SD.3-60 Var.100	SH.3762	N162CN N162SB/G-BRMX	26.10.95	BAC Express Airlines Ltd	(Horley)	26. 3.03T
G-OCFC	Robin R2160	374		21. 6.02	Cornwall Flying Club Ltd	Bodmin	11. 7.05T
G-OCHM	Robinson R44 Raven	1055		4. 5.01	Westleigh Developments Ltd	Whetstone, Leics	30. 5.04T
G-OCJK	Schweizer Hughes 269C (300C)	S.1294	N69A	10.12.87	P.Crawley *(New CofR 5.02)*	(Shipley)	27. 5.00
G-OCJW	Cessna 182R Skylane II	18268316	G-SJGM N357WC	18. 4.97	C.J.Ward	Wellesbourne Mountford	24.10.04
G-OCMJ	Aérospatiale SA341G Gazelle 1	1301	G-HTPS G-BRNI/YU-HBI	5.10.01	Gazelle Investments Ltd	(Belize)	24. 7.03
G-OCMM	Agusta A109A II	7347	G-BXCB F-GJSH/G-ISEB/G-IADT/G-HBCA	20. 3.01	Castle Air Charters Ltd	Trebrown, Liskeard	28. 4.03T
G-OCOV	Robinson R22 Beta	3217		23. 5.01	Flight Training Ltd	Coventry	14. 6.04T
G-OCPC	Reims/Cessna FA152 Aerobat	FA15200343		20. 1.78	Westward Airways (Lands End) Ltd	St.Just	12. 8.05T
G-OCPF	Piper PA-32-300 Cherokee Six	32-7640082	G-BOCH N9292K	22. 9.97	Syndicate Clerical Services Ltd	Exeter	8. 9.03T
G-OCRI	Colomban MC-15 Cri-Cri	524 & PFA 133-12288		24. 6.92	M.J.J.Dunning *(Amended CofR 8.02)*	(Stockport)	
G-OCST	Agusta-Bell 206B-3 JetRanger III	8694	N39AH VR-CDG/G-BMKM	14.12.94	J.R.Fuller	(Dorking)	8. 1.04T
G-OCTI	Piper PA-32-260 Cherokee Six	32-288	G-BGZX 9XR-MP/5Y-ADH/N3427W	26. 7.88	D.G.Williams	Blackbushe	14. 5.04T
G-OCUB	Piper J-3C-90 Cub (L-4J-PI) *(Frame No.13078)*	13248	OO-JOZ PH-NKC/PH-UCH/45-4508	21. 4.81	C.A.Foss & P.A.Brook tr Florence Flying Group *"Florence"*	Shoreham	14. 2.03P

(Official c/n of 13215 is 45-4475/PH-UCW and was rebuilt as PH-UCH)

Reg	Type	C/n	Prev ID	Date	Owner/Operator	Location	Date2
G-ODAC	Reims/Cessna F152 II	F15201824	G-BITG	19.12.96	T.M. & M.L.Jones *(Op Derby Aero Club)*	Eggington, Derby	9. 8.04T

(Rebuilt with cockpit/front fuselage of G-BITG 6.96)

Reg	Type	C/n	Prev ID	Date	Owner/Operator	Location	Date2
G-ODAD	Colt 77A HAB	2001		20. 2.91	K.Meehan *"Odyssey"*	Much Wenlock	20. 7.03A
G-ODAE*	American Aviation AA-5A Cheetah	AA5A-0374	G-OBSF G-ODSF/G-BEUW/N6158A	17.11.97	Not known	Elstree	

(Cancelled as WFU 14.9.98: wreck noted 5.00: appears that restoration as G-ODAE did not proceed as second fuselage abandoned alongside G-OBSF qv)

Reg	Type	C/n	Prev ID	Date	Owner/Operator	Location	Date2
G-ODAK	Piper PA-28-236 Dakota	28-7911162	D-EXMA OH-SMO/N386WT/N22328	29. 2.0	Airways Aero Associations Ltd	Booker	16. 3.03T
G-ODAM	Gulfstream AA-5A Cheetah	AA5A-0818	G-FOUX N8488H	16.11.88	Stop & Go Ltd	Elstree	22. 3.02T

(Lost power on take-off Biggin Hill 25.1.02 & force landed in nearby field, breaking off n/wheel & damaging prop, engine, wing & fuselage: dumped 8.02)

Reg	Type	C/n	Prev ID	Date	Owner/Operator	Location	Date2
G-ODAT	Aero L-29 Delfin	194227	ES-YLV Estonian AF/Soviet AF	28. 7.99	Graniteweb Ltd	North Weald	15.12.03P
G-ODBN	Lindstrand Flowers SS HAB	389		22. 5.96	Magical Adventures Ltd *"Sainsbury's Flowers"* Oswestry		12.10.03A
G-ODCS	Robinson R22 Beta-II	2828		19. 5.98	V.E.Nalbantis	Panshanger	1. 6.04T
G-ODDY	Lindstrand LBL-105A HAB	042		15. 7.93	P.& T.Huckle	Oakwood	1. 6.03A
G-ODEB	Cameron A-250 HAB	4328		23. 4.98	A.Derbyshire	(Stafford)	25. 7.03T
G-ODEE	Van's RV-6	PFA 181-13173		14. 4.00	D.Powell	Lichfield	9. 6.03P
G-ODEL*	Falconar F-11-3	PFA 32-10219		14. 8.78	G F Brummell	Jubilee Farm, Bedford	17. 7.89P

(Damaged Little Gransden 4.9.88: cancelled 15.11.00 by CAA: on rebuild 2000)

Reg	Type	C/n	Prev ID	Date	Owner/Operator	Location	Date2
G-ODEN	Piper PA-28-161 Cadet	2841282	N92004	22.11.89	J.Appleton, t/a Holmes Rentals *(Op Denham School of Flying)*	Denham	18.12.04T
G-ODES	Robinson R44 Astro	0722		9. 2.00	Eagle Distribution Ltd	Bourn	2. 3.03
G-ODGS	Jabiru Jabiru UL	PFA 274A-13472		2. 8.99	D.G.Salt	(Ashbourne)	
G-ODHG	Robinson R44 Raven	1024		19. 4.01	Driver Hire Group Services Ltd	Leeds-Bradford	22. 4.04T
G-ODIN	Mudry CAARP CAP-10B	192	F-GDTH	16.12.93	R.P.W.Steele	Sandown	11. 4.04T
G-ODJD	Raj Hamsa X'Air 582	559 & BMAA/HB/151		25. 4.01	D.J.Davis	(Bideford)	4. 8.03P
G-ODJG	Europa Aviation Europa (Rotax 912S) *(Monowheel u/c)*	167 & PFA 247-12889		3. 5.96	D.J.Goldsmith *(F/f 30.8.97)*	(Edenbridge)	
G-ODJH	Mooney M.20C Ranger	690083	G-BMLH N9293V	19. 1.93	R.M.Schweitzer	Hilversum, The Netherlands	15. 9.05
G-ODLY	Cessna 310J	310J0077	G-TUBY G-ASZZ/N3077L	21. 3.88	Card Tech Ltd	Booker	18. 6.03
G-ODMC	Aérospatiale AS350B1 Ecureuil	2200	G-BPVF	17.10.89	D.M.Coombs t/a DM Leasing Co	Denham	25.10.04T
G-ODNH	Schweizer 269C-1 (300)	0112	N41S	5. 9.00	DNH Helicopters Ltd *(Op Kent Helicopters)*	Biggin Hill	14. 9.03T
G-ODOC	Robinson R44 Astro	0372		27. 8.97	Gas & Air Ltd	Booker	12.10.03T
G-ODOD	MD Helicopters MD 600N	RN052	N3204S	5.10.00	HPM Investments Ltd	Bournemouth	12.10.03T
G-ODOG	Piper PA-28R-200 Cherokee Arrow II	28R-7235197	EI-BPB G-BAAR/N11C	2. 8.96	Advanced Investments Ltd	Sibson	22.10.02

Reg	Type	C/n	Prev id	Date	Owner/Operator	Location	Status
G-ODOT	Robinson R22 Beta-II	2779		23. 1.98	Farm Aviation Ltd	Booker	8. 3.04T
G-ODSK	Boeing 737-37Q	28537		23. 7.97	British Midland Airways Ltd	East Midlands	27. 7.03T
					(Op bmibaby) "baby dragon fly"		
G-ODTW	Europa Aviation Europa	215 & PFA 247-12890		7. 9.95	D.T.Walters	(Longfield, Kent)	
	(Monowheel u/c)				*(Current status unknown)*		
G-ODUB*	Embraer EMB-110 P1 Bandeirante	110.217	PH-FVC	7. 2.00	Comed Aviation Ltd	Leeds-Bradford	6.2.01T
			G-BNIX/N8536J		*(Cancelled 9.10.02 by CAA)*		
G-ODUS	Boeing 737-36Q	28659	D-ADBX	17. 3.98	Go Fly Ltd *(Easyjet titles)*	Stansted	15. 4.04T
G-ODVB	CFM Shadow DD	300-DD	G-MGDB	3.11.98	D.V.Brunt	Plaistows Farm, St Albans	24. 4.03P
	(Rotax 582)						
G-OEAC	Mooney M.20J (201)	24-1636	N57656	16. 6.88	D.Teece & R.Hodges t/a DR Airgroup	Nottingham	5. 4.03
G-OEAT	Robinson R22 Beta	0650	G-RACH	8. 1.98	C.Y.O.Seeds Ltd	(Didcot)	24. 1.05T
G-OECH	Gulfstream AA-5A Cheetah	AA5A-0836	G-BKBE	24. 1.89	Plane Talking Ltd	Cranfield	10. 5.03T
			(G-BJVN)/N26952		*(Op London School of Flying)*		
G-OEDB	Piper PA-38-112 Tomahawk	38-79A0167	G-BGGJ	9. 5.89	Metropolitan Services Ltd	Hawarden	15. 6.03T
			N9694N				
G-OEDP	Cameron N-77 HAB	2189		28.12.89	M.J.Betts "Eastern Counties Press"	Norwich	12. 6.01A
G-OEGG*	Cameron Egg 65SS HAB	2140		4.12.89	Virgin Airship & Balloon Co Ltd	Telford	25. 3.00A
	(Cadbury's Creme Egg shape)				"Cadburys Creme Egg" *(Cancelled 30.12.02 as wfu)*		
G-OEGL	Christen Eagle II	001	N46JH	12. 1.98	R.Dauncey,	Shoreham	11. 4.03P
	(Lycoming IO-360)				tr The Eagle Flight Syndicate		
G-OEJA	Cessna 500 Citation	500-0264	G-BWFL	2. 8.96	Eurojet Aviation Ltd	Birmingham	20. 7.03T
			F-GLJA/N205FM/N5264J				
G-OELD	Pegasus Quantum 15-912	7765		20.12.00	T H Filmer	Newtownards, Co.Down	16. 3.03P
G-OERR	Lindstrand LBL-60A HAB	469		30. 6.97	Lindstrand Balloons Ltd	Oswestry	12. 4.03
G-OERX	Cameron O-65 HAB	4004		23. 1.96	R.Roehsler	Vienna, Austria	27. 2.97A
G-OEST	British Aerospace Jetstream Srs.3202	836		18. 6.99	Air Kilroe Ltd *(Op Eastern Airways)*	Humberside	20 .6.03T
			OH-JAD				
			N836JX/C-FGLH/G-31-836/N332QJ/G-31-836				
G-OESY	Flying K Enterprises Easy Raider J22	0005 & BMAA/HB/193		16.11.01	P.C.Bell	(Maidstone)	16. 6.03P
G-OETI	Bell 206B-3 Jet Ranger III	2533	G-RMIE	23. 7.02	Elec-Track Installations Ltd	(Hythe)	5.12.04T
			G-BPIE/N327WM				
G-OEWA	de Havilland DH.104 Dove 8	04528	G-DDCD	10. 6.98	D.C.Hunter	Kemble	AC
			G-ARUM		*(On rebuild 2001 for East West Airlines)*		
G-OEYE	Rans S-10 Sakota	PFA 194-11955		25. 4.91	I.M.J.Mitchell	Otherton, Cannock	8.10.03P
	(Rotax 582-2V)						
G-OEZI	Flying K Enterprises Easy Raider J22	0007 & BMAA/HB/216		31. 5.02	M.A.Claydon	(Farnham)	
G-OEZY	Europa Aviation Europa	042 & PFA 247-12590		8. 8.95	A.W.Wakefield	Conington	22. 6.03P
	(Rotax 912UL) (Monowheel u/c)				*(F/f 13.6.96)*		
G-OFAS	Robinson R22 Beta	0559		17. 6.86	J.L.Leonard t/a Findon Air Services	Shoreham	25. 4.05T
G-OFBJ	Thunder Ax7-77A HAB	2050		2. 9.91	N.D.Hicks "Blue Horizon"	Alton	25. 9.99A
G-OFBU	Comco Ikarus C42 FB UK	PFA 322-13653		28. 8.01	Ikarus Ultralights Ltd	Old Sarum	10.12.03P
G-OFCH	Agusta-Bell 206B JetRanger II	8337	HB-XUI	15. 5.00	Fleet Coast Helicopters Ltd	Shoreham	11. 7.03T
			G-BKDA/LN-OQX				
			(Rolled over & main rotor struck ground Morn Farm, Chickerell 4.1.02: damaged beyond repair)				
G-OFCM	Reims/Cessna F172L	F17200839	G-AZUN	21.10.81	FCM Aviation Ltd	Guernsey	24. 4.03
			(OO-FCB)				
G-OFER	Piper PA-18-150 Super Cub	18-7709058	N83509	29.12.89	Mary S.W.Meagher	Shenington	11. 5.03
G-OFFA	Pietenpol Aircamper	PFA 47-13181		3.11.98	D.J. Street tr Offa Group	(Chinnor)	
G-OFIL	Robinson R44 Astro	0555		15. 1.99	W. & W.Potter Ltd	(Sowerby Bridge)	10. 4.05T
G-OFIT	SOCATA TB-10 Tobago	938	G-BRIU	11. 9.89	P.Hennessy tr GFI Aviation Group	White Waltham	20. 3.05T
G-OFJC	Eiri Pik-20E	20291	OH-641	19. 3.93	M.J.Aldridge	Tibenham	3. 6.02
G-OFLG	SOCATA TB-10 Tobago	11	G-JMWT	11.12.91	Westward Airways (Lands End) Ltd	St.Just	2. 8.01T
			F-GBHF		*(Dismantled 4.02)*		
G-OFLT	Embraer EMB-110P1 Bandeirante	110.211	G-MOBL	11.12.90	Flightline Ltd	Southend	1. 1.02T
			(G-BGCS)/PT-GMD		*(Open store 2.03)*		
G-OFLY	Cessna 210M Centurion II	21061600	(D-EBYM)	13.10.79	A.P.Mothew	Southend	3. 6.04
			N732LQ				
G-OFMB	Rand Robinson KR-2	7808	N5337X	29. 4.97	F M & S I Burden	(Gloucester)	
	(Built M.A.Shepard)						
G-OFOA	British Aerospace BAe 146 Srs.100	E1006	G-BKMN	3. 3.98	Formula One Adminstration Ltd	Biggin Hill	14. 7.03
			EI-COF/SE-DRH/G-BKMN/G-ODAN				
G-OFOM	British Aerospace BAe 146 Srs.100	E1144	N3206T	16. 3.00	Formula One Management Ltd	Biggin Hill	2.10.03
			PK-DTA/G-BSLP/(PK-DTA)/G-6-144/G-11-144/(G-BRLM)				
G-OFOX	Denney Kitfox	PFA 172-11523		1.11.89	P.R.Skeels	Barton	
G-OFRA	Boeing 737-36Q	29327		5. 5.98	Go Fly Ltd *(Easyjet titles)*	Stansted	17. 5.03T
G-OFRB	Everett Gyroplane Srs.2 (Rotax 503)	006	(G-BLSR)	7. 8.85	M.P.James	(Burton Joyce)	14.10.03P
G-OFRT	Lockheed L.188CF Electra	1075	N347HA	29.10.91	Dart Group plc	Coventry	28.10.01T
			N423MA/N23AF/N64405/SE-FGC/N5537 *(Corrosion found and WFU - noted 4.02)*				
G-OFRY	Cessna 152 II	15281420	G-BPHS	8. 2.93	Devon School of Flying Ltd	Dunkeswell	8. 1.05T
			N49971				
G-OFTI	Piper PA-28-140 Cherokee Cruiser	28-7325201	G-BRKU	11. 6.90	P.E.Richardson	King's Farm, Thurrock	8.10.05T
			N15926				
G-OGAN	Europa Aviation Europa	100 & PFA 247-12734		28. 7.94	B.W.Rendall tr G-OGAN Group	Wombleton	9. 4.03P
	(Rotax 912) (Tri-gear u/c)				*(F/f 19.11.99)*		
G-OGAR	PZL SZD-45A Ogar	B-601	SP-0004	29. 1.90	N.C.Grayson	Boscombe Down	9. 6.00
G-OGAS*	Westland WG.30 Srs.100	008	G-17-1	23. 3.83	Westland Helicopters Ltd	Yeovil	19. 5.88T
			G-OGAS/G-BKNW				
			(Cancelled 3.6.92 as WFU: dumped 4.00 in BA Helicopters c/s (navy boom/tail, white cabin & red diagonal stripe))				
G-OGAV	Lindstrand LBL-240A HAB	074		4. 2.94	Airborne Balloon Management Ltd	Tonbridge	22. 6.04T
G-OGAZ	Aérospatiale SA341G Gazelle 1	1274	G-OCJR	12. 1.94	I.M. & S.M.Graham t/a Killochries Fold	Edinburgh	22. 2.04T
			G-BRGS/F-GEQA/N341SG/(N341P)N341SG/N47295 *(Op Forth Helicopters Ltd)*				
G-OGBB	Boeing 737-34S	29108		27. 1.98	GB Airways Ltd *(Colum t/s)*	Gatwick	26. 1.04T

Regn	Type	C/n	Prev id	Date	Owner/Operator	Base	Date
G-OGBC	Boeing 737-34S	29109	N1787B	26. 2.98	GB Airways Ltd (Koguty Lowickie t/s)	Gatwick	25. 2.04T
G-OGBD	Boeing 737-3L9	27833	OY-MAR	16. 3.98	GB Airways Ltd (Ndebele Martha t/s)	Gatwick	12. 3.04T
			D-ADBJ/OY-MAR				
G-OGBE	Boeing 737-3L9	27834	OY-MAS	24.11.98	GB Airways Ltd (Crossing Borders t/s)	Gatwick	17.12.04T
G-OGCA	Piper PA-28-161 Warrior II	28-8016262	N8154L	16. 8.90	Cardiff-Wales Aviation Services Ltd	Cardiff	23. 8.05T
G-OGEE	Christen Pitts S-2B Special	5200	OH-SKY	1. 6.95	P.M.Ambrose	Popham	28. 6.04T
	(Lycoming AEIO-540)						
G-OGEM	Piper PA-28-181 Archer II	28-8190226	N83816	10. 3.88	GEM Rewinds Ltd	Coventry	24. 5.03T
G-OGEO	Aérospatiale SA341G Gazelle 1	1417	G-BXJK	28. 1.02	MW Helicopters Ltd	Stapleford	17. 8.03
			F-GEHC/N341AT/N49536				
G-OGES	Enstrom 280FX Shark	2078	G-CBYL	15.11.02	G.N.Ratcliffe	Barton	10.11.05T
			HB-XAJ				
G-OGET*	Piper PA-39 Twin Comanche C/R	39-87	G-AYXY	14. 3.83	P.G.Kitchingman	White Waltham	12 9.05
			N8930Y		(Cancelled 17.1.03 by CAA)		
G-OGHH	Enstrom 480	5015		14. 2.96	Silver Lining Finance SA	(Luxembourg)	12. 3.05T
G-OGJM	Cameron C-80 HAB	4869		21.11.00	G.J.Madelin	(Farnham)	22.10.02A
G-OGJP	Hughes 369E	0512E	N685F	23. 1.01	Motortrak Ltd	(Thames Ditton)	30. 1.04T
			N5223X				
G-OGJS	Rutan Puffer Cozy	PFA 159-11169		27. 1.89	G.J.Stamper	Carlisle	14. 9.98P
	(Lycoming O-360)						
G-OGOA	Aérospatiale AS350B Ecureuil	1745	G-PLMD	16. 1.90	Lomas Helicopters Ltd Lake	Bideford	20. 6.05T
			G-NIAL				
G-OGOB	Schweizer Hughes 269C (300C)	S.1315	G-GLEE	2.10.90	Kingfisher Helicopters Ltd	Longdown	11. 4.05T
			G-BRUW/N86G				
G-OGOG	Robinson R22 Beta	1475	G-TILL	2. 7.97	D.Thomas t/a Lake Services	Exeter	9.10.02T
G-OGOH	Robinson R22 Beta-II	2738	G-IPDM	25.11.02	Lomas Brothers Ltd	(Bideford)	15. 5.04T
			G-OMSG		t/a Lomas Helicopters		
G-OGOS	Everett Gyroplane	004	7Q-YES	30. 7.84	N.A.Seymour	(Norwich)	12. 9.90
	(Volkswagen 1834)		G-OGOS				
G-OGPN	Cassutt Special	PFA 126-10778	G-OMFI	1. 5.01	S.Alexander	Bidford	28. 8.02P
	(Continental C90)		G-BKCH				
G-OGRK	Aérospatiale AS355F1 Twin Squirrel	5185	G-BWZC	26. 3.99	Anglia Aviation plc	(Ipswich)	8. 2.03T
			(G-MOBZ)/N107KF/N5799R				
G-OGSA	Jabiru Jabiru UL	300? & PFA 274A-13540		10. 2.00	G.J.Slater & W.Moultrie Lower Upham Farm, Chiseldon		11. 3.03P
	(Jabiru 2200A)						
G-OGSS	Lindstrand LBL 120A HAB	683		19. 5.00	R.Klarer	Erbach, Germany	6. 8.03A
G-OGTS	Air Command 532 Elite	0432 & PFA G/104-1125		19.12.88	GTS Engineering (Coventry) Ltd	Coventry	1.10.90P
	(Rotax 532)				t/a GTS Cars		
G-OGTX	Cessna T310R	310R1209	N37600	10.12.01	I.M.& S.M.Graham	Perth	16.1.05T
G-OHAC	Reims/Cessna F182Q Skylane	F18200048	D-ENCM	11. 7.01	The RAF Halton Aeroplane Club	RAF Halton	8. 8.04T
G-OHAJ	Boeing 737-36Q	29141		2. 6.98	Go Fly Ltd (Easyjet titles)	Stansted	30. 8.03T
G-OHAL	Pietenpol Aircamper	PFA 47-12840		25.11.96	H.C.Danby	(Sudbury)	
G-OHCP	Aérospatiale AS355F1 Twin Squirrel	5249	G-BTVS	14. 3.94	Plane Talking Ltd	Elstree	20. 2.04T
			G-STVE/G-TOFF/G-BKJX				
G-OHEA*	Hawker Siddeley HS.125 Srs.3B/RA	25144	G-AVRG	25.11.86	Cranfield University	Cranfield	7. 8.92T
			G-5-12		(Cancelled 23.6.94 as WFU) (Fuselage dumped 6.02 as "G-DHEA")		
G-OHFT	Robinson R22 Beta	1040	G-TYPO	18.12.01	Heliflight (UK) Ltd	Wolverhampton	14. 3.05T
			G-JBWI				
G-OHHI	Bell 206L-1 LongRanger II	45552	G-BWYJ	30. 4.98	Big Heli-Charter Ltd	Manston	6. 3.03T
			D-HOBD/D-HGAD				
G-OHIG*	Embraer EMB.110-P1 Bandeirante	110.235	G-OPPP	29..3 95	Air Salvage International	Alton	26. 5.98T
			XC-DAI/PT-SAB (Cancelled 11.4.01 by CAA) (Fuselage noted 4.02 at Air Salvage International yard)				
G-OHKS	Pegasus Quantum 15(HKS)	7505		24. 3.99	York Microlight Centre Ltd	Rufforth	8. 5.03T
	(HKS 700E s/n 99030A)				(C/n checked and confirms original allocation)		
G-OHMS	Aérospatiale AS355F1 Twin Squirrel	5194	N367E	15. 6.90	South Western Electricity plc	Farnborough	23. 6.05T
					(WPD Electricity titles)		
G-OHRH	Lindstrand LBL 150A HAB	754		12. 2.01	A.Holly t/a Exclusive Ballooning	Bristol	5. 2.03T
					(The Prince's Trust titles)		
G-OHSA	Cameron N-77 HAB	4269		2. 2.98	D.N. & L.J.Close (HSA Healthcare titles)	Andover	15. 4.01A
G-OHSL	Robinson R22 Beta	0967	G-BPNF	4. 7.01	Astons of Kempsey (Holdings) Ltd	Shobdon	24. 8.04T
			N8029Y				
G-OHVA	Mainair Blade 912	1189-0199-7 & W992		6.11.98	M C Metatidj	(La Baule, France)	13. 3.03P
G-OHWV	Raj Hamsa X'Air 582	474 & BMAA/HB/121		18.11.99	H.W.Vasey	(Newquay)	13. 5.03P
G-OIAN*	Morane Saulnier MS.880B Rallye Club	5116	PH-MSB	17. 5.82	Not known	Sewell, Dunstable, Beds	
					(Did not aspire to a CofA & cancelled 2.9.91 by CAA) (Noted dumped 5.01)		
G-OIBM	Rockwell Commander 114	14295	G-BLVZ	14.10.88	I.Rosewell	Blackbushe	4. 7.03
			SX-AJO/N4957W				
G-OIBO	Piper PA-28-180 Cherokee C	28-3794	G-AVAZ	21. 1.87	Britannia Airways Ltd	Wellesbourne Mountford	26. 3.03T
			N11C				
G-OICV*	Robinson R22 Beta	0991	G-BPWH	11. 2.93	Helicentre Ltd	Blackpool	18. 3.01
					(Damaged Blackpool 18.7.99: cancelled 19.11.99 as WFU) (Wreck stored 12.01)		
G-OIDW	Cessna F150G	F150-0188	N70163	24. 4.90	T.S.Sheridan-McGinnitty	Sherlowe	24. 5.03
	(Built Reims Aviation SA)		D-EGTI				
G-OIFM	Cameron Dude 90SS HAB	2841		18. 6.92	Magical Adventures Ltd	West Bloomfield, Mi., USA	29. 5.99A
	(Radio One FM DJ's Head & Earphones)				"Cool Dude"		
G-OIIO	Robinson R22 Beta	2444	G-ULAB	27. 3.02	J.W.Lanchbury	Shobdon	21. 9.03T
			N8311Z				
G-OIMC	Cessna 152 II	152-85506	N93521	15. 5.87	East Midlands Flying School Ltd	East Midlands	26. 6.03T
G-OINK	Piper J-3C-65 Cub	12613	G-BILD	22. 3.83	A.R.Harding	Newton Farm, Sudbury	19. 7.99P
	(L-4J-PI) (Frame No.12443)		G-KERK/F-BBQD/44-80317				
G-OINV	British Aerospace BAe 146 Srs.300	E3171	VH-EWI	17. 2.00	British Airways Citiexpress Ltd	Inverness	15. 5.03T
			G-6-171/VH-EWI/G-6-171		"Chatham Historic Dockyard"		
G-OIOZ	Thunder AX9-120 S2 HAB	4434		17.11.98	The Flying Doctors Hot Air Balloon Co Ltd	Salisbury	23.10.03T
					(Spire FM titles)		

G-OISO	Reims/Cessna FA150 Aerobat *(Built as FRA150L)*	FRA1500213	G-BBJW	3. 4.90	V J Wilce & D A Miller	Great Ashfield	26. 8.05T
G-OITN	Aérospatiale AS355F1 Twin Squirrel	5088	N400HH N5788B	3.10.89	Independent Television News Ltd	Redhill	13.12.04T
G-OITV	Enstrom 280C Shark	1038	G-HRVY G-DUGY/G-BEEL	9. 4.96	C.W.Brierley Jones	(Warrington)	24. 9.04T
G-OIZI	Europa Aviation Europa XS T-G	474 & PFA 247-13615		9.10.00	K.S.Duddy	(Malvern)	
G-OJAB	Jabiru Jabiru SK *(Jabiru 2200A)*	PFA 274-13031		19. 9.96	P.A.Brigstock	Leicester	9. 5.03P
G-OJAC	Mooney M.20J (201)	24-1490	N5767E	20. 8.90	Hornet Engineering Ltd	Biggin Hill	27. 1.03T
G-OJAE	Hughes 269C	90-0966	N1101W	12. 2.90	J.A. & C.M.Wilson	Slaithwaite, Huddersfield	20.10.05
G-OJAN	Robinson R22 Beta	2012	G-SANS G-BUHX	22. 5.01	Heliflight (UK) Ltd	Wolverhampton	5. 9.04T
G-OJAS	Auster J/1U Workmaster	3501	F-BJAS F-WJAS/(F-OBHT)	21. 3.00	K.P.& D.S.Hunt *(On rebuild 5.01)*	Shoreham	
G-OJAV	Fairey Britten-Norman BN-2A Mk.III-2 Trislander	1024	G-BDOS (4X-CCI)/G-BDOS	6. 6.90	Lyddair Ltd	Lydd	19.12.03T
G-OJBB	Enstrom 280FX	2084		14. 6.99	Pendragon (Design & Build) Ltd	Gloucestershire	1. 7.05T
G-OJBM	Cameron N-90 HAB	2899		28. 9.92	P.Spinlove	Chalfont St.Giles	23. 9.93A
G-OJBS	Cameron N-105 HAB	4733		8. 3.00	Up and Away Ballooning Ltd	High Wycombe	4. 5.03T
G-OJBW	Lindstrand J & B Bottle SS HAB	436		26. 8.97	Justerini & Brooks Ltd	London SW1	20. 5.02A
G-OJCW	Piper PA-32RT-300 Lance II	32R-7985062	N3016K	9. 1.80	P.G.Dobson tr CW Group	Blackbushe	6. 6.04
G-OJDA	EAA Acrosport 2 *(Lycoming O-360-A4A)*	PFA 72-11067		1. 4.98	D.B.Almey	(Spalding)	2. 6.03P
G-OJDC	Thunder Ax7-77 HAB	875		9. 1.89	Julia Crosby	Brighton	1. 8.02A
G-OJDR	Yakovlev Yak-50	792006	LY-JDR DOSAAF	24. 7.02	A.M.Holman-West *(As "JD-R/J-DR" in US c/s)*	Wellesbourne Mountford	20. 8.03P
G-OJEG	Airbus Industrie A321-231	1015	D-AVZN	14. 5.99	Monarch Airlines Ltd	Luton	13. 5.05T
G-OJEH	Piper PA-28-181 Archer II	28-8690051	D-EDPA N9125Y	17.12.02	J.E. Howe	Compton Abbas	AC
G-OJEM*	Hawker Siddeley HS.748 Srs.2B/378	1791	ZK-MCH G-BKAL/(9N-ADF)/G-BKAL/V2-LDK/D-AHSD/G-BKAL	22. 3.96	Air Salvage International	Alton	14. 4.99T
	(Damaged in forced landing Stansted 31.3.98 & broken up 6.98) (Cancelled 27.7.98 as WFU) (Nose only 1.00)						
G-OJEN	Cameron V-77 HAB	3302		26. 5.94	D.J.Geddes *(New CofR 3.02 & active 8.02)*	High Wycombe	18. 7.96A
G-OJGT	Maule M-5-235C Lunar Rocket	7285C	LN-AEL (LN-BEK)/N5635V	30. 6.98	J.G.Townsend	Draycott Farm, Chiseldon	8. 8.04
G-OJHB	Colt Flying Ice Cream Cone SS HAB	2591		23. 6.94	Benedikt Haggeney GmbH	Ennigerloh, Germany	17. 4.03A
G-OJHL	Europa Aviation Europa *(Rotax 912-UL) (Monowheel u/c)*	311 & PFA 247-13039		12. 5.97	J.H.Lace *"Lady Lace"* *(F/f 19.8.99)*	Prestwick	3. 9.03P
G-OJIL	Piper PA-31-350 Navajo Chieftain	31-7625175	OY-BTP	28. 5.97	Redhill Aviation Ltd *(Op Redhill Charters)*	Redhill	10.1.04T
G-OJIM	Piper PA-28R-201T Turbo Cherokee Arrow III	28R-7703200	N38299	4. 8.86	Grey Fox Investigations Ltd	(Tonbridge)	5. 2.05
G-OJJB	Mooney M.20K (252TSE)	25-1161		12. 8.88	G Italiano	Roma-Urbe, Italy	4. 7.04
G-OJJF	Druine D.31 Turbulent *(Volkswagen 1300)*	378 & 31	OO-30	6. 1.97	J.J.Ferguson *(Wings noted Eaglescott 10.00)*	(Bideford)	
G-OJKM	Rans S-7 Courier	PFA 218-12982		5. 3.01	M.Jackson *(Under construction 1.02)*	Southend	
G-OJLH	TEAM mini-MAX 91 *(Rotax 447)*	PFA 186-12164	G-MYAW	12.12.01	J.L.Hamer	(Hartpury)	13. 4.03P
G-OJMB	Airbus Industrie A330-243	427	F-WWYH	8.11.01	JMC Airlines Ltd	Manchester	8.11.04T
G-OJMC	Airbus Industrie A330-243	456	F-WWKI	5. 3.02	JMC Airlines Ltd	Manchester	4. 3.05T
G-OJMF	Enstrom 280FX	2086	G-DDOD	12. 6.01	JMF Ltd	(Ballymoney)	9 .12.02
G-OJMR	Airbus Industrie A300B4-605R	605	F-WWAY	3. 5.91	Monarch Airlines Ltd	Luton	2. 5.05T
G-OJNB	Lindstrand LBL-21A HAB	085		14. 2.94	Justerini & Brooks Ltd	London SW1	19. 5.02A
G-OJOD	Jodel D.18	PFA 169-12774		20. 6.02	D.Hawkes & C.Poundes	(Milton Keynes)	
G-OJON	Taylor JT.2 Titch III *(Continental C90)*	PFA 3208		6.10.78	J.H.Fell	(RAF Marham)	18. 5.01P
G-OJPB	Hawker Siddeley HS.125 Srs.F600B	25258	VP-CJP VR-CJP/G-BFAN/G-AZHS	25. 9.97	Widehawk Aviation Ltd	Cambridge	9.11.01T
G-OJRH	Robinson R44 Astro	0321		11. 4.97	Holgate Construction Ltd	Emley Moor, Huddersfield	10. 4.03
G-OJRM	Cessna T.182T Turbo Skylane	T18208007	N72778	19. 7.01	SPD Ltd	Old Sarum	31. 7.04T
G-OJSH	Thruster T600N 450 Jab	0061-T600N-052		29. 5.01	S.A.Lewis tr November Whiskey Flying Club	Shobdon	23. 9.03P
G-OJTA	Stemme S-10V	14-018	D-KGDA	18. 9.95	O.J.Truelove t/a OJT Associates	RAF Halton	5. 6.05
G-OJTW	Boeing 737-36N	28558	(G-JTWF)	26. 4.97	British Midland Airways Ltd *(Op bmibaby) "rock-a-bye baby"*	East Midlands	1. 5.03T
G-OJVA	Van's RV-6	PFA 181-12292		6. 9.96	J.A.Village	Moorgreen Farm, Barlow	6.11.03P
G-OJVH	Cessna F150H *(Built Reims Aviation SA)*	F150-0356	G-AWJZ	27. 3.81	A.W.Cairns	RAF Brize Norton	23. 5.04T
G-OJVL	Van's RV-6	PFA 181-12441		28.10.02	S.E.Tomlinson	(Bournemouth)	
G-OJWS	Piper PA-28-161 Cherokee Warrior II	28-7816415	N6377C	13. 7.88	P.J.Ward	Denham	11. 7.03
G-OKAG	Piper PA-28R-180 Cherokee Arrow	28R-30075	N3764T	15. 4.88	N.F. & B.R.Green	Stapleford	13. 4.03T
G-OKAY	Pitts S-1E Special *(Lycoming IO-360)*	12358	N35WH	27. 5.80	D S T Eggleton	Waits Farm, Belchamp Walter	10. 4.03P
G-OKBT	Colt 25A Sky Chariot Mk.II HAB	2301		10.11.92	British Telecommunications plc *"Skypiper II"*	Thatcham	18. 4.03A
G-OKCC	Cameron N-90 HAB	1741		6. 5.88	D.J.Head	Newbury	25. 7.00A
G-OKED	Cessna 150L	15074250	N19223	29.1.93	L A Maynard *(Op Old Sarum Flying Club)*	Old Sarum	31. 1.03T
G-OKEN	Piper PA-28R-201T Turbo Cherokee Arrow III	28R-7703390	N47518	20.10.87	W.B.Bateson	Blackpool	12. 4.03T
G-OKES	Robinson R44 Astro	0053		16. 3.94	Hecray Co Ltd t/a Direct Helicopters	Southend	25. 5.03T
G-OKEV	Europa Aviation Europa *(Rotax 912-UL) (Tri-gear u/c)*	328 & PFA 247-13091		11. 6.97	K.A.Pilcher *"Freedom"* *(F/f 15.7.98)*	Wolverhampton	17 10.03P

Reg	Type	C/n	Prev identity	Date	Owner/Operator	Base	C of A
G-OKEY	Robinson R22 Beta	2004		14. 1.92	Key Properties Ltd	Denham	25. 6.05
G-OKGB	IAV-Bacau Yakovlev Yak-52	9010407	LY-AGU	16.10.02	W.Hanekom	(Bedford)	16.10.03P
G-OKIS	Tri-R Kis (CAM.100)	PFA 239-12248		15. 6.92	M.R.Cleveley *(Noted 2002)*	(Halesworth)	17. 7.03P
G-OKJN	Boeing 727-225RE *(Converted to freighter configuration 2001)*	21453	N8880Z N380KP/N8880Z	3. 5.00	Cougar Leasing Ltd *(Op TNT)*	Stansted	8.10.04TC
G-OKMA	Tri-R Kis	PFA 239-12808		22.11.95	K.Miller	(Coventry)	
G-OKPW	Tri-R Kis (Continental O-200-A)	PFA 239-12359		17. 8.93	K.P.Wordsworth	Shoreham	7. 6.03P
G-OKYA	Cameron V-77 HAB *(Replacement envelope c/n 3331)*	1259		4. 3.87	D.J.B.Woodd tr Army Balloon Club *"Fly Army II"*	BFPO.17, Germany	
G-OKYM	Piper PA-28-140 Cherokee	28-23303	G-AVLS N11C	10. 5.88	B.Marshall	Humberside	5.11.03
G-OLAU	Robinson R22 Beta	1119		5. 9.89	Thistle Aviation Ltd	Southend	17. 7.05T
G-OLAW	Lindstrand LBL-25A Cloudhopper HAB	170		9.12.94	George Law Plant Ltd *"Law Hopper"*	Kidderminster	24. 4.97A
G-OLCP	Eurocopter AS355N Twin Squirrel	5580	G-CLIP	18. 2.02	Charterstyle Ltd	Blackbushe	11. 4.04T
G-OLDC	Learjet Learjet 45	45-156	N3017F	12.10.01	Gold Air International Ltd	Cambridge	11.10.03T
G-OLDD	British Aerospace BAe 125 Srs.800B	258106	PK-RGM PK-WSJ/G-5-580	11. 3.99	Gold Air International Ltd	Cambridge	19..8.03T
G-OLDF	Learjet Learjet 45	45-055	G-JRJR N45LR/N63MJ	3. 1.03	Gold Air International Ltd	Biggin Hill	23. 1.03T
G-OLDG	Cessna T182T Turbo Skylane	T18208127	G-CBTJ N5170R	17.10.02	Gold Air International Ltd	Cambridge	22. 8.05T
G-OLDJ	Learjet Learjet 45	45-138	N5018G	24. 5.01	Gold Air International Ltd	Biggin Hill	23. 5.03T
G-OLDL	Learjet Learjet 45	45-124	N4003Q	19. 2.01	Gold Air International Ltd	Cambridge	18. 2.03T
G-OLDM	Pegasus Quantum 15-912	7589		10.12.99	P.Simpson	(Cuffley)	15.12.01P
G-OLDN	Bell 206L LongRanger	45077	G-TBCA G-BFAL/N64689/A6-BCL	2.10.84	Von Essen Aviation Ltd	Thruxton	26. 7.03T
G-OLDR	Learjet Learjet 45	45-161	N3000S	18. 1.02	Gold Air International Ltd	Cambridge	17. 1.03T
G-OLDX	Cessna 182T Skylane	18280967	G-IBZT N3536W	26. 4.02	Gold Air International Ltd	Cambridge	25. 1.04T
G-OLEE	Reims/Cessna F152 II	F15201797		11. 9.80	Redhill Air Services Ltd	Redhill	6. 4.03T
G-OLEL	American Blimp Corp A-60+ Airship	016	N606LG	9. 3.01	Lightship Europe Ltd *("www.mazda.de" titles)*	(Rednal)	22. 3.04T
G-OLEM	Jodel D.18 (Revmaster R2100)	PFA 169-11613	G-BSBP	11. 2.02	D.G.H.Oswald	(Cupar)	
G-OLEO	Thunder Ax10-210 Srs.2 HAB	3974		9. 1.97	P.J.Waller	Norwich	11. 6.03T
G-OLEZ	Piper J-3C-65 Cub	18432	G-BSAX N98260/NC98260	8. 8.01	L.Powell *(For restoration)*	(Canterbury)	
G-OLFB	Pegasus Quantum 15-912	7767		2. 3.01	A.J.Boyd	Newtownards, Co.Down	16. 3.03P
G-OLFC	Piper PA-38-112 Tomahawk	38-79A0995	G-BGZG N9658N	6.12.85	M.W.Glencross	Luton	29. 5.04T
G-OLFT	Rockwell Commander 114	14274	G-WJMN N4954W	28. 3.85	D.A.Tubby	(Warrington)	16. 5.05
G-OLGA	CFM Starstreak Shadow SA.II (Rotax 618)	K.288 & PFA 206-13164		15.10.97	N.F.Smith	Halstead	13 02.03P
G-OLIZ	Robinson R22 Beta	0779		29. 9.88	R S Forsyth & L T W Alderman	Cambridge	16. 8.04T
G-OLJT	Mainair Gemini/Flash IIA (Rotax 503)	570-887-5 & W359	G-MTKY	16. 9.98	A Wraith	(Huddersfield)	13. 3.03P
G-OLLI	Cameron O-31 HAB (Golly Special shape)	196		11. 5.76	N.A.Robertson *"Golly III"* *(Op British Balloon Museum & Library 2002)*	Newbury	17. 7.97A
G-OLMA	Partenavia P.68B	159	G-BGBT	15. 4.85	C.M.Evans	Bodmin	16.10.05T
G-OLOW	Robinson R44 Astro	0100		3.10.94	J.E.Morris t/a Morris Transport	(Oswestry)	14. 6.04T
G-OLPG	Colt 77A HAB	2568		11. 3.94	D.J.Farrar	Leeds	16. 2.03
G-OLRT	Robinson R22 Beta	1378	N4014R	21. 5.90	S.Farmer t/a First Degree Air	Tatenhill	12. 8.05T
G-OLSF	Piper PA-28-161 Cadet	2841284	G-OTYJ G-OLSF/N92008	23.11.89	Bflying Ltd *(Op Bournemouth Flying Club)*	Bournemouth	23. 1.05T
G-OLVR*	Clutton FRED Srs.II (Continental A65)	PFA 29-10321		17.11.78	C.P.Whitwell *(Cancelled 23.12.99 by CAA: dismantled 1.00)*	Dunkeswell	2. 6.00P
G-OLYD	Beech 58 Baron	TH-1427	N7255H ZS-LYC/N7255H	12. 9.97	I.G.Lloyd	Gamston	1.11.03
G-OLYN	Sky 260-24 HAB	088		24. 4.98	Airborne Balloon Management Ltd	Tonbridge	27. 3.03T
G-OMAC	Reims FR172E Rocket	FR17200022	PH-HAI (PH-KRC)/D-EDDC	3. 7.84	S.G.Shilling	Manston	15.11.04T
G-OMAF	Dornier 228-200	8112	D-CAAD	16. 2.87	Cobham Leasing Ltd *(Op DEFRA/Fisheries Patrol)*	Bournemouth	22. 6.05T
G-OMAK	Airbus Industrie A319-132 CJ	913	F-WWIF G-OMAK/F-WWIF/G-OMAK/D-AVYL	7. 1.99	Twinjet Aircraft Sales Ltd	Luton	7. 1.06T
G-OMAL	Thruster T600N 450	0061-T600N-050		16. 5.01	M Howland	Wickenby	15.11.02P
G-OMAP	Rockwell Commander 685	12036	F-GIRX F-OCGX/F-ZBBU/N6525V	4.11.94	Cooper Aerial Surveys Ltd	Gamston	14. 5.05A
G-OMAT	Piper PA-28-140 Cherokee D	28-7125139	G-JIMY G-AYUG/N11C	27. 8.87	R.B.Walker t/a Midland Air Training School	Coventry	9.11.03T
G-OMAX	Brantly B.2B	473	G-AVJN	7. 8.87	P.D.Benmax	Denham	16.11.03
G-OMDB	Van's RV-6A	25735		14. 8.02	D.A.Roseblade	(Dubai, UAE)	
G-OMDD	Cameron Thunder AX8-90 S2 HAB	4345		2. 4.98	M.D.Dickinson	(Bristol)	24. 3.03T
G-OMDG	Hoffmann H-36 Dimona	3510	OE-9215	19.11.98	D. Coulson tr Ards Dimona Group	Newtownards	9. 1.05
G-OMDH	MD Helicopters Hughes 369E (500E)	0293E		14.11.88	Stiltgate Ltd	Booker	15. 2.04T
G-OMDR	Agusta-Bell 206B-3 JetRanger III	8610	G-HRAY G-VANG/G-BIZA	8.12.97	Anglia Aviation plc	Norwich	15.12.03T
G-OMEC	Agusta-Bell 206B-3 JetRanger III	8716	G-OBLD	16. 1.90	Kallas Ltd	(Monaco)	21.10.01
G-OMEL	Robinson R44 Astro	0073	G-BVPB	30. 9.96	Nedair Ltd	Blackpool	2.11.03T
G-OMEX	Zenair CH.701 STOL	PFA 187-13556		11.12.01	S.J.Perry	(Woodhall Spa)	
G-OMEZ	Zenair CH.601HDS Zodiac	PFA 162-13552		16. 7.01	C.J.Gow	Perth	6.11.03P
G-OMFG	Cameron A-120 HAB	4965		7. 2.01	M.F.Glue	Hertford	5. 2.02T

Regn	Type	C/n	Prev. identities	Date	Owner/Operator	Base	Expiry
G-OMGE	British Aerospace BAe 125 Srs.800B	258197	G-5-696 / G-BTMG	1. 7.91	Marconda Services Ltd	Luton	22. 5.03T
G-OMGG	British Aerospace BAe 125 Srs.800B	258058	N125JW / G-5-637/N125JW/VH-NMR/ZK-EUI/(ZK-EUR)/G-5-510	21.11.94	Aviation One Co. Ltd (George Town, Cayman Islands)		23.11.03T
G-OMHC	Piper PA-28RT-201 Arrow IV	28R-7918105	N3072Y	10. 2.81	Tatenhill Aviation Ltd	Tatenhill	27. 5.05T
G-OMHI	Mills MH-1	MH.001		8.10.97	J.P.Mills	Barton	
G-OMHP	Jabiru Jabiru UL	PFA 274A-13584		23. 5.00	M.H.Player	(Shepton Mallet)	
G-OMIA	SOCATA MS.893A Rallye Commodore 180	12074	D-ENME / F-BUGE/(D-ENMH)	21. 7.98	P.W.Portelli	Elstree	19.12.04
G-OMIK	Europa Aviation Europa (Rotax 914) (Monowheel u/c)	270 & PFA 247-12991		12. 1.98	M.J.Clews (F/f 13.8.01)	White Waltham	27. 8.03P
G-OMJT	Rutan LongEz (Lycoming O-235)	968 & PFA 74A-10703		14.10.92	M.J.Timmons	Prestwick	4. 9.03P
G-OMMG	Robinson R22 Beta	1041	G-BPYX	25. 2.94	Preston Associates Ltd	Yearby	24. 1.04T
G-OMMM	Colt 90A HAB	2328		20. 1.93	V.Trimble	Henley-on-Thames	3. 5.03A
G-OMMT	Robinson R44 Astro	0315	G-IBKA / G-USTE	10. 6.02	Morrison Motors (Turriff)	(Turriff)	6. 4.03T
G-OMNH	Beech 200 Super King Air	BB-108	N108BM / RP-C1979/TR-LWC	19. 8.98	Maynard & Harris Holdings Ltd	Stapleford	20. 8.03T
G-OMNI	Piper PA-28R-200 Cherokee Arrow II	28R-7335130	G-BAWA / N11C	3. 1.84	Avon Leasing Ltd t/a The Blue Book	Gloucestershire	16. 7.03T
G-OMOG*	Gulfstream AA-5A Cheetah	AA5A-0793	G-BHWR / N26892	4. 3.88	Solent Flight Aircraft Ltd (Cancelled 23.7.01 by CAA)	Southampton	15. 4.02T
G-OMOL	Maule MX-7-180C Star Rocket	28012C		15. 8.00	Aeromarine Ltd	Owlesbury	2.10.03
G-OMRB	Cameron V-77 HAB	2184		29. 8.90	I.J.Jevons "Harlequin"	Bristol	14. 6.03A
G-OMRG	Hoffmann H-36 Dimona	36132	G-BLHG	15.11.88	M.R.Grimwood	Kemble	21. 1.06
G-OMST	Piper PA-28-161 Warrior III	2842121	G-BZUA / N53363	1. 8.01	Mid-Sussex Timber Co Ltd	Biggin Hill	11. 6.04T
G-OMUC	Boeing 737-36Q	29405		29. 6.98	Go Fly Ltd (Easyjet titles)	Stansted	22.11.03T
G-OMUM	Rockwell Commander 114	14067	PH-JJJ / (PH-MMM)/N4737W	24. 1.97	C.E.Campbell	Blackbushe	7. 3.03
G-OMWE	Zenair CH.601HD Zodiac (Mid-West AE.100R)	PFA 162-12740	G-BVXU	21. 3.97	Mid-West Engines Ltd	Egelsbach, Germany	14. 7.01P
G-ONAF	Naval Aircraft Factory N3N-3 (Wright Whirlwind R.760)	--	N45192 / Bu.4406	31. 1.89	R.P.W.Steele & J.D.Hutchinson	Sandown	30. 8.02
G-ONAV	Piper PA-31 Navajo C	31-7812004	G-IGAR / D-IGAR/N27378	29. 1.93	Panther Aviation Ltd	Elstree	31. 5.03T
G-ONCB	Lindstrand LBL-31A HAB	393		4. 6.96	R.J.Mold	High Wycombe	17. 9.02A
G-ONCL	Colt 77A HAB	1637		4. 4.90	D.R.Pearce	Slimbridge	16. 6.02A
G-ONCM	Partenavia P.68C	217	I-CITT / G-TELE/G-DORE/OY-CAD	5.12.01	M.Arnell	Aberdeen	13. 1.05T
G-ONEB	Westland Scout AH.1	F.9761	G-BXOE / XW798	21. 1.98	E.R.Meredith & E M Smith	Draycott Farm, Chiseldon	26. 6.03P
G-ONES	Slingsby T.67M-200	2046	SE-LBB / LN-TFB/G-7-122	12.11.01	L.J.Jones	(Martock)	AC
G-ONET	Piper PA-28-180 Cherokee E	28-5802	G-AYAU / N11C	3. 6.98	J.Blackburn	Elstree	22 8.05T
G-ONFL	Murphy Maverick (Rotax 503)	402 & PFA 259-12750	G-MYUJ	27.11 98	M.J.Whiteman-Haywood	Pound Green, Buttonoak, Kidderminster	2. 5.03P
G-ONGC	Robin DR400/180R Remorquer	1385	EI-CKA / SE-GHM	11.11.98	Norfolk Gliding Club Ltd	Tibenham	26.3.05
G-ONHH	Forney F-1A Aircoupe	5725	G-ARHA / N3030G	13.12.89	R.D.I.Tarry "Easy Rider"	Pytchley Grange	14. 3.04
G-ONIX	Cameron C-80 HAB	4411		12. 8.98	Hillwalk Ltd	Weston-super-Mare	11. 6.03A
G-ONKA	Aeronca K (Lycoming O-145)	K283	N19780 / NC19780	21.10.91	N.J.R.Minchin "Aggnes"	Hill Top Farm, West Sussex	28. 6.03P
G-ONMT	Robinson R22 Beta-II	2963		20. 7.99	Redcourt Enterprises Ltd	Kintore	2 .8.05T
G-ONON	Rotary Air Force RAF 2000 GTX-SE	PFA G/13-1313		13. 8.99	M.S.R.Allen	(Oakham)	
G-ONOW	Bell 206A JetRanger	605	G-AYMX	8. 8.88	J.Lucketti	(Rochdale)	27. 4.00T
G-ONPA(2)	Piper PA-31-350 Navajo Chieftain	31-7952110	N89PA / N35225	6. 5.98	West Wales Airport Ltd	Shobdon	15.10.04T
G-ONSF	Piper PA-28R-201 Cherokee Arrow III	28R-773708	G-EMAK / D-EMAK/N38180	17 .1.01	Northamptonshire School of Flying Ltd	Sywell	17. 4.04T
G-ONTV	Agusta-Bell 206B-3 JetRanger III	8733	D-HUNT / TC-HKJ/(D-HSAV)/I-GPFP/I-PIEF	1. 4.98	Castle Air Charters Ltd	Liskeard	19. 4.04T
G-ONUN	Van's RV-6A	PFA 181-12976		20. 2.96	R.E.Nunn	Maypole Farm, Chislet	22 .5.03P
G-ONUP	Enstrom F-28C	348	G-MHCA / G-SHWW/G-SMUJ/G-BHTF	18. 1.00	R.E.Harvey	(West Deeping)	20. 6.02
G-ONYX	Bell 206B-3 JetRanger III	4160	G-BXPN / N18EA/D-HOBA/(D-HOBE)	22. 1.98	N.C.Wheelwright	Gloucestershire	15. 3.04T
G-ONZO	Cameron N-77 HAB (Regd initially as "O-77")	1089		13.11.84	K.Temple "Gonzo"	(Rickinghall)	19. 7.99A
G-OOAE	Airbus Industrie A321-211	852	(G-UNIF) / D-AVZG	14. 7.98	Air 2000 Ltd	Manchester	13. 7.04T
G-OOAF	Airbus Industrie A321-211	677	G-UNID / G-UKLO/D-AVZO	4.12.98	Air 2000 Ltd	Mancheste	r6. 5.03T
G-OOAH	Airbus Industrie A321-211	781	G-UNIE / D-AVZK	4. 1.99	Air 2000 Ltd	Mancheste	r2. 3.04T
G-OOAI	Airbus Industrie A321-211	1006	D-AVZJ	30. 4.99	Air 2000 Ltd	Manchester	29. 4.05T
G-OOAJ	Airbus Industrie A321-211	1017	D-AVZM	12. 5.99	Air 2000 Ltd	Manchester	11. 5.05T
G-OOAL	Boeing 767-38AER	29617		29. 3.99	Air 2000 Ltd "Sunrise"	Manchester	29 .3.02T
G-OOAM	Boeing 767-38AER	29618		10. 5.00	Air 2000 Ltd	Manchester	8 .5.03T
G-OOAN	Boeing 767-39HER	26256	G-UKLH	26. 1.99	Air 2000 Ltd "Caribbean Star"	Manchester	4 .4.03T

Registration	Type	C/n	Prev id	Date	Owner/Operator	Location	Date
G-OOAP	Airbus Industrie A320-214	1306	F-WWBY	23.10.00	Air 2000 Ltd	Manchester	22.10.03T
G-OOAR	Airbus Industrie A320-214	1320	F-WWDT	3.11.00	Air 2000 Ltd	Manchester	2.11.03T
G-OOAU	Airbus Industrie A320-214	1637	F-WWDM	10. 1.02	Air 2000 Ltd	Manchester	9. 1.05T
G-OOAV	Airbus Industrie A321-211	1720	D-AVXA	29. 4.02	Air 2000 Ltd	Manchester	28. 4.05T
G-OOAW	Airbus Industrie A320-214	1777	F-WWDM	27. 5.02	Air 2000 Ltd	Manchester	26. 5.05T
G-OOAX	Airbus Industrie A320-214			R	Air 2000 Ltd	Manchester	
G-OOBA	Boeing 757-28A	32446	N446GE (N558NA)	9. 2.01	Air 2000 Ltd	Manchester	4. 4.04T
G-OOBB	Boeing 757-28A	32447	N447GE (N559NA)	9. 2.01	Air 2000 Ltd	Manchester	11. 4.04T
G-OOBC	Boeing 757-28A	33098		2.03R	Air 2000 Ltd *(For delivery 2.03)*	Manchester	
G-OOBD	Boeing 757-28A	33099		3.03R	Air 2000 Ltd *(For delivery 3.03)*	Manchester	
G-OOBE	Boeing 757-28A	33100		4.03R	Air 2000 Ltd *(For delivery 4.03)*	Manchester	
G-OODE	SNCAN Stampe SV-4C (DH Gipsy Major 10)	500	G-AZNN F-BDGI	9. 5.77	A.R.Radford	Redhill	5. 9.05T
G-OODI	Pitts S-1D Special (Lycoming IO-360)	KH.1	G-BBBU	23.12.80	R.M.Buchan *"Little Bumble"*	North Weald	7. 5.03P
G-OODW	Piper PA-28-181 Archer II	28-8490031	N4332C	14. 7.87	Goodwood Road Racing Co Ltd	Goodwood	19. 5.05T
G-OOER	Lindstrand LBL-25A Cloudhopper HAB	125		15. 8.94	Airborne Adventures Ltd	Skipton	18.10.95A
G-OOFT	Piper PA-28-161 Warrior III	2842083	N170FT	25. 5.00	Lyrical Computing Ltd *(Op Denham School of Flying)*	Denham	22. 6.03T
G-OOGA	Gulfstream GA-7 Cougar *(C/n correct but duplicates that for YV-1334P)*	GA7-0111	SE-IEA N758G	3. 2.86	Cougar Aviation Ltd	Elstree	25.11.04T
G-OOGI	Gulfstream GA-7 Cougar	GA7-0077	G-PLAS G-BGHL/N789GA	16. 1.95	Plane Talking Ltd	Biggin Hill	23. 8.03T
G-OOGO	Grumman-American GA-7 Cougar	GA7-0049	N762GA	12.11.97	Leonard F.Jollye (Brookmans Park) Ltd	Elstree	7.12.03T
G-OOGS	Gulfstream American GA-7 Cougar	GA7-0105	G-BGJW N737G	19. 6.98	Bflying Ltd *(Op Bournemouth Flying Club)*	Bournemouth	23 .5.02T
G-OOHO	Bell 206B-3 JetRanger III	3370	G-OCHC G-KLEE/G-SIZL/G-BOSW/N2063T	4. 7.01	Into Space Ltd	Leicester	26. 6.04T
G-OOIO	Eurocopter AS350B3 Ecureuil	3463		17.10.01	Hovering Ltd	(Douglas, Isle of Man)	19.11.04T
G-OOJC	Bensen B.8MR *(Converted ex Air Command)*	PFA G/101-1303		4.12.98	J.R.Cooper *(Noted11.02)*	Henstridge	
G-OOJP	Commander Aircraft Commander 114B	14567	D-EYCA N92JT	24.12.99	Plato Management Ltd	Oxford	19..1.03
G-OOLE	Cessna 172M Skyhawk II	17266712	G-BOSI N80714	25. 8.89	P.S.Eccersley	Humberside	30. 1.04
G-OONE	Mooney M.20J (205)	24-3039		31. 7.87	J.H.Donald & K.B.Moore	Cumbernauld	11. 5.03
G-OONI	Thunder Ax7-77 HAB	1534		9. 3.90	Fivedata Ltd *"Bridesnightie"*	Todmorden, Lancs	31. 3.01A
G-OONY	Piper PA-28-161 Warrior II	28-8316015	N83071	26. 7.89	D.A.Field & P.B.Jenkins	Compton Abbas	23.10.04T
G-OOOB	Boeing 757-28A	23822	C-FOOB G-OOOB (x9)	19. 2.87	Air 2000 Ltd	Manchester	28. 4.04T
G-OOOC	Boeing 757-28AER	24017	C-FRYL C-FXOC/G-OOOC (x7)	19. 1.88	Air 2000 Ltd	Manchester	27. 4.05T
G-OOOD	Boeing 757-28A	24235	C-GRYU G-OOOD (x4)/C-FXOD (x4)	28.10.99	Air 2000 Ltd	Manchester	27.10.05T
G-OOOG	Boeing 757-23AER	24292	C-FOOG G-OOOG (x5)	29. 3.89	Air 2000 Ltd *(TCS Expeditions titles)*	Manchester	29.10.04T
G-OOOI	Boeing 757-23AER	24289	N510SK EC-EMV/EC-247	19.10.89	Air 2000 Ltd	Manchester	19.10.05T
G-OOOJ	Boeing 757-23AER	24290	N510FP EC-EMU/EC-248	19.10.89	Air 2000 Ltd	Manchester	1.11.05T
G-OOOK	Boeing 757-236	25054	SE-DUK (G-JOEM)/SE-DUK/N100FS/EI-CMA/XA-MMX/N3502P/N5002K/(EC-668)/(G-BSNB)	9.10.02	Air 2000 Ltd	Manchester	31.10.05T
G-OOOM	Boeing 757-225	22612	SE-DUN G-OOOM/N523EA	19.10.89	Air 2000 Ltd	Manchester	13.12.05T
G-OOON	Piper PA-34-220T Seneca III	34-8533024	N822CB ZS-LWI/N2431Q/N9513N	8. 1.03	N.Cooper *(Noted 2.03 @ Kemble)*	(London SW18)	
G-OOOS	Boeing 757-236ER	24397	G-BRJD EC-ESC/EC-349/G-BRJD	14. 5.91	Air 2000 Ltd	Manchester	18.10.05T
G-OOOU	Boeing 757-2Y0ER	25240		30. 8.91	Air 2000 Ltd *(TCS Expeditions titles)*	Manchester	24.10.05T
G-OOOX	Boeing 757-2Y0ER	26158		24. 2.93	Air 2000 Ltd	Manchester	22. 3.03T
G-OOOY	Boeing 757-28AER	28203		21. 5.98	Air 2000 Ltd	Manchester	20. 5.04T
G-OOOZ	Boeing 757-236	25593	N593RA C-GRYK/N593KA/SE-DSL/N593KA/G-BUDZ/C-FNXY/G-BUDZ	5. 4.02	Air 2000 Ltd	Manchester	9. 5.05T
G-OOSE	Rutan VariEze	1536 & PFA 74-10326		7.12.78	B.O.Smith & J.A.Towers *(Stored dismantled 1.02)*	Yearby	
G-OOSI	Cessna 404 Titan	404-0855	VT-DAT N404N/F-WQFV/F-ZBDB/F-BRGN/N68104	31. 1.03	Cooper Aerial Surveys Ltd	Gamston	
G-OOSY	de Havilland DH.82A Tiger Moth *(Composite rebuild)*	85831	F-BGFI Fr AF/DE971	6. 9.94	M.Goosey *(On rebuild 9.94: current status unknown)*	Eccleshall, Stafford	
G-OOTC	Piper PA-28R-201T Turbo Cherokee Arrow III	28R-7703086	G-CLIV N3011Q	18. 1.94	R.Noble Ltd	Seething	9. 1.03
G-OOUT	Colt Flying Shuttlecock SS HAB	1938		16. 5.91	Shiplake Investments Ltd *"Shuttlecock"*	Guernsey	18.11.00A
G-OOXP	Aero Designs Pulsar XP (Rotax 912)	PFA 202-11915		25.10.90	T.D.Baker *(Current status unknown)*	Corby	18. 4.96P
G-OPAG	Piper PA-34-200 Seneca	34-7250348	N506DM G-BNGB/F-BTQT/F-BTMT	16.10.90	A.H.Lavender	Biggin Hill	10. 4.03
G-OPAL	Robinson R22 Beta	0535	N23750	11. 2.86	Heli Air Ltd Leasowes Farm, Oxhill, Warks *(Op The Leamington Hobby Centre Ltd)*		20. 2.04T
G-OPAM	Reims/Cessna F152 II	F15201536	G-BFZS	5. 9.86	PJC (Leasing) Ltd *"Little Red Rooster"*	Stapleford	17. 6.03T
G-OPAT	Beech 76 Duchess	ME-304	G-BHAO	6.12.82	R.D.J.Axford	Booker	7. 2.03
G-OPAZ	Pazmany PL-2	PFA 69-10673		20. 3.98	K.Morris *"Y Myddryg Bach Melyn"*	Boscombe Down	18.12.02P
G-OPCG	Cessna 182T Skylane	18280948	N2451Y	18. 2.02	Pye Consulting Group Ltd	Blackpool	25. 2.05T

G-OPCS	Hughes 369E	0333E	CS-HBN N500AH	31. 1.01	Productivity Computer Solutions Ltd	(Ossett)	10. 4.04T
G-OPDM	Enstrom 280FX Shark	2021	N8627Q PH-GBL/N650PG	7. 1.98	Lamindene Ltd	Goodwood	15. 5.04T
G-OPDS	Denney Kitfox Model 4 PFA 172A-12259 (Rotax 582)			8. 1.93	D.A.Lord	Shoreham	23. 7.03P
G-OPEP	Piper PA-28RT-201T Turbo Arrow IV 28R-7931070		OY-PEP N2217Q	3.12.97	Oxford Aviation Services Ltd	Oxford	5. 3.04T
G-OPET	Piper PA-28-181 Cherokee Archer II 28-7690067		OH-PET OY-BLC	3. 1.02	It's Just Plane Fun Ltd	(Wirral)	26. 2.05T
G-OPFT*	Cessna 172R Skyhawk II	17280316	N9491F	11. 3.98	Rankart Ltd	Lydd	19. 3.01T
	(Overran runway landing Newtownards 14.11.2000: damage to undercarriage) (Cancelled 20.11.02 as temp. wfu)						
G-OPFW	Hawker Siddeley HS.748 Srs.2A/266	1714	G-BMFT	1. 7.98	Emerald Airways Ltd	Liverpool	16. 2.04T
	VP-BFT/VR-BFT/G-BMFT/5W-FAO/G11-10 *(Parcel Force titles)*						
G-OPHA	Robinson R44 Astro	0359	CS-HDW G-OPHA	17. 7.97	Simax Services Ltd *(Op Red Aviation)*	Bournemouth	2. 3.03T
G-OPHR	Diamond DA40 Star	40066		8.11.01	MC Air Ltd	Wellesbourne Mountford	5. 3.05T
G-OPHT	Schleicher ASH 26E	26105		6. 2.97	Scheibler Filters Ltd "T1" *(Stored in trailer 4.01)*	Gloucestershire	21. 6.04
G-OPIC	Reims/Cessna FRA150L Aerobat FRA15000234		G-BGNZ PH-GAB/D-EIQE	20. 6.95	S.J.Burke t/a Peak Aviation Photography	Bodmin	4. 9.03T
G-OPIK	Eiri PIK-20E Srs.1	20233	PH-651	27. 1.82	A.J.McWilliam	Newtownards, Co.Down	18.10.02
G-OPIT	CFM Streak Shadow K.126-SA & PFA 161A-11624 (Rotax 532)			22.11.89	I.Sinnett	Bodmin	8. 7.03P
G-OPJC	Cessna 152 II	15282280	N68354	7. 6.88	PJC (Leasing) Ltd	RAF Henlow	17.10.03T
G-OPJD	Piper PA-28RT-201T Turbo Arrow IV 28R-8231028		N8097V	2.10.89	J M McMillan	(Hook)	16.12.04T
G-OPJH	Rollason Druine D.62B Condor	RAE/619	G-AVDW	15. 4.97	P.J.Hall	Oaksey Park	9.12.01
G-OPJK	Europa Aviation Europa 017 & PFA 247-12487 (Rotax 912UL) *(Monowheel u/c)*			29. 4.93	P.J.Kember Fowle Hall Farm, Laddingford *"The First of the Many" (F/f 14.10.95)*		24. 4.03P
G-OPJS	Pietenpol Aircamper	PFA 47-12834		10.11.00	P.J.Shenton	(Brackley)	
G-OPKF	Cameron Bowler-90 SS HAB	2314		12. 6.90	D.K.Fish *(New CofR 8.02)*	Burbage	2. 8.03A
G-OPLB	Cessna 340A II	340A0486	G-FCHJ G-BJLS/(N6315X)	11. 7.95	Ridgewood Ltd	Jersey	19. 6.03
G-OPLC	de Havilland DH.104 Dove 8	04212	G-BLRB VP962	10. 1.91	W.G.T.Pritchard *(Op Mayfair Dove)*	Redhill	9. 5.03T
G-OPME	Piper PA-23-250 Aztec D	27-4099	G-AZGB/N878SH/N9...N	31. 3.94	Portway Aviation Ltd	Shobdon	14. 4.04T
G-OPMN	Boeing 727-225RE	21578	N8881Z	28. 4.00	Cougar Leasing Ltd	Stansted	24. 5.03T
	N381KP/N8881Z/(PP-ARR)/N8881Z *(Op Cougar Airlines)*						
G-OPMT	Lindstrand LBL-105A HAB	052		30. 9.93	Pace Micro Technology plc "Pace"	Shipley	31. 7.99A
G-OPNH	Stoddard-Hamilton Glasair IIRG PFA 149-13011		G-CINY	14.10.98	P N Haigh	Crosland Moor	19. 6.03P
G-OPPL	Gulfstream AA-5A Cheetah	AA5A-0867	G-BGNN	11.10.85	Plane Talking Ltd	Elstree	8. 8.03T
G-OPRC	Europa Aviation Europa XS 378 & PFA 247-13281 *(Tri-gear u/c)*			22. 6.01	M.J.Ashby-Arnold *(F/f 14.2.02)*	Wombleton	17. 4.03P
G-OPSF	Piper PA-38-112 Tomahawk	38-79A0998	EI-BLT G-BGZI/N9664N	13.10.82	Panshanger School of Flying Ltd	High Cross, Ware	17. 8.00T
G-OPSL	Piper PA-32R-301 Saratoga SP	32R-8013085	G-IMPW N8186A	4. 1.99	Photonic Science Ltd	Lydd	23. 3.03
G-OPST	Cessna 182R Skylane II	18267932	OO-HFF N9317H	16. 6.88	Lota Ltd	Shoreham	2. 6.03T
G-OPTS	Robinson R22 Beta-II	2712		16. 7.97	T.A.Knox (Shopfitters) Ltd	(Woodley, Stockport)	17. 8.03T
G-OPUB	Slingsby T.67M-160 Firefly	2002	G-DLTA G-SFTX	18.10.96	P.M.Barker	Wombleton	24. 7.04T
G-OPUP	Beagle B.121 Pup 2	B121-062	G-AXEU (5N-AJC)	31.10.84	A.Brinkley Standalone Farm, Meppershall t/a Brinkley Light Aircraft Services		26. 4.04
G-OPUS	Jabiru Jabiru SK PFA 274-13343 (Jabiru 2200A)			16. 7.98	H.H.R.Lagache	Leicester	2. 5.03P
G-OPWK	Grumman-American AA-5A Cheetah AA5A-0663		G-OAEL N26706	26. 5.92	A.H.McVicar *(Op Prestwick Flight Centre)*	Prestwick	6. 9.02T
G-OPWS	Mooney M.20K (231)	25-0663	N1162W	12. 4.91	A.R.Mills	Fowlmere	17. 7.03
G-OPYE	Cessna 172S Skyhawk	172S8059	N653SP	19. 2.99	Far North Aviation	Wick	25 .2.02T
G-ORAC*	Cameron Van-110SS HAB	4577		22. 6.99	Virgin Airship & Balloon Co Ltd *(RAC titles) (Cancelled 8.10.02 by CAA)*	Telford	21 .5.02A
G-ORAF	CFM Streak Shadow K.134-SA & PFA 161A-11627 (Rotax 532)			18. 5.90	A.P.Hunn	Swanton Morley	1.11.00P
	(PFA c/n duplicates MW6 G-MYCU) (Dismantled 5.00)						
G-ORAL	Hawker Siddeley HS.748 Srs.2A/334	1756	G-BPDA G-GLAS/9Y-TFS/G-11-8	13. 8.99	Emerald Airways Ltd *(Reed Aviation titles) "John J Goodhall"*	Liverpool	12.11.05T
G-ORAR	Piper PA-28-181 Archer II	2890224	N9255G	6. 6.95	P.N. & S.M.Thornton	Goodwood	26. 6.01T
G-ORAS	Clutton FRED Srs.2	PFA 29-11002		14. 6.01	A.I.Sutherland *(Under construction 2001)*	(Edderton)	
G-ORAY	Reims/Cessna F182Q Skylane II	F18200132	G-BHDN	18. 3.94	G A Barret	Gamston	9.10.04
G-ORBD	Van's RV-6A PFA 181-12677 (Lycoming O-320)		G-BVRE	23. 7.01	O.R.B.Dixon	Barton	17. 9.03P
G-ORBS	Mainair Blade 1336-0802-7 & W1131 (Rotax 582)			19. 8.02	J.W.Dodson	(Oakham)	19. 8.03P
G-ORCP	Hawker Siddeley HS.748 Srs.2A	1647	ZS-OCF ZK-CWJ	2. 1.03	Emerald Airways Ltd	Liverpool	AC
G-ORDB	Cessna 550 Citation Bravo	550-1042	N51869	11.12.02	Coalpower Ltd	Gamston	12.12.05T
G-ORDN*	Piper PA-28R-200 Cherokee Arrow II 28R-7235294		G-BAJT N11C	21. 7.93	Not known	Stapleford	4. 9.99
	(Damaged Stapleford 27.5.96: cancelled 18.4.97 by CAA) (Open store 6.00)						
G-ORDO	Piper PA-30 Twin Comanche B	30-1648	N8485Y	19. 4.91	Avcorp Ltd	Jersey	31. 5.03
G-ORED	Pilatus Britten-Norman BN-2T Islander	2142	G-BJYW	10. 1.85	Red Devils Aviation Ltd	AAC Netheravon	25. 9.03A
G-OREV	Revolution Helicopters Mini 500	0112		8. 8.96	R.H.Everett	Thruxton	AC
G-ORFC	Jurca MJ.5 Sirocco PFA 2210 (Lycoming O-290)			16. 5.85	D.J.Phillips	Lasham	3. 7.03P

Regn	Type	C/n	Prev id	Date	Owner/Operator	Location	Expiry
G-ORFE*	Cameron Golf 76SS HAB	2474		2. 7.91	Not known "Dimples"	(USA)	
	(Cancelled 2.12.98 on sale to USA: flying as "G-ORFE" Albuquerque, NM, USA 10.00)						
G-ORFH	Aérospatiale/Alenia ATR-42-300	346	F-WWEI	29.12.93	Aeronautix Leasing Ltd *(Stored 10.01)*	Dinard, France	28.12.02T
G-ORGY	Cameron Z-210 HAB	10320		9. 7.02	A.M.Holly *(Go Ballooning.co.uk titles)*	Berkeley	2. 7.03T
G-ORHE	Cessna 500 Citation	500-0220	(N619EA)	25. 3.96	R.H.Everett	Thruxton	22. 5.03T
	G-OBEL/G-BOGA/N932HA/N93WD/N5220J						
G-ORIG	Glaser-Dirks DG-800A	8-39-A29	BGA4972/KBY	5. 4.94	I.Godfrey "386"	Lasham	4. 2.04
			G-ORIG				
G-ORIX	ARV K1 Super 2	034 & PFA 152-12424	G-BUXH	16. 9.93	T.M.Lyons	Egginton, Derby	18.12.03P
	(Norton AE.100R)		(G-BNVK)				
G-ORJB	Cessna 500 Citation	500-0364	G-OKSP	2. 7.92	Personal Airliner Ltd	(Guernsey)	20.10.04T
	N40DA/N20WP/(N221JB)/N221AC/HB-VFF/N36892						
G-ORJW	Laverda F.8L Falco Srs.4	403	(PH-...)	2.12.85	W.R.M.Sutton	(Hilversum, The Netherlands)	1. 9.01
			G-ORJW/D-ELDV/D-ELDY				
G-ORJX*	BAE Systems Avro 146-RJX85	E2376		16. 2.00	BAE Systems (Operations) Ltd	Woodford	
	(Cancelled 12.12.02 as wfu)						
G-ORMA	Aérospatiale AS355F1 Twin Squirrel	5192	G-SITE	9.11.98	Stratton Motor Co (Norfolk) Ltd	Long Stratton	7. 6.04T
			G-BPHC/N365E				
G-ORMB	Robinson R22 Beta	1607		14.12.90	CHC Scotia Ltd	Cumbernauld	19. 4.03T
G-ORMG	Cessna 172R Skyhawk II	17280344	N9518F	25. 9.98	J.R.T.Royle	Andrewsfield	8.10.04
G-OROB	Robinson R22 Beta	0965	G-TBFC	11. 6.90	R.Culff t/a Corniche Helicopters	Redhill	25. 6.95T
			N80287		*(Spares use 9.97: current status unknown)*		
G-OROD	Piper PA-18-150 Super Cub	18-7856	SE-CRD	27. 6.89	B.W.Faulkner	(Petersfield)	10. 3.05
G-ORON	Colt 77A HAB	1149		8. 3.88	J.Charley tr Orion Hot Air Balloon Group	Wymeswold	1.10.00A
G-ORPR	Cameron O-77 HAB	2341		26. 6.90	T.Strauss & A.Sheehan "Batman"	London SW1	10. 8.01A
G-ORRR	Hughes H369HS	114-0673S	G-STEF	20. 6.01	The Lower Mill Estate Ltd	(Cirencester)	4. 3.04
			G-BKTK/OY-HCL/OO-JGR				
G-ORSP	Beech A36 Bonanza	E-2723	N56037	26.10.92	C.W.Makin t/a Makins	Garforth	15. 1.05
G-ORTM	Glaser-Dirks DG-400	4-209		6. 3.87	M.A.Recht	Aboyne	29. 4.03
G-ORVB	McCulloch J.2	039	(G-BLGI)	2. 8.89	R.V.Bowles *(Rebuilt 2000)*	(Rugby)	AC
			(G-BKKL)/Bahrain Public Security BPS-3/N4329G				
G-ORVG	Van's RV-6	PFA 181A-13509		2. 1.01	R J Fray *(F/f 15.12.01)*	Sibson	13. 1.03P
G-ORVR	Partenavia P68 Victor	115	G-BFBD	2.10.95	Cheshire Flying Services Ltd t/a Ravenair	Liverpool	1. 4.05T
	(Officially regd as P68B Victor)						
G-OSCC	Piper PA-32-300 Cherokee Six	32-7540020	G-BGFD	27.11.84	BG & G Airlines Ltd	Jersey	17. 4.05
			D-EOSH/N32186		*(Made heavy landing Fairoaks 12.8.01: substantial damage to starboard wing spar)*		
G-OSCH	Cessna 421C Golden Eagle III	421C0706	G-SALI	13. 9.95	Sureflight Aviation Ltd	(Birmingham)	8.11.32
			N26552				
G-OSCO*	TEAM mini-MAX 91	PFA 186-12878		24.12.96	P.J.Schofield	(Sproston, Crewe)	20. 8.02P
	(Rotax 447)				*(Cancelled 8.7.02 by CAA)*		
G-OSDI	Beech 58 Baron	TH-1111	G-BHFY	27. 7.84	D.Darling	Wellesbourne Mountford	18. 5.11
G-OSEA	Pilatus Britten-Norman BN-2B-26 Islander	2175	G-BKOL	27. 8.85	W.T.Johnson & Sons (Huddersfield) Ltd	Crosland Moor	23. 3.04
G-OSEE	Robinson R22 Beta	0917		11. 1.89	Aero-Charter Ltd	Manston	13.10.02T
G-OSEP	Mainair Blade 912	1340-0902-7-W1135		29.10.02	J.D.Smith	Baxby Manor, Husthwaite	28.10.03P
G-OSFA	Diamond HK.36TC Super Dimona	36649		15. 6.99	Oxfordshire Sportflying Ltd	Enstone	23. 7.05T
G-OSFC	Reims/Cessna F152 II	F15201872	G-BIVJ	31. 1.86	Stapleford Flying Club Ltd	Stapleford	12. 6.03T
G-OSGB	Piper PA-31-350 Navajo Chieftain	31-7952155	G-YSKY	25. 1.99	Gold Air International Ltd	Blackpool	1. 5.03T
			N3529D		*(Ordnance Survey titles)*		
G-OSHL	Robinson R22 Beta	1000		19. 4.89	Sloane Helicopters Ltd	Sywell	6. 9.04T
G-OSIC	Pitts S-1C Special	1921-77	G-BUAW	7.10.02	J.A.Dodd	(Windsor)	1.12.00P
	(Lycoming O-320)		N29DH				
G-OSII	Cessna 172N Skyhawk II	17267768	G-BIVY	17.10.95	K.J.Abrams	Andrewsfield	14. 3.05T
			N73973				
G-OSIP	Robinson R22 Beta-II	2916		9. 2.99	Heli Air Ltd	Tatenhill	3. 3.02T
G-OSIS	Pitts S-1S Special	PFA 09-12043		19. 9.94	C.Butler *(Current status unknown)*	Netherthorpe	
G-OSIT	Pitts S-1T Special	1023	N96JD	7.12.01	P.Shaw	Breighton	9.12.04
G-OSIX	Piper PA-32-260 Cherokee Six	32-499	G-AZMO	5. 8.86	A.E.Whittie	Blackpool	29. 5.05T
			SE-EYN				
G-OSKP	Enstrom 480	5002	F-GSOT	6. 6.94	Churchill Stairlifts Ltd	Hawarden	9. 8.04T
			G-OSKP/N480EN				
G-OSKR	Best Off Skyranger 912	UK/162 & BMAA/HB/249		14. 1.03	Skyranger UK Ltd	Sywell	
G-OSKY	Cessna 172M Skyhawk II	17267389	A6-KCB	27. 2.79	Skyhawk Leasing Ltd	Wellesbourne Mountford	8. 7.03T
			N73343				
G-OSLD	Europa Aviation Europa XS	485 & PFA 247-13641		23. 8.00	Opus Software Ltd	Black Spring Farm, Castle Bytham	7. 3.03P
	(Rotax 914) *(Tri-gear u/c)*				*(F/f 18.2.02)*		
G-OSLH	Boeing 737-76Q	30283		18. 6.02	EasyJet Airline Co Ltd	Luton	20. 6.05T
G-OSLO	Schweizer Hughes 269C	S.1360	N7507L	15. 3.89	AH Helicopter Services Ltd	Newton Abbot	4. 3.04T
G-OSMD	Bell 206B JetRanger II	2034	G-LTEK	12. 2.99	Stuart Aviation Ltd	White Waltham	6. 2.04T
			G-BMIB/ZS-HGH				
G-OSMS	Robinson R22 Beta	1528	G-BXYW	22. 2.99	Heliflight (UK) Ltd	Wolverhampton	13. 5.05T
			HA-MIU/N528SH				
G-OSMT*	Europa Aviation Europa	079 & PFA/247-12705		15. 6.94	S.M.Thomas	(Stockton-on-Tees)	
	(Monowheel u/c)				*(Cancelled 12.12.00 by CAA -no PtoF issued)*		
G-OSND	Reims/Cessna FRA150M Aerobat	FRA1500272	G-BDOU	16.10.84	Wilkins & Wilkins (Special Auctions) Ltd t/a Henlow Flying Club	RAF Henlow	30. 1.03T
G-OSNI	Piper PA-23-250 Aztec C	27-3852	G-AWER	2. 7.98	Marham Investments Ltd	Belfast	22. 5.04T
			N6556Y				
G-OSOE	Hawker Siddeley HS.748 Srs.2A/275	1697	G-AYYG	17.11.97	Emerald Airways Ltd	Liverpool	10.11.05T
			ZK-MCF/C-GRCU/ZK-MCF/G-AYYG/(x3)/G-11-9		*(Securicor Omega Express titles)*		
G-OSPS	Piper PA-18 Super Cub 95	18-1555	OO-SPS	9. 7.92	T.Gale, J.Morrissey, F.Keegan & D.Curtis	(Dublin)	17.11.02
	(L-18C-PI) *(Frame No.18-1527)*		G-AWRH/OO-HMI/?ALAT 51-15555				
G-OSSF	Gulfstream AA-5A Cheetah	AA5A-0863	G-MELD	1. 2.00	Hecray Co Ltd, t/a Direct Helicopters	Southend	22. 1.04T
			G-BHCB		*(Op Southend School of Flying)*		
G-OSST	Colt 77A HAB	737		28.10.85	British Airways plc "Concorde II"	Heathrow	10.10.96A

Regn	Type	c/n	Prev id	Date	Owner	Location	Expiry
G-OSTA	Auster V J/1 Autocrat	1957	G-AXUJ PH-OTO	22. 7.99	D & M Nelson	Coldharbour Farm, Willingham	1. 4.01
G-OSTC	Gulfstream AA-5A Cheetah	AA5A-0848	N26967	22. 4.91	5th Generation Designs Ltd	White Waltham	5.10.03T
G-OSTU	Gulfstream AA-5A Cheetah	AA5A-0807	G-BGCL	18. 4.95	Hecray Co Ltd t/a Direct Helicopters *(Op Southend School of Flying)*	Southend	3. 7.03T
G-OSTY	Cessna F150G *(Built Reims Aviation SA)*	F150-0129	G-AVCU	21. 3.97	C.R Guggenheim	Bournemouth	15.12.02T
G-OSUP	Lindstrand LBL-90A HAB	098		17. 3.94	T.J.Orchard tr British Airways Balloon Club *"Goes Up"*	Booker	19. 7.01T
G-OSUS	Mooney M.20K (231)	25-0429	OY-SUS (N3597H)	7.11.94	J.B. & M.O.King	Goodwood	21. 1.04
G-OTAC	Robinson R22 Beta-II	2737		8.10.97	Hecray Co Ltd t/a Direct Helicopters	Southend	23.10.03T
G-OTAF	Aero L-39ZO Albatros	232337	N40VC N159JC/(N4321X)/Chad AF TT-ROB/Libyan Arab AF 2337	9. 2.95	P.D.Jackson *(As "111")*	(Edenbridge)	4. 8.03P
G-OTAL	ARV1 Super 2 *(Rotax 912)*	024	G-BNGZ	10. 9.87	N.R.Beale	Shotteswell	26.11.03P
G-OTAM	Cessna 172M Skyhawk II	17264098	N29060	13. 2.89	G.V.White	Norwich	6.12.04T
G-OTAN	Piper PA-18-135 Super Cub *(L-21B-PI) (Frame No.18-3850)*	18-3845	OO-TAN (OO-DPD)/R.Neth AF R-155/54-2445	28.10.96	S.D.Turner	Andrewsfield	29. 5.03
G-OTBA	Hawker Siddeley HS.748 Srs.2A/242	1712	A3-MCA ZK-MCA/G-11-7	14. 3.01	Emerald Airways Ltd	Liverpool	3. 5.04T
G-OTBY	Piper PA-32-300 Six	32-7940219	N2932G	14. 2.91	M.J.Willing	Jersey	5. 4.03
G-OTCH	CFM Streak Shadow *(Rotax 582)*	K.207 & PFA 206-12401		28.10.93	H.E.Gotch	Redhill	3. 9.02P
G-OTDB	MD Helicopters Hughes 369E	0204E	G-BXUR HA-MSC	7. 4.98	D.E.McDowell	(Wantage)	23.1.05T
G-OTED*	Robinson R22HP	0209	G-BMYR ZS-HLG	17. 1.96	Andrews Heli-Lease Ltd *(Cancelled 26.3.02 as WFU)*	Denham	17. 2.02T
G-OTEL	Thunder Ax8-90 HAB	1790		13. 6.90	D.N.Belton	Chard	31 7.03A
G-OTFT	Piper PA-38-112 Tomahawk	38-78A0311	G-BNKW N9274T	14. 3.97	N.Papadroushotis	Panshanger	25. 4.03T
G-OTGA	Piper PA-28R-201 Cherokee Arrow III	28R-7837281	ZS-KFI	21. 2.01	TG Aviation Ltd	Manston	29. 3.04T
G-OTHE	Enstrom 280C-UK Shark	1226	G-OPJT G-BKCO	22. 9.87	GTS Engineering (Coventry) Ltd	Coventry	24. 11.05
G-OTIB	Robin DR400/180R Remorqueur	1545	D-EGIA	26. 4.00	Norfolk Gliding Club Ltd	Tibenham	27. 4.03
G-OTIG	Gulfstream AA-5B Tiger	AA5B-0996	G-PENN (I-TIGR)/N3756L	28. 7.00	D H Green	Elstree	30. 9.04T
G-OTIM	Bensen B.8MV	PFA G/101-1084		5. 6.90	T.J.Deane	(Tilehurst, Reading)	
G-OTIS	Cessna 550 Citation II	550-0672	N550PF PT-OMB/N6763C	19. 4.00	The Streamline Partnership Ltd	(High Wycombe)	19. 4.03T
G-OTJB	Robinson R44 Raven	0813		4. 8.00	Heli Air Ltd	Wellesbourne Mountford	16. 8.03T
G-OTJH	Pegasus Quantum 15-912	7791		20. 3.01	T.J.Hector	(Royston)	8. 4.03P
G-OTOE	Aeronca 7AC Champion	7AC-4621	G-BRWW N1070E/NC1070E	24. 4.90	J.M.Gale *(Damaged Coombe Farm 31.5.95: new CofR 6.01)*	Coombe Farm, Spreyton, Crediton	10. 5.95P
G-OTOO	Stolp SA.300 Starduster Too	PFA 35-13352		26. 8.98	I.M.Castle	(Market Harborough)	
G-OTOY	Robinson R22 Beta	0888	G-BPEW	5. 9.97	Tickstop Ltd	Kimpton Park, Hitchin	24. 9.03T
G-OTRG	Cessna TR182 Turbo-Skylane RG II	R18200766	(N736SU)	14. 3.79	P.Mather	(Saffron Walden)	16.12.04
G-OTRV	Van's RV-6 *(Lycoming O-360-A1A)*	PFA 181-13302		27. 5.98	W.R.C.Williams-Wynne	Talybont	18. 6.03P
G-OTSP	Aérospatiale AS355F1 Twin Squirrel	5177	G-XPOL G-BPRF/N363E	31. 3.98	Anglia Aviation plc *(Op Essex Police Air Support Unit)*	Boreham, Essex	20. 3.03T
G-OTTI	Cameron OTTI 34SS HAB	3490		23. 3.95	Ballonverbung Hamburg GmbH	Kiel, Germany	3. 9.03A
G-OTTO	Cameron Katalog 82SS HAB *(New envelope 1999 - c/n 4382)*	2843		15. 6.92	Ballonverbung Hamburg GmbH *"Otto Versand Katalog"*	Kiel, Germany	6. 7.03A
G-OTUG	Piper PA-18-150 Super Cub *(Frame No.18-5424)*	18-5352	(G-BKNM) PH-MBA/ALAT 18-5352/N10F	17. 2.83	B.F.Walker	Nympsfield	22. 7.04
G-OTUI	SOCATA TB-20 Trinidad	1096	G-KKDL G-BSHU	7. 3.03	P.F.Rothwell	Luton	22.8.05T
G-OTUN	Aerotechnik EV-97 Eurostar	PFA 315-13865		15. 5.02	E.O.Otun	(Maidenhead)	24. 6.03P
G-OTUP	Lindstrand LBL-180A HAB	111		28. 3.94	Airborne Adventures Ltd	Skipton	18. 3.03T
G-OTWO	Rutan Defiant *(Lycoming O-320)*	114		24. 6.87	A.J.Baggarley	Shoreham	14.10.03P
G-OTYE	Aerotechnik EV-97 Eurostar	PFA 315-13858		15. 4.02	A.B.Godber & J.Tye	(Ashbourne)	23. 5.03P
G-OUCH	Cameron N-105 HAB	4830		3. 5.00	Flying Pictures Ltd *(Elastoplast titles)*	Chilbolton	26. 3.03A
G-OUEL	Robinson R44 Raven	1235	N71112	31. 7.02	Universal Energy Ltd	(High Wycombe)	4. 9.05T
G-OUHI	Europa Aviation Europa XS T-G	488 & PFA 247-13684		7. 6.01	Europa Aircraft Co Ltd	Wombleton	
G-OUMC	Lindstrand LBL 105A HAB	724		14. 9.00	A.Holly t/a Executive Ballooning *(Uphill Motor Company titles)*	Bristol	18. 9.03T
G-OURA	British Aerospace BAe 125 Srs.800B	258050	G-ICFR N9LR/G-5-503/I-OSLO/G-5-503/G-BUCR/HZ-OFC/G-5-503	28.11.02	Ourjet Ltd	Farnborough	1.12.02T
G-OURB	British Aerospace HS.125 Srs.700B	257054	G-NCFR G-BVJY/RA02802/G-BVJY/C6-BET	28.11.02	Ourjet Ltd	Farnborough	
G-OURO	Europa Aviation Europa *(NSI EA-81/100) (Tri-gear u/c)*	016 & PFA 247-12522		13.12.93	K.D.Taylor *(F/f 21.6.96)*	Eddsfield	2. 4.03P
G-OURS	Sky 120-24 HAB *(Bear's Head shape)*	168		22.12.99	M P A Sevrin *"Victor"*	Albuquerque, NM, USA	26. 7.03
G-OUVI	Cameron O-105 HAB	1766		4. 5.89	P.Spellward *"Uvistat II"* tr Bristol University Hot Air Ballooning Society	Bristol	31. 3.94A
G-OVAX	Colt AS-80 Mk II Hot-Air Airship *(Reported as AS-105GD - new envelope?)*	1501		3. 7.89	Gefa-Flug GmbH *"Vax Airship"*	Aachen, Germany	9. 2.03A
G-OVBF	Cameron A-250 HAB	3494		1. 3.95	Airxcite Ltd t/a Virgin Balloon Flights *"Virgin Oscar"*	Wembley	27. 9.01T
G-OVBL	Lindstrand LBL 105A HAB	875		10.10.02	R.J.Henderson	Churchdown, Glos	21.10.03A
G-OVET	Cameron O-56 HAB	3939		25. 6.96	E.J.A.Macholc	Saltburn-by-the-Sea	5. 7.03A

Reg	Type	C/n	Prev id	Date	Owner	Location	Date
G-OVFM	Cessna 120 (Continental O-200-A)	14720	N2119V NC2119V	29.4.88	R.B.& E.G.Woods	(Thatcham)	3.10.02P
G-OVFR	Reims/Cessna F172N Skyhawk II	F17201892		23.5.79	Western Air (Thruxton) Ltd	Thruxton	11.6.04T
G-OVID	Avid Flyer (Rotax 532)	NMFC.11760	N879UP	31.5.91	A.J.Dunlop	Long Acre Farm, Sandy	14.7.03P
G-OVLA	Comco Ikarus C42 FB-UK	PFA 322-14028		4.2.03	Fly Buy Ultralights Ltd	(Bedford)	
G-OVMC	Reims/Cessna F152 II	F15201667		29.5.79	J.A.Lyons t/a Staverton Flying School	Gloucestershire	19.8.04T
G-OVNR	Robinson R22 Beta	1634		24.12.90	Helicopter Training & Hire Ltd	Newtownards, Co.Down	14.5.03T
G-OWAC	Reims/Cessna F152 II	F15201678	G-BHEB (OO-HNW)	25.2.80	K.McDonald	Compton Abbas	10.4.04T
G-OWAK	Reims/Cessna F152 II	F15201677	G-BHEA	25.2.80	A.S.Bamrah t/a Falcon Flying Services	Rochester	23.11.04T
G-OWAL	Piper PA-34-220T Seneca III	3448030	D-GAPN N9163K	7.7.98	R.G.& W.Allison	Gamston	25.9.04
G-OWAR	Piper PA-28-161 Warrior II	28-8616054	TF-OBO N9521N	18.2.88	Bickertons Aerodromes Ltd (Op The Pilot Centre)	Denham	27.3.03T
G-OWAX	Beech 200 Super King Air	BB-302	N86Y N300BW/N600CP	4.1.00	Context GB Ltd	Blackpool	10.2.03T
G-OWAZ	Pitts S-1C Special (Lycoming O-320)	43JM	G-BRPI N199M	22.11.94	P.E.S.Latham "Tiny Dancer"	Sleap	5.3.03P
G-OWCG	Bell 222	47041	G-VERT G-JLBZ/G-BNDB/A40-CH	12.8.94	Von Essen Aviation Ltd	(Taunton)	12.3.03T
G-OWCS	Cessna 182J Skylane	18257009	D-EFSA N2909F	25.11.02	P.Ragg	(Weerberg, Austria)	AC
G-OWDB	Hawker Siddeley HS.125 Srs.700B	257040	G-BYFO HB-VMD/VP-BPE/VR-BPE/N47TJ/EC-ETI/EC-375/G-OWEB/HZ-RC1	18.2.99	Bizair Ltd	Jersey	25.4.03
G-OWEL	Colt 105A HAB	1773		18.5.90	S.R.Seager	Aylesbury	16.3.98T
G-OWEN	K & S Jungster 1 (Continental C90)	PFA 44-10124		13.11.78	R.C.Owen	Danehill	
G-OWET	Thurston TSC-1A2 Teal	037	C-FNOR (N1342W)	28.9.94	D.Nieman	Hinton in the Hedges	10.5.02
G-OWFS	Cessna A152 Aerobat	A1520805	G-DESY G-BNJE/N7386L	21.5.02	MAMM Ltd (Op Westair Flying Services)	Blackpool	19.4.03T
G-OWGC	Slingsby T.61F Venture T.2	1875	XZ555	14.8.91	Wolds Gliding Club Ltd	Pocklington	1.11.03
G-OWLC	Piper PA-31 Turbo Navajo	31-679	G-AYFZ N6771L	13.6.91	Channel Airways Ltd	Guernsey	14.8.03T
G-OWND	Robinson R44 Astro	0644		26.8.99	W.N.Dore	Wellesbourne Mountford	7.9.05T
G-OWOW	Cessna 152 II	15283199	G-BMSZ N47254	10.5.95	A.S.Bamrah t/a Falcon Flying Services	Rochester	15.11.04T
G-OWRC	Cessna 525 Citation Jet	525-0177	G-OCSB N1280A/(RP-C717)/N1280A/N5163C	13.12.00	Softbreeze Ltd	Oxford	4.2.03T
G-OWRT	Cessna 182G Skylane	18255077	G-ASUL N3677U	24.8.00	Blackpool & Fylde Aero Club Ltd	Blackpool	17.5.04
G-OWWW	Europa Aviation Europa XS T-G	051 & PFA 247-12683		9.6.94	R.F.W.Holder & N.F.Harrison tr Whisky Group (F/f 26.2.03)	(Ware)	
G-OWYE	Lindstrand LBL 240A HAB	645		27.4.00	Wye Valley Aviation Ltd	Ross-on-Wye	17.6.03T
G-OWYN	Aviamilano F.14 Nibbio	208	HB-EVZ I-SERE	2.2.87	D.Kynaston	Cambridge	31.5.01P
G-OXBC	Cameron A-140 HAB	4981		2.2.01	J.E.Rose	(Abingdon)	5.1.03T
G-OXBY	Cameron N-90 HAB	1993		9.6.94	C.A.Oxby "The Zit"	Doncaster	
G-OXKB	Cameron Jaguar XK8 Sports Car 110SS HAB	3941		9.7.96	Flying Pictures Ltd "Jaguar XK8"	Chilbolton	17.4.02A
G-OXTC	Piper PA-23-250 Aztec D	27-4344	G-AZOD N697RC/N6976Y	31.5.89	A.S.Bamrah t/a Falcon Flying Services	Biggin Hill	15.6.98T
G-OXVI	Supermarine 361 Spitfire LF.XVIe	CBAF.IX.4262	7246M TD248	22.8.89	Silver Victory BVBA (As "TD248/D" in 41 Sqdn c/s)	Duxford	7.7.03P
G-OYAK	SPP Yakovlev C.11 (C/n quoted as 1701139 and/or 690120)	171205	EAF 705 OK-KIH	25.2.88	A.H.Soper (As "27" in Soviet AF c/s)	North Weald	3 5.03P
G-OYES	Mainair Blade 912 (Rotax 912-UL)	1186-1198-7 & W989		12.11.98	J.Crowe	East Fortune	29 3.03P
G-OYST	Agusta-Bell 206B JetRanger III	8440	G-JIMW G-UNIK/G-TPPH/G-BCYP	9.10.02	Oyster Leasing Ltd	(Ipswich)	16.4.04T
G-OZAR	Enstrom 480	5007	G-BWFF	31.7.95	Lancroft Air Ltd	RAF Shawbury	1.11.04T
G-OZBD	Airbus Industrie A321-231	1202	D-AVZN	19.4.00	Monarch Airlines Ltd	Luton	18.4.03T
G-OZBE	Airbus Industrie A321-231	1707	D-AVZH	27.3.02	Monarch Airlines Ltd	Luton	26.3.05T
G-OZBF	Airbus Industrie A321-231	1763	D-AVZB	20.6.02	Monarch Airlines Lt.d	Luton	19.6.05T
G-OZEE	Avid Speed Wing Mk.4	PFA 189-12308		18.4.94	S.C.Goozee	Bow, Totnes	11.9.03P
G-OZOI	Cessna R182 Skylane RG II	R18201950		31.5.85	J.R. & F.L.Gibson Fleming t/a Ranston Farms	Ranston, Blandford Forum	28.6.04
G-OZOO	Cessna 172N Skyhawk II	17267663	G-BWEI N73767	17.11.99	Atlantic Air Bridge Ltd	Lydd	27.8.04T
G-OZRH	British Aerospace BAe 146 Srs.200	E2047	N188US N364PS	29.1.96	Flightline Ltd (Op Croatia Airlines)	Zagreb, Croatia	1.2.05T
G-OZZI	Jabiru Jabiru SK (Jabiru 2200A)	PFA 274-13176		15.8.97	A.H.Godfrey	(Weston-Super-Mare)	22.6.03P

G-PAAA - G-PZZZ

Reg	Type	C/n	Prev id	Date	Owner	Location	Date
G-PACE	Robin R1180T Aiglon	218		16.10.78	Millicron Instruments Ltd	Denham	21.11.03
G-PACL	Robinson R22 Beta	1893	N2314S	17.12.91	R.Wharam	(Rotherham)	14.2.04
G-PADI	Cameron V-77 HAB	1809		18.8.88	R.F.Penney	Watford	23.4.01A
G-PADS	Commander Aircraft Commander 114B	14637	N60987	15.1.98	New Media Holdings Ltd	Guernsey	29.1.04T
G-PAGS	Aérospatiale SA341G Gazelle 1	1155	G-OAFY G-SFTH/G-BLAP/N62406	11.3.96	P.A.G.Seers	Willingale	2.12.02T

Reg	Type	c/n	Prev id	Date	Owner	Location	CofA
G-PAIZ	Piper PA-12 Super Cruiser	12-2018	N3215M / NC3215M (Carries "NC3215M" on tail)	11. 4.94	B.R.Pearson	Eaglescott	14. 6.04T
G-PALL	Piper PA-46-350P Malibu Mirage	4636091	G-RMST	4. 3.99	Pressurised Aircraft Leasing Ltd	Booker	4. 4.03
G-PALS	Enstrom 280C-UK-2 Shark	1191	N5688M	17. 7.80	J.A.Sullivan	(Stockport)	31. 1.03
G-PAPS	Piper PA-32R-301T Turbo Saratoga SP	32R-8529005	F-GELX / N4385D	8. 7.97	W.J.Forrest	(New Mills)	25. 9.03
G-PARI	Cessna 172RG Cutlass II	172RG0010	N4685R	19.11.79	Applied Signs Ltd	Tatenhill	7. 4.05
G-PART	Partenavia P68 Victor (Officially regd as P68B Victor)	62	F-GMPT G-PART/OY-CEY/D-GATE/PH-EEO/(N718R)	19.12.84	Springbank Aviation Ltd	Coventry	21. 1.05
G-PASF	Aérospatiale AS355F1 Twin Squirrel	5033	G-SCHU / N915EG/N5777H	7. 3.91	M.F.Sheardown	Manston	30. 1.05T
G-PASG	MBB Bö.105DBS/4	S.819	G-MHSL / D-HFCC	7.12.92	Police Aviation Services Ltd	Gloucestershire	30. 5.05T
G-PASH	Aérospatiale AS355F1 Twin Squirrel	5040	F-GHLI / LX-HUG/F-GHLI/N356E (Op Polo Aviation)	17. 5.96	Police Aviation Services Ltd	Bristol	24. 3.04T
G-PASV	Pilatus Britten-Norman BN-2B-21 Islander	2157	G-BKJH / HC-BNR/G-BKJH	26. 2.92	Police Aviation Services Ltd	Gloucestershire	18. 7.03T
G-PASX	MBB Bö.105DBS/4	S.814	D-HDZX	20.12.89	Police Aviation Services Ltd	Shoreham	13. 2.05T
G-PATF	Europa Aviation Europa (Rotax 912S) (Monowheel u/c)	107 & PFA 247-12757		5. 1.99	E P Farrell (Current status unknown)	(Beaconsfield)	
G-PATG	Cameron O-90 HAB	3856		13. 3.96	P.A. & A.J.A.Bubb "Purple Rain"	Guildford	29. 8.03A
G-PATI	Reims/Cessna F172M Skyhawk II	F17201311	G-WACZ / G-BCUK	20. 4.00	Nigel Kenny Aviation Ltd	(Lymm)	8. 5.05T
G-PATN	SOCATA TB-10 Tobago	307	G-LUAR	25. 3.97	N Robson	(North Ferriby)	23.11.03T
G-PATP	Lindstrand LBL-77A HAB	471		8. 7.97	P.Pruchnickyj	Weston Turville, Bucks	3. 9.03
G-PATS	Europa Aviation Europa (Rotax 912) (Monowheel u/c)	216 & PFA 247-12888		19. 7.95	D.J.G.Kesterton (Current status unknown)	(Milton Keynes)	
G-PATX	Lindstrand LBL 90A HAB	778		19. 6.01	P.A.Bubb	Guildford	9. 8.03A
G-PATZ	Europa Aviation Europa (Rotax 912) (Monowheel u/c)	069 & PFA 247-12625		2. 6.98	H.P.H.Griffin (F/f 9.7.99)	White Waltham	1. 8.03T
G-PAVL	Robin R3000/120	170		22.11.96	Newcharter (UK) Ltd	Biggin Hill	10. 2.03T
G-PAWL	Piper PA-28-140 Cherokee	28-24456	G-AWEU / N11C	8. 9.82	A.E.Davies tr G-PAWL Group	Barton	14. 6.04
G-PAWN	Piper PA-25-260 Pawnee C	25-5207	G-BEHS / OE-AFX/N8755L (New owner 3.01)	12. 3.01	A.P.Meredith	Lasham	25. 6.93A
G-PAWS	Gulfstream AA-5A Cheetah	AA5A-0806	N2623Q	8. 2.82	Hecray Co Ltd t/a Direct Helicopters (Op Southend School of Flying)	Southend	24. 5.04T
G-PAXX	Piper PA-20-135 Pacer	20-1107	N135XX / G-PAXX/(G-ARCE)/F-BLLA/CN-TDJ/F-DADR	20. 5.83	D.W.Grace	(St.Austell)	17. 9.05
G-PAYD	Robin DR400/180 Regent	847	D-EAYD	14. 1.03	A.Head	Bicester	
G-PAZY	Pazmany PL-4A (Continental A65)	PFA 17-10378	G-BLAJ	20.11.89	C.R.Nash	(Fordingbridge)	3.10.95P
G-PBEE	Robinson R44 Raven	0829		11. 9.00	P.Barnard	Guernsey	21. 9.03T
G-PBEL	CFM Shadow DD	305-DD		27.10.98	P.C.Bell	(Maidstone)	3.10.03P
G-PBES	Robinson R22 Beta	1491	G-EXOR / G-CMCM	17. 3.95	M.Horrell	Conington	28. 3.04T
G-PBUS	Jabiru Jabiru SK (Jabiru 2200A)	PFA 274-13269		18. 8.98	G.R.Pybus	Morgansfield, Fishburn	7. 5.03P
G-PBYY	Enstrom 280FX Shark	2077	G-BXKV / D-HHML	15. 8.97	J.J.Woodhouse	Sandown, Isle of Wight	9. 4.04T
G-PCAF	Pietenpol Aircamper	PFA 47-12433		1. 6.94	C.C. & F.M.Barley (Under construction 2000)	(Farnborough)	
G-PCAM	Fairey Britten-Norman BN-2A Mk.III-2 Trislander	1052	G-BEPH/S7-AAG/G-BEPH (ABN AMRO Bank titles)	26. 9.01	Aurigny Air Services Ltd	Guernsey	14. 6.04T
G-PCAR	Piper PA-46-500TP Malibu Meridian	4697078	N51151	30. 7.01	J.A.Carr	Bournemouth/Guernsey	30. 7.04T
G-PCDP	Moravan Zlin Z.526F Trener Master	1163	SP-CDP	24.10.94	M.A.N.Newall	White Waltham	23. 4.05
G-PDGE	Eurocopter EC120B	1211	F-WQPD	20. 7.01	Cadenza Helicopters Ltd	(London W1)	10. 9.04
G-PDGG	Aeromere F.8L Falco Srs.3	208	OO-TOS / I-BLIZ	6. 1.98	P.D.G.Grist	Sibson	17. 5.04
G-PDGN	Aérospatiale SA365N Dauphin 2	6074	PH-SSU / 5N-ATX/PH-SSU/(G-BLDR)/G-TRAF/G-BLDR	5. 4.01	PLM Dollar Group Ltd	Inverness	19. 7.04
G-PDHJ	Cessna T182R Turbo Skylane II	T18268092	N6888H	3. 1.85	P.G.Vallance Ltd	Redhill	28.12.03
G-PDOC	Piper PA-44-180 Seminole	44-7995090	G-PVAF / N2242A	17.12.85	T.White t/a Medicare	Newcastle	8.10.04T
G-PDOG	Cessna O-1E Bird Dog (Regd as Cessna 305C)	24550	F-GKGP / ALAT (As "24550/GP" in South Vietnamese AF c/s)	25. 9.98	N.D.Needham	Old Manor Farm, Anwick	7. 5.04
G-PDSI	Cessna 172N Skyhawk II	17270420	N739BU	4. 1.88	A.J.Clements & C.I.Bateman tr DA Flying Group	Frensham/Wishanger	26. 2.04T
G-PDWI	Revolution Helicopters Mini-500	0248		14. 2.97	P.Waterhouse	(Stockport)	
G-PEAK	Agusta-Bell 206B JetRanger II	8242	G-BLJE / SE-HBW	7. 3.94	Techanimation Ltd	(Stansted)	16. 5.03T
G-PEAL	Aerotek Pitts S-2A Special (Lycoming AEIO-360)	2048	N81LF / N48KA	11. 5.88	Plymouth Executive Aviation Ltd (Damaged nr Kidderminster 28.6.91: uncovered airframe complete 2.01)	Plymouth	21. 2.92T
G-PEGA	Pegasus Quantum 15-912	7700		14. 8.00	J.J.Bowen	(Stockport)	9. 8.03P
G-PEGG	Colt 90A HAB	1550		28. 6.89	Ballon Vole Association	Fontaine Les Dijon, France	5. 4.03A
G-PEGI	Piper PA-34-200T Seneca II	34-7970339	N2907A	27.11.89	Tayflite Ltd	Perth	20. 7.04T
G-PEGY	Europa Aviation Europa (Rotax 914) (Tri-gear u/c)	096 & PFA 247-12713		16. 5.00	M.T.Dawson (F/f 27.10.00)	(Ilkley)	28. 2.03P
G-PEJM	Piper PA-28-181 Archer III	2843355	N41860	28. 6.00	E.J.Moorey	Bournemouth	29..6.03
G-PEKT	SOCATA TB-20 Trinidad	532	N24AS	28. 7.89	A.J.Dales	Mount Airey Farm, South Cave	7. 3.05
G-PEPL	MD Helicopters MD 600N	RN047	N3047L	5. 2.01	Helidirect UK Ltd	Peplow Hall, Peplow	26. 4.04T
G-PERC	Cameron N-90 HAB	10127		29. 8.01	Stanton Marris Ltd	(London W1)	16. 7.02A
G-PERE	Robinson R22 Beta	3382	N70881	24. 2.03	Wentworth Asset Management Ltd	(Thames Ditton)	
G-PERI	Agusta A109A II	7393	G-EXEK / G-SLNE/G-EEVS/G-OTSL	18.10.02	Aston Pierpoint Ltd	(Hounslow)	3 .7.03T

Reg	Type	C/n	Prev identity	Date	Owner/Operator	Location	CofA
G-PERZ	Bell 206B-3 JetRanger III	4411	N6272T	7. 1.97	C.P.Lockyer	Coventry	27. 2.03T
G-PEST	Hawker Tempest II *(Built Bristol Aeroplane Co Ltd) (Regd with c/n "1181")*	12202	HA604 Indian AF/MW401	9.10.89	Tempest Two Ltd *(Rebuild nearing completion 8.00)*	Hemswell	AC
G-PETR	Piper PA-28-140 Cherokee Cruiser	28-7425320	G-BCJL N9591N	23. 9.85	A.A.Gardner	(Port St.Mary, Isle of Man)	22. 1.06
G-PFAA	EAA Model P2 Biplane *(Continental PC90)*	PEB/03 & PFA 1338		19. 9.78	S.Alexander & M.Coffee	Bidford	2. 1.03P
G-PFAF	Clutton FRED Srs.II	PFA 29-10310		30.10.78	M.S.Perkins Stoke	Golding	29. 7.03P
G-PFAG	Evans VP-1 *(Volkswagen 1600)*	PFA 7022		13.11.78	J.A.Hatch	Netherthorpe	30. 6.89P
G-PFAH	Evans VP-1 *(Volkswagen 1834)*	PFA 7004		23.11.78	J.A.Scott	Chestnut Farm, Tipps End	1. 7.03P
G-PFAL	Clutton FRED Srs.II *(Volkswagen 1600)*	PFA 29-10243		7.12.78	J.M.Robinson *(Stored 4.96)*	Bann Foot, Lough Neagh	27. 7.88P
G-PFAO	Evans VP-1	PFA 7008		12.12.78	P.W.Price	(Cheadle)	
G-PFAP	Phoenix Currie Wot *(Continental O-200-A) (Built as an SE-5A rep)*	PFA 58-10315		12.12.78	J.H.Seed *(As "C1904/Z" in RFC c/s)*	Black Spring Farm, Castle Bytham	17.12.96P
G-PFAR	Isaacs Fury II *(Continental O-200-A)*	PFA 11-10220		18.12.78	J.W.Hale & R.Cooper *(As "K2059" in 25 Sqdn RAF c/s)*	Netherthorpe	6. 6.03P
G-PFAT	Monnett Sonerai II *(Volkswagen 1834)*	PFA 15-10312		26.10.78	H.B.Carter *(Stored Newcastle 5.93: current status unknown)*	(St.Clement, Jersey)	24.10.92P
G-PFAW	Evans VP-1 *(Volkswagen 1834)*	PFA 62-10183		18.12.78	R.F.Shingler	Forest Farm, Welshpool	28. 4.03P
G-PFAY	EAA Biplane	PFA 1525		18.12.78	A.K.Lang & A.L.Young *(Project abandoned 5.98: valid CofR 4.02)*	(Stoke-sub-Hamdon)	
G-PFFN	Beech 200 Super King Air	BB-456	N456CD N861D/N124BB/C6-BFP/C6-CAA/N80NF/N80NE/N100FB	7. 4.00	The Puffin Club Ltd	Carlisle	17. 4.04T
G-PFML	Robinson R44 Astro	0082		9. 9.94	D.J.Parker t/a Skyscraper Aviation	(Llandyssil)	30.10.03T
G-PFSL	Reims/Cessna F152	F15201746	PH-TWF D-ENAX	30. 8.00	P.A.Simon	Biggin Hill	17. 1.04T
G-PGAC	Dyn'Aéro MCR-01 Ban-bi	PFA 301-13186		27. 1.99	D.T.S.Walsh & G.A.Coatesworth	Cambridge	4. 7.03P
G-PGFG	Tecnam P92-EM Echo	PFA 318-13772		30.10.01	P.G.Fitzgerald	Clench Common	30. 5.03P
G-PGSA	Thruster T600N *(Rotax 582)*	0080-T600N-046		11. 8.00	A.J.A.Hitchcock	Clench Common	7. 1.03T
G-PGSI	Robin R2160 Alpha Sport	309	F-GSAF	9. 3.00	P.Spencer	Shoreham	17. 4.03
G-PGUY	Sky 70-16 HAB	131	G-BXZJ	13.12.99	J L Guy t/a Black Sheep Balloons	Skipton	18. 4.03
G-PHAA	Reims/Cessna F150M	F15001159	G-BCPE	19. 6.97	PHA Aviation Ltd	Elstree	11. 4.04T
G-PHEL	Robinson R22 Beta	1669	G-RUMP N2405T	15. 8.96	Focal Point Communications Ltd	Gamston	4. 5.03T
G-PHIL	Brookland Hornet *(Volkswagen 1600)*	17		7. 7.78	A.J.Philpotts *(Stored 5.90: current status unknown)*	St.Merryn	11. 8.89P
G-PHOT*	Cameron Thunder & Colt Film Cassette SS HAB	4507		3. 2.99	Flying Pictures Ltd *(Agfa titles) (Cancelled 16.12.02 as wfu)*	Chilbolton	23. 3.02A
G-PHSI	Colt 90A HAB	2181		12. 5.92	P.H.Strickland & Simpson (Piccadilly) Ltd *(Daks titles)*	Bedford	21. 7.01A
G-PHTG	SOCATA TB-10 Tobago	1008		15.11.89	A.J.Baggarley	Goodwood	14.10.05
G-PHXS	Europa Aviation Europa XS *(Tri-gear u/c)*	523 & PFA 247-13876		22. 7.02	P.Handford	(Wellingborough)	
G-PHYL	Denney Kitfox Model 4	PFA 172A-12189		14. 9.98	J.Dunn	Siege Cross Farm, Thatcham	5. 6.03P
G-PHYS	Jabiru Jabiru SP-470	PFA 274B-13926		19. 2.03	P.C.Knight	(Stafford)	
G-PIAF	Thunder Ax7-65 HAB	1885		19.11.90	L.Battersey *"No Regrets/La Vie en Rose"*	Newbury	24. 3.94A
G-PICT	Colt 180A HAB	1723		22. 3.90	J.L.Guy	Skipton	9. 9.02T
G-PIDG	Robinson R44 Astro	0678		23.11.99	P.J.Rogers	(Lichfield)	11.12.05T
G-PIDS	Boeing 757-225	22155	N505EA	9. 1.95	MyTravel Airways Ltd	Manchester	23. 2.04T
G-PIEL	Menavia Piel CP.301A Emeraude	218	G-BARY F-BIJR	17.11.88	P.R.Thorne	Cublington	5. 3.03P
G-PIET	Pietenpol Air Camper	PFA 47-12267		1. 4.93	N.D.Marshall	RAF Halton	14..5.05P
G-PIGG	Lindstrand Flying Pig SS HAB	473		18. 8.97	Iris Heidenreich	Remscheid, Germany	18. 3.03A
G-PIGS	SOCATA Rallye 150ST	2696	G-BDWB	13. 6.88	D.Hodgson tr Boonhill Flying Group	Wombleton	17. 5.03
G-PIGY	Short SC.7 Skyvan 3A-100	SH.1943	LX-JUL 5T-MAM/(G-14-111)	21.12.95	Babcock Support Services Ltd t/a Babcock HCS	Oxford	21.11.03T
G-PIII	Pitts S-1D Special *(Lycoming O-320)*	7-0314 & PFA 09-10156	G-BETI	11. 1.02	N.A.Scully tr On A Roll Aerobatics Group	(Navenby)	9. 5.01P
G-PIIX	Cessna P210N Pressurised Centurion II	P21000130	G-KATH (N4898P)	12. 6.95	J.R.Colthurst	(Hungerford)	21. 3.05
G-PIKE	Robinson R22 Mariner	1718M		18. 3.91	Sloane Helicopters Ltd	Sywell	6.12.03T
G-PIKK	Piper PA-28-140 Cherokee	28-22932	G-AVLA N11C/(N9509W)	19. 8.88	S J Woodfield tr Coventry Aviators Flying Group	Coventry	16. 9.04
G-PILE	Rotorway Executive 90 *(Rotorway RI 162)*	5143		27. 7.93	J.B.Russell	Magheramorne, Co.Antrim	5.11.98P
G-PILL	Avid Flyer Mk.4 (Rotax 912-UL)	PFA 189-12333		12. 8.97	D.R.Meston	Old Sarum	16. 4.03P
G-PING	Gulfstream AA-5A Cheetah	AA5A-0878	G-OCWC G-WULL/N27153	6.12.95	Plane Talking Ltd *(Op London School of Flying)*	Cranfield	4. 6.03T
G-PINT	Cameron Barrel 60 SS HAB *(Wells Brewery Beer Barrel shape)*	794		4. 1.82	D.K.Fish *"Charles Wells"*	Bedford	13. 2.98A
G-PINX	Lindstrand Pink Panther SS HAB	032		23. 4.93	Magical Adventures Ltd	West Bloomfield, Mi., USA	30. 5.99A
G-PIPR	Piper PA-18 Super Cub 95 *(Frame No.18-832)*	18-826	G-BCDC 4X-ANQ/IDF/AF/4X-ADE	11.10.96	D.S.Sweet	Dunkeswell	29. 8.04T
G-PIPS	Van's RV-4 *(Lycoming O-320-D1A)*	PFA 181-11836		3. 8.90	C.J.Marsh	Whitwell	26. 4.03P
G-PIPY	Cameron Scottish Piper 105SS HAB	3815		30. 1.96	Cameron Balloons Ltd *(Op M.Moffat) "Pipy"*	Almondsbury, Glos	5. 1.03A
G-PITS	Pitts S-2AE Special *(Lycoming IO-360)*	PFA 09-11001		4. 7.85	P.F.van Lonkhuyzen & E.Goggins tr The Eitlean Group	Weston, Dublin	20. 7.03P

Reg	Type	C/n	Prev id	Date	Owner	Location	Date
G-PITZ	Pitts S-2A Special (Lycoming AEIO-360)	100ER	N183ER	2.10.87	A.K.Halvorsen	Barton	19. 6.03P
G-PIXE	Colt 31A HAB	4883		11. 7.00	N.D.Eliot	London SW19	25. 9.03A
G-PIXI	Pegasus Quantum 15-912	7557		27. 8.99	G.R.Craig	Insch	12. 9.03P
G-PIXS	Cessna 336 Skymaster	336-0130	N86648	9. 9.88	Atlantic Bridge Aviation Ltd *(Stored 10.01)*	Lydd	29. 1.95T
G-PIZZ	Lindstrand LBL 105A HAB	629		27. 7.99	HD Bargain SRL	Firenze, Italy	4. 8.03A
G-PJMT	Neico Lancair 320 *(Tricycle u/c)* (Lycoming IO-320-D1B)	PFA 191-12348		8. 5.98	M.T.Holland	Perth	25. 6.03P
G-PJTM	Reims/Cessna FR172K Hawk II	FR17200611	EI-CHJ G-BFIF	13.10.98	P J McNamara t/a Jane Air	Haverfordwest	14.11.04T
G-PKPK	Schweizer Hughes 269C (300C)	S.1454	EI-CAR N69A	3. 8.93	C.H.Dobson	(Louth)	26. 9.05T
G-PLAC	Piper PA-31-350 Chieftain	31-8052038	G-OLDA G-BNDS/N131PP/N3550N	23.12.98	D.B.Harper	Biggin Hill	26. 2.05T
G-PLAH	British Aerospace Jetstream Srs.3102	640	G-LOVA G-OAKA/G-BUFM/G-LAKH/G-BUFM/N410MX/G-31-640 *(Ceased trading 11.01) (Noted 11.02)*	1.11.99	Vale Aviation PLAH Ltd	Blackpool	26. 7.02T
G-PLAJ	British Aerospace Jetstream Srs.3102	738	N2274C C-GJPH/N331QB/G-31-738 *(Ceased trading 11.01)*	30. 3.00	Vale Aviation PLAJ Ltd	Southampton	18. 5.02T
G-PLAN	Reims/Cessna F150L	F15001066	PH-SPR	11. 8.78	D.A.Johnson tr G-PLAN Flying Group	Barton	23.12.05
G-PLAY	Robin R2112	170	F-ODIT	1. 8.79	D.R.Austin	High Cross, Ware	28. 8.04
G-PLBI	Cessna 172S Skyhawk	172S8822	N35368	8. 5.01	Grandfort Properties Ltd	Booker	12. 6.04T
G-PLEE	Cessna 182Q Skylane II	18266570	N95538	4.12.87	Sunderland Parachute Centre Ltd t/a Peterlee Parachute Centre	Shotton Colliery	25. 4.03
G-PLIV	Pazmany PL-4A (Continental A65-8)	PFA 17-10155		19.12.78	B.P.North	RAF Halton	17. 6.03P
G-PLMB	Aérospatiale AS350B Ecureuil	1207	G-BMMB C-GBEW/(N36033)	26. 3.86	PLM Dollar Group Ltd	Inverness	15. 2.04T
G-PLMH	Eurocopter AS350B2 Ecureuil	2156	F-WQDJ G-PLMH/HB-XTE/F-WQPK/HB-XTE	9. 1.95	PLM Dollar Group Ltd	Inverness	25. 2.04T
G-PLMI	Aérospatiale SA365C1 Dauphin 2	5001	F-GFYH F-WZAE	19. 6.95	PLM Dollar Group Ltd	Cumbernauld	8. 7.04T
G-PLOW	Hughes 269B	67-0317	G-AVUM	13. 9.83	Sulby Aerial Surveys Ltd *(Cockpit section only stored 12.01)*	Sywell	29.11.92
G-PLPC	Schweizer Hughes 269C (300C)	S.1558	G-JMAT	14. 4.97	Power Lines, Piper & Cables Ltd	(Carluke)	3. 6.04
G-PLPM	Europa Aviation Europa XS 383 & PFA 247-13287 (Rotax 912S) *(Monowheel u/c)*			17. 5.00	P.L.P.Mansfield	(Hartley Wintney)	
G-PLXI	British Aerospace ATP *(Development a/c with PW 127D engines)*	2001	G-MATP (G-OATP)	26. 8.94	BAE Systems (Operations) Ltd *(Stored 12.01)*	Woodford	2.12.92P
G-PMAM	Cameron V-65 HAB	1155		29. 5.85	P.A.Meecham *"Tempus Fugit"*	Milton-under-Wychwood	28. 9.03A
G-PMAX	Piper PA-31-350 Navajo Chieftain	31-7305006	G-GRAM G-BRHF/N7679L	7. 7.99	AM & T Aviation Ltd	Bristol	18. 9.03T
G-PMNF	Supermarine 361 Spitfire HF.IX	CBAF.10372	SAAF?? TA805	29. 4.96	P.R.Monk *(On rebuild 1995 as "TA805")*	(Maidstone)	
G-PNEU	Colt Bibendum 110SS HAB	4223		5. 1.98	The Aerial Display Co Ltd *(Op Balloon Preservation Group) (Michelin titles)*	Lancing	26. 6.02A
G-POAH	Sikorsky S-76B	760399		30. 3.92	Lynton Aviation Ltd t/a Signature Aircraft Charter	Blackbushe	17. 5.04T
G-POAJ	Canadair CL604 Challenger	5442	N604PS C-GLWR	9. 6.00	P & O Containers (Assets) Ltd	Stansted	8..6.05T
G-POGO	Flight Design CT2K	01-06-02-12		30. 7.01	P.A.& M.W.Aston	Exeter	29. 7.03P
G-POLY	Cameron N-77 HAB	428		13. 7.78	D.M.Barnes, N.F.Biggs, J.L.Hinton, M.A.C.Life & D.J.Thornley tr The Empty Wallets Balloon Group *"Polywallets"*	Bristol	4. 8.00A
G-POND	Oldfield Baby Lakes (Continental A80)	01	N87ED	2.10.90	C.Bellmer	Landshut, Germany	30. 6.03P
G-POOH	Piper J-3C-65 Cub *(Frame No.7015)*	6932	F-BEGY NC38324	17.10.79	P. & H.Robinson	Upper Harford Farm, Bourton-on-the-Water	9. 8.04
G-POOL	ARV1 Super 2	025	G-BNHA	28. 8.87	P.A.Dawson *(Fuselage stored 1.01)*	RAF Keevil	9. 9.90T
G-POOP	Dyn'Aéro MCR-01 Ban-bi (Rotax 912 ULS)	PFA 301-13190		5.11.97	K.& E.Nicholson t/a Eurodata Computer Supplies	Leicester	6.10.03P
G-POPA	Beech A36 Bonanza	E-2177	N7007F N7204R	20. 5.92	C.J.O'Sullivan	Southend	28. 1.05
G-POPE	Eiri PIK.20E Srs.1	20257		5. 3.80	C.J.Hadley *"PE"*	Bidford	6. 6.04
G-POPI	SOCATA TB-10 Tobago	315	G-BKEN (G-BKEL)	20. 4.90	C.J. Earle tr G-POPI Flying Group	Seething	27. 3.04
G-POPS	Piper PA-34-220T Seneca III	34-8133150	N8407H	11. 6.90	Alpine Ltd	Jersey	12. 5.05
G-POPW	Cessna 182S Skylane	18280204	N9451F	10. 7.98	D.L. Price	Little Staughton	19. 7.04
G-PORK	Grumman-American AA-5B Tiger	AA5B-0625	EI-BMT G-BFHS	28. 2.84	C.M.M.Grange & D.Thomas	Southampton	3. 2.05T
G-PORT	Bell 206B-3 JetRanger III	2784	N37AH N39TV/N397TV/N2774R	23. 8.89	J.Poole	(Romsey)	7. 8.04T
G-POSE	Sud SE.313B Alouette II	1430	G-BZGG EI-CTH/F-GKML/ALAT	3.12.01	Alouette Aviation Ltd	Booker	17. 9.04T
G-POSH	Colt 56A HAB	822	G-BMPT	10. 6.86	B.K.Rippon	Didcot	27. 3.03A
G-POTT	Robinson R44 Astro	0383		21.11.97	Ranc Care Homes Ltd	Stapleford	10.12.03T
G-POWL	Cessna 182R Skylane II	18267813	N9070G D-EOMF/N6265N	11.11.82	Hillhouse Estates Ltd	Bowldown Farm, Tetbury	27. 4.04
G-PPPP	Denney Kitfox Model 3 771 & PFA 172-11830 (Rotax 582)			9. 1.91	R.Powers	Otherton, Cannock	10. 7.03P
G-PPTS	Robinson R44 Clipper *(Float equipped)*	0664		14.10.99	Superstore Ltd	Cannes	14. 5.05T
G-PRAG	Brugger MB.2 Colibri (Volkswagen 1835)	PFA 43-10362		29.11.78	D.Frankland tr Colibri Flying Group	RAF Mona	28.11.02P
G-PRAH	Flight Design CT2K	01-06-01-12		31. 7.01	P.R.A.Hammond	London Colney	14. 8.03P
G-PRET	Robinson R44 Astro	0381		8.10.97	J.A.& C.M. Wilson	Folly Farm, Cop Hill, Slaithwaite	26.10.03T
G-PREY	Pereira Osprey II 88 & PFA 70-10193 (Lycoming IO-320)		G-BEPB	28. 9.99	D.W.Gibson	(Doseley)	8. 6.98P

Reg	Type	C/n	Prev id	Date	Owner/Operator	Location	Expiry
G-PREZ	Robin DR400/500	0038		26. 7.02	M.A.Wilkinson	Spanhoe	22. 8.05P
G-PRII	Hawker Hunter PR.Mk.11	41H-670690	N723WT A2616/WT723	14. 7.99	Stick & Rudder Aviation Ltd	Ostend, Belgium	5. 9.03P
	(As "WT723" in RN c/s)						
G-PRIM	Piper PA-38-112 Tomahawk	38-78A0669	N2398A	28. 1.87	Braddock Ltd	Chilbolton	25.12.01T
G-PRIT	Cameron N-90 HAB	1375	G-HTVI G-PRIT	6.11.86	B.J.Hammond	Chelmsford	9. 5.02A
G-PRLY	Jabiru Jabiru SK	PFA 274-13385	G-BYKY	11. 3.02	N.C.Cowell	Tatenhill	30. 8.02P
	(Jabiru 2200A)						
G-PRNT	Cameron V-90 HAB	2819		23. 3.92	E.K.Gray	Droitwich	17. 6.03A
G-PROB	Eurocopter AS350B2 Ecureuil	2825	G-PROD	25. 6.01	Irvine Aviation Ltd	Denham	29. 3.04T
G-PROF	Lindstrand LBL 90A HAB	740		14. 2.01	S.J.Wardle *(Sunbank.com titles)*	Thrapston	4 .3.03A
G-PROM	Aérospatiale AS350B Ecureuil	1486	G-MAGY G-BIYC	11.10.96	Peadar Hughes	Dungannon, Co.Tyrone	23.10.05T
					t/a General Cabins & Engineering		
G-PROP	Gulfstream AA-5A Cheetah	AA5A-0845	G-BHKU (OO-HTF)	16. 2.84	Fortune Technology Ltd	Panshanger	28. 5.01T
G-PROV	Hunting P.84 Jet Provost T.52A (T.4)	PAC/W/23905		13.12.83	Hollytree Management Ltd	(Sutton)	15. 5.03P
	Sing AF 352/ South Yemen AF104 /G-27-7/XS228 tr Provost Group						
G-PROW	Aerotechnik EV-97 Eurostar	PFA 315-13968		30.10.02	G.M.Prowling	(Leeds)	
G-PRSI	Pegasus Quantum 15-912	7492		17.12.98	M H Rollins	(Birmingham)	16.12.02P
G-PRTT	Cameron N-31 HAB	1374		6.11.86	J.M.Albury *"Baby Pritt"*	Cirencester	13.11.00A
G-PRXI	Supermarine 365 Spitfire PR.XI	6S/583003	PL983 G-15-109/N74138/PL983	6. 6.83	Propshop Ltd	Duxford	11. 6.01P
	(Official c/n is HAI 6S-501431)				*(As "PL983/JV-F" in 4 Sqdn, 2 TAF c/s) (New owner 2.03)*		
G-PSIC	North American P-51C-10 Mustang	103-26778	N51PR 43-25147	16. 4.98	Patina Ltd *"Princess Elizabeth"*	Duxford	AC
	(Composite of P-51D IDF/AF 13 major components)				*(Op The Fighter Collection) (Under rebuild 6.00)*		
G-PSON	Colt Cylinder One SS HAB	1780	PH-SON	14. 3.95	R.S.& A.D.Kent	Kirdford	7. 8.99A
	(Panasonic Battery shape)				tr Balloon Preservation Group *(Panasonic Battery titles)*		
G-PSRT	Piper PA-28-151 Cherokee Warrior	28-7615225	G-BSGN N9657K	18. 3.99	P.A.S.Dyke	Little Gransden	13. 6.99T
G-PSST	Hawker Hunter F.58A	HABL-003115	J-4104 G-9-317/A2568/XF947	12. 2.97	Heritage Aviation Developments Ltd	Kemble	30.10.03P
					"Miss Demeanour"		
G-PSUE	CFM Shadow CD	K.139	G-MYAA	1. 4.99	P.F.Lorriman	Middle Stoke, Kent	19. 5.03P
	(Rotax 503)						
G-PTAG	Europa Aviation Europa	337 & PFA 247-13121		14.12.98	R.C.Harrison	Wickenby	20. 2.03P
	(Jabiru 3300) (Tri-gear u/c)				*(F/f 6.9.00)*		
G-PTRE	SOCATA TB-20 Trinidad	762	G-BNKU	14. 6.88	Trantshore Ltd	Lydd	21. 4.04
G-PTWB	Cessna T303 Crusader	T30300306	G-BYNG G-PTWB/N6312V	6.12.84	F.Kratky t/a FK Global Aviation	Denham	3. 4.03
G-PTWO	Pilatus P.2-05	600-30	U-110 A-110	26. 2.81	Bulldog Aviation Ltd	Earls Colne	17. 7.03P
					(As "U-110" in Swiss AF c/s)		
G-PTYE	Europa Aviation Europa	001 & PFA 247-12496		22. 1.96	P.J.Carnes	(Stoke-on-Trent)	1. 9.03P
	(Rotax 912-UL) (Monowheel u/c)				t/a Hitech International *(F/f 29.2.96)*		
G-PUDL	Piper PA-18-150 Super Cub	18-7292	SE-CSE	24. 2.98	R.A.Roberts	Sparr Farm, West Sussex	22. 5.04
G-PUDS	Europa Aviation Europa	253 & PFA 247-12999		9.10.97	I.Milner	Carlisle	2. 4.03P
	(Rotax 914-UL) (Tri-gear u/c)				*(F/f 10.9.99)*		
G-PUFF	Thunder Ax7-77 Bolt HAB	165		17.11.78	C.A.Gould	Ipswich	20. 8.99A
					tr Intervarsity Balloon Club *"Puffin II"*		
G-PUFN	Cessna 340A II	340A0114	N532KG N532KC/N5477J	4.12.96	G.R.Case	Guernsey	15.12.02T
G-PUGS	Cessna 182H Skylane	18256480	SE-ESM N8380S	15. 5.00	N.C.& M.F.Shaw	Great Massingham	12. 6.03T
G-PULL*	Piper PA-18-150 Super Cub	18-5356	PH-MBB ALAT 18-5356/N10F	17. 2.83	R.A.Yates	Sibsey	2. 4.89A
	(Frame No.18-5429)				*(Crashed Eaglescott 13.6.86: cancelled 25.11.87 as WFU: stored 8.90: current status unknown)*		
G-PUMA	Aérospatiale AS332L Super Puma	2038	F-WMHB	31. 1.83	CHC Scotia Ltd	Aberdeen	12. 4.03T
G-PUMB	Aérospatiale AS332L Super Puma	2075		31. 1.83	CHC Scotia Ltd	Aberdeen	15. 5.03T
G-PUMD	Aérospatiale AS332L Super Puma	2077	F-WXFD	31. 1.83	CHC Scotia Ltd	Aberdeen	23. 8.05T
G-PUME	Aérospatiale AS332L Super Puma	2091		3. 8.83	CHC Scotia Ltd	Aberdeen	6. 9.03T
G-PUMG(2)	Aérospatiale AS332L Super Puma	2018	F-ODOS	3. 8.83	CHC Scotia Ltd	Aberdeen	14. 5.05T
G-PUMH	Aérospatiale AS332L Super Puma	2101		3. 8.83	Bristow Helicopters Ltd	Aberdeen	22. 5.04T
G-PUMI	Aérospatiale AS332L Super Puma	2170		27. 1.86	Bristow Helicopters Ltd	Aberdeen	21. 5.05T
G-PUMK	Aérospatiale AS332L Super Puma	2067	LN-OMF G-PUMK/LN-OMF/F-WXFP	23. 3.90	CHC Scotia Ltd	Aberdeen	2. 8.03T
G-PUML	Aérospatiale AS332L Super Puma	2073	LN-ODA G-PUML/LN-OMG	20. 7.90	CHC Scotia Ltd	Aberdeen	4. 7.03T
G-PUMM	Eurocopter AS332L-2 Super Puma	2477		29. 7.98	CHC Scotia Ltd	Aberdeen	21. 9.05T
G-PUMN	Eurocopter AS332L-2 Super Puma	2484	LN-OHF	16. 7.99	CHC Scotia Ltd	Aberdeen	26. 7.03T
G-PUMO	Eurocopter AS332L-2 Super Puma	2467		30. 9.98	CHC Scotia Ltd	Aberdeen	25.10.05T
G-PUMS	Eurocopter AS332L-2 Super Puma	2504		18. 8.00	CHC Scotia Ltd	Aberdeen	30. 1.05T
G-PUNK	Thunder AX8-105 HAB	1719		28. 3.90	S.C.Kinsey *(CofR restored 4.02)*	Amersham	
G-PUPP	Beagle B.121 Pup 2	B121-174	G-BASD (SE-FOG)/G-BASD	23.11.93	P.A.Teichman	Elstree	21.5.05T
G-PUPY	Europa Aviation Europa XS	499 & PFA 247-13694		10. 9.02	P.G.Johnson	(Leeds)	
	(Monowheel u/c)						
G-PURR	Gulfstream AA-5A Cheetah	AA5A-0794	G-BJDN N26893	22. 2.82	N.Bass t/a Nabco Retail Display	Elstree	2. 9.05T
G-PURS	Rotorway Executive (Rotorway RW 152)	3827		19. 1.90	J.E.Houseman	Clitheroe	5. 6.96P
G-PUSH	Rutan LongEz	PFA 74A-10740		11. 7.83	E.G.Peterson	(Nottingham)	
G-PUSI	Cessna T303 Crusader	T30300273	N3479V	26. 7.88	Crusader Aviation Ltd	Oxford	18. 5.03T
G-PUSK	Piper PA-32R-301 Satatoga II HP	3246143	N237TB	24. 8.01	H.Nathanson	Elstree	30. 8.04T
G-PUSS	Cameron N-77 HAB	1577		6.10.87	L.D.Thurgar *"Dick Whittington"*	Bristol	18. 6.01A
G-PUSY	Tiger Cub RL-5ALW Sherwood Ranger	PFA 237-12964	G-MZNF	25. 6.99	B.J.Chester-Master	Moccas	11.11.02P
	(Rotax 582)						
G-PUTT	Cameron Golfball 76SS HAB	2060	LX-KIK	8. 8.95	D.P.Hopkins	Pidley, Huntingdon	
					t/a Lakeside Lodge Golf Centre		

G-PVBF	Lindstrand LBL-260S HAB	504		7. 4.98	Virgin Balloon Flights Ltd	London SE16	30. 4.03T
G-PVCU	Cameron N-77 HAB	4376		22. 5.98	R.G.March & T.J.Maycock	Market Harborough	17 8.03A
					(Coldseal titles)		
G-PVET	de Havilland DHC.1 Chipmunk 22	C1/0017	WB565	23. 5.97	Connect Properties Ltd	Kemble	12.11.03T
					(As "WB565/X" in Army c/s)		
G-PVST	Thruster T600N 450	0122-T600N-074		29.10.02	Thruster Air Services Ltd	Ginge Farm, Wantage	
G-PWBE	de Havilland DH.82A Tiger Moth	LES.1	VH-KRW	23. 7.99	P.W.Beales	White Waltham	11. 8.03P
	(Built Lawrence Engineering & Sales Pty Ltd, Camden, NSW, Australia ex-RAAF spares)						
G-PWER	Agusta A109E Power	11092		6.11.00	Powersense Ltd	Fairoaks	16. 1.04T
G-PWIT	Bell 206L-1 LongRanger II	45193	D-HHSW	18. 5.00	Formal Graphics Ltd	Gloucestershire	13. 7.03T
			G-DWMI/N18092				
G-PWUL	Van's RV-6	PFA 181-12773		3. 7.02	P.C.Woolley	(Woodhall Spa)	
G-PYNE	Thruster T600N 450	0072-T600N-067		27. 8.02	R.Dereham	(Bungay)	27. 8.03P
G-PYRO	Cameron N-65 HAB	567		8. 1.80	A.C.Booth "Pyromania"	Bristol	27. 6.02A
G-PZAZ	Piper PA-31-350 Navajo Chieftain	31-7405214	G-VTAX	18. 1.95	Air Medical Ltd	Oxford	22. 5.03T
			(G-UTAX)/N54266				
G-PZIZ	Piper PA-31-350 Navajo Chieftain	31-7405429	G-CAFZ	30.10.98	Air Medical Ltd	Oxford	22. 3.05T
			G-BPPT/N54297/N9655N				

G-RAAA - G-RZZZ

G-RACA*	Hunting-Percival P.57 Sea Prince T.1	P57/49	WM735	2. 9.80	Not known	Long Marston	4.11.80P
					(Cancelled 28.11.95 by CAA) (Derelict 3.02)		
G-RACO	Piper PA-28R-200 Cherokee Arrow II	28R-7535300	N1498X	12. 9.91	Graco Group Ltd	Barton	12. 3.04
G-RACY	Cessna 182S Skylane	18280588	N7273Y	19.10.99	N.J.& P.D.Fuller	Cambridge	29.12.05
G-RADA	Soko P-2 Kraguj	024	Yugoslav AF 30140	25. 9.96	Steerworld Ltd	Fairoaks	29. 6.01P
G-RADI	Piper PA-28-181 Archer II	28-8690002	N2582X	6. 5.98	G.S. & D.V.Foster	Tatenhill	7. 6.04
			N9608N				
G-RAEM	Rutan LongEz	557 & PFA 74A-10638		15. 3.82	G.F.H.Singleton tr Easy Group	(Matlock)	18. 6.93P
	(Lycoming O-235)						
G-RAES	Boeing 777-236ER	27491	(G-ZZZN)	10. 6.97	British Airways plc (Delftblue Daybreak t/s)	Heathrow	9. 6.03T
G-RAFA	Grob G-115A	8081	D-EGVV	2. 3.89	RAF College Flying Club Ltd	RAF Cranwell	30. 3.04T
G-RAFB	Grob G-115A	8079	D-EGVV	2. 3.89	RAF College Flying Club Ltd	RAF Cranwell	2. 4.04T
G-RAFC	Robin R2112 Alpha	192		19. 5.80	J.E.Churchill tr RAF Charlie Group	Conington	25. 6.04
G-RAFE	Thunder Ax7-77 Bolt HAB	176		18.12.78	L.P.Hooper	Bristol	7. 9.02A
					tr Giraffe Balloon Syndicate "Giraffe"		
G-RAFG	Slingsby T.67C Firefly	2076		2.11.89	Arrow Flying Ltd	Denham	18. 4.05T
G-RAFH	Thruster T600N 450	0032-T600N-063		10. 4.02	R.H.Braithwaite	RAF Halton	9. 4.03P
					tr RAF Microlight Flying Association		
G-RAFI	Hunting-Percival P.84 Jet Provost T.4		8458M	18.12.92	R.J.Everett	North Weald	11. 3.00P
		PAC/W/17641	XP672		(As "XP672/03")		
G-RAFT	Rutan LongEz	PFA 74A-10734		9. 8.82	B.Wronski	Gloucestershire	27.11.03P
	(Continental O-240-A)				"A Craft of Graft"		
G-RAFW	Mooney M.20E Super 21	805	G-ATHW	14.11.84	Vinola (Knitwear) Manufacturing Co Ltd	Leicester	4.10.04
			N5881Q				
G-RAFZ	Rotary Air Force RAF 2000 GTX-SE			7. 5.02	John Pavitt (Engineers) Ltd	(Torrington)	
		PFA G/13-1295					
G-RAGS	Pietenpol Aircamper	PFA 47-11551		8. 6.94	R.F.Billington	(Kenilworth)	
G-RAID	Douglas AD-4NA Skyraider	7722	F-AZED	7. 6.93	Patina Ltd (Op The Fighter Collection)	Duxford	22. 3.02P
	(SFERMA c/n 42)		TR-K.../Fr AF 42/Bu.126922		(As "26922/AK/402" in VA-176 Sqdn USN c/s)		
G-RAIL	Colt 105A HAB	1434		31. 3.89	Ballooning World Ltd "Railfreight"	London NW1	2. 1.03A
G-RAIN	Maule M-5-235C Lunar Rocket	7262C	N5632J	26. 7.79	D.S.McKay & J.A.Rayment	Hinton in the Hedges	10.10.04
G-RAIX	CCF T-6J Texan (Harvard 4)	CCF4...	G-BIWX	16. 2.98	M.R.Paul & P.A.Shaw	Lee-on-Solent	3. 4.03P
	(Possibly c/n CCF4-409 ex 51-17227)		MM53846/RM-22/51-17...		(As "KF584")		
G-RAJA	Raj Hamsa X'Air 582	456 & BMAA/HB/118		13. 9.99	S.R.Roberts tr Priory Flyers	Priory Farm, Tibenham	11.10.03P
G-RALD	Robinson R22HP	0218	G-CHIL	25. 1.96	Heli Air Ltd	Wellesbourne Mountford/Denham	1. 2.06T
			(G-BMXI)/N9074K				
G-RAMI	Bell 206B-3 JetRanger III	2955	N1080N	18.10.90	M.D.Thorpe	Coney Park, Leeds	11. 9.03T
					t/a Yorkshire Helicopters		
G-RAMP	Piper J-3C-65 Cub	6658	N35941	5. 7.90	J.Whittall	Brickhouse Farm, Frogland Cross	31. 8.01P
			NC35941				
G-RAMS	Piper PA-32R-301 Saratoga SP	32R-8013134	N8271Z	17.10.80	Air Tobago Ltd	Gamston	26. 6.05
G-RAMY	Bell 206B JetRanger II	1401	N59554	22. 9.95	Lincair Ltd	(Brigg)	30.10.04T
G-RANS	Rans S-10 Sakota	PFA 194-11537		17. 8.89	J.D.Weller	Egginton, Derby	23. 6.00P
	(Rotax 532)						
G-RANZ	Rans S-10 Sakota	PFA 194-11536		2.11.89	O.M.Dismore	(Corsham)	27. 6.03P
	(Rotax 532)						
G-RAPH	Cameron O-77 HAB	1673		21. 3.88	M.E.Mason "Walsal Litho"	Bristol	28. 5.00T
G-RAPP	Cameron H-34 HAB	2380		16. 8.90	Cameron Balloons Ltd	St.Louis, USA	23. 4.03A
G-RARB	Cessna 172N Skyhawk II	17272334	G-BOII	4. 6.96	Cristal Air Ltd	Lydd	27. 6.03T
			N4702D				
G-RASC*	Evans VP-2	V2-1178 & PFA 63-10422		14.12.78	Not known	Breighton	
					(Crashed on take-off from Bagby 9.7.95) (Cancelled 19.9.95 as TWFU: on rebuild 12.02)		
G-RATE	Gulfstream AA-5A Cheetah	AA5A-0781	G-BIFF	11. 6.84	J.Appleton t/a Holmes Rentals	Blackbushe	14.11.04T
			(G-BIBR)/N26879				
G-RATZ	Europa Aviation Europa	037 & PFA 247-12582		16. 6.95	W.Goldsmith	Morgansfield, Fishburn	23. 8.03P
	(Rotax 912UL) (Monowheel u/c)				(F/f 8.4.97)		
G-RAVE	Southdown Raven X/Mercury Trike	SN2232/0219	G-MNZV	22.12.98	M.J.Robbins	Tunbridge Wells	16. 3.03P
	(Trike is a Mainair Gemini with Rotax 582 [538-0487]: sailwing is from G-MNCV [2000/0219] but not as officially registered. Original trike fitted with						
	Rotax 462 & initially sold to Portugal but then sold to Swiss owner & attached to used Raven sailwing [T.15])						
G-RAVN	Robinson R44 Raven	1022		23. 3.01	Heli Air Ltd	Wellesbourne Mountford	5. 4.04T
G-RAWS	Rotorway Executive 162F	6492		14.11.00	Raw Sports Ltd (Noted 2.03)	Street Farm, Takeley	AC
G-RAYA	Denney Kitfox Model 4	PFA 172A-12403		14.12.92	A.K.Ray	(Stone)	

Registration	Type	c/n	Previous ids	Date	Owner	Location	Status
G-RAYC	Robinson R44 Raven	0771		5. 5.00	TJD Trade Ltd	Cranfield	22. 6.03T
G-RAYE	Piper PA-32-260 Cherokee Six	32-460	G-ATTY / N11C	30. 5.96	G.R.Silver tr G-RAYE Group	Panshanger	8. 8.03
G-RAYS	Zenair CH.250	RED.001 & PFA 24-10460		26.10.78	M.J.Malbon	(Stafford)	
	(Lycoming O-235)				(New owner 9.01)		
G-RBBB	Europa Aviation Europa	073 & PFA 247-12664		6. 5.94	T.J.Hartwell	Sackville Lodge, Riseley	7. 5.99P
	(Rotax 912UL) (Monowheel u/c)				(F/f 10.3.97)		
G-RBCI	Fairey Britten-Norman BN-2A Mk.III-2 Trislander	1035	G-BDWV / 8P-ASF/G-BDWV	16. 3.01	Aurigny Air Services Ltd	Guernsey	15. 4.05T
					(Royal Bank of Canada titles)		
G-RBIN*	Robin DR400 2+2	1225	D-EEVT	25.10.78	(Southern Sailplanes)	Membury	
	(Crashed near Rochester 21.5.93: cancelled 7.9.93 by CAA) (Wreck noted 10.01)						
G-RBMV	Cameron O-31 HAB	4658		27. 7.99	P.D.Griffiths	Romsey	10. 7.03A
G-RBOW	Thunder Ax7-65 HAB	1439		24. 4.89	A.C.Hall "Rain-Beau-Lune"	Melton Mowbray	30. 5.03A
G-RBSG	Dassault Falcon 900EX	113	F-WWFL	21.10.02	The Royal Bank of Scotland plc	Edinburgh	22.10.03T
G-RCED	Rockwell Commander 114	14241	VR-CED / N4917W	19. 6.92	Echo Delta Ltd	Guernsey	13. 5.04
G-RCEJ	British Aerospace BAe 125 Srs.800B	258021	VR-CEJ / G-GEIL/G-5-15	15. 6.95	Aravco Ltd	Farnborough	14. 6.03T
G-RCMC	Murphy Renegade 912	485 & PFA 188-12483		1. 2.93	R.C.M.Collisson	Turweston	30. 6.03P
G-RCMF	Cameron V-77 HAB	1618		23.11.87	J.M.Percival (New owner 2.02)	Burton-on-the-Wolds	19. 8.97A
G-RCML	Sky 77-24 HAB	148		9. 3.99	R.C.M.Sarl	Luxembourg	10 .3.02
G-RCOM	Bell 206L-3 Long Ranger III	51599	TC-HZT	24.10.02	3GRComm Ltd	(Hereford)	AC
G-RDBS	Cessna 550 Citation II	550-0094	G-JETA / (N26630)	7. 5.99	Albion Aviation Management Ltd	Biggin Hill	21. 6.03T
G-RDCI	Rockwell Commander 112A	345	G-BFWG / ZS-JRX/N1345J	15. 5.85	H & W Developments Ltd	Humberside	8. 3.04T
G-RDEL	Robinson R44 Raven	1071		5. 6.01	J A R Allwright	Jaggards House, Weeley Heath	27. 6.04T
					t/a Jara Aviation		
G-RDHS	Europa Aviation Europa XS	549 & PFA 247-13887		31. 5.02	R.D.H.Spencer	(Braintree)	
	(Tri-gear u/c)						
G-RDVE	Airbus Industrie A320-231	0163	OY-CND / F-WWDU	26. 2.97	MyTravel Airways Ltd	Manchester	2. 3.03T
G-READ	Colt 77A HAB	1158	EI-BYI / G-READ	16.11.87	J.Keena	Athlone, Co.Westmeath	13. 9.03A
					(Flying as "EI-BYI" 9.98)		
G-REAH	Piper PA-32R-301 Saratoga SP	32R-8413017	G-CELL / (G-BLRI)/N4361D	15. 8.94	M.Q.Tolbod & S.J.Rogers	Blackbushe	17. 8.03
G-REAP	Pitts S-1S Special	PFA 09-11557		7. 2.90	R.Dixon	Netherthorpe	13. 5.03P
	(Lycoming O-360)				"The Grim Reaper"		
G-REAS	Van's RV-6A	PFA 181-12188		16. 8.94	T.J.Smith	(Ellesmere)	22.10.03P
	(Lycoming O-320)						
G-REAT	Grumman-American GA-7 Cougar	GA7-0033	N29699	6.10.78	Goodtechnique Ltd	Leeds-Bradford	20. 7.03T
G-REBA	Rotary Air Force RAF 2000 GTX-SE	PFA G/13-1334		5.10.01	D.J.Pearce	Henstridge	6. 6.03P
G-REBK	Beech B200 Super King Air	BB-1202	D-IHAP / N44VM/N7207M	22. 5.97	Planstable Enterprises Ltd	Blackpool	28. 7.05T
G-REBL	Hughes 269B	67-0318	N9493F	25. 7.89	Farmax Ltd (Current status unknown)	(Maidstone)	9.10.95
G-RECK	Piper PA-28-140 Cherokee B	28-25656	G-AXJW / N11C	17. 3.88	R.J.Grantham & D.Boatswain Clutton Hill Farm, Clutton		12. 8.04
G-RECO	Jurca MJ-5L2 Sirocco	96	F-PYYD / F-WYYD	30. 9.91	J D Tseliki	Shoreham	
					(Stored 6.93: current status unknown)		
G-RECS	Piper PA-38-112 Tomahawk	38-81A0118	N5824H / D-EFFX/N23138	23. 4.02	S.H.& C.L.Maynard	(Middlesbrough)	2. 5.05T
G-REDA	Robinson R22 Beta	3172		12. 2.01	Simax Services Ltd (Op Red Aviation)	Bournemouth	7. 3.04T
G-REDB	Cessna 310Q	310Q0811	G-BBIC / N69600	17. 6.93	Red Baron Haulage Ltd	Full Sutton	9. 7.04T
G-REDC	Pegasus Quantum 15-912	7572		30. 9.99	Red Communications Ltd	Sutton Meadows, Ely	28.10.03P
G-REDD	Cessna 310R II	310R1833	G-BMGT / ZS-KSY/(N2738X)	2.10.96	G.Wightman	Blackpool	25. 3.05
G-REDI	Robinson R44 Raven	0817		2. 8.00	Redeye.com Ltd	Sheffield City	24. 8.03T
G-REDS	Cessna 560XL Citation Excel	560-5167	N250SM / N5188N	10.10.02	Ferron Trading Ltd	Jersey	9.10.05T
G-REDX	Experimental Aviation Berkut	002 & PFA 252-12481		27. 1.95	G.V.Waters	Norwich	23. 6.03P
	(Lycoming O-360-A1A)						
G-REEC	Sequoia F.8L Falco	654	LN-LCA	2. 7.96	J.D.Tseliki	Kittyhawk Farm, Deanland	17. 8.03P
	(Lycoming IO-320)						
G-REED	Mainair Blade 912S	1282-0501-7 & W1077		11. 6.01	P.A.B.Morgan	(Cambridge)	13. 7.03P
G-REEF	Mainair Blade 912S	1285-0501-7 & W1080		15. 6.01	G.B.Shaw	(Pwllheli)	9. 7.03P
G-REEK	Grumman-American AA-5A Cheetah	AA5A-0429		12. 9.77	J.& A.Pearson	Dundee	10.12.01
G-REEM	Aérospatiale AS355F1 Twin Squirrel	5175		9. 3.98	Heliking Ltd	Redhill	17.12.03T
	G-WEKR/G-CHLA/N818RL/C-FLXH/N818RL/N818R/N5798U						
G-REEN	Cessna 340	340-0063	G-AZYR / N5893M	2. 2.84	E. & M.Green	Guernsey	6.11.05
G-REES	SAN Jodel D.140C Mousquetaire III	156	F-BMFR	23. 4.80	W.H.Greenwood	Swanborough Farm, Lewes	20. 6.04
G-REKO	Solar Wings Pegasus Quasar IITC	SW-TQC-0073 & SW-WQT-0467	G-MWWA	14.11.01	G.S.Stokes Pound Green, Buttonoak, Kidderminster		26.10.03P
	(Rotax 503)						
G-RENE	Murphy Renegade 912	PFA 188-12030		6.11.91	P.M.Whitaker	(Ilkley)	26. 6.03P
G-RENO	SOCATA TB-10 Tobago	249		10.12.81	Lamond Ltd	Birmingham	21. 5.04T
G-RENT	Robinson R22 Beta	0758	N2635M	17. 3.88	Rentatruck (Self Drive) Ltd	Newtownards, Co.Down	12. 6.94T
	(Op Helicopter Training & Hire) (Damaged Newtownards 30.9.92: current status unknown)						
G-REPH	Pegasus Quantum 15-912	7785		6. 2.01	R.S.Partridge-Hicks	(Bury St. Edmunds)	3 .5.03P
G-REPM*	Piper PA-38-112 Tomahawk	38-79A0354	N2528D	8. 1.87	Nultree Ltd	Chilbolton	9.10.95T
	(Cancelled 16.3.01 as destroyed) (Forward fuselage & wings noted 3.02)						
G-REST	Beech P35 Bonanza	D-7171	G-ASFJ	14.12.82	C.R.E.S.Taylor	Biggin Hill	8.10.03
G-RETA	CASA I-131E Jungmann 2000	2197	E3B-305	24. 3.80	N.S.C.& G.English	North Weald	21. 4.02P

G-REXS	Piper PA-28-181 Archer II	28-8090102	N8093Y	14. 1.80	Tatenhill Aviation Ltd	Tatenhill	28. 6.04T
G-REYS	Canadair CL-604 Challenger	5467	N467RD C-GLWX	17. 9.01	Greyscape Ltd	Farnborough	16. 9.04T
G-RFDS	Agusta A109A II	7411	N1YU VP-CLA/VR-CLA/G-BOLA/VR-CMP/G-BOLA	24. 5.99	Castle Air Charters Ltd	Liskeard	22. 7.05T
G-RFIO	Aeromot AMT-200 Super Ximango	200-048		6. 3.95	M.D.Evens	Dunstable	30. 6.04
G-RFSB	Sportavia Fournier RF5B Sperber	51045	N55HC	2.12.88	S.W.Brown	Sibson	1. 4.04
G-RFUN	Robinson R44 Raven	1239		17. 7.02	Heli Air Ltd	Wellesbourne Mountford	29. 7.05T
G-RGEE	Extra EA.300/L	091	D-ESEW	25. 6.01	Skylane Aviation Ltd	Sherburn-in-Elmet	23. 7.04T
G-RGEN	Cessna T337D Turbo Super Skymaster	3371062	G-EDOT G-BJIY/9Q-CPF/PH-JWL/N86056	24. 5.96	Legoprint SPA	(Lavis, Italy)	30.11.02
G-RGUS	Fairchild 24R-46A Argus III (UC-61K-FA)	1145	(PH-) G-RGUS/ZS-UJZ/ZS-BAY/KK527/44-83184 (As "44-83184/7" in USAAC c/s)	16. 9.86	Fenlands Ltd	Sturgate	19. 2.05
G-RHCB	Schweizer 269C-1	0036	N201WL	20. 3.98	S.J. Skilton t/a Aviation Rentals (Op Bournemouth Helicopters)	Bournemouth	9. 4.04T
G-RHHT	Piper PA-32RT-300 Lance II	32R-7885190	N36476	3. 7.78	R.W. & M.Struth	Southend	19. 3.03
G-RHYM	Piper PA-31 Turbo Navajo B	31-815	G-BJLO F-BTQG/(F-BTDV)/N7428L	24. 4.02	Rhymer Aviation Ltd c/o Palmer Aviation Ltd	Fairoaks	30. 1.05T
G-RHYS	Rotorway Executive 90 (Rotorway RI 162)	5140		8.11.93	A.K.Voase & K.Matthews	(Hornsea)	9. 1.02P
G-RIAN	Agusta-Bell 206A JetRanger	8056	G-SOOR G-FMAL/G-RIAN/G-BHSG/PH-FSW	16. 9.87	Thorneygrove Ltd	Wardley	22.12.02
G-RIAT	Robinson R22 Beta-II	2684		27. 5.97	R.Cove & J.P.Gordon t/a RMJ Helicopters	Cranfield	29. 6.03T
G-RIBS	Diamond DA.20-A1 Katana	10143	G-BWWM	7. 7.97	R.Butterfield & A.Dyson t/a Principle Air	(Holmfirth)	28.11.05T
G-RIBV	Cessna 560 Citation Ultra	560-0506	N50820	17. 3.99	Houston Air Taxis Ltd	Oxford	16. 3.03T
G-RICC	Aérospatiale AS350B2 Ecureuil	2559	G-BTXA	30.10.91	Specialist Helicopters Ltd	Nairn	8. 2.04T
G-RICE	Robinson R22 Beta	2509	N93MK	14. 3.97	Heli Air Ltd	Wellesbourne Mountford	3. 4.03T
G-RICK	Beech 95-B55 Baron	TC-1472	G-BAAG	23. 5.84	James Jack (Invergordon) Ltd	Wick	7. 5.03T
G-RICO	American-General AG-5B Tiger	10162	N130U	14. 5.99	Dynasty Trading Ltd	(London SE10)	31. 5.05T
G-RICS	Europa Aviation Europa 125 & PFA 247-12747 (Subaru EA81) (Conventional u/c)			19. 3.96	R.G.Allen t/a The Flying Property Doctor (F/f 27.4.98)	Kemble	16. 9.03P
G-RIDE	Stephens Akro (Lycoming AIO-360)	111	N81AC N55NM	10. 8.78	R.Mitchell t/a Mitchell Aviation (PSA c/s) (Stored 4.02)	RAF Cosford	13. 8.92P
G-RIDL	Robinson R22 Beta	3194		30. 3.01	Peterborough Helicopter Hire Ltd	Conington	23. 4.04T
G-RIET	Hoffmann H 36 Dimona	36224	I-RIET	6. 8.02	L.J.McKelvie tr Dimona Gliding Group	(Lisburn, Co.Down)	16.12.05
G-RIFB	Hughes 269C	116-0562	N7428F	17. 5.90	J.C.McHugh & Son (Civ Eng) Contractors Ltd	Romford	6. 3.03
G-RIFN	Mudry CAP.10B	276		6. 6.96	S.A.W.Becker	Goodwood	30. 6.02T
G-RIGB	Thunder Ax7-77 HAB	1201		16. 3.88	N.J.Bettin	Farnham	27. 8.03A
G-RIGH	Piper PA-32R-301 Saratoga	3246123	N41272 G-RIGH/N41272	23.12.98	G M R & I H L Graham t/a Rentair	Fowlmere	22.12.04T
G-RIGS	Piper Aerostar 601P	61P-0621-7963281	N8220J	18. 5.79	G G Caravatti & P G Penati	Monza, Italy	4.10.03
G-RIIN	WSK PZL-104M Wilga 2000	00010010	SP-WEI	27. 6.01	E.A.M.Austin	(Cirencester)	22.7.04T
G-RIKI	Mainair Blade 912	1280-0401-7 & W1075		29. 8.01	R.Cook	East Fortune	7.10.03P
G-RIKS	Europa Aviation Europa XS 393 & PFA 247-13329 (Rotax 912S) (Tri-gear u/c)			18.10.01	R.Morris	Cambridge	17. 6.03P
G-RILY*	Monnett Sonerai IIL (Volkswagen 1834)	PFA 15-10353		20.12.78	Not known (Cancelled 26.3.97 by CAA) (Stored 5.00)	Hill Farm, Nayland	5.10.89P
G-RIMB	Lindstrand LBL 105A HAB	827		15. 3.02	D.Grimshaw	Leyland	27. 2.03T
G-RIMM	Westland Wasp HAS.Mk.1 (Official records quote "ex NZ3907")	F9605	NZ3908 XT435	11. 3.99	M.P.Grimshaw & T.Martin (As "XT435/430")	RNAS Yeovilton	7. 8.03P
G-RINN	Mainair Blade	1261-1000-7 & W1055		2. .1.01	J.P.Lang	(Chester)	1. 1.03P
G-RINO	Thunder Ax7-77 HAB	975		24. 6.87	D.J.Head "Cerous"	Newbury	5. 3.94T
G-RINS	Rans S-6ESD Coyote II (Rotax 582)	PFA 204-13361		15. 3.99	D.Watt Ladthwaite Farm, Kirkby Steven (Struck hedge on take-off Soulby, Cumbria 30.12.01: major damage)		14. 5.02P
G-RINT	CFM Streak Shadow K199-SA & PFA 206-12251 (Rotax 582)			7.12.93	D. & J.S.Grint	Shoreham	24.11.03P
G-RISE	Cameron V-90 HAB	2395		21. 9.90	D.L.Smith "Rise N' Shine"	Newbury	21.11.98T
G-RIST	Cessna 310R II	310R1294	G-DATS (N6128X)	28. 4.81	F B Spriggs	Bournemouth	5. .2.05
G-RIVR	Thruster T.600F (Hirth H2706)	9029-T600N-031		3.12.99	Thruster Air Services Ltd (Operates on floats) (Noted 12.01)	Farm, Wantage	7.12.00P
G-RIVT	Van's RV-6 (Lycoming O-320) PFA 181-12743			31. 7.95	N.Reddish	Netherthorpe	26. 3.03P
G-RIXS	Europa Aviation Europa XS 533 & PFA 247-13822 (Rotax 912S) (Tri-gear u/c)			2. 7.02	R.Iddon	(Leyland)	
G-RIZE	Cameron O-90 HAB	3163		13.12.93	S.F.Burden	Noordwijk, The Netherlands	25 9.03A
G-RIZI	Cameron N-90 HAB	3080		12. 5.93	R.Wiles	Wadhurst	4. 5.01A
G-RIZZ	Piper PA-28-161 Cherokee Warrior II	28-7816494	D-EMFW N9563N	11. 2.99	Northamptonshire School of Flying Ltd	Sywell	21. 3.05T
G-RJAH	Boeing-Stearman D75N1 (PT-27BW) Kaydet (Continental W670)	75-4041	N75957 RCAF FJ991/42-15852	6. 4.90	R.J.Horne (As "44" in US Army c/s)	Kemble	11. 4.04
G-RJAM	Sequoia F.8L Falco	PFA 100-11665		26. 7.00	R.J.Marks	(Bridgwater)	
G-RJCP	Commander Aircraft Commander 114B	14606	N6001M	3. 7.96	Heltor Ltd	Exeter	30. 8.05
G-RJGR	Boeing 757-225	22197	N701MG N507EA	22.11.94	MyTravel Airways Ltd	Manchester	1. 2.04T
G-RJMS	Piper PA-28R-201 Arrow III	28R-7837059	N6223H	19. 1.88	M.G.Hill	Crosland Moor	21. 5.03
G-RJTT	Bell 206B-3 JetRanger III	4551	C-GJLE	28.11.01	J.A.Robson t/a Air Deluxe	Gloucestershire	20.12.04T
G-RJWW	Maule M-5-235C Lunar Rocket	7250C	G-BRWG N5632H	6.10.87	PAW Flying Services Ltd	Sandtoft	25. 9.03T
G-RJWX	Europa Aviation Europa XS 359 & PFA 247-13197 (Rotax 912S) (Monowheel u/c)			11. 9.00	J.R.Jones (F/f 11.9.01)	(Wrexham)	26. 9.02P
G-RJXA	Embraer EMB-145EP	145.136		18. 6.99	British Midland Airways Ltd (Op bmi Regional)	East Midlands	17. 6.05T

G-RJXB	Embraer EMB-145EP	145.142		23. 6.99	British Midland Airways Ltd	East Midlands	27. 6.05T	
					(Op bmi Regional)			
G-RJXC	Embraer EMB-145EP	145.153	PT-SEE	15. 7.99	British Midland Airways Ltd	East Midlands	14. 7.05T	
					(Op bmi Regional)			
G-RJXD	Embraer EMB-145EP	145.207		4. 2.00	British Midland Airways Ltd	East Midlands	3. 2.03T	
					(Op bmi Regional)			
G-RJXE	Embraer EMB-145EP	145.245		10. 4.00	British Midland Airways Ltd	East Midlands	9. 4.03T	
					(Op bmi Regional)			
G-RJXF	Embraer EMB-145EP	145.280		29. 6.00	British Midland Airways Ltd	East Midlands	28. 6.03T	
					(Op bmi Regional)			
G-RJXG	Embraer EMB-145EP	145.390		20. 2.01	British Midland Airways Ltd	East Midlands	19. 2.04T	
					(Op bmi Regional)			
G-RJXH	Embraer EMB-145EP	145.442	PT-SVD	1. 6.01	British Midland Airways Ltd	East Midlands	31. 5.04T	
					((Op bmi Regional) Star Alliance c/s)			
G-RJXI	Embraer EMB-145EP	145.454	PT-SVD	22. 6.01	British Midland Airways Ltd	East Midlands	21. 6.04T	
					(Op bmi Regional) (Star Alliance c/s)			
G-RJXJ	Embraer EMB-145ER	145.473		23. 7.01	British Midland Airways Ltd	East Midlands	22. 7.04T	
					(Op bmi Regional)			
G-RJXK	Embraer EMB-135ER	145.494	PT-SXN	14. 9.01	British Midland Airways Ltd	East Midlands	13. 9.04T	
					(Op bmi Regional) (Star Alliance c/s)			
G-RJXL	Embraer EMB-135ER	145.494	PT-SXN	14. 9.01	British Midland Airways Ltd	East Midlands	13. 9.04T	
					(Op bmi Regional)			
G-RJXM	Embraer EMB-135ER	145.494	PT-SXN	14. 9.01	British Midland Airways Ltd	East Midlands	13. 9.04T	
					(Op bmi Regional))			
G-RKEL	Agusta-Bell 206B-3 JetRanger III	8617	HB-XPR	2. 8.01	Nunkeeling Ltd	(Brough)	26. 3.05T	
			F-GCVE					
G-RKET	Taylor JT.2 Titch	PFA 3223	G-BIBK	25. 8.99	P.A.Dunley	RAF Valley		
G-RLFI	Reims/Cessna FA152 Aerobat	FA15200340	G-DFTS	17. 1.90	Tayside Aviation Ltd	Dundee	5. 2.03T	
G-RLMC	Cessna 421C Golden Eagle II	421C0118	PH-SBI	9. 3.88	R.D.Lygo	Farnborough	26. 5.03	
			D-IMAZ/I-CCNN/N3849C					
G-RLON	Fairey Britten-Norman BN-2A Mk.III-2 Trislander		G-ITEX	26. 4.02	Aurigny Air Services Ltd	Guernsey	16 12.04T	
		1008	G-OCTA/VR-CAA/(G-OLPL)/VR-CAA/DQ-FCF/G-BCXW *(Royal London Asset Management titles)*					
G-RMAC	Europa Aviation Europa	109 & PFA 247-12717		3. 7.97	P.J.Lawless	Kemble		
	(Monowheel u/c)				*(Under construction 2.03)*			
G-RMAN	Aero Designs Pulsar	PFA 202-13071		6. 6.97	M.B.Redman	Old Sarum	22. 5.03P	
G-RMAX	Cameron C-80 HAB	4705		6.12.99	M Quinn & D Curtain	Dublin	22. 9.03A	
G-RMIT	Van's RV-4	PFA 181-12207		4. 9.96	J.P.Kloos	Truleigh Manor Farm, Edburton	25. 5.03P	
	(Lycoming O-302-E3D)							
G-RMUG	Cameron Nescafe Mug 90SS HAB	3450		3. 5.95	Nestle UK Ltd *"Nescafe"*	Croydon	12. 7.03A	
G-RNAS*	de Havilland DH.104 Sea Devon C.20	04473	XK896	16.11.82	Not known	Filton	3. 7.84	
					(Cancelled 17.4.97 by CAA) (For spares 9.01)			
G-RNBW	Bell 206B JetRanger II	2270	F-GQFH	9. 1.98	Rainbow Helicopters Ltd	Whimple	22. 2.04T	
			F-WQFH/HB-XUF/F-GFBP/N900JJ/N16UC					
G-RNGO	Robinson R22 Beta	3035		19. 1.00	B.E.Llewellyn	Swansea	10. 2.03T	
G-RNIE	Cameron Ball 70SS HAB	2333		3. 8.90	N.J.Bland *"Schwarzenegger"*	Didcot	14. 8.03A	
G-RNLI	Supermarine 236 Walrus 1	S2/5591	W2718	13.12.90	R.E.Melton	Great Yarmouth		
					(As "W2718/AA5Y" in 751 Sqdn RN c/s: on rebuild 6.95: new CofR 8.02)			
G-RNME	Bell 206B Jet Ranger III	947	G-CBDF	18.11.02	R & M International Engineering Ltd	North Creake	7. 3.05T	
			N211KR/JA9119/N58064					
G-RNRM	Cessna A185F Skywagon	A18502541	N1826R	20. 1.87	Skydive St.Andrews Ltd	Sorbie Farm, Kingsmuir	20. 2.03	
					"Thunderchild"			
G-ROAR	Cessna 401	401-0166	G-BZFL	8. 3.82	Special Scope Ltd	Blackpool	16. 9.02	
			G-AWSF/N4066Q					
G-ROBD	Europa Aviation Europa	078 & PFA 247-12671		23. 2.94	R.D.Davies	(Cowbridge)		
	(Monowheel u/c)				*(Current status unknown)*			
G-ROBN	Robin R1180T Aiglon	220		16. 8.78	Bustard Flying Group Ltd	Boscombe Down	13. 8.03T	
G-ROBT	Hawker Hurricane I	--	P2902	19. 9.94	R.A.Roberts	Moat Farm, Milden		
	(Built Gloster Aircraft)				*(On rebuild by Hawker Restorations Ltd from remains salvaged in 1988 from wreck site at Dunkirk Beach: to be "P2902/DX-X")*			
G-ROBY	Colt 17A Cloudhopper HAB	483		7. 2.83	Virgin Airship & Balloon Co Ltd *"Cloudhopper"*	Telford	26. 9.92A	
G-ROCH	Cessna T303 Crusader	T30300129	N4962C	29. 3.90	R.S.Bentley	Cambridge	7. 6.05	
G-ROCK	Thunder Ax7-77 HAB	781		25. 2.86	M.A.Green *"Rocky"*	Rednal	16. 6.03A	
G-ROCR	Schweizer Hughes 269C	S.1336	N219MS	14. 6.90	Oxford Aviation Services Ltd	Oxford	14. 2.03T	
G-RODC	Steen Skybolt	4568	N10624	20. 2.02	R.G.Cameron	(Dundee)	28. 8.03P	
	(Built R.H. Williams)							
G-RODD	Cessna 310R II	310R0544	G-TEDD	2.10.89	R J Herbert Engineering Ltd	Cranfield	1. 8.02	
			G-MADI/N87396/G-MADI/N87396					
G-RODG	Jabiru Jabiru UL (Jabiru 2200A)	PFA 274A-13379		14. 4.99	P.C.Appleton	(Blazey)	9. 5.03P	
G-RODI	Isaacs Fury	PFA 11-10130		22.12.78	M.R.Baker	Westfield Farm, Hailsham	17. 8.95P	
	(Lycoming O-290)				*(As "K3731" in 43 Sqdn c/s: stored 3.97: current status unknown)*			
G-ROGY	Cameron Concept 60 HAB	3055		11. 5.93	S.A.Laing	(Banchory)	8. 9.02A	
G-ROLA	Piper PA-34-200T Seneca II	34-7670066	N4537X	4.12.85	R.A.Denton	Sherburn-in-Elmet	23.11.04T	
			G-ROLA/N4537X					
G-ROLF	Piper PA-32R-301 Saratoga SP	32R-8113018	N83052	7. 1.81	P.F.Larkins	High Cross, Ware	23. 5.05	
G-ROLL	Aerotek Pitts S-2A Special	2175	N31444	20. 2.80	N.Lamb t/a Aerial & Aerobatic Services	Booker	13. 8.04A	
	(Lycoming AEIO-360)							
G-ROME	III Sky Arrow 650TCC	011		26. 5.99	Sky Arrow (Kits) UK Ltd	Old Sarum	16. 6.05T	
G-ROMS	Lindstrand LBL-105G HAB	401		13. 9.96	T D Donnelly *"Gromit"*	Doncaster	13. 9.00A	
					tr Gromit Balloon Group			
G-ROMW	Cyclone AX2000 (HKS 700E V3)	7486		4. 2.99	Financial Planning (Wells) Ltd	Wells	14. 5.03P	
G-RONA	Europa Aviation Europa	043 & PFA 247-12588		17. 1.95	C.M.Noakes	Shenstone	17. 6.03P	
	(Rotax 912UL) (Monowheel u/c)				*"Mr Jake" (F/f 8.3.97)*			
G-ROND	Short SD.3-60 Var.100	SH.3604	EI-CWG	1.11.01	Emerald Airways Ltd	Liverpool	26.11.05T	
			G-OLAH/G-BPCO/G-RMSS/G-BKKU					
G-RONG	Piper PA-28R-200 Cherokee Arrow II 28R-7335148		N16451	14. 6.90	E.Tang	Elstree	7.11.05	

Reg	Type	C/n	Prev ID	Date	Owner/Operator	Base	Date
G-RONI	Cameron V-77 HAB	2349		27. 7.90	R.E.Simpson *"Roni"*	Great Missenden	15. 8.02A
G-RONN	Robinson R44 Astro	0267	N770SC	8. 1.98	R Hallam & S E Watts	Leicester	15. 2.04
			G-RONN/D-HIRR				
G-RONS	Robin DR400/180 Regent	2088		17. 7.91	R. & K.Baker	Newcastle	10. 8.03
G-RONW	Clutton FRED Srs.II	PFA 29-10121		18.12.78	K.Atkinson	Haverfordwest	29. 3.03P
	(Volkswagen 1834)						
G-ROOK	Reims/Cessna F172K Skyhawk II	F17202081	PH-TGY	12. 1.81	Rolim Ltd	Aberdeen	18.11.05T
			G-ROOK		*(Op Bon Accord Flying Group)*		
G-ROOV	Europa Aviation Europa XS 354 & PFA 247-13214			16. 7.98	E.Sheridan & P.W.Hawkins	Biggin Hill	7. 5.03P
	(Rotax 914-UL) *(Tri-gear u/c)*				*(F/f 12.12.99)*		
G-RORI	Folland Gnat T.1	FL.549	8621M	18.10.93	Delta Engineering Aviation Ltd	Kemble	16.12.03P
			XR538		*(As "XR538/01")*		
G-RORY	Focke-Wulf Piaggio FWP.149D	014	G-TOWN	2. 8.88	Bushfire Investments Ltd	Booker	6.10.02
	(Piaggio c/n 338)		D-EFFY/90+06/BB+394				
G-ROSE	Evans VP-1	PFA 7031		22. 1.79	A.P.M.Long	(Leighton Buzzard)	
G-ROSI	Thunder Ax7-77 HAB	1284		29. 6.88	J.E.Rose *"Rosi"*	Abingdon	21. 9.96A
G-ROTI	Luscombe 8A	2117	N45590	18. 4.89	R.Ludgate & A.L.Chapman	Old Hay, Paddock Wood	9.10.97P
	(Continental A65)		NC45590		*(CofR restored 4.02)*		
G-ROTR	Brantly B.2B	403	N2192U	9.12.91	P.G.R.Brown	Trenchard Farm, Eggesford	17.11.02
G-ROTS	CFM Streak Shadow			21.12.89	G.K.Kenealy	Warrington	11. 3.03P
	(Rotax 582) K.120-SA & PFA 161A-11603						
G-ROUP	Reims/Cessna F172M Skyhawk II	F17201451	G-BDPH	23. 5.84	Stapleford Flying Club Ltd	Stapleford	23. 4.03T
G-ROUS	Piper PA-34-200T Seneca II	34-7870187	(G-BFTB)	26. 4.78	Oxford Aviation Services Ltd	Oxford	10. 2.03T
			N9412C				
G-ROUT	Robinson R22 Beta	1241	N8068U	23. 1.90	Preston Associates Ltd	(Guisborough)	16.10.03T
G-ROVE	Piper PA-18-135 Super Cub	18-3846	PH-VLO	6. 5.82	S.J.Gaveston	Headcorn	13. 8.04T
	(L-21B-PI) *(Frame No.18-3853)*		(PH-DKF)/R-156/54-2446		*(As "54-2446/R-156")*		
G-ROVY	Robinson R22 Beta-II	2957		9. 7.99	R.Rice	Wellesbourne Mountford	23. 9.05T
G-ROWE	Reims/Cessna F182P Skylane II	F18200007	OO-CNG	18.12.95	D.Rowe	St.Just	4 3.05
G-ROWI	Europa Aviation Europa XS 435 & PFA 247-13482			16. 6.99	R.M.Carson	(Cheltenham)	
	(Wilksch WAM-120) *(Monowheel u/c)*				*(Current status unknown)*		
G-ROWL	Grumman-American AA-5B Tiger	AA5B-0595	(N28410)	26.10.77	Airhouse Corporation Ltd	Elstree	10. 5.04T
G-ROWN	Beech 200 Super King Air	BB-684	G-BHLC	13.10.87	Valentia Air Ltd	Oxford	10. 4.05T
			N27L/N8511L/G-BHLC				
G-ROWR	Robinson R44 Raven	1036		17. 4.01	R.A.Oldworth	(Petworth)	4. 6.04T
G-ROWS	Piper PA-28-7715296 Cherokee Warrior	28-7715296	N8949F	15. 9.78	Mustarrow Ltd	Manchester	9. 3.03
G-ROZI	Robinson R44 Astro	0252		26. 3.96	Milford Garage Ltd	(Sheffield)	29. 4.05T
G-ROZY	Cameron R-36 Gas/HAB	1141		20. 5.85	Jacques W.Soukup Enterprises Ltd	Florida, USA	18. 9.96A
G-RPEZ	Rutan LongEz	PFA 74A-10746		3. 4.84	B.A.Fairston & D.Richardson	Booker	
					(Stored uncomplete 5.00)		
G-RPBM	Cameron Z-210 HAB	10230		6. 3.02	The Balloon Co Ltd, t/a First Flight	Bristol	4. 3.03T
					(Robert Price Builders Merchants titles)		
G-RRCU	CEA DR221B Dauphin	129	F-BRCU	9.12.99	Merlin Flying Club Ltd	Hucknall	4..9.03T
G-RRFC	SOCATA TB-20 Trinidad GT	2053	F-OILV	9. 5.01	A.T.Paton	Blackbushe	15. 5.04
G-RRGN	Supermarine 390 Spitfire PR.XIX	6S/594677	G-MXIX	23.12.96	Rolls-Royce plc	Filton	3. 9.03P
			PS853		*(As "PS853/C" in 2nd TAF/PRU c/s)*		
G-RROB	Robinson R44 Raven II	10011		6.12.02	Heli Air Ltd	Wellesbourne Mountford	AC
G-RROD	Piper PA-30 Twin Comanche B	30-1221	G-SHAW	20. 6.00	R.P.Coplestone	Thruxton	7. 5.04P
			LN-BWS/N10F				
G-RSCJ	Cessna 525 Citation Jet	525-0298		15. 1.99	Pektron Group Ltd	(Derby)	19. 2.03T
G-RSKR	Piper PA-28-161 Warrior II	28-7916181	G-BOJY	27. 4.95	R.Sherwin-Smith tr Krown Group	Slinfold	26.10.03T
			N3030G				
G-RSSF	Denney Kitfox Model 2	PFA 172-12125		9.10.92	R.W.Somerville	Comber, Co.Down	15. 5.97P
					(Current status unknown)		
G-RSVP	Robinson R22 Beta-II	2788		5. 2.98	Pearce Enterprise Ltd	Brands Hatch	8. 3.04T
G-RSWO	Cessna 172R Skyhawk II	17280206	N9401F	25. 2.98	AC Management Associates Ltd	Kemble	11. 3.04T
G-RSWW	Robinson R22 Beta	1775	N40815	16. 5.91	R.S.Weston-Woods,	Brands Hatch, Dartford	6. 7.03T
					t/a Woodstock Enterprises		
G-RTBI	Thunder Ax6-56 HAB	2584		19. 4.94	P.J.Waller	Norwich	8. 7.02A
G-RTWW	Robinson R44 Astro	0438		20. 3.98	R.Woods t/a Rotorvation	(Longfield)	7. 5.04T
G-RUBB	Gulfstream AA-5B Tiger	AA5B-0928	(G-BKVI)	20. 9.83	D.E.Gee	Blackbushe	23.11.04
			OO-NAS/(OO-HRC)				
G-RUBI	Thunder Ax7-77 HAB	1051		27. 2.87	G.Warren *"Rubicon Computer Systems"*	Norwich	20.11.93A
					t/a Warren & Johnson		
G-RUBY	Piper PA-28RT-201T Turbo Arrow IV	28R-8331037	G-BROU	5. 1.90	R.Harman tr Arrow Aircraft Group	Tatenhill	26. 6.05
			N4306K				
G-RUDD	Cameron V-65 HAB	844		19. 5.82	N.A.Apsey *"Smilie"* (Kodak titles)	High Wycombe	20. 5.00A
G-RUES	Robin HR100/210 Safari	185	F-BVCH	31. 7.02	R.H.R.Rue	(Oxford)	23. 9.05
G-RUFF	Mainair Blade 912	1203-0799-7 & W1006		18. 6.99	C.G.P.Holden	(Chesterfield)	17 .6.03P
G-RUFS	Jabiru Jabiru UL	PFA 274A-13359		19.11.99	J.W.Holland	Kemble	21. 3.03P
G-RUGS	Campbell Cricket Mk.4	PFA G/103-1307		11. 2.99	J.L.G.Mclane	(York)	
G-RUIA	Reims/Cessna F172N Skyhawk II	F17201856	PH-AXA(3)	4.10.79	Knockin Flying Club Ltd	Knockin, Shropshire	13. 7.04
G-RUMI	Noble Hardman Snowbird Mk.IV	SB-018	G-MVOI	9. 9.02	G.Crossley	Tarn Farm, Cockerham	13. 6.02P
	(Rotax 532)				*(Noted as "G-MVOI" 2.03)*		
G-RUMM	Grumman F8F-2P Bearcat	D.1088	NX700HL	20. 3.98	Patina Ltd *(Op The Fighter Collection)*	Duxford	5. 7.03P
			NX700H/N1YY/N4995V/Bu.121714		*(As "21714/201B" in USN c/s)*		
G-RUMN	Grumman-American AA-1A Trainer	AA1A-0086	N87599	30. 5.80	M.T.Manwaring	(Barking)	17. 3.03
			D-EAFB/(N9386L)				
G-RUMT	Grumman F7F-3P Tigercat	C.167	N7235C	6. 4.98	Patina Ltd *(Op The Fighter Collection)*	Duxford	5. 7.03P
			BuA.80425		*(As "80425/WT-4" in US Marines c/s)*		
G-RUMW	Grumman FM-2 Wildcat	5765	N4845V	15. 4.98	Patina Ltd *(Op The Fighter Collection)*	Duxford	28. 6.03P
			BuA.86711		*(As "F" in FAA c/s)*		
G-RUNG	SAAB-Scania SF.340A	340A-086	F-GGBV	3. 6.97	Aurigny Air Services Ltd	Guernsey	5. 6.03T
			SE-E86				

G-RUNT	Cassutt Racer IIIM	161149 & PFA 34-10860		12. 4.83	N.A.Scully	RAF Wyton	12. 9.03P
	(Lycoming O-235)						
G-RUSA	Pegasus Quantum 15-912	7517		7. 4.99	A.D.Stewart	Perth	14..4.03P
G-RUSL	Van's RV-6A	PFA 181-13522		22.10.01	G.R.Russell	(Crewkerne)	
	(Regd by PFA as RV-6 Plans No.181A-13522)						
G-RUSO*	Robinson R22 Beta	1387		25. 5.90	R.M.Barnes-Gorell	Thruxton	6. 4.02T
	(Damaged Thruxton 27.3.00: cancelled 8.6.00 as WFU)						
G-RUUD	Hawker Hunter F.MK.58	41H-697440	J-4073	1. 8.02	Skyline Historical Flight Soesterberg, The Netherlands		
G-RUVI	Zenair CH.601UL	PFA 162A-13933		8.11.02	P.G.Depper	(Kidderminster)	
G-RUVY	Van's RV-9A	PFA 320-13807		4. 1.02	R Taylor	(Wincanton)	
G-RVAL	Van's RV-8	PFA 303-13532		23. 7.01	R.N.York	(Pulborough)	
G-RVAN	Van's RV-6	PFA 181-12657		25. 4.97	D.Broom	Benington	22. 4.03P
	(Lycoming IO-320)						
G-RVAW	Van's RV-6	PFA 181-13234		24.11.97	P.E.Bates High Flatts Farm, Chester Le Street		21. 5.03P
					tr High Flatts RV Group		
G-RVBA	Van's RV-8A	PFA 303-13309		26.10.99	S.Hawksworth (Under construction 2000)	(Nuneaton)	
G-RVBC	Van's RV-6A	PFA 181-12618		16. 2.00	T G Gibbs	(Radstock	
G-RVCE	Van's RV-6A	PFA 181-13372		28. 6.01	M.D.Barnard & C.Voelger	(Welwyn)	
G-RVCG	Van's RV-6A	PFA 181A-13602		26. 4.01	C.J.Griffin	(Stratford-upon-Avon)	
G-RVCL	Van's RV-6	PFA 181A-13439		18. 2.99	C.T.Lamb	(Stamford)	
G-RVDJ	Van's RV-6	PFA 181-12938		8. 2.99	J.D.Jewitt	(Selby)	3.10.03P
	(Lycoming O-360-A4A)						
G-RVDP	Van's RV-4	PFA 181-13416		10. 5.00	D.H.Pattison Lower Upham Farm, Chiseldon		
G-RVDR	Van's RV-6A	PFA 181-13098		15. 5.00	T M Norman	Nottingham	25 .4.03P
G-RVDS	Van's RV-4	PFA 181-12270		28.10.02	D.F.Sargant	(Ludham)	
G-RVEE	Van's RV-6	PFA 181-12262		16. 2.93	J.C.A.Wheeler	Perth	18. 2.03P
	(Lycoming O-360-A1AD)						
G-RVET	Van's RV-6	PFA 181-12852		9. 3.98	D.R.Coleman	Rochester	11. 2.03P
	(Lycoming O-300-D2A)						
G-RVGA	Van's RV-6A	PFA 181-13079		11. 5.98	D.P.Dawson	Rush Green	2. 5.02P
	(Lycoming IO-320-D2A)						
G-RVHT	Cessna 550 Citation II	550-0441	N221GA	17.11.99	Ravenheat Manufacturing Ltd	Leeds-Bradford	22.11.03T
			HB-VKS/VR-CCE/N56PC/N50LM/N1220J				
G-RVIA	Van's RV-6A	PFA 181-12289		13. 8.97	A.N.Tyers	Cumbernauld	26.10.03P
	(Lycoming O-320-E2A))						
G-RVIB	Van's RV-6	PFA 181-13220		22. 6.99	I.M.Belmore	Slinfold	13. 6.03P
G-RVII	Van's RV-7	PFA 181A-13576		13. 9.01	P.H.C.Hall	(Swindon)	
	(Project conceived originally as a RV-6, hence the '181A' prefix)						
G-RVIN	Van's RV-6	PFA 181-13236		28.11.97	R.G.Jones	Rednal	9. 6.02P
	(Lycoming O-320-D1A)						
G-RVIT	Van's RV-6	PFA 181-12422		1. 5.95	P.J.Shotbolt	Ingthorpe	2. 9.03P
	(Lycoming O-360-A1D)						
G-RVIV	Van's RV-4	PFA 181-12366		31.12.97	G.S.Scott Truleigh Manor Farm, Edburton		20 .5.03P
	(Lycoming O-320-D3G)						
G-RVIX	Van's RV-9A	PFA 320-13779		11. 9.01	R.E.Garforth	(Hockley)	
G-RVJM	Van's RV-6	PFA 181A-13861		4.12.02	M.D.Challoner	(Sturminster Newton)	
G-RVMJ	Van's RV-4	PFA 181-13433		16. 2.99	M.J.de Ruiter	(Craigavon)	
G-RVMT	Van's RV-6	PFA 181A-13644		30. 1.01	M R Tingle	Ludham	8. 5.03P
G-RVMZ	Van's RV-8	PFA 303-13395		12.11.99	M.W.Zipfell Hollow Lane Farm, Thurston		21. 1.03P
G-RVRA	Piper PA-28-140 Cherokee Cruiser	28-7625038	G-OWVA	14. 1.97	Mona Aviation Ltd	RAF Mona	19. 4.03T
			N4459X		t/a Mona Flying Club		
G-RVRB	Piper PA-34-200T Seneca II	34-7970440	G-BTAJ	24. 2.97	Cheshire Flying Services Ltd	Manchester	11. 7.04T
			N22MJ/N45113		t/a Ravenair		
G-RVRC	Piper PA-23-250 Aztec E	27-7405336	G-BNPD	14.10.97	Cheshire Flying Services Ltd	Manchester	23. 1.04T
			N101VH/N40591		t/a Ravenair		
G-RVRD	Piper PA-23-250 Aztec E	27-4634	G-BRAV	16. 3.98	Cheshire Flying Services Ltd	Manchester	17.12.05T
			G-BBCM/N14021		t/a Ravenair		
G-RVRF	Piper PA-38-112 Tomahawk	38-78A0714	G-BGEL	21.11.97	Cheshire Flying Services Ltd	Liverpool	24. 5.03T
			N9723N		t/a Ravenair		
G-RVRG	Piper PA-38-112 Tomahawk	38-79A1092	G-BHAF	3. 8.98	Cheshire Flying Services Ltd	Manchester	15. 8.03T
			N9703N		t/a Ravenair		
G-RVRH	Van's RV-3B	PFA 99-10821		17. 2.03	R.Hodgson	(Guildford)	
G-RVRS	Robinson R22 Beta	1478	G-XTEC	31. 1.01	Holly Aviation Ltd	Duxford	11.11.01T
			G-BYCK/N1O1EJ				
	(Struck ground & bounced during autorotational landing Duxford 26.10.01: main rotor damaged & tail boom broken off)						
G-RVRV	Van's RV-4	PFA 181-13024		29. 9.98	P Jenkins (Amended CofR 8.02)	(Inverness)	
G-RVSA	Van's RV-6A	PFA 181-12574		19. 5.99	W.H.Knott (Under construction 2001)	(Inverness)	
G-RVSH	Van's RV-6A	PFA 181-13026		20. 9.02	S.J.D.Hall (Under construction 1.03)	Blackbushe	
G-RVSX	Van's RV-6	PFA 181-13090		18. 9.97	R.L. & V.A.West	(Worthing)	
G-RVVI	Van's RV-6	PFA 181-12418		26. 1.93	J.E.Alsford & J.N.Parr	Sibson	17.10.01P
G-RWHC	Cameron A-180 HAB	2700		16. 4.92	J.J.Rudoni & A.C.K.Rawson	Stafford	13. 4.00T
					t/a Wickers World Hot Air Balloon Co		
G-RWIN	Rearwin 175 Skyranger	1522	N32391	12. 9.90	G.Kay Yew Tree Farm, Lymm Dam		18. 7.03P
	(Continental A75)		NC32391				
G-RWLY	Europa Aviation Europa XS	469 & PFA 247-13701		22. 3.01	C.R.Arkle	(Ascot)	
	(Tri-gear u/c)						
G-RWRW	Ultramagic M-77 HAB	77/221		11.11.02	Flying Pictures Ltd	Chilbolton	
G-RWSS	Denney Kitfox Model 2	PFA 172-12008		16. 4.91	R.W.Somerville	Comber, Co.Down	14. 6.93P
					(Current status unknown)		
G-RXUK	Lindstrand LBL-105A HAB	232		29. 3.95	P.A.Hames "Rank Xerox"	Reading	19. 5.02A
G-RYAL	Jabiru Jabiru UL	PFA 274A-13365		6. 7.99	A.C.Ryall	Cardiff	3.10.02P
G-RYPH	Mainair Blade 912	1248-0500-7 & W1041		8. 6.00	I.A.Cunningham	(Doune)	3. 8.03P
G-RZPH	CFM Streak Shadow SLA	PFA 206-13736		1. 5.01	CFM Aircraft Ltd (Current status unknown) Parham Park		

G-SAAA - G-SZZZ

Reg	Type	C/n	Prev id	Date	Owner	Location	Date
G-SAAB	Rockwell Commander 112TC	13002	G-BEFS / N1502J	5.12.79	P.J.Clothier	Compton Abbas	13. 7.03
G-SAAM	Cessna T182R Turbo Skylane II	18268200	G-TAGL / G-SAAM/N2399E	23. 5.84	M.D.Harvey, M.A.Tokley & J.R.Partner	Earls Colne	22.11.04
G-SABA	Piper PA-28R-201T Turbo Cherokee Arrow III	28R-7703268	G-BFEN / N38745	22. 8.79	D.Booth	Sherburn-in-Elmet	3. 5.04
G-SABR	North American F-86A-5NA Sabre *(Regd with c/n 151-083)*	151-43547	N178 / N68388/48-178	6.11.91	Golden Apple Operations Ltd *(Op The Old Flying Machine Co) (As "8178/FU-178" in 4th Fighter Wing USAF c/s)*	Duxford	18. 6.03P
G-SACB	Reims/Cessna F152 II	F15201501	G-BFRB	7. 3.84	Flight Ltd	(Ashton-under-Lyne)	12. 4.03T
G-SACD	Cessna F172H *(Built Reims Aviation SA)*	F172-0385	G-AVCD	13. 6.83	Northbrook College of Design & Technology *(Op Sky Leisure Aviation)*	Shoreham	27. 7.00T
G-SACF*	Cessna 152 II	15283175	G-BHSZ / N47125	21. 3.85	Derby Aero Club Ltd	Egginton, Derby	8. 6.98T
					(Damaged landing Egginton 21.3.97: cancelled 11.8.97 by CAA) (Wreck dumped 9.02)		
G-SACH	Stoddard-Hamilton GlaStar	PFA 295-13088		27. 8.99	R.S.Holt	(Evesham)	29.10.03P
G-SACI	Piper PA-28-161 Warrior II	28-8216123	N81535	26. 7.89	PJC (Leasing) Ltd	Stapleford	2. 5.05T
G-SACK	Robin R2160	316		2. 5.97	Sherburn Aero Club Ltd	Sherburn-in-Elmet	6. 6.03T
G-SACO	Piper PA-28-161 Warrior II	28-8416065	N4358Z	1. 6.89	D.C.& M.Brooks t/a The Barn Gallery	Oxford	16. 7.04
G-SACR	Piper PA-28-161 Cadet	2841046	N91618	6. 2.89	Sherburn Aero Club Ltd	Sherburn-in-Elmet	20. 2.04T
G-SACS	Piper PA-28-161 Cadet	2841047	N91619	6. 2.89	Sherburn Aero Club Ltd	Sherburn-in-Elmet	20. 2.04T
G-SACT	Piper PA-28-161 Cadet	2841048	N9162D	6. 2.89	Sherburn Aero Club Ltd	Sherburn-in-Elmet	25. 2.04T
G-SACU*	Piper PA-28-161 Cadet	2841049	N9162X	6. 2.89	Sherburn Aero Club Ltd	Sherburn-in-Elmet	19. 2.98T
					(Damaged landing Sherburn-in-Elmet 29.6.96: cancelled 7.6.01 as WFU: wrecked fuselage stored 10.02)		
G-SACZ	Piper PA-28-161 Warrior II	28-7916258	N2098N	26. 7.89	Lima Delta Aviation Ltd	Shoreham	21. 5.05T
G-SADE	Reims/Cessna F150L	F15000752	G-AZJW	28. 5.91	N.E.Sams *(Stored engineless 6.02)*	Cranfield	21. 9.97T
G-SAFE	Cameron N-77 HAB	511		14. 2.79	P.J.Waller "The High Flyer"	Norwich	21. 4.91A
G-SAFI	Piel CP.1320	PFA 183-12103		23. 7.01	C.S.Carleton-Smith	(Great Missenden)	
G-SAFR	SAAB 91D Safir	91-382	PH-RLR	10.10.95	Sylmar Aviation & Services Ltd	Lower Wasing Farm, Brimpton	AC
G-SAGA	Grob G-109B	6364	OE-9254	28. 6.90	G-GROB Ltd	Booker	16. 7.05
G-SAGE	Luscombe 8A Silvaire *(Continental A65)*	2581	G-AKTL / N71154/NC71154	15. 8.90	R.J.P.Herivel	Alderney	10. 4.03P
G-SAHI	FLS Sprint 160 *(Lycoming O-235) (Design known originally as Trago Mills SAH-1)*	001		21.10.80	Aces High Ltd *(Amended CofR 3.02)*	North Weald	30. 4.94P
G-SAIR	Cessna 421C Golden Eagle III	421C0471	G-OBCA / N6812C	1. 4.86	Air Support Aviation Services Ltd	Aberdeen	21. 4.03
G-SAIX	Cameron N-77 HAB	626	N386CB	14. 1.99	C.Walther, B.Sevenich, B. & S.Harren	Aachen, Germany	21. 2.00A
G-SALA	Piper PA-32-300 Six	32-7940106	(G-BHEJ) / N2184Z	17.10.79	Stonebold Ltd	Elstree	16. 3.04
G-SALL	Reims/Cessna F150L	F15000682	PH-LTY / D-ECPH	19. 1.79	D.& P.A.Hailey	Thruxton	7. 8.03
G-SAMG	Grob G-109B	6278		16. 5.84	T.Holloway tr RAFGSA	Bicester	16. 4.05
G-SAMI	Cameron N-90 Sainsbury Strawberry SS HAB	3907	G-BWSE	21. 8.96	Flying Pictures Ltd	Chilbolton	15. 7.02A
G-SAMJ	Partenavia P68B Victor *(C/n indicates P68 model)*	101	D-GERA / CS-AYB/D-GERA	27. 4.01	S.M.Jack tr G-SAMJ Group	Sherburn-in-Elmet	4. 6.04T
G-SAMM	Cessna 340A II *(RAM-conversion)*	340A0742	N37TJ / N2671A	7. 3.88	M.R.Cross	Exeter	5. 7.03
G-SAMY	Europa Aviation Europa *(Tri-gear u/c)*	221 & PFA 247-12901		17. 8.95	K.R.Tallent *(Project partially finished kit @ 4.01)*	(Farnborough)	
G-SAMZ	Cessna 150D	15060536	G-ASSO / N4536U	19. 4.84	Bonus Aviation Ltd	Cranfield	12.12.03P
G-SAND	Schweizer Hughes 269C (300C)	S.1399		17. 8.89	R.C.Hields t/a Hields Aviation	Sherburn-in-Elmet	7.11.04T
G-SARA	Piper PA-28-181 Archer II	28-7990039	N21270	6. 4.81	R.P.Lewis	Full Sutton	2. 5.04T
G-SARH	Piper PA-28-161 Warrior II	28-8216173	N8232Q	18. 2.91	Sussex Flying Club Ltd	Shoreham	18. 2.04T
G-SARK	British Aircraft Corporation BAC.167 Strikemaster Mk.84	EEP/JP/1931	N2146S / Sing.AF 311/G-27-140	13. 1.95	Sark International Airways Ltd *(Op A.Gjertsen Classic Jets Aircraft) (Noted 8.02)*	North Weald	AC
G-SARO	Saro Skeeter AOP.12	S2/5097	XL812	17. 7.78	B.Chamberlain (As "XL812")	Otley, Ipswich	1. 8.01P
G-SARV	Van's RV-4	PFA 181-12606		2.10.00	S.N.Aston	Bicester	4. 6.03P
G-SASA	Eurocopter EC135-T1	0147		12.10.00	Bond Air Services Ltd *(Op Scottish Ambulance Service)*	Inverness/Glasgow City Heliport	22.10.03T
G-SASB	Eurocopter EC135-T1	0151		29. 9.00	Bond Air Services Ltd *(Op Scottish Ambulance Service)*	Inverness/Glasgow City Heliport	5.10.03T
G-SASK	Piper PA-31P Pressurised Navajo	31P-39	G-BFAM / SE-GLV/OH-PNF/N6834L	30.10.97	Middle East Business Club Ltd *(Noted as "G-BFAM" 12.00 qv)*	(Guernsey)	30. 8.91T
G-SATL	Cameron Sphere 105SS HAB	2696		5.12.91	Ballonverbung Hamburg GmbH	Kiel, Germany	29. 4.97A
G-SAUF	Colt 90A HAB *(New envelope c/n 2492 c.1990/1)*	1497		25. 5.89	K.H.Medau	Baden, Germany	7. 6.03A
G-SAWI	Piper PA-32RT-300T Turbo Lance II	32R-7887069	OY-CJJ / N36719	23. 6.99	S.A.& K.J.Williams	Brine Pits Farm, Wychbold	25. 4.05
G-SAXO	Cameron N-105 HAB	3864		1. 4.96	Flying Pictures Ltd *(Citroën Saxo titles)*	Chilbolton	25. 5.00A
G-SAYS	Rotary Air Force RAF 2000 GTX-SE	PFA G/13-1322		4. 9.00	The Aziz Corporation Ltd	(Winchester)	9. 7.03P
G-SAZZ	Piel CP.328 Super Emeraude	PFA 216-11940		4. 7.01	D.J.Long *(Under construction 11.02)*	(Gloucestershire)	
G-SBAE	Reims/Cessna F172P Skyhawk	F17202200	D-EOCD(3)	3. 6.98	BAE Systems (Operations) Ltd	Blackpool	25. 7.04T
G-SBAS	Beech B200 Super King Air	BB-1007	SE-IVZ / N777GA/G-BJJV	16.11.90	Gama Aviation Ltd	Aberdeen	20.12.03T
G-SBHH	Schweizer 269C (300C)	S.1314	G-XALP / N41S	7. 5.02	Hughes Helicopter Co Ltd t/a Biggin Hill Helicopters	Biggin Hill	8.10.03T
G-SBIZ	Cameron Z-90 HAB	10348		12.12.02	Snow Business International Ltd	Stroud, Glos	1.12.03A

Reg	Type	c/n	Prev id	Date	Owner/Operator	Location	Date
G-SBLT	Steen Skybolt	MH-01		14. 4.92	S.D.Arnold tr Skybolt Group *(Current status unknown)*	Coventry	
G-SBMM	Piper PA-28R-180 Cherokee Arrow	28R-30877	G-BBEL SE-FDX	8. 2.02	K.S.Kalsi	Conington	26. 4.04T
G-SBMO	Robin R2160I	116	EI-BMO SE-GSZ	12. 2.99	D.Henderson, U.Simpson & M.Mannion	Waterford	26. 4.02T
G-SBUS	Britten-Norman BN-2A-26 Islander *(Built PADC)*	3013	G-BMMH RP-C578	31.10.86	Isles of Scilly Skybus Ltd	St.Just	17. 4.03T
G-SBUT	Robinson R22 Beta-II	2739	G-BXMT	18. 5.98	Princepro Ltd	(Alfreton)	12.11.03T
G-SCAN	Vinten Wallis WA-116 Srs.100/R *(Rotax 532)*	001		5. 7.82	K.H.Wallis *(Stored 8.01)*	Reymerston Hall, Norfolk	10. 7.91P
G-SCAT	Cessna F150F *(Built Reims Aviation SA) (Wichita c/n 15063455)*	F150-0054	G-ATRN (G-ATMN) *(Tail-wheel u/c)*	15. 9.86	Westward Airways (Lands End) Ltd	Lands End	10. 4.05T
G-SCBI	SOCATA TB-20 Trinidad	1908	F-OIGV	10. 8.99	S.C.Brown t/a Ace Services	Enstone	17. 8.05T
G-SCFO	Cameron O-77 HAB	1131		3. 5.85	M.K.Grigson *(Op Balloon Preservation Group) "Southern Counties"*	Kidford	24. 5.95A
G-SCHI	Eurocopter AS350B2 Ecureuil	3337	F-WQOQ	5. 2.01	Patriot Aviation Ltd	(Birmingham)	22. 3.04T
G-SCIP	SOCATA TB-20 Trinidad GT	2014	F-OILO	19. 9.00	J.C.White	Oxford	24..9.03
G-SCLX	FLS Aerospace Sprint 160	002	G-PLYM	14. 7.94	Aces High Ltd	Dunsfold Park	16. 7.03T
G-SCOI	Agusta A.109E Power	11051	G-HPWH G-HWPH	16. 8.02	B.K.Scowcroft	Belle Isle, Lake Windermere	23. 6.05T
G-SCOO	Bell 206B JetRanger II	1129	G-CORC G-CJHI/G-BBFB/N18094	23. 6.00	Hughes Helicopter Co Ltd t/a Biggin Hill Helicopters	Biggin Hill	12. 7.03T
G-SCPL	Piper PA-28-140 Cherokee Cruiser	28-7725160	G-BPVL N1785H	4. 5.89	Aeros Leasing Ltd	Gloucestershire	19. 8.04T
G-SCRU	Cameron A-250 HAB	3935	G-BWWO	30. 9.96	Societe Bombard SARL	Meursanges, France	6.10.03A
G-SCTA	Westland Scout AH.1	F.9701	XV126	18.12.95	G.R.Harrison *(As "XV126/X" in AAC c/s)*	(Guildford)	7. 7.03P
G-SCUB	Piper PA-18-135 Super Cub *(L-21B-PI) (Frame No.18-3849)*	18-3847	PH-GAX R.Neth AF R-157/54-2447	13.12.78	N.D. & Mrs.C.L.Needham t/a N.D.Needham (Farms) *(As "54-2447" in US Army c/s)*	Old Manor Farm, Anwick	23. 8.03
G-SCUD	Montgomerie-Bensen B.8MR	PFA G/101-1294		18. 8.97	D.Taylor	Belper	
G-SCUL	Rutan Cozy	PFA 159-13212		28. 5.98	K.R.W.Scull	(Usk)	
G-SCUR	Eurocopter EC120B	1090		1. 3.00	JS Aviation Ltd	Luton	18..5.03T
G-SDCI	Bell 206B JetRanger II	925	G-GHCL G-SHVV/N72GM/N83106	24. 2.00	S.D.Coomes	(Auldhouse, East Kilbride)	3. 6.05T
G-SDEV	de Havilland DH.104 Sea Devon C.20	04472	XK895	29. 3.90	Wyndeham Press Group plc *(As "XK895/CU19" in 771 Sqdn RN c/s)*	Kemble	17. 9.01
G-SDFM	Aerotechnik EV-97 Eurostar	PFA 315-13884		23. 8.02	A.K.Paterson	(Sleaford)	22.10.03P
G-SDLW	Cameron O-105 HAB	2460		11. 3.91	P.J.Smart	Bath	15. 5.99A
G-SEAI	Cessna U206G Stationair 6 *(Amphibian)*	U20604059	N756FQ	20. 3.92	K.O'Connor	Weston, Dublin	8. 3.03T
G-SEAT	Colt 42A HAB	817		28. 5.86	Virgin Airship & Balloon Co Ltd *"Virgin Atlantic"*	Telford	7. 4.95A
G-SEED	Piper J-3C-90 Cub *(L-4H-PI) (Frame No.10932)*	11098	EI-BAP F-BFBZ/44-80203/43-29807	28. 1.80	J.H.Seed Black Spring Farm, Castle Bytham *(Official identity is c/n 12499/44-80203 & probably rebuilt 1945)*		9. 6.03P
G-SEEK	Cessna T210N Turbo-Centurion II	21064579	N9721Y	14.10.83	A.Hopper	Little Shelford	21. 3.03
G-SEJW	Piper PA-28-161 Cherokee Warrior II	28-7816469	N9557N	19. 4.78	Keen Leasing Ltd	Belfast	26. 4.03T
G-SELF	Europa Aviation Europa *(Jabiru 3300) (Monowheel u/c)*	279 & PFA 247-12996		10. 8.01	N.D.Crisp, A.H.Lames & E.J.Hatcher	(Leigh-on-Sea)	
G-SELL	Robin DR400/180 Regent	1153	D-EEMT	7. 3.85	C.Morris tr G-SELL Regent Group	Bidford	10. 4.03
G-SELY	Agusta-Bell 206B-3 JetRanger III	8740		26. 7.96	GR8 Developments Ltd *(Op G Riddel)*	Glenrothes	15. 9.05T
G-SEMI	Piper PA-44-180 Seminole	44-7995052	G-DENW N21439	23. 2.99	T.Hiscox	Wolverhampton	22.12.02T
G-SENA	Rutan LongEz	1325	F-PZSQ F-WZSQ	11.11.96	G.Bennett	(Great Yarmouth)	
G-SEND	Colt 90A HAB	2100		2.12.91	B.Nigrowsky	Bouzille, France	28. 1.03T
G-SENX	Piper PA-34-200T Seneca II	34-7870356	G-DARE G-WOTS/G-SEVL/N36742	15. 5.95	Katotech Ltd	Cardiff	2. 7.04T
G-SEPA	Eurocopter AS355N Twin Squirrel	5525	G-METD G-BUJF/F-WYMF	25. 7.96	Metropolitan Police Authority Fairoaks/Lippitts Hill, Loughton		4. 8.05T
G-SEPB	Eurocopter AS355N Twin Squirrel	5574	G-BVSE	1. 2.95	Metropolitan Police Authority Fairoaks/Lippitts Hill, Loughton		1. 3.04T
G-SEPC	Eurocopter AS355N Twin Squirrel	5596	G-BWGV	29.11.95	Metropolitan Police Authority Fairoaks/Lippitts Hill, Loughton		20. 3.05T
G-SEPT	Cameron N-105 HAB	1880		22.11.88	P.Gooch *"Septodont"*	Alresford	12. 4.03A
G-SERA	Enstrom F-28A-UK	103	G-BAHU EI-BDF/G-BAHU	14. 3.91	W.R.Pitcher t/a Enstrom Associates	Leatherhead	1. 5.03T
G-SERL	SOCATA TB-10 Tobago	109	G-LANA EI-BIH	28. 5.92	R.J.Searle	Rochester	19. 4.03
G-SETI	Cameron Sky 80-16 HAB	4853		25. 9.00	R.P.Allan	Chinnor	30.12.02A
G-SEVA	Replica Plans SE.5A *(Continental C90)*	PFA 20-10955		19. 6.85	I.D.Gregory *(As "F-141/G" in 141 Sqdn RFC c/s)*	Boscombe Down	2. 1.03P
G-SEVE	Cessna 172N Skyhawk II	17269970	N738GR	10. 1.90	MK Aero Support Ltd	Andrewsfield	13. 2.05T
G-SEVN	Van's RV-7	PFA 323-13795		13. 9.01	N.Reddish	(Kirkby-in-Ashfield)	
G-SEWP	Aérospatiale AS355F2 Twin Squirrel	5480	G-OFIN G-DANS/G-BTNM	14. 8.00	Veritair Ltd	Cardiff Heliport	14. 6.05T
G-SEXI	Cessna 172M Skyhawk II	17263806	N1964V	21. 4.92	Willowair Flying Club (1996) Ltd	Southend	5. 9.04T
	(Bounced landing Nayland 2.2.02 & overran: struck hedge & came to rest inverted: damaged beyond repair)						
G-SEXY*	American American AA-1 Yankee *(Regd incorrectly as c/n 0042)*	AA1-0442	G-AYLM	30. 6.81	Not known *(Damaged landing Burscough, Lancs 11.2.94: stored 1.01)*	Liverpool	17. 3.95
G-SFHR	Piper PA-23-250 Aztec F	27-8054041	G-BHSO N2527Z	24. 6.82	Comed Aviation Ltd	Blackpool	22.11.01T
G-SFOX	Rotorway Executive 90 *(Rotorway RI 162)*	5059	G-BUAH	11.10.93	Magpie Computer Services Ltd Crabtree Farm, Crowborough		29.10.02P

G-SFPA	Reims/Cessna F406 Caravan II	F406-0064		11.11.91	Secretary of State for Scotland/Dept of Agriculture & Fisheries		
					(Op Direct Flight for Fisheries Protection Agency)	Prestwick	12. 3.03T
G-SFPB	Reims/Cessna F406 Caravan II	F406-0065		11.11.91	Secretary of State for Scotland/Dept of Agriculture & Fisheries		
					(Op Direct Flight for Fisheries Protection Agency)	Prestwick	26. 4.03T
G-SFRY	Thunder Ax7-77 HAB	1667		23. 1.90	M.Rowlands	Wigan	21. 5.03A
G-SFSL	Cameron Z-105 HAB	10308		31. 7.02	A.M.Holly t/a Exclusive Ballooning	Berkeley	10. 6.03T
					(Somerfield titles)		
G-SFTZ	Slingsby T.67M-160 Firefly	2000		7. 2.83	Western Air (Thruxton) Ltd	Thruxton	7. 2.05T
G-SGAS*	Colt 77A HAB	2073		31.10.91	SGL Ltd t/a Shellgas South West Area	Barton	26. 4.01A
					"Shell Gas" (Cancelled 9.11.01 by CAA) (Stored)		
G-SGSE	Piper PA-28-181 Archer II	28-7890332	G-BOJX N3774M	2.12.96	I.R.Chaplin	(Colchester)	12. 9.03
G-SHAA	Enstrom 280-UK Shark	1011	N280Q	8. 7.88	C.J.& D.Whitehead t/a ELT Radio Telephones	(Burnley)	9. 4.05T
G-SHAH	Reims/Cessna F152 II	F15201839	OH-IHA SE-IHA	7. 2.97	I.R.Chaplin	Andrewsfield	17. 5.03T
G-SHAM	Beech C90 King Air	LJ-819	N2063A	12. 4.99	Aerospeed Ltd	Southampton	3. 7.02T
G-SHAY	Piper PA-28R-201T Turbo Arrow III	28R-7703365	G-JEFS G-BFDG/N47381	17. 9.01	R.J.Shay	Andrewsfield	2.10.04
G-SHCB	Schweizer Hughes 269C-1	0038	N41S	28. 6.96	Oxford Aviation Services Ltd	Oxford	27.10.05T
G-SHED	Piper PA-28-181 Cherokee Archer II	28-7890068	G-BRAU N47411	12. 6.89	R B Kay	Gloucestershire	16. 8.04
G-SHEP	SOCATA TB-20 Trindad GT	2061	F-OILU F-WWRB	16. 7.01	L.W.Shepherd	(Heathfield)	31. 7.04T
G-SHIM	CFM Streak Shadow K.228-SA & PFA 206-12501			19. 5.93	K.R.Anderson	Shobdon	25. 8.01P
	(Rotax 582) (C/n duplicates G-MURR)						
G-SHIV	Gulfstream GA-7 Cougar	GA7-0092	N713G	22.11.84	Westley Aircraft Ltd	Cranfield	18. 1.98T
					(Stored outside 6.02 with nose-cone & cowlings missing)		
G-SHOG	Colomban MC-15 Cri-Cri	001	G-PFAB F-PYPU	3.10.96	V.S.E.Norman	Rendcomb	24. 6.02P
	(JPX PUL-212)				(Mitsubishi Shogun titles)		
G-SHPP	Hughes 269A (TH-55A)	36-0481	N80559 64-18169	24. 7.89	R.P.Bateman	White Waltham	15.12.02T
G-SHRK	Enstrom 280C-UK Shark	1173	N373SA	6. 1.97	D.R.Kenyon t/a Aviation Bureau	Redhill	26. 9.02T
			G-SHRK/G-BGMX/EI-CCS/G-SHXX/G-BGMX/EI-BHR/G-BGMX/(F-GBOS)				
G-SHSH	Europa Aviation Europa 113 & PFA 247-12722			7. 4.98	D.G.Hillam	(Birkenhead)	
	(Rotax 912) (Monowheel u/c)				(Current status unknown)		
G-SHSP	Cessna 172S	172S8079	N6535P N9552Q	25. 3.99	Shropshire Aero Club Ltd	Sleap	15. 4.05T
G-SHUF	Mainair Blade	1241-0200-7 & W1034		10. 3.00	J.A.Shufflebotham	Macclesfield	24. 3.03P
	(Rotax 582)						
G-SHUG	Piper PA-28R-201T Turbo Cherokee Arrow III		N1026Q	17. 5.88	G-SHUG Ltd	(Watford)	10. 7.03T
		28R-7703048					
G-SHUU	Enstrom 280C-UK-2 Shark	1221	G-OMCP G-KENY/G-BJFG/N8617N	16.10.89	D.Ellis	Hawarden	20. 5.03
G-SHUV	Aerosport Woody Pusher	PFA 07A-13960		20. 9.02	J.R.Wraight	(Chatham)	
G-SIAI	SIAI-Marchetti SF.260W	361/31-005	F-GVAB(2) OO-XCP/FAB-184	15. 1.01	D Gage	Booker	23. 7.03P
					(As "FA Boliviana FAB-184" 7.00)		
G-SIAL	Hawker Hunter F.58	41H-697457	J-4090	2.10.95	Classic Aviation Ltd	Duxford	21. 3.01P
					(Op The Old flying Machine Co) (As "J4090")		
G-SIAM	Cameron V-90 HAB	4096		7. 3.01	D Tuck "Warners"	London NW1	13.11.03A
G-SIGN	Piper PA-39 Twin Comanche C/R	39-8	OY-TOO N8853Y	9. 2.78	D.Buttle	Blackbushe	20. 1.03
G-SIIA	Aerotek Pitts S-2A	2127	D-ECKC N8073	14.11.01	A.P.Crumpholt	(Baldock)	9.12.04
G-SIIB	Aviat Pitts S-2B Special	5218	G-BUVY N6073U	24. 3.93	G.Ferriman	Horsford	30. 4.05
	(Lycoming AEIO-540)						
G-SIIC	Aviat Pitts S-2C	6021	N16JV	7. 4.00	Technoforce Ltd	Biggin Hill	26. 4.03T
					(Op Gold Air) (Alpine titles)		
G-SIII	Extra EA.300	058	D-ETYE	10. 1.95	Callmast Ltd	Hawarden	1. 8.03T
G-SIIS	Pitts S-1S Special	PFA 09-13485	G-RIPE	3. 7.02	I.H.Searson	(Mansfield)	
G-SIJW	Scottish Aviation.Bulldog Srs.120/121	BH120/295	XX630	31. 3.00	M.Miles (As "XX630/5")	Shenington	2..9.04
G-SILS	Pietenpol Air Camper	PFA 47-13331		29. 6.98	D.Silsbury (On build 8.02)	Dunkeswell	
G-SIMI	Cameron A-315 HAB	3391		10. 3.95	Balloon School (International) Ltd	Petworth	17. 7.03T
					t/a Balloon Safaris		
G-SIMN	Robinson R22 Beta-II	2769		10.12.97	Flight Training Ltd	Coventry	18. 1.04T
G-SIMP	Jabiru Jabiru SP	PFA 274B-13794		4. 1.02	J C Simpson	(Pulborough)	
G-SION*	Piper PA-38-112 Tomahawk II	38-81A0146	N23661	30. 1.91	Not known	Enstone	28.12.00
					(Noted 7.02) (Cancelled 9.9.02 by CAA)		
G-SIPA	SIPA 903	63	G-BGBM F-BGBM	31. 5.83	G.K.Brothwood & P.R.Tonks	Liverpool	14. 2.89F
					tr Mersey SIPA Group (Current status unknown)		
G-SIRR	North American P-51D-25NA Mustang	122-39798	N51RR	3. 2.97	D.J.Gilmour t/a Intrepid Aviation Co	Duxford	10. 6.03P
			(N151MC)/TNI-AU F-3../44-73339 (As "474008/IF-R" in 4th FG/1336th FS USAAF c/s)				
	(Adopted identity of c/n 122-40548/44-74008/RCAF 9274/N8676E/N76AF/(N151MC) during 1982-84 rebuild)						
G-SIRS	Cessna 560XL Citation Excel	560-5185	N51042	1. 8.01	Amsail Ltd (Op London Executive Aviation)	Stansted	1. 8.04T
G-SITA	Pegasus Quantum 15-912	7797		18. 6.01	A.R.Oliver	Dunkeswell	15. 6.04P
G-SIVC	Agusta A109E Power	11115		10. 5.01	Mandarin Aviation Ltd	Redhill	14. 5.04T
G-SIVJ	Westland SA.341C Gazelle HT.Mk2	2012	G-CBSG ZB649	26. 6.02	C.J.Siva-Jothy	(London SE1)	19. 9.03P
G-SIVR	MD Helicopters MD.900	900-00102	N7002S	20. 8.02	Mandarin Aviation Ltd	Redhill	5. 9.05T
G-SIVW	Lake LA-250 Renegade	233	N8553T	6. 2.03	Mandarin Aviation Ltd	Redhill	
	(Built Aerofab Inc)						
G-SIVX	Robinson R22 Beta	3241		23. 7.01	Mandarin Aviation Ltd	Redhill	30. 7.04T
G-SIXC	Douglas DC-6A/B	45550	N93459 N90645/B-1006/XW-PFZ/B-1006	20. 3.87	Atlantic Air Transport Ltd	Coventry	4. 4.05T

Reg	Type	c/n	Prev id	Date	Owner/operator	Base	Date
G-SIXD	Piper PA-32-300 Cherokee Six D	32-7140007	HB-OMH N8615N	25. 3.98	M.B.Payne & I.Gordon	King's Farm, Thurrock	9.10.04
G-SIXX	Colt 77A HAB	1327		21.10.88	M.Dear & M.Taylor	Marlow	19. 5.02A
G-SIXY	Van's RV-6	PFA 181-13368		9. 3.99	C.J.Hall & C.R.P.Hamlett	(Cambridge)	
G-SJCH	Pilatus Britten-Norman BN-2T-4S Islander	4006	G-BWPK	18.11.99	Hampshire Police Authority *"Sir John Charles Hoddinott"*	Lee-on-Solent	26. 2.05T
G-SJDI	Robinson R44 Astro	0626		16. 7.99	HJV Ltd	(Brighton)	7. 8.05T
G-SJKR	Lindstrand LBL 90A HAB	756		26..1.01	S J Roake	(Camberley)	29. 8.03A
G-SJMC	Boeing 767-31KER	27205	N6038E	16. 3.94	MyTravel Airways Ltd	Manchester	15. 3.03T
G-SKAN	Reims/Cessna F172M Skyhawk II	F17201120	G-BFKT F-BVBJ	8. 7.85	Bustard Flying Club Ltd	Boscombe Down	5. 4.04T
G-SKCI	Rutan VariEze	PFA 74-12081		30. 3.01	S.K.Cockburn	(Stanford-le-Hope)	
	(Landed short of runway Biggin Hill 16.2.02 due to engine problems on first flight: substantial damage to nose u/c & a/c nose)						
G-SKID	Lake LA-4-200 Buccaneer	680	G-BMGY N39RG/G-BWKS/G-BDDI/N1087L	4.11.99	J.G.McAllister	Hawarden	20. 9.03T
G-SKIE	Steen Skybolt	AACA/357	ZK-DEN	29. 8.97	S.Gray	Redhill	12. 9.02P
G-SKIL	Cameron N-77 HAB	2264		19. 3.90	S.P.Johnston *"Skillball"*	Longfield	29. 5.03T
G-SKOT	Cameron V-42 HAB	4813		27. 6.00	S.A.Laing	(Banchory)	8. 9.02A
G-SKYC	Slingsby T.67M Firefly	2009	G-BLDP	13. 6.97	T.W.Cassells	Bagby	7.10.05T
G-SKYD	Christen Pitts S-2B Special	5057	N5331N	15.10.92	J.G.Johnston	(Seaford)	17. 6.05
	(Lycoming AEIO-540)						
G-SKYE	Cessna TU206G Turbo Stationair 6 II	U20604568	(G-DROP) N9783M	1. 8.79	P.M.Hall tr RAF Sport Parachute Association	RAF Weston-on-the-Green	5. 7.04
G-SKYF	SOCATA TB-10 Tobago	1589	VH-YHG	1. 5.01	Air Touring Ltd	Goodwood	24. 5.04T
G-SKYG	III Sky Arrow 650 TC	C008		15.12.98	R.Jones	Membury	20. 2.05
G-SKYK	Cameron A-275 HAB	4879		31. 7.00	Cameron Flights Southern Ltd *(Cameron Balloons titles)*	Pewsey	14. 7.03T
G-SKYL	Cessna 182S Skylane	18280176	N4104D	19. 6.98	Skylane Aviation Ltd	Sherburn-in-Elmet	12. 6.04
G-SKYO	Slingsby T.67M-200 Firefly	2264		20. 9.00	E.D.Fern	Truro	28. 9.03T
G-SKYR	Cameron A-180 HAB	2826		31. 3.92	Cameron Flights Southern Ltd *"Candy Floss"*	Pewsey	29. 4.00T
G-SKYT	III Sky Arrow 650TC (Rotax 912)	C.004		6. 9.96	J.D.Scott	Top Farm, Croydon, Royston	7. 3.03
G-SKYU	Cameron A-210 HAB	10129		28. 8.01	Cameron Flights Southern Ltd *(Evening Advertiser titles)*	Pewsey	5. 8.03T
G-SKYX	Cameron A-210 HAB	4613		22. 6.99	Cameron Flights Southern Ltd *(Whitely Village titles)*	Pewsey	5. 6.02T
G-SKYY	Cameron A-250 HAB	3402		9. 3.95	Cameron Flights Southern Ltd *"City of Southampton"*	Pewsey	9. 3.01T
G-SLCE	Cameron C-80 HAB	4022		24. 2.97	A.M.Holly	Berkeley	20. 5.03T
G-SLEA	Mudry/CAARP CAP.10B	124		19.12.80	P.D.Southerington	Cranwell North	28. 6.03
G-SLII	Cameron O-90 HAB	2388		20. 9.90	R.B. & A.M.Harris *"Mad Dash"*	Huntingdon	17. 8.03A
G-SLIP	Flying K Enterprises Easy Raider BMW R100	0004 & BMAA/HB/215		21. 5.02	J.S.Harris	(Porton)	
G-SLOW	Pietenpol Aircamper	PFA 47-13488		8.10.99	C.Newton	(Brackley)	
G-SLTN	SOCATA TB-20 Trinidad	763	HB-KBR	6. 8.99	Oceana Air Ltd	Elstree	27. 8.05T
G-SLYN	Piper PA-28-161 Warrior II	28-8116204	N161WA N8373K	12. 4.89	Haimoss Ltd	Old Sarum	31. 5.04
G-SMAF	Sikorsky S-76A	760149	N130TL N5425U	6. 9.88	Air Harrods Ltd	Stansted	3.10.05T
G-SMAN	Airbus Industrie A330-243	261	F-WWKR	26. 3.99	Monarch Airlines Ltd	Luton	25. 3.05T
G-SMBM	Pegasus Quantum 15-912	7602		24. 1.00	P.J.Caterer	(Tewkesbury)	13. 2.03P
G-SMDH	Europa Aviation Europa XS	403 & PFA 247-13367		8.10.98	S.W.Pitt *(Current status unknown)*	(Petersfield)	
	(Rotax 912S) *(Tri-gear u/c)*						
G-SMDJ	Eurocopter AS350B2 Ecureuil	3187		21. 4.99	M.Ziani de Ferranti	(Llanfairfechan)	12. 8.05
G-SMIG	Cameron O-65 HAB	922		6. 6.83	R D Parry *(New owner 12.01)*	Stroud	28. 7.87A
G-SMJH	Robinson R44 Astro	0024	G-NTEE	22.11.01	J.Moodie t/a Jim Moodie Racing	(Hamilton)	4. 5.03T
G-SMJJ	Cessna 414A Chancellor II	414A0425	N2694H	24. 3.81	Gull Air Ltd	Guernsey	31. 5.03
G-SMTC	Colt Flying Hut SS HAB	1828		7. 1.91	Shiplake Investments Ltd	(Switzerland)	18.11.00A
G-SMTH	Piper PA-28-140 Cherokee C	28-26916	G-AYJS N11C	28. 9.90	Rangecycle Ltd t/a Masonair	Kemble	13. 2.05
G-SNAK	Lindstrand LBL-105A HAB	404		23. 9.96	Ballooning Adventures Ltd	Hexham	18. 5.03T
G-SNAP	Cameron V-77 HAB	1217		29.11.85	C.J.S.Limon *"Snapshot"*	Great Missenden	5. 4.03A
G-SNAZ	Enstrom F-28F	761	G-BRCP	31.10.94	Thornhill Aviation Ltd	Barton	15. 4.05T
G-SNEV	CFM Streak Shadow SA K.283 & PFA 206-13042			17. 9.96	N.G.Smart	(Feltham)	1. 4.03P
	(Rotax 582) *(Official c/n duplicates G-BZNW qv)*						
G-SNOG	Air Creation Kiss 400-582	FL011, A02048-2045/T02033 & BMAA/HB/219		2. 5.02	B.H.Ashman	Buttermilk Hall Farm, Blisworth	
G-SNOW	Cameron V-77 HAB	541	(G-BGWA)	21. 6.79	M.J.Ball	Clitheroe	16. 7.03A
	(Fitted with replacement envelope 1989 - c/n 2050 which was the original G-BSDX)						
G-SNUZ	Piper PA-28-161 Warrior II	28-8416021	G-PSFT G-BPDS/N4328P	19.12.01	J.C.O.& C.A.Adams	Biggin Hill	6.11.03T
G-SOAR*	Eiri PIK-20E	20214		21. 6.79	F.W.Fay *"AR"* (Cancelled 2.9.02 by CAA)	Bidford	7. 6.02
G-SOAY	Cessna T303 Crusader	T30300060	OH-AIL EC-ETD/N1426C	5. 9.00	Bulldog Aviation Ltd	Jersey	18.10.03
G-SOBI	Piper PA-28-181 Archer II	28-7690212	D-EAQL N9542N	3. 5.00	D.J.Gibney tr SOBI Flying Group	Top Farm, Croydon, Royston	8. 8.03T
G-SOEI	Hawker Siddeley HS.748 Srs.2A/242	1689	ZK-DES	25. 2.98	Emerald Airways Ltd *(Securicor Omega Express titles)*	Liverpool	17. 4.04T
G-SOFT	Thunder Ax7-77 HAB	1339		5.12.88	A.J.Bowen *"Enterprise Software"*	Edinburgh	11. 9.99A
G-SOHI	Agusta A109E Power	11045		23. 4.99	Tri-Ventures Group Ltd	Elstree	2. 5.05T
G-SOIF	Piper PA-44-180 Seminole	44-7995179	G-HSFT EI-CCB/N2093K	22. 2.02	Hub'Air SPRL	(Saint-Hubert, Belgium)	11.11.05T
G-SOKO	Soko P-2 Kraguj	033	G-BRXK Yugoslav Army 30149	6. 1.94	A.G.& G.A.G.Dixon	Bournemouth	11. 3.03P

Reg	Type	C/n	Prev id	Date	Owner	Location	Status
G-SOLA	Star-Lite SL-1 (Rotax 447)	203TG & PFA 175-11311		9. 6.88	J.P.Roberts-Lethaby "A Star Is Born" (Stored 6.93: current status unknown)	(Lynton)	31. 3.93P
G-SOLD	Robinson R22 Alpha	0471	N8559X	16. 5.85	J.F.H.James	Banbury	15. 6.03
G-SOLH	Bell 47G-5	2639	G-AZMB CF-NJW	5. 3.97	Sol Helicopters Ltd	Elstree	9. 3.03T
G-SOLO	Anvil-Pitts S-2S Special (Lycoming AEIO-540)	AA/1/1980		30. 5.80	Landitfast Ltd (Current status unknown)	Denham	6. 4.96P
G-SONA	SOCATA TB-10 Tobago	151	G-BIBI	24.10.80	M.Kelly	Sherburn-in-Elmet	25. 9.03
G-SOOC	Hughes 369HS (500C)	111-0354S	G-BRRX N9083F	6.10.93	J.Rawding t/a Helicopter Experience	(Lincoln)	14.10.02
G-SOOE	Hughes 369E (500E)	0227E		27. 4.87	R.W.Nash	Rochester	26. 5.05
G-SOOS	Colt 21A Cloudhopper HAB	1263		7. 6.88	P.J.Stapley	Redcar	25. 3.95A
G-SOOT	Piper PA-28-180 Cherokee C	28-4033	G-AVNM N11C	19. 8.88	J.A.Bridger	Exeter	22. 8.04T
G-SOOZ	Rans S-6ES Coyote II	PFA 204-13543		27. 4.01	A.Batters	(Ilkley)	31. 7.03P
G-SOPH	Best Off Skyranger 912	UK/286 & BMAA/HB/259		25. 2.03	N A Read	Nunnington, York	
G-SOPP	Enstrom 280FX	2024	G-OSAB N86259	23.10.97	F.P. & M.Sopp & L.A.Moore	Jefferies Farm, Billingshurst	5.11.04T
G-SORT	Cameron N-90 HAB	2878		13. 7.92	A.Brown "Streamline"	Bristol	20. 7.03A
G-SOUL	Cessna 310R II	310R0140	N5020J	27. 6.88	Atlantic Air Transport Ltd	Coventry	10. 6.04T
G-SPAM	Avid Aerobat	829 & PFA 189-12074		9. 5.91	J.Lee	(Full Sutton)	19. 7.02P
G-SPDR	de Havilland DH.115 Sea Vampire T.Mk.35	15641	VH-RAN RAN N6-766/XG766	19. 5.00	M.J.Cobb (Noted 9.99: current status unknown)	Swansea	
G-SPEE	Robinson R22 Beta	0939	G-BPJC	20. 7.94	Verve Systems Ltd	Shobdon	21. 9.03T
G-SPEL	Sky 220-24 HAB	045		26. 7.96	T.G.Church t/a Pendle Balloon Co (Pendle titles)	Blackburn	30.12.02T
G-SPEY	Agusta-Bell 206B-3 JetRanger III	8608	G-BIGO	1. 4.81	Castle Air Charters Ltd	Liskeard	15. 9.05T
G-SPFX	Rutan Cozy	PFA 159-13113		30. 4.97	B.D.Tutty	(Gillingham, Kent)	
G-SPHU	Eurocopter EC135T2	0245	D-HKBA	12.11.02	McAlpine Helicopters Ltd	Oxford	AC
G-SPIT	Supermarine 379 Spitfire FR.XIVe	6S/649205	(G-BGHB) Indian AF T-20/MV293	2. 3.79	Patina Ltd (Op The Fighter Collection: as "MV268/JE-J")	Duxford	18. 6.03P
G-SPOG	San Jodel DR.1050 Ambassadeur	155	G-AXVS F-BJNL	25. 9.95	A.C.Frost (Damaged Stonacre Farm, Bredhurst 17.2.91: on rebuild 1995)	(Ware)	13. 6.77S
G-SPOL	MBB Bö.105DBS-4	S-392	VR-BGV	23. 3.90	Bond Air Services Ltd (Op Thames Valley EMS)	White Waltham	5. 6.05T
G-SPOR	Beech B200 Super King Air	BB-1557	N57TL N57TS	3. 9.99	Select Plant Hire Co Ltd (Op Platinum Airways)	Southend	19 .9.05T
G-SPUR	Cessna 550 Citation II	550-0714	N593EM N12035	27.10.98	Banecorp Ltd (Op London Executive Aviation)	Stansted	15.11.04T
G-SPYI	Bell 206B-3 JetRanger III	3689	G-BVRC G-BSJC/N3175S	9. 5.96	K.H.Bott	Blackpool	18. 7.05T
G-SRII	Flying K Enterprises Easy Raider 503 (Originally regd as Sky Raider II 503(1) until 8.01)	BMAA/HB/163		2. 3.01	Reality Aircraft Ltd (Trailered to Old Sarum for operation)	(Amesbury)	14. 8.02P
G-SROE	Westland Scout AH.1	F.9508	XP907	26.10.95	Bolenda Engineering Ltd (As "XP907")	Ipswich	31.10.01P
G-SRVO	Cameron N-90 HAB	3551		10. 4.95	Servo & Electronic Sales Ltd (Servo titles)	Lydd	5. 8.03A
G-SRWN	Piper PA-28-161 Warrior II	28-8116284	G-MAND G-BRKT/N8082Z	30. 7.02	S.Smith	(Alton)	3.12.01T
G-SRYY	Europa Aviation Europa XS T-G	530 & PFA 247-13806		19. 9.02	S.R.Young	(Seaton)	
G-SSAS	Airbus Industrie A320-231	0230	C-GTDO D-AFRO/G-BYFS/D-AFRO/A4O-MA/N230RX/SX-BSJ/N230RX/F-WWDI	4. 4.02	MyTravel Airways Ltd	Manchester	3. 4.05T
G-SSCL	MD Helicopters Hughes 369E (500E)	0491E	N684F	25. 4.98	Shaun Stevens Contractors Ltd	Rochester	30. 5.04
G-SSFT	Piper PA-28-161 Warrior II	28-8016069	G-BHIL N80821	16. 7.86	Plane Talking Ltd	Elstree	15. 3.04T
G-SSIX	Rans S-6-116 Coyote II (Rotax 582) (Tailwheel u/c)	PFA 204A-12749		5. 9.94	T.J.Bax	Henstridge	25. 5.03P
G-SSKY	Pilatus Britten-Norman BN-2B-26 Islander	2247	G-BSWT	11. 5.92	Isles of Scilly Skybus Ltd	St.Just	29. 4.03T
G-SSLF	Lindstrand LBL 210A HAB	649		29. 2.00	A.M.Holly t/a Exclusive Ballooning (Somerfield titles)	Berkeley	28. 8.03T
G-SSPP	Sky Science Powerhawk L70/500	SS001		18. 7.00	Sky Science Powered Parachutes Ltd	(Tidworth)	
G-SSSC	Sikorsky S-76C	760408		26.10.93	CHC Scotia Ltd	Aberdeen	13. 1.04T
G-SSSD	Sikorsky S-76C	760415		26.10.93	CHC Scotia Ltd	Aberdeen	22.12.05T
G-SSSE	Sikorsky S-76C	760417		23.11.93	CHC Scotia Ltd	Aberdeen	2. 2.03T
G-SSTI	Cameron N-105 HAB	3238		30. 3.94	British Airways plc "Concorde"	Heathrow	17.12.01T
G-SSWA	Short SD.3-30 Var.100	SH.3042	D-CTAG G-BHHU/OY-MUC/G-BHHU/N181AP/N332MV/G-BHHU/G-14-3042	15.10.99	Streamline Aviation (SW) Ltd (Stored 12.01)	Exeter	14.12.03T
G-SSWB	Short SD.3-60 Var.100	SH.3690	C6-BFT N690PC/G-BMLE/G-14-3690	17. 8.00	Freshleave Ltd (Op Streamline Aviation)	Exeter	25. 9.03T
G-SSWC	Short SD.3-60 Var.100	SH.3686	SE-LGE G-BMHX/G-14-3686	2.11.00	Streamline Aviation (SW) Ltd	Exeter	14.11.03T
G-SSWE	Short SD.3-60 Var.100	SH.3705	SE-IXE (G-BNBA)/G-14-3705	15. 7.02	Streamline Aviation (SW) Ltd "Laura"	Exeter	22. 8.03T
G-SSWM	Short SD.3-60 Var.100	SH.3648	SE-KCI G-OOAS/G-BLIL/OY-MMB/G-BLIL/G-14-3648	28. 9.01	Freshleave Ltd	Exeter	14.10.03T
G-SSWO	Short SD.3-60 Var.100	SH.3609	SE-KLO N343MV/(G-BKMY)/G-14-3609	8.10.01	Streamline Aviation (SW) Ltd	Exeter	4.12.03T
G-SSWP	Short SD.3-30 Var.100	SH.3030	CS-DBY (5N-OJU)/G-BGNB/N330MV/G-BGNB/G-14-3030	21. 6.00	Freshleave Ltd	Exeter	3. 8.03T
G-SSWR	Short SD.3-60 Var.100	SH.3670	SE-KGV HR-IAT/N108PS/B-3603/G-BLWJ/G-14-3670	2.10.01	Freshleave Ltd	Exeter	13.11.03T
G-SSWT*	Short SD.3-30 Var.100	SH.3095	4X-CSQ G-BNYA/G-BKSU/G-14-3095	2. 6.98	Hanningfield Metals (Noted dismantled 8.02: cancelled 21.10.02 as wfu)	Templewood, Stock	18. 6.01T

G-SSWV	Sportavia Fournier RF5B Sperber	51032	N55WV	31. 5.90	E.C.Neighbour & J.A.Melville	Camphill	4. 9.03P
					tr Skylark Flying Group		
G-SSWX	Short SD.3-60 Var.200	SH.3715	N711PM	19.10.99	Streamline Aviation (SW) Ltd	Exeter	2.12.03T
			G-BNDL/G-14-3715				
G-STAF	Van's RV-7A	PFA 323-13875		15. 2.02	A.F.Stafford	(Melbourne, Derbyshire)	
G-STAT	Cessna U206F Stationair II	U20603485	A6-MAM	20. 2.79	Wingglider Ltd	Hibaldstow	17.10.04
			N8732Q				
G-STAY	Reims/Cessna FR172K Hawk XP	FR17200620	D-EOVX	15.12.00	Staywhite UK Ltd	Rochester	20. 2.04
			OE-DVX				
G-STEA	Piper PA-28R-200 Cherokee Arrow II		HB-OIH	18. 6.02	D.J.Brown	(Horley)	26. 6.05
		28R-7235096	N4569T				
G-STEM	Stemme S-10V	14-027		2. 7.97	Warwickshire Aerocentre Ltd	Husbands Bosworth	26.10.03
G-STEN	Stemme S-10	10-32	D-KGCH	9. 1.92	J P Lyell tr G-STEN Syndicate	(Winchester)	24. 5.04
G-STEP	Schweizer Hughes 269C	S.1494		1.10.90	M.Johnson	Neath	29.11.03T
G-STER	Bell 206B-3 JetRanger III	4116	OO-EGA	23. 3.94	Maintopic Ltd	(Boroughbridge)	18. 4.03T
G-STEV	CEA Jodel DR-221 Dauphin	61	F-BOZD	9. 3.82	S.W.Talbot	Long Marston	17. 4.05
G-STMP	SNCAN Stampe SV-4A	241	F-BCKB	11. 3.83	A.C.Thorne	(Yelverton)	
					(On overhaul Ivybridge 5.93: current status unknown)		
G-STOK	Cameron Colt 77B HAB	4791		4. 5.00	M.H.Read & J.E.Wetters	(Altrincham)	27..6.02A
G-STOO	Stolp Starduster Too	PFA 35-13870		30. 1.03	K.F.Crumplin	Franklyn's Field, Chewton Mendip	
G-STOW	Cameron Wine Box-90 SS HAB	4420		2.10.98	I.Martin & D.Groombridge	Bristol	19. 8.99A
					t/a Flying Enterprises Partnership (Stowells of Chelsea titles)		
G-STOX	Bell 206B JetRanger II	1513	G-BNIR	27. 4.89	Burman Aviation Ltd	Cranfield	4. 7.05T
			N59615				
G-STPI	Cameron A-250 HAB	4102		26. 2.97	A.D.Pinner (Central Auto Supplies titles)	Northampton	13. 7.03T
G-STRA	Boeing 737-3S3	24059	G-OBWY	25. 3.02	Astraeus Ltd	Gatwick	9. 5.03T
			N202KG/G-DEBZ/RP-C4006/EC-FGG/EC-711/G-BNPB/C-FGHT/G-BNPB				
G-STRB	Boeing 737-3Y0	24255	G-OBWX	27. 3.02	Astraeus Ltd	Gatwick	13. 6.03T
			SE-DUS/HB-IID/EI-CFQ/OO-IID/XA-RJP/G-MONL				
G-STRC	Boeing 737-7BX	30736	N361ML	30. 5.02	Astraeus Ltd	Gatwick	29. 5.05T
			N1785B				
G-STRD	Boeing 737-7BX	30737	N362ML	31. 5.02	Astraeus Ltd	Gatwick	30. 5.05T
			N1786B				
G-STRG	Cyclone AX2000	7837		24. 7.01	D.Young	Kemble	23. 7.03P
	(HKS 700E)				tr Pegasus Flight Training (Cotswolds)		
G-STRK	CFM Streak Shadow SA			4. 4.90	E.J.Hadley	(Arch, Switzerland)	17. 4.03P
	(Rotax 582)	K.143-SA & PFA 161-11762		(Type c/n should be '161A-...)			
G-STRM	Cameron N-90 HAB	3568		3. 7.95	B.G.Jones t/a High Profile Balloons	Devizes	19. 7.02T
G-STRO	Robinson R22 Mariner	3262M	G-MIKK	29. 5.02	G.Stroud	(Mallorca, Spain)	10.10.04T
G-STUA	Aerotek Pitts S-2A Special	2164	N13GT	6. 3.91	Rollquick Ltd	White Waltham	21. 3.03T
	(Lycoming AEIO-360)						
G-STUB	Christen Pitts S-2B Special	5163	N260Y	5. 5.94	P.T.Borchert	(Salisbury)	13. 8.03
	(Lycoming AEIO-540)						
G-STUS	Robinson R44 Raven II	10023		3. 1.03	Heli Air Ltd	Wellesbourne Mountford	AC
G-STWO	ARV1 Super 2	002 & PFA 152-11048		24. 4.85	G.E.Morris	Dunkeswell	18. 2.03P
	(Hewland AE75)						
G-STYL	Pitts S-1S Special (Lycoming-O-320)	GJSN-1P	N665JG	26. 1.88	C.A.Wills	(Ely)	5. 9.03P
G-STYX	Pegasus Quik	7932		28. 1.03	T.A.E.M.Stewart tr G-STYX Flying Group	(Orpington)	
G-SUCH	Cameron N-77 HAB	676	G-BIGD	3. 9.01	D.G.Such	Redditch	4. 1.84A
	(Originally regd as V-77)						
G-SUCK	Cameron Z-105 HAB	10280		16. 5.02	Virgin Airship & Balloon Co Ltd	Telford	15. 4.03A
					(Halls Soothers titles)		
G-SUEB	Piper PA-28-181 Archer III	2843466	N5330M	18. 7.01	GYTO Ltd	Great Ashfield	18. 7.04T
G-SUED	Thunder Ax8-90 HAB	1546	G-PINE	22.10.02	E.C.Lubbock & S.A.Kidd	Billericay	31.10.03A
G-SUEE	Airbus Industrie A320-231	0363	G-IEAG	23. 9.93	MyTravel Airways Ltd	Manchester	18. 3.03T
			F-WWBX				
G-SUSE	Europa Aviation Europa XS T-G			25. 6.02	P.R.Tunney	(Sale)	
	(BMW1100RS)	507 & PFA 247-13905					
G-SUEZ	Agusta-Bell 206B JetRanger II	8319	SU-YAE	16. 9.98	Aerospeed Ltd	Manston	3. 7.05T
			YU-HAZ				
G-SUFF	Eurocopter EC135-T1	0118		1. 2.00	Suffolk Constabulary Air Support Unit	Beccles	23. 8.03T
G-SUKI	Piper PA-38-112 Tomahawk	38-79A0260	G-BPNV	22. 5.91	Western Air (Thruxton) Ltd	Thruxton	5. 6.03T
			N2313D				
G-SUMT	Robinson R22 Beta	2147	G-BUKD	24. 9.92	EK Aviation Ltd	Cambridge	23. 9.04T
			N23381				
G-SUMX	Robinson R22 Beta	3274		1.11.01	Frankham Brothers Ltd	Leicester	28.11.04
G-SUPA	Piper PA-18-150 Super Cub	18-5395	PH-BAJ	13.12.78	D.Sutton tr G-SUPA Owners Group	(Maidstone)	2.12.04
	(Frame No.18-5512)		PH-MBF/ALAT 18-5395/N10F				
G-SURG	Piper PA-30 Twin Comanche B	30-1424	G-VIST	18. 6.90	A.R.Taylor	Turweston	26. 3.05T
			G-AVHZ/N8287Y				
G-SURV	Pilatus Britten-Norman BN-2T-4S Defender 4000		G-BVHZ	14. 4.94	Atlantic Air Transport Ltd	Coventry	7. 7.05T
		4005					
G-SUSI	Cameron V-77 HAB	1133		22. 7.85	J.H.Dyden "Susi"	Okehampton	10. 8.02A
G-SUSX	MD Helicopters MD.900	900-00065	N3065W	19. 1.00	Sussex Police Authority	Shoreham	18. 2.04T
G-SUSY	North American P-51D-25NA Mustang	122-39232	N12066	23. 7.87	E.A.Morgan "Susy"	Sywell	20. 5.01P
			FAN GN120/44-72773		(As "472773/AJ-C" in 354th FG USAF c/s)		
G-SUTN	III Sky Arrow 650TC	C007		27. 8.98	G.C.Sutton	Headcorn	4.11.04
G-SUZI	Beech 95-B55 Baron	TC-1574	G-BAXR	11. 3.84	Bebecar (UK) Ltd	Elstree	25. 7.04
G-SUZN	Piper PA-28-161 Warrior II	28-8016187	N3573C	16. 1.91	E.Reed t/a St.George Flight Training	Teesside	29. 3.03T
			N9540N				
G-SUZY	Taylor JT.1 Monoplane	PFA 55-10395		1.12.78	N.Gregson	RAF Kinloss	24. 9.02P
	(Volkswagen 1600)						
G-SVBF	Cameron A-180 HAB	3587		2. 6.95	Airxcite Ltd "Virgin Sierra"	Wembley	20. 8.02T
					t/a Virgin Balloon Flights		

Reg	Type	C/n	Prev id	Date	Owner	Location	Expiry
G-SVEA	Piper PA-28-161 Warrior II	28-7916082	N30299	16.12.98	A.Hastings & E.Lowery t/a Avion Aviation	Coventry	15.12.01T
G-SVIP	Cessna 421B Golden Eagle II	421B0820	G-BNYJ N4686Q/D-IMVB/N1590G	12. 3.97	Stephenson Marine Co Ltd	Southampton	26.12.03T
G-SVIV	SNCAN Stampe SV-4C (DH Gipsy Major)	475	N65214 F-BDBL	7. 8.90	R.Taylor	Vendee Air Park, France	12. 6.05
G-SWAT	Robinson R44 II	10041		24. 2.03	Heli Air Ltd	Wellesbourne Mountford	
G-SWEB	Cameron N-90 HAB	2413		1.10.90	South Western Electricity plc "SWEB"	Bristol	1. 8.01T
G-SWEL	Hughes 369HS	61-0328S	G-RBUT C-FTXZ/CF-TXZ	18. 7.96	M A Crook & A E Wright	Barton	27. 3.03
G-SWIF	Supermarine 552 Swift F.7	VA.9597	XF114	1. 6.90	Heritage Aviation Developments Ltd *(Stored 9.98)*	Scampton	AC
G-SWJW	Airbus Industrie A300B4-203	302	OH-LAB F-WZMY	19. 5.98	OY Air Scandic International Aviation AB	Manchester	18. 5.04T
G-SWOT	Phoenix Currie Super Wot (Continental O-200-A)	PFA 3011		10. 9.80	P.M.Flint *(As "C3011/S" in SE.5A guise)*	Sibson	30 9.03P
G-SWPR	Cameron N-56 HAB	829		16. 3.82	A.Brown *"Post Code"*	Bristol	5. 7.95A
G-SWUN	Pitts S-1M Special (Lycoming O-320)	338-H	G-BSXH N14RM	18. 4.95	T.G.Lloyd	Little Gransden	5. 9.02P
G-SYCO	Europa Aviation Europa (NSI EA-81/118) *(Conventional u/c)*	031 & PFA 247-12540		27.11.95	R Oliver *(F/f 15.3.97)*	Rayne Hall Farm, Rayne	8. 6.03P
G-SYFW	WAR Focke-Wulf 190 replica (Continental O-200-A)	269 & PFA 81-10584		28. 2.83	T.A.S.Rayner & G.Hunter *(As "WNo.7334/2+1" in Luftwaffe c/s)*	East Fortune	4. 8.03P
G-SYPA	Aérospatiale AS355F2 Twin Squirrel	5193	LV-WHC F-WYMS/G-BPRE/N366E	25. 9.96	South Yorkshire Police Authority	Sheffield City	2. 4.03T
G-SYTN	Robinson R44 Raven	1156	N70575	11. 2.02	F.G.Synter	Leicester	3. 5.05T

G-TAAA - G-TZZZ

Reg	Type	C/n	Prev id	Date	Owner	Location	Expiry
G-TAAL	Cessna 172R Skyhawk	17280733	N9535G	11. 8.99	Eagle Cruise Aviation Ltd	Booker	18. 9.05T
G-TABS	Embraer EMB.110P1 Bandeirante	110.212	G-PBAC F-GCLA/F-OGME/F-GCLA/PT-GME	18. 8.98	Skydrift Ltd *(Op Keenair)*	Liverpool	21.10.03T
G-TACE*	Hawker Siddeley HS.125 Srs.403B	25223	G-AYIZ F-BSSL/PJ-SLB/G-AYIZ/G-5-15	23. 1.81	British Airways Aircraft Recovery Unit *(Cancelled 9.1.90 as WFU) (Dumped 3.00)*	Dunsfold	16. 7.86F
G-TACK	Grob G-109B	6279		30. 5.84	A.P.Mayne	Exeter	22 5.05
G-TADC	Aeroprakt A22 Foxbat	PFA 317-13883		16. 4.02	R.J.Sharp	(Sidcup)	
G-TAFF	CASA I-131E Jungmann	1129	G-BFNE E3B-148	7. 9.84	A.J.E.Smith	Breighton	11. 6.03P
G-TAFI	Dornier Bücker Bü.133C Jungmeister	24	N2210 HB-MIF/SwAF U-77	27. 1.93	R.J.Lamplough	Manor Farm, East Garston	5. 7.01P
G-TAGR	Europa Aviation Europa XS	317 & PFA 247-13061		23. 8.02	A.G.Rackstraw	(Nottingham)	
G-TAGS	Piper PA-28-161 Warrior II	28-8416026	N4329D	6. 5.88	Oxford Aviation Services Ltd	Oxford	12.10.03T
G-TAIL	Cessna 150J	15070152	N60220	21. 4.89	L.I.D.Denham-Brown *(New owner 10.01: on rebuild 12.01)*	Blackpool	15. 1.98T
G-TAIR	Piper PA-34-200T Seneca II	34-7970055	N3059H	17.11.87	D.I.G. & J.de Souza t/a Branksome Dene Garage	Bournemouth	12. 3.03T
G-TAIT	Cessna 172R Skyhawk II	17280781	G-DREY N23726	23. 7.02	D.S.J.Tait	(Cobham)	2.12.05T
G-TAMR	Cessna 172S Skyhawk	172S8480	N2458J	7. 6.00	C.Durbidge t/a Tamair Leasing	Oxford	11. 7.03T
G-TAMS	Beech A23-24 Musketeer Super	MA-190	OY-DKF	30. 6.00	Aerograde Ltd	Old Buckenham	23.11.03T
G-TAMY	Cessna 421B Golden Eagle	421B0512	SE-FNS N2BH/N69865	14.11.77	Charniere Ltd	Truro	15.11.03
G-TAND	Robinson R44 Astro	0478		12. 6.98	Global Air Charter Ltd	(Ascot)	12. 7.04T
G-TANI	Gulfstream GA-7 Cougar	GA7-0107	G-VJAI G-OCAB/G-BICF/N8500H/N29707	18. 5.95	S.Spier	Elstree	6. 2.05T
G-TANJ	Raj Hamsa X'Air 582	629 & BMAA/HB/171		21. 6.01	R.Thorman	(Abernethy)	15. 9.03P
G-TANK	Cameron N-90 HAB	3625		20. 6.95	Hoyers (UK) Ltd *(DFDS/Hoyer titles)*	Huddersfield	14. 6.03A
G-TANS	SOCATA TB-20 Trinidad	1870		25. 9.98	K.& G.Threfall t/a Tettenhall Leisure	Wolverhampton	30.10.04
G-TAOS	McDonnell Douglas DC-10-10	47832	F-GRBX OY-CNU SE-DHU//N914WA	30. 8.00	MyTravel Airways Ltd	Manchester	21. 9.03T
G-TAPE	Piper PA-23-250 Aztec D	27-4054	G-AWVW OY-RPF/G-AWVW/N6799Y/N9654N	7.10.83	D.J.Hare *(Op Merlix Air)*	Fairoaks	5. 4.03T
G-TARN	Pietenpol Air Camper	PFA 47-13349		3. 8.98	P.J.Heilborn	(Guildford)	
G-TART	Piper PA-28-236 Dakota	28-7911261	N2945C	18.12.90	Prescot Planes Ltd	(Godalming)	18. 6.03T
G-TARV	ARV.1 Super 2	PFA 152-12627		1. 6.94	M.F.Filer	Dunkeswell	29. 5.02P
	(Hewland AE75) *(Originally G-OARV c/n 001 crashed 1986: rebuilt with ARV fuse c/n 008 & remnants of c/n 001: subsequently rebuilt as PFA project)*						
G-TASH	Cessna 172N	17270531	PH-KOS N739GL	4.11.98	A.Ashpitel	Popham	30.11.04T
G-TASK	Cessna 404 Titan II	404-0829	PH-MPC SE-IHL/N6806Q	10. 3.93	Bravo Aviation Ltd *(Op DEFRA)*	Coventry	8. 7.03T
G-TASS	Schweizer 269CS	1600	PH-HPL N69A	14. 8.02	A.Tasker	Coney Park, Leeds	10. 9.05T
G-TATS	Aérospatiale AS350BA Ecureuil	1905	F-GHSN N37AW	14. 5.01	Air Medina Ltd	Battersea Power Station	7..6.04T
G-TATT	Gardan GY-20 Minicab	PFA 56-10347		30.11.78	P.W.Tattershall tr Tatt's Group	(Clitheroe)	
G-TATY	Robinson R44 Astro	0627		27. 7.99	W.R.Walker	Denham	22. 8.05T
G-TAWE	Aérospatiale/Alenia ATR-42			3.03R	Air Wales *(For delivery 3.03)*		
G-TAXI	Piper PA-23-250 Aztec E	27-7305085	N40270	6. 4.78	M.L.Levi, S.Waite & R.Murgatroyd t/a SWL Leasing	Leeds-Bradford	17.12.04T
G-TAYI	Grob G.115	8008	(D-ENFT) G-TAYI/G-DODO/D-ENFT	12. 9.90	K.P.Widdowson & K.Hackshall	Sandtoft	8. 2.04
G-TAYS	Reims/Cessna F152 II	F15201697	G-LFCA	28.10.91	Tayside Aviation Ltd	Dundee	19. 6.04T
G-TBAE	British Aerospace BAe 146 Srs.200	E2018	G-JEAR G-HWPB/G-6-018/G-BSRU/G-OSKI/N603AW	6. 1.03	BAE Systems (Corporate Air Travel) Ltd	Warton	7. 4.04T

Reg	Type	c/n	Prev id	Date	Owner	Location	Expiry
G-TBAG	Murphy Renegade 912 (Rotax 912)	PFA 188-11912		11.12.90	M.R.Tetley	Newton-on-Rawcliffe, Yorks	12.10.03P
G-TBAH	Bell 206B JetRanger II	2051	G-OMJB	10.12.01	Murray Galloway Ltd	(Ascot)	20.11.04T
			N315JP/N712WG/N712WC/N9989K				
G-TBBC	Pegasus Quantum 15-912	7583		6.12.99	Big Bamboo Co Ltd	Eshott	11.5.03P
G-TBEE	Dyn'Aéro MCR-01 Ban-bi	PFA 301-13514		30.11.99	A.D.S.Baker	Shoreham	17.2.03P
G-TBGL	Agusta A109A II	7412	G-VJCB	6.1.99	Bulford Holdings Ltd	(Jersey)	22.3.04T
			G-BOUA				
G-TBGT	SOCATA TB-20 Trinidad GT	2027	F-OILF	1.12.00	A J Maitland-Robinson	(Jersey)	7.12.03T
G-TBIC	British Aerospace BAe 146 Srs.200	E2025	N167US	15.1.97	Flightline Ltd	Aberdeen	16.1.06T
			N349PS				
G-TBIO	SOCATA TB-10 Tobago	340	F-BNGZ	10.2.83	Kilo Aviation Ltd	Liverpool	9.5.05T
G-TBLY	Eurocopter EC120B	1192	F-WQOV	12.3.01	A.D.Bly Aircraft Leasing Ltd	(Knebworth)	28.6.04T
G-TBMW	Murphy Renegade Spirit	PFA 118-11725	(G-MYIG)	20.10.98	S J & M J Spavins	(St Albans)	
G-TBOK	SOCATA TB-10 Tobago	1111	SX-ABF	26.6.02	P.Albrow & J.Brabrook	Dunkeswell	24.9.05T
			F-GKUA				
G-TBRD	Canadair CL-30 (T-33AN) Silver Star Mk.3	T33-261	N33VC	18.12.96	Golden Apple Operations Ltd	Duxford	10.2.03P
			G-JETT/G-OAHB/CF-IHB/CAF 133261/RCAF 21261				
						(Op The Old Flying Machine Co) (As "21261" in RCAF c/s)	
G-TBXX	SOCATA TB-20 Trinidad	276		16.3.82	D.A.Phillips & C.S.Swaine	Headcorn	12.6.03
G-TBZI	SOCATA TB-21 Trinidad TC	871	N21HR	25.7.96	M D Bond	(Rugby)	21.11.05
G-TBZO	SOCATA TB-20 Trinidad	444		8.8.84	D.L.Clarke & M.J.M.Hopper	Shoreham	27.4.03
G-TCAN	Colt 69A HAB	1996		19.7.91	H.C.J.Williams *"Toucan"*	Bristol	3.5.03A
G-TCAP	British Aerospace BAe 125 Srs.800B	258115	G-5-599	24.4.96	BAE Systems (Operations) Ltd	Warton	28.8.03
			104 RSAF/G-5-665/104 RSAF/G-BPGR/G-5-599				
G-TCAS	Cameron Z-275 HAB	10343		28.2.03	The Ballooning Business Ltd	Northampton	
G-TCDI	Hawker Siddeley HS.125 Srs.F400B	25248	N792A	10.10.96	Aravco Ltd	Farnborough	16.1.04T
			G-5-707/G-SHOP/G-BTUF/G-5-707/D-CFCF				
G-TCMP*	Robinson R22 Beta	0890		3.11.88	Not known	Thruxton	19.2.01T
			(Crashed on take-off Thruxton 30.6.00 & severely damaged: cancelled 6.12.00 as WFU) (Wreck stored 5.01)				
G-TCNM	Tecnam P92-EA Echo	PFA 318-13922		12.8.02	J.Quaife	(Etchingham)	
G-TCOM	Piper PA-30 Twin Comanche C	30-1967	N555JC	29.1.96	C.A.C.Burrough	Jersey	11.4.05
			N8810Y				
G-TCTC	Piper PA-28RT-201T Turbo Arrow IV	2831001	N9130B	1.12.89	T.Haigh	Wellesbourne Mountford	26.3.05
	(Built as N9524N [28R-8631006])						
G-TCUB	Piper J-3C-65 Cub	13970	N9039Q	31.7.87	C.Kirk	(Lincoln)	28.5.04
	(Frame No.13805)		N67666/NC67666/Bu.29684/45-55204				
G-TDOG	Scottish Aviation Bulldog Srs.120/121	BH120/230	XX538	17.9.01	G.S Taylor (As *"XX538/O"*)	Shobdon	25.4.05
G-TDTW	McDonnell Douglas DC-10-10	46983	OY-CNY	25.10.00	MyTravel Airways Ltd	Manchester	29.11.03T
			SE-DHY/N909WA				
G-TDVB	Dyn'Aero MCR-01 ULC Banbi	PFA 301B-14015		23.1.03	D.V.Brunt	Plaistowes Farm, St. Albans	
G-TEAL*	Thurston TSC-1A1 Teal	15	C-GDQD	8.12.92	K.Heeley	Crosland Moor	
			(Damaged Crosland Moor 3.93: on rebuild 4.00) (Cancelled 24.5.02 by CAA)				
G-TEBZ	Piper PA-28R-201 Cherokee Arrow III	28R-7737050	N105CC	7.1.00	R.W.Tebby	Bristol	7.6.03T
					t/a S.F.Tebby & Son *(Op Bristol Flying Centre)*		
G-TECC	Aeronca 7AC Champion	7AC-5269	N1704E	26.6.91	G.S.Claybourn	Walton Wood, Doncaster	20.11.03P
			NC1704E				
G-TECH	Rockwell Commander 114	14074	G-BEDH	8.8.85	P.A.Reed	Elstree	7.8.03
			N4744W				
G-TECK	Cameron V-77 HAB	625		21.3.86	G.M.N.Spencer *"Spring Fever"*	Watford	5.8.02A
G-TECM	Tecnam P92-EM Echo	PFA 318-13667		1.12.00	D A Lawrence	(Swindon)	29.8.03P
G-TEDF	Cameron N-90 HAB	2634		8.8.91	Fort Vale Engineering Ltd	Nelson	12.7.03A
G-TEDS	SOCATA TB-10 Tobago	57	G-BHCO	29.3.83	E.W.Lyon	Wolverhampton	28.5.05
G-TEDY	Evans VP-1	PFA 62-10383	G-BHGN	4.10.90	N.K.Marston *"The Plank"*	(Harrow)	1.7.97P
	(Volkswagen 1834)				*(Current CofR @ 4.02)*		
G-TEFC	Piper PA-28-140 Cherokee F	28-7325088	OY-PRC	18.6.80	P.M.Havard	Andrewsfield	18.4.05
			N15530				
G-TEHL	CFM Streak Shadow M	185	G-MYJE	20.11.98	A.K. Paterson	Sleaford	13.8.03P
	(Rotax 503)						
G-TELY	Agusta A109A II	7326	N1HQ	10.3.89	Castle Air Charters Ltd	Liskeard	24.7.05T
			N200SH				
G-TEMP	Piper PA-28-180 Cherokee E	28-5806	G-AYBK	15.5.89	M.J.Groome tr Bev Piper Group	Andrewsfield	23.8.04T
			N11C				
G-TEMT	Hawker Tempest II	420	HA586	9.10.89	Tempest Two Ltd	(Hemswell)	AC
			(RIAF)/MW763		*(On rebuild 11.96: to be "MW763/HF-A" in 183 Sqdn c/s)*		
G-TENS	HOAC DV20 Katana 100	20148	G-BXBW	28.2.01	Ewan Ltd	Gloucestershire	18.6.03T
			D-ESHM				
G-TENT	Auster J/1N Alpha	2058	G-AKJU	1.2.90	R.C.Callaway-Lewis	Goodwood	26.8.05
			TW513				
G-TERN	Europa Aviation Europa	106 & PFA 247-12780		18.7.97	J.E.G.Lundesjo	White Waltham	25.10.02P
	(NSI EA81/100) (Monowheel u/c)				*(F/f 31.8.98)*		
G-TERR	Pegasus Quik	7925		6.1.03	T.R.Thomas	(Stroud, Glos)	6.1.04P
G-TERY	Piper PA-28-181 Archer II	28-7990078	G-BOXZ	13.1.89	J.R.Bratherton	Wombleton	26.2.05T
			N22402		*(New owner 4.02)*		
G-TEST	Piper PA-34-200 Seneca	34-7450116	OO-RPW	28.7.89	Stapleford Flying Club Ltd	Stapleford	23.12.04T
			G-BLCD/PH-PLZ/N41409				
G-TETI	Cameron N-90 HAB	2877	D-OBMW	9.2.00	Teti SpA	(Florence, Italy)	
G-TEWS	Piper PA-28-140 Cherokee B	28-25128	G-KEAN	23.5.88	M.J.Tew tr G-TEWS Flying Group	Liverpool	30.9.04T
			G-AWTM/N11C				
G-TFCI	Reims/Cessna FA152 Aerobat	FA15200358		25.10.79	Tayside Aviation Ltd	Dundee	21.6.04T
G-TFOX	Denney Kitfox Model 2	PFA 172-11817		3.6.91	F.A.Bakir	Barton	11.3.03P
G-TFUN	Valentin Taifun 17E	1011	D-KIHP	28.12.83	G.F.Wynn & D.H.Evans	Blackpool	10.5.04
					tr North West Taifun Group		
G-TFYN	Piper PA-32RT-300 Lance II	32R-7885128	N5HG	28.4.00	M.D.Parker	Bourn	5.7.04T
			D-ELAE/N31740				

Reg	Type	C/n	Prev id	Date	Owner	Location	Date
G-TGAS	Cameron O-160 HAB	1315		12. 8.87	Zebedee Balloon Service Ltd	Hungerford	26. 5.00T
G-TGER	Gulfstream AA-5B Tiger	AA5B-0952	G-BFZP	20. 2.86	P.J.Haldenby	Rochester	5.11.03T
G-TGRA	Agusta A109A	7201	D-HEED	15. 2.01	Tiger Helicopters Ltd	Shobdon	8. 2.04T
			N3983H/HB-XNF/I-PATZ				
G-TGRR	Robinson R22 Beta	1235	G-BSZS	4.12.02	Tiger Helicopters Ltd	Shobdon	3. 4.03T
			N8058J				
G-TGRS	Robinson R22 Beta	1069	G-DELL	5.11.97	Tiger Helicopters Ltd	Shobdon	9. 10.04T
			N80466		*(Rolled over landing Duxford 18.11.01 & damaged)*		
G-TGRZ	Bell 206B JetRanger II	2288	G-BXZX	15. 6.00	Tiger Helicopters Ltd	Shobdon	21.11.04T
			N27EA/N286CA/N93AT/N16873				
G-THAI	CFM Shadow E 912	33<u>6</u> & BMAA/HB/239	(G-PIXY)	28. 8.02	D.L.Hendry	(Appin)	
			G-85-26				
G-THAT	Raj Hamsa X'Air Falcon 912	<u>613</u> & BMAA/HB/221		27. 5.02	M.G.Thatcher	(Chirk Bank)	
G-THEA	Boeing-Stearman E75 (N2S-5) Kaydet	75-5736A	(EI-RYR)	18. 3.81	C.M.Ryan	(Leixlip, Co.Kildare)	5.12.05
	(Lycoming R-680)		N1733B/USN Bu.38122		*(As "33" in Navy c/s)*		
G-THEL	Robinson R44 Astro	0159	G-OCCB	2. 9.98	N.Parkhouse	Elstree	3. 5.04T
			G-STMM				
G-THEO	TEAM mini-MAX 91	PFA 186-13099		9. 2.99	T.Willford	Blandford Forum	18. 6.03P
	(Rotax 447) *(Built up rear fuselage)*						
G-THIN	Reims FR.172E Rocket	FR17200016	G-BXYY	4.12.02	I.A.C.Slight	(Andover)	13. 6.04T
			OY-AHO/ F-WLIP				
G-THLS	MBB Bö.105DBS-4	S.80/859	G-BCXO	20. 2.92	Bond Air Services	RAF St.Mawgan	27. 2.04T
	(Rebuilt with new pod c/n S.859 c.1992)		D-HDCE		*(Op Trinity House Lighthouse Service)*		
G-THOM	Thunder Ax6-56 HAB	366		14. 7.81	T.H.Wilson *"Macavity"*	Diss	21. 8.03A
G-THOS	Thunder Ax7-77 HAB	769		20. 2.86	C.E.A.Breton	Bristol	14. 3.01A
G-THOT	Jabiru Jabiru SK	PFA 274-13159		16. 9.97	D J & S C Reed	Booker	17. 6.02P
	(Jabiru 2200A)						
G-THRE	Cessna 182S Skylane	18280454	N2391A	6. 5.99	S.J.G.Mole	Wolverhampton	5. 5.05
G-THSL	Piper PA-28R-201 Arrow III	28R-7837278	N36396	11. 9.78	D.M.Markscheffel	Elstree	28. 4.03
G-THUN	Republic P-47D Thunderbolt		N47DD	18. 6.99	Patina Ltd	Duxford	7. 7.03P
					(Op The Fighter Collection as "226671/MH-X/LH-X")		
	(Note 1: Composite re-build from wreck of original N47DD plus new P-47N fuselage identification unknown)						
	(Note 2: "Original" N47DD is c/n 399-55731 ex Peruvian AF 119/Peruvian AF 545/45-49192 & is static exhibit in American Air Museum, Duxford)						
G-THZL	SOCATA TB-20 Trinidad	534	F-GJDR	9. 5.96	Thistle Aviation Ltd	Booker	16. 4.05
			N65TB				
G-TICH	Taylor JT.2 Titch	PFA 60-3213		12. 2.01	A.J.House, C.J.Wheeler & R.Davitt	(Reading)	
	(Project no originally allocated as PFA 3213)				*(40% complete in 1973! : current status unknown)*		
G-TICL	Airbus Industrie A320-231	0169	OY-CNG	10.12.96	MyTravel Airways Ltd	Manchester	11.12.05T
			F-WWIH				
G-TIDS	SAN Jodel 150 Mascaret	44	OO-GAN	15. 4.86	M.R.Parker	Sywell	20.11.03P
G-TIGA	de Havilland DH.82A Tiger Moth	83547	G-AOEG	5. 6.85	D.E.Leatherland	Nottingham	20. 8.04T
			T7120				
G-TIGB	Aérospatiale AS332L Super Puma	2023	G-BJXC	31. 3.82	Bristow Helicopters Ltd *"City of Aberdeen"*	Aberdeen	27. 4.04T
			F-WTNM				
G-TIGC	Aérospatiale AS332L Super Puma	2024	G-BJYH	14. 4.82	Bristow Helicopters Ltd	Aberdeen	17. 5.05T
			F-WTNJ		*"Royal Burgh of Montrose"*		
G-TIGE	Aérospatiale AS332L Super Puma	2028	G-BJYJ	15. 4.82	Bristow Helicopters Ltd *"City of Dundee"*	Aberdeen	7. 6.04T
			F-WTNM				
G-TIGF	Aérospatiale AS332L Super Puma	2030	F-WKQJ	15. 4.82	Bristow Helicopters Ltd *"Peterhead"*	Aberdeen	27. 6.03T
G-TIGG	Aérospatiale AS332L Super Puma	2032	F-WXFT	15. 4.82	Bristow Helicopters Ltd *"Macduff"*	Aberdeen	1. 8.04T
G-TIGH*	Aérospatiale AS332L Super Puma	2034	F-WXFL	15. 4.82	Bristow Helicopters Ltd	Aberdeen	24. 8.92T
					(Damaged 100m NE of Shetland Isles 14.3.92: cancelled 3.8.92 as destroyed) (Instruction use 2001)		
G-TIGI	Aérospatiale AS332L Super Puma	2036	F-WTNP	15. 4.82	Bristow Helicopters Ltd *"Fraserburgh"*	Shenzhen, China	5. 9.05T
G-TIGJ	Aérospatiale AS332L Super Puma	2042	VH-BHT	15. 4.82	Bristow Helicopters Ltd *"Rosehearty"*	Aberdeen	29. 6.05T
			G-TIGJ				
G-TIGL	Aérospatiale AS332L Super Puma	2050		15. 4.82	Bristow Helicopters Ltd *"Portsoy"*	Aberdeen	9.12.05T
G-TIGM	Aérospatiale AS332L Super Puma	2045		15. 4.82	Bristow Helicopters Ltd *"Banff"*	Shenzhen, China	1. 8.03T
G-TIGO	Aérospatiale AS332L Super Puma	2061	PP-MIM	18. 2.83	Bristow Helicopters Ltd	Aberdeen	22. 8.04T
			G-TIGO/F-WMHH		*"Royal Burgh of Arbroath"*		
G-TIGP	Aérospatiale AS332L Super Puma	2064		11. 3.83	Bristow Helicopters Ltd *"Carnoustie"*	Shenzhen, China	8. 5.03T
G-TIGR	Aérospatiale AS332L Super Puma	2071	F-WTNW	11. 3.83	Bristow Helicopters Ltd *"Stonehaven"*	Aberdeen	19. 5.05T
G-TIGS	Aérospatiale AS332L Super Puma	2086		6. 5.83	Bristow Helicopters Ltd *"Findochty"*	Aberdeen	27. 6.05T
G-TIGT	Aérospatiale AS332L Super Puma	2078		6. 5.83	Bristow Helicopters Ltd *"Portknockie"*	Aberdeen	2. 5.04T
G-TIGV	Aérospatiale AS332L Super Puma	2099	LN-ONC	12. 1.84	Bristow Helicopters Ltd *"Burghead"*	Aberdeen	25. 6.04T
			G-TIGV/LN-ONC/G-TIGV/LN-OPF/G-TIGV				
G-TIGZ	Aérospatiale AS332L Super Puma	2115	C-GQKK	8. 8.84	CHC Scotia Ltd	Aberdeen	14.10.03T
			G-TIGZ				
G-TIII	Aerotek Pitts S-2A Special	2196	G-BGSE	27. 2.89	S.B.Janvrin tr Treble India Group	(Cuckfield)	14. 7.04
	(Lycoming AEIO-360)		N947				
G-TIKO	Hatz CB-1	PFA 143-13396		9. 7.99	K.Robb t/a Tiko Architecture	(Yeovil)	
G-TILE	Robinson R22 Beta	1100		4. 8.89	M.J.Webb & C.R.Woodwiss	Coventry	12. 8.05T
G-TILI	Bell 206B JetRanger II	2061	F-GHFN	6. 3.96	C.I.Threlfall Ream Hill Farm, Weeton, Preston		22. 4.02
			N7037A/XC-BOQ		t/a CIM Helicopters		
G-TIMB	Rutan VariEze	PFA 74-10795	G-BKXJ	11. 6.85	T.M.Bailey *"Kitty"*	Shoreham	22. 7.03P
	(Continental O-200-A)						
G-TIME	Piper PA-61P Aerostar 601P	61P-0541-230	N8058J	21. 7.78	T & G Engineering Co Ltd	(West Byfleet)	21.12.02
G-TIMG	Beagle Terrier 3	"PFA 00-318"		7. 3.01	T.J.Goodwin	(Manningtree)	
G-TIMK	Piper PA-28-181 Archer II	28-8090214	OO-TRT	25. 8.81	T.Baker	Wolverhampton	5. 6.03
			PH-EAS/OO-HLN/N8142H				
G-TIMM	Folland Gnat T.1	FL.519	8618M	19. 2.92	T.J.Manna t/a Kennet Aviation	North Weald	26. 2.03P
			XP504		*(As "XM693")*		
G-TIMP	Aeronca 7BCM Champion	7AC-3392	N84681	14. 8.92	M G Rumney *"Nancy"*	(Chichester)	5. 8.02P
	(Continental C85)		NC84681				
G-TIMS	Falconar F-12A	PFA 22-12134		1.10.91	T.Sheridan	Wellingborough	

Reg	Type	C/n
G-TIMY	Gardan GY-80-160 Horizon	36
G-TINA	SOCATA TB-10 Tobago	67
G-TING	Cameron O-120 HAB	4007
G-TINK	Robinson R22 Beta	0937
G-TINS	Cameron N-90 HAB	1626
G-TINY	Moravan Zlin Z.526F Trener Master	1257
G-TIPS	Tipsy Nipper T.66 Srs.5	PFA 25-12696
	(Jabiru 2200A) *(Rebuild of Fairey c/n 50)*	
G-TJAL	Jabiru Jabiru SPL-430	PFA 274-13360
G-TJAY	Piper PA-22-135 Tri-Pacer	22-730
G-TKAY	Europa Aviation Europa	179 & PFA 247-12804
	(Rotax 912) (Monowheel u/c)	
G-TKGR	Lindstrand Racing Car SS HAB	380
G-TKIS	Tri-R Kis	029 & PFA 239-12358
	(Lycoming O-290-D2) (Tail-wheel variant)	
G-TKPZ	Cessna 310R II	310R1225
G-TLDK	Piper PA-22-150 Tri-Pacer	22-4726
G-TLEL	American Blimp Corp. A-60+ Airship	003
G-TMCC	Cameron N-90 HAB	4327
G-TMDP	Airbus Industrie A320-231	0168
G-TMKI	Percival P.56 Provost T.1	PAC/F/268
G-TMOL	SOCATA TB-20 Trinidad	2103
G-TNTN	Thunder Ax6-56 HAB	1991
G-TOAD	SAN Jodel D.140 Mousquetaire	27
G-TOAK	SOCATA TB-20 Trinidad	468
G-TOBA	SOCATA TB-10 Tobago	625
G-TOBE*	Piper PA-28R-200 Cherokee Arrow II	28R-7435148
G-TOBI	Reims/Cessna F172K	F17200792
G-TOBY*	Cessna 172B	47852
G-TODD	ICA IS-28M2A	59
G-TODE	Ruschmeyer R90-230RG	016
G-TOFT	Thunder & Colt 90A HAB	1693
G-TOGO	Van's RV-4	PFA 181A-13447
G-TOHS	Cameron V-31 HAB	10267
G-TOLL	Piper PA-28R-201 Arrow III	28R-7837025
G-TOLY	Robinson R22 Beta-II	2809
G-TOMC	North American AT-6D Harvard III	88-14602
G-TOMM	Robinson R22 Beta	3384
G-TOMS	Piper PA-38-112 Tomahawk	38-79A0453
G-TOMZ	Denney Kitfox Model 2	PFA 172-11977
G-TOOL	Thunder Ax8-105 HAB	1670
G-TOOT	Dyn'Aéro MCR-01 Ban-bi	PFA 301-13542
G-TOPC	Aérospatiale AS355F1 Twin Squirrel	5313
G-TOPS	Aérospatiale AS355F1 Twin Squirrel	5151
G-TORE*	Hunting-Percival P.84 Jet Provost T.3A	PAC/W/9212
G-TORS	Robinson R22 Beta	3021
G-TOSH	Robinson R22 Beta	0933
G-TOTO	Reims/Cessna F177RG Cardinal	F177RG0049
G-TOUR	Robin R2112	187
G-TOWS	Piper PA-25-260 Pawnee C	25-4853
	(Hoffman 4 x blade propeller)	
G-TOYZ	Bell 206B-3 JetRanger III	3949
G-TPSL	Cessna 182S	18280398
G-TRAC	Robinson R44 Astro	0598
G-TRAM	Pegasus Quantum 15-912	7552
G-TRAN	Beech 76 Duchess	ME-408
G-TRCY	Robinson R44 Astro	0668
G-TRDM	SOCATA TB-20 Trinidad GT	2032
G-TREC	Cessna 421C Golden Eagle III	421C0838
G-TRED	Cameron Colt Bibendum 110SS HAB	4222
G-TREE	Bell 206B-3 JetRanger III	2826

Prev Reg	Date	Owner	Location	Cert
I-TIKI	17. 1.00	R.G.Whyte	Dunstable	AC
	30.10.79	A.Lister	Shipdham	13. 9.04
	4.10.96	Floating Sensations Ltd	Thatcham, Berks	12.11.03T
G-NICH	22. 5.01	N.T.Burton	Costock	5. 5.04T
	27. 1.88	J.R.Clifton	Brackley	11.10.03A
		(Carling Black Label titles)		
OK-CMD	10. 5.95	D.Evans	Little Gransden	17. 8.98
G-TINY/YR-ZAD				
OO-VAL	27. 3.95	R.F.L.Cuypers	Grimbergen, Belgium	3. 7.03P
9Q-CYJ/9O-CYJ/(OO-CYJ)/(OO-CCD)				
	21. 2.03	T.J.Adams-Lewis	(Cardigan)	
N730TJ	11. 5.93	D.D.Saint	Garston Farm, Marshfield	28. 8.05
N2353A				
	2. 6.99	A.M.Kay	Nuthampstead	1. 8.03P
		(F/f 25.7.99)		
	28. 8.96	Brown & Williamson Tobacco Corporation (Export) Ltd		
		"Team Green"	Louisville, KY, USA	20. 8.99A
	23.12.93	J.L.Bone	Biggin Hill	15.12.02P
G-BRAH	19. 3.90	Air Charter Scotland Ltd	Edinburgh	1. 4.05T
N1909G				
N6072D	27. 1.97	A.M.Thomson	Phoenix Farm, Lower Upham	
		(Noted 12.99: current status unknown)		
I-TIRE	17. 5.02	Lightship Europe Ltd	Telford	26. 5.05T
N2017A		*(Nescafe titles)*		
	30. 3.98	Prudential Assurance Co Ltd	Bristol	7. 6.02A
		(The Mall/Cribbs Causeway titles)		
OY-CNF	19.11.96	MyTravel Airways Ltd	Manchester	19.11.05T
(D-ADSL)/OY-CNF/F-WWIF				
WW453	1. 7.92	B.L.Robinson	(Clevedon)	
		(As "WW453/W-S" in RAF c/s)		
F-OJBQ	24.12.01	West Wales Airport Ltd	Gloucestershire	13. 1.05T
	25. 4.91	H.M.Savage & J.F.Trehern	Edinburgh	10 9.03A
F-BIZG	27. 9.88	J.H.Stevens	Headcorn	25. 6.03
N83AV	5.12.89	C.Wade & A.Young tr Phoenix Group	Belfast	11. 1.05
N600N	4. 4.91	E.J.Downing	Farley Farm, Romsey	17. 9.03
G-BNRO	25.11.87	Not known	Headcorn	6. 3.94
N40979	*(Damaged near Cranbrook, Kent 6.3.92: cancelled 6.5.92 as WFU) (Stored 7.00)*			
G-AYVB	5. 1.84	G.Hall	Henstridge	14. 7.05
G-ARCM	4. 4.81	Northbrook College	Shoreham	28. 4.85
N6952X	*(Damaged Sandown 15.10.83: cancelled 27.2.90 by CAA) (Instructional airframe 2.01)*			
	18. 4.86	C.I.Roberts & C.D.King	Shobdon	7. 9.01
D-EEAX	20. 6.94	A.I.D.Rich	Elstree	6. 8.03
	8. 3.90	C.S.Perceval *"Bumble"*	Great Missenden	20. 5.03A
	6. 4.99	G.Schwetz *(Under construction 7.02)*	Nympsfield	
	4.11.02	J.P.Moore	Great Missenden	19. 9.03P
N52HV	12.10.00	Plymouth School of Flying Ltd	Plymouth	16.11.03T
D-ECIW/N9007K				
G-NSHR	8. 2.01	Heli Air Ltd	Wellesbourne Mountford	27. 6.04T
114700	22. 4.02	A.A.Marshall tr Texan Restoration	(Bruntingthorpe)	
French AF/42-44514				
	5.11.02	Helisport UK Ltd	Earls Colne	2.12.05T
N9658N	22. 1.79	Juno Estates Ltd	Wellesbourne Mountford	11. 7.04T
	15.11.00	P.T.Knight	Leicester	17. 6.03P
	29. 3.90	W.J.Honey *"Trademaster"*	Bristol	7. 4.03A
	1. 3.01	E.K.Griffin	(Bicester)	
I-LGOG	29. 7.97	Bridge Street Nominees Ltd	Stapleford	6.11.03T
3A-MCS/D-HOSY/OE-BXV/D-HOSY				
G-BPRH	7. 5.91	Sterling Helicopters Ltd	Norwich	24. 1.05T
N360E/N5794F				
XM405	14. 6.91	R.J.Everett	Sproughton	5. 5.95P
		(As "42" (Cancelled 25.2.00 by CAA) (Noted 10.01)		
	4. 1.00	GT Investigations (International) Ltd	(Sligo, Co.Sligo)	12. 1.03T
N2629S	14. 3.97	Heli Air Ltd	Leicester	20. 3.03T
LV-RBD/N8012T				
G-OADE	29. 8.89	Horizon Flyers Ltd	Denham	11. 7.04
G-AZKH				
	9.10.79	Mardenair Ltd	Goodwood	12. 3.04T
PH-VBT	17. 7.91	Lasham Gliding Society Ltd	Lasham	23.12.03
D-EAVI/N4370Y/N9722N				
G-RGER	21.11.96	A.R.Pocock	(Glasgow)	24.10.03T
N75EA/JA9452/N32018				
N23700	11.12.98	A.N.Purslow	Blackbushe	15. 1.05T
	10. 5.99	C.Sharples	Newbury	22. 5.05T
	29. 7.99	T.F.J.Roach	Knapthorpe Lodge, Caunton	28. 7.03P
G-NIFR	15. 3.93	Multiflight Ltd	Leeds-Bradford	25. 9.04T
N1808A				
	22.10.99	T.Fletcher	Collingham, Newark	18.11.02T
F-OILX	2. 1.01	West Wales Airport Ltd	Aberporth	8. 1.04T
G-TLOL	2. 7.96	Sovereign Business Integration plc	(Barnet)	6. 3.05T
(N2659K)				
	12.12.97	The Aerial Display Co Ltd	Looe	11. 2.02A
N2779U	15. 6.87	LGH Aviation Ltd	Fairoaks	18.12.05T
		(Op Alan Mann Helicopters)		

Reg	Type	Serial	Prev ID	Date	Owner	Location	Status
G-TREK	Jodel D.18 (JPX 4TX @ 65hp)	182 & PFA 169-11265		1. 5.92	R.H.Mole	Leicester	7. 8.03P
G-TRIB	Lindstrand HS-110 Hot Air Airship (Rotax 582)	174	(N....)	23. 1.95	J Addison	Melton Mowbray	2. 5.03A
G-TRIC	de Havilland DHC.1 Chipmunk 22A	C1/0080	G-AOSZ WB635	18.12.89	D.M.Barnett tr Landpro *(As "18013" in RCAF c/s)*	High Cross, Ware	26.10.03
G-TRIM	Monnett Moni	00258T & PFA 142-11012		16. 2.84	J.E.Bennell	(High Wycombe)	
G-TRIN	SOCATA TB-20 Trinidad	1131		25. 6.90	TL Aviation Ltd	Jersey	9. 3.03
G-TRIO	Cessna 172M Skyhawk II	17266271	G-BNXY N9621H	30. 7.91	C.M.B.Reid	Rochester	17. 1.03T
G-TROP	Cessna T310R II	T310R1381	N4250C	31.12.86	D E Carpenter	Shoreham	29. 4.05T
G-TROY	North American T-28A Fennec	142/174-545	F-AZFV FrAF No 142/51-7692	21. 4.99	S.G.Howell & S.Tilling *(As "51-7692")*	Duxford	22. 3.03P
G-TRUD	Enstrom 480	5022	XT-BOK	27. 2.01	Sussex Aviation Ltd	Shoreham	1. 3.04T
G-TRUE	MD Helicopters Hughes 369E	0490E	N6TK ZK-HFP	12. 9.94	Bailey Employment Services Ltd	(Melksham)	20. 3.04T
G-TRUK	Stoddard-Hamilton Glasair IIRG (Lycoming O-320)	575R & PFA 149-11015		23. 7.84	M.P.Jackson	Fairoaks	22. 5.04P
G-TRYG	Robinson R44	0960		4. 1.01	Productive Investments Ltd	(Guildford)	25. 6.03T
G-TRYK	Air Creation Kiss 400-582 FL004, A01157-1163/T01098 & BMAA/HB/191			31.10.01	S.Elsbury	(Brentwood)	
G-TSAM	British Aerospace BAe 125 Srs.800B	258028	G-5-12	31. 1.85	BAE System (Operations) Ltd	Warton	5. 9.03
G-TSGJ	Piper PA-28-181 Archer II	28-8090109	N8097W	12. 9.88	A.Dove & A.D.S.Peat tr Golf Juliet Flying Club	Teesside	7. 1.04
G-TSIX	North American AT-6C-1NT Harvard IIA	88-9725	FAP1535 SAAF7183/EX289/41-33262	19. 3.79	J.M.& B.E.Adams *(As "111836/JZ/6" in USN c/s)*	Eggington, Derby	24. 5.03P
G-TSKD	Raj Hamsa X'Air J22	633 & BMAA/HB/165		8. 5.01	T.Sexton & K.B.Dupuy *(Constructed 2002)*	(Westcliff-on-Sea)	
G-TSKY	Beagle B.121 Pup Srs.2	B121-010	OE-CFM HB-NAA/G-AWDY/HB-NAA/G-AWDY	6. 4.98	R.G.Hayes	Elstree	7. 5.04T
G-TSOL	EAA Acrosport 1 (Lycoming O-320)	PFA 72-11391	G-BPKI	18. 7.00	A.G.Fowles	(Shrewsbury)	31. 3.00P
G-TTAC	SOCATA TB-20 Trinidad GT	2121	F-OIMD (N212GT)	8. 5.02	AC Aviation Ltd	Shoreham	23. 5.05T
G-TTDD	Zenair CH.701 STOL (Jabiru 2200A)	PFA 187-13106		1. 9.97	D.B.Dainton & V.D.Asque	Sackville Farm, Riseley	2. 1.03T
G-TTFN	Cessna 560 Citation V	560-0537	N5181V	19.11.99	Corporate Administration Management Ltd	Shoreham	12.12.05T
G-TTHC	Robinson R22 Beta	1196		21.12.89	Multiflight Ltd	Leeds-Bradford	28. 5.05T
G-TTIA	Airbus Industrie A321-231	1428	D-AVZA	19. 2.01	GB Airways Ltd	Gatwick	18. 2.04T
G-TTIB	Airbus Industrie A321-231	1433	D-AVZC	27. 2.01	GB Airways Ltd	Gatwick	26. 2.04T
G-TTIC	Airbus Industrie A321-231	1869 D-AVZZ		12.12.02	GB Airways Ltd	Gatwick	11.12.05T
G-TTMC	Airbus Industrie A300B4-203	299	OH-LAA (LX-LGP)/F-WZMX	25. 4.98	OY Air Scandic International Aviation AB	Manchester	29. 4.04T
G-TTOA	Airbus Industrie A320-232	1215	F-WWDB	18. 5.00	GB Airways Ltd	Gatwick	17. 5.03T
G-TTOB	Airbus Industrie A320-232	1687	F-WWIM	11. 2.02	GB Airways Ltd	Gatwick	13. 2.05T
G-TTOC	Airbus Industrie A320-232	1715	F-WWDB	6. 3.02	GB Airways Ltd	Gatwick	5. 3.05T
G-TTOD	Airbus Industrie A320-232	1723	F-WWBH	14. 3.02	GB Airways Ltd	Gatwick	13. 3.05T
G-TTOE	Airbus Industrie A320-232	1754	F-WWDH	11. 4.02	GB Airways Ltd	Gatwick	10. 4.05T
G-TTOF	Airbus Industrie A320-232	1918	F-WWIS	13. 2.03	GB Airways Ltd	Gatwick	
G-TTOG	Airbus Industrie A320-232	1969		4.03R	GB Airways Ltd *(For delivery 4.03)*	Gatwick	
G-TTOH	Airbus Industrie A320-232	1993		5.03R	GB Airways Ltd *(For delivery 5.03)*	Gatwick	
G-TTOI	Airbus Industrie A320-232			12.03R	GB Airways Ltd *(For delivery 12.03)*	Gatwick	
G-TTOJ	Airbus Industrie A320-232			2.04R	GB Airways Ltd *(For delivery 2.04)*	Gatwick	
G-TTOY	CFM Streak Shadow SA (Rotax 618)	K.233 & PFA 206-12805		15. 4.96	S.Marriott	Old Sarum	27. 8.03P
G-TUBB	Jabiru Jabiru UL-450 (Jabiru 2200A)	PFA 274A-13484		1.10.99	A.H.Bower	Kemble	20.11.02P
G-TUCH	Bell 206B JetRanger II	969	G-OCBB G-BASE/N18093	4. 4.01	P.Dobson t/a Touchdown	Redhill	30.10.03T
G-TUDR	Cameron V-77 HAB	1135		20. 5.85	Jacques W.Soukup Enterprises Ltd *"Tudor Rose/HVIIIR"*	(USA)	24.10.03A
G-TUGG	Piper PA-18-150 Super Cub (Lycoming O-360-A3) *(Frame No.18-8497)*	18-8274	PH-MAH N5451Y	10. 1.83	Ulster Gliding Club Ltd	Bellarena	9. 4.04
G-TUGY	Robin DR400/180 Regent	2052	D-EPAR	27. 4.98	J.M.Airey	Tibenham	19. 5.04T
G-TULP	Lindstrand LBL Tulips SS HAB	662	(PH-AJT) (PH-TLP)/PH-ORA)	16.10.00	Oxford Promotions (UK) Ltd *(Op F Prell)*	Kentucky, USA	3. 4.03A
G-TUNE	Robinson R22 Beta	0818	N60661 G-OJVI/(G-OJVJ)	12. 1.99	Ecurie Ecosse (Scotland) Ltd *(Op Scotia Helicopters)*	Cumbernauld	6. 2.05T
G-TURF	Reims/Cessna F406 Caravan II	F406-0020	PH-FWF (EI-CND)/PH-FWF/F-WZDS	17.10.96	Atlantic Air Transport Ltd *(Op Marine & Coastal Agency) "Lord of the Isles"*	Inverness	20. 1.05T
G-TURN	Steen Skybolt (Lycoming IO-360)	003 & PFA 64-11349		14. 7.88	R.Bentley	(Congleton)	29. 5.03P
G-TUSA	Pegasus Quantum 15-912	7841		9. 8.01	C.J.Cullen	Dunkeswell	16. 8.02P
G-TUSK	Bell 206B-3 JetRanger III	4406	G-BWZH N53114	13. 1.97	Heli Aviation Ltd	Blackbushe	23. 2.03T
G-TVAA	Agusta A109E Power	11052		24. 9.99	Agusta SpA	(Cascina, Italy)	7.11.02T
G-TVAC	Agusta A109E Power	11090		26.10.00	Sloane Helicopters Ltd *(Op Thames Valley Air Ambulance)*	White Waltham	12.11.03T
G-TVBF	Lindstrand LBL-310A HAB	439		2. 4.97	Airxcite Ltd t/a Virgin Balloon Flights	Wembley	17. 6.03T
G-TVII	Hawker Hunter T.7	41H-693834	XX467 RJordAF 836/RSAF 70-617/G-9-214/XL605 *(As "XX467" in TWU c/s)*	8.12.97	G.R.Montgomery	Kemble	AC
G-TVIJ	CCF Harvard 4 (T-6J-CCF Texan)	CCF4-442	G-BSBE Moz PLAF 1730/FAP 1730/AA+652/52-8521 *(As "28521/TA-521" in USAF c/s)*	10.12.93	R.W.Davies	Little Robhurst Farm, Woodchurch	17. 6.03P
G-TVIP	Cessna 404 Titan Courier II	404-0644	G-KIWI G-BHNI/LN-LGM/SE-IFV/G-BHNI/(N5302J)	16. 8.00	Capital Trading (Aviation) Ltd	Filton	5. 2.03T

G-TVTV	Cameron TV 90SS HAB	2357		14. 9.90	J.Krebs	Erfstadt, Germany	2. 6.99A
G-TWEL	Piper PA-28-181 Archer II	28-8090290	N81963	12. 6.80	International Aerospace Engineering Ltd	Cranfield	15. 5.05T
G-TWEY	Colt 69A HAB	700		24. 7.85	N.Bland	Didcot	12. 1.02A
G-TWIG	Reims/Cessna F406 Caravan II	F406-0014	PH-FWD	21.10.98	Highland Airways Ltd *"Wee Dram"*	Inverness	22.10.04T
			F-WZDS				
G-TWIN	Piper PA-44-180 Seminole	44-7995072	N30267	6.11.78	Bonus Aviation Ltd	Cranfield	22. 5.03T
G-TWIZ	Rockwell Commander 114	14375	SE-GSP	9. 5.90	B.C.& P M Cox	Redhill	17. 6.05
			N5808N				
G-TXSE	Rotary Air Force RAF 2000 GTX-SE			1. 3.96	G.J.Layzell	(Quedgeley)	1. 1.98P
		PFA G/113-1271			*(New owner 2.02)*		
G-TYAK	IAV-Bacau Yakovlev Yak-52	899907	RA01038	23.12.02	S.J.Ducker	Breighton	AC
			LY-AIE/DOSAAF 94 (yellow)				
G-TYER	Robin DR400/500	0021	F-GTZB	25. 4.00	Alfred Graham Ltd	Southend	14. 5.03
G-TYGA	Gulfstream AA-5B Tiger	AA5B-1161	G-BHNZ	22. 2.82	D H & R J Carman	Rochester	29. 1.04T
			(D-EGDS)/N4547L				
G-TYKE	Jabiru Jabiru UL	PFA 274A-13739		8. 6.01	A.Parker	(Bingley)	2. 7.03P
	(Jabiru 2200A)						
G-TYNE	SOCATA TB-20 Trindad	1523	F-GRBM	6.11.97	D.T.Watkins	Newcastle	26.11.03
			F-WWRW/CS-AZH/F-OHDE				
G-TYRE	Reims/Cessna F172M Skyhawk II	F17201222	OY-BIA	16. 2.79	J.A.Lyons	Willington Court, Sandhurst	2. 9.03T
					t/a Staverton Flying School		
G-TZEE	SOCATA TB-10 Tobago	727	F-GFQG	9. 1.03	Zytech Ltd	Earls Colne	
G-TZII	Thorp T.211B	PFA 305-13285		2. 6.99	AD Aviation Ltd	Barton	

G-UAAA - G-UZZZ

G-UANT	Piper PA-28-140 Cherokee F	28-7325568	OO-MYR	12. 4.02	Air Navigation & Trading Co Ltd	Blackpool	AC
			N56084				
G-UAPA	Robin DR400/140B Major	2213	F-GMXC	11. 1.95	Carlos Saraiva Lda	(Alges, Portugal)	3.10.04
G-UAPO	Ruschmeyer R90-230RG	019	D-EECT	2. 3.95	S.J.Green	Lagoa, Portugal	2. 7.04
G-UCCC	Cameron Sign 90SS HAB	3918		5. 7.96	B.Conway	Wheatley, Oxon	6. 9.99A
G-UDAY	Robinson R22 Beta	1101		4. 8.89	Newmarket Plant Hire Ltd	Cambridge	29. 5.05T
G-UDGE	Thruster T.600N (Rotax 503UL)	9099-T600N-037	G-BYPI	17. 9.99	L.J.Appleby	Leicester	17.10.02P
G-UDOG	Scottish Aviation.Bulldog Srs.120/121	BH.120/204	XX518	24. 1.02	Gamit Ltd *(As "XX518/S")* *(Open storage 11.02)*	Sleap	AC
G-UEST	Bell 206B JetRanger II	1484	G-RYOB	8. 9.89	Summit Aviation Ltd	Oxford	1. 2.03T
			G-BLWU/ZS-PAW				
G-UESY	Robinson R22 Beta-II	2801		13. 3.98	Plane Talking Ltd *(Op London Helicopters)*	Redhill	2. 4.04T
G-UFAW	Raj Hamsa X'Air 582	582 & BMAA/HB/167		24. 7.01	J.H.Goddard	Dunkeswell	16. 6.03P
G-UFCA	Cessna 172S Skyhawk	172S8313	N2461P	26. 1.00	Ulster Flying Club (1961) Ltd	Newtownards, Co.Down	9. 2.03T
G-UFCB	Cessna 172S Skyhawk	172S8318	N455SP	25. 1.00	Ulster Flying Club (1961) Ltd	Newtownards, Co.Down	3. 2.03T
G-UFCC	Cessna 172S Skyhawk	172S8611	N2466X	8. 1.01	Ulster Flying Club (1961) Ltd	Newtownards, Co.Down	8. 1.04T
G-UFCD	Cessna 172S Skyhawk	172S8443	G-OYZK	4. 1.01	Ulster Flying Club (1961) Ltd	Newtownards, Co.Down	12. 7.03T
					(Swung on landing Newtownards 22.8.01, damaging propeller & starboard wing tip)		
G-UFCE	Cessna 172S Skyhawk	172S9305	N5318Y	20. 2.03	Oxford Aviation Services Ltd	Oxford	
G-UFCF	Cessna 172S Skyhawk	172S9306	N5320Y	20. 2.03	Oxford Aviation Services Ltd	Oxford	
G-UFLY	Cessna F150H	F150-0264	G-AVVY	29. 9.89	Westair Flying Services Ltd	Blackpool	11. 3.05T
	(Built Reims Aviation SA)						
G-UGLY	Sud SE.313B Alouette II	1500	G-BSFN	7. 6.00	L.Smith t/a Helicopter Services	Booker	16. 7.04T
			XP967				
G-UILD	Grob G-109B	6419		28. 1.86	Runnymede Consultants Ltd	Blackbushe	30. 4.04
G-UILE	Neico Lancair 320	PFA 191-12538		17. 1.94	R.J.Martin	(Alresford, Hants)	
G-UILT	Cessna T303 Crusader	T30300280	G-EDRY	3. 7.00	W.J.Forrest tr G-UILT Group	Barton	10. 4.05
			N4817V				
G-UINN	Stolp SA.300 Starduster Too	HB.1980-1	EI-CDQ	16. 3.98	J.D.H.Gordon	Charterhall	2.12.03P
	(Lycoming O-360)		C-GTLJ		*(Also carries "EI-CDQ")*		
G-UIST	British Aerospace Jetstream Srs.3102	750	N190PC	15. 3.02	Highland Airways Ltd	Inverness	27. 5.05T
		(N331QH)/N840JS/G-31-750					
G-UJAB	Jabiru Jabiru UL	PFA 274A-13373		27. 1.99	C.A.Thomas	Top Farm, Croydon, Royston	23. 8.03P
G-UJGK	Jabiru Jabiru UL	PFA 274A-13558		17. 4.00	W.G.Upton & J.G.Kosak	RNAS Culdrose	7. 5.03P
G-UKAC	British Aerospace BAe 146 Srs.300	E3142	G-5-142	25.10.89	KLM UK Ltd *(Op Buzz)*	Stansted	19.11.04T
G-UKAG	British Aerospace BAe 146 Srs.300	E3162	G-6-162	28.11.90	KLM UK Ltd *(Op Buzz)*	Stansted	11.12.04T
G-UKFA	Fokker F.28 Mk.0100	11246	N602RP	1. 7.92	KLM Cityhopper UK Ltd	Stansted	12.10.05T
			C-FICY/PH-EZB				
G-UKFB	Fokker F.28 Mk.0100	11247	N602TR	1. 7.92	KLM Cityhopper UK Ltd	Stansted	12. 8.05T
	(Fokker 100)		C-FICW/PH-EZC				
G-UKFC	Fokker F.28 Mk.0100	11263	N602DG	1. 7.92	KLM Cityhopper UK Ltd	Stansted	27. 7.05T
	(Fokker 100)		C-FICL/PH-EZF				
G-UKFD	Fokker F.28 Mk.0100	11259	C-FICP	22. 7.92	KLM Cityhopper UK Ltd	Stansted	9.11.05T
	(Fokker 100)		PH-EZJ				
G-UKFE	Fokker F.28 Mk.0100	11260	C-FICQ	22. 7.92	KLM Cityhopper UK Ltd	Stansted	30.11.05T
	(Fokker 100)		PH-EZK				
G-UKFF	Fokker F.28 Mk.0100	11274	PH-ZCK	9.11.93	KLM Cityhopper UK Ltd	Stansted	8.11.03T
	(Fokker 100)		(G-FIOB)/PH-ZCK/PH-EZB/(PH-KLK)				
G-UKFG	Fokker F.28 Mk.0100	11275	PH-ZCL	19.11.93	KLM Cityhopper UK Ltd	Stansted	18.11.03T
	(Fokker 100)		(G-FIOC)/PH-ZCL/PH-EZV/(PH-KLL)				
G-UKFH	Fokker F.28 Mk.0100	11277	PH-ZCM	29. 9.93	KLM Cityhopper UK Ltd	Stansted	28. 9.03T
	(Fokker 100)		(G-FIOD)/PH-ZCM/PH-EZW/(PH-KLN)				
G-UKFI	Fokker F.28 Mk.0100	11279	PH-ZCN	12.10.93	KLM Cityhopper UK Ltd	Stansted	11.10.03T
	(Fokker 100)		(G-FIOE)/PH-ZCN/PH-EZX/(PH-KLO)				
G-UKFJ	Fokker F.28 Mk.0100	11248	F-GIOV	30. 1.96	KLM Cityhopper UK Ltd	Stansted	22. 2.05T
	(Fokker 100)		C-FICB/PH-INC/PH-EZD				
G-UKFK	Fokker F.28 Mk.0100	11249	F-GIOX	19. 2.96	KLM Cityhopper UK Ltd	Stansted	1. 4.05T
	(Fokker 100)		C-FICO/PH-INA/PH-EZE				

Reg	Type	C/n	Prev id	Date	Owner/Operator	Base	Date2
G-UKFM	Fokker F.28 Mk.0100 *(Fokker 100)*	11269	PH-KLD F-GIDQ/PH-KLD	27.10.98	KLM Cityhopper UK Ltd	Stansted	25.11.04T
G-UKFN	Fokker F.28 Mk.0100 *(Fokker 100)*	11270	PH-KLE F-GIDP/PH-KLE	16. 6.97	KLM Cityhopper UK Ltd	Stansted	21. 7.03T
G-UKFO	Fokker F.28 Mk.0100 *(Fokker 100)*	11271	PH-KLG F-GIDO/PH-KLG	20.10.97	KLM Cityhopper UK Ltd	Stansted	20.10.03T
G-UKFR	Fokker F.28 Mk.0100 *(Fokker 100)*	11273	PH-KLI F-GIDM/F-OGQB/PH-KLI	21. 3.97	KLM Cityhopper UK Ltd	Stansted	26. 3.03T
G-UKHP	British Aerospace BAe 146 Srs.300	E3123	G-5-123	26.10.88	KLM UK Ltd *(Op Buzz)*	Stansted	26. 2.05T
G-UKID	British Aerospace BAe 146 Srs.300	E3157	G-6-157	28. 2.90	KLM UK Ltd *(Op Buzz)*	Stansted	6. 3.05T
G-UKOZ	Jabiru Jabiru SK	PFA 274-13310		16. 6.99	D.J.Burnett	Hinton in-the Hedges	15. 8.03P
G-UKRC	British Aerospace BAe 146 Srs.300	E3158	G-BSMR G-6-158	14. 2.91	KLM UK Ltd *(Op Buzz)*	Stansted	24. 2.05T
G-UKSC	British Aerospace BAe 146 Srs.300	E3125	G-5-125	26.10.88	KLM UK Ltd *(Op Buzz)*	Stansted	9. 3.05T
G-UKTA	Fokker F.27 Mk.050 *(Fokker 50)*	20246	PH-KXF	22. 2.95	KLM UK Ltd *"City of Norwich"*	Norwich	21. 2.04T
G-UKTB	Fokker F.27 Mk.050 *(Fokker 50)*	20247	PH-KXG	21. 3.95	KLM UK Ltd *"City of Aberdeen"*	Norwich	21. 3.04T
G-UKTC	Fokker F.27 Mk.050 *(Fokker 50)*	20249	PH-KXH	25. 1.95	KLM UK Ltd *"City of Bradford"*	Norwich	25. 1.04T
G-UKTD	Fokker F.27 Mk.050 *(Fokker 50)*	20256	PH-KXT	20. 1.95	KLM UK Ltd *"City of Leeds"*	Norwich	19. 1.04T
G-UKTE	Fokker F.27 Mk.050 *(Fokker 50)*	20270	PH-LXJ	14. 2.95	KLM UK Ltd *"City of Hull"*	Norwich	14. 2.04T
G-UKTF	Fokker F.27 Mk.050 *(Fokker 50)*	20271	PH-LXK	31. 1.95	KLM UK Ltd *"City of York"*	Norwich	31. 1.04T
G-UKTG	Fokker F.27 Mk.050 *(Fokker 50)*	20276	PH-LXP	28. 2.95	KLM UK Ltd *"City of Durham"*	Norwich	28. 2.04T
G-UKTH	Fokker F.27 Mk.050 *(Fokker 50)*	20277	PH-LXR	28. 3.95	KLM UK Ltd *"City of Amsterdam"*	Norwich	28. 3.04T
G-UKTI	Fokker F.27 Mk.050 *(Fokker 50)*	20279	PH-LXT	17. 3.95	KLM UK Ltd *"City of Stavanger"*	Norwich	16. 3.04T
G-UKTM	Aérospatiale/Alenia ATR 72-202	508	F-WWLU	23. 4.98	KLM UK Ltd *(Op British Regional)*	Jersey	22. 4.04T
G-UKTN	Aérospatiale/Alenia ATR 72-202	496	F-WWLT	4. 6.98	KLM UK Ltd	Norwich	3. 6.04T
G-UKUK	Head Ax8-105 HAB	248	N8303U	1. 9.97	P.A.George *"Union Jack"*	Princes Risborough	14. 8.03A
G-ULAS	de Havilland DHC.1 Chipmunk 22	C1/0554	WK517	14. 6.96	ULAS Flying Club Ltd *(As "WK517")*	Denham	11. 9.02
G-ULIA	Cameron V-77 HAB	2860		20. 5.92	J.M.Dean	Oswestry	16. 5.03A
G-ULLS	Lindstrand LBL-90A HAB	434		18. 2.97	J.R.Clifton	Brackley	11.10.03A
G-ULPS	Everett Gyroplane Srs.1 *(Volkswagen 1835)*	007	G-BMNY	13. 7.93	C.J.Watkinson	(Goole)	10. 7.01P
G-ULTR	Cameron A-105 HAB	4100		24. 2.97	P.Glydon *(Ultrafilter titles)*	Birmingham	9. 9.03T
G-UMMI	Piper PA-31 Navajo C	31-7912060	G-BGSO N3519F	11. 8.92	J.A, G.M, D.T.A.& J.A.Rees t/a Messrs Rees of Poynston West	Haverfordwest	1. 8.03T
G-UNDD	Piper PA-23-250 Aztec E	27-4832	G-BATX N14271	22. 3.00	G.J.& D.P.Deadman	Goodwood	13. 9.04T
G-UNGE	Lindstrand LBL-90A HAB	122	G-BVPJ	6.12.96	M.T.Stevens tr Silver Ghost Balloon Club	Solihull	18. 7.03A
G-UNGO	Pietenpol Aircamper	PFA 47-13951		16. 9.02	A.R.Wyatt	(Buntingford)	
G-UNIV	Montgomerie-Parsons Two-Place Gyroplane	PFA G/08-1276	G-BWTP	3. 8.99	Department of Aerospace Engineering, University of Glasgow	(Glasgow)	1. 3.00P
G-UNNY	British Aircraft Corporation BAC.167 Strikemaster Mk.87 *(Or PS.170?)*	EEP/JP/2872 & PS.164	G-AYHR/Botswana DF OJ4/Kenya AF 601/G-27-141/G-AYHR/G-27-191 *(As "OJ4/Z-2" in Botswana c/s)*	19. 3.98	Strikemaster Films Ltd	(South Africa)	27. 4.03P
G-UNYT	Robinson R22 Beta	0985	G-BWZV G-LIAN	17.11.97	Heli Air Ltd	Wellesbourne Mountford	16.11.03T
G-UPHL	Cameron Concept 80 HAB	3002		23. 2.93	CSM (Weston) Ltd t/a Uphill Motor Co *(Uphill Motors titles)*	Weston-super-Mare	8. 9.00T
G-UPPP	Colt 77A HAB	852		4. 8.86	M.Williams *"Nugget"*	Wadhurst	25. 3.95A
G-UPPY	Cameron DP-80 Hot-Air Airship	2274		29. 3.90	Jacques W.Soukup Enterprises Ltd *"Jacques Soukup"* Beaulieu Court, Wilts/Great Missenden		27. 8.94A
G-UPUP	Cameron V-77 HAB	1828		21. 7.89	S.R.Burden *"Fantasia"*	Noordwijk, The Netherlands	8. 6.03T
G-URCH	Rotorway Executive 162F *(Rotorway RI 162F)*	6414		1.10.99	D.L.Urch	(Winscombe)	AC
G-UROP	Beech B55 Baron	TC-2452	N64311	17. 9.90	Pooler International Ltd	Sleap	15. 3.03
G-URRR	Air Command 582 Sport	0630 & PFA G/04-1200		13. 6.90	L.Armes	(Basildon)	
G-USAM	Cameron Uncle Sam SS HAB *(Uncle Sam head shape) (New envelope c/n 4526 c.3.99)*	1120		20. 5.85	Corn Palace Balloon Club Ltd	Tyndale, South Dakota, USA	27. 6.00A
G-USIL	Thunder Ax7-77 HAB	1587		22. 8.89	Window on the World Ltd *"Mantis"*	London SE1	27. 5.99A
G-USMC	Cameron Chestie 90SS HAB *(US Marine Corps Bulldog shape)*	1251		24. 4.86	Jacques W.Soukup Enterprises Ltd	Tyndale, South Dakota, USA	15. 6.00A
G-USSR	Cameron Doll 90SS HAB *(Russian Doll shape)*	2273		29. 3.90	Corn Palace Balloon Club Ltd *"Matrioshka"*	Tyndale, South Dakota, USA	9. 6.00A
G-USSY	Piper PA-28-181 Archer II	28-8290011	N8439R	7.11.88	Western Air (Thruxton) Ltd	Thruxton	18. 2.04T
G-USTA*	Agusta A109A	7170	G-MEAN G-BRYL/G-ROPE/G-OAMH	3.12.96	Markoss Aviation Ltd	Biggin Hill	21. 4.00T
			(Damaged Bedlam Street, Hurstpierpoint 27.3.99: cancelled 5.8.99 as WFU) (Stored w/o boom 12.00)				
G-USTB	Agusta A109A	7163	D-HEEG (D-HEEF)/VR-CKN/HB-XKM	9. 6.97	Newton Aviation Ltd	Redhill	19. 7.03T
G-USTY	Clutton FRED Srs.III *(Volkswagen 1834)*	PFA 29-10390		11.10.78	R.T.Mosforth tr GUSTY Group	Netherthorpe	25. 6.03P
G-UTSI	Rand Robinson KR-2	KBG-01		2.10.89	K.B.Gutridge *(Stored 12.00)*	Biggin Hill	
G-UTSY	Piper PA-28R-201 Cherokee Arrow III	28R-7737052	N3346Q	29. 8.86	Arrow Aviation Ltd	Southend	8. 2.05
G-UTTS	Robinson R44 Raven	0865	G-ROAP	20.10.00	Heli Hire Ltd	Gamston	12.10.03T
G-UTZY	Aérospatiale SA341G Gazelle 1	1307	G-BKLV N341SC	21.12.87	Richer Jet Ltd *(New owner 4.02)*	(London SE1)	26. 3.05T
G-UVIP	Cessna 421C Golden Eagle III	421C0603	G-BSKH N88600	23.11.98	Capital Trading Aviation Ltd	Filton	2.11.04T
G-UVNR	British Aircraft Corporation BAC.167 Strikemaster Mk.87 *(Or PS.174?)*	EEP/JP/2876 & PS.168	G-BXFS/Botswana DF OJ10/Kenyan AF 605/G-27-195 *(As "OJ-10")*	4. 5.01	Global Aviation Services Ltd	Humberside	23.12.03P
G-UZEL	Aérospatiale SA341G Gazelle 1	1413	G-BRNH YU-HBO	21.11.89	MCC Ltd	Kirk Michael, Isle of Man	3. 7.04
G-UZLE	Colt 77A HAB	2021		1. 8.91	Flying Pictures Ltd *"John Courage"*	Chilbolton	25. 5.00A

G-VAAA - G-VZZZ

Reg	Type	c/n	Prev id	Date	Owner	Location	Expiry
G-VAEL	Airbus Industrie A340-311	015	F-WWJG	15.12.93	Virgin Atlantic Airways Ltd "Maiden Toulouse"	Gatwick	14.12.05T
G-VAGA	Piper PA-15 Vagabond (Lycoming O-145-B2)	15-248	N4458H NC4458H	14.11.80	I.M.Callier	(Windsor)	29. 8.98P
G-VAIR	Airbus Industrie A340-313	164	F-WWJA	21. 4.97	Virgin Atlantic Airways Ltd "Maiden Tokyo"	Gatwick	20. 4.03T
G-VALS	Pietenpol Aircamper	PFA 47-13157		30. 7.97	I.G.& V.A.Price	(Liphook)	
G-VALZ	Cameron N-120 HAB	4998		9. 1.01	D Ling	(Nottingham)	26 11.03T
G-VANS	Van's RV-4 (Lycoming O-320)	355	N16TS	7. 9.92	M.Swanborough & D.Jones	Breighton	14. 2.02P
G-VANZ	Van's RV-6A	PFA 181-12531		15. 7.93	S.J.Baxter (Under construction 2000)	(Macclesfield)	
G-VARG	Varga 2150A Kachina	VAC 157-80	OO-RTY N80716	14. 5.84	A.C.Fletcher	Sherburn-in-Elmet	23. 6.03
G-VASA	Piper PA-34-200 Seneca	34-7350080	G-BNNB (N...)/G-BNNB/N15625	29. 3.96	V.Babic	Bournemouth	5. 7.03T
G-VAST	Boeing 747-41R	28757		17. 6.97	Virgin Atlantic Airways Ltd "Ladybird"	Heathrow	16. 6.03T
G-VATL	Airbus Industrie A340-642	376	F-WWCC	9.03R	Virgin Atlantic Airways Ltd "Atlantic Angel" (For delivery 9.03)		
G-VAUN	Cessna 340 II	340-0538	D-IOFW N5148J	25.11.77	White Falcon Enterprises Ltd	(Sheffield)	25.11.04
G-VBAC	Short SD.3-60 Var.100	SH.3736	VH-MJU G-BOEJ/G-14-3736	15. 9.97	BAC Leasing Ltd (Op BAC Express) "City of Norwich"	Exeter	15. 9.03T
G-VBIG	Boeing 747-4Q8	26255		10. 6.96	Virgin Atlantic Airways Ltd "Tinker Belle"	Gatwick	9. 6.05T
G-VBUS	Airbus Industrie A340-311	013	F-WWJE	26.11.93	Virgin Atlantic Airways Ltd "Lady in Red"	Gatwick	25.11.03T
G-VCAT	Boeing 747-267B	22872	TF-ATK G-VCAT/B-HIE/VR-HIE	16.10.98	Virgin Atlantic Airways Ltd (Stored 10.02)	Mojave-Kem Co, Ca, USA	21.10.04T
G-VCED	Airbus Industrie A320-231	0193	OY-CNI F-WWIX	21. 1.97	MyTravel Airways Ltd	Manchester	30. 1.03T
G-VCIO	EAA Acrosport 2	PFA 72-12388		9.10.97	V Millard	Crowfield	27. 5.03P
G-VCML	Beech 58 Baron	TH-1346	N2289R	31.10.97	St.Angelo Aviation Ltd (Noted 11.01)	Dunkeswell	10. 1.04T
G-VDIR	Cessna 310R II	310R0211	N5091J	31. 1.91	J.Driver	(Pinner)	13. 6.04T
G-VECD	Robin R1180T Aiglon II	234	F-GCAD	22. 6.00	Mistral Aviation Ltd	Goodwood	21. 9.03T
G-VECE	Robin R2120U	355		11. 5.01	Mistral Aviation Ltd	Goodwood	8. 7.04T
G-VECG	Robin R2160 Alpha Sport	322	F-GSRD	6. 2.02	Mistral Aviation Ltd	Goodwood	17. 2.05T
G-VEIL	Airbus Industrie A340-642		F-WW..	9.03R	Virgin Atlantic Airways Ltd "Dancing Girl!" (For delivery 9.03)		
G-VELA	SIAI-Marchetti S.205-22R (Confirmed as S.208A Waco Vela)	4-149	N949W	30.10.89	K.R.Allen t/a G-VELA Partnership	Gamston	29. 4.05
G-VELD	Airbus Industrie A340-313	214	F-WWJY	16. 3.98	Virgin Atlantic Airways Ltd "African Queen"	Gatwick	15. 3.04T
G-VENI	de Havilland DH.112 Venom FB.50 (FB.1) (Built F + W)	733	J-1523	8. 6.84	Lindsay Wood Promotions Ltd (As "VV612" in silver RAF c/s) (Stored1.03)	Bournemouth	25. 7.01P
G-VENM	de Havilland DH.112 Venom FB.50 (FB.1) (Built F + W)	824	G-BLIE J-1614	16. 6.99	T.J.Manna (As "WK436" in 11 Sqdn c/s)	North Weald	17. 1.03P
G-VENT	Schempp-Hirth Ventus 2CM	3/17	D-KBTL	25. 9.01	D.Rance	(Kemberton)	5.11.04
G-VERA	Garden GY-201 Minicab	PFA 56-12236		7. 6.94	D.K.Shipton	(Peterborough)	
G-VETA	Hawker Hunter T.7	41H-693751	G-BVWN XL600	2. 7.96	Veta Ltd	Kemble	18. 4.03P
G-VETS	Enstrom 280C-UK Shark	1015	G-FSDC G-BKTG/OY-HBP	11. 9.95	C.Upton	Barton	28. 7.02
G-VEYE	Robinson R22	0140	G-BPTP N9056H	8. 2.00	J.B.Errington (Hangared less rotors 8.01)	Shobdon	2. 6.01T
G-VEZE	Rutan Varieze	PFA 74-10285		2. 9.77	S.D.Brown, S.Evans & M.Roper	(West Wickham/Haywards Heath)	
G-VFAB	Boeing 747-4Q8	24958		28. 4.94	Virgin Atlantic Airways Ltd "Lady Penelope"	Gatwick	27. 4.03T
G-VFAR	Airbus Industrie A340-313X	225	(G-VPOW) F-WWJZ	12. 6.98	Virgin Atlantic Airways Ltd "Diana"	Gatwick	11. 6.04T
G-VFLY	Airbus Industrie A340-311	058	F-WWJE	24.10.94	Virgin Atlantic Airways Ltd "Dragon Lady"	Gatwick	23.10.03T
G-VFOX	Airbus Industrie A340-642	449	F-WWCM	23.12.02	Virgin Atlantic Airways Ltd "Silver Lady"	Heathrow	22.12.05T
G-VFSI	Robinson R22 Beta	1785	N4081L	19.12.96	M.N.Cowley t/a Dragonfly Aviation	(Towcester)	14. 6.03T
G-VGAL	Boeing 747-443	32337	(EI-CVH)	26. 4.01	Virgin Atlantic Airways Ltd "Jersey Girl"	Gatwick	25. 4.04T
G-VGOA	Airbus Industrie A340-642	371		7.03R	Virgin Atlantic Airways Ltd "Indian Princess" (For delivery 7.03)		
G-VHOL	Airbus Industrie A340-311	002	F-WWAS	30. 5.97	Virgin Atlantic Airways Ltd "Jetstreamer"	Gatwick	29. 5.03T
G-VHOT	Boeing 747-4Q8	26326		12.10.94	Virgin Atlantic Airways Ltd "Tubular Belle"	Gatwick	11.10.03T
G-VIBA	Cameron DP-80 Hot Air Airship	1729		28. 5.91	Jacques W.Soukup Enterprises Ltd	Beaulieu Court, Wilts/Great Missenden	3. 2.99A
G-VIBE	Boeing 747-219B	22791	ZK-NZZ 9M-MHH/ZK-NZZ/N6108N	24. 9.99	Virgin Atlantic Airways Ltd "Spirit of New York" (Stored 12.02)	Marana-Pinal Airpark, AZ, USA	23. 9.02T
G-VICC	Piper PA-28-161 Warrior II	28-7916317	G-JFHL N2249U	3. 3.92	J.R.Green tr Charlie Charlie Syndicate	Hinton in the Hedges	5. 8.04T
G-VICE	MD Helicopters Hughes 369E (500E)	0365E	D-HLIS	16. 5.95	Bramington Properties Ltd	Wolverhampton	21. 8.04
G-VICI	de Havilland DH.112 Venom FB.50 (FB.1) (Built F + W)	783	HB-RVB (G-BMOB)/J-1573	6. 2.95	Lindsay Wood Promotions Ltd (As "J-1573" in Swiss AF c/s) (Stored1.03)	Bournemouth	24.11.99P
G-VICM	Beech F33C Bonanza	CJ-136	PH-BNG	3. 7.91	Velocity Engineering Ltd	Booker	20. 5.03
G-VICS	Commander Aircraft Commander 114B	14655	N655V	3. 2.98	Millennium Aviation Ltd	Guernsey	17. 4.04
G-VICT	Piper PA-31 Turbo Navajo B	31-7401211	G-BBZI N7590L	10. 9.99	Heliquick Ltd	(Salisbury)	13. 8.05T
G-VIEW	Vinten Wallis WA-116/L (Limbach L2000)	002		5. 7.82	K.H.Wallis (Stored 8.01)	Reymerston Hall, Norfolk	6.10.85P
G-VIIA	Boeing 777-236ER	27483	N5022E (G-ZZZF)	3. 7.97	British Airways plc (Waves of the City t/s)	Gatwick	2. 7.03T
G-VIIB	Boeing 777-236ER	27484	N5023Q (G-ZZZG)	23. 5.97	British Airways plc	Heathrow	22. 5.03T
G-VIIC	Boeing 777-236ER	27485	N5016R (G-ZZZH)	6. 2.97	British Airways plc	Heathrow	20. 8.05T
G-VIID	Boeing 777-236ER	27486	(G-ZZZI)	18. 2.97	British Airways plc	Heathrow	15. 9.05T

Reg	Type	C/n	Prev id	Date	Owner/Operator	Base	Date
G-VIIE	Boeing 777-236ER	27487	(G-ZZZJ)	27. 2.97	British Airways plc	Heathrow	23. 9.05T
G-VIIF	Boeing 777-236ER	27488	(G-ZZZK)	19. 3.97	British Airways plc	Heathrow	1.11.05T
G-VIIG	Boeing 777-236ER	27489	(G-ZZZL)	9. 4.97	British Airways plc	Heathrow	8. 4.03T
G-VIIH	Boeing 777-236ER	27490	(G-ZZZM)	7. 5.97	British Airways plc	Heathrow	6. 5.03T
G-VIIJ	Boeing 777-236ER	27492	(G-ZZZP)	29.12.97	British Airways plc (Benyhone Tartan t/s)	Gatwick	21.12.03T
G-VIIK	Boeing 777-236ER	28840		3. 2.98	British Airways plc (Animals & Trees t/s)	Gatwick	2. 2.04T
G-VIIL	Boeing 777-236ER	27493		13. 3.98	British Airways plc (Wings t/s)	Heathrow	12. 3.04T
G-VIIM	Boeing 777-236ER	28841		26. 3.98	British Airways plc (Waves & Cranes t/s)	Gatwick	13. 9.03T
G-VIIN	Boeing 777-236ER	29319		21. 8.98	British Airways plc (Whale Rider t/s)	Heathrow	20. 8.04T
G-VIIO	Boeing 777-236ER	29320		26. 1.99	British Airways plc (Chelsea Rose t/s)	Gatwick	25. 1.05T
G-VIIP	Boeing 777-236ER	29321		9. 2.99	British Airways plc (Colum t/s)	Heathrow	8. 2.05T
G-VIIR	Boeing 777-236ER	29322		18. 3.99	British Airways plc (Benyhone Tartan t/s)	Gatwick	17. 3.05T
G-VIIS	Boeing 777-236ER	29323		1. 4.99	British Airways plc (Chelsea Rose t/s)	Heathrow	31. 3.05T
G-VIIT	Boeing 777-236ER	29962		26. 5.99	British Airways plc (Rendezvous t/s)	Heathrow	25. 5.05T
G-VIIU	Boeing 777-236ER	29963		28. 5.99	British Airways plc (Delftblue Daybreak t/s)	Heathrow	27. 5.05T
G-VIIV	Boeing 777-236ER	29964		29. 6.99	British Airways plc	Gatwick	28. 6.05T
G-VIIW	Boeing 777-236ER	29965		30. 7.99	British Airways plc	Heathrow	29. 7.05T
G-VIIX	Boeing 777-236ER	29966		11. 8.99	British Airways plc	Gatwick	10 .8.05T
G-VIIY	Boeing 777-236ER	29967		22.10.99	British Airways plc	Heathrow	21.10.05T
G-VIKE	Bellanca 17-30A Super Viking 300A	79-30911	N302CB	8. 7.80	W.G.Prout	(Lee-on-Solent)	16. 6.05
G-VIKY	Cameron A-120 HAB	3068		27. 4.93	N.A.Fishlock	(Malvern)	31. 8.02A
G-VILA	Jabiru Jabiru UL (Jabiru 2200A)	PFA 274A-13364	G-BYIF	18. 7.02	R.W.Sage & T.R.Villa	Priory Farm, Tibenham	23. 6.03P
G-VILL	Carmichael Lazer Z.200 (Lycoming AEIO-360)	10	G-BOYZ	10. 6.96	M.G.Jefferies (Global Village titles)	Little Gransden	12. 7.03P
G-VINO	Sky 90-24 HAB	102		25. 2.98	Fivedata Ltd (Lambrini Bianco titles)	Todmorden	31.5.03A
G-VIPA	Cessna 182S Skylane	18280720	N148ME	13. 9.00	Rollright Aviation Ltd	(Chipping Norton)	19.10.03T
G-VIPH	Agusta A109C	7643	EI-CUV G-BVNH/G-LAXO	21. 9.01	Sloane Helicopters Ltd	Sywell	23. 9.04T
G-VIPI	British Aerospace BAe 125 Srs.800B	258222	G-5-745	27. 7.92	Yeates of Leicester Ltd	Southampton	16. 9.03T
G-VIPP	Piper PA-31-350 Navajo Chieftain	31-7952244	G-OGRV G-BMPX/N3543D	6. 8.93	Capital Trading Aviation Ltd	Filton	28. 8.03T
G-VIPY	Piper PA-31-350 Navajo Chieftain	31-7852143	EI-JTC G-POLO/(EI-...)/G-POLO/N27750	10.10.97	Capital Trading Aviation Ltd	Filton	12.10.03T
G-VITE	Robin R1180T Aiglon	219		16.10.78	D.C.Perrett & D.T.Scrutton tr G-VITE Flying Group	Stapleford	14. 9.03
G-VITL	Lindstrand LBL 105A HAB	720		24. 8.00	Actionsolus Ltd t/a Vital Resources (Vital Resources titles)	Manchester	8..2.03A
G-VIVA	Thunder Ax7-65 Bolt HAB	190		28.11.78	R.J.Mitchener (Inflated 4.02)	Andover	18. 3.99A
G-VIVI	Taylor JT.2 Titch	PFA 60-12405		4.11.96	D.G.Tucker	Hill Farm, Nayland	12.11.02P
G-VIVM	British Aircraft Corporation P.84 Jet Provost T.5	PAC/W/23907	G-BVWF XS230	25. 3.96	K.Lyndon-Dykes	North Weald	4.12.03P
G-VIXN	de Havilland DH.110 Sea Vixen FAW.2 (TT)	10145	8828M XS587	5. 8.85	P.G.Vallance Ltd (Gatwick Aviation Museum as "XS587 in RN c/s)	Charlwood, Surrey	
G-VIZZ	Sportavia RS.180 Sportsman	6018	D-EFBK	25.10.79	J.D.Howard & S.J.Morris tr Exeter Fournier Group	Exeter	23. 7.04
G-VJAB	Jabiru Jabiru UL (Jabiru 2200A) (PFA prefix "274" indicates model SK: a model UL shold be "274A")	PFA 274-13322		25. 6.98	ST Aviation Ltd	Southery	24. 3.03P
G-VJET	Avro 698 Vulcan B.2	-	XL426	7. 7.87	R.J.Clarkson tr The Vulcan Restoration Trust (As "XL426/G-VJET") (Noted 12.02)	Southend	
G-VJIM	Thunder & Colt Jumbo SS HAB (Registered as Colt Jumbo-2)	1298	(G-BPJI)	7. 8.89	Magical Adventures Ltd West Bloomfield, Mi., USA "Jumbo Jim" (Virgin Atlantic titles)		14.10.02A
G-VKIT	Europa Aviation Europa (Rotax 912S) (Monowheel u/c)	163 & PFA 247-12783		11. 6.01	T.H.Crow	(Bicester)	
G-VLAD	Yakovlev Yak-50	791502	D-EIVR N51980/DDR-WQR/DM-WQR	14.11.88	M.B.Smith	Top Farm, Croydon, Royston	11. 9.02P
G-VLCN	Avro 698 Vulcan B.2		XH558	6. 2.95	C.Walton Ltd (As "XH558") (Noted 3.02)	Bruntingthorpe	
G-VLIP	Boeing 747-443	32338	(EI-CVI)	15. 5.01	Virgin Atlantic Airways Ltd "Hot Lips"	Gatwick	14. 5.04T
G-VMCO	Agusta A109E Power	11123		31. 7.01	Unique Aviation Group Ltd	Jacobstowe, Devon	30. 7.04T
G-VMDE(2)	Cessna P210N Pressurised Centurion II	P21000088	(N4717P)	20. 7.78	Just Plane Trading Ltd Top Farm, Croydon, Royston		4. 4.04
G-VMEG	Airbus Industrie A340-642	391		5.10.02	Virgin Atlantic Airways Ltd "Mystic Maiden"	Heathrow	3.10.05T
G-VMJM	SOCATA TB-10 Tobago	1361	G-BTOK	21. 4.92	Cardonstar Ltd	Enstone	2. 5.04T
G-VMPR	de Havilland DH.115 Vampire T.11	15621	8196M XE920	13. 3.95	de Havilland Aviation Ltd (As "XE920/A" in 603 (County of Edinburgh) Sqdn c/s)	Bournemouth	3. 4.01P
G-VMSL	Robinson R22 Alpha	0483	G-KILY N8561M	5. 2.98	L.L.F.Smith (Force landed & rolled over near Turweston 4.6.01)	Booker	26.12.03T
G-VNOM	de Havilland DH.112 Venom FB.50 (FB.1) (Built F + W)	842	J-1632	13. 7.84	T.J.Manna (As "J-1632") (On loan to De Havilland Heritage Museum)	London Colney	
G-VNUS	Hughes 269C (300)	122-0175	G-BATT	20. 9.00	Heli Air Ltd	Wellesbourne Mountford	21.11.03T
G-VOAR	Piper PA-28-181 Archer III	2843011	N9256Q	3.11.95	S.J.Skilton t/a Aviation Rentals (Op Solent Flight Training)	Bournemouth	7.1.05T
G-VODA	Cameron N-77 HAB (New envelope c/n 4164 @ 12.97)	2208		8. 2.90	Vodafone Group plc (Vodafone titles)	Newbury	14. 6.01A
G-VOGE	Airbus Industrie A340-642	416	F-WWCF	29.11.02	Virgin Atlantic Airways Ltd "Cover Girl"	Heathrow	28.11.05T
G-VOID	Piper PA-28RT-201 Arrow IV	28R-8118049	ZS-KTM (G-GCAA)/ZS-KTM/N83232	17. 8.87	Newbus Aviation Ltd	Shoreham	13. 1.03T
G-VOLH	Airbus Industrie A321-211	0823	(EC-) D-AVZX	15. 5.98	MyTravel Airways Ltd	Manchester	27. 6.04T
G-VOLK	Bell 206L-1 LongRanger II	45565	G-GBAY G-CSWL/G-SIRI/G-CSWL/F-GDAD	21. 5.02	Chester Air Maintenance Ltd	Hawarden	20. 6.03T
G-VOTE	Ultramagic M-77 HAB	77-164		10. 3.99	Window on the World Ltd	London SE1	10. 4.03A
G-VPCB	Evans VP-1 Srs 2	PFA 62-13901		28. 2.03	Claudine A.Bloom	Shoreham	
G-VPSJ	Europa Aviation Europa (Rotax 912S) (Monowheel u/c)	023 & PFA 247-12520		29. 7.93	J.D.Bean (Current status unknown)	(Oxford)	

G-VPUF	Boeing 747-219B	22725	ZK-NZY N6005C	21. 3.00	Virgin Atlantic Airways Ltd Mojave-Kem Co, Ca, USA *"High as a Kite" (Stored 10.02)*		21 .3.03T
G-VROE	Avro 652A Anson T.21	3634	G-BFIR 7881M/WD413	3. 3.98	Air Atlantique Ltd	Coventry	1. 7.03P
G-VROM	Boeing 747-443	32339	(EI-CVJ)	29. 5.01	Virgin Atlantic Airways Ltd *"Barbarella"*	Gatwick	28. 5.04T
G-VROS	Boeing 747-443	30885	(EI-CVG)	22. 3.01	Virgin Atlantic Airways Ltd *"English Rose"*	Heathrow	21. 3.04T
G-VROY	Boeing 747-443	32340	(EI-CVK)	18. 6.01	Virgin Atlantic Airways Ltd *"Pretty Woman"*	Gatwick	17. 6.04T
G-VRST	Piper PA-46-350P Malibu Mirage	4636189		7.12.98	Winchfield Development Ltd	Fairoaks	24. 2.05
G-VRTX	Enstrom 280FX	2044	G-CBNH Chilean Army H-180	8. 7.02	Unison (1000) Ltd	(Selby)	11.12.05T
G-VRUM	Boeing 747-267B	23048	TF-ATV G-VRUM/B-HIF/VR-HIF/N6066U	2.11.98	Virgin Atlantic Airways Ltd *"Calypso Queen"* *(Stored 10.02)* Mojave-Kem Co, CA, USA		1.11.04T
G-VRVI	Cameron O-90 HAB	2522		27. 2.91	Cooling Services Ltd *(Daikin VRV titles)*	Portishead	29. 3.03A
G-VSBC	Beech B200 Super King Air	BB-1290	N3185C JA8859/N3185C	17. 6.93	Vickers Shipbuilding & Engineering Ltd Walney Island		21. 6.03
G-VSEA	Airbus Industrie A340-311	003	F-WWDA	7. 7.97	Virgin Atlantic Airways Ltd *"Plain Sailing"*	Gatwick	6. 7.03T
G-VSGE	Cameron O-105 HAB	2382	I-VSGE G-BSSD	14. 8.02	G.Aimo	Mondovi, Italy	18. 9.03A
G-VSHY	Airbus Industrie A340-642	383	F-WWCD	26. 7.02	Virgin Atlantic Airways Ltd *"Madam Butterfly"* Heathrow		25. 7.05T
G-VSKY	Airbus Industrie A340-311	016	F-WWJH	21. 1.94	Virgin Atlantic Airways Ltd *"China Girl"*	Gatwick	20. 1.03T
G-VSSH	Airbus Industrie A340-642		F-WW..	.03R	Virgin Atlantic Airways Ltd *"Sweet Dreamer" (On order 2003)*		
G-VSUN	Airbus Industrie A340-313	114	F-WWJI (F-GLZJ)	30. 4.96	Virgin Atlantic Airways Ltd *"Rainbow Lady"*	Gatwick	29. 4.05T
G-VTAL	Beechcraft V35 Bonanza	D-7978	HB-EJB D-EFTH	27. 2.03	R.Chamberlain Wellesbourne Mountford t/r Wellesbourne Bonanza Group		
G-VTAN	Airbus Industrie A320-214	0764	G-BXTA F-WWDF	29. 4.99	Virgin Atlantic Airways Ltd *"Sunshine Girl"* *(Stored 10.02)*	Dublin	29. 4.04T
G-VTEN*	Vinten-Wallis WA.117 Venom (Continental O-200-B)	UMA-01 & 003		22. 4.85	K.H.Wallis Reymerston Hall, Norfolk *(Cancelled 12.6.89 as WFU) (Stored unmarked 8.01)*		3.12.85P
G-VTII	de Havilland DH.115 Vampire T.11 *(Fuselage No.DHP40273)*	15127	WZ507	9. 1.80	Vampire Preservation Ltd Bournemouth *(As "WZ507")*		15. 7.03P
G-VTOP	Boeing 747-4Q8	28194		28. 1.97	Virgin Atlantic Airways Ltd *"Virginia Plain"*	Gatwick	17. 3.03T
G-VUEA	Cessna 550 Citation II	550-0671	G-BWOM N671EA/9M-TAA/(N6761L)	20. 6.02	AD Aviation Ltd	(Warrington)	18. 4.04T
G-VULC*	Avro 698 Vulcan B.2A	-	N655AV G-VULC/XM655	27. 2.84	Radarmoor Ltd Wellesbourne Mountford *(As "XM655") (Cancelled 25.3.02 as WFU) (Noted 4.02)*		
G-VVBF	Colt 315A HAB	4058		3. 3.97	Airxcite Ltd t/a Virgin Balloon Flights	Wembley	2. 5.03T
G-VVBK	Piper PA-34-200T Seneca II	34-7570303	G-BSBS G-BDRI/SE-GLG	26. 1.89	The Mann Organisation Ltd	Gloucestershire	15. 8.04T
G-VVIP	Cessna 421C Golden Eagle III	421C0699	G-BMWB N2655L	7. 7.92	Capital Trading Aviation Ltd	Filton	30. 4.04T
G-VWOW	Boeing 747-41R	32745		31.10.01	Virgin Atlantic Airways Ltd *"Cosmic Girl"*	Heathrow	12.12.04T
G-VXLG	Boeing 747-41R	29406		30. 9.98	Virgin Atlantic Airways Ltd *"Ruby Tuesday"*	Heathrow	29. 9.04T
G-VYGR	Colt 120A HAB	2479		24. 9.93	A.van Wyk	Caxton	23. 6.02T
G-VZZZ	Boeing 747-219B	22722	ZK-NZV	7. 7.99	Virgin Atlantic Airways Ltd Mojave-Kem Co, CA, USA *"Morning Glory" (Stored 10.02)*		6 .7.02T

G-WAAA - G-WZZZ

G-WAAC	Cameron N-56 HAB	492		14. 2.79	N.P.Hemsley Crawley tr Whacko Balloon Group *"Whacko"*		26. 6.97A
G-WACB	Reims/Cessna F152 II	F15201972		16. 9.86	Wycombe Air Centre Ltd	Booker	24. 2.05T
G-WACE	Reims/Cessna F152 II	F15201978		16. 9.86	Wycombe Air Centre Ltd	Booker	23. 4.05T
G-WACF	Cessna 152 II	15284852	N628GH (LV-PMB)/N628GH	20. 1.87	Wycombe Air Centre Ltd	Booker	24.11.03T
G-WACG	Cessna 152 II	15285536	ZS-KXY (N93699)	4.11.86	Wycombe Air Centre Ltd	Booker	3. 4.03T
G-WACH	Reims/Cessna FA.152 Aerobat	0425		18. 6.87	Wycombe Air Centre Ltd	Booker	4. 8.05T
G-WACI	Beech 76 Duchess	ME-289	N6703Y	26. 7.88	Wycombe Air Centre Ltd	Booker	14.11.03T
G-WACJ	Beech 76 Duchess	ME-278	N6700Y	3. 1.89	Wycombe Air Centre Ltd	Booker	7. 5.05T
G-WACL	Reims/Cessna F172N Skyhawk II	F17201912	G-BHGG	19. 6.89	The Exeter Flying Club Ltd	Exeter	21. 4.04T
G-WACM	Cessna 172S Skyhawk	172S9005	N35526	21.12.01	Wycombe Air Centre Ltd	Booker	7. 2.05T
G-WACO	Waco UPF-7	5400	N29903 NC29903	28. 1.87	R.G.Vincent t/a RGV (Aircraft Services) & Co Glos *(Damaged Liverpool 15.4.89: stored 4.01)*		13. 5.90
G-WACP	Piper PA-28-180 Cherokee Archer	28-7405007	G-BBPP N9559N	5. 4.89	Wycombe Air Centre Ltd	Booker	10. 7.04T
G-WACR	Piper PA-28-180 Cherokee Archer	28-7505090	G-BCZF N9517N	18.12.86	Lees Avionics Ltd	Booker	9. 7.03T
G-WACT	Reims/Cessna F152 II	F15201908	G-BKFT	24. 6.86	The Exeter Flying Club Ltd	Exeter	5.10.03T
G-WACU	Reims/Cessna FA152 Aerobat	FA1520380	G-BJZU	10. 7.86	Wycombe Air Centre Ltd	Booker	9. 6.03T
G-WACW	Cessna 172P Skyhawk II	17274507	N5307K	16. 5.88	Wycombe Air Centre Ltd	Booker	16. 6.03T
G-WACY	Reims/Cessna F172P Skyhawk II	F17202217	F-GDOZ	3.10.86	Wycombe Air Centre Ltd	Booker	21. 1.05T
G-WADI	Piper PA-46-350P Malibu Mirage	4636205		8. 5.99	H.J.D.S.Baioes	Cranfield	2. 6.05T
G-WADS	Robinson R22 Beta	1224	G-NICO	25. 4.96	M & S Tarpaulins Ltd	(Accrington)	3. 3.05T
G-WAGG	Robinson R22 Beta-II	2960		7. 7.99	J.B.Wagstaff t/a N.J.Wagstaff Leasing	Costock	28 .7.05T
G-WAHL	QAC Quickie	PFA 94-10619		20. 9.00	A.A.M.Wahlberg	(Lee-on-Solent)	
G-WAIR	Piper PA-32-301 Saratoga	32-8506010	N2607X N9577N	14. 1.91	P.H.Burtwhistle Thorne, Doncaster t/a Thorne Aviation		13. 5.03
G-WAIT	Cameron V-77 HAB	2390		20.11.90	C.P.Brown	Ely	24. 7.99A
G-WAKE	Mainair Blade 912	1244-0300-7 & W1037		6. 3.00	J.G.Lloyd	Willingale	6. 3.03P
G-WAKY	Cyclone AX2000	7890		5. 4.02	G.C.Weighell	Enstone	14. 4.03P
G-WALS*	Cessna A152 Aerobat	A1520843	N4614A	27. 9.88	Redhill Aviation Ltd Redhill t/a Redhill Flying Club *(Cancelled 23.8.02 as WFU)*		5. 2.01T

Reg	Type	C/n	Prev id	Date	Owner/Operator	Location	Expiry
G-WALY	Maule MX-7-180 Super Rocket	11028C	N5668H	23. 1.03	A.J.West	Sywell	
G-WARB	Piper PA-28-161 Warrior III	2842034	N41286 (G-WARB)/N41286	4. 9.98	Muller Aircraft Leasing Ltd	Biggin Hill	7. 9.04T
G-WARC	Piper PA-28-161 Warrior III	2842035	N41244 (G-WARC)/N41244	11. 9.98	Plane Talking Ltd	Elstree	13. 9.04T
G-WARD	Taylor JT.1 Monoplane (Volkswagen 1834)	WB.VI & PFA 1407		1.12.80	R.P.J.Hunter (Damaged Redhill 17.9.99)	Redhill	22. 2.00P
G-WARE	Piper PA-28-161 Warrior II	28-8416080	N4357L ("N4354Z")	21. 7.89	W.B.Ware	Filton	27. 3.05
G-WARH	Piper PA-28-161 Warrior III	2842063	N4177Y G-WARH	4. 2.00	Newcastle upon Tyne Aero Club Ltd	Newcastle	10. 2.03T
G-WARK	Schweizer Hughes 269C (300C)	S.1354		13.11.89	K.Sutcliffe	(Halifax)	15. 4.05
G-WARP	Cessna 182F	18254633	G-ASHB N3233U	6. 6.95	G.Burton tr Army Parachute Association	AAC Netheravon	16. 8.04
G-WARR	Piper PA-28-161 Warrior II	28-7916321	N3074U	15. 9.88	T.J. & G.M.Laundy (Op RAF Halton Aeroplane Club)	RAF Halton	5. 2.04T
G-WARS	Piper PA-28-161 Warrior III	2842022	N9281X (G-WARS)/N9281X	7.11.97	Blaneby Ltd	Biggin Hill	6.11.03T
G-WARV	Piper PA-28-161 Warrior III	2842036	N41247 (G-WARV)/N41247	9.10.98	Plane Talking Ltd	Elstree	13.10.04T
G-WARW	Piper PA-28-161 Warrior III	2842037	N41254 (G-WARW)/N41254	17.11.98	C.J.Simmonds	St.Just	1. 1.05T
G-WARX	Piper PA-28-161 Warrior III	2842038	N4126D (G-WARX)/N4126D	15.12.98	C.M.A.Clark	Wellesbourne Mountford	15. 1.05
G-WARY	Piper PA-28-161 Warrior III	2842024	N9287X (G-WARY)/N9287X	13.11.97	Armstrong Aviation Ltd	Blackpool	29.11.03T
G-WAVA	Robin HR200/120	B352		10. 7.00	Wellesbourne Flyers Ltd t/a Wellesbourne Aviation	Wellesbourne Mountford	3. 8.03T
G-WAVE(2)	Grob G-109B	638		11. 8.85	M.L.Murdoch	Park Farm, Eaton Bray	11. 3.04
G-WAVI	Robin HR200/120B	346	G-BZDG	8. 5.01	Wellesbourne Flyers Ltd	Wellesbourne Mountford	12. 4.03T
G-WAVN	Robin HR200/120B	344	G-VECA	2. 5.02	Wellesbourne Flyers Ltd t/a Wellesbourne Aviation	Wellesbourne Mountford	9. 3.03T
G-WAZZ	Pitts S-1S Special (Lycoming O-360)	7-0332	G-BRRP N3TD	17. 6.94	D.T.Knight	White Waltham	13. 7.00P
G-WBAT	Wombat Gyrocopter (Rotax 532)	CJ-001	G-BSID	31. 5.90	M.R.Harrison	(Guernsey)	
G-WBMG	Cameron N Ele 90SS HAB	3086	G-BUYV	5. 7.93	M.Sevrin	Court St.Etienne, Belgium	22. 6.02A
G-WBPR	British Aerospace BAe 125 Srs.800B	258085	G-5-551	29. 9.87	Granada Group plc	RAF Northolt	13.11.03
G-WBTS	Falconar F-11W-200 (Continental O-200-A)	PFA 32-10070	G-BDPL	22.10.90	W.C.Brown	White Waltham	15. 7.03P
G-WCAO	Eurocopter EC135-T1	0204		8. 4.02	Avon & Somerset Constabulary & Gloucestershire Constabulary (Op Western Counties Air Operations Unit)	Filton	13. 6 05T
G-WCAT	Colt Flying Mitt SS HAB	1744		30. 5.90	I.Chadwick tr Balloon Preservation Flying Group "Washcat"	Kirdford	19..8.00A
G-WCEI	SOCATA MS.894E Rallye 220GT	12141	G-BAOC	28. 5.85	R.A.L.Lucas	Walney Island	23. 7.04
G-WCRD	Aérospatiale SA.341G Gazelle	1390	F-GEHD N6KT/N49527	25.10.02	Wickford Aviation Services Ltd	Wickford	10.12.05T
G-WCUB	Piper PA-18-150 Super Cub	18-8278	HB-OLR N5514Y	11. 5.01	P.A.Walley	Croft Farm, Defford	6. 8.04T
G-WDEB	Thunder Ax7-77 HAB	1606		26. 9.89	N.C.Glaysher "Landplan"	(Malpas)	21. 7.03A
G-WDEV	Westland SA.341G Gazelle 1	1098	G-IZEL G-BBHW	30. 9.98	M W Helicopters Ltd	Stapleford	9. 3.03T
G-WEAC	Fairey Britten-Norman BN-2A Mk.III-2 Trislander	1042	5H-AZD G-BEFP (4X-CCL)/G-BEFP/N30WA/JA6401/G-BEFP	16.12.94	Keen Leasing Ltd (Op Woodgate Executive Air Services)	Belfast	12.12.02T
G-WELI	Cameron N-77 HAB	1078		26. 9.84	M.A.Shannon "Wellie"	Southampton	18. 8.01A
G-WELL	Beech E90 King Air	LW-198	N202CC (N7PB)/N202CC	18. 7.85	Colt Transport Ltd	Goodwood	5. 6.03T
G-WELS	Cameron N-65 HAB	1297		7. 4.86	K.J.Vickery "Talisman"	Billingshurst	26. 6.92A
G-WEND	Piper PA-28RT-201 Arrow IV	28R-8118026	PH-SYL N8296L	8.11.82	Tayside Aviation Ltd	Perth	20. 5.05T
G-WERY	SOCATA TB-20 Trinidad	305		2. 4.82	Fastour Aviation Ltd	(Tadcaster)	11. 5.03
G-WEST	Agusta A109A	7213		21. 1.81	Westland Helicopters Ltd	Yeovil	28. 3.05
G-WESX	CFM Streak Shadow K.116-SA & PFA 161A-11561 (Rotax 582)			2. 2.90	K.Kerr	(Wirral)	16.12.05P
G-WFFW	Piper PA-28-161 Warrior II	28-8116161	N8342A	26.10.93	N.F.Duke	Bournemouth	27. 1.03
G-WFOX	Robinson R22 Beta-II	2826		2. 6.98	Heli-Air Ltd	Wolverhampton	27. 6.04T
G-WGAL	Bell 206B-3 JetRanger III	3165	G-OICS N678TM	22. 3.93	Watkiss Group Aviation Ltd	Keysoe	27. 3.04T
G-WGCS	Piper PA-18 Super Cub 95 (L-18C-PI) (Frame No.18-1500)	18-1528	(G-BLSV) ALAT F-MBCH/51-15528	21.12.84	S.C.Thompson	Newells Farm, Bolney	8. 7.03P
G-WGHB	Canadair (CL-30) T-33AN Silver Star Mk.3	T33-640	CF-EHB CAF 133640/RCAF 21640	9. 5.74	R.H.& G.C Cooper (Stored 5.00) (Valid CofR 9.02)	Hibaldstow	13. 6.77P
G-WGSC	Pilatus PC-6/B2-H4 Turbo-Porter	848	OE-ECS	2. 1.90	D.M.Penny (Op Wild Geese Parachute Centre)	Movenis, Co.Londonderry	23. 3.04
G-WHAM	Eurocopter AS350B3 Ecureuil	3494		18. 1.02	B.M.Christie t/a Horizon Helicopter Hire	Goodwood	21. 4.05T
G-WHAT	Colt 77A HAB	1911		15. 3.91	M.A.Scholes "Chad"	London SE25	10.10.03T
G-WHAZ	Agusta-Bell 206A JetRanger	8112	OH-HRE G-WHAZ/OH-HRE	26. 6.97	Heli Charter Ltd	Manston	31.10.03
G-WHEE	Pegasus Quantum 15-912	7510		26. 3.99	D.Young tr PFT (Cotswolds)	Kemble	4 .3.03P
G-WHEN	Tecnam P92-EM Echo	PFA 318-13679		7. 2.01	C.D.Marsh	(Camberley)	
G-WHIM	Colt 77A HAB	1476		10. 4.89	D.L.Morgan	Ilford	14. 8.01A
G-WHOG	CFM Streak Shadow K.253-SA & PFA 206-12776 (Rotax 618)			21. 9.94	B.R.Cannell "Wart Hog"	Old Sarum	4. 9.02P

Reg	Type	C/n	Prev id	Date	Owner	Base	Exp
G-WHOO	Rotorway Exec 162F	6495		5. 6.01	C.A.Saul (Noted 2.03)	Street Farm, Takeley	AC
G-WHRL	Schweizer 269CS	1453	EC-GGX CS-HDG/G-WHRL/N41S	19. 4.90	G.Wood t/a Graham Wood Decorators	(York)	26 .8.05T
G-WHST	Eurocopter AS350B2 Ecureuil	2915	G-BWYA	9. 8.96	Hawkrise Ltd	Wishaw, Warks	26. 9.05T
G-WIBB	Jodel D.18 (Subaru EA81)	PFA 169-11640		18. 6.96	D.Dobson	Little Staughton	5. 6.03P
G-WIBS	CASA I-131E Srs.2000	2005	E3B-401	25. 3.99	C Willoughby	(Ashford)	
G-WIFE	Cessna R182 Skylane RG II	R18200244	G-BGVT N3162C	11.12.01	J.Brennan tr Wife Group	(Sligo, Co.Sligo)	29. 1.05
G-WILD	Aerotek Pitts S-1T Special (Lycoming AEIO-360)	1017	ZS-LMM	6.12.85	A McClean	White Waltham	12. 1.04
G-WILG	WSK PZL-104 Wilga 35A	62153	G-AZYJ	15. 4.97	M.H.Bletsoe-Brown	Sywell	4. 4.04
G-WILS	Piper PA-28RT-201T Turbo Arrow IV	28R-8431005	PH-DPD N4330W	16. 1.96	B. Walker & Co (Dursley) Ltd	Gloucestershire	14. 4.05T
G-WILY	Rutan LongEz (Lycoming O-320)	1200 & PFA 74A-10724		8. 6.83	W.S.Allen "Time Flies"	Gloucestershire	28. 3.00P
G-WIMP	Colt 56A HAB	755		13. 2.86	T.& B.Chamberlain	York	23.11.03A
G-WINK	Grumman-American AA-5B Tiger	AA5B-0327	N74658	14.12.90	B.S.Cooke	Elstree	19. 3.03
G-WINS	Piper PA-32-300 Cherokee Six	32-7640065	N8476C	24. 4.91	Cheyenne Ltd	Jersey	14. 3.03
G-WIRE	Aérospatiale AS355F1 Twin Squirrel	5312	G-CEGB G-BLJL	22. 1.90	National Grid Co plc	Oxford	12. 6.03T
G-WIRL	Robinson R22 Beta	0671		27. 7.87	Rivermead Aviation Ltd	(Vaude, Switzerland)	20. 6.05T
G-WISH	Lindstrand Cake SS HAB (Birthday Cake shape)	006		14.12.92	Oxford Promotions (UK) Ltd (Op F Prell)	Kentucky, USA	3. 4.03A
G-WIXI	Avions Mudry CAP.10B	279		27. 1.98	J.M. & E.M.Wicks Boones Farm, High Garrett, Braintree		2. 8.04
G-WIZA	Robinson R22 Beta	0861	G-PERL N90815	16.11.94	Patriot Aviation Ltd	Cranfield	14. 11.05T
G-WIZB	Grob G.115A	8104	EI-CAD	2. 9.98	R.N.R.Bellamy	Gloucestershire	22.10.04T
G-WIZD	Lindstrand LBL-180A HAB	066		12.11.93	T.H.Wilson	Diss	19. 8.03T
G-WIZI	Enstrom 280FX	2040	Chilean Army H-177	8. 7.02	Rotary Energy Droplet Company International Ltd (Newport, Isle of Wight)		2.12.05T
G-WIZO	Piper PA-34-220T Seneca III	34-8133171	N8413U	16.12.86	B.J.Booty	Bristol	26. 4.04T
G-WIZR	Robinson R22 Beta-II	2799		9. 3.98	J.L.Leonard t/a Findon Air Services	Shoreham	5. 4.04T
G-WIZY	Robinson R22 Beta	0566	G-BMWX N24196	26. 8.97	Heli Air Ltd	Wellesbourne Mountford	18. 6.03T
G-WIZZ	Agusta-Bell 206B JetRanger II	8540		7.12.77	Rivermead Aviation Ltd	(Reading)	3.11.02T
G-WJAN	Boeing 757-21KER	28674		18. 3.97	MyTravel Airways Ltd	Manchester	19. 3.03T
G-WKRD	Eurocopter AS350B2 Ecureuil	2668	G-BUJG G-HEAR/G-BUJG	16. 3.99	Wickford Aviation Services Ltd	Wickford	22. 9.04T
G-WLAC	Piper PA-18-150 Super Cub	18-8899	G-HAHA G-BSWE/N9194P	2. 6.98	White Waltham Airfield Ltd	White Waltham	11. 7.04T
G-WLGA	WSK PZL-104 Wilga 80	CF21910932	EC-FYY F-GMLR	8.11.96	A.J.Renham	Teesside	10. 4.03
G-WLLY	Bell 206B JetRanger II	405	G-OBHH G-WLLY/G-RODY/G-ROGR/G-AXMM/N1469W	24. 3.93	Blue Five Aviation Ltd	Redhill	8. 8.05T
G-WLMS	Mainair Blade 912	1223-0999-7 & W1016		23. 9.99	J.R.North	Ince Blundell	10 10.03P
G-WMAA	MBB Bö.105DBS-4 (Rebuilt with new airframe S.914 1994 - see G-PASB)	S.135/914	G-PASB VH-LSA/G-BDMC/D-HDEC	8. 9.94	Bond Air Services Ltd (Op West Midlands Air Ambulance)	RAF Cosford	29. 9.03T
G-WMAN	Aérospatiale SA341G Gazelle 1	1277	ZS-HUR N4491R/YV-54CP	4. 8.99	J.Wightman	(Ballynahinch)	4. 7.03
G-WMAS	Eurocopter EC135-T1	0174		18. 6.01	Bond Air Services Ltd	RAF Cosford	26 .7.04T
G-WMID	MD Helicopters MD.900	900-00062	N3063T	12.10.99	West Midlands Police Authority "Miss Molly Collins"	Birmingham	13 .1.03T
G-WMLT	Cessna 182Q Skylane II	18266689	G-BOPG N95962	23. 4.02	G.Wimlett	Blackpool	20. 3.04T
G-WMPA	Aérospatiale AS355F2 Twin Squirrel	5401		7. 2.89	Police Aviation Services Ltd	Gloucestershire	25. 6.04T
G-WMTM	Gulfstream AA-5B Tiger	AA5B-1035	N4517V	8. 1.91	A.Allen (Carries "4517V" on fin)	Insch	10. 8.05T
G-WMWM	Robinson R44 Raven	0767		27. 4.00	K.Cummins	Cambridge	1. 6.03T
G-WNGS	Cameron N-105 HAB	4385		15. 7.98	R M Horn (Motorola Wings titles)	Chelmsford	16. 9.03A
G-WOLF	Piper PA-28-140 Cherokee Cruiser	28-7425439	OY-TOD	20. 3.80	Aircraft Management Services Ltd	Elstree	12. 2.05T
G-WOOD	Beech 95-B55A Baron	TC-1283	SE-GRC G-AYID/SE-EXK	17. 9.79	T.D.Broadhurst t/a Baron Aviation	Sleap	7. 1.05
G-WOOF	Enstrom 480	5027		3. 3.98	Netcopter.co.uk Ltd	(Knutsford)	9. 5.04T
G-WOOL	Colt 77A HAB	2044		23. 2.93	T.G.& C.L.Pembrey & N.P.Helmsley tr Whacko Balloon Group	Steyning	20. 6.02
G-WORM	Thruster T600N (Rotax 582 UL)	9109-T600N-039		5.10.99	J.R.North (Op West Lancashire Mircolight School)	Ince Blundell	7.12.03P
G-WOSY	MBB Bö.105DBS/4	S.656	G-PASD G-BNRS/N14ES/N4572Q/D-HDTZ	28.11.01	Redwood Aviation Ltd	(Newport, Isle of Wight)	26. 9.03T
G-WOTG	Pilatus Britten-Norman BN-2T Islander	2139	(ZF444) G-WOTG/G-BJYT	10.11.83	P.M.Hall tr RAF Sport Parachute Association	RAF Weston-on-the-Green	16. 2.03
G-WOWW	Robinson R44 Raven II	10038		14. 2.03	Heli Air Ltd	Wellesbourne Mountford	7.11.04T
G-WPAS	MD Helicopters MD.900	900-00053		1. 7.98	Police Aviation Services Ltd (Op Wiltshire Police/Ambulance Authority)	Devizes	7.11.04T
G-WREN	Aerotek Pitts S-2A Special (Lycoming AEIO-360)	2229	N9472	8. 1.81	Northamptonshire School of Flying Ltd	Sywell	10. 4.05T
G-WRFM	Enstrom 280C-UK Shark	1202	G-CTSI G-BKIO/(G-BKHN)/SE-HLB	21. 4.89	A.J.MacFarlane t/a Skywalker Enterprises	Goodwood	6. 6.04
G-WRIT	Colt 77A HAB	1328		15. 9.88	G.Pusey "Legal Eagle"	Seville, France	7. 8.03A
G-WRLY	Robinson R22 Beta	0699	G-OFJS G-BNXJ	22.11.00	Burman Aviation Ltd	Gloucestershire	26.10.02T
G-WRWR	Robinson R22 Beta-II	2964		20. 7.99	Air Foyle Ltd	Luton	22. 8.05T
G-WSEC	Enstrom F-28C	398	G-BONF N51661	19.12.88	AJD Engineering Ltd (Op Helicopter Aviation Sales)	Weston, Dublin	3. 2.05

Reg	Type	c/n	Prev id	Date	Owner	Location	Date
G-WSKY	Enstrom 280C-UK-2 Shark	1037	G-BEEK	25. 7.83	M.I.Edwards	Brandon, Suffolk	6.12.03
G-WUFF	Europa Aviation Europa (Rotax 912) *(Monowheel u/c)*	235 & PFA 247-12942		19. 1.99	M.A.Barker *(F/f 11.8.01)*	Gamston	
G-WULF	WAR Focke-Wulf 190 (Continental O-200-A)	204 & PFA 81-10328		24. 2.78	A.Howe *(As "8+-" in Luftwaffe c/s)*	(Birmingham)	22. 6.01P
G-WUSH	Eurocopter EC120B	1290		15. 5.02	S Farmer t/a First Degree Air	Tatenhill	15. 8.05T
G-WVBF	Lindstrand LBL-210A HAB	312		6.12.95	Airxcite Ltd t/a Virgin Balloon Flights	Wembley	11. 6.03T
G-WWAL	Piper PA-28R-180 Cherokee Arrow	28R-30461	G-AZSH N4612J	23.10.98	C.& G.Clarke	White Waltham	19. 9.05T
G-WWAS	Piper PA-34-220T Seneca III	34-8133222	G-BPPB N83270/(N707WF)/N83270/N9579N	2. 3.95	D.Intzevidis	Athens, Greece	6. 3.05
G-WWBB	Airbus Industrie A330-243	404	F-WWKP	30. 5.01	British Midland Airways Ltd *(Op SAA)*	Johannesburg, RSA	29. 5.04T
G-WWBC	Airbus Industrie A330-243	455		R	British Midland Airways Ltd	Manchester	
G-WWBD	Airbus Industrie A330-243	401	F-WWKN	9. 5.01	British Midland Airways Ltd *(Op SAA)*	Johannesburg, RSA	8. 5.04T
G-WWBM	Airbus Industrie A330-243	398	F-WWKL	27. 4.01	British Midland Airways Ltd	Manchester	26. 4.04T
G-WWII	Supermarine 379 Spitfire F.XIVe	6S/663452	F-AZSJ G-WWII/Indian AF/SM832	9. 7.79	The Fighter Collection Ltd *(New CofR 3.02)*	Duxford	5. 6.03P
G-WWIZ	Beech 58 Baron	TH-429	G-GAMA G-BBSD	18.10.96	Scenestage Ltd	Bournemouth	23. 6.05T
G-WWWG	Europa Aviation Europa (Wilksch-Airmotive WAM120) *(Monowheel u/c)*	040 & PFA 247-12597	"G-DSEL"	31. 7.95	Chloe F.Williams-Wynne *(F/f 31.7.96)*	Talybont, Gwynedd	10.11.98P
G-WYAT	CFM Streak Shadow SA (Rotax 618)	K.279 & PFA 206-12993		9. 6.97	M.G.Whyatt	(High Peak, Derbyshire)	20. 6.03P
G-WYCH	Cameron Witch 90SS HAB	1330		30. 9.86	Corn Palace Balloon Club Ltd "Hilda"	Tyndale, South Dakota, USA	13. 7.99A
G-WYMP	Cessna F150J (Built Reims Aviation SA)	F150-0521	G-BAGW SE-FKM	26. 2.82	R.Hall	Full Sutton	18. 8.99T
G-WYMR	Robinson R44 Astro	0439		15. 4.98	Heli Air Ltd *(Heli-Air Flying Training Schools titles)*	Thruxton	3. 5.04T
G-WYND	Wittman W.8 Tailwind	PFA 31-12407		2. 8.99	R.S.Marriott & C.Clark tr Forge Group	(Scunthorpe)	
G-WYNN	Rand Robinson KR-2 *(Originally regd as c/n PFA 129-11093: probably composite of both projects)*	PFA 129-11141		28. 8.85	W.Thomas	(Wrexham)	
G-WYNS	Aero Designs Pulsar XP (Rotax 912)	PFA 202-11976		22. 2.91	S.L.Bauza	(Palma de Mallorca)	27. 4.98P
G-WYNT	Cameron N-56 HAB	1038		3. 4.84	S.L.G.Williams "Gwyntoedd Dros Cymru/Winds over Wales"	Bristol	14. 4.02A
G-WYPA	MBB Bö.105DBS/4	S.815	D-HDZY	27.10.89	Police Aviation Services Ltd	Gloucestershire	9. 1.05T
G-WYSP	Robinson R44 Astro	0657		17. 9.99	Calderbrook Estates Ltd	(Sowerby Bridge)	28 .9.05T
G-WZOL	Tiger Cub RL5B LWS Sherwood Ranger (Jabiru 2200A)	PFA 237-12887	G-MZOL	20. 1.99	G.W.F.Webb	Coldharbour Farm, Willingham	13.12.02P
G-WZZZ	Colt AS-42 Hot Air Airship *(Rebuilt 1984/85 using new AS-56 envelope c/n 607)*	459		10.12.82	Lindstrand Balloons Ltd *"Kit Kat"*	Oswestry	4. 9.01A

G-XAAA - G-XZZZ

Reg	Type	c/n	Prev id	Date	Owner	Location	Date
G-XARV	ARV1 Super 2	010	G-OPIG G-BMSJ	8.11.95	D.J.Burton	Damyn's Hall, Upminster	2. 4.03P
G-XATS	Aerotek Pitts S-2A	2147	CS-AZE N338BD	29. 3.01	Air Training Services Ltd	Duxford	8.11.04T
G-XAXA	Fairey Britten-Norman BN-2A-26 Islander	530	G-LOTO G-BDWG/(N90255)/(C-GYUF)/G-BDWG	22. 8.00	AirX Ltd *(Op Le Cocq)*	Bournemouth	28.11.03A
G-XAYR	Raj Hamsa X'Air 582	471 & BMAA/HB/122		4. 1.00	R.V.Barber	(Saffron Walden)	19. 4.03P
G-XBHX	Boeing 737-36N	28572		21. 5.98	British Airways plc *(Grand Union t/s)*	Gatwick	5. 9.03T
G-XCCC	Extra EA.300/L	142		20. 8.01	P.T.Fellows	Rochester	20. 9.04T
G-XCEL	Aérospatiale AS355F1 Twin Squirrel	5324	G-HBAC G-HJET/F-GEOX/F-WYMC/OY-HDL	16. 5.95	Von Essen Aviation Ltd	Thruxton	5. 6.03T
G-XCUB	Piper PA-18-150 Super Cub	18-8109036	N9348T	1. 5.81	M.C.Barraclough	(Selborne, Alton)	26. 4.04
G-XENA	Piper PA-28-161 Cherokee Warrior II	28-7716158	N3486Q	29. 6.98	Braddock Ltd	Blackbushe	16. 5.05T
G-XFLY	Lambert Aircraft Mission M212-100	PFA 306-13380		3. 2.00	Lambert Aircraft Engineering BVBA	(Kortrijk, Belgium)	
G-XIOO	Raj Hamsa X'Air Floats	681 & BMAA/HB/247		27. 1.03	R.Paton	(Winchester)	
G-XKEN	Piper PA-34-200T Seneca II	34-7970003	N3036A	5. 9.01	Choicecircle Ltd	(Rugby)	16. 9.04T
G-XLAA	Boeing 737-8Q8	28226		13. 3.01	Excel Airways Ltd	Gatwick	26. 7.04T
G-XLAB	Boeing 737-8Q8	28218		14. 5.01	Excel Airways Ltd	Gatwick	10.12.04T
G-XLAC	Boeing 737-81Q	29051	G-OJSW N8254G/N1786B	26. 4.01	Excel Airways Ltd	Gatwick	17. 2.03P
G-XLAD	Boeing 737-81Q	29052	G-ODMW N8254Q)	27. 2.01	Excel Airways Ltd	Gatwick	23. 5.03T
G-XLAE	Boeing 737-8Q8	30637	D-ABAA G-OKJW/N1787B	9.11.01	Air Berlin GmbH & Co.Luftverkers KG	Berlin, Germany	8.11.04T
G-XLAF	Boeing 737-86N	29883		15. 3.02	Air Europa Lineas Aereas SAU	Palma, Mallorca	14. 3.05T
G-XLAG	Boeing 737-86N	33003		29. 4.02	Excel Airways Ltd	Gatwick	28. 4.05T
G-XLAH	Boeing 737-86N	29833		R	Excel Airways Ltd	Gatwick	
G-XLIV	Robinson R44 Raven	0810		11. 7.00	Defence Products Ltd	Redhill	25. 7.03T
G-XLMB	Cessna 560XL Citation Excel	560-5259	N52526	25. 6.02	Aviation Beauport Ltd	Jersey	25. 6.05T
G-XLTG	Cessna 182S Skylane	18280234	N9571L	17. 7.98	GX Aviation Ltd	Denham	30. 7.04
G-XLXL	Robin DR400/160 Knight	813	G-BAUD	3. 1.92	L.R.Marchant	(Sittingbourne)	5. 5.03
G-XMAN	Boeing 737-36N	28573		18. 6.98	British Airways plc *(Golden Khokhloma t/s)*	Manchester	16.10.03T
G-XMEN	Eurocopter AS350B3 Ecureuil	3362	G-ZWRC F-GPNE	7. 6.02	Corporate Estates Ltd	Booker	5. 7.04T
G-XMGO	Aeromot AMT-200S Super Ximango	200127		18. 4.01	R.P.Beck & G.McLean	Rufforth	3. 5.04
G-XMII	Eurocopter EC135-T1	0215		15. 4.02	Merseyside Police Authority	RAF Woodvale	6. 8.05T

Reg	Type	C/n	Prev id	Date	Owner	Location	Permit
G-XPBI	Letov LK-2M Sluka (Rotax 447)	PFA 263-13341		4.12.98	K.Harness	North Coates	25. 4.03P
G-XPSS	Short SD.3-60 Var.100	SH.3713	EI-CPR G-OBOH/G-BNDJ/G-14-3713	2. 5.01	BAC Express Airlines Ltd *"City of Derby"*	Gatwick	7. 5.03T
G-XPXP	Aero Designs Pulsar XP (Rotax 912) *(Tail-wheel u/c)*	218 & PFA 202-11958		30. 3.92	B.J.Edwards	Belle Vue Farm, Yarnscombe	18. 6.03P
G-XRAF	Raj Hamsa X'Air 582	513 & BMAA/HB/132		7. 4.00	M.E.Howard tr X'Air Syndicate	RAF Halton	28. 7.03P
G-XRAY	Rand Robinson KR-2	PFA 129-11227		30. 4.87	R.S.Smith *(Under construction 2001)*	Barthol Chapel	
G-XRLD	Cameron A-250 HAB	4820		25. 4.00	Red Letter Days Ltd *(Red Letter Days titles)*	London N127	28. 7.03T
G-XRXR	Raj Hamsa X-Air 582	431 & BMAA/HB/102		13. 9.99	M.J.Whiteman-Haywood *(New owner 3.02)*	Bewdley	
G-XSAM	Van's RV-9A	PFA 320-13797		18. 9.02	D.G.Lucas	(Bodmin)	
G-XSDJ	Europa Aviation Europa XS (Rotax 914) *(Monowheel u/c)*	402 & PFA 247-13378		3. 2.99	D.N.Joyce *(F/f 2.5.02)*	(Berkeley)	13. 6.03P
G-XSFT	Piper PA-23-250 Aztec F	27-7754103	G-CPPC G-BGBH/N63773	18. 6.86	T.L.B.Dykes	Bournemouth	1. 6.03T
G-XSKY	Cameron N-77 HAB	2508		26. 3.91	T.D.Gibbs *(Op D Hempleman-Adams)*	Corsham	11. 8.00A
G-XTEK	Robinson R44 Astro	0647		11. 8.99	PLM Properties plc	(Burton-on-Trent)	29. 9.03T
G-XTOR	Fairey Britten-Norman BN-2A Mk.III-2 Trislander *(Fuselage ex N3266G [1065] fitted 2.96)*	359	G-BAXD	1. 4.96	Aurigny Air Services Ltd	Guernsey	5. 7.03T
G-XTRR	Extra EA.300/200	018	D-EVNO	25.10.00	B.J.De Haan	Stoke Golding	19.12.03
G-XTUN	Westland-Bell 47G-3B1	WA/382	G-BGZK XT223	11. 5.99	R.C.Hields t/a Hields Aviation *(As "XT223" in Army Air Corps c/s)*	Sherburn-in-Elmet	29. 5.03T
G-XVOM	Van's RV-6	PFA 181-12894		6. 4.01	A.Baker-Munton	(Leicester)	
G-XXEA	Sikorsky S-76C	760492		21.12.98	T.C.Hewlett, Director of Royal Travel *(Op Queen's Flight)*	Blackbushe	4. 1.04T
G-XXIV	Agusta-Bell 206B-3 JetRanger III	8717		27. 4.89	A.N.Onn	Headcorn	4. 7.04T
G-XXTR	Extra EA 300/L	126	G-ECCC D-EDGE	13. 8.02	Airpark Flight Centre Ltd	Coventry	13. 3.04T
G-XXVI	Sukhoi Su-26M	04-10	RA0410	2. 4.93	A.N.Onn *(As "39")*	Headcorn	26. 2.03P

G-YAAA - G-YZZZ

Reg	Type	C/n	Prev id	Date	Owner	Location	Permit
G-YACB	Robinson R22 Beta	3092	G-VOSL	24. 1.02	A.C.Barker t/a ACB Hydraulic Services	(Stoke-on-Trent)	27 .6.03A
G-YAKA	Yakovlev Yak-50	822303	LY-ANJ DOSAAF 80	10.11.94	B.Brown & E.Evans	Breighton	26. 6.03P
G-YAKB	Aerostar Yakovlev Yak-52	9211517	RA44491	25.11.02	Kemble Air Services Ltd	Kemble	AC
G-YAKC	IAV-Bacau Yakovlev Yak-52	867212	LY-AKC DOSAAF	25. 6.02	P.Doggett & P.A.Gray	Andrewsfield	4. 7.03P
G-YAKH	IAV-Bacau Yakovlev Yak-52	899915	RA01948 LY-AFV/DOSAAF 102 (yellow)	24.12.02	Plus7Minus5 Ltd	RAF Halton	AC
G-YAKI	IAV-Bacau Yakovlev Yak-52	866904	LY-ANM DOSAAF 100	20. 9.94	Yak One Ltd *"100" (DOSAAF c/s)*	Popham	27. 2.03P
G-YAKK	Yakovlev Yak-50	853104	RA01293	5.11.02	K.J.Pilling	(Chesham)	7.11.03P
G-YAKM	Yakovlev Yak-55M	820506	RA01333R DOSAAF 40	R	Mrs B.Abela	White Waltham	
G-YAKO	IAV-Bacau Yakovlev Yak-52	822203	RA01493(1)	8. 5.99	M.K.Shaw	Norwich	20. 6.03P
G-YAKR	IAV-Bacau Yakovlev Yak-52	899803	LY-AOV Ukraine AF 75 (Yellow)/DOSAAF 75 (Yellow)	15.11.02	A.S.Nottage & R.A.Alexander	North Weald	19.11.03P
G-YAKS	Aerostar Yakovlev Yak-52	9311708		16.12.93	Two Bees Associates Ltd *"2"*	North Weald	2. 5.03P
G-YAKT	IAV-Bacau Yakovlev Yak-52	8910302	RA01564 DOSAAF 149 (yellow)	21. 1.03	I.G. Parker tr Flying Collies	White Waltham	
G-YAKW	IAV-Bacau Yakovlev Yak-52	855601	LY-AKW DOSAAF 56	15.11.02	D.R Keene & A.Hunt tr Cuddesdon Fying Group	(Cuddesdon)	1.12.03P
G-YAKX	Aerostar Yakovlev Yak-52	9111307	RA44473 G-YAKX/RA9111307/DOSAAF 27	13. 3.96	The X-Fliers Ltd	White Waltham	16.12.03P
G-YAKY	Aerostar Yakovlev Yak-52	844109	LY-AKX DOSAAF 24 (red)	26. 2.96	W.T.Marriott	(Market Rasen)	7. 3.02P
G-YAMS	Yakovlev Yak-52	844306	LY-AMS DOSAAF 51 (red)	3.03R	Willowair Flying Club *(Noted 9.02 as LY-AMS)*	Southend	
G-YANK	Piper PA-28-181 Archer II	28-8090163	N81314	19. 3.93	Janet A.Millar-Craig tr G-YANK Flying Group	Tatenhill	3. 5.05
G-YARR	Mainair Rapier (Rotax 503)	1255-0700-7 & W1049		14. 8.00	D.Yarr	St.Michaels	31. 8.03P
G-YARV	ARV1 Super 2 *(Built Hornet Aviation Ltd)* (Hewland AE75)	K.004 & PFA 152-11127	G-BMDO	15.10.01	P.R.Snowden *(Current status unknown)*	(Bury St.Edmunds)	12. 6.97P
G-YAWW	Piper PA-28RT-201T Turbo Arrow IV	28R-8031024	N2929Y	15.11.90	Barton Aviation Ltd	Barton	9. 7.03
G-YBAA	Reims FR172J Rocket	FR17200579	5Y-BAA	15.11.84	A.Evans	Bourn	21. 6.03
G-YCII	LET Yakovlev C.11	2511108	F-AZPA Egyptian AF	13. 1.00	R.W.Davies	(Woodchurch, Kent)	3..8.01
G-YCUB	Piper PA-18-150 Super Cub	1809077	N4993X N4157T	23. 8.96	F.W.Rogers Garage (Saltash) Ltd	Bodmin	9. 3.03
G-YEAR	Revolution Helicopters Mini-500 (Rotax 582)	0050		6.10.95	D.J.Waddington	(Preston)	
G-YELL	Murphy Rebel	PFA 232-12381		1. 5.95	A.D.Keen *(Noted 10.02)*	Bodmin	
G-YEOM	Piper PA-31-350 Chieftain	31-8352022	N41108	3. 1.89	Foster Yeoman Ltd	Bristol	21. 3.02
G-YEWS	Rotorway Exec 152	DGP-1 & 3850		22. 6.89	R.Turrell & P.Mason	(Wickford)	17. 6.93P
G-YFLY	VPM M-16 Tandem Trainer (Arrow GT1000R)	VPM16-UK114	G-BWGI	14.10.96	A.J.Unwin	Kemble	4. 9.03P
G-YFUT	IAV Bacau Yakovlev Yak-52	888410	LY-FUT Ukraine AF 22 (yellow)/DOSAAF 22	6. 2.03	J.A.Griffin	(Galway, Co.Galway)	
G-YIII	Reims/Cessna F150L	F15000827	PH-CEX	5. 6.80	Sherburn Aero Club Ltd	Sherburn-in-Elmet	31. 8.03T

Reg	Type	C/n	Prev id	Date	Owner	Location	Date
G-YIIK	Robinson R44 Astro	0640		9. 8.99	The Websiteshop (UK) Ltd	Denham	4 .9.05T
G-YJBM	Airbus A320-231	362	G-IEAF	28. 9.93	MyTravel Airways Ltd	Manchester	26. 1.03T
			F-WWIN				
G-YJET	Montgomerie-Bensen B.8MR	PFA G/01-1072		25. 9.96	A.Shuttleworth	Barton	19. 9.02P
	(Rotax 582)						
G-YKCT	Aerostar Yakovlev Yak-52	9010307	LY-ATI	29. 5.02	C.R.Turton	(Ashford)	29. 5.03P
			Ukraine AF 04/DOSAAF 04				
G-YKEN	Robinson R22 Beta-II	2875		22.10.98	R.L.Moody	Bennett's Field, Denham	5.11.01
					(Crashed near Beaune, France 5.5.01)		
G-YKSO	Yakovlev Yak-50	791506	LY-APT	8. 4.02	Classic Display (Scotland) Ltd	Perth	22. 5.03P
G-YKSS	Yakovlev Yak-55M	901103	RA44525	3.03R	Not known	Headcorn	
			DOSAAF 96		(As RA44525 @ 9.02)		
G-YKSZ	Aerostar Yakovlev Yak-52	9311709		16.12.93	J.N. & C.J.Carter	Poplar Hall Farm, Elmsett	25. 9.03
					(As "01" in Soviet AF c/s)		
G-YLYB	Cameron N-105 HAFB	4482		15. 1.99	Virgin Airship & Balloon Co Ltd	Telford	14.11.02A
					(Lloyds TSB titles)		
G-YMBO	Robinson R22 Mariner	2054M	OY-HFR	21. 8.95	Helicentre Blackpool Ltd	Blackpool	20. 9.04T
G-YMMA	Boeing 777-236ER	30302	N5017Q	7. 1.00	British Airways plc	Heathrow	6. 1.06T
G-YMMB	Boeing 777-236ER	30303		18. 1.00	British Airways plc	Heathrow	17. 1.06T
G-YMMC	Boeing 777-236ER	30304		4.2.00	British Airways plc	Heathrow	3. 2.03T
G-YMMD	Boeing 777-236ER	30305		19. 2.00	British Airways plc	Heathrow	17. 2.03T
G-YMME	Boeing 777-236ER	30306		16. 4.00	British Airways plc	Heathrow	14. 4.03T
G-YMMF	Boeing 777-236ER	30307		17. 5.00	British Airways plc	Heathrow	16. 5.03T
G-YMMG	Boeing 777-236ER	30308		28. 9.00	British Airways plc	Heathrow	26..9.03T
G-YMMH	Boeing 777-236ER	30309		14.10.00	British Airways plc	Heathrow	13.10.03T
G-YMMI	Boeing 777-236ER	30310		2.11.00	British Airways plc	Heathrow	1.11.03T
G-YMMJ	Boeing 777-236ER	30311		8.12.00	British Airways plc	Heathrow	7.12.03T
G-YMMK	Boeing 777-236ER	30312		8.12.00	British Airways plc	Heathrow	7.12.03T
G-YMML	Boeing 777-236ER	30313		10. 4.01	British Airways plc	Heathrow	13. 4.04T
G-YMMM	Boeing 777-236ER	30314		31. 5.01	British Airways plc	Heathrow	30 .4.04T
G-YMMN	Boeing 777-236ER	30316		15. 6.01	British Airways plc	Heathrow	14. 6.04T
G-YMMO	Boeing 777-236ER	30317		17. 9.01	British Airways plc	Heathrow	13. 9.04T
G-YMMP	Boeing 777-236ER	30315		30.10.01	British Airways plc	Heathrow	29.10.04T
G-YNOT	Rollason Druine D.62B Condor	RAE/649	G-AYFH	10.11.83	A.Littlefair	Lymington	4. 9.03P
G-YOGI	Robin DR.400/140B Major	1090	G-BDME	1.10.86	A Titmus	(Huntingdon)	19. 4.04
G-YORK	Reims/Cessna F172M Skyhawk II	F17201354	PH-LUY	14.12.78	H-R.A.E.Waetjen	(Athboy, Co.Meath)	10.10.03
			F-WLIT				
G-YOYO	Pitts S-1E Special	PFA 09-10885	G-OTSW	22. 5.96	J.D.L.Richardson	Exeter	24. 7.03P
	(Lycoming O-360)		G-BLHE				
G-YPOL	MD Helicopters MD.900	900-00078	N7038S	4.10.00	West Yorkshire Police Authority	(Wakefield)	25. 1.04T
G-YPSY	Andreasson BA.4B	PFA 038-10352		7. 6.78	R.W.Hinton	Poplar Hall Farm , Elmsett	25. 2.03P
	(Continental O-200-A)						
G-YRAF	Rotary Air Force RAF 2000 GTX-SE			1. 6.01	C.V.King	Henstridge	23. 8.03P
		PFA G13/1289					
G-YRIL	Luscombe 8E Silvaire	5945	N1318B	3. 2.92	C.Potter	North Weald	12.10.03P
	(Continental O-200-A)		NC1318B				
G-YROI	Air Command 532 Elite (Rotax 532)	0002	N532CG	3. 9.87	W.B.Lumb (New CorR 6.02)	(Manchester)	17.12.90P
G-YROO	Rotary Air Force RAF 2000 GTX-SE			27.11.01	K.D.Rhodes & C.S.Oakes	(Wimborne)	22.10.03P
		PFA G/13-1341					
G-YROS	Montgomerie-Bensen B.8M	PFA G/101-1004		29. 1.81	N.B.Gray	(Wardley, Manchester)	6. 6.97P
	(HAPI 60-6M)				(Current status unknown)		
G-YROY	Montgomerie-Bensen B.8MR	PFA G/101A-1145		12. 9.89	S.Brennan	Carlisle	2. 5.03P
	(Rotax 532)						
G-YSON	Eurocopter EC120B	1068		14. 1.00	Heli-Express Ltd	Elstree	2. 3.03T
G-YSPY	Cessna 172Q Skyhawk	17275932	N917AT	4. 2.03	J.Henderson	Blackbushe	
			N917ER/(N65957)				
G-YSTT	Piper PA-32R-301 Saratoga IIHP	3246056	N848T	4. 8.97	A.W.Kendrick	Wolverhampton	5. 8.03
			N9282D				
G-YTUK	Cameron A-210 HAFB	4640		30. 9.99	Societe Bombard SRL	Beaune, France	6.10.03A
G-YUGO*	Hawker Siddeley HS.125 Srs.1B/R-522	25094	G-ATWH	25. 8.88	British Airways Aircraft Recovery Unit	Biggin Hill	19. 4.91
			HZ-BO1/G-ATWH		(Cancelled 29.3.93 as WFU: fuselage noted 3.01)		
G-YULL	Piper PA-28-180 Cherokee E	28-5603	G-BEAJ	30. 3.79	G. Watkinson-Yull	Guernsey	2.10.03
			9H-AAC/N2390R				
G-YUMM	Cameron N-90 HAFB	2723		12.12.91	Wunderbar Ltd "Boulevard"	York	31.12.02A
G-YUPI	Cameron N-90 HAFB	1602		12. 1.88	MCVH SA	Brussels, Belgium	22.11.98A
G-YURO*	Europa Aviation Europa	001 & PFA 220-11981		6. 4.92	Not known	Wombleton	9. 6.95P
	(Rotax 912UL)				(F/f 12.9.92) (Cancelled 22.4.98 as WFU) (Noted 7.02)		
G-YVBF	Lindstrand LBL-317S HAFB	505		2. 4.98	Airxcite Ltd t/a Virgin Balloon Fights	Wembley	26. 3.03T
G-YVET	Cameron V-90 HAFB	3182		11.10.93	K.J.Foster	Coleshill, Birmingham	16. 4.02A
G-YYAK	Aerostar Yakovlev Yak-52	878101	LY-AOM	18. 4.02	Ensecon Laboratories Ltd	Teesside	29. 5.03P
			DOSAAF 118				
G-YYYY	Max Holste MH.1521 C1 Broussard	208	F-GDPZ	10. 3.00	P.F. Burrow	Trenchard Farm, Eggesford	29..3.03
			French Air Force		tr Eggesford Heritage Flight		

G-ZAAA - G-ZZZZ

Reg	Type	C/n	Prev id	Date	Owner	Location	Date
G-ZAAZ	Van's RV-8	PFA 303-13279		2. 7.02	P.A.Soper	Ipswich	
G-ZABC	Sky 90-24 HAFB	062		10. 4.97	J.A.Lister "Bart"	Malaga, Spain	12. 8.03A
G-ZACE	Cessna 172S Skyhawk SP	172S8808	F-HAMC	3. 9.02	M.J.Foggo	Shoreham	3. 9.05T
			N3527P				
G-ZACH	Robin DR.400/100 Cadet	1831	G-FTIO	20.10.92	A.P.Wellings	Sandown	5. 9.04
G-ZAIR	Zenair CH.601HD Zodiac	PFA 162-12194		21. 2.92	Speedfreak Ltd	Crosland Moor	4. 7.03P
	(Rotax 912UL)						

Reg	Type	c/n	Prev id	Date	Owner/Operator	Location	Expiry
G-ZAPH	Bell 206B-3 JetRanger III	4401	G-DBMW / C-GAJH	6. 2.01	Titan Airways Ltd	Stansted	3. 7.05T
G-ZAPJ	ATR-42-312	113	EI-CIQ / DQ-FEQ/F-WWEJ	17. 5.96	Titan Airways Ltd	Stansted	19. 5.05T
G-ZAPK	British Aerospace BAe 146 Srs.200QC	E2148	G-BTIA / ZS-NCB/G-BTIA/G-6-148/G-PRIN	25. 4.96	Titan Airways Ltd	Stansted	17. 4.03T
G-ZAPM	Boeing 737-33A	27285	DQ-FJD / N102AN/CS-TKG	2. 6.99	Titan Airways Ltd	Stansted	2 .6.05T
G-ZAPN	British Aerospace BAe 146 Srs.200QC	E2119	ZK-NZC / G-BPBT	20. 9.99	Titan Airways Ltd	Stansted	15.11.05T
G-ZAPO	British Aerospace BAe 146 Srs.200QC	E2176	F-GMMP / G-BWLG/VH-NJQ/G-PRCS	28. 7.00	Titan Airways Ltd	Stansted	3. 8.03T
G-ZAPT	Beechcraft B200C Super King Air	BL-141	N200KA / N5141Y	24. 9.01	Titan Airways plc	Stansted	23. 9.05T
G-ZAPY	Robinson R22 Beta	0788	G-INGB	8. 7.98	Heli Air Ltd	Wellesbourne Mountford	9. 8.04T
G-ZARI	Grumman-American AA-5B Tiger	AA5B-0845	G-BHVY / N28835	7. 3.86	ZARI Aviation Ltd	Biggin Hill	23. 2.04
G-ZARV	ARV1 Super 2	PFA 152-13035		26. 2.97	P.R.Snowden	Cambridge	22. 6.03P
G-ZAZA	Piper PA-18 Super Cub 95 (L-18C-PI)	18-2041	D-ENAS / R.Neth AF R-66/52-2441	1. 5.84	Airborne Taxi Services Ltd *(Op Adrian Swire)*	Wantage	11. 4.03P
G-ZBED	Robinson R22 Beta	1684	N63993 / F-GHHM	18.11.99	P.D.Spinks	Stream Farm, Sherburn-in-Elmet	22.11.05T
G-ZBLT	Cessna 182S Skylane	18280910	N72764	6. 7.01	Entee Global Services Ltd	(Abingdon)	17. 7.04T
G-ZEBO	Thunder Ax8-105 Srs.2 HAFB	2197		22. 5.92	S.M.Waterton *"Gazebo"*	Borehamwood	3. 5.03T
G-ZEIN	Slingsby T.67M-260 Firefly	2234		19. 7.95	RV Aviation Ltd	Blackbushe	22. 8.05T
G-ZENA	Zenair CH.701UL	PFA 187-13637		16.10.00	A.N.Aston	(Wolverhampton)	
G-ZEPI	Colt GA-42 Gas Airship (RR Continental O-200B)	878	G-ISPY / (G-BPRB)	9. 4.92	P A Lindstrand	Oswestry	12. 5.93A
G-ZERO	Grumman-American AA-5B Tiger	AA5B-0051	OO-PEC	3. 9.80	D.M.Ashford tr G-ZERO Syndicate	Southampton	26. 3.05T
G-ZHWH	Rotorway Exec 162F	6596		19.11.01	B.Alexander	(Canterbury)	AC
G-ZIGI	Robin DR.400/180 Regent	2107		19.11.91	R.J.Dix	Bodmin	8. 3.04
G-ZIPA	Rockwell Commander 114A (Laid down as c/n 14436)	14505	G-BHRA / N5891N	3. 9.98	M.F.Luke	Goodwood	15. 2.04T
G-ZIPI	Robin DR.400/180 Regent	1557		22. 2.82	H.U. & D.C.Stahlberg	Rochester	14. 5.04
G-ZIPY	Wittman W.8 Tailwind (Lycoming O-235)	PFA 031-11339		29. 5.91	M.J.Butler	Ranksborough Farm, Langham	8. 7.03P
G-ZIZI	Cessna 525 Citationjet	525-0345	N5185V	10.11.99	Ortac Air Ltd	Guernsey	17.11.05T
G-ZLIN	Moravan Zlin Z.326 Trener Master (Modified to Z.526 standard)	916	G-BBCR / OH-TZF	30. 6.81	N.J.Arthur *(C/n confirmed but duplicates I-ETRM)*	Finmere	6.10.01
G-ZLLE	Aérospatiale SA341G Gazelle 1	1012	N504KH / JA9098	4.10.01	G-ZLLE Ltd	Stapleford	8.11.04T
G-ZLOJ	Beechcraft A36 Bonanza	E-1677	ZS-LOJ / N6748J	11. 9.98	W.D.Gray	Bournemouth	20.12.04
G-ZLYN	Moravan Zlin Z.526F Trener Master	1255	OK-CMC / YR-ZAB	4. 8.95	H.G.Philippart	(London N1)	24.10.03
G-ZMAM	Piper PA-28-181 Archer II	28-7890059	G-BNPN / N47379	3.11.00	Z.Mahmood	Elstree	6. 2.03T
G-ZOBA	Cessna 208B Caravan	208B0957	N5268M	20. 6.02	Centeline Air Charter Ltd	Bristol	27. 6.05T
G-ZODI	Zenair CH.601UL Zodiac (Rotax 912UL)	PFA 162A-13585		13. 3.00	B.McFadden	Mount Airey Farm, South Cave	18. 1.03P
G-ZONK	Robinson R44 Astro	0179	G-EDIE	16. 7.97	CCB Aviation Ltd	Thruxton	25. 6.04T
G-ZOOL	Reims/Cessna FA152 Aerobat	FA15200357	G-BGXZ	11.11.94	G.G.Hammond	(South Croydon)	9. 5.04T
G-ZORO	Europa Aviation Europa (Monowheel u/c)	074 & PFA 247-12672		20. 6.95	N.T.Read *(Current status unknown)*	(Gillingham, Kent)	
G-ZTED	Europa Aviation Europa (Monowheel u/c)	015 & PFA 247-12492		30. 4.96	J.J.Kennedy & E.W.Gladstone *(Part built 7.01)*	(Edinburgh)	
G-ZULU	Piper PA-28-161 Warrior II	28-8316043	N4292X	25. 2.88	R.W.Tebby t/a S.F.Tebby & Son *(Op Bristol Flying Centre)*	Bristol	29. 6.03T
G-ZUMI	Van's RV-8 PFA	303-13527		6. 3.02	P.M.Wells	(Aylesbury)	
G-ZVBF	Cameron A-400 HAFB	4280		21. 1.98	Airxcite Ltd t/a Virgin Balloon Flights	Wembley	13.12.02T
G-ZWAR	Eurocopter EC120B	1024	D-HVIP	14. 4.00	Hedgeton Trading Ltd	Marbella, Spain	22. 5.03
G-ZYAK	IAV Bacau Yakovlev Yak-52	877415	LY-AFK / DOSAAF 27	14. 2.03	R.C Amer	(Haywards Heath)	
G-ZZAG	Cameron Z-77 HAFB	4588		6. 4.99	T.Charlwood *"Zig Zag"*	Chichester	27 12.01A
G-ZZIP	Mooney M.20J (205)	24-3167	N1086N	14. 6.91	H.T.El-Kasaby & A.Rogerson	Southend	3. 7.04T
G-ZZOE	Eurocopter EC120B	1196	F-WQOX	21. 3.01	McAlpine Helicopters Ltd	Oxford	9. 7.04T
G-ZZWW	Enstrom 280FX	2052	G-BSIE / HA-MIN/G-BSIE	22. 2.00	DB International (UK) Ltd	(Ipswich)	27. 3.04T
G-ZZZA	Boeing 777-236	27105	N77779	20. 5.96	British Airways plc	Heathrow	19. 5.05T
G-ZZZB	Boeing 777-236	27106	N77771	28. 3.97	British Airways plc	Heathrow	3.12.05T
G-ZZZC	Boeing 777-236	27107	N5014K	11.11.95	British Airways plc	Heathrow	10.11.04T

           Civil Aircraft & Glider Registers

SECTION 2 – IRELAND

Pete Hornfeck has again compiled the Irish Register and we extend our thanks for his sterling efforts. The latest basic source information comes from Ian Burnett''s monthly Overseas Register section included in Air-Britain News. Other infortmation has been supplied by Miike Cain, Ian Callier, Antoin Daltun, Ken Hearns, Paul Hewins, Ken Parfitt and Tony Pither. My thanks to one and all.

As no official C of A data is available it is difficult to determine the status of aircraft so we are grateful to the numerous reports which appear in the "Round and About" section of Air-Britain News. This information is used to update the notation system which indicates if an aircraft has been seen as either active (A) or noted (N) throughout the year. This year I have included the notation system for all commercial airline aircraft. Previous editions have included many aircraft which have not been reported for several years. Accordingly, this year I have removed many non commercial aircraft aircraft not sighted prior to January 2000. Any that re-emerge will be re-introduced in the next edition. A number of contentious entries remain and these are included in italics. If there are no reported sightings during 2003 they will be removed from next year's edition.

Regn	Type	C/n	P/I	Date	Owner/Operator	Probable Base	CA Expy
EI-ABI(2)	de Havilland DH.84 Dragon 2	6105	EI-AFK	12. 8.85	Aer Lingus plc	Dublin	A 6.00
			G-AECZ/AV982/G-AECZ		*"Iolar"*		
EI-ADV	*Piper PA-12 Super Cruiser*	12-3459	NC4031H	11. 5.48	R.E.Levis	Weston	N 7.99
	(Lycoming O-235)				*(Badly damaged in force landing Maynooth, Weston 8.7.99)*		
EI-AFE	Piper J-3C-90 Cub	16687	OO-COR	11. 3.49	J.Conlon	Kildare	N 4.96
			D-ELAB/N9954F/EI-AFE/NC79076		*(On rebuild)*		
EI-AFF	BA L.25C Swallow II	406	G-ADMF	18. 5.49	J.Molloy, J.J.Sullivan & B.Donoghue	Ashbourne	N 4.96
	(Pobjoy Cataract II)				*(Damaged Coonagh 24.10.61: on rebuild)*		
EI-AGJ	Auster V J/1 Autocrat	2208	G-AIPZ	3.11.53	T.G.Rafter *(On rebuild)*	(Ballyboughal)	
EI-AHI(2)	de Havilland DH.82A Tiger Moth	85347	G-APRA	17. 9.93	High Fidelity Flyers	Birr	A 8.02
			DE313				
EI-ALH	*Taylorcraft Plus D*	106	G-AHLJ	5. 5.60	N.Reilly	Ballyjamesduff	
			HH987/G-AFTZ				
EI-ALP	Avro 643 Cadet	848	G-ADIE	12. 9.60	J.C.O'Loughlin	(Ballybougal)	N2002
	(Genet Major)				*(Engine seizure 12.6.77: awaiting spares & stored)*		
EI-AMF*	Taylorcraft Plus D	157	G-ARRK	26. 4.62	C J Baker	Carr Farm,Thorney, Newark	N 1.03
			G-AHUM/LB286		*(Fuselage partly restored)*		
EI-ANT	Champion 7ECA Citabria	7ECA-38		13. 1.65	T.Croke, H.Sydner, D.Foley & E.Lennon	Gorey	A 6.01
EI-ANY	Piper PA-18 Super Cub 95	18-7152	G-AREU	18.11.64	The Bogavia Group	Weston	N 1.03
			N3096Z				
EI-AOB	Piper PA-28-140 Cherokee	28-20667		28. 4.65	J.Surdival, L.Moran, J.Kilcoyne & J.Cowell	Waterford	A 5.01
EI-AOK(2)	Cessna F172G	F172-0208		14. 3.66	D.Bruton	Abbeyshrule	N 7.01
	(Built Reims Aviation SA)				*(Stripped hulk noted)*		
EI-APF	*Cessna F150G*	F150-0112		6. 3.66	Sligo Aero Club Ltd	Strandhill	A 8.98
	(Built Reims Aviation SA)						
EI-APS(2)	*Schleicher ASK 14*	14008	(EI-114)	24.11.69	SLG Group	Gowran Grange	
			G-AWVV/D-KOBB				
EI-ASR(2)	*McCandless M.4 Gyroplane*	M.4/5	G-AXHZ	29. 9.69	G.J.J.Fasenfeld	Sion Mills, Strabane	N 4.96
	(Volkswagen) (C/n M4/4 quoted also)				*(Sold to R.McGregor: stored)*		
EI-AST	Cessna F150H	F150-0273		30. 1.68	Ormand Flying Group	Birr	N 1.03
	(Built Reims Aviation SA)						
EI-ASU*	Beagle A.61 Terrier 2	B.633	G-ASRG	10. 1.68	C Lebroda & Pntrs	Trim	N 1.03
			WE599		*(Stored)*		
EI-ATJ	Beagle B.121 Pup 2	B121-029	G-35-029	10. 2.69	L.O'Leary	Waterford	N 1.02
EI-ATK*	Piper PA-28-140 Cherokee	28-24120	G-AVUP	18.10.68	Mayo Flying Club	Abbeyshrule	N 1.03
			N11C		*(Damaged Connaught 14.2.87: stripped hulk noted)*		
EI-ATS	*SOCATA MS.880B Rallye Club*	1582		20. 4.70	ATS Group *(Stored)*	Abbeyshrule	N 4.96
EI-AUE	SOCATA MS.880B Rallye Club	1359	G-AXHU	1. 4.70	Kilkenny Flying Club Ltd	Kilkenny	N 1.03
EI-AUG	SOCATA MS.894A Rallye Minerva 220	11080		17. 6.70	K.O'Leary	Rathcoole	N 1.03
EI-AUM	*Auster V J/1 Autocrat*	2612	G-AJRN	11. 9.70	T.G.Rafter *(On rebuild)*	(Ballyboughal)	N 6.96
EI-AUO	Reims/Cessna FA150K Aerobat	FA1500074		2. 3.70	Kerry Aero Club Ltd	Waterford	A10.02
EI-AUS	*Auster J/5F Aiglet Trainer*	2779	G-AMRL	17.11.70	T.Stevens & T.Lennon *(On rebuild)*	Powerscourt	N 4.95
EI-AUT	Forney F-1A Aircoupe	5731	G-ARXS	21.12.70	Joyce Aviation Ltd Bann Foot, Lough Neagh		N 8.97
			D-EBSA/N3037G		*(Stored) (To N.Glass & A.Richardson?)*		
EI-AVB	Aeronca 7AC Champion	7AC-1790	7P-AXK	14. 6.71	J D Cooper	Thonotosassa, Florida, USA	N10.99
	(Continental A65)		ZS-AXK		*(Regd in USA as N151JC [7AC-71790]*		
EI-AVC	Reims/Cessna F337F Super Skymaster		N4757	26. 8.71	Christy Keane (Saggart) Ltd	Castlerock	N10.01
	(Wichita c/n 337001355)	F33700032			*(Stored Abbeyshrule & used as spares source)*		
EI-AVM	Reims/Cessna F150L	F15000745		3. 3.72	T.Carter & Partners	Abbeyshrule	A 7.01
EI-AWE	Reims/Cessna F150L	F15000877		22. 2.73	D.Bruton *(Fuselage stored)*	(Dublin)	N 4.01
EI-AWH	Cessna 210J Centurion	21059067	G-AZCC	19. 1.73	Rathcoole Flying Club Ltd	Rathcoole	
			(EI-AWH)/G-AZCC/5N-AIE/N1734C/(N6167F)				
EI-AWP	de Havilland DH.82A Tiger Moth	85931	F-BGCL	4. 7.72	Anne.P.Bruton	Abbeyshrule	N 1.03
	(Regd with c/n 19577)		Fr.AF/DF195				
EI-AWR	Malmo MFI-9 Junior	010	LN-HAG	12. 6.73	M.Whyte & J.Brennen	Galway	N 1.03
			(SE-EBW)				
EI-AWU	*SOCATA MS.880B Rallye Club*	880	G-AVIM	12. 1.74	Longford Aviation Ltd	Rosnakil	N 8.98
EI-AYA	SOCATA MS.880B Rallye Club	2256	G-BAON	27. 7.73	Limerick Flying Club (Coonagh) Ltd	Coonagh	A 8.02
EI-AYB	Gardan GY-80-180 Horizon	156	F-BNQP	5.10.73	J.B.Smith	Abbeyshrule	N 1.03
EI-AYD	*Grumman-American AA-5 Traveler*	0380	G-BAZE	9. 7.73	P.Howick, H.Martini & V.O'Rourke	Powerscourt	
			N5480L				
EI-AYF	Reims/Cessna FRA150L Aerobat	FRA1500218		26. 3.74	Limerick Flying Club (Coonagh) Ltd	Coonagh	N 1.03
EI-AYI	Morane MS.880B Rallye Club	189	F-OBXE	21.11.73	J.McNamara	Cloncameel	A 9.02
EI-AYK	Reims/Cessna F172M Skyhawk II	F17201092		25. 3.74	D.Gallagher	Trim	N 1.03
EI-AYN	IRMA BN-2A-8 Islander	704	G-BBFJ	26. 3.74	Galway Aviation Services Ltd	Connemara	A2003
					t/a Aer Arann Express *"Inis-Mor"*		
EI-AYR	Schleicher ASK 16	16022	(EI-119)	5. 4.74	Brian O'Broin	Kilrush	N 1.03
EI-AYT(2)	SOCATA MS.894A Rallye Minerva 220	11065	G-AXIU	6. 8.74	K.A.O'Connor	Abbeyshrule	N 5.00
					(Damaged Palklasmore 12.11.89: wreck only)		

Reg	Type	c/n	Prev id	Date	Owner	Location	Code
EI-AYY	Evans VP-1 (Volkswagen W 1500)	MD-01 & SAAC-03		18.8.75	M.Donoghue	Newcastle	A10.98
EI-BAJ	SNCAN Stampe SV-4C	171	F-BBPN	17.10.74	Dublin Tiger Group (Being rebuilt at Abbeyshrule)	Trim	N 1.03
EI-BAS	Reims/Cessna F172M Skyhawk II	F17201262		2.5.75	Falcon Aviation Ltd	Waterford	A10.02
EI-BAT	Reims/Cessna F150M	F15001196		2.5.75	K.A.O'Connor	Weston	N 1.03
EI-BAV	Piper PA-22-108 Colt	22-8347	G-ARKO	30.4.75	Edmond Finnamore & Jerry Deegen	Birr	N 1.03
EI-BBC	Piper PA-28-180 Cherokee B	28-1049	G-ASEJ	18.6.75	Vero Beach Ltd (New owner 11.01)	Strandhill	N 8.01
EI-BBD	Evans VP-1 (Volkswagen 1600)	VP-1-No.2 & SAAC-02		13.8.76	The Volksplane Group (Damaged 12.9.81: on rebuild)	Celbridge	N 1.03
EI-BBE	Champion 7FC Tri-Traveler (Tail-wheel conversion to 7EC Traveler status)	7FC-393	G-APZW	7.9.75	Randal McNally & Cormac Carey	Carnmore, Galway	N 2.03
EI-BBG	SOCATA Rallye 100ST	2592		27.10.75	Weston Ltd (Dismantled fuselage)	Weston	N 4.01
EI-BBI	SOCATA Rallye 150ST	2663		13.10.75	Kilkenny Airport Ltd	Kilkenny	A 8.02
EI-BBJ	SOCATA MS.880B Rallye 100S	2361	F-BUVX	7.11.75	Weston Ltd	Weston	N 1.03
EI-BBO	SOCATA MS.893E Rallye 180GT	12522	F-BVNM	8.3.76	G.P.Moorhead	Hacketstown	N 1.03
EI-BBV	Piper J-3C-65 Cub (L-4J-PI) (Frame No.12888)	13058	D-ELWY F-BEGB/44-80762	14.6.76	F.Cronin (As "480762" in USAAF c/s)	Weston	N 1.03
EI-BCE	Britten Norman BN-2A-26 Islander	519	G-BDUV	14.9.76	Galway Aviation Services Ltd t/a Aer Arann Express "Inis-Meain"	Connemara	A2003
EI-BCF	*Bensen B-8M Gyrocopter (McCullough O-100)*	*47941*	*N....*	*24.8.76*	*P.Flanagan (Stored)*	*(Kilrush)*	*N1997*
EI-BCH	GEMS MS.892A Rallye Commodore 150	10561	G-ATIW	17.9.76	Limerick Flying Club (Coonagh) Ltd	Coonagh	A 9.01
EI-BCJ(2)	Aeromere F.8L Falco 3	204	G-ATAK D-ENYB	19.1.77	D.Kelly (On rebuild)	Abbeyshrule	N 1.03
EI-BCK	Reims/Cessna F172N Skyhawk II	F17201543		22.11.76	K.A.O'Connor	Weston	A10.02
EI-BCL	Cessna 182P Skylane II (Reims assembled with c/n F1820045)	18264300	N1366M	22.11.76	L.Burke	Newcastle	A12.01
EI-BCM	Piper J-3C-65 Cub (L-4H-PI)	11983	F-BNAV N9857F/44-79687	26.11.76	Kilmoon Flying Group	Trim	N 1.03
EI-BCN	Piper J-3C-65 Cub (L-4H-PI)	12335	F-BFQE OO-PIE/44-80039	26.11.76	Snowflake Flying Group	Trim	A 1.00
EI-BCP	*Rollason Druine D.62B Condor*	*RAE/618*	*G-AVCZ*	*27.1.77*	*A.Delaney*	*Dolla*	
EI-BCS	SOCATA MS.880B Rallye 100T	2550	F-BVZV	4.2.77	Organic Fruit & Vegetables of Ireland Ltd	Kilkenny	A 4.02
EI-BCU	SOCATA MS.880B Rallye 100T	2595	F-BXTH	10.2.77	Weston Ltd (Derelict)	Weston	N 1.03
EI-BDK	*SOCATA MS.880B Rallye 100T*	*2561*	*F-BXMZ*	*10.8.77*	*Limerick Flying Club (Coonagh) Ltd (Airframe stored)*	*Abbeyshrule*	*N 9.99*
EI-BDL	Evans VP-2 (Volkswagen)	V2-2101/PFA 7213 & SAAC-04		7.9.77	P.Buggle	Kildare	N 1.03
EI-BDR	Piper PA-28-180 Cherokee C	28-3980	G-BAAO LN-AEL/SE-FAG	8.12.77	Cherokee Group	Farranfore	A10.02
EI-BEA	SOCATA Rallye 100ST	3007		28.2.78	Weston Ltd (Dismantled fuselage hangared)	Weston	N 4.01
EI-BEN	Piper J-3C-65 Cub (L-4J-PI) (Frame No.12376)	12546	G-BCUC F-BFMN/44-80250	28.4.78	J.J.O'Sullivan	Weston	A 8.00
EI-BEP	SOCATA MS.892A Rallye Commodore 150	11947	F-BTJT	14.4.78	H.Lynch & J.O'Leary (Stripped hulk noted)	Abbeyshrule	N 1.03
EI-BFE	Cessna F150G (Built Reims Aviation SA)	F150-0158	G-AVGM	3.8.78	Joyce Aviation Ltd (Stored dismantled)	Waterford	N 1.02
EI-BFF	Beech A23-24 Musketeer Super III	MA-352	G-AXCJ	20.8.78	P.McCoole	Coonagh	N 1.03
EI-BFI	SOCATA Rallye 100ST	2618		10.8.78	J O'Neill (Crashed 14.12.85: stripped hulk noted)	Abbeyshrule	N 1.03
EI-BFM	SOCATA MS.893E Rallye 180GT	12958	F-GARN	12.10.78	Limerick Flying Group (Coonagh) Ltd (Stripped hulk noted)	Abbeyshrule	N 1.03
EI-BFO	*Piper J-3C-90 Cub (L-4J-PI) (Frame No.12531) (Regd as c/n 8911)*	*12701*	*F-BFQJ N79856/NC79856/44-80405*	*11.9.78*	*D.Gordon*	*Weston*	
EI-BFP	SOCATA Rallye 100ST	2942	F-GARR	6.10.78	Weston Ltd	Weston	A 1.03
EI-BFR	SOCATA Rallye 100ST	2429	F-OCVK	9.11.78	J.Power	Waterford	A 1.02
EI-BGA	SOCATA Rallye 100ST	2549	G-BCXC F-OCZQ	23.11.78	J.J.Frew	Mullaghmore	N 7.01
EI-BGD	SOCATA MS.880B Rallye Club	2287	F-BUJI	18.12.78	N.Kavanagh (Stripped hulk noted)	Abbeyshrule	N 1.03
EI-BGG	SOCATA MS.892E Rallye 150GT	12824	F-GAFS	30.1.79	J.Dowling & M.Martin	Abbeyshrule	N 1.03
EI-BGJ	Reims/Cessna F152 II	F15201664		14.5.79	Sligo Aeronautical Club Ltd	Strandhill	A10.02
EI-BGT	Colt 77A HAB (New envelope c/n 1092 - original to EI-BBM)	041		14.5.79	M.J.Mills "Spirit of Ireland" (Ryan Air titles) (New owner 9.01)	Navan	
EI-BHB*	*SOCATA MS.887 Rallye*	*2162*	*F-BUCH*	*7.6.79*	*Hotel Bravo Flying Club Ltd (Open store: cancelled 29.11.99)*	*Abbeyshrule*	*N 5.99*
EI-BHC	Reims/Cessna F177RG Cardinal (Wichita c/n 17700117)	F177RG0010	G-AYTG	11.7.79	B.J.Palfrey & Partners "Hot Chocolate/90"	Dublin	A 5.01
EI-BHI	*Bell 206B JetRanger II*	*906*	*G-BAKX*	*14.8.79*	*George Tracey*	*Dublin*	
EI-BHK	Socata MS.880B Rallye Club	1307	F-BRJE	20.8.79	Not known (Noted derelict)	Kilkenny	N 4.02
EI-BHN	SOCATA MS.893A Rallye Commodore 180	11422	F-BRRO	11.10.79	T.Garvan (On overhaul)	Hacketstown	N 1.03
EI-BHP	*SOCATA MS.893A Rallye Commodore 180*	*11459*	*F-BSAA*	*12.10.79*	*Spanish Point Flying Club*	*Spanish Point*	
EI-BHT	Beech 77 Skipper	WA-77		17.10.79	Waterford Aero Club Ltd	Waterford	A 1.02
EI-BHV	Aeronca 7EC Traveler	7EC-739	G-AVDU N9837Y	30.10.79	E.P.O'Donnell & Partners	Clonmel	N 1.03
EI-BHW	*Cessna F150F (Built Reims Aviation SA) (Wichita c/n 15062671)*	*F150-0013*	*G-ATMK*	*22.11.79*	*R.Sharpe*	*Weston*	
EI-BHY	SOCATA Rallye 150ST	2929	F-GARL	19.11.79	Limerick Flying Club (Coonagh) Ltd	Coonagh	N 1.03
EI-BIB	Reims/Cessna F152 II	F15201724		30.11.79	Galway Flying Club Ltd	Carnmore, Galway	A 2.03
EI-BIC	Reims/Cessna F172N Skyhawk II	F17201965	(OO-HNZ)	15.2.80	Oriel Flying Group Ltd (Wreck in open storage)	Abbeyshrule	N 1.03
EI-BID	Piper PA-18 Super Cub 95 (L-18C-PI)	18-1524	D-EAES ALAT 18-1524/51-15524	30.11.79	S.Coghlan & P.Ryan	Carnmore, Galway	N 2.03
EI-BIG	*Moravan Zlin 526 Trener Master*	*1086*	*D-EBUP OO-BUT*	*7.12.79*	*P A Colman (Damaged 9.91 & acquired for spares?) Luxters Farm, Hambleden, Henley-on-Thames*		*N2002*

Reg	Type	c/n	Prev id	Date	Owner/Operator	Location	Code
EI-BIJ	Agusta-Bell 206B JetRanger II	8432	G-BCVZ	29. 1.80	Medavia Properties Ltd	Dublin Heliport	A12.01
					(Op Celtic Helicopters Ltd)		
EI-BIK	Piper PA-18-150 Super Cub	18-7909088	N82276	1. 2.80	Dublin Gliding Club Ltd	Gowran Grange	N10.01
	(Modified to 180hp)						
EI-BIO	Piper J-3C-65 Cub	12657	F-BGXP	27. 5.80	Monasterevin Flying Group		
	(L-4J-PI)		OO-GAE/44-80361			Harristown Nurney, Monasterevin	A 8.00
EI-BIR	Reims/Cessna F172M Skyhawk II	F17201225	F-BVXI	24. 3.80	B.Harrison, K.Brereton, P.Rogers & F.Maher		
						Clonbullogue	A11.00
EI-BIS	Robin R1180TD Aiglon	268		14. 5.80	The Robin Aiglon Group	Abbeyshrule	N 1.03
EI-BIT	SOCATA MS.887 Rallye 125	2169	F-BULQ	18. 3.80	Spanish Point Flying Club	Spanish Point, Co.Clare	A 1.00
EI-BIV	Bellanca 8KCAB Super Decathlon	464-79	N5032Q	3. 6.80	Aerocrats Flying Group Ltd	Abbeyshrule	N 7.01
EI-BJB	Aeronca 7DC Champion	7AC-925	G-BKKM	16. 4.80	W.Kennedy	Killenaule	N12.00
	(Continental C85)		EI-BJB/N82296/NC82296		*(Stored incomplete)*		
EI-BJC	*Aeronca 7AC Champion*	*7AC-4927*	*N1366E*	*2. 4.80*	*E.Griffin*	*Blackwater*	
	(Continental A65)		*NC1366E/SE-FBW/OY-DKN*		*(Crashed Edenderry 9.82: probably scrapped pre 1990)*		
EI-BJJ	*Aeronca 15AC Sedan*	*15AC-226*	*(G-BHXP)*	*6. 6.80*	*O.Bruton*	*Abbeyshrule*	*N 3.98*
			EI-BJJ/N1214H		*(Stored)*		
EI-BJK	SOCATA Rallye 110ST	3226	F-GBKY	8. 7.80	Malachy Keenan	Weston	A 1.03
EI-BJM	Cessna A152 Aerobat	A1520936	N761CC	18. 9.80	Leinster Aero Club Ltd	Abbeyshrule	A 9.01
EI-BJO	Cessna R172K Hawk XP II	R1723340	N758TD	6. 8.80	P.Hogan & G.Ryder	Carnmore, Galway	N 2.03
EI-BJS	Gulfstream AA-5B Tiger	AA5B-0979	G-BFZR	3. 9.80	P.Morrissey	Newcastle	A 6.01
EI-BJT	Piper PA-38-112 Tomahawk	38-78A0818	G-BGEU	16.10.80	S.Corrigan & W.Lennon	Abbeyshrule	N 1.03
			N9650N				
EI-BKC	Aeronca 15AC Sedan	15AC-467	N1394H	5.11.80	G.Hendrick, M.Farrell & J.Keating	Birr	N 1.03
EI-BKE*	Morane MS.885 Super Rallye	278	F-BKUN	9. 2.81	Not known	Abbeyshrule	N 1.03
			F-WKUN		*(Crashed Ballyclumack, Wexford 5.4.81: stripped hulk noted)*		
EI-BKF	Cessna F172H	F172-0476	G-AVUX	4.12.80	Malcolm D N Fisher	Abbeyshrule	N 7.01
	(Built Reims Aviation SA)						
EI-BKK	Taylor JT.1 Monoplane	PFA 1421	G-AYYC	2. 2.81	Waterford Aero Club	Waterford	N 1.02
	(Volkswagen 1500)				*(Stored dismantled)*		
EI-BKN	SOCATA Rallye 100ST	3035	F-GBCK	18. 2.81	Weston Ltd *(Stored)*	Weston	N 8.02
EI-BKT	Agusta-Bell 206B-3 JetRanger III	8562	D-HAFD	6. 4.81	Irish Helicopters Ltd	Dublin	A12.02
			HB-XIC				
EI-BLD	MBB Bö.105DB	S.381	D-HDLQ	21. 7.81	Irish Helicopters Ltd	Dublin	A 1.03
EI-BMA	SOCATA MS.880B Rallye Club	1965	F-BTJR	26. 1.82	W.Rankin & M.Kelleher *(Wings only noted)* Abbeyshrule		N 1.03
EI-BMB	SOCATA MS.880B Rallye 100T	2505	G-BJCO	5. 1.82	Glyde Court Developments Ltd	Weston	N 1.03
			F-BVLB				
EI-BMF	Laverda F.8L Super Falco Srs.IV	416	G-AWSU	28. 1.82	M.Slazenger & H.McCann	Powerscourt	A 8.02
EI-BMI	SOCATA TB-9 Tampico	203	F-GCOV	12. 5.82	Ashford Flying Group	Weston	N 1.03
EI-BMJ	SOCATA MS.880B Rallye 100T	2594	F-BXTG	10. 3.82	Weston Ltd	Weston	N 9.02
EI-BMM	*Reims/Cessna F152 II*	*F15201899*		*10. 3.82*	*P.Redmond*	*Weston*	
EI-BMN	Reims/Cessna F152 II	F15201912		10. 3.82	Sligo Light Aviation Club Ltd	Strandhill	N 8.02
EI-BMU	Monnett Sonerai IIL	01224		19. 5.82	A.Fenton	Ballyshannon	N 7.01
	(Volkswagen 2100)						
EI-BMV	American Aviation AA-5 Traveler	AA5-0200	G-BAEJ	28. 7.82	E.Tierney & K.A.Harold	Abbeyshrule	N 1.03
					(Damaged Brittas Bay 3.93: stripped hulk noted)		
EI-BMW	*Maddock Skytrike/Hiway Vulcan LM-100*			*1. 6.82*	*L.Maddock*	*Carlow*	
	(Fuji-Robin)						
EI-BNA	McDonnell-Douglas DC-8-63CF	45989	LX-ACV	15. 4.83	Aer Turas Teoranta	Marana-Pinal, AZ, USA	A2002
			(CX-BOU)/TF-ACV/LX-ACV/N779FT t/a Irish Cargo Airlines "City of Dublin"				
EI-BNH	*Hiway Skytrike*	*AS.09*		*18.10.82*	*M.Martin*	*Tullamore*	
	(Fuji-Robin EC-25-PS)						
EI-BNK	Cessna U206F Stationair	U20601706	G-HILL	23.12.82	Irish Parachute Club Ltd	Clonbulloge	A 1.03
			PH-ADN/D-EEXY/N9506G				
EI-BNL	Rand Robinson KR-2	-		13. 1.83	K.Hayes	Birr	N 1.03
	(Volkswagen 2000)				*(Under construction)*		
EI-BNT	Cvjetkovic CA-65	-		23. 3.83	B.Tobin & P.G.Ryan	(Tallaght)	
EI-BNU	SOCATA MS.880B Rallye Club	1204	F-BPQV	7. 4.83	P.A.Doyle	Coonagh	N 1.03
EI-BOE	SOCATA TB-10 Tobago	301	F-GDBL	12. 9.83	P.Byron, K.Lawford, L.Naye, E.Murtagh,		
					G.Haughey, M.Verling & J.Byron	Weston	N 1.03
EI-BOV	*Rand Robinson KR-2*	*SAAC-11*		*7. 5.84*	*G.O'Hara & G.Callan "Kitty Hawk"*	*NK*	
	(Volkswagen 1835)				*(Damaged Carnmore 3.91 on re-build 1999)*		
EI-BPE	Viking Dragonfly	SAAC-16		15.10.84	G.G.Bracken	Castlebar	N 1.01
	(Volkswagen 1835)				*(Not completed & stored)*		
EI-BPL	Reims/Cessna F172K	F17200758	G-AYSG	28. 3.85	Phoenix Flying Ltd	Shannon	A12.01
EI-BPN	*Flexiform Striker*	*-*		*12. 3.85*	*P.H.Collins*	*Dunlaoghaire*	
	(Fuji Robin)						
EI-BPO	*Southdown Puma*	*1923*		*12. 3.85*	*A.Channing*	*Clane*	
	(Fuji-Robin EC-44-PM - E/No.82-00108) (Also quoted as Southdown Sailwing c/n 1924)						
EI-BPP	Eipper Quicksilver MX	3207		12. 3.85	J.A.Smith	Abbeyshrule	N 1.03
	(Cuyana 430)				*(Stored)*		
EI-BPU	Hiway Demon	-		26. 3.85	A.Channing	Abbeyshrule	N 5.00
	(Fuji-Robin EC-25-PS)						
EI-BRS	Cessna P172D	P17257173	G-WPUI	2. 9.85	D.& M.Hillary	Weston	N 1.03
			G-AXPI/9M-AMR/N11B/(N8573X) *(In poor condition)*				
EI-BRU	Evans VP-1	V-12-84-CQ & SAAC-18		5.11.85	Home Bru Flying Group	Weston	N 6.02
	(Volkswagen 1600)						
EI-BSB	Wassmer Jodel D.112	1067	G-AWIG	23. 6.87	Estartit Ltd	Kilrush	A 1.03
			F-BKAA				
EI-BSC	Reims/Cessna F172N Skyhawk II	F17201651	G-NIUS	10.12.85	S.Phelan	Weston	N 1.03
EI-BSF*	Avro 748 Srs.1/105	1544	EC-DTP	28. 5.86	Ryanair Ltd "Spirit of Tipperary"	Dublin	N 4.01
			G-BEKD/LV-HHF/LV-PUM		*(Fuselage used as cabin trainer for fire training in all-white c/s)*		
EI-BSG	*Bensen B-80 Gyrocopter*	*HB*		*30. 1.86*	*J.Todd*	*(Riverstick)*	*N 3.90*
	(McCullough 4318)				*(Stored)*		

Reg	Type	c/n	Prev id	Date	Owner/Operator	Location	Status
EI-BSK	SOCATA TB-9 Tampico	618		9. 4.86	Weston Ltd	Weston	N 1.03
EI-BSL	Piper PA-34-220T Seneca III	34-8233041	N8468X	27. 6.86	P Greenan	Weston	A 6.02
EI-BSN	Cameron O-65 HAB	1278		14. 4.86	Carol O'Neill & Tracy Hooper *"Erin-Go-Bragh"*	Cavan	A 10.02
EI-BSO	Piper PA-28-140 Cherokee B	28-25449	C-GOBL N8241N	16. 4.86	H.M.Hanley	Waterford	A 1 02
EI-BSV	SOCATA TB-20 Trinidad	579	G-BMIX	15. 8.86	J.Condron	Abbeyshrule	N 1.03
EI-BSW	Solar Wings Pegasus XL-R (Rotax 447) SW-TB-1124 & SW-WA-1122			22. 6.87	E.Fitzgerald	Waterford	A 10.02
EI-BSX	*Piper J-3C-65 Cub* (Frame No.8999) (Official c/n 13255 is incorrect as a/c probably rebuilt c.1945)	*8912*	*G-ICUB F-BEGT/NC79805/45-4515/42-36788*	*25. 3.86*	*J. & T.O'Dwyer*	*Gowran Grange*	
EI-BTX	McDonnell Douglas DC9-82 (MD-82)	49660	(N59842)	23. 3.88	Airplanes Holdings Ltd (Op Aeromexico) Mexico City-Benito Juarez, Mexico		A2003
EI-BTY(2)	McDonnell Douglas DC9-82 (MD-82)	49667	(N12844)	6. 5.88	Airplanes Holdings Ltd (Op Aeromexico) Mexico City-Benito Juarez, Mexico		A2003
EI-BUA	Cessna 172M Skyhawk II	17265451	N5458H	8. 8.86	Skyhawks Flying Club	Weston	N 1.03
EI-BUC	Jodel D.9 Bebe (Volkswagen 1500)	PFA 929	G-BASY	20. 1.87	Bernard Lyons & Michael Blake	Thurles	A 7.01
EI-BUF	Cessna 210N Centurion II	21063070	G-MCDS G-BHNB/N6496N	18.12.86	210 Group	Abbeyshrule	N 1.03
EI-BUG	SOCATA ST-10 Diplomate	125	G-STIO OH-SAB	4. 2.87	J.Cooke (Derelict)	Weston	N 1.03
EI-BUH	Lake LA-4-200 Buccaneer	543	G-PARK G-BBGK/N39779	27. 5.87	T.Henderson	Lough Derg Marina, Killaloe	N.1.03
EI-BUL	*Whittaker MW.5 Sorcerer* (Citroen 602cc)	*1*		*4. 3.87*	*J.Culleton*	*Mountmellick*	
EI-BUN	Beech 76 Duchess	ME-371	(EI-BUO) N37001	26. 6.87	K.A.O'Connor	Weston	A10.02
EI-BUR	Piper PA-38-112 Tomahawk	38-79A0363	G-BNDE N2541D	10. 7.87	Westair Aviation Ltd	Shannon	A 4.01
EI-BUS	Piper PA-38-112 Tomahawk	38-79A0186	G-BNDF N2439C	10. 7.87	Westair Aviation Ltd	Shannon	A 3.01
EI-BUT	GEMS MS.893A Rallye Commodore 180	10559	SE-IMV F-BNBU	30. 7.87	T.Keating (Galerien c/s)	Weston	A 9.02
EI-BVB	Whittaker MW.6 Merlin (Rotax)	1		14. 9.87	R.England	Watergrasshill	N 9.00
EI-BVJ(2)	*AMF Chevvron 2-32* (Konig SD570)	*009*		*16. 2.88*	*S.J.Dunne*	*Bolybeg, Ballymore Eustace*	
EI-BVK	Piper PA-38-112 Tomahawk	38-79A0966	OO-FLG OO-HLG/N9705N	2. 3.88	James Dowling & Michael Martin	Trim	N 1.03
EI-BVT	Evans VP-2 V2-2129/PFA 7221 & SAAC-20 (Volkswagen 1834)		G-BEIE	29. 4.88	P.Morrison (Under construction)	(Cobh)	N 1.01
EI-BVY	Heintz Zenith CH.200AA-RW (Lycoming O-320)	2-582		7. 6.88	J.Matthews, M.Skelly & T.Coleman	Abbeyshrule	A 7.01
EI-BWH	Partenavia P.68C	212	G-BHJP	11.12.87	K.Buckley	Cork	A10.02
EI-BXD	Boeing 737-448	24866		1. 6.90	Aer Lingus Ltd *"St.Colman"*	Dublin	A2003
EI-BXI	Boeing 737-448	25052		29. 4.91	Aer Lingus Ltd *"St.Finnian"*	Dublin	A2003
EI-BXK	Boeing 737-448	25736		14. 4.92	Aer Lingus Ltd *"St.Caimin"*	Dublin	A2003
EI-BXL	*Polaris FIB OK350* (Rotax 503)	*M.561628*		*27. 6.91*	*M.McKeon*	*Lough Gowna*	
EI-BXO	*Fouga (Valmet) CM-170 Magister* (C/n FM-28 also quoted)	*213*	*N18FM*	*21.11.88*	*G.W.Connolly* (Stored)	*Saggart, Dublin*	*N 4.96*
EI-BXT	Rollason Druine D.62B Condor	RAE/626	G-AVZE	24. 8.88	The Condor Group	Abbeyshrule	A 1.03
EI-BXX	Agusta-Bell 206B-3 JetRanger III	8560	G-JMVB G-OIML	15.11.88	Westair Aviation Ltd	Shannon	A10.02
EI-BYF	Cessna 150M Commuter	15076654	N3924V	20.11.89	Twentieth Air Training Group Ltd	Dublin	A10.02
EI-BYG	SOCATA TB-9 Tampico Club	928		23. 8.89	Weston Ltd	Weston	A 9.02
EI-BYJ	Bell 206B JetRanger II	1897	N49725	23. 6.89	Medeva Properties Ltd	Dublin Heliport	N 1.03
EI-BYL	Heintz Zenith CH-250 (Lycoming O-320) (C/n quoted as c/n A2-866)	MS/FAS 2866	(EI-BYD)	14. 6.89	M.McLoughlin	Kilrush	N 1.03
EI-BYO	Aérospatiale/Alenia ATR 42-310	161	OY-CIS EI-BYO/F-WWEH	20. 12.02	GPA-ATR Ltd. (Op Aer Arann Express)	Dublin	A 1.03
EI-BYR	Bell 206L-3 LongRanger III	51284	(EI-LMG) EI-BYR/D-HBAD	15. 8.89	H.S.S.Ltd (New owner 9.01)	Rathcoole	A 8.01
EI-BYX	Champion 7GCAA Citabria	7GCAA-40	N546DS	4. 4.90	P.J.Gallagher	Abbeyshrule	N 1.03
EI-BYY	Piper J-3C-85 Cub (Frame No.12322) (Regd with c/n 22288 and officially ex G-AKTJ/N3595K/NC3595K)	12494	EC-AQZ HB-OSG/44-80198	12. 4.90	The Cub Club	Galway	A12.01
EI-BZE	Boeing 737-3Y0	24464		2. 8.89	Paloma Developments (PAL) (Op Philippine Airlines) Manila-Nino Aquino, Philippines		A2003
EI-BZF	Boeing 737-3Y0	24465		7. 8.89	Pergola Ltd Manila-Nino Aquino, Philippines (Op Philippine Airlines)		A2003
EI-BZJ	Boeing 737-3Y0	24677		29. 3.90	Pergola Ltd Manila-Nino Aquino, Philippines (Op Philippine Airlines)		A2003
EI-BZL	Boeing 737-3Y0	24680		4.10.90	GECAS Technical Services Ltd (Op Philippine Airlines) Manila-Nino Aquino, Philippines		A2003
EI-BZM	Boeing 737-3Y0	24681		15.10.90	GECAS Technical Services Ltd Subic Bay, Philippines (Leased Air Philippines)		A2003
EI-BZN	Boeing 737-3Y0	24770		30.10.90	Airplanes Finance Ltd Subic Bay, Philippines (Leased Air Philippines)		A2003
EI-CAA*	Reims FR172J Rocket	FR17200486	G-BHTW 5Y-ATO	17. 8.89	O.Bruton	Abbeysrule	N 9.00
	(Damaged 1993/94: cancelled 27.11.98 as WFU: open store)						
EI-CAC	Grob G-115A	8092		22.10.89	G.Tracey	Weston	A 1.03

Reg	Type	c/n	Prev id	Date	Owner/Operator	Location	Code
EI-CAE	Grob G-115A	8105		5. 4.90	Kieran A.O'Connor	Weston	A 1.02
EI-CAN	Aerotech MW.5(K) Sorcerer (Rotax 447)	5K-0011-02	(G-MWGH)	15. 6.90	V.Vaughan	Mulinahone	
EI-CAP	Cessna R182 Skylane RGII	R18200056	G-BMUF N7342W	27. 4.90	M.J.Hanlon	Weston	A 8.02
EI-CAU	*AMF Chevvron 2-32 (Konig SD32)*	*022*		*14.11.90*	*J.Farrant*	*Rathcoole*	
EI-CAW	Bell 206B JetRanger II	780	N2947W	11. 7.90	Celtic Helicopters (Maintenance Services) Ltd (Dismantled)	Dublin Heliport	N 5.00
EI-CAX	Cessna P210N Pressurized Centurion II	P21000215	(EI-CAS) G-OPMB/N4553K	9. 7.90	J.Rafter	Abbeyshrule	N 1.03
EI-CAY	Mooney M.20C Ranger	690074	N9272V	14.11.90	Ranger Flights Ltd (Stored dismantled)	Hacketstown	N 1.03
EI-CBK	Aérospatiale/Alenia ATR 42-310	199	F-WWEM	25. 7.90	GPA-ATR Ltd (Op Aer Arran Express)	Connemara	A 1.03
EI-CBR	McDonnell Douglas DC-9-83 (MD-83)	49939		3.12.90	Airplanes 111 Ltd (Leased Avianca) "Ciudad de Bucaramanga"	Bogota, Colombia	A2002
EI-CBS	McDonnell Douglas DC-9-83 (MD-83)	49942		10.12.90	GECAS Technical Services Ltd (Leased Avianca) "Ciudad de Cucuta"	Bogota, Colombia	A2002
EI-CBY	McDonnell Douglas DC-9-83 (MD-83)	49944		30. 7.91	GECAS Technical Services Ltd (Leased Avianca) "Ciudad de Barranquilla"	Bogota, Colombia	A2002
EI-CBZ	McDonnell Douglas DC-9-83 (MD-83)	49945		13. 8.91	GECAS Technical Services Ltd (Leased Avianca) "Ciudad de Santiago de Cali"	Bogota, Colombia	A2002
EI-CCC	McDonnell Douglas DC-9-83 (MD-83)	49946		27. 9.91	Airplanes 111 Ltd (Leased Avianca) "Ciudad de Pereira"	Bogota, Colombia	A2002
EI-CCD	Grob G-115A	8108	D-EIUD or D-EIWD ?	15. 8.90	MOD Aviation Ltd	Weston	A 1.03
EI-CCE(2)	McDonnell Douglas DC-9-83 (MD-83)	49947		19. 9.91	GECAS Technical Services Ltd (Leased Avianca) "Ciudad de Medelin"	Bogota, Colombia	A2002
EI-CCF	Aeronca 11AC Chief (Continental A65)	11AC-S-40	N3826E NC3826E	10. 1.91	L.Murray & Partners	Trim	A 1.03
EI-CCH	Piper J-3C-65 Cub	7278	N38801 NC38801	24. 1.91	J.Matthews & Partners	Trim	N11.00
EI-CCJ	*Cessna 152 II*	*15280174*	*N24251*	*9.10.90*	*M.P.Cahill (Stored)*	*Dublin*	*N 2.95*
EI-CCK	*Cessna 152 II*	*15279610*	*N757BM*	*9.10.90*	*M.P.Cahill (Damaged pre 1995)*	*Newcastle*	
EI-CCM	*Cessna 152 II*	*15282320*	*N68679*	*9.10.90*	*E Hopkins*	*Newcastle*	
EI-CCV	*Cessna R172K Hawk XPII*	*R1723039*	*N758EP*	*2. 3.91*	*Kerry Aero Club Ltd*	*Farranfore*	
EI-CDA	Boeing 737-548	24878	YR-BGZ EI-CDA/EI-BXE	31.5.01R	Aer Lingus Ltd "St.Columba/Colum"	Dublin	A2003
EI-CDB	Boeing 737-548	24919	EI-BXF	27. 5.91	Aer Lingus Ltd "St.Albert/Ailbhe"	Dublin	A2003
EI-CDC	Boeing 737-548	24968	EI-BXG	19. 6.91	Aer Lingus Ltd "St.Munchen/Maincin"	Dublin	A2003
EI-CDD	Boeing 737-548	24989	EI-BXH	3. 7.91	Aer Lingus Ltd "St.Macartan/Macarthain"	Dublin	A2003
EI-CDE	Boeing 737-548	25115	PT-SLM EI-CDE/(EI-BXJ)	21. 5.91	Aer Lingus Ltd "St.Jarlath/Iarflaith"	Dublin	A2003
EI-CDF	Boeing 737-548	25737		23. 3.92	Aer Lingus Ltd "St.Cronan"	Dublin	A2003
EI-CDG	Boeing 737-548	25738		7. 4.92	Aer Lingus Ltd "St.Moling"	Dublin	A2003
EI-CDH	Boeing 737-548	25739		14. 4.92	Aer Lingus Ltd "St.Ronan"	Dublin	A2003
EI-CDP	Cessna 182L	18258955	G-FALL OY-AHS/N4230S	20. 5.91	Irish Parachute Club Ltd	Clonbulloge	N 1.03
EI-CDV	Cessna 150G	15066677	N2777S	17. 7.91	K.A.O'Connor	Weston	A.1.03
EI-CDX	Cessna 210K Centurion	21059329	G-AYGN N9429M	14. 8.91	Falcon Aviation Ltd	Waterford	A 6.02
EI-CDY	McDonnell Douglas DC-9-83 (MD-83)	49948		27. 9.91	GECAS Technical Services Ltd (Op Avianca) "Ciudad de Santa Maria"	Bogota, Colombia	A2003
EI-CEG	*SOCATA MS.893E Rallye 180GT*	*13083*	*SE-GTS*	*31.10.91*	*M.Farrelly*	*Powerscourt*	
EI-CEK	McDonnell Douglas DC-9-83 (MD-83)	49631	EC-FMY EC-113/EI-CEK/EC-EPM/EC-261	13.12.91	Airplanes IAL Finance Ltd (Op Nouvelair)	Monastir, Tunisia	A2003
EI-CEN	*Thruster T.300 (Rotax 582)*	*9012-T300-500*		*2. 3.92*	*P.J.Murphy*	*Macroom*	
EI-CEP	McDonnell Douglas DC-9-83 (MD-83)	53122		14. 4.92	GECAS Technical Services Ltd (Op Avianca) "San Andres Isla"	Bogota, Colombia	A2003
EI-CEQ	McDonnell Douglas DC-9-83 (MD-83)	53123		14. 4.92	GECAS Technical Services Ltd (Op Avianca) "Ciudad de Leticia"	Bogota, Colombia	A2003
EI-CER	McDonnell Douglas DC-9-83 (MD-83)	53125	N9017P	20. 5.92	Airplanes 111 Ltd (Op Avianca) "Ciudad de Monteria"	Bogota, Colombia	A2003
EI-CES	Taylorcraft BC-65	2231	G-BTEG N27590/NC27590	25. 3.92	N.O'Brien	Kilkenny	N 9.00
EI-CEX	Lake LA-4-200 Buccaneer	1115	N8VG N3VC/N8544Z	18. 5.92	Derg Developments Ltd Lough Derg Marina, Killaloe		A10.01
EI-CEY	Boeing 757-2Y0	26152		10. 8.92	Pergola Ltd (Leased Avianca)	Bogota, Colombia	A2003
EI-CEZ	Boeing 757-2Y0	26154		18. 9.92	Airplanes Holdings Ltd (Op Avianca)	Bogota, Colombia	A2003
EI-CFE	Robinson R22 Beta	1709	G-BTHG	15. 5.91	Crinstown Aviation Ltd	Weston	A 9.02
EI-CFF	Piper PA-12 Super Cruiser (Lycoming O-235)	12-3928	N78544 NC78544	23. 5.91	J.O'Dwyer & J.Molloy	Gowran Grange	N 1.03
EI-CFG	Rousseau Piel CP.301B Emeraude	112	G-ARIW F-BIRQ	1. 6.91	Southlink Ltd (Stored complete)	Waterford	N 1.02
EI-CFH	*Piper PA-12 Super Cruiser (Lycoming O-320)*	*12-3110*	*(EI-CCE) N4214M/NC4214M*	*1. 6.91*	*G.Treacy*	*Shinrone*	*A10.99*
EI-CFN	Cessna 172P Skyhawk II	17274113	N5446K JA4172/N5446K	10. 5.92	B.Fitzmaurice & G.O'Connell	Weston	N 1.03
EI-CFP	Cessna 172P Skyhawk II	17274428	N52178	15. 7.91	K A O'Connor	Weston	N 1.03
EI-CFV*	SOCATA MS.880B Rallye Club	1850	G-OLFS G-AYYZ	13. 5.92	Not known	Abbeyshrule	N.1.03
					(Cancelled 15.11.00 as scrapped) (Stripped hulk noted)		
EI-CFX	Robinson R22 Beta	0793	G-OSPI§	16. 6.92	Ballaugh Motors Ltd	Galway	A 8.02
EI-CFY	Cessna 172N Skyhawk II	17268902	N734JZ	18. 6.92	K.A.O'Connor	Weston	N 1.03

Reg	Type	C/n	Reg2	Date	Owner/Operator	Location	Ref
EI-CFZ	McDonnell Douglas DC-9-83 (MD-83)	53120	N6206F	29. 7.92	Airplanes 111 Ltd (Op Avianca) "Ciudad de San Juan de Pasto"	Bogota, Colombia	A2002
EI-CGB	*TEAM miniMAX*	*SAAC-36*		20. 8.92	*M.Garvey*	*Abbeyshrule*	
EI-CGC	Stinson 108-3 Station Wagon	108-5243	OO-IAC OO-JAC/N3B	17. 7.92	Anne P.Bruton	Kildare	N 1.03
EI-CGD	Cessna 172M Skyhawk II	17262309	OO-BMT N12846	30. 7.92	J Murray	Weston	A10.02
EI-CGE*	*Hiway Demon/Skytrike* (Fuji-Robin EC-25PS-04) (C/n is engine type)	*EC-25PS-04K*		19. 8.92	*T Carr* (Temp unregd 11.2.97)	*Kilpedder*	
EI-CGF	Phoenix Luton LA-5 Major	PAL-1124/PFA 1208 & SAAC-19	G-BENH	31. 7.92	F.Doyle & J.Duggan	(Newlands)	A 4.01
EI-CGG	Ercoupe 415C (Continental C75)	3147	N2522H NC2522H	10. 9.92	Irish Ercoupe Group (Derelict)	Weston	N 1.03
EI-CGH	Cessna 210N Centurion II	21063524	N6374A	16.11.92	J.J.Spollen	Abbeyshrule	A 9.01
EI-CGN	Solar Wings Pegasus XL-R (Rotax 447)	SW-WA-1529	G-MWXM	14.11.92	V.Power	Donamore, New Ross	A 8.00
EI-CGO	McDonnell Douglas DC-8-63AF	45924	N353AS (N791AL)/SE-DBH/OY-SBM/HS-TGZ/SE-DBH t/a Irish Cargo Airlines	25. 4.89	Aer Turas Teoranta	Dublin	A2002
EI-CGP	Piper PA-28-140 Cherokee C	28-26928	G-MLUA G-AYJT/N11C	25.11.92	G.Cashman (Op Euroair Training)	Cork	A10.02
EI-CGQ	Aérospatiale AS350B Ecureuil	2076	G-BUPK JA9740	21. 1.93	Corporate Helicopters Ireland Ltd	Dublin Heliport	A10.01
EI-CGT	*Cessna 152 II*	15282331	G-BPBL N16SU/N68715	10.12.92	*J.Rafter*	*Seven Parks Farm, Naul*	
EI-CGV	Piper J-5A Cub Cruiser	5-624	G-BPKT N35372/NC35372	11.12.92	J5 Grp	(Trim)	A 9.02
EI-CHK	*Piper J-3C-65 Cub Special*	23019	C-FHNS CF-HNS/N1492N/NC1492N	10. 3.93	*N.Higgins*	*Longwood*	*A 7.99*
EI-CHM	Cessna 150M Commuter	15079288	G-BSZX N714MU	2. 3.93	K.A.O'Connor	Weston	N 1.03
EI-CHN	SOCATA MS.880B Rallye Club	901	G-AVIO	22. 2.93	Limerick Flying Club (Coonagh) Ltd (Wreck in open storage)	Abbeyshrule	N 1.03
EI-CHP	de Havilland DHC-8-103 Dash Eight	258	VH-FNQ C-GFRP	7. 4.93	Airplanes Jetprop Finance Ltd (Op Allegheny Airlines)	(Canada)	N2002
EI-CHR	CFM Shadow BD (Rotax 447)	063	G-MTKT	20. 5.93	Fergus Maughan	Ardclough, Straffan	A 1.03
EI-CHS	Cessna 172M Skyhawk II	17266742	G-BREZ N80775	26. 4.93	Kerry Aero Club Ltd	Farranfore	A10.02
EI-CHT	Solar Wings Pegasus XL-R	SW-WA-1568	G-MWCU EI-CHT/G-BZXU	27. 3.02	Enda Spain	Monasterevin	A 1.03
EI-CHV	Agusta A109A II	7149	VR-BMM HB-XTJ/D-HASV	10. 6.93	Celtic Helicopters Ltd	Dublin Heliport	N 1.03
EI-CIA	SOCATA MS.880B Rallye Club	1218	G-MONA G-AWJK	26. 4.93	G.Hackett & C.Mason	Thurles	A 8.02
EI-CIF	Piper PA-28-180 Cherokee C (Rebuilt 1967 with spare frame c/n 28-3808S)	28-2853	G-AVVV N8880J	12. 6.93	AA Flying Group	Weston	N 1.03
EI-CIG	Piper PA-18-150 Super Cub (Frame No.18-7360)	18-7203	G-BGWF ST-AFJ/ST-ABN	12. 6.93	K.A.O'Connor	Weston	A 1.03
EI-CIJ	Cessna 340	3400304	G-BBVE N69451	2. 7.93	Airlink Airways Ltd	Sligo	A10.02
EI-CIK	Mooney M.20C Mk 21	2620	G-BFXC 9H-ABD/G-BFXC/OH-MOA/N1349W	2. 7.93	T.G.Gordon	Connemara	N 5.00
EI-CIM	Avid Flyer mk.IV	1125D		17. 8.93	P.Swan	Weston	A 1.03
EI-CIN	Cessna 150K	15071728	G-OCIN EI-CIN/G-BSXG/N6228G	6. 9.93	K.O'Connor	Weston	A 1.03
EI-CIR(2)	Cessna 551 Citation II (Built as Cessna 550 EI-CIR(1) c/n 550-0128)	551-0174	N60AR EI-CIR(1)/F-WLEF/9A-BPU/RC-BPU/YU-BPU/N220LA/N536M/N2631V	29.11.93	Air Group Finance Ltd	Dinard, France	A12.01
EI-CIV	Piper PA-28-140 Cherokee Cruiser	28-7725232	G-BEXY N9648N	20.11.93	G.Cashman & E.Callanan	Cork	A10.02
EI-CIW	McDonnell Douglas DC-9-83 (MD-83)	49785	HL-7271	30.12.93	Carotene Ltd (Op Meridiana)	Olbia, Italy	A2002
EI-CIZ	Steen Skybolt (Lycoming IO-360)	001	G-BSAO N303BC	12.12.93	J.Keane	Coonagh	N 1.03
EI-CJC	Boeing 737-204ADV	22640	G-BJCV CS-TMA/G-BJCV/C-GCAU/G-BJCV/C-GXCP/G-BJCV (Hertz Car Rental titles)	25. 1.94	Ryanair Ltd	Dublin	A2003
EI-CJD	Boeing 737-204ADV	22966	G-BKHE (G-BKGU)	18. 2.94	Ryanair Ltd (Eirecell titles)	Dublin	A2003
EI-CJE	Boeing 737-204ADV	22639	G-BJCU EC-DVE/G-BJCU	10. 3.94	Ryanair Ltd (Jaguar titles)	Dublin	A2003
EI-CJF	Boeing 737-204ADV	22967	G-BTZF G-BKHF/(G-BKGV)	24. 3.94	Ryanair Ltd	Dublin	A2003
EI-CJG	Boeing 737-204ADV	22058	G-BGYK PP-SRW/G-BGYK/(G-BGRV)	25. 3.94	Ryanair Ltd	Dublin	A2003
EI-CJH	Boeing 737-204ADV	22057	G-BGYJ (G-BGRU)/N8278V	30. 3.94	Ryanair Ltd	Dublin	A2003
EI-CJI	Boeing 737-2E7	22875	G-BMDF (PK-RI.)/G-BMDF/4X-BAB/N4570B	8. 7.94	Ryanair Ltd	Dublin	A2003
EI-CJR	SNCAN Stampe SV-4A	318	G-BKBK OO-CLR/F-BCLR	28. 2.94	C.Scully, P.Ryan & P.McKenna	Carnmore	N 1.03
EI-CJS	Jodel Wassmer D.120A Paris-Nice	339	F-BOYF	28. 2.94	Anthony Flood	Birr	N 1.03
EI-CJT	*Slingsby Cadet III* (Volkswagen 1835)	830 & PCW-001	G-BPCW XA288	25. 2.94	*J.Tarrant*	*Rathcoole*	
EI-CJV	Moskito 2 (Rotax 582)	004	D-MBGM	12. 3.94	Peril, Kingston, Hanly & Fitzgerald (Dismantled)	Coonagh	N 1.03

EI-CJZ	Whittaker MW-6S Fatboy Flyer (Rotax 503)	PFA 164-11493	G-MWTW	24. 3.94	M.McCarthy	Watergrasshill	N 9.00
EI-CKH	Piper PA-18 Super Cub 95	18-7248	G-APZK N10F	3. 6.94	G.Brady & C.Keenan	Weston	N 1.03
EI-CKI	Thruster TST Mk.1 (Rotax 503)	8078-TST-091	G-MVDI	3. 6.94	S.Pallister	Brannockstown	A 8.02
EI-CKJ	*Cameron N-77 HAB*	*3305*		6. 7.94	*F.Meldon "Goodfellas"*	*Blackrock*	
EI-CKM	McDonnell Douglas DC-9-83 (MD-83)	49792	TC-INC	10. 8.94	Airplanes Finance Ltd	Olbia, Italy	A2002
	EI-CKM/(D-ALLW)/EI-CKM/XA-RPH/EC-FFP/EC-733/XA-RPH *(Op Meridiana)*						
EI-CKN	*Whittaker MW-6S Fatboy Flyer* *(Rotax 462)*	*BCA.8942*		29. 7.94	*F.Byrne & M.O'Carroll*	*Kilrush*	
EI-CKP	Boeing 737-2K2ADV	22296	PH-TVS	7.10.94	Ryanair Ltd	Dublin	A2003
	PP-SRV/PH-TVS/LV-RBH/PH-TVS/LV-RAO/PH-TVS/EC-DVN/PH-TVS						
EI-CKQ	Boeing 737-2K2ADV	22906	PH-TVU	20. 2.95	Ryanair Ltd	Dublin	A2003
	G-BPLA/PH-TVU/C-FCAV/PH-TVU						
EI-CKR	Boeing 737-2K2ADV	22025	PH-TVR	4. 5.95	Ryanair Ltd	Dublin	A2003
	C-FICP/PH-TVR/(D-AJAA)/PH-TVR						
EI-CKS	Boeing 737-2T5ADV	22023	PH-TVX	1. 6.95	Ryanair Ltd	Dublin	A2003
	OE-ILE/PH-TVX/G-BGTW						
EI-CKT	*Mainair Gemini/Flash*	*307-585-3 & W47*	G-MNCB (EC-44-PM)	27. 9.94	*C.Burke*	*Bartlemy*	
EI-CKU	*Solar Wings Pegasus XL-R* *(Rotax 447)* *SW-TB-1434 & SW-WA-1500*		G-MWVB	14.10.94	*M.O'Regan*	*Edenderry*	
EI-CKX	Wassmer Jodel D.112	1166	G-ASIS F-BKNR	7.12.94	W.R.Prescott	Riverstown	A 6.00
EI-CLA	HOAC DV-20 Katana	20106		24. 3.95	Weston Ltd	Weston	N 1.03
EI-CLB	Aérospatiale/Alenia ATR 72-212	423	F-WWEB	23. 2.95	Tarquin Ltd	Rome-Fiumicino, Italy	A2003
					(Op Alitalia Express) "Lago di Bracciano"		
EI-CLC	Aérospatiale/Alenia ATR 72-212	428	F-WWEF	24. 2.95	Tarquin Ltd	Rome-Fiumicino, Italy	A2003
					(Op Alitalia Express) "Fiume Simeto"		
EI-CLD	Aérospatiale/Alenia ATR 72-212	432	F-WWEL	3. 3.95	Tarquin Ltd	Rome-Fiumicino, Italy	A2003
					(Op Alitalia Express) "Fiume Piave"		
EI-CLG	British Aerospace BAe 146 Srs.300	E3131	G-BRAB	7. 6.95	Aer Lingus Ltd "St.Finbar/Fionnbar"	Dublin	A2003
	HS-TBL/G-BRAB/G-11-131						
EI-CLH	British Aerospace BAe 146 Srs.300	E3146	G-BOJJ	2. 6.95	Aer Lingus Ltd "St.Aoife"	Dublin	A2003
	I-ATSC/G-BOJJ/G-6-146						
EI-CLI	British Aerospace BAe 146 Srs.300	E3159	G-BVSA	19. 4.95	Aer Lingus Ltd "St.Eithne"	Dublin	A2003
	I-ATSD/G-6-159/G-5-159						
EI-CLL	*Whittaker MW-6S Fatboy Flyer* *(Rotax 503)*	*1069*		2. 4.95	*F.Stack*	*Midleton, Co Cork*	
EI-CLQ	Reims/Cessna F172N Skyhawk II	F17201653	G-BFLV	26. 5.95	K.Dardis & Partners	Abbeyshrule	N 1.03
EI-CLW	Boeing 737-3Y0	25187	XA-SAB	10. 6.95	Airplanes Finance Ltd *(Op Air One)*	Pescara, Italy	A2003
EI-CLY	British Aerospace BAe 146 Srs.300	E-3149	G-BTZN	16. 4.97	Aer Lingus Ltd "St.Eugene/Eoghan"	Dublin	A2003
	N146PZ/ZP-CCY/N146PZ/G-BTZN/HS-TBN/G-11-149						
EI-CLZ	Boeing 737-3Y0	25179	XA-RJR N3521N	27. 7.95	Airplanes Finance Ltd *(Op Air One)*	Pescara, Italy	A2003
EI-CMB	Piper PA-28-140 Cherokee Cruiser	28-7725094	G-BELR N9541N	5. 9.95	Kestrel Flying Group Ltd	Dublin	A 8.02
EI-CMI	Robinson R.22 Beta	1129	G-BRRZ N8050N	30.11.95	Santail Ltd	Leeds-Bradford	A 7.00
EI-CMJ	Aérospatiale/Alenia ATR 72-210	467	F-WWLU	21.12.95	Tarquin Ltd	Rome-Fiumicino, Italy	A2003
					(Op Alitalia Express) "Fiume Volturno"		
EI-CMK	*Eurowing Goldwing ST* *(Fuji-Robin EC-PM-34)*	*76 & SAAC-57*		22.12.95	*M.Garrigan*	*Clondara, Longford*	
EI-CML	Cessna 150M	15076786	G-BNSS N45207	5. 1.96	K.A.O'Connor	Weston	A 1.03
EI-CMN	Piper PA-12 Super Cruiser (Lycoming O-235)	12-1617	N2363N NC2363M	26. 1.96	D.Graham & Partners	Birr	N 1.03
EI-CMR	Rutan LongEz (Lycoming O-235)	1716		2. 5.96	F. & C.O'Caoimh	Waterford	A 1.02
EI-CMS	British Aerospace BAe 146 Srs.200A	E2044	N184US N361PS	24. 4.96	Cityjet Ltd *(Op Air France)*	Paris, France	A2003
EI-CMT	Piper PA-34-200T Seneca II	34-7870088	G-BNER N2590M	23. 4.96	Atlantic Flight Training Ltd	Cork	A10.02
EI-CMU	Mainair Mercury (Rotax 462)	1071-0296-7 & W873		3. 5.96	L.Langan & L.Laffan *(Restored)*	Wexford/Waterford	N 8.01
EI-CMV	Cessna 150L	150-72747	G-MSES N1447Q	17. 5.96	K.A.O'Connor	Weston	N 1.03
EI-CMW	*Rotorway Executive* *(Rotorway RW 162D)*	*3550*		13. 5.96	*B.McNamee*	*Dunboyne*	
EI-CMY	British Aerospace BAe 146 Srs.200A	E2039	N177US N356PS	19. 6.96	Cityjet Ltd *(Op Air France)*	Paris, France	A2003
EI-CMZ	McDonnell Douglas DC-9-83 (MD-83)	49390	9Y-THN	20. 7.96	Airplanes Finance Ltd *(Op Eurofly)*	Milan-Malpensa, Italy	A2003
EI-CNA	Letov LK-2M Sluka (Rotax 447)	8295S005		28. 6.96	G.Doody	Portlaoise	A 7.00
EI-CNB	British Aerospace BAe 146 Srs.200A	E2046	(EI-CMZ) N187US/N363PS	3. 8.96	Cityjet Ltd *(Op Air France)*	Paris, France	A2003
EI-CNC	Team miniMax 1600 (Rotax 447)	514		10. 9.96	A.M.S.Allen	Enniskillen	A 7.01
EI-CNG	Air & Space 18-A Gyroplane	18-75	G-BALB N6170S	10. 9.96	P.Joyce	Waterford	A 1.02
EI-CNI	British Aerospace BAe 146 Srs.200 (Avro RJ85)	E2299	G-6-299	26.11.96	Peregrine Aviation Leasing Co Ltd *(Op Azzurra Air) "Lombardia"*	Bergamo, Italy	A2003

Reg	Type	c/n	Prev id	Date	Owner/Operator	Location	Source
EI-CNJ	British Aerospace BAe 146 Srs.200 (Avro RJ85)	E2300	G-6-300	2.12.96	Peregrine Aviation Leasing Co Ltd (Op Azzurra Air) "Piemonte"	Bergamo, Italy	A2003
EI-CNK	British Aerospace BAe 146 Srs.200 (Avro RJ85)	E2306	G-6-306	8. 5.97	Peregrine Aviation Leasing Co Ltd (Op Azzurra Air) "Lazio"	Bergamo, Italy	A2003
EI-CNL	Sikorsky S-61N Mk.II	61746	G-BDDA ZS-RBU/G-BDDA/N91201/G-BDDA	19.12.96	CHC Ireland Ltd (Op Irish Marine Emergency Service)	Cork	A2003
EI-CNM	Piper PA-31-350 Navajo Chieftain	31-7305107	N1201H G-BBNT/N74958	16.12.96	M.Goss (Op Air Atlantic)	Dublin	A 1.03
EI-CNN	Lockheed L.1011-385-1 Tristar	1024	VR-HHV G-BAAA	30. 1.97	Aer Turas Teoranta t/a Irish Cargo Airlines	Dublin	A2002
EI-CNO	McDonnell Douglas DC-9-83 (MD-83)	49672	EC-FTU EC-487/EC-EJQ/EC-150	19. 2.97	Airplanes Finance Ltd (Op Nouvelair)	Monastir, Tunisia	A2002
EI-CNQ	British Aerospace BAe 146 Srs.200	E2031	G-OWLD N173US/N353PS	2. 7.97	Cityjet Ltd (Op Air France)	Paris, France	A2002
EI-CNR	McDonnell Douglas DC-9-83 (MD-83)	53199	SE-DLU N13627	10. 4.97	Aircraft Finance Trust Ireland Ltd (Op Eurofly)	Milan-Malpensa, Italy	A2002
EI-CNT	Boeing 737-230ADV	22115	D-ABFC	5.12.96	Ryanair Ltd (Vodaphone titles)	Dublin	A2003
EI-CNU	Pegasus Quantum 15-912	7326		10. 4.97	M.Ffrench	Donamore, New Ross	A 6.01
EI-CNV	Boeing 737-230ADV	22128	D-ABFX (D-ABFW)	26. 3.97	Ryanair Ltd	Dublin	A2003
EI-CNW	Boeing 737-230ADV	22133	D-ABHC (B-)/D-ABHC/(D-ABHB)	31. 5.97	Ryanair Ltd	Dublin	A2003
EI-CNX	Boeing 737-230ADV	22127	D-ABFW N5573K/(D-ABFU)	4. 7.97	Ryanair Ltd	Dublin	A2003
EI-CNY	Boeing 737-230ADV	22113	D-ABFB N5573K	10.10.97	Ryanair Ltd (Kilkenny - Cream of Irish Beer titles)	Dublin	A2003
EI-CNZ	Boeing 737-230ADV	22126	D-ABFU (D-ABFT)	5.11.97	Ryanair Ltd	Dublin	A2003
EI-COA	Boeing 737-230ADV	22637	CS-TES D-ABHX	16.12.97	Ryanair Ltd	Dublin	A2003
EI-COB	Boeing 737-230ADV	22124	D-ABFR	16. 1.98	Ryanair Ltd	Dublin	A2003
EI-COE	Europa Aviation Europa (Jabiru 2200) (Monowheel u/c)	286		29. 5.97	F.Flynn (Under construction)	(Urlanmore)	N 1.01
EI-COG	Gyroscopic Gyroplane	G.120		11. 3.98	R.C.Fidler & D.Bracken	Letterkenny	A 8.98
	(Imported from Australia 1996 and flown without marks 8.97: design is 2-seat side by side open cockpit gyro: the quoted c/n may be type designation)						
EI-COH	Boeing 737-430	27001	D-ABKB (VT-S)/D-ABKB	6. 6.97	Flightlease (Ireland) Ltd (Op Air One)	Pescara, Italy	A2003
EI-COI	Boeing 737-430	27002	D-ABKC	13.11.97	Challey Ltd (Op Air One)	Pescara, Italy	A2003
EI-COJ	Boeing 737-430	27005	D-ABKK (D-ABKF)	13.11.97	Challey Ltd (Op Air One)	Pescara, Italy	A2003
EI-COK	Boeing 737-430	27003	F-GRNZ EI-COK/D-ABKD	22. 4.02	Flightleases (Ireland) Ltd (Op Air One)	Milan, Italy	A2003
EI-COM	Whittaker MW-6S Fatboy Flyer (Rotax 582)	1		10.10.97	M.Watson (Under construction)	Clonbullogue	N 1.01
EI-CON	Boeing 737-2T5	22396	PK-RIW EI-CON/PK-RIW/VT-EWF/A40-BM/C-GVRE/(EI-B)/G-BHVH	21. 7.97	Ryanair Ltd	Dublin	A2003
EI-COO	Carlson Sparrow II (Rotax 532)	302		13. 8.97	D.Logue	Weston	
EI-COP	Reims/Cessna F150L	F15001058	G-BCBY PH-TGI/(G-BCBY)	26. 6.97	High Kings Flying Group Ltd	Greigs, Navan	A 5.01
EI-COQ	British Aerospace BAe 146 Srs.100 (Avro RJ70)	E1254	9H-ACM (9H-ABW)/G-BVRJ/G-6-254	17.10.97	Peregrine Aviation Leasing Co Ltd (Op Azzurra Air) "Puglia"	Bergamo, Italy	A2003
EI-COT	Reims/Cessna F172N Skyhawk II	F17201884	D-EIEF	24.11.97	Kawasaki Distributors (Ireland) Ltd	Newcastle	N 1.03
EI-COX	Boeing 737-230ADV	22123	D-ABFP	9. 1.98	Ryanair Ltd	Dublin	A2003
EI-COY	Piper J-3C-65 Cub Special	22519	N3319N NC3319N	5.11.97	P.McWade	Abbeyshrule	N 1.03
EI-COZ	Piper PA-28-140 Cherokee C	28-26796	G-AYMZ N11C	5.11.97	G Cashman	Cork	A10.02
EI-CPB	McDonnell Douglas DC-9-83 (MD-83)	49940	TC-IND G-TTPT/N30016	27.11.97	Irish Aerospace Ltd (Op FreeAir)	Palermo, Italy	N2002
EI-CPC	Airbus Industrie A321-211	815	D-AVZT	8. 5.98	ILFC (Op Aer Lingus) "St.Fergus/Faergus"	Dublin	A2003
EI-CPD	Airbus Industrie A321-211	841	D-AVZA	19. 6.98	ILFC (Op Aer Lingus) "St.Davnet/Damhnat"	Dublin	A2003
EI-CPE	Airbus Industrie A321-211	926	D-AVZQ	11.12.98	ILFC (Op Aer Lingus) "St.Enda/Eanna"	Dublin	A2003
EI-CPF	Airbus Industrie A321-211	991	D-AVZE	9. 4.99	Aer Lingus Ltd "St.Ida/Ide"	Dublin	A2003
EI-CPG	Airbus Industrie A321-211	1023	D-AVZR	28. 5.99	Aer Lingus Ltd "St.Aidan/Aodhan"	Dublin	A2003
EI-CPH	Airbus Industrie A321-211	1094	F-WWDD D-AVZA	22.11.99	Aer Lingus Ltd "St.Dervilla/Dearbhile"	Dublin	A2003
EI-CPI	Rutan LongEz (Lycoming O-235)	17		18.12.97	D.J.Ryan "Lady Elizabeth"	Waterford	A 1.02
EI-CPJ	British Aerospace BAe 146 Srs.100 (Avro RJ70)	E1258	9H-ACN (9H-ABX)/G-6-258	27. 3.98	Peregrine Aviation Leasing Co Ltd (Op Azzura Air) "Puglia"	Bergamo, Italy	A2003
EI-CPK	British Aerospace BAe 146 Srs.100 (Avro RJ70)	E1260	9H-ACO (9H-ABY)/G-6-261	27. 3.98	Peregrine Aviation Leasing Co Ltd (Op Azzurra Air) "Calabria"	Bergamo, Italy	A2003
EI-CPL	British Aerospace BAe 146 Srs.100 (Avro RJ70)	E1267	9H-ACP (9H-ABZ)/G-6-267	31. 3.98	Peregrine Aviation Leasing Co Ltd (Op Azzurra Air) "Veneto"	Bergamo, Italy	A2003
EI-CPN	Auster J/4	2073	G-AIJR	1. 4.98	E.Fagan	Abbeyshrule	N12.00
EI-CPO	Robinson R.22B2 Beta	2775	G-BXUJ	23. 9.98	Santail Ltd	Weston	A 4.01
EI-CPP	Piper J-3C-65 Cub (L-4H-PI) (Rebuilt Glasthule, Dublin 1994/1998)	12052	G-BIGH F-BFQV/OO-GAS/OO-GAZ/44-79756	23. 3.98	E.Fitzgerald	Newcastle	A10.02
EI-CPS	Beech 58 Baron	TH-862	G-BEUL	21. 5.98	F.Doherty	Carrickfinn	A10.02
EI-CPT	Aérospatiale/Alenia ATR 42-300	191	C-GIQS (ZS-NYP)/C-GIQS/F-WWEA	12. 6.98	GPA-ATR Ltd (Op Aer Arran Express)	Connemara	A2003
EI-CPX	III Sky Arrow 650T	K.122 & SAAC-67		24. 6.98	N.Irwin	Watergrasshill	N.8.00
EI-CRB	Lindstrand LBL-90A HAB	550		23. 9.98	J.& C.Concannon	Tuam	
EI-CRD	Boeing 767-31BER	26259	B-2565	29.10.98	ILFC Ireland Ltd (Op Alitalia)	Rome-Fiumicino, Italy	A2003

Reg	Type	c/n	Prev id	Date	Owner/Operator	Location	Source
EI-CRE	McDonnell Douglas DC-9-83 *(MD-83)*	49854	D-ALLL	11.12.98	AAR Ireland Ltd *(Op Meridiana)*	Olbia, Italy	A2003
EI-CRF	Boeing 767-31B	25170	B-2566	4.12.98	ILFC Ireland Ltd	Rome-Fiumicino, Italy	A2003
					(Leased Eurofly & Op Alitalia)		
EI-CRG	Robin DR400-180R	2021	D-EHEC	11.12.98	D & B Lodge	Waterford	A 1.02
EI-CRH	McDonnell Douglas DC-9-83 *(MD-83)*	49935	HB-IKM G-DCAC/N3004C	10. 2.99	Airplanes 111 Ltd *(Op Meridiana)*	Olbia, Italy	A2003
EI-CRJ	McDonnell Douglas DC-9-83 *(MD-83)*	53013	D-ALLP	27. 1.99	C A Aviation Ltd *(Op Meridiana)*	Olbia, Italy	A2003
EI-CRK	Airbus Industrie A330-301	070	(EI-NYC) F-WWKV	18.11.94	Aer Lingus Ltd "St Patrick/Padraig"	Dublin	A2003
EI-CRL	Boeing 767-343ER	30008	(I-DEIB)	22. 3.99	GECAS Technical Services Ltd	Rome-Fiumicino, Italy	A2003
					(Op Alitalia TEAM) "Leonardo da Vinci"		
EI-CRM	Boeing 767-343	30009		8. 4.99	GECAS Technical Services Ltd	Rome-Fiumicino, Italy	A2003
					(Op Alitalia TEAM) "Amerigo Vespucci"		
EI-CRO	Boeing 767-3Q8ER	29383		16. 4.99	ILFC Ireland Ltd	Rome-Fiumicino, Italy	A2003
					(Op Alitalia TEAM) "Francesco de Pinedo"		
EI-CRR	Aeronca 11AC Chief	11AC-1605	OO-ESM (OO-DEL)/OO-ESM	13. 4.99	L.Maddock & Partners	Killamaster	N 1.03
EI-CRS	Boeing 777-2Q8ER	29908		15. 7.99	ILFC (Ireland) Ltd St Denis-Gilot, Reunion, France		A2003
					(Op Air Austral 4.03.- reserved as F-OPAR 11.02)		
EI-CRT	Boeing 777-2Q8ER	28676		8.10.99	ILFC (Ireland) Ltd St Denis-Gilot, Reunion, France		A2003
					(Op Air Austral 5.03)		
EI-CRU	Cessna 152	15285621	G-BNSW N94213	21. 9.99	W.Reilly	Inis Mor	
EI-CRV	Hoffman H.36 Dimona	3674	OE-9319 HB-2081	2. 6.99	Falcon Aviation Ltd	Waterford	A 1.02
EI-CRW	McDonnell Douglas DC-9-83 *(MD-83)*	49951	HB-IKN G-GMJM/N13627	8. 4.99	Airplanes IAL Ltd *(Op Meridiana)*	Olbia, Italy	A2003
EI-CRX	SOCATA TB-9 Tampico	1170	F-GKUL	21. 5.99	Hotel Bravo Flying Club Ltd	Weston	A 9.02
EI-CRY	Medway EclipseR	160/138		2. 6.99	G.A.Murphy	Rathcoole	
EI-CRZ	Boeing 737-36E	26322	EC-GGE EC-798	14. 4.99	ILFC Ireland Ltd *(Op Air One)*	Pescara, Italy	A2003
EI-CSA	Boeing 737-8AS	29916	N5537L N1786B	12. 3.99	Ryanair Ltd	Dublin	A2003
EI-CSB	Boeing 737-8AS	29917	N1786B	16. 6.99	Ryanair Ltd	Dublin	A2003
EI-CSC	Boeing 737-8AS	29918	N1786B	25. 6.99	Ryanair Ltd	Dublin	A2003
EI-CSD	Boeing 737-8AS	29919	N1786B	9. 8.99	Ryanair Ltd	Dublin	A2003
EI-CSE	Boeing 737-8AS	29920	N1786B	31. 8.99	Ryanair Ltd	Dublin	A2003
EI-CSF	Boeing 737-8AS	29921	N1786B	24. 5.00	Ryanair Ltd	Dublin	A2003
EI-CSG	Boeing 737-8AS	29922	N1786B	31. 5.00	Ryanair Ltd	Dublin	A2003
EI-CSH	Boeing 737-8AS	29923	N1787B	9. 6.00	Ryanair Ltd	Dublin	A2003
EI-CSI	Boeing 737-8AS	29924	N1796B	12. 6.00	Ryanair Ltd	Dublin	A2003
EI-CSJ	Boeing 737-8AS	29925	N1786B	20. 6.00	Ryanair Ltd	Dublin	A2003
EI-CSK	British Aerospace BAe 146 Srs.200A	E2062	N810AS N880DV/G-5-062/N406XV/(G-BNDR)/G-5-062	3. 4.98	Cityjet Ltd *(Op Air France)*	Paris, France	A2003
EI-CSL	British Aerospace BAe 146 Srs.200A	E2074	N812AS N881DV/G-5-074/G-BNND/HS-TBQ/G-BNND/N146SB/N192US/N368PS/(G-BNND)/G-5-074	8. 5.98	Cityjet Ltd *(Op Air France)*	Paris, France	A2003
EI-CSM	Boeing 737-8AS	29926	N...	7.12.00	Ryanair Ltd	Dublin	A2003
EI-CSN	Boeing 737-8AS	29927	N...	11.12.00	Ryanair Ltd	Dublin	A2003
EI-CSO	Boeing 737-8AS	29928	N...	11. 1.01	Ryanair Ltd	Dublin	A2003
EI-CSP	Boeing 737-8AS	29929	N...	25. 1.01	Ryanair Ltd	Dublin	A2003
EI-CSQ	Boeing 737-8AS	29930	N...	26. 1.01	Ryanair Ltd	Dublin	A2003
EI-CSR	Boeing 737-8AS	29931	N...	5.12.01	Ryanair Ltd	Dublin	A2003
EI-CSS	Boeing 737-8AS	29932	N...	14.12.01	Ryanair Ltd	Dublin	A2003
EI-CST	Boeing 737-8AS	29933	N...	19.12.01	Ryanair Ltd	Dublin	A2003
EI-CSU	Boeing 737-36E	27626	EC-GGZ EC-799	14. 4.99	ILFC Ireland Ltd *(Op Air One)*	Pescara, Italy	A2003
EI-CSV	Boeing 737-8AS	29334		18. 1.02	Ryanair Ltd	Dublin	A2003
EI-CSW	Boeing 737-8AS	29935		4. 2.02	Ryanair Ltd	Dublin	A2003
EI-CSX	Boeing 737-8AS	32778		21. 5.02	Ryanair Ltd	Dublin	A2003
EI-CSY	Boeing 737-8AS	32779		25. 6.02	Ryanair Ltd	Dublin	A2003
EI-CSZ	Boeing 737-8AS	32780		15. 7.02	Ryanair Ltd	Dublin	A2003
EI-CTA	Boeing 737-8AS	29936		19. 11.02	Ryanair Ltd *(For delivery 2003)*	Dublin	
EI-CTB	Boeing 737-8AS	29937		19. 11.02	Ryanair Ltd *(For delivery 2003)*	Dublin	
EI-CTC	Medway EclipseR	158/137		2. 6.99	C.Brogan	Kilrush	N 1.03
EI-CTD	Airbus Industrie A320-211	0085	F-GJVZ F-WWDF	6. 5.99	Aerco Ireland Ltd *(Op VolareAirlines)*	Verona, Italy	A2003
EI-CTG	Stoddard-Hamilton SH-2R Glasair RG		N721WR	3. 6.99	K.Higgins	Carnmore, Galway	N 2.03
EI-CTI	Reims/Cessna FRA150L	FRA1500261	G-BCRN	29. 4.99	D.Bruton	Abbeyshrule	N 1.03
EI-CTL	Aerotech MW-5B Sorcerer *(Fuji-Robin EC-44-PM)*	SR102-R440B-07	G-MTFH	21. 5.99	M.Wade	Kilrush	N 1.03
EI-CTM	British Aerospace BAe 146 Srs.300	E3129	G-JEAL G-BTXN/HS-TBM/G-5-129	23. 3.99	Trident Aviation Leasing Services (Jersey) Ltd *(Op Aer Lingus)* "St.Fiacre/Fiacra"	Dublin	A2003
EI-CTN	British Aerospace BAe 146 Srs.300	E3169	G-BSNS EC-FHU/EC-839/G-6-169/G-BSNS/N887DV/G-BSNS/(N887DV)/G-6-169	4. 7.00	Trident Aviation Leasing Services (Jersey) Ltd *(Op Aer Lingus)* "St Cormac"	Dublin	A2003
EI-CTO	British Aerospace BAe 146 Srs.300	E3193	G-BUHC G-BTMI/(N883DV)/G-6-193	30. 5.00	Aer Lingus Ltd "St.Ciara/Ciara"	Dublin	A2003
EI-CTT	Piper PA-28-161 Cherokee Warrior II	28-7716305	N38974	14. 7.99	M.Farrell	Connaught	A12.01
EI-CTW	Boeing 767-341ER	30342		8.12.99	GECAS Technical Services Ltd *(Op Alitalia TEAM)*	Rome-Fiumicino, Italy	A2003
EI-CUA	Boeing 737-4K5	24901	D-AHLR	29. 9.99	Gustav Leasing XI Ltd *(Op Blue Panorama Airlines)*	Rome-Fiumicino, Italy	A2003
EI-CUD	Boeing 737-4Q8	26298	TC-JEI	13. 3.00	ILFC Ireland Ltd *(Op Blue Panorama Airlines)*	Rome-Fiumicino, Italy	A2003

EI-CUE	Cameron N-105 HAB	4683		16. 9.99	Bord Telecom Eireann *"EIRCOM"*	Dublin	A 9.01
EI-CUG	Bell 206B JetRanger II	4177	N248BC	21.10.99	J.O'Reilly & B.McNamara	Dublin	A2003
			N118GC				
EI-CUI	Robinson R44 Astro	0110	G-JANI	3. 3.00	Santail Ltd	Weston	A 1.03
			D-HIMM				
EI-CUJ	Cessna 172N Skyhawk II	17271985	G-BJGO	19.11.99	M.Casey & Partners	Cork	N 1.03
			N6038E				
EI-CUL	Boeing 737-36N	28559	PH-OZC	16. 2.00	Aircraft Finance Trust (Ireland) Ltd		
					(Op Philippine Airlines) Manila-Nino Aquino, Philippines		A2003
EI-CUN	Boeing 737-4K5	27074	D-AHLS	13. 4.00	Gustav Leasing XI Ltd Rome-Fiumicino, Italy		A2003
			(D-AHLG)		*(Op Blue Panorama Airlines)*		
EI-CUP	Cessna 335	335-0018	N2706X	5. 5.00	J.Greany	Kerry	A11.02
EI-CUQ	Airbus Industrie A320-214	1259	F-WWIZ	24. 7.00	Lumehavi Finance Ltd (Flightlease (Ireland) Ltd)		
					(Op Volare Airlines)	Verona, Italy	A2003
EI-CUS	Agusta-Bell 206B-3 JetRanger III	8721	G-BZKA	24. 8.00	Emerald Helicopter Consultants	Castleknock	A 7.01
			(EI-...)/G-OONS/G-LIND/G-OONS				
EI-CUT	Maule MX 7-180A	21080C		6. 4.01	Cosair Ltd	Trim	N 1.03
	(Nosewheel u/c)						
EI-CUW	Pilatus BN-2B-20 Islander	2293	G-BWYW	8.11.00	Galway Aviation Services Ltd	Connemara	A2003
					t/a Aer Arann Express		
EI-CVA	Airbus Industrie A320-214	1242	F-WWIT	22. 6.00	Aer Lingus Ltd *"St Schira/Scire"*	Dublin	A2003
EI-CVB	Airbus Industrie A320-214	1394	F-WWIV	8. 2.01	Aer Lingus Ltd *"St Mobhi"*	Dublin	A2003
EI-CVC	Airbus Industrie A320-214	1443	F-WWBG	6. 4.01	Aer Lingus Ltd *"St Kealin/Caoilfhionn"*	Dublin	A2003
EI-CVD	Airbus Industrie A320-214	1467	F-WWDK	10. 5.01	Aer Lingus Ltd *"St Kevin/Caoimhin"*	Dublin	A2003
EI-CVL	Ercoupe 415CD	4754	G-ASNF	??	Bernard Lyons & Jerry Hackett	Thurles	N10.01
			PH-NCF/NC94647				
EI-CVM	Schweizer Hughes 269C	S1328	G-GIRO	7.11.00	W.Moloney	Tralee, Co.Kerry	A 1.03
			N41S				
EI-CVN	Boeing 737-4YO	24684	TC-AFK	21.11.00	Airplanes Finance Ltd		
					(Op Philippine Airlines) Manila-Nino Aquino, Philippines		A2003
EI-CVO	Boeing 737-4S3	25594	SP-LLH	28.10.00	Aerco Ireland Ltd		
			N2423N/TC-AVA/9M-MLJ		*(Op Philippine Airlines)* Manila-Nino Aquino, Philippines		A2003
EI-CVP	Boeing 737-4YO	26081	TC-AFU	22.12.00	Airplanes Finance Ltd		
					(Op Philippine Airlines) Manila-Nino Aquino, Philippines		A2003
EI-CVR	Aérospatiale/Alenia ATR 42-310	022	F-GGLK	17. 1.01	Comhfhorbairt (Gaiiimh) Teo	Dublin	A2003
			OH-LTB/F-WWEI		*(Op Aer Arann Express)*		
EI-CVS	Aérospatiale/Alenia ATR 42-310	033	F-GIRC	16. 3.01	Comhfhorbairt (Gaiiimh) Teo	Dublin	A2003
			F-WIAF/OH-LTC/F-WWEO		*(Op Aer Arann Express)*		
EI-CVT	Gulfstream Gulfstream IV-SP	1419	N419GA	5. 4.01	AC Executive Aircraft Leasing	Farnborough	A 7.02
					(Op International Jet Club)		
EI-CWA	British Aerospace BAe 146 Srs.200	E2058	G-ECAL	7. 11.02	Cityjet Ltd	Dublin	
			N699AA/G-ECAL/(G-BMXE)/N148AC/G-5-058				
EI-CWB	British Aerospace BAe 146 Srs.200	E2051	SE-DRE	29. 3.01	Cityjet Ltd	Paris, France	A2003
			N694AA/N141AC/G-5-003/N141AC/G-5-003 *(Op Air France)*				
EI-CWC	British Aerospace BAe 146 Srs.200	E2053	SE-DRC	27. 4.01	Cityjet Ltd	Paris, France	A2003
			N695AA/N142AC/G-5-053/N142AC/G-5-053 *(Op Air France)*				
EI-CWD	British Aerospace BAe 146 Srs.200	E2108	SE-DRK	13. 6.01	Cityjet Ltd	Paris, France	A2003
			N295UE/G-5-108		*(Op Air France)*		
EI-CWE	Boeing 737-42C	24232	N941PG	18. 5.01	Rockshaw Ltd	Milan, Italy	A2003
			PH-BPE/G-UKLD		*(Op Air One)*		
EI-CWF	Boeing 737-42C	24814	PH-BPG	16. 5.01	Rockshaw Ltd	Milan, Italy	A2003
			G-UKLG		*(Op Air One)*		
EI-CWH	Agusta A109E	11106		17. 7.01	Lochbrea Aircraft Ltd	Carnmore, Galway	A2.03
EI-CWL	Robinson R22 Beta	0885	G-BXCX	19. 9.01	J.McLoughlin	Dunboyne	
			G-MFHL				
EI-CWP	Robinson R22 Beta	3233	G-CBBK	23.10.01	Santail Ltd	Weston	A 1.03
EI-CWR	Robinson R22 Beta	3234	G-CBDB	2.11.01	Inflight Aviation Ltd	Weston	N 1.03
EI-CWS	Schweizer 269C-1	0129	G-CBCN	27.11.01	Bob Scanlon (European Helicopter Academy) Dunboyne		N 1.03
EI-CWW	Boeing 737-4YO	24906	EC-GAZ	19.12.01	Airplanes Holdings Ltd	Milan, Italy	A2003
			EC-850/9M-MJO		*(Op Air One)*		
EI-CWX	Boeing 737-4YO	24912	EC-GBN	6.12.01	Airplanes Holdings Ltd	Milan, Italy	A2003
			EC-851/9M-MJQ		*(Op Air One)*		
EI-CXB	Boeing 767-3P6ER	24484	SP-LPD	26. 9.02	Pembroke 767 Ltd	USA	
			EI-CXB/HA-LHD/A40-GH		*(Stored)*		
EI-CXC	Raj Hamsa X'Air 502T	333	44SU)	6. 9.02	M.Treanor	Scotstown	
EI-CXD	Boeing 737-76N	29885		30. 4.02	GECAS Technical Services	Milan, Italy	A2003
					(Op Azzura Air)		
EI-CXE	Boeing 737-76N	32737			GECAS Technical Services	Milan, Italy	A2003
					(Op Azzura Air)		
EI-CXI	Boeing 737-46Q	28661	EC-GPI	5. 4.02	Bellevue Aircraft Leasing Ltd *(Op Air One)*	Milan, Italy	A2003
EI-CXJ	Boeing 737-4Q8	25164	G-BUHJ	22. 3.02	ILFC Ireland Ltd *(Op Air One)*	Milan, Italy	A2003
			N164LF				
EI-CXK	Boeing 737-4S3	25596	G-OGBA	9. 4.02	Skynet Airlines Ltd	Shannon	A2003
			G-OBMK				
EI-CXL	Boeing 737-46N	28723	G-SFBH	1. 5.02	Monroe Aircraft Ireland Ltd *(Op Air One)*	Milan, Italy	A2003
EI-CXM	Boeing 737-4Q8	26302	VH-VOZ	17. 5.02	ILFC Ireland Ltd *(Op Air One)*	Milan, Italy	A2003
			TC-JEM				
EI-CXN	Boeing 737-329	23772	OO-SDW	1. 5.02	Embarcadero Aircraft Securitization Trust Ireland Ltd		
			N506GX/OO-SDW		*(Op Transaero Airlines)* Moscow-Domodedovo, Russia		A2003
EI-CXO	Boeing 767-3GS	28111	N581LF	12. 4.02	ILFC Ireland Ltd	Milan, Italy	A2003
			D-AMUJ		*(Op Blue Panorama)*		
EI-CXP	Boeing 737-883	30467	LN-RPO	26. 4.02	Challey Ltd *(Op Air One)*	Milan, Italy	A2003
EI-CXR	Boeing 737-329	24355	OO-SYA	31. 5.02	Embarcadero Aircraft Securitization Trust Ireland Ltd		
			(OO-SQA)		*(Op Transaero Airlines)* Moscow-Domodedovo, Russia		A2003

EI-CXS	Sikorsky S.61N	61816	G-CBKZ	18. 10.02	CHC Ireland Ltd	Sligo	A 1.03
			LN-OQU		*(Op Irish Maritime Emergency Service)*		
EI-CXT	Boeing 737-883	30468	OY-KKT	7. 6.02	Challey Ltd *(Op Air One)*	Milan, Italy	A2003
			LN-RPR/SE-DTP/N1787B				
EI-CXU	Boeing 737-883	28323	LN-RPD	8. 5.02	Challey Ltd *(Op Air One)*	Milan, Italy	A2003
			SE-DYA/(SE-DTO)/(LN-RPM)/N1786B				
EI-CXV	Boeing 737-8CX	32364		3. 7.02	Jackson Leasing Ireland Ltd	Ulan Bator, Mongolia	A2003
					(Op Mongolian Airlines)		
EI-CXW	Boeing 737-883	30194	LN-RPP	22. 5.02	Challey Ltd *(Op Air One)*	Milan, Italy	A2003
			(SE-DTO)/(OY-KKN)				
EI-CXX							
EI-CXY	Evektor EV-97 Eurostar	(20000701)	OK-FUR	31. 10.02	Gerard Doody & Edward McEvoy	Portlaoise	A 1.03
EI-CXZ	Boeing 767-216ER	24973	N502GX	25. 7.02	Embarcadero Aircraft Securitization Trust Ireland Ltd		
			VH-RMM/N483GX/CC-CEF		*(Op Transaero Airlines)*	Moscow-Domodedovo, Russia	A2003
EI-CZA	HOAC DV-20 Katana	NK			Not known	Carnmore, Galway	N 2.03
EI-CZC	CFM Streak Shadow	K269SA11	G-BWHJ	16. 7.02	Michael Devane	Kerry Airport	
EI-CZD	Boeing 767-216ER	23623	N762TA	2. 9.02	Embarcadero Aircraft Securitization Trust Ireland Ltd		
			CC-CJU/N4529T		*(Op Transaero Airlines)*	Moscow-Domodedovo, Russia	A2003
EI-CZF	Airbus Industrie A319-112	1160	OO-SSG	7. 8.02	Ensor Aircraft Leasing	Bremen	
			D-AVWL				
EI-CZG	Boeing 737-400	25740	VH-VGB	8. 10.02	ILFC Ireland Ltd *(Op Air One)*	Milan, Italy	A2003
			N257BR/SU-PTA/EC-HAN/TC-JED				
EI-CZH	Boeing 767-3G5ER	29435	D-AMUO	9. 8.02	ILTU Ireland Ltd *(Op Blue Panorama)*	Milan, Italy	A2003
EI-CZI	Robinson R22B Beta	3374	N71849	10. 12.02	Lacken Agricultural Machinery Ltd	New Ross	
EI-CZJ	CFM Shadow Srs.B	012	G-MNSV	19. 9.02	F.Lynch	Fermoy	
EI-CZK	Boeing 737-4YO	24519	N519AP	10. 1.03	Skynet Airlines Ltd	Shannon	A2003
			TC-ACA/VR-CAB				
EI-CZL	Schweizer 269C-1	0147	N86G	19.12.02	E.Dunican Holding Ltd	Weston	
EI-CZM							
EI-CZN							
EI-CZO	British Aerospace BAe 146 Srs.200	E2024	G-CLHA	3.03R	CityJet Ltd *(Op Air France)*	Paris, France	
			(G-GNTX)/G-DEBC/N168US/N348PS				
EI-CZP							
EI-CZR	Airbus Industrie A330-200	290	OO-SFQ	6. 1.03	Calliope Ltd	Dublin	
			F-WWKQ				
EI-CZS	Airbus Industrie A330-200	296	OO-SFR	6. 1.03	Calliope Ltd	Dublin	
			F-WWYC/F-WWKO				
EI-CZT	Airbus Industrie A330-200	300	OO-SFS	6. 1.03	Calliope Ltd	Dublin	
			F-WWYG/(PT-MVE)				
EI-DAA	Airbus Industrie A330-202	397	F-WWKX	17. 4.01	Aer Lingus Ltd *"St Keeva/Caoimhe"*	Dublin	A2003
EI-DAB	Cessna 550 Citation Bravo	550-0917	N5100V	4. 4.00	D.Colgan/Eurojet	Biggin Hill	A11.01
EI-DAC	Boeing 737-8AS	29938		2. 12.02	Ryanair Ltd	Dublin	A2003
EI-DAD	Boeing 737-8AS	33544		3. 12.02	Ryanair Ltd	Dublin	A2003
EI-DAE	Boeing 737-8AS	33545		9. 12.02	Ryanair Ltd	Dublin	A2003
EI-DAF	Boeing 737-8AS	29939		9. 1.03	Ryanair Ltd	Dublin	A2003
EI-DAG	Boeing 737-8AS	29940		17. 1.03	Ryanair Ltd	Dublin	A2003
EI-DAH	Boeing 737-8AS	33546		22. 1.03	Ryanair Ltd	Dublin	
EI-DAI	Boeing 737-8AS	33547		02R	Ryanair Ltd	Dublin	
EI-DAJ	Boeing 737-8AS	33548		02R	Ryanair Ltd	Dublin	
EI-DHL	Airbus Industrie A300B4-203F	274	PH-SFM	21. 6.01	Air Contractors (Ireland) Ltd *(Op DHL)*	Dublin	A2003
			N227KW/N14977/N235EA/F-GDVC				
EI-DLA	McDonnell Douglas DC-10-30	46958	N883LA	22. 6.94	GECAS Technical Services Ltd	Mojave, Colorado, USA	N10.00
			EI-DLA/RP-C2003/(RP-C2000)/(PH-DTM) *(Stored)*				
EI-DLP	Agusta A109C	7657	N611VA	8.02R	Sloane Helicopters Inc	Shannon	
			N97CN				
EI-DMG	Cessna 441 Conquest	441-0165	N140MP	4. 7.01	Dawn Meats Group	Waterford	A 1.03
			N27214				
EI-DUB	Airbus Industrie A330-301ER	055	F-WWKP	6. 5.94	Aer Lingus Ltd *"St.Brigid/Brighid"*	Dublin	A2003
EI-ECA	Agusta A109A II	7387	N109RP	28. 2.97	Backdrive Ltd *(Op Ace Helicopters Ltd)*	Drogheda	A12.01
			JA9662				
EI-EDR	Piper PA-28R-200 Cherokee Arrow II		G-BCGD	19.11.87	Kestrel Flying Group Ltd	Dublin	A 8.02
		28R-7435265	N9628N				
EI-EEC	Piper PA-23-250 Aztec E	27-7554045	G-SATO	6. 2.92	Westair Aviation Ltd	Shannon	A 9.01
			G-BCXP/N54257				
EI-ELL	Medway EclipseR	157/136		2. 6.99	Microflex Ltd	Kilrush	N 1.03
EI-EUR	Eurocopter EC 120B	1138	G-BZMK	14.12.00	Atlantic Helicopters Ltd	Dublin	N 1.03
			F-WQOE				
EI-EWR	Airbus Industrie A330-202	330	F-WWKV	9. 5.00	Aer Lingus Ltd	Dublin	A2003
					"Laurence O'Toole / Lorcan O'Tuathail"		
EI-EXP*	Short SD.3-30 Var.100	SH.3092	G-BKMU	23. 7.92	Ireland Airways Holdings Ltd	Alton, Hants	N 4.00
			SE-IYO/G-BKMU/G-14-3092/EI-BEH/EI-BEG/G-BKMU/G-14-3092 *(Cancelled as scrapped 22.8.00)*				
EI-FBG	Reims/Cessna F182Q Skylane	F18200032	D-EFBG	4. 7.00	Messrs Tunney, Helly & Spelman	Weston	A 1.03
			(F-GAGU)				
EI-FKC	Fokker F.27 Mk 050	20177	PH-EXC	23. 2.90	Aer Lingus Ltd	Woensdrecht, The Netherlands	N 2.01
	(Fokker 50)				*"St.Fidelma" (Stored)*		
EI-FKD	Fokker F.27 Mk 050	20181	PH-EXG	12. 4.90	Aer Lingus Ltd	Woensdrecht, The Netherlands	N 2.01
	(Fokker 50)				*"St.Mel" (Stored)*		
EI-FKE	Fokker F.27 Mk 050	20208	PH-EXA	28. 1.91	Aer Lingus Ltd	Woensdrecht, The Netherlands	N 2.01
	(Fokker 50)				*"St.Pappin" (Stored)*		
EI-FKF	Fokker F.27 Mk 050	20209	PH-EXE	8. 2.91	Aer Lingus Ltd	Woensdrecht, The Netherlands	N 4.01
	(Fokker 50)				*"St.Ultan" (Stored)*		
EI-GER	Maule MX-7-180A Star Rocket	20006C		7. 1.94	P.J.L.Ryan	Trim	N 1.03
	(Tail-wheel u/c)						
EI-GFC	SOCATA TB-9 Tampico	141	G-BIAA	9.10.93	B.McGrath, J.Ryan & D.O'Neill	Waterford	A 1.02

EI-GSE	Cessna F.172M	1105	D-EDXO	12. 4.02	Frank Doherty	Donegal	
EI-GSM	Cessna 182S	18280188	N9541Q	17. 6.98	Westpoint Flying Group	Dublin	N 1.03
EI-GWY	Cessna 172R Skyhawk	17280162	N9497F	31.12.97	Galway Flying Club Ltd	Galway	A 1.03
EI-HAM	*Light-Aero Avid Flyer (Rotax 582)*	*1072-90*		18.11.96	*H.Goulding*	*Bray*	
EI-HCA	Boeing 727-225F	20382	N8839E	15. 4.94	Air Contractors (Ireland) Ltd	Singapore	A2003
EI-HCB	Boeing 727-223F	19492	N6817	2. 9.95	Air Contractors (Ireland) Ltd	Kemble	A2003
			EI-HCB/N6817		*(For scrapping 1.03)*		
EI-HCI	Boeing 727-223F	20183	N6830	23. 5.95	Air Contractors (Ireland) Ltd	Singapore	A2003
EI-HCS	Grob G-109B	6414	G-BMHR	18. 8.95	H.Sydner	Boleybeg, Ballymore Castle	A 9.01
EI-HER	Bell 206B-3 JetRanger III	3408	G-HIER	1. 7.94	Irish Helicopters Ltd	Dublin	A10.02
			G-BRFD/N2069N				
EI-HXM	Bell 206B JetRanger II	4105	ZS-HXM	28. 7.00	Euprepia Enterprises Ltd	Celtic/Knocksedan	N 1.03
			N7131J				
EI-IAU	Learjet Learjet 60	190	N190LJ	11.12.00	Irish Air Transport	Prestwick	A 1.03
			N5012K				
EI-IAW	Learjet Learjet 60	218	N8084J	14. 6.01	Irish Air Transport	Prestwick	A11.01
			N50157				
EI-IPC	Fairey Britten-Norman BN-2A-26 Islander	2011	G-CHES	24. 1.02	Irish Parachute Club	Clonbulloge	A 1.03
			G-PASY/G-BPCB/G-BEXA/G-MALI/(ZB503)/G-DIVE/G-BEXA				
EI-IRE	Canadair CL.600-2B16 Challenger	5515	N515DM	20. 8.02	Starair (Ireland)Ltd	Dublin	A 1.03
			C-GLXF				
EI-IRV	Aérospatiale AS350B Ecureuil	1713	D-HENY	7.10.96	Rathalope Ltd	Barberston House	A12.01
EI-IZO	Eurocopter EC 120B	1191	G-BZUS	26. 7.01	Cloud Nine Helicopters Ltd	Carlow	A12.01
			F-WQOU				
EI-JBC	Agusta A109A	7126	F-GATN	24. 7.97	Medeva Properties Ltd	Dublin Heliport	N 5.00
EI-JFD	Robinson R44	0969		13. 3.01	New World Plant Ltd	Galway	N 1.03
EI-JFK	Airbus Industrie A330-301	086	F-GMDE	11. 7.95	Aer Lingus Ltd *"St.Colmcille"*	Dublin	A2002
EI-JIV	Lockheed L.382G Hercules	4673	ZS-JIV	15. 11.02	Air Contractors (Ireland) Ltd	Dublin	
			D2-THE/ZS-JIV				
EI-JVL	Lockheed L.382G-35C Hercules	4676	ZS-JVL	30. 8.02	Air Contractors (Ireland)Ltd	Dublin	N 1.03
			PH-RMH/D2-TAA/ZS-JVL/D2-TAA/ZS-JVL				
EI-JWM	Robinson R.22 Beta	1386	G-BSLB	21.11.92	C.Shiel	Weston	A10.00
EI-LAX	Airbus Industrie A330-202	269	F-WWKV	29. 4.99	Aer Lingus Ltd *"St.Mella/Mella"*	Dublin	A2003
EI-LCH	Boeing 727-281F	20466	N903PG	6. 2.95	Air Contractors (Ireland) Ltd	Dublin	A2002
			N527MD/HL7355/JA8332				
EI-LIT	MBB Bö.105S	S.434	A6-DBH	20. 2.96	Irish Helicopters Ltd	Cork	A 9.01
			Dubai 105/D-HDMH				
EI-LKS	Eurocopter EC.130B4	3643	F-WQDQ	20. 1.03	WIGAF Leasing Co.Ltd *(Op Links Helicopters)*	Shannon	N 1.03
EI-LNX	Eurocopter EC-130B4	3498	N460AE	10. 6.02	WIGAF Leasing Co.Ltd *(Op Links Helicopters)*	Shannon	N 1.03
EI-LRS	*Schweizer Hughes 269C*	*S.1701*	*N41S*	6. 3.95	*Lynch Roofing Systems Ltd*	*Galway*	
EI-MAG	Robinson R22 Beta	2592	G-DHGS	3. 8.01	Airo Helicopters Ltd	Bagnelstown, Carlow	A 1.03
EI-MCF	Cessna 172R	172080799	N2469D	20. 1.00	Galway Flying Club	Carnmore, Galway	A 2.03
EI-MEL	Agusta A109C	7672	LV-WXA	20. 6.00	Ballymore Properties Ltd	Dublin Heliport	N 1.03
			N27ET/LV-WXA/N4NM				
EI-MER	Bell 206B	4513	N60507	28. 9.99	Gaelic Helicopters Ltd	Westpoint	A10.02
EI-MES	Sikorsky S-61N	61776	G-BXAE	27. 3.97	CHC Ireland Ltd	Cork	A2003
			LN-OQO		*(Op Irish Marine Emergency Service)*		
EI-MIK	Eurocopter EC 120B	1104	G-BZIU	22. 6.01	Bachir Ltd	Oranmore	N 1.03
EI-MIP	Aérospatiale SA.365N Dauphin 2	6119	G-BLEY	20. 3.96	CHC Ireland Ltd	Cork	A2003
			F-WTNM				
EI-MIT	Agusta A109E	11162		17. 1.03	Mercury Engineering Ltd	Dublin	A 1.03
EI-MON	Boeing 757-2YO	26151	4X-BAY	4.02	Monarch Airlines (Lease)	Lasham	
			SE-DUL/SX-BBY/XA-KWK/XA-SCB *(Stored 1.03 - for export as G-ZAPU)*				
EI-MUL	Robinson R44 Raven	1074		29. 8.01	Cotton Box Design Group Ltd	Galway	
EI-MYO	AS.350BA	1903		10. 1.02	SELC Ireland Ltd	Belmullet	
EI-ONE	Bell 206B JetRanger II	1761	EI-CJM	30. 5.96	Helicopter Sales Leasing Ltd	Weston	A 8.02
			N281C/N49582				
EI-ORD	Airbus Industrie A330-301	059	(EI-USA)	6. 6.97	Aer Lingus plc *"St.Maeve/Maedh"*	Dublin	A2003
			F-GMDD				
EI-OZA	Airbus Industrie A300B4-103	148	F-GOZA	5. 4.02	Air Contractors (Ireland) Ltd	Dublin	
EI-OZB	Airbus Industrie A300B4-103	184	F-GOZB	5. 4.02	Air Contractors (Ireland) Ltd	Dublin	
EI-OZC	Airbus Industrie A300B4-103	189	F-GOZC	8. 2.02	Air Contractors (Ireland) Ltd	Dublin	
EI-PAL	Cessna 550 Citation Bravo	550-0935	N5264A	31. 8.00	Pacific Aviation Ltd *(Op Eurojet Aviation Ltd)*	Dublin	A 7.02
EI-PAM	Boeing 737-4Q8	24069	G-BNNK	21.12.01	IAI Marichan Ltd *(Op Panair)*	Palermo, Italy	A2003
EI-PAR	Boeing 737-308	24300	F-OMAL	13. 7.01	IAI Bailey Ltd *(Op Panair)*	Palermo, Italy	A2003
			N737FA/XA-AMH/N737FA/B-2980/G-OBML/SE-DLA/G-KKUH				
EI-PAT	British Aerospace BAe.146 Srs.200	E2030	G-ZAPL	11.10.99	Brimstage Ltd *(Op Cityjet & op Air France)*	Paris, France	A2003
			G-WLCY/N172US/N352US				
EI-PAX	Cessna 560XL	5228			Pacific Aviation Ltd *(Op Eurojet Ireland Ltd)*	Dublin	A2003
EI-PCI	Bell 206B Jet Ranger			R			
EI-PMI	*Agusta-Bell 206B-3 JetRanger III*	*8614*	*EI-BLG*	19. 9.96	*Ping Golf Equipment Ltd*	*Dublin*	*A 8.99*
			G-BIGS				
EI-POD	Cessna 177B Cardinal	177B02729	N1444C	3. 8.95	Trim Flying Club Ltd	Trim	N 1.03
EI-PRI	Bell 206B Jet Ranger	4523	N6389V	29. 2.00	Brentwood Properties Ltd	Castleknock	A10.02
			C-GLZM				
EI-RCG	Sikorsky S.61N	61807	G-BZSN	25. 9.01	CHC Ireland Ltd	Shannon	A2003
			LN-OQB				
EI-REA	Aérospatiale/Alenia ATR 72-201	441	F-WQNC	30. 5.02	Comhfhorbairt (Gaillimh) Teo	Dublin	A2003
			G-BWTL/F-WWLG		*(Op Aer Arann Express*		
EI-REB	Aérospatiale/Alenia ATR 72-201	470	F-WONH	17. 5.02	Comhfhorbairt (Gaillimh) Teo	Dublin	A2003
			F-WQOL/F-WQOF/G-BWTM/F-WWED *(Op Aer Arann Express)*				
EI-RMC	Bell 206B Jet Ranger	488	G-BWLO	16.12.99	Westair Aviation Ltd	Shannon	A 7.01
			N2290W				

Reg	Type	c/n	Prev id	Date	Owner/Operator	Base	Source
EI-RNJ	British Aerospace BAe 125 Srs.800	258414	N800XM N800XP/N30742	11. 6.02	Westair Aviation Ltd	Shannon	A 1.03
EI-RZZ	Robinson R.22B2 Beta	2982	G-PWEL	6. 6.02	Ultimate Flight Ops.Ltd	Galway	
EI-SAC	Cessna 172P Skyhawk	17276263	N98149	22. 9.00	Sligo Aeronautical Club	Strandhill	A 8.02
EI-SAF	Airbus Industrie A300B4-203F	220	PH-SFL N860PA/SE-DSF/N74989/N231EA/F-GBNY *(Op DHL)* *(Reserved as OO-DIC 12.02)*	26. 7.01	Air Contractors (Ireland) Ltd	Dublin	A2003
EI-SAM	Extra EA.300/200	031	(D-EDGE (5))	19. 7.01	S & D Bruton	Abbeyshrule	N 1.03
EI-SAR	Sikorsky S-61N *(Mitsubishi c/n M61-001)*	61-143	G-AYOM N4585/JA9506/N94565 *(Op Irish Marine Emergency Service)*	26. 6.98	CHC Ireland Ltd	Cork	A 1.03
EI-SAT	Steen Skybolt	1	N52DH	22.10.99	Capt B.O'Sullivan	Trim	N 1.03
EI-SBP	Cessna T.206H	T20608159	N2354M N4234H	16. 8.00	P.Morrissey	Dublin	N 1.03
EI-SKT	Piper PA-44-180 Seminole	44-7995004	G-BGSG N36538	27. 11.02	Shemburn Ltd	Waterford	N 1.03
EI-SLF	Aérospatiale/Alenia ATR 72-202	210	OY-RUA B-22703/F-WWEH	26. 11.02	Air Contractors (Ireland) Ltd	Dublin	
EI-SQG	Agusta A109E Power	11084		1. 8.00	Quinn Group Ltd *(Slieve Russel Hotel titles)*	Dublin	A12.01
EI-STR	Bell 407	53282	N44504	19. 5.00	Barkisland (Developments) Ltd	Dublin Heliport	N 1.03
EI-STT	Cessna 172M	17266228	D-EVBB N9557H	30 .8.00	Garda Aviation Club Ltd	Weston	N 1.03
EI-TAA	Airbus Industrie A320-233	912	N458TA F-WWDU *(Op Cubana De Aviacion)*	20. 9.01	Rockshaw Ltd	Havana, Cuba	A2003
EI-TAB	Airbus Industrie A320-233	1624	(N485TA) F-WWIZ	27. 6.02	CIT Ireland Leasing Ltd *(Op TACA International Airlines)* San Salvador-Comalapa, El Salvador		
EI-TAC	Airbus Industrie A320-233	1676	F-WWBX (N486TA)/F-WWBX	18. 10.02	CIT Ireland Leasing Ltd *(Op TACA International Airlines)* San Salvador-Comalapa, El Salvador		
EI-TAI	Airbus Industrie A320-233	916	N459TA F-WWDX *(Op TACA International Airlines)*	19. 9.01	Rockshaw Ltd	San Salvador-Comalapa, El Salvador	A2002
EI-TBM	SOCATA TBM.700	232		3. 7.02	Folens Management Services Ltd	Weston	N 1.03
EI-TIP	Bell 430	49074	N430MK N9151Z/C-GAHJ	12. 6.02	Starair (Ireland) Ltd	Cloughran	
EI-TKI	Robinson R.22 Beta	1195	G-OBIP	22. 8.91	J.McDaid	Weston	A10.00
EI-TOY*	Eurocopter EC120B	1257		6.02R	NTU - remained as G-CBJF -see SECTION 1		
EI-UFO	Piper PA-22-150 Tri-Pacer *(Tail-wheel conversion)*	22-4942	G-BRZR N7045D	12. 2.94	W.Treacy	Trim	N 9.00
EI-VNE	Eurocopter EC.120B	1253	G-CBHS	17. 5.02	Seafield Demesne Management Ltd	Weston	A11.02
EI-WAC	Piper PA-23-250 Aztec E	27-4683	G-AZBK N14077	26. 5.95	Westair Aviation Ltd	Shannon	A 7.01
EI-WAV	Bell 430	49028	N4213V	24.12.97	Westair Aviation Ltd	Shannon	A12.01
EI-WDC	Hawker Siddeley HS.125 Srs.3B	25132	G-OCBA EI-WDC/G-OCBA/G-MRFB/G-AZVS/OY-DKP	2. 7.94	Westair Aviation Ltd	Shannon	A11.01
EI-WGV	Gulfstream G.1159 Gulfstream V	505	N505GV	21.11.97	Westair Aviation Ltd *"Born Free"*	Shannon	A12.01
EI-WJN	Hawker Siddeley HS.125 Srs.700A	257062	N416RD N26EA/RA02809/G-5-708/RA02809/((G-BWJX)/G-5-708/N7062B/HB-VGF/G-5-708/HB-VGF/G-5-16	30. 5.00	Westair Aviation Ltd	Shannon	A12.01
EI-WMN	Piper PA-23-250 Aztec F	27-7954063	G-ZSFT G-SALT/G-BGTH/N2551M/N9731N	12.10.00	Westair Aviation Ltd	Shannon	A 9.01
EI-WRC	Bell 222A	47029	EI-TAR N121NN/N121NC/N120NC	4. 5.00	Westair Aviation Ltd	Shannon	A 8.00
EI-WRN	Piper PA-28-151 Cherokee Warrior	28-7615212	G-BDZX N9559N	5.10.99	Waterford Aero Club Ltd	Waterford	A 6.01
EI-WSN	Bell 206B JetRanger II	1669	G-CHGL G-BPNG/G-ORTC/G-BPNG/N20EA/C-GHVB	24. 3.00	Westair Aviation Ltd	Shannon	A 9.01

Registrations awaited

Reg	Type	c/n	Prev id	Date	Owner/Operator
EI-...	Aerial Arts Chaser S	CH723	G-MVGI	1.03	Not yet known
EI-...	Bell 206B	407	N208M JA9850/C-GAJN	12.02	Not yet known

SECTION 3

UNITED KINGDOM & IRELAND REGISTRATIONS ADDED & REMOVED DURING 2002/3

Regn	Type	C/n	P/I	Date	Owner/Operator	Cancellation Details	
G-BACM	Reims/Cessna FRA150L	FRA1500160	EI-BRX	27. 5.02	J.H.A.Clarke	Sold as EI-...	29. 5.02
			G-BACM				
G-BZYJ	Westland SA.314B Gazelle AH.1	1152	XW885	3. 4.02	Military Helicopters Ltd	To G-ZZEL	25.11.02
G-CBKZ	Sikorsky S.61N	61816	LN-OQU	30. 4.02	CHC Scotia Ltd	Sold as EI-CXS	17.10.02
G-CBLC	Cameron A-530 HAB	10170		11. 3.02	Cameron Balloons Ltd	Sold as PH-NGN	7. 5.02
G-CBND	Sikorsky S-76C	760375	B-HZG	12. 4.02	Nash Group Ltd	Sold as N775AB	20. 8.02
			VR-HZG/HKG-20				
G-CBNE	Sikorsky S-76C	760376	B-HZH	12. 4.02	Nash Group Ltd	Sold as N776AB	20. 8.02
			VR-HZH/HKG-21/N7600A				
G-CBMN	Cessna 182P Skylane	18261643	ZS-KJS	16. 5.02	E.W.Guess (Holdings) Ltd	To G-GUMS	11.11.02
			N21458				
G-CBNH	Enstrom 280FX Shark	2044	Chilean Army	17. 4.02	Eastern Atlantic Helicopters Ltd	To G-VRTX	8. 7.02
			H-180				
G-CBNP	Bombardier BD-700-1A10 Global Express	9032	G-52-26	18. 4.02	Marshall of Cambridge Aerospace Ltd	Sold as OY-MSI	19. 8.02
			N700HE/C-GFAK				
G-CBOH	Airbus Industrie A319-112	1068	OO-SSB	19. 6.02	Magritte Aircraft Leasing Ltd	Sold as F-...	16. 9.02
			D-AVWD				
G-CBOI	Airbus Industrie A321-211	1012	OO-SUC	19. 6.02	Magritte Aircraft Leasing Ltd	Sold as F-...	19. 9.02
			D-AVZH				
G-CBOJ	Airbus Industrie A319-112	1145	OO-SSF	19. 6.02	Magritte Aircraft Leasing Ltd	Sold as F-...	26. 9.02
			D-AVWH				
G-CBRS	Cameron Mikey-90 SS HAB	10301		18. 6.02	Cameron Balloons Ltd	Sold as VH-	21. 2.03
G-CBSG	Westland Gazelle HT.Mk2	2012	ZB649	6. 6.02	London Helicopter Centres Ltd	To G-SIVJ	26. 6.02
G-CBSY	Airbus Industrie A319-112	1388	OO-SSM	11. 7.02	Magritte Aircraft Leasing Ltd	Sold as F-...	26. 9.02
			D-AVYG				
G-CBTJ	Cessna T182T	T18208127	N5170R	5. 8.02	Oxford Aviation Services Ltd	To G-OLDG	17.10.02
G-CBTP	Airbus Industrie A319-112	1336	OO-SSK	6. 8.02	Magritte Aircraft Leasing Ltd	Sold as F-...	26. 9.02
			D-AVYL				
G-CBUT	Cameron Z-315 HAB	10290		5. 8.02	Cameron Balloons Ltd	Sold as C-	7. 2.03
G-CBVJ	Boeing 737-2T4	22802	UR-GAD	28. 8.02	Elasis Leasing IV Ltd	Sold as N203YT	12. 2.03
			B-610L/B-2501/N6009F/N4561K/(N88AF)				
G-CBYG	Lindstrand LBL 77A HAB	885		2.12.02	R.J.Henderson	Transferred to Hong Kong	28. 2.03
G-CBYK	Beech B60 Duke	P-544	N3669D	6.12.02	N.J.Vetch	Sold as N3669D	13. 1.03
G-CBYL	Enstrom 280FX	2078	HB-XAJ	22.10.02	Eastern Atlantic Helicopters Ltd	To G-OGES	15.11.02
G-CCAI	British Aircraft Corporation BAC.167 Strikemaster Mk.80A	EEP/JP/3688	R Saudi AF 1121/G-27-232	28. 1.03	R.J.Everett	Sold as N799PS	4. 2.03
G-CELW	Boeing 737-377	23659	VH-CZG	4. 7.02	Dart Group plc	Sold as N659DG	15. 8.02
G-LOFH	Lockheed L-188C Electra	1140	N9744C	28. 8.02	European Aero Leases Ltd	Sold as N4HG	17. 2.03
G-OSMA	SOCATA TB-20 Trinidad	1809	F-WWRS	5. 3.02	Societe de Motorisations Aeronautiques B-N Group Ltd	Sold as F-...	5. 8.02
G-OXLA	Boeing 737-81Q	30619	N733MA	1. 6.01	Excel Airways Ltd	To N733MA	(See note)
			G-OXLA/N733MA				

(The entry was omitted from SECTION 3 of 2002 Edition being allocated @ 1.6.01 & cancelled to N733MA @ 5.11.01. it was since restored from N733MA on 31.5.02 but reverted to N733MA on 27.10.02)

G-VINS	Cameron N-90 HAB	4731		18. 3.02	Les Montgolfieres du Sud SARL	Sold as F-GVIN	7. 5.02

(Cancelled 27.2.02 by CAA, restored 18.3.02)

SECTION 4

PART 1 – MUSEUMS & PRIVATE COLLECTIONS

The introduction of this Section was foreshadowed last year. The sole qualification for inclusion is that all entries were originally allocated either United Kingdom and Ireland registrations, BGA and BAPC allocations or "B" Conditions markings and remain in existence. Furthermore, these registrations are now officially cancelled and details are shown. All entries are usually available to the public being Gate Guardians or located within Museums and private collections and these can be made accessible, in some cases, by prior permission. Some are held in Museum stores and may not be available for viewing: these are annotated. As a consequence, this allows numerous entries formerly within Section 1 to be located in a more suitable setting. Beware that some Museums and private collections also hold specimens which retain current Certificates of Registration and remain pertinent to Section 1, therefore.

It is hoped to extend to the Section next year to cater for the numerous formerly registered United Kingdom & Ireland aircraft still to be found elsewhere in Museums & collections world-wide but which have not featured in our Registers for many years, if at all. Indeed, some are included this year. In addition, the listing will include those aircraft which were only allocated CAA's "B" Conditions before being sold abroad. As such, entries will be located under their original G- & EI- registration with details of subsequent markings now carried. Accordingly, I invite readers to submit new candidates for inclusion next year. In compiling this new Section I am grateful for Ken Ellis and his 18th Edition of "Wrecks & Relics" and, also, to Bernard Martin for reviewing and updating certain information.

Regn	Type	C/n	P/I	Date	Remarks	CA Expiry

UNITED KINGDOM

BEDFORDSHIRE
Stondon Transport Museum, Lower Stondon SG16 JN (www.transportmuseum.co.uk)

Regn	Type	C/n	P/I	Date	Remarks	CA Expiry
G-AXOM	Penn-Smith Gyroplane	DJPS.1		26. 9.69	Cancelled 11.10.74 as WFU	24. 2.71P
	(Volkswagen 1600)					
BAPC.77	Mignet HM.14 Pou-Du-Ciel	--			*(As "G-ADRG")*	
	(Citroën 425cc) *(Modern reproduction)*					

The Shuttleworth Collection, Old Warden SG18 9EP (www.shuttleworth.org)

Regn	Type	C/n	P/I	Date	Remarks	CA Expiry
BAPC 1	Roe Triplane rep	--			See G-ARSG in SECTION 1	
BAPC 2	Bristol Boxkite rep	--			See G-ASPP in SECTION 1	
BAPC 3	Bleriot XI	--			See G-AANG(2) in SECTION 1	
BAPC 4	Deperdussin	--			See G-AANH(2) in SECTION 1	
BAPC 5	Blackburn monoplane	--			See G-AANI(2) in SECTION 1	
BAPC.8	Dixon Ornithopter					
BAPC11	English Electric Wren	--			See G-EBNV in SECTION 1	

BERKSHIRE
British Balloon Museum & Library, Newbury

Regn	Type	C/n	P/I	Date	Remarks	CA Expiry
G-ATGN	Thorn K-800 Coal Gas Balloon	2		12. 7.65	Cancelled 23.6.81 as WFU *"Eccles"*	
G-ATXR	Abingdon Gas Balloon HAB	A.F.B.1		22. 7.66	Cancelled 14.7.86 by CAA *(Basket only)*	1. 9.76
G-AVTL	Brighton Ax7-65 HAB	01		17. 8.67	Cancelled 11.9.81 as WFU	
	(Orig regd as Hot-Air Group/FB with c/n 1)					
G-AWCR	Piccard Ax6 HAB	6204		29. 1.68	Cancelled 24.5.78 as WFU *"London Pride 1"*	
G-AWJB	Brighton MAB-65 HAB	MAB-3		3. 5.68	Cancelled 4.12.70 on sale to Italy	
					(To HB-BOU(1) 2.73) (As "HB-BOU")	
G-AWMO	Omega O-84 HAB	01		31. 7.68	Cancelled 13.5.69 *(To OY-BOB 5.69) "Blue Strike"*	
G-AWOK	Sussex Gas (Free) Balloon	SARD.1		7. 8.68	Cancelled 29.2.84 as WFU *(Withdrawn 1970) "Sardinia"*	
G-AXMD	Omega O-20 HAB	06		7. 8.69	Cancelled 7.12.89 as WFU *"Nimble"*	
	(Acquired second envelope c/n 07 c.1969/70 but not known which one BBML holds)					
G-AXVU	Omega 84 HAB	09		7. 1.70	Cancelled 22.8.89 as WFU *"Henry VIII"*	28. 4.77
G-AXXP	Bradshaw HAB-76 (Ax7) HAB	RB.001		20. 2.70	Cancelled 9.9.81 *(WFU 2.77) "Ignis Volens"*	
G-AYAJ	Cameron O-84 HAB	11		31. 3.70	Cancelled 1.2.90 as WFU *"Flaming Pearl"*	
G-AYAL	Omega 56 HAB	10		2. 4.70	Cancelled 18.10.84 by CAA *"Nimble II"*	25. 8.76
G-AYJZ	Cameron (Ax8) O-84 HAB	16		30. 9.70	Cancelled 21.5.75 *"Godolphin"*	
	(Original canopy replaced by c/n 433)				*(To EI-BAY 5.75) (As "EI-BAY")*	
G-AZBH	Cameron O-84 HAB	23		8. 7.71	Cancelled 30.8.85 as WFU *"Serendipity"*	10. 5.81
G-AZER	Cameron O-42 (Ax5) HAB	26		9. 9.71	Cancelled 25.3.92 by CAA *"Shy Tot"*	15. 5.81A
G-AZJI	Western O-65 HAB	007		2.12.71	Cancelled 19.5.93 by CAA *"Peek-A-Boo"*	
G-AZSP	Cameron O-84 HAB	43		18. 4.72	Cancelled 11.1.82 as WFU *"Esso"*	22. 3.82
G-AZUV	Cameron O-65 HAB	41		12. 5.72	Cancelled 6.1.82 *"Icarus"*	23. 6.83
					(Damaged & WFU Rendham Green, Suffolk)	
G-AZUW	Cameron A-140 HAB	45		12. 5.72	Cancelled 7.6.73 *"Cumulonimbus"*	
					(To F-WTVO 6.73, F-BTVO, 5Y-SIL)	
G-AZYL	Portslade School HAB	MK17		10. 7.72	Cancelled 25.4.85 as WFU	
G-BAMK	Cameron D-96 HA Airship	72		11. 1.73	Cancelled 16.8.00 by CAA *"Isibidbi"*	24. 4.90A
G-BAVU	Cameron A-105 HAB	66		11. 4.73	Cancelled 6.12.01 by CAA	5.10.84A
G-BAXF	Cameron O-77 HAB	74		3. 5.73	Cancelled 5.9.95 by CAA *"Granna"*	
G-BAXK	Thunder Ax7-77 HAB	005		9. 5.73	Cancelled 7.9.01 as WFU *"Jack O'Newbury"*	2. 7.91A
G-BBFS	Van Den Bemden K-460 (Gas) FB	VDB-16	OO-BGX	10. 8.73	Cancelled 19.5.93 by CAA *"Le Tomate"*	
G-BBLL	Cameron O-84 HAB	84		2.10.73	Cancelled 19.5.93 by CAA *"Boadicea"*	25. 5.81A
G-BBYU	Cameron O-56 HAB	96		19. 2.74	Cancelled 9.8.89 as WFU *"Chieftain"*	28. 2.82A
G-BCAR	Thunder Ax7-77 HAB	019		5. 3.74	Cancelled 2.4.92 by CAA *"Marie Antoinette"*	
G-BCFD	West Ax3-15 HAB	JW.1		16. 5.74	Cancelled 30.1.87 by CAA *"Hellfire"*	
G-BCFE	Byrne Odyssey 4000 MLB	AJB-2		20. 5.74	Cancelled 19.9.85 as WFU *"Odyssey"*	
G-BCGP	Gazebo Ax6-65 HAB	1		13. 6.74	Cancelled 18.12.79 as WFU *"Aries"*	
G-BDVG	Thunder Ax6-56A HAB	067		2. 4.76	Cancelled 3.4.92 by CAA *"Argonaut"*	
G-BEEE	Thunder Ax6-56A HAB	070		20. 8.76	Cancelled 19.5.93 by CAA *"Avia"*	11. 5.84A
G-BEPO	Cameron N-77 HAB	279		1. 4.77	Cancelled 14.5.98 as WFU *"Sungas"*	
G-BEPZ	Cameron D-96 HA Airship	300		13. 4.77	Cancelled 28.4.94 as WFU *"Zanussi"*	12. 2.90A
					(Damaged Warren Farm, Savernake Forest 8.1.94 & DBR during recovery)	

Reg	Type	c/n	prev id	Date	Status	Date
G-BETF	Cameron Champion 35SS HAB	280		17. 5.77	Cancelled 24.1.92 as WFU *"Champion"*	6. 4.84A
	(Champion Spark Plug shape)					
G-BETH	Thunder Ax6-56A HAB	113		27. 5.77	Cancelled 11.5.93 as WFU *"Debenhams"*	31. 5.78
G-BEVI (3)	Thunder Ax7-77A HAB	125		30. 5.77	Cancelled 8.1.92 as WFU *"Prime Bang"*	
G-BFAB	Cameron N-56 HAB	297		15. 8.77	Cancelled 21.4.92 by CAA *"Phonogram"* *(On loan from A.Gibson)*	
G-BFOZ	Thunder Ax6-56 Plug HAB	144		20. 3.78	Cancelled 16.4.92 by CAA *"Motorway"* *(Current status unknown)*	
G-BGAS	Colting Ax8-105A HAB	001		27. 6.78	Cancelled *(Destroyed Flims, Switzerland 20.9.80)* *(Basket only)*	
G-BGOO	Colt Flame 56SS HAB	039		27. 4.79	Cancelled 19.5.93 by CAA *"Mr Gas"*	
	(Smiling Flame shape)					
G-BGPF	Thunder Ax6-56Z HAB	206		13. 7.79	Cancelled 21.11.89 as WFU *"Pepsi"*	27. 6.82A
					(On loan from P.J.Bish)	
G-BHKN	Colt 14A Cloudhopper HAB	068		17. 1.80	Cancelled 5.12.89 as WFU *"Green Ice 2"*	
	(Officially regd as Colt 12A)					
G-BHKR	Colt 14A Cloudhopper HAB	071		17. 1.80	Cancelled 5.12.89 as WFU *"Green Ice 5"*	
	(Officially regd as Colt 12A)					
G-BIAZ	Cameron AT-165 (Helium/Hot-Air) FB	400		7. 2.78	Cancelled 27.5.80 *"Zanussi"*	31.10.78
	(Used for 1978 Atlantic attempt)				*(Hot Air envelope destroyed Trubenbuch, Austria 14.1.80) (Inner helium cell envelope only)*	
G-BIDV	Colt 17A Cloudhopper HAB	789		29. 1.79	Cancelled 20.5.93 by CAA *"Smirnoff"*	
	(Originally. was Colt 14A c/n 034)					
G-BIGT	Colt 77A HAB	078		28. 2.80	Cancelled 4.2.87 by CAA *"Big T"*	20. 2.83A
					(Damaged Belton Hall, Grantham 23.8.81)	
G-BKES	Cameron Bottle 57 SS HAB	846		25. 6.82	Cancelled 1.5.90 by CAA *"Robinsons Barley Water"*	
	(Robinsons Barley Water Bottle)					
G-BKMR	Thunder Ax3 Maxi Sky Chariot HAB	497		12. 1.83	Cancelled 23.4.98 as WFU *"The Weasel"*	
G-BLIO	Cameron R-42 Gas/HAB	1015		17. 4.84	Cancelled 24.1.90 as destroyed	17. 5.84P
G-BLKU	Colt Flame 56SS HAB	572		17. 7.84	Cancelled 1.5.92 as WFU *"Mr.Wonderful II"*	
G-BMEZ	Cameron DP-70 HA Airship	1130		18. 9.85	Cancelled 20.6.91	4. 5.89A
	(Originally regd as D-50)				*(Sold as EC-FUS)* *(Envelope only)*	
G-BNHN	Colt Ariel Bottle SS HAB	1045		30. 3.87	Cancelled 24.1.92 as WFU *"Ariel"*	
G-BOGR	Colt 180A HAB	1183		11. 5.88	Cancelled 28.4.97 as WFU *"Britannia"*	13. 3.92T
G-BOTL	Colt 42A SS HAB	466		23.11.82	Cancelled 21.11.89 as WFU *"Bottle"*	
G-BPKN	Colt AS-80 Mk.II HA Airship	1297		11. 1.89	Cancelled 7.1.91 by CAA *"Fuji"*	14. 3.91A
G-BRZC	Cameron N-90 HAB	2227		8. 2.90	Cancelled 29.4.97 as WFU *"Unipart II"*	2.12.92A
G-BUBL	Thunder Ax8-105 HAB	1147		10.12.87	Cancelled 16.6.98 as WFU *"Mercier/l'Espit D'Adventure"*	
G-BUUU	Cameron Bottle 77SS HAB	2980		11. 2.93	Cancelled 22.10.01 by CAA *"Bells Whisky"*	4. 3.94A
	(Bells Whisky Bottle shape)					
G-BVBX	Cameron N-90M HAB	3102		10. 8.93	Cancelled 10.2.97 as temporary WFU *"Mercury"*	27. 9.95A
G-CHUB	Colt Cylinder Two N-51 HAB	1720		11. 4.90	Cancelled 12.12.01 as WFU *"Chubb Fire Extinguisher"*	19.12.95A
	(Fire Extinguisher shape)					
G-FTFT	Colt Financial Times 90SS HAB	1163		14. 1.88	Cancelled 13.5.98 as WFU *"Financial Times"*	5. 6.95A
					(On loan from Financial Times Ltd)	
G-FZZZ	Colt 56A HAB	507		23. 2.83	Cancelled 29.4.97 as WFU *"Alka Seltzer 1"*	
G-LCIO	Colt 240A HAB	1381		23. 1.89	Cancelled 25.5.94 as WFU *"Star Flyer 2"*	
					(Damaged landing after first overflight Mt Everest by HAB 21.10.91)	
G-LOAG	Cameron N-77 HAB	359		10.11.77	Cancelled 31.3.93 as destroyed *"Famous Grouse"*	6. 4.84A
					(Envelope only)	
G-OBUD	Colt 69A HAB	698		26. 6.85	Cancelled 29.4.97 as WFU *"Budweiser"*	1. 2.90A
G-OFIZ	Cameron Can 80SS HAB	2106		30.10.89	Cancelled 10.2.97 as temporary WFU *"Andrews Can"*	2.12.91A
G-OLLI	Cameron O-31 HAB				See SECTION 1	
G-PARR	Colt Bottle 90SS HAB	1953		15. 3.91	Cancelled 10.2.97 as temporary WFU *"Old Parr"*	29. 9.94A
	(Old Parr Whisky bottle shape)					
G-PERR	Cameron Bottle 60SS HAB	699		28. 1.81	Cancelled 24.1.92 as WFU *"Perrier"*	3. 6.84A
G-PLUG	Colt 105A HAB	1958		17. 4.91	Cancelled 23.7.96 by CAA	14. 8.95T
G-PUBS	Colt Beer Glass 56SS HAB	037		7. 6.79	Cancelled 1.12.95 by CAA	
G-ZUMP	Cameron N-77 HAB	377		18. 1.78	Cancelled 8.4.98 as WFU *"Gazump"*	
	(Rebuilt 1985 with new canopy c/n 1107)					
BAPC.258	Adams Balloon (15,000 cu.ft)	--			Built GQ Parachutes	

Museum of Berkshire Aviation / Royal Berkshire Aviation Society & The Herald Society (+) ,Woodley RG5 4UF

Reg	Type	c/n	prev id	Date	Status	Date
G-AJJP	Fairey FB.2 Jet Gyrodyne	F.9420 & FB.2		1. 3.47	Cancelled 9.11.50	
					(To RAF as XD759 in 11.50) (As "XJ389")	
G-AKKY	Miles M.14A Hawk Trainer 3	2078	T9841	23. 6.48	Cancelled 12.4.73 as WFU	6.11.64
	(Also allocated BAPC.44 to reflect rebuild status from various parts)				*(WFU 11.60) (As "L6906")*	
G-APLK	Miles M.100 Student 2	100/1008		11. 3.58	Cancelled 31.8.84 to G-MIOO *(See SECTION 1)*	
G-APWA	Handley Page HPR.7 Dart Herald 100 (+)		PP-SDM	28. 9.59	Cancelled 29.1.87 as WFU	6. 4.82T
				149	G-APWA/PP-SDM/PP-ASV/G-APWA *(BEA titles)*	
BAPC.233	Broburn Wanderlust Sailplane	--			Built 1946	
BAPC.248	McBroom Hang-Glider	--			Built 1974	

BRISTOL
City Museum & Art Gallery, Clifton BS8 1RL (www.bristol-city.gov.uk/museums)

Reg	Type	c/n	prev id	Status
BAPC.40	Bristol Boxkite rep	BOX 3--	BM.7281	*("Those Magnificent Men in Their Flying Machines" film)*
	(Gnome)			

CAMBRIDGESHIRE
Imperial War Museum, Duxford CB2 4QR (www.iwm.org.uk)

Reg	Type	c/n	prev id	Date	Status	Date
G-ACUU	Avro 671 Cierva C.30A Autogiro	726	(G-AIXE)	26. 6.34	Cancelled 14.11.88 as WFU	30. 4.60
	(AS Civet)		HM580/G-ACUU		*(WFU 4.60) (As "HM580")*	
G-AFBS	Miles M.14A Hawk Trainer 3	539	(G-AKKU)	17. 9.37	Cancelled 22.12.95 by CAA	25. 2.63
			BB661/G-AFBS			
G-AHTW	Airspeed AS.40 Oxford 1	3083	V3388	6. 6.46	Cancelled 3.4.89 by CAA *(As "V3388")*	15.12.60
G-ALCK	Percival P.34A Proctor 3	H.536	LZ766	18. 6.48	WFU *(As "LZ766")*	19. 6.63
G-AMDA	Avro 652A Anson 1	--	N4877	20. 7.50	Cancelled 9.9.81 by CAA *(As "N4877")*	14.12.62

G-ASKC	de Havilland DH.98 Mosquito TT.35	--	TA719	8. 7.63	Crashed 27.7.64 *(As "TA719")*	18. 1.64
G-BCYK	Avro (Canada) CF-100 Canuck Mk.IV	--	RCAF 18393	18. 3.75	Cancelled 15.9.81 as WFU	
					(As "18393" in RCAF c/s)	
G-BEDV	Vickers 668 Varsity T.1	--	WJ945	26. 7.76	Cancelled 15.6.89 by CAA *(As "WJ945/21")*	15.10.87P
G-BESY	British Aircraft Corpn BAC.167 Strikemaster Mk.80A		G-27-299	26. 4.77	Cancelled 7.77	
	(Officially regd as Mk.88)	PS.364	Saudi AF 1133/G-27-299		*(As "1133" in Saudi c/s)*	
G-LANC	Avro 683 Lancaster B.X	--	RCAF KB889	31. 1.85	Cancelled 2.9.91 by CAA	
	(Built Victory Aircraft, Canada)				*(As "KB889/NA-I" in 428 Sqdn c/s)*	
G-LIZY	Westland Lysander III	"504/39"	RCAF 1558	20. 6.86	Cancelled 18.4.89 as WFU	
	(C/n also quoted as "Y1351")		V9300		*(As "V9673/MA-J" in 161 Sqdn c/s)*	
G-USUK	Colt 2500A HAB	1100		1. 6.87	Cancelled 21.8.90 as WFU *"Virgin Atlantic Flyer"*	19. 8.87P
					(On loan from Virgin Atlantic Airways Ltd) (Gondola displayed - remainder stored)	
EI-AUY	Morane-Saulnier MS.502 Criquet	338	F-BCDG	30.11.70	Cancellation details not known	
	(Argus AS.10)		Fr.Mil		*(On loan from G Warner) (As "CF+HF" in Luftwaffe c/s)*	
BAPC.90	Colditz Cock rep	--			*(BBC "The Colditz Story" film)*	
BAPC.93	Fieseler Fi 103 (V-1)	--				
BAPC.267	Hawker Hurricane fsm	--			*(As "R4115/LE-X" in 243 Sqdn c/s)*	
BGA.4757	Colditz Cock rep	--	"JTA"	1.00	Built Southdown Aero Services & J.Lee	

American Air Museum, Duxford

G-BFYO	SPAD XIII rep	0035	D-EOWM	16.11.78	Cancelled 14.10.86 as WFU	21. 6.82P
	(Built Williams Flugzeugbau) (Lycoming AIO-360)				*(As "1/4513" in 3rd Escadrille French AF c/s)*	
G-BHUB	Douglas C-47A-85DL Dakota	19975	"G-AGIV"	30. 4.80	Cancelled 19.10.81 as WFU	
			Span.AF T3-29/N51V/N9985F/SE-BBH/43-15509 *(As "315509/W7-S" in USAAF c/s)*			
G-BHDK	Boeing TB-29A-45-BN Superfortress	11225	44-61748	27. 9.79	Cancelled 29.2.84 as WFU *"Hawg Wild" (As "461748/Y" in USAF c/s)*	
BAPC.255	NA P-51D Mustang fsm	--			Built Rialto, Ca, USA 1990 *(As "463209/WZ-S" in 78th FG c/s)*	

Duxford Aviation Society, Duxford

G-ALDG	Handley Page HP.81 Hermes IV	HP.81/8		27.10.49	WFU 9.62 *"Horsa" (BOAC titles) (Fuselage only)*	9. 1.63
G-ALFU	de Havilland DH.104 Dove 6	04234		14.12.48	Cancelled 14.11.72 as WFU	4. 6.71
G-ALWF	Vickers 701 Viscount	5		2. 1.50	Cancelled 18.4.72 as WFU	16. 4.72
G-ALZO(2)	Airspeed AS.57 Ambassador 2	5226	R Jordan AF 108	5. 4.50	Cancelled 10.9.81 as WFU	14. 5.71
			G-ALZO/(G-AMAD)			
G-ANTK	Avro 685 York C.1	---	MW232	23. 7.54	WFU Lasham 30.4.64 *(Dan Air titles)*	29.10.64T
G-AOVT	Bristol 175 Britannia 312	13427		23. 6.58	Cancelled 21.9.81 as WFU *(Monarch titles)*	11. 3.75T
G-APDB	de Havilland DH.106 Comet 4	6403	9M-AOB	2. 5.57	Cancelled 18.2.74 as WFU *(Dan-Air titles)*	7.10.74
			G-APDB			
G-APWJ	Handley Page HPR.7 Dart Herald 201	158		28. 9.59	Cancelled 10.7.85 as WFU *(Air UK titles)*	21.12.85
G-ASGC	Vickers Super VC-10 Srs.1151	853		11. 4.63	WFU 15.4.80 *(BOAC-Cunard titles)*	20. 4.80
G-AVFB	Hawker Siddeley HS.121 Trident 2E	2141	5B-DAC	1. 2.67	Cancelled 9.7.82	30. 9.82
			G-AVFB		*(WFU 27.3.82) (BEA titles)*	
G-AVMU	British Aircraft Corporation One-Eleven 510ED		BAC.148	11. 5.67	Cancelled 12.7.93 as WFU	8. 1.95T
					(British Airways titles) "County of Dorset"	
G-AXDN	British Aircraft Corporation-Aérospatiale Concorde			16. 4.69	Cancelled 10.11.86 as WFU	30. 9.77
		13522 & 01				
G-OPAS	Vickers 806 Viscount	263	G-AOYN	5.10.94	Cancelled 28.7.97 as destroyed	26. 3.97T
					(WFU 6.96 Southend & broken up) (Parcelforce titles) (Nose only)	

CHESHIRE
Hooton Park Trust, Hooton Park L65 1BQ

G-AGPG	Avro 652A Anson 19 Srs.2	1212		15. 6.45	Cancelled 5.11.75	13. 2.71
	(Originally regd as Anson XII, to Anson XIX 1.47 & to 19 Srs.2 5.52)				*(On loan from The Aeroplane Collection)*	
G-AJEB	Auster J/1N Alpha	2325		14. 3.47	Cancelled 9.6.81 as WFU	27. 3.69
					(On loan from The Aeroplane Collection)	
BAPC.68	Hawker Hurricane fsm	--	"P3975"		*(As "H3426") ("Battle of Britain" film)*	

CORNWALL
Flambards Village Theme Park, Helston TR13 0QA (www.flambards.co.uk)

G-BDDX	Whittaker MW2B Excalibur 001 & PFA 041-10106			28. 5.75	WFU 1976
	(Volkswagen 1500)				

Land's End Theme Park, Land's End TR19 7AA

G-BCXO	MBB Bö.105DD	S.80	D-HDCE	27. 2.75	Cancelled 4.3.92 as WFU
	(C/n S.80 is the original pod, replaced @1992 and subsequently rebuilt as display piece "G-CDBS")				

CUMBRIA
Solway Aviation Museum & Edward Haughey Aviation Heritage Centre, Carlisle CA6 4NW (www.solway-aviation-museum.org.uk)

G-APLG	Auster J/5L Aiglet Trainer	3148		4. 3.58	Cancelled 11.2.99 by CAA	26.10.68
G-AYFA	Scottish Aviation Twin Pioneer Mk.3	538	G-31-15	15. 6.70	Cancelled 16.5.91 as WFU	24. 5.82
	(Originally regd as a CC.2)		XM285		*(Nose only)*	
G-BJWY	Sikorsky S-55 (HRS-2) Whirlwind HAR.21	55???	A2576	25. 1.82	Cancelled 23.2.94 by CAA	
			WV198/Bu.130191		*(As "WV198/K") (On loan from D.Charles)*	

RAF Millom Museum, Haverigg LA18 4NA

BAPC.231	Mignet HM.14 Pou-Du-Ciel	--			*(On loan from South Copeland Aviation Group)*
	(Thought originally built @ Ulverston 1936 with Anzani engine)				*(As "G-ADRX")*
BAPC.260	Mignet HM.280	--			

Windermere Steamboat Centre, Windermere LA23 1BN (www.steamboat.co.uk)

BGA.266	Slingsby T.1 Falcon 1 Waterglider	237A		29. 5.36

DORSET

Bournemouth Aviation Museum, Bournemouth BH23 6SE (www.aviation-museum.co.uk)

G-BEYF	Handley Page HPR.7 Dart Herald 401	FM1022	175	13. 7.77	Cancelled 18.11.99 as WFU *(On loan from Dart Group plc)*	11. 3.01T
G-BRFC	Hunting Percival P.57 Sea Prince T.1	P57/71	WP321	10. 9.80	Cancelled 12.11.99 as sold abroad *(To N7SY 11.99)*	
G-NATY	Folland Gnat T.1	FL.548	8642M	19. 6.90	Cancelled 23.8.02 by CAA	
			XR537		*(No UK PtoF issued) (As "XR537/T")*	

ESSEX

Aces High Flying Museum, North Weald CM16 6AA

G-AMSN	Douglas C-47B-35DK Dakota IV	16631/33379	N3455	28. 4.52	Cancelled 25.1.00 as WFU	3. 1.68
			G-AMSN/EI-BSI/SU-BFZ/G-AMSN/KN673/44-77047 *(Dismantled 9.02)*			
(G-BKXW)	North American NA.82 B-25J Mitchell	108-35186	"HD368"	83R	NTU & remained as N9089Z *"Bedsheet Bomber"*	
			N9089Z/"N908"/N9089Z/44-30861 *(As "430861" in USAAF c/s)*			
G-CSFT	Piper PA-23-250 Aztec D	27-4521	G-AYKU	20. 9.84	Cancelled 5.6.96 as WFU	3.12.94T
			N13885		*(Fuselage only)*	

GLOUCESTERSHIRE

Bristol Aero Collection, Kemble GL7 6BA(www.bristolaero.com)

G-ALBN	Bristol 173 Mk.1	12871	7648M	22. 7.48	Cancelled	
			XF785		*(To RAF as XF785 in 1953)*	
G-ALRX	Bristol 175 Britannia Srs.101	12874	(WB473)	25. 6.51	Cancelled 5.4.54 as Withdrawn	
			(VX447)		*(On loan from Britannia Aircraft Preservation Trust)*	
					(DBR landing Littleton-upon-Severn 4.2.54) (Nose only)	
G-ANCF	Bristol 175 Britannia Srs.308F	12922	5Y-AZP	3. 1.58	Cancelled 21.2.84 as WFU	12. 1.81
	(Originally regd as Srs.305)		G-ANCF/LV-GJB/LV-PPJ/(G-ANCF)/G-14-1/G-18-4/G-ANCF/(N6597C)			
					(On loan from Britannia Aircraft Preservation Trust) (Fuselage only)	
G-ARRM	Beagle B.206X	B.001		23. 6.61	Cancelled 9.4.74 as PWFU	23.12.64
	(Originally regd as Beagle B.2 Srs.1 [B2/1010]: re-designated 9.61)				*(WFU 1965?)*	
G-ATDD	Beagle B.206 Srs.1	B.013	(VH-...)	27. 4.65	Cancellation details not known	
	(Originally regd as Beagle B.206R - to Srs.1 1966)		G-ATDD		*(U/c collapsed Sherburn 6.73: nose only)*	
BAPC.87	Bristol 30/46 Babe III rep	1			*(Built W.Sneesby) (As "G-EASQ")*	

Britannia Aircraft Preservation Trust, Kemble

G-BDUP	Bristol 175 Britannia Srs.253	13508	XM496	31. 3.76	Cancelled 9.8.84 as sold abroad.	
			G-BDUP/CU-T120/EL-WXA		*(To CU-T120 8.84) (As "XM496" in RAF c/s)*	

HAMPSHIRE

Farnborough Air Sciences Trust, Farnborough GU16 6DH

G-BKIK	Cameron DG-19 Helium Airship	776		23. 8.82	Cancelled 5.9.00 as WFU "B & Q"	4. 9.88A
	(Rotax 400)				*(On loan from Balloon Preservation Group)*	

Prince's Mead Shopping Centre, Farnborough

BAPC.208	RAF SE.5A rep	--			*(Built AJD Engineering) (As "D276/A")*	

Dakotas American Bistro, Fleet

G-AGYX	Douglas C-47A-10DK Dakota 3	12472	5N-ATA	15. 1.46	Sold as PH-MAG	
			PH-MAG/G-AGYX/KG437/42-9264 *(Subsequently N9050T) (Nose only)*			

Second World War Aircraft Preservation Society, Lasham

G-APXX	de Havilland DHA.3 Drover 2	5014	VH-EAS	15.12.59	Cancelled 26.11.73 as WFU	
			VH-EAZ		*(Regn not taken up) (As "VH-FDT")*	
G-APIT	Percival P.40 Prentice T.1	PAC/016	VR192	28.11.57	Cancelled 8.11.79 as WFU *(As "VR192")*	7. 9.67

Museum of Army Flying, AAC Middle Wallop SO20 8DY (www.flying-museum.org.uk)

G-ABOX(2)	Sopwith Pup	--			See SECTION 1	
G-AKKR	Miles M.14A Hawk Trainer 3	1995	"T9967"	23. 6.48	Cancelled 16.7.69 as PWFU	10. 4.65
	(May be T9967 [2160] from 1943 rebuild)		8378M/G-AKKR/T9708		*(As "T9707")*	
G-AKOW	Taylorcraft J Auster 5	1579	PH-NAD(2)	23.12.47	Cancelled 5.8.87 as WFU	26. 6.82
	(Regd as c/n TJ569A after rebuild in Holland)		PH-NEG/G-AKOW/TJ569		*(As "TJ569")*	
G-APXW	Lancashire Aircraft EP-9 Prospector	43		22.12.59	Cancelled 20.5.82	22. 5.76
					(Composite rebuild ex G-APWZ & others) (As "XM819" in Army c/s)	
G-ARYD	Auster AOP.6	--	WJ358	8. 3.62	Cancelled 5.8.87 as WFU *(Conversion abandoned 9.63)* (As "WJ358")	
G-AXKS	Westland-Bell 47G-4A	WA.723	G-17-8	22. 7.69	Cancelled 22.4.82 as WFU	21. 9.82
BAPC.80	Airspeed AS.58 Horsa II				*(Composite from LH208, TL659 & 8569M) (As "KJ351")*	
BAPC.163	Hafner AFEE 10/42 Rotabuggy rep	--			*(On loan from Wessex Aviation Society) (As "B-415")*	
BAPC.185	WACO CG-4A Hadrian	--			*(Fuselage only) (As "243809")*	
BAPC.261	GA Hotspur rep *(Composite from anonymous cockpit of Mk.1 & rear of Mk.II, HH379)* (As "HH379")					

Hall of Aviation, Southampton SO1 1FR (www.spitfireonline.co.uk)

G-ADWO	de Havilland DH.82A Tiger Moth	3455	BB807	9.12.35	Cancelled 15.9.58 as destroyed	
			G-ADWO		*(As "BB807")*	
	(Restored @ 3.51 & overhauled with fuselage of BB860 (ex G-ADXT): damaged landing Christchurch 31.7.58 & WFU: fuselage/parts ex G-AOAC					
	& parts ex G-AOJJ] used in composite rebuild 1987/90: completed to static condition 1990)					
G-ALZE	Britten-Norman BN-1F	1		16. 3.50	Cancelled 8.6.89 as WFU	
G-BRDV	Supermarine Spitfire Prototype rep			3. 7.89	Cancelled 19.5.00 as WFU	18. 2.95P
	(Jaguar V-12 350hp) HD36/001 & PFA 130-10796				*(As "K5054" in RAF c/s) (On loan from Replica Spitfire Ltd)*	
BAPC.7	SUMPAC	--			*(Southampton University Manpowered Aircraft)*	
BAPC.164	Wight Quadruplane Type 1 rep	--			*(As "N546")*	
BAPC.210	Avro 504J rep	--			Built AJD Engineering	
	(Gnome Monosoupape 100hp)				*(As "C4451")*	
BAPC.215	Airwave Hang Glider prototype	--				
BAPC.253	Mignet HM.14 Pou-Du-Ciel rep	--			*(Built 1990s) (On loan from H.Shore) (As "G-ADZW")*	

HERTFORDSHIRE

Galleria Mall, Hatfield

BAPC.257	de Havilland DH.88 Comet fsm				*(As "G-ACSS") "Grosvenor House"*	

De Havilland Heritage Museum, London Colney AL2 1BU (www.dehavillandmuseum.co.uk)

Reg	Type	c/n	ID	Date	Remarks	Date
G-ABLM	Cierva C.24	710		22. 4.31	Cancelled as WFU 12.34	16. 1.35
	(DH Gipsy III)				*(On loan from Science Museum)*	
G-ADOT	de Havilland DH.87B Hornet Moth	8027	X9326	?.11.35	Cancelled as WFU	15.10.59
			G-ADOT			
G-AMXR	de Havilland DH.104 Dove 6	04379	D-CFSB	21. 1.53	Cancelled 22.7.54 as sold abroad	
			G-AMXR/N4280V		*(To D-CFSB 7.54 & subsequently D-IFSB(1))*	
G-ANRX	de Havilland DH.82A Tiger Moth	3863	N6550	25. 5.54	WFU 20.6.61 *"Border City"*	20. 6.61
G-AOJT	de Havilland DH.106 Comet IXB	06020	F-BGNX	11. 5.56	Cancelled 9.7.56 as WFU	5. 7.56
					(Fuselage only) (As "F-BGNX" in Air France titles)	
G-AOTI	de Havilland DH.114 Heron 2D	14107	G-5-19	25. 7.56	Cancelled 17.10.95 as WFU	24. 6.87T
G-AREA	de Havilland DH.104 Dove 8	04520		3. 8.60	Cancelled 19.9.00 by CAA	18. 9.87
G-ARYC	de Havilland DH.125 Srs.1	25003		1. 3.62	Cancelled 31.3.76 as WFU *(WFU 1.8.73)*	1. 8.73
G-AVFH	Hawker Siddeley HS.121 Trident 2E	2147		1. 2.67	Cancelled 12.5.82	18. 5.83T
					(WFU 24.10.81) (Forward fuselage only)	
G-AWJV	de Havilland DH.98 Mosquito TT.35	--	TA634	21. 5.68	Cancelled 19.10.70 as WFU *(As "TA634/8K-K" in 571 Sqdn c/s)*	
G-BBNC	de Havilland DHC-1 Chipmunk T.10	C1/0682	WP790	12.10.73	Cancelled 23.9.74 as WFU *(As "WP790/T") (Used for spares)*	
BAPC.186	de Havilland DH.82B Queen Bee	--	"K3584"		*(As "LF789/R2-K") (Correct identity not known)*	
BAPC.216	de Havilland DH.88 Comet fsm	--			*(As "G-ACSS")*	
BAPC.232	Airspeed AS.58 Horsa I/II	--			*(Composite airframe from unidentified components)*	

KENT

Brenzett Aeronautical Museum Trust, Brenzett TN29 0EE

G-AMSM	Douglas C-47B-20-DK Dakota	15764/27209	KN274	28. 4.52	Cancelled 11.9.78 as WFU	
			43-49948		*(Ground-looped on take-off Lydd 17.8.78) (Nose only)*	

Kent Battle of Britain Museum, Hawkinge CT18 7AG

BAPC.36	Fieseler Fi 103 V-1 fsm	--			*("Operation Crossbow" film)*
BAPC.63	Hawker Hurricane fsm	--	"L1592"		*("Battle of Britain" film) (As "P3208/SD-T" in 501 Sqdn c/s)*
BAPC.64	Hawker Hurricane fsm	--			*("Battle of Britain" film) (As "P3059/SD-N" in 501 Sqdn c/s)*
BAPC.65	Supermarine Spitfire fsm	--			*("Battle of Britain" film) (As "N3289/DW-K" in 610 Sqdn c/s)*
BAPC.66	Messerschmitt Bf109 fsm	1480			*("Battle of Britain" film)*
	(Hispano HA.1112)				
BAPC.67	Messerschmitt Bf109 fsm	--			*("Battle of Britain" film)*
	(Hispano HA.1112)				
BAPC.69	Supermarine Spitfire fsm	--			*("Battle of Britain" film) (As "N3313/KL-B" in 54 Sqdn c/s)*
BAPC.74	Messerschmitt Bf109 fsm	6357			*("Battle of Britain" film)*
	(Hispano HA.1112)				
BAPC.133	Fokker DR.1 model	--			*(As "425/17")*
BAPC.272	Hawker Hurricane fsm	--			*(As "N2532/GZ-H" in 32 Sqdn c/s)*
BAPC.273	Hawker Hurricane fsm	--			*(As "P2921/GZ-L" in 32 Sqdn c/s)*
BAPC.278	Hawker Hurricane fsm	--			*(As "P3679/GZ-K" in 32 Sqdn c/s)*

Lashenden Air Warfare Museum, Headcorn TN27 9HX

BAPC.91	Fieseler Fi 103R-IV	

RAF Manston History Museum, Manston CT12 5DF (www.raf-manston.fsnet.co.uk)

G-AZCM	Beagle B.121 Pup Srs.150	B121-155	G-35-155	30. 7.71	Cancelled 4.5.72 as sold abroad *(To HB-NAV 5.72)*
G-BWJZ	de Havilland DHC.1 Chipmunk 22	C1/0653	WK638	23.11.95	Cancelled as WFU 4.4.00

Medway Aircraft Preservation Society, Rochester ME5 9TX

(G-ALSP)	Bristol 171 Sycamore 3	12900	17.11.50		Cancelled 26.3.52
					(NTU - to RAF as WV783 in 4.52) (As "WV783")
G-36-1	Short SB.4 Sherpa	SH.1604	G-14-1		Cancelled
	(Short & Harland Experimental & Research Aircraft)				*(WFU 5.66) (Fuselage only)*

LANCASHIRE

Botany Bay Village, Chorley PR6 9AF

BAPC.176	RAF SE.5A scale rep	--			*(Built Slingsby Sailplanes for "The Blue Max" film)*
	(Currie Wot basic airframe)				*(As "A4850")*

Bygone Times Antique Warehouse, Eccleston PR7 5PD

G-BAYV	SNCAN 1101 Noralpha	193	F-BLTN	22. 5.73	Cancelled 28.4.83 as WFU 2. 8.75
			Fr.AF		*(Crashed Longbridge Deverill 23.2.74) (On loan from P.Smith) (As "F-OTAN-6")*

LEICESTERSHIRE

Snibston Discovery Park, Coalville LE67 3LN

G-AFTN	Taylorcraft Plus C2	102	HL535	2. 5.39	Cancelled 13.1.99 by CAA	1.11.57
			G-AFTN			
G-AGOS	Reid & Sigrist RS.4 Desford Trainer	3	VZ728	?. 5.45	Cancelled 9.11.81 as WFU	28.11.80P
			G-AGOS		*(As "VZ728")*	
G-AIJK	Auster V J/4	2067		13.11.46	CofA expired & WFU	24. 8.68

Charnwood Museum, Loughboough LE11 3QU

G-AJRH	Auster J/1N Alpha	2606		12. 5.47	Cancelled 18.1.99 by CAA	5. 6.69

East Midlands Aeropark, East Midlands Airport

G-APES	Vickers 953C Vanguard Merchantman	721		9. 9.57	Cancelled 28.2.97 as WFU *(Nose only) "Swiftsure"*	2.10.95T

G-BAMH	Westland S-55 Whirlwind Srs.3	WA.83	VR-BEP	10. 1.73	Cancelled 31.10.73	
			G-BAMH/XG588		*(To VR-BEP 10.73) (As "XG588 in SAR c/s)*	
G-BEOZ	Armstrong-Whitworth AW.650 Argosy 101	6660	N895U	28. 3.77	Cancelled 19.11.87 as WFU	28. 5.86T
			N6502R/G-1-7		*(Elan c/s) "Fat Albert"*	
(G-BLMC)	Avro 698 Vulcan B.2A	--	XM575	R	Reservation @ 8.84 not taken up *(As "XM575")*	
G-FRJB	Britten SA-1 Sheriff	0001		18. 5.81	Cancelled 6.2.87 by CAA	
					(Not completed: unfinished airframe without marks)	

Percy Pilcher Museum, Stanford Hall, Stanford LE17 6DH (www.stanfordhall.co.uk)

| BAPC.45 | Pilcher Hawk glider rep | -- | | | *(Built Armstrong-Whitworth Aviation apprentices 1957/58)* | |

LINCOLNSHIRE
Lightning Association, Binbrook LN8 6DR

| G-BTSY | English Electric Lightning F.6 | 95207 | XR724 | 25. 7.91 | Cancelled 26.5.92 as TWFU | |
| | | | | | *(No Permit issued) (As "XR724")* | |

Battle of Britain Memorial Flight, RAF Coningsby LN4 4SY

G-AISU	Supermarine 349 Spitfire LF.VB	CBAF.1061	AB910	25.10.46	Cancelled as transferred to Military Marks	
					(As "AB910/ZD-C" in 222 Sqdn c/s)	
G-AMAU	Hawker Hurricane IIc	--	PZ865	1. 5.50	Cancelled 19.12.72 as transferred to Military Marks	
	(12,780th & final Hurricane built)				*(As "PZ865/Q" in RAFSEAC c/s)*	
G-AWIJ	Supermarine 329 Spitfire IIA	CBAF.1	P7350	25. 4.68	Cancelled 29.2.84 to MOD *"Blue Peter"*	
					(Returned to RAF) (As "P7350/XT-D" in 603 Sqdn c/s)	

Royal Air Force, RAF Cranwell

| BAPC.225 | Supermarine Spitfire IX fsm | -- | | | *(As "P8448/"UM-D" in 52 Sqdn c/s)* | |

Royal Air Force, RAF Digby

| BAPC.229 | Supermarine Spitfire IX fsm | -- | "L1096" | | *(As "MJ832/DN-Y" in 416 Sqdn c/s) "City of Oshawa"* | |

Lincolnshire Aviation Heritage Centre, East Kirkby (www.lincsaviation.co.uk)

G-ASXX	Avro 683 Lancaster B.VII	--	(8375M)	22.10.64	Cancelled 16.2.79 as WFU	
			Fr.Navy WU-15/NX611			
	("NX611/LE-C" in 630 Sqdn c/s "City of Sheffield" [starboard] & "NX611/DX-C" in 57 Sqdn c/s "Just Jane" [port])					
BAPC.90	Colditz Cock rep	--			*(BBC "The Colditz Story" film)*	

Bomber County Aviation Musem, Hemswell (www.lineone.net/~bcam)

| BAPC.120 | Mignet HM.14 Pou-Du-Ciel | TLC.1 | G-AEJZ | 9. 6.36 | Cancelled 31.12.38 in census *(As "G-AEJZ")* | |

Aerial Application Collection, Wainfleet

G-BFBP	Piper PA-25-235 Pawnee D	25-7756033		7. 9.77	Cancelled 21.6.78 as destroyed	
					(Crashed near Comberton, Cambs 11.5.78) (Cockpit only)	
G-BFEY	Piper PA-25-235 Pawnee D	25-7756039		20.10.77	Cancelled 17.7.90 as WFU *(Fuselage frame only)*	19.1.87

GREATER LONDON
Royal Air Force HQ 11/18 Groups, RAF Bentley Priory

| BAPC.217 | Supermarine Spitfire I fsm | -- | | | *(As "K9926/JH-C" in 317 Sqdn c/s)* | |
| BAPC.218 | Hawker Hurricane IIc fsm | -- | "P3386" | | *(As BN230/FT-A"in 43 Sqdn c/s)* | |

Royal Air Force Memorial Chapel, Biggin Hill

| BAPC.219 | Hawker Hurricane I fsm | -- | | | *(As "L1710/AL-D" in 79 Sqdn c/s)* | |
| BAPC.220 | Supermarine Spitfire I fsm | -- | | | *(As "N3194/GR-Z" in 92 Sqdn c/s)* | |

Croydon Airport Visitor Centre, Croydon (www.croydon.gov.uk/airport-soc/)

G-ANKV	de Havilland DH.82A Tiger Moth	84166	T7793	30.12.53	Cancelled 9.56	
	(Provenance uncertain)				*(Not converted) (As "T7793" in RAF c/s)*	
G-ANUO	de Havilland DH.114 Heron 2D	14062		27. 9.54	Cancelled 9.8.96 as WFU	12. 9.86T
					(As "G-AOXL" in Morton Air Services c/s)	

Trident Preservation Society, Heathrow (www.hs121.org.uk)

| G-AWZK | Hawker Siddeley HS.121 Trident 3B Srs.101 | | | 14. 1.69 | Cancelled 29.5.90 as WFU | 14.10.86T |
| | | 2312 | | | *(WFU 1.11.85) (BEA "Quarter Union Jack" titles)* | |

Royal Air Force Museum, Hendon NW9 5LL (www.rafmuseum.com)

G-EBIC	R.A.F. SE.5A	688/2404	"B4563"	26. 9.23	Cancelled 31.12.38	3. 9.30
	(Wolseley Viper 200hp) (Regd with c/n 687/2404)		9208M/G-EBIC/F937		*(WFU 9.30) (As "F938")*	
G-EBJE	Avro 504K	927	(9205M)	??. 7.24	Cancelled ?.12.34	29. 9.34
	(Includes components of Avro 548A G-EBKN ex E449)				*(As "E449")*	
G-ABBB	Bristol 105A Bulldog IIA	7446	"K2227"	12. 6.30	Cancelled 22.9.61 as PWFU	
			G-ABBB/R-11/G-ABBB		*(As "K2227")*	
G-ABMR	Hawker Hart	H.H-1	"J9933"	28. 5.31	Cancelled 2.2.59 on transfer to Military Marks	11. 6.57
			G-ABMR		*(To "J9933" & later "J9941") (As "J9941" in 57 Sqdn c/s)*	
G-AETA	Caudron G.III	7487	OO-ELA	29. 1.37	Sold to RAF 1972	
	(Anzani 90hp)		O-BELA/(9203M)		*(As "3066" in RNAS c/s) (Also reported as either c/n 5019 or 5021)*	
G-AFDX	Hanriot HD.1	"HD.1"	N75	4. 5.38	Cancellation details not known	
			OO-APJ/Belgian AF H-1/Belgian AF N75 *(As "HD-75")*			
	(DBR landing Old Warden 17.6.39: wings destroyed in air raid Brooklands 1940, fuselage survived & rebuilt 1968)					
G-AITB	Airspeed AS.40 Oxford 1	--	MP425	1.11.46	C of A expired & WFU *(As "MP425" in 1536 BATF c/s)*	24. 5.61
G-APUP	Sopwith Pup rep	B.5292 & PFA 1582	9213M	13. 2.59	Cancelled 4.10.84 by CAA	28. 6.78
	(Le Rhone)		G-APUP/N5182		*(As "N5182")*	
G-ATVP	Vickers FB.5 Gunbus rep	VAFA-01 & FB.5		31. 5.66	Cancelled 27.2.69 as WFU	6. 5.69
	(Gnome Monosoupape 100 hp)				*(As "2345" in RFC c/s)*	
G-AWAU	Vickers FB.27A Vimy rep	VAFA-02	"H651"	8. 1.68	Cancelled 19.7.73 as WFU *"Triple First" (As "F8614")*	4. 8.69

Reg/Ref	Type	c/n	Prev ID	Date	Notes	Date
G-BEOX	Lockheed 414 Hudson IIIA	414-6464	VH-AGJ	25. 3.77	Cancelled 22.12.81 as WFU	
	(A-29A-LO)		VH-SMM/R.Australian AF A16-199/FH174/41-36975 (As "A16-199/SF-R")			
G-BFDE	Sopwith Tabloid Scout rep	168 & PFA 067-10186		22. 9.77	Cancelled 8.12.86 as WFU	4. 6.83P
	(Continental PC.60)				(As "168" in RNAS c/s)	
G-BIDW	Sopwith "1f1" Strutter rep	WA/5	"9382"	24. 9.80	Cancelled 4.2.87 by CAA	29.12.80P
	(Built Westward Airways) (Le Clerget)				(As "A8226" in 45 Sqdn RFC c/s)	
G-BLWM	Bristol M.1C rep	PFA 112-10892	"C4912"	12. 3.85	Cancelled 12.5.88 by CAA	12. 8.87P
	(110 hp Gnome)				(As "C4994" in RFC c/s)	
G-OIOI	EH Industries EH-101 Heliliner	50008		23.11.88	Cancelled 1.4.96 - to MOD	5. 5.94P
	(Airframe No.PP8)				(To RAF as "ZJ116")	
G-OTHL	Robinson R22 Beta	0738	G-DSGN	28.11.94	Cancelled 8.2.00 as WFU (As "G-RAFM")	27. 4.03T
G-USTV	Messerschmitt Bf.109G-2/Trop	---	8478M	26.10.90	Cancelled as PWFU 24.9.98	30. 5.98P
	(Built Erla Maschinenwerk GmbH)	10639	RN228/Luftwaffe		(As "10639/6" in Luftwaffe III/JG77 c/s)	
BAPC.92	Fieseler Fi 103 (V-1)	--				
BAPC.100	Clarke Chanute biplane glider	--			(On loan from Science Museum)	
BAPC.165	Bristol F.2b	--			(As "E2466" in 22 Sqdn c/s)	
	(RR Falcon rep)					
BAPC.181	RAF BE.2b rep	--			(As "687")	
	(Renault V8)				(Restoration from original components)	
BAPC.205	Hawker Hurricane IIc fsm	--			(As "BE421/XP-G" in 174 Sqdn c/s)	
BAPC.206	Supermarine Spitfire IX fsm	--			(As "MH486/FF-A" in 132 Sqdn c/s)	

Royal Air Force, RAF Northolt

Reg/Ref	Type	c/n	Prev ID	Date	Notes	Date
BAPC.221	Supermarine Spitfire LF.IX fsm	--			(As "MH777/RF-N" in 303 Sqdn c/s)	

Science Museum, South Kensington, London SW7 2DD (www.sciencemuseum.org.uk)

Reg/Ref	Type	c/n	Prev ID	Date	Notes	Date
G-EBIB	R.A.F.SE.5A	687/2404	"F939"	26. 9.23	Cancelled 1.12.46	8. 8.35
	(Regd with c/n 688/2404)		G-EBIB/F937		(WFU)	
G-AAAH	de Havilland DH.60G Moth	804		30. 8.28	Cancelled 12.31	23.12.30
	(Original but note two BAPC.reproductions depicted as "G-AAAH" exist –see below)				"Jason"	
G-ACWP	Avro 671 Cierva C.30A Autogiro	728	AP507	24. 7.34	Cancelled 1.6.40 on sale (Impressment)	6. 3.41
			G-ACWP		(As "AP507/KX-P" in 529 Sqdn c/s)	
G-ASSM	Hawker Siddeley HS.125 Srs.1/522	25010	5N-AMK	5. 5.64	Cancelled 28.5.80 as sold in Nigeria	
			G-ASSM			
G-AWAW	Reims/Cessna F150F	F150-0037	OY-DKJ	5. 1.68	Cancelled 16.5.90 as WFU	8. 6.92T
	(Wichita c/n 15063167)					
G-AZPH	Pitts S.1S Special	S1S-001-C	N11CB	13. 3.72	Cancelled 8.1.97 as WFU "Neil Williams"	4. 9.91P
	(Lycoming IO-360)				(Ground-looped landing Little Snoring 10.5.91)	
G-LIOA	Lockheed 10A Electra	1037	N5171N	6. 5.83	Cancelled 26.4.02 as WFU	
			NC243/NC14959		(As "NC5171N")	
BAPC.50	Roe Triplane Type I	--			(1909 original)	
	(JAP 9hp)					
BAPC.51	Vickers FB.27 Vimy IV	13			(Rebuild of 1919 original)	
	(RR Eagle VIII 360hp)					
BAPC.53	Wright Flyer rep	--			(Built Hatfield)	
BAPC.54	JAP/Harding Monoplane	--			(Modified Bleriot XI built J.A.Prestwich & Co 1910)	
	(JAP Anzani 45hp)					
BAPC.55	Levasseur-Antoinette developed Type VII Monoplane				(1909 original)	
	(Antoinette V8 50hp)	--				
BAPC.56	Fokker E.III	--			(Captured @ Somme, France 4.1916)	
	(Oberusal 100hp)				(Skeletal airframe) (As "210/16")	
BAPC.62	Cody Type V Bi-plane	--			(1912 original)	
	(Austro-Daimler 120hp)				(As "304")	
BAPC.124	Lilienthal Glider Type XI rep	--			(Display reproduction of BAPC.52 qv)	
BAPC.199	Fieseler Fi 103 (V-1)	--			(As "442795")	
BGA.2097	Schempp-Hirth Cirrus	--			(As "DFY")	
	(Note: SECTION 6 states BGA.2097 = DGE & DFY = BGA.2091 – both have current CofAs!!)					

Imperial War Museum, South Lambeth, London SE1 6HZ (www.iwm.org.uk)

Reg/Ref	Type	c/n	Prev ID	Date	Notes	Date
BAPC.198	Fieseler Fi 103 (V-1)	--				

Royal Air Force, RAF Uxbridge

Reg/Ref	Type	c/n	Prev ID	Date	Notes	Date
BAPC.222	Supermarine Spitfire IX fsm	--			(As "BR600/SH-V" in 64 Sqdn c/s)	

GREATER MANCHESTER

Museum of Science & Industry in Manchester, Castlefield, Manchester M3 4JP (www.msim.org.uk)

Reg/Ref	Type	c/n	Prev ID	Date	Notes	Date
G-EBZM	Avro 594A Avian IIIA	R3/CN/160		??.7.28	Cancelled 1.12.46 by Sec of State	20. 1.38
	(ADC Cirrus)				(Fitted with parts from G-ABEE) (On loan from The Aeroplane Collection)	
G-ABAA	Avro 504K	--	9244M	11. 9.30	Cancelled 1939?	11. 4.39
			"H2311"/G-ABAA			
G-ADAH	de Havilland DH.89 Dragon Rapide	6278		30. 1.35	WFU 1969 "Pioneer"	9. 6.47
					(Allied Airways (Gandar Dower) c/s) (On loan from The Aeroplane Collection)	
G-APUD	Bensen B-7Mc	1		11. 5.59	Cancelled 27.2.70 as WFU	27. 9.60
					(On loan from The Aeroplane Collection)	
G-AYTA	SOCATA MS.880B Rallye Club	1789		19. 2.71	Cancelled 12.5.93 as WFU	7.11.88
G-AWZP	Hawker Siddeley HS.121 Trident 3B Srs.101	2317		14. 1.69	Cancelled 27.6.86 as destroyed (Nose section only)	14. 3.86T
G-MJXE	Mainair Tri-Flyer 330/Hiway Demon 175			17. 5.83	Cancelled 19.10.00 as TWFU	21. 3.95P
		102-131082 & HS-001			(On loan from The Aeroplane Collection)	
BAPC.6	Roe Triplane Type IV rep (JAP 9hp)	--			(As "14") "Bullseye Avroplane"	
BAPC.12	Mignet HM.14 Pou-Du-Ciel (Scott A2S)	--				
BAPC.98	Yokosuka MXY7 Ohka 11		8485M		(As "997")	

BAPC.175	Volmer VJ-23 Swing-wing (McCulloch 9hp)	--				
BAPC.182	Wood Ornithopter	--				
BAPC.251	Hiway Spectrum Hang-Glider	--			*(Built 1980)*	
BAPC.252	Flexiform Wing Hang-Glider	--			*(Built 1982)*	
BGA.1156	EoN AP.10 460 Srs.1	EoN/S/007	BGA.2666	26. 1.64	*(As "BQT")*	18. 4.97
			AGA.6/BGA.1156			

WEST MIDLANDS
Boulton Paul Association/Boulton Paul Heritage Project, Bilbrook, Wolverhampton WV8 1EU

G-AVVR	Avro 652A Anson 19 Srs.2	"34530"	VP519	6.10.67	Cancelled by CAA 16.9.72 *(Not converted & scrapped in early 1970)*	
					(Nose only) (On loan from The Aeroplane Collection)	
BAPC.274	Boulton & Paul P.6 fsm	--			*(As "X-25")*	
BGA.1759	Slingsby T.8 Tutor ——	--	RAFGSA.178	10.72		
BGA.1992	Hirth Go IV Goevier 3	557	D-5233	13. 7.74	*(As "DBU")*	19. 7.87

NORFOLK
Royal Air Force, RAF Coltishall

BAPC.223	Hawker Hurricane I fsm	--			*(As "V7467/LE-D"in 242 Sqdn c/s)*	

City of Norwich Aviation Museum, Norwich Airport NR10 3JE

G-ASKK	Handley Page HPR.7 Dart Herald 211	161	PP-ASU	17. 7.63	Cancelled 29.4.85 as WFU	19. 5.85T
			G-ASKK/PI-C910/CF-MCK			
G-AWON	English Electric Lightning F.53	95291	G-27-56	9. 8.68	Cancelled 9.68 *(To R.Saudi AF as 53-686 4.69 then 223)*	
G-BEBC	Westland WS-55 Whirlwind HAR.10	WA.371	8463M	25. 6.76	Cancelled 5.12.83 as WFU	
			XP355		*(Not converted) (As "XP355/A")*	
G-BHMY	Fokker F-27 Friendship 600	10196	F-GBDK(2)	6. 5.80	Cancelled as PWFU 22.3.03	22. 5.99T
			(F-GBRV)/PK-PFS/JA8606/PH-FDL *(Donated by KLM (UK) Ltd - less engines)*			

NORTHUMBERLAND & TYNESIDE
Military Vehicle Museum, Newcastle upon Tyne NE2 4PZ (www.military-museum.org.uk)

G-ANFU	Taylorcraft J Auster 5	1748	TW385	31.10.53	Cancelled 3.8.76 as WFU	17. 2.71
					(On rebuild with frame of un-identified Auster 5.93) (As "NJ719" with starboard wing ex G-AKPH)	

North East Aircraft Museum, Usworth, Sunderland SR5 3HZ

G-APTW	Westland WS-51/2 Widgeon	WA/H/150		27. 4.59	Cancelled 24.8.77 as WFU	26. 9.75
G-ARAD	Phoenix Luton LA-5A Major PAL/1204 & PFA 836			29. 4.60	Cancelled 16.10.02 as WFU	
					(Completed but not flown)	
G-ASOL	Bell 47D-1	4	N146B	31. 1.64	Cancelled 5.12.83 as WFU	6. 9.71
G-AWRS	Avro 652A Anson C.19 Srs.2	"33785"	TX213	14.10.68	Cancelled 30.5.84 as PWFU *(WFU 5.2.73)*	10. 8.73
G-BEEX	de Havilland DH.106 Comet 4C	6458	SU-ALM	10. 9.76	Cancelled 19.5.83	
					(Not converted & broken up Lasham 8.77: nose section only)	
G-SFTA	Westland SA.341G Gazelle 1	1039	G-SFTA	10. 9.82	Cancelled 21.5.86 as WFU	24. 2.86
			HB-XIL/G-BAGJ/(XW858)		*(Crashed near Alston, Cumbria 7.3.84) (As "G-BAGJ")*	
G-MBDL	Striplin (AES) Lone Ranger	109		21.10.81	Cancelled 13.6.90 by CAA	
G-OGIL	Short SD.3-30 Var.100	SH.3068	G-BITV	23. 1.89	Cancelled 12.11.92 as WFU	21. 4.93T
			G-14-3068		*(Damaged Newcastle 1.7.92)*	
BAPC.96	Brown Helicopter	--				
BAPC.97	Luton LA.4 Minor (JAP J99)	--			*(As "G-AFUG")*	
BAPC.119	Bensen B.7 Gyroglider	--				
BAPC.211	Mignet HM.14 Pou-Du-Ciel	--			*(As "G-ADVU")*	
	(Built Ken Fern/Vintage & Rotary Wing Collection 1993)					
BAPC.228	Olympus Hang Glider	--				

NOTTINGHAMSHIRE
Newark Air Museum, Winthorpe NG24 2NY (www.newarkairmuseum.co.uk)

G-AHRI	de Havilland DH.104 Dove 1B	04008	4X-ARI	11. 7.46	Cancelled 18.5.72 as WFU	
			G-AHRI			
G-AMBB	de Havilland DH.82A Tiger Moth	85070	T6801	1. 5.50	Cancellation details not known *(Composite rebuild - as "G-MAZY")*	
G-ANXB	de Havilland DH.114 Heron 1B	14048	G-5-14	3.12.54	Cancelled 2.11.81 as PWFU	25. 3.79
					(BEA Scottish Airways titles) "Sir James Young Simpson"	
G-APIY	Percival P.40 Prentice T.1	PAC/075	VR249	28.11.57	Cancelled 19.4.73	18. 3.67
					(WFU 18.3.67) (As "VR249/FA-EL" in RAFC c/s)	
G-APVV	Mooney M.20A	1474	N8164E	30. 7.59	Cancelled 3.4.89 by CAA *(Crashed at Barton 11.1.81)*	19. 9.81
G-AVVO	Avro 652A Anson C.19 Srs.2	34219	VL348		Cancelled 16.9.72 by CAA *(As "VL348")*	6.10.67
G-AYZJ	Westland WS-55 Whirlwind HAS.7	WA.263	XM685	24. 5.71	Cancelled 29.12.80 as WFU	
	(Also c/n WAG/34)				*(As "XM685/PO-513")*	
G-BFTZ	SOCATA MS.880B Rallye Club	1269	F-BPAX	2. 6.78	Cancelled 14.11.91 by CAA	19. 9.81
					(On loan from The Aeroplane Collection)	
G-BJAD	Clutton FRED Srs.II CA.1 & PFA/29-10586			11. 6.81	Cancelled 9.9.97 by CAA	
					(No Permit issued, probably not completed)	
G-BKPG	Luscombe P3 Rattler Strike	003		7. 3.83	Cancelled 31.7.91 by CAA *(No Permit issued)*	
G-BKPY	SAAB 91B/2 Safir	91321	R NorAF 56321	23. 3.83	Cancelled 8.2.02 as WFU *(As "56321" in R.NorAF c/s)*	
G-MBBZ	Volmer VJ-24W	7		23. 9.81	Cancelled 29.11.95 as WFU	
G-MBUE	MBA Tiger Cub 440	MBA-001		29. 4.82	Cancelled 6.9.94 by CAA *(Originally regd as Micro-Bipe c/n 001)*	
BAPC.43	Mignet HM.14 Pou-Du-Ciel (Scott A2S)	--				
BAPC.101	Mignet HM.14 Pou-Du-Ciel	--				
BAPC.183	Zurowski ZP.1 (Panhard 850cc)	--			*(Polish AF c/s)*	
BAPC.204	McBroom Hang-Glider	--				

OXFORDSHIRE
Royal Air Force, RAF Benson

BAPC.226	Supermarine Spitfire XI fsm	--			*(As "EN343" in PRU c/s)*	

SHROPSHIRE

Royal Air Force Museum including Michael Beetham Restoration Centre ($), RAF Cosford TF11 8UP (www.rafmuseum.com)

G-EBMB	Hawker Cygnet I **($)**	1	No.14	29. 7.25	Cancelled 30.11.61	30.11.61
	(Bristol Cherub III)		Lympne 1924			
G-AAMX(2)	Moth Corporation DH.60GM Moth	125	NC926M	11. 9.86	Cancelled 19.8.95 as WFU	7. 5.94P
	(DH Gipsy II)					
G-ADMW	Miles M.2H Hawk Major **($)**	177	DG590	30. 7.35	Cancelled 16.9.86 by CAA	30. 7.65
			8379M/G-ADMW			
G-AEEH	Mignet HM.14 Pou-Du-Ciel	EGD.1		13. 3.36	Cancelled 8.46 in census *(WFU 15.5.38)*	15. 5.38
G-AEKW	Miles M.12 Mohawk **($)**	298	HM503	14. 7.36	Crashed Spain 1.1.50	1. 3.50
			G-AEKW/"G-AEKN"			
G-AGNV	Avro 685 York C.1	1223	"MW100"	20. 8.45	WFU 9.10.64	6. 3.65
			"LV633"/G-AGNV/TS798			
G-AHED	de Havilland DH.89A Dragon Rapide 6 **($)**	6944	RL962	27. 2.46	Cancelled 3.3.69 *(WFU)*	17. 4.68
G-AIXA	Taylorcraft Plus D **($)**	134	LB264	13. 1.47	Cancelled 13.12.02 by CAA	21. 2.02P
G-AIZE	Fairchild F.24W-41A Argus II	565	N9996F	18.12.46	Cancelled 6.4.73	6. 8.66
	(UC-61A-FA)		G-AIZE/43-14601		*(WFU)* *(As "FS628")*	
G-AMOG(2)	Vickers 701 Viscount	7	(G-AMNZ)	23. 5.52	Cancelled 17.5.76 as WFU	14. 6.77
					(BEA c/s) *"RMA Robert Falcon Scott"*	
G-AOVF	Bristol 175 Britannia Srs.312F	13237	9Q-CAZ	13. 2.57	Cancelled 21.11.84 as WFU	
			G-AOVF		*(BOAC c/s)*	
G-APAS	de Havilland DH.106 Comet 1A	06022	8351M	23. 5.57	Cancelled 22.10.58	
			XM823/G-APAS/G-5-23/F-BGNZ		*(BOAC c/s)* *(As "XM823" @ 30.1.58)*	
G-APFJ	Boeing 707-436	17711		7. 8.59	WFU 12.6.81 *(British Airtours titles)*	16. 2.82T
G-ARPH	de Havilland DH.121 Trident 1C	2108		13. 4.61	WFU 26.3.82 *(British Airways titles)*	8. 9.82T
G-ARVM(2)	Vickers VC-10 Srs.1101	815	(G-ARVJ)	16. 1.63	WFU 22.10.79 *(British Airways titles)*	5. 8.80
G-AVMO	British Aircraft Corporation One-Eleven 510ED			11. 5.67	Cancelled 12.7.93 as WFU	3. 2.95T
		BAC.143			*(British Airways titles)* *"Lothian Region"*	
G-BBYM	Handley Page HP.137 Jetstream 200	243	G-AYWR	13. 2.74	Cancelled 7.6.00 as WFU	20. 9.98A
			G-8-13			
BAPC.82	Hawker Afghan Hind **($)**	41H/81899			*(R.Afghan AF c/s)*	
	(RR Kestrel)					
BAPC.83	Kawasaki Ki 1001b	--	8476M		*(As "24")*	
BAPC.84	Mitsubishi Ki 46III (Dinah)	--	8484M		*(As "5439")*	
BAPC.94	Fieseler Fi 103 (V-1)	--	8483M			
BAPC.99	Yokosuka MXY7 Ohka 11	--	8486M			
BAPC.106	Bleriot XI (Anzani 40hp)	--	9209M		*(1910 original)* *(As "164")*	
BAPC.107	Bleriot XXVII **($)**	--	9202M		*(1911 original)* *(As "433")*	
BAPC.108	Fairey Swordfish IV **($)**	--	HS503		*(As "HS503")*	
BGA.572	Slingsby T.21B Sedbergh TX.1 **($)**	539	8884M		*(As "VX275")*	
			VX275/BGA.572			

Wartime Aircraft Recovery Group Aviation Museum, Sleap (www.wargroup.homestead.com)

BAPC.148	Hawker Fury II rep	--		*(As "K7271" in 1 Sqdn c/s)*
BAPC.234	Vickers FB.5 Gunbus fsm	--		*(Built 1985 for "Gunbus" film)* *(As "GBH-7")*

SOMERSET

The Helicopter Museum, Weston-super-Mare BS24 8PP (www.helicoptermuseum.co.uk)

G-ACWM	Avro 671 Cierva C.30A Autogiro	715	(G-AHMK)	24. 7.34	Cancelled 17.3.59 as Withdrawn	13. 7.40
			AP506/G-ACWM		*(On loan from E.D.ap Rees)* *(No external marks)*	
G-ALSX	Bristol 171 Sycamore 3	12892	G-48/1	17.11.50	CofA expired & WFU	24. 9.65
			G-ALSX/VR-TBS/G-ALSX		*(On loan from E.D.ap Rees)*	
G-ANFH	Westland WS.55 Whirlwind 1	WA.15		27.10.53	Cancelled 2.9.77 as WFU	17. 7.71
					(On loan from E.D.ap Rees) *(No external marks)*	
G-ANJV	Westland WS-55 Whirlwind 3	WA.24	VR-BET	14.12.53	Cancelled 8.1.74 on sale in Bermuda	
			G-ANJV		*(On loan from E.D.ap Rees)* *(No external marks)* *(Stored 3.02)*	
G-AODA	Westland WS-55 Whirlwind 3	WA.113	9Y-TDA	13. 5.55	Cancelled 23.9.93 by CAA *"Dorado"*	23. 8.91A
			EP-HAC/G-AODA		*(Bristow Helicopters c/s)*	
G-AOUJ	Fairey Ultralight Helicopter	F.9424	XJ928	1. 8.56	Cancelled 26.2.69 as Destroyed	29. 3.59
					(WFU) *(On loan from E.D.ap Rees)*	
G-AOZE	Westland WS-51/2 Widgeon	WA/H/141	5N-ABW	11. 1.57	Cancelled 20.6.62 on sale in Nigeria	
			G-AOZE		*(On loan from E.D.ap Rees)*	
G-ARVN(2)	Servotec Rotorcraft Grasshopper 1	1		16. 2.63	Cancelled 14.3.77 as WFU	18. 5.63
					(On loan from E.D.ap Rees)	
G-ASCT	Bensen B.7Mc	DC.3		14. 8.62	Cancelled 20.9.73 as PWFU	11.11.66P
	(McCulloch 4318E)				*(Built D.Campbell)* *(WFU)* *(Stored 3.02)*	
G-ASHD	Brantly B.2A	314		2. 4.63	Cancelled 22.6.67 as Destroyed	5. 6.67
					(Crashed into River Colne, Brightlingsea, Essex 19.2.67)	
					(Stored 3.02)	
G-ASTP	Hiller UH-12C	1045	N9750C	4. 6.64	Cancelled 24.1.90 by CAA	3. 7.82
G-ATBZ	Westland WS-58 Wessex 60 Srs.1	WA/461		22. 3.65	Cancelled as TWFU 23.11.82	15.12.81
					(WFU 5.12.81 - to G-17-4) *(Stored 3.02)*	
G-ATKV	Westland WS-55 Whirlwind Srs.3	WA/493	VR-BEU	11.11.65	Cancelled 8.1.74	
			G-ATKV/EP-HAN(1)/G-ATKV		*(To VR-BEU 1.74)* *(Stored 3.02)*	
G-AVKE	Gadfly HDW-1	HDW-1		19. 4.67	Cancelled 12.10.81 as WFU	
	(Continental IO-340A)				*(On loan from E.D.ap Rees)*	
G-AVNE	Westland WS-58 Wessex 60 Srs.1	WA.561	G-17-3	15. 5.67	Cancelled 23.11.82 as TWFU	7. 2.83
			G-AVNE/5N-AJL/G-AVNE/9M-ASS/VH-BHC/PK-HBQ/G-AVNE/(G-AVMC) *(As "G-AVNE" & "G-17-3")*			
G-AWRP	Cierva Rotorcraft CR.LTH.1 Grasshopper III	GB.1		14.10.68	Cancelled 5.12.83 as WFU	12. 5.72P
G-AXFM	Cierva Rotorcraft CR.LTH.1 Grasshopper III	GB.2		19. 5.69	Cancelled 5.12.83 as WFU	
					(Completed as Ground-Running Rig) *(Stored 3.02)*	
G-AYXT	Westland WS-55 Whirlwind HAS.7 (Srs.2)	WA.167	XK940	28. 4.71	Cancelled 8.8.00 by CAA *(As "XK940")*	4. 2.99P
G-AZAU	Cierva Rotorcraft CR.LTH.1 Grasshopper III	GB.3		21. 6.71	Cancelled 5.12.83 as WFU *(Incomplete Rig)* *(Stored 3.02)*	

G-AZYB	Bell 47H-1	1538	LN-OQG	4. 7.72	Cancelled 22.4.85 as destroyed	8. 9.84
			SE-HBE/OO-SHW		*(Crashed St.Mary Bourne, Thruxton 21.4.84)*	
					(On loan from E.D.ap Rees) (As "OO-SHW")	
G-BAPS	Campbell Cougar Gyroplane	CA/6000		14. 2.73	Cancelled 21.1.87 by CAA	20. 5.74
	(Continental O-240-A)				*(On loan from A.M.W.Curzon-Howe-Herrick)*	
G-BGHF	Westland WG.30 Srs.100-60	WA.001.P		4. 1.79	Cancelled 29.3.89 as WFU	1. 8.86
G-BKFD	Westland WG.30 Srs.100	004	G-17-28	22. 6.82	Cancelled 6.12.82 *(To N5820T) (Stored 3.02)*	
G-BKFF	Westland WG.30 Srs.100	006	G-17-30	22. 6.82	Cancelled 6.12.82 *(To N5840T) (Stored 3.02)*	
G-BKGD	Westland WG.30 Srs.100	002	(G-BKBJ)	15. 7.82	Cancelled 15.4.93 as WFU	6. 7.93
G-BRMA	Westland WS-51 Dragonfly HR.5	WA/H/50	WG719	15. 6.78	Cancelled 30.3.89 as WFU	
					(On loan from E.D.ap Rees) (As "WG719")	
G-BRMB	Bristol 192 Belvedere HC.1	13347	7997M	15. 6.78	Cancelled 3.7.96 as WFU	
			XG452		*(On loan from E.D.ap Rees) (As "XG452")*	
G-EFIS	Westland WG.30 Srs.100	014	G-17-18	24. 6.84	Cancelled 27.11.84 *(To N114WG 11.84) (As "N114WG")*	
G-EHIL	EH Industries EH-101	50003	ZH647	9. 7.87	Cancelled 28.4.99 as PWFU	9. 7.87
	(Airframe No.PP3)				*(To MoD as ZH647 9.93 & restored 8.98)*	
G-ELEC	Westland WG.30 Srs.200	007	G-BKNV	17. 6.83	Cancelled 27.2.98 as WFU	28. 6.95P
G-HAUL	Westland WG.30-300	020	G-17-22	3. 7.86	Cancelled 22.4.92 as WFU	27.10.86P
G-LYNX	Westland WG.13 Lynx 800	WA/102	(ZA500)	6.11.78	Cancelled 27.2.98 as WFU	
			G-LYNX/ZB500		*(As "ZB500")*	
G-PASB	MBB Bö.105D	S.135	VH-LSA	2. 3.89	Cancelled 9.8.94 as WFU	
			G-BDMC/D-HDEC		*(Original pod from 1994 rebuild)*	
G-RWWW	Westland WS-55 Whirlwind HCC.12	WA/418	8727M	21. 6.90	Cancelled 10.7.00 as WFU	25. 8.96P
			XR486		*(As "XR486" in Queens Flight c/s)*	
BAPC.10	Hafner R.II Revoplane (Salmson 45hp)	--				
BAPC.60	Murray M.1 helicopter (JAPJ99 36hp)	--				
BAPC.128	Watkinson CG-4 rotorcraft	--				
BAPC.153	Westland WG-33	--			*(Engineering mock-up)*	
BAPC.212	Bensen B.6 Gyrocopter	--			*(Stored 3.02)*	
BAPC.213	Cranfield Vertigo MP helicopter	--				
BAPC.264	Bensen B8M	--			*(Built 1984)*	

Fleet Air Arm Museum/FAAM Cobham Hall ($), RNAS Yeovilton BA22 8HT (www.fleetairarm.com)

G-AIBE	Fairey Fulmar 2	F.3707	N1854	29. 7.46	Cancelled 30.4.59 as transferred to Mil Markings	6. 7.59
			G-AIBE/N1854		*(As "N1854")*	
G-AIZG	Supermarine VS.236 Walrus 1	6S/21840	EI-ACC	20.12.46	Cancelled 1963	
			IAC N-18/L2301		*(As "L2301")*	
G-AOXG	de Havilland DH.82A Tiger Moth ($)	83805	XL717	3.10.56	Cancelled as sold as XL717 10.56	
			G-AOXG/T7291		*(As "G-ABUL")*	
G-APNV	Saunders-Roe P.531-1	S2/5268		24. 6.58	Cancelled 1.10.59 *(To RN as XN332 10.59) (As "XN332/759")*	
G-ASTL	Fairey Firefly 1	F.5607	SE-BRD	1. 6.64	WFU 3.2.82	
			Z2033		*(As "Z2033/275/N" in 1771 Sqdn RN c/s)*	
G-AWYY	Slingsby T.57 Sopwith Camel F.1 rep	1701	"C1701"	14. 2.69	Cancelled 25.11.91 as WFU	1. 9.85P
	(Clerget)		N1917H/G-AWYY		*(As "B6401")*	
G-AZAZ	Bensen B.8M ($)	RNEC.1		2. 7.71	Cancelled 19.9.75 as WFU	
G-BEYB	Fairey Flycatcher rep	WA/3		11. 7.77	Cancelled 12.7.96 as WFU	
	(Built Westward Airways)					
G-BFXL	Albatros D.Va rep	0034	D-EGKO	24. 8.78	Cancelled 10.3.97 as WFU	5.11.91P
	(Ranger 6-440-C5)				*(Built Williams Flugzeugbau) (As "D5397" in German c/s)*	
G-BGWZ	Eclipse Super Eagle ($)	ESE.007		29. 6.79	Cancelled 5.12.83 as WFU *(No external marks)*	
G-BIAU	Sopwith Pup rep	EMK/002		4. 1.83	Cancelled 10.3.97 as WFU	13. 9.89P
	(Le Rhone 80hp)				*(As "N6452" in RNAS c/s)*	
G-BMZF	WSK-Mielec LIM-2	1420	Polish AF	18.12.86	Cancelled 23.2.90 as WFU	
	(MiG-15bis)		1B-01420		*(As "01420" in North Korean c/s)*	
G-BSST	British Aircraft Corporation-Sud Concorde SST			6. 5.68	Cancelled 21.1.87 as WFU	31.10.74P
		13520 & 002			*(WFU 4.3.76) (On loan from Science Museum)*	
BAPC.58	Yokosuka MXY7 Ohka 11	--			*(As "15-1585") (On loan from Science Museum)*	
BAPC.88	Fokker DR.1 5/8th rep	--			*(Modified Lawrence Parasol airframe) (As "102/17")*	
BAPC.111	Sopwith Triplane rep	--			*(As "N5492") "Black Maria"*	
BAPC.149	Short S.27 rep ($)	--				

SUFFOLK

Norfolk & Suffolk Aviation Museum, Flixton, Bungay NR35 1NZ (www.aviationmuseum.net)

G-ANLW	Westland WS-51 Srs.2 Widgeon	WA/H/133	"MD497"	23. 3.54	Cancelled 15.11.02 as WFU	27. 5.81A
			G-ANLW		*(On loan from Sloane Helicopters Ltd)*	
G-AWSA	Avro 652A Anson C.19/2	"293483"	(N5054)	21.10.68	Cancelled 18.8.69 as sold in USA	
			G-AWSA/VL349		*(Not delivered) (As "VL349/V7-Q")*	
G-AZLM	Reims/Cessna F172L	F17200842		31.12.71	Cancelled 15.4.91 as destroyed	
					(Crashed on take off Badminton 23.3.91) (Fuselage only)	
G-BDVS	Fokker F-27 Friendship 200	10232	S2-ABK	20. 4.76	Cancelled 19.12.96 as WFU	
			PH-FEX/PH-EXC/9M-AMM/PH-FEX		*(Scrapped 12.96 - nose only) "Eric Gandar Dower"*	
G-BFIP	Wallbro Monoplane rep	WA-1		16.12.77	Cancelled 28.3.01 as TWFU	22. 4.82P
	(McCulloch/Wallis)				*(On loan from K.H.Wallis) (No external marks)*	
G-MTFK	Moult Trike/Flexiform Striker	DIM-01		23. 3.87	Cancelled 13.6.90 by CAA	
G-MJSU	MBA Tiger Cub 440	SO.75/1		2. 2.83	Cancelled 23.6.93 by CAA	31. 1.86E
	(Officially regd with c/n SO.175)					
BAPC.71	Supermarine Spitfire fsm	--	"P9390"		*("Battle of Britain" film) "Nuflier"*	
			"N3317"		*(As "P8140/ZP-K" in 74 Sqdn c/s)*	
BAPC.115	Mignet HM.14 Pou-Du-Ciel (Douglas 500cc)	--			*(On loan from I Hancock)*	
BAPC.147	Bensen B7 Gyroglider	--			*(As "LHS-1")*	
BAPC.239	Fokker D.VIII 5/8th scale rep	--				
BGA.1461	EoN AP.7 Primary	NK			*(As "CDN")*	

Wings Of Liberty Memorial Park, USAF Lakenheath

BAPC.269	Supermarine Spitfire V fsm		--		*(As "BM631/XR-C" in 71 Sqdn c/s)*

SURREY

Brooklands Museum, Brooklands, Weybridge KT13 0QN (www.motor-software.co.uk/brooklands

Reg	Type	C/n	Prev id	Date	Notes	Fate
G-AEKV	Kronfeld (BAC) Drone de luxe	30		13. 1.37	Cancelled 14.1.99 as WFU	6.10.60P
					(On loan from M.L.Beach) (Allocated BGA.2510 5.79)	
G-AGRU	Vickers 657 Viking 1	112	VP-TAX	8. 5.46	WFU 9.63 *"Vagrant"*	9. 1.64
			G-AGRU		*(BEA c/s)*	
G-APEJ	Vickers 953C Vanguard Merchantman	713		9. 9.57	Cancelled 15.11.96 as WFU *"Ajax"*	
					(WFU 24.12.92: broken up 1.6.95: nose section only)	
G-APEP	Vickers 953C Vanguard Merchantman	719		9. 9.57	Cancelled 28.2.97 as WFU *"Superb"*	1.10.98T
					(Hunting Cargo Airlines c/s)	
G-APIM	Vickers 806 Viscount	412		19.11.57	Cancelled *"Viscount Stephen Piercey"*	19. 7.88T
					(DBR struck by Short SD.3-30 G-BHWT on 11.1.88) (British Air Ferries c/s)	
G-ASIX	Vickers VC-10 Srs.1103	820		29. 5.63	Cancelled 10.10.74 *(To A40-AB 10.74) (As "A40-AB")*	
G-ASYD	British Aircraft Corporation One-Eleven 475AM			9.11.64	Cancelled 25.7.94 as WFU	13. 7.94
		BAC.053			*(Originally regd as Srs.400AM: converted to prototype Srs.500 1967: to Srs.475EM 1970)*	
G-BFCZ	Sopwith Camel F.1 rep	WA2		12.10.77	Cancelled 23. 1.03 as WFU	23. 2.89P
	(Built Westward Airways) (Clerget 9B)				*(As "B7270")*	
G-BJHV	Voisin Scale rep	MPS-1		1. 9.81	Cancelled 4.7.91 by CAA *(On loan from M.P.Sayer)*	
G-BNCX	Hawker Hunter T.7	41H/695454	XL621	9. 1.87	Cancelled 1.3.93 as WFU	28. 3.87P
					(On loan from J Hallett) (As "XL621")	
G-MJPB	Manuel Ladybird	WLM-14		9.11.82	Cancelled 13.6.90 by CAA *(On loan from Estate of W.L.Manuel)*	
G-VTOL	Hawker Siddeley Harrier T.52	B3/41H/735795	ZA250	27. 7.70	Cancelled 3.90 by CAA	2.11.86S
			G-VTOL/(XW273)			
BAPC.29	Mignet HM.14 Pou-Du-Ciel (Anzani "V")	--			*(Built P.D.Roberts, Swansea 1960/78) (As "G-ADRY")*	
BAPC.114	Vickers 60 Viking IV rep	--	"R4"		*(As "G-EBED") ("The Land Time Forgot" film)*	
BAPC.177	Avro 504K rep (Clerget 130hp)	--	"G1381"		*(Brooklands School of Flying c/s) (As "G-AACA")*	
BAPC.187	Roe Type I Biplane rep (ABC 24hp)	--			*(Built M.L.Beach)*	
BAPC.249	Hawker Fury I fsm	--			*(As "K5673" in 1 Sqdn 'A' Flight c/s)*	
BAPC.250	RAF SE.5A rep	--			*(As "F5475/A") "1st Battalion Honourable Artillery Company"*	
BAPC.256	Santos Dumont Type 20 Demoiselle rep	--			*(Built J Aubot 1996/97)*	
BGA.162	Manuel Willow Wren			9.34	*"The Willow Wren"*	
BGA.643	Slingsby T.15 Gull III	364A	TJ711	11.49	*(As "ATH")*	9.94
BGA.3922	Abbott-Baynes Scud I rep.	001		R	*(As "HFZ")*	

Gatwick Aviation Museum, Charlwood, Surrey RH6 0BT (www.gatwick-aviation-museum.co.uk)

G-TURP	Aérospatiale SA341G Gazelle 1	1445	G-BKLS	21. 1.88	Cancelled 17.8.92 as WFU	2.12.91T
			N17MT/N14MT/N49549		*(No external marks)*	
					(Damaged Stanford-le-Hope 9.9.91: restored as G-BKLS 5.11.91 for rebuild but cancelled)	

SUSSEX

Gatwick Hilton Hotel, Gatwick Airport

BAPC.168	de Havilland DH.60G Moth rep	8058			*(As "G-AAAH") "Jason"*

British Airports Authority Skyview Visitors Centre, South Terminal, Gatwick Airport

G-CEXP	Handley Page HPR.7 Dart Herald 209	195	I-ZERC	29.10.87	Cancelled 22.3.96 by CAA	7.11.96T
			G-BFRJ/4X-AHO		*(WFU 8.3.96)*	

Balloon Preservation Group, Kirdford (www.balloons.flyer.co.uk/bpg1.htm)

Reg	Type	C/n	Prev id	Date	Notes	Fate
G-AYVA	Cameron O-84 HAB	17		30. 3.71	Cancelled 19.5.93 by CAA *"April Fool"* *(Located Alfriston)*	6. 9.76
G-BAKO	Cameron O-84 HAB	57		18.12.72	Cancelled 19.5.93 by CAA *"Pied Piper"*	12. 7.76
G-BAND	Cameron O-84 HAB	52		22. 1.73	Cancelled 17.4.98 as WFU *"Clover"* *(Located Southampton)*	
G-BAOW	Cameron O-65 HAB	59		6. 2.73	Cancelled 15.10.01 by CAA *"Winslow Boy"*	9. 5.74S
					(Located Southampton)	
G-BAST	Cameron O-84 HAB	70		15. 3.73	Cancelled 19.5.93 by CAA *"Honey"*	2. 5.84A
G-BBDJ	Thunder Ax7-65 HAB	006		20. 7.73	Cancelled 11.5.93 by CAA *"Jack Tar"* *(Located Southampton)*	
G-BBYR	Cameron O-65 HAB	97		14. 2.74	Cancelled 30.1.87 by CAA *"Phoenix"*	15. 7.81
G-BCAP	Cameron O-56 HAB	92		5. 3.74	Cancelled 30.3.93 as WFU *"Honey Child"*	
G-BCAS	Thunder Ax7-77 HAB	018		5. 3.74	Cancelled 30.11.01 by CAA *"Drifter"*	9. 4.91A
					(Located Southampton)	
G-BCCH	Thunder Ax6-56A HAB	024	G-BCCH	4. 4.74	Cancelled 15.11.82 as sold Belgium but NTU *"Wrangler"*	
G-BCRE	Cameron O-77 HAB	128		30.10.74	Cancelled 19.5.93 by CAA *"Snapdragon"*	6.10.83A
					(Located Aylesbury)	
G-BDGO	Thunder Ax7-77 HAB	048		16. 7.75	Cancelled 12.6.02 by CAA *"J & B"*	2. 2.82A
G-BDMO	Thunder Ax7-77 HAB	053	(EC-...)/G-BDMO	25.11.75	Cancelled 8.3.95 as WFU *"Flash Harry"*	
G-BEIF	Cameron O-65 HAB				See SECTION 1	
G-BEJB	Thunder Ax6-56A HAB	096		31.12.76	Cancelled 10.5.02 by CAA *"Baby J & B"*	21. 5.87A
	(Original canopy destroyed by fire @ Latimer 4.9.77: replacement c/n not known)					
G-BGST	Thunder Ax7-65 Bolt HAB	217		14. 5.79	Cancelled 7.12.01 by CAA *"Black Fred"*	23. 3.91A
G-BHAT	Thunder Ax7-77 Bolt HAB	250		28. 1.80	Cancelled 29.4.93 as WFU *"Witter"*	6. 2.83A
G-BJZC	Thunder Ax7-65Z HAB	416		5. 3.82	Cancelled 8.7.98 as WFU *"Greenpeace Trinity"*	17. 6.94A
G-BKIY	Thunder Ax3 Sky Chariot HAB	464		7.10.82	Cancelled 15.11.01 as WFU *"Michaelangelo"*	
G-BKOW	Colt 77A HAB	505		6. 9.84	Cancelled 29.4.97 as WFU *(Elle titles) "Lady Di"*	14. 2.88A
G-BLDL	Cameron Truck 56 SS HAB	990		10. 1.84	Cancelled as WFU *"Europa"*	21.10.96
G-BLIP	Cameron N-77 HAB	1031		17. 4.84	Cancelled 23.6.98 as WFU *"Systems 80"*	26. 3.94A
G-BLJF	Cameron O-65 HAB				See SECTION 1	
G-BLJH	Cameron N-77 HAB				See SECTION 1	
G-BLKJ	Thunder Ax7-65 HAB	580		18. 7.84	Cancelled 22.5.97 as PWFU *"Up & Coming"*	3. 2.96A
G-BLSH	Cameron V-77 HAB	1085		7.12.84	Cancelled 30.3.98 as WFU *"Compass Rose"*	14. 1.95A
G-BLUE	Colting Ax7-77A HAB	77A-011		2. 5.78	Cancelled 30.11.01 by CAA	20. 9.99
	(Regd as Colt 77A c/n 11)					

G-BLZB	Cameron N-65 HAB	1164		21. 5.85	Cancelled 22.11.01 as WFU *"Pro-Sport"*	25. 4.90A
G-BMKX	Cameron Elephant 77SS HAB	1196		6. 2.86	Cancelled 21.10.96 as WFU *"Benjamin I"*	19. 2.89A
G-BMST	Cameron N-31 HAB	1317		4. 6.86	Cancelled 1.5.92 as WFU *"B&Q"*	
					(Badly damaged & for spares 12.01)	
G-BMWU	Cameron N-42 HAB				See SECTION 1	
G-BMUR	Cameron Zero 25 HA Airship	1169		11. 6.86	Cancelled 21.10.96 as WFU *"Zero 25"*	
G-BNHL	Colt Beer Glass 90SS HAB	1042		24 .3.87	Cancelled 22.6.98 as WFU *"Gatzweiler"*	4. 3.97A
G-BOGT	Colt 77A HAB	1212		21. 3.88	Cancelled 9.5.97 as WFU *"British Gas"*	2.12.94A
G-BONK	Colt 180A HAB	1167		14.12.87	Cancelled 28.11.01 as WFU *"Bonkette"*	2.11.94T
G-BONV	Colt 17A Cloudhopper HAB	1238		3. 5.88	Cancelled 22.11.01 as WFU *"Bryant Group"*	1. 4.93A
G-BOOP	Cameron N-90 HAB	1702	(G-BOMX)	11. 5.88	Cancelled 31.10.95 by CAA *"Betty Boop"*	28. 9.95A
					(Unipart titles) (Located Aylesbury)	
G-BORA	Colt 77A HAB	1233		19. 5.88	Cancelled 17.9.98 as WFU *"Carla"*	24. 8.94A
G-BOTE	Thunder Ax8-90 HAB	555		14. 6.88	Cancelled 12.12.95 as WFU *"Barge Fox"*	16. 2.95T
G-BPAH	Colt 69A HAB	512		2. 6.83	Cancelled 13.5.02 by CAA *"J & B Phil"*	15. 8.88A
G-BPDF	Cameron V-77 HAB				See SECTION 1	
G-BPFJ	Cameron Can 90SS HAB	1834		14.11.88	Cancelled 9.5.97 as WFU *"Budweiser Can I"*	10.12.93A
	(Budweiser Beer Can shape)					
G-BPFX	Colt 21A Cloudhopper HAB	1348		7.11.88	Cancelled 23.12.98 as WFU *"Budweiser Hopper"*	
G-BPSZ	Cameron N-180 HAB	1911		14. 3.89	Cancelled 9.5.01 as WFU *"Park Furnishers"*	30. 4.01T
G-BRFR	Cameron N-105 HAB	2042		14. 7.89	Cancelled 9.5.97 as WFU *"Rover"*	6.12.93A
					(Badly damaged, spares use only)	
G-BRLX	Cameron N-77 HAB	2095		13. 9.89	Cancelled 23.10.01 by CAA *"National Power"*	1. 6.96A
G-BSBM	Cameron N-77 HAB	2229		8. 3.90	Cancelled 15.7.98 as WFU *"Nuclear Electric 1"*	21.11.96A
G-BSWZ	Cameron A-180 HAB				See SECTION 1	
G-BTML	Cameron Rupert Bear 90SS HAB	2533		16. 5.91	Cancelled 29.4.97 as WFU *"Rupert Bear"*	31.12.94A
G-BTPV	Colt 90A HAB	1956		14. 6.91	Cancelled 25.3.99 as PWFU *"Mondial"*	1. 8.97A
G-BUET	Colt Flying Drinks Can SS HAB	2162		30. 3.92	Cancelled 29.4.97 as WFU *"Bud King Can"*	10.12.93A
	(Budweiser Can shape)					
G-BUEU	Colt 21A Cloudhopper HAB	2163		30. 3.92	Cancelled 29.4.97 as WFU *"Bud King Hopper"*	2.12.94A
G-BUIZ	Cameron N-90 HAB *(Telecoms Shape)*	2850		12. 6.92	Cancelled 19.10.00 as WFU *"Hutchinson"*	7. 8.95A
G-BUKC	Cameron A-180 HAB	2870		3. 7.92	Cancelled 11.10.99 as WFU *"Cloud Nine"* (Located Malpas)	
G-BUXA	Colt 210A HAB	2400		28. 4.93	Cancelled 20.12.01 as WFU *"Buxam"*	7. 4.99T
G-BVBJ	Colt Flying Coffee Jar 1 SS HAB	2427		27. 7.93	Cancelled 29.4.97 as WFU *"Maxwell House I"*	21.11.96A
	(Maxwell House Jar)					
G-BVBK	Colt Flying Coffee Jar 2 SS HAB	2428		27. 7.93	Cancelled 29.4.97 as WFU *"Maxwell House II"*	14. 2.97A
	(Maxwell House Jar)				(Located Malpas)	
G-BVFY	Colt 210A HAB				See SECTION 1	
G-BVIO	Colt Flying Drinks Can SS HAB	2538		4. 2.94	Cancelled 6.11.01 as WFU *"Budweiser Can II"*	9. 6.00A
	(Budweiser Can shape)					
G-BVWH	Cameron N-90 Lightbulb SS HAB	3404		8.12.94	Cancelled 17.12.01 as WFU *"Phillips Light Bulb"*	2. 9.98A
G-BVWI	Cameron Light Bulb 65SS HAB	3405		8.12.94	Cancelled 17.12.01 as WFU *"Phillips Energy Saver"*	2. 6.97A
G-BWAN	Cameron N-77 HAB	3499		24. 3.95	Cancelled 6.11.01 as WFU *"Wanda"*	16. 8.97A
G-BWGA	Lindstrand LBL-105A HAB	295		2. 8.95	Cancelled 14.5.99 as WFU *"Asda"*	24. 3.97A
G-BWPL	Airtour AH-56 HAB	011	G-OAFC	19. 3.96	Cancelled 17.9.01 as WFU *"Paul J Donnellan"*	
					(As *"G-OAFC"* - qv) (Located Wokingham)	
G-BWUR	Thunder Ax10-210 Srs.2 HAB				See SECTION 1	
G-BXAL	Cameron Bertie Bassett 90SS HAB					
G-BXAX	Cameron N-77 HAB	2010		25. 5.89	Cancelled 31.1.02 as WFU *"Citroen"*	21.11.96A
G-BXHM	Lindstrand LBL-25A Cloudhopper HAB	466		30. 5.97	Cancelled 6.11.01 as WFU *"Bud Ice/Michelob"*	7. 5.00A
G-BXHN	Lindstrand Budweiser Can SS HAB	465		30. 5.97	Cancelled 6.11.01 as WFU *"Budweiser Can III"*	8. 3.01A
G-BXND	Cameron Thomas The Tank Engine 110SS HAB				See SECTION 1	
G-BZIH	Lindstrand LBL 31A HAB	700		7. 6.00	Cancelled 6.11.01 as WFU *"Budweiser""Budweiser"*	11. 6.01A
G-CBPG	The Balloon Works Firefly 7 HAB					
G-COLR	Colt 69A HAB	780		8. 4.86	Cancelled 21.5.93 as WFU *"Bubble"*	
G-COMP	Cameron N-90 HAB	1564		24. 9.87	Cancelled 18.12.01 by CAA *"Computacentre I"*	20. 5.97
G-COOP	Cameron N-31 HAB	382		2. 3.78	Cancelled 22.10.01 by CAA *"Co-op"*	13. 5.87A
G-CURE	Colt 77A HAB	1424		3. 7.89	Cancelled 29.4.97 as WFU *"Alka Seltzer III"*	21.11.96A
	(Standard shape plus Tablet blisters)					
G-DHLI	Colt World 90SS HAB	2603		2. 6.94	Cancelled 9.4.99 as WFU *"DHL World"*	17.12.98A
G-DHLZ	Colt 31A Air Chair HAB	2604		2. 6.94	Cancelled 9.4.99 as WFU *"DHL Parcel"*	23. 7.99A
G-ETFT	Colt Financial Times SS HAB	1792	G-BSGZ	11. 1.91	Cancelled 10.12.02 by CAA *"Financial Times II"*	14.10.00A
G-FZZY	Colt 69A HAB	779		19. 2.86	Cancelled 29.4.97 as WFU *"Alka-Seltzer II"*	16. 2.90A
G-GEUP	Cameron N-77 HAB	880		8.12.82	Cancelled 9.5.01 as WFU *"Gee-Up"*	19. 7.96
G-GURL	Cameron A-210 HAB	2387		3. 9.90	Cancelled 2.12.98 as WFU *"Hot Airlines"* (Located Austria)	9. 8.96T
G-HELP	Colt 17A Cloudhopper HAB	902		16. 2.87	Cancelled 27.3.99 as PWFU *"Mondial Cloudhopper"*	7. 8.95A
G-HENS	Cameron N-65 HAB	740		8. 7.81	Cancelled 8.4.93 by CAA *"Free Range"*	
G-HLIX	Cameron Helix Oilcan 61SS HAB	1192		20. 9.85	Cancelled 29.4.97 as WFU *"Helix Oil Can"*	25. 4.90A
	(Originally regd as 80SS)					
G-HOFM	Cameron N-56 HAB				See SECTION 1	
G-IAMP	Cameron H-34 HAB	2541		11. 3.91	Cancelled 6.11.01 as WFU *"National Power"*	14. 6.97A
G-IGEL	Cameron N-90 HAB	2726		7. 4.92	Cancelled 18.12.01 by CAA *"Computacentre II"*	12. 5.97A
G-IMAG	Colt 77A HAB	1718		9. 3.90	Cancelled 31.1.02 as WFU *"Agfa"*	19. 1.00A
	(Second envelope c/n 2254 as original dbf 6.92)					
G-JANB	Colt Flying Bottle SS HAB	1643		16. 2.90	Cancelled 20.12.01 by CAA *"J & B Bottle"*	30. 9.96A
	(J & B Whisky Bottle shape)					
G-KORN	Cameron Berentzen Bottle 70SS HAB				See SECTION 1	
G-LLAI	Colt 21A Cloudhopper HAB	519	(G-BKTX)	18. 7.83	Cancelled 16.7.90 by CAA *"Llama"*	
					(Lowndes Laing Insurance titles)	
G-MAAC	Advanced Airship Corporation ANR-1	01		16. 1.89	Cancelled 15.11.00 by CAA *"ANR-1"* (Located Malpas)	
G-MAPS	Sky Flying Map SS HAB	105		20. 7.98	Cancelled 31.7.01 as WFU *"OS Map"*	28. 2.01A
					(On loan from The Balloon Advertising Co Ltd)	
G-MHBD	Cameron O-105 HAB	1021		23. 2.84	Cancelled as WFU 17.4.98 (Dawsons Toys titles)	
G-MOLI	Cameron A-250 HAB				See SECTION 1	

G-NPNP	Cameron N-105 HAB	2959	G-BURX	18. 1.93	Cancelled 6.11.01 as WFU *"National Power III"*	18. 8.98A
G-NPWR	Cameron RX-100 HAB	2849		13. 7.92	Cancelled 15.7.98 as WFU *"Nuclear Rozier"*	21.11.96A
					(Located Malpas)	
G-NWPB	Thunder Ax7-77Z HAB	278		13. 5.80	Cancelled 27.4.90 by CAA *"Post Office"*	
G-OAFC	Airtour AH-56 HAB			15. 6.89	Re-registered G-BWPL - qv	
G-OCND	Cameron O-77 HAB	1020		6. 2.84	Cancelled 19.5.95 by CAA *"CND Airborne"*	
G-OHDC	Colt Film Cassette SS HAB	2633		8. 8.94	Cancelled 31.1.02 as WFU *"Agfa HDC Can"*	26. 8.99A
	(Agfa Film Can shape)					
G-OLDV	Colt 90A HAB	2592		5. 5.94	Cancelled 29.6.99 as WFU *"LDV"*	10.11.98A
G-OSVY	Sky 31-24 HAB	104		28. 5.98	Cancelled 31.7.01 as WFU *"OS Hopper"*	11. 3.00A
G-OXRG	Colt Film Can SS HAB	2138		17. 1.92	Cancelled 29.4.97 as WFU *"Agfa XRG Can"*	
	(Agfacolor Film Can shape)					
G-PONY	Colt 31A Air Chair HAB	434		23. 8.82	Cancelled 19.5.95 by CAA *"Neddie"*	
G-POPP	Colt 105A HAB	1776		1. 3.91	Cancelled 5.2.99 as WFU *"Mercier"*	21.11.96A
G-PSON	Colt Cylinder One SS HAB				See SECTION 1	
G-PURE	Cameron Can 70SS HAB *(Guinness Can)*	1913		18. 1.89	Cancelled 29.4.97 as WFU *"Guinness Can"*	
G-PYLN	Cameron Pylon 80SS HAB	2958	G-BUSO	18. 1.93	Cancelled 6.11.01 as WFU *"Essex Girl"*	25. 4.97A
	(Electricity Pylon shape)					
G-RARE	Thunder Ax5-42 SS HAB	266		20. 2.80	Cancelled 14.5.02 by CAA *"J & B Hamish"*	7. 4.95A
	(J & B Rare Whisky Bottle shape)					
G-RIPS	Cameron Action Man/Parachutist 110SS HAB	4092		29. 4.97	Cancelled 23.7.02 as WFU *"Action Man"*	25. 5.00A
					(Located Stockport)	
G-SCAH	Cameron V-77 HAB	788		18. 1.82	Cancelled 30.11.01 by CAA *"Orpheus"*	24. 7.87A
					(Located Southampton)	
G-SCFO	Cameron O-77 HAB				See SECTION 1	
G-SEGA	Cameron Sonic 90SS HAB	2896		16. 9.92	Cancelled 26.6.00 as WFU *"Sonic"*	29. 6.00A
	(Sonic The Hedgehog shape)					
G-SEUK	Cameron TV 80SS HAB	3810		12. 4.96	Cancelled 31.1.02 as WFU *"Samsung Monitor"*	24. 3.00A
	(Samsung Computer shape)					
G-TTWO	Colt 56A HAB	087		14. 5.80	Cancelled 14.11.95 as WFU *"Tea 4 Two"*	1. 9.87A
G-UNIP	Cameron Oil Container SS HAB	2532		15. 3.91	Cancelled 31.1.02 as WFU *"Unipart Can"*	7.11.96A
	(Unipart Sureflow Oil Can)					
G-VOLT	Cameron N-77 HAB	2157		8.11.89	Cancelled 23.10.01 as WFU *"National Power II"*	25. 4.97A
G-WATT	Cameron Cooling Tower SS HAB	2158		8.11.89	Cancelled 23.10.01 as WFU *"Cooling Tower"*	22. 8.96A
G-WCAT	Colt Flying Mitt SS HAB				See SECTION 1	
G-WINE	Thunder AX7-77Z HAB	472		25.11.82	Cancelled 10.4.02 by CAA *"Gemini"*	17. 6.97A
G-WORK	Thunder Ax10-180 Srs.2 HAB	2396	DQ-PBF	12. 5.93	Cancelled 3.11.97 *(Sold as DQ-HBF 11.97) (As "DQ-PBF")*	
			G-WORK		*(Paradise Balloon Flights titles) (Located Malpas)*	

Museum of D-Day Aviation, Shoreham Airport BN43 5FJ

BAPC.209	Supermarine Spitfire LF.IXC fsm			*(As "MJ751/DU-V" in 321 Sqdn c/s) ("Piece of Cake" film)*	

Visitor Centre & Archive, Shoreham Airport BN43 5FF (www.thearchivesshoreham.co.uk)

BAPC.20	Lee-Richards Annular Biplane rep	--		*("Those Magnificent Men in Their Flying Machines" film)*	
BAPC.277	Mignet HM.14 Pou-Du-Ciel				

Tangmere Military Aviation Museum, Tangmere PO20 6ES (www.tangmere-museum.org.uk)

BAPC.214	Supermarine Spitfire prototype fsm	--		*(As "K5054")*	
BAPC.241	Hawker Hurricane I fsm	--		*(As "L1679/JX-G" in 1 Sqdn c/s)*	
	(Built Aerofab 1994)				
BAPC.242	Supermarine Spitfire VB rep	--		*(As "BL924/AZ-G" in 234 Sqdn c/s) "Valde Maar Atterdag"*	
	(Built TDL Reps 1994)				

Foulkes-Halbard Collection, Filching Manor, Wannock BN26 5QA

G-BHNG	Piper PA-23-250 Aztec E	27-7405432	N54125	13. 5.80	Cancelled 12.12.86 by CAA	
	(Badly damaged following collision with Cessna F152 G-BFRB on take-off Shoreham 19.12.81) (Fuselage only)					
BAPC.127	Halton Jupiter MPA					
IAHC.2	Aldritt Monoplane					

WARWICKSHIRE
Midland Air Museum, Coventry CV8 3AZ (www.midlandairmuseum.org.uk)

G-EBJG	Parnall Pixie III	--	No.17/18	?. 9.24	Cancelled 1.12.46 by Sec of State	2.10.36
	(Lympne 1924)				*(Components only for long term rebuild 4.96)*	
G-ABOI	Wheeler Slymph	AHW.1		17. 7.31	Cancelled 1.12.46 by Sec of State	
					(Dismantled components on loan from A.H.Wheeler)	
G-AEGV	Mignet HM.14 Pou-Du-Ciel	EMAC.1		22. 4.36	Cancelled 12.37 *(WFU 26.5.37)*	26. 5.37
G-ALCU	de Havilland DH.104 Dove 2B	04022	VT-CEH	3. 8.48	Cancelled 8.9.78 as WFU	16. 3.73
G-AOKZ	Percival P.40 Prentice 1	PAC/238	VS623	20. 4.56	Not converted *(Became instructional airframe) (As "VS623")*	
G-APJJ(2)	Fairey Ultralight Helicopter	F.9428		4.12.57	Cancelled 2.3.73 as WFU	1. 4.59
G-APRL	Armstrong-Whitworth 650 Argosy Srs.101		N890U	2. 1.59	Cancelled 19.11.87 as WFU *"Edna"*	23. 3.87T
		AW.6652	N602Z/N6507R/G-APRL		*(Elan titles)*	
G-APWN	Westland WS-55 Whirlwind 3	WA.298	VR-BER	8. 9.59	Cancelled 25.6.81 as WFU *"Skerries"*	17. 5.78
			G-APWN/5N-AGI/G-APWN		*(Bristow Helicopters c/s)*	
G-ARYB	de Havilland DH.125 Srs.1	25002		1. 3.62	Cancelled 4.3.69	22. 1.68
G-MJWH	Chargus Vortex 120			R		
	(Regn reserved 1983 for Chargus T.250 & engine: fitted to 1974 Vortex hang glider: abandoned & only wing on display)					
BGA.804	Slingsby Cadet TX.1	931?	XE761?	5.57?	*(As "BAA")*	9. 3.97?
			VM589			
BAPC.9	Bleriot XI Monoplane rep (Humber)	--			*(Converted to 1911 Humber Bleriot Monoplane)*	
BAPC.32	Crossley Tom Thumb				*(Not completed Banbury 1937)*	
BAPC.126	Rollason-Druine D.31 Turbulent	--			*(Static airframe)*	
BAPC.179	Sopwith Pup rep	--			*(As "A7317")*	

Jet Aviation Preservation Group, Long Marston

G-ANUW	de Havilland DH.104 Dove 6	04458		16. 5.55	Cancelled 5.6.96 as WFU	22. 7.81

WILTSHIRE

Royal Air Force, RAF Lyneham

G-AMPO	Douglas C-47B-30DK Dakota 3	16437/33185	LN-RTO	25. 2.52	Cancelled 18.10.01 as WFU	29. 3.97A
	(Regd as c/n 16438/33186)		G-AMPO/KN566/44-76853		*(As "FZ625")*	

Science Museum Air Transport Collection & Storage Facility, Wroughton SN4 9NS (www.sciencemuseum.org.uk/wroughton)

G-AACN	Handley Page HP.39 Gugnunc	1	K1908	2.11.28	Cancelled 12.30 on transfer to RAF	19.9.30
			G-AACN			
G-AEHM	Mignet HM.14 Pou-Du-Ciel	HJD.1		30. 4.36	Cancelled in 3.39 census *"Blue Finch"*	
	(ABC Scorpion @ 35 hp)					
G-ALXT	de Havilland DH.89A Dragon Rapide	6736	4R-AAI	24. 1.50	Cancelled 5.7.51 on sale to CY-AAI *"Star of Scotia"*	
			CY-AAI/G-ALXT/NF865		*(Railway Air Service titles)*	
G-ANAV	de Havilland DH.106 Comet 1A	06013	CF-CUM	15. 8.53	Cancelled 1.7.55 as WFU	
					(Broken up RAE Farnborough 1955: nose section)	
G-APWY	Piaggio P.166	362		16.12.59	Cancelled 20.10.00 by CAA	14. 3.81
G-APYD	de Havilland DH.106 Comet 4B	6438	SX-DAL	21. 1.60	Cancelled 23.11.79 as WFU	3. 8.79T
			G-APYD		*(Dan-Air titles)*	
G-ATTN	Piccard HAB (62,000 cu ft)	15 & 1352		27. 4.66	Cancelled 5.12.77 as PWFU *"The Red Dragon"*	
					(Envelope/basket stored 6.94)	
G-AVZB	LET Z-37 Cmelak	04-08	OK-WKQ	30.11.67	Cancelled 21.12.88 as WFU	5. 4.84A
G-AWZM	Hawker Siddeley HS.121 Trident 3B Srs.101			14. 1.69	Cancelled 18.3.86 as WFU	13.12.85T
		2314			*(WFU 13.12.85) (British Airways titles)*	
G-BBGN	Cameron A-375 HAB	90		23. 8.73	Cancelled 22.8.89 as WFU	
G-BGLB	Bede BD.5B (Hirth 230R) 3796 & PFA 14-10085			2. 3.79	Cancelled 21.11.91 by CAA	4.8.81P
G-CONI	Lockheed 749A-79 Constellation	2553	N7777G	12. 5.82	Cancelled 13.6.84 as WFU	
			N173X)/N7777G/TI-1045P/PH-LDT/PH-TET	*(As "N7777G" in TWA c/s)*		
G-MMCB	Huntair Pathfinder II	136		13. 7.83	Cancelled 23.11.88 as WFU	
G-RBOS	Colt AS-105 HA Airship	390		9. 2.82	Cancelled 3.4.97 by CAA	6. 3.87A
EI-AYO(2)	Douglas DC-3A-197	1911	N655GP			5. 3.76
			N65556/N255JB/N8695E/N333H/NC16071			
BAPC.52	Lilienthal Glider Type XI	--			*(1895 original)*	
BAPC.162	Goodhart MPA	--			*"Newbury Manflier"*	
BAPC.172	Chargus Midas Super E Hang-Glider	--				
BAPC.173	Birdman Grasshopper Hang-Glider	--				
BAPC.174	Bensen B.7 Gyro-Glider	--				
BAPC.188	McBroom Cobra 88 Hang-Glider	--				
BAPC.276	Hartman Ornithopter	--				

YORKSHIRE

Museum of Army Transport, Beverley HU17 0NG (www.museum/armytransport.co.uk)

G-AOAI	Blackburn Beverley C.1	1002	XB259	15. 3.55	Cancelled 30.3.55 *(Restored to RAF as XB259) (As "XB259")*	

AeroVenture, Doncaster DN4 5EP

G-ALYB	Taylorcraft J Auster 5	1173	RT520	3. 2.50	Cancelled 29.2.84 by CAA	26. 5.63
G-AOKO	Percival P.40 Prentice 1	PAC/234	VS621	13. 4.56	Cancelled 9.10.84 as WFU	23.10.72
					(On loan from Atlantic Air Transport Ltd)	
G-APMY	Piper PA-23-160 Apache	23-1258	EI-AJT	15. 5.58	WFU 1.11.81 *(On loan from W.Fern)*	1.11.81
G-ARGI(2)	Auster 6A Tugmaster	2299	VF530	8.12.60	WFU at Heathfield in 7.73 *(Fuselage stored)*	4.7.76
G-ARHX	de Havilland DH.104 Dove 8	04513		11. 1.61	WFU 8.9.78	8. 9.78
G-AVAA	Reims/Cessna F150G	F150-0164		14.10.66	Cancelled 16.4.96 by CAA *(Fuselage only)*	5. 7.96
G-BOCB	Hawker Siddeley HS.125 Srs.1B/522	25106	G-OMCA	14. 9.87	Cancelled as WFU 22.2.95	16.10.90
			G-DJMJ/G-AWUF/5N-ALY/G-AWUF/HZ-BIN	*(WFU Luton 1994 for spares) (Cockpit only)*		
G-DELB	Robinson R-22 Beta	0799	N26461	18. 5.88	Cancelled 20.4.95 by CAA *(DBR Sherburn-in-Elmet 27.12.94)*	
G-MJKP	Hiway Skystrike/Super Scorpion	PEB-01		7. 9.82	Cancelled 9.12.94 as WFU	
	(Fuji-Robin EC-25)					
BAPC.207	Austin Whippet rep	--			*(On loan from D Charles) (As "K.158")*	
	(Built Ken Fern/Vintage & Rotary Wing Collection c.1993)					
BGA.2517	Slingsby T.30B Prefect TX.1	--	WE987		*(No external marks)*	

Museum & Art Gallery, Doncaster DN1 2AE (www.doncaster.gov.uk)

G-AEKR	Mignet HM.14 Pou-Du-Ciel	CAC.1		26. 6.36	WFU & cancelled 31.7.38	22. 6.37
	(Stored Doncaster 1938/1960: dbf RAF Finningley 4.9.70: rebuilt Claybourn Co @ c/n CAC.1 with original engine & components: allocated BAPC.121)					
BAPC.275	Bensen B.7 (Volkswagen 1600)	--			*(Built S J R Wood)*	

Yorkshire Air Museum, Elvington YO41 4AU (www.yorkshireairmuseum.gov.uk)

G-AJOZ	Fairchild F.24W-41A Argus 1	347	FK338	21. 4.47	Cancelled	15.12.63
	(UC-61-FA)		42-32142		*(Crashed Rennes, France 16.8.62)*	
G-AMYJ	Douglas C-47B-25DK Dakota 6	15968/32716	SU-AZF	23. 2.53	Cancelled 12.12.01 as WFU	4. 4.97A
			G-AMYJ/XF747/G-AMYJ/KN353/44-76384			
G-ASCD	Beagle A.61 Terrier 2	B.615	PH-SFT	23. 7.62	Cancelled 5.10.89 as WFU	26. 9.71
			(PH-SCD)/G-ASCD/VW993		*(As "TJ704/JA")*	
G-AVPN	Handley Page HPR.7 Dart Herald 213	176	I-TIVB	22. 6.67	Cancelled 8.12.97 as WFU	14.12.99T
			G-AVPN/D-BIBI/(HB-AAK)		*(Channel Express c/s)*	
G-BDBZ	Westland WS-55 Whirlwind 2 (HAR.10)	WA.62	XJ398	23. 4.75	Cancelled 28.3.85 by CAA *(Not converted) (As "XJ398")*	
		(Regd with c/n WA.386)	(XD768)		*(On loan from Yorkshire Helicopter Preservation Group)*	
G-BKDT	RAF SE.5A rep	278 & PFA 080-10325		26. 5.82	Cancelled 11.7.91 by CAA	
					(No Permit issued) (As "F943" - as carried by G-BIHF also)	
G-HNTR	Hawker Hunter T.7	HABL-003311	8834M	7. 7.89	Cancelled 11.10.91 as WFU	
			XL572		*(As "XL571/V" in "Blue Diamonds" c/s)*	
G-MJRA	Mainair Tri-Flyer 250/Hiway Demon	PRJM-01		21.12.82	Cancelled 24.1.95 by CAA	28. 6.91

G-MVIM	Noble Hardman Snowbird Mk.IV	SB-015		6. 2.89		
G-TFRB	Air Command 532 Elite Sport	0628 & G/04-1167		26. 4.90	Cancelled 7.6.01 by CAA	6. 8.98P
BAPC.28	Wright Flyer rep	--				
BAPC.41	RAF BE.2C rep	--	"6232"			
BAPC.42	Avro 504K rep	--			(As "H1968")	
BAPC.76	Mignet HM.14 Pou-Du-Ciel (Scott)	--			(Modern reproduction) (As "G-AFFI")	
BAPC.89	Cayley Glider rep	--				
BAPC.130	Blackburn 1911 Monoplane rep	--			"Mercury" (Built for TV Srs."The Flambards")	
BAPC.157	WACO CG-4A Hadrian	--			(As "237123") (Fuselage frame section only & tail pieces ex 456476)	
BAPC.240	Messerschmitt Bf.109G fsm	--			(Built D.Thorton 1994)	
BAPC.254	Supermarine Spitfire 1 fsm	--			(As "R6690/PR-A" in 1 Sqdn/RCAF c/s)	
BAPC.265	Hawker Hurricane fsm	--			(As "P3873/YO-H" in 609 Sqdn c/s)	
BAPC.270	de Havilland DH.60 Moth fsm	--			(As "G-AAAH") "Jason"	

Eden Camp Modern History Theme Museum, Malton YO17 6RT (www.edencamp.co.uk)

BAPC.230	Supermarine Spitfire fsm	--	"AA908"		(Built TDL Replicas 1993) (As "AB550/GE-P" in 349 Sqdn c/s)
BAPC.235	Fieseler Fi 103 (V-1) fsm)	--			(Built TDL Replicas 1993)
BAPC.236	Hawker Hurricane fsm	--			(Built TDL Replicas 7.93) (As "P2793/SD-M" in 501 Sqdn c/s)

SCOTLAND

Dumfries & Galloway Aviation Museum, Dumfries DG2 9PS (www.members.xoom.com/dgamuseum)

G-AHAT	Auster J/1N Alpha	1849	(HB-EOK)	11. 2.46	Cancelled 7.7.75 as WFU (Crashed 31.8.74) (Frame only)	6. 2.75
G-AWZJ	Hawker Siddeley HS.121 Trident 3B Srs.101	2311		14. 1.69	Cancelled 7.3.86 as WFU (Forward fuselage only)	12. 9.86T

National Museums of Scotland - Museum of Flight, East Fortune EH39 5LF (www.nms.ac.uk/flight)

G-ABDW	de Havilland DH.80A Puss Moth	2051	VH-UQB	23. 8.30	Cancelled 12.33 WFU & 21.1.82 PWFU	
			G-ABDW	26. 6.34	(To VH-UQB 27.5.31 & restored 25.3.77) (As "VH-UQB")	
G-ACVA	Kay Gyroplane 33/1 (Pobjoy R 75hp)	1002		26. 6.34	Cancelled 9.58 (On loan from Glasgow Museum of Transport)	
G-ACYK	Spartan Cruiser III	101		2. 5.35	Crashed Largs, Ayrshire 14.1.38 (Remains recovered 7.73)	2. 6.38
G-AFJU	Miles M.17 Monarch	789	X9306	25. 8.38	Cancelled 18.11.74 as PWFU	18. 5.64
			G-AFJU		(On loan from Aircraft Preservation Society of Scotland)	
G-AGBN	General Aircraft GAL.42 Cygnet 2	111	ES915	4.10.40	Cancelled 15.11.88 as WFU	28.11.80P
			G-AGBN			
G-AHKY	Miles M.18 Srs.2	4426	HM545	26. 4.46	Cancelled 19.3.92 as WFU	20. 9.89P
			U-0224/U-8			
G-ANOV	de Havilland DH.104 Dove 6	04445	G-5-16	11. 3.54	Cancelled 6.7.81 as WFU (Civil Aviation Authority c/s)	31. 5.75
G-AOEL	de Havilland DH.82A Tiger Moth	82537	N9510	27. 9.55	WFU 18.7.72	18. 7.72
G-APHV	Avro 652A Anson C.19 Srs.2	—	VM360	19. 9.57	Cancelled 21.1.82 as PWFU (As "VM360")	15. 6.73
G-ARCX	Gloster Meteor NF.14	AW.2163	WM261	8. 9.60	Cancelled 25.10.73 as WFU (WFU 2.69)	20. 2.69S
	(Built Armstrong-Whitworth Aircraft)					
G-ASUG	Beech E18S-9700	BA-111	N575C	3. 7.64	WFU 12.5.75	23. 7.75
			N555CB/N24R		(Loganair c/s)	
G-ATFG	Brantly B.2B	448		16. 6.65	Cancelled 25.9.87 as WFU	25. 3.85
	(Composite with parts from G-ASLO/G-AXSR)				(On loan from Aircraft Preservation Society of Scotland)	
G-ATOY	Piper PA-24-260 Comanche B	24-4346	N8893P	7. 2.66	Crashed near Elstree 6.3.79 "Myth Too" (Fuselage only)	
G-AXEH	Beagle B.125 Bulldog 1	B.125-001		25. 4.69	Cancelled 15.1.77 as WFU	15. 1.77
G-BBBV	Handley Page HP.137 Jetstream	234	N14234	26. 6.73	Cancelled 21.8.74	
	(Fuselage used by BAe as Jetstream 31 mock-up)		N102SC/N1BE/(N200SE)/G-BBBV/G-8-12 (To N200SE 8.74) (As "N14234")			
G-BBVF	Scottish Aviation Twin Pioneer 3	558	7978M	17.12.73	Cancelled 8.8.83	14. 5.82
			XM961			
G-BDFU	PMPS Dragonfly MPA Mk.1	01		14. 7.75	Cancelled 12.83 as WFU (On loan from R.J.Hardy & R.Churcher)	
G-BDIX	de Havilland DH.106 Comet 4C	6471	XR399	1. 9.75	Cancelled 2.9.91 by CAA (Dan-Air titles)	11.10.81T
G-BDYG	Percival P.56 Provost T.1	PAC/F/056	7696M	25. 5.76	Cancelled 4.11.91 by CAA	28.11.80P
			WV493		(As "WV493/29/A-P")	
G-BIRW	Morane-Saulnier MS.505 Criquet	695/28	OO-FIS	10. 4.81	Cancelled 15.11.88 as WFU	3. 6.83P
			F-BDQS/French AF 695		(As "FI+S" in Luftwaffe c/s)	
G-JSSD	Handley Page HP.137 Jetstream 1	227	N510F	14. 6.79	Cancelled 4.1.96 by CAA	9.10.90
	(Conv to BAe Jetstream Srs.3001 prototype.1979/80)		N510E/N12227/G-AXJZ			
G-MBJX	Hiway Skytrike I/Hiway Super Scorpion	MM-01		2. 2.82	Cancelled 13.6.90 by CAA	
	(Valmet SM160 s/n 15108)					
G-MBPM	Eurowing Goldwing	EW-21		14. 4.82	Cancelled 30.8.00 as WFU	21. 8.98P
	(Fuji-Robin EC-34-PM)					
G-MMLI	Mainair Tri-Flyer 250/Solar Wings Typhoon S	BAPC.244		26. 3.84	Cancelled 7.9.94 by CAA	
	RPAT-01 & T484-423L				(Originally regd as Hiway Skytrike Mk.II 250)	
BAPC.49	Pilcher Hawk glider (1896 original)	--			(Rebuilt after fatal crash Stanford Hall, Leics 30.9.1899)	
BAPC.59	Sopwith F1 Camel rep	--	"D3419"		(As "B5577/W")	
			"F1921"			
BAPC.70	Auster AOP.5	TAY/33153	"GALES"		(As "TJ398") (On loan from Aircraft Preservation Society of Scotland)	
BAPC.85	Weir W-2 (Weir Dryad II 50hp)	--			(As "W-2") (On loan)	
BAPC.160	Chargus 18/50 Hang-Glider	--				
BAPC.195	Birdman Sports Moonraker 77 Hang-Glider	--			(Built c.1977)	
BAPC.196	Southdown Sailwings Sigma 2m Hang-Glider	--			(Built c.1980)	
BAPC.197	Scotkites Cirrus III Hang-Glider	--			(Built 1977)	
BAPC.244	Solar Wings Typhoon S Hang-Glider	--			(Wing for G-MMLI - see above ?)	
BAPC.245	Electraflyer Floater Hang-Glider	--			(Built 1979) (Wing only)	
BAPC.246	Hiway Cloudbase Hang-Glider	--			(Built 1978)	
BAPC.247	Albatros ASG.21 Hang-Glider	--			(Built 1977)	
BAPC.262	(Eurowing) Catto CP-16	--				
BGA.852	Slingsby T.8 Tutor	--	TS291	2. 7.58	(As "TS291")	
BGA.902	Slingsby T.12 Gull I			15. 5.59	(As "BED") "G-ALPHA"	
BGA.1014	Slingsby T.21B	556	SE-SHK	1.62	(As "BJV")	

City of Edinburgh Council, Edinburgh Airport
BAPC.227   Supermarine Spitfire IA fsm   --   (As "L1070/XT-A" in 603 Sqdn c/s)

Museum of Transport, Kelvin Hall, Glasgow G3 8DP
BAPC.48   Pilcher Hawk glider rep   --   (Built No.2175 Sqdn ATC, Glasgow 1966)

WALES

Caernarfon Air Museum, Caernarfon, Gwynedd LL54 5TP (www.caeairparc.com)

Reg	Type	c/n	prev id	date	status	date
G-ALFT	de Havilland DH.104 Dove 6	04233		14.12.48	Cancelled 11.2.77 as WFU	13. 6.73
G-AMLZ	Percival P.50 Prince 6E	P.46	(VR-TBN)	23.11.51	Cancelled 9.10.84 as WFU	18. 6.71
G-AWUK	Reims/Cessna F150H	F150-0344		25.11.68	Cancelled 13.4.73 as WFU	3. 9.73
					(Crashed Shoreham 4.9.71) (Cockpit only)	
G-MBEP	American Aerolights Eagle 215B	2877		9.11.81	Cancelled 16.5.96 as WFU	8. 4.96E
	(Chrysler 820)					
BAPC.201	Mignet HM.14 Pou-Du-Ciel	--				

National Museum & Gallery, Cardiff CF10 3NP
BAPC.47   Watkins CHW Monoplane (Watkins 40hp)   --

IRELAND

Ulster Folk & Transport Museum, Holywood, Belfast BT18 0EU (www.nidex.com/uftm)

Reg	Type	c/n	prev id	date	status	date
G-ACUX	Short S.16 Scion 1	S.776	VH-UUP	26. 6.34	Cancelled 2.38 & 7.81 (Stored)	
			G-ACUX	(To VH-UUP 2.10.35 & restored 25.3.77) (Not rebuilt following import) (As "VH-UUP")			
G-AJOC	Miles M.38 Messenger 2A	6370		23. 4.47	Cancelled 5.1.82 as WFU (Stored)	18. 5.72
G-AKEL	Miles M.65 Gemini 1A	6484		8. 9.47	Cancelled 30.5.84 as WFU (Components only) (Stored)	29. 4.72
G-AKGE	Miles M.65 Gemini 3C	6488	EI-ALM	18.10.47	Cancelled 30.5.84	7. 6.74
			G-AKGE		(Stored)	
G-AKLW	Short SA.6 Sealand 1	SH.1571	(USA)	26.11.47	Sold abroad 8.51	
			R Saudi AF/SU-AHY/G-AKLW		(Stored)	
G-BKMW	Short SD.3-30 Sherpa Var.100	SH3094	G-14-3094	13.12.82	Cancelled 14.11.96 as WFU (Broken up 3.96) (Cockpit only)	14.9.90
G-AOUR	de Havilland DH.82A Tiger Moth	86341	NL898	14. 8.56	Crashed Newtownards 6.6.65 (Stored)	19.11.66
G-ARTZ (1)	McCandless M.2 Gyrocopter	M2/1		?.10.61	Replaced by G-ARTZ(2) – see SECTION 1	
	(Triumph 650cc)				(Stored)	
G-ATXX	McCandless M.4 Gyrocopter	M4/3		27. 7.66	Cancelled 9.9.70 as WFU	
	(Volkswagen 1600)				(Stored)	
BGA.470	Short Nimbus	S.1312		.47	(As "ALA")	8.75
IAHC.6	Ferguson Monoplane rep (Original engine)				(Built Capt J.Kelly Rogers 1974)	
IAHC.9	Ferguson Monoplane rep				(Built L.Hannah 1980) (Stored)	

Ulster Aviation Heritage, Langford Lodge, Belfast BT16 1WQ (www.ulsteraviationsociety.co.uk)

Reg	Type	c/n	prev id	date	status	date
G-BDBS	Short SD.3-30 UTT	SH.1935 & SH.3001	G-14-3001	21. 4.75	Cancelled 1.7.93 as WFU	28. 9.92S
	(Airframe originally laid down as SC.7 Skyvan c/n SH.1935)					
G-BTUC	Embraer EMB-312 Tucano	312.007	G-14-007	19. 6.86	Cancelled 20.12.96 as WFU	11. 9.93
			PP-ZTC			
G-MJWS	Eurowing Goldwing (Fuji-Robin EC-34-PM)	EW-22		16. 5.83	Cancelled 23.6.97 by CAA	
EI-BAG	Cessna 172A	47571	G-ARAV	7. 8.74	(Damaged 3.10.76)	26. 6.79
			N9771T			
EI-BUO	Aero Composites Sea Hawker	80		25. 8.87		
	(Aka Glass S.005E)					
BAPC.263	Chargus Cyclone	--			(Built 1979)	
BAPC.266	Rogallo Hang-glider	--				

Nutgrove Shopping Centre, Churchtown, Dublin
EI-124   Grob G.102 Astir Standard CS 77   1761   D-...   .80

Meath Aero Museum, Ashbourne, Co.Meath
IGA.6   Slingsby T.8 Tutor   --   IAC.6   .56
                                      VM657

South East Aviation Enthusiasts Group c/o Cavan & Leitrim Railway, Dromod, Leitrim, Co.Leitrim

Reg	Type	c/n	prev id	date	status	date
G-ALCS(2)	Miles M.65 Gemini 3C	WAL/C/1001		7.11.49	Cancelled 30.5.84 by CAA	
	(Originally regd as Srs.3A with c/n 6534)				(WFU 1983) (Cockpit only) (Provenance suspect)	
G-AMDD	de Havilland DH.104 Dove 6	04292		8. 8.50	Cancelled 26.9.68 (As "IAC 176")	
	(Originally regd as Srs.2, then 2B)				(To VQ-ZJC 9.68, 3D-AAI, VP-YKF & IAC 176)	
G-AOGA	Miles M.75 Aries 1	75/1007	EI-ANB	9.11.55	Cancelled 30.5.84	10.10.69
			G-AOGA		(To EI-ANB 18.5.63, restored 10.9.65: damaged Cork 8.8.69)	
G-AOIE	Douglas DC-7C	45115	PH-SAX	27. 8.56	Cancelled 31.3.70 as WFU	
			G-AOIE		(To PH-SAX 10.4.67, restored 18.11.69)	
					(Scrapped 10.97: fuselage only)	
G-AYAG	Boeing 707-321	18085	N759PA	26. 3.70	Cancelled 8.12.72 (As "VP-BDF") (Nose only)	
			(To G-41-2-72, (CS-BDG) (N435MA) & VP-BDF 12.72)			
EI-BDM	Piper PA-23-250 Aztec D	27-4166	G-AXIV	10.10.77	(WFU & scrapped Shannon 4.85) (Fuselage only)	
			N6826Y			
IAHC.1	Mignet HM.14 Pou-Du-Ciel	--			"Patrick"	

AUSTRALIA

Sir Ross & Sir Keith Smith War Memorial, Adelaide

Reg	Type	c/n	prev id	date	status	date
G-EAOU	Vickers FB.27A Vimy IV	--	(A5-1)	23.10.19	Cancelled 1920	31.10.20
			G-EAOU/F8630		(As "G-EAOU")	

Queensland Cultural Centre, Brisbane

G-EACQ	Avro 534 Baby	534/1	VH-UCQ	29. 5.19	Sold 6.21 & regd G-AUCQ 12.7.21	
			G-AUCQ/G-EACQ/K-131		*(To VH-UCQ 10.30) (As "G-EACQ")*	
G-EBOV	Avro 581E Avian	5116	No 9	7. 7.26	Cancelled 14.1.30 as sold in Australia	
			(Lympne 1926)	30. 1.29	*(Orig regd as Avro 581, to 581A in 1927 & mod. to 581E)*	

Australian War Memorial, Canberra

G-EAQM	Airco DH.9	--	F1278	31.12.19	Cancelled 8.1.20	1. 1.21
	(AS Puma)				*(NTU & to Australia 1920) (As "G-EAQM")*	

Moorabin Air Museum, Melbourne, Victoria

G-AJKG(2)	Miles M.38 Messenger 2A	6373		30. 5.47	Cancelled 17.8.53 as sold to Australia	
					(To VH-AVQ) (Stored)	

Temora Aviation Museum, Temora, New South Wales, Australia

G-BURM	English Electric Canberra TT.18	--	WJ680	11.12.92	Cancelled 3.7.02	2.12.02P
	(Built Handley Page Ltd)				*(Delivered 5.02)*	

AUSTRIA

McDonald's Restaurant, Vienna-Schwechat Airport, Vienna

G-AGRW	Vickers 639 Viking 1	115	XF640	8. 5.46	WFU 8.64	9. 7.68
	(Originally registered as 498 Viking 1A)		G-AGRW		*(Noted 9.01)*	

BELGIUM

Koninklijk Leger Museum/Musée Royal de l'Armée, Brussels

G-ACGR	Percival P.1C Gull Four IIA	D.29		11. 5.33	Cancelled 12.34	20. 6.35
	(DH Gipsy Major I)				*(Originally regd as P.1B) (Crashed Waterloo, Belgium 12.34)*	
G-AFJR	Tipsy Trainer 1	2		20. 8.38	Cancelled 12.4.89 as TWFU	10. 9.64
	(Converted to Belfair)				*(Stored for static rebuild with remains of G-AFRV)*	
G-AFRV	Tipsy Trainer I	10		15. 7.39	Cancelled 10.2.87 by CAA	
					(Damaged landing Herrings Farm, Cross-in-Hand, Sussex 15.9.79) (Used for spares for rebuild of G-AFJR)	
G-AFVH	Tipsy S.2	29	OO-ASB	7. 6.39	Cancelled 27.7.49 (As "OO-TIP") (To OO-TIP 7.49)	
G-AKIS	Miles M.38 Messenger 2A	6725		19. 9.47	Cancelled 24.2.70 as WFU	5. 8.70
G-AKNV	de Havilland DH.89A Dragon Rapide	6458	G-AKNV	2.12.47	Cancelled 27.9.55 (As "OO-CNP")	
			EI-AGK/G-AKNV/R5922		*(To OO-AFG 9.55 then OO-CNP 4.64))*	
G-AMJD	de Havilland DH.82A Tiger Moth	83728	T7238	9. 4.51	Cancelled 11.11.52 (To OO-SOI 10.52) (As "T-24/UR-!")	
G-AOJX	de Havilland DH.82A Tiger Moth	3272	K4276	18. 4.56	Cancelled 5.6.56 (To OO-EVS 7.56) (As "OO-EVS")	
G-APPT	de Havilland DH.82A Tiger Moth	84567	T6100	24.10.58	Cancelled 2.1.59 (To (OO-SOK)/OO-SOW 1.59) (As "OO-SOW")	
G-BDPU	Fairey Britten-Norman BN-2A-21 Islander	510		5. 2.76	Cancelled 19.11.76	
	(Originally regd as BN-2A-26)				*(To B-06/OTA-LF Belgium Army 8.76) (As "B-06")*	
BAPC.19	Bristol F2b	--			*(As "66" in Belgian AF c/s)*	
	(Rebuilt to static condition by Skysport Engineering 6.89 with parts from J8264)					

Waarschoot, Flemish Region (Route N9)

G-AZNA	Vickers 813 Viscount	350	(G-AZLU)	8. 2.72	Cancelled 17.6.92 by CAA	
			ZS-CDX/(ZS-SBX)/ZS-CDX		*(WFU & stored Waarschoot) (On display 12.01)*	

CANADA

National Aviation Museum, Rockcliffe, Ottawa, Ontario

G-AIKR	Airspeed AS.65 Consul	4338	PK286	25. 9.46	CofA expired & WFU (As "G-AIKR")	14. 5.65

DENMARK

Danmarks Flyvemuseum, Kongelunden, Billund

G-AKDK	Miles M.65 Gemini 1A	6469		22. 8.47	Cancelled 5.11.73 as WFU	27. 3.70
					(For rebuild with parts from G-AJWA c/n 6290)	

Dansk Veteranflysamling, Stauning

G-BLPZ	de Havilland DH.104 Devon C.2	04270	WB534	18.10.84	Cancelled 12.3.86 - to OY-BHZ (As "OY-BHZ") (Stored 5.01)	

FINLAND

Keski-Suomen Ilmailumuseo, Tikkakoski

G-EBNU	Avro 504K	--	E448	19. 3.26	To Finnish AF as AV-57 in 9.26 & cancelled (As "AV-57" 6.01)	

FRANCE

Forbes Balloon Museum, Balleroy, Normandy

G-BMUN	Cameron Harley 78SS HAB	1188		10. 6.86	Cancelled 12.11.01 as WFU	23. 5.99
	(Harley Davidson Motorcycle shape)					

Concorde Supermarket, Lempdes, Clermont Ferrand

G-ARER	Vickers 708 Viscount	12	F-BGNM	19. 9.60	Cancelled 27.6.66. To F-BOEA in 8.66	
					(Crashed 28.12.71) (As "F-BOEA" 9.97)	

Musée National de l'Automobile, Mulhouse

G-AIVG	Vickers 610 Viking 1B	220		18.11.46	Crashed Le Bourget 12.8.53 (Airframe only)	12. 2.54

Musee de l'Air et de l'Espace, Le Bourget, Paris

G-EBYY	Avro 617 Cierva C.8L Mk.2 (AS Lynx 180hp)	--		21. 6.28	Sold 4.30 abroad?	13. 7.29

Ailes Anciennes Toulouse, Blagnac, Toulouse

G-ALWC	Douglas C-47A-25-DK Dakota	13590	KG723	10. 1.50	To F-GBOL in 11.82 but NTU	6.2.83
			42-93654		*(Cancelled 29.2.84 by CAA, restd 1.5.84, cancelled by CAA 3.4.89)*	

GERMANY

Hubschrauber Museum, Sableplatz, Bückeburg

G-AYNP	Westland WS-55 Whirlwind Srs.3	WA/71	ZS-HCY	14.12.70	Cancelled 22.2.94 by CAA	27.10.85T
			G-AYNP/XG576			

Luftfahrt Museum, Laatzen, Hannover

G-FXIV	Supermarine 379 Spitfire FR.XIVc	---	T44	11. 4.80	Cancelled 5.2.85 as WFU	
			Indian AF HS.../MV370		*(As "MV370")*	

Flugausstellung L und P Junior Museum, Hermeskeil, Trier

G-ARVF	Vickers VC-10-1101	808		16. 1.63	Cancelled as WFU 11.4.83 *(UAE c/s)*	23. 7.81
G-BDIW	de Havilland DH.106 Comet 4C	6470	XR398	1. 9.75	Cancelled 23.2.81 to Germany *(Dan-Air c/s)*	6.6.81
G-BKLZ	Vinten Wallis WA-116MC	UMA-01		8.12.82	Cancelled 8.6.89 as destroyed	16.12.83P
	(Aka Vinten VJ-22 Autogyro)				*(As "G-55-2")*	
G-BXSL	Westland Scout AH.Mk.1	F.9762	XW799	17. 2.98	Cancelled 7.5.02 by CAA *(As "XW799")*	19. 8.02P
G-NAVY	de Havilland DH.104 Sea Devon C.20 (Dove 6)		XJ348	6. 1.82	Cancelled 2.7.91 as WFU	
		04406	G-AMXX		*(As "XJ348") (Stored 9.01)*	

Luftfahrt und Tecknik Museumpark, Merseburg

G-DEVN	de Havilland DH.104 Devon C.2/2	04269	WB533	26.10.84	Cancelled 16.11.90 by CAA	4.2.85P

Auto und Technik Museum, Sinsheim

G-AKLL	Douglas C-47A-30-DK Dakota	14005/25450	KG773	18.11.47	Cancelled 6.6.50 - to EC-AEU	
			43-48189		*(To Span AF T.3-62/N8041A/"D-CORA") (As "D-CADE")*	
G-ARUE(2)	de Havilland DH.104 Dove 7	04530	IAC-194	7.10.80	Cancelled 17.7.86 by CAA	
			Irish Air Corps/(G-ARUE)		*(To D-IKER 10.83)*	
G-AWHS	Hispano HA.1112-Mil	228	Span AF C4K-170	14. 5.68	Cancelled 17.2.69 on sale to Spain	
	(Daimler-Benz.605D)				*(To N170BG) (As "4+-" in Luftwaffe c/s)*	
G-BFHF	CASA C.352L	166	Span AF T2B-275	23.11.77	Cancelled 30.4.90 as WFU	
	(Junkers Ju 52/3m)		Span AF "721-15"		*(Sold West Germany 1.86) (As "RJ+NP")*	
	(Provenance unconfirmed – museum version also reported as ex T2B-140 [50] and later N9012P)					

Stuttgart Airport, Stuttgart

G-BGGR	North American AT-6A Harvard	77-4176	Portuguese AF	17. 1.79	Cancelled 20.4.79	
			1608/41-217		*(D-FOBY reserved 4.79) (As "D-FOBY")*	
G-AVHE	Vickers 812 Viscount	363	(G-AVGY)	20. 2.67	Cancelled 14.2.73 as destroyed	
			N251V		*(WFU 30.3.70 & broken up 8.72) (Forward fuselage only)*	

ITALY

Italian Air Force Museum, Vigna di Valle

G-FIST	Fiesler Fi.156C-3 Storch	156-5802	D-EDEC	23.11.83	Cancelled 4.12.90 by CAA	
			I-FAGG/MM12822		*(Restored 25.2.91 & canc 24.4.95 on sale to Italy) (As "MM12822/20")*	

MALTA

Malta Aviation Museum, Ta'Qali

G-ANFW	de Havilland DH.82A Tiger Moth	85660	DE730	5.11.53	Cancelled 10.3.00 by CAA	21. 7.01
	(Built Morris Motors) (Regd with Fuselage No.3737)				*(As "DE730")*	

THE NETHERLANDS

Aviation Shop, Aalsmeerderbrug

G-BPMP	Douglas C-47A-50-DL Dakota	10073	N54607	2. 2.89	Cancelled 18.4.95 as WFU *(Cockpit only 3.02)*	
			(N9842A)/N54607/Morocco AF 20669/CN-CCL/F-BEFA/42-24211			

Museum Bevrijdende Vleugels/Wings of Liberation Museum, Best, Noord-Brabant

G-AMPP	Douglas C-47B-15-DK Dakota 3	15272/26717	"G-AMSU"	4. 3.52	Cancelled 7.2.71	7. 2.71
			XF756/G-AMPP/KK136/43-49456			

Aviodome & Stichting Koolhaven Vliegtuigen ($), Schiphol Centrum

G-EACN	BAT FK.23 Bantam 1 **($)**	FK23/15	K-123	22. 7.19	NTU - No CofA issued	
	(ABC Wasp)		F1654		*(K-123 regd 29. 5.19 & cancelled 7.19)*	
G-BVOL	Douglas C-47B-40-DL Dakota	9836	ZS-NJE(2)	14. 6.94	Cancelled 16.5.96 on sale to Netherlands as spares	
			SAAF 6867/FD938/42-23974		*(As "PH-TCB" 3.02)*	
BAPC.22	Mignet HM.14 Pou-Du-Ciel (Scott A2S)	WM.1			*(As "G-AE0F")*	

NEW ZEALAND

Jean Batten Memorial, Terminal Building, Auckland International Airport, Auckland

G-ADPR	Percival P.3 Gull Six	D.55	AX866	29. 8.35	Cancelled 14.3.95	1. 8.95P
			G-ADPR		*(To ZK-DPR) (As "ZK-DPR")*	

NORWAY
Forsvarsmuseet/Norwegian Armed Forces Museum, Gardermoen

G-BMEW	Lockheed 18-56 Lodestar	18-2444	OH-SIR		30. 9.85	Cancelled 15.7.86 on sale to "Canada"
	(C-60A-5-LO) *(Gulfstar conversion c.4.59)*		(N283M)/OH-MAP/N283M/N9223R/N105G/N69898/NC69898/42-55983			
						(Allocated N283M but ntu) (As "G-AGIH")

Flyhistorick Museum Sola, Stavangar

G-AKKA	Miles M.65 Gemini 1A	6528			21.10.47	Cancelled 27.4.48 - to LN-TAH 4.48
G-AOXL	de Havilland DH.114 Heron 1B	14015	(LN-BFY)		5. 4.57	To (LN-BFY) 13.9.71
			G-AOXL/PK-GHB			*(NTU & restored 21.9.71: cancelled 11.10.71 - to LN-BFY 2.72)*
						(As "LN-PSG" 10.01)
G-BBZL	Westland-Bell 47G-3B1	WA/583	S Yemen AF 404		26. 2.74	Cancelled 2.6.82- to SE-HME 6.82
						(Became "LN-ORB" but as "G-BBZL" 11.02)
G-BCZS	Fairey Britten-Norman BN-2A-21 Islander	441			1. 4.75	To LN-MAF 5.75. Cancelled 19.8.77. *(Stored 11.02)*

REPUBLIC of SOUTH AFRICA
South African Air Force Museum, Pretoria

G-EAML	Airco DH.6	--	C9449		8. 9.19	Cancelled 19.9.19: to South Africa	18. 9.20
						(Components only preserved as "G-EAML")	
G-AITF	Airspeed AS.40 Oxford 1	--	ED290		1.11.46	Cancelled 31.10.61 as PWFU *(As "G-AITF")*	8. 6.60

SPAIN
Hotel Las Americas, Tenerife

G-AOYM	Vickers 806 Viscount	262			20.12.56	Cancelled 29.10.85 - to EC-DYC 10.85 *(Nose only stored 12.99)*

SWEDEN
High Chapperal Park, Hillerstorp

G-AVJB	Vickers 815 Viscount	375	(LX-LGD)		21. 3.67	Cancelled 28.10.86 - to SE-IVY "Big Airland"
			G-AVJB/AP-AJF			*(Noted 8.01)*

Flyvapenmuseum, Malmen, Linköping

G-ANVU	de Havilland DH.104 Dove 1B	04082	VR-NAP		12.11.54	Cancelled 20.6.85 by CAA	14.9.77
	(Originally regd as Srs.1)					*(WFU 1977: restored 15.4.86: cancelled 16.9.86 on sale to Sweden) (Stored 5.01)*	

Arlanda Aerospace Expo, Stockholm

G-AGIJ	Lockheed 18-56 Lodestar II	2593	43-16433		4. 3.44	Cancelled 9.7.45
	(C-60A-5-LO)					*(To R.Norwegian AF as 2593/T-AE in 7.45, to OH-VKP & SE-BZE) (Stored 5.01)*

Svedinos Bil Och Flymuseum

G-AIZW	Auster J/1 Autocrat	2230			31. 1.47	Cancelled 14.8.58 - to SE-CGR 8.58
G-AKAO	Miles M.38 Messenger 2A	6703			27. 6.47	Cancelled 7.9.53 - to SE-BYY 9.53 *(As "L-H")*
G-ANSO	Gloster Meteor T.7	G5/1525	G-7-1		12. 6.54	Cancelled 11.8.59 - to SE-DCC 8.59
	(Originally built as Meteor F.8 G-AMCJ)					*(As "WS774/4")*

SWITZERLAND
Technorama Museum, Winterthur

G-AHPB	Vickers 639 Viking 1	132			4. 9.46	Cancelled?? *(To XF638 ?? & restored ??) (As "D-BABY")*	20.5.68
	(Originally regd as Type 614)					*(Also reported as broken up between 1988 & 1993: current status unknown)*	

UNITED ARAB EMIRATES
Al Mahata Museum, The Sharjah Aviation Museum, Sharjah

G-ARDE	de Havilland DH.104 Dove 6	04469	I-TONY		15.11.60	Cancelled 30.5.01 by CAA *(As "G-AJPR" in Gulf Air c/s)*	25. 8.91

UNITED STATES OF AMERICA
United States Army Aviation Museum, Fort Rucker, Alabama

G-BLXT	RAF SE.5A	--	N4488		2.10.85	Cancelled 28.9.89 by CAA
			USAAS 22-296			*(To USA in 1994)*
G-BSKS	Nieuport 28C-1	6531	"N5246"		27. 6.90	Cancelled 1.4.93 on sale to USA
			US Navy			*(As "6531/5" in 94 Aero Sqn AEF c/s)*

Miami International Airport, Miami, Florida

G-ASCY	Phoenix Luton LA-4A Minor	PAL/1124			5. 9.62	Cancelled 8.69 *(Sold as EI-ATP 29.8.69)*
						(Displayed in Concourse E as EI-ATP/N924GB @ 10.94)

Valiant Air Command Museum, Tico, Florida

G-AGWE	Avro 19 Srs.2	1286	TX201		28.12.45	Cancelled as sold 17.5.73 to USA *(Stored 6.94)*	5. 3.73

Cavanaugh Flight Museum, Addison, Texas

G-CCMV	Chance Vought FG-1D Corsair	3660	N448AG		21.11.00	Cancelled 5.9.02 on sale in USA as N451FG
	(Built Goodyear)		N4717C/Bu.92399			

National Air & Space Museum, Washington DC

G-AARO(2	Arrow Sport A2-60	341	N932S		17. 9.79	Cancelled in 6.83 on sale as N280AS
			NC932S			*(Now N9325 in 1.85: noted as "G-AARO" 10.00 @ Paul E Garber Facility)*
G-BFHD	CASA C.352L	146	T2B-255		23.11.77	Cancelled 21.1.88 on sale to West Germany
:			"721-8"			*(To NASM as "D-ODLH" in Lufthansa c/s)*

PART 2 – BRITISH AVIATION PRESERVATION COUNCIL

The British Aviation Preservation Council (BAPC) was formed in 1967 and is the national body for the preservation of aviation related items. It is a voluntary staffed body which undertakes a representation, co-ordination and enabling role. BAPC membership includes national, local authority, independent and service museums, private collections, voluntary groups and other organisations involved in the advancement of aviation preservation in the UK. A number of overseas aircraft preservation organisations have affiliated membership. The Secretary is Nick Foster c/o Museum of Science & Industry, Liverpool Road, Castlefield, Manchester M3 4FP (Tel: 0161 8322244), email: curatorial@mussci.u-net.com.

The BAPC register of historic aircraft was started in the 1980s to identify and record the many aircraft which were never allocated an official military or civil identity. These include hang gliders, RAF "plastic replicas", film replicas, German & Japanese aircraft and homebuilts. Most exhibits held in Museums are usually on display and the identities shown in the Comments column are carried. With the publication of the 18th edition of Ken Ellis' "Wrecks & Relics" I have taken the opportunity to update the information. We are very grateful to Ken for this and to Barry Taylor for additional information. Further information about many of these aircraft, their various locations and the availabilty of Museums can be found in "Wrecks & Relics" and in Part 1 above. Do not forget that access to the London collections of the Imperial War, Science, and RAF Museums is free of charge.

BAPC No.	Type	C/n	P/I	Owner/Operator	Location
1	Roe Triplane rep			See PART 1 above	
2	Bristol Boxkite rep			See PART 1 above	
3	Bleriot XI			See PART 1 above	
4	Deperdussin			See PART 1 above	
5	Blackburn Monoplane			See PART 1 above	
6	Roe Triplane Type IV rep			See PART 1 above	
7	SUMPAC			See PART 1 above	
8	Dixon Ornithopter			See PART 1 above	
9	Bleriot XI Monoplane rep			See PART 1 above	
10	Hafner R.II Revoplane			See PART 1 above	
11	English Electric Wren			See PART 1 above	
12	Mignet HM.14 Pou-Du-Ciel			See PART 1 above	
13	Mignet HM.14 Pou-Du-Ciel			Brimpex Metal Treatments Ltd	Sheffield
	(Douglas 600cc)			(Under restoration 3.98)	
14	Addyman Standard Training Glider			A.Lindsay & N.H.Ponsford (Stored 2.00)	Selby
15	Addyman Standard Training Glider			N.H.Ponsford	Wigan
	(Yorkshire Aeroplanes rebuild)	YA2		(Stored 2.00)	
16	Addyman Ultralight			A.Lindsay & N.H.Ponsford	Selby
				(Stored incomplete 2.00)	
17	Woodhams Sprite			BB Aviation (Stored incomplete 2.00)	Canterbury
18	Killick Gyroplane			A.Lindsay & N.H.Ponsford (Stored 2.00)	Selby
19	Bristol F2b			See PART 1 above	
20	Lee-Richards Annular Biplane rep			See PART 1 above	
21	Thruxton Jackaroo			M.J.Brett	Not known
	(Used as spares in rebuild of G-APAL)			(Current status unknown)	
22	Mignet HM.14 Pou-Du-Ciel			See PART 1 above	
23	Allocation cancelled – originally used by fi scale SE.5 rep at Newark Air Museum				
24	Allocation cancelled – originally used by 2/3rd scale Currie Wot rep at Newark Air Museum				
25	Nyborg TGN.III Sailplane			P Williams (Stored 1.92)	Warwick
26	Auster AOP.9			(Fuselage frame only - since scrapped Swansea)	
27	Mignet HM.14 Pou-Du-Ciel			M J Abbey (Under construction 1988)	Not known
28	Wright Flyer rep			See PART 1 above	
29	Mignet HM.14 Pou-Du-Ciel			See PART 1 above	
30	DFS Grunau Baby			Not known (Destroyed by fire Swansea 1969)	
31	Slingsby T.7 Tutor			Not known (Believed scrapped Swansea)	
32	Crossley Tom Thumb			See PART 1 above	
33	DFS 10849 Grunau Baby IIB		VN148	Russavia Collection	Bishops Stortford
			LN+ST	(On rebuild as BGA.2400 1978: status unknown)	
34	DFS 10849 Grunau Baby IIB	030892	RAFGSA281	D.Elsdon	Hazlemere, Bucks
			RAFGGA GK.4/LZ+AR		
				(Originally on rebuild as BGA.2362: status unknown but possibly used for spares)	
35	EoN AP.7 Primary	EoN/P/063		Not known (ex Russavia Collection)	Pocklington
				(On rebuild as BGA.2493 8.89)	
36	Fieseler Fi 103 V1 model			See PART 1 above	
37	Blake Bluetit			See G-BXIY in SECTION 1	
38	Bristol Scout D rep			K Williams & M Thorn	Solihull
	(Gnome 80 hp)			(As "A1742") (On rebuild 11.99)	
39	Addyman Zephyr Sailplane			A Lindsay & N.H Ponsford	Selby
				(Parts held for eventual rebuild 2.00)	
40	Bristol Boxkite rep			See PART 1 above	
41	RAF BE.2C rep			See PART 1 above	
42	Avro 504K rep			See PART 1 above	
43	Mignet HM.14 Pou-Du-Ciel			See PART 1 above	
44	Miles M.14A Magister			See PART 1 above	
45	Pilcher Hawk Glider rep			See PART 1 above	
46	Mignet HM.14 Pou-Du-Ciel			Not known	Tump Farm, Coleford
				(Status unknown: probably scrapped)	
47	Watkins CHW Monoplane			See PART 1 above	
48	Pilcher Hawk Glider rep			See PART 1 above	
49	Pilcher Hawk Glider			See PART 1 above	
50	Roe Triplane Type I			See PART 1 above	
51	Vickers FB.27 Vimy IV			See PART 1 above	
52	Lilienthal Glider Type XI			See PART 1 above	
53	Wright Flyer rep			See PART 1 above	
54	JAP/Harding Monoplane			See PART 1 above	
55	Levasseur-Antoinette Developed Type VII Monoplane			See PART 1 above	

56	Fokker E.III			See PART 1 above	
57	Pilcher Hawk Glider rep			E Littledike	(St Albans)
	(Built Martin & Miller, Edinburgh 1930)				
58	Yokosuka MXY7 Ohka 11			See PART 1 above	
59	Sopwith F1 Camel rep			See PART 1 above	
60	Murray M.1 Helicopter			See PART 1 above	
61	Stewart Ornithopter			North Coates Flyng Club	North Coates
				"Bellbird II" (Stored 12.00)	
62	Cody Type V Biplane			See PART 1 above	
63	Hawker Hurricane fsm			See PART 1 above	
64	Hawker Hurricane fsm			See PART 1 above	
65	Supermarine Spitfire fsm			See PART 1 above	
66	Messerschmitt Bf109 fsm			See PART 1 above	
67	Messerschmitt Bf109 fsm			See PART 1 above	
68	Hawker Hurricane fsm			See PART 1 above	
69	Supermarine Spitfire fsm			See PART 1 above	
70	Auster AOP.5			See PART 1 above	
71	Supermarine Spitfire fsm			See PART 1 above	
72	Hawker Hurricane fsm			Jet Age Museum	(Gloucester)
				(Gloucestershire Aviation Collection) (As "V6779" of 501 RAAF Sqdn c/s)	
73	Hawker Hurricane rep			Not known	Bishops Stortford
				(Displayed "Queens Head" Public House: current status unknown)	
74	Messerschmitt Bf109 fsm			See PART 1 above	
75	Mignet HM.14 Pou-Du-Ciel			See G-AEFG in SECTION 1	
76	Mignet HM.14 Pou-Du-Ciel			See PART 1 above	
77	Mignet HM.14 Pou-Du-Ciel			See PART 1 above	
78	Hawker Afghan Hind			See G-AENP in SECTION 1	
79	Fiat G.46-4b	71	FHE	Not known	La Ferte Alais
			MM53211	*(Stored as "MM53211/ZI-4" 9.00)*	
80	Airspeed AS.58 Horsa II			See PART 1 above	
81	RFD (Hawkridge) Dagling	10471	BGA.493	Russavia Collection	Hemel Hempstead
				(On rebuild)	
82	Hawker Afghan Hind			See PART 1 above	
83	Kawasaki Ki 1001b			See PART 1 above	
84	Mitsubishi Ki 46III (Dinah)			See PART 1 above	
85	Weir W-2			See PART 1 above	
86	DH.82A Tiger Moth			*(Current status unknown)*	
87	Bristol 30/46 Babe III rep			See PART 1 above	
88	Fokker DR.1 5/8th rep			See PART 1 above	
89	Cayley Glider rep			See PART 1 above	
90	Colditz Cock rep			See PART 1 above	
91	Fieseler Fi 103R-IV			See PART 1 above	
92	Fieseler Fi 103 (V-1)			See PART 1 above	
93	Fieseler Fi 103 (V-1)			See PART 1 above	
94	Fieseler Fi 103 (V-1)			See PART 1 above	
95	Gizmer Autogyro			F.Fewsdale	Darlington
				Current status unknown	
96	Brown Helicopter			See PART 1 above	
97	Luton LA.4 Minor			See PART 1 above	
98	Yokosuka MXY7 Ohka 11			See PART 1 above	
99	Yokosuka MXY7 Ohka 11			See PART 1 above	
100	Clarke Chanute Biplane Glider			See PART 1 above	
101	Mignet HM.14 Pou-Du-Ciel			See PART 1 above	
102	Mignet HM.14 Pou-Du-Ciel			Not constructed - parts to BAPC.75	
103	Hulton Hang-Glider			Personal Plane Services Ltd	Booker
	(Built E.A.S.Hulton, London 1969)				
104	Bleriot XI		G-AVXV	Sold as F-AZIN 1992	
105	Bleriot XI		54	Arango Collection	Los Angeles
	(Anzani "V" 25hp)				California, USA
	(Composite from original components including c/n 54: built by L.D.Goldsmith in 1976 @ RAF Colerne)				
106	Bleriot XI			See PART 1 above	
107	Bleriot XXVII			See PART 1 above	
108	Fairey Swordfish IV			See PART 1 above	
109	Slingsby T.7 Cadet	28	8599M	Current status unknown	
			BGA.679		
110	Fokker D.VII rep			Current status unknown *(ex Leisure Sport)*	
				(As "5125/18") (Sold 10.87)	
111	Sopwith Triplane rep			See PART 1 above	
112	de Havilland DH.2 rep			See G-BFVH in SECTION 1	
113	RAF SE.5A rep			Current status unknown *(ex Leisure Sport) (As "B4863")*	
114	Vickers 60 Viking IV rep			*See PART 1 above*	
115	Mignet HM.14 Pou-Du-Ciel			*See PART 1 above*	
116	Santos-Dumont Demoiselle XX rep			Current status unknown	
	(JAP J99)			*(ex Flambards Theme Park)*	
117	RAF BE.2C rep			P Smith	(Hawkinge)
	(Gipsy Major)			*(Built Ackland & Shaw for BBC TV "Wings" 1976)*	
118	Albatros D.V static rep			Current status unknown *(As "C19/15")*	
119	Bensen B.7 Gyro-Glider			See PART 1 above	
120	Mignet HM.14 Pou-Du-Ciel			See PART 1 above	
121	Mignet HM.14 Pou-Du-Ciel			See PART 1 above	
122	Avro 504 rep			Current status unknown	
	(Ford 1300)			*(Built PPS for BBC TV "Wings" 1976) (As "1881")*	
123	Vickers FB.5 Gunbus rep	1186/2	ZS-UHN	A.Topen *(As "P641")*	Cranfield
	(Built IES Projects Ltd 1975 for "Shout at the Devil" film: small components only remain & stored 3.90)				

124	Lilienthal Glider Type XI rep		See PART 1 above	
125	Clay Cherub ground trainer		Not known	(Coventry)
126	Rollason-Druine D.31 Turbulent		See PART 1 above	
127	Halton Jupiter MPA		See PART 1 above	
128	Watkinson CG-4 rotorcraft		See PART 1 above	
129	Blackburn 1911 Monoplane rep		Current status unknown	
	(Built for TV Srs."The Flambards")		*"Mercury" (Sold 1993)*	
130	Blackburn 1911 Monoplane rep		See PART 1 above	
131	Pilcher Hawk Glider rep		C.Paton	London E
	(Built C.Paton for film 1972)		*Current status unknown (Probably stored)*	
132	Bleriot XI EMK010 & PFA/8810864		Current status unknown	
	(Anzani 25hp) (Built L.D.Goldsmith 1976 from original components: rebuilt again by EMK in 1982 & initially allotted G-BLXI: reported as sold to unidentified Musee de l'Automobile, France in 1986: possibly the same a/c as BAPC.189)			
133	Fokker DR.1 model		See PART 1 above	
134	Pitts S.2A	"G-RKSF"	Toyota Cars	Northampton
			(See "G-CARS" in SECTION 4)	
135	Bristol M.1C Monoplane rep		Current status unknown	
			(ex Leisure Sport) (As "C4912") (Sold 10.87)	
136	Deperdussin 1913 Floatplane rep		National Air Race Museum	Sparks,
			(As "619")	Nevada, USA
137	Sopwith Baby Floatplane rep		Current status unknown	
	(Built FEM Displays Ltd 1978)		*(ex Leisure Sport) (As "8151") (Sold 10.87)*	
138	Hansa Brandenberg W.29 rep		Current status unknown	
	(Ford 1300)		*(ex Leisure Sport) (As "2292") (Sold prior to 10.87)*	
139	Fokker DR.1 Triplane rep		Current status unknown	
			(ex Leisure Sport) (As "DR1/17") (Sold 10.87)	
140	Curtiss 42A R3C2 rep		National Air Race Museum	Sparks,
			(As "3" in US Army c/s)	Nevada, USA
141	Macchi M.39 rep		National Air Race Museum	Sparks,
	(Gipsy Queen)		*(As "5")*	Nevada, USA
142	RAF SE.5A rep		Current status unknown	Switzerland
			(As"F5459/Y") (Sold 1.5.93)	
143	Paxton MPA		R.A.Paxton	Gloucestershire
			(Current status unknown: presumed stored)	
144	Weybridge MPA		Current status unknown	Cranwell
	(Previously "Dumbo" rebuilt)		*"Mercury"*	
145	Oliver MPA		Current status unknown	Warton
			(Possibly scrapped)	
146	Pedal Aeronauts MPA		Current status unknown *"Toucan"*	
			(Centre section/power train only departed London Colney 1995)	
147	Bensen B7 Gyro-Glider		See PART 1 above	
148	Hawker Fury II rep		See PART 1 above	
149	Short S.27 rep		See PART 1 above	
150	BAC/Sepecat Jaguar GR.1 fsm	"XX718"	RAF Exhibition Production & Transportation Team	
		"XX732"	*(As "XX725/GU" in 54 Sqdn c/s)*	Oman
150	BAC/Sepecat Jaguar GR.1 fsm	"XX718"	RAF Exhibition Production & Transportation Team	
		"XX732"	*(As "XX725/GU" in 54 Sqdn c/s)*	Oman
151	BAC/Sepecat Jaguar GR.1A fsm	"XX824"	RAF Exhibition Production & Transportation Team	
			(As"XZ363/A")	RAF Cranwell
152	BAe Hawk T.1A fsm	"XX262"	RAF Exhibition Production & Transportation Team	
		"XX162"	*(As "XX226/74" in 74 Sqdn c/s)*	RAF Cranwell
153	Westland WG-33		See PART 1 above	
154	Druine D.31 Turbulent	PFA 1654	Lincolnshire Aviation Society	East Kirkby
			(Unfinished: stored 3.96)	
155	Panavia Tornado GR.1 model	"ZA368"	RAF Exhibition Production & Transportation Team	
		"ZA446/ZA600/ZA322"	*(As "ZA556/AJ-P")*	RAF Cranwell
156	Supermarine S.6B rep		National Air Race Museum	Sparks,
			(As "S1595")	Nevada, USA
157	WACO CG-4A Hadrian		See PART 1 above	
158	Fieseler Fi 103 (V1)		Defence Explosives Ordnance Disposal School	
				Chattenden
159	Yokosuka MXY7 Ohka 11		Defence Explosives Ordnance Disposal School	
				Chattenden
160	Chargus 18/50 Hang-Glider		See PART 1 above	
161	Stewart MP Ornithopter		A Stewart *"Coppelia" (Stored 8.98)*	Louth
162	Goodhart MPA		See PART 1 above	
163	Hafner AFEE 10/42 Rotabuggy rep		See PART 1 above	
164	Wight Quadruplane Type 1 rep		See PART 1 above	
165	Bristol F.2b		See PART 1 above	
166	Bristol F.2b		See G-AANM in SECTION 1	
167	RAF SE.5A rep		TDL Replicas Ltd *(Exported 12.97)*	USA
168	DH.60G Moth rep		See PART 1 above	
169	BAC/Sepecat Jaguar GR.1		RAF/No.1 School of Technical Training	RAF Cosford
	(Engine systems static demonstration airframe)		*(As "XX110")*	
170	Pilcher Hawk Glider rep		A Gourlay	Strathallan
	(Built A.Gourlay 1983)		*("Kings Royal" BBC film) (Current status unknown: stored 3.93)*	
171	BAe Hawk T.1 fsm	"XX297"	RAF Exhibition Production & Transportation Team	
		"XX262"	*(As "XX253")*	RAF Cranwell
172	Chargus Midas Super E Hang-Glider		See PART 1 above	
173	Birdman Grasshopper Hang-Glider		See PART 1 above	
174	Bensen B.7 Gyro-Glider		See PART 1 above	
175	Volmer VJ-23 Swing-wing		See PART 1 above	
176	RAF SE.5A scale rep		See PART 1 above	
177	Avro 504K rep		See PART 1 above	

178	Avro 504K rep	"E373"	By-gone Times Antique Warehouse Eccleston, Lancs
			(German c/s)
179	Sopwith Pup rep		See PART 1 above
180	McCurdy Silver Dart rep		Reynolds Pioneer Museum Wetaskiwin, Alberta, Canada
			(Delivered 4.94)
181	RAF BE.2b rep		See PART 1 above
182	Wood Ornithopter		See PART 1 above
183	Zurowski ZP.1		See PART 1 above
184	Supermarine Spitfire IX fsm		R.J.Lamplough/Fighter Wing Display Team
	(Built Specialised Mouldings Ltd 1985)		*(As "EN398")* North Weald
185	WACO CG-4A Hadrian		See PART 1 above
186	DH.82B Queen Bee		See PART 1 above
187	Roe Type I Biplane rep		See PART 1 above
188	McBroom Cobra 88 Hang-Glider		See PART 1 above
189	Bleriot XI rep		Current status unknown *(See BAPC.132)*
	(Anzani) (Some original parts ex Goldsmith Trust)		*(Sold @ Christies 31.10.86, probably to France)*
190	Supermarine Spitfire prototype fsm	"K5054"	P.Smith (Hawkinge)
191	BAe Harrier GR.7 fsm	"ZD472"	RAF Exhibition Production & Transportation Team
			(As "ZH139/01") RAF Cranwell
192	Weedhopper JC24		M J Aubrey Kington, Herts
193	Hovey WDII Whing Ding		M J Aubrey Kington, Herts
194	Santos Dumont Type 20 Demoiselle rep	24 bis	RAF Museum Reserve Collection RAF Stafford
	(ABC Scorpion 30hp) PPS/DEM/1		*("Those Magnificent Men in Their Flying Machines" film)*
195	Birdman Sports Moonraker 77 Hang-Glider		See PART 1 above
196	Southdown Sailwings Sigma 2m Hang-Glider		See PART 1 above
197	Scotkites Cirrus III Hang-Glider		See PART 1 above
198	Fieseler Fi 103 (V-1)		See PART 1 above
199	Fieseler Fi 103 (V-1)		See PART 1 above
200	Bensen B.7 Gyroglider		Current status unknown Leeds
	(Composite three airframes)		*(Last noted stored 11.93)*
201	Mignet HM.14 Pou-Du-Ciel		See PART 1 above
202	Supermarine Spitfire V fsm		Current status unknown DERA Llanbedr
			("A Piece of Cake" film) (As "MAV467/"RO")
203	Chrislea LC.1 Airguard rep		The Aeroplane Collection Wigan
			(As "G-AFIN") (Current status unknown: burnt 1998?)
204	McBroom Hang-Glider		See PART 1 above
205	Hawker Hurricane IIc fsm		See PART 1 above
206	Supermarine Spitfire IX fsm		See PART 1 above
207	Austin Whippet rep		See PART 1 above
208	RAF SE.5A rep		See PART 1 above
209	Supermarine Spitfire LF.IXC fsm		See PART 1 above
210	Avro 504J rep		See PART 1 above
211	Mignet HM.14 Pou-Du-Ciel		See PART 1 above
212	Bensen B.6 Gyrocopter		See PART 1 above
213	Cranfield Vertigo MP Helicopter		See PART 1 above
214	Supermarine Spitfire prototype fsm		See PART 1 above
215	Airwave Hang Glider prototype		See PART 1 above
216	DH.88 Comet fsm		See PART 1 above
217	Supermarine Spitfire I fsm		See PART 1 above
218	Hawker Hurricane IIc fsm		See PART 1 above
219	Hawker Hurricane I fsm		See PART 1 above
220	Supermarine Spitfire I fsm		See PART 1 above
221	Supermarine Spitfire LF.IX fsm		See PART 1 above
222	Supermarine Spitfire IX fsm		See PART 1 above
223	Hawker Hurricane I fsm		See PART 1 above
224	Supermarine Spitfire V fsm		AJD Engineering/Hawker Restorations Ltd Sudbury
	(Built TDL Replicas)		*(As "BR600")*
225	Supermarine Spitfire IX fsm		See PART 1 above
226	Supermarine Spitfire XI fsm		See PART 1 above
227	Supermarine Spitfire IA fsm		See PART 1 above
228	Olympus Hang Glider		See PART 1 above
229	Supermarine Spitfire IX fsm		See PART 1 above
230	Supermarine Spitfire fsm		See PART 1 above
231	Mignet HM.14 Pou-Du-Ciel		See PART 1 above
232	Airspeed AS.58 Horsa I/II		See PART 1 above
233	Broburn Wanderlust Sailplane		See PART 1 above
234	Vickers FB.5 Gunbus fsm		See PART 1 above
235	Fieseler Fi 103 (V-1 fsm)		See PART 1 above
236	Hawker Hurricane fsm		See PART 1 above
237	Fieseler Fi 103 (V-1)		Royal Air Force Museum Reserve Collection
			RAF Stafford
238	Waxflatter Ornithopter rep		Personal Plane Services Ltd Booker
			(Built PPS for "Young Sherlock Holmes")
239	Fokker D.VIII 5/8th scale rep		See PART 1 above
240	Messerschmitt Bf.109G fsm		See PART 1 above
241	Hawker Hurricane I fsm		See PART 1 above
242	Supermarine Spitfire VB rep		See PART 1 above
243	Mignet HM.14 Pou-Du-Ciel	"A-FLEA"	P.Ward Malvern Wells
	(Scott A2S) (Built Bill Francis)		*(As "G-ADYV") (Stored 8.95)*
244	Solar Wings Typhoon Hang-Glider		See PART 1 above
245	Electraflyer Floater Hang-Glider		See PART 1 above
246	Hiway Cloudbase Hang-Glider		See PART 1 above
247	Albatros ASG.21 Hang-Glider		See PART 1 above
248	McBroom Hang-Glider		See PART 1 above

249	Hawker Fury I fsm	See PART 1 above	
250	RAF SE.5A rep	See PART 1 above	
251	Hiway Spectrum Hang-Glider	See PART 1 above	
252	Flexiform Wing Hang-Glider	See PART 1 above	
253	Mignet HM.14 Pou-Du-Ciel rep	See PART 1 above	
254	Supermarine Spitfire 1 fsm	See PART 1 above	
255	NA P-51D Mustang fsm	See PART 1 above	
256	Santos Dumont Type 20 Demoiselle rep	See PART 1 above	
257	DH.88 Comet fsm	See PART 1 above	
258	Adams Balloon (15,000 cu.ft)	See PART 1 above	
259	Gloster Gamecock fs rep	Jet Age Museum	(Gloucester)
		(Under construction by Gloucestershire Aviation Collection 2.00)	
260	Mignet HM.280	See PART 1 above	
261	GA Hotspur rep	See PART 1 above	
262	Catto CP-16	See PART 1 above	
263	Chargus Cyclone	See PART 1 above	
264	Bensen B8M	See PART 1 above	
265	Hawker Hurricane fsm	See PART 1 above	
266	Rogallo Hang-Glider	See PART 1 above	
267	Hawker Hurricane fsm	See PART 1 above	
268			
269	Supermarine Spitfire V fsm	See PART 1 above	
270	de Havilland DH.60 Moth fsm	See PART 1 above	
271			
272	Hawker Hurricane fsm	See PART 1 above	
273	Hawker Hurricane fsm	See PART 1 above	
274	Boulton & Paul P.6 fsm	See PART 1 above	
275	Bensen B.7	See PART 1 above	
276	Hartman Ornithopter	See PART 1 above	
277	Mignet HM.14 Pou-Du-Ciel	See PART 1 above	
278	Hawker Hurricane fsm	See PART 1 above	
279			
280			
281			
282			
283			
284			
285			
286			
287			
288			
289			
290			
291			
292			
293			
294			
295			
296			
297			
298			
299			
300			
301			
302			
303			
304			
305			
306			
307			
308			
309			
310			
311			
312			
313			
314			
315			
316			
317			
318			
319			
320			

PART 3 – IRISH AVIATION HISTORICAL COUNCIL

The IAHC Register came into existence with similar objectives to the BAPC. Thanks to Ken Ellis for new information this year.

IAHC No.	Type	C/n	P/I	Remarks	Location
1	Mignet HM.14 Pou-Du-Ciel			See PART 1 above	
2	Aldritt Monoplane			See PART 1 above	
3	Mignet HM.14 Pou-Du-Ciel *(Built 1937 but unflown)*			M.Donohoe *(Last noted 4.96)*	Delgany
4	Hawker Hector		IAAC....	D.McCarthy *(Believed components on rebuild Florida, USA)*	NK
5	Not known			Not known	
6	Ferguson Monoplane rep			See PART 1 above	
7	Sligo Concept			G.O'Hara Current status unknown *(Was stored incomplete 8.91)*	Sligo
8	O'Hara Autogyro			G.O'Hara Current status unknown *(Was stored unflown 8.91)*	Sligo
9	Ferguson Monoplane rep			See PART 1 above	

SECTION 5

PART 1 – FOREIGN CIVIL REGISTERED AIRCRAFT LOCATED IN UK & IRELAND

There are some changes to this Section this year. Foreign registered specimens with a UK & Irish provenance have been transferred to the new Museum listing introduced iin SECTION 4, Part 1. Those museum aircraft with no UK history are now shown in a new Part 2 below. Aircraft removed from the 2002 edition are shown in Part 3.

Once again I am very grateful to Paul Hewins for his detailed examination of the Section during the year and continued supply of updates. Other valuable contributions have come from Peter Budden, Mike Cain - particularly his monthly listings and annual review of "foreign" movements, Bernard Martin & Ken Tilley. Many thanks to you all.

Underlining indicates a significant change to previously published information while an asterisk denotes the registration no longer appears on the relevant country register.

Regn	Type	C/n		Owner/Operator	Probable Base
UNITED ARAB EMIRATES					
A6-ALG*	MBB Bö.105	S-94		Bond Air Services Ltd (On rebuild 2.00)	Bourn
A6-ESH(2)	Airbus Industrie A319-133X	910		Ruler of Sharjah (Noted 10.02)	Farnborough/Sharjah
A6-HHH	Gulfstream Gulfstream IV	1011	(A6-DLF)	Government of Dubai	Farnborough/Dubai
			N17581	(Noted 10.02)	
A6-HRS	Boeing 737-7EO	29251		Dubai Royal Flight (Noted 10.02)	Farnborough/Dubai
A6-SHK*	British Aerospace BAe 146 Srs.100	E1091	G-BOMA	Air Salvage International	Alton
			G-5-091	(Fuselage noted 4.02)	
MUSCAT & OMAN					
A40-AB*	Vickers VC-10 Srs.1103	820		See G-ASIX in SECTION 4	
A4O-CT(1)*	Britten Norman BN-2T Islander	2201	G-51-2201	Britten-Norman Group	Bembridge
			G-BOMC	(Original fuselage derelict 1.02)	
CANADA					
CF-EPV*	Aviation Traders ATL.98 Carvair	10448/8	EI-AMR	Old Airfield Estate	Halesworth
			N88819/42-72343	(Cockpit section only 3.02)	
C-FQIP	Lake LA-4-200 Buccaneer	679	N1068L	P J Molloy (Noted 9.02)	Elstree
C-GWJO	Boeing 737-2A3	20299	HR-SHO	Westjet	Newcastle
			HR-TNR/CX-BHM/N1797B/N1787B (Instructional use 2.03)		
PORTUGAL					
CS-AZY	de Havilland DHC.1 Chipmunk T.20	40	FAP1350	Not known (Noted 6.01)	Bourn
	(Built OGMA)				
CS-HBK*	Hughes 369E	0165E	N5233N	March Helicopters (Wreck noted 9.02)	Sywell
CS-HBL*	Hughes 369E	0377E		March Helicopters (Wreck noted 12.01)	Sywell
CS-HCE*	Hughes 369D	120-0856D	G-JIMI	March Helicopters	Sywell
			N1109T	(Noted dismantled 12.01)	
GERMANY					
D-ABNE	Boeing 757-230	24749	N35153	Condor (Stored 10.02)	Lasham
D-CALM	Dornier Do 228-101	7051		Not known (Noted 2.03)	Fairoaks
D-CAOA	Embraer EMB.120RT Brasilia	120.013	N122AM	Air Omega	Coventry
			PT-SII	(Op Atlantic Express) (Noted 2.03)	
D-CAOB	Embraer EMB.120RT Brasilia	120.012	N120AM	Air Omega	Coventry
			PT-SIG	(Op Atlantic Express) (Noted 1.03)	
D-CBIG	Beech 1900D	UE-288	N11320	Avanti Air	Cardiff
			TC-CNK/N11320	(Op Air Wales 11.02)	
D-EALX(2)	Cessna F150L	F15000766	OE-ALX	S A Young (Noted 4.02)	Hill Farm, Nayland
D-EAWD*	Reims/Cessna F150M	F15001259		Not known	Andrewsfield
				(Noted w/o engine, damaged fin, wings & rear fuselage 7.02)	
D-EAXX*	SEEMS MS.885 Super Rallye	260	F-BKUI	P Garcia (Noted 2.00)	King's Farm, Thurrock
D-EBLI	Bölkow Bö.207	223		Not known (Noted 1.03)	Crowfield
D-EBLO	Bölkow Bö.207	224		Not known (Noted 9.02)	Popham
D-CBSF	Beech 1900D	UE-8	N55778	Avanti Air	Cardiff
				(Op Air Wales)	
D-EBWE	Piper PA-28-235 Cherokee	28-10431	N8874W	Not known (Noted 8.02)	North Weald
D-ECDL	Navion Rangemaster H	NAV-4-2522	N2520T	G Spooner (Noted dismantled12.02)	Earls Colne
				(Acquired as spares source for long-term restoration of Navion N3864 qv)	
D-ECDU(1)*	Reims/Cessna F172E	F172-0068		M Dunn	Longside, Peterhead
				(Carries fictitious marks "G-ASOK" 6.00)	
D-EDEQ	Beech B24R Sierra 200	MC-239		Not known (Noted 12.02)	Shoreham
D-EEAH	Bölkow Bö.208C Junior	658	(D-EJMH)	J Webb	Bourne Park, Hurstbourne Tarrant
				(Noted active 7.02)	
D-EELY	Piper PA-28-161 Warrior II	28-8216121	N9636N	Small World Aviation Inc (Noted 8.01)	North Weald
D-EEPC	Reims/Cessna F182P Skylane	F18200005		Small World Aviation Inc (Noted 8.01)	North Weald
D-EEPI	Wassmer WA.54 Atlantic	151		E S Davison (Noted 2.02)	Shoreham
D-EFFA(4)	Ruschmeyer RG90-230RG	018	D-ELVY(2)	H-J Krebs	Old Buckenham
			(D-EEBY(2))	(Noted 10.02)	
D-EFJD	Bölkow Bö.209 Monsun 160RV	126		W Williams-Wynne (Noted 7.01)	Old Sarum
D-EFJG	Bölkow Bö.209 Monsun 160RV	129		R.Truesdale (Noted 6.02)	Newtownards
D-EFNO*	Bölkow Bö.208A-1 Junior	604		Aero Engines & Airframes	Yearby
				(For composite rebuild with G-ASFR 3.02)	
D-EFTI	Bölkow Bö.207	219		Mark Hayles (Noted 8.02)	Turweston

Reg	Type	C/N	Prev id	Owner/Operator	Location
D-EFZO	Reims Cessna F172F	F172-0156		Not known *(Noted 10.02)*	Stapleford
D-EGEU	Piper PA-22-108 Colt	22-9055	EL-AEU	Not known	Fenland
			5N-AEH	*(Badly damaged by storms 27.10.02 Farley Farm, Romsey)*	
D-EGJD	Reims FR172J Rocket	FR17200420		Small World Aviation Inc *(Noted 8.01)*	North Weald
D-EHJL	Piaggio FWP.149	045	90+31	C A Tyers/Windmill Aviation	Spanhoe
			AC+441/AS+441/GA+394/D-EGEW/GA+394	*(Noted 5.02)*	
D-EHKY	Bölkow Bö 207	272		Not known *(Noted 10.02)*	Haverfordwest
D-EHLA	Bölkow Bö.207	273		J Webb *(Noted 3.03)*	Popham
D-EHUQ	Bölkow Bö.207	207		Not known *(Noted 9.02)*	Nuthampstead
D-EHYX	Bölkow Bö.207	209		Not known *(Noted 8.02)*	Haverfordwest
D-EIAL	Piper PA-28-161 Warrior II	28-8116076	N8291D	Not known *(Noted 1.02)*	Alderney
D-EIAR	CEA DR.250/160 Capitaine	98		D G Holmann *(Noted 11.01)*	Leicester
D-EIIA	Robin R3000/160	164		Not known *(Noted 12.02)*	Shennington
D-EJBI	Bölkow Bö.207	242		E J Jonker	Biggin Hill
				(Substantially damaged landing Lowden Farm, Cranbrook 4.5.02)	
D-EKGD(3)*	Rockwell Commander 114	14397		Not known	Fairoaks
				(Landed wheels-up Portoroz, Slovenia 21.1.01, cancelled & on rebuild 3.02)	
D-EKKO	Reims FR172G Rocket	FR17200185		Not known *(Noted 2002)*	Croft Farm, Defford
D-EMUH	Bölkow Bö.208C Junior	623		M Pitcher *(Noted 1.03)*	Rayne Hall Farm, Rayne
D-EMZC	Reims FR.172G Rocket	FR17200154		Small World Aviation Inc *(Noted 9.02)*	North Weald
D-EOLW	Maule MX.7-180 Star Rocket	11050C	N6118L	Not known	Not known
				(Badly damaged by storms 27.10.02 Farley Farm, Romsey)	
D-EPUD	Bölkow Bö.209 Monsun 160FV	196	HB-UED	Not known	Lydd
			D-EAIL	*(Noted 9.01)*	
D-EQQQ	Cessna 172N	17273670	N4725J	Small World Aviation Inc *(Noted 8.01)*	North Weald
D-EXGC	Extra EA.200	027		Not known *(Noted 9.02)*	Andrewsfield
D-EXLH	Extra EA.400	06		Not known *(Noted 7.02)*	Seething
D-EZAP	Cessna 152	15283078	N46598	Not known *(Noted 1.02)*	Stapleford
D-FKMA	Antonov An-2T	117411	LSK440	Not known	Wellesbourne Mountford
				(Noted 10.02) (Aero Troika titles)	
D-FLOH	Cessna 208B Grand Caravan	208B0576	N1041F	Not known *(Noted 8.01)*	Langar
D-GDCO	Piper PA-23-160 Apache	23-1800	SE-EDG	Not known *(Noted 8.02)*	Panshanger
			D-GABA/N4369P		
D-GIFR	Partenavia P.68B	57	LN-LMS	L Bax *(Noted 10.02)*	Old Sarum
D-HCKV	Agusta A109A-11	7345	N109C	The Global Travel Group plc	Sywell
			N2GN	*(Damaged near Newby Bridge, Cumbria 2.1.00: wreck stored 8.02)*	
D-HGBX*	Enstrom F.280	1189	SE-HKX	Not known *(Gutted pod noted 9.01)*	North Weald
D-HMED*	MBB Bö.105S	S.341		Bond Air Services Ltd	Bourn
				(Pod stored 12.99 - white/green & carries "Polizei" titles)	
D-HMUR*	MBB Bö.105C	S.91		Bond Air Services Ltd *(Pod stored 5.00)*	Bourn
D-HOXQ	Mil Mi-8T	105103	DDR-SJA	Pinewood Studios *(Noted 1.02)*	(Denham)
				(Marked as North Korean "P-71" for James Bond film)	
D-HSUN	Eurocopter EC120B	1272		Not known	Dublin
D-IFSB(1)*	de Havilland DH.104 Dove 6	04379		See G-AMXR in SECTION 4	
D-KMDP	Fournier RF-3	37	F-BMDP	Not known *(Noted 2.03)*	Galway
D-MVMM	WDL Fascination			Not known *(Noted 9.02)*	Gloucestershire
D-NFBA	Hang-glider *(Type?)*	NK		Not known *(Noted 3.00)*	Edburton
D-0369	Glasflugel H201 Standard Libelle	289		Not known "J" *(Noted 8.99)*	Dunstable

FIJI

DQ-PBF*	Thunder Ax10-180 Srs.2 HAB			See G-WORK in SECTION 4	

SPAIN

Reg	Type	C/N	Prev id	Owner/Operator	Location
EC-AOY*	Aero-Difusion Jodel D.1190-S Compostela	E.56		G.Janney	Sibsey
				(Water damaged remains 2001- thought unuseable)	
EC-CFI	Boeing 727-256	20819		Iberia *(Stored 2.03)*	Bournemouth
EC-DDX	Boeing 727-256A	21779		Iberia *(Stored 1.03)*	Bournemouth
(EC-FVM)	FLS OA.7 Optica 301	021		See G-BOPO in SECTION 1	
EC-HDE	Rockwell Commander 680V	1684-65	N10TG	Not known	Fairoaks
			N1UT/N1BA/N81D	*(Noted 10.02)*	

LIBERIA

Reg	Type	C/N	Prev id	Owner/Operator	Location
EL-AKJ	Boeing 707-321C	19375	(N2NF)	Omega Air *(Open store 2.03)*	Southend
			EL-AKJ/(PP-BRR)/EL-AKJ/9Q-CSW/5N-TAS/N864BX/OB-R-1243/HK-2473/HK-2473X/N473RN/N473PA		
EL-AKL	Boeing 707-351C	18922	EL-AKF	Omega Air *(Open store 1.03) (All white c/s)*	Shannon
			HR-AME/5N-JIL/5N-ASY/N82TF/VR-HGP/(VR-HGQ)/N362US		
EL-WXA	Bristol 175 Britannia 253F			See G-BDUP in SECTION 4	

ESTONIA

Reg	Type	C/N	Prev id	Owner/Operator	Location
ES-NOB	Antonov An-72	36572070695	CCCP72931	Enimex	Bournemouth
				(Op Channel Express) (Noted 1.03)	
ES-YLK	Aero L-29A Delfin	194521	Est.AF	R Patton	Cork, Co.Cork
			Sov AF	*(Noted 10.01)*	

FRANCE

Reg	Type	C/N	Prev id	Owner/Operator	Location
F-BBGH*	Brochet MB.100	01		Not known *(Frame stored 2001)*	Sibsey
F-BBSO*	Taylorcraft Auster 5	1792		D.J.Baker	Carr Farm, Thorney, Newark
			TW452	*(Dismantled frame 1.03)*	
F-BGNR*	Vickers 708 Viscount	35	(OY-AFO)	Skysport Engineering	Rotary Farm, Hatch
			(OY-AFN)/F-BGNR	*(Stored 7.01)*	

Reg	Type	Serial	Prev ID	Owner / Notes	Location
F-BGNX*	de Havilland DH.106 Comet 1XB			See G-AOJT in SECTION 4	
F-BKRK	Piper PA-24 250 Comanche	24-3034	N7814P	Not known *(Noted 11.02)*	Farley Farm, Romsey
F-BMCY*	Potez 840	02	N840HP	Highlands & Islands Airports Ltd	Sumburgh
			F-BJSU/F-WJSU	*(Damaged Sumburgh 29.3.81: Fire Service use 2002)*	
F-BOJP	Mooney M.20F Executive	670216	N9639M	Not known *(Noted 2002)*	Bournemouth
F-BOXQ*	Piper PA-23-250 Aztec C			See N2209P below	
F-BRHN*	Bölkow Bö.208C Junior	688	D-EEAK	Not known *(Noted stored 11.02)*	Farley Farm, Romsey
F-BRII	Cessna U206D Skywagon	U206-1318	N72204	Not known *(Noted 1.03)*	Sorbie Farm, Kingsmuir
F-BTMM	Piper PA-31 Turbo Navajo	31-480	N449TA	Alarm Service France SA *(Noted 9.02)*	Elstree
F-CARF	Fournier RF-9	02	F-WARF	Not known *(Wrecked 8.02)*	Nympsfield
F-GCCZ	Aérospatiale SA.342J Gazelle	1393	(KAF-401)	MW Helicopters Ltd *(Noted 7.01)*	Stapleford
F-GCOF	SOCATA TB-10 Tobago	135		Not known *(Noted 11.02)*	Cambridge
F-GEHA*	Aérospatiale SA.341G Gazelle	1064	N7721Y	MW Helicopters Ltd	(Stapleford)
			N6952/F-WMHG	*(Spares use 8.01)*	
F-GFDG	Aérospatiale SA.342 Gazelle	1204	TG-KOV	P Holder	Blackpool
				(Op MW Helicopters) (Noted 10.02)	
F-GFEB	Aérospatiale SA.341G Gazelle	1491	N9002L	Not known *(Noted unmarked 9.02)*	Stapleford
F-GFLD*	Beech C90 King Air	LJ-741	HB-GGW	RFS Aircraft Engineering	Southend
			I-AZIO	*(Stored unmarked 2.03)*	
F-GFNO	Robin ATL	16	F-WFNO	B Walker *(Noted 1.03)*	RAF Mona
F-GFOR	Robin ATL	42		M Godsell *(Noted 6.01)*	Haverfordwest
F-GFRO	Robin ATL	64		B Sharpen *(Noted 9.02)*	North Weald
F-GFVE	Cessna 305C (L-19E) Bird Dog	24541	F-WFVE	T Mould	Redhill
			ALAT	*(As "24541" in US Marines c/s) (Noted 7.02)*	
F-GGHZ	Robin ATL	123		D.R.G.Whielaw *(Noted 3.02)*	North Connel, Oban
F-GGTJ	Aérospatiale SA.342J Gazelle	1473	C-GVWC	M W Helicopters Ltd	Bristol
	(Converted from SA.341G to SA.342J @ 3.92)		F-WXFX	*(Noted 9.02)*	
F-WGTX	Heli Atlas	01		Intora Firebird plc *(Stored 2002 -unconfirmed)*	Southend
F-WGTY	Heli Atlas	02		Intora Firebird plc *(Stored 2002 -unconfirmed)*	Southend
F-GIBU	Aérospatiale SA.342J Gazelle	1470	HB-XMU	Global Aviation Services Ltd	Hawarden
			N9000A	*(Noted 9.01)*	
F-GJQI	Robin ATL L	133		C Fox *(Noted 8.02)*	Wing Farm, Longbridge Deverill
F-GJSL	Aérospatiale SA.342J Gazelle	1052	C-GPGO	MW Helicopters Ltd	Stapleford
	(Converted from SA.341GJ)		N8350	*(Noted 4.02)*	
F-GKKI	Avions Mudry CAP.231EX	02	(G-BVXL)	D Kaberry	Barton
			F-GKKF/F-WGZC	*(Noted 8.02)*	
F-GMPA	Aérospatiale AS350B Ecureuil	1749	D-HSAN	MW Helicopters Ltd	Ashford, Kent
			SE-HUV/D-HCHL	*(Noted 2.03)*	
F-GNGH	Schweizer 269C	S-1535	D-HLIL	March Helicopters	Sywell
			N86G	*(Noted dismantled 11.00)*	
F-GOTC	Mudry CAP.232	15		T Cassells *(Noted 6.02)*	Bagby
F-WWGM*	Thunder & Colt AS-261 HA Airship			See G-BPLD in SECTION 4	
F-WWMX	Aerotech Europe CAP.222	CO3		A Cassidy *(Noted 6.01)*	White Waltham
F-GXDB	Mudry CAP.232	33		Diana Britten *(Noted 8.02) "Diana"*	Fairoaks
F-GYRO	Mudry CAP.232	25		A Cassidy *(Securicor titles) (Noted 5.01)*	White Waltham
F-PAGD	Auster V J/1 Autocrat	2218	G-AJID	J Guerin	Trenchard Farm, Eggesford
				(Noted 8.02)	
F-PFUG*	Adam RA-14	11		Not known *(Stored 2001)*	Sibsey
F-PYOY	Heintz Zenith 100	52		B L Featherstone *(Noted 2.03)*	Southend
31-WI	Twinstarr Gyrocopter	--		Woody de Saar *(Noted 11.02)*	Shipdham
50-BH	Fisher FP-202 Super Koala	--		K.Riches	(Guernsey)
				t/a MUL International (Stored 12.01)	
51-HU	Ultralair Ax-3 HAB	C3103163		Not known	Belle Vue Farm, Yarnscombe
				(Noted 2002)	

HUNGARY

Reg	Type	Serial	Prev ID	Owner / Notes	Location
HA-ABP	WSK-PZL Antonov An-2R	1G-185-52	RA54885	Not known	Hinton in the Hedges
			CCCP54885	*(Noted 7.01)*	
HA-ACL	Dornier Do.28D-2 Skyservant	4125	D-IDRC	Not known	Sherburn-in-Elmet
		58+50		*(Crashed 1.00: stored 8.00)*	
HA-ACO	Dornier Do.28D-2 Skyservant	4335	G-BWCN	Not known	Hibaldstow
HA-LAQ	Letovlev LET L-410UVP-E4	841332	5N-AYE/D-ILID/9V-BKL/D-ILID	*(Op Wingglider Ltd) (Noted 10.02)*	
			HAF-332	Farnair Hungary	Hinton in the Hedges
			HA-YFB	*(Noted 8.02)*	
HA-MKE	WSK-PZL Antonov An-2R	1G-158-34	UR-07714	Air Foyle	White Waltham
			CCCP-07714	*(Noted 2.03)*	
HA-MKF	WSK-PZL Antonov An-2TP	1G-233-43	OM-248	Transair	White Waltham
			OM-UIN/OK-UIN	*(Noted 2.03)*	
HA-PPY	SOKO SO341 Gazelle	021	HA-LFR	J R Saul	Brierley,
	(Aérospatiale c/n 1118)		HA-VLA/YU-HDN/JRV	*(Noted 5.00)*	South Yorks
HA-YDF	Technoavia SMG-92 Finist	01-0005		G-92 Kereskedelmi.Kft	Hibaldstow
				(Op Wingglider Ltd) (Noted 9.02)	
HA-YFC	Letovlev LET L-410-FG	851528		Farnair Hungary	Cark
				(Farner Air/Farnair titles) (Noted 9.02)	

SWITZERLAND

Reg	Type	Serial	Prev ID	Owner / Notes	Location
HB-BOU(1)*	Brighton MAB-65 HAB			See G-AWJB in SECTION 4	
HB-FOU	Pilatus PC-12/45	368		Not known *(Noted 9.02)*	Fairoaks
HB-IBX	Gulfstream Gulfstream IV/SP	1183	VR-BDC	Jet Club SA	Farnborough
			N476GA	*(Noted 8.02)*	
HB-IVR	Canadair CL604 Challenger	5318	HB-IKQ	Sintec SA	Luton
			(TC-DHE)/C-FYYH/C-GLXO	*(Noted 10.02)*	
HB-LTG	de Havilland DHC-6 Twin Otter 300	628	D-IFLY	Zimex Aviation	Weston on the Green
			LN-BNT	*(Noted 4.01)*	

HB-NAV*	Beagle B.121 Pup Srs.150			See G-AZCM in SECTION 4	
HB-UXL	Bölkow Bö.207	208	(D-EHUM)	Not known *(Noted 10.01)*	Bideford
HB-XMO	Enstrom F280C Shark	1213	N5697N	Eastern Atlantic Helicopters	Shoreham
				(Tail boom noted 5.00)	
HB-XOV	Bell 214ST	28129	N13158	SETI *(Stored 9.02)*	Redhill

SAUDI ARABIA

HZ-123	Boeing 707-138B	17696	"17696"	Not known *(Open store 1.03)*	Southend
			HZ-123/N138MJ/N220M/N138TA/(N112TA)/C-FPWV/CF-PWV/VH-EBA/N31239		
HZ-AB3	Boeing 727-2U5AR	22362	V8-BG1	Al Anwa Establishment	Lasham
			V8-HM2/V8-HM1/V8-UB1/V8-HM1/JY-HNH *(Stored 11.02)*		
HZ-KAA	Gulfstream Gulfstream IV/SP	1294	N416GA	Mawarid Ltd	Farnborough
			HZ-MAL/N416GA	*(Noted 10.02)*	
HZ-OFC4	Dassault Falcon 900EX	31	F-GSAI	Olayan Finance Co	Luton
			F-WWFC	*(Noted 12.02)*	
HZ-SJP3	Canadair CL604 Challenger	5346	N604JP	Jouannou & Parskevaides	Farnborough
			C-GLXS	*(Noted 8.02)*	

ITALY

I-EIXM*	Piper PA-18-135 Super Cub	18-3572	MM54-2372	Not known	Kesgrave, Ipswich
			54-2372	*(As "EI-184") (Open store 3.02)*	
I-ISAK*	SIAI-Marchetti SF.260D	839		Not known *(Noted 2.03)*	Old Sarum
I-JULI	Beech 95-B55 Baron	TC-629	HB-GBH	Not known *(Noted 6.01)*	Elstree
I-LELF	SIAI-Marchetti SF.260C	568/41-004		Not known *(Noted 9.02)*	Elstree
I-RALY	Agusta A.119 Koala	14013		Sport Ltd *(Noted 10.02)*	Cockermouth
				(Op Malcom Wilson Motorsport)	
I-VFAN*	Agusta Bell AB.206B3	8670	VF-26	Not known *(Noted 8.02)*	Redhill
I-6052	Jabiru Jabiru UL	—		Not known *(Noted 7.02)*	Lower Mountpleasant, Chatteris

NORWAY

LN-AMY	North American AT-6D Harvard	88-16849	(LN-LCS)	The Old Flying Machine Co *"Amy"*	Duxford
			(LN-LCN)/N10595/42-85068	*(Breitling Fighter Team titles) (Noted 10.02)*	
LN-FOI(3)*	Lockheed L-188C Electra	2005	(LN-MOF)	Not known *(DHL c/s)*	Coventry
			N31231/ZK-TEA/(ZK-BMP)/N9724C *(Stored derelict 10.02)*		
LN-RDU*	Bombardier DHC-8Q Srs.402	4044	C-GDIU	SAS Norge ASA *(Stored 10.02)*	Exeter
LN-RDW*	Bombardier DHC-8Q Srs.402	4040	N384BC	SAS Norge ASA *(Stored 10.02)*	Exeter
			C-FDHZ		
LN-RDX*	Bombardier DHC-8Q Srs.402	4041	N385BC	SAS Norge ASA *(Stored 10.02)*	Exeter
			(SE-LRI)		

ARGENTINA

LV-RIE	Nord 1002 Pingouin	240		R.J.Lamplough *(Stored 8.02)*	North Weald

LUXEMBOURG

LX-TLB	Douglas DC-8-62F	45925	N822BV	Cargo Lion *(Stored 9.02)*	Manston
			CX-BQN/CX-BQN-F/C-GMXR/N922CL/HB-IDG		

LITHUANIA

LY-ABW	Antonov An-2	1G-195-26	DOSAAF	Not known	Wickenby
			CCCP-68121	*(Noted 8.02)*	
LY-ABZ	Yakovlev Yak-52	9611914		Not known *(Noted 6.02)*	Panshanger
LY-AFA	Yakovlev Yak-52	822608	DOSAAF 110	Not known	Little Gransden
				"110" (Noted 3.03 - to become G-LYFA 2003)	
LY-AFB	Yakovlev Yak-52	822610	DOSAAF 112	Termikas Co *"112" (Last noted 9.02)*	Little Gransden
LY-AFO	Antonov An-2R	1G-211-42	LY-ADL	Not known	Cork
			CCCP-32683	*(Noted 10.01)*	
LY-AHB	Yakovlev Yak-52	9812106	DOSAAF	Not known *(Noted 9.02)*	North Weald
LY-AHD	Yakovlev Yak-12	30119	SP-CXW	Not known	Little Gransden
			PLW....	*(Noted 8.01)*	
LY-AIG	Yakovlev Yak-52	8910106	Ukraine AF 23 (yellow)	Not known *(Noted 4.01)*	Weston
LY-AJR	Yakovlev Yak-52	9812108		Not known *(Noted 2001)*	Little Gransden
LY-ALJ	Yakovlev Yak-52	8910115	DOSAAF 132	D.Hawkins *(Wreck noted 12.01)*	Little Gransden
LY-ALS	Yakovlev Yak-52	855509	DOSAAF 69	M.Jefferies *"69"*	Little Gransden
			DOSAAF 49	*"Once a Knight" (Noted 3.03 - to become G-KOMI 2003)*	
LY-ALT	Yakovlev Yak-52	822704	DOSAAF 121	Titan Airways Ltd *(Noted 9.02)*	Elmsett
LY-AMJ	Yakovlev Yak-18T	22202047812	DOSAAF	Not known *(Noted 9.02)*	Earls Colne
LY-AMS	Yakovlev Yak-52	844306	DOSAAF 51(red)	Willowair Flying Club	Southend
				(Noted 9.02 - to become G-YAMS 2003)	
LY-AOO	Yakovlev Yak-18T	22202040425	LY-AOG	Not known *(Damaged 5.01)*	Wickenby
LY-AOT	Yakovlev Yak-50	853101		Not known	White Waltham
				(Noted 11.01 - to become G-CBPO 2003)	
LY-APP	Yakovlev Yak-18T	01-03	LY-AOG	A Hyatt *(Noted 9.02)*	Leicester
LY-ARH	Yakovlev Yak-18T	22202040114		Nerka Ltd *(Noted 10.02)*	Guernsey
LY-FKD	Yakovlev Yak-12M	210999	SP-FKD	M Jefferies	Oaksey Park
			SP-AAD(3)/PLW...	*(Noted 7.02)*	
LY-IOO	Yakovlev Yak-50	NK		Not known *(Noted 11.01)*	NK

UNITED STATES OF AMERICA

Reg	Type	Serial
N1FD	SOCATA TB-200 XL Tobago	1614
N1FY	Cessna 421C Golden Eagle I	421C1067
N2CL	Piper PA-28RT-201T Turbo Arrow IV	28R-8131054
N2FU	Learjet Learjet 31	31-027
N2MD	Piper J3C-65 Cub	17521
N3TQ	Cessna 310Q	310Q0752
N4H	Eurocopter AS365N2	6450
N5LL	Piper PA-31 Navajo C	31-7812041
N6FL	Latulip LM-3X	LM-3X-1001
	(Rotax 377) (Aeronca 7AC scale rep)	
N6NE	Lockheed Jetstar 731	5006/40
N7AG	Agusta A109A Mk.II	7436
N7SY*	Hunting Percival P.57 Sea Prince	
N7UK	Cirrus Design SR-22	0200
N9AY	Cessna 421C Golden Eagle III	421C0844
N9VL	Agusta A109A-II	7325
N11FV(2)	Cessna T303 Crusader	T30300133
N11ZP	American Blimp Corp A-60+ Airship	011
N12ZP	American Blimp Corp A-60+ Airship	012
N15CK	Maule MX-7-235 Star Rocket	10012C
N15FH	Cessna 340A II	340A0722
N18V	Beech UC-43-BH Traveler	6869
N19F	Cessna 337A Super Skymaster	33700289
	(Robertson STOL conversion)	
N19GL	Brantly B.2B	2004
N20RJ	Beech H35 Bonanza	D-5193
N20UK	Mooney M.20F Executive	22-1380
N22CG	Cessna 441 Conquest II	441-0119
N25PJ	Cessna 340A II	340A0912
N25PR	Piper PA-30-160 Twin Comanche B	30-1511
N26HE	Cessna 421C Golden Eagle II	421C0687
N26PJ	Piper PA-30-160 Twin Comache B	30-1477
N27BG	Cessna 340A	340A0656
N27MW	Beech B58 Baron	TH-995
N28TE	Raytheon 58 Baron	TH-1951
N29KF	SOCATA TB-20 Trinidad	2003
N30NW	Piper PA-30-160 Twin Comanche	30-312
N31NB	Piper PA-31 Turbo Navajo B	31-7401239
N31RB	Grumman-American AA-5B Tiger	AA5B-0156
N33CJ	Cessna 525 CitationJet	525-0245
N33EW	Mitsubishi MU-2B-60	1519SA
N34FA	SOCATA TB-20 Trinidad	866
N35AL	Piper PA-34-220T Seneca IV	3447014
N36NB	Beech A36 Bonanza	E-2274
(N36TH*)	Canadair T-33AN Silver Star	
N37US	Piper PA-34-200T Seneca II	34-8070111
N37WC	Cessna 401	401-0183
N39N	Cessna 560 Citation V	560-0243
N40D	Stolp SA-100 Starduster 1	4258549
N41AK	Beech F90 King Air	LA-188
N41FT	PiperPA-39 Twin Comanche C/R	39-59

Reg / Previous identities	Owner / Operator	Base
	Siek Aviation Inc *(Noted 10.02)*	Blackbushe
N345TG	Southern Aircraft Consultancy Inc *(Noted 10.02)*	Guernsey
N8333S	Southern Aircraft Consultancy Inc	Elstree
N9649N	*(Noted 6.02)*	
N30LJ	Wilmington Trust Company	Biggin Hill
N91201	*(Op Formula One Administration) (Noted 6.01)*	
N70515	Merlin Aire Limited	Rendcomb
NC70515	*(Op V.S.E.Norman) (Kia Cars titles) (Noted 4.02)*	
N1534T	American Aviation Ltd *(Noted 5.00)*	(Blackbushe)
ZS-RLI	Otter Corp	Oxford
G-BUTR	*(Noted 9.02)*	
N27495	Southern Aircraft Consultancy Inc	Guernsey
	(Noted 9.02)	
	M J Aubrey	KIngton, Hereford)
	(Stored 2002)	
(VR-CCC)	Aerospace Finance Leasing Inc	Southampton
N6NE/N222Y/N731JS/N227K/N12R/N9280R		
	(Damaged Southampton 27.11.92: on fire dump 2.02)	
I-AXLE	Helijet Inc *(Noted 5.02)*	Stapleford
	See G-BRFC in SECTION 4	
	Southern Aircraft Consultancy Inc	Bournemouth
	(Noted 9.02)	
G-NSGI	Sooty Aviation Inc	Jersey
N421EL/XA-RAE/N421EB/(N21MW)/N421EB/N2659Z *(Noted 9.02)*		
OO-AHE	Castle Helicopters Inc	Liskeard
OO-XHE/N109LA	*(Noted 9.02)*	
G-BXRI	Auster Aviation	Guernsey
HB-LNI/(N5143C)	*(Noted 12.01)*	
	Virgin Lightships Inc	Wolverhampton
	(Lotto titles) (Noted 6.02)	
	Virgin Lightships Inc	Wolverhampton
	"Spirit of Europe 2" (Lotto titles) (Noted 5.02)	
	Rossendale Air *(Noted 1.03)*	East Winch
G-CMAC	Kestrelair Inc	Liverpool
G-JIMS/G-PETE/N2667N	*(Op F.R.Foran & D.Hanley) (Last noted 4.00)*	
NC18	R.J.Lamplough	North Weald
Bu 32898/FT507/44-67761	*(As "DR828/PB1") (Noted 8.02)*	
N6289F	Southern Aircraft Consultancy Inc	Fakenham
	(Noted 4.01)	
	Southern Aircraft Consultancy Inc	
	(Noted 9.02)	Hill Top Farm, Hambledon
N7945D	Tickton Inc *(Noted 3.02)*	Shobdon
N9155J	R D Garretson	Biggin Hill
G-BDVU	*(Noted 2.02)*	
	Jubilee Airways Inc	Prestwick
	(Op M.Klinge) (Noted 12.02)	
HB-LNM	Southern Aircraft Consultancy Inc	Guernsey
LN-TEA/N27026	*(Noted 1.02)*	
G-AVPR	PSL Aviation	Gloucestershire
N8395Y	*(Noted 3.01)*	
	Wells Fargo Bank Northwest NA	Fairoaks
	(Noted 9.02)	
G-BAWU(2)	Southern Aircraft Consultancy Inc	Guernsey
(G-BAWV)(1)/9J-RFW/ZS-FAM/N8332Y *(Noted 12.01)*		
	Traca Inc *(Op B Gregory) (Noted 6.02)*	Cardiff
	B58 Aviation Inc *(Noted 10.02)*	Fairoaks
	Ecosse Aviation Inc *(Noted 9.02)*	Blackbushe
	Southern Aircraft Consultancy Inc *(Noted 10.02)*	Jersey
G-ASON	R S Barnett	Norwich
N7273Y	*(Noted 4.02)*	
G-OSFT	Navajo Aviation Inc	Old Buckenham
G-MDAS/5N-AEP/G-BJCZ/N61427 *(Op N.Brown) (Noted 6.02)*		
	Southern Aircraft Consultancy Inc	Bournemouth
	(Op Forest Aviation Ltd) (Noted 9.02)	
N5214J	William Aviation Inc *(Noted 12.02)*	Blackpool
N331W	Florida Express Corp	Southend
N33TW/N434MA	*(Op King Aviation) (Noted 2.03)*	
G-BPFG	Southern Aircraft Consultancy Inc *(Noted 1.03)*	Elstree
D-GLPE	Able Liston Aviation *(Noted 9.02)*	Jersey
F-GKTZ	Air Bickerton Inc	Biggin Hill
N7249H	*(Noted 5.02)*	
	See G-BYOY is SECTION 1	
G-PLUS	Southern Aircraft Consultancy Inc *(Noted 5.02)*	Jersey
N917WS	Flywest Inc	Blackpool
N4083Q	*(Op Durston Air Service) (Noted 12.02)*	
N12890	Longborough Aviation *(Noted 10.02)*	Gloucestershire
	Southern Aircraft Consultancy Inc	Rochester
	(Noted 5.01)	
N41CK	Southern Aircraft Consultancy Inc	Guernsey
N6429M	*(Noted 10.02)*	
G-BZLW	Southern Aircraft Consultancy Inc	Biggin Hill
ZS-NLF/ZS-MRH/ZS-IKG/N8904Y *(Noted 9.02)*		

Reg	Type	c/n
N42FW	Beech E33 Bonanza	CD-1199
N44DN	Piper PA-46-350P Malibu Mirage	4622116
N45AW	Piper PA-28RT-201T Turbo Arrow IV	28R-8431003
N45CD(2)	Piper PA-28-161 Warrior II	28-7916467
N47DG*	Republic P-47G Thunderbolt	21962
N47FK	Douglas C-47A-35-DL Dakota 3	9700
N48NS	Cessna 550 Citation Bravo	550-0939
N55AE	Beech 95-C55 Baron	TE-84
N55BN	Beech 95-B55 Baron	TC-1572
N55EN	Beech 95-E55 Baron	TE-942
N55RZ	British Aerospace BAe 125 Srs.400A	25262/NA764
N58GT	Beech B58 Baron *(winglets)*	TH-1090
N58SA	Schweizer 269C	S-1317
N59VT	Beech K35 Bonanza	D-5897
N60GM	Cessna 421C Golden Eagle III	421C0828
N60NB	Mitsubishi MU-2B-60 Marquise	1528SA
N60VB	Ted Smith Aerostar 600A	60-0182-080
	(Machen Superstar conversion)	
N61HB(2)	Piper PA-34-220T Seneca V	3449217
N64MS	Piper PA-28-180 Cherokee Challenger	28-7305466
N65JF	Piper PA-28-181 Archer II	28-7990140
N65TD	IAI 1125A Astra-SPX	093
N66SG	Learjet Learjet 45	45-073
N66SW	Cessna 340	340-0011
N67TC	Rockwell Turbo Commander 690A	11233
N70AA	Beech 70 Queen Air	LB-35
N70VB	Ted Smith Aerostar 600A	60-0446-150
N70XA	Cessna 550 Citation II	550-0008
N71VE	Rockwell Commander 690A	11043
N74DC	Pitts S-2A Special	2228
N74PM	Agusta A109C	7636
N75*	Hanriot HD.1	
N75TL	Boeing-Stearman A75N1 (N2S-4) Kaydet	75-3616
N76JN	Piper PA-31-350 Navajo Chieftain	31-7652176
N76TH	Sikorsky S-76A	76-0373
N77XB	Piper PA-31-310 Navajo	31-583
N77YY	Piper PA-32R-301T Saratoga II TC	3257120
N78HB	Aviat A-1B Husky	2066
N79AP	Beech 58P Baron	TJ-206
N79EL	Beech 400A Beechjet	RK-214
N79YK	Yakovlev Yak-50	791602
N80JN	Mitsubishi MU-2J	626
N80RF	Beech 60 Duke	P-17
N88PL	Piper PA-46-310P Malibu	46-8508099
N90SA	Reims Cessna F172M	F17201402
N90U	Piper PA-46-350P Malibu Mirage	4622106
	(DLX Jet Prop conversion)	
N91ME	SOCATA TB-20 Trinidad	2152
N93GS	Grumman G.21A Goose	B-76
	(Pratt & Whitney R-985)	
N94SA	Citabria 7ECA Champion	227
N95D	Piper PA-34-220T Seneca V	3449060

Reg	Owner/Operator	Location
N7682N	Southern Aircraft Consultancy Inc	Kirknewton
	(Op Feroz Wadia) (Noted 12.02)	
	Convergance Aviation *(Stored 2.02)*	Bournemouth
N43230	Andair Inc	Turweston
N9548N	*(Op Powersway Aviation) (Noted 2.03)*	
PH-AND	Hill Air Inc	Sigwells, Somerset
N2841J	*(Noted 9.02)*	
N42354	Flying A Services	North Weald
42-25068	*(Stored in container 8.02)*	
EC-FNS	Kilo Aviation Inc	North Weald
EC-187/N2669A/C-FEEX/CF-EEX/N308FN/N3PG/N3W/N7V/NC49538/42-23838		
	(Op The Dakota Club) (As "292912/NF-L") (Noted 10.02)	
VP-BNS	Tower House Investments	Jersey
(N939BB)/N5076K	*(Noted 5.02)*	
OH-BBF	Sam Agro Aviation Inc	Bruntingthorpe
SE-EUT	*(Noted 12.02)*	
G-KCAS	Snowadam Inc	Cranfield
G-KCEA/N2840W	*(Op C.Butler) (Noted 10.02)*	
	Monckton Byng Inc *(Noted 11.02)*	Elstree
XB-CUX	Roc Air Service	Liverpool
N59BH	*(Noted 7.02)*	
HB-GIK	Swiftair Inc *(Noted 6.02)*	Elstree
G-BXUP	Southern Aircraft Consultancy Inc *(Noted 11.02)*	Redhill
SE-HTB		
D-EMEF	Southern Aircraft Consultancy Inc *(Noted 5.02)*	Kemble
	Southern Aircraft Consultancy Inc *(Noted 10.01)*	Ronaldsway
5Y-VIZ	Dogfox Airways Inc *(Noted 2.03)*	Dublin
N7513S	Southern Aircraft Consultancy Inc	Henstridge
	(Noted 4.02)	
G-CBAA	HBC Aviation Inc	Jersey
N53445	*(Noted 2.03)*	
D-EHBH	M.Swan	Andrewsfield
N55782	*(Noted 1.03)*	
N2087C	Southern Aircraft Consultancy Inc	Nottingham
	(Noted 9.02)	
	Helios Inc *(Noted 4.02)*	Luton
N65U	C E Rodriguez *(Op Sagesoft) (Noted 10.02)*	Luton
N5035Q	Cabledraw Inc *(Noted 9.02)*	Elstree
N9192N	Aircraft Guaranty Title Corp	Southend
HR-AAJ/N9192N	*(Noted 2.03)*	
G-KEAA	Metals & Alloys International	Southend
G-REXP/G-AYPC	*(Op Trygon Ltd) (Noted 2.03)*	
C-GVHQ	Southern Aircraft Consultancy Inc	Thruxton
N9805Q	*(Noted 12.01)*	
N70X	Wells Fargo Bank Northwest NA	Gloucestershire
N550JF/(N108AJ)/OE-GIW/N575W/N98840 *(Noted 12.02)*		
N71VT	Airbourne Inc	Gamston
N2VQ/N2VA	*(Noted 7.01)*	
I-ALAT	H J Seery *(Op D.Cockburn) (Noted 8.02)*	Norwich
I-SEIN	Ortac Inc *(Op Huktra UK Ltd) (Noted 7.02)*	Hawarden
	See G-AFDX in SECTION 4	
N5148N	Pluto Inc	Headcorn
Bu.37869	*(As "669" in US Army c/s: noted 8.02)*	
	Aviation Leasing Inc *(Noted 9.02)*	East Midlands
VR-CWH	Turbine Helicopters Inc	Leeds-Bradford
I-DVRM	*(Noted 10.02)*	
G-AXXB	Spacetronics Inc	Oxford
N7XB/N6645L/G-AXXB/N6645L *(Noted 4.02)*		
G-LLYY	Flying Start Aviation Inc	Guernsey
N4165C	*(Op M J Start) (Noted 9.02)*	
N115BB	HBC Aviation Inc	King's Farm, Thurrock
G-FOFF/N115BB	*(Op T Holding) (Noted 10.01)*	
VH-ORP	Aircraft Guaranty LLC	Enstone
ZK-TML/N6648Z	*(Op R & B Services Ltd) (Noted 2.03)*	
	Edra Lauren Leasing Corp	East Midlands
	(Op DFS Furniture) (Noted 10.02)	
SE-LBR	Windjammer Aviation	Rochester
DOSAAF	*(Noted 12.02 still marked "SE-LBR")*	
EC-GLU	Aircraft Guaranty Title Group	Waterford
OY-ATZ/SE-GHY/N476MA	*(Noted 4.02)*	
(G-BMSO)	Goldwing Aviation Inc	Fairoaks
I-DUKA/F-BRAX/HB-GDO	*(Op MLP Aviation/E.Lundquist) (Noted 10.00)*	
N9605N	Clarkco Ltd *(Noted 10.02)*	
	(Op D.Clark) Grove Fields Farm, Wellesbourne Mountford	
PH-TWS	W F Chmura	St Just
OY-BUL	*(Noted 5.02)*	
	Speedair Inc	Gloucestershire
	(Noted 7.02)	
	Komfort Aviation *(Noted 9.02)*	Denham
C-FBAE	Caribbean Clipper Inc *"Caribbean Clipper"*	(Isle of Islay)
CF-BAE/CF-FEM/RCAF 392/Bu.37823 *(Op T.Friedrich) (Noted 7.01)*		
OY-AUG	Southern Aircraft Consultancy Inc	Kilkeel, Co.Down
D-EFLO	*(Noted 6.02)*	
N9506N	Zeta Aviation Inc *(Noted 9.02)*	Welshpool

Reg	Type	c/n	Previous identities	Owner / Operator	Location
N99ET	SOCATA TB-10 Tobago	226	G-BJDG / F-BNGR	E.A.Terris *(Noted 6.00)*	Oxford
N101UK	Mooney M.20K	25-0631		Southern Aircraft Consultancy Inc *(Noted 12.02)*	Blackpool
N104WF	Cessna P210N Centurion	P21000033		D O Miller *(Noted 7.02)*	Exeter
N105LF	Dassault Falcon 2000	105	N220EJ / F-WWVZ	Wells Fargo Bank Northwest NA *(Op Krystel Air Charter) (Noted 1.02)*	Cranfield
N109AB	Agusta A109E Power	11015		Monument Aircraft Services Inc *(Noted 8.01)*	Rhyader
N109AN	Agusta A109A-II	7348		Andorran Aviation Inc *(Noted 7.02)*	Stapleford
N109AR	Agusta A109A	7390		Adrian Raymond Aviation Inc *(Op Castle Air Charters) (Noted 9.02)*	Liskeard
N109GR	Agusta A109E Power	11043		Castle Helicopters Inc *(Op Castle Air Charters) (Noted 9.02)*	Liskeard
N109TF	Agusta A109A-II	7328	VH-NWD	Chestham Park Inc *(Op Castle Helicopters Inc) (Noted 1.03)*	Liskeard
N109TW	Agusta A109C	7650	D-HCKM	TWR Aviation Inc *(Op Tom Walkinshaw Racing) (Noted 8.02)*	Oxford
N109UK	Agusta A109A-II	7304	F-GKGV / N109PS/(N109FS)/N109FM *(Noted 9.01)*	M W Helicopters Inc	Stapleford
N109WF	Agusta A109A-II	7298		Agusta 109 LLC *(Op Lenham Racing) (Noted 9.02)*	Elstree
N110PR	Raytheon 390 Premier I	RB-29	N747BK	Wells Fargo Bank Northwest NA *(Noted 1.03)*	Jersey
N111HH	Neico Lancair IV-P	HHF001		Wells Fargo Bank Northwest NA *(Noted 2.03)*	Turweston
N111HT	Cirrus Design SR-22	0232		Aircraft Guaranty Management *(Noted 8.02)*	Gloucestershire
N111SX	Piper PA-46-350P Malibu Mirage	4636286	EC-HPP	Saxon Aviation *(Noted 11.02)*	Elstree
N114WG*	Westland WG-30-100			See G-EFIS in SECTION 4	
N116WG*	Westland WG-30-100	016	(G-BLLG)	Cogent plc? *(Op Oil Petroleum Training Industry Board) (Noted 12.02)*	Montrose
N121MT	Britten Norman BN-2T Turbine Islander *(Build IRMA)*	880	N200LQ / USAF 88-0916/N5097R/N73413/(YV-2173P)/N413JA/G-BFNX *(Noted 2.03)*	Swiftair Inc	Booker
N121ZR	Beech 1900C-1	UC-121	F-GPYV / N121ZR/N528LX	Raytheon Aircraft Credit Corporation *(Noted stored 11.02)*	Blackbushe
N123AX	Piper PA-32R-301 Saratoga IIHP	3246060	G-LLTT / N9283P	Axis Aircraft Leasing Inc *(Noted 8.02)*	Gloucestershire
N123CU	Aero Commander 200D	358	N3044U / G-SONY	R D Garretson *(Noted 8.02)*	(Nayland)
N123SA	Piper PA-18-150 Super Cub	18-1372		Southern Aircraft Consultancy Inc *(Noted 9.02)*	North Weald
N123SX	Piper PA-46-500TP Meridian	4697050		Saxon Aviation Inc *(Noted 2.03)*	Elstree
N125GP	Learjet Learjet 31A	31A-162	N162LJ / N525GP	TR Airways Inc *(Op Damon Hill) (Noted 9.01)*	Dublin
N125XX	Hawker Siddeley HS.125 Srs.700A	257075/NA0254	N124AR / N125TR/N125AM/(G-BHKF)/G-5-13	Surewings Inc *(Last noted 10.02) (Op Aviation/Ambrion Aviation)*	Luton
N125YY	British Aerospace BAe 125 Srs.700B	257115	G-BMIH / G-5-502/5N-AMX/G-BMIH/G-5-502/HZ-DA3	Perastra Inc *(Noted 10.02)*	Luton
N126SE	Boeing Stearman E75	75-5498		Not known *(Noted 5.02)*	Kemble
N128M	Dassault Falcon 50EX	276	N159M / F-WWHB	Motorola Inc *(Noted 10.02)*	Farnborough
N129SC	Piper PA-32-300 Cherokee Six	32-7440057		Manx Orthopaedic Services *(Noted 11.02)*	Ronaldsway
N132CK	Cessna 421A	421A0038	EI-TCK / G-AXAW/(EI-TCK)/G-AXAW/N2238Q	Southern Aircraft Consultancy Inc *(Noted 10.02)*	Weston, Dublin
N133H	Agusta A109C	7609	N1NQ	Thames Aviation Inc *(Op Graff Aviation Ltd) (Noted 9.02)*	Fairoaks
N136SA	American General AG-5B	10164	G-RICA	Southern Aircraft Consultancy Inc *(Noted 1.03)*	Henstridge
N139DB	Piper PA-23-250 Aztec E	27-4611	G-AYUL / N13992	Pyramis Inc *(Op Earlsfield Investments) (Noted 10.02)*	White Waltham
N139JV	Commander Aircraft Commander 114TC	20034		LCM Airways *(Noted 9.02)*	St Just
N142TW	Beech 58 Baron		TH-1841	Specialized Aircraft Services Inc *(Noted 7.02)*	Fairoaks
N145DF(2)	Cessna S550 Citation II	S550-0018	N1AF / N814CC/N501NB/(N1259K) *(Noted 11.02)*	Star Aviation Ltd	Luton
N145DR	Piper PA-34-220T Seneca	3449240		Cleevewood Aviation Inc *(Noted 10.02)*	Gloucestershire
N146FL	Beech F90 King Air	LA-59	G-FLTI / N7P	Keep Holdings *(Operated Flightline) (Noted 2.03)*	Guernsey/Southend
N147CD	Cirrus Design SR-20	1043		Free Flight Aviation Ltd *(Noted 12.02)*	Glasgow
N147DC	Douglas C-47A-75-DL Dakota	19347	G-DAKS / TS423/"108841"/"KG374"/"G-AGHY"/TS423/42-100884 *(As "07") (Noted 12.02)*	Aces High US Inc	Dunsfold
N150JC	Beech A35 Bonanza	D-2084	N8674A	R.M.Hornblower *(Open store, dismantled 2.03)*	Southend
N151CG	Cirrus Design SR-22	0344		Central Chiswick Surveying Inc *(Noted 11.02)*	White Waltham
N153H	Bell 222B	47138		Spansky Aviation Inc *(Noted 8.02)*	Castleknock, Co.Dublin
N154CD	Cirrus Design SR20	1053		Blue Morning Aviation *(Noted 6.02)*	Biggin Hill
N154DJ	Cessna T303	T30300230		Jane Fortier Inc *(Noted 2.03)*	Denham
N156LG	American Blimp Corp A-1-50 Airship	106		American Blimp Corp *(Noted 4.01)*	Cardington
N156RH	Cessna 421C Golden Eagle	421C-0008		Soft Air Service Inc *(Noted 1.03)*	Cambridge
N170AZ	Cessna 170A	19674	HB-CAZ / N5720C	Southern Aircraft Consultancy Inc *(Noted under restoration 12.02)*	Perth
N172AM	Cessna 172M Skyhawk II	17264993	G-BXHG	Southern Aircraft Consultancy Inc *(Noted 9.02)*	Norwich

Reg	Type	c/n	Prev id	Owner/Operator	Location
N176AF	Cessna 650 Citation III	650-0176		General Electric Capital Corp (Noted 10.02) (Op Ilmor Engineering)	Coventry
N177MA	Piper PA-46-350P Malibu Mirage	4622177		Southern Aircraft Consultancy Inc (Noted 8.02)	Weston, Dublin
N177SA	Reims/Cessna F177RG Cardinal RG	F177RG0171	F-GBFI	Southern Aircraft Consultancy Inc (Noted 2.03)	Southend
N180BB	Cessna 180K	18053103		Southern Aircraft Consultancy Inc (Noted 9.02)	Humberside
N180FN	Cessna 180K	18053201		Noise Abroad Inc (Noted 2.03)	Fordham, Newmarket
N181WW	Beagle B.206 Srs.1	B.018	G-BCJF N181WW/G-BCJF/XS773	Southern Aircraft Consultancy Inc (Noted 10.02)	Biggin Hill
N184CD	Cirrus Design SR20	1087		Plane Holdings Inc (Noted 2.03)	Turweston
N185UK	Cessna A185F Skywagon II (Floatplane)	18504367	SE-KOC N96DS/N9903N	Jet Blades & Engineering Inc (Op Seaflite) (Noted 12.02)	Lochearnhead
N187SA	Piper PA-28R Cherokee Arrow II	28R-7235139	G-BOJH N2821T	Southern Aircraft Consultancy Inc "Knight of the Thistle" (Noted 12.02)	Glasgow
N189SA	Piper PA-31-325 Turbo Navajo	31-7512045	G-BMGH ZS-LEU/N8493/A2-CAT	Southern Aircraft Consultancy Inc (Stored 2.03)	Southend
N191ME	Cessna T206H	T20608188		Anglo Irish Air Services (Noted 10.02)	Weston, Dublin
N201CV	Mooney M.20J	24-0084		K Knut (Noted 9.02)	Weston, Dublin
N201YK	Mooney M.20J	24-0518		ASA International of Central Florida Inc (Op W Fraser) (Noted 12.02)	Cumbernauld
N202AA	Cessna 421C Golden Eagle	421C1015		Simply Living Ltd (Noted 10.02)	Elstree
N202MC	Mitsubishi MU-2B-26A	369SA	N755MA	Southern Aircraft Consultancy Inc (Noted 10.02)	Bournemouth
N203SA	Piper AE-1 Cub Cruiser	5-1477	G-BWUG (ZK-USN)/N62073/NC62073/Bu30274 (As "Bu30274" in US Navy c/s) (Noted 4.02)	Southern Aircraft Consultancy Inc	Henstridge
N206HE	Bell 206B Jet Ranger	2880	N316JP	Southern Aircraft Consultancy Inc (Noted 9.02)	Bournemouth
N206NS	Bell 206B-3 JetRanger III	4474		Biztech International Inc (Noted 9.02)	(Swindon)
N210AD	Cessna 210G Centurion	21058835	OE-DES	Aerodynamics Worldwide (Noted 6.02)	Jersey
N210CP	Cessna 210M Centurion	21062034		D A Mann (Op Willowair Flying Club) (Noted 2.03)	Southend
N210SA	Maule M.7-235B	23062C		Southern Aircraft Consultancy Inc (Noted 9.01)	(St Just)
N213CT	Beech C90-1 King Air	LJ-1028	VP-CCT VR-CCT/N6420H/G-BKFY	Southern Aircraft Consultancy Inc (Op Corgi Toys) (Noted 10.02)	Oxford
N218SA	Piper PA-24-250 Comanche	24-1877	G-OJOK PH-DZE/D-EIEI/N6749P	Southern Aircraft Consultancy Inc (Noted 10.02)	Boonhill Farm, Fadmoor
N220SC	Piper PA-31T Cheyenne II	31T-8120041	N79CA N8361T/N816SW/N818SW/N2604X	Entrechato Inc (Op Sark International Airways) (Noted 2.02)	Guernsey
N220TW(2)	Canadair CL601-3A Challenger	5067	9A-CRT 9A-CRO/N603CC/C-GLXF	TWR Aero Inc (Noted 4.02)	Oxford
N228CX	SOCATA TBM-700	084		Turbine Aviation Inc (Op B.Holmes) (Noted 2.03)	Southend
N228TM	Raytheon Hawker 800XP	258458		Wells Fargo Bank Northwest NA (Op EMC Corporation)(Noted 11.02)	Cork, Co.Cork
N232N	Beech F33A Bonanza	CE-971	G-BYRT ZS-LFB/N18384	Hughston Aircraft Corp (Noted 1.03)	North Weald
N234SA	Cessna T310R	310R1805	F-GGGG N310AF/N2642B	Southern Aircraft Consultancy Inc (Noted 7.02)	Nottingham
N235PF	Piper PA-28-235 Pathfinder	28-7410083	OO-DDC	Southern Aircraft Consultancy Inc (Noted 1.03)	Southend
N237TD	Beech 95 Travelair	TD-237	HB-GOC	Southern Aircraft Consultancy Inc (Noted 8.02)	Cardiff
N240SE	Airbus Industrie A320-211	024	VH-HYC F-WWDT	Wells Fargo Bank Northwest NA (Stored 1.03)	Cambridge
N250AC	Piper PA-31 Navajo C	31-7612040	G-NWAC G-BDUJ/N59814	North West Air Inc (Noted 10.02)	Liverpool
N250MD	Piper PA-31-310 Navajo	31-742	D-ICHY F-BTCK/N7222L	Oilsearch Aviation (Noted 9.02)	Gloucestershire
N250TB	Piper PA-23-250 Aztec D	27-4577	G-VHFA G-BZFE/G-AZFE/EI-BPA/G-AZFE/N13962 c/o Computaplane (Stored 12.02)	Motor City Aviation LLC	Prestwick
N250TP	Beech A36TP Bonanza (Allison 250-B17)	E-2408	N416HC N600TT/N3107K	Minster Enterprises Inc (Noted 9.02)	Tatenhill
N251JS	Gulfstream G1159 Gulfstream II	251	N36GS N567A/N9PY/N9PG/N944H (Noted 2.01)	Eurolynx Corporation	Stansted
N257SA	Piper PA-32-300 Cherokee Six	32-40755	OY-PCF OH-PCF	Southern Aircraft Consultancy Inc (Noted 8.02)	Henstridge
N260SE	Airbus Industrie A320-211	0026	VH-HYE F-WWDV	Wells Fargo Bank Northwest NA (Stored 1.03)	Cambridge
N261SA	Reims FR172E Rocket	FR1720046	D-ECLY	Southern Aircraft Consultancy Inc (Noted 2.03)	Lower Wasing Farm, Brimpton
N270SE	Airbus Industrie A320-211	027	VH-HYF F-WWDD	Wells Fargo Bank Northwest NA (Stored 1.03)	Cambridge
N273TB	Beech 58 Baron	TH-305		Rogers Aviation Inc (Noted 9.02)	Welshpool
N275NM	Cessna 750 Citation X	750-0178	N5152X	II Leone Inc (Op Nigel Mansell) (Noted 10.02)	Jersey
N276SA	Brantly B.2B	474	G-AXSR G-ROOF/G-AXSR/N2237U	Southern Aircraft Consultancy Inc (Noted 9.02)	(Bedford)
N277CD	Cessna 210L Centurion	21059663	SE-IGY N1163Q	Bonner-Davies Aviation Inc (Noted 6.02)	White Waltham
N277SA	Piper PA-28-140 Cherokee	28-21661	SE-EYG	Southern Aircraft Consultancy Inc (Noted 12.02)	Blackpool
N280SA	Maule MX-7-180 Star Rocket	11070C	G-BSKT	Southern Aircraft Consultancy Inc (Noted 2.03)	Carnmore, Galway

Reg	Type	c/n	Prev id	Owner/Operator	Location
N282CJ	Cessna 525A CitationJet CJ2	525A-0082		CJ Airways	Guernsey
				(Op C I Automobiles Ltd) (Noted 7.02)	
N285F	Lockheed L.188CF Electra	1107	N5012K	JBQ Aviation Corp (Untitled hulk dumped 1.03)	Shannon
N285RA	Consolidated PBY-6A Catalina	2087	N212DM	Randsburg Corporation (Noted 12.02)	North Weald
	G-BPFY/N212DM/G-BPFY/N212DM/C-FHNH/CF-HNH/F-BAV/N5555H/N2864D/Bu.64017				
N290SE	Airbus Industrie A320-211	029	VH-HYG	Wells Fargo Bank Northwest NA	Cambridge
			F-WWDF	(Stored 1.03)	
N295S	Piper PA-46-350P Malibu Mirage	4636174	N295SS	Not known	(Jersey)
	(Jetprop DLX conversion)			(Noted 12.02)	
N295SA	Cessna F172G	F172-0278	EI-BAO	Southern Aircraft Consultancy Inc	Skegness
	(Built Reims Aviation SA)		G-ATNH	(On rebuild 8.02)	
N310QQ	Cessna 310Q	310Q0695	G-BAUE	Veryord Inc	Elstree
			N8048Q	(Op H Gold) (Noted 2.03)	
N312CJ	Cessna 525A CitationJet	525A0031		JCT Inc (Noted 5.02)	Ronaldsway
N314BG	North American P-51D-20NA Mustang	--	C-GZQX	Ice Strike Corporation	North Weald
				(Op Flying A Services/David Arnold) (Stored 8.02)	
	(Regd with c/n 122-39599 ex C-FBAU/44-73140: this crashed & dbf 7.7.84: possibly a composite rebuild)				
N320MR	Piper PA-30 Twin Comanche C	30-1917	G-CALV(2)	N320MR Inc	Elstree
	(Modified to PA-39 C/R status)		G-AZFO/N8761Y	(Noted 9.02)	
N321KL	Mooney M.20J (201)	24-1102	G-BPKL	Southern Aircraft Consultancy Inc	Stapleford
			N1008K	(Noted 10.02)	
N322MC	MD Helicopters MD 369E	0224E		AAA Flight Inc	Blackpool
				(Op Jepar Rotorcraft) (Noted 10.02)	
N322RJ	Beech 60 Duke	P-322		Aircraft Guaranty Title Corp (Noted 10.02)	Leeds-Bradford
N324JS	SOCATA TBM-700	230		Flamingo 700 Inc (Noted 2.03)	Fairoaks
N338DB	Piper PA-46-500TP Meridian	4697111		Oakfield Aviation (Noted 10.02)	Jersey
N340BR	Cessna 340A	340A1532		Soaring Eagle LLC (Noted 12.02)	(Biggin Hill)
N340SC	Cessna 340	340-0363		E C Rodriguez (Noted 2.03)	North Weald
N340YP	Cessna 340A II	340A0990	VR-CHR	ILEA Inc	Biggin Hill
			G-OCAN/D-ICIC/(N3970C)	(Noted 6.02)	
N341D	Beech 60 Duke	P-397		Mentor Adi Recruitment (Noted 10.02)	Teesside
N345TB	SOCATA TB-20 Trinidad	1914		Monty 345TB Llc (Noted 5.02)	Biggin Hill
N346X	Maule M5-210C Strata Rocket	6156C		Southern Aircraft Consultancy Inc	East Winch
				(Noted stored 7.02)	
N350UK	Aérospatiale AS350B Ecureuil	1244	F-GJYG	Starbuc Ltd (Noted 2.03)	(Brentwood)
N359DW	Piper PA-30 Twin Comanche C	30-770	G-ATET	L W Durrell	Jersey
			N230ET	(Noted 4.02)	
N369AN	Cessna 182S	18280696		Air View Ltd (Noted 4.02)	Jersey
N370SA	Piper PA-23-250 Aztec F	27-8054005	G-BKVN	Southern Aircraft Consultancy Inc	
			N6959A	(Op B K Pugh) (Noted 2.03)	Guernsey/Southend
N372SA	Cessna 172RG Cutlass II	172RG0550	G-BHVC	Southern Aircraft Consultancy Inc	High Cross
			N5515V	(Noted 4.02)	
N375SA	Piper PA-34-200T Seneca II	34-7670002	G-BMWP	Southern Aircraft Consultancy Inc	Gamston
			N3946X	(Noted 6.02)	
N395TC	Commander Aircraft Commander 114TC	20003		BNZ Aviation Inc	Denham
				(Noted 6.02)	
N409SA	Reims/Cessna FR182 Skylane RG	FR18200046	G-BJDI	Southern Aircraft Consultancy Inc	Leicester
			N8062H	(Noted 2.03)	
N412MD	Pilatus PC12		HB-FSI	Not known	Bournemouth
				(Noted 12.02 with reserved marks)	
N414FZ	Cessna 414RAM	414-0175	G-AZFZ	Lizard Aviation Inc	Jersey
			N8245Q	(Noted 9.02)	
N417RK	Piper PA-46-350P Malibu Mirage	4636249	G-BYSO	K-Air Aviation Inc	Jersey
			N9533N	(Noted 8.02)	
N418WS	Beech 58 Baron	TH-1967	N4467N	Millburn World Travel Services Two Inc	Edinburgh
				(Op W Scott & Partners Ltd) (Noted 12.02)	
N421CA	Cessna 421C Golden Eagle III	421C0153		USA Marine Inc (Noted 10.02)	Ronaldsway
N421N	Cessna 421C Golden Eagle III	421C1235		IMVA Aviation Inc (Noted 11.02)	Humberside
N423RS	Consolidated-Vultee PBY-5A Catalina	1785	C-FJJG	Southern Aircraft Consultancy Inc	Lee-on-Solent
			CF-JJG/N4002A/BuAer48423 (Op Super Catalina Restoration) (Noted 3.03)		
				(As "JV828" of 210 Sqdn in RAF c/s)	
N425DR	Cessna 425 Conquest I	425-0199	VP-BDR	Intercity Co Inc (Noted 6.01)	Booker
N425RR	Rockwell Commander 690A	11259	VP-BRR	Rami Aviation Inc	Fairoaks
			SE-KYY/OY-BEO/SE-IYX/OY-BEO/N57090 (Op Mann Aviation) (Noted 9.02)		
N425TV	Cessna 425 Corsair	425-0176	ZS-LDR	Conquest Aircraft Leasing	Aberdeen
			N6873T	(Op Apex Tubulars Ltd) (Noted 1.02)	
N429PK	Cessna 525 CitationJet	525-0429		E C Rodriguez (Noted 5.02)	Oxford
N430CE	Bell 430	49064		Wells Fargo Bank Northwest NA	Blackpool
				(Op JJC Sports) (Noted 10.02)	
N431WH	Bell 430	49066		Southern Aircraft Services	Shannon
				(Op Westair) (Noted 8.01)	
N432A	Raytheon B36TC Bonanza	EA-666		Sales Force Management Inc	King's Farm, Thurrock
				(Op Arrow Flying Associates) (Noted 2.03)	
N442BJ	Reims/Cessna F177RG Cardinal RG	F177RG0094	F-BVBC	Hughston Aircraft Corp	Seething
				(Noted 9.02)	
N448JC	Cessna 525 CitationJet	525-0448		Jet-Care Aviation (Noted 8.02)	Bournemouth
N454CC	Bell UH-1E	6200	Bu155344	S W Firczak (Noted 12.02)	Howth, Co Dublin
	(C/n 6199 quoted also)			(Op Independent Helicopters Ltd)	
N456JR	Piper PA-46-350P Malibu Mirage	4636311		Southern Aircraft Consultancy Inc	Liverpool
				(Noted 8.02)	
N473BS	Piper PA-28RT-201T Turbo Arrow IV	28R-8631003	G-BNYY	Sales Force Management Inc	Southend
			N25WA/N77860/G-BNYY/N9129X/N9517N (Op B.Strickland) (Noted 10.02)		
N480DS	Enstrom 480	5045		Eastern Atlantic Helicopters (Noted 7.02)	Gloucestershire

Reg	Type	Serial
N480E	Enstrom F480	5001
N484CJ	Cessna 525 CitationJet	525-0484
N485A	Enstrom F480	5029
N485ED	Piper PA-23-250 Aztec C	27-3864
N492PA	Beech B90 KingAir	LJ492
N494AT	British Aerospace BAe 125 Srs.-800XP	258103/NA0404
N499MS	Piper PA-28-181 Archer III	2843166
N500AV	Piper PA-24-260 Comanche	24-4805
N500LN	Howard 500	500-113
	(Lockheed PV-1 Ventura [5560] conversion)	
N502TC	Piper PA-30-160 Twin Comanche	30-881
N510PS	Cessna 310N	310N0054
N511VA	MD Helicopters MD 600N	RN-023
N519MC	Piper PA-28-140 Cherokee Cruiser	28-7325519
N524SF	Cessna 525 CitationJet	525-0240
N525CM	Cessna 525 CitationJet	525-0093
N527EW	Cessna 501 Citation 1	501-0322
N535CE	Cessna 560 Citation Ultra	560-0635
N554RB	Beech E55 Baron	TE-1141
N559C	Piper PA-34-220T Seneca V	3449238
N560S	Cessna 560XL Citation Excel	560-5190
N560TH	Cessna 560XL Citation Excel	560-5215
N565F	Aérospatiale SA.341G Gazelle	1182
N565G	SOCATA TB-20 Trinidad	2140
N580HE	Boeing 737-76N	28580
N582HE	Boeing 737-76N	28582
N583HE	Boeing 737-76N	28583
N584SR	Boeing 737-76N	28584
N585D	Gulfstream Gulfstream IV/SP	1258
N585HE	Boeing 737-76N	28585
N600MG	MD Helicopters MD.600N	RN-049
N600HV	MD Helicopters MD.600N	RN-058
N600PV	MD Helicopters MD.600N	RN-048
N600RN	MD Helicopters MD.600N	RN-015
N600SY	MD Helicopters MD.600N	RN-031
N605LG	American Blimp Corp A-60+ Airship	015
N611VA	Agusta A109C	7657
N620LH	Aérospatiale AS355F Twin Squirrel 2	5463
N620PL	Piper PA-32R-301 Saratoga SP	3213078
N625LH	Eurocopter AS355N Twinstar	5577
N637CG	Agusta A109C	7619
N642P	Piper PA-31 Turbo Navajo	31-761
N646JR	Piper PA-32RT-300T Turbo Lance II	32R-7987019
N656AG	Piper PA-34-220T Seneca III	34-8333087
N656JM	Reims Cessna FR182 Skylane RGII	FR1820049
N665CH	Cessna 525 CitationJet	0504
N666AW	Piper PA-31 Navajo C	31-7612061
N666GA	Gulfstream AA-5B Tiger	AA5B-1136
N666HM	SOCATA TB-20 Trinidad	1073
N666JH	Cessna 182T	18281025
N669MM	Bellanca 8KCAB-180 Super Decathlon	825-99
N671B	Raytheon A36 Bonanza	E-3409
N685TT	Rockwell Commander 685	12043
N700AR	SOCATA TBM-700	23
N700KH	SOCATA TBM-700	210

Reg	Owner / Operator	Location
HB-XUX	Eastern Atlantic Helicopters (Noted 10.02)	Jersey
N5211F	Cross Aviation (Noted 10.02)	Kerry, Co.Kerry
	Eastern Atlantic Helicopters (Noted 9.02)	Shoreham
G-BAED	Southern Aircraft Consultancy Inc	Waterford
N6567Y	(Noted 8.02)	
	Personal Airliner Ltd (Noted 12.01)	Jersey
	Vodaphone Americas Asia Inc	Farnborough
	(Noted 10.02)	
G-EPJM	MS Aviation	Jersey
N41268	(Noted 12.01)	
OO-SAP	Southern Aircraft Consultancy Inc	Blackbushe
	(Noted 10.02)	
N381RD	Western Aviation Leasing Inc	Exeter
N206G/N200G/N539N/SAAF 6417/FP579/Bu.34670 (Op Baker Petroleum) (Noted 7.01)		
G-BMSX	Southern Aircraft Consultancy Inc	Prestwick
N502TC/N7802Y	(Noted 10.02)	
G-AWTA	Island Seaplane Inc	Walton Wood,
EI-ATB/N4154Q	(Op Heliscott Ltd) (Noted 9.02)	Pontefract
G-SIVB	Marks Parks Inc (Noted 10.02)	Shoreham
G-BBID	R Lobell	Elstree
	(Noted 9.02)	
N525GM	C P Lockyer Inc (Noted 8.02)	Coventry
I-IDAG	Wells Fargo Bank Northwest NA	Edinburgh
N5151S	(Op Airmac Ltd) (Noted 12.02)	
(N769EW)	Rockville Aero Inc	Jersey
(N669DM)/N314GS/N374GS/N2663J (Noted 9.02)		
	Latium Jet Services (IOM) (Noted 2.03)	Gloucestershire
G-BNRH	Rodney Badham Inc	Coventry
N7855E	(Noted 9.02)	
	Chiswell Aviation Inc (Noted 6.02)	Fowlmere
	Sisma Aviation (Noted 8.02)	Jersey
VP-CPC	TJH Air Inc	Blackpool
N5091J/N560TH	(Noted 12.02)	
	Quay Contracts Inc (Noted 7.02)	Booker
	Ginsberg Aviation (Noted 10.02)	Blackpool
PP-VQA	Wells Fargo Bank Northwest NA	Lasham
	(Stored 10.02)	
PP-VQB	Wells Fargo Bank Northwest NA	Lasham
	(Stored 10.02)	
PP-VQC	Wells Fargo Bank Northwest NA	Lasham
	(Stored 10.02)	
PP-VQD	Lift VG Brasil Llc (Stored 10.02)	Lasham
N400UP	E I Dupont de Nemours & Co	Teesside
N416GA	(Noted 12.01)	
PP-VQE	Wells Fargo Bank Northwest NA	Lasham
	(Stored 10.02)	
N3266A	Paul Bundy Aviation Inc	Wolverhampton
	(Op Metafin Group) (Noted 10.02)	
N70470	Cumbrian Seafoods Inc	Hexham, Northumberland
	(Noted 10.02)	
	Southern Aircraft Consultancy Inc	
	(Noted 8.02)	Maryport, Cumbria
	Alan Smith Aviation (Noted 5.02)	Gloucestershire
N9211F	Eastern Atlantic Helicopters	Gloucestershire
	(Noted 10.02)	
	Lightship Group (Noted 2.00)	Wolverhampton
N97CN	Sloane Helicopters Inc (Noted 8.02)	(Oranmore)
	(Op Executive Helicopters) (Reserved as EI-DLP)	
	MJD Aviation Inc (Noted 10.02)	Redhill
	Marcella Thiel (Noted 6.02)	Booker
RP-C3688	Lloyd Helicopters US Inc (Noted 10.02)	Redhill
D-HARI	Castle Air Services Inc (Noted 6.02)	Denham
N500UD	Universal Direct Inc (Noted 1.03)	Sleap
G-EEAC/G-SKKA/G-FOAL/G-RMAE/N7239L (The World Gas Corporation titles)		
PH-LFD	Southern Aircraft Consultancy Inc	Kemble
N3032A	(Noted 8.02)	
F-GLMB	Southern Aircraft Consultancy Inc	Popham
N42996	(Noted 10.02)	
G-BHEO	JM Aviation Inc	Old Sarum
	(Noted 10.02)	
	Volante Aviation (Noted 12.02)	Cranfield
	Atlantic International Air Charter Inc	Biggin Hill
	(Noted 10.02)	
	Southern Aircraft Consultancy Inc	Enniskillen, Co.Fermanagh
	(Op Mr.Fasano) (Noted 10.02)	
OO-PDV	Euro Air Inc Trustee (Noted 11.02)	NK
	Hoggair Inc (Noted 1.03)	Rochester
	Gypsy Flyers Ltd (Noted 7.02)	White Waltham
	N671B Inc (Noted 11.02)	Ronaldsway
	RPM Family Limited Partnership	Gamston
	(Op Coopers Aerial Surveys) (Noted 1.01)	
F-GLBF	Air Touring Inc	Biggin Hill
F-WNGO/N700XL	(Noted 4.02)	
	TBM 700 Leasing Inc (Noted 10.02)	Liverpool

Reg	Type	c/n	Previous identities	Owner/Operator (Notes)	Base
N700PK	SOCATA TBM-700	52	F-OHEV VH-PTG/(VH-FIS)/F-OHBH	Sky High Aviation Inc *(Noted 6.01)*	Ronaldsway
N700S	SOCATA TBM-700	193		Speedbird Aviation *(Noted 10.02)*	Fairoaks
N700VA	SOCATA TBM-700	233	F-OIKI	Wells Fargo Bank Northwest NA *(Noted 2.03)*	Biggin Hill
N700VB	SOCATA TBM-700	237	F-OIKJ	Wells Fargo Bank Northwest NA *(Noted 2.03)*	Biggin Hill
N703JS	Dassault Falcon 10	157		Wickhaven Aviation Inc *(Op Medusa International) (Noted 4.02)*	Farnborough
N707LD	Piper PA-E23-250 Aztec C	27-2754	G-JANK EI-BOO/G-ATCY/N5640Y	Southern Aircraft Consultancy Inc *(Op I A Qureshi) (Keenair titles) (Noted 1.03)*	Shoreham
N707TJ	Boeing-Stearman A75N1 (N2S-1) Kaydet (Pratt & Whitney R-985 450hp)	75-950	N9PK N50057/Bu.3173	M G Plaskett *(Utterly Butterly titles)* "Honey" *(Op V.S.E.Norman t/a Aerosuperbatics Ltd) (Noted 8.02)*	Rendcomb
N708SP	Learjet Learjet 45	45-014		E C Rodriguez *(Op Hamlin Jet) (Noted 10.02)*	Luton
N709AT	Agusta A109E Power	11017	HB-XQM	Associated Technologies *(Noted 10.02)*	(Turweston)
N709EL	Beech 400A Beechjet	RK-52	(N709EW) N709JB	GAL Air Inc *(Op DFS Furniture) (Noted 10.02)*	East Midlands
N711TL	Piper PA-60 Aerostar 700P	60-8423017	N700SX N15GK/XB-EXQ/N6906Y	Southern Aircraft Consultancy Inc *(Noted 9.02)*	Biggin Hill
N719CD	Cirrus Design SR-22	0051		Southern Aircraft Consultancy Inc *(Noted 9.02)*	Exeter
N719CS	Piper PA-18S-135 Super Cub (L-21C)	18-3569	G-BWUC SX-ASM/EI-181/I-EIYB/MM54-2369/54-2369	Southern Aircraft Consultancy Inc *(Op Caledonian Seaplanes Ltd) (Under restoration 5.02)*	Cumbernauld
N720B	Bell 206L-1 LongRanger II	45452	G-DALE G-HBUS	Omega Air Inc *(Noted 8.02)*	Dublin
N735CX	Cessna 182Q Skylane II *(Modified to Advanced Lift 260 STOL)*	18265329		Wilmington Trust Company *(Op B.Holmes) (Noted 10.02)*	Barnard Farm, Thurrock
N736GX	Cessna R172K Hawk XP *(Tail-wheel u/c)*	R1722526		Project Air Inc *(Op MAF Europe) (Noted 5.02)*	Headcorn
N741CD	Cirrus Design SR-22	0137		Southern Aircraft Consultancy Inc *(Noted 10.02)*	Cambridge
N745HA	Agusta A109A-II	7413		Helix Aviation *(Noted 10.02)*	Prees, Shropshire
N747MM	Piper PA-28R-200 Arrow II	28R-7335445	PH-MLP N56489	Rivers Air Inc *(Noted 11.02)*	Coventry
N747SD	Cessna 414	4140934		N747SD Inc *(Noted 6.02)*	NK
N747WW	Piper PA-23-250 Aztec D	27-4330	G-AXOG N6965Y	Southern Aircraft Consultancy Inc *(Noted 10.02)*	Biggin Hill
N750NS	Cessna 750 Citation X	750-0172	N5066U	Sealpoint Aviation USA *(Op Aviation Beauport) (Noted 10.02)*	Jersey
N754AM	Agusta A109A	7154	I-CELB	Capital Helicopters London Inc *(Op Biggin Hill Helicopters Ltd) (Noted 10.02)*	Biggin Hill
N758BK	Cessna R172K Hawk XP	R1722963		Eros Inc *(Noted 8.01)*	Jersey
N766AM	Aérospatiale AS355N Twin Sqirrel	5601		E C Rodriguez *(Op Beacon Energy (Aviation) Ltd) (Noted 9.02)*	Beacon Farm, Leicestershire
N767CW	SOCATA TBM-700	96		High Sierra Inc *(Noted 4.01)*	Biggin Hill
N769JS	SOCATA TBM-700	187		Jato Aviation Inc *(Noted 9.02)*	Biggin Hill
N770RM	SOCATA TB-9 Tampico	131	PH-CAG	Simply Living Ltd *(Noted 11.02)*	Ronaldsway
N773DC	Beech 58 Baron	TH-755	G-BDWK (G-BEET)	DC Aviation Inc *(Op DC Energy Ltd) (Noted 7.01)*	Gamston
N777NG	Cessna 550 Citation Bravo	550-0992		Tazio Aviation Inc *(Noted 10.02)*	Hawarden
N797HG	Piper PA-46-310P Malibu	46-8408064		Rocol Aviation *(Noted 10.02)*	Shoreham
N799JH	Piper PA-28RT-201T Turbo Arrow IV	28R-8231051	HB-PNE PH-HJM/N8206B	Southern Aircraft Consultancy Inc *(Op J Havers) (Noted 1.03)*	King's Farm, Thurrock
N800C	Cirrus Design SR-22	0367		Context GB Inc *(Noted 12.02)*	Blackpool
N800HL	Bell 222	47054		Yorkshire Helicopters USA Inc *(Noted 9.02)*	(Coney Park, Leeds)
N800UK	Raytheon Hawker 800XP	258577	N51027	Wells Fargo Bank Northwest NA *(Op Liberty Aviation) (Noted 10.02)*	Leeds/Bradford
N800VM	Beech 76 Duchess	ME-318	G-BHGM	Southern Aircraft Consultancy Inc *(Noted 4.01)*	Gloucestershire
N808NC	Gulfstream 695B Commander 1200	96085		Wilmington Trust Co *(Op Coopers Aerial Surveys) (Noted 1.01)*	Gamston
N816RL	Beech E90 King Air	LW-187	N66BP N816EP/N900MH/N2187L	Springair Inc *(Op English Braids Ltd) (Noted 11.01)*	Gloucestershire
N818MJ	Piper PA-23-250 Aztec B	27-2486	G-ASNH	Retail Management Associates *(Noted 1.03)*	Charlton Park, Malmesbury
N818Y	Piper PA-30 Twin Comanche B	30-1458	ZS-CAO ZS-EYB/A2-ZFE/ZS-EYB/VQ-ZIY/ZS-EYB/N8318Y	One Eight Yankee Aviation Inc *(Noted 6.02)*	Guernsey
N822DE	Lockheed L.1011-385-1 Tristar 1	193A-1152	3C-QQX LZ-TPC/LZ-PTC/D-AERP/N337EA	Duane A Egli *(Stored 2.03)*	Manston
N829CB	Cessna 550 Citation Bravo	550-0829	N5096S	Wells Fargo Bank Northwest NA *(Op JJB Sports) (Noted 2.03)*	Blackpool
N836TP	Beech A36TP Bonanza	E-2124	N6770M	Hastingwood Aviation Inc *(Op Velcourt East plc) (Noted 1.03)*	Tatenhill
N840LE	Rockwell Commander 690C	11709	N690BA ZS-KZM/N5961K	Wells Fargo Bank Northwest NA *(Op O.Henriksen) (Noted 9.02)*	Guernsey
N841WS	Cessna 550 Citation Bravo	550-0841	N5086W	Millburn World Travel Services Inc *(Op Walter Scott & Ptnrs) (Noted 12.02)*	Edinburgh
N852FT*	Boeing 747-122F	19757	N4712U	PIK Ltd *(Noted 12.02 for fire service use)*	Prestwick
N853CD	Cirrus Design SR-22	0348		Assegai Aviation *(Noted 11.02)*	Denham
N866C	Cirrus Design SR-22	0397		Aircraft Guaranty Trust *(Noted 2.03)*	Turweston
N866CD	Cirrus Design SR-20	1235		Great Falls Associates Inc *(Noted 2.03)*	Turweston
N866LP	Piper PA-46-350P Malibu Mirage	4636130	N666LP N92928	TLP Aviation Inc *(Noted 8.02)*	Guernsey
N874RA	Gulfstream G1159A Gulfstream III	361	(N875E)	Banc of America Leasing & Capital LLC *(Noted as N874RA c.2000 although N874RR reserved)*	Stansted
N882	SOCATA TB-20 Trinidad GT	2161	F-OIMA	Harland Aviation *(Noted 11.02)*	Newcastle

Reg	Type	c/n	Reg 2	Owner/Operator	Location
N882JH	Maule M.7-235B	23056C		Everbright Aviation Inc *(Noted 1.03)*	Henstridge
N900CB	Cessna 421C Golden Eagle III	421C0837	VP-CPR	Southern Aircraft Consultancy Inc	Guernsey
			VR-CPR/N2659F	*(Op Fifty North) (Noted 10.02)*	
N909WJ	Grumman FM-2 Wildcat	—	BuAer 16203	Iron Baron Corp	North Weald
				(Op Flying A Service/Wizzard Investments Ltd) (Noted 8.02)	
N915TC	Aeronca 15AC Sedan	15AC-429	EI-ETC	Southern Aircraft Consultancy Inc	Athboy, Co.Meath
			G-CETC/HB-ETC	*(Op H.Moreau) (Noted 6.00)*	
N916CD	Cirrus Design SR-22	0318		Farnborough Aircraft Inc *(Noted 11.02)*	Blackbushe
N918Y	Piper PA-30-160 Twin Comanche	30-736	ZS-NLH	Southern Aircraft Consultancy Inc	Shobdon
			N31RK/ZS-NLH/ZS-FZR/CR-AJR/ZS-EIU/VQ-ZIS/N7658Y *(Noted 2.03)*		
N920RP	Cessna T310R	310R0877		Avalon Air Services *(Noted 8.01)*	Biggin Hill
N950H	Dassault Falcon 50EX	307		Island Aviation Inc *(Noted 10.02)*	Farnborough
N951SF	Beech 56TC Baron	TG-83	N23PB	Timcar Inc *(Noted 10.02)*	Elstree
N957JK	Piper PA-24-250 Comanche	24-1931	OE-DEU	Trek-Air BV	Bournemouth
			N6798P	*(Noted 12.02)*	
N961JM	Piper PA-46-500TP Meridian	4697122	N53450	Blackbrook Aviation	Bournemouth
			OY-LAW	*(Crashed Dunkeswell 1.03 & noted 17.1.03)*	
N966SW	Cessna 560 Citation V Ultra	560-0284	N5108G	Terry Coleman Inc *(Noted 7.02)*	Liverpool
N971CT	Diamond DA20-C1	C0124		Diamond Aircraft Sales *(Noted 8.02)*	Gamston
N971RJ	Piper PA-39 Twin Comanche C/R	39-111	G-AZBC	Aircraft Guaranty Corporation	
			N8951Y	*(Noted 8.02)*	Wellcross Grange, Slinfold
N973BB	Mitsubishi MU-2B-60 Marquise	1509SA		Romeo Aviation Inc *(Noted 9.02)*	Jersey
N980HB	Rockwell Commander 695	95006		HBC Aviation Inc *(Noted 12.02)*	Guernsey
N991RV(2)	IAI 1125 Astra	011	N705MA	E I Aviation Inc	Dublin
			N450BM/N450PM/4X-CUK	*(Op Eddie Irvine) (Noted 9.02)*	
N997JB	Partenavia P.68C-TC	288-20-TC	F-GROG	Pangaea Air Service	Little Staughton
			HB-LSB/F-GEQD/N60CH/YV-2318P *(Noted 2.01)*		
N999BE	Dassault Falcon 2000	147	F-WWVB	Formula One Management	Biggin Hill
				(Op Bernie Ecclestone) (Noted 10.02)	
N999F	Beech F33A Bonanza	CE-1282		N T N Fox Systems Inc *(Noted 4.02)*	Newcastle
N999MH	Cessna 195B	7168	OH-CSE	E Detiger *(Noted 10.02)*	Compton Abbas
N999PJ	Morane-Saulnier MS.760 Paris 2	89	F-BJLY	R.J.Lamplough *(Noted 12.02)*	North Weald
N1024L	Beech 60 Duke	P-78	C-FOPH	Flytru Aviation Inc	North Weald
			CF-OPH/N1024L/CF-OPH	*(Op R.Ogden) (Noted 8.02)*	
N1027G	Maule M.7-235B	23032C		Southern Aircraft Consultancy Inc	Elstree
				(Noted 9.02)	
N1089D	Hughes 369D	51-0966D		Sky Dock Helicopter Holdings *(Noted 6.01)*	
				(Op Nunkeeling Ltd)	Elloughton, Humberside
N1092H	Beech C90A King Air	LJ-1454		Park Close Aviation Inc *(Noted 9.02)*	Blackbushe
N1120Z	Raytheon B200 Super King Air	BB-1570		Air Direct Inc *(Noted 10.02)*	Guernsey
N1158V	Cessna 310J	310J0172		Southern Aircraft Consultancy Inc	Sandtoft
				(Noted 7.02)	
N1172X	Piper PA-34-200T Seneca II	34-7570228		Southern Aircraft Consultancy Inc	Shoreham
				(Noted 2.02)	
NC1328	Fairchild F24R-46KS Argus	3310		Eastern Stearman Inc	Priory Farm, Tibenham
				(Op Blackbarn Aviation) (Frame noted 4.02)	
N1344	Ryan PT-22-RY Recruit	2086	41-20877	Flying Heritage Inc	RAF Cosford
				(Op Mrs.H.Mitchell t/a PT Flight) (Noted 4.02)	
N1350J	Rockwell Commander 112B	516		Southern Aircraft Consultancy Inc	Elmsett
				(Op G.Richards) (Noted 9.02)	
N1364V	Boeing E75	75-8672		Tranzair Inc *(Noted 9.01)*	North Weald
N1407J	Rockwell Commander 112A	407		Blue Lake Aviation Inc *(Noted 10.02)*	Popham
N1551D	Cessna 190	7773		Southern Aircraft Consultancy Inc	Seething
				(Noted 9.02)	
N1565B	Beech 400 Beechjet	RJ-65		International Aviation Leasing Inc	Leeds-Bradford
				(Op A.Ogden & Sons plc) (Noted 10.02)	
N1731B	Boeing A75N-1 Stearman	75-5716		Eastern Stearman Inc	Priory Farm, Tibenham
				(Under rebuild 4.02)	
N1745M	Cessna 182P Skylane II	18264424		D Thomas *(Noted 8.02)*	Cardiff
N1778X	Cessna 210L Centurion	21060798		Central Investment Corporation *(Noted 9.02)*	Denham
N1835W	Beech 95-B55 Baron	TC-1513	ZS-ING	Virginia Aircraft Trust Corp	Kemble
			N1835W	*(Noted 2.03)*	
N1937Z	Cessna 172RG Cutlass RG	172RG0908	EI-BVS	Virginia Aircraft Trust Corp *(Noted 8.02)*	Ronaldsway
N1944A	Douglas DC-3C-47A-80-DL	19677	(N5211A)	Wings Venture Ltd	Kemble
			N3239W/RDanAF K-683/RnorAF/43-15211 *(As "315211/JB-Z") (Noted 7.02)*		
N2061K	Beech 58P Pressurised Baron	TJ-161		R Wagstaff *(Noted 9.02)*	Oxford
N2121T	Gulfstream AA-5B Tiger	AA5B-1031		J.Siebols *(Noted 2.03)*	Southend
N2209P	Piper PA-23-250 Aztec C	27-3788	G-BYRW	E Walsh	Elstree
			F-BOXQ/N6500Y	*(Noted as "F-BOXQ" 9.02)*	
N2216X	Cessna 337 Super Skymaster	3370116		Euram Inc *(Noted 9.02)*	(Lee-on-Solent)
N2273Q	Piper PA-28-181 Cherokee Archer II	28-7790389		Minwriston Inc	Marley Hall
				(Noted 10.02)	
N2326Y	Beech 58P Baron	TJ-83	F-GALL	Southern Aircraft Consultancy Inc	Gamston
				(Noted 11.02)	
N2341S	Raytheon B300 Super King Air	FL-241		Specsavers Aviation Inc *(Noted 10.02)*	Guernsey
N2366D	Cessna 170B	20518		Southern Aircraft Consultancy Inc	Turweston
				(Noted 7.02)	
N2379C	Cessna R182 Skylane RG	R18200170		West Country Aviation Inc *(Noted 6.02)*	Ledbury
N2401Z	Piper PA-23-250 Aztec B	27-8054034		Pan Maritime Inc *(Noted 2.03)*	Filton
N2423C	Piper PA-38-112 Tomahawk	38-79A0177		Phoenix East Aviation Inc *(Stored 2.00)*	Bristol
N2454Y	Cessna 182S	18280918		Seima Aviation *(Noted 1.03)*	Great Massingham
N2480X	Piper PA-31T1 Cheyenne I	31T-8104026		Jane Air *(Noted 2.02)*	Southampton
N2548T	Navion Model H Rangemaster	NAV-4-2548		Navion Airways Inc *(Noted 8.02)*	Guernsey
N2612	Stinson Junior R	8754	NC2612	A.L.Young *(Stored 8.02 as "NC2612")*	Henstridge

Reg	Type	C/n	Prev	Owner	Location
N2652P	Piper PA-22-135 Tri-Pacer	22-2992		J L Morris *"Jeff Jeff"*	Weston
				(Op Anne Lait) (Noted 8.01)	
N2923N	Piper PA-32-300 Cherokee Six	32-7940207		S W Freeborn *(Noted 3.03)*	Buttermilk Hall Farm, Blisworth
N2929W	Piper PA-28-151 Cherokee Warrior	28-7415457	OO-GPE	Funair Inc	Elstree
			N9619N	*(Op R.Lobell) (Noted 10.02)*	
N2941W	Christen A-1 Husky	1040		Southern Aircraft Consultancy Inc *(Noted 10.02)*	Sherlowe
N2943D	Piper PA-28RT-201 Arrow IV	28R- 7918231	G-BSLD	Southern Aircraft Consultancy Inc	Barton
			N2943D	*(Op E.Gawronek) (Noted 10.02)*	
N2967N	Piper PA-32-300 Six	32-7940242		Aerotechnics Aviation Inc *(Stored 7.02)*	Guernsey
N2975K*	Luscombe 8E	5702		Not known	Westland Zoyland
				(Noted 10.01 for UK registration)	
N3018C	Raytheon B200 Super KingAir	BB-1718		Wells Fargo Bank Northwest NA	Blackbushe
				(Noted 8.02)	
N3023W	Beech V35B Bonanza	D-9517		M A Sargent *(Noted 8.02)*	Guernsey
N3043L	Beech 1900C-1	UC-163		Raytheon Aircraft Credit Corp	Blackbushe
			N163AM/N163YV	*(Stored 1.03)*	
N3044B	Piper PA-34-200T Seneca II	34-7970012		Aerotechnics Aviation Inc *(Noted 9.02)*	Alderney
N3536N	Mooney M.20F	68-0088		J E M Williams *(Noted 7.01)*	North Weald
N3586D	Piper PA-31-325 Navajo C/R	31-8012065		L. W.Durrell *(Noted 2.03)*	Jersey
N3839H	Piper Aerostar 601P	61P-0569-7963247	F-GKCL	Southern Aircraft Consultancy Inc	Jersey/Southend
			N3839H/G-RACE/N8083J	*(Op J.Reynolds) (Noted 2.03)*	
N3864	Ryan Navion B	NAV-4-2285B		Southern Aircraft Consultancy Inc	Earls Colne
				(Under rebuild by G Spooner 12.02)	
N3922B	Boeing-Stearman E75 (PT-17) Kaydet		42-17642	Eastern Stearman Inc	Priory Farm, Tibenham
	(Continental W670)	75-5805		*(Noted 4.02)*	
N3995W	Piper PA-32-260 Cherokee Six	32-963		E W Wells	Bournemouth
				(Crashed Le Rignolent, France 31.5.98: fuselage stored 5.00)	
N4085E	Piper PA-18-150 Super Cub	18-7809059		R N Hall *(Noted 8.01)*	Goodwood
N4168D	Piper PA-34-220T Seneca V	3449158		AAL Inc *(Noted 10.02)*	Plymouth
N4173T	Cessna 320D Skyknight	320D0073		N4173T Inc *(Op J.Irwin) (Noted 6.02)*	Cranfield
N4178W	Piper PA-32R-301T Saratoga II	TC 3257178		Meridian Aircraft Ferrying Inc *(Noted 10.01)*	Jersey
N4232Y	Reima Cessna F150G	F1500098	D-EBYW	F Acevedo *(Noted 10.02)*	Stapleford
N4306Z	Piper PA-28-161 Warrior II	28-8316073		Thomas Stuer Aviation Inc	Stapleford
				(Op USAF Flying Club) (Noted 10.02)	
N4337K	Cessna 150K	15071583	G-BTSA	T L Crook	Branscombe
			N6083G	*(Noted 9.02)*	
N4422P	Piper PA-23-160 Geronimo	23-1936		W J Armstrong Inc *(Noted 7.01)*	Thruxton
N4545	Learjet Learjet 45	45-045		P N C Leasing *(Noted 1.01)*	Jersey
N4575C	Grumman G.21A Goose	B-120		Aerofloat G21A Inc *(Noted 8.02)*	Weston, Dublin
N4596N	Boeing-Stearman E75 (PT-13D) Kaydet			Phil Dacy Aviation *(US Mail c/s) (Noted 3.02)*	Goodwood
	(Lycoming R680-7)	75-5945	42-17782	*(Op N.Mason & D.Gilmour t/a Intrepid Aviation Co)*	
N4599W	Rockwell Commander 112TC	13089		Skyfast Inc *(Noted 3.00)*	Haverfordwest
N4698W	Rockwell Commander 112TC-A	13274		Syston Aviation Inc *(Noted 9.02)*	Denham
				(Op W.Haynes)	
N4712V	Boeing Stearman PT-13D Kaydet	75-5094	42-16931	Southern Aircraft Consultancy Inc	Chalmington
				(Stored 7.01 with Wessex Aviation & Transport)	
N4770B	Cessna 152	15283626		Walkwitz Aviation *(Noted 10.02)*	Panshanger
N5010X	Raytheon 390 Premier 1	RB-10		Wells Fargo Bank Northwest NA	Luton
				(Op Ambrion Aviation) (Noted 1.03)	
N5052P	Piper PA-24-180 Comanche	24-56	G-ATFS	T A G Randell	Farley Farm, Romsey
			N5052P	*(Noted under restoration 9.01)*	
N5057V	Boeing-Stearman PT-13D Kaydet	75-5598	42-17435	M G Plaskett *"Charlie Brown"*	Rendcomb
				(Op V.S.E.Norman) (Utterly Butterly titles) (Noted 9.02)	
N5064L	Raytheon B90B King Air	LJ-1664		Specialized Aircraft Services Inc	Blackbushe
				(Noted 1.03)	
NC5171N	Lockheed 10A Electra			See G-LIOA in SECTION 4	
N5180Y	Piper PA-23-250 Aztec B	27-2226		Southern Aircraft Consultancy Inc	Glasgow
				(Noted 4.01)	
N5240H	Piper PA-16 Clipper	16-44		Southern Aircraft Consultancy Inc *(Noted 5.02)*	
				(Op D.Hillier)	Wellcross Grange, Slinfold
N5264Q	MD Helicopters MD.369E	0126E		Trafficopters Inc *(Noted 11.02)*	Donegal
N5277T	Piper PA-32-260 Cherokee Six	32-7200031		K R Denman *(Noted 6.02)*	Goodwood
N5315V	Hiller UH-12C	757		Southern Aircraft Consultancy Inc	Sancreed, Cornwall
				(Noted 5.01)	
N5345N	Boeing Stearman PT-13D Kaydet	75-5718	42-17555	Eastern Stearman Inc	Priory Farm, Tibenham
				(On rebuild 4.02)	
N5346S	Piper PA-32R-301T Saratoga II TC	3257257		Saxon Aviation *(Noted 1.03)*	Elstree
N5428C	Cessna 170A	19462		28 Charlie Inc *(Op P.Norman) (Noted 8.02)*	Audley End
N5632R	Maule M-5-235C Lunar Rocket	7244C		Southern Aircraft Consultancy Inc	Stowes Farm
				(Op RD Group) (Noted 8.01)	Tillingham
N5644L	American AA-1 Yankee	AA1-0044		Southern Aircraft Consultancy Inc	Biggin Hill
				(Noted 10.02)	
N5647S	Maule M-5-235C Rocket	7345C		Virginia Aircraft Trust Corp	
				(Noted 8.00)	Yeatsall Farm, Abbotts Bromley
N5675Z*	Piper PA-22-108 Colt	22-9501		Not known *(Noted 5.00)*	Kilrush, Co.Clare
N5730H	Piper PA-16 Clipper	16-342		Southern Aircraft Consultancy Inc	
				(Noted 8.02)	Cork Farm, Streethay
N5736	Raytheon Hawker 800XP	258471	N43642	Wells Fargon Bank Northwest NA *(Noted 7.00)*	Luton
N5820T	Westland WG-30-100			See G-BKFD in SECTION 4	
N5834N*	Rockwell Commander 114	14383		W F Chmura	Peterstone
				(Crashed 23.10.98 - cancelled by FAA 7.99 - hulk noted 2.02)	
N5840T	Westland WG-30-100			See G-BKFF in SECTION 4	
N5880T	Westland WG-30-100	009	G-17-31	Offshore Fire & Survival Training Centre	Norwich
				(Noted 3.02)	

Reg	Type	Serial	Prev id	Owner/Operator	Location
N5900H	Piper PA-16 Clipper	16-520		Southern Aircraft Consultancy Inc *(Noted 8.02)*	Shenstone
N5915V	Piper PA-28-161 Cherokee Warrior II	28-7716215		Southern Aircraft Consultancy Inc *(Noted 9.02)*	North Weald
N5966D	Zenair CH-801	8-4152		D A Defelici *(Noted 9.01)*	Shoreham
N6003F	Commander Aircraft Commander 114B	14590		Deskey Aviation Inc *(Noted 9.02)*	Exeter
N6010Y	Commander Aircraft Commander 114B	14589		Camrose Inc *(Noted 2.03)*	Biggin Hill
N6095A	Commander Aircraft Commander 114B	14635		Bonbois Aviation *(Noted 12.01)*	Guernsey
N6107Y	Commander Aircraft Commander 114B	14627		Tamboti Aviation Inc *(Noted 10.02)* *(Op IPP Aviation)*	Guernsey
N6182G	Cessna 172N Skyhawk II	17273576		Southern Aircraft Consultancy Inc *(Noted10.02)*	Andrewsfield
N6302W	Government Aircraft Factory N22B Nomad	F-159	VH-HWB	Chatteris Aviation Inc *(Op London Parachute Centre) (Noted 7.02)*	Lower Mt.Pleasant, Chatteris
N6315X	Cessna 421C	421C-1003		Transatlantic Flyers Ltd *(Noted 7.01)*	Oxford
N6339U	Piper PA-28-236 Dakota	28-8011089	OO-JFD	Thistle Aviation In	Southend
			F-GCMU or V?/OO-HLM/N8152S *(Op JRB Aviation) (Noted 2.03)*		
N6498V	Cessna T303 Crusader	T30300313	G-CRUS N6498V	Southern Aircraft Consultancy Inc *(Noted 9.02)*	Guernsey
N6593W	Cessna P210N	P210-00801		Southern Aircraft Consultancy Inc *(Noted 10.02)*	Stapleford
N6601Y	Piper PA-23-250 Aztec C	27-3905	XC-DAZ N6601Y	3 Greens Aviation *(Noted 12.02)*	Blackpool
N6602W	Piper PA-23-250 Aztec C	27-3799	G-AYSA N6509Y	Hughston Aircraft Corp *(Noted 2.03)*	Norwich
N6602Y	Piper PA-28-140 Cherokee	28-21943	G-ATTG N11C	T.P.Hughston *(Noted 10.02)*	Little Staughton
N6632L	Beech C23 Musketeer	M-2188		W J Forrest *(Noted 9.02)*	Enstone
N6690D	Piper PA-18-135 Super Cub	18-3848	PH-KNK	6688 Delta Inc *(Op S Gruver) (Noted 6.00)*	Netherley
N6819F	Cessna 150F	15063419		W J Davis *(Noted 2.02)*	Shoreham
N6830B	Piper PA-22-150 Tri-pacer	22-4128		Vintage Aircraft Lelystad Inc *(Noted 4.02)*	Leicester
N6834L	Cessna T310R II	310R2137		NL Aviation Inc *(Op P.Basch/Tropair Engineering Ltd) (Noted 10.02)*	Leeds-Bradford
N6907E	Cessna 175A Skylark	56407		Southern Aircraft Consultancy Inc *(Noted 10.02)*	Popham
N6954J	Piper PA-32R-300 Cherokee Lance	32R-7680394		Matrix Aviation Inc *(Op Avionicare) (Noted 2.03)*	Southend
N7027E	Hawker Tempest V	---	EJ693	K Weeks *(On rebuild 6.01)*	Booker
N7070A	Cessna S550 Citation II	S550-0068	N4049 N404G/N1272Z	Omega Air Inc *(Noted 8.02)*	Dublin
N7148R	Beech B55 Baron	TC-2028	N2198L	Air Services Holdings Corp	Guernsey
			C-GWFD/N2198L/D-IGRW/N2198L *(Noted 6.02)*		
N7214Y	Beech A36 Bonanza	E-2169		Southern Aircraft Consultancy Inc *(Noted 3..03)*	Gloucestershire
N7219L	Beech B55 Baron	TC-717		Southern Aircraft Consultancy Inc *(Noted 5.02)*	Kemble
N7263S	Cessna 150H	15067963		Cesna Inc *(On rebuild 7.02)*	Plaistows Farm, St Albans
N7348P	Piper PA-24-250 Comanche	24-2526		Southern Aircraft Consultancy Inc *(Op J.Bown) (Noted dismantled 7.02)*	Netherthorpe
N7374A	Cessna A150M Aerobat 135 *(Tail-wheel conversion)*	A1500726		J A Thomas "Turnin' Tricks" *(Noted 9.02)*	Branscombe
N7423V	Mooney M.20E Chapparal	21-1163		Southern Aircraft Consultancy Inc *(Noted 7.02)*	Hinton in the Hedges
N7564J*	Piper PA-28R-180 Cherokee Arrow	28R-30942		Southern Aircraft Consultancy Inc *(Noted as "N7564J" 2.01)*	Thruxton
N7640F	Piper PA-32R-300 Cherokee Lance	32R-7780069	ZS-OGX N7640F	Southern Aircraft Consultancy Inc *(Noted 12.02)*	Wellesbourne Mountford
N7777G*	Lockheed L.749A-79 Constellation			See G-CONI in SECTION 4	
N7813M	Piper PA-28-180 Cherokee D	28-5227	G-AZYF 5Y-AJK/N7813N	Southern Aircraft Consultancy Inc *(Noted 9.02)*	Leicester
N7832P	Piper PA-24-250 Comanche	24-3052		Three Two Papa Inc *(Noted 10.02)*	White Waltham
N7976Y	Piper PA-30 Twin Comanche B	30-1075		Southern Aircraft Consultancy Inc *(Noted 7.02)*	Guernsey
N8153E	Piper PA-28RT-201T Turbo Arrow IV	28R-8131185	N9561N N84205	P B Payne *(Noted 1.03)*	RAF Mona
N8241Z	Piper PA-28-161 Warrior II	28-8316079		Pett Air Inc *(Noted 5.01)*	Goodwood
N8258F	Beech B36TC Bonanza	EA-513		Millfore Aviation Inc *(Noted 7.02)*	Elstree
N8403Y	Piper PA-30-160B Twin Comanche	30-1552	4X-AVY N8403Y	D Yoshpe *(Noted 9.02)*	Elstree
N8471Y	Piper PA-28-236 Dakota	28-8211019		Turbo Arrow Inc *(Noted 10.02)*	Panshanger
N8754J	Aviat A-1 Husky *(Built Christen Industries)*	1160		Southern Aircraft Consultancy Inc *(Op A.Febrache) (Noted 9.02)*	Guernsey
N8829P	Piper PA-24-260 Comanche	24-4285		Southern Aircraft Consultancy Inc *(Noted 6.02)*	(Filton)
N8911Y	Piper PA-39 Twin Comanche C/R	39-66	G-AYFT N8911Y	Southern Aircraft Consultancy Inc *(Noted 9.02)*	Popham
N9050T*	Douglas C-47A-10DK Dakota 3			See G-AGYX in SECTION 4	
N9089Z	North American TB-25J-25NC Mitchell			See G-BKXW in SECTION 4	
N9122N	Piper PA-46-310P Malibu	4608097		Libra Air Inc *(Noted 10.00)*	Oxford
N9123X	Piper PA-32R-301 Saratoga	3229003		Vector Sky Service Inc *(Noted 7.02)*	Shoreham/Hilversum
N9146N	Cessna 401B *(RAM conversion)*	401B0010		A J Air Ltd Inc *(Noted 9.02 in derelict condition)*	Weston, Dublin
N9201U	MD Helicopters MD.900	900-00042		MD Helicopters Inc *(Noted 1.02)*	Shoreham
N9208V	MD Helicopters MD.900	900-00010		Explorer Aviation Inc *(Noted 10.02)*	Shoreham

Reg	Type	Serial	Prev identity	Owner/Operator	Location
N9232Y	Piper PA-31P-350 Mojave	31P-8414018		Saratoga Air Club Inc *(Op Anglo American Airmotive) (Noted 8.00)*	Bournemouth
N9239Y	Piper PA-31P-350 Mojave	31P-8414040		Castle Aviation Inc *(Noted 9.02)*	Guernsey
N9308V	Mooney M.20F	69-0086		Southern Aircraft Consultancy Inc *(Noted 4.02)*	Biggin Hill
N9325N	Piper PA-28R-200 Cherokee Arrow *(Lopresti version)*	28R-35025		Southern Aircraft Consultancy Inc *(Op Hiam Mercado) (Noted 10.02)*	Panshanger
N9381P	Piper PA-24-260 Comanche C	24-4882		Southern Aircraft Consultancy Inc *(Noted 7.02)*	Elstree
N9469P	Piper PA-24-260 Comanche C	24-4979		Southern Aircraft Consultancy Inc *(Noted 9.02)*	Guernsey
N9521C	Consolidated 28-5ACF (PBY-5A) Catalina		Bu48294	Training Services Inc *(Noted 10.02)*	North Weald
N9533Y	Cessna T.210N	21064539		Simply Living Ltd *(Noted 10.02)*	Liverpool
N9727G	Cessna 180H	18052227	G-FESC N9727G	Simply Living Ltd *(Op B Richardson) (Noted 1.03)*	Wellcross Grange, Slinfold
N9766N*	Hughes 369C	NK		Chieftain Trailers Ltd *(Reserved 5.02)*	Donegal
N9861M	Maule M.4-210C	1058C		Southern Aircraft Consultancy Inc *(Noted 7.02)*	Fairoaks
N9950	Curtiss P-40N Warhawk	33723	44-7983	Ice Strike Corp *(Stored in container 8.02)*	North Weald
N9999M	Gulfstream Gulfstream IV	1090	VP-CYM N9999M/VP-CYM/VR-CYM/N466GA	Wells Fargo Bank Northwest NA *(Op Jet Fly Aviation) (Noted 1.03)*	Luton
N11824	Cessna 150L	15075652		Southern Aircraft Consultancy Inc *(Noted 10.01)*	Manor Farm, Glatton
N12739(3)	de Havilland DH.83 Fox Moth	4026(2)		J M Hirtle *(Airframe noted 1.02)*	Denford Manor, Hungerford
N13253	Cessna 172M	17262613		Anglia Aviation Inc *(On rebuild 9.02)*	Plaistows Farm, St Albans
N14113	North American T-28B Trojan	174-398	Haiti AF 1236 N14113/FrAF 119/51-7545	Radial Revelations Ltd *"Little Rascal"* *(As "119" in French AF/AdlA c/s) (Noted 12.01)*	Duxford
N14152	Piper PA-23-250 Aztec E	27-4715	G-AZMK OY-AJA/G-AZMK/N14152	Western Aviation Leasing Inc *(Noted 7.01)*	Exeter
N14234*	Handley Page HP.137 Jetstream			See G-BBBV in SECTION 4	
N15486	Beech 1900C	UC-131	F-GNAH N15486	Raytheon Aircraft Credit Corp *(Stored 10.02)*	Blackbushe
N15750	Beech D.18S	A-850	G-ATUM D-IANA/N20S	S Quinto *(Nose only preserved 2002?)*	Strathdon
NC16403*	Cessna C.34 Airmaster	322		Alan House *(Stored 1.02)*	Lower Wasing Farm, Brimpton
N18028	Beech D17S Staggerwing	147	NC18028	P.H.McConnell *(Noted 6.02)*	Popham
N21381	Piper PA-34-200 Seneca	34-7350274	F-BUTM F-ETAL	Tickton Inc *(Noted 4.00)*	Dunkeswell
N23659	Beech B58 Baron	TH-893		S W Freeborn *(Noted 7.02)*	Guernsey
N24136	Beech A36 Bonanza	E-1233		Dickens Aviation Inc *(Noted 2.03)*	Panshanger
N26634	Piper PA-24-250 Comanche	24-3551	G-BFKR PH-BUS/D-ELPY/N8306P	J A McMahon *(Noted 8.00)*	Ronaldsway
N27597	Piper PA-31-350 Navajo Chieftain	31-7852073		Matthew Airlines Inc *(Noted 2.03)*	Southend/Fairoaks
N29566	Piper PA-28R-201T Arrow IV	28R-7918146		Southern Aircraft Consultancy Inc *(Noted 9.02)*	North Weald
N31356	Douglas DC-4-1009	42914	C-FTAW EL-ADR/N6404	Aces High US Inc *(As "42-42914") (Noted 10.02)*	North Weald
N32625*	Piper PA-34-200T Seneca II	34-7570039		Guernsey Airport Fire Service *(Hulk only 12.01)*	Guernsey
N33870	Fairchild M62A (PT-19-FA) Cornell	T40-237	G-BTNY N33870/US Army	Ice Strike Corp *(Op R.M Lamplough) (As "02538" in US Army c/s)*	North Weald
NC33884*	Aeronca 65CA Chief	CA.14101		N.A.Evans *(Noted 7.02)*	Branscombe
N36362	Cessna 180 Skywagon	31691	G-BHVZ F-BHMU/N4739B	Southern Aircraft Consultancy Inc *(Op W Burgess) (Noted 8.01)*	Sibson
N38049	Beech A36TC Bonanza	EA-178		T B Ellison Inc *(Noted 8.01)*	Old Sarum
N38273	Piper PA-28R-201 Cherokee Arrow III	28R-7737086		S W Freeborn *(Op L.Slater) (Noted 10.02)*	Blackbushe
N38940	Boeing-Stearman A75N1 (PT-17) Kaydet (Continental R670)	75-1822	(G-BSNK) N38940/N55300/41-8263	Eastern Stearman Inc *(Op R.W.Sage t/a Blackbarn Aviation) (Noted 8.02) (As "18263/822" in US Army c/s)*	Priory Farm, Tibenham
N39132*	Piper PA-38-112 Tomahawk	38-82A0065	(G-NCFD) D-EIIS/N2477V	Not known *(Noted derelict 7.01)*	Swanton Morley
N39605	Piper PA-34-200T Seneca	34-7870397		Heliquick Aviation *(Noted 1.03)*	Biggin Hill
N41098	Cessna 421B Golden Eagle	421B0448		M C I Inc *(Noted 9.02)*	Elstree
N41762	Raytheon Hawker 800XP	258456		Wells Fargo Bank Northwest NA *(Op J Max Air Services) (Noted 12.02)*	Blackpool
N44914	Douglas C-54D Skymaster	10630	Bu56498 42-72525	Aces High US Inc *(As "56498") (Noted 10.02)*	North Weald
N47914	Piper PA-32-300 Six	32-7840018		Southern Aircraft Consultancy Inc *(Noted 12.01)*	Alderney
N49272	Fairchild M.62/PT-23-HO Cornell (Continental W670)	HO-437	42-.....	Flying Heritage Inc *(Noted 4.02) (Op R.E.Mitchell t/a PT Flight) (As "23" in USAAC c/s)*	RAF Cosford
N50029	Cessna 172	28807	LX-AIB N6707A	Southern Aircraft Consultancy Inc *(Op E.Byrd) (Noted 7.02)*	Exeter
N50429	Fairchild M-62A Cornell	T43-5205	42-34539	Southern Aircraft Consultancy Inc *"63"* *(Noted 9.02)*	(Cot Valley, St Just, Cornwall)
N52485	Boeing-Stearman A75N1 (PT-17) Kaydet	75-4494		Roland Stearman Aviation *(Noted 9.02) (Op V S E Norman) (As "169" in US Navy c/s)*	Rendcomb
N53486	Piper PA-34-220T Seneca V	3449235		Branksome Aviation Inc *(Op Meridian Aviation) (Noted 1.03)*	Bournemouth

Registration	Type	C/n	Prev identity	Owner/Operator	Location
N53595	Piper PA-31 Turbo Navajo	31-544		C Sada *(Noted 7.02)*	Panshanger
N54211	Piper PA-23-250 Aztec E	27-7554006	G-ITTU D-IKLW/G-BCSW/N54211	Southern Aircraft Consultancy Inc *(Noted 9.02)*	Elstree
N54922	Boeing-Stearman A75N1 (N2S-4) Kaydet (Pratt & Witney 985-14B)	75-3491	Bu.30054	M G Plaskett *"Sweetie"* *(Op V.S.E.Norman) (Utterly Butterly titles) (Noted 8.02)*	Rendcomb
N56421	Ryan PT-22-RY Recruit	1539	41-15510	Flying Heritage Inc *(Noted 4.02)* *(Op R.E.Mitchell t/a PT Flight) (As "855" in US Army c/s)*	RAF Cosford
N56462	Maule M.6-235 Rocket	7409C		Avocet (US) Inc *(Noted 4.02)*	Old Buckenham
N56643	Maule M.5-180C	8086C		Southern Aircraft Consultancy Inc *(Noted 6.02)*	Duxford
N58093	Mooney M.20K Srs.231	25-0877		Aircraft Sales International Inc *(Noted 3.02)*	Coventry
N58566	Consolidated-Vultee BT-15-VN Valiant	10670	42-41882	Flying Heritage Inc *(Noted 4.02)* *(Op R.E.Mitchell t/a PT Flight) (US Army c/s)*	RAF Cosford
N59101	Airbus Industrie A300B4-203F	101	EC-HND N59101/I-BUSB/F-WZEA	Wells Fargo Bank NW NA *(Noted 11.02)*	Bournemouth
N59269	Boeing Stearman A75L3	75-3867		R W Hightower *"817" (Noted 9.02)*	North Weald
N60256	Beech C35 Bonanza	D-3346	OO-DOL OO-JAN	R.M.Hornblower *(Noted 2.03)*	Southend
N60526	Beech E55 Baron	TE-1159		E Walsh *(Noted 1.03)*	Elstree
N61422	Piper PA-31 Turbo Navajo B/Panther	31-7401236		Southern Aircraft Consultancy Inc *(Noted 9.02)*	Elstree
N61970	Piper PA-24-250 Comanche	24-3364	OO-GOE F-OCBM/5R-MVA/N8198P/N10F *(Noted 6.02)*	Southern Aircraft Consultancy Inc	Gamston
N62171	Hiller Felt UH-12C	GF-2		Southern Aircraft Consultancy Inc *(Noted 10.02)*	Shoreham
N62840*	Boeing-Stearman PT-17 Kaydet	--	??	Blackbarn Aviation *(Stored 4.00)*	Priory Farm, Tibenham
N63560	Piper PA-31 Turbo Navajo	31-188	HB-LFW N9141Y	Southern Aircraft Consultancy Inc *(Noted 9.02)*	Coventry
N63590	Boeing-Stearman N2S-3 Kaydet	75-7143	Bu.07539	Eastern Stearman Inc *(As "07539/143" in US Navy c/s) (Noted 6.02)*	North Weald
N65200	Boeing-Stearman D75N1 Kaydet	75-3817		Eastern Stearman Inc *(Stored 8.02)*	Swanton Morley
N65565	Boeing-Stearman B75N1 Kaydet	75-7463	FJ767	Ortac Inc *(Noted 9.02)*	Rednal
N67548	Cessna 152	15281906		Southern Aircraft Consultancy Inc *(Noted 4.02)*	Norwich
N70154	Piper J-3C-65 Cub	17139		R Long *(Noted 7.01)*	Rendcomb
N70457*	MD Helicopters MD.600N	RN-057		NK *(Cancelled 10.01) (Noted 9.02 as "511" for film)*	North Weald
N70526	MD Helicopters MD.369E	0556E		Eastern Atlantic Helicopters *(Noted 12.02)*	Kintore
N72127	Cessna U206D Skywagon *(Robertson STOL conversion)*	U2061368	G-AXJY N72326	R D Garetson *(Noted 5.01)*	Hill Farm, Nayland
N73410	Boeing-Stearman B75N1 (N2S-3) Kaydet	75-7761	Bu.38140	Eastern Stearman Inc *(As "N73410/29") (Noted 5.02)*	Kemble
N74189	Boeing Stearman PT-17	75-717		M G Plaskett *(Noted 9.02)* *(Op Aerosuperbatics Ltd) (Utterly Butterly titles)*	Rendcomb
N76402*	Cessna 140	10828	NC76402	(C.Murgatroyd)	Blackpool
	(W/O near Meppershall 9.8.98 per AAIB 12.98: cancelled FAA 3.99?) (Wreck noted 12.02)				
N80388	Beech D18S	A-288		Kingfisher Aviation *(Noted 5.01)*	North Weald
N80533	Cessna 172M Skyhawk	17266640		Southern Aircraft Consultancy Inc *(Noted 10.02)*	Alderney
N82507	Piper PA-28RT-201 Arrow IV	28R-8018100		Ronair Inc *(Noted 10.02)*	Stapleford
N83196	Piper PA-28RT-201 Arrow IV	28R-8118045	N9646N	P C Laine *(Noted 2.03)*	Shoreham
N90724	Hiller UH-12C	810		Southern Aircraft Consultancy Inc *(Noted 5.01)*	Sancreed, Cornwall
N91384	Rockwell Commander 690A	11118	SE-FLN	Airbourne Data Inc *(Noted 3.02)*	Gamston
N92001	MD Helicopters MD.900	900-00040		Wells Fargo Bank Northwest NA *(Op Signature Helicopters) (Noted 11.02)*	Blackbushe
N92562	Piper PA-46-350P Malibu Mirage	4636010		Trevair Inc *(Noted 10.02)*	Ronaldsway
NC92782	Piper PA-12 Super Cruiser	12-228		Southern Aircraft Consultancy Inc *(Noted 9.02)*	Bibberne Farm, Stalbridge
N93938	Erco 415C	1261		Merkado Holdings *(Noted 10.02)*	Panshangar
N96240	Beech D18S (3TM)	CA-159	G-AYAH N6123/RCAF 1559	M L & C E Edwards *(Noted 11.02)*	North Weald
N97121*	Embraer EMB-110P1 Bandeirante	110.334	PT-SDK	Guernsey Airport Fire Service *(Hulk only 12.01)*	Guernsey
N97821	Mooney M.20J	24-1080		Southern Aircraft Consultancy Inc *(Noted 10.02)*	Panshanger

CZECH REPUBLIC

Registration	Type	C/n	Prev identity	Owner/Operator	Location
OK-EUU 15	Urban Air UFM-13 Lambada	3/11		M.Tormey *(Noted 8.02)*	Abbeyshrule
OK-EUU 24	Urban Air UFM-13 Lambada	NK		Not known	Abbeyshrule
OK-EUU 55	Urban Air UFM-13 Lambada	11/11		Not known *(Noted 9.01)*	Abbeyshrule
OK-EUU 56	Urban Air UFM-13 Lambada	12/11		M.Tormey *(Noted 7.01)*	Abbeyshrule
OK-FUA 05	Urban Air UFM-10 Samba	NK	OK-EUU-02	Not known *(Noted 9.01)*	Waterford
OK-FUA 09	Urban Air UFM-13 Lambada	NK		Not known *(Noted 2.03)*	Carnmore, Galway
OK-FUU 31	Urban Air UFM-10 Samba	NK		Not known *(Noted 7.01)*	Abbeyshrule
OK-GUA 16	Urban Air UFM-10 Samba	NK		Not known *(Noted 8.02)*	Abbeyshrule
OK-GUA 19	Urban Air UFM-10 Samba	NK		Not known *(Noted 5.02)*	Abbeyshrule
OK-GUA 28	Urban Air UFM-10 Samba	21/10		Not known *(Noted 6.02)*	Abbeyshrule

BELGIUM

Registration	Type	C/n	Prev identity	Owner/Operator	Location
OO-DHN	Boeing 727-31	20113	N260NE N97891	Not known *(Stored 10.02)*	Lasham
OO-DHO	Boeing 727-31	20112	N250NE N7890	Not known *(Stored 10.02)*	Lasham
OO-MHB*	Piper PA-28-236 Dakota	28-8011143	G-BMHB D6-PAD/N81321/N9593N	R W H Watson *(Damaged Southend 20.10.90: wreck stored 12.02)*	Blackpool

OO-NAT	SOCATA MS.880B Rallye Club	2253	G-BAOK	R W H Watson	Grimmet Farm, Maybole
				(Fuselage stored 12.02)	
OO-RTC	Reims FR172H Rocket	FR17200265	F-BSHK	Not known	(Surrey)
	(Damaged Brussels 5.99 & exported to UK: noted road running on M25, Surrey 6.4.01 in damaged state)				
"OO-SDK"	Boeing 707-329C	20916		European Aviation Air Charter Ltd	Bournemouth
				(G-BYYK stored as "OO-SDK 12.02)	
OO-WIO*	Reims/Cessna FRA150L Aerobat		F-BUMG	Department of Engineering, Salford University	Salford
		FRA1500183		*(Instructional Airframe 2001)*	

DENMARK

OY-ALW	Miles M.28 Mercury 6	6268	D-EHAB	Not known	Little Staughton
			G-AHAA	*(Noted 2.01)*	
OY-BNM*	Embraer EMB.110P2 Bandeirante	110.200	N5071N	Air Salvage International	Alton
			(N892AC)/N5071N/G-BFZK/PT-GLS *(Noted 7.00)* (See G-AWMO in SECTION 4)		
OY-ELW	Mooney M.20R Ovation	29-0045	G-BVZY	Hansengroup *(Noted 6.02)*	Liverpool
OY-JRI	Beech 1900C-1	UC-44	SE-KXX	Danish Air Transport A/S	Aberdeen
			N31261/(N144GP)/N31261/JA8864/N31261 *(Noted 12.02)*		
OY-JRR	de Havilland DHC.2 Turbo Beaver III		N911CC	Not known	Headcorn
		1632/TB-18	C-FUKK/CF-UKK	*"Black Beaver" (Noted 2.03)*	
OY-JRW	GAF N-24A Nomad	117	VH-KNA	Not known	Weston on the Green
			ZK-ECM/VH-PGW/(N415NE)/VH-PGW/(VH-AUR) *(Damaged on take off 13.4.02)*		
OY-MUB*	Short SD.3-30 Var.200	SH.3069	G-BITX	Air Salvage International	Alton
			G-14-3069	*(Noted 6.02)*	
OY-NMH	GAF N-24A Nomad	74FA	ZK-NMH	Not known	Hinton in the Hedges
			N870US/PH-HAG/(PH-DHL)/N5579K/VH-PNF *(Noted 2.03)*		
OY-PBA	Pilatus PC-6/B-4-H2 Turbo-Porter	678	LN-VIT	Not known	Langar
			HB-FEY/I-ALPJ/HB-FEY	*(Noted 7.00)*	
OY-PBH(2)	LET L-410UVP-E20	972736	OK-DDC	Benair A/S *(Noted 12.02)*	Inverness/Sumburgh
OY-PBI(2)	LET L-410UVP-E20	871936	OK-SDM	Benair A/S	Inverness/Sumburgh
			Sov.AF 1936	*(Noted 12.02)*	
OY-SES*	Boeing 727-251	19977	N258US	Cougar Airlines	Southend
			(N258KP)/N258US	*(Being scrapping commenced 2.03)*	
OY-SET	Boeing 727-227F	21245	EI-PAK	Not known	Southend
			N16762/N569PE/(N443PS)/N444BN *(Open store 2.03)*		
OY-SEY	Boeing 727-224F	20659	N29730	Sterling European/TNT	Southend
			(N24730)	*(Open store 2.03)*	

ARUBA

P4-FAZ	Gulfstream Gulfstream V	572	N472GA	Not known	Gloucestershire
				(Op Zephyr Investment Management) (Noted 1.03)	

THE NETHERLANDS

PH-ABL	Piper PA-28-235 Cherokee	28-10648	F-BNFY	Not known	Gloucestershire
			N9054W	*(Noted 12.02)*	
PH-END	Bölkow Bö.208A Junior	515	D-ENDA	M Palfreman	Bagby
			VH-UES/D-ENDA	*(Noted 10.02)*	
PH-NLH*	Hawker Hunter T.7	41H-695342		Not known	Eaglescott
	(Forward fuselage noted 10.00: wings @ Long Marston as part of "XJ714")				
PH-NLK*	Piper PA-23-160 Apache	23-1694	OY-DCG	Not known	Water Leisure Park,
			SE-CKW/N10F	*(Wreck stored for spares 3.02)*	Skegness
PH-PAB	Neico Lancair 360	766		D C Ratcliffe *(Noted 10.02)*	Shoreham
PH-RAR	Beech 1900D	UE-372	ZS-ONS	Rossair Europe	Ronaldsway
			N30287	*(Op Euro Manx) (Noted 1.03)*	
PH-RAT	Beech 1900D	UE-350	N23481	Rossair Europe	Ronaldsway
				(Op Euromanx) (Noted 1.03)	

RUSSIA

RA01096	Yakovlev Yak-50	NK		Not known	Bourne Park, Hurstbourne Tarrant
				"Sasha" (Noted 5.02)	
RA01153	Yakovlev Yak-18T	22202047817		Not known *(Noted 6.01)*	Haverfordwest
RA01274	Yakovlev Yak-55	910103	DOSAAF 03	Not known *"03" (Noted 2.03)*	Wolverhampton
RA01294	Yakovlev Yak-50	853104		Not known *(Noted 8.02)*	North Weald
RA01333	Yakovlev Yak-55M	920506	DOSAAF 40	Mrs B.Abela	White Waltham
				(G-YAKM reserved) (Noted 5.01)	
RA01370	Yakovlev Yak-18T	NK		F.M.Govern	Old Sarum
				(Crashed 5.01: wrecked stored 8.01)	
RA01491	Yakovlev Yak-50	NK		Not known *(Noted 9.01)*	Thruxton
RA01555	Yakovlev Yak-18T	NK		Not known *(Noted 10.02)*	Old Sarum
RA01607	Sukhoi Su-29	77-02	RA7702	S Jones *(Noted 6.01)*	White Waltham
RA01609	Sukhoi Su-29	75-03	RA7503	Mr Moshe *(Noted 9.01)*	White Waltham
RA01610	Sukhoi Su-29	78-02	RA7802	P.Williams *(Noted 2.02)*	White Waltham
RA01813	Yakovlev Yak-52	NK		Not known *("13" (Noted 10.02)*	Wolverhampton
RA01949	Yakovlev Yak-52	800708	LY-ALN	Not known *"52/N" (Noted 7.02)*	Rochester
RA02041	Yakovlev Yak-52	822603	LY-AID	Not known	Gloucestershire
			DOSAAF 105	*(Noted 10.02)*	
RA02080	Yakovlev Yak-52	9010508	DOSAAF 35 (yellow)	Not known *"35" (Noted 1.01)*	White Waltham
RA02090	Yakovlev Yak-52	9111205	DOSAAF 10 (grey)	O Hutcheon *"10" (Noted 10.02)*	White Waltham
RA02209	Yakovlev Yak-52	9111311	DOSAAF 31	P.Scandrett *"31" (Noted 6.02)*	Rendcomb
RA02293	Yakovlev Yak-52	9011013	DOSAAF 115	A.Tyler *(Noted 2.00)*	Wolverhampton
RA02622	Yakovlev Yak-52	9612001	LY-AFH	Not known *(Noted 9.01)*	White Waltham
RA02933	Yakovlev Yak-18T	NK		Not known *"2" (Noted 5.02)*	Wickenby

Reg	Type	C/n	Prev id	Owner/Operator	Location
RA02974	Antonov An-2T	1G-108-55	SP-FBO(3) PLW-0855	Not known	Priory Farm, Tibenham
RA22521	Yakovlev Yak-52	9211612	DOSAAF 04	D.Squires *"04" (Noted 6.00)*	Wellesbourne Mountford
RA44400	Yakovlev Yak-18T	11-35		Richard Goode Aerobatics *(Noted 6.00)*	White Waltham
RA44435	Yakovlev Yak-52	NK		Not known *(Noted 8.00)*	Wolverhampton
RA44444	Sukhoi Su-26	04-05		Not known *(Noted 8.02)*	White Waltham
RA44445	Yakovlev Yak-55	911209		D Samuels *(Noted 10.02)*	White Waltham
RA44454	Yakovlev Yak-52	822807		Not known *(Noted 11.02)*	White Waltham
RA44455	Yakovlev Yak-52	877902		D.Samuels *(Noted 12.02)*	Southend
RA44459	Yakovlev Yak-50	822210	LY-AGG DOSAAF 107	Not known *"107"* *(Op Yakolev Team) "Svetlana" (Noted 2.03)*	White Waltham
RA44460	Yakovlev Yak-52	822710	LY-AHE DOSAAF 100	Not known *(Noted 3.02)*	Rochester
RA44461	Yakovlev Yak-50	NK		NK *(Op Yakolev Team) (Noted 1.03)*	Compton Abbas
RA44463	Yakovlev Yak-52	888912	DOSAAF 99	Not known *(As "N/123" in FAA Sea Fury c/s) (Noted 9.02)*	RNAS Yeovilton
RA44465(2)	Yakovlev Yak-18T	NK	LY-AOL(?)	Yak UK *(Noted 8.02)*	Leicester
RA44466(2)	Yakovlev Yak-52S	855905		NK *(Op Yakolev Team) (Noted 9.02)*	Compton Abbas
RA44469(2)	Yakovlev Yak-52	899413	LY-AFX	D Noble *(As "DOSAAF 69") (Noted 1.03)*	Compton Abbas
RA44470	Technoavia Yak-18T	18-33		B.Austen *(Noted 8.02)*	Oaksey Park
RA44478	Sukhoi Su-29	76-031		Richard Goodes Aerobatics *(Noted 7.02)*	White Waltham
RA44480	Technoavia Yak-18T	08-34		Not known *(Noted 9.02)*	North Weald
RA44484	Technoavia SM-92 Finist	NK		Not known *(Noted 9.01)*	RAF Benson
RA44502(3)	Aerostar Yak-52	9411711	LY-ANE G-BVJR/Romanian AF 48	Not known *(Noted 6.01)*	White Waltham
RA44506	Yakovlev Yak-18T	22202034139	HA-JAC FLA-02159	Not known *(Noted 9.02)*	Tilstock
RA44508(2)	Sukhoi Su-31	03-01		Not known *(Noted 8.02)*	Oaksey Park
RA44510	Yakovlev Yak-55M	930707	DOSAAF 59	T Shears *"Lady Venise" (Noted 10.02)*	White Waltham
RA44514	Yakovlev Yak-52	9111413	DOSAAF 48	Not known *"48" (Noted 7.02)*	Manston
RA44515	Yakovlev Yak-52	9111515	DOSAAF 56	M.Stebbing *"65" (Noted 5.02)*	Poplar Hall Farm, Elmsett
RA44525	Yakovlev Yak-55M	901103	DOSAAF 96	Not known *(Noted 9.02 - to become G-YKSS 2003*	Headcorn
RA44527	Yakovlev Yak-18T	15-35		Not known *(Noted 2.03)*	White Waltham
RA44531	Sukhoi Su-26	01-04	PK-SDM	Goldair Aerobatic *(ALPINE titles) (Noted 9.02)*	Biggin Hill
RA44532	Yakovlev Yak-18T	14-35		Not known *(Noted 11.02)*	White Waltham
RA44533	Yakovlev Yak-50	853206		Not known *(Op Yakolev Team) (Noted 1.03)*	Compton Abbas
RA44536	Yakovlev Yak-18T	22202034143	LY-AMI DOSAAF	M Webb *(Noted 2.01)*	Popham
RA44537	Yakovlev Yak-55M	910104	HA-JAM	Not known *(Noted 3.02)*	White Waltham
RA44538	Yakovlev Yak-18T	22202052122		Not known *(Noted 10.02)*	White Waltham
RA44544	Yakovlev Yak-18T	11-33		Not known *(Noted 6.02)*	White Waltham
RA44545	Yakovlev Yak-18T	22202034023	LY-AIH ES-FYE	Not known *(Noted 2.02)*	White Waltham
RA44547	Technoavia SP-55M	0101-0007		Richard Goodes Aerobatics *(Noted 2.03)*	White Waltham
RA44548	Technoavia SP-55M	NK		Not known *(Noted 8.02)*	White Waltham
RA44549	Yakovlev Yak-50	822305	G-BXNO LY-ASD/DOSAAF 82	*(Op Yakolev Team) (Noted 2.03)*	Compton Abbas
RA44550	Yakovlev Yak-52	877409	LY-AKF	Not known *(Noted 2.03)*	White Waltham
RA44553	Yakovlev Yak-50	NK		Not known *(Noted 9.01)*	NK
RA44777	Yakovlev Yak-18T	12-35		V S E Norman *(Noted 8.00)*	Rendcomb
RA81584	Yakovlev Yak-18T	22202054812		Mr Newman *(Noted 9.02)*	Elstree

SWEDEN

Reg	Type	C/n	Prev id	Owner/Operator	Location
SE-BZP	Stinson V-77 Reliant	6375	OO-NUT FB536	M Hales *(Noted 6.00)*	Little Staughton
SE-GPU	Piper PA-28-161 Cherokee Warrior II	28-7716200		Not known *(Noted 8.02 unmarked)*	East Winch
SE-GVD	Piper PA-28-161 Cherokee Warrior II	28-7816196		Not known *(Noted 9.02)*	East Winch
SE-GVH	Piper PA-38-112 Tomahawk	38-78A0053		Not known *(Fuselage noted 2.00)*	Little Staughton
SE-HXF*	Rotorway Scorpion	SE-1		Not known *(Noted stored 9.02)*	Earls Colne
SE-IIV	Piper PA-24-260 Comanche C	24-4970	HB-OHZ N9462P	Not known *(Noted 12.02)*	Netherthorpe
SE-KBU	Christen A-1 Husky	038		A Allan? *(Stored 12.02)*	Perth
SE-KGR	Piper PA-28RT-201T Turbo Arrow IV	28R-8031020	OY-PEI N8117G	Not known *(Noted 1.03)*	Bournemouth
SE-LAX	Fairey Britten-Norman BN-2A-21 Islander	431	LN-MAC G-BCWO	Cormack (Aircraft Services) Ltd *(Noted 12.02)*	Cumbernauld
SE-LLF	Scottish Aviation Bulldog Srs.100 BH.100/132		Swedish Arm Fv61026 G-BZIT	Not known *(Noted 2.03)*	East Winch
SE-LLI	Scottish Aviation Bulldog Srs.100 BH.100/146		Swedish Arm Fv61037 G-BZMR	Not lknown *(Noted 2.03)*	East Winch
SE-LLK	Scottish Aviation Bulldog Srs.100BH.100/148		Swedish Arm Fv61038 G-BZMS	Not lknown *(Noted 2.03)*	East Winch
SE-RAA	Embraer EMB.135ER	145.210		Investment AB Janus *(Op Eastern Airways) (Noted 2.03)*	Aberdeen
SE-RAB(2)	Embraer EMB.135ER	145.453		SEB Finans AB *(Op British Midland/Eastern Airways) (Noted 8.02)*	Edinburgh

POLAND
SP-CHD*	PZL-101A Gawron	74134		Not known *(On rebuild 8.02)*	North Weald

SUDAN
ST-AHZ	Piper PA-31 Turbo Navajo	31-473	G-AXMR	Not known	Elstree
			N6558L	*(Fire practice: burnt-out fuselage remains 6.00)*	

GREECE
SX-BFM	Piper PA-31-350 Chieftain	31-8052204	N4504J	Not known	Bournemouth
				(Fuselage stored unmarked & derelict 12.02)	
SX-HCF	Agusta A109A-II	7207	N71PT	Castle Air Charters Ltd	Liskeard
			N4263A	*(Spares use 6.01)*	
SX-OAD	Boeing 747-212B	21684	9V-SQI	Not known *(Noted 6.02)*	Bruntingthorpe

SLOVENIA
S5-CAI	Rockwell Commander 690A	11121	D-IGAF	Not known	Fairoaks
			(N57121)	*(Noted 6.02)*	

SEYCHELLE ISLANDS
S7-AAW	Airbus Industrie A300C4-103	033	HS-THH	Not known	Filton
			HS-TAX/HS-TGH/F-WNDC	*(Stored 2.03)*	

TURKEY
TC-ALM*	Boeing 727-230	20431	TC-IKO	Fire Services	East Midlands
			TC-JUH/TC-ALB/N878UM/D-ABDI	*(Trainer noted 3.02)*	

ICELAND
TF-ABP*	Lockheed L.1011-385-100 Tristar	1045	VR-HOG	Not known	North Weald
			N323EA	*(Nose only 3.02)*	
TF-ATP	Boeing 767-204ER	24239	G-BOPB	Air Atlanta Iceland	Gatwick
			N6009F	*(Op Excel Airways in full c/s) (Noted 11.02)*	
TF-ATR	Boeing 767-204ER	24457	EC-GHM	Air Atlanta Iceland	Gatwick
			EC-276/G-BPFV	*(Op Excel Airways in full c/s) (Noted 9.02)*	
TF-ELJ	Aérospatiale / Alenia ATR-42-310	118	C-FIQN	Not known	Exeter
			F-WWEO	*(Stored 10.02)*	
TF-ELL	Boeing 737-210C	20138	N41026	Islandsflug	Stansted
			F-GGFI/N4906	*(Stored 9.02 in ATA Brasil c/s)*	
TF-ELP	Boeing 737-330QC	23522	D-ABXA	Islandsflug	Stansted
			N1786B	*(Op Channel Express) (Noted 10.02)*	
TF-ELR	Boeing 737-330QC	23523	D-ABXB	Islandsflug	Stansted
				(Op Channel Express (Noted 9.01)	

UKRAINE
UR-67199	Letovlev Let L410UVP Turbolet	790305	CCCP-67199	Air Ukraine *(Noted 9.02)*	Langar
UR-67439	Letovlev LET L-410UVP Turbolet	841204		Not known *(Universal Avia c/s) (Noted 4.02)*	Headcorn
UR-67477	Letovlev LET L-410UVP Turbolet	841302	CCCP-67477	Not known *(Universal Avia c/s) (Noted 4.02)*	Sibson
UR-74057	Antonov An-74-200	36547098960		RAF Avia	Coventry
				(Op Atlantic Air Transport) (Noted 1.03)	
UR-82070	Antonov An-124	97730513559127		Not known *(Stored 9.02)*	Manston

AUSTRALIA
VH-DHS	Beech 58 Baron	TH-1386	VH-NSN	Global Aviation	(Filton)
			N6921Y	*(Noted 9.01)*	
VH-UQB*	de Havilland DH.80A Puss Moth			See G-ABDW in SECTION 4	
VH-UUP*	Short S.16 Scion 1			See G-ACUX in SECTION 4	
VH-ZIC	American Blimp Corp A-60+ Airship	010		Not known *(Noted 6.02) (Lotto titles)*	White Waltham

BERMUDA (new series)
VP-BAT	Boeing 747SP-21	21648	VR-BAT	Worldwide Aircraft Holding (Bermuda)	Bournemouth
			N148UA/N539PA	*(Noted 10.02)*	
VP-BBG	Piaggio P.180 Avanti	1037	F-GUAE	Not known *(Noted 10.02)*	Fairoaks
VP-BBT	Boeing 737-705	29089	LN-TUB	Ford Motor Co	Stansted
			(LN-SUB)	*(Noted 10.02)*	
VP-BBU	Boeing 737-705	29090	LN-TUC	Ford Motor Co	Stansted
			(LN-SUC)	*(Noted 10.02)*	
VP-BBW	Boeing 737-7BJ	30076	N737BF	GAMA Aviation	Farnborough
			P4-CZT/VP-CZT/N737MC/D-AXXL/N374MC/N1784B/N1786B *(Noted 2.03)*		
VP-BCC	Canadair CL600-2B19	7717	C-GZSQ	Consolidated Contractors (UK) Ltd	
	(CRJ200			*(Noted 2.03)*	Farnborough/Athens
VP-BCE	Eurocopter AS355N Twin Squirrel	5663		Sioux Corporation *(Noted 12.01)*	Jersey
VP-BCI	Canadair CL601 Challenger	5193	VR-BCI	Consolidated Contractors (UK) Ltd	Farnborough/Athens
			N604D/C-GLYK	*(Noted 8.02)*	

Reg	Type	Serial	Prev ids / Owner	Location
VP-BCO	Canadair CL604 Challenger	5420	N603CC / C-GLWR — Consolidated Contractors (UK) Ltd *(Noted 8.02)*	Farnborough/Athens
VP-BDB	Cessna 560 Citation V	560-0503	(ZS-FCB) / N52059 — Fegotila Ltd *(Noted 10.01)*	Gloucestershire
VP-BDF	Boeing 707-312		See G-AYAG in SECTION 4	
VP-BDL	Dassault Falcon 2000	111	F-WWVF — Sioux Corporation *(Noted 5.01)*	Luton
VP-BGE	Cessna 500 Citation I	500-0287	N287AB / PT-WHZ/N31LH/OY-CGO/N57MB/N73LL/N287CC/(N5287J) *(Noted 2.03)* — Not known	Filton
VP-BIE	Canadair CL601 Challenger 1A	3016	N601CL / N1107Z/N4562Q/C-GLWV — Inflite Aviation *(Noted 8.02)*	Stansted
VP-BJT	Cessna 425 Corsair	425-0027	VP-BNM / VR-BNM/N181AA/HI-598SP/N97DA/(N711EF)/N97DA/N67720 *(Noted 11.01)* — Rig Design Services Group Ltd	Booker
VP-BKH	Gulfstream Gulfstream IV	1029	VP-BKI / VR-BKI/N429GA — Specialised Transportation *(Noted 9.02)*	Ronaldsway
VP-BKK	Hawker Siddeley HS.125-Srs.400A/731	25238	VR-BKK / N808V/N125GC/G-TOPF/G-AYER/9K-ACR/G-AYER *(Noted 10.02)* — Air 125 Ltd/Business Real Estates	Southampton
VP-BKQ	Bell 430	49008	N62833 — Jud Investments Co Ltd *(Noted 7.02)*	Blackbushe
VP-BKZ	Gulfstream Gulfstream V	602	N602GV / N538GA — Dennis Vanguard International (Switchgear) *(Noted 9.02)*	Birmingham
VP-BLA	Gulfstream Gulfstream V	654	N960AV — ISPAT Group *(Noted 10.02)*	Luton
VP-BLD	Lockheed 329-731 Jetstar	5117/35	(N858SH) / VP-BSH/VR-BSH/N310CK/N210EK/N7962S *(Noted 1.03)* — Wings Ventures Ltd	Luton
VP-BLK	Rockwell Turbo Commander 690C *(Built Gulfstream American)*	11672	VR-BLK / OE-FIT/D-IKOM/(N5924K) *(Noted 7.02)* — Control Techniques (Bermuda) Ltd	Welshpool
VP-BLS	Pilatus PC-XII	176	N176BS / VP-BLS/HB-FSL *(Noted 10.02)* — B.L.Schroeder	Fairoaks
VP-BMD	British Aerospace BAe 125 Srs.700B	257200	VR-BMD / G-MSFY/G-5-14 *(Noted 1.03)* — D Mannios Shipping	Luton
VP-BMZ	Rockwell Turbo Commander 690D *(Built Gulfstream Aerospace)*	15033	VR-BMZ / G-MFAL/N49GA/(N5925N) *(Noted 9.01)* — Aviatica Trading Co Ltd/Marlborough Fine Art Ltd	Fairoaks
VP-BPS	Consolidated 28-5ACF (PBY-5A) Catalina	1997	Not known *(On rebuild 2002)* / G-BLSC/C-FMIR/N608FF/CF-MIR/N10023/Bu.46633 *(Op Super Catalina Restoration)*	Lee-on-Solent
VP-BPW	Dassault Falcon 900B	135	VR-BPW / F-WWFJ — Tower House Consultants Ltd *(Noted 12.01)*	Jersey
VP-BRD	Eurocopter EC120B	1155	F-WQDK — Not known *(Noted 7.01)*	Redhill
VP-BRS	Boeing 747-2B5B(SCD)	22485	N285SW / HL7458 — Air Freight Express *(Stored 12.02)*	Heathrow
VP-BUS	Gulfstream Gulfstream IV	1127	VR-BUS / VR-BLR/N427GA — U Schwarzenbach *(Noted 10.02)*	Farnborough

CAYMAN ISLANDS

Reg	Type	Serial	Prev ids / Owner	Location
VP-CAD	Cessna 525 CitationJet	525-0297	N316MJ — Reynard Motorsport *(Noted 11.01)*	Oxford
VP-CAS	British Aerospace BAe 125 Srs.800A	258167	VR-CAS / N125AS/G-5-662/N125AS/G-5-662 *(Noted 8.02)* — Cavalier Air Corporation	Southampton
VP-CAT	Cessna 501 Citation 1	501-0232	VR-CAT / VR-CHF/N35TL/N853KB/N2616C/(N2616G) *(Noted 11.02)* — Kestrel Aviation/Aviation Jet	Guernsey
VP-CBM	Cessna 550 Citation II	550-0729	VR-CBM / N1210V — Bernard Matthews plc *(Noted 10.02)*	Norwich
VP-CBW	Gulfstream Gulfstream IV	1096	VR-CBW / (G-...)/N17589 — Rolls-Royce plc *(Noted 10.02)*	Farnborough
VP-CBX	Gulfstream Gulfstream V	511	N511GA — Aravco *(Noted 10.02)*	Farnborough
VP-CCO	Cessna 550 Citation II	550-0321	N321GN / TC-COY/N321SE/N5430G — Not known *(Noted 2.03)*	Biggin Hill
VP-CCP	Cessna 550 Citation Bravo	550-0857	VP-CNM(1) / N51246 — Not known *(Op Trustair) (Noted 12.02)*	Blackpool
VP-CCW	MD Helicopters MD 600N	RN030	N9203Q — Weetabix plc *(Noted 9.02)*	Sywell
VP-CED	Cessna 550 Citation Bravo	550-0870	N50612 — Iceland Foods *(Noted 10.02)*	Hawarden
VP-CFG	Cessna 501 Citation I/SP	501-0176	VR-CFG / (VR-CIA)/N49LC/N44LC/N6779L *(Noted 3.02)* — Alpha Golf Aviation Ltd	Gloucestershire
VP-CGE	Cessna 650 Citation VII	650-7077	(N582JF) / N532JF/N877CM/N5203J — Not known *(Op Grosvenor Estates) (Noted 7.02)*	Hawarden
VP-CGP	Dassault Falcon 900	163	VP-BEH — Williams Grand Prix Engineering Ltd *(Noted 9.02)*	Oxford
VP-CHJ	Agusta A109C	7634	VR-CHJ / VR-CEC/3A-MSG — Estate of F.Hackett-Jones *(Stored 12.01)*	Guernsey
VP-CHM	British Aircraft Corporation One-Eleven 492GM	BAC.260	HZ-KA7 / G-BLHD/G-16-25 — Mercury Aviation *(Noted 2.03)*	Southend
VP-CIC	Canadair CL601 Challenger	5011	VR-CIC / N602UK/N611MH/JA8283/N603CC/C-GLXD *(Noted 9.02)* — TGC Aviation Ltd/Fakhar Ltd	Stansted
VP-CIS	Cessna 525 CitationJet	525-0252	N740JV / (N5223P) — Flightline Ltd *(Noted 2.03)*	Southend/Guernsey
VP-CJR	Cessna 550 Citation II	550-0354	VR-CJR / N121C/N121CG — Broome & Wellington (Aviation) Ltd *(Noted 9.02)*	Manchester
VP-CLA	Beech F90	LA-231	N27PA / N7220T — Claessons International Ltd *(Noted 10.02)*	Farnborough
VP-CLD	Cessna 550 Citation II	550-0323	N323AM / TC-YZB/TC-FMB/TC-FAL/OE-GCP/(N5703C) *(Op Dovey Aviation) (Noted 2.03)* — Not known	Filton
VP-CLM	British Aircraft Corporation One-Eleven 401AK	BAC.072	N119DA / N119GA/N310EL/N5030 — TAG Aviation *(Noted 1.03)*	Bournemouth
VP-CMF	Gulfstream Gulfstream IV	1062	VR-CMF / N688H/N462GA/N17583 — Aravco Ltd/Sheikh Mohammed Fakhry *(Noted 10.02)*	Luton
VP-CMS	Cessna 560 Citation Ultra	560-0457	N59HA / N51564 — Redbus Group *(Op Redbus Charter) (Noted 10.02)*	Luton

VP-CNF	Cessna 525 CitationJet	525-0153	(N525EF) N551Q/N551G/N5090V	Foster Aviation *(Noted 9.02)*	Biggin Hill
VP-CNP	Gulfstream G1159A Gulfstream III	496	N843HS (N99SU)/N99SC/N89AB/N89AE/N21NY/N310SL/N327GA *(Noted 10.02)*	Fitzwilton plc	Dublin
VP-COM	Cessna 500 Citation I	500-318	VR-COM N944B/N518CC/N5318J	Rapid 3864 Ltd *(Noted 10.02)*	Biggin Hill
VP-CPT	British Aerospace BAe 125 Srs.1000B	259004	VR-CPT G-LRBJ/G-5-779	Reno Investments Inc *(Noted 7.01)*	Biggin Hill
VP-CRB	Learjet Learjet 60	60-125	N60LR	Lisane Ltd *(Noted 9.02)*	Guernsey
VP-CSN	Cessna 560 Citation Ultra	560-0401	N401CV N5197A	Scottish & Newcastle Breweries Ltd *(Noted 12.02)*	Edinburgh
VP-CTJ	Cessna 550 Citation II	F550-0073	F-GBTL N4621G	Flight Consultancy Services *(Noted 10.02)*	Biggin Hill
VP-CWA	Agusta A109C	7628	JA6610	Williams Grand Prix Engineering Ltd *(Op Alan Mann Helicopters) (Noted 1.03)*	Oxford

FALKLANDS ISLANDS & DEPENDENCIES

VP-FAZ	de Havilland DHC.6-310 Twin Otter	748	C-GEOA (FAP-2029)/C-GEOA	British Antarctic Survey *(Noted 8.01)*	Oxford
VP-FBB	de Havilland DHC.6-310 Twin Otter	783	C-GDKL	British Antarctic Survey *(Noted 9.02)*	Coventry
VP-FBC	de Havilland DHC.6-310 Twin Otter	787	C-GDIU	British Antarctic Survey *(Noted 9.01)*	Oxford
VP-FBL	de Havilland DHC.6-310 Twin Otter	839	C-GDCZ	British Antarctic Survey *(Noted 9.02)*	Coventry
VP-FBQ	de Havilland DHC-7-110	111	G-BOAX C-GDNG	British Antarctic Survey *(Noted 10.02)*	Coventry

ZIMBABWE formerly SOUTHERN RHODESIA

VP-YKF	de Havilland DH.104 Dove 6			See G-AMDD in SECTION 4	

BERMUDA (old series)

VR-BEB	British Aircraft Corporation One-Eleven 527FK	BAC.226	RP-C1181 PI-C1181	European Aviation Ltd *(Fire Compound 10.01 - all white & no marks)*	Bournemouth
VR-BEP	Westland WS-55 Whirlwind 3			See G-BAMH in SECTION 4	
VR-BEU	Westland WS-55 Whirlwind 3			See G-ATKV in SECTION 4	
VR-BMB	Hawker Siddeley HS.125 Srs.400B	25240	VR-BKN I-GJBO/G-AYLI/G-5-11	Not known *(Open storage 9.02)*	Stansted

INDIA

VT-EKE*	Westland WG.30-160	021	G-BLPR G-17-17	Turbine World *(Reported mid 2000)*	Honeycrock Farm, Redhill
VT-EKK*	Westland WG.30-160	025	G-17-13	Turbine World *(Reported mid 2000)*	Honeycrock Farm, Redhill
VT-EKL*	Westland WG.30-160	028	G-17-14	Turbine World *(Reported mid 2000)*	Honeycrock Farm, Redhill
VT-EKM*	Westland WG.30-160	027	G-17-15	Turbine World *(Reported mid 2000)*	Honeycrock Farm, Redhill
VT-EKT*	Westland WG.30-160	035	G-17-23	Turbine World *(Reported mid 2000)*	Honeycrock Farm, Redhill
VT-EKW*	Westland WG.30-160	038	G-17-26	Turbine World *(Reported mid 2000)*	Honeycrock Farm, Redhill
VT-EKX*	Westland WG.30-160	039	G-17-27	Turbine World *(Reported mid 2000)*	Honeycrock Farm, Redhill

MEXICO

XA-NAA	MBB Bö.105CBS/4	S-759		Bond Air Services Ltd	Bourn
	(Non-airworthy pod with "Pegasus" logo as operated by Transportes Aereos Pegaso) (Noted 5.00)				
XA-TLJ	Boeing 737-2H6	20926	PK-IJE 9M-MBH/9M-ASR	European Aviation *(Stored for spares 11.02)*	Bournemouth
XB-RIY	Boeing PT-17 Stearman	75-7275		Not known *(Stored 8.02)*	Rendcomb

LATVIA

YL-BAK	British Aerospace BAe 146 Srs 100 *(Avro RJ70A*	E1223	EI-CUO G-BZFA/VH-NJW/YL-BAK/VH-NJW/YL-BAK/N832BE/G-6-223 *(Stored 2.03)*	Not known	Exeter
YL-LEU*	WSK-PZL Antonov An-2R	1G-165-45	CCCP19731 SP-ZFP/CCCP19731	Hawarden Air Services *(As "CCCP-19731") (Noted dismantled 2.02)*	Hawarden
YL-LEV*	WSK-PZL Antonov An-2R	1G-148-29	CCCP07268	Hawarden Air Services *(As "CCCP07268") (Noted 5.00)*	Hawarden
YL-LEW*	WSK-PZL Antonov An-2R	1G-182-28	CCCP56471	Hawarden Air Services *(As "CCCP56471") (Noted 5.00)*	Hawarden
YL-LEX*	WSK-PZL Antonov An-2R	1G-187-58	CCCP54949	Hawarden Air Services *(As "CCCP54949") (Noted 5.00)*	Hawarden
YL-LEY*	WSK-PZL Antonov An-2R	1G-173-11	CCCP40784	Hawarden Air Services *(As "CCCP40784") (Noted 5.00)*	Hawarden
YL-LEZ*	WSK-PZL Antonov An-2R	1G-165-47	CCCP19733	Hawarden Air Services *(As "CCCP19733") (Noted 10.00)*	Hawarden
YL-LFA*	WSK-PZL Antonov An-2R	1G-172-20	CCCP40748	Hawarden Air Services *(As "CCCP40748") (Noted 5.00)*	Hawarden
YL-LFB*	WSK-PZL Antonov An-2R	1G-173-12	CCCP40785	Hawarden Air Services *(As "CCCP40785") (Noted 5.00)*	Hawarden

YL-LFC*	WSK-PZL Antonov An-2R	1G-206-44	CCCP17939	Hawarden Air Services	Hawarden
				(As "CCCP17939") (Noted 5.00)	
YL-LFD*	WSK-PZL Antonov An-2R	1G-172-21	CCCP40749	Hawarden Air Services	Hawarden
				(As "CCCP40749") (Noted 5.00)	
YL-LHN*	Mil Mi-2	524006025	CCCP20320	Hawarden Air Services	Hawarden
				(As "CCCP20320") (Noted 2.00)	
YL-LHO*	Mil Mi-2	535025126	CCCP20619	Hawarden Air Services	Hawarden
				(As "CCCP20619") (Noted 2.00)	

NICARAGUA

YN-CCN	Boeing 707-123B	18054	5B-DAO	Omega Air	Shannon
			G-BGCT/N7526A	*(Stored 8.02)*	

SERBIA

YU-DLG	UTVA 66		JRV51109	Shuttle Air *(Noted 10.02)*	Biggin Hill
YU-DMN(2)	UTVA-66		JRV51182	M Roberts /a F C S	(Biggin Hill)
				(As "51182" in Serbia AF c/s) (Noted 7.01 @ Oshkosh)	
YU-HCC	Agusta Bell AB.212	5712		Not known *(Stored 1.03)*	Redhill
YU-HEH	Soko/Aérospatiale SA.341G Gazelle	011	JRV12619	Kestrel Shipping *(Noted 9.02)*	Redhill
YU-YAB	SOKO G-2A Galeb (Seagull)	NK	JRV23170	Shuttle Air *(Noted 9.02)*	North Weald
YU-YAG	SOKO G-2A Galeb	NK	JRV23194	Shuttle Air *(Noted 5.02)*	Biggin Hill

NEW ZEALAND

ZK-BMI*	Auster B.8 Agricola Srs.1	B.101	(G-ANYG)	D.J.Baker	Carr Farm, Thorney, Newark
			G-25-3	*(Fuselage frame only 1.03)*	
ZK-RMH	Curtiss P-40E-CU Kittyhawk	19669	NZ3009	The Old Flying Machine Co	Duxford
			ET482/41-25158	*(Breitling Fighter Team titles) (Noted 10.02)*	
				(As "663/P11151/88" in Chinese AF c/s)	

REPUBLIC of SOUTH AFRICA

ZS-JIY	Lockheed L-100-30	4691	D2-THS	Safair	Shannon
			ZS-JIY/9Q-CZS/ZS-JIY/A2-ABZ/ZS-JIY *(Op Air Contractors 2.03)*		
ZS-RSI	Lockheed L-100-30	4600	F-GIMV	Safair	Shannon
			ZS-RSI/F-GDAQ/F-WDAQ/ZS-RSI/C-FNWY/ZS-RSI *(Op Air Contractors 12.02)*		

EQUATORIAL GUINEA

3C-GIG	Boeing 707-373C	19179	3D-CSB	Koda Air Cargo	Southend
			9Q-CSB/CS-TBJ/N372WA	*(Impounded 2.03)*	
3C-QSB	Fokker Friendship 200MAR	10612	M-1	Trygon	Southend
			PH-EXC	*(Stored 2.03)*	
3C-QSC	Fokker Friendship 200MAR	10622	M-2	Trygon	Southend
			PH-FSI/PH-EXD	*(Stored 2.03)*	

CYPRUS

5B-HAC	Rutan Defiant	162		Not known *(Noted 9.02)*	Enstone

NIGERIA

5N-AAN*	British Aerospace BAe 125 Srs.F3B/RA		F-GFMP	Air Atlantic Nigeria Ltd	Biggin Hill
		25125	G-AVAI/LN-NPA/G-AVAI	*(Stored 10.02)*	
5N-AJT	Bell 212	30636	G-BCLG	Bristow Helicopters Ltd	Redhill
			EP-HBY/VR-BFK/G-BCLG/9M-ATV/VR-BFK/G-BCLG/N18091 *(Stored 1.03)*		
5N-AJU	Bell 212	30632	G-BFDJ	Bristow Helicopters Ltd	Redhill
			EP-HCA/VR-BGP/G-BFDJ/9V-BGE/B-2309/9V-BGE *(Stored 9.02)*		
5N-AJV	Bell 212	30868	G-BGMK	Bristow Helicopters Ltd	Redhill
			EP-HCC/VR-BGR/N18096	*(Stored 9.02)*	
5N-AJW	Bell 212	30601	G-BGML	Bristow Helicopters Ltd	Redhill
			EP-HBL/VR-BEX	*(Stored as hulk 9.02)*	
5N-AWD	Hawker Siddeley HS.125 Srs.1	25008	G-ASSI	Not known *(Noted 10.00 on fire dump)*	Luton
5N-BAK	Aérospatiale AS355F1 Twin Squirrel	5112	G-BUFW	Bristow Helicopters Ltd	Redhill
			N57904	*(Stored 1.03)*	
5N-BCE	Sikorsky S-76A+	760083	G-BIBG	Bristow Helicopters Ltd *(Stored 1.03)*	Redhill
5N-BHM	Bell 212	32134	G-BJJO	Bristow Helicopters Ltd	Redhill
				(On rebuild 1.03 to become ZJ966)	
5N-BHN	Bell 212	32135	G-BJJP	Bristow Helicopters Ltd	Redhill
			N5736D	*(Stored 9.02)*	
5N-BEG	Boeing 727-256A	20602	EC-GCJ	Dasab Air	Lasham
			EC-CBH	*(Stored 10.02)*	
5N-HHH	British Aircraft Corporation One-Eleven 401AK	BAC.064	HZ-NB2	Kabo Air	Southend
			N5024	*(Open store 2.03)*	
5N-HTC	British Aircraft Corporation One-Eleven 208AL	BAC.049	EI-ANE	Hanningfield Metals	Stock, Essex.
				(Dismembered hulk in yard 6.02)	

KENYA

5Y-SIL	Cameron A-140 HAB			See G-AZUW in SECTION 4	

SENEGAL
6W-SAF	Douglas C-47A-65-DL 19074	42-100611	F-GEFU	Not known *"Lilly Belle"*		North Weald
				(As "42-100766") (Nose section only 9.02)		

MALAWI
7Q-YDF	Piper J3C-65 Cub	18711	5Y-KEV	Not known		Pent Farm, Postling
			VP-KEV/VP-NAE/ZS-AZT	*(Stored 6.02)*		

GHANA
9G-LCA	Conroy CL-44-O	16	(P4-GUP)	Not Known		Bournemouth
			4K-GUP/EI-BND/N447T	*(Noted 1.03)*		
9G-MKA	Douglas DC-8F-55	45804	N855BC	MK Airlines		Manston
			CX-BLN/C-GMXP/N855BC/HP-927/PH-DCZ/OY-KTC *(Stored 9.02)*			
G108	Scottish Aviation Bulldog Srs.120/122		G-BCUP	Aerofab Restorations	Bourne Park, Hurstbourne Tarrant	
		BH120-372		*(Stored 7.02)*		

SIERRA LEONE
9L-LCD	Letovlev LET L-410UVP Turbolet	810611	C5-LES	Sierra National Airways		Bruntingthorpe
			"010"/UR-67010/CCCP67010 *(To 9XR-RC @ 2001/02?)*			
9L-LCI	Letovlev LET L-410UVP Turbolet	831036	C5-LET	Sierra National Airways		Bruntingthorpe
			"67408"/UR-67408/CCCP67408 *(Stored 2.02)*			
9L-LDA	Beech A90 King Air	LJ-281	RP-C3318	Not known *(Noted 2.03)*		Southend

MALAYSIA
9M-BCR	Dassault Falcon 20C	35	N809P	(FR Aviation) *(Stored 2002)*		Bournemouth
			(N1777R)/N809F/F-WMKG			

PART 2 – FOREIGN CIVIL REGISTERED AIRCRAFT LOCATED IN COLLECTIONS

Regn	Type	C/n		Owner/Operator	Location

CANADA

CF-BXO*	Supermarine 304 Stranraer	CV-209	RCAF 920	RAF Museum *(As "920/QN-" in RCAF c/s)*	Hendon
CF-EQS*	Boeing-Stearman A75N1 (PT-17-BW) Kaydet	41-8169	75-1728	American Air Museum *(As "217786/25" in USAAF c/s)*	Duxford
CF-KCG*	Grumman TBM-3E Avenger AS.3	2066	RCN326 Bu.69327	American Air Museum *(As "46214/X-3" in USN c/s)*	Duxford
C-GYZI*	Cameron O-77 HAB	269		Balloon Preservation Group *"Aeolus"*	Southampton

GERMANY

D-CATA*	Hawker Sea Fury T.20S	ES.8503	D-FATA G-9-30/VZ345	Royal Naval Historic Flight *(As "VZ345": crashed 19.4.85 & stored)*	RNAS Yeovilton
D-HMQV*	Bolkow Bö.102 Helitrainer	6216		The Helicopter Museum *(Development aircraft)*	Weston-super-Mare
D-HOAY*	Kamov Ka.26	7001309	DDR-SPY DM-SPY	The Helicopter Museum	Weston-super-Mare
D-Opha*	Fire Balloons 3000 HAB	057	D-TALCID	Balloon Preservation Group *"Talcid"*	Kirdford
D-Pamgas*	Cameron N-90 HAB	1288		Balloon Preservation Group *"Pamgas"*	Kirdford

FRANCE

F-BDRS*	Boeing B-17G-95DL Flying Fortress	—	N68269 32376/NL68269/44-83735	American Air Museum *"Mary Alice"* *(As "231983/IY-G" in 401st BG/615th BS USAAF c/s)*	Duxford
F-BGEQ*	de Havilland DH.82A Tiger Moth	86305	Fr.AF NL846	Brooklands Museum *(Under restoration 3.02)*	Denford Manor, Hungerford
F-BTGV*	Aero Spacelines 377SGT Super Guppy	201001	N211AS	British Aviation Heritage-Cold War Jets Collection *(As "1")*	Bruntingthorpe
F-BTRP*	Sud SA.321F Super Frelon *(Converted from SA.321 c/n 116)*	01	F-WMHC F-BTRP/F-WKQC/F-OCZV/F-RAFR/F-OCMF/F-BMHC/F-WMHC	The Helicopter Museum *(As "F-OCMF" in Olympic Airways c/s)*	Weston-super-Mare
F-HMFI*	Farman F.40 *(Modified to F141 Status)*	6799	9204M	RAF Museum	RAF Cosford

NORWAY

LN-BNM*	Noorduyn AT-16-ND Harvard IIB	14-639	31-329 R.Dan AF/FE905/42-12392	RAF Museum *(As "FE905" in RAF/RCAF c/s)*	Hendon

ARGENTINA

LQ-BLT*	MBB Bö.105/CBS *(Non-airworthy pod is original airframe which crashed 13.6.96: shipped to UK and rebuilt with airframe c/n S.915)*	S.863		North East Aircraft Museum	Sunderland

UNITED STATES OF AMERICA

N18E*	Boeing 247D	1722	NC18E NC18/NC13340	Science Museum Air Transport Collection & Storage Facility	Wroughton
N46EA*	Percival P.66 Pembroke C.1 *(Regd with c/n K66-046)*	P66/83	8452M XK885	P.G.Vallance Ltd *(Gatwick Aviation Museum)*	Charlwood, Surrey
N47DD(2)*	Republic P47D-30-RA Thunderbolt	399-55731	N47DD Peru AF FAP119/45-49192	Imperial War Museum Collection/American Air Museum *"Oregon's Britannia" (As "226413/UN-Z")*	Duxford
N112WG*	Westland WG-30-100	012		The Helicopter Museum	Weston-super-Mare
N118WG*	Westland WG-30-100	018		The Helicopter Museum	Weston-super-Mare
N196B*	North American F-86A-5-NA Sabre	151-43611	48-0242	American Air Museum *(As "48-0242/242" in USAF c/s)*	Duxford
NC285RS*	North American Navion	NK		South East Aviation Enthusiasts Group *"My Way"* *(Crashed 11.6.79: fuselage only 3.02)*	Dromod, Leitrim, Co.Leitrim
N413JB	Cameron O-84 HAB	723		Balloon Preservation Group *"Autumn Fall"*	Kirdford
N2138J	English Electric Canberra TT.18 *(Built A V Roe & Co)* EEA/R3/EA3/6640		WK126	S D Picatti *(Stored 7.02)* *(Loaned to Gloucestershire Aviation Collection as "WK126/843")*	Gloucestershire
N2700*	Fairchild C-119G-FA	10689	3C-ABA Belg AF CP-9/51-2700	Aces High Flying Museum *(Nose only noted 9.02)*	North Weald
N3188H*	ERCO 415C Ercoupe	3813	NC3188H	AeroVenture *(Damaged c7.92: rebuild 9.02)*	Doncaster
N4519U*	Head AX9-118 HAB	184		Northern Light Balloon Expeditions *"Ground Hog" (Op Balloon Preservation Group)*	Kirdford
N4565L	Douglas DC-3-201A	2108	(N3TV) LV-GYP/LV-PCV/N129H/N512/N51D/N80C/NC21744	390th BG Memorial Air Museum *(Damaged in gales 10.87 & 25.1.90: on rebuild 3.02)*	Framlingham/Parham Park
N4990T*	Thunder Ax7-65B HAB	123		British Balloon Museum & Library *"Stormy Weather"*	Newbury
N5023U*	Avian Magnum IX HAB	169		Balloon Preservation Group *"Tumbleweed"*	Kirdford
N5237V*	Boeing B-17G-95-DL Flying Fortress	32509	(N6466D) N5237V/Bu.77233/44-83868	RAF Air Museum *(As "44-83868/N" in 94th BG USAAF c/s)*	Hendon
N5419*	Bristol Scout D rep *(Built Leo Opdycke 1983)*	01		FAA Museum *(Frame only)*	RNAS Yeovilton
N6526D*	North American P-51D-25NA Mustang *(Composite)*	122-39874	RCAF 9289 44-73415	RAF Museum *"Little Friend"* *(As "413573/B6-K" in 361st FS/357th FG USAAF c/s)*	Hendon
N6699D	Piasecki HUP-3 Retriever	51	RCN 622 USN/51-16622	Not known *(Loaned The Helicopter Museum) (As "622" in RCN c/s)*	Weston-super-Mare

N7614C*	North American B-25J/PBJ-1J Mitchell		44-31171		Imperial War Museum/American Air Museum	
		108-37246			*(As "31171" in US Marines c/s)*	Duxford
N9115Z*	North American TB-25N-20NC Mitchell		44-29366		RAF Museum *"Hanover Street/Catch 22"*	Hendon
		108-32641			*(As "34037" in USAAF c/s: allotted 8838M)*	
N12006	Raven S.50A HAB	111			R Higbie *"Cheers"*	Newbury
					(On loan to British Balloon Museum & Library)	
N16676	Fairchild F.24CR-C8F Argus	3101	NC16676		A Langendal	Flixton
			(		*(On loan to Norfolk & Suffolk Aviation Museum)*	
N33600*	Cessna L-19A-CE Bird Dog	22303	51-11989		Museum of Army Flying	AAC Middle Wallop
					(As "111989" in US Army c/s)	
N66630	Schweizer TG-3A	63	42-52983		Imperial War Museum *(P/i not confirmed)*	Duxford
					(As "252983" in USAAC c/s)	
N99153	North American T-28C Trojan	252-52	Zaire AF FG-289		W R Montague	Flixton
	(FAA quote c/n 226-93)		Congo AF FA-289/Bu.146289 *(On loan tp Norfolk & Suffolk Aviation Museum)*			
			(Crashed Limoges, France 14.12.77: fuselage only as "146289/2W")			

BELGIUM

OO-ARK(2)	Cameron N-56 HAB	276		Balloon Preservation Group	Kirdford
				(Spares use) "Princess Alex"	
OO-BDO(2)*	Cameron N-90 HAB	1960	(LX-PRO)	Balloon Preservation Group	Kirdford
				(Spares use) "Profi 2"	
OO-BFH*	Piccard Gas Balloon	—		Science Museum South Kensington, London SW.7	
				(Gondola only)	
OO-JAT*	Cameron Zero 25 Airship	1407		Balloon Preservation Group	Farnborough
				(On loan to Farnbrough Air Sciences Trust)	

DENMARK

OY-BOW(2)*	Colting 77A HAB	77A-014	SE-ZVB	British Balloon Museum & Library *"Circus"*	Newbury

RUSSIA

RA01277	Sukhoi Su-29	80-02	RA8002	Yorkshire Air Museum *(Noted 7.02)*	Elvington
RA01378	Yakovlev Yak-52	833004	DOSAAF 14	Wellesbourne Wartime Museum	
	(Composite with c/n 833805/DOSAAF 134 which is now N54GT)			*(Noted 4.02)*	Wellesbourne Mountford
RA01641	Antonov An-2R	1G-190-47		Black Country Aircraft Collection	Wolverhampton
				"3":(Crashed Milton 2.11.99) (Forward fuselage extant 2.00)	

SWEDEN

SE-AZB*	Avro 671 Cierva C.30A Autogiro	R3/CA.954	K4232	RAF Museum *(As "K4232")*	Hendon

POLAND

SP-SAY*	Mil Mi-2	529538125		The Helicopter Museum	Weston-super-Mare

ICELAND

TF-SHC*	Miles M.25 Martinet TT.1	--	MS902	Museum of Berkshire Aviation	Woodley
				(Crashed 18.7.51: on rebuild with Master components 2.02)	

AUSTRALIA

VH-ALB*	Supermarine 228 Seagull V	--	A2-4	RAF Museum *(As "A2-4")*	Hendon
VH-ASM*	Avro 652A Anson I	72960	W2068	RAF Museum *(As "W2068/68" in RAF c/s)*	Hendon
VH-AYY	Kavanagh D-77 HAB	KB136		Balloon Preservation Group *"Carlsberg"*	Kirdford
VH-BRC*	Short S.24 Sandringham IV	SH.55C	N158C	Science Museum *"Beachcomber"*	Southampton
			VP-LVE/N158C/VH-BRC/ZK-AMH/JM715 *(On loan to Hall of Aviation)*		*(Ansett c/s)*
VH-SNB*	de Havilland DH.84A Dragon	2002	VH-ASK	National Museums of Scotland/Museum of Flight	
			A34-13		East Fortune
VH-UTH*	General Aircraft Monospar ST-12	ST12/36		Newark Air Museum	Innsworth
				(On rebuild by Cotswold Aircraft Restoration Group 2.00)	

KENYA

VP-KJL*	Miles M.38 Messenger 4A	--	G-ALAR	The Miles Aircraft Collection	Not known
			RH371	*(For rebuild off-site 3.02)*	

PART 3 – ENTRIES REMOVED FROM 2002 EDITION

Regn	Type	C/n	Reason for removal

PORTUGAL

CS-AZS	de Havilland DHC.1 Chipmunk T.20	55	To G-DHPM 3.02
CS-AZT	de Havilland DHC.1 Chipmunk T.20	63	To G-CBJG 2.02
CS-HBN	Hughes 369E	0333E	To G-OPCS 1.01

GERMANY

D-CFLX	Short SD.3-60 Var.300	SH3735	Restored as G-BOEI 2.02
D-ECLY*	Reims FR172E Rocket	FR17200046	To N261SA 12.02 - see PART 1 above
D-EHBH	Piper PA-28-180 Cherokee Challenger	28-7305466	Now N64MS – see PART 1 above
D-EMIX(2)	Piper PA-32R-300 Lance	32R-7780225	To N9786F 2.02
D-ERAC	Piper PA-28-161 Warrior II	28-8116103	To EC-IFP 2002
D-ERCH*	Mooney M.20M TLS	27-0210	To N68FB

SPAIN

EC-AXZ*	Bell 47J	2079	No recent reports
EC-GSI	British Aerospace BAe ATP	2044	Restored as G-BTPN 1.02
EC-HFM	British Aerospace BAe ATP	2015	Restored as G-BTPH 1.02
EC-HND	Airbus Industrie A300B4-203F	101	To N59101 10.02

LIBERIA

EL-AKU	Boeing 707-347C	19964	Scrapped by 7.02

ESTONIA

ES-YLB	Aero L-39 Albatros	730932	To G-BZVL 4.02

FRANCE

F-CCHG	Wassmer WA.21 Javelot II	19	No reports since 6.99
F-GDPA*	Cessna 172RG Cutlass	172RG1091	No reports since 8.98
F-GEHD	Aérospatiale SA.341G Gazelle	1390	To G-WCRD 10.02
F-GGGG	Cessna T310R	310R1805	To N234SA – see PART 1
F-GGKR	Holste MH.1521M Broussard	316	No reports since 11.99
F-GHOB*	Chaize CS.2200-F12 HAB	30	No reports since 6.97
F-GJGM	Mudry CAP.232	07	Displayed in Terminal 5, Stockholm Arlanda Airport 5.02
F-GNVB	Sud-Est SE.3130 Alouette II	1920	To OO-ASM 6.01
F-GPYV	Beech 1900C-1	UC-121	To N121ZR 3.02 - see PART 1
F-GPYX	Beech 1900C-1	UC-111	To N111YV 3.02
F-WQKF	Aérospatiale AS.365N Dauphin 2	6219	To F-GVFE 5.01
F-PYYV(2)	Rutan LongEz	1046	To G-CBLZ 6.02

SWITZERLAND

HB-CAZ	Cessna 170A	19674	To N170AZ 11.01 - see PART 1
HB-EZR	SOCATA TB-10 Tobago	129	To G-CBPE 6.02
HB-XFH*	Bell 206 Jet Ranger	1051	Mis-sighting - pod is D-HGBX – see PART 1
HB-ZCD	Agusta A109C	7663	To N109BS 5.02

THAILAND

HS-TFS	Boeing 707-321C	19372	To 9G-JET 6.02

ITALY

I-TOMI*	Nardi FN.305D	--	No reports since 7.99

NORWAY

LN-RDN*	Bombardier DHC-8Q Srs.402	4043	Left UK storage as N535DS 2.03

LITHUANIA

LY-ABV	Yakovlev Yak-52	8910004	To RA02956 but became G-CBPX 12.02
LY-AFK	Yakovlev Yak-52	877415	To G-ZYAK 2.03
LY-AFV	Yakovlev Yak-52	899915	To RA01948 but became G-YAKH 12.02
LY-AFZ	Yakovlev Yak-50	842706	To G-IIYK 10.02
LY-AGL*	Yakovlev Yak-55	870406	Now based in Germany
LY-AGN	Yakovlev Yak-52		To G-LYAK 12.02
LY-AHE	Yakovlev Yak-52	822710	To RA44460 but became G-CBMD 11.02
LY-AHF	Yakovlev Yak-52	888615	To RA44472 then G-CBLJ 4.02
LY-AID	Yakovlev Yak-52	822603	Now RA02041 – see PART 1
LY-AIE	Yakovlev Yak-52	899907	To RA01038 but became G-TYAK 12.02
LY-AIJ	Yakovlev Yak-52	833707	To RA44475 then G-CBSS 2.03
LY-AKC	Yakovlev Yak-52	867212	To G-YAKC 6.02
LY-AKW	Yakovlev Yak-52	855601	To G-YAKW 11.02
LY-ALO	Yakovlev Yak-52	844815	To G-CBRH 9.02
LY-ALU	Yakovlev Yak-52	9011107	To G-HYAK 8.02
LY-AMP	Yakovlev Yak-52	800708	To RA44474 but became G-CBPY 1.03
LY-AMU	Yakovlev Yak-52	833901	To G-LENA 11.02
LY-ANG	Yakovlev Yak-50	832409	To G-HAMM 10.02

LY-ANI	Yakovlev Yak-52	9411812	No reports since 7.98
LY-ANU	Yakovlev Yak-52	867110	To G-CBLI 4.02
LY-AOB	Yakovlev Yak-52	9211517	To RA44491 but became G-YAKB 11.02
LY-AOC	Yakovlev Yak-52	811308	To G-CBOZ 11.02
LY-AOK	Yakovlev Yak-52	877404	To G-LAOK 1.03
LY-AOM	Yakovlev Yak-52	878101	To G-YYAK 4.02
LY-AOV	Yakovlev Yak-52	899803	To G-YAKR 11.02
LY-AOX	Yakovlev Yak-52	833708	To RA44468 but became G-CBRL 12.02
LY-AOZ	Yakovlev Yak-52	855907	To G-CBMI 7.02
LY-APT	Yakovlev Yak-50	791506	To G-YKSO 4.02
LY-ASG	Yakovlev Yak-50	812101	To G-CBPM 7.02
LY-FUT	Yakovlev Yak-52	888410	To G-YFUT 2.03
LY-JDR	Yakovlev Yak-50	792006	To G-OJDR 7.02

UNITED STATES OF AMERICA

N12FU	Learjet Learjet 60	60-027	To N69LJ 4.02
N12NM	Cessna 501 Citation I	501-0257	Sold North Carolina, USA 8.02
N18SF	Agusta A109A Mk.II	7275	To G-MKSF 12.01
N21PM	SNCAN Stampe SV-4C	556	To G-BXSV 10.02
N32LE	Piper PA-32R-301T Turbo Saratoga SP	32R-8329016	Based abroad - Bratislava?
N47SA	Brantly B.2B	451	No recent reports
N52NW	Gulfstream G1159 Gulfstream II	52	Sold Indiana, USA 1.03
N59SD	MDH MD 369E	0019E	No recent reports
N61AN	Reims/Cessna F182Q Skylane	F18200127	Restored as G-IFAB 12.02
N64GA	Beech 200 Super King Air	BB-790	Sold Texas, USA 6.02
NX71MY	Vickers Vimy rep	01	Returned to USA - scheduled to revisit UK 6.03
N74BF	Stoddard-Hamilton Glasair	2274	Sold Missouri, USA 8.02
N79GW	Cessna 340A	340A-0680	To New Zealand 2.02
N80BA	Pitts S-1A Special	648-4	No report since 12.99
N83WA	Gulfstream 695B	96063	Sold Oregon, USA 11.02
N97RJ	Piper PA-31 Turbo Navajo	31-7300956	Restored as G-BBDS 1.02
N100UP	Dassault Falcon 900B	44	Sold Connecticut, USA 4.02
N101AP	Beech B200 King Air	BB-1004	No report since 10.99
N124CD	Cirrus Design SR-20	1011	To Antwerp, Belgium 12.01
N135XX	Piper PA-20-135 Pacer	20-1107	Restored as G-PAXX 6.02
N141CA	Piper Aerostar 601P	61P-0711-7963343	To Germany 5.02
N147BK	Piper PA-46-350P Malibu Mirage	4636236	Sold Washington State, USA 3.02
N158JC	Aero Vodochody L-39ZO	831201	Sold Minnesota, USA 9.02
N167B	Douglas A-26B Invader	27881	No longer based in UK
N167F	North American P-51D Mustang	122-40417	No longer based in UK
N182VV	Cessna 182P	18264973	Sold Florida,USA 7.02
N195AL	Beech 300 Super King Air	FA-102	Sold Texas, USA 4.02
N198SL	Cessna 550 Citation Bravo	550-0835	Sold Nevada, USA 1.02
N200LQ	IRMA Britten-Norman BN-2T Islander	880	To N121MT 1.03 -see PART 1
N200UP	Dassault Falcon 50	55	Now based Amsterdam
N201XJ	Mooney M.20J	24-0494	Sold Spain 9.02
N210MP	Cessna T210N Turbo Centurion II	21063193	Sold Colorado, USA 10.01
N240JS	Aérospatiale/Alenia ATR 42-320	240	To ZS-OWU 7.02
N240SA	Cessna 337D Super Skymaster	337-1070	To USA 6.02
N243SA	Piper PA-22-108 Colt	22-8376	To France by 10.02
N250SM	Cessna 560XL Citation Excel	560-5167	To G-REDS 10.02
N260QB	Aerotek Pitts S-2S Special	3002	No report since 12.99
N281Q	Enstrom F.28A	266	No report since 1999
N287AB	Cessna 500 Citation I	500-0287	To VP-BGE 6.02 – see PART 1
N295SS	Piper PA-46-350P Malibu Mirage	4636174	To N295S 6.02 - see PART 1
N300GB	Beechjet 400A	RK-262	Sold North Carolina, USA 10.02
N363DG	SOCATA TB-10 Tobago	1901	Sold Iceland 5.02
N385AT	Cessna T303	T303-00195	Sold Idaho, USA 12.01
N402R	Cessna 402B II	402B1364	No report since 1.97
N500UD	Piper PA-31 Turbo Navajo	31-761	Now N642P – see PART 1
N501VH	Cessna 500 Citation I	500-0044	To ZS-DSA 6.02
N508MV	Beech B200 Super King Air	BB-877	Sold New Jersey, USA 3.02
N521JS	Aérospatiale/Alenia ATR 42-320	205	Sold South Africa 7.02
N525AD	Cessna 525 CitationJet	525-0435	To G-CJAD 6.02
N601UK	Ted Smith Aerostar 601P	61P-0183-012	Sold Florida,USA 5.02
N666EX	Piper PA-32R-301T	3257241	Last noted 10.01
N670AT	Beech B90 King Air	LJ-481	Sold Florida,USA 10.01
N800VP	Beech 95-B55	TC-1805	To N600VP 12.02
N844F	Dassault Falcon 100	201	Sold Montana, USA 5.02
N850FT	Boeing 747-122F	19755	Broken up Prestwick 9.02
N864AE	British Aerospace Jetstream Srs.3201	864	To SE-LHK 9.02
N909RM	Mooney M.20J (201)	24-0636	Crashed Thurrock 14.5.01: wreck shipped to USA 2002
N913PM*	Lockheed L-1011 Tristar 200	1223	Scrapped c.2001
N991RV(1)	Dassault Falcon 10	24	To N230RS 2.02
N1061Y	Navion Rangemaster H	NAV-4-2531	To USA 7.02
N1062U	Piper PA-32-300 Cherokee Six	32-40070	Sold California, USA 3.02
N1325M	Boeing-Stearman E75 (N2S-5) Kaydet	75-8484	No report since 6.99
N2000M	Cessna 560 Citation V	560-0146	To N500AT 3.02
N2099L	Beech 95B55 Baron	TC-1983	Sold Texas, USA 8.00
N2495Q	Piper PA-34-200T Seneca II	34-7770188	To G-CBWB 10.02
N2937A*	Cessna 180	30137	Cancelled FAA 8.11.01 as destroyed

N4647J	Piper PA-28R-180 Cherokee Arrow	28R-30541	To G-CSWH 4.02
N5107N	Boeing B75N1 Stearman	75-7166	No report since 2.99
N5129U	Beechjet BJ.400A	RK-329	Returned to USA 11.02
N5360H	Piper PA-16 Clipper	16-167	Based in The Netherlands
N5824H	Piper PA-38-112 Tomahawk II	38-81A0118	To G-RECS 4.02
N5339Z	Piper PA-32R-301 Saratoga IIHP	3246193	Sold in Spain 11.02
N5668H	Maule MX-7-180 Star Rocket	11028C	To G-WALY 1.03
N6268	Travelair 2000	707	No report since 7.96
N7133J	Mooney M.20C Mk 21	3116	W/O Bodmin 14.3.99 per AAIB 5.99: cancelled FAA 5.02 as destroyed)
N7801R	Bell 47G-5	7801	No report since 12.99
N8075U	Cessna 150G	15065381	No report since 7.97
N8360Y	Piper PA-28-181 Archer II	28-8190195	Sold New Jersey, USA 10.02
N8862V	Bellanca 17-31ATC Turbo Viking	31022	No report since 9.99
N9045C	Barnes SS Condom HAB	FS7-001	To G-CBPG 6.02
N9143C	Aero Commander 685	12040	No report since 11.99
N9303W	Piper PA-28-235 Cherokee B	28-10981	No report since 3.99
N9606H	Fairchild M.62A-4 Cornell	T43-4361	No report since 7.99
N24730	Piper PA-38-112 Tomahawk	38-80A0004	To G-BTIL 3.91
N37600	Cessna T310R	310R1209	To G-OGTX 12.01
N46294	Steen Skybolt	SB-1990	No report since 9.99
N53091	Boeing-Stearman A75N1 (PT-17) Kaydet	75-2795	No report since 5.99
N61787	Piper J3C-65 Cub	13624	No report since 8.99
N67501	Beech A36 Bonanza	E-2116	To G-LOLA 2.02
N68427	Boeing-Stearman A75N1 (N2S-4) Kaydet	75-5008	No report since 7.98

AUSTRIA

OE-DPC	Piper PA-32-300 Cherokee Six	32-40070	To N1062U 9.01

FINLAND

OH-LBS	Boeing 757-2Q8	27623	Returned to Finnair

CZECH REPUBLIC

OK-DUU 15	Urban Air UFM-13 Lambada	3/11	Error - see OK-EUU 15
OK-EUU 55	Urban Air UFM-13 Lambada	NK	Error - see OK-EUU 15
OK-JIY*	Yakovlev C.11	172673?	No reports since 3.96
OK-PDO	Letovlev LET L-410UVP Turbolet	851411	Returned to Czech Republic by 8.02
OK-XTA	Extra EA.300/S	004	Exported 7.02

BELGIUM

OO-FAN	Beech 56TC Baron	TG-10	Exported – N2046Q reserved
OO-JAL*	Jodel D.120A Paris-Nice	59	To G-CCBR 2.03
OO-VPC	Cessna 182P Skylane II	18263928	No report since 1.96

DENMARK

OY-ANZ*	Maule M.5-210C Strata Rocket	6027C	No report since 2.99
OY-MBS	Canadair CL600-2B19 (CRJ 200)	7283	To N785BC 2002

ARUBA

P4-ESP	Boeing 707-328C	19292	Scrapped by 7.02

THE NETHERLANDS

PH-DUC	Stoddard-Hamilton Glasair IIRG-S	2069	Returned to Netherlands 2002

RUSSIA

RA1765	Piper PA-28-181 Archer II	2890093	Restored as G-BTAM 6.02
RA4147	Reims/Cessna FA.337G Super Skymaster	F33700070	Restored as G-BOYR 11.02
RA01038	Yakovlev Yak-52	899907	To G-TYAK 12.02
RA01193	Yakovlev Yak-50	801804	To G-EYAK 2.03
RA01293	Yakovlev Yak-50	853104	To G-YAKK 11.02
RA01493	Yakovlev Yak-50	853001	To G-JYAK 11.02
RA01564	Yakovlev Yak-52	8910302	To G-YAKT 1.03
RA01596	Yakovlev Yak-52	NK	Not confirmed - believed misread registration
RA01948	Yakovlev Yak-52	899915	To G-YAKH 12.02
RA02042	Yakovlev Yak-52	888911	To G-CBRU 1.03
RA02135	Aeropract A-21M Solo	01	No report since 3.97
RA02149	Yakovlev Yak-52	8910001	To G-IMIC 8.02
RA02246	Yakovlev Yak-50	852905	To G-GYAK 12.02 (Note corrected c/n)
RA02705	Yakovlev Yak-52	866915	To France 2002
RA02956	Yakovlev Yak-52	8910004	To G-CBPX 12.02
RA44464	Yakovlev Yak-52	9111415	To G-CBRW 2.03
RA44468	Yakovlev Yak-52	833708	To G-CBRL 12.02
RA44473	Yakovlev Yak-52	9111307	Restored as G-YAKX 11.02
RA44474	Yakovlev Yak-52	800708	To G-CBPY 1.03
RA44491	Yakovlev Yak-52	9211517	To G-YAKB 11.02
RA44518	Yakovlev Yak-50	832601	To N227W 10.02
RA44534	Yakovlev Yak-52	822013	To G-CBSL 1.03
RA44546	Yakovlev Yak-52	889012	Destroyed 11.8.01 near Compton Abbas

SWEDEN

SE-BNN	Saab 91A Safir	91130	Returned to Sweden by 5.02
SE-DXA	Hawker Hunter F.Mk.58	41H-679995	No longer UK based
SE-DXY	de Havilland DH.100 Vampire FB.Mk.6	693	No longer UK based
SE-LBR*	Yakovlev Yak-50	791602	To N79YK 5.02 - see PART 1

POLAND

SP-FBO(3)	Antonov An-2T	1G-108-55	To RA02974 2002 – see PART 1

ICELAND

TF-ATO	Boeing 767-204ER	24013	Lease ended 11.02
TF-TOA	Piper PA-28R-200 Cherokee Arrow III	28R-7635029	No reports since 8.99

CENTRAL AFRICAN REPUBLIC

TL-ADJ	Boeing 707-329C	20200	Left UK 12.02
TL-ALM	Boeing 707-329C	20200	To TL-ADJ 8.02 - see above

AUSTRALIA

VH-YOT	Skyfox Gazelle CA25N	CA25N030	No reports since 8.97

SEYCHELLE ISLANDS

VQ-SAC	Britten Norman BN-2A Islander	287	No reports since 3.94

BERMUDA (new series)

VP-BCN	British Aerospace BAe 125 Srs.600B	256035	To N128YT 5.02
VP-BFE	Boeing 737-7CP	30753	To N754BC 8.02
VP-BFO	Boeing 737-7CP	30755	To N752BC 8.02
VP-BIS	Gulfstream Gulfstream IV	1150	To N386AG 7.02
VP-BJV	Gulfstream G1159 Gulfstream II	186	No report since 3.98
VP-BMF	Dassault Falcon 50	206	To N801DL 12.02
VP-BNS	Cessna 550 Citation Bravo	550-0939	To N48NS 5.02 - see PART 1
VP-BNU	Robin DR400/180 Regent	2047	To G-NFNF 11.02
VP-BNZ(3)	Gulfstream Gulfstream V	509	To N509GV 4.02

CAYMAN ISLANDS

VP-CAM	Canadair CL601 Challenger	5090	To HB-ITK 12.02
VP-CEO	Eurocopter EC.135	0031	To F-GSMB 5.01
VP-CNM(2)	Cessna 560XL Citation Excel	560-5070	To N507VP 3.02
VP-CPC	Cessna 560 XL Citation Excel	560-5215	To N560TH 5.02 - see PART 1
VP-CRY	Gulfstream Gulfstream IV	1176	Now N9253V
VP-CSC	Cessna 560 Citation Ultra	560-0439	To N6NY 10.02

BERMUDA (old series)

VR-BPS	Consolidated (PBY-5A) Catalina	1997	To VP-BPS – see SECTION 5, PART 1

MEXICO

XA-NAN	MBB Bö.105CBS/4	S-761	To SE-JDJ 11.02
XA-PBA	Boeing 737-2H6	20631	Broken up Bournemouth 9.02

LATVIA

YL-CBH*	Yakovlev Yak-50	832507	No report since 11.97
YL-CBI*	Yakovlev Yak-52	811202	No report since 11.97
YL-CBJ*	Yakovlev Yak-52	790404	No report since 11.97
YL-VIP(2)	British Aerospace BAe 125 Srs.800B	258078	Returned to Latvia 6.02
YL-YAK*	Yakovlev Yak-50	832507	No report since 11.95

SERBIA

YU-DMT	UTVA-66	--	No report since 11.97
YU-HCE	Agusta-Bell 212	5713	Returned to Serbia 2000
YU-HEI	Soko/Aérospatiale SA.341G Gazelle	008	No report since 11.99
YU-HEK	Soko/Aérospatiale SA.341G Gazelle	012	No report since 11.99

NEW ZEALAND

ZK-MKV	Supermarine Spitfire Vc	--	To G-LFVC 9.99

REPUBLIC of SOUTH AFRICA

ZS-JVL	Lockheed L-100-30 Hercules	4676	To EI-JVL 8.02
ZS-KCT	Beech A36 Bonanza	E-1280	Now N3030S
ZS-LWI	Piper PA-34-220T Seneca	34-8533024	To N822CB 10.02 and G-OOON 1.03
ZS-OGX	Piper PA-32R-300	32R-7780069	Restored as N7640F 10.02 - see PART 1
ZS-SDA	Airbus Industrie A300B2K-3C	032	Scrapped Bournemouth 9.02
ZS-SDD	Airbus Industrie A300B2K-3C	040	Scrapped Bournemouth 2.02

SWAZILAND

3D-HVW	Westland Gazelle HT.3	WA/1906	Restored as G-BZDW 2.02
3D-HXL	Westland Gazelle HT.2	WA/1150	Restored as G-BZDV 2.02

AZERBAIJAN
4K-AZ3*   Boeing 707-341C   19321   Scrapped 4.02

ISRAEL
4X-AVY   Piper PA-30-160B Twin Comanche   30-1552   Restored as N8403Y – see PART 1

CYPRUS
5B-DBE   Boeing 727-30   18371   Returned to Cyprus by 9.02

NIGERIA
5N-ABJ   Boeing 707-3F9C   20474   Scrapped 1998
5N-ALQ   Bell 212   30670   Wreck destroyed mid 2001
5N-AQW   Bell 212   30600   Wreck destroyed mid 2001
5N-ATU   Beech A90 King Air   LJ-136   Scrapped by 2001

SENEGAL
6W-SAE   Douglas C-47A-25-DK   13430   No reports since 8.94

MALTA
9H-AAJ*   Agusta Bell 206A   8185   Registered G-DNCN in 11.97!

DEMOCRATIC REPUBLIC of KINSHASA
9Q-CBW   Boeing 707-329C   20200   Became TL-ALM 5.02 then TL-ADJ 8.02 – see above

SECTION 6

PART 1 – BRITISH GLIDING ASSOCIATION

The Register includes the Certificate of Airworthiness reference number as issued by the British Gliding Association (BGA). This is usually found below the tailplane in small characters. We include, as a primary reference, the corresponding three-letter coding (or trigraph (TG) system) frequently marked on the tails. If gliders are known to be wearing their respective trigraphs then we have indicated this and/or any other identity in the first composite column, for example BGA Competition Numbers are shown if carried with further details contained in SECTION 7. The official BGA list is extended by including non-current gliders and those with recently lapsed Certificates of Airworthiness (CA) for which no cancellation details are known but which may survive. These are identified by * in the CA expiry column. In this edition, to be consistent with the presentation used in the powered aircraft sections, we have shown the complete expiry dates for Certiifcates of Airworthiness, and the complete date for the first issue of a CofA where this information is known. Where the latter information is not readily available, efforts will be made to add the missing data in future editions. Where a BGA CofA number has been reserved for future use, the reservation date is now shown, prefixed by the letter 'R'. The non-current gliders include many examples known to be in storage or under restoration in the ownership of members of the Vintage Glider Club (VGC).

We are grateful to Phil Butler for updating the BGA register and to Richard Cawsey, Wal Gandy, Barry Taylor and Tony Morris for additional comments. Once again, special appreciation is given to the BGA's Secretary, Barry Rolfe, for his valued assistance whilst for the VGC data we owe thanks to Peter Chamberlain. Information is current to the end of January 2003.

TG/BGA/Code		Type	C/n	P/I	Date	Owner/Operator	Probable Base	CA Expy
162		Manuel Willow Wren			9.34	Brooklands Museum	Brooklands	*
						"The Willow Wren" (Stored)		
AAA 231		Abbott-Baynes Scud II	215B	G-ALOT	8.35	(Under repair)	Dunstable	22. 4.01
		(Built Slingsby)		BGA.231		*(On display 3.96)*		
AAF 236		Slingsby T.6 Kite 1	27A	G-ALUD	14.11.35	Not known	Dunstable	*
				BGA.236/(BGA.222)		*(Stored pending rebuild 12.95)*		
AAX 251		Slingsby T.6 Kite 1	227A	(ex RAF)	30. 3.36	R.Boyd	Rivar Hill	7.12.02
				BGA.251				
ABG 260		Schleicher Rhönsperber	32-16		4. 5.36	F.K.Russell tr Rhönsperber Syndicate	Dunstable	18.11.03
(ABN)266		Slingsby T.1 Falcon 1 Waterglider	237A		29. 5.36	Windermere Steamboat Museum	Windermere	*
						(On display 5.95)		
ABZ 277		Grunau Baby 2	?	RAFGSA.270	25. 8.36	J.L.Smoker & Ptnrs	Hinton in the Hedges	22. 7.95*
		(Built F.Coleman)		BGA.277/G-ALKU/BGA.277				
ACF 283		Abbott-Baynes Scud III	2	G-ALJR	18.12.36	L.P.Woodage	Dunstable	14.6.03
				BGA.283				
ACH 285	E	Slingsby T.6 Kite 1	247A	G-ALNH	30.12.36	E.B.Scott	AAC Middle Wallop	5.99*
				BGA.285		*(On loan The Museum of Army Flying) (As "G285/E" in 1 GTS RAF c/s)*		
ADJ 310		Slingsby T.6 Kite 1	258B	RAFGSA182	9. 2.37	A.M.Maufe	Tibenham	17. 7.01
				VD218/BGA.310		*(Rebuilt 1982 with components from BGA.327 c/n 285A)*		
AEM 337		Schleicher Rhönbussard	620	G-ALME	25. 4.38	C.Wills & S.White	Booker	31. 5.02
				BGA.337				
(AFW)	370	Grunau Baby 2	1		11.10.38	Not known	Saltby	
		(Built J.Hobson)				*(Under restoration 2000)*		
AGE 378		Slingsby T.12 Gull I	312A	G-ALPJ	14. 9.38	ML Beach	Dunstable	21.6.03
				BGA.378				
AHC 400	F	Slingsby T.6 Kite 1	336A	VD165	6. 5.39	R.Hadlow & Ptnrs	Thame	27. 4.97
		(Wings from Special T.6 c/n 355A)		BGA.400		*(In 1 GTS RAF c/s)*		
AHU 416	G-ALRD	Scott Viking 1	114	G-ALRD	19. 6.39	M.L.Beach	Dunstable	2.7.03
				BGA.416				
AJW 442	AJW	Slingsby T.8 Tutor	MHL/RC/8	G-ALMX	8.46	M.Hodgson	Dunstable	14. 8.98
				BGA.442				
AKC 448		DFS 108-68 Weihe	000348	G-ALJW	6.47	D.Philips	Snitterfield	*
				BGA.448/LO+WQ		*(Damaged Thun, Switzerland 20.7.79: on rebuild 1994)*		
AKD 449		DFS/70 Olympia-Meise	227	LF+VO	7.47	L.S.Phillips *(Stored and for sale)*	Perranporth	5.85*
AKW 466		Slingsby T.8 Tutor	MHL/RT/7		11.46	D.Kitchen	Tibenham	6. 7.96
ALA 470		Short Nimbus	S.1312		.47	Ulster Folk & Transport Museum	Holywood, Belfast	8.75*
						(Stored 6.97)		
ALR 485		Slingsby T.8 Tutor	513	G-ALPE	11.46	M.H.Birch	Booker	14. 6.97
				BGA.485		*(Stored)*		
ALW 490	G-ALRK	Hutter H-17A		G-ALRK	8.48	N.I.Newton	Booker	3. 5.03
		(Built D.Campbell)		BGA.490				
ALX 491		Hawkridge Dagling	08471		2.47	N.H.Ponsford *(Stored 1.98)*	(Breighton)	*
(ALZ) 493		Hawkridge Nacelle Dagling	10471		7.47	P. & D.Underwood	Eaton Bray	*
		(Also allotted BAPC.81)				*(On rebuild 2000)*		
AMK 503	AMK	EoN AP.5 Olympia 2	EoN/O/003	G-ALJP	5.47	D.T.Staff	Booker	28. 5.95*
				BGA.503		*(Under restoration)*		
AMM 505		EoN AP.5 Olympia 2	EoN/O/006	G-ALJV	5.47	I.Hodge	RAF Marham	31. 5.03
				BGA.505				
AMP 507		EoN AP.5 Olympia 2	EoN/O/008	G-ALJO	6.47	M.Briggs	Cranfield	25. 6.95*
				BGA.507				
AMR 509	AMR	EoN AP.5 Olympia 2	EoN/O/011	G-ALLA	5.47	K.J.Nurcombe	Husbands Bosworth	4. 8.03
				BGA.509				
AMT 511	AMT	EoN AP.5 Olympia 2	EoN/O/005	G-ALLM	5.47	E.W.Burgess	Lyveden	25. 7.97
				BGA.511				
AMU 512		EoN AP.5 Olympia 2	EoN/O/012			Not known *(Under rebuild 2000)*	Challock	
AMV 513		EoN AP.5 Olympia 2	EoN/O/014	G-ALNB		Not known	Camphill	
				BGA.513		*(Under refurbishment 2000)*		
AMW 514	AMW	EoN AP.5 Olympia 2	EoN/O/015	G-ALKM	6.47	M.R.Fox	Pocklington	16. 4.03
				BGA.514				
AND 521		Slingsby T.26 Kite II	MHL/RK.5			Not known *(Stored)*	Chalfont St.Giles	ANW 538

ANW 538	ANW	EoN AP.5 Olympia 2B	EoN/O/040	G-ALNE BGA.538	7.47	E.A.Barnacle	Snitterfield	14. 7.03
ANZ 541		EoN AP.5 Olympia 2	EoN/O/043		9.47	Not known (Under restoration)	RAF Halton	
APC 544	APC	EoN AP.5 Olympia 2	EoN/O/046	G-ALMJ BGA.544	9.47	N.G.Oultram	Seighford	19. 7.03
APV 561		EoN AP.5 Olympia 2B	EoN/O/032	G-ALKN BGA.561	6.47	A.Kepley t/a Fenland & West Norfolk Aviation Museum (Stored 8.97)	Crowland	8.78*
APZ 565		Slingsby T.25 Gull 4	505	G-ALPB (BGA.565)		E.A.Arthur	Lasham	12. 8.01
AQE 570		Slingsby T.21B	538	G-ALNJ BGA.570		Not known (Stored pending rebuild 10.97)	Camphill	*
AQG 572		Slingsby T.21B Sedbergh TX.1	539	8884M VX275/BGA.572		RAF Museum (Stored 11.01)	RAF Cosford	*
AQN 578	AQN	Hawkridge Grunau Baby 2B	G.3348	G-ALSO BGA.578	.48	R G Hood	Lasham	18. 6.02
AQQ 580		EoN AP.7 Primary	EoN/P/003	G-ALPS BGA.580		Imperial War Museum (Stored)	Duxford	*
AQY 588		EoN AP.7 Primary	EoN/P/011			N.H.Ponsford (Stored 1.98)	(Breighton)	*
AQZ 589		EoN AP.7 Primary	EoN/P/012	G-ALMN BGA.589		Not known (Stored 1992)	(Farnborough)	4.51*
ARK 599	ARK	Slingsby T.30A Prefect	548	PH-1 BGA.599/G-ALLF/BGA.599	.	K.M.Fresson	RNAS Yeovilton	31.7.03
ARM 601	ARM	Slingsby T.21B	543	G-ALKX BGA.601	8.48	South London Gliding Centre	Kenley	10. 8.03
ASB 614	T42	Slingsby T.21B	549	RNGSA G-ALLT/BGA.614	9.48	J.L.Rolls & Ptnrs	Talgarth	26. 7.03
ASC 615		Grunau Baby 2B (Built Hawkridge)	G-4848	G-ALMM BGA.615	2.49	C.D.Stainer & Ptnrs (Stored 8.95 - sold in Germany)	Rufforth	8.94*
ASN 625		Slingsby T.30B Prefect	567	G-ALPC BGA.625	1.49	G.Martin	Rhigos	24. 5.99
ASR 628		EoN AP.8 Baby	EoN/B/004	G-ALRU BGA.628	3.49	Not known (Crashed Bardney 28.5.71; stored Aston Down 8.02)	Aston Down	*
AST 629	G-ALRH	EoN AP.8 Baby	EoN/B/005	G-ALRH BGA.629	3.49	EoN Baby Syndicate "Liver Bird" (Extant 2000)	Chipping	9.96
ATH 643		Slingsby T.15 Gull III	364A	TJ711	11.49	Brooklands Museum	Brooklands	9.94*
ATL 646		Slingsby T.21B	536	G-ALKS	6.50	G.Markham (Stored 2.01)	Enstone	7.96
ATR 651		Slingsby T.13 Petrel 1	361A	EI-101 IGA.101/IAC.101/BGA.651/G-ALPP	7.50	G.Saw	Booker	3. 5.03
ATV 655	OK-8592	Zlin 24 Krajanek	101	G-ALMP OK-8592	4.50	N.Barr	Booker	3. 5.03
AUD 663	663	Slingsby T.26 Kite 2B	727		1.52	R.S.Hooper	Lasham	19. 5.03
AUG 666		Slingsby T.21B	643		6.51	Cambridge University GC	Gransden Lodge	13. 5.03
AUJ 668		Slingsby T.21B (Built Aero & Engineering)	639		6.51	Not known (Damaged Feshiebridge 16.7.85: stored 7.97)	Rufforth	6.86*
AUP 673	N21	Slingsby T.21B	636		7.51	The Solent T21 Group	Lee-on-Solent	10. 4.03
AUU 678	AUU	EoN AP.5 Olympia	EoN/0/076		4.52	J.M.Lee	Parham Park	19. 8.00
AUW 680		Avia 40P	117		8.52	F.Ragot	(St.Auban, France)	27. 7.98
AVA 684		Abbott-Baynes Scud III	3		1.53	E.A.Hull	Dunstable	29. 5.03
AVB 685	AVB	Slingsby T.34 Sky	644	G-644	2.53	R.Moyse	Lasham	25. 7.03
AVC 686	AVC	Slingsby T.34 Sky	670		3.53	P.J.Teagle "Kinder Scout II"	Camphill	28. 8.03
AVD 687	AVD	Eon AP.5 Olympia 2	EoN/O/092		3.53	A.C.Jarvis	Parham Park	26. 7.98
AVF 689	AVF	Slingsby T.26 Kite 2A	728	RAFGSA.294 BGA.689	4.53	C.P.Raine	Dunstable	28. 6.03
AVG 690		Slingsby T.31B	717		4.53	A.R.Worters (Refurbishing: previously reported as becoming G-BMDD)	North Connel	
AVL 694		Slingsby T.34 Sky	671	G-671	5.53	M.P.Wakem	Long Mynd	29. 5.03
AVQ 698	AVQ G46	Slingsby T.34 Sky	645	G-645	8.53	Miss A.G.Veitch & B.Middleton "Gertie"	Easterton	22. 6.03
AVT 701		Slingsby T.30B Prefect	857	AGA... BGA.701	1.53	Booker GC	Booker	14. 5.00
AWD 711	AWD	Slingsby T.21B	950		30. 9.54	D.B.Brown tr T.21 Syndicate	Chipping	25. 6.01
AWS 724	AWS	Slingsby T.41 Skylark 2S	997		6.55	D.M.Cornelius	Dunstable	25. 5.03
AWU 726		EoN AP.5 Olympia	EoN/O/082		5.55	M J Riley	Sackville Farm, Riseley	14. 4.03
AWX 729	AWX	Slingsby T.41 Skylark 2	946		1.56	A.G.Leach	Cranfield	24. 4.01
AWZ 731	AWZ	Slingsby T.7 Cadet	SSK/FF/169	RA847	8. 1.57	R.Moyse	Lasham	31.10.03
AXB 733	AXB	Slingsby T.41 Skylark 2	926		2.55	A.L.Shaw	Lyveden	30. 6.02
AXD 735	AXD	Slingsby T.43 Skylark 3	1014		.55	F.G.T.Birlison	Aston Down	1. 5.03
AXE 736	AXE	Slingsby T.43 Skylark 3	1029		24. 3.57	C.J.Bushell	Snitterfield	21. 8.01
AXJ 740	AXJ	Slingsby T.42A Eagle 2	994		.55	P.C.Horn tr The Eagle Syndicate	Parham Park	12. 7.03
AXL 742		Slingsby T.43 Skylark 3	1030		6.56	M.Chalmers & Ptnrs	Kingston Deverill	14. 4.02
AXP 745	AXP	Slingsby T.41 Skylark 2	949		4.55	M.Sanderson	Milfield	16. 3.99
AXR 747	AXR	Slingsby T.41 Skylark 2	945		.56	Kilham	Crowland	31.3.00
AXU 750	AXU	Slingsby T.41 Skylark 2	944		3.55	M.A.Langhurst	Halesland	24. 6.95*
AXV 751		Slingsby T.26 Kite 2A	.		4.56	Not known (Refurbishing)	Booker	
AYD 759	AYD	Slingsby T.41 Skylark 2	1048		.56	B.Milburn	Currock Hill	17. 6.01
AYF 761	AYF	Slingsby T.43 Skylark 3B	1058		9.56	A.A.Jenkins	Hinton in the Hedges	26. 4.03
AYH 763	AYH	Slingsby T.43 Skylark 3B	1066		.56	A.D.Griffiths	Lyveden	8. 6.03
AYK 765		Slingsby T.21B	1080		.	Not known (Stored 2002)	RAF Keevil	
AYN 768		Slingsby T.41 Skylark 2	996			Not known (Stored)	NK	
AYY 778	33	Slingsby T.41 Skylark 2C	1073		.56	H.Johnson	Long Mynd	12. 6.96*
AZA 780	AZA	Slingsby T.42 Eagle 3	1085	RNGSA BGA.780	2-08	J.M.Crewe	Hinton-in-the-Hedges	23. 7.01

AZC	782	782	Slingsby T.21B	1096		5.57	C.Stachulla	(Augsberg)	28. 7.03
AZF	785		Slingsby T.30B Prefect	1100		.56	L.J.Smith tr The Prefect Syndicate RNAS Culdrose		26. 3.96*
AZK	789		Slingsby T.8 Tutor		VM650	6.57	Not known *(Stored 5.93)*	Croft, Skegness	7.90*
AZP	793	136	Slingsby T.41 Skylark 2	999		1.57	G.Dixon & Ptnr	Currock Hill	13. 8.97
AZQ	794	VM687	Slingsby T.8 Tutor		VM687	.57	J.M.Brookes	Strubby	7. 6.02
AZR	795	AZR	EoN AP.5 Olympia 2	EoN/O/101		7.58	Not known *(Under restoration)*	Syerston	28. 7.95*
AZT	797	AZT	EoN AP.5 Olympia 2	EoN/O/063	ZS-GCM	3.57	N.C.Kerr	Winthorpe	10. 8.02
AZX	801	AZX	Slingsby T.41 Skylark 2	995	BGA.1909	4.57	B.J.Griffin	Saltby	
					AGA.4/BGA.801		*(Under rebuild)*		
AZY	802	AZY	Slingsby T.41 Skylark 2	963		16. 4.57	A.J.Jackson	Burn	29. 6.97*
BAA	804	BAA	Slingsby T.8 Tutor	931	XE761	5.57	A.Chadwick *(Stored 6.02)*	RAF Keevil	9. 3.97*
					VM589		*(Note Cadet TX.1 as "BGA.804 ex VM589" @ Midland Air Museum, Coventry)*		
BAC	806		Slingsby T.43 Skylark 3B	1101	RNGSA CU19	6.58	M.Stokeld	Carlton Moor	27. 5.97
					BGA.806				
BAH	810	BAH	Slingsby T.41 Skylark 2	1104		7.58	B.Jackson	Cranfield	7. 9.97
BAL	813		Slingsby T.43 Skylark 3B	1111		11.57	S.G. Blair	Carlton Moor	28. 1.03
BAM	814	BAM	Slingsby T.41 Skylark 2	1108		1.58	B.H.Thwaites	Wormingford	2. 6.02
BAN	815		Slingsby T.30B Prefect	1120		1.58	J.S.Allison	RAF Halton	15. 5.00
BAV	822	BAV	Slingsby T.41 Skylark 2B	1113		2.58	M.H.Simms	Rattlesden	16. 4.02
BAW	823	BAW	Slingsby T.43 Skylark 3B	1126		2.58	G.E.Sarjeant	Halesland	.4. 9.03
BAY	825	BAY	Slingsby T.42B Eagle 3	1116		3.58	M.Lodge	Ringmer	15. 8.00
BAZ	826	BAZ	Slingsby T.41 Skylark 2	1112		3.58	W.Fuller	Currock Hill	17. 5.03
BBA	827	BBA	Slingsby T.41 Skylark 2	1128		3.58	M.Bosher	Winthorpe	1. 5.99
BBB	828	BBB	Slingsby T.42B Eagle 3	1118		4.58	I.K.Mitchell	North Hill	22.10.03
BBD	830		Slingsby T.42B Eagle 3	1119		6.58	D.Williams & M.Lodge *(Stored 12.02)*	Ringmer	
BBG	833		Slingsby T.8 Tutor	-	VW535	3. 9.57	R.H.Short	Husbands Bosworth	27. 7.03
BBH	834	BBH	EoN Olympia 2	EoN/O/041	BGA.539	8.57	J.W.Bonham	Cranfield	17. 6.99
BBP	840		Slingsby T.43 Skylark 3	1125		6.58	Not known *(Under repair 2000)*	NK	
BBQ	841	BBQ	Slingsby T.42B Eagle 3	1115		5.58	Eagle Syndicate	Milfield	5. 7.03
BBT	844	BBT	Slingsby T.43 Skylark 3B	1134	RAFGSA.234	.58	J.P.Gilbert	Wormingford	11. 5.02
					BGA.844				
BBU	845	BBU	Slingsby T.41 Skylark 2B	1135		.58	J.A.Timpany	Bicester	27. 6.03
BCB	852	TS291	Slingsby T.8 Tutor	----	TS291	2. 7.58	National Museums of Scotland/Museum of Flight	East Fortune	*
BCF	856		Slingsby T.21B	1		10.58	P.Underwood	Eaton Bray	*
			(Built Leighton Park School)				*(Stored 2000)*		
BCH	858	BCH	Slingsby T.8 Tutor	SSK/FF/489	VM547	9.58	N.James	Lyveden	13. 8.02
BCL	861	BCL	Slingsby T.43 Skylark 3B	1139		9.58	R.Aylett	Bidford	18. 5.96*
BCP	864	BCP	Slingsby T.43 Skylark 3B	1140		11.58	K.I.Latty	Milfield	13. 4.02
BCS	867	BCW	Slingsby T.43 Skylark 3B	1144		12.58	M.Wright & Ptnrs	Rattlesden	24. 3.01
BCU	869	2	Slingsby T.21B	1148		1.59	Not known *(Stored 2002)*	North Connel	*
BCV	870	BCV/155	Slingsby T.43 Skylark 3B	1195		4.59	W R Davis	Challock	15. 7.03
BCW	871	BCW	Slingsby T.43 Skylark 3B	1147		3.59	I.Tittensor	Bidford	15. 3.03
BCX	872		Slingsby T.41 Skylark 2B	1197		4.59	G W Haworth	Tibenham	20. 5.00
BCY	873	T45	Slingsby T.45 Swallow	1198		4.59	D.C.Unwin	Talgarth	16. 7.00
BDA	875		Slingsby T.21B	1205	AGA.7	6.59	W Grobkinsky	Dahlemer Binz, Germany	4. 7.02
					BGA.875				
BDF	880	BDF	Slingsby T.42B Eagle 3	1213		9.59	D.C.Phillips	Snitterfield	11. 7.03
BDM	886		Slingsby T.21B	1216		11.59	D.G.Cooper	Wormingford	15. 7.98
BDR	890	BDR	Slingsby T.45 Swallow	1243		6.60	R.J.Shallcrass	Challock	18. 5.03
BDW	895		Slingsby T.8 Tutor TX.2	---	VM637	4.59	R.Patrick & Ptnrs	Winthorpe	6.93*
							(On rebuild 1.96: probably to be VM637)		
BDX	896	BDX	Slingsby T.41 Skylark 2	CH.095/1		6.59	H D Maddams	Wormingford	17. 4.03
			(Built C Hurst)						
BEA	899	BEA	Slingsby T.41 Skylark 2	1194		7.59	M.L.Ryan	RAF Keevil	25.12.01
BED	902		Slingsby T.12 Gull I	---		15. 5.59	National Museums of Scotland/Museum of Flight	East Fortune	
BEF	904	BEF	Slingsby T.8 Tutor	---	(ex RAF)	10.59	D.Chaplin	Sutton Bank	2. 5.96*
			(Frame No.SSK/FF 934)				*(Tutor Syndicate)*		
BEL	909	BEL	EoN AP.5 Olympia 2B	EoN/O/126		12.59	J.G.Gilbert & Ptnrs	Wormingford	24.11.02
BEM	910		Slingsby T.45 Swallow	1221		5. 2.60	D. Wood	Kingston Deverill	24. 7.03
BER	914	BER	Slingsby T.43 Skylark 3B	1225		3.60	K.V.Payne	Llantisilio	3. 2.99
BET	916	600	Slingsby T.43 Skylark 3B	1227		3.60	A.C.Robertson & Ptnrs	Feshiebridge	31. 5.98
BEX	920	BEX	Slingsby T.43 Skylark 3F	1229		4.60	S. Barber	Rivar Hill	27. 9.03
BEY	921	BEY	Slingsby T.45 Swallow	1230		4.60	G.P.Hayes	Kenley	1. 6.03
BEZ	922	BEZ	Slingsby T.43 Skylark 3F	1232		4.60	R.G.Gillow	Perranporth	31. 3.03
BFB	924		Slingsby T.45 Swallow	1235		5.60	Essex & Suffolk GC	North Weald	16. 6.01
							(Crashed at Ridgewell 18.6.00)		
BFC	925	BFC	Slingsby T.43 Skylark 3F	1239		20. 5.60	Strathclyde GC	Strathaven	.9. 4.03
BFD	926		Slingsby T.21B	1240	RAFGSA	5.60	B.Jaessing	(Hamburg)	26. 7.96*
					BGA.926				
BFE	927	BFE	Slingsby T.43 Skylark 3F	1244		6.60	Essex Skylark Gliding Syndicate (I.F.Barnes)	North Weald	.4. 6.03
BFG	929	BFG	Slingsby T.43 Skylark 3F	1245		8. 7.60	T.J.Wilkinson	Sackville Lodge, Riseley	15. 6.02
BFL	933	BFL	Slingsby T.41 Skylark 2B	1249		5.60	D G Coats	Milfield	31. 8.99
BFN	935		EoN AP.5 Olympia 2B	EoN/O/125		2. 3.60	Not known *(Being refurbished during 2000)*	NK	
BFP	936		Schleicher Ka7 Rhönadler	702/60		5.60	Dartmoor GC	Brent Tor	28. 4.96*
							(Damaged Brent Tor 15.11.95)		
BFS	939		SZD-8ter-ZO Jaskolka	235		3.60	Not known *(Stored during 2002; damaged by fire)*	NK	
BFY	945	BFY	Slingsby T.21B	1251	RAFGGA.515	9.60	D.M.Hayes & Ptnrs	Sutton Bank	29. 9.03
					RAFGSA.286/BGA.945				

BGB	948		Slingsby T.21B (Robin EC-33)	1274	RAFGSA.282 BGA.948	11.60	Shenington GC (Stored 6.00)	Edgehill	9.12.97
BGD	950	BGD	Slingsby T.43 Skylark 3F	1276		26.11.60	Essex University GC	Wormingford	9. 8.99
BGG	953		Slingsby T.21B	1294		12.60	West Wales Gliding Trust	Templeton	31. 3.98
BGH	954	BGH	Slingsby T.43 Skylark 3F	1295		12.60	Denbigh GC (Written-off Denbigh 8.1.00)	Lleweni Parc	23. 5.00
BGL	957	BGL	Slingsby T.43 Skylark 3F	1296		3.61	C.Willey & Ptnrs	Perranporth	11. 7.02
BGP	960	BGP	Slingsby T.21B	1297	RAFGSA.283 BGA.960	1.61	Bannerdown GC	RAF Keevil	29. 6.02
BGR	962	BGR	EoN AP.5 Olympia 2B	EoN/O/124		6.60	M.H.Gagg	RAF Cosford	5. 1.00
BGS	963		Grunau Baby II		RAFGSA RNGSA 1-14	19. 6.60	Not known (Stored during 2000 – previously reported sold as N20GB)	NK	
BGT	964		DFS/30 Kranich II (Built AB Flygplan)	087	SE-STF Fv.8226	29.10.6	C.Wills	Booker	.9. 7.03
BGX	968		EoN AP.5 Olympia 2	EoN/O/123	(BGA.892)	8.60	C.Kaminski	Eaglescott	7. 7.97*
BHC	973	BHC	EoN AP.5 Olympia 2B	EoN/O/138		1.61	M.Pedwell (Damaged beyond repair in hangar)	Bidford	15. 5.01
BHQ	985	760	Slingsby T.43 Skylark 3F	1304		4.61	R.Furness	Cranfield	1. 5.96*
BHS	987		Slingsby T.43 Skylark 3F	1305	RAFGSA293 BGA.987		Not known (Under repair during 2000)	NK	
BHT	988	BHT	Slingsby T.43 Skylark 3F	1306		4.61	K.Chichester & Ptnrs	Hinton in the Hedges	13. 5.02
BHV	990	BHV	Slingsby T.45 Swallow	1308	NEJSGSA.4 BGA.990	4.61	M.G.Dawson	Spilsby	27. 3.01
BHY	993		Slingsby T.31B	1292	Pakistan AF	5.61	Not known (Stored 2000)	NK	
BJB	996	BJB	Slingsby T.43 Skylark 3F (Built Jones, Pentelow & Saint)	SSK/JPS/1		4.61	R.A.Mills	Turweston	21. 7.03
BJC	997	BJC	EoN AP.5 Olympia 2B	EoN/O/135		4.61	P.J.Devey	Lyveden	.4. 8.03
BJD	998		SZD-9 bis Bocian 1D	P-391		5.61	D.L.Martlew (Bocian Syndicate)	Lasham	11. 6.03
BJF	1000	BJF	Slingsby T.21B	1309		6.61	Sedbergh Syndicate	Wormingford	18. 7.03
BJK	1004		Slingsby T.43 Skylark 3F	1311		7.61	D.A.Wiseman & Ptnrs	Andreas	20. 7.03
BJP	1008	BJP	Slingsby T.45 Swallow	1316		9.61	G. Winch	Stow Maries	.6. 4.03
BJQ	1009	BJQ	Slingsby T.49A Capstan	1314		NK	L.A. Glover & Ptnrs	Husbands Bosworth	27. 5.03
BJV	1014		Slingsby T.21B	556	SE-SHK	1.62	National Museums of Scotland/Museum of Flight	East Fortune	*
BJW	1015	198	Slingsby T.43 Skylark 3G	1321		3.62	J.B.Strzebrakowski (Written-off Melton Mowbray 16.04.00)	Lyveden	31. 3.01
BJY	1017	BJY	Slingsby T.45 Swallow	1324		3.62	D.A.Wiseman	Andreas	29. 9.03
BJZ	1018		Slingsby T.45 Swallow	1325		3.62	J.P.Marshall	North Connel	20.11.96*
BKA	1019	BKA	Slingsby T.50 Skylark 4	1326	EI-117 BGA.1019	28. 5.62	Staffordshire GC	Seighford	17. 7.03
BKC	1021	BKC	DFS 108-68 Weihe (Built AB Flygindustri)	231	SE-SNE Fv.8312	4.61	B.Briggs	RAF Cranwell	24. 2.03
BKE	1023	BKE	Slingsby T.43 Skylark 3F (Built C Ross)	1715/CR/1		13. 7.61	D.H.Clack	Kingston Deverill	.8. 5.03
BKJ	1027	BKJ	Schleicher Ka6CR	565/59	9G-AAR	7.61	P.M.Hogan	Sandhill Farm, Shrivenham	15. 4.02
BKK	1028		EoN AP.5 Olympia 2	EoN/O/139	RNGSA.CU11 BGA.1028	7.61	J.Bradley	Thruxton	24. 7.99
BKL	1029	BKL	EoN AP.5 Olympia 2B	EoN/O/134		6.61	J.S.Orr	Lasham	20. 5.02
BKN	1031	BKN	Schleicher Ka7 Rhönadler	1091/61		9.61	East Sussex GC	Ringmer	11. 8.01
BKP	1032	BKP	Slingsby T.45 Swallow	1203		10.61	E.Traynor	Easterton	9. 5.02
BKS	1035	BKS	EoN AP.5 Olympia 2B	EoN/O/144		11.61	N W Woodward	Booker	14. 6.03
BKU	1037	BKU	EoN AP.5 Olympia 2B	EoN/O/153		1.62	D.N.MacKay	Aboyne	29. 4.03
BKW	1039	BKW	Schleicher Ka6 Rhönsegler	295	OH-RSA	10.62	I.M.Hembling	Rattlesden	2. 5.01
BKX	1040	BKX	EoN AP.5 Olympia 2B	EoN/O/148		3.62	D.J.Allibone	Gallows Hill	22. 6.03
BLA	1043	327	Slingsby T.50 Skylark 4	1331		5.62	I.A.Masterton	Portmoak	15. 5.00
BLE	1047	BLE	Slingsby T.50 Skylark 4	1335	RNGSA 1-228 BGA.1047	6.62	S.Frank	Easterton	29. 3.03
BLH	1050	BLH	Slingsby T.50 Skylark 4	1338	RAFGSA BGA.1050	7.62	M.D.Cohler	Rufforth	25. 9.02
BLJ	1051	BLJ	EoN AP.6 Olympia 419X	EoN/4/009		3.62	G.Balshaw & Ptnrs "Big Bird"	Lleweni Parc	10.10.96*
BLK	1052	67	EoN AP.6 Olympia 419X	EoN/4/007	G-APSX	4.62	C.J.Abbott & Ptnrs	Long Mynd	17. 7.03
BLN	1055	BLN	EoN AP.5 Olympia 2B	EoN/O/152		5.62	M.R.Derwent	RAF Cranwell	.5. 4.03
BLP	1056		EoN AP.5 Olympia 2B	EoN/O/149		3.62	D.Birtwhistle & Ptnrs (Being refurbished during 2000)	Chipping	25. 5.95*
BLQ	1057		EoN AP.5 Olympia 2 Special	EoN/O/042	RAFGSA 145 BGA.540	7.62	R.J.McAdam	Winthorpe	14. 5.03
BLS	1059		EoN AP.5 Olympia 2B (EoN rebuild of BGA.897 [EoN/O/128])	EoN/O/151		7.62	D.J.Wilson	Seighford	26. 4.03
BLU	1061		Slingsby T.45 Swallow	1340		7.62	J.M. Brookes	Strubby	.6. 8.03
BLW	1063	BLW	Slingsby T.50 Skylark 4	1342		8.62	S.R.A.Trusler	Weston-on-the-Green	19. 6.03
BLZ	1066		Slingsby T.50 Skylark 4	1346		11.62	R.M Lambert	Feshie Bridge	19. 5.03
BML	1077		Slingsby T.45 Swallow	1328		6.62	Dartmoor GS	Burnford Common	9. 7.97*
BMM	1078		SZD-9bis Bocian 1	P-397		8.99	D.R.Wilcox	Crowland	20. 7.03
BMQ	1081	BMQ	Slingsby T.21B	1351		11.62	W.Masterton	(Jamaica)	16.12.02
BMU	1085		Slingsby T.21B (T) (Rotax 503)	1355	9G-ABD BGA.1085	12.62	D.Woolerton & Ptnrs "Spruce Goose" (Noted dismantled 7.02)	North Coates	27. 9.97
BMW	1087	BMW	Slingsby T.50 Skylark 4	1357		12.62	M.Williams	RAF Halton	13.11.02
BMX	1088	739	Slingsby T.50 Skylark 4	1358	RAFGSA.308 BGA.1088	1.63	R.O.Linee (739 Syndicate)	Kingston Deverill	.4. 5.03
BMY	1089	163	Slingsby T.50 Skylark 4	1361		1.63	N.Dickenson	Chipping	7. 4.98
BNA	1091		Shenstone Harbinger Mk.2	1		12.62	S.Edyvean	Winthorpe	.5. 4.03

BNC	1093		DFS 108-68 Weihe	1	SE-SHU	3.63	K.S.Green	Lasham	22. 9.02
			(Built AB Kockums Flygindustri)						
BND	1094	BND	Schleicher Ka6CR	1157		3.63	K.Alan & ptnrs.	Saltby	27. 8.03
BNE	1095	BNE	Slingsby T.50 Skylark 4	1375		4.63	T.Davies	Usk	15. 8.03
BNH	1098	BNH	Schleicher Ka6CR	6115		3.63	Bath, Wilts & North Dorset GC	Kingston Deverill	14. 4.03
BNK	1100	BNK	Slingsby T.50 Skylark 4	1362		2.63	E.D.Weekes & Ptnrs	Weston-on-the-Green	10. 3.03
BNM	1102		Slingsby T.50 Skylark 4	1367		3.63	D.Hertzburg	North Weald	.1. 2.03
							(Reported as BMN)		
BNN	1103	BNN	Slingsby T.50 Skylark 4	1366		3.63	J R Robinson	Pocklington	6.12.98
BNP	1104	653	Slingsby T.50 Skylark 4	1368		3.63	A.R.Worters	North Connel	22. 7.01
BNQ	1105	BNQ	Slingsby T.50 Skylark 4	1369		3.63	R Pye	North Connel	29. 4.00
BNR	1106	BNR	Slingsby T.49B Capstan	1370		8.63	C.M.Hurst	Gransden Lodge	.2. 3.03
BNS	1107	XS652	Slingsby T.45 Swallow	1373	XS652 BGA.1107	20. 3.63	York GC Swallow Syndicate	Rufforth	30. 6.02
BNU	1109		Slingsby T.45 Swallow	1377		5.63	P.Cammish	Sutton Bank	15. 6.02
BPA	1115	BPA	Slingsby T.50 Skylark 4	1383		5.63	D.Penney	Lasham	17. 2.02
BPB	1116	255	Slingsby T.50 Skylark 4	1384	RNGSA BGA.1116	6.63	G. Robertson	Lasham	13. 4.03
BPC	1117	BPC	Slingsby T.50 Skylark 4	1389		7.63	J.L.Grayer & Ptnr	Ringmer	.5. 5.03
BPD	1118	N55	Slingsby T.49B Capstan	1390		22. 7.63	Culdrose GC	RNAS Culdrose	30. 3.03
BPE	1119	BPE	Slingsby T.50 Skylark 4	1391		6.63	D.H.Scales	Currock Hill	25. 5.03
BPG	1121	741	Slingsby T.50 Skylark 4	1393		7.63	R.M.Neill & Ptnrs	Long Mynd	21. 5.03
BPJ	1123	809	Slingsby T.50 Skylark 4	1360		4.63	M.Cooper *(Damaged Challock 26.3.97)*	Challock	6. 3.98*
BPK	1124	BPK	Slingsby T.50 Skylark 4	1381		6.63	D.Crowhurst	Crowland	14. 8.02
BPL	1125	BPL	EoN AP.5 Olympia 2B	EoN/O/136	G-APXC	6.63	D.Harris & Ptnrs *(Stored)*	(Essex)	19. 5.97*
BPN	1127		Oberlerchner Standard Austria	003	OE-0496	6.63	R.K.Avery & Ptnrs	Eaglescott	10. 6.03
BPS	1131		Slingsby T.49B Capstan	1399		9.63	Capstan Gliding Group	Aboyne	18. 4.03
BPT	1132		Slingsby T.49B Capstan	1400		10.63	J.E.Neville *(Stored 2002)*	Laurencekirk	11. 2.95*
BPU	1133		Slingsby T.49B Capstan	1402		11.63	I.T.Godfrey	Dunstable	17. 3.98
							tr Capstan Syndicate *(Under repair)*		
BPV	1134	BPV	Slingsby T.49B Capstan	1404		20.12.63	G.L.Barrett	Weston on the Green	22. 9.03
BPW	1135		Slingsby T.49B Capstan	1408		1.64	Ulster GC	Bellarena	6. 6.02
BPX	1136	859	Slingsby T.45 Swallow	1397	XS859 BGA.1136	1. 1.64	F.Pape & Ptnrs	Rufforth	5. 7.98
BPZ	1138	BPZ	Slingsby T.50 Skylark	41406		3.64	A.Pattermore & Ptnrs	Old Sarum	10. 7.00
BQA	1139		Slingsby T.51 Dart 15	1421		4.64	*(Stored RAF Odiham 2000; being refurbished)*		
BQE	1143	RA905	Slingsby T.7 Cadet	RAFGSA.273	RA905	8.63	M.L.Beach	Aston Down	14. 3.00
BQF	1144	1	Slingsby T.21B	1168	XN189	10.63	Connel GC	North Connel	13. 4.02
BQJ	1147		DFS/30 Kranich II	821	RAFGSA.215	11.63	M.C.Russell	Bishops Stortford	*
			(Built Schleicher)				*(As "D-11-3224") (Stored 3.96)*		
BQK	1148	BQK	Schleicher Ka7 Rhönadler	7120		12.63	R.B Armitage *(Damaged 21.8.95)*Waldershare Park		21. 6.96*
BQL	1149		Schleicher Ka6CR	725/60	D-7117	12.63	R.O.Toop	Eaglescott	15. 7.00
BQM	1150	BQM	EoN AP.10 460 Srs.1B	EoN/S/002	RAFGSA.276	12.63	A.Duncan	Portmoak	5. 6.01
BQP	1152	BQP	Slingsby T.30B Prefect	646	RAFGSA.159	9.99	A.Downie	Dunstable	9. 9.00
BQQ	1153		EoN AP.5 Olympia 2B	EoN/0/121	RAFGSA.244	2.64	P.R.Brinson	Nympsfield	18. 4.03
			(Rebuilt 1993 using wings from BGA.678)				"Dopey"		
BQS	1155	BQS	EoN AP.10 460 Srs.1	EoN/S/008		3.64	P.Williams	Bidford	6. 4.97*
BQT	1156	BQT	EoN AP.10 460 Srs.1	EoN/S/007	BGA.2666 AGA.6/BGA.1156	26. 1.64	J.H.May	Manchester	18. 4.97*
							(On display Museum of Science & Industry 3.01)		
BQU	1157	BQU	Schleicher Ka7 Rhönadler	7141	RNGSA AR66 BGA.1157	4.64	A.J.Pellatt	Llantisilio	1. 4.03
BQZ	1162	BQZ	Slingsby T.50 Skylark 4	1416		4.64	G.Colledge	Edgehill	3. 8.02
BRA	1163	BRA	Slingsby T.49B Capstan	1417		4.64	K.R.Brown	Nympsfield	29. 5.03
BRB	1164	T51	Slingsby T.51 Dart 15	1423	RAFGSA.334 BGA.1164	4.64	M.Sansom	North Hill	27. 2.03
BRC	1165	BRC	Slingsby T.45 Swallow 1	1407		5.64	J.R.Smalley	Kirton-in-Lindsey	26. 3.03
BRD	1166	BRD	Slingsby T.51 Dart 15	1425	RAFGSA.335 BGA.1166	5.64	V.Day	Lyveden	6. 5.02
BRE	1167		Slingsby T.45 Swallow 2	1415		5.64	A.Swannock & Ptnrs	Gamston	19. 5.01
BRG	1169		Slingsby T.45 Swallow	1410		5.64	A.W.F.Edwards	Gransden Lodge	7. 6.03
BRH	1170		EoN AP.5 Olympia 2B	EoN/O/154		3.64	A.Shallcrass *(For refurbishment)*	Challock	
BRK	1172	243	EoN AP.10 460 Standard Srs.1A	EoN/S/001	G-APWL	4.99	D.G.Andrew	Eaglescott	26. 4.00
					BGA.1172/G-APWL/RAFGSA.268/G-APWL *(Restored as G-APWL 10.02)*				
BRL	1173		EoN AP.5 Olympia 2B	EoN/O/132		NK	A.Cutts & Ptnrs	Ridgewell	27. 3.99
BRM	1174	BRM	Schleicher Ka7 Rhönadler	776/60	D-4635	5.64	D.S.Driver	Currock Hill	4. 5.03
BRQ	1177	BRQ	EoN AP.10 460 Srs.1C	EoN/S/003	G-ARFU	6.64	J.Steel & Ptnrs *(Stored 2002)*	Falgunzeon	4. 8.96*
BRT	1180		Slingsby T.51 Dart 15	1430		6.64	H.E.Birch & Ptnrs	AAC Dishforth	5. 5.01
BRU	1181	BRU	Slingsby T.51 Dart 15	1429		6.64	G.M.Polkinghorne	Currock Hill	16. 8.03
BRW	1183	BRW	Slingsby T.49B Capstan	1413		6.64	A.West & Ptnrs	Lasham	22.11.03
BRY	1185	BRY	Slingsby T.51 Dart 15	1434		7.64	S.R.Wilkinson & Ptnrs	Kirton-in-Lindsey	23. 5.03
BSA	1187	BSA	Slingsby T.51 Dart 15	1405		7.64	N G Oultram	Seighford	12. 7.01
BSC	1189	H23	Slingsby T.50 Skylark 4	1422		8.64	A.Etchells	Bidford	10. 2.03
BSE	1191	BSE	Slingsby T.49B Capstan	1414		9.64	D.A Bullock	Bicester	9. 4.03
BSG	1193	BSG	Slingsby T.50 Skylark 4	1436		9.64	Denbigh GC	Llantisilio	22. 7.01
BSH	1194	BSH	Slingsby T.50 Skylark 4	1444		11.64	M Mathieson	Wormingford	14. 7.99
BSK	1196	BSK	Slingsby T.49B Capstan	1418		10.64	Kermit Syndicate	Lleweni Parc	17. 4.00
BSL	1197	BSL	Slingsby T.51 Dart 17	1445		10.64	C.J.Owles	Tibenham	26. 7.03
BSM	1198	597	Slingsby T.51 Dart 15	1439		10.64	D. Tait	Camphill	3. 5.03
BSQ	1201	463	EoN AP.10 460 Srs.1	EoN/S/014		5.64	K.G.Ashford	Husbands Bosworth	5. 8.02
BSR	1202	BSR	Slingsby T.50 Skylark 4	1443		12.64	D.Johnstone	Rattlesden	31. 5.03
BSS	1203	T49	Slingsby T.49B Capstan	1449		12.64	Black Mountains GC	Talgarth	17. 8.03

BST	1204		Slingsby T.49 Capstan	1451		1.65	P H Pickett	Snitterfield	24. 4.03
BSV	1206	BSV	Slingsby T.51 Dart 15	1454		7.65	G.G.Butler	Snitterfield	11. 2.97*
BSW	1207	BSW	Slingsby T.51 Dart 15	1459		2.65	B.L.Owen	Tibenham	19. 8.01
BSX	1208	BSX	Slingsby T.45 Swallow	1461	OO-ZWC	4.65	P.Brownlow & Ptnrs	Sackville Lodge, Riseley	30. 5.01
					F-OTAN-C5/BGA.1208				
BSY	1209	BSY	Slingsby T.50 Skylark 4	1448		4.65	G B Dennis	Nympsfield	9. 2.00
BSZ	1210	BSZ	Slingsby T.50 Skylark 4	1460		4.65	J.Farley	Lleweni Parc	18. 5.02
BTA	1211	BTA	Slingsby T.45 Swallow	1473		6.65	M.Morley	RAF Odiham	26. 8.01
BTD	1214	BTD	DFS/49 Grunau Baby 2C	?	(ex RAFGSA)	8.64	Bidford Gliding Centre	Bidford	14. 5.97*
BTE	1215		Slingsby T.21B	557	OH-KSA	1.65	Not known	NK	
					SE-SHL		*(Stored)*		
BTG	1217	BTG	EoN AP.10 460 Srs.1	EoN/S/024		2.65	J.Libell	Strubby	19. 3.02
BTH	1218	WB981/	Slingsby T.21B	JHB/2		3.65	P.Gilmore	Aston Down	2. 9.03
		BTH	*(Built J.Hulme) (Restored 1995 with wings from BGA.3238/WB981)*						
BTJ	1219	BTJ	Schleicher Ka6CR	6367		3.65	D.Keith	Kingston Deverill	3.10.03
BTK	1220	BTK	Slingsby T.50 Skylark 4	1364	SE-SZW	3.65	J.M.Hall	Llantisilio	27. 8.03
BTM	1222	211	Schleicher Ka6CR	6174		3.65	P.D.Maller	Aston Down	6. 1.03
BTN	1223	BTN	EoN AP.10 460 Srs.1	EoN/S/022	AGA.15	4.65	S.C.Thompson	Parham Park	17. 6.03
					BGA.1223				
BTQ	1225	BTQ	EoN AP.10 460 Srs.1	EoN/S/029		4.65	P.L.Storey	Burn	18.10.03
BTV	1230		DFS/68 Weihe	000358	RAFGGA	7. 5.65	B.Briggs *(Being refurbished)*	RAF Cranwell	23. 5.93*
BUC	1237	BUC	Slingsby T.49B Capstan	1472		6.65	Lakes GC	Walney Island	19. 8.03
BUE	1239	BUE	Slingsby T.50 Skylark 4	1468		7.65	I.H.Davies	Seighford	14. 3.03
BUF	1240	366	Slingsby T.51 Dart 17R	1469		7.65	C.H.Brown & Ptnrs	Chipping	16. 3.03
BUG	1241	BUG	EoN AP.10 460 Srs.1	EoN/S/028		5.65	A.Rowson & Ptnrs	Long Mynd	5. 3.97*
BUH	1242		EoN AP.10 460 Srs.1	EoN/S/021	G-ASMP	.65	A.E.Lawrence	Sackville Lodge, Riseley	19. 5.96*
			(Damaged Gransden Lodge 29. 6.95)						
BUK	1244		EoN AP.10 460 Srs.1	EoN/S/027		5.65	M.Hodgson	Booker	28. 6.97*
BUL	1245	BUL	Slingsby T.51 Dart 17R	1470		7.65	A.Parrish & Ptnr	Lyveden	17.12.02
BUP	1247	837	Slingsby T.51 Dart 17R	1478		9.65	D.S.Carter	Enstone	10. 6.99
BUR	1249	BUR	Slingsby T.49B Capstan	1482		11.65	Denbigh GC	Llantisilio	8. 7.00
BUT	1251	BUT	Slingsby T.43 Skylark 3F	VRT.1		7.65	I.Bannister tr Sky Syndicate	Chipping	29. 4.03
			(Built V.R.Tull & Ptnrs)						
BUV	1253		EoN AP.10 460 Srs.1	EoN/S/030		7.65	S.H.Gibson	Gransden Lodge	26. 6.03
BUW	1254	BUW	Slingsby T.21B	?	RAFGSA.242	8.65	J.N.Wardle *"Lucy"*	Lasham	19. 9.00
BUZ	1257	BUZ	Schleicher Ka6CR	6418		8.65	R.Leacroft	Lyveden	29.12.02
BVB	1259	BVB	Schleicher Ka7 Rhönadler	7230	RAFGSA R75	9.65	York Gliding Centre	Rufforth	7. 3.03
			(Modified to ASK 13 standard)		BGA1259				
BVE	1262	61	Slingsby T.51 Dart 17R	1483		11.65	P.Leach & Ptnr	Sandhill Farm, Shrivenham	2. 9.01
BVF	1263	BVF	Slingsby T.45 Swallow	1481		11.65	Pershore Flying Club	Bidford	13. 8.03
BVH	1265	BVH	Slingsby T.51 Dart 17R	1485		12.65	D.J.Simpson	Halesland	6. 7.03
BVJ	1266	BVJ	Slingsby T.51 Dart 17R	1486		1.66	R.& M.Weaver	Usk	3. 1.03
BVL	1268	404	Slingsby T.51 Dart 15	1487		1.66	D.Stabler & Ptnrs	Tibenham	16. 8.99
BVM	1269	150	Slingsby T.51 Dart 17R	1492		1.66	N.H.Ponsford *(Stored 12.99)*	(Breighton)	5.89*
BVN	1270		EoN AP.10 460 Srs.1	EoN/S/023		3.65	F J Clarke & Ptnrs	North Hill	25. 9.02
BVR	1273	BVR	Schleicher Ka6CR	6441		5.10.65	R.C Cannon & Ptnrs	Lasham	11. 3.03
BVS	1274		SZD-9 bis Bocian 1D	F-831			Spilsby Soaring	Spilsby	28. 7.01
BVW	1278		EoN AP.6 Olympia 403	EoN/4/001	RAFGSA.306	8.65	J.B. & K.D.Dumville	Camphill	29. 5.01
					G-APEW				
BVX	1279	BVX	Schleicher Ka6CR	6439		10.65	C.G.Stoves	Burn	9.10.03
BVY	1280	BVY	LET L-13 Blanik	173121		17.10.65	Strathclyde GC	Strathaven	9. 3.03
BVZ	1281		Schleicher Ka6CR	6446		10.65	L.Blair	Bellarena	13. 6.03
BWB	1283	B96	EoN AP.10 460 Srs.1	EoN/S/036		12.65	S Metcalfe	Tibenham	17.12.03
BWC	1284	BWC	Schleicher Ka6CR	6449		12.65	M.E.Hazlewood	Lasham	20. 7.03
BWE	1286	BWE	EoN AP.10 460 Srs.2	EoN/S/035		12.65	C.Hughes	Nympsfield	1. 8.03
BWG	1288	465	EoN AP.10 465 Srs.2	EoN/S/038		7.12.65	K.S.Green & Ptnr *(Being refurbished)*	Lasham	27. 4.97*
BWJ	1290	377	Slingsby T.51 Dart 17R	1495		2.66	D.Godfrey & Ptnrs	Edgehill	8.10.02
BWK	1291		Slingsby T.45 Swallow	1493		2.66	K.Hubbard & Ptnrs	North Hill	5. 6.03
BWM	1293	18	Slingsby T.51 Dart 17R	1500		4.66	P.L. & L.E.Poole	Lasham	12. 5.03
BWP	1295	861	Slingsby T.51 Dart 17R	1501		3.66	D Champion	Parham Park	9. 3.03
BWQ	1296	BWQ	Slingsby T.51 Dart 15	1505		3.66	C.Uncles	Halesland	14. 6.03
BWS	1298	517	Slingsby T.51 Dart 17R	1502		4.66	R.D.Broom & E.A.Chalk	Hinton-in-the-Hedges	13. 5.02
BWT	1299	163	Slingsby T.51 Dart 15R	1508		4.66	R.Parker *(Stored)*	AAC Dishforth	29. 8.96*
BWU	1300		EoN AP.10 460 Srs.11	EoN/S/034		1.66	P.W.Berridge	Ridgewell	18. 6.03
BWX	1303		EoN AP.5 Olympia 2B	101		2.66	P.Kent *(Built from spares)*	Seighford	13. 9.03
BXB	1307		EoN AP.10 460 Srs.1	EoN/S/040		3.66	J.M.Lee	Parham Park	30.10.02
BXC	1308	BXC/781	EoN AP.10 460 Srs.1	EoN/S/006		4.66	D.D.Copeland	Dunstable	15. 4.96*
BXE	1310	BXE	Slingsby T.51 Dart 15R	1509		5.66	M.P.Holburn	Currock Hill	23.10.02
BXG	1312	686	Slingsby T.51 Dart 17R	1512		5.66	B.W.Compton	Usk	5. 3.03
BXH	1313		Slingsby T.51 Dart 17R	1516		6.66	S.A.Stokes	Usk	23. 3.03
BXK	1315		Slingsby T.21B	1510		6.66	Not known	Rufforth	*
			(Damaged Falgunzeon 18.5.80; being refurbished 2000)						
BXL	1316	121	Slingsby T.51 Dart 17R	1517		6.66	W.R.Longstaff & Ptnr	Feshiebridge	24. 5.98
BXM	1317	9	Slingsby T.51 Dart 17R	1521		7.66	P.R.Davie	Dunstable	20. 7.03
BXP	1319		Slingsby T.45 Swallow 2	1522		7.66	Carlton Moor GC	Carlton Moor	25.10.02
BXR	1321		LET L-13 Blanik	173301	G-ATPX	5.66	Not known *(Stored 7.98)*	Cranfield	12.92*
BXT	1323	BXT	Schleicher Ka6CR	6492		4.66	J.& A.Briggs	Tibenham	3. 1.03
BXV	1325	G-ATRA	LET L-13 Blanik	173304	G-ATRA	12. 5.66	Blanik Syndicate (P.Martin)	Husbands Bosworth	30. 1.03
BXW	1326	BXW	LET L-13 Blanik	173305	G-ATRB	16. 6.66	R Chapman	Bidford	27. 9.03
BXY	1328	BXY	EoN AP.10 460 Srs.1	EoN/S/042		6.66	G.K.Stanford	Brent Tor	26. 7.03
BYA	1330	BYA	Slingsby T.51 Dart 17R	1518		7.66	G.A.Chalmers	Easterton	29. 3.03

BYB	1331	352	Slingsby T.45 Swallow	1525		7.66	Surrey Hills GC		Kenley	8. 7.97*
BYC	1332	BYC	Slingsby T.51 Dart 17R	1526		8.66	D.J.Ireland	Sandhill Farm, Shrivenham		10. 4.03
BYE	1334	BYE	EoN AP.10 463 Srs.1	EoN/S/044		9.66	C.J.Bushell		Snitterfield	29. 4.01
BYG	1336	225	Slingsby T.51 Dart 17R	1535	RAFGSA BGA.1336	11.66	W.T.Emery		Rufforth	28. 4.03
BYJ	1338		Slingsby T.45 Swallow	1568		2.67	D.I.Johnstone tr Swallow Soaring Group		Strathaven	18.11.96*
BYK	1339		Slingsby T.45 Swallow	1566		1.67	G.E.Williams		Seighford	19. 9.02
BYL	1340		Schleicher Ka6CR	6517		7.66	D.Heaton		Llantisilio	21.11.03
BYM	1341	558	Schleicher Ka6CR	6518	RAFGSA.381 BGA.1341	7.66	K.S.Smith		Wormingford	12. 9.03
BYU	1348	350	Schleicher Ka6CR	6525	XW640 BGA.1348	9.66	R.N.John		Haylesland	15. 2.02
BYX	1351	BYX	Schleicher Ka6E	4055		12.66	J.Dent & D.B.Andrews		Chipping	13. 4.03
BYY	1352	BYY	Slingsby T.21B	628	RAFGSA.338 BGA.1352/WB967	11.66	T.Akerman		Bicester	28. 6.02
BZA	1354	BZA	Slingsby T.21B	1162	RAFGSA.318 XN183	11.66	A Hill		Bicester	16. 8.03
BZB	1355	BZB	EoN AP.10 460 Srs.1	EoN/S/047		10.66	D.C.Ratcliffe Syndicate		Parham Park	3. 5.03
BZC	1356	BZC	Slingsby T.51 Dart 17R	1563		2.67	A.N.Ely		Strubby	23. 9.02
BZF	1359	311	Slingsby T.51 Dart 17R	1570		3.67	P.C.Gill & Ptnrs		Ridgewell	1.10.03
BZG	1360	N54	Slingsby T.49B Capstan	1581		28. 4.67	Culdrose GC		RNAS Culdrose	11. 8.03
BZH	1361	406	Slingsby T.51 Dart 17R	1580		4.67	C.Long		Bidford	19.12.00
BZJ	1362	362	Slingsby T.51 Dart 17R	1567		4.67	D.M.Steed "Anastasia"		Enstone	13. 8.98
BZL	1364	BZL	Slingsby T.45 Swallow	1596		7.67	Cairngorm Swallow Syndicate		Feshiebridge	14. 8.00
BZM	1365		Slingsby T.45 Swallow	1597		7.67	F.Webster		Drumshade	22. 5.97*
BZP	1367	F4	SZD-24-4A Foka 4	W-301		1.67	I.K.Mitchell		North Hill	16. 3.03
BZQ	1368	453	Schleicher Ka6CR	6551		2.67	A.Holland		North Hill	24. 8.99
BZR	1369	471	EoN AP.10 460 Srs.1	EoN/S/049		2.67	G.Wardell		Camphill	6. 7.02
BZS	1370	BZS	EoN AP.10 460 Srs.1	EoN/S/052		2.67	R.Hutchinson		Carlton Moor	25. 4.97*
BZV	1373	BZV	EoN AP.10 460 Srs.1	EoN/S/046		2.67	I.F.Smith		Lasham	15. 7.02
BZW	1374	Z11	EoN AP.10 460 Srs.1	EoN/S/053		3.67	J.Bradley & Ptnrs		Lleweni Parc	12. 4.97*
							(De-registered 27.2.02 - to spares use at Lasham)			
BZX	1375		Schleicher Ka6CR		6571	3.67	Leeds University GC		Rufforth	15. 2.03
BZY	1376		Slingsby T.31B	SSK/FF1817	BGA.1175	3.67	A.L.Higgins		Dunstable	3. 5.03
			(Rebuild of BGA.1175)				tr The Blue Brick Syndicate			
BZZ	1377	77	SZD-24-4A Foka 4	W-308		3.67	M.Hudson & Ptnrs		Lasham	18. 5.03
CAB	1379	CAB	EoN AP.10 460 Srs.1	EoN/S/033	RAFGSA.344	3.67	P.Green & Ptnr		Enstone	21.10.98
CAC	1380	994	Schleicher Ka6E	4054		3.67	M. Burridge		Crowland	8. 3.03
CAE	1381	575	Schleicher Ka6E	4076		8. 4.67	D.Craven		Long Mynd	11. 4.03
CAF	1382		EoN AP.5 Olympia 2B	EoN/O/131	RAFGSA.254	5. 4.67	A.J.Davey	Kiel, Germany		27. 4.03
CAG	1383	715	Schleicher Ka6E	4080		4.67	S.L.Beaumont		Crowland	10. 6.03
CAK	1386	117	EoN AP.5 Olympia 2B	EoN/O/122	RAFGSA.246	3.67	P.Hatfield tr Olympia 2B Syndicate		Rufforth	28. 4.03
CAN	1389		EoN AP.10 460 Srs.1	EoN/S/050		3.67	I.L.Pattingdale		Booker	3. 5.03
CAQ	1391	812	Schempp-Hirth SHK	37		3.67	M.A.Thorne		Old Sarum	9. 7.03
CAR	1392	422	Schempp-Hirth SHK-1	40		4.67	P.Gentil & M.Gresty		Aston Down	24. 3.01
CAS	1393	372	Schleicher Ka6E	4029	RAFGSA.372	5.67	R.F.Tindall		Gransden Lodge	22. 8.02
CAT	1394	CAT	EoN AP.10 460 Srs.1	EoN/S/051		5.67	D.C.Phillips & Ptnrs		Snitterfield	2. 7.03
CAV	1396	CAV	Schleicher ASK13	13015		5.67	M.Cuming		Edgehill	3. 8.00
CAW	1397	357	LET L-13 Blanik	173202	RAFGSA.357 G-ASZK	5.67	Not known		Enstone	2.83*
							(Stored - spares use 6.96)			
CAX	1398	CAX	Slingsby T.45 Swallow	1598		7.67	G.M. Hicks		Waldershare Park	17. 8.02
CAZ	1400	702	Slingsby T.51 Dart 17WR	1611		7.68	J.M.Young & Ptnrs		Easterton	31. 5.98
CBA	1401	679	Slingsby T.51 Dart 17WR	1612		7.68	D.R.Bennett & P.H.Pickett		Snitterfield	19. 4.03
CBK	1410		Grunau Baby III	----	RAFGSA.378 D-4676	5. 9.67	N.H.Ponsford		Breighton	4.83*
			(Built Sfg.Schaffin)				_(Op Real Aeroplane Club)_ _(Stored 1.98)_			
CBM	1412	343	Schleicher Ka6CR	6607		7.67	R.H.Moss		Nympsfield	28. 2.03
CBN	1413	CBN	SZD-30 Pirat	W-320		5.67	B.C.Cooper		Portmoak	12.11.01
CBP	1414	CBP	SZD-24C Foka	W-198	OY-BXR	7.67	G.Sutton		Sutton Bank	18. 6.01
CBR	1416	CBR	Aeromere M.100S	044		7.67	G.Viglione		Rattlesden	21. 9.02
CBS	1417		EoN AP.5 Olympia 2B	EoN/O/143	RAFGSA.291	7.67	G.Moden & Ptnrs		Edgehill	4. 9.94*
			(Possibly kit-built - c/n incorrect - EoN/O/143 became BGA.1034 & sold to Zambia) _(Stored 6.95)_								
CBU	1419	905	Schempp-Hirth SHK-1	53	D-8441	17.10.67	M.J.Dodd		Shobdon	26.12.99
CBV	1420	362	EoN AP.10 460 Srs.1	EoN/S/055		6.67	J.Sharples & Ptnr		Burn	13.10.96*
CBW	1421	CBW	Schleicher ASK13	13034		8.67	Stratford-upon-Avon GC		Snitterfield	24. 1.03
CBY	1423	475	Schleicher Ka6CR	960	RAFGSA.322 D-3222	10.67	G.Martin		Chipping	27. 7.03
CCA	1425	CCA	Schleicher Ka6E	4126		10.67	R.K.Forrest		Feshiebridge	7.12.03
CCB	1426	CCB	Schempp-Hirth SHK-1	52		7.67	R.M.Johnson		Milfield	22. 9.03
CCC	1427		Schleicher ASK13	13035	RAFGSA.R83 BGA.1427	6.99	Shenington GC		Edgehill	18. 1.03
CCD	1428	373	Schleicher Ka6E	4127		12.67	M.H.Phelps		Husbands Bosworth	4. 4.03
CCE	1429	CCE	Schleicher ASK13	13047		12.67	Oxford GC		Weston-on-the-Green	5. 4.03
CCF	1430	CCF	Schleicher ASK13	13042		12.67	Norfolk GC		Tibenham	27. 2.03
CCG	1431		Schleicher Ka6E	4125		12.67	G.A.Fudge		Thame	21. 6.02
CCJ	1433	878	Schleicher Ka6CR	6145	RAFGSA.323	10.67	P.Green		Weston-on-the-Green	8. 4.99
CCL	1435	47	Schleicher Ka6E	4129		3.68	M.T.Stanley		Sutton Bank	9. 1.03
CCM	1436	CCM	Schleicher ASK13	13053		2.68	Burn GC		Burn	23. 4.03
CCN	1437	CCN	SZD-9 bis Bocian 1E	P-431		3.68	South London Gliding Centre		Kenley	26. 4.00
CCP	1438	L99	Schleicher ASK13	13052		2.68	DRA GC		RAF Odiham	1.2.03
CCR	1440	CCR	Schleicher Ka6E	4149		2.68	A. Shaw		Enstone	2. 3.03
CCS	1441	CCS	Slingsby T.41 Skylark	21008	PH-230	3.68	S.L.Benn		Cranwell	28.5.03

Reg	No	Code	Type	S/n	Prev id	Date	Owner	Location	Date
CCT	1442	CCT	Schleicher ASK13	13057		3.68	Stratford-upon-Avon GC	Snitterfield	
17.12.02									
CCU	1443	CCU	Schleicher Ka6E	4122		3.68	D.C.Findlay	RAF Keevil	20. 4.03
CCV	1444		Schleicher Ka6E	4160		3.68	C.J.Nicholas	Ridgewell	17. 7.03
CCW	1445	CCW	Schleicher ASK13	13051		3.68	J E.Hart & Ptnrs	Sutton Bank	16. 2.03
CCX	1446	CCX	Schleicher ASK13	13054		3.68	Trent Valley GC	Kirton-in-Lindsey	16. 4.03
CCY	1447	CCY	Schleicher ASK13	13050		3.68	Devon & Somerset GC	North Hill	11. 3.03
CCZ	1448	CCZ	Schleicher ASK13	13070		3.68	Trent Valley GC	Kirton-in-Lindsey	2. 9.03
CDA	1449		Schleicher Ka6E	4136		3.68	F.T.Bick & Ptnrs	Aboyne	3. 5.03
CDB	1450		Schleicher Ka6E	4137		3.68	K.L.Holburn	Currock Hill	23.10.02
CDC	1451	CDC	Schleicher K8B	8743		3.68	Enstone Eagle GC (Stored 7.01)	Rivar Hill	15. 3.99
CDD	1452		Schleicher Ka6E	4165		3.68	D.T.Staff	Booker	29. 3.99
CDF	1454	683	Schleicher Ka6E	4162		3.68	J.Reid & Ptnrs	Rivar Hill	12. 5.03
CDG	1455		FFA Diamant 18	35		3.68	J.A.Luck	Cranfield	7. 4.02
CDH	1456	619	Schempp-Hirth HS.2 Cirrus	10		4.68	A.A.Jenkins	Enstone	14. 1.03
CDK	1458		Schleicher K8B	8747		5.68	Burn GC	Burn	15. 2.03
CDN	1461		EoN AP.7 Primary	---		NK	Norfolk & Suffolk Aviation Museum	Flixton	7.00
CDQ	1463		Grunau Baby III	R161		6.68	Not known (Under repair 2000)	NK	
CDR	1464	CDR	Scheibe Bergfalke III	5625		8.68	N.M Neil	Hinton in the Hedges	24. 4.01
CDV	1468	CDV	Schleicher Ka6E	4159		5.68	Not known (Wreck stored 7.97)	Cranfield	4.87*
CDW	1469		FFA Diamant 18	033		8.68	J.L.McIver	Falgunzeon	3.11.03
CDX	1470	303	SZD-30 Pirat	W-392		5.68	S.Cynalski	Rufforth	19. 6.00
CDZ	1472	CDZ	Schleicher Ka6E	4177		5.68	J R Minnis	North Weald	16. 7.03
CEA	1473	CEA	Schempp-Hirth HS.2 Cirrus	21	XZ405 BGA.1473/D-8437	8.68	M.S.Whitton	Long Mynd	2. 4.03
CEB	1474	CEB	SZD-9 bis Bocian 1E	P-433		5.68	Bath, Wilts & North Dorset GC	Kingston Deverill	23. 6.03
CEC	1475	18	Schempp-Hirth HS.2 Cirrus	22		7.68	C.R.Ellis	Long Mynd	15. 1.03
CED	1476	814	Schleicher Ka6E	4196		6.68	H.G.Williams & Ptnrs	Snitterfield	9. 3.03
CEG	1479		Schleicher Ka6E	4203		6.68	J.C.Boley	Halesland	21. 3.96*
CEH	1480	CEH	Wassmer WA.22 Super Javelot	68	F-OTAN-C6 F-CCLU	7.68	N.A.Mills	Lasham	14. 4.03
CEJ	1481	CEJ	Schleicher ASK13	13102		8.68	Devon & Somerset GC	North Hill	11. 2.03
			(Written-off in accident North Hill 17. 7.02)						
CEK	1482		Slingsby T.21B (T)	1151	RAFGSA.369 XN147	7.68	D.Woolerton	North Coates	3. 2.03
			(Fuji-Robin EC34PM s/n 82-00391)						
CEL	1483	JD	Schleicher Ka6E	4174		8.68	Essex & Suffolk GC	Wormingford	27.12.03
CEM	1484	CEM	Schleicher Ka6E	4212		8.68	G.D.Bowes	Pocklington	22. 6.03
CEN	1485	CEN	SZD-30 Pirat	W-393	SP-2520	7.68	A.Bogan	Kirton-in-Lindsey	8. 3.03
CEQ	1487	458	Schleicher Ka6E	4230		8.68	C.L.Lagden & Ptnrs	Ridgewell	6. 8.03
CEV	1492		Scheibe Bergfalke II	184	???	8.68	A.Lewis (Stored 10.96)	Jurby, Isle of Man	17.12.93*
CEW	1493	CEW	Schleicher Ka6E	4209		8.68	J.W.Richardson	Dunstable	9. 5.03
CEX	1494	CEX	Schleicher ASK13	13108		9.68	Newcastle & Teesside GC	Carlton Moor	25.10.02
CEY	1495	CEY	Schleicher Ka6E	4222		8.68	S.N.Longland & Ptnrs	Gransden Lodge	26. 3.03
CFA	1497	CFA	Schleicher ASK13	13113		10.68	Booker GC	Booker	3. 4.03
CFB	1498		Schleicher ASK13	13110		10.68	Not known (Wrecked)	Burn	*
CFC	1499	CFC	Schleicher Ka7 Rhönadler	470	RAFGSA.387 F-OTAN-C1	11.68	K.F.Marchant	Edgehill	20.11.03
CFD	1500	B1	LET L-13 Blanik	173214	G-ATCG	10.68	M D White	Burn	19. 3.01
			(De-registered 10.6.02, to Ireland as EI-154 – initially allotted EI-153 in error)						
CFF	1502	CFF	Schleicher K8B	8765		10.68	Norfolk GC	Tibenham	24. 5.03
CFG	1503	CFG	Schleicher ASK13	13115		10.68	Staffordshire GC	Seighford	7. 3.03
CFK	1506		Schempp-Hirth HS.2 Cirrus	38		11.68	C.V Webb & Ptnrs	Sleap	16.12.02
CFL	1507	CFL	Schleicher Ka6E	4215		10.68	Bath, Wilts & North Dorset GC	Kingston Deverill	29. 4.03
CFM	1508	CFM	Schleicher ASK13	13121		7.12.68	Vale of The White Horse GC	Sandhill Farm Shrivenham	21.11.02
CFS	1513	CFS	Glasflugel H.201 Standard Libelle	83		4.70	J.L.H.Pegman	Milfield	19. 7.03
CFT	1514	62	Slingsby T.59A Kestrel 17	1729		3.73	J.A.Kane	Carlton Moor	21. 7.03
CFX	1518	CFX	Glasflugel H.201 Standard Libelle	274		2.72	D.F.Porter	Seighford	4. 4.03
CFY	1519	862	Glasflugel H.201 Standard Libelle	27		3.72	C.W.Stevens	Rufforth	6. 5.03
CGB	1522	CGB	Schleicher Ka6E	4247		12.68	M.J.Huddart	Winthorpe	18. 5.03
CGD	1524	418	Schleicher Ka6E	4202		1.69	I F Smith	Lasham	29. 9.02
CGE	1525		Schleicher Ka6E	4246		1.69	C.Weir	Bellarena	.4 .4.03
CGH	1528	153	Schleicher K8B	8772		23. 2.69	I.G.Brice	Lasham	21. 4.03
CGJ	1529	CGJ	Schleicher K8B	8773		2.69	Nene Valley GC	Upwood	8. 2.03
CGK	1530	124	Schleicher Ka6E	4261		3.69	J.E. Hampson	Wormingford	24. 9.03
CGM	1532	CGM	FFA Diamant 18	053		4. 4.69	J.G.Batch	Hinton in the Hedges	29. 6.03
CGN	1533	309	Schleicher Ka6E	4173		3.69	K.R Brown & Ptnr	Nympsfield	18. 4.01
CGQ	1535	CGQ	Schleicher ASK13	13153		7. 4.69	Oxford GC	Weston-on-the-Green	14. 5.03
CGR	1536	913	Schleicher ASK13	13142		31. 3.69	Bristol & Glos GC	Nympsfield	1.12.96*
			(Damaged near Nympsfield 2.6.96)						
CGS	1537	CGS	FFA Diamant 18	055		7.69	C.J.Wimbury	Talgarth	23. 6.03
CGT	1538	449	Schempp-Hirth SHK-1	38	D-1966	4.69	B.W.Svenson	Pocklington	16.12.03
CGU	1539	CGU	EoN AP.5 Olympia 2B	EoN/O/115	RAFGSA.228	4.69	M.Skinner & Ptnrs	Pocklington	30. 8.97*
CGV	1540	CGV	PIK-16C Vasama	48		4.69	D.J.Osborne & Ptnrs	Currock Hill	15. 9.03
CGX	1542	CGX	Bolkow Phoebus C	869		4.69	W.N.Smith & Ptnrs	Sackville Lodge, Riseley	26. 5.03
CGY	1543	CGY	Schempp-Hirth HS.2 Cirrus	51		18. 4.69	R.Munday & Ptnrs	Eaglescott	31. 5.02
CGZ	1544	CGZ	Schempp-Hirth SHK	39		5.69	M.C.Ridger	Saltby	3. 3.03
CHB	1546	577	Schleicher Ka6E	4235		5.69	D.L.Jones	Weston-on-the-Green	13. 2.03
CHC	1547		Bolkow Phoebus C	858		5.69	D.Garner Syndicate	Rhigos	7. 9.00
CHE	1549	CHE	Slingsby T.41 Skylark 2	DSS.002		6.69	M.S.Howey	Burn	19. 4.03
			(Built Doncaster Sailplane Services)						

CHF	1550	CHF	SZD-9 bis Bocian 1E	P-432		5.69	T.J.Wilkinson	Sackville Lodge, Riseley	2. 8.96*
						(Damaged Sackville Lodge 27. 8.95)			
CHG	1551	N52	SZD-30 Pirat	B-294		27. 6.69	Culdrose GC	RNAS Culdrose	20. 4.03
CHJ	1553	CHJ	Bolkow Phoebus 17C	879		6.69	D.C.Austin	Sutton Bank	30. 4.02
CHK	1554	CHK	EoN AP.5 Olympia 2B	?	RAFGSA	6.69	Oly Gliding Syndicate	Halesland	28. 9.03
CHL	1555	CHL	SZD-30 Pirat	B-295		6.69	W.Sage & Syndicate	Rufforth	4. 6.03
CHQ	1559		Slingsby T.31B	1186	XN247	6.69	N.H.Ponsford *(Stored 1.98)*	Wigan	7.82*
CHT	1562	846	Schleicher ASW15	15013		8.69	N.A.Kelly & Ptnrs	Lasham	11. 2.03
CHU	1563	CHU	Schleicher K8B	8794		10. 8.69	H B Chalmers *(Highland GC Syndicate)* Easterton		26. 4.03
CHW	1565	CHW	Schleicher ASK13	13187		8.69	Dorset GC	Gallows Hill	6. 5.03
CHY	1567	CHY	Slingsby T.45 Swallow	RG.103		9.69	J.L.H.Pegman & Ptnrs	Currock Hill	27. 6.02
			(Built R.Greenslade from kit)						
CHZ	1568	857	Schleicher Ka6E	4153	N6916	9.69	M.Uphill	Usk	2. 3.03
CJB	1570	764	Bolkow Phoebus C	919		12.69	T.J.Wilkinson	Sackville Lodge, Riseley	1. 6.01
CJC	1571		Ginn-Lesniak Kestrel	1		10.69	P.G.Fairness & K Burns	Milfield	25. 3.02
CJD	1572	S14	Schleicher ASK13	13182		19.10.69	Shenington GC	Edgehill	7. 1.03
CJF	1574	474	Schleicher K8B	8803		29.11.69	Surrey & Hants GC	Lasham	11. 8.02
CJG	1575	CJG	Wassmer WA.21 Javelot II	38	F-OTAN-C4	1.70	R S Hanslip	Burn	31. 5.03
					F-CCEZ				
CJJ	1577	CJJ	Bolkow Phoebus C	913		15. 1.70	P Maddocks	Falgunzeon	4. 5.03
CJK	1578	CJK	Schempp-Hirth SHK	35	RAFGSA	25 2.70	R.H.Short	Lyveden	8. 9.03
CJL	1579	222	Schempp-Hirth SHK-1	42	OO-ZLG	2.70	M.F.Brook	Camphill	.3. 6.03
CJM	1580	CJM	Schleicher K8B	8814		8. 3.70	Surrey & Hants GC	Lasham	10. 3.03
CJN	1581	CJN	Schempp-Hirth SHK-1	55		3.70	G.Kench	Dunstable	14. 7.03
CJP	1582		Schleicher ASW15	15041		3.70	C.Pain	Cranfield	2. 6.03
CJR	1584	83	Schempp-Hirth HS.2 Cirrus	87		3.70	J.H.Stanley	Lasham	11. 1.03
CJY	1591	CJY	Schleicher Ka6CR	555	(RAFGSA)	4.70	Bristol & Glos GC	Nympsfield	16. 5.03
CKC	1595	CKC	Bolkow Phoebus C	936	(BGA.1590)	21. 4.70	S.J.Bennett	Bidford	18. 7.02
CKD	1596	CKD	SZD-30 Pirat	B-327		4.70	L.D.Crisp	Bidford	2. 1.02
CKF	1598	961	Glasflugel H.201 Standard Libelle	101		4.70	S.M.Turner	Crowland	21. 6.03
CKJ	1601		Slingsby T.30B Prefect	740	PH-197	4.71	Not known *(Stored)*	Crosshill	14. 4.90*
CKL	1603	CKL	Schleicher Ka6E	4336		4.70	I.Lowes & Ptnrs	Milfield	11. 8.03
CKN	1605	CKN	SZD-9 bis Bocian 1E	P-496		5.70	Strubby GC "Enola Gay"	Strubby	10. 8.03
CKP	1606	CKP	Schleicher ASW15	15058		7.70	M.G.Shaw & Ptnrs	Portmoak	16. 1.03
CKR	1608		Schleicher ASK13	13247		7.70	Essex GC	North Weald	9. 7.03
CKT	1610		Scheibe Bergfalke II	E.03	D-9208	7.70	Not known *(Being restored)*	Thame	
CKU	1611	CKU	Schleicher ASK13	13243		11. 8.70	Essex GC	North Weald	22. 5.03
CKV	1612	T10	Schleicher ASK13	13253		8.70	Black Mountain GC	Talgarth	21. 7.03
CKW	1613	CKW	Schleicher K8B	8836		9.70	D.R Crompton	Bidford	14. 6.98
CKY	1615	743	Glasflugel H.201 Standard Libelle	139		22. 8.70	G. Herbert	Bidford	13. 5.03
CKZ	1616	724	Schempp-Hirth HS.4 Standard Cirrus	52	RAFGSA	8.70	M.E.Kingston	Dunstable	9. 2.03
					BGA.1616				
CLA	1617	CLA	Schempp-Hirth HS.4 Standard Cirrus	63		11.70	J.A.Wight & D.Dye	Nympsfield	5.10.03
CLC	1619		Slingsby T.21B	1200	RNGSA 2-07	11.70	Not known *(Stored 2000)*	NK	
CLF	1622	CLF	Schleicher Ka7 Rhönadler	931	D-5062	5. 1.71	P.M.Morgan & Ptnrs	Tibenham	15. 5.03
CLG	1623	CLG	Schempp-Hirth HS.4	36	RAFGSA.27	9. 1.71	J.E.Kenny	Bembridge	4. 5.03
CLH	1624	252	Schempp-Hirth HS.4 Standard Cirrus	77		??	P.C.Bray & Ptnrs	Nympsfield	13. 2.03
CLJ	1625		EoN AP.7 Primary	EoN/P/035	WP267	8. 2.71	T Ackerman *(On rebuild 2000)*	Bicester	2.72*
CLK	1626	CLK	Schleicher Ka7 Rhönadler	607	D-5714	2.71	Cornish GC	Perranporth	7. 5.03
			(Partly modified to ASK-13 standard)						
CLM	1628	535	Glasflugel H.201 Standard Libelle	178		2.71	J.N.Cochrane	North Hill	24. 3.03
CLN	1629	142	Glasflugel H.201 Standard Libelle	175		4.71	J.N.Wardle	Lasham	19. 5.03
CLP	1630	948	Glasflugel H.201B Standard Libelle	176		2.71	A.Jelden	Booker	7. 3.03
CLQ	1631	CLQ	Schempp-Hirth HS.2 Cirrus	99		29. 1.71	K.Bastenfield	Brent Tor	9. 1.03
CLR	1632	284	Glasflugel H.201B Standard Libelle	173		4.71	R.A. Christie	Easterton	8. 3.03
CLT	1634		Schleicher Ka7 Rhönadler	251	D-5529	4.71	R.Spencer tr The Syndicate	Rhigos	7.12.02
CLV	1636		Glasflugel H.201 Standard Libelle	180		3.71	J.M.Sherman	Parham Park	26. 4.03
CLW	1637	937	Glasflugel H.201 Standard Libelle	174		12. 3.71	N.A.Dean & Ptnrs	Kirton-in-Lindsey	31.12.03
CLX	1638	CLX	Schleicher K8B	8851		12. 3.71	Midland GC	Long Mynd	9. 1.03
CLY	1639		Hirth Go.III Minimoa	378	PH-390	20. 3.72	Not known	Dunstable	1.79*
					D-5076		*(On rebuild 2000)*		
CLZ	1640	799	Schleicher Ka6E	4056	AGA.2	2. 4.71	H.N.Craven	Pocklington	23. 8.03
CMF	1646	CMF	SZD-32A Foka 5	W-534		7.71	D J Linford	Lasham	26. 6.03
CMG	1647	CMG	Schleicher Ka7 Rhönadler	462	D-8116	7.71	P.M.Williams "Fledermaus"	Lasham	8. 2.03
CMH	1648	165	Glasflugel H.201B Standard Libelle	224		12. 7.71	D.N Greig	North Hill	17. 3.03
CMK	1650		Schleicher ASK13	13305		8.71	South Wales GC	Usk	11. 4.03
CML	1651	CML	Schleicher K8B	8862		8.71	Vectis GC	Bembridge	13. 3.01
							(Collided with Super Cub G-BAFS at Bembridge 8.10.00)		
CMN	1653	CMN	Schleicher K8B	8870		23. 8.71	Bristol & Glos GC	Nympsfield	4. 3.03
CMQ	1655	CF	Glasflugel H.201 Standard Libelle	233		13. 8.71	J.A. Murdock	Ridgewell	28. 7.03
CMR	1656	CMR	Glasflugel H.201 Standard Libelle	225		15. 8.71	J.A.Dandie & Ptnrs	Portmoak	25. 8.03
CMS	1657	602	Glasflugel H.201 Standard Libelle	234		8.71	D.Manser & Ptnrs	Challock	9. 5.03
CMT	1658		Scheibe Bergfalke II	124	D-6012	22. 8.71	Not known *(Stored 2000)*	NK	
CMV	1660	184	Glasflugel H.201 Standard Libelle	235		11. 8.71	S.E.Evans & Ptnrs	Weston on the Green	25. 4.03
CMW	1661	CMW	Glasflugel H.201B Standard Libelle	242		9.71	A M Dalton	Dunstable	26. 2.03
CMX	1662	226	Glasflugel H.201 Standard Libelle	232		9.71	W D Johnson	Burn	22. 3.03
CMY	1663		Grunau Baby IIIC	1	RAFGSA.373	22. 1.72	Not known	Manor Farm, Glatton	*
			(Built LSV Fussen)		D-1090		*(Stored for rebuild 7.95)*		

CMZ	1664	CMZ	Schleicher Ka7 Rhönadler	323	D-5589	11. 6.72	Cornish GC	Perranporth	29. 5.03
CND	1668	CND	SZD-9 bis Bocian 1E	P-428	RAFGSA.392	1.72	Angus GC	Drumshade	27. 4.03
CNE	1669	525	Glasflugel H.201 Standard Libelle 266			1.72	E.T.Melville	Portmoak	16. 2.03
CNF	1670	709	Glasflugel H.201B Standard Libelle	271		1.72	D.F.Mazingham	Pocklington	18. 3.03
CNG	1671	622	Glasflugel H.201 Standard Libelle 265			2.72	C.F.Smith & Ptnr	Nympsfield	6.11.03
CNH	1672	442	Glasflugel H.201 Standard Libelle 269			2.72	A.D'Otreppe	Lasham	28. 7.03
CNJ	1673	CNJ	Glasflugel H.201 Standard Libelle 272			9. 2.72	R.Thornley	Crowland	24. 4.03
CNK	1674	CNK	SZD-30 Pirat	B-459		3.72	R.C.T.Birch	Portmoak	17. 2.03
CNM	1676	CNM	SZD-9 bis Bocian 1	EP-551		2.72	M.Williamson & Ptnrs	Crowland	22. 6.02
CNN	1677		Schempp-Hirth HS.4 Standard Cirrus	173		2.72	R.W.Asplin	Camphill	15. 4.03
CNP	1678	CNP	Glasflugel H.201 Standard Libelle 264			3.72	S. & J.McKenzie	Camphill	11. 7.03
CNS	1681		Slingsby T.59A Kestrel 17	1724		4.72	J.R.Greenwell	Carlton Moor	1. 5.02
CNV	1683	229	Slingsby T.59F Kestrel 19	1790		6.72	P.H.Fanshawe & E.A.Smith	Snitterfield	4. 1.03
CNW	1684	625	Slingsby T.59F Kestrel 19	1791		7.72	S.R.Watson	Camphill	28. 3.03
CNX	1685	818	Slingsby T.59F Kestrel 20	1792		27. 7.72	D.Starer	Dunstable	13. 2.02
CNY	1686	151	Glasflugel H.201 Standard Libelle 322			9.72	S.B.Marshall & Ptnrs	Portmoak	26.10.03
CPA	1688	466	Glasflugel H.201B Standard Libelle	328		9.72	K.Hampson	Kenley	23. 2.03
CPB	1689	858	Slingsby T.59D Kestrel 19	1796		10.72	A.T.Videon	North Weald	2. 3.03
CPD	1691	402	Schleicher ASW17	17026		3.74	A.S. Raffan	Long Mynd	7. 6.03
CPE	1692	CPE	EoN AP.5 Olympia 2B	EoN/O/120	RAFGSA.233	3.72	Not known	Edgehill	9. 8.95*
							(W/O Arbroath 10. 9.94; stored 5.97)		
CPF	1693	T15	Glasflugel H.201 Standard Libelle 267			3.72	J.M.Norman & P.Elvidge	Pocklington	9. 3.03
CPG	1694	CPG	Schleicher Ka7 Rhönadler	7036	D-4029	15. 4.72	Queens University GC	Bellarena	7.12.02
CPJ	1696	CPJ	Schleicher Ka6E	4059	OO-ZDA	9. 4.72	J.Herd & Ptnrs	Feshie Bridge	9. 4.03
CPL	1698		Slingsby T.8 Tutor	FF477	RAFGSA183	26. 4.72	Not known *(Being refurbished 2001)*	Lasham	
CPM	1699	CPM	Glasflugel H.201 Standard Libelle 179			4.72	M.J.Wilson	Dunstable	14. 4.03
CPU	1706	761	Schempp-Hirth HS.4 Standard Cirrus	194		4.72	J.P.J.Ketelaar	Feshiebridge	6.11.02
CPV	1707	CPV	SZD-30 Pirat	B-470		3.72	G.Hall	Portmoak	6. 4.03
CPX	1709	CPX	SZD-30 Pirat	B-460		4.72	J.Murphy	Usk	5. 6.03
CQC	1714	CQC	SZD-30 Pirat	B-472		15. 4.72	A.White	Winthorpe	18. 5.03
CQD	1715	CQD	Schleicher K8B	419/58	D-5625	4.72	E.McCaig	Challock	19. 4.01
CQG	1718	CQG	EoN AP.5 Olympia 2B	EoN/O/044	RAFGSA.206 BGA.542	4.72	L.McKenzie	Sutton Bank	20. 2.03
CQJ	1720	K17	Slingsby T.59A Kestrel 17	1727		5.72	A.Shelton	Portmoak	27. 7.02
CQL	1722	339	Schempp-Hirth HS.5 Nimbus 2	11		5.72	M N Erlund	East Kirkby	28.12.03
CQM	1723	234	Slingsby T.59F Kestrel 19	1765		22. 5.72	J.A.Knowles	RAF Odiham	25. 5.03
CQN	1724	CQN	Schempp-Hirth HS.4 Standard Cirrus	204G		19. 5.72	M.G.Sankey & Ptnrs	Lasham	22. 4.03
CQP	1725	918	Schempp-Hirth HS.5 Nimbus 2	4		4.72	D.Caunt & Ptnrs	Booker	23. 2.03
CQQ	1726	139	Schempp-Hirth HS.5 Nimbus 2	5		4.72	M.D.J.White	Camphill	24. 3.03
CQR	1727	703	Schempp-Hirth HS.4 Standard Cirrus	220G		28. 5.72	B.E.Richards Sandhill Farm, Shrivenham		1. 5.03
CQT	1729	CQT	Schleicher Ka7 Rhönadler	603	D-5712	6.72	Shenington GC	Edgehill	6. 7.96*
							(Stored Kemble 7.97: current status unknown)		
CQW	1732	342	SZD-36A Cobra 15	W-572		6.72	W.Alexander	Portmoak	6.10.02
CQX	1733	789	SZD-30 Pirat	B-483		9. 6.72	The B Syndicate	Lleweni Parc	6. 7.01
CQY	1734	D49	Schempp-Hirth HS.4 Standard Cirrus	214		16. 6.72	S.R.Blackmore	Edgehill	24. 3.03
CRA	1736	CRA	Schleicher Ka7 Rhönadler	7009	???	7. 7.72	Welland GC	Lyveden	19. 5.02
CRB	1737	241	Glasflugel H.201 Standard Libelle 243			6.72	A.I.Mawer	Winthorpe	29. 5.03
CRD	1739		SZD-36A Cobra 15	W-578		8. 7.72	J.Durman	Pocklington	13. 6.94*
CRF	1741		Birmingham Guild BG-135	001		2.72	C D Stevens	Lee-on-Solent	6. 4.02
CRH	1743	650	Schempp-Hirth HS.4 Standard Cirrus	233G		8.72	D.Thompson	Portmoak	27. 3.03
CRJ	1744		Slingsby T59A Kestrel 17		1728	7.72	M.Krap	Nordhorn, Germany	30. 3.03
CRK	1745		Slingsby T.8 Tutor	930	XE760 VM539	25. 7.72	I.D.Smith	Nympsfield	8.82*
							(Stored 8.01)		
CRL	1746	CRL	Schleicher ASK13	13013	???	4. 8.72	Midland GC	Long Mynd	25. 2.03
CRM	1747		Grunau Baby III	1	RAFGSA.361 D-8061	27. 7.72	R.Wasey & Ptnrs	Sandown	26. 11.96*
							"Grumpy"		
CRN	1748	566	Schempp-Hirth HS.4 Standard Cirrus	234G		4. 8.72	M.G.Woollard	Dunstable	29. 3.03
CRQ	1750	CRQ	Glasflugel H.201B Standard Libelle	326		10. 8.72	K.G.Counsell & Ptnrs	Usk	2. 4.03
CRS	1752		Glasflugel H.201B Standard Libelle	325		13. 8.72	S.Biggs	Husbands Bosworth	24. 6.03
CRT	1753	CRT	Schleicher ASK13	13396		1. 8.72	Bowland Forest GC	Chipping	4. 1.04
CRV	1755		Glasflugel H.201B Standard Libelle	329		22. 8.72	P.Arthur & Ptnr	Perranporth	30. 5.03
CRW	1756	417	Glasflugel H.201 Standard Libelle 324			10.72	M.Buick	Nympsfield	22. 3.03
CRZ	1759		Slingsby T.8 Tutor	----	RAFGSA.178	10.72	Boulton Paul Museum	Wolverhampton	
CSA	1760	182	Slingsby T.59F Kestrel 20	1797		11.72	P.L Poole	Parham Park	9. 5.03
CSB	1761	CSB	Slingsby T.59F Kestrel 19	1798		17.11.72	N.D.Paveley	Pocklington	25. 3.03
CSD	1763	53	Slingsby T.59D Kestrel 19	1800		1.12.72	M.J.Silver	Pocklington	30. 4.03
CSF	1765	347	Slingsby T.59F Kestrel 19	1802		1.73	G.R.Glazebrook	Dunstable	14. 2.03
CSG	1766	217	Slingsby T.59D Kestrel 19	1804		3.73	A.Swann & D.Williams	Lasham	5. 6.99
							(Mid-air collision with BGA.1943 Bidford 27.7.98)		

CSJ	1768	CSJ	Glasflugel H.201B Standard Libelle	372		26. 1.73	S.N.Croner	Challock	15. 4.03
CSK	1769	387	Slingsby T.59D Kestrel 20	1806		3.73	H.A. & J.E.Torode	RAF Odiham	14. 2.03
CSL	1770		Slingsby T.8 Tutor	928	XE758 VF181	15.10.72	W.D.Baars	(The Netherlands)	19. 9.00
CSN	1772	CSN	Pilatus B4 PC-11	021		12.72	M.Hine	North Hill	23. 9.02
CSP	1773	CSP	Pilatus B4 PC-11	027		3.73	I.T.Ashton	Chipping	22. 6.03
CSR	1775	808	Glasflugel H.201 Standard Libelle	368		14. 1.73	W.G.Miller & Ptnrs	North Connel	18. 5.02
CSU	1778		Manuel Hawk	1		11.72	Not known (Stored)	Sackville Lodge, Riseley	
CSV	1779	CSV	SZD-30 Pirat	B-515		3.12.72	P.Uden & Ptnrs	Gamston	31. 8.02
CSW	1780	CSW	Pilatus B4 PC-11	022		12.72	I.H.Keyser	Waldershare Park	11. 3.03
CTA	1784	CTA	EoN AP.5 Olympia 2B	EoN/O/146	RAFGSA.285	12.72	P.N.Tolson	Wormingford	30. 9.00
CTB	1785	579	Schempp-Hirth HS.4 Standard Cirrus	264G		1.73	M.J.Gibbons & Ptnrs	Weston-on-the-Green	.7. 2.03
CTD	1787		Yorkshire Saiplanes YS-53	1721		4.74	P.Older	Andreas, Isle of Man	
			(Under restoration in 2000 after heavy landing)						
CTE	1788	40	Schleicher ASW17	17012		1.73	D.Edwards & S.Blackmore	Lasham	25. 2.03
CTF	1789		Schleicher Ka4 Rhönlerche	01	D-3574	1.73	M.Goodman	Winthorpe	9. 2.02
			(Owner quotes p/i D-4346, but unconfirmed)						
CTJ	1792	CTJ	Slingsby T.59D Kestrel 19	1810		14. 3.73	H.B.Walrond & Ptnrs	Rattlesden	18. 3.03
CTL	1794	CTL	Slingsby T.59D Kestrel 19	1812		28. 3.73	P.G.Codd	Wormingford	18. 4.03
CTM	1795	254	Slingsby T.59D Kestrel 19	1813		3.73	G.P.Emsden	Dunstable	21. 3.03
CTN	1796	CTN	Slingsby T.59D Kestrel 19	1814		4.73	J.T Goodall	Sutton Bank	28. 3.02
			(Written-off in landing accident, Elkington, Northants, 23.6.01)						
CTP	1797	49	Slingsby T.59D Kestrel 19	1815		14. 4.73	D.C.Austin	Sutton Bank	.3. 6.03
CTQ	1798	924	Slingsby T.59D Kestrel 20	1816		27. 4.73	K.A.Moules	Bicester	14. 6.03
CTR	1799	402	Slingsby T.59D Kestrel 19	1817		5.73	D.J.Marpole	Kingston Deverill	18. 3.03
CTS	1800	CTS	EoN AP.5 Olympia 2B	EoN/O/157	RNGSA	13. 1.73	M.D.Smith	Parham Park	6. 9.02
CTT	1801	873	Schempp-Hirth HS.4 Standard Cirrus	277G		17. 2.73	S.M.L.Young	Nympsfield	19. 3.03
CTU	1802	501	Glasflugel H.201 Standard Libelle	371		2.73	J.R.Humpherson	Camphill	15. 5.03
CTV	1803		SZD-30 Pirat	B-528		2.73	B.Fantham	Rhigos	30.10.02
CTW	1804	1	SZD-9 bis Bocian 1E	P-598		2.73	Mendip GC	Halesland	1. 9.01
CTX	1805	CTX	SZD-30 Pirat	B-527		2.73	P.Goulding	Crowland	19. 7.03
CTZ	1807	CTZ	Schleicher K8B	8035/B5	D-KOCU D-5203	3. 4.73	Scottish Gliding Union Ltd	Portmoak	12. 6.03
CUB	1809	CUB	Pilatus B4 PC-11	047		31. 3.73	P.Noonan & D.Wardell	Enstone	26. 7.03
CUC	1810		Pilatus B4 PC-11	003	HB-1102	5.73	H.M.Pantin & Ptnrs	AAC Dishforth	28. 3.03
CUD	1811	CUD	Yorkshire Sailplanes YS-53 Sovereign	02		7.72	D R Bricknell	Saltby	20. 5.01
			(Built from Slingsby T.53B XV951 [1574] w/o 11.4.72)						
CUF	1813	331	Yorkshire Sailplanes YS-55 Consort	04		9.11.73	C.G.Taylor & Ptnrs	Sutton Bank	21. 7.00
CUJ	1816	706	Glasflugel H.201B Standard Libelle	370		13. 2.73	T.G.B.Hobbis & Ptnrs	Lasham	22. 3.03
CUK	1817	380	Glasflugel H.201 Standard Libelle	367		3.73	G.R.Brown	Dunstable	9. 8.01
CUL	1818	550/10	Schempp-Hirth HS.4 Standard Cirrus	265G		7. 4.73	L.G.Watts	Husbands Bosworth	20. 7.98
CUM	1819	CUM	SZD-30 Pirat	B-534		24. 2.73	E.Hughes	Pocklington	18. 1.03
CUQ	1821	CUQ	Pilatus B4 PC-11	040		2.73	A.E.Hayes & Ptnrs	Aston Down	26. 5.03
CUS	1822	842	Schempp-Hirth HS.2 Cirrus VTC 126Y			3.73	G.F.Wearing	Chipping	14. 6.03
CUT	1823		Pilatus B4 PC-11	041		3.73	N.R.Cawte	Gamston	11.10.95*
			(On repair 1997: current status unknown)						
CUZ	1829	CUZ	LET L-13 Blanik	025409		4.73	East Sussex GC	Andreas, Isle of Man	11.98
			(Damaged 7.7.98, to Andreas GC as spares)						
CVA	1830	CVA	LET L-13 Blanik	025418		3.73	D.Wiseman	Andreas, Isle of Man	12. 4.03
			"Boggles the Blanik"						
CVB	1831	CVB	LET L-13 Blanik	025419		3.73	W.N.Smith	Sackville Lodge. Riseley	26. 5.03
CVC	1832	CVC	SZD-30 Pirat	B-535		3.73	J.P.Batty	Dunstable	22. 6.03
CVE	1834	BZ	Schempp-Hirth HS.2 Cirrus VTC 127Y			15. 3.73	B.Roberts	Gransden Lodge	5. 4.03
CVF	1835	CVF	Schempp-Hirth HS.2 Cirrus VTC 127Y			16. 3.73	I.Hamilton *(Damaged at Chipping 4.9.99)* Chipping		7. 5.00
CVG	1836	656	Pilatus B4 PC-11	045		19. 3.73	I H Keyser	Waldershare Park	23. 4.99
CVH	1837	CVH	Schempp-Hirth SHK	34	N6524A	30. 3.73	J.C.Fletcher	Dunstable	16. 8.03
CVJ	1838	CVJ	Breguet Br.905S Fauvette	37	F-CCJH	29. 6.73	I.C.Gutsell	Burn	22. 5.02
CVK	1839	92	Pilatus B4 PC-11	048		22. 3.73	R.R.Stoward	Dunstable	18. 7.03
CVL	1840	253	Glasflugel H.201B Standard Libelle	369		2.73	N.A.Dean	Kirton-in-Lindsey	2. 3.03
CVM	1841		Pilatus B4 PC-11 *(Powered)*	036		23. 3.73	J.A.Mace	Old Sarum	26. 3.03
CVN	1842		SZD-36A Cobra 15	W-608		3.73	N.Bickham	Dunkeswell	21. 9.96*
CVP	1843	CVP	SZD-9 bis Bocian 1E	P-597		17. 3.73	M.Boyle	Aboyne	22. 5.02
CVQ	1844	428	Glasflugel H.201 Standard Libelle	374		23. 3.73	C.J.Taunton & Ptnrs	Dunstable	28. 4.03
CVR	1845	CVR	SZD-30 Pirat	B-538		27. 3.73	M.Langford	Weston-on-the-Green	13. 5.03
CVS	1846	CVS	SZD-36A Cobra 15	W-610		3.73	B. Mossop	Pocklington	.2. 7.03
CVT	1847		SZD-36A Cobra 15	W-609		27. 3.73	J.Amor	Ridgewell	1.95*
CVV	1849	CVV	Pilatus B4 PC-11	028		27. 3.73	F.R.Wolff & Ptnrs	Brent Tor	16. 3.03
CVW	1850	423	Slingsby T.59D Kestrel 19	1818		29. 5.73	P.B.Hogarth	Halesland	23. 5.02
CVX	1851	3	Slingsby T.59D Kestrel 19	1823		7.73	Not known	Aston Down	*
			(Crashed Portmoak 6.9.80: wreck stored 7.99)						
CVY	1852	355	Slingsby T.59D Kestrel 19	1821		4. 7.73	J.Ainsworth *(Damaged Upavon 15.6.97)*	Sleap	19. 6.98*
CVZ	1853	269	Slingsby T.59D Kestrel 19	1824		3. 8.73	T.R.F.Gaunt & Ptnrs	Kingston Deverill	12. 3.03
CWA	1854	539	Slingsby T.59D Kestrel 19	1825		9.73	I.B.Kennedy	Usk	28.12.02
CWB	1855		Slingsby T.59D Kestrel 19	1833		9. 1.74	K.Fairness	Milfield	2. 7.03
CWD	1857	998	Slingsby T.59D Kestrel 19	1835		1.74	J.R.Dransfield	Aboyne	26. 7.03
CWE	1858	468	Glasflugel H.201 Standard Libelle	482		31. 1.74	T.W.S.Stoker	Rufforth	4. 5.03

CWF	1859	CWF	Slingsby T.59D Kestrel 19	1838		2.74	P.F.Nicholson	Thame	17. 4.03
CWG	1860	322	Glasflugel H.201 Standard Libelle 391			7. 4.73	G.Pledger	Currock Hill	13. 8.03
CWH	1861	CWH	Schleicher ASK13	13424		12. 4.73	York Gliding Centre	Rufforth	11. 3.03
CWJ	1862	CWJ	Schleicher Ka7 Rhönadler	630	D-6057	27. 4.73	Wolds GC	Pocklington	10. 8.03
					D-5723				
CWL	1864		Schempp-Hirth HS.2 Cirrus VTC 125Y			4.73	J.Richardson	Chipping	26. 1.98*
							(Damaged Hornsea 15.8.97)		
CWN	1866	CWN	Glasflugel H.201B Standard Libelle			4.73	R.B.Petrie	Portmoak	26. 3.03
			386						
CWR	1869	917	Schempp-Hirth HS.2 Cirrus VTC 133Y			4.73	S.T.Bonser	Dunstable	24. 1.03
CWS	1870	CWS	Schempp-Hirth HS.2 Cirrus VTC 129Y			19. 4.73	R.W.Cassels & Ptnrs	Ridgewell	.3. 5.03
CWT	1871	978	Glasflugel H.201B Standard Libelle 384			4.73	C.Lawrence	Husbands Bosworth	28. 3.03
CWU	1872		Schleicher Ka4 Rhönlerche II	390	D-5627	22.4.73	Not known *(Under restoration 2001)* (West Sussex)		
CWV	1873	Z	Schleicher Ka4 Rhönlerche II	123	D-8226	22. 4.73	11th Bristol (Headley Park) Scout Troop		
							(Stored 8.02)	Aston Down	5.94*
CWX	1875	832	Glasflugel H.201 Standard Libelle 36		RAFGSA.132	4.73	C.A.Weyman & Ptnrs	Gallows Hill	.9. 3.03
CWY	1876	146	Glasflugel H.201 Standard Libelle 387			14. 4.73	J Dixon	Portmoak	27. 1.03
CWZ	1877	CWZ	Glasflugel H.201 Standard Libelle 392			30. 4.73	Derby & Lancs GC	Camphill	21. 9.02
CXH	1885	CXH	SZD-36A Cobra 15	W-619		10. 6.73	C D Street	Parham Park	25. 9.03
CXJ	1886	791	SZD-36A Cobra 15	W-618		6.73	S R Bruce	Feshiebridge	18. 7.00
CXK	1887		Glasflugel H.201 Standard Libelle 383			6.73	C.A Turner	Cross Hayes	10. 1.03
CXL	1888	CXL	SZD-30 Pirat B-	548		6.73	J.A. Barnes	Wormingford	5.11.03
CXM	1889	532	Slingsby T.59D Kestrel 19	1820		7.73	R.P.Beck & Ptnrs	AAC Dishforth	15. 4.03
CXN	1890	508	Yorkshire Sailplanes YS-55 Consort			21.12.73	A.A.Priestley & Ptnrs	Sutton Bank	13. 3.02
			05						
CXP	1891		Yorkshire Sailplanes YS-55 Consort		BGA.1892	5.76	A.D.Coles	North Hill	19. 4.03
			07						
CXV	1897	CXV	Yorkshire Sailplanes YS-53 Sovereign			7.74	C.Wright	Chipping	.7. 6.03
			03						
CXW	1898		Yorkshire Sailplanes YS-53 Sovereign			7. 3.74	The Tin Bird Syndicate	Aboyne	7.93*
			1654				*(Wreck stored 5.94)*		
CYA	1902	503	Pilatus B4 PC-11	072		7.73	E.J.Bromwell & Ptnrs	North Hill	4.11.03
CYC	1904	CYC	Pilatus B4 PC-11	029	N47247	7.73	D.F.Barley	Ringmer	25. 7.03
CYD	1905		SZD-30 Pirat	B-559		25. 7.73	I.Johnstone	Portmoak	.9. 7.03
CYG	1908	YG	Glasflugel H.201 Standard Libelle 441			8.73	D.J.Cooke	Husbands Bosworth	23. 1.03
CYJ	1910	CYJ	DFS/49 Grunau Baby 2B	031000	D-6021	11. 8.73	C.Bird	Dunstable	1.90*
			(Built Petera 1943)				*(Under restoration during 2000)*		
CYK	1911	248	Pilatus B4 PC-11	078		8.73	I.M.Trotter tr Pilatus Soaring Syndicate	Portmoak	19.10.02
CYM	1913	299	Schempp-Hirth HS.4 Standard Cirrus		RAFGSA	9.73	L.J.Hartfield	Lasham	4. 4.03
			48		D-0578				
CYN	1914	N4	Slingsby T.59D Kestrel 19	JP.054		10.74	S.J.Cooke & Ptnrs	Gransden Lodge	22.12.02
			(Built D Jones & T Pentelow)						
CYP	1915	982	Schempp-Hirth HS.4 Standard Cirrus			9.73	O.Stuart-Menteth	Cranfield	25. 3.00
			369						
CYQ	1916	477	Schempp-Hirth HS.4 Standard Cirrus			27.9.73	B.M.Reeves	Nympsfield	22. 2.03
			364						
CYR	1917	CYR	LET L-13 Blanik	025610		9.10.73	Not known	Cranfield	12.90*
			(Damaged near Bidford 8.7.90; rebuilt using fuselage of BGA.2958 c/n 025817) *(Stored 7.97)*						
CYT	1919	CYT	Schempp-Hirth HS.4 Standard Cirrus			9.73	G.Royle	Llantisilio	13. 5.03
			357G						
CYW	1922		Birmingham Guild BG-135	6		1.10.73	Not known *(Stored 2000)*	NK	
CYY	1924		Schleicher Ka4 Rhönlerche	---	AGA.19	4.11.73	Not known *(Stored 2000)*	NK	
CYZ	1925	CYZ	Schleicher K8B	8882	RAFGSA	8. 9.74	Oxford GC	Weston-on-the-Green	28. 1.01
CZD	1929	CZD	Pilatus B4 PC-11	081		12.73	S.E. Marples	Currock Hill	23. 8.03
CZE	1930	CZE	SZD-30 Pirat	S-0114		23.12.73	M.Pedwell	Bidford	13. 2.03
CZG	1932	CZG	SZD-30 Pirat	S-0116		31.12.73	J.T.Pajdak	Kenley	.9. 5.03
CZJ	1934	CZJ	SZD-30 Pirat	S-0115		29.12.73	C.L Groves & Ptnrs	Husbands Bosworth	.2. 5.03
CZL	1936	504	Glasflugel H.201 Standard Libelle 483			31. 1.74	L P Woodage	Dunstable	29.11.02
CZM	1937	CZM	Munchen Mu-13D-III	10/52	D-1488	9.74	M.Chapple	Bicester	23. 4.03
CZN	1938	CZN	Schleicher ASW15B	15329		13. 3.74	P.C.Tuppen & Ptnrs	Bembridge	18. 5.03
CZQ	1940	CZQ	Slingsby T.59D Kestrel 19	1840		5. 4.74	J.P.Walker & Ptnrs	Husbands Bosworth	8.4.03
CZR	1941	CZR	Slingsby T.59D Kestrel 19	1842		4.74	R.P.Brisbourne	Rufforth	31. 1.03
CZS	1942	CZS	Slingsby T.59D Kestrel 22	1844		3. 5.74	P.Glennie	Portmoak	22. 3.97*
CZT	1943	A3	Slingsby T.59D Kestrel 19	1848		30. 5.74	G.W.Camp	Enstone	1. 3.99
CZU	1944	826	Slingsby T.59D Kestrel 19	1849		14. 6.74	K.R.Merrett & P.F.Croote	Halesland	11. 5.03
CZV	1945	415	Slingsby T.59D Kestrel 19	1850		16. 7.74	V.F.G.Tull	Dunstable	15. 6.03
CZW	1946	CZW	Slingsby T.59D Kestrel 20	1846		17.10.76	C.D Berry	Cranfield	14. 4.03
CZZ	1949		Slingsby T.59D Kestrel 19	1739		6.74	R.M.Grant	Lasham	19.11.96*
DAA	1950	DAA	SZD-9 bis Bocian 1	EP-639		10. 3.74	Highland GC	Easterton	24. 9.01
DAC	1952		SZD-36A Cobra 15	W-656		3.74	C.D.Peacock	Husbands Bosworth	16. 7.03
DAF	1955		LET L-13 Blanik	025825		4.74	Not known *(Stored 2000)*	NK	
DAJ	1958	14	Schempp-Hirth HS.5 Nimbus 2	50		21. 3.74	J.D.Jones	Nympsfield	13. 4.03
DAL	1960	DAL	EoN AP.6 Olympia 419	EoN/4/010	RAFGSA.301	4.74	D.M.Judd & Ptnrs	Snitterfield	5. 9.99
DAM	1961	675	ICA IS-29D	27		4.74	W.T.Barnard	Strathaven	24. 9.00
DAN	1962		SZD-30 Pirat	S-0145		23. 3.74	W.Pottinger & Ptnrs	Ridgewell	4. 5.03
DAP	1963	DAP	SZD-30 Pirat	S-0147		4.74	N.Crawford	Currock Hill	4. 5.03
DAQ	1964	DAQ	SZD-36A Cobra 15	W-657		4.74	C.Bigwood & Ptnrs	Lyveden	3. 7.97*
DAR	1965	DAR	Slingsby T.21B	---	RAFGSA.404	1. 6.74	D.Bourne	Upwood	27. 5.03
DAS	1966	DAS	Schempp-Hirth HS.4 Standard Cirrus		(BGA.1925)	4.74	G.Goodenough	Burn	19. 4.03
			378						
DAT	1967		SZD-30 Pirat	S-0149		27. 4.74	The Borders GC *(Crashed Milfield 1.8.99)*	Milfield	3. 5.00

Reg	No	Code	Type	c/n	Prev id	Date	Owner	Location	Date
DAU	1968		SZD-30 Pirat	S-0150		4.74	W.Fisher	Winthorpe	4. 4.03
DAV	1969	240	SZD-38A Jantar-1	B-608		4.74	R.M.Roberts	Brent Tor	4.10.03
DAW	1970	DAW	Schleicher Ka6CR	951	RAFGSA D-2025	8. 6.74	P.S.Holmes	Bellarena	23. 3.03
DBA	1974	207	EoN AP.5 Olympia 2B	EoN/O/156	RNGSA.208	25. 5.74	W.R.Williams	RAF Halton	11. 7.01
DBB	1975	DBB	Slingsby T.51 Dart 17R *(Built Greenfly Aviation)*	DG/51/01		5. 2.76	S.D.Codd	Crowland	31. 5.03
DBC	1976	DBC	Pilatus B4 PC-11	135		6.74	J.H.France & Ptnrs	Shobdon	17. 5.03
DBD	1977	DBD	SZD-30 Pirat	S-0202		6.74	E W Burgess	Cranfield	14. 7.03
DBF	1979	DBF	Schleicher Ka7 Rhönadler	179	RAFGS RAFGGA.552/D-5473	6.74	Welland GC *(Crashed at Lyveden 10.9.00)*	Lyveden	3. 3.01
DBG	1980	DBG	ICA IS-29D	31		6.74	G.V.Prater	Lasham	24. 6.03
DBJ	1982	691	Slingsby T.59D Kestrel 22	1856	BGA.1892 BGA.1982	19.10.74	P L Sanderson	RAF Syerston	23. 5.03
DBK	1983	523	Slingsby T.59D Kestrel 22	1861		2.12.74	R.E.Perry & C.Crabb	North Hill	19.12.03
DBN	1986	617	Slingsby T.59D Kestrel 19	1857		25. 3.75	A.C.Wright	Sutton Bank	.9. 2.03
DBP	1987	551	Glasflugel H.205 Club Libelle	51		1. 5.75	N.A.White	Rattlesden	27. 3.03
DBQ	1988	101	Slingsby T.59D Kestrel 22	1863		17. 4.75	P.Ramsden	Rufforth	15. 5.03
DBR	1989	95	Slingsby T.59D Kestrel 19	1858		22. 4.75	J.G.Bell	Parham Park	30.10.00
DBS	1990	DBS	Slingsby T.59D Kestrel 22	1864		24. 4.75	J.W.Rice	Kirton-in-Lindsey	10. 6.02
DBT	1991	11	Schempp-Hirth Standard Austria S 35		F-CCPQ	7.74	F.J.Tucker	Parham Park	20. 8.00
DBU	1992		Hirth Go IV Goevier 3	557	D-5233	13. 7.74	Boulton & Paul Museum	Wolverhampton	19. 7.87*
DBV	1993	DBV	SZD-30 Pirat	S-0227		1. 7.74	M.H.Bryan & Ptnrs	Usk	27. 4.03
DBW	1994	DBW	SZD-9 bis Bocian 1E	P-641		12. 7.74	Sackville GC	Sackville Lodge, Riseley	3. 4.99
DBX	1995	DBX	SZD-9 bis Bocian 1E	P-642		20. 7.74	Miss A.G.Veitch *tr Highland Bocian Syndicate*	Easterton	9. 2.03
DCA	1998	DCA	SZD-36A Cobra 15	W-686		18. 9.74	M.J.North	Husbands Bosworth	15. 8.01
DCC	2000	324	Glasflugel H.201B Standard Libelle	585		11.74	J.Warbey & M.Hutchinson	Shobdon	21. 3.03
DCE	2002		Slingsby T.41 Skylark 2B	1003	RAFGGA.540 PH-225	11.74	C.P.Race	Winthorpe	25. 8.02
DCF	2003		Schleicher Ka6CR	6520	RAFGSA.356	11.74	R.Spencer	Burn	17. 7.95*
DCG	2004		Schleicher Ka2B	2	D-7064	12.74	Not known *(Stored)*	Falgunzeon	*
DCH	2005	DCH	SZD-30 Pirat	S-0315		11.74	Spilsby Soaring	Spilsby	31. 8.96*
DCJ	2006		SZD-30 Pirat	S-0316		11.74	N.Jones *(Crashed near North Hill 29.3.97)*	North Hill	25. 3.98*
DCL	2008		LET L-13 Blanik	026154		11.74	Not known *(Wreck noted 2001)*	Strathaven	7. 8.92*
DCN	2010		Slingsby T.21B	1250	RAFGGA.501 RAFGSA.287/BGA.943	31.12.74	A.R.Worters	North Connel	16. 7.95*
DCR	2013	DCR	SZD-9 bis Bocian 1E	P-670		1.75	Mendip GC *(Crashed Halesland 13.6.96)*	Halesland	23.10.96*
DCS	2014	DCS	Slingsby T.45 Swallow	1538	RAFGGA.544	4.74	A.B.Dickenson	Chipping	23. 8.01
DCW	2018	DCW	Schleicher Ka6CR	1076	D-5228	2.75	Trent Valley GC	Kirton-in-Lindsey	11. 7.01
DCY	2020	DCY	Swales SD.3-15V *(Rebuild of incomplete Yorkshire Sailplanes YS-55 Consort c/n 09)*	01		2.75	T.R.Edwards	Chipping	16. 5.97*
DCZ	2021	DCZ	King-Elliott-Street Osprey *(Believed to be converted Slingsby T.51 Dart but c/n conflicts with BGA.1245)*	1470		10.75	G.R.Burkert	Lasham	28. 5.00
DDA	2022	DDA	Schempp-Hirth HS.4 Standard Cirrus	532G		2.75	R.G.Johnson	Parham Park	3. 5.03
DDB	2023	DDB	Schleicher ASK13	13493		2.75	Shenington GC	Edgehill	22.10.03
DDC	2024		Slingsby T.21B	1157	RAFGSA.313 XN153	3.75	J.S.Shaw & Ptnrs	Perranporth	30. 4.03
DDD	2025	695	Schempp-Hirth HS.5 Nimbus 2	84	G-BKPM BGA.2025	3.75	D.D.Copeland	Dunstable	9. 3.03
DDE	2026	DDE	SZD-38A Jantar-1	B-641		4.75	B.Jones	Bidford	19. 3.98
DDJ	2030	DDJ	ICA IS-29D	37		3.75	P.Andrews	Lyveden	7.98*
			(Written-off Lyveden 8.97 : to East Surrey College, Redhill as instructional airframe 10.97)						
DDK	2031		SZD-30 Pirat	S-0408		4.75	T.A.Buckley	Bembridge	.3 6.03
DDL	2032	DDL	Schleicher K8B	218/61	D-5156	4.75	Ouse GC	Rufforth	29. 5.03
DDM	2033	959	Schempp-Hirth HS.2 Cirrus VTC	164Y		3.75	J.J.Smith	Wormingford	14. 3.03
DDN	2034	DDN	SZD-9 bis Bocian 1E	EP-429	RAFGSA.393	3.75	Bath, Wilts & North Dorset GC	Kingston Deverill	19. 5.03
DDR	2037	680	Schempp-Hirth HS.4 Standard Cirrus	531G		3.75	J.Smith	Pocklington	12. 2.03
DDV	2041	536	SZD-38A Jantar	1	B-664	4.75	G.V.McKirdy	Edgehill	11. 5.98*
DDW	2042	DDW	SZD-30 Pirat	S-0433		4.75	C.P.Offen	Parham Park	2. 3.03
DDY	2044	DDY	Schleicher Ka6CR	678	D-8841	4.75	Needwood Forest GC	Cross Hayes	12. 5.03
DEB	2047	DEB	Slingsby T.59D Kestrel 19	1866		24.10.75	T.Moss	Weston-on-the-Green	30. 6.03
DEG	2051	DEG	ICA IS-28B2	48			P.S. & H.Whitehead	Sutton Bank	10. 9.03
DEN	2057	588	ICA IS-29D	41		4.75	S.E.Marples	Feshiebridge	13. 3.01
DEP	2058	DEP	Schleicher Ka6CR	6452	AGA... BGA.2058/RAFGSA.350	4.75	S.J.Aldridge	Saltby	5. 3.03
DEQ	2059	716	Glasflugel H.205 Club Libelle	97		4.75	J.A.Holland & Ptnrs	Kingston Deverill	2. 3.01
DEV	2064	DEV	Schleicher Ka6CR	6453	RAFGSA.354	5.75	P.J.Groves & Ptnrs	Long Mynd	31. 7.03
DEW	2065	DEW	ICA IS-29D	40		12. 6.75	M.D.Smith	Lee on Solent	19.10.02
DEX	2066	DEX	LET L-13 Blanik	026348	RAFGSA.R4 BGA.2066	1. 7.75	L.Wright	Talgarth	14. 9.03
DEY	2067	DEY	LET L-13 Blanik	026352	RAFGSA.R12 BGA.2067	10. 7.75	Bath, Wilts & North Dorset GC	Kingston Deverill	9. 9.03
DEZ	2068	977	ICA IS-29D	43		6.75	R.J.Everett *(Damaged Lewknor 7.3.90: stored 12.95)*	Sproughton	19. 4.91*
DFC	2071	128	Schempp-Hirth HS.4 Standard Cirrus	592G		7.75	R.J.Marriott & A.Weatherhead	Cranfield	15. 2.03
DFE	2073	DFE	Molino PIK-20B	20052		7.75	M.Roff-Jarrett	Parham Park	19.12.02

DFK	2078	DFK	Molino PIK-20	20039	OH-500	14. 9.75	M.J Fairclough	North Hill	19. 2.03
DFL	2079	DFL	SZD-38A Jantar-1	B-682		9.75	J.Howlett	Crowland	9. 6.03
DFN	2081		Glaser-Dirks DG-100	30		9.75	D.J.Clarke	Wormingford	2. 8.03
DFP	2082	DFP	Aeromere M.100S	029	I-LSUO	9.75	D.& J.Lee	Pocklington	23. 2.03
DFR	2084	906	Grob G.102 Astir CS	1038		10.75	P.Gee	Lasham	8. 1.04
DFU	2087	30	SZD-38A Jantar-1	B-685		3.12.75	J.E.New & Ptnrs	Lasham	13. 3.96*
DFV	2088	164	SZD-38A Jantar-1	B-684		7.12.75	R.R.Rodwell	Bellarena	15.12.01
DFW	2089	DFW	SZD-30 Pirat	S-0545		26.11.75	R.G.Skerry	Strubby	1. 2.03
DFX	2090	767	SZD-41A Jantar Standard	B-691		10.75	J.C.Tait & Ptnrs	Easterton	29. 4.03
DFY	2091		Schempp-Hirth HS.4 Standard Cirrus	AGA...		5.11.75	M.H.Challans	Booker	9. 5.02
				396					
DFZ	2092	774	Molino PIK-20	20080		27.11.75	M.J.Leach & J.P.Ashcroft		
								Sandhill Farm, Shrivenham	15. 4.03
DGA	2093	DGA	Schleicher K8B	8587	RAFGSA	11.75	Welland GC	Lyveden	4. 9.03
					BGA.1926/D-...				
DGB	2094	DGB	LET L-13 Blanik	026459		27.11.75	Black Mountains GC	Bidford	2.96*
			(Rebuilt with fuselage from BGA.2061 pre 1995)				*(Damaged Bidford 21.10.95; stored 5.98)*		
DGE	2097		Schempp-Hirth HS.4 Standard Cirrus 75			12.75	T.E.Snoddy	Bellarena	17. 7.03
				606					
DGG	2099	DGG	Schleicher Ka6E	4061	RAFGSA.263	15.12.75	N.F.Holmes & Ptnrs	Long Mynd	6. 7.03
DGH	2100	DGH	SZD-30 Pirat	B-533	RNGSA	12.75	E.Lowne	Snitterfield	19. 2.03
					BGA.2100				
DGK	2102	DGK	Schleicher Ka6CR	6287	D-3224	21.12.75	IBM GC *"Betty Blue"*	Lasham	25. 4.03
DGM	2104		Slingsby T.45 Swallow	1506	RAFGGA	12.75	Not known *(Being refurbished 2000)*	North Hill	8.11.93
DGP	2106	DGP	LET L-13 Blanik	026560		26. 5.76	J.M.Purves	Rufforth	16. 7.01
DGT	2110		Schleicher Ka2B	181	D-5469	5.76	Not known *(Stored 2002)*	Falgunzeon	23.10.93*
DGV	2112	DGV	Brequet Br.905S Fauvette	2	HB-632	5.76	R.M.Cust & Ptnrs	Burn	19. 4.03
DGX	2114	610	Schempp-Hirth HS.4 Standard Cirrus 75	AGA.3		11. 5.76	G.R.Seaman & Ptnrs	Lasham	29. 5.03
				619	BGA.2114				
DGY	2115	195	Schempp-Hirth HS.5 Nimbus 2	105		11. 5.76	J.H.Taylor	Nympsfield	27. 2.03
DHA	2117	DHA	Schleicher K8B	1055	D-8848	23. 6.76	Booker GC	Booker	5. 1.04
			(C/n conflicts with D-8616)		D-5148				
DHB	2118	DHB	SZD-30 Pirat	S-0643		9. 6.76	J.T.Winsworth	Tibenham	11. 4.00
DHC	2119	811	SZD-41A Jantar Standard	B-710	(BGA.2109)	9. 6.76	M.C.Burlock	Aston Down	18. 2.03
DHG	2123	517	Schleicher Ka6CR	1131	D-5170	23. 6.76	Angus GC	Drumshade	3. 8.03
DHH	2124	116	Molino PIK-20B	20124		5.76	D.M.Steed	Dunstable	28.11.02
DHJ	2125	DHJ	Glaser-Dirks DG-100	48		1.76	H.D.Armitage	Usk	1. 4.03
DHK	2126	A30	Glaser-Dirks DG-100	50		1.76	R.Dell & B.J.Griffin	Saltby	3. 4.03
DHL	2127	DHL	Glaser-Dirks DG-100	52		1.76	K.J.Adam	Aboyne	23. 8.03
DHM	2128	DHM	Schleicher Ka6E	4124	RAFGSA.26	6. 2.76	J.G.Heard	Seighford	18. 4.03
DHN	2129	824	Molino PIK-20B	20082		1.76	G J Bass	Challock	11. 6.03
DHP	2130		Slingsby T.45 Swallow	45176		5. 2.76	Dumfries & Galloway GC	Falgunzeon	10.89*
			(Components ex BGA.1041 [1329]: c/n = type/year)				*(W/o 3.4.64 with parts from BGA.1032; sold for rebuild 2002)*		
DHR	2132	DHR	Slingsby T.53B	1718		2.76	E.MacDonald	Portmoak	29. 9.00
DHT	2134	DHT	Schleicher Ka6E	4065	???	2.76	D.Wilkinson	Nympsfield	13. 1.03
DHV	2136	DHV	Molino PIK-20B	20111		3.76	J.D.& G.J.Walker	Booker	28. 6.03
DHW	2137	951	Schempp-Hirth HS.5 Nimbus 2	106		23. 4.76	A.J.Bauld	Portmoak	. 7. 5.03
DHY	2139	DHY	Schleicher Ka7 Rhönadler	1137	RAFGSA.266	14. 4.76	G.Whittaker	Chipping	28. 4.03
					D-5162				
DHZ	2140	DHZ	SZD-30 Pirat	S-0641		23. 4.76	Peterborough & Spalding GC	Crowland	1. 3.03
DJA	2141	DJA	SZD-30 Pirat	S-0642		23. 4.76	J.Young	Lyveden	18. 5.03
DJB	2142	N11	Schleicher K8B	8879	(RAFGSA.N11)	7. 4.76	Portsmouth Naval GC	Lee-on-Solent	14.11.03
					AGA.17/BGA.2142/RAFGSA.R97(1)/RAFGSA.R98(2)/RAFGSA.397(1)				
DJD	2144	DJD	Grob G.102 Astir CS	1226		5. 8.76	P.Gascoigne & Ptnrs	Kingston Deverill	15 4.03
DJE	2145	DJE	Schleicher Ka6CR	6412	D-3682	15. 7.76	M.Burton	Shobdon	10. 5.03
DJF	2146	500	Halford JSH Scorpion	001		7.77	R.G.Greenslade	(Doncaster)	
							(Previously at South Yorkshire Air Museum – for restoration)		
DJG	2147	K2	Schleicher Ka2B Rhönschwalbe	231	D-6179	6.76	J.Harmer	Lasham	10. 6.01
DJJ	2149	DJJ	Schleicher ASK18	18029		16. 7.76	Mendip GC	Halesland	28. 7.03
DJK	2150	DJK	Schleicher ASK18	18030		15. 7.76	Booker GC	Booker	22. 5.03
DJL	2151	DJL	SZD-41A Jantar Standard	B-714		16. 7.76	A.M.Cooper	Llantisilio	17. 2.03
DJM	2152	DJM	SZD-41A Jantar Standard	B-715		17. 8.76	T.E.Betts	Cross Hayes	26. 5.03
DJN	2153	407	Molino PIK-20B	20140C		16. 7.76	S.L.Cambourne	Lasham	17. 3.03
DJP	2154	DJP	Schleicher K8B	8588	RAFGSA.335	21. 7.76	Sackville GC	Sackville Lodge, Riseley	17. 6.03
DJQ	2155	214	Grob G.102 Astir CS	1258		17.10.76	H.Evans & D.J.Jeffries	Usk	16. 3.03
DJR	2156		Schleicher Ka6CR	680	D-8423	4. 8.76	J.A.Walker	Rivar Hill	29. 5.03
DJS	2157	608	Schempp-Hirth SHK-1	51	SE-TNF	16. 7.76	S.J.Collins	Nympsfield	23.11.01
					OY-MFX/HB-898				
DJT	2158	DJT	Schleicher Ka7 Rhönadler	?	RAFGSA	7.76	Enstone Eagles GC	Enstone	1.12.03
					(BGA.4271 is marked "DJT" also)				
DJU	2159		Scheibe Bergfalke II/55	204	D-....	7.76	Not known	*(Stored 2000)*	
DJW	2161		Manuel Condor	1		7.76	C.V. & R.C.Inwood	Booker	18. 5.98
DJX	2162	614	Grob G.102 Astir CS	1259		17.11.76	R.Duke	Lyveden	11. 1.03
DJZ	2164	989	Eiri PIK-20B	20144		4. 8.76	D.S.Puttock	Halesland	26. 9.03
DKB	2166	DKB	Schempp-Hirth Standard Austria S 32	F-CCPR		4. 8.76	J R Parr	Burn	25.10.03
DKC	2167	DKC	Schleicher K8B	8261	D-1431	8.76	Yorkshire GC	Sutton Bank	13. 5.03
DKD	2168	759	Glasflugel H.206 Hornet	67	(BGA.2165)	8.76	I.M.Evans	Long Mynd	.6. 5.03
DKE	2169	DKE	Schleicher ASK13	13548		28. 9.76	South Wales GC	Usk	26. 3.03
DKG	2171	DKG	Schleicher Ka6CR	6233	D-4327	8.76	C.Nunn & Ptnrs	Wormingford	10. 3.03
DKH	2172	769	LET L-13 Blanik	026644		8. 9.76	H.E.Birch	Rufforth	12. 6.00
DKK	2174	884	Schempp-Hirth SHK-1	32	HB-864	8. 9.76	C.Buzzard & D.J.Deacon	Husbands Bosworth	29. 5.95*

BGA	No.	Comp	Type	c/n	Prev ID	Date	Owner	Location	Date
DKL	2175	444	Schempp-Hirth HS.5 Nimbus 2	086	D-2111	8. 9.76	G.J.Croll	Snitterfield	24. 3.03
DKM	2176	DKM	Glasflugel H.206 Hornet	49	(BGA2213) BGA2176/D-7816	9.76	M.Lee	Rattlesden	1. 6.03
DKN	2177	DKN	Schleicher Ka6CR	6456	D-9358	12 .3.77	D.Lees & Ptnrs	Wormingford	8. 6.02
DKQ	2179	DKQ	Glaser-Dirks DG-100G	91G11		9.76	G.Peters	North Hill	10. 2.03
DKR	2180	360	Grob G.102 Astir CS	1327		9.76	Oxford GC	Weston-on-the-Green	28.11.02
DKS	2181	788	Grob G.102 Astir CS	1330		23.12.76	C.K.Lewis	Lasham	14. 8.02
DKT	2182	DKT	Eiri PIK-20B	20155		4.11.76	G.Barnham	Rufforth	6. 4.03
DKU	2183	DKU	Grob G.102 Astir CS	1326		11.76	G.Jennings	Lasham	2. 4.03
DKV	2184	391	Grob G.102 Astir CS	1328		9.76	T.J.Ireson	Sandhill Farm, Shrivenham	31. 1.99
DKW	2185	DKW	Grob G.102 Astir CS	1329		9.76	J.H.C.Friend	Llantisilio	21. 6.03
DKX	2186	353	Grob G.102 Astir CS	1331		9.76	L.R. & J.M.Bennett	Usk	19. 3.03
DKY	2187	DKY	Schleicher Ka7 Rhönadler	7187	RAFGSA.342	4.11.76	Defford Aero Club	Bidford	14. 8.02
DKZ	2188	DKZ	Glasflugel H.205 Club Libelle	111	RAFGSA.774	4.11.76	P.Jackson & C.Parsons	Bidford	17. 5.02
DLA	2189	DLA	Pilatus B4 PC-11	149	RAFGSA	17.10.76	P.R.Seddon	Chipping	6. 4.03
DLB	2190	DLB	Schleicher ASK18	18040		17.10.76	Vale of The White Horse GC	Sandhill Farm, Shrivenham	17.12.03
DLC	2191	C	Schleicher ASK13	13549		4.11.76	Lasham Gliding Society	Lasham	15. 9.03
DLD	2192	DLD	Schleicher K8B	8766	RAFGSA.383	17.11.76	Shalbourne SG	Rivar Hill	9. 2.03
DLE	2193	433	Schleicher Ka6E	4074	AGA.8 RAFGSA	10.76	D.C.Unwin	Snitterfield	29. 6.02
DLG	2195	DLG	Schempp-Hirth HS.4 Standard Cirrus	579	AGA.2	17.10.76	S.Naylor	Burn	7. 5.03
DLH	2196	378	Grob G.102 Astir CS77	1646		2.77	B.Bamber & R.Smith	Lasham	28. 2.03
DLJ	2197	DLJ	Molino PIK-20B	20157		16.12.76	M.S Parkes	Milfield	25. 7.03
DLM	2200	266	Grob G.102 Astir CS	1260	(BGA.2163)	1.12.76	Highland GC	Easterton	18. 4.03
DLP	2202	DLP	Schleicher Ka6CR	6519	RAFGSA.355	11.76	J.R Crosse	Crowland	22. 4.03
DLR	2204	DLR	Scheibe L-Spatz 55 *(Quoted as ex D-3659 but unconfirmed)*	647	BGA.2654 BGA.2204/D-5638	17.11.76	Dumfries & District GC *(Crashed near Falgunzeon 3.1.99)*	Falgunzeon	30. 8.99
DLS	2205	DLS	Schleicher K8B	8650	D-5718	1.12.76	D.B.Rich	Eaglescott	23. 3.03
DLT	2206	DLT	ICA IS-28B2	32		12.76	A.Woodrow	Tibenham	3. 7.03
DLU	2207	R93	ICA IS-28B2	33	RAFGSA.R93 NEJSGSA.3/EI-141/BGA.2207	12.76	Crusaders GC	Kingsfield, Dhekelia	19.11.03
DLW	2209	DLW	SZD-30 Pirat	B-467	PH-433	12.76	G.Bryce & Ptnrs	North Connel	29. 4.96*
DLX	2210		Slingsby T.45 Swallow	1494	RAFGGA.539	12.76	M.Sanderson	Milfield	29. 5.95*
DLY	2211		Eiri PIK-20D	20509		5. 1.77	M.Conrad	Dunstable	23. 2.03
DLZ	2212		Swales SW.3-15T	03		12.76	R.Harris	Thruxton	27. 6.01
DMB	2214	831	Schleicher K8B	8209	D-4331	18. 1.77	DRA GC *"Kate"*	RAF Odiham	.2.10.03
DMD	2216	251	Glaser-Dirks DG-100	75		12.76	N. Hill	Weston-on-the-Green	1. 4.03
DMF	2218	DMF	Schleicher Ka7 Rhönadler	7073	D-4313	2. 3.77	Staffordshire GC	Seighford	22. 8.02
DMG	2219	DMG	Schleicher K8B	8763	RAFGSA.382	19. 3.77	Dorset GC	Gallows Hill	2. 6.02
DMH	2220	DMH	Grob G.102 Astir CS	1511		23. 4.77	Oxford GC	Weston-on-the-Green	15. 1.03
DMJ	2221	DMJ	Schleicher K8B	8077	PH-290	19. 3.77	Not known (*Stored*)	Strathaven	23. 9.93*
DMK	2222	593	Schempp-Hirth SHK	25	D-5401	5. 4.77	P.Gray	Aston Down	29. 3.03
DML	2223	DML	Schleicher Ka7 Rhönadler	929	D-6194 D-5005	4. 2.77	Newark & Notts GC	Winthorpe	18. 2.03
DMM	2224	74	Schempp-Hirth HS.5 Nimbus 2	125		4. 2.77	T.E.Linee	Gallows Hill	3. 5.03
DMN	2225	DMN	Glasflugel H.303 Mosquito	20		2.77	R.P.Brecknock	Booker	27. 3.03
DMP	2226	233	Grob G.102 Astir CS	1239	ZS-GKF	28. 2.77	D.G.Nisbet	Dunstable	24. 1.03
DMQ	2227	DMQ	Schleicher Ka6E	4062	RAFGSA.264	12. 3.77	A.R.Bushnell & Ptnr	Crowland	25. 5.03
DMR	2228	511	Grob G.102 Astir CS	1435		19. 3.77	L.A.Beale & Ptnrs	Parham Park	15. 4.03
DMS	2229	259	Glasflugel H.201B Standard Libelle	385	RNGSA	19. 3.77	D.J.White & Ptnrs	Burn	7. 5. 03
DMU	2231	392	Eiri PIK-20D	20524		3.77	A.C.Walford & Ptnrs	Gransden Lodge	2. 3.03
DMV	2232	DMY	Eiri PIK-20D	20526		12. 4.77	F.S.Parkhill	Bellarena	3. 1.04
DMX	2234	DMX	Schleicher ASK13	13567		5. 4.77	Kent GC *(Incorrectly marked as BGA.2294)*	Challock	4. 1.03
DMY	2235	371	Eiri PIK-20D	20532		3.77	G.A.Piper	Parham Park	9. 4.00
DNB	2238		DFS/49 Grunau Baby 2B *(Built Flg.u.Arbeitsg.Hall)*	2	RAFGSA.380 D-5766	2.77	P.Underwood *(On rebuild 2000; to be in Luftwaffe c/s)*	Eaton Bray	*
DNC	2239	588	Grob G.102 Astir CS	1428		13. 4.77	A.J.Carpenter *"Natural High"*	Edgehill	27. 6.99
DND	2240	DND	Pilatus B4 PC-11AF	136		19. 3.77	R J Happs	Lasham	14. 4.03
DNE	2241	DNE	Grob G.102 Astir CS77	1631		3.77	S P Woolcock	Cranfield	8. 3.03
DNF	2242	DNF	SZD-9 bis Bocian 1D	P-354	HB-657	23. 4.77	M.G.Shaw	Portmoak	31. 5.03
DNG	2243	265	Schempp-Hirth HS.5 Nimbus 2	126		5. 4.77	A.O.Harkins & A Brown	Gallows Hill	19. 6.03
DNJ	2245	DNJ	Schleicher ASK18	18042		13. 4.77	Derby & Lancs GC	Camphill	17.12.03
DNK	2246	745	Grob G.102 Astir CS	1434		3. 5.77	745 Syndicate	Wormingford	22.11.03
DNL	2247	DNL	Glasflugel H.201 Standard Libelle	82	RAFGSA.742 RAFGSA 16/G-AXZH	23. 4.77	P.J.Luckhurst *(Owner reports c/n as 82, not 382 as previously recorded)*	Tibenham	6. 4.02
DNQ	2251	307	Rolladen-Schneider LS-3	3035		1.77	M.Cooper	Challock	1. 3.03
DNT	2254	DNT	SZD-30 Pirat	S-0712		25. 5.77	M.Davidson & Ptnrs	Drumshade	11. 5.00
DNU	2255	U2	SZD-42-1 Jantar 2	B-783		4.77	C.D.Rowland & Ptnrs	Booker	1. 8.03
DNV	2256	DNV	Schleicher ASK13	13568		4.77	Buckminster GC	Saltby	3. 5.03
DNW	2257	DNW	Schleicher Ka6CR	829	???	5.77	F.G.Broom	Rhigos	27. 6.03
DNX	2258		Schleicher Ka6CR	6094Si	D-5107	14. 6.77	C.J.Riley	Burn	15.11.02
DNZ	2260	DNZ	Schleicher K8B	8095	???	5.77	North Wales GC	Llantisilio	17. 5.00
DPA	2261	DPA	Schleicher ASK18	18044		25. 5.77	Vectis GC	Bembridge	17. 7.03
DPD	2264	DPD	LET L-13 Blanik *(Incorporates major portions of BGA2121)*	026860		14. 6.77	E.McCaig	Challock	27. 8.01
DPG	2267	DPG	Munchen Mu-13D III	005	D-1327	14. 6.77	G.J.Moore	Dunstable	12. 5.03
DPH	2268	287	Schempp-Hirth HS.7 Mini Nimbus	009		5.77	J.W.Murdoch	Strathaven	23. 5.03

DPJ	2269	DPJ	Grob G.102 Astir CS77	1641		8. 7.77	J.Liddiard & Ptnrs	Lasham	14. 3.03
DPK	2270		Glasflugel H.303 Mosquito	27		6.77	G.Lawley	Cross Hayes	17. 7.03
DPL	2271	437	Eiri PIK-20D	20549		26. 6.77	D.W.Standen	Dunstable	20. 8.02
DPP	2274	DPP	Schleicher Ka2B Rhönschwalbe	105	D-1880	1. 7.77	B.G.Hoekstra	Breda, The Netherlands	8. 7.02
DPQ	2275	DPQ	Grob G.102 Astir CS77	1632		8. 7.77	J.Bone	Wormingford	19. 9.03
DPR	2276	D-1265	Scheibe L-Spatz	05	D-1265	8. 7.77	V.W.Jennings *"Sparrowfahrt"*	Thame	25. 7.01
DPT	2278		Scheibe L-Spatz 55	01	???	25. 8.77	B.V.Smith	AAC Dishforth	12. 7.98
DPU	2279	DPU	EoN AP.5 Olympia 2B	EoN/O/142	RAFGSA.274	6. 9.77	J.M.Turner	Challock	12. 4.03
DPX	2282	440	Schleicher ASW19	19126		7.77	S.L.Morecraft	Nympsfield	8. 4.03
DPY	2283	375	Grob G.192 Astir CS77	1652		8.77	D S Burton	Lasham	7. 6.03
DPZ	2284	DPZ	Slingsby T.34A Sky	822	HB-561	9. 8.77	N McLaughlin	Saltby	3. 7.00
DQA	2285	DQA	Schleicher ASK13	13582		8.77	Essex & Suffolk GC	Wormingford	2. 2.03
DQB	2286	844	Grob G.102 Astir CS77	1653		8.77	G.R.Davey	Kirton-in-Lindsey	26. 3.03
DQC	2287	DQC	Schleicher Ka6CR	6373Si	D-5725	26. 9.77	I.F.Smith	Lasham	27. 3.03
DQD	2288	DQD	Slingsby T.8 Tutor	---		25. 8.77	K.J.Nurcombe	Husbands Bosworth	10.10.03
			(Built from parts by F.Breeze)						
DQE	2289	480	Grob G.102 Astir CS77	1636		8.77	Heron GC	RNAS Yeovilton	11. 5.03
DQF	2290	DQF	Schleicher Ka6CR	6417	D-5827	9.77	P.James	Saltby	15. 2.03
DQG	2291	770	Grob G.102 Astir CS77	1649		6. 9.77	Miss A.G.Veitch	Easterton	8. 7.03
DQH	2292		Schmetz Condor IV	2	D-8538	7. 7.78	M.H.Birch	Utersen, Germany	16. 7.03
DQJ	2293	DQJ	Schleicher Ka6CR	228	D-5467	7.10.77	K.Whitworth	Kenley	27. 1.02
DQK	2294	542	Schleicher Ka6E	4341	D-0541	15.10.77	S.Y.Duxbury & R.S.Hawley *(See BGA.2234)* Camphill		28. 6.03
DQL	2295	DQL	Schleicher Ka8	509	D-5675	15.11.77	Lakes GC	Walney Island	23. 5.03
DQM	2296		Pilatus B4 PC-11	138	RAFGSA	15.10.77	A.R.Dearden	Ringmer	29. 9.03
DQP	2298	DQP	Schleicher K8B	1181	???	15.11.77	Soaring Centre	Husbands Bosworth	27. 5.03
DQR	2300	556	Grob G.102 Astir CS77	1667		10.77	N.R.Warren & Ptnrs	Kingston Deverill	1. 1.04
DQS	2301	DQS	Schleicher Ka6CR	1065	D-5144	23.11.77	L.Hill	North Hill	14. 3.03
DQU	2303	DQU	Eiri PIK-20D	20579		10.77	A.Duncan	Portmoak	28. 6.02
DQX	2306	DQX	Schleicher Ka7 Rhönadler	743	D-9127	15.11.77	Scottish Gliding Union Ltd	Portmoak	3. 4.02
DQY	2307		Schleicher K8B	647	D-4375	11.77	Mendip GC	Halesland	23. 8.03
DRA	2309		Schleicher Ka6CR	1118	D-9041	11.77	P Davis	Bidford	22.11.02
DRB	2310	86	Glaser-Dirks DG-100	31	PH-532	11.77	J.D.Peck	Bicester	26. 3.03
DRD	2312	DRD	Schleicher Ka6CR	6377Si	D-9080	11.77	Essex & Suffolk GC	Wormingford	23. 3.03
DRE	2313	DRE	Schleicher Ka6CR	6197	D-8558	25. 1.78	J.H.Jowett	North Hill	11. 3.03
DRF	2314	DRF	Schleicher Ka6CR	943	D-8600	11.77	Devon & Somerset GC	North Hill	11. 4.98*
			(Damaged North Hill 14.7.97)						
DRG	2315	DRG	Schleicher Ka6CR	6157	D-4090	11.77	WE Smith t/a Summer Wine Syndicate Gallows Hill		14. 8.01
DRJ	2317	D	Schleicher ASK13	13583		11. 1.78	Lasham Gliding Society	Lasham	3.10.03
DRK	2318	DRK	Grob G.102 Astir CS77	1686		12.77	N.Toogood	Lasham	17. 5.03
DRL	2319	DRL	Scheibe SF-26 Standard	5040	D-7073	15.12.77	T McKinley	Kirton-in-Lindsey	16. 2.02
DRM	2320	DRM	Schleicher Ka7 Rhönadler	7017	D-4666	1. 2.78	L.G.Cross & Syndicate	Dunstable	3. 8.03
DRN	2321	821	Glasflugel H.303 Mosquito	082		11. 2.78	A.Roberts	North Hill	28. 3.03
DRP	2322	DRP	Pilatus B4 PC-11	080	RAFGSA BGA.1927	5. 1.78	M.C.Moxon	Weston-on-the-Green	7. 3.03
DRQ	2323	258	Grob G.103 Twin Astir	3027		25. 1.78	V.C.Carr & Ptnrs	Sleap	23. 4.03
DRR	2324	DRR	Schleicher Ka2B Rhönschwalbe	49	D-8108	11. 1.78	Dumfries & District GC	Falgunzeon	16. 7.03
DRS	2325	DRS	SZD-9 bis Bocian 1E	P-783		1. 2.78	Mendip GC	Halesland	25. 5.03
DRT	2326	688	Eiri PIK-20D	20587		5. 1.78	P F Fowler	Sleap	2. 4.03
DRU	2327	334	Grob G.102 Astir CS77	1685		5. 1.78	J.R.Goodenough	Wormingford	27. 1.03
DRV	2328	DRV	Schleicher K8b	8026	D-6169	1.78	P.G.Clayton	Portmoak	23. 4.03
DRW	2329	798	Grob G.102 Astir CS	1081	D-3311	23. 2.78	P.A.Brooks	Lasham	16. 4.03
DRY	2331		Schleicher Ka6BR	370	D-5533	11. 2.78	A.May	RAF Marham	25. 7.99
DRZ	2332	DRZ	Schleicher K8B	668	D-4622 D-KANB/D-4622	1. 2.78	East Sussex GC	Ringmer	9. 3.03
DSA	2333		Slingsby T.30 Prefect	575	WE985	11. 2.78	R.J.Sharman	Crowland	15. 6.03
DSB	2334	DSB	Schleicher Ka6E	4300	D-0263	15. 3.78	M H Yates	Ridgewell	18.10.03
DSE	2337	227	Schempp-Hirth HS.7 Mini Nimbus	36		2.78	G Binnie	Portmoak	11. 1.97*
DSF	2338	DSF	Schleicher K8B	8220	D-7114	2.78	Edinburgh University GC *"Snoopy"*	Portmoak	4. 1.04
DSG	2339		Schleicher Ka6CR	6395	D-5696	13. 4.78	R P Maddocks	Booker	11. 8.00
DSH	2340	648	Grob G.102 Astir CS77	1696		13. 4.78	R B Petrie	Portmoak	20. 4.03
DSJ	2341		Grob G.103 Twin Astir	3050		8. 3.78	L J Kaye	Shobdon	18. 7.03
DSL	2343	447	Grob G.103 Twin Astir	3041		2. 3.78	J.G.Hampson	Enstone	11. 7.03
DSM	2344		Fauvel AV.22S	3	F-CCGM	4.78	I.Dunkley	Camphill	1. 8.95*
DSN	2345	893	Grob G.102 Astir CS77	1698		23. 3.78	J.J.M.Riach	Feshiebridge	.9. 6.03
DSP	2346	270	Schempp-Hirth HS.7 Mini Nimbus	33		9. 3.78	R.I.Hey & Ptnrs	Nympsfield	1. 3.03
DSR	2348	DSR	Schleicher Ka6CR	970	D-5040	31. 5.78	Cornish GC	Perranporth	21. 4.02
DST	2350	972	Schleicher ASW20L	20059		24. 8.78	J.G.Haines	Dunstable	27. 2.03
DSU	2351	DSU	Grob G.102 Astir CS77	1663		19. 4.78	Bowland Forest GC	Chipping	22. 2.03
DSV	2352	718	Pilatus B4 PC-11	134	RAFGSA.718 RAFGGA.518	23.3.78	Staffordshire GC	Seighford	11.95*
DSW	2353	533	Schempp-Hirth HS.7 Mini Nimbus	37	RNGSA.N33	3.78	S.C.Fear	Crowland	8. 3.03
DSX	2354	877	Schleicher ASW19	19188		13. 4.78	R.Grundy	Kingston Deverill	29. 3.03
DSY	2355	DSY	Schleicher Ka6CR	561	D-5702	28. 4.78	D.J.L.Smith	Chipping	30.11.02
DTA	2357	699	Glaser-Dirks DG-2002-	27		9. 5.78	R P Hardcastle	Camphill	19. 5.03
DTC	2359		Schempp-Hirth HS.6 Janus B	63	RAFGSA.R9 RAFGSA 16/BGA.2359	4.78	Dukeries GC	Gamston	14. 7.03
DTD	2360	DTD	Schleicher ASW19	19187		4.78	R.K.Warren	Cross Hayes	21. 3.03
DTE	2361	DTE	Schleicher ASW19	19185		28. 4.78	G.R.Purcell	Lasham	2. 3.03
DTG	2363	DTG	Schempp-Hirth SHK-1	012	D-2034	9. 5.78	M.A.T.Jones & F.A.W.Elliott	Rattlesden	.5. 6.03
DTK	2366	760	Glasflugel H.303 Mosquito B	109		4.78	P.France	Usk	14. 5.03
DTM	2368		Glaser-Dirks DG-200	2-34		31. 5.78	C. Neil	Rattlesden	12. 5.03

DTN	2369	DTN	Schleicher K8B	117/58	???	1. 6.78	F.McKeegan	Wormingford	22. 2.03
DTP	2370	915	Schleicher ASW20	20078		5.78	T.S.Hills & Ptnrs	Lasham	20. 1.03
DTQ	2371	DTQ	Schleicher ASW20	20054		31. 7.78	D.H.Garrard	Cranfield	26. 4.00
DTR	2372	DTR	EoN AP.6 Olympia 401	EoN/4/005	NEJSGSA.7	31. 5.78	B.D.Clarke	Ringmer	15. 5.02
					RAFGSA.252/G-APSI				
DTS	2373	DTS	CARMAM M.100S Mésange	031	F-CCST	18. 5.78	R.C.Holmes	Llantisilio	20. 9.01
DTU	2375	DTU	Schempp-Hirth HS.5 Nimbus 2B	167		9. 5.78	R.E.Wooler	Chipping	25. 3.03
DTV	2376	704	Glasflugel H.303 Mosquito B	110		7. 6.78	S.R.Evans	Nympsfield	21. 6.03
DTW	2377	DTW	SZD-30 Pirat	S-0711		7. 6.78	C Kaminski	North Hill	7. 7.03
DTX	2378	320	Glasflugel H.303 Mosquito B	111		18. 5.78	K.D.Hook	Portmoak	23 .1.02
DTY	2379	766	Glasflugel H.303 Mosquito B	112		18. 5.78	R.Ward	Gransden Lodge	13. 3. 03
DTZ	2380	S30	Slingsby T.30 Prefect	573	WE983	21. 6.78	C.Hughes	Nympsfield	3.12.03
DUB	2382	911	Glasflugel H.303 Mosquito B	113		31. 5.78	A.G.Reid & Ptnrs	Kenley	6. 5.03
DUC	2383		CARMAM M.100S Mésange	012	F-CCSA	7. 6.78	Not known *(Stored 5.94)*	Carlton Moor	5.88*
DUD	2384		Grunau Baby III		BGA.2074	7. 6.78	Not known	(West Sussex)	
					RAFGSA.374/D-9142		*(Under restoration 2001)*		
DUE	2385	A11	Schleicher ASK-13	13591	AGA.15	4. 7.78	Kestrel GC	RAF Odiham	23.3.02
					BGA.2385				
DUF	2386		Schleicher K8B	8296A	D-5294	11. 7.78	Essex GC	Ridgewell	5. 6.03
DUH	2388	DUH	Scheibe L-Spatz	760	NK	28. 7.78	R.J. Aylesbury	Upwood	31. 5.03
DUK	2390	DUK	Schleicher K8B	752	D-4048	21 6.78	Bristol & Glos GC	Nympsfield	14. 3.03
DUL	2391	642	Grob G.102 Astir CS77	1720		21.6.78	J. Warren	Long Mynd	26. 3.03
DUQ	2394	DUQ	Glaser-Dirks DG200	2-43		7.78	D.M. Cottingham	North Hill	9.12.02
DUR	2395	DUR	Schleicher Ka6CR	6273	OY-DLX	15. 8.78	Rattlesden GC	Rattlesden	14. 6.03
DUS	2396	638	Schleicher Ka6E	4263	OY-XCB	.8.78	M. O'Brien	Tibenham	27. 9.03
DUT	2397	T34	Schleicher ASW20	20089		24. 8.78	T.J.Murphy	Portmoak	11. 7.03
DUW	2400		DFS 108/49 Grunau Baby 2B	---	VN148	12.77	C.Tonks	(North Wales)	*
			(Also allocated BAPC.33)		LN+ST		*(On rebuild 2000)*		
DUX	2401	885	Grob G.102 Club Astir	2140		7.78	B.T.Spreckley	Le Blanc, France	15.10.02
DUY	2402	652	Glaser-Dirks DG-100	24	PH-525	13.10.78	A.C.Saxton & Ptnrs	Carlton Moor	14. 7.02
DVB	2405		Schleicher ASK13	13596		8.78	Essex & Suffolk GC	Wormingford	14. 3.03
			(Components, incl c/n plate, donated to BGA.3493 & possibly discarded parts from crash Dunstable 5.6.82)						
DVC	2406	DVC	Schleicher ASK13	13597		31. 8.78	Southdown GC	Parham Park	29. 3.03
DVD	2407	DVD	LET L-13 Blanik	027021	RNGSA.N22	9. 9.78	Vectis GC	Bembridge	14. 4.03
DVE	2408	879	Schleicher Ka6E	4226	RAFGSA.379	15. 8.78	H.F.Young	Sandhill Farm, Shrivenham	25.11.02
DVG	2410	DVG	Schleicher Ka6CR	003	D-1916	22.11.78	R.F.Warren	Ringmer	22. 6.03
			(Built Holzmann-Drespack)						
DVH	2411	DVH	Schleicher Ka6E	4117	RAFGSA	31. 8.78	P.Brett	Perranporth	6. 8.03
DVJ	2412	869	Eiri PIK-20D	20638		9. 9.78	M.C.Hayes	Bidford	29. 5.03
DVK	2413	732	SZD-48 Jantar Standard 2	W-868		22. 9.78	G.P. Nuttall	Gransden Lodge	20. 6.03
DVL	2414	X96	Schleicher ASW19	19222		10.10.78	P.T Healy & Ptnrs	Lasham	2. 6.03
DVM	2415	DVM	Glasflugel H.205 Club Libelle	52	RAFGGA.581	12. 9.78	M.J.Gooch	Rattlesden	13. 4.03
DVN	2416	DVN	Eiri PIK-20D	20641		22.11.78	P.J.Goulthorpe	Husbands Bosworth	1. 6.03
DVP	2417	971	Schleicher ASW19	19220		23. 9.78	E.F.Davies	Booker	27. 8.03
DVQ	2418	DVQ	Schleicher K8B	8134	D-0288	16. 9.78	Staffordshire GC	Seighford	6. 6.99
					D-KICE/D5235				
DVR	2419		Scheibe L-Spatz 55	663	D-1565	23. 9.78	J.Young	Lyveden	6.96*
DVS	2420	VS	Schempp-Hirth HS.4 Standard Cirrus		RAFGSA.824	26. 9.78	D.S.Hands & Ptnr	Parham Park	9. 4.03
			(C/n duplicates VH-GGC)	380					
DVV	2423	810	Schleicher ASW20L	20100		9.78	Mrs A.F.Coppen	Lasham	29. 4.03
DVW	2424	590	Schleicher ASW20	20099		9.78	Not known	Aston Down	2.85*
						(Damaged in collision with BGA.2618 Lasham 17.8.84; wreck stored 7.99)			
DVX	2425	S13	Schleicher ASK13	13598		5.10.78	Shenington GC	Edgehill	15. 6.03
DVY	2426	272	Schempp-Hirth HS.2 Cirrus	52	OO-ZIR	10.78	M.G.Ashton	Perranporth	5. 8.03
DVZ	2427	Z25	Glasflugel H.303 Mosquito B	133		31.10.78	B.H.Shaw	Husbands Bosworth	4. 5.03
DWB	2429	733	Glasflugel H.303 Mosquito B	135		10.11.78	C.G.Salt & Ptnrs	Lasham	26. 3.03
							(As "BGA.2924")		
DWC	2430	DWC	Schleicher Ka6E	4111	AGA.11	24.10.78	D.Jones	Wormingford	22. 5.03
DWE	2432	DWE	Schleicher Ka7 Rhönadler	7132	D-5427	3.11.78	N.T.Large	Llantisilio	24.10.02
DWF	2433	DWF	DFS/49 Grunau Baby 2B	-	AGA.16	11.78	L.P.Woodage	Dunstable	9. 1.02
			(Built RNAY Fleetlands)		RNGSA 1-13/VW743				
DWG	2434		Schleicher K8B	165/60	D-5750	11.78	Newark & Notts GC	Winthorpe	18. 3.02
DWH	2435	DWH	Schleicher K8B	1	D-8614	11.78	Essex GC	Ridgewell	9.96*
			(Built by Gebr.Huber)		D-8331				
DWJ	2436	191	Glaser-Dirks DG-200	2-59		11.78	P.R.Desmond	Chipping	19. 4.03
DWL	2438	755	Glasflugel H.303 Mosquito B	141		2.12.78	A.Stanford & Ptnrs	Husbands Bosworth	1. 7.03
DWN	2440	DWN	Schleicher Ka7 Rhönadler	7101	D-5360	12.78	L.R.Merritt	Edgehill	14. 4.03
DWP	2441	DWP	Glasflugel H.303 Mosquito B	136		15.12.78	N.E.Whiteman	Lasham	20.10.03
DWQ	2442	DWQ	Grob G.102 Astir CS77	1758		9. 1.79	J.O.Davies	Seighford	25. 5.03
DWR	2443	P9	Glasflugel H.303 Mosquito B	134	(BGA.2428)	23. 1.79	C.D.Lovell	Lasham	14. 3.03
DWS	2444	728	Eiri PIK-20D	20652		7. 3.79	D.G.Slocombe	Camphill	21. 5.03
DWT	2445	886	Slingsby T.65A Vega	1898		28. 3.79	A.P.Grimley	Husbands Bosworth	28. 9.00
DWU	2446	DWU	Grob G.102 Astir CS	1201	D-7269	30. 1.79	G.V.McKirdy	Parham Park	9. 5.98
DWW	2448	DWW	Slingsby T.65A Vega	1896		2. 3.79	J.Sorrell	Usk	15. 5.03
DWZ	2451	DWZ	Schleicher ASW19	19243		14. 2.79	J.A.Stirk & Ptnrs	Burn	4. 5.02
DXA	2452	483	Glasflugel H.303 Mosquito B	137		14. 2.79	S H Gibson	Dunstable	13. 3.03
DXB	2453	81	Schleicher ASW20	20142			J.A.Timpany & Ptnrs	Nympsfield	5. 3.03
DXD	2455	132	Slingsby T.65A Vega	1901		20. 4.79	T.C.Harrington & Ptnrs	Bicester	5. 5.03
DXE	2456		Slingsby T.65A Vega	1902		16. 5.79	H.K. Rattray	Usk	16. 3.03
DXF	2457	DXF	Slingsby T.65A Vega	1903		16. 5.79	P.Goulding	Crowland	4. 2.03
DXG	2458	46	Slingsby T.65A Vega 17L	1906		2. 6.79	M.H.Pope	Bidford	29. 4.00

DXH	2459	DXH	Schleicher Ka6E	4198	RAFGSA.489 D-4093	28. 3.79	B.Hughes	Bicester	7. 3.03
DXJ	2460	DXJ	Grob G.102 Astir CS77	1762		2. 3.79	B.Meech	Gransden Lodge	7. 2.03
DXK	2461	160	Centrair ASW20F	20108		15. 5.79	A.Townsend	Booker	23. 6.03
DXL	2462	DXL	Schempp-Hirth HS.4 Standard Cirrus	203G	AGA.1	6. 3.79	P. & A.Gelsthorpe	Lasham	9. 5.03
DXM	2463	DXM	Schleicher Ka7 Rhönadler	626	RAFGGA.551 D-5707	20. 3.79	Vale of Neath GC	Rhigos	13. 7.02
DXN	2464	267	Glaser-Dirks DG-200	2-63		17. 3.79	J.A.Johnston	Gransden Lodge	2. 2.03
DXP	2465	DXP	Schleicher K8B	8646A	D-8537	24. 3.79	Stratford-upon-Avon GC	Snitterfield	24. 2.02
DXQ	2466	147	Schempp-Hirth HS.7 Mini Nimbus C 96 *(Build No.MN97)*			13. 3.79	T.Lamb & P.Hawkins	Weston-on-the-Green	31. 5.03
DXR	2467		Slingsby T.65A Vega	1905		21. 6.79	D.R.Sutton	Sutton Bank	29. 8.94*
DXT	2469	286	Schempp-Hirth HS.7 Mini Nimbus C 97			14. 3.79	C.Chapman	Booker	20.10.03
DXU	2470	DXU	Slingsby T.59J Kestrel 22	1867	G-BDWZ	11. 4.79	D.R. Wilkinson	Riseley	9. 4.03
DXV	2471	DXV	Schleicher ASK13	13602		16. 3.79	Cambridge University GC	Gransden Lodge	22. 2.99
DXW	2472	354	Glasflugel H.303 Mosquito B	142		7. 4.79	P.Newmark & Ptnrs	Burn	15. 2.03
DXX	2473	580	Schleicher ASW19B	19245		17. 3.79	P.F.Whitehead	Bicester	6. 1.03
DXY	2474	HB-474	Muller Moswey III	---	HB-474	20. 4.79	G.M.Bacon & Ptnrs	Gransden Lodge	22. 7.01
DYB	2477		Schleicher Ka7 Rhönadler	167/59	D-5775	29. 3.79	South London Gliding Centre "6" *(Reported as "DYN")*	Kenley	28. 4.03
DYC	2478	DYC	Schleicher Ka6CR	6390	D-1545	20. 3.79	F.J.Smith	Burn	7. 5.03
DYE	2479	828	Schleicher ASW20L	20143		27. 3.79	T.A.Sage	Dunstable	15. 2.03
DYF	2480	850	Grob G.102 Astir CS77	1805		7. 4.79	York Gliding Centre	Rufforth	18. 4.03
DYG	2481	592	Slingsby T.59H Kestrel 22	1868	G-BDZG	31. 3.79	R.E.Gretton & R.L.Darby	Crowland	19. 7.03
DYH	2482	DYH	Glaser-Dirks DG-200	2-75		5. 4.79	W.A.Urwin	Milfield	26. 5.96*
DYJ	2483	DYJ	Schleicher Ka6CR	6583	D-5838	15. 5.79	R.M.Morris	Dunstable	7. 6.03
DYL	2485	DYL	CARMAM JP/15-36A Aiglon	37		4.79	M.P.Edwards	Crowland	23. 5.03
DYN	2486		Schleicher Ka6CR	6129Si	D-8458	1. 5.79	C.N.Harder *(See BGA.2477)*	Lasham	24. 4.03
DYP	2487	BR	Schleicher Ka6BR	191	OO-ZXL D-5482	15. 5.79	D.S.Ling *(Crashed Ridgewell 31.5.97)*	Ridgewell	23. 3.98*
DYQ	2488	DYQ	Schleicher Ka6CR	6178	D-5328	9. 5.79	Dorset GC	Gallows Hill	20. 8.00
DYR	2489	DYR	Schleicher Ka7 Rhönadler	766	D-5220	12. 4.79	Avon Soaring Centre	Bidford	19.12.03
DYT	2490	537	Eiri PIK-20D	20657		18. 5.79	P.J.Hampshire *(Damaged near Parham 12.4.97)*	Parham Park	9. 3.98*
DYU	2491	531	Schempp-Hirth HS.5 Nimbus 2C	181		18. 4.79	A.Pickles	Lasham	7. 7.01
DYX	2494	102	Schleicher ASW20	20135		23. 6.79	J.C.Bailey	Challock	27.11.03
DYZ	2495	943	Schempp-Hirth HS.5 Nimbus 2C	180		24. 4.79	P.M.Molley	Rivar Hill	17. 2.03
DZA	2496	DZA	Slingsby T.65A Vega 17L	1907		26. 6.79	M.P.Garrod	Lasham	21. 2.03
DZB	2497	639	Slingsby T.65A Vega	1908		10. 7.79	A.N.Christie	Drumshade	8. 9.03
DZC	2498	DZC	Scheibe L-Spatz 55	642	RAFGGA D-5629	4. 5.79	G.A.Ford	Nympsfield	23.10.98
DZD	2499	573	Schleicher ASW19B	19268		30. 5.79	J.Anderson	Llantisilio	10.10.03
DZF	2501	152	Schempp-Hirth HS.4 Standard Cirrus	421G	RAFGSA.27	15. 5.79	L.S.Hood	Bicester	27. 5.03
DZG	2502	909	Schleicher ASW19B	19267		10. 5.79	S.P.Wareham	Gallows Hill	17. 2.03
DZJ	2504	576	Grob G.102 Club Astir	2230		11. 5.79	J. & R.Acreman	Halesland	14. 5.03
DZK	2505	957	Schempp-Hirth HS.5 Nimbus 2C 198 *(Fuselage No.195)*			10. 5.79	R Hudson	Sutton Bank	3.12.02
DZM	2507	DZM	Slingsby T.65A Vega	1909		10. 7.79	D.G.MacArthur	Long Mynd	11. 3.03
DZN	2508	990	Slingsby T.65A Vega 17L	1910		13. 7.79	D.A.White	Aboyne	17.12.02
DZP	2509	DZP	Slingsby T.65A Vega	1911		17.11.79	M.T.Crews	Currock Hill	18. 5.03
DZR	2511	DZR	ICA IS-28B	287		13. 6.79	Lakes GC	Walney Island	2. 2.03
DZS	2512	DZS	SZD-8bis-0 Jaskolka	183	HB-583	30. 5.79	N.A Clark	Parham Park	3. 6.03
DZT	2513	106	Eiri PIK-20D	20661		9. 6.79	A.C.Garside	Challock	24. 2.03
DZU	2514	DZU	Grob G.102 Astir CS	1076	D-3308	6. 6.79	P.F.Clarke	Booker	29. 1.03
DZV	2515	839	Scheibe SF-27A Zugvogel V	6065	D-5839	17. 7.79	A.P.Montague	Nympsfield	2. 5.03
DZW	2516	DZW	Schleicher Ka6CR	6628	D-1045	11. 7.79	A.Wildman	Husbands Bosworth	18. 7.03
DZY	2518	757	Schleicher ASW19B	19275		13. 6.79	M.C.Fairman & T.Marlow	Dunstable	8. 4.03
EAC	2522	367	Grob G.102 Astir CS77	1803		14. 6.79	B.T.Pratt	Husbands Bosworth	21. 4.03
EAD	2523	EAD	Slingsby T.65A Vega	1912		30.11.79	I.McCague	Pocklington	2.10.03
EAE	2524	107	Schleicher ASW20L	20224		20. 6.79	L.Clayton	Challock	5. 4.03
EAF	2525	EAF	Grob G.102 Astir CS77	1830		12. 7.79	J.Bell	Milfield	22. 9.03
EAG	2526		Slingsby T.65A Vega	1913		4. 9.79	D.R.Moore	Gransden Lodge	.5.12.02
EAH	2527	EAH	Schleicher Ka6E	4085	D-7542 D-7142	12. 7.79	M.Lodge	Lasham	14. 5.03
EAJ	2528	79	Schempp-Hirth HS.5 Nimbus 2	7	D-0699	28.6.79	G.Harvey	Currock Hill	25.11.03
EAK	2529	594	Glasflugel H.303 Mosquito B	155		29.6.79	T. Barnes	Aston Down	2. 5.03
EAL	2530		Schleicher Ka4 Rhönlerche II	3051/BR	PH-331	7.79	Newcastle & Teesside GC *(Stored 2000)*	Carlton Moor	13. 9.91*
EAM	2531	EAM	Schempp-Hirth HS.5 Nimbus 2B	93	D-2787	10. 7.79	C.H.Brown	Chipping	14. 4.03
EAP	2533	R31	Schleicher ASK-13	13609	RAFGSA.R31 BGA.2533	19. 7.79	RAFGSA Centre	Bicester	9. 2.03
EAR	2535	EAR	Eiri PIK-20D	---		28. 7.79	D.Coker	RAF Syerston	20.12.02
EAT	2537	786	Eiri PIK-20D	20664		22. 8.79	P.T.Reading & Ptnrs	Lasham	6.10.03
EAU	2538	EAU	Schleicher Ka7 Rhönadler	7092	PH-304	7.79	Welland GC *(Part modified to ASK13)*	Upwood	23. 3.03
EAV	2539		Schempp-Hirth HS.7 Mini Nimbus C 136			31. 7.79	G.D.Crawford	Lasham	13. 4.03
EAW	2540	EAW	Grob G.102 Astir CS77	1831		21. 7.79	W.Severn	Cross Hayes	11. 7.03
EBA	2544	EBA	Slingsby T.65A Vega 17L	1914		1.11.79	F.T.Bick	Aboyne	11.11.03
EBB	2545	881	Grob G.102 Speed Astir IIB	4040		28. 7.79	M.Malcolm & A.F.Grinter	Pocklington	14. 5.03

			Type	c/n	Prev id	Date	Owner	Location	Date
EBC	2546	EBC	Slingsby T.30B Prefect	583	RAFGSA.33	1. 8.79	K.R.Reeves	RAF Syerston	10. 4.00
			(Built from parts ex BGA.808 & BGA.1618?) WE993				*"Jonathan Livingstone Prefect"*		
EBD	2547		Scheibe Bergfalke IV	5822	D-1005	4. 9.79	D.Clarke	Burn	31. 3.03
EBE	2548	EBE	Issoire E78 Silene	07		20.11.79	B.A.Burgess	Husbands Bosworth	26. 4.03
EBF	2549	EBF	Schempp-Hirth HS.7 Mini Nimbus C	138		17. 8.79	M.J.Gooch	Rattlesden	12. 4.03
EBG	2550		Eiri PiK-20D	20662		4. 9.79	P.F.Woodcock	Camphill	19. 5.00
			(Assembled from BGA.2550 [fuselage] & BGA.2490 [wings])						
EBJ	2552	h11	Schleicher ASW19B	19282		21. 8.79	J.D.Hill	Sutton Bank	26.11.03
EBK	2553	552	Schempp-Hirth HS.7 Mini Nimbus C	139	AGA.2 BGA.2553	17. 8.79	J.B.Burgoyne	Lyveden	27. 6.03
EBL	2554	EBL	Schleicher ASK13	13610		7. 9.79	Bristol & Glos GC	Nympsfield	25.10.02
EBM	2555	807	Grob G.102 Astir CS77	1843		8.79	P.K. Hayward	Ringmer	2. 4.03
EBN	2556	37	Centrair ASW20F	20118		22. 8.79	K.W.Blake & Ptnrs	Camphill	19. 6.03
EBP	2557	EBP	Allgaier Geier I	3/4	D-9025	4. 9.79	D.P.Raffan	RAF Marham	21. 7.01
EBQ	2558		Schleicher Ka6CR	6051Si	D-5237	3.10.79	Not known *(Under repair 2000)*	Tibenham	
EBR	2559	EBR	Glaser-Dirks DG-200/17	2-89/1706	D-6893	6. 9.79	M.D.Parsons	Lee-on-Solent	25. 5.03
EBS	2560	EBS	Scheibe Zugvogel IIIA	1054	LX-CAF D-8363	21.11.79	I.D.McLeod	Challock	1. 6.03
							"Schwarzhornfalke"		
EBX	2565	644	Schleicher ASW20	20058	D-7973	21. 9.79	J P Davies	Gransden Lodge	11.11.03
EBZ	2567	EBZ	Schleicher ASK13	13614		9.79	Booker GC	Booker	10.12.02
ECA	2568		Wright Falcon	1		9.79	P.W.Wright	Saltby	22. 8.98
ECC	2570	ECC	Schleicher Ka6CR	60/01	D-5080	10.10.79	A.Allison & Ptnrs	Burn	23. 4.03
ECF	2573	ECF	Schleicher Ka6CR	856	D-5808	10.79	D.Goldup	Aston Down	18. 3.03
ECG	2574		Schempp-Hirth SHK	19	D-5359 D-1329	10.10.79	M.F.Hardy	AAC Upavon	17. 3.03
ECH	2575	ECH	Glasflugel H.303 Mosquito B	173		24. 1.80	A.Walker & Ptnrs	Rattlesden	12. 3.03
ECJ	2576	ECJ	Slingsby T.65A Vega	1916		21.12.79	J.E.B.Hart & Ptnrs	Sutton Bank	18. 4.03
ECK	2577	ECK	Slingsby T.65A Vega	1917		13.12.79	B. Chadwick	Lyveden	28. 3.03
ECL	2578		Slingsby T.65A Vega 17L	1918		2. 2.80	J.B.Strzebrakowski	Gransden Lodge	19. 6.03
ECM	2579	ECM	Slingsby T.65A Vega	1919		15. 1.80	F.L.Wilson	Aston Down	24. 6.03
ECN	2580	645	Slingsby T.65A Vega 17L	1920		20.11.79	C.Claxton Syndicate	Booker	1. 2.03
ECP	2581	ECP	Rolladen-Schneider LS-3-17	3426		26. 3.80	D.Crowhurst	Lyveden	7. 4.03
ECQ	2582	ECQ	Grob G.102 Astir CS77	1837		25.10.79	N.Harrison	Tibenham	22. 2.03
ECS	2584	955	Glasflugel H.303 Mosquito B	166		26.10.79	R.C.Adams & P.Robinson	Wormingford	13. 3.03
ECT	2585	604	Glasflugel H.604	2	I-FEVG D-0279	4.10.79	F.K.Russell	Dunstable	31. 3.03
ECW	2588	ECW	Schleicher ASK21	21008		2. 3.80	Norfolk GC	Tibenham	26. 1.03
ECX	2589	600	Schleicher ASW20L	20315		10. 6.80	A.C.Robertson	Feshiebridge	17. 5.03
ECY	2590	ECY	Glasflugel H.201B Standard Libelle	530	RAFGGA.557	13.11.79	E.W.Fry	Bidford	17.5.02
ECZ	2591	ECZ	Schleicher ASK21	21009		26. 4.80	Booker GC	Booker	15. 4.03
EDA	2592	647	Slingsby T.65A Vega 17L	1888	G-BFYW	30.11.79	A.R.Worters	North Connel	17. 9.01
EDB	2593	EDB	CARMAM JP-15-36AR Aiglon	40		1. 2.80	P.J.Martin & Ptnrs	Crowland	14. 4.03
EDC	2594		Schleicher Ka7 Rhönadler	244	D-8527	13. 2.80	J.C.Shipley	Camphill	25. 6.03
EDD	2595	EDD	Schleicher ASW17	17043	D-6865	12.79	C.Curtiss	Crowland	25. 3.03
EDE	2596	750	Centrair ASW20F	20128		27. 2.80	G.M.Cumner	Aston Down	17. 5.00
EDF	2597	530	Schempp-Hirth HS.7 Mini Nimbus C	149		8. 1.80	C.W.Boutcher	Snitterfield	17.10.03
EDG	2598	EDG	Schleicher Ka6CR	6512	RAFGSA	9. 1.80	M.Wood	Saltby	29. 3.03
EDH	2599		Glasflugel H.303 Mosquito B	184		25. 3.80	D.G.Cooper	Tibenham	21. 7.03
EDJ	2600	EDJ	Glasflugel H.303 Mosquito B	185		4. 4.80	A.J.Leigh & Ptnrs	Camphill	.3. 4.03
EDK	2601	EDK	Schleicher Ka7	7791	D-1633	13. 2.80	York Gliding Centre	Rufforth	3. 4.03
EDL	2602		Focke-Wulf Weihe 50	4	D-0893 HB-555	26. 1.80	F.K.Russell	Dunstable	14.10.96*
							(Being restored during 2000)		
EDM	2603	EDM	Glaser-Dirks DG-2002-	98		17. 2.80	A.H.St Pierre	Sutton Bank	21. 3.03
EDN	2604	820	Glaser-Dirks DG-100G Elan	E12G6		14. 2.80	A.P.Scott & Ptnrs	Currock Hill	5. 7.03
EDP	2605	448	Glaser-Dirks DG-100G Elan	E19G7		12. 2.80	B.Jenkinson	Nympsfield	11. 3.03
EDS	2608	EDS	Scheibe SF-26 Standard	5038	RAFGGA.??? D-8454	1. 2.80	I.Davidson	Long Mynd	28. 3.96*
			(Probably ex RAFGGA.548)						
EDU	2610	EDU	Schleicher ASK13	13613		22. 3.80	Kent GC	Challock	8. 2.03
EDV	2611	541	Slingsby T.65A Vega 17L	1893	G-BGCU	8. 2.80	J.L.Clegg	Aston Down	18. 4.03
EDW	2612	EDW	Schleicher ASK21	21010		5. 4.80	UCLU GC	RAF Halton	2. 8.03
EDX	2613	EDX	Slingsby T.65D Vega	1928		20. 5.80	A.James	Usk	27. 4.03
EDY	2614	EDY	Slingsby T.65D Vega	1929		23. 5.80	C.J.Steadman	Husbands Bosworth	8. 4.03
EDZ	2615	EDZ	Slingsby T.65C Sport Vega	1931		18. 6.80	R.C.Copley	Chipping	11. 1.04
EEA	2616	EEA	Slingsby T.65C Sport Vega	1932		27. 6.80	Peterborough & Spalding GC	Crowland	4. 7.03
EEC	2618	EEC	Schleicher ASW20L	20311	(G-BSTS)	27. 6.80	D.M.Cushway	Challock	5. 3.03
EED	2619	R91	Schleicher K8B	590	RAFGSA.R91 NEJSGSA/BGA.2619/D-5703	1. 3.80	R.D.Welsh	Bicester	9. 2.02
EEE	2620	EEE	Schleicher ASW20L	20312		4. 4.80	T E MacFadyen	Nympsfield	7. 4.03
EEF	2621	EEF	Rolladen-Schneider LS-3-17	3441		13. 6.80	G.J.Nicholas	Rivar Hill	22.10.02
EEG	2622	EEG	Slingsby T.65C Sport Vega	1922	EI-129 BGA.2622	3.80	G.Harris	Rufforth	9. 4.03
EEH	2623	166	Schleicher ASW19	19042	RAFGSA	27. 2.80	K Kiely	AAC Dishforth	19. 6.03
EEJ	2624	EEJ	Schleicher ASW20L	20314		20. 9.80	R.R.Stoward	Dunstable	4. 9.02
EEK	2625	141	Schempp-Hirth HS.5 Nimbus 2C	201		23. 2.80	R.E.Cross	Lasham	22.11.02
EEM	2627	EEM	Schleicher K8B	8688AB	D-0254	28. 2.80	South Wales GC	Usk	29. 5.03
EEN	2628		Schempp-Hirth HS.4 Standard Cirrus 75	621	RAFGSA 87 (BGA.2609)	1. 3.80	J.Hanlon	Weston-on-the-Green	30. 3.03
EEP	2629	EEP	Wassmer WA.26P Squale	36	F-CDSX	3.80	R.H.Parker	Aston Down	11. 3.03

Reg	BGA	Comp	Type	c/n	Prev id	Date	Owner	Location	Date
EEQ	2630	EEQ	Grob G.102 Standard Astir II	5015S	RNGSA.N12	3.80	S.W.Bradford	Dunstable	7. 5.03
EER	2631		Schempp-Hirth HS.7 Mini Nimbus	150		14. 3.80	D.J.Uren	Perranporth	20. 4.03
EES	2632	50	Rolladen-Schneider LS-3-17	3248		26. 3.80	J.Illidge & Ptnrs	Camphill	15.10.03
EEU	2634	456	Issoire E78 Silene	08		3.80	M.B.Jefferyes & Ptnrs	Ridgewell	8. 8.98
EEV	2635	129	Centrair ASW20FL	20145		15. 5.80	J.P.Lyell & Ptnr	Lasham	11. 8.03
EEW	2636	EEW	Schleicher Ka6CR	6188	RAFGGA D-6151	26. 3.80	P.E.Lowden	Winthorpe	20. 6.03
EEX	2637	EEX	Rolladen-Schneider LS-3-17	3442		5. 7.80	W A.Dallimer & Ptnr	Aston Down	12. 6.03
EEZ	2639	157	Rolladen-Schneider LS-3A	3458		10. 6.80	J.P. Gilbert	Wormingford	7.12.03
EFA	2640	470	Schleicher ASW20L	20326		2. 7.80	B.Middleton	Dunstable	23. 4.03
EFB	2641	EFB	Schempp-Hirth HS.5 Nimbus 2C	216		3. 4.80	N.Revell & Ptnrs	Gamston	19. 5.03
EFC	2642	EFC	Siebert Sie-3	3018	D-0811	3.4.80	M.S.A.Skinner	Cross Hayes	11. 7.03
EFD	2643	EFD	Schleicher Ka7 Rhönadler	7007	PH-277	15.7.80	South London Gliding Centre	Kenley	19. 1.99
EFE	2644	586	Centrair ASW20F	20139		1. 5.80	J.A.Quartermaine & Ptnrs	Sutton Bank	31. 1.03
EFF	2645	737	Schempp-Hirth HS.5 Nimbus 2C	208		10. 4.80	E.R.Duffin & D.L.Jobbins	Rhigos	16. 4.03
EFG	2646	EFG	Schleicher K8B	?	RAFGGA	10. 4.80	Rattlesden GC	Rattlesden	7. 2.98
EFH	2647	939	Schleicher ASW20	20308		18. 4.80	M B Judkins	Lasham	27. 2.03
EFJ	2648	CW	Centrair ASW20F	20127		12. 4.80	D.E.Ball	Booker	18. 8.03
EFK	2649	643	Centrair ASW20FL	20140		15. 5.80	G.B.Mounslow	Long Mynd	29. 3.03
EFL	2650	297	Centrair ASW20FL	20133		15. 5.80	D.J.Connolly	Kingston Deverill	16. 4.99
							(Believed w/o North Hill 15.5.98)		
EFM	2651	GAZ	Schleicher Ka6E	4103	RAFGSA	4. 6.80	G.S.Foster	Parham Park	6. 8.03
EFN	2652	EFN	Scheibe L-Spatz 55	635	D-1617	17. 5.80	D.J. Edwardes	RAF Odiham	25. 5.03
EFP	2653		Schleicher K8B	E.01	D-8859	13. 5.80	Not known *(Stored 3.95)*	Portmoak	7.88*
EFR	2655	EFR	Scheibe L-Spatz	320	RAFGGA	4.80	H. & A.Purser	Cranfield	25. 9.98
EFS	2656	636	Rolladen-Schneider LS-3	3022	HB-1356	14. 5.80	G.I Boswell	Dunstable	11. 6.99
EFT	2657	J45	Schempp-Hirth HS.5 Nimbus 2B	26	HB-1160	23. 4.80	S.A.Adlard	Long Mynd	26. 5.03
EFV	2659		Schleicher ASW20	20041	OE-5162	12. 6.80	A.R McKillen	Bellarena	4. 9.03
EFW	2660	EFW	Slingsby T.65C Sport Vega	1938		18. 7.80	Dukeries GC	Gamston	21. 6.03
EFX	2661		LET L-13 Blanik	026460	AGA.21	24. 2.80	Enstone Eagles GC	Edgehill	10.11.94*
					RAFGSA.R7/BGA.2095 *(Crashed Enstone 25.6.94; parts to BGA.3666; wreck stored 6.95)*				
EFZ	2663	EFZ	Rolladen-Schneider LS-3A	3273		21.7.80	D.H.Gardner & J.Higgins	Aston Down	18. 4.03
EGD	2667	D3	Schleicher ASW17	17028	D-2343	25. 6.80	W.J.Dean	Booker	22.12.03
EGE	2668	EGE	Rolladen-Schneider LS-3A	3465		31. 7.80	D.Barker	Nympsfield	11. 1.02
EGF	2669	EGF	Slingsby T.65C Sport Vega	1936		28. 6.80	A.P.Aitken	Ringmer	2. 3.03
EGG	2670	JH	Slingsby T.65C Sport Vega	1939		23. 9.80	J.Milsom	Usk	24. 3.03
EGH	2671	EGH	Slingsby T.65C Sport Vega	1943		28.11.80	M.J Davies & Ptnrs	Winthorpe	4. 6.03
EGJ	2672	672	Slingsby T.65C Sport Vega	1944		12.12.80	K.J.Towell & Ptnrs	Lasham	22.11.02
EGK	2673	569	Schempp-Hirth HS.4 Standard Cirrus	542G	RAFGSA.569 RAFGSA.R2(2)	1. 7.80	I.M.Deans & Ptnrs	Lasham	28.11.03
EGL	2674	EGL	Schleicher Ka6CR	6330	D-6037	6.80	G.B.Dennis	Halesland	24.11.97*
							tr Mendip K6 Syndicate *(Damaged North Hill 9.7.97)*		
EGN	2676	EGN	Grob G.103 Twin II	3542		19. 8.80	Enstone Eagles GC	Enstone	20. 3.03
EGP	2677	172	Schleicher ASW20L	20336		17. 9.80	A.W.Gillett & Ptnrs	Nympsfield	2. 3.03
EGR	2679	EGR	Breguet Br.905SA Fauvette	18	F-CCGT	22. 8.80	P.Parker	Dunstable	15. 2.03
EGS	2680	2	Schempp-Hirth HS.5 Nimbus 2CS	192	D-2111	21. 7.80	P.G.Myers	Chipping	27. 4.03
EGT	2681	EGT	Slingsby T.65D Vega	1933		28. 7.80	D.M.Badley & Ptnrs	Sleap	9. 2.03
EGU	2682	EGU	Slingsby T.65A Vega	1921		28. 7.80	M.N.Bishop	Challock	22. 4.03
EGW	2684	EGW	Schempp-Hirth HS.7 Mini Nimbus B	78	HB-1447	1. 8.80	I F Barnes	Ridgewell	28. 8.03
			(Modified to Mini Nimbus C?)						
EGX	2685	EGX	Slingsby T.65C Sport Vega	1937	RAFGSA.R23 BGA.2685	15.10.80	M.D.Organ	Weston-on-the-Green	7. 2.03
EGZ	2687	EGZ	Schleicher ASK21	21030		28.10.80	Needwood Forest GC	Cross Hayes	16. 3.03
EHA	2688		Schleicher K8B	136/59	D-5084	6. 9.80	NK *(Stored as "D-5084" 1.97)*	Fairwood Common	*
EHB	2689	K3	Schleicher Ka3	3	????	23.10.80	L.S.Hood	Cranwell	5. 7.03
EHC	2690	EHC	Eichelsdorfer SB-5B	5017	D-9310	14. 8.80	R.I.Davidson	Husbands Bosworth	8. 8.02
EHD	2691	891	Schleicher ASW20L	20386		10.80	B.Lumb	Burn	18. 4.03
EHE	2692	WE992	Slingsby T.30B Prefect	582	WE992	29. 9.80	A.P.Stacey tr A.T.C.Syndicate	RAF Keevil	5. 3.98
EHF	2693		Caudron C.801	320/4	F-CBTE	11. 5.89	Dutch Aircastle Society	Loosdrecht, The Netherlands	5. 3.03
EHG	2694	453	Slingsby T.65C Sport Vega	1940		21.10.80	M.J.Vickery & Ptnrs	Lasham	7 .2.01
EHH	2695	V7	Schempp-Hirth Ventus A	07		5.11.80	P.G.Sheard & A.Stone	Lasham	5. 3.03
EHK	2697	490	Rolladen-Schneider LS-4	4068		15. 3.81	S.J.C.Parker	Nympsfield	9. 2.03
EHL	2698	138	Rolladen-Schneider LS-4	4024		24. 4.81	C.J.Evans	Booker	26. 3.03
EHM	2699	EHM	Schleicher Ka6E	4118	RAFGSA.318	28. 3.81	D.J.Pengilly	Kingston Deverill	13. 8.03
EHN	2700	EHN	Slingsby T.65C Sport Vega	1942	G-BILH BGA.2700	17.12.80	G.D.Hayter	Challock	14. 3.03
EHP	2701	EHP	Schempp-Hirth HS.5 Nimbus 2C	234		11.80	R.Hudson	Sutton Bank	28. 2.03
EHQ	2702	431	Schleicher ASK21	21035		21.11.80	University of Surrey GC	Lasham	27. 1.03
EHS	2704	EHS	ICA IS-28B	289		3.12.80	M.Terry	Winthorpe	1. 9.03
EHT	2705	EHT	Schempp-Hirth HS.5 Nimbus 2C	235		12.80	P.M.Kirschner	Cranfield	19. 4.03
EHU	2706	849	Glasflugel H.304	209		5.11.80	F.& J.M.Townsend	Camphill	3.12.03
EHV	2707	481	Schleicher ASW20L	20385		6. 1.81	G.S.Neumann & Ptnrs	Booker	24. 3.03
EHW	2708	EHW	ICA IS-28B	286		9. 1.81	M Sanderson	Milfield	23. 6.03
EHX	2709	1128	DFS/49 Grunau Baby 2B	134	D-1128	21.12.80	J.A.Knowles	RAF Odiham	10. 3.98
EHY	2710		Slingsby T.65D Vega	1941		8. 1.81	R.Spear	Ringmer	15. 3.03
EHZ	2711	413	Schleicher ASW20L	20388		29. 1.81	D.Hoolahan	Challock	8. 7.03
EJA	2712		ICA IS-28B	288		16. 1.81	DRA GC	RAF Odiham	15.12.00
EJB	2713	EJB	Slingsby T.65C Sport Vega	1945		23. 1.81	I.G.Walker & Ptnrs	Camphill	4. 5.03
EJC	2714	EJC	Slingsby T.65C Sport Vega	1946		9. 2.81	A M.Raper & Ptnrs	Rattlesden	14. 4.03
EJD	2715	261	Slingsby T.65D Vega 17L	1930		29. 6.81	A.J.French	Rufforth	28. 5.97*
							(Damaged Dunstable 28.3.97: wreck noted 5.99)		

EJE	2716	EJE	Slingsby T.65C Sport Vega	1947		16. 2.81	DRA GC	RAF Odiham	20. 4.03
EJF	2717	EJF	Schleicher K8B	8966	D-2328	15. 1.81	Cambridge University GC	Gransden Lodge	5. 1.04
EJG	2718		Schleicher K8B	01	D-5679	30. 1.81	Kent GC	Challock	28. 2.99
EJH	2719	EJH	Eichelsdorfer SB-5E	5041A	D-5430	14. 1.81	H.J.McEvaddy	Husbands Bosworth	11. 6.01
					D-0087				
EJJ	2720	EJJ	Slingsby T.21B	618	RAFGSA.120	1. 3.81	N.P.Marriott	Parham Park	17. 4.03
					BGA.662/WB957				
EJK	2721	76	Centrair ASW20FLP	20172		15. 4.81	A.M.Blackburn		4. 5.01
							(Crashed Camphill 21.7.00 and written-off)		
EJL	2722	904	Centrair ASW20FL	20183		27. 4.81	S.R.Jarvis	Bidford	8. 5.03
EJQ	2726	EJQ	Centrair ASW20FL	20184		20. 4.81	J. Bayford	Gransden Lodge	7. 4.03
EJR	2727	193	Schleicher ASW19B	19334		12. 4.81	A.R.P.Charters	Nympsfield	21. 3.03
EJS	2728	319	Slingsby T.65C Sport Vega	1948		20. 3.81	A.D.McLeman	Portmoak	9. 9.02
EJT	2729	890	Slingsby T.65A Vega	1889	G-VEGA	5. 3.81	W.A.Sanderson	Rattlesden	3.12.03
					(G-BFZN)				
EJW	2732		Issoire D77 Iris	04		30. 4.81	T.Hurley	Husbands Bosworth	27. 2.95*
EJY	2734	EJY	SZD-9 bis Bocian 1D	P-351	D-1587	13. 4.81	The Borders GC	Milfield	15. 9.03
EKA	2736	EKA	Glaser-Dirks DG-200/17	2-128/1730		3. 8.81	M J Lindsey	Tibenham	20. 3.03
EKB	2737	710	Schempp-Hirth HS.6 Janus C	129		16. 4.81	D.A.Head	Bicester	21. 2.99
							(Reported damaged RAF Halton 1.3.98)		
EKC	2738	EKC	Schleicher Ka6E	4079	OO-ZDV	18. 6.81	S L Benn	RAF Cranwell	16. 3.03
					OE-0813				
EKD	2739	EKD	Schleicher ASK13	13539	OH-494	21. 4.81	Bristol & Glos GC	Nympsfield	16. 6.03
EKE	2740	20L	Schleicher ASW20L	20387		15. 4.81	A.G.Mackenzie	Ringmer	29. 4.03
EKF	2741	EKF	Grob G.102 Club Astir III	5519C		14. 6.81	Bristol & Glos GC	Nympsfield	30. 3.03
EKG	2742	EKG	Schleicher ASK21	21067	AGA.8	11.99	Wyvern GC	AAC Upavon	29.12.03
					BGA.2742				
EKH	2743	714	Schempp-Hirth Ventus B	32		1. 5.81	R Bottomley	Lasham	22.12.02
EKJ	2744	186	Schempp-Hirth Ventus B	36		7. 5.81	I.J.Metcalfe	Nympsfield	17. 8.03
EKK	2745	EKK	SZD-48 Jantar Standard 2	W-853		9. 5.81	S.Nutley	Portmoak	31. 8.02
EKM	2747	EKM	Schleicher K8B	647	PH-258	28. 5.81	Not known *(Wreck stored 8.02)*	Aston Down	
EKP	2749	EKP	Glaser-Dirks DG-100G Elan	E71G46		3.10.81	P.J.Masson	Lasham	8. 3.03
EKR	2751	117	Schempp-Hirth HS.5 Nimbus 2C	195	D-4904	25. 6.81	J.W.Evans	Bidford	15 2.03
EKS	2752	EKS	Scheibe SF-27A Zugvogel V	6096	D-8166	28. 4.81	J.C. Johnson	Parham Park	12. 3.03
EKT	2753		Wassmer WA30 Bijave	241	F-CDML	11. 5.81	D.C.Austin	Dishforth	1.10.02
EKU	2754	408	Schleicher ASW20L	20384		19. 5.81	A.Gilson	Sleap	5. 1.03
EKV	2755	EKV	Rolladen-Schneider LS-4	4102		12. 7.81	M.Ray	Lasham	15.11.02
EKW	2756	430	Schempp-Hirth HS.5 Nimbus 2B	111	D-7245	7. 6.81	R.S.Jobar	Lasham	3. 5.03
EKX	2757	D1221	Schleicher Ka6E	4027	D-1221	20. 6.81	A.Coatsworth	Gallows Hill	10. 8.03
EKY	2758	EKY	Slingsby T.65C Sport Vega	1949		17. 6.81	Essex & Suffolk GC	Wormingford	26. 3.03
ELA	2760	ELA	Schleicher ASW19B	19346		28. 7.81	A.G.Stark	Portmoak	4. 5.03
ELC	2762	ELC	Slingsby T.45 Swallow	1474	AGA	25. 5.81	J.Povall	AAC Dishforth	15. 3.03
					RAFGSA.346				
ELD	2763	ELD	Slingsby T.65C Sport Vega	1950		17. 8.81	D.J Clark & Ptnrs	Challock	15. 1.03
ELE	2764	ELE	Schleicher ASK21	21065		1. 7.81	Midland GC	Long Mynd	27. 4.03
ELG	2766	ELG	Schempp-Hirth Ventus B	46		19. 8.81	H.Forshaw	Burn	4. 4.03
ELH	2767		Slingsby T.21B	---	RAFGSA.314	16. 9.81	Not known	Enstone	7.91*
			(Possibly ex WB966 [627])		(RAF)		*(Stored 3.97)*		
ELJ	2768	ELJ	Breguet Br.905SA Fauvette	21	F-CCGU	20. 8.81	E.A.Hull	Dunstable	16. 2.03
ELK	2769		Slingsby T.9 King Kite rep.			8.83	D.G.Jones	Husbands Bosworth	26. 5.99
ELL	2770	L01	Vogt Lo-100 Zwergreiher	25	HB-591	27. 7.81	I.E.Tunstall	RAF Syerston	14. 5.01
ELN	2772	ELN	Grob G.102 Astir CS Jeans	2024	???	12. 8.81	J.M.Hughes	Dunstable	1. 6.03
ELQ	2774	ELQ	Slingsby T.65D Vega	1934		3. 9.81	J.Bell	Milfield	23. 9.03
ELR	2775	188	Schleicher ASW19B	45		19. 8.81	I.D.Smith	Nympsfield	1. 3.03
ELS	2776		EoN AP.10 460 Srs.1	EoN/S/020	RAFGGA.530	8.81	D.G.Shepherd	Easterton	6.11.02
ELT	2777	ELT	Rolladen-Schneider LS-4	4186		9.81	P.D.MaCarthy	Lasham	21. 2.03
ELU	2778	696	Schleicher ASW20L	20462		9.81	D. Briggs	Aston Down	3. 1.04
ELV	2779	ELV	Scheibe Zugvogel IIIB	1088	F-CCPX	5. 9.81	C.R.W.Hill	Crowland	12. 4.03
ELX	2781		Schleicher Ka7 Rhönadler	928	D-4023	18. 9.81	Rattlesden GC	Rattlesden	14. 6.03
ELY	2782	ELY	Schleicher Ka6CR	6485Si	D-5172	28. 9.81	P.F.Richardson & Ptnrs	Bellarena	3. 4.03
ELZ	2783	719	Schleicher ASW20L	20310		4.10.81	D.A.Ogden	Booker	25. 2.03
EMB	2785	L11	Rolladen-Schneider LS-4	4185		10.81	M.E.Lee	Winthorpe	9. 2.03
EME	2788	515	Glaser-Dirks DG-202/17C	2-176CL18		11.81	E.D.Casagrande	Usk	14. 2.03
EMF	2789	452	Rolladen-Schneider LS-4	4187		11.81	E.R.Smith & Ptnrs	Thruxton	1. 3.03
EMG	2790	EMG	Rolladen-Schneider LS-4	4242		8. 5.82	R C Bowsfield	Nympsfield	25. 3.03
EMJ	2792	EMJ	Slingsby T.65C Sport Vega	1951		1. 2.82	Staffordshire GC	Seighford	2. 5.03
EMK	2793		Slingsby T.45 Swallow	1514	RAFGGA.545	12.81	A.Povey & Ptnrs	RAF Syerston	5.00
EML	2794	218	Slingsby T.65A Vega	1892	G-BGCB	8.12.81	P.W.Williams	North Hill	30 5.03
EMN	2796	EMN	Slingsby T.65D Vega	1935		25. 1.82	C.D Sword	Currock Hill	28. 7.03
EMP	2797		Slingsby T.65C Sport Vega	1952		2. 2.82	D.R Freehold	Kenley	18. 3.03
EMR	2799		Slingsby T.65C Sport Vega	1954		10. 2.82	P.Greenway & Ptnrs	Shobdon	15. 8.03
EMS	2800	T65	Slingsby T.65A Vega 17L	1890	G-BGBV	26. 1.82	M.P.Day	Kenley	12.10.02
EMT	2801	55	Rolladen-Schneider LS-4	4243		12.81	D.B.Eastell	Challock	3. 2.03
EMU	2802	606	Glaser-Dirks DG-202/17	2-162/1753		1.82	P.B.Gray & Ptnrs	Camphill	4. 5.03
EMV	2803	EMV	Schleicher Ka7 Rhönadler	---	AGA.13	1. 1.82	Shalbourne Soaring Group	Rivar Hill	11. 7.02
					BGA.2803				
EMW	2804	17	Grunau Baby III	---	D-1373	5. 7.89	M.T.A.Sands	(France)	27. 9.99
EMY	2806	264	Rolladen-Schneider LS-4	4189		15. 4.82	N.V.Parry	Nympsfield	16. 3.03
EMZ	2807	EMZ	Slingsby T.65A Vega	1891	G-BGCA	5. 2.82	F.S.Smith	Portmoak	18. 4.03
ENA	2808	288	Rolladen-Schneider LS-4	4191		31. 5.82	J.D.Collins & Ptnr	Bidford	12. 4.03

ENC	2810	ENC	Schleicher Ka7 Rhönadler	384	D-8111	2. 3.82	I.H.Keyser	Waldershare Park	23. 4.02
			(Modified to ASK13 status)						
ENE	2812	281	Rolladen-Schneider LS-4	4271		1. 6.82	D.M.Abbey	Husbands Bosworth	26. 2.03
ENG	2814	ENG	Focke-Wulf Kranich III	79	D-5420	8. 3.82	P.R.Davie & Ptnrs	Dunstable	18. 7.03
ENJ	2816	771	Schempp-Hirth Ventus B	62		25. 3.82	S.J.Boyden	Lasham	11. 9.03
ENK	2817	ENK	Schleicher ASK21	21106		12. 4.82	H Jakeman	Aston Down	7. 3.03
ENN	2820	345	Schempp-Hirth Nimbus 3	9		5. 4.83	R.Kalin & Ptnrs	Gransden Lodge	1. 1.03
ENP	2821	626	Schempp-Hirth Nimbus 3	10		12.11.82	L.Bleaken	Aston Down	19. 4.03
ENT	2825	902	Glasflugel H.304	210		13. 5.82	P.D.Light	Dunstable	8. 4.02
ENU	2826	435	Glaser-Dirks DG-100G Elan	E108G78		8. 8.82	R.D.Platt	Camphill	12. 4.03
ENV	2827	181	Schleicher ASW20L	20554		27. 5.82	R.D.Hone	Booker	15. 7.03
ENW	2828	ENW	Schleicher ASW20L	20567		28. 5.82	A.Hunter	Pocklington	21. 3.03
ENX	2829		SZD-48 Standard Jantar 2	W857	(BGA.2746)	6.82	J.M. Hire	Currock Hill	14. 6.03
ENY	2830	ENY	Schleicher ASK13	13606	RAFGSA.R17	22. 7.82	Aquila GC	Hinton in the Hedges	3. 5.03
ENZ	2831		Schleicher ASW19B	19366		29. 6.82	O.Pugh	Booker	13. 5.03
EPD	2835	EPD	Schleicher ASK21	21119		29. 8.82	J.E.Ashcroft	Chipping	21. 4.03
EPE	2836	EPE	Schleicher ASW19B	19335	RAFGSA.R18	29. 6.82	J.Horner	Pocklington	22. 3.03
					BGA.2836				
EPF	2837	323	Centrair ASW20FLP	20515		1. 7.82	D.J.Howse	Gransden Lodge	14. 3.03
EPG	2838		CARMAM M.100S Mésange	3	F-CCPB	7.82	P.Shanahan	Templeton	24. 2.95*
EPJ	2840		Nord 2000 (Olympia)	10399/69	F-CACX	8.82	B.V.Smith	Sutton Bank	1. 5.02
EPK	2841	742	Centrair 101A Pégase	101-012		16. 1.83	742 Syndicate	Bicester	14. 3.02
EPM	2843	EPM	Scheibe SFH-34 Delphin	5115		22.10.82	Angus GC	Drumshade	19. 6.03
EPN	2844		Breguet Br.905SA Fauvette	11	F-CCIO	18. 7.82	P.F.Woodcock	Camphill	31. 7.95*
EPP	2845	EPP	Schleicher ASK13	1609		28.12.82	Mendip GC	Halesland	3. 7.03
			(Rebuild of PH-368 c/n 13064: c/n is spare fuselage no.)						
EPR	2847		Hutter H-17	-	(Kenya)	30. 9.82	D.Shrimpton	Halesland	29. 6.97
					PH-269				
EPS	2848	765	Schleicher ASW20L	20245	RAFGSA.87	5. 7.85	D.Richardson	Booker	30. 4.98
EPT	2849	EPT	Schleicher K8B	---	RAFGGA.504	14. 9.82	Trent Valley GC	Kirton-in-Lindsey	21. 1.03
EPU	2850		Glaser-Dirks DG-100G Elan	E116G85	(BGA.2833)	31.10.82	J.F.Rogers	Booker	23. 3.03
EPV	2851	EPV	Schleicher Ka7 Rhönadler	7148	D-5468	8.10.82	Surrey Hills GC	Kenley	6. 7.03
EPW	2852	EPW	Schleicher Ka6CR	6537	(Kenya)	21. 3.83	J.Kitchen	Strubby	12. 3.03
EPX	2853	EPX	Schempp-Hirth Ventus B/16.6	107		20.10.82	D.L. Slobom	Dunstable	11. 4.03
EPZ	2855		Scheibe Bergfalke II/55	370	D-4012	15. 1.83	G.W.Sturgess *(Being refurbished 2000)*	Upavon	11. 8.96*
EQA	2856	279	Rolladen-Schneider LS-4	4259		24. 6.83	R.L.Smith	Booker	1. 2.03
EQB	2857		SZD-30 Pirat	S-0648	D-2702	31.10.82	R.Firman	Booker	6. 7.03
EQD	2859	EQD	Grob G.102 Astir CS77	1614	PH-570	14. 1.83	D.S.Fenton & Ptnrs	Rhigos	10. 5.03
EQE	2860	EQE	Schleicher ASK13	13627		14. 4.83	Essex GC	Ridgewell	9. 4. 03
EQF	2861		Schleicher ASK13	13626		8. 3.85	Essex GC	Ridgewell	27. 5.03
EQG	2862	239	Schleicher ASW19B	19265	PH-665	16.12.82	C.M.Whittington & Ptnrs	Challock	15. 3.03
EQJ	2864	968	Centrair ASW20FL	20512		21. 1.83	R.Grey	Lasham	26. 3.03
EQK	2865	EQK	Centrair 101A Pégase	101-054		30. 5.83	F.G.Irving & Ptnrs	Lasham	20. 4.03
EQL	2866		Avialsa (Rocheteau) CRA-60 Fauconnet	F-CDNR 03K		18. 1.86	J.James	Saltby	30. 6.01
EQM	2867		CARMAM M.100S Mésange	81	F-CDKQ	20. 3.83	R.Boyd	Rivar Hill	25. 7.03
EQN	2868	340	Schempp-Hirth Nimbus 3	31		21. 2.83	A.D.Purnell	Lasham	5. 2.03
EQQ	2870	451	Schleicher Ka6CR	6541	AGA.24 BGA.1353	6. 3.83	G.H.Costin & Ptnrs	Challock	2. 2.03
EQR	2871	EQR	Schleicher ASK21	21157		25. 4.83	London GC	Dunstable	26.11.03
EQT	2873	R58	Grob G.103A Twin II Acro	3787-K-65	RAFGSA.R58 BGA.2873	15. 4.83	R.Tyrell	Bidford	28.10.02
EQU	2874	EQU	Pilatus B4 PC-11	201	PH-535	2. 4.83	G.A.Settle	Chipping	26. 4.03
EQV	2875		Schempp-Hirth Janus C	169	ZD974 BGA.2875	8. 3.83	Burn GC	Burn	17.10.03
EQW	2876	383	Schempp-Hirth Janus C	171	ZD975 BGA.2876	24. 4.83	J.N.Mills	Lasham	7. 4.03
EQX	2877	EQX	CARMAM M.200 Foehn	54	F-CDKR	11.4.83	C.A.McLay & Ptnrs	Chipping	15. 3.03
EQY	2878		BAC.VII rep	01		8. 9.91	M.H.Maufe	Sutton Bank	21. 5.96P*
			(Rebuild of BAC Drone using wings of G-AEJR & new fuselage; being refurbished)						
EQZ	2879	EQZ	Schleicher K8B	8113A	D-8763	13. 4.83	Cotswold GC	Aston Down	7. 4.03
ERA	2880	283	Centrair ASW20FL	20526		4.83	D.A.Adams	Booker	2. 5.03
ERB	2881		Slingsby T.50 Skylark 4 Special	001		25. 4.83	B.V.Smith *(Built C.Almack)*	Sutton Bank	16. 5.03
ERH	2887	ERH	Schleicher ASK21	21147	ZD647 BGA.2887	28. 4.83	Burn GC	Burn	23. 4.03
ERJ	2888	R35	Schleicher ASK21	21148	RAFGSA.R35 ZD648/BGA.2888	28.4.83	Cranwell GC	RAF Cranwell	20.12.03
ERP	2893	SH5	Schleicher ASW-19B	19348	ZD657 BGA.2893	28. 4.83	Surrey & Hants GC	Lasham	19. 1.03
ERQ	2894		Schleicher ASW-19B	19381	ZD658 BGA.2894	28. 4.83	G.Lane	Riseley	4. 4.03
ERR	2895	ERR	Schleicher ASW-19B	19382	ZD659 BGA.2895	28.4.83	D.M. Hook	Lasham	15. 3.03
ERS	2896	ERS	Schleicher ASW-19B	19383	ZD660 BGA.2896	28. 4.83	J.C.Marshall	Kingston Deverill	14. 1.03
ERU	2898	ERU	Schempp-Hirth Nimbus 3	13	RAFGSA.R26 D-6330	4. 5.83	L.Urbani	Rieti, Italy	31. 5.03
ERV	2899	854	Rolladen-Schneider LS-4	4257		19. 5.83	R E Francis	Nympsfield	7.11.03
ERW	2900		Slingsby T.21B	1130	RAFGSA.237 BGA.842	24. 5.83	High Moor GC *"The Spruce Goose"*	Hafotty Bennett	10.11.02
ERX	2901	180	Centrair 101A Pégase	101-058		3. 8.83	C.N.Harder	Lasham	10.5.03

ERY	2902	983	Slingsby T.59D Kestrel 19	1839	EI-125	14. 6.83	R.J.Hart & Ptnr	Crowland	15. 3.03
					D-9253				
ERZ	2903		Oberlerchner Mg19a Steinadler	015	OE-0324	1. 6.83	C.Wills	Booker	4. 5.02
ESA	2904	ESA	SZD-9 bis Bocian 1E	P-750		21. 6.83	The Soaring Centre	Husbands Bosworth	17.10.03
ESB	2905	ESB	Schleicher ASK21	21176		2. 9.83	A.L.Garfield	Dunstable	10.12.03
ESC	2906	379	Rolladen-Schneider LS-4	4261		25. 6.83	J.M.Staley	Bicester	28. 7.03
ESE	2908	LS4	Rolladen-Schneider LS-4	4260		26. 6.83	P.C.Fritche	Parham Park	21.12.03
ESH	2911	118	Centrair 101A Pégase	101-069		2. 7.83	J.E. Moore	Booker	16. 3.03
ESJ	2912	ESJ	Schleicher K8B	8730	D-5010	13. 7.83	Bowland Forest GC	Chipping	26.11.03
ESK	2913		Schleicher Ka2B	697	RAFGGA.594	23. 7.83	W.R.Williams	RAF Halton	20. 5.00
					D-5947				
ESM	2915	ESM	Breguet Br.905SA Fauvette	30	F-CCJA	14.10.83	A C Jarvis	Parham Park	7.10.03
ESP	2917	ESP	SZD-48-3 Jantar Standard 3		B-1294	19. 4.84	J.Durman	Pocklington	18. 3.03
ESQ	2918	231	Glaser-Dirks DG-300 Elan	3E10		4.84	G.R.Brown	Sandhill Farm, Shrivenham	29. 6.03
ESU	2922	ESU	Schleicher ASK21	21180	RAFGSA.R40	12.11.83	Aquila GC	Hinton in the Hedges	25. 3.03
			(Composite with RAFGSA.R28 c/n 21154)		BGA.2922				
ESV	2923		LET L-13 Blanik	173328	EI-110	22. 5.84	Herefordshire GC	Shobdon	17. 4.98
					IGA,110/G-ATWW		*(Noted as wreck 8.99)*		
ESW	2924	590	Centrair 101A Pégase	101-068		20. 3.84	D.A.Brown	Usk	23. 1.03
ESX	2925	ESX	Schleicher K8B	8805	RAFGGA.553	10. 9.83	Wolds GC	Aston Down	31.12.96*
							(W/o Pocklington 2. 2.96 ; stored 7.02)		
ESY	2926	ESY	Rolladen-Schneider LS-4	4334		4. 2.84	K.Jenkins & Ptnrs	North Hill	18. 2.03
ETA	2928	ETA	Schleicher ASK21	21181		19.11.83	R W Collings	Husbands Bosworth	12. 7.03
ETB	2929	ETB	Schleicher Ka6E	4365	HB-1021	20.11.83	A.J.Padgett	Tibenham	24. 9.03
ETD	2931	R44	Schleicher K8B	8918	RAFGSA.R44	30.12.83	RAFGSA Centre	Bicester	7.12.03
					BGA2931				
ETE	2932		Fauvel AV.36C	214	RAFGSA.R53	25. 8.87	J.F.Beringer *"The Budgie"*	Wormingford	7. 6.98
					D-5353/D-8259				
ETG	2934	ETG	Rolladen-Schneider LS-4	4349		7. 2.84	M.W.Rebbeck & Ptnrs	Rattlesden	18. 7.03
ETH	2935	ETH	Schleicher K8B	120	D-5755	23. 3.84	North Wales GC	Llantsilio	3. 9.03
ETJ	2936	223	Centrair 101A Pégase	101A-0110		8. 8.84	K.J.Bye	Wormingford	17. 1.03
ETK	2937	215	SZD-48 Jantar Standard 2	W-876	OY-XJO	14. 2.84	J.A.Cowie	Portmoak	26. 6.03
ETL	2938		Jansson BJ-1B Duster	01		1.85	I.Beckett	North Hill	28. 3.96*
ETM	2939	M7	Centrair 101 Pégase	101-111		11. 4.84	M.D. Evans	Booker	24. 6.03
ETN	2940		CARMAM M.100S Mésange	23	F-CCSL	24. 2.84	T.E.Betts	Seighford	27. 8.96*
ETP	2941	WB943	Slingsby T.21B	610	WB943	7.84	P.Hepworth t/a Ouse T.21 Syndicate	Rufforth	5. 8.03
ETR	2943	S7	Schleicher Ka7 Rhönadler	3	D-8339	21. 2.84	Shenington GC	Edgehill	26. 3.02
ETS	2944		Schleicher ASK13	13635AB		3. 3.84	Upward Bound Trust	Thame	11.11.02
ETU	2946	ETU	Schleicher Ka7 Rhönadler	---	RAFGSA R.8	24. 3.84	R.Cullum	Strubby	30. 3.03
ETV	2947	ETV	Rolladen-Schneider LS-4	4314	(BGA.2919)	23. 3.84	T.A.Meaker	Kirton-in-Lindsey	9. 7.03
ETY	2950	249	Rolladen-Schneider LS-4	4368		16. 4.84	R.Harris	Booker	8. 1.04
ETZ	2951	20	Schleicher ASW20CL	20730		20. 3.84	N.L.Clowes	Lasham	22. 3.03
EUC	2954	EUC	Schleicher ASK13	13104	AGA.12	15. 4.84	Bristol & Glos GC	Nympsfield	21. 2.03
EUD	2955	56	Schleicher ASW20C	20734		3. 6.84	J.E.Gilbert	Lasham	2. 3.03
EUE	2956	EUE	Scheibe SF-27A Zugvogel V	6106	D-5342	6. 4.84	Newark & Notts GC	Winthorpe	19. 2.03
EUF	2957		SZD-50-3 Puchacz	B-1090		30. 5.84	D.B.Meeks tr Bidford Gliding Centre	Bidford	31. 3.00
EUG	2958		LET L-13 Blanik	025817	RAFGSA.R56	14. 5.84	Avon Soaring Centre	Bidford	31. 5.93*
					RAFGSA.426/BGA.1953		*(Wreck stored 8.94)*		
			(Composite rebuild - fuselage/tail: BGA.1917 [025610], port [025817] & starboard wings (BGA.2028 [026257])						
EUH	2959	446	Rolladen-Schneider LS-4	4382		14. 4.84	A.R.Turner	Nympsfield	19. 3.03
EUJ	2960	210	Schempp-Hirth Ventus B/16.6	162		9. 4.84	T.Paterson & Ptnrs	Portmoak	13. 1.03
EUK	2961	992	Centrair ASW20FL	20530		20. 5.84	J.L.Caton	Lasham	24. 3.03
EUM	2963		Scheibe SF-26A Standard	5039	RAFGSA	20. 4.84	Vale of Neath GC	Rhigos	14. 7.97*
EUN	2964		Slingsby T.21B	588	RAFGSA.R92	20. 4.84	Booker GC	Booker	6. 6.03
					RAFGSA.212/WB925				
EUQ	2966	EUQ	Schleicher Ka7 Rhönadler	863	D-4639	8. 5.84	Kent GC	Challock	14. 3.03
EUS	2968	443	Schempp-Hirth Ventus B/16.6	192		19. 5.84	J.C.Bastin	Rivar Hill	24. 1.03
EUT	2969		Schleicher Ka4 Rhönlerche	---	RAFGSA.R89	4. 5.84	G.DeOrfe & Ptnrs	Gransden Lodge	30.11.99
			(Both p/is need confirmation)		D-1789				
EUV	2971		SZD-42-2 Jantar 2BB-	934		29. 5.84	G.V.McKirdy	Edgehill	9. 5.98
EUX	2973	EUX	Schleicher ASK18	18005	D-3988	28. 5.84	Southdown GC	Parham Park	5.11.03
EUY	2974	88	Schleicher ASW20BL	20645		8. 6.84	D.G.Roberts & Ptnrs	Aston Down	25.11.03
EUZ	2975		Slingsby T.21B	620	WB959	24. 6.84	Dartmoor Gliding Association	Brent Tor	23. 7.03
EVB	2977	EVB	Schleicher Ka7 Rhönadler	7004	D-5109	12. 6.84	R.Armitage t/a Channel GC	Waldershare Park	21. 3.03
EVC	2978	EVC	CARMAM M.200 Foehn	55	F-CDKT	20. 6.84	W.Young & Ptnrs	Pocklington	13. 8.03
EVD	2979	382	Rolladen-Schneider LS-3	3024	N63LS	11. 8.84	C.H.Appleyard	Lasham	15. 4.03
					D-7914				
EVE	2980	491	Centrair 101A Pégase	101A-0141		19. 6.84	B.M.Chaplin	Lasham	10. 4.03
EVF	2981	90	Schempp-Hirth Nimbus 3T	15/76	D-KHIJ	19. 3.85	R.A.Foot & Ptnrs	Lasham	11. 4.03
EVG	2982	EVG	Schleicher Ka7 Rhönadler	396	D-0018	17. 7.84	Derby & Lancs GC	Camphill	16. 1.03
EVH	2983	EVH	Schleicher Ka10	10008	HB-791	26. 5.86	J.W Bolt	Brent Tor	21. 8.03
EVJ	2984	H	Schleicher ASK13	13637AB		14. 7.84	Lasham Gliding Society	Lasham	5.12.01
EVK	2985	EVK	Grob G.102 Astir CS	1397	PH-546	20.12.86	Peterborough & Spalding GC	Crowland	22.12.02
EVL	2986	SA1	Grob G.102 Astir CS77	1638	PH-575	26. 7.84	Southdown Aero Service	Lasham	11. 5.03
EVM	2987	N51	Centrair 101A Pégase	101A-0157		17. 8.84	Culdrose GC	RNAS Culdrose	22. 3.03
EVP	2989	K	Schleicher ASK13	13638AB		23. 8.84	Lasham Gliding Society	Lasham	10. 1.03
EVQ	2990	682	Centrair 101A Pégase	101A-0149		19. 8.84	R.J.Dann & Ptnr	Rivar Hill	5. 7.03
EVR	2991	EVR	LET L-13 Blanik	172604	G-ASVS	30. 8.84	D.Latimer	Hinton-in-the-Hedges	19.10.03
					OK-3840				
EVS	2992		SZD-50-3 Puchacz	B-1091		6. 9.84	Connel GC	North Connel	25. 5.02
EVT	2993	EVT	Scheibe Bergfalke IV	5807	D-0730	24. 9.84	J.Selman	(Limerick)	18.11.01

Reg	BGA	Tri	Type	c/n	Prev ID	Date	Owner	Location	Date
EVU	2994		Raab Doppelraab	515	RAFGSA.666	R	Not known	Bicester	*
			(Built Wolf Hirth 1952)		D-5223		*(Frame stored 9.94)*		
EVV	2995	EVV	Schleicher ASK23	23004		21.11.84	Midland GC	Long Mynd	1. 2.03
EVW	2996	EVW	Schleicher ASK23	23006		4. 1.85	London GC	Dunstable	28.11.03
EVX	2997	EVX	Schleicher ASK23	23007		7. 1.85	London GC	Dunstable	8. 1.03
EVY	2998	EVY	Schleicher ASK23	23008		31. 1.85	London GC	Dunstable	9.10.02
EWP	3013		Grob G.103A Twin II Acro	33892-K-130	ZE523 BGA.3013	3.11.84	Cambridge University GC	Gransden Lodge	13. 5.03
EWR	3015	R70	Grob G.103A Twin II Acro	33894-K-132	RAFGSA.R70 ZE525/BGA.3015	9.11.84	Anglia GC	RAF Wattisham	4. 5.03
EYS	3064	R71	Grob G.103A Twin II Acro	33961-K-194	RAFGSA.R71 ZE612/BGA.3064	3.99	Fenland GC	RAF Marham	7. 3.03
EZE	3076		Grob G.103A Twin II Acro	33981-K-214	ZE634 BGA.3076	3. 5.85	Oxford GC	Weston-on-the-Green	25. 1.00
FAF	3101	271	Schleicher ASW20	20214	RAFGSA.271 RAFGSA.R27	5.10.84	M.S.Armstrong	Gallows Hill	30.6.03
FAJ	3103	FAJ	Glaser-Dirks DG-300 Elan	3E50		3.10.84	B.A.Brown	Lyveden	9. 3.03
FAK	3104	FAK	Avialsa A.60 Fauconnet	104K	F-CDFG	12. 5.85	I.D.Gumbrell	Kingston Deverill	9. 5.01
FAM	3106	J15	Schempp-Hirth Nimbus 3/24.5	79		16. 3.85	I.M.Stromberg	Camphill	17. 6.03
FAN	3107	202	Centrair 101A Pégase	101A-0161		25.10.84	M Heslop	Parham Park	12. 3.03
FAP	3108		Monnett Monerai	123		1. 5.87	D.B Rich	Eaglescott	29. 5.99
FAQ	3109	631	Rolladen-Schneider LS-4	4465		9. 3.85	C.H.Meir	Camphill	24.11.02
FAR	3110	FAR	Glasflugel H.205 Club Libelle	58	HB-1262	5. 6.85	G.A.Gair	Kenley	8. 5.03
FAT	3112	FAT	Schleicher ASK13	13528	PH-456	22. 1.85	Dorset GC	Gallows Hill	8.11.03
FAV	3114	FAV	ICA IS-32A	05		27.12.84	Black Mountains GC	Talgarth	10. 5.03
FAW	3115	333	Schempp-Hirth Ventus B/16.6	26	D-6768	23. 3.85	P.Stafford-Allen	Crowland	18. 1.03
FAZ	3118	FAZ	Schleicher K8B	8558	D-1043	2. 3.85	Southdown GC *"Katie"*	Parham Park	3. 3.01
							(Crashed Parham 19.7.00)		
FBA	3119	178	Schleicher ASW20BL	20665		23. 1.85	R.H.Prestwich	Sleap	7.12.03
FBB	3120	822	Schempp-Hirth HS.4 Standard Cirrus	327G	RAFGGA.312	1.85	R.Andrewartha	Bidford	14. 1.03
FBC	3121	FBC	Schleicher ASW15B	15356	OH-439	19. 5.85	C.Knock	Sandhill Farm, Shrivenham	1. 4.03
FBD	3122		Schleicher ASW15B	15407	OH-445	19. 5.85	R.Pettifer & C.A.McLay	Chipping	10. 8.03
FBE	3123	1	Rolladen-Schneider LS-6	6028	D-9384	2. 6.85	T.J.Wills	New Zealand/Booker	3. 8.02
FBF	3124	175	Glaser-Dirks DG-300 Elan	3E9	BGA.2952	16. 1.85	A.L.Garfield	Dunstable	21. 3.02
FBG	3125		SZD-50-3 Puchacz	B-1081		14. 2.85	Not known	NK	27. 3.90*
							(Wrecked in gales Booker 25.1.90; stored Rivar Hill 5.94; removed by 5.99)		
FBH	3126	177	Glaser-Dirks DG-100G Elan	E156G123		1. 4.85	IBM (S.Hants) GC	Lasham	24. 4.03
FBJ	3127	FBJ	Schleicher K8B	8221	D-6340	18. 2.85	Bidford GC	Bidford	26. 6.03
FBL	3129		Schleicher Ka2B Rhönschwalbe	373	HB-606	17. 2.85	J.D.Melling	Andreas	2. 5.96*
FBM	3130	727	Schempp-Hirth Nimbus 3/24.5	73		28. 2.85	D.K.Gardiner	Portmoak	5. 7.03
FBN	3131	FBN	Glasflugel H.303 Mosquito B	160	D-6364	1. 5.85	S.R.Nash	Lasham	19. 2.03
FBQ	3133	464	Schleicher ASW20BL	20669		16. 4.85	D.W.Gosden	Usk	31. 3.03
FBR	3134	773	Grob G.102 Astir CS77	1701	SE-TSV	5. 3.89	G.Smith & Ptnrs	Pocklington	16. 6.03
FBT	3136	488	Schempp-Hirth Ventus BT	218/35		12. 3.85	S.M.Young	Easterton	11.10.03
FBV	3138	FBV	Schleicher ASK21	21223		2. 5.85	London GC	Dunstable	3. 1.03
FBW	3139	395	Glaser-Dirks DG-101G Elan	E174G140		11. 4.85	Surrey & Hants GC	Lasham	19.11.02
FBY	3141	780	Schempp-Hirth Discus B	20		12. 4.85	D Latimer	Dunstable	29. 8.03
FBZ	3142	D4667	Schleicher Ka6CR	6016	D-4667 D-KIMN/D-4667	12. 5.85	R.H. Martin & Ptnrs	Booker	21. 2.03
FCB	3144	FCB	Centrair 101 Pégase	101-0178	F-CGEA	15. 4.85	N.Stratton	Portmoak	2. 1.03
FCC	3145	XN243	Slingsby T.31B	1182	XN243	6. 5.85	D.A.Head & Ptnrs	Bicester	17. 8.03
FCD	3146	641	Centrair 101A Pégase B	101A-0207		1. 5.85	G.J.Bass	Challock	19. 4.03
FCF	3148		Slingsby T.21B	MHL.017	WB990	12. 5.85	N. R. Worrell	Lasham	1. 4.03
FCG	3149	WT871	Slingsby T.31B	681	WT871	5.85	J.Desmond	RAF Marham	11. 1.99
FCH	3150	FCH	CARMAM M.100S Mésange	72	F-CDKD	29. 5.85	D. Laidlaw	Saltby	26. 1.03
FCJ	3151	571	Grob G.102 Astir CS	1231	D-4205	19. 5.85	M.Levitt & G.Fellows	Aston Down	16. 2.03
FCK	3152	671	Schempp-Hirth Ventus B/16.6	241		6. 5.85	L.J.Scott	Llantisilio	25. 5.03
FCL	3153		Schleicher K8B	8045E	D-5225	20. 5.85	M.Jackson	Challock	20. 4.98
							(Reported damaged Lasham 14.2.98)		
FCM	3154	411	Glaser-Dirks DG-300 Elan	3E94		17. 5.85	R.B.Coote	Parham Park	29.11.03
FCN	3155	920	Schempp-Hirth HS.4 Standard Cirrus	131G	D-0191	18. 6.85	S.M.Robinson	Nympsfield	9. 2.03
FCP	3156	721	Rolladen-Schneider LS-6	6030		2. 7.85	R.E.Robertson	Lasham	21. 6.03
FCQ	3157		Schleicher K8B	1	RAFGGA..2 D-8322 or D-0322?	7. 4.85	M.W.Meagher	Edgehill	28. 3.98
			(Built Bayer)						
FCR	3158	113	Schleicher Ka6E	4223	OH-375 OH-REC	10. 6.85	R.F.Whitaker & Ptnrs	Lasham	23. 2.03
FCS	3159	2R	Schempp-Hirth HS.5 Nimbus 2C	233/81	D-5993	7. 7.85	R.W.Hawkins	Parham Park	1. 5.03
FCT	3160	FCT	Slingsby T.21B	611	WB944	16.12.86	A.Dyer	Haddenham/Thame	2. 6.01
FCV	3162		Schleicher ASW20	20076	RAFGSA.R24	7. 6.85	M.J.Davis & Ptnrs	RAF Cosford	17. 4.02
FCW	3163	L	Schleicher ASK13	13642AB		27. 6.85	Lasham Gliding Society	Lasham	14.12.02
FCX	3164		Schleicher ASK23	23011		7. 7.85	Midland GC	Long Mynd	29. 1.98*
							(Damaged Long Mynd 26.7.97 & w/o)		
FCY	3165	FCY	Schleicher ASW15	15122	D-0748	29. 6.85	M.D.Evershed & Ptnrs	Dunstable	26. 2.01
FCZ	3166		Slingsby T.1 Falcon 1 rep	-		7.85	D.D.Knight & J.Harber	RAF Halton	N/E(P)
			(Built Southdown Aero Services)						
FDA	3167	7D	Schleicher ASW15	15050	D-0511	2. 7.85	N W Woodward	Booker	7. 1.03

FDB	3168		ICA IS-30	07		23. 9.85	Black Mountains GC	Talgarth	19. 6.00
FDC	3169	FDC	CARMAM JP-15/34 Kit Club			10. 3.87	T.A.Hollins	Rufforth	20. 7.03
				TAH.50/60					
FDD	3170	FDD	Schleicher K8B	8972	AGA.5	11. 7.85	Shalbourne Soaring Society	Rivar Hill	26. 3.03
FDE	3171	510	Schempp-Hirth Ventus BT	256/53		8.85	P.Clay	Camphill	4. 4.03
FDF	3172	FDF	Grob G.102 Astir CS	1321	D-7338	2. 9.85	R.H.Davies	Aston Down	23. 6.03
FDG	3173	FDG	ICA IS-29D2 Club	02		23. 8.85	D.Mole	Sackville Lodge, Riseley	1. 6.02
FDK	3176		Slingsby T.59 Kestrel 19	1832	(BGA.4927)	8.85	T.Gauder	NK	28. 2.03
					G-BBVC				
FDL	3177		Schleicher Ka8	Liz.105/58	D-4650	9. 9.85	G.F.Millar & Ptnrs	Cranfield	25.11.95*
FDP	3180	996	ICA IS-30	08		24. 5.86	C.H.Bolton	Llantisilio	24. 9.03
FDQ	3181		Slingsby T.31B	710	WT915	19. 9.85	J.F.J.M.Forster *"Chris Wills"*	Maastricht	18. 5.03
FDR	3182	FDR	Schleicher Ka6CR	6119	D-8456	18.11.85	P.Hill & R.J.Grayling	Burnford Common	10. 3.03
FDT	3184	W22	Schleicher ASW22	22025	D-7709	28.10.85	O.Riccius	(Switzerland)	13. 4.02
							(De-registered 3.7.02 and sold as HB-3353)		
FDU	3185	H20	Schempp-Hirth Discus B	87		23. 5.86	J.L.Whiting	Long Mynd	22. 1.03
FDV	3186		LET L-13 Blanik	173333	D-5826	8. 4.86	T.Wiltshire	East Kirkby	4. 7.98
					D-KOEB/D-5826				
FDW	3187	FDW	Glaser-Dirks DG-300 Elan	3E143		26. 1.86	N Kelly	Enstone	22. 6.03
FDX	3188	FDX	SZD-48-1 Jantar Standard 2	B-1251	(BGA.2916)	22.12.85	A.P.Twort	Ringmer	9.10.03
FDY	3189		Slingsby T21B	MHL.005	WB978	26. 1.86	R.B.Armitage	Waldershare Park	28. 5.03
FEA	3191	FEA	Grob G.103 Twin Astir	3151	RAFGSA.R83	6.12.85	M.Boyle	Rufforth	25. 4.03
					RAFGSA 833				
FEB	3192	398	Grob G.102 Club Astir III	5643C		15.11.85	Surrey & Hants GC	Lasham	6. 3.03
FEE	3195		Slingsby T.21B	MHL.016	WB989	20. 1.86	K.Schickling	Aschaffenburg, Germany	28. 7.03
FEF	3196	FEF	Grob G.102 Astir CS	1164	OY-XGC	9. 2.86	Oxford University GC	Bicester	26. 3.03
FEG	3197	120	Schempp-Hirth Ventus B/16.6	279		12. 2.86	K.Moorhouse & Ptnr	Rivar Hill	15. 3.03
FEH	3198	318	Centrair 101A Pégase Club	101A-0268		1. 5.86	Booker GC	Booker	17. 2.03
			(Rebuilt with new fuselage c/n 01304: original fuselage rebuilt as BGA.3560)						
FEJ	3199	538	Schempp-Hirth Discus B	76		22. 2.86	J.W.White	Thame	17.12.03
FEL	3201	FEL	Schleicher Ka7 Rhönadler	7231	RAFGGA..	22. 9.86	Burn GC	Burn	23. 5.02
			(See BGA.3231)		D-???				
FEN	3203	FEN	SZD-50-3 Puchacz	B-1326		24. 3.86	Northumbria GC	Currock Hill	27. 5.03
FEP	3204	209	Schempp-Hirth Ventus BT	284/69		1. 4.86	R.J.Nicholls	Husbands Bosworth	22. 1.03
FEQ	3205	M	Schleicher ASK13	13650AB		7. 4.86	Lasham Gliding Society	Lasham	4. 2.03
FER	3206	FER/370	Schempp-Hirth Discus B	75		27. 3.86	D.R.Campbell & Ptnr	Booker	26. 3.03
FES	3207	564	Schempp-Hirth Discus B	88		4. 4.86	N.G.Storer	Lasham	23. 2.03
FEW	3209	499	Schleicher ASW22	22030	D-8888	12. 4.86	D.P.Taylor	Sutton Bank	24. 5.01
							(Crashed, Sierra de Guadarrama, Spain, 4.8.00)		
FEX	3210	ZS-GFZ	Glasflugel H.301B Libelle	100	ZS-GFZ	5.86	T.J.Wills	(New Zealand)	5.10.03
FEX	3212	FEX	Grob G.102 Astir CS77	1660	D-7492	6. 4.86	J.Taylor	Upwood	9. 4.03
FEZ	3214	FEZ	EoN AP.7 Primary	EoN/P/037	RAFGSA.R13	19. 9.86	G.J.Moore	Dunstable	3. 6.01
					RAFGSA 113/WP269				
FFA	3215	FFA	Schleicher ASK13	13651AB		15. 5.86	Staffordshire GC	Seighford	19. 4.03
FFB	3216	R9	Grob G.102 Astir CS	1123	RAFGSA.R9	10. 6.86	RAF GSA Centre	Bicester	7.11.03
					RAFGSA.R97/BGA.3216/D-6977				
FFC	3217	FFC	Centrair 101A Pégase	101A-0255		30. 5.86	C.A Hitchin	Kingston Deverill	19. 6.03
FFG	3221	WB920	Slingsby T.21B	559	WB920	2. 6.86	J.H.Wisselink	Roosendaal, The Netherlands	11. 5.03
FFH	3222	FFH	Schleicher ASW20	20037	D-7947	4. 4.87	J.Hayes	AAC Dishforth	11. 5.03
FFJ	3223	623	Grob G.103A Twin II Acro	34075-K-305		6. 6.86	Derby & Lancs GC	Camphill	24.11.99
							(Mid-air collision Camphill, 31.5.99)		
FFK	3224	7	Schempp-Hirth Nimbus 3			11. 4.87	Dr. D.Brennig-James	Booker	18. 4.03
FFL	3225	FFL	Slingsby T.21B	MHL.020	WB993	28. 6.87	J.P.Visser	Zwolle, The Netherlands	5. 4.03
FFN	3227	987	ICA IS-29D	21	D-9223	13. 8.86	A.Sutton & Ptnrs	Snitterfield	11. 6.00
FFP	3228	93	Schleicher ASW19B	19317	RAFGSA.R19	12. 6.86	K.A.Ford	Lasham	7. 3.03
FFQ	3229		Slingsby T.31B	913	XE800	18. 8.86	K.J. Grosse	Lasham	26. 3. 03
FFS	3231	FFS	Centrair 101A Pégase	101A-0265		27. 6.86	W Murray *(Carries BGA.3201)*	Gransden Lodge	23. 2.03
FFT	3232		Schempp-Hirth Discus B	110		30. 6.86	R.Maskell & Ptnrs	Ridgewell	22.12.03
FFU	3233	FFU	Glaser-Dirks DG-100G Elan	E200G166		11. 1.87	S.Robinson	Chipping	9. 4.03
FFV	3234		SZD-51-1 Junior	B-1616	F-WGJA	26. 8.86	Herefordshire GC	Shobdon	28.11.02
FFW	3235		Slingsby T21B	1155	XN151	2.10.87	S.C.Luck *(Sold in Germany during 2000)* Cranfield		25. 6.00
FFX	3236	627	Schempp-Hirth Discus B	109		12. 7.86	P.J.Tiller	Crowland	19. 4.03
FFY	3237	FFY	SZD-51-1 Junior	W-938		24.11.86	Cornish GC	Perranporth	14. 5.03
FFZ	3238		Slingsby T.21B	MHL.008	WB981	21. 8.86	M.Lake *(Under restoration 2002)*	RAF Keevil	5. 6.95*
FGA	3239	WT913	Slingsby T.31B	708	WT913	26.10.86	J.M.Brookes & Ptnrs *(Being refurbished)*	Strubby	21. 7.96*
FGB	3240		Slingsby T.21B	654	WJ306	23. 8.86	Oxford GC	Weston-on-the-Green	8. 7.03
FGC	3241		Slingsby T.31B	713	WT918	24. 8.86	E.Woefeel	Jena, Germany	13. 4.03
FGF	3244	141	Schempp-Hirth Nimbus 3T	25/91		16. 8.86	R.E.Cross	Lasham	5. 2.03
FGG	3245	WG498	Slingsby T.21B	665	WG498	29. 9.86	G.A.Ford & Ptnrs	Aston Down	28. 9.03
FGJ	3247	FGJ	Schleicher Ka6CR	6634	D-1041	22. 9.86	JCB Syndicate	Lleweni Parc	19.10.03
FGK	3248	FGK	Grob G.102 Astir CS	1323	RAFGSA.R61	9.86	P. Allingham	Rivar Hill	16. 3.03
					RAFGSA.316				
FGM	3250	FGM	Slingsby T.21B	1160	XN156	19. 7.87	R.B.Petrie	Strathaven	6. 6.03
			(Modified with 330cc engine)						
FGP	3252	FGP	Schleicher ASW19	19121	C-GJXG	1.11.86	C.I.Sullivan	Gransden Lodge	31. 3.03
FGR	3254	N29	Schleicher ASK13	13655AB		24.10.86	Portsmouth Naval GC	Lee-on-Solent	26. 2.03
			(Built Jubi)						
FGS	3255	XN157	Slingsby T.21B	1161	XN157	11.10.86	D.W.Cole & Ptnrs	Long Mynd	30. 7.95*
			(Fuselage No.SSK/FF/1745)						
FGT	3256	FGT	Glaser-Dirks DG-300 Elan	3E217		6. 3.87	S.C.Williams	Booker	4.11.03

FGU	3257	806	Schempp-Hirth HS.4 Standard Cirrus	147	D-0193	27. 4.87	L.E.Ingram	Snitterfield	11. 3.03
FGV	3258	FGV	Schleicher Ka7 Rhönadler	?	OO-Z..	15.12.86	Nene Valley GC	Upwood	6. 4.03
			(Hybrid using ex Belgian Ka7 fuselage & wings from Ka2 BGA.2662)						
FGW	3259	701	Centrair 101A Pégase	101A-0275		23. 6.87	L.P.Smith	Nympsfield	24. 3.03
FGY	3261	527	Schleicher ASW22	22027	D-3527	3.12.86	M.J.Bird	Dunstable	4. 4.03
FGZ	3262	D2	Schleicher Ka7 Rhönadler	7238	D-5376	17. 1.87	Dartmoor GC	Brent Tor	9.10.99
FHB	3264		Slingsby T.21B(T)	MHL.018	WB991	17. 2.87	G.Traves	East Kirkby	22. 8.03
			(Fuji-Robin EC-34PM)						
FHC	3265		Slingsby T.21B	MHL.013	WB986	7. 6.87	G.Traves	East Kirkby	5. 7.97
FHD	3266	196	Schleicher ASW20BL	20694	RAFGGA..	15. 2.87	K.J.Hartley	Bicester	1. 6.03
FHE	3267		Scheibe L-Spatz III	817	LX-CLM	3.87	C.W.Matten & Ptnrs	RNAS Culdrose	23. 3.98
FHF	3268		SZD-51-1 Junior	W-952		20. 3.87	Black Mountains GC	Talgarth	11. 5.03
FHG	3269	187	Schempp-Hirth HS.7 Mini Nimbus C	140	(BGA.3213) ZS-GNI	22. 3.87	R.W.Weaver	Usk	20. 1.03
FHJ	3271	987	Centrair 101A Pégase	101A-0278		13. 5.87	Booker GC	Booker	11. 2.03
FHK	3272	FHK	Slingsby T.31B	695	WT900	22. 4.87	N.A.Scully & Ptnrs "Tweety"	Saltby	9. 6.01
FHL	3273	136	Rolladen-Schneider LS-4	4633		17. 4.87	I.P.Hicks	Cranfield	19. 2.03
FHM	3274	P	Schleicher ASK13	13662AB		7. 6.87	Lasham Gliding Society	Lasham	30. 4.03
FHN	3275	FHN	Schleicher K8B	?	RAFGSA.R85 RAFGSA.385/RAFGSA.360	5. 6.87	B.F.Cracknell	Crowland	27. 2.03
FHQ	3277		Hols-der-Teufel replica	-	-	6.87	M.L.Beach	Brooklands	N/E
			(Built M.L.Beach)		*(Sold to Germany in 1998- on display at Deutsches Segelflugmuseum, Wasserkuppe 5.02)*				
FHR	3278	Q5	Schempp-Hirth Discus B	152		8. 6.87	P.Tratt & Syndicate	Parham Park	19.12.02
FHS	3279	154	Schempp-Hirth Ventus CT	326/82		11. 6.87	R.Andrews	Long Mynd	25. 7.03
FHT	3280	FHT	Grob G.102 Astir CS	1234	D-4208	12. 6.87	A.C.Howells	Rattlesden	9. 2.03
FHU	3281	FHU	Schleicher Ka7 Rhönadler	629	RAFGSA.R15 RAFGGA/D-5722	17. 6.87	Dartmoor GC	Brent Tor	28. 3.03
			(Modified to ASK13 standard)						
FHV	3282	FHV	SZD-48-1 Jantar Standard 2	B-1036	D-4516	25. 6.87	R.A.Williams & Ptnrs	Long Mynd	26. 4.03
FHW	3283	698	Grob G.102 Astir CS	1087	D-6987	30. 6.87	P.R.J.Halliday	Lasham	18. 3.03
FHY	3285	H5	Scheibe SF-27A Zugvogel V	6045	D-1868	28. 6.87	J.M.Pursey	North Hill	21.10.03
FHZ	3286	FHZ	Schleicher Ka6CR	949	D-4661	20. 8.87	J.Hiley	Husbands Bosworth	21. 4.03
FJA	3287	FJA	Slingsby T.21B	1152	XN148	8. 7.87	M.Steiner	Sembach, Germany	3. 5.03
FJB	3288	FJB	Slingsby T.21B	MHL.002	WB975	8. 7.87	Angus GC (As "WB975")	Drumshade	19. 6.03
FJD	3290	FJD	Slingsby T.21B	MHL.007	WB980	29. 8.87	R.H.Short & Ptnrs	Lyveden	10.12.02
FJE	3291	744	Schleicher ASW20BL	20953		1. 8.87	B.Pridal	Booker	2.12.03
FJF	3292	FJF	Slingsby T.21B	586	WB923	7. 9.87	R.L.Hill	Snitterfield	15. 5.03
			(Frame No.SSK/FF 1085)						
FJH	3294	FJH	Grob G.102 Astir CS77	1763	AGA.7	11. 7.87	Shalborne Soaring Society	Rivar Hill	1. 3.03
FJJ	3295	134	Schempp-Hirth Ventus BT	344.93		20. 8.87	A.D.Purnell	Lasham	15. 2.03
FJK	3296	FJK	Centrair 101A Pégase	101-070	N4429W	30. 4.88	D.J.Ingledew	Lee on Solent	29. 5.03
FJM	3298	143	Rolladen-Schneider LS-4A	4665	D-1431	4.12.87	G.C.Beardsley & Ptnr	Dunstable	13. 2.03
FJN	3299	WT903	Slingsby T.31B	698	WT903	17. 2.88	R.R.Beazer	Husbands Bosworth	29. 4.03
FJQ	3301	FJQ	Schempp-Hirth Ventus CT	104/365		24. 3.88	B.Rood	Hinton-in-the-Hedges	9. 4.03
FJR	3302	950	Glaser-Dirks DG-300 Club Elan	3E270C2		12. 2.88	G Smith	(France)	20. 3.03
FJS	3303	257	Glaser-Dirks DG-300 Club Elan	3E271C3		28. 5.88	Yorkshire GC	Sutton Bank	19.12.03
FJT	3304	997	Centrair 101A Pégase	101A-0284		20. 2.88	D.M.Smith & A.Marlow	Booker	29. 5.03
FJU	3305	FJU	Schleicher K8B	976	OH-240 OH-RTC	1.11.87	Northumbria GC	Currock Hill	24. 6.02
					(De-Registered as 'written-off', 7.10.02 following accident at Currock Hill 15. 9.02)				
FJV	3306	713	Schleicher ASW15	15109	D-0710	3.11.87	G.N.Turner & Ptnr	Sandhill Farm, Shrivenham	14. 5.01
FJW	3307	FJW	Schleicher Ka7	980	OH-241 OH-KKF	15.11.88	A.J.Pettitt & Syndicate	Rivar Hill	10. 9.03
FJX	3308	FJX	Glaser-Dirks DG-300 Elan	3E261		6. 2.88	D.S Jones	North Hill	15. 7.03
FJZ	3310	FJZ	Schempp-Hirth SHK	14		2. 4.88	R H.Hanna & A.& R.Willis	Bellarena	14.12.02
FKA	3311	FKA	Schleicher Ka6CR	6239	D-7037 D-5435	21. 2.88	S.T.Dry & B.Davies	Kingston Deverill	23. 6.01
FKB	3312	FKB	Glaser-Dirks DG-600	6-08		10.88	J.A.Watt	Dunstable	28. 1.03
FKE	3315	G2	Schleicher ASW15	15146	D-0794	6. 3.88	D.G.Lloyd & Syndicate	Bidford	21. 2.03
FKG	3317	125	Rolladen-Schneider LS-4A	4673		18. 5.88	B.A.Pocock	Kingston Deverill	13. 5.02
FKH	3318	FKH	Schleicher Ka6CR	6343	EI-109 IGA.106	3.88	F.McGuigan	Bellarena	11. 7.03
FKJ	3319	FKJ	Schleicher K8B	8032	OH-264 OH-RTE	4. 4.88	Aquila GC	Hinton in-the-Hedges	5. 7.02
					(Collided with free-fall parachutist over Hinton in the Hedges 1.6.02 & destroyed)				
FKK	3320	406	Schempp-Hirth Discus B	219		12. 3.88	D.J.Eade	Lasham	27. 3.03
FKL	3321	152	Schleicher ASW20BL	20954		21. 3.88	J.M.Ley & J.Rollason	Ridgewell	27. 3.03
FKM	3322	399	Schempp-Hirth Discus B	212		19. 3.88	Surrey & Hants GC	Lasham	16. 1.03
FKN	3323	13	Schleicher ASH25	25042	(BGA.3491) BGA.3323	19. 7.88	M Bird	Dunstable	11. 4.03
FKP	3324	WB971	Slingsby T.21B	632	WB971	28. 2.88	M.Powell	Tibenham	25. 4.01
FKQ	3325	FKQ	Scheibe SFH-34 Delphin	5119	D-1412	22. 4.88	Bristol & Glos GC	Nympsfield	30. 3.01
			(Suffered structural failure at Nympsfield in 2000; fuselage used for crash test .02)						
FKT	3328	FKT	Schleicher K8B	8382	D-5366	8. 5.88	P.Willock	Shobdon	21. 5.03
FKU	3329	FKY	Schleicher Ka6CR	822	D-0025	6. 4.88	J.A.Timmis	Camphill	25. 5.03
FKV	3330		CARMAM M.100S Mésange	60	F-CDDV	3. 5.88	G.G Hunt	Bidford	29. 7.97*
FKW	3331	FKW	Schleicher Ka7 Rhönadler	7145	OH-302 OH-KKJ	2. 4.88	Welland GC	Lyveden	14. 6.03
FKX	3332	FKX	Schleicher Ka6CR	6433	D-4316	30. 4.88	D Bowtell & Ptnrs	Lasham	30. 4.02
FLB	3336		Slingsby T.31B	837	XA295	23 .8.88	Not known *(Stored 2000)*	NK	
FLC	3337	368	Glaser-Dirks DG-300 Elan	3E310		26. 9.88	J.L. Hey	Camphill	8. 3.03

			Type	Serial	Prev. ID	Date	Owner	Location	Date
FLE	3339	314	Schempp-Hirth Discus B	207		7. 5.88	Booker GC	Booker	1.12.03
FLF	3340	Z4	Rolladen-Schneider LS-4A	4694		20. 3.88	D.E.Lamb	Booker	20. 3.03
FLG	3341	A25	Schleicher ASH25E (Turbo)	25044		6.88	D.S.McKay	Enstone	16. 4.03
FLH	3342	FLH	Schleicher K8B	22	OH-361	12. 5.88	South Wales GC	Usk	9. 7.03
			(Built KK Lehtovaara O/Y)		OH-RTW				
FLK	3344		Schleicher Ka7 Rhönadler	985	D-5047	12. 1.89	Dukeries GC	Gamston	20. 4.03
FLL	3345		SZD-9 bis Bocian 1D	F-877	OH-336	30. 7.88	Bath, Wilts & North Dorset GC	Kingston Deverill	12. 5.03
					OH-KBP				
FLP	3348	FLN	Schleicher K8B	07	OH-316	7. 5.88	Bath, Wilts & North Dorset GC	Kingston Deverill	4. 5.02
			(Built KK Lehtovaara O/Y)		OH-RTP				
FLQ	3349	FLQ	Schleicher K8B	8195A	D-8887	15. 8.88	F.J.Glanville	Long Mynd	20. 4.03
FLS	3351	FLS	Schleicher Ka6CR	6180	D-4001	16.11.88	P.B.Arms	RAF Halton	12.11.02
FLT	3352		Glasflugel H.201B Standard Libelle	41	D-0211	11.12.88	C.Glover	Husbands Bosworth	20. 8.00
FLU	3353	DJ2	Glasflugel H.201B Standard Libelle	52	D-0298	22. 6.88	C.D.Duthy-James	Talgarth	3. 6.03
FLV	3354	3354	LET L-13 Blanik	173312	D-1335	30. 7.88	North Devon GC "Jenny"	Eaglescott	10. 5.96*
FLW	3355	127	Schempp-Hirth HS.4 Standard Cirrus 75	656	F-CEMT	3. 7.88	J.R.Taylor	Perranporth	17.12.02
FLX	3356		Glaser-Dirks DG-300 Club Elan	3E304C19		19.10.88	R.Emms	Gransden Lodge	2. 5.03
FLY	3357	B21	Schleicher ASW24	24012		7.88	I.J.Lewis	North Weald	4.01
			(De-registered 6.8.01, sold in the USA)						
FLZ	3358	FLZ	Scheibe SF-27A Zugvogel V	6061	D-5378	14. 7.88	R Russon	Long Mynd	19. 4.03
FMA	3359		Slingsby T.38 Grasshopper	793	WZ797	8. 8.88	Not known (On rebuild 8.98)	Edgehill	7. 8.89
FMC	3361	68	Rolladen-Schneider LS-6B	6184		27. 7.88	B.L.Cooper	Booker	19. 2.03
FMD	3362	FMD	Schleicher Ka7 Rhönadler	343	D-2877	23. 7.88	Not known	Aston Down	1.12.92*
					HB-603		(Damaged Ringmer 6.5.92: stored at Aston Down 3.02)		
FME	3363	927	Schleicher ASW15	15164	D-0825	1. 8.88	T.J.Stanley	Rufforth	19. 2.03
FMG	3365	969	Schempp-Hirth Discus B	242		3. 8.88	J.Melvin	Nympsfield	14. 3.03
FMH	3366	B	Schleicher ASK13	13673AB		22. 8.88	Lasham Gliding Society	Lasham	14. 3.03
FMK	3368	FMK	Centrair 101 Pégase	101-0293		20. 1.90	A.Bailey	Bidford	30. 3.03
			(Model 101B?)						
FML	3369	FML	Schleicher ASW15B	15294	F-CEGR	21.11.89	A.D.Duke & Ptnrs	Nympsfield	11. 4.03
FMM	3370	FMM	Schleicher Ka6CR	6328	D-1260	20.10.88	K.E Hebdon	Gamston	3. 8.02
FMN	3371	CKF	Schempp-Hirth Ventus CT	123/397		12. 9.88	S.C.Kovac	Lasham	13. 3.03
FMP	3372	328	Schleicher ASW24	24023		21. 1.89	D.S.Pitman	Booker	8. 1.04
FMQ	3373	158	Schempp-Hirth Discus B	243		1.10.88	A.L Harris	Nympsfield	17. 3.03
FMR	3374	FMR	Neukom Standard Elfe	S-2 05	HB-801	8.11.88	M.Powell & Ptnrs	Camphill	19. 5.03
FMS	3375	519	Schleicher ASW15	15061	N111SP	11.88	A.J.Pettit	Lasham	26. 3.03
FMT	3376	FMT	Schempp-Hirth HS.4 Standard Cirrus 249		N2HM	10.89	S.R.Westlake	Nympsfield	8. 6.03
FMU	3377	FMU	Schempp-Hirth HS.4 Standard Cirrus 236		N3LB	14. 7.90	S.A Manktelow	Aston Down	7. 3.03
FMW	3379	XA229	Slingsby T.38 Grasshopper	862	XA229	R	NTU (Stored)	Burn	
FMX	3380	FMX	Schleicher ASW24	24014		5. 3.90	D.T.Reilly	North Hill	30. 3.03
FMY	3381	371	Rolladen-Schneider LS-7	7004	D-1256	18.12.88	M.Newman	Camphill	26. 6.03
FMZ	3382	FMZ	Schleicher Ka7 Rhönadler	7018	D-6035	22.11.88	Nene Valley GC	Upwood	29. 3.03
FNA	3383	FNA	Schleicher K8B	8499	D-5670	13.11.88	Bowland Forest GC	Chipping	16. 3.03
FNC	3385		Slingsby T.21B	601	WB934	5.11.88	P.Hoffmann	(The Netherlands)	8. 6.02
FND	3386	FND	Schleicher Ka6E	4069	PH-366	14.11.88	J.M.Smith	North Hill	30. 3.00
FNE	3387	FNE	SZD-38A Jantar-1	B-612	HB-1215	20.12.88	D.A Salmon & Ptnrs	Camphill	14. 6.03
FNF	3388	461	Schleicher ASW22B	22053		20.12.88	T.J.Parker	Dunstable	14. 2.03
FNG	3389	104	Schleicher ASW24	24015		10. 5.89	P.H.Pickett	Snitterfield	31. 1.03
FNH	3390	A19	Schleicher ASW19	19174	D-7969	9. 2.89	P.W.Roberts	Lasham	2. 3.03
FNK	3392	FNK	Slingsby T.65A Vega	1897	N9023H	10.12.88	A.P.Brown	Kenley	22. 3.03
FNL	3393	705	Schempp-Hirth Discus B	253		28.11.88	P.A.Holland	Kirton-in-Lindsey	15. 3.03
FNM	3394	FNM	Centrair 101B Pégase	101B-0289	F-CGSE	30. 3.89	R.Harrison	Sleap	21. 2.03
FNN	3395		Schempp-Hirth Ventus CT	130/407		8.12.88	C.A.Marren	Aston Down	20. 1.03
FNP	3396	FNP	Schleicher Ka6CR	567	D-4657	16. 1.89	Trent Valley GC	Kirton-in-Lindsey	24. 6.03
FNQ	3397	282	Schempp-Hirth Discus B	259		18.12.88	R.J. Hart	Tibenham	5. 1.04
FNR	3398	130	Schempp-Hirth Discus B	255		20. 3.89	R.Lemin	Nympsfield	24. 2.03
FNS	3399		Glaser-Dirks DG-300 Club Elan	3E314C23		2. 4.89	P.E.Williams	Portmoak	4. 6.03
FNT	3400	674	Glaser-Dirks DG-600	6-12		12.88	D.M.Hayes	Rufforth	30. 3.03
FNU	3401	190	Rolladen-Schneider LS-4A	4732	D-1376	9. 4.89	R J Simpson	Nympsfield	16. 2.03
FNW	3403	FNW	Schleicher Ka6CR	598	HB-634	20. 3.89	Cotswold GC	Aston Down	17. 1.99
			(Crashed near Aston Down 5.8.98)						
FNX	3404	FNX	Wassmer WA.30 Bijave	84	F-CCTJ	2. 1.89	The Borders GC	Milfield	11. 1.04
FPB	3408	FPB	Schleicher ASW15B	15243	D-2068	18.12.88	R C Tatlow	Winthorpe	21. 7.03
FPD	3410	973	Rolladen-Schneider LS-77	033	D-5178	14. 1.89	P.H.Rackham	Dunstable	11.12.03
FPE	3411	238	Schempp-Hirth Ventus CT	131/408		14. 1.89	P.Whitt & N.Francis	Shobdon	7. 3.03
FPF	3412	FPF	Scheibe L-Spatz 55	2720	RAFGGA...	11. 2.89	P.Saunders	Usk	18. 5.01
FPG	3413		Scheibe Bergfalke II/55	----	C-....	18. 1.89	Not known (Stored 2000)		
FPH	3414	FPH	Centrair ASW 20F	20132	F-CFFX	29. 1.89	R.Gibson & Ptnrs	Bidford	9. 7.03
FPJ	3415	459	Schleicher ASW19	19001	D-1909	29. 1.89	F.W.Pinkerton	Lyveden	30. 4.01
FPK	3416	Y1	Glaser-Dirks DG-300 Elan	3E6	D-1233	21. 1.89	G.C.Keall & Ptnrs	Husbands Bosworth	13. 2.03
FPL	3417	242	Schempp-Hirth Ventus C	409		27. 1.89	R.V Barrett	Nympsfield	22. 3.03
FPM	3418	FPM	SZD-51-1 Junior	B-1788		6. 3.89	Kent GC	Challock	17.12.03
FPN	3419	69	Schleicher ASW20	20376	RAFGGA.545	5. 3.89	E C Wright	RAF Syerston	4. 7.03
					D-8780				
FPP	3420	N2	Schempp-Hirth HS.5 Nimbus 2B	142	D-6779	26. 3.89	R.Jones	Walney Island	1. 6.03
					D-2111				
FPQ	3421	FPQ	Schleicher Ka7 Rhönadler	EB180/61	D-5184	15. 2.89	East Sussex GC	Ringmer	13. 1.03
FPT	3424	574	Schleicher ASW20	20007	D-7574	18. 2.89	L.Hornsey & Ptnrs	RAF Halton	15. 3.03

FPU	3425	FPU	Schleicher Ka2B Rhönschwalbe	-	HB-698	17. 2.89	T.J.Wilkinson	Sackville Lodge, Riseley	30 3.03
			(Built Segelfluggruppe Zwingen)						
FPV	3426	FPV	Schleicher Ka6E	4123	N29JG	10. 3.89	J.E.Stewart	Bembridge	11. 5.03
					G-AWTP				
FPW	3427	39	Glaser-Dirks DG-600	6-17		13. 4.89	W.S.Stephen	Aboyne	25. 1.03
FPX	3428		Schleicher ASK13	13325	F-CDYR	21. 6.89	M.O.Breen	Booker	27. 8.03
FQB	3432	FQB	Schleicher ASW15B	15340	D-2345	10. 8.89	P.Usborne	Dunstable	31.10.02
FQC	3433	201	Glaser-Dirks DG-202/17c	2-178CL19	HB-1645	8. 3.89	A.T.MacDonald	Ridgewell	10. 2.03
FQD	3434	FQD	Schleicher K8B	8289	D-1908	6. 3.89	Kent GC	Challock	11. 2.03
FQE	3435	FQE	Schleicher K8	3	D-6329	3. 4.89	Cotswold GC	Aston Down	9. 4.01
FQF	3436		Scheibe SF-27A Zugvogel V	6025	D-0009	19. 2.89	S.Maddox	Winthorpe	26. 3.03
FQG	3437	952	Rolladen-Schneider LS-7	7050	D-1712	4. 6.89	R.W.Spiller	Sutton Bank	23. 3.03
FQH	3438	A98	Rolladen-Schneider LS-7	7029	D-1316	15. 4.89	P.J.Lazenby	Rufforth	29.11.03
FQK	3440	FQK	Grob G.103C Twin III Acro	34123		15. 8.89	P.O'Donald	Gransden Lodge	13. 3.03
FQL	3441	772	Schleicher Ka6CR	6235	HB-772	18. 3.89	P.R. Alderson	Lasham	1. 4.03
FQM	3442	FQM	Scheibe SF-27A Zugvogel V	6098	D-9421	19. 2.89	R.D.Noon	Winthorpe	13. 4.03
FQN	3443	479	Schempp-Hirth Ventus B/16.6	141	D-8772	26. 3.89	R.Parsons & Ptnrs	Challock	14. 2.03
					D-KHIB				
			(Composite rebuild of D-8772 - ex Ventus BT D-KHIB (10/141): w/o 27.5.85 & possibly HB-1626 (91) as 3443 has build plate V91)						
FQQ	3445	656	Glaser-Dirks DG-600	6-11		3.89	M.B.Jefferyes & Ptnr	Ridgewell	5. 6.03
FQR	3446	FQR	Schleicher K8B	8537	PH-349	9. 3.89	Dorset GC	Gallows Hill	18. 3.03
FQT	3448	484	SZD-48-3 Jantar Standard 3	B-1891	(BGA.3409)	28. 3.90	T H Greenwood	Sandhill Farm, Shrivenham	16. 4.02
FQU	3449	FQU	Schleicher Ka7 Rhönadler	1139	D-8614	13. 3.89	J.E.Harber	RAF Halton	1. 5.03
					HB-709				
FQV	3450	P	CARMAM JP-15/36AR Aiglon	28	F-CETX	20. 3.89	K.H.Withey	Perranporth	11. 4.98
FQX	3452		Schleicher K8B	8037	D-5205	5. 4.89	Burn GC	Burn	6. 1.96*
FQY	3453	785	Schempp-Hirth Discus B	274		16. 4.89	P.Studer	Nympsfield	29. 3.03
FQZ	3454		Rolladen-Schneider LS-1F	391	F-CEKH	12. 6.89	G.P.Hibberd	Sleap	15. 3.03
FRA	3455	79	Rolladen-Schneider LS-6B	6151	D-8081	20. 4.89	M.Randle	Aston Down	7. 3.03
FRB	3456	FRB	Schempp-Hirth Ventus C	404		4 .3.89	C.J.Ratcliffe	Cross Hayes	2. 3.03
FRC	3457	988	Schempp-Hirth HS.5 Nimbus 2B	151	D-4980	15. 5.89	C.F.Whitbread	Challock	15. 3.03
FRD	3458	JPB	Centrair 101A Pégase	101A-0311		15. 4.89	A.Kangars	Husbands Bosworth	15. 5.03
FRE	3459	FRE	Schleicher Ka6E	4349	F-CDTL	13. 4.89	D.J.Stewart	Parham Park	19. 5.03
FRF	3460	FRF	Schleicher Ka7 Rhönadler	450/58	D-5653	7. 4.89	P.Roberts & Co	Dunstable	6. 9.01
FRG	3461		Siebert Sie-3	3009	D-0739	7. 4.89	I.R.Taylor & Co	Cross Hayes	1. 8.03
FRH	3462	634	Schleicher ASW20CL	20740	D-9229	2. 4.89	J.N.Wilton & Ptnr	Husbands Bosworth	13. 5.03
FRJ	3463	FRJ	Schempp-Hirth HS.4 Standard Cirrus	103G	HB-1041	23. 4.89	P.D.Oswald & Ptnrs	Portmoak	30. 1.03
FRK	3464	FRK	Schleicher ASW15B	15214	D-0941	21. 3.89	A.D.Smith	Booker	7.12.03
FRL	3465	609	Grob G.102 Astir CS	1373	D-7402	22. 4.89	South Wales GC	Usk	21. 5.03
FRM	3466		Scheibe SF-27A Zugvogel V	6040	D-3644	22. 4.89	Burn GC	Burn	14. 5.98
FRP	3468	995	Schempp-Hirth Nimbus 3/24.5	43	N697L	28. 7.89	T.R.Gardner & J.Mardon	Aston Down	9.10.95*
					D-2518				
FRQ	3469		Slingsby T.45 Swallow	1420	XT653	27. 4.89	D.Shrimpton	Halesland	4. 7.02
FRR	3470	495	Centrair 101A Pégase	101A-0034	(BGA.3451)	16. 4.89	P.A.Lewis	Walney Island	30. 4.03
					F-CFQA		"Scoundrel"		
FRS	3471	FRS	Scheibe Zugvogel IIIB	1097	D-2171	27. 4.89	S.W.Vallei	Rivar Hill	15. 6.03
					HB-749				
FRT	3472	S9	Schempp-Hirth Ventus CT	137/421		26. 4.89	S.Edwards	Dunstable	11. 3.03
FRV	3474	FRV	Centrair 101A Pégase	101A-0325		28.10.89	D.G.Every	Gallows Hill	6. 4.03
FRW	3475	268	Schleicher ASW20L	20202	D-5981	5. 5.89	D.Cooper	Booker	4. 3.03
FRX	3476	FRX	Centrair 101A Pégase	101A-0315		30. 5.89	BBC Gliding Group	Booker	29. 1.03
FRZ	3478	H6	Schempp-Hirth HS.4 Standard Cirrus	348G	HB-1194	15. 5.89	N.A.Maclean	Lasham	24. 3.03
					D-2172				
FSA	3479	498	Grob G.102 Astir CS	1277	D-7371	9. 4.89	L. Wells	Dunstable	5. 3.03
FSC	3481		Slingsby T.38 Grasshopper	751	WZ755	27. 4.90	Not known (Stored 5.98)	Gallows Hill	30. 4.93
FSD	3482	N28	Schleicher ASK13	13367	D-0863	24. 5.89	Portsmouth Naval GC	Lee-on-Solent	22. 3.03
FSE	3483		Schleicher Ka6CR	6021	D-1946	19. 8.89	G.W.Lobb	North Hill	15 .8.02
FSF	3484	FSF	Schleicher Ka2	120	D-1688	31. 5.89	B.T.Spreckley	Le Blanc, France	1.10.99
FSH	3486	FSH	Grob G.102 Astir CS Jeans	2090	D-7532	9. 5.89	Buckminster GC	Saltby	4. 2.03
FSJ	3487	WT908	Slingsby T.31B	703	WT908	22. 5.89	R.J.Abraham	Dunstable	8. 1.99
FSL	3489	F11	Schempp-Hirth HS.7 Mini Nimbus	52	HB-1413	9. 6.89	S.C.Waddell	Booker	13. 3.02
							(De-registered 3.10.02, reason unknown)		
FSQ	3493		Schleicher ASK13	13596		13. 6.89	London GC	Dunstable	12. 1.99
			(Composite containing c/n plate from BGA.2405; crashed at Dunstable 9.7.98)						
FSR	3494	FSR	Glaser-Dirks DG-300 Elan	3E343		24. 8.89	E.J.Dent	Nympsfield	1.11.03
FSS	3495	FSS	Schleicher Ka6E	4019	D-5260	19. 8.89	C.Davies	Lasham	11. 5.03
FST	3496	FST	Schleicher ASH25E	25073	(BGA.3530)	12.10.89	K.H.Lloyd & Ptnrs	Aston Down	1. 5.03
					(BGA.3496)				
FSU	3497	FSU/55	Scheibe Zugvogel IIIA	1060	D-9055	30. 6.89	P.W.Williams	Brent Tor	28. 6.03
FSV	3498	WZ819	Slingsby T.38 Grasshopper	800	WZ819	26. 6.89	P.D.Mann	RAF Halton	18. 6.02
FSX	3500	405	Glaser-Dirks DG-300 Elan	3E344		11. 7.89	C.Hyett	Lasham	24. 1.03
FSY	3501	162	Schleicher ASH25	25064	D-1578	14. 7.89	B.T.Spreckley	Le Blanc, France	14.10.03
FSZ	3502	FSZ	Grob G.102 Astir CS77	1841	D-2908	29. 7.89	D.Gardiner & Ptnr	Aston Down	11. 3.03
FTA	3503	FTA	Schleicher K8B	8702	D-0048	15. 7.89	Lincolnshire GC (Crashed Strubby 1996)	Strubby	29. 3.97*
FTB	3504	FTB	Schleicher Ka6CR (Built Bitz)	019	D-8900	22. 7.89	P.J.Blair	Bidford	19 .2.03
FTC	3505	N56	SZD-51-1 Junior	B-1860		23. 7.89	Culdrose GC	RNAS Culdrose	8. 3.03
FTD	3506	FTD	Schleicher ASW15B	15191	D-0872	23. 8.89	A.E. Stephenson	Walney Island	19. 4.03
FTF	3508	FTF	Schleicher Ka6CR	6294	D-6081	5. 9.89	A.Sparrow	Parham Park	25. 4. 03
FTG	3509	FTG	Schleicher Ka7 Rhönadler	535	D-8321	18.10.89	Angus GC	Drumshade	26. 3.00
FTH	3510	FTH	SZD-50-3 Puchacz	B-1881		24. 8.89	Buckminster GC	Saltby	28.11.03

FTJ	3511	FTI	SZD-48 Jantar Standard 2	W-889	HB-1472	25. 8.89	D.P. Bieniasz	Kirton-in-Lindsey	13. 3.03
FTK	3512	518	Grob G.102 Astir CS Jeans	2059	OE-5152	10.89	R.Lapsley	Bellarena	10. 5.03
FTL	3513	FTL	Schleicher ASW20CL	20751	D-3564	2. 9.89	J.S.Shaw	Dunstable	30. 3.03
FTM	3514		Schleicher K8B	513	D-5708	30. 8.89	West Wales GC	Usk	10. 8.02
FTN	3515	853	Schleicher K8B	996	D-8539	11. 3.89	Vale of The White Horse GC		
					D-KAEL/D-8539			Sandhill Farm,Shrivenham	24. 4.03
FTP	3516	332	Schleicher ASW20CL	20733	D-3640	4. 1.90	A J Mainwaring	Dunstable	18. 3.03
FTQ	3517	FTQ	Centrair ASW20FL	20123	F-CFFR	12. 8.89	C.Wilby	Camphill	13.11.99
FTR	3518	FTR	Grob G.102 Astir CS77	1606	D-4807	6.10.89	Lakes GC	Walney Island	20 .1.03
FTS	3519	FTS	Glaser-Dirks DG-300 Club Elan			12.10.89	Southdown GC	Parham Park	30. 3.03
				3E349C38					
FTU	3521	FTU	Schleicher Ka7 Rhönadler	302	HB-599	25. 9.89	Dartmoor GS *"Fondue"*	Brent Tor	25. 3.03
FTV	3522	944	Rolladen-Schneider LS-7	7073		9.10.89	D.Hilton & S.White	Booker	15. 3.03
FTW	3523	230	Schempp-Hirth Discus B	292		4.10.89	N.H.Wall & Ptnrs	Nympsfield	9. 2.03
			(Rebuilt with new fuselage after accident 21.6.91; original fuselage rebuilt as BGA.3879)						
FTY	3525	753	Rolladen-Schneider LS-7	7075		8.10.89	A.M.Burgess	Easterton	6. 2.03
FUB	3528		Schleicher Ka6CR	6007	D-8573	6.11.89	D.E.Hooper	Brent Tor	23. 7.99
FUD	3529	2	SZD-9 bis Bocian 1E	P-689	SP-2807	2.11.89	Mendip GC	Halesland	3. 8.02
FUF	3531	FUF	Scheibe SF-27A Zugvogel V	6089	D-6068	30. 9.89	East Sussex GC	Ringmer	15. 5.03
FUG	3532	BB	Schleicher ASH25	25074	(BGA.3526)	20.10.89	J.P.Gorringe & D.S.Hill	Lasham	11. 2.02
FUH	3533	192	Schempp-Hirth Ventus C	438		12.10.89	M.A.Gale & Ptnrs	Gallows Hill	9. 3.03
FUJ	3534	FUJ	Glaser-Dirks DG-300 Elan	3E353		5.12.89	J.D.Cook & Ptnrs	Portmoak	4. 3.03
FUL	3535	803	Schempp-Hirth Discus B	293		14. 3.90	R.Banks	Dunstable	11.12.03
FUM	3536	FUM	Schleicher Ka6CR	808	D-6289	25. 3.90	S. Stanley	Dunstable	25. 5.03
FUN	3537	FUN	Schleicher ASW20CL	20813	D-3432	5. 4.91	W.H.Parker	Dunstable	1. 3.03
FUP	3538	397	Schempp-Hirth Discus B	291		18.10.89	Surrey & Hants GC	Lasham	20.12.02
FUQ	3539	FUQ	Scheibe SF-27A Zugvogel V	6090	D-5196	1. 4.90	G.Elliott & Ptnrs	Ringmer	10. 5.03
FUR	3540	256	Schempp-Hirth Ventus CT	145/446		15. 3.90	D.S.Towson	Shobdon	6. 4.03
FUS	3541	FUS	SZD-51-1 Junior	B-1912		20.11.89	Scottish Gliding Union Ltd	Portmoak	18. 2.03
FUT	3542	612	Glaser-Dirks DG-300 Club Elan			11. 3.90	A.Eltis	Gransden Lodge	16. 6.03
				3E350C39					
FUU	3543	FUU	Glaser-Dirks DG-300 Club Elan			4. 3.90	P.J.Dixon-Clarke	Lasham	11. 6.03
				3E360C45					
FUV	3544	194	Rolladen-Schneider LS-7	7068		4.11.89	E.Alston	Brent Tor	18.12.02
FUW	3545	XE807	Slingsby T.31B Cadet TX.3	920	XE807	20.11.89	D.Shrimpton	Halesland	25. 1.03
FUY	3546	FUY	SZD-50-3 Puchacz	B-1983		30.11.89	M.G.Ashton	Eaglescott	15. 5.03
FVA	3548	N15	Schleicher K8B	1051	D-5117	13. 4.90	Portsmouth Naval GC	Lee-on-Solent	27. 9.02
FVB	3549	228	Schempp-Hirth Ventus CT	144/445		13. 1.90	D.J.Barke	Camphill	23. 4.03
FVC	3550	FVC	Schleicher ASK13	13682AB		11.12.89	Devon & Somerset GC	North Hill	30. 1.03
			(Built Jubi)						
FVD	3551	FVD	Scheibe Bergfalke IV	5806	D-0729	9.12.89	North Wales GC	Llantisilio	26.11.03
FVE	3552	FVE	Rolladen-Schneider LS-4	4190	RAFGSA232	12. 1.90	R.J.Rebbeck	Edgehill	28. 4.03
					RAFGSA R30/D-4542				
FVF	3553	FVF	Schempp-Hirth HS.5 Nimbus 2C	202	D-2880	3. 3.90	L.C.Mitchell & J.Wood	Chipping	2. 4. 03
FVG	3554	660	Glaser-Dirks DG-600	6-41		17.12.89	R.G.Tomlinson	Winthorpe	23. 4.03
FVH	3555	246	Rolladen-Schneider LS-7	7067	(BGA.3527)	18.12.89	B.R.Forrest & A.Hallum	Booker	2. 4.03
FVL	3558	FVL	Scheibe Zugvogel IIIB	1082	D-5224	29.12.89	T.G. Homan	Kirton-in-Lindsey	24. 8.03
FVM	3559	369	Centrair 101A Pégase	101A-0345		15. 3.90	S.H.North	RNAS Yeovilton	26. 4.03
FVN	3560	FVN	Centrair 101A Pégase	101A-0268/2		16. 1.90	G.G.Butler	Snitterfield	5. 2. 03
			(Rebuild of BGA.3198 and carries c/n 10100268)						
FVP	3561	FVP	Centrair 101A Pégase	101A-0350		22. 4.90	J.R.Parry & Ptnr	Long Mynd	9. 3.03
FVQ	3562	FVQ	Rolladen-Schneider LS-7	7079		18. 1.90	P.Harvey	Gransden Lodge	27. 3.03
FVS	3564	FVS	Schempp-Hirth HS.4 Standard Cirrus		D-2168	25. 3.90	P.A Clark	Lasham	21. 2.03
				359G					
FVT	3565	760	Schempp-Hirth HS.5 Nimbus 2	18	N795	17. 5.90	I.Dunkley	Camphill	29. 7.98
FVU	3566	FVU	Schleicher ASK13	13062	D-1348	17. 4.90	Edinburgh University GC	Portmoak	12. 7.03
FVV	3567	FVV	Centrair 101A Pégase	101A-0353		27. 4.90	Cambridge University GC	Gransden Lodge	27. 3.03
FVW	3568	FVW	Schempp-Hirth Ventus BT	252/51	D-KORN	26. 1.90	I.Champness	Lasham	10. 3.03
FVY	3570	FVY	Scheibe Zugvogel IIIA	1046	D-8323	21. 2.90	S.C.Ottner & Ptnrs	Rivar Hill	16. 5.99
FVZ	3571	PS	Schleicher Ka6E	4007	D-4104	27. 2.90	R.C.Fisher	Booker	14. 6.03
FWA	3572	FWA	Schleicher Ka6CR	6227	D-1062	26. 3.90	D.Cousins	Usk	23. 8.03
FWB	3573	FWB	Schleicher ASK13	13224	HB-989	2. 4.90	Cotswold GC	Aston Down	13.10.03
FWC	3574	45	Grob G.103C Twin III Acro	34154		5. 4.90	Lasham Gliding Society Ltd	Lasham	8.11.02
FWD	3575	FWD/888	Schempp-Hirth Ventus CT	148/468		10. 5.90	R.S.Maxwell-Fendt	Lasham	5. 4.03
FWE	3576		SZD-50-3 Puchacz	B-1984	(BGA.3547)	5. 2.90	Deeside GC	Aboyne	18. 1.03
FWF	3577	L57	Rolladen-Schneider LS-7	7097		28. 2.90	G.P.Hibberd	Sleap	24. 3.03
FWG	3578	FWG	Centrair 101A Pégase	101A-0252	PH-793	22. 2.90	Devon & Somerset GC	North Hill	11. 4.03
FWH	3579	FWH	Scheibe SF-27A Zugvogel V	6024	D-4733	10. 2.90	R.Sampson	Husbands Bosworth	17. 6.03
FWJ	3580	S3	Rolladen-Schneider LS-7WL	7078		22. 3.90	J.P.Popika	Gransden Lodge	15. 3.03
FWK	3581	29	Schempp-Hirth Nimbus 3DT	32		22. 3.90	J.D.Glossop	Gransden Lodge	20. 6.03
FWL	3582		Schleicher K8B	106/58	D-7151	24. 2.90	Dukeries GC	Gamston	3. 1.04
FWM	3583	FWM	Glaser-Dirks DG-300 Club Elan			15. 6.90	N.Clements	Snitterfield	26. 3.03
				3E373C50					
FWN	3584	FWN	Schleicher ASK13	13285	HB-1023	20. 4.90	Booker GC	Booker	23. 3.03
FWP	3585	980	Schleicher ASW19B	19262	D-5980	4. 4.90	K.Harris & Ptnrs	Dunstable	28. 3.03
FWQ	3586	FWQ	Schleicher ASK21	21460		15. 5.90	Midland GC	Long Mynd	4. 1.03
FWR	3587	277	Glasflugel H.303 Mosquito	34	N77RL	26. 3.90	S.J.Ferguson	Aston Down	12. 5.03
FWS	3588	662	Schleicher ASW20C	20765	D-6623	18. 2.90	P.C.Gill	North Weald	27.11.03
FWT	3589	FWT	SZD-50-3 Puchacz	B-1988		24. 3.90	The Soaring Centre	Husbands Bosworth	4. 3.03
FWU	3590	768	Rolladen-Schneider LS-7	7080		19. 3.90	C.Brown	Husbands Bosworth	3. 5.03
FWW	3592	FWW	Schleicher ASH25E	25093		19. 6.90	A.T.Farmer	Weston-on-the-Green	9. 4.03

FWX	3593	B38	Centrair 101A Pégase	101A-033	F-CFRZ	27. 3.90	I.R.Stanley	Booker	21. 6.03
FWY	3594	FWY	Centrair 101A Pégase	101A-071	F-CFXE	23. 3.90	C.G.Gilbert	Lasham	27. 3.03
FWZ	3595	FWZ	Schleicher ASW19B	19342	D-2603	14. 4.90	C.Fowler	Camphill	13.12.03
FXA	3596	567	Grob G.102 Speed Astir IIB	4083	D-2671	16. 4.90	A.D.Duke	Nympsfield	3.11.03
FXB	3597		Schleicher K8B	8193/A	D-5597	29. 3.90	R.J.Morris	Brent Tor	21. 6.03
FXC	3598	FXC	Schleicher Ka6E	4268	D-0150	9. 8.90	B.Laverick-Smith	Challock	10. 4.03
FXD	3599	285	Centrair 101A Pégase	101A-0346	(BGA.3563)	31. 3.90	The Soaring Centre	Husbands Bosworth	13.10.03
FXE	3600	35	Rolladen-Schneider LS-7	7090		23. 3.90	J.C.Kingerlee	Weston-on-the-Green	28. 9.01
FXF	3601	FXF	Slingsby T.50 Skylark 4	1455	HB-812	7. 5.90	S.White	Booker	13. 5.02
FXG	3602	FXG	Schempp-Hirth HS.2 Cirrus	23	N1216	23. 8.90	G.F.King	Kingston Deverill	15. 2.00
						(Crashed North Hill 15.9.99; at Rufforth 5.01 for potential rebuild)			
FXH	3603		Schleicher Ka7 Rhönadler	353	D-4040	10. 4.90	Vale of Neath GC	Rhigos	19.12.00
FXJ	3604	247	Schleicher ASW24	24086		4. 5.90	A.K.Laylee	Booker	8. 5.03
FXL	3606	108	Schleicher ASH25	25088		11. 4.90	R.H.Blackmore	Husbands Bosworth	11.11.03
FXM	3607	173	Schempp-Hirth Discus BT	16/301	D-KHIA	12. 4.90	R.J.H.Fack	Shobdon	6. 7.03
FXN	3608	FXN	CARMAM M.200 Foehn	4	OO-ZNI	14. 4.90	I.C.Gutsell & Ptnrs	Burn	9. 9.01
					(OO-ZXS)/F-CCXS				
FXP	3609	FXP	LET L-23 Super Blanik	907609		17. 7.90	Dill Faulke Education Trust	Sutton Bank	24. 6.03
FXQ	3610	954	Schempp-Hirth Nimbus 3DT	31		21. 4.90	D.G.Tanner	Kingston Deverill	13. 3.03
FXR	3611	L12	LAK-12 Lietuva	6162		9.90	S R Blackmore	Enstone	11. 4.03
FXS	3612	FXS	Schleicher Ka6E	4228	D-0073	7. 5.90	R.Woodhouse & B.C.Wade	Tibenham	25. 5.03
FXT	3613		Centrair 101A Pégase	101A-0056	F-CFQV	4.90	K.Ludlow	Viterbo, Italy	8. 4.02
FXU	3614	FXU	Schleicher Ka6E	4071	OH-343	8. 6.90	M E Mann Syndicate	Lasham	18. 4.03
					OH-RSY				
FXW	3616	FXW	Schleicher K8B	8651	D-7203	5. 4.90	South Wales GC	Usk	25. 9.03
					D-KOLA/D-7203				
FXX	3617		Scheibe L-Spatz 55	756	D-3598	1. 9.91	P.Brown	Ridgewell	19. 6.00
FXY	3618	723	Schleicher ASW15B	15348	F-CEJL	21. 5.90	C.I.Willey	Dunstable	26.12.03
FYA	3620	FYA	SZD-50-3 Puchacz	B-2022		9. 5.90	Cairngorm GC	Feshiebridge	15. 4.02
FYB	3621	779	Rolladen-Schneider LS-7	7102		2. 5.90	J.T.Hitchcock	Sandhill Farm, Shrivenham	5.11.03
FYC	3622	A10	Schempp-Hirth Ventus B	83		1. 6.90	D.B.Meeks	Sutton Bank	19. 9.03
FYD	3623	942	Schleicher ASH25	25095		19. 5.90	C.C.Lyttleton	Challock	15. 2.03
FYE	3624	FYE	Scheibe Zugvogel IIIB	1067	OY-MHX	20. 5.90	R.J.Hawley	Brent Tor	27. 6.03
					SE-TCE/OY-EFX/D-1814				
FYF	3625	FYF	Schleicher ASK21	21470		4. 8.90	London GC	Dunstable	27. 3.03
FYG	3626	FYG	Glasflugel H.205 Club Libelle	22	OH-545	13. 5.90	I.H Shattock	Usk	10. 8.03
FYH	3627	224	Rolladen-Schneider LS-4A	4804		4. 7.90	G.W.Craig	Weston-on-the-Green	7. 8.02
FYJ	3628		Schempp-Hirth HS.4 Standard Cirrus	581G	D-8931	12. 7.90	T.D.Winn	Pocklington	16. 5.03
FYK	3629	34	Rolladen-Schneider LS-7	7108		1. 6.90	J.C.Ferguson	Portmoak	16. 2.03
FYL	3630		SZD-50-3 Puchacz	B-1990		6.90	Deeside GC	Aboyne	21. 5.03
FYM	3631	326	Schempp-Hirth Discus BT	31/328		1. 6.90	J.A.Denne	Enstone	18. 4.03
FYN	3632	J3	Schempp-Hirth Discus B	179	N75J	14. 7.90	P.Foulger	Wormingford	5. 4.03
FYP	3633		LET L-23 Super Blanik	907620		4. 8.90	Needwood Forest GC	Cross Hayes	30. 3.03
FYR	3635	FYR	LET L-23 Super Blanik	917816		2. 7.92	North Wales GC	Llantisilio	24. 6.00
FYU	3638	M5	Glaser-Dirks DG-100 Elan	E111	OY-XMR	28. 6.90	J.L Bugbee	North Hill	6. 5.03
					SE-TYO				
FYV	3639	FYV	Schleicher ASK21	21468		25. 7.90	Booker GC	Booker	1. 4.03
FYW	3640	Z7	Rolladen-Schneider LS-7	7111		6. 6.90	J.D.Williams	Saltby	22. 1.03
FYX	3641	208	Schempp-Hirth Discus bT	32/333		3. 7.90	M.P.Brockington	Talgarth	28. 4.03
FYY	3642	S	Schleicher ASK13	13685AB		9. 7.90	Lasham Gliding Society	Lasham	18. 7.03
FYZ	3643	171	Schleicher ASH25	25097		18. 7.90	M.G.Thick	Sutton Bank	5. 8.03
FZA	3644	FZA	SZD-51-1 Junior	B-1913		23. 7.90	Booker GC	Booker	31. 3.03
FZB	3645	669	Glasflugel H.201B Standard Libelle 112		OH-388	31. 7.90	C.Thomas & J.E.Herring	Lasham	8. 3.03
					OH-GLA				
FZC	3646	FZC	Schempp-Hirth SHK-1	58	OH-357	30. 8.91	J.F Mills	RAF Cranwell	20. 7.02
					OH-SHA				
FZF	3649	FZF	SZD-51-1 Junior	B-1861		21. 7.90	Devon & Somerset GC	North Hill	4. 4.03
FZG	3650	FZG	SZD-9 bis Bocian 1D	F-859	SP-2450	24. 9.90	The Borders GC	Milfield	16. 6.02
FZH	3651	FZH	Schempp-Hirth Ventus C	455		26. 7.90	G.D.Clack	Rivar Hill	5. 2.03
FZK	3653	FZK	Schempp-Hirth HS.4 Standard Cirrus	81G	HB-967	2. 9.90	J.L.Rodgers & Syndicate	Aston Down	7. 8.03
FZL	3654	Z6	Schleicher ASW20CL	20764	D-5937	12. 7.90	R.M.Housden	Aston Down	21. 3.03
FZM	3655	FZM	Scheibe SF-27A Zugvogel V	6103	D-1772	7. 8.90	N.Dickenson	Camphill	17. 4.02
FZN	3656	K13	Schleicher ASK13	13045	D-5759	9. 8.90	Black Mountains GC	Talgarth	20. 6.03
FZP	3657	N16	SZD-51-1 Junior	B-1926		9. 8.90	Portsmouth Naval GC	Lee-on-Solent	11. 1.03
FZQ	3658	FXQ	SZD-50-3 Puchacz	B-2024	(BGA.3637)	9. 8.90	Coventry GC	Husbands Bosworth	18.12.02
FZR	3659	FZR	Schleicher Ka6CR	6136	D-8459	17.12.90	P.S.Huggins	North Hill	24.11.03
FZS	3660	L13	LET L-13 Blanik	025609	NEJSGSA.8	28. 8.90	B.J.Shackell & A.Pattemore	Gallows Hill	7. 4.99
			(Rebuild with parts from BGA.2661)						
FZU	3662		Slingsby T.38 Grasshopper	761	WZ765	8.8.91	H.Chapple	Berlin	26.12.96*
			(Probably composite wings ex WZ765 & spare fuselage c/n SSK/FF2069: as "WZ765": to Luftwaffen Museum 1996)						
FZV	3663	480	Rolladen-Schneider LS-7	7116		16.12.90	R.N.Boddy	Booker	2.10.03
FZW	3664	FZW	Glaser-Dirks DG-300 Club Elan	3E378C53		23. 9.90	Mr & Mrs S.L.Barter	Ringmer	8. 1.03
FZX	3665	FZX	SZD-51-1 Junior	B-1925		18. 9.90	Nene Valley GC	Upwood	23. 2.03
FZY	3666		LET L-33 Solo	940206		19. 3.94	A.W.Cox	Bicester	18. 3.95*
FZZ	3667	FZZ	LET L-33 Solo	940220		28. 4.95	D.A Wiseman	Andreas	12. 4.03
GAB	3669		LAK-12 Lietuva	6170		12. 1.91	M.J. Wilshere	RAF Halton	4. 4.03

GAC	3670	GAC	Schleicher Ka6CR	6301	(BGA.3647) RAFGGA.557(2)/D-5572	17.11.90	York Gliding Centre *(Crashed Rufforth 25.11.98)*	Rufforth	2. 2.99
GAD	3671	L5	Rolladen-Schneider LS-3	3032	HB-1363	19.11.90	M.J.Towler	Bidford	7. 6. 03
GAF	3673	778	Schleicher ASK21	21152	ZD652 BGA.2892	8.11.90	Lasham Gliding Society	Lasham	11. 3.03
GAG	3674	GAG	Schleicher ASK21	21143	ZD645 BGA.2885	24. 1.91	Stratford-upon-Avon GC	Snitterfield	17.12.03
GAH	3675	GAH	Schempp-Hirth HS.4 Standard Cirrus	572	HB-1240	3.12.90	M.G.Harris	Nympsfield	26.11.03
GAJ	3676	GAJ	Glaser-Dirks DG-300 Club Elan	3E385C56		10.12.90	M.R Wooley & Ptnrs	Long Mynd	16. 7.02
GAK	3677	GAK	LET L-13 Blanik	174522	2-84 (Lithuania)	7.97	North Wales GC	Llantisilio	26.10.02
GAL	3678	GAL	Schempp-Hirth HS.4 Standard Cirrus	335	HB-1150	3. 4.91	D.Reynolds & S.Cooke *(Collided with Pawnee G-ASLK Aston Down 14.9.01)*	Aston Down	8. 2.02
GAM	3679	GAM	Schleicher ASK21	21144	ZD646 BGA.2886	21.11.90	Oxford University GC	Bicester	17.11.03
GAN	3680	83	Glasflugel H.301 Libelle	8	D-4111	12.12.90	W.J.Dean	Long Mynd	12. 8.03
GAP	3681	GAP	Schempp-Hirth Ventus bT	14/150	OH-774 N416DP	28. 4.91	J.R.Greenwell	Currock Hill	30. 3.03
GAQ	3682	GAQ/K7	Schleicher Ka7 Rhönadler	3	PH-788 D-5550	19. 4.91	York Gliding Centre	Rufforth	23. 6.01
GAR	3683	148	Rolladen-Schneider LS-6C	6205		2.11.90	A.J.Burton	Shobdon	22. 8.02
GAS	3684	GAS	Schempp-Hirth Ventus CT	157/509		30. 5.91	M W Edwards	Kingston Deverill	18. 3.03
GAT	3685	GAT	Grob G.102 Astir CS	1130	D-4176	23.11.90	R.S.Scott	Lasham	26. 7.03
GAU	3686	725	Glasflugel H.201B Standard Libelle	498	F-CELA	11. 6.93	D.R.Pickett	Crowland	11. 4.03
GAV	3687	GAV	Scheibe SF-27A Zugvogel V	6073	D-5287	18.11.90	W.Waite	Lleweni Parc	23. 2.03
GAW	3688	GAW	Schleicher Ka6CR	61/08	D-6320	30.12.90	B.D.Floyd	Saltby	6. 4.03
GAX	3689	302	SZD-55-1	551190008		30. 4.91	Rattlesden GC	Rattlesden	14. 4.03
GBA	3692	GBA	Schleicher ASK13	13417	D-2114	4.12.90	Burn GC	Burn	7. 8.03
GBB	3693		Schleicher ASK21	21073	D-3239	11.12.90	B.T.Spreckley	Le Blanc, France	22. 3.03
GBD	3695	GBD	SZD-50-3 Puchacz	B-2028		27. 4.91	Northumbria GC	Currock Hill	22.12.03
GBE	3696		Schleicher Ka6CR (Pe)	6133A	D-4085	23.12.90	J.Swannock	Gamston	7. 9.02
GBF	3697	GBF	Schleicher ASK21	21142	ZD644 BGA.2883	3. 2.91	BBC Gliding Group	Booker	20. 1.03
GBG	3698	S21	Rolladen-Schneider LS-6c	6214		12.12.90	C.M.Greaves	Rufforth	11. 1.03
GBJ	3700	GBJ	Grob G.102 Astir CS	1107	D-4167	5. 1.91	Aquila GC	Hinton-in-the-Hedges	1. 6.03
GBK	3701	GBK	Grob G.102 Astir CS	1461	D-7451	5. 1.91	R.J.Thacker *"Mountain Man"*	Cross Hayes	4. 3.03
GBL	3702	720	Rolladen-Schneider LS-7	7119		12.11.90	C.Sutton	Winthorpe	18. 3.03
GBM	3703	GBM	Scheibe SF-27A Zugvogel V	6060	RAFGGA D-5409	2. 1.91	G.Cook t/a BFMT Syndicate	North Hill	23. 7.03
GBN	3704	843/MD	Schleicher ASK21	21141	ZD643 BGA.2884	14.3.91	Essex & Suffolk GC	Wormingford	26. 11.03
GBP	3705	GBP	Schleicher ASK21	21150	ZD650 BGA.2890	29. 1.91	London GC *(Destroyed by mid-air lightning strike 4.99)*	Dunstable	30.11.99
GBQ	3706	630	Rolladen-Schneider LS-6	6082	D-3725	6. 2.91	A. & P.R.Pentecost	Kingston Deverill	3. 2.03
GBR	3707	218	Rolladen-Schneider LS-6C	6196	D-3482	25.11.90	S.Hurd	Dunstable	7. 3.03
GBS	3708	206	Glaser-Dirks DG-300 Club Elan	3E389C58		15. 3.91	Yorkshire GC	Sutton Bank	9. 2.03
GBT	3709	IV	Rolladen-Schneider LS-4A	4355	N220BB	8. 4.91	S.A.Adlard	Long Mynd	25. 2.03
GBU	3710	922	Centrair 101A Pégase	101A-0394		3. 4.91	S.I.Ross	Parham Park	13. 2.03
GBV	3711	649	Schleicher ASK21	21149	ZD649 BGA.2889	23. 4.91	Wolds GC	Pocklington	15. 4.03
GBX	3713	290	Schleicher ASW22	22029	D-4325	27. 2.91	E.J.Rogers & Ptnrs	Gransden Lodge	7. 3.03
GBY	3714	425	Rolladen-Schneider LS-7	7121		21. 1.91	W.J.Morecraft & Ptnrs	Saltby	9. 2.03
GBZ	3715	GBZ	Glaser-Dirks DG-500 Elan Trainer	5E34T10		10. 8.91	Needwood Forest GC	Cross Hayes	13. 4.03
GCA	3716		Schleicher ASW19B	19281	D-3179	2. 3.91	Deeside GC	Aboyne	21. 3.03
GCB	3717	637	LAK-12 Lietuva	647		29. 3.91	B.Middleton	Dunstable	10. 7.01
GCC	3718	GCC	SZD-51-1 Junior	B-1928		10. 3.91	The Soaring Centre	Husbands Bosworth	5. 3.03
GCD	3719	507	Schempp-Hirth HS.4 Standard Cirrus	476	PH-507	21. 2.91	B.Van Woerden	Chipping	9. 5.03
GCE	3720	8	Schleicher ASH25	25105		19. 2.91	C.L.Withall	Dunstable	11. 3.03
GCF	3721	GCF	Schleicher ASK23	23010	AGA.9	8. 2.91	Needwood Forest GC	Cross Hayes	5. 3.03
GCG	3722	S81	Schleicher K8B	8186	D-5227	5. 2.91	Shenington GC	Edgehill	4. 9.02
GCH	3723	438	Schleicher ASW15B	15212	PH-438 D-0950	17. 4.91	M.D.Woodman-Smith & Ptnr	Dunstable	24. 4.99
GCJ	3724	GCJ	LAK-12 Lietuva	626		30. 3.91	P.Crowhurst *(New wings with reconditioned 1982-built fuselage)*	Crowland	31.10.03
GCK	3725	GCK	SZD-50-3 Puchacz	B-2025	(G-BTJV) BGA.3725	8. 3.91	Kent GC	Challock	28. 3.03
GCL	3726	GCL	Grob G.102 Astir CS	1194	D-7311	10. 3.91	C.P.Offen	Burn	28. 2.03
GCM	3727	Z29	Rolladen-Schneider LS-6C	6216		12. 3.91	M.H.Hardwick	Enstone	11.12.03
GCN	3728	B35	Centrair 101A Pégase	101A-0035	(BGA.3694) F-CFQB	12. 3.91	B.T.Spreckley *(Damaged Nympsfield 18.6.95)*	Le Blanc, France	14. 3.96*
GCP	3729	GCP	Schleicher Ka6CR	6416	D-6369	3. 5.91	D.Clarke	Burn	19. 4.03
GCQ	3730	GCQ/845	Schempp-Hirth HS.2 Cirrus VTC	135Y	D-2945	2. 4.91	Dumfries & Galloway GC	Falgunzeon	28. 6.03
GCR	3731	748	Schleicher ASW15B	15447	D-6887	23. 3.91	K.A.Harrison	Dunstable	25.11.03
GCS	3732	H12	Glasflugel H.205 Club Libelle	159	F-CEQL	7. 7.91	N.Stainton	Bidford	24. 6.02
GCT	3733	GCT	Schempp-Hirth Discus B	360		22. 3.91	J.C.Leonard	Bembridge	6. 5.03
GCU	3734	GCU	SZD-50-3 Puchacz	B-2023	(BGA.3619)	19. 3.91	Buckminster GC	Saltby	18. 3.03

GCX	3736	N6	Schleicher ASW15	15034	D-0420	21. 5.91	A.S.Edlin	Husbands Bosworth	8. 3.03
GCY	3737	GCY	Centrair 101A Pégase	101A-0392		22. 4.91	G.R. Hudson	Lasham	23. 4.03
GCZ	3738		Rolladen-Schneider LS-7WL	7130		23. 3.91	*(De-registered 18.9.00 – sold as EC-...)*		
GDA	3739	546	Rolladen-Schneider LS-3-17M	3448	RAFGGA.546	20. 5.91	C.J. Davison	Winthorpe	24. 5.03
GDB	3740	GDB	Schleicher K8B	8152	HB-738	23. 3.91	Welland GC	Lyveden	28. 3.03
GDC	3741	GDC	Slingsby T.38 Grasshopper	FF.1795		11. 5.91	F.K.Russell & Ptnrs	Dunstable	2. 5.97*
			(Built from spare frame - also carries marking SSK/RF.3107)						
GDD	3742	GDD	Bolkow Phoebus 17C	836	D-0060	18. 4.91	I.D.McLeod	Challock	2. 6.02
GDE	3743	GDE	Schleicher Ka6CR	6570Si	D-5306	26. 4.91	D.N.Jones	North Hill	5. 4.03
GDF	3744		Schleicher Ka6BR	389	D-8544	17. 4.91	A.D.Chapman	Burn	30. 6.03
GDJ	3747	450	Rolladen-Schneider LS-4A	4832		27. 4.91	A Clark	Aboyne	11. 5.03
GDK	3748	GDK	Schleicher K8B	8240	D-5381	15. 4.91	East Sussex GC	Ringmer	25. 4.03
					D-KANU/D-5381				
GDM	3750	668	Glasflugel H.201B Standard Libelle	597	D-6666	29. 4.91	K.Fear & Syndicate	Crowland	15. 3.03
GDN	3751	294	Rolladen-Schneider LS-3-17M	3291	D-6932	28. 4.91	S.J Pepler	Sandhill Farm, Shrivenham	11. 7.03
GDP	3752	GDP	Schleicher ASW19B	19285	D-3160	2. 5.91	P. Heywood	Parham Park	19. 4.03
GDQ	3753	GDQ	Grob G.102 Astir CS	1145	D-7229	11. 5.91	J.T.Harrison	Camphill	19. 7.03
GDR	3754		Schempp-Hirth Discus CS	016CS		5. 5.91	R.H.Wright	Husbands Bosworth	9. 6.03
			(Built Orlican)						
GDS	3755	GDS	Schleicher ASW15B	15205	D-0902	20. 6.91	J.Edwards	Dunstable	11. 9.03
GDT	3756	T54	Schleicher ASW24	24120		10. 5.91	A.Ditchfield	Camphill	5. 4.03
GDU	3757	801	Schleicher ASW24	24118		8. 6.91	G.J.Moore	Dunstable	28. 4.03
GDV	3758	GDV	Schleicher Ka6E	4099	OO-ZWQ	20. 6.91	L.D.Howell	Snitterfield	29. 4.03
					I-NEST/OE-0807				
GDW	3759		Scheibe SF-27A Zugvogel V	6116	D-1997	16. 5.91	M.W.Hands	Camphill	22. 5.03
GDX	3760	896	Schempp-Hirth Discus CS	023CS		2. 7.91	The Soaring Centre	Husbands Bosworth	5. 3.03
GDY	3761	GDY	Schleicher ASW15B	15220	D-0947	6. 5.91	J Archer	Bidford	26.11.03
GDZ	3762	524	Schleicher ASW24	24116		17. 5.91	I.C.Lees	Pocklington	14. 3.03
GEA	3763	GEA	Schleicher Ka6CR	849	(BGA.3605)	7. 6.91	M Wood	Rufforth	19. 5. 03
					D-5801				
GEB	3764	GEB	Grob G.102 Astir CS77	1628	PH-576	7. 6.91	J.O.Lavery	Bellarena	30. 6.02
GEE	3767	928	Glasflugel H.201B Standard Libelle	94	D-0928	6. 6.91	C.Metcalfe	Gamston	23. 5.03
GEF	3768	GEF	Schleicher Ka6CR	6459	D-1068	24. 5.91	J.B Christie	Nympsfield	4. 7.98
GEG	3769		Schleicher K8B	689	HB-639	27. 4.91	Newark & Notts GC	Winthorpe	29. 1.03
GEH	3770	219	Schleicher ASW15B	15276	D-2124	9. 7.91	K.G.Vincent & Ptnrs	Challock	22. 3.03
GEL	3772	N23	SZD-50-3 Puchacz	B-2030		29. 5.91	Portsmouth Naval GC	Lee-on-Solent	3. 4.03
GEM	3773	GEM	Schleicher Ka6CR	6249	D-8486	4. 6.91	E.R.V.Nash	Rivar Hill	17. 6.03
GEN	3774	GEN	Slingsby T.21B	1154	RAFGGA.550	16. 5.92	A.Harris	RAF Bruggen	13. 7.03
					XN150				
GEP	3775	GEP	Schempp-Hirth HS.4 Standard Cirrus	205G	D-0917	10. 6.91	G.S.Wadforth	Pocklington	24. 4.03
GEQ	3776	2001	SZD-12A Mucha 100A	462	SP-2001	6. 6.91	T.Slater *(Stored 11.01)*	(Bury St.Edmunds)	
HAA	3777	263	Glasflugel H.201B Standard Libelle	356	HB-1090	20. 6.91	T.J.Mormin & Ptnrs	Gransden Lodge	14. 3.03
HAB	3778	HAB	Schleicher Ka6CR	6596	D-1596	1.92	M Greenwood	Rhigos	9. 3.03
HAC	3779		SZD-50-3 Puchacz	B-2035		29. 6.91	Peterborough & Spalding GC	Crowland	27. 3.03
HAD	3780	429	Glasflugel H.201 Standard Libelle	3	D-8914	5. 7.91	G.S Roe & Ptnrs	Lasham	18. 3.03
HAE	3781	HAE	Glasflugel H.205 Club Libelle	75	D-8687	5. 7.91	J.P.Kirby	Lee on Solent	6. 5.03
HAF	3782	N53	SZD-50-3 Puchacz	B-2031		4. 7.91	Culdrose GC	RNAS Culdrose	15. 3.03
HAG	3783	HAG	Schleicher Ka7 Rhönadler	834	D-5795	21. 5.92	Denbigh GC	Lleweni Parc	31. 5.03
HAJ	3785	391	Schempp-Hirth Ventus C	517		19. 7.91	Surrey & Hants GC	Lasham	30. 1.03
HAK	3786	XA302	Slingsby T.31B	844	XA302	17. 8.91	W.Walker	RAF Syerston	24. 5.96*
HAL	3787	HAL	Schleicher ASK1313	690AB		7. 9.91	Cotswold GC	Aston Down	17.12.03
HAN	3789	278	Schempp-Hirth HS.4 Standard Cirrus	130	D-0326	14. 8.91	M.Hastings & Syndicate	Weston-on-the-Green	28. 3.03
HAP	3790	HAP	Schleicher Ka6E	4335	HB-985	29. 8.91	T.Turner	Dunstable	26. 8.03
HAQ	3791	114	Rolladen-Schneider LS-6B	6150	D-8079	2. 9.91	A R Hughes	Gransden Lodge	3. 5.03
HAR	3792	HAR	Schleicher K8B	8151	D-8453	4. 9.91	G.Weale	Brent Tor	4. 7.97*
HAS	3793	HAS	SZD-50-3 Puchacz	B-2043		17. 8.91	The Soaring Centre	Husbands Bosworth	16. 1.03
HAT	3794	HAT	Glaser-Dirks DG-200/17	2-93/1709	D-6843	26. 8.91	D.Simon	Carlton Moor	15.12.02
HAU	3795	HAU	Grob G.102 Astir CS Jeans	2043	D-3887	11. 9.91	Yorkshire GC	Sutton Bank	20. 3.03
HAV	3796	HAV	Glasflugel H.201B Standard Libelle 40		HB-950	25. 8.91	P.W.Andrews	Husbands Bosworth	20. 5.03
HAX	3798	HAX	Schempp-Hirth HS.4 Standard Cirrus	02	ZS-GHZ	10.10.91	P.J.Mortimer	Rivar Hill	5. 4.03
					ZS-TIM/ZS-GGR/D-0302				
HAY	3799		Rolladen-Schneider LS-7	7154		15.10.91	N.Leaton & Ptnrs	Challock	14. 7.96*
HBA	3801	729	Rolladen-Schneider LS-7	7156	D-6041	12.10.91	P.O'Donald	Gransden Lodge	23.11.03
HBB	3802		Schleicher ASW24	24132		19. 9.91	London GC	Dunstable	24.10.03
HBC	3803	HBC	Rolladen-Schneider LS-6C	6209	D-...	20. 9.91	J.Burry	Lasham	7. 5.03
HBD	3804	HBD	Glaser-Dirks DG-2002-	12	HB-1384	5.10.91	R.W. Brown	Rattlesden	22. 8.02
HBE	3805	356	Glaser-Dirks DG-300 Elan	3E237	SE-UFB	21. 5.92	A.W.Cox & Ptnrs	Enstone	16.12.03
HBF	3806	HBF	Schempp-Hirth HS.5 Nimbus 2C	191	D-3369	5.10.91	T.Cauldwell	Sackville Lodge, Riseley	21. 7.00
HBG	3807	96	Schleicher ASW24	24133		10.12.91	Imperial College GC	Lasham	1. 8.03
HBH	3808	496	Grob G.103C Twin III	36006		14.10.91	Imperial College GC	Lasham	13.12.02
HBJ	3809	949	Rolladen-Schneider LS-6C-18	6230		26. 9.91	D.J.Hill	Tibenham	3. 3.03
HBK	3810	HBK	Grob G.103 Twin Astir	3254-T-31	RAFGGA.550	29. 9.91	R.W.Idle	Burn	19. 9.02
					D-2389				
HBL	3811	HBL	Grob G.102 Astir CS77	1626	RAFGSA R78	17.10.91	J.McCormick	Bidford	15. 6.03
					RAFGSA.778				

HBM	3812	HBM	Grob G.102 Astir CS77	1633	RAFGSA R65	3.12.91	A.Fox	RAF Syerston	13. 4.03
					RAFGSA.R66/RAFGSA.546				
HBP	3814	522	Glaser-Dirks DG-500/22 Elan	5E36S8		10.91	A.Taverna	Florence, Italy	15. 6.03
HBQ	3815		Schleicher Ka6CR	6611	D-5616	22.11.91	P.N.Jones	Dunstable	14. 4.03
HBR	3816	PM	Schempp-Hirth Nimbus 4T	3/6	(BGA.3784)	1. 8.92	P S Hawkins	(Australia)	16. 5.03
HBS	3817	HBS	SZD-41A Jantar Standard	B-852	D-4160	2.12.91	A.Henderson	Milfield	9. 7.03
HBT	3819		Grob G.102 Club Astir	2235	PH-675	9. 2.92	M.D.Evans	Winthorpe	29. 3.03
HBU	3820	605	Centrair ASW20F	20527	F-CFSI	22.11.91	R.Palmer & R.Mann	Bidford	28. 1.03
HBV	3821	667	Schempp-Hirth HS.5 Nimbus 2B	143	D-7850	11.91	C.J.Teagle	Sutton Bank	12. 2.03
HBW	3822	829	Glaser-Dirks DG-300 Club Elan			15.12.91	P.C.Cannon	Lasham	19. 4.00
				3E405C64					
HBX	3823	HBX	Slingsby T.45 Swallow	1386	8801M	16. 5.93	C.D.Street & Ptnrs	Lasham	26. 9.02
					XS650				
HBY	3824	664	Rolladen-Schneider LS-7	7148		7.11.91	K.W.Payne	Husbands Bosworth	11. 6.03
HBZ	3825	HBZ	Slingsby T.15 Gull III rep	---		28. 6.92	P.R.Philpot	Chipping	19. 6.03
HCA	3826	HCA	Grob G.103 Twin Astir	3289	D-0094	24.12.91	M.Wright	Rattlesden	18. 4.03
					OO-ZOH/D-3063				
HCB	3827	754	Schempp-Hirth Nimbus 3DT	47		24.12.91	P.A.Green	Lasham	7. 4.03
HCC	3829		SZD-50-3 Puchacz	B-2048		4. 1.92	Heron GC	RNAS Yeovilton	20.12.03
HCD	3830	HCD	SZD-50-3 Puchacz	B-2049		7. 1.92	The Soaring Centre	Husbands Bosworth	1. 5.03
HCE	3831	346	Schleicher ASW19B	19305	D-6527	6. 1.92	N.J.Morgan	Dunstable	14. 2.03
HCF	3832	HCF	SZD-50-3 Puchacz	B-2047		20.12.91	Shalbourne Soaring Society	Rivar Hill	8. 2.03
HCG	3833	HCG	Maupin Woodstock One	---		10.92	R.Harvey	Swanton Morley	6.11.03
			(Built R.Harvey)						
HCH	3834	355	Centrair ASW20FP	20178	F-CEUL	20. 3.92	A.Henderson	Saltby	8. 9.03
HCJ	3835	HCJ	Grob G.103 Twin II	3709	D-2611	21. 4.92	Peterborough & Spalding GC	Crowland	14. 6.03
HCK	3836	WB962	Slingsby T.21B	623	RAFGGA5..	2. 1.92	V.Mallon	Laarbruch, Germany	21. 9.03
					WB962				
HCL	3837	144	Schempp-Hirth Discus B	136	D-4682	13. 3.92	M.A.Powell-Brett	Snitterfield	20. 3.03
HCM	3838	HCM	Schleicher Ka7 Rhönadler	498	D-5669	4. 3.92	M.Barnard	Dunstable	29. 8.02
HCN	3839	HCN	CARMAM M.200 Foehn	24	F-CDDR	21.12.92	J S Shaw	Perranporth	19. 7.99
HCP	3840	HCP	Avialsa A.60 Fauconnet	123K	F-CDLA	3.93	C.Kaminski *(Being refurbished)*	Eaglescott	31. 7.95*
HCQ	3841	HCQ	Glasflugel H.201B Standard Libelle		HB-999	28. 1.92	E.K.Harris	Dunstable	1. 3.03
				197					
HCR	3842	394	SZD-51-1 Junior	B-2003		28. 4.92	Surrey & Hants GC	Lasham	1.12.03
HCS	3843	HCS	Grob G.102 Astir CS77	1727	RAFGSA.R84	5. 2.92	Buckminster GC	Saltby	26. 4.97*
					RAFGSA.884				
HCU	3845	78	Glaser-Dirks DG-300 Club Elan			7. 2.92	M.S Smith & Ptnrs	Aston Down	14. 4.03
				3E407C66					
HCV	3846	X19	Schleicher ASW19B	19084	D-4486	14. 5.93	A.B. Laws	Syerston	17. 5.03
HCW	3847	HCW	SZD-51-1 Junior	B-2002	(BGA.3844)	1. 2.92	Deeside GC	Aboyne	24. 2.03
HCX	3848	HCX	Schleicher ASK21	21541		16. 5.92	Devon & Somerset GC	North Hill	23. 6.03
HCY	3849	HCY	Glaser-Dirks DG-300 Club Elan			10. 5.94	S.T.Dry	RAF Keevil	5. 8.03
				3E413C67					
HCZ	3850	HCZ	Schleicher K8B	8114A	D-4675	21. 2.92	South London Gliding Centre	Kenley	18. 5.03
HDA	3851	HDA	Pilatus B4 PC-11AF	017	D-0964	18. 3.92	P.Bois	(Jersey)	2. 7.03
HDB	3852	HDB	SZD-51-1 Junior	B-1997		4. 3.92	Stratford-upon-Avon GC	Snitterfield	23.12.03
HDC	3853	HDC	Schleicher ASK13	13308	D-0750	19. 3.93	Bowland Forest GC	Chipping	22.11.03
HDD	3854	591	Centrair 101B Pégase	101B-0425		5. 4.92	Scottish Gliding Union	Portmoak	5.12.03
HDE	3855		Pilatus B4 PC-11AF	223	VH-XOZ	12. 4.92	A.J.Hamilton	Shobdon	4. 7.01
					VH-WQP				
HDF	3856	910	Schempp-Hirth Discus B	404		21. 2.92	T.M.Lipscombe	Lasham	19.12.03
HDH	3858	991	Glaser-Dirks DG-202-15	2-197	???	24. 5.92	A.J. Millson	Rattlesden	13. 3.03
HDJ	3859	HDJ	Schleicher ASW20CL	20828	D-8442	4. 3.92	G.E.Lambert	Booker	2. 3.03
HDL	3861	137	Schleicher ASW20	20082	D-1617	13. 4.92	S.Thackray	Booker	12. 6.03
					OH-495				
HDM	3862	HDH	SZD-12A Mucha 100A	448	SP-1987	15. 4.92	T.J.Wilkinson	Sackville Lodge, Riseley	22. 4.02
HDN	3863	HDN	Schleicher K8B	2	D-8017	17. 3.92	Upward Bound Trust	Thame	30. 4.03
HDP	3864	N36	SZD-50-3 Puchacz	B-2050		3.92	Heron GC	RNAS Yeovilton	31. 5.03
HDR	3866	467	Glaser-Dirks DG-300 Elan	3E95	RAFGSA R30	14. 3.92	C.J.Cornish	Booker	9. 5.03
HDT	3868	291	Schempp-Hirth Discus BT	76/405		18. 3.92	J.D.J.Glossop & Ptnrs	Gransden Lodge	23. 4.03
HDU	3869	HDU	SZD-51-1 Junior	B-1996		25. 3.92	Cambridge University GC	Gransden Lodge	23. 2.03
HDV	3870	882	Schleicher ASW19B	19345	D-2876	20. 4.92	R.J.Hinley	Long Mynd	19. 4.03
HDW	3871	HDW	Centrair 101A Pégase	101A-0179	F-CGEE	21. 3.92	T.Head	Husbands Bosworth	27. 6.03
HDX	3872	A2	Rolladen-Schneider LS-7	7161		27. 3.92	P.W.Rodwell	Crowland	6. 4.03
HDY	3873		Schleicher K8B	8277	D-4094	24. 3.92	M.A Everett	Crowland	21. 4.01
HDZ	3874	W1	Schempp-Hirth Discus CS	078CS		7. 7.92	J.P.Wright & G.Bennett	Challock	19. 2.03
HEA	3875	HEA	Slingsby T.38 Grasshopper		(ex RAF)	4. 7.92	R.L.McLean	Rufforth	19.11.01
				'SSK/FF529'					
HEB	3876	HEB	Schleicher Ka6CR	6289	HB-773	6. 5.92	J.W.Watt	North Hill	22. 6.02
HEC	3877	308	SZD-55-1	551191019		10. 5.92	G.P Davis	Nympsfield	28. 2.03
HED	3878	840	Schempp-Hirth Ventus A	17	D-2524	18. 4.92	M.R.Dawson	RAF Keevil	27. 4.03
HEE	3879	316	Schempp-Hirth Discus B	292		19. 4.92	Booker GC	Booker	11. 2.03
			(Rebuild of BGA.3523 after accident 21.6.91 but see BGA.4047)						
HEF	3880	HEF	Glaser-Dirks DG-500 Elan Trainer			24. 5.92	Yorkshire GC	Sutton Bank	17. 4.03
				5E53T20					
HEG	3881	HEG	LAK-12 Lietuva	6206		27. 6.92	R.Kmita & Ptnrs	Kirton-in-Lindsey	7. 3.03
HEH	3882	795	Rolladen-Schneider LS-7WL	7163	D-6078	24. 6.92	P.D.Candler	Gransden Lodge	17. 2.03
HEJ	3883	687	Schleicher ASW15B	15441	D-6871	5.92	R.Bickerton	Weston on the Green	10. 2.03
HEK	3884	HEK	SZD-51-1 Junior	B-2009	BGA.3893	29. 5.94	Cambridge University GC	Gransden Lodge	15. 1.03
					(BGA.3884)				

HEL	3885	A9	Rolladen-Schneider LS-4	4027	(BGA.3896) BGA.3885/D-6431	26. 5.92	J. Ballard	Long Mynd	23. 3.03
HEM	3886	473	Schempp-Hirth Discus CS	073CS		22. 5.92	G.G. Lee	Lasham	1. 3.03
HEN	3887	735	Schempp-Hirth Discus B	422		5. 6.92	A.R.Verity & Ptnrs	Challock	25. 1.03
HEP	3888		SZD-50-3 Puchacz	B-2057		30. 5.92	Peterborough & Spalding GC	Crowland	5. 2.03
HEQ	3889	611	Schleicher ASW20L	20410	D-6747	6. 6.92	M.Chant	Brent Tor	3. 3.03
HER	3890	HER	Schleicher ASW19	19240	F-CERR	1. 4.93	B.T.Spreckley	Le Blanc, France	23. 3.03
HES	3891	HES	Centrair 101A Pégase	101A-039	F-CFQF	13. 2.93	B.T.Spreckley	Le Blanc, France	22. 3.03
HET	3892	335	Rolladen-Schneider LS-6C	6263		26. 5.92	M.P.Brooks	Lasham	7. 3.03
HEV	3894	HEV	Schempp-Hirth HS.2 Cirrus	41	OO-ZXY (OO-ZOZ)/D-0104	26. 5.92	D.A Clempson	Portmoak	10. 4.03
HEW	3895	486	Rolladen-Schneider LS-6C	6250		29. 4.92	R.M.Underhill	Bicester	21. 1.03
HEY	3897		Hutter H-17A	02		6.92	J.M.Lee	Parham Park	17. 5.00
			(Built J.M.Lee - possibly ex BGA.3661)						
HEZ	3898	607	Rolladen-Schneider LS-6C	6264		16. 7.92	J.E.Cruttenden	Lasham	11. 6.03
HFA	3899	495	Schempp-Hirth Ventus B/16.6	251	RAFGSA.R24	26. 6.92	D.R.Stewart	Winthorpe	25. 6.95*
HFB	3900	HFB	Schleicher Ka6CR	6344Si	D-5825	13. 7.92	S.Tomlinson	Winthorpe	3.11.03
HFC	3901	WB924	Slingsby T.21B	587	WB924	7.92	M.G.Stringer	Dunstable	25.11.02
HFD	3902	289	Grob G.102 Astir CS Jeans	2229	D-5912	29. 6.92	East Sussex GC	Ringmer	26. 8.97*
							(Damaged Ringmer15.6.97 & w/o)		
HFE	3903	XN187	Slingsby T.21B	1166	XN187	23. 6.92	A.J.Oultram	Seighford	10. 1.04
HFF	3904	870	Schempp-Hirth Standard Cirrus	539	D-8916	14. 2.93	R.S.Morrisroe	Upwood	23. 2.03
HFG	3905	HFG	Slingsby T.21B	1165	XN186	28. 6.92	A.M.Thompson	RAF Marham	2. 5.00
HFH	3906	HFH	SZD-50-3 Puchacz	B-2059		4. 8.92	Trent Valley GC	Kirton-in-Lindsey	21. 4.03
HFJ	3907		SZD-42-1 Jantar 2A	B-792	RAFGGA... OO-ZDE	5. 4.92	P.Stein	RAF Bruggen	9. 3.02
							(De-registered 18. 6. 02 Sold abroad as OO-ZDE)		
HFL	3909	925/SSC	Schleicher ASH25	25147		18. 7.92	Scottish Gliding Union	Portmoak	21. 2.03
HFM	3910	747	Rolladen-Schneider LS-6C	6266		8. 7.92	F.J.Sheppard	Booker	26. 6.03
HFN	3911		Wassmer WA-26P Squale	18	F-CDQP	24. 6.92	C.Duthy-James	Talgarth	22. 8.96*
HFP	3912		CARMAM M.100S Mésange	87K	F-CDPQ	24. 6.92	D.Patrick & Ptnr	Falgunzeon	28. 9.96*
HFQ	3913	126	Rolladen-Schneider LS-6C	6260	(BGA.3908)	23. 6.92	M.E.Baker	Gamston	4. 3.03
HFU	3917	HFU	SZD-9 bis Bocian 1D	P-334	SP-2038	22. 6.94	T.Wiltshere	(Spilsby)	15. 8.96*
HFV	3918	F2	Schempp-Hirth Ventus B 16.6	204	D-5235	1.10.92	A.Cliffe	Camphill	23. 3.03
HFW	3919	HFW	Schleicher K8B	8108	HB-705	24. 9.92	Oxford GC	Weston-on-the-Green	19. 2.03
HFX	3920	82	Schempp-Hirth Nimbus 4T	12		3. 7.92	R.Jones	Lasham	19.12.02
HFY	3921	940	Schempp-Hirth Ventus CT	168/554	(BGA.3916) (BGA.3867)	21. 7.92	M.T.Day & D.J.Ellis	Lasham	27. 2.03
HFZ	3922		Abbott-Baynes Scud I rep.	001		R	Brooklands Museum *(Noted 4.99)*	Brooklands	
HGA	3923	HGA	Wassmer WA-26P Squale	43	F-CDUH	30. 3.93	E.C.Murgatroyd	Sackville Lodge, Riseley	30. 5.03
HGB	3924	509	Grob G.102 Astir CS	1356	D-7386	16.11.92	P.J.Hollamby & Ptnrs	Lee-on-Solent	23. 5.03
							(Rebuilt with wings & components from RAFGGA.587)		
HGC	3925	HGC	Schleicher Ka7 Rhönadler	540	D-5689	6. 3.94	T.A.Joint	Lasham	27. 8.00
HGF	3928	HGF	Schleicher ASW15B	15264	D-2128	25. 8.92	K.E. Singer	Camphill	24. 4.03
HGG	3929		Schempp-Hirth HS.4 Standard Cirrus	362	HB-1172	31.12.92	P.W. Cooper	Camphill	25. 4.03
HGH	3930	HGH	Schleicher ASW19B	19351	D-1199	26. 8.92	A.Wood	Brent Tor	19. 4.01
HGJ	3931		CARMAM M.200 Foehn	33	F-CDHG	28. 9.92	M.Skinner	Cross Hayes	11.95*
HGK	3932	HGK	Schempp-Hirth Discus BT	96/435		30.10.92	C.T.Skeate	Parham Park	16. 1.03
HGL	3933	583	Schempp-Hirth Discus B	431		30. 7.92	P.J.Ward	Aston Down	16. 3.03
HGM	3934	HGM	Scheibe SF-27A Zugvogel V	6017	D-9351	26. 9.92	S.R.Algeo	Lyveden	6. 9.02
HGN	3935	808	Schempp-Hirth Ventus CT	172/562		18. 9.92	D.J. Scholey	Lasham	5. 8.03
HGP	3936	HGP	Rolladen-Schneider LS-6C	6270		3.11.92	D.Elrington	Camphill	28. 2.03
HGQ	3937	637	LAK-12 Lietuva	6208		1.12.92	R.A.M.Lovegrove	Dunstable	7. 9.02
HGR	3938	HGR	LAK-12 Lietuva	6186		22. 3.93	R.G.Stevens	Husbands Bosworth	29. 4.03
HGS	3939	730	Schempp-Hirth Discus B	439		6.11.92	P.J.Bramley	Challock	7. 2.03
HGT	3940		FFA Diamant 16.5	40	HB-929	12. 4.94	R.W.Collins	Burn	31. 3.03
HGU	3941	HGU	Avionautica Rio M.100S	048	HB-1038 I-RIKI	3. 6.93	R.D.Colman	Old Sarum	7. 5.98
HGV	3942	HGV	Glaser-Dirks DG-500/22 Elan	5E70S11		26. 2.93	B.H.Bryce-Smith	Gransden Lodge	19. 2.03
HGW	3943	HGW	Centrair ASW20F	20102	F-CFFB	1. 1.93	C.Smith	Husbands Bosworth	6. 3.03
HGX	3944	783	LAK-12 Lietuva	6201		3. 5.93	K.Pickering	Parham Park	7. 6.03
HGY	3945		SZD-24C Foka	W-180	SP-2385	16.12.92	Peterborough & Spalding GC	Crowland	3. 6.02
HGZ	3946	502	Schempp-Hirth Discus BT	95/434		18.12.92	G.D.Coppin	Lasham	16. 4.03
HHA	3947	HHA	SZD-50-3 Puchacz	B-2058		18. 2.93	Derby & Lancs GC	Camphill	6. 2.03
HHC	3949	HHC	SZD-50-3 Puchacz	B-2080		16. 4.93	Derby & Lancs GC	Camphill	18. 4.03
HHD	3950	HHD	SZD-51-1 Junior	B-2010		19. 3.93	Derby & Lancs GC	Camphill	17. 5.03
HHE	3951	HHE	SZD-51-1 Junior	B-2008		30. 6.93	Derby & Lancs GC	Camphill	9. 4.03
HHG	3953	WT910	Slingsby T.31B	705	WT910	9. 1.93	P.Wickwar & Ptnr	Challock	30. 5.97*
HHH	3954	963	Rolladen-Schneider LS-6C	6289		11.12.92	B.R.Wise	Booker	2. 3.03
HHJ	3955	97	Glaser-Dirks DG-500/22 Elan	5E71S12		9. 2.93	British Gliding Association	Bicester	24. 2.03
HHK	3956	838	Schleicher ASW19B	19384	ZD661 BGA.2897	14. 3.93	A.J.Peters Syndicate	Lasham	13. 4.03
HHL	3957	HHL	Schleicher Ka7 Rhönadler	446	OY-XCK D-5619	30. 7.93	Lincolnshire GC *"Buttercup"*	Strubby	9. 6.03
HHM	3958	HHM	LAK-12 Lietuva	6195		9. 8.93	R.Parayre	(France)	27. 3.03
HHN	3959	979	Schempp-Hirth Ventus B/16.6	205	RAFGSA.R27	6. 2.93	N.A.C.Norman	Feshiebridge	11. 5.03
			(Build No. V-204)						
HHP	3960	KL	Schempp-Hirth Discus B	399	SE-UKL	12. 2.93	D.J.Knowles	Camphill	23.10.03
HHQ	3961	97Z	Schempp-Hirth Discus BT	106/453		12. 2.93	J.P.Galloway	Portmoak	28. 4.03

HHR	3962	100	SZD-55-15	51191020		18. 4.93	R.T.Starling	Nympsfield	27. 1.03
HHS	3963	HHS	Schleicher ASW20	20008	SE-TTU	3. 3.93	P.J.Rocks	Kirton-in-Lindsey	13. 9.03
HHT	3964	855	Rolladen-Schneider LS-6C	6292		18. 7.93	R.C.Bromwich	Kingston Deverill	15. 5.03
HHU	3965	23	Rolladen-Schneider LS-6C	6296		15. 2.93	J.S.Weston	Bellarena	10. 1.04
HHW	3967	237	LAK-12 Lietuva	6212		19. 3.93	A.J.Dibdin	Dunstable	22. 2.03
HHX	3968	HHX	Wassmer WA-26P Squale	14	F-CDQJ	27. 2.93	M.H.Gagg	Chauvigny, France	27. 2.03
HHY	3969	HHY	Glasflugel H.201B Standard Libelle	119	SE-TIU	1. 5.93	R.Tietma & M.Ainsworth	Husbands Bosworth	25. 3.03
HJA	3971	HJA	VFW-Fokker FK-3	0008	D-0409	9. 8.93	M.A Johnson & Ptnrs	Sackville Lodge, Riseley	2. 6.03
HJC	3973	25	Rolladen-Schneider LS-6C	6290		17. 3.93	F.J Davies & I.C.Woodhouse	Enstone	15.12.03
HJD	3974	HJD	Schleicher Ka6E	4141	D-.... OH-505/SE-TFM	4. 2.94	J.P. Stafford	Snitterfield	22. 5.03
HJE	3975	505	Schleicher K8B	8259	(BGA.3926) RAFGGA.505 (&/or RAFGGA.971)	16. 4.93	Denbigh GC	Lleweni Parc	7. 8.03
HJF	3976	245	Rolladen-Schneider LS-6C	6291		29. 4.93	J.L.Bridge	Gransden Lodge	19. 2.03
HJH	3978	HJH	Schempp-Hirth Discus BT	65/391	N224WT	22. 4.93	P.J.Goulthorpe	Crowland	5.12.03
HJJ	3979		Slingsby T.38 Grasshopper	797	WZ816	R	J.Wilkins (On rebuild 2000)	Redhill	
HJK	3980	HJK	Schleicher Ka7 Rhönadler	795	RAFGSA.R5 D-5791	14. 6.93	Leeds University GC	Rufforth	1. 5.03
HJL	3981	306	Schempp-Hirth Discus BT	105/451		3. 5.93	A.R.MacGregor	Kingston Deverill	15. 1.03
HJM	3982	HJM	Hutter H.28-III rep (Built E.R.Duffin; being refurbished)	ED.02		25. 5.93	E.R.Duffin	Nympsfield	12. 6.99
HJN	3983	HJN	Grob Standard Cirrus	440G	HB-1206	2. 6.93	D.F Marlow	Aston Down	23. 5.03
HJR	3986	HJR	Glasflugel H.201B Standard Libelle	102	SE-TIO	26. 5.95	B.Magnani	Wormingford	9. 5.03
HJT	3988	292	Centrair ASW20F	20115	F-CFFL	3. 6.93	C.I Roberts & Ptnrs	Snitterfield	6. 5.03
HJU	3989	HJU	Schempp-Hirth Standard Cirrus	134	EC-DNE D-0327	8. 7.93	A M Cooper (Crashed Usk 15.7.01 on take-off)	Usk	7. 7.01
HJV	3990	HJV	Grob G.102 Astir CS	1007	D-7000	7. 6.93	Cotswold GC	Aston Down	10.12.03
HJX	3991	203	Rolladen-Schneider LS-6C	6271		28. 5.93	R.S.Hatwell & M.Haynes	Swanton Morley	26. 5.03
HJY	3992	HJY	Schempp-Hirth Standard Cirrus	459	HB-1207	23. 6.93	W.W Turnbull & Ptnrs	Currock Hill	23. 7.02
HJZ	3993	865	Schleicher ASW15B	15190	OH-408	15. 5.94	R.R.Beezer	Camphill	19. 9.02
HKA	3994	135	Schempp-Hirth Discus CS	120CS		20. 5.93	The Soaring Centre	Husbands Bosworth	21. 2.03
HKB	3995	HKB	Grob G.102 Astir CS77	1658	D-7491	26.10.93	K.J.McPhee	RAF Keevil	22. 2.03
HKC	3996	HKC	Grob Standard Cirrus	520G	D-3268	28. 8.93	L.White	Dunstable	11. 5.03
HKD	3997	C34	Grob Standard Cirrus	576G	F-CEMF	7. 7.93	J.A.Clark	Edgehill	17. 5.03
HKE	3998		CARMAN JP-15/36AR Aiglon	6	F-CETD	9. 7.93	M.F.Cuming (W/o Bidford 9.7.95: wreck stored 8.99 as "CETD")	Bidford	
HKF	3999	HKF	CARMAM JP-15/36AR Aiglon	23	F-CETU	31. 7.93	K. & C.Vincent	Bidford	26. 7.00
HKJ	4002		Penrose Pegasus 2 (Built J.M.Lee)	001		7.93	J.M.Lee	Parham Park	15. 9.98
HKK	4003	HKK	Schleicher K8B	8886	D-0866	16. 1.94	R.K.Lashly	Easterton	23. 4.03
HKL	4004	919	Schempp-Hirth Discus bT	120/476		2.94	M.A.Thorne	Rivar Hill	19. 1.03
HKM	4005	HKM	Grob G.102 Astir CS Jeans	2108	D-7636	3.94	D.Simpson	Ridgewell	27. 2.03
HKN	4006	HKN	Centrair 101C Pégase	101-902	N101CR F-WFXB	23. 7.93	J.A.Sutton (Crashed at Milfield 23.1.99)	Currock Hill	19. 2.99
HKP	4007	HKP	Schleicher ASK23B	23100	D-2935 HB-1935	9. 8.93	Midland GC	Long Mynd	5. 3.03
HKQ	4008	970	Schempp-Hirth Nimbus 3DT	63		7. 8.93	R.I.Hey & Syndicate	Nympsfield	6.11.03
HKR	4009	985	Jastreb Standard Cirrus G/81	276	OH-663	15.10.93	J.Evans	Lyveden	24. 4.03
HKS	4010	HKS	Jastreb Standard Cirrus G/81	361	SE-TZS	11.11.93	E.W.Richards	Booker	27. 4.03
HKT	4011	HKT	Schleicher ASW19	19168	D-7958	4.10.93	A.Birkenshaw & Ptnr (C/n conflicts with OE-5174 but believed correct)	Burn	12. 9.03
HKU	4012	C29	Grob Standard Cirrus	513G	F-CEMA	5.12.93	T.J Wheeler & Ptnr	Lyveden	31. 3.03
HKV	4013		Scheibe Zugvogel IIIA	1034	D-8294	6.10.93	Dartmoor GC	Brent Tor	21.10.02
HKW	4014	HKW	Marco J-5 (Built D.Austin - regd with c/n 001)	009	G-BSBO	2. 6.94	G.K Owen ("Flying Penguin II")	Seighford	17. 2.03
HKX	4015	HKX	Rolladen-Schneider LS-4B	4933		18.12.93	D.J Hughes	Long Mynd	1. 2.03
HKY	4016	JA	Schempp-Hirth Discus B	461		14.10.93	J.G Arnold	RAF Keevil	7. 4.03
HKZ	4017	P31	CARMAM JP-15/36AR Aiglon	31	F-CFGA	27. 9.93	R.Borthwick	Milfield	16. 7.02
HLB	4019	365	Rolladen-Schneider LS-4	4935		27. 4.94	E.G.Leach	Gransden Lodge	9. 8.03
HLC	4020	HLC	Pilatus B4 PC-11	177	SE-UFX OH-455	10. 3.94	E.A.Lockhart	Wormingford	2. 5.03
HLD	4021	462	Schempp-Hirth Discus BT	122/479		30.10.93	C.M.Robinson & Ptnrs (Damaged Parham 7.5.95 & w/o)	Kenley	21.10.95*
HLG	4024	HLG	Schleicher ASK21	21596		1. 4.95	London GC	Dunstable	27. 1.03
HLH	4025	HLH	Schleicher K8B (See BGA.4162)	8637	RAFGGA.569 D-5691	26. 2.94	R.Das	Usk	25. 7.03
HLK	4027	HLK	Glasflugel H.301 Libelle	85	SE-TFS	11. 4.95	E.Sweetland	Dunstable	6. 7.03
HLM	4029	819	Schleicher ASW19B	19269	OH-538	10. 2.94	R.A.Colbeck	Booker	24. 7.03
HLN	4030	805	Schempp-Hirth Discus CS	143CS		18. 1.94	Portsmouth Naval GC	Lee-on-Solent	29.11.02
HLP	4031	HLP	Schleicher ASK21	21597		24. 3.94	Yorkshire GC	Sutton Bank	26. 4.03
HLQ	4032	381	Schempp-Hirth Discus bT	128/490		22.12.93	J.F.Goudie	Portmoak	27. 3.03
HLR	4033		Slingsby T31B	899	XE786	18.12.93	D.Thomson	Arbroath	30.11.00
HLS	4034	V5	Schempp-Hirth Discus B	114	RAFGSA.R11	28. 1.94	R.A.Lennard	Dunstable	15. 1.03
HLT	4035		LAK-12 Lietuva	6190		8. 2.94	Baltic Sailplanes Ltd (Damaged Rufforth 16.7.94; stored 7.97)	Rufforth	7 .2.95*
HLU	4036	HLU	Scheibe SF-27A Zugvogel V	6101	SE-TGP	22. 2.94	T.R.Bainbridge	Booker	14. 7.03
HLV	4037	UIM	Schleicher K8B	8760	SE-UIM D-5005	24. 2.94	M.Cuming (Damaged Chedworth 18.7.96: wreck stored)	Edgehill	12. 1.97*
HLW	4038	HLW	Schleicher ASW19B	19325	D-8799	3. 4.94	F.J.Hayden	Gransden Lodge	15. 1.03

HLX	4039	260	Schleicher ASH25	25124	D-3988	27. 2.94	P.Pozerskis	Husbands Bosworth	5. 4.03
HLY	4040	565	Schempp-Hirth Discus CS	161CS		15. 6.94	F.G.Birlison	Aston Down	28.11.03
HLZ	4041	359	Schleicher ASW20BL	20951	D-8188	19. 3.94	T Vines	Dunstable	18. 3.03
HMA	4042		SZD-51-1 Junior	B-2132		30. 3.94	The Soaring Centre	Husbands Bosworth	3.12.03
HMB	4043	HMB	Glaser-Dirks DG-300 Elan	3E105	D-4676	31. 3.94	A.D.Langlands	Thame	4. 2.03
HMG	4044	HMG	ICA IS-28B2	353	HA-....	20. 4.94	J.W.Courchee	Tibenham	3. 4.03
HMH	4045	S82	Schleicher K8B	5	D-5735	15. 4.94	Shenington GC	Edgehill	22. 7.03
			(Officially regd as c/n 2330)						
HMK	4046	121	Rolladen-Schneider LS-6-18W	6324	D-1245	18. 3.94	A.S.Decloux	Gransden Lodge	27. 1.03
HML	4047	38	Schempp-Hirth Discus CS	114CS	OO-ZTU	16. 3.94	M.E.Hahnefeld	Parham Park	11. 2.03
			(Composite with wings from BGA.3879)						
HMM	4048	D19	Glasflugel H.304B	322	SE-UGZ D-1005	31. 3.94	R.N.Cook	Husbands Bosworth	15. 3.03
HMP	4050	297	Schempp-Hirth Discus B	497		13. 3.94	D.J.Connolly	North Hill	6. 5.03
HMQ	4051	364	Schempp-Hirth Discus CS	099CS	D-7160	8. 3.94	S.A.Hindley	Edgehill	28. 3.03
HMR	4052	CCZV	Wassmer WA.30 Bijave	140	F-CCZV	4. 4.94	Bidford GC	NK	3. 4.95*
			(Wreck stored 9.97 Bidford but gone by 8.99)						
HMS	4053	HMS	Glaser-Dirks DG-100	40	D-2579	8. 4.94	B.Walton-Knight	Cross Hayes	18.11.03
HMT	4054	380	Glasflugel H.303 Mosquito B	153	F-CEDY	20. 3.94	B.T.Spreckley	Le Blanc, France	13. 2.03
HMU	4055		CARMAM JP-15/36AR Aiglon	22	F-CETT	7. 5.94	J.R.Holmes	Kingston Deverill	15. 4.03
HMV	4056	N26	Schleicher ASK13	13177	D-0268	9. 5.94	Portsmouth Naval GC	Lee-on-Solent	30. 6.03
HMX	4058	V19	Rolladen-Schneider LS.4B	4230	OO-ZNN F-CEIO	14. 5.94	D.Robson	Currock Hill	6. 5.03
HMY	4059	HMY	Schempp-Hirth HS.4 Standard Cirrus	121	HB-1034	29. 4.94	C.P.Woodcock / B.J.Thomas Weston-on-the-Green		13. 2.03
HMZ	4060	469	Federov Me-7 Mechta	M.004		4.94	R.Ellis	Rufforth	12. 2.96*
			(Crashed Camphill 12.6.96 & major components stored 7.97)						
HNA	4061	HNA	Glaser-Dirks DG-500/20 Elan	5E128W3		14. 7.94	J.P.Boneham	Winthorpe	19.12.02
HNB	4062	563	Schempp-Hirth HS.6 Janus C	215	D-4149	16. 4.94	C.M.Fox	Lleweni Parc	9. 3.03
HNC	4063		Schleicher ASW19B	19297	OH-515	18. 4.94	J. Lawn	Tibenham	14. 6.03
HND	4064	HND	Scheibe Zugvogel IIIA	1044	HB-735 D-9119	23. 5.94	D.Spillane	Lyveden	26. 4.03
HNE	4065	708	Schempp-Hirth HS.5 Nimbus 2B	91	D-2786	10. 5.94	S.Noad & Ptnrs	Challock	4. 1.03
HNF	4066	315	Schempp-Hirth Duo Discus	11		11. 5.94	Booker GC	Booker	1.12.03
HNG	4067	HNG	Schleicher K8B	132/59	D-8378	5. 5.94	Bidford GC	Bidford	25. 7.03
HNH	4068	599	Schempp-Hirth HS.5 Nimbus 2C	187	D-2830	31. 3.94	A.P.Hatton	Winthorpe	1. 4.03
HNJ	4069	HNJ	Schleicher Ka7 Rhönadler	7031	D-1667 RAFGGA??/D-6233	6. 5.94	N.J.Orchard-Armitage	Waldershare Park	11. 1.03
HNK	4070	HNK	SZD-51-1 Junior	B-1496	SP-3299 (SP-3290)	20. 5.94	Booker GC	Booker	19. 2.03
HNM	4072	167	Jastreb Standard Cirrus G/81	360	SE-TZT	2. 7.94	V.L.Brown & Ptnr	Snitterfield	14. 2.03
HNN	4073	HNN	Schempp-Hirth Duo Discus	21		15. 9.94	M.R.Smith	Aboyne	21. 1.03
HNS	4077	XN185	Slingsby T.21B	1164	8942M XN185	21. 6.94	B.Walker	RAF Syerston	17. 7.02
HNT	4078	105	Schleicher ASW15	15167	F-CEAQ	27. 4.94	A.P.Moulang	Challock	11. 6.03
HNU	4079	48	Schempp-Hirth Nimbus 4DT	3/5	D-KHIA	25. 5.94	D.E.Findon	Bidford	18. 4.03
HNV	4080	692	Rolladen-Schneider LS-4B	4960		11.12.94	P.W.Armstrong	Kirton-in-Lindsey	4. 6.03
HNW	4081	2UP	Schempp-Hirth Duo Discus	25		21.11.94	J.L.Birch	Dunstable	23. 3.03
HNX	4082	585	Rolladen-Schneider LS-4B	4937		6. 7.94	C.S.Crocker	Long Mynd	26. 3.03
HNY	4083	HNY	Centrair 101A Pégase	101A-020	F-CFRP	12.10.95	M.O. Breen	Booker	22. 7.03
HNZ	4084	RY	Centrair 101A Pégase	101A-032	F-CFRY	14. 7.94	R.H.Partington	Kirton-in-Lindsey	9.12.03
HPA	4085		Issoire E78 Silene	4	F-CFEA	R	T.M.Perkins	Dunstable	
HPB	4086		Hutter H.28 II replica	---		24. 8.94	D.G.Jones	Husbands Bosworth	8.95P*
HPC	4087	HPC	Schleicher ASW20CL	20787	D-3424	20. 7.94	D.R.Sutton	Pocklington	10. 4.03
HPD	4088	717	Rolladen-Schneider LS-6C-18	6331	D-1054	24.10.94	S.A. Hughes	Camphill	19.11.03
HPE	4089	HPE	Schleicher ASK13	13510	D-3992	2.10.94	Nottingham University GC	RAF Syerston	5. 3.03
HPF	4090	HPH	SZD-9 bis Bocian 1E	P-740	OH-508	3. 8.94	Bath, Wilts & North Dorset GC	Kingston Deverill	23. 2.01
HPG	4091	HPG	Maupin Woodstock	551	VR-HKI	8.94	J.M.Stockwell *(Built J.M.Stockwell)*	Perranporth	19. 3.03
HPH	4092	73	Schempp-Hirth Discus CS	174CS		21. 9.94	M.T.Burton	Ridgewell	19. 9.03
HPJ	4093	HPJ	Edgley EA9 Optimist	EA9/001		5.94	Edgley Aeronautics Ltd	Lasham	11. 8.01
			(C/n reported by John Edgely as '004')						
HPK	4094		Bibby G.1	1		R	K.Bibby		
HPL	4095	655	Rolladen-Schneider LS-4B	4959	(BGA.4071)	28. 7.94	P.G.Mellor	Booker	10. 4.02
HPM	4096	HPM	Grob G.102 Astir CS	1072	D-3304	21.11.94	S.K.Moeller	Lasham	14. 3.03
HPP	4098		Slingsby T.38 Grasshopper	863	XA230	5. 2.95	S.Butler	Gransden Lodge	12. 8.02
HPQ	4099	HPQ	Schleicher Ka6CR	6200	D-1933	5.10.94	M.Ewer	Crowland	4. 3.03
HPR	4100	150	Schempp-Hirth Discus B	532		20. 2.95	J.S.McCullagh	Dunstable	17.10.03
HPS	4101	HPS	Federov Me-7 Mechta	M.005		30. 5.95	R.Ellis *(W/o Tibenham 23.5.98)*	(Bellarena?)	16. 6.98
HPT	4102	HPT	Federov Me-7 Mechta	M.006		29. 3.96	A E.Griffiths	Long Mynd	15. 1.03
HPU	4103	848	Glaser-Dirks DG-800S	8-38S9	(BGA.4074)	20.11.94	R.J.Middleton	Portmoak	30. 4.03
HPV	4104	HPV	Schleicher ASK21	21608		13.10.94	Scottish Gliding Union Ltd	Portmoak	31. 1.03
HPW	4105	HPW	Schleicher ASK21	21609		25.11.94	Scottish Gliding Union Ltd	Portmoak	9. 3.03
HPX	4106	693	Schempp-Hirth Discus CS	177CS		12. 4.95	P.C.Whitmore & M.A.Whitehead	Gransden Lodge	28. 2.03
HPY	4107		ASC Spirit	EUR.001		5.95	Repclif Aviation Ltd	(Crewe)	2. 6.98
HPZ	4108		ASC Falcon	EUR.002		1.96	Repclif Aviation Ltd	(Crewe)	26.11.97
HQB	4110	HQB	Slingsby T.21B	602	WB935	1.10.94	C.E.Anson	(Germany)	23.11.02
			(Officially regd with c/n 1099 which is a corruption of fuselage no.SSK/FF/1099)						
HQC	4111	HQC	Scheibe Bergfalke II/55	322	D-9004	20.12.94	S.H.Gibson *(Being refurbished)*	Gransden Lodge	1. 5.99
HQD	4112	A20	Schleicher ASW20	20288	SE-ULA OH-548	1.11.94	D.G.Brain & Ptnrs	Dunstable	25. 5.02

			Type	c/n	Prev id	Date	Owner	Location	Date
HQE	4113	3D	Schempp-Hirth Duo Discus	29		19. 2.95	3D Syndicate	Aboyne	7. 3.03
HQF	4114	HQF	CARMAM M.100S Mésange	26	F-CCSO	3.11.94	R.E.Stokes	Rhigos	9. 6.01
HQG	4115	HQG	LAK-12 Lietuva	6222		30. 4.95	M.Boyle & Ptnrs	Rufforth	26. 4.03
HQH	4116	HQH	Schleicher Ka4 Rhönlerche II	3072/Br	(BGA.4097) HB-877	5.95	D.Fulchiron	Bellechasse, France	24. 7.03
							(D-4116 reserved 12.02, not yet de-registered in UK)		
HQJ	4117	762	Schempp-Hirth Discus B	336	D-1762	10. 2.95	D.G.Lingafelter	Dunstable	3. 3.03
HQK	4118	S2	Schleicher ASW20CL	20854	D-3366	18. 1.95	S.D.Minson	Halesland	31. 3.03
HQL	4119	LS6	Rolladen-Schneider LS-6C-18W	6352	D-0794	3. 3.95	D.P.Masson	Lasham	1. 5.03
HQM	4120	HQM	Schempp-Hirth Discus B	44	RAFGSA.R10	23. 1.95	Cambridge University GC	Gransden Lodge	7. 1.03
HQN	4121	D64	Schempp-Hirth HS.5 Nimbus 2B	139	D-6494	29. 1.95	D.Peters	Burn	15. 2.03
HQR	4123	19	Schempp-Hirth Discus B	531		26. 4.95	British Gliding Association	Bicester	17.12.02
HQS	4124	HQS	Grob G.103 Twin Astir	3155	OO-ZEG	26. 2.95	Essex & Suffolk GC	Wormingford	16. 5.03
HQT	4125	A77	Grob G.102 Astir CS77	1678	RAFGGA.561	12. 2.95	D.F.Bailey	Kenley	19. 6.03
HQU	4126		SZD-9 bis Bocian 1D	F-848	SP-2439	9. 7.97	T.Wiltshere	(Spilsby)	8. 7.98
HQV	4127		SZD-51-1 Junior	B-2139		20. 3.95	The Soaring Centre	Husbands Bosworth	21. 4.03
HQW	4128	329	Schempp-Hirth Discus B	538		9. 3.95	J.E.May	Nympsfield	7.11.02
HQX	4129	HQX	Schleicher ASW15B	15326	D-2315	13. 3.95	P. Ridgill	Dunstable	8. 3.03
HQY	4130	487	Schempp-Hirth HS.7 Mini Nimbus C	328	D-....	14. 3.95	A.H Sparrow	Lasham	7. 5.03
HQZ	4131	U2	Rolladen-Schneider LS-6C-18W	6353	D-1486	6. 3.95	N.P.Marriott	Lasham	20. 4.03
HRA	4132	N19	Grob G.102 Astir CS	1109	D-4169	21. 4.95	Portsmouth Naval GC	Lee-on-Solent	7. 8.02
HRB	4133		LAK-12 Lietuva	6223		3.95	J.E.Neville	Aboyne	11. 1.03
HRC	4134	390	Glaser-Dirks DG-500-20 Elan Trainer	5E136W5		15. 5.95	N.J.Allcoat	Portmoak	4. 3.01
HRD	4135		Slingsby T.21B	634	WB973	18. 3.95	U.Seegers	(Germany)	6. 6.03
HRE	4136	HRE	Schleicher Ka6CR	572	D-9326	26. 4.96	R.J.Playle	Edgehill	23. 5.03
HRF	4137	JM	Schleicher Ka6E	4272	OO-ZJR D-0165	12. 5.95	J.F.Morris	Gransden Lodge	27.11.03
HRG	4138	HRG	SZD-51-1 Junior	B-2013		25. 4.95	Scottish Gliding Union Ltd	Portmoak	24. 1.03
HRJ	4139	504	Schleicher K8B	8093Ei	D-5048	26. 4.95	M.Barnard	Turweston	23.11.03
HRK	4140	HRK	Centrair 101A Pégase	101A-048	F-CFQJ	16. 5.95	I.P Bramley	Dunstable	16. 5.03
HRL	4141	HRL	Schempp-Hirth HS.4 Standard Cirrus	525	D-3099	26. 4.95	M.Harbour	Camphill	19. 3.03
HRN	4143	HRN	Schleicher ASK18	18026	HB-1308	7. 4.95	Stratford-upon-Avon GC	Snitterfield	31. 1.03
HRP	4144	HRP	SZD-51-1 Junior	B-1807	SP-3442	19. 5.95	Wolds GC	Pocklington	28. 2.03
HRQ	4145	169	Schempp-Hirth HS.7 Mini Nimbus C	123	(BGA.4122) SE-TVB	17.4.95	C.Buzzard	Husbands Bosworth	9. 5.03
HRR	4146	D70	Schleicher ASK21	21033	D-7083	2. 2.95	Lakes GC	Walney Island	20. 1.03
HRS	4147	B33	Schempp-Hirth Discus CS	100CS	D-5100	1. 5.95	M.E.Hughes	Husbands Bosworth	14. 5.03
HRT	4148		Schleicher K8B	8390A	D-5599	9. 3.96	Heron GC	RNAS Yeovilton	2. 6.03
HRU	4149	FK	Centrair ASW20F	20114	F-CFFK	27. 7.95	European Soaring Club	Le Blanc, France	14.10.02
							(De-registered 10.6.02 , sold abroad as ZK-GYR)		
HRV	4150		SZD-55-1	551195076		2.11.95	R.W.Southworth	Warsaw, Poland	24.11.01
HRW	4151	802	Schempp-Hirth Duo Discus	43	(BGA.4160) BGA.4151	22. 6.95	A.J.Davis	Nympsfield	6.12.03
HRX	4152	P5	Schempp-Hirth Discus A	545		24. 5.95	P.G.Sheard	Dunstable	24.11.02
HRY	4153	L8	Rolladen-Schneider LS-6C-18W	6362		2. 6.95	F.K.Russell	Dunstable	19. 2.03
HSA	4155	A1	Rolladen-Schneider LS-6C-18W	6361		8. 8.95	D.A.Benton	Long Mynd	20. 3.03
HSB	4156	HSB	Glaser-Dirks DG-300 Elan	3E461		20. 7.95	J.S.Forster	Parham Park	16. 3.03
HSC	4157	99	SZD-50-3 Puchacz	B-2079		15. 8.95	British Gliding Association	Bicester	24. 1.03
HSD	4158	D15	Schempp-Hirth Discus B	258/1	(BGA.4142)	19. 6.95	J.R.Reed	Dunstable	25. 2.03
			(Rebuild of BGA.3406 c/n 258 w/o 26.8.94)						
HSE	4159	HSE	Grob G.102 Astir CS77	1635	RAFGSA.R68 RAFGSA.548	2. 9.95	R.G.Tait	Easterton	29. 3.03
HSG	4161	7827	Scheibe SF-27A Zugvogel V	1705/E	D-7827 OE-0827	11. 7.95	Welland GC	Lyveden	30. 8.03
HSH	4162	HSH	Scheibe Zugvogel IIIB	7/1041	D-6558	12. 7.95	J.E.Harman *"Brigitta" (Also wears "6558")*	Bidford	16. 7.03
HSJ	4163	D54	Schempp-Hirth Discus B	546		3. 7.95	K.L.Rowley	Pocklington	11. 7.02
HSK	4164	751	Schleicher ASW20CL	20827	D-3499	18. 7.95	T.M.World	Lasham	29. 5.03
HSL	4165	213	Schempp-Hirth Ventus 2C	1/2	(BGA.4154)	4. 7.95	H.G.Woodsend	Aston Down	17. 4.03
			(Incomplete airframe assembled by Southern Sailplanes)						
HSM	4166	HSM	Schleicher ASK13	13145	D-0168	18. 7.95	Stratford-upon-Avon GC	Snitterfield	13. 2.03
HSN	4167		Schleicher Ka6CR	6218	OO-ZZF D-8546	1. 8.95	Needwood Forest GC	Cross Hayes	20. 8.03
HSP	4168	385	Schempp-Hirth HS.6 Janus C	112	RAFGSA.R1 BGA.2723/D-7013	R	D.H.Garrard *(Active)*	Gransden Lodge	
HSQ	4169	493	Schempp-Hirth Discus B	99	D-2943	8. 8.95	Midland GC	Long Mynd	1. 2.03
HSR	4170	313	LAK-12 Lietuva	6178		3. 8.95	J.F.Morris & Ptnr	Gransden Lodge	29. 3.03
HSS	4171		Schleicher Ka7 Rhönadler	7015	RAFGSA.R29 D-5241	29. 8.95	M.Cuming	Edgehill	28. 8.96*
HSU	4173	K18	Schleicher ASK18	18025	AGA.16	R	R.C.Martin *(Being refurbished)*	NK	
HSV	4174		Schempp-Hirth HS.4 Standard Cirrus	195	D-0785	14. 3.96	C.D.Morrow	Rivar Hill	3. 4.03
HSW	4175	895	Schempp-Hirth Duo Discus	48		25. 8.95	C.R.Simpson	Husbands Bosworth	1. 4.03
HSX	4176	HSX	Scheibe SF-27A Zugvogel V	6031	SE-TDT	26. 9.95	S.D.Jones	Wormingford	27. 3.03
HSY	4177	A15	Pilatus B4 PC-11	050	SE-UFF OH-431	22. 9.95	A.L.Dennis	Walney Island	19. 9.00
HSZ	4178	V8	Rolladen-Schneider LS-8a	8030		9.95	C.L.Withall	Dunstable	4.11.03
HTA	4179		Centrair C-201B1 Marianne	201-014	F-CGMM	21.10.95	E.Crooks	Kirton-in-Lindsey	31.10.00
HTB	4180	HTB	Schempp-Hirth HS.6 Janus A	007	D-3114	27. 7.95	P.J.Gibbs & Ptnrs	Edgehill	26. 1.03
HTC	4181	HTC	Schleicher ASW15B	15188	OE-0930	26.10.95	N.A.Page	Camphill	25. 3.01

HTD	4182	VMC	Grob G.102 Astir CS	1012	D-6508	20. 5.96	G.V.McKirdy	Edgehill	15. 4.00
HTE	4183	HTE	Grob G.102 Astir CS77	1716	RAFGSA.R82 RAFGSA.882	23.11.95	J.R.Whittington	Challock	7. 3.03
HTF	4184	HTF	LAK-12 Lietuva	6180		1. 6.96	D.Stidwell	Cross Hayes	22. 5.02
HTG	4185	HTG	Grob G.102 Astir CS	1510	RAFGSA.R59(2) RAFGSA.R69(2)/RAFGSA.519	30.10.95	Trent Valley GC	Kirton-in-Lindsey	1. 8.03
HTH	4186	C4	Schempp-Hirth Janus CT	185/2	N137DB D-KHIE	13.11.95	D. Bramwell *(Cambridge Aero Instruments research vehicle)*	Long Mynd	3. 7.03
HTJ	4187	HTJ	Schleicher ASK13	13125	D-6048	2.12.95	Ulster GC	Bellarena	26. 4.03
HTL	4189	LS	Rolladen-Schneider LS-8-18	8038	D-3156	10.95	A. & L.Wells	RAF Keevil	5.12.03
HTM	4190	Z8	Rolladen-Schneider LS-8-18	8036		10.95	W.Payton	Sutton Bank	9. 4.03
HTN	4191	S22	Schleicher ASW22	22013	ZS-GLN	16. 4.96	J.B.Giddins	Edgehill	28.10.02
HTP	4192	L58	Rolladen-Schneider LS-8-18	8039	D-3175	11.95	R.A.Browne	Crowland	22. 3.03
HTQ	4193	C64	Rolladen-Schneider LS-8-18	8037	D-2993	11.95	P.G. & S.J.Crabb *(De-registered 14. 3.02 and sold as D-8047, then OH-935)*	Sandhill Farm, Shrivenham	20. 9.02
HTR	4194	HTR	Grob G.102 Astir CS	1190	D-7307	20.11.95	I.Wright	Kingston Deverill	24. 2.03
HTS	4195	H8	Rolladen-Schneider LS-8-18	8040		22.11.95	D.J.Howse	Gransden Lodge	29.11.02
HTT	4196	HTT	Schleicher ASW20CL	20627	D-2410	24.11.95	J.Potter	Camphill	26. 3.03
HTU	4197	HTU	Schempp-Hirth HS.2 Cirrus	88	D-0478	29.12.95	S.Kochanowski	Lasham	7. 5.03
HTV	4198	HTV	Schleicher ASK21	21624	D-8355	3. 3.96	Cambridge University GC	Gransden Lodge	31. 3.03
HTW	4199		Pottier JP15-34 Kit Club	50-39	F-CFGF	4.12.95	R.P Halton	Bidford	16. 3.99
HTX	4200	900	Schleicher ASW20	20239	D-3180	3. 3.96	C.Ramshorn	Gransden Lodge	18. 2.02
HTY	4201		LET L-13 Blanik	026318	LY-GDT DOSAAF	1. 4.96	North Devon GC	Brent Tor	6. 6.03
HTZ	4202	833	Bolkow Phoebus 17C	908	OO-ZDJ BGA.1573	9.12.95	A.de Tourtoulon *(De-registered 27. 8 .02, to Ireland as EI-158)*	Wormingford	3 .8.02
HUA	4203		Schleicher ASW19	19091	D-3840	29.12.95	M.T Davenport	Lasham	20. 8.02
HUB	4204		SZD-48-3 Jantar Standard	B-1527	DOSAAF	17. 3.96	C.F.Sermanni	Strathaven	7. 1.03
HUC	4205	HUC	Schempp-Hirth Janus CE	170	(BGA.4188) D-3189	24. 2.96	C.W.Price	Wormingford	16.12.03
HUD	4206	HUD	Schleicher ASK13	13018	D-9203	21. 2.96	London GC	Dunstable	11. 1.03
HUE	4207	N5	Schleicher ASW27	27022		10.96	E.H.Downham	Dunstable	21. 2.03
HUF	4208	HUF	Schleicher ASK13	13109	OO-ZWE	10. 3.96	Welland GC	Lyveden	1.11.02
HUH	4210	D31	Schempp-Hirth HS.6 Janus	15	D-3116	9. 5.96	B.A.Fairston	Husbands Bosworth	18. 3.03
HUJ	4211	HUJ	Centrair ASW20F	20170	F-CFLY	5. 3.96	M. Manning	Rattlesden	25. 4.03
HUK	4212	HUK	Schleicher Ka6CR	6385	SE-TCN	15. 4.96	T.J Donovan & Ptnr	Lyveden	21. 7.03
HUL	4213	624	Schempp-Hirth HS.2 Cirrus	V3	HB-900	26. 2.96	I.Ashton & Ptnrs	Chipping	20. 4.03
HUM	4214	241	Rolladen-Schneider LS-6C	6267	OO-ZXS D-4350	25. 3.96	A.Hall	Lasham	9. 5.03
HUN	4215	HUN	Grob G.102 Astir CS Jeans	2089	D-7531	27. 2.96	D P.Manchett	Lleweni Parc	11.10.03
HUP	4216	170	Schempp-Hirth Ventus 2CT	4/11		16. 2.96	C G Corbett	Tibenham	19. 2.03
HUQ	4217		Federov Me-7 Mechta	007		21. 6.96	J S Fielden	Brent Tor	2. 5.02
HUR	4218	HUR	Schempp-Hirth HS.2 Cirrus	12	HB-927	20. 4.96	M. Rossiter	Usk	29. 4.03
HUS	4219	HUS	Scheibe SF-27A Zugvogel V	6010	D-1035	6. 8.97	C J Palmer	Booker	1. 3.03
HUT	4220	HUT	Centrair ASW20F	20187	F-CEUQ	14. 4.96	G.A MacFadyen	Nympsfield	4. 4.03
HUU	4221		Schleicher ASK13	13527AB	D-7506 D-8945	15. 4.96	Upward Bound Trust	Thame	18.12.02
HUV	4222	64	Rolladen-Schneider LS-8A-18	8056	D-3823	4.96	C.P.Jeffery	Gransden Lodge	19. 3.03
HUW	4223	S8	Rolladen-Schneider LS-8A	8058		3.96	S.E.Bort	Kenley	2. 4.03
HUX	4224	58	Schempp-Hirth Ventus 2C	7/12		17. 3.96	E.R.Lysakowski *(Crashed Cavenham 11.7.98 after midair collision)*	Lasham	16. 3.99
HUY	4225	HUY	Schempp-Hirth Ventus CT	84/329	D-KILZ	3. 4.96	M A Challans	Lasham	25. 2.03
HUZ	4226	200	Schempp-Hirth Discus BT	158/559		2. 3.96	J.Lynchenhaun	Lleweni Parc	3. 7.03
HVA	4227	HVA	SZD-59 Acro	B-2169		2. 5.96	T.Williams *(Sold as N459TW 14.11.02, not yet de-registered in the UK)*	Lasham	17. 6.03
HVB	4228	HVB	Slingsby T.31B	850	(BGA.3249) XA308	27. 4.96	M.Hoogenbosch *"Top Less"*	Hilversum, The Netherlands	10. 5.03
HVC	4229		Slingsby T.38 Grasshopper	766	WZ770	4. 5.01	J.F.Forster	Hilversum, The Netherlands	27. 9.03
HVD	4230	304	SZD-55-1	551193052		23. 4.96	M.Drecka	Booker	7. 4.03
HVE	4231	W54	Schempp-Hirth Ventus 2CT	8/19	D-KHIA	28. 3.96	Glyndwr Soaring Club	Lleweni Parc	9. 4.03
HVF	4232	321	Rolladen-Schneider LS-8-18	8059	D-1683	4.96	M.D.Wells	Bidford	9. 5.03
HVG	4233	RP1	Schleicher ASK21	21062	D-2606	17. 4.96	Rattlesden GC	Rattlesden	30. 9.03
HVH	4234	HVH	Pilatus B4 PC-11	067	D-2156	21. 5.96	C.Cain	Lasham	6. 6.00
HVJ	4235	962	Scheibe SF-27A Zugvogel V	6012	OE-0762	1. 6.96	C.P.Bleaden	Kirton-in-Lindsey	5. 7.98
HVK	4236	HVK	Grob G.102 Astir CS	1161	D-4182	26. 4.96	F.R.Panter	Tibenham	23. 3.03
HVL	4237	LS8	Rolladen-Schneider LS-8-18	8060		4.96	J.Allison	Bidford	3. 2.03
HVM	4238	393	Glaser-Dirks DG-300 Elan	3E177	D-4314	17. 5.96	Surrey & Hants GC	Lasham	16.12.02
HVP	4240	930	Schleicher ASW20	20374	D-1961 BGA.4076/EC-DLN	3. 5.96	E.J.Smallbone	Lasham	29. 1.03
HVQ	4241	HVQ	Schleicher ASK13	13251	D-0605	27. 4.96	R.B.Brown	Edgehill	21. 4.03
HVR	4242	HVR	Schempp-Hirth Discus B	560		3. 5.96	Yorkshire Gliding Club (Pty) Ltd	Sutton Bank	6. 4.03
HVT	4244	210	Schempp-Hirth Ventus 2B	37		10. 5.96	P.R.Jones	Booker	29. 4.03
HVU	4245	59	Rolladen-Schneider LS-8A	8066		4.96	European Soaring	(France)	9. 5.03
HVV	4246	HVV	Rolladen-Schneider LS-4B	41009		5. 1.97	A.J.Bardgett	Currock Hill	17.12.03
HVW	4247	HVW	Schleicher ASK13	13431	D-2140	14. 4.96	Rattlesden GC	Rattlesden	5. 4.03
HVX	4248		Centrair ASW20F	20528	F-CFSJ	13. 6.96	A.S Goldsmith	Camphill	24. 6.99
HVY	4249	584	Schempp-Hirth Ventus 2C	9/21		17. 5.96	R.Ashurst	Lasham	19.12.03
HVZ	4250	HVZ	Schempp-Hirth HS.4 Standard Cirrus	567G	HB-1269	5. 6.96	J.Bennett	Gransden Lodge	22. 2.03
HWA	4251	31	Schempp-Hirth Ventus 2C	8/20		7. 6.96	C.Garton	Lasham	19. 9.03
HWB	4252	775	Schempp-Hirth Duo Discus	84		25. 5.96	Lasham Gliding Society	Lasham	15. 1.03

HWC	4253	L18	Glasflugel H.201B Standard Libelle	310	HB-1076	7. 7.96	J.C.Rogers	Winthorpe	23. 2.03
HWD	4254	HWD	Schempp-Hirth HS.4 Standard Cirrus	97	HB-987	3. 6.96	M.R. Hoskins	Rivar Hill	21. 6.03
HWE	4255	HWE	Schleicher K8B	1151	HB-700	31. 5.96	J.P.Brady	Brent Tor	25. 3.03
HWF	4256	ZC	Jastreb Standard Cirrus G/81	281	SE-TZC	12. 6.96	M.Langford	Booker	25. 6.03
HWG	4257	HWG	Glasflugel H.201B Standard Libelle	259	HB-1051	19. 6.96	S.C.J.Barker	Pocklington	13.10.03
HWH	4258	712	Schempp-Hirth Ventus CT	182/599	RAFGGA.506	7. 7.96	H.R.Browning	Lasham	6.11.02
HWK	4260		Grob G.104 Speed Astir IIB	4070	OO-ZVQ LX-CRT	14.7.96	P.Gilbert	Tours, France	13. 7.97*
HWL	4261	84	Rolladen-Schneider LS-8A	8076		15. 6.96	M.Coffee	Bidford	28. 3.03
HWM	4262	D7	Rolladen-Schneider LS-8A	8079		7.96	C.D.Marsh	Bidford	27. 3.03
HWN	4263	598	Schempp-Hirth Nimbus 3T	8/60	D-KHIF	5. 7.96	H.Hampel	(Germany)	24. 6.03
HWP	4264	HWP	Glaser-Dirks DG-100G Elan	E24G13	D-3772	12. 7.96	J.D.Neaves	SuttonBank	3. 3.03
HWQ	4265	HWQ	Scheibe L-Spatz 55	607	D-6195	7.96	A.Gruber	Usk	2. 3.03
HWS	4267	75	Rolladen-Schneider LS-8-18	8080		14. 2.97	E.A.Coles	Dunstable	16.12.03
HWT	4268	S83	Schleicher K8B	8780	HB-958	13. 7.96	Shenington GC	Edgehill	.2. 8.02
HWV	4270	526	Schempp-Hirth Discus B	561		12. 8.96	J.R.Martindale	Walney Island	23. 4.03
			(Rebuild of fuselage from AGA.4 c/n 206 with new wings c/n 561)						
HWW	4271	DJT	Grob G.103 Twin II Acro	3658-K-27	OE-5285	23. 8.96	T.Gage	Lasham	25. 2.03
HWX	4272	HWX	SZD-59 Acro	B-2170		3. 9.96	D.W.Gosden	Usk	8. 8.03
HWY	4273	168	Jastreb Standard Cirrus VTC G/81	359	LN-GAL	6. 9.96	D.D.Copeland	Booker	23. 9.03
HWZ	4274	HWZ	Schleicher ASW19B	19316	HB-1524	6. 9.96	K.Commins & L. Keegan	Dublin	29. 5.02
			(To owners in Ireland as EI-153, but not yet de-registered in UK)						
HXA	4275	HXA	Scheibe Zugvogel IIIB	1107	D-2005	17. 3.97	B W Millar	North Connel	21. 4.01
HXB	4276	HXB	Grob G.102 Astir CS77	1819	D-6755	29. 9.96	K.S.Wells	Crowland	30. 8.03
HXC	4278	M8	Rolladen-Schneider LS-8A	8094		24. 2.97	S.M.Smith	Gransden Lodge	19. 2.03
HXD	4279	HXD	Schleicher ASW27	27030		8. 3.97	M.Jerman	Wormingford	9. 1.03
HXE	4280	Y4	Schleicher ASW19B	19053	D-6699	25. 9.96	M.Lloyd-Owen	Lasham	29. 5.03
HXH	4283	HXH	Schempp-Hirth Discus B	573	BGA.4375	6.98	Deeside GC	Aboyne	15.11.03
			(Originally NTU then re-allotted as BGA.4375 and finally reverted to BGA.4283)		(BGA.4283)				
HXJ	4284	HXJ	Schleicher ASK13	13216	D-0417	29.11.96	Cotswold GC	Aston Down	7.11.03
HXL	4286	OK-0927	Letov LF-107 Lunak	39	OK-0927 OK-0827	1.11.96	G.P.Saw	Booker	22. 3.03
HXM	4287	HXM	Grob G.102 Astir CS	1272	D-7367	15.11.96	C.Fretwell	Challock	30. 5.03
HXN	4288	57	Rolladen-Schneider LS-8-18	8095		28. 1.97	J.L Birch	Dunstable	8. 3.03
HXP	4289	HXP	Schleicher ASK13	13023	D-3656	19.11.96	K.E.Ballington	Cross Hayes	16. 4.03
HXQ	4290	156	Schleicher ASH25B	25187	OH-874	23.11.96	M.Chant	Brent Tor	28. 1.03
HXR	4291	560	Schempp-Hirth Ventus CT	88/333	D-KESH	20. 2.97	J.W.A'Court	Lasham	9.12.03
HXS	4292	V11	Schempp-Hirth Ventus 2CT	10/41		27.11.96	I.R.Cook	Rivar Hill	5. 3.03
HXT	4293	LS4	Rolladen-Schneider LS-4A	4325	ZS-GNV	21. 3.97	B.T.Spreckley	Le Blanc, France	22. 3.03
HXU	4294	HXU	Schleicher ASW19B	19359	SE-TXN	14. 4.97	G.A.Chalmers	Easterton	15. 3.03
HXV	4295	HXV	Schleicher ASK13	13080	D-5462	5.12.96	Aquila GC	Hinton-in-the-Hedges	29.11.03
HXW	4296	325	Rolladen-Schneider LS-8-18	8097		7. 3.97	W.Aspland	Dunstable	14. 3.03
HXX	4297	HXX	Schempp-Hirth HS.4 Standard Cirrus	154G	D-0363	29. 1.97	E J Winning	Usk	29. 1.03
			(Built Grob)						
HXY	4298	HXY	Grob G.102 Astir Jeans	1781	D-7689	8.12.96	P. Barnes	Bidford	28. 2.03
HXZ	4299	S5	Rolladen-Schneider LS-4	4249	SE-TXF	30. 3.97	E.J.Foggin	Sandhill Farm, Shrivenham	18. 3.03
HYA	4300	DD	Rolladen-Schneider LS-6	634B		28. 2.97	R.H.Dixon	Parham Park	21. 2.03
			(Probably c/n 6349 ex D-2162)						
HYB	4301	T5	Schempp-Hirth Discus B	140	D-4684	19. 4.97	K.A.Boost	Lasham	9. 3.03
HYD	4303	HYD	Schleicher ASW24	24039	OE-5460	13. 2.97	M.Makari	Lasham	3. 3.03
HYE	4304	913	Glaser-Dirks DG-505 Elan Orion	5E167X22		22.12.96	Bristol & Glos GC	Nympsfield	29.11.02
HYF	4305	KM	Rolladen-Schneider LS-8-18	8106		15. 3.97	A.T.Johnstone	Dunstable	8.12.03
HYH	4307	HYH	Rolladen-Schneider LS-3-17	3186	D-6650	18. 1.97	J.Lamb	Bellarena	4. 4.03
HYJ	4308	HYJ	Schleicher ASK21	21066	D-2724	17. 1.97	Highland GC	Easterton	19. 4.03
HYK	4309		Centrair ASW20FLP	20176	F-CEUN	25. 9.97	J.C.Riddell	Rufforth	14. 6.01
HYL	4310	K4	Schempp-Hirth Ventus 2A	44		31. 5.97	A J Stone	Booker	31. 1.03
HYM	4311	PW5	DWLKK PW-5 Smyk	17.06.020		28. 2.97	T.A.Joint	Lasham	11. 5.02
			(C/n is officially recorded as "100")				"Iceman"		
HYN	4312	HYN	Schleicher K8B	8310A	D-1018	11.97	G.Brook	Crowland	16. 7.03
HYP	4313	HYP	SZD-50-3 Puchacz	B-2082		22. 2.97	Rattlesden GC	Rattlesden	9. 4.03
HYR	4315	432	Schleicher ASW27	27013	D-8733	11. 3.97	A.R.Hutchings	Dunstable	5. 3.03
HYS	4316	A14	Schleicher ASK21	21519	RAFGGA.514	6.99	RAFGSA	Bicester	8. 2.03
HYT	4317	HYT	Schleicher ASK21	21568	AGA.20 RAFGGA.515	1.99	Wyvern GC	AAC Upavon	9. 3.03
HYU	4318	A61	Schempp-Hirth Discus CS	192CS	RAFGSA.R61 RAFGGA.561	6.99	Anglia GC	Wattisham	27. 6.03
HYW	4320	HYW	Schleicher K8B	8163A	D-5316 D-3202	13. 3.97	Lincs GC	Strubby	9. 6.03
HYX	4321	HYX	Schleicher K8B	686	D-5742	???	Oxford University GC	Bicester	13. 4.03
HYY	4322	A26	Schempp-Hirth Nimbus 3DT	21	RAFGSA.R26 D-KAFA	1. 3.97	N.J.Wright	Bidford	4. 4.03
HYZ	4323	L88	Rolladen-Schneider LS-8-18	8104		12. 4.97	P J Coward	Crowland	19. 8.03
HZA	4324	374	Schempp-Hirth Nimbus 3/24.5	94	SE-UFO	27. 4.97	P.J. Kite	Lasham	5. 2.03
HZB	4325	HZB	DWLKK PW-5 Smyk	17.06.021		28. 2.97	J.D.Scott	Gransden Lodge	2. 8.03
HZC	4326	216	Grob G.102 Astir CS	1092	D-6991	24. 3.97	K.G.Laws	Lasham	27. 1.03
HZD	4327	HZD	Schleicher ASW15B	15327	D-2191	20. 3.97	C.P.Ellison	Booker	20. 4.03

HZE	4328	T3	Schempp-Hirth Discus CS	121CS	D-6946	24. 3.97	A.D.Irving	Kenley	15. 9.03
HZF	4329	G7	Centrair 101A Pégase	101A-0262	PH-796	6. 5.97	B.R.George	Gransden Lodge	23. 2.03
HZG	4330	X7	Rolladen-Schneider LS-8-18	8118		10. 3.97	N.G.Hackett	Husbands Bosworth	18. 6.02
HZH	4331	HZH	Schleicher Ka6CR	6461	HB-836	1. 6.97	M.E.de Torre	Gamston	22. 6.02
HZJ	4332	HZJ	Schempp-Hirth HS.4 Standard Cirrus 23		HB-981	18. 3.97	A.B.Stokes	Enstone	17.12.03
HZL	4334	HZL	Schempp-Hirth HS.4 Standard Cirrus 304		D-2060	5. 4.97	P.Conran	Lasham	14. 4.01
HZM	4335	U1	Rolladen-Schneider LS-4A	4762	D-1394	14. 4.97	J.M.Bevan	Crowland	19. 3.03
HZN	4336	D6173	Schleicher Ka2B Rhönschwalbe	195	D-6173	28. 3.97	R.A.Willgoss	Booker	20. 6.03
HZP	4337	56	Rolladen-Schneider LS-8-18	8117		12. 3.97	S.J.Redman	Gransden Lodge	31.10.03
HZQ	4338	K5	Schleicher ASW27	27018	D-4499	10. 5.97	M.D.Rogers	Dunstable	3. 1.03
HZR	4339	HZR	Schleicher ASK21	21079	D-4491	1. 5.97	A.Roseberry	Aston Down	1. 3.03
HZS	4340	K1	Schempp-Hirth Ventus 2A	43		3.97	A.E.Kay	Weston-on-the-Green	23. 4.03
HZT	4341	X50	Centrair ASW20F	20150	F-CFLL	19. 8.97	T.J.Banks	Ringmer	14.10.02
HZU	4342	B11	Schempp-Hirth HS.4 Standard Cirrus 366		HB-1258 N71KW	30. 4.97	D.R.Piercy	Winthorpe	16. 2.03
HZV	4343	P61	Schempp-Hirth HS.4 Standard Cirrus 305		VH-GFZ BGA.4343/HB-1457/D-2061	30. 4.97 *(Restored 5.8.02 ex VH-GFZ)*	P.R.Cox	Tibenham	4. 8.03
HZW	4344	112	Schempp-Hirth Nimbus 3T	22/88	D-KILO	1. 6.97	J.Ellis	Sutton Bank	9. 4.03
HZX	4345	476	Schleicher K8B	8257	D-8476	12.4.97	G.E.W.Woodward	Upwood	14. 6.03
HZY	4346	EN	Rolladen-Schneider LS-4A	4479	D-3458	19.4.97	N.P.Wedi	Booker	31. 1.03
HZZ	4347	LD	Schleicher ASW20L	20273	N727AM	27.4.97	P.E.Rice	Wormingford	24. 5.03
JAA	4348	JAA	Schempp-Hirth HS.6 Janus B	163	D-3147	18. 4.97	A.A.Baker	Lasham	11.12.03
JAB	4349	JAB	Glaser-Dirks DG-300 Elan	3E320	OY-XTC	24. 4.97	I.G. Johnston	Sutton Bank	21. 3.03
JAC	4350	98	Schempp-Hirth Duo Discus	128		24. 5.97	British Gliding Association	Bicester	7. 4.03
JAD	4351		Schleicher ASK21	21659		10.97	Borders GC	Milfield	6.10.03
JAE	4352	N8	Glaser-Dirks DG-200/17C	2-62	HB-1443	21. 4.97	S.A.White	Hinton-in-the-Hedges	19. 2.02
JAF	4353	620	Schempp-Hirth Ventus 2B	33	(BGA.4306)	24. 4.97	D.K.McCarthy	Gransden Lodge	28. 1.03
JAG	4354	JAG	Schleicher ASW20L	20136	HB-1474	15. 7.97	654 Syndicate	Currock Hill	13. 5.03
JAH	4355	921	Schempp-Hirth Discus B	572		30. 5.97	K.Neave	Nympsfield	29. 5.03
JAJ	4356	916	Glaser-Dirks DG-202/17	2-150/1744	D-4154	8. 5.97	T.R Dews	Kingston Deverill	24. 3.03
JAK	4357		Schleicher Ka6E	4301	F-CDRJ	R			
JAL	4358	JAL	Schleicher Ka6E	4360	F-CDTX	19. 6.97	N.Gilkes	Lasham	22. 4.03
JAM	4359	777	Schleicher ASW15B	15353	D-2360	5.97	T.J.Beckwith	Sackville Lodge, Riseley	20. 1.00
JAN	4360	JAN	Schempp-Hirth Discus B	575		10.97	Wolds GC	Pocklington	20.12.03
JAP	4361		Slingsby T.38 Grasshopper *(Thought to be ex WZ818 [799])*	779	WZ783	R	R.H.Targett	Nympsfield	
JAQ	4362	823	Schempp-Hirth Discus B	190	D-0960	2. 6.97	P.D.Duffin	Wormingford	15. 4.03
JAR	4363	P3	Schempp-Hirth Discus BT	83/417	D-KHEI	16. 5.97	C.J.Partridge	Lasham	14. 2.03
JAS	4364	7Q	Glasflugel H.201 Standard Libelle	109	SE-TIS	29. 5.97	M.D.Wells	Enstone	28. 5.98
JAT	4365	JAT	Schleicher K8B	8150	D-4390	6. 6.97	Wolds GC	Pocklington	5. 4.03
JAU	4366	WB922	Slingsby T.21B	585	WB922	27. 5.97	J.Priddle	Kingston Deverill	1. 7.02
JAV	4367	JAV	Schleicher ASK21	21662		1.97	Wolds GC	Pocklington	3.12.03
JAW	4368	M4	Glaser-Dirks DG-200/17	2-180/1759	D-5618	12. 6.97	C.J.Walker	Lasham	20. 2.03
JAX	4369	JAX	Schleicher ASK21	21665		1.98	Wolds GC	Pocklington	16.11.03
JAY	4370	123	Schleicher ASW20	20034	D-7941	19. 6.97	D.A.Smith	Kingston Deverill	17. 5.03
JAZ	4371	JAZ	Grob G.102 Astir Jeans	2073	D-7586	28. 8.97	Bath, Wilts & North Dorset GC	Kingston Deverill	13. 9.03
JBA	4372	JBA	Slingsby T.38 Grasshopper *(Assembled from components; p/i is starboard wing only)*	1262	XP463	6.98	J A Northen & Pntr	Challock	5. 8.00
JBB	4373	B3	Rolladen-Schneider LS-8	8003	D-8023	22. 8.97	R F Thirkell	Lasham	16.12.02
JBC	4374	2B	Schempp-Hirth Ventus 2CT	15/61		20. 6.97	B.A.Bateson	Ringmer	7. 5.01
JBE	4376	LX	ISF Mistral C	MC.020/79	OY-XLX PH-667	4. 7.97	H.H.Crowther	Aston Down	25. 7.03
JBF	4377		Glasflugel H.201 Standard Libelle	246	F-CDPV	22. 7.97	L.Coles	Booker	26. 3.03
JBG	4378	U9	Schempp-Hirth Ventus B	135	OE-5315	20. 7.97	W.R.Longstaff	Feshiebridge	16.10.03
JBH	4379	537	Eiri PIK-20D	20621	OH-529	6. 7.97	537 Syndicate (P.J.Holloway)	Parham Park	1. 2.03
JBJ	4380	G81	Jastreb Standard Cirrus G/81	280	SE-TZD	8. 7.97	T.Rendell	Lasham	30. 7.03
JBK	4381	L3	Schleicher ASW19B	19204	D-4099 PH-602	11.97	P.M. Sharpe	Dunstable	4. 1.03
JBM	4383	S21	Schleicher ASK21	21089	D-6391	26. 7.97	Staffs GC	Seighford	2. 5.03
JBN	4384		Schempp-Hirth Discus B	94	D-7175	R			
JBP	4385	B2	Rolladen-Schneider LS-6-18W	6378		25. 7.97	I.C.Baker	Nympsfield	27. 3.03
JBQ	4386	LH7	Rolladen-Schneider LS-8-18	8148		24. 9.97	L.Hill	North Hill	11. 9.03
JBR	4387	AB	Schempp-Hirth Discus B	90	F-CGGD F-WGGD	8. 8.97	A.A.Baker	RAF Odiham	14. 4. 03
JBS	4388	JBS	LAK-12 Lietuva	6115	???	10. 8.97	I.G.Smith & Ptnrs	Ringmer	5. 5.03
JBT	4389	JBT	Schleicher ASW19	19075	D-4477	2. 8.97	Aquila GC	Hinton-in-the-Hedges	3. 5.03
JBU	4390	HL	Rolladen-Schneider LS-6-18W	6350	D-0462	23. 9.97	J.Gorringe	Lasham	9. 9.03
JBV	4391		Monnett Monerai *(Built J.Foxson & B.Niblett)*	----		7.97	W.B.Niblett	Kingston Deverill	19. 7.98
JBW	4392	710	Schempp-Hirth Discus BT	34/337	D-KBJR	8.97	N.C.Pringle	Lasham	28. 1.03
JBX	4393	JBX	Rolladen-Schneider LS-4A	4293	D-9111	4.98	P.W.Lee & Ptnr	Aston Down	15. 4.03
JBY	4394	960	LAK-12 Lietuva	6185		12. 8.97	C.J.Nicholas	Gransden Lodge	30. 5.03
JBZ	4395	JBZ	Grob G.102 Astir CS	1492	D-4794	30. 8.97	K.R.Bryer	RAF Keevil	12. 1.03
JCA	4396	JCA	Schleicher ASW15B	15202	(BGA.4049) OH-410	11. 9.97	R.H. & A.Moss	Nympsfield	4.10.02
JCB	4397	JCB	Rolladen-Schneider LS-6C-18WL	6234	D-6116	4.98	A.Binks	Dunstable	16.12.03
JCD	4399	H5	Schleicher ASW24	24101	D-6091	10.97	M.D.Evershed	Crowland	27. 1.03
JCE	4400	911	Schempp-Hirth Ventus BT	46/240	D-KFMS	15. 9.97	A.G.Reid	Kenley	19. 2.03

JCF	4401	JCF	Grob G.102 Astir CS77	1705	PH-1012 D-7634	23. 9.97	Northumbria GC	Currock Hill	9.12.02
JCG	4402	JCG	DWLKK PW-5 Smyk	17.09.003		9.97	H.V. Jones	Crowland	28. 5.03
JCH	4403	FOX	MDM-1 Fox	218		97	C.Cain (De-regd 18.12.01 – sold in USA)	Lasham	24. 8.01
JCJ	4404	C7	Grob Standard Cirrus	434G	SE-TNC	5.98	M R Garwood	Crowland	2. 6.03
JCK	4405	DC	Schempp-Hirth Discus BT	92/430	D-KIDE	10.97	D.Coppin	Lasham	4. 3.03
JCL	4406	T2	Rolladen-Schneider LS-8-18	8147		10.97	T.W.Slater	Aboyne	10. 4.03
JCM	4407	JCM	Schleicher ASW27	27064		12.97	M.J.Clayton	Snitterfield	29. 3.03
JCN	4408	JCN	Schempp-Hirth HS.4 Std Cirrus	646	D-7247	10.97	P.W.Reavill	Camphill	17.10.03
JCP	4409	36	Rolladen-Schneider LS-8-18	8146		10.97	A.J.Emck	Lasham	19.12.02
JCQ	4410	W19	Schleicher ASW19B	19086	PH-562	12.97	A.J.Preston	Dunstable	19. 4.03
JCR	4411	JCR	Grob G.102 Astir CS	1181	OE-5188	10.97	B Harrison	Kingston Deverill	28.11.03
JCS	4412	WT898	Slingsby T.31B	693	BGA.3284 WT898	10.97	M.Steiner	(Germany)	29.10.01
JCT	4413	176	Schempp-Hirth Nimbus 4T	21	D-KKKL	10.97	D S Innes	Lasham	9. 5.03
JCU	4414	616	Schempp-Hirth HS.4 Std Cirrus 75	688	D-6604	10.97	N.Swinton	RAF Halton	26.11.03
JCV	4415	IM	Schleicher ASH25E	25069	D-KAIM	11.97	B.R.George	Gransden Lodge	31. 3.03
JCW	4416	JCW	Grob G.102 Astir CS77	1612	PH-573	10.97	C.R.Phipps	Llantisilio	11. 1.03
JCX	4417	JCX	Schempp-Hirth Discus BT	93/432	D-KJOB	10.97	J.E.Bowman	Bidford	4.11.03
JCY	4418	F3	Rolladen-Schneider LS-8-18	8171		12.97	R.Starey	Lasham	18.12.03
JCZ	4419	JCZ	Schleicher Ka6CR	6108	D-7152	11.97	N.W.Hanney	Kingston Deverill	2. 3.03
JDA	4420	GR	Schempp-Hirth Nimbus 3/24.5	8	D-1788	11.97	G.R.Ross	Lasham	1. 7.02
JDB	4421	WZ828	Slingsby T.38 Grasshopper	809	WZ828	11.97	H.Chapple	Bicester	23. 4.03
JDC	4422	A27	Schleicher ASW27	27010	D-6209	12.97	P.J.Henderson	Challock	7. 3.03
JDD	4423	JDD	Glaser-Dirks DG-200 / 17C	2-171 / CL17	PH-717	12.97	J.W. Richardson	Chipping	9. 2.03
JDE	4424	543	Rolladen-Schneider LS-8-18	8151		5.98	M.N.Davies	Snitterfield	16. 5.03
JDF	4425	907	Schleicher ASH25E	25150	D-KPAS	11.97	W. Young	Pocklington	3.10.03
JDG	4426	KW	Rolladen-Schneider LS-6B	6145	D-5675	2.98	A.Moss	Nympsfield	9. 1.03
JDH	4427	2F	Rolladen-Schneider LS-6C-18W	6287	D-9128	2.98	F.Schlafke	(Germany)	14.10.03
JDJ	4428	434	Rolladen-Schneider LS-3	3010	D-7729	11.97	J.C.Burdett	Chipping	30.12.02
JDK	4429	841	Rolladen-Schneider LS-8-18	8153		3.98	G.K. Drury	Challock	16. 3.03
JDL	4430	JDL	Schempp-Hirth Discus BT	165/578		4.98	S Robinson	Chipping	2. 6.03
JDM	4431	JDM	Schleicher ASW15B	15280	F-CEGL	1.98	D C Blyth	Tibenham	8. 3.03
JDN	4432	JDN	Glaser-Dirks DG-505 Elan Orion	5E180X31		3.98	Devon & Somerset GC	North Hill	10. 4.03
JDP	4433	JDP	Glaser-Dirks DG-200/17	2-136/1734	D-0152	12.97	J.J.Benton	Camphill	9. 1.04
JDQ	4434	JDQ	Schleicher ASW19	19106	D-3862	2.99	Surrey & Hants. GC	Lasham	20. 3.02
			(Written-off in take-off accident at Lasham, 25.5.01)						
JDR	4435	JDR	Schleicher ASW15A	15053	D-6910	2.98	L Whitaker	Booker	12.12.03
JDS	4436	JDS	Schempp-Hirth HS.4 Std Cirrus 75	638	D-4057 OY-XCZ	3.98	I.P. Santos	Usk	15. 2.03
JDT	4437	232	Rolladen-Schneider LS-8a	8172		1.98	R.J.Rebbeck	Dunstable	19. 6.03
JDU	4438		LET L-13 Blanik	026301	D-8919	12.97	Herefordshire GC	Shobdon	28. 2.03
JDV	4439	JDV	Glaser-Dirks DG-303	3E481A24		3.98	I.N.Busby	Booker	14. 3.03
JDW	4440	JDW	DWLKK PW-5 Smyk	17.09.018		12.97	G.Pledger	Currock Hill	14.12.00
			(Damaged Charterhall 11.8.00)						
JDX	4441		Wassmer WA-28F Espadon	101	F-CDZU	12.97	S.S.Turner	Upwood	26. 2.01
JDY	4442	P2	Rolladen-Schneider LS-8-18	8173		2.98	P.O.Paterson	Booker	30. 4.03
JDZ	4443	N1	Schempp-Hirth Nimbus 4T	18	D-KOLF	1.98	A.J.French	Lasham	21. 3.03
JEA	4444	D4	Rolladen-Schneider LS-8-18	8159	D-2411	3.98	R.I.Davidson	Husbands Bosworth	28. 4.03
JEB	4445	JEB	Schleicher ASW24	24172	D-9344	2.98	M.A.& J.Taylor	Rattlesden	8.11.03
JEC	4446	JEC	SZD-50-3 Puchacz	B-2197		4.98	Cambridge University GC	Gransden Lodge	25. 1.03
JED	4447		Schleicher ASW15B	15427	D-3976	1.98	P.R.Williams	Lyveden	1. 3.03
JEE	4448	787	Schleicher ASW20L	20073	(BGA.4456) D-7666	2.98	C.J.Bailey	Wormingford	28. 9.01
JEF	4449	M2	Schempp-Hirth Ventus CT	126/400	D-KFWH	1.98	M.R.Emmett	Booker	24. 9.03
JEG	4450	685	Rolladen-Schneider LS-8-18	8150		1.98	J.R.Luxton	Booker	11.12.02
JEH	4451	KE	Glasflugel H.303 Mosquito B	172	OY-XKE	2.98	I.T.Vickery	Lasham	27. 3.03
JEJ	4452	F1	Rolladen-Schneider LS-7WL	7074	OE-5477	3.98	I.Mountain	Dunstable	5. 4.03
JEK	4453		Grob G.102 Astir CS	1374	(BGA.4398) D-7403	8.99	S.R.Allen	Thame	5. 8.00
JEL	4454	W2	Schleicher ASW24	24044	PH-866	2.98	D.Robson	Currock Hill	15. 4.03
JEM	4455	570	Schempp-Hirth Duo Discus	146		3.98	H.Kindell	Lasham	9. 1.03
JEP	4457	JEP	Rolladen-Schneider LS-4B	41021		3.99	C.F.Carter	Long Mynd	6. 5.03
JEQ	4458	OZ	Schempp-Hirth Nimbus 3D	1/6	OO-ZOZ HB-1921/D-7695	2.98	M.Pocock	Kingston Deverill	28. 9.03
JER	4459	JH	Schempp-Hirth Standard Cirrus 75	654	D-6475 OO-ZBM	4.98	J.W.Hoskins	AAC Upavon	21. 1.02
JES	4460	V4	Schleicher ASW19B	19119	SE-TTV	3.98	J.A.Crowhurst	Sutton Bank	21. 3.03
JET	4461	JET	Schempp-Hirth Ventus cT	161/521	RAFGSA.R38	2.98	B.H.Bryce-Smith	Gransden Lodge	28. 3.03
JEU	4462	JEU	Glasflugel H201 Std Libelle	55	SE-TIC	4.98	D.Johns	Bidford	16. 3.03
JEV	4463	JEV	Schempp-Hirth Std Cirrus B	650	OE-5072	2.98	G.F.King	Brent Tor	11.12.03
JEW	4464	D41	Schleicher Ka6CR	6493	D-4116	2.98	J.McLaughlan	Sleap	26. 3.03
JEX	4465	DW	Schempp-Hirth Ventus 2A	64	-	3.98	D.S.Watt	Bicester	11. 3.03
JEY	4466	T7	Schempp-Hirth Std Cirrus	456G	D-3255	3.98	R.J.Lockett	North Weald	3. 3.03
JEZ	4467	274	Glaser-Dirks DG-100	3	PH-792 D-3721	3.98	S.Parramore	Booker	3. 4.03
JFA	4468	JFA	Schempp-Hirth Std Cirrus	225	D-0974	4.98	P.M.Sheahan	Lasham	22. 3.03

JFB	4469	S6	Rolladen-Schneider LS-8-18	8152		3.98	J.A.Clark	Lyveden	16. 4.03
JFC	4470	R55	Schempp-Hirth Discus CS	054CS	RAFGSA.R55	3.98	RAFGSA Fenland GC	RAF Marham	6. 2.03
JFD	4471	R8	Grob G.102 Astir CS	1379	RAFGSA.R8	3.98	RAFGSA Centre	Bicester	30.10.03
					OY-XGE				
JFE	4472	16	Schempp-Hirth Janus Ce	21/299	RAFGSA.R16	3.98	RAFGSA Centre	Bicester	22.12.03
JFF	4473	26	Schempp-Hirth Duo Discus	131	RAFGSA.R26	3.98	RAFGSA Centre	Bicester	12.12.03
JFH	4475	R1	Schempp-Hirth Duo Discus	118	RAFGSA.R1	3.98	RAFGSA Centre	Bicester	16. 3.03
JFJ	4476	JFJ	Schleicher ASW20CL	20830	D-8307	4.98	W.R.Mills	Usk	1. 3.03
					F-CGCS				
JFK	4477	JFK	Schleicher ASW20L	20201	D-5979	4.98	M.K.Field	Sleap	5. 6.03
JFL	4478	42	Rolladen-Schneider LS-8-18	8178		3.98	G.N.Smith	Dunstable	3.12.02
JFM	4479	JFM	Schleicher ASK13	13222	D-0396	3.98	Newark & Notts GC	Winthorpe	29. 1.03
JFN	4480	M25	Schleicher ASH25E	25060	D-KCOH	6.98	R.J.Baker	Cranfield	28. 4.03
JFP	4481	HB	Schempp-Hirth Ventus A	19	PH-707	3.98	S.J.Harris	Dunstable	24. 2.03
JFQ	4482	651	Schempp-Hirth Nimbus 4DT	9/40		5.98	P.Whitt	Camphill	23. 3.03
JFR	4483	221	Schempp-Hirth Ventus cT	170/560	RAFGSA.R24	12.97	J.G.Allen	Bicester	20. 3.03
JFS	4484	528	Schempp-Hirth Ventus cT	147/456	RAFGSA.R28	7.98	M.J.Towler	Snitterfield	28. 7.00
JFT	4485	JFT	Schleicher K8B	8451	D-1883	3.98	South London Gliding Centre	Kenley	7. 5.03
JFU	4486	JFU	Schleicher ASW19	19038	D-4531	3.98	East Sussex GC	Ringmer	2. 2.00
JFV	4487	WA1	Schleicher ASK21	21675		6.98	Scottish GU	Portmoak	24. 6.03
JFW	4488	JFW	LAK-12 Lietuva	6192	LX-CDM	4.98	A.M.Hatfield	Crowland	6. 7.03
JFX	4489	144	Rolladen-Schneider LS-8A	8174		3.98	P.E.Baker	Gransden Lodge	19. 2.03
JFY	4490		Federov Me-7b	8		10.98	D.S.Adams	Booker	22.10.02
JFZ	4491		Federov Me-7b	9		10.98	M.Powell-Brett	Long Mynd	16.11.00
JGA	4492		Federov Me-7b	10		10.98	N.Wilkinson	Challock	19.12.03
JGB	4493	CU	Schleicher K8B	AB.02	D-8868	5.98	Cambridge UGC	Gransden Lodge	17. 3.03
JGC	4494	CC	Rolladen-Schneider LS-6A	6031	D-6699	4.98	Gliding Expeditions Ltd	Les Ages, France	11. 5.03
					PH-763				
JGD	4495	JGD	Schleicher K8B	8214A-SH	D-??..	4.98	R.E.Pettifer	Chipping	15. 3.03
JGE	4496	K21	Schleicher ASK21	21068	RAFGSA.R21	2.98	N.Wall	Long Mynd	17. 6.03
JGF	4497	JGF	Neukom Elfe S4D	416	D-4820	5.98	C.V.Inwood	Lasham	14. 5.02
					BGA.3316				
JGG	4498	JGG	Schleicher ASW15B	15332	D-2325	4.98	L.R.Groves	Ringmer	30. 4.03
JGH	4499		Schempp-Hirth Nimbus 2c	188	OO-ZZM	4.98	J.Swannack	Gamston	20. 7.03
					D-2834				
JGJ	4500	JGJ	Schleicher ASK21	21039	RAFGSA.R22	4.98	Midland GC	Long Mynd	25. 2.03
JGK	4501	JGK	Molino Pik-20D	20571	OO-ZDL	4.98	R.Cassidy	Milfield	22. 4.03
					D-6707				
JGL	4502	27	Schempp-Hirth Discus CS	148CS	RAFGSA.R27	4.98	Chilterns GC	RAF Halton	24. 3.03
JGM	4503	R53	Schempp-Hirth Discus CS	036CS	RAFGSA.R53	4.98	Chilterns GC	RAF Halton	22. 2.03
JGN	4504	JGN	Schempp-Hirth Std Cirrus	554	D-8674	4.98	F.G.Wilson	Pocklington	13. 5.03
JGP	4505	E8	Schempp-Hirth Ventus 2cT	3/10	N200EE	4.98	C.Morris	Bidford	27. 3.03
					D-KHIA				
JGQ	4506	JGQ	LET L-13 Blanik	026224	HB-1282	6.98	Joint Aviation Services	Lasham	19. 3.02
JGR	4507	BT	Schempp-Hirth Discus bT	10/275	D-KGPS	5.98	J.A.Horne	Wormingford	8. 4.03
					D-5461				
JGS	4508	L2	Rolladen-Schneider LS-8-18	8180		5.98	M.D.Allan	Shobdon	7. 1.03
JGT	4509	JGT	Scheibe SF27	6021	D-1126	4.98	South London Gliding Centre	Kenley	28. 4.99
JGU	4510	JGU	Schempp-Hirth Mini Nimbus	69	HB-1427	5.98	P.Etherington	Husbands Bosworth	3. 3.03
JGV	4511	LGC	Schempp-Hirth Duo Discus	173	D-4020	4.00	London GC	Dunstable	2.12.02
JGW	4512		Schleicher ASK13	13146	D-0169	5.98	Newark & Notts GC	Winthorpe	24. 5.03
JGX	4513	JGX	Schleicher K8B	753	D-1878	5.98	J.Fisher	Andreas	12. 4.03
JGY	4514	C3	Schempp-Hirth Std Cirrus	333	SE-TMU	5.98	P.A.Chapman	Husbands Bosworth	31. 3.03
JGZ	4515	JGZ	Glasflugel H-201 Std Libelle	193	D-0697	5.98	J.H.Edwards	Pocklington	16. 6.03
JHA	4516	EU	Schempp-Hirth Std Cirrus	645	D-4240	5.98	J.Lee	Pocklington	17. 4.03
JHB	4517	JHB	Scheibe L-Spatz 55	552	D-1618	8.98	A.Gruber	Rhigos	24. 7.00
JHC	4518	JHC	Schleicher ASW19B	19304	OO-ZBN	8.98	Scottish GU	Portmoak	17. 8.00
							(Written-off Portmoak 25.9.99)		
JHD	4519	JHD	Schleicher Ka6E	4307	OY-XGS	5.98	M.A. King	Gransden Lodge	30. 6.03
					D-0272				
JHE	4520	JHE	Grob G.102 Astir CS Jeans	2189	CS-PBI	5.98	AC de Portugal	Lisbon	22. 2.03
					BGA3977/D-7764				
JHF	4521	VW	Schempp-Hirth Nimbus 4T	30/44		5.98	P.S.Kurstjens-Hawkins	(Australia)	14. 5.03
JHG	4522	51	Grob G.102 Astir CS	1084	D-6984	5.98	J.K.G.Pack	Kingston Deverill	11. 2.03
JHH	4523	JHH	Schempp-Hirth Std Cirrus	349G	D-3006	5.98	R.J.Lodge	Rufforth	10. 5.02
JHJ	4524		Glasflugel H-201 Std Libelle	495	HB-1187	30. 6.01	A.C.Jarvis	Parham	20.12.03
JHK	4525	JHK	Schleicher K8B	558	(BGA4319)	8.98	Stratford GC	Snitterfield	19. 3.03
					AGA.21/RAFGGA.558				
JHL	4526	JHL	Schleicher Ka6E	4073	SE-TFB	6.98	N.J.Banks	Tibenham	1.11.02
JHM	4527	JHM	Schempp-Hirth Discus b	373	???	6.98	J.H.May	Camphill	16. 6.03
JHN	4528	JHN	Grob G.102 Astir Jeans CS	2110	D-7638	5.98	B.Niblett	Kingston Deverill	30. 1.03
JHP	4529	JHP	Valentin Mistral C	MC048-82	D-4948	5.98	R.H.Targett	Nympsfield	13. 2.01
JHQ	4530	R43	Schleicher ASK18	18021	RAFGSA.R43	9.98	RAFGSA Centre	Bicester	15.11.03
					RAFGSA.713/RAFGSA.113				
JHR	4531	JHR/A34	Centrair Alliance SNC-34c	34026		6.98	Borders GC	Milfield	16. 6.03
JHS	4532	JHS	Schleicher ASW19B	19047	D-6716	3.99	B.Crow	Usk	8. 9.03
JHT	4533	D2	Schempp-Hirth Discus 2A	2	- ? -	5.98	R.Jones	Membury	30. 4.03
JHU	4534	868	Rolladen-Schneider LS-8-18	8197		7.98	J.H.Russell	Sutton Bank	17. 5.03
JHW	4536	JHW	Glaser-Dirks DG-200	2-19	HB-1400	6.98	P.I.Fenner	Lasham	25. 9.03
JHX	4537	JHX	Bolkow Phoebus C	930	OO-ZYN	6.98	M.Dunlop	Usk	19. 2.03
					F-CDON				

JHY	4538	LT	Rolladen-Schneider LS-8a-18	8181	D-9988	7.98	L.E.N.Tanner	Aboyne	24. 2.03
JHZ	4539	G41	Schleicher ASW20	20313	D-6532	6.98	T.J. Stanley	Camphill	17.10.03
JJA	4540	JJA	Schempp-Hirth Cirrus	13	D-8114	7.98	P.Tolson *(Crashed Falgunzeon 29.5.99)*	Saltby	3. 7.99
JJB	4541	615	Rolladen-Schneider LS-4	4542	D-2397	6.98	M.Tomlinson	Rhigos	18. 3.03
JJC	4542	JJC	Schleicher ASK13	13661AB	D-1503	7.98	East Sussex GC *(W/o Ringmer 12.8.00)*	Ringmer	9. 7.01
JJD	4543	K11/SUF	Schempp-Hirth Discus bT	5/262	D-KIHS	7.98	D.Wilson	Burn	2. 8.03
JJE	4544	JO1	Schempp-Hirth Discus a	379	OE-5530 VH-XQT	7.98	N.Braithwaite	Walney Island	31. 7.03
JJF	4545	G1	Schleicher ASW27	27086		6.98	G.F.Read	Booker	10.11.03
JJG	4546	V1	Schempp-Hirth Nimbus 4T	3	D-KIXL	7.98	P.G.Sheard	Dunstable	25. 2.03
JJH	4547	899	Glaser-Dirks DG-800S	8-137S30		4.99	W.R.Brown	Husbands Bosworth	31. 3.03
JJJ	4548	JJJ	Schempp-Hirth Standard Cirrus	284	D-2946	7.98	F.R.Stevens	Bidford	31. 3.03
JJK	4549	K8	Rolladen-Schneider LS-8-18	8199		8.98	J.E.C.White	Dunstable	25. 2.03
JJL	4550	JJL	Schleicher ASW19B	19302	D-4227	4.99	Newark & Notts GC	Winthorpe	2. 2.03
JJM	4551	JJM	Schempp-Hirth Standard Cirrus	403G	D-2933	7.98	S.A.Young	Husbands Bosworth	18. 7.03
JJN	4552	JJN	Slingsby T.38	1267	XP490	7.98	Swanton Morley Collection	Swanton Morley	21. 7.99
			(Regd as '2067', from Frame no.SSK/FF/2067)						
JJP	4553	494	Schempp-Hirth Duo Discus	180		7.98	R.J.Fack	Long Mynd	26. 3.03
JJQ	4554	JJQ	SZD-51-1 Junior	B-2191		9.98	Norfolk GC	Tibenham	22. 9.01
JJR	4555	R73	Schleicher ASK21	21054	RAFGSA.R73 RAFGGA.513	8.98	RAFGSA Centre	Bicester	3. 3.03
JJS	4556		Slingsby T.38	873	XA240	R	Not known *(Stored 6.02)*	RAF Keevil	
JJT	4557	933	Schleicher ASW27	27070	D-6209	8.98	T.M.World	Booker	9. 3.03
JJU	4558	H2	Rolladen-Schneider LS-8a	8200		8.98	P.J.Harvey	Cranfield	14. 3.03
JJV	4559	JJV	Schleicher Ka6CR	1001	D-1719	8.98	C.J. Huck	Aston Down	7. 4.03
JJX	4561	T9	Schleicher ASW15B	15323	D-2312	9.98	T.J.Davies	Portmoak	16. 2.03
JJY	4562	JJY	Schempp-Hirth Ventus bT	273/61	PH-981 D-KMIH	9.98	I.H.Molesworth	Challock	15. 3.03
JJZ	4563	15	Schempp-Hirth Discus bT	156/556	OO-ZQX	9.98	S.Walker	Nympsfield	28. 1.03
JKA	4564	JKA	Schleicher ASK21	21059	D-8835	10.98	E Sussex GC	Ringmer	27. 3.03
JKB	4565	JKB	DWLKK PW-5	17.10.08		9.98	J.C.Gibson	Chipping	4. 9.03
JKC	4566	FOX	MDM-1 Fox	224	SP-P632	9.98	G.C.Westgate & Ptnr	Ringmer	29.10.03
JKD	4567	P1	Rolladen-Schneider LS-8-18	8215		10.98	R.J.Large	Lyveden	3. 1.03
JKE	4568	JKE	DWLKK PW-5	17.11.025		10.98	Burn GC	Burn	20. 4.03
JKF	4569		Glaser-Dirks DG-200	2-35	D-6069	10.98	R.Hutchinson	Sutton Bank	29. 9.03
JKG	4570	R48	Schleicher ASK18	18036	RAFGSA.R48 RAFGSA.448	3.99	RAFGSA Centre	Bicester	17. 1.03
JKH	4571	P30	Schempp-Hirth Ventus cT	174/566	RAFGSA.R30	10.98	E.Fitzgerald	Usk	28.11.03
JKJ	4572	R21	Schleicher ASK21	21679	RAFGSA.R21	10.98	RAFGSA Centre	Bicester	29.11.03
JKK	4573	A7	Schleicher ASK21	21182	AGA.11	10.98	AGA Kestrel GC	RAF Odiham	31. 5.03
JKL	4574	W8	Rolladen-Schneider LS-8-18	8218		4.99	R.J.Welford	Gransden Lodge	31. 3.03
JKM	4575	Z10	Glaser-Dirks DG-202-17M	2-148/1746	D-4155	10.98	A.H.Brown	Portmoak	11. 1.03
JKN	4576	790	Rolladen-Schneider LS-8-18	8214		10.98	D.A.Booth	Crowland	8. 1.04
JKP	4577	PH1	Rolladen-Schneider LS-4B	41000	PH-1089	12.98	D.M.Hope	Booker	20. 3.03
JKQ	4578	R20	Schleicher ASK21	21098	RAFGSA.R20	1.99	RAFGSA Bannerdown GC	RAF Keevil	22. 3.03
JKR	4579	P12	Schempp-Hirth Discus b	151	RAFGSA.R12	11.98	RAFGSA Wrekin GC	RAF Cosford	23. 5.03
JKS	4580	S19	Schleicher ASW19B	19362	D-1273	11.98	P.R.Taverner	Tibenham	17.12.03
JKT	4581	R7	Schleicher ASK13	13615	RAFGSA.R7	8.99	Clevelands GC	AAC Dishforth	27. 4.03
JKU	4582	R33	Schleicher ASK18	18022	RAFGSA.R33 RAFGSA.223	6.99	Clevelands GC	AAC Dishforth	8. 6.03
JKV	4583	R52	Grob G103A Twin II Acro	34042-K-273	RAFGSA.R52	5.99	Clevelands GC	AAC Dishforth	23. 5.03
JKW	4584	R60	Grob G.102 Astir CS 77	1666	RAFGSA.R60 RAFGSA.560	1.99	Clevelands GC	AAC Dishforth	19. 5.03
JKX	4585	R17	Schempp-Hirth Discus B	247	RAFGSA.R17	8.99	Clevelands GC	AAC Dishforth	23. 7.03
JKY	4586	24	Schempp-Hirth Ventus cT	181/597	RAFGSA.R24 RAFGGA.557	11.98	Clevelands GC	AAC Dishforth	11.11.03
JKZ	4587	R25	Schleicher ASK21	21123	RAFGSA.R25	12.98	RAFGSA Centre	Bicester	27.11.02
JLA	4588	JLA	Schempp-Hirth Ventus 2cT	26/94	PH-1129	11.98	E.C.Neighbour	Camphill	17. 9.03
JLB	4589	70	Schempp-Hirth Ventus 2A	74		11.98	R.J.Knight	Usk	30. 8.01
							(De-registered 18. 2..02 and sold as N777UN)		
JLC	4590	R10	Schempp-Hirth Discus CS	193CS	RAFGSA.R10	11.98	RAFGSA Centre	Bicester	25. 2.03
JLE	4592	JLE	Schleicher ASK13	13245	RAFGSA.R90 NEJSGSA.1	10.98	AGA Kondor GC	Bruggen	15. 2.03
JLF	4593	JLF	Schleicher ASK13	13150	AGA.14	12.98	Wyvern GC	AAC Upavon	22.11.03
JLG	4594	JLG	SZD-51-1 Junior	B.1933	AGA.5 BGA.3699	2.99	Wyvern GC	AAC Upavon	8. 3.03
JLH	4595	JLH	Rolladen-Schneider LS-4	4256	AGA.1	3.99	Wyvern GC	AAC Upavon	4. 1.03
JLJ	4596	A8	Rolladen-Schneider LS-4B	4997	AGA.2	12.98	Wyvern GC	AAC Upavon	8. 3.03
JLK	4597	12	Rolladen-Schneider LS-7	7112	AGA.3	4.99	A.R.Mountain	Llantisilio	30. 3.03
JLL	4598	N25	Schleicher ASK13	13144	HB-952	11.98	Portsmouth Naval GC	Lee-on-Solent	1.12.02
JLM	4599	R2	Schempp-Hirth HS.6 Janus C	210	RAFGSA.R2	5.99	RAFGSA Cranwell GC	RAF Cranwell	23.11.03
JLN	4600	R4	Rolladen-Schneider LS-8-18	8169	RAFGSA.R4	3.99	RAFGSA Centre	Bicester	10. 1.04
JLP	4601	R39	Schempp-Hirth Discus CS	034CS	RAFGSA.R39	4.99	RAFGSA Cranwell GC	RAF Cranwell	5. 2.03
JLQ	4602	R40	Schleicher ASK13	13608	RAFGSA.R40 RAFGSA.R4	4.99	RAFGSA Cranwell GC	RAF Cranwell	23. 2.03
JLR	4603	R57	Grob G.102 Astir CS	1509	RAFGSA.R57 RAFGSA.507	2.99	RAFGSA Cranwell GC	RAF Cranwell	2.11.03
JLS	4604	R75	Schleicher K8B	8950	RAFGSA.R75(2) RAFGSA.285(2)	3.99	RAFGSA Cranwell GC	RAF Cranwell	11.12.02
JLT	4605	JLT	Schleicher Ka6E	4115	D-6082	11.98	M.Thompson	Husbands Bosworth	3.12.03

Reg	No	Code	Type	C/n	Prev ID		Owner	Location	Date
JLU	4606	11	Schempp-Hirth Ventus 2cT	37/126		3.99	J.C.Mitchell	Chipping	23. 3.03
JLV	4607	JLV	Schleicher Ka6E	4192	OY-XEU	1.99	M.S.Neal	Crowland	16. 3.03
					D-4424				
JLW	4608	87	Schempp-Hirth Discus CS	033CS	RAFGSA.R87	12.98	RAFGSA Centre	Bicester	14. 2.03
JLX	4609	JLX	Grob Standard Cirrus	279G	OO-ZGL	11.98	M.W.Fisher	Edgehill	8. 4.03
					D-1985				
JLY	4610	JLY	Schleicher ASW27	27111		6.99	P.C.Piggott	Husbands Bosworth	30. 5.03
JLZ	4611	21	Grob G.103A Twin II Acro	3633-K-15	D-7912	12.98	R.A.Walker	Kingston Deverill	19. 1.03
JMA	4612	R36	Schleicher ASK18	18038	RAFGSA.R36	6.99	RAFGSA Centre	Bicester	22. 3.03
					RAFGSA.236				
JMB	4613	R5	Rolladen-Schneider LS-8-18	8130	RAFGSA.R5	2.99	RAFGSA Centre	Bicester	10. 2.02
JMC	4614	R22	Schleicher ASK21	21681	(RAFGSA.R22)	12.98	RAFGSA Wrekin GC	RAF Cosford	14.12.02
JMD	4615	P23	Schempp-Hirth Discus b	241	RAFGSA.R23	4.99	R.C.Oliver	Kenley	18. 4.03
JME	4616	JME	Schleicher Ka7	5	D-8867	12.98	W.Masterson	Kingston, Jamaica	17. 1.03
JMG	4618	JMG	SZD-51-1 Junior	B.2192		4.99	Kent GC	Challock	15. 2.03
JMH	4619	JMH	Schempp-Hirth Standard Cirrus	571	HB-1263	12.98	F.Davidson	Rufforth	6.12.02
JMJ	4620	R46	Schleicher ASK13	13616	RAFGSA.R46(2)	9.99	RAFGSA Fenlands GC	RAF Marham	12. 9.03
					RAFGSA.R16				
JMK	4621	R49	Schleicher ASK18	18023	RAFGSA.R49	1.99	RAFGSA Fenlands GC	RAF Marham	21. 2.03
					RAFGSA.318(2)				
JML	4622	R63	Grob G.102 Astir CS 77	1718	RAFGSA.R63	1.99	RAFGSA Fenlands GC	RAF Marham	27. 4.03
					RAFGSA.883				
JMM	4623	JMM	Schempp-Hirth Discus b	254	BGA.4474	12.98	M.R.Fox	Pocklington	22. 4.03
					RAFGSA.R15				
JMN	4624	636	Schempp-Hirth Nimbus 2	38	D-1129	12.98	R.A.Holroyd	Pocklington	15.12.02
					HB-1159				
JMO	4625	781	Rolladen-Schneider LS-8-18	8225		12.98	D.J.Langrick	Husbands Bosworth	20. 2.03
JMP	4626	JMP	Schleicher ASK13	13436	D-2984	1.99	East Sussex GC	Ringmer	29. 7.02
JMQ	4627	KR	Schleicher ASW20L	20499	F-CADB	1.99	S.G.Back	Crowland	20.12.03
					D-2026				
JMR	4628	628	Rolladen-Schneider LS-8-18	8198	D-0280	12.98	D.Williams	Lasham	19. 6.03
JMS	4629	R23	Schleicher ASK21	21212	RAFGGA.521	11.98	RAFGSA Centre	Bicester	9. 6.03
JMT	4630	301	Rolladen-Schneider LS-8-18	8223		2.99	J.Burry	Lasham	15.12.03
JMU	4631	140	Rolladen-Schneider LS-8-18	8246		3.99	R.D.Payne	Nympsfield	23. 2.03
JMV	4632	EW	Schempp-Hirth HS.5 Nimbus 2C	179	D-6738	1.99	K.R.Walton	Lasham	6. 3.03
JMW	4633	R61	Schleicher ASK13	13688AB	RAFGSA.R59(3)	1.99	RAFGSA Bannerdown GC	RAF Keevil	30.11.02
					RAFGGA.567				
JMX	4634	JMX	Schleicher ASK13	13107	RAFGSA.R86	2.99	Shalbourne SG	Rivar Hill	29. 3.03
					RAFGSA.R46/RAFGSA.386				
JMY	4635	JMY	SZD-51-1 Junior	W-959	OO-ZRH	3.99	Highland GC	Easterton	26. 4.03
JMZ	4636	R37	Schleicher ASK13	13099	RAFGSA.R37(2)	1.99	RAFGSA Wrekin GC	RAF Cosford	14. 3.03
					RAFGSA.378(2)				
JNA	4637	JNA	Grob G.102 Astir CS Jeans	2160	D-4556	2.99	Shenington GC	Edgehill	5. 4.03
JNB	4638	D1	Rolladen-Schneider LS-8-18	8227		2.99	Tatenhall Aviation	Cross Hayes	18. 3.03
JNC	4639	Z22	Schempp-Hirth Standard Cirrus	322	HB-1157	2.99	S.M.Veness	Bicester	5. 5.03
JND	4640		Slingsby T38 Grasshopper	(ex ?)		R	S.Williams		NK
			(C/n given as 'SSK/OW2987', which is a part number)						
JNE	4641	JNE	Schempp-Hirth Discus 2A	18	D-4499	2.99	J.R.W.Kronfeld	Lasham	2.12.02
JNF	4642	80	Schempp-Hirth Discus 2A	12		2.99	A.J.Davis	Nympsfield	22. 3.03
JNG	4643	JNG	Glasflugel H.201B Standard Libelle	6	SE-TFU	3.99	P.K.Spencer	Edgehill	21. 7.03
JNH	4644	E3	Schleicher ASW27	27102		3.99	E.Drew	Crowland	23. 6.02
			(De-registered 12.12.01 – sold in the USA)						
JNJ	4645	601	Rolladen-Schneider LS-8-18	8226		2.99	J.D.Spencer	Dunstable	30. 3.03
JNK	4646	676	Rolladen-Schneider LS-8-18	8244		2.99	M.J.Jordy	Enstone	17. 2.03
JNL	4647	DR7	Schempp-Hirth HS.6 Janus	25	HB-1313	2.99	D.M.Ruttle	Saltby	14. 2.03
JNM	4648	P4	Rolladen-Schneider LS-8-18	8232	(BGA.4617)	3.99	P.Onn	Dunstable	13. 3.03
					D-8217				
JNN	4649	JNN	Schleicher K-8B	8744	D-8583	3.99	Buckminster GC	Saltby	26.10.02
JNP	4650		Rolladen-Schneider LS-6B	6109	D-5853	R	P.Fink		
JNQ	4651	441	Glaser-Dirks DG-300 Elan	3E-341	SE-UHO	4.99	F.C.Roles	Camphill	1. 4.03
JNR	4652	JNR	Glasflugel H.303 Mosquito B	159	D-5908	3.99	I.Agutter	Wormingford	1. 2.03
JNS	4653	D48	Schleicher ASW27	27103		3.99	B.H.Owen	Lasham	3. 1.03
JNT	4654	SC	Schleicher ASW19B	19371	D-2233	4.99	S.Cheshire	Booker	1.11.03
JNU	4655	R69	Rolladen-Schneider LS-6-18W	6345	RAFGSA.R69(3)	3.99	RAFGSA Chilterns GC	RAF Halton	6. 4.03
					RAFGSA.553/D-8037				
JNV	4656	E2	Schleicher ASW22BL	22079		4.99	R.A.Cheetham	Husbands Bosworth	14. 3.03
JNW	4657	L4	Rolladen-Schneider LS-8	8217		3.99	P.C. Fritche	Ringmer	29. 3.03
JNX	4658	JNX	LET L-13 Blanik	027408	OK-2712	5.99	Vectis GC	Bembridge	3. 5.03
JNY	4659	CZ	Schempp-Hirth Discus 2B	17	D-4498	3.99	D.H.Conway	RAF Keevil	4. 4.03
JNZ	4660	813	Glaser-Dirks DG-100	70	(D-7324)	3.99	P.F.Gleeson	Husbands Bosworth	10. 5.03
					HB-1324				
JPA	4661	HB1	Schempp-Hirth Duo Discus	201		3.99	The Soaring Centre	Husbands Bosworth	16. 1.03
JPB	4662	A5	Schleicher ASK23	23005	AGA.18	4.99	Kestrel GC	RAF Odiham	5.01
			(De-registered 05.09.01 – sold in The Netherlands)						
JPC	4663	R51	Schleicher ASK13	13256	RAFGSA.R51	3.99	Anglia GC	RAF Wattisham	29. 3.03
JPD	4664	V2T	Schempp-Hirth Ventus 2cT	39/129		3.99	P.A.Hearne	Challock	20. 3.03
JPE	4665	L77	Rolladen-Schneider LS-1f	488	F-CESC	5.99	A.A.Darlington	Lasham	12. 6.03
JPF	4666	JPF	Glaser-Dirks DG-100	22	D-3735	5.99	H.G.Burkert	Rivar Hill	7. 6.03
JPG	4667	520	Schempp-Hirth Ventus 2cT	2/3	D-KLYC	4.99	P.Naegeli	Rivar Hill	14.11.02
			(De-registered 14.12.01 – sold in Denmark)						
JPH	4668	CB	Rolladen-Schneider LS-8-18	8259		7.99	J.P.Ben-David	Lasham	22. 9.02

JPJ	4669	SA	Grob G.104 Speed Astir IIB	4089	OE-5352	4.99	R.J.Maisonpierre	Rattlesden	17. 5.02
JPK	4670		Slingsby T34 Sky	672	RAFGSA.876 XA876/G-672	5.99	J.Tournier	Booker	17. 5.03
JPL	4671	RW	Rolladen-Schneider LS-8-18	8249	D-2562	4.99	I.Reekie	Thame	4. 3.03
JPM	4672	JPM	Grob G.102 Astir CS Jeans	2209	D-3825	5.99	J.Thorpe	Cross Hayes	15. 5.03
JPN	4673	280	Schleicher ASW27	27117		6.99	M.Strathern	Nympsfield	3. 8.02
					(De-registered 9 .9.02 and sold as ZK-GKW)				
JPP	4674	388	Schempp-Hirth Discus B	206	AGA.4	4.99	Kestrel GC	RAF Odiham	2. 5.03
JPQ	4675	R32	Schleicher ASK18	18002	RAFGSA.R32 RAFGSA.213/D-3978	5.99	RAFGSA Fulmar GC	Easterton	26.12.02
JPR	4676	161	Rolladen-Schneider LS-8-18	8245		4.99	D.M.Byass	Dunstable	24. 4.03
JPS	4677	CL	Schleicher ASW27	27108		5.99	C.C.Lyttleton	Dunstable	19. 2.03
JPT	4678	JPT	Schleicher ASW27	27113		10.99	R & W Willis-Fleming	North Hill	16. 9.03
JPU	4679	TL2	Schempp-Hirth Discus CS	257CS		4.99	K.Armitage	Camphill	11.12.03
JPV	4680	R88	Schleicher ASK13	13312	RAFGSA.R88 RAFGSA.186	5.99	RAFGSA Centre	Bicester	28. 3.03
JPW	4681	JPW	Glaser-Dirks DG-200	2-48	D-2201	5.99	J.P.Goodison	Burn	27. 5.03
JPX	4682	JPX	Schleicher ASW15	15160	D-0823	5.99	P.Seymour	Cranfield	1. 3.03
JPY	4683	R59	Schleicher ASK13	13653AB	RAFGGA.509	5.99	RAFGSA Cranwell GC	Cranwell	8. 3.03
JPZ	4684	R56	Schleicher ASK18	18027	RAFGGA.563	4.99	RAFGSA Phoenix GC	Bruggen	30.11.03
JQA	4685	547	Schempp-Hirth Discus b	265	BGA.4535 RAFGGA.547/RAFGGA.500	4.99	Bannerdown GC	RAF Keevil	2. 3.03
JQB	4686	JQB	Schleicher K8B	8880	RAFGSA.R98 RAFGSA.398	5.99	A.J.Taylor & Ptnrs	Lee on Solent	14. 4.03
JQC	4687	JT	Schempp-Hirth Discus bT	127/488	D-KITT(3)	5.99	J.C.Taggart	Bellarena	7. 6.03
JQD	4688	R3	Rolladen-Schneider LS-8-18	8224		5.99	RAFGSA Bannerdown GC	RAF Keevil	26.11.03
JQE	4689	JQE	Schempp-Hirth HS4 Standard Cirrus 75	25	OO-ZRS D-0483	6.99	C.Nunn	Rattlesden	4. 4.03
JQF	4690	5GC	Glaser-Dirks DG-505 Elan Orion	5E194X38	S5-7516	6.99	Scottish Gliding Union	Portmoak	4. 5.03
JQG	4691	R50	Grob G.103A Twin II Acro	33964-K-197	RAFGSA.R50	5.99	RAFGSA Fulmar GC	Easterton	14. 4.02
JQH	4692		LAK-12 Lietuva	6188		5.99	S.R.Brown	Snitterfield	4. 4.03
JQJ	4693	JQJ	Schleicher K8B	8795	RAFGSA.R47 BGA.1564	5.99	Staffordshire GC	Seighford	8.11.03
JQK	4694	506	Schempp-Hirth Discus CS	075CS	RAFGGA.501	5.99	Phoenix GC	RAF Bruggen	10. 3.03
JQL	4695	W2	Schempp-Hirth Ventus 2A	79		5.99	M.L.Dawson	RAF Keevil	16. 4.03
JQM	4696	Z9	Schleicher ASW-27	27114		6.99	A.Heynor	Weston-on-the-Green	12.12.03
JQN	4697	R67	Grob G.102 Astir CS 77	1634	RAFGSA.R67 RAFGSA.547	6.99	RAFGSA Centre	Bicester	18. 7.03
JQP	4698	JQP	Centrair 101A Pégase	101-066	F-CFQY	6.99	J.Rees	Usk	12. 6.03
JQQ	4699	185	Schempp-Hirth Duo Discus	227		3.00	K.G.Reid & Ptnrs	RAF Keevil	16. 3.03
JQR	4700	JQR	Schempp-Hirth Ventus 2cT	49/152		10.99	M.C.Costin	Crowland	15.12.03
JQS	4701	JQS	Schempp-Hirth Standard Cirrus	251G	D-1147	6.99	M.Charlton	Currock Hill	5. 7.03
			(Built by Grob)						
JQT	4702	JQT	Grob G.102 Astir CS Jeans	2076	D-7589	6.99	Southdown GC	Parham Park	7. 2.03
JQU	4703	L17	LAK-17A	102		6.99	A Pozerskis	Husbands Bosworth	28. 4.03
JQV	4704	Z12	Schleicher ASW27	27112		7.99	I.N.Lingham	Booker	13.11.03
JQW	4705	JQW	Schempp-Hirth HS.2 Cirrus 18	47	D-0186	7.99	GE.Smith	Parham Park	4. 1.03
JQX	4706	JQX	Schleicher ASK21	21702		9.99	Southdown GC	Parham Park	23.10.03
JQY	4707	R92	Slingsby T21 Sedbergh	666	RAFGSA.R92 NEJSGSA.4/WG499	6.99	Crusaders GC	Kingsfield, Dhekelia	29. 6.03
JQZ	4708	JQZ	Schleicher K8B	8854	RAFGSA.R42 RAFGSA.323	7.99	Bowland Forest GC	Chipping	31. 3.03
JRA	4709	E11	Rolladen-Schneider LS-8-18	8263		7.99	S.R.Ell	Sutton Bank	13. 1.03
JRB	4710	S33	Schleicher ASW19B	19227	D-2713	7.99	K.F.Bell	Lasham	4. 1.03
JRC	4711	JRC	Glaser-Dirks DG300 Club Elan 3E-20		HB-1718	8.99	D.P.Sillett	Rattlesden	28. 7.03
JRD	4712	R18	Grob G102 Astir CS	1487	RAFGSA.R18 RAFGSA.540/D-4791	6.99	RAFGSA Centre	Bicester	23. 4.03
JRE	4713	JP	Schleicher ASW-15	15048	LN-GGL OH-391/OH-RWA/D-4391	8.99	J.D.Pride	Long Mynd	13. 8.03
JRF	4714	JRF	SZD-50-3 Puchacz	B-1395	OO-ZTX D-8213/SP-3285	8.99	Derby & Lancs GC	Camphill	7. 3.03
JRG	4715	◂G	Schempp-Hirth Standard Cirrus	146	D-0297	8.99	D.Draper	Rivar Hill	20. 3.03
JRH	4716	T27	Schleicher ASW27	27118		8.99	P.C.Jarvis	Booker	8. 1.04
JRJ	4717	JRJ	SZD-50-3 Puchacz	503199327		8.99	Bidford GC	Bidford	14. 7.03
JRK	4718	618	Rolladen-Schneider LS-8-18	8267		9.99	D.King	Snitterfield	18. 9.03
JRL	4719	F84	Glaser-Dirks DG-100G Elan	E185G151	D-1246	2.00	A.McKay	Sleap	18. 5.03
JRM	4720	212	Grob G102 Astir CS	1332	AGA.6 BGA.4314	9.99	Kestrel GC	RAF Odiham	23.11.02
JRN	4721	PT	Glaser-Dirks DG-202/17C	2-118CL01	D-7267	9.99	T.G.Roberts	Lasham	20. 3.03
			(C/n 2-118CL04?)						
JRP	4722	JRP	Grob G102 Astir CS Jeans	22494	D-5951	9.99	Borders GC	Milfield	22. 9.03
JRQ	4723	PM3	Neukom Elfe PM3	001	N6351U N63514/HB-526	11.99	G.Mclean	Lleweni Parc	23. 8.03
JRR	4724	LA	Schempp-Hirth Discus bT	50/367	PH-1087 D-KBHM	3.00	C.R.Lear	RAF Keevil	25. 3.03
JRS	4725	AT	Valentin Mistral C	MC021/79	D-4921	3.00	A.Towse	RAF Wattisham	1. 5.03
JRT	4726		Schempp-Hirth Standard Cirrus	99	D-0734	10.99	S.Hutchinson	Husbands Bosworth	28.10.03
JRU	4727	MB	Schleicher ASW-24	24168	D-7085	1.00	M.Bull	Lasham	10. 3.03

			Type	Serial	Prev ID	Date	Owner	Location	Date
JRV	4728	B19	Schleicher ASW19B	19233	D-2644	10.99	M.Roome	Lasham	14.12.02
JRW	4729	R95	Grob G103A Twin II Acro	34040-K-271	RAFGGA.556	10.99	RAFGSA Centre	Bicester	7.12.03
JRX	4730	R41	Schleicher ASK13	13375	RAFGSA.R41 RAFGSA.241(2)	10.99	Chilterns GC	RAF Halton	22. 2.03
JRZ	4732		Colditz Cock rep *(Under construction by M.Francis)*	--			R M.Francis	Camphill	
JSA	4733		Scheibe SF-27MB	6303	(G-BSUM) D-KIBE	R	M.Davies	NK	
JSB	4734	JSB/UWE	Rolladen-Schneider LS-4	4424	D-4541	2.00	H.Vare	Speyer, Germany	7. 3.03
JSC	4735	827	Schempp-Hirth Nimbus 3dT	10	F-CFUE F-WFUE/D-KFUE	11.99	D.P.Taylor & P.J.Teagle	Sutton Bank	7. 1.03
JSD	4736	R77	Grob G102 Astir CS	1133	RAFGSA.R77 D-4177	2.00	RAFGSA Wrekin GC	RAF Cosford	23. 4.03
JSE	4737	296	Schempp-Hirth Discus b	365	PH-918	3.00	Imperial College GC	Lasham	2. 3.03
JSF	4738	414	Rolladen-Schneider LS-1f	383	LN-GGE SE-TOU	3.00	R.C. Godden	North Weald	5. 5.03
JSG	4739	500	Schleicher K-6E	4248	D-0090	2.00	J.S.Halford	Kingston Deverill	15. 6.03
JSH	4740	396	Grob G102 Astir IIIB	5504CB	D-6470	11.99	Surrey & Hants GC	Lasham	14. 3.03
JSJ	4741	7X	Rolladen-Schneider LS-7WL	7058	D-5774	10.99	T.Moyes	Camphill	15. 3.03
JSK	4742	JSK	Grob G102 Astir CS	1521	D-7455	11.99	J.W.Bolt	North Hill	5. 4.03
JSL	4743	JSL	Schempp-Hirth Ventus cT	121/395	D-KIFL	11.99	B.Ingles	Bidford	7.11.03
JSN	4745	R45	Schleicher K8B	8916	RAFGSA.R45 RAFGSA.245	11.99	Chilterns GC	RAF Halton	29.11.02
JSP	4746		Slingsby T31B	909	XE796	R			
JSQ	4747		Rolladen-Schneider LS-8T	8301	D-KKAF	5.00	P.G. Wright	Gransden Lodge	14.12.03
JSR	4748	JSR	SZD-50-3 Puchacz	B-1386	OY-XRV SP-3283	3.00	Bidford GC	Bidford	14. 4.03
JSS	4749	JB	Schleicher ASW27B	27121		12.99	J.H.Belk	Dunstable	18.12.03
JST	4750	X5	Rolladen-Schneider LS-1c	86	OO-ZPA D-0766	1.00	L.Gerrard	Husbands Bosworth	6. 4.03
JSU	4751	95	Rolladen-Schneider LS-8-18	8297	D-0543	3.00	J.G.Bell	(Chichester)	11. 3.03
JSV	4752	R80	Schleicher ASK13	13127	RAFGSA.R80 BGA.1509	1.00	RAFGSA Centre	Bicester	18.11.03
JSW	4753	H4	Rolladen-Schneider LS-4	4262	ZS-GOP	10.00	European Soaring	(France)	23. 3.03
JSX	4754	JSX	Glaser-Dirks DG-505 Elan Orion	5E200X44		5.00	Oxford GC	Weston on the Green	23. 4.03
JSY	4755		Pilatus B4 PC-11	127	D-3055 D-5787/PH-578	1.00	A.de Tourboulon & ptnr.	Wormingford	17. 2.03
JSZ	4756	JSZ	Schleicher ASK-18	18012	D-6878	4.00	C.J.N.Weston	Challock	9. 7.03
JTA	4757	-	Colditz Cock rep *(Built Southdown Aero Services & J.Lee)*	---		1.00	Southdown Aero Services	Duxford	*
JTB	4758	V17	Schleicher ASW-24	24017	D-3465	2.00	P.Shaw	RAF Keevil	1. 3.03
JTC	4759	JTC	Glaser-Dirks DG-100G	84G5	(BGA.4744) HB-1335	5.00	A.Burger	Nunstadt, Germany	23. 5.03
JTD	4760	103	Rolladen-Schneider LS-6-18W	6371	D-2571	2.00	C.J.Mayhew	Lasham	18.12.03
JTE	4761	JTE	Schempp-Hirth Standard Cirrus	470G	D-3718	2.00	G.Reeves	Parham Park	11. 6.03
JTF	4762	Z3	Schleicher ASW-27B	27125		3.00	P.M.Wells		26. 3.03
JTG	4763	D55	SZD-55	551197100	N4364R	3.00	N.A.McLean	Booker	12. 3.03
JTH	4764	H3	Schleicher ASW-24	24218	D-7681	3.00	R.H.Yarney	Lasham	25. 3.03
JTJ	4765		Schempp-Hirth Mini Nimbus b	73	D-7620	3.00	A.Richards	North Hill	23. 2.03
JTK	4766	JTK	Glaser-Dirks DG-303 Elan	3E487A28		5.00	B.J.Edwards	Booker	4. 1.04
JTL	4767	352	Rolladen-Schneider LS-8-18	8317		3.00	L.S.Hood	Cranwell	13. 4.03
JTM	4768	205	Rolladen-Schneider LS-8-18	8268		2.00	M.Young & Ptnr	Dunstable	6. 3.03
JTN	4769	E5	Glaser-Dirks DG-300	3E19	HB-1717	3.00	M.J.Chapman	Seighford	13. 3.03
JTP	4770	JTP	Schleicher ASW-20L	20569	D-4688	3.00	C.A.Sheldon	Rufforth	9. 3.03
JTQ	4771	JTQ	Glasflugel H303 Mosquito	88	OO-ZYL	4.00	I.Hamilton	Chipping	19. 3.03
JTR	4772		Rolladen-Schneider LS-7	7104	D-5309	3.00	B.L.Anson	Booker	2. 5.03
JTS	4773	JTS	Schempp-Hirth Cirrus VTC	108	S5-3059 SL-3059/YU-4200	3.00	S.J.Smith	(Sutton)	21. 3.03
JTU	4775	377	Schempp-Hirth Duo Discus	234		3.00	R.Starmer Syndicate	Burn	28. 2.03
JTV	4776	666	Schempp-Hirth Ventus 2cT	52/173		3.00	A.P.Moulang	Challock	25. 1.03
JTW	4777	AV8	Glasflugel H303 Mosquito	199	F-CELX	4.00	M.Wright	AAC Wattisham	27. 3.03
JTX	4778	JTX	Start+Flug H101 Salto	47	D-9260	3.00	C.Schneeberger	Maxdorf, Germany	14. 3.03
JTY	4779	JTY	Rolladen-Schneider LS-8A	8102	SE-USA	4.00	BBC Club	Booker	22. 1.03
JTZ	4780	GC	Schempp-Hirth Ventus 2B	23	OO-ZQS	2.00	G.Costacurta	Asiago, Italy	8. 6.03
JUA	4781	Y2K	Schempp-Hirth Discus 2B	48		2.00	C.Costa	(Italy)	30. 6.03
JUB	4782	894	Schempp-Hirth Discus CS	268CS		4.00	D.F.Wass	Lasham	14. 2.03
JUC	4783	X1	Rolladen-Schneider LS-8-18	8305		4.00	G.P.Stingemore	Winthorpe	10. 9.02
JUD	4784	Z19	Rolladen-Schneider LS-8-18	8309		3.00	D.S.Haughton	Camphill	22. 2.03
JUE	4785	X15	Rolladen-Schneider LS-8-18	8295		3.00	R.Arkle	Aboyne	31. 7.03
JUF	4786	46	Schempp-Hirth Ventus 2cT	53/174		4.00	M.H.Pope	Bidford	8. 4.03
JUG	4787	FE	Issoire E78 Silene	9	F-CFED	7.00	Essex & Suffolk GC	Wormingford	31.10.02
JUH	4788	R6	Schleicher ASW-27B	27129		4.00	RAFGSA Centre	Bicester	27. 1.03
JUJ	4789	370	Schleicher ASW-27B	27127		4.00	D.R.Campbell	Booker	8. 5.03
JUK	4790	554	Grob G102 Astir CS	1430	PH-552	6.00	C.Shepherd	Booker	13. 2.03
JUL	4791	621	Schleicher ASW-27B	27132		4.00	T.Stuart	Nympsfield	24. 4.03
JUM	4792	2UP	Schempp-Hirth Duo Discus	243		4.00	B.A.Bateson	Parham Park	7. 6.03
JUN	4793	M19	Schleicher ASW-19B	19096	D-3844	5.00	M.P.Roberts	Gransden Lodge	3. 5.03
JUP	4794	183	Schempp-Hirth Discus 2b	60		5.00	P.J.Ward	Aston Down	29. 4.03
JUQ	4795	250	Schempp-Hirth Ventus 2cT	55/179		5.00	W.J.Murray	Rivar Hill	5. 5.03
JUR	4796	JUR	Valentin Mistral C	MC042/81	HB-1596	5.00	Essex & Suffolk GC	Wormingford	25. 8.03

Reg	BGA	Code	Type	Serial	Prev id	Date	Owner	Location	Date
JUS	4797	JUS	Grob G102 Astir CS	1403	(BGA.4774) D-4269	5.00	Rattlesden GC	Rattlesden	25. 4.03
JUU	4799	JUU	Schempp-Hirth Standard Cirrus	450	PH-500	5.00	J.Simpson	Rufforth	13. 7.03
JUV	4800	SH2	Schempp-Hirth Discus b	551	D-8257	6.00	Surrey & Hants GC	Lasham	5. 3.03
JUW	4801	4T	Schleicher ASW-19B	19074	D-4476	5.00	E.Cole	RAF Keevil	29. 6.03
JUX	4802	CD1	Avia Stroitel AC-4c	051		5.00	C.J.Davison	Winthorpe	27. 1.03
			(Formerly known as Federov Me-7)						
JUY	4803	JUY	Valentin Mistral C	MC041/81	D-4941	5.00	C.A.Pennifold	Lee-on-Solent	31. 3.03
JUZ	4804	SH6	Schleicher ASW-19B	19146	D-7932	6.00	Surrey & Hants GC	Lasham	27. 3.03
JVA	4805		Schempp-Hirth Ventus 2cT	66		8. 1.02	N.A.Leigh	Camphill	12. 2.03
JVB	4806	DF	Schempp-Hirth Discus bT	111/462	D-KUNK	5.00	D.J.Fawcett	Lasham	20 .3.03
JVC	4807	JVC	SZD-51-1 Junior	B-1799	SP-3434	6.00	Yorkshire Gliding Centre	Rufforth	5. 5.03
JVE	4809	JVE	Eiri PiK-20D	20631	OY-XJC	6.00	S.R.Wilkinson	Kirton-in-Lindsey	23. 6.03
JVF	4810	JH1	Schempp-Hirth Discus CS	271CS		6.00	J.Hodgson	Wormingford	16. 5.03
JVG	4811	420	Schempp-Hirth Discus bT	121/477	D-KSOP	6.00	P.J.Charnell	Lasham	11. 6.03
JVH	4812	AC4	Avia Stroitel AC-4c	052		6.00	R.Hurley	Shobdon	29. 7.02
JVJ	4813	JS	LAK-17A	108		6.00	J.A.Sutton	Currock Hill	24. 2.03
JVK	4814	CP	Rolladen-Schneider LS-6c-15/18	6236	D-6417	7.00	M.F.Collins	Lasham	16. 7.03
JVL	4815	400	Glaser-Dirks DG-300	3E158	HB-1833	7.00	A.M.Blackburn	Camphill	5. 6.03
JVM	4816	GP	Schleicher ASW-27B	27138		6.00	G.K.Payne	Booker	20.12.02
JVN	4817	T4	Schleicher ASW-27B	27134		6.00	N & R Tillett	Dunstable	14. 1.03
JVP	4818	JVP	Glaser-Dirks DG-200	2-1	D-8200	7.00	M.P.Ellis & Ptnrs	Rufforth	21. 6.03
JVQ	4819	275	Schleicher ASW-27B	27136		7.00	M.R.Fountain	Booker	4. 7.03
JVR	4820	540	Schempp-Hirth Discus 2b	72		7.00	P.Davies	Lasham	8. 7.03
JVS	4821	Z1	Schleicher ASW-28	28003	D-4008	9.00	S.J.Steinberg	Gransden Lodge	12.11.03
JVT	4822	JE	Schempp-Hirth Nimbus 3-25	5 37	D-3176	7.00	J.R.Edyvean	Winthorpe	1. 8.02
JVU	4823		Lanverre Cirrus CS11-75L	28	F-CEVT	7.12.00	C.R.Coates	Snitterfield	23. 1.03
JVV	4824	J50	Sch-Hirth Janus Ce	176	D-4150	8.00	G.R.Jenkins	Lasham	21. 2.03
JVW	4825		Schleicher ASW-15A	15042	HB-992	20. 2.01	G.J.Armes	Rattlesden	28.10.03
JVX	4826	163	Schempp-Hirth Discus CS	087CS	D-0263	8.00	L.Marks	Lasham	7. 8.03
JVY	4827	F6	Schempp-Hirth Discus b	175	RAFGSA.R6	8.00	M.R.Garwood	Crowland	24. 7.03
JVZ	4828	JVZ	Schleicher ASK-21	21721		12.00	Yorkshire GC *"Sharpe's Classique"*	Sutton Bank	17.12.03
JWA	4829	E1	Schleicher ASW-28	28005		10.00	R.A.Cheetham	Winthorpe	31.10.03
JWB	4830	JWB	Schleicher ASK-13	13671	D-1066	12.00	East Sussex GC	Ringmer	17. 2.03
JWC	4831	900	Schleicher ASW-27B	27142		10.00	C.Starkey	Lasham	2.12.03
JWD	4832	GWD	Schleicher ASK-21	21724		16. 2.00	London GC	Dunstable	28. 2.03
			(Reported marked as "GWD")						
JWE	4833		Slingsby T.21B	1159	XN155	1. 7.00	M.Selss	Bad Tolz	11. 7.03
JWF	4834	S27	Schleicher ASW-27B	27144		11.00	B.A.Fairston	Husbands Bosworth	6.11.03
JWG	4835	111	Schempp-Hirth Nimbus 3DT	11	D-KMGD	11. 2.01	T.P.Browning	Lasham	28. 2.03
JWH	4836		Schempp-Hirth Standard Cirrus	256	SE-TMZ	14. 6.01	M.F.Cuming	Edgehill	13. 6.02
JWJ	4837	R38	Schleicher ASK-13	13599	RAFGSAR3	11.00	RAFGSA	Bicester	7.11.03
JWK	4838	722	Schempp-Hirth Discus bT	106	HB-1860	11.00	D.E.Barker	Aston Down	14.11.02
JWL	4839	D4	Schempp-Hirth Ventus B	125	D-6667	11.00	S Weber	(Germany)	17.11.03
JWM	4840		Grob G.103 Twin II	3536	D-8730	11.00	Norfolk GC	Tibenham	9.12.03
JWN	4841	UY	Rolladen-Schneider LS.4	4728	D-7008	24. 2.01	D. Bartek	Speyer, Germany	24. 2.03
JWQ	4843	310	Schempp-Hirth Discus 2A	82		11.00	P.S.Sheard	Dunstable	13.11.02
JWR	4844	NJ1	Grob G.102 Astir CS	1271	D-7366	1.01	N.J.Irving	Portmoak	29. 1.03
JWS	4845		Schleicher ASW-15B	15098	D-4656	14. 4.01	P Lyons	NK	19. 3.03
JWT	4846	JWT	Glaser-Dirks DG-200	2-42	D-6560 D-6660	11.00	A Farr	Kingston Deverill	4. 5.03
JWU	4847		Schempp-Hirth Ventus bT	19/159	ZS-GOW	10.00	G Tabbner	Gransden Lodge	9.10.02
JWV	4848	S60	Glasflugel Standard Libelle	411	OY-XBG	14. 3.01	G.K.Drury	Challock	18. 2.03
JWW	4849		Schleicher ASW-19	19381	ZD658 BGA.2894	R8.12.00	G Lane	--	
			(Restored as BGA.2894 qv)						
JWX	4850	63	Schempp-Hirth Ventus 2cT	66		20.12.00	S.G.Olender	(Spain)	28. 3.03
JWY	4851	JWY	Schleicher ASK-13	13504	D-3977	12. 1.01	Southdown GC	Parham Park	11. 1.02
			(Written-off in crash at Parham 23.5.01)						
JWZ	4852		Schleicher ASW-22	22037	D-3422	22. 1.01	D.Prosolek	Gamston	9.12.03
JXA	4853	Y44	Schempp-Hirth Nimbus 3dT	9	D-KKYY D-4444	3. 2.01	B.C.Morris	Booker	9. 2.03
JXB	4854		Centrair 201 Marianne	201-015	F-CGMN	27. 1.01	M.J.Thompson	Rufforth	11.12.03
JXC	4855		Wassmer WA.28F	102	F-CDZV	27. 3.01	A.P.Montague	Nympsfield	26. 3.02
JXD	4856		Slingsby T.21B	---	?	20. 1.01	F.Brune	Eudenbach	6. 1.03
JXE	4857		SZD-22C Mucha Standard	F-717	SP-2330	12. 8.01	C.E.Harwood	Challock	11. 8.02
JXF	4858		Bolkow Phoebus B	875	(BGA.4842) D-0128	R18. 1.01	P.A.Hearne	NK	
JXG	4859	W5	Eiri PIK-20D	20660	PH-670	23. 2.01	T.J.Clubb	Lasham	17. 2.03
JXH	4860	W20	Schleicher ASW-20L	20067	D-7657	17. 2.01	G.M.Brightman	Dunstable	27. 4.03
JXJ	4861	W7	Schleicher ASW-28	28012		29. 1.01	E.W.Johnston	Dunstable	20. 1.03
JXK	4862		Schempp-Hirth Ventus bT	49	D-KLOE	25. 1.01	P.L.Manley	Wormingford	21. 2.03
JXL	4863	SG1	Schempp-Hirth Discus CS	278CS		5. 4.01	Southdown GC	Parham Park	19. 4.03
JXM	4864	R34	Schleicher ASK-13	13542	RAFGSA.R34 F-CERF	25. 2.01	RAFGSA Chilterns GC	RAF Halton	13. 4.03
JXN	4865	JXN	Centrair 201B Marianne	201B-035	F-CBLI	21. 2.01	E.Crookes	Kirton-in-Lindsey	9. 3.03
JXP	4866	H52	Glaser-Dirks DG-100	18	PH-320	16. 5.01	P.W.Butcher	Husbands Bosworth	28. 6.03
JXQ	4867		Wassmer WA.26P	19	F-CDQQ	26. 9.01	J.A.French	Nympsfield	25. 9.02
JXR	4868	DM	Schempp-Hirth Discus B	540	D-9152	8. 4.01	Cambridge GC	Gransden Lodge	31. 3.03
JXS	4869		Schleicher K8B	8778	RAFGSA.R95 RAFGSA.395	R6. 3.01	Stratford GC	Snitterfield	
JXT	4870	CT	Schleicher ASW-24B	24233	D-6706	9. 3.01	C.Thwaites	Rufforth	20.11.03

JXU	4871	646	Rolladen-Schneider LS-8	8354		10. 3.01	C.J. Alldis	Long Mynd	2. 4.03
JXV	4872	JXV	Glaser-Dirks DG-100	63	PH-543	24. 3.01	R.Vos	Challock	22. 3.03
JXW	4873	871	Schempp-Hirth Duo Discus T	7		11. 5.01	C.Bainbridge	Wormingford	10. 4.03
JXX	4874	JXX	Pilatus PC-11 B4	13	HB-1112	28. 5.01	K.J.Sleigh	Rattlesden	27. 5.02
JXY	4875	JXY	Neukom Standard Elfe	68	HB-1267	29. 5.01	K.J.Sleigh	Rattlesden	28. 5.02
JXZ	4876	27B	Schleicher ASW-27B	27152		16. 3.01	M.Fryer	Rufforth	19.11.03
JYA	4877	JYA	Slingsby T.21B	MHL015	WB988	31. 3.01	C.Bravo	Madrid, Spain	9. 4.03
JYB	4878	IZ	Glaser-Dirks DG-202/17	2-143/1738	D-1086	1. 5.01	N.Wood	Rufforth	4. 5.03
JYC	4880	R19	Grob G102 Astir CS	1429	RAFGSA.R19	9. 4.01	RAFGSA Centre	Bicester	24. 3.02
					RAFGGA 742/D-7425				
JYD	4881	T6	Schleicher ASW-27B	27155		25. 3.01	J.E. Gatfield	Booker	29.10.03
JYE	4882		Schleicher ASK-13	13191	D-0347	11. 4.01	Ulster GC	Bellarena	12. 4.03
JYF	4883	N55	Schempp-Hirth Discus CS	281CS		11. 4.01	D.Bradley	Rufforth	10. 4.03
JYG	4884		Letov LF107 Lunak	49	OK-0833	R17. 4.01	M.Laurner	(Germany)	
JYJ	4886	JYJ	Schempp-Hirth Ventus 2cT	64		1. 5.01	J.A.Evans	Chipping	26. 4.03
JYK	4887	115	Glaser-Dirks DG-800B	8-194B116	(G-BZEM)	2. 5.01	I.M.Stromberg	Camphill	4. 5.03
JYL	4888		LAK-12 Lietuva	6197	(Slovenia)	9. 5.01	C.Arrigo	Udine, Italy	30. 6.03
JYM	4889	LR	Schempp-Hirth Discus 2A	86		9. 5.01	S.Meriziola	Rome, Italy	30. 6.03
JYN	4890		Schempp-Hirth Discus 2B	94		9. 5.01	S.R.L. Aliman	Briauzo, Italy	30. 6.03
JYP	4891	B12	Grob G102 Astir IIB	5018C	D-8743	19. 5.01	Norfolk GC	Tibenham	8. 5.03
JYQ	4892	485	Glaser-Dirks DG-100G	E181G147	D-1485	15. 6.02	A.M.Booth	Wormingford	14. 6.03
JYR	4893	B20	Schempp-Hirth Duo Discus T	16/267	D-KOZX	3. 7.01	B.F.Walker	Nympsfield	26. 7.03
JYS	4894	878	Schempp-Hirth Mini Nimbus C	106	HB-1437	6. 6.01	A.Jenkins	Shobdon	19. 6.03
JYT	4895	E4	Schempp-Hirth Ventus 2B	114	(BGA.4884)	15. 6.01	J.C.Bastin	Booker	21. 3.03
JYU	4896	R11	Schempp-Hirth Ventus 2cT	70/216		15. 6.01	RAFGSA Centre	Bicester	13. 3.03
JYV	4897	JYV	Schleicher K8B	133	D-8395	18. 6.01	European Soaring Club	Le Blanc, France	3. 7.03
JYW	4898	JYW	Schleicher K8B	8432A	D-5682	18. 6.01	European Soaring Club	Le Blanc, France	3. 7.03
JYX	4899	JYX	Rolladen-Schneider LS-3-17	3289	D-3517	18. 6.01	D.M. Beck	Dunstable	15. 6.03
JYY	4900	PB	Schleicher ASW-28	28029		21. 6.01	P.F.Brice	Dunstable	18.10.02
							(De-registered 4.11.02; sold in Denmark)		
JYZ	4901		Bolkow Phoebus B	855	OE-0872	R26. 6.01	K.Sleigh	Rattlesden	
JZA	4902	JZA	Start+Flug H101 Salto	27	D-2997	10. 7.01	C.J. Pollard	Rattlesden	25. 4.03
JZB	4903	JZB	Glaser-Dirks DG-505 Orion	5E223X61		28. 7.01	Faulkes Flying Foundation	NK	28. 8.03
JZC	4904	M9	Rolladen-Schneider LS-8-18	8395		11.3.02	M.H.Patel	Dunstable	10.3.03
JZD	4905	GZD	Dittmar Condor IV	018	(D-0125)	7.3.02	P.J.Underwood	Dunstable	6.3.03
					LV-DHV				
JZE	4906	SG2	Schleicher ASK-13	13423	OY-XPJ	11.11.01	Southdown GC	Parham Park	16.12.03
					D-2125				
JZF	4907	SOOM	Glaser-Dirks DG-500-22	5E42M20	G-SOOM	9. 7.01	G.W.Kirton	Husbands Bosworth	31. 7.02
JZG	4908	SM	Schempp-Hirth Discus bT	9	D-KISM	9. 7.01	R.J.Middleditch	Nympsfield	8. 8.03
JZH	4909	JZH	Schleicher ASW-20CL	20754	D-5932	10. 7.01	C.P.Gibson	Lasham	24.11.03
JZJ	4910		Schleicher ASW-15	15147	D-0791	R12. 7.01	K.Sleigh	Rattlesden	
JZK	4911	JZK	Glaser-Dirks DG-505 Orion	5E225X63		1. 9.01	Faulkes Flying Foundation	NK	27. 8.03
JZL	4912	BS	Schempp-Hirth Mini Nimbus B	92	HB-1453	25. 8.01	S.J.Ware & Ptnr.	Kirton-in-Lindsey	12. 8.03
JZM	4913	110	Schempp-Hirth Ventus 2A	117		24. 8.01	Southern Sailplanes	Membury	8. 9.03
JZN	4914	JZN	Schleicher ASW-28	28038		19.12.01	I.C.Lees	Rufforth	19.12.03
JZP	4915	JZP	Marganski Swift S1	119	F-CIAB	26. 9.01	I.E.Tunstall	Winthorpe	25. 9.02
JZQ	4916		Edgely EA9 Optimist	006		R3. 9.01	T.Henderson	NK	
JZR	4917		Edgely EA9 Optimist	008	(BGA.4731)	R3. 9.01	University of London	NK	
JZS	4918		Schempp-Hirth Ventus	3	?	R3. 9.01	*(Believed not taken up - registered as G-VENT)*		
JZT	4919	L30	Schleicher ASW-27	27163	D-4115	22. 8.01	L.Brigliadori	Sirtori, Italy	21. 8.02
							(De-registered 15. 7.02, sold as ZS-GWP)		
JZU	4920		Glaser-Dirks DG-101G	E64G39	HB-1579	R12. 9.01	M.Robinson	NK	
JZV	4921	V2C	Schempp-Hirth Ventus 2cT	72/225		14. 9.01	P.McLean	Tibenham	13. 9.02
JZW	4922	JZW	Grob G102 Astir CS	1208	D-7281	27. 9.01	R.Theil	Cranwell	26. 9.03
JZX	4923		Schleicher ASW-27	27166		22. 9.01	P.R.Barley	Bicester	9.10.03
JZY	4924		Grob G104 Astir III	5600	D-6951	2.10.01	T.R.Dews	Kingston Deverill	6.12.03
JZZ	4925		Rolladen-Schneider LS-7WL	7128	SE-UIU	28.3.02	J.H.Tucker	Gransden Lodge	27. 3.03
KAA	4926	XE790	Slingsby T31B	903	XE790	14. 9.02	N.Stalpers	Castricum, The Netherlands	13. 9.03
KAB	4927		Slingsby T59 Kestrel 19	1832	G-BBVC	R27. 9.01	T.Gauder		
					BGA.3176		*(Restored as BGA.3176 instead, qv.)*		
KAC	4928		Glaser-Dirks DG-200	2-159	HB-1611	3.10.01	C.Morton-Fincham	Kirton-in-Lindsey	10.10.03
KAD	4929		Glaser-Dirks DG-300 Elan	3E259	D-8411	5.10.01	N.G.Maxey	Challock	4.10.02
					OE-5420				
KAE	4930	KAE	Centrair Pégase	101-0152	F-CGBN	4.6.02	Rattlesden GC	Rattlesden	3. 6.03
KAF	4931		Schempp-Hirth Duo Discus T	49		R10.10.01	M.R.Smith	Feshiebridge	23. 7.03
KAG	4932	EE	Schempp-Hirth Nimbus 3T	23	D-KMHF	15.11.01	K. Engelherdt	Berlin	23.10.03
KAH	4933	KAH	Schempp-Hirth Discus Bt	464/112	D-KNZZ	13.11.01	R.M.Brown	Bicester	12.11.02
KAJ	4934	KAJ	Schempp-Hirth Ventus 2cT	86		18.5.02	A.N.Reddington	Perranporth	17. 5.03
KAK	4935	J1	Schleicher ASW-28	28032		1.11.01	R.A.Johnson	Husbands Bosworth	31.10.02
KAL	4936	A28	Schleicher ASW-28	28031		13.11.01	A.Smith	Nympsfield	12.11.02
KAM	4937	TS2	Glasflugel H205 Club Libelle	83	D-8928	10.12.02	M.W.Black	Wormingford	9.12.02
KAN	4938	KAN	SZD-50-3 Puchacz	B2106	PH-1104	10.12.01	Bath, Wilts & North Dorset GC	Kingston Deverill	9.12.02
KAP	4939	KAP	Schempp-Hirth Discus CS	290CS		16.2.02	A.A.Stewart	Portmoak	15. 2.03
KAQ	4940	BG	LAK-17A	125		8.12.01	LAK Deutschland	Musbach, Germany	7.12.02
KAR	4941	977	Schempp-Hirth Duo Discus T	35	D-KHAF	3.12.01	J.P.Galloway	Portmoak	2.12.02
KAS	4942		Schempp-Hirth Ventus cT				*See BGA.4995*		
KAT	4943	520?	Schempp-Hirth Ventus 2cT	82		22.3.02	P.C.Naegeli	Lasham	21. 3.03
KAU	4944	KAU	Glaser-Dirks DG-303 Elan	3E500A35		20.4.02	G.Earle	Lasham	19. 4.03
KAV	4945	GG	Rolladen-Schneider LS-4A	4996	D-2975	11. 2.02	G.S.Goudie	Gransden Lodge	10. 2.03
KAW	4946		Glaser-Dirks DG-505 Orion	5E228X66		10.3.02	Faulkes Flying Foundation	NK	9. 3.03

Code	No.	Trigraph	Type	Serial	Prev ID	Date	Owner	Location	Date
KAX	4947		Glaser-Dirks DG-505 Orion	5E229X67		12.4.02	Faulkes Flying Foundation	NK	11.4.03
KAY	4948		Grob G102 Astir CS	1452	D-7433	7.2.02	D.A.Woodforth	Saltby	6.2.03
KAZ	4949		Glaser-Dirks DG-600	6-5	VH-GHS	19.3.02	M.Geisen	Dunstable	18.3.03
KBA	4950	KBA	Centrair 101 Pégase	101A-0435	HB-3096	28.3.02	K.Sleigh	Rattlesden	27.3.03
KBB	4951		Schempp-Hirth Mini Nimbus C	147	HB-1508	12.2.02	K.E.Ballington	Cross Hayes	11.2.03
KBD	4953	NU	Grob G102 Astir CS	1217	D-7290	4.4.02	Notts U'versity GC	Syerston	3.4.03
KBE	4954	SP	LAK-17A	130		14.3.02	C.Triebel	(Germany)	13.3.03
KBF	4955	ALG	Glaser-Dirks DG-303	3E498		10.4.02	A.L.Garfield	Dunstable	9.4.03
KBG	4956	71	Schempp-Hirth Ventus 2cT	83		15.3.02	J.F.D'Arcy	Strathaven	14.3.03
KBH	4957	H1	Rolladen-Schneider LS-6	6072	D-7798	4.4.02	J. French	Nympsfield	3.4.03
KBJ	4958		Rolladen-Schneider LS-8-18	8422		8.4.02	W.Schneider	Enstone	7.4.03
KBK	4959	409	Schempp-Hirth Ventus 2cT	79/244		15.4.02	R.J. Nicholls	Husbands Bosworth	19.8.03
KBL	4960	N12	Grob G102 Astir CS	1464	D-7436	13.4.02	Norfolk GC	Tibenham	12.4.03
KBM	4961	Z1	Schleicher ASW-28	28046	D-0001	29.3.02	Zulu Glastek &P.Wells		24.4.03
KBN	4962	NH	SZD-55	551190004	SE-ULV	26.3.02	K.Davis	Dunstable	25.3.03
KBP	4963	KBP	Slingsby T.31B	852	XA310	20.4.02	A.P.Stacey	Hullavington	19.4.03
KBQ	4964	Y2	Schempp-Hirth Discus A	279	OH-807	5.4.02	R.Priest	Booker	4.4.03
KBR	4965		Glasflugel Libelle	57		R15.4.02	M.Geisen	NK	
KBS	4966	KBS	Glaser-Dirks DG-600	6-42	OO-YPH D-4882	20.4.02	H.Altmann	Booker	19.4.03
KBT	4967	633	Schempp-Hirth Standard Cirrus 561G		D-4755	3.6.02	P R Johnson	Rattlesden	2.6.03
KBU	4968	104	Schleicher ASW-28	28040		18.4.02	G C Metcalfe	Lasham	17.4.03
KBV	4969	MM	Schleicher ASW-28	28045		24.4.02	M P Mee	Booker	23.4.03
KBW	4970	KBW	Letov LF107 Lunak	22	OM-0973	9.6.02	K Sleigh (Wears "OM-0973")	Rattlesden	8.6.03
KBX	4971	FF	Schleicher ASW-27	27092	PH-1146 OK-0973	11.5.02	C Colton	Gransden Lodge	10.5.03
KBY	4972	386	Glaser-Dirks DG-800A	8-39-A29	G-ORIG	4.5.02	I Godfrey	Lasham	3.5.03
KBZ	4973	C64	Rolladen-Schneider LS-8	8425		12.5.02	P G Crabb	Husbands Bosworth	11.5.03
KCA	4974	C65	Rolladen-Schneider LS-8	8424		3.5.02	S J Crabb	Husbands Bosworth	2.5.03
KCB	4975		Rolladen-Schneider LS-4A	4776	PH-887	7.6.02	Bristol & Glos GC	Nympsfield	6.6.03
KCC	4976	V26	Schempp-Hirth Ventus 2cT	90/266		13.5.02	F.B.Jeynes	Bidford	12.5.03
KCD	4977	66	Schempp-Hirth Ventus 2cT	91/267		20.5.02	J.Delafield	Bicester	19.5.03
KCE	4978	24	Schempp-Hirth Ventus 2cT	85/...		28.5.02	RAFGSA Centre	Bicester	27.5.03
KCF	4979	72	Schempp-Hirth Duo Discus T	48		13.5.02	J.L.Birch	North Weald	12.5.03
KCG	4980	T99	Schleicher ASW-27B	27182		31.5.02	T.N.McGee	Dunstable	17.12.03
KCH	4981	EA	Schempp-Hirth Ventus 2cT	56/186	PH-1191	12.7.02	L.Marks & W.Pridell	Lasham	11.7.03
KCJ	4982	V8	Schleicher ASW-28	28051		16.7.02	S.L.Withall	Dunstable	15.7.03
KCK	4983	RA	Schempp-Hirth Ventus 2cT	../272		5.7.02	R.F.Aldous	Booker	4.7.03
KCL	4984	KCL	Rolladen-Schneider LS-4	4123	D-4239	12.7.02	R.L.Fox	Rufforth	11.7.03
KCM	4985	J8	Glasflugel H201 Standard Libelle	104	HB-968	17.7.02	G.A.Cox	Kingston Deverill	16.7.03
KCN	4986	700	Schleicher ASW-27B	27188	D-0001	11.7.02	W.J.Head & Ptnr	Dunstable	10.7.03
KCP	4987	NG1	Grob G102 Astir CS	1094	OY-XDB	7.8.02	Norfolk GC	Tibenham	26.11.03
KCQ	4988		DWLKK PW-5	17-04-010	OY-XYE	R15.7.02	Go Soaring	NK	
KCR	4989	LEO	LAK-17A	132		3.6.02	R.A.Bickers	Lasham	2.6.03
KCS	4990	KCS	Grob G103A Acro	3691-K-42	D-6940 OH-645	7.7.02	Cairngorm GC	Feshiebridge	30.11.03
KCT	4991		Schleicher ASK-21	21751		R18.7.02	Kent GC	Challock	
KCU	4992	KCU	Schempp-Hirth Standard Cirrus	100	D-0741	7.7.02	G.Carruthers	Sutton Bank	6.8.03
KCV	4993	WE4	Schempp-Hirth Duo Discus T	54	D-KOZZ	7.8.02	T.W.Slater	Wormingford	6.8.03
KCW	4994	KCW	Glaser-Dirks DG-200-17	2-137/1735	D-0153	6.9.02	R.W.Adamson	Portmoak	5.9.03
KCX	4995		Schempp-Hirth Ventus 2cT	93/582	(BGA.4942) D-KREB	R 2.8.02	J E Bowman	(Bidford)	
KCY	4996	KCY	Schleicher ASW-20	20068	PH-597	14.11.02	J Epple	Camphill	13.11.03
KCZ	4997		Schleicher ASK-21	21749		R 8.02	Booker GC	Booker	
KDA	4998		Schempp-Hirth Ventus 2BX	138		R10. 9.02	D.Eade (To KDL/BGA.5008 11.02)		
KDB	4999		Schleicher Ka-6CR	6431	HB-805	R11. 9.02	Aquila GC	Hinton in the Hedges	
KDC	5000		Schleicher ASW-20	20254	C-GRKX	R13. 9.02	K Sleigh	Rattlesden	
KDD	5001		Avia Stroitel AC-5T	027		26. 9.02	Russia Sailplanes	NK	25. 9.03
KDE	5002	SI	Schempp-Hirth Duo Discus	193	PH-1141	29.10.02	C R Emson	Enstone	28.10.03
KDF	5003	E7	Schleicher ASK-21	21006	D-6539	29. 9.02	Portsmouth Naval GC	Lee-on-Solent	28. 9.03
KDG	5004	6S	Glasflugel H205 Club Libelle	119	OO-YHL D-2473	22.10.02	T.W.Slater	Wormingford	21.10.03
KDH	5005	KDH	Schleicher K-8B	E4	D-8428	3.1. 03	Midland GC	Long Mynd	2.1.04
KDJ	5006		Schempp-Hirth Ventus 2cT	102		R	M.Nash	NK	
KDK	5007		Rolladen-Schneider LS-4A	4352	D-4106	9.11.02	M.C.Ridger	Long Mynd	8.11.03
KDL	5008		Schempp-Hirth Ventus 2BX	138	(BGA4998)	R11.11.02	D.Eade	NK	
KDM	5009		Schleicher ASH-25WL	25139	F-CHAY	R21.11.02	R.Browne	NK	
KDN	5010		Schleicher ASW-27	27196?		R22.11.02	R.Payne	NK	
KDP	5011		Schleicher ASK-21	21760		R25.11.02	Kent GC	Challock	
KDQ	5012	808	Schempp-Hirth Ventus 2cT	97		29.11.02	A.Milne	Kingston Deverill	28.11.03
KDR	5013		SZD-48-3 Standard Jantar 3	B1642	DOSAAF	R6.12.02	S.J.Kochanowski	Lasham	
KDS	5014		Schleicher ASW-27B	27207		R13.12.02	G.Morris	NK	
KDT	5015		Letov LF107 Lunak	12	OK-0975	.... 12.02	I.H.Keyser (Wears "OK-0975")	Challock	28. 9.03
KDU	5016		Glaser-Dirks DG-202-17	2-161/1752	D-6000	R18.12.02	P.Nouen	NK	
KDV	5017		Schempp-Hirth Ventus B	224	HB-1770	R .3. 1.03	R.Theil	Cranwell	
KDW	5018		Schleicher ASW-27B	27196		R 6. 1.03	A.J.Kellarman	NK	
KDX	5019		Glaser-Dirks DG-500	2-11	D-7218	R11. 1.30	B.Searle	NK	
KDY	5020		Glaser-Dirks DG-100	78	D-2591	R14. 1.03	N.Claidon	NK	
KDZ	5021		Schempp-Hirth Standard Cirrus 75	696	OO-ZKB	R27. 1.03	M.Williams	NK	

PART 2 – IRISH GLIDING & SOARING ASSOCIATION

The system is similar to the British Glider Association and the register is maintained by the Irish Gliding & Soaring Association. Originally this was kept by the Irish Aviation Club using the prefix "IAC". From 1960 until 1967 gliders were allocated with a number prefixed "IGA". The IGSA listing is updated from Air-Britain sources. We have decided to expand the data this year and include some historical entries. Thanks to Richard Cawsey for this and the new information.

No/Code	Type	C/n	P/I	Date	Owner/Operator	Probable Base	CA Expy
IGA.6	Slingsby T.8 Tutor	-	IAC.6	.56	Meath Aero Museum Ashbourne, Co.Meath		
			VM657		*(Noted 3.01)*		
EI-100	SZD-12A Mucha 100A	494	OY-XAN	.95	J.Finnan & M.O'Reilly	Gowran Grange	1. 7.97
EI-101	Slingsby T.13 Petrel	361A	IGA.101	54	*To BGA 651 1973*		
			IAC.101/BGA 651/G-ALPP				
EI-102	Slingsby T.26 Kite 2	?	IGA.102	.54	Dublin GC	Gowran Grange	
			IAC.102/BGA...		*(Stored 5.99)*		
EI-103	Chilton Olympia	CAH/OL/7	IGA 103	.61	*EI- marks not taken up - damaged 1966 & scrapped*		
			BGA434/G-ALJN/BGA 434				
EI-104	Schleicher Ka4 Rhönlerche II	?	IGA 104?	.61	*Fate unknown*		
EI-105	Schleicher Ka7 Rhönadler	775	IGA.7	.60	Dublin GC *(Noted 5.99)*	Gowran Grange	14. 6.97
EI-106	Schleicher K 8B	1099	IGA 8	.61	*To BGA 1695 4.72*		
EI-107	Scheibe Bergfalke II	190	IGA	.61	*To BGA 2571 10.79*		
			OY-AXP				
EI-108 08	Schleicher K8B	8486		.65	Dublin GC	Gowran Grange	13. 4.97
	(Logbook shows c/n 8468)				*(Active 10.01)*		
EI-109	Schleicher Ka 6CR	6343	IGA 106	.64	*To Ulster GC as BGA 3318 3.88*		
EI-110	LET L-13 Blanik	173328	IGA 110	.66	*To BGA 2923 4.84*		
			G-ATWW				
EI-111 11	Schleicher Ka6CR	6565	IGA.9	.67	Not known *(Noted 5.99)*	Gowran Grange	30. 3.97
EI-112	Schleicher ASK13	13131		.69	Dublin GC *(Noted 5.99)*	Gowran Grange	9. 3.97
EI-113	Schleicher ASK13	13189		.69	Clonmel GC	Kilkenny	17. 7.97
EI-114	Schleicher ASK14	14008	EI-APS	.69	SLG Group	Gowran Grange	
			G-AWVV/D-KOBB		*(Not used; see EI-APS in SECTION 2)*		
EI-115	EoN AP.5 Olympia 2B	EoN/O/155	BGA.1097	.70	S.Cashin *(Active 5.99)*	Kilkenny	
EI-116	Scheibe Mü 13E	305	D-1127	.71	*Kerry GC; fate unknown*		
EI-117	Slingsby T.50 Skylark 4	1326	BGA 1019	.73	*To BGA 1019 5.84*		
EI-118	EoN AP.8 Baby	EoN/B/001	BGA.608	.73	B.Douglas	Gowran Grange	
			RAFGSA.217/BGA.608/G-ALLU/BGA.608 *(Stored 6.95)*				
EI-119	Schleicher ASK16	16022	EI-AYR	??	*(Not used - remained as EI-AYR)*		
EI-120	LET L-13 Blanik	175205	RAFGSA	.75	Private Syndiate	Gowran Grange	
			BGA.1730		*(Active 10.01)*		
EI-121	Pilatus B4 PC11AF	199		.77	Clonmel GC *(Stored 6.95)*	Kilkenny	
EI-122	Scheibe SF 28A Tandem Falke	5739	G-BBGA	.78	*Not used - to EI-BFD 2.80*		
			D-KOEI				
EI-123	Bölkow Phoebus C	840	D-0057	??	*Crashed*		
EI-124	Grob G.102 Astir Standard CS 77	1761	D-...	.80	Nutgrove Shopping Centre Churchtown, Dublin		
					(Noted 5.99)		
EI-125	Slingsby T.59D Kestrel 19	1839	D-9253	.80	*To BGA 2902 6.83*		
EI-126	Centrair ASW 20FL	20107	F-CFFG	.81	*Damaged 27 May 82 - to F-CFTA*		
EI-127	Schleicher Ka6CR	662	PH-259	??	Not known *(Current 1993)*	NK	
EI-128	Schleicher Ka6CR	6649	D-1393	??	Dublin GC *(On rebuild 4.96)* Gowran Grange		
EI-129	Slingsby T.65C Sport Vega	1922	BGA 2622	.87	*To BGA 2622 9.94*		
EI-130	Scheibe L-Spatz	200	BGA.2199	??	J.J.Sullivan	Gowran Grange	
			D-4707		*"White Cloud"*		
EI-131	Schleicher Ka 2	133	BGA 1418	.90	*Crashed near Bellarena 3 Jun 95*		
			RAFGSA/D-4327				
EI-132 TK	Schleicher ASW17	17031	D-2365		Not known	Gowran Grange	17. 6.97
EI-133 33	Schleicher K8B	8557	D-8517	.91	Dublin GC	Gowran Grange	14. 6.97
			D-9367		*(Active 10.01)*		
EI-134 34	Schleicher ASW15B	15249	D-1087	.91	Not known	Gowran Grange	7. 5.97
EI-135	Slingsby T.38 Grasshopper	758	WZ762	.91	(Syndicate)	Gowran Grange	
	(Wings from WZ756 or WZ768)				*(Stored as "WZ762" 5.99)*		
EI-136	Schleicher ASK18	18007	BGA.2945	.91	Dublin GC	Gowran Grange	30. 7.97
			D-6868		*(Noted 5.99)*		
EI-137	Rolladen-Schneider LS3-17	3308	D-3521	.92	Not known	Gowran Grange	1. 3.97
					(Sold abroad to USA 1.02)		
EI-138 BR	Schempp-Hirth Discus CS	089CS		.92	B.Ramseyer	Gowran Grange	
					(Sold to N189HH 12.00)		
EI-139	Slingsby T.31B	902	BGA.3485	.93	P.Bedford Syndicate	Gowran Grange	2. 8.97
			G-BOKG/XE789				
EI-140	SZD-12A Mucha 100A	491	HB-647	.93	D.Mongey	Gowran Grange	
EI-141	ICA IS-28B	233	BGA 2207	.93	*To Crusaders GC, Cyprus 6.95*		
EI-142	Scheibe SF-27A Zugvogel V	6049	D-1444	.94	Not known	Gowran Grange	19. 7.97
					(Active 5.99, to EI-144 qv)		
EI-143	Schleicher ASK13	13112	BGA.1501	.94	Dublin GC	Gowran Grange	
EI-144	Scheibe SF-27A Zugvogel V	6049	(EI-142)	.94	Not known	Gowran Grange	
			D-1444				
EI-145	Glaser-Dirks DG-200	2-88	PH-930	.95	Not known	Gowran Grange	
			D-7610		*(Noted 5.99)*		
EI-146 TK	Scheibe Zugvogel IIIB	1085	D-4096	.96	N Short & T Daly *(Active 10.01)*	Gowran Grange	
EI-147	Glaser-Dirks DG-200	2-22	D-6760	.97	Not known *(Active 6.00)*	Gowran Grange	

EI-148	Not yet allocated					
EI-149	Not yet allocated					
EI-150 `	Schleicher ASK-21	21002	D-6957	12.02	Dublin GC	Gowran Grange
EI-151 51	Schleicher ASW-27B	27174		.02	K.Houlihan	Gowran Grange
EI-152 52	Schempp-Hirth Ventus 2cT	88/263		.02	B.Ramseyer	Gowran Grange
EI-153	Schleicher ASW-19B	19316	BGA.4274/HWZ HB-1524	.02	K.Commins & L.Keegan	Gowran Grange
EI-154	LET L-13 Blanik	173214	BGA.1500/CFD G-ATCG	6.02	J Selman	Ardagh
EI-155	Not yet allocated					
EI-156	Not yet allocated					
EI-157	Slingsby T.21B	1158	BGA.1465 RAFGSA.333/XN154	.02	Dublin GC *(Active 10.01)*	Gowran Grange
EI-158	Bolkow Phoebus	908	BGA.4202 OO-ZDJ/BGA.1573	.02	Not known	Gowran Grange

Notes:
1)   *Blanik EI-154 was initially allotted EI-153 in error and this identity was reported to the BGA at the time of its cancellation in the UK.*
2)   *Apart from ASK 13 EI-113 & Pilatus B4 EI-121 all current gliders are based with the Dublin Gliding Club, Gowran Grange, near Naas.*
3)   *Ulster Gliding Club aircraft are registered with the British Gliding Association.*

PART 3 – BGA COMPETITION NUMBERS & TAIL CODES

BGA Competition Numbers are issued to members/pilots and not to individual gliders but, beware, they change frequently. There is no formal list of Competition Numbers and little control over other gliders wearing similar or past numbers, or other (tail) codes- see below. The listing is a composite based on BGA information and reported sightings. The missing numbers are not allocated. Competition Numbers marked with an asterisk indicate where gliders have been noted with the numbers shown, although not listed in the current BGA record. In some cases because joint (syndicate) ownership is common this means that the Competition Number belongs to a member of a syndicate other than the one whose name appears as owner in the BGA's records. The member's name/glider type is shown where the glider concerned is not identified. This sub-section also includes a separate Alpha-Numeric (tail)-code listing.

No.	BGA No.	No.	BGA No.	No.	BGA No.	No.	BGA No.
1	1144*/1804*/3123	75	4267*	150	4100/1269*	229	1683
2	869*/2680/3529*	76	2721*	151	1686	230	3523
3	(JD Bally	77	1377	152	2501/3321*	231	2918*/(G Huggins)
4	(WA Kahn)	78	3845	153	1528	232	4437
5	(G.D.Green)	79	3455/2528*	154	3279	233	2226*
7	3224	80	4642	155	(JM Turner)/870*	234	1723
8	3720	81	2453*	156	4290*/(JM Airey)	236	(HB Middleton)
9	1317*	82	3920	157	2639*	237	3967
10	1818	83	3680/1584*	158	3373	238	3411
11	1991*/4606*	84	4261	159	3321	239	2862
12	4597	85	(DJ Robertson)	160	2461	240	1969*
13	3323*	86	2310	161	(JA McCoshim)/4676*	241	4214/1737*
14	1958	87	4608	162	4653/3501*	242	3417
15	(S.J.Parker)/4563*	88	2974	163	1089*/1299*/4826	243	1172*/(MP Osborne)
16	4472	89	(JA Millar)	164	2088	244	(SG Olender)
17	2804	90	2981	165	1648	245	3976
18	1475	91	(GP Stingemore)	166	2623	246	3555
19	4123	92	1839	167	4072	247	3604*/(GG Dale)
20	2951	93	3228	168	4273	248	1911
21	(MI Gee) 4611*	94	(RC Bromwich)	169	4145	249	2950*/(JA Johnston)
22	TS Zealley	95	1989/4751	170	4216	250	4795
23	(PR Redshaw)/3965*	96	3807	171	3643	251	2216
24	4586*/4978	97	3955	172	2677*/(GD Morris)	252	1624
25	3973	98	4350	173	3607	253	1840
26	4473	99	4157	175	3124	254	1795
27	4502	100	3962	176	4413	255	1116
28	3341	101	1988	177	3126	256	3540
29	3581	102	2494	178	3119	257	3303
30	2087	103	4760	180	2901	258	2323
31	4251	104	4968	181	2827	259	2229*/(BI Stoddart)
32	PJ Haseler	105	(AP Moulang)	182	1293/1760	260	4039
33	778	106	2513	183	3933/4794	261	2715*
34	3629*	107	(GO Avis)/2524*	184	1660	262	(DW Allison)
35	3600	108	3606	185	4699	263	(RN Turner)/3777*
36	4409	109	(MJ Botwinski)	186	2744	264	2806
37	(S MacArthur)/2556*	110	4913	187	3269	265	2243
38	4047*	111	4835	188	2775	266	(IA Davidson)/2200*
39	3427	112	4344	189	3401	267	2464
40	1788*	113	3158	190	2436	268	3475
41	RF Aldous	114	3791	191	2436	269	1853
42	4478	115	4887	192	3533	270	2346
43	1949	116	2124	193	2727	271	3101
44	(TB Sarjeant)	117	1386*/2751*/(KS Wells)	194	3544	272	(G Martin)/2426*
45	3574	118	2911	195	2115	273	(JH Fox)
46	2458/4786	119	4010	196	3266	274	4467
47	1435*	120	3197	198	1015	275	4819
48	4079	121	1316	199	(J Fuchs)	277	3587*
49	1797	122	4046	200	4226	278	3789
50	2632	123	4370	201	3433*	279	2856
51	4522	124	1530	202	3107	280	(M Strathern)
52	(CP Jeffery)	125	3317	203	3991	281	2812*/(RJ Harraway)
53	1763	126	3708	205	4768	282	3397
54	(R Jones)	127	(AJ Barnes)/3355*	206	3708	283	(DJ Maynard)/2880*
55	2801/3497*	128	2071	207	1974	284	1632
56	4337/2955*	129	2635	208	3641	285	3599
57	4288*	130	3398	209	3204	286	(JM Beattie)/2469*
58	4224	131	(WJ Dean)	210	2960*/4244	287	2268
59	(BT Spreckley)	132	2455	211	(GA Childs)/1222*	288	2808
60	(SH Marriott)	134	3295	212	4720	289	3902*
61	1262	135	3994	213	4165	290	3713
62	1514	136	793*/3273	214	2155*/(NS Jones)	291	3868
63	4850	137	(SJ Parsonage)/3861*	215	2937*/(MH Jones)	292	3988*
64	4222	138	2698	216	4326	294	(SC Foggin)/3751
65	(AK Lincoln)	139	1726	217	(RJ Clement)/1766*	295	(RM Hitchin)
66	4977	140	4631	218	2794*/3707	296	4737
67	1052	141	2625/3244	219	(CJ Ireland)/3770*	297	4050/2650*
68	3361	142	1629	221	4483	298	(G Lane)
69	3419	143	3298	222	1579	299	1913
70	(RJ Knight)	144	3837*/4489	223	2936	301	(KM Draper)/4630*
71	4956	145	(NL Jennings)	224	3627	302	3689
72	4979	146	1876	225	1336	303	(SG Olender)/1470*
73	4092*	147	2466	226	(DM Bellamy)/1662*	304	4230*/Z. Marcynski
74	2224	148	3683	227	2337*/(AT Farmer)	305	(AC De Tourtoulon)
				228	3549		

306	3981	405	3500	504	(NM Claiden)/1936*/4139*	604	2585/(PT Nash)
307	2251	406	3320	505	3975*	605	3820
308	3877	407	2153	506	4694	606	2802
309	(GF Fisher)/1533	408	2754*	507	3719	607	3898
310	4843	409	4959	508	1890*/(T. McKinley)	608	2157*
311	1359	410	(R Jones)	509	3924	609	3465
313	4170	411	3154	510	3171	610	2114
314	3339	413	2711	511	(BG Cooper)/2228*	611	3889
315	4066	414	4738	512	(AK Mitchell)	612	3542*
316	3879	415	1945	514	4738*	614	2162*
317	(P Bell)	417	(PM Dunster)/1756*	515	2228*/2788	615	4541
318	3198	418	1524*	517	1298	616	4414
319	2728	419	(ML Boxall)	518	3512*/(T. Busby)	617	1986
320	2378	420	4811	519	(AF Brind)/3375	618	4718
321	4232	422	1392	520	4943	619	1456
322	1860*	423	1850	521	(CM Greaves)	620	4353
323	2837	425	3714	522	3814	621	4791
324	2000	427	(PF Brice)	523	1983*	622	1671
325	4296	428	1844	524	3762*/(MY Haddon)	623	3223*
326	3631	429	(SM Sagun)/3780	525	1669	624	4213
327	1043	430	2756	526	4270	625	1684
328	3372	431	2702*	527	3261*/(P Shrosbree)	626	2821
329	4128	432	4315	528	4484	627	3236
331	1813	433	2193	529	(JA Tanner)	628	4628
332	3516	434	4428/G-OAPW*	530	(AA Maitland)/2597*	630	3706
333	3115	435	2826	531	2491*	631	3109
334	2327*/(AR Wilkinson)	437	2271*/(HA Schuricht)	532	1889	633	4967
335	3892	438	3723*	533	2353	634	3462
337	(PE Kettle)	440	2282*	535	1628*	636	2656*/4624
339	1722*/(LI Rigby)	441	4651	536	2041*	637	3717*/3937*
340	2868	442	1672	537	2490*/4379	638	2396*/(M Toon)
342	1732*	443	(RJ Whitaker)/2968*	538	3199*	641	3146
343	(IR Starfield)/1412*	444	2175	539	1854	642	2391*/(WJ Tolley)
345	2820	445	(JS Weston)	540	(MF Evans)/4820*	643	(GB Monslow)
346	(GG Pursey)/3831*	446	2959	541	2611	644	2565
347	1765	447	(N Whiteman)/2343*	542	2294	645	2580*/(BA Walker)
350	1348	448	2605*/(JF Beach)	543	4424	646	4871
351	1741	449	1538	544	(PW Copland)	647	2592*
352	1331*/4767	450	3747	546	3739	648	2340
353	2186	451	(CR Reese)/2870*	547	4685	649	3711
354	2472	452	2789	549	(A Towse)	650	1743
355	1852*/3834	453	1368*/2694	550	1818	651	4482
356	3805	456	2634	551	1987	652	2402*/(MA Fellis)
357	(MP Brooks)/1397*	458	1487	552	2553	653	1104*
359	(CC Watt)/4041*	459	3415	554	4790	655	4095
360	2180*	461	3388	555	(RM Fendt)	656	1836*/3445
362	1362*/1420*	462	4021*	556	(RG Wardell)/2300*	660	3554
364	4051	463	1201	558	1341	661	(JRW Kronfeld)
365	4019	464	(RA Robertson)/3133	560	4291	662	3588
366	1240	465	1288	561	4641*/(JA Hallam)	663	663*
367	2522	466	1688*	563	4062	664	3824
368	3337	467	3866*	564	3207	665	(JB Dalton)
369	3559	468	1858	565	4040	666	4776
370	3206/4789	469	4060*	566	1748	667	(RJ Strarup)/3821
371	2235*/3381	470	2640*	567	3596	668	3750
372	1393	471	1369	569	2673	669	3645
373	1428	473	3886	570	4455	671	3152
374	4324	474	1574	571	3151	672	(MJ Henegan)/2672
375	2283	475	1423	572	(AR Parker)	674	3400
376	(CJ Short)	476	4345	573	2499*/(J Farley)	675	1961
377	1290*/4775	477	1916	574	3424	676	4646
378	2196/(MD Saunders)	479	3443	575	1381*	677	1855
379	2906	480	3663/2289*	576	2504*	678	1810
380	1817*/4054*/(RJ Pirie)	481	2707	577	1546	679	1401
381	4032	483	(KS Whiteley)/2452*	579	(IM Young)/1785	680	2037
382	2979*	484	3448	580	2473*/(PG Bateman)	682	2990
383	2876*	485	(AM Booth)	581	(PT Worth)	683	1454
385	4168*	486	3895	583	3933/(D Nichols)	685	4450
386	4972	487	4130*	584	4249	686	(SJ Jenkins)/1312*
387	1769	488	3136	585	4082	687	3883
388	4674	490	(RT Starling)/2697*	586	2644	688	(L Dent)/2326
390	4134	491	(JW North)/2980*	588	2057*/2239*	691	1982
391	2184*/3785	492	G-BRRG*	590	2424*/2924	692	4080
392	2231	493	4169	591	3854	693	4106
393	4238	494	4553	592	2481	695	2025
394	3842	495	3470/3899*	593	2222	696	(ER Walker)/2778*
395	3139*	496	3808	594	2529	698	3283
396	4740	497	(AL Green)	595	(SW Bennett)	699	2357
397	3538	498	3479	597	1198	700	4986
398	3192	499	3209	598	4263*	701	3259
399	3322	500	2146*/4739	599	4068	702	1400
400	4815	`501	(AB Dickinson)	600	916*/2589	703	1727
402	1799	502	1802*/3946	601	4645	704	2376
404	1268	503	1902*/(NM Claiden)	602	1657	705	3393

706	1816	771	(GE Wick)/2816*	841	4429	918	1725
707	1752	772	3441	842	1822	919	4004
708	4065*	773	3134	843	3704	920	3155*/(K Neave)
709	1670	774	2092	844	2286	921	4355
710	(M Dowding)/2737*/4392	775	4252	845	(MK Field)	922	3710
711	(M Chant)	777	4359*	846	1562	924	1798
712	4258	778	3673	848	4103	925	3909
713	3306	779	3621	849	2706	927	3363
714	(RG Johnson)/2743*	780	3141	850	2480	928	3767
715	1383	781	4625/1308*	853	3515	930	4240
716	2059*	782	782	854	2899	933	4164/4557
717	4088	783	3944	855	3964*/(GO Humphries)	937	(J Williams)/1637*
718	2352*	785	3453	857	(PD Everett)/1568*	939	(RJ Williams)/2647*
719	2783	786	(MJ Crawley)/2537	858	(P Ryland)/1689	940	3921
720	3702	787	4448	859	1136*	941	(RJ Smith)
721	3156	788	2181	861	1295	942	3623
722	4838	789	1733	862	1519	943	2495*/(MJ Slade)
723	(N Climpson)/3618	790	4576	865	3993	944	3522
724	(RN Johnston)/1616*	791	1886	866	(HS Franks)	948	1630*
725	3686	795	3882	868	4534	949	(GJ Lyons)/3809*
727	3130*/(TP Docherty)	798	2329	869	2412	950	3302*/(WJ Palmer)
728	2444	799	(M Pagram)/1640	870	3904	951	2137*/(MJ Carruthers)
729	3801	800	(CA Marren)	871	4873	952	(DW Smith)/3437*
730	3939	801	3757	873	(C Osgood)/1801*	954	3610*/(MC Foreman)
732	2413*	802	4151	877	2354	955	2584
733	2429	803	3535	878	1433*/4894	957	2505
734	(FG Bradney)	805	4030	879	2408	959	2033
735	3887	806	3257	880	(TP Browning)	960	4394
737	2645	807	2555	881	2545	961	1598
739	(SR Stanwix)/1088*	808	1775*/3935*/5012	882	3870	962	4235*
741	1121	809	1123*	884	2174*	963	3954
742	2841	810	2423*	885	2401	968	2864
743	1615	811	2119	886	2445	969	3365
744	3291	812	1391*/(M Clarke)	888	3575	970	(P Harper-Little)/4008
745	2246	813	4660	890	2729	971	2417
746	(DP Holdcroft)	814	1476	891	2691	972	2350*
747	3910	815	(AB Laws)	893	2345	973	3410
748	3731*/(H MacLean)	818	1685	894	4782	977	2068*/4941
750	2596	819	4029	895	4175	978	1871
751	4164*/(C Ramshorn)	820	(SM Hall)/2604*	896	3760	979	3959
753	3525	821	2321	899	4547	980	(AG Kefford)/3585*
754	3827	822	3120	900	4200*/4831	982	1915
755	2438*	823	4362	902	2825	983	(SW Bradford)/2902*
757	2518	824	2129	904	2722	985	4009*
758	(J Nash)	826	1944	905	1419*	986	(P Winter)
759	2168*	827	4735	906	2084*/(WT Craig)	987	3227*/3271
760	985*/2366/3565*	828	2479	907	4425*	988	3457
761	1706	829	3822	909	2502	989	2164
762	4117	830	916	910	3856	990	2508
764	1570*	831	(L Bradford)	911	2382/4400	991	3858
765	2848*	832	1875	912	(FB Reilly)	992	2961
766	2379	833	4202	913	1536/4304	993	(JL Caton)
767	2090	837	1247	914	(J Archer)	994	1380
768	3590*	838	3956	915	2370	995	3468*
769	2172*	839	2515	916	(PI Fenner)/4356*	996	3180/(MN Erlund)
770	2291	840	3878*/(SJ Ayres)	917	(AI Galbraith)/1869*	997	3304

PART 4 – ALPHA / NUMERIC TAIL CODES

Code	Reg	Code	Reg	Code	Reg	Code	Reg
1Z	4878	C29	4012	G46	698	L13	3660
2A	(B Flewett)	C34	3997	G81	4380	L17	4703
2B	4374*	C64	4973	GA	4847	L18	4253
2C	(D Heslop)	C65	4974	GC	4780	L55	2652
2CS	2680	C74	4823	GG	4945	L57	3577
2F	4427*	CB	4668	GP	4816	L58	4192
2R	3159	CC	4494	GR	4420	L77	4665
2UP	4081*/4792	CD1	4802	H	2984	L88	4323
3D	4113	CF	1655	H1	4957	L99	1438
4T	4801	CJ	(M Wright)	H2	4558	L01	2770
5GC	4690	CL	4677	H3	4764	LA	4724
5U	(SK Armstrong)	CP	(LG Blows)/4814*	H4	4753*	LD	4347
6S	5004	CT	4870	H5	3285	LH7	4386
7D	3167*	CU	4493	H6	3478	LR	4889*
7H	4377	CW	2648	H8	4195	LS	4189
7Q	4364*	CZ	4659	H11	2552	LS1	(I Craigie)
7X	4741	D	2317	H12	3732	LS4	2908/4293
17K	4720	D1	4638	H20	3185	LS6	4119
20L	2740	D2	3262/4533	H23	(LBlick)/1189*	LS7	4452
27B	4876	D3	2667	H52	4866	LS8	4237
97Z	3961	D4	4444	HB	4481	LT	4538
A1	4155	D5	(DH Smith)	HB1	4461	LX	4376*
A2	3872	D7	4262	HL	4390	M	3205
A3	1943*	D8	(DS Lodge)	HS	4399	M2	4449
A7	4573	D9	(DJ Scholey)	IH4	(BTSpreckley)	M4	4368
A8	4596	D15	4158	IM	4415	M5	3638
A9	3885	D19	4048*	IV	3709	M6	(P Richer)
A10	3622	D31	(SA Young)/4210*	IZ	(see 1Z)*	M7	2939
A11	2385	D41	4464	J1	4935	M8	4278
A14	4316	D48	4653	J3	3632	M9	4904
A15	4177	D49	1734	J4	(PG Sheard)	M19	4793
A19	3390	D53	4772	J6	(CA Marren)	M25	4480
A20	4112	D54	4163	J8	4985	MB	4727
A23	(PR Redshaw)	D55	4763	J15	3106	MD	4704*
A25	3341	D64	4121	J45	2657	MF	(SR Ell)
A26	4322	D70	4146	J50	4824	MM	4969
A27	4422	DC	4405	JA	4016	MY	(Bristol & Glos GC)
A28	4936	DD	4300	JB	4749	N1	4443
A30	2126	DD2	(MR Smith)	JD	1483	N2	(R Murfitt)/3420*
A34	4531	DF	4806	JE	4822	N4	1914
A61	4318*	DH	3809	JG	(J Gorringe)	N5	4207
A77	4125*	DJ2	3352*	JH	4459	N6	3736*
A98	3438	DM	4868	JH1	4810	N8	4352
AB	4387	DR7	4647	JJ	4562	N11	2142
AC4	4812	DT	(RB Witter)	JM	4137	N12	4960
AC5	(S Kotomin)	DV8	(P Thelwall)	JO1	4544	N15	3548
AL	(AD Purnell)	DW	4465	JP	4713	N16	3657
AT	4725	E	285*	JS	4813	N19	4132
AV	(J Epple)	E1	4829	JT	4687	N21	673
AV8	4777	E2	4656	JW	(BC Morris)	N23	3772
AW	(A Warbrick)	E4	4895	K	2989	N25	4598
B	3366	E5	4769	K1	4340	N26	4056
B2	4385	E7	5003	K2	2147	N28	3482
B3	4373	E8	4505	K3	2689*	N29	3254
B9	(BO Marcham)	E11	4709	K4	4310	N36	3864*
B11	4342	EA	4981	K5	(RA King)/4338*	N51	2987
B12	4891*	EB	(J Rees)	K7	3682*	N52	1551*
B19	4728	EE	4932	K8	4549	N53	3782*
B20	4893	EN	4346	K11	4543	N54	1360*
B33	4147	EO	4862	K13	3656	N55	1118*/4883
B35	3728*	ET	1784	K17	1720*	N56	3505
B38	3593	EU	4516	K18	4173	NG1	4987
B96	1283	EW	4632	K21	4496	NH	4962
BA	4929	EZ	2168	KE	4451	NJ1	4844
BB	(MJ Wells)/3532	F	400*	KL	3960	NT	(N Toogood)
BD	4113*	F1	(AJ Clarke)/4452	KM	4305	NU	4953
BG	4940	F2	(DP Francis)/3918*	KR	4627	OP8	4534
BIT	4522	F3	4418	KS	(K Stewart)	OZ	(R Lynch)/4458
BJ	(JA Hallam)	F4	(JH Mare)/1367	KT	(KA Meadows)	P	3274
BK	(M Holmes)	F6	4827	KW	4426	P1	4567
BR	2487*	F11	3489	L	3163	P2	4442
BS	4912	F84	4719	L1	2770	P3	4363
BT	4507	FE	4787	L2	4508	P4	4648
BZ	1834	FF	4971	L3	4381	P5	4571
C	2191	FOX	4566	L4	4657	P9	2443
C1	(D Tagg)	FTI	3511	L5	3671	P10	4923
C3	4514	G1	4545	L8	4153	P12	4579*
C4	4186	G2	3315	L10	(CJ Davison)	P19	(G Hall)
C7	4404	G7	4329	L11	2785	P23	4615
C8	(C Bradley)	G41	4539	L12	3611	P30	4571

P31	4017	R53	4503	SA1	2986	V26	4976
P61	4343	R55	4470	SC	4654	V2C	4921
PB	4900	R56	4684*	SG1	4863	V2T	4664
PH1	4577	R57	4603	SG2	4906	VMC	4182*
PK	(Cairngorm GC)	R58	2873*	SH2	4800	VS	2420*
PM	3816	R59	4683	SH5	2893	VW	4521*
PM3	4723	R60	4584	SH6	4804	W1	3874
PW5	4311	R61	4633	SI	5002	W2	4695
PN	4943	R63	4622	SK1	4429	W4	(D Keith)
PS	3571	R67	4697	SM	4908	W5	4859
PT	4721	R69	4655	SP	4954	W7	4861
PW5	4311	R70	3015*	SR	(SC Rishton)	W8	4574
PZ	(IM Evans)	R71	3064	SSC	3909	W19	4410
Q5	3278	R73	4555	T1	(PH Turner)	W20	4860
R1	4475	R75	4604*	T2	4406	W22	4852
R2	4599	R77	4736	T3	4328	W54	4231
R3	4688	R80	4752*	T4	4817	WA1	4487
R4	4600	R88	4680*	T5	4301	WE4	4993
R5	4613	R91	2619*	T6	4881	X1	4783
R6	4788	R92	4707*	T7	4466	X3	(RM Fendt)
R7	4581	R93	2207*	T8	(PG Wright)	X5	4750
R8	4471	R95	4729*	T9	4561	X7	4330
R9	3216	RA	3946	T10	1612	X15	4785
R10	4590	RC	(RA Browne)	T12	(Norfolk GC)	X19	3846
R11	4896	RP1	4233	T15	1693	X50	4341
R17	4585	RW	4671	T27	4716	X96	2414
R18	4712	RY	4084	T34	2397	XL5	(SR Ell)
R19	4880	S	3642	T42	614	Y1	(MA Edmonds)/3416
R20	4578*	S1	4821	T45	873	Y2	4964
R21	4572	S2	4118	T49	1203	Y2K	4781
R22	4614	S3	3580	T51	1164	Y4	4280
R23	4629	S4	(BT Spreckley)	T54	3756	Y44	4853
R25	4587	S5	4299	T65	2800	Z	1873
R31	2533*	S6	4469	T99	4980	Z1	4961
R32	4675*	S7	2943*	TL2	4679	Z2	(P Wells)
R33	4582*	S8	4223	TS2	4937	Z3	4762
R35	2888*	S9	3472	U1	4335	Z4	3340
R36	4612*	S10	(BC Marsh)	U2	4131/2255*	Z6	3654*
R37	4636	S11	(M Geisen)	U9	4378	Z7	3640
R38	4837	S13	2425	UIM	4037	Z8	4190
R39	4601	S14	1572	V1	4546	Z9	4696
R40	4602*	S19	4580	V2	(R Jones)	Z10	4575
R41	4730*	S21	3698*/4383*	V2T	4664	Z11	1374
R43	4530*	S22	4191	V3	(PG Sheard)	Z12	4704
R44	2931*	S27	4834	V4	4460	Z19	4784
R45	4745*	S30	2380	V5	4034	Z22	4639
R46	4620*	S33	4710	V6	(M Nash)	Z25	2427
R48	4570	S60	4848	V7	2695	Z29	3727
R49	4621*	S81	3722	V8	4178 & 4982	Z35	(RG Parker)
R50	4691*	S82	4045	V11	4292	ZC	4256*
R51	4663*	S83	4268	V17	4758		
R52	4583*	SA	4669	V19	4058		

Notes:

(i)   Codes "SY" to "ZZ" are allocated to the Air Cadets Central Gliding School

(ii)   A few gliders wear foreign identities but without any nationality mark, namely: CCZV = BGA.4052, 1128 = BGA.2709 & 7827 = BGA.4161.

(iii) Some imported, or ex British civil and military, gliders still carry their previous marks. Known examples include:

D-1221	= BGA.2757	RA809	= BGA.1143	WT903	= BGA.3299
D-1265	= BGA.2276	TS291	= BGA.852	WT908	= BGA.3487
D-4667	= BGA.3142	VM687	= BGA.794	WT910	= BGA.3953
D-5084	= BGA.2688	WB920	= BGA.3221	WT913	= BGA.3239
D-6173	= BGA.4336	WB922	= BGA.4366	WZ819	= BGA.3498
D-8538	= BGA.2292	WB924	= BGA.3901	WZ828	= BGA.4421
G-ALRD	= BGA.416	WB926	= BGA.3520	XA229	= BGA.3379
G-ALRH	= BGA.629	WB943	= BGA.2941	XA240	= BGA.4556
G-ALRK	= BGA.490	WB962	= BGA.3836	XA302	= BGA.3786
G-ATRA	= BGA.1325	WB971	= BGA.3324	XE807	= BGA.3545
G285	= BGA.285	WB981	= BGA.1218	XN157	= BGA.3255
HB-474	= BGA.2474	WE992	= BGA.2692	XN185	= BGA.4077
OK-0927	= BGA.4286	WG498	= BGA.3245	XN187	= BGA.3903
OK-8592	= BGA.655	WT871	= BGA.3149	XN243	= BGA.3145
ZS-GFZ	= BGA.3210	WT898	= BGA.4412	XS652	= BGA.1107

SECTION 7

PART 1 – ALPHABETICAL TYPE INDEX (UNITED KINGDOM) – COVERS SECTIONS 1 & 4

Abingdon
GAS BALLOON
G-ATXR

ACRO
ADVANCED
G-BPAA

ADAM
RA.14 LOISIRS
G-BHIK

ADVANCED AIRSHIP CORPORATION
ANR-1
G-MAAC

ADVANCED TECHNOLOGIES INC
FIREBIRD CH1 ATI
G-BXZN
AT-10
G-OATG

AERIAL ARTS LTD including CYCLONE
110/130SX (wing)/ALPHA/AVENGER (combi)
G-MMSZ MMYL MMZI MNDE MNEK MNEL MNJV MNMY MNTT MNWL MNZS MVBC
CHASER
G-MNTD MNYD MNYE MNYF MTCP MTDD MTDE MVDK MVDL MVDN MVDP MVDR MVGA MVGF MVGG MVGH MMGJ MVHA MVHN MVID MVIE MVJF MVJG MVJH MVJI MVJJ MVJK MVKY MVKZ MVLA MMLB MVLC MVLD MVLE MVLF MVLG MVLH MVLS MVLT MVLW MVML MVMM MVOA MVOD MVOP MVRG MVRL MVSG MVSK MVTL MVTM MVUS MVUT MVVU MVYY MVZM MVZY MWGO MWWZ MWXW MWXX MWXY MWXZ MWYM MYBU MYCB MYEI MYEJ MYFO MYGI MYGK MYIL MYIT MYJO MYJW MYKD MYLJ MYMY MYSA MYSV MYWN MYWS MYYD MYZW MYZX MZCB MZTS

AERO COMMANDER INC
including ROCKWELL & GULFSTREAM production
500S SHRIKE
G-BDAL
680/685/690
G-AWOE OMAP

AERO DESIGNS
PULSAR
G-BSFA BTDR BTRF BTWY BUDI BUJL BULM BUOW BUSR BUYB BUZB BVJH BVSF BVTW BXDU BYJL CBLA CCBZ EPOX IIAN LEEN LUED LWNG MCMS NEVS OOXP RMAN WYNS XPXP

AERO DIFUSIÓN see JODEL

AERO DYNAMICS LTD
SPARROWHAWK
G-BOZU

AERO VODOCHODY see CZL/LET
L-29 DELFIN
G-BYCT BZNT DELF DLFN ODAT
L-39 ALBATROS
G-BZDI OALB OTAF
SB LIM-2
G-OMIG

AEROCAR including TAYLOR
MINI IMP
G-BLWW
SOOPER COOT
G-COOT

AERODYNE see RAVEN

AEROFAB see LAKE

AEROMERE see AVIAMILANO

AEROMOT INDUSTRIA MECANICO
AMT-200 SUPER XIMANGO
G-BWNY JTPC KHOM LLEW RFIO XMGO

AERONCA see CHAMPION
C-3/100
G-ADRR ADYS AEFT AESB AEVS AEXD
K
G-ONKA
11AC CHIEF/11CC SUPER CHIEF
G-AKTK AKUO AKVN BJEV BJNY BPRA BPRX BPXY BRCW BRFJ BRWR BRXF BRXL BSTC BTFL BTRI BTSR BUAB BUTF IIAC IVOR
15AC SEDAN
G-AREX
A65TAC/65C SUPER CHIEF/O-58B/L-3 GRASSHOPPER
G-BRHP BRPR BTRG BTUV

AEROPRAKT
A22 FOXBAT
G-CBGJ CBJH CBYH CCCE CHAD FBAT FOXB FXBT TADC

AEROSPACE DEVELOPMENTS
AD.500/Skyship 50
G-BECE BIHN

AÉROSPATIALE see AÉROSPATIALE, ALENIA, ATR, SOCATA
& SUD AVIATION & including EUROCOPTER production
AS332 SUPER PUMA
G-BKZE BKZG BLPM BLRY BLXR BMCW BMCX BRXU BUZD BWMG BWWI BWZX CHCF JSAR PUMA PUMB PUMD PUME PUMG PUMH PUMI PUMK PUML PUMM PUMN PUMO PUMS TIGB TIGC TIGE TIGF TIGG TIGH TIGI TIGJ TIGL TIGM TIGO TIGP TIGR TIGS TIGT TIGV TIGZ
AS350B ECUREUIL
G-BMAV BRVO BVJE BVXM BWFY BXGA BXNE BXNJ BXNY BXOG BXOK BXPG BXPJ BYZE BZVG CBHL COPT CWIZ DOIT DRHL EJOC FIBS FROH IANW IIPM JBBZ JOSS JTCM LHPL ODMC OGOA OOIO NUTY PLMB PLMH PROB RICC SCHI SMDJ TATS WHAM WHST WKRD XMEN
AS355 TWIN SQUIRREL
G-BOOV BPRI BPRJ BPRL BSTE BSYI BTIS BVLG BXBT BYPA BYZA BZGC BZVZ CAMB CCAO CPOL DANZ DOOZ ECOS EMAN EMHH EPOL FFRI FTWO GMPA GONN GRID HARO HEMH HOOT ICSG JARV JETU JPAL LCON LECA LENI LINE LOUN LUVY MOBI NAAS NMHS OASP OGRK OHCP OHMS OITN OLCP OROM ORMA OTSP PASF PASH REEM SASU SEPA SEPB SEPC SEWP SYPA TOPC TOPS WIRE WMPA XCEL
SA365 DAUPHIN 2
G-MLTY PLMI

AÉROSPATIALE/ALENIA
ATR-42
G-BUPS BVJP BXEH IONA KNNY ORFH TAWE ZAPJ
ATR-72
G-BVTJ BVTK BXTN BYTO BYTP UKTM UKTN

AEROSPORT
SCAMP
G-BKFL BKPB BOOW
WOODY PUSHER
G-AWWP AYVP BSFV SHUV

AEROSTAR SA see TED SMITH & YAKOVELEV

AEROTEC/AEROTEK INC see PITTS

AEROTECH see WHITTAKER

AESL see VICTA

AGUSTA S.p.A see BELL HELICOPTER
A109
G-BVCJ BWNZ BWZI BXIV BXWD BZEI DATE DPPH JERL JMXA MKSF MOMO OCMM PERI PWER RFDS SCOI SIVC SOHI TBGL TELY TGRA TVAA TVAC USTA USTB VIPH VMCO WEST

AHERNE
BARRACUDA
G-BZSV

AIR & SPACE
18A
  G-BVWK BVWL

AIR COMMAND MANUFACTURING
503 COMMANDER
  G-BMZA BOAS BOIK
532 ELITE/582 SPORT
  G-BOGV BOJF BOKF BOOJ BPAO BPGC BPPR BPPU BPRS BPUE BPUG
  BPUI BREM BRGO BRLB BRSP BSCB BSND BSRZ BTCB KENB OGTS TFRB
  URRR YROI

AIR CREATION
KISS 400/BUGGY
  G-BZXP CBEB CBJA CBJL CBKE CBKS CBLX CBMX CBNY CBRZ CBSX
  CHKN SNOG TRYK
ULTRAFLIGHT FUN 18 GT
  G-MYMM MYOL MYTZ MYUA MYVI MYXF

AIRBUS INDUSTRIE
A300
  G-CEAA CEAB CEXH CEXI CEXJ CEXK HLAA HLAB HLAB MAJS MONR
  MONS OJMR SWJW TTMC
A319
  G-CBTU EUOA EUOB EUOC EUOD EUOE EUOF EUOG EUOH EUOI EUOJ
  EUPA EUPB EUPC EUPB EUPC EUPD EUPE EUPF EUPG EUPH EUPJ EUPK
  EUPL EUPM EUPN EUPO EUPP EUPR EUPS EUPT EUPU EUPV EUPW
  EUPX EUPY EUPZ OMAK
A320
  G-BXKA BXKB BUSB BUSC BUSD BUSE BUSF BUSG BUSH BUSI BUSJ
  BUSK BXKC BXKD BYTH COEZ CRPH CVYD CVYE CVYG DJAR EUOK EUOL
  EUOM EUON EUOO EUOP EUOR EUOS EUOT EUOU EUOV EUOW EUOX
  EUOY EUOZ EUUA EUUB EUUC EUUD EUUE EUUF EUUG EUUH EUUI EUUJ
  EUUK EUUL EUUM EUUN EUUO EUUP EUUR EUUS EUUT EUUU EUUV
  FHAJ JDFW MEDA MEDB MEDD MEDE MEDH MIDK MIDP MIDR MIDS MIDT
  MIDU MIDV MIDW MIDX MIDY MIDZ MONW MONX MPCD OOAI OOAJ OOAP
  OOAR OOAU OOAW OOAX OUZO RDVE SSAS SUEE TICL TMDP TTOA
  TTOB TTOC TTOD TTOE TTOF TTOG TTOI TTOJ UNIH VCED VTAN
A321
  G-CTLA DHJH JSJX MEDF MEDG MIDA MIDC MIDE MIDF MIDH MIDI MIDJ
  MIDK MIDL MIDM MIDN MIDO MIDR MIDT MIDU NIKO OOAE OOAF OOAH
  OOAV OZBD OZBE OZBF TTIA TTIB TTIC VOLH YJBM
A330
  G-EOMA MDBD MLJL MOJO OJMB OJMC SMAN WWBB WWBC WWBD
  WWBM
A340
  G-VAEL VAIR VATL VBUS VEIL VELD VFAR VFLY VFOX VGOA VHOL VMEG
  VOGE VSEA VSHY VSKY VSUN

AIRCO
DH.2
  G-BFVH
DH.6
  G-EAML
DH.9
  G-EAQM

AIRMARK see CASSUTT
TSR.3
  G-AWIV

AIRSHIP INDUSTRIES see AEROSPACE DEVELOPMENTS

AIRSPEED LTD
AS.40 OXFORD
  G-AHTW AITB AITF
AS.57 AMBASSADOR
  G-ALZO

AIRSPEED
300 MLB
  G-FYGJ

AIRTOUR BALLOONS
Hot Air Balloons:
AH-31
  G-BKVY
AH-56
  G-BKVW BKVX BLVA BLVB BSGH BWPL OAFC
AH-77
  G-BLYT BOBH IVAC OAAC

AIRWAVE GLIDERS LTD
MERLIN (wing)
  G-MMIJ
NIMROD (wing)
  G-MBCX MBJG MBJL MNIW MNZY

ALON INC see ERCOUPE

ALLPORT
MLB variants
  G-BJIA BJSS

AMD-BA see DASSAULT

AMERICAN AEROLIGHTS including ELECTRAFLYER
EAGLE/DOUBLE EAGLE
  G-MBCU MBEP MBFS MBHE MBJD MBJK MBKY MBNK MBRB MBRD MBRS
  MBWE MBZV MJAE MJBL MJBV MJCX MJEO MJNM MJNO MMTV

AMERICAN BLIMP CORPN
A-60+ AIRSHIP
  G-OLEL TLEL

AMERICAN AVIATION CORPN see GRUMMAN-AMERICAN

AMETHYST BALLOONS
AX6 srs.
  G-BFLP

AMF MICROFLIGHT LTD
CHEVVRON
  G-MNFL MTFG MVGC MVGD MVGE MVIP MVOO MVUO MVVV MVXX MVZZ
  MWNO MWNP MWPW MWRZ MWUI MWZB MYYP MZDP MZFH

ANDERSON
EA-1 KINGFISHER AMPHIBIAN
  G-BUTE BXBC

ANDREASSON including CROSBY
BA.4B
  G-AWPZ AYFV BEBS BFXF JEDS YPSY

ANEC
II
  G-EBJO
IV MISSEL THRUSH
  G-FBPI

ARBITER SERVICES
TRIKE
  G-MNWL

ARKLE see MITCHELL

ARMSTRONG-WHITWORTH AIRCRAFT see GLOSTER
SEAHAWK
  G-JETH
AW.650 ARGOSY
  G-APRL BEOZ

ARROW AIRCRAFT (LEEDS) LTD
ACTIVE
  G-ABVE

ARROWFLIGHT LTD see CGS

ARV AVIATION LTD
ARV1 SUPER 2
  G-BMOK BMWE BMWF BMWM BNGV BNGW BNGY BNHB BNHD BNHE BNVI
  BOGK BPMX BSRK BWBZ COWS DEXP ERMO OARV ORIX OTAL POOL
  STWO TARV XARV YARV ZARV

AUSTER AIRCRAFT LTD including TAYLORCRAFT production
PLUS C/D
  G-AHCR AHGW AHGZ AHSD AHUG AHWJ AHXE AIXA
Model E III
  G-AHLK AREI BUDL
Model G/H 4/5/5D/ALPHA 5
  G-AGLK AIKE AJGJ AJXC AJXV AJXY AKOW AKSY AKSZ AKWS AKWT AKXP
  ALBJ ALBK ALFA ALNV ALXZ ALYB ALYG AMVD ANFU ANHR ANHS ANHU
  ANHW ANHX ANIE ANIJ ANRP AOCP AOCR AOCU AOFJ AOVW APAF APAH
  APBE APBW APRF APTU BDFX BICD BXKX

J/1 AUTOCRAT/J/1N ALPHA & KINGSLAND/CROFTON SPECIAL
G-AGTO AGTT AGVN AGXN AGXU AGXV AGYD AGYK AGYT AHAL AHAM
AHAP AHAT AHAU AHAV AHCK AHCL AHHH AHHT AHSO AHSP AHSS AHST
AIBH AIBM AIBR AIBW AIBX AIBY AIFZ AIGD AIGF AIGR AIGT AIGU AIJI AIPV
AIRC AIZU AIZW AIZY AJAE AJAJ AJAS AJEB AJEE AJEH AJEM AJIH AJIS
AJIT AJIU AJIW AJRB AJRC AJRE AJUD AJUE AJUL AJYB AMTM APIK APJZ
APKM APKN APTR ARRL ARUY BLPG BRKC BVGT GINO JAYI OJAS OSTA
TENT
J/1B AIGLET
G-AMKU ARBM
J/1U WORKMASTER
G-AGVG APMH APSR
J/2 ARROW
G-AJAM BEAH
J/4
G-AIJK BIJM BIJT BIPR
J/5B/G/P/V AUTOCAR
G-AOFM AOHZ AOIY APUW ARKG ARLY ARNB ARUG ASFK AXMN
J/5F/K/L AIGLET TRAINER
G-AMMS AMRF AMTA AMYD AMZI AMZT AMZU AOFS APVG
J/5Q/R ALPINE
G-ANXC AOGV AOZL APCB
6A/AOP.6/TUGMASTER
G-ARGB RGI ARHM ARIH ARRX ARXU ARYD ASNB ASOC ASTI BKXP BNGE
AOP.9/11/BEAGLE E.3
G-ASCC AVHT AVXY AXRR AXWA AYUA AZBU BDFH BGKT BGTC BKVK
BUCI BWKK BXON
B.4
G-AMKL
B.8 AGRICOLA
G-CBOA

AUTOMOBILOVE ZAVODY MRAZ
M.1 SOKOL
G-AIXN

AVENGER
MLB variants
G-BHMJ BHMK BIGR BIPW BIRL

AVIA
FL.3
G-AGFT

AVIAMILANO SRL including AEROMERE, LAVERDA& SEQUOIA production
F.8L FALCO
G-BVDP BWYO BYLL CWAG FALC FALO GANE KYNG LMOCAD OCDS
ORJW PDGG REEC RJAM
F.14 NIBBIO
G-OWYN

AVIASUD ENGINEERING SA
MISTRAL
G-MGAG MVSJ MVUP MVWW MVWZ MVXN MVXV MVZR MWIB MYSL MZJB

AVID AIRCRAFT INC
AVID FLYER/SPEEDWING/AEROBAT
G-BSPW BTGL BTHU BTKG BTMS BTNP BTRC BUFV BUIR BUJJ BUJV BULC
BULY BUON BUZE BUZM-BVAA BVBR BVBV BVFO BVHT BVIV BVLW BVSN
BVYX BWLW BWRC BWZD BXNA CURV EFRY ELKS FOLD IJAC IMPY LAPN
LORT OVID OZEE PILL SPAM

AVIONS MAURICE BROCHET see BROCHET

AVIONS MAX HOLSTE see MAX HOLSTE

AVIONS MUDRY ET CIE see CAARP & MUDRY

AVIONS PIERRE ROBIN see ROBIN

AVRO AIRCRAFT LTD see ENGLISH ELECTRIC & HAWKER

A V ROE & CO LTD including HSA & BAe production
TRIPLANE - *see ROE*
504K/L
G-EASD EBJE EBNU
G-ABAA ADEV
534 BABY
G-EACQ
581/594 AVIAN
G-EBOV, EBZM
G-ACGT

621 TUTOR
G-AHSA
652A ANSON/NINETEEN
G-AGPG AGWE AHKX AMDA APHV AVVO AWRS AWSA AYWA BFIR VROE
683 LANCASTER
G-ASXX BVBP LANC
685 YORK
G-AGNV ANTK
694 LINCOLN
G-APRJ
698 VULCAN
G-BLMC VJET VLCN VULC
748
G-ARAY ATMI ATMJ AVXI AVXJ AYIM BEJD BGMN BGMO BIUV BORM BVOU
BVOV CLEW OJEM OPFW ORAL ORCP OSOE OTBA SOEI

AVRO (CANADA)
CF-100 CANUCK
G-BCYK

BA see BRITISH KLEMM & KLEMM
EAGLE 2
G-AFAX
SWALLOW 2
G-ADPS AFCL AFGC AFGD AFGE

BAC including KRONFELD & PROCTOR
DRONE
G-ADPJ AEDB
L.25 SWALLOW
G-ACXE

BAC-SUD see BRITISH AIRCRAFT CORPORATION & AÉROSPATIALE

BAE SYSTEMS (OPERATIONS) LTD including
BRITISH AEROSPACE plc, BRITISH AEROSPACE (REGIONAL AIRCRAFT) Ltd, HANDLEY-
PAGE & SCOTTISH AVIATION production
JETSTREAM variants to Srs.32
G-AXUM BBYM BKUY BLKP BRGN BTXG BUIO BURU BUTW BUUZ BUVC
BUVD BWWW BXLM BYMA BYRA BYRM BYYI BZYP CBCS CBDA CBEA
CBEP CBER EEST IJYS JSSD JURA LOVB NFLC OAKJ OEST PLAH PLAJ
UIST
JETSTREAM Srs.41 variants
G-BWUI GCJL JMAC MAJA MAJB MAJC MAJD MAJE MAJF MAJG MAJH MAJI
MAJJ MAJK MAJL MAJM MSKJ
ATP/JETSTREAM 61
G-BTNI BTPA BTPC BTPD BTPE BTPF BTPG BTPJ BTPK BTPL BTPN BTTO
BTUE BTZG BTZH BTZK BUKJ BUUP BUUR BUWM BUWP CORP MANA
MANB MANC MANE MANF MANG MANH MANJ MANL MANM MANO MANP
MANU MAUD OBWP OBWR OEDJ PLXI WISS
146 (including Avro variants)
G-BKMN BLRA BPNT BSNR BSXZ BTNU BTTP BTUY BTVO BVCE BXAR
BXAS BZAT BZAU BZAV BZAW BZAX CBAE CBFL CBMF CBMG CBMH CBXY
CFAA CFAB CFAC CFAD CFAE CFAF CFAH CLHD DEBE DEFK DEFL DEFM
FLTA FLTB GNTZ IRJX JEAJ JEAK JEAM JEAO JEAS JEAT JEAU JEAV JEAW
JEAX JEAY JEBA JEBB JEBC JEBD JEBE LUXE MABR MANS MIMA NBAA
NJIC NJIE OFOA OFOM OINV ORJX OZRH TBAE TBIC UKAC UKAG UKHP
UKID UKRC UKSC ZAPK ZAPL ZAPN ZAPO

(THE) BALLOON WORKS
FIREFLY 7
G-CBPG

BARKER
CHARADE
G-CBUN

BARNES
AVON (Trike)
G-MJGO

BARNETT ROTORCRAFT
BARNETT J4B
G-BRVR BRVS BWCW

BAT
FK-23 BANTAM
G-EACN

BEAGLE AIRCRAFT LTD
A.109 AIREDALE
G-ARNP AROJ ARRO ARXB ARXC ARXD ARYZ ARZS ASAI ASBH ASBY
ASRK ASWB ASWF ATCC AVKP AWGA

B.121 PUP
G-AVDF AVLM AVLN AVZN AVZP AWKM AWKO AWVC AWWE AWYJ AWYO AXCX AXDU AXDV AXDW AXEV AXHO AXIA AXIE AXIF AXJH AXJI AXJJ AXJO AXMW AXMX AXNL AXNM AXNN AXNP AXNR AXNS AXOJ AXOZ AXPA AXPB AXPC AXPM AXPN AXSC AXSD AXUA AZCK AZCL AZCN AZCP AZCT AZCU AZCV AZCZ AZDA AZDG AZEU AZEV AZEW AZEY AZFA AZGF AZSW BAKW BASP BDCO IPUP JIMB OPUP PUPP TSKY
B.206
G-ARRM ATDD BSET HRHI FLYP

BEAGLE-AUSTER AIRCRAFT LTD
A.61 TERRIER
G-ARLP ARLR ARNO ARSL ARTM ARUI ASAJ ASAK ASAN ASAX ASBU ASCD ASDK ASDL ASKJ ASMZ ASOI ASOM ASUI ASYG ASZE ASZX ATBU ATDN ATHU AVYK AYDX TIMG
D.4
G-ARLG
D.5 HUSKEY
G-ASNC ATCD ATMH AVSR AWSW AXBF
D.6
G-ARCS ARDJ

BEDE see BROOKMOOR BEDE AIRCRAFT

BEECH AIRCRAFT CORPORATION
17 TRAVELER/UC-43
G-BRVE BUXU
18/3NM, 3TM & C-45
G-ASUG AYAH BKGL BKGM BKRN BSZC
23/24 MUSKETEER/SUNDOWNER/SIERRA
G-ASJO ASWP ATBI AWFZ AWTS AWTV AYYU BAHO BARH BASN BBSB BBSC BBTY BBVJ BUXN BYDG CBCY BZPG GUCK TAMS
33 DEBONAIR/33 BONANZA
G-BGSW BTHW BTZA COLA ENSI GRYZ HOPE JUST MOAC OAHC VICM
35 BONANZA/("V" tail)
G-APTY ARKJ ARZN ASJL ATSR BBTS BONZ EHMJ NEWT REST VTAL
36 BONANZA
G-BMYD BSEY JLHS LOLA MAPR ORSP POPA ZLOJ
55/56/58 BARON
G-ASOH AWAH AWAJ AYPD AZDK AZXA BFLZ BLJM BLKY BMLM BNBY BNUN BNVZ BTFT BWRP BXDF BXNG BXPM BYDY BZIT DAFY FABM FLAK FLTZ IOCO MOSS OLYD OSDI RICK SUZI UROP VCML WOOD WWIZ
60 DUKE
G-IASL
65/70/80 QUEEN AIR
G-AVDS KEAB KEAC TUBS WJPN
76 DUCHESS
G-BGHP BGRG BGVH BIMZ BMJT BNTT BNUO BNYO BODX BOFC BRPU BXHD BXMH BXWA BXXT BYNY BZNN BZOY BZPJ BZRT CBBF GBSL GCCL JLRW OADY OBLC OPAT TRAN WACI WACJ
90 KING AIR
G-BMKD DEXY ERAD SHAM WELL
95 TRAVEL AIR
G-ASMF ASYJ ATRC
200/300/350 SUPER KING AIR
G-BGRE BPPM BVMA BYCK BYCP BZNE CEGP CEGR CLOW FPLA FPLB FPLD FRYI HAMA IMGL KMCD KVIP MAMD MOUN OMNH OWAX REBK ROWN SBAS SPOR VSBC WRCF ZAPT

BELL
MLB
G-BITY

BELL HELICOPTER TEXTRON INC including AGUSTA, BELL HELICOPTER CO, BELL HELICOPTER TEXTRON CANADA & WESTLAND production
47D/G (WESTLAND)
G-ARXH ASOL AXKO AXKS AXKX AXKY BAXS BBRI BEGA BFEF BFYI BGID BGMU BGZK BHAR BHBE BHNV BLGR BPAI CHOP CIGY GGTT MASH SOLH XTUN
47H/47J (AGUSTA-BELL)
G-ASLR ATFV AZYB BFPP EURA
206A/206B JETRANGER I/II/III
G-AVII AVSZ AYMW BAML BARP BBCA BBNG BBOR BODH BEWY BKEW BKZI BLGV BLZN BNYD BOLO BOTM BPWI BSBW BTFX BTFY BTHY BUZZ BVGA BWZW BXAY BXDS BXKL BXLI BXNS BXNT BXRY BXUF BYBA BYBC BYBI BYSE BZEE BZNI CCLY CLAY CODE COIN CORN CORT CPTS CTPW CVIP DNCN DOFY DORB ELLI FINS FOXM GAND GSJH GUST HANY HEBE HELE HMPH HMPT HMSS HPAD HSDW HSLB IBIG INVU JAHL JBDB JETX JLEE JWBI JWLS LILY MCPI MFMF MILI MOTA NEWS NEWZ OAMG OAMI OBAM OBAY OBYT OCST OETI OFCH OMDR OMEC ONOW OOHO OOOW ONTV ONYX OSMD OYST PEAK PORT RAMI RAMY RIAN RJTT RKEL RNBW RNME SCOO SDCI SELY SPEY SPYI STER STOX SUEZ TBAH TGRZ TILI TOYZ TREE TUCH UEST WGAL WHAZ WIZZ WLLY XXIV ZAPH

206L LONG RANGER
G-CBXD ELIT EYLE EYRE IANG JGBI LEEZ NEUF OHHI OLDN PWIT RCOM VOLK
212
G-BCMC BGLJ BFER BIXV BJGV
214ST SUPER TRANSPORT
G-BKFN
222
G-NOIR OWCG
407
G-DCDB GAJW
412EP
G-CBST CBUB CBVP CBWT CBXN CBYR
UH-1H IROQUOIS
G-HUEY

BELLANCA-AIRCRAFT CORPORATION see CHAMPION
17-30 SUPER VIKING
G-VIKE

BENSEN AIRCRAFT CORPORATION including CAMPBELL-BENSEN & MONTGOMERIE-BENSEN
B.7/B.8 GYROCOPTER
G-APUD ARTJ ASCT ASME ASWN ASYP ATLP ATOZ AWDW AWPY AXBG AZAZ BCGB BGIO BHEM BHKE BIFN BIGP BIGU BIHX BIPY BIVK BIZT BJAO BJSU BKBS BKUS BLLA BLLB BMBW BMOT BMYF BMZW BNBU BNJL BOUV BOWZ BOZW BPCV BPIF BPNN BPOO BPSK BPTV BRBS BRCF BREA BREU BRFW BRHL BRXN BSBX BSJB BSMG BSMX BSNL BSNY BSPJ BSZM BTAH BTBL BTFW BTIG BTJN BTJS BTST BTTD BUJK BUPF BVAZ BVIF BVJF BVKJ BVMG BVPX BWAH BWEY BWJN BWSZ BXCL BYTS BZID BZJR CBFW CBNX CBSV HAGS JOEL OOJC OTIM SCUD YJET YROS YROY

BEST OFF
SKYRANGER 912)
G-CBIV CBVR CBVS CBWL CBWW CBXS CCAF CCBA CCBG CCBJ CCCK CCDH CRAB LDAH OSKR SOPH

BETTS
TB.1
G-BVUG

BINDER AVIATIK GmbH see PIEL

BIRDMAN ENTERPRISES LTD
WT-11 CHINOOK
G-MMKE

BLACKBURN AEROPLANE & MOTOR CO LTD
B.2
G-ADFV AEBJ
MONOPLANE
G-AANI

BLAKE
BLUETIT
G-BXIY

BLERIOT
XI
G-AANG BPVE BWRH LOTI

BOEING AIRCRAFT CO including BOEING COMPANY
B-17G FLYING FORTRESS
G-BEDF
B-29 SUPERFORTRESS
G-BHDK
707-300 srs.
G-AYAG
707-400 srs.
G-APFG APFJ
727-200 srs.
G-BNNI BPND OKJN
737-200 srs.
G-BYYF BYYK BZKP CEAC CEAD CEAE CEAF CEAG CEAH CEAI CEAJ
737-300 srs.
G-BYZJ BZZA BZZB BZZE BZZF BZZG BZZH BZZI BZZJ CELS CELU CELV CELX ECAS EZYB EZYC EZYD EZYF EZYG EZYH EZYI EZYJ EZYK EZYL EZYP EZYR EZYT IGOA IGOB IGOC IGOE IGOF IGOG IGOH IGOI IGOJ IGOK IGOL IGOM IGOO IGOP IGOR IGOS IGOT IGOU IGOV IGOW IGOX IGOY IGOZ LGTE LGTF LGTG LGTH LGTI LGTJ LGTK LGTL OBWZ ODSK ODUS OFRA OGBB OGBC OGBD OGBE OHAJ OJTW OMUC STRA STRB XBHX XMAN ZAPM

737-400 srs.
G-BSNV BSNW BUHK BVNM BVNN BVNO DOCA DOCB DOCD DOCE DOCF DOCG DOCH DOCI DOCL DOCM DOCN DOCO DOCP DOCR DOCS DOCT DOCU DOCV DOCW DOCX DOCY DOCZ GBTA GBTB OBMM

737-500 srs.
G-BVKA BVKB BVKC BVKD BVZE BVZG BVZH BVZI GFFA GFFB GFFC GFFD GFFE GFFF GFFG GFFH GFFI GFFJ

737-700 srs.
G-EZJA EZJB EZJC EZJD EZJE EZJF EZJG EZJH EZJI EZJJ EZJK EZJL EZJM EZJN EZJO EZJP EZJR EZJS EZJT EZJU EZJV EZJW EZJX EZJY EZJZ EOSLH STRC STRD

737-800 srs.
G-OBBJ OBMP XLAA XLAB XLAC XLAD XLAE XLAF XLAG XLAH

747-200 srs.
G-BDXB BDXE BDXF BDXG BDXH BDXI BDXJ BDXN BDXO GAFX INTL VCAT VIBE VPUF VRUM VZZZ

747-400 srs.
G-BNLA BNLB BNLC BNLD BNLE BNLF BNLG BNLI BNLJ BNLK BNLL BNLM BNLN BNLO BNLP BNLR BNLS BNLT BNLU BNLV BNLW BNLX BNLY BNLZ BYGA BYGB BYGC BYGD BYGE BYGF BYGG CIVA CIVB CIVC CIVD CIVE CIVF CIVG CIVH CIVI CIVJ CIVK CIVL CIVM CIVN CIVO CIVP CIVR CIVS CIVT CIVU CIVV CIVW CIVX CIVY CIVZ GSSA GSSB VAST VBIG VFAB VGAL VHOT VLIP VROM VROS VROY VTOP VWOW VXLG

757-200 srs.
G-BIKC BIKF BIKG BIKI BIKJ BIKK BIKM BIKN BIKO BIKR BIKS BIKT BIKU BIKV BIKW BIKY BIKZ BMRA BMRB BMRC BMRD BMRE BMRF BMRH BMRI BMRJ BPEC BPED BPEE BPEF BPEI BPEJ BYAD BYAE BYAF BYAH BYAI BYAJ BYAK BYAL BYAN BYAO BYAP BYAS BYAT BYAU BYAW BYAX BYAY CDUO CDUP CPEL CPEL CPEM CPEN CPEO CPEP CPER CPES CPET CPEU CPEV DAJB FCLA FCLB FCLC FCLD FCLE FCLF FCLG FCLH FCLI FCLJ FCLK JALC JMAA JMAB JMCD JMCE JMCF LCRC MCEA MONB MONC MOND MONE MONJ MONK CCMY OOBA OOBB OOBC OOBD OOBE OOOB OOOC OOOD OOOG OOOI OOOJ OOOK OOOM OOOS OOOU OOOX OOOY OOOZ PIDS RJGR WJAN ZAPU

767-200 srs.
G-BYAA BYAB

767-300 srs.
G-BNWA BNWB BNWC BNWD BNWH BNWI BNWM BNWN BNWO BNWR BNWS BNWT BNWU BNWV BNWW BNWX BNWY BNWZ BRIF BRIG BZHA BZHB BZHC DAJC DIMB OBYB OBYC OBYE OBYG OBYH OBYI OBYJ OOAM OOAN SJMC UKLI

777-200 srs.
G-RAES VIIA VIIB VIIC VIID VIIE VIIF VIIG VIIH VIIJ VIIK VIIL VIIM VIIN VIIO VIIP VIIR VIIS VIIT VIIU VIIV VIIX VIIY VIIZ YMMA YMMB YMMC YMMD YMME YMMF YMMG YMMH YMMI YMMJ YMMK YMML YMMM YMMN YMMO YMMP ZZZA ZZZB ZZZC

BOEING AIRPLANE CO
75 KAYDET/N2S/PT-13/PT-17 STEARMAN:
G-AROY AWLO AZLE BAVO BIXN BNIW BRHB BRSK BRTK BRUJ BSDS BSGR BSWC BTFG ERIX IIIG ILLE ISDN NZSS RJAH

BOLAND
52 HAB
G-BYMW

BÖLKOW including MALMO & MBB production
Bö.207
G-EFTE
Bö.208 JUNIOR
G-ASFR ASZD ATDO ATRI ATSI ATSX ATTR ATUI ATVX AVKR AVLO AVZI BIJD BSME CLEM ECGO
Bö.209 MONSUN
G-AYPE AZBB AZDD AZOA AZOB AZRA AZTA AZVA AZVB BLRD

BOMBARDIER INC including CANADAIR production
CL604 CHALLENGER
G-POAJ REYS
CRJ 200 REGIONAL JET
G-ELNX JECA JECB JECC JECD MSKK MSKR MSKS MSKT MSKU MSKV
CRJ 700 REGIONAL JET
G-MRSG MRSH MRSI MRSJ MRSK
BD-700 GLOBAL EXPRESS
G-LOBL

BONSALL
DB-1 MUSTANG
G-BDWM

BOWERS
FLY BABY
G-BFRD BNPV BUYU

BRADSHAW
HAB-76
G-AXXP

BRANDLI
BX-2 CHERRY
G-BXUX

BRANTLY HELICOPTER CORPORATION
B.2
G-ASHD ASXD ATFG AVIP AWDU BPIJ OAPR OMAX ROTR
305
G-ASXF

BREMNER see MITCHELL WING

BRIGHTON
Ax7-65 HAB
G-AVTL AWJB

BRISTOL AEROPLANE CO LTD
BOXKITE
G-ASPP
BABE
G-EASQ
F.2B FIGHTER
G-AANM ACAA AEPH
M.1C REP
G-BLWM BWJM
105 BULLDOG
G-ABBB
149 BOLINGBROKE (BLENHEIM)
G-BPIV MKIV
156 BEAUFIGHTER
G-DINT
171 SYCAMORE
G-ALSX HAPR
173
G-ALBN
175 BRITANNIA
G-ANCF AOVS AOVT
192 BELVEDERE
G-BRMB

BRITISH AIRCRAFT CORPN/AÈROSPATIALE
CONCORDE
G-AXDN BBDG BOAA BOAB BOAC BOAD BOAE BOAF BOAG SSST

BRITISH AIRCRAFT CORPORATION (BAC) see HUNTING
ONE-ELEVEN
G-ASYD AVMJ AVMK AVMN AVMO AVMP AVMS AVMT AVMU AVMY AVMZ AWYV AZMF MAAH OBWD

BRITTEN
SHERIFF
G-FRJB

BRITTEN-NORMAN LTD including FAIREY BRITTEN-NORMAN LTD, IRMA & PILATUS (BN-2) production
BN.1F
G-ALZE
BN.2A/B/T ISLANDER/DEFENDER
G-AWNT AXHE AXUB AXZK AYRU BCEN BCWO BCZS BDPU BEEG BELF BFNU BIIP BJOP BJWO BLDV BLNJ BLNL BOMG BPCA BPLR BSWR BUBN BVFK BVHX BVHY BVSJ BVSL BWPM BWPR BWPV BWPW BWPX BWYZ BWZF CHES CHEZ CIAS ISLA GMPB JSAT JSPC LEAP MAFF NESU ORED OSEA PASV RAPA RLON SBUS SJCH SSKY SURV WOTG XAXA
BN.2A/III TRISLANDER
G-AZLJ BBYO BDOT BDTN BDTO BEDP BEVR BEVT BEVV FTSE JOEY LCOC OJAV PCAM RBCI WEAC XTOR

BROCHET
MB.50 PIPISTRELLE
G-AVKB
MB.84
G-AYVT

BROOKLAND
HORNET
G-BRPP MIKE PHIL
MOSQUITO
G-AWIF

BROOKLANDS AIRCRAFT CO see OPTICA

BROOKMOOR BEDE AIRCRAFT
BD-4
  G-BEKL BKZV BOPD BYLS
BD-5
  G-BCLV BCOX BGLB BJPI BYFH

BRÜGGER
MB.2/MB.3 COLIBRI
  G-BKCI BKRH BNDP BNDT BPBP BRWV BSUJ BUDW BUTY BVIS BVVN BXVS HRLM KARA PRAG

BÜCKER including CASA & DORNIER production
Bü.131 JUNGMANN (CASA 1.131)
  G-BECT BECW BEDA BHPL BHSL BIRI BJAL BPDM BPTS BPVW BRSH BSAJ BSFB BSLH BTDT BTDZ BUCC BUCK BUOR BUTA BUVN BUVP BVPD BWHP BXBD BYIJ BZJV BZVS CBCE CDRU DUDS EHBJ EMJA JGMN JUNG RETA TAFF WIBS
Bü.133 JUNGMEISTER
  G-AEZX AXMT AYSJ BSZN BUKK BUTX BVXJ BZTJ TAFI
Bü 181 BESTMANN
  G-CBKB

BUSHBY-LONG see LOEHLE
MIDGET MUSTANG
  G-AWIR BDGA MIDG

BYRNE
ODYSSEY 4000 MLB
  G-BCFE

CAARP including AVIONS MUDRY, CAP AVIATION & PIEL production
CAP.10
  G-BECZ BKCX BLVK BRDD BXBK BXBU BXFE BXRA BXRB BXRC BYFY CAPI CAPX CPZC CZCZ GDTU LORN MOZZ ODIN RIFN SLEA WIXI
CAP.20/21
  G-BIPO BPPS

CAB see GARDAN

CALL AIRCRAFT CO see IMCO

CAMBRIDGE HOT-AIR BALLOONING ASSOCIATION
HAB
  G-BBGZ

CAMERON BALLOONS LTD see CAMERON-COLT & CAMERON-THUNDER
Gas Airship:
DG-19
  G-BKIK
Gas Balloons:
R-15
  G-CICI
R-36
  G-ROZY
R-42
  G-BLIO
R-77
  G-BUFA BUFC BUFE
R-150
  G-BVUO
Gas/Hot Air Balloon
RN-9
  G-BVOG
Hot Air Airships:
Zero 25
  G-BMUR
DP-50
  G-BMEZ
DP-70
  G-BNXG-BPFF BRDT
DP-80
  G-BTBR UPPY VIBA
D-96
  G-BAMK BEPZ
Hot Air Balloons:
20 variants
  G-BIBS BJUV BOYO BPRU BRCJ BRCO
24 srs.
  G-BSCK BVCY

31 variants
  G-BEJK BEUY BGHS BKIX BMST BPUB BRMT BVFB BZYR CBIH CBLN COOP LEAU NOMO PRTT RBMV TOHS
34 variants
  G-BRKL BRWY BUCB BVZX BYNW BZBT EZER FZZI IAMP OBLU RAPP
42 variants
  G-BZER BCDL BISH BKNB BMWU BPHD BUPP BVLC BWEE BWGX BXJH BXTG BYRK CCAY HOPI SKOT
56 variants
  G-AZKK BBYU BCOJ BDPK BDSF BDUI BDUZ BDYH BECK BEEH BELX BEND BENN BERT BEXX BEXZ BFAB BFFT BFKL BFME BGLX BGOI BGUY BHGF BHSN BICU BKRS BKZF BNIF BOWM BRIR BRSA BTHZ BUVG BYSL BZKK HOFM HOOV LENN OVET SWPR WAAC WYNT
65 variants
  G-AZIP AZUP AZUV AZXB BAOW BAYC BBGR BBYR BCAP BCFN BCRI BDFG BDRK BDSK BEIF BETP BGJU BHKH BHNC BHND BHOT BHOU BIBO BIGL BIGY BIWK BIWU BIYI BJAW BJWJ BJZA BKGR BKJT BKWR BKXX BLEP BLJF BLZB BMCD BMJN BMKY BMPD BMVW BMYJ BNAN BNAU BNAW BOAL BOOB BOWV BPGD BPPA BPXF BREH BRMI BROE BROG BSAS BSGP BTUH BWBA BWHB BWHG BXGY BXUU BYZL GLUE HENS KAFE MUIR NATX OERX PMAM PYRO RUDD SMIG WELS
77 variants
  G-BAXF BBCK BBOC BCNP BCRE BCZO BDBI BDCU BDSE BEEI BEPO BFUG BFYK BGAZ BGHV BHDV BHHB BHHK BHHN BHII BHYO BIDU BIEF BIET BJGK BKNP BKPN BKTR BKWW BKZB BLFY BLIP BLJH BLLD BLPP BLSH BLXF BLZS BMAD BMCK BMKJ BMKP BMKW BMLJ BMLW BMOH BMPP BMTN BMTX BMZB BNCB BNCJ BNDN BNDV BNEO BNES BNFG BNFO BNGJ BNGN BNHI BNIN BNIU BNJG BNKT BNMA BNMG BNNC BNNE BNPE BNTW BNTZ BNUC BOAU BOBR BOEK BOFF BOGP BOJB BOJD BOJU BOOZ BORB BORN BOSV BOTW BOVV BOWB BOWL BOXG BOYS BOZN BPBU BPBV BPBY BPDF BPDG BPHH BPHJ BPLF BPLV BPPP BPSH BPSR BPTD BPVC BPVM BPWC BPYI BPYS BPYT BPYV BRAJ BRBO BRFE BRFO BRHC BRIE BRKW BRLX BRMU BRMV BRNW BROB BRRF BRRO BRRR BRRW BRTV BRUE BRUV BRZA BRZT BSBI BSBM BSBR BSDX BSEV BSGY BSHO BSHT BSIC BSIJ BSLI BSKD BSMS BSUV BSWV BSWY BSXM BTAG BTIX BTJH BTKZ BTOI BTOP BTPT BTRX BTWJ BTWM BTWX BTZV BUAF BUAM BUDU BUEV BUGD BUGP BUGS BUHM BUNG BUOX BUPI BUTJ BUWU BUWY BUZK BVBS BVBU BVDR BVFF BVHK BVLI BVMF BVUK BVXB BWAJ BWAN BWHC BWKV BWPB BWPC BWTJ BWYN BXAX BXSX BXTJ BXVT BYBN BYHY BYLY BYNJ BYRF BZPU BZPW CBHX CBKV CCAR CEJA CGOD CHOK CHUK CRAK CTGR CXHK DASU DRYI EIIR ENNY EPDI ERIK FABB FELT FUZY GEES GEEZ GEUP GUNS HARE HENY HORN HOST JLMW KEYY KODA KTEE LAZR LEGO LEND LEXI LIDD LIOT LOAG LOAN LOLL LUBE MAMO MILE MOFF MOKE MRTY NWPR OATH OCND OEDP OHSA OJEN OKYA OMRB ONZO ORPR PADI POLY PUSS PVCU RAPH RCMF RONI SAFE SAIX SCAH SCFO SKIL SNOW SUCH SUSI TECK TUDR UPUP ULIA VODA VOLT WAIT WELI XSKY ZUMP ZZAG
84 srs.
  G-AYAJ AYJZ AYVA AZBH AZDF AZNT AZRN AZSP BZVT BAAX BAGY BAKO BALD BAND BAST BBLL BCEZ BNET BNFP BNXR BOWU BOYM BRGD BSKE BSKU BSMK BUYN BVXD BWLN KEYB MOSY
90 variants
  G-BMFU BMJZ BNII BOOP BPSO BPUJ BROH BROY BRPJ BRZC BSCA BSNJ BSSO BSWX BTBP BTCM BTFU BTHF BTJU BTNJ BTTB BTTL BTWV BTXF BUAJ BUFJ BUFX BUGY BUIE BUIU BUIZ BUOE BUUO BUVW BVBX BVDX BVEJ BVFP BVHO BVHR BVKV BVMR BVOC BVOP BVPK BVTN BWAU BWBC BWDU BWIP BWJI BWNO BWNS BWPT BWUU BWVU BWYC BXAM BXCS BXJO BXVV BYDT BYHC BYIU BYJC BYKX BYMY BYNN BYOK BYOX BYTW BYZX BZFD BZIX BZJH BZKX BZLJ BZMX BZOX BZRU BZTK BZOU BZXR BZYW BZYY CBAT CBED CBJI CBJK CBKK CBUO CCBBCOMP CONC CPSF CTEL CXCX DHLB DIAL DRYS ELLE FBNW FOGG GLAW GOCX GOGW HBUG IBLU IGEL IGLE INSR ITOI IWON JULU LAGR LTSB MANI MFLI MOFZ OJBM OJBW OXBY PATG PERC PKCC PRIT PRNT RISE RIZE RIZI SBIZ SIAM SLII SORT SRVO STRM SWEB TANK TEDF TEEL TETI TINS TMCC VRVI YUMM YUPI YVET
100 srs.
  G-NPWR
105 variants
  G-BAVU BMEE BMOV BMVI BNFN BOTD BOTK BPBW BPJE BRFR BRLL BRZB BSNZ BTEA BTFM BTIZ BTKW BTPB BTRL BTOU BUAV BUHU BULD BUPT BUWF BVCA BVEU BVHV BVNR BVUA BVXA BWDH BWEW BWKF BWOW BWPZ BWRY BWSU BXBM BXBR BXBY BXEN BXGC BXXG BXXL BYFJ BYHU BYIL BYMX BYNX BYPD BZDJ BZKU BZVU BZXO CAMP CBEC CBHW CBMC CBNW CITR CLIC DRGN ELEE ENRY FOWS GFAB HONK JOSH JSON KSKS LOSI MHBD NPNP NYLB NZGL OAML OJBS OUCH OUVI SAXO SDLW SEPT SFSL SSTI SUCK ULTR VSGE WNGS YLYB
120 variants
  G-BNEX BOBB BOHL BOZY BPSS BPTX BPZK BRXA BSRD BSYB BTEE BTKN BTUU BTXS BUDV BUFT BURN BVSO BVXF BWAG BWKD BWLD BWYS BXVJ BXWI BYSV CBFF CBMK CBOW CBVV FLOA GHIA HOTT LOBO MEUP MOFB OMFG TING VIKY VALZ
133 srs.
  G-BWAA BZVE CBUW
140 variants
  G-AZUW BVPU BVYU BWTE FLTG OXBC

145 srs.
G-DENT HIBM
160 variants
G- BPCN BPLE BRIM BYHW CBHD TGAS
165 srs.
G-BIAZ
180 variants
G-BPPJ BRTH BRVC BRZI BSWD BSWZ BSYD BSZY BTCW BTYE BUAU BUJR BUKC BVKL BWBR BWHW BXMM OBRY RWHC SKYR SVBF
200 srs.
G-BXOS BZJU
210 srs.
G-BTXV BUEE BUHY BUOC BVBN BWZK BXBA BXJC BXNM BXRM BXZG BXZH BYDI BYJV BYMG BYSM BZBE BZXF CBFY CBKX CVBF FLYE JOJO LGLG LPGI ORGY RPBM SKYU SKYX YTUK
250 srs.
G-BUBR BUXE BUXR BUZY BVIG BVYR BWKU BWKX BWZJ BXPK BYHX BYYD BZIK HIUP LORA MOLI OBUN ODEB OVBF SCRU SKYY STPI
275 srs.
G-BWML BXIC BXKJ BXMW BXTE BXYL BYSK BYZG BZTE BZTT CBZZ SKYK TCAS
300 srs.
G-BZSU CBAW SIMI
315 srs.
G-BZNU
340 srs.
G-BZUO KVBF KYBF RANG
375 srs.
G-BWNH
400 srs.
G-ZVBF
CONCEPT srs.
C-60
G-BTZU BVDM BVDY BWRT BXJZ CBJS CBVD ROGY
C-70
G-BXOT BYJX BZEK CBKP
C-80
G-BUYC BVEK BVEN BVGJ BVSV BVSW BVUU BVWE BVZN BWAO BWGP BXJP BXLG BXSC BXSJ BYER BYJJ BYTJ BZMV BZPK CBEY EVET MCAP NMOS OARG OBTS OGJM ONIX RMAX SLCE UPHL
C-90
G-CBLU CBRV

SPECIAL SHAPES

SHAPE	REGISTRATION(S)
ACTION MAN PARACHUTIST	G-RIPS
APPLE	G-BWSO
BALL	G-RNIE
BEER BARREL	G-PINT
BEER CAN	G-IBET
BEETHOVEN BUST	G-BNJU
BELLS WHISKY BOTTLE	G-BUUU
BELLOWS	G-BIUL
BENIHANA	G-BMVS
BERENTZEN BOTTLE	G-KORN
BERTIE BASSETT	G-BXAL BZTS
BIERKRUG	G-BXFY
BOWLER	G-OPKF
BRADFORD AND BINGLEY	G-BWMY
BUDWEISER CAN	G-BPFJ
BULB	G-BVWI
BULL	G-BZOH CBON
BUS	G-BUSS
CADBURY'S CARAMEL BUNNY	G-BUNI
CADBURY'S CRÈME EGG	G-OEGG
CAN	G-BXPR G-OFIZ
CARROTS	G-BWSP HUCH
CART	G-BYDU
CHAMPION SPARK PLUG	G-BETF
CHATEAU DE BALLEROY	G-BTCZ
CHESTIE	G-USMC
CHICK	G-BYEI
CLUB	G-BWNP
COCA COLA BOTTLE	G-BXSA BYIV BYIW BYIX
COOLING TOWER	G-WATT
COTTAGE	G-COTT
DOLL	G-BVDF
DOUGLAS LURPAK BUTTERMAN	G-BXCK
DUDE	G-OIFM
EAGLE	G-BVMJ
ELEPHANT	G-BLRW BMKX BPRC
EXPANSION JOINT	G-BIUL

FABERGE EGG	G-BNFK
FIRE EXTINGUISHER	G-BZJA
FILM CASSETTE	G-PHOT
FLAME	G-CBIU
FORBES' MAGAZINE	G-BPOV
FURNESS BUILDING	G-BSIO
GOLFBALL	G-ORFE PUTT
GOLLY	G-OLLI
GRAND ILLUSION	G-MAGC
HARLEY DAVIDSON MOTORCYCLE	G-BMUN
HELIX OILCAN	G-HLIX
HOFMEISTER LAGER BEAR	G-HEYY
HOME SPECIAL	G-BWZP
ICE CREAM CONE	G-BZTL
JAGUAR XK8 SPORTS CAR	G-OXKB
KATALOG	G-OTTO
KOOKABURRA	G-CHKL
KP CHOC DIPS TUB	G-DIPI
LIGHTBULB	G-BVWH LAMP
LIPS	G-LIPS
MACAW	G-BRWZ
MICKEY MOUSE	G-MOUS
MONSTER TRUCK	G-BWMU
MUG	G-RMUG
N ELE	G-WBMG
OIL CAN	G-UNIP
OTTI	G-OTTI
PERRIER BOTTLE	G-PERR
PIG	G-HOGS
POT	G-CHAM
PRINTER	G-BYFK
ROBINSON'S BARLEY WATER	G-BKES
RUPERT BEAR	G-BTML
RUSSIAN DOLL	G-USSR
SAMSUNG COMPUTER	G-SEUK
SANTA MARIA SHIP	G-BPSP
SATURN	G-DREX
SAUCER	G-GUFO
SCOTTISH PIPER	G-PIPY
SIGN	G-UCCC
SONIC THE HEDGEHOG	G-SEGA
SPARKASSE BOX	G-BXKH
SPHERE	G-BVFU BYJW IBBC SATL
STRAWBERRY	G-BXTF SAMI
SUGAR BOX	G-BZDX BZDY BZKR
TEMPLE	G-BMWN
TENNENT'S LAGER GLASS	G-BTSL
THOMAS	G-BXND
TISSUE PACK	G-LOOS
TRAINER'S SHOE	G-BUDN
TRUCK	G-BLDL DERV
TV	G-TVTV
UNCLE SAM	G-USAM
VAN	G-ORAC
WITCH	G-WYCH
WINE BOX	G-STOW

CAMPBELL AIRCRAFT including BENSEN & EVERETT production
COUGAR
G-BAPS
CRICKET
G-AXPZ AXRC AXVM AYCC AYPZ BHBA BKVS BORG BRLF BSRL BTEI BTMP BUIG BVDJ BVIT BVLD BVOH BWSD BWUA BWUZ BXCJ BXHU BXUA BYMO BYMP BZKN CBWN GYRO RUGS

CARLSON
SPARROW
G-BSUX BVVB

CASA see BUCKER *(1.131)*, HEINKEL *(2.111)* & JUNKERS *(C.352L)*

CASSUTT including MUSSO/SPECIAL
RACER
G-BDTW BEUN BNJZ BOMB BOXW BPVO BUFK BXMF CXDZ FRAY NARO OGPN RUNT

CAUDRON
G.III
G-AETA

CCF see HAWKER & NORTH AMERICAN

CEA see JODEL/ROBIN

CENTRAIR
MOTO-DELTA
G-MBPJ

CESSNA AIRCRAFT COMPANY including REIMS AVIATION SA production
(F.prefix)

C.165 AIRMASTER
G-BTDE

120/140
G-AHRO AJJS AJJT AKTS AKUR AKVM ALOD ALTO ANGK BHLW BJML BOCI
BPHW BPHX BPKO BPUU BPWD BPZB BRJC BRPE BRPF BRPG BRPH
BRUN BRXH BSUH BTBV BTBW BTEW BTOS BTVG BTYW BTYX BUHO
BUHZ BUJM BVUZ BYCD GAWA HALJ JOLY OVFM

150
G-APXY APZR ARFI ARFO ARSB ASMS ASMU ASMW ASST ASUE ASYP
ASZB ASZU ATEF ATHV ATHZ ATKF ATMC ATML ATMM ATMN ATMY ATNE
ATNL ATRK ATRM ATUF ATYM ATZY AVAA AVAR AVCU AVEM AVEN AVER
AVGU AVHM AVIA AVIB AVIT AVJE AVMD AVMF AVNC AVPH AVUG AVUH
AVVL AVVX AVZU AWAW AWAX AWBX AWCM AWCP AWES AWFF AWGK
AWLA AWMT AWOT AWPJ AWPP AWPU AWRK AWTJ AWTX AWUG AWUJ
AWUK AWUL AWUN AWUO AWUT AWUU AXGG AXPF AYBD AYGC AYKL
AYRF AZLH AZLY AZLZ AZXC BABB BABC BABH BAEU BAHI BAIK BAIP
BAMC BAXU BAXV BAYO BAYP BAZS BBBC BBCI BBDT BBJX BBKA BBKB
BBKE BBKY BBNJ BBTT BBTZ BCBX BCCC BCRT BCUH BCUJ BCZN BDBU
BDFJ BDFZ BDOD BDSL BDTX BDUM BDUO BDZC BEIG BELT BEOK BEWP
BFFY BFGW BFIY BFOG BFSR BFVU BFWL BGBI BGEA BGOJ BHIY BIFY
BIOC BJOV BLVS BMBB BMLX BMXJ BNFI BOBV BOIV BOMN BORY BOTP
BOUJ BOUZ BOVS BOVT BPAB BPAW BPAX BPCJ BPEM BPGY BPGZ BPNA
BPOS BPWG BPWM BPWN BRBH BRJT BRLR BRNC BRTJ BSBZ BSEJ BSJU
BSJZ BSKA BSSB BSYV BSYW BSZU BSZV BTES BTGP BTHE BTSN BTTE
BTYC BUCS BUCT BUGG BUNS BURH BWGU BWII BWVL BZTE CSBM CSFC
DENA DENB DENC DEND ECBH EJMG FAYE FFEN FINA GBLR GCNZ GFLY
GLED HCFB HFCI HIVE HULL IANJ JHAC JWDS LFSF LUCK MABE NSTG
OIDW OJVH OKED OSTY PHAA PLAN SADE SALL SAMZ SCAT TAIL UFLY
WYMP YIII

A150 AEROBAT
G-AXRT AXRU AXSW AXUF AYCF AYOZ AYRO AZID AZJY AZLL AZOZ AZUZ
BACC BACN BABD BACO BACP BAEP BAEV BAEZ BAII BAIN BAOP BAPI
BAPJ BBEO BBKF BBKU BBNY BBTB BBTK BBXB BCDY BCFR BCKU BCKV
BCUY BCVG BCVH BDAI BDEX BDOW BDRD BEIA BEKN BEMY BEOE BEOY
BFGG BFGX BFGZ BFIE BFRR BHRH BIBN BJTB BLPH BMEX BOFW BOFX
BOYU BPJW BTFS BUCA BUTT CLUB FMSG HFCA JAGS OISO OPIC OSND

152
G-BFEK BFFC BFFE BFFW BFHT BFHU BFHV BFKH BFLU BFOE BFOF
BGAA BGAB BGAD BGAE BGFX BGGO BGGP BGHI BGIB BGLG BGNT BHAA
BHAI BHAV BHCP BHCX BHDM BHDR BHDS BHDW BHEC BHFC BHFI
BHHG BHIN BHSA BHPY BHRB BHRM BHRN BHSA BHUI BHWA BHWB
BHYX BHZH BICG BIDH BIJV BIJW BIJX BILR BILS BIOK BIOM BITF BITH
BIUM BIXH BIZG BJKY BJNF BJVJ BJVT BJWH BJYD BKAZ BKFC BKGW
BKTV BKWY BLJO BLWV BLZE BLZH BLZP BMCN BMFZ BMGD BMJC
BMJD BMMM BMSU BMTA BMTB BMTJ BMVB BMXA BMXB BMXC BMXX
BNAJ BNDO BNFR BNFS BNHJ BNHK BNID BNIV BNJB BNJC BNJD BNJH
BNKC BNKI BNKP BNKR BNKS BNKV BNMC BNMD BNME BNMF BNNR
BNOZ BNPY BNPZ BNRK BNRL BNSI BNSM BNSN BNSU BNSV BNUL BNUS
BNUT BNXC BNYL BNYN BOAI BODO BOFL BOFM BOGC BOGG BOHI BOHJ
BOIO BOIP BOIR BOKY BOLV BOLW BONW BOOI BORI BORJ BORO BOTG
BOYL BOZR BPBG BPBJ BPBK BPEO BPFZ BPGM BPHT BPIO BPJL BPME
BPTF BPTU BRBP BRND BRNE BRNK BRNN BRPV BRTD BRTP BRUA BSCP
BSCZ BSDO BSDP BSFP BSFR BSRC BSTO BSTP BSWH BSZI BSZO BSZW
BTAL BTCE BTDW BTFC BTGH BTGR BTGW BTGX BTIK BTVW BTVX BTYT
BUEF BUEG BVTM BWEU BWEV BWNB BWNC BWND BXGE BXJM BXTB
BXVB BXVY BXWC BXYU BYFA BYMH BYMJ BZAE BZEB BZED BZSW
CHIK CPFC CWFY DACF DRAG ENTT ENTW FIGA FIGB HART HFCL HFCT
IAFT IBRO IRAN KATT LAMS LSMI MASS OAFT OBEN ODAC OFRY OIMC
OLEE OPAM OPJC OSFC OVMC OWAC OWAK OWFS OWOW PFSL RICH
SACB SACF SHAH TAYS WACB WACE WACF WACG WACT

A152 AEROBAT
G-BFGL BFKF BFMK BFRV BFZN BFZT BFZU BGAF BGLN BHAC BHAD
BHED BHEN BHMG BHMH BIHE BILJ BIMT BLAC BLAX BMUO BMYG BOPX
BOSO BOYB BRCD BRUM BZEA FIFE FLAP FLIP JEET JONI LEIC MPBH
OCPC RLFI TFCI WACH WACU WALS ZOOL

170
G-AORB APVS AWOU BCLS

172/SKYHAWK
G-ARID ARMO ARMR AROA ARWH ARWO ARWR ARYI ARYK ARYS ARZE
ASFA ASIB ASMJ ASNW ASOK ASSS ASUP ASVM ASWL ATAF ATFX ATFY
ATGO ATKT ATKU ATLM ATSL ATWJ AVEC AVHH AVIC AVJF AVKG
AVTP AVVC AVZV AWGD AWLF AWMP AWUX AWUZ AWVA AXBH AXBJ
AXDI AXSI AXVB AYCT AYRG AYRT AYUV AZJV AZKW AZKZ AZLM AZLV
AZTK AZTS AZUM AZXD AZZV BAAL BAEO BAEY BAIW BAIX BANX BAOB
BAOS BAVB BAXY BAZT BBDH BBJY BBJZ BBKI BBKZ BBNZ BBOA BBTG
BBTH BCCD BCEC BCHK BCOL BCPK BCRB BCUF BCVJ BCYR BCZM BDCE
BDNU BDZD BEHV BEMB BENK BEUX BEWR BEZK BEZO BEZR BEZV BFGD

BFKB BFMX BFOV BFPH BFPM BFRS BFTH BFTX BFZV BGAG BGBR BGHJ
BGIU BGIY BGLO BGMP BGND BGRO BGSV BHAW BHCC BHCM BHDX
BHDZ BHIH BHMI BHPZ BHSB BHUG BHUJ BHVR BHYP BHYR BIBW BIDF
BIGJ BIHI BIIB BIIE BING BIOB BITM BIZF BJDE BJDW BJGY BJVM BJWI
BJWW BJXZ BKCE BKEP BKEV BKII BKIJ BKLO BLHJ BLVW BMCI BMHS
BMIG BMTS BNKD BNKE BNRR BNST BNTP BNXD BNYM BOEN BOHN BOIL
BOIX BOIY BOJR BOJS BOLI BOLX BOLY BOMS BOMT BONO BONR BONS
BOOL BORW BOUE BOUF BOVG BOYP BPML BPRM BPTL BPVA BPVY
BPWS BRAK BRBI BRBJ BRCM BRWX BRZS BSCR BSEP BSNG BSOG
BSOO BSPE BSTM BTMA BTMR BTRE BUAN BUJN BULH BUOJ BURD BUZN
BWJP BXGV BXHG BXOI BXSD BXSE BXSM BXSR BXXK BYBD BYEA BYEB
BYES BYET BYNA BZBF BZKB BZZD BZGH BZPM CBFO CBME CBOR CBXJ
CCCC CFLY CLUX COCO CSCS CURR DCKK DEMH DENR DODD DRAM
DRBG DUVL ECGC EGEG ENII ENNK ENOA EOFM ETDC FACE FNLD FNLY
GBFF GBLP GRAY GWYN GYAV GZDO HERC HILS ICOM IZSS IZZY JFWI-
JMKE JONE JONZ LANE LAVE LENX LICK MALK MELT MFAC MICK MILA
OBMS OFCM OOLE OPFT OPYE ORMG OSII OSKY OTAM OVFR OZOO PDSI
PLBI RARB ROOK ROUP RSWO RUIA SACD SBAE SEVE SEXI SHSP SKAN
TAAL TAIT TASH TOBI TOBY TRIO TYRE UFCA UFCB UFCC UFCD UFCE
UFCF WACL WACM WACW WACY WACZ YORK YSPY ZACE

172RG CUTLASS
G-BHYC BILU BIXI PARI

FR172 HAWK/REIMS ROCKET
G-AWCN AWDR AWWU AWYB AXBU AYGX AYJW BARC BBKG BBXH BCTK
BDOE BEZS BFFZ BFIG BFIU BFSS BHYD BLPF BPCI BPWR BTMK BZVB
DAVD DIVA EDTO FANL JANS LOYA MFEF OMAC PJTM STAY THIN YBAA
YIPI

175/SKYLARK
G-ARCV ARFG ARFL ARML ARMN AROC ARRG ARRI ARUZ ARWS OTOW

177(RG) CARDINAL
G-AYPG AYPH AYSX AYSY AZTF AZTW AZVP BAGN BAIS BAJA BAJB BAJE
BBHI BBJV BCUW BEBN BFIV BFMH BPSL BRDO BRPS BTSZ BUJE FIJJ
LNYS OAMP TOTO

180/SKYWAGON
G-ARAT ASIT AXZO BETG BNCS BOIA BTSM BUPG DAPH

182/SKYLANE variants
G-ARAW ASRR ASSF ASXZ ATCX ATLA ATPT ATTD AVCV AVDA AVGY AVID
AXNX AXZU AYOW AYWD AZNO BAAT BAFL BAHD BAHX BAMJ BBGX BBYH
BBYS BCWB BDBJ BDIG BEKO BFOD BFSA BFZD BGAJ BGFH BGPA BHDP
BHIB BHIC BHVP BHYA BJVH BKHJ BKKN BKKO BLEW BMMK BMUD BNMO
BNOX BNRY BOPH BOTH BOWO BPUM BRKR BRRK BSDW BSRR BTHA
BUVO BWMC BWRR BXEZ BXZM BYEM BZVF BZVO CCAN CBIL CBMP CBVX
DATG DOVE DRGS EEZS EIRE EIWT EOHL GCYC GHOW GUMS HRNT HUFF
IATU IBZS IFAB IOPT IRPC ISEH IZZI JBRN JENI JOON KWAX LEGG LVES
MICI MILN MISH NLEE NOCK OBBO OCJW OHAC OJRM OLDG OLDX OPCG
OPST ORAY OTRG OWCS OWRT OZOI PDHJ PLEE POWL PUGS RACY
ROWE SAAM SKYL THRE TPSL VIPA WARP WIFE WMLT XLTG ZBLT

185 SKYWAGON/AG CARRYALL
G-AYNN BBEX BDKC BKPC BLOS BWWF BXRH BYBP RNRM

(T)188 AG WAGON/AG TRUCK/AG HUSKY
G-AZZG

190/195
G-BSPK BTBJ

205
G-ASNK ASOX

206 SUPER SKYLANE/SUPER SKYWAGON/STATIONAIR
G-ASVN ATCE ATLT AWUA AYCJ AZRZ BAGV BFCT BGED BGWR BMHC
BMOF BOFD BPGE BRID BSMB BSUE BXDB BXRO BYIC CTFF DROP EESE
MGMG SEAI SKYE STAT

207 SKYWAGON/STATIONAIR 8
G-NJAG PARA

208/B (GRAND) CARAVAN
G-BZAH EELS EORD ETHY ZOBA

210 CENTURION
G-ASXR BBRY BENF BEYV BNZM BSGT BVZM DECK IKIS MANT MPRL
OFLY PIIX SEEK VMDE

T303 CRUSADER
G-BSPF CRUZ CYLS DOLY GAME IKAP INDC JUIN OAPE PTWB PUSI ROCH
SOAY UILT

305 BIRD DOG (L-19)
G-PDOG

310
G-APNJ ARCI AVDB AXLG AYGB AYND AZRR AZUY AZYM BALN BARG
BARV BBBX BBXL BCTJ BGTT BHEH BIFA BJMR BKSB BMMC BODY BPIL
BRIA BTFF BTYK BWYE BWYG BWYH BXUY BXYG EGEE EGLT FFWD FISH
IMLI MIWS MPBI ODLY OGTX REDB REDD RIST RODD SOUL TKPZ TROP
VDIR

335
G-FITZ

336 SKYMASTER
G-PIXS

337 SUPER SKYMASTER
G-ATCU ATSM AXHA AZKO AZLO BCBZ BFGH BFJR BMJR BOWDBOYR
BTVV HIVA NYTE RGEN

340
G-BISJ BVES FEBE LAST LIZA OPLB PUFN REEN SAMM VAUN
401/402
G-AVKN AWWW AZFR AZRD BXJA DACC EYES MAPP NOSE ROAR
404 TITAN/AMBASSADOR/COURIER
G-BWLF BYLR EXEX MIND OOSI TASK TVIP
406 CARAVAN II
G-BVJT DFLT LEAF MAFA MAFB SFPA SFPB SURF TWIG
414/CHANCELLOR
G-DYNE SMJJ
421/GOLDEN EAGLE
G-BAGO BBUJ BDYF BDZU BFTT BHKJ BKNA BLST CSNA CJEA FTAX GILT
HASI HIJK JACK KWLI MUVG OSCH RLMC SAIR TAMY TREC UVIP VVIP
425/441 CONQUEST I/II
G-BNDY FPLC FRAX
500/501 CITATION 1
G-CITI DJAE LOFT OEJA ORHE ORJB
525 CITATIONJET
G-BVCM CJAD GRGG HMMV IUAN OWRC RSCJ ZIZI
550/CITATION BRAVO/551 CITATION II
G-BJIR CBTU EJEL ESTA FIRM FCDB FJET FLVU GHPG JETC JETJ ORDB
RDBS RVHT SPUR VUEA
560 CITATION EXCEL/ULTRA
G-CBRG CFRA CJAE KDMA NETA REDS RIBV SIRS TTFN XLMB
650 CITATION III
G-HNRY

CFM METAL-FAX
(STREAK) SHADOW
G-BONP BROI BRSO BRWP BRZZ BSMN BSOR BSPL BSRX BSSV BTDD
BTEL BTGT BTKP BTZZ BUGM BUIL BULJ BUOB BUTB BUVX BUWR BUXC
BVDT BVFR BVLF BVOR BVPY BVTD BWAI BWCA BWOZ BWPS BXFK BXVD
BXWR BXZV BXZY BYAZ BYCI BYFI BYOO BZDF BZEZ BZLF BZMZ BZWJ
BZWY CAIN CBCZ CBGI CBNO DARK DMWW ENEE FAME GORE HLCF
LYNK MEOW MGGT MGPH MGTW MGUY MJVF MMWT MNCM MNER MNIS
MNTK MNTP MNVJ MNVK MNWK MNWY MNXX MNZJ MNZP MNZR MNZZ
MTBE MTCA MTCT MTDU MTDX MTFU MTFZ MTGN MTGV MTGW MTHS
MTHT MTHV MTKR MTMX MTMY MTSG MTTH MTWH MTWK MTWL MTWN
MTXR MVAC MVAM MVAN MVBB MVCC MVCW MVEI MVEN MVFH MVHD
MVIG MVLJ MVLP MVOH MVPK MVRE MVRO MVRP MVRR MVRT MVVT
MVYZ MWAE MWDB MWDN MWEN MWEZ MWFB MWIZ MWJF MWJJ MWLD
MWMU MWON MWOW MWPN MWPP MWRL MWRY MWSZ MWTJ MWTN
MWTP MWUA MWVG MWVH MWYD MYBC MYBL MYCM MYDD MYDE MYEP
MYGO MYIF MYIP MYKE MYLV MYNA MYNX MYOH MYON MYOS MYPL
MYPT MYSM MYTH MYTY MYUS MYWF MYWM MYZP MZBE MZBN
MZBS MZCT MZGS MZKH MZRS MZLO MZLP MZNH MZOM ODVB OLGA
OPIT ORAF OTCH PBEL PSUE RINT ROTS RZPH SHIM SNEV STRK TEHL
THAI TTOY WESX WHOG WYAT

CGS including ARROWFLIGHT
HAWK
G-MWYS MYTP MZGU

CHAMPION including AERONCA & BELLANCA production
7AC/7DC CHAMPION
G-AJON AKTO AKTR AOEH ATHK AVDT AWVN BGWV BPFM BPGK BRAR
BRCV BRER BRFI BRWA BRXG BTGM BTNO BTRH BUYE BVCS CHMP
HAMP JTYE LEVI OTOE TECC
7BCM (L-16)
G-BFAF TIMP
7FC TRI-TRAVELER
G-APYT ARAS
CITABRIA/DECATHLON/SCOUT
G-AYXU BBEN BBXY BDBH BFHP BGGA BGGB BGGC BGGD BITA BIZW
BKBP BOID BOLG BOTO BPMM BRJW BSLW BTXX BUGE BVLT CIDD EXPL
HUNI IGLZ

CHANCE-VOUGHT see VOUGHT

CHARGUS
T.225/T.250 (Trike)
G-MBEU MBJG MMRY

CHICHESTER-MILES
LEOPARD
G-BRNM

CHILTON AIRCRAFT
DW.1/1A/1B/2
G-AESZ AFGH AFGI AFSV AFSW BWGJ DWIA DWIB

CHRISLEA AIRCRAFT CO LTD
LC.1 AIRGUARD
G-AFIN
CH.3 SUPER ACE
G-AKUW AKVF
CH.3 Srs.4 SKYJEEP
G-AKVR

CHRISTEN INDUSTRIES INC see PITTS & Including AVIAT
EAGLE
G-EEGL EGAL EGLE EGUL ELKA IXII OEGL
A-1/18 HUSKY
G-BUVR HUSK

CHRIS TENA
MINI COUPE
G-BPDJ

CIERVA
C.24
G-ABLM
C.30A AUTOGIRO (AVRO 671)
G-ACUU ACWM ACWP

CIVILIAN AIRCRAFT CO
CAC.1 COUPE
G-ABNT

CLUTTON-TABENOR
FRED
G-BBBW BDBF BDSA BGFF BGHZ BISG BITK BKAF BKDP BKEY BKVF BKZT
BLNO BMAX BMMF BMSL BNZR BOLS BPAV BVCO BWAP BYLA MANX
OLVR ORAS PFAF PFAL RONW USTY

COLT BALLOONS LTD see COLTING & including CAMERON production
Gas Airship:
GA-42
G-MATS ZEPI
Hot Air Airships:
AS-42
G-WZZZ
AS-56
G-BTXH NOVO
AS-80
G-BPCF BPGT BPKN BROL BTSW OVAX
AS-105
G-BROL BTFD BUKV BWKE BWMV BXEY BXNV BXYF RBOS
AS-120
G-BXKU BZWF
Gas Balloon:
AA-1050
G-BWVM
Hot Air Balloons:
12A Cloudhopper
G-BHOJ
14A Cloudhopper
G-BHKN BHKR BHPN BVKX
17A Cloudhopper
G-BIDV BIYT BJWV BKBO BKXM BLHI BONV BOSG BPXH BRBU HELP ROBY
21A Cloudhopper
G-BKSH BLXG BMKI BNFM BOLN BOLP BOLR BPFX BSAK BSIG BTNN BTXM
BUEU BWBJ LLAI MLGL SOOS
H-24
G-BZUV
25A Sky Chariot
G-BSOF BUPH BVAO OKBT
31A Air Chair
G-BHIG BLOB BROJ BSDV BSMM BVTL BXXU DNGR DHLZ DOWN HOUS
IMAN MUTE PIXE PONY
42 variants
G-BJZR BVHP SEAT
56 variants
G-BGIP BHEX BHGX BHRY BICM BISX BIXW BJXP BJYF BKSD BLCH BLLW
BLOT BMYA BPWV BTZY BUGO BVOZ BVUC BVYL CFBI ILEE FZZZ MERC
POSH TTWO WIMP
69 srs.
G-BLEB BLUE BOSF BOVW BPAH BSHC BSHD BTMO BVDD COLR FZZY
JBJB OABC OBUD ODIY TCAN TWEY
77 variants
G-BGOD BIGT BKOW BLSK BLTA BMYN BNGP BOCF BOGT BOHD BORA
BORE BORT BPEZ BPFB BPJK BRLT BRVF BRVU BSCI BSUB BTDS
BTTS BTVH BTXB BTZR BTZS BUJH BUKS BULF BURG BUVB BUVE BUVS

BUVT BUYO BUZF BVAX BXFN BXIE BYFX CHEL CURE DING DRAW DURX FLAG GGOW GOBT HOME HOTI HOTZ HRZN IMAG JONO LOWA LSHI MAUK MKAK OAWS OCAR ODAD OLPG ONCL ORON OSST READ SGAS SIXX STOK TRUX UPPP UZLE WHAT WHIM WOOL WRIT

90 srs.
G-BLWE BOBU BPUW BRFH BRHG BRRU BSIU BTCS BTMH BTPV BVEI BXUW EXPR FOWL IRLY JNNB OBBC OLDV OMMM PEGG PHSI SAUF SEND TOFT

105 srs.
G-BGAS BLHK BLMZ BMBS BNAG BPZS BRUH BSBK BSCC BSHS BSNU BTHX BURL BUSV BWMA BWRM BXOV BXOW BYIO DYNG HSSH PLUG RAIL TIKI

120 srs.
G-BXAI BXCO BYDJ BYPV BZIL BZNF CBEJ OBIB VYGR

180 srs.
G-BOGR BONK CUCU PICT

210 srs.
G-BTYZ BUGN BULN BUXA BVFY BZYO

240 srs.
G-BNAP IGLA LCIO

260 srs.
G-HUGO

300 srs.
G-RAPE

315 srs.
G-KAUR VVBF

2500 srs.
G-USUK

SPECIAL SHAPES

SHAPE	REGISTRATION(S)
AGFA FILM CASSETTE	G-OHDC
APPLE	G-BRZV
ARIEL BOTTLE	G-BNHN
BEER GLASS	G-BNHL PUBS
BIBENDUM	G-GRIP PNEU TRED
BLACK KNIGHT	G-BNMI
BOTTLE	G-BOTL BUEL BVHU
BUDWEISER CAN	G-BUET BVIO
CLOWN	G-GWIZ
DRACHENFISCH	G-BMUJ
EGG	G-BWWL
FINANCIAL TIMES	G-ETFT FTFT
FIRE EXTINGUISHER	G-CHUB
FLAME	G-BLKU
FLYING MITT	G-WCAT
FLYING YACHT	G-AXXJ
GAS FLAME	G-BGOO
GOLF BALL	G-BJUY
GORDON'S GIN BOTTLE	G-BUYG
HOP	G-MALT
HUT	G-SMTC
ICE CREAM CONE	G-BWBE BWBF OJHB
J & B WHISKY BOTTLE	G-JANB
KINDERMOND	G-BMUL
MAXWELL HOUSE COFFEE JARS	G-BVBJ BVBK
MICKEY MOUSE	G-BTRB
OLD PARR WHISKY BOTTLE	G-PARR
PANASONIC BATTERY	G-PSON
PIG	G-BUZS
PIGGY BANK	G-BWBV BXVW
SANTA CLAUS	G-HOHO
SATZENBRAU BOTTLE	G-BIRE
SHUTTLECOCK	G-OOUT
STORK	G-BRGP
UFO	G-BMUK
WORLD	G-DHLI

COLOMBAN including ZENAIR
MC.12/15 CRI-CRI
G-BOUT BWFO CRIC MCXV OCRI SHOG

COMCO IKARUS
IKARUS C42
G-CBFV CBGP CBIJ CBJW CBKU CBOD CBPD CBRF CBTG CBVY CBXC DUGE EGGI GNJW GSCV ICRS IKRS ILRS MROY MSKY OFBU OVLA

COMMANDER AIRCRAFT COMPANY see ROCKWELL

COMMONWEALTH see NORTH AMERICAN

COMPER AIRCRAFT CO
CLA.7 SWIFT
G-ABUS ACTF KBWW LCGL

CONSOLIDATED-VULTEE see STINSON
L-13A
G-BGHE

CONVAIR
CV-440-54
G-CONV

COSTRUZIONI AERONAUTICHE GIOVANNI AGUSTA S.p.A see AGUSTA

COOK
ARIES P
G-MYXI

COPE
BUG
G-BXTV

CORBEN
BABY ACE
G-BTSB BUAA
JUNIOR ACE
G-BSDI

CORBY
CJ-1 STARLET
G-BVVZ CBHP ILSE

COSMOS
TRIKE
G-MVCK

COUGAR
(Wing)
G-MMUJ

CRANFIELD
A.1-400 EAGLE
G-COAI

CREMER
MLB variants
G-BJLX BJLY BJRP BJRR BJRV BJVB

CROSBY see ANDREASSON

CUB PROSPECTOR see PIPER

CULVER
LCA CADET
G-CDET

CURRIE including TURNER
WOT
G-APNT ARZW ASBA AVEY AYNA BANV BDFB BFAH BFWD BKCN BLPB BXMX CWBM CWOT PFAP SWOT

CURTISS AEROPLANE & MOTOR CO
JN-4D
G-ECAB

CURTISS-WRIGHT CORPORATION
TRAVEL AIR 12Q
G-AAOK
P-40 KITTYHAWK / TOMAHAWK
G-KITT TOMA

CURTISS ROBERTSON
ROBIN C.2
G-BTYY HFBM

CUTLASS see SKYHOOK

CVJETKOVIC
CA-65 SKYFLY HAB
G-BWBG

CYCLONE AIRSPORTS LTD see AERIAL ARTS, CHARGUS, PEGASUS AVIATION & SOLAR WINGS (AVIATION)

70 (Trike)
  G-MMYL MNMY

AX3
  G-BVJG MYFI MYFV MYFW MYFY MYFZ MYGD MYHG MYHH MYHJ MYHM
  MYHR MYIJ MYIU MYKA MYKF MYKT MYME MYMF MYMW MYMZ MYOY
  MYPM MYPR MYRO MYRU MYRV MYSO MYTM MYUI MYVN MYXH MYYL
  MYZC MYZF MYZG MZDO MZDS ZELE

AX2000
  G-BYJM CBGS CBHC CBIT CBMB CBUX JONY MGUN MYER MZER MZFA
  MZFX MZGA MZGB MZGC MZGM MZGP MZHR MZIV MZJF MZJL MZJR
  MZKC MZLS MZLU MZMX MZOE OAJB ROMW STRG WAKY YROO

Cyclone (Wing)
  G-MBOK

TS.440 (Wing)
  G-MBDU

Vortex (Wing)
  G-MJWH

Titan 38 (Trike)
  G-MBDU MYZH

CZAL

AERO 45/145
  G-APRR ATBH AYLZ

DAN RIHN

DR.107 ONE DESIGN
  G-IDDI IIID LOAD

DART AIRCRAFT LTD

KITTEN
  G-AEXT

DASSAULT

FALCON 20/200
  G-FFRA FRAF FRAH FRAI FRAJ FRAK FRAL FRAM FRAO FRAP FRAR FRAS
  FRAT FRAU FRAW FRBA

FALCON 50
  G-JPSI

FALCON 900
  G-EVES CBHT DAEX MLTI JCBG JCBX JJMX LYCA OPWH RBSG

FALCON 2000
  G-GEDI IBSF

DAVIS

DA-2
  G-BPFL

DE HAVILLAND AIRCRAFT CO LTD see AIRCO & HAWKER SIDDELEY AVIATION & including F + W, MORANE, MORRIS MOTORS, MOTH CORPORATION & OGMA production

DH.51
  G-EBIR

DH.53 HUMMING BIRD
  G-EBHX EBQP

DH.60/60G/60M/60X MOTH
  G-EBLV EBWD EBZN
  G-AAAH AADR AAEG AAHI AAHY AAMX AALY AAMY AANL AANV AAOR
  AAWO AAZG ABAG ABDX ABEV ABSD ABYA ATBL

DH.60GIII MOTH MAJOR
  G-ABZB ACGZ ACNS ACXB ADHD BVNG

DH.71 TIGER MOTH
  G-ECDX

DH.80A PUSS MOTH
  G-AAZP ABLS AEOA

DH.82A TIGER MOTH
  G-ABUL ACDA ACDC ACDI ACDJ ACMD ADGT ADGV ADGZ ADIA ADJJ
  ADNA ADPC ADWJ ADWO ADXT AFGZ AFVE AFWI AGEG AGHY AGNJ
  AGPK AGYU AGZZ AHAN AHIZ AHLT AHOO AHPZ AHUF AHUV AHVU AHVV
  AIDS AIRI AIRK AIXJ AJHS AJHU AJOA AJTW AJVE AKUE AKXS ALBD ALIW
  ALJL ALNA ALND ALRI ALTW ALUC ALVP ALWS ALWW AMBB AMCK AMCM
  AMHF AMIU AMIV AMJD AMNN AMTF AMTK AMTV AMVS ANCS ANCX
  ANDE ANDM ANDP ANEH ANEL ANEM ANEN ANEW ANEZ ANFC ANFI
  ANFL ANFM ANFP ANFV ANFW ANHK ANJA ANJD ANKK ANKT ANKV ANKZ
  ANLD ANLH ANLS ANMO ANMV ANMY ANNB ANNE ANNG ANNI ANNK
  ANOH ANOM ANON ANOO ANPE ANPK ANRF ANRM ANRN ANRX ANSM
  ANTE ANZU ANZZ AOAA AOBH AOBO AOBX AODT AOEI AOEL AOES AOET
  AOGI AOGR AOHY AOIL AOIM AOIS AOJJ AOJK AOJX AOUR AOZH APAL
  APAM APAO APAP APBI APCC APFU APGL APIH APJO APLU APMX APPN
  ARAZ AREH ARMS ARTL ASKP ASPV AVPJ AXAN AXBW AXBZ AXXV AYDI
  AYIT AZDY AZGZ AZZZ BAFG BBRB BEWN BFHH BHLT BHUM BJAP BJZF
  BMPY BNDW BPAJ BPHR BRHW BTOG BWIK BWMK BWMS BWVT BXMN

  BYLB BYTN DHTM DHZF EMSY ERDS ISIS MOTH OOSY PWBE TIGA

DH.82B QUEEN BEE
  G-BLUZ

DH.83/C FOX MOTH
  G-ACCB ACEJ AOJH

DH.84 DRAGON
  G-ACET ACIT ECAN

DH.85 LEOPARD MOTH
  G-ACLL ACMA ACMN ACOJ ACUS AIYS APKH

DH.87B HORNET MOTH
  G-ADKC ADKK ADKL ADKM ADLY ADMT ADND ADNE ADOT ADRH ADUR
  AELO AESE AHBL AHBM

DH.88 COMET
  G-ACSP ACSS

DH.89A DRAGON RAPIDE
  G-ACZE ADAH AEML AGJG AGSH AGTM AHAG AHED AHGD AIDL AIUL AIYR
  AJBJ AJCL AKDW AKIF AKNV AKOE AKRP ALXT

DH.90 DRAGONFLY
  G-AEDU

DH.94 MOTH MINOR
  G-AFNG AFNI AFOB AFOJ AFPN

DH.98 MOSQUITO
  G-ASKC AWJV

DH.100 VAMPIRE
  G-DHXX FBIX MKVI

DH.104 DOVE/(SEA) DEVON
  G-AHRI ALCU ALFT ALFU AMDD AMXT ANOV ANUW ANVU APSO ARBE
  ARDE AREA ARHW ARHX ARJB ARUE AVVF BLPZ BLRN BVXR DHDV DVEN
  DVON HBBC KOOL OEWA OPLC NAVY RNAS SDEV

DH.106 COMET
  G-ALYW AOJT APAS APDB APDF APMB APYD BDIW BDIX BEEX CPDA

DH.110 SEA VIXEN
  G-CVIX VIXN

DH.112 VENOM
  G-BLID BLSD DHSS DHTT DHUU GONE VENI VENM VICI VNOM

DH.114 HERON
  G-ANUO ANXB AORG AOTI AOXL HRON

DH.115 VAMPIRE TRAINER
  G-BZRC BZRD DHVV DHWW DHYY DHZZ DUSK HELV OBLN SPDR VMPR
  VTII

DH.121 TRIDENT – see HAWKER SIDDELEY
DH.125 – see HAWKER SIDDELEY

DE HAVILLAND (AUSTRALIA)

DHA.3 DROVER
  G-APXX

DE HAVILLAND (CANADA) including BOMBARDIER & OGMA production

DHC-1 CHIPMUNK
  G-AKDN ALWB AMUF ANWB AOFE AOJR AORW AOSF AOSK AOSO AOSU
  AOSY AOTD AOTF AOTR AOTY AOUO AOUP AOZP APLO APPA APPM
  APYG ARGG ARMB ARMC ARMD ARMF ARMG ARWB ATHD ATVF BAPB
  BARS BAVH BBMN BBMO BBMR BBMT BBMV BBMW BBMX BBMZ BBNA
  BBNC BBND BBRV BBSS BCAH BCCX BCEY BCGC BCHL BCIH BCKN BCOI
  BCOO BCOU BCOY BCPU BCRX BCSA BCSL BCXN BCYJ BCYM BCZH
  BDCC BDDD BDEU BDRJ BFAW BFAX BFDC BHRD BNZC BPAL BTWF BVTX
  BVWP BVZZ BWHI BWJY BWMX BWNK BWNT BWOX BWTG BWTO BWUN
  BWUT BWUV BWWY BWVZ BXCP BXCT BXCV BXDA BXDG BXDH BXDI
  BXDM BXDP BXEC BXGL BXGM BXGO BXGP BXGX BXHA BXHF BXIA BXIM
  BXNN BYHL BYSJ BYYW BZDU BZGA BZGB BZXE CBAJ CBJG CHPY CPMK
  DHCC DHCI DHPM HAPY JAKE MAJR OACP PVET TRIC ULAS

DHC-2 BEAVER
  G-BUCJ BVER

DHC-6 TWIN OTTER
  G-BIHO BVVK BZFP CBML

DHC-8 DASH EIGHT variants
  G-BRYH BRYI BRYJ BRYU BRYV BRYW BRYY BRYX BRYZ JEDC JEDD
  JEDE JEDF JEDG JEDI JEDJ JEDK JEDL JEDX JEDY JEDZ NVSA NVSB

DEMON see HIWAY

DENNEY AEROCRAFT COMPANY

KITFOX
  G-BNYX BONY BPII BPKK BRCT BSAZ BSCG BSCH BSCM BSFX BSFY
  BSGG BSHK BSIF BSIK BSMO BSNO BSRT BSSF BSUZ BSVK BTAT BTBG
  BTBN BTDC BTDN BTFA BTIF BTIR BTKD BTMT BTMX BTNR BTOL BTSV
  BTTY BTVC BTWB BUDR BUIC BUIP BUKF BUKP BULZ BUNM BUOL BUPW
  BUWS BUYK BUZA BVAH BVCT BVEY BVGO BWAR BWHV BWSJ BWSN
  BWWZ BWYI BXCW BXWH BZAR BZLO CBDI CBTX CJUD CRES CTOY DJNH
  ELIZ EYAS FOXC FOXD FOXF FOXG FOXI FOXS FOXZ FSHA HOBO HUTT
  KAWA KFOX KITF KITY LACR LEED LESJ LESZ LOST OFOX OPDS PHYL
  PPPP RAYA RWSS RSSF RWSS TFOX TOMZ

DEPERDUSSIN
MONOPLANE
  G-AANH

DESIGNABILITY see JORDAN

DESOUTTER
DESOUTTER 1
  G-AAPZ

DIAMOND AIRCRAFT INDUSTRIES GmbH see HOAC

DORNIER-WERKE AG see BUCKER
EKW C-3605
  G-DORN
DO.27
  G-BMFG BNMK
DO.28/SKYSERVANT
  G-ASUR BWCO BXTK
228
  G-BUXT MAFE MAFI OMAF
328
  G-BWIR BWWT BYHG BYMK BYML BYTY BZIF BZOG

DOUGLAS AIRCRAFT COMPANY INC including DOUGLAS AIRCRAFT
CORPORATION & also see McDONNELL DOUGLAS
AD-4 SKYRAIDER
  G-RAID
DC-3/C-47 DAKOTA/SKYTRAIN
  G-AKLL ALWC AMCA AMHJ AMPO AMPP AMPY AMPZ AMRA AMSM AMSN
  AMSV AMYJ ANAF BHUB BPMP BVOL DAKK DAKS
DC-6
  G-APSA SIXC
DC-7C
  G-AOIE

DRAGON BALLOONS
G77
  G-BKRZ

DRAGON LIGHT AIRCRAFT CO LTD
DRAGON Srs.150/200/250
  G-MJLK MJSL MJUZ MJVY MMAC MMAE MMAI MMML MMNH MNJF

DRAYTON BALLOONS
DRAYTON B-56 HAB
  G-BITS

DRUINE including ROLLASON production
D.5 TURBI
  G-AOTK APBO APFA
D.31 TURBULENT
  G-AJCP APIZ APNZ APOL APTZ APUY APVN APVZ APWP ARBZ ARGZ ARIM
  ARJZ ARLZ ARMZ ARNZ ARRZ ASFX ASHT ASMM ASPU ASSY ASTA ATBS
  AWBM AWDO AWFR AWMR AWWT BFXG BGBF EGMA BKXR BLTC BUKH
  BVLU BWID OJJF
D.62 CONDOR
  G-ARHZ ARVZ ASEU ASRB ASRC ATAU ATAV ATOH ATUG ATVW AVAW
  AVEX AVJH AVKM AVMB AVOH AVXW AWAT AWEI AWFN AWFO AWFP
  AWSN AWSP AWSS AWST AXGS AXGU AXGV AXGZ AYFC AYFD AYFE
  AYFF AYFG AYZS BADM BUOF OPJH YNOT

(SOCIÉTÉ) DYN'AÉRO
CR100
  G-BZGY
MCR-01 BAN-BI/CLUB
  G-BYEZ BYTM BZXG CBNL CBZX CUTE LMLV PGAC POOP TBEE TDVB
  TOOT

EAA
ACROSPORT
  G-BJHK BKCV BLCI BPGH BSHY BTAK BTWI BVVL OJDA TSOL VCIO
BIPLANE
  G-ATEP AVZW BBMH BPUA BRUU PFAA PFAY

EAGLE see AMERICAN AEROLIGHTS

EAVES (EUROPEAN)
MLB variants
  G-BJDK BJFC BJIC FYDN FYFI

ECLIPSE
SUPER EAGLE
  G-BGWZ

EDGAR PERCIVAL including LANCASHIRE AIRCRAFT COMPANY production
EP.9 PROSPECTOR
  G-APXW ARDG

EDGLEY including BROOKLANDS & OPTICA production
OPTICA
  G-BMPL BOPM BOPN BOPO BOPR TRAK

EDWARDS
GYROCOPTER
  G-ASDF

EH INDUSTRIES
EH-101
  G-EHIL

EIPPER AIRCRAFT INC
QUICKSILVER
  G-MBBM MBCK MBFO MBYM MJAM MJDU MJDW MJHX MJIR MJJK MJKH
  MJPV MJUO MJVP MJVU MJZL MMAH MMBU MMIL MMMG MMNB MMND
  MMWC MMYR MNCO MTDO MWDZ

EIRI.EINO RHIELA KY
PIK-20E
  G-BGZL BHFR BHNP OFJC OPIK POPE SOAR

ELECTRAFLYER see AMERICAN AEROLIGHTS

ELLIOTTS OF NEWBURY (EoN)
AP.10 460
  G-APWL

ELMWOOD
CA-05 CHRISTAVIA
  G-MRED

EMBRAER
EMB-110 BANDEIRANTE
  G-BGYT FLTY LOOT OBPL ODUB OFLT TABS
EMB-145 variants
  G-EMBA EMBB EMBC EMBD EMBE EMBF EMBG EMBH EMBI EMBJ EMBK
  EMBL EMBM EMBN EMBO EMBP EMBS EMBT EMBU EMBV EMBW EMBX
  EMBY ERJA ERJB ERJC ERJD ERJE ERJF ERJG RJXA RJXB RJXC RJXD
  RJXE RJXF RJXG RJXH RJXI RJXJ RJXK RJXL RJXM
EMB-312 TUCANO
  G-BTUC

ENGLISH ELECTRIC CO LTD including AVRO production
WREN
  G-EBNV
CANBERRA
  G-BURM BVIC BVWC BVXC
LIGHTNING
  G-BTSY

ENSTROM HELICOPTER CORPORATION
F-28
  G-BAAU BBHE BBIH BBPN BBPO BDKD BHAX BRZG BSHZ BURI BWOV
  BXXB BXXW BYKF BZHI MHCE MHCJ OABO SERA SNAZ WSEC
280 SHARK
  G-BEYA BGWS BIBJ BPXE BRPO BSDZ BSLV BXEE BXFD BXRD BYSW CBYL
  CKCK COLL ECHO GKAT HDIX HYST IDUP MEYO MHCB MHCD MHCF MHCG
  MHCH MHCI MHCK MHCL OGES OITV OJBB OJMF ONUP OPDM OTHE PALS
  PBYY SHAA SHRK SHUU SOPP VETS VRTX WIZI WRFM WSKY ZZWW
480
  G-BWMD GUAY HADA IGHH IJBB JPTT LADD LIVR OGHH OSKP OZAR PBTT
  TRUD WOOF

ERCO including ALON & FORNEY production
ERCOUPE 415
  G-ARHB ARHC ARHF AROO AVIL AVTT BKIN BZKS BZNO COUP EGHB
  ERCO HARY ONHH

EUROCOPTER see AÉROSPATIALE, SUD AVIATION & MBB
EC120
  G-BXYD CBJF CBNB DEVL ECZZ EMCM FEDA IBRI IGPW ISSY MODE PDGE
  SCUR TBLY WUSH YSON ZZOE

EC135
G-BZRS CCAU CHSU CPSH EMAS ETHU IWRC KRNW LASU NESV NWPS SASA SASB SPHU SUFF WCAO WMAS XMII

EUROPA AVIATION
EUROPA
G-BVGF BVIZ BVJN BVKF BVLH BVLV BVOS BVOW BVRA BVUV BVVH BVVP BVVM BWCV BWDP BWDX BWEG BWFH BWFX BWIJ BWIV BWJH BWKG BWNL BWON BWRO BWUP BWVS BWWB BWYD BWRA BWZT BXCH BXDY BXEF BXFG BXGG BXHY BXII BXIJ BXLK BXLZ BXNC BXOB BXTD BXUM BYFG BYIK BYPM BYJI BYSA BZAM BZNY BZTH BZTI BZTN CBES CBHI CBOF CBWF CBWP CBXW CBYN CHAV CHEB CHET CHUG CLAV COPY CROB CROY CUTY DAMY DAYI DAYS DDBD DEBR DLCB DONZ DRMM EENI EESA EIKY EMIN EMSI EOFS EORJ EURX EZZA FELL FIZY FLOR FLOX FLYT GBXS GCAC GIWT HOFC IANI IBBS IGII IKRK ILUM IMAB INAV IOWE IVER IVET JAMY JERO JHYS JOST JULZ JXWS KIMM KITS KITZ LABS LACE LAMM LEBE LILP MAAN MFHI MIME MEGG NDOL NEAT NESA NHRJ NIGL OBEV OBJT ODJG ODTW OEZY OGAN OIZI OJHL OKEV OMIK OPJK OPRC OSLD OSMT OUHI OURO OWWW PATF PATS PATZ PEGY PHXS PLPM PTAG PTYE PUDS PUPY RATZ RBBB RDHS RICS RIKS RIXS RJWX RMAC ROBD RONA ROOV ROWI RWLY SAMY SELF SHSH SMDH SRYY SUES SYCO TAGR TERN TKAY VKIT VPSJ WUFF WWWG XSDJ YURO ZORO ZTED

EUROWING LTD
GOLDWING
G-MBDG MBFZ MBPM MBPX MBZH MJAJ MJAY MJDP MJEG MJGK MJOE MJRL MJRO MJRS MJSY MJUU MJWB MJWS MMBN MMLE MMTZ MMWL MNNS MNZU

EVANS
VP-1
G-AYUJ AYXW BAAD BAJC BBXZ BCTT BDAH BDAR BDTB BDTL BDUL BEHX BEIS BEKM BFAS BFHX BFJJ BGEE BGFK BGLF BHMT BHYV BICT BIDD BIFO BKFI BLCW BLKK BLWT BMJM BVAM BVEL BVJU BVUT BWFJ GVPI PFAG PFAH PFAO PFAW ROSE TEDY VPCB
VP-2
G-BCVE BEHX BEYN BFYL BGFC BGPM BJVC BJZB BMSC BTAZ BTHJ BTSC BUGI BUKZ BVPM BXOC RASC

EVEKTOR-AEROTECHNIK
EV-97 EUROSTAR
G-CBIY CBJR CBMZ CBNK CBRR CBVM CBWE CBWG CCAC CCBK CCBM CCDX CCEM CSMK DATH GHEE NIDG OTUN OTYE PROW SDFM

EVERETT ENGINEERING see CAMPBELL
GYROPLANE
G-BIPI BMZN BMZP BMZS BSJW BTMV BTVB BUAI BULT BUZC BWCK MICY OFRB OGOS ULPS

EXPERIENCE
TRIKE
G-MYLU

EXPERIMENTAL AVIATION
BERKUT
G-REDX

EXTRA FLUGZEUGBAU GmbH
EA.230/260
G-CBUA EXTR
EA.300
G-BZFR BZII DUKK EIII EXEA IICM IIDI IILI IIMI IISI IITI IIZI IXTI KAYH MIII RGEE SIII XCCC XTRR XXTR

EXTREME SARL
EXTREME/SILEX
G-BZKG

FAIRCHILD
24/ARGUS
G-AIZE AJOZ AJPI BCBH BCBL FANC RGUS

FAIREY AVIATION
FLYCATCHER
G-BEYB
FIREFLY
G-ASTL
FULMAR
G-AIBE
GANNET
G-BMYP

FB.2 JET GYRODYNE
G-AJJP
SWORDFISH
G-AJVH BMGC
ULTRA-LIGHT HELICOPTER
G-AOUJ OPJJ

FAIRTRAVEL see PIEL

FALCONAR
F-9/F-11/F-12
G-AWHY AYEG BGHT CBWV ODEL TIMS WBTS

FARNELL
TRIKE
G-MJKO

FEWSDALE TIGERCRAFT
GYROPLANE
G-ATLH

F + W see DE HAVILLAND

FIAT
G.46
G-BBII

FIESLER
Fi/156c-3 STORCH
G-FIST

FISHER
FP202U KOALA/SUPER KOALA
G-BTBF BUVL MMTY

FLAGLOR
SKY SCOOTER
G-BDWE

FLEET
80 CANUCK
G-FLCA

FLEXIFORM see MAINAIR
HILANDER (Wing)
G-MJAN
SEALANDER (Wing)
G-MBBY MBGA MBIA MMFL MMGU
STRIKER (Wing)/SOLO & DUAL STRIKER
G-MBHK MBWF MBZO MJER MJFB MJFI MJIA MJIC MJIF MJMN MJMX MJTP MJVN MJYP MJZO MJZU MMAL MMAN MMAW MMAX MMCZ MMDK MMDN MMEJ MMFD MMFE MMFG MMFH MMFV MMFY MMGH MMGI MMJG MMKM MMMR MMNT MMPL MMRW MMWG MMWN MMWS MMYV MTFK
TRIKE
G-MBGL

FLIGHT DESIGN GmbH
CT2K
G-CBAI CBDH CBDJ CBEW CBEX CBIB CBIE CBLV CBNA CBUF CBVZ CBWA CTCT DMCT GGCT IDSL KATZ MCOY NULA POGO PRAH

FLYING K ENTERPRISES
EASY RAIDER
G-CBKF CBXE CBXF OESY OEZI SLIP SRII

FLYING PICTURES LTD
ELSON APOLY1 44000 HAB
G-CBTH CBTI

FLYLIGHT AIRPORTS LTD
DOODLE BUG/TARGET
G-BZKH BZKI BZKJ CBZY

FLS
SPRINT
G-BVNU BXWU BXWV FLSI SAHI SCLX

FOCKE WULF see PIAGGIO
FW 189
G-BZKY

FOKKER AIRCRAFT BV including FOKKER VFW NV & FAIRCHILD-HILLER production
D.VII
  G-BFPL
D.VIII
  G-BHCA
DR.1
  G-ATJM BVGZ
E.III
  G-AVJO
S.11 INSTRUCTOR
  G-BEPV BIYU
F-27 FRIENDSHIP/FH-227
  G-BHMW BHMY BMXD BNCY BNIZ BVOB CEXA CEXB CEXD CEXE CEXF
  CEXG JEAD JEAE JEAH JEAI
F.27-050 (Fokker 50)
  G-UKTA UKTB UKTC UKTD UKTE UKTF UKTG UKTH UKTI
F.28-0100 (Fokker 100)
  G-BVJA BVJB BVJC BVJD BXWE BXWF BYDN BYDO UKFA UKFB UKFC
  UKFD UKFE UKFF UKFG UKFH UKFI UKFJ UKFK UKFM UKFN UKFO UKFR

FOLLAND
GNAT
  G-BVPP FRCE GNAT MOUR NAAT NATY RORI TIMM

FORNEY see ERCOUPE

FOSTER-WIKNER
GM.1 WICKO
  G-AFJB

(AVIONS) FOURNIER
RF3
  G-ATBP AYJD BCWK BFZA BHLU BIIA BIPN BLXH BNHT
RF4D
  G-AVHY AVKD AVLW AVNX AVNZ AVWY AWBJ AWEL AWEM AWGN AWLZ
  AYHY BHJN IIF BUPJ BXLN IVEL
RF5/RF5B SPERBER
  G-AYME AZJC AZPF AZRK AZRM BACE BEVO BJXK BPWK CBPC KCIG
  RFSB SSWV
RF6B
  G-BKIF BLWH BOLC
RF7
  G-LTRF

FRED see CLUTTON

FUJI HEAVY INDUSTRIES LTD
FA.200
  G-BBGI BBNV BBRC BBZN BBZO BCFF BCKS BCKT BCNZ BDFR BDFS
  BFGO HAMI KARI MCOX

GADFLY
HDW-1
  G-AVKE

GAERTNER
AX4 SKYRANGER HAB
  G-BSGB

GARDAN including CAB & BARRITAULT production
GY-20 MINICAB
  G-ATPV AVRW AWEP AWUB AWWM AZJE BANC BBFL BCER BCNC BCPD
  BDGB BGKO BGMJ BGMR BRGW TATT VERA
GY-80 HORIZON
  G-ASJY ASZS ATGY ATJT AVMA AVRS AWAC AZAW AZRX AZYA BFAA
  BJAV BKNI BYBL BYME BYPE GYAT GYBO TIMY

GARDNER
T-M SCOUT
  G-MJTD

GARLAND-BIANCHI see PIEL

GAZEBO
AX6-65 HAB
  G-BCGP

GAZELLE see SOUTHERN MICROLIGHT

GEFA-FLUG
AS.105GD AIRSHIP
  G-BZUR

GEMINI see MAINAIR

GENERAL AIRCRAFT
GAL.42 CYGNET
  G-AGBN

GENERAL AVIA
F22
  G-FZZA

GLASER-DIRKS FLUGZEUGBAU GmbH including DG FLUGZEUGBAU
DG-400
  G-BLJD BLRM BNXL BPIN BPXB BRTW BYTG SBOM DGDG DIRK HAJJ INCA
  LEES OAPW ORTM
DG-500M/MB
  G-BRRG BZYG
DG-600
  G-BZEM KOFM
DG-800
  G-BVJK BXSH BXUI BYEC DGCL DGIV IANB MSIX ORIG

GLOBE
GC-1B SWIFT
  G-ARNN

GLOSTER AIRCRAFT CO LTD including ARMSTRONG-WHITWORTH production
GAMECOCK rep
  G-CBTS
GLADIATOR
  G-AMRK CBHO GLAD
METEOR variants
  G-ANSO ARCX BWMF JETM LOSM

GOLD MARQUE SPORTS
GYR (Wing)
  G-MJKO

GOULD-TAYLORCRAFT see TAYLORCRAFT

GRANGER
ARCHEOPTERYX
  G-ABXL

GRASSHOPPER including SERVOTEC
GRASSHOPPER
  G-ARVN AWRP AXFM AZAU

GREAT LAKES see OLDFIELD
2T-1A SPORT TRAINER
  G-BIIZ BUPV

GREEN
S-25 HAB
  G-BSON

GREGA see PIETENPOL

GRIFFITHS
GH.4
  G-ATGZ

GROB-WERKE GMB & CO KG
G.109
  G-BIXZ BJVK BJZX BLMG BLUV BMCG BMFY BMGR BMLK BMLL BMMP
  BRCG BXSP BXXG BYJH CBLY CHAR DKDP IPSI KEMC KNEK LULU NDGC
  SAGA SAMG TACK UILD WAVE
G.115//TUTOR
  G-BOPT BOPU BPKF BVHC BVHD BVHE BVHF BVHG BYDB BYFD BYUA
  BYUB BYUC BYUD BYUE BYUF BYUG BYUH BYUI BYUJ BYUK BYUL BYUM
  BYUN BYUO BYUP BYUR BYUS BYUT BYUU BYUV BYUW BYUX BYUY
  BYUZ BYVA BYVB BYVC BYVD BYVE BYVF BYVG BYVH BYVI BYVJ BYVK
  BYVL BYVM BYVN BYVO BYVP BYVR BYVS BYVT BYVU BYVV BYVW BYVX
  BYVY BYVZ BYWA BYWA BYWB BYWC BYWD BYWE BYWF BYWG BYWH
  BYWI BYWJ BYWK BYWL BYWM BYWN BYWO BYWP BYWR BYWS BYWT
  BYWU BYWV BYWW BYWX BYWY BYWZ BYXA BYXB BYXC BYXD BYXE
  BYXF BYXG BYXH BYXI BYXJ BYXK BYXL BYXM BYXN BYXO BYXR BYXS
  BYXT BYXX BYXY BYXZ BYYA BYYB MERF RAFA RAFB TAYI WIZB

GRUMMAN AIRCRAFT ENGINEERING
F-6F HELLCAT
  G-BTCC

F-7F TIGERCA
G-RUMT
F-8F BEARCAT
G-RUMM
FM-2 WILDCAT
G-RUMW
TBM-3 AVENGER
G-BTDP

GRUMMAN-AMERICAN AVIATION CORPN including AMERICAN AVIATION, AMERICAN-GENERAL & GULFSTREAM-AMERICAN CORPORATION production
AA-1 YANKEE/TRAINER/LYNX
G-AYHA AYLP AZKS BBFC BBWZ BCIL BCLW BDLS BDNW BDNX BERY BEXN BFOJ BTLP RUMN SEXY
AA-5/AG-5 TRAVELER/CHEETAH/TIGER
G-AZMJ AZVG BAFA BAJN BAJO BAOU BASG BASH BAVR BBBI BBCZ BBDL BBDM BBLS BBRZ BBSA BBUE BBUF BCCJ BCCK BCEE BCEF BCEO BCEP BCIJ BCIK BCLI BCLJ BCPN BCRR BDCL BDFY BDLO BEBE BEZC BEZF BEZG BEZH BEZI BFIJ BFIN BFLW BFLX BFPB BFTF BFTG BFVS BFXW BFXX BFZO BGCM BGFG BGFI BGPH BGVV BGVW BGVY BHLX BHZK BHZO BIAY BIBT BIPA BIPV BIVV BIWW BJAJ BJDO BKPS BLFW BLSF BMYI BNVB BOXU BOZO BOZZ BPIZ BSTR BTII BTUZ BXHH BXOO BXOX BXTT BYDX CCAT CHTA DAVO DINA DOEA DONI ERRY ESTE GAJB GIRY IFLI IRIS JAJB JAZZ JENN JNAS JUDY KINE LSFI MALC MILY MOGI MSTC NGBI NODE NODY NONI OABR OBMW OBSF OCAM ODAE ODAM OECH OMOG OPPL OPWK OSSF OSTC OSTU OTIG PAWS PING PORK PROP PURR RATE REEK RICO ROWL RUBB TGER TYGA WINK WMTM ZARI ZERO
GA-7 COUGAR
G-BGNV BGON BGSY BLHR BOGS BOOE BOXR CYMA EENY FLII GABD GENN GOTC HIRE OOGA OOGI OOGO REAT SHIV TANI

GRYPHON SAILWINGS see WASP & WILLGRESS
GRYPHON
G-MMYC

GULFSTREAM AEROSPACE CORPORATION
G159 GULFSTREAM I
G-BNCE
GULFSTREAM IV/V
G-DNVT EVLN HARF

GULFSTREAM-AMERICAN CORPORATION see GRUMMAN-AMERICAN

GYROFLIGHT see BROOKLAND

Hadland
WILLOW
G-MMMH

HALLAM
FLECHE
G-FLCT

HANDLEY PAGE LTD
O/400 Rep
G-BKMG
HP.39 GUGNUNC
G-AACN
HP.81 HERMES
G-ALDG

HANDLEY PAGE (READING) LTD
HPR.7 DART HERALD
G-APWA APWJ ASKK ASVO ATIG AVPN BAZJ BEYF BEYK CEXP

HANRIOT
HD.1
G-AFDX

HAPI
CYGNET SF-2A
G-BRZD BWFN BXCA BXHJ BYYC

HARKER
DH/WASP
G-MJSZ

HATZ
CB-1
G-BRSY BXXH CBYW HATZ TIKO

HAWKER AIRCRAFT LTD see W.A.R & including AVRO/CCF production
CYGNET
G-CAMM EBJI EBMB
AUDAX
G-BVVI
DEMON
G-BTVE
FURY (Biplane)
G-BKBB
TOMTIT
G-AFTA
HART
G-ABMR
HIND
G-AENP CBLK
NIMROD
G-BURZ BWWK
HURRICANE
G-AMAU BKTH BWHA BYDL CBOE HRLI HUPW HURI HURR HURY KAMM ROBT
TEMPEST
G-PEST TEMT
FURY/SEA FURY
G-AGHB BUCM BWOL CBEL
HUNTER
G-BNCX BUEZ BVGH BVVC BWAF BWFR BWFT BWGK BWGL BWGM BWGN BWOU BXFI BXKF BZPB BZPC BZSE BZSF BZSR EGHH FFOX GAII HHAB HHAC HHAD HHAE HHAF HNTR HPUX HVIP KAXF PRII PSST RUUD SIAL TVII VETA

HAWKER SIDDELEY AVIATION including DE HAVILLAND, BAe & RAYTHEON HAWKER production
HS.121 TRIDENT
G-ARPH ARPK ARPL ARPO ARPP AVFB AVFE AVFG AVFH AVFJ AVFK AVFM AWZJ AWZM AWZO AWZP AWZR AWZS AWZU AWZX
HS.125
G-ARYB ARYC ASSM ATPD AWYE AXDM BOCB BTAB BWSY BYHM BZNR CJAA DEZC ETOM FANN GDEZ GIRA GMAB IFTE JETI MKSS OHEA OJPB OLDD OMGE OURA OURB OWDB RCEJ SUFC SVLB TACE TCAP TCDI TSAM VIPI WBPR YUGO
BUCCANEER
G-HHAA
HARRIER
G-CBCU CBGK VTOL

HEAD
Ax8-105 HAB
G-UKUK

HEINKEL
CASA C.2111D (He.111H-16)
G-AWHB

HEINTZ see ZENAIR

HELIO
SUPER COURIER
G-BAGT BGIX

HELTON
LARK 95
G-LARK

HILL see MAXAIR

HILLER
UH-12 (360)
G-ASAZ ASTP ATKG BBAZ

HINDUSTAN
PUSHPAK
G-AVPO BXTO

HISPANO see MESSERSCHMITT

HIWAY HANG GLIDERS LTD
DEMON (Wing)
G-MBEU MBFK MBIT MBUA MJAV MJDJ MJDR MJHV MJKF MJMD MJNK MJRP MJSO MJXY MJYX MJYY MMHD MMLH MMNW MMTD MTHD MWXE MYBN
EXCALIBUR (Wing)
G-MBAA

SKYTRIKE
G-MBAA MBCL MBDD MBFK MBIA MBIT MBJF MBKZ MBLM MBPU MBTE MBVS MBVV MBXF MBXJ MJAN MJAV MJDJ MJDR JMHV MJMA MJMD MJMS MJMT MJMU MJNK MJNT MJOU MJPE MJPP MJSO MJUM MJXY MMBS MMCV MMEF MMEI MMHG MMHL MMHP MMLH MMOO MMRH MMUR MNME MYBN
SUPER SCORPION (Wing)
G-MBGW MBJX MBVS MJCW MJKP MMEF MMHK MMHL
VULCAN (Wing)
G-MBIZ MJAP

HOAC FLUGZEUGWERKE including DIAMOND AIRCRAFT INDUSTRIES production
DA20/DV-20 KATANA
G-BWEH BWFD BWFE BWFI BWFV BWGY BWGZ BWLP BWLS BWLT BWLV BWPY BWTA BWYM BXGH BXJV BXJW BXMZ BXOF BXPB BXPC BXPD BXPE BXTP BXTR BXTS BYFL BYMB OBDA OSFA RIBS TENS
DA40 STAR
G-CBFA CBFB CBFC EMDM MOPB OPHR

HOFFMANN FLUGZEUGBAU FRIESACH
H-36 DIMONA/HK-36 SUPER DIMONA
G-BKPA BLCV BNUX IMOK KOKL LIDA LIDR LYDA OMDG OMRG RIET

HORNET MICROLIGHTS LTD
TRIKE
G-MBCX MBJL MJDA MJWN MMHD MMNM
INVADER (Trike)
G-MMHY
DUAL TRAINER/RAVEN (Combi)
G-MNRI MNRK MNRL MNRM MTGX MTJX MTMP MTMR MTRL MTXE MTXY MVHZ
R/RS (Combi)
G-MVUR MVYI MVYJ MVYK MVYL MVYN MVZW MWBM MWBN MWBP MWBR MWBS MWBU MWBW MWBY- MWDE MWDI MWEU MWEY MWKE

HOVEY
BETA BIRD
G-BKRV
WD-II/III WHING DING
G-MBAB MNVO

HOWARD
SPECIAL T-MINUS
G-BRXS

HOWES
AX6 HAB
G-BDWO

HUGHES TOOL CO/HUGHES HELICOPTERS INC including SCHWEIZER
AIRCRAFT CORPORATION (269 wef 1986) & McDONNELL DOUGLAS (369 wef 1983) production
269 (Srs.300)
G-BAUK BAXE BMWA BOVX BOXT BPJB BPPY BRTT BSML BSVR BUEX BWAV BWDV BWNJ BWZJ BXMY BXRP BXTL BZXJ CBYA DRKJ ECLI GNXZ HFLA IBHH JMDI MARE OCBI OCJK ODNH OGJP OGOB OJAE OPCS OSLO OZAP PKPK PLOW PLPC REBL RHCB RIFB ROCR SAND SBHH SHCB SHPP STEP TASS VNUS WARK WHRL ZBHH
369 (Srs.500)
G-AZVM BIOA BPLZ BRTL BTRP CSPJ DIZZ ERIS GASC GSPG HAUS HKHM HMAC HSOO HUKA IDWR JETZ JIVE LIBS LINC LOGO MRAJ NIPY OMDH ORRR OTDB SOOC SOOE SSCL SWEL TRUE VICE

HUNT
WING/AVON/EXPERIENCE/PEGASUS
G-BZRG BZTW BZUZ MGTR MMGT MNCA MWPT MYTV MYUR MYWE MYWH MYYE MYYJ MZCX MZCZ MZDZ-MZFE MZFF MZGH MZLB MZLK

HUNTAIR LTD
PATHFINDER
G-MBWG MBYL MJBZ MJDE MJDH MJFM MJJA MJOC MJTY MJUV MJWK MJXS MMBV MMCB MMDR

HUNTING PERCIVAL AIRCRAFT LTD see PERCIVAL & including BRITISH
AIRCRAFT CORPORATION (BAC) production
P.84 JET PROVOST/BAC.145/167 STRIKEMASTER
G-AOBU AYHR BESY BKOU BVEZ BVSP BVTC BWBS BWCS BWDR BWEB BWGF BWGS BWGT BWOF BWOT BWSG BWSH BWUW BWZE BWZZ BXBH BXBI BXDL BXFP BXFU BXFV BXFW BYED BZRE BZRF CBPB FLYY JPRO JPTV JPVA KNOT PROV RAFI SARK TORE-UNNY UNVR VIVM

HYBRED see MEDWAY

IAV-BACHAU see YAKOVLEV

ICA
IS.28B2/M2
G-BKXN BMMV BMOM TODD

I.C.P srl
MXP-740 SAVANNAH J(1)
G-CBBM

III (INIZIATIVE INDUSTRIALE ITALIANE)
SKY ARROW
G-BXGT BYCY BYZR BZVT CBTB CIAO FINZ GULP IXIX ROME SKYG SKYT SUTN

ILYUSHIN
Il-2
G-BZVW BZVX

INTERAVIA
HAB
70TA
G-BUUT
80TA
G-BZYT

ISAACS
FURY
G-ASCM AYJY BBVO BCMT BEER BIYK BKFK BKZM BMEU BTPZ BWWN BZAS BZNW PFAR RODI
SPITFIRE
G-BBJI BXOM

JABIRU AIRCRAFT (PTY) LTD
JABIRU SK/SPL/UL
G-BXAO BXNU BXSI BYBM BYBZ BYCZ BYFC BYIA BYIM BYJD BYJF BYNL BYNR BYNS BYSF BYTK BYTV BYYL BYYT BYZS BZAP BZDZ BZEN BZFI BZGT BZHR BZIV BZLV BZMC BZST BZSZ BZTY BZUL BZWK BZXN BZYK CBFZ CBGR CBIF CBJM CBJY CBKY CBOP CBPP CBPR CBSU CBZM CCAE CCBY CCEL CNAB COVE CSDJ DJAY DMAC DWMS ENRE EWBC GPAS HINZ IZDD JABA JABS JABY JACO JAJP JAXS JBSP JPMA JSPL JUDD KKER LEEE LOIS LUMA LYPG MGCA MITT NIGC ODGS OGSA OJAB OMHP OPUS OZZI PBUS PHYS PRLY RODG RUFS RYAL SIMP THOT TJAL TUBB TYKE UKOZ UJAB VILA VJAB

JACKAROO AIRCRAFT SEE THRUXTON

JODEL see FALCONAR & ROBIN & including CEA, SAN & WASSMER production
D.9/D.92 variants
G-AVPD AWFT AXYU AZBL BAGF BDEI BDNT BGFJ BURE BZBZ KDIX
D.11/D.112/D.117/D.119 & AERO D.1190S variants
G-ARDO ARNY ASJZ ASXY ATIN ATIZ ATJN ATWB AVPM AWFW AWMD AWWB AWVZ AWWI AXAT AXCG AXCY AXFN AXHV AXWT AXXW AXZT AYBP AYBR AYCP AYEB AYGA AYHX AYKJ AYKK AYKT AYMU AYWH AYXP AZFF AZHC AZII AZKP AZVL BAAW BAKR BAPR BARF BATJ BAUH BAZM BBPS BCGL BCGW BCLU BDBV BDDG BDIH BDJD BDMM BEDD BEZZ BFEH BFGK BFNG BFXR BGTX BGWO BHCE BHEL BHFF BHHX BHKT BHNL BHNX BIAH BIDX BIEO BIOU BIPT BITO BIVW BIWN BIYW BIZY BJOT BKAO BKIR BMIP BOOH BPFD BRCA BRVZ BVEH BVPS BVVE BWMB DAVE
D.18
G-BODT BRZO BSYA BTRZ BUAG BUPR BWVC BWVV BXFC CBRC CBRD OLEM TREK WIBB
D.120 PARIS-NICE
G-ASPF ASXU ATLV AVLY AVYV AXNJ AYGG AYLV AYRS AZEF AZGA AZLF BACJ BANU BCGM BDDF BDEH BDWX BFOP BGZY BHGJ BHNK BHPS BHXD BHXS BHZV BICR BIEN BJFM BJOE BJYK BKAE BKCW BKCZ BKGB BKJS BKPX BMDS BMID BMLB BMYU BOWP BYBE CCBR DIZO
D.140 MOUSQUETAIRE
G-ARDZ ARLX AROW ARRY ATKX AYFP BJOB BSPC BWAB DCXL JRME OBAN REES TOAD
150 variants
G-ASKL ASRT AVEF AZBI BACL BFEB BHEG BHEZ BHVF BIDG BKSS BLAT BLXO BMEH BVSS BVST BZXH DISO EDGE FARR IEJH JDLI MASC OABB TIDS
DR.100/105/1050/1051 variants
G-ARFT ARRD ARRE ARXT ASXS ATAG ATEV ATFD ATGE ATIC ATJA ATLB ATWA AVGZ AVHL AVJK AVOA AWEN AWUE AWVE AWWN AWWO AXLS AXSM AXUE AXUK AYEH AYEJ AYEV AYEW AYGD AYJA AYKD AYLC AYLF AYLL AYUT AYYO AYYT AZBI AZCX AZOU AZWF BAEE BDMW BEAB BEYZ BFBA BGBE BGRI BHHE BHOL BHSY BHTC BHUE BIOI BKDX BLKM BLRJ BLUL BOBG BPLH BTHH BXIO BXYJ BYCS BYFM DANA IOSI IOSO JODL JWBB JWIV SPOG

DR.200/220/221 variants
G-AVOM AYDZ BANA BFHR BHRW BLCT BLLH BMKF BUTH CPCD GOSS RRCU STEV
DR.250/253 variants
G-ATTM AWKP AWYL AXWV AYUB BJBO BKPE BOSM BSZF BUVM BXCG BYEH BYHP
DR.315/340/360 variants
G-AXDK AYCO AZIJ AZJN BGVB BICP BLAM BLGH BLHH BOEH BOZV BVYG BVYM BXOU DRSV DRZF KIMB

JORDAN AVIATION
DUET
G-MBWH MMKY MNIN

JURCA
MJ.2 TEMPETE
G-ASUS AYTV
MJ.5 SIROCCO
G-AZOS CLAX ORFC RECO

K & S
SA.102.5 CAVALIER
G-AZHH BCKF BCRK BDKJ BDLY

KAY
GYROPLANE
G-ACVA

KEN BROCK
KB-2
G-BSEG BUYT BUZV BVMN BVUJ

KENSINGER
KF
G-ASSV

KIRK
SKYRIDER MLB
G-BJTF

KLEMM see BA & BRITISH KLEMM
L.25
G-AAUP AAXK
KL.35
G-BWRD

KNIGHT see PAYNE

KOLB
TWINSTAR
G-BUZT CYRA KOLB BYTA MWWM MYDP MYIK MYKB MYLN MYLP MYMI MYNY MYOG MYOO MYOR MYPC MYVA MYWP MYXS MZGJ MZZT

KRONFELD see BAC

L A MOUETTE
PROFIL (Wing)
G-MVCK

LAFAYETTE
HI-NUSKI Mk.1
G-MBWI

LAKE AIRCRAFT CORPORATION INCL AEROFAB INC
LA-4 BUCCANEER/SKIMMER
G-BASO BOLL SKID
LA-250 RENEGADE
G-LAKE SIVW

LAMBERT AIRCRAFT ENGINEERING
MISSION M212-100
G-XFLY

LANCAIR see NEICO

LANCASHIRE
MICRO-TRIKE
G-MJXX MJYW MJZO MMFG MMPL

LANCASHIRE AIRCRAFT see EDGAR PERCIVAL

LAVERDA see AVIAMILANO

LAZAIR see ULTRAFLIGHT

LAZER see STEPHENS

LEARJET CORPORATION INC
LEARJET 35A
G-HUGG JETG LEAR LJET MURI
LEARJET 45
G-GMAA OLDC OLDF OLDJ OLDL OLDR

LEDERLIN
38OL LADYBUG
G-AYMR

LEOPOLDOFF
L-6
G-BYKS
L-7
G-AYKS

LET NARODNI PODNIK KUNOVICE see YAKOVLEV & ZLIN
L-200A/D MORAVA
G-ASFD BNBZ
Z-37 CMELAK
G-AVZB KDLN

LETOV AIR
LK-2M SLUKA
G-MYRP MYRR MYUP MYVG MYVT MYXO MZBF MZBK MZDX MZES MZFC MZGF MZLY MZNZ MZOI MZOT MZOX XPBI

LE VIER
COSMIC WIND
G-ARUL BAER

LIGHTNING see SOUTHDOWN

LILLIPUT BALLOONS UK
TYPE 1 MLB
G-HONY

LINDSTRAND BALLOONS LTD
Gas Balloon:
AS-2
G-BYPC

Hot Air Airship:
HS-110
G-LRBW TRIB

Hot Air Balloons:
LBL-9
G-BVRP
LBL-14
G-BWBB BWEO BWER BXAJ BXEP
LBL-21/RR-21
G-BVRL BYEY CBYS OJNB
LBL-25 CLOUDHOPPER
G-BVUI BXHM BYYJ BZKZ CBZJ EECO OLAW OOER
LBL-31 AIR CHAIR
G-BVOJ BWHD BXIZ BXUH BZIH BZNV BZUK ELLE FFFT ONCB
LBL-42
G-BWCG CBLO
LBL-56
G-COSY
LBL-60
G-CCBP OERR
LBL-69
G-BVDS BVGG BVIR BYKA BZJY CBBX LBLI
LBL-77
G-BUBS BUWI BUZR BVPV BVRR BWAW BWBO BWEP BWFK BWKZ BWMH BWTU BXDR BYJG BYKW BYLW BYRZ BYYE BYYR BZBJ BZKE ERRI HERD HUNK ICEY ICKY MERE PATP
LBL-90
G-BVAG BVWW BVXG BVZT BWBT BWRV BWTN BWWE BWZU BXLF BXXO BXZF BXZI BYEP BZLU BZNA CBIM CBNI DUGI FLEW JEMY JIGS MINN MRKT OBJB OSUP PATX PROF SJKR ULLS UNGE
LBL-105
G-BUUN BUYJ BUZJ BVDO BVON BVOO BVRU BWGA BWOK BWRZ BWSB BWTB BWWY BXHE BXHP BXJG BXUO BYFU BYIY BYJN BYJZ BYLX BZAG BZPV BZUD CBPH CBPW ENRI FLGT GULF HAPI ICOI LPAD OAER ODDY OPMT OUMC PIZZ ROMS RIMB RXUK SNAK VITL

LBL-120/A
G-BVLZ BWDM BWEA BZBL CBTR CBVH OGSS

LBL-150
G-BVEW BXCM CBXB IRTH OHRH OVBL

LBL-180
G-BVBM BVIX CBNS EVNT GVBF CBZU KNOB OTUP WIZD

LBL-203
G-BXGK

LBL-210
G-BVLL BVML BXNX BZDE DVBF FVBF HVBF JVBF NVBF OCBS SSLF WVBF

LBL-240
G-BXBL OGAV

LBL-260
G-PVBF

LBL-310
G-BZPE CBIW TVBF

LBL-317
G-YVBF

LBL-330
G-BXVE

SPECIAL SHAPES

SHAPE	REGISTRATION(S)
ARMCHAIR	G-LAZY
BABY BEL	G-BXUG
BEAR	G-BWTF
BIRTHDAY CAKE	G-WISH
BUDWEISER CAN	G-BXHN
BUNNY	G-FLUF
CAKE	G-BZNZ
FLOWERS	G-ODBN
J & B BOTTLE	G-OJBW
NEWSPAPER	G-FFTT
PIG	G-PIGG
PINK PANTHER	G-PINX
RACING CAR	G-TKGR
SUN	G-BZIC
SYRUP BOTTLE	G-BXUB
TELEWEST SPHERE	G-BXHO
TULIPS	G-TULP

LOCKHEED AIRCRAFT CORPORATION including LOCKHEED-CALIFORNIA CO & CANADAIR production

10 ELECTR
G-LIOA

18 LODESTAR
G-AGIJ BMEW

414 HUDSON
G-BEOX

L.188 ELECTRA
G-CEXS CHNX FIJR FIJV FIZU LOFB LOFC LOFD LOFE LOFF LOFG OFRT

L.749 CONSTELLATION
G-CONI

L.1011 TRISTAR
G-IOIT

T-33A
G-BYOY TBRD WGHB

LORIMER

IOLAIRE
G-MZFI

LOVEGROVE see BENSEN

AV-8 GYROPLANE
G-BXXR

LUSCOMBE AIRPLANE CORPORATION

8 SILVAIRE/MASTER/RATTLER
G-AFUP AFYD AFZK AFZN AGMI AHEC AICX AJAP AJJU AJKB AKPG AKTI
AKTN AKTT AKUF AKUG AKUH AKUI AKUJ AKUK AKUL AKUM AKUP AKVP
BNIO BNIP BPOU BPPO BPVZ BPZA BPZC BPZE BRDJ BRGF BRGG BRHX
BRHY BRJA BRJK BRKA BROO BRPZ BRRB BRSW BRUG BSHH BSHI BSNE
BSNT BSOE BSOX BSSA BSTX BSUD BSYF BSYH BTCH BTCJ BTDF BTIJ
BTJA BTJB BTJC BUAO BUKT BUKU BULO BVEP BVGW BVGY BVMD BWOB
DAIR EITE KENM LUSC LUSI LUST NIGE ROTI SAGE YRIL

LVG

C.VI
G-AANJ

LYNDEN

AURORA
G-CBZS

M<small>c</small>CANDLESS

M.4 GYROPLANE
G-ARTZ ATXX AXVN BVLE

M<small>c</small>CULLOGH

J.2
G-ORVB

McDONNELL DOUGLAS CORPORATION

DC-10
G-BYDA DMCA DPSP TAOS TDTW

McDONNELL DOUGLAS HELICOPTER CO see HUGHES & MD HELICOPTERS

MACAIR

MERLIN
G-BWEN

MAINAIR SPORTS LTD see PEGASUS/FLASH

BLADE
G-BYHN BYHO BYHS BYJB BYKC BYKD BYNM BYON BYOS BYOW BYRO
BYRP BYRR BYTL BYTU BZAA BZAL BZDC BZDD BZEG BZEL BZHY BZFO
BZFS BZIR BZJL BZJN BZLM BZMS BZNS BZPA BZPN BZPZ BZRB BZRW
BZTM BZTR BZTU BZTV BZTX BZUB BZUM BZUN BZWB BZXM BZXT CBAD
CBBG CBDD CBDL CBDN CBDP CBEM CBET CBGM CBGT CBGY CBHG
CBHJ CBHM CBJT CBKM CBKN CBKO CBLD CBLM CBLT CBMM CBNC
CBOG CBOL CBOM CBOO CBOV CBRE CBRJ CBRM CBSM CBSZ CBTE
CBTM CBTW CBVG CBWM CBXM CBXV CBYF CBYM CBZA CBZB CBZD
CCAB CCAG CCAM CCAW CLFC EEYE ENVY FERN JAIR JBEN JMAN JOOL
MAIN MYRC MYRD MYTD MYTG MYTL MYTU MYUC MYUM MYUN MYVB
MYVE MYVH MYVO MYVY MYVZ MYXJ MYXM MYXN MYYA MYYG MYYH
MYYW MYYY MZAA MZAB MZAE MZAF MZAG MZAI MZAJ MZAL MZAM
MZAP MZAR MZAS MZAT MZAY MZAZ MZBA MZBL MZCC MZCD MZCE
MZCG MZCN MZCU MZDF MZDK MZDT MZEB MZED MZEG MZEJ MZEW
MZFB MZFS MZFZ MZGI MZGW MZIH MZIR MZIS MZIT MZIW MZJA MZJD
MZJK MZJV MZJX MZJZ MZKG MZKJ MZKK MZKM MZKO MZKV MZKZ MZLC
MZLZ MZMB MZMD MZMJ MZMM MZMP MZMV MZMY MZNC MZNI MZNI
MZNJ MZNK MZNL MZNO MZOC MZOF MZOP MZOR MZPH MZSD MZSM
MZZY NNON NOOK OBMI OHVA ORBS OSEP OYES REED REEF RIKI RINN
RUFF RYPH SHUF WAKE WLMS

GEMINI/FLASH (Combi)
G-MJYF MJZD MMDP MMKL MMOW MMPO MMSP MMTG MMUO MMUT
MMUW MMVP MMWA MMXD MMXG MMXJ MMXK MMXL MMXT MMXU MMXV
MMZA MMZB MMZC MMZF MMZJ MMZK MMZM MMZV MNAC MNAE MNBD
MNBF MNBG MNBN MNBP MNBR MNBS MNBT MNBV MNBW MNCF MNCG
MNCJ MNDC MNDF MNEF MNEG MNEH MNET MNEV MNEY MNFE MNFF
MNFH MNFM MNFN MNFP MNGK MNGL MNGM MNGN MNGT MNGU MNGW
MNHZ MNIA MNIE MNIF MNIG MNIH MNII MNIP MNIX MNIZ MNJU MNLI MNLX
MNLY MNMG MNMI MNMJ MNMV MNNF MNNI MNNJ MNNL MNNR MNNV
MNPC MNPG MNRW MNRX MNRY MNSA MNSI MNSJ MNSR MNTI MNTS
MNTU MNTV MNTX MNTZ MNUA MNUF MNUG MNUO MNUR MNUY MNVT
MNVU MNVV MNVW MNWD MNWI MNWZ MNXS MNXU MNYJ MNZB MNZC
MNZD MNZE MNZF MTAB MTAC MTAE MTAF MTAG MTAH MTAR MTBD
MTBH MTBI MTBJ MTBW MTBX MTBY MTCC MTCE MTCU MTCW MTDF
MTDR MTDW MTDY MTEJ MTEK MTEN MTEY MTFF MTFI MTFJ MTGA MTGO
MTGO MTHW MTHZ MTIA MTIB MTIL MTIM MTIN MTJA MTJB MTJC MTJD
MTJE MTJK MTJL MTJM MTJT MTJV MTJW MTJZ MTKN MTKV MTKW MTKX
MTKZ MTLB MTLC MTLD MTLL MTMA MTMC MTML MTMT MTMW MTMW
MTNC MTNG MTNH MTNI MTNJ MTNL MTNM MTNX MTNY MTPA MTPB
MTRA MTRZ MTSC MTTI MTTM MTTP MTTR MTTW MTUU MTUV MTVG
MTVH MTVI MTVJ MTWF MTWG MTWR MTWS MTWX MTXM MTXP MTXS
MTXZ MTZG MTZH MTZL MTZM MTZO MTZV MTZW MTZX MTZY MTZZ MVAA
MVAB MVAD MVAO MVAP MVBD MVBF MVBG MVBI MVBK MVBL MVBM
MVBN MVBO MVCE MVCF MVCY MVCZ MVDA MVDT MVEH MVEJ MVEK
MVEL MVEO MVEP MVER MVES MVET MVEV MVEW MVGM MVHE MVHF
MVHG MVHH MVIB MVIC MVLH MVIX MVIY MVIZ MVJA MVJC MVJE MVJL
MVKC MVLL MVLR MVMO MVMR MVMT MVMU MVMV MVMX MVMY MVMZ
MVNM MVNW MVNX MVNY MVNZ MVOB MVOF MVON MVOR MVPA MVPB
MVPD MVPE MVPI MVPO MVRA MVRB MVRC MVRD MVRM MVSN MVSO
MVSP MVST MVSV MVTC MVUA MVXB MVXC MVXR MVXS MVYS MVZS
MWAB MWAU MWCE MWCW MWDJ MWEL MWGG MWHO MWHR MWIA
MWIG MWIH MWIV MWJY MWLP MWLT MWLX MWMM MWMS MWMT MWMX
MWMY MWNE MWNS MWNT MWNU MWOJ MWOK MWOL MWPA MWPB
MWPC MWPD MWPF MWPO MWRB MWRC MWRD MWRE MWRF MWRG
MWRH MWRI MWRJ MWRR MWSL MWSM MWTG MWTH MWTO MWTR
MWTY MWTZ MWVN MWVO MWVR MWVS MWVT MWVW MWVY MWVZ
MWWB MWWC MWWK MWWN MWXB MWXC MWXL MWXN
MWXN MWXO MWXU MWXV MWYA MWYG MWYH MWYL MWYT MWYV
MWZC MWZG MWZL MWZN MYAO MYAS MYAU MYBJ MYCK MYCR MYCS
MYDV MYEU MYFP MYFR MYGJ MYHF MYHJ MYHN MYHX MYIH
MYIV MYIY MYJB MYJC MYJM MYKC MYKG MYKH MYKV MYLG MYLR MYMK
MYMO MYMV MYND MYOM MYOW MYPE MYPW MYSJ OLJT

GEMINI *(Trike)*
G-MBST MBTE MJYP MMAJ MMAR MMIR MMIV MMJT MMKM MMMD MMOB MMRP MMRW MMSC MMSO MMTL MMTX MMXW MNGB MNMC MNUM MTBY

MERCURY
G-MWVK MWXF MWXJ MWXK MWZA MYAI MYAV MYCJ MYCL MYCN MYCV MYDC MYGJ MYJR MYKI MYKW MYKX MYKY MYLS MYML MYMT MYNC MYNF MYNJ MYOB MYOF MYOV MYOX MYPD MYPV MYRW MYSG MYSZ MYTB MYTK MYTX MYUB MYUD MYUE MYUK MYUW MYVL MYVS MYWA MYYU MZAK MZCO

RAPIER
G-BYBV BYOZ BZAB BZUF BZWR MZEP MZEV MZFD MZGL MZHJ MZHL MZIL MZIM MZJE MZKN MZND MZNU MZON YARR

SCORCHER SOLO
G-MNDD MNNM MNPV MNPY MNPZ MNRE MNRF MNRG MNRZ MYFT MZKI MZKN

STARLET
G-MYLT

TRI-FLYER *(Trike)*
G-MBCJ MBGA MBHK MBIZ MBPG MBPZ MBUK MBZA MBZO MJEE MJEY MJFK MJHR MJIF MJJO MJMN MJMR MJPE MJTP MJXE MJYV MJYX MJZU MMAL MMAN MMCZ MMDK MMDN MMDT MMEJ MMFD MMFE MMFK MMJG MMKR MMLI MMMB MMNW MMTD MMUH MMWG MMWN MMYV MNIW MNJD MNJG MNUI MNXB MVBC

MAINAIR/FLEXIFORM
RAPIER 1+1 *(Combi)*
G-MJYV

MALMO see BÖLKOW

MANNING-FLANDERS
MF.1
G-BAAF

MANTA
PFLEDGE *(Wing)*
G-MBNY

MANUEL
LADYBIRD
G-MJPB

MARQUART
MA.5 CHARGER
G-BHBT BVJX

MASQUITO
M.58
G-MASX MASY MASZ

MAULE AIRCRAFT CORPORATION
M-5 LUNAR ROCKET
G-BHJK BICX BIES BPMB BVFT BVFZ CBVW CCBF FMGG KRIS OJGT RAIN RJWW
M-6 SUPER ROCKET
G-BKGC MOUL
M(XT)-7 SUPER/STAR ROCKET/STARCRAFT
G-BSKG BSKO BTMJ BTWN BTXT BUEP BUXD BVIK BVIL BZDT CROL GROL HIND ITON JREE LOFM OMOL WALY

MAX HOLSTE
MH.1521M BROUSSARD
G-BWGG BWLR CBGL YYYY

MAXAIR
DRIFTER
G-MYBB
HUMMER
G-MBYH MJCF MMZZ MNIM

MBB
Bö.105
G-AZOR BAMF BATC BCXO BFYA BTHV BTKL BUXS CDBS DNLB ESAM EYNL NAAA NAAB PASB PASG PASX SPOL THLS WMAA WOSY WYPA
BK.117
G-DCPA

MD HELICOPTERS INC
MD.500N
G-NOTR
MD.600N
G-BZTZ ODOD PEPL

MD.900
G-BXZK EHMS GMPS HPOL KAAT LNAA SIVR SUSX WMID WPAS YPOL

MEA
MISTRAL TRAINER
G-MBET MBOH MBUS MMIB

MEDWAY MICROLIGHTS LTD see RAVEN/SOUTHDOWN
ECLIPSER
G-BYBO BYXV BYXW BZGE BZWI CBMR CBMS CCCI OBRI
HALF PINT *(Trike)*
G-MMSZ MMZI MNDE MNEK MNLW MNTT MNVL
HYBRED *(Trike/Combi/R44XLR)*
G-BYBJ BYRH MGOM MJVE MMEK MMKG MMKH MNCU MNCV MNEI MNFW MNJK MNMN MNXO MTFC MTJG MTJP MTLX MTNE MTNF MTUX MVCD MVDB MVDJ MVEE MVGB MVGL MVGY MVKB MVPF MVPG MVPL MVRY MVRZ MVSI MVSR MVUD MVVH MVVI MVVR MVVV MVXD MVXE MVXI MVXJ MVXM MVYP MVYR MVZO MWBJ MWCX MWCY MWCZ MWGC MWIL MWJP-MWJR MWJX MWLB MWLS MWRM MWSS MWST MWSU MWVU MYRI MYVV MYVX MZGE MZME
PUMA SPRINT
G-MMJM MWBI
RAVEN
G-MVIF
REBEL
G-BYPP BYSS

(SOCIÉTÉ) MENAVIA see PIEL

MESSERSCHMITT see NORD & including HISPANO production
Bf.109/HA.1112
G-AWHS BWUE BYDS

MICKLEBURGH
L107
G-BZVC

MICRO AVIATION
B-22 BANTAM
G-BXZU BZYS MZEY MZLX

MICRO BIPLANE AVIATION (MBA)
TIGER CUB
G-MJRU MJSP MJSU MJSV MJUF MJUH MJUW MJWF MJWJ MJXF MJYD MJYJ MJZE MMAG MMBH MMBT MMCX MMFN MMFS MMGF MMGL MMHN MMIE MMIH MMIM MMIX MMJV MMKP MMLB MMOI MMUM MNJC MNKM MWFT

MICROFLIGHT AIRCRAFT LTD
SPECTRUM
G-MVJM MVSU MVWX MWCG MWHD MWKW MWKX MWOF MWPG MWPH MWTD MWTE MWWR MWWX MYAY

MIDLAND ULTRALIGHTS LTD
FIREFLY/SX130
G-MNUL
SIROCCO
G-MNDU MNDW MNRT MTJN MTRC MVSM

MIGNET
HM.14/HM.19 POU-DU-CIEL
G-ADRG ADRX ADRY ADVU ADYV ADZW AEBB AEEH AEFG AEGV AEHM AEJZ AEKR AEMY AEOH AFFI BWRI MYSI
HM.293
G-AXPG
HM-1000 BALERIT
G-MRAM MYDZ MYXL MZIX MZLI MZMW MZPB MZTA

MIKOYAN AVIATION including WSK-PZL
MiG-15 (Lim-2)
G-BMZF
MiG-17 (Lim 5)
G-MIGG
MiG-21
G-BRAM

MILES AIRCRAFT LTD
M.2H HAWK MAJOR
G-ADMW
M.2L HAWK SPEED SIX
G-ADGP
M.3 FALCON
G-AEEG

M.5 SPARROWHAWK
G-ADNL
M.11A WHITNEY STRAIGHT
G-AERV AEUJ
M.12 MOHAWK
G-AEKW
M.14A HAWK TRAINER 3
G-AFBS AHUJ AIUA AJRS AKAT AKKR AKKY AKPF ANWO
M.17 MONARCH
G-AFJU AFLW AFRZ
M.18
G-AHKY
M.38/48 MESSENGER
G-AGOY AIEK AJOC AJOE AJWB AKAO AKBO AKEZ AKIN AKIS AKVZ ALAH
M.65 GEMINI
G-AKDK AKEL AKER AKGD AKGE AKHP AKHW AKHZ AKKA AKKB AKKH
ALCS
M.75 ARIES
G-AOGA
M.100 STUDENT
G-APLK MIOO

MILLS
MH-1
G-OMHI

MIRAGE see ULTRAFLIGHT

MITCHELL
WING B-10
G-MMJA
WING U-2
G-MMNS

MITCHELL-PROCTER see PROCTER
KITTIWAKE
G-ATXN BBRN BBUL

MONG
SPORT
G-BTOA

MONNETT
MONI
G-BMVU CBTL NOW MONI TRIM
SONERAI
G-BGEH BGLK BICJ BJBM BJLC BKDC BKNO BLAI BMIS BOBY BSGJ BVCC
CCOZ LOWE PFAT RILY

MONOCOUPE
90A
G-AFEL

MONTGOMERIE-BENSEN see BENSEN & PARSONS

MOONEY AIRCRAFT CORPORATION
M.20/M.252
G-APVV ASUB ATOU AWLP BCJH BDTV BHBI BHJI BIBB BIWR BJHB BKMA
BKMB BPCR BPFC BSXI BVZY BWJG BWTW BXML BYDD BYEE CERT DBYE
DESS DEST EKMW FLYA GCKI GJKK JAKI JDIX JENA MALS MUNI OBAL
ODJH OEAC OJAC OJJB OONE OPWS OSUS RAFW ZZIP

MORANE-SAULNIER see DE HAVILLAND & FIESELER & inc GEMS, MORANE, SEEMS
& SOCATA production
TYPE N
G-AWBU
MS.315
G-BZNK
MS.502/505
G-BIRW BPHZ
MS.733 ALCYON
G-MSAL
MS.880/MS.885/MS.887/MS.892/MS.894 RALLYE/GALERIEN/GALOPIN
G-ARXW ASAT ASAU AVIN AVTV AVVJ AVZX AWAA AWKT AWOA AWXY
AWYX AXCL AXCM AXGC AXGE AXHS AXHT AXOH AXOS AXOT AYRH
AYTA AYYX AZEE AZGI AZGL AZKC AZKE AZMZ AZUT AZVF AZVH AZVI
AZYD BAAI BAOG BAOH BAOJ BAOM BBED BBGC BBLM BCLT BCOR BCST
BCUL BCVC BCXB BDEC BDWH BECA BECB BECC BEIL BERA BERC BETO
BEVB BEVC BEVW BFAK BFDF BFGS BFTZ BGKC BGMT BGPZ BGSA BHWK
BIAC BIIK BIOR BJDF BKBF BKGA BKGT BKJF BKOA BKUT BKVA BKVB
BLGS BLIY BOJL BPJD BRDN BTIU BTOW BTUG BUKR BVAN BVWA BWWG
BXZT BYPN BZNX EISO EXIT FARM FOSY GIGI HENT HHAV KHRE MELV
OACI OIAN OMIA PIGS WCEI

MORAVAN NARODNI PODNIK see ZLIN

MORRIS MOTORS LTD see DE HAVILLAND

MOSSCRAFT
MA.1/MA.2
G-AFHA AFJV

MOTH CORPORATION see DE HAVILLAND

MOTO-DELTA see CENTRAIR

MOULT
(Trike)|
G-MTFK

MOYES ULTRASPORTS LTD
MEGA (Wing)
G-MZCL

MSS see EUROWING

MUDRY see CAARP

MURPHY AIRCRAFT MANUFACTURING LTD
ELITE
G-CBRT
MAVERICK
G-BYCV MZJJ MZJS MZLE ONFL CBVF
REBEL
G-BUTK BVHS BWCY BWFZ BWLL BWFZ BYBK BZFT CBFK DIKY LJCC YELL
RENEGADE/SPIRIT
G-BTHN BTKB BWPE BYBU FIRZ MGOO MVZP MVZX MWAJ MWDM MWKA
MWMW MWNF MWNR MWOO MWPS MWPZ MWUH MWVP MWWD MYAM
MYAZ MYCO MYFM MYJP MYRK MYUF MYXR MZIZ NINE RCMC RENE
TBAG TBMW

NANCHANG see YAKOVLEV

NASH see PROCTER

NAVAL AIRCRAFT FACTORY
N3N-3
G-ONAF

NEICO
LANCAIR 235/320/IV
G-BSPX BSRI BUNO CBAF FOPP PJMT UILE

NICOLLIER
HN.700 MENESTREL
G-BVHL CCCJ MINS

NIEUPORT
SCOUT 17/23
G-BWMJ
28C-1
G-BSKS

NIMROD see AIRWAVE

NOBLE HARDMAN AVIATION LTD
SNOWBIRD
G-BZYV MTXL MTXU MVCI MVCJ MVIL MVIM MVIN MVIO MVOJ MVOL MVYT
MVYU MVYV MVYW MVYX RUMI

NOORDUYN AVIATION LTD see NORTH AMERICAN

NORD see SNCAC
1002 PINGOUIN
G-ASTG ATBG
1101 NORALPHA
G-ATDB ATHN BAYV SMD
1203 NORECRIN
G-BAYL BEDB
3202
G-BIZK BIZM BPMU
3400
G-BOSJ

NORMAN
NAC-1 FREELANCE
  G-NACA NACI
NDN-1 FIRECRACKER/TURBO FIRECRACKER
  G-NDNI
NAC-6 FIELDMASTER/FIREMASTER
  G-NRDC

NORTH AMERICAN see LOEHLE & including CCF & FENNEC production
B-25 MITCHELL
  G-BKXW BWGR BYDR
F-86 SABRE
  G-SABR
P-51 MUSTANG
  G-BIXL BTCD CBNM HAEC MSTG PSIC SIRR SUSY
NA-64 YALE
  G-BYNF
OV-10B BRONCO
  G-BZGK BZGL
T-6/AT-16 HARVARD/TEXAN
  G-AZBN AZSC BBHK BDAM BGGR BGHU BGOR BGPB BHTH BICE BIWX
  BJST BKRA BRLV BRVG BSBG BTXI BWUL BZHL CTKL DDMV ELMH HRVD
  JUDI RAIX TOMC TSIX TVIJ
T-28/A TROJAN/FENNEC
  G-TROY

NOSTALGAIR
N.3 PUP
  G-BVEA

NOTT
NAZCA II
  G-CBWH

NOTT-CAMERON
ULD-1/2/3
  G-BLJN BNXK NOTT

NOVA VERTRIEBSGESELLSCHAFT GmbH
VERTEX
  G-BYLI BYZT BZVI
PHOCUS
  G-BZYI
PHILOU
  G-BZXI
X LARGE 37
  G-BZJI

OLDFIELD
BABY LAKES
  G-BBGL BGEI BGLS BKCJ BKHD BMIY BRKO BTZL BWMO POND

OMEGA BALLOONS
O-20
  G-AXMD
56
  G-AYAL
84
  G-AWMO AXJB AXVU

OPTICA see EDGLEY

ORD-HUME see LUTON

ORIENTAL
MLB
  G-BINY

ORLICAN
L-40 META-SOKOL
  G-APUE APVU AROF

OSPREY (CHOWN)
MLB variants
  G-BJID BJLE BJND BJNH BJPL BJRA BJRG BJTN BJTY BJUE BJUU FYAV
  FYBD FYBE FYBF FYBG FYBH FYBI FYBJ FYCL FYCV FYCZ FYDF FYDO
  FYDS FYEV FYFN

PAKES
JACKDAW
  G-MBOF

PANTHER see MAINAIR/SOLAR WINGS/ULTRASPORTS

PARKER
CA-4
  G-AFIU

PARNALL
ELF
  G-AAIN
PIXIE
  G-EBJG

PARSONS including MONTGOMERIE production
GYROCOPTER/GYROPLANE
  G-BPIF BTFE BUWH CBOU IIXX IVYS UNIV

PARTENAVIA COSTRUZIONI AERONAUTICHE S.p.A
P.64B OSCAR
  G-BMDP
P.68B/C VICTOR
  G-BCDK BFBU BGXJ BHBZ BHJS BIFZ BMOI ENCE FJMS HUBB KIMK KWIK
  OLMA ONCM ORVR PART SAMJ

PAYNE
AX6-62 HAB
  G-AZRI BFMZ

PAYNE KNIGHT
TWISTER
  G-BRAX

PAZMANY
PL-2
  G-OPAZ
PL-4/A
  G-BMMI BRFX FISK PAZY PLIV

PEARSON
MLB
  G-BIXX

PEGASUS AVIATION see CYCLONE AIRSPORTS
QUANTUM 15 variants
  G-BYEU BYDM BYDZ BYEW BYFF BYFG BYIS BYIZ BYJK BYKT BYLC BYMF
  BYMI BYMT BYND BYNO BYOG BYOV BYPB BYPJ BYPL BYRJ BYRU BYSR
  BYSX BYTC BYYN BYYP BYYY BZAI BZBR BZED BZGZ BZHN BZHO BZIM
  BZIW BZJF BZJO BZJZ BZKT BZLL BZLX BZLZ BZMI BZMW BZNB BZNC BZNM
  BZOC BZOD BZOE BZOO BZOU BZOV BZRJ BZRP BZSA BZSG BZSI BZSM
  BZSS BZSX BZUC BZUE BZUI BZUX BZVJ BZVV BZWS BZWU BZXV BZXX
  BZYN CBAY CBBB CBBN CBBP CBBZ CBCD CBCF CBCX CBDX CBDZ CBEN
  CBEU CBEV CBGG CBHK CBHN CBHY CBIZ CBJO CBKW CBLL CBMV CBNT
  CBOY CBSP CBTD CBTZ CBUD CBUS CBUU CBUZ CBYI CBYV DINO DSLL
  EDMC EMLY EOFW FFUN JAWC JGSI KICK MCEL MCJL MDBC MGDL MGDM
  MGEF MGFK MGGG MGGV MGMC MGTG MROC MSPY MYLC MYLE MYLH
  MYLI MYLK MYLL MYLM MYLZ MYMB MYMC MYMD MYMX MYNB MYNK
  MYNL MYNN MYNO MYNP MYNR MYNS MYNT MYNV MYNZ MYOU MYPH
  MYPI MYPN MYPX MYPY MYRF MYRM MYRN MYRS MYRT MYRY MYRZ
  MYSB MYSC MYSR MYSW MYSX MYSY MYTI MYTJ MYTN MYUO MYUU
  MYUV MYVC MYVJ MYVK MYVM MYVR MYWG MYWI MYWJ MYWL MYWL
  MYWO MYWR MYWT MYWU MYWW MYWX MYWY MYXE MYXT MYXW MYXX
  MYXZ MYYB MYYC MYYI MYYK MYYN MYYX MYZB MYZJ MYZK MYZL MYZM
  MYZY MZAN MZAW MZAX MZBB MZBC MZBI MZBM MZBO MZBT MZBY MZCI
  MZCJ MZCM MZCR MZCV MZCY MZDB MZDC MZDD MZDE MZDH MZDN
  MZDU MZDV MZDY MZEC MZEE MZEH MZEM MZET MZEX MZEZ MZFG
  MZFM MZFV MZGG MZGK MZGN MZGO MZGV MZHI MZHK MZHN MZHP MZIB
  MZIC MZIE MZIF MZIJ MZIK MZIU MZJG MZJH MZJN MZJO MZJT MZJW MZJY
  MZKA MZKD MZKF MZKL MZKX MZKY MZLA MZLD MZLF MZLH MZLJ MZLN
  MZLT MZLV MZLW MZMC MZMF MZMG MZMH MZNP MZMN MZMT MZNB
  MZNG MZNR MZNS MZNT MZOD MZOG MZOJ MZOS MZOV MZOW MZPD
  MZRC MZRH MZRM MZSC NAPO OAKS OAMF OBJP OELD OLDM OLFB OTJH
  PEGA PIXI PRSI REDC REPH RUSA SITA SMBM TBBC TRAM TUSA WHEE
QUASAR variants
  G-MWHT MWHU MWIM MWIU MWIW MWIX MWIY MWJD MWJH MWJI MWJJ
  MWJK MWJS MWJT MWJU MWJV MWLH MWLI MWLJ MWLK MWMI MWMJ
  MWMK MWML MWMM MWNK MWNL MWOM MWOP MWPU MWSH MWSI MWTK
  MWTL MWVM MWXG MWXH MWYI MWYJ MWZD MWZE MWZF MWZO
  MWZP MWZR MWZS MYAK MYBD MYBE MYBT MYCE MYCF MYEK MYEM
  MYEN MYEO MYFK MYFL MYIM MYIN MYIO MYJJ MYJK MYJS MYJT MYJU
  MYKP MYKR MYKS MYTR MYXD MZMA MZPW REKO
QUIK
  G-CBRY CBVN CBYE CBYO CBZH CBZT CCAD CCAS CCAW CCAZ EZAR
  MRJJ SYTX TERR

PENN-SMITH
GYROPLANE
G-AXOM

PERCIVAL AIRCRAFT CO/LTD see HUNTING
P.1/P.3 GULL
G-ACGR ADPR
P.6 MEW GULL
G-AEXF
P.10 VEGA GULL
G-AEZJ
P.16 Q SIX
G-AFFD
P.28/P.31/P.34/P.44 PROCTOR
G-AHTE AKIU AKZN ALCK ALJF ANPP ANXR
P.40 PRENTICE
G-AOKH AOKL AOKO AOKZ AOLK AOLU APIT APIY APJB APPL
P.56 PROVOST
G-AWPH AWRY AWVF BDYG BKFW BLIW KAPW MOOS TMKI
P.57/P.66 PRINCE/SEA PRINCE/PEMBROKE
G-AMLZ BNPH BNPU BXES DACA GACA RACA

PEREIRA
OSPREY
G-BEPB BVGI GEOF PREY

PHANTOM see SKYRIDER

PHILLIPS
ST.1 SPEEDTWIN
G-DPST EMNI GPST

PHOENIX see CURRIE WOT & ROLLASON
LUTON LA-4/A MINOR/PARKER CA-4/PHOENIX DUET
G-AFIR AMAW ARIF ARXP ASAA ASEA ASEB ASML ASXJ ATCJ ATCN ATFW ATKH AVDY AVUO AWIP AWMN AXGR AXKH AYDY AYSK AYTT AZHU AZPV BANF BBCY BBEA BCFY BDJG BIJS BKHR BRWU
LA-5A MAJOR
G-ARAD

PIAGGIO including FOCKE WULF production
P.149
G-BRKD RORY
P.166
G-APWY

PICCARD
Hot Air Balloon
G-ATTN
AX6
G-AWCR AZHR

PIEL including COOPAVIA, MENAVIA, ROUSSEAU, SCINTEX production & BINDER / FAIRTRAVEL variants
CP.301/328 EMERAUDE
G-APNS ARDD ARRS ARUV ASCZ ASLX ASMT ASVG ASZR AXXC AYCE AYEC AYTR AZGY AZYS BBKL BCCR BDCI BDDZ BDKH BHRR BIDO BIJU BIVF BKFR BKNZ BKUR BLRL BPRT BSVE BXAH BXYE DENS PIEL SAZZ
CP.1310/1315/1320 SUPER EMERAUDE
G-ASMV ASNI BANW BCHP BGVE BHEK BJCF BJVS BLXI BXRF SAFI

PIETENPOL
AIRCAMPER
G-ADRA BBSW BKVO BMDE BMLT BNMH BPOL BRXY BSVZ BUCO BUXK BUZO BVYY BWAT BWWB BXZO BYFT BYKG BYLD BYZY DAYZ ECOX EDFS IMBY OFFA OHAL OPJS PCAF PIET RAGS SILS SLOW TARN UNGO VALS

PIK see EIRI & SIREN

PILATUS AIRCRAFT LTD
P.2
G-BLKZ BONE CJCI PTWO
P.3
G-BTLL
PC.6 PORTER
G-BYNE WGSC

PIPER AIRCRAFT CORPORATION see TED SMITH & including TAYLOR AIRCRAFT CO LTD & THE NEW PIPER AIRCRAFT INC production
J-2 CUB
G-AEXZ AFFH JTWO
J-3C CUB (L-4/O-59)
G-AFDO AGAT AGIV AGVV AHIP AIIH AISS AISX AJAD AJES AKAZ AKIB AKRA AKTH AKUN ASPS ATKI ATZM AXGP AXHP AXHR AYCN AYEN BAET BBHJ BBLH BBUU BBXS BCNX BCOB BCOM BCPH BCPJ BCUB BCXJ BDCD BDEY BDEZ BDHK BDJP BDMS BDOL BECN BEDJ BEUI BFBY BFDL BFHI BFZB BGPD BGSJ BGTI BGXA BHPK BHVV BHXY BHZU BIJE BILI BJAF BJAY BJSZ BJTO BKHG BLPA BMKC BOTU BOXJ BPCF BPUR BPVH BPYN BREB BROR BSBT BSFD BSNF BSTI BSVH BSYO BTBX BTET BTSP BTUM BTZX BVAF BVPN BWEZ CCUB COPS CUBS CUBY FRAN HEWI KIRK LIVH LOCH NCUB OCUB OINK OLEZ POOH RAMP SEED TCUB
J-4A CUB COUPE
G-AFGM AFWH AFZA BSDJ BUWL
J-5A CUB CRUISER
G-BRIL BRLI BSDK BSXT BTKA
PA-12 SUPER CRUISER
G-AMPG ARTH AWPW AXUC BCAZ BOWN BSYG PAIZ
PA-15/PA-17 VAGABOND
G-AKTP ALEH ALGA ALIJ AMYL ASHU AWKD AWOF AWOH BCVB BDVA BDVB BDVC BIHT BLMP BOVB BRJL BRPY BRSX BSFW BSMV BSWG BTBY BTCI BTFJ BTOT BUKN BUXX FKNH VAGA
PA-16 CLIPPER
G-BAMR BBUG BIAP BSVI BSWF
PA-18/PA-18A SUPER CUB (L-18/L-21)
G-AMEN APZJ ARAM ARAN ARAO ARCT AREO ARGV ARVO ASCU ATRG AVOO AWMF AXGA AXLZ AYPM AYPO AYPR AYPS AYPT AZRL BAFT BAFV BAKV BBOL BBYB BCFO BCMD BEOI BEUA BEUU BFFP BGPN BGWH BGYN BHGC BHOM BHPM BIDJ BIDK BIID BIJB BIMM BIRH BITA BIYJ BIYR BIYY BIZV BJBK BJCI BJEI BJFE BJVI BJLH BJTP BJWX BJWZ BKET BKJB BKRF BKTA BKVM BLGT BLHM BLIH BLLN BLLO BLMI BLMR BLMT BLPE BLRC BMAY BMEA BMKB BNXM BOOC BPJG BPJH BPUL BROZ BRRL BSHV BTBU BTDX BTUR BVIE BVIW BVMI BVRZ BWHH BWOR BWUB BZHT CBFI CUBB CUBI CUBJ CUBP FUZZ GCUB GDAM HACK HELN JCUB KAMP LION NESY NETY NNAC OFER OROD OSPS OTAN OTUG PIPR PUDL PULL ROVE SCUB SUPA TUGG WCUB WGCS WLAC XCUB YCUB ZAZA
PA-20 PACER/PA-22 conversions
G-APTP APYI ARBS ARGY ARNK ATBX AVDV ATXA BFMR BIYP BSED BTLM BUDE BUOI BUXV BWWU BXBB GGLE PAXX
PA-22 TRI-PACER/CARIBBEAN/COLT
G-APUR APXR APXT APXU APYN APZL APZX ARAI ARAX ARBV ARCC ARCF ARDS ARDT ARDV AREL ARET AREV ARFB ARFD ARGO ARHN ARHP ARHR ARHU ARIK ARIL ARJE ARJF ARJH ARKK ARKM ARKN ARKP ARKS ARND ARNE ARNG ARNJ ARNL ARON ARSU ARSW ARYH ASSE AWLI AZRS BMCS BNED BRNX BTKV BTWU BUVA CBEI HALL TJAY TLDK
PA-23/PA-27 APACHE/AZTEC
G-APMY ARBN ARCW ARHL ARJS ARJT ARJU ARJV ARYF ASEP ASHH ASHV ASMO ASMY ASND ATFF ATMU ATOA AXZP AYBO AYMO AZRG AZSZ AZXG AZYU BADI BADJ BAPL BATN BAUJ BAUW BAVL BAVZ BBCC BBDO BBEY BBGB BBHF BBIF BBMJ BBRA BBTJ BBVG BCBG BCBM BCCE BCEX BCRP BEXO BFBB BFVP BFWE BGTG BGWW BICY BJNZ BJXX BKJW BKVT BMFD BNUV BRAV BSVP BXPS BYRW CALL CSFT ESKY FOTO HFTG JTCA KEYS LIZZ MLFF MOLY NRSC OART OPME OSNI OXTC RVRC RVRD SFHR TAPE TAXI UNDO XSFT
PA-24/PA-26 COMANCHE
G-APUZ APXJ ARBO ARDB ARFH ARHI ARIN ARLK ARUO ARXG ARYV ASCJ ASEO ATIA ATJL ATNV ATOY AVCM AVGA AXMA AXTO AYED AZKR AZWY BAHG BAHJ BRDW BRXW BUTL BWNI BYTI DISK KSVB MOTO
PA-25 PAWNEE
G-ASIY ASKV ASVP ATFR AVPY AVXA AXED AZPA BAUC BCBJ BDDS BDDT BDPJ BDWL BEII BETL BETM BFBP BFEV BFEW BFEY BFPR BFPS BFRY BFSC BFSD BHUU BILL BLDG BNZV BPWL BSTH BUXY BVYP BXST CMGC DSGC LYND NYMF PAWN TOWS
PA-28-140/160 CHEROKEE/CHALLENGER/CRUISER/FLITE-LINER
G-ARUR ARVT ARVU ARVV ASLV ASPK ASSW ASVZ ATDA ATEZ ATIS ATJG ATMW ATOI ATOJ ATOK ATOL ATOM ATON ATOO ATOP ATOR ATOS ATPN ATRO ATRP ATRR ATTF ATTI ATTK ATTV ATUB ATUD ATVK ATVL ATVO AVFP AVFR AVFX AVFZ AVGC AVGD AVGE AVGG AVGI AVLB AVLC AVLD AVLE AVLF AVLG AVLH AVLI AVLJ AVLT AVSI AVUS AVUT AVUU AVVO AVWD AVWE AVWG AVWI AVWJ AVWL AVWM AVYP AVYR AWBE AWBG AWBH AWBS AWEV AWEX AWPS AWSM AWTM AXAB AXIO AXJV AXJX AXSZ AXTA AXTC AXTH AXTJ AXTL AYAT AYIG AYJP AYJR AZWB AZWD AZWE AZZO BAFU BAFW BAGX BAHE BAHF BAKH BAMM BASL BATW BAWK BAXZ BBBK BBBY BBDC BBEF BBEV BBHY BBIL BBIX BBYP BBZF BCDJ BCGI BCGJ BCGN BCGT BCJM BCJN BCJP BDGY BDSH BDWY BEAC BEEU BEFF BEYO BEYT BFBF BFXK BGAX BGPU BGRC BHXK BIFB BIYX BOFY BOSR BOSU BRBW BRPK BRPL BRWO BSER BSLM BSLU BSSE BSTZ BTEX BTGO BTON BTVR BULR BWYB BXPL BXVU BXYM BYCA BZWG CGHM COLH DAKS DENE DIAT FIAT GCAT JAKS JDJM KATS LFSC LFSI LIZI LTFC MATZ MIDD MKAS NHRH OFTI OKYM OMAT PAWL PETR PIKK RECK SCPL SMTH TEFC TEWS UANT WOLF
PA-28-151/161 CHEROKEE WARRIOR/CADET
G-BCIE BCIR BCRL BCTF BDGM BDPA BEBZ BEFA BELP BFBR BFDK BFMG BFNI BFNJ BFNK BFWB BFWK BGKS BGOG BGPJ BGPL BGVK BHFK BHIL BHJO BHOR BHRC BHVB BICW BIEY BIFB BIUW BJBW BJBX BJBY BJCA BJSV BJYG BLEJ BLVL BMFP BMKR BMTR BMUZ BNCR BNEL BNJM BNJT BNMB BNNO BNNS BNNT BNNY BNNZ BNOE BNOF BNOG BNOH BNOJ

BNOK BNOM BNON BNOP BNOS BNOT BNOV BNRG BNSY BNSZ BNTD
BNXE BNXT BNXU BNZB BNZZ BOAH BODA BODB BODC BODD BODE BODF
BODR BOER BOFZ BOHA BOHO BOHR BOIG BOJG BOJZ BOKB BOKK BOKL
BOKP BOKS BOKT BOKX BOMY BOPC BORK BORL BOSP BOTF BOTI BOTN
BOUP BOUR BOVK BOXA BOXB BOXC BOYH BOYI BOZI BPAC BPAF BPBM
BPCK BPDT BPDU BPEL BPFH BPHB BPHL BPID BPIU BPJO BPJP BPJR
BPJU BPKM BPKR BPMF BPMR BPOM BPPK BPRN BPRY BPWA BPWE
BRBA BRBB BRBD BRBE BRDF BRDG BRDM BRFM BRJV BRRN BRSE BRSG
BRTM BRTX BRUB BRXC BSAW BSBA BSCV BSCY BSFK BSGL BSJX BSLE
BSLK BSLT BSMZ BSOK BSOZ BSPI BSPM BSSC BSSW BSSX BSVG BSVM
BSXA BSXB BSXC BSYZ BSZT BTAW BTBC BTDV BTFO BTGY BTID BTIM
BTIV BTKT BTNE BTNT BTNV BTRK BTRS BTRY BTSJ BTUW BUFH BUFY
BUIF BUIJ BUIK BUJO BUJP BUKK BURT BVIH BVJZ BVTO BXAB BXJX BXLY
BXNH BXTX BXTY BXTZ BYHH BYHI BYKN BYKO BYKR BYXU BYZM BZBS
BZDA BZLH BZMT CBAL CBKR CBWD CBXP CBYU CDON CLAC CLEA CPTM
CWFZ DENH DOME EDGI EEGU EGLD EGTR EKIR EKKL ELZY EMSL EOLD
ERFS ESFT ESSX ETDA FIZZ FLAV FLEN FMAM FNPT FOXA FPIG FPSA
GALB GBRB GFCA GFCB GFCF GFTA GFTB GRRC GURU GUSS GYTO
HMED HMES IKBP ISDB JACA JAMP JASE JAVO KART KBPI KDET KNAP
LACA LACB LAZL LBMM LFSJ LORC LSFT LUSH MAYO MSFT NINA NSFT
OAAA OANI OBFC ODEN OGCA OJWS OMST OOFT OONY OTYJ OWAR
PSRT RIZZ RSKR ROWS SACI SACO SACR SACS SACT SACU SACZ SARH
SEJW SLYN SNUZ SRWN SUZN TAGS VICC WARB WARC WARE WARH
WARR WARS WARV WARW WARX WARY WFFW XENA ZULU

PA-28-180/181 CHEROKEE/CHALLENGER/ARCHER
G-ARYR ASFL ASHX ASII ASIJ ASIL ASKT ASRW ASUD ASWX ATAA ATAS
ATEM ATHR ATNB ATOT ATTX ATUL ATVS ATXM ATYS ATZK AVAX AVBG
AVBH AVBS AVGK AVNN AVNO AVNP AVNS AVNU AVNW AVOZ AVPV AVRK
AVRU AVRY AVRZ AVSA AVSB AVSC AVSD AVSE AVSF AVSP AVYL AVYM
AVZR AWDP AWET AWIT AWSL AWTL AWXR AWXS AXOR AXSG AXTP
AXZD AXZF AYAB AYAR AYAS AYAW AYEE AYEF AYPJ AYUH AYUI AZDX
AZLN BABG BAJR BASJ BATV BBBN BBEC BBKX BBPY BCCF BCLL BDSB
BEIP BEMW BEXW BEYL BFDI BFSY BFVG BGBG BGTJ BGVZ BGWM BHNO
BHWZ BHZE BIIV BIUY BJAG BJOA BKCC BLFI BMIW BMPC BMSD BNGT
BNPO BNRP BNVE BNYP BOBZ BODM BOEE BOHM BOJM BOMP BOMU
BOOF BOPA BORS BOSE BPAY BPFI BPGU BPOT BPTE BPXA BPYO BRBG
BRBX BRGI BRME BRNV BRUD BRXD BSCS BSEF BSEU BSGD BSIM BSIZ
BSKW BSNX BSVB BSXS BSZJ BTAM BTGZ BTKX BTYI BUMP BUTZ BUUX
BUYY BVNS BVOA BWPH BWUH BXEX BXIF BXJD BXOZ BXRG BXRJ BXTW
BXWO BYFP BYHK BYKL BYSP BZHK BZHV CBMO CBSO CBTT CHAS CHIP
CIFR CJBC DEVS DIXY DJJA DLTR EFIR EGLS EHGF EHLX EMAZ ERNI
FBRN FLUX GALA GASP GBRB HARN HOCK IBBO ILLY ISAX ITUG JACB
JACC JACS JADJ JANA JANT JCAS JJAN JJEN JOYT JOYZ KAIR KEES KEMI
KEVB KITE LACD LFSG LKTB LORR MALA MASF MDAC MERI NERI NIKE
NINB NINC NITA NOTE OBFS OBUS OGEM OIBO OJEH ONET OODW OPET
ORAR PEJM PIPA RADI REXS SARA SGSE SHED SOBI SOOT SUEB SVEA
TEMP TERY TIMK TSGJ TWEL USSY VOAR WACP WACR YANK YULL ZMAM

PA-28-235/236 CHEROKEE/DAKOTA
G-BGXS BHTA BNYB BOKA BPCX BRKH BXCC BZEH CCBH DAKO FRGN
FWPW KOTA LEAM ODAK TART

PA-28R/PA-28RT CHEROKEE ARROW
G-AVWN AVWO AVWW AVWU AVWV AVXF AVYS AVYT AWAZ AWBA
AWBB AWBC AWEZ AWFB AWFC AWFD AWFJ AXCA AXWZ AYAC AYII AYPU
AYRI AZAJ AZDE AZFI AZFM AZNL AZOG AZSF AZRV AZWS BAHS BAIH
BAMY BAPW BAWG BBDE BBEB BBFD BBIA BBZH BBZV BCGS BCJO BCPG
BEOH BEWX BFDO BFLI BFTC BFZH BGKU BGKV BGOL BGVN BHAY BHEV
BHFJ BHGY BHIR BHWY BIDI BIKE BIZO BKFZ BKXF BLXP BMGB BMHT
BMIV BMJG BMKK BMLS BMNL BMOE BMPR BNEE BNJR BNNX BNSG BNTC
BNTS BNVT BNZG BOBA BOET BOGM BOIC BOJI BONC BOOG BOWY BOYV
BPBO BPXJ BPZM BRLG BRMS BRRJ BSNP BSPN BTLG BTRT BUND BUNH-
BUUM BVDH BWMI BWNM BXVC BXYO BXYP BXYR BXYT BYHJ BYKP BZKL
CBEE CBPI CBVU CBZR CSWH DAAH DAAZ DDAY DIZY DMCS DNCS DONS
DORA DSFT ECJM EDVL EPTR EVVA FBWH FULL GDOG GEHP GHRW
GPMW GYMM HALC HERB IBFW IJOE IRKB ISCA JANO JESS JMTT LAOL
LBRC LZZY MACK MEAH MEGA MEME MERL MRST NELI OARI OARO OARU
OBAK ODOG OJIM OKAG OKEN OMHC OMNI ONSF OOTC OPEP OPJD
ORDN OTGA RACO RJMS RONG RUBY SABA SBMM SHAY SHUG STEA
TCTC TEBZ THSL TOBE TOLL UTSY VOID WEND WILS WWAL YAWW

PA-30/PA-39 TWIN COMANCHE
G-ASMA ASON ASRO ASSB ASSP ASWW ATEW ATMT ATSZ ATWR ATXD
AVAU AVCX AVCY AVJJ AVKL AVPS AVUD AWBN AWBT AYSB AYZE AZAB
BAKJ BAWN BKCL BLOR BZRO COMB LADI LARE OAJS OGET ORDO RROD
SIGN SURG TCOM

PA-31/PA-31T NAVAJO/CHIEFTAIN/CHEYENNE
G-AYEI BBDS BBZI BEZL BFAM BFIB BFOM BLFZ BPYR BVYF BWDE BWHF
BXKS CBGF CBTN CITY EEJE EHJM EMAX EPED FILL GLTT GLUG GURN
HVRD IFIT ILEA ISFC JAJK LIDE LYDD MOHS MRMR NERC NEWR OAMT
OJIL ONAV ONPA OSGB OWLC PLAC PMAX PZAZ PZIZ RHYM SASK UMMI
VICT VIPP YEOM

PA-32/PA-32R CHEROKEE SIX/LANCE/SARATOGA
G-ATES ATJV ATRW ATRX AVFU AVTK AVUZ AZDJ BAGG BAXJ BBFV
BBSM BDWP BEHH BEZP BFUB BFYC BGUB BHBG BHGO BHWL BJCW
BKEK BKMT BMDC BMJA BOGO BOON BOTV BPVI BPVN BRGT BRHA BRNZ
BSTV BSUF BSYC BTCA BVBG BVWZ BXWP BYFR BYPU CBCA CCST

CCSW CDUX CEYE CSIX CTCP DCAV DENI DIGI DIWY EENA ELDR ELLA
ETAV ETBY FLJA FRAG GOTO HDEW HERO HYLT IFFR ILTS IMPW JPOT
JUPP KFRA KNOW LADE LUNA MAIE MOLL MOVI NIOS NROY NEAL OCPF
OCTI OJCW OSCC OSIX OTBY PAPS PUSK RAMS RAYE REAH RHHT RIGH
ROLF SALA SAWU SIXD WAIR WINS WYST

PA-34 SENECA
G-AZIK AZOL AZOT AZVJ BABK BACB BAIG BAKD BASM BATR BBLU BBNH
BBNI BBPX BBXK BBZJ BCID BCVY BDUN BEAG BEHU BEJV BETT BEVG
BFKY BFLH BGFT BGLW BHFH BHYE BHYF BHYG BLWD BLYK BMDK BMJO
BMUT BNEN BNRX BOCG BOCP BOCR BOCS BOCT BOCU BOCX BOFE
BRHO BRXO BSDN BSGK BSHA BSII BSOY BSPG BSUW BTGU BTGV BUBU
BVDN BVEV BWDT BXPV BXPW BYBH BZTG CAHA CBWB CDAV CEGA
CHEM CLOS CLUE CTWW CVLH DARA DAZY DCEA DSID ELBC EMER EXEC
EZYU FILE FLYI GAFA GFCD GUYS HCSL HMJB HTRL IEIO IFLP JANN
JDBC JLCA LENY LORD MAIK MAXI MAXI MPWT NESW NSUK OACG OBNA
OOON OPAG OWAL PEGI POPS ROLA ROUS RVRB SENX TAIR TEST VASA
VVBK WIZO WWAS XKEN

PA-38 TOMAHAWK
G-BFVF BGBK BGBN BGBW BGBY BGEK BGGE BGGG BGGI BGGL BGGM
BGGN BGIG BGKY BGLA BGRL BGRM BGRN BGRR BGRX BGSH BGSI
BGWN BGWU BGXB BGXO BGZF BGZJ BGZW BHCZ BJNN BJUR BJUS
BJYN BKAS BKCY BLWP BMKG BMML BMNP BMSF BMTO BMVL BMVM
BMXL BNCO BNEK BNGR BNGS NBHG BNIM BNKH BNNU BNPL BNPM
BNSL BNUY BNVD BNXV BNYK BNYV BOBL BOCC BODP BODS BOHN
BOHS BOHT BOHU BOLD BOLE BOLF BOMO BOMZ BOUD BPER BPES BPHI
BPIK BPJF BPPD BPPE BPPF BRFL BRFN BRHR BRHT BRJR BRLO BRLP
BRMJ BRML BRNJ BRSJ BSFE BSKK BSKL BSOT BSOU BSVV BSVW BSVX
BSYK BSYL BSYM BTAP-BTAR BTAS BTFP BTIL BTJK BTJL BTND BTOD
BVHM BVLP BWNR BWNU BWSC BXET BXZA BYLE BYMC BYMD CHER
CWFA CWFB CWFD CWFE DFLY-DTOO DYOU EDNA EMMS EORG EGNR
GALL GTHM LFSA LFSB LFSD LFSH MSFC NCFC NCFE OATS OEDB OLFC
OPSF OTFT PRIM RECS REPM PVRF PVRG SION SUKI TOMS

PA-44 SEMINOLE
G-BGCO BGJB BGTF BHFE BHRP BOHX BRUI BRUX DENZ FSFT GAFT
GHSI GISO OACB OACC PDOC SEMI SOIF TWIN

PA-46 MALIBU/MERIDIAN
G-BXER BYLM BZSD CREW CUPN DIPM DNOP DODI HITS JCAR OACA
PALL PCAR VRST WADI

PIPER
CP.1 METISSE
G-BVCP

PITTS including AEROTECK, AVIAT & CHRISTEN INDUSTRIES INC
S-1/2 SPECIAL
G-AXNZ AZCE AZPH BADW BADZ BBOH BHSS BIRD BKDR BKPZ BKVP
BLAG BMTU BOEM BOXH BOXV BOZS BPDV BPLY BPRD BPZY BRAW
BRBN BRCE BRCI BRJN BRRS BRVL BRVT BRZL BRZX BSDB BSRH BTEF
BTOO BTTR BTUK BTUL BUWJ BVSZ BXAF BXAU BXFB BXTI BYIP BYIR
BYJP BZSB EWIZ FCUK FLIK FOLY FORZ GOMD HISS ICAS IICI IIDY IIII IIIL
IIIR IIIT IIIX ITII JAWZ KITI LITZ LOOP MAGG MAXG MINT OGEE OKAY OODI
OSIC OSIS OSIT OWAZ PEAL PIII PITS PITZ REAP ROLL SIIA SIIB SIIS SKYD
SOLO STUA STUB STYL SWUN TIII WAZZ WILD WREN XATS YOYO

PIXIE see SKYHOOK

PLUMB
BGP.1 BIPLANE
G-BGPI FUNN

PMPS
DRAGONFLY MPA Mk 1
G-BDFU

POBER
P-9 PIXIE
G-BUXO

PORTERFIELD
CP-50
G-AFZL
CP-65
G-BVWY

PORTSLADE SCHOOL
HAB
G-AZYL

PORTSWOOD
HAB
G-FYBS FYBX

(AVIONS) POTTIER
P.80S
G-BTYH

POWERCHUTE SYSTEMS INTERNATIONAL LTD
KESTREL
G-MVRV MWCI MWCJ MWCK MWCN MWCO MWCP MWCS MWFL MWGT
MWGU MWGW MWGY MWGZ MWMB MWMC MWMD MWMG MWMH MWNV
MWNX MWOC MWOD MWOE MYCW MYCX MYCY MYDA MYEW MYEX
MYFA MYHS
RAIDER
G-MVHB MVHC MVMD MVNA MVNC MVNI MVNK MVNL MVNM MVVZ MVWH
MVWJ

PRACTAVIA
PILOT SPRITE
G-AZZH BALY BCVF BCWH

PRICE
AX7-77 HAB
G-BMDJ
TPB.2 HAB
G-BULE

PRIVATEER see SLINGSBY

PROCTER see MITCHELL
PETREL
G-AXSF

PROTECH
PT-2C SASSY
G-EWAN

PTERODACTYL LTD see SOLEAIR
PFLEDGLING/PTRAVELER
G-MBAW MBHZ MBPB MJST MMPI

(ALFONS) PUTZER KG
ELSTER B
G-APVF BMWV LUFT

PZL
PZL-104 WILGA variants
G-BTNS BUNC BWDF BXBZ BXMU RIIN WILG WLGA
PZL SZD-45A OGAR
G-BEBG BKTM BMFI OGAR

QAC
QUICKIE/TRI-Q
G-BKFM BKSE BMFN BMVG BNCG BNJO- BPMW BPNL BPUC BSPA BSSK
BVYT BXOY FARY IMBI KUTU KWKI WAHL

QUAD CITY
CHALLENGER
G-BYKU CAMR CBDU IBFC MGAA MGRH MVZK MWFU MWFV MWFX MWFY
MWFZ MYAG MYDN MYDS MYFH MYGM MYIA MYIX MYOZ MYPZ MYRH
MYRJ MYSD MYTO MYTT MYUL MYXC MYXK MYXV MYYF MZAC MZBW
MZBZ MZEA MZHO MZKW MZNA

RAF -see REPLICA PLANS & SLINGSBY
SE-5
G-EBIA EBIB EBIC
G-BKDT

RAJ HAMSA
X'AIR variants
G-BYCL BYHV BYJU BYLN BYLT BYMM BYMR BYNT BYOH BYOJ BYOR BYPO
BYPW BYRV BYSY BYTW BYTT BYTZ BYYM BYYR BYZF BYZW BZAF BZAK
BZBP BZDK BZEJ BZER BZEX BZFF BZGX BZIA BZIS BZIY BZKC BZLD BZLT
BZMR BZNG BZUP BZVH BZVK BZVR BZWC BZXA BZYM BZYX CBAH CBAV
CBBH CBCI CBCM CBDO CBDV CBDW CBDY CBFE CBFT CBHB CBHV CBIC
CBII CBIS CBJX CBKL CBLF CBLH CBLP CBLW CBMA CBNJ CBOC CBPU CBTK
CBTY CBUC CBUJ CBVC CBVE CBVO CBWY CBXA CCAX CCBI CCBU CCDJ
HARI HITM ODJD OHWV RAJA TANJ THAT TKSD UFAW XAYR XIOO XRXR

RAND-ROBINSON
KR-2
G-BETW BFKC BLDN BMFL BMMD BNAD BNML BOLZ BPRR BRJY BRSN
BTGD BUDF BUDS BURF BUWT BVIA BVZJ BXXE BYLP BSTL CBAU CBPK
DGWW JCMW KISS KRII OFMB UTSI WYNN XRAY

RANGO including RANGO-SAFFERY
MLB variants
G-BJAS BJRH FYEU FYFW FYFY FYGI FYGK

RANS
S-4/S-5 COYOTE
G-MVPJ MVXW MWBO MWEP MWES MWFF MWFW MWGA MWGN MWIO
MWLA MWLZ MWWP MYDO MYWV MZGD
S-6 COYOTE variants
G-BSMU BSSI BSTT BSUA BSUT BTNW BTXD BUEW BUOK BUTM BUWK
BVCL BVFM BVIN BVOI BVPW BVRK BVUM BVZO BVZV BWHK BWWP
BWYR BXCU BXRZ BXWK BYBR BYCM BYCN BYCO BYIB BYID BYJO BYKE
BYMN BYMU BYMV BYNP BYOT BYOU BYPZ BYRG BYRS BYSN BYZO
BZBC BZBX BZEW BZKD BZKO BZLE BZMJ BZNH BZNJ BZRA BZRY BZUH
BZVM BZYA BZYL CBAS CBAZ CBFX CBNV CBOK CBOS CBTO CBUY CBXZ
CBYD CBZG CBZN CCDC CLEE IZIT MGEC MGND MWCH MWMF MWIF
MWRK MWSC MWTT MWUK MWUL MWUN MWVL MWWL MWYE MWYN
MYHI MYHK MYHP MYIR MYIS MYJD MYJY MYKN MYLD MYLF MYLO MYLW
MYMH MYMP MYMR MYMS MYNE MYNH MYOA MYOI MYOT MYPA MYPJ
MYSP MYSU MYTE MYUZ MYVP MYXB MYXG MYXP MYYV MYZR MZAH
MZBD MZBH MZBU MZCA MZDA MZDG MZDM MZDR MZEN MZEO
MZEU MZFL MZFN MZFY MZIY MZJI MZJM MZKE MZLG MZLL MZMP MZMS
MZMU MZNV MZOZ MZUB RINS SOOZ SSIH
S-7 COURIER
G-BVNY BWKJ BWMN CBNF KATI OJKM
S-9 CHAOS
G-BPUS BSEE
S-10 SAKOTA
G-BRPT BRSC BRZW BSBV BSGS BSMT BSNN BSWB BTCR BTGG BTJX
BTWZ BUAX BUGH BUKB BULW BVCB BVFA BVHI BWIA BWIL BYRE OEYE
RANS RANZ
S-12
G-BZAO

RAVEN AIRCRAFT INTERNATIONAL see MEDWAY & SOUTHDOWN
VECTOR
G-MBTW MJAZ

RAYTHEON HAWKER see HAWKER SIDDELEY AVIATION

REARWIN
175 SKYRANGER
G-BTGI RWIN
8125 CLOUDSTER
G-BVLK
8500 SPORTSTER
G-AEOF
9000L SPORTSTER
G-BGAU

REECE
SKY RANGER
G-MJRR

REID & SIGRIST
RS.4 DESFORD
G-AGOS

REIMS AVIATION SA see CESSNA

RENEGADE see MURPHY

REPLICA PLANS
SE-5A
G-BDWJ BIHF BKER BMDB BUOD BUWE INNY SEVA

REPUBLIC
P-47 THUNDERBOLT
G-THUN

REVOLUTION HELICOPTERS
MINI-500
G-BWCZ OREV PDWI YEAR

RH7B
TIGER LIGHT
G-MZGT

RIDOUT
MLB variants
G-BIRP BIWF BIWG BJMX BJMZ BJNA

RIGG
MLB variants
G-BHLJ BIAR

(AVIONS PIERRE) ROBIN
DR400/500 variants
G-BAEB BAEM BAEN BAFP BAFX BAGC BAGR BAGS BAHL BAJY BAJZ
BAKM BALF BALG BALH BALI BALJ BAMS BAMU BAMV BANB BAPV BAPX
BAZC BBAX BBAY BBCH BBCS BBDP BBJU BBMB BCXE BDUY BEUP BFJZ
BGRH BGWC BHAJ BHFS-BHJU BHLE BHLH BHOA BIHD BIZI BJUD BKDH
BKDI BKDJ BKVL BNFV BNXI BOGI BPHG BPZP BRBK BRBL BRBM BRNT
BRNU BSDH BSFF BSLA BSSP BSVS BSZD BTRU BUGJ BUYS BXRT
BYHT BYIT BZIJ BZMM CBBA CBEZ CBMT CBVB CBZK CHIX CONB DUDZ
EGGS EHMM ELEN ELUN ETIV EYCO FCSP FTIL FTIM FTIN FUEL GBUE
GOSL HAIR HANS-HXTD IEYE IOOI IYCO JBDH JEDH JMTS JUDE KENW
KIMY LARA LEOS LISE MIFF MOTI NBDD NFNF ONGC PAYD PREZ RBIN
RONS SELL TUGY UAPA XLXL YOGI ZACH ZIGI ZIPI
HR100 ROYALE/SAFARI/TIARA
G-AZHB AZHK AZKN BAEC BAPY BAWR BAYR BBAW BBCN BBIO BEUD
BLHN BLWF BXWB CBFN HRIO MPWI RUES
HR200/CLUB
G-BBOE BCCY BETD BFBE BGXR BLTM BNIK BUWZ BVMM BWFG BWPG
BXDT BXGW BXOR BXVK BYLG BYLH BYNK BYSG BZLG BZXK GORF JPAT
NSOF WAVA WAVI WAVN
R1180T AIGLON
G-BGHM BIRT BJVV GBAO GDER GEEP PACE ROBN VECD VITE
R2100/2112/2120/2160 variants
G-BGBA BICS BIVA BKXA BLWY BVYO BWZG BYBF BYOF BZFB CBLE CBLG
CBNG MATT OCFC PGSI PLAY RAFC SACK SBMO TOUR VECE VECG
R3000
G-BLYP BOLU BZOL ENNI PAVL

ROBINSON AIRCRAFT CO
REDWING
G-ABNX

ROBINSON HELICOPTER CO INC
R22 ALPHA/BETA/MARINER
G-BJUC BLDK BLME BLTF BOAM BOCN BODZ BOEW BOEZ BOVR BOYC BOYX
BPGV BPIT BPNI BPTZ BRBY BROX BRRY BRVI BRWD BRXV BSCE BSEK BSGF
BSXN BTBA BTHI BTNA BTOC BTVU BUBW BVGS BVPR BWHY BWTH BXLA
BXOA BXSG BXSY BXTU BXUC BXXN BXYK BYCF BYCK BYCU BYHE BYTD
BYTE BYZP BYZZ BZBU BZJJ BZJK BZMO BZYE CBOT CBPT CBVL CBWZ CBXK
CCAP CRAY CBXN CBXO CBZF CBZO CHIS CHYL CHZN CNDY DAAM DABS
DEER DELT DERB DLDL DMCD DODB DODR EFGH EIBM EPAR ERBL EROM
ETIN FEBY FIRS FLYH FOGY FOLI GEGE GJCD GOUP GSFC HBMW HERA HIEL
HIPO HONI HRHE HSLA HUGS HUMF HURN IAGD IBED ICCL IHSB IIFR IIPT INIS
IORG ISMO JARA JERS JHEW JNET JONH JSAK JWFT KENN KNIB KRAY KUKI
LAIN LAND LEDA LHCA LIDS LIPE LYNC MAVI MDKD MFHT MICH MIGK MOGY
MRSN MUFY NJSH NORT OASH OAVA OBIL OBIO OCOV ODCS ODOT OEAT
OFAS OGOG OGOH OHFT OHSL OICV OIIO OJAN OKEY OLAU OLIZ OLRT
OMMG ONMT OPAL OPTS ORMB OROB OSEE OSHL OSIP OSMS OTAC OTED
OTHL OTOY OVNR PACL PBES PERE PHEL PIKE RALD REDA RENT RIAT RICE
RIDL RNGO ROUT ROVY RSVP RSWW RUSO RVRS SBUT SIMN SIVX SOLD
SPEE STRO SUMT SUMX TOMM TCMP TGRR TGRS TINK TILE TOLY TORS
TOSH TTHC TUNE UDAY UESY UNYT VEYE VFSI VMSL WADS WAGG WFOX
WIRL WIZA WIZR WIZY WRLY WRWR YACB YKEN YMBO ZAPY
R44 ASTRO/CLIPPER/RAVEN
G-BVMC BWVH BXPY BXUK BYCE BYKK BZIN BZLP BZMG BZOP BZPL BZRN
BZTA BZXY CBAK CBEG CBFJ CBKH CBRO CBVI CBXX CBYY CBZC CEEE
CHAP CHUM CLKE DCSE DSPI EKKO ESSY EUGN EYET FABI GLIB HALE
HEPY HMPF HRHS HRPN HTEL ICAB IFDM IFTS INDY IVIV JBBS JBKA JEFA
JILY JJWL KAZZ KPAO KTOL KYDD KYNT LATK LNDS LOTA LRSN LUKI LUKY
LWAY MAMK MAPL MGAN MGWI MURY NIOL NSEW NUDE OBBY OBHI OCHM
ODES ODHG ODOC OFIL OJRH OKES OLOW OMEL OMMT OPHA OTJB OUEL
OWND PBEE PFML PIDG POTT PPTS PRET RAVN RAYC RDEL REDI RFUN
RONN ROZI RROB RTWW SJDI SMJH STUS SWAT SYTN TAND TATY THEL
TPTS TRAC TRCY TRYG UTSS WOWW WYMR WYSP XLIV XTEK YIIK ZONK

ROCKWELL INTERNATIONAL CORPORATION see AERO COMMANDER
& including COMMANDER AIRCRAFT CORPN (114)
COMMANDER 112/114
G-BDAK BDFW BDIE BDKW BDLT BDYD BEBU BEDG BENJ BEPY BERI
BERW BFAI BFPO BFRA BFXS BFZM BGBZ BHRO BHSE BIOJ BIUO BKAY
BLTK BMJL BMWR BOLT BPTG BUSW BVNL BYKB CRIL DANT DASH DIME
EHXP ERIC FATB FLPI GRIF HILO HMBJ HPSB HPSE HROI IMPX JILL JURG
LADS LITE NATT NOOR OIBM OMUM OOJP PADS RCED RDCI RJCP
SAAB TECH TWIZ VICS ZIPA

ROE
TRIPLANE
G-ARSG

ROGERSON
HORIZON 1
G-DOGZ

ROLLASON AIRCRAFT & ENGINES LTD see DRUINE
BETA
G-AWHX BADC BETE BUPC

ROMAIN
COBRA BIPLANE
G-MNLH

ROOSTER see LIGHTWING

ROTARY AIR FORCE INC
RAF 2000
G-BUYL BVSM BWAD BWAE BWHS BWTK BWWS BXAC BXEA BXEB BXGS
BXKM BXMG BYDW BYIN BYJA CBCJ CBHZ CBIT CBJE CBJN CBMJ HOWL
IRAF JEJE ONON RAFZ REBA SAYS YRAF

ROTEC
RALLY 2B
G-MBAZ MBGS MBMG MJPA MVRF

ROTORWAY
SCORPION/EXEC
G-BHHZ BNZL BNZO BPCM BRGX BSRP BSUR BUJZ BURP BUSN BVOY
BVTV BWJK BWLY BWUJ BYNI BYNJ BZBW BZES BZOM BZXD CBWO
CBWU CBYB CBZI CHTG ESUS FLIT KENI MAMC NEEL PILE PURS RAWS
RHYS SFOX URCH WHOO YEWS ZHWH

ROUSSEAU see PIEL

ROYAL AIRCRAFT FACTORY
SE.5A
G-ALXT

RUSCHMEYER LUFTFAHRTTECHNIK GmbH
RUSHMEYER R90
G-EERH TODE UAPO

RUTAN
COZY
G-BXDO BXVX COZI OGJS SCUL SPFX
DEFIANT
G-OTWO
LONG-EZ
G-BKXO BLLZ BLMN BLTS BMHA BMIM BMUG BNCZ BOOX BPWP BRFB
BSIH BUPA BZMF CBLZ HAIG ICON LEZE LUKE MUSO OMJT PUSH RAEM
RAFT RPEZ SENA WILY
VARIEZE
G-BEZE BEZY BIMX BKST BNUI BVAY BVKM EMMY EZOS IPSY LASS OOSE
SKCI TIMB VEZE

RYAN AERONAUTICAL CORPN
ST3KR/PT-22
G-AGYY BTBH BYPY

SAAB-SCANIA AB including SVENSKA AEROPLAN AB (SAAB)
32 LANSEN
G-BMSG
91 SAFIR
G-ANOK BCFW BKPY HRLK SAFR
SF.340
G-GNTB GNTC GNTF GNTG LGNA LGNB LGNC LGND LGNE LGNF LGNG
RUNG

SABRE see SKYHOOK
(Wing)
G-MJFX MJIB MJNY

SAFFERY
MLB variants
G-BERN BFBM BIHU FYGM

SAI
KZ.VIII
G-AYKZ

SAN see JODEL

SAUNDERS-ROE (SARO)
SKEETER
   G-APOI AWSV BJWC BKSC BLIX SARO
P531-2
   G-APVL

SCALLAN
MLB variants
   G-FYEO FYEZ

SCHEIBE-FLUGZEUGBAU GmbH
SF.23 SPERLING
   G-BCHX
SF.24 MOTORSPATZ
   G-BBKR BZPF
SF.25 FALKE & SLINGSBY T.61 variants
   G-AVIZ AXEO AXIW AXJR AYBG AYSD AYUM AYUN AYUP AYUR AYYL
   AYZU AYZW AZHD AZIL AZMC AZMD AZPC AZYY BADH BAIZ BAKY BAMB
   BDZA BECF BEGG BFPA BFUD BGMV BHSD BIGZ BKVG BLCU BLTR BLZA
   BMBZ BMVA BODU BPIR BPZU BRRD BRWT BSEL BSUO BSWL BSWM
   BTDA BTRW BTTZ BTUA BTWC BTWD BTWE BUDA BUDB BUDC BUDT
   BUED BUEK BUFG BUFN BUFR BUGL BUGT BUGV BUGW BUGZ BUHA
   BUHR BUIH BUJA BUJB BUJI BUJX BUNB BUXJ BVKK BVKU BVLX BWTR
   BXAN BXMV FEFE FHAS FLKE FLKS GBGA HBOS KAOM KDEY KDFF KFAN
   KGAO KWAK MFMM OWGC
SF.28 TANDEM FALKE
   G-BARZ BYEJ

SCHEMPP-HIRTH FLUGZEUBAU GmbH
3DM/4DM
   G-HJSM
JANUS CM
   G-BMBJ BXJS
NIMBUS 4DM
   G-IVDM
VENTUS 2CM
   G-KTCC VENT

(ALEXANDER) SCHLEICHER GmbH & CO
ASK-14
   G-BKSP BSIY KOHF
ASK-16
   G-BCHT BCTI
ASH-26E
   G-BWBY DAVT OPHT

SCHWEIZER AIRCRAFT CORPN see HUGHES

SCOBLE see SOUTHERN MICROLIGHT

SCINTEX see PIEL

SCOTTISH AVIATION
BULLDOG
   G-ASAL AXEH AXIG BCUO BCUS BCUV BDOG BHXA BHZR BHZS BHZT
   BPCL BULL BWIB BZDP BZEP BZND BZME BZMH BZML BZON BZPS BZXC
   BZXS BZXZ CBAB CBAN CBBC CBBL CBBR CBBS CBBT CBBU CBBW CBCB
   CBCO CBCR CBCT CBCV CBDK CBDS CBEF CBEH CBEK CBFP CBGX CBID
   CBJJ CBJK DAWG DDOG DOGG EDAV GGRR GRRR JWCM KDOG KKKK
   SIJW TDOG UDOG
TWIN PIONEER
   G-APRS AYFA BBVF

SCRUGGS
MLB variants
   G-BILE BILG BINI BINL BINM BINX BIPH BISL BISM BISS BIST BIWB BIWC

SE see R.A.F./SLINGSBY/REPLICA PLANS

SEEMS see MORANE-SAULNIER

SEQUOIA see AVIAMILANO

SERVOTEC see CIERVA

SHARP & SONS
TARTAN (Trike)
   G-MBDE

SHAW
TWIN-EZE
   G-IVAN

SHERRY
BUZZARD
   G-MMNN

SHERWOOD RANGER see TIGER CUB

SHIELD
XYLA
   G-AWPN

SHORT BROTHERS LTD see EMBRAER
S.16 SCION
   G-ACUX AEZF
SA.6 SEALAND
   G-AKLW
SC.5 BELFAST
   G-BEPS HLFT
SC.7 SKYVAN
   G-BEOL BVXW PIGY
SD.3-30
   G-BDBS BITW BJLK BKIE BKMW BNTX DACS OGIL ROND SSWA SSWP
   SSWT XPSS
SD.3-60
   G-BKMU BKMX BLZT BMLC BNMU BOEG BOEI BPFN BPFR BPKZ CEAL
   CLAS EXPS OBHD OBLK SSWB SSWC SSWE SSWM SSWO SSWR SSWX
   UBAC VBAC

SCHROEDER FIRE BALLOONS GmbH
G
   G-BCVK

SIAI-MARCHETTI S.p.A
S.205
   G-AVEH AYXS BBRX BFAP VELA
SF.260
   G-BAGB IGIE MACH NRRA SIAI

SIGMA see SOUTHDOWN

SIKORSKY AIRCRAFT see VERTICAL AVIATION TECHNOLOGIES (S-52) & WESTLAND
S-61
   G-ATBJ ATFM AYOY BBHL BBVA BCEA BCEB BCLC BCLD BDIJ BDOC BEJL
   BFFJ BFFK BFRI BGWJ BGWK BHOG BHOH BIMU BPWB CBWC LAWS
S-76
   G-BHBF BHGK BIEJ BISZ BITR BJFL BJGX BMAL BOYF BURS BUXB BVKR
   BWDO BXZS BYDF BYOM CBJB CBNC CHCD DRNT EWEL HARH JCBA JCBJ
   POAH SMAF SSSC SSSD SSSE UKLS XXEA

SIPA
901/903/91
   G-AMSG ASXC ATXO AWLG BBBO BBDV BDAO BDKM BGME BHMA SIPA

SKY BALLOONS LTD including CAMERON BALLOONSI
Hot Air Balloons:
21
   G-BYCB
25
   G-BXWX BZSL
31
   G-BWOY BXVP OSVY
56
   G-BWYP
65
   G-BWUS BXFZ BXKO BXUS DUNG
70
   G-PONY
77
   G-BWSL BXHL BXVG BXXP BZLS CLRK KSKY LOWS MAGL OBET RCML
80
   G-BYBS BYOI SETI
90
   G-BWKR BXGD BXJT BXJU BXLP BXPP BXVR BXWL BYZV BZKV CLOE
   CZAG GPEG LEAS VINO ZABC
105
   G-BWDZ BWOA BWPP BWUM BXCN BXDV BXIW BXVN BXXS BYNV
120
   G-BWIX BWJR BWPF BWYU BXLC BXWG BYEX OURS
140
   G-BWHM BYKZ
160
   G-BWUK BXZZ BYHZ
180
   G-BWIW BXVL

200
G-BWEL BWST BXIH
220
G-BWRW BXDH EGUY SPEL
240
G-BXUE MRLN
260
G-KTKT OLYN

SPECIAL SHAPES

SHAPE	REGISTRATION(S)
FLYING MAP	G-MAPS

SKYCRAFT see WHEELER

SKYFOX
CA-25N GAZELLE
G-IDAY

SKYHOOK
SAILWINGS TR1 (Trike)/PIXIE
G-MJFX MJNU MJNY MMVS MNGH MNBJ
SAILWINGS CUTLASS (Wing)
G-MBHJ MBVW MJNU MNUI
SAILWINGS ZEUS (Wing)
G-MMVS MNGH

SKYRAIDER
GYROCOPTER
G-BUUS

SKYRIDER
AIRSPORTS PHANTOM
G-MJKX MJSE MJSF MJTE MJTX MJTZ MJUX MJVX MMKX MNCS MTTN

SKY SCIENCE POWERED PARACHUTES LTD
POWERHAWK L70/500
G-SSPP

SKYTRIKE see HIWAY

SLEPCEV
STORCH
G-BZOB

SLINGSBY AIRCRAFT CO LTD see TIPSY

SLINGSBY SAILPLANES LTD see FOURNIER, SCHEIBE & SOPWITH
T.21/T.29/T.31 MOTOR CADET/TUTOR
G-AYAN AZSD BCYH BDSM BEMM BMDD BNPF BODG BODH BOKG BOOD
BPIP BRTZ BRVJ BUAC BVFS BZLK
T.67/T.67M FIREFLY
G-BIOW BJIG BJNG BJXA BJXB BJZN BKAM BKTZ BLLP BLLR BLLS BLPI
BLRF BLRG BLTT BLTU BLTV BLTW BLUX BLVI BNSO BNSP BNSR BOCL
BOCM BONT BONU BUUA BUUB BUUC BUUD BUUE BUUF BUUG BUUI
BUUJ BUUK BUUL BWGO BWXA BWXB BWXC BWXD BWXE BWXF BWXG
BWXH BWXI BWXJ BWXK BWXL BWXM BWXN BWXO BWXP BWXR BWXS
BWXT BWXU BWXV BWXW BWXX BWXY BWXZ BXKW BYBX BYOA BYOB
BYOD BYRY BYYG CBHE CBWX EFSM FLYG FORS HONG KONG ONES
OPUB RAFG SFTZ SKYC SKYO ZEIN

SMD see SOUTHERN MICROLIGHT

SMITH
DSA-1 MINIPLANE
G-BTGJ

SMYTH
SIDEWINDER
G-BRVH JOPF

SNCAC including NORD production
NC854/858
G-BCGH BDJR BDXX BGEW BIUP BJEL BJLB BPZD NORD

SNCAN/STAMPE including AIA production
SV-4A/B/C
G-AIYG AMPI ASHS ATIR AWEF AWIW AWXZ AXCZ AXHC AXNW AXRP
AYCG AYCK AYDR AYGE AYIJ AYJB AYWT AYZI AZCB AZGE AZNK AZSA
AZTR BAKN BALK BEPC BEPF BHFG BHYI BIMO BKRK BKSX BMNV BNYZ
BPLM BRXP BTIO BWEF BWRS BYDK BXSV BZSY EEUP FORC FORD GMAX
HJSS OODE STMP SVIV

SNIAS see SUD & AÉROSPATIALE

SOCATA see MORANE-SAULNIER
ST-10 DIPLOMATE
G-AZIB HOLY
TB-9 TAMPICO/TB-10 TOBAGO
G-BGXC BGXD BGXT BHDE BHER BHGP BHIT BHJF BHOZ BIAK BIBA BITE
BIXA BIXB BIZE BIZR BJDT BJKF BJUG BKBN BKBV BKBW BKCR BKIA BKIB
BKIS BKIT BKUE BKVC BLCG BLCM BLYE BMEG BMYC BMZE BNDR BNIJ
BNRA BOIT BOIU BPGX BRIV BSDL BTHR BTIE BTWX BTZP CBGC CBHA
CBPE CFME CMED COCL CONL DAND EDEN GBHI GHZJ GMSI GOLF HALP
HILT IANH IGGL JURE MOOR MRTN OFIT OFLG PATN PHTG POPI RENO
SERL SONA SKYF TBIO TBOK TEDS TINA TOBA TZEE VMJM
TB-20/TB-21 TRINIDAD & TB.200 TOBAGO GT/XL
G-BLXA BLYD BNXX BPAS BPFG BPTI BSCN BTEK BTZO BXLT BXVA BYJS
BYTB BZLI BZPI CBFM CORB CPMS CTIO CTZO DLOM DMAH EGHR EGJA
EWFN FITI FIFI GDGR GOOD HGPI HOOD JDEE KKES KPTT KUBB OALD
OBEI OBGC OTUI PEKT PTRE RRFC SCBI SCIP SHEP SLTN TANS TBGT
TBXX TBZI TBZO THZL TMOL TOAK TRDM TRIN TTAC TYNE WERY

SOKO
P-2 KRAGUJ
G-BSXD RADA SOKO

SOLAR WINGS LTD/SOLAR WINGS AVIATION LTD
including HOLD CONTOL plc & see CYCLONE & PEGASUS
XL-P
G-MMYA
XL-Q
G-BZWM DEAN MGCB MNKO MTNO MTNP MTPN MTPS MTRU MTRV MTTD
MTTE MTTX MTTZ MTUP MTUR MTUS MTUT MTUY MTVX MTXH MTXI MTXJ
MTXK MTYA MTYC MTYD MTYE MTYF MTYI MTYL MTYP MTYR MTYS MTYT
MTYU MTZP MTZR MTZS MTZT MVAW MVAX MVAY MVCL MVCM MVCN MVCP
MVCR MVCS MVCT MVCV MVEX MVEZ MVFA MVFB MVFC MVFD MVFE MVFF
MVFG MVGT MVGU MVGW MVHO MVHP MVHR MVHS MVHT MVHU MVHW
MVHX MVHY MVIA MVJD MVJN MVJO MVJP MVJR MVJS MVJT MVJU MVJW
MVKF MVKG MVKL MVKN MVKO MVKP MVKS MVKT MVKU MVKV MVKW
MVKX MVLX MVLY MVMC MVPR MVPS MVPU MVPW MVPY MVRH MVRI
MVRJ MVRU MVRW MVRX MVSB MVSD MVSE MVSW MVSX MVSY MVSZ
MVTA MVTI MVTJ MVTK MVUF MVUG MVUH MVUI MVUJ MVUL MVUM MVVN
MVVO MVVP MVYC MVYD MVZJ MVZL MVZT MVZU MVZV MWAC MWAD
MWAL MWAT MWBK MWCB MWCF MWCV MWDD MWDK MWDL MWEE MWEF
MWEG MWEH MWER MWFS MWGL MWGM MWGR MWHC MWHF MWHG
MWHL MWHW MWHX MWIE MWIR MWIS MWIT MWJN MWJO MWKO MWKP
MWKY MWKZ MWLL MWLM MWMN MWMO MWMP MWMZ MWNA MWNB
MWNC MWNG MWOR MWOX MWOY MWPE MWPJ MWPK MWRV MWRW
MWRX MWSD MWSJ MWSK MWTA MWTB MWTC MWTI MWUO MWUX MWUY
MWUZ MWVA MWWG MWWH MWWV MWXP MWXR MWYB MWYC MWYU
MWYY MYAC MYAD MYAE MYAF MYBF MYBG MYBS MYBV MYBW MYBY
MYBZ MYEA MYEC MYED MYFX MYTC MYTH MYUH MZCP MZLR
XL-R
G-MGPD MMOH MMTA MMTC MMTR MNAO MNAR MNAW MNAX MNAY
MNAZ MNBA MNBB MNBC MNGG MNHB MNHC MNHD MNHE MNHI MNHJ
MNHK MNHL MNHM MNHN MNHR MNHS MNHT MNHU MNHV MNMK MNUX
MTAI MTAJ MTAO MTAT MTAV MTAW MTAX MTAY MTAZ MTBA MTBL MTBU
MTCG MTCH MTCN MTCO MTCR MTCX MTDG MTDH MTDI MTDS MTEB
MTEC MTED MTEE MTER MTES MTET MTEU MTEW MTEX MTFA MTFB
MTFE MTFM MTFO MTFP MTFR MTFT MTGJ MTGK MTGL MTGM MTHG
MTHH MTHI MTHJ MTHN MTIE MTIH MTIJ MTIO MTIP MTIR MTIS MTIU MTIV
MTIW MTIX MTIY MTIZ MTJH MTJS MTKG MTKH MTKI MTLG MTLI MTLJ
MTLT MTLU MTLV MTLY MTME MTMF MTMG MTMH MTMI MTOA MTOB
MTOD MTOE MTOG MTOH MTOI MTOJ MTOK MTOL MTOM MTON MTOO
MTOP MTOR MTOS MTOT MTOU MTOX MTOY MTOZ MTPP MTPR MTRM
MTRN MTRO MTRS MTSN MTSO MTSP MTSR MTSS MTSV MTSX
MTSY MTSZ MTTA MTTB MTTU MTUA MTUI MTUJ MTUK MTUL MTVB MTVK
MTVL MTVM MTVN MTVO MTWA MTWB MTWC MTWD MTYY MTZK MVAR
MVAT MVAV MVBJ MVBY MVBZ MVCA MVCB MVDU MVDV MVDW MVDX
MVDY MVDZ MVEC MVED MVEF MVEG MVFP MVFR MVFS MVFT MVFV
MVFW MVGN MVGO MVGP MVGS MVKH MVKJ MVKK MVKM MVKK MVVM
MWAF MWAG MWAI MWAV MWBL MWCC MWCU MWDE MWFA MWJG
MWLE MWLF MWLG MWLU MWMR MWMV MWOH MWOI MWPX MWRN
MWRP MWRT MWRU MWSE MWSF MWSO MWSP MWSR MWTM MWTU
MWUB MWUC MWUD MWUF MWUP MWUR MWUS MWUU MWUV MWVE
MWVF MWZH MWZI MWZJ MWZT MWZU MWZV MWZW MWZX MWZY MWZZ
MYAB MYBO MYBP MYDI MYDJ MYEG MYEH MYGT MYGU MYGV
XL-S
G-MNAH MNAI MNAK MNBI MNHH MJWZ MMJF MMMN MMOK MMRK MMRL
MMRZ MMSA MMSG MMSH MMTT MMVC MMZG
FLASH
G-MNDO MNGF MNJH MNJJ MNJL MNJN MNJO MNJR MNKP MNKR MNKS
MNKV MNKW MNKX MNNY MNNZ MNPA MNPB MNSH MNSN MNUD MNUE
MNVG MNVH MNWP MNWU MNWV MNXP MNYA MNYK MNYZ MNZO MTCK

PHOTON
  G-MNIK MNIU MNKB MNKC MNKD MNKE MNKG MNKI MNKK MNNG MNVZ
  MNXB MTAL
STORM (Wing)
  G-MMUR
TYPHOON (Wing)
  G-MBCI MBCJ MBCL MBGP MBJS MBOK MBPG MBTJ MJCU MJEE MJMR
  MJPP MJVE MMBJ MMBZ MMCV MMKG MMKH MMLI MMPU MMTK MMUG
  MNCU MNCV MNEI MNFA MNFR MNGD MNSD MZLK

SOMERS-KENDAL
SK.1
  G-AOBG

SOPWITH AVIATION CO
CAMEL
  G-AWYY BFCZ BPOB BZSC
PUP/DOVE
  G-EAGA EAVX EBKY
  G-ABOX APUP BIAU BZND
TABLOID SCOUT
  G-BFDE
TRIPLANE
  G-BOCK BWRA
"1½" STRUTTER REP
  G-BIDW

SORRELL
SNS-7 HYPERBIPE
  G-HIPE

SOUTHDOWN AEROSTRUCTURE LTD
PIPISTRELLE
  G-MJTM

SOUTHDOWN SAILWINGS LTD see MEDWAY
& including SOUTHDOWN INTERNATIONAL LTD
LIGHTNING (Wing)
  G-MBGX MBLK MBLU MBMT MJEY MJHC MJHR MJZH MMAS MMDF MMIZ
  MMKR MMKZ MMMI
PUMA/PUMA SPRINT (Combi-unit)
  G-MBZJ MJCE MJEB MJHZ MJRT MJTR MJVN MJYT MMAO MMAR MMAZ
  MMBL MMCI MMCM MMIR MMIW MMJD MMJT MMKV MMPG MMPH MMRN
  MMTI MMTM MMTZ MMUA MMUV MMVI MMVO MMVX MMVZ MMWX MMXN
  MMXO MMYF MMYO MMYT MMYU MMYY MMYZ MMZR MMZW MMZX MNAV
  MNBE MNBM MNCI MNCP MNDG MNDY MNDZ MNFB MNFG MNFX MNGS
  MNGX MNHL MNJD MNJG MNJS MNKU MNMC MNSB MNUM MVAF MWCR
RAVEN/HORNET DUAL TRAINER
  G-MGOD MMVH MNFD MNJB MNJT MNKZ MNLB MNLE MNLK MNLM MNLN
  MNLT MNLU MNLV MNLZ MNMD MNMU MNNA MNNB MNNC MNNO MNRP
  MNRS MNSL MNSX MNSY MNTC MNTE MNTM MNTN MNTY MNUU MNVN
  MNVP MNWA MNWG MNXA MNXE MNXF MNXI MNYG MNYL MNYM MNYP
  MNYS MNZW MNZX MTAP MTBB MTBK MTBN MTBO MTBZ MTCM MTHC
  MTID MTIK MTMK MTMO MTPC MTRT MTRW MTSD MTYV MTYW MTYX
  MVOS MYKL MYLX MYLY MYMJ MYVW MYYZ MYZO MZBR MZDJ RAVE
SIGMA (Wing)
  G-MBDM
SPRINT (Wing)/PUMA
  G-MBST MBTF MBTG MMDP MMHR MMKU MMLP MMMB MMOB MMRO
  MMRP MMSO MMTB MMTG MMTL MMTO MMTX MMUH MMXW MWTF
WILD CAT (Trike)
  G-MJUE MMDF

SOUTHERN
FLYER
  G-MJCN
MICROLIGHT (SMD) GAZELLE (Trike)
  G-MMGU MMPT
MICROLIGHT (SMD) VIPER
  G-MMHS

SOUTHERN
MARTLET
  G-AAYX

SPAD
XIII
  G-BFYO

SPARTAN AIRCRAFT LTD
ARROW
  G-ABWP
CRUISER
  G-ACYK

SPEZIO
DAL-1 TUHOLER/SPORT
  G-NGRM NOBI

SPORTAVIA see FOURNIER
RS.180 SPORTSMAN
  G-VIZZ

SPP see YAKOVLEV

SQUIRES
LIGHTFLY
  G-MNNG

STAAKEN
Z-1/Z-21A FLITZER
  G-BVAW BYYZ ERDA FLIZ FLZR

STARCK
AS.80
  G-BJAE

STAR-LITE
SL-1
  G-BUZH FARO SOLA

STEARMAN see BOEING-STEARMAN

STEEN AERO LAB INC
SKYBOLT
  G-BGRT BIMN BRIS BUXI BVXE BZWV ENGO BWPJ CBYJ KEST RODC SBLT
  SKIE TURN

STEMME GmbH & Co.KG
S-10
  G-BVYZ BXGZ BXHR BZSP CBLR CHLT EXPD JCKT JULL OJTA STEM STEN

STEPHENS
AKRO/LAZER 200
  G-BRHZ BWKT CBHR LAZA RIDE VILL

STERN
ST.80 BALADE
  G-BWVI

STEVENDON
SKYREACHER MLB
  G-BIWA

STINSON AIRCRAFT CORPORATION
RELIANT
  G-BUCH
HW-75/105 VOYAGER
  G-AFYO BMSA
108 STATION WAGON
  G-BHMR BPTA BRZK

STITS
SA.3A PLAYBOY
  G-BDRL BGLZ BVVR

STODDARD-HAMILTON
GLASAIR
  G-BMIO BODI BOVU BSAI BUBT BUHS BZBO CINY ICBM IIRG KRES KSIR
  LAIR LASR OPNH TRUK
GLASTAR
  G-BYEK BZDM CBAR CBCL CBJD CTEC ETCW GERY IARC LAZZ LEZZ LSTR
  SACH

STOLP
SA.100 STARDUSTER
  G-BSZG
SA.300 STARDUSTER TOO
  G-BNNA BOBT BRVB BSZB BTGS BUPB BZKD DUST JIII KEEN OTOO STOO
  UINN
SA.500 STARLET
  G-AZTV
SA.750 ACRODUSTER TOO
  G-BLES BUGB
SA.900 V-STAR
  G-BLAF

STRIKER see FLEXIFORM

STRIPLIN
LONE RANGER
G-MBDL MBJM
SKY RANGER
G-MJKB MMFZ

STROJNIK
S-2A
G-BMPS

SUD AVIATION see GARDAN & SOCATA & including AÉROSPATIALE, SOKO & WESTLAND production
SE.3130 ALOUETTE II/SA.315 LAMA
G-BVSD LAMA POSE UGLY
SA.341 GAZELLE
G-BAGL BCHM BXTH BXZD BZDV BZDW BZLA BZYB BZYC BZYD CBBV CBFD CBGZ CBJZ CBKA CBKC CBKD CBSA CBSB CBSC CBSD CBSE CBSF CBSH CBSI CBSJ CBSK CBXT CBZL DFKI DMSS EHUP EROL EZEL GAZA GAZI GAZL GAZZ GZLE LOYD MANN OCMJ OGAZ OGEO PAGS SFTA SIVJ TURP UTZY UZEL WCRD WDEV WMAN ZLLE ZZEL
SA.365 DAUPHIN 2
G-BKXD BLEZ BLUM BLUN BTEU BTNC BTUX BXLL BXPA MLTY PDGN PLMI

SUKHOI
Su-26M
G-XXVI

SUPER SCORPION see HIWAY

SUPERMARINE
WALRUS/SEAGULL
G-AIZG RNLI
SPITFIRE/SEAFIRE
G-AIST AISU ALGT AWII AWIJ BKMI BMSB BRAF BRDV BRMG BRRA BRSF BSKP BUAR BUOS BWEM BXVI BYDE CBNU CCCA CCIX CCVV CTIX FXII FXIV ILDA LFIX LFVB LFVC MKIA MKVB MXVI OXVI PMNF PRXI RRGN SPIT WWII
SWIFT
G-SWIF

SUSSEX
GAS BALLOON
G-AWOK

SWALLOW AEROPLANE CO
SWALLOW B
G-MJBK

SWEARINGEN
SA-227 METRO III
G-BUKA

SZD see PZL

TARJANI
(Trike)
G-MJCU

TAYLOR
JT.1 MONOPLANE
G-APRT AWGZ AXYK AYSH AYUS BBBB BDAD BDAG BDKU BDNC BDNG BDNO BEUM BEVS BEYW BFBC BFDZ BFOU BFRF BGCY BGHY BILZ BJMO BKEU BKHY BLDB BMAO BMET BNAR BRUO BUXL BVDE BXTC BYAV CDGA CRIS DIPS DRAY SUZY WARD
JT.2 TITCH
G-BABE BARN BCSY BDRG BFID BGMS BIAX BKWD BVNI BZJS MISS MOLE OJON RKET TICH VIVI

TAYLOR see AEROCAR

TAYLOR-WATKINSON
DINGBAT
G-AFJA

TAYLOR AIRCRAFT CO INC see PIPER

TAYLORCRAFT see AUSTER

TAYLORCRAFT AIRCRAFT CORPN
BC-12D/BL-65/DF-65/DCO-65
G-AHNR AKVO BIGK BOLB BPHO BPHP BPPZ BREY BRIH BRIY BRPX BRXE BSCW BSDA BTFK BVDZ BVRH-BVXS BWLJ
F-19/F-21/F-22
G-BPJV BRIJ BVOX BWBI

TEAM
HI-MAX
G-CCAJ MZHM MZIA
MINI-MAX
G-BVSB BVSX BVYK BXCD BXSU BYBW BYFV BYII BYJE BYYX BZDR BZTC CBIN CBNZ CBPL CBXU MWFC MWFD MWHH MWLW MWSA MWWE MWZM MYAT MYBM MYCT MYDF MYGF MYGL MYII MYIZ MYKJ MYKZ MYLB MYNI MYRG MYRL MYSK MYXA MYYR MYYS MYZE MZCS MZII MZMO MZNM MZNN MZOY MZPJ NADS OJLH OSCO THEO

TECNAM (CONSTRUZIONI AERONAUTICHE TECNAM SRL)
P92 ECHO
G-BZHG BZWT CBAX CBDM CBGE CBLB CBUG CBYZ CCAL DWPF OALH PGFG TECM TCNM WHEN

TED SMITH including PIPER production
AEROSTAR 601
G-MOVE RIGS TIME

TEMAN
MONO-FLY
G-MMJX MMPZ

TEVERSON
BISPORT
G-CBGH

THORN
COAL GAS BALLOON
G-ATGN

THORP including VENTURE
T-18
G-BLIT BSVN BYBY HATF
T-211
G-BTHP BXPF BXPO BYJF TZII

THRUSTER AIR SERVICES LTD incl THRUSTER AIRCRAFT (UK) LTD
TST
G-CBBC CBVA CCBC CSAV DRUM MCCF MGTV MTGB MTGC MTGD MTGE MTGF MTGP MTGR MTGS MTGT MTGU MTKA MTKB MTKD MTKE MTLM MTLN MTLR MTNR MTNS MTNT MTNU MTNV MTPT MTPU MTPV MTPW MTPX MTPY MTSH MTSJ MTSK MTSM MTUB MTUC MTUD MTUF MTVP MTVR MTVS MTVT MTVV MTWY MTWZ MTXA MTXB MTXC MTXD MTZA MTZB MTZC MTZD MTZE MTZF MVAG MVAH MVAI MVAJ MVAK MVAL MVBP MVBT MVDD MVDE MVDF MVDG MVDH MVFJ MVFK MVFL MVFM MVFN MVFO MVHI MVHJ MVHK MVHL MVIR MVIT MVIU MVIV MVIW MVME MVMG MVMH MVMI MVOT MVOU MVOV MVOW MVOX MVOY MVXL-MVYE MWDP MYWZ MYEE NDOT OBAX OJSH OMAL PYNE
T.300/SUPER T300
G-MGWH MVUB MVWN MVWR MVWS MVZA MVZB MVZC MVZD MVZG MVZI MWAN MWAP MWAR MWDS MWWS MYAP MYAR MYDR MYDU MYJF MYJG MYXU
T.600
G-BYFN BYPF BYPG BYPH BYPI BZDB BZJC BZJD BZNP BZTD CBGU CBGV CBGW CBIO CBIP CBIR CBKG CBPN CBWI CBWJ CBXG CBXH CBYT CCCB CCCF CCCH EVEY INGE MYWD MYWE MZFO MZFP MZFR MZFU MZGX MZGY MZGZ MZHA MZHC MZHD MZHE MZHF MZHS MZHU MZHV MZHW MZHY MZHZ MZKP MZKR MZKS MZKT MZKU MZNX MZNY PGSA PVST RAFH RIVR UDGE WORM

THRUXTON see JACKAROO AIRCRAFT
JACKAROO
G-ANZT AOEX AOIR

THUNDER BALLOONS LTD including THUNDER & COLT LTD
Airship
AS-33
G-ERMS
AS-120
G-BZWF
Gas Balloon:
AA-1050
G-BSRJ

Hot Air Balloons:
AX3 SKY CHARIOT
  G-BHUR BJGE BJVF BKBD BKFG BKIY BKMR NEIL
AX4 srs.
  G-LORY
AX5 srs.
  G-BDAY BEEP BEMU BLOV
AX6 srs.
  G-BBCP BBOO BCCH BCFU BDVG BEEE BEJB BERD BECS BETH BFIT
  BFOS BFOZ BGPF BGWY BGZZ BHAM BHTG BIIG BIIL BJVU BKUJ BLWB
  BPSJ BPUF BUSY BVRI BVUH DICK LDYS LIFE RTBI THOM TNTN
AX7 srs.
  G-BAXK BBDJ BBOX BCAN BCAR BCAS BCCG BCIN BCSX BCZI BDGH
  BDGO BDMO BDON BEVI BFIX BGRS BGST BHAT BHEU BHHH BHIS BHOO
  BHSP BHZX BIGF BJHT BJSW BJZC BKDK BKUU BLAH BLCY BLET BLGX
  BLKJ BLTN BLUI BLZF BMCC BMHJ BMJS BMMW BMMY BMOG BMUU BMVT
  BMYS BNBL BNBV BNBW BNCC BNCU BNGO BNHO BNMX BNXZ BNZK
  BOAO BOIJ BORD BOSB BPBZ BPGF BPHU BPNU BPVU BPYK BPYZ BRDC
  BRDE BRLS BROA BRVN BRWF BRXB BRZE BSAV BSBN BSCF BSCO BSOJ
  BSZH BTAN BTAU BTHK BTRR BTSX BTTW BTVA BTXK BUDK BUIN BUKI
  BULB BUNV BUPU BUYI BVDB BWED BYNU BZBH CBWR GASS GGGG
  GHIN HOWE LENS LYTE MLWI NEGS NIGS NWPB OFBJ OJDC OONI ORDY
  PIAF PUFF RAFE RBOW RIGB RINO ROCK ROSI RUBI SFRY SOFT THOS
  USIL VIVA WDEB WINE
AX8 srs.
  G-BJMW BOHF BORR BOTE BPZZ BRTT BRVY BSCX BSKI BSPB BSTK
  BSTY BTBB BTHM BTJD BTPX BTRO BTTK BUBL BUBY BUEI BUJW BUXW
  BUYD BVDW BVGB BVKH BVLS BVPA BVWB BWKW BYLV CBFG CBFH
  GEMS HAZE HOPS INGA ISTT KBKB OMDD OTEL PUNK SUED THOR TOOL
  ZEBO
AX9 srs.
  G-BGHW BTJO BTMN BTOZ BTRN BTUJ BUAT BULK BVKZ BVSY BZBL IOAZ
AX10 srs.
  G- G-BTJF BTNL BTYF BUNZ BUOZ BUVZ BWNX BWUR OLEO WORK
AX11 srs.
  G-BXAD BXVF BZHX BZRZ
MLB
O.5
  G-BBOD

SPECIAL SHAPES	
SHAPE	REGISTRATION(S)
FILM CASSETTE	G-PHOT
FORK LIFT TRUCK	G-BWBH
ICE CREAM	G-ICES
JUMBO JET	G-VJIM
WHISKY BOTTLE	G-RARE

THURSTON
TEAL
  G-OWET TEAL

TIGER
T.200 MLB
  G-BIMK

TIGER CUB see MBA
RL5A SHERWOOD RANGER
  G-BZUG CBHU CCBW GKFC HVAN MWND WZOL PUSY

TIPSY including COBELAVIA & SLINGSBY production
TRAINER/B/BELFAIR
  G-AFJR AFRV AFSC AFVH AFVN AFWT AISA AISC APIE APOD
JUNIOR
  G-AMVP
T.66 NIPPER
  G-APYB ARBG ARBP ARDY ARFV ASXI ASZV ATBW ATKZ ATUH AVKI AVKK
  AVKT AVXC AVXD AWDA BWHR AWJE AWJF AWLR AWLS AXLI AXZM AZBA
  BLMW BRIK BRPM BWCT BYLO CBCK CORD ENIE NIPA NIPP TIPS

TRAGO MILLS see FLS

TREKKING see AIRWAVE

TRI-FLYER see MAINAIR

TRI-R TECHNOLOGIES
KIS
  G-BVTA BVZD BXJI BZDR CBTV MANW OKIS OKMA OKPW TKIS
KIS CRUISER
  G-BYZD

TRIDENT see SHEFFIELD

TRIPACER see ULTRASPORTS

TROTTER
AX3-90 HAB
  G-BRBT

TURLEY see RAVEN

TURNER
SUPER T-40A
  G-BRIO

TURNER see CURRIE

TWAMLEY
TRIKE
  G-MBGF MJWI

Uas
SOLAR/STORM BUGGY (Trike)
  G-MJBS

ULTIMATE AIRCRAFT
10 DASH 200
  G-BOFO

ULTRAFLIGHT
LAZAIR
  G-MBYI MNRD MTDN MTFL MVGZ
MIRAGE
  G-MBRH MBSX MBXX

ULTRAMAGIC SA
Hot Air Balloons:
H-31
  G-BZIZ BZPY
77 variants
  G-BXPT BZKW BZSH BZSO CBRK CBWK DAIV DWPH RWRW VOTE
M-90
  G-CSFD
105 variants
  G-BZPX BZRX CBRB
S-130
  G-CBKK
M-145
  G-BZGI
N-210
  G-BZPR BZPT
N-250
  G-BZJX CBUE
N-300
  G-CBPZ

ULTRASPORTS see SOUTHDOWN
TRIPACER
  G-MBAL MBFU MBLU MBPY MBTJ MBZA MJER MJFB MJFI MJHC MJHM
  MJHZ MJIA MJIC MJIZ MJTC MMEO MMMR MMPU MMUK MNGD MNSD
  MTTL
(Combi PANTHER/TRIPACER/TYPHOON)
  G-MBZK MJIY MMBY MMDE MMGS MMKA MMRR MMTC MMTS MMTT MMVF
  MMYN MMZP

ULTRAVIA
SUPER PELICAN
  G-MWRS
PELICAN CLUB
  G-BWWA

UNICORN
MLB variants
  G-BINR BINS BINT BIWJ BJGM BJLF BJLG FYEK

Vahdat
SEMICOPTER GYROPLANE
  G-BZEV

VALENTIN
TAIFUN 17E
  G-BMSE OACE TFUN

VAN'S

RV-3
G-BVDC RVRH

RV-4/4A
G-BOHW BROP BULG BVDI BVLR BVRV BVUN BVVS BXPI BXRV BZPH CBGN FTUO MAXV PIPS RMIT RVMJ RVDP RVDS RVRV SARV VANS

RV-6/6A
G-BUEC BUTD BVCG BXJY BXVM BXVO BXWT BXYN BXYX BYDV BYEL BZOZ BZRV BZUY BZVN BZWZ BZXB CBCP CBUK EDRV EERV ESTR EYOR GDRV GLUC GPAG GRIN HOPY JAEE KELL NPKJ OJVA OJVL OMDB ONUN ORBD ORVG OTRV PWUL REAS RIVT RUSL RVAN RVAW RVBC RVCE RVCG RVCL RVDJ RVDR RVEE RVET RVGA RVIA RVIB RVIN RVIT RVIV RVJM RVMT RVSA RVSH RVSX RVVI SIXY TOGO VANZ XVOM

RV-7
G-CBJU KELS RVII SEVN STAF

RV-8
G-BZWN DUDE LEXX RVAL RVBA RVMX ZAAZ ZUMI

RV-9A
G-DUGS RUVY RVIX XSAM

VAN DEN BEMDEN

GAS BALLOON
G-BBFS BDTU BIHP BWCC

VARGA

2150A KACHINA
G-BLHW BPVK CHTT DJCR VARG

VENTURE see THORP

VICKERS

FB-5 GUNBUS
G-ATVP

FB.27 VIMY (including rep)
G-EAOU
G-AWAU

600 Srs.VIKING
G-AGRW, AIVG

668 VARSITY
G-BEDV BHDD

700/800 Srs.VISCOUNT
G-ALWF AMOG AOHL AOYM APIM ARER AVHE AVJB AZLP AZLS AZNA AZNC OPAS

953 VANGUARD / MERCHANTMAN
G-APEJ APEP APES

(SUPER) VC-10
G-ARVF ARVM ASGC ASIX

VICKERS SUPERMARINE LTD see SUPERMARINE

VICTA including AESL production

AIRTOURER
G-ATCL ATEX ATHT ATJC AWMI AWWG AXIX AYLA AYWM AZBE AZHI AZHT AZMN AZOE AZOF AZRP

VIKING

DRAGONFLY
G-BKPD BNEV BRKY DKGF

VOISIN

REP
G-BJHV

VOLMER

VJ.22 SPORTSMAN
G-BAHP

VOUGHT

F4U CORSAIR
G-BXUL FGID

VPM SNC

M-14 SCOUT
G-BUEN

M-16 TANDEM TRAINER
G-BUPM BUZL BVWX BXEJ BXIX BZJM BZXW CBUP CVPM DBDB POSA YFLY YROW

WACO

UPF-7
G-WACO

YKS-7
G-BWAC

WAG-AERO INC

CUBY ACROTRAINER
G-BLDD BTWL CUBW

CUBY SPORT TRAINER
G-BVMH BZHU

WAG-A-BOND
G-BNJA

WALLBRO

MONOPLANE
G-BFIP

WALLINGFORD (WMB)

MLB variants
G-BIAI BIBX BILB

WALLIS including BEAGLE-WALLIS & VINTEN production

WA.116/WA.122
G-ARRT ARZB ASDY ATHM ATTB AVJV AVJW AXAS AYVO BAHH BGGU BGGV BGGW BKLZ BLIK BMJX SCAN VIEW VTEN

WA.201
G-BNDG

W.A.R.

FOCKE-WULF FW190
G-BSLX JABO SYFW WULF

REPUBLIC P-47 THUNDERBOLT
G-BTBI

VOUGHT F-4U CORSAIR
G-BJNB

WARD

ELF
G-MMUL

GNOME
G-AXEI

WASP

GRYPHON (Wing)
G-MBPY MJYW

(SOCIETE) WASSMER see JODEL

WA.41 SUPER BALADOU
G-ATSY ATZS AVEU

WA.52 PACIFIC/EUROPA
G-AZYZ BTLB

WA.81 PIRANHA
G-BKOT

WATKINSON see TAYLOR-WATKINSON

WEEDHOPPER OF UTAH INC

JC-24
G-BHWH MJMB MTNK

WEST

AX3-15 HAB
G-BCFD

WESTERN

Hot Air Balloons:
20
G-AYMV
O-31
G-AZPX
O-65
G-AZJI AZOO BBCB BBUT

WESTLAND AIRCRAFT LTD incl WESTLAND (HELICOPTERS) LTD & SIKORSKY production - also see SUD AVIATION

LYSANDER
G-AZWT LIZY

WS.51 DRAGONFLY
G-BRMA

WS.51/2 WIDGEON
G-ANLW AOZE APTW

WS.55 WHIRLWIND
G-ANFH ANJV AODA APWN AYNP AYXT AYZJ BAMH BDBZ BEBC BJWY BVGE RWWW

WS.58 WESSEX
G-ATBZ AVNE AWOX BYRC HANA
WG.13 LYNX
G- BFDV LYNX
WG.30
G-BGHF BKGD HAUL OGAS
SCOUT
G-BWHU BWJW BWLX BXOE BXRR BXRS BXSL BYKJ BYRX BZBO CBUH
CBUI CRUM KAXL NOTY ONEB SCTA SROE
WASP
G-BMIR BZPP KAWW KAXT RIMM

WESTLAND-AGUSTA see EH INDUSTRIES

WESTLAND-BELL see BELL

WHE
AIRBUGGY
G-AXYZ AXZA

WHEELER see FLYLITE
SCOUT/SKYCRAFT
G-MBBB MBRE MBUZ MNKN

WHEELER
SLYMPH
G-ABOI

WHITTAKER including AEROTECH
MW2B EXCALIBUR
G-BDDX
MW4/5/SORCERER
G-BZWX BZXL CBBO MBTH MMGV MNXZ MTAS MTBP MTBR MTBS MTDK
MTFN MTHB MTLZ MTRX MVNN MVNO MVNP MVNR MVNS MVNT MVNU
MWEK MWEO MWGI MWGJ MWGK MWIC MWJW MWLN MWSX MWSY
MYAH MYAN MYDL MYDW MYJZ MYRB MZEI MZOH
MW6 MERLIN/MW6-S FATBOY FLYER/MW6-T
G-BUOA BYTX BZYU CBMU CBWS CBYP MNMW MTTF MTXO MURR MVPH
MVPM MVPN MVTD MVXA MWAW MWHM MWIP MWLO MWOV MWPR
MWSW MYCA MYCP MYCU MYDM MYET MYEV MYGE MYIE MYKO MYMN
MYPP MYPS MYZA MYZN MZBG MZBX MZCH MZDI MZDL MZFK MZFS
MZHG MZHT MZID MZJP MZNE MZOK
MW7
G-BOKH BOKJ BPUP BREE BRMW BSXX BTFV BTUS BWVN BZOW

WILD
BVS SPECIAL MLB
G-BJUB

WILLGRESS see GRYPHON
GRYPHON
G-MBPS

WILLIAMS
KFZ-1 TIGERFALCK
G-KFZI

WILLIAMS (WESTWIND)
MLB variants
G-FYAN FYAO FYAU FYDI FYDP FYFJ

WILLS
AERA 2
G-BJKW

WINDSOR
MLB
G-BJGD

WITTMAN
TAILWIND
G-BCBR BDAP BDBD BDJC BJWT BMHL BNOB BOHV BOIB BPYJ CIPI JBPR
WYND ZIPY

WITTY
SPHINX HAB
G-BJLV

WOLF
W-II BOREDOM FIGHTER
G-BNAI

WOMBAT
GYROCOPTER
G-BWLZ WBAT

WOODS – see AEROSPORT

WSK-PZL – see MIKOYAN
PZL-110 KOLIBER 150A/160A
G-BUDO BVAI BXLR BXLS BYSI BZAJ BZLC CBGA KOLI LOKM
MIELEC TS-11 ISKRA
G-BXVZ ISKA

YAKOVLEV including ACROSTAR, IAV-BACHAU, LET NANCHANG & SPP production
Yak-1
G-BTZD
Yak-3
G-BTHD BWOE
Yak-11
G-BTUB BTZE BZMY IYAK KYAK OYAK YCII
Yak-18
G-BMJY BVVG BVVX BXZB
Yak-50
G-BTZB BVVO BWFM BWJT BWWH BWWX BWYK CBPM CBPO CBRH EYAK
FUNK GYAK HAMM IIYK IVAR JYAK OJDR VLAD YAKA YAKK YKSO
Yak-52
G-BVMU BVOK BVVA BVVW BVXK BWFP BWOD BWSV BWVR BXAK BXAV
BXID BXJB BZJB BZTF CBLI CBLJ CBMD CBMI CBOZ CBPX CBPY CBRL
CBRU CBRW CBSL CBSR CBSS CBVT CCCP HYAK IMIC KOMI LAOK LENA
LYAK LYFA OKGB TYAK YAKB YAKC YAKH YAKI YAKO YAKR YAKS YAKT
YAKW YAKX YAKY YAMS YFUT YKCT YKSZ YYAK ZYAK
Yak-55
G-YAKM

ZEBEDEE
V-31 HAB
G-BXIT

ZENAIR see HEINTZ/COLOMBAN
CH.200/250 ZENITH variants
G-BIRZ BTXZ DUNN GFKY RAYS
CH.600/601 ZODIAC variants
G-BRII BRJB BUTG BUZG BVAB BVAC BVPL BVVM BVZR BYEO BYJT BYLF
BYPR BZFV CBAP CBCH CBDG CBDT CBGB CBIX CBJP CBPV CBRX CBUR
CCAK CLEO OANN OMEZ OMWE RUVI ZAIR ZODI
CH.701 STOL/UL variants
G-BRDB BTMW BXIG BZJP BZVA CBGD CBMW CBZW EOIN FAMH OMEX
TTDD ZENA

ZLIN
226/326/526 TRENER/TRENER MASTER/AKROBAT
G-AWJX AWJY AWSH BEWO BKOB BLMA BPNO BUPO EJGO PCDP TINY
ZLIN ZLYN
Z.242
G-BWTC BWTD EKMN
Z.50L
G-MATE

PART 2 – ALPHABETICAL TYPE INDEX (IRELAND) - COVERS SECTION 2

AERONCA
11AC CHIEF
  EI-CCF CRR
15AC SEDAN
  EI-BJJ BKC

AÉROSPATIALE
AS.350B ECUREUIL
  EI-CGQ IRV MYO
SA.365 DAUPHIN 2
  EI-MIP

AÉROSPATIALE/ALENIA
ATR-42
  EI-BYO,CBK CPT CVR CVS
ATR-72
  EI-CLB CLC CLD CMJ REA REB SLF

AGUSTA S.p.A
A109
  EI-CHV DLP ECA JBC MEL MIT SQG

AIR & SPACE
18A
  EI-CNG

AIRBUS INDUSTRIE
A.300
  EI-CEB DHL OZA,OZB OZC SAF
A319
  EI-CZF
A.320
  EI-CTD CUQ CVA CVB CVC CVD TAA TAB TAC TAI
A.321
  EI-CPC CPD CPE CPF CPG CPH
A330
  EI-CRK CZR CZS CZT DAA DUB EWR JFK LAX ORD

AMF MICROFLIGHT LTD
CHEVVRON
  EI-BVJ CAU

AUSTER AIRCRAFT LTD including TAYLORCRAFT production
PLUS C/D
  EI-ALH
J/1 AUTOCRAT/J/1N ALPHA
  EI-AGJ AUM
J/4
  EI-CPN
J/5F AIGLET TRAINER
  EI-AUS

AVIAMILANO SRL
F.8L FALCO
  EI-BCJ BMF

AVID AIRCRAFT INC
AVID SPEEDWING
  EI-CIM

A V ROE & CO LTD
643 CADET
  EI-ALP
748
  EI-BSF

BA
SWALLOW 2
  EI-AFF

BAE SYSTEMS (OPERATIONS) LTD
BAe 146 including Avro variants
  EI-CLG CLH CLI CLY CMS CMY CNB CNI CNJ CNK CNQ COF COQ CPJ CPK
  CPL-CPY CSK CSL CTM CTN CTO CWA CWB CWC CWD CZO PAT

BEAGLE AIRCRAFT LTD
B.121 PUP
  EI-ATJ

BEAGLE-AUSTER AIRCRAFT LTD
A.61 TERRIER
  EI-ASU

BEECH AIRCRAFT CORPORATION
23 MUSKETEER
  EI-BFF
58 BARON
  EI-CPS
76 DUCHESS
  EI-BUN CMX
77 SKIPPER
  EI-BHT

BELL HELICOPTER TEXTRON INC
206A/B JET RANGER I/II
  EI-BHI BIJ BKT BXX BYJ CAW CLT CUG CUS HER HXM MER ONE PMI PRI
  RMC WSH WSN
206L LONG RANGER
  EI-BYR CHL CIO
407
  EI-STR
430
  EI-WAV

BENSEN AIRCRAFT CORPORATION
B.8 GYROCOPTER
  EI-BCF BSG

BOEING AIRCRAFT CO including BOEING COMPANY
727-200 srs
  EI-HCA HCB HCI LCH
737-200 srs
  EI-CJC CJD CJE CJF CJG CJH CJI CKP CKQ CKR CKS CNT CNV CNW CNX
  CNY CNZ COA COB CON COX
737-300 srs
  EI-BZE BZF BZJ BZL BZM BZN CLW CLZ CRZ CUL CXN CXR
737-400 srs
  EI-BXD BXI BXK COH COI COJ COK CUA CUD CUN CVN CVO CVP CWE
  CWF CWW CWX ,CXI CXJ CXK CXL CXM CZG CZK PAM PAR
737-500 srs
  EI-CDB CDC CDD CDE CDF CDH CHH
737-700 srs
  EI-CXD,CXE
737-800 srs
  EI-CSA CSB CSC CSD CSE CSF CSG CSH CSI-CSJ CSM CSN CSO CSP CSR
  CSS CST CSU CSV CSW CSX CSY CSZ CTA CTB CXP CXT CXU CXV CXW
  DAC DAD DAE DAF DAG DAH DAJ
757-200 srs
  EI-CEY CEZ
767-300 srs
  EI-CRD CRF CRL CRO CRM CTW CXB CXO CXZ CZD CZH
777-200 srs
  EI-CRS CRT

BRITTEN-NORMAN LTD
BN.2A ISLANDER
  EI-AYN BCE CUW IPC

CAMERON BALLOONS LTD
65 variants
  EI-BSN BVC
77 variant
  EI-CKJ
105 variant
  EI-CUE

CANADAIR LTD
CHALLENGER 604
  EI-IRE

CARLSON
SPARROW
  EI-COO

CESSNA AIRCRAFT COMPANY
including REIMS AVIATION SA production (F.prefix)
150
  EI-APF AST AVM AWE BAT BFE BHW BYF CDV CHM CIN CML CMV COP

A150 AEROBAT
  EI-AUO AYF CTI
152
  EI-BGJ BIB BMM BMN CCJ CCK CCM CGT CRU
A152 AEROBAT
  EI-BJM
172/SKYHAWK
  EI-AYK BAS BCK BIC BIR BKF BPL BRM BRS BSC CFN CFP CFY CGD CHS
  CLQ COT GWY MCF EI-SAC STT
172RG CUTLASS
  EI-BPC
R172 HAWK XP/FR172 ROCKET
  EI-BJO CCV
177(RG) CARDINAL
  EI-BHC POD
(R)182/SKYLANE (RG)
  EI-AOD BCL CAP CDP GSM
206 SUPER SKYLANE/STATIONAIR
  EI-BGK BNK SBP
210 CENTURION
  EI-AWH BUF CAX CDX CGH
335
  EI-CUP
337 SUPER SKYMASTER
  EI-AVC
340
  EI-CIJ
441
  EI-DMG
550 CITATION BRAVO/551 CITATION II
  EI-CIR DAB PAL
560XL CITATION EXCEL
  EI-PAX

CFM METAL-FAX
(STREAK) SHADOW
  EI-CHR CZC CZJ

CHAMPION including AERONCA & BELLANCA production
7AC/7DC CHAMPION
  EI-ATL AVB BJB BJC
7EC TRAVELER
  EI-BBE BHV
CITABRIA
  EI-ANT BYX
SUPER DECATHLON
  EI-BIV

COLT BALLOONS LTD
77A HAB
  EI-BGT

DE HAVILLAND AIRCRAFT CO LTD
DH.82A TIGER MOTH
  EI-AHI AWP
DH.84 DRAGON
  EI-ABI

DE HAVILLAND (CANADA)
DHC-8 DASH EIGHT
  EI-CHP

DRUINE
D.62 CONDOR
  EI-BCP BXT

EIPPER
QUICKSILVER
  EI-BPP

ERCO
ERCOUPE 415
  EI-AUT CGG CVL

EUROCOPTER
EC.120
  EI-EUR MIK IZO TOY VNE
EC.130B
  EI-LKS LNX

EUROPA AVIATION
EUROPA
  EI-COE

EUROWING LTD
GOLDWING
  EI-CMK

EVANS
VP-1
  EI-AYY BBD BRU
VP-2
  EI-BVT

EVEKTOR AEROTECHNIK
EUROSTAR
  EI-CXY

EXTRA
EA.300/200
  EI-SAM

FLEXIFORM see MAINAIR
STRIKER
  EI-BPN

FOKKER AIRCRAFT BV
including FOKKER VFW NV & FAIRCHILD-HILLER production
F.27-050
  EI-FKC FKD FKE FKF

FOUGA
CM-170 MAGISTER
  EI-BXO

GARDAN
GY-80 HORIZON
  EI-AYB

GROB-WERKE GmbH & CO KG
G-109
  EI-HCS
G-115
  EI-CAC CAE CCD

GRUMMAN-AMERICAN AVIATION CORPN
AA-5 TRAVELER/TIGER
  EI-AYD BJS BMV

GULFSTREAM AEROSPACE CORPORATION
GULFSTREAM IV/V
  EI-CVT WGV

GYROSCOPIC
GYROPLANE
  EI-COG

HAWKER-SIDDELEY AVIATION including BRITISH AEROSPACE production
HS/BAe.125
  EI-RNJ WDC WJN

HIWAY HANG GLIDERS LTD
DEMON (Wing) SKYTRIKE
  EI-BNH BPU CGE
VULCAN (Wing)
  EI-BMW

HOAC FLUGZEUGWERKE including DIAMOND production
DV-20 KATANA
  EI-CLA CZA

HOFFMANN FLUGZEUGBAU FRIESACH
H-36 DIMONA
  EI-CRV

HUGHES TOOL CO/HELICOPTERS INC
including SCHWEIZER AIRCRAFT CORPN
269 (Srs 300)
  EI-CVM CWS CZL LRS

Iıı (INIZIATIVE INDUSTRIALE ITALIANE)
SKY ARROW
  EI-CPX

Jodel including CEA, SAN & WASSMER production
D.9 BEBE
  EI-BUC
D.112
  EI-BSB CKX
D.120 PARIS-NICE
  EI-CJS

Lake AIRCRAFT CORPORATION
LA-4 BUCCANEER
  EI-BUH CEX

LEARJET CORPORATION INC
LEARJET 60
  EI-IAU IAW

LETOV AIR
LK-2M SLUKA
  EI-CAN

LINDSTRAND BALLOONS LTD
LBL-90A
  EI-CRB

LOCKHEED-CALIFORNIA CO
L.1011 TRISTAR
  EI-CNN

McCANDLESS
M.4 GYROPLANE
  EI-ASR

McDONNELL DOUGLAS CORPORATION
DC-8
  EI-BNA CGO
DC-9-82/83
  EI-BTX BTY BWD CBR CBS CBY CBZ CCC CCE CDY CEK CEP CEQ CFZ CIW CKM CMZ CPB CRE CRH CRJ CRW CTJ
DC-10
  EI-DLA

MAINAIR SPORTS LTD
GEMINI/FLASH (Combi)
  EI-CKT
MERCURY
  EI-CMU

MALMO
MFI-9 JUNIOR
  EI-AWR

MAULE AIRCRAFT CORPORATION
MX-7
  EI-CUT GER

MBB
Bö.105
  EI-BLD LIT

MEDWAY MICROLIGHTS LTD
ECLIPSE R
  EI-CRY CTC ELL

MONNETT
MONI
  EI-BMU

MOONEY AIRCRAFT CORPORATION
M.20
  EI-CAY CIK

MORANE-SAULNIER
MS.880/885/887/892/894 RALLYE variants
  EI-ATS AUE AUG AWU AYA AYI AYT BBG BBI BBJ BBO BCH BCS BCU BCW

  BDH BDK BEA BEP BFI BFM BFP BFR BGA BGG BHK BHN BHP BHY BIT BIW BJK BKE BKN BMA BMB BMJ BNG BNU BUT CEG CHN CIA

MOSKITO
MOSKITO 2
  EI-CJV

Partenavia COSTRUZIONI AERONAUTICHE S.p.A
P.68
  EI-BWH

PEGASUS AVIATION
QUANTUM
  EI-CNU

PHOENIX
LUTON LA-5A MAJOR
  EI-CGF

PIEL
CP.301 EMERAUDE
  EI-CFG

PIPER AIRCRAFT CORPORATION
J-3C CUB
  EI-AFE BBV BCM BCN BEN BFO BIO BSX BYY CCH CHK COY CPP
J-5A CUB CRUISER
  EI-CGV
PA-12 SUPER CRUISER
  EI-ADV CFF CFH
PA-18 SUPER CUB
  EI-ANY BID BIK CIG CKH
PA-22 TRI-PACER/COLT
  EI- AV UFO
PA-23 AZTEC
  EI-EEC WAC WMN
PA-28-140/160 CHEROKEE/CRUISER
  EI-AOB ATK BSO CGP CIV CMB COZ
PA-28-151/161 CHEROKEE/WARRIOR
  EI-CTT WRN
PA-28-180/181 CHEROKEE
  EI-BBC BDR CIF
PA-28R CHEROKEE ARROW
  EI-EDR
PA-31 NAVAJO CHIEFTAIN
  EI-CNM
PA-34 SENECA
  EI-BSL CMT
PA-38 TOMAHAWK
  EI-BJT BUR BUS BVK
PA-44 SEMINOLE
  EI-SKT

POLARIS MOTOR SRL
FIB OK350
  EI-BXL

PTERODACTYL LTD
MICROLIGHT
  EI-BOA

Rand-ROBINSON
KR-2
  EI-BNL BOV

(AVIONS PIERRE) ROBIN
DR400/180R REMORQUER
  EI-CRG
R.1180T AIGLON
  EI-BIS

ROBINSON HELICOPTER CO INC
R22 BETA
  EI-CFE CFX CMI CPO CWL CWP CWR CZI JWM MAG RZZ TKI
R44 ASTRO
  EI-CUI JFD MUL

ROTORWAY
EXECUTIVE
  EI-CMW

RUTAN
LONG-EZE
  EI-CMR CPI

SCHLEICHER
ASK14
  EI-APS
ASK16
  EI-AYR

SHORT BROTHERS LTD
SD.3-30
  EI-EXP

SIKORSKY AIRCRAFT
S-61
  EI-BLY CNL MES RCG SAR

SLINGSBY SAILPLANES LTD
T.21 CADET
  EI-CJT

SNCAN STAMPE including AIA production
STAMPE SV.4A/C
  EI-BAJ CJR

SOCATA
ST.10 DIPLOMATE
  EI-BUG
TB.9 TAMPICO
  EI-BMI BSK BYG CRX GFC
TB.10 TOBAGO
  EI-BOE
TB.20 TRINIDAD
  EI-BSV

SOLAR WINGS LTD
XL-R
  EI-BSW CGN CHT CKU

SOUTHDOWN SAILWINGS LTD
PUMA
  EI-BPO

STEEN AERO LAB.INC
SKYBOLT
  EI-CIZ SAT

STINSON AIRCRAFT CORPORATION
108 STATION WAGON
  EI-CGC

STODDARD-HAMILTON
GLASAIR
  EI-CTG

STOLP
SA.300 STARDUSTER TOO
  EI-CDQ

TAYLOR
JT.1 MONOPLANE
  EI-BKK

TAYLORCRAFT AIRCRAFT CORPN
Plus D
  EI-AMF
BC-65
  EI-CES

TEAM
MINIMAX
  EI-CGB CNC

THRUSTER AIR SERVICES LTD
T.300
  EI-CEN
TST
  EI-CKI

THUNDER BALLOONS LTD
AX8 variant
  EI-BAR

VIKING
DRAGONFLY
  EI-BPE

WHITTAKER
MW5
  EI-BUL CAN CTL
MW6 MERLIN/MW6-S FATBOY FLYER
  EI-BVB CJZ CKN CLL COM

ZENAIR see HEINTZ & COLOMBAN
CH.200/250 ZENITH variants
  EI-BVY BYL

ZLIN
526 TRENER MASTER
  EI-BIG

PART 3 – AIRCRAFT WEARING MILITARY & OTHER MARKINGS

In certain circumstances the Civil Aviation Authority may permit the operation of an aircraft without the need to carry regulation size national registration letters. These conditions are referred to as "exemptions". The CAA will issue to each operator an Exemption Certificate which is usually valid for two years. The basic requirements are that the owner undertakes to notify the CAA of the markings carried and may not, without specific permission of the overseas country, fly overseas. In the case of aircraft wearing military marks the authority of the relevant department at the Ministry of Defence is required for UK markings whilst an equivalent establishment must sanction any overseas markings to be carried.

Below are current details of all aircraft and gliders which are known to be wearing military or, in a very few cases, "B" Conditions markings, see Part 6. The information is compiled from member's observations and includes any BAPC & "B" Conditions identities and overseas registered aircraft known to be based in the UK & Ireland. Full details of BAPC markings are carried in SECTION 4 and c/ns for all can be found in their respective Sections. We should point out that some of the serials used below are spurious - these are annotated with asterisks.

Country	Serial	Code	Regn	Type
UNITED KINGDOM (RAF unless otherwise shown)				
	168		G-BFDE	Sopwith Tabloid Scout rep (RNAS)
	304*		BAPC.62	Cody Biplane (RFC)
	687*		BAPC.181	RAF BE.2b (RFC)
	1701*		BAPC.117	RAF BE.2c rep (RFC)
	2345		G-ATVP	Vickers FB.5 Gunbus rep (RFC)
	2882*		BAPC.234	Vickers FB.5 Gunbus rep (RFC)
	3066		G-AETA	Caudron G.III (RNAS)
	5964*		BAPC.112	DH.2 rep (RFC)
	5964		G-BFVH	DH.2 rep
	6232*		BAPC.41	RAF BE.2c rep (RFC)
	A1742*		BAPC.38	Bristol Scout D rep (RFC)
	A4850*		BAPC.176	SE.5A rep (RFC)
	A7317*		BAPC.179	Sopwith Pup rep (RFC)
	A8226		G-BIDW	Sopwith "1fi" Strutter Rep (RFC)
	B415*		BAPC.163	AFEE 10/45 Rotabuggy rep
	B595	W	G-BUOD	SE.5A rep (RFC)
	B1807	A7	G-EAVX	Sopwith Pup (RFC) - intended marks
	B2458	R	G-BPOB	Sopwith Camel rep (RFC)
	B3459	2	G-BWMJ	Nieuport Scout 17/23 rep (RFC)
	B5577*		BAPC.59	Sopwith F1 Camel rep
	B6401		G-AWYY	Sopwith Camel rep (RFC)
	B7270		G-BFCZ	Sopwith Camel rep (RFC)
	C1904	Z	G-PFAP	SE.5A (Currie Wot) (RFC)
	C3011	S	G-SWOT	SE.5A (Currie Wot) (RFC)
	C4451*		BAPC.210	Avro 504J rep (RFC)
	C4918		G-BWJM	Bristol M.1C rep
	C4994		G-BLWM	Bristol M.1C rep (RFC)
	C9533	M	G-BUWE	SE.5A rep (RFC)
	D276*	A	BAPC.208	SE.5A rep (RFC)
	B5577*		BAPC.59	Sopwith Camel rep (RFC)
	D7889		G-AANM	Bristol F.2b
	D8084*	S	G-ACAA	Bristol F.2b
	D8096		G-AEPH	Bristol F.2b
	E449		G-EBJE	Avro 504K
	E2466*		BAPC.165	Bristol F2b
	F141	G	G-SEVA	SE.5A rep (RFC)
	F235	B	G-BMDB	SE.5A rep (RFC)
	F904	H	G-EBIA	SE.5A (RFC)
	F938		G-EBIC	SE.5A (RFC)
	F943		G-BIHF	SE.5A rep (RFC)
	F943		G-BKDT	SE.5A rep (RFC)
	F5447	N	G-BKER	SE.5A rep (RFC)
	F5459	Y	G-INNY	SE.5A rep (RFC)
	F5459*	Y	BAPC.142	SE.5A rep (RFC)
	F5475*		BAPC.250	SE.5A rep (RFC)
	F8010	Z	G-BDWJ	SE.5A rep (RFC)
	F8614		G-AWAU	Vickers FB.27A Vimy rep
	H1968*		BAPC.42	Avro 504K rep
	H3426*		BAPC.68	Hawker Hurricane rep
	H5199		G-ADEV	Avro 504K
	J7326		G-EBQP	DH.53 Humming Bird - intended marks
	J9941		G-ABMR	Hawker Hart II
	K1786		G-AFTA	Hawker Tomtit
	K1930		G-BKBB	Hawker Fury II
	K2050		G-ASCM	Hawker (Isaacs) Fury
	K2059		G-PFAR	Hawker (Isaacs) Fury
	K2060		G-BKZM	Hawker (Isaacs) Fury
	K2075		G-BEER	Hawker (Isaacs) Fury
	K2227		G-ABBB	Bristol Bulldog IIA
	K2567		G-MOTH	DH.82 Tiger Moth
	K2572		G-AOZH	DH.82A Tiger Moth
	K2587		G-BJAP	DH.82A Tiger Moth
	K3215		G-AHSA	Avro Tutor
	K3731		G-RODI	Hawker (Isaacs) Fury
	K4232		SE-AZB	Cierva C.30A (Avro Rota)
	K-4259	71	G-ANMO	DH.82A Tiger Moth
	K5054		G-BRDV	Supermarine Spitfire prototype rep

K5054*		BAPC.190	Supermarine Spitfire rep
K5054*		BAPC.214	Supermarine Spitfire rep
K5414	XV	G-AENP	Hawker Hind
K5600		G-BVVI	Hawker Audax
K5673*		BAPC.249	Hawker Fury I rep
K5673		G-BZAS	Hawker Fury I rep
K7271*		BAPC.148	Hawker Fury rep
K8203		G-BTVE	Hawker Demon I
K8303	D	G-BWWN	Hawker (Isaacs) Fury
K9926*	JH-C	BAPC.217	Supermarine Spitfire rep
L1070*	XT-A	BAPC.227	Supermarine Spitfire rep
L1679*	JX-G	BAPC.241	Hawker Hurricane 1 rep
L1710*	AL-D	BAPC.219	Hawker Hurricane rep
L2301		G-AIZG	Supermarine Walrus 1 (RN)
L6906		G-AKKY	Miles Magister
N500		G-BWRA	Sopwith Triplane rep (RNAS)
N546*		BAPC.164	Wight Quadruplane rep
N185		G-AIBE	Fairey Fulmar 2 (RN)
N2276*		G-GLAD	Gloster Gladiator II
N3194*	GR-Z	BAPC.220	Supermarine Spitfire rep
N3289*	QV-K	BAPC.65	Supermarine Spitfire rep
N3313*	KL-B	BAPC.69	Supermarine Spitfire rep
N4877		G-AMDA	Avro 652A Anson 1
N5182		G-APUP	Sopwith Pup (RNAS)
N5195		G-ABOX	Sopwith Pup (RNAS)
N5492*	B	BAPC.111	Sopwith Triplane rep (RNAS)
N6181		G-EBKY	Sopwith Pup (RNAS)
N6290		G-BOCK	Sopwith Triplane rep (RNAS)
N6452		G-BIAU	Sopwith Pup rep (RNAS)
N6466		G-ANKZ	DH.82A Tiger Moth
N6740		G-AISY	DH.82A Tiger Moth
N-6797		G-ANEH	DH.82A Tiger Moth
N6847		G-APAL	DH.82A Tiger Moth
N6965	FL-J	G-AJTW	DH.82A Tiger Moth
N6985		G-AHMN	DH.82A Tiger Moth
N9191		G-ALND	DH.82A Tiger Moth (RN)
N9192	RCO-N	G-DHZF	DH.82A Tiger Moth
N9389		G-ANJA	DH.82A Tiger Moth
P2793*	SD-M	BAPC.236	Hawker Hurricane rep
P2902	DX-X	G-ROBT	Hawker Hurricane I
P3059*	SD-N	BAPC.64	Hawker Hurricane rep
P3208*	SD-T	BAPC.63	Hawker Hurricane rep
P6382	C	G-AJRS	Miles Magister
P7350	XT-D	G-AWIJ	Supermarine Spitfire F.IIA
P8140*	ZF-K	BAPC.71	Supermarine Spitfire rep
P8448*	UM-D	BAPC.225	Supermarine Spitfire rep
R1914		G-AHUJ	Miles Magister
R3821	UX-N	G-BPIV	Bristol Blenheim IV
R4897		G-ERTY	DH.82A Tiger Moth
R4959	59	G-ARAZ	DH.82A Tiger Moth
R5136		G-APAP	DH.82A Tiger Moth
R4115*	LE-X	BAPC.267	Hawker Hurricane fsm
S1287	5	G-BEYB	Fairey Flycatcher rep (FAA)
S1579	571	G-BBVO	Hawker Nimrod (Isaacs Fury) (RN)
S1581	573	G-BWWK	Hawker Nimrod 1 (FAA)
T5672		G-ALRI	DH.82A Tiger Moth
T5854		G-ANKK	DH.82A Tiger Moth
T-5879	RUC-W	G-AXBW	DH.82A Tiger Moth
T6313		G-AHVU	DH.82A Tiger Moth
T-6562		G-ANTE	DH.82A Tiger Moth
T6818		G-ANKT	DH.82A Tiger Moth
T6953		G-ANNI	DH.82A Tiger Moth
T-7230		G-AFVE	DH.82A Tiger Moth
T7281		G-ARTL	DH.82A Tiger Moth
T7328		G-APPN	DH.82A Tiger Moth
T7404	04	G-ANMV	DH.82A Tiger Moth
T7471		G-AJHU	DH.82A Tiger Moth
T-7842		G-AMTF	DH.82A Tiger Moth
T7909		G-ANON	DH.82A Tiger Moth
T8191		G-BWMK	DH.82A Tiger Moth
T9707		G-AKKR	Miles M.14A Hawk Trainer
T9738		G-AKAT	Miles M.14A Hawk Trainer
V1075		G-AKPF	Miles M.14A Hawk Trainer
V3388		G-AHTW	Airspeed Oxford 1
V6028	GB-D	G-MKIV	Bristol Blenheim IV
V6799*		BAPC.72	Hawker Hurricane rep
V7476*	LE-D	BAPC.223	Hawker Hurricane rep
V9367	MA-B	G-AZWT	Westland Lysander IIIA
V9545	BA-C	G-BCWL	Westland Lysander IIIA
V9673*	MA-J	G-LIZY	Westland Lysander III
W2718	AA5Y	G-RNLI	Supermarine Walrus (RN)
W5856	A2A	G-BMGC	Fairey Swordfish II
W9385	YG-L	G-ADND	DH.87B Hornet Moth
Z2033	N/275	G-ASTL	Fairey Firefly TT.1

Z5053		G-BWHA	Hawker Hurricane IIB
Z5252	GO-B	G-BWHA	Hawker Hurricane IIB
Z7015	7-L	G-BKTH	Hawker Sea Hurricane IB (RN)
Z7197		G-AKZN	Percival Proctor III
Z7381	XR-T	G-HURI	Hawker Hurricane IIB
AA908*	UM-W	BAPC.230	Supermarine Spitfire rep
AB910	ZD-C	G-AISU	Supermarine Spitfire LF.Vb
AP507	KX-P	G-ACWP	Cierva C.30A (Avro Rota)
AR213	PR-D	G-AIST	Supermarine Spitfire IA
AR352*	RF-C	G-MKVB	Supermarine Spitfire Vb - see BM597
AR501	NN-A	G-AWII	Supermarine Spitfire Vc
AR614	DU-Z	G-BUWA	Supermarine Spitfire Vc
AR654*	RF-T	G-BKMI	Supermarine Spitfire VIIIc - see MT928
AR3185*	RF-M	G-LFVB	Supermarine Spitfire V - see EP120
AR4474*	RF-Y	G-AWII	Supermarine Spitfire Vc - see AR501
BB807		G-ADWO	DH.82A Tiger Moth
BE417	AL-X	G-HURR	Hawker Hurricane IIB
BE421*	XP-G	BAPC.205	Hawker Hurricane rep
BL924*	AZ-G	BAPC.242	Supermarine Spitfire Vb rep
BM597	JH-C	G-MKVB	Supermarine Spitfire Vb
BN230*	FT-A	BAPC.218	Hawker Hurricane rep
BR600	SH-V	BAPC.222	Supermarine Spitfire rep
BR600	JP-A	BAPC.224	Supermarine Spitfire rep
BW881		G-KAMM	Hawker Hurricane XIIA
CB733		G-BCUV	SA Bulldog
DE208		G-AGYU	DH.82A Tiger Moth
DE470	16	G-ANMY	DH.82A Tiger Moth
DE623		G-ANFI	DH.82A Tiger Moth
DE673		G-ADNZ	DH.82A Tiger Moth
DE730		G-ANFW	DH.82A Tiger Moth
DE970		G-AOBJ	DH.82A Tiger Moth
DE992		G-AXXV	DH.82A Tiger Moth
DF112		G-ANRM	DH.82A Tiger Moth
DF128	RCO-U	G-AOJJ	DH.82A Tiger Moth
DF155		G-ANFV	DH.82A Tiger Moth
DG590		G-ADMW	Miles Hawk Major
DR628	PB-1	N18V	Beech Traveler
EM720		G-AXAN	DH.82A Tiger Moth
EN224		G-FXII	Supermarine Spitfire XII – intended marks
EN343		BAPC.226	Supermarine Spitfire rep
EN398		BAPC.184	Supermarine Spitfire IX rep
EP120	AE-A	G-LFVB	Supermarine Spitfire Vb
FB226	MT-A	G-BDWM	N-A Mustang (Bonsall Mustang)
FE695	94	G-BTXI	N-A Harvard IIB
FE905		LN-BNM	N-A Harvard IIB
FE992	K-T	G-BDAM	N-A Harvard IIB
FJ777		G-BIXN	Boeing-Stearman Kaydet
FR886*		G-BDMS	Piper Cub
FR887*		G-BWEZ	Piper L-4 Cub (US Army)
FS628*		G-AIZE	Fairchild Argus
FT323	GN	FAP 1513	N-A Harvard III
FT375		G-BWUL	N-A Harvard IIB
FT391		G-AZBN	N-A Harvard IIB
FX301*	FD-NQ	G-JUDI	N-A Harvard III
FZ625*		G-AMPO	Douglas Dakota 3
HB275		G-BKGM	Beech Expeditor
HB751		G-BCBL	Fairchild Argus III
HM580		G-ACUU	Cierva C.30A (Avro Rota)
JV828		N423RS	Consolidated-Vultee PBY-5A Catalina
KB889	NA-I	G-LANC	Avro Lancaster X
KD345	A-130	G-FGID	Vought FG-1D Corsair (RN)
KF584		G-RAIX	N-A Harvard IV
KJ351		BAPC.80	Airspeed Horsa II
KZ321		G-HURY	Hawker Hurricane IV
LB312		G-AHXE	Taylorcraft Plus D (Auster I)
LB367		G-AHGZ	Taylorcraft Plus D (Auster I)
LB375		G-AHGW	Taylorcraft Plus D (Auster I)
LF789		BAPC.186	DH.82B Queen Bee
LF858		G-BLUZ	DH.82B Queen Bee
LS326	L/2	G-AJVH	Fairey Swordfish II
LZ766		G-ALCK	Percival Proctor III
MAV467	R-O	BAPC.202	Supermarine Spitfire V rep
MH434	ZD-B	G-ASJV	Supermarine Spitfire IXB
MH486	FF-A	BAPC.206	Supermarine Spitfire rep
MH777	RF-N	BAPC.221	Supermarine Spitfire rep
MJ627	9G-P	G-BMSB	Supermarine Spitfire IX
MJ730	GZ-?	G-HFIX	Supermarine Spitfire IXe
MJ751	DU-V	BAPC.209	Supermarine Spitfire rep
MJ832	DN-Y	BAPC.229	Supermarine Spitfire rep
MK732	3W-17	G-HVDM	Supermarine Spitfire IXc
MK805*	SH-B	*	Supermarine Spitfire IX rep

* Built by TDL Rep Aircraft, in 64 Sqn c/s, as SH-B/"Peter John III"

MK912	SH-L	G-BRRA	Supermarine Spitfire IX
ML407	OU-V/NL-D	G-LFIX	Supermarine Spitfire IX

Serial	Code	Registration	Type
ML417	2I-T	G-BJSG	Supermarine Spitfire IXe
MP425		G-AITB	Airspeed Oxford I
MT438		G-AREI	Auster III
MT928	ZX-M	G-BKMI	Supermarine Spitfire VIIIc
MV262		G-CCVV	Supermarine Spitfire XIV - intended marks
MV268	JE-J	G-SPIT	Supermarine Spitfire XIVe
MV370		G-FXIV	Supermarine Spitfire XIVc
MW763	HF-A	G-TEMT	Hawker Tempest II
MW800	HF-V	G-BSHW	Hawker Tempest II
NH238	D-A	G-MKIX	Supermarine Spitfire IX
NJ633		G-AKXP	Auster 5
NJ673		G-AOCR	Auster 5
NJ695		G-AJXV	Auster 4
NJ703		G-AKPI	Auster 5
NJ719		G-ANFU	Auster 5 - intended marks
NL750		G-AOBH	DH.82A Tiger Moth
NL772		G-BXMN	DH.82A Tiger Moth
NL985		G-BWIK	DH.82A Tiger Moth
NM181		G-AZGZ	DH.82A Tiger Moth
NS519*		G-MOSI	DH.98 Mosquito 35 (RAF/USAAF)
NX534		G-BUDL	Auster III
NX611	LE-C/DX-C	G-ASXX	Avro Lancaster B.VII
PL344	Y2-B	G-IXCC	Supermarine Spitfire IXe
PL965	R	G-MKXI	Supermarine Spitfire PR.XI
PL983	JV-F	G-PRXI	Supermarine Spitfire XI
PP972		G-BUAR	Supermarine Seafire III
PR772		G-BTTA	Hawker Iraqi Fury FB.11
PS853	C	G-RRGN	Supermarine Spitfire PR.XIX
PT462	SW-A	G-CTIX	Supermarine Spitfire IX
PV202	5R-Q	G-TRIX	Supermarine Spitfire IX
PZ865	Q	G-AMAU	Hawker Hurricane IIc
RG333*		G-AIEK	Miles Messenger
RM221		G-ANXR	Percival Proctor IV
RN201		G-BSKP	Supermarine Spitfire XIV
RN218	N	G-BBJI	Isaacs Spitfire
RR232		G-BRSF	Supermarine Spitfire IXc
RT486	PF-A	G-AJGJ	Auster 5
RT610		G-AKWS	Auster 5A
RX168		G-BWEM	Supermarine Seafire L.III - intended marks
SM520		G-BXHZ	Supermarine Spitfire HF.IX
SM845	GZ-J	G-BUOS	Supermarine Spitfire XVIIIe
SM969	D-A	G-BRAF	Supermarine Spitfire XVIII
SX336		G-BRMG	Supermarine Seafire XVII
TA634	8K-K	G-AWJV	DH.98 Mosquito TT.35
TA719		G-ASKC	DH.98 Mosquito TT.35
TA805		G-PMNF	Supermarine Spitfire IX
TB252	GW-H	G-XVIE	Supermarine Spitfire XVIe
TD248	D	G-OXVI	Supermarine Spitfire XVIe
TE184	D	G-MXVI	Supermarine Spitfire XVIe
TE517		G-CCIX	Supermarine Spitfire IXe - intended marks
TJ398*		BAPC.70	Auster 5
TJ534		G-AKSY	Auster 5
TJ565		G-AMVD	Auster 5
TJ569		G-AKOW	Auster 5
TJ672		G-ANIJ	Auster 5
TS291*		BGA.852	Slingsby T.8 Tutor
TS423	YS-L	G-DAKS	Douglas Dakota 3
TS798		G-AGNV	Avro 685 York C.1
TW439		G-ANRP	Auster 5
TW467	ROD-F	G-ANIE	Auster 5
TW511		G-APAF	Auster 5 (Army)
TW536	TS-V	G-BNGE	Auster AOP.6
TW591		G-ARIH	Auster AOP.6 (Army)
TW641		G-ATDN	Auster AOP.6
TX183		G-BSMF	Avro Anson C.19
VF512	PF-M	G-ARRX	Auster AOP.6
VF516		G-ASMZ	Auster AOP.6
VF526	T	G-ARXU	Auster AOP.6 (Army)
VF581		G-ARSL	Auster AOP.6
VL348		G-AVVO	Avro Anson C.19/2
VL349		G-AWSA	Avro Anson C.19/2
VM360		G-APHV	Avro Anson C.19/2
VP955		G-DVON	DH.104 Devon C.2/2
VP981		G-DHDV	DH.104 Devon C.2/2
VR192		G-APIT	Percival Prentice T.1
VR249	FA-EL	G-APIY	Percival Prentice T.1
VR259	M	G-APJB	Percival Prentice T.1
VS356		G-AOLU	Percival Prentice T.1
VS610	K-L	G-AOKL	Percival Prentice T.1
VS623		G-AOKZ	Percival Prentice T.1
VT871		G-DHXX	DH.100 Vampire FB.6
VV612		G-VENI	DH.112 Venom FB.1
VX118		G-ASNB	Auster AOP.6
VX147*		G-AVIL	Ercoupe 415

VX653		G-BUCM	Hawker Sea Fury FB.11
VX926		G-ASKJ	Auster AOP.6
VZ345		D-CATA	Hawker Sea Fury T.20 (RN)
VZ467	A	G-METE	Gloster Meteor F.8
VZ638		G-JETM	Gloster Meteor T.7 (RN/FRU)
VZ728		G-AGOS	Reid & Sigrist Bobsleigh
WA591		G-BWMF	Gloster Meteor T.7 - intended marks
WB188		G-BZPB	Hawker Hunter GA.Mk.11
WB188		G-BZPC	Hawker Hunter GA.Mk.11
WB531		G-BLRN	DH.104 Devon C.2/2
WB533		G-DEVN	DH.104 Devon C.2/2
WB565	X	G-PVET	DHC.1 Chipmunk T.10 (Army)
WB569		G-BYSJ	DHC.1 Chipmunk T.10
WB571	34	G-AOSF	DHC.1 Chipmunk T.10
WB585	M	G-AOSY	DHC.1 Chipmunk T.10
WB588	D	G-AOTD	DHC.1 Chipmunk T.10
WB615	E	G-BXIA	DHC.1 Chipmunk T.10
WB652		G-CHPY	DHC.1 Chipmunk T.10
WB654	U	G-BXGO	DHC.1 Chipmunk T.10
WB660		G-ARMB	DHC.1 Chipmunk T.10
WB671	910	G-BWTG	DHC.1 Chipmunk T.10 (RN)
WB697	95	G-BXCT	DHC.1 Chipmunk T.10
WB702		G-AOFE	DHC.1 Chipmunk T.10
WB703		G-ARMC	DHC.1 Chipmunk T.10
WB711		G-APPM	DHC.1 Chipmunk T.10
WB726	E	G-AOSK	DHC.1 Chipmunk T.10
WB763		G-BBMR	DHC.1 Chipmunk T.10
WD286	J	G-BBND	DHC.1 Chipmunk T.10
WD288		G-AOSO	DHC.1 Chipmunk T.10
WD292		G-BCRX	DHC.1 Chipmunk T.10
WD305		G-ARGG	DHC.1 Chipmunk T.10
WD310		G-BWUN	DHC.1 Chipmunk T.10
WD331		G-BXDH	DHC.1 Chipmunk T.10
WD347		G-BBRV	DHC.1 Chipmunk T.10
WD363		G-BCIH	DHC.1 Chipmunk T.10
WD373	12	G-BXDI	DHC.1 Chipmunk T.10
WD379*	K	G-APLO	DHC.1 Chipmunk T.10
WD390		G-BWNK	DHC.1 Chipmunk T.10
WE569		G-ASAJ	Beagle Terrier (Auster T.7)
WE591	Y	G-ASAK	Beagle Terrier (Auster T.7)
WF118		G-DACA	Percival P.57 Sea Prince T.1
WG307		G-BCYJ	DHC.1 Chipmunk T.10
WG316		G-BCAH	DHC.1 Chipmunk T.10
WG321		G-DHCC	DHC.1 Chipmunk T.10
WG348		G-BBMV	DHC.1 Chipmunk T.10
WG350		G-BPAL	DHC.1 Chipmunk T.10
WG407	67	G-BWMX	DHC.1 Chipmunk T.10
WG422		G-BFAX	DHC.1 Chipmunk T.10
WG465		G-BCEY	DHC.1 Chipmunk T.10
WG469		G-BWJY	DHC.1 Chipmunk T.10
WG472		G-AOTY	DHC.1 Chipmunk T.10
WG719		G-BRMA	Westland Dragonfly HR.5
WJ358		G-ARYD	Auster AOP.6
WJ680	CT	G-BURM	EE Canberra TT.18
WJ945	21	G-BEDV	Vickers Varsity T.1
WK126	843	N2138J	EE Canberra TT.18
WK163		G-BVWC	EE Canberra B.2(mod)
WK436*		G-VENM	DH.112 Venom FB.50 (FB.1)
WK512	A	G-BXIM	DHC.1 Chipmunk T.10 (Army)
WK514		G-BBMO	DHC.1 Chipmunk T.10
WK517		G-ULAS	DHC.1 Chipmunk T.10
WK522		G-BCOU	DHC.1 Chipmunk T.10
WK549		G-BTWF	DHC.1 Chipmunk T.10
WK585		G-BZGA	DHC.1 Chipmunk T.10
WK586	V	G-BXGX	DHC.1 Chipmunk T.10 (Army)
WK590	69	G-BWVZ	DHC.1 Chipmunk T.10
WK609	93	G-BXDN	DHC.1 Chipmunk T.10
WK611		G-ARWB	DHC.1 Chipmunk T.10
WK622		G-BCZH	DHC.1 Chipmunk T.10
WK624	M	G-BWHI	DHC.1 Chipmunk T.10
WK628		G-BBMW	DHC.1 Chipmunk T.10
WK630		G-BXDG	DHC.1 Chipmunk T.10
WK633	B	G-BXEC	DHC.1 Chipmunk T.10
WK640	C	G-BWUV	DHC.1 Chipmunk T.10
WK642		G-BXDP	DHC.1 Chipmunk T.10
WL505		G-FBIX	DH.100 Vampire FB.9
WL505		G-MKVI	DH.100 Vampire FB.6
WL626	P	G-BHDD	Vickers Varsity T.1
WM167		G-LOSM	AW Meteor NF.11
WP308	572	G-GACA	Hunting Percival P.57 Sea Prince T.1
WP788		G-BCHL	DHC.1 Chipmunk T.10
WP790	T	G-BBNC	DHC.1 Chipmunk T.10
WP795	901	G-BVZZ	DHC.1 Chipmunk T.10 (RN)
WP800	2	G-BCXN	DHC.1 Chipmunk T.10

WP803		G-HAPY	DHC.1 Chipmunk T.10
WP808		G-BDEU	DHC.1 Chipmunk T.10
WP809	78	G-BVTX	DHC.1 Chipmunk T.10 (RN)
WP840	9	G-BXDM	DHC.1 Chipmunk T.10
WP844		G-BWOX	DHC.1 Chipmunk T.10
WP856	904	G-BVVP	DHC.1 Chipmunk T.10 (RN)
WP857	24	G-BDRJ	DHC.1 Chipmunk T.10
WP859		G-BXCP	DHC.1 Chipmunk T.10
WP860	6	G-BXDA	DHC.1 Chipmunk T.10
WP896	M	G-BWVY	DHC.1 Chipmunk T.10
WP901		G-BWNT	DHC.1 Chipmunk T.10
WP903		G-BCGC	DHC.1 Chipmunk T.10 (Queens Flight)
WP920		G-BXCR	DHC.1 Chipmunk T.10
WP925	C	G-BXHA	DHC.1 Chipmunk T.10 (ARMY)
WP928	D	G-BXGM	DHC.1 Chipmunk T.10 (ARMY)
WP929	F	G-BXCV	DHC.1 Chipmunk T.10
WP930	J	G-BXHF	DHC.1 Chipmunk T.10
WP971		G-ATHD	DHC.1 Chipmunk T.10
WP977		G-BHRD	DHC.1 Chipmunk T.10
WP983	B	G-BXNN	DHC.1 Chipmunk T.10
WP984	H	G-BWTO	DHC.1 Chipmunk T.10
WR360		G-DHSS	DH.112 Venom FB.1
WR410		G-DHUU	DH.112 Venom FB.1
WR421		G-DHTT	DH.112 Venom FB.1
WT327		G-BXMO	EE Canberra B.6
WT333		G-BVXC	EE Canberra B(I).8
WT722	878/VL	G-BWGN	Hawker Hunter T.8C (RN)
WT723		G-PRII	Hawker Hunter PR.11 (RN)
WV198	K	G-BJWY	Sikorsky Whirlwind HAR.21
WV318	D	G-FFOX	Hawker Hunter T.7B
WV372	R	G-BXFI	Hawker Hunter T.7
WV493	29/A-P	G-BDYG	Percival Provost T.1
WV666	O-D	G-BTDH	Percival Provost T.1
WV740		G-BNPH	Hunting Percival Pembroke C.1
WW453	W-S	G-TMKI	Percival Provost T.1
WZ507		G-VTII	DH.115 Vampire T.11
WZ553	40	G-DHYY	DH.115 Vampire T.11
WZ589		G-DHZZ	DH.115 Vampire T.55
WZ662		G-BKVK	Auster AOP.9 (Army)
WZ706		G-BURR	Auster AOP.9 (Army)
WZ711		G-AVHT	Auster AOP.9 (Army)
WZ729		G-BXON	Auster AOP.9
WZ819		BGA.3498	Slingsby T.38 Grasshopper
WZ847		G-CPMK	DHC.1 Chipmunk T.10
WZ868*	H	G-ARMF	DHC.1 Chipmunk T.10
WZ879	73	G-BWUT	DHC.1 Chipmunk T.10
WZ882	K	G-BXGP	DHC.1 Chipmunk T.10 (Army)
XA880		G-BVXR	DH.104 Devon C.2 (RAE)
XD693	Z-Q	G-AOBU	Percival Jet Provost T.1
XE489		G-JETH	Armstrong-Whitworth Sea Hawk FGA.6
XE665	876/VL	G-BWGM	Hawker Hunter T.8C (RN)
XE685	861/VL	G-GAII	Hawker Hunter GA.11 (RN)
XE689	864/VL	G-BWGK	Hawker Hunter GA.11 (RN)
XE897		G-DHVV	DH.115 Vampire T.55
XE920	A	G-VMPR	DH.115 Vampire T.11
XE956		G-OBLN	DH.115 Vampire T.11
XF114		G-SWIF	Supermarine Swift F.7
XF515	R	G-KAXF	Hawker Hunter F.6A
XF516	19	G-BVVC	Hawker Hunter F.6A
XF597	AH	G-BKFW	Percival Provost T.1
XF603	H	G-KAPW	Percival Provost T.1
XF690		G-MOOS	Percival Provost T.1
XF836		G-AWRY	Percival Provost T.1
XF877	J-X	G-AWVF	Percival Provost T.1
XG232		G-HHAC	Hawker Hunter F.6
XG452		G-BRMB	Bristol Belvedere HC.1
XG547	T-S/S-T	G-HAPR	Bristol Sycamore HR.14
XG775		G-DHWW	DH.115 Vampire T.11 (RN)
XH558		G-VLCN	Avro Vulcan B.2
XH568		G-BVIC	English Electric Canberra B.2/B.6
XJ389		G-AJJP	Fairey Jet Gyrodyne
XJ615		G-BWGL	Hawker Hunter T.8C (representing T.7 prototype)
XJ729		G-BVGE	Westland Whirlwind HAR.10
XJ763	P	G-BKHA	Westland Whirlwind HAR.10
XJ771		G-HELV	DH.115 Vampire T.55
XK416		G-AYUA	Auster AOP.9
XK417		G-AVXY	Auster AOP.9
XK895	CU-19	G-SDEV	DH.104 Sea Devon C.20 (RN)
XK940		G-AYXT	Westland Whirlwind HAS.7
XL426		G-VJET	Avro Vulcan B.2
XL502		G-BMYP	Fairey Gannet AEW.3 (RN)
XL571	V	G-HNTR	Hawker Hunter T.7 (Blue Diamonds)
XL573		G-BVGH	Hawker Hunter T.7
XL602		G-BWFT	Hawker Hunter T.8M

XL613		G-BVMB	Hawker Hunter T.7A
XL616	D	G-BWIE	Hawker Hunter T.7A
XL621		G-BNCX	Hawker Hunter T.7
XL714		G-AOGR	DH.82A Tiger Moth
XL-716		G-AOIL	DH.82A Tiger Moth
XL809		G-BLIX	Saro Skeeter AOP.12 (Army)
XL812		G-SARO	Saro Skeeter AOP.12
XL929		G-BNPU	Hunting Percival Pembroke C.1
XL954		G-BXES	Hunting Percival Pembroke C.1
XM223		G-BWWC	DH.104 Devon C.2
XM365		G-BXBH	Hunting Jet Provost T.3A
XM376	27	G-BWDR	Hunting Jet Provost T.3A
XM420	12	G-BWZZ	Hunting Jet Provost T.3A
XM424		G-BWDS	Hunting Jet Provost T.3A
XM470		G-BWZZ	Hunting Jet Provost T.3A
XM478		G-BXDL	Hunting Jet Provost T.3A
XM479	54	G-BVEZ	Hunting Jet Provost T.3A
XM553		G-AWSV	Saro Skeeter AOP.12
XM575		G-BLMC	Avro Vulcan B.2A
XM655		G-VULC	Avro Vulcan B.2A
XM685	PO/513	G-AYZJ	Westland Whirlwind HAS.7
XM693		G-TIMM	Folland Gnat T.1
XM819		G-APXW	Lancashire Aircraft EP.9 (Army)
XN351		G-BKSC	Saro Skeeter AOP.12 (Army)
XN437		G-AXWA	Auster AOP.9
XN441		G-BGKT	Auster AOP.9
XN459		G-BWOT	Hunting Jet Provost T.3A
XN470		G-BXBJ	Hunting Jet Provost T.3A
XN498	16	G-BWSH	Hunting Jet Provost T.3A
XN510		G-BXBI	Hunting Jet Provost T.3A
XN629	49	G-KNOT	Hunting Jet Provost T.3A
XN637	03	G-BKOU	Hunting Jet Provost T.3
XP242		G-BUCI	Auster AOP.9 (Army)
XP254		G-ASCC	Auster AOP.11
XP279		G-BWKK	Auster AOP.9 (Army)
XP282		G-BGTC	Auster AOP.9
XP355	A	G-BEBC	Westland Whirlwind HAR.10
XP672	03	G-RAFI	Hunting Jet Provost T.4
XP772		G-BUCJ	DHC.2 Beaver AL.1 (Army)
XP907		G-SROE	Westland Scout AH.1
XP924		G-CVIX	DH.110 Sea Vixen D.3
XR240		G-BDFH	Auster AOP.9 (Army)
XR241		G-AXRR	Auster AOP.9 (Army)
XR246		G-AZBU	Auster AOP.9
XR486		G-RWWW	Westland Whirlwind HCC.12 (Queens Flight c/s)
XR537	T	G-NATY	Folland Gnat T.1
XR538	01	G-RORI	Folland Gnat T.1 (RAF Training c/s)
XR595	M	G-BWHU	Westland Scout AH.1 (Army)
XR673		G-BXLO	Hunting Jet Provost T.4
XR724		G-BTSY	EE Lightning F.6
XR944		G-ATTB	Wallis WA.116
XR991		G-MOUR	Folland Gnat T.1 (Yellowjacks c/s)
XR993		G-BVPP	Folland Gnat T.1 (Red Arrows c/s)
XS101	1	G-GNAT	Folland Gnat T.1 (Red Arrows c/s)
XS165	37	G-ASAZ	Hiller UH-12E-4
XS587		G-VIXN	DH.110 Sea Vixen FAW.2 (RN
XS765		G-BSET	Beagle Basset CC.1
XS770		G-HRHI	Beagle Basset CC.1 (Queens Flight c/s)
XT223		G-XTUN	Westland Sioux AH.1 (Army)
XT435	430	G-RIMM	Westland Wasp HAS.1 (RN)
XT634		G-BYRX	Westland Scout AH.1 (Army)
XT653		BGA.3469	Slingsby T.45 Swallow
XT781	426	G-KAWW	Westland Wasp HAS.1 (RN)
XT782	316	G-BMIR	Westland Wasp HAS.1 (RN)
XV121		G-BYKJ	Westland Scout AH.1 (Army)
XV126	X	G-SCTA	Westland Scout AH.1 (Army)
XV130	R	G-BWJW	Westland Scout AH.1 (Army)
XV134		G-BWLX	Westland Scout AH.1 (Army)
XV137		G-CRUM	Westland Scout AH.1
XV140	K	G-KAXL	Westland Scout AH.1 (Army)
XV238*	41	G-ALYW(2)	de Havilland DH.106 Comet 1
XV268		G-BVER	DHC.2 Beaver (Army)
XW281	U	G-BYNZ	Westland Scout AH.1 (Royal Marines)
XW289	73	G-JPVA	BAC Jet Provost T.5A
XW293	Z	G-BWCS	BAC Jet Provost T.5
XW310	37	G-BWGS	BAC Jet Provost T.5A
XW324		G-BWSG	BAC Jet Provost T.5
XW325	E	G-BWGF	BAC Jet Provost T.5A
XW333		G-BVTC	BAC Jet Provost T.5A
XW422		G-BWEB	BAC Jet Provost T.5A
XW423	14	G-BWUW	BAC Jet Provost T.5A
XW431	A	G-BWBS	BAC Jet Provost T.5A
XW433		G-JPRO	BAC Jet Provost T.5A (CFS)
XW635		G-AWSW	Beagle Husky

XW784	VL	G-BBRN	Mitchell-Procter Kittiwake (RN)
XW858		G-DMSS	Westland Gazelle HT.3
XW895	51	G-BXZD	Westland Gazelle HT.2 (RN)
XX110		BAPC.169	BAC/Sepecat Jaguar GR.1
XX226*	74	BAPC.152	BAe Hawk T.1A fsm
XX253*		BAPC.171	BAe Hawk T.1 (Red Arrows)
XX467	86	G-TVII	Hawker Hunter T.7 (TWU)
XX513	10	G-KKKK	SA Bulldog
XX514*		G-BWIB	SA Bulldog
XX515	4	G-CBBC	SA Bulldog
XX518	S	G-UDOG	SA Bulldog
XX521	H	G-CBEH	SA Bulldog
XX522	06	G-DAWG	SA Bulldog
XX524	04	G-DDOG	SA Bulldog
XX525	6	G-CBJJ	SA Bulldog
XX528	X	G-BZON	SA Bulldog
XX534	B	G-EDAV	SA Bulldog
XX537	C	G-CBCB	SA Bulldog
XX538	O	G-TDOG	SA Bulldog
XX543	F	G-CBAB	SA Bulldog
XX546	03	G-CBCO	SA Bulldog
XX549	6	G-CBID	SA Bulldog
XX550	Z	G-CBBL	SA Bulldog
XX551	E	G-BZDP	SA Bulldog
XX554	09	G-BZMD	SA Bulldog
XX561	7	G-BZEP	SA Bulldog
XX611		G-CBDK	SA Bulldog
XX612	A03	G-BZXC	SA Bulldog
XX614	V	G-GGRR	SA Bulldog
XX619	T	G-CBBW	SA Bulldog
XX621	H	G-CBEF	SA Bulldog
XX622	B	G-CBGX	SA Bulldog
XX624	E	G-KDOG	SA Bulldog
XX625	01	G-CBBR	SA Bulldog
XX628	9	G-CBFU	SA Bulldog
XX629	V	G-BZXZ	SA Bulldog
XX630	5	G-SIJW	SA Bulldog
XX631	W	G-BZXS	SA Bulldog
XX636	Y	G-CBFP	SA Bulldog
XX638		G-DOGG	SA Bulldog
XX658	03	G-BZPS	SA Bulldog
XX667	16	G-BZFN	SA Bulldog
XX668	I	G-CBAN	SA Bulldog
XX692	A	G-BZMH	SA Bulldog
XX693	07	G-BZML	SA Bulldog
XX694	E	G-CBBS	SA Bulldog
XX695	3	G-CBBT	SA Bulldog
XX698	9	G-BZME	SA Bulldog
XX699	F	G-CBCV	SA Bulldog
XX700	17	G-CBEK	SA Bulldog
XX702	P	G-CBCR	SA Bulldog
XX707	4	G-CBDS	SA Bulldog
XX711	X	G-CBBU	SA Bulldog
XX713	2	G-CBJK	SA Bulldog
XX725	GU	BAPC.150	BAC/Sepecat Jaguar GR.1
XZ329		G-BZYD	Westland Gazelle AH.1
XZ363*	A	BAPC.151	BAC/Sepecat Jaguar GR.1A
ZA556*		BAPC.155	Panavia Tornado GR.1
ZA634	C	G-BUHA	Slingsby T-61F Venture T.2
ZB500		G-LYNX	Westland WG.13 Lynx 800 (Army)
ZH139	01	BAPC.191	BAe Harrier GR.5
	42	G-TORE	Hunting Jet Provost T.3A
	AL-K	G-HURR	Hawker Hurricane XII
	F	G-RUMW	Grumman FM-2 Wildcat (RN/FAA)
SR-XP020*		G-BZUG	Tiger Cub RL7A XP Sherwood Ranger
	VO-B	G-BYDR	N-A B-25D Mitchell II

"B" Conditions markings

G-17-3		G-AVNE	Westland Wessex 60
G-29-1		G-APRJ	Avro Lincoln
G-48/1		G-ALSX	Bristol Sycamore
U-0247		G-AGOY	Miles Messenger - intended marks
W-2		BAPC.85	Weir W-2
X-25		BAPC.274	Boulton & Paul P.6 fsm

OTHER ARMED FORCES
AUSTRALIA

A2-4		VH-ALB	Supermarine Seagull
A16-199	SF-R	G-BEOX	Lockheed Hudson IIIA
A17-48		G-BPHR	DH.82A Tiger Moth

BELGIUM

HD-75		G-AFDX	Hanriot HD.1

BOLIVIA

FAB-184		G-SIAI	SIAI-Marchetti SF.260W (FA Boliviana)

BOTSWANA

OJ-1		G-BXFU	BAC.167 Strikemaster 83
OJ-4	Z-2	G-UNNY	BAC.167 Strikemaster 87
OJ-7	Z-28	G-BXFX	BAC.167 Strikemaster 83
OJ-8		G-BXFV	BAC.167 Strikemaster 83
OJ10		G-UNVR	BAC.167 Strikemaster 87

CANADA

622		N6699D	Piasecki HUP-3 Retreiver (RCN)
920	QN-	CF-BXO	Supermarine Stranraer
3349		G-BYNF	NA Yale
16693*	693	G-BLPG	Auster J/1N (AOP.6 c/s)
18013		G-BNZC	DHC.1 Chipmunk
18013		G-TRIC	DHC.1 Chipmunk
18393		G-BCYK	Avro Canada CF.100 Canuck IV
20310	310	G-BSBG	N.A. Harvard IV
21261		G-TBRD	Lockheed T-33A

PEOPLES' REPUBLIC OF CHINA (inc HONG KONG)

663/P11151	88	ZK-RMH	Curtiss P-40E Kittyhawk (Chinese AF)
2751219	88	G-BVVG	Nanchang CJ-6A
HKG-5		G-BULL	SA Bulldog
HKG-6		G-BPCL	SA Bulldog
HKG-11		G-BYRY	Slingsby T.67M-200 Firefly
HKG-13		G-BXKW	Slingsby T.67M-200 Firefly

FRANCE

120	3	G-AZGC	Stampe SV-4C
124		G-BOSJ	Nord 3400
143		G-MSAL	Morane-Saulnier MS.733 (Aeronavale)
185	44-CA	G-BWLR	Max Holste Broussard
316	315-SN	F-GGKR	Max Holste Broussard
394		G-BIMO	Stampe SV-4C
MS.824		G-AWBU	Morane-Saulnier N rep
1/4513		G-BFYO	SPAD XII rep
	315-SQ/20	G-BWGG	Max Holste Broussard
F-OTAN-6		G-ATDB	SNCAN 1101 Noralpha
F-OTAN-6*		G-BAYV	SNCAN 1101 Noralpha

GERMANY

1+4		G-BSLX	WAR FW190 scale rep
2+1	7334	G-SYFW	WAR FW190 Scale rep
3		G-BAYV	Nord 1101 (Messerschmitt guise)
8+-		G-WULF	WAR FW190 scale rep
10	KG+EM	G-ETME	Nord 1002 Pingouin
14		BAPC.67	Messerschmitt Bf.109 rep
+14		G-BSMD	Nord 1101 (Messerschmitt guise)
28+10		G-BWTT	Aero L-39ZO Albatros
50	CW+BG	G-BXBD	CASA I-131 Jungmann
97+04		G-APVF	Putzer Elster B
99+32		G-BZGK	North American OV-10B Bronco
99+26		G-BZGL	North American OV-10B Bronco
124		G-BHCA	Fokker D.VIII rep
152/17		G-ATJM	Fokker DR.1 rep
422/15		G-AVJO	Fokker E-III rep
425/17		BAPC.133	Fokker DR.1 rep
626/8		N6268	Fokker D.VII (Travel Air 2000)
1227	DG+HO	G-FOKW	Focke-Wulfe FW190A-5
1480	6	BAPC.66	Messerschmitt Bf.109 rep
6357	6	BAPC.74	Messerschmitt Bf.109 rep
7198/18		G-AANJ	LVG C.VI
10639	6 (Black)	G-USTV	Messerschmitt Bf.109G-2
D604		G-FLIZ	Staaken Flitzer
D692		G-BVAW	Staaken Flitzer
D5397/17		G-BFXL	Albatros D.VA rep
	BU+CC	G-BUCC	CASA I-131E Jungmann
	BU+CK	G-BUCK	CASA I-131E Jungmann
	CC+43	G-CJCI	Pilatus P.2 (Arado Ar.96B guise)
	CF+HF	EI-AUY	Morane-Saulnier MS.502 Criquet
	F+IS	G-BIRW	Morane-Saulnier MS.505 Criquet
	LG+01	G-AYSJ	Bucker 133 Jungmeister
	LG+03	G-AEZX	Bucker 133 Jungmeister
	NJ+C11	G-ATBG	Messerschmitt Bf.108 (Nord 1002)
	RJ+NP	G-BFHF	CASA 352L (*Identity unconfirmed*)
	S4+A07	G-BWHP	CASA I-131E Jungmann
	S5+B06	G-BSFB	CASA I-131E Jungmann
	TA+RC	G-BPHZ	Morane-Saulnier MS.505 Criquet

HUNGARY

503		G-BRAM	MiG 21PF (Russian c/s)

IRELAND

177		G-BLIW	Percival Provost T.51

ITALY

	W7	G-AGFT	Avia FL.3
MM12822	20	G-FIST	Fiesler Fi.156C-3 Storch

JAPAN

24	BAPC.83	Kawasaki Ki 100-1b

THE NETHERLANDS

BI-005	G-BUVN	CASA I-131E Jungmann
E-15	G-BIYU	Fokker S.11 Instructor
R-55	G-BLMI	Piper L-18C Super Cub (R Neth A/F)
R-151	G-BIYR	Piper L-21B Super Cub
R-156	G-ROVE	Piper L-21B Super Cub
R-163	G-BIRH	Piper L-21B Super Cub
R-167	G-LION	Piper L-21B Super Cub
174	G-BEPV	Fokker S.11.1 Instructor (Navy)

NEW ZEALAND

NZ6361	G-BXFP	BAC.167 Strikemaster 87

NORTH KOREA

01420	G-BMZF	MiG-15

NORTH VIETNAM

1211	G-MIGG	WSK PZL-Mielec Lim-5 (MiG-17F)

NORWAY

321	G-BKPY	Saab Safir
423 & 427	G-AMRK	Gloster Gladiator

PORTUGAL

85	G-BTPZ	Hawker (Isaacs) Fury
1377*	G-BARS	DHC.1 Chipmunk
1747	G-BGPB	CCF Harvard 4

RUSSIA

01	G-YKSZ	Yakovlev Yak 52
07 (Yellow)	G-BMJY	Yakovlev Yak 18
09	G-BVMU	Yakovlev Yak 52 (DOSAAF)
11 (White)	G-BZMY	SPP Yakovlev Yak C-11
12 (Red)	G-DELF	Aero L-29A Delfin
26	G-BVXK	Yakovlev Yak 52 (DOSAAF)
27	G-OYAK	Yakovlev Yak 11
39	G-XXVI	Sukhoi Su-26M
50	G-CBRW)	Yakovlev Yak-52 (DOSAAF)
52	LY-AMP	Yakovlev Yak-52 (DOSAAF)
55	G-BVOK	Yakovlev Yak 52 (DOSAAF)
69	G-BTZB	Yakovlev Yak 50 (DOSAAF)
69*	RA44469(2)	Yakovlev Yakovlev Yak-52
72	G-BXAV	Yakovlev Yak 52 (DOSAAF)
139	G-BWOD	Yakovlev Yak 52 (DOSAAF)
6247	G-OMIG	MiG-15 (Korean War c/s)
853007	G-BVVO	Yakovlev Yak 50

REPUBLIC OF SOUTH AFRICA

92	G-BYCX	Westland Wasp HAS.Mk.1 (Navy)

SAUDI ARABIA

1133	G-BESY	BAC 167 Strikemaster Mk.80A

SPAIN

E3B-153	781-75	G-BPTS	CASA I.131 Jungmann
E3B-350	05-97	G-BHPL	CASA I.131 Jungmann
E3B-369	781-32	G-BPDM	CASA I.131 Jungmann
	781-25	G-BRSH	CASA I.131 Jungmann

SWITZERLAND

A 10	G-BECW	CASA I-131E Jungmann
A 50	G-CBCE	CASA 1-131E Jungmann rep
A 57	G-BECT	CASA I-131E Jungmann
A 125	G-BLKZ	Pilatus P.2-05
A 806	G-BTLL	Pilatus P.3
C-552	G-DORN	EKW C-3605
J-1149	G-SWIS	DH.100 Vampire FB.6
J-1573	G-VICI	DH.112 Venom FB.50
J-1605	G-BLID	DH.112 Venom FB.50
J-1611	G-DHTT	DH.112 Venom FB.50
J-1632	G-VNOM	DH.112 Venom FB.50
J-1758	G-BLSD	DH.112 Venom FB.50
J-4031	G-BWFR	Hawker Hunter F.58

J-4058		G-BWFS	Hawker Hunter F.58
J-4066		G-BXNZ	Hawker Hunter F.58
J-4090		G-SIAL	Hawker Hunter F.58
U-80		G-BUKK	Bucker Jungmeister
U-95		G-BVGP	Bucker Jungmeister
U-99		G-AXMT	Bucker Jungmeister
U-110		G-PTWO	Pilatus P.2
U-1234		G-DHAV	DH.115 Vampire T.11
V-54		G-BVSD	SE.3130 Alouette II

UNITED NATIONS

001		G-BFRI	Sikorsky S-61N Mk.II

UNITED STATES OF AMERICA

2		G-AZLE	Boeing-Stearman Kaydet (US Army)
5		G-BEEW	Taylor Monoplane (Boeing P-26A) (US Army)
14		G-ISDN	Boeing-Stearman Kaydet (US Army)
23		N49272	Fairchild PT-23 Cornell (USAAC)
26		G-BAVO	Boeing-Stearman Kaydet (US Army)
27		G-AGYY	Ryan PT-21 (USAAC)
27		G-BRVG	NA SNJ-7 Texan (US Navy)
28		N8162G	Boeing-Stearman Kaydet (US Army)
33		G-THEA	Boeing-Stearman Kaydet (US Navy)
43	SC	G-AZSC	NA AT-16 Texan (USAAF)
44		G-BWHH	Piper L-21B Super Cub (US Army)
44		G-RJAH	Boeing-Stearman Kaydet (US Army)
49		G-KITT	Curtiss TP-40M Kittyhawk (US Army)
54		G-BCNX	Piper L-4H (USAF)
85		G-BTBI	Republic P-47 Thunderbolt Scale rep (USAF)
112		G-BSWC	Boeing-Stearman Kaydet (US Army)
118		G-BSDS	Boeing-Stearman Kaydet (US Army)
379		G-ILLE	Boeing-Stearman Kaydet (US Army)
441		G-BTFG	Boeing-Stearman Kaydet (US Navy)
526		G-BRWB	NA T-6G Texan (USAF)
624	D-39	G-BVMH	Piper L-4 (Wag-Aero Cuby) (USAAC)
669		N75TL	Boeing-Stearman Kaydet (US Army)
854		G-BTBH	Ryan PT-22 (US Army)
855		N56421	Ryan PT-22 (US Army)
897E		G-BJEV	Aeronca Chief (US Navy)
985		G-ERIX	Boeing-Stearman Kaydet (US Navy)
1164		G-BKGL	Beech C-45 (US Army)
2807	V-103	G-BHTH	NA T-6G Texan (US Navy)
7797		G-BFAF	Aeronca L-16A (US Army)
8178	FU-178	G-SABR	NA F-86A Sabre (USAF)
8242	FU-242	N196B	NA F-86A Sabre (USAF)
02538		N33870	Fairchild PT-19 Cornell (USAAC)
07539	143	N63590	Boeing-Stearman Kaydet (US Navy)
14863	TA-863	G-BGOR	NA AT-6D Texan (USAAF)
16136	205	G-BRUJ	Boeing-Stearman Kaydet (US Navy)
18263	822	N38940	Boeing-Stearman Kaydet (USAAC)
21714	201B	G-RUMM	Grumman F8F-2P Bearcat (USN)
28521	TA-521	G-TVIJ	NA T-6J Harvard (USAF)
26922	AK-402	G-RAID	Douglas AD-4NA Skyraider (US Navy)
29261		G-CDET	Culver Cadet (USAAF)
30274		N203SA	Piper AE-1 Cub Cruiser
31145	G-26	G-BBLH	Piper L-4B (US Army)
31171		N7614C	NA B-25J Mitchell (US Marines)
31952		G-BRPR	Aeronca L-3C Grasshopper (US Army)
38674		G-MTKM	Thomas-Morse S4 Scout Scale rep (USASC)
40467	19	G-BTCC	Grumman F6F Hellcat (US Navy)
41386		G-MJTD	Thomas-Morse S4 Scout Scale rep (USASC)
46214	X-3	CF-KCG	Grumman TBM-3E Avenger (USN)
53319	RB/319	G-BTDP	Grumman TBM-3R Avenger (US Navy)
54137	69	G-CTKL	Noorduyn Harvard IIB (US Navy)
56498		N44914	Douglas C-54D Skymaster
80425	WT-4	G-RUMT	Grumman F7F-3P Tigercat (USN)
80480	E-44	G-BECN	Piper L-4J (USAAC)
91007	TR-007	G-NASA	Lockheed T-33A (USAF)
92844	8	G-BXUL	Vought FG-1D Corsair (US Navy)
93542	LTA-542	G-BRLV	NA T-6 Texan (USAF)
111836	JZ/6	G-TSIX	NA AT-6C Texan (US Navy)
111989		N33600	Cessna L-19A Bird Dog (US Army)
115042	TA-042	G-BGHU	NA T-6G Texan (USAF)
115302	TP	G-BJTP	Piper L-18C Super Cub (US Marines)
115684	VM	G-BKVM	Piper L-21A Super Cub (US Army)
124485	DF-A	G-BEDF	Boeing B-17G Flying Fortress (USAAC)
122351		G-BKRG	Beech C-45G
126603		G-BHWH	Weedhopper JC-24C (US Navy)
151632		G-BWGR	NA TB-25N Mitchell (USAF)
217786	25	CF-EQS	Boeing-Stearman Kaydet (USAAF)
224319	L4-D	N147DC	Douglas C-47A-75-DL Dakota (USAAF)
226413	ZU-N	N47DD	Republic P-47D Thunderbolt (USAAF)
226671	MX-X/LH-X	G-THUN	Republic P-47D Thunderbolt (USAAF)
231983	IY-G	F-BDRS	Boeing B-17G Flying Fortress (USAAF)

237123		BAPC.157	Waco CG-4A Hadrian
238410	A-44	G-BHPK	Piper L-4A (USAAF)
243809		BAPC.185	Waco CG-4A Hadrian
252983		N66630	Schweizer TG-3A
292912	LN-F	N47FK	Douglas C-47A-35-DL Dakota 3 (USAAF)
314887		G-AJPI	Fairchild UC-61 Forwarder (USAAF)
315211	JB-Z	N1944A	Douglas C-47A
315509	W7-S	G-BHUB	Douglas C-47A Dakota (USAAF)
329405	A-23	G-BCOB	Piper L-4H (USAAC)
329417		G-BDHK	Piper L-4A Cub (USAAC)
329471	F-44	G-BGXA	Piper L-4H (USAAC)
329601	D-44	G-AXHR	Piper L-4H (USAAC)
329854	R-44	G-BMKC	Piper L-4H (USAAC)
329934	B-72	G-BCPH	Piper L-4H (USAAC/French)
330238	A-24	G-LIVH	Piper L-4H (USAAC)
330485	C-44	G-AJES	Piper L-4H (USAAC)
343251	27	G-NZSS	Boeing-Stearman Kaydet (USAAC)
413573	B6-V	N6526D	NA P-51D Mustang (USAAC)
413704	B7-H	G-BTCD	NA P-51D Mustang (USAAF)
414419	LH-F	G-MSTG	NA P-51D Mustang (USAF)
454467	J-44	G-BILI	Piper L-4J (US Army)
454537	J-04	G-BFDL	Piper L-4J (US Army)
461748	Y	G-BHDK	Boeing B-29A Superfortress (USAF)
463209*	WZ-S	BAPC.255	NA P-51D Mustang (USAAF)
472216	HO-M	G-BIXL	NA P-51D Mustang (USAAF)
472218	WZ-I	G-HAEC	NA P-51D Mustang (USAAF)
472773	AJ-C	G-SUSY	NA P-51D Mustang (USAAF)
473877		N167F	NA P-51D Mustang (USAAF)
474008	IF-R	G-SIRR	NA P-51D Mustang (USAAF)
479609	PR-L4	G-BHXY	Piper L-4H (USAAC)
479744	M-49	G-BGPD	Piper L-4H (USAAC)
479766	D-63	G-BKHG	Piper L-4H (USAAC)
480015	M-44	G-AKIB	Piper L-4H (USAAC)
480133	B-44	G-BDCD	Piper L-4J (USAAC)
480321	H-44	G-FRAN	Piper L-4J (USAAC)
480636	A-58	G-AXHP	Piper L-4J (USAAC)
480752	E-39	G-BCXJ	Piper L-4J (USAAC)
483868	N	N5237V	Boeing B-17G Flying Fortress (USAF)
493209		G-DDMV	NA T-6G Texan (Calif ANG)
517962		G-TROY	NA T-28B Trojan
607327	L-09	G-ARAO	Piper (L-21B) Super Cub (US Army)
3-1923		G-BRHP	Aeronca O-58B Grasshopper (US Army)
18-2001		G-BIZV	Piper L-18C Super Cub (US Army)
18-5395	CDG	G-CUBJ	Piper L-18C Super Cub (ALAT)
41-33275	CE	G-BICE	NA AT-6C Texan (USAAC)
42-42914		N31356	Douglas DC-4-1009
42-58678	IY	G-BRIY	Taylorcraft L-2A (USAAC)
42-78044		G-BRXL	Aeronca L-3F (US Army)
42-84555	EP-H	G-ELMH	NA AT-6D Harvard (USAAC)
44-30861		N9089Z	NA B-25J Mitchell (USAAC)
44-63507		NL51EA	NA P-51D Mustang
44-80594		G-BEDJ	Piper L-4J (USAAC)
44-80723	J-E5	G-BFZB	Piper L-4J (USAAC)
44-83184	7	G-RGUS	Fairchild UC-61K Forwarder (USAAC)
51-7545		N14113	NA T-28B Trojan
51-11701A	AF258	G-BSZC	Beech C-45H (USAF)
51-15227	10	G-BKRA	NA T-6G Texan (US Navy)
51-15319	A-319	G-FUZZ	Piper L-18C Super Cub (US Army)
54-2446		G-ROVE	Piper L-21B Super Cub (US Army)
54-2447		G-SCUB	Piper L-21B Super Cub (US Army)
146-11042	7	G-BMZX	SPAD rep (Wolf W.II) (US Army/AEF)
146-11083	5	G-BNAI	SPAD rep (Wolf W.II) (US Army/AEF)
	H-57	G-AKAZ	Piper L-4A (USAAF)
	K-33	G-BJLH	Piper L-18C Super Cub (US Army)

YUGOSLAVIA

30140		G-RADA	Soko Kraguj
30146		G-BSXD	Soko Kraguj
30149		G-SOKO	Soko Kraguj

UNATTRIBUTED

001		G-BYPY	Ryan ST3-KR
111		G-OTAF	Aero L-39ZO Albatros

PART 4 – FICTITIOUS CIVIL MARKINGS & AUTHENTIC, REPRODUCTION & MOCK-UP SPECIMENS

The majority of the aicraft listed below have originated from within the BAPC ranks. We welcome any amendments.

Regn	Type	Comments
"K.158"	Austin Whippet rep	See BAPC.207 in SECTION 4
"EI-ABH"	HM.14 Pou-du-Ciel rep (1)	Under construction @ Meath Aero Museum 2001
"F-OCMF"		See F-BTRP in SECTION 5, PART 1
"G-EASQ"	Bristol 30/46 Babe III rep	See BAPC.87 in SECTION 4
"G-EBED"	Vickers 60 Viking IV rep	See BAPC.114 in SECTION 4
"G-AAAH"	DH.60 Moth rep	Located at Yorkshire Aircraft Museum, Elvington
"G-AAAH"	DH.60G Moth rep	See BAPC.168 in SECTION 4
"G-AACA"	Avro 504K rep	See BAPC.177 in SECTION 4
"G-ABUL"	DH.82A Tiger Moth	See G-AOXG in SECTION 1, PART 2
"G-ACDR"	DH.82A Tiger Moth	US regd as N9295 [c/n 86536]
"G-ACSS"	DH.88 Comet model	See BAPC.216 in SECTION 4
"G-ACSS"	DH.88 model	See BAPC.257 in SECTION 4
"G-ADRG"	Mignet HM.14 Pou-Du-Ciel	See BAPC.77 in SECTION 4 PARTS 1 & 2
"G-ADRX"	Mignet HM.14 Pou-Du-Ciel	See BAPC.231 in SECTION 4
"G-ADRY"	Mignet HM.14 Pou-Du-Ciel	See BAPC.29 in SECTION 4
"G-ADVU"	Mignet HM.14 Pou-Du-Ciel	See BAPC.211 in SECTION 4
"G-ADYV"	Mignet HM.14 Pou-Du-Ciel	See BAPC.243 in SECTION 4
"G-ADZW"	Mignet HM.14 Pou-Du-Ciel	See BAPC.253 in SECTION 4
"G-AEAJ"	DH.89 Dragon Rapide rep	Marriott Hotel South, Liverpool Airport
		(Railway Air Services titles) (Static FSM)
"G-AEOF"	Mignet HM.14 Pou-Du-Ciel	See BAPC.22 in SECTION 4
"G-AFAP"	CASA 352L (Ju52/3m)	Ex Sp AF T2B-272 (c/n 163) @ RAF Museum, Cosford
		(Original British Airways titles)
"G-AFFI"	Mignet HM.14 Pou-Du-Ciel	See BAPC.76 in SECTION 4
"G-AFUG"	Luton LA.4 Minor	See BAPC 97 in SECTION 4
"G-AJOV"	Westland WS-51 Dragonfly HR.3	ex WP495 (c/n WA/H/80) @ RAF Museum, Cosford
		(BEA titles)
"G-AJOZ"	Fairchild F.24W-41A Argus 1	The Thorpe Camp Preservation Group Woodhall Spa
		(Full-scale replica)
"G-AMSU"	Douglas C-47A Dakota 3	See G-AMPP in SECTION 1, PART 2
"G-AMZZ"(2)	Douglas C-47A-DK Dakota [12254,]	Al Mahata Museum/The Sharjah Avin Museum, Sharjah,UAE
	(ex 42-92452 - to RCAF FZ669, CAF12943, C-GCXE, HI-502, N688EA) (Noted 1.03)	
"G-AOXL"	DH.114 2	See G-ANUO in SECTION 1, PART 2
"G-ASOK"	Cessna F172E Rocket	See (D-ECDU) in SECTION 5, PART 1
"G-CARS"	Pitts S-2A Special	See BAPC.134 in SECTION 4
"G-CDBS"	MBB Bo.105D	See G-BCXO in SECTION 1, PART 2
"G-DRNT"	Sikorsky S-76A	Petak Offshore Industry Training Centre, Norwich
"G-ESKY"	Piper PA-23-250 Aztec	Is G-BADI (qv)- used 1999 for TV work as "G-BADF"
"G-MAZY"	DH.82A Tiger Moth	H.Hodgson, Winthorpe *"Maisie"*
	(On loan from Cotswold Aircraft Restoration Group) (Rebuilt for static display & loaned Newark Air Museum)	
	Composite ex Newark components & G-AMBB/T6801; also reported as ex DE561 [lost at sea 1942]	
"G-RAFM"	Robinson R22 Beta	See G-OTHL in SECTION 1, PART 2
"G-SHOG"	Colomban MC-15 Cri-Cri	V.S.E.Norman, Rendcomb *(Static model 1999)*

PART 5 – AIRCRAFT WITH NO EXTERNAL MARKINGS CARRIED

These are listed by Type to ease identification! Amendments and alterations are always welcome.

Regn	Type	Comments
G-AANI	Blackburn Monoplane	See SECTION 1
G-AANG	Bleriot XI	See SECTION 1
G-BWJM	Bristol M.1C rep	See SECTION 1
G-MYBL	CFM Shadow CD	See SECTION 1
G-AANH	Deperdussin Monoplane	See SECTION 1
G-EBNV	English Electric Wren	See SECTION 1
G-BAAF	Manning-Flanders MF.1	See SECTION 1
G-ARSG	Roe Triplane IV rep	See SECTION 1
G-BFIP	Wallbro Monoplane	See SECTION 1

PART 6 – ALPHABETICAL TYPE INDEX (UK & IRELAND GLIDERS)

Herewith a summary of BGA No/Tri-graph tie-ups but note the letters I and O are not used except in the case of JMO.

BGA No.	Tri-graph		BGA No.	Tri-graph
101 – 230	None		3535 – 3545	FUL – FUW
231 – 246	AAA – AAR		3546 – 3735	FUY – GCV
247 – 605	AAT – ARR		3736 – 3770	GCX – GEQ
606 – 628	ART – ASR		3771 – 3776	GEK – GEQ
629 – 806	AST – BAC		3777 – 3817	HAA – HBS
807 – 1245	BAE – BUL		3818	Not used
1246 – 1380	BUN – CAC		3819 – 3827	HBT – HCB
1381 – 1681	CAG – CNS		3828	Not used
1682 – 1819	CNU – CUM		3829 – 3990	HCC – HJV
1682 – 1819	CNU – CUM		3991 – 4043	HJX – HMB
1820 – 1821	CUP – CUQ		4044 – 4045	HMG – HMH
1822 – 2048	CUS – DEC		4046 – 4122	HMK – HQP
2049 – 2391	DEE – DUL		4123 – 4138	HQR – HRG
2392 – 2478	DUN – DYC		4139 – 4276	HRJ – HXB
2479 – 2485	DYE – DYL		4277	Not used
2486 – 2489	DYN – DYR		4278 – 4624	HXC – JMN
2490 – 2494	DYT – DYX		4625	JMO
2495 – 3101	DYZ – FAF		4626 – 4878	JMP – JYB
3102 – 3528	FAH – FUB		4880 – 5023	JYC – KEB
3529 – 3534	FUD – FUJ			

ABBOTT-BAYNES SAILPLANES LTD
SCUD I
  HFZ
SCUD II
  AAA
SCUD III
  ACF AVA

AEROMERE see CARMAM

ALLGAIER
GEIER
  EBP

ASC
FALCON
  HPZ
SPIRIT
  HPY

AVIA
40P
  AUW

AVIASTROITEL see FEDEROV
AC-4
  JUX JVH
AC-5
  KDD

AVIALSA see SCHEIBE

AVIONAUTICA RIO see CARMAM

BAC
VII rep
  EQY

BIBBY
G.1
  HPK

BIRMINGHAM GUILD LTD see SWALES & YORKSHIRE SAILPLANES
BG.135
  CRF CUF CYW CXN CXP DCY DLZ

BOLKOW
PHOEBUS C
  CGX CHC CHJ CJB CJJ CKC GDD HTZ JHX JVH JWP JYZ EI-123 EI-158

BREGUET
905 FAUVETTE
  CVJ DGV EGR ELJ EPN ESM

CARMAM (SOCIETE CARMAM) see AEROMERE/AVIONAUTICA RIO
M.100S MÉSANGE
  CBR CLU DFP DTS DUC EPG EQM ETN FCH FKV HFP HGU HQF
M.200 FOEHN
  EQX EVC FXN HCN HGJ
JP.15/34 KIT-CLUB/15/36A AIGLON
  DYL EDB FDC FQV HKE HKF HKZ HMU HTW

CAUDRON
C.801
  EHF

(SA) CENTRAIR see SCHLEICHER
101 PÉGASE
  EPK EQK ERX ESH ESW ETJ ETM EVE EVM EVQ FAN FCB FCD FEH FFC
  FFS FGW FHJ FJK FJT FMK FNM FRD FRR FRV FRX FVM FVN FVP FVV FWG
  FWX FWY FXD FXT GBU GCN GCY HDD HDW HES HKN HNY HNZ HRK HZF
  JQP KAE KBA
201 MARIANNE
  HTA JXB JXN
ALLIANCE SNC-34
  JHR

CHARD see KING-ELLIOTT-STREET

CHILTON
OLYMPIA
  EI-103

COLDITZ
COCK REP
  JRZ JTA - both designs are unrelated

DFS see GRUNAU, EoN, NORD, FOCKE-WULF, WEIHE & SCHLEICHER production
KRANICH
  BGT BQJ
OLYMPIA-MEIS
  AKD
108-68 WEIHE
  AKC BKC BNC BTV BWR EDL

DITTMAR
CONDOR IV
  JZD

DWLKK
PW-5 SMYK
  HYM HZB JCG JDW JKB JKE KCQ

EDGLEY
EA.9
  HPJ JZQ JZR

EICHELSDORFER

SB.5
EHC EJH

EIRI

PIK-20
DFE DFK DFZ DHH DHN DHV DJN DJZ DKT DLJ DLY DMU DMV DMY DPL
DQU DRT DVJ DVN DWS DYT DZT EAR EAT EBG JBH JGK JVE JXG

EoN see DFS/NORD

AP.5 OLYMPIA
AMK AMM AMP AMR AMT AMU AMV AMW ANW ANZ APC APV AUU AVD
AWU AZR AZT BBH BEL BFN BGR BGX BHC BJC BKK BKL BKS BKU BKX BLN
BLP BLQ BLS BNG BPL BQQ BRH BRL BWX CAF CAK CBS CGU CHK CPE
CQG CTA CTS DBA DPU EI-115
AP.6 OLYMPIA 401/403/419
BLJ BLK BVW CDW DAL DTR
AP.7 PRIMARY/ETON TX.1
AQQ AQY AQZ CLJ FEZ
AP.8 BABY
ASS AST G-ALRH EI-118
AP.10 460/463/465
BQM BQS BQT BRK BRQ BSQ BTG BTN BTQ BUG BUH BUK BUV BVN BWB
BWE BWG BWU BXB BXC BXY BYE BZB BZR BZS BZV BZW CAB CAN CAT
CBV ELS

FAUVEL

AV.22S
DSM
AV.36C
ETE

FEDEROV see AVIA STROITEL

Me-7 MECHTA
HMZ HPS HPT HUQ JFY JFZ JGA

FFA FLUGZEUGWERKE AG

DIAMANT
CDG CDW CGM CGS HGT

FOCKE-WULF see DFS WEIHE

KRANICH III
ENG

GINN-LESNIAK

KESTREL
CJC

GLASER-DIRKS

DG-100/DG-101
DFN DHJ DHK DHL DKQ DMD DRB DUY EDN EDP EKP ENU EPU FBH FBW
FFU FYU HMS HWP JEZ JNZ JPF JRL JSM JTC JXP JXV JYQ JZU KDY
DG.200/DG.202
DTA DTM DUQ DWJ DXN DYH EBR EDM EKA EME EMU EQP FQC HAT HBD
HDH JAE JAJ JAW JDD JDP JHW JKF JKM JPW JRN JVP JXG JYB KAC KCW
KDU KDY EI-145 EI-147
DG.300/DG.303 ELAN
ESQ FAJ FBF FCM FDW FGT FJR FJS FJX FLC FLX FNS FPK FSR FSX FTS
FUJ FUT FUU FWM FZW GAJ GBS HBE HBW HCU HCY HDR HMB HSB HVM
JAB JDV JNQ JRC JTK JTN JVL KAD KAU KBF
DG-500/DG-505 ELAN
GBZ HBP HEF HGV HHJ HNA HRC HYE JDN JQF JSX JZB JZF JZK KAW KAX
DG-600
FKB FNT FPW FQQ FVG KAZ KBS
DG-800
HPU JBL JJH JYK KBY

GLASFLUGEL

H.201 STANDARD LIBELLE
CFS CFX CFY CKF CKY CLM CLN CLP CLR CLV CLW CMH CMQ CMR CMS
CMV CMW CMX CNE CNF CNG CNH CNJ CNP CNY CPA CPF CPM CRB CRQ
CRS CRV CRW CSJ CSR CTU CUJ CUK CVL CVQ CWE CWG CWN CWT CWX
CWY CWZ CXK CYG CZL DCC DMS DNL ECY FLT FLU GAU GDM GEE HAA
HAD HAV HCQ HHY HJR HWC HWG JAS JBF JEU JGZ JHJ JNG JVW KBR
KCM
H.205 CLUB LIBELLE
DBP DEQ DKZ DVM FAR FYG GCS HAE KAM KDG
H.206 HORNET
DKD DKM
H.301 LIBELLE
FEV GAN HLK

H.303 MOSQUITO

DMN DPK DRN DTK DTV DTX DTY DUB DVZ DWB DWL DWO DWR DXA DXW
EAK ECH ECS EDH EDJ FBN FWR HMT JEH JNR JTQ JTW
H.304
EHU ENT HMM
H.604
ECT

GROB (BURKHART GROB LUFT und RAUMFAHRT GmbH) see SCHEMPP-HIRTH

G.102/G.104 SPEED ASTIR
DFR DJD DJQ DJX DKR DKS DKU DKV DKW DKX DLH DLM DMH DMP DMR
DNC DNE DNK DPJ DPQ DPY DQB DQE DQG DQR DRK DRU DRW DSH DSN
DSU DUL DUX DWQ DWU DXJ DYF DZJ DZU EAC EAF EAW EBB EBM ECQ
EEQ EKF ELN EQD EVK EVL FBR FCJ FDF FEB FEF FEX FFB FGK FHT FHW
FJH FRL FSA FSH FSZ FTK FTR FXA GAT GBJ GBK GCL GDQ GEB HAU HBL
HBM HBT HCS HFD HGB HJV HKB HKM HPM HQT HRA HSE HTD HTE HTG
HTR HUN HVK HWK HXB HXM HXY HYQ HZC JAZ JBZ JCF JCR JCW JEK JFD
JHE JHG JHN JKW JLR JML JNA JPJ JPM JQN JQT JRD JRM JRP JSD JSH
JSK JTT JUK JUS JWR JYC JYP JZW JZY KAY KBD KBL KCP EI-124
G.103 TWIN ASTIR/ACRO
DRQ DSJ DSL EGN EQT EWP EWR EYS EZE FEA FFJ FQK FWC HBH HBK
HCA HCJ HQS HWW JKV JLZ JQG JRW KCS

GRUNAU including DFS,FOKKER &HAWKRIDGE production

BABY
ABZ AFY AQN ASC BGS BTD CBK CDQ CMY CRM CYJ DNA DNB DUD DUW
DWF EHX EMW HJB

HALFORD

JSH SCORPION
DJF

HAWKRIDGE

DAGLING
ALX ALZ

HIRTH

Go.III MINIMOA
CLY
GOEVIER
DBU

HOLS-DER-TEUFEL

REPLICA
FHQ

HUTTER

H.17
ALW EPR HEY
H.28
HJM HPB

ICA (INTREPRINDERA DE CONSTRUCTII AERONAUTICE OF CIAR 1968)

IS-28B2
DEG DLT DLU DZR EHS EHW EJA HMG EI-141
IS-29D
DAM DBG DDJ DEN DEW DEZ FDG FFN
IS-30
FDB FDP
IS-32A
FAV

ISF

MISTRAL C
JBE JRS

ISSOIRE (SOCIÉTÉ ISSOIRE-AVIATION)

D77 IRIS
EET EJW
E78 SILENE
EBE EEU HPA JUG

JANSON

BJ-1B DUSTER
ETL

JASTREB see SCHEMPP-HIRTH

KING-ELLIOTT-STREET

OSPREY
DCZ

LAK

LAK-12 LIETUVA
FXR GAB GCB GCJ HEG HGQ HGR HGX HHM HHW HLT HQG HRB HSR HTF
JBS JBY JFW JQH JYL
LAK-17
JQU JVJ KAQ KBE KCR

LANAVERRE see SCHEMPP-HIRTH

LET

L-13 BLANIK
BVY BXR BXV BXW CAW CFD CUZ CVA CVB CYR DAF DCL DEX DEY DGB
DGP DKH DPD DVD EFX ESV EUG EVR FDV FLV FZS GAK HTY JDU JGQ JNX
EI-120 EI-154
L-23 SUPER BLANIK
FXP FYP FYR
L-33 SOLO
FZY FZZ

LETOV (VOJENSKÁ továrna na letadla LETOV)

LF-107 LUNAK
HXL JYF KBW KDT

MANUEL

CONDOR
DJW
HAWK
CSU
WILLOW WREN
BGA.162

MARCO

J-5
HKW

MARGANSKI

SWIFT S1
JZP

MAUPIN

WOODSTOCK
HCG HPG

MDM

MDM-1 FOX
JCH JKC

MOLINO see EIRI

MONNETT

MONERAI
FAP JBV

MÜLLER

MOSWEY III
DXY

MÜNCHEN

MÜ-13D
CZM DPG

NEUKOM

STANDARD ELFE S-2
FMR JGF JXY
ELFE PM3
JRQ

NORD see EoN

2000
EPJ

OBERLERCHNER see SCHEMPP-HIRTH

Mg19a STEINADLER
ERZ

PENROSE

PEGASUS
HKJ

PIK see EIRI

PIK-16C VASAMAss
CGV

PILATUS FLUGZEUGWERKE

B4 PC-11
CSN CSP CSW CUB CUC CUQ CUT CVG CVK CVM CVV CYA CYC CYK CZD
DBC DLA DND DQM DRP DSV EQU HDA HDE HLC HSY HVH JSY JXX
EI-121

POTTIER see CARMAM

RAAB

DOPPELRAAB
EVU

ROLLADEN-SCHNEIDER

LS1F
FQZ JPE JSF JST
LS3
DNQ ECP EEF EES EEX EEZ EFS EFZ EGE EVD GAD GDA GDN HYH JDJ JYX
EI-137
LS4
EHK EHL EKV ELT EMB EMF EMG EMT EMY ENA ENE EQA ERV ESC ESE
ESY ETG ETV ETY EUH FAQ FHL FJM FKG FLF FNU FVE FYH GBT GDJ HEL
HKX HLB HMX HNV HNX HPL HVV HXF HXT HXZ HZM HZY JBX JEP JJB JKP
JLH JLJ JSB JSW JWN KAV KCB KCL KDK
LS6
FBE FCP FMC FRA GAR GBG GBQ GBR GCM HAQ HBC HBJ HET HEW HEZ
HFM HFQ HGP HHH HHT HHU HJC HJF HJX HMK HPD HQL HQZ HRY HSA
HUM HYA JBP JBQ JBU JCB JDG JDH JGC JNP JNU JTD JVK KBH
LS7
FMY FPD FQG FQH FTV FTY FUV FVH FVQ FWF FWJ FWU FXE FYB FYK
FYW FZV GBL GBY GCZ HAY HBA HBY HDX HEH JEJ JLK JSJ JTR JZZ
LS8
HSZ HTL HTM HTP HTQ HTS HUG HUV HUW HVF HVL HVU HWL HWM HWS
HXC HXN HXW HYF HYZ HZG HZP JBB JCL JCP JCY JDE JDK JDT JDY JEA
JEG JFB JFL JFX JGS JHU JHY JJK JJU JKD JKL JKN JLN JMB JMO JMR JMT
JMU JMW JNB JNJ JNK JNM JNW JPH JPL JPR JQD JRA JRK JSQ JSU JTL
JTM JTY JUC JUD JUE JXU JZC KBJ KBZ KCA

SCHEIBE-FLUGZEUBAU including AVIALSA/ROCHETAU production

BERGFALKE
CDR CEV CKT CMT DJU EBD EPZ EVT FPG FVD HQC EI-107
L-SPATZ
DLR DPR DPT DUH DVR DZC EFN EFR EQL FAK FHE FPF FXX HCP HWQ
JHB EI-130
ZUGVOGEL III
EBS ELV FRS FSU FVL FVY FYE HKV HND HSH HXA EI-146
MÜ-13E
EI-116
SF-26 STANDARD
DRL EDS EUM
SF-27A ZUGVOGEL V
DZV EKS EUE FHY FLZ FQF FQM FRM FUF FUQ FWH FZM GAV GBM GDW
HGM HLU HSG HSX HUS HVJ JSA EI-142
SF-28A TANDEM FALKE
EI-122
SFH-34 DELPHIN
EPM FKQ

SCHEMPP-HIRTH OHG including GROB, JASTREB & OBERLERCHNER production

STANDARD AUSTRIA
BPN DBT DKB
SHK/SHK-1
CAQ CAR CBU CCB CGT CGZ CJK CJL CJN CLG CVH DJS DKK DMK DTG
ECG FJZ FZC
HS.2 CIRRUS/CIRRUS VTC
CDH CEA CEC CFK CGY CJR CLQ CUS CVE CVF CWL CWR CWS DDM DVY
FXG GCQ HEV HTU HUL HUR JJA JQW JTS KEA
HS.4 STANDARD CIRRUS
CKZ CLA CLH CNN CPU CQN CQR CQY CRH CRN CTB CTT CUL CYM CYP
CYQ CYT DAS DDA DDR DFC DFY DGE DGX DLG DVS DXL DZF EEN EGK
FBB FCN FGU FLW FMT FMU FRJ FRZ FVS FYJ FZK GAH GAL GCD GEP
HAN HAX HFF HGG HJN HJU HJY HKC HKD HKR HKS HKU HMY HNM HRL
HSV HVZ HWD HWF HWY HXX HZJ HZL HZU HZV JBJ JCJ JCN JCU JDS JER
JEV JEY JFA JGN JGY JHA JHH JJJ JJM JLX JMH JNC JQS JRG JRT JTE JUU
JVU JWH KBT KCU KDZ KEB
HS.5 NIMBUS 2
CQL CQP CQQ DAJ DDD DGY DHW DKL DMM DNG DTU DYU DYZ DZK EAJ
EAM EEK EFB EFF EFT EGS EHP EHT EKR EKW FCS FPP FRC FVF FVT HBF
HBV HNE HNH HQN JGH JMN JMV JQE

HS.6 JANUS
DTC EKB EQV EQW HNB HSP HTB HTH HUC HUH JAA JFE JLM JNL JVV
HS.7 MINI NIMBUS
DPH DSE DSP DSW DXQ DXT EAV EBF EBK EDF EER EGW FHG FSL HQY HRQ JGU JTJ JYS JZL KBB
NIMBUS 3/4
ENN ENP EQN ERU EVF FAM FBM FFK FGF FRP FWK FXQ HBR HCB HFX HKQ HNU HWN HYY HZA HZW JCT JDA JDZ JEQ JFQ JHF JJG JSC JVT JWG JXA KAG
DISCUS A/B/CS
FBY FDU FEJ FER FES FFT FFX FHR FKK FKM FLE FMG FMQ FNL FNQ FNR FQY FTW FUL FUP FXM FYM FYN FYX GCT GDR GDX HCL HDF HDT HDZ HEE HEM HEN HGK HGL HGS HGZ HHP HHQ HJH HJL HKA HKL HKY HLD HLN HLQ HLS HLY HML HMP HMQ HPH HPR HPX HQJ HQM HQR HQW HRS HRX HSD HSJ HSQ HUZ HVR HWV HXH HYB HYU HZE JAH JAN JAQ JAR JBD JBN JBR JBW JCK JCX JDL JFC JFG JGL JGM JGR JHM JHT JHV JJD JJE JJZ JKR JKX JLC JLP JLW JMD JMM JPP JPU JQA JQC JQK JRR JSE JUB JUV JVB JVF JVG JVX JVY JWK JXL JXR JYE JZG KAH KAP KBQ EI-138
DISCUS 2
JNE JNF JNY JUA JUP JVR JWQ JYM JYN
DUO DISCUS
HNF HNN HNW HQE HRW HSW HWB JAC JEM JFF JFH JGV JJP JPA JQQ JTU JUM JXW JYR KAF KAR KCF KCV KDE
VENTUS A/B/C
EHH EKH EKJ ELG ELR ENJ EPX EUJ EUS FAW FBT FCK FDE FEG FEP FHS FJJ FJQ FMN FNN FPE FPL FQN FRB FRT FUH FUR FVB FVW FWD FYC FZH GAP GAS HAJ HED HFA HFV HFY HGN HHN HUY HVE HWH HXR HYG JBG JCE JEF JET JFP JFR JFS JJY JKH JKY JLA JLU JSL JWL JWU JXK JZS KAS KDV
VENTUS 2
HSL HUP HUX HVE HVT HVY HWA HXS HYL HZS JAF JBC JEX JGP JLB JLU JPD JPG JQL JQR JTV JTZ JUF JUQ JVA JWX JYH JYJ JYT JYU JZM JZV KAJ KAT KBG KBK KCC KCD KCE KCH KCK KCX KDA KDJ KDL KDQ EI-152

SCHLEICHER including CENTRAIR production

RHÖNBUSSARD
AEM
RHÖNSPERBER
ABG
Ka2B RHÖNSCHWALBE
DCG DGT DJG DPP DRR ESK FBL FPU FSF HZN EI-131
Ka3
EHB
Ka4 RHÖNLERCHE II
CTF CVY CWU CWV CYY EAL EUT HQH EI-104
Ka6/BR/CR RHÖNSEGLER
BKJ BKW BND BNH BQL BTJ BTM BUZ BVR BVX BVZ BWC BXT BYL BYM BYU BZQ BZX CBM CBY CCJ CJY DAW DCF DCW DDY DEP DEV DGK DHG DJE DJR DKG DKN DLP DNW DNX DQC DQF DQJ DQS DRA DRD DRE DRF DRG DRY DSG DSR DSY DUR DVG DYC DYJ DYN DYP DYQ DZW EBQ ECC ECF EDG EEW EGL ELY EPW EQQ FBZ FDR FGJ FHZ FKA FKH FKU FKX FLS FMM FNP FNW FQL FSE FTB FTF FUB FUM FWA FZR GAC GAW GBE GCP GDE GDF GEA GEF GEM HAB HBQ HEB HFB HPQ HRE HSN HUK HZH JCZ JEW JJV KDB EI-109 EI-111 EI-127 EI-128
Ka6E
BYX CAC CAE CAG CAS CCA CCD CCG CCL CCR CCU CCV CDA CDB CDD CDF CDV CDZ CED CEG CEL CEM CEQ CEW CEY CFL CGB CGD CGE CGK CGN CHB CHZ CKL CLZ CPJ DGG DHM DHT DLE DMQ DQK DSB DUS DVE DVH DWC DXH EAH EFM EHM EKC EKX ETB FCR FND FPV FRE FSS FVZ FXC FXS FXU GDV HAP HJD HRF JAK JAL JHD JHL JLT JLV JSG
Ka7 RHÖNADLER
BFP BKN BQK BQU BRM BVB CFC CLF CLK CLT CMG CMZ CPG CQT CRA CWJ DBF DHY DJT DKY DMF DML DQX DRM DWE DWN DXM DYB DYR EAU EDC EDK EFD ELX EMV ENC EPV ETR ETU EUQ EVB EVG FEL FGV FGZ FHU FJW FKW FLK FMD FMZ FPQ FQU FRF FTG FTU FXH GAQ HAG HCM HGC HHL HJK HNJ HSS JME EI-105
K8B
CDC CDK CFF CGH CGJ CHU CJF CJM CKW CLX CML CMN CQD CTZ CYZ DDL DFQ DGA DHA DJB DJP DKC DLD DLS DMB DMG DMJ DNZ DQL DQP DQY DRV DRZ DSF DTN DUF DUK DVQ DWG DWH DXP EAZ EED EEM EFG EFP EHA EJF EJG EKM EPT EQZ ESJ ESX ETD FAZ FBJ FCL FCQ FDD FDL FHN FJU FKJ FKT FLH FLP FLQ FNA FQD FQE FQR FQX FTA FTM FTN FVA FWL FXB FXW GCG GDB GDK GEG HAR HCZ HDN HDY HFW HJE HKK HLH HLV HMH HNG HRJ HRT HWE HWT HYN HYV HYW HYX HZX JAT JFT JGB JGD JGX JHK JLS JNN JQB JQJ JQZ JSN JXS JYV JYW KDH
EI-106 EI-108 EI-133
Ka10
EVH
ASK13
CAV CBW CCC CCE CCF CCM CCP CCT CCW CCX CCY CCZ CEJ CEX CFA CFB CFG CFM CGQ CGR CHW CJD CKR CKU CKV CMK CRL CRT CWH DDB DKE DLC DMX DNV DQA DRJ DUE DVB DVC DVX DXV EAP EBL EBZ EDU EKD ENY EPP EQE EQF ETS EUC EVJ EVP FAT FCW FEQ FFA FGR FHM FHU FMH FPX FSD FSQ FVC FVU FWB FWN FYY FZN GBA HAL HDC HMV HPE HSM HTJ HUD HUF HUU HVQ HVW HXJ HXP HXV JFM JGW JJC JKT JLE JLF JLL JLQ JMJ JMP JMW JMX JMZ JPC JPV JPY JRX JSV JWB JWJ JWY JXM JYD JZE EI-112 EI-113 EI-143
ASW15
CHT CJP CKP CZN FBC FBD FCY FDA FJV FKE FME FML FMS FPB FQB FRK FTD FXY GCH GCR GCX GDS GDY GEH HEJ HGF HJZ HNT HQX HTC HZD JAM JCA JDM JDR JED JGG JJX JPX JRE JVW JWS JZJ EI-134
ASK16
EI-119
ASW17
CPD CTE EDD EGD EI-132
ASK18
DJJ DJK DLB DNJ DPA EUX HRN HSU JHQ JKG JKU JMA JMK JPQ JPZ JSZ EI-136
ASW19
DPX DSX DTD DTE DVL DVP DWZ DXX DZD DZG DZY EBJ EEH EJR ELA ENZ EPE EQG ERP ERQ ERS FFP FGP FNH FPJ FWP FWZ GCA GDP HCE HCV HDV HER HGH HHK HKT HLM HLW HNC HUA HWZ HXE HXU JBK JBT JCQ JDQ JES JFU JHC JHS JJL JKS JNT JRB JRV EI-153
ASW20
DST DTP DTQ DUT DVV DVW DXB DXK DYE DYX EAE EBN EBX ECX EDE EEC EEE EEJ EEV EFA EFE EFH EFJ EFK EFL EFV EGP EHD EHV EHZ EJK EJL EJQ EKE EKU ELU ELZ ENV ENW EPF EPS EQJ ERA ETZ EUD EUK EUY FAF FBA FBQ FCV FFH FHD FJE FKL FPH FPN FPT FRH FRW FTL FTP FTQ FUN FWS FZL HBU HCH HDJ HDL HEQ HGW HHS HJT HLZ HPC HQD HQK HRU HSK HTT HTX HUJ HUT HVP HVX HYK HZT HZZ JAG JAY JEE JEN JFJ JFK JHZ JMQ JTP JXH JZH KCY KDC EI-126
ASK21
ECW ECZ EDW EGZ EHQ EKG ELE ENK EPD EQR ERH ERJ ESB ESU ETA FBV FWQ FYF FYV GAF GAG GAM GBB GBF GBN GBP GBV HCX HLG HLP HPV HPW HRR HTV HVG HYJ HYS HYT HZR JAD JAV JAX JBM JFV JGE JGJ JJR JKA JKJ JKQ JKZ JMC JMS JQX JVZ JWD KCT KCZ KDF KDP EI-150
ASW22
FDT FEU FGY FNF GBX HTN JNV JWZ
ASK23
EVV EVW EVX EVY FCX GCF HKP JPB
ASW24/E
FLY FMP FMX FNG FXJ GDT GDU GDZ HBB HBG HYD JCD JEB JEL JRU JTC JXT
ASH25
FKN FLG FST FSY FUG FWW FXL FYD FYZ GCE HFL HLX HXQ JCV JDF JFN KDM
ASW27
HUE HXD HYR HZQ JCM JDC JJF JJT JLY JNH JNS JPN JPS JPT JQM JQV JRH JSS JTF JUH JUJ JUL JVM JVN JVQ JWC JWF JXZ JYD JZT JZX KBX KCG KCN KDN KDS KDW EI-151
ASW28
JVS JWA JXJ JYY JZN KAK KAL KBM KBU KBV KCJ

SCHMETZ

CONDOR
DQH

SCOTT

VIKING
AHU

SHENSTONE

HARBINGER
BNA

SHORT

NIMBUS
ALA

SIEBERT

SIE 3
EFC FRG

SLINGSBY SAILPLANES LTD including YORKSHIRE SAILPLANES production

T.1 FALCON 1
ABN FCZ
T.6 KITE 1
AAF AAX ACH ADJ AHC
T.7 CADET
AWZ BQE
T.8 TUTOR
AJW AKW ALR AZK AZQ BAA BBG BCB BCH BDW BEF CPL CRK CRZ CSL DQD IGA.6
T.9 KING KITE REP
ELK
T.12 GULL I
AGE BED

T.13 PETREL
ATR EI-101
T.15 GULL III
ATH HBZ
T.21
AQE AQG ARM ASB ATK AUG AUJ AUP AWD AYK AZC BCF BCU BDA BDM
BFD BFY BGB BGG BGP BJF BJV BMQ BMU BQF BTH BUW BXK BYY BZA
CEK CLC DAR DCN DDC EJJ ELH ERW ETP EUN EUZ FCF FCT FDY FEE FFG
FFL FFW FFZ FGB FGG FGM FGS FHB FHC FJA FJB FJD FJF FKP FNC GEN
HCK HFC HFE HFG HNS HQB HRD JAU JQY JXD JYA EI-157
T.25 GULL 4
APZ
T.26 KITE 2
AND AUD AVF EI-102
T.30B PREFECT
ARK ASN AVT AZF BAN BQP CKJ DSA DTZ EBC EHE
T.31B
AVG BHY BZY CHQ FCC FCG FDQ FFQ FGA FGC FHK FJN FLB FSJ FUW
HAK HHG HLR HVB JCS JSP JWE KAA KBP EI-139
T.34 SKY
AVB AVC AVL AVQ DPZ JPK
T.38 GRASSHOPPER
FMA FMW FSV GDC HEA HJJ HPP HVC JAP JBA JDB JJN JJS JND EI-135
T.41 SKYLARK 2
AWS AWX AXB AXP AXR AXU AYD AYY AZP AZX AZY BAH BAM BAV BAZ
BBA BBU BCX BDY BEA BFL CCS CHE DCE
T.42 EAGLE
AXJ AZA BAY BBB BBD BBQ BDF
T.43 SKYLARK 3
AXD AXE AXL AYF AYH BAC BAW BBP BBT BCM BCP BCS BCV BCW BER BET
BEX BEZ BFC BFE BFG BGD BGH BGL BHQ BHS BHT BJB BJK BJW BKE BUT
T.45 SWALLOW
BCY BDR BEM BEY BFB BHV BJP BJY BJZ BKP BLU BML BNS BNU BPX BRC
BRE BRG BSX BTA BVF BWK BXP BYB BYJ BYK BZL BZM CAX CHY DCS
DGM DHP DLX ELC EMK FRQ HBX
T.49 CAPSTAN
BJQ BNR BPD BPS BPT BPU BPV BPW BRA BRW BSE BSK BSS BST BUC
BUR BZG
T.50 SKYLARK 4
BKA BLA BLE BLH BLW BLZ BMW BMX BMY BNE BNK BNM BNN BNP BNQ
BPA BPB BPC BPE BPG BPJ BPK BPZ BQZ BSC BSG BSH BSR BSY BSZ BTK
BUE ERB FXF EI-117
T.51 DART
BQA BRB BRD BRT BRU BRY BSA BSL BSM BSV BSW BUF BUL BUP BVE
BVH BVJ BVL BVM BWJ BWM BWP BWQ BWS BWT BXE BXG BXH BXL BXM
BYA BYC BYG BZC BZF BZH BZJ CAZ CBA DBB
T.53
CUD CXV CXW DHR
T.59 KESTREL
CFT CNS CNV CNW CNX CPB CQJ CQM CRJ CSA CSB CSD CSF CSG CSK
CTJ CTL CTM CTN CTP CTQ CTR CVW CVX CVY CVZ CWA CWB CWD CWF
CXM CYN CZQ CZR CZS CZT CZU CZV CZW CZZ DBJ DBK DBN DBQ DBR
DBS DEB DXU DYG ERY FDK KAB EI-125
T.65 VEGA
DWT DWW DXD DXE DXF DXG DXR DZA DZB DZM DZN DZP EAD EAG EBA
ECJ ECK ECL ECM ECN EDA EDV EDX EDY EDZ EEA EEG EFW EGF EGG
EGH EGJ EGT EGU EGX EHG EHN EHY EJB EJC EJD EJE EJS EJT EKY ELD
ELQ EMJ EML EMN EMP EMR EMS EMZ FNK EI-129

STANDARD AUSTRIA see SCHEMPP-HIRTH

START+FLUG
H101 SALTO
JTX JZA

SWALES see BIRMINGHAM GUILD

SZD
SZD-8 JASKOLKA
BFS DZS
SZD-9 BOCIAN
BJD BMM BVS CCN CEB CHF CKN CND CNM CTW CVP DAA DBW DBX DCR
DDN DNF DRS EJY ESA FLL FUD FZG HFU HPF HQU
SZD-12A MUCHA
GEQ HDM EI-100 EI-140
SZD-22C MUCHA STANDARD
JXE
SZD-24/SZD-32 FOKA
BZP BZZ CBP CMF HGY
SZD-30 PIRAT
CBN CDX CEN CHG CHL CKD CNK CPV CPX CQC CQX CSV CTV CTX CUM
CVC CVR CXL CYD CZE CZG CZJ DAN DAP DAT DAU DBD DBV DCH DCJ
DDK DDW DFW DGH DHB DHZ DJA DLW DNT DTW EQB FKD

SZD-36A COBRA 15
CQW CRD CVN CVS CVT CXH CXJ DAC DAQ DCA
SZD-38A JANTAR-1
DAV DDE DDV DFL DFU DFV FNE
SZD-41A/SZD-48 JANTAR-STANDARD
DFX DHC DJL DJM DVK EKK ESP ETK FDX FHV FQT FTJ HBS HUB KDR
SZD-42 JANTAR-2
DNU EUV HFJ
SZD-50-3 PUCHACZ
EUF EVS FBG FEN FTH FUY FWE FWT FYA FYL FZQ GBD GCK GCU GEL
HAC HAF HAS HCC HCD HCF HDP HEP HFH HHA HHC HSC HYP JEC JRF
JRJ JSR KAN
SZD-51-1 JUNIOR
FFV FFY FHF FPM FTC FUS FZA FZF FZP FZX GCC HCR HCW HDB HDU HEK
HHD HHE HMA HNK HQV HRG HRP JJQ JLG JMG JMY
SZD-55
GAX HEC HHR HRV HVD JTG KBN
SZD-59 ACCRO
HVA HWX

VFW-FOKKER GmbH
FK-3
HJA

VALENTIN
MISTRAL
JHP JUR JUY

VOGT
LO-100 ZWERGREIHER
ELL

WASSMER (SOCIETE DES ETABLISHMENTS BENJAMIN WASSMER)
WA21 JAVELOT II
CJG
WA22 SUPER JAVELOT
CEH
WA26P SQUALE
EEP HFN HGA HHX JXQ
WA28F ESPADON
JDX JXC
WA30 BIJAVE
EKT FNX HMR

WRIGHT
FALCON
ECA

YORKSHIRE SAILPLANES see BIRMINGHAM GUILD

ZLIN (ZLINSKA LETECKNA AKCIOVA)
24 KRAJANEK
ATV

PART 7 (i) – "B CONDITIONS" ORIGINAL SERIES MARKINGS

The latest Air Navigation Order (ANO2000) continues to promulgate the specific circumstances under which aerospace maufacturers can pursue the conduct of aircraft trials without the need for valid Certificates of Airworthiness. ANO2000 establishes both "A" & "B" conditions but we are only concerned here with the latter requirements which stipulate the use of identity marks as approved by the CAA for the purposes of "B Conditions" flight.

In brief, under "B Conditions" an aircraft must only fly for the purpose of:
(a) experimenting with or testing the aircraft (including any engines installed thereon) or any equipment installed or carried in the aircraft;
(b) enabling it to qualify for the issue of a certificate of airworthiness or the validation thereof or the approval of a modification of the aircraft or the issue of a permit to fly;
(c) demonstrating and displaying the aircraft, any engines installed thereon or any equipment installed or carried in the aircraft with a view to the sale thereof or of other similar aircraft, engines or equipment;
(d) demonstrating and displaying the aircraft to employees of the operator;
(e) the giving of flying training to or the testing of flight crew employed by the operator or the training or testing of other persons employed by the operator; or
(f) proceeding to or from a place at which any experiment, inspection, repair, modification, maintenance, approval, test or weighing of the aircraft, the installation of equipment in the aircraft, demonstration, display or training is to take place or at which installation of furnishings in, or the painting of, the aircraft is to be undertaken.

The flight must be operated by a person approved by the CAA for the purposes of these Conditions and subject to any additional conditions which may be specified in such an approval. If not registered in the United Kingdom the aircraft must be marked in a manner approved by the CAA for the purposes of these Conditions. The aircraft must carry such flight crew as may be necessary to ensure the safety of the aircraft. No person can act as pilot in command of the aircraft except a person approved for the purpose by the CAA.

In May 1978 the erstwhile Merseyside Aviation Society published an excellent booklet "Under B Conditions" by D S Revell and edited by Phil Butler. The book detailed the background to "B Conditions" flights, explained the role of the Society of British Aircraft Constructors (SBAC) in stimulating the identity listing, and aimed to identify every known aircraft which had carried "B Conditions" identities from 1929 up to that time. Readers who wish to know more should note that plans are in hand for Air-Britain to revise and re-publish this book with the above gentlemen still at the helm! Both listings in the last Register has been revised in accordance with Phil Butler's article and his further comments in the Summer & Autumn 2002 editions of Air-Britain Digest.

Prefix	Company	Period	Remarks	
A	The Sir W G Armstrong Whitworth Aircraft Ltd	1929-1948	Issued 23.12.29	
B	Blackburn Aeroplane & Motor Co.Ltd	1929-1948	Issued 23.12.29	
C	Boulton & Paul Ltd	1929-1948	Issued 23.12.29	
D	Bristol Aeroplane Co.		Not taken up	
D	Cunliffe Owen Aircraft		Proposal not taken up	
D	Portmouth Aviation Ltd	1947-1948	Issued 1947	
E	de Havilland Aircraft Co Ltd	1929-1948	Issued 23.12.29	
F	The Fairey Aviation Co Ltd	1929-1948	Issued 23.12.29	
G	Gloster Aircraft Ltd	1929-1948	Issued 23.12.29	
H	Handley Page Ltd	1929-1948	Issued 23.12.29	
I	H G Hawker Engineering Co Ltd	1929-1948	Issued 23.12.29	
J	George Parnall & Co (to Parnall Aircraft Ltd)	1929-1946	Issued 23.12.29	Cancelled 1946
J	Reid & Sigrist Ltd	1947-1948	Issued 1947	
K	A V Roe & Co Ltd	1929-1948	Issued 23.12.29	
L	Saunders-Roe Ltd	1929-1948	Issued 23.12.29	
M	Short Bros (Rochester & Bedford) Ltd	1929-1948	Issued 23.12.29	
N	Supermarine Aviation Works (Vickers) Ltd	1929-1948	Issued 23.12.29	
O	Vickers (Aviation) Ltd	1929-1948	Issued 23.12.29	
P	Westland Aircraft Works	1929-1948	Issued 23.12.29	
R	The Bristol Aeroplane Co.Ltd	1929-1948	Issued 23.12.29	
S	Spartan Aircraft Ltd	1930-1936	Issued 30.8.30	Cancelled 29.2.36
S	Heston Aircraft Ltd	1936-1948	Issued 15.5.36	
S	Comper Aircraft		Not taken up	
T	General Aircraft Ltd	1933-1948	Issued 8.5.33	
U	Phillips & Powis Aircraft Ltd	1934-1948	Issued 5.2.34	
V	Airspeed (1934) Ltd	1934-1948	Issued 27.6.34	
W	G & J Weir Ltd	1933-1948	Issued 8.5.33	Cancelled 1946
X	Percival Aircraft Ltd	1936-1948	Issued 21.1.36	
Y	The British Aircraft Manufacturing Co.Ltd	1936-1938	Issued 1936	Cancelled 1938
Y	Cunliffe-Owen Aircraft Ltd	1940-1948	Issued 28.10.40	
Z	Taylorcraft Aeroplanes (England) Ltd	1946-1948	Issued 12.1.46	
AA	Believed not allocated			
AB	Slingsby Sailplanes Ltd	1947-1948	Issued 1947	

PART 7 (ii) – "B CONDITIONS" CURRENT SERIES MARKINGS

Prompted by the SBAC a radically new system was introduced in 1948. In essence, this remains in existence today. Whilst deemed "current" many Companies included have long merged with each other or ceased to trade and so, by coincidence, the table below encapsulates in miniature the absorbing changes within the UK aircraft industry which have occured during the period 1948 to 2002. The same can also be said for the earlier table covering the period from 1929 to 1948.

Prefix	Company	Period	Remarks	
G-1-	Sir W G Armstrong-Whitworth Aircraft Ltd	1948-1967	Issued 1.1.48	Cancelled c.1967
G-1-	Rolls-Royce Ltd (Bristol Engines Division)	1949-19xx	Issued 9.4.69	Cancelled
G-2-	Blackburn Aircraft Ltd	1949-1967	Issued 1.1.48	Cancelled c.1967
G-3-	Boulton Paul Aircraft Ltd	1948-1973	Issued 1.1.48	Cancelled 31.12.73
G-03	BAe Systems (Operating) Ltd	19xx- Current		
G-4-	Portsmouth Aviation Ltd	1948-1949	Issued 1.1.48	Cancelled 23.5.49
G-4-	Miles Aviation & Transport (R&D) Ltd	1969-19xx	Issued 1.5.69	Cancelled
G-04	BAe Systems (Operating) Ltd	19xx- Current		
G-5-	The de Havilland Aircraft Co Ltd (Current as Raytheon Services Ltd)	1948-	Issued 1.1.48	
G-6-	Fairey Aviation Ltd	1948-1969	Issued 1.1.48	Cancelled 17.1.69
G-7-	Gloster Aircraft Ltd	1948-1961	Issued 1.1.48	Cancelled c.1961
G-7-	Slingsby Sailplanes (Current with Slingsby Aviation Ltd)	1971-	Issued 21.10.71	
G-8-	Handley Page Ltd	1948-1970	Issued 1.1.48	Cancelled 28.2.70
G-08	BAe Systems (Operating) Ltd	19xx-	Current	
G-9-	Hawker Aircraft Ltd (later British Aerospace Defence Ltd)	1948-1996	Issued 1.1.48	Cancelled c.1996
G-10-	Reid and Sigrist Ltd	1948-1953	Issued 1.1.48	Cancelled 1.4.53
G-11-	A.V.Roe & Co. Ltd (Current as BAe Systems (Operations) Ltd)	1948-	Issued 1.1.48	
G-12-	Saunders-Roe Ltd	1948-1967	Issued 1.1.48	Cancelled 9.6.67
G-13-	Not allocated		Issued 1.1.48	
G-14-	Short Brothers & Harland Ltd (Current as Short Brothers plc)	1948-	Issued 1.1.48	
G-15-	Vickers Armstrong Ltd, Supermarine Division	1948-1968	Issued 1.1.48	Cancelled 17.10.68
G-16-	Vickers Armstrong Ltd, Weybridge Division (later British Aerospace Airbus Ltd)	1948-1999	Issued 1.1.48	Cancelled c.1999
G-17-	Westland Aircraft Ltd (Current as GKN Westland Helicopters Ltd)	1948-	Issued 1.1.48	
G-18-	The Bristol Aeroplane Co.Ltd	1948-1975	Issued 1.1.48	Cancelled 31.7.75
G-19-	Heston Aircraft Ltd	1948-1960	Issued 1.1.48	Cancelled 4.2.60
G-20-	General Aircraft Ltd	1948-1949	Issued 1.1.48	Cancelled 23.5.49
G-21-	Miles Aircraft Ltd (H P Reading Ltd)	1948-1963	Issued 1.1.48	Cancelled 11.2.63
G-22-	Airspeed Div, de Havilland Aircraft Co Ltd	1948-1952	Issued 1.1.48	Cancelled 23.5.52
G-23-	Percival Aircraft Ltd	1948-1966	Issued 1.1.48	Cancelled 31.5.66
G-24-	Cunliffe-Owen Aircraft Ltd	1948-1949	Issued 1.1.48	Cancelled 23.5.49
G-25-	Auster Aircraft Ltd	1948-1962	Issued 1.1.48	Cancelled c.1962
G-26-	Slingsby Sailplanes Ltd	1948-1949	Issued 1.1.48	Cancelled 19.12.49
G-27-	English Electric Co Ltd Aircraft Division (later British Aerospace Military Aircraft Division Ltd)	1948-1991	Issued 1.1.48	Cancelled c.1991
G-28-	British European Airways Corp (Helicopters) (Current as Brintel Helicopters Ltd)	1948-	Issued 1.1.48	
G-29-	D Napier & Son Ltd	1948-1962	Issued 1.1.48	Cancelled 9.11.62
G-30-	Pest Control Ltd	1952-1957	Issued 1.1.48	Cancelled 4.3.57
G-31-	Scottish Aviation Ltd (Current as BAe Systems (Operations) Ltd)	1948-	Issued 1.1.48	
G-32-	Cierva Autogiro Co. Ltd	1948-1951	Issued 1.1.48	Cancelled 9.3.51
G-33-	Flight Refuelling Ltd			
G-34-	Chrislea Aircraft Ltd	1948-1952	Issued 1.1.48	Cancelled c.1952
G-35-	F.G.Miles Ltd (later Beagle Aircraft Ltd)	1951-1970	Issued 9.8.54	Cancelled 29.6.70
G-36-	College of Aeronautics (Current as Cranfield Aerospace Ltd)	1954-	Issued 9.8.54	
G-37-	Rolls-Royce Ltd	1954-1971	Issued 9.8.54	Cancelled 17.9.71
G-38-	de Havilland Propellers Ltd (later Hawker Siddely Dynamics)	1954-1975	Issued 9.8.54	Cancelled 22.10.75
G-39-	Folland Aircraft Ltd	1954-1965	Issued 9.8.54	Cancelled 2.4.65
G-40-	Wiltshire School of Flying Ltd		Not taken up	
G-41-	Aviation Traders (Engineering) Ltd	1956-1976	Issued 3.10.56	Cancelled 27.2.76
G-42-	Armstrong Siddeley Motors Ltd	1956-1959	Issued 13.11.56	Cancelled 28.8.59
G-43-	Edgar Percival Aircraft Ltd	1956-1959	Issued 21.11.56	Cancelled 26.6.59
G-44-	Agricultural Aviation Ltd	1959-1959	Issued 17.4.59	Cancelled 14.12.59
G-45-	Bristol Siddeley Engines Ltd	1959-1969	Issued 27.5.59	Cancelled 8.4.69
G-46-	Saunders-Roe Ltd, Helicopter Division	1959-1962	Issued 15.6.59	Cancelled 3.5.62
G-47-	Lancashire Aircraft Co. Ltd	1960-19xx	Issued 8.2.60	Cancelled ???
G-48-	Westland Aircraft Ltd, Bristol Division	1960-1969	Issued 7.7.60	Cancelled 28.2.69

G-49-	F.G.Miles Engineering Ltd	1965-1969	Issued 23.7.65	Cancelled c.1969
G-50-	Alvis Ltd	1967-1975	Issued 16.2.67	Cancelled 1975???
G-51-	Britten-Norman Ltd *(Current as BN Group Ltd)*	1967-	Issued 20.9.67	
G-52-	Marshalls of Cambridge (Engineering) Ltd *(Current as Marshalls of Cambridge Aerospace Ltd)*	1968-	Issued 18.1.68	
G-53-	Norman Aeroplane Co. Ltd	1977-19xx	Issued 23.5.77	Cancelled???
G-54-	Cameron Balloons Ltd	197x-	Issued ???	
G-55-	W.Vinten Ltd	19xx-19xx	Issued ???	Cancelled 1999??
G-56-	Edgley Aircraft Ltd	19xx-19xx	Issued ???	Cancelled???
G-57-	Airship Industries (UK) Ltd	19xx-19xx	Issued ???	Cancelled???
G-58-	ARV Aviation (later Island Aircraft)	19xx-19xx	Issued ???	Cancelled???
G-59-	Mainair Sports	19xx-19xx	Issued ???	
G-60-	FR Aviation Ltd *(Current together with G-71)*	19xx-	Issued ???	
G-61-	Aviation Enterprises Ltd	19xx-	Issued ???	
G-62-	Curtiss & Green Ltd	19xx-19xx	Issued ???	Cancelled???
G-63-	Thunder & Colt Balloons	1994-19xx	Issued c.1994	Cancelled???
G-64-	Brooklands Aerospace Group plc	19xx-19xx	Issued ???	Cancelled???
G-65-	Solar Wings Aviation Ltd	19xx-1995	Issued ???	Cancelled c.1995
G-66-	Aerial Arts Ltd	19xx-19xx	Issued ???	Cancelled???
G-67-	Atlantic Aerengineering Ltd	19xx-	Issued ???	
G-68-	Medway Microlights	19xx-	Issued ???	
G-69-	Cyclone Airsports Ltd	19xx-	Issued ???	
G-70-	FLS Aerospace (Lovaux) Ltd	19xx-1997	Issued ???	Cancelled c.1997
G-71-	FR Aviation Ltd	19xx-	Issued ???	
G-72-	Lindstrand Balloons Ltd	19xx-	Issued ???	
G-73-	Aviation (Scotland) Ltd	19xx-1995	Issued ???	Cancelled c.1995
G-74-	Fleaplanes UK Ltd	19xx-2001	Issued ???	Cancelled c.2001
G-75-	Chichester Miles Consultants	19xx-	Issued ???	
G-76-	Police Aviation Services Ltd	19xx-	Issued ???	
G-77-	Thruster Air Services Ltd	19xx-	Issued ???	
G-78-	Bristow Helicopters	19xx-	Issued ???	
G-79-	McAlpine Helicopters Ltd	19xx-	Issued ???	
G-80-	British Microlight Aircraft Association	19xx-	Issued ???	
G-81-	Cooper Aerial Services	19xx-19xx	Issued ???	Cancelled???
G-82-	European Helicopters Ltd	19xx-1999	Issued ???	Cancelled c.1999
G-83-	Mann aviation Group (Engineering) Ltd	19xx-	Issued ???	
G-84-	Intora-Firebird plc	19xx-19xx	Issued ???	Cancelled???
G-85-	CFM Aircraft Ltd	19xx-	Issued ???	
G-86-	Advanced Technologies Group Ltd	19xx-	Issued ???	
G-87-	CHC Scotia Ltd	19xx-	Issued ???	
G-88-	Air Hanson Engineering	19xx-	Issued ???	

PART 8 (i) – ICAO HISTORICAL AIRCRAFT NATIONALITY AND REGISTRATION MARKS

To help the discerning reader decipher the many and varied origins of UK & Irish registered aircraft have decided to include a list of foreign aircraft markings. Both lists are based on member Roger House's web-site and expanded with reference to Tony Pither's "Airline Fleets" and Ian Burnett's Overseas Registers section in "Air-Britain News". Any amendments will be welcomed.

Regn Prefix	Prev Prefix	Country	Period	Remarks
A-		Austria	1929-1939	Changed to OE-
AN-		Nicaragua	1936-	Changed to YN-
BR-		Burundi	1962-1965	Changed to 9U-
C-		Colombia	1929-1946	Changed to HK-
CB-		Bolivia	1929-1954	Changed to CP-
CCCP-		Soviet Union	1929-	Changed to RA-
CF-		Canada	1929-1974	Changed to C-
CH-		Switzerland	1929-1936	Changed to HB-
CR-A		Mozambique	1929-1975	Changed to C9-
CR-B		Mozambique	1971-1975	Changed to C9-
CR-C		Cape Verde Islands	1929-	Changed to D4-
CR-G		Portuguese Guinea/Guinea Bissau	1929-1975	Changed to J5-
CR-I		Portuguese India	1929-1961	Changed to VT-
CR-L		Angola	1929-1975	Changed to D2-
CR-S		Sao Tome and Principe	1929-	Changed to S9-
CR-T		Timor	1929-1975	Changed to PK-
CV-		Romania	1929-1936	Changed to YR-
CY-	VP-C	Ceylon	1948-1954	Changed to 4R-
CZ		Monaco	1929-1949	Changed to MC-
DDR-		East Germany	1945-1956	Changed to DM-
DM-		East Germany	1956-	Changed to D-
ES-		Estonia	1929-1939	Merged into Soviet Union CCCP-
EZ-		Saar Territory	1929-1933	Changed to SL-
FC-		Free French	1940-1944	Changed to F-
F-D		French Morocco	1929-1952	Changed to CN-
F-KH		Cambodia	1945-1954	Changed to XU-
F-L		Laos	1945-1954	Changed to XW-
F-O		Dahomey/Benin	1929-1960	Changed to TY-
F-O		Algeria	1929-1962	Changed to 7T-
F-O		Upper Volta	1929-1960	Changed to XT-
F-O		Ubangi-Shari	1929-1960	Changed to TL-
F-O		Tunisia	1929-1956	Changed to TS-
F-O		Cameroon	1929-1960	Changed to TJ-
F-O		Chad	1929-1960	Changed to TT-
F-O		Senegal	1929-1960	Changed to 6V-
F-O		Congo	1929-1960	Changed to TN-
F-O		Mauritania	1929-1960	Changed to 5T-
F-O		Gabon	1929-1960	Changed to TR-
F-O		Guinea	1929-1958	Changed to 3X-
F-O		Cote D'Ivoire	1929-1960	Changed to TU-
F-O		Madagascar	1929-1960	Changed to 5R-
F-O		Niger	1929-1960	Changed to 5U-
F-O		Mali	1929-1960	Changed to TZ-
F-VN		French Indochina (Vietnam)	1929-1954	Changed to XV-
J		Japan	1929-1945	
JZ-		Dutch East Indies	1945-	
K-		Kuwait	1967-1968	Interim - Changed to 9K-
KA-		Katanga	1961-1963	Unoffical - Changed to 9O-
KW-		Cambodia	1954	Changed to XU-
LG-		Guatemala	1936-1948	Changed to TG
LI-		Liberia	1929-1952	Changed to EL-
LR-		Lebanon	1944-1954	Changed to OD-
LY-		Lithuania	1929-1939	Merged into Soviet Union CCCP-
M-		Spain	1929-1933	Changed to EC-
MC-		Monaco	1949-1959	Changed to 3A-
OA-		Peru	1929-1950	Changed to OB-
OO-C		Belgian Congo	1929-1960	Changed to 9O-
PI-		Philippines	1941-1975	Changed to RP-
R-		Argentina (three digits)	1929-1932	Changed to LV-
R-		Panama (two digits)	1929-1943	Changed to RX-
RV-		Persia (Iran)	1929-1944	Changed to EP-
RX-		Panama	1943-1952	Changed to HP-
RY-		Lithuania	1929-1939	Merged into Soviet Union CCCP-
SL-	EZ-	Saar Territory	1947-1959	Changed to D-
SN-		Sudan	1929-1959	Changed to ST-
TJ-		Transjordania	1946-1954	Changed to JY-
TS-		Saar Territory	1930-1931	Unoffical - Changed to EZ-
UH-		Saudi Arabia	1945	Interim - Changed to HZ-
UL-		Luxembourg	1929-1939	Changed to LX-
UN-		Yugoslavia	1929-1935	Changed to YU-
VO-		Newfoundland	1929-1939	Merged into Canada CF-
VP-A		Gold Coast (Ghana)	1929-1957	Changed to 9G-
VP-B		Bahamas	1929-1975	Changed to C6-
VP-C		Ceylon	1929-1948	Changed to CY-
VP-G		British Guiana	1929-1967	Changed to 8R-

VP-H	British Honduras (Belize)	1947-	Changed to V3-
VP-J	Jamaica	1930-1964	Changed to 6Y-
VP-K	Kenya	1929-1963	Changed to 5Y-
VP-L	Leeward and Windward Islands	1929-	Now Antigua V2-
VP-LKA-LLZ	St. Kitts and Nevis		Changed to V4-
VP-M	Malta	1929-1968	Changed to 9H-
VP-N	Nyasaland	1929-1953	Changed to VP-Y
VP-P	Western Pacific Islands	1929-	Now Solomon Islands H4-
VP-R	Northern Rhodesia	1929-1953	Changed to VP-Y
VP-S	Somliland	1929-1960	Changes to 6OS-
VP-T	Trinidad and Tobago	1931-1965	Changed to 9Y-
VP-U	Uganda	1929-1962	Changed to 5X-
VP-V	St. Vincent and Grenadines	1959-	Changed to J8-
VP-W	Rhodesia	1971-	Changed to Z-
VP-W	China (Wei-Hai-Wei)	1929-1939	
VP-X	Gambia	1929-1945	
VP-Y	Southern Rhodesia, Rhodesia & Nyasaland	1929-1964	Changed to 7Q-, 9J-
VP-Z	Zanzibar	1929-1964	Changed to 5H-
VQ-B	Barbados	1952-1968	Changed to 8P-
VQ-C	Cyprus	1952-1960	Changed to 5B-
VQ-F	Fiji/Tonga/Friendly Isles	1929-1971	Changed to DQ-
VQ-G	Grenada	1962-	Changed to J3-
VQ-L	St. Lucia	1965-	Changed to VQ-L
VQ-M	Mauritius	1929-1968	Changed to 3B-
VQ-P	Palestine	1930-1948	Changed to either TJ- or 4X-
VQ-S	Seychelles	1929-1977	Changed to S7-
VQ-ZA, -ZD	Basutoland	1929-1967	Changed to 7P-
VQ-ZE, -ZH	Bechuanaland	1929-1968	Changed to A2-
VQ-ZI	Swaziland	1929-1975	Changed to 3D-
VR-A	Aden	1939	
VR-B	Bermuda	1931-	Changed to VP-B
VR-C	Caymen Islands	1968-	Changed to VP-C
VR-G	Gibraltar	1929-1939	Changed to G-
VR-H	Hong Kong	1929-	Changed to B-H
VR-J	Johore	1929-1963	Changed to 9M-
VR-L	Sierra Leone	1929-1961	Changed to 9L-
VR-N	British Cameroons	1929-1958	Changed to either TJ- or 5N-
VR-O	Sabah (North Borneo)	1929-1963	Changed to 9M-
VR-R	Malaya	1929-1963	Changed to 9M-
VR-S	Singapore	1929-1965	Changed to 9V-
VR-U	Brunei	1929-	Changed to V8-
VR-W	Sarawak	1929-	
XH-	Honduras	1929-1960	Changed to HR-
XT-	China	1929-1949	
XV- 3W-	South Vietnam	1959-1975	
XW-	Laos	1954-	Changed to RDPL-
YE-	Yemen	1955-1969	Changed to 4W-
YL-	Latvia	1929-1939	Merged in Soviet Union CCCP-
YM-	Danzig Free State	1929-1939	Changed to D-
YN-	Nicaragua	1929-1936	Changed to AN-
ZM-	New Zealand	1929-1939	
3W-	Vietnam	1954-1959	Interim - Changed to XV-
4W-	Yemen	1969-	Merged into 7O-
6OS-	Somalia	1960-1969	Changed to 6O-
9O-	Zaire	1960-1966	Changed to 9Q-

PART 8 (ii) – ICAO CURRENT AIRCRAFT NATIONALITY AND REGISTRATION MARKS

Regn Prefix	Prev Prefix	Country	Period	Remarks
AP-		Pakistan	1947-	
A2-	VQ-ZE, -ZH	Botswana	1972-	
A3-		Tonga		
A40-		Oman	1974-	
A5-		Bhutan		
A6-		United Arab Emirates	1977-	
A7-		Qatar	1975-	
A9C-		Bahrain	1977-	
B-	XT-	China, Republic of	1975-	
B-		Taiwan	1949-	
B-H	VR-H	Hong Kong, China		
C-	CF-	Canada	1974-	
CC-		Chile	1929-	
CN-		Morocco	1952-	
CP-	CB-	Bolivia	1954-	
CS-	CR-	Portugal	1929-	
CU-		Cuba	1945-	
CX		Christmas Islands		
CX-		Uruguay	1929-	
C2-		Nauru	1971-	
C3-		Andorra		
C5-	VP-X	The Gambia	1978-	
C6-	VP-B	Bahamas	1975-	
C9-	CR-A, CR-B	Mozambique	1975-	
D-	DM-, DDR-	Germany	1929-	
D2-	CR-L	Angola	1975-	
D4-	CR-C	Cape Verde Islands		
D6-		Comoro Islands	1977-	
DQ	VQ-F	Fiji	1971-	
EC-	M	Spain	1929	
EI-		Ireland	1929	Also EJ- but not used
EK-	CCCP-	Armenia		
EL-	LI-	Liberia	1952-	
EP-	RV-	Iran	1944-	
ER-	CCCP-	Moldova, Republic of		
ES-	CCCP-	Estonia		
ET-		Ethiopia	1929-	
EW-	CCCP-	Belarus		
EX-	CCCP-	Kyrgyzstan		
EY-	CCCP-	Tajikistan		
EZ-	CCCP-	Turkmenistan		
E3-		Eritrea		
F-		France	1929-	
F-O		Frech Overseas Territories		
G-		United Kingdom	1929-	
GL-		Greenland		
HA-		Hungary	1935-	
HB-	CH-	Switzerland	1935-	
HC-		Ecuador	1929-	
HH-		Haiti	1929-	
HI-		Dominican Republic	1929-	
HK-	C-	Colombia, Republic of	1946-	
HL		Korea, Republic of	1948-	
HP-	RX-	Panama	1952-	
HR-	XH-	Honduras	1961-	
HS-		Thailand	1929-	
HV-		Vatican City		
HZ-	UH-	Saudi Arabia	1945-	
H4-	VP-P	Solomon Islands		
I-		Italy	1929-	
JA	J	Japan	1948-	
JU-	MT	Mongolia		
JY-		Jordan	1954-	
J2-		Djibouti		
J3-	VQ-G	Grenada		
J5-	CR-G	Guinea Bissau		
J6-	VQ-L	St. Lucia		
J7-		Dominica		
J8-	VP-V	St. Vincent and Grenadines		
LN-		Norway	1931-	
LQ-		Argentina (Government)	1932-	
LV-	R-	Argentina	1932-	
LX-	UL-	Luxembourg	1946-	
LY-		Lithuania		
LZ-		Bulgaria	1929-	
N	NC,NL,NR.NS,NX	United States of America	1929-	
OB-	OA-	Peru	1950-	
OD-	LR-	Lebanon	1954-	
OE-	A-	Austria	1945-	

OH-		Finland	1931-	
OK-		Czech Republic	1929-	
OM-	OK-	Slovakia		
OO-		Belgium	1929-	
OY-		Denmark	1929-	
P-		Korea, Democratic Peoples Rep.of		
PJ-		Netherlands Antilles	1945-	
PK-		Indonesia	1929-	
PP-		Brazil	1932-	
PR-		Brazil		
PT-		Brazil	1950-	
PZ-		Suriname	1929-	
P2-		Papua New Guinea	1974-	
P4-		Aruba		
RA-	CCCP-	Russian Federation		
RDPL-	F-L, XW-	Laos	1975-	
RP-	PI-	Philippines	1975-	
SE-		Sweden	1929-	
SP-		Poland	1929-	
ST-	SN-	Sudan	1959-	
SU-		Egypt	1931-	
SX-		Greece	1929-	
S2-		Bangladesh	1972-	
S3-		Bangladesh	1976	
S5-	SL-	Slovenia		
S7-	VQ-S	Seychelles	1977-	
S9-	CR-S	Sao Tome Island		
TC-		Turkey	1929-	
TF-		Iceland	1937-	
TG-	LG-	Guatemala	1948-	
TI-		Costa Rica	1931-	
TJ-	F-O, VR-N	Cameroon	1960-	
TL-	F-O	Central African Republic	1960-	
TN-	F-O	Congo Brazzaville	1960-	
TR-	F-O	Gabon	1960-	
TS-	F-O	Tunisia	1956-	
TT-	F-O	Chad	1960-	
TU-	F-O	Ivory Coast	1960-	
TY-	F-O	Benin	1960-	
TZ-	F-O	Mali	1960-	
T3-		Kiribati		
T7-		San Marino		
T9-	YU-	Bosnia Herzegovina		
UK-	CCCP-	Uzbekistan		
UN-	CCCP-	Kazakstan		
UR-	CCCP-	Ukraine		
V8-	VR-U	Brunei		
VH-		Australia	1929-	
VN-	XV-	Vietnam		
VP-A		Anguilla		
VP-B	VR-B	Bermuda		
VP-C	VR-C	Caymen Islands		
VP-F		Falkland Islands	1929-	
VP-L-		British Virgin Islands	1971-	
VQ-H		St. Helena	1929-	
VQ-T		Turks & Caicos Islands		
VT-		India	1930-	
V2-	VP-L	Antigua		
V3-	VP-H	Belize		
V4-	VP-LKA-LLZ	St.Kitts & Nevis		
V5-		Namibia		
V6-		Micronesia		
V7-		Marshall Islands		
XA-		Mexico	1929-	Commercial
XB-		Mexico	1929-	Private
XC-		Mexico	1929-	Government
XT-	F-O	Burkina Faso		
XU-	F-KH, KW-	Kampuchea	1954-	
XY-		Myanmar	1948-	
XZ-		Myanmar		
YA-		Afghanistan	1929-	
YI-		Iraq	1931-	
YJ-		Vanuatu	1929-	
YK-		Syria	1952-	
YL-		Latvia		
YN-	AN-	Nicaragua		
YR-	CV-	Romania	1936-	
YS-		El Salvador, Republic of	1939-	
YU-	UN-	Yugoslavia (Serbia & Montenegro)	1935-	
YV-		Venezuela	1931-	
Z-	VP-W, VP-Y	Zimbabwe		
Z3-		Macedonia		
ZA-		Albania	1946-	
ZK-		New Zealand	1929-	

ZL-		New Zealand		
ZP-		Paraguay	1929-	
ZS-		South Africa	1929-	
ZT-		South Africa		
ZU-		South Africa		
3A-	CZ, MC	Monaco	1959-	
3B-	VQ-M	Mauritius	1968-	
3C-	VQ-ZI	Equatorial Guinea	1975-	
3D-		Swaziland	1975-	
3X-	F-O	Guinea	1958-	
4K-		Azerbaijan		
4L-		Georgia		
4R-	VP-C, CY-	Sri Lanka	1954-	
4X-		Israel	1948	
5A-		Libya	1951-	
5B-	VQ-C	Cyprus	1960-	
5H-	VP-Z	Tanzania	1964-	
5N-	VR-N	Nigeria	1961-	
5R-	F-O	Malagasy Republic	1960-	
5T-	F-O	Mauritania	1960-	
5U-	F-O	Niger	1960-	
5V-		Togo	1976-	
5W-		Samoa	1962-	
5X-	VP-U	Uganda	1962-	
5Y-	VP-K	Kenya	1963-	
6O-	6OS-	Somalia	1969-	
6V-	F-O	Senegal	1960-	
6W-		Senegal		
6Y-	VP-J	Jamaica	1964-	
7O-	YE-, 4W-	Yemen	1974-	
7P-	VQ-ZA,-ZD	Lesotho	1967-	
7Q-	VP-Y	Malawi	1964-	
7T-	F-O	Algeria	1962-	
8P-	VQ-B	Barbados	1968-	
8Q-		Maldives	1976-	
8R-	VP-G	Guyana	1967-	
9A-	RC-	Croatia		
9G-	VP-A	Ghana	1957-	
9H-	VP-M	Malta	1968-	
9J-	VP-Y	Zambia	1964-	
9K-	K-	Kuwait	1961-	
9L-	VR-L	Sierra Leone	1961	
9M-	VR-J, VR-O, VR-R	Malaysia	1963-	
9N-		Nepal	1961-	
9Q-	9O-	Democratic Republic of Congo	1966-	Formerly Zaire
9U-	BR-	Burundi	1962-	
9V-	VR-S	Singapore	1970-	
9XR-		Rwanda	1962	
9Y-	VP-T	Trinidad and Tobago	1965-	

AIR-BRITAIN SALES

Companion volumes to this publication are also available by post-free mail order from

Air-Britain Sales Department (Dept UKI03)
41 Penshurst Road, Leigh,
Tonbridge, Kent TN11 8HL

For a full list of current titles and details of how to order, visit our e-commerce site at www.air-britain.com
Visa / Mastercard / Delta / Switch accepted - please give full details of card number and expiry date.

ANNUAL PUBLICATIONS - 2003 - NOW AVAILABLE

UK & IRELAND QUICK REFERENCE 2003 £5.95 (Members) £6.95 (Non-members)
New, basic easy-to-carry registration and type listing, UK-based foreign aircraft, current military serials, aircraft museums and base index. A5 size, 136 pages.
Buy this together with Airline Fleets Quick Reference for a £1.00 combined price reduction.

BUSINESS JETS QUICK REFERENCE 2003 £4.50 (Members) £4.95 (Non-members)
The latest addition to the Quick Reference range, listing all purpose-built business jets, in both civil and military use, in registration or serial order by country. Easy-to-carry A5 size, 72 pages.

AIRLINE FLEETS QUICK REFERENCE 2003 £5.95 (Members) £6.95 (Non-members)
New pocket guide now expanded to airliners of over 19 seats of major operators likely to be seen worldwide; regn, type, c/n, fleet nos. Listed by country and airline. A5 size, 176 pages.
Buy this together with UK & Ireland Quick Reference for a £1.00 combined price reduction.

BUSINESS JETS INTERNATIONAL 2003 (*Prices to be announced, available April*)
Complete production listings of all business jet types in c/n order, giving full identities, fates and a comprehensive cross-reference index. Available in hardback or softback at approx 400 pages.

AIRLINE FLEETS 2003   £18.00 (Members) £22.50 (Non-members)
Almost 3000 fleets listed by country plus numerous appendices including airliners in non-airline service, IATA and ICAO airline and base codes, operator index, short-lived airlines, etc. 768 pages A5 size hardback.

EUROPEAN REGISTERS HANDBOOK 2003   (*Prices to be announced, available April/May*)
Current civil registers of 42 European countries, all powered aircraft, balloons, gliders, microlights. Full previous identities and many extra permit and reservation details. Now in new A4 softback format approx 580 pages.

OTHER PUBLICATIONS AVAILABLE NOW:

JET AIRLINERS OF THE WORLD 1949-2001   £16.00 (Members) £20.00 (Non-members)
Detailed production lists of over 70 jet airliner types with expanded coverage of Russian-built types and purely military jet transports. Full cross-reference index containing over 56,000 registrations and serials.

BUSINESS TURBOPROPS INTERNATIONAL 2000   £15.00 (Members) £19.00 (Non-members)
Complete production lists of over 75 types including all B-N Islanders, with 42,000+ cross-reference index. 360 pages, hardback.

WORLD MILITARY TRANSPORT FLEETS 2002   £15.00 (Members) £19.00 (Non-members)
The complete country-by-country guide of all the fixed-wing military and government operated transport and patrol aircraft. C/ns, units and bases are given where known. Over 10,000 entries including future plans. 280 pages.

Air-Britain also publishes a comprehensive range of military titles, please check for latest details of RAF Serial Registers, detailed RAF aircraft type "Files", Squadron Histories and Royal Navy Aircraft Histories.

IMPORTANT NOTE – Members receive substantial discounts on prices of all the above Air-Britain publications. For details of membership see the following page or visit our website at http://www.air-britain.com

AIR-BRITAIN MEMBERSHIP

Join on-line at www.air-britain.co.uk

If you are not currently a member of Air-Britain, the publishers of this book, you may be interested in what we have on offer to provide for your interest in aviation.

About Air-Britain

Formed over 50 years ago, we are the world's most progressive aviation society, and exist to bring together aviation enthusiasts with every type of interest. Our members include aircraft historians, aviation writers, spotters and pilots – and those who just have a fascination with aircraft and aviation. Air-Britain is a non-profit organisation, which is independently audited, and any financial surpluses are used to provide services to the ever-growing membership. In the last 7 years, our membership has increased annually, and our current membership now stands at over 4,200.

Membership of Air-Britain

Membership is open to all. A basic membership fee is charged and every member receives a copy of the quarterly house magazine, Air-Britain Aviation World, and is entitled to use all the Air-Britain specialist services and to buy **Air-Britain publications at discounted prices**. A membership subscription includes the choice to add any or all of our other 3 magazines, News &/or Archive &/or Aeromilitaria. Air-Britain publishes 10-20 books per annum (around 70 titles in stock at any one time). Membership runs January - December each year, but new members have a choice of options periods to get their initial subscription started.

Air-Britain Aviation World is the quarterly 48-page house magazine containing not only news of Air-Britain activities, but also a wealth of features, often illustrated in colour, on many different aviation subjects, contemporary and historical, contributed by our 4,200 members.

Air-Britain News is the world aviation news monthly, containing data on Aircraft Registrations worldwide, and news of Airlines and Airliners, Business Jets, Local Airfield News, Civil and Military Air Show Reports and International Military Aviation. An average 160 pages of lavishly–illustrated information for the dedicated enthusiast.

Air-Britain Archive is the quarterly 40-48 page specialist journal of civil aviation history. Packed with the results of historical research by Air-Britain specialists into aircraft types, overseas registers and previously unpublished photographs and facts about the rich heritage of civil aviation. Up to 100 photographs per issue, some in colour.

Air-Britain Aeromilitaria is the quarterly 48-page unique source for meticulously researched details of military aviation history edited by the acclaimed authors of Air-Britain's military monographs, featuring British, Commonwealth, European and U.S. Military aviation articles. Illustrated in colour and black & white.

Other Benefits

Additional to the above, members have exclusive access to the Air-Britain e-mail Information Exchange Service (ab-ix) where they can exchange information and solve each other's queries, and to an on-line UK airfield residents database. Other benefits include numerous Branches, use of the Specialists' Information Service; Air-Britain trips and access to black & white and colour photograph libraries. During the summer we also host our own popular FLY-IN. Each autumn, we host an Aircraft Recognition Contest.

Membership Subscription Rates – from £10 per annum.

Membership subscription rates start from as little as £10 per annum, and this amount provides a copy of 'Air-Britain Aviation World' quarterly as well as all the other benefits covered above. Subscriptions to include any or all of our other three magazines vary between £18 and £50 per annum (slightly higher to overseas).

Join on-line at www.air-britain.co.uk   or, write to 'Air-Britain' at 1 Rose Cottages, 179 Penn Road, Hazlemere, High Wycombe, Bucks HP15 7NE, UK, or telephone/fax on 01394 450767 (+44 1394 450767) and ask for a membership pack containing the full details of subscription rates, samples of our magazines and a book list.